ENCYCLOPEDIC DICTIONARY OF RELIGION

ENCYCLOPEDIC

Edited by

Paul Kevin Meagher, OP, S.T.M.

Thomas C. O'Brien

Sister Consuelo Maria Aherne, SSJ

THE SISTERS OF ST. JOSEPH OF PHILADELPHIA

Volume **O-Z**

DICTIONARY
OF RELIGION

CORPUS PUBLICATIONS: WASHINGTON, D.C.

Nihil Obstat:

John P. Whalen S.T.D., J.D.
Censor Deputatus

Imprimatur:

✠ William Cardinal Baum
Archibishop of Washington D.C.
February 7, 1978

Prepared by an

Editorial Staff at Corpus Publications, Inc. (1966–1970)
Washington, District of Columbia, and at
Mt. St. Joseph (1973–1979) Chestnut Hill,
Philadelphia, Pennsylvania.

Production Manager: Gerard G. Mayer

Composition: Lexigraphics Inc.
                 150 Fifth Avenue
                 New York, N.Y. 10011

Sales Manager: Jack Heraty and Associates, Inc.
                 P. O. Box 875
                 Palatine, Illinois 60067

Encyclopedic Dictionary of Religion

Library of Congress Catalog Number: 78-62029

ISBN 0-9602572-2-5 (Volume O-Z)   ISBN 0-9602572-3-3 (Set)

O

O ANTIPHONS, seven antiphons, each beginning with the interjection "O," which consecutively introduce the *Magnificat* in the Liturgy of the Hours for the 7 days preceding the vigil of Christmas (Dec. 17–23). The antiphons are addressed to the Messiah and contain recognition of some messianic attribute along with an appeal to the Messiah that he come. The texts have their source in the OT prophetic and sapiential literature but also manifest a loose compilation of other scriptural material. BIBLIOGRAPHY: M. Huglo, NCE 10:587–588.

[B. ROSENDALL]

OAK, SYNOD OF THE, an assembly convened in 403 at a place called The Oak, a short distance to the SE of Chalcedon, to depose St. *John Chrysostom. In 402 *Theophilus, patriarch of Alexandria, was summoned to Constantinople to appear before a synod presided over by St. John Chrysostom to answer charges made against him by some Egyptian monks. But in July of the following year, with the connivance of the Empress, a group of Chrysostom's enemies made up of 36 bps. (all but 7 from Egypt), led by Theophilus, Severian of Gabala, and Acacius of Beroea, met at The Oak and condemned John on 29 ridiculous charges (PG 103:105–113). Chrysostom refused to appear before the synod, packed as it was with his known enemies. The Emperor Arcadius accepted the decision and exiled John to Bithynia. This action stirred the wrath of the city mobs which, aided by the coincidence of an earthquake, forced the quick return of John a few days later. BIBLIOGRA - PHY: Quasten 3:426–427; C. Baur, *John Chrysostom: His Life and Times* (2 v., orig. Ger. 1929–30, Eng. tr. 1959–60); D. Attwater, *St. John Chrysostom* (1939).

[R. B. ENO]

OATES PLOT, scheme alleged by Titus Oates (1649–1705) to have been devised by English Catholics for the assassination of Charles II. An Anglican clergyman, Oates entered the RC Church as a spy and attended Jesuit schools.

In 1678 he and another Anglican clergyman, I. Tonge (1621–80), brought allegation of the plot to London magistrate E. B. Godfrey, who was later found murdered. A scare developed, and from 1678 to 1681 numerous trials were held and more than 25 Catholics executed. In 1685 Oates was found guilty of perjury and imprisoned. On the abdication of James II he was released and pensioned by William III. The plot is also known as the Popish Plot.

[T. EARLY]

OATH AGAINST MODERNISM, formula promulgated in the *motu proprio, Sacrorum antistitum,* of Pope Pius X (Sept. 1, 1910). The oath had to be sworn by clerics before receiving the subdiaconate, and by priests upon appointment to various offices and dignities (CIC c.1406–08). The oath was a formal affirmation of the principal doctrines proposed by the *magisterium of the Church, esp. with regard to the possibility of human reason's proving the existence of God, the external signs of divine revelation, the establishment of the Church by Christ, the immutability of dogma, and the nature of faith. The oath included a formal, explicit rejection of *modernism. The oath is no longer imposed; on May 31, 1967, the Congregation for the Doctrine of the Faith substituted a very brief, concise affirmation of faith. BIBLIOGRAPHY: D 3537–50; J. J. Heaney, NCE 9:995–996.

[J. H. ROHLING]

OATHS, formal affirmations that call upon God or some aspect of divine power as a witness that what one asserts is the truth, or what one pledges will be performed. Oaths have been used in most societies, and they are mentioned, e.g., in the Code of Hammurabi. Among the Jews the custom developed of taking hold of the Scriptures while taking an oath, a practice that has continued in the modern practice of swearing on the Bible. The historian Josephus reports opposition to swearing among the Essenes. In Christian history several groups have opposed all oaths, in literal obedience to the words of Jesus (Mt 5.33–7) and James (5.12). Opposition has come particularly from such groups as Anabaptists and Quakers, who were in tension with the authorities of Church and State that employed oaths. Mennonites have also been noted for their refusal to take oaths, a stand taken by their founder, *Menno Simons, incorporated in their Confession of Waterland (Art. 38), and still maintained in the *Mennonite Confession of 1963 (Art. 17).

The basic point of Jesus' teaching is generally considered to be the necessity for a character of such total honesty that any formal assertion that one is making a true statement would be superfluous. The implication is that the moral demand for truth is absolute, and no distinction can be drawn between ordinary speech and special occasions when an oath is used. Most Christians have regarded Jesus' statement as an example of his use of hyperbole, comparable to such assertions as that a disciple should hate his father and mother (Lk 14.26), and not to be interpreted with absolute literalness. The main authorities of the Churches, therefore, have approved oaths as a necessity for government, both secular and ecclesiastical. Supporters of oaths point out that such OT figures as Abraham swore (Gen 21.24), that Yahweh is said to swear (Is 62.8), and that Paul used oaths (2 Cor 1.23). Although some of the Fathers opposed swearing (see Chrysostom, Homilies 8 and 9 on Acts), St. Thomas Aquinas approved (ThAq ST 2a2ae, 89), and RC canon law regulates the use of oaths (CIC c. 1307–21). The main Churches of the Reformation, in contrast to Anabaptists, also supported the use of oaths. The last of the *Thirty-Nine Articles of the Church of England approves oaths, as does c. 22 of the *Westminster Confession.

Most Christians today do not make an issue of taking oaths, though they may agree that ideally they should be unnecessary for Christians. In secular courts, oaths are now primarily a means to forestall false testimony under penalty for perjury and alternative forms of affirmation have been devised not only for such groups as object to swearing but also for atheists, whose lack of belief makes traditional oaths meaningless. In general, it may be doubted whether oaths have a significant effect in an increasingly secularized society. BIBLIOGRAPHY: MennEnc 4:2–8.

[T. EARLY]

OATHS, ENGLISH ECCLESIASTICAL, a series of oaths and subscriptions required of clergymen during the English Reformation in an endeavor to achieve unity in doctrine and practice. After successive alterations in the content and administration of these, the present requirements in the C of E are: an oath of allegiance to the sovereign, a declaration of assent to the doctrines and rites of the C of E, and an oath of canonical obedience. In the Act of Supremacy of 1534, Parliament declared the king to be "the only supreme head in earth of the Church of England" and at the same session made it treasonable to deny the king any of his dignities or titles. In order to receive new commissions from the king, bps. were required in 1535 to re-

pudiate the papacy and to aid in the enforcement of the laws. All except John Fisher, Bp. of Rochester, took the oath and proceeded to bring the clergy of their dioceses to accept the new situation. Fisher was executed for treasonably denying the king's supremacy. In 1550, during the reign of Edward VI, the oath of supremacy was incorporated in the new ordination service, where it remained until 1865, except during the Marian and Cromwellian periods. Declaring the king to be the head of the C of E, it also explicitly repudiated the usurped power and authority of the bp. of Rome. The Act of Supremacy, enacted in 1559, included an oath of supremacy that had to be taken by all persons in ecclesiastical office. It required clerics to swear allegiance to Queen Elizabeth I and her successors and to acknowledge her as the supreme governor of the realm, in matters spiritual as well as temporal. The reference to the usurped power of the bp. of Rome was altered to a renunciation of all foreign jurisdictions, powers, and authorities. William and Mary, in 1689, further modified the form of the oath, in which the ordained swore to "abhor, detest, and abjure . . . that damnable doctrine" that princes excommunicated or deprived by Rome may be deposed or murdered by their subjects, and denied any jurisdiction to foreign powers, ecclesiastical or spiritual. In 1865, a Clerical Subscriptions Act removed the oath from the ordination service, requiring it to be taken beforehand. The form of the oath was altered in 1868, and at present it is a simple oath of allegiance to the ruling sovereign and his successors, with no mention being made of the king's supremacy.

Other declarations and subscriptions were designed to secure uniformity of doctrine and practice. The adoption of the *Book of Common Prayer, in 1549, was accompanied by an Act of Uniformity. Compliance with its forms was mandatory, and heavy penalties were attached for nonconformity; but no oath was included. The same was true of similar Acts of 1552 and 1559. The Act of Uniformity of 1662, however, required "every Parson, Vicar, or other Minister" to declare before his congregation "unfeigned assent and consent" to the use of everything in the Prayer Book. An oath also had to be taken before the bp. to the same end. With respect to doctrine, the *Forty-Two Articles were published in 1553, and all clerics licensed to preach or instituted to benefices were to subscribe them. They were revised and published in 1563 as the *Thirty-Nine Articles, without any provision concerning subscription. In 1571, however, a Subscription Act was passed, making subscription obligatory upon all clerics. By the Clergy Subscriptions Act of 1865 and subsequent Acts of 1868 and 1871, the required oath and subscription were reduced to a single declaration of assent to the Thirty-Nine Articles and the Prayer Book, and affirming a belief that the doctrine of the C of E is agreeable to the word of God. The declaration is made before the ordination service. The oath of canonical obedience (or due obedience) was originally only for bps. to make in relation to their abps., and it was a part of the Edwardine Ordinal of 1550. Eventually, it was extended to apply to all clerics being licensed to a curacy or instituted to a benefice. It is not a promise of unlimited obedience to a person, but signifies willingness to submit to the administrative authority of bp. or abp. insofar as he officially requires what is in accord with the laws of the Church. BIBLIOGRAPHY: Hughes RE; *Prayer Book Dictionary* (ed. G. Harford and M. Stevenson, 1925).

[N. H. MARING]

OBADIAH (Abdias), common OT name meaning servant of Yahweh: (1) chief official of Ahab's household and a loyal supporter of Yahweh (1 Kg 18.3–16); (2) descendant of David (1 Chr 3.21); (3) chief in the tribe of Issachar (1 Chr 7.3); (4) son of Azel, of the tribe of Benjamin (1 Chr 8.38; 9.44); (5) Levite, son of Shemaiah (1 Chr 9.16; cf. Neh 11.17); (6) Gadite in David's army (1 Chr 12.10); (7) father of Ishmaiah, a Zebulunite official (1 Chr 27.19); (8) prince sent by Jehoshaphat with the "book of the law" to teach "through all the cities of Judah" (2 Chr 17.7–9); (9) Levite who supervised temple repairs under Josiah (2 Chr 34.12); (10) one of those accompanying Ezra to Jerusalem (Ezra 8.9; Neh 10.5); (11) gatekeeper under Nehemiah and Ezra (Neh 12.25).

It is not known whether any of the above produced the oracles recorded in the Book of Obadiah.

[T. EARLY]

OBADIAH (ABDIA), BOOK OF, the shortest of the OT prophetic books, comprising only 21 verses. Of the prophet himself nothing is known. In Hebrew his name means "slave of Yahweh." The name is not unique, since it appears elsewhere in the Old Testament. The book is preoccupied with two main themes: a denunciation of Edom, peopled according to OT folklore by the descendants of Esau (2–14), and the restoration of Judah (16–21). The passage on Edom appears shocking for its gloating and triumphant tone over Edom's destruction. But the language in these verses is found elsewhere in the OT Prophets (Is 34.5–17; Lam 4.21–22; Mal 1.2–5; Ezek 35.4–15) and is rather intended to invoke the justice of Yahweh. Scholars are unable to fix the date of Obadiah, since its material finds plausible settings in the conflict between Judah and Edom in the 9th cent. B.C., in Edom's forays into Judah after the fall of Jerusalem in 587 B.C., and in Edom's own downfall in the 4th cent. B.C.

[C. P. CEROKE]

OBAZINE (AUBAZINE), ABBEY OF, a monastery founded near Limoges, France, early in the 12th cent. by a priest turned hermit, St. Stephen (d. 1159). The growing community adopted the Benedictine rule, founded six other monasteries, and in 1147 merged with the Cistercians. After 2 cent. of prosperity the abbey was repeatedly devastated by wars and under the misrule of commendatory abbots was unable to recover. In the 18th cent. it supported only six monks and was suppressed by the Revolution in 1791. The surviving portion of the late 12th–cent. church is a fine example of Cistercian architecture. BIBLIOGRAPHY: A. Dimier, *L' Art cistercien* (1962) 159–184.

[L. J. LEKAI]

OBEDIENCE, in RC theology, the virtue by which a person does what he is commanded to do by one possessing legitimate authority. Since all true authority comes from God (Rom 13.1), whether in the State, the family, or the Church, obedience to legitimate authority is obedience to God. The perfection of the virtue is to act according to the will and mind of the superior without being commanded. A strict obligation in conscience to obey is present only when the superior uses his authority to command in a strict and formal way. There can be no legitimate authority to command anything contrary to the law of God. Nor will there be any obligation to obey a superior who is commanding something beyond the limits of his authority. Further, there is no strict obligation in conscience to obey when the superior is merely directing or suggesting a course of action. In all cases of authority-obedience, if the superior becomes physically or mentally incompetent, the next in line takes over the authority. These general conditions apply to all the fields of authority discussed below.

Some moderns object that obedience is proper only to children who need help in knowing what to do. The obedience of children certainly differs from that of adults. The former is ordered toward bringing the child to proper maturity; but for adults, authority and obedience are necessary for coordinating the efforts of many toward a common goal. All use of authority must be reasonable and ordered to the proper goal or end. It need not express the most perfect way. But someone must decide, if many are to attain a common goal.

Family. The first basic unit in which authority occurs is in the family. Scripture teaches that children must obey their parents, as a part of the command of the decalogue "Honor your father and your mother" (Eph 5.1–3; Col 3.20). Theologians explain the basis of parental authority over children as required to bring the children to the proper maturity to lead their own lives. Therefore, it applies to most matters except the choice of a state in life or whatever would hinder their legitimate choice in adult life. The obligation to obey remains with the child until "emancipation," which theology and civil law recognize as occurring by reaching the age of 21, or before, with consent of the parents or by marriage. Theologians formerly added: or entrance into religious life. This is no longer practical since religious institutes will not accept an unemancipated minor without parental consent. Parents reasonably consent to earlier emancipation when the son or daughter shows sufficient maturity to direct his or her own life.

Within the family, according to SS. Peter (1 Pet 3.1) and Paul (Eph 5.22–23; Col 3.18), wives should also obey their husbands in all things, which theologians interpret as meaning in all things pertaining to the family as a social unit: the place to live, the level of life, etc. The same passages in Scripture stress that the relationships in the family, between husband and wife, and between parents and children, should be ruled by love.

Teachers may share in the parents' authority over their children as far as the parents give that authority. Mere disciplinary matters in class conduct as well as work assignments are generally considered purely penal regulations and not directly binding in conscience.

Older theologians, following Scripture, also spoke of obedience of servants or slaves to their masters and of employees to employers. However, with the abolition of slavery, and outside of the case of a very young servant's being committed to a family, these relations are matters of contract or mutual agreement and do not pertain strictly to the virtue of obedience. Charity demands that everyone treat his fellowman with love, recognizing him as a child of God made in his image and likeness.

State. As recorded in the Gospels (Mt 22.21; Jn. 19.11), Our Lord and SS. Peter (1 Pet 2.13–17) and Paul (Rom 13.1–7) clearly teach that a civil government has true authority from God. The Church (John XXIII, *Pacem in terris* 46; Vat II ChurchModWorld 74) explains that by this authority the State can bind its citizens in conscience to whatever is within its competence, namely to whatever is necessary or notably conducive to the common material welfare of the people. How and to what extent such an obligation in conscience applies to present–day civil laws is greatly debated. It would be hard to find widespread agreement in stating any strict obligation of obedience to specific civil laws, although all agree that justice certainly obliges all citizens to do their fair share and part in promoting the common welfare and respecting the rights of their fellowmen.

Church. In Scripture, teaching and governing authority in religious matters are not clearly distinguished. But whatever may be said of the nature of these functions, Jesus clearly taught that the people should do what the legitimate religious authority stated as obligatory, even though the leaders did not give good example (Mt 23.2: "Upon the chair of Moses. . . .") This same kind of authority Jesus gave to the Apostles (Mt 16.19; 28.18). The Church has traditionally held that this authority passes on to the successors of the Apostles, the pope and the bps. (Vat II Const Church 20–22, 25, 27). The authority to make laws or give precepts obliging in conscience belongs to the pope for the whole Church and each bp. for his own diocese. Pastors per se do not have such authority. And before a bp.'s precept entails a strict obligation in conscience, he must make it clear that he intends such an obligation.

Religious Communities. Members of religious institutes bind themselves by vow to obey the laws of their institute and the orders of their superiors, in accordance with the constitutions of the institute. The constitutions of all religious institutes now state that the laws or orders of superiors strictly bind in conscience only when the vow is explicitly

and clearly invoked. Otherwise, obedience can still be virtuous but not of strict obligation. BIBLIOGRAPHY: K. V. Trular, NCE 10:602–606; E. Roelker, *Precepts* (1955); J. J. Farraher, "Is Religious Disobedience Always a Sin?" *Review for Religious* 19 (1960) 215–224; A. Plé et al., *Obedience* (1953).

[J. J. FARRAHER]

OBEDIENTIAL POTENCY, the passive capacity of every creature to receive from God a higher mode of existence or of activity than would naturally pertain to that creature. The term is used in scholastic theology to reconcile two seemingly contradictory notions—God's continuing intervention in history and the fixity of the natural order—by affirming the fundamental openness of all creation to any divine action whatsoever. The obediential potency is of course limited by the principle of contradiction: God cannot affect anything which would be contrary to his prior creative act. For example, man may be given the gift of inspiration but a stone may not.

Prior to the scholastic age, this concept (if not the term itself) expressed nature's conformity to God's will in both creation and miracle. Increasingly, however, obediential potency was applied to man and human nature's ability to receive infused *knowledge, the *hypostatic union, *prophecy, etc. Thomists seem to agree that Thomas Aquinas did not use this purely passive potency to express man's capacity for the supernatural, even though some 16th-cent. commentators (esp. Cajetan) have interpreted Thomas in this way. BIBLIOGRAPHY: H. De Lubac, *Mystery of the Supernatural* (tr. R. Sheed, 1967); K. Rahner, *Nature and Grace* (tr. D. Wharton, 1964). *NATURAL ORDER; *SUPERNATURAL EXISTENTIAL; *SUPERNATURAL ORDER.

[T. M. MCFADDEN]

OBEDIENTIARY, in monastic nomenclature, an official with a relatively permanent appointment within the monastery, e.g., master of novices, sacristan, bursar; or the appointed prior of a dependent house that does not have status as a conventual priory, and so does not have an elected superior.

[T. C. O'BRIEN]

OBERAMMERGAU, village in S Bavaria, famous for wood carving and for its Passion play, which has been presented with much regularity every 10 years since its inauguration in 1634 as a thanksgiving for deliverance from plague. Performance was halted during World War II but was resumed in 1950. BIBLIOGRAPHY: E. H. Corathiel, *Oberammergau and Its Passion Play* (1960).

[M. F. MCCARTHY]

OBERLIN CONFERENCE, the first North American conference on *faith and order, held at Oberlin, Ohio, Sept. 3–10, 1957. The general theme, "The Nature of the Unity We Seek," was considered in relation to three main areas:

the gospel, the organized structures conducive to unity, and the sociocultural pressures that affect unity. The Conference, attended by RC observers authorized by the local diocese, produced a statement on the Eucharist (not accepted by all the participating Churches) that declared that "this commemoration . . . is more than the mere recollection of a past event . . . [it is] an action in which Christ mediates himself to us in the present moment" and that "in the entire eucharistic action Christ is personally present." In an attempt to define the unity of Christ's Church that was sought, the conference stressed a unity of ministry and members "bound together in a worshipping and sacramental community"—a concept further elaborated in later studies and formulations, notably that of the *New Delhi Assembly (1961). BIBLIOGRAPHY: *Nature of the Unity We Seek* (ed. P. S. Minear, 1958).

[D. CODDINGTON]

OBERLIN THEOLOGY, system of Christian thought that flourished in the 19th cent. at Oberlin College in Ohio under the leadership of Asa Mahan (1799–1889), Charles G. *Finney (1792–1875), and James H. Fairchild (1817–1902). The doctrine, first advanced by Mahan and continued by Finney, emphasized Christian *perfectionism and *sanctification. Influenced by the *New England Theology, Finney repudiated the traditional Calvinist doctrines of the determinism of the will and the imputation of Adam's guilt but retained the notion of *total depravity. Especially distinctive of the Oberlin movement was the principle of the simplicity of moral action, a view that maintained each moral choice to be either totally sinful, as self-gratifying, or holy, as surrendered to the general good. Fairchild's *Elements of Theology, Natural and Revealed* (1892) presented similar views in less formal terms. The system proved adaptable to a common-sense view of the Christian life and was a departure from orthodox Calvinism. BIBLIOGRAPHY: G. F. Wright, *Charles Grandison Finney* (1891); F. H. Foster, *Genetic History of the New England Theology* (1907); R. S. Fletcher, *History of Oberlin College* (2 v., 1943).

[C. A. HOLBROOK]

OBERZELL, ST. GEORGE, German church on the island of Reichenau, having one of the best-preserved cycles of late Ottonian–pre-Romanesque (mid-10th cent.) style, depicting the miracles of Christ, with prophets and other figures, the greater expanse of decorative pattern presaging Romanesque work.

[M. J. DALY]

OBJECT, MORAL, a term used by classical moral theology, which considers that every power, capability, or faculty of activity responds to an object (from *obiicere,* to set against, confront, offer) or reality other than itself; and that this determines its appropriate dispositions, habits (*habitos*) and activities or operations. It is, as it were, what they are

up against, and only by attaining it do they become fully actual. As directly engaging their specific interest, it is called the formal object; as offering the more undifferentiated material about which they act, it is called the material object: thus color and sound are the formal objects of sight and hearing respectively, while a physical thing is the material object of both.

Speaking at depth and breadth, God is the object of the knowing and loving of intelligent beings, and from this springs a real relationship to him which, to Christian theology, is not just the causal one of creatures to creator; it is also objectual, in that ultimately they will see and rejoice with him face to face, and already by charity can live in immediate friendship with him. To the will he is at once end and object. Here lies the paramount importance of a man's fundamental intention. But now we are set in a world of real beings which, although wholly from and to God, are also true and real in themselves, and therefore objects, and not just means (*media*), of our knowing and loving.

Here we have to reason and come to deliberate choices. The things about us are classified into different kinds—the recognition of this is an early condition of finding our way around—and they offer objects for different kinds of activity, and in particular of moral activity. Of course, virtue can be left as a diffused and generalized godliness ready to improvise in any situation, but it is better to be more specific about the opportunities and challenges it encounters. Sex has promises and dangers which are not those of citizenship; loving one's neighbor has problems which are not those of controlling one's appetite. And so the systematic moralist proceeds to set out different types of virtue, and also of vice, according to their different kinds of object. Thus what is owing to another is the concern of justice, keeping one's head in danger that of courage, having well-tempered desires for pleasure that of courage, and so forth. It may be felt that the process has sometimes been carried too far and has resulted in rather niggling distinctions; nevertheless the method is sound, indeed essential, if morals are to make a science. Yet the masters, at least, keep recurring to the singleness of human life in the concrete.

It is important to observe that while a moral object depends on, it is not to be resolved into a physical or psychological object; the submoral, says St. Thomas Aquinas, provides a genus for the act, but not its moral species. Thus you cannot render the due of justice as a special virtue merely in the imagination; or be brave unless you have fears; or be chaste if you have no desires. On the other hand, you are not really just if you pay but without good will; or brave if you are just fighting mad; or chaste if you are acting purely therapeutically. Moral objects are constituted by their position in their proper system of reference, namely the order of all human acts to final happiness and God. It is only in this context that their type can be defined, some as right of their kind, thus smiling at your wife, some as wrong of their kind, thus swearing at her, others as morally neutral, thus watching TV together. The definition is only of a nature and does not indicate an individual action. For a less incomplete assessment of the morality of an individual deed, the circumstances or situation and the motives or intention must also be taken into account. Nevertheless if moral science loses its base on the object or *finis operis,* the immediate goal to be expected from the sort of deeds men perform, it becomes merely opinionative. BIBLIOGRAPHY: ThAq ST (Lat-Eng v. 18 app. 2, 3, 5, 10–11; v. 31, app. 1; v. 33, app. 4).

[T. GILBY]

OBJETS TROUVÉS (Found objects), inanimate objects manipulated in surrealist and Dada constructions. Appearing exactly as they are, but removed from their natural context they effect provocative and at times disturbing juxtapositions, intensifying discrete, ontological essences or communicating aesthetic values through realities of the commonplace. With ultimate origin in collage, "found objects" moved through "junk" works and assemblage to the "combine" paintings of Rauschenberg, and Paolozzi's rusty machine parts from automobile graveyards—asserting the creative truth of concept.

[M. J. DALY]

OBLATE MISSIONARIES OF MARY IMMACULATE (OMMI), a secular institute of women dedicated to a life of bearing witness to the charity of Christ. The institute was founded at Grand Falls, N. B., Canada, in 1952 by Rev. Louise Marie Parent, O.M.I. It received papal approval in 1962. The members take the three vows, renewing them each year and in this way making spiritual formation a continuous life work. The Oblates live alone or in groups, and in whatever profession or occupation they are engaged, their primary purpose is to make known and communicate the love of God to all mankind. For this reason, the Oblate pledges to support the apostolic effort of the Church, to cooperate in building Christ's kingdom in love, justice, and peace, and to bear responsibilities by participation in Christian social action. Their apostolate has spread to about 23 countries on each of the continents and the international membership is approximately 670. To maintain a fraternal charity and unity, the Oblates meet in groups each month and hold district meetings 4 or 5 times a year. The government of the institute is collegial and is presided over by a president. The headquarters are at Trois-Rivières, P.Q., Canada.

[R. A. TODD]

OBLATE SISTERS OF PROVIDENCE (OSP), a diocesan foundation established in 1829 in Baltimore, Md., by a Sulpician, Jacques Nicholas Joubert. It is the first congregation of Negro women to take vows in the U.S.; it received approbation from Rome in 1831. The sisters are primarily active in the education of black youth but they also serve wherever there are other needs. They conduct elementary and secondary schools, a junior college, and are engaged in social service and nursing. Their missions are located throughout the southern and middle regions of the U.S., covering 12 states, and in Costa Rica. In 1977 the total membership was 204 professed sisters in 26 houses. The motherhouse is in Baltimore.

[R. A. TODD]

OBLATE SISTERS OF ST. FRANCIS DE SALES (OSFS), a community of religious founded at Troyes, France, in 1866 by Rev. Louis Brisson and Mother Francis de Sales Aviat. Its purpose is to educate youth, maintain houses for working girls and students, and give retreats. The congregation was approved by the Holy See in 1911. It is divided into regions and has missions in Europe, Africa, S. America, and in 1951 established a house in the U.S. with headquarters at Childs, Maryland. In 1975, the congregation had 57 houses and 503 members. The motherhouse is located at Troyes. BIBLIOGRAPHY: K. Burton, *So Much, So Soon* (1953).

[R. A. TODD]

OBLATE SISTERS OF THE ASSUMPTION (OA), a religious congregation of French origin with its motherhouse in Paris, co-founded in 1865 by Emmanuel d'Alzon and Mother Emmanuel Marie Correnson. The institute observes the rule of St. Augustine and in 1893 received papal approbation. The sisters work to bring about church unity, particularly in the countries of Eastern Europe. Their apostolate spread to foreign missions in the Near East, S. America, Africa, and the U.S. in 1956. The community engages in education and social work and maintains printing presses. In 1975 they had a total of 52 houses and 506 professed sisters.

[R. A. TODD]

OBLATE SISTERS OF THE MOST HOLY REDEEMER (OSSR), a congregation established in Spain in 1865 for the purpose of maintaining homes for wayward girls. It was founded by Mother Antonia María de Oviede y Schontal and José Benito Serra, a Benedictine missionary. The community later extended its work from social service to teaching in academies and schools of art. Soon the missions spread from Spain through Portugal and Italy and then to foreign missions in Latin America and in the U.S. at Jamaica Plain, Massachusetts. In 1975 the community had 63 houses and 874 members. The superior general resides at Madrid.

[R. A. TODD]

OBLATES (from the Lat. *oblati,* persons offered, made over to), a term that has been used in different senses. (1) In the early history of monasticism it was applied to children committed by their parents to a monastery. Until the 12th cent. this offering of a child was sometimes rigorously interpreted to obligate the one committed to the monastic state for life. (2) In the early Middle Ages the term was also applied to *conversi* (lay brothers) associated with monasteries; they entered in varying degrees into the life and activities of the monastery, but were concerned with the care of the monastery's temporal interests rather than with assistance at choral services. (3) From the 13th cent. onward the term was also applied to persons who remained in the world but donated their possessions to a monastery. Often such oblates lived under a quasi-monastic rule and received direction from the abbot. "Oblates" as applied to the modern Oblates of St. Benedict is derived from this use of the term. So also the term as applied to the Oblates of Mary, a society founded by St. *Frances of Rome (later, the Oblates Regular of St. Benedict), in which, under a mother president, women live according to the Rule of St. Benedict but without vows and without the surrender of their property. (4) The term has been adopted by a number of post-Tridentine religious congregations as part of their official title. They are "oblates" in the sense that they are given or dedicated to the service of God. BIBLIOGRAPHY: J. C. Almond, CE 11:188–189; L. E. Boyle, NCE 10:610–611.

[J. C. WILLKE]

OBLATES OF MARY IMMACULATE (OMI), a missionary congregation of men religious established in France in 1816. The rule, drawn up by the founder, Bl. Charles Joseph Eugène de *Mazenod, received episcopal approval in 1818, and in 1826 the society was approved by Rome. By 1850, the work of preaching missions and establishing seminaries had spread from France to most of Western Europe and countries of Latin America, Africa, and the major islands of the Far East. Foreign missions were established also in Canada (1841), and the Oblates evangelized most of Western Canada and in the U. S. (1842), where the congregation took special care of numerous Marian shrines. In 1976 there were 5 U.S. provinces, with a membership of 811 priests and 79 brothers. The world membership of the society in 1976 was 6,491, of whom 5,009 are priests. Today, the community maintains about 913 houses and their apostolate is chiefly educational and mission work. The superior general resides at Rome. BIBLIOGRAPHY: G. Carrière, *Histoire documentaire de la Congrégation des Missionaires Oblats de Marie Immaculeé dans l'est du Canada* (5 v., 1957–63); J. Leflon, *Eugène de Mazenod, Bishop of Marseilles, Founder of Oblates of Mary Immaculate* (tr. F.D. Flanagan, 1961).

[R. A. TODD]

OBLATES OF ST. BENEDICT, men and women affiliated to a Benedictine abbey, who undertake to live in the world in accordance with the spirit of the Rule of St. Benedict. The statutes and regulations which they observe are approved by the Holy See. They make no formal vows, but they do make an act of oblation, which is a promise made in the presence of the abbot of the monastery to which they are affiliated. They promise to reform their lives and to live in keeping with their rules and statutes. The status of the Oblate of St. Benedict is much like that of the secular tertiary of an order (e.g., Franciscan, Dominican, Carmelite, Augustinian) that has an affiliated *third order secular.

[J. C. WILLKE]

OBLATES OF ST. CHARLES, WESTMINSTER (OSC), a community of diocesan priests founded in London in 1857 by H. E. Manning, later card. abp. of Westminister. The need for such an institute came as the result of a great increase in the Catholic population brought about by the *Oxford Movement. The community was patterned after the Oblates of Milan, a group founded by St. Charles Borromeo. The rule, a modified form of that of St. Charles, received papal approbation in 1877. Under Manning's direction as the first superior, the Oblates lived in communities and were engaged in pastoral and domestic mission work. The apostolate grew, and soon four parishes and primary and secondary schools were established. Some communities of sisters were introduced into the archdiocese to assist the Oblates. Members of the community also labor in the Diocese of Brentwood. BIBLIOGRAPHY: E.S. Purcell, *Life of Cardinal Manning, Archbishop of Westminster* (2 v., 1896, repr. 1974).

[R. A. TODD]

OBLATES OF ST. FRANCES OF ROME, one of several communities of sisters affiliated to the Olivetan Benedictines, attached to the church of Sta. Maria Nova in Rome, and established around the time of the 15th-cent. reform movements. These Oblates were founded in Rome in 1425 by St. Frances of Rome. At first, they were a group of noble Roman ladies who did not live as a community but later, after some reorganization, adopted the communal life and dedicated themselves to works of mercy. In 1433 the constitution received the approval of the Pope. The Oblates of Mary, as they were originally called, lived in a convent in the Tower of Specchi near the Campidoglio, where St. Frances retired after the death of her husband. Presently they have foundations in Switzerland and the United States. In 1975 the Oblates of St. Frances had 3 houses and a total membership of 35 religious.

[R. A. TODD]

OBLATES OF ST. FRANCIS DE SALES (OSFS), a religious congregation of men founded at Troyes, France, about 1871 by Rev. Louis Brisson. The institute was formed in the spirit of St. Francis de Sales, who centuries before had desired to establish such a society. Its constitutions, based chiefly on the writings of St. Francis esp. his "Spiritual Directory," received approval by Rome in 1897. In their apostolate of education, foreign missions, and pastoral ministry the Oblates direct a house of studies, seminaries, private and diocesan high schools, colleges, parishes, and boys' camps. The congregation is divided into provinces located in France, Austria, the U.S., Germany, Holland, Switzerland, and Italy. The motherhouse is in

Rome. In 1975 the Oblates of St. Francis had 132 houses and a total membership of 1,015, of whom approximately 742 members are priests. BIBLIOGRAPHY: K. Burton, *So Much, So Soon: Father Brisson, Founder of the Oblates of St. Francis de Sales* (1953).

[R. A. TODD]

OBLATES OF ST. JOSEPH (OSJ), a religious congregation of men established for the purpose of humbly serving the Church through whatever work was assigned them by the bishop. The Oblates were founded at Asti, Italy, by Giuseppe Marello, bp. of Acqui, in 1878, and were given final approval by the Holy See in 1909. The members are engaged in parochial and educational work and, besides foundations in Italy and Belgium, they have foreign missions in the U.S., Latin America, and the Philippine Islands. In the U.S., the Oblates have a W and E province. The superior general resides at Rome. In 1975 the congregation had a total of 88 foundations and 394 members, of whom 275 were priests.

[R. A. TODD]

OBLATION, an offering made to God in reverence and worship; thus an outward act prompted by the virtue of *religion. The term applies to all the various offerings and sacrifices of the OT; *sacrifice, however, is a narrower term, denoting the change or consumption of the offering; oblation is more generic. The term serves also as a general description of the Mass; more particularly for the Offertory of the Mass as an expression of the oblation of all participating; and most specifically for one aspect of the Consecration, as this is both an oblation and an immolation (see EUCHARIST).

[T. C. O'BRIEN]

OBLATORIUM (Prothesis), area in the early Christian basilica where the bread and wine were blessed before their introduction in the Mass.

OBLIGATION, MORAL. Since the time of Kant the problem of duty and obligation (the acknowledgment of what we ought to do) has become central in moral philosophy and theology. The ideal of the moral life, lived in full accord with rational dignity, is represented as doing one's duty for duty's sake. To do justice to this position it must be recalled that Kant distinguished two kinds of imperatives, the hypothetical, which founds the practical necessity of a possible way of acting on its being a means toward an end that in fact is willed or at least may be legitimately willed; and secondly, the categorical, which for him as the only truly moral imperative, commands an act as being good in itself without reference to any ulterior end. He thus wishes to exclude every semblance of utilitarianism from the moral ideal. An act is such when it appears to me as a duty to the fulfillment of which I am obliged by law or precept. Here Kant lays himself open to being misun-

derstood, as indeed he was in the later climate of legal and political positivism. However he further distinguishes a twofold hypothetical imperative, and in doing so he appears somewhat ill at ease with his general theory. Some concrete ends are open to the choice of individuals, and simple hypothetical imperatives show the means toward their attainment. But there is one end that all in fact desire and that all must desire, and that is *happiness. The hypothetical imperative that declares the practical necessity of positing an action as a means to this purpose he calls an assertoric imperative. It is here that we become conscious of certain gaps in his moral synthesis. A thorough analysis of *law is missing. If an action is good in itself because declared by law, the question arises: by what law? So, too, a satisfying analysis of the key notion of happiness is lacking.

In contrast Scripture and RC theology see things almost the other way round. The matter might be put like this: because an action is good in itself and presents itself as such to me here and now, it becomes a duty and consequently obliges me. Duty and obligation are two aspects of the same reality—duty indicates the objective reality (to be realized and put into execution by me) and obligation the necessity my freedom adopts when faced with it existentially. The roots of all duty and obligation lie in the fact of creation. For all things created are by that very fact participated beings, and as such belong to the Supreme Being from which they proceed. Man moves and guides himself into the perfection (that is, happiness or beatitude) that the Creator has destined for him. Obligation understood in this way is not a force imposed from without, hampering growth and freedom, but rather an exigency from within. Man's first and fundamental duty is the perfection appointed him by God, and his first and fundamental obligation is that of coming to that divinely appointed consummation in being. In the history of salvation God has entered into a covenant with men, at first through the law, then renewed and fulfilled in Christ Jesus. Under the New Alliance obligations, on the visible and outward level, lie in general ecclesial life and practice, but at the deeper level are rooted in the new spirit of sonship and friendship—truly a matter of *noblesse oblige*; and indeed St. Paul insists on this (see Eph 5.3; 4.1–3; Col 3.12; Gal 5.22; Rom 6.22). Ultimately, then, it is not a question of duty for duty's sake, but rather duty for goodness sake, and for God's sake who calls his human creatures back to himself and whose glory is achieved in their perfection and happiness. BIBLIOGRAPHY: ThAq ST 1a2ae, 18–21 (esp. in ed. Lat-Eng v. 18, ed. T. Gilby); H. Rashdall, *Theory of Good and Evil* (2 v., 2d ed. 1924); H. R. Niebuhr, *Responsible Self* (1963).

[C. WILLIAMS]

OBRECHT, JAKOB (Hobrecht, Obertus, Opprecht, Uberto; 1452–1505), leading Flemish composer who held positions as music master, chaplain, music teacher, and music director throughout the Low Countries (1484–1502) and in Italy (1504). His compositions include 24 Masses, inspired by Frye, Busnois, Okeghem, and Agricola, 22 motets and hymns. A setting of St. Matthew's Passion, an important contribution ascribed to O., may have been written by Longueval. Chief among his works are settings of *Alma Redemptoris Mater, Ave Regina Caelorum* and *Salve Regina.*

[R. J. LITZ]

OBREGONIANS (POOR INFIRMARIANS), congregation of Hermanos Minimos, an order of nursing brothers. It was founded in Madrid (1568) by Bernadino Obregón, converted nobleman-officer of Philip II. The revised constitution (1594) incorporated the rule of the Third Order of St. Francis of Paola and the three usual vows, plus a vow of hospitality. Their work spread throughout the Spanish Empire, but the congregation disappeared during the French Revolution. BIBLIOGRAPHY: M. P. Trauth, NCE 10:617–618.

[R. I. BURNS]

OBREPTION, in canon law on *rescripts, a falsification of the narrative portion of a petition for a rescript that alters facts or circumstances presented. Obreption is contrasted with subreption, the omission of information in the petition. While unlawful, neither obreption nor subreption necessarily nullifies the rescript granted; the validity of the rescript simply requires that the essential purpose be truly stated in the petition and that the rescript itself be in accord with the usual procedures of law.

[T. C. O'BRIEN]

O'BRIEN, MATTHEW ANTHONY (1804–71), Irish-born American Dominican preacher, pastor, provincial. He came to the U.S. at the age of 21 and for several years before entering the Order of Preachers was a schoolmaster in Kentucky. He was received and made profession as a Dominican at St. Rose Priory, Springfield, Ky., in 1837, where 2 years later he was ordained. Most of his life was spent giving parish missions throughout the Midwest, even during his term as provincial (1850–54). He was pastor of St. Rose parish, where his memory has continued to be revered; he built its still-impressive parish church and the "rosary walk" on the hillside before the church is associated with him. He also established St. Joseph's College, Somerset, Ohio, and reopened St. Thomas Aquinas College at St. Rose. BIBLIOGRAPHY: V. F. O'Daniel, *Very Rev. Fr. Matthew Anthony O'Brien, An American Apostle* (1923).

[T. C. O'BRIEN]

O'BRIEN, TERENCE ALBERT (1600–51), Irish Dominican bp. and martyr. He was educated in Limerick and Toledo where he was ordained (*c.*1628). In 1630, he returned to Ireland, became prior of the Limerick Dominicans, Irish provincial of his order (1643), and bp. of Emly (1647). He opposed Ormond, and exhorted resistance to the end against Cromwell's forces during the siege of Limerick (1651). He was condemned and executed as an original incendiary of the rebellion. BIBLIOGRAPHY: J. Baqwell, DNB 14:773–774.

[T. M. MCFADDEN]

O'BRIEN, WILLIAM VINCENT (1740–1816), missioner. An Irish Dominican, he served as a preacher in Dublin and received the rank of preacher general. In 1787 he went to the U.S. working in Philadelphia and New Jersey. He supported Bp. Carroll in his efforts to establish an episcopal see in Baltimore, Maryland. In 1887 he was named pastor of St. Peter's in New York City, then threatened by schism. He was the strongest force in the Church in the state of New York as a leader and unifier of Catholics. In 1800 he established the first free school and Catholic school in New York State. BIBLIOGRAPHY: V. O'Daniel, *Dominican Province of St. Joseph* (1942).

[J. R. AHERNE]

OBSCENITY, filthiness, lewdness, impurity (from Lat. *caenum*, filth, mire). In this sense it categorizes any word, gesture, action, or mode of dress that is against chastity, purity, or modesty. The claim is often made that it is not such things that constitute obscenity, but poverty, war, oppression. Such outrages against human justice and dignity are damnable; their immorality, however, does not negate the reality of obscenity as sexual immorality. Puritanical attitudes have often exaggerated the extension of obscenity to repress perfectly warranted artistic expression, or even to make the obscene and the sexual synonymous. Such exaggerations are false. What obscenity does include is either the public display of matters that are private and personal, or actions that are themselves contrary to chastity and purity. Such a description presupposes that not every form of sexual expression is right, nor every opportunity for sexual gratification an inalienable personal freedom. Indulgence in obscenity can be a sexual sin, a form of cooperation in *sin, or of *scandal, or of the specific scandal consisting in corrupting the young. As a general principle civilized society has accepted the need of constraints on public obscenity. The U.S. civil law has evolved in the direction of narrowing the meaning and thus towards less constraint. A landmark Supreme Court decision (Roth vs. United States, 354 U.S. 476 [1957]), denied that obscenity as such is protected by the constitutional rights of free speech and press; but set norms for determining what is obscene that have made laws against obscenity almost unenforceable: those matters are obscene which, judging from contemporary standards, appeal predominantly to prurient interest. As far as civil society is concerned, then, there is both a strong aversion for censorship and perplexity about standards for constraining obscenity. Obscenity in an objective and concrete sense also is taken to mean the so-called four–letter words or gestures related to them. Obscenities in this sense have become a symbol of rebellion, of morally anarchic counterculture of many young people. Their very attraction is their moral offensiveness, their crudeness, flagrance, and vulgarity.

The Christian standard for such things is guided by the NT: Col 3.8, "But now put them all away, anger . . . foul talk from your mouth"; Eph 5.3, "But immorality and impurity . . . must not even be named among you." See *PORNOG-RAPHY.

[T. C. O'BRIEN]

OBSCURANTISM, opposition to enlightenment, scholarship, and intellectual progress, particularly on the grounds of maintaining religious orthodoxy. Use of the term perhaps derives from the *Epistolae obscurorum virorum (Letters of Obscure Men,* 1515–17). In the conflicts of religion with contemporary philosophy, historical studies, and science (including scientific criticism of the Bible) obscurantism has been a term of reproach against those who reject the validity of these movements. It is applied esp. to those who reject them without serious study and who try to keep others from having the opportunity to consider them. Obscurantism implies a deliberate refusal to examine evidence or arguments that might lead to a change of outlook. It is associated with such features as censorship of books, dismissal of teachers with liberal views, opposition to an educated clergy, and general indifference to scholarship and other intellectual values.

OBSECRATION, one of the components of a prayer of petition according to the theological interpretation of 1 Tim 2.1 in the Vulg, tr. as "supplication": "I urge that supplications (*obsecrationes*), prayers, intercessions and thanksgivings be made for all men." The Lat. *obsecratio* has the specific force of an entreaty solemnly addressed to God in the name of his own holiness in general, and in particular through Jesus in the names of the divine persons, as in the endings of the Collects of the Liturgy (ThAq ST 2a2ae, 83.17). It expresses an attitude of humility, making God's goodness and mercy, not one's own worth, the sole grounds for asking favors (ThAq *In Rom.* 12, lect. 1). The prayers of the Mass prior to the Consecration come under the heading of obsecration, the invocation of the sacred (*idem, In 1 Tim.* 2, lect.1).

[T. C. O'BRIEN]

OBSEQUIOUS SILENCE, an external compliance that cloaks an inner dissent. In church history it refers to the manner of the Jansenist subscription to a formulary imposed by Alexander VII in 1665 (D 2020) on all ecclesiastics and professors of theology: they were to swear their agreement with the condemnation of five Jansenistic propositions by Innocent X in 1653 (D 2001–06) and by Alexander in 1656 (D 2010–12). Condemnation of the Jansenists' obsequious silence towards the formulary came in 1705 with Clement X's *Vineam Domini Sabaoth* (D 2390). Later theology, esp. after Vatican Council I, drew from the condemnation the conclusion that an interior *obedience is required with regard to doctrinal, authentically approved propositions or decrees of the Church, esp. towards those made by the pope.

In practice it is not always clear which teachings are authentically proposed. The kind of acceptance required where the issue is clear is an obedient and internal assent; it is not, however, an act of theological faith.

[T. C. O'BRIEN]

OBSERVANCE. (1) Commonly observance may be taken in the sense of a monastic *rule or *custom with the related meaning of the assiduous keeping of that rule. Thus the adjective *observant refers to a stricter living, but common or even relaxed observance is not always pejorative; observance is to be judged in relation to its purpose and to the real ability of the person to live the observance undertaken. (2) In the classical sense observance is a virtue annexed to justice and concerned with paying the debt of honor and reverence to other persons in positions of dignity. This spirit of *reverence was taken over by Christian authors from Cicero (Augustine, *Sententiae Ciceronis* PL 40, 21; ThAq ST 2a2ae, 102), but with Pauline authority (Rom 13.7). BIBLIOGRAPHY: N. B. Joseph, *Virtue of Observance* (1954); W. Farrell, "Virtues of the Household," *Thomist* 9 (1946) 337–378.

[U. VOLL]

OBSERVANTS, OBSERVANTINES, those members of a religious order, usually Franciscan but sometimes Benedictine, Dominican, or others, who strictly follow the rule of their order. The Franciscan Observants were the successors of the Spiritual *Franciscans. In the 16th cent., the Observants, as opposed to the Conventual Franciscans, attempted to follow the primitive rule. Other bodies appeared among them with the ideal of greater austerity; such were the Reformed Franciscans, *Recollects, *Alcantarines. All these bodies were subject to the minister general of the Observants. In 1897 Pope Leo XIII by the bull *Felicitate quadam* abolished all these differences in the practice of the rule and abrogated the name Observants, giving the Franciscans their original title of Friars Minor. BIBLIOGRAPHY: Hughes HC 3:451–452.

[U. VOLL]

OBSESSION, generally, a preoccupation of abnormal intensity and persistent frequency with some image, feeling, or even idea that the victim declares he does not want. Contemporary psychology inclines to an explanation in terms of compulsive neuroses and *repression, particularly of sexual feeling or the drive for self-assertion. In fact, when external stimulation seems insufficient, such temptations (if and when they are that) may often be interpreted as some form of auto-suggestion, even though this is unconscious. Nevertheless Catholic thought does not exclude another possibility, that of diabolic attack. The Bible depicts Adam, Job, Christ himself, and the early Christian Church undergoing the onslaughts of the devil. Thus, mystical theologians confronted with the data in the lives of the saints categorized internal (images and feelings) and external (visions, noises, odors, levitations, blows) obsession over against *possession in which the devil was supposed to have entered into the body to manipulate it as a machine. Just as the more refined techniques of modern medical and psychological diagnosis have discovered natural causes for conditions once thought preternatural, parapsychology has investigated some external phenomena which can be attributed to causes not yet completely understood, and in that sense preternatural, without these causes being necessarily diabolical. BIBLIOGRAPHY: C. W. Baars, NCE 10:622; A. Royo and J. Aumann, *Theology of Christian Perfection* (1962) 244–248.

[C. CORCORAN]

OBSESSION, DIABOLICAL, see DIABOLICAL OBSESSION.

O'CALLAGHAN, EDMUND BAILEY (1799–1880), physician and historian. Born in Ireland, he studied medicine in Paris, emigrated to Canada, and began a practice in Quebec in 1823. His interest in writing showed early when he edited the *Vindicator* in Montreal. A partisan of the rebels in the revolution of 1837, he fled Canada and lived for many years in Albany, New York. His early historical journal contributions led him to explore the records of Dutch influence in New York State. Mastering the Dutch language he began publication of records hitherto unread. *The History of New Netherland* (2 v., 1846–48) was a landmark. At the request of the state he gave up his medical practice and devoted the years 1848 to 1870 to researching records and publishing the history of the Dutch in New York. His knowledge and scholarly precision were phenomenal. Among significant works were *Documentary History of the State of New York* (4 v., 1849–51) and *Documents Relative to the Colonial History of the State of New York* (11 v., 1853–61). In 1870 Mayor Hall of New York City persuaded O'C. to move there and research the common-council minutes of the city. He edited fifteen volumes before support was suspended in the financial reforms following the Boss Tweed scandal.

[J. R. AHERNE]

O'CALLAGHAN, JEREMIAH (1780–1861), missioner, writer. Born in Ireland and ordained there in 1805, he led a stormy life. He was a fanatical opponent of usury and interest and was censured by his bp. for his statements accusing the Irish Church of silence on the subject. For 10 years he wandered, going to Paris, to New York where Bp. Connolly refused to accept him, to Baltimore, and to Montreal. In that city he wrote *Usury or Interest, Proved to be Repugnant to the Divine and Ecclesiastical Laws . . . .* (1824). Rome demanded that O'C. make peace with his bp., but the latter refused. In 1830 Bp. Fenwick accepted him in Boston and he was assigned to Vermont. O'C. was a zealous and hard-working missionary, founding the first Catholic Church in Vermont at Burlington. He continued to publish

controversial works such as a new edition of his *Usury* (1834), *Banks and Paper Money* (1852), and *Exposure of the Vermont Banking Companies* (1854). BIBLIOGRAPHY: W. Byrne, *History of the Catholic Church in the New England States* (2 v., 1890).

[J. R. AHERNE]

O'CALLAGHAN, ROGER (1912–1954), Orientalist. A Jesuit with extensive background in Oriental studies, O'C. taught biblical studies at the Pontifical Biblical Institute in Rome. In 1953 he was engaged in the American excavation project in Nippur, Iraq. He died in an automobile accident near Baghdad the next year. O'C. published significant studies, most notable being *Aram Naharaim: a Contribution to the History of Upper Mesopotamia in the Second Millennium, B.C.* (1948).

[J. R. AHERNE]

O'CASEY, SEAN (1884–1964), Irish dramatist and prose writer. One of the greatest writers of the Celtic Renaissance, reputed with J. M. *Synge as the two best playwrights, O'C. was born in the slums of Dublin and knew at first hand the miseries of the poor, which he was later to dramatize in grim, satiric comedies usually considered his masterpieces. Self-educated, he received his knowledge from books he borrowed or stole. His early readings in Marx and Engels led to his lifelong belief that communism had the answers to the social and economic problems of the world; this conviction is reflected in his plays. *The Shadow of a Gunman* (1923) was his first play in the series of three powerful, realistic dramas set against the background of the Dublin slums. It was a great financial success. The other two are *Juno and the Paycock* (1924), a fine tragicomedy, and *The Plough and the Stars* (1926). All three plays were written for the Abbey Theatre and performed there with great success. They have in common the superiority of the women characters over the men, who are represented as ne'er-do-wells. In this sense they have been called "hymns of praise to women." When the Abbey Theatre rejected *The Silver Tassie* (1928) an experimental play dealing with World War I, O'C. terminated his connections and went to England where he remained for the rest of his life. His later plays were also more experimental and diffuse. They include *Within the Gates* (1934), *Purple Dust* (1940), *Red Roses for Me* (1942), and *The Bishop's Bonfire* (1955). In addition he wrote a six-volume autobiography, collectively published as *Mirror in My House* (1956) and *The Green Crow* (1956), drama criticism. O'C. was a master of dialogue and characterization. His language was powerful, at times even virulent. He was acidly anti-Catholic. He reveals, however, moral integrity in the handling of subject matter, and the ability to show the effect of major events on the lives of the poor and downtrodden. BIBLIOGRAPHY: D. Krause, *Sean O'Casey: The Man and His Work* (1960).

[S. A. HEENEY]

OCCASIONALISM, the philosophical doctrine that creatures do not exercise true causality but are only occasions for God's causal action in their relations with one another. In its denial of secondary causality occasionalism is closely allied with empiricism. The senses report only a succession of phenomena, not causality as such. Continuous repetition of the same series of data conditions the mind to conclude to a necessary, or causal, connection between them. But this conclusion goes beyond the empirical evidence. In positing God as the only cause occasionalism departs from pure empiricism and introduces questions that are fundamentally metaphysical and theological. In essaying to secure the position of God and his creative activity as totally above and apart from nature, proponents of the system have often fallen into crypto-pantheism. To explain human knowledge they have had to seek some identity of the soul with the divine, while professedly inveighing against the overt pantheism of the metacosmic deity of Spinoza, the apotheosis of nature by Giordano Bruno, the world-soul of the Platonists, or the Arabic misconception of Aristotelian substance as a completely self-contained and self-sufficient mechanism. Against the last the 10th-cent. Muslims known as *Mutākallimūn* (disputants) introduced the idea that the whole universe is constantly being recreated by God, that no part of it endures for more than a mere moment of time. Algazel (al-Ghazzālī, 1058–1111) proposed a completely arbitrary God whose will alone is the reason for the patterns in the world visible at any given moment of time. Through his absolutizing of the individual and denial of the reality of relations William of Ockham also advocated a kind of occasionalism and influenced the thought of G. Biel, P. d'Ailly and N. d'Autrecourt. The doctrine reaches its classical expression in the works of A. Geulincx and N. Malebranche. Following the line of Descartes they taught that true causes must know themselves as such. Nothing can cause unless it can demonstrate how it causes, and so only God can be a cause. Since human ideas cannot be caused by objects encountered nor by the soul itself, Malebranche had to defend some kind of vision of all things in God and the consequent union of the soul with him.

The assertions of its defenders notwithstanding, the doctrine of occasionalism logically undermines the traditional philosophical arguments for the existence of God and man's responsibility for man's acts. BIBLIOGRAPHY: M. R. Holloway, NCE 10:624–625; Copleston, 5:2–4.

[R. T. MEYER]

OCCASIONIST, in pastoral theology, a penitent in a situation that is an *occasion of sin. At issue is the person's own moral self-evaluation and the confessor's judgment of dispositions for sacramental absolution. An intent to live rightly and a true purpose of amendment as part of *contrition include the will to avoid occasions of sin. Clearly these occasions are incompatible with a virtuous and contrite intent if they are, either objectively or by the penitent's experience, proximate and voluntary associations. As to "remote occasions of sin," to risk them must be warranted by reasons proportionate to the risk. More perplexing problems, however, arise over personal associations or circumstance over which the penitent has no control. They are situations or associations not sinful in themselves, but constitute a risk for the particular penitent. He and the confessor must be sure of an honest intent to guard against the necessary risk and to strive to minimize its influence.

[T. C. O'BRIEN]

OCCULTISM, belief in or practice of such pseudosciences as astrology, magic, alchemy, theosophy, and spiritism. The term is used broadly to designate attempts at achieving contact with supposed mysterious powers of nature or the supernatural world and to gain benefit from them. Those practicing occultism also allegedly seek the harm of their enemies. It refers to practices that are neither scientific nor religious, and the Church, along with other official institutions, has generally opposed occult practices as harmful to society, even when church leaders shared the belief of their time that such things could be done. The persistence of occultism is sometimes interpreted as a survival of pre-Christian pagan religions. With varying degrees of seriousness, some groups in recent years have promoted occultism as a way of overcoming an objective, impersonal view of reality.

[T. EARLY]

OCCUPANCY, one of the legitimate titles to *ownership: taking possession, with the intent of keeping, a material object that either belongs to no one or has been abandoned. Practically speaking legal hunting and fishing are examples; maritime laws concerning the rights of salvage determine another form of legitimate occupancy. Theoretically the concept is connected with the legitimation of the right of private *property, i.e., that ownership of the material goods of the earth safeguards their care and fruitful use. The discoveries and colonization of other lands by European countries were considered a case of occupancy; the native peoples were regarded as savages, their lands, therefore, belonging to no one.

[T. C. O'BRIEN]

OCEANIA, the collective name of the islands of the central and S Pacific, lying E of the *Philippines, *Indonesia, and *Australia. Its main divisions are *Polynesia, *Micronesia, and *Melanesia.

[M. J. SUELZER]

OCHINO, BERNARDINO (1487–1564), Italian Reformer. A native of Siena, of the 'Oca quarter, whence came his name, O. became first an Observantine Franciscan (*c.*1512), then a Capuchin (1534). He held high office among the Capuchins and until his defection was considered the most powerful preacher in Italy. Through contacts with Juan de *Valdés and *Peter Martyr Vermigli in Naples in

1536, he began to accept Lutheran teachings and to insinuate them into his sermons, e.g., in a series at Venice in 1539. He fled to Geneva in 1542, his departure being a great blow to his order. His life as a Protestant was spent continually moving about; he lived in Geneva, Augsburg, Strassburg, England (1547–55; he was a prebendary at Canterbury), Zurich, and Poland. As a Catholic he published *Dialoghi sette* (1540 and 1542) on Christian perfection and *Prediche nove* (1541), a collection of sermons. His Protestant writings were translated into many languages; two in English were *The Usurped Primacy of the Bishop of Rome* and the *Labyrinth,* in which he opposed Calvinist teaching on predestination. O. derided celibacy and the religious state; but his theories were also considered excessive by the Reformers. He was expelled from Zurich for his *Dialoghi XXX* (1563), which seemed to attack both the Trinity and monogamy. He found brief refuge in Poland, then in Slavkov (Austerlitz), Moravia, where he died in misery. His thought became more and more skeptical with regard to dogma, and he made the individual conscience the supreme norm of morality. BIBLIOGRAPHY: R. H. Bainton, *Bernardino Ochino* (1940); F. C. Church, *Italian Reformers 1534–1564* (1932).

[T. C. O'BRIEN]

OCHOZIAS, see AHAZIAH.

OCKEGHEM, JOANNES (Johannes, Jean de Ockenheim, Ockenheim, Okenghem, Okeghem; 1430–*c*.1495), Flemish composer, contrapuntalist, founder of the new Netherland School. He served in Antwerp as choir boy (1443–44), in Moulins to the Duke of Bourbon (1446–48), in Paris under Charles VII (1453), as treasurer in Tours at St. Martin's Abbey (1459), and as maitre de chappelle to Louis XI (1465). His work, characterized by an imaginative and flowing style, comprised Masses, chansons, canons, and motets. He was a renowned teacher whose pupils included Josquin des Prés and Pierre de La Rue.

[R. J. LITZ]

O'CLERY, MICHAEL (*c*.1590–1643), Irish Franciscan lay brother, historian, and hagiographer. He entered the order (1622) at Louvain where Gaelic scholars, H. Ward, P. Fleming, and others at the College of St. Anthony, were beginning their work on the lives of the Irish saints. O'C. was sent to Ireland (1626–37) to collect hagiographical material. In addition to this research, he wrote and edited other works on Irish history and religion. With other scholars' assistance, he produced the *Annals of the *Four Masters* (1632–36), which covered Irish history up to 1616. Much of the historical and hagiographical material that O'C. transcribed, discovered, and preserved was used in subsequent Irish histories and lives of the saints.

[R. J. LITZ]

O'CONNELL, ANTHONY, SISTER (1814–97), Civil War nurse. Born in Ireland, she was brought to the U.S. as a child. In 1835 she joined St. Elizabeth Seton's Sisters of Charity in Emmitsburg, Maryland. Sent to Cincinnati in 1837, she administered hospitals and homes for children, founding St. John's Hotel for Invalids, the first such facility in the city. In 1852 she became one of the founders of the Sisters of Charity of Cincinnati. During the Civil War she gave outstanding nursing service to soldiers and was called "the Florence Nightingale of America." After the Civil War her community was given a hospital in Cincinnati by the government, which was renamed Good Samaritan. Her congregation in 1873 opened St. Joseph's Infant Home, the first institution of its kind in Cincinnati, to care for unwed mothers and foundlings. BIBLIOGRAPHY: M. McCann, *History of Mother Seton's Daughters* (3 v., 1917–1923).

[J. R. AHERNE]

O'CONNELL, DANIEL (1775–1857), Irish patriot, called "the Liberator." He was the most powerful figure in 19th-cent. Irish political life and one of the most influential members of the British Parliament. His service to Catholics of England as well as Ireland was monumental. One of the great orators and lawyers of his time, he has become a legend in his own country. Forced to interrupt his studies at Douai English College (no Catholic could attend English universities) by the French Revolution, he studied law in London and was called to the Irish bar. Though a member of the United Irishmen he refused to take part in the uprisng of 1798 and in fact resisted violence as a way to freedom for Ireland all his life. The Act of Union in 1800 abolished the Irish Parliament, whereupon O'C. agitated for repeal of the anti-Catholic laws that kept Catholics from public office. In 1823, with Richard Sheil, he founded the Catholic Association which drew so many members that the British government dared not suppress it. He was elected to Parliament (1828) though not eligible as a Catholic; his victory convinced the Duke of Wellington that the time had come to grant rights to the Irish Catholics. The Emancipation Act of 1829 gave Catholics the right to hold public office, including seats in Parliament; O'C. thus took his seat in the House of Commons. In 1835 he aided in the overthrow of Sir Robert Peel's Conservative ministry and entered a successful alliance with the Whig government. When it became apparent that the Whigs would do nothing for Ireland he founded the Repeal Association, which aimed at ending the Anglo-Irish union. O'C. went through Ireland addressing mass meetings until his arrest on charges of sedition in 1844. After 3 months in prison he was released, but failing health prevented his prosecuting the reform movement. He died suddenly in Genoa, while on a pilgrimage to Rome. Flamboyant, a brilliant orator, and skilled statesman, O'C. left a legacy of nonviolent but effective resistance to British tyranny. BIBLIOGRAPHY: D. Gwynn, *Daniel O'Connell, the Irish Liberator* (1930).

[J. R. AHERNE]

O'CONNELL, DENIS JOSEPH (1849–1927), bp. of Richmond, Virginia. Ordained in Rome (1877), he first served in the Diocese of Richmond under his friend J. *Gibbons, its bishop. O'C. had an important part in the Third Plenary Council of Baltimore (1883) as one of its secretaries, and was a member of the committee sent to Rome to gain approval of its decrees. From 1885 he was rector of the North American College in Rome and representative of some American bps., esp. of Gibbons, by then abp. of Baltimore. In this function he became embroiled in controversy; sympathetic to Gibbons, J. *Ireland, and J. *Keane on such issues as the *Knights of Labor, The Catholic Univ. of America, H. George and the single tax, the school question, and *Americanism, O'C. antagonized the more conservative American bishops. They forced his resignation from the North American College in 1895; he remained in Rome as rector of Gibbon's titular church, Sta. Maria in Trastevere until appointed rector of The Catholic Univ. in 1903. His attempts at academic and financial improvements were somewhat thwarted by a financial scandal in 1904. In 1907 O'C. was made titular bp., then left the Univ. in 1908 to become auxiliary bp. of San Francisco. He was named bp. of Richmond in 1912; the expectation that he would become bp. of some larger diocese was not fulfilled; he remained at Richmond until 1926, when ill health caused him to resign.

[J. R. AHERNE]

O'CONNELL, JOHN PATRICK (1918–60), priest of the Chicago archdiocese, editor, zealous promoter of the liturgy. Despite his editorial responsibilities he found time and energy to contribute to the liturgical movement by writing many articles for different publications and by lecturing to varied groups. He served the National Liturgical Conference as secretary (1946–47), treasurer (1949–52), and editor of its proceedings (1946, 1957–59). BIBLIOGRAPHY: F. R. McManus, YBLS 1 (1960) xi–xiv.

[N. KOLLAR]

O'CONNELL, WILLIAM HENRY (1859–1954), card. abp. of Boston. A native of Lowell, Mass., where Protestant opposition made him more aware of his Catholic heritage, O'C. was ordained in Rome in 1884. The controversies within the American hierarchy centering on Abp. J. *Ireland forced the retirement of D. *O'Connell, the rector of the North American College in Rome, and O'C. was named the new rector (1895). His able administration of the institution drew the attention of Leo XIII, who in 1901 named O'C. bp. of Portland, Maine. O'C. ably headed his new diocese, expanding its parishes, promoting active work by the laity, and bettering relations between Protestants and Catholics. Commissioned by the Vatican to visit Japan and prepare the way for diplomatic relations between the Empire and the Vatican, he was highly successful. As a result he was named coadjutor of Boston with the right of succession, and in 1907 he became abp. of that diocese.

He was a strong administrator, who insisted that all work with financial aspects be brought under his direction. He improved the efficiency of his diocese, though this effort seemed to earn him the reputation of being a cold manager. The archdiocese in his time grew into one of the largest in the U.S.; he fostered schools and hospitals, the Holy Name Society and the League of Catholic Women. He consistently supported the reforms in church music initiated by Pius X. O'C. took positive stands on public issues that he saw as affecting morality and the freedom of the Church. He alienated many by his opposition to such Irish Catholic politicians as James Michael Curley. Because of his Roman training, he was not sympathetic to the Americanization efforts of some in the American Church. O'C. was a consistent opponent of what he saw as federal encroachment on state and local rights. He was a powerful and dominant figure in New England, but not the national figure that Card. Gibbons was. He was essentially devoted to a strong Roman influence and its echo in a centralized diocesan administration. He was a renowned orator; his addresses fill 11 volumes. *Recollections of Seventy Years,* his autobiography, appeared in 1934.

[J. R. AHERNE]

O'CONNOR, EDWIN (1918–68), novelist. A native of Rhode Island, he began his career in radio and commentary on radio and television. He chose to live and work in Boston and began there a long association with the *Atlantic Monthly* and its publisher, Little, Brown and Company. His first widely accepted novel, *The Last Hurrah* (1956), was an exuberant story of Boston Irish politicians. A second study, *The Edge of Sadness* (1961), regarded by many as his best work, deals with three generations of an Irish middle class family; its narrator, Father Hugh Kennedy, is one of the few believable clerics in modern fiction. It won the Pulitzer Prize for fiction in 1962. O'C. is a master of rich characterization, a gentle satirist, possessing an extraordinary ear for the speech of his characters. His own profoundly held Catholicism shows clearly in his novels.

[J. R. AHERNE]

O'CONNOR, FRANK (MICHAEL O'DONOVAN; 1913–66). One of the most gifted of the brilliant Irish short-story writers, he was born Michael O'Donovan, a native of Cork. He took part in the Irish civil war as a republican and spent some time in prison as a result. From early years he was a student of Gaelic and his stories reflect the influence of the old tales and poetry. Through ''AE'' (George W. Russell) he became associated with the *Irish Statesman.* For many years O'C. was on the board of directors of the Abbey Theater. His early collections of short stories: *Bones of Contention* (1936), *Guests of the Nation* (1931), and *Crab Apple Jelly* (1944), established him as a significant voice in fiction. *Stories by Frank O'Connor* (1952) and *More Stories by Frank O'Connor* (1954) are representative of his best work. He also published criticism, biography, and translations. O'C. had a special ability to tell his stories as spoken narrative. One hears rather than merely reads the tales. He demonstrates compassion as well as anger and a fine wit. BIBLIOGRAPHY: V. Mercier, *Great Irish Short Stories* (1964); Autobiography, *An Only Child* (1961).

[J. R. AHERNE]

O'CONNOR, MARY FLANNERY (1925–64), novelist and short story writer. The brief life of O'C. was long enough to create for her a permanent place in American fiction. She wrote essentially from a Christian viewpoint. She was born in Georgia, and her stories are set in the South. Her realism, stark but not shocking, is conditioned by the conviction that even the alienated live in a world redeemed by Christ; even if they fail to live by that vision, the vision remains. Her best work is in the field of the short story. *A Good Man Is Hard to Find* (1955), *The Violent Bear It Away* (1960), and *Everything That Rises Must Converge* (posth., 1965) contain some of the most masterly writing of the age. Her novel *Wise Blood* (1952) caused critics to recognize a strange new talent in American writing.

[J. R. AHERNE]

O'CONNOR, MICHAEL (1810–72), first bp. of Pittsburgh, Pennsylvania. A native of Ireland, he was ordained in 1833. Teaching in Rome he became a friend of Gregory XVI. After several years in Ireland he went to Philadelphia at Bp. F. P. *Kenrick's invitation, as rector of St. Charles Seminary. In 1841 he became vicar general of Pittsburgh. O'C. went to Rome to request transfer to the Jesuits, but while there was named first bp. of Pittsburgh (1843). His tenure as bp. saw tremendous growth in churches and schools, the advent of the Sisters of Mercy, a great increase in clergy, and the founding of the *Pittsburgh Catholic,* the diocesan newspaper. When the diocese was divided in 1853, he was briefly transferred to Erie, Pa., but soon restored. In 1860 he returned to Rome to petition acceptance in the Society of Jesus, which he joined after resigning his see. From 1862 until 1872 he labored as a Jesuit missionary, retreat master, pastor; built St. Francis Xavier Church in Baltimore for blacks, and volunteered to work among the slaves in Cuba. His own apostolate took him from Canada to Louisiana and Cuba.

[J. R. AHERNE]

O'CONNOR, THOMAS FRANCIS (1899–1950), American church historian. A teacher and historiographer of the diocese of Syracuse and the archdiocese of New York, O'C. published a number of journal articles but unhappily left little in writing to reflect his extensive knowledge of American church history, perhaps because of his premature death.

[J. R. AHERNE]

OCOTLÁN, SANCTUARY OF, pilgrimage church near Tlaxcala, Mexico, on the site of a miraculous spring (16th cent.) dedicated to the Virgin of Ocotlán. The exterior (1760) in the style of Mexico City with local decorative and symbolic additions, shows striking red-orange "lizard skin" tower bases. The interior, attributed to Francisco Miguel, has impressive retables and triumphal arch (restored 1939–40) and a fine image-niche *(camarín)* behind the high altar.

[M. J. DALY]

OCTATEUCH, 12th-cent. Byzantine MS, illustrated text of the first eight books of the Bible, probable source for Italo-Byzantine mosaic cycles of OT subjects. Very few survive. BIBLIOGRAPHY: C.R. Morey, *Mediaeval Art* (1942).

[M. J. DALY]

O'CULLENAN, GELASIUS (Glaisne; 1554–80), Irish Cistercian martyr. Born in County Donegal, he entered a Cistercian monastery at a tender age, later going to the Sorbonne in Paris to complete his studies and theological training. Upon his return to Ireland, he became abbot of the Abbey of Boyle, which the English had suppressed (c.1569), ministered to the faithful, but was arrested in 1580. Together with a Premonstratensian colleague, John Kieran of Tuam, he was imprisoned in Dublin Castle and there tortured for his religious beliefs prior to his sentencing and execution.

[E. M. GATES]

O'DALY, DANIEL (1595–1662), Dominican priest and diplomat. He was a teacher and superior (1624) at the Irish Dominican college in Louvain and founded a similar college in Lisbon. With the restoration of the Portuguese monarchy (1640), he became the queen's confessor and acted on various diplomatic missions. After King John's death, he was chief advisor to the queen-regent. He died as bp.-elect of Coimbra. BIBLIOGRAPHY: M. B. MacCurtain, NCE 10:641–642.

[V. SAMPSON]

O'DANIEL, VICTOR FRANCIS (1868–1960), American Dominican, historian. A Dominican from 1883, ordained in 1891, O'D. in his earlier career was professor of theology in houses of his order. From 1907 he was Dominican archivist in Washington, D.C., and after 1913 spent his life in historical research. He was co-founder (with Peter Guilday) of the *Catholic Historical Review* (1915) and served as associate editor for six years. He wrote extensively for the *Review* and published *Dominican Province of St. Joseph* (1930) and *Dominicans in Early Florida* (1942), as well as biographies of several prominent Dominicans in American church history. While he amassed valuable documentation for the Dominican archives, he wrote in an oddly antiquarian style, and was often severely biased in interpretation.

[J. R. AHERNE]

ODD FELLOWS, INDEPENDENT ORDER OF (IOOF), a secret, fraternal society. The IOOF traces its history to several convivial and mutual benefit societies that started in 18th-cent. England. A reorganization and reform undertaken by the Manchester lodge in 1812 led to a federation of Odd Fellows lodges. Thomas Wildey, a member of an English lodge, came to the U.S. in 1817 and established the first Odd Fellows lodge in Baltimore in 1819; lodges were founded in Boston in 1820, and in Philadelphia in 1821. In 1842 the American lodges declared their independence of the English lodges.

IOOF lodges have four degrees: Initiatory, Friendship, Love, and Truth. A higher Encampment lodge confers three additional degrees: Patriarchal, Golden Rule, and Royal Purple. A uniformed parade unit is known as the Patriarchs Militant. The Odd Fellows ritual has undergone many revisions; the most recent was in 1954. The Ancient Order of Samaritans serves as the "fun" organization for the Odd Fellows; female relatives may join the Rebekah lodge. About 1,400,000 men belong to 22,000 lodges in the U.S., Canada, Australia, Germany, Switzerland, the Netherlands, Mexico, Cuba, and Sweden. Membership has declined since the 1920s, and the lodge has difficulty attracting young men or college graduates. The order maintains a chain of homes for the aged and for orphans. Baltimore, Md., is its headquarters. Blacks are not eligible for initiation; they have organized a separate lodge, the Grand United Order of Odd Fellows in America, which is not recognized by the IOOF. Because of its oaths and naturalistic philosophy, the IOOF was condemned by the Holy Office (now Congregation for the Doctrine of the Faith) in 1894. Roman Catholics who joined the IOOF were denied the sacraments but not excommunicated; the religious position of the Odd Fellows was not regarded to be as opposed to Christian teaching as was that of the Freemasons. Individual lay Catholics are no longer forbidden membership in such societies as the IOOF. Some Lutheran bodies and other Protestant churches also forbid membership in the lodges. BIBLIOGRAPHY: W. J. Whalen, *Handbook of Secret Organizations* (1966) 117–125.

[W. J. WHALEN]

O'DEVANY, CORNELIUS (*c.* 1532–1612), Irish bp. and martyr. O'D. became a Franciscan in Donegal and was consecrated bp. of Down and Connor (1583). He was imprisoned in Dublin castle (1588–90) for treason but released for lack of evidence. He returned to his bishopric and escaped arrest until 1611 when he was accused of complicity in Tyrone's rebellion and of visiting the Pope and the King of Spain at the request of Hugh O'Neill. He was convicted and executed for treason. BIBLIOGRAPHY: J. T. Gilbert, DNB 14:864–865.

[T. M. MCFADDEN]

ODILIA, ST. (d. *c.*720), patroness of Alsace and widely venerated in France and Germany. Daughter of Aldaric, duke of Alsace, O. became abbess of Mont-Sainte-Odile and foundress of Niedermünster. According to a 10th-cent. biography, O., born blind, received sight at her baptism. Her intercession is invoked for diseases of the eye. She was celebrated during World Wars I and II because of an apocryphal prophecy attributed to her. BIBLIOGRAPHY: Butler 4:551–553; R. Van Doren and A. M. Raggi, BiblSanct 9:1110–16.

[P. K. MEAGHER]

ODILO OF CLUNY, ST. (962–1049), abbot from 994. Entering the clerical state as a canon of St. Julien at Brioude, he transferred to the monastery of Cluny and became its fifth abbot. O. strengthened internal discipline, increased the number of dependent houses, and formed them into an order. He introduced liturgical innovations such as the Feast of All Souls and sponsored extensive building projects. He stood on close personal terms with important rulers such as Henry II, Conrad II, and Robert II, and travelled widely, thus spreading Cluny's fame over all Europe. BIBLIOGRAPHY: R. Grégoire, NCE 10:643; J. Hourlier, BiblSanct 9:1115–19; *idem, Saint Odilon, abbé de Cluny* (1964); *Cluny, Beiträge zur Gestalt und Wirkung der Cluniazen–Sischen Reform* (ed. H. Richter, 1975).

[R. H. SCHMANDT]

ODIN, JOHN MARY (1801–70), first bp. of Galveston, Texas; abp. of New Orleans. A native of France and a volunteer for mission work in Louisiana, O. came to St. Louis as a subdeacon, joined the Vincentians, and was ordained in 1823. He served on the Arkansas missions and later became rector of the Vincentian seminary, the Barrens, at Cape Girardeau, Missouri. In 1841 he became assistant to the vicar apostolic of Texas, the Vincentian Bp. J. *Timon, and labored there as a missionary for the next 20 years. O. ministered to the Indians and scattered Catholics, cared for the Mexicans in exile, built churches, restored Spanish missions, promoted emigration, and won esteem from the Texans. In 1842 he himself was made vicar apostolic. In 1846 Texas became a diocese and he was appointed bp. of Galveston. With keen awareness of the need for Catholic schools, he brought in the Ursulines, the Ladies of the Incarnate Word, the Oblates of Mary Immaculate, Brothers of Mary, Conventual Franciscans, and Benedictines to serve in the diocese. In 1861 he was named abp. of New Orleans, where he guided the archdiocese through the difficult days of the Civil War and Reconstruction. He became ill while in attendance at Vatican Council I and died in his hometown, Ambierle, France.

[J. R. AHERNE]

ODIUM THEOLOGICUM, lit. "theological hatred," used, however, not of *hatred for God, but to characterize the acrimony, even vilification that occurs at times between disputants in a theological controversy (e.g., in the history of *Jansenism). Sometimes the term may refer to hostility based on religious differences.

[T. C. O'BRIEN]

ODO OF BAYEUX (*c*.1036–97), bishop. O. was a half brother of William the Conqueror, who gave him the see of Bayeux in his youth. Mainly his career was that of soldier and statesman, founding the Priory of St.-Vigor and fighting in the Battle of Hastings. O. was imprisoned, apparently for having led an expedition to Italy, until after the death of William. He rebuilt the Bayeux Cathedral, and it is supposed that he commissioned the famous Bayeux tapestry. An active supporter of the First Crusade (1096), O. died on the way to Palermo. BIBLIOGRAPHY: ODCC 976; B. W. Scholz, NCE 10:644.

[M. C. BRADLEY]

ODO OF CAMBRAI, BL. (Odo of Tournai; d. 1113), abbot, bp., scholar, whose teaching at Toul and Tournai gave new impetus to realism. For 13 years he was abbot of Saint-Martin where he introduced the Cluniac reform. When he was made bp. of Cambrai in 1105 he refused lay investiture from Henry V. BIBLIOGRAPHY: H. Platelle, BiblSanct 9:1100–01; Butler 2:586–587.

[V. BULLOUGH]

ODO OF CANTERBURY, ST. (Oda; d. 958), archbishop. Born of pagan Danish parents, O. became a monk, was made bp. of Ramsbury in 927 and abp. of Canterbury in 942. He restored the bishopric of Elmham, ordered annual visitations in his ecclesiastical province, and founded parish churches. He is known as Odo the Good. His life was written by Eadmer of Canterbury (PL 133:933–944) and by William of Malmesbury, *Gesta pontificum* (Rolls Series 52) 20–24, 30, 248. BIBLIOGRAPHY: W. F. Hook, *Lives of the Archbishops of Canterbury* 1 (1860) 360–381; W. Hunt, DNB 41:421–423; H. Farmer, BiblSanct 9:1092–93; Butler 3:15–16.

[J. L. GRASSI]

ODO OF CHÂTEAUROUX (*c*.1208–73), Cistercian monk, card.-bp. of Frascati. O. studied theology at Paris, becoming chancellor of the Univ. in 1238. He preached the Sixth Crusade in France and accompanied (1248–54) King Louis IX to Egypt and Palestine. Several theological treatises attributed to Odo are of doubtful authenticity. BIBLIOGRAPHY: J. E. Wrigley, NCE 10:645.

[J. E. WRIGLEY]

ODO OF CLUNY, ST. (*c*.878–942) abbot from 927. A native of Aquitaine, O was a canon of St. Martin of Tours, then a monk at Beaume. He transferred to Cluny, became its second abbot, and developed the *ordo* or regimen of Cluniac observance that became a model for the *Cluniac Reform. Zealous for the ideals of Benedictine monasticism, he had a hand in the reform of many older houses that had fallen into decay. He enjoyed the confidence of Popes John XI, Leo VII, and Stephen VIII and carried out missions at their request. A prolific writer, O. composed commentaries on Scripture, poetry, two biographies, and a collection of lectures. BIBLIOGRAPHY: J. Hourlier, BiblSanct 9:1101–04; J. Evans, *Monastic Life at Cluny* (repr. 1968).

[R. H. SCHMANDT]

ODO OF KENT (d. 1200), Benedictine theologian and abbot. Prior of Christ Church, Canterbury, he was active in ecclesiastical politics. He helped to elect *Richard of Canterbury to the primatial see. Instead of being appointed to that see when Richard died in 1184, he was elected abbot of Battle Abbey. BIBLIOGRAPHY: C. L. Kinsford, DNB 14:871–873; Knowles MOE 305–306; M. Chibnall, NCE 10:646.

[J. A. WEISHEIPL]

ODO RIGALDUS (Eudes de Rigaud; d. 1275), Franciscan theologian, abp. of Rouen. At Paris he was the student of *Alexander of Hales and became the regent master of the Franciscan house there (1245–48). He was named abp. in 1248 and was a saintly and zealous pastor. He was a collaborator with Alexander of Hales and others in a commentary on the rule of the Franciscans, *Expositio regulae quattuor magistrorum*; his commentaries on the first three books of Peter Lombard's *Sentences* were unedited, as well as a group of *quaestiones disputatae*. O. *Lottin has shown the considerable influence and importance of O. in the development of medieval moral theology.

[T. C. O'BRIEN]

O'DONNELL, EDMUND (1542–75), first Jesuit martyred by the English government. Irish–born, he became a Jesuit in Rome but died before ordination. He taught in Limerick at the school of David Woulfe, SJ, (1564–68), and raised funds in Madrid for Woulfe's release from prison. He returned to Ireland (1570) but later went back to Spain. Again in Ireland, he was arrested, condemned, and executed. It is probable that during his journeys he acted as messenger in bringing to James Fitzmaurice Pius V's bull excommunicating Elizabeth. BIBLIOGRAPHY: F. Finegan, NCE 10:646

[V. SAMPSON]

ODORIC OF PORDENONE, BL. (d. 1331), Franciscan missionary. After his entrance into the order *c*.1280 and his ordination 10 years later, he began a remarkable career that for 35 years took him to many countries of the Middle and Far East. Working as a missionary in the Balkans and S Russia, he set out through Turkey, Iran, and Iraq to the Persian Gulf for China to join in the apostolate of Abp. *John of Monte Corvino. He touched India and Ceylon before sailing for Canton, China, whence he traveled overland to Peking. After 3 years assisting John of Monte Corvino, he returned by land to Italy, hoping to recruit other Franciscan missionaries for the Orient. At Udine in May 1330 he dictated his journal, one of the famous travel books of the Middle Ages, plagiarized by the author of *Travels of Sir John Mandeville*. Benedict XIV approved his cult in 1775. BIBLIOGRAPHY: A. Van den Wyngaert, *Sinica Fran-*

ciscana (1929) 1:413–495; M. A. Habig, *In Journeyings Often* (1953) 80–108; C. da Langasco, BiblSanct 9:1120–21.

[O. J. BLUM]

ODYSSEUS, chief figure in Homer's *Odyssey*, celebrated in the Latin tradition as Ulysses. He was regarded in early Greek tradition as a symbol of deceit; his heroic image as a man overcoming evil emerged among later Greeks. In Virgil's *Aeneid* O. is portrayed as a deceiver, but Horace's *First Epistle* portrays him as the heroic figure. In the early Christian tradition O. became a type of the Christian in his voyage through life, contending against the forces of evil. In the medieval *Gesta Romanorum* he became a symbol of Christ.

[J. R. AHERNE]

OECOLAMPADIUS, JOHANNES (Gr. form of his surname, Husschyn or Hussgen; 1482–1531), German humanist and reformer of Basel. O. studied at Heidelberg and Bologna, was ordained in 1510, and then studied Greek and Hebrew at Tübingen and Stuttgart, where he first met *Melanchthon. In 1515 he helped *Erasmus with his editing of Jerome and of the NT, and began his own lifelong task of editing and translating the Greek Fathers. After serving as cathedral preacher in Basel and Augsburg, he suddenly retired (1520) to the Brigittine monastery of Altomünster to clarify his thinking. There he wrote *Paradoxon,* a treatise on confession. The tension created in the monastery by his views caused him to leave. He returned to Basel, where he was named professor of Scripture. In 1525 he was made pastor at St. Martin's as well. In his dual role as pastor and professor O. guided the church reform of Basel, drafting its *church order (*Ordinances of the City of Basel,* 1529) and its liturgy. His reform measures helped form Calvin's idea of church discipline. O. participated in conferences at Baden (1526), Bern (1528), and Marburg (1529), where he defended the eucharistic teaching of his friend *Zwingli (see MARBURG ARTICLES). BIBLIOGRAPHY: H. R. Guggisberg, RGG 4:1567–68; Léonard HistProt 1:146–151; 155–160.

[M. J. SUELZER]

OEDIPUS COMPLEX, a psychological phenomenon described by *Freud and incorporated into *psychoanalytic theory as a key concept. Its acceptance is a cornerstone of strict psychoanalytic orthodoxy. In the oedipal period from the 4th to 6th years of life, the male child's strongest love is for his mother. This is a yearning, passionate love seeking exclusive love and admiration in return, and according to orthodox Freudians, connected with feelings of genital excitement. With this love goes jealousy toward the father, who seems to share the mother's love in intimate ways, which jealousy prompts fierce wishes for the father's annihilation; hence the name oedipus after Sophocles' hero who unwittingly killed his father and married his mother. These jealous, murderous wishes arouse conflict because retaliat-

ory punishment is feared and the father is also loved and admired. The punishment feared by the boy is mutilation, particularly castration, which fear becomes so intense that he eventually *represses or abandons the passionate yearnings for his mother which began the conflict. In the case of a girl, the resolution is more complicated; she realizes the lack of male organs (already castrated) and feels shame and rage against her mother who gave her birth with this deficiency. She turns then to her father as the prime love object, and since she cannot possess him exclusively, must also renounce her passionate yearnings. The situation is further complicated by the fact that the boy has a secondary yearning for the father's love and jealousy of the mother, and the girl similar yearning for the mother and jealousy of the father. The oedipal period ends when the child abandons or represses the yearning, jealous, murderous wishes, and passes into the phase of libidinal latency, rebuilding his love and admiration for his parents on less passionate bases. To the degree the wishes are effectively renounced, they will not disturb later emotional development. To the degree that they are only repressed and remain active as unconscious fantasies and strivings, they will tend to be restimulated after puberty when the physical maturing of the sex organs arouses libidinal drives, and will complicate the formation of mature sexual relationships. The unresolved yearnings, jealousies, and rages will attach themselves inappropriately to prospective sexual partners, or will suffer repression as they originally did, with a consequent inhibition of normal sexual attitudes and feelings. According to Freudians, the oedipus complex is a universal human phenomenon, and in most people, the decisive crisis in their psychosexual development. BIBLIOGRAPHY: C. Brenner, *Elementary Textbook of Psychoanalysis* (1957)

[M. E. STOCK]

OEGG, JOHANN GEORG (1703–80), Austrian ironsmith working in Vienna for Prince Eugene of Savoy and introduced by the famous architect B. Neumann to the prince bishop of Würzburg for whom O. wrought the most magnificent grilles in German rococo style: Hofgarten gates (*c.*1734–54), Würzburg, Residenz.

[M. J. DALY]

OENGUS, ST. (Aengus, Oengus mac Oengobann), a saint who is traditionally supposed to have composed the Old Irish martyrology, or more properly Festology (*Félire Oengusso*) *c.*800 A.D. He was one of the Culdees or hermits who later became a monk at Tallaght, of which monastery we also have an early monastic rule and a penitential. BIBLIOGRAPHY: L. Boyle, BiblSanct 9:1128–30.

[R. T. MEYER]

OERTEL, JOHN JAMES MAXIMILIAN (1811–82), editor. O. came to New York as a Lutheran minister in 1837. After moving to St. Louis he became a Catholic (1840) and served for a time as instructor in German at St.

John's College, Fordham, New York. He then became editor of *Wahrheitsfreund* in Cincinnati. In 1846 he founded a newspaper, *Kirchenzeitung*, which became the most influential German-language paper in the U.S. BIBLIOGRA - PHY: J. L. Morrison, NCE 10:648.

[M. J. SUELZER]

OESTERREICHER, JOHN M. (1904–   ), scholar, priest, and administrator. Born of Jewish parents in Stadt Liebau, Austria, after studying medicine and theology at the Univ. of Vienna and Graz, he was ordained (1927) and later served as pastor and professor of religion in Vienna (1928–38). In 1940, O. came to the U.S., and at first worked in the New York Archdiocese. In 1953 he founded the Institute of Judaeo-Christian Studies at Seton Hall Univ., South Orange, N.J. He inaugurated a program of graduate studies with a master's degree (1975), and edited the Institute's organ, *The Bridge*, Vol. I-V (1955–70). Among his writings are: *Racisme-Antisémitisme-Antichristianisme* (1940–43); *Walls are Crumbling* (1952); *Auschwitz, the Christian, and the Council* (1965); *The Rediscovery Of Judaism* (1971); *Anatomy of Contempt: Critique of Rosemary Reuther's Faith and Fratricide* (1975). O. is considered the main architect of the declaration of Vatican Council II on non-Christians that sought to reshape the Church's relationship to the Jewish people.

[R. A. TODD]

OF FAITH, a technical term used to identify three kinds of infallible teaching of the Catholic Church. Depending on the immediate motive for acceptance, a doctrine may be of divine faith, of divine and Catholic faith, or of Catholic faith.

There are truths of revelation that the Church has not (or not yet) declared to be formally revealed in Scripture or tradition. Yet they are objectively doctrines ''of faith,'' and call for this kind of response from the believer insofar as he recognizes their revealed character. The motive for his faith is God, who is infinitely true and therefore will neither deceive nor be deceived. Prior to papal definition, the doctrine of the Immaculate Conception belonged to this category.

Other truths are both revealed and actually proposed by the Church as revealed dogmas. The subjective faith that corresponds to this type of teaching is divine and Catholic. Classic examples are the definitions of Ephesus and Chalcedon on the two natures and one Person in Christ.

Finally, a large body of truth has not been actually revealed by God, except in the generic sense that he gave man the native capacity for knowledge by the right use of his reason. Such truth may belong to the order of principles (metaphysical) or facts (physical) or personalities (moral) and, taken alone, would not come under the scope of Christian belief. But when, for a variety of reasons, any form of this truth touches on the economy of salvation, the Church has the right to pass infallible judgment and declare that a certain principle, or fact, or personality is (or is not) whatever the circumstances of a given situation demand to be certainly known.

This kind of definitive teaching becomes ''of Catholic faith.'' Yet even here the underlying motive for accepting the Church's authority is the revealed word of God that he wants his Church to exercise such authority. BIBLIOGRAPHY: Vat II DivRev; Pius XII, *Humani generis* (tr. and comp. A.C. Cotter, 1951); S. Cartechini, *De valore notarum theologicarum* (1951); E. G. Kaiser, *Sacred Doctrine* (1958) 275–314.

[J. A. HARDON]

OFFA (d.796), **KING OF MERCIA** from 757, the greatest English monarch of his century. O. established Mercian supremacy south of Northumbria, built Offa's Dyke against the Welsh, and negotiated on equal terms with Charlemagne. He received papal approval of a new archbishopric, Lichfield, lessening Canterbury's power (787). BIBLIOGRAPHY: F. M. Stenton, *Anglo-Saxon England* (1947).

[W. A. CHANEY]

OFFENSIVE TO PIOUS EARS (*piarum aurium offensiva*), a theological censure, i.e., a pejorative judgment concerning a theological thesis, indicating that the proposition is obnoxious to the sensitivities of the devout. It was used, for instance, in the rejection of *Fénelon's position (D 2374), also in that of the errors of Quesnel (D 2502), as well as earlier in the condemnation of Baius (D 1980), and elsewhere. The censure *male sonans* (bad sounding; D 1690) is an example of related judgment.

[E. A. WEIS]

OFFERING OF HOLY COMMUNION. One receiving holy communion performs a good and meritorious work with, among other special values, special impetratory value, because it is the reception of the very Author of sanctity (D 1639) and the Bestower of all good. The object of such impetration may be a favor for oneself or the spiritual or temporal welfare of another. To this, oral and mental prayer of petition may be added during the sacred moments of the eucharistic presence. The reception of holy communion is the most intimate way of participating in the Holy Sacrifice of the Mass. One may during such participation have in mind, in particular ways, the other ends of sacrifice also: adoration, thanksgiving, and reparation.

[E. A. WEIS]

OFFERTORY, the part of the Roman Mass where the gifts of bread and wine are presented, placed on the altar, and offered as gifts by the celebrant. In ancient times those to receive communion presented bread and wine in an offertory procession. A sufficient portion of the *oblata* was placed on the altar by the priest who then recited a prayer (prayer over the gifts, later called the ''secret'') which concluded this rite, just as a prayer concluded the other processions of the Mass (entrance and communion). Gallican influences complicated this simple rite with various gestures and prayers which anticipated the element of sacrifice or offering proper to the Eucharistic Prayer. The procession itself gradually disappeared. Recent reforms have simplified the rite, trying to return it to its proper, subordinate place. A symbolic procession, with representatives of the congregation presenting bread and wine, has been restored. The rite is once more called simply "the preparation of the gifts." A collection is generally taken at this time of the Mass on Sundays. BIBLIOGRAPHY: J. A. Jungmann, *Mass of the Roman Rite* (tr. F. A. Brunner, 2 v., 1951–55) 2:1–100. 2:1–100.

[J. DALLEN]

OFFERTORY ANTIPHON, the remnant of the antiphon and psalm (both variable according to occasion) sung during the procession of the ancient Roman Mass as the people who were to receive communion presented gifts of bread and wine. With the disappearance of the procession only the antiphon remained. In the present Roman Mass this antiphon is omitted if it is not sung; other hymns may be used in its place.

[J. DALLEN]

OFFICE, daily prayers and liturgical services of the Church, more specifically, the Divine Office (*Liturgy of the Hours) of the Western Church as the public prayer of the Church for praising God and sanctifying the day. Its daily celebration is required as a sacred obligation by men in holy orders and by men and women religious who have professed solemn vows. Among the community of the faithful its celebration is commended and encouraged. Divided into *canonical hours it consists of the Office of Readings (*Matins); Morning (*Lauds) and Evening Prayer (*Vespers); Daytime Prayer (*Little Hours); and Night Prayers (Compline).

[C. J. NOONE]

OFFICE, ABUSE OF (CANON LAW). In its Book V on penalties, the CIC (c. 2404–14) lists the following as abuses of ecclesiastical authority and attaches appropriate penalties: purloining, destroying, mutilating episcopal documents; falsifying episcopal or parochial registers; bribery, real or attempted, of officials to omit their duties; extortion by raising legal taxes; issuing *dimissorial letters illegally; religious superiors' violation of a bp.'s right to ordain; religious superiors' illegally admitting candidates to novitiate or to profession; a superioress' unlawful use of a candidate's *dowry or her failure to notify the diocesan bp. of reception or profession of candidates; a superioress' interference with the procedures and her subjects' freedom in a canonical visitation; a superioress' encroachment on a subject's freedom of sacramental confession.

[T. C. O'BRIEN]

OFFICE, DIVINE, see LITURGY OF THE HOURS.

OFFICE, ECCLESIASTICAL, a notion which, as defined in CIC c.145.1 involves three elements: (1) a function; (2) determination of range and limits provided by Christ or his Church; and (3) participation of authority by those who exercise it.

From the beginning there was, as St. Paul amply testifies, a distinction of activities in the Church as there is in every body, physical or moral. The Apostle developed at length the notion of the Church as the Body of Christ partly at least to explain and justify the diversity of functions in the Church; a diversity that had given rise to envy and dispute among some of the early Christians.

If the presence of diverse functions is something to be expected, it may not be equally clear that there should be functions fixed by Christ or by the Church and thus institutionalized by stable arrangements. Could not Christ have so disposed that the functions necessary for the Church's life be quite temporary ones, carried out by those who for the moment were charismatically endowed? For the Catholic mind this question is to be answered, not alone by an appeal to the unnaturalness or inconvenience of such an arrangement in a permanent group or body (nor to the confusion that could so easily result), but mainly by an appeal to the intention of Christ in instituting the original apostolate. The Church holds that Jesus selected and separated and specially prepared the Twelve to bear his person and continue his saving action till the end of time; and it is convinced that the stable functions of the Apostles themselves and certain subordinate functions are sufficiently attested by data to be found in the Pauline Epistles and in the Acts of the Apostles.

The third element in the concept is that of participation of ecclesiastical authority. The function is not merely a service, a duty, to meet the needs of others as would be the service of a waiter, an usher, a clerk, but a ministration that maintains the life of the community. Consequently, the one who holds an office does truly serve, but in the way that a father serves the family. The one who holds the office recreates in the community the function of Christ himself, who though he came to minister to others never failed to recall that he was Lord and teacher (Jn 13.13–14). In the light of his example there is no necessary conflict or incompatibility between service and pastoral power, and in the light of the events of the apostolic age, no necessary conflict between such institutionalized functions and the fruitful activity of those charismatically called in every age to tasks of reformation and renewal. BIBLIOGRAPHY: R. Naz, DDC 6:1074–1105; D. E. Heintschel, *Medieval Concept of an Ecclesiastical Office* CUA CLS 363 (1956).

[S. E. DONLON]

OFFICE CATHOLIQUE INTERNATIONAL DU CINÉMA, see ORGANISATION CATHOLIQUE INTERNATIONALE DU CINÉMA.

OFFICE OF READINGS, see MATINS.

OFFICE OF THE DEAD, a variation of the Liturgy of the Hours used on All Souls' Day (2 November) and sometimes, in whole or in part, on the occasion of a funeral, particularly of a cleric or religious. Originally it consisted of Matins, Lauds, and Vespers; its antiquity (at least 7th cent.) and Roman origin were evident in the psalm arrangement and the lack of such monastic and Gallican elements as hymns and introductory prayers. But Pius X added the "little hours" (daytime sections) and the 1971 reform of the Liturgy of the Hours made the Office of the Dead consistent in form with other offices. During the Middle Ages this votive office was often prayed in addition to the office of the day. In recent years a vernacular wake service modelled on the office has become increasingly popular and its use is recommended in the 1970 Rite of Funerals.

[J. DALLEN]

OFFICIALIS (JUDICIAL VICAR), a priest in the diocesan *curia, in modern Catholic practice, who with the diocesan bp. acts as a judge in the diocesan court or tribunal, which decides for or against nullity pleas in marriage cases. This is practically the only remaining role of the office whose roots go back centuries. In the 12th cent. bps. began to adopt the Roman custom of appointing a vicar general and an *officialis* to counteract the quasi-independent powers of archdeacons. The Council of Trent reduced the office of archdeacon to virtually nil, thus paving the way for the evolution of the roles of the post-Tridentine vicar general and *officialis*. The Code of Canon Law (1918) made it an obligation of common law for each diocese to have, in addition to a vicar general, an *officialis* with ordinary jurisdiction for noncriminal cases coming before the diocesan court (curia). The *officialis* is removable at the will of the bp., but his office perdures during the vacancy of the see. He is appointed by the bp. and except in small dioceses cannot also be vicar general; if needs be the bp. may also appoint assistants, *vice-officiales*. The *officialis* and his assistants must be priests of high repute, at least 30 years of age, and hold a doctorate in canon law, or at least possess equivalent canonical knowledge. (CIC, c. 1573).

[E. J. DILLON]

OGILVIE, JOHN, ST. (*c.*1579–1615), Scottish Jesuit, the only officially recognized martyr in post-Reformation times in Scotland. Of noble family, O. was brought up a Calvinist but converted to Catholicism while a student on the Continent (1596). He became a Jesuit (1599), was ordained in Paris (1610), and sought permission to go on the mission in Scotland. His request was granted in 1613. His missionary activity lasted a little less than a year. He was betrayed to the Protestant abp. of Glasgow by a prospective convert, was arrested, and after an imprisonment of about 6 months (during which he was subjected to cruel torture), was condemned to death and hanged at Glasgow Cross (1615). He was beatified in 1929 and canonized in 1976.
BIBLIOGRAPHY: W. E. Brown, *John Ogilvie* (1925); T. Collins, *Martyr in Scotland: The Life and Times of John Ogilvie,* (1955); Butler 1:552–556; N. Del Re, BiblSanct 9:1132–35.

OGNISSANTI, CHURCH OF, Franciscan church in Florence (1251). Rebuilt with Baroque façade in 17th and 18th cent. it boasts impressive Renaissance frescoes: *Madonna of Mercy* (*c.*1470) by Domenico and Davide Ghirlandajo, *St. Augustine* (1480) by Botticelli, and *St. Jerome* (1480) and a *Last Supper* in the refectory, both by Domenico Ghirlandajo.

[M. J. DALY]

O'GORMAN, THOMAS (1843–1921), bp. of Sioux Falls, South Dakota. Ordained in 1863, O'G. served in St. Paul, Minn., until 1878 when he joined the Paulists in New York; from there he travelled throughout the U.S. as preacher. In 1885 his friend Bp. John *Ireland appointed him first rector of St. Thomas College in St. Paul. In 1890 he assumed the chair of church history at The Catholic University of America, where he published in 1895 *A History of the Roman Catholic Church in America*. In 1896 he was named bp. of Sioux Falls. Theodore Roosevelt, after the Spanish–American War, sent him to Rome with Justice Taft to negotiate the settlement of religious order land claims in the Philippines. O'G. was a great builder and brought his diocese many new parishes, schools, and hospitals.

[J. R. AHERNE]

O'HANLON, JOHN (1821–1905), Irish historian, folklorist, and hagiographer. Coming to the U.S. with his parents (1842), ordained at St. Louis (1847), he worked among the Irish immigrants in his diocese until he returned to Ireland (1853) for reasons of health. In and around Dublin he served several parishes and was pastor of Sandymount. Besides his *Life and Scenery in Missouri* (1890), a memoir of his years at St. Louis, he wrote an *Irish American History of the United States* (1903). His *Lives of Irish Saints* (9 v.; 1875–1905), begun in 1856, was a popular work and more valuable hagiographically than his numerous shorter individual lives.

[R. J. LITZ]

O'HARA, EDWIN VINCENT (1881–1956), bp. of Great Falls, Mont., and of Kansas City, Mo., pioneer of Catholic rural life movement. Ordained for Oregon in 1905, O'H. played a major role in the Oregon school case that vindicated the right of parents to send their children to Catholic schools. His work on behalf of minimum wages for women resulted in his appointment by the governor of Oregon as chairman of the State Industrial Welfare Commission. During most of his career O'H. was a force in the Catholic rural life movement. Through his influence, the

Catholic Rural Life Bureau was established by the American bps. in 1920 and O'H. named its first chairman. He published *A Program of Catholic Rural Action* (1922) and *The Church and the Country Community* (1927). Under his direction, the first National Catholic Rural Life Conference was held in 1923. His advancement to the position of bp. of Great Falls, in 1930 led him into intense promotion of the Archconfraternity of Christian Doctrine. Through him, a national headquarters was established at The Catholic University of America, and a decree from Rome ordered the setting up of the Confraternity in every diocese. He was instrumental in revising the Baltimore Catechism, which had been unchanged since the Council of 1884. Through his influence, a revision of the Bible was undertaken in the mid-1930s. In 1952 the first volume of the revision was published by the Confraternity. Named bp. of Kansas City, Mo., in 1939, O'H. embarked on an ambitious program of building, which resulted in 42 churches and 24 educational institutions. In 1954, O'H. was named abp. *ad personam.* BIBLIOGRAPHY: J. G. Shaw, *Edwin Vincent O'Hara, American Prelate* (1957).

[J. R. AHERNE]

O'HARA, JOHN FRANCIS (1888–1960), educator, bp. of Buffalo, N.Y., abp. of Philadelphia, cardinal. A member of the Congregation of the Holy Cross from 1912, he was ordained in 1916. A professor at the Univ. of Notre Dame, he established and served as dean of the College of Commerce. In later years he became the spiritual director of the University, where he achieved fame as an influence on students; in 1934 he became president of Notre Dame. His tenure in that position was marked by improvement and enlargement of faculty and erection of new buildings. In 1939 he was named a titular bp. and military delegate to Abp. F. *Spellman, vicar for the armed forces. During World War II O'H. administered the central office of the military ordinariate, supervised 5,000 chaplains, and visited the camps and stations of the armed forces. In 1943 he was created bp. of Buffalo and in 1952 named to the See of Philadelphia. There he followed an ambitious program of parish and school development, establishing 55 new parishes and 14 new high schools. John XXIII created him a cardinal in 1958. He was never robust, and his labors resulted in poor health in his final years. BIBLIOGRAPHY: T. T. McAvoy et al., RACHS 64, 1 (1953) 3–56.

[J. R. AHERNE]

O'HELY, PATRICK (d. *c.*1578), Irish bp. and martyr. Little is known of his life beyond the facts that he was educated in Spain and Italy by the Franciscans, that he was ordained priest, and that *c.*1576 he was consecrated bp. of Mayo. With a number of clerical companions, he eluded the watch, which the government maintained at all Irish harbors, and gained entrance to Ireland. A few weeks after his arrival he was arrested. Because he refused to deny his Catholic faith or to recognize Elizabeth I as head of the Church, he was condemned and executed. BIBLIOGRAPHY: A. F. Pollard, DNB 14:959.

OHIO, a Midwestern state admitted to the Union (1803) as the 17th state. Robert Cavelier, Sieur de *la Salle, probably discovered the Ohio River (1669–70) and he was followed (1692) by Arnout Viele, an agent of Albany traders. In 1750 the area was explored by Christopher Gist, an agent of the Ohio Company, and the British took firm control of the region after the defeat of Pontiac's Conspiracy (1763–64). With American independence, Ohio became part of the Old Northwest Territory and began to attract Scotch-Irish Presbyterian and New England Congregationalist settlers. Methodism was spread throughout the Ohio Valley by zealous circuit riders, while Baptists and Disciples of Christ could be found throughout the territory. Episcopalians located mostly in urban centers.

Although Jesuits worked as missionaries among the Indians during the period of French control, few Catholics lived in Ohio until the 19th cent. when an influx of Irish and German Catholic immigrants occurred. In 1821 the Diocese of Cincinnati was erected and E. *Fenwick named as its first bishop. Fenwick became embroiled in a controversy over diocesan and Dominican property ownership, but the problem was solved by the Congregation of the Propagation of the Faith, and *trusteeism never became a major issue in the diocese. With 6,000 Catholics in his diocese, Fenwick constructed a cathedral, opened a seminary, and welcomed European priests and financial aid. He also founded the *Catholic Telegraph* the year before his death in 1832. He was succeeded by J. B. *Purcell, former president of Mt. St. Mary's College, Emmitsburg, Maryland. Purcell consecrated a new cathedral, St. Peter in Chains (1845), and 5 years later Cincinnati was raised to archdiocesan status. Its five suffragan sees are now the Dioceses of Toledo, Cleveland, Youngstown, Columbus, and Steubenville.

Purcell's brother, Rev. E. *Purcell, became involved in a banking operation which failed. Not until the administration of Abp. H. J. Moeller (1904–25) did the archdiocese recover from the Purcell bank crisis. Moeller established new parishes, a seminary, the Fenwick Club for Catholic men, and St. Rita's School for the Deaf. In the field of social action, he coordinated charitable efforts under a Bureau of Catholic Charities and supported the Catholic Students' Mission Crusade.

The episcopacy of John T. *McNicholas, Cincinnati's fourth abp., was marked by institutional growth. He opened 50 new parishes, provided mission chapels for rural areas, doubled the number of priests, and introduced the Catholic Youth Organization into the archdiocese. After his death (1950), Abp. K. J. Alter continued his work by engaging the archdiocese in some 350 projects, including reconstruction of the Cathedral of St. Peter in Chains and completion of St. Gregory's preparatory seminary.

In 1976 Ohio's Catholics numbered 2,359,724, or 21.8% of the total state population. The major Protestant sects are the Methodist Church, with 7.9% of the population in 1971, and the Presbyterian Church, with 2.9%. Other Protestant denominations comprised 16.4%. The Jewish population (1968) was 160,715 or 1.5%.

There are 13 Catholic colleges in Ohio, with a total enrollment of 24,647 students. Some 63,471 students attend the state's 88 Catholic high schools. Its 547 Catholic elementary schools are attended by almost 175,291 pupils. BIBLIOGRAPHY: E. H. Roseboom and F. P. Weisenburger, *History of Ohio* (1953); G. F. Houch and M. W. Carr, *A History of Catholicity in Northern Ohio and in the Diocese of Cleveland from 1749 to 1900* (2v., 1903); D. W. Johnson, P.R. Picard, B. Quinn, *Churches and Church Membership in U.S.* (1974).

[J. L. MORRISON; R. M. PRESTON]

OHOLAH AND OHOLIBAH (Oolla, Ooliba), two sisters representing Samaria and Jerusalem respectively in the allegory of Ezek ch. 23. Continuing a tendency begun in Egypt, they "played the harlot" with the Assyrians. Citing the fate of Oholah as God's punishment, Ezekiel warned of a similar coming judgment on Oholibah, i.e., Jerusalem.

[T. EARLY]

OHRMAZD, see AHURA MAZDA.

O'HURLEY, DERMOT (1519–84), abp. of Cashel and martyr. O'H. received a liberal education in Europe, taught philosophy at Louvain and canon and civil law at Reims. Although he was not a priest, O'H. was appointed abp. by Gregory XIII in Rome (1581). He returned to Ireland in 1583, was imprisoned in Dublin castle, tortured on instructions from Walsingham (Elizabeth I's secretary), and hanged in Dublin when he refused to renounce his religion. BIBLIOGRAPHY: J. Hurley, NCE 10:666.

[T. M. MCFADDEN]

OIL OF CATECHUMENS, see OILS, HOLY.

OIL OF THE SICK, see OILS, HOLY.

OILS, HOLY, the oils consecrated by bps. during the Mass of the Oils (Chrism Mass) on Holy Thursday or another suitable day, and by priests under certain conditions, for use in certain sacraments and consecrations. (1) The oil of catechumens (O.S., *oleum sanctum*) is olive or vegetable oil used at baptism and the ordination of priests. It was originally used for the one or more anointings of catechumens in the exorcisms that preceded baptism, but later came to be employed also in the anointing of the hands in the ordination of priests, and in the anointing that was part of the coronation ceremony of Christian kings. (2) Chrism (S.C., *sanctum chrisma*), olive or vegetable oil mixed with balm, used at baptism, in confirmation, at the ordination of a bp., in the consecration of churches, altars, altarstones, sacred vessels, and in the blessing of bells. (3)

The oil of the sick (O.I., *oleum infirmorum*), olive or vegetable oil used in the anointing of the sick.

[C. J. NOONE]

OJETTI, BENEDETTO (1862–1932), Italian Jesuit, moralist and canonist at the Gregorian Univ., Rome, from 1896; author of *Synopsis rerum moralium et juris pontificii* (4 v., 1899–1904) and works on canonical jurisprudence.

[T. C. O'BRIEN]

O'KELLY, JAMES (c.1735–1826), one of the founding fathers of the Christian Churches, which, in 1931, merged with the Congregational Church. A Methodist *lay preacher from c.1775, he was ordained in 1785 and became a presiding elder in southern Va. (1785–92). During much of this time he contended with Bp. F. *Asbury in opposition to Asbury's episcopal authority. Failing to gain the right of ministerial appeal for appointments in the *general conference of 1792, O'K. and his followers withdrew. They at first formed the Republican Methodist Church (1793), which they renamed the Christian Church at a meeting in Surry Co., Va., in 1794. At the same meeting they took the Bible as their only creed and ruled for a single order of the clergy, congregational *independency, and government by the laity. O'K. continued as an itinerant preacher through the remainder of his long life. His followers merged with those of Elias Smith and Abner Jones to form the Christian Denomination, later renamed the Christian Churches. They also felt close affinity with Barton W. *Stone, until in 1832 he merged his followers with those of Alexander *Campbell. BIBLIOGRAPHY: C. F. Kilgore, *James O'Kelly: Schism in the Methodist Episcopal Church* (1963), with complete bibliog. of original sources.

[D. E. STEVENSON]

OKETUS, see HOCKET.

OKLAHOMA, a southwestern state, admitted to the Union (1907) as the 46th state. Most of the territory was acquired by the U.S. through the Louisiana Purchase (1803). Two Catholic tribes, the Osage and Potawatomi, settled in Oklahoma in the 19th century. Not until the arrival of French Benedictines (1875), however, did missionaries reside in the area on a permanent basis. Isidore *Robot, OSB, became the first prefect apostolic for the territory (1876). In 1905 the Diocese of Oklahoma was established, with T. Meerschaert, former vicar apostolic, as its first bishop. His successor, Francis C. *Kelley (1924–48), was founder of the Catholic Church Extension Society. During his episcopate the name of the diocese was changed to Oklahoma City and Tulsa. Kelley was succeeded by E. J. McGuinness (1948–57). Since 1958 Victor J. Reed has been bishop. The diocese is a suffragan of the Archdiocese of San Antonio, Texas. In 1976 Oklahoma's Catholics numbered 106,934, or 4.1% of the total state population. The major Protestant denominations are the Southern Baptist Convention, with

26.3% of the total population in 1971, and the Methodist Church, with 11.6%. Other Protestant denominations accounted for 13.2% of the population. The Jewish population (1968) was 6,480, or 0.25%. There is one Catholic junior college in Oklahoma, with an enrollment of 376 students. Some 2,177 students attend the state's 5 Catholic high schools, and more than 5,273 pupils attend the 30 Catholic elementary schools. BIBLIOGRAPHY: G. Foreman, *History of Oklahoma* (1942); M. V. Thomas, *Catholic Church on the Oklahoma Frontier* (1940).

[J. L. MORRISON; R. M. PRESTON]

OKTOICHOS, see OCTOECHOS.

OLAF I TRYGGVESSON (*c.*964–1000), **KING OF NORWAY** from 995. The *Anglo-Saxon Chronicle* mentions the Battle of Maldon where O. killed Byrhtnod. He later attacked London unsuccessfully. Once he was Christianized, O. forced his new religion upon all alike. Because of his influence Iceland was Christianized about the year 1000 A.D. He met his death by treachery after a visit to Poland.

[R. T. MEYER]

OLAF II, KING OF NORWAY, ST. (995–1030). The patron saint of Norway was son of Harald and king of Norway from 1016. Converted to Christianity at Rouen after a stormy career, he went back to Norway to become its king. He brought priests and religious from England and organized the Church in Norway on English lines. He was more successful in planting Christianity in Norway than his predecessor Olaf I who had used force. A cult in his honor soon sprang up there after his death in battle. BIBLIOGRAPHY: H. L. Sibilia, BiblSanct 9:1138–43.

[R. T. MEYER]

OLÁH, MIKLÓS (1493–1568), Hungarian ecclesiastic and humanist. Ordained in 1516, he was secretary to Louis II, King of Hungary and Bohemia, and a member of the royal council at the time of the king's defeat and death (1526) in the battle of Mohács against the Turks. In 1531 he accompanied the widowed queen to Belgium after Emperor Charles V appointed her his lieutenant in the Lowlands. Here he made the acquaintance of *Erasmus of Rotterdam and other noted humanists. After O.'s return to Hungary, Ferdinand of Habsburg (later Emperor Ferdinand I), who had inherited the crowns of Hungary and Bohemia, made him chancellor of Hungary (1543), bp. of Eger (1548). In 1553 he became abp. of Gran (Esztergom) and primate of Hungary, and in 1562 served for a time as the king's lieutenant. As primate, O. attempted to reform the Church on Tridentine lines by reorganizing the education of priests and by calling in the Jesuits to combat the inroads of Protestantism. He was the author of two works: *Hungaria,* a history of his native land up to the disaster of Mohács; and *Attila,* a biography of the barbarian king.

[E. M. GATES]

OLAVIDE Y JAUREGUI, PABLO DE (1725–1803), Peruvian statesman and economist who, in a varied career, was at one time a leader in the movement against traditionalism in Spain, and then later an apologist for the Catholic faith against secular Enlightenment. He went to Spain in 1752, became chief officer of justice of Seville (1767), and later superintendent of the colonization of Sierra Morena in Peru. In these posts he tried to change the scholastic orientation of the University of Seville and in Peru bring about bold agrarian reform. In 1776 he ran afoul of the Inquisition and after a grueling imprisonment escaped to France (1780). He was at first a friend and translator of the Encyclopedists, later he survived Jacobean imprisonment, and eventually recovered his Catholic faith and became its defender. He returned to Spain the same year (1798) that appeared his autobiographical *El evangelo en triunfo o historia de un filósofo desengañado,* considered a precursor of Chateaubriand's *Le génie du christianisme.*

[E. J. DILLON]

OLD ACADEMY, the school of Plato and his immediate successors, esp. *Speusippus and Xenocrates. *GREEK PHILOSOPHY.

[M. R. P. McGUIRE]

OLD BELIEVERS, Russian Christians who broke with the Orthodox Church over liturgical changes introduced by Patriarch Nikon (1653). He sought to make the ritual conform with Constantinople's, and though only minor details were involved, the new practices were denounced as alien imports. In councils of 1666–67, resisters were anathematized as schismatics (*raskolniki*). Despite severe persecution for many years, they have survived as a conservative, nationalistic group. The *popovtsi* (having priests) maintained a priesthood and grew in importance. The *bezpopovtsi* (priestless) split into various sects.

[T. EARLY]

OLD CALENDARISTS, see PALAIOMEROLOGITES.

OLD CATHOLIC CHURCH OF THE NETHERLANDS, the *Little Church of Utrecht (OBC), which entered the *Old Catholic communion in 1889.

[T. C. O'BRIEN]

OLD CATHOLIC-ORTHODOX RELATIONS. Discussions between *Old Catholics and the Orthodox patriarchates of Constantinople and Moscow, begun in the 19th cent., were interrupted by World War I and the Russian Revolution but were resumed later by Constantinople. Although a Russian synodal committee recommended recognition of the Old Catholic Communion in 1892, areas of disagreement have subsequently increased and become more serious. The Old Catholic-Anglican accord of 1931 regarding inter-communion raised major difficulties for Orthodoxy. The most important meetings between the two Churches were the *Bonn Reunion Congresses of 1874,

1875, and the Bonn Conference of 1931. A commission established by the third *Pan-Orthodox Conference at Rhodes held an initial meeting in 1966.

[T. BIRD]

OLD CATHOLICS, members of a religious body that arose in the 19th cent. as an organized secession from the RC Church in protest against its teaching on papal primacy and infallibility. They accuse the RC Church of deserting traditional Catholicism in the following instances: the Council of Trent, centralizing power in the papacy; the bull *Unigenitus* (1713), demanding blind obedience to the pope's word; Pius IX's issuing the dogma of the Immaculate Conception (1854) without a council; the *Syllabus of Errors* (1864), manifesting papal despotism; and Vatican Council I, proclaiming under constraint the dogma of the infallibility and universal episcopate of the pope.

Denial of papal supremacy by the celebrated canonist Z. B. van Espen (1646–1728) led to the *Schism of Utrecht's inaugurating the independent Little Church of Utrecht (1724), which ultimately became the Old Catholic Church (OCC) of the Netherlands. Van Espen's idea was expanded by J. N. von Hontheim (1701–90), coadjutor bp. of Trier (pseudonym, J. Febronius). He asserted that bps. must govern the Church and that Scripture contained no basis for papal claims to divine right (see FEBRONIANISM). Febronius's ideas were put into practice successfully in the Diocese of Constance by Vicar-General I. H. von Wessenberg (1774–1860), who became the forerunner of the OCC in Central Europe. Vatican Council I aroused German professors including I. von *Döllinger, F. *Reusch, and J. von *Schulte, who issued the *Nuremberg Declaration (1870) that sparked the Old Catholic movement. J. H. Reinkens, elected bp. of the German OCC, was consecrated (1874) by Bp. H. Heykamp of Utrecht. Humanism and rationalism contributed to the birth of the Swiss Christkatholiken, chiefly a lay movement; Reinkens consecrated the first bp., E. Herzog (1878). The Austrian OCC began in 1872, but the government allowed it no bp. until 1925. Also traceable to the late Habsburg era and belatedly obtaining a bp. (1924) was the OCC of Czechoslovakia. Disputes with Italy and traditions of independence brought forth the Yugoslav OCC (1923). The Old Catholic Communion, the *Union of Utrecht, dates from 1889. Members are: the Dutch, German, Swiss, Austrian, Czech, and Yugoslav (Croatian anti-Kalogjera segment) OCC; the *Polish National Catholic Church in America and Poland (founded by F. *Hodur); the largest, the *Philippine Independent Catholic Church was accepted as a member in 1965. These Churches include about 2,400,000 persons (see MARIAVITES). Several British and European Churches style themselves Old Catholic but are not recognized by the Utrecht Union. This is also true of the following in the U.S.: *American Catholic: Archdiocese of New York, American Catholic (Syro-Antiochean), Christ Catholic, and the two North American Old Roman Catholic Churches. The Liberal Catholic Church traces its apostolic succession through the Dutch OCC. The *Bonn Agreement (1931) established intercommunion between the Utrecht Union and the *Anglican Communion.

The doctrinal standard is the *Declaration of Utrecht. Scripture is the primary rule of faith, and genuine tradition is an authoritative source of teaching. The bp. of Rome is recognized solely as "first among equals." Faith working by love is the means of man's justification. The Declaration accepts the seven sacraments (auricular confession is optional for adults), *apostolic succession, the obligation to hear Mass on Sundays and holy days, and commemoration of the faithful departed. The eucharistic *Real Presence is professed, but not transubstantiation. Divorce is forbidden. Old Catholics reject the treasury of merits of saints; the Immaculate Conception and Assumption of Mary as well as the title "mediatrix of all graces"; compulsory days of fast; indulgences; pilgrimages; processions; veneration of the saints, relics, and images; sacramentals; the Roman Index of Forbidden Books; male religious orders; obligatory reading of the Breviary by priests; and temporal power and privilege for Church and clergy. Clerical marriage, mixed marriages, cremation, and communion under both kinds by *intinction are allowed. The Polish National Catholic Church and the Philippine Independent Catholic Church have minor variations in doctrine and practice.

Church edifices and ornaments are similar to those of the RC Church, but simpler. Liturgy for services and sacraments is based on the Roman rite and uses the vernacular except for the formula "Receive the Holy Ghost," which is said in Latin at a bp.'s consecration. In the Creed the *filioque* is omitted. Rites are recited aloud with the congregation participating. Sunday readings are spread over a 5-year cycle. Each OCC is a national Church; its bp. (abp. in the case of Utrecht) rules as a constitutional monarch. The supreme government is the synod, comprising the bp. and synodal council members (priests and lay representatives of the parishes). Meeting annually, the synod is chaired in Germany by the bp., but in Austria and Switzerland by a layman; it legislates but may not alter or add dogma; by majority vote it elects the bp. who (in Europe) must seek approval by the civil government. The synod chooses members of an executive body, composed of the bp., three priests, and five laymen, which is responsible to the synod. The synod also elects four jurymen of the synodal court; the bp., an ex-officio member, appoints three judges; cases may be appealed to the synod. Each parish elects its own pastor. BIBLIOGRAPHY: V. Conzemius, "Catholicism: Old and Roman," *Journal of Ecumenical Studies* 4 (1967) 426–445; C. B. Moss, *Old Catholic Movement* (1966); F. Dvornik, *Ecumenical Councils* (1961) 100–101.

OLD LATIN VERSION (*Vetus Latina*), designation for Latin translations of the Bible prior to St. Jerome (*c.*342–420). Though such translations existed from the 2d cent., the translators are unknown and no complete Old Latin Bible survives. Parts are found in the *deuterocanonical portions of the Vulgate OT, in lectionaries, quotations in works of Latin authors, and some codices. Scholars distinguish two principal types of Old Latin text—African and European. The *Collectanea biblica latina* (1912–), and the *Vetus Latina* (1956–) of the Abbey of Beuron are modern editions of the Old Latin.

[T. EARLY]

OLD ORDER AMISH, the most conservative of the *Amish Mennonites. The designation "Old Order" came into use between 1850 and 1870, to connote the resistance of these Amish to modernization either in church life or in manner of living. They continue to wear plain, 18th-cent. dress, live apart, and resist the use of modern machinery and appliances. Because they worship in private homes, they are sometimes called "House Amish," while more progressive Amish Mennonites are called "Church Amish." The Old Amish use German in worship services; in daily life among themselves they use a German dialect, "Pennsylvania Dutch." They object to education above an elementary level. There are settlements in Pennsylvania, Ohio, Indiana, and Iowa. The main organized body is the Old Amish Mennonite Church; there are some Unaffiliated Conservative and Amish Mennonite Churches. Baptized (i.e., adult) members in the U.S. and Canada number nearly 25,000. BIBLIOGRAPHY: MennEnc 1:43–47.

OLD-ROMAN CHANT, a repertory of liturgical *chant surviving in five musical MSS (three *Graduals and two *Antiphonaries) written in Rome between 1071 and *c*.1250. Comparison with the *Gregorian chant repertory reveals essentially the same Mass and Office structure, calendar, and texts. Noteworthy in the Old-Roman are the absence of a Mass for the fourth Sunday of Advent, a special *Vespers during Easter week, lack of hymns, use of only eight responsories in *Matins, and a "double" Matins for Christmas and the Feast of SS. Peter and Paul. The musical differences are more basic, showing two distinct yet cognate traditions. In general, one finds similar melodic shapes but independent stylistic development, the Old-Roman generally being more *melismatic. Perhaps more interesting is the historical relationship of the two repertories, all the more intriguing because of the MS evidence. While all five Old-Roman sources are definitely Roman and pre-1250, not one MS of Gregorian chant is known to have been written or used in Rome before the mid-13th century.

Many theories have been proposed to explain the liturgical and musical disagreement as well as the MS situation. Dom *Mocquereau focused attention on the Old-Roman chant (which he called Vatican) as early as 1891, concluding from a study of three of its sources that the Old-Roman melodies constituted a post-Gregorian transformation. Dom Andoyer's slightly later studies revealed a more ancient liturgical practice in the Old-Roman and the absence of feasts added to the Gregorian after *c*.800; he therefore classified the repertory as pre-Gregorian. A summary of the current state of research follows.

On the basis of historico-liturgical evidence (Andrieu, *Les Ordines Romani* 3 [1951] 211–227), B. Stäblein believes that both chants are of Roman origin and that Old-Roman is earlier, revised into Gregorian in the late 7th century. J. Smits van Waesberghe points to veiled references in the *Liber pontificalis* to a struggle for liturgical primacy between Roman monks and clergy in the 7th cent. as further testimony that two chants may have existed in Rome at this time, one for each group. Other historico-liturgical evidence has attracted still other scholars to this view; but examined critically, the documents are subject to various interpretations. However probable the theory may be, no substantial evidence for it has yet been found.

Some musicologists have sought answers from the music itself. H. Hucke, for example, comparing the gradual chants of both repertories, concludes that the more direct Gregorian melodies are arrangements of the Old-Roman, made not in Rome but in a different stylistic environment with different esthetic preferences—in Carolingian France. W. Lipphardt, however, sees the Old-Roman as the later version, produced not by deliberate revision but by a presumed oral tradition in Rome. Taking into account the appearance of Gregorian chant MSS in Carolingian domains around the end of the 9th cent. but the total lack of any chant MSS in Rome before 1071, he suggests the chant that accompanied the Roman liturgy into France in the 9th cent. was the Gregorian, orally transmitted in Rome but written down and fixed in France. The Old-Roman is the result of two more centuries of oral transmission of those same melodies in Rome. Lipphardt proposes, then, that we have the Roman chant in two stages of development: in the 9th cent. form as recorded in France, and in the 11th-cent. form as recorded in Rome.

All theories advanced so far, however, must be considered inconclusive. The historico-liturgical evidence is of questionable value; the musical studies are incomplete. At present we are unable to determine whether the melodic differences can be attributed to evolution in an oral tradition, or if the simpler version means an early stage of development or a late revision. Clearly what is needed most now is a systematic and exhaustive musical comparison of the Old-Roman and Gregorian chants. Perhaps then it will be possible to describe more exactly their relationship and to trace more clearly the development of each. BIBLIOGRAPHY: M. Huglo, "Le chant *vieux-romain*: Liste des manuscrits et témoins indirects," *Sacris erudiri* 6 (1954) 90–124; H. Hucke, "Zu einigen Problemen der Choralforschung," *Die Musikforschung* 11 (1958) 385–414; P. F. Cutter, "Question of the 'Old-Roman' Chant: A Reappraisal," *Acta musicologica* 39 (1967) 2–20.

[P. F. CUTTER]

OLD TESTAMENT, division of the Christian Bible, a term first used *c*.170 A.D. by Melito of Sardis. The word testament, from the Lat. *testamentum,* last will, is a mistranslation of the Greek *diathēkē,* which in the Bible means "covenant." The *Hebrew Bible falls into three main divisions, the Law (Gen, Ex, Lev, Num, and Dt), the Prophets, subdivided into the Former Prophets (Jos, Jg, 1–2 Sam, 1–2 Kg) and the Latter Prophets, comprising the Major Prophets (Is, Jer, and Ezek) and the 12 Minor Prophets (Hos to Mal), and finally the Writings, comprising Ps, Job, Pr, Ru, S of S, Ec, Lam, Est, Dan, 1–2 Chr, and Ezra-Neh. This completes the official Hebrew canon. The OT in the Protestant Bible corresponds, but Catholics also accept the following *deuterocanonical books: Tob, Jdt, Wis, Sir, Bar, 1–2 Macc, and additions to Est and Dan. The composition of the OT was a process extending from *c.* 1200 to *c.* 100 B.C. (see CANON, BIBLICAL).

The Law or Pentateuch. The evolution of the Law or Pentateuch has been admirably described by G. von Rad. Its heart and center is constituted by two broad complexes of tradition. The first of these commemorates the events of the exodus and the entry into the promised land, and is epitomized in the ancient cultic "credo" as preserved, for instance in Dt 26.5–10. The second tradition complex is centered upon the *covenant. It displays the basic structure of the Hittite vassal treaty: a solemn proclamation of Yahweh's name is followed by a reminder of his past favors as a motive for the people's gratitude and future faithfulness. This leads on to the solemn proclamation of Yahweh's will in law and the sealing of the covenant, in which the people commit themselves to obey this law. A list of blessings for obedience and cursings for disobedience is then appended. Into this structure various further law-codes associated with the covenant were later inserted.

These two basic complexes are then united and further expanded by the inclusion of a number of previously independent units and complexes of tradition—some very ancient—relating to the patriarchs and centered primarily upon the promise of land and seed. This patriarchal history too is seen as orientated toward the covenant promises as the goal of Yahweh's plan and purpose, in which his own glory and his people's happiness are to be achieved. A further stage in the process of development is the prefixing of one version of the primordial history (Gen Ch. 1–11), which makes the implementation of the divine plan begin not merely with the promise to Abraham but with the Creation of the world. Finally the whole body of tradition acquires a fresh level of interpretation when the 10th-cent.–*Yahwist (J) writer, who was probably attached to Solomon's court, aligns the whole with the accession of Solomon himself and the glories of his kingdom. These are now seen as implementing and fulfilling Yahweh's plan and purpose right from the Creation onwards.

The strand of tradition thus unified and re-orientated constitutes the earliest and the chief of the four major strands of which our present Pentateuch is composed. A second strand, the *Elohist (E), was written perhaps some 100–200 years later. The author of E, perhaps disillusioned by the corruptions of the northern kingdom in which he seems to have lived, appears concerned to relate the events in such a way as to revive the spirit and values of Moses and the patriarchs. Hence his story begins with Abraham. The third main component of the Pentateuch, the Deuteronomist (D), is mainly confined to Deuteronomy. This again preserves ancient traditions but seems to have come to its full flowering in the 7th cent. under the reforming king Josiah. It is characterized by a concept of worship which consists primarily in cherishing, heeding, and obeying Yahweh's words, remembering his past favors and being dedicated to his service to the absolute exclusion of all alien or idolatrous influences. It also lays special emphasis on the duty of caring for the poor and defenseless. A fourth tradition strand, the Priestly (P), belongs to the late 5th century. It retells the story from the creation onwards in such a way as to show the whole of creation converging in space and time upon the moment when Yahweh actually descends upon the shrine in the midst of his people and makes it his dwelling. Round this shrine the people are ranged in an ordered hierarchy to express their worship through the medium of their priests in a ceaseless round of ritual and sacrifice. Elaborate and detailed laws governing the building and decoration of the shrine itself, the vestments, ordination, privileges, and obligations of the priests, the forms of worship and the ritual purity which the people must constantly preserve, are included in Ex, Lev, and Numbers.

Probably the whole Pentateuch acquired substantially its present form in the 4th century. The existing division into five books may be prompted by liturgical considerations connected with synagogue worship.

The Former Prophets. Underlying traditions date from the 12th cent.; the books were probably completed between 600 and 560. The high points of this section are unquestionably the choosing of David and of Zion, the inauguration of Solomon, and the building of the temple. The rest of the tradition material incorporated—the stories of heroes, judges, and prophets, the accounts of wars, and the annals of the kings, etc.—all tends to be secondary. But a further level of interpretation has been superimposed upon the whole complex by Deuteronomist editors in such a way that it now displays a recurrent pattern of sin, chastisement, repentance, and deliverance until the increase in sin, for which the later kings are chiefly blamed, finally leads to the ruin and Exile of 587.

Latter Prophets. Composition was from 750 (Amos) to the 3d cent. (the *Minor Prophets). The message here is primarily and basically concerned with the judgment of Yahweh. This is to fall either on the people or on specific classes for their sins (chiefly pre-Exilic Prophets) or else upon those who ill-treat the Israelites or triumph over their misfortunes (chiefly post-Exilic Prophets). But the Prophets also predict the survival and restoration of an Israel purged and renewed. This is to be achieved through a "righteous remnant" led by a divinely inspired *Messiah (First Isaiah) through a new covenant greater and more glorious than the old one, which the people have so radically betrayed (Jer), in a new and more glorious land reorganized and repeopled after the Exile with a new Zion and a new temple at its center to supply it with miraculous fruitfulness and healing (Ezek). All this is to take place when the people return from Babylon in a new and more glorious Exodus (Deutero-Isaiah). Salvation and restoration are to come through a supreme charismatic figure, a ''prototype'' Israelite who is to proclaim Yahweh's Law to all the Gentiles, to suffer vicariously for his people's sins, and at last to receive glory and honor from all (the *Servant of the Lord Oracles). The basic themes of judgment and restoration are continued with variations in the *Minor Prophets.

The Writings. Sources date from the 10th cent.; composition extended to the 2d century. These are obviously more heterogeneous in character, and their function in the OT as a whole is correspondingly more difficult to define. Broadly speaking, however, they do not express God's dynamic will and plan for his people in the same direct sense as do the Law and the Prophets, but rather the people's own reaction to that will and their inspired reflections upon the significance of its workings. The Psalms, most of which were composed in the context of the Temple and its cult, express, in a manner recognized as sacred in the ancient Near East, the basic attitudes of the prayer with which Israel responds to, appeals to, or praises her covenant God. Proverbs, Sir, and Wis teach that the wisdom that enables man to live harmoniously and happily in all departments of human life comes from God and is a charism bestowed upon his people by him. Job and Ec, without solving it, reflect on the problem of evil as it bears upon the individual Israelite's relationship with his covenant God.

The deuterocanonical books were all composed in the last 2 pre-Christian centuries.

If there is one supreme and all-pervasive characteristic of the OT, it is, as W. Eichrodt asserts, its essentially forward movement, dynamic, purposive and irresistible, and its inexorable demand for a fulfillment that lies beyond itself. BIBLIOGRAPHY: A. Robert, A. Feuillet, *Introduction to the Old Testament* (Eng. tr. 1968); O. Eissfeldt, *Old Testament: An Introduction* (Eng tr. 1965); A. Weiser, *Old Testament: Its Formation and Development* (Eng tr. 1961); H. H. Rowley, *Growth of the Old Testament* (1950); J. L. McKenzie, *Two-Edged Sword* (1959); G. Von Rad, *Old Testament Theology* (Eng tr., 2 v., 1962, 1965).

[D. J. BOURKE]

OLD TESTAMENT POETRY, see POETRY OF THE OLD TESTAMENT.

OLDCASTLE, JOHN (d. 1417), *Lollard. O. took part in military expeditions to Scotland (1400), Wales (1401), France (1411); he also served as a member of Parliament from Herts (1404). Sometime before 1410 he embraced Lollard teaching; before *Convocation under Abp. T. *Arundel in 1413 he denied transubstantiation and auricular confession. Imprisoned, he escaped from the Tower of London, took part in the Lollard uprising of 1414 and in subsequent conspiracies until he was captured and executed. A cent. later he was given a place in *Foxe's *Book of Martyrs.* Falstaff in the original version of Shakespeare's *Henry IV* was called Sir John Oldcastle, but O. was not the model for Shakespeare's character. BIBLIOGRAPHY: K. B. McFarlane, *John Wycliffe and the Beginnings of English Nonconformity* (1953); J. Tait, DNB 42 (1895) 68–93.

[T. C. O'BRIEN]

OLDEGAR, ST. (Oleguer, Ollegarius; 1060–1137), abp. of Tarragona. Ordained in Barcelona, O. became prior of Saint-Adrian (Provence, 1099), abbot of Saint-Ruf (Avignon, 1113), bp. of Barcelona (1116), and first abp. of the restored Tarragona metropolitanate (1118). As political counselor, preacher of the Spanish crusade, and symbol, he helped prepare Catalonia's later union with Aragon. BIBLIOGRAPHY: R. I. Burns, NCE 10:677–678; M. Rodés, BiblSanct 9:1172.

[R. I. BURNS]

OLDHAM, HUGH (d.1519). He studied arts, canon and civil law at Oxford, and served as bp. of Exeter 1504–19. Chaplain to Margaret Beaufort, Countess of Richmond, O. was king's clerk and chaplain by 1503. He was a benefactor of Corpus Christi College, Oxford, and chief benefactor in the endowment of Manchester Grammar School. BIBLIOGRAPHY: Emden Ox 2:1396–97.

[C. D. ROSS]

OLDMEADOW, ERNEST AMES (1867–1949), English novelist, editor, and journalist. He had been a minister in Nova Scotia when he was converted from Methodism to Catholicism in 1897. He edited the London *Musical Times* until 1923, when he took James Milburn's place as editor of the *Tablet,* a Catholic paper. In his columns he strove to maintain an apologetic and polemical Catholic line against the C of E, but popular interest continued to wane and O.'s editorship ended in 1936. *Antonio* (1909) was the most notable of his many Edwardian romantic novels; in addition to his fiction he wrote several studies of composers, and a two-volume biography *Francis Cardinal Bourne* (1940–44).

[R. J. LITZ]

OLDOINI, AGOSTINO (1612–83), Italian Jesuit, historian of the papacy, notably in his *Vitae et res gestae pontificum Romanorum et s.r.e. cardinalium* (4 v., 1670–77), a revision of an earlier work of Alfonso Ciacconius up to the pontificate of Clement IX (1667–69).

[T. C. O'BRIEN]

O'LEARY, HENRY JOSEPH (1879–1938), Canadian bishop. He was ordained (1901) and consecrated bp. of Charlottetown, Prince Edward Island (1913), where he devoted much concern to St. Dunstan's Univ. and to questions of social justice. In 1920 he was transferred to Edmonton, Alberta, where his interest in social action found considerable scope in labor problems and in the agricultural depression and drought relief in the 1930's.

[R. K. MacMASTER]

OLEGUER, ST., see OLDEGAR, ST.

OLEVIANUS, CASPAR (Olevian; 1536–87), *Reformed theologian. O. was a doctor of law when he became interested in Calvinism. He studied theology at Geneva and Zurich (1557), and became a preacher and teacher at Trier until 1560. At the invitation of the Calvinist Elector Frederick III, O. went to Heidelberg. There as professor, pastor, and church councilor (1560–71), he was one of those principally responsible for the *Heidelberg Catechism (1561), a ritual (1563), and a Genevan type of church discipline (1570). After Frederick's death and the reestablishment of Lutheranism in the Palatinate, O. labored successfully for the Calvinist cause in the Hesse-Nassau region of Germany. His theological writings were an expression of the characteristic teachings of John Calvin and the *covenant theology of J. *Bullinger. BIBLIOGRAPHY: J. F. G. Goeters, RGG 4:1626; J. Ney, EncRelKnow 8:235; bibliog. for Heidelberg Catechism.

[T. C. O'BRIEN]

OLGA, ST. (Helga, d. 969), wife of the Russian Prince Igor, at whose death (945) she became regent for her son Svyatoslav. She sought an alliance with Byzantium through the introduction of Christianity and was baptized at Constantinople in 957. To appease the Scandinavian boyars she requested a bp. for Kiev from the German Emperor Otto. But Bp. Adalbert did not reach Kiev until after O. had been forced to cede power to her son who shared none of his mother's interest in Christianity. Although she failed to Christianize her country, O. is recorded in Russian annals as the first Kievan saint and has been venerated there and in Bohemia from 1072. Unfortunately, details of her life are not recorded. BIBLIOGRAPHY: G. Vernadsky, *Kievan Russia* (1948); A. Koren, BiblSanct 9:1149–52.

[L. NEMEC]

OLIER, JEAN JACQUES (1608–57), mystic, founder of the Sulpicians and the seminary of St.-Sulpice in Paris; leading author of the French school of spirituality, Parisian-born, he was son of Jacques Olier de Verneuil, secretary of Henry IV and later intendant at Lyons, where the son studied with the Jesuits, 1617–24 (there Francis de Sales encouraged him to be a priest). In Paris, at the Collège d'Harcourt until 1627, the Sorbonne until 1629; in Rome for Hebrew, he lost his sight, restored only after a Loreto pilgrimage. Student for the licentiate in Paris, he was ordained priest in 1633. Embarrassed by benefices given him, he used them to do God's work. His missions (1634–39) in the

Auvergne and Brittany were very fruitful, but the attempt to found a seminary at Chartres failed. He refused St. Vincent de Paul's urging to accept the Langres bishopric, but C. de *Condren through the mystic Marie Rousseau pointed the way for O. to renew the priesthood as Trent decreed. He began a seminary at Vaugirard, transferred it in a year to Paris where as pastor, with his new Society, he revivified the tumultous parish of St.-Sulpice. The model Sulpician seminary trained priests who went to other dioceses to direct clerical formation. Notable are seminaries he undertook at Nantes (1649), Viviers (1650), LePuy (1652), and Clermont (1653). O.'s mission spirit embraced England (Charles II profited from his spiritual counsel, 1653) and Canada where to honor Mary he sent Sulpicians to Montreal. Migne edited his *Oeuvres* (1856–57); influential today, they amplify his priestly work of but 24 years, and with his *Mémoires* (written for his director) and *Lettres spirituelles* (1672) manifest his zeal for souls, his love of Mary, his respect for the poor, and his spiritual teaching (see SULPICIAN SPIRITUALITY.) Suffering marked his final days. St. Vincent assisted at his death at Issy. BIBLIOGRAPHY: *Life:* M. Faillon (3 v. 1861, 4th and enlarged ed. 1873; E.H. Thompson (1885); P. Pourrat (Eng. tr. W.S. Reilly, 1932); Bremond 3:419–507

[M. R. BROWN]

OLIGARCHY (from Gr. *oligos*, few, and *archein*, to rule), government by the few, but not because of their political merits, for in that case it would be *aristocracy. In industrial countries managers of large units geared to mass production, communication, and consumption, not landowners, increasingly tend to exercise great political power.

[T. GILBY]

OLIGER, LIVARIUS (1875–1951), Franciscan historian. O. held the chair of Franciscan history at the Antonianum, Rome (1906–50), was associate editor of the *Archivum Franciscanum historicum* (1911–15) and founder of the journal, *Antonianum* (1926–   ). He was the author of numerous works in Franciscan history, biography, and hagiography, producing pioneer studies of the Fraticelli, Franciscan Spirituals, and Brethren of the Free Spirit. BIBLIOGRAPHY: L. Spatling, "P. L. Oliger," *Franziskanische Studien* 32 (1950) 362–381; O. J. Blum, NCE 10:680.

[O. J. BLUM]

OLIGON, in *Byzantine chant notation, one of the *somata, or signs indicating a note one scale step higher than the previous note. This is the commonest of the three signs indicating a scale step higher. Oligon is used with unaccented notes.

[A. DOHERTY]

OLIVA, ABBEY OF, Cistercian monastery near Danzig. Founded in 1178, it served as a center of German expansion and missionary activity among the pagan Prussians. In 1224

it was destroyed by the Prussians. The rebuilt abbey suffered much during recurrent wars but was each time reconstructed. In the 18th cent. the abbey's gigantic Gothic church (over 300 feet long) was redecorated in Baroque. Oliva was suppressed in 1831 but its church continued to serve the local parish; in 1925 it became the cathedral of the new Diocese of Danzig. In 1945 the monastery was revived by Polish Cistercians.

[L. J. LEKAI]

OLIVAINT, PIERRE (1816–71), French Jesuit martyr under the Commune. Superior of the Jesuit residence at Rue de Sèvres from 1851, he distinguished himself as a preacher. He was an able spiritual director and showed great zeal in his retreat and sodality work and in the field of social action. His cause was introduced in Rome in 1937. BIBLIOGRAPHY: Fliche-Martin (1952) 21:7–8, 373 and *passim*; Sommervogel 11:1841–42; P. Molinari, BiblSanct 9:1169–71.

[J. P. REID]

OLIVER, BERNARD, see BERNARD OLIVER.

OLIVÉTAN, PIERRE ROBERT (c.1506–38), early French Reformer, and translator of the Bible; he signed himself "Louis Olivier." O. was a cousin of John *Calvin and had been won over to the Protestant reforms in the 1520s. Theodore *Beza in his *Life of Calvin* stresses O.'s influence on the young Calvin when the latter was a student at the Univ. of Paris. O. fled France for Strassburg in 1528, where he continued his study of Greek and Hebrew. Later at Neuchâtel, where he was principal of a school, he undertook a French translation of the Bible at the request of the Waldenses of Piedmont. This work, based on the earlier translation of *Lefèvre d' Étaples, was published at Neuchâtel in 1535. Calvin, then a new convert to the Protestant cause, contributed two prefaces to it. O.'s translation, later somewhat revised, was used by French-speaking Protestants well into the 19th century.

[J. C. OLIN]

OLIVETANS, see BENEDICTINES, OLIVETAN.

OLIVI, PETER JOHN, see PETER JOHN OLIVI.

OLLÉ-LAPRUNE, LÉON (1839–98), professor of philosophy at L'École supérieure normale, master of Blondel. Opposing the rigorous rationalism of, e.g., Malebranche, O.-L. conceives the universe in dynamic and spiritual terms, seeing reality as developing harmoniously in dependence on the First Cause. O.-L. was a profoundly convinced believer, a fact that inspires another marked feature of his philosophical position: the role of the will in man's certitude. Good will is an essential condition for the knowledge of truth. The will does not give truth, but disposes man so that the reason can attain it. O.-L. may best be

described as a Christian philosopher who recognized the distinction of the natural and supernatural orders, but constructed his thought autonomously.

[W. B. MAHONEY]

OLLEGARIUS, ST., see OLDEGAR, ST.

OLSSON, ERIK (c.1422–86), Swedish theologian, historian. Educated at Rostock, he became a canon in Uppsala around 1459 and from 1477 onward professor of theology at the newly founded university there. Called the father of Swedish historiography, he is best known for his *Chronica regni Gothorum*, written in the last third of the 15th cent. and based on a large assortment of Latin- and Scandinavian-language sources.

[E. M. GATES]

OLYMPIAN GODS, heavenly deities who, according to Greek mythology, lived on Mount Olympus, a lofty mountain in N Greece. According to the traditional list, which admitted some variations, there were 12 greater Olympians: Zeus, his brother Poseidon, his sister and wife Hera, his sister Hestia, his 7 sons and daughters, Hermes, Apollo, Ares, Hephaestus, Athena, Artemis, and Aphrodite, and the grain-goddess Demeter. Alongside these there were other important deities such as Selene, Leto, Dionysus, and Themis, and others of lesser rank such as Hebe, Ganymede, and the Graces, Muses, and Horae, who could attend to the needs of the more important deities. The gods were believed to possess human qualities (including numerous defects) but superhuman powers along with immortality. They spent much of their time in merrymaking or in quarreling among themselves. With the passage of time Zeus, who is already described by Homer as "the father of gods and men," takes on more and more the character of a supreme and beneficent being upon whom all the other gods and men depend. Contrasted with the Olympian gods were the chthonic deities of the Lower World, who were worshiped with different rites. BIBLIOGRAPHY: Höfer, *W. H. Roscher, Lex. der griech. und röm. Mythologie* (1902; 1965 reprint) 3.1:838–840.

[M. J. COSTELLOE]

OLYMPIAS, ST. (c.368–408), honored widow and deaconess of the Church of Constantinople, called by St. Gregory of Nazianzus "the glory of the widows of the Eastern Church." She was to John Chrysostom what Paula was to Jerome, the most eminent of the holy women whom he gathered around him. At a very early age she was orphaned and became the heiress of an immense fortune. She married young, but soon found herself a widow without children. She had to struggle against the will of the Emperor Theodosius who kept urging her to marry again. She was finally allowed to dedicate her life and fortune to the poor and sick, and to render hospitality to ecclesiastics. Her lifestyle was marked by great austerity; her garb was coarse and worn. She was consecrated a deaconess by the Patriarch

*Nectarius and established herself in a large house with a number of women dedicated to the service of God. She fell into disgrace and exile shortly after Chrysostom was exiled. Her last years were marked by sickness, slander, and the dispersion of her community of dedicated women. She died in Nicomedia. Knowledge about her comes from various writings of that era, including the correspondence between herself and Chrysostom, which continued during their exiles, from such writers as Palladius of Helenopolis, and a 5th-cent. account of her life. BIBLIOGRAPHY: R. Janin, BiblSanct 9:1154–58; Butler 4:577–579.

[E. J. DILLON]

OLYMPIEION, AKRAGAS (Temple of the Giants; 500–600 B.C.). Most colossal Doric temple in Sicily, heptastyle and pseudoperipteral, named for colossal figures of giants as caryatids of the architrave.

[M. J. DALY]

OLYMPIEION, ATHENS, huge temple of Zeus Olympus begun in the Doric order by Peisistratus in the 6th cent. B.C., continued in the Corinthian order by Antiochus Epiphanes (215–163 B.C.), and finished under the Roman emperor Hadrian c. 125 A.D.

[M. J. DALY]

OLYMPIODARUS (1st half of 6th cent. A.D.), Neoplatonic philosopher of the Alexandrian school. He was a pupil of *Ammonius Hermion. He and his own pupils, Elias and David, produced a series of commentaries that are extant on works of Plato, Aristotle, and Porphyry's *Eisagōgē*. O. remained a pagan. BIBLIOGRAPHY: CHGMP 482–483; Ueberweg 1:643.

[M. R. P. McGUIRE]

OMAN, JOHN WOOD (1860–1939), Scottish Presbyterian theologian. Educated at Edinburgh (1877–82), at the theological college of the United Presbyterian Church in Scotland, and at continental universities in Erlangen, Heidelberg, and Neuchâtel, O. served as minister at Alnwick, Northumberland (1889–1907), professor of systematic theology and apologetics (1907–35) and principal (1925–35) of Westminister College, Cambridge. In 1893 he published a translation of Schleiermacher's *Speeches on Religion*. Schleiermacher's belief that man has immediate awareness of the supernatural deeply influenced O.'s subsequent theology. His treatment of the supernatural and sacred, antedating Otto's study of the "holy," was later elaborated philosophically in *The Natural and the Supernatural* (1931). His concern for the sincerity of the believer, the idea of freedom, and the inner authority of revealed truth color his entire theology. Among his other works are *Vision and Authority* (1902), *The Problem of Faith and Freedom* (1906), *The Church and Divine Order* (1911).

[R. J. LITZ]

OMAN, see MUSQAT AND OMAN.

OMAR KHAYYAM (fl. 11 cent.), great Persian astronomer, mathematician, freethinker, and poet. Little is known of his early life. Khayyam (meaning tentmaker) derives from his father's trade. He wrote, among other treatises, a standard work on algebra. This work as well as those of a similar nature raised him to the foremost rank among other mathematicians of his time. As a result, Sultan Malik-Shah summoned him in 1074 to initiate works in astronomy on a large scale, and to be one of a group of eight to aid him in reforming the Muslim calendar. O.'s fame in the West, however, rested upon his book of poetry, *The Rubaiyat*, paraphrased in English by Edward Fitzgerald (1859). O. is known because of it in almost all parts of the world. *The Rubaiyat* (quatrains) is not a single poem of many parts; there is no continuity in them, each stanza being a distinct thought expressed in musical verse. Its impact was significant. It has been said that it "helped to shape the melancholy hedonism and moral uncertainty of late 19th-cent. England." BIBLIOGRAPHY: *Rubaiyat of Omar Khayyam* (tr. E. Fitzgerald, 1937); A. J. Arberry, *Omar Khayyam* (1952).

[S. A. HEENEY]

OMBRELLINO, a small, white silk canopy made in the shape of an ordinary umbrella, sometimes held over the Blessed Sacrament when it is carried in procession.

[J. DALLEN]

OMEGA, see ALPHA AND OMEGA.

OMEGA POINT, a pivotal reality in the evolutionary theology of Pierre Teilhard de Chardin. The term omega point has two sources: the use of Greek letters for points in a geometric diagram, and the biblical title for God, Alpha and Omega. As the last letter of the Greek alphabet, omega is here used by Teilhard to denote (1) the final stage of cosmic evolution, (2) the encounter, at that stage, between the matured universe and God as transcendent center, and (3) God himself precisely as the divine center of attraction—the primal source and ultimate end of evolution. BIBLIOGRAPHY: P. Teilhard de Chardin, "La Centrologie," (1944) in *Oeuvres de P. Teilhard de Chardin* (1963) 7:103–134; idem, *Phenomenon of Man* (1959), 260–272.

[M. D. MEILACH]

OMEN, a word or occurrence that is arbitrarily interpreted as foreboding evil or forecasting good fortune. Making or taking such an interpretation seriously would be a sin of *divination, contrary to the virtue of *religion (ThAq ST 2a2ae, 95.3). The familiar, folkloric superstitions about good and bad luck signs would not ordinarily come under the heading of divination.

[T. C. O'BRIEN]

OMER OF THÉROUANNE, ST. (Audomarus; d. *c.*670), bishop. Probably of Anglo-Saxon origin, he and his father became monks at Luxeuil after the death of O.'s mother. As Bp. of Thérouanne, O. effected a spiritual renewal in his diocese with the help of three companions from Luxeuil. Together they established the monastery of Sithiu (later Saint-Bertin), which became a center of learning in France. BIBLIOGRAPHY: H. Platelle, BiblSanct 2:586–587; Butler 3:516–517.

[G. M. COOK]

OMISSION, SIN OF, culpable failure to place an act called for by the demands of virtue, or prescribed by *positive law. Lack of action can be voluntary, thus have a moral quality, when a person who can and should act, either wills not to act, or does not will to act (ThAq ST 1a2ae, 6. 3). Every sin requires an act of will. In the case of a sin of omission, when a person does not will to do what he can and should do, the omission itself is a nonwilling; yet that results from another act of will, incompatible with the act omitted (*ibid*. 71.5). Comparison between the two kinds of omission indicates that to will not to do what is required involves greater contempt for virtue or for law. It is worse to will not to go to Mass on Sunday, than simply to go fishing.

[T. C. O'BRIEN]

OMNIBONUS (Omnibene; d. 1185), bp. of Verona (1157), *decretist, author of a minor canonical work, *Abbreviatio Decreti* on Gratian's *Decretum.*

OMNIPOTENCE, literally, the possession of all power, in Christian theology an attribute of God. The idea of omnipotence is not an object of sense experience, but a mental extension of the concept of God's nature as infinite and absolute being. As understood in theology, omnipotence is the power of the Divine Being to do anything not inherently contradictory. So understood the idea represents some degree of metaphysical sophistication. It cannot be reasonably claimed that omnipotence has been explicitly recognized in all religions, or in all stages of religious development, as a necessary attribute of divinity. In neither Old nor New Testament is omnipotence affirmed of God as a metaphysical attribute. The OT *El Shaddai,* commonly translated into English as God almighty, probably meant God of the mountain, and the *pantokratōr* of Revelation is simply the LXX's rendition of *El Shaddai.* However, in the Bible something like omnipotence is attributed to God in the concrete manifestations of his power—creation, his sway over nature and nations, the Incarnation, the work of Redemption, and so on; all these testify to the greatness of his power, which, at work within us, can do more abundantly than we ask or think (Eph 3.20), so that it can be said indeed that with God nothing is impossible (Lk 1.37). BIBLIOGRAPHY: ThAq ST 1a, 25.

[N. SHARKEY]

OMNIPRESENCE OF GOD, the causal immediacy of God as conserving and governing every being whatsoever; negatively, the denial of God's containment either in a physical place (see LOCATION) or by restriction of his causality to any single sphere of reality; thus also the divine transcendence over any limiting measure, the divine immensity. The divine omnipresence also means God's immanence in creation in a way consistent with *transcendence over all creation. St. Thomas Aquinas expresses the truth of God's presence in all things by the phrase *inest quia adest* (ThAq ST 1a, 8.1), and summarizes the force of that in a formula taken from St. Gregory the Great, "God exists in everything by power inasmuch as everything is subject to his power; by presence inasmuch as everything is naked to his gaze; and by substance inasmuch as he exists in everything as causing their existence" (*ibid*. 3). The truth and reality of God's presence in all things is the truth and reality of the creatures' own existence. For that existence is an actual dependence on the divine reality (*ibid*. 44.1 ad 1); without that sustaining causality no single being could exist but would, again in Gregory's words, fall into nothingness (*ibid*. 104.1). This is the implication of the truth that being, *esse* (see ESSENCE AND EXISTENCE) is the proper effect of God alone (*ibid*.). But God's sustaining causality does not, like an electric current, pass out of God as an intermediate between God and the effects he sustains; the divine causality is God, his mind, and his will; it is the creature that, as it were, passes out of God; God is his own, immanent action and even this is not an intermediary between himself and his created effects (*ibid*. 14.2; 25.1; 54.1 ad 3). The fact of God's presence is the fact that anything whatsoever exists; God remains transcendent, because wherever anything at all exists his causality is the prime reason, he is immanent in all things. Because his causality is himself, it is limitless; no matter how much there is besides God, there can always be more: the finite cannot exhaust the infinite. Staggering as the full import of God's omnipresence is, in the context of its development by classical theology it stood in contrast with the greater wonder of God's presence to those who share in his grace. That is true in St. Augustine, St. Gregory the Great, in Peter Lombard and his commentators, and above all in St. Thomas. The presence of God by grace may well be the primary truth that the whole *Summa theologiae* is shaped to teach. Following the tradition, St. Thomas points out that while God reaches all things by his causality, they do not reach him; they do not have to do with God in their being or actions. Their relationship to him is through intermediaries: the created goods that de facto are shared reflections of the divine good. Even man in his purely natural knowledge, e.g., philosophy, would not have mental contact with God himself, but only with created effects that might hint at, allow an inference of God's reality. But by grace God is present in an unmediated way to man. First, one man is united in being with the divine: in the Person of Christ a human nature exists by the substantial divine existence of the Word; this is *hypostatic union. Secondly, to those who by grace are made like Christ God is immediately united as the known united to the knower and the beloved to the lover (*ibid.*, 1a.8,3;43,3). That presence of God begins with the indwelling of the Trinity here and now and is consummated in the beatific vision. BIBLIOGRAPHY: ThAq ST (Lat-Eng v.7, *Father, Son, and Holy Ghost,* ed. T.C. O'Brien) 259–265; v. 14 (*idem, Divine Government*) 169–175. *CHARITY; DIVINE NATURE, PARTAKER OF; *FAITH; *GRACE, SUBSTANTIAL; *IMAGE OF GOD.

[T. C. O'BRIEN]

OMNIS UTRIUSQUE SEXUS, opening words of the decree of Lateran Council IV (1215) requiring as a condition for good-standing in the Church at least annual communion at Easter time as well as prior confession of any mortal sins. (The wording of the decree is still present in CIC, c. 859, 1.) Confession was to be made to the person's pastor; confession to any other priest required the pastor's consent. *COMMUNION, FREQUENCY OF.

[T. C. O'BRIEN]

OMNISCIENCE, the knowledge of all things; a transcendent, nonfinite manner of knowing which Christian theology considers an attribute of God. Omniscience transcends human sense experience but can be predicated of God by the *via negativa,* i.e., by eliminating any limitation from positive divine qualities such as knowledge. Basically, this omniscience is based upon God's knowledge of his own essence by which all things move and have their being. Scripture gives abundant reference to God's omniscience, characteristically in its presentation of him as a personal being rather than merely a principle of energy. Man has a living experience of a sovereign Lord who is a God of knowledge (1Sam 2.3). Before him no creature is hidden; no act goes unnoticed. Everything lies open (Heb 4.13). Through his encounter with men, God reveals his transcendent manner of knowing (Ex 32. 13; Rom 1. 19; 11. 33; Gal 4. 9). In this confrontation man realizes that he is in the presence, and under the saving closeness, of an all-knowing Absolute (Ps 139. 7–18). Divine wisdom which in the OT came to be seen as a subsistent quality of God, ultimately manifests itself in the person of Christ as the image of the Father who carries out the plan for our salvation (Col 1. 15).

Speculative theology also recognizes the totality of God's knowledge. Since he causes all things as an intelligent agent, he must know them in their individual actuality (ThAq ST 1a, 14.11). Indeed he knows not only what is but also every possible way of being (*scientia simplicis intelligentiae*). Much theological controversy has centered around God's knowledge of the future, esp. the free acts of man. From the 16th cent. *predestination and divine foreknowledge became a central issue debated protractedly among the adherents of *Molinism and *Bâñezianism. Many contemporary theologians refuse to support either

school, maintaining that the controversy has proceeded from a basic misunderstanding of the relationship between instrumental causality and divine transcendent causality. BIBLIOGRAPHY: E. M. Burke, NCE 10:690–694 with bibliog.

[T. M. MCFADDEN]

OMONT, HENRI AUGUSTE (1857–1940), French paleographer and librarian. He studied under L. Delisle and A. Giry at the École des Chartes. From 1905 until 1935 O. served as *conservateur* of the Department of Manuscripts at the Bibliothèque Nationale and also as inspector-general of French libraries. Author of many erudite studies, he added much prestige to the Bibliothèque Nationale. BIBLIOGRAPHY: É. Brouette, NCE 10:694; G. Brunel, *Bibliothèque de l'École des Chartes* 102 (1941) 371–378.

[F. D. LAZENBY]

OMOPHRION, in some Eastern Churches, the counterpart of a Latin abp.'s *pallium; a band of silk worn round the neck in the manner of a scarf.

[T. C. O'BRIEN]

OMRI (AMRI), KING OF ISRAEL, founder of the fourth dynasty of the northern kingdom (876–869 B.C.). He built Samaria for his capital and was one of the strongest of the Israelite kings, although his reign is treated only briefly in Kg 16.15–23. He is held up as a symbol of wickedness in Mic 6.16, since idolatry was permitted in his kingdom through the marriage of his son Ahab to Jezabel of Tyre.

[T. C. O'BRIEN]

ONAN, son of Judah, commanded by him to take Tamar, the widow of his brother Er, and give her offspring according to the law of the levirate marriage. Onan evades this duty by "spilling his seed on the ground" at the moment of intercourse, and is killed by Yahweh for this crime (Gen 38.4–10). In the minds of the biblical writers his crime consists less probably in sexual withdrawal, than in his refusal to fulfil his obligations according to the law of the levirate marriage.

[D. J. BOURKE]

ONANISM, prevention of conception by male withdrawal before emission in sexual intercourse. This is regarded in RC teaching as an immoral act. It derives its name from *Onan, but the biblical condemnation is probably not for a sexual sin but for the violation of the law of *levirate marriage (Gen 38.4–10). Onanism has also been used as a term for masturbation.

[T. C. O'BRIEN]

ONEIDA COMMUNITY, also called Perfectionists, the best-known American communal movement of the 19th cent., established by John Humphrey Noyes (1816–86). He was converted at New Haven, Conn., during the revivals inspired by C. G. *Finney. After association with those perfectionists who believed that Christ's second coming had already occurred, and who carried their idea of *sanctification to the limit of *antinomianism, esp. with regard to sexual matters, Noyes established his community at Putney, Vt. (1845); public outcry forced a move to Oneida, N.Y. 2 years later. The community considered itself the kingdom of God on earth, living in the millennium according to a pattern of life that was communitarian both in its economic organization and in its sexual practice. In the arrangement called "complex marriage," monogamy was repudiated; eugenic theories of Noyes, including the control of the sexual embrace, were also practiced. Because of public opinion, the community life was abandoned in 1880, but a corporation was formed (1881) to carry on its manufacturing enterprises, and remains famous for its silverware. BIBLIOGRAPHY: M. Holloway, *Heavens on Earth: Utopian Communities in America 1630–1880* (1951).

O'NEILL, EUGENE (1888–1953), American dramatist. O'N.'s religious roots were Catholic; he attended Catholic boarding schools, but sometime in his 15th year he refused to attend Mass. Though preparation for Princeton was successful, his work at the university was less than adequate, and he became a drifter of sorts between 1907 and 1913, working as seaman, miner, reporter, and finally writer. His life in Greenwich village encouraged his experiences; a bout with tuberculosis (1913) made him consider writing as a career. The 1920s projected into literature a kind of disenchantment: H. L. Mencken, Sinclair Lewis, Sherwood Anderson were contemporary iconoclasts. O'N. was stirred to action in such dramas as *Anna Christie* (1921) and *Strange Interlude* (1928). He portrayed characters resisting and collapsing under circumstances beyond their control. Such dramas as *The Emperor Jones* (1920), *The Great God Brown* (1926), *Strange Interlude* (1928), and others carried this pessimistic strain. His plays reflect in a sense the modern milieu: the tragedy of circumstance. O'N. saw 20th-cent. man growing perhaps increasingly dehumanized. Despite Jansenistic overtones, O'N. brought compassion and integrity to American theater goers. He wrote 47 plays, many of these dealing with the sea, to him an all-pervasive power. O'N. won four Pulitzer Prizes and in 1936 the Nobel Prize for *Anna Christie*. BIBLIOGRAPHY: B. Clark, *Eugene O'Neill: The Man and His Plays* (1947).

[R. M. FUNCHION]

O'NEILL, SARA BENEDICTA (1869–1954), lay apostle. A Chicago teacher and librarian, she was moved by admiration for the Benedictine tradition to become an Oblate (lay affiliate) of St. Benedict in 1902. O'N. planned and brought to completion a project to establish a library to provide cultural, religious, and intellectual service to the Chicago Loop. St. Benedict's Library, opened in 1931, became a meeting place for writers and others and a center of intellectual life. She was also an early champion of the liturgical movement.

[J. R. AHERNE]

ONESIMUS, slave whom Paul sent back to his master Philemon (Philem; Col 4.9). Presumably a runaway converted by Paul, O. had been assisting the Apostle, who was in prison.

[T. EARLY]

ONESIPHORUS, benefactor of the Apostle Paul (2 Tim 1. 16–18; 4.19). On coming to Rome. he found Paul, who was then in chains, and "refreshed" him. O. had also served at Ephesus.

[T. EARLY]

ONIAS, name of several high priests in the Hellenistic era of Jewish history. Onias I (d. *c*.300 B.C.) is mentioned in 1 Macc 12.7–20; Onias II (d. *c*.227 B.C.) is identified in Sir 50.1 as the father of the high priest Simon II. Onias III (d. *c*.171 B.C.) according to 2 Macc ch. 3 was defender of the temple treasury against Heliodorus; later he was treacherously murdered at Antioch (2 Macc 4.7–38); he appeared with Jeremiah in a vision to Judas Maccabaeus before the victory over Nicanor (2 Macc 15.11–16). Onias IV, son of Onias III, is not mentioned in the OT, but in the *Antiquities* (12.9.7; 13.3.1–3) of Josephus; he built a temple in honor of Yahweh at Leontopolis in Egypt. Some scholars, however, identify Onias III as the builder of this temple.

[T. C. O'BRIEN]

ÔNÎTĀ, East Syrian poetic strophe, usually assembled in a series, loosely associated with fragmentary psalm-verses.

[A. CODY]

ONLY BEGOTTEN (SCRIPTURE). There is some doubt as to whether the Greek word *monogenēs* should be rendered "only begotten"—thus stressing what is known in Trinitarian theology as the divine procession, or "unique"—thus describing a quality of Jesus, esp. in the Johannine texts (Jn 1.14, 18; 3:16,18; 1 Jn 4.9). In the LXX, Psalms 21 (22).20; 24(25).16; and 34(35).17 seem to favor the second rendering of the Hebrew *yaḥid*. However, the LXX does contain passages where *monogenēs* means "only child" (Jg 11.34; Tob 3.15; 6.11). To complicate matters further, Hebrew *yaḥid* is many times translated in the LXX by *agapētos,* meaning "beloved" or "precious," without necessarily implying "only child" or "only begotten" (Gen 22.2,12,16; Jer 6.26; Am 8.10; Zech 12.10). In NT usage, *monogenēs* in Lk 7.12; 8.42 and 9.38 has been traditionally understood as meaning "only child." However, in Heb 11.17 the word means "unique" or "uniquely precious," since Isaac was Abraham's uniquely precious son, but not his only begotten. Only the fourth Evangelist uses *monogenēs* to describe the relationship of Jesus to God. The synoptics prefer *huios mou ho agapētos,* "uniquely precious son,'' while in the Pauline literature *protótokos,* ''first born'' is found (Rom 8.29; Col 1.15,18). The Old Latin version rendered *monogenēs* in the Johannine passages by *unicus,* but Jerome, to answer the Arian charge that Jesus was not begotten but made, translated the word by the Latin *unigenitus,* ''only begotten.'' The subsequent influence of the Vulgate on the AV made ''only begotten'' the accepted English translation. However, in all probability, *monogenēs* describes a quality of Jesus in the Johannine passages, namely, his uniqueness. According to the fourth Evangelist, Jesus is the unique and only revealer of the Father because of the Incarnation. God from all eternity, the Son came into the world in the Incarnation (Jn 1.14; 5.43; 6.38; 8.14, 42; 10.10) at the sending of the Father (Jn 12.44; 13.20; 20.21). Secondly, *monogenēs* stresses that Jesus Son of God is the unique and only Redeemer of men. The work of the unique Son of God is declared in Jn 3.16 and the person of the only Son is declared in Jn 3.18. Because Jesus is the unique Son of God, his sending into the world is both the supreme demonstration of God's love for the world, and the only way the world can achieve salvation. BIBLIOGRAPHY: R. E. Brown, *Gospel According to John,* (1966) v. 1:13–14; F. Büchsel, *Theological Dictionary of the New Testament,* s.v. *monogenēs,* 4:745–750; D. Moody, JBL 72 (1953) 213–219.

[T. J. RYAN]

ONOLATRIA, worship of the ass (donkey), a legendary cult known to the Greeks in the 2 cent. preceding the Christian era and attributed disparagingly to the Jews. The origin and purpose of the legend is obscure. The donkey's head figured prominently in the religion of ancient Egypt in the cult of the Lord of the Underworld. BIBLIOGRAPHY: H. Leclercq, DACL 12.2:2147–48.

[E. J. DILLON]

ONOMASTICON, an alphabetical list of places mentioned in the Bible with appropriate descriptions of their history and geography written by Eusebius of Caesarea sometime before the death of Bp. Paulinus of Tyre (331) who requested it. In its still extant Latin translation by St. Jerome and its original Greek text, it remains an important source for the topography of Palestine. BIBLIOGRAPHY: Quasten 3:336.

[F. H. BRIGHAM]

ONTOLOGICAL ARGUMENT, since the 18th cent., designation for a way of reasoning about God's existence, esp. that of St. Anselm of Canterbury. The argument has a vigorous history. St. Anselm in ch. 2 of the *Proslogion* addresses these words to God: ''We believe that thou art a being such that a greater cannot be thought of'' (*aliquid quo nihil majus cogitari potest*). He proceeds to show that no one having this idea of God and accepting what the terms mean, can deny that God really and necessarily exists. Such a denial involves a contradiction. God could not be defined as that than which no greater can be conceived, and at the same time exist only as an idea, since to exist in reality is greater than to exist only as an idea. The idea of God, then, necessarily includes his real existence. Ever since Anselm's contemporary Gaunilo, some critics have rejected the argument as a fallacious transition from the logical to the real: the ''real existence'' affirmed remains a mental predicate not existence in reality (cf. ThAq ST 1, 2. 1 ad 2). Others, however, defend the value of Anselm's exposition because of the theological premise of the *Proslogion*: ''to understand in some degree Thy truth, which my heart believes and loves. For I do not seek to understand in order that I may believe; but I believe that I may understand.'' The dialectic on God's existence gives intelligibility to the truth of God's necessary existence, accepted by faith, through the idea of God given by faith, that he is a being than which no greater can be conceived.

Descartes proposed his adaptation of the ontological argument as a pure proof by reason. Kant, calling the Cartesian version ontological (as distinct from a posteriori, cosmological arguments), rejected its validity: the existence affirmed could only be a mental or verbal definition, not real, extramental existence. Anselm's argument has continued to fascinate. In contemporary thought J. N. Findlay uses its central elements to argue to God's non-existence. Charles Hartshorne and Norman Malcolm see a valid line of argument in the *Proslogion* for the logical necessity of God's existence. Karl Barth viewed Anselm's dialectic not as a proof but as a believer's reflection on God's revealed word. BIBLIOGRAPHY: A. Nemetz, NCE 10:699–701, bibliog.; J. Hick, EncPhil 5:538–542 bibliog.; e.g., *Ontological Argument from St. Anselm to Contemporary Philosophers* (ed. A. Plantenga, pa., 1965); K. Barth, *Anselm's Fides quaerens intellectum* (tr. I. W. Robertson, 1960).

[T. C. O'BRIEN]

ONTOLOGISM, a generic term which in general signifies a philosophic position maintaining that God or the divine ideas in God constitute the primary object of human intellectual knowledge and that the first act of the human intellect is the intuition of God or his ideas. Every variety of the theory has as its point of departure the recognition that man has an idea of the Infinite which cannot be gleaned from finite things insofar as they are finite; moreover, man's concepts and judgments are characterized by their universality, eternity, and necessity whereas finite things are particular, temporal, and contingent. Hence, the need exists for an act of intuition by man wherein he directly confronts God and/or the divine ideas to explain human concepts. The following are three variations of ontologism: (1) Nicolas *Malebranche in his *Recherche de la verité* (1674), develops his theory of a vision of God according to which man has true knowledge of things, not through ideas that are the product of the mind's activity, but in the eternal archetypes or divine ideas in the divine mind, i.e., the models after which the things of reality are formed. Insofar as man is aware of these exemplars in his own cognitions, he sees all things in God, who is thus ever present to the human intellect. This view is an aspect of M's doctrine of occasionalism, which holds God's direct causal intervention in the activities of the universe, in this case causing the perfect coincidence of the known object and its idea in God. (2) Vincenzo *Gioberti, the Italian philosopher, states his version of ontologism in his *Introduzione allo studio della filosofia* (1840), which maintains that man's first act of intellectual knowledge is an intuition that Being creates existences ex nihilo. In this intuitive act, the human mind knows God directly and immediately as the one necessary Being, and also knows the created existences as contingent beings and the creative act uniting the Creator and the created. Only God is Being whereas all else is a mere existent or the divine ideas in finite and individual form. God is thus the source of all human knowledge as apprehended in intuition, and this knowledge is the beginning of philosophy. (3) Casimir *Ubaghs, the Belgian philosopher and leader of the Ontologico-Traditionalist School at Louvain, asserts in his *Essai d'idéologie ontologique* (1860) that man's universal concepts having the marks of necessity and eternity as well as his idea of the infinite cannot exist unless they exist in God, and thus an intuition of God is necessary to make him present to our minds as the divine archetype of all being. The human intellect contemplates God directly and beholds in him the truths or objective ideas of which our knowledge is a weak reflection. BIBLIOGRAPHY: L. Olle-Laprune, *La philosophie de Malebranche* (1870); B. Spavema, *La Filosofia di Gioberti* (1863); M. De Wulf, *Histoire de la philosophie en Belgique* (1910).

[J. T. HICKEY]

ONTOLOGY, literally, the study of being (Gr. *to ōn*). Use of the term became widespread in the 18th cent. through the circulation of C. *Wolff's philosophy textbooks. For him philosophy, the study of how being is possible, begins with a study of general laws about being; this is ontology; the study of specific kinds of being forms the other parts of philosophy, cosmology, psychology, theology. Scholastic manuals of philosophy accepted this division, and ontology was equivalent to general, as against special, metaphysics. The term is still used currently in its etymological sense to refer to the study of being, as in the philosophy of M. *Heidegger.

[T. C. O'BRIEN]

OOLLA AND OOLIBA, see OHOLAH AND OHOLIBA.

OOST, VAN, FAMILY OF. Jacob van Oost I (1601–1671), Flemish painter of religious subjects, master in Bruges (1621). In Italy he studied with Annibale Carracci, painting in a Caravaggesque and later in the Venetian mode. His son **Jacob van Oost II** combined Italian and French Baroque styles in religious works. A second son **Willem van Oost** was a Dominican lay brother who probably painted (1671) the St. Dominic in a landscape by Achtschellinck.

[M. J. DALY]

OPEN BRETHREN, those of the Plymouth Brethren who regard as acceptable association with non-Brethren. The division into Open and Exclusive Brethren began in 1848. *PLYMOUTH BRETHREN.

[T. C. O'BRIEN]

OPEN COMMUNION, term for the practice whereby a Church admits to the Lord's Supper Christians who are not members; the opposite of close, or closed, communion. In the RC Church under certain conditions Eucharistic sharing with Orthodox Churches is permitted and the issue of Eucharistic sharing with other Churches is under consideration by theologians and ecumenists. Among Protestant Churches open communion has become general. The issue of open vs. closed communion has had particular prominence in Baptist history; the Baptists who accept open communion still distinguish it from open membership, i.e., acceptance as members without rebaptism those who already had been baptized as infants in another Church. *CLOSED COMMUNION; *INTERCOMMUNION.

[T. C. O'BRIEN]

OPEN HOUSING, freedom from *discrimination in buying, renting, or leasing a residence. In the U.S. this is regarded as a civil right and a legal obligation to respect; it rests on those who sell, rent, or lease, and particularly requires the avoidance of racial discrimination. The moral vindication of the right and obligation involved has one immediate basis: the open-housing laws are just laws, framed for the sake of the common good in the concrete conditions of American society: *legal justice dictates both the enactment and the observance of such just laws. A more radical moral vindication, of even the rightness of such laws, is the meaning of *equality. This does not mean uniformity or a classless society. But equality of opportunity rests fundamentally on the natural right to live in society in a way conducive to the attainment of a decent way of self-preservation, the rearing of a family, cultural and educational betterment. Race or color are not determinants of that right, but solely of being a human person. Open housing is the right to human opportunity, and any form of discrimination is in violation of that right. No segment of society has a moral right to keep another segment in a ghetto. The kind of housing typical of a given society is in fact made possible by the dynamics of the society itself. The issue of who is to share in adequate housing cannot be decided on the sole basis of private ownership of a given piece of property. Anyone who offers to sell, rent, or lease does so also as a member of the collective whole, as a participant in and a contributor to the good of the whole. Anyone who has the means to buy, rent, or lease a residence offered does so also as a member of that same whole, and so as an equal. Justice requires that that equality be the sole basis for any possible transaction. The moral rights and obligations at issue, however, do not prohibit a given community, in keeping with the common good, from determining the quality of its own life, by zoning laws, self-limitation in growth, the acreage required for residency, the kind of schools to be maintained. But open housing does mean that no one able to enter the community can be excluded on discriminatory grounds. It seems widely agreed that this avoidance of discrimination also includes the willingness of communities to create positive opportunities for low-cost housing within their boundaries. There is the conviction that the common good of the wider civic community requires the achievement of economic and racial balance throughout; that affluent suburban enclaves create de facto ghettos.

[T. C. O'BRIEN]

OPEN SHOP, a place of work where employees are said to be free to join or not to join a union as a condition of employment, the opposite of a closed shop, where only union members may be employed. The term is frequently used in a deprecatory sense, as implying that the operator of such a shop, by employing non-union workers, is in effect discriminating against trade unions, and hampering their advancement. An open shop is usually understood as favoring the right-to-work principle and opposing the mandatory trade union approach.

[F. T. RYAN]

OPERATIONALISM, a tendency and movement within the philosophy of science that seeks to verify the content of all scientific concepts by grounding all definitions in experimental procedures, e.g., defining temperature in terms of the altered electrical resistance of platinum in a platinum-wire thermometer, i.e., in terms of physical changes in the measuring device. Operationalism is a more severe and special mode of the general philosophical movement of logical positivism or logical empiricism. Where logical positivists were satisfied with verification of statements by observation, operationalists demanded that scientific statements not only be verified by observation but that the actual physical process of the observation be verified as well. Since R. Carnap's "The Methodological Character of Theoretical Concepts," operationalism has become less stringent in its demands and has become the particularly scientific strand of contemporary empiricism. Physicist P. W. Bridgman first articulated the tenets of operationalism in his *The Logic of Modern Physics* (1927). Bridgman's initial emphasis upon exhaustive definition in terms of performable physical (as opposed to theoretical) procedures was criticized for being trivial in cases of simple measurement of length, and inadequate in cases where the presumably accurate functioning of the measuring device depends upon the validity of a theory, as in the case of a platinum-wire thermometer constructed to perform in keep-

ing with an accepted theory of variable electrical resistance according to temperature. Operationalism has been adopted widely in the behavioral and social sciences to achieve more precise terminology and definitions.

[R. J. LITZ]

OPHIR, a gold-producing region, probably in SE Arabia bordering on the Persian Gulf; according to many biblical passages, its gold was synonymous with the finest of that metal. Attempts to locate Ophir exactly have resulted in widely differing hypotheses. The Septuagint and Josephus posit a location in the Far East. Some recent theorists follow their lead and locate it either on the E side of the delta of the Indus, or along the coasts of Malabar, or in the Malay peninsula. Such speculation is triggered by the list of exotic goods listed in 1 Kg as precious cargo brought to King Solomon from Ophir by the "ships of Tarshish" which Hiram of Tyre had built and manned for Solomon at Ezion-geber in the Gulf of Aqaba (I Kg 10.11,22; cf. I Kg 9.26–28). Even in these passages, however, it is the gold which is emphasized as the product of Ophir. Costly wood and precious stones are described as coming also from Ophir. But the silver, ivory, apes, and peacocks are linked with the ships of Tarshish. The latter sailed the seas of the known world and picked up exotic goods wherever they found them. It is reasonable to assume they would unload exotic cargo from the Far East at the Persian Gulf coastlands of Arabia (Ophir), to be then transported by land caravan to such cities as Jerusalem. Attempts to locate Ophir in Africa, accompanied by notions that "Ophir" and "Africa" have the same root (meaning "land of the south") are themselves rooted in the same mistaken need to find a place in which all or most of the list of exotic goods would be native. A location in SE Arabia bordering the Persian Gulf makes more sense. That was the gold-producing area known to Israel, and it squares well with the geneology in Gen 10.29, in which Ophir is listed among the eastern Semites.

[E. J. DILLON]

OPHITES (from Gr. *ophis*, serpent), an early syncretistic Gnostic sect, possibly identified with the Naassenes. Their name comes from their use of the serpent in their worship. They held the God of the OT, the Creator, in abomination. Epiphanius (*Haer.*, 26) described a form of eucharistic rite in which they released a serpent to entwine itself around the elements. BIBLIOGRAPHY: R. M. Grant, *Gnosticism and Early Christianity* (1959).

OPHRAH (OPHRA), name of: (1) a son of Meonothai and descendant of Judah (1 Chr 4.14); (2) a city allotted to Benjamin, perhaps NE of Jerusalem (Jos 18.23); (3) a city of Manasseh, site of Gideon's commission to deliver Israel from the Midianites (Jg 6.11–18), and of his burial (Jg 8.27–32).

[T. EARLY]

OPICINUS DE CANISTRIS, Italian scribe (1296–c.1350) attached to the papal court at Avignon, the author of the Vatican Codex (Pal. Lat. 1993) containing drawings, illuminations, and biographical comments.

[M. J. DALY]

OPINION. (1) In *epistemology opinion describes the quality of an assent given to one side of an issue on the basis of probability, rather than of conclusive evidence; this state of mind, more than *doubt but less than certitude, includes an awareness that the opposite of what is affirmed or denied might be true. Used in an objective sense, an opinion is a proposition that has *probability. Thus (2), in moral theology and canon law, an opinion is an author's resolution of a moral or legal doubt that has some degree of probability; so used, it belongs to the history of *probabilism and the other moral systems. (3) In theology generally, opinion has an analogous usage: it describes the teaching or statement of a private theologian (even if he be a pope) as meriting an assent inferior in quality to adherence by faith. This certitude rests upon the motive of faith, the word of God; an authentic dogmatic teaching of the Church declares what God's word guarantees and what therefore merits the assent of faith. The teaching of the theologian, while sound and possessing a reasoned certitude, remains an opinion when compared to an object of faith.

[T. C. O'BRIEN]

OPPENHEIM, PHILIPP (1899–1949), German Benedictine liturgical scholar. He taught at San Anselmo in Rome from 1928, at the Lateran Univ. from 1945, and at Propaganda from 1946. He was a consultor for the Congregation of Rites and served as a member of its liturgical commission. His writings are listed in Kapsner BB 1:428–429. BIBLIOGRAPHY: A. Roth, NCE 10:705.

[N. KOLLAR]

OPPOSITION, in Aristotelico-scholastic analysis, the type of difference between two elements that excludes their both being in the same subject at the same time and under the same aspect, or the formal relation between a pair of propositions having the same subject and predicate but differing in quantity and quality. Although the two senses of the term are intimately interrelated and overlap, the philosophical tradition has analyzed them separately. There are four species of the first opposition, that of natures and, consequently, terms. The first is that of contradiction, the opposition of a nature and its simple and complete negation, as in man and not-man. The second is that of contrariety, the opposition between a species and the diametrically opposed species of the same genus, as in man and brute, species of the genus animal; here the negation is of the specific difference. The third species of opposition is privation or lacking and possession or having, the relation between that which lacks something it can and should naturally have and that which possesses it. The fourth species is that of relative

opposition, the opposition or difference between the subject and the term of a relation. Opposition between propositions too has diverse species. Having the same subject and predicate, they can be either affirmative or negative and they can be either universal, about all things named by the subject, or particular, about at least some. Propositions differing in both quantity and quality are contradictories; they cannot both be true and they cannot both be false. The universal affirmative and universal negative propositions are contraries; they can both be false but cannot both be true. The particular affirmative and particular negative propositions are subcontraries; they can both be true but cannot both be false. The universal and particular affirmatives are related, as are the universal and particular negative propositions, in two ways. First, the universals are related to the particulars of the same quality as subalternates; if the universal is true, then the particular is, but the falsity of the universal permits no inference. Second, if the particular is false, then the universal of the same quality is false, while the truth of the particular permits no inference.

[R. E. HENNESSEY]

OPTATUS OF MILEVIS, ST. (fl. 2d half of 4th cent.), bp., Catholic champion against the Donatists. His work, today called *Contra Parmenianum Donatistam*, was both a doctrinal refutation of Donatist teaching and a conciliatory proposal for their return. The work first appeared in six books, c.367; a revision with the addition of Book VII appeared c.385 (CSEL 56.1893). Though incomplete and badly mutilated, the appendix to the work (called a "Donatist dossier") is valuable for its documents on Donatist history. Augustine's response to Donatism relied on O.'s teaching, esp. on the *ex opere operato* power of the sacraments, the distinction between personal holiness and ministerial office in their administration, and on the unity of the Church through the sacraments, the bp.'s office, and the chair of Peter. BIBLIOGRAPHY: Altaner, 435–436; *Work of St. Optatus against the Donatists* (ed., O. R. Vassall-Phillips, 1917).

[R. B. ENO]

OPTIMISM, a term sometimes used in reference to a religious position to describe a hopeful outlook on life and the world despite the undeniable presence of evil both physical and moral. It is not to be identified with a temperamental disposition to see the bright side of things and to trust that all will be well in the end. It is based on a doctrine holding that goodness, right order, and truth prevail at the final outcome of history, even though they are not always apparent in the course of history. The Christian message of salvation includes such a doctrine. It gives the certainty that evil does not triumph forever and that under God's guidance history is the unfolding of his sovereign saving plan, however ambiguously or confusedly that plan may be understood at different points of time and by different people. Good is indestructible even now and will triumph in the end. This trust rests on God's saving presence, however hidden, his love, infinite power, and righteousness. All religions of salvation mean to be the basis of a relative optimism. BIBLIOGRAPHY: P. Siwek and Z. Alszegy, NCE 10:707–709; O. Much, LTK 7:1181–83; L. E. Loemker, EncPhil 6:114–121.

[P. De LETTER]

OPUS, term designating Roman, early Christian, and Byzantine masonry: *opus albarium,* polished Roman cement and stucco surfaces; *opus lithostratum,* mosaic pavements, etc.

[M. J. DALY]

OPUS DEI (Societas Sacerdotalis Sanctae Crucis et Opus Dei), a worldwide association of RC faithful, who devote themselves to the practice of Christian virtues and give witness to Christ by leading intensely spiritual lives in their own various environments; members are not religious, do not take vows, or live in community. The association was founded in Madrid in 1928 by Msgr. José María *Escrivá de Balaguer; he was succeeded in 1975 by Fr. Alvaro del Portillo. He also founded a women's branch (1930) within Opus Dei. In 1950, the Sacerdotal Society of the Holy Cross and Opus Dei were granted final approval by Rome. Priests also belong to the society, and in 1975, 54 of its members of various professions and from 19 countries were ordained to the priesthood in Spain. The men's and the women's branches have independent government and specific apostolates, but the two are united under one president general. Apostolic works include educational institutions in Spain, Kenya, Japan, Mexico and more than 200 student residences throughout the world. Opus Dei maintains centers for conferences, technical training of farmers and workers, clinics and nursing schools, as well as numerous charitable centers in underprivileged areas. It has over 60,000 members from 80 nations; its general council has headquarters in Rome. U.S. directors of Opus Dei are located in New York City.

[R. A. TODD]

OR SAN MICHELE, Florence. Originally an Italian Gothic grain market (1290), the first floor open loggia was enclosed as a church (1337–80), with exterior niches boasting statues by Donatello, Ghiberti, and Giovanni Bologna; a white marble tabernacle on the interior by Orcagna (1349–59); an upper story for grain storage becoming repository for national archives (1569).

[M. J. DALY]

ORACLE BONES, inscribed bones of the Chinese Shang dynasty from An-yang (excavated 1928). The cracks in heated animal bones or carapace (of tortoise) were inscribed as answers and used to determine propitious dates for sacrifices. They are important in the study of the Bronze Age in China.

[M. J. DALY]

ORACLES. (1) In Greek and Roman religion, the occult pronouncements of a deity about future events or courses of action; thus a form of *divination. The oracles were usually to be sought in special, sacred places, and through the mediation of priests, priestesses, or seers, who, usually in an ecstatic trance, interpreted sounds to convey the oracle. Among the celebrated oracles of antiquity were the Oracle of Delphi and the Sibyls, esp. the Sibyl of Cumae, near Naples. The persecution of Christians by the Emperor Diocletian followed upon consultation of an oracle. (2) The term is also used as a general description of the sayings of Yahweh in the Bible in response to priests or Prophets. To consult Yahweh on courses of action was one of the priests' chief offices. Such consultation corresponded to the pattern set by Moses during the Exodus (Ex 18.15–16; 33.7–16; cf. 28.30; Lev 8.8; Jg 18.5–6; Deut 17.8–12). The practice, "seeking the Law (Torah)," was in keeping with Israel's dependence on Yahweh's guidance, and excluded *superstition or *divination. The Prophets' oracles announcing divine decisions are frequently marked in the Bible by the phrase, "Thus saith the Lord" (1 Sam 9. 9,11.18–20; 2 Sam 7.17; 1 Kg 18.36–39; 2 Kg 8.7–15; Is 38.1–6). Under the heading of oracles are also grouped divine messages given in dreams, as well as special occurrences taken for signs of Yahweh's will, on which all depended (e.g., Gen 37.5–10; Dan 2.1; 1 Sam 24.1–5).

[T. C. O'BRIEN]

ORAISON, MARC (1914–   ), French psychiatrist. O. received his medical degree from the Univ. of Bordeaux, then studied theology at the Institut Catholique in Paris and was ordained in 1948. He pursued further research into Freudian psychology and sought to reconcile Freudian insights and Christian morality. Roman ecclesiastical authorities have censured some of his writings, but O. continues to publish extensively. Works include *Morality for Our Time* (tr. Nels Challe, 1968), *Being Together* (tr. R. Sheed, 1970), *Strange Voyage: The Autobiography of a Non-Conformist* (tr. J.F. Bernard, 1970).

[T. MCFADDEN]

ORANGE, COUNCILS OF, early synods held at Orange in what is now southern France. The city was an episcopal see from the 4th till the 18th cent.; it is particularly known in the history of theology for two councils, one held in 441, the other in 529. The first, under St. Hilary of Arles, was attended by 16 bps. and enacted 30 canons concerning disciplinary matters, such as the celibacy of deacons. What is historically known as the Second Council of Orange (529), is of doctrinal importance. It did for the ending of *Semi-Pelagianism what the 15th (16th) Council of Carthage did for Pelagianism. St. Caesarius of Arles, with a view to putting an end to the opposition of the school of Lérins to the teaching of St. Augustine on the need of grace for the beginning of faith and for perseverance in good works, composed what are now known as the *Decrees of the Sec-*

ond *Council of Orange,* drawing from a Roman list (or composing himself) the first 8 canons (D 371–378) and adding 17 propositions selected from the *Sententiae Augustini* of Prosper of Aquitaine (D 379–395). He prefaced the document with an introduction of his own and appended a profession of faith (D 370, 396–398). This document was promulgated at Orange, on the occasion of the blessing of a basilica, and signed by 14 bps. and 8 laymen. It apparently had not been submitted to any conciliar discussion. It was sent to Rome for approval and went by the name of *Decrees of the Second Council of Orange.* The following year, at the request of Caesarius, Pope Boniface II confirmed the decrees, particularly the profession of faith (D 398–400). Orange was not included in conciliar collections through several centuries. Aquinas changed his teaching on grace in his later works after seeing the Council decrees; they also influenced the Council of Trent (D 1551–53). BIBLIOGRAPHY: C. M. Aherne, NCE 10:712.

[P. De LETTER]

ORANGE, MARTYRS OF, thirty-two sisters guillotined July 6–26, 1794. At the height of the Revolution's Reign of Terror, refusal to take the Oath of Liberty and Equality led to condemnation by the local tribunal and the scaffold. Such was the lot of these sisters—13 Sacramentines, 16 Ursulines, 2 Bernadines, and 1 Benedictine. They had been ejected from their convent in Bollène in 1792; subsequently regrouped, they subsisted by knitting, embroidering, and sewing. They were arrested and imprisoned May 2, 1794, in Orange near Avignon. Their condemnation to death followed upon their refusal to take the oath. They were beatified in 1925. BIBLIOGRAPHY: H. LeClercq, *La Révolution, 1794–1798* (1913), includes names and bibliog.; M. Lawlor, NCE 10:712.

[R. J. MARAS]

ORANGEMEN, an organized group of northern Irish Protestants claiming to protect their liberties against encroachments by Roman Catholics. The Loyal Orange Institution was founded in 1795 in County Armagh, Ulster, to maintain the Protestant constitution and counteract the United Irishmen, and called after William of Orange—King Billy—who defeated James II at the Battle of the Boyne, July 12, 1690. The day is celebrated by processions with fife and drum, and sometimes by insults hurled at the pope. A historic irony is that by a poetic turn of political fortune, William was backed by the Pope of the day, Bl. Innocent XI. After Gladstone declared in favor of home rule for Ireland, the movement, organized in lodges, became civically respectable, at least with respect to the Unionist establishment, though it remains associated with an aggressively violent fringe of bigots or hooligans or both, for which reason responsible Protestant ministers view it with reservations. The movement, though losing some of its tribal ethos, has spread outside Ireland, to Merseyside, Clydeside, and Ortana. It was involved in the Philadelphia riots of 1844.

ORANS (ORANT), praying posture, in early Christian art showing the figure with hands raised. In Byzantine art a Madonna orant in such posture carries a medallion of the Christ Child around her neck.

[M. J. DALY]

ORARION, the Greek name, of uncertain origin, of the diaconal stole (Sl. *orar*) in the Byzantine Church. It is a narrow band of silk, brocade, or velvet about 4 yards long and marked in three places with crosses and the word *agios* (Gr., holy). The orarion is worn over the deacon's *sticharion.* The Greeks drape it in front from the left shoulder down under the right arm; but in back, the other extremity hangs down straight to the ground. Others, among them the Russians, place it over the left shoulder and let it hang straight down both in front and in back. The deacon always holds the front extremity of the orarion between the fingers of his right hand and gestures with it, e.g., toward the icon of Christ or of the Mother of God when mentioning their names. At the Lord's Prayer he undoes the orarion and girds himself with it, crossing it over his back and chest, so as to keep it from encumbering his movements during the Communion. After the Communion of the people, he rearranges it as before. The orarion is the distinguishing vestment of the deacon and is common to all the Eastern rites, but with slight variations. Subdeacons wear a shorter and less ornate form of the orarion around the waist, crossed on the back and hanging down in front. This is often used also by altar boys.

[A. J. JACOPIN]

ORATORIANS (CO), priest and lay-brother members of the Institute of the Oratory of St. Philip Neri founded by him in Rome, in 1575. The members of each congregation live in community life but take no vows (see SOCIETIES OF COMMON LIFE). The constitutions of the Institute were approved by Rome in 1612, and were reapproved in 1942 when the Oratorians became a confederation of congregations in which each house was completely autonomous. Besides the priestly ministry, the members pursue personal holiness through prayer and the practice of the evangelical counsels. The Institute has no central government, nor superior general, but a procurator-general represents the congregations to the Holy See, which may issue directives and rules for the independent houses. Each congregation becomes known by the name of the city in which it is located and only by exception does a large modern city have two houses. The Oratorians are located in England (where J. H. *Newman founded the Birmingham Oratory), Spain, Italy, Poland, Germany, Latin America, and the U.S. (in the dioceses of Charleston, S.C., and Gallup, New Mexico). In 1975 there were 60 houses and a total of 452 members, of whom 361 were priests. BIBLIOGRAPHY: M. Jouhandeau, *St. Philip Neri* (tr. G. Lamb, 1960); R. Addington, *Idea of the Oratory* (1966).

[R. A. TODD]

ORATORIES (CANON LAW), places of worship set aside for a specific group or particular person, not for the general community of the faithful (CIC, c. 1188, §1). Oratories are public, semipublic, or private. A public oratory, however, is one to which the general community does have a general right of access for divine services. Among public oratories are permanent shipboard chapels; chapels of an apostolic nuntiature or delegation; chapels in the room of a saint's birth or death. Semipublic oratories are of more restricted access; the chapels of religious houses or of a cardinal or bishop are of this class. A private oratory is restricted to use by a private person or his household. In no case can an oratory be used for any but sacred functions. The distinction has primary practical importance in regard to the precept of hearing Mass on Sundays and holy days. This can be satisfied by anyone attending Mass in a public or semipublic oratory; or in a cemetery chapel, even though these are private oratories. In other private chapels only members of the household can fulfill the obligation to hear Mass.

[T. C. O'BRIEN]

ORATORY OF DIVINE LOVE, see DIVINE LOVE, ORATORY OF.

ORBAIS, JEAN D', 13th-cent. French Gothic architect, first master of Reims Cathedral (1210–c. 1225) who is recorded as having begun the chevet.

[M. J. DALY]

ORCHIOTOMY, more precisely, orchiectomy, the surgical removal of the testicles, i.e., male *castration. The moral justification rests on the principle of *totality: therapeutic castration is permissible when the diseased testicles are a threat to life. Since they are endocrine glands, their removal upsets hormonal balance and so medically is a serious procedure. A man who, before marriage, has had both testicles removed is considered canonically to have the *impediment of *impotence; he cannot enter a valid marriage.

[T. C. O'BRIEN]

ORDEAL, a word of Teutonic origin translated into medieval Lat. *ordalium*, thence into Elizabethan English, though there is an early instance of it in Chaucer. The term refers to a mode of trial in which a suspect is required to perform certain acts ordinarily harmful or even fatal and if he emerges unscathed is declared innocent. Trial by ordeal is connected with magic and may be considered as a process of divination turned to legal purposes. It may also rely on occult sympathetic influences in nature, as in the conviction, which still lingers among countryfolk, that if the suspected murderer is brought into the presence of the corpse it will manifest certain signs. While not widespread in the Near East, this sort of test is mentioned in the Code of Hammurabi. Among primitive peoples of Europe and Asia,

methods of ordeal included plunging the suspect into deep water, or forcing him to grasp red hot iron, or walk on glowing coals. The OT contains one clear description of ordeal, in Num 5.11–31: a woman suspected of adultery must drink a prescribed potion, which will bring a curse upon her if she is guilty, or leave her unharmed if she is innocent. There are perhaps allusions to ordeal in other OT passages (e.g., Jos 7.13–26; 1 Sam 14.36–45; Jer 8.14; 9.15; Ezek 23.31–34). Among the tests used in the early Middle Ages were walking through fire or over red-hot ploughshares, carrying red-hot irons, plunging an arm into molten lead, being bound and ducked into water (customarily applied to witches), a trial slice of blessed bread-and-cheese, over which a guilty person would choke. Immunity from harm was a sign of God's judgment. Sacramentals and even the sacraments also might be used. With the growth of civilization and the revival of the Roman law by canonists and civilians with its more rational and controlled procedures—and also the calculated application of *torture to extract the truth—the practice diminished. The Council of the Lateran II in 1215 prohibited the clergy from blessing trials by ordeal; and this influenced abolition of the practice in England, Denmark, and elsewhere, though trial by combat or wager in battle continued. Savanarola refused to undergo trial by ordeal.

[T. GILBY]

ORDER. (1) as a philosophical term, order is the pattern or sequence of priorities among several elements having a common point of reference or source. The sequence may mean that one thing comes after another in time; or that one thing is prior in meaning to another: the meaning of one presupposes the other, even where they exist simultaneously (the egg comes before the chicken in time; the chicken before the egg in meaning). (2) Order as the proper arrangement and subordination of parts in a whole is a concept involved in the understanding of the *order of the universe. (3) In theology, the Lat. terms *ordo* and *ordines* refer also to the sacrament of *holy orders. Latin theology, dependent here esp. on Pseudo-Dionysius, referred also to the choirs of angels as ''orders'' (tr. of the Gr. *taxēs*) within the angelic hierarchies. The two uses were sometimes connected because in Dionysius the earthly hierarchy, constituted by orders in the Church, is patterned on the heavenly hierarchies.

[T. C. O'BRIEN]

ORDER, RELIGIOUS, see RELIGIOUS INSTITUTES.

ORDER, SUPERNATURAL, see SUPERNATURAL ORDER.

ORDER OF CHRIST, now a papal order of honorary knighthood conferred, rarely, on Catholic heads of state or on the commandment of the Noble Guard. The name dates from 1319 when in Portugal a military order was founded and given some of the properties of the suppressed Knights Templar. This religious military order was until 1542 under the oversight of the abbot of the Cistercians of Alcobaca; then it was put under the power of the king and gradually became a purely secular and honorary order.

[T. C. O'BRIEN]

ORDER OF THE SWAN, a sodality of great prestige founded in Germany in 1440 by Elector Frederick II of Brandenberg. Membership at first was restricted to nobility, but in 1452, the founder revised the statutes and admitted commoners as well. The purpose of the order was to increase devotion to the Virgin Mary and promote charity. At the time of Reformation, the order died out. In 1843 it was revived by King Frederick William IV of Prussia as a secular association of members of all social classes with social welfare as its goal.

[R. A. TODD]

ORDER OF THE UNIVERSE, the complex of relationships joining all created beings to one another and to God. The universe (Gr., *kosmos*), displays a divine plan, a constant theme from *Plato (e.g., *Timaeus* 27A–34A) through the Fathers to *Teilhard de Chardin, which is realized under one divine government neither as a monolithic structure nor as a *chance assemblage of units, but as possessing a singleness in diversity. Each of these notes will be glanced at in turn.

First, the unity. This lies in the mind of the maker, and in his providence. The general design may escape the philosopher in terms of external finality, for he may well be at a loss to explain, for instance, "Why poison ivy?" or "What is the use of a pneumonia virus?", yet he may still recognize internal finality within the appetite of beings by participation, that is things deriving from one font of good and converging to one supreme good beyond the totality they form together. The position of Christian theologians is more secure, because of the revelation of the Word of God, the *Logos in whom all things were made, and who now, made flesh, is the head of all creation (cf. Col 1.15–20).

Next, the variety. Christian theology rejects monism or pantheism by its doctrine of *creation; the world is other than God. Yet with divine transcendence goes divine immanence, for he is most intimately present to it down to the least particularity. And this distinctiveness of things, natures, traits, and twirls is because he willed it so the less inadequately to reflect and communicate his own inexhaustible resources. Hence the unity of the world is not that of one single organism, but is composed of a pluralism of irreducible substances. These for a theologian are *persons above all, and to this he is committed both by dogma and morals, e.g., the personal existence of Christ and of his mother, our personal response through charity, and our personal guilt through sin. For the rest, he is uncommitted; as a natural philosopher he may have his own convictions, for instance, as to whether an entomological biologist be right

in maintaining that the substantial unit is the ant-hill, not each particular ant; the question, however, does not arise for the City of Reason and the People of God.

The general view is that the unity of the universe consists in direct and indirect relationships, mutual and reciprocal, between diverse things all conspiring to one end, which is represented as the *common good. The problem of *evil is here the chief stumbling block, both for the philosopher and the theologian. Neither can claim to solve it; what they can do is to show how it is not irreconcilable with the doctrine that God's world-order is good, and even perhaps go further, though modestly, with recommending reasons for its being pictured as a chiaroscuro. Yet it is a mystery for reason and for faith alike, and the only glimmer of its real explanation comes through the Passion of Christ.

The interrelation of things in the cosmic order is held in the activities of mind and will, of God's first of all and then of created beings who become partakers of and co-operators in his providence, and is executed through the four types of causality, material, formal, efficient, and final. The last two closely correspond, and created substances can be active and attractive causes under the embracing First Cause and Ultimate Good. As secondary causes they can be either principal or instrumental; as entering into final causality, they can be either intermediate ends or means. They form a hierarchy of beings, pure spirits, embodied spirits, animated bodies, non-living things. All, as it were, belong together, for all belong to God. BIBLIOGRAPHY: ThAq ST 1a, 47–49; 1a, 111–119; (esp. in ed. Lat-Eng, v. 8, *Creation and Variety,* ed. T. Gilby, 1967, and v. 15, *World Order,* ed. M. J. Charlesworth, 1970).

[T. GILBY]

ORDERICUS VITALIS (1075–1142), historian, Benedictine priest. O. received the tonsure from Mainier, abbot of St. Évroult and the Norman name Vitalis. He passed his whole life as a monk of Évroult and was possibly present at the Council of Reims in Oct. 1119 and later at a great assembly of Cluniac monks at Cluny. His work *Historia ecclesiastica* is a general history, beginning with the preaching of the gospel and extending to 1141. It is divided into 13 books, which were not composed in the order in which they now stand. From him we get a detailed picture of life as seen by one who lived in a Norman monastery. O. was thoroughly read in all available literature, in theology, in the Fathers, and in Latin classics. He aimed to give truth without flattery, and his vivid imagination makes the history lively although sometimes inaccurate. The work begins to be of value after the Norman Conquest. O. also had a reputation as a poet. BIBLIOGRAPHY: C. L. Kingsford, DNB 14:1135–36; B. La Croix, NCE 10:724–725; PL 188.

[M. C. BRADLEY]

ORDERS, see HOLY ORDERS.

ORDERS, ANGLICAN, see ANGLICAN ORDERS.

ORDERS AND PRAYERS FOR CHURCH WOR-SHIP, a manual primarily for the use of British Baptist ministers, first published in 1960 (2d ed., 1965). Having no official denominational sanction, the book was prepared by E. A. Payne and S. F. Winward, and its use is purely voluntary. Payne is a church historian and has served as secretary of the Baptist Union of Great Britain and Ireland; he has also been president of the World Council of Churches. Winward is a London pastor and author of *The Reformation of Our Worship* (1964). The manual has been widely used in Great Britain. Baptists usually have had simple, informal services of worship, stressing freedom and spontaneity. The editors of *Orders and Prayers* maintain that freedom does not preclude preparation of prayers and utilization of forms used by other communions. As is explained in the "Introduction," they wished to avoid the extremes of an inflexible, fixed liturgy and the "uninspired disorder" that often results from disregard of traditional forms. Endeavoring to combine freedom and order, they disclaim any intention of offering a Baptist equivalent of the *Book of Common Prayer; they are providing a Book of Common Order. The eight main parts of the book include orders of service; Scripture passages; and prayers for regular public worship, for baptism and the Lord's Supper, and for special occasions. The last section has a lectionary for ordinary and systematic reading of the Scriptures at public services of worship.

[N. H. MARING]

ORDINALS, ANGLICAN, see ANGLICAN ORDINALS.

ORDINALS, ROMAN, books giving the *ordo,* i.e., the ritual and rubrics, for liturgical ceremonies. The formal development and editing of such books began during the Carolingian renaissance. By the 10th cent. from the various Gallic and Roman elements in practice the Roman ordinal developed, and its disposition of the liturgy became the basic usage of the Latin Church. The ordinals are thus important to the history of the Roman rite. The modern reconstruction of the Roman ordinals and their development was largely the work of Michel *Andrieu (1886–1956).

ORDINANCE, a term common among Mennonites, Baptists, and other nonliturgical Churches, used instead of "sacrament." The preference is based on the objection to magical connotations of the latter term (see SACRAMEN-TALISM). Early Baptists used both terms but preferred ordinances, and later Baptists used it almost exclusively. With reference to baptism and the Lord's Supper, no biblical precedent exists for calling these rites either sacraments or ordinances. The latter, however, is an OT term (e.g., Ex 29.9; Lev 6.18), which was interpreted to mean something divinely instituted and of perpetual validity. BIBLIOGRAPHY: W. R. McNutt, *Polity and Practice in Baptist Churches* (rev. ed., 1959); MennEnc 4:72–73.

ORDINARIES (ECCLESIASTICAL), in canon law (CIC, c. 198) a cleric with primary *jurisdiction over another individual in both the internal forum of conscience and the external forum as judge. Local ordinaries include the pope himself, residential bishops, and other prelates who exercise a territorial jurisdiction. Personal or religious ordinaries are the *major superiors of exempt religious orders. The authority of a local ordinary is limited geographically, while that of a religious ordinary is limited to those individuals specifically subject to him.

[R. A. ARONSTAM]

ORDINARY OF THE MASS, the collective name applied to the nonvariable parts of the Roman Mass, distinguishing them from parts (esp. scripture readings and some prayers) variable according to day or season. For many of these prayers (found in the part of the *Sacramentary* titled Order of Mass) various forms or options are provided. An agreed-upon ecumenical translation of several of these elements (e.g., Gloria, Creed, Sanctus) is now available and in use in several denominations in the English-speaking world.

[J. DALLEN]

ORDINARY TEACHING OF THE CHURCH, a phrase used in Vatican Council I to describe one manner in which the teaching authority of the Church (*magisterium*) is exercised. (1) That Council indicates that the Church proposes certain matters as revealed truths, and as such to be believed, either by "solemn judgment" or "by its ordinary and universal magisterium" (D 3011). The solemn judgment may refer to the infallible teaching of a council of bps. assembled in union with the pope, or to a papal *ex cathedra* pronouncement. Exercise of the ordinary and universal magisterium refers to extraconciliar teachings on matters of faith and morals assented to by the college of ruling bps. in union with the pope; the infallible guidance of the Holy Spirit guarantees that such unanimity in teaching cannot be in error. Theologians agree, however, that it is not easy to determine that a specific truth is so authenticated. But it is clear that, for example, the Nicene Creed is authentically sustained by the present ordinary teaching authority, and not merely by the historical act of the councils that formulated it (see also MIND OF THE CHURCH). (2) As the pope exercises his own privileged teaching authority, it is universal, since he is the pastor over the whole Church. The ordinary exercise of that office occurs apart from *ex cathedra* pronouncements; nor is it exercised in virtue of union with the college of bishops. Teachings so proposed are thus not infallible; they do call for respectful docility. *ENCYCLICALS.

[T. C. O'BRIEN]

ORDINATION, IMPEDIMENTS TO, see HOLY ORDERS, IMPEDIMENTS TO.

ORDINATION, TITLE OF, the canonical requirement for lawful ordination that the ordinand have an assured, steady income, sufficient for his lifetime support in keeping with his station (CIC, c.979). For secular clergy the canonical titles are: title of *benefice, largely obsolete; title of patrimony, i.e., the private means of the ordinand; title of pension, i.e., a subsidy from State, Church or other source; title of perpetual service to a diocese, i.e., one based on the lifelong service to be rendered by the ordinand, and on the guarantee of the bp. or mission superior to support him; this title also requires the ordinand's oath swearing lifelong service. In the case of members of clerical religious, the canonical title for *regulars is the title of poverty, i.e., based on their solemn religious profession; for members of religious congregations, it is the title of the community table; in both instances the religious institute stands as the guarantor of support. For other religious the titles for seculars apply (*ibid.*, c.982).

[T. C. O'BRIEN]

ORDINATIONS IN THE ROMAN RITE, the liturgical actions which establish a man in the hierarchy of orders. Broadly speaking, there are three historical stages in the development of the present ceremonies. In the ancient Roman rituals as described by Hippolytus (d.*c.*235) in the *Apostolic Tradition,* the ordination rites for the bp., priest, and deacon are extremely simple and unadorned. They consist of two essential elements: an imposition of hands upon the head of the ordinand, and an appropriate consecratory prayer. Beginning in the 6th cent., the ordination rites were somewhat expanded. The imposition of hands and accompanying blessing remained, but additional actions (examination of the bp.'s or priest's worthiness, presentation of the ordinand to the people, prostrations, the kiss of peace, and various prayers) were appended. The third stage represents a complete departure from earlier Roman simplicity, and results from the combination of the Roman ritual with that of the *Gallican rite. This fusion was first accomplished in the 9th cent. but adapted by William *Duranti the Elder (d. 1296), and finally imposed on the Latin Church in 1596. Emphasis was placed upon the visible expression of the prayer texts; anointings with oil became highly important; vestments and various insignia of office (miter and crozier, chalice, or book of the gospels) were handed over; and several concluding blessings were added. It is this ritual which forms the basis for contemporary ordination rites. According to the Apostolic Constitution, *Sacramentum ordinis* (1947) of Pius XII, the laying on of hands and the consecratory formula within the ordination-rite preface constitute the essential sacramental sign of holy orders for bps., presbyters, and deacons. In accordance with the directives of the Vatican II ConstChurch these three are the ordained ministers in the Church. Revised rites for their ordination were promulgated by Paul VI's Apostolic Constitution, *Pontificalis Romani* (June 18, 1969); Paul VI's *motu proprio, Ministeria quaedam* (Aug. 15, 1972) suppressed subdiaconate and the minor orders. On the same day the *motu proprio, Ad pascendum* decreed a rite of commission to

celibacy prior to ordination as deacons. Entrance into the two universal liturgical lay ministries of reader and acolyte the same document designated as "institution." The rites of institution for these ministries serve as model for the rite of institution of extraordinary (or special) ministers of the Eucharist and for particular ministries, e.g., in the U.S. that of the minister of music, which are recognized by the Holy See on petition by episcopal conferences. BIBLIOGRAPHY: A. Martimort, *Signs of the New Covenant* (1963); N. J. O'Shea, NCE 10:727–734; *Ordination of Deacons, Priests, and Bishops* (USCC, 1975); *Institution of Readers and Acolytes, Admission to Candidacy for Ordination As Deacons and Priests, Commission to Celibacy* (USCC, 1976); USCC *Study Text III, Ministries in the Church (Ministeria quaedam and Ad pascendum;* n.d.).

[J. J. FLOOD]

ORDO, ROMAN, a calendar with directions for the celebration of Mass and the office throughout the Roman Rite. An outgrowth of local and monastic calendars and their special liturgical offices, it became a means of promulgating a uniform liturgy in accord with the decrees of Trent. The Roman Calendar of 1969 replaced the former Roman Ordo. The term *ordo* refers properly to the disposition of and directions for liturgical rites.

[F. H. BRIGHAM]

ORDÓÑEZ, BARTOLOMÉ (d.1520), sculptor. "Eagle of the Spanish Renaissance," whose style shows a masterly command of Donatello and Michelangelo, he collaborated with Diego de Siloe on the *Caraccioli Altarpiece* (1514–15), doing the principal panel *Adoration of the Magi.* For Barcelona cathedral (1519) O. carved reliefs in wood for the choir stalls and in marble for the *trascoro* (screen across the nave), and the sepulchres of Joan the Mad and Philip the Handsome (Royal Chapel, Granada).

[M. J. DALY]

ORÉ, LUIS GERÓNIMO DE (1554–1630), Franciscan missionary, linguist, and bishop. Born in Ayacucho, Peru, of a numerous family, O. was ordained in Lima in 1582 and from 1584 to 1598 served as a missionary to the Collaguas Indians in the S part of the country. His *Símbolo católico indiano* (1598), containing hymns and teaching material, was the fruit of this labor. After returning to Lima as vicar, O. taught his brethren at the convent the Quechua and Aymara tongues, which he had known since childhood. He next took in hand the religious instruction to be given the Indians of the Cuzco, Arequipa, La Paz, and Charcas dioceses. A long trip to Rome (1604–1610), saw the appearance of several works, the most important of which was *Rituale seu manuale peruanum* (1607), principally a guide for missionaries working in Peru but printed in three European and five different Indian languages. A mission to Spain following the death of St. Francis *Solano in 1610 led to the publication in 1614 of O.'s *Relación de la vida y milagros* *del Venerable P. Fray Francisco Solano,* while the *Relación de los mártires de la Florida* (1618, tr. *Martyrs of Florida,* ed. and tr. J. M. Geiger, 1937) grew out of a trip to Florida and Cuba in 1614 to investigate the Franciscan missions there. Named bishop of Concepción, Chile, by the King of Spain, O. arrived in his new post in 1622 and thereafter devoted himself to the conversion of the Indians.

[E. M. GATES]

OREGON, a state of the Pacific NW, admitted to the Union (1859) as the 33d state. British and American fur traders occupied the region through the early 19th cent., with the Hudson's Bay Company conducting the larger trading operation. The territory up to the 49th parallel was conceded to the U.S. by England in a treaty of 1846. Catholicism came to the area with the French-Canadian fur traders of the Hudson's Bay Company; and J. *McLoughlin, the company's chief factor in the territory before the boundary settlement, became a Catholic in 1842. In 1838 F. N. *Blanchet was sent as vicar general from Quebec to minister to the Catholics of the territory. With his assistant, M. Demers, Blanchet worked among the Indian and French Canadian population. They established several missions, among which were Fort Vancouver and Oregon City. Pierre J. *De Smet, SJ, was also active in missionary work in E Oregon during the 1840s. With the influx of immigrants the Archdiocese of Oregon City was created (1846), and Blanchet was appointed its first archbishop. Although Indian attacks and the gold rush to California depleted the population, Blanchet developed Catholic facilities, aided by funds from South America and the teaching skills of the Sisters of the Holy Names of Jesus and Mary. In 1862 Blanchet moved to Portland, where he encouraged the foundation of the *Catholic Sentinel* and St. Vincent's Hospital. After Blanchet's resignation (1880), he was succeeded by C. *Seghers (1880–84), and W. *Gross (1884–98). Gross stressed education, founded the Sisters of St. Mary, and invited the Christian Brothers and other teaching orders to Oregon. His successor, A. Christie, established numerous schools and supported the foundation of the present Univ. of Portland (1901). During Christie's administration, the so-called Oregon School Law, requiring that all children attend public schools, was passed in 1922; this was declared unconstitutional by the U.S. Supreme Court in 1925. E. D. Howard became abp. in 1926 and devoted himself to institutional reorganization. He expanded the school system and coordinated the archdiocesan Catholic Charities. In 1928 the official title of the see was changed from Oregon City to Portland in Oregon. Abp. Robert Dwyer was appointed in 1966 and resigned in 1974. The archdiocese is now (1978) administered by Abp. Cornelius M. Power. Its suffragan sees are the Dioceses of Helena and Great Falls, Mont., Boise, Idaho, and Baker, Oregon.

Oregon's Catholics numbered 299,360 in 1976 or 12.3% of the total population. The major Protestant denominations represented are the Methodists, with 2.8% of the population and the Church of Jesus Christ of the Latter-Day Saints with 2.8%. Other Protestant denominations comprised 17.2% of the population. The Jewish population (1968) amounted to 0.4%. There are two Catholic colleges in Oregon, with a total enrollment of 2,855 students. Some 3,937 students attend the state's 10 Catholic high schools, and 11,092 the 55 Catholic elementary schools. BIBLIOGRAPHY: E. V. O'Hara, *Pioneer Catholic History of Oregon* (4th ed., 1939); *Early Catholic Missions in Old Oregon* (ed. C. B. Bagley, 2 v., 1932).

[J. L. MORRISON; R. M. PRESTON]

OREGON SCHOOL CASE (*Pierce v. Society of Sisters,* 268 U.S. 510), U.S. Supreme Court case in 1925 resulting in a decision upholding parental rights in the education of children. In the upsurge of nativist sentiment and religious bigotry of the early 1920s, private denominational schools were under strong attack. An Oregon law of 1922, passed by initiative procedure, made attendance of children at public schools compulsory. Opponents of the law, principally Catholic forces aided by Episcopalians, Seventh Day Adventists, Jews, and other religious groups, waged a 2-year battle through the courts, which assumed national significance because similar legislation was pending in other states. By unanimous verdict the U.S. Supreme Court declared the Oregon law unconstitutional. The decision referred to the precedent of *Meyer v. Nebraska* (1923), which had involved limitations on private schools, wherein the Court associated the right to educate with religious freedom protected by the 14th Amendment. The Oregon decision squarely asserted the right of parents to direct the upbringing and education of their children. It also recognized the property rights of those involved in private education. The decision served to protect the existence of private and denominational schools and also their future development. It subsequently influenced the statement in the United Nations Declaration of Human Rights on parental rights in the education of children. BIBLIOGRAPHY: *Oregon School Cases: Complete Record* (1925); G. E. Reed, NCE 10:738–740.

[J. C. WILLKE]

O'REILLY, BERNARD (1803–56), second bp. of Hartford, Connecticut. Born in Ireland, he studied for the priesthood in Montreal and St. Mary's Seminary, Baltimore, Maryland. Ordained in 1831, he served in New York State, becoming vicar general of Buffalo, N.Y., in 1847. Named bp. of Hartford in 1850, he was a vigorous builder of churches and did much to increase the number of clergy in his diocese, both by recruitment from Ireland and by founding St. Mary's Seminary in Providence, R.I. (then part of the Hartford diocese). On a voyage of recruitment to Europe, he was lost at sea when the ship went down with all aboard.

[J. R. AHERNE]

O'REILLY, EDMUND (1606–69), abp. of Armagh. He left Dublin (1633) to study at Louvain, returned in 1641 to serve as vicar general of the Dublin diocese (1642–48), and during the rebellion against England, served as governor of Wicklow (1642). He was accused of betraying the Irish and English troops of Ormond and Purcell to Michael Jones. Promoted to the archbishopric of Armagh (1654), he was consecrated at a Jesuit chapel in Brussels, and after numerous escapes and near arrests in England, he arrived at his diocese in 1659. After Charles II's restoration, the Pope ordered O'R. to leave Ireland. He went to Rome and later returned to Ireland for a national synod in Dublin (1666), where he opposed the pro-English faction. Arrested, then exiled by Ormond after the synod, O'R. went to the Continent where he visited Irish colleges at Paris, Brussels, and Louvain; he died at Saumur in France.

[R. J. LITZ]

O'REILLY, JOHN BOYLE (1844–90) Irish-born journalist and poet. He first worked on newspapers in Ireland and England, then decided that the cause of Irish freedom called for a more active role. He joined the Fenians, an organization of men in Ireland and abroad pledged to free Ireland from British rule. Infiltrating a British regiment in Dublin, he worked against the Crown, was arrested, tried before a military court, and sentenced to be hanged. The commutation to life imprisonment meant Dartmoor, the most dreaded of English prisons. A second commutation sent him into exile in the penal colony of Australia. Assigned to work in the mahogany forests, he managed to escape and board an American sailing vessel and reached Boston. There he became a celebrated lecturer and journalist, ultimately (1870) editor of *The Pilot,* the diocesan weekly. Under him, it attained an astounding readership—at one time of over a million people. An autobiographical novel *Moondyne Joe* (1879) and his considerable poetry, published in 1878 under the title *Songs, Legends and Ballads,* showed him as a competent man of letters. His best book of verse is *In Bohemia* (1886). O'R. was ahead of his age in fighting anti-Semitism, and in his espousal of rights for blacks he became a fellow-worker and friend of Wendell Phillips. His editorials in the 1880s read like liberal statements of the 1960s on the civil rights question. When he died, a man in his prime, there was an outpouring of praise from President Harrison and former President Cleveland, and other public figures. BIBLIOGRAPHY: W. G. Schofield, *Seek for a Hero* (1956).

[J. R. AHERNE]

O'REILLY, POTOMIAN, BROTHER (1847–1917), educator, scientist. An Irish-born immigrant to the U.S., O'R. became a Brother of the Christian Schools in 1859. His teaching assignments included schools in the U.S., Canada, England, and Ireland. He served at St. Joseph's College, London, as professor and president from 1870 to 1893, and was the first Catholic to receive a doctorate in science from the Univ. of London (1883). O'R. was also the first to apply the recently discovered X-ray to medicine in Ireland. At Manhattan College in New York from 1896 to 1917, he did his most notable work in electrical science, contributing to scientific journals and publishing a pioneer work, *Catalogue of the Wheeler Gift of Books, Pamphlets and Periodicals in the Library of the American Institute of Electrical Engineering* (1909), an annotated survey of the monumental collection.

[J. R. AHERNE]

ORGANIC ARTICLES, a French law attached unilaterally by *Napoleon Bonaparte to the Concordat of 1801 between France and the Holy See. In essence the Articles were a civil code regulating the French Church in the interest of the government. The 74 provisions restored many of the principles of *Gallicanism and practices that Napoleon had agreed to abolish, and thus they contradicted the spirit of the Concordat. Their effect was to legalize the civil authority's control of the Church in administrative matters, in its contact with Rome, its cult and catechism; they even required seminaries to teach the doctrines of the *Declaration of the French Clergy. Pope Pius VII's protest went unheeded, and the Articles remained the law of France until 1905.

[R. H. SCHMANDT]

ORGANIC TRANSPLANTS. The morality of supplying the lack or remedying the defect of a bodily part in a living human being by a surgical operation which grafts a working equivalent excised from another is governed by principles. Some are common to both cases of a living and of a dead donor; some are proper to each. We take them in turn.

(1) Obviously the matter engages the public interest, and on it, therefore, the State may have a policy. Prohibitory laws in this matter would seem to bind in conscience even if, on grounds of the prevailing sentiment, they forbid a practice that a private individual or group may find defensible. This is the whole proscribing what a section does not think to be wrong, not prescribing what a section thinks to be wrong. The cases are quite different. Accordingly, organic transplants, even when morally allowable under the conditions to be indicated below, might well be outlawed if they are repugnant to people as a whole. It would be otherwise, however, were the State to act more positively and to enforce compulsory transplantation at need, for that would be an invasion of personal and family rights, which could victimize the living or affront feelings of reverence for the dead which still survive as more than archaisms.

Then also, since it concerns illness and health, what doctors themselves think must be taken into a moral account. A consensus of the medical profession, more esp. if it forms a free association and not a department of State, will be of great weight, and all the more if it represents general physicians accustomed to treat persons in the round, not just one specialist class of surgeons.

(2) If a man is praised for losing his limbs from pushing a child off the line in front of a train, it would seem at first

sight that he may submit to the excision of a part of his own body in order to save the life of another. But the question is not so simple as that. Some moral theologians emphasize the old teaching that man is not the proprietor but the administrator of his body, and may lawfully choose *mutilation only for the sake of the health of his whole body. Others, however, take a more corporate view of human associations, and argue that within limits we may save others directly through some loss of our physical integrity, and more lasting than that of a blood-transfusion or skin-graft. This seems to have the authority of what moralists call a "probable opinion." The limits are largely those set by a sense of proportion; no man may choose to be killed or, it seems, to be sterilized, or to lose one leg that another may have two. The question admits of easier solution in the case of paired organs such as kidneys, or organs that are not functioning in the giver but will function in the receiver. Most of the specific rules here will be subject to the judgment of *prudence, in which, as indicated, the physician will play a part, as to what will be to the true advantage of both donor and recipient. It should be made clear throughout the discussion we are dealing, not with what a man is obliged to do, but with what he may do, and be admired for it.

The transplantation of a living foetus would seem to be inadmissible as breaking the proper reciprocation between the unitive and fruitful values in human sexuality. Some people might feel that, after *Humanae vitae,* an encyclical on the subject would redress the balance.

(3) There are no moral difficulties about a person's willing his body to be used for medical purposes after his death. In the absence of any testamentary disposition on the part of the deceased, and in the absence of legal custodians entitled to make the decision, there is no reason why the law must prevent the body from being disposed of for the benefit of others; though in this connection Pius XII warned us against acquiescing in one law for the rich and another law for the poor.

No small problem here arises from our lack of knowledge about the exact moment of death, which causes hesitation about giving hospital authorities too forthright and immediate powers to perform what might be a lethal operation. The Church, which has been in the business of death longer than any other group, must certainly be represented among experts who draw up the proper regulatory safeguards.

There is no question of the human person in the philosophical and theological sense of their being radically changed by any feasible operation, or of any eschatological embarrassment being caused at the general resurrection. Advances in the techniques of engrafting some centers from one organism to another may produce problems of personality-changes in respect of certain psychosomatic manifestations. We need not strive officiously to stay alive; we might be better dead than surviving under some conditions. The same consideration will affect organic transplants from animals were they to affect serious psychic derange-

ment. Otherwise, that is when they procure a true human benefit, they are lawful. *TOTALITY, PRINCIPLE OF.

[T. GILBY]

ORGANICISM, a philosophical approach which finds an essential integrative design in all events and sequences of events. The organicist, given facts and fragments of experience, discovers implied connections (nexuses) among these fragments. These connections suggest that the process of which these fragments are a part is organized in an orderly holistic fashion. The presumption that fragments are indeed part of a process and that there is an "inner form" to this process is what immediately distinguishes organicism from other philosophies. Contradictions and apparent irregularities among facts in a nexus are resolved in a greater organic unity, a whole that transcends those contradictions without sacrificing any facts or fragments. This greater organic whole, the organicist maintains, was implicit in the fragmentary facts of experience: what appeared as fragmentary was really an organic unity, an ideal toward which events were proceeding. Thus the organicist solution to the problem of the One and the Many is basically that the totality composed of many distinct parts is implicitly an organic whole, greater than and prior to its parts. The living organism, whose continued life processes cannot be explained in terms of its elements and parts, is the guiding metaphor for organicist speculations on the whole range of philosophical, social, psychological, and theological issues. Besides the development and evolution of living things, individual works of art that are conceived as wholes but necessarily grow by parts and pieces, any change of which alters the whole, are another class of items fruitfully described by organic philosophy. Thus, organicism has always been an attractive philosophy for those whose primary interest is aesthetics. Among the more notable thinkers whose philosophies fall within this general description of organicism may be numbered: G. W. F. Hegel, F. von Schelling, A. W. Schlegel, T. H. Green, A. C. Bradley, B. Bosanquet, J. Royce, A. N. Whitehead, and other philosophers whose thought is pragmatic yet colored by idealism.

[R. J. LITZ]

ORGANISATION CATHOLIQUE INTERNATIONALE DU CINÉMA (OCIC), a papally approved federation of national Catholic film offices and other international Catholic organizations with similar objectives, founded at The Hague in 1928. OCIC consists of 58 national members, 5 international members, with 10 nations to be recommended for membership at the 1977 general assembly at Munich. It has a network of specialized services and operates through regional secretariats situated in countries of Africa, Asia, Europe, Latin America, North America, and Oceania. In view of the growing influence of the film in mission countries, a missionary service of the OCIC was instituted in 1958 with headquarters at Vatican

City. OCIC pursues four principal objectives: to collaborate in the development of cinema as an art form and as an instrument for social communication fulfilling the cultural, informational, and leisure needs of mankind; to contribute to the human and spiritual growth of film professionals and spectators; to further the production and distribution of films and of audio-visual media in view of evangelization and promotion of human development; to help in the organization of film directors and users of audio-visual media for purposes of education and the expression of faith. OCIC conducts a large variety of film-related activities, meetings and congresses, which in turn give impetus to Catholic cinematographic work throughout the world and contribute in forming the Church's attitude toward the cinema. Since 1944, the federation has awarded prizes at many international film festivals for fine quality films that contribute to the development of spiritual and human values. Amongst the winners of the Grand Prize, awarded annually since 1955, are *The Diary of Anne Frank, Dialogue des Carmé-lites, A Man for All Seasons,* and *Godspell.* OCIC's administration is carried on by a directory committee of members representative of the various world regions. A general council of delegates representing all affiliated national offices meets every three years. The legal seat and general secretariat of the federation is in Brussels, Belgium. Among its publications are a journal, *Revue Internationale du Cinéma* (in English, French, and Spanish) and the *Newsletter.*

[R. A. TODD]

ORGANIZATION OF AMERICAN STATES (OAS), an association of most of the nations of the Western hemisphere to protect themselves against aggression from the outside, to facilitate the settlement of their own disputes, and to promote the welfare of their people through cooperative effort. The OAS was established in 1948 as an outgrowth of the periodical meetings of the Pan-American Union and a century of diplomatic effort to safeguard mutual interests. It transformed the Monroe Doctrine into a mutual defense pact, with Communism seen as the principal threat. The evolution of the Castro regime in Cuba presented the OAS with its most serious internal challenge. The OAS comprises a regional agency within the United Nations. Its chief organ is the Inter-American Conference, meeting every five years, with each member state having a single vote in the formulation of basic policies and the determination of areas of concern. The Meeting of Consultation of Ministers of Foreign Affairs convenes only in emergencies that threaten hemispheric peace. The Council of the OAS is a permanent body, with headquarters in Washington under an elected secretary general, which handles emergency issues and whatever other duties the Conference assigns to it. The Advisory Defense Committee, also in Washington, counsels the OAS on military matters. The Pan-American Union serves as the secretariat. Additional specialized agencies include the Inter-American Council of Jurists, the Inter-American Economic and Social Council, and the Inter-American Cultural Council. Other lesser bodies coordinate or formulate projects in the area of child, women's or Indian welfare, agriculture, health and history. The Alliance for Progress (1961) was the OAS's most comprehensive program of a non-political nature, including many projects in the areas of social concern or health improvement, with the U.S. as the chief source of resources and the Latin American states the beneficiaries.

[R. H. SCHMANDT]

ORICELLARIUS, BERNARD (RUCELLAI; 1448–1514), historian, politician. Member of a prominent family, married to Nannina, sister of Lorenzo de' Medici, he held important posts in the government of Florence. He opposed Pietro II de' Medici for his disregard of republican forms. This resulted in his choice as a committee member to effect a change of government in Florence which by 1512 was wracked by dissension and corruption. During the interregnum period of discord, O. concentrated on his literary works. In his *De bello italico* (1733), the term balance of power made its first appearance in political writings. BIBLIOGRAPHY: M. G. McNeil, NCE 10:761–762.

[J. M. O'DONNELL]

ORIENTAL CHURCHES, see EASTERN CHURCHES.

ORIENTAL CHURCHES, CONGREGATION FOR THE, one of nine congregations of the *Curia Romana and charged with care of Eastern-rite Catholics and their Churches in all matters administered by the other congregations for the Latin Church. This congregation has jurisdiction over regions where the greater number of Christians are members of the Oriental rite Churches: as in southern Albania, Bulgaria, Cyprus, Greece, Eritrea, Lebanon, Turkey, part of Thrace subject to Turkey, Palestine, Jordan, Sinai Peninsula, Egypt, N Ethiopia, Afghanistan, Iran, Iraq, and also over smaller communities of Orientals no matter where they reside. Historically, the congregation had its beginning in 1573, when Gregory XIII established a Congregation of Affairs of the Greeks, which was commissioned to deal with matters concerning Greek-rite Catholics and to promote the faith among other Eastern Christians. From the 17th cent. these matters were under the Congregation for the Propagation of the Faith; it was not until 1917 that Benedict XV created the autonomous Congregation for the Oriental Churches. In March 1963, John XXIII appointed five Eastern-rite patriarchs and one Roman-rite patriarch, giving each the same privileges as cardinals enjoy. In November of the same year, Paul VI designated representatives of all Eastern-rite bodies to serve as advisors of the Congregation for the Oriental Churches.

[R. A. TODD]

ORIENTAL CODE (CANON LAW), the canonical legislation for members of the 18 Eastern Catholic rites (see EASTERN RITES). On Jan. 5, 1929 the Sacred Congregation for the *Oriental Churches directed all ordinaries of the Eastern rites to submit proposals for the compilation of an Oriental Code to a commission appointed by Pope Pius XI. Under the presidency of Card. P. Gasparri, and later of Acacius Coussa, the commission began codification. The text of the proposed 2,666 canons was fixed by a special commission called the Pontifical Commission for the Redaction of the Code of Oriental Canon Law (CICO). The Code was promulgated by way of four *motu proprios* from 1949 to 1957. The decree of Vatican Council II on the Eastern Catholic Churches (1964) has already changed certain parts of the CICO as it is summarized below.

(1) Crebrae allatae, promulgated Feb. 22, 1949 (AAS 41:89–119), in force May 2, 1949, contains 131 canons in great part identical with the Latin rite CIC. About 30 canons differ from the Latin Code to any degree; e.g., matrimonial banns are legislated by particular law, local ordinaries, and patriarchs, and major archbishops have wide powers of dispensation.

(2) Sollicitudinem nostram, promulgated Jan. 6, 1950 (AAS 42:5–120), in force Jan. 6, 1951, contains 567 canons dealing with the law of procedure for the Oriental Church. It establishes the membership and power of various patriarchal tribunals, and provides for lower courts as well as for eparchies of several rites.

(3) Postquam apostolicis, promulgated Feb. 9, 1952 (AAS 44:65–152), in force Nov. 12, 1952, contains three sections: cc. 1–231 on religious; cc. 232–301 on the temporal property of the Church; cc. 302–325 on the definition of a number of legal terms. The section on religious gives each institute the right to retain a Latin rite form of organization or return to the original monastic state. The majority chose the former.

(4) Cleri sanctitati, promulgated June 2, 1957 (AAS 49:433–603), in force Nov. 25, 1958, contains 550 canons divided into four sections: cc. 1–15 deal with the acquisition and change of rite; cc. 16–158 provide legislation regarding age, domicile, consanguinity and affinity, moral and physical persons; cc. 38–526 treat the nature of hierarchical and parochial organization with special emphasis on the patriarchs; cc. 527–558 deal with the laity and their associations.

Vatican Council II's *Orientalium ecclesiarum* and other decrees have already modified what has appeared of CICO and further promulgation of the planned code has ceased since a major revision of both Latin and Oriental canon law is forthcoming. BIBLIOGRAPHY: A. Coussa, *Epitome praelectionum de iure ecclesiastica orientali* (3 v., 1941–50; suppl. 1958); F. Galtier, *La Procédure judiciaire en droit oriental* (1954); V. J. Pospishil, NCE 10:763–767.

[F. T. RYAN]

ORIENTAL INSTITUTE, PONTIFICAL, see PONTIFI-CAL INSTITUTE FOR ORIENTAL STUDIES.

ORIENTALIUM DIGNITAS, an encyclical letter issued by Pope Leo XIII on Nov. 30, 1894 asserting that the preservation of the *Eastern rites is vital for the universal Church. The variety of these rites and their apostolic origin illustrate the divine unity of the Catholic faith. For these reasons Leo XIII declared that it is the duty of the Roman pontiff to keep these various ecclesial groups intact and he warned Latin rite missionaries who work among Eastern rite people to respect their venerable traditions instead of attempting to change them. In this document Leo XIII entrusted the care of the Eastern rite people living outside the limits of their patriarchates or Eastern regions to the local Latin bishops. The encyclical inaugurated a new era of appreciation and understanding of the Eastern rites in the West. BIBLIOGRAPHY: ASS 27:257–264.

[E. EL-HAYEK]

ORIENTALIUM ECCLESIARUM, the decree on the Eastern Catholic Churches of Vatican Council II, promulgated Nov. 21, 1964, which defined principles that should determine the attitude and relationship of Catholics toward Catholic and non-Catholic Eastern Christianity. The 30 articles describe the attitude of the Catholic Church, esp. the Roman See, toward the Eastern Churches, reemphasizing that the various Eastern rites are equal parts of the Church, not less genuine than the Latin rite (1–3). The document supports the genuine tradition of the Eastern rites against the extraneous influence of the Western Church, which had replaced authentic Eastern traditions, forms, institutions (6, 12, 21, 22, 23). It also regulates the legal relationship among the various rites, esp. the transfer of individuals from one to another (4). The importance of the offices of patriarch and archbishop major is stressed, and thereby also the institutions of particular Churches against the centralizing tendency of the Roman See (5, 7–11). The decree reestablishes the right of all priests to administer confirmation (13, 14); permits the transfer of the Sunday obligation where it exists to Saturday evening or to parts of the divine services other than Mass (15); confers jurisdiction for confession to any priest in all Churches and places of any rite within the territory of his original jurisdiction (16); reestablishes a permanent diaconate (17); declares as valid, marriages of Catholics before a non-Catholic Eastern priest (18). Finally, it establishes principles of ecumenical relationships, e.g., a common date for Easter (20) and common participation in sacramental worship of Catholics and Eastern Orthodox (24–29).

The decree made few definitive decisions about problems affecting the relationship between the Roman See and the Eastern Churches, and a number of articles are somewhat vaguely and equivocally worded. This lack of juridical precision, it is felt, was probably intentional since the canon law for the Eastern Catholic Churches is in the process of recodification. BIBLIOGRAPHY: V. J. Pospishil, *Orientalium Ecclesiarum. The Decree on the Eastern Catholic Churches* (1965); M. Wojnar, in *Jurist* (April 1965) 173–255.

[V. J. POSPISHIL]

ORIENTATION, the practice adopted by Christians in earlier centuries of facing toward the *East in prayer, of building their churches with their portals or apse toward the East, and of burying the dead with feet toward the East. The custom survived down to the Middle Ages and in some cases even beyond, but gave way as other considerations made the E-W positioning of churches impractical; and as the fixed altar in the churches became more generally accepted as the symbol of Christ. BIBLIOGRAPHY: Podhradsky 151.

[P. K. MEAGHER]

ORIGEN (185–253), most distinguished representative of the school of Alexandria, a pupil of *Clement of Alexandria. Born at Alexandria, O. was trained first by his father *Leonides, martyred in 202 or 203. At age 18 he was appointed in 204 by Bp. *Demetrius to succeed Clement as head of the catechetical school of Alexandria. During his tenure he continued his studies, attending the lectures of the Neoplatonist *Ammonius Saccas, learning Hebrew, and meditating on the Scriptures. He spent the years 212–215 in Rome. He then traveled to Palestine where he taught Scripture in the churches at the suggestion of Theoctistis, bp. of Caesarea, and Alexander, bp. of Jerusalem. In 218–219, he returned to Alexandria to continue teaching at the request of Bp. Demetrius. With added secretaries, he was able to increase his literary output.

While in Palestine in 230, O. was ordained by Theoctistis and Alexander without the required canonical permission of Demetrius, who removed him from his post as head of the catechetical school and forbade him to exercise his priestly function. These pronouncements were promulgated in two synods held by Demetrius in 231. Herclas, successor to Demetrius, repeated the penalties.

O. then settled in Caesarea where he began a new school of theology sponsored by the bp. of Caesarea. His pupil there, *Gregory Thaumaturgus, indicated in his panegyric that the course included an introduction to philosophy with stress on logic, dialectic, natural science, geometry, and astronomy, then a course on ethics and theology. Origen's students were required to read the ancient classical philosophers.

In 244, while in Arabia, he helped restore Bp. Beryllus of Bostra from *Monarchianism. During the Decian persecution, he suffered great tortures, according to Eusebius, never fully recovered, and died in Tyre, Phoenicia in 253.

Unfortunately, the Origenist controversies of subsequent generations occasioned the loss of most of his writings (see ORIGENISM). Latin translations are for the most part the best that tradition has to offer of those works which have survived.

While his approach reflects the learning of a universalist, his extant writings are on biblical, apologetic, dogmatic, and ascetical subjects. Of his biblical writings, the most important was the *Hexapla. His exegetical works included scholia, (see SCHOLIUM), commentaries, and homilies. Complete scholia have not survived. Some excerpts are contained in the *Philokalia* and in *catenae*. No complete text of the commentaries is available. Of 25 books of the commentary on St. Matthew, 8 remain (10–17), as do 8 of his 32 books of commentary on St. John. Only fragments of his 15–book commentary on the *Epistle to the Romans* can be found in the *Philokalia,* in St. Basil, (the) *catenae,* and in a Bible MS discovered by E.v.p. Goltz on Mt. Athos. Rufinus made the Latin translation of 10 of these books. Of his commentary on the OT, only the first part of his commentary on the Canticle of Canticles (Song of Solomon) has come down to us through the translation of Books 1–4 by Rufinus. Of his homilies, which he preached on practically all books of Scripture, very few have survived either in the original Greek or in the translations by Rufinus and St. Jerome. They are of more interest as a contribution to the history of Christian spirituality than to biblical studies. Foremost a biblical scholar, O. preferred the allegorical interpretation of Scripture to the moral and the literal. He was thereby able to examine the higher spiritual meaning of Scripture, in keeping with the classical Jewish-Hellenistic exegesis of his time and his own tendency toward mysticism.

In the field of apologetics, Origen is best remembered for his *Against *Celsus*. In it he shows the broad range of his scholarship as he refutes the arguments of his opponent one by one.

His most significant theological work, *On First Principles (Peri Archōn),* reaches us in the rather liberal translation of Rufinus and the fragmentary literal translation of St. Jerome. In it he approaches the subject of God, angels, the creation, the fall, the redemption, and last things, freedom of the will, sin, and Scripture in its three senses and as a source of faith.

Two surviving ascetical works *On Prayer* and *Exhortation to Martyrdom* reveal the inner piety of the author. His personal life was marked by great austerity; in his great earnestness he exposed himself to martyrdom with more fervor than prudence and was even led by his literal interpretation of Mt 19.12 to self-mutilation.

His teachings on the nature of God take into account the Trinity. But because of some of his statements on the inferiority of the Son to the Father he has been accused by some of *Subordinationism. He taught that creation was eternal. His most controverted teaching concerns the ultimate goal for all souls, and he saw the possibility of continuing rise and fall even after death until the final *apocatastasis.

The loss of O.'s writings and his exclusion from the calendar of saints are lasting effects of the Origenistic controversies and the resulting condemnation of his alleged teaching (see ORIGENISM). Recent scholarship has revealed his significant positive influence as a mystical writer and exegete. BIBLIOGRAPHY: Quasten 2:37–101; H. Crouzel, NCE 10:767–774; idem, Origène et la connaissance mystique (1961); idem, "Origen," in ed. J. Walsh, Spirituality through the Centuries (n.d.); Origen on First Principles (ed. G. W. Butterworth, pa. 1966).

[F. H. BRIGHAM]

ORIGEN THE NEOPLATONIST (3d cent. A.D.), philosopher, and one of the more important pupils of *Ammonius Saccas. He has often been identified, but erroneously, with the Christian *Origen. He is mentioned favorably by *Plotinus, Cassius Longinius, and, later, by *Proclus. He made his first principle of reality, not the One beyond intellect and being, but the supreme intellect and primary being. Thus, unlike Plotinus, he continued to adhere closely to the traditional teaching of Middle Platonism in this respect. BIBLIOGRAPHY: CHGMP 196–200; K. O. Weber, Origines der Neuplatoniker (1962).

[M. R. P. MCGUIRE]

ORIGENISM, a complex of theories, many of a controversial nature, attributed to Origen by later writers. Although these teachings met with much condemnation and led to serious divisions, Origen's doctrine as a whole exerted a strong influence on Christian writers of the 4th cent. and also of later generations. There is textual evidence to vindicate Origen's personal orthodoxy with respect to some of the doctrines he was accused of holding, among which were the pre-existence of souls, metempsychosis, the inferiority of the Son to the Father or Subordinationism, the equivocation of the word and the spirit with creatures, the spherical form of glorious bodies, and a pantheistic *apocatastasis or universalism.

Origen, from the beginning, was defended by many notable religious leaders, among whom were SS. Pamphilus, Athanasius, Basil, Gregory Nazianzus, and Didymus; and, in the latter half of the 4th cent., Evagrius Pontus, Isidore of Pelusium, Palladius, Ammonius, Melania, and Rufinus. The monks of Palestine and Egypt, under the leadership of Evagrius, systematized some of the teachings of Origen, blending them with some Platonic and Gnostic tenets in the predominantly spiritual yet orthodox setting of monastic life. From this arose the first serious Origenist controversy, one phase of which took place in Jerusalem where *Epiphanius openly censured Origen's followers while he preached in the Church of the Resurrection whose Bp. John was a strong supporter of Origen. In this disagreement, Jerome, a former adherent of Origen, aligned himself with Epiphanius, while Rufinus supported Bp. John. Theophilus, bp. of Alexandria, effected a temporary reconciliation in 397 between these two friends; but when Rufinus quoted Jerome's praise of Origen in the introduction of his translation of the Peri Archōn, Jerome's antagonism flared up anew and he remained thereafter a bitter critic of Rufinus.

About the same time, a second and more serious phase of the first controversy was beginning in Egypt. Theophilus, under pressure from the monks of the desert of Scete, whose anthropomorphic tendencies he had criticized, condemned Origen in a synod held in 400. Three hundred Nitrian monks, together with their four leaders known as the *Tall Brothers, were expelled, some to Palestine and others to Constantinople. Because he supported them, St. *John Chrysostom was banished from his see by the Synod of the *Oak in 403 at the instigation of the politically motivated Theophilus.

The second important Origenist controversy occurred at the beginning of the 6th century. This time, the Origenist monks of the New *Laura near Jericho in Palestine were opposed by St. Sabbas, abbot of the Old or Great Laura near Jerusalem and superior of all Palestinian monks. He tried unsuccessfully to induce Justinian I to censure the monks. In 543, about 10 years after the death of Sabbas, Justinian issued a decree condemning nine points of doctrine drawn from Origen's Peri Archōn, and listed his name with heretics to be anathematized by newly appointed bishops and abbots. The document repeats the objections raised in the first controversy with respect to Subordinationism and the spherical shape of glorious bodies. This edict was known as the Letter to Mennas—Mennas was patriarch of Constantinople. It seems to have had the approval of the Pope and four patriarchs. A later letter to bishops prior to the Council of Constantinople II (553) is more concerned in its anathemas with Origenist monks and the Christology of Evagrius of Pontus. Origen's name is mentioned in Canon 11 of the council together with other heretics but not in the Emperor's opening statement nor in Pope Vigilius' letter Constitutum (see D 416–420) which gave post factum approval to the council. Because of these facts, scholars do not consider Origen a formal heretic. Yet, the confusion of events surrounding the Council of Constantinople II caused later councils to regard the extra conciliar letter of Justinian to the bishops (553) condemning Origenism as an act of the council and on that basis they repeated the condemnation. It is for this reason that most of Origen's writings in the original were destroyed. Despite these condemnations, Origen's mystical and exegetical writings were widely read through the 12th century. Aristotelianism caused their eclipse until Erasmus and others awakened new interest during the Renaissance. Scholars of the 19th cent. were preoccupied with Origen's witness to Platonic philosophy, but the 20th cent. has acknowledged the importance of his spiritual doctrine and exegesis. BIBLIOGRAPHY: G. Fritz, DTC 11:2:1565–88; A. Guillaumont, Les "Kephalaia Gnostica" d'Évagre le Pontique (1963); H. Crouzel, NCE 10: 767–774.

[F. H. BRIGHAM]

ORIGINAL JUSTICE, "the rightness in which God made man in his first state" (ThAq ST 1a, 95.1). The terminology derives from St. Anselm, who takes original sin to mean primarily the loss of an original rightness (*justitia*) of will (*De conceptu virginis* 1–7; 27; PL 158, 433–442,461). In St. Thomas's understanding the term original here has a meaning parallel to what it has in the term original sin. The gift of righteousness was an endowment to human nature as such in the person of the first man, one to be derived to others in virtue of the origin of their nature (*ibid*. 1a,100.1;1a2ae, 81.2). Because this is the case, original justice is taken to be a state of human nature, i.e., a fixed and stable disposition favorable to moral uprightness. This state of harmony or balance of parts means first and above all the right relation of the will in submissiveness to God, then the inner harmony of all human moral powers, including the emotions, with that orientation of will, and even freedom from bodily death and suffering. The relationship to God is a grace-relationship, in which man receives God's self-communication and shares in the divine life as a friend and son. All the secondary elements in the primordial state derived from and depended on grace; thus the loss of grace by sin brought about the loss of all the other gifts of the original state. The correlation with the meaning of original sin, then, is that in essence it is the condition of the absence (*privation) of the original grace-relationship with God; and in its secondary consequences, the loss of the concomitants of grace in the original state (see CONCUPISCENCE). Baptism remedies the first lack; the second is the meaning of abiding concupiscence and also the condition in which the Christian imitates Christ by struggle against sin and comes to complete restoration by sharing in Christ's Resurrection. BIBLIOGRAPHY: ThAq ST (Lat-Eng v. 26, ed. T. C. O'Brien, *Original Sin*, 1965) 144–153.

[T. C. O'BRIEN]

ORIGINAL SIN, in Christian teaching a sinful condition common to every member of the human race. The term original denotes a traditional explanation of the community of this condition, namely, that it is derived by reason of origin, and specifically because of carnal descent from Adam. Both RC and Protestant *doctrinal standards have affirmed the fact of original sin in this sense; they have differed on the nature of the sinful condition as it affects each individual. New biblical and theological interpretations are being sought.

Source of Original Sin. The articulation of the universal sinfulness of mankind as a sin through origin from Adam came with St. Augustine. His teaching was reflected in the second canon of the Council held at Carthage in 418 against *Pelagianism (D 223), and in canons 1 and 2 of the Second Council of Orange, held in 529 (D 371–372). These canons were revised and incorporated at the Council of Trent in the decree on original sin, which stands as the normative statement of RC teaching (D 1511–16). The decree speaks of a particular person, Adam, sinning and losing grace and other gifts not only for himself but for all mankind, and of his passing on not only punishment but also sin to his descendants. The sin is described as one in kind because of its one source and as present in each person because of descent from Adam, not because of a personal act imitating his sin. The most recent authoritative comment on this decree is the encyclical of Pius XII, *Humani generis* (1950), which states that it is in no way apparent how the denial of monogenism, the origin of the human race from a single couple, can be reconciled with Tridentine teaching.

The classical Protestant *confessions of faith for the most part simply assumed the explanation of man's sinful condition as a "birth sin." The Lutheran *Augsburg Confession states that all men begotten after the common course of nature are born with sin (Art. II). The *Reformed confessions repeat that original sin is "an hereditary evil" but also introduce the idea of a covenant by which Adam acted for all, and his sin was thus imputed to all (*Gallican Confession, Art. X; *Westminster Confession, Ch. VI and VII; *Westminster Catechism, Q. 16). The Westminster Confession is echoed in the *Savoy Declaration of Congregationalism and in the Baptists' *Philadelphia Confession. For Anglicanism the *Thirty-Nine Articles speak of "the fault and corruption of the nature of every man that naturally is engendered of the offspring of Adam" (Art. IX); the *Twenty-Five Articles of Methodism repeat these words (Art. VII).

Pelagianism was a denial of the hereditary sin of mankind. Unitarian rationalism rejected the concept of the Fall and of hereditary guilt. The Anabaptist and Mennonite traditions with their stress on salvation as a personal experience paid little heed to original sin. The *Apology* of R. *Barclay of the Religious Society of Friends recognized no causal connection between Adam's sin and the fallen condition of every man, nor did it recognize any sinful quality in this condition anterior to personal consent. In the preaching of the *Holiness movement original sin is inbred but involuntary and guiltless. Mormons, or Latter-day Saints, simply reject original sin. Even where the Churches officially maintained the traditional acceptance of original sin, actual adherence to the doctrine diminished. Under the influence of the *Enlightenment, rationalism, and higher biblical criticism, Protestants, except for fundamentalists, largely dismissed the doctrine. Liberal theology, with its subjectivism, optimism, and obliteration of the supernatural, had no place for it. In the theology of Karl *Barth and in *neo-orthodoxy, original sin was reasserted basically as a condition of man's creatureliness and egocentricity; there is scant connection with the traditional explanation. Many RC theologians have been directing their efforts to explanations more in keeping with modern biblical exegesis and evolutionary theory and to an understanding of the doctrine that would not make carnal descent from Adam essential in RC teaching on human community in sin. No consensus has been achieved.

Nature of Original Sin. The decrees of Trent did not

resolve continuing differences among RC theologians as to whether original sin consists essentially simply in the absence of an original righteousness or in *concupiscence. Canon 5 states that all that is of sin, not just its imputation, is taken away by baptism; concupiscence is not sin in a proper sense (D 1515). Canon 2 refers to a loss of sanctity and righteousness, as well as death and other penalties, derived to all men from Adam's sin (D 1512). The moral plight of man, however, does not mean loss of free will (D 1521, 1535, 1941, 1966, 2003); nor does it mean complete incapacity for moral good (1537, 1961, 1962, 1965, 2001, 2401). For Luther original sin is the "capital sin," looming larger than actual sins; it is an abiding condition of blindness, rebellion, and concupiscence besetting human nature; its dominance makes critical the need of grace saving through faith. The Calvinistic tradition speaks of human *total depravity; *Arminianism rejected this idea and extolled man's power to consent to grace. In this vein J. *Wesley accepted the Thirty-Nine Articles' statement that man is "very far gone from original righteousness," but denied that there is true guilt in inbred sin, and proposed the ideal of a sinless Christian perfection. Holiness teaching on *sanctification also extolls the moral capacities of man; concupiscence is not an insuperable sinfulness. Rationalist or liberalist tendencies in theology, of course, did not recognize any basic deterioration in human nature. The classic "pessimism" of the Reformation was reformulated by Barth and neo-orthodoxy.

Catholic Theology. The dogma of original sin, an article of Catholic faith, means that sin is passed on to every human being; that there is a sinful condition that is universal, present in every man, and truly hereditary. The practice of infant baptism from the 2d cent. suggests an ancient belief in hereditary sinfulness. Catholic teaching recognizes that original sin is the loss of a holiness and moral rectitude once given to mankind; that it is a deterioration of human powers for moral good, but not a total depravity. The primary difficulty in the mystery, however, is hereditary guilt, a moral condition that is not sinful as a personal sin is, yet is sinful in some sense.

Scripture. As a history of salvation the whole Bible and esp. the NT proclaims the universal need of saving grace (cf. Tit 2.11), and thus the universality and community of human sinfulness. The account of the Fall in Genesis (ch. 2–3) points out in particular that God created man good; it was man who by sin introduced moral evil. The idea of racial community, as well as of hereditary guilt and punishment enter the Biblical range of vision, namely that the present human plight is connected with man's introduction of sin into God's work; the account does not say more. The central NT text, *Romans* ch. 5, is similar. It contrasts the universal, baneful presence of sin and death in the world, introduced by Adam's sin, with the universal saving grace of Christ. The text points to the appearance and universality of sin in man's world; the Vulgate reading of v. 12, "in whom (Adam) all have sinned," is not faithful to St. Paul's own words ("because all men have sinned," cf. CCD).

Theological Formulations. Beginning with the opposition to Gnostic dualism, the Greek Fathers affirmed the scriptural explanations that pervasive moral evil is connected with the Fall, which introduced sin into God's creation. But the Latin Fathers, particularly St. Augustine, formulated the idea of a sin that by definition is hereditary. The classic theories of original sin explain the human community of sin affirmed in Scripture by that special sinful condition present in all men because they share one origin. In all such theories there are at least two essential presuppositions, which were certainly taken for granted by the fathers of Trent, whether or not they entered their actual pronouncements. The first is monogenism, an essential because the explanations of the specific condition, original sin, sought to show how it is not merely imputed to each individual, but also in some way has the quality of voluntary moral fault. The second presupposition is that some divine endowment (called *original justice in traditional terminology) was possessed and lost by humanity in Adam.

Augustine resisted Manichaeism by tracing moral evil to the Fall; he rejected Pelagian optimism by asserting the universal need of grace to save man from original sin. In defending the true sinfulness of original sin, he inaugurated a type of argumentation that explains the guilt or voluntariness of original sin through participation by every man in the sinful act of Adam. According to Augustine this participation was a consequence of each man's being contained in Adam the protogenitor. The sin of Adam is manifested and communicated in sexual libido or *concupiscence. The dominance of "vitiated" or "infected" flesh over the conjugal act is the communication of true sin to each man "born of Adam." From this line of thought the identity of original sin with concupiscence and the imagery of it as a stain or disease in the soul were developed. St. Anselm, seeing all of humanity as subsistent and thus acting in Adam, introduced a more restrained view, that original sin is humanity's loss of an original rectitude of will. Another form of the argument for participation in Adam's act took a juridic line: Alexander of Hales and St. Bonaventure spoke of a divine decree empowering Adam to act for all; from the 16th cent. theologians conceived of a pact constituting Adam the moral head acting in the name of all men (the theory of a covenant or of federal headship also was common among Calvinist theologians).

St. Thomas Aquinas's argumentation is quite different. He largely rejects the whole Augustinian line. The voluntariness of original sin is explained not by a participation in Adam's act, but by the *de facto* continuity of human nature. In each person human nature exists as deprived of its original divine endowments, and the deprivation is voluntary by the sin of Adam. In the presumed *de facto* continuity of all men with Adam, he is simply the first. This first parent initiated the process of human generation, the transmittal of human nature; Adam as sinner took away a gift given to nature. Each man comes to be because the process of generation initiated by Adam continues; he comes to be in a condition of sin because the nature involved in his generation and birth is lacking something it should have; that privation is original sin and is voluntary solely by the will of Adam, by his sin. Because each man comes to be by communication of a nature with this kind of historic antecedent, he comes to be in sin.

Contemporary thought. In contemporary theology, the classical theories are widely repudiated. The presuppositions of monogenism and of a pristine state of human perfection are regarded as unwarranted by biblical exegesis and inconsistent with evolution. Original sin is viewed as original or hereditary not because of origin from Adam, but as inherited from mankind; it is a sin of the race, "the sin of the world" (Jn 1.29). This sin is not simply an imitation of the Genesis episode through personal sins; it is a sin by propagation in the sense that by birth every man comes under the power of iniquity pervading human history and environment. There is in humanity a unity in sinfulness, which every man and the community of men have ratified by personal sins. The sin of the race is upon every man not through a biological lineage, but through the toll of his human heritage, an environment of accumulating guilt. Being born into a community of sin, each man is heir to sin and needs salvation. BIBLIOGRAPHY: S. Trooster, *Evolution and the Doctrine of Original Sin* (1968); ThAq ST (Lat-Eng v. 26, 1965); P. DeRosa, *Christ and Original Sin*; A. M. DuBarle, *Biblical Doctrine of Original Sin* (tr. E. M. Stewart, 1965). P. Schoonenberg, *Man and Sin* (1965).

[T. C. O'BRIEN]

ORIOL, JOSEPH, ST. (1650–1702), Spanish priest and doctor of theology known for his humility and simplicity. An unexceptional preacher, he journeyed to Rome seeking an appointment to a foreign mission, but he fell ill en route and was directed in a vision to return to his native Barcelona. Predicting his death, he distributed all of his earthly goods to the poor without indicating the cause of his generosity. He was beatified in 1806 and canonized in 1909.

[R. J. LITZ]

ORIONE, LUIGI (1872–1940), Italian charity worker and organizer. After leaving the Franciscans because of poor health and after a period at Turin in the Salesian Oratory, O. returned (1890) to study at the seminary at his native Tortona. Ordained in 1895, he created a house, the Piccola Opera della Divina Providenza (Little Work of Divine Providence), for needy seminarians, orphans, the elderly, the poor, and the needy. In order to further this work, he also founded the Sons of Divine Providence, the Little Missionary Sisters of Charity, the Hermits of Divine Providence, the Brothers of Divine Providence, and the Sacramentine Sisters. As temporary vicar general of Messina, he was instrumental in Sicily's recovery from the 1908 earthquake.

He went to Latin America in 1921 and again in 1934 to visit his disciples.

[R. J. LITZ]

ORISSA, SCHOOL OF (10th–13th cent.), most important school of medieval N Indian temple architecture with center at Bhuvaneśvara, capital of Orissa state in NE India, and at Purī. Exteriors are lavishly decorated, interiors unadorned, with finest example at Lingarāja (*c.* 1000 A.D.), its four halls and *śikhara* of elaborate silhouette curving inward in a final Orissan form. Noteworthy are the Temple of Viṣṇu-Jagannatha, Purī, and the Temple of the Sun, Konarak with twelve enormous splendidly decorated wheels of the chariot of Sūrya (sun god), one of the largest and most magnificent temples in India with an ecstatic proliferation of figural sculpture inferring a tantric cult.

[M. J. DALY]

ORLANDO DE' MEDICI, ST. (d. 1386), hermit at Salsmaggiore near Parma, whose cult developed from miracles attributed to his intercession after his death. O. was not a member of the Florentine Medici family.

ORLÉANS, CHARLES D' (1391–1465), a nephew of Charles VI of France, and a major lyric poet of the Middle French period. Captured at Agincourt, he spent a luxurious captivity of 25 years in England; this period produced tender and nostalgic verse, anticipating Du Bellay. The poems after his release, topical and trivial *ballades* and *rondeaux,* pale next to those of his vagabond contemporary, *Villon.

[J. P. WILLIMAN]

ORLEY, BERNARD VAN (Barent van Brussel; *c.* 1492–1542), leading 16th-cent. painter in Brussels, designer of stained glass and tapestry. He showed influences of Raphael and Dürer in mannered figures awkwardly articulated, excessive architectural decorative details, and bizarre costumes. Early works include portraits of *Charles V* and *Ferdinand I,* and *Dr. Zelle* (1519), *Hanneton Triptych* (1522)), *Last Judgment Altarpiece* (1525) and a depiction of Charlemagne's return with relics of the Passion from the Holy Land for the Brothers of the Holy Cross. In Brussels O. supervised the weaving of tapestries from Raphael's cartoons depicting the life of Christ for the Vatican and painted the important triptych of *Trials of Job* for Margaret of Austria, later the basis of tapestries for Marie of Hungary, eight of which are now at Hampton Court. Twelve attributed stained glass works for Ste. Gudule are disputed. BIBLIOGRAPHY: C.D. Cutler, *Northern Painting* (1968).

[M. J. DALY]

ORMAZD, see AHURA MAZDA.

ORNAMENTALISM, the dominant stylistic trend in Russian prose of the 1920s. Its followers, among them Bely,

Remizov, Babel, Bulgakov, and Ivanov, stressed style for its own sake and strove for unusual and striking linguistic and syntactical effects. BIBLIOGRAPHY: W. E. Harkins, *Dictionary of Russian Literature* (1959).

[M. F. MCCARTHY]

ORNAMENTS, the individual items which comprise the material setting of divine worship. These include the vestments of clerics as well as the appointments of the sanctuary and altar: crucifix, candlesticks, altar cloths, etc.

[R. B. ENO]

OROSIUS (fl. early 5th cent.), Spanish priest, historian. In Africa in 414, O. presented to St. *Augustine a work he had written against the *Priscillianists and Origenists. Augustine informed him of the incipient Pelagian controversy and persuaded him to go to Palestine to win the support of St. *Jerome against the new doctrine. When the decision of *John of Jerusalem favored Pelagius and cast doubt on O.'s own orthodoxy, O. wrote a *Liber apologeticus contra Pelagianos* in defense of himself and in justification of his stand against Pelagius. He then returned to the West, going to Africa rather than to Spain (then suffering from the ravages of the barbarian invasions), where he found Augustine completing the 11th book of the *City of God*. At Augustine's urging he wrote his *Historiarum adversus paganos libri VII,* a work intended to supplement the *City of God* by showing that the disasters suffered by the empire under Christian leadership were not worse than those of pagan times. This work, very popular during the Middle Ages, attempts a sketch of all history down to his own time. It is considered to be superficial and without historical value except for its record of events of O.'s own time. Works: PL 31 (crit. ed. C. Zangemeister, CSEL 5, 1882); I. W. Raymond (with Eng. tr., 1936); *Seven Books of History against the Pagans,* FathCh 50 (1964). BIBLIOGRAPHY: *Church Historians* (ed. P. Guilday, 1926).

[R. B. ENO]

O'ROURKE, JOHN JOSEPH (1875–1958), American Jesuit, scripture scholar. A member of the Society from 1895, he was ordained in 1910. Most of his career was spent in Rome at the Biblical Institute, where he taught and which he headed from 1924 to 1930. As rector he broadened the curriculum, established the doctoral program, and opened a subsidiary house in Jerusalem, where he was himself superior (1947–49). BIBLIOGRAPHY: E. Vogt, *Biblica* 39 (1958) 397–399.

[J. R. AHERNE]

OROZCO, JOSÉ CLEMENTE (1883–1949), Mexican painter considered preeminent among the "Great Four" (with Rivera, Siqueiros, Tamayo). In his *House of Tears* series (1911–13) rooted in German Expressionism, O. made initial use of his prostitute symbol. Following a visit to the U.S. (1917) he cofounded Mexico's mural renaissance, painting frescoes of heroic monumentality at the National Preparatory School (1923–26). O. exhibited in the U.S. (1928); illustrated M. Azuela's *The Underdogs* (1929); painted murals for Pomona College, California (1930) depicting a terrible "Prometheus" in a symbolism of purifying, liberating fire; another at the New School of Social Research, New York (1930–31); and a formidable project in Baker Library, Dartmouth College, N. H. (1932), juxtaposing an aboriginal paradise vs. a capitalist Christianity. His masterpieces in Guadalajara (1936–39)—a ferocious castigation of society—present sacrificial victims as in Aztec rites, and Father Hidalgo who led Mexico to independence. O's testaments of despair were followed by a spiritual *detente,* except in the Chapel of Jesus Nazarene (1942). Experiments in medium and abstract forms mark his last works. His contact with Posada rendered O.'s strong black and white graphics ineluctable and uncompromising. BIBLIOGRAPHY: M. Helm, *Man of Fire: José Clemente Orozco* (1953); J. C. Orozco, *An Autobiography* (1962).

[M. J. DALY]

ORPHISM, a religious current of thought traced to the Greek archaic period (c.650–480 B.C.). Although it is uncertain that Orpheus ever existed, many writings and doctrines were attributed to him, and legends about him as a wondrous singer and lyre player were widespread. Beliefs associated with his name include particularly an explanation of original evil in man's make-up, the possibility of purification, the passage of the individual soul on a wheel of birth (probably including belief in the transmigration of souls), the expectation of punishment or bliss in the afterlife, denigration of the body as an evil, and abstinence from killing and eating of animals. An elaborate Orphic mythology told how the universe of gods and men was created. Its two most striking features were, first, the egg formed in the Aither (Sky) by Chronos (Time), from which came forth Phanes (Shining One), creator and first king of the gods; and second, the devouring of the child Zagreus by the Titans, their destruction by Zeus's lightning, and the creation of man from their ashes. Man thus contains within himself the evil of the Titans and the divinity of their victim. Spreading particularly in the Greek cities of Sicily and south Italy, Orphism is reflected in early philosophers, in certain odes of Pindar, in Aristophanes, and in Plato. Earlier devotees were often despised as charlatans. In late antiquity it enjoyed a revival along with Pythagoreanism, to which it was closely related. BIBLIOGRAPHY: E. R. Dodds, *Greeks and the Irrational* (pa. 1957) 135–178; W. K. C. Guthrie, *Orpheus and Greek Religion* (1967).

[Z. STEWART]

ORPHREY (from *auriphrygium,* a Latin term used for gold Phrygian embroidery), a piece or strip of embroidery employed in decorating chasubles, dalmatics, and copes.

Probably these were originally used as devices to improve the appearance of borders or to hide seams. Sometimes they assumed symbolic designs, as in the cross often seen on the back (and occasionally on the front) of chasubles.

[N. KOLLAR]

ORSI, GIUSEPPE AGOSTINO (1692–1761), Dominican theologian and cardinal. After teaching philosophy and theology at San Marco, Florence, where he was also prior, he worked in the Casanatense library (Rome) after 1732. He was appointed secretary to the Congregation of the Index (1738), master of the Sacred Palace (1749), and cardinal priest of San Sisto (1759). His chief work was a 21–volume *Istoria ecclesiastica* written to counteract Gallicanism. BIBLIOGRAPHY: M. M. Gorce, DTC 11.2:1612–19; A. D'Amato, EncCatt 9:369–370: S. Olivieri, NCE 10:786.

[J. A. WEISHEIPL]

ORSINI, one of the oldest and most powerful noble families in Rome and the Papal States during the Middle Ages. The Orsini led the Guelf party which sought to insure the existence of a papacy free of pressure from secular rulers. The Guelf aim was the creation of a truly independent papal state in Central Italy. The Ghibelline party, headed by another powerful and ancient Roman family, the Colonna, opposed this policy. The history of the city of Rome and of the papacy during the Middle Ages is very largely the story of the conflict between the Orsini and the Colonna. Although Orsini family tradition traces the family back to the 5th cent., the Orsini only appeared as a powerful force in Roman politics during the 12th century. The extent of the family's power during the next 6 cent. can be gauged by the fact that between 1144 and 1789 there were 22 Orsini cardinals and three Orsini popes, Celestine III (1191–98), Nicholas III (1277–80), and Benedict XIII (1724–30). In addition, numerous other members of the family held important posts in the government of the Papal States. The family's rise to power coincided with the period of church reform directed by a series of reform-minded popes. The wealth and power of the Orsini were tied directly to the fate of these popes and their Guelf allies. The pontificate of Nicholas III marked the apex of Orsini power. Nicholas attempted to complete the work, begun by his reforming predecessors, of centralizing the government of the papal territories. In this work he relied heavily on his family for support. After his death the policy collapsed, largely because of the difficulties inherent in attempting such a program based primarily on the resources of a single family. Even under the French dominated Avignon papacy of the 14th cent., however, the Orsini remained an important force in Roman and papal politics. In the late 15th cent., marriage alliances were made with the ruling families of Naples and Tuscany, an indication of the prestige which the Orsini still retained. BIBLIOGRAPHY: Mann 10, 16; Pastor, 1, 4, 5, 6, 9; D. Waley, *Papal State in the Thirteenth Century* (1961).

[J. MULDOON]

ORSISIUS, ST. (also Orsiesius, or Horsiesi; d. *c*.380), Egyptian monk, outstanding disciple and successor of St. *Pachomius who founded the monastic community of Tabennisi. He was still quite young when Pachomius made him abbot of Chenoboskion. When sometime after, he succeeded Pachomius at Tabennisi, the strictness of his rule threatened a schism in the community (*c*.350); he made Theodore, who had been a fellow disciple with him under Pachomius, his coadjutor, and the two ruled jointly until Theodore's death, when O. resumed full supervision. A Latin translation of his treatise on the monastic life (*De doctrina de institutione monachorum*) has survived (PG 40:869–894; PL 103:453–476), as well as two letters to him from his friend St. *Athanasius (PG 26:977–980). BIBLIOGRAPHY: Quasten 3:159–160; Butler 2:547; M. C. McCarthy, NCE 10:853.

[R. B. ENO]

ORTEGA Y GASSET, JOSÉ (1883–1955), Spanish philosopher, journalist, humanist. Born in Madrid, O. was educated at a Jesuit college near Malaga, at the Univ. of Madrid, and at German universities. He was professor of metaphysics at Madrid (1910–36) and was also active as a journalist and politician, aiding in the overthrow of Alphonso XIII in 1931 and serving as a deputy in the Spanish Cortes (1931–36). He left Spain at the outset of the Civil War, taught in Argentina, Peru, and Portugal, returning to Madrid after World War II to found the Institute of Humanities, where he lectured until his death. He was mainly concerned with the analysis of art forms and political and social theory. He described his philosophy as ''the metaphysics of vital reason,'' and saw it as a vitalism purged of the antirationalism which had characterized that theory in its earlier forms. His thought can also be called existentialist, though he claimed his existentialism predated the French, which he criticized for its sentimentalism. Man is not a thing, but a project, an authentic self to be realized through interaction with his circumstances. No egalitarian, O. stressed the importance of the role of an intellectual aristocracy. In his view of truth he tended to relativism. He looked to a gradual emergence of a nonreligious secular society. Among his works best known to the English-speaking world are: *Revolt of the Masses* (tr. 1931), *Modern Theme* (tr. J. Cleugh, 1933), and *Invertebrate Spain* (tr. M. Adams, 1937). BIBLIOGRAPHY: N. McInnes, EncPhil 6:2–5; F. Alluntis, ''Vital and Historical Reason of José Ortega y Gasset,'' FrancStudies 15 (1955) 60–78.

[J. T. HICKEY]

ORTHODOX BAPTISTERY, RAVENNA, 5th-cent. domed octagonal building of plain exterior, with interior rich in marbles and mosaics relating to baptism, with a crowning medallion of the baptism of Jesus. Redecorated by Bp. Neon, it is an important source of Byzantine decoration and iconography. BIBLIOGRAPHY: W. Deichmann, *Frühchristliche Bauten und Mosaiken von Ravenna* (1958).

[M. J. DALY]

ORTHODOX CHURCH IN AMERICA, successor to Russian Orthodox Greek Catholic Church of America. It took the present name in 1970 on receiving autocephalous status from the Moscow Patriarchate (an action not recognized by all Eastern Orthodox Churches). The history of the OCA dates to 1794, when Russian missionaries arrived in Alaska, then owned by Russia. An Alaska diocese was established in the following century, moved to San Francisco in 1872, was upgraded to an archdiocese in 1903, and transferred to New York in 1905. In the pre-World War I period, the Church was greatly enlarged by the gain of numerous Carpatho-Russian parishes that had been Uniate. And it provided oversight to other Orthodox groups until they organized separately after World War I. Following the Russian Revolution, when the Patriarchate sent a new bp. to replace Metropolitan Platon, a critic of the communist regime, the American Church refused to accept the change, and at a 1924 *sobor* declared itself self-governing. In 1935 this body, commonly called the Metropolia, became affiliated with the Russian Orthodox Church Abroad (see RUSSIAN ORTHODOX CHURCH OUTSIDE RUSSIA), but ended the relationship in 1946. The Metropolia was also in rivalry with a group of parishes that remained loyal to a patriarchal exarch (see RUSSIAN ORTHODOX CHURCH IN THE USA; PATRIARCHAL PARISHES). The OCA reports a membership of 1 million in 500 parishes of North and South America.

[T. EARLY]

ORTHODOX CHURCHES, see EASTERN ORTHODOX CHURCH.

ORTHODOX CHURCHES IN THE U.S. (excluding Russian Orthodox) are organized in jurisdictions submitted to patriarchs who reside in the Eastern hemisphere and are the heads of autocephalic and several other autonomous Churches organized along lines of nationality and/or language. The largest Orthodox body in the U.S., the Greek Orthodox Archdiocese of North and South America under the Ecumenical Patriarch of Constantinople, Dimitrios I, is headed by Archbishop Jakovos, with an estimated membership of some 1.5 million. An additional 650,000 or more Orthodox belong to smaller national and language jurisdictions. The Orthodox (non-Russian) jurisdiction in North America with their affiliated autonomous Churches are: Albanian with 22 parishes, Bulgarian (22 parishes), Estonian (3), Greek (384), Syrian Antiochene (81), Romanian (74), Ruthenian (67), Serbian (73), Ukrainian (246), White Russian (17), Western rite (6). Heads of Orthodox jurisdictions hold membership in the Standing Conference of Canonical Orthodox Bishops in the Americas, established in 1960 to achieve cooperation among the various ethnic Churches. Member Churches of the conference are the following: Albanian, Carpatho-Russian, Antiochian, Bulgarian, Greek Orthodox of North and South America, Orthodox Church of America, Romanian Episcopate, Serbian, Ukrainian (Ecumenical Patriarchate), Holy Ukrainian Autocephalic. The Orthodox of North America are in communion with World Orthodoxy except for three splinter groups. The three jurisdictions not in communion with the other Orthodox branches are: the synodal Russian Church with the Romanian Missionary Episcopate of Canada; the Ukrainian Orthodox Church of the U.S.A.; and finally the Ukrainian Autocephalic jurisdiction.

[L. PEANO]

ORTHODOX CREED, drafted in 1678 by *General Baptists as "an essay to unite and confirm all true Protestants." It was intended to clear the General Baptists of charges of *Socinianism and to demonstrate their fundamental accord with *Particular Baptists and other *dissenters. Its most notable features were: (1) the preoccupation of its drafters with Christology; the first eight articles of the Creed are devoted to this subject, and the preface states, "We are sure that the denying of baptism is a less evil than to deny the Divinity or Humanity of Christ"; (2) a desire to harmonize differences regarding *Arminianism and *Calvinism among Baptists through the articles on "Predestination and Election," "Original Sin," "Perseverance," "The Invisible Church," and "The Covenants"; (3) the declaration in the article entitled "Of General Councils or Assemblies" that representatives from local churches met in general assembly "make up one church" and that these assemblies have power to deal with heresies or grievances of members of local congregations; (4) the statement of Article 38 that "The three Creeds, viz, Nicene creed, Athanasius' creed, and the Apostles' creed, . . . ought thoroughly to be received, and believed"; this is the only known Baptist confession that includes such a statement. The Orthodox Creed was adhered to by many General Baptist Churches as a *doctrinal standard but was not as widely accepted as the Standard Creed of 1660. BIBLIOGRAPHY: *Baptist Confessions of Faith* (ed. W. L. Lumpkin, 1959).

ORTHODOX SUNDAY, or Feast of Orthodoxy, a celebration in the Greek Church commemorating the restoration of icons which had been removed by the Iconoclasts. The celebration first took place by order of the Empress Theodora on the first Sunday of Lent in 842 A.D. In the Greek Church it is still observed on that day.

[P. K. MEAGHER]

ORTHODOXY (Gr. *orthos,* straight, right; *dōxa,* opinion), a term with several Christian uses: (1) Adherence to established or traditional belief or practice. Since most Christian Churches profess fidelity to the teachings of Christ and the Apostles, and many adhere to *confessions of faith or *doctrinal standards, orthodoxy means the claim to doctrinal fidelity, in opposition to heresy or heterodoxy. (2) A body of established beliefs or practices. (3) Conservatism or conformity as opposed to liberalism with regard to doctrine or practice. (4) In Lutheran history, the scholastic systematization of doctrine pursued by Lutheran theologians for a cent. after Luther's death; *Pietism arose as a reaction. (5) Capitalized, a concrete, collective term for Eastern Churches. Byzantine, Jacobites, Armenian, and Coptic Christians originally classified themselves as Orthodox because of fidelity to the Council of Chalcedon and in opposition to Monophysites and Nestorians. (6) In a cognate abstract sense, conformity to the tradition, thought, practice, etc., of the Eastern or Orthodox Churches.

ORTHOGENESIS, a biological term describing the process by which micro-molecules join together to form megamolecules, setting the platform for the leap to first cells. Through this process, therefore, individual units of matter unite with other individual units to form an aggregate whose whole is greater than its parts. According to *Teilhard de Chardin, orthogenesis applied to living cells is that force which gives to living matter not just the capability of multiplying and spreading out, but of ascending upward into more complex and conscious forms. Consequently, orthogenesis is an essential force within the process of evolution and is responsible for the forward thrust of evolution. Applied to the human species, orthogenesis will give individual particles of thinking matter the ability to unite, forming a total organism capable of a hyperpersonal consciousness. BIBLIOGRAPHY: Teilhard de Chardin, *Phenomenon of Man* (1959); *Future of Man* (1964). *OMEGA POINT.

[W. J. DUGGAN]

ORTHROS, liturgical office of the Byzantine rite corresponding to Matins.

[P. K. MEAGHER]

ORTIZ DE ZÁRATE, PEDRO (1622–83), Argentinian priest and martyr. He came of a wealthy colonial family, married and had two daughters, and after his wife's death became a priest (1659). Zealous for the conversion of the Indians, he financed and led, in company with two Jesuits, an expedition to Chaco (1682). Two settlements were founded there and friendly relations with the Indians appeared to be established. However, the following year O. and one of the Jesuits, Fr. Salinas, were slain. He was held in high esteem for the holiness of his life.

[P. DAMBORIENA]

ORTLIEB OF STRASSBURG (13th cent.), founder of the Ortliebarians. The teaching of O., condemned by Innocent III, was an asceticism that appealed to inner experience against church authority, denied the divinity of Christ, and condemned marriage. His followers, called Ortliebarians, did not survive the 13th century. BIBLIOGRAPHY: Bihlmeyer-Tüchle 2:306–307.

ORTOLANA, BL. (d. before 1238), mother of Clare of Assisi. Descended from the noble Fiumi family, she was a devout young woman who undertook pilgrimages to Rome, Monte Gargano, and in 1192 to the Holy Land. By her marriage to Count Favarone di Offreducio of Assisi, she bore four children, among them Clare and Agnes of Assisi. After her husband's death she joined her daughters among the Poor Clares. BIBLIOGRAPHY: L. Bracaloni, *S. Chiara d'Assisi* (1949); Englebert-Brady-Brown; B. J. Comaskey, NCE 10:803.

[O. J. BLUM]

ORTON, WILLIAM AYLOTT (1889–1952), Englishborn philosopher and economist. He was educated at Cambridge and the University of London. He came to the U.S. and taught at Smith College, Bryn Mawr, and the University of California at Berkeley. His books include *The Economic Role of the State* (1949) and *The Liberal Tradition* (1945). O.'s economic philosophy was based on a positive role for Christianity and the liberal approach in influencing world development.

[M. A. MCFADDEN]

ORVAL, ABBEY OF, located in Luxembourg, one of the three great Cistercian abbeys in Belgium. Founded *c.*1070 by Arnould II, count of Chiny, it was first occupied by Benedictines from Calabria; then in 1110, by Canons Regular of Trèves; and finally, from 1131, by Cistercian monks from the abbey of Trois-Fontaines. It suffered destruction by fire (1258), and the monks were dispersed. Later it prospered, enjoying wealth and power. Under a great abbot, Bernard de Mongaillard (1605–28), order was restored after the upheavals of the Reformation and religious wars. Again, however, misfortune overtook them when the Huguenot troops of Maréchal de Chatillon completely burned down the abbey (1637) and the monks had to retire to Montmédy. Little by little, reconstruction was undertaken. In 1680 the church of Notre Dame was restored. In the second half of the 18th cent., work was begun to rebuild the abbey in contemporary style, but the French Revolution intervened, and the abbey was burned down again in 1793. The monks withdrew to the priory of Conques and in 1796 were finally dispersed. The ruins were sold early in 1797. Exploited in the 19th cent., the last remains were better protected as the Commission of Monuments and Sites undertook some repairs and funding. A Trappist priory was built at Orval in 1926. BIBLIOGRAPHY: E. Michel, *Abbayes et Monastères de Belgique* (1923) 225–230.

[S. A. HEENEY]

ORVIETO, CATHEDRAL OF, Sienese Gothic structure begun in 1290 and continued by Lorenzo Maitani (1308–30); noted for scenes from the Old and New Testament on the façade delicately carved by M. and assistants, and important paintings of eschatological theme in the S. Brizio

Chapel by L. Signorelli (1499–1504, at first assisted by Fra Angelico). Sculptures by G. and Nino Pisano, Arnolfo di Cambio, gold and silverwork, a *Madonna* and polyptych by S. Martini, treasures from the Cathedral, are now located in the adjacent Palace of the Popes.

[M. J. DALY]

OSBALD (d. 799), **KING OF NORTHUMBRIA**, abbot. O. was made king after the murder of Aethelred (796). Twenty-seven days later, deserted by the nobles, he fled. Suspected of plotting Aethelred's murder, he received a letter from Alcuin urging him to "flee the company of crime" and fulfill his promise to become a monk; O. complied. BIBLIOGRAPHY: W. Hunt, DNB 14:1167; E. S. Duckett, *Alcuin, Friend of Charlemagne* (1951) 165, 168–169.

[A. WARDLE]

OSBERN OF GLOUCESTER (*fl.* 1150), English Benedictine exegete, lexicographer. One of his unpublished commentaries, on Judges, was dedicated to Gilbert Foliot, one-time abbot of Gloucester. His *Liber derivationum*, used by Huguccio of Pisa (d. 1210) for his glossary, was alphabetically arranged within an allegorical framework. BIBLIOGRAPHY: R. B. Palmer, NCE 10:804.

[F. D. BLACKLEY]

OSBERT OF CLARE (*fl.* 1136–60), English hagiographer, poet, and prior of Westminster (from 1136). He took his rhymed prose *Life of Edward the Confessor* to Rome (1139), seeking Edward's canonization. He was a zealous proponent of the doctrine of the Immaculate Conception and his letters have some historical importance. BIBLIOGRAPHY: *Letters of Osbert of Clare* (ed. E. W. Williamson, 1929); H. Thurston, *Month* (1904) 449–465.

[F. D. BLACKLEY]

OSCOTT (St. Mary's College), founded in 1793 by Catholic gentry in England as a school for their sons, Oscott has had a varied history of success and failure. The school produced many leaders of Catholic life in England. At Oscott in 1852 the first provincial synod of Westminster was held, the first meeting of the restored hierarchy in England and the occasion for J. H. *Newman's celebrated address, "Second Spring". In 1889 the college became the diocesan seminary for Birmingham and in 1897 a central seminary for seven dioceses. In 1909 Oscott returned to the status of diocesan seminary for Birmingham.

[J. R. AHERNE]

OSEBERG, SHIP OF, mid-9th-cent. A.D. royal funeral barge, some 70 feet in length, containing the burial of a queen, found in 1904 preserved in clay on the W side of Oslo Fjord, Norway. Remarkable for the woodcarving of its stempost, and of the bed, wagons, sledges, etc., and unique fragmentary tapestries of the burial deposit, it is now in the Viking Ship-Museum, Oslo.

[R. L. S. BRUCE-MITFORD]

OSEE, see HOSEA.

OSEE, BOOK OF, see HOSEA, BOOK OF.

OSIANDER, ANDREAS (1498–1552), controversial German Reformer. O. studied at Leipzig, Altenburg, and Ingolstadt and was ordained in 1520, then taught Hebrew in the Augustinian monastery at Nuremberg. By 1522 he had accepted Lutheran teaching. He worked with Lazarus Spengler, Wenceslaus Linck, and Willibald Pirkheimer to introduce Lutheranism into Nuremberg, and he helped write the Brandenburg-Nuremberg *church order (1533). In 1548 he accepted an appointment as pastor at Königsberg (now Kaliningrad) and chief professor on the theological faculty. His inaugural address gave rise to the controversy sometimes called the Osiandric Controversy on the doctrine of justification. O. rejected *forensic justification and taught that righteousness is the indwelling divine nature of Christ in the believer. He was bitterly opposed by M. *Flacius Illyricus, M. *Chemnitz, P. *Melanchthon, and others. O.'s teaching is dealt with and rejected in the *Formula of Concord (Art. 3). In spite of the opposition O. was able, because of Duke Albert's friendship, to stay on the Königsberg faculty until 1551, when he was made superintendent of Samland. At his death the Duke accorded him a royal funeral. BIBLIOGRAPHY: E. Bizer, RGG 4:1730–31; E. G. Schwiebert, NCE 10:806–807.

[M. J. SUELZER]

OSIRIS, Egyptian god of vegetation and growth. Killed by the evil god Seth, O. was resurrected by his wife Isis and his son Horus through magical formulae—believed to confer eternal life on all dead thereafter. As supreme judge of the dead, O. carries a crook and a flail.

[M. J. DALY]

OSMUND OF SALISBURY, ST. (d. 1099), churchman and chancellor. He was a nephew of William the Conqueror, whom he served as chancellor 1072–78, and became bp. of Salisbury in 1078. His compilation of liturgical services formed the basis of the Sarum rite, which was generally used throughout medieval England. He was canonized in 1457. BIBLIOGRAPHY: William of Malmesbury, *Gesta pontificum* (Rolls 78–79, ed. W. H. R. Jones); H. Farmer, BiblSanct 9:1283–84; W. J. Torrance, *St. Osmund of Salisbury* (1920), written from an Anglican point of view; Butler 4:492–493.

[J. L. GRASSI]

OSONA, THE ELDER, RODRIGO DE (fl. *c.*1476–1510), Spanish painter in Valencia. O. signed the *Retable of *the Crucifixion* (1476), worked for Cardinal Borgia (1483–84). His style relating to Hugo van der Goes and the Paduan Squarcione, shows a strong Valencian elegance and verticality. His works are in Madrid, Barcelona, and Philadelphia, Pennsylvania.

[M. J. DALY]

OSRHOENE, a small kingdom between the Euphrates and Tigris rivers, capital Edessa, incorporated as a province into the Roman Empire in 216 A.D. Christianity had been introduced into Osrhoene from Antioch by Jewish Christians. There is no reliable evidence that the synonymous Osrhoene was the first king to become a Christian. Eusebius (*Hist eccl.,* 5.24) witnesses to the fact that counsel was sought from the Diocese of Osrhoene in the matter of the fixing of the date for Easter. The Christians of Osrhoene wrote in Syriac; St. Ephrem was their brilliant representative.

[L. PEANO]

OSSAT, ARNAUD D' (*c.*1537–1604), French churchman and diplomat in Rome who negotiated with Pope Clement VIII on behalf of Henry IV of France. Through O.'s efforts, Henry's conversion was accepted and the King absolved. O.'s letters became a model for diplomatic correspondence.

[R. J. LITZ]

OSSERVATORE ROMANO, the daily newspaper published from Vatican City which serves principally as the vehicle for formal and informal papal statements, and for other Vatican documents. Founded in 1861 and at first privately edited, it was taken over by the Holy See in 1873 and became the papacy's chief polemical instrument in the conflict with the Kingdom of Italy over the *Roman Question and in other controversies, e.g., with Mussolini in the Fascist era. The editor-in-chief has always been a layman, but ultimate supervision rests with the papal *Secretariat of State. Though carrying agency reports on Italian and world political events, the paper is considered to be a semi-official organ of the Holy See, and to reflect, within limits, Vatican views on current issues concerning the Church and world problems. The *Osservatore Romano* is to be distinguished from *Acta Apostolicae Sedis,* which is the official gazette of the Holy See. The illustrated weekly magazine *Osservatore della Domenica,* published from the same office and often cited in stories of religious interest, is editorially independent and without any official standing. An English edition of *Osservatore Romano* has been issued since April 4, 1968.

[R. A. GRAHAM]

OSSETS, see ALANS.

OSSUARIES, small rectangular receptacles in which the bones of the dead were kept after the flesh had decayed. Made of soft limestone, clay or wood, they were found in Jerusalem, Haderah, Bene-Berak, Azor and other places in Palestine. Their significance has been enhanced by the inscriptions usually of the name of deceased written in Hebrew, Aramaic, or Greek or in two languages. Several decorated in variations of a rosette motif on paneled framework or with reproduction of plants, gates and buildings are a source of Jewish folk art of the Second Temple period. BIBLIOGRAPHY: M. A. Hofer, NCE 10:809; A. G. Barrois, *Manuel d'archéologie biblique* 2 (1953) 308; R. Motte, DB Suppl 6:940–948; R. North, LTK 7:1270–71; EDB 1683–84.

[F. H. BRIGHAM]

OSTENSORIUM, another name for the *monstrance.

OSTIARY (doorkeeper or porter), the first of the now obsolete minor orders preparatory for priesthood. In the beginning (early 3d cent. A.D.) the principal responsibility of the ostiary was to protect the entrance of the Church and prevent unauthorized persons from attending the Eucharist. The office had become entirely symbolic before it was abolished by Paul VI's *motu proprio* of 1972, *Ministeria quaedam.* BIBLIOGRAPHY: A. Michel DTC 12.2:2600–02; H. Leclerq, DACL 14.2:1525–33.

[F. H. BRIGHAM]

OSTRACON, a potsherd, or pottery fragment, used in antiquity as a writing surface. In Greece, and esp. Athens, ostraca marked with the names of politicians thought to constitute a danger to the democratic state figured as ballots in the voting process which led to banishment, called therefore "ostracism." The citizen who received the largest number of votes was then exiled, usually for a period of 10 years, without however losing either his citizenship or property. A precautionary rather than a juridical measure, ostracism was utilized in Athens from 487 to 417 B.C., numbering among its more important victims Aristides, Themistocles, and Cimon. Ostraca inscribed with these famous names, unearthed by 20th-cent. archaeologists, can now be seen in Athens' Agora Museum. Palestinian ostraca have been discovered, and their inscriptions have been important to biblical studies. *LACHIS LETTERS.

[E. M. GATES]

OSTROVSKI, ALEXANDER NIKOLAYEVICH (1823–86), leading Russian playwright of the realistic period, creator of the Russian national drama, reformer of the theater. His masterpiece, *The Storm* (1860), and most of his other plays depict the religious beliefs and superstitions, the patriarchal manners and customs, the *samodurstvo* ("blind obstinacy"), the daily anxieties, even the language, of what Dobrolyubov has called the "Kingdom of Darkness," i.e., the life of the Moscow merchants of his era. His pedagogical purpose is obvious in such titles as *Poverty Is No Crime* (1854) and *Even a Wise Man Stumbles* (1868). *The Snow Maiden* (1873), a fairy tale in verse, was made into an opera by Rimsky-Korsakov (1880–81). BIBLIOGRA -

PHY: M. Slonim, *Soviet Russian Literature* (1964) 181–183; idem, *Outline of Russian Literature* (1958) 93–102.

[M. F. MCCARTHY]

O'SULLIVAN, ADELAIDE FRANCES, see ADELAIDE OF ST. TERESA.

O'SULLIVAN-BEARE, PHILIP (*c*.1590–*c*.1660), Irish historian, author of *Historiae catholicae Iberniae compendium* (1621). The section on the Elizabethan wars contains observations of participants, but otherwise the work is considered overly partisan and inaccurate. Other works include a life of St. Patrick, polemics against Irish Protestants, and numerous lives of the saints.

[R. J. LITZ]

OSWALD, KING OF NORTHUMBRIA, ST. (604–642), martyr. Left an orphan after the death of King Aethelfrith, O. was educated in the monastery of Iona. In 634 he waged battle against Cadwallon who had allied himself with Penda in killing his cousin, King Edwin of Northumbria. O. won the battle through the help of a holy cross but found the country lapsed from Christianity. O. secured the help of St. Aidan of Lindisfarne in reconverting the people. Later he was killed by Penda and his body brought finally to Gloucester, though many continental churches still claim part of his relics. A great cult in his honor sprang up soon after his death, and he is revered as a martyr. BIBLIOGRAPHY: Butler 3:293–295; H. Farmer, BiblSanct 9:1290–95.

[R. T. MEYER]

OSWALD OF YORK, ST. (Oswald of Worcester; d. 992), bp. of Worcester (961), abp. of York (972). O. helped establish the 10th-cent. Anglo-Saxon monastic revival. He introduced the reform practices of Fleury into England, founding monasteries (e.g., Ramsey) and monasticizing Worcester. O. helped crown three kings. BIBLIOGRAPHY: E. John, *Orbis Britanniae* (1966); Butler 1:439–440; Knowles MOE 40–56; H. Farmer, BiblSanct 9:1296–97.

[W. A. CHANEY]

OSWIN, ST. (d. 651), the Christian king of Deira, which he governed well for 7 years. When Oswy, the King of Bernicia, attacked the kingdom, O. dismissed his army and sought haven with Hunvald. This ealdorman betrayed him, and he was murdered at Oswy's order. Deira was then united with Bernicia, and the kingdom of Northumbria formed. At Gilling, where O. was killed, Oswy, repentant, founded a monastery. BIBLIOGRAPHY: Bede, *Ecclesiastical History* 4: 14, 24; Butler 3:366–367; H. Farmer, BiblSanct 9:1297–98.

[A. WARDLE]

OTFRIED OF WEISSENBURG (*c*.800–*c*.870), North Alsatian monk, pupil of Rabanus Maurus; first German poet known to us by name and, in the **Evangelienbuch (Krist)*,

the first to use rhyme. BIBLIOGRAPHY: D. A. McKenzie, *Otfrid von Weissenburg: Narrator or Commentator?* (1946).

[M. F. MCCARTHY]

OTHLO OF SANKT EMMERAM (1010–*c*.1070), Benedictine writer. Educated at the abbeys of Tegernsee and Hersfeld, O. entered Sankt Emmeram in 1032. Devotion to Cluniac ideals led him to renounce his love for classical literature and to give himself to patristic and scriptural studies. His writings include religious poetry and prose works on Church reform, Christian education, and theology. He viewed with disfavor the dialectical approach to theology then beginning to appeal to some theologians. Works: PL 146:9–434. BIBLIOGRAPHY: R. H. Schmandt, NCE 10:811.

[M. S. TANEY]

OTHMAR, ST. (Audemar, Audomar; *c*.689–759), abbot. O. prepared for the priesthood in Chur, Switzerland, and exercised his priestly duties in the Church of St. Florinus in Chur or Remüs. At the request of the tribune, Waltram of Arbon, he undertook the direction of a band of monks dwelling near the grave of St. Gall. O. built a monastery that was to follow the Benedictine Rule and also set up the first house for lepers in Switzerland. For upholding the property rights of the monastery and its exemption, he was imprisoned and then exiled. His relics were transferred to the abbey of Sankt Gallen in 769 and in 867 were placed in the church that bears his name. BIBLIOGRAPHY: B. D. Hill, NCE 10:811–812; J. Duft, BiblSanct 9:1300–01.

[J. M. O'DONNELL]

OTHNIEL (Othoniel), first of the deliverers or judges of Israel (Jg 3.7–11). He received Caleb's daughter Achsah as wife in return for capturing Kiriath-sepher (Jos 15.15–17).

[T. EARLY]

O'TOOLE, GEORGE BARRY (1886–1944) educator. Ordained for Cleveland in 1911, O'Toole spent most of his career in university work, teaching philosophy in a variety of Catholic institutions, esp. The Catholic Univ. of America. He became cofounder of the Catholic Univ. of Peking in 1925, and taught there until 1933. He edited the *China Monthly* from 1939 to 1944.

[J. R. AHERNE]

OTT, MICHAEL (1870–1948), Benedictine abbot. He became a Benedictine in 1889 in St. John's Abbey, Collegeville, Minn., and spent 25 years there. Ordained in 1894, he taught at the abbey's university. In 1919 he was named abbot of St. Peter's abbey, Saskatchewan, Canada, and the first abbot-ordinary in 1921 when it became an abbey *nullius*. O. established a secondary school and a junior college at the abbey. He resigned in 1931 and served as chaplain to Benedictine nuns in Crookston, Minnesota.

[J. R. AHERNE]

OTTERBEIN, PHILIP WILLIAM (1726–1813), founder of the United Brethren in Christ (see EVANGELICAL UNITED BRETHREN CHURCH). Born in Dillenberg, Germany, O. entered the ministry of the Reformed Church. He received a classical education at Herborn, center of *Pietism. Ordained in 1749, he was one of the six young pastors who 3 years later followed Michael Schlatter overseas to mission work among the spiritually needy Pennsylvania Germans. He served pastorates at Lancaster, York, and Reading, Pa., and Frederick, Md., before going to the German Evangelical Reformed Church in Baltimore in 1774, where he served until his death. O.'s Pietism, plus a profound religious experience, led him to react against a prevailingly formalized, confessional churchmanship. In 1767, upon hearing Martin Boehm, a Mennonite layman, preach, O. embraced him with the words "We are brethren." This incident ultimately gave rise to the creation of the Church of the United Brethren in Christ, with the two as superintendents of this initially nondenominational, revivalistic society that in 1800 began to meet regularly. Just before his death, O. "ordained" three men for this ministry. Combining this Pietism with true ecumenism, he never left the Reformed Church; he led the United Brethren in his day not as a separate Church but as a society given to unity and mission. BIBLIOGRAPHY: A. C. Core, *Philip William Otterbein: Pastor-Ecumenist* (1968).

[K. J. STEIN]

OTTO I (Otto the Great; 912–973), **ROMAN EMPEROR** from 962; German king from 936, first of the Holy Roman Emperors. The Western Empire of *Charlemagne had broken up into three main parts, Italy, France, and Germany (Lombardy and Lorraine being debatable lands); but Germany was now organized on a strong Saxon basis, and Otto its ruler, having consolidated his realm and filled its subordinate principalities and duchies with relatives, was invited by Pope John XII to renew once more the Roman Empire and was crowned at Rome. Thus began a political institution that was to endure until 1806, though the term "Holy Empire" seems not to have been used until *Frederick Barbarossa; and in the course of its history it was to prove neither holy nor Roman nor an empire. O. himself was a successful soldier, a just and vigorous ruler, and a worthy heir to the Carolingian tradition: missionary bishoprics were established in the Elbe and Oder basins, church discipline was strengthened, and the study of the humanities encouraged, largely through his brother, Bruno, abp. of Cologne. He was the founder of the Ottonian Renaissance. O.'s marriage to St. Adelaide gave him his title to Lombardy and opened the way to Rome. There he intervened, to the resentment of the Roman people, in the shifty politics of the papacy, nominated the blameless Leo VIII, and upheld him against an antipope, whom he deported to Hamburg. BIBLIOGRAPHY: M. Uhlirz, NCE 10:814–817.

[T. GILBY]

OTTO II (955–983), **ROMAN EMPEROR** from 973, German King. He was the son and successor of Otto I the Great, under whom the Western Empire, now resting on an East Frankish and Saxon basis, became in effect the Holy Roman Empire, and the policy was begun of integrating Italy with Germany. O. married Theophano, daughter of the Byzantine Emperor, and proved a strong and not unsuccessful ruler: Lorraine was held against the French; Bavaria and Bohemia were kept to their allegiance; only on the Italian mainland were the inroads made by a temporary alliance between the Saracens and Greeks not repaired.

[T. GILBY]

OTTO III, (980–1002), **ROMAN EMPEROR** from 996, German King, King of the Lombards. Carefully trained by his mother, Theophano, the widow of Otto II; by Bernward of Hildesheim and Gerbert of Aurillac; and protected during his minority by his grandmother, St. Adelaide, a sagacious and imperious woman of unusual beauty, he did much in his short life to strengthen the Empire and clean up the Roman stable from the squalor of the *Crescentii period. His cousin, Otto of Carinthia, was raised to the chair of Peter as Gregory V, and on his death, Gerbert, O.'s old tutor, was appointed (Sylvester II). Splendor and piety marked the Ottonian Renaissance, together with a missionary zeal that saw the beginning of the Christianization of Poland and Hungary.

[T. GILBY]

OTTO IV, (c.1175–1218), **ROMAN EMPEROR** from 1207, opponent of Philip of Swabia. The son of Henry the Lion and of Matilda, daughter of Henry II of England, he was reared at the English court and was a pawn in the diplomatic maneuvering between France and England. He was elected king of the Germans and crowned at Aachen (1198), a step toward the imperial throne. He was favored over his opponent by Innocent III, and his cause was greatly enhanced by Philip's murder (1208). He was crowned emperor by the Pope in 1209. O.'s attacks on papal fiefs in Italy and Sicily later led the Pope to abandon him in favor of young Frederick. The French victory over John of England and O. at Bouvines (1214) proved his undoing, and O. died a deserted man. BIBLIOGRAPHY: G. Barraclough, *Origins of Modern Germany* (2d ed., 1957); A. L. Poole, CMedH 6:44–79.

[O. J. BLUM]

OTTO OF BAMBERG, ST. (c.1062–1139), bishop. A Swabian, O. entered the service of Emperor Henry IV, to whose attention he came while serving as chaplain to Henry's sister, the duchess of Poland. In the investiture struggle O. managed to retain the respect of both sides. Though loyal to the Emperor, he gave no countenance to Henry's antipope; when named bp. of Bamberg (1102), he would not accept consecration until he could receive it at the hands of Pascal II at Anagni (1106). He was a successful mediator and played an important part in arranging for the Concordat of Worms (1122). O. was an active builder of monasteries, churches, and castles for the fortification of the diocese. At the request of Boleslaus III of Poland, O. headed two effective missionary campaigns in Pomerania, and because of his success in this enterprise is sometimes called the Apostle of Pomerania. He was canonized in 1189 by Pope Clement III. BIBLIOGRAPHY: G. L. M. Zannini, BiblSanct 9:1316–18; Butler 3:8–9.

OTTO OF CAPPENBERG, BL. (d. 1171), Premonstratensian. Along with his brother Godfrey, O. gave his ancestral land to Norbert of Xanten in order to establish the first Premonstratensian abbey in Germany in 1122. He served as fourth prior of Cappenberg from 1156 to his death. O. preserved the relics of his blessed brother at Cappenberg. BIBLIOGRAPHY: S. Schneider, *Cappenberg* (1949); J. B. Valvekens, BiblSanct 9:1318–19.

[B. F. SCHERER]

OTTO OF FREISING (*c*.1111–58), bp., historian. A member of the Babenberg family, O. was the son of St. Leopold III of Austria, grandson of Emperor Henry IV. After studying in Paris (*c*.1127), he entered the Cistercian Order, and in 1137 was made bp. of Freising. He served as advisor and diplomat at the German court under King Conrad III and his nephew Frederick I Barbarossa. His *Historia de duabus civitatibus* established his reputation as the leading philosophical historian of the 12th century. Like St. Augustine, O. saw history as the unfolding in time of the principles of good and evil. The conflict between Church and State tinged O.'s account with pessimism, but the movement toward peace and order that came with the accession of Barbarossa inspired a more optimistic tone in his biography of Frederick, *Gesta Friderici imperatoris,* which was undertaken at the Emperor's request and expense. O. died after completing only two books of the biography; his secretary Rahewin added two more. BIBLIOGRAPHY: *Deeds of Frederick Barbarossa,* (tr. C. C. Mierow, 1953) 3–14, 341–346.

OTTO OF SANKT BLASIEN (d. 1223), probably abbot of the Benedictine monastery of Sankt Blasien (Black Forest). Little is known about his life. He continued the *Chronica* of Bp. Otto von Freising and considered the German emperors the rightful successors of the Roman Caesars. O.'s annals deal with the period from 1146 to 1209 i.e., the reign of Conrad III to the murder of Philip of Swabia and the coronation of Otto IV (1175–1218), at which point the chronicle abruptly ends.

[S. A. SCHULZ]

OTTO, RUDOLF (1869–1937), a German Protestant theologian and philosopher of religion. O. taught at the Univ. of Göttingen (1897–1914), Breslau (1914–17), and Marburg (1917–29). He was strongly attracted by theologians like *Ritschl and *Schleiermacher who emphasized emotion (*Gefül; Gemüt*) as the practical reality of religion, but was also interested in the philosophical problems presented particularly by *Kant and *Fries (see his *Philosophy of Religion,* 1931). His deep knowledge of religious phenomena caused O. to reject all attempts to reduce religion either to a biological-social-psychological disposition (materialism) or to a particular function of the mind (idealism). Instead O. interpreted the religious phenomenon, esp. in his famous book *The Idea of the Holy* (1923), as a synthesis of a transcendental a priori and as a reality beyond any merely sociological or psychological interpretation. Religion begins in itself and remains related to the wholly Other, i.e., the numinous, a term coined by O. to emphasize the nonrational uniqueness of the sacred. The sacred or holy is an a priori category independent from other categories such as the good or value. It is ambivalent insofar as man experiences it as *fascinosum,* (attracting), *tremendum* (awe-inspiring), or both. The world of the sacred is distinct from the profane; is expressed in myth or ideogram; and evokes the feeling of createdness which is at the root of religion. Within this horizon, O. did extensive work interpreting religious forms and phenomena. In 1921, he founded the Religious Confederation of Mankind (*Religiöser Menschheitsbund*), which in 1956 was associated with the World Congress of Faith as its German branch. BIBLIOGRAPHY: R. Otto, *Mysticism East and West* (1932); *idem, India's Religion of Grace and Christianity* (1930); R. F. Davidson, *Rudolf Otto's Interpretation of Religion* (1947). *RELIGION, COMPARATIVE STUDY OF.

[W. DUPRÉ]

OTTOBEUREN, ABBEY OF, a Benedictine monastery, one of the most beautiful in the world. It was founded (764) by a certain Toto, who became its first abbot. St. Ulrich, bp. of Augsburg, was a monk of Ottobeuren. In the 15th cent. it fell into some decay, but in the turbulent times of the 16th cent., Ottobeuren was a stronghold of discipline and faith. Its intellectual level was always high and it was the main contributor to the foundation of the Benedictine Univ. of Salzburg. The 17th and 18th centuries were a time of enormous prosperity for it. The abbey was independent, imperial, and ruled a small territory (Reichsabtei). A huge abbey and church were constructed (1735–66) and these were masterpieces of the baroque art, decorated by the most famous artists of the time (Fischer, Feichtmayer). It was suppressed in 1802, but the monks were allowed to continue common life; in 1834 the monastery was restored by King Lewis I as a dependent priory of St. Stephen's Abbey, Augsburg. In 1918 it again became an abbey and the monks today operate a college. For the 1200–year jubilee (1964), which was celebrated with splendor, the abbey was thoroughly renovated. BIBLIOGRAPHY: J. Hemmerle, *Die Benediktinerklöster Bayerns* (1951) 95–98, with full bibliography.

[F. N. BACKMUND]

OTTOBONI, PIETRO VITO, see ALEXANDER VIII, POPE.

OTTOBUONO FIESCHI, see ADRIAN V, POPE.

OTTOMAN EMPIRE, empire created by a militant dynasty of Turcomans from Anatolia (modern Turkey). Its name derives from the Arabic form of the name of its founder Osman (d. 1324), who is credited with unifying the scattered Turcoman tribes centered in Anatolia. At the height of its power the empire encompassed such European territories as the Balkan states, Greece, Crete, Cyprus, parts of Hungary, Austria, and S Russia. Outside of Europe and Anatolia, it included Iraq, Palestine, Egypt, North Africa W to Algeria, and parts of Arabia. It endured for 6 cent., coming to a definitive end only after World War I. The peak of Ottoman power occurred during the rule of the sultan Süleyman I, the Magnificent (1520–66), the last in a succession of 10 long-lived, militarily effective rulers. Hungary was annexed, Austria invaded, and Vienna besieged. If it were not for concurrent war with Persia, the Ottomans could have made further inroads into Europe, whose emerging nation states were about to embark on a protracted era of nationalist strife buttressed by deeply felt differences in religion. The Ottoman conflict with Persia incidentally insured that the Ottomans would be the militant leaders of Sunnite Islam, in opposition to the Shiite Safavid dynasty of Persia. The Crusades had left the Greeks and Slavs with residual hostility to the Franks and the Latin Church, so that popular sentiment probably preferred domination by the sultan over that of Western Europe. Besides, Ottoman civilization arose on the frontier between the Byzantine and the Seljuk cultures and borrowed freely from both. On the folk level there was not much difference in religious practice between the two cultures. Folk religion was at an equal distance from the orthodoxy of either Christianity or Islam. Greek Orthodox, Armenians, and Jews were allowed to govern themselves as autonomous communities. The Orthodox clergy may have had more real autonomy under the Ottomans than in the late Byzantine period, even though it became law that the patriarch of Constantinople be appointed by the sultan as a consequence of the Ottoman capture of that city in 1453. The second siege of Vienna in 1683 signaled an era of decline marked by occasional military defeat for the Ottomans. A European anti-Ottoman coalition was sparked by the Polish King Jan Sobieski (1674–96) and included the military might of Russia, Austria, and Venice. Only France and Sweden supported the sultan, with Britain and Holland remaining neutral to protect the commercial privileges they had gained from the sultans. Later, under the growing pressure of 19th-cent. nationalism in the Balkans and elsewhere, the sultan gradually came to be viewed as the "sick man" of Europe. The imperial system disintegrated until its complete rejection after World War I (1922), and the establishment of the National Turkish Republic in Anatolia.

[E. J. DILLON]

OTTONIAN ART, the flowering of the arts in Germany under the Saxon emperors, from Henry I (919–936) and Otto I (936–973) to the death of Henry III (1056). The marriage of Otto II to Princess Theophano (972) added Byzantine influence, manifest in Ottonian architecture—a combination of highly sophisticated Carolingian and classical style with Byzantine rhythm and color (St. Michael's, Hildesheim, St. Cyriacus, Gernrode; and the Chapel of St. Bartholomew, Paderborn, 1018). Illuminated MSS produced in the royal schools at Reichenau, Mainz, Regensburg, and Echternach include the famous *Codex aureus Epternacensis* and *Wermgerode Gospels* showing patterning from Byzantine textiles. Sumptuous goldwork in the Byzantine manner numbers the proto-Romanesque *Essen Madonna,* silver-gilt, jeweled and enameled bookcovers (*Pericopes* of Henry II) and famous reliquaries (*Stavelot Triptych,* New York). Masters Renier of Huy, Godefroy de Claire, and Roger von Helmarshausen produced sculptures in bronze and gold, small but monumental. Renier's world famous bronze baptismal font (c. 1107–18) resting on twelve oxen, in St. Barthélemy, Liège, evidences his dramatic and masterful skill. BIBLIOGRAPHY: L. Grodecki, *L'Architecture Ottonienne* (1958); H. Jantzen, *Ottonische Kunst* (2d ed., 1959).

[R. C. MARKS]

OTTONIAN RENAISSANCE, the period of recovery and stability in Central Europe which began under Henry I (919–936) and ended with the investiture struggle. Imperial authority was asserted through resistance to Magyar, Slav, and Viking attacks, the suppression of German provincialism, and control of the Church. The emperors also supported religious reform, and at a number of monasteries and cathedrals, particularly in Saxony and Lorraine, this fact led to the emergence of brilliant schools of learning. Moreover, the great revival in the arts during this period can be largely considered a by-product of the reform movement and also owed much to imperial patronage. BIBLIOGRAPHY: G. Barraclough, *Origins of Modern Germany* (2d ed., 1947).

[R. C. MARKS]

OUDENBURG (ALDENBURG), ABBEY OF, a former Benedictine abbey near Ostend, Belgium. It was founded c. 1084 by Bp. Arnould (Arnulf) of Soissons. Though destroyed in 1579 by the Calvinists, it was rebuilt (1628–30). When it was suppressed in 1797, the buildings were razed with the exception of the abbot's manor. The new Benedictine abbey of Steenbrugge near Brugge obtained in 1934 the title, arms, and privileges of the old abbey of Oudenburg.

BIBLIOGRAPHY: *Monasticon Belge* 3:49–85; Cottineau 2157.

[N. BACKMUND]

OUEN OF ROUEN, ST. (Owen, Audoenus, Dado; d. 684), bishop. From a wealthy Frankish family, he was educated at the court of Chlotar II and served as chancellor to both Dagobert I and Clovis II. Under Dagobert he established the monastery of Rebais; under Clovis he was ordained priest and shortly thereafter made bp. of Rouen (641). As bp. he founded monasteries, sent missionaries to the remaining pagans of his diocese, and encouraged scholarship. BIBLIOGRAPHY: H. Platelle, BiblSanct 2:586; Butler 3:393–394.

[G. M. COOK]

OUR LADY, a frequent designation for the Blessed Virgin Mary. It seems to have been first used in English by Cynewulf (8th cent.) in his poem "Christ." The words often precede some Marian attribute or association, e.g., Our Lady of Perpetual Help, Our Lady of Lourdes.

[T. M. MCFADDEN]

OUR LADY, MOTHER OF MERCY, BROTHERS OF, a congregation of teaching religious, sometimes known as Brothers of Tilburg, founded in the Netherlands in 1844 by Fr. Joannes Zwijsen, who later became abp. of Utrecht. The institute received approval of the Holy See in 1870 and, after restricting membership to brothers only, was reapproved in 1927. The brothers take perpetual vows, and their work is chiefly that of education and Christian instruction of young boys. Presently the congregation has about 720 brothers who conduct their apostolate from 62 houses located in the Netherlands, Belgium, Ireland, Africa, Indonesia, Latin America, and the U.S. The superior general resides at Tilburg in the Netherlands.

[R. A. TODD]

OUR LADY OF CHARITY OF REFUGE, SISTERS OF (OLCR), an order of religious women founded by St. John *Eudes at Caen, France, in 1641. The members keep the Rule of St. *Augustine and use a modified form of the constitution of the Visitation nuns. In addition to the three simple vows, the sisters take a vow of zeal for souls. The original purpose of their foundation was to provide shelter for fallen women, but later the congregation took care of and trained neglected and dependent young girls. Their apostolate spread from France to England, Ireland, and the U.S., and later houses were established in Spain, Portugal, Italy, Canada, Mexico, and Kenya in Africa. As an aid in strengthening the contemplative and apostolic life of its members, the houses in the U.S., though autonomous, united to form a federation in 1944. Soon other houses in Europe followed the same pattern. In 1975 the total membership was 555 with 31 houses.

[R. A. TODD]

OUR LADY OF GOOD COUNSEL, an ancient title of the Blessed Virgin *Mary and the name of a noted church in her honor at Genazzano, Italy. The church houses the famous fresco of Our Lady of Good Counsel which, according to legend, was miraculously imprinted there in 1467. Because of the legend and several cures, which are reported to have occurred there, the church has become a center of Marian pilgrimages. Several popes approved of the devotion to Mary under this title; Leo XIII established the scapular of Our Lady of Good Counsel, inserted the title into the Litany of Loreto, and declared the church a minor basilica. Recent investigations have shown that the fresco was painted in the early 15th cent., was covered over with plaster, and was suddenly revealed again in the course of further construction on the church.

[T. M. MCFADDEN]

OUR LADY OF MERCY, DAUGHTERS OF, a community of religious women founded in 1837 in Italy by St. Mary Joseph *Rossello. The constitutions follow the Franciscan rule. The apostolate of the institute includes educational and hospital work. In 1919, a foundation was opened in Springfield, Mass.; there is now an American motherhouse at Newfield, New Jersey. In 1975, the congregation maintained 245 houses and had a membership of 1,691 sisters. The generalate is located at Savona, Italy.

[R. A. TODD]

OUR LADY OF PERPETUAL HELP, a title in honor of the Blessed Virgin *Mary in view of her constant willingness to assist men toward the love of Christ. The title is connected with a 14th– or 15th–cent. Byzantine painting which was stolen, brought to Rome, and (upon the instructions of Mary who appeared in a vision to a young girl) placed in the Augustinian church of St. Matthew in Rome. After that church was destroyed (1798), the painting was given (1866) to the Redemptorists, who placed it in the church of Sant' Alfonso which had been built on the original site of St. Matthew's. Devotion to Mary under this title is popular throughout the world.

[T. M. MCFADDEN]

OUR LADY OF THE GARDEN, DAUGHTERS OF (GIANELLINE), a congregation of religious cofounded in 1829 by St. Anthony *Gianelli and Sr. Caterina Podestà at Chiavari in Liguria, Italy. The members take simple vows, and the goal of the institute is the sanctification of the sisters, eternal salvation, and corporal service toward the neighbor. The Daughters were esp. distinguished for their charity at the time of the Ligurian plague in 1835–37. The congregation received papal approbation in 1882. The sisters engage in activities of social charity, and their apostolate has spread to five countries in South America, Jordan, Spain, and the U.S. The superior general resides at Rome, Italy. In 1975 the congregation had 159 foundations and a total membership of 1,380 sisters.

[R. A. TODD]

OUR LADY OF THE MISSIONS, SISTERS OF, religious congregation founded by Mother Marie du Coeur de Jésus (Euphrasie Barbier, 1829–93) at Lyons, France, in 1861. The foundation, established mainly for educational work in the mission field, received approval from Rome in 1906. The sisters take simple, perpetual vows, and their apostolate engages them in mission activities located in 12 countries, covering 4 continents. In 1975, the congregation had 126 houses and 1,202 members, with motherhouse at Castel Gandolfo at Rome. BIBLIOGRAPHY: R. Rios, *Teaching Nations 100 Years* (1961).

[R. A. TODD]

OUR LADY OF THE SACRED HEART, DAUGHTERS OF, a congregation of religious founded in 1882 at Issoudun, France, by Jules *Chevalier in collaboration with Mother Marie Louise Hartzer. The sisters take simple, perpetual vows and have special devotion in offering homage, love, and reparation to the Sacred Heart, after the example of Mary, whom they honor as Our Lady of the Sacred Heart. In 1928, papal approval was given the constitutions of the institute. The members are primarily engaged in the mission fields of Oceania, Indonesia, and Africa, where they are active in educational and hospital work. Their apostolate has spread through eight countries of Europe, Brazil, and the U.S. The congregation has an approximate membership of 1,839 sisters and 228 houses (1976). The generalate is in Rome.

[R. A. TODD]

OUR LADY OF THE SNOW, a title given to *Mary based upon the legend that she appeared to a Roman couple, instructing them to build a church in her honor. The site was designated by a midsummer snowfall on the Esquiline Hill in Rome and confirmed in a dream to Pope Liberius (352–366). There has been a Marian church on that spot since that time; it is now known as the Basilica of St. Mary Major. The legend appears to have been unknown before the 10th cent. and does not seem worthy of credence.

[T. M. MCFADDEN]

OUR LADY OF VICTORY MISSIONARY SISTERS (OLVM), a community of religious commonly called Victory Noll sisters, who are engaged in religious educational and social work. They are members of a pontifical congregation founded in 1922 in Chicago, Ill., by Rev. John J. Sigstein. The motherhouse and novitiate, located in Huntington, Ind., was built by Bp. John F. *Noll of Fort Wayne, Indiana. The members are also active in parish visitations, clinical work, and the Newman aapostolate. Recent statistics show that the congregation has 338 sisters and 79 houses.

[R. A. TODD]

OURAR, Armenian diaconal stole, worn over the left shoulder with the ends falling loosely in front and back.

Armenian Catholics often call the sacerdotal stole (the *porourar*) an *ourar*.

[A. CODY]

OUSIA, a noun derived from the Gr. *einai* (to be), the equivalent of the Latin *substantia* and the English "substance." It is the first of the Aristotelian categories and signifies that which is capable of existing in and by itself, and serving as the subject for accidents and accidental changes. Like substance, *ousia* may also signify the nature or essence of a thing, and in this sense the word was important in the gradual clarification of Trinitarian dogma.

[M. J. COSTELLOE]

OUTER COURT, that large section of Ezekiel's Temple where the common people gathered, as distinct from the inner court reserved for priests. The outer court was comparatively free of buildings but had 30 cells arranged along its outer walls. Ezekiel uses the phrase 12 times in describing the Temple (Ez Ch:40–43).

[T. M. MCFADDEN]

OUTLER, ALBERT COOK (1906–), United Methodist theologian and educator. He was born at Thomasville, Ga. He received his higher education at Wofford College, Emory University, and Yale. He is the recipient of eight honorary degrees including an LL.D. degree from Notre Dame in 1966. After serving various pastorates in the Southern Georgia Conference, he became in 1938 Instructor and later professor of theology at Duke University until 1945, when he became associate professor and in 1948 Timothy Dwight Professor of Theology at Yale University. In 1951 he became professor of theology at Southern Methodist University, where he currently is research professor of theology at the University's Perkins School of Theology. He has filled lectureships at forty-six different colleges and universities and is the author or editor of nine different books in addition to numerous articles, chapters, reviews etc. in learned journals and symposia. A member of numerous international church councils and assemblies, he became a world figure through his work as co-chairman of the Theological Study Commission on Tradition and Traditions of the *World Council of Churches (1952–63) and as a delegate-observer from the World Methodist Council to the Vatican Council II and his subsequent involvement in the Roman Catholic-United Methodist Bilateral Consultations (the first of these from 1965–72; a five year series has been projected, beginning in Germany October 3 to 7, 1977). In his own denomination O. is chiefly noted for his leadership as chairman of the Theological Study Commission on Doctrine and Doctrinal Standards (1968–72), whose report became a part of the *United Methodist Disciplines of 1972 and 1976. In addition, he is a member of the editorial board planning a new and critical edition of John *Wesley's works, his particular assignment being a critical edition of John Wesley's *Sermons.* He holds membership in thirteen professional societies including the American Catholic Historical Association of which he was Vice President 1970–71 and President from 1971–72. In 1973 he became a member of the Board of directors of the *National Catholic Reporter*. He has been honored by the establishment of an endowed professorship in his name at Wofford College, South Carolina, his undergraduate alma mater.

[F. E. MASER]

OUWATER, ALBERT VAN (fl. *c*.1460–75), Dutch painter, "founder" of the Haarlem school, teacher of Geertgen tot Sint Jans (1478) and sometimes identified with "Hand G" of the *Turin-Milan Hours*. O.'s *Raising of Lazarus* (Berlin) bears a relation to Dirk Bouts.

[M. J. DALY]

OVALLE, ALONSO DE (1601–51), Chilean Jesuit and historian. He became a Jesuit in 1618, studied at Córdoba de Tucumán, achieved some distinction as a preacher, taught philosophy, and directed the seminary of Santiago. Sent to Rome in the interests of his province, he stopped in Madrid where he engaged in important conversations with the King and the Council of the Indies. Seeing the importance of making more accurate information available to Europeans, he wrote his *Histórica relación del reino de Chile* (1646), which was translated into several languages and became a standard source of information concerning colonial Latin America and a classic of Chilean literature.

[P. DAMBORIENA]

OVARIOTOMY, the removal of one or both ovaries; more exact medical terms are ovariectomy or oophorectomy. The removal by surgery or irradiation is justified morally when the ovaries themselves are cancerous or when their functioning worsens breast cancer (see TOTALITY, PRINCIPLE OF). Since the ovaries are endocrine glands, their removal upsets hormonal balance and so is a medical procedure not taken lightly. Canonically, a woman who has had both ovaries removed, although sterile, is still capable of contracting a valid marriage; she does not have the impediment of *impotence in the canonical sense.

[T. C. O'BRIEN]

OVERBECK, JOHANN FRIEDRICH (1789–1869), German painter and leading *Nazarene. O. founded in Vienna the Lukasbund for the renewal of art, which became (1810) the Brotherhood of S. Isidoro (called "Nazarenes"). O.'s frescoes in churches in Italy, murals in the Villa Giustiniani-Massimo, Rome (1829) and the *Rose Miracle of Mary* in the Portiuncula Chapel, Assisi, show the influence of Perugino and Raphael.

[M. J. DALY]

OVERBERG, BERNARD (1754–1826), German priest, Catholic educator, and spiritual advisor. Ordained in 1779, he was asked by vicar general F. von Fürstenberg to direct the organization of Münster's normal school. There he developed a pedagogical system that combined the learning of teaching skills and subject matter with religious and moral training. O. promoted the role of laywomen in what he described as the "vocation" of teaching. As rector of the Münster seminary (1809), he continued to stress the moral development of the seminarians in addition to their regular training. His most important book on education, which presents his program and method in detail, is *Anweisung zum zweckmässigen Schulunterricht für die Schullehrer im Fürstentum Münster* (1793, 1835; ed. J. Esterhues, 1957); he also published numerous catechetical works. O. was an influential advisor to Amalia *Gallitzin and her son and to the mystic Anne Catherine *Emmerich.

[R. J. LITZ]

OVIEDO, FRANCISCO DE (1601–51), Spanish Jesuit theologian at Madrid and Alcalá, author of *Tractatus theologici scholastici et morales* (1646) and *Tractatus de virtutibus fide, spe et charitate* (1651).

[T. C. O'BRIEN]

OVIEDO, STA. MARIA DE NARANCO, small 9th-cent. Mozarabic Spanish church, with barrel-vaulted nave, side entrances, and crypt beneath.

OWEN, ST., see OUEN OF ROUEN, ST.

OWEN, NICHOLAS, ST. (d. 1606), English Jesuit lay brother, martyr. O. was probably Edmund *Campion's servant and was first imprisoned for defending Campion's innocence. He later worked with Henry *Garnet and John *Gerard for 18 years. An excellent carpenter, he constructed hiding places for priests throughout England. A few authentic examples survive: Sawston Hall near Cambridge; Huddington Court, Worcestershire; Coughton Hall, Warwickshire. He saved literally hundreds of clerics and laymen. He was captured (1605), tortured in the Tower of London, and died on the rack. He was beatified in 1929 and canonized in 1970. BIBLIOGRAPHY: Butler 1:579–581; N. Del Re, BiblSanct 9:1327–28.

[T. M. MCFADDEN]

OWL AND THE NIGHTINGALE, THE, most distinguished piece of Middle English literary debate, dating from *c*.1200. The poet, wandering into a quiet valley, overhears the arguments of an owl and a nightingale about which is the better singer and therefore which serves man best. Bitter vituperation follows until the wren suggests arbitration, and the birds seek Master Nicholas of Guildford. No verdict is given. Interpretation of the poem varies from the birds as representative of the religious love poetry of the time vs. secular love poetry; the threatening God of the OT and the forgiving Redeemer; philosophy against art; contemplative vs. active life. Authorship is uncertain. The author reveals a fine sense of comedy, lively characterization, presents English scenes from monastery, cathedral, and parish life as well as secular scenes.

[M. M. BARRY]

OWNERSHIP (Lat. *dominium*), the right (see RIGHT AND RIGHTS) of possessing and so of using, destroying, or otherwise disposing of something. Primarily it is understood of property, but it is also recognized with reference to the body, its parts and its life (see LIFE, RISKS TO; MUTILATION), and such intangibles as reputation gained by work done. In the case of material possessions ownership is in principle a natural right because man finds in material realities the means necessary to sustain life and to provide for children and his own betterment (see NATURAL LAW). The right is not absolute, since it must be exercised with *justice, i.e., in harmony with the rights of others and in a way that contributes to the common good of the society in which a person lives; thus individual ownership must at times give way to the state's right of eminent domain. In a more particularized analysis, ownership is classified as complete, which means radical dominion over both the substance and use of a possession; or as partial ownership, i.e., a control over the usufruct; thus the difference between owning an automobile and leasing one (see also POVERTY, VOW OF.) The ways of acquiring ownership recognized in moral theology are: *occupancy, natural increase (e.g., a harvest from land owned); personal *labor; *prescription according to law; *contract; and finding (see LOST PROPERTY AND OWNERSHIP). Not only an individual but also a moral person, can acquire and exercise ownership (see CHURCH PROPERTY).

[T. C. O'BRIEN]

OXEIA, in *Byzantine chant notation, one of the somata, or signs indicating a note one scale step higher than the previous note. This is used with accented notes.

[A. DOHERTY]

OXFORD, UNIVERSITY OF, the oldest English university, a federation of independent colleges, founded at different times and separately governed, each by its own master and fellows. Its origins are obscure. Perhaps it sprang from the flourishing schools attached to local religious houses, or it may have begun with the English students forced to leave the University of Paris (1167). By 1300 Oxford had a university with a large number of scholars. The scholars and their masters, deeply resented by the townspeople, banded together to live in halls. These were the forerunners of the colleges. The first colleges—Merton, Balliol, and University—were established in the 13th cent., each with its own statutes, charter, library, hall, and chapel.

Many abbeys sent monks to Oxford to study, but it was *Robert Grosseteste (c. 1175–1253) and the friars such as Roger *Bacon (c. 1214–92) who introduced new thought from Europe and first made Oxford the equal of Paris and Padua.

After various town–and–gown riots and one massacre the university's rights and privileges over the town were confirmed. More colleges were founded and richly endowed. The university, established and assured of its authority, now influenced every part of national life and was itself developing in line with the rest of Christian Europe. The study of Greek was introduced. Literary humanism was slowly replacing scholasticism under teachers like *Grocyn, the mentor of *Erasmus, Thomas *More, and T. *Linacre, later founder of the College of Physicians (1518). Duke Humphrey established his library in 1480. This, the nucleus of the great Bodleian, lost all its treasures at the Reformation, during which time the whole university suffered great confusion. It had always been a religious institution. Its scholars clerks in holy orders, its colleges conceived as religious houses though their scope had been widened, its chief purpose the education of those intending to take holy orders, it was thrown into chaos by the suppressions and confiscations of the Reformation. Still, Oxford remained the citadel of Catholicism. Scholars began to leave only under Elizabeth when members of the university were required to subscribe to the Thirty-Nine Articles. Louvain, Douai, and the English College in Rome recruited them.

The Reformers and their successors endowed Oxford, in their turn, with new colleges and with the treasures of the dissolved monasteries. Sir Thomas Bodley restored Duke Humphrey's library (1598–1602) and founded the Bodleian. The reformed statutes of the Stuart chancellor of the university, Abp. *Laud, bound the university firmly to the Established Church; and during the Civil War Oxford, loyal to Church and King, housed Charles I, his army and his Parliament.

There followed in the late 17th and early 18th cent. a generation of able and energetic men who devoted great wealth and intelligence to the interests of the university. They employed the architects Christopher Wren (1632–1723), himself a fellow of All Souls, and Nicholas Hawksmoor (1661–1736). They built, and they improved, and many of Oxford's noblest buildings date from this time.

Later 18th-cent. Oxford was, by comparison, lethargic. Condemned for its idleness and frivolity by Jeremy Bentham, Gibbon, and Adam Smith, Oxford yet saw the invention of *Methodism by John and Charles *Wesley when they founded the Holy Club, to read the Scriptures and visit the sick and imprisoned. The movement did not make many converts in Oxford, however; its influence was more felt elsewhere. A later age of reform split Oxford and deeply affected the C of E when Victorian seriousness fathered the Oxford Movement. The movement, started to defend Church against State, went on to claim the apostolic foundation of the Church, and the tracts in which its leaders, *Pusey, *Keble, and *Newman, published these views electrified England. The movement failed, Newman became a RC later a cardinal.

A great liberalization of Oxford followed these dissensions. Dons were no longer obliged to be clergymen; fellows could marry; Dissenters and Catholics were admitted to the university. The first women's college was founded in 1878. The Jesuits founded their college, Campion Hall, in 1897. The last considerable religious movement to originate in Oxford was the *Oxford Group. Founded in 1921 by Frank Buchman, it was later called Moral Rearmament and seems to have no continuing connection with Oxford. BIB - LIOGRAPHY: W. Gaunt, *Oxford* (1965); *Bibliography of Printed Works Relating to the University of Oxford* (ed. E. H. Cordeaux and D. H. Merry, (1967); A. A. Wood, *Athenae Oxonienses: An Exact History of All Writers and Bishops Who Had Their Education in the University of Oxford* (5 v. 1820, 3d ed. 4 v. 1968); V. H. Green, *History of Oxford University* (1975); Emden Ox.

[J. OGDEN]

OXFORD CONFERENCE, a world conference of the *Life and Work movement, held at Oxford, England, July 12–26, 1937, under the title Conference on Church, Community, and State. The ferment initiated by the *Stockholm Conference in 1925 had led to a number of similar international conferences in the early 1930s; and in 1934 the Universal Christian Council for Life and Work, meeting on the Danish island of Fano, issued a call for a world conference of Churches on social, economic, and political problems. The Oxford Conference itself was only one part of a continuing process of ecumenical thinking that extended over several years. There were intensive studies preparatory to the Conference, and its own reports led to additional works of theologians, economists, sociologists, and statesmen. The stated purpose of the Conference was neither to pronounce authoritatively nor to express a consensus of the Churches, but to provide "as comprehensive and balanced a statement as possible . . . of the present mind of the Church" and to define the points in the contemporary situation at which Christian effort was crucial. The issues were considered under four aspects: Church and community; Church and State; Church, community, and State in relation to education; and the universal Church and the world of nations. The question of the nature of the Church was seen as so central that two comprehensive studies were published for the Conference: *The Church and Its Function in Society* and *Kirche, Staat und Mensch,* the latter representing the Orthodox viewpoint. At the Conference itself, reports drafted by the various sections were submitted to the general session, which studied, discussed, and extensively revised them. The six large collections of papers eventually issued became landmarks of Christian social thought. Not without some dissension, the Oxford Conference approved a proposal for a merger of Life and Work with *Faith and Order, which led eventually to creation of the *World Council of Churches. BIBLIOGRAPHY: *Oxford Conference* (ed. J. H. Oldham, 1937).

OXFORD GROUP, the name appropriated by F. *Buchman in 1929 for the religious movement now called

*Moral Rearmament. Many of Buchman's followers were Oxford University people. Others at Oxford tried to prevent this use of the university name, and the movement was sometimes referred to as The Group or as Buchmanism.

OXFORD MOVEMENT (1833–45), an attempt by Anglican clergymen of Oxford Univ. to renew the C of E by a return to 17th-cent. *high-church ideals and ritual. It drew strength from the Catholic roots of the C of E, which had been respected by the Elizabethan settlement, had put forth new growth under the Stuarts, but seemed likely to be killed by the patronage of a latitudinarian state under the Hanoverians. Nevertheless, in 1833 a tradition of Catholic-minded learning and piety persisted, esp. among the country gentry and the clergy, whose social prestige outweighed their political power. Looking forward, the Oxford movement should be seen as opening out into the *Anglo-Catholicism that, in the face of decades of opposition from the bps., the press, and Parliament, has influenced the spirit and focus of Anglican worship. In addition, it has provided the RC Church with many of its most capable recruits, although many mid-Victorian converts were not in direct contact with the movement, e.g., the future Cardinal Manning, who in fact had joined in the general attack on John Newman's *Tract 90 and also had been rebuked by E. *Pusey for attacking the Romanizers.

The history of the movement is taken to start with J. *Keble's not very striking assize sermon on "National Apostasy" (1833), which was part of the high-church flurry produced by the *Catholic Emancipation Act (1829), and by the alliance of Daniel O'Connell with the Whigs, and of dissenters with Benthamites. A more considerable manifestation was the first of the *Tracts for the Times, begun by Newman in 1829; they were pamphlets and treatises to recall the Church to its beginnings, to be faithful to the Christian dogmas, to keep its continuity through *apostolic succession, and to work for a unity transcending national boundaries. They spoke for a band of friends, who included R. I. Wilberforce, C. Marriott, and I. Williams; they were reinforced by the weight of Pusey, later joined by W. G. Ward of Balliol and his circle. All agreed in pulling down the idols of the Reformation; not all agreed in looking to Rome. Keble had no liking for Rome, but Froude, the true spark of the movement, turned Newman's eyes in that direction. Yet it was still the time of the *via media,* between the excess of too much articulation of doctrine and the defect of softening it out of existence. The *Library of the Fathers* was begun in 1836, and the corpus of *Caroline Divines in the *Library of Anglo-Catholic Theology* in 1841, with the purpose of drawing the attention of the Church of England to essentials of its authentic patristic and properly Anglican tradition. Opposition to the Tractarians took the form of honest anger, stupefaction, abuse, and ridicule (the subterfuges typical of vested interests when threatened) and the obscurantism that often goes with liberalism. In 1843 things came to a head with *Tract 90;* only a friendly proctor's *non* *placet* prevented the imposition of an oath of reprobation. In 1845 Ward's exuberant logic drove him to Rome, and Newman took the step, with more agony. Many followed his example. But Pusey and many more stood firm. It was the parting of friends; the last chapter of a volume, but not the end of a series. BIBLIOGRAPHY: R. W. Church, *Oxford Movement* (1891, repr. 1970); *Oxford Movement* (ed. E. Fairweather, 1964); M. R. O'Connell, *Oxford Conspirators: A History of the Oxford Movement, 1833–45* (1969).*TRACTARIANISM; *EVANGELICAL ALLIANCE.

[T. GILBY]

OXNAM, GARFIELD BROMLEY (1891–1963), Methodist bp. and ecumenist. His education included studies both in the U.S. and abroad. He was president of De Pauw Univ., Greencastle, Ind. (1928–36), then was elected bishop. He served in Omaha (1936–39), Boston (1939–44), New York (1944–52), and Washington, D.C. (1952–60). He supported the union of the three largest Methodist bodies in the U.S. in 1939 (see METHODIST CHURCH); was president of the *Federal Council of Churches (1944–46); and was a member of the six-man praesidium of the newly organized *World Council of Churches (1948–54). He was a founder (1947) and officer of *Protestants and Other Americans United for Separation of Church and State (POAU). In 1953 he appeared at his own request before the House Un-American Activities Committee to defend liberal clergymen charged with Communist sympathies. His numerous publications centered on preaching, social reform, and international and industrial subjects. BIBLIOGRAPHY: HistAmMeth 3:555–556; 569–571.

OXYRHYNCHUS PAPYRI, an immense collection of papyri discovered in the late 19th cent. at Oxyrhynchus, an important Egyptian town from 300 B.C. to 600 A.D. and a Christian center in the 4th century. Among the papyri are thousands of fragments of classical literature: gospels, apocrypha, Greek and Hebrew hymns, patristic texts, calendars, and inventories of church property. BIBLIOGRAPHY: *Oxyrhynchus Papyri,* (ed. B. F. Grenfell et al., 29 v., 1898–1963).

OXYRHYNCHUS SAYINGS OF JESUS, see APOCRYPHA (NT), 39.

OYEND, ST. see EUGENDUS OF CONDAT, ST.

OZANAM, ANTOINE FRÉDÉRIC (1813–53), French social thinker, historian, literary critic, and founder of the St. Vincent de Paul Society. Born in Milan and reared in Lyons, O. early became interested in social problems and in 1831 published a critique of the social theories of Saint-Simon. In the same year he went to Paris to study law and literature, and in 1833, with some fellow students, founded the *St. Vincent de Paul Society, devoted to the personal service of the poor in their homes and the spiritual development of the members through prayer and study. He held a chair in the law faculty at Lyons before becoming professor of literature at the Sorbonne in 1844. He won renown for his doctoral thesis on Dante (1839), for *La Civilisation chrétienne chez les Francs* (1849), and for his edition of the 13th-cent. Franciscan poets (1852), and twice won the Prix Gobert. In the social ferment of the mid-century, O. advocated that Catholics play an active part in democratic political processes. His law lectures expounded a social doctrine that foreshadowed *Rerum novarum,* and the St. Vincent de Paul Society, today spread all over the world, anticipated some of the methods of modern social work. BIBLIOGRAPHY: *Oeuvres complètes* (11 v., 1859–65); C. A. Ozanam, *Vie de Frédéric Ozanam* (1879); G. Goyau, *Frédéric Ozanam* (1925).

[D. CODDINGTON]

P

PACCA, BARTOLOMEO (1756–1844), Italian card. and papal nuncio. Sent to Cologne in 1786 in order to suppress the movement for ecclesiastic independence that had sprung up among the bp. electors in the Rhineland, P. proved a skillful diplomat on behalf of the pope's right to intervene in spiritual affairs, though his mission was cut short by invading French Revolutionary armies in 1794. In Lisbon as nuncio from 1794 to 1801 he struggled against a different problem: the role of the Portuguese monarchy in ecclesiastical matters. He became a cardinal in 1801. An uncompromising supporter of the Old Regime, P. opposed the pragmatic Concordat with Napoleon in 1801 and, as prosecretary of State (1808–09), following the French occupation of Rome, was arrested and taken together with Pope Pius VII into French custody for the next 4 years. After their return to the Eternal City in 1815, P. set himself against the conciliatory policy of Secretary of State *Consalvi and even against the reforms proposed by the pope. His memoirs, somewhat biased, offer a valuable picture of his turbulent times.

[E. M. GATES]

PACCANARISTS, religious institute of priests established as the Society of the Faith of Jesus to reinstitute Jesuit life during the suppression period (1773–1814). The society was called Paccanarists after the founder, Niccolò Paccanari, who with four companions—one a former Jesuit—established the congregation at Rome in 1797. They were pledged to live by the Jesuit rule and took the fourth vow of special obedience to the pope. Pius VI approved the institute in 1798, permitted members to recite the Breviary with Jesuit supplements and to admit former Jesuits; in 1799 he directed a merger with the Society of the Sacred Heart of Jesus, a group of identical character founded by É. *Tournély. The society was noted for its various pastoral and educational works and it soon extended from Italy and Austria (where the Society of the Sacred Heart had established itself) to England, France, Holland, Switzerland, and Germany. Paccanari himself was of unstable character, came under suspicion, and was imprisoned in 1808; nothing is known of his whereabouts after 1810. After restoration of the Jesuits in 1814 most of the Paccanarists joined the Jesuits, and the interim body ceased to exist.

[R. A. TODD]

PACE, EDWARD ALOYSIUS (1861–1938), psychologist, philosopher, educator at The Catholic University of America. P. was ordained for the diocese of St. Augustine, Florida, in 1885, where he became chancellor of his diocese and rector of the cathedral. Named to the faculty of CUA in 1888 by Bp. *Keane, first rector, P. studied in Paris and Louvain and received his doctorate in psychology at Leipzig in 1891. From that year until his retirement in 1935, P. was a powerful influence at the University, serving as professor of psychology (1891–94) and of philosophy (1894–1935), dean of the school of philosophy, and vice-rector. In 1891 P. established one of the first psychology laboratories in the U.S. An editor of *The Catholic Encyclopedia* (1907–1914), cofounder of the *Catholic Educational Review* (1911), he also edited *Studies in Psychology and Psychiatry* (1926). From 1927 to 1936 he was an editor of *The New Scholasticism*. P. served as chairman of the American Council on Education in 1925–26. He was also the outstanding U.S. representative of Neo-Scholasticism. His awareness of the place of psychology in the field of learning was a pioneering stance which caused him some difficulties with conservative forces in the American Church. His contributions to Catholic education cannot be exaggerated.

[J. R. AHERNE]

PACE, RICHARD (1482–1536), English diplomat and humanist, awarded (1519) the position of dean of St. Paul's by Henry VIII for diplomatic services on the Continent on behalf of Henry and Card. Wolsey. Friend of Thomas More and correspondent of Erasmus, P. established chairs in

2639

Greek at both Oxford and Cambridge to further renaissance humanism.

[R. J. LITZ]

PACEM IN TERRIS (Eng., Peace on Earth), the encyclical of John XXIII advocating human freedom and dignity as the basis for world order and peace (1963). The document is divided into four parts. (1) The foundation for all human affairs is the preeminent value and worth of the individual person. The human rights which belong to each man are specifically listed, and their basis in the creative act of God is noted. (2) The relationship of the individual to the State is basically one of subjection to authority insofar as the State is a moral entity which must legislate for the common well-being of its citizens. This section contains an extended consideration of a proper philosophy of law based upon the necessary conformity between human legislation and the laws of God. (3) The rights and duties of States are considered. All States are equal in dignity, no matter what their stage of cultural development. States must abide by the moral law in their relationships with each other, and here, as well as in personal affairs, love rather than fear must be the guiding force. The pope makes specific reference to world peace, pleads that the arms race cease, that nuclear weapons be banned, and that a general disarmament be negotiated. (4) The reality of greater interdependence among modern States is pointed out. Modern technology has made the absolute sovereignty and isolation of one nation from another a reality of the past. Nations must cooperate in the achievement of their individual goals.

[T. M. MCFADDEN]

PACHECO, FRANCISCO (1564–1654), Spanish painter, studying copies and prints of works of Raphael, Michelangelo, and Lucas van Leyden, associated with the young Velasquez, later his son-in-law. Scholar, teacher, writer, and official censor of the Inquisition, interested in academic form and iconography, P. promoted realism in the expression of religious ideals in his book *El Arte de la pintura, su antigüedad y grandeza.* BIBLIOGRAPHY: M. B. Rodriguez, *Pacheco, su tierra y su tiempo* (1963).

[M. J. DALY]

PACHER, MICHAEL (*c.*1435–98), woodcarver and painter of the leading S Tyrol school whose art combines the N Gothic tradition, in which he was trained, with Italian developments in perspective. His painting suggests contact with the works of Mantegna, Donatello, and Bellini. His masterpiece is the large carved and painted polyptych altarpiece (1481) for the church of St. Wolfgang near Salzburg, a highpoint in S German carving full of innovations of great significance to art history. The *Four Fathers of the Church* (1480, Munich) and *Mystic Marriage of St. Catherine* (1490) are attributed to P. who introduced Italian Renaissance style into Austria, Switzerland, and Germany. BIBLIOGRAPHY: O. Schürer, *Michael Pacher* (1940).

[R. E. FLEISCHER]

PACHOMIUS, ST. (also Packom; *c.*290–*c.*346), Egyptian abbot and founder of cenobitic monasticism. It is said that he was born at Sne of pagan parents and, after serving in the army, was converted to Christianity. He became a hermit under Palemon (*c.*314), but after 6 years became dissatisfied with eremitic life. He then settled in *Tabennisi where he founded a monastic community based on strict common life (cenobite). In contrast to Nitrian practices, austerities were moderate, a matter of personal initiative. Work was not penitential but for community support. Adequate food and clothing were provided for each monk. Obedience to the abbot *(apa)* was absolute. Pachomius founded a second monastery at Pbou which became the central headquarters of a close federation of nine monasteries and two convents. Composed in Coptic, the rules of Pachomius were translated into Greek, Latin and Ethiopian, and in some degree influenced all subsequent monastic rules. BIBLIOGRAPHY: AS May 3:282–356; Palladius of Helenopolis, *Lausiac History* (ed. C. Butler, 1896–1904); Quasten 3:154–160.

[D. W. JOHNSON]

PACHOMIUS, RULE OF ST., a document, written in Coptic, which marks the beginnings of monastic common life. St. Basil modeled his monastic foundations on its precepts. St. Jerome, using a Greek text, made a Latin translation (*c.*404) which is the only surviving text of the complete Rule, and as such has had a significant influence on Western Monasticism, e.g., the Rules of SS. Caesarius of Arles, and Benedict, and the reform of St. Benedict of Aniane. It contains four groups of monastic regulations prescribing the daily routine of prayer and manual labor. These directives, allegedly dictated by an angel, were the fruit of practical experience. Their enduring value lies in the fact that they laid the spiritual and economic foundations on which the common life is based. BIBLIOGRAPHY: L. T. Lefort, *Pachomiana Latina* (1932); Quasten 3:154–158; D. Knowles, *From Pachomius to Ignatius* (1966) 3–4.

PACHYMERES, GEORGE (1242–*c.*1310), Byzantine historian. G. held high positions in both state and Church, and his intellectual interests and writings covered a broad range. His *History,* the chief source on the 2d half of the 13th cent., is esteemed for its impartiality (ed. in PG 143:443–996; 144:15–716).

PACIAN OF BARCELONA, ST. (4th cent.), bishop. The chief source of information about P. is *Jerome's De viris illustribus,* a book dedicated to P.'s son, Dexter, the praetorian prefect. Jerome praised P. for his sanctity and pastoral zeal. His authentic extant writings are: an exhortation to penance; three letters to Sympronian, an adherent of the Novatian heresy, on the Catholic doctrine of the forgiveness of sins; and a sermon on baptism. These works are of great value for the history of the sacrament of *penance. It was in his first letter to Sympronian that P. wrote the famous line: "My name is Christian; my surname,

Catholic.'' Works: PL 13:1051–94. BIBLIOGRAPHY: Butler 1:533; G. Madoz, EncCatt 9:504–505.

[R. B. ENO]

PACIFERI, see CAPUTIATI.

PACIFICATION OF GHENT, treaty of November 8, 1576 between Catholic and Calvinist provinces in the Netherlands against Spain. In the early 1570s attempts to unite Calvinist Zeeland and Holland with Catholic Brabant, Hainault, and Flanders proved unsatisfactory. Yet the hatred of Spanish troops supplied a common rallying point. On November 4, 1576 unruly and unpaid Spanish troops rebelled and sacked Antwerp. This so-called Spanish Fury convinced wavering Catholics and Calvinists that an alliance was necessary. According to the Pacification reached at Ghent they agreed to unite against Spanish oppression; edicts against heresy were temporarily suspended; and Holland and Zeeland promised not to extend the persecution of Catholics outside their borders. The alliance was shortlived. Religious differences remained unsolved and the victories of the Duke of Parma, Alexander Farnese, largely divided the Catholic South from the Calvinist North. BIBLIOGRAPHY: P. Geyl, *Revolt of the Netherlands* (1958); J. H. Elliott, *Europe Divided, 1559–1598* (1968).

[C. T. EBY]

PACIFICUS OF NOVARA, BL. (Pacific of Cerano [Ceredano]; *c.* 1420–82), Franciscan Observant preacher. Educated by the Benedictines, P. entered the Franciscans in 1445. He preached popular missions (1452–71) and (from 1480) the Crusade against the Turks proclaimed by Sixtus IV. His *Sommetta della coscienza* (1474), a casuist manual for confessors, was known as the *Somma Pacifica*. BIBLIOGRAPHY: O. J. Blum, NCE 10:854; V. G. Gremigni, BiblSanct 10:4–5.

[O. J. BLUM]

PACIFISM, doctrinal and practical dedication to peace. Its positive motivation is a faith that all things worth doing can be done through love; negatively, it is expressed by the refusal to use violence or to feel hatred in accomplishing any end in life. It is older than Christianity, going back to Lao Tse and Buddha in the Orient. Christian pacifism is rooted in the teachings of Jesus on love as a way of life. The early Christian Church was predominantly pacifist until the time of the Emperor Constantine in the 4th century. In the era of the Reformation, the Anabaptists of Switzerland, the Swiss Brethren, taught a form of pacifism perhaps better called *nonresistance. Anabaptists refused to accept public office because it might require the use of force, and many Anabaptist leaders died under persecution without making any effort to defend themselves. Their religious testimony of nonresistance was passed on to their successors, the Mennonites, whose leader *Menno Simons declared: ''The regenerated do not go to war. They are the children of peace who have beaten their swords into plowshares and their

spears into pruning hooks, and know of no war.'' Mennonites have continued to maintain this teaching, and the German *Brethren Churches have held to similar belief since their origin. In the 17th cent. in England the founder of the Religious Society of Friends (Quakers), George *Fox, insisted that the Lord told him inwardly that he must live ''in the virtue of that life and power that took away the occasion of all war.'' For more than 3 cent. Friends have at least officially upheld this religious testimony. The worldwide humanitarian work of the American Friends Service Committee is based on this conviction, and young Friends have conscientiously objected to military service during every war in which their countries have been involved since the mid-17th century. In recent years, they have been joined by an increasing number of individuals from other Protestant denominations and some from the RC Church. Most of these conscientious objectors have been convinced by their own reflections that the use of force against other human beings is wrong and that what is usually accomplished by violent means can be better accomplished through love.

In World War II the U.S. government set up a program of Civilian Public Service for drafted conscientious objectors; nearly 12,000 men were distributed among large camps, where they did manual labor for such government projects as the Soil Conservation, Forest, and National Park Services. Many went from these camps to mental hospitals or training schools, where they served as attendants, and others performed additional types of ''detached service'' work. In all, about 25,000 men were willing to be drafted into military service if they were allowed to do noncombatant work; most of these were attached to the Medical Corps. About 5,500 men were much more radical: they either refused to register for the draft under Selective Service or, having been drafted, ''walked out'' of camps and special service units. Only in war time, when there is conscription, is a man forced to declare himself as a pacifist. In the second half of the 20th cent., with the frightening development of atomic weapons, the number of both religious and secular pacifists and near-pacifist organizations, e.g., the International Fellowship of Reconciliation, the War Resisters' International, and the Women's International League for Peace and Freedom, all reflect this growth.

The antiwar movement of the 1960s throughout the Western world and markedly in the U.S. was a protest against the Viet Nam War itself as unjust. Many of those who fled the U.S. rather than serve in the military did so in protest of that war. But in the antiwar movement there was certainly an element of pacifism, a repudiation of war and violence as such. Many of the Churches and church organizations supported the antiwar movement and moved closer to pacifism. There was a strong minority at Vatican Council II that sought the condemnation of modern warfare as such; the conciliar statement, influenced by the U.S. hierarchy and other bps., succeeded in getting a more mitigated condemnation (Vat II ChurchModWorld 82). In the face of the meaning of nuclear warfare, however, papal and other ecclesiastical statements seem to support the practical meaninglessness of the "just war" theory; nuclear terror is almost imposing pacifism as a necessary position. Guerilla warfare and "conventional war," however, seem to be acceptable even to Christian leaders as a means to remedy political and social injustices. A "theology of revolution" is espoused by some liberation theologians; nor would all rule out even political terrorism. Thus it cannot be said that there is any Christian consensus on pacifism, as though it were an intrinsic component of the gospel message. How the victims of violence benefit from its use, even for the cause of their liberation, is not clear. Nor is the perennial and haunting suspicion quieted that the advocates of violence for a cause are not exploiting the cause in the interest of their own passions and ambitions. *BOMB, ATOMIC.

There are many differences of opinion among religious and secular pacifists. The basic one questions whether pacifism is a means or is an end in itself. Is love the best means of achieving any goal, or is it rather a way of life desirable in and of itself, quite apart from its practical effectiveness? Another major difference relates to what the pacifist should do under conscription. Some pacifists will do noncombatant work under the military; others will accept work "of national importance" under civilian auspices; still others will do no form of alternative service under the government and must suffer the legal penalties for following the dictates of their conscience. BIBLIOGRAPHY: L. L. McReavy, NCE 10:855–857, and bibliog.

[F. B. TOLLES]

PADERBORN CATHEDRAL, N German Romanesque Ottonian structure, begun (1009) by Bp. Meinwerk. Burned (1058), rebuilt under Bp. Imad, the cathedral has the largest Romanesque W tower in Germany, recalling the Chapel of the Savior in St. Riquier, France.

[M. J. DALY]

PADILLA Y ESTRADA, IGNACIO DE (1695–1760), Augustinian bishop. Born in Mexico City, he spent time in Rome as a representative of his Augustinian province. In 1745 he was consecrated abp. of Santo Domingo, and led a reformation of the clergy and restored many churches. In 1753, he assumed the bishopric of Mérida, Yucatán and become known for his concern about the welfare of the Indians.

[M. A. MCFADDEN]

PADRE, Italian or Spanish, father; used in English to refer to a military chaplain, or more generally to designate or address any clergyman informally, sometimes with a note of discomforting familiarity.

[T. C. O'BRIEN]

PADROADO, see PATRONATO REAL.

PADUA, UNIVERSITY OF, a medieval Italian institution of higher learning, originally an offshoot and rival of the Univ. of Bologna. Although officially erected as a *studium generale* in 1222 to accommodate professors and students emigrating from the Univ. of Bologna as a result of town-and-gown struggles, and approved by Emperor Frederick II in 1225, the university had its roots in the 12th cent. when the famous jurist, Gerardus Pomadelli, later bp. of Padua, and other professors of law taught there, probably *c*.1165. In 1274, the university received status from the Council of Lyons II equal to Paris and Bologna; it was reconfirmed in 1346 by Clement VI as a *studium generale*. In 1363 Urban V issued a bull granting the power to confer the doctorate in theology and this led to the uniting the schools of theology that had been operating under Dominicans, Franciscans, and Augustinians. During the 15th and 16th cent., under the Venetian government, the university enjoyed unusual prosperity, with Galileo, G. Fallopius, and A. Vesalius among its greatest professors. It suffered a decline in the 17th cent. but regained its academic vigor in the 18th cent. when G. B. Morgagni occupied the chair of anatomy for nearly 60 years. With the fall of the Venetian Republic (1797), the university, under French control, was reorganized and its schools combined under one rector. In 1814, under the Austrian government, the faculty of theology was transferred to the seminary, and the different faculties were reestablished as separate schools. Following the insurrection against Austria (1848) and ultimate return to Italian rule (1866), the university resumed its academic activities. Today Padua's teaching staff averages about 1,035; its enrollment, 21,000. The library, founded in 1629, houses 414,021 volumes and 2,579 MSS. BIBLIOGRAPHY: H. Rashdall, *Universities of Europe in the Middle Ages,* (ed. F. M. Powicke and A. B. Emden, 3 v. 1936).

[M. B. MURPHY]

PADUAN SCHOOL, one of the first N centers of Italian Renaissance style, rivaling Venice (13th to 15th centuries). Padua, rich in works of Donatello, Lippi, Uccello, and Mantegna, boasts Giotto's great fresco cycle (1305) in the Scrovegni (Arena) Chapel; the bronze reliefs (1444–50) of the high altar of the Basilica of St. Anthony ("Il Santo"; 1232–1307) in the Piazza del Santo and the famous bronze (1445–50) of Erasmo da Narni ("Gattamelata"), the first equestrian statue of the Renaissance, both by Padua's native son and genius, Donatello; a marble Madonna by G. Pisano; and Mantegna's St. Christopher frescoes (*c*.1455) in the church of the Eremitani, damaged in World War II (1944). The Paduan school declined in a vulgarization of Mantena's style.

[M. J. DALY]

PAEDOBAPTISM, see INFANT BAPTISM.

PAEDOBAPTISTS (Pedobaptists; Gr. *pais,* child, and *baptizein,* baptize), a term used to designate those who practice *infant baptism. It was coined in the polemic carried on in 17th-cent. England by Presbyterians and Congregationalists against the Baptists.

[N. H. MARING]

PAESTUM, TEMPLES AT (7th century B.C.), best-preserved Greek architecture in Italy at Poseidonia (Paestum) on the Gulf of Salerno. They are three great Doric temples: a basilica (540 B.C.), Temple of Neptune (450 B.C.) and Temple of Ceres (520 B.C.). From a Latin colony (237 B.C.), the Roman remains show baths, gymnasium, amphitheater and an Italic temple (3d cent. B.C.). Murals in Lucanian tombs (400 B.C.) and, from the neighboring sanctuary of Hera at Foce del Sele, splendid sculptures from a temple and ''treasury'' preserved in the Paestum museum, are noteworthy. BIBLIOGRAPHY: P. C. Sestieri, *New Museum of Paestum* (1956).

[M. J. DALY]

PAGAN (from Lat. *paganus,* civilian or resident of a rural area), person not a Jew, Christian, or (in some usages) Muslim. Opinion is divided concerning which meaning lies behind the current usage of pagan. Some scholars assert that because Christianity spread first in the cities, with rural areas the last to be converted, rural residents came to be equated with adherents of the old Roman religions. Others believe the term derived from the Christian's understanding of himself as a soldier of Christ, others being civilians. The earliest Christian term for nonbelievers was gentiles, following OT usage. Augustine refers to the term pagan as in popular use, and it was first used officially by Valentinian I in 370. It has come to be more broadly used for a person who is not religious and is concerned only with the enjoyment of this world without thought of any ultimate judgment.

[T. EARLY]

PAGAN, TEMPLES OF (9th–13th cent.), evidences of Classical architecture of the Mon-Khmer people who established their capital at Pagan, the cultural center of Burma, erecting 5,000 temples and stupas in Indian style. Of the remaining structures the Buddhist Ananda Temple is the most impressive.

[M. J. DALY]

PAGI, family name of two Conventual Franciscans, uncle and nephew, church historians. **Antoine** (1624–99) entered the Conventual Franciscans at Arles and in his lifetime was provincial three times. Though he wrote historical treatises on the Roman consuls (1682) and on St. Martin of Tours and also published a Latin edition of St. Anthony of Padua's sermons, much of his life was devoted to a massive, critical gloss on Card. *Baronius's Annales ecclesiastici.* During his own life Antoine published only the first of this four-volume work (1689). **François** (1654–1721), nephew, also a church historian, is best known for his *Pontificum Romanorum gesta* (1719–27), which carried papal history up to 1447. He edited and published the rest of his uncle's work, under the title, *Critica historico-chronologica* (1705).

[E. M. GATES]

PAGNINI, SANTES (1470–1536), Dominican, philologist, biblical scholar whose Latin translation of the Hebrew Bible (1528), the first since Jerome, introduced the numbering of verses still in use. In Lyons, 1524, he successfully preached against both Waldensians and Lutherans. P.'s translation influenced some early English versions of the OT.

[R. J. LITZ]

PAGODA, term coined by Portuguese traders for S Asian Hindu towered temples which they used as beacons (*Black Pagoda* at Māmallapuram). The Chinese term refers to the rectangular tall towers, with marked, gracefully curved projecting rooflines, dating from the Han period and used as observatories and pleasure towers. Small ceramic ''spirit houses'' from Han tombs are ''pagoda'' forms and we know of observatory towers at central Asian stations of Chinese soldiers in Han times. The Buddhist White Goose Pagoda, Ch'ang-an, 652 was modeled on the Indian form at Bodh-gayñ. The Japanese pagoda is related to Chinese forms (five-story Pagoda, Horyuji, Nara).

[M. J. DALY]

P'AI LOU (Pailoo; Pailow), Chinese memorial gateway to the dead, related to the Indian *torana* and the Japanese *torii* and built of wood or stone, similar to the Roman commemorative arch. The *p'ai lou,* supporting an ornamental projecting roof, may also be erected across a city street to honor a faithful widow.

[M. J. DALY]

PAIDEIA, CHRISTIAN, the formal instruction in the truths of the faith and the formation of a definite Christian culture through the combination of what was best in the classical tradition, whether literary or philosophical, with the revealed truths of Scripture (cf. Phil 4.8). *Paideia* both as a system of education and as its consequent type of civilization was a commonplace among the Greeks. The expression ''Christian paideia'' is first found in Clement of Rome (1 Cor 21.6, 8). This concept, which was taken up by later writers, was elaborated by Clement of Alexandria in his *Paidagogos* where he gives detailed instructions on the Christian way of life. Practical instructions for those preparing for baptism are to be found in the *Catecheses* of St. Cyril of Jerusalem and Theodore of Mopsuestia and in the *De catechizandis rudibus* of St. Augustine. In Gregory of Nyssa, Christian *paideia* is a kind of *deificatio,* a divine anabasis through which a Christian comes to an ever greater contemplation of God and an ever more perfect union with him through a *morphosis* brought about through the imitation of Christ. BIBLIOGRAPHY: W. Jaeger, *Early Christianity and Greek Paideia* (1961); H. Fuchs, RAC 5:390–398.

[M. J. COSTELLOE]

PAIN BÉNIT, see EULOGIUM.

PAIN OF LOSS, a phrase used by scholastic theology to describe the negative aspect of the dual punishment of hell, the positive part of which was called *pain of sense. In scholasticism it is related to that element of sin which is expressed as a turning away from God, the last end of man and of all things. Pain of loss is an extension of this aversion. The damned are eternally turned away from the presence of God and excluded from the beatifying union with him which is expressed principally, but not exclusively, as the beatific vision. The man who has freely turned from God during life is deprived eternally of the divine illumination by means of which he could know God as his total fulfillment. BIBLIOGRAPHY: A. Winklhofer, *Coming of His Kingdom* (tr. A. V. Littledale, 1963). *HELL.

[J. CORDOUE]

PAIN OF SENSE, a phrase used by scholastic theology to describe the positive aspect of the dual punishment of hell, the negative part of which was called *pain of loss. In scholasticism it is related to that element of sin which is expressed as a turning toward creatures (see SIN, PERSONAL.) Creatures now serve as an external material agent of suffering for sin under the principal metaphor of *hellfire. St. Thomas understood this infliction of punishment by material things as a subjection to or restriction by them. This view presupposes the notion of a final harmony between the total created universe and the will of God, thus the damned are condemned to remain outside of this harmony, subject to it, and constricted in their chosen isolation from it. Contemporary theology, therefore, tends to extend this Thomistic notion of subjection and restriction to the entire material universe, with respect to which the damned are in a state of disharmony. BIBLIOGRAPHY: A. Winklhofer, *Coming of His Kingdom* (tr. A. V. Littledale, 1963). *HELL.

[J. CORDOUE]

PAINE, JOHN, ST. (Payne; d. 1582), English martyr during the reign of Elizabeth I. P. studied at Douai College where he was ordained (1576). He immediately set out for England and lived at the home of Lady Petre in Ingratistone, Essex, until his first arrest and brief imprisonment (1577). He returned to Ingratistone where he worked until again betrayed in 1581. After being questioned by Walsingham (Elizabeth's secretary), he was imprisoned for 8 months in the Tower, then taken to Chelmsford gaol, tried, found guilty on flimsy evidence, and executed. He was beatified in 1886 and canonized in 1970. BIBLIOGRAPHY: Butler 2:16–17; N. Del Re, BiblSanct 10:424–425.

[T. M. MCFADDEN]

PAINE, THOMAS (1737–1809), exponent of revolutionary political and religious ideas. Born in Suffolk, England, he was confirmed in the Anglican Church, his mother's faith, but was also influenced by his Quaker father. Largely self-educated, he achieved great influence through the vigor and clarity of his writings. Dismissed from his post in the excise as an agitator, he sailed to America in 1774, where he supported the cause of independence by joining the army

and writing a series of pamphlets on *The Crisis.* In 1787 he returned to Europe to promote his invention for an iron bridge. His famous *Rights of Man* (1791–92) was a reply to E. *Burke's *Reflexions on the French Revolution.* He was elected a member of the French Convention, but fell foul of Robespierre and was imprisoned for a time. While in prison he completed *The Age of Reason,* an attack on the Bible and Christianity. A *deist, he affirmed his belief in God and humanity, but called Christianity an invention of mythmakers. This was among the causes of his ostracism in the U.S., to which he returned in 1802. BIBLIOGRAPHY: H. Pearson, *Tom Paine* (1937).

[T. EARLY]

PAISIELLO, GIOVANNI (1740–1816), Italian composer of church music and, more notably, of opera. While studying with Durante in Naples (1754–1763), P. composed primarily church music—oratorios, Masses, Requiems, *Te Deum* for two choruses, *Miserere,* and a Christmas pastoral. After 1763, he turned successfully to opera with *L'idolo cinese* (1767) and *La Frascatana* (1774), and *Il barbiere di Siviglia* (1782), which reigned until Rossini's setting of the story (1816). All were well received by contemporaries. P. held positions on the courts of Catherine the Great (1776–84), Ferdinand IV (1784–1802), and Napoleon Bonaparte (1802–03). He composed 100 operas, known for their simplicity, expressiveness, and structural innovation, and symphonies, concertos, church and chamber music.

[R. J. LITZ]

PAISLEY ABBEY, a large and impressive Cluniac monastery in the heart of Paisley, Renfrewshire, Scotland, and founded *c.*1163 by Walter, son of the Steward of Scotland, badly damaged by the English in 1307 and by the Reformers in 1561. Its church is still in use today. BIBLIOGRAPHY: *Registrum monasterii de Passelet* (Maitland Club, 1832); D. E. Easson, *Medieval Religious Houses: Scotland* (1957) 57.

[L. J. MACFARLANE]

PAISSI OF CHILANDAR, ST. (1722–*c.*81), Bulgarian monk of Mt. Athos, first at the Serbian monastery of Chilandar and later at the Bulgarian one of Zographou. He is credited with the revival of the Bulgarian national conscience after several cent. of Turkish oppression through the impact made by his *Slavo-Bulgarian History* (1762), a compilation mainly from Western sources (notably Baronius and Mauro Orbini). The work was circulated through the country in MS form and was copied by hand for several decades. In 1962 the Bulgarian Orthodox Church canonized Paissi a confessor of the Church.

[G. ELDAROV]

PAKEGH (Phakel'), a stiff black hat worn in public by Armenian clerics of priestly rank or higher, except when they are wearing hieratic vestments. The lower part is cylindrical, but the upper part is in the form of a low cone. Over the *pakegh* members of the celibate clergy wear the *veghar*.

[A. CODY]

PAKISTAN, an Islamic republic in SW Asia (310,000 sq mi, pop. *c*.60,000,000). It is called the Islamic Republic because 80% of the people are Islamic in religion and culture, the Hindus constituting 10% and Christians 4% of the remainder. Pakistan's N areas were the seat of a rich central Asiatic civlization. Islamization began in the 8th cent. and reached its zenith under the Mongul Empire in the 16th. The territory was united to India under British rule. Mohammedans, however, formed the Muslim League in order to resist Hindu influence. Independence was achieved in 1947, but was accompanied by violence and the migration of millions of people from Pakistan to India and vice versa. Relations between the two countries have been strained, chiefly because of the controversy over Kashmir. The masses are culturally backward (the illiteracy rate is 85%), but a serious effort is being made to promote education. The Christian traders who were active in the area in the 6th and 7th cent. disappeared, leaving few traces of their presence. In the W section the Jesuits began a short-lived mission at the court of Akbar in 1594. They were followed in Sind by Augustinians and Carmelites, but in both regions success was limited, and the work came to a stand-still during the 18th century. Catholic missions were reopened at the time of the British occupation, and Lahore became a vicariate apostolic in 1881. The E region, (approx. 55,000 sq mi with *c*.45 million pop.) which is located nearly 1,000 mi from the W section and which became an independent nation (Bangladesh) in 1971, was entrusted to Dominicans, Jesuits, and Augustinians. In 1834 a vicariate apostolic was created for Bengal. With the independence, Pakistan was divided into two ecclesiastical provinces: Karachi, with suffragans at Lahore, Rawalpindi, Hyderabad, Lilliapur, and Multan (where U. S. Dominicans work); and Dacca, Bangladesh, with the Sees of Chittagong, Dinajpur, and Khulna. The first Pakistani abp. was consecrated in 1953. The Catholic population numbers 365,718 (1976) baptized (0.5% of the pop.) and 82,000 catechumens. There are 219 priests, 226 religious men, and 578 religious women. Religious freedom is guaranteed by law, but the Muslim population is staunchly opposed to conversions. Protestant missionaries, the principal groups being the C of E and the Punjab Synod of the United Presbyterian Reformed Church, have been active in the country from the mid-19th century. There is an All Pakistan Christian Council, and steps have been taken to form the Church of N India and Pakistan on the model of that of the Church of S India Union. The total Protestant membership is reckoned at 416,000, with 732 foreign missionaries, and 544 ordained Pakistani ministers.

[P. DAMBORIENA]

PALA D'ORO, most famous screen of 86 of the finest late-Byzantine cloisonné enamel plaques mounted in a gold and silver framework enriched with precious stones, commissioned in Constantinople during the 10th cent., enriched after 1204 with enamels taken from the Monastery of the Pantocrator, and again altered by mounting in a Gothic frame (1345) and used as the retable of the high altar at St. Mark's, Venice. BIBLIOGRAPHY: C. R. Morey, *Medieval Art* (1942); J. F. Schuler, *100 Kostbarkeiten,* (1963).

[M. J. DALY]

PALACE SCHOOLS, see RENAISSANCE COURT SCHOOLS.

PALAEOLOGIAN ART (1258–1453), a Byzantine art style under the Palaeologian rulers noted esp. for textiles, mosaics at Kahrie-Djami, Istanbul, and frescoes in many churches in Mistra characterized by attenuated figures in expressive color. BIBLIOGRAPHY: A. Grabar, *Byzantine Painting* (1953). *BYZANTINE ART.

[M. J. DALY]

PALAFOX Y MENDOZA, JUAN DE, Spanish churchman who became bp. of Puebla, Mexico. The illegitimate son of Jaime Palafox, P. served in various government offices and in the Council of the Indies. After his ordination to the priesthood, he was elected bp. of Puebla, in which office he was active in pastoral, educational, and cultural affairs. For a time he served as viceroy of Mexico. P. was involved in a long controversy with the Jesuits, whom he attacked with bitter and at times, unjust reports. He was, however, an upright and saintly man. He died as bp. of Osma, Spain. BIBLIOGRAPHY: H. Pereña, NCE 10:872.

[P. DAMBORIENA]

PALAIOIMEROLOGITES (Gr. for Old Calendarists), a term for the 200,000 Greek Orthodox who have broken ecclesiastical ties with the main Greek Orthodox Church because of the official Church's change in 1924 from the Julian to the Gregorian calendar. In the late 30s they split to form two separate hierarchies. There are about 250 Old Calendar Greek priests who keep alive among the simple people the burning conviction that there is an immense importance in maintaining the 13 days that separate the liturgical cycle (the Kingdom of God) from the official state calendar (the Kingdom of this world). The Old Calendarists consider the other Greek Orthodox who follow the Gregorian calendar as heretical and refuse to communicate with them. All the monks on Mt. Athos except those of Vatopedi follow the Old Calendar. There are two such parishes in the United States. The majority of Slav Orthodox still retain the Julian Calendar which is 13 days behind the Gregorian or Western calendar.

[G. A. MALONEY]

PALAMAS, GREGORY (1296–1359), Byzantine theologian, abp. of Thessalonica, and a saint of the Orthodox Church. Born in Asia Minor, he received his education in Constantinople before becoming a monk on Mt.

Athos *c.*1316. For over 20 years, he pursued a rather classical monastic career and authored several treatises of spirituality. Beginning in 1337, he became involved in a theological controversy with Barlaam the Calabrian, who claimed that communion with God was a matter of intellectual contemplation, and not of real "deification" (*theōsis*). He also attacked the spiritual practices of the Byzantine monks, known as the *Hesychasts* (*hesychia,* "spiritual quietude"), who used psychosomatic methods to achieve attention in mental prayer. In addition to a series of letters addressed to Barlaam, P. published nine treatises known as the *Triads for the Defense of the Hesychasts,* where he justified the psychosomatic practices and also developed the doctrine of "deification," as real vision of God in Christ and as communion with the "uncreated light," the very light seen by the Apostles on the mount of Transfiguration.

Supported by the monks of Mt. Athos, P. succeeded in having Barlaam condemned by a council in Constantinople (1341). During the civil war that followed these events (1341–47), a confused struggle involving both political and theological factors, led Patriarch John Calecas to oppose P. and to give his support to Gregory Akindynos, a theologian who fiercely criticized P.'s doctrines on "uncreated light" and the divine "energies." Theological polemics against Akindynos and also against the philosopher Nicephorus Gregoras, who started his opposition to Palamism after 1347, represent another major section of P.'s theological legacy. Vindicated at the end of the civil war (councils of 1347 and 1351), P. became abp. of Thessalonica and left an important collection of sermons. He died on Nov. 14, 1359. In 1368, he was canonized and special celebration in his memory was established for the second Sunday of Lent.

The essential message of Palamite theology consists in the affirmation that man, created according to the image and likeness of God, can fulfill his humanity only in communion with his Creator. This communion, which involves the spiritual and physical life of man and which is achieved in Christ and the Holy Spirit, makes true knowledge of God possible, liberates man from slavery to mortality and sinfulness, and restores him in his true position of leadership in the created world. However, P. also maintains that God, in his essence, is absolutely transcendent: only the three Divine Persons possess the essence of God and are God "by nature." Creatures can be "deified," but only "by grace," entering into communion with God's "energies," i.e., his existence *ad extra*. In his polemics with his adversaries, P. takes pains in affirming that his distinction between God's transcendent essence and his energies does not presuppose Neoplatonic emanationism, or a division in God: personally and existentially, God is fully present in his energies, because he desires to give himself to his creatures, while he also remains, by essence, totally above anything which is a result of his creative will. BIBLIOGRAPHY: G. Palamas, *Works* (in Gr.) I–III (1962–); *Defense of the Holy Hesychasts* (ed. J. Meyendorff, in Gr. with Fr. tr., 2d ed., 1974); J. Meyendorff, *Study of Gregory Palamas* (2d. ed., 1974).

A helpful review of the very vast modern literature on Palaminism in D. Stiernon, "Bulletin sur le palamisme," *Revue des études Byzantines* 30 (1972) 231–341.

[J. MEYENDORFF]

PALAMITE RENAISSANCE, 20th-cent. renewal of interest in the Greek exponent of Hesychasm, Gregory Palamas (*c.*1296–1359); sometimes called neo-Palamism. It has been led by Russian theologians working in the West. They view the Palamite tradition as an authentic development of patristic Orthodoxy and as a theology suited to meet the intellectual and spiritual requirements of the contemporary world. Among the leaders of this movement have been G. Florovsky, Vasily Krivoshein, Cyprian Kern, and John Meyendorff. Since many of the writings of Gregory Palamas had never been published, the precise nature of his thought was little known, particularly in the West. Some of these works have now been published, though others remain in manuscript. Meyendorff asserts that the thought of Palamas, taken as a whole, provides "a personalist and existentialist theology and a spirituality which, freed from Platonic spiritualizing, integrates the whole man in the new life" (*Gregory Palamas,* 1959; Eng. tr. 1964).

[T. EARLY]

PALANCO, FRANCISCO (1655–1720), theologian. A Spanish Franciscan, P. was twice provincial of his province and later vicar general of his order. In 1717 he became bp. of Jacca. In theology he wrote in defense of St. Thomas Aquinas's doctrine on the Eucharist. His writings comprise 14 volumes.

[J. R. AHERNE]

PALATINE, the most important of the seven hills of Rome, the site, tradition says, where Romulus built his fortified city. There is only scanty evidence of early settlement on the hill, but primitive cemeteries in the Forum suggest a contemporary settlement on the adjacent Palatine. In republican times indigenous deities like Luna Noctiluca and Febris were worshiped here, and temples were built to Victoria (294 B.C.) and to Cybele (*c.*204). From the 4th cent. B.C. on the hill were the residences of many famous Romans, e.g., Cicero, Crassus, and Marc Antony. Here Augustus built a temple to Apollo, and his own mansion was the first of many imperial palaces on the Palatine that continued to be used into the 6th century. A number of churches and monasteries built in the 8th cent. and later, as well as villas constructed in the late Middle Ages by great Roman families, are today among the hill's many antiquities.

[F. J. MURPHY]

PALATINE CHAPEL, PALERMO, founded by Roger II of Sicily in 1132, consecrated in 1140. The palace chapel based on a Greek cross plan, with nave attached, is Saracenic in the stalactite vaulting of the choir, Byzantine in the magnificent mosaic decoration (Virgin in main apse; SS. Peter and Paul in the side apses, etc.) later modified to provide a suitable view from the royal tribune, placed in the N transept. BIBLIOGRAPHY: O. Demus, *Mosaics of Norman Sicily* (1950).

[S. D. MURRAY]

PALATINE GUARD, former guard of honor of the pope, made up of citizens of Rome. Established in 1850, it was disbanded in 1970 by Paul VI's *Pontificalis domus,* reorganizing the papal household.

PALENCIA, UNIVERSITY OF, a medieval institution of higher learning, the first in Spain. It was founded at Palencia by Alfonso VIII in 1208–09 (or, acc. to some, 1212). The endowment of professorships encouraged masters from famous universities to teach in Palencia. The university was unique in having neither formal royal foundation charter nor papal bull. Probably it was simply an expansion of the cathedral school under the cathedral *magister scholarum* where *c.*1184 St. Dominic had studied arts and theology. After the death of the founder (1214) the growth of the rival university at Salamanca attracted many of Palencia's students and masters and the university showed signs of decline. To forestall its collapse, Ferdinand III in 1220 obtained from Honorius III permission to use a certain portion of the church revenues for professors' salaries; he also won the pope's protection for masters and scholars although no bull was issued or special privilege conferred. At a synod in Valladolid in 1228 the cardinal legate made a further effort to bolster the university, but neither these measures nor a bull obtained from Urban IV in 1263 granting professors and students the privileges of the Univ. of Paris availed against the lack of financial support and the proximity of Salamanca. The university was transferred to Valladolid *c.*1264. BIBLIOGRAPHY: H. Rashdall, *Universities of Europe in the Middle Ages* (ed. F. M. Powicke and A. B. Emden, 3 v., 1936).

[M. B. MURPHY]

PALENCIA CATHEDRAL, Spanish church boasting a crypt (673), chevet (1321), transepts (1440–50) by Pedro Jalopa, western bays by Bartolomé de Solorzano (1450–1516), choir screen (*trascoro*) by Simon de Colonia, many 16th-cent. retables, and a *St. Sebastian* by El Greco.

[M. J. DALY]

PALÉOGRAPHIE MUSICALE, collection of facsimiles and studies of chant in 19 volumes, edited by the Benedictines of Solesmes under Dom André Mocquereau to 1930 and under Dom Joseph Gojard since 1931. The collection, which comprises the principal MSS of the Gregorian, Ambrosian, Mozarabic, and Gallican plainsong, was published in phototype facsimile in quarterly fascicles beginning in 1889. By a comparison and criticism of these medieval MSS, which were gathered from all the important libraries

and monasteries of Europe, Solesmes has, in a manner similar to that of scripture scholars, endeavored to restore the authentic reading and true rhythm of the ancient melodies.

[M. T. LEGGE]

PALEOGRAPHY AND DIPLOMATICS, VATICAN SCHOOL OF, an institute of higher learning established by Leo XIII in 1889; with a two-year course in the study of documents and archival methods, leading to a certification of the student as "paleographic archivist."

PALEOLITHIC ART (40,000–10,000 B.C.), art of the last Ice Age, made possible by the invention of a blade tool (flint) for carving and making tools for engraving and painting, found in three main areas: (1) region of SW Asia, N Africa, and S Spain from which a few rock engravings remain; (2) in Central and Eastern Europe into Siberia an East Aurignacian culture of impressive sculptured animals and female figures (the renowned *Venus of Willendorf,* Austria) and more than 130 others from the Pyrenees to Lake Baikal, Siberia; (3) in Western Europe famous cave paintings and engravings from a fusing of French and Franco-Cantabrian groups with migrating peoples of plastic tradition resulting in late Perigordian or Upper Aurignacian naturalistic forms of the famous cave at Lascaux. A Solutrean culture hunting herds of wild horses, probably creating the animal sculptures of Charente, was followed by the Magdalenian period of polychrome paintings at Font-de-Gaume and Altamira which with figural and animal rock sculptures was the most brilliant phase at the end of the Ice Age. BIBLIOGRAPHY: H. Breuil, *Four Hundred Centuries of Cave Art* (1952).

[M. J. DALY]

PALESTINE, in ordinary usage, the land of the Bible. It is roughly the area occupied by modern Israel and part of Syria, the land once occupied by the kingdoms of Israel and Judah.

Geology. In the geological past the Mediterranean sea extended for long periods of time over and beyond the Jordan valley. Significant is the great longitudinal fissure in the Nubian sandstone that forms the lowest area in the world, the Jordan Valley and the Dead Sea. The coastal plain has fertile alluvial soil. The central highland is mostly composed of limestone. The region has always been subject to earth tremors with serious earthquakes approximately every 50 years.

Physical Geography. The four main regions are the coastal plain, the highlands, the Jordan Valley, and Transjordan. The fertile coastal plain, from 2 to 20 miles wide extends from Accho in the N to Gaza in the S, where it gradually becomes desert. The unbroken coast provides no natural seaports. The highlands extend E from the coastal plain increasing in altitude through a series of foothills. To the N, they are broken by the valley of Esdraelon and contiguous valleys separating Galilee from Samaria. In the W they are broken by the cleft of the Jordan valley. The arid western slopes form the desert of Judea. The Jordan valley is part of a great rift extending from above Lake Huleh, through the lake of Galilee, along the river Jordan to the Dead Sea, 1,275 feet below sea level. Along the river, it is from 1 to about 12 miles wide. Once jungle region, the fertile land is now extensively cultivated. The Transjordan region is a high plateau E of the Jordan. To the E it gradually merges with the Arabian desert. It is divided by four notable river valleys, the *Zered, the *Arnon, the *Jabbok, and the *Yarmuk.

Because of the unique geographical features of Palestine, there are wide ranges in climate and rainfall. The annual rain falls mostly between late October and early April. The only really abundant unfailing water supply is the river Jordan. In the rainy season, the dry river beds become raging torrents. Springs, wells, and cisterns tap the winter rains absorbed through the abundant limestone.

Political Geography. Only for short periods has Palestine been a united country. In pre-Israelite times, there was a mixed population with numerous independent city states. In the period of Joshua and the Judges, the land was roughly divided according to Jos ch. 13–21. Yet Israelite power was only gradually extended in each area, and only a common outside threat such as the Philistines brought the various tribes together. In the period of the monarchy, Saul and David united the tribes and extended Israelite territory to its furthest limits. After Solomon, they split into two independent kingdoms, Israel in the N, and Judah in the S. Israel was annexed as an Assyrian province in 722 B.C. The kingdom of Judah was terminated by the Babylonians in 587 B.C. After the Persian conquest, Judea became a Persian province until the Greek conquest under Alexander the Great (333 B.C.) The Maccabean revolt (166–135 B.C.) brought independence once more until the beginning of the Roman period with the victory of Pompei (63 B.C.). The Arabs (640), followed by the Turks (1071), dominated Palestine until the Crusades (1099). The Mamelukes of Egypt (1250) governed the country until the Ottoman Turks' conquest (1517). From 1917 to 1948 Palestine was under British mandate. Displacement of the Palestinians by the 1948 establishment of the State of Israel is central in the tensions between Arabs and Israelis.

Economic-Cultural Geography. The principal products of Palestine were wheat, barley, olives, and grapes. Flour was made from wheat and barley; olive oil was used for lamp fuel, cooking, and ointments. Grapes were eaten, or pressed to make wine. Other products were dates, figs, and pomegranates. Sheep, cattle, and goats were raised both for meat, milk, butter, and cheese as well as for wool and hides. They also were used in liturgical sacrifices. Most of the commerce was local, products being exchanged at the city gates. There was also some exchange with the people of Phoenicia and Tyre for tools, textile, and other manufactured goods.

Natural History. The large forests of Lebanon and Basan supplied lumber necessary for building temples, palaces, and other large structures. The most extensive pasture lands were found in Basan, across the Jordan. The Negeb was also principally used for pasture. The Bible names about 100 plants. It also gives about 110 animal names: mammals (39), birds (38), reptiles etc. (13), insects etc. (20). Most of the wild animals have disappeared in modern times. Camels, goats, sheep, and pigs were domesticated at least as far back as 5000 B.C. The ass and the mule were important, rather than the horse. Chickens were raised from the period of the monarchy.

Archeology. In the Stone Age, during the Paleolithic period (c.500,000 to c.10,000 B.C.) deposits indicate human remains in the earliest period. In the Mesolithic period (c.10,000 B.C. to c.6000 B.C.) we find small blades and tools, hooks and harpoons of fishers; sickles show the beginning of agriculture. Carvings of animals and a human head are examples of early art. Amulets and pendants suggest religious beliefs. In the Neolithic period (c.6000 to c.4500 B.C.), excavations at Jericho show man's transition from a hunter to a settled community member. Jericho finds indicate the beginning and development of pottery manufacture. From the Chalcolithic period (c.4500 to 3100 B.C.) there is evidence of the manufacture of copper articles, along with the continued use of stone implements.

In the Bronze Age (c.3100 to c.1200 B.C.), villages developed into walled cities, of which a number have been excavated. In the late Bronze Age (c.1600 to 1200 B.C.), archeological evidence shows that many cities were destroyed, among them Jericho and Tel-Beit-Mirsim, by the invading Israelites. Written sources become more numerous in this last period. Outstanding among them are the Tel-el Amarna letters found in Egypt. Some 350 of these in the form of cuneiform tablets have been found, most of them being official correspondence from Palestine to Egypt. The beginning of the Iron Age (c.1200 to 600 B.C.) approximately coincides with the beginning of Israelite settlement. Extensive archeological material is available from this period. Many inscriptions have been found. Many Astarte figurines have been unearthed, evidence of religious practices. Abundant materials are also available from the Persian period (6th to 4th cent. B.C.), the Greek period (4th to 1st cent. B.C.), and the Roman period (1st cent. B.C. to 4th cent. A.D.). Most important in these last two periods are the Qumran manuscripts.

Pre-Israelite Ethnology. Prominent pre-Israelite Semitic groups were the Canaanites and the Amorites. Evidence of Canaanites' presence goes back to the 4th millennium B.C. The Amorites were present in northern Syria in the 2d millennium B.C., and spread out through the fertile crescent. The less numerous non-Semitic population was composed of the Hurrians, Hittites, Hevites, Jebusites and Pherezites.

Holy Places. For Christians, these are places hallowed by the presence of Jesus, Mary, and the Apostles. The construction of sanctuaries goes back to the 4th century. However, there were earlier Jewish-Christian traditions esp. about the place of the Annunciation in Nazareth, the Cenacle, the cave of Gethsemane, and the site of the Holy Sepulcher. Other notable sanctuaries are at Mt. Tabor, Bethany, the Mount of the Beatitudes, the Mount of the Ascension, the cave of the Nativity, and the tomb of the Virgin in Jerusalem. BIBLIOGRAPHY: EDB 1691–1700; E. Lussier et al., NCE 10:891–921, with maps, illustrations, and bibliography.

[J. A. GRASSI]

PALESTINE, EARLY CHURCH IN. Despite the fact that Jerusalem was the cradle of Christianity, the site of the first church council (49 or 50 A.D.), and an object of solicitude to the other Churches of the Roman world, as is indicated by the collections taken up for its poor (Acts 24.17; Rom 15.26; 1 Cor 16.1–4; 2 Cor 8–9; Gal 2.10), the Church in Palestine never attained the prominence that might have been expected. This was due to the continued hostility of the Jews, to the twofold destruction of Jerusalem by the Romans (in 70 and 135 A.D.), and esp. to the Gnostic and Judaizing tendencies within the Christian communities themselves that eventually led many of them into heresy.

The daily increase of converts (Acts 2.47) after the descent of the Holy Spirit upon the Apostles soon brought their number to 5,000 men (Acts 4.4). Though these primitive Christians followed most of the customs of the Mosaic Law, their preaching and meeting together for their own services aroused the anger of the Jews and led to the eventual stoning of Stephen (c.33). Many of the Christians then fled to the country districts of Judea and Samaria, thus introducing the new faith into those areas. Some 10 years later James the Elder was executed under Herod Agrippa; James the Younger, the first bp. of Jerusalem, suffered a similar fate by order of the Sanhedrin (c.63). His successor, Simeon, saved his flock by taking them across the Jordan to Pella before the investing of Jerusalem by the Roman army under Vespasian and Titus. Some of these must have returned to the Holy City after the reestablishment of peace, and some of their descendants may have been able to remain there after the expulsion of the Jews (135) though many migrated to Kokhaba in Transjordania, to Nazareth, and to Beroea (modern Aleppo) in northern Syria (Epiphanius, *Haer.* 29.7).

The Judaeo–Christians of Palestine retained a strong attachment to the relatives of Christ (Eusebius, *Eccl. Hist.* 3.12, 19–20). Their stubborn retention of Jewish customs and attempts to impose these upon converts from paganism, however, and the development of their own literature (notably the Gospel according to the Hebrews, which resembles that of St. Matthew, and the Pseudo-Clementine *Homilies* and *Recognitions*) separated them from the general run of Christians. By the mid-2d cent. many converts from paganism would not associate with them (Justin, *Dialog*

47); and by the end of the cent. there were some who were obviously heretical in their beliefs and came to be known as Ebionites or Nazarenes. Their rigorism may possibly be traced to the conversion of the Essenes to Christianity after the destruction of Qumran.

Christians of gentile origins undoubtedly began to play a more important role in Palestine after the reconstruction of Jerusalem as a Hellenistic city with the name of Aelia Capitolina. In the council held there (190) to discuss the date of Easter, the local Church was represented by its bp., Narcissus, who seems to have been of Greek descent. At this time his see was subject to the metropolitan of Caesarea. It was only at the Council of Chalcedon (451) that Jerusalem became an independent patriarchate. Other cities in Palestine with bishoprics before 325 were Maximianopolis, Scythopolis, Sebaste, Flavia Neapolis, Ascalon, Diospolis (or Lydda), Nicopolis, Gadara, Azotus, Ascalon, Eleutheropolis, Jericho, Capitolias, Alia, and Gaza. A council held at Tyre and Jerusalem in 335 espousing the cause of Arianism deposed Athanasius and repudiated the term *homoousios*.

Both Eastern and Western monasteries were erected in Palestine in the early 4th cent., the latter largely under the initiative of St. Jerome. In this same cent. the Holy Land became an extremely popular place of pilgrimage; and its liturgy, a description of which has been preserved in the *Peregrinatio ad loca sancta* of *Etheria from the end of the 4th cent., had a wide influence throughout the Church because of the pilgrims who took part in it. After suffering from a Persian invasion in 614, Palestine fell to the Muslims with the capture of Jerusalem by the Caliph Omar in 637. BIBLIOGRAPHY: Bihlmeyer Tüchle 1:48–55, 71, 143–146; J. J. Gavigan, NCE 10:921–923; E. Testa, *Il simbolismo dei giudeo-cristiani* (1962).

[M. J. COSTELLOE]

PALESTRINA (*c*.1525–94), the composer whose polyphony at its origin and in St. Pius X's *Tra le sollecitudini,* the 19th-cent. reform *motu proprio,* is the model, along with Gregorian chant, for liturgical music. Born Giovanni Pierluigi Sante, he came to be called "da Palestrina" from his birthplace, one of the *castelli* or hill towns near Rome. He began his musical life as a choirboy in the Palestrina cathedral, then at Saint Mary Major's in Rome. He completed his musical studies in Rome (1544) and went home to become master of the cathedral choir there. From 1551 he was choirmaster of the Julian Choir at the Vatican; then (1555) at the Lateran; at St. Mary Major's (1561); and from 1571 he finished his career at the Vatican. He also directed the music at the Collegio Romano (from 1564). He suffered the loss of two sons and his wife in the plague. As a widower he took minor orders, but married again rather than going on to the priesthood. His most famous Mass, the *Mass of Pope Marcellus* was one of three written at the express commission of the Council of Trent, 1564. His music was intended as a corrective to the abuse of adopting the melody of profane street songs as the setting for liturgical texts. The reform of the Caecilian movement in the 19th cent., which culminated in Pius X's reform, was directed against the operatic or theatrical and the vulgarly sentimental types of music that had crept into the liturgical services. P.'s work is characterized by a simplicity, reverence, and quiet exaltedness that are suited to liturgical worship and to the primacy of the word of God in liturgy. Although in execution not appealing to all tastes, the Sistine Choir is the most conspicuous practitioner of the Palestrina repertoire, which is enormous, much of it even yet unedited. He published Masses and motets all during his career; one of his sons published more after P.'s death. One collection of his works has reached 33 volumes. BIBLIOGRAPHY: H. K. Andrews, *Introduction to the Technique of Palestrina* (1958); C. Angoff, *Palestrina, Saviour of Church Music* (1944); K. Jeppesen, *Style of Palestrina and the Dissonance* (repr. 1970).

[T. C. O'BRIEN]

PALESTRINA, SANCTUARY OF, see PRAENESTE.

PALEY, WILLIAM (1743–1805), Anglican theologian and philosopher. A fellow of Christ College, Cambridge from 1766, he won recognition for his clear and forceful lectures on ethics, metaphysics, and the New Testament. In 1776 he became rector of Musgrave and in 1782 archdeacon of Carlisle. His first book, *The Principles of Moral and Political Philosophy* (1785), admirably expressed the utilitarian doctrines common to his age and soon became a standard text. More original was the *Horae paulinae* (1790), in which he set out to prove the truth of the NT by comparing the Pauline Epistles with Acts. P.'s fame, however, rests on two apologetic works, *A View of the Evidences of Christianity* (1794) and *Natural Theology* (1802), in both of which he argued for the existence of God from the evidences of design in the universe. P.'s common-sense, rationalist approach was most influential in the C of E during its latitudinarian heyday, but could not withstand the onslaughts of either the *Oxford Movement or the development of higher criticism.

[E. M. GATES]

PALI CANON, the canon or authoritative collection of Theravada Buddhist texts (usually called the *Tripitaka*), first an oral tradition, then receiving written form probably in the 1st cent. B.C. in Sri Lanka (Ceylon). The language is Pali, apparently a literary dialect that originated in western India. Religiously, this collection is normative for Theravada Buddhists, whose tradition claims that it goes back to the teachings of the Buddha. Historically, there seem to be equally early texts, now preserved in Sanskrit, Chinese, and Tibetan collections, which were just as important to other early schools of Buddhism and which are not part of the Pali canon. BIBLIOGRAPHY: E. Conze, *Thirty*

Years of Buddhist Studies (1968) 1–13; R. H. Robinson, *Buddhist Religion* (1970) 36–37, 125–28.

[D. P. EFROYMSON]

PALIMPSEST (Gr. *palim,* again; *psaō,* rub), a MS on which one text has been effaced and the vellum or parchment reused for another text. It was common practice to rub out an earlier piece of writing by means of washing or scraping in order to replace it with a later one. It is usually possible, esp. with the aid of modern methods of infra-red photography, to discern substantial parts of the earlier writing, which is usually more valuable than the later writing. Among several notable examples of palimpsests the most important is the *Codex Ephraemi Rescriptus* of which only 209 leaves have survived. Over the original 5th-cent. text of the Bible sermons of St. Ephrem were written in the 12th cent. BIBLIOGRAPHY: F. G. Kenyon, *Our Bible and the Ancient Manuscripts* (2d ed., 1912) 85–87.

[D. J. BOURKE]

PALIOTTO, early medieval antependium (altar frontal) of gold, silver, and ivory decorated with religious designs. Outstanding is the 9th-cent. paliotto of silver-gilt plaques with precious stones and enamel made by the goldsmith Wolvinus and given by Abp. Angilbert of St. Riquier to S. Ambrogio, Milan (824–835). The silver paliotto of Città di Castello (1144) is also noteworthy.

[M. J. DALY]

PALL, (1) a large piece of cloth used to cover the coffin during the funeral Mass; hence, figuratively, the coffin itself. Formerly black or purple, colors of mourning, the cloth, where used, is now generally white, the color of hope and resurrection, and is often ornamented with a cross and/or baptismal symbols. It is symbolic of "being clothed with Christ" at baptism, the Christian's hope of eternal life. (2) a stiffened square of linen placed on the chalice during the Roman Mass to keep out foreign objects. Originally a corner of the corporal or altarcloth was used for this purpose; the small, separate pall ("covering") developed later. Its use is now optional.

[J. DALLEN]

PALLADINO, LAWRENCE BENEDICT (1837–1927), missionary. An Italian who entered the Jesuits and was ordained in 1863, P. volunteered for the California mission. After teaching at San Francisco and Santa Clara he was sent to the Rocky Mountain Indian missions. He worked among the Flatheads in Montana, heading a mission and Indian school which taught industrial and agricultural skills. From Helena, where he went in 1873, P. made extensive trips through Montana to minister to Indians, soldiers, and frontiersmen. Returning to his first mission, he worked there from 1884 until 1894, when he became rector of Gonzaga College, Spokane, Washington. His last years were spent in Missoula, Montana. In 1894 P. published *Indian and White* *in the Northwest,* a primary source of the history of Montana.

[J. R. AHERNE]

PALLADIO, ANDREA DI PIETRA (1508–80), Italian architect of the Venetian School, leading architect of the High Renaissance in N Italy, P.'s lucid, classicizing style influenced tremendously 17th- and 18th-cent. architecture in England and America. Avidly studying ancient architecture and the architectural theories of Vitruvius and Alberti, P. published his own treatise, *I quattro libri dell'architettura* in 1570. Designing extraordinary country residences in the Veneto, his most famous, the Villa Rotonda (Vicenza, 1550) shows Roman temple porticoes on four sides of a square building radiating from a central dome. In Venice his two great church designs, S. Giorgio Maggiore (begun 1566) and Il Redentore (begun 1558) epitomize P.'s ideal of a harmonious unity of all parts to the whole. BIBLIOGRAPHY: J. Ackerman, *Palladio* (1966); R. Wittkower, *Palladio and Palladianism* (1974).

[S. CONWAY]

PALLADIUS, ST. (fl. 430), a missionary of uncertain national origin reported by Prosper of Aquitaine in his *Chronicon* to have been sent to the Irish people as their first bp. by Pope Celestine I. The events of his life are shrouded in the conflicting legends that have grown up about his name and that of St. Patrick. He appears to have worked for a time in Ireland but without great success, although he is credited with founding three churches. He departed for Scotland (or Britain?) *c.*432 where he died soon afterwards. The story accepted in medieval Scotland that he spent 23 years on a mission in that country is regarded by scholars as without historical foundation. BIBLIOGRAPHY: AS July 2:286–290; J. Carney, *Problem of St. Patrick* (1961); P. Roche, NCE 10:927; Butler 3:33.

[R. B. ENO]

PALLADIUS (*c.*363–after 431), bp. **OF HELENOPOLIS,** historian of early *monasticism. A native of Galatia and a disciple of *Evagrius Ponticus, P. spent about 9 years with the monks of Egypt and Palestine. On his return to Asia Minor he was consecrated bp. of Helenopolis in Bithynia by St. *John Chrysostom. When John was banished by the Synod of the *Oak, P. went to Rome to ask for justice from the Pope. His support of Chrysostom led to his own exile in Egypt, where he wrote a life of the saint. He was allowed to return in 412, and 5 years later was made bp. of Aspuna where he wrote his *Lausiac History.* Works: PG 34:991–1262; 47:5–82. BIBLIOGRAPHY: *Lausiac History* (tr. and ed. R. T. Meyer, ACW 34, 1965); Quasten 3:176–180; R. T. Meyer, NCE 10:927–928.

[R. B. ENO]

PALLAVICINO, PIETRO SFORZA (1607–67), Italian Jesuit, card. from 1659, historian of the Council of Trent. He began his career in the service of the *Curia Romana, fell into disfavor with Urban VIII in 1632. A doctor in theology from 1628, he became a Jesuit in 1637 and taught at the Collegium Romanum from 1639, succeeding F. de *Lugo in the chair of theology in 1643. In 1652 he was a member of the commission that condemned the five Jansenist propositions (see JANSENISM). He published some theological treatises, but his greatest work, done at the command of the Jesuit general and a standard source for centuries, was *Istoria del Concilio di Trento* (2 v., 1656–57). P. himself referred to it as a history mixed with apologetics, or vice versa. Begun in 1652, it was based on 25 years of research by the Jesuit Terenzio Alciati (d. 1651), P. was also able to include the findings from his consultation of the *acta* of the Council in the archives of the Castel Sant' Angelo. The work was meant as a refutation of P. *Sarpi's *Istoria del Concilio Tridentino* (1619), which strongly insinuated that the Council was convoked and conducted to aggrandize the power of the papacy. P. also wrote a life of Pope Alexander VII, and a defense of the Jesuits, *Vindicationes Societatis Jesu* (1649).

[T. C. O'BRIEN]

PALLEN, CONDÉ BENOIST (1858–1929), writer, editor of the *Catholic Encyclopedia* (CE). Born in St. Louis, Mo., P. edited *Church Progress* from 1887 to 1897. He was Catholic editor of the *New International Encyclopedia* and the *Encyclopedia Americana.* One of the first to recognize the need for a Catholic general reference work, P. was a guiding force of *The Catholic Encyclopedia* (16 v. 1907–14), serving from 1904 to 1920 as its managing editor. As editor of the Universal Knowledge Foundation he supervised the encyclopedia *Universal Knowledge* in its first two volumes (1927–28) and the *New Catholic Dictionary* (1929). P. was a well-known lecturer to Catholic groups. He wrote a number of books, among them the *Philosophy of Literature* (1897), *Collected Poems* (1915), *As Man to Man: the Adventures of a Commuter* (1927).

[J. R. AHERNE]

PALLIUM, a vestment of disputed origins (perhaps borrowed from Roman imperial use), probably a scarf or folded mantle, which has taken various forms in the Eastern and Western Churches as a symbol of superior episcopal authority and dignity. Given only by the pope (or the patriarch in the East), it is worn over the chasuble by archbishop-metropolitans and by patriarchs. In its present form in the Latin Church, it is a circular band of white wool about two inches wide with two vertical bands, one in front and one in back, ornamented with six black crosses. The wool is from two lambs blessed at a Roman basilica on the feast of St. Agnes. Once made and blessed, the pallia are kept near the tomb of Peter until sent by the pope to a new patriach or archbishop metropolitan as a symbol of communion as well as of dignity. The metropolitan-elect must ask for the pallium within three months (CIC c. 275); its use is enjoined for metropolitan and other jurisdictional or sacramental junctions or ceremonies (*ibid.* c.276).

[J. DALLEN]

PALLOTTA, MARIA ASSUNTA, BL. (1878–1905), missionary. Born in the Marches of Ancona, she went to work at an early age to help support her poor family. After joining the Franciscan Missionaries of Mary in Rome in 1898, she was stationed in various houses of the congregation in Italy, taught catechism, cared for the sick, and did gardening. In 1904 she was sent to the congregation's orphanage in China. While tending the sick during a typhus epidemic, she contracted the disease and died. She was beatified in 1954 by Pius XII. BIBLIOGRAPHY: G. Fabiani, BiblSanct 10:65–66.

[E. A. CARRILLO]

PALLOTTI, VINCENT, ST. (1795–1850), religious founder. Son of a wealthy family, P. developed an intense interest in the poor. Ordained in 1818, he taught theology at Sapienza Univ. before becoming spiritual director at the Roman College, founded the Society of the Catholic Apostolate (Pallottine Fathers) in 1835 and the Pallottine Missionary Sisters in 1843. The Oxford Movement encouraged him to believe that England was ripe for conversion to Roman Catholicism, and he sent priests to England to carry on the apostolate. The Mill Hill Missionaries owed their foundation to P.'s inspiration. John XXIII canonized him in 1963. BIBLIOGRAPHY: E. Weber, *Vincent Pallotti: Apostle and Mystic* (1964); J. Frank, *Vincenz Pallotti* (2 v., 1952–65).

[E. A. CARRILLO]

PALLOTTINE MISSIONARY SISTERS (MP), religious congregation, official name Missionary Sisters of the Catholic Apostolate, "Pallottine," a branch of the Pallottine Sisters of the Catholic Apostolate founded in Rome in 1843 by St. Vincent *Pallotti. Originally the institute was established to take care of orphaned children, but in 1891 when the Pallottine Fathers began to evangelize the German colony of the African Camaroons, the help of the sisters was requested. Sister-candidates from Germany were invited and trained in the novitiate at Rome to prepare them for the African mission. In 1895 a motherhouse was founded in Limburg, Germany, and the mission activities (mainly educational and hospital work) spread to England, Switzerland, Poland, Central America, South Africa and the U.S. in 1912. When papal approval was given to this branch in 1964, the congregation received its official title. Headquarters in Rome give statistics (1975) showing the community to have 69 houses and a total membership of 757 sisters. BIBLIOGRAPHY: J. Gaynor, *Life of St. Vincent Pallotti* (1963).

[R. A. TODD]

PALLOTTINE SISTERS OF THE CATHOLIC APOSTOLATE (CSAC), a community of religious founded in Rome in 1843 by St. Vincent Pallotti for the purpose of taking care of young children orphaned by the cholera plague. The spirit of the congregation was such as to enable the sisters to engage in any activity in support of the needs of the mission they served. In 1889, members were sent to the U.S. to assist Italian immigrants. Their apostolate includes educational, catechetical and various social works, and their houses are located in Brazil, Argentina and the U.S., as well as in Italy. In 1975 the institute had a membership of 642 sisters and maintained 76 houses. The generalate is located in Rome. BIBLIOGRAPHY: E. Weber, *Vincent Pallotti; Apostle and Mystic* (1964).

[R. A. TODD]

PALLOTTINES (SAC; official title, the Society of the Catholic Apostolate), a society of common life, made up of priests and lay brothers, commonly known as the Pallottine Fathers, founded by St. Vincent Pallotti at Rome in 1835, first as a pious union of laity and clergy. The purpose of the institute was to revive faith and charity among Catholics and to spread the faith through the entire universe by means of prayer and labor. Pallotti soon formed a congregation of priests for this work, without religious vows, but living a common life. The official title caused much controversy among other groups involved in similar apostolic work, and in 1854 was temporarily changed to Pious Society of Missions; the original title was restored in 1947. The institute was approved in the same year it was founded. The members make promises of poverty, chastity, obedience, and perseverance. Their apostolate engages them in a special way with home and foreign missions, retreats, publications, spiritual care of immigrants, and other works of mercy. The Pallottines maintain approximately 342 houses in about 21 countries and have 1,431 priests out of a total number of 2,137 members.

[R. A. TODD]

PALM, a princely tree, highly prized in desert borderlands for its beauty, stately dignity, shelter, and shade. Considered holy in Babylon and sacred to the god Apollo at Delos, it typically provided décor for the ornamentation of temples in the ancient Near East. A branch of the date-bearing palm tree was carried in joyful and triumphal processions by ancient Romans and Jews as a symbol of victory and well-being. They were given as victory emblems by Romans at their public games and carried by exulting throngs of Jews on pilgrimage in joyful anticipation of liberation on the Feast of Tabernacles. Jews also offered them on other festive occasions as part of the bouquet (*lulab*) given as a sign of homage to a hero or to celebrate victory. Palms strewn along the path of Jesus' triumphal entry into Jerusalem paved the way for their decorative and liturgical use among Christian peoples. In the NT they are connected with martyrdom (Rev 7.9); they were used to decorate tombs in the catacombs as a memorial of the triumphal death of the martyrs. In the Psalms (92.12–13) the palm was already the symbol of the just man who flourishes like the palm tree: strong and supple and graceful. On early Christian sarcophagi and in mosaics, Christ and the Apostles are pictured amid palms or carrying palms, which have become a symbol of paradise. BIBLIOGRAPHY: H. Leclercq, DACL 13.1:947–961.

[E. J. DILLON]

PALM SUNDAY, the Sunday before Easter which is now known as Sunday of the Passion, or Passion Sunday. The day's liturgy is characterized by contrast: the joy and triumph of the blessing and procession of the palms which reenacts Christ's entry into Jerusalem (Jn 12.12–16), and the sorrow of the Mass of the Passion. The ceremony of the blessing of and procession with palms originated in Jerusalem by at least the 4th cent. and was gradually introduced into the West, first in Gaul and then in Rome. In the Middle Ages, the rite acquired a distinctly dramatic character with an elaborate rite for blessing the palms and a procession from one church to another. The Holy Week restoration of Pius XII (1955) emphasizes the central place of the triumphal procession in honor of Christ the King and provides for greater participation by all the faithful. This Sunday also marks the beginning of *Holy Week. BIBLIOGRAPHY: W. J. O'Shea, NCE 10:934–935; J. Gaillard, *Holy Week and Easter* (tr. W. Busch, 2nd and rev. ed., 1957) 31–43.

[B. ROSENDALL]

PALMA, BIAGIO (1577–1635), spiritual writer. P. was a Barnabite priest, a well-known spiritual director, and author of several significant treatises on the spiritual life. Most famous is his *Atti virtuosi interni dell'anima cristiana* (Rome, 1616). He contributed to the usage of the title "Mother of Divine Providence" for Mary. BIBLIOGRAPHY: V. M. Colciago, EncCatt 9:650–651.

[T. M. MCFADDEN]

PALMA, RICARDO (1833–1919), Peruvian poet and writer. Because of his liberal and anticlerical views, P. spent a good part of his early life in exile in Chile and various European countries. In 1883 he was recalled to Peru and made director of the National Library. His main literary work is a series of volumes called *Tradiciones Peruanas* (1872–1918) in which he dealt in a humorous and satirical way with customs and events of colonial Peru. The historical value of the work is slight, esp. where P. concerns himself with ecclesiastical topics, but it ranks as a masterpiece of Latin American literature.

[P. DAMBORIENA]

PALMA DE MALLORCA, CATHEDRAL OF, Spanish Gothic structure begun by James I of Aragon (1230) with additions through the 15th cent.: in the sea façade the beautiful Puerta del Mirador (1380–97) by G. Morey with portal figures by Guillem Sagrera (1422). The interior vaults are higher and wider than those of Amiens. There are two fine sculptured pulpits (1526–35) by Juan de Salas, with restorations and additions by A. Gaudi (1904–14). BIBLIOGRAPHY: F. P. Verrié, *Mallorca* (1948); R. A. Cram, *Cathedral of Palma De Mallorca* (1932).

[M. J. DALY]

PALMER, WILLIAM (1803–85), English theologian of the Tractarian school. A fellow of Worcester College, Oxford, from 1831, he first came into contact with the future leaders of the *Oxford Movement—J. Keble, H. J. Rose, J. H. Newman, and W. G. Ward—through his learned *Origines liturgicae* (1832). Always the high churchman, he nevertheless remained unsympathetic to the Roman tendencies of this group. His own conception of Anglican doctrine was spelled out in the *Treatise on the Church of Christ* (1838), wherein he argued for the C of E's equality with the Roman and Orthodox branches of the Catholic Church. His *Narrative of Events connected with the Publication of Tracts for the Times* (1843), further expressing his differences with Tractarian tendencies, served as a catalyst in converting Newman and Ward to Roman Catholicism. P.'s last book, *Doctrine of Development, and Conscience considered in relation to the Evidences of Christianity and of the Catholic System* (1846), was in fact a reply to Newman's *Development of Christian Doctrine* (1845).

[E. M. GATES]

PALMER, WILLIAM (1811–79), English divine and archeologist. A fellow of Magdalen College, Oxford, from 1832 and tutor in classics there from 1838 to 1843, P. was a high churchman principally interested in the possibility of intercommunion between the Anglican and Eastern Orthodox Churches. For this purpose he twice visited Russia, where he vigorously but unsuccessfully pushed the Anglican claim. He was also personally attracted to joining the Orthodox, but the Russians made this too difficult, and in 1855 P. instead became a Roman Catholic. He thereafter devoted himself to archeological pursuits in Rome. His publications include *Harmony of Anglican Doctrine with the Doctrine of the Eastern Church* (1846), *Dissertations on Subjects relating to the Orthodox or Eastern Catholic Communion* (1853), and *Notes of a Visit to the Russian Church in the Years 1840, 1841* (ed. J. H. Newman; 1882).

[E. M. GATES]

PALMETTE, ornament related to the Egyptian lotus, the Greek anthemion, and, with special relevance to the sacred tree-of-life motif spreading from Mesopotamia by way of the Sassanians, and recurring on the chancel of St. Peter in the Citadel of Metz, the cenotaph of St. Dizier (7th cent.), the reliquary casket in the cathedral of Chur (8th cent.?), in hybrid plants on the tomb of the Abbess Theodata at Pavia (720), on balustrade panels of the font (737) of the cathedral of Cividale, and on the *Harbaville Triptych* (10th cent.) in combination with the cross which is thus identified as the Christian tree of life and salvation.

[M. J. DALY]

PALMIERI, AURELIO (1870–1926), author of Italian books and articles, esp. in DTC and the review *Bessarione* on the history and theology of the Eastern Churches. He was ordained an Augustinian (1902) but was later laicized.

[T. C. O'BRIEN]

PALMIERI, DOMENICO (1829–1909), Italian Jesuit philosopher and theologian. His *Institutiones philosophiae* (3 v. 1874–76) expressed many anti-Thomistic philosophical positions. He also published several works of dogmatic theology, and a commentary on the philosophical and theological aspects of Dante's *Divina commedia*.

[T. C. O'BRIEN]

PALMYRA, city *c.*120 miles NE of Damascus. Known as Palmyra by the Greeks and Romans, its Arab name was Tadmor (Tadmar, Tadmur). It achieved considerable prosperity from its strategic location on caravan routes, reaching its height under Odenathus (255–67 A.D.). His widow Zenobia asserted the city's independence from Rome, but was defeated by Aurelian. According to one account (2 Chr 8.4) Solomon built Tadmor. The parallel passage (1 Kg 9.18), however, has Tamar, possibly the Tamar in S Judah (Ezek 47.18–19; 48.28).

[T. EARLY]

PALMYRA (TADMOR), RUINS AT, impressive Greco-Roman ruins: the Temple of Bel (principal shrine); Temple of Belshamin; a caravansary; agora; a great colonnaded avenue 36 ft by 3600 ft with a *decumanus-cardo* (two main streets crossing at right angles), the columns with corbels once supporting portrait statues of merchants identified by inscriptions. Christian mosaics mark churches built in the Temple of Bel and also in the Temple of Belshamin. Tower tombs on hills are remarkable for sculptured gods, scenes of ritual, and high-relief portraits of the dead in Palmyrene hieratic, frontal, immobile style. Scholars differ citing Greco-Persian, Roman, and Byzantine relevances. BIBLIOGRAPHY: P. Collart, "Le Sanctuaire de Baalshamin à Palmyre," *Les Annales archéologique de Syrie* (v. 6, 1956).

[M. J. DALY]

PALOMAR, JOHN OF (fl. 1431–43) Spanish theologian, leading figure at the Council of Basel and in the controversy with the *Hussites over the Church's jurisdiction in temporal matters and its right to own property; an opponent of *conciliarism.

[R. J. LITZ]

PALÓU, FRANCISCO (1723–89), Spanish Franciscan missionary, founder (1776) of Arroyo de los Dolores, the beginning of San Francisco, companion and biographer (1787) of Junípero *Serra (*Life of Fray Junípero Serra,* tr. M. J. Geiger, 1955). With Serra P. began his mission work in Mexico City in 1749; labored in Baja California from

1767, and in Alta California from 1773. He returned to Mexico City in 1785 and died as superior of Colegio S. Fernando there.

[T. C. O'BRIEN]

PAMMACHIUS, ST. (*c.*340–410), a Roman of the distinguished Furian family, a senator, and a close friend and correspondent of SS. *Jerome and *Paulinus of Nola. In 385 he married Paulina, second daughter of St. *Paula, and after her death (397) he devoted his time and wealth to works of charity and religion, esp. the hospital and hospice at Porto that he, together with St. *Fabiola, had founded, and the church (*titulus Pammachii*) in his house on the Caelian, the site of the present church of SS. John and Paul. The mild-tempered P. objected to the violence of Jerome's attacks on *Jovinian and *Rufinus. He died during the siege of Rome by Alaric. BIBLIOGRAPHY: T. Lawler, NCE 10:937; Butler 3:446–447; E. Romanelli, EncCatt 9:666–667.

[R. B. ENO]

PAMMAKARISTOS, CONGREGATION OF, a group of Catholic nuns of the Greek Byzantine rite founded in 1921 at Cospli in Turkey by Bp. George Calavassy and dedicated to the Theotokos Pammakaristos (The Most Blessed Mother of God). In 1922 the new community moved to Greece and in 1945 opened the Pammakaristos Hospital in Athens. Numbering only 25 they operate two centers for young women workers and students and at Nea Macri an orphanage and school for Greek refugee children.

[G. A. MALONEY]

PAMPHILUS, ST. (d. 310), martyr, teacher of *Eusebius of Caesarea. Born of a distinguished family in Berytus (Beirut), Syria, P. studied in the school of Alexandria under *Pierius, from whom he learned to hold Origen in great esteem. After his ordination (*c.*290) P. reestablished the school at Caesarea in Palestine that Origen had founded, and devoted special attention to the preservation and expansion of its library. In the persecution of Maximinus Daia he was beheaded after an imprisonment of 2 years. Information of his life is derived from Eusebius who considered him the most illustrious martyr of his day. While in prison, P. wrote an *Apology for Origen* in five books with the aid of Eusebius. Only the first book has survived in the Latin translation of Rufinus. In it P. defends Origen's essential orthodoxy, discounting his stranger teachings as speculation. Works: PG 17:541–616. BIBLIOGRAPHY: Butler 2:437–438; H. Crouzel, NCE 10:937–938; Quasten 2:144–146.

[R. B. ENO]

PAMPHYLIA, the name, which means "all tribes," of a Roman province along the S coast of Asia Minor between Lycia on the W and Cilicia on the E and Pisidia on the North. Its capital was Perga and its main port Attalia. On their missionary journey Barnabas and Paul visited the region and passed through these cities (Acts 13.13; 14.24). On the first Pentecost Jews from Pamphylia were among those who heard the Apostles speaking in their own tongue.

[S. MUSHOLT]

PAMPLONA, FRANCISCO DE (Tiburcio de Redin; 1597–1651), military officer in Spain, Capuchin lay brother from 1637, missionary in the Congo in 1645, and from 1647 in Panama and Venezuela, where he died.

[T. C. O'BRIEN]

PANAETIUS OF RHODES (*c*.185–109 B.C.), with Posidonius of Apamea (*c*.135–51 B.C.), the founder of Middle Stoicism. He is esp. important for his success in adapting Stoic ethics to suit the needs and temperament of the Roman intellectual class. *STOICISM.

[M. R. P. MCGUIRE]

PANAGIA (Gr., the all-holy one), a favorite term used in the Byzantine Church for the all-holy Mother of God. The word is also applied derivatively: (1) to the *encolpion* bearing the image of the Mother of God worn as the distinctive sign of prelates; and (2) to a loaf of bread blessed by Greek monks and who pronounce over it an invocation of the Most Holy Trinity and the Mother of God. It is eaten during morning meal prayers and probably had its origin in a fashion similar to that of the *antidoron* or *artoklasia*.

[A. J. JACOPIN]

PANAKÉ (Panagué), Armenian equivalent of the Greek *encolpion*.

PANAMA, a republic occupying the narrowest portion of the isthmus connecting N and S America (including the Canal Zone, 29,306 sq mi; pop. [est. 1976] 1,630,000, over 1 million Catholic; ethnic distribution: 65% mixed [mestizo, mulatto, mestizo-mulatto], 13% Negro, 11% white, 10% Indian, 1% Oriental; illiteracy rate, 25%). Discovered by Rodrigo de Bastidas (1501), Panama's coast was skirted by Columbus on his fourth voyage in 1502. Balboa organized the first settlements in 1513; in 1514 Pedrarias Dávila was appointed governor. An *audiencia* was established in 1535, and Panama was put under the viceroyalty of Peru (1542) but was joined to that of New Grenada in 1717. With independence from Spain (1821), Panama remained united with Colombia. It enjoyed some autonomy (1855–85), after which Colombia resumed closer control and retained it till Panama gained its independence in 1903. In that same year a treaty with the U.S. was signed providing for the building of a canal (completed 1914) across the isthmus and leasing in perpetuity to the U.S. a strip of land five miles in width on either side of the canal. Despite the lease, Panama's sovereignty over this zone was acknowledged in principle by the U.S. in 1959 and the treaty signed by both countries in June 1978 returns the Canal Zone to Panama in

a process to be completed Dec. 31, 1999. The evangelization of Panama was first committed to Franciscans and Dominicans, who were followed by Mercedarians and Jesuits. Dominicans and Jesuits established a number of educational centers, the latter founding (1749) the Univ. of San Javier. In the concordat of 1886 the union of Church and State was recognized but this was dissolved by Panama's separation from Colombia. Relations with the Vatican were not resumed until 1929. In 1925 Panama (City) became an archiepiscopal see. The constitution of 1946 declared that Catholicism was the religion of the majority, but accorded it no privileges on that account. Religion may be taught in public schools; the schools operated by the Church receive no subsidy from the State and are in fact obliged to pay taxes. The suffragan sees are David (1955), Chitré (1962), and Santiago (1963). A prelature *nullius* was established at Bocas del Toro in 1962, and a vicariate apostolic at Darién in 1925. Among the problems to be faced by the Church in Panama are the religious ignorance of the masses and the low standard of family morality that prevails in many homes. About 30% of the marriages contracted are civil only; about 46% of the births are illegitimate. Too little can be done toward the re-Christianization of the people because of the shortage of priests. There are only 76 diocesan and 212 religious priests, and 442 religious women. In the Canal Zone (pop. 42,000, of which number about 20% are Catholic) the Church is served by 32 priests. Among the encouraging signs are the attention being given to social problems, various pastoral projects, the better preparation of catechists, and the founding (1965) of the Catholic Univ. of Santa María de la Antigua. Among the Protestant denominations active in the republic are the Episcopalian Church, the International Foursquare Gospel, and the Methodist Missionary Society. The total membership of the Protestant community numbers *c*.70,000; it is served by 327 national and 255 foreign missionaries. BIBLIOGRAPHY: E. J. Castillero, NCE 10:939–942.

[P. DAMBORIENA]

PANATHENAIC PROCESSION, climactic feature of the festival honoring Athena. The procession wound through Athens to the Acropolis hill where in the Parthenon the sacred robe (*peplos*) on the cult statue of Athena was changed every 4 years, and rich sacrifices were offered. The procession is the subject of the monumental Parthenon frieze on the cella wall beyond the portico, where water-carriers on foot, bulls for sacrifice, youths on horseback, and enthroned gods and goddesses exemplify the Greek genius through isocephaly (placing of all heads in the same zone), attaining the ideal serenity of Classicism.

[M. J. DALY]

PANBABYLONIANISM, theory that the teachings of the OT and even the NT were derivations from Babylonian religion. This interpretation of the Bible, proposed by Friedrich Delitzsch (1850–1922) and other German scholars, was popular in the early 20th cent.,but has been discarded by all biblical scholars.

[T. C. O'BRIEN]

PANCHRISTIANITY, a designation used by Pius XI in his encyclical *Mortalium animos* (1928) for any ecumenical efforts that would be based upon the belief that the Church is merely a loose federation of ecclesial bodies without a unity of faith and hierarchical order. In the encyclical, the Pope sought to explain why Catholics did not participate in the Lausanne Conference (1927), stating that Catholics could not take part in any meeting whose principles contradicted the very nature of the Church. BIBLIOGRAPHY: G. Weigel, *Catholic Primer on the Ecumenical Movement* (1960) 35–37.

[T. M. MCFADDEN]

PANCRAS, ST. (early 4th cent.?), boy martyr. That there was a martyr of this name seems certain, for Pope Symmachus *c*.500 built a church over his tomb. But all the particulars told of him come from worthless legendary *acta*. According to these he was an orphan of Phrygian or Syrian origin who was taken to Rome by his uncle. There they both became Christians. Only a month after his conversion, when he was not yet 14 years of age, P. was martyred by decapitation and buried on the Via Aurelia. The first church built at Canterbury was dedicated in his honor and a portion of his relics sent by Pope Vitalian helped to popularize his cult in medieval England. The railway station in London that bears his name was so called from its location in the district embracing the old cemetery of St. Pancras. BIBLIOGRAPHY: Butler 2:285; E. Josi, EncCatt 9:674–675.

[R. B. ENO]

PANDULF (d. 1226), Roman ecclesiastic; papal legate to England; Bp. of Norwich (1222). Representing Innocent III in the dispute over Stephen Langton's election, P. excommunicated John (1211), negotiated with his French enemies, and received his submission (1213), thereafter supporting him against Langton and the barons. After the death of William Marshall, Henry III's regent (1219), P. became virtual ruler. His efficient administration ended civil hostilities, but enemies persuaded Honorius III to replace him with Langton (1221). BIBLIOGRAPHY: R. S. Hoyt, NCE 10:943 (bibliog.)

[R. W. HAYS]

PANENTHEISM, a philosophic doctrine maintaining that the universe exists in God without being identical with God or exhausting the infinitude of his Being. There are many variations of the central theme but the first use of the term is accredited to the German philosopher, Karl C. F. Krause (1781–1832), in describing his own version, in some ways the most notable. Striving to articulate the definitive position of I. *Kant, Krause adopted an extremely mystical and spiritualistic approach in his effort to reconcile theism and pantheism, the former accepting a transcendent and personal God and the latter holding for the identity of God and the universe. Krause's mediation between the two is such that God is not outside the world and he is not the world but rather is it in him who himself extends beyond its limits. Thus, from the Greek *pan-en-theos,* meaning literally everything in God, Krause's coinage was readily suggested. Moreover, from this basic conception, he developed a philosophic outlook regarding man and his history as a moral animal, idealizing the attainment of a human federation (*Menschheitsbund*) as the goal of man's earthly striving.

Individual self-consciousness as the key to the nature of all reality considers its own finitude and concludes to the necessary existence of an Absolute Being on whom all others depend and whose nature is beheld by man in an intuitive vision as the ground of all other knowledge. God is the primordial being *(Urwesen),* containing the universe but apart from and superior to it in a relation of the whole to the part. Men should seek after an imitation of the divine in their own interior lives, striving to participate in the goodness which God is, and this inner union with God (*Gottesinnigkeit*) is the foundation of morality and the core of all religion. And the gradual evolution of humanity in the ethical sphere is the unfolding realization of this ideal.

Apart from Krause's system, panentheism represents any of a number of views in which a fundamental duality is expressed in the concept of God as both eternal and temporal, as embracing creation and yet remaining aloof from it. Depending upon one's interpretation, elements of the doctrine can be found in widely different contexts as, for instance, in Plato's being and becoming, in Nicholas of Cusa's Infinite reconciling all opposites, in Nicholas de Malebranche's Vision of God, in The Absolute Spirit of Georg Hegel, and more recently, in Pierre Teilhard de Chardin's fusion of The One and the Many, and in A. N. Whitehead's process philosophy. BIBLIOGRAPHY: See Krause's most important work, *Das Urbild der Menschheit* (1812); C. Macauley, *K. C. F. Krause, Heroic Pioneer for Thought and Life* (1925); on panentheism generally, see F. Thonnard, *Short History of Philosophy* (tr. E. Maziarz, 1955); J. Collins, *God in Modern Philosophy* (1959); and P. Weiss, *Modes of Being* (1958).

[J. T. HICKEY]

PANIGAROLA, FRANCESCO (1548–94), Italian Franciscan preacher, bp. of Asti from 1587. He was converted from a dissolute life and joined the Friars Minor Observant in 1567. His chief work was as preacher in the Tyrol from 1583, under commission of St. *Charles Borromeo, against Reformation doctrine. As a bp. P. continued to combat the Reformation and to promote church discipline in his own diocese. His *Lettioni sopra dogmi dette calviniche* (1583) were read widely and translated into other languages; other works include *Conciones 100 supra Christi passionem* (1585), and the posthumous *Rhetorica ecclesiastica* (1605).

[T. C. O'BRIEN]

PANNINI, GIOVANNI PAOLO (1691 or 1692–1765), Italian fresco painter of decorative landscapes whose classical *capricci*, treated as stage settings peopled with elegant figures, influenced French rococo *fêtes galantes* and the fantasies of Piranesi. P.'s paintings of royal and ecclesiastical ceremonies show accurate views of existing buildings in real and imaginary topography. BIBLIOGRAPHY: R. Wittkower, *Art and Architecture in Italy, (1600–1750)* (1958).

PANNONHALMA, ABBEY OF, archabbey *nullius* and center of the Hungarian Benedictine Congregation. Established in 996 near Györ, it served as a stronghold of Christian civilization throughout the Middle Ages. In the 16th and 17th cent. it was a fortress against the Turks. The abbey was suppressed by Joseph II (1786) but was revived in 1802. In the 19th cent. the monks turned to secondary education and eventually operated eight gymnasia of high reputation. In 1948 the Communist regime secularized most institutions of the congregation. Pannonhalma has been preserved but with severely curtailed membership and activity. BIBLIOGRAPHY: L. J. Lekai, NCE 10:946.

[L. J. LEKAI]

PANOFSKY, ERWIN (1892–1968), German historian of art, from 1931 in the United States. A man of encyclopedic learning and keen respect for the rational, he introduced synthesis rather than analysis or contextual studies in history, religion, philosophy, and literature for exploring and illuminating the meaning of works of art. A master of iconography, he contributed greatly to the better understanding of medieval and Renaissance art. P.'s studies are intensive and masterful historical explications in which great learning is brought to bear, with skill and taste, on the elucidation of enigmatic works of art. His *schema* for interpretation is intensively philosophic, scholarly, and intuitive. His *Studies in Iconology* (1939), *Gothic Architecture and Scholasticism* (1951), relating articulation in cathedrals to the scholastic working habit, are expositions of these theories. BIBLIOGRAPHY: E. Panofsky, *Studies in Iconology* (1939).

[P. P. FEHL]

PANORMITANUS, see TUDESCHIS, NICHOLAUS DE.

PAN-ORTHODOX CONFERENCES, a series of meetings held since 1961 by the various Orthodox patriarchates and autocephalous and autonomous Orthodox Churches to discuss such questions as the relations between the local Orthodox Churches, points of dogma, Orthodox spirituality, and ecclesiastical administration. The First Rhodes Conference (Sept. 24 to Oct. 1, 1961) was called by the

Committee for Pan-Christian Relations of the Ecumenical Patriarchate to draw up an agenda for the second meeting or pro-synod. It was planned that a third meeting or synod would formally promulgate the decisions reached at the pro-synod. The agenda worked out at the 1961 meeting (each item requiring the unanimous consent of the Churches for inclusion) contained eight major headings: (1) faith and dogma; (2) worship; (3) administration and ecclesiastical discipline; (4) inter-Orthodox relations; (5) relations between Orthodox and other Christian Churches; (6) Orthodoxy in the world; (7) theological questions; and (8) social questions. In fact, the Second Rhodes Conference (Sept. 26–28, 1963) limited itself to a discussion of whether or not to send observers to Vatican Council II. The Ecumenical Patriarchate wanted the Church as a whole to send observers, but the final vote left the decision up to the local Churches, acting independently. In addition, agreement in principle was reached on the establishment of a permanent commission to study the obstacles to reunion with Rome. The Third Rhodes Conference (Nov. 1–14, 1963) also limited discussion to the question of how and when to initiate the dialogue with Rome. One faction favored immediate commencement of such conversations with formal notification of the Vatican concerning this decision, while another group preferred to await the conclusion of Vatican II before taking such a step, with this decision to be released to the press only and not communicated to Rome. The compromise achieved contained a commitment to dialogue, but no action was to be taken until after the Council, although the decision was to be communicated to the Pope at once. On Feb. 7, 1968, in an attempt to return to the original purpose of the Rhodes meetings, Patriarch Athenagoras asked for the convocation of an Inter-Orthodox Commission (later called the Fourth Pan-Orthodox Conference) to resume preparations for the Synod agreed upon in 1961, and, to continue the discussion of problems concerning relations between the Orthodox and other Christian Churches. Because of the political situation in Greece, this meeting took place at Chambesy, Switzerland (June 8–15, 1968). The outcome of this commission was contained in the resolutions of four sub-committees accepted in plenary session: (1) A series of presynodal meetings was agreed upon at which the topics accepted in 1961 would be examined by theologians. This resolution amounted to a strong reaffirmation of the Churches' commitment to a synod. (2) Concerning relations with Rome, no agreement could be reached on the actual beginning of dialogue; the two factions that had emerged earlier limited this resolution to a statement on the desirability of informal contacts with Rome by the local Churches. It was hoped that this would eventually create the climate for dialogue. (3) It was agreed that the local Orthodox Churches should set up theological groups to study questions that might arise in future dialogues with the Anglicans, Old Catholics, Monophysites, and Lutherans. Informal contacts were encouraged here, too, but it was agreed that any substantive, official theological discussions were to be undertaken only by the Orthodox Church as a whole. (4) It was resolved that pressure should be brought to bear on the World Council of Churches to afford the Orthodox a greater role in that body's undertakings. Overall it can be seen that these four meetings have demonstrated the extent of the desire for renewal within the Orthodox Churches, including a shift towards the restoration of conciliar practice and a marked increase in interest in ecumenical matters.

The first of the presynodal conferences was held at Chambesy, Switzerland, Nov. 21–28, 1976. Participants agreed on an agenda of ten topics for the Synod, and on preparatory procedures. The conference dealt with two matters in addition to the Synod: relations with non-Orthodox Churches and with the World Council of Churches; proposals for securing agreement on the date of Easter. Delegates concluded that existing dialogues should continue with the non-Chalcedonian Orthodox, Lutherans, and Anglicans, despite the Anglican decision to ordain women, and that pan-Orthodox dialogue should begin with the Roman Catholic Church. On the WCC, they recommended that participation continue, but with efforts to secure greater Orthodox influence in decision making. It was decided to take no immediate action on the Easter question, but to plan for studies and include it among the ten agenda items for decision by the Synod. The other nine agreed upon were fasting regulations, obstacles to marriage, Orthodoxy in the "diaspora," relations with non-Orthodox Christians, ranking of autocephalous Churches, autocephaly and autonomy, terms for granting autonomy, the ecumenical movement, and the Church and the world. BIBLIOGRAPHY: R. H. Marshall, "Renewal at Rhodes," *Diakonia* 1.2 (1966) 61–70.

[R. H. MARSHALL; T. EARLY]

PANPSYCHISM, a philosophic theory of nature according to which not only man and animals but all beings of the objective universe have some form of psychic experience or power, variously referred to in terms of sensation, consciousness, or psychological being sometimes called soul. Depending upon the version of the hypothesis, it extends from the tiniest particles of matter through inanimate nature, commonly so-called, to all species of plant and animal, usually described in terms of a hierarchical scale with ascending degrees of psychic endowment up to man himself. The position is in some respects a revival on the part of modern science of the theories of animism and hylozoism as held in antiquity, or at least, it is related to these. Animism maintains that all natural bodies are animate, ensouled, or spirit-directed from within, and that the soul is the cause of all psychical phenomena, whereas hylozoism asserts that all matter is literally animated or alive, life being conceived as a property of matter. Panpsychism, with these associated schools, persists in early Greek thought among the pre-Socratic cosmologists, is found in a revived form in the Renaissance thought of G. Bruno, B. Telesio, and T. Campanella, and permeates the thinking of the 19th-cent. German philosophers, Leibnitz and Schopenhauer. In its more definitive scientific expression, however, it is prominent in the works of the German thinkers—Gustav Fechner, Freidrich Paulsen, and Rudolf Lotze, and the American philosopher, Josiah Royce.

As an example of a specific brand of panpsychism, the view of Fechner is one which reasons from man's mental life to the existence of psychic awareness in descending degrees of clarity among brutes, plants, and inorganic matter. For Fechner, the entire universe moreover is made up of minds, and man does not have the highest form of psychic life therein. The earth and the other planets have souls but all such psychic forms of existence are in some manner contemplated by the world-soul which is the highest or the soul of God. BIBLIOGRAPHY: G. S. Kirk and J. E. Raven, *Pre-Socratic Philosophers* (1957); S. Greenberg, *Infinite in Giordano Bruno* (1950); G. Fechner, *Nanna: oder über das Seelenleben der Pfanzen* (3d ed. 1903); Eng. tr. selections of Fechner's works by W. Lowrie, *Religion of a Scientist*, (1946); R. Lotze's *Mikrokasmus* (v. 1, 1856–64; tr. by E. Hamilton and E. E. Jones 1890).

[J. T. HICKEY]

PANSELINOS, MANUEL (fl. early 14th cent.), Greek painter from Salonika working at Mt. Athos, known from 17th- and 18th-cent. sources, chiefly from the *Painter's Manual of Mount Athos* by Dionysius of Fourna, who termed P. the model for all Byzantine painters. He executed frescoes in the Protaton Monastery (14th cent.) in the Macedonian style of the Paleologian period. *BYZANTINE ART.

PAN-SLAVISM, an international movement esp. prevalent in the 19th cent. advocating unity of all Slavs for cultural and political purposes. Emphasis at first was on academic collaboration among Slavs, notably urged by scholars including the Czechs Frantisek Palacky and Paul Safarik, and the Slovak Jan Kollar. The first formalized attempt for a more extensive unity in the face of German and Russian expansion was expressed at the Prague Pan-Slav Congress in June 1848 under the chairmanship of Palacky. As a result of the Crimean War the momentum of the movement grew apace and shifted to Russia. It became more aggressive, particularly under the influence of the publicist Michael Pogodin, the activist-writer I. S. Aksakov, F. Dostoyevsky, and the scientist Danilevsky. The latter saw a future Russia as hub of a new world civilization succeeding the "rotting West." Despite many pious statements on the themes of solidarity and common heritage at various conventions and exhibitions, Russia's bid for hegemony over its brother Slavs was thwarted. In the 20th cent. Pan-Slavist ideology faded, not however, without Russia's seizing parts of Czechoslovakia and Poland in the name of racial brotherhood. BIBLIOGRAPHY: F. Fadner, *Seventy Years of Pan-Slavism in Russia* (1962); H. Kohn, *Pan-Slavism; Its His-*

tory and Ideology (1960); M. Petrovich, *Emergence of Russian Panslavism, 1856–1870* (1956).

[D. DIRSCHERL]

PANTAENUS, ST. (d. *c*.190), first known head of the celebrated catechetical school at Alexandria. Eusebius speaks of him as a man of great learning and zeal. He appears to have contributed much to the formation of St. *Clement of Alexandria, who was his pupil at the school and who succeeded him as its head. He left no writings, but his teaching seems to have been in the Platonist tradition. According to less reliable reports, he may have been of Sicilian origin and may have traveled to India (Arabia?) as a missionary. BIBLIOGRAPHY: PG 5:1327–32; Quasten 2:4–5; Butler 3:32–33; F. Tamburini, BiblSanct 10:119–121.

PANTALEON, ST. (d. *c*.305), martyr. Legend has made him a physician in the court of the Emperor Galerius at Nicomedia. Though he was brought up a Christian, the evil example of the palace led him to apostasy, but he returned to the faith through the influence of a Christian named Hermolaos. Shortly after this, persecution broke out and P., denounced by jealous associates, was grievously tortured and beheaded (after six other attempts to take his life had failed). He was greatly honored in the Middle Ages and is a patron of physicians. BIBLIOGRAPHY: Butler 3:192–193; A. Amore, EncCatt 9:684; J-M. Sauget, BiblSanct 10:107–118.

[R. B. ENO]

PANTANASSA, MONASTERY OF, MISTRÁ, Byzantine monastery in Mistrá, Greece, built (1428) by John Frangopoulos, its church of rough stone and brick in decorative patterns consists of a cruciform upper church supporting five cupolas, a columnar portico on the east side, and rich frescoes in a late Paleologian style.

[M. J. DALY]

PANTHEISM, the doctrine that, in some sense more than merely metaphorical, God is all there is or all is God. It is doubtful that any major religious thinker ever defended a strictly literal pantheism; the overwhelming emphasis in the historical pantheist positions has been on the universal immanence of God and the permeation of the natural by the divine. This involves a redefinition of God and the divine in ways unacceptable to theism and an exclusion of divine transcendence. In *Spinoza pantheism expresses the perfect systematic and mechanical order which the world possesses. There is a difficulty in explaining the possibility of natural or moral evil or the meaningfulness of human freedom. The pantheist wants his God so close that he willingly denies all distance between divinity and the world of man. Pantheism itself comprises two apparently divergent components: (1) the swallowing up the world of nature in God, whose reality is thus made to engulf all, to the point of negating what is not God, and (2) the banishing of God from the world as a ridiculous and superfluous hypothesis. Pantheism has persisted in the history of thought with remarkable tenacity, assuming an amazing variety of forms. The spirit of pantheism has pervaded a segment of Western literature, esp. during periods of romantic sentimentalism. Once the transcendence of God is eliminated, man has at least an ostensible claim to the sole mastery of his destiny. Pantheism is a univocalist error, attributing to the being of our immediate experience the substantial perfections of an infinite, absolutely perfect being. BIBLIOGRAPHY: D. J. B. Hawkins, *Essentials of Theism* (1949); R. Garrigou-Lagrange, *God, His Existence and His Nature* (tr. B. Rose, 2 v. 1934–36).

[J. P. REID]

PANTHÉON, LE (Paris), French Neoclassical structure, originally the church of Ste. Genevieve, designed by Soufflot (1757) and finished by his pupil Rondelet. The church is a Greek cross plan with Corinthian façade and tall dome, the interior solemn, spacious, colonnaded. Designated as a mausoleum for ''great citizens'' in 1791, it was returned as a church in 1806, became the *panthéon* in 1830, Ste. Genevieve in 1852, and finally the *panthéon* for the funeral of Victor Hugo in 1885. Voltaire, Diderot, Rousseau, and Soufflot himself with many others are buried here. Impressive historical and mythological reliefs, portraits, mosaics, and valuable paintings by P. de Chavannes enrich the interior. The *panthéon* is a perfect exposition of the Neoclassical theories of the Abbé Laugier (*Essai sur l' architecture,* 1753) avoiding as it does unclassical Renaissance deviations. BIBLIOGRAPHY: M. Petzet, *Soufflots Sainte-Genevieve und der französische Kirchenbau des 18 Jahrhunderts* (1961).

[M. J. DALY]

PANTHEON, ROME, impressive circular Roman temple (120–124 A.D.) built by Hadrian on the site of an earlier temple dedicated to all the gods by Agrippa in 27 B.C. as attested by the inscription on the portico. The immense rotunda 142 ft by 140 ft high, supported by a wall 20 ft thick and with Greek Corinthian octastyle portico, boasts a magnificent low Roman dome—a dramatic interior note—with oculus at center, lightened by the distinctive Roman coffered ceiling, false windows with Greek pedimental and Roman-arch frames, the dynamic and varied string courses confirming the swinging rhythms. An entablature supported by pilasters framing recesses with two columns runs along the interior wall. The temple rededicated to the Blessed Virgin in 609 is known as Sta. Maria Rotonda.

[M. J. DALY]

PANTOCRATOR (Gr., ruler of all), a representation of Christ usually filling the dome of Byzantine churches. Christ is generally portrayed with a stern countenance holding in one hand the roll of the law while the other is raised in a gesture of command. Originally it signified God the Father, the awesome ruler, lawgiver and judge of all, and was meant to instill a sense of fear of judgment in the poor sinner below. Since the Father is invisible he cannot be pictured, but he was made visible in his Incarnate Son, and so can be represented by Christ.

[G. T. DENNIS]

PANVINIO, ONOFRIO (1530–68), Augustinian, "father of modern church history." P.'s study of history began with his entrance at the age of 12 into the Augustinian Order. From 1554 he enjoyed the patronage of Card. Alexander Farnese and accompanied him into the conclave of 1559. His historical investigations brought him the acquaintance of Delfino, Sirleto, Maffei, and Latini. For his planned history of the ancient Church and Christian Rome, P. indefatigably gathered material that filled 68 volumes. His works were concentrated on Roman antiquity, the history of the ancient Church and its cult, as well as on the history of the popes and cardinals. He edited an edition of Platina's *Lives of the Popes*. Scholarly and untiring in his researches, he never accomplished his projected refutation of the Magdeburg Centuriators. BIBLIOGRAPHY: H. Jedin, LTK 8:31; F. Roth, NCE 10:950–951; G. de Libero, "Panvinio Onofrio," *Roma* 21 (1943) 98–111.

[J. M. O'DONNELL]

PANZANI, GREGORIO (d. 1662), papal agent in England. Pope Urban VIII sent P. as a personal emissary to Queen Henrietta Marie, Urban's goddaughter, to assess the situation of the English Catholics, to reconcile differences between the secular and regular clergy, and to probe the possibility of reunion with Rome. P. was successful in bringing about an official exchange of emissaries between Pope and Queen, but was over-optimistic in his reports of Anglican readiness to move toward reunion with Rome. In 1640 P. became Bp. of Mileto. BIBLIOGRAPHY: G. Albion, *Charles I and Court of Rome* (1935).

[V. SAMPSON]

PANZUTI, BIAGIO (1775–1846), theologian. An Italian Redemptorist, P. was named procurator general of his congregation. A follower of St. Alphonsus Liguori he published in 1824 a systematization of Liguorian theology much admired throughout Europe. Accused by some as presenting a laxist view of the theology of St. Alphonsus, P. was vindicated by the Congregation of the Index. In 1842 he published two volumes on casuistry according to St. Alphonsus.

[J. R. AHERNE]

PAOLO VENEZIANO (fl. *c*.1333–62), master Venetian painter extending the Byzantine tradition. His *Death of the Virgin* (1333) is conventional in gold-threaded drapery and flattened space. The heavily restored panels of the *Pala d'oro* (St. Mark's, 1344–45) are more dynamically spatial.

A *Coronation of the Virgin* signed by P. and his son Giovanni shows Gothic influence in fluid linear drapery and gesture.

[M. J. DALY]

PAOLO, GIOVANNI DI (1403–82), leading Italian painter of the Sienese School during the *quattrocento*. P. typifies the conservatism of Renaissance painting in Siena with its strong affinity to the International Style. However, his style is enlivened by a mystical intensity achieved through elegantly costumed, weightless figures drifting through exquisite fantasy landscapes filled with delicately detailed plants and animals *St. John in the Wilderness* (*c*.1450, Art Institute of Chicago), *Paradise* (1445, Metropolitan Museum of Art, N.Y.) BIBLIOGRAPHY: J. Pope-Hennessey, *Giovanni di Paolo* (1937).

[S. CONWAY]

PAOLUCCI, GIUSEPPE (1726–76), Italian Franciscan composer and theorist, who studied under Martini. He was choirmaster in Venice, Sinigaglia, and Assisi (1771). He is remembered for his treatise, *Arte pratica di contrappunto dimostrata con esempi di varii autori e con osservazioni* (1765).

[R. J. LITZ]

PAPACY. This article considers the papacy through the careers of some 90 popes; it is based on certain historical presuppositions. In its early history the Roman see resembled the Eastern episcopate, although the bp. of Rome was always *primus inter pares*. Changing political conditions forced the pope to protect Italy when the emperor in Constantinople could not. This responsibility became permanent when the Papal States appeared with Pepin's donation of land in 756. Medieval feudalism affected churchmen: as feudal lords they were responsible for benefices endowed with governmental functions important to their overlords. The papacy struggled thereafter to establish its autonomy. By the 19th cent. the Holy See, though crushed politically, rose to a new spiritual preeminence. This article will suggest how individual popes reveal the politico-ecclesiastical aspects of the papacy; how historical forces shaped it; what authority is regarded as intrinsic to the papacy; and what is accidental, historical accretion.

Papacy to Gregory I. Whatever the proper setting of Mt 16.16–19, the fact is that Peter after Christ's Ascension appears in Acts 1–15 as the undisputed leader of the Church. From these circumstances, the primacy of the Roman see derives: whoever is bp. of Rome is therefore successor to St. Peter and, like him, head of the Church. The early history of the papacy is uncertain; even the listing of the first successors of Peter is disputed. The famous letter of Clement, Bp. of Rome *c*.95, establishes him in that role, but it does not indicate—as earlier attested—that he was acting with special authority over the Church of Corinth or that he had been asked to do so. (See H. Dressler, NCE

3:926–927. Hereafter authors cited, unless otherwise noted, are from NCE.) Only a few popes in the 2d cent. are noteworthy: Pius I, brother of Hermas, author of *The Shepherd*, received at Rome men more famous than himself, e.g., Hegesippus, Justin, Polycarp, and Irenaeus (see E. G. Weltin, 11:193). Victor I (d. 198?) was deeply involved in controversy over the date of Easter. He was tempted to excommunicate Eastern bps., but St. Irenaeus, bp. of Lyons, dissuaded him. The struggle itself is significant as "the first evidence of a move by the Roman Church to influence the internal affairs of Eastern Churches" (Weltin, 14:646). Pope Callistus (*c*.217–*c*.222) is important because his election was followed by that of Hippolytus, the first antipope. Historians now doubt that Callistus issued the decree permitting adulterers forgiveness through penance (*exomologesis*) hitherto forbidden them. Of Pope Fabian I (d. 250) Emperor Decius allegedly said that he would lose a legion rather than hear that another bp. of Rome had been elected. Pope Cornelius (251–253) faced a schism headed by Novatian when the Pope permitted *exomologesis* for apostates, a relaxation begun by Cyprian of Carthage. The letter communicating Cornelius's decision to Bp. Fabius of Antioch describes vividly the 3d-cent. Roman Church (J. Chapin, 3:333–334).

Dramatic changes in relations between Church and Empire were introduced by Constantine (306–337). Sylvester I, Constantine's contemporary, was largely overlooked. Constantine's way of handling Donatism and his role at Nicaea (325) seemed to reduce Sylvester to the position of a concerned onlooker. Medieval legends compensated for Sylvester's insignificance, esp. the 5th-cent. *Acts of Blessed Sylvester*, which recount his baptism of Constantine (J. Chapin, 13:857–858). Julius I (337–352) inherited the struggle over Arianism. After Nicaea Arian bps. undermined the key phrase *homooúsion to patrî* (of one substance with the Father), in the creed of Nicaea and deposed the stanchly orthodox Athanasius of Alexandria. Julius vigorously asserted his authority: "Why were we not written to about the Church of the Alexandrians? Are you ignorant that the custom was first to write to us, and then for justice to be determined from here?" At Sardica (354) the assembled bps. witnessed to the Roman primacy, which they said honored the memory of blessed Peter (J. Chapin, 8:51–52). Liberius (352–366), the first pope who described Rome as the Apostolic See, suffered sharp persecution under the Arian Emperor Constantius II. He exiled the Pope to Thrace (355) but recalled him when Liberius agreed to sign a vague creed. Athanasius, Jerome, Hilary of Poitiers, all contemporaries, condemned Liberius, who nevertheless continued to teach Catholic doctrine and to oppose Arianism. His successor, Damasus (366–384), was harassed by Arianism until 381, when Emperor Theodosius I outlawed the heresy at Constantinople I. Less happy in the Pope's eyes was the council's elevation of Constantinople as the New Rome to a primacy second only to Old Rome. Innocent I (401–417) asserted his authority on doctrinal matters: "The bishops, our brothers, should refer [them] to Peter, the founder of the episcopate to provide for the common good of all the Churches" (*Epist:* 30.2; P. Camelot, 7:519–520).

The new problem of Nestorianism beset Celestine I (422–432), who entrusted its solution almost totally to Cyprian of Alexandria. In Celestine's reign, African bps. led by Augustine asserted their independence on the provincial level. Leo I the Great (440–461) fought Monophysitism, convoking (449) the abortive synod of Ephesus; he later designated it, "Not a council but a den of thieves." He agreed to the Council of Chalcedon (451) and its decrees, except canon 28, which transformed Constantinople's primacy of honor into one of jurisdiction. He described his authority as a *plenitudo potestatis*, superior to any bishop's. Leo established the juridical structure on which the primacy has since rested. When Leo's doctrinal statement, the *Tome*, was read at Chalcedon, the bps. cried: "Thus through Leo Peter has spoken," a cry that exactly expressed Leo's own concept of his office (F. X. Murphy, 8:637–639). Gelasius I (492–496), the first pope to be described (495) as "vicar of Christ" (J. Chapin, 6:315–316), addressed a famous letter on the two powers, sacred and secular to Emperor Anastasius I, whose duty it was "to learn from bishops." Hormisdas (514–523), like his predecessors, fought Monophysitism, officially condemned in 451 but constantly revived. The Formulary of Hormisdas imposed by the Emperor healed the Acacian schism between Rome and Constantinople (484–519) and is "the most strongly pro-Roman and pro-papal statement ever signed by Byzantine bishops" (J. Chapin, 7:148). John I (523–526) journeyed to Constantinople to plead in vain for persecuted Arians. Taken prisoner by Theodoric, Arian king of the Ostrogoths, he died in Ravenna. Pope Vigilius (537–555) also had to face recurring Monophysitism; he succumbed in 554 to unbearable pressures in the complicated Three Chapters controversy (F. X. Murphy, 14:664–667). Pelagius was appointed by the Emperor Justinian to succeed Vigilius as pope—a procedure that horrified the West and set the bad precedent that popes seek imperial approval. Elected pope by popular acclaim, Gregory I the Great (590–604) already had wide experience as prefect of Rome and later as papal representative (*apocrisiarius*) at the court of Constantinople. He protected Rome, abandoned by Constantinople and Ravenna: Gregory's position as *de facto* ruler aroused Emperor Maurice. Gregory claimed universal jurisdiction over bps. since the Roman see "is set over all the Churches." Though he respected the internal autonomy of dioceses, he objected to the epithet "ecumenical" for the patriarch of Constantinople. His theological, pastoral, and liturgical writings contributed to Gregory's image "as a bridge-builder between the ancient and the medieval world." By 600 the papacy clearly appeared as an institution consciously possessing extensive spiritual, ecclesiastical, and quasi-political powers.

Medieval Papacy. Monophysitism in its variant forms (Monothelitism, Monoenergism) continued to harass the popes. Honorius I (625–638) failed to distinguish adequately the orthodox from the heretical formulation, emphasizing instead the harmony of wills in Christ (H. G. J. Beck, 7:123–125). Martin I (649–653 or 655) in the Lateran Synod also condemned Monophysitism. He was exiled and died for orthodoxy. This synod was the basis of Constantinople III (690), where Monophysitism in all its form was officially repudiated (C. M. Aherne, 9:300–301). About 730 the popes began a rapprochement to Western rulers, which made them increasingly independent of Constantinople. Gregory II (715–731) threatened Leo III for his iconoclasm, Gregory III (731–741) excommunicated iconoclasts in the Roman synod (731), and both popes asked Charles Martel for help. Pope Zachary (741–752) fostered papal political influence by recognizing Pepin's assumption of the royal title (M. C. McCarthy, 14:1106). Stephen II (752–757), threatened by the Lombards, appealed to Pepin, who defeated them and made over the conquered lands to the Pope (756). Thus were established the Papal States (756–1870). Adrian I (772–795) defended Rome before being forced to appeal to Charlemagne (J. E. Bresnahan, 1:144). Leo III (795–816) was attacked, wounded, and vilified by Adrian's nephews; the Pope cleared himself of their accusations by taking a solemn oath to his own innocence (Dec. 23, 800) for "the first see can be judged by no one." He rejected the addition of *filioque* to the creed as unauthorized (not as untrue). He also crowned Charlemagne emperor. However, Charlemagne objected to the Pope's seizing the initiative in the coronation (R. E. Sullivan, 8:640). Nicholas I the Great (858–867) is noteworthy for daring to censure Lothair II's adultery, for the Pope felt he had a right to judge rulers. Nicholas was deeply involved with Photius, Patriarch of Constantinople (858–867), following Patriarch Ignatius' resignation. Photius sent the Pope letters of introduction seeking recognition. He was at first accepted by papal legates, then repudiated by Nicholas, who disavowed their actions (862, 863), and finally was ordered to Rome for a reexamination of the whole matter (865). In anger Photius summoned a synod (867), which declared Nicholas deposed. Photius showed in this confrontation considerable respect for the papal office. A later pope recognized him (879; see H. G. J. Beck, 10:441; F. Dvornik, *Photian Schism*, 1946).

The nadir of papal prestige was reached in the 10th and 11th cent., an era ushered in by the tragic reign of Formosus (891–896), involved in the bitter rivalry of two Carolingians, Arnulf and Lambert. After the Pope's death, Lambert tried him, exhuming his corpse, condemning it in the famous "cadaverous trial" to be stripped of papal insignia and thrown into the Tiber. The domination of the papacy for 150 years by Roman nobility began with Sergius III (904–911), who had tried to seize the papacy in 897 and with the aid of Alberic I of Spoleto succeeded in 904; his immediate predecessors, Leo V and antipope Christopher, both had been murdered. Sergius invalidated Formosus' ordinations. He may have been the father of the future John XI by Marozia,

a notorious Roman woman. She imprisoned John X and perhaps caused his death. John XII (955–964), son of Alberic II of Spoleto, civil head of Rome, was only 18 when his father forced his election. Even allowing for the virulence of contemporary accounts. John was a most unworthy pope. Otto I's aid against the Pope's enemies resulted in John's crowning him as Holy Roman Emperor (962). Otto tried to become suzerain of the Papal States, but John refused. He died soon after this crisis under scandalous circumstances (S. McKenna, 7:1011). The reign of Sylvester II was a relief from the sordidness of his predecessors. Involved in the power struggle between Carolingians and Capetians, Gerbert (the future pope) supported Hugh Capet. He was censured for accepting a bishopric from Hugh, and fled to the court of Otto III, who appointed him abp. of Ravenna and later pope. As pope he unfortunately fostered the Germanizing policy of Otto among the Slavic peoples but denounced simony, nepotism, and concubinage; he supported provincial councils.

The Church continued to suffer until the unworthy Benedict IX (1033–44) was persuaded to retire by his successor, Gregory VI (1045–46), for an enormous sum of money—a transaction that naturally provoked accusations of simony. Henry III called a synod at Sutri, which persuaded Gregory to resign and then elected—not surprisingly—a German of Henry's choice, Clement II (O. J. Blum, 6:772). Another royal nominee, Leo IX (1048–54), brought the reform movement flowing from Cluny to the papacy itself. He liberated the papacy from the Roman nobility and from the German emperor. But a mission he dispatched to Constantinople to deal with the Patriarch Michael Cerularius contributed to, rather than healed, the breach. His military actions against the Normans in S Italy failed, although they later became vassals of the pope. Nicholas II (1058–61) further freed the papacy by the electoral law of 1059, which limited the electorate—formerly the people and clergy of Rome—to the cardinal bishops (later expanded to include all the cardinal clergy of Rome), thus freeing the election of political manipulation, at least on the local level.

High and Late Medieval Papacy. The most important medieval pope is Gregory VII (1073–85). A Roman monk, he served Gregory VI, Leo IX, and his successors. His election was obvious, tumultuous, and almost illegal. He considered the papacy as "primarily governmental and as such felt that it presupposed law." The *Dictatus papae*—considered the strongest statement of papal authority ever made—are, Ullmann thinks, chapter headings of a lost collection of canons. His epochal struggle with Henry IV, the German emperor, grew from the latter's blatant violations of Gregory's reforming decrees. His well-timed repentance at Canossa, though of doubtful sincerity, saved him his throne. Henry again "deposed" Gregory in 1084 (as he had in 1076), this time with more success. Gregory fled to the Castle of Sant' Angelo. His Norman vassals rescued him and took him to Salerno, where he died (1085). Henry was in control of Rome in the reigns of Victor III (1087) and Urban II (until 1194). Urban's situation made him a traveling pope, and one conciliatory toward recalcitrant bishops. His reforming activity and growing prestige are evident in the Council at Piacenza (April 1095), where envoys from the Eastern Roman Emperor appealed for aid. At Clermont (Nov. 1095) Urban launched the first crusade. Henry IV finally repudiated his own antipopes, but the investiture conflict continued under his son, Henry V (1106–25). Paschal II (1099–1118) offered at Sutri (1111) to surrender the *regalia* attached to all sees in the Empire in return for Henry's surrender of investiture. The bps. objected violently, and Paschal surrendered to Henry. A positive gain was the realization that the *regalia* were not in themselves sacred, a new concept emphasized by Ivo of Chartres. He proposed what in fact underlay the Concordat of Worms (1122), recognition of the mutual rights of Church and State in ecclesiastical feudal estates (D. D. McGarry, 2:1081). Lateran Council I (1123) ratified the concordat.

As desire for reform seized even secular rulers, Innocent II (1130–43) begged for peace and ecclesiastical independence, as did his rival, the antipope Anacletus (J. R. Sommerfeldt, 7:520–521). Eugene III (1145–53), a product of the Cistercian movement and a submissive disciple of Bernard, was a zealous reforming pope. The revolutionary Arnold of Brescia forced the Pope to leave Rome (1146–48). Adrian IV (1154–59) interdicted the rebellious Romans (1155). He had to deal with the incident of Besançon: a papal document used the word *beneficia* (benefits) for papal favors to the Holy Roman Empire. Antipapal churchmen at the imperial court pretended that the Pope was claiming that the Empire was a benefice from the Pope. Adrian, the only English pope, in the bull *Laudabiliter* authorized Henry II of England's expedition to reform Ireland. The struggle between the Emperor, the papacy, and the northern Italian towns organized into the Lombard League benefited Alexander III (1159–81), who supported them. The League triumphed at Legnano (1176), and Frederick I capitulated. Alexander had to deal with Henry II in his conflict with Thomas Becket. Concerned with education in general, he insisted that teachers secure a license to teach. The redoubtable Alexander was succeeded by several aged popes. Celestine III (1191–98) was the last and weakest. Eighty-five at his accession, he was an easy prey of Henry VI, who bullied the Pope into crowning him emperor, invaded Sicily, permitting the capture of the crusader Richard I, and arranged for the murder of a bishop. For the last two crimes he was not even censured by the Pope (W. H. Principle, 3:365).

The ruins of papal prestige lay all around when Innocent III (1198–1216) made ''the exercise of papal plenitude of power his hallmark'' (W. Ullmann, 7:521–524). The Hohenstaufen problem in Sicily was alleviated by the deaths of Henry VI and, a year later, his wife Constance. She committed her son (the future Frederick II) to the Pope's care, making Innocent regent for Sicily, a task the Pope

found impossible to discharge after 1208. The Pope's dream of a crusade materialized in 1202. However, it was diverted into intervention in a civil war in Constantinople. Crushed by such deviousness, the Pope nevertheless approved the establishment of a western dynasty (Eastern Latin Empire, 1204–61) to heal the Eastern Schism. But relations between the Churches worsened seriously as a result. Innocent was an efficient administrator, establishing sound finances; he worked against heresy and encouraged St. Dominic. Lateran Council IV (1215) brought the medieval Church to the zenith of its influence with a definition of transubstantiation, disciplinary decrees against heresy, and legislation for the Easter duty; it even revived the dream of a new crusade. Innocent III was a statesman: suzerain for about ten medieval kingdoms, including England after 1213, he took his role seriously, e.g., by repudiating Abp. Stephen Langton in favor of John, the Pope's former enemy become his vassal.

Honorius III (1216–27) like Innocent a lawyer, published *Compilatio quinta* (1226), the first official book of canon law (S. Williams, 7:126–127). Both the Dominican and Franciscan Orders were approved by him and were to play a significant role in the subsequent reign of Gregory IX (1227–41). Gregory inaugurated the papal Inquisition (1233), fought Frederick II because he failed his crusader's vow, and dominated N Italy. Gregory vigorously affirmed the primacy of Rome in negotiations—understandably unsuccessful—for reunion with the Eastern Church. Innocent IV (1243–54) broke the Hohenstaufen power forever—a questionable achievement. His successors continued his policy and supported the worthless Charles of Anjou as ruler of Sicily, for anything was preferable to encirclement by the dreaded German emperors. Urban IV (1261–65) continued to support Charles of Anjou, bestowing on him the ''vacant'' Sicilian throne against the claims of Manfred, Frederick's illegitimate son. Charles' ambitions were boundless, and included Constantinople itself. His actions alienated the East still more, negating Urban's efforts at reunion (H. Wieruszowski, 14:478). Gregory X (1271–76), after a 3-year delay in his election, established rules to shorten subsequent conclaves. In 1274 he convoked the Council of Lyons II (to which St. Thomas Aquinas was summoned to answer for errors in his writings; luckily he died in route, for 241 errors were discovered!). The Pope's attempts to reunite Eastern and Western Christendom failed. Martin IV (1281–85) continued to support Charles' erratic schemes in the East and in Sicily until 1282, when Charles was expelled from this island and 80,000 Frenchmen residing there were murdered as the Vesper bells were ringing, the infamous Sicilian Vespers.

Charles II of Anjou, with the Orsini and Colonna families, dominated the election of Celestine V (1294), a saintly recluse totally unfit to be pope. After a chaotic reign of 5 months he resigned with strong encouragement from the person who succeeded him as Boniface VIII (J. J. Smith, 3:365–366). Boniface's reign was a disaster. A student of canon law, he was sensitive to the Church's rights and to his own. His chief opponent was Philip IV of France, who was intent upon a policy of greater centralization, financial and political. Boniface wrote a series of letters: *Clericis laicos* (against taxing the clergy), the less demanding *Asculta fili*, then, in 1303, *Unam sanctam*, a very strong papal stance. The redoubtable Philip pursued the humiliated and defeated Pope even to the grave and beyond. For it was Clement V (1305–14) whose agony it was to resist the posthumous condemnation of Boniface only at the price of consenting to the destruction through the Council of Vienne (1311–12) of the Knights Templar. He was responsible also for the move to Avignon (1309) because of dangerous conditions in Italy and out of deference to Philip IV, whom he even absolved from all blame for Boniface's death. The residence of the popes at Avignon (1309–77) was a great scandal. All seven popes were French, as were 113 of 135 cardinals created by them. Accusations of extravagance are true principally of Clement VI, John XXII (1316–34) was involved in a struggle between rival emperors. One of them, Louis of Bavaria, attracted to his court John of Jandun and Marsilius of Padua, author of *Defensor pacis*, a vindication of council over pope. John XXII left a full treasury of 800,000 florins, which was squandered by his successors, esp. Clement VI (D. L. Douie, 3:1014–15). His reign was troubled by a revolution in Rome led by Cola di Rienzi. The English and French kings defeated his attempt to appoint all bps. from Avignon (1344) by seizing benefices held by foreigners. The unsuccessful attempt to return to Rome by Urban V (d. 1370) was realized under Gregory XI (1370–78). However, the anti-French sentiment in Rome made the subsequent papal election difficult. The threatening populace demanded a Roman or at least an Italian. The Abp. of Bari, Bartolomeo Prignani, was elected Urban VI. Although some doubt the validity of this election, others believe that eye-witness accounts definitely validate Urban VI. However, his choleric and unpredictable conduct forced the French cardinals (13 out of 16) to Avignon (1378), where they declared the April election invalid and chose a Frenchman as Clement VII.

Thus began the *Great Western Schism (1378–1415) with its two obediences, two popes, two curias, and two colleges of cardinals. The Council of *Pisa (1409) declared both popes deposed and elected a third, Alexander V. The Council of *Constance, convoked (1415) by Emperor Sigismund, deposed the Pisan pope; Gregory XII (successor in the Roman line) also officially convoked a council and resigned to it, whereupon Martin V (1417–31) was elected. He devoted himself to restoring papal prestige, to reform through periodic councils decreed by Constance (Pavia, 1423; Basel, 1431). Conciliarist himself at Pisa, Martin resisted *conciliarism as pope (K. A. Fink, 9:301–302). His successor, Eugene IV (1431–47), struggled against recalcitrants at Basel and convoked the Council of Ferrara-Florence (1438–45), which perceived that variety in rites could coexist with identity in faith. Statements favorable to

Roman doctrines on the *filioque*, purgatory, and papal primacy were accepted by East and West. The Council of Basel, now removed to Lausanne, continued into the reign of Nicholas V (1447–55), who won over the recalcitrant conciliarists. He used the jubilee of 1450 to reestablish papal prestige and devoted himself to Renaissance pursuits (J. Gill, 10:443–445). Constantinople fell to the Ottoman Turks in Nicholas's reign (1453), and he was unable to arouse crusading zeal to rescue her, nor were Pius II and Callistus III successful. Pius (1458–64) was a great humanist before and after his elevation. Renaissance popes of the 15th and 16th cent. (J. G. Rowe, 11:393–394) placed themselves at the head of the Renaissance movement in Italy and so identified the Church with it, including its worldliness and corruption. Nepotism and involvement in Italian politics characterized Sixtus IV (1471–84). Through his nephew, Riario, he participated in a scandalous and unsuccessful *coup* to overthrow the Medici family's control of Florence. Innocent VIII (1484–92) and Alexander VI (1492–1503) notoriously exemplified election through simony in the political advancement of their illegitimate children. Innocent VIII made feeble efforts at reform and on his deathbed implored the cardinals to elect a better man. Alexander tried to unite and strengthen the Papal States, trusting too much to his Machiavellian son, Cesare Borgia. He made real contributions to missionary developments in Spanish and Portuguese overseas empires, yet nothing he did could adequately compensate for the iniquity of his politics and his life (M. Battlore, 1:290–292).

The Papacy After 1500. Julius II (1503–13), responsible for the simony of Innocent VIII's election, tried to correct that evil, to reduce nepotism, and to render the papacy financially solvent. Though attached to pomp, he was concerned with reform and convoked Lateran Council V (1512–1517). Supporter of creative arts, in his reign he checked the worst excesses of the Renaissance papacy. His successors, the De' Medici, Leo X (1513–21), and Clement VII (1523–34) reigned disastrously. The former closed Lateran V, urging peace, crusade, and reform. He made a concordat with Francis I unbelievably favoring the monarch. He was incapable of evaluating the impact of Luther at its full strength when he signed the bull excommunicating him (J. G. Gallagher, 8:643–645). The 20-month reign of the Dutchman, Adrian VI (1522–23), last non-Italian pope, was marred by a language barrier and a lack of sympathy with Renaissance culture. Clement VII, as inept as his cousin in handling great affairs, lost England by temporizing over Henry VIII's divorce of Queen Catherine. Complications in Habsburg-Valois rivalry found Clement again on the losing side.

Paul III (1534–49), considered the first pope of the Catholic reform, appointed several exemplary cardinals (John Fisher, Reginald Pole, Caraffa, later Paul IV), approved the Jesuits (1540) and the Ursulines (1544), revived the Inquisition in Rome (1542), and published an Index (1543). Above all he worked for a council of reform, which finally met at Trent in three extended sessions (1545–1563; C. L. Hohl, Jr., 11:13–14). Julius III (1550–55) also championed reform, calling the second session of the Council of Trent (1551–52), appointing good cardinals, and encouraging the Jesuits. Paul IV (1555–59), severe, ascetic, identified the papacy indelibly with reform. He attacked simony and nepotism, abjuring forever his nephews when he discovered they had betrayed papal interests. Pius IV (1559–65) brought Trent to conclusion. His nephew, Charles Borromeo, exemplified its decrees in the Archdiocese of Milan. Pius V (1566–72) continued the implementation of Trent, revising the Roman Missal and Breviary and publishing the *Catechism of the Council of Trent* (1566). His international relations were poor, however: he excommunicated Elizabeth I and supported Catherine de Médicis against the Huguenots; on news of the *St. Bartholomew's Day Massacre (1572) he offered a solemn *Te Deum* of thanksgiving. Gregory XIII (1572–85) actualized the aims of the Council of Trent and introduced the Gregorian calendar (D. R. Campbell, 6:779–781). Clement VIII (1592–1605) recognized the *Edict of Nantes (1598), accepting the then-revolutionary principle of religious toleration. Kiev and the Ruthenian bishops were united to Rome under him (1595; J. C. Willke, 3:933–934).

The Jesuits, one of the principal agents of the Catholic reform, aroused jealousy in other religious orders. Urban VII (1623–44) opened China to all missionaries (1633) rather than to Jesuits only; Benedict XIV (1740–58) suppressed the special rites that Jesuits had requested as expressive of Chinese culture; Clement XIII (1778–69) had to face the hostility of Catholic kings toward Jesuits who were expelled from Portugal (1759), France (1762), and Spain (1767); their worldwide suppression was demanded in 1769. Clement XIV (1769–74) inherited the problem: having promised Charles III of Spain and Louis XV of France, he suppressed the Society (1773) with its 11,000 Jesuits, 266 colleges, 103 seminaries, and 88 residences (E. D. McShane, 3:940–942). The order survived in Prussia and Russia, although Pius VI (1775–99) tried to extinguish it. Weak and indecisive, Pius fatally identified church interests with those of the *ancien régime*, bitterly opposing the French Revolution, which in turn became violently anticlerical. Napoleon Bonaparte protected the Pope, but Pius was taken captive to France and died there during Bonaparte's Egyptian campaign. Papal authority deteriorated rapidly through *Josephinism in Austria, *Febronianism in Germany, and the Tuscan priests' revolt at the Synod of *Pistoia (1786). Pius VII (1800–23), upon Napoleon's return, signed the Concordat of 1801, unfortunately negated by the strongly Gallican Organic Articles. Pius accepted many like humiliations for a measure of spiritual freedom. After Napoleon's fall Pius reestablished control in the Papal States, negotiated with new states in a conciliatory spirit, and most important, reestablished the Society of Jesus (1814; J. Leflon, 11:400–404).

The Church reestablished by Metternich's Congress of Vienna reacted against change under Leo XII (1823–29) by restoring control in the Papal States to clergy and nobles, by anti-Semitic measures in Rome, censorship of press, and an encyclical against Freemasonry and the *Carbonari*, thus striving to check the forces of liberalism and to support the restored monarch (T. F. Casey, 8:646–647). The ideology of the French Revolution affected all Europe. A circle of French Catholic intellectuals led by Félicité de Lamennais, attempting to reconcile political liberalism with a deep devotion to the Church, denounced the Church's servitude under the *ancien régime,* advocated complete separation of Church and State, and thereby evoked condemnation of Gregory XVI (1831–46), who confused the divine mission of the Church with the status quo both in France and in Italy. This condemnation resulted in Lamennais' defection from the Church. Stopgap measures of reform were insufficient, and the Pope left a very difficult legacy to his successor, Pius IX.

The Papacy in the Modern World. Pius IX's reign (1846–78) is described as the longest and stormiest in the Church's history (A. Simon, 6:782–788). He manifested an initial liberalism, then a reactionary conservatism after the Revolution of 1848 resulted in the absorption, into the newly established Kingdom of Italy, of Romagna (1860), the Marches (1860), and Rome itself (1870). Rejecting all monetary compensation from the Italian state, Pius became the "prisoner of the Vatican"; the impasse was known as the Roman Question. Pius IX convoked Vatican Council I (1869–70), which defined papal infallibility, to the bitter displeasure of Protestants, and pronounced on the role of reason in faith. The Council was abruptly terminated by the war, which ended the pope's political independence. Pius IX's many dogmatic and doctrinal pronouncements (e.g., Immaculate Conception in 1854), his condemnation of various errors (*Syllabus of Errors*, 1864) are important. Pius was popular: his warmth, humor, even his sufferings, endeared him to Catholics (R. Aubert, 11:405–408). The next pope was a great contrast to his predecessor; Leo XIII (1878–1903) urged the Church to become involved, encouraged French Catholics to participate in political life and accepted the term "Christian democracy" (1901). Intransigent on the Roman Question, he nevertheless favored liberal governments in Belgium, Germany, France, and the U.S. (*Testem benevolentiae*, 1899). An intellectual, he revived the study of Thomistic philosophy (1879) and emphasized biblical studies (1893). His encyclical on labor (*Rerum novarum*, 1891) indicated the Church's concern for the working class, which had been too long ignored.

Pius X (1903–14) was deeply disturbed by doctrinal aberrations, condemning *modernism and thus alienating Catholic scholars (*Lamentabili*, 1907; *Pascendi*, 1907). Noted for personal sanctity and concern for liturgy, he legislated for frequent and early communion (1905, 1910). He was slightly less intransigent on the Roman Question; he also encountered bitterly anticlerical legislation, loss of church property, and secularization of schools in France (C.

Ledre, 11:408–411). The efforts of Benedict XV (1914–22) to help all victims of World War I and at the same time maintain strict neutrality were alike misconstrued. He contributed to the solution of the Roman Question, published the Code of Canon Law, and established a special congregation for the Oriental Churches. His attempts to mediate for peace (1914, 1917, 1919) were repulsed, but he aided Catholics in some newly established countries. Pius XI (1922–39) faced the bitter aftermath of World War I in the rise of totalitarian regimes in Mexico, Italy, Spain, Nazi Germany, and Eastern Europe. He addressed vigorous encyclicals, notably one on atheistic communism (1937), to the faithful in each country except Russia. He indicated social dimensions of Christianity (*Quadragesimo anno*, 1931) that would be advanced by Pius XII and even more dramatically by John XXIII in *Mater et magistra* (1961). Pius XI succeeded in solving the Roman Question by agreeing to establish Vatican City (109 acres) through the Lateran Treaty of 1929, receiving "a little corner of the earth where I may be master." Thus the Church surrendered the Papal States, yet retained political independence. Pius XI's encyclicals on moral questions, *Casti connubii* (1930), *Christian Education* (1929), and on mass media, *Vigilanti cura* (1936) are important. The reign of Pius XII (1939–58) began with the horrors of World War II (1939–45), which he had tried to prevent. He set up a Vatican Information Center for locating missing persons and worked in behalf of the Jews of Rome and Germany. He laid the intellectual foundations of Vatican Council II. He was the most accessible of popes, meeting more than 10 million persons, making over 3,000 pronouncements in his discourses and encyclicals. His successor, John XXIII (1958–63), can be described as the most popular pope who ever lived. His reign was an extraordinary event marked by two great encyclicals, *Mater et magistra* (1961) and *Pacem in terris* (1963), and by the convoking of Vatican Council II (1962–65), which restored the Church to the world. His impact was enormous; indeed "He put his arm around the world." By contrast his successor, Paul VI (1963–78), had a hard and painful pontificate. The accelerated pace of change, the problems of *aggiornamento* in a world torn by war, poverty, and racism, have demanded solutions with unprecedented urgency. Internally the Church is anguished by challenges to her authority over birth control, celibacy, obedience, and the right to freedom of inquiry. The prestige of the papacy has suffered a sharp decline; a pilgrim indeed, the Church in the late 20th cent. faces cruel dilemmas: more anguish than certitude, more losses than gains, more hope than happiness. BIBLIOGRAPHY: H. Grisar, *History of Rome and the Popes in the Middle Ages* (tr. L. Capadelta, 3v., 1912, repr. 1975); L. Hertling, *Communio: Church and Papacy in Early Christianity* (tr. J. Wicks, pa. 1972); Y. Renouard, *Avignon Papacy*, 1305–1403 (tr. D. Bethell, 1970); F. A. Ridley, *Papacy and Fascism: The Crisis of the Twentieth Century* (1937, repr. AMS); Mann; Pastor; Duchesne LP.

[C. M. AHERNE]

PAPADOPOULOS, CHRYSOSTOMOS (1868–1938), Greek Orthodox abp. of Athens from 1923. He had been a professor of theology and ecclesiastical history at the Orthodox seminary in Athens, 1911–23, and also at the Univ. of Athens from 1914. He published many historical works throughout his life. As abp. he was influential in political affairs; favored the ecumenical movement, but strongly disapproved of Greek Uniates.

[T. C. O'BRIEN]

PAPADOPOULOS, ISAIA (1852–1932), Catholic bp. of the Greek rite, who worked toward unification of Catholics in Greece. In 1883 he was sent as a young priest to the village of Malgara in N Greece, where, under difficult circumstances, he formed a community of Greek Catholics, which was soon recognized by civil authority. He established a temporary church, a school, and a rectory. His work extended to the Greek villages in the vicinity of Dandeli and likewise to the Bulgarians of Lisgar. In 1907, P. was appointed vicar general to the Byzantine rite Catholics by Abp. Giovanni Tacci, apostolic delegate to Constantinople. Pius X established an ordinariate for Byzantine rite Catholics (1911) and a year later, named P. the first bishop. In 1917 he was made the first assessor to the newly organized Sacred Congregation of the Oriental Churches. As bishop, he was succeeded in 1920 by Bp. George Calavassy. BIBLIOGRAPHY: OrientCatt 215–217.

[R. A. TODD]

PAPAL BLESSING, see APOSTOLIC BLESSING.

PAPAL BULL, see BULL, PAPAL.

PAPAL CEREMONY AND VESTURE. As bp. of Rome the pope generally celebrates the liturgy in the Roman rite. Differences from the ceremonial generally followed by bps. include the following items. Proper liturgical vestments include the *fanon*, related to the amice, though worn over the chasuble, and the *subcinctorium*, related to the maniple. A *cope* or large mantle is worn in solemn entries, as is the *tiara* or papal crown, although it is not part of the liturgical insignia. In the solemn entry the pope is generally carried in the *sedes gestatoria*, a type of sedan chair. Notable differences in his Mass include the chanting of the Gospel in both Latin and Greek and the reception of communion at the throne, with the wine generally received through a silver straw. Apart from the liturgy the pope generally wears a white cassock and zuchetto (skullcap), although the proper papal color is red. Ceremonies reserved to the pope include canonization, opening and closing of ecumenical councils, opening of the Holy Door in a Holy or Jubilee Year, blessing of the abp.'s pallium, and the blessing of the golden rose.

[J. DALLEN]

PAPAL CHAMBERLAIN, the title for monsignors who are attendants of the pope. *PAPAL HOUSEHOLD.

PAPAL COMMISSIONS, see COMMISSIONS, PAPAL.

PAPAL DOCUMENTS, see DOCUMENTS, PAPAL.

PAPAL ELECTIONS, the method of naming a pope. Since the primacy of St. Peter the Apostle has been continued in the person of the bp. of Rome, it is not surprising that in the beginning and until the 4th cent. the manner of choosing the pope was much the same as the manner of choosing other bps.: an election in which it seems that the bps. of the region, the local clergy, and adult laity participated. Beyond this general description of the elections little else is known. From the 4th to the 11th cent. Christian emperors and princes (e.g., Roman, Ostrogoth, Carolingian) very frequently influenced and directed the selection of the pope. If this arrangement reduced the tumult and turbulence that might otherwise have ensued, it had the marked disadvantage of raising to the supreme pontificate men likely to be too amenable to the civil rulers to whom they owed their election. In the 11th cent., at about the time of the Gregorian reform, church law began the transfer of the right of election to the college of cardinals. The decrees of Nicholas II in 1059, of Alexander III in 1179, and of Gregory X in 1274 (providing for the conclave) introduced a form of election that has remained substantially the same down to the present. But the last vestiges of direct secular intervention were not removed until the beginning of the present century (St. Pius X, 1904). At present Papal elections in the 20th cent. have been regulated by the *Vacantis apostolicae sedis*.

The actual regulation of a papal election, however, was set out in Paul VI's apostolic constitution, *Romano Pontifici eligendo* (Oct. 1, 1975). The number of electors is limited to no more than 120 cardinals (cardinals over 80 years of age were made ineligible by the *motu proprio* of that same Pope, *Ingravescentem aetatem*, Nov. 21, 1970). New norms for the conclave esp. to preserve secrecy are laid down, e.g., safeguards against electronic listening devices. The three modes of election—by acclamation, compromise, or ballot—are retained, but election by ballot requires for election that a candidate receive two-thirds of the votes plus one (John XXIII's *Summi Pontificis electio* stipulated simply two-thirds).

As the procedure for choosing the Pope is a matter within the competence of the Church, changes are always possible and may at times be desirable. It has been suggested that the choice of the pope be in the hands of the whole episcopal college, but if the bps. were to choose through a smaller committee set up for this purpose, the actual electoral body might not be too different from the present one, esp. if the Holy See continues the trend to widen and internationalize the college of cardinals. Whether a pope may name his successor (as two 6th-cent. popes are said to have done) is a disputed point among canonists and theologians. The general tradition of the Church seems opposed to it. BIBLIOGRAPHY: A. Swift, NCE 11:572–574; B. Forshaw, *ibid.* 4:114.

[S. E. DONLON]

PAPAL FLAG. (1) The flag symbolic of the papacy is, since the Concordat of 1929 with Italy, the state flag of Vatican City. It consists of two equal, vertical stripes, yellow at the hoist and white at the fly; the white displays the papal arms, crossed keys—gold for spiritual, silver for temporal power—bound together with red ribbon and surmounted by the *tiara. Before 1929 the flag was the pope's personal flag. In many church sanctuaries, not by requirement but as a symbol of loyalty, the papal flag stands along with the national flag of the country. The state arms of Vatican City are the tiara surmounting the gold and silver keys crossed in saltire (i.e., as a St. Andrew's cross) on a red field. The personal arms of the pope are the same, but with his personal coat of arms as the shield, behind which are the keys and tiara (Paul VI's arms are three silver *fleurs de lis* in the form of a triangle and six rounded pillars, also in a triangle). (2) The flag bestowed by medieval popes was known as the *vexillum S. Petri*. It was a banner of the gonfalon or flag type, usually a gold cross on a bordered silver field, cantoned by four disks, and signified papal power in secular and often military matters. In 1044 Benedict IX endowed Henry III with this papal flag, making Henry's campaign against the Hungarians a holy war. Many medieval rulers, including William of Montreuil, Roger I, and William the Conqueror, bore the papal flag to indicate papal support of their causes. Innocent III, under whom papal power reached its zenith, explained the flag's symbolism of sacred and secular power in a letter to the Czar of the Bulgars.

[R. J. LITZ]

PAPAL HOUSEHOLD, the lay and clerical officials with specific titles and functions at the personal service of the pope. During the time of the *States of the Church, the pope was traditionally surrounded by a court often quite similar to that of any sovereign in the European monarchic tradition. With the loss of the papal states and the European movement toward more democratic forms of government, many of these offices became purely honorific and anachronistic. Pope Paul VI reorganized the system in 1968, noting that at the Vatican Council II the bps. had been more in favor of the simple and the functional than the exterior and the decorative. The former papal court assumed an earlier designation as the papal or pontifical household (*Casa pontificia*) and is now divided into two sections, the papal family and the papal chapel, under the direction of the prefect of the Apostolic Office. Posts are held for a normal term of 5 years. The *Cappella pontificia* consists of those persons who function at religious services presided over by or in the presence of the pope. These include the cardinals themselves and other high members of various papal agencies. The papal family (*Famiglia pontificia*) consists of the immediate personal aides of the pope and include the substitute secretary of state, the secretary for the Council for the Public Affairs of the Church, the papal almoner, the vicar general for Vatican City and the president of the Pontifical

Ecclesiastical Academy. It also includes persons with such honorary titles as prothonotaries apostolic, prelates of honor of his holiness (formerly called domestic prelates), and chaplains of his holiness (formerly called papal chamberlains). Lay members of the papal family include the commandants of the Palatine and Swiss guards, of the papal gendarmerie, the delegate of Vatican City, and other administrative aides. BIBLIOGRAPHY: H. Scharp. *How the Catholic Church Is Governed* (tr. A. Derrick, 1960) 112–134.

[R. A. GRAHAM]

PAPAL LINE OF DEMARCATION (1494) was an imaginary line running N—S 370 leagues W of the Cape Verde Islands at longitude 46° 36' West. Its purpose was not an effort to divide the world between the two leading explorer-nations of the day, Spain and Portugal, but to settle the dispute raging about the spheres of influence of each. After the discovery of the New World, Spain was quick to lay claim to all lands explored or to be explored, providing they belonged to no other Christian ruler. Pope Alexander VI confirmed this claim in a papal bull of May 3, 1483. But Ferdinand V of Spain wanted more. Under pressure from this monarch, the Pope issued a bull, predated May 4, 1493, which set up a line of demarcation 100 leagues W of the Azores, as suggested by Columbus. Another bull, issued Sept. 26, 1493, unjustly revoked papal grants given to Portugal concerning lands it was in the process of exploring. The irate King John II of Portugal began war preparations, forcing Ferdinand and Isabella to relent and modify the line of demarcation to 370 leagues W of the Cape Verde Islands. The Treaty of Tordesillas (June 7, 1494) confirmed the revision. The new line of demarcation gave Portugal a larger portion of what is now Brazil and a share in the riches of the New World. BIBLIOGRAPHY: H. Vander Linden, "Alexander VI and the Demarcation of the Maritime and Colonial Domains of Spain and Portugal," *American Historical Review* 22 (1916–17) 1–20.

[D. G. NUGENT]

PAPAL PEACE PLAN, August 1, 1917. The peace proposal of Pope Benedict XV coincided with the third anniversary of the outbreak of World War I, which seemed a favorable opportunity for mediation. Although the casualties had already far exceeded those of any previous war, a military stalemate existed that offered little hope to either side for a complete realization of its objectives. In addition, war weariness and popular agitation for an end to the war had intensified during 1917, particularly among Socialists opposed to the established order. The Papal Peace Plan therefore went beyond the frequently expressed papal desire for peace to include "more concrete and practical proposals" that might serve as the basis for negotiations among the belligerents. The plan stipulated the "reciprocal restitution of occupied territories," including the evacuation of Belgium and of French territory, in return for the restitution of German colonies. Other territorial questions could then be settled in a conciliatory spirit of equity and justice. It is noteworthy that the papal plan also incorporated several principles of the so-called new diplomacy. These proposals proceeded from the fundamental point that "the moral force of right should take the place of the material force of arms." Thus the papal message advocated mutual disarmament, arbitration of international disputes, and freedom of the seas. Finally the plan suggested the principle of "a complete and reciprocal condonation" as a means of settling war costs and damages. In spite of repeated urging from the papal nuncio in Berlin, Eugenio Pacelli, the future Pius XII, the German government avoided any direct mention of Belgium, the restitution of which the Allies had demanded as a precondition for any negotiations. Thus the papal mediation effort failed, but the publication of the plan contributed to the growing sentiment for peace in the world. BIBLIOGRAPHY: H. Johnson, *Vatican Diplomacy in the World War* (1933).

[R. J. GIBBONS]

PAPAL PRIMACY, see PRIMACY OF THE POPE.

PAPAL REGISTERS, the letters and papers of popes preserved in the Vatican Archives. There are three series: the Vatican Registers, covering the pontificates from Innocent III (1198) to Clement VIII (1592–1605); the Avignon Registers covering the Avignonese papacy (1316–1415); and the Lateran Registers, covering the period 1389–1897. The Registers are neither complete nor exhaustive, but they are an obviously important resource. From canonical collections and other documents it is known that such registers were kept as early as the 4th century. BIBLIOGRAPHY: J. Gilchrist, NCE 10:977–978.

PAPAL STATES, see STATES OF THE CHURCH.

PAPAL VOLUNTEERS FOR LATIN AMERICA (PAVLA), a program for Catholic lay missionaries between the ages of 21 and 45 who volunteer to serve the Church in Latin America in education, medicine, and community development, usually for a minimum of 3 years. It was established in response to John XXIII's request, and approved by the Pontifical Commission for Latin America in April 1960. In the U.S. it is under the Bishops' Committee for Latin America and is administered by the Latin American Bureau of the U.S. Catholic Conference. Volunteers are recruited by PAVLA diocesan directors appointed by their bp. or by other Catholic organizations of priests and sisters dedicated to the lay apostolate. Fordham Univ. in New York operates two independent training institutions through the Center for International Formation: one, for the Spanish language, in Cuernavaca, Mexico; the other, for the Portuguese language at Petropolis, Brazil.

[M. B. MURPHY]

PAPAS, the Gr. word for father (Sl. *otcha, batoushka*), the general term of address for priests in the Byzantine tradition. Among the Russians the term "pope" (*pop*) derived from the Gr. *papas* and is sometimes used to address priests, although this is considered to be in poor taste. The patriarch of Alexandria is called pope, but since the 11th cent. the term generally refers to the distinctive title of the bp. of Rome.

[R. K. GOLINI]

PAPCZYŃSKI, STANISLAUS (1631–1701), Polish cleric who founded the Marian Fathers. A Piarist novice from 1654, he was ordained in 1661, and following his removal to Warsaw in 1663 became well-known both for his teaching and preaching. He was secularized in 1669 in order to found the Society of the Marian Clerics of the Immaculate Conception. The new congregation, with P. at its head, got under way at Korabiew in 1673, continuing after 1677 in Nowa Jerozolima outside Warsaw. Thereafter, until his death, he devoted his energies to the formal establishment of the Marians in conformity with the rule, the *Norma Vitae* (published 1687), he had devised. Approval was secured from the Holy See in 1701. P. also wrote *Prodromus Reginae Artium* (1669) and *Templum Dei Mysticum* (1675).

[E. M. GATES]

PAPEBROCH, DANIEL VON (1628–1714), Belgian Jesuit and Bollandist. He was appointed in 1659 to collaborate with J. van *Bolland and G. *Henschen in order to hasten the publication of the *Acta sanctorum*. He journeyed about Europe with Henschen in search of MSS (1660–62) and again in 1668 and 1680. He became involved in an acrimonious dispute with the Carmelites whose hostility he aroused by questioning their claim that their order had originated with the Prophet Elia. The Spanish Inquisition took the part of the Carmelites and in 1695 condemned the 14 volumes of the *Acta* published up to that time. Rome, however, did not confirm the decree of the Inquisition, which was revoked (1715) after P.'s death. BIBLIOGRAPHY: H. Delehaye, *A travers trois siècles, L'oeuvre des Bollandistes de 1615–1915* (1920).

[R. B. ENO]

PAPHNUTIUS, ST. (d. *c.*360), once a monk of the desert under the direction of St. *Anthony, bp. of a city in the Upper Thebaid. In the persecution under Maximinus Daza (308–313) P. was deprived of his right eye, hamstrung in his left leg, and forced to labor in the mines. At the Council of Nicaea (325), in the deliberations of which he took a prominent part, his mutilations made him an object of wonder and veneration to Constantine and the conciliar bishops. He is reputed to have turned the tide at the Council against a proposal to forbid clerics, married before their ordination, to continue living with their wives. At the Council of Tyre (335) he stood firmly by St. *Athanasius and rallied other Egyptian bps. to the cause of orthodoxy. BIBLIOGRAPHY: Butler 3:538–539; M. M. Hasset, CE 11:457; H. Leclercq, DACL 13:1358–61.

PAPIAS (d. *c.*130), bp. **OF HIERAPOLIS** in Asia Minor. What little is known of him is provided by Irenaeus and Eusebius. As described by Irenaeus he was a hearer of John, a companion of Polycarp, and a man of old times. He wrote, in five books, an exposition of the sayings (*logia*) of the Lord of which only a few fragments preserved in quotations by Irenaeus and Eusebius are extant. These are important as evidence of a tradition regarding the origins of the Gospels of Matthew and Mark. He held millenarian opinions like those of SS. Justin and Irenaeus. There are, accordingly, conflicting views on his value as an example of Christian thought. Irenaeus thought well of him, but Eusebius, who looked with disfavor on chiliastic speculation, considered him a man of small intelligence and wanting in critical judgment. Works: tr. and ed. J. Kleist, ACW 6 (1948). BIBLIOGRAPHY: Quasten 1:82–85; J. Chapman, CE 11:457–459; Lex AW 2215, bibliog.

PAPIAS THE LOMBARD (fl. *c.*1050), lexicographer. Probably a married cleric, P. dedicated his works to his two sons. He is credited with a Latin grammar and the *Elementarium doctrinae rudimentum*, an alphabetic glossary that served for centuries as an encyclopedic manual of reference, important in the development of medieval lexicography. BIBLIOGRAPHY: Manitius 2:717–724; 3:191–192, 790; O. J. Blum, NCE 10:980.

[O. J. BLUM]

PAPINI, GIOVANNI (1881–1956), Italian writer. The first half of his life was devoted to literary and philosophic pursuits in the attempt to discover and promote a system of founded humanistic values that would transcend positivist reductionism. For this purpose he inaugurated the review *Il Leonardo* (1903) and wrote several philosophical works exploring possibilities. In despair of philosophy he next turned to literature and literary criticism. World War I shattered any hopes in a humanist solution; he turned to a study of the Gospels, became a convert to Catholicism (1921), and spent most of the rest of his life publishing religious works to advance Christian ideas. Among his translated publications are: *Life of Christ* (tr. D. C. Fisher, 1923); *St. Augustine* (tr. M. P. Agnetti, 1930); *Laborers in the Vineyard* (tr. A. Curtayne, 1930, repr. 1970); *Letters of Pope Celestine VI to All Mankind* (tr. L. Murnasee, 1948); *Dante vivo* (tr. E. H. Broadus and A. Benedetti, 1969). P.'s most controversial work was *Il Diavolo* (1953; *The Devil*, tr. A. Foulke, 1954); it was put on the Index because it proposed *universalism or restorationism according to which in the end even Satan would be restored to grace.

[T. C. O'BRIEN]

PAPINI TARTAGNI, NICCOLÒ (1751–1834), historian, minister general of the Franciscan Conventuals

(1803–09). His historical contribution was principally in Franciscana, most important of which are: *Etruria francescana* (part 1ª, 1787; part 2ª unpublished); *Notizie sicure della morte, sepoltura, canonizzazione e traslazione di s. Francesco e del ritrovamento del di lui corpo* (1822; 1824); *Storia del Perdono di Assisi* (1824); *Storia di s. Francesco d'Assisi* (2 v. 1825–27); "Index Fratrum Minorum Conventualium qui scientias et artes, conducti, publice tradiderunt," *Miscellanea Francescana* 31 (1931), 32 (1932). His unpublished bibliographical works can be found in the archives of the general curia of the Franciscan Conventuals in Rome, among which is a supplement to Sbaraglis's *Scriptores.* BIBLIOGRAPHY: D. Sparacio, "Gli studi di storia e i minori conventuali," *Miscellanea Francescana* 20 (1919) 56–64; J. J. Smith, NCE 10:981.

[J. J. SMITH]

PAPIST, like papish and popish, a hostile epithetic, which became almost onomatopoetic, with echoes of apish and knavish, applied from the 16th cent. onwards to those who upheld the supremacy of the Roman Pontiff, and later adopted by some Roman Catholics in England in jocular mock-disparagement or as a mark of honor. The first use is in St. John Fisher's reference to Luther's calling them "so often in derisyon papistas, papastros, papanos, and papenses."

[T. GILBY]

PAPUA–NEW GUINEA: Independent (Sept. 16, 1975), a section of SE Guinea (pop. 2,600,000). Portions of Papua were explored and annexed by Germany and Great Britain in the late 19th century. In 1903 Britain transferred its section to Australia; and after World War I Germany did the same. Marists began mission work in Papua in 1847, helped for a time by priests from Milan. In 1889 the country became part of the Vicariate Apostolic of New Guinea. World War II greatly damaged the missions. Papua is now divided into the vicariates of Port Moresby, Samarai, and Yule Island; and the prefectures of Daru and Mendi. The division exists because of the variety of languages, the difficulty of transportation, and the scattered location of the Christians. Capuchins, Picpus Fathers, Monfortians, and Christian Brothers, together with several congregations of sisters, are at work. In 1976 there were 789,202 Catholics cared for by 481 priests, 694 brothers, and 904 sisters. Protestants have long worked in Papua: Anglicans, Methodists, Lutherans, Congregationalists, and the London Missionary Society. The total Protestant membership reported in 1968 was 198,637. BIBLIOGRAPHY: G. Goyau, *Le Christ chez les Papous* (1938); *Bilan du Monde* 2:670–671.

[P. DAMBORIENA]

PAPYRUS, a type of biblical MS named from the material on which it is written (see CODEX). The papyrus reed belongs primarily to Egypt. The reed was first cut into strips that were then laid parallel to one another. A second layer of the same material was then laid over the first, but now with the strips at right angles to those of the first layer, and the whole was pressed together (perhaps with a little glue) and smoothed with pumice-stone. Although only one side was normally used for writing, the finished papyrus was nearly as good as paper, and in dry climates has survived for many centuries. The important biblical papyri discovered in the last century are designated by the letter P plus a number, according to the time of discovery. BIBLIOGRAPHY: M. David and P. A. van Groningen, *Papyrological Primer* (4th ed. 1965). *CHESTER BEATTY PAPYRI; *NASH PAPYRUS; *DEAD SEA SCROLLS.

[D. J. BOURKE]

PARABLES OF JESUS. The English word "parable" is from the Greek *parabolē,* whose root meaning involves the placing of things side by side for the sake of comparison. The *parabolē* of the NT is the equivalent of Hebrew *mashal,* a word that covers such forms as proverbs (Lk 4.23), maxims (Lk 14.7–11), riddles (Mk 7.15–17), examples (Lk 12.15–21), figurative speech (Mk 4.33), similes (Mt 13.33), metaphors (Mt 5.14), and finally parables themselves. Contemporary research into the NT parable form has established some general certitudes about it, despite the fact that interpretations of specific parables differ. First, Jesus taught in parables, which the early Church readily translated into allegories. The parable makes its point as a totality, and the point is never exhausted by any one apprehension of it but can be apprehended afresh as the parable is retold in different situations. In an allegory the parts of the metaphor count and each individual part bears a one-to-one relationship with what it represents, as in the allegorization of the Sower parable in Mk 4.13–20. Secondly, both the allegorizing of the parables and their present context and application in the Gospels are the work of the Church and the Evangelists. To interpret a parable as a parable of Jesus, one must first reconstruct the original nonallegorical form of the parable and then interpret it as a parable in the context of the message of Jesus. Thirdly, the fundamental element in a parable is the element of metaphor, the comparison of the lesser known with the better known, so that, for example, as the Kingdom of God is the lesser known, aspects of its meaning are illuminated by something better known or more readily envisaged (e.g., Mt 13.44–46). Fourthly, the purpose of a parable at the time of Jesus was normally pedagogical; Jewish rabbis used them extensively to illuminate, illustrate, and instruct. In the case of Jesus, however, this normal use of the parable was subordinated to another and different use, namely, the proclamation of the presence and approach of the Kingdom of God. As employed by Jesus the parables of the kingdom challenged hearers to say what should not be said (Lk 10.30–36, the "Good" Samaritan), to applaud what should not be applauded (Lk 16.1–13, the Unjust Steward), and to recognize in the reversal of human judgments and human situations the sign of the in-breaking of God's kingdom (Lk 16.19–31; 18.10–14; 14.7–11).

Jesus' transformation of the parable into a vehicle of proclamation indicates the presence of a power to mediate to his hearers the experience of the kingdom. Such a power is particularly indicated in the parables of the Hidden Treasure and the Pearl (Mt 13.44–46), that "a man can suddenly be confronted by the experience of the kingdom of God and find the subsequent joy overwhelming and all-determinative" (Perrin *New Testament*). Just as the kingdom is a present reality in the teaching of Jesus, so also does it have a future aspect, as indicated by a group of parables: the Sower (Mk 4.3–9); the Mustard Seed (Mk 4.30–32); the Leaven (Mt. 13.33); the Seed growing of itself (Mk 4.26–29). All challenge the hearer to look to the future result. Jesus also employed the parable form for instruction or teaching, that is, to instruct the hearer to respond in various ways to the experience mediated by the proclamation, as in the Friend at Midnight (Lk 11.5–8) and the Importuned Judge (Lk 18.1–8). The emphasis placed upon the kingdom by the Synoptics is put in the Johannine tradition on the sending of Jesus by the Father. The challenge presented in the Synoptic tradition by the kingdom of God is presented in John by the person of Jesus (Jn 3.16–21). BIBLIOGRAPHY: C. H. Dodd, *Parables of the Kingdom* (1961); J. Jeremias, *Parables of Jesus* (1963); J. D. Crossan, NTS 18 (1972) 285–307; N. Perrin, *Rediscovering the Teaching of Jesus* (1967); *idem, New Testament: An Introduction* (1974); *idem, Jesus and the Language of the Kingdom* (1975).

[T. J. RYAN]

PARACELSUS, PHILIPPUS AUREOLUS (Philippus Theophrastus Bombastus von Hohenheim; 1493?–1541), German physician, alchemist, metallurgist, who also interested himself in philosophy, theology, and the occult. Having studied in Italy, P. traveled much in various countries as an army surgeon; later he practiced medicine and lectured in Strassburg, Basel, Nuremberg, Vienna, and Salzburg. He made important contributions to medicine by his discovery of some of the pharmaceutical uses of opium and of various metals. The antagonism aroused by his abrasive personality as well as his strange philosophical and theological views accounts for his many changes of residence. *Rosicrucianism in its earliest known form is traceable to the circle of his disciples, if not to P. himself. There is no truth in the claim that "bombast" in the sense of turgid and pretentious speech is derived from one of P.'s given names. BIBLIOGRAPHY: W. Pagel, *Paracelsus: An Introduction to Philosophical Medicine in the Era of the Renaissance* (1958).

[P. K. MEAGHER]

PARACLESIS (Gr. intercession), in Byzantine liturgy: (1) the *paraklētikos kanōn,* comprising nine odes (biblical canticles), a Gospel reading, and various prayers, to be sung in time of great need; (2) dispensation from fasting on certain feasts; (3) as an extension of the first meaning, prayers which someone requests from a priest either for himself or for someone else, common in Orthodox Greece.

[A. CODY]

PARACLETE, the advocate in heaven for Christ's followers who is also at work in behalf of the Christian community on earth. As a specific term, the word appears only five times in the NT and is peculiar to John. Although its sense varies, it has the active connotation of a helper, mediator, or intercessor; the translation comforter is unwarranted. John applies the term both to Christ (1 Jn 2.1) and to the Spirit (Jn 14.26), hence paraclete should not be taken as a name but as a functional designation. The meaning of these functions becomes clear only upon an inquiry into each Johannine pericope. In 1 Jn 2.1, the sinless Christ intercedes for man's forgiveness in heaven. John 14.16, however, speaks of "another advocate" who, in addition to Christ and after his departure, continues Christ's work, defends the Church, and accuses a sinful world. John 14.26 continues this presentation of the Spirit as a defender. The Spirit's role in Jn 15.26 is as a witness to the truth, testifying that Jesus is truly the one sent by the Father. A climax is reached in Jn 16.7 where a triple task is described: the Spirit will prove the world guilty of the innocent Christ's death, testify to that innocence through the Resurrection, and condemn *Satan, the prince of this world. BIBLIOGRAPHY: J. Behm, Kittel TD 5:800–814; EDB 1717–20; D. M. Crossan, NCE 10:989–990.

[T. M. MCFADDEN]

PARACLETE, SERVANTS OF THE HOLY (SP), a diocesan congregation of professed priests and clerics founded for the purpose of assisting and caring for priests, esp. those experiencing vocation crises. The institute was established at Jemez Springs, New Mexico, in 1947 by Fr. Gerald of the Holy Spirit (Gerald M. C. Fitzgerald) and was energetically supported by Card. Spellman, Abp. Edwin V. Byrne and Abp. William D. O'Brien. It was formally erected by Abp. Byrne in 1952. The common life is shared by both the Paracletes and their retreatants, and they participate with deep devotion in activities honoring the Eucharist, as by all day and night adoration and the offering of Masses around the clock on First Fridays. The generalate is located at Sunset Hills, Missouri, while the procurator general resides in Rome. The congregation has 10 houses and 54 members of whom 45 are priests.

[R. A. TODD]

PARADISE, the abode of the blessed. The word came to the Hebrews and the Greeks from a Persian word for "wooded park or enclosure." Through the influence of the LXX it came to be used in Hellenized Jewish circles to refer to the Garden of Eden. In apocalyptic literature it came to mean the abode of the righteous after death as they await the final judgment and resurrection. *Sheol came to be segregated into Paradise and Gehenna, with Paradise still retaining, however, its identity with Eden. There is lack of agreement as to actual location: whether on earth, in heaven, or in the third heaven (cf. 2 Cor 12.2–3). During the period of apocalyptic Judaism beliefs were in transition, as hope in the resurrection of the just gradually reshaped the symbolism of death and Sheol. First, Paradise was the original Garden of Eden; then it was that same Garden as the abode of the righteous dead awaiting their resurrection; finally, it was that garden as the eternal home of the righteous. The words of Jesus to the thief on the cross (Luke 23.43) reflect the second phase, and express his belief that on that day (''Today'') they would be together in that part of Sheol (Hades; Hell) reserved for the just awaiting resurrection. New Testament confidence in life beyond death is based upon Christ's Resurrection, and such life is called life with Christ. All such language was known to be symbolic, pointing in the direction of ultimate reality.

[E. J. DILLON]

PARAGUAY, an inland republic in S central South America (159,827 sq mi; pop. [est. 1972] 2,500,000; ethnic distribution: mestizo, with the Indian strain predominant, 82%; creole, 10%; foreigners, 3%). The illiteracy rate has been reduced to *c.* 20%. The region was discovered in 1524 by Alejo García and its conquest and colonization began in 1536. The city of Asunción was founded in 1541 and the territory was detached from the Buenos Aires *audiencia* in 1620. In the four decades that followed the declaration of independence from Spain (1811), Paraguay was ruled by dictators José Gaspar Rodríguez Francia (1814–40) and Carlos Antonio López (1840–62). During the regime of Francisco Solano López, who succeeded his father in 1862, the country became involved in the disastrous War of Triple Alliance (1864–70) in which López lost his life and Paraguay half of its population, which had numbered about 1 million. The Chaco War with Bolivia (1932–35) resulted in a military victory but also in heavy losses in men and resources. Since 1954 the government has been in the hands of Gen. A. Stroessner. Missionaries accompanied the conquistadors. Franciscans, Mercedarians, Hieronymites, Dominicans, and Jesuits were active in the field and did important work in languages and in defending the exploited Indians as they organized their missions and evangelized the people. For their unique achievement see PARAGUAY *RE-DUCTIONS OF. Asunción was made a suffragan see of Lima in 1547, but Pedro de la Torre, who was named bp., did not arrive until 1556. Because of its geographical isolation the country suffered much from episcopal absenteeism; only half the bps. appointed took actual charge of their sees. During the regime of José Francia there was confiscation of church property and expulsion of religious orders. Political tensions have contributed to the development of anti-clericalism among some segments of the population. Beginning in the 1920s there was some renewal in the life of the Church, mainly as the result of the work of different religious orders and congregations. Redemptorists, Francis-

cans, Servites, Salesians, and Jesuits, as well as a number of sisterhoods, have been active in missionary, parochial, educational, and social work. Catholic education is progressing, and the Catholic Univ. of Asunción, established in 1960, is beginning to exercise some influence upon public opinion. The Franciscans operate a popular radio station *Caritas*. There has been some effective activity among lay groups. Paraguay has one archiepiscopal see, Asunción, with three suffragan dioceses, Concepción (1929), Villarrica (1929), and San Juan Bautista (1957). There are two vicariates apostolic, Pilcomayo and Chaco Paraguayo, and three prelatures *nullius*, Encarnación y Alto Paraná, Caacupé, and Coronel Oviedo. In 1976 Paraguay had 2,310,000 Catholics, 447 priests, 236 parishes, 274 Catholic schools, and 106 charitable organizations. The principal Protestant denominations active in Paraguay are the Southern Baptist Convention, the New Testament Union, and the Mennonites; and more recently Mormons, Adventists, and Jehovah Witnesses have entered the field. Church membership of Protestant groups amounts to 36,000, with 200 missionaries and 285 national ministers.

[P. DAMBORIENA]

PARALIPOMENON, BOOKS OF, see CHRONICLES, BOOKS OF.

PARAMYSTICAL, an adjective used in reference to an authentic religious experience which has such intensity and such emotional and sensible content that it has a profound effect upon the person experiencing it, not unlike the effect produced by *mystical experience properly so called. The difference lies in the agent or efficient cause, a strictly mystical experience has God for its direct and immediate cause, whereas the paramystical is in large measure the immediate work of man. The effect in the life and conduct of the man is also different in that the true mystical experience will always produce spiritual growth while the paramystical may be vitiated by unworthy human motivation. Finally, the paramystical is ordinarily a transient experience while true mysticism may develop into a perduring state of life. *MYSTICAL PHENOMENA.

[M. B. PENNINGTON]

PARAN (PHARAN), DESERT OF, a desert mentioned several times in the OT, whose precise localization is difficult. According to Gen 21.21 it is the home of Ishmael and his descendants. Numbers 10.12; 13.3,26 (P tradition) list it as a step in Israel's journey from Sinai to Canaan, and as the site from which scouts set out and to which they returned. Deuteronomy 1.1 is extremely vague regarding its position. Going from Midian to Egypt, Hadad of Edom passed through Paran (1 Kg 11.18). In Dt 33.2 and Hab 3.3 it is the site of a theophany patterned on Israel's desert march. Genesis 14.6 is not clear. One can only say that Paran is S of Judah, in the Negeb, and S of Kadesh-barnea, perhaps extending down as far as Elath.

[I. HUNT]

PARANOIA, a psychotic disorder usually occurring later in life (after 30), characterized by elaborate and logically worked out systems of delusional thinking, usually centering on ideas of personal grandeur or of persecution. In true paranoia, the delusional system is usually kept separate from the person's normal, realistic thinking; there is little personality disorganization and such a person can often live a productive life. The condition however is chronic and virtually incurable. In paranoid states there are delusions often associated with schizophrenic symptoms of personality disorganization. These attacks are often of short duration and the illness may go undetected. Paranoids are generally not dangerous in society unless their delusions generate hostility which centers on one or a few people. Paranoia and paranoid states are probably of psychological origin, stemming from frustrated ambitions, the pressure of anxiety-producing internal drives, deeply injured self-esteem, etc. The paranoid tends to handle these problems by rationalization and the projection of hostile impulses and hates upon other people. When the force of his defensive needs drives these processes to the point at which he loses contact with reality, i.e., when facts contrary to his rationalizations can no longer correct his thinking but are subject to being worked into the delusional system by any kind of distortion, the person is paranoid. As in all psychoses, the moral responsibility of the subject is minimal; he lacks the capacity to evaluate the delusional thought processes rationally and the freedom to make decisions based on reality. Since however he can profit from a congenial environment, the counselor or clergyman who can use his influence in this direction can provide genuine, effective support. BIBLIOGRAPHY: F. J. Braceland and M. Stock, *Modern Psychiatry: A Handbook for Believers* (1963).

[M. E. STOCK]

PARAPSYCHOLOGY (sometimes called "metaphysics"), the term used to designate the serious study of physical and psychological phenomena which are apparently inexplicable in terms of generally accepted scientific laws and principles. These phenomena, called psi-phenomena, include the psychological capacities for extrasensory perception (ESP), either as mental telepathy, *clairvoyance or premonition, and physical phenomena (called psychokinesis), i.e., physical actions caused by the power of the mind. The scientific study of these phenomena (for which J. B. Rhine is most famous in America) involves statistical analysis of the results produced by subjects trying to exercise paranormal capacities under controlled conditions, in order to detect patterns which cannot be explained as random effects. BIBLIOGRAPHY: C. P. Svoboda, NCE 10:994–997; R. Omez, *Psychical Phenomena* (tr. R. Haynes, 1958).

[M. E. STOCK]

PARASCEVE, from the Gr. meaning preparation, a term applied by Hellenistic Jews to the evening before the sabbath, or to the day of preparation for the Sabbath. In Christian usage it was until 1955 the liturgical name for *Good Friday, which was known as *feria sexta in parasceve*, but the preparation was understood to refer not to the Sabbath but to the Resurrection of the Lord.

[P. K. MEAGHER]

PARAVICINO Y ARTEAGO, HORTENSIO FÉLIX (1580–1633), pulpit orator. A native of Madrid, P. entered the Trinitarians in 1600. His oratorial powers caused Philip III and Philip IV to name him court preacher. His discourses are esteemed among the great masterpieces of Spain's golden age. A lyric poet, P. wrote among other poems "The Divine Passion", "To Our Lady of Guadalupe" and "Sonnet on the Tomb of the Painter Who Was 'El Greco' of Toledo."

[J. R. AHERNE]

PARAY-LE-MONIAL, a city in the Burgundy section of France (Saône-et-Loire department). A *Cluniac foundation was established there (973), and Christ appeared to St. Margaret Mary Alacoque (1673–75) at the Visitation Convent within the city. The relics of this saint and a shrine in honor of the Sacred Heart are a popular object for religious pilgrimages. BIBLIOGRAPHY: M. L. Lynn, NCE 10:997–998.

[T. M. MCFADDEN]

PARCLOSE, a screen that in many ancient, medieval and Baroque churches divided a side chapel from the rest of the church, or the choir from the aisles on either side of it. *CHOIR SCREEN.

[T. C. O'BRIEN]

PARDON, see FORGIVENESS OF SINS.

PARDONER, in English church history, name for a priest empowered to grant indulgences. The often disparaging use of the term reflects the abuses connected with indulgences and their "sale" (see OED).

PARDOW, WILLIAM O'BRIEN (1847–1909), preacher, educator. Descendant on both sides of families long associated with Catholic struggles in Ireland, P. was born in the U.S. and entered the Society of Jesus in 1865. In 1877 he was ordained in France at a time when the Jesuits were being expelled. Returning to the U.S. he taught and administered a parish before being elected in 1893 as provincial of the New York-Maryland Province. Succeeding years saw P. as teacher and pastor, his last assignment as pastor of St. Ignatius in New York. P. was a fiery preacher known from coast to coast. His notes were published in 1916 under the title *Searchlights of Eternity*.

[J. R. AHERNE]

PAREDES Y FLORES, MARIANNA DE JESÚS, ST. (1618–45, "the Lily of Ecuador"). Descended from a noble Castilian family, she was placed under the care of relatives, the De Caso family, after the death of her parents. Spiritually mature, she dedicated her life to God at the age of 10. A spiritual advisor of her choice, Hernando de la Cruz, was appointed; her confessor was Alonso de Rojas. Remaining a lay person, she joined the Third Order of St. Francis, but wore a black Jesuit garb. She fed the poor, taught little children including poor Indians in the bright upper room set aside for her prayer. Her models were SS. Rose of Lima, Catherine of Siena, and Teresa of Ávila. After a life of prayer, suffering, and mortification, she died having offered her life publicly in reparation to stop the ravages of an earthquake. She is buried in nearby Jesuit grounds. As she predicted, her house is now a Carmelite convent. She was canonized by Pope Pius XII in 1950. BIBLIOGRAPHY: F. P. Keyes, *Rose and the Lily* (1961); J. I. Tellechea, BiblSanct 8:1034–35; Butler 2:401.

[A. P. HANLON]

PAREJA, FRANCISCO DE (d. 1628?), Franciscan missionary. A Castilian. P. joined the Franciscans working in Florida. Elected provincial of the missionary area of Cuba, Georgia, and Florida, he was known for his zeal and for his writings. Four works in Spanish and the language of the Timucuan Indians were published in Mexico. Two of these were *Catecismo en lengua castellana y timuquana* (1612) and *Arte y pronunciación en lengua timuquana y castellana* (1614).

[J. R. AHERNE]

PAREKKLESIA (Gr., beside the church), in some cathedrals and larger churches a side chapel with its own altar, prothesis, diaconicon and icon screen which forms in effect a separate church. This allows for the celebration of a second Liturgy and the placement of a second altar which is legally forbidden in Orthodox tradition. The term is also applied to a small separate building consecrated for divine worship near a larger church.

[J. FRANCAVILLA]

PARGOIRE, JULES (1872–1907), French Assumptionist, author of the important *L'Église byzantine de 527 à 847* (1905). He also contributed numerous articles to Byzantine publications and to encyclopedias of liturgy, archeology, and history.

[M. J. SUELZER]

PARHAM, CHARLES FOX (1873–1937), a chief founder of Pentecostalism. P. was a preacher in the *Holiness movement when he opened Bethel Bible College at Topeka, Kans., in 1900. There early in 1901 he and his students became convinced by their experience that *baptism with the Holy Spirit was essentially connected with, and manifested by *glossolalia. Efforts to spread the message failed, however, until in 1903 at Galena, Kans., he included *divine healing. The Apostolic Faith movement, as he called

it, spread throughout Kansas, Missouri and Texas; it was not unified because he opposed any form of ecclesiastical organization. One of P.'s disciples at Houston, Tex., was W. J. Seymour, who later led the Azusa Street Revival. Because of alleged sexual deviation, P. has sometimes been ignored even by Pentecostal writers, but he must be recognized as a pioneer of modern Pentecostalism. BIBLIOGRAPHY: J. T. Nichol, *Pentecostalism* (1966), 26–32; N. Bloch-Hoell, *Pentecostal Movement* (1964) 18–29.

[T. C. O'BRIEN]

PARIS, UNIVERSITY OF, a state institution of medieval origin, one of the 19 comprising the National Univ. of France. The university developed (1150–70) from the cathedral school of Notre Dame, the abbey school of Ste. Geneviève, and the school of St. Victor, which together made Paris a center of attraction for masters and scholars from the whole of Europe. The schools were under the jurisdiction of the chancellor of the Île de Cité, who alone had the right to issue the license to teach. To offset this authority, which was widely resented, and to guarantee more educational autonomy, the students and professors formed a union or *conjuratio*, later called *universitas*, for which they sought papal protection. King Philip Augustus granted the *conjuratio* certain privileges in 1200; in 1208 Innocent III allowed the students and professors to draw up their own regulations; and in 1215, through his legate, Robert de Courçon, the Pope freed them from the control of the cathedral chancellor. In the 1220s the mendicant orders—Dominicans and Franciscans, and later Carmelites and Augustinians—established colleges in Paris for the theological education of their own brethren and also began teaching at the university. In 1231 Gregory IX's bull *Parens scientiarum*, defined relations between the bishop and the university, granted the university extensive privileges, reconfirmed its autonomy, and recognized it as a fully developed *studium generale* composed of four faculties, theology, canon law, medicine, and arts. This last was divided into four nations of students and professors: French, Picard, Norman, and English (which later became German). Each faculty had a dean, each nation a proctor. The dean of the faculty of arts from as early as 1244 was possibly also the rector of the university. By 1250 conflict began between the friars and secular masters, and a bitter controversy raged between Averroists and moderate Aristotelians. The secular masters addressed an appeal to the monarchy and papacy. Louis IX sided with the friars; and although Innocent IV supported the seculars, his successor, Alexander IV, revoked Innocent's bull and in 1255 issued his own, *Quasi lignum vitae*, which favored the friars. As a result the secular declared the dissolution of the university and promoted a boycott against the friars—a disturbance that, despite several papal bulls, did not end until the accession of Urban IV. From the mid-13th cent. to the late 14th, the university was an acknowledged intellectual center, esp. in theology. Among its outstanding scholars were Roger Bacon, Alexander of Hales, Bonaventure, Albert the Great, Thomas Aquinas, Duns Scotus, William of Ockam, and Jean Gerson. The university's involvement in the Western Schism (1378–1417) which caused students and masters to seek other intellectual centers, its political entanglements and reverses, its scholastic mediocrity during the Renaissance, and the ravages of the Protestant Reformation, contributed to the undermining of its prestige in the 15th and 16th centuries. The 17th cent. found in it little response to the prevailing philosophical currents or the first stirrings of scientific vigor. With the election of Card. Richelieu as headmaster of the *Sorbonne in 1622, the university became an active theological center and the hub of Parisian intellectual life. An edict of 1679 reformed and reorganized French universities, Paris among them. Again political involvement, the neglect of research, and an unwillingness to make a place in the curriculum for subjects of contemporary importance, caused the glory of the university to decline. Like other French universities, it disappeared during the French Revolution, which aimed at annihilating all institutions of the *ancien régime*. Its faculties were revived (1804–08) but they functioned in considerable isolation from each other until 1898 when they were federated again into a university. The present status of the university as a part of the National Univ. of France dates from 1920. BIBLIOGRAPHY: H. Rashdall, *Universities of Europe in the Middle Ages* (ed., F. M. Powicke and A. B. Emden, 3 v., 1936); P. Kibre, *Nations in the Medieval University* (1948); *Scholastic Privileges in the Middle Ages* (1962).

[M. B. MURPHY]

PARIS FOREIGN MISSION SOCIETY, a religious institute of secular priests who take no vows but promise to serve for life in the foreign missions; founded in France *c*.1660 by François Pallu, later vicar apostolic in SW China, with the active collaboration of his colleague Pierre Lambert de la Motte. Already in that day some farsighted missionaries, notably the Jesuit Alexandre de Rhodes, saw the need for a native clergy in the Far East. Pious French clergy and laity, such as members of the Compagnie du Saint-Sacrement, were eager to aid in evangelizing newly discovered lands. For different reasons, both Louis XIV and the newly created Curial Congregation Propaganda Fidei wanted to wrest control of the foreign missions away from the Spanish and Portuguese crowns. The combined efforts of these forces led to the regular appointments of vicars apostolic in the Far East charged with the formation of a native clergy, and a seminary was founded in Paris in 1663 to prepare missionaries to advance these goals. The Society's activities centered at first in Tonkin, Cochinchina, Siam, and W China; they were later extended to include S India (1776), Japan, and Korea (1831), Manchuria (1838), Tibet (1846), the Chinese provinces of Koang-Tong, Koang-Si, the Hainan (1848), Burma (1855), and Malaysia (1899). Seminaries for native clergy were opened in Siam (1665), Cochinchina (1665), Tonkin (1666), and China

(1703 and again in 1777). There were 19 such seminaries in 1845; 41 in 1900; 75 in 1939. The year 1909 was the peak year for the Society's membership which included 38 bishops, 1,377 priests, and could claim 783 native priests formed by the Society. In 1920 Propaganda had entrusted to the Society territories comprising 250 million peoples. In 1963 its membership included 24 bp., but its 849 priests also served 21 native bishops. In 1977 the Society's 683 priests served only native bishops. In its long history, 16 of its members (in China, Korea, and Tonkin) eventually came to be numbered among the beatified martyrs. BIBLIOGRAPHY: J. Guennou, NCE 10:1016–; cf. H. Prouvost, NCE 10:932–933; A. da Silva Rego, NCE 10:1114–15; W. M. Porras, NCE 10:1115–16; AnnPont (1977) p. 1228.

[E. J. DILLON]

PARISH, in ecclesiastical usage, a term with several meanings: (1) a subdivision of a diocese, which has its own church building and is under the authority of a rector, parish priest, or pastor responsible for the care of souls (the parish as a civil unit—e.g., in England equivalent to a township, in Louisiana, to a county—corresponds to older ecclesiastical divisions); (2) any local church or congregation and its sphere of activity; (3) a collective word for members of a parish in either of the above senses; (4) the charge of a pastor.

Meanings (1) and (2) have certain ecclesiological connotations. Etymologically the word comes, through the Lat. *paroecia,* or *parochia,* from the Gr. *paroikia,* a word used in early Christian times, like *ekklēsia,* to designate the local Christian community under the care of a bishop. Until the 6th cent. the terms parish and diocese were interchangeable. The roots of differentiation go back to the 2d cent., when multiplication of places of worship served by priests of the bishop's household became necessary; by the 4th cent. the stationing of priests in rural areas began (see ARCHDEACON, ARCHPRIEST). By the 5th cent. the fixing of boundaries started; the bishop's control, however, was always maintained. The territorial principle remained constant as parishes were established where abbeys or feudal lords built churches for the populace. The parish system during the Middle Ages was beset by the abuses of lay investiture and plural benefices. With the Council of Trent reform was initiated that remained the basis of the modern RC parochial system. The parish in its first, territorial meaning, presupposes that all the people in a given area are members of the Church universal as one, visible society; it implies their juridic assignment to the care of a pastor in order to provide for their spiritual needs. That meaning (2) has no such connotations is based ultimately on a different conception of the Church and *membership in the Church. While the territorial parish continued in the Lutheran and English Reformation, in other traditions it did not. The Reformed, or Presbyterian, Congregationalist, Baptist, and Methodist traditions have, in various ways, conceived of the Church as embodied in the local congregation. Members, as it were, make the Church to exist by gathering or covenanting together; they are not thought of as first belonging to the Church universal, then being assigned to a local jurisdiction. (See INVISIBLE CHURCH; GATHERED CHURCH.) The Anabaptists, Mennonites, Quaker, and similar groups also spiritualized the meaning of the Church as the voluntary union of those who share a similar inner Christian experience.

Distinction between the two uses of the term is diminishing, however. The territorial sense of parish is less and less significant in the circumstances of modern mobility and psychology. More importantly, theology has given new prominence to the Church as the assembled community of Christ. The parish is thus thought of as the active, voluntarily gathered community in which the Church is actually expressed and concretely present, esp. as the community actively participates in the Eucharistic celebration. BIBLIOGRAPHY: *Parish* (tr. R. Kress, ed. H. Rahner, 1954); C. Floristan Semanes, *Parish, Eucharistic Community* (tr. J. F. Byrne, 1964).

PARISH, TERRITORIAL, see TERRITORIAL PARISH.

PARISH COUNCILS, a mechanism devised to attempt to bring the reforms of Vatican Council II to the parish level. Vatican Council II made a recommendation of pastoral councils with a broad mandate to investigate and weigh matters that bear on pastoral activity and to formulate pastoral strategies (VatII BpPastOff 27). These were to include priests, religious, and lay persons. It was natural to apply this general directive to the parish structure. The effect to date has not been impressive, at least in regard to more mature lay participation. Also for such nourishment as that provided by the cursillo, marriage encounter, and charismatic prayer groups, parishioners often go outside the parish structure. In addition, priests, religious, and esp. women religious have shown themselves far more adept at organizing to place their agenda before the church leadership, than have the laity. BIBLIOGRAPHY: J. P. Boyle, AER 169 (1975) 592–609.

[E. J. DILLON]

PARISH CENSUS, a pastoral instrument intended to aid in ministering to the spiritual needs of the congregation. Canon law (CIC, c. 470) requires each pastor to maintain a register of the spiritual condition of all individuals or families within parish boundaries (*Liber de statu animarum*). The census should include names, addresses, and information about the ages, occupations, and religious practice of all family members. With this information, the pastor should be better able to offer meaningful guidance to each family. The compilation of the census, either by parish clergy or by seminarians or members of religious orders, affords opportunities for dialogue with those whose attendance at church is not frequent, as well for ecumenical encounters.

[R. A. ARONSTAM]

PARISH CHURCH, see CHURCHES.

PARISH PRIEST, or pastor, the priest or moral person, e.g., a religious order, having title to a parish and responsibility for the souls therein, subject to the jurisdiction of the local ordinary. (CIC c. 451.1; ClerSanct c. 489.1). Legal division of dioceses into separate parishes did not take place throughout the Church until the Council of Trent (1545–63). In his parish, the parish priest has specified disciplinary and administrative responsibilities, which include administering the sacraments as needed, making himself known to the faithful, teaching Christian doctrine to the young and adults, preventing anything dangerous to faith and morals, ministering to the troubled and those in need, and encouraging all activities that enhance the Christian life. BIBLIOGRAPHY: B. M. Kelly, NCE 10:1075; F. Claeys-Bouuaert, DDC 4:900–941; C. J. Koudelka, *Pastors: Their Rights and Duties According to the New Code of Canon Law* (CUA CLB Washington, 1921).

[F. H. BRIGHAM]

PARISH REGISTERS, the records that, according to CIC, c. 470§1, the pastor is required to keep on baptisms, confirmations, marriages, deaths; also the parish census (*liber de statu animarum*). Each year copies of all but the last must be sent to the bishop. These records are to be kept, with other documents essential to the history and status of the parish, in the parish archives; they are inspected at the time of the bp.'s official visitation (*ibid*. §4). The baptismal record of each person is kept up to date by the notation of confirmation, marriage, solemn religious vows, or sacred ordination; such notations are to be included on a requested baptismal certificate (*ibid*. §2).

[T. C. O'BRIEN]

PARISH VISITORS OF MARY IMMACULATE (PVMI), contemplative women religious dedicated to restoring the spirit of the Holy Family to the home. Mother Mary Teresa (Julia Teresa) Tallon (1867–1954) founded the congregation in New York City in 1920. After diocesan approval was given, the institute was canonically established in 1927. Working with the pastor and his associates, the visitors take the *parish census, make spiritual surveys of the parish and in this way assess the spiritual, psychological, social and material needs of the family and the individuals in it. The sisters introduce CCD programs in parishes and also visit orphanages, jails, and homes for the aged and the physically and mentally handicapped. In 1976 the congregation had a membership of 118 sisters engaged in mission work in nine archdioceses and dioceses. The motherhouse is located at Monroe, New York.

[R. A. TODD]

PARISHIONER, a Christian who resides in that portion of the diocese under the authority of the pastor or parish priest who is responsible for his or her welfare. BIBLIOGRAPHY: C. K. Riepe, NCE 10:1017–19; H. Rahner ed. *The Parish* (tr.

R. Kress, 1958); C. Floristan Semanes, *The Parish Eucharistic Community* (tr. J. F. Byrne, 1964).

[F. H. BRIGHAM]

PARISIS, PIERRE LOUIS (1795–1866), French bp. prominent in the Catholic liberal movement sparked by *Montalembert and H. de *Lamennais. Ordained in 1819, P. served as bp. of Langres from 1834 to 1851, then, until his death, as bp. of Arras. An anti-Gallican from the start, he is known chiefly for his struggle on behalf of the Church's liberties, esp. in the area of education. He was an early supporter of Montalembert, while his *Cas de conscience* (1847) reflected Lamennais' liberal position. As a member of the National Assembly during the life of the Second Republic, he opposed the government-sponsored Falloux educational bill, even though it favored the Church, but otherwise supported Louis Napoleon until the Emperor's propapal policy was dropped as inexpedient. In the meantime, P. had dissociated himself from the Catholic liberals to embrace *ultramontanism. His *Cas de conscience sur les libertés publiques* (1865) conformed to Rome's needs.

[E. M. GATES]

PARK (LE PARC), MONASTERY OF, Premonstratensian abbey at Louvain, Belgium, founded in 1128 by Duke Godfrey of Brabant and by the abbey of St. Martin, Laon. This important monastery served many parishes; its abbots were mitred since 1462. A center of reform in the 17th cent., it was suppressed in 1789 and 1797, but was restored in 1834 and became an abbey again in 1872. Since 1896 it has dependent houses and serves parishes in Brazil. The church (12th cent.) and the beautiful monastery (16th-18th cent.) are monumental; its archives are rich. BIBLIOGRAPHY: Hugo 2:473 ff.; Backmund 2:317–322.

[N. BLACKMUND]

PARKER, MATTHEW (1504–75), abp. of Canterbury, born at Norwich, and educated at Cambridge. Appointed chaplain to Anne Boleyn in 1535, and to Henry VIII 2 years later, much of his career was devoted to academic administration as dean of Stoke-by-Clare College, master of Corpus Christi College at Cambridge, and for a time vice-chancellor at Cambridge. While an undergraduate he had imbibed some ideas of reform from Lutheran writings, but he adopted only a few basic Reformation principles. Relatively conservative but broadly tolerant, he was well fitted as Elizabeth I's abp. of Canterbury to lead in the development of a Church representing a *via media*. He helped to fashion Anglican doctrine by sharing in the formulation of the *Thirty-Nine Articles, and he firmly adhered to the *Book of Common Prayer with its required ceremonies and vestments. Although he wrote some books, his chief scholarly contribution was the preservation of hundreds of ancient MSS. His episcopal ordination has been a key issue in the controversies over Anglican Orders. BIBLIOGRAPHY: V. J. K. Brook, *Life of Archbishop Parker* (1962). *ANGLICAN ORDERS.

PARKER, THEODORE (1810–60), American Unitarian minister. After graduating from Harvard Divinity School in 1836, he became a Unitarian minister. Ralph Waldo *Emerson and American transcendentalism exercised lasting, but not determinative influence on his thought; Kant, Schleiermacher, and H. T. Buckle were also important sources of his philosophical development. His South Boston sermon, "The Transient and the Permanent in Christianity" (1841), and the publication of *A Discourse of Matters Pertaining to Religion* (1842) aroused the hostility of the Boston Unitarian clergy against his rationalistic views of religion. Parker was a scholar, proficient in the use of many languages; a forceful preacher; and a firm advocate of social reform, esp. abolition of slavery. He ranks with William Ellery *Channing as one of the two greatest leaders of American Unitarianism. BIBLIOGRAPHY: *Collected Works of Theodore Parker* (ed F. Cobbe, 12 v., 1863–65); *Works of Theodore Parker* (centenary edition, 15 v., 1907–11); H. S. Commager, *Theodore Parker* (1936); J. E. Dirks, *Critical Theology of Theodore Parker* (1948); W. R. Hutchison, *Transcendentalist Ministers* (1959).

[J. C. GODBEY]

PARKINSON, ANTHONY (1667–1728), English Franciscan and historian. A teacher of philosophy at the Franciscan college in Douai (France) from 1692, he returned to his native England in 1698, serving first as superior of his order at Warwick and then at Birmingham. He was twice the Franciscan provincial (1713–16 and 1722–25). He is principally remembered for his historical work the *Collectanea Anglo-Minoritica, or a Collection of the Antiquities of the English Franciscans or Friars' Minor Commonly Called Gray Friars* (1726).

[E. M. GATES]

PARKMINSTER, St. Hugh's Charterhouse, a Carthusian monastery in Horsham, Sussex, England. Founded in 1873 it served as a refuge for religious orders expelled from France. There are cells for 36 choir monks and 50 lay brothers and a valuable library. Parkminister is the only charterhouse remaining in England today. Its spire is a well-known landmark.

[M. A. MCFADDEN]

PARLER, family of 14th-cent. German masons and stone sculptors in S Germany and Bohemia. **Heinrich,** master mason probably from Cologne, designed the famous late Gothic Holy Cross Church at Schwäbisch-Gmünd and the chancel at Ulm Cathedral (1377). His son, **Peter** (c. 1330–99) the most important master, designed the major part of St. Vitus cathedral, Prague (1353–85), directing construction after the death of Matthew of Arras until 1385, and planned St. Bartholomew, Kolín, and St. Barbara, Kutná

Hora. In his cathedral carvings Peter injected a new rugged realism into Bohemian sculpture. **Johannes** worked on the cathedral in Freiburg-im-Breisgau (1354), and **Heinrich** of Gmünd advised on the Milan Cathedral.

[M. J. DALY]

PARLIN, CHARLES COOLIDGE (1898–), lawyer and influential lay person who, from 1940 to 1970, was elected to and actively participated in nine separate sessions of the General Conference, the highest legislative body of the *United Methodist Church. He was born in Wausau, Wis., he received his higher education at the Univ. of Pennsylvania and Harvard. After serving in World War I, he was admitted to the bar in 1923, eventually becoming senior partner of Shearman and Sterling, New York City in 1945. He has served on numerous church committees and commissions and has been active in the work of the National Council of Churches of Christ. He was chairman of the committee in the U.S. to raise money for the founding of the *World Council of Churches. He attended the founding, Amsterdam Assembly in 1948 as well as succeeding Assemblies in 1954, 1961 and 1968. In addition, he was one of the Presidents of the *World Methodist Council (1970–71) and a member of the Praesidium of the World Council of Churches 1961–68. In 1970 he was honored by a testimonial dinner at the General Conference of the *United Methodist Church at their sessions in St. Louis. Nearly the entire conference attended. BIBLIOGRAPHY: *Encyclopedia of World Methodism* (1974).

[F. E. MASER]

PARMENIAN (d. 391 or 392), Donatist primate, orator, and theologian. He was born in Gaul or Spain, where he came to know Donatus in exile, and was consecrated a bp. in 355. He went to Carthage in 362, where he became Donatus's successor. He brought the Donatist Church through a series of internal crises, and under his rule it reached the height of its power and prosperity. P. wrote one work, consisting of five treatises, on the Donatist view of the Church; and a similar public letter to which Augustine wrote a rebuttal. BIBLIOGRAPHY: W. H. C. Frend, *Donatist Church* (1952) 193–207.

[M. J. COSTELLOE]

PARMENIDES OF ELEA (c.515–c.445 B.C.), founder of the Eleatic School and one of the greatest of the Presocratics. He presented his ideas in an allegorical poem describing his chariot-journey from the House of Night to the House of Day, where he meets a goddess whom he makes the expounder of his teaching. His fundamental doctrine is that Being, the One, is, and that becoming, change, is an illusion. In religion, he accepted the monistic view of divinity advanced by *Xenophanes of Colophon. He held that there are three ways of thought, that It is, that It is not, that It is and is not. His approach to cosmology and cosmogony is based on human belief and experience. His analysis of the ways of thought introduced method into philosophy and led him to discover the principle of contradiction and to point the way to the possibility of strict logical proof. His distinction between reason and sense and between truth and appearance, his emphasis on the One, and his denial of becoming and change, exercised a deep influence on all subsequent Greek philosophy. Despite his stimulation to the development of idealism, he is not to be classed as an idealist himself, but rather as a materialistic monist. BIBLIOGRAPHY: OCD 648; Lex AW 2223–24; Copleston 1:47–53; Guthrie 2:1–80.

[M. R. P. MCGUIRE]

PARMIGIANINO (PARMIGIANO), really Girolamo Francesco Maria Mazzola (1503–41). Virtuoso Emilian mannerist artist whose supremely elegant style shows the influence of Correggio and Raphael in self-portrait in a convex mirror, *Marriage of St. Catherine,* and an "aristocratic" *Vision of St. Jerome.* His major works are *Madonna with St. Zachary, Cupid Sharpening His Bow,* and the famous *Madonna of the Long Neck* (1535). More important than his paintings for the development of 16th-cent. art are P.'s numerous drawings and etchings. BIBLIOGRAPHY: S. J. Freedberg, *Parmigianino: His Works in Painting* (1950).

[L. A. LEITE]

PARNELL, CHARLES STEWART (1846–1891), Irish nationalist and leading proponent of Home Rule. Born in County Wicklow the son of a wealthy Protestant landowner and educated at Cambridge, P. was drawn to the cause of Irish parliamentary independence and agrarian reform despite his unlikely background. Elected a member of Parliament from Meath in 1875, he brought new life to the hitherto lackluster Home Rule League by the skillful obstructionist tactics he employed in the House of Commons to bring Irish grievances to the fore. His success won him support both among British advocates of a Home Rule policy and among Fenian nationalists in Ireland and America. But it was the depressed economic situation in Ireland, with near-famine conditions, rack rents, and the threat of evictions hanging over tenant farmers, that contributed most to P.'s growing power. His assumption in late 1879 of the presidency of the National Land League, whose long-term aim was to convert tenant farmers into landowners, brought him to national prominence, as did his handy reelection to Parliament from Cork in 1880, which led to his becoming chairman of the Parliamentary Home Rule party. This gave him two levers of pressure—one agricultural, the other legislative—in his struggles on behalf of the Irish peasantry. The Land League's boycott campaign and the disorders in Ireland that accompanied it, however, led the Gladstone government to imprison P. and his followers at Kilmainham in late 1881. To retaliate the Land League urged a no-rent policy, which in turn led to further repression on the part of the government. When the country refused to quiet down, Gladstone was forced to come to terms: P. was released in the spring of 1882 in return for a promise to back Liberal party policy once its Irish land legislation was altered in a pro-tenant direction. In fact, over the next few years, P.'s party functioned so efficiently that it controlled the balance of power between the Tories and Liberals, inducing Gladstone finally to embrace Home Rule. Even after the defeat of Gladstone's Home Rule Bill of 1886, the two political leaders continued to work together, but difficult times now lay ahead for Parnell. In 1887, he was accused by the *Times* of complicity in Irish terrorist murders that had taken place in 1882; he was acquitted in 1890 by the commission set up to investigate the charges and even recovered substantial damages from London's foremost newspaper. What he could not survive was being named corespondent in the divorce suit which was brought by Captain O'Shea against his wife and which neither party contested. P. subsequently married Katharine O'Shea and tried to treat the affair as a purely private matter; but this neither Victorian Ireland nor England would tolerate and his own party deserted him in 1891, after Gladstone threatened to withdraw Liberal support for Home Rule if P. remained titular leader of the cause. P. fought hard against the verdict in an attempt to win back popular support in Ireland, but in this last political trial the Irish Catholic clergy, who a decade earlier had in large measure contributed to his success—despite Rome's disapproval—were no longer with him. Rheumatic fever on top of otherwise failing health killed him 10 months later. One of the most effective and popular leaders in Ireland's turbulent history, P. succeeded—his final personal failure notwithstanding—in forging a dynamic coalition that made self-government for Ireland a persistent, because thereafter realizable, cause. BIBLIOGRAPHY: R. B. O'Brien, *Life of Charles Stewart Parnell* (1899, repr. 1969).

[E. M. GATES]

PAROCHIAL SCHOOLS, U.S. Elementary and secondary schools as an integral part of the teaching mission of the Church in the U.S. have been a constant concern since colonial times. Early examples were the academies for boys and girls and the first parish free school established by St. Elizabeth Seton in Emmitsburg, Md., in 1810. A parochial school system in its current form was created by St. John Neumann in the Diocese of Philadelphia in the mid-19th century. The Third Plenary Council of Baltimore in 1884 decreed that every parish should have a parochial school. The decision to provide a separate system for Catholic children developed over a long period of time and not without sharp controversy. It was the hope of Catholics early in the history of the Republic that a common school system could be developed, but experience proved that public schools grew progressively more secularistic. The only way to give Catholic children a Christian viewpoint was to set up a Catholic system. There were a few local successes in persuading School Boards to give financial support to the parochial school, but these were short-lived and infrequent,

leaving the burden of support with the Catholic community. In the 1870s the Republican Party made an issue of the matter, condemning any support of nonpublic schools. When the Council of Baltimore made mandatory the building of parish schools, the more extreme Protestant groups attacked the attitude of the Church as divisive. The climax of the bitter controversy came on the heels of a speech by the stormy and flamboyant Abp. John Ireland of St. Paul. The oratorical flourishes in the speech of July 1890 to the National Education Association meeting in St. Paul, Minn., more than the substance of his proposals earned the enmity of many Catholics and a number of militant Protestants. Ireland proposed a compromise: the public schools should teach the religion of the majority; Catholic schools should provide Catholic instruction but be supported by school boards in their instruction in secular subjects. In his discourse, Ireland praised the public schools as the schools of the nation, but acknowledged that Catholics had a right to schooling in their faith. Fanned by irresponsible journalists, Catholic and non-Catholic alike, the controversy over Ireland's views grew more savage. It pitted Ireland, Card. Gibbons, Bp. Keane, and The Catholic Univ. of America against the Jesuits, Abp. Corrigan of New York, Bp. McQuaid of Rochester, and to a lesser extent Abp. Patrick J. *Ryan of Philadelphia. The matter died down in 1893 with a letter from Pope Leo XIII to Card. Gibbons.

It is not strange that Abp. Ryan should have been in opposition to Ireland's views, since he was creating the most complete network of parochial schools in Philadelphia that the American Church provided. His successor Card. Dennis *Dougherty made notable additions on both elementary and secondary levels. Philadelphia became the showplace of parochial and diocesan Catholic schools. By the mid-1960s there were in the U.S. more than 4,500,000 students in parochial elementary schools and several hundred thousand in secondary schools.

In 1977 there were in the U.S. 2,478,229 students in parochial elementary schools and 563,411 students in diocesan and parochial high schools. The decline of vocations to sisterhoods and congregations of men, plus defections, both phenomena of the American Church after Vatican Council II, have created serious staffing and financial problems for parochial and diocesan schools. Nevertheless, a recent survey conducted by Andrew Greeley, director of the Center for the Study of American Pluralism, National Opinion Research Center, Univ. of Chicago, has proved that Catholics are convinced of the need for Catholic schools and are willing to make extensive efforts to continue them. As a result of his survey, Greeley claims that "even as use of the parochial schools declines, we find that only ten percent of the Catholic population believes that the Catholic school system has had its day and should be allowed to sink into nonexistence. Rather, the great majority of the Catholic population believes the Catholic school system should be getting financial assistance from the federal government in order to assure its continued existence''.

Commitment to Catholic education was reflected in the deliberations and discussions of the 75th Meeting of the National Catholic Education Association held in March, 1978. Educators were exhorted to take a total view of education as a lifelong learning experience which involves Catholic schools, CCD, parents, pastors, education committees, and all concerned parties in the educational process. Commitment to an inexhaustible quest for excellence emerged as a goal for Catholic educators. Educators were urged to assume a major role of leadership in American education and to learn from the past how to deal creatively with the future. Catholic educators were commended for the value dimension of the schools, the moral authority of the teachers, and for their caring and committed response to students in keeping with their philosophy of educating the whole person. BIBLIOGRAPHY: J. Burns and B. Kohlbrenner, *A History of Catholic Education in the United States* (1937); J. T. Ellis, *Life of James Cardinal Gibbons* (2 v, 1952); J. Hughes, *Education in America* (1960); A. Greeley, *Catholic Schools in a Declining Church* (1976).

[J. R. AHERNE]

PAROUSIA, a transliteration of the classical Greek word for presence or arrival; it is used in the NT to denote the return of Christ in glory to judge the living and the dead. *SECOND COMING.

[T. M. MCFADDEN]

PARRAS, PEDRO JOSÉ (c.1710–84), missionary. A Spanish Franciscan, P. volunteered for the missions of Río de la Plata (1748). Adviser to the bp. of Paraguay as well as to the governor of Paraguay he influenced the policy of both. After a sojourn in Spain, P. returned to La Plata. Named rector of the Univ. of Córdoba, Argentina, he served with distinction until his death. His most important work was *Gobierno de los regulares de la América* (2 v., 1783) a presentation of the legal position of religious in Spanish America.

[J. R. AHERNE]

PARRENIN, DOMINIQUE (1665–1741), missionary. A French Jesuit, P. went to Peking in 1697. His knowledge of Chinese ingratiated him with Emperor K'ang-hi, and through that friendship he was able to discuss science and Christianity with the court. P. was a masterly cartographer and his map of China was a real service to China. The letters of P. were published in France in two collections (1711 and 1735).

[J. R. AHERNE]

PARSCH, PIUS (1884–1954), Austrian Canon Regular of St. Augustine who did pioneer work in developing the concepts of pastoral liturgy and the necessity of Bible study for the understanding of the liturgy. He founded the periodical *Bibel und Liturgie* to help translate these concepts into action. Largely through his efforts his monastery (Kloster-

neuburg) became an important center of the Austrian and German liturgical movement. His work, which he called the Popular Liturgical Apostolate, was aimed at bringing Christians into closer participation in the liturgy. Among his best known works are *Das Jahr des Heiles* (1923), which has appeared in English under the title *The Church's Year of Grace* (5 v., tr. W. G. Heidt, 1963–65); *The Liturgy of the Mass* (tr. F. C. Eckhoff, rev. ed., 1957); *Breviary Explained* (tr. W. Nayden and C. Hoegerl, 1952), and *Seasons of Grace* (tr. H. E. Winstone, 1963).

[N. KOLLAR]

PARSEES, the descendents of the Persians in Iran, but esp. of the Persian immigrants to the Bombay region of India, who have preserved the ancient Persian religion but with some modifications. They number c.20,000 in Iran and c.120,000 in India. They worship the god *Ormazd* (*Mazda*) and revere his prophet *Zadusht* or Zoroaster. They are dualists, but under the influence of Islam, Christianity, and Hinduism, *Ahriman* has become reduced largely to a symbol of man's evil inclinations. They still maintain an elaborate fire ritual, which entails the recitation of large portions of the *Avesta*. They retain also the custom of exposing corpses in "towers of silence." The Parsees never marry outside their group and never attempt to win converts. They are noted for their prosperity, for their charities which ignore the barriers of race or creed, and for fostering education. BIBLIOGRAPHY: J. Duchesne-Guillemin, *La Religion de l'Iran ancien* (1962) 367–383; *idem*, NCE 10:1040–41.

[M. R. P. MCGUIRE]

PARSIFAL, see PARZIVAL.

PARSON, an ecclesiastical term, which in English legal terminology means the *rector of a church. Originating from the Latin *persona*, as early as the 12th cent. the word signified the holder of a parochial benefice; the parson was the *persona ecclesiae*, i.e., the representative of the Church in the parish. Strictly speaking, parson signifies only the rector, but in popular usage it came to designate any clergyman. The parson has life tenure in the parsonage, glebe lands, and other rights attached to the benefice. The term came to be applied to *Nonconformist ministers, but in this sense often had a derogatory implication. In the American colonies the word was used esp. by Anglicans; it survives only as a colloquialism.

PARSONS, ROBERT, see PERSONS, ROBERT.

PARSONS, WILFRED (1887–1958), American Jesuit, editor and writer. A native of Philadelphia, he entered the Society and was ordained in 1918, after teaching assignments at Boston College and Holy Cross. Appointed editor of the weekly *America* in 1925, P. took strong positions on economic and moral issues. He was a moderate supporter of the New Deal, but critical of some of its philosophy. In

1935 he offered trenchant criticism of Father Charles E. Coughlin's social doctrine. P. was the founder of the quarterly journal *Thought,* a cultural review. In 1936 he became professor of political science at Georgetown Univ. and in 1940 occupied the same position at The Catholic Univ. of America. At Georgetown he published *Early Catholic Americana,* a work which listed Catholic writings in the U.S. from 1729 to 1830. Other works were *The Pope and Italy* (1929) and *Which Way, Democracy?* (1940).

[J. R. AHERNE]

PARTHENIUS, 1st-cent. B.C. Greek grammarian and poet. P. was born in Bithynia, and was taken as a prisoner to Rome after the war against Mithridates. *Love's Woes,* his only surviving work, is a collection of 36 love stories.

[T. M. MCFADDEN]

PARTHENIUS (d. *c.*360), a saint of the Eastern Church. Son of a deacon in Miletopolis (Hellespont) and gifted with healing power, he was ordained for the priesthood and later on consecrated bp. of Lampsakos by the metropolitan of Kyzikos. Supported by Constantine the Great, he worked with zeal as a missionary. He participated in the Council of Nicea, but since he was not an outstanding theologian he refrained from any statement pertinent to the controversy; P. cannot be qualified as a "semi-Arian." On his life see PG 114:1345–66.

[L. PEANO]

PARTICIPATION. The doctrine of participation is concerned first of all with the philosophical problem of classification and is proposed by Plato and his followers as a way of explaining how it is possible for there to be both one genus and many individuals not identical with one another within that one genus. Essentially it is the affirmation that wherever there exists a many (a multiplicity of individuals) which is thought to constitute a group or class by virtue of their possession of a common attribute, there must at the same time be a single source, superior to all these individuals, possessing the same attribute in perfection. From this single superior source all individuals in the multiplicity derive the attribute, and derive it in an imperfect or diminished form. This doctrine leads Plato to postulate the reality of a world of forms to explain the one source of each shared attribute possessed by a multiplicity. As Plato himself says in discussing the notion of participation: "There is absolute beauty and absolute good, and of other things to which the term 'many' is applied there is an absolute; for they may be brought under a single idea, which is called the essence of each." (*Republic* 507b)

The major difficulty with Plato's position was that it was vague and indefinite as to the exact nature of this participation. The notion of a limited participation in an infinite perfection was a notion closed to Plato since he, like Aristotle, accepted the idea that the finite was superior to the infinite. Plotinus' restatement of the Platonic position on participation changes this because Plotinus introduces into the participation doctrine the concept of the infinite as a plenitude of perfection, thus establishing the infinite as something superior to the finite and permitting the participation doctrine to be explained in terms of a limited participation in an infinite perfection.

The participation doctrine was eventually taken over by St. Thomas Aquinas who, in his theory, preserved the basic insight of the participation theory, namely, the common possession of an attribute by many individuals is to be explained in terms of a reference to a higher source from which the individuals receive this attribute. Thomas insisted, however, that certain conditions must be present for the participation theory to have application. A source must be identified which possesses the perfection to an unlimited degree; a participant subject must be present possessing the same attribute in a limited way; and the attribute possessed must be received from a higher source. It is thus necessary, Thomas insisted, in applying the notion of participation, that there be certainty that the attributes discussed be shared by both superior and inferior beings, and that they are in some way relevant to the perfection of the beings.

This concept is of use in theology in discussing, for example, the nature and attributes of God, because it forms the basis for reasoning by analogy about the source of perfection. If, for example, it is possible to identify in a finite being some perfection which that being possesses in common with other beings and which is a positive perfection (i.e., something which might be viewed from the perspective of the infinite without contradiction), then it is possible to argue through the participation doctrine that God possesses this perfection in its fullness, as source of the shared perfection. This is, of course, precisely the use to which Thomas Aquinas put the participation doctrine, arguing that the Aristotelian categories of potency and act are applicable to the participation doctrine, that finite participants are in a state of both potency and act, but that, since act is superior to potency, God, as the source of perfection, must be viewed as pure act. Potency then represents for Aquinas the limitation placed on the creatures in their participation in the perfection of God. BIBLIOGRAPHY: C. P. Bigger, *Participation: A Platonic Inquiry* (1968).

[F. J. CUNNINGHAM]

PARTICULAR BAPTISTS, those so named in contrast to *General Baptists, because they believed in a *limited atonement. They held that God had decreed in advance who were to be "elect" and who "reprobate." Since God is infinitely wise, they reasoned, he would not make provision for Christ's atonement to cover persons who could not be saved. Therefore Christ's atoning death was sufficient only for the sins of the particular persons whom God had chosen to save. Arising in England in the 1630s, the Particular Baptists became the main body in Baptist life. BIBLIOGRAPHY: R. G. Torbet, *History of the Baptists* (rev. ed., 1963).

PARVATI, Indian goddess, "daughter of the mountain," consort of *Siva (Rudra). Unlike another consort, the destructive *Kali, Parvati is gentle and sometimes restrains Siva's destructiveness. Her relationship to Siva is ambivalent, since as lord of asceticism Siva overcomes passion, but as lord and symbol of masculine sexuality and as Parvati's consort he must at times make love to her. She is known esp. as mother of the popular elephant-headed god Ganesha, born miraculously (without sexual contact) to her and Siva. BIBLIOGRAPHY: W. D. O'Flaherty, *Hindu Myths* (1975) 154–73; 261–69.

[D. P. EFROYMSON]

PARZIVAL, medieval German courtly epic, composed *c.*1210 by Wolfram von Eschenbach (*c.*1170–*c.*1220). Though Wolfram names as his source a still unidentified *Kyot der Provenzale,* he is clearly indebted, though not slavishly bound, to Chrétien de Troyes' uncompleted *Li Contes del Graal.* Wolfram's *Parzival* contains almost 25,000 lines (16 books) of short rhymed couplets; its language is mystical and allegorical and, consequently, often difficult and obtuse; its structure, centering on the thematically important ninth book, is nearly symmetrical. Often referred to as the first German *Entwicklungsroman* (developmental novel), the epic represents Wolfram's attempt to reconcile the secular world of Arthurian knighthood with the spiritual world of the Grail. BIBLIOGRAPHY: W. von Eschenbach, *Parzival* (tr. H. M. Mustard and C. E. Passage, 1961); H. Sacker, *Introduction to Wolfram's Parzival* (1963).

[M. F. MCCARTHY]

PASCAL, BLAISE (1623–62), mathematician, physicist, and Christian apologist. His father, a mathematician, brought him into early contact with learned circles in Paris. By 1640, several major factors in P.'s life were manifest: a grave malady that plagued him all his life; the influence of his two sisters; and his versatile genius, which began to be recognized in 1639 when he wrote his *Essai pour les coniques.* In 1642 he became famous through the invention of the first known calculating machine. By 1647 he had proved the existence of a vacuum and the weight of air. At Rouen in 1646, P. and his entire family had been converted to *Jansenism by followers of the Abbé de *Saint-Cyran. For P. this step entailed the renunciation of fame, but he continued his research in the field of physics. Aggravation of his illness then caused him to seek diversion, and he entered upon a brief worldly period. Yet at that time he laid the foundations for the calculus of probabilities, became familiar with Montaigne, and came to center his attention on man himself. In 1648 his younger sister, Jacqueline, became a religious at the Jansenistic monastery of *Port-Royal-des-Champs. P.'s second conversion is marked by the *Memorial* composed after a religious experience in 1654. He became associated with the solitaries of Port-Royal and put his genius at their service in their quarrel with the Jesuits. In 1656–57 he composed, probably with the assistance of A. *Arnauld, the pamphleteering masterpiece known as the *Provincial Letters (*Lettres écrites par Louis de Montalte à un provincial*). Their mordant satire of Jesuit casuistry, and their high literary quality made them an effective defense of the Jansenist cause. Soon after publication the Letters were placed on the Index. With a view to the conversion of free-thinking friends, he began to prepare an apologetic, the pieces of which were organized after their writer's death and published under the title *Pensées.* After 1658 P.'s illness became more acute and, while continuing some religious and philosophical work, he retired to the home of his older sister, Gilberte. Without renouncing allegiance to Jansenism, which was not at the time generally recognized as a departure from orthodoxy, he did withdraw from all controversy and died, as he had always thought to live, a devout Catholic. Pascal saw truth, under different aspects, as attainable through two means: (1) geometric reasoning (*esprit de géométrie, raison*) and (2) a certitude of faith, which comes from the heart (*esprit de finesse, coeur*). Reason can do no more than point to those things that surpass it. Corrupted by the Fall, it cannot resolve the difficulties of faith and Christian morality. Only the light of revelation can do this. Reason can, however, grasp the historicity of revelation, and it can realize both the weakness and the greatness of man, who is "a thinking reed." An exploratory hypothesis, based on some facts, has therefore a certain apologetic validity. The *Pensées* were intended not to form a rational demonstration but rather to assist the reader gradually to accept the light of revelation. Pascal opposed any compromise between humanism and Christianity. His profound insight and penetrating style rank him high in the history of literature. Works: *Oeuvres complètes* (ed. L. Brunschvicg and P. L. Boutroux, 14 v., 1904–14); *Pensées* (ed. L. Lafuma, 3 v., 1951). BIBLIOGRAPHY: J. Mesnard, *Pascal: His Life and Works* (tr. G. S. Fraser, 1952).

[L. TINSLEY]

PASCENDI DOMINICI GREGIS, an encyclical letter of Pope Pius X (Sept. 10, 1907) analyzing the basic principles and tendencies of *modernism, which it characterizes as "the synthesis of all heresies." It discusses the trend of modernism toward agnosticism, its distortion of religious history, and its teachings about vital immanence, religious sense, and the origin, nature, symbolism, and evolution of dogma. Among the causes of modernism it mentions the arrogance, ignorance, and rashness of its proponents. It concludes with some disciplinary remedies. BIBLIOGRAPHY: ASS 40 (1907) 593–650; D 3475–3500 (Eng. tr. V. A. Yzermans, *All Things in Christ,* 1954).

[J. H. ROHLING]

PASCH (from LXX *páscha,* a transliteration of the Aramaic *pashā*). (1) The Jewish feast of *Passover. (2) The Christian feast of Easter considered as superseding the Jewish Passover, Christ in his death taking the place of the

Jewish paschal lamb. Some form of this word is used in the Romance languages for Easter, for example, *Pâques* in French.

[R. B. ENO]

PASCHAL I, ST. (d. 824), **POPE** from 817. He came of a lower class Roman family and was a priest and an official of the papal curia when he was elected pope by the forces that had dominated in the reign of Leo III (795–816). His reign began peacefully. The Emperor Louis the Pious granted his request for a reconfirmation of the privileges granted the Church by Pepin the Short and Charlemagne. Louis' decree, the *Pactum Ludovicianum,* affirmed the freedom of papal elections and the independence of the pope in governing the States of the Church, but nevertheless granted the pope's subjects a right of appeal to the emperor. Yet Louis deferred to the pope's position by requesting his blessing on a division of the Empire (817), and when Louis' son Lothair became co-emperor (823), he was crowned by Paschal. Certain nobles, dissatisfied with the Pope because of his humble birth and his authoritarian manner, charged P. with complicity in the murder of two Roman nobles. As in the case of *Leo III (800), the Pope was obliged to deny the charge under oath. P. sought to win the Eastern Emperor away from the heresy of Iconoclasm, and he provided refuge in Rome for those who fled from the iconoclastic persecution. He contributed to the evangelization of the land beyond the Elbe in the direction of Denmark and Scandinavia by commissioning Abbo, abp. of Reims to head a mission that enjoyed some success. P. was noted for his zeal for the building of churches. He was not, however, a popular pope, and when he died the Romans would not permit his burial in St. Peter's. He was never canonized and there is little evidence to show he was honored with an early cult. How his name came to be included in the Roman Martyrology is unknown. BIBLIOGRAPHY: Mann 2:122–135; Butler 1:311; P. Rabikausas and M. C. Celletti, BiblSanct 10:353–358.

[P. F. MULHERN]

PASCHAL II (Rainerius; d. 1118) **POPE** from 1099. The death of the antipope Clement III (d. 1100), the capture and imprisonment of two other claimants to the papacy: Theoderic (d. 1100) and Albert (d. 1102), and the demise of Sylvester IV (d. 1111) freed this pontificate from the danger of schism. P.'s chief problem was the investiture struggle. In this conflict the Emperor Henry IV was excommunicated and lay investiture again forbidden in 1102. Henry V caused more serious trouble. In August 1110 he began his march on Rome determined to obtain imperial coronation and the right of investiture. However, on February 9, 1111, it was announced at Sutri that the Emperor would renounce investiture (bestowal of ring and crozier), the Church would forego the *regalia,* and bps. and abbots would henceforth be content with tithes and offerings. On February 12 when the agreements were read as the coronation ceremonies began,

there was an uproar and the Pope was taken prisoner. Two months later, April 13, the Pope granted the Emperor the "privilege" of investiture and bestowed the imperial crown. P., however, repudiated the "privilege" in 1112 and explicitly condemned lay investiture once more in 1116. In spite of reverses the Pope's attitude toward the temporalities was ideally correct. BIBLIOGRAPHY: Jedin-Baus 3.1 (1966).

[H. DRESSLER]

PASCHAL CANDLE, esp. in the RC Church, a large, sometimes decorated candle, symbolic of the risen Christ, blessed at the beginning of the Easter Vigil, and kept near the altar or pulpit throughout the Easter season and lighted during Mass. In the renewal of the liturgy the Paschal candle is kept for use also at baptisms and the rites for funerals recommend its being carried in the funeral procession and left burning at the bier during the Eucharistic Liturgy.

[J. DALLEN]

PASCHAL CHRONICLE, known also as *Chronicon Alexandrinum* and *Chronicon Constantinopolitanum,* a medieval Greek chronicle from the Creation (5509 B.C.) to 627 A.D.; it originally extended to 629. It was written in Constantinople in the reign of Heraclius (610–641) by a cleric to harmonize the calendar with civil and ecclesiastical chronology. To calculate the dates of Easter it used a solar and lunar cycle of 532 years and the common assumption that the Creation took place in the mid-6th millennium B.C. This chronology was the basis for the Byzantine system, effective from the 7th century. Dating was also by Olympiads, consuls, and indictions. It contains original material only for the last decades. Its sources included the Bible, Sextus Julius Africanus, Eusebius, Epiphanius, John Malalas, Acts of the Martyrs, and consular *fasti.* The work was very popular in the Middle Ages. Ed. L. Dindorf, 1832 and reprinted in PG 92; no critical edition. BIBLIOGRAPHY: H. Gelzer, *Sextus Julius Africanus und die byzantinsche Chronographie* (1885) 2:138–176; G. Moravscik, *Byzantinoturcica*² (1958) 241–243; V. Grumel, *La Chronologie* (1958) 73–85.

[M. A. MOFFATT]

PASCHAL LAMB, the central symbol of the sacrificial aspect of the ancient observance of Passover, appropriated by Christians as a symbol of Christ in his Crucifixion. Passover combined two pre-Israelite traditions: an agricultural feast of thanksgiving when the new grain appeared (unleavened bread); and a pastoral festival centered probably on the firstborn of herd and flock. The rituals of both traditions were given a historical reference: commemorating the liberation of Israel from Egypt. Similarly, the sacrifice of the passover lamb or kid carried with it a long evolution of meaning. It may originally have been a sacred family observance with the lamb being slaughtered in the doorway of each house, with the blood serving as a sign that the house has entered into a covenant with the Lord and has passed into his protection and possession. The blood also served as an apotropaic sign: to ward off some evil spirit, demon, or destroyer (Ex 12.21–23). It was also an acknowledgement that the firstborn of man, herd, and flock belonged to the Lord and must be sacrificed or redeemed (Ex 13). Some such pastoral observance at a very early stage of development may actually have served as a pretext or occasion for the Hebrews to leave the land of Goshen and go out into the wilderness to keep festival. The biblical text on the institution of Passover (Ex 12) is placed at this point of escape from Egypt and made to commemorate that event. The ritual surrounding the Passover victim is prescribed in careful detail. Either a sheep or goat will suffice. On the 10th day of the month of Abib ("Ears," first ears of grain), each head of household selects the lamb or kid for the feast. It must be a yearling male, without blemish. On the 14th day (the full moon) the victim is slaughtered between dusk and dark amid the assembled community. Some of the blood is to be smeared on the lintel and doorposts of every house in which the lamb is eaten. The lamb must be eaten that night, roasted whole on the fire, head, shins, and entrails; eaten with unleavened bread and bitter herbs. If anything is left over until morning, it must be destroyed by fire. Those partaking of the meal must eat in urgent haste, with loins girded, sandals on feet, and with staff in hand. The rite is still observed minutely, even down to this last detail, by the dwindling Samaritan community at Nablus, Jordan, a sect that broke away from the official Judaism of Jerusalem around the 4th cent. B.C. At the time of Jesus Passover was a great pilgrimage festival rivaled only by Tabernacles. With the help of the *Mishna we can reconstruct the ritual of the lamb at that time. The first concern of the head of a "company" or family group upon arrival in Jerusalem was to procure a sizable room for the feast (Mk 14.15) and then purchase a sheep for sacrifice. The minimum number permitted for a group was ten, and since the entire lamb had to be eaten, the size of it should correspond to the size of the group. At about 3 in the afternoon, the slaughtering of the Passover sacrifices would begin in the Temple. The Levites signaled the moment with three loud blasts on the trumpet. While some Levites sang the Hallel, others slew the sacrificial animals and bled them in gold and silver trays held by the priests. The Levites then flayed and dressed the animals to be given back to the people for roasting, while the priests tossed the blood against the great altar and burned portions of fat on the altar. This was a means of declaring God's redeeming action in past history and of releasing it new on the occasion of the feast. With the destruction of the Temple in 70 A.D., the sacrificial aspect of the observance of Passover ceased and it became simply Israel's festival of freedom. Paul, in 1 Cor 5.7, refers to Christ as the sacrifice of Passover, in a passage whose principal reference is to Christians being unleavened Passover bread, full of sincerity and truth, from whom the old leaven of corruption has been purged. The Gospels make a point of mentioning that Christ died at 3 in the afternoon, the hour when the slaughtering of

Passover sacrifices would have begun (Mk 15.33ff). The centurions who came to break the bones of the three who had been crucified, so that the bodies would not be left on the cross throughout Passover, broke the legs of the two crucified with Jesus, but when they saw that Jesus was already dead, one of them merely pierced his side with a lance. Thus the text detailing the ritual of the sacrificial lamb was fulfilled: no bone of his shall be broken (Jn 19.31–37). These allusions must reflect an acknowledgement of the redeeming, liberating effects of Jesus' bloody death, viewed in the light of his Resurrection.

[E. J. DILLON]

PASCHAL PRECEPT, see EASTER DUTY.

PASCHAL TIME, in the U.S. the period from the beginning of Lent until Trinity Sunday, during which the church commandment that all the faithful receive holy communion at least once a year (Easter duty) must be fulfilled (CIC c. 859). Power to extend the period is granted to ordinaries by the law; without the extension Paschal time is the week preceding and the week following Easter (*ibid.* §2).

[T. C. O'BRIEN]

PASCHASINUS (fl. mid-5th cent.), bp. of Lilybaeum, a Sicilian diocese at a time when Sicily was being devastated by Vandal raids. Pope Leo I the Great sent him money and became a kind of patron. There was considerable correspondence between the two. When Leo consulted him about the Paschal cycle, P. at first replied in favor of the Alexandrian computation against the Roman. Later he was sent as one of Leo's legates to the Council of Chalcedon (451), presided in Leo's name, and opposed Dioscorus, bp. of Alexandria. No more is known about him after Chalcedon.

[E. J. DILLON]

PASCHASIUS OF DUMIO, a monk of Dumio who died toward the end of the 6th century. At the suggestion of his abbot, Bl. Martin of Prague, he translated into Latin a Greek collection of Oriental monastic ascetical instructions. The Latin title is *Verba seniorum.*

[E. J. DILLON]

PASCHASIUS RADBERTUS, ST. (*c.*785–*c.*860), abbot, theologian. Reared by nuns at Soissons and tonsured in their presence, professed at Corbie before 812, and ordained deacon, he became disciple and biographer of Adalard and Wala, cousins of Charlemagne. In 822 he participated in establishing New Corvey. After 10 years as abbot of Corbie, he resigned *c.*852. Except for a time at St. Riquier, he spent his latter years at Corbie. In addition to biographies, his writings were biblical commentaries, treatises on theological virtues and on Mary, some poetry, and his most famous work, *De corpore et sanguine Domini,* attacked by his colleague Ratramnus. BIBLIOGRAPHY: A. Cabaniss, *Charlemagne's Cousins* (1967).

[A. CABANISS]

PASCHINI, PIO (1878–1962), church historian. After seminary studies in Treviso and Udine he was ordained in Rome and took a degree in canon law (1900). He taught in Udine (1900) and Rome (1913), where he was made rector of the Pontifical Lateran Univ. (1932–57). He influenced church history studies in Italy also through many articles in journals and encyclopedias and through his founding of the *Rivista di storia della chiesa in Italia* (1947) and by his work as president of the directive committee of the *Enciclopedia cattolica* (1948).

[E. P. COLBERT]

PASQUALIGO, ZACCARIA (1600–64), Theatine moral theologian and canonist. He taught philosophy at Padua and from 1649 until his death, theology at Rome. His *De statu supernaturali humanae naturae sacra moralis doctrina* (1650) was placed on the Index for *laxism in 1655, but taken off the next year after P. corrected the work. His moral *Decisiones . . .* was put on the Index after his death for the same laxist tendencies (1683). P. also published several casuistic collections. His *De sacrificio Novae Legis quaestiones theologico-iuridico-morales* (2 v. 1662) is of some interest to Eucharistic theology for its proposal that the Offertory is a distinct and separate rite in itself.

[T. C. O'BRIEN]

PASQUIER, ÉTIENNE (1529–1615), French lawyer and humanist. *Avocat* at the Paris *parlement* (1549), P. distinguished himself in various court cases, but esp. by his defense of the Univ. of Paris (1565) against the Jesuits to whom the university attempted to deny the right to teach. *Commissaire* at the *Grands Jours* (courts of assizes) at Poitiers (1579) and Tours (1583), he was appointed advocate-general at the Paris Chambre des Comptes (1585). Although he opposed the extremes of the Catholic Holy League, he remained faithful to Henry III, and then Henry IV. His publications include: poetry and letters; *Le Monophile* (1554), on marriage, fidelity, and love; *Pour parler du prince* (1560), on the best form of government; *Le Cathéchisme des Jésuites ou examen de leur doctrine*, a satirical polemic continuing his controversy with the Jesuits whom he considered dangerous; and his best-known encyclopedic work, *Recherches de la France* (1560–1621), an examination of the origins of French history, institutions, and customs, for which he was attacked by the Jesuit Garasse (1622). BIBLIOGRAPHY: M. J. Moore, *E. Pasquier, historien de la poésie et de la langue françaises* (1934).

[R. N. NICOLICH]

PASQUINO (PASQUINADES), the popular name for the remains of an ancient Roman statue unearthed in Rome in 1501. The name supposedly was borrowed from a local shopkeeper near whose house or shop the statue was discovered. It became the custom to attach to the statue's torso highly quotable satirical comments lampooning contemporary leaders or ridiculing current national affairs. A relatively safe way of circulating the barbed comment was to use the introductory formula: Pasquino says. These anonymous or pseudonymous lampoons came to be called *pasquinate* in Italian, *pasquinades* in French and were collected and ascribed to contemporary writers of note and published. When the vogue of posting the barbed comment died out, the word pasquinade acquired a more general meaning referring to any brief, anonymous satirical political commentary.

[E. J. DILLON]

PASSAGIANI (Passagini), a short-lived Judaizing sect that arose in 12th-cent. Lombardy and was condemned by the Council of Verona in 1184 (D 760). Its principal characteristic was insistence on certain OT practices, esp. circumcision, as necessary for salvation. Some Christian beliefs were retained, but like other contemporary reform groups the Passagiani preached against the sacraments and against the authority of the Church. BIBLIOGRAPHY: É. Amann, DTC 11:2206–07; I. da Milano, *L'eresia di U. Speroni nella confutazione del maestro Vacario* (1945) 27–32, 436–444; *idem,* EncCatt 9:907–908; L. I. Newman, *Jewish Influence on Early Christian Reform Movements* (1925) 255–302.

[C. J. LYNCH]

PASSAGLIA, CARLO (1812–87), Italian priest and patriot. A Jesuit from 1827, he became professor of dogmatic theology at the Collegio Romano in 1844, and to this period belong his major preparatory work on the dogmatic definition of Mary's Immaculate Conception (1854), and his publishing, with K. Schrader, *De immaculato Deiparae Virginis conceptu* (3 v., 1854). With the permission of the Holy See he left the Society in 1854 and Pius IX appointed him professor of philosophy at the Sapienza. P. became a mediator for the party of C. *Cavour in an attempt to persuade papal renunciation of the territory known as the Legations. He also wrote *Pro causa italica ad episcopos catholicos, auctore presbytero catholico* (1861); the Italian translation was put on the Index, Oct. 9, 1861. P. had to flee Rome in secular clothes, and went to Turin, where he became a professor at the university. He wrote a further work of petition, asking that Pius IX give Rome up so that it could become the capital of Italy, *Petizione di novemila sacerdoti italiani à Sua Santità Pio IX e ai vescovi cattolici con esso uniti* (1862); he also founded a newspaper to further the Italian cause. Suspended from the ministry, he lived the rest of his life as a layman; before his death he renounced his errors and was formally reconciled with the Church. Among P.'s theological works of merit were his new edition of *Enchiridion de fide, spe, et charitate S. Augustini* (1847); and his own *Commentariorum theologicorum partes tres* (3 v., 1850–51); *De ecclesia Christi* (2 v., 1853–56). Even during his estrangement he wrote in defense of Catholic teaching on marriage, against Renan, and a commentary on Leo XIII's encyclical *Aeterni Patris*.

[T. C. O'BRIEN]

PASSAIC (N.J.) EPARCHY OF, Byzantine rite see established in 1963 as a suffragan of the Metropolitan Ruthenian See of Pittsburgh (established in 1924). The eparchy ministers to Hungarian and Croatian Byzantine Catholics. Ruthenians, or Carpatho-Russians (Rusins) returned to Catholic Unity in the Union of Brest-Litovsk, 1596, and the Union of Uzhorod, 1646. Liturgical languages are Old Slavonic, English. The first eparch (bishop) of Passaic was Stephen Kocisko, 1963–68; Michael J. Dudick, has been eparch since 1968.

[L. PEANO]

PASSARION OF EGYPT, see BESSARION OF EGYPT.

PASSEONE, DOMENICO (1682–1761), cardinal. A complex figure in troubled times for the Church, R. was a rigorist of the Augustinian school of moral theology. A friend of Montesquieu and Voltaire, he demonstrated both rationalistic and Jansenist proclivities. In diplomatic service of the Holy See from 1706 until 1738, P. was created cardinal in the latter year. A violent foe of the Jesuits, he played a part in their suppression. P.'s liberal views often embarassed the Holy See.

[J. R. AHERNE]

PASSIO, the suffering of a martyr as recorded in the early Church by another from the testimony of eye witnesses (St. Polycarp, SS. Perpetua and Felicitas). Later authors developed accounts replete with miraculous details which were in many cases fictional, thereby beclouding history with legend (SS. Hippolytus, Cecilia, Agnes, Sebastian). After the 5th century several so called passio's were written which have no other historical foundation than a name of a martyr and location of the martydom. Passios are distinct from Acts of the Martyrs, official shorthand accounts of the event. BIBLIOGRAPHY: F. X. Murphy NCE 10; 1052; R. Aigrain, L'Hagiographie (1953).

[F. H. BRIGHAM]

PASSION, a term with several religious and philosophical meanings. (1) In material logic it is one of Aristotle's ten categories of real being (Gr. *paschein*); it is the condition of being acted upon or of being affected by an external agent: hence the correlatives *action-passion. (2) In psychological philosophy it means the feeling induced by being acted upon (Gr., *pathos*). (3) It is sometimes used in a broad sense to include spiritual and intentional reception of activity; thus the mind is affected by what it knows, the will by what it desires. (4) In its most proper sense it is synonymous with *emotion and implies the causal production of an effect in the sensitive appetite of an animal, human or otherwise. By common usage, passion in this sense refers esp. to strong emotions of desire or anger. (5) The psychosomatic alteration implied in the preceding sense may spell either gain or loss: gain, as in pleasure after hope deferred; loss, when it means suffering or undergoing an evil. This is passion in its most pointed sense; it is used of the endurance of martyr-

dom (see PASSIO), and above all of martyrdom's chief exemplar, the Passion of Christ.

[T. GILBY]

PASSION OF CHRIST, a traditional designation for the last events of Jesus' life, and title for the gospel narratives that tell of these events. Besides being essential to the theology of Redemption, the fact of the Passion provides theological reflection on the Incarnation with data of the first importance. Christian devotional life and spirituality have found nourishment in the Passion of Christ through the ages.

In the Bible. A cursory glance at the general outline of the four Gospels discloses that the Passion narrative unquestionably constitutes their most important part. In Mark the Passion accounts for almost a third of the text. It is, moreover, noteworthy that the four Gospels agree more closely in the sequence of the events of the Passion story than they do in any other portion of their contents. This indicates that the Evangelists are depending on a fixed form of telling the story of these last days that was already a tradition in the preaching of the primitive Church. The fact of Christ's Passion is of such fundamental significance for the Church's faith and preaching that the whole story of how the event of the Crucifixion took place was recounted—it was not enough to proclaim it as the object of that faith and confession. The reason for this attention to the Passion is, first of all, because together with the Resurrection the Passion is the central theme of the apostolic kerygma. The Gospel narratives are theologically structured to show that, contrary to contemporary Jewish expectations, Christ's death for man's sins is "in accordance with the Scriptures" (1 Cor 15.3–5). Second, the Passion narrative holds a privileged place in Christian worship. Traces of it are found in the hymns of Phil 2.6–11; 1 Tim 3.16; 1 Pet 1.18–21, and in the heavenly liturgy of Rev 5.6–14, while explicit references to the Passion are made in the rites of Eucharist and baptism. Third, the Passion narrative presents Jesus' self-sacrifice as a model for Christian living that one finds applied in the apostolic writing (e.g., Rom 8.17; 2 Cor 1.5; Phil 3.10; Eph 5.1–2; 1 Pet 4.13).

In Theology. The fact of the Passion confronts the believer with the full mystery of the Incarnation. This man, who is in his person the consubstantial Son of the Father, is fully a man like other men. The Passion narrative catalogs the reality of his bodily suffering: he sweated blood, was scourged, crowned with thorns, and crucified; he experienced torturing thirst, and gasped a last breath in death. Even more significantly, he experienced the psychological tortures of anguish, revulsion, and dread in anticipation of his death, sorrow over the disloyalty of his friends, sadness at the rejection by his people, and instinctive conflict with the severe demands of his Father's will. Theology has wrestled with the mystery of the psychology of the suffering God-man from the beginning. An earlier theology attributed a perfection of human knowledge to Christ that made the full reality of this suffering struggle hard to account for (see ThAq ST 3a, 15.10; 15.7). Contemporary theology tends rather to limit the impact of Christ's divine being on his human mode of knowing and acting in a way that accounts better of his being "tempted in every way that we are, though he is without sin" (Heb 4.15).

In Devotion. While always a part of the Christian experience, the remembrance of the Passion has been marked by different emphases throughout history. Some emphases have been legitimate developments, while others have shown signs of distorting the paschal mystery. Already in the Scriptures, the characteristics of a Passion devotion are present, even if not dominant. The amplitude of the Passion narratives is witness to the reverent reflection of the first Christians on this mystery. Giving a glimpse into his own heart, St. Paul marvels at him "who loved me and who sacrificed himself for my sake" (Gal 2.20). If the Christian, dead to sin by his death and born to newness of life through his Resurrection, is to be one with his master, he must live crucified (Gal 5.24), carrying his cross (Lk 9.23; 14.27), suffering with him while in the flesh that he might be glorified with him (Rom 8.17). The reality of this discipleship unto blood finds poignant expression in the plea of Ignatius of Antioch to the Romans while looking forward to his martyrdom: "Permit me to follow the example of the Passion of my God" (*To the Romans*, 6.3).

The great Fathers of the Church exhibit a genuine personal devotion to Christ in the mystery of his sufferings in their sometimes surprisingly tender sermons on the Passion. But it is in the 12th cent. that the writings of St. Bernard turned hearts toward the mysteries of the earthly life of Jesus, esp. those of his birth and Passion. The popular preachers of the mendicant orders expanded the trend. The reticence of the Gospels was supplemented with imaginative and dramatic embellishments culled from apocryphal gospels and personal fancy. Emotional elements were very prominent but at their best were so channeled that a genuine experience of faith was nurtured by the experience of felt compassion. This pre-Reformation era gave rise to the cult of the wounds of the Savior, the pierced heart, and the precious blood of Jesus. The devotion of the Way of the Cross became popular. There were also aberrations. Liturgical life was at a low ebb, and devotional experience tended to become divorced from sound theology, esp. Christology. He who made himself loving sacrifice for our sin could become in popular thought, preaching, and ultimately in a new theology their scapegoat, the object of God's wrath accepting alienation from God in the place of sinners. A compassion for the sufferings of the Savior risked blocking out his glorious victory, abetting a pessimistic world view, and even opening the way to enthusiastic excesses like those of the Flagellants. A devout awareness of the Passion of Christ is essential if the integral paschal mystery is to be lived in a renewed Church pledged to walk the road Christ walked: "a road of poverty and obedience, of service and self-sacrifice to the death, from which death

He came forth a victor by His resurrection" (Vat II Miss-Act 5). BIBLIOGRAPHY: M. Judge et al., NCE 10:1052–59; X. Léon-Dufour, DBSuppl 6:1419–92; Th Aq ST 3a, 46–52; C. Marmion, *Christ in His Mysteries* (1926).

[C. REGAN]

PASSION PLAYS, a genre of medieval religious drama focusing on the suffering, death, and Resurrection of Christ. The relatively late development of the Passion play may be attributed to the Church's liturgical emphasis on the Resurrection rather than on the death of Christ—on peripety and theophany rather than on agon and pathos. Apart from an Italian fragment of the 14th cent., the only extant Latin plays in which the death of Christ is enacted are two plays found in the 13th-cent. Benediktbeuern MS—the longer of the two including such prior episodes as the anointing of Mary Magdalen, the last supper, and the betrayal. In both plays the crucifixion is enacted without violence. Among suggested influences on the formation of the Passion play, other than the Mass itself, are the following: the already developed liturgical plays, the Good Friday veneration of the cross together with the 12th-cent. custom of chanting a long lyrical *planctus* or lament of the Blessed Virgin, the dramatic homily on the Passion, and such long narrative poems on the death of Christ as the *Passion des jongleurs*. Vernacular Passion plays appear early in the 14th cent. in Germany and France. These Continental plays, which include OT episodes and episodes of Christ's ministry and Resurrection, are to be distinguished from the English *Corpus Christi cycle, which adds to these a group of episodes on the Nativity. The oldest surviving German Passion play is found in a Sankt Gallen MS probably of the early 14th century. A Vienna play of slightly later date expands the action to include the Fall of Adam. By the late 15th and 16th cent. the plays had so expanded that the action required 3 days for performance. In France, the Passion play had a similar development. Notable early plays are *La Passion du Palatinus,* the *Passion d'Autun,* and the *Passion de Semur*—all associated with the Burgundian area. The really great French plays, however, are those of Eustache Mercadé and Arnoul Greban, both of the 15th century. The Passion plays of London and Southern England have disappeared but they were, according to Craig, the great contemporary rival of the Corpus Christi play. Their loss has, in consequence, put undue stress on the Corpus Christi cycles as the typical drama of medieval England. The Cornish Passion is alone extant. Performances of Passion plays continued long into modern times esp. in Austria and Germany and continue spasmodically—but the only one to become famous is that of Oberammergau which since 1634 has been performed every 10 years. BIBLIOGRAPHY: H. Craig, *English Religious Drama of the Middle Ages* (1955); G. Frank, *Medieval French Drama* (1954); O. B. Hardison, *Christian Rite and Christian Drama in the Middle Ages* (1965); C. J. Stratman, *Bibliography of the Medieval*

Drama (1954); K. Young, *Drama of the Medieval Church* (2 v., 1933).

[M. N. MALTMAN]

PASSION SUNDAY, the 5th Sunday of Lent, so called because it marked the beginning of *Passiontide. Since 1956 this Sunday has been designated the First Sunday of the Passion, and the following Sunday (*Palm Sunday) the Second Sunday of the Passion.

PASSIONIST SISTERS (CP), religious congregation of pontifical right, and a branch of the Passionist Congregation founded by St. Paul of the Cross in 1720. The congregation under the full title, Sisters of the Most Holy Cross and Passion of Our Lord Jesus Christ, was established in Lancashire, England in 1852 by Gaudentius Ross, C.P. and Mother Mary Joseph Prout. The rule of the Passionists was adopted by the community, whose main apostolate was the conversion of England. The sisters also conduct schools, hospitals, retreat houses, and hostels; they are active in parish visitation and social work. The general motherhouse is in Bolton, England. In 1975, the congregation totalled 607 members and 58 foundations, located in the countries of the British Isles, Spain, and North and South America. BIB - LIOGRAPHY: *Sisters of the Cross and Passion* (1960).

[R. A. TODD]

PASSIONISTS (CP), clerical religious institute, officially the Congregation of the Discalced Clerics of the Most Holy Cross and Passion of Our Lord Jesus Christ, founded by St. Paul of the Cross in Italy in 1720. The members take simple perpetual vows and the brothers and professed priests share the common life on the same level. The rule and constitutions written by the founder were granted papal approval in 1741, and both were reapproved by John XXIII. The spirit of the congregation, as stressed in its documents, is one of prayer, penance, and solitude. The institute was founded primarily for the purpose of spreading devotion to the Passion of Our Lord Jesus Christ through the medium of parish missions and other sacred ministries. Their specific apostolic mission work includes preaching missions and giving retreats. A monthly magazine, the *Sign,* is published by the order at Union City, N.J., the location of the U.S. motherhouse. The Passionists maintain 449 houses throughout Europe, Japan, the Philippines, West Indies, and the U.S.; they total 3,288 members, of whom 2,495 are priests. The generalate is in Rome.

[R. A. TODD]

PASSIONTIDE, previously the 2-week interval between the First Sunday of the Passion (Passion Sunday) and Easter Sunday. This designation of these last 2 weeks in Lent prevailed since the 11th century, until the recent liturgical changes of Vatican II. The reenactment of Christ's Passion, Crucifixion, and Resurrection sets the theme for the liturgical celebrations of this period. Crucifixes and statues in the churches were veiled in purple, and recitation of the doxology in the Mass and Office was discontinued to convey a spirit of sorrow. The Gospels during this period stressed the growing conflict between Christ and the Jewish leaders, whereas the hymns of the Breviary reflected the triumph of the Cross. Presently Palm Sunday (now called Passion Sunday), the beginning of Holy Week, ushers in this period of solemn and renewed liturgical celebrations.

[B. ROSENDALL]

PASSIVE RESISTANCE, see NONVIOLENT RESISTANCE.

PASSOVER, FEAST OF, in contemporary Judaism the festivities that begin at the full moon of the vernal equinox, the 14th of Nisan in the lunar calendar, and continue for the following week to the 21st, thus including also the Feast of Unleavened Bread. In ancient Israel the two feasts were separate and the Passover referred only to the first day, the 15th of Nisan, which began the evening before at sunset, the Passover Lamb being eaten in its early hours. In 2 Sam 4.4, *pesah* is connected with the Hebrew root *psh,* ''to limp'' or ''jump,'' referring to the action of Yahweh killing the firstborn of the Egyptians but skipping the houses of the Israelites where the Passover was celebrated (Ex 12.13). This is a later addition, however, the etymology being debated by scholars. The Vulgate generally uses *phase* in the OT and *pascha* in the NT, the latter being a transliteration of the Septuagint rendering of *pesah;* hence the English adjective *paschal*. The Passover was very probably celebrated by the Israelites before the Exodus, being a rite practiced by shepherds, and resembling more than any other the sacrifices offered by the ancient nomadic Arabs. These were offered in the spring for the fertility and welfare of the flocks as they moved to new pastures. The blood of the sacrifice on the stiles of the doors was intended to drive away evil powers (cf. the ''destroyer'' in Ex 12.23). The nomadic features of the feast were evident in such details as the roasting and eating of the lamb without utensils, the eating of unleavened bread—still part of the Bedouins' diet—and bitter herbs (such as may be found in the desert), and the participants clad for a journey.

As celebrated in Israel, the original nature feast was transformed into a historical memorial of the Exodus to remind the participants of the origins of their national identity in the liberation from slavery that provided the freedom of later generations. The ritual of the Passover is described in the Bible by the Priestly source in Ex 12.1–14, 40–51; Lev 23.5–8; Num 28.16–25 (cf. Num 9.1–14) and by Dt 16.1–8. The details differ somewhat in the different traditions. In its origins the Passover was a family feast—no priest or altar are mentioned: it was a domestic affair. With the Deuteronomic reform and the centralization of cult, esp. under Josiah (d. 609 B.C.), the Passover became a pilgrimage feast for which men came to the sanctuary: the animal was to be slain, cooked, and eaten during the night in the sanctuary. In NT times, the number of pilgrims was so great that only the ritual slaughter of the animals and the sprinkling of the blood against the altar took place in the Temple, and the rest of the ritual was done in the home. Excommunication resulted for the Jew who omitted the Passover celebration (Num 9.13). All the circumcized and only they could take part in it (Ex 12.43–49); in case of necessity it could be put off a month, e.g., if a person were ritually unclean from touching a corpse necessarily (Num 9.10–11). The Passover celebration, therefore, became a rallying point of Jewish independence; often national feelings ran high, at times ending in bloodshed. It was a Feast of hope; some speculated that during this night the Messiah would come. Since the Passover was a celebration of the deliverance from slavery and the beginning of Israel as God's people, it looked also to the future, to the definitive redemption and the making of the new covenant of which the Prophets had spoken. Christians saw this accomplished in the life and death of Christ that brought liberation from sin and so was a new Exodus. For Christians the weekly Sunday and the annual Easter Eucharist is a sacramental representation of Christ's Exodus and the liberation it brought. In this rite the liberation is both celebrated and appropriated by the followers of Jesus as they look for the consummation of history when they will fully enter into Christ's Passover by being conformed to his death, Resurrection, and glorification at the parousia, the permanent presence of the Lord. BIBLIOGRAPHY: De Vaux AncIsr 484–493; E. G. Hirsh, JE 9:548–556; InterDB.

[A. J. TKACIK]

PASSOVER MEAL, the ritual meal eaten on the eve of the feast of the *Passover, whose origins are lost in the pastoral cultic ritual of Semitic Bedouins but which now recalls for Israel the historic events of the Exodus. The rite is described according to the Priestly tradition in Ex 12.1–13 where it is a family celebration, and in Dt 16.1–8 and 2 Chr 35. 10–15 according to the "D" tradition, where the meal is eaten in the temple area. In NT times, because of the large number of pilgrims, the meal was eaten at home or in a room obtained for the occasion by the pilgrims even though the lambs were slaughtered ritually in the Temple. According to Ex 12.1–4, the meal was eaten by families, and neighboring households joined to eat the meal according to the size of the lamb, since nothing of it was to remain until the next day. If away from home, a man joined a group of friends and the oldest acted as father. Slaves and resident aliens could join in the meal if they were circumcised. The meal was begun with the blessing over the first of four cups of wine each mixed with a little water, the meal being thus divided into four parts. When the first cup was drunk, the leader of the group said a blessing over unleavened bread and green herbs and distributed them. The Passover lamb was brought, the Exodus meaning of the meal explained, and Psalms 113 and 114.1–8 were sung. After another cup of wine and a prayer of praise, the Passover lamb was eaten with bitter herbs and unleavened bread dipped in *haroset*, a

sauce made of spices and vinegar. The "cup of blessing," the third cup of wine blessed in thanksgiving for the Passover meal was drunk, followed by a fourth cup and the singing of the second part of the Hallel, Psalms 115–118, which express trust in God's covenant love. By the celebration of the Passover and esp. in the eating of the meal each succeeding generation in Israel entered personally into the Exodus and appropriated the benefits and responsibilities flowing from it. The blood of the lamb represented God's deeds of liberation in Egypt, esp. the slaying of the first-born; the bitter herbs were herbs of the desert and represented the hardships in Egypt as well as those of the journey; the reclining at table as princes symbolized the freedom which each Israelite enjoyed.

According to the Synoptics, the last supper Jesus shared with his Disciples was a Passover, with Jesus as leader (Mt 26.2, 17–19; Mk 14.12–17; Lk 22.7–15), but according to John, the Jews had not yet eaten the Passover meal when they stood before Pilate on Friday to accuse Jesus. In Lk 22.15–18, the Passover meal seems to be indicated as a type of the Eucharist by which the Church, the people of God, is called into existence and each succeeding generation shares in the experience through participation in it. BIBLIOGRAPHY: *Passover Haggadah* (ed. N. N. Glatzer, 1953); EDB 1752.

[A. J. TKACIK]

PASTERNAK, BORIS LEONIDOVICH (1890–1960), Russian poet and novelist in the U.S.S.R. His early poems, which appeared in several collections: *A Twin in the Clouds* (1913), *Above the Barriers* (1917), *My Sister, Life* (1922), *Themes and Variations* (1923), *The Second Birth* (1932), are romantic in their cosmic feeling for nature, but intellectual in their esoteric imagery, unusual syntax, and elliptical phraseology. With some notable exceptions (e.g., *Adolescence of Zhenya Luvers*), the prose works published between 1925 and 1927 are unsuccessful attempts to write positively on revolutionary themes. *Safe Conduct* (1931), also in prose, is a spiritual autobiography of his early years. Accused by Soviet authorities of alienation from the masses and lack of understanding for the Revolution, P. published almost nothing but translations (e.g., of Shakespeare and Goethe) between 1932 and 1943, when he published the volume of poems entitled *On Early Trains*. Though he was encouraged by the so-called thaw in Soviet policy to publish more poems after 1954, his greatest work, *Dr. Zhivago*, appeared first in Italian (1957) and has not yet been published in Soviet Russia. Like the *Divine Comedy*, the novel must be read on several levels. On one level, it is the life story of a Russian intellectual caught in the conflicting political and social currents before and after 1917; on another, it is the record of a spiritual struggle toward a kind of optimism (the name *Zhivago*, derived from the Russian verb "to live," suggests the concept of resurrection). Though the NT has inspired the main imagery of the novel, the Christianity that it reflects is not orthodox, and the symbolism is, in consequence, often obscure. In 1958, P. was awarded the

Nobel Prize for literature, but was forced to refuse it. BIB-LIOGRAPHY: G. Reavey, *Poetry of Boris Pasternak* (1969); R. Payne, *Three Worlds of Boris Pasternak* (1962).

[M. F. MCCARTHY]

PASTEUR, LOUIS (1822–1895), French scientist whose studies of fermentation and spontaneous generation led to his theory that each fermentative process is associated with a specific microorganism. From his theory, P. developed the process of pasteurization by which these microorganisms were eliminated by sterilization. His theory of fermentation became the foundation for a "germ" theory of disease, an area which he researched for the last 20 years of his life. P. always publicly insisted upon a separation of scientific and religious matters; he remained a practicing Catholic throughout his life.

[R. J. LITZ]

PASTOR, LUDWIG VON (1854–1928), ecclesiastical historian. Born at Aachen, P. studied in many institutions before receiving his doctorate at Graz. He taught at the Univ. of Innsbruck, Austria, from 1881 to 1901 and then became director of the Austrian Historical Institute in Rome; in 1920 Austria's ambassador to the Vatican. P. was the first historian to work extensively in the secret Vatican Archives, and was largely responsible for their being opened to scholars. Except for popular biographies of Austrian military heroes, all his voluminous writings pertain to Catholic figures—Johannes Janssen, August Reichensperger, Max von Gagern—or to the Reformation period. His masterpiece is the monumental *History of the Popes since the Close of the Middle Ages* (16 v., 1886–1926 in German; 40 in the Eng. tr., 1891–1953). It rests solidly on his Roman researches. P.'s other important works include *Geschichte des deutschen Volkes,* with J. *Janssen (8 v., 1893–1926), and *Katholische Reformatoren* (1924).

[R. H. SCHMANDT]

PASTOR, in the U.S. the term commonly used for the priest or minister in charge of a RC or a Protestant parish or congregation; sometimes a designation for any clergyman. In Continental languages the same term or its equivalent is restricted to designate a Protestant minister. Among the gifts of Christ to his Church, according to Eph 4.11, are "pastors and teachers." The imagery involved in the biblical term (Gr. *poimen*; Lat. *pastor,* shepherd) made it natural to apply the word to those in the Church responsible for the care of souls—bps. and elders. In the nomenclature proper to the various Churches, another title is often used to designate the one in charge of a local church (e.g., the Methodist "preacher in charge," the Anglican "rector," the RC Lat. term *parochus*).

[N. H. MARING]

PASTOR AETERNUS, title of two documents: (1) bull of Leo X, Dec. 19, 1516, at Lateran Council V, formalizing a concordat with Francis I of France, and notable for its repudiation of *conciliarism; (2) the dogmatic constitution of Vatican Council I on the Church. Its ch. 1–3 define the universal, jurisdictional primacy of St. Peter and of the Roman Pontiff as his successor (D 3055, 3058, 3064); ch. 4 contains the statement of the Council on papal *infallibility, its solemn definition as a dogma of faith (D 3074).

[T. C. O'BRIEN]

PASTORAL EPISTLES, 1 Timothy, 2 Timothy and Titus, three letters traditionally attributed to the Apostle Paul. They are called "Pastoral" because they contain instructions for carrying out the pastoral or ministerial office of the Church. These instructions are directed to two of Paul's associates known from other letters and from Acts. As a group, the Pastorals present a number of distinct peculiarities and problems. The style and language differ somewhat from that of the acknowledged letters of Paul, and yet closely resemble each other, representing a single stylistic and linguistic grouping. The Pastorals presuppose a historical setting found neither in Acts nor in the other letters. They seem to presume a situation in which Paul had been released from his Roman imprisonment (Acts 28; cf. 2 Tim 4.16–18) for further work in the East. Apparently, he was then rearrested, and is not expected to be released a second time (2 Tim 4.6–18). Further, the church situation is peculiar in two respects. First, the danger of heresy to the one faith is now acute. Secondly, a regular ministry and system of ordination seems to exist (1 Tim 3.1–13; 4.14). The distinction between ministry and laity represents a development beyond that found in other Pauline letters. Because of this complex of peculiarities and problems, scholars differ sharply both on the tradition of Pauline authorship and chronology. First Timothy and Titus are concerned with ecclesiastical organization, order, and doctrine, and somewhat secondarily with heresy. Second Timothy on the other hand is primarily concerned with the threat posed by false doctrine. BIBLIOGRAPHY: M. Dibelius - H. Conzelmann, *Pastoral Epistles* (1972); A. T. Hanson, *Pastoral Letters* NEB (1966); B. Easton, *Pastoral Epistles* (1947). *TIMOTHY, LETTERS TO; *TITUS, LETTER TO.

[T. J. RYAN]

PASTORAL PSYCHOLOGY, that branch of applied psychology that enables the religious counselor to understand the client and to develop techniques in a counseling relationship that will free the client's capacity to live the spiritual life more fully, with greater openness to reality and inner harmony. Pastoral psychology is informed by dogmatic and moral theology, but utilizes the rapidly growing body of psychological knowledge to assist the individual who comes to a religious director for assistance. It is generally based on a person-centered rather than problem-centered approach. Pastoral psychology is employed first to enable the "pastor" to understand the client as to: the stages of emotional development, motivation, personality, types, and possible behavior deviations. But pastoral psychology also trains the religious director in the various techniques of guidance, esp. in the counseling situation that relies not on giving advice but on enabling the client to come to greater self-awareness. An important aspect of pastoral psychology is the counselor's ability to recognize psychotic or deeply neurotic behavior so that the client might be referred to a suitable psychotherapist. BIBLIOGRAPHY: A. L. Van Kaam, *Religion and Personality* (1964); R. Vaughan, *Introduction to Religious Counseling* (1969); M. J. O'Brien, *Introduction to Pastoral Counseling* (1968); C. A. Curran, *Religious Values in Counseling and Psychotherapy* (1969).

[T. M. MCFADDEN]

PASTORAL THEOLOGY, the practical discipline which formulates guidelines for the effective exercise of the Church's ministry of salvation. These guidelines and the principles of pastoral action which they imply reflect the essential function of the Church and are rooted in the dogmas of faith, but they are also historically conditioned by the cultural situation in which the gospel is proclaimed. Thus pastoral theology applies the good news of salvation in the light of cultural, psychological, and sociological analyses. In one sense, pastoral theology has been present in the Church from its beginnings, e.g., in Jesus' instruction of his disciples and the advice of Paul in the Pastoral Epistles. Insofar as pastoral theology is understood as the guidance given priests for their ministry, many patristic writings are devoted to the problem. St. Gregory the Great's *De cura pastorali* (590) is the most noted. The Middle Ages witnessed a steady decline in the quality of and importance assigned to pastoral ministry by the clergy, so that both the Protestant Reformation and the Council of Trent sought to bring about widespread reform. Emphasis in the Counter Reformation was placed upon the holiness of the clergy, their intellectual and moral formation, and their commitment to a pastoral office through catechetics, parish visitation, and the regular celebration of the sacraments. Classical proponents of pastoral reform at this time were Sts. Vincent de Paul, Francis de Sales, Alphonsus Liguori, and Charles Borromeo. The contemporary training and formation of the priest for his pastoral care continues to stress personal holiness, the effective dispensation of the sacraments, and intellectual awareness, but seek to do this in a way that reflects developments in the social sciences, especially psychology.

The ecclesiology reflected in Vatican II, however, rejects any cleric-centered view of the Church's mission and even the name pastoral theology itself insofar as it implies a passive congregation which is to be "shepherded" by the priest. Instead, a broadly-conceived practical theology is proposed whereby the saving mission of the whole Church is encompassed. In this sense, pastoral theology would be a subdivision (dealing with priestly ministry) of a practical theology whose aim would be to examine the principles and modes of the Church's evolving presence in the world. BIBLIOGRAPHY: J. H. Brennan, NCE 10:1080–84; H. Schuster, SacMund 4:365–368; M. Pfliegler, *Pastoral Theology* (1966).

[T. M. MCFADDEN]

PATANAZZI family of Italian majolica potters and painters whose workshop in Urbino (1580–1620) was begun by **Antonio,** pupil of Orazio Fontana, and continued by **Alfonso, Francesco,** and **Vincenzo.** Their work—carrying biblical and mythological scenes—is inferior to that of the Fontanas.

[M. J. DALY]

PATARINES (Patarenes, Patarelli), members of a movement at Milan (*c.* 1050) against the simony and concubinage of the clergy. The quarter of the city where they met, Pataria, is probably the origin of the name. Most of the members were simple laymen, and in their zeal against abuses of the clergy they had the support of Popes Stephen IX and Alexander II. Patarines refused to receive the sacraments from simoniacal bps. or priests; sometimes they used physical force to remove unworthy clergy. In their struggles against the abps. of Milan appointed by the Emperor Henry IV they became opponents of lay investiture. Their leaders SS. Arialdus and Erlembaldus were martyred by agents of the archbishops. The spirit of the movement spread to other parts of Italy and contributed to the Gregorian Reform. By the end of the 11th cent. the Patarines ceased to be active. For uncertain reasons the same name was applied in the 12th cent. to the *Bogomils; Lateran Council IV (1179; D 760) used it as practically synonymous with *Cathari; and in the 13th and 14th cent. it often designated any sort of heretic. BIBLIOGRAPHY: S. Runciman, *Medieval Manichee* (1961) 94–115; C. Violante, *La pataria milanese e la riforma ecclesiastica* I (1955); *idem,* NCE 10:1084–85; E. Werner, *Pauperes Christi* (1956) 111–164.

[C. J. LYNCH]

PATEN, dish or plate used in the Mass to hold the communion bread. With a decline in frequency of communion on the part of the people, this became small and held only the wafer to be received by the priest; a ciborium held the people's wafers. Liturgical instructions on the Mass now suggest a large paten able to hold all the communion bread.

[J. DALLEN]

PATER, WALTER (1839–94), an English essayist and one of the major Victorian critics, educated at Cambridge and Oxford. His literary career began with the publication of an essay, *Winckelmann* (1867), which contains the characteristics of style that gave P. his unique distinction: precision and refinement. He was the somewhat reluctant leader of the Aesthetic Movement. A man of scrupulous conscience and high moral standards, P. was associated only with the doctrine of the movement and not with the extravagance to which the creed of beauty degenerated because of "fanatics" who distorted its ends, even to the point of relaxing the principles of morality, with the result that certain members ended in complete "moral and social shipwreck." P.'s *Studies in the History of the Renaissance* (1873) established his reputation. *Marius the Epicurean* (1885), a romance, is considered his finest work and the greatest of all his contributions to literature. Other works are *Child in the House* (1894), clearly reminiscent of his own early childhood; and two posthumous publications, *Greek Studies* (1895) and *Gaston Latour* (1896). BIBLIOGRAPHY: A. C. Benson, *Walter Pater* (1906); A. Symons, *Walter Pater: Studies in Prose and Verse* (1904).

[S. A. HEENEY]

PATER NOSTER PLAYS, an extinct genre of medieval play, regarded as a predecessor of the morality plays. Surviving records and allusions indicate that the different petitions of the Lord's Prayer were illustrated by using allegorical characterizations for the ideas involved, probably as virtues and vices personified. One historian, Hardin Craig, has suggested that the Pater Noster play was a cycle of saints' lives, each component featuring a saint outstanding for one of the virtues opposed to the seven deadly sins.

[E. C. DUNN]

PATERIKON, in Eastern monasticism, a book about a particular monastery that includes a chronicle of the monastery and an account of the lives of abbots and monks renowned for their saintly lives. Paterikons printed in more recent times include, in addition to descriptions of the monastery involved, maps showing its location, and pictures of it and its recent superiors. Devotional material such as exhortations for Christians to lead a more devout life and appeals to the faithful to consider whether they were called to the monastic life are sometimes included.

[S. SURRENCY]

PATERNIANS (Venustians), a sect teaching that the lower parts of the body were created not by God but by the devil. They made this doctrine an excuse for lives of flagrant sexual license. Augustine (*Haer.* 85) says little of their origin, name, or diffusion. Augustine probably derived his information from the Pelagian *Julian of Eclanum, who accused Augustine of a similar teaching on the origin of human sexuality. No doubt the name *Venustiani,* indicating dedication to Venus, was given them because of their excesses. The *Praedestinatus* (1.85) claims that they were condemned by Pope Damasus and that a subsequent civil law made them liable to prosecution on a capital charge. But the *Praedestinatus* is not a reliable source. BIBLIOGRAPHY: É. Amann, DTC 11:2246-47.

[L. G. MÜLLER]

PATERNITY DIVINE, the fatherhood that exists in God on a twofold level, the natural and the adoptive, both being intimately related; in conventional theological parlance paternity refers only to the former. It designates in the mystery of the divine life the eternal relationship of the Father to the Son. The Father begets the Son eternally. Since all that exists in God is God and there is in him no plurality other than of relationships, the relationship of paternity is identical with the person of the Father. This means that the Father is constituted as person by the relationship of paternity; he is Father essentially. Correlated to that of paternity, there exists in God a relationship of *filiation, identical to the Son, who in turn subsists only as related to the Father. Mutually distinct, the relationships of paternity and filiation are respectively identical with the divine nature. Thus, though Father and Son are two distinct persons, both are one God. BIBLIOGRAPHY: R. L. Richard, NCE 10:1086.

[J. DUPUIS]

PATIENCE, the virtue of Christian suffering. Among the moral virtues patience alone is the one that, according to St. Thomas Aquinas, cannot exist without grace and charity: that someone should put the good which grace gives above all else that the human heart holds dear, and sustain the grief of their loss requires that charity which loves God above all (ThAq ST 2a2ae, 136.3). This peculiarly Christian quality of patience does not mean that only the Christian suffers pain bravely; but the emphasis is on the totality implied by charity: the preferential love of God above all means negatively the will to accept the loss of everything rather than be separated from God's love. The love of God is the sole effective motive for suffering total loss without despair, without terror, without rebellion against God. The distinctive meaning of patience is exemplified in the total sacrifice of Christ, in the ordeal of the martyrs. St. Thomas's teaching reflects the tradition deriving from antiquity through Augustine (*De patientia*). Patience is the highest disposition for the total surrender that marks the child of God relying on the loving will and hidden ways of the Father; it permits imitation of Christ's atonement in the face of life's hardships. Its full development is not a matter of course, but a measure of highest growth in spiritual maturity.

[T. C. O'BRIEN]

PATINIR (PATINIER), JOACHIM DE, (*c.*1485–1524), Flemish painter from the Meuse valley, master of the Antwerp guild (1515). He excels through a distinctive landscape style, even collaborates as scenery specialist with Massys (*Temptation of St. Anthony,* Prado) and others. With a high station point he creates grandiose panoramic landscapes filling three-quarters of space with brown foreground, green middleground, and blue distance, the figures small and incidental. Early signed paintings: *St. Jerome, Rest on the Flight into Egypt* (Antwerp) and *Baptism of Christ* with details by Metsys and Joos van Cleve. P.'s four greatest works are the Prado *Rest on the Flight into Egypt* with warm romantic setting, *Charon Crossing the Styx,* with Boschlike, weird beasts and *Temptation of St. Anthony* with its "ship of fools" after Brueghel. P. evidences a "prophetic intuition in his landscapes" as M. J. Friedländer wrote. BIBLIOGRAPHY: B. Koch, *Joachim Patinir* (1968); M. J. Friedländer, *From Van Eyck to Bruegel* (1956).

[R. BERGMANN]

PATMORE, COVENTRY (1823–96), English poet and prose writer. Privately tutored by his father, P. had no formal education except for 6 months in the Collège de France at the age of 16. He worked for 20 years as a librarian in the British Museum, writing poetry on the side. His *Poems* (1844) made him known to various men of letters such as Gabriel Rossetti. He was thus drawn to the Pre-Raphaelite movement and contributed his poem *The Seasons* to *The Germ,* their publication. In 1854 the first part of his best-known poem, *Angel in the House,* appeared. It exalts the sanctity of married love and was continued in *Espousals* (1856), *Faithful Forever* (1860), and *Victories of Love* (1863). P. became a convert to Roman Catholicism (1864) and in 1877 published *Unknown Eros,* a series of 43 odes that reflect the spiritual change effected by his conversion, considered by some as his finest work. BIBLIOGRAPHY: E. W. Gosse, *Coventry Patmore* (1905, repr. 1973); J. C. Reid, *Mind and Art of Coventry Patmore* (1957).

[S. A. HEENEY]

PATRIARCH, a term applied in the OT to the chiefs of the tribes of Israel and in the NT also to Abraham and David; and used in the Christian Church as a title of respect, first for all bps. without consideration of hierarchical rank, and gradually reserved to the bps. of the principal centers of Christianity (Rome, Constantinople, Alexandria, Antioch, Jerusalem). This practice was stated in a letter of Justinian II to Pope John V (687). The Roman pontiff was understood to be the first patriarch, but this title was absorbed in his higher rank as head of the entire Church. The patriarch is the father and head of his Church or rite, with ordinary power over metropolitans, bps., clergy, religious, and faithful. However, he is only the first among otherwise equal bishops. The authority of a Catholic is greater than that of an Orthodox patriarch, despite the fact that the Orthodox patriarchate as such is independent of any higher ecclesiastical authority. The law covering the Catholic Eastern patriarchs is codified in ClerSanc (cc. 216–314) and in Vat II EastCath. Although he is head of his Church, the patriarch can exercise his authority only together with his hierarchy. Affairs of lesser importance he resolves alone—e.g., dispensations and encyclical letters. For more important matters the advice or consent of the permanent synod is needed—e.g., to dispense the entire patriarchate, establish exarchies, grant the *stauropegium. The election of bps., the establishment of dioceses and the transfer of bps., etc. are reserved to the patriarchal synod under the presidency of the patriarch, although in all these matters the initiative is in his hands. The patriarch is elected by a synod composed of all the bps. of the patriarchate. Confirmation of a secular ruler may be needed in Orthodox Churches; Catholic patriarchs can be enthroned at once and then only request

ecclesiastical communion with the pope. The patriarch is addressed as His Holiness or Beatitude. He sometimes wears a white supracamelaucium (*epanokamilovkion, klobuk*). He consecrates the holy myron (chrism) for the entire Church. The major Catholic patriarchs (Alexandria, Antioch) are now appointed cardinals, ranking after the cardinal bishops.

Catholic Patriarchal Titles. The pope, as bp. of Rome is patriarch of the West. The patriarch of Alexandria is known as the patriarch of the Copts. Antioch has Byzantine (Melchite), Maronite, and Syrian patriarchs; the Melchite patriarch of Antioch has also the personal title of patriarch of Alexandria and Jerusalem. At Baghdad there is the Chaldean patriarch of Babylon; in Lebanon there is the Armenian patriarch of Cilicia. Latin rite patriarchs are merely titular; they include the Latin rite patriarch of Jerusalem (1847), of Venice (Aquileia-Grado 607; transferred 1451), Lisbon (1716), West Indies (ordinary of the Spanish armed forces, 1540), and East Indies (the abp. of Goa, 1886).

Orthodox Patriarchal Titles. The archbishop of Constantinople is the Byzantine or ecumenical patriarch (i.e., of the entire Byzantine Empire) and first prelate of the Eastern Orthodox Churches. There is also an Armenian patriarch of Constantinople. At Alexandria there is a Byzantine pope and patriarch, and a Coptic patriarch. Antioch has Byzantine and Syrian patriarchs; Jerusalem, Byzantine and Armenian. The patriarchal title is also accorded to the heads of the following Churches: Bulgarian (1235; reestablished 1953); Serbian (1346; reestablished 1920); Russian (patriarch of Moscow and all Russia, 1589); Romanian (1925); Armenian (catholicos-patriarch at Etchmiadzin and patriarch of Cilicia); Nestorian (catholicos-patriarch of the Chaldeans of the East, who resides in Los Angeles, Cal.); Ethiopian (1959). BIBLIOGRAPHY: V. J. Pospishil, *Law on Persons* (1960); idem, *Der Patriarch in der Serbisch-Orthodoxen Kirche* (1966); E. Eid, *La Figure juridique du patriarche* (1962); G. Salem et al., NCE 10:1088–96.

[V. J. POSPISHIL]

PATRIARCH, LATIN. During the period of the *Crusades, Latin bps. were given, or assumed, the jurisdiction and title of patriarch of Jerusalem, Antioch, and Constantinople, thereby displacing the legitimate Oriental patriarchs. A Latin patriarch of Alexandria was never installed and remained merely titular. After the Crusades the Latin patriarchs usually resided in Rome as titulars, but gradually this was done away with and Orientals resumed actual jurisdiction. These abuses, arising chiefly from Western ignorance, have been understandably offensive to Eastern Christians. In 1847 a residential Latin patriarch was named for Jerusalem with jurisdiction over the Latin faithful in Palestine and Jordan. In addition the Catholic bps. of Venice, Lisbon, and Goa bear the strictly honorary title of patriarch.

[G. T. DENNIS]

PATRIARCHATE OF THE WEST, that part of the RC Church under the patriarchal jurisdiction of the bp. of

Rome, as distinguished from the areas under the similar jurisdiction of the various Eastern patriarchs. This designation presupposes the distinction between the papal power of the pope and his patriarchal power. Those who belong to the Western patriarchate are bound by the Roman Code of Canon Law and worship according to the Latin Rite. Although originally a territorial division, its members are now found throughout the world.

[T. M. MCFADDEN]

PATRIARCHS (BIBLE). The title is applied to the great figures of Israel's history, but is more generally restricted to the three, Abraham, Isaac, and Jacob whose stories are related in Gen 12–50. The substance of these accounts is the migration of Abraham from Mesopotamia to Canaan, his wandering in the hill country, the birth and marriage of Isaac, the birth and marriages of Jacob, his 12 sons, the taking of Joseph to Egypt and the later descent of the whole family to that land. As they now stand, the stories of the patriarchs serve as an introduction to the story of Israel. They have undergone some theological transformation to that end. The covenantal observations and particularly the promises of a great posterity and of future possession of the land are the principal areas of this transformation by the three traditions (Yahwist, Elohist, and Priestly) responsible for the material. Varying cultic and moral emphases can also be attributed to these traditions. For the most part, however, the authors respected their sources and presented them as they found them. But before they adopted them, the stories had already experienced a long period (some 800 years or more) of oral transmission, during which elaboration took place. This is not history in the modern sense of the word. Nevertheless, archeology and other sciences have shown that the patriarchal narratives are an authentic reflection of the period attributed to them, the first half of the 2d millennium B.C. Originally independent stories about individuals, peoples, and holy places, they were gradually developed as cycles of stories centering on an individual patriarch and preserved at various sanctuaries. These were then taken over by the later Israelites when they conquered the land and were affixed to their history of salvation. Because of the elaboration and adaptation, it is impossible to answer specific questions about the historical character of particular events and persons. But the evidence would justify the theological use made of the stories by Israel. The Exodus from Egypt had definite historical antecedents in the movements of the patriarchs in Canaan some 400 years earlier. Israel's faith saw these as under the direction of the same God that brought it out of the land of Egypt. BIBLIOGRAPHY: P. Trible, "Depatriarchalizing in Biblical Interpretation," *Journal, American Academy of Religion* 41 (1973) 1, 30–48; T. L. Leishman, *Continuity of the Bible: The Patriarchs* (1968).

[E. H. MALY]

PATRICIAN BROTHERS (FSP), members of a religious community entitled the Congregation of the Brothers of St. Patrick, founded in Ireland in 1808 by Bp. Daniel Delaney. The brothers take simple perpetual vows and are engaged in the Christian education and instruction of youth. The congregation received papal approbation in 1893. There are about 241 Patrician Brothers serving in Ireland, Africa, India, Pakistan, Australia, and the United States. They are divided into three provinces and have 36 houses. The superior general resides at Tullow, County Carlow, Ireland.

[R. A. TODD]

PATRICIUS ROMANORUM, an honorary title first conferred by Emperor Constantine I. It was bestowed on important imperial officers, and in the West became part of the title of the exarch of Ravenna. After the end of the exarchate in the 8th cent. the popes bestowed the title on the Frankish kings and it became a distinction of the Holy Roman Emperor as protector of the papacy. Henry IV, however, used the title as deriving from the Roman people to assert his rights against Gregory VII in the *investiture struggle. The patriciate was abolished by the commune of Rome in its revolt (1143) against the papacy and restoration of a Roman republic under *Arnold of Brescia.

[T. C. O'BRIEN]

PATRICK, ST., apostle of Ireland, 5th-cent. bp. who preached the gospel in the North and West of Ireland where no Christian evangelist had yet entered. The entire chronology of his life is subject to dispute. It is even seriously conjectured that there were others, esp. Palladius, the first bp. sent to Ireland by Pope Celestine I in 431, who evangelized Ireland in the 5th cent., and that their accomplishments have been absorbed into the legends surrounding P. because of the eventual prestige of Armagh and its claim to be his see. There are two authentic writings of P. that have survived: his *Confessio* and the letter (*Epistola*) to Coroticus; although these remarkable documents are only accidentally concerned with chronology and biography, they do give a credible account of his religious vocation and ministry in Ireland. The *Confessio* was written in old age as an account of God's mercy to the author and as an answer to his critics. In it he mentions his birth at "Bannavem Taberniae" in Roman Britain; which may mean (1) near Dumbarton on the Clyde; (2) in Cumberland to the S of Hadrian's Wall; or (3) at the mouth of the Severn—to mention just the three places most favored by scholars. His grandfather was a Christian priest. His father was a deacon and, at the time of P.'s birth, an official of the Roman Empire in Britain. At the age of 16 P. was kidnapped (by Irish raiders) from his father's estate and sold as a slave in Ireland. He served his master as a shepherd for 6 years before escaping by ship and then wandering over desolate terrain for days, and eventually returning to his kinfolk. He spent years in Gaul where he entered the religious life and prepared for a mandate to evangelize in the land of his former captors "who dwelt beside the wood of Foclut . . . near the western sea." It was during his captivity that he wished he had not neglected the warnings of the priests, and that he learned to pray night and day, in forest and on the mountain, in snow and frost and rain. His name was Magonus Sucatus, and may have taken or been given the name Patricius (meaning nobleman) on his ordination as a kind of cancellation of his slave background and deficient education. Upon returning to Ireland, perhaps already in late maturity, he was able to gain the support of local kings, oppose the Druids, travel extensively, baptize multitudes, and receive many into the religious life, including sons and daughters of chieftains. His ecclesiastical innovations were adapted to the Irish clan structure, with monastic communities playing an important role. Even at the end of his life he expected daily a violent death, to be robbed or reduced to slavery. In his letter to Coroticus he demanded the excommunication of the British prince Coroticus for a raid on Ireland in which some of P.'s new Christians were killed and others sold into slavery. He was homesick for Britain and for Gaul, but decided he should stay in Ireland until death. Like Abraham he merited the title of Father of a new nation in a strange and foreign land. P. summed up his own life in words that echo the Magnificat of Mary: "I was a stone lying deep in the mire; and he who is mighty came and scooped me up, lifted me high, and set me atop the wall" (PL 53:805). BIBLIOGRAPHY: J. B. Bury, *Life of St. Patrick* (1905); L. Bieler NCE 10:1099–1102; idem, *Life and Legend of St. Patrick* (1949); PL 53:789–840; Butler 1:612–617.

[E. J. DILLON]

PATRIMONY, one of the titles of *ordination, meaning that the candidate has a secure, life-long source of income for his support as a priest.

PATRIMONY OF ST. PETER. (1) the lands that came under papal dominion after the *Peace of the Church (313) under *Constantine the Great; (2) the *States of the Church after the campaigns of 754 and 756 by Pepin against the Lombards (see also *DONATION OF CONSTANTINE); (3) within the States of the Church, the territory of the duchy of Rome or province of Lazio, the last lost by the papacy in the Risorgimento. BIBLIOGRAPHY: P. Partner, *Lands of St. Peter* (1972).

[T. C. O'BRIEN]

PATRIOTISM (from late Lat. *patriota,* fellow-countryman [St. Gregory uses the term]; Gr. *patrios,* of one's fathers), the love of one's country and the will to promote its welfare. At first patriot was usually qualified good, true, sound, or the like; when unqualified it could refer disparagingly to a Parliament man who claimed he was supporting his country against the king and court.

In medieval moral theology the nearest category is *pietas,* which in classical Latin meant a sense of duty toward the gods, one's kin, benefactors, or country. It is ranged under justice, the virtue of rendering what is objectively due in fairness, but it is not a type of pure justice because its service is not given to an equal or to another who is altogether distinct; for these reasons also it is not contractual. Patriotism is shown to what is above you and of which you are part, to your home, even though it may have been a bad home, to a *connaturale principium,* as St. Thomas Aquinas says, a cause to which you are, or should be, attached by a sympathy deeper than choice, a *principium essendi,* the stock that gave you life. It is a particular sense of justice not possible if you are rootless, and though in his day nationalism was not the social and political force it afterwards became, Aquinas did recognize that patriotism toward your own provided the social cohesion underlying the distinct and more formalized virtue of respect for the dignity of office and obedience toward superiors.

Racial identity may be an element, and one not to be despised, and nationality "by birth" is justly esteemed; nevertheless explicitly patriotic communities, such as the U.S. and United Kingdom show a remarkable capacity of assimilating strangers who respond to their adoption with the authentic spirit.

Patriotism goes deeper than the good citizenship of serving the State, which is a more artificial construction than country, and certainly deeper than supporting the government in power. Indeed it may prompt opposition, as in the case of public demonstrations against current policies, where participants actuated by love of country can be discerned pretty readily from those who are not. It persists, even as family piety does (even when most that has been learned with profit has often been from bad example) in the stubborn feeling, "my country right or wrong," though this should not extend to condoning or cooperating in its misdeeds, or to jingoism or xenophobia. Patriotism, exclaimed Dr. Johnson, the last refuge of a scoundrel. Still, a refuge is something, and a saving grace is more. For a devotion that claims no rights, a local patriotism or one that spreads beyond the frontiers of one's country, a partisanship for a team or a good cause, is truly a gracious and supernatural virtue. All the same we may end with the simple words of Nurse Cavell who died for it; they are carved on the plinth of her statue, "Patriotism is not enough." BIBLIOGRAPHY: ThAq ST 2a2ae, 101, esp. Lat-Eng, v. 41, ed. T. C. O'Brien.

[T. GILBY]

PATRIPASSIANISM, also called Sabellianism, one of the early Trinitarian heresies closely related to the heterodox teachings of monarchianism and modalism. To safeguard the unity of the Godhead, the patripassianists held that Father, Son, and Holy Spirit were different manifestations of a single divine person. Consequently the Father became man and suffered (whence the name patripassianism). This teaching originating with Noetus of Smyrna was propagated esp. by Epigonus, Cleomenes, Praxeas, and Sabellius. BIBLIOGRAPHY: J. N. D. Kelly, *Early Christian Doctrine* (2d ed. 1960) 120–123; Daniélou-Marrou 1:106–108; 144–151; H. Crouzel, LTK 8:180–181.

[H. DRESSLER]

PATRISTIC PHILOSOPHY, the philosophical elements discernible in the writings of the Fathers of the Church. The Fathers were not philosophers, but apologists and exponents of the teachings of faith. The philosophers were, in a sense, their antagonists, since the philosophers were pagans whose world-view had to cede to the vision of creation and of man given by Christ as revelation of the Father. Yet early in Christian history the conviction manifested itself that faith and revelation did give a *gnōsis,* a wisdom illumining the meaning of existence and that surpassed the wisdom of the philosophers. Further there was the position that whatever of truth the philosophers had enuntiated was theirs as "unjust possessors." The more "intellectualist" (rather than the moralists) among the Fathers appropriated philosophical concepts and language from their own milieu. The philosophy of the Fathers can thus be taken to mean elements of the main currents of thought in antiquity, assimilated and adapted to serve the faith. These elements were, in brief, from Plato, the Neoplatonists, Aristotle, the Stoics. As far as the influence of the Fathers on the development of Christian philosophy is concerned Augustine's work is, of course, preeminent. BIBLIOGRAPHY: G. Prestige, *God in Patristic Thought* (1936); Y.-M. Congar, *History of Theology* (H. Guthrie, tr., 1968) 37–49.

[T. C. O'BRIEN]

PATRISTIC THEOLOGY, that part of Christian theological activity that endeavors to discover, examine, and synthesize the content of revelation by investigating the insights and structuring the analyses and understandings that have been achieved in the period of history from NT times to the close of the 8th cent. (although the limits of the period of patristic witness are not determined). It has its beginning as a discipline separate from biblical, dogmatic, and speculative theology in the 17th century. It is related to patrology, since both study the extensive literature of the Fathers; to the history of dogmas, since both examine the truths of revelation in historical context and seek to discern and explain the development of revelation and show the historical continuity of present Christian forms with the witness found in the doctrinal expositions, biblical commentaries, and sermons of the Fathers. As a theological endeavor it moves from within the community of faith and looks to a true and fuller contemporary apprehension of revelation by enriching current theological understanding with the self-understanding of the early Christian period. This theological concern for faith to some degree limits patristic theology to the writings of the Fathers and ecclesiastical writers, who wrote from the community of faith with the purpose of making known revealed truth and to be witnesses of the Christian faith. To be accepted as such a witness of biblical faith, orthodox doctrine, holiness of life, antiquity, and recognition in some way by the Church provided some criteria for the Church's judgment. BIBLIOGRAPHY: F. X. Murphy, NCE 10:1107–11; H. Musurillo, "New Horizons in Patristic Theology," *Traditio* 14 (1958) 33–61.

[E. F. MALONE]

PATRIZI, FRANCESCO SAVERIO (1797–1881), biblical scholar. P. was professor of Scripture and Hebrew at the Roman College. He wrote numerous exegetical works; his *De interpretatione scripturarum sacrarum* (2v., 1844) was a skilled and frequently used hermeneutical treatise, and his *De Evangeliis* (3v., 1853) sought to refute the rationalistic interpretation of the New Testament. BIBLIOGRAPHY: W. Drum, CE 11:559–560.

[T. M. MCFADDEN]

PATROCLUS, ST. (d. 2d half of 3d cent.), martyr. According to Gregory of Tours, P. was buried at Troyes and near his tomb stood an oratory; there his cult developed after the discovery of the *passio* recounting the story of his martyrdom. In 960 the relics of P. were given by the bp. of Troyes as a gesture of gratitude to St. Bruno, bp. of Cologne, who had them deposited in the church of Soest in Wesphalia. The inhabitants of that place attributed their deliverance from siege in 1447 to this saint's intercession. BIBLIOGRAPHY: J.-C. Didier, BiblSanct 10:417–418.

[H. DRESSLER]

PATROCLUS OF ARLES (d. 426), bishop. According to the report of Prosper of Aquitaine, P. became bp. of Arles in 412 after the people of that city expelled their bp., Heros, a disciple of St. Martin of Tours. P. caused discord among the bps. of Gaul. In 417 Pope Zosimus, despite objections from Proclus, bp. of Marseilles, and Simplicius, bp. of Vienne, declared P. primate of Gaul, but Pope Boniface I, successor of Zosimus, did not renew the privilege. In 426 P. was murdered by the tribune Barnabas. BIBLIOGRAPHY: MGHS Auct. ant. 9:466, 471; É. Griffe, *La Gaule chrétienne* (2d ed., 1966) 2:146–157.

[H. DRESSLER]

PATROLOGY, a term first used by the Lutheran theologian Johann Gerhard (1582–1637) in his posthumously published *Patrologia* (1653). In current usage it generally designates the scientific study of the life and works of ancient Christian authors both orthodox and heretical. In the West "ancient" designates writers from the subapostolic age to Isidore of Seville (d. 636); in the East it extends to John Damascene (d. 749). In the scientific study of writers included in these time limits patrology not only designates their works as genuine, doubtful, or spurious, but also indicates their doctrinal significance, their relations to their cultural heritage and to their contemporaries within and without the Church. The beginnings of patrology reach back to the *Ecclesiastical History* of Eusebius of Caesarea and to St. Jerome's *De viris illustribus.* Interest in the writings of the Fathers continued throughout the Middle Ages and received new impetus through the editions of the Maurists and the works of Tillemont and Ceillier. A new era in patrology began in mid-19th cent. with J. P. Migne's two series of texts: *Patrologia Graeca* and *Patrologia Latina* (1844–66). These were quickly followed by the critical editions in Latin and Greek: *Corpus scriptorum ecclesiasticorum latinorum*

(1866–), *Die griechischen christlichen Schriftsteller der ersten drei Jahrhunderte* (1897–). The 20th cent. witnessed the resurgence of Oriental patrology in the *Corpus scriptorum orientalium Christianorum* (1903–) and the continuing interest in Greek and Latin texts in the editions *Sources chrétiennes* (1942–) and the *Corpus Christianorum* (1953–). BIBLIOGRAPHY: Quasten 1:1–22; Altaner 1–44; A. Hamman, LTK 8:183–187.

[H. DRESSLER]

PATRON SAINT, a saint whose heavenly protection and intercession are invoked by a particular place, person, profession, institution, or other social or economic category. The selection of patron saints in early Christian times presumably rested on the association of the saint in question with a specific locale or activity, whether historical or legendary; but patron saints are still chosen by individuals—for instance, by parents when naming their children at baptism, by children when taking an additional name at confirmation, and by religious in adopting a new name at the time of entrance into religious life. In more recent times, the Church itself has officially designated certain saints as the patrons of enterprises or occupations that could be appropriately related to some event or aspect of their lives. Tutelary deities were of course common throughout the pagan world, so that the custom of choosing patron saints may be simply a continuation of an antique and almost ubiquitous practice. The theological justification for the practice among Christians, however, can be found in the doctrine of the communion of saints. Certainly by the early 4th cent., Christians were naming their children after the Apostles and martyrs, and soon thereafter began the custom of dedicating churches to saints, the patron chosen often being the martyr over whose tomb the church was erected. The custom increased with time, reaching its apogee in the Middle Ages, when not only many of Europe's greatest cathedrals were dedicated to patron saints but most of the newly arising towns bore saints' names as well, and nearly every nation, guild, fraternity, condition or complaint in life was assigned its special saintly protector. Some of the more celebrated patron saints of countries are: Patrick (Ireland); Andrew (Scotland); David (Wales); George (England); Joan of Arc (France); Catherine of Siena (Italy); Stephen (Hungary); Cyril and Methodius (South Slavs); and Casimir (Poland and Lithuania). Patrons of cities include SS. Geneviève and Denis (Paris), Peter and Paul (Rome), Gennaro (Naples), Mark (Venice), and Anthony (Lisbon). St. Luke is the patron of physicians; St. Francis de Sales, of writers and journalists; St. Thomas Aquinas, of scholars; St. Francis Xavier, of Christian missionaries; St. Cecilia, of sacred music; St. Vincent de Paul, of charitable works; St. Christopher, of travelers; St. Valentine, of lovers; St. Monica, of wives and mothers; and St. Nicholas, of children.

[E. M. GATES]

PATRONAGE (CANON LAW), the rights, privileges, and responsibilities that the Church concedes to individual founders of churches, chapels, or benefices (CIC, c. 1448). Once widespread, patronage has all but disappeared; in 1917 the Code of Canon Law abolished the right to patronage (CIC c. 1450, §2) and stressed the obligations rather than the privileges of patrons. To implement Vat II BpPastOff 28, Paul VI in 1966 with the *motu proprio, Ecclesiae sanctae,* 18, further curtailed the right or privilege of presenting priests to a parochial office or benefice; the bp.'s right of freedom in this regard was strengthened.

[R. A. ARONSTAM]

PATRONATO REAL, Spanish term meaning royal patronage, but referring more specifically to the system of Church-State relations under which the Church operated in the American colonies and elsewhere in the Spanish empire. Because of the dominant administrative and fiduciary role played by the monarch in the overseas Spanish Church, *patronato real* in practice made for a somewhat parochial institution far removed from Rome's restraining influence. The Portuguese *padroado* operated similarly in Portugal's empire in India, the Far East, Africa, and Brazil. The system of patronage developed throughout Europe in the early Middle Ages as the result of the Church's need for lay support in the founding of churches and other ecclesiastic institutions. In return for their help, patrons enjoyed the privilege of appointing the incumbent of the benefice and of collecting the revenues derived therefrom. Though the institution had declined in Europe by the 15th cent., it was to find new life, and its most extended expression, in the world empires then being created by the monarchs of Spain and Portugal. Initially, the papacy saw only advantages in a system that would spare it the enormous expenses connected with converting the native populations of several continents; Spanish and Portuguese gold could instead be entrusted with the enterprise. Thus, after Columbus returned from his first voyage to America in 1493, Alexander VI readily affirmed Ferdinand and Isabella's claims to the territory discovered along with their self-imposed Christianizing mission, for which purpose they received a wide variety of apostolic privileges. This almost unconditional grant was seconded by Pope Julius II, who in 1508 assigned to the rulers of Castile and Léon in perpetuity the right to authorize ecclesiastical construction and to propose the personnel for the offices and benefices pertaining to all such cathedrals, churches, monasteries, and related establishments—their choices then to be passed on by the pope or his bishops. In time, the monarchy began to look at this right of patronage, by which the king acted as the pope's delegate in the New World, as irrevocable and even as an inherent regal right. In operation, the system allowed the king, aided by the Council of the Indies in Spain, and the vice patrons in the colonies (which included the viceroys, presidents of *audiencias,* and provincial governors) to rule over the Spanish Church with an iron hand throughout the colonial period. Though theoretically patronage embraced only the right to present candidates for offices and benefices, in actuality the king and his surrogates assumed many others which seriously prejudiced the freedom of the Church and made of its hierarchy little more than civil servants. For instance, nominees had to go through the same bureaucratic procedures that were imposed on other public officials, while the very qualifications of those entering the priesthood were also determined by the *patronato real–mestizos* being forbidden ordination through the 17th century. In addition, the Council of the Indies prevented direct contact between the Vatican and the Spanish Church in America by censoring or altering communications from the Holy See and by forbidding bps. to report directly to Rome. The upshot of this heavy-handed control was to stunt the growth of the Church by preventing its development along lines most appropriate to its task in the New World. Thus, even after the Spanish colonies (Mexico, Central and South America) broke away from the mother country in the 19th cent., the Church still lacked the experience and personnel to establish fully its independence vis-à-vis the new republican governments and therefore remained subject to pressure from the State. The system of royal patronage was not finally ended in the Spanish colonies until the end of the century when Cuba became independent and Puerto Rico and the Philippines were acquired by the United States. Portugal, on the other hand, maintained the *padroado* in India until 1953; but at least in India and Southeast Asia the Portuguese patronage system, unlike the Spanish, had from the 17th cent. through the 19th experienced some very stiff competition from the missionaries sent out by the Congregation for the Propagation of the Faith.

[E. M. GATES]

PATTADAKAL, TEMPLES AT. In the 7th and 8th cent. in Pattadakal, capital of the Chālukya dynasty, among numerous temples the important Pāpanātha (northern type) and Virūpāksha (southern type) show perfection in interior development: the open porch, *mandapam* (assembly hall) with ceiling supported by elaborate columns, the devotee moving from the brilliant exterior to the darkness of the shrine (*garbhagriha*, womb chamber). The exterior aesthetic of these temples, marred by awkward transitions, was later to be solved by architects of N India.

[M. J. DALY]

PATTON, FRANCIS LANDEY (1843–1932), Presbyterian clergyman and educator. A native of Bermuda, Patton was educated in Toronto and at Princeton Theological Seminary, graduating and being ordained to the ministry in 1865. After serving pastorates and teaching at what is now McCormick Theological Seminary, Chicago, he was called in 1883 to Princeton Seminary to teach about the relationship of philosophy and science to the Christian religion. In 1888 he became president of the College of New Jersey (now Princeton Univ.), where he was successful as an administrator, an exponent of theism, a teacher of Christian ethics, and an imaginative and witty lecturer. He was involved in the theological controversies of the Presbyterian

Church in the U.S.A. in the post-Civil War period. His continued interest in theological matters is indicated by one of his most important books, *Fundamental Christianity* (1926).

[J. H. SMYLIE]

PATUZZI, GIOVANNI VINCENZO (d. 1769), Dominican preacher and moralist at Venice. He was a disciple of D. *Concina and wrote against the moral systems of *probabilism and *equiprobabilism, esp. that of St. Alphonsus Liguori, in his *Trattato della regola prossima delle azioni umane nella scelta delle opinioni* (1758) and in *La causa del probabilismo*. BIBLIOGRAPHY: T. Deman, DTC 13:579–580 s.v. "Probabilisme."

[T. C. O'BRIEN]

PAUL, ST., APOSTLE, author of several NT writings, Apostle of the Gentiles.

Life. Two sources within the NT itself provide information: first, the account of his early hostility, conversion, missionarh journeys, and captivity in Acts 7.58; 9.1–30; 11.25–30; 12.25; 13.1–28.31; second, the biographical references in the Pauline Epistles, chiefly Gal 1.11–2.14; Phil 3.4–7 and 4.16; 1 Cor 7.7; 16.5–9; 2 Cor 2.1–4, 9–13; 11.32–33; 12.2–9, 14, 17, 21; 13.1, 10; Rom 11.1; 15.19–28. From references to the appointments of certain Roman officials, notably that of Gallo, proconsul in Achaia, as well as to the famine that occurred in A.D. 46 (see Acts 11.28–30) and to the expulsion of the Jews from Rome in A.D. 49 (see Acts 18.2), a reasonably accurate chronology of Paul's life can be reconstructed. He was born at Tarsus (Acts 22.3) *c*.5–10 A.D. He had the privileges of Roman citizenship from birth (Acts 16.37–40; 21.39), and learned the trade of tent-making (Acts 18.3) by which he was to support himself throughout his apostolic journeys (1 Cor 9.11–18). A student of the rabbi *Gamaliel (Acts 22.3) he was, in his early years, a rigid Pharisee (Acts 23.6; 1 Cor 15.9; Gal 1.13; Phil 3.6), and as such actively supported those who stoned Stephen to death (Acts 7.58). He received authority from the Sanhedrin to harass, imprison, and possibly to extradite Christians (Acts 9.1–2). While he was actually engaged in this *c*.34–36, he experienced the conversion (Acts 9; 22.6–16; 26.12–18) that decided the entire course of his life. He received from Jesus himself equal status and authority with the Twelve (1 Cor 9.1–18) and the gospel which he was to preach and develop throughout his ministry. Three years later he began to preach in the synagogues of Damascus, but soon had to flee from his former Jewish associates to Jerusalem, where he met the other Apostles, *c*.37–39 (Gal 1.18–24).

After returning to Tarsus Paul was taken to the newly founded Church at Antioch in 43–44, and commissioned by that Church to undertake his first missionary journey accompanied by Barnabas. This first journey, *c*.45–49, extended through Cyprus, Perga, Antioch of Pisidia, and the cities of Lycaonia (Acts ch. 13–14). Next P. went to

Jerusalem where he was instrumental in securing the exemption of gentile Christians from the specifically Jewish obligations of the Old Law. Shortly after returning to Antioch, where Paul rebuked Peter for supporting the Judaizers in spite of the decision taken at Jerusalem (Gal 2.11–14), P. set out on his second missionary journey (Acts 15.36–18.21), accompanied by Silas. He visited Cilicia, Lycaonia, Phrygia, and Galatia, and founded Churches at Philippi, Thessalonica, and Beroea. At Philippi he and Silas were imprisoned for a time, until they were miraculously delivered, converting their jailer in the process (Acts 16.25–40). Hostility from the Jews forced them to leave Beroea also; in Athens the unsuccessful discourse on the Areopagus took place (Acts 17.22–28). P. went on to Corinth, founded the most famous of his Churches, and probably wrote the first two of the canonical Epistles, 1–2 Thess (51–52 A.D.). The third of P.'s missionary journeys is chiefly notable for the founding of the Church at Ephesus. There Gal and 1 Cor were written (54 A.D.) and 2 Cor followed during the next stage of the journey, to Macedonia (57). From there he went on to Corinth to deal with problems already treated in 1–2 Cor, and it was while staying at Corinth in 57–58 that he wrote Romans. Finally he went to Jerusalem via Achaia, apparently hoping to secure recognition of his gentile converts as full Christians, equal in status to Jewish Christians. But at Jerusalem itself his appearance in the Temple caused a riot on the part of his bitter enemies, the Jews, and was the occasion of his arrest and transference to Caesarea, where he was imprisoned for 2 years. In order to avoid being returned to Jerusalem and tried in the bitterly hostile atmosphere there, he used his privileges as a Roman citizen to appeal to Caesar. Accordingly he was sent to Rome to be tried, but was shipwrecked on the way at Malta, only landing in Italy in the spring of 61. For the next 2 years he was kept under arrest, but in easy circumstances and apparently with fairly free access to his friends (c.61–63). The captivity Epistles, Col, Phil, Eph and Philem, are to be assigned to this period. There is some evidence of two further short missionary journeys before a further period of captivity culminating in his condemnation and execution c.67–68 A.D.

Theology. The primary source of St. Paul's theology is his vision on the road to Damascus and the commission and message he received from the risen Lord. Even from the brief account of Acts 9.3–6, certain elements stand out as definitive for P.'s thought. First, Jesus, who had recently been crucified and was now risen to a state of glory, speaks from the midst, it seems, of the *shekinah,* the radiant light associated with the immediate presence of God himself (see v. 3); this may be taken as a sign of the closeness of his present union with God. The immediate outcome of this was that P. proclaimed "He is the Son of God," and "proved that Jesus was the Christ" (Acts 9.20–22). Second, while actually in this risen and glorified state in heaven, Jesus also identifies himself with his followers on earth (see v. 5). Third, he directs P. to receive instruction from Christians in

Damascus as to what he is to do (v. 6). These three points, therefore, determine the shape of Paul's future. He is to preach the gospel of Jesus Christ, Son of God and Messiah, risen from the dead to a state of union with the Father, and, from his place of glory in heaven, actively uniting himself as Savior to all who believe in him. Paul is to preach this as an Apostle of the Church, commissioned and instructed by the Church (initially represented by Ananias, Acts 9.10–19). His gospel, though received directly from the risen Lord, is in fact substantially identical with the gospel of the Church.

To proclaim Jesus as the Christ, then, is to say that his death and Resurrection are the fulfillment for which the Jews, the privileged recipients of the promises of the Old Covenant, have been waiting, even though all except a remnant of them have refused to recognized it now that it has come (Rom 11.1–2). The gentiles are to inherit these promises, and only when the gospel has been preached to them will the Jews follow (Rom 11.25–32). Thus the "salvation event" of Christ's passion, death and Resurrection fulfills the promises to Israel, and itself looks forward to a further fulfillment in the future. In the death and Resurrection of Christ the eschatological age has dawned, but still awaits its final fulfillment at the *parousia. The world's history falls into three great ages: first, the age before the Law, from Adam to Moses, when sin had entered the world but was still present only latently and implicitly beneath the surface of man's conscious life; second, the age of the Law, which had the effect of making sin explicit and conscious, but without providing any remedy; third, the age from the salvation event to the second coming, during which the salvation event is in process of pervading all mankind and the whole of creaturehood until all things are brought under the rule of Christ and made over by him to the Father (1 Cor 15.24–28).

This salvation event is the central point of God's secret plan, counsel or "mystery" for the whole of Creation and history, a plan foreordained from the beginning of time and now partially revealed. The salvation event fulfills the past, pervades the present, summoning all, gentile and Jew alike, to respond to it with faith, and is working toward its predestined consummation when Christ comes again.

This is P.'s vision in its breadth. Its depths are suggested by his answers to the following vital questions: How does Christ's death and Resurrection save man? How is it extended into the life of the individual? How are the individuals who have been so saved united among themselves? What should their attitude be to God and Christ? How ought they to regard their world, made up of both Jews and gentiles? The death and Resurrection of Jesus are salvific because they constitute that event in which the love of God is made present by the sending of his Son into the world with his power to re-create, to heal, and to rescue man. The forces of sin and death are met with the counterforce of God's love; the Son of God takes upon his own person the curse of the Law, thereby averting its effects. Christ reconciles believers, restoring them to peace and union with the Father (2 Cor 5.18–20; Rom 5.10–11; Col 1.20–21; Eph 2.16). He blots out, wipes away, or expiates their sins (Rom 3.25; 1 Cor 15.3; Col 1.14; Eph 1.7). He redeems them (1 Cor 6.14; 7.22; Gal 3.13; 4.5) by freeing them from the bondage of sin and death. He justifies them (Rom 4.25; 5.18; 1 Cor 4.4; 6.11, etc.), not merely juridically declaring them to be just but actually constituting them so and causing them to be so.

P.'s conception of human nature is deeply conditioned by these basic ideas. He tends to think of man as subject to forces from without, esp. those of sin and death, and when this is in the forefront of his mind he usually refers to him as *sōma,* body (Rom 6.12–13; 1 Cor 9.27, etc.) or, to express his extreme weakness, frailty, and subjection to earthly tendencies instead of heavenly ones, as *sarx,* flesh (1 Cor 1.29; Rom 8.5, 8; Gal 5.19–21, etc). When P. wishes to advert to man as an intelligent being, capable of decision, he tends to designate him as *psychē* (1 Thess 2.8; Phil 2.30; 2 Cor 1.23; 12.15; Rom 11.3; 16.4) or, concentrating more particularly on man's faculties of mind and will, as *pneuma* (Phil 1.27; 2 Cor 12.18).

Mind and will are the immediate subject of faith. With them man responds to God made present to him in the gospel words by hearing those words and deciding to yield himself up totally and unreservedly to their divine truth. Hearing, *akoē,* develops into total obedience, *hypakoē* (2 Thess 1.8; Rom 6.16–17). The worship of the mind develops into the worship of all-embracing self-commitment, the appropriate response to God who makes himself present initially through the medium of a spoken message. The power to make this response is itself a free grace of God (Eph 2.8), but he who fails to respond is disobedient and subject to the power of "the god of this age" (2 Cor 4.4; cf. Phil 1.27; 1 Cor 9.26–27; Eph 2.2).

Faith leads on to baptism "into" Christ, which for Paul is essentially the mode in which the Christian becomes united to him precisely in the saving event of his death and Resurrection. Thus baptism is not merely a cleansing and purifying rite (Eph 5.26), but also, and more importantly, a way of being buried with Christ and rising again with him into a new life (Rom 6.4–5) and a "new creation" (Gal 6.15; 2 Cor 5.17). Through baptism, then, or more properly through Christ, the Christian dynamically identifies himself with Christ, and the union thus achieved has to be maintained and intensified. He is engrafted into Christ, and achieves a state of being in Christ to the point where he can say: "I live now not I, but Christ lives in me" (Gal 2.20). By his Resurrection Christ becomes "a life-giving spirit" (1 Cor 15.45), extending his life into all believers. The Christian is immediately associated with Christ in the redemptive act of his death and Resurrection, suffering with, dying with, being crucified with him, and is also associated with him in the achievement of his eschatological glory, the goal of Christian living.

Union with one and the same Lord in his single redemptive act has the further effect of uniting Christians among themselves, "for we have all—Jews or Greeks, slaves or free men—been baptized in one Spirit to form one body" (1 Cor 12.13; cf. Gal 3.28; Eph 2.15). The individual Christians are the various members of this body, all deriving their unity, their coordination and their basic life-force from the single head which is Christ (Eph 4.16). This corporate unity is at once effected, maintained, and expressed by participation in the eucharistic meal. "Because there is one loaf we, many as we are, are one body; for we all share the one loaf" (1 Cor 10.16–17). This union, and this corporate life in the risen and glorified Christ, must grow and extend until all creaturehood is subsumed under it and pervaded by it (Eph 1.23). This is the goal and purpose of the Church and its accomplishment will entail apostolic sufferings which supplement or "fill up" the sufferings of Christ himself (Col 1.24). These fruitful and creative sufferings will continue until Christ comes again to hand over the kingdom thus achieved to his Father (1 Cor 15.24–25). BIBLIOGRAPHY: F. Amiot, *Key Concepts of St. Paul* (tr. J. Dingle, 1962); L. Cerfaux, *Christ in the Theology of St. Paul* (tr. G. Webb and A. Walker, 1959); *idem, Church in the Theology of St. Paul* (tr. G. Webb and A. Walker, 1959); *idem, Christian in the Theology of St. Paul* (tr. L. Soiron, 1968); D.E.H. Whiteley, *Theology of St. Paul* (1964); E. E. Ellis, *Paul and His Recent Interpreters* (1961); B. Rigaux, *Saint Paul et ses lettres* (1962); D. Balboni and M. Liverani, BiblSanct 10:164–228.

[D. J. BOURKE]

PAUL I, ST. (d. 767), **POPE** from 757. A brother of *Stephen II, his immediate predecessor, P. had taken an important part in the deliberations between the papal curia and the Frankish court that led to the foundation of the states of the Church in 752. His pontificate was beset with difficulties. Immediately he had to face *Desiderius, King of the Lombards, who allied himself with the Eastern Emperor, Constantine V, in order to recover the lands that *Aistulf, his predecessor, had been forced by Pepin to cede to Rome. In the outcome, however, the influence of the Franks cost the Lombards the loss of yet more territory to the papal states. Meanwhile, P. was using every means to turn Constantine from his *iconoclasm. The Emperor sought to win the devout Pepin, friend of the Holy See, to his own heretical stand. In this he failed, but P.'s other efforts against the heresy availed little. He has been considered a firm, even a harsh, ruler, but the times were disorderly, and his reputation was due in part to the tyrannical activities of subordinate officials. Nothing else is known of his activities except that he is credited with the transfer of relics from the catacombs to the churches of Rome. BIBLIOGRAPHY: Mann 1.2:331–360; R. Sullivan, NCE 11:12; Butler 2:659.

[P. F. MULHERN]

PAUL II (Pietro Barbo; 1417–71), **POPE** from 1464. A Venetian, P. was created cardinal at the age of 23 by his uncle, Eugene IV. He succeeded Pius II and refused to publish a bull confirming the articles agreed on before his election; they included the reform of the curia and the calling of a general council. He was ostentatious, pompous, and luxurious; but his achievements included the founding at Subiaco of the first printing-house in Italy, the energetic prosecution of the war against the Turks, and the support of the Albanians under *Scanderbeg.

PAUL III (Alexander Farnese; 1468–1549), **POPE** from 1534 to 1549, responsible for the opening of the Council of Trent. His rise in the church hierarchy was favored by his wealthy background and by Pope Alexander VI. Although his earlier life was marked by scandalous behavior, P. experienced a spiritual revival in 1513 after which he became a moderate reformer. When elected pope in October 1534, he faced serious opposition against the calling of a council, not only from such political powers as Charles V and Francis I, but also from his own cardinals. An earlier council at Mantua in 1537 was cancelled, but P. persisted until in Dec. 1545 the reform council was opened at Trent. He also raised to the rank of card. such important figures as G. Contarini, R. *Pole and G. P. *Carafa. Finally, it was during P.'s pontificate that the first steps towards the recognition of the Society of Jesus were made. BIBLIOGRAPHY: Pastor v. 12; M. O'Connell, *Counter Reformation* (1974).

[C. T. EBY]

PAUL IV (Gian Pietro Carafa; 1476–1559), **POPE** from 1555, reformer. He had been a member of the circle of reform card. favored by Paul III. Elected in May 1555 at the age of 79, P. already possessed a remarkable record of church reform. His efforts as abp. of Naples were significant and he was also famous as the founder of the Theatines. Unfortunately as pope his personal austerity and sternness often led to rigidity and unreasonableness. He tolerated no opposition even if it were well-intended, as exampled in his mistreatment of such capable men as Giovanni *Morone and Reginald *Pole. Moreover, his belief in a personal reform of the Church influenced his decision not to reconvene the Council of Trent. His greatest mistake might have been his appointment of his nephew Carlo, as the papal political adviser. The blunders of Carlo eventually became so flagrant that even P. turned against him. While in hindsight he aided the progress of church reform, his pontificate proved to be one of the most unpopular of this period. BIBLIOGRAPHY: Pastor, v. 14 and 15; M. O'Connell, *Counter Reformation* (1974).

[C. T. EBY]

PAUL V (Camillo Borghese; 1552–1621), **POPE** from 1605. P., trained in law, brought to the papacy a zeal for reform in regard to episcopal absenteeism but not to nepotism. He encouraged scholarship among the religious orders and assisted the Vatican Library. To terminate fruitless and acerbic controversy, he banned further recriminations over the issue of grace and free will by Catholic theologians (see CONGREGATIO DE AUXILIIS; D 1997). P. strove to improve the government of the Church and of the Papal State; within Rome he commissioned numerous public works. With Venice he had a bitter quarrel over the rights of the Church. In the political arena he condemned a new English oath of allegiance, supported the False Dmitri in Russia, and maintained neutrality in the Thirty Years' War while acclaiming Ferdinand II's victory in Bohemia.

[R. H. SCHMANDT]

PAUL VI (Giovanni Battista Montini; 1897–78), **POPE** from 1963. After ordination in 1920 and advanced studies in Rome he entered the Vatican diplomatic service, from 1924 to 1954 working in the Secretariate of State, undersecretary after 1937. In 1954 he became abp. of Milan, in 1958 a cardinal, and in 1963 pope. P. has stood between powerful currents of change and equally strong pressures emphasizing preservation of past achievements. He identified with neither and in part endorsed both. In social and political matters he has been open and progressive, dealing with Communist governments whenever improvement of relations has seemed possible. Very aware of the Third World, he issued *Progressio populorum* (1967), a call for justice in the evolution of undeveloped lands, and he traveled more than any other pope, visiting South America, Africa, India, the United Nations in New York, the Holy Land, Geneva, and Constantinople. P.'s ecumenical gestures include reconciliation with Orthodox Patriarch Athenagoras and meetings with heads of the Anglican, Armenian, and Jacobite Churches and with the Protestant World Council of Churches. Within the Roman Curia he diminished Italian influence, deprived aged cardinals of voting rights in papal elections, and effected bureaucratic reorganizations. He granted bps. more evident roles in church affairs but set a retirement age of 75. P. allowed Vatican Council II to continue and promulgated its decrees; yet in theology he was conservative, as evidenced in the encyclicals *Mysterium fidei* on the Eucharist (1965) and *Humanae vitae* on birth control (1968). He reaffirmed ancient discipline in his encyclical on priestly celibacy, *Sacerdotalis celibatus* (1967) and approved the 1977 declaration against women's ordination by the Congregation for the Doctrine of the Faith. The apostolic exhortation *Evangelii nuntiandi,* Dec. 8, 1975, which resulted from the 1974 Synod of Bishops, was his last major document and gave impetus to the progress of evangelization in the Catholic Church.

[R. H. SCHMANDT]

PAUL II, PATRIARCH OF CONSTANTINOPLE (641–653). He entered upon his office at a time when Monophysitism was causing grave division in the Byzantine Church. He soon (646–647) accepted the Monothelite position defended by the preceding patriarchs, Sergius and Pyrrhus. In 648 he supported the *Typos* of the Emperor Constans II (641–668) which forbade all further discussions of Christology. In 649, along with Sergius and Pyrrhus he was excommunicated by the Lateran synod summoned by Pope Martin I. The Emperor for this and for Martin's failure to secure imperial sanction for his elevation exiled the Pope to the Chersonesus in 653—the year of P.'s death. Owing to the failure to resolve the Monophysite controversy and to the Arab conquests of the strongly Monophysite provinces of the Empire, the Monothelite compromise was repudiated and subsequently condemned by the Sixth General Council, Constantinople III (680–681), Paul among others being denounced as heretical. BIBLIOGRAPHY: Fliche-Martin 5:165–168; Hefele-Leclercq 3:398–400, 426–432.

[M. R. P. MCGUIRE]

PAUL IV, ST. (724–784), **PATRIARCH OF CONSTANTINOPLE** (780–784). Born in Cyprus, he is known also as Paul the Younger of Salamis and Paul of Cyprus. Selected by Emperor Leo IV in 780 for the See of Constantinople, he accepted the Emperor's condition to take an oath to pursue the imperial policy of *iconoclasm; yet he cannot be counted as a fanatic iconoclast. Emissaries were sent in 784 to him by Empress Irene, regent from 780, who had changed the religious policy of the empire, repudiating iconoclasm. P. gave them a solemn retraction of his errors, pronounced an anathema against iconoclasm and resigned from his office; he died soon afterwards. The Empress obtained his canonization from the pope so that he might serve the cause of the veneration of images better by his death than by his life.

[L. PEANO]

PAUL OF BURGOS (c. 1351–1435), Spanish bp., biblical scholar, and apologist. Through studying Scripture and Thomas Aquinas, P. was converted from Judaism to Christianity. After his wife's death, he was ordained, named bp. of Cartagena (1405) and Burgos (1415), and chancellor of Castile (1416). He published his *Additiones* (1429–31) to *Nicholas of Lyra's important commentary on the Bible, and a *Dialogus . . . contra perfidiam Judaeorum* which went through several editions.

[T. M. MCFADDEN]

PAUL OF CANOPUS, Egyptian monk, patriarch of Alexandria, 536–539, succeeding the deposed Monophysite patriarch Theodosius. Recommended by the deacon (and future pope) Pelagius, P. was consecrated at Constantinople by Patriarch Mennas. On returning to Egypt, Paul used military force to take possession of his see, and resorted to such violence against the Monophysites that the unrest intensified until finally P. himself was forced to flee to Gaza, where a synod was convened at the initiative of Justinian in 539. The patriarchs of Antioch, Jerusalem, and Ephesus were there, in addition to the imperial official Eusebius and the same deacon Pelagius. The result was that P. was deposed and exiled, and another monk was named patriarch in his place.

[E. J. DILLON]

PAUL, OF CONSTANTINOPLE, ST. (d. c. 351). In 337 he succeeded Alexander, bp. of Constantinople who had previously ordained him. In 339 P. was exiled to Sing-

ara in Mesopotamia and was replaced by Eusebius of Nicomedia, an ambitious Arian. Upon Eusebius' death, in late 341, P. was recalled by the group of orthodox Christians, but the Arians elected Macedonius. This was the occasion for an open fight among rival factions during which Hermogenes, the *Magister militum* in charge of his exile, was killed. Finally the Emperor Constantius II exiled P. and reinstated Macedonius. Through the support of Constans I, P. was called back in 346 to occupy his see. However after Constans' death P. was driven into exile in 351 by the Arians and choked to death. His relics during the reign of Theodosius were transferred to Constantinople.

[L. PEANO]

PAUL OF THE CROSS, ST. (Paolo Francesco Danei; 1694–1775), mystic and founder of the Passionists. After the age of 20, a series of mystical experiences prompted P. to found a congregation of men totally dedicated to a life of prayer and to preaching, esp. in parishes, sanctification through the remembrance of the Passion of Christ. He was ordained in 1722 and began a lifetime of preaching on the mystery of the Cross. Final papal approval of the new congregation was not received until 1741. P. established the first two provinces with 12 foundations. He also was founder of a contemplative community of women Passionists. Through his letters and teachings he is recognized for his personal mysticism and as a master on the mystical life. He was canonized in 1867.

[T. C. O'BRIEN]

PAUL THE DEACON (c. 730–799), historian, poet, grammarian. After receiving a sound education under Flavianus at Pavia and serving for a time as tutor to the daughter of Desiderius, king of the Lombards, P. entered Monte Cassino c. 774. In 782 he addressed an appeal in verse to Charlemagne on behalf of a brother implicated in a revolt at Friuli. Impressed by P.'s learning and culture, Charlemagne invited him to Aachen, where he spent several years as an honored member of the court circle. Among his writings are: an abridgement of the *De verborum significatione* of Festus; many poems (some of which rank among the best of the Carolingian era); a life of Gregory the Great. He also gathered and edited lessons for the office and a homilarium at the request of Charlemagne. His historical works include a history of the diocese of Metz, a *Historia Romana* in which he edited and supplemented the *Breviarium ab urbe condita* of Eutropius, bringing it up to the year 553. But his chief work was his *Historia gentis Langobardorum,* in the six books of which he gave an account of the history of the Lombards from legendary times to the death of Liutprand in 744. This, despite some chronological vagueness, is a valuable work for it is based on documents not available to subsequent historians, and it sheds considerable light on a period and a people that without it would be relatively unknown to history. The commentary on the Rule of St. Benedict, long attributed to P., is no longer thought to be his work. Works: PL 95:433–1710; Eng. tr. of the *His-*

toria Langobardorum, L. Bethmann and G. Waitz (1907). BIBLIOGRAPHY: C. M. Aherne, NCE 11:24–25.

[M. S. TANEY]

PAUL THE HERMIT, ST. (known also as Paul of Thebes; d. *c*.340), commonly accounted the first Christian hermit. He was a native of the Lower Thebaid, orphaned at an early age, who while still in his youth fled to the desert to escape the persecution of Decius. What began as an escape became a cherished way of life. For 90 years he dwelt in a cave, giving himself to prayer and mortification, and subsisting at first on the fruit of a nearby palm tree and later on bread brought regularly to him by ravens. Toward the end of his life he was visited by St. *Anthony who was on quest for a solitary more perfect than himself. When he died at the age of 112 St. Anthony buried him in a cloak that was the gift of St. Athanasius. His life, edited and translated into Latin by St. Jerome (PL 23:17–28), makes a gentle and edifying story that has been a favorite of Christian art and piety, although the improbable detail with which it abounds is now regarded as legendary, despite the fact that the original documents were written not long after P.'s death. BIBLIOGRAPHY: Butler 1:91–93; H. Waddell, *Desert Fathers* (1936) 35–63; G. Caliò, BiblSanct 10:269–276.

[R. B. ENO]

PAUL OF MIDDLEBURG (1455–1534), bp. of Fossombrone 1494–1524, scientist. After ordination at Middleburg, P. was professor of astronomy and mathematics at Padua. As bp., he became convinced of the need for calendar reform, esp. the correct calculation of Easter; hence, his chief work, *Paulina, sive de recta paschae celebratione.* His studies, presented to popes and emperor, to scholars including Copernicus, were instrumental in bringing the project to the Fifth Lateran Council, preparing for the Gregorian calendar reform. BIBLIOGRAPHY: A. Condit, NCE 11:26.

[M. E. DUFFY]

PAUL OF ST. FRANCIS, see ATKINSON, MATTHEW.

PAUL OF SAMOSATA, bp. of Antioch (260), deposed by the third synod of Antioch (268) mainly for holding modalist views (see MODALISM). In his *Hist. eccl.* 7.27, Eusebius reports that soon after his consecration Paul became suspect of "low and mean views as to Christ . . . namely that he was in his nature an ordinary man." There also seems to have been some question about his personal character, liturgical innovations, and financial interests (while bp. he was governor of the Syrian province of Commagene and secretary of the treasury to Queen Zenobia of Palmyra). Since P.'s teachings are known only from fragments of the stenographic record of his debate with the priest Malchion and from passing references in later authors, it is difficult to determine the extent and nature of his errors. According to Leontius of Byzantium, "he gave the name of Father to God who created all things, that of Son to

him who was purely man, and Spirit to the grace which resided in the Apostles" (*De sectis* 3.3). He is also said to have maintained that Jesus was greater than Moses and the Prophets but that he was not God. He would thus have been Monarchian in his explanation of the Trinity and Adoptionist in his Christology. The synod which deposed him also rejected the word *homoousios* (later accepted as the orthodox term explaining the divine equality of Christ and the Father) probably because P. had given it a modalist interpretation. BIBLIOGRAIHY: Quasten 2:140–142. *MONARCHISM; *ADOPTIONISM.

[M. J. COSTELLOE]

PAUL THE SIMPLE, ST. (*c*. 339), an anchorite monk (not to be confused with St. Paul, the first hermit). He became one of the most eminent followers of St. Anthony in the Egyptian Thebaïd. The surname The Simple was given on account of his childlikeness. Upon a long journey into the desert to become a disciple of St. Anthony, he was repulsed by the great patriarch who judged him to be too old to enter a hermit's life. Because of his perseverance and humility, Anthony admitted P. rather reluctantly. He was subjected to a rough course of training, but whatever he was told to do he did cheerfully and promptly. Anthony recognized in the old man singular spiritual gifts and certain powers of healing and reading men's thoughts, and held him up to all his disciples as a model. It is likely that Palladius' account in his *Lausiac History,* written *c*.60 years after the death of Paul the Simple, was embellished by some legendary accretions. BIBLIOGRAPHY: Butler 1:513–514; J. M. Sauget, BiblSanct 10:264–265.

[L. PEANO]

PAUL OF VENICE (Paolo Veneto [Nicoletti]; *c*.1369–1428), Venetian Augustinian philosopher and theologian who studied at Oxford (1390–93), took his doctorate at Padua, was Venetian ambassador to Poland (1413), and was forbidden to attend the Council of Constance (1414–18) where his presence might have embarrassed the Venetian government. In philosophy his position was Averroistic; in logic, Ockhamist. BIBLIOGRAPHY: Gilson HCP 798; U. Viglino, EncCatt 9:747.

PAUL, ACTS OF, see APOCRYPHA (NT), 40.

PAUL, APOCALYPSE OF, see APOCRYPHA (NT), 41.

PAUL, MARTYRDOM OF ST., a legendary account dating from the 2d cent. of the trial and execution of St. Paul in Rome during the persecution of Nero. The *passio* or *martyrium,* which is preserved in two Greek MSS and with incomplete Latin, Syriac, Coptic, Ethiopic, and Slavonic versions, forms the concluding sections of the apocryphal Acts of Paul. The description of his death had an important influence on Christian art and liturgy. BIBLIOGRAPHY: Quasten 1:132; *Acta apostolorum apocrypha* (eds. R. A. Lipsius and M. Bonnet, 1891) 1:104–117.

[M. J. COSTELLOE]

PAUL, PASSION OF, see APOCRYPHA (NT), 42.

PAUL AND SENECA, CORRESPONDENCE OF ST., see SENECA AND ST. PAUL, CORRESPONDENCE OF.

PAUL AND THECLA, ACTS OF, an apocryphal work of the 2nd cent. narrating St. Paul's conversion of the virgin Thecla and their subsequent adventures. Though later propagated as a separate treatise, it originally formed a part of the *Acts of Paul* along with the *Correspondence of Paul with the Corinthians* and the *Martyrdom of Paul.* According to these Acts Paul, after fleeing from Antioch in Pisidia, arrived at Iconium, where he preached in the house of Onesiphorus on the advantages of chastity. Converted by his words, Thecla renounced her engagement with Thamyris. Paul was arrested and later banished. T. was condemned to death, but when the fire that had been kindled about her was quenched by a miraculous rain, she was set free. Later she met Paul on the road to Daphne and was taken by him to Antioch. After more impossible adventures and assisting Paul in his missionary labors, she retired to Seleucia, where she peacefully passed away. According to Tertullian these acts were composed by an Asian presbyter through a love for St. Paul, but when his authorship was discovered he was deposed for his pains (*De bapt.* 17). The popularity of this work, which reflects the traditions of the Hellenistic novel, is proved by its survival in the original Greek, in five different Latin, and Coptic, Syriac, Armenian, Slavonic, and Arabic versions. Its influence on Christian art and literature, esp. in its description of St. Paul, has been extensive. BIBLIOGRAPHY: Quasten 1:130–131; B. Kötting, LTK 10:18–19; *Acta apostolorum apocrypha* (ed. R. A. Lipsius and M. Bonnet, 1891) 1:235–269.

[M. J. COSTELLOE]

PAULA, ST. (347–404), illustrious Roman matron, wife and mother, widow and penitent, friend of St. Jerome, founder of a monastery for men, a convent for women, and a hospice for travelers, all in Bethlehem. In 362 she married Toxotius, also of noble family; they had one son and four daughters. Eventually one of her daughters, a son-in-law, and a granddaughter would also be numbered among the saints. Widowed in 379, P. led a penitential life of good works and hospitality. She came to know Jerome during his stay in Rome during the days of Pope St. Damasus I. She left with him to return to Palestine where she ended her days. What is known of her is derived from Jerome's writings, esp. a letter, written as a eulogy, that serves as a biography. BIBLIOGRAPHY: Butler 1:171–172; G. Del Ton, BiblSanct 10:123–136.

[E. J. DILLON]

PAULICIANS, a dualistic sect originating in obscure circumstances in Asia Minor during the second half of the 8th century. Their first known leader was a certain Constantine, who established a Paulician community at Kibossa in Armenia in the time of Emperor Constantine IV (641–668). They were called Paulicians either because of their great love for the writings of St. Paul or because of certain similarities of their doctrine to that of Paul of Samosata. Their theology is a close elaboration of Manichaeism, with its central tenet of the two supreme principles of good and evil in eternal conflict over the created world, with visible and material things (including Church ritual and organization) representing the power of evil, the invisible and spiritual ones (as the soul of man) expressing the power of good. Compared to other forms of dualism, Paulicianism is rated as absolute dualism, for it has no view of a clear-cut final victory of good over evil. In conflict with the Byzantine State the Paulicians suffered persecution and exile, and as a consequence were eager to ally themselves with the external enemies of the empire, particularly with the Arabs, a circumstance which later led many of them to embrace Islam. A sizeable Paulician colony was resettled by the Byzantine Emperor John Tzimisces (969–976) in the newly occupied Bulgarian territory around Plovdiv, where they mixed with the Bogomils, with whose history and fate they were closely linked thereafter, till their final extinction as a separate sect, probably during the 12th century. BIBLIOGRAPHY: R. Janin, DTC 12:56–62; S. Runciman, *Medieval Manichee* (1947).

[G. ELDAROV]

PAULINE FATHERS (SSP), religious congregation of priests and brothers engaged in the apostolate of manifesting Christ to the world by means of the press, cinema, radio, and television. The institute, its formal title the Society of St. Paul for the Apostolate of Communications, was founded by Very Rev. James *Alberione in Alba, Italy, in 1914; it was granted approval by Rome in 1949. The work of the Paulines has spread to 26 countries, and in Italy alone they operate 10 printing plants. *Christian Family,* a weekly magazine of wide circulation, is one of their publications. The society maintains 20 Catholic bookstores and information centers and also supports 400 parish libraries. In Rome, St. Paul Films, the largest distributor of educational and entertainment films in Italy and of catechetical films around the world, is owned and operated by the society. The U.S. office for St. Paul Films is at Brookline, Mass. In the U.S., where the society was established in 1932, it publishes the *Catholic Home Messenger,* part of an international monthly published in 6 languages, with a circulation of 5 million in 12 countries. Among other American publications are *Pastoral Life, The Word of God,* and the *Voice of the People.* Alba House is a publishing company of the Paulines. The American province of the society is in Derby, N.Y., and the generalate is in Rome. It also runs a chain of theaters in Japan and manages and controls the largest radio station in Tokyo. The Pauline Fathers maintain 75 houses, and of its 1,215 members, 516 are priests.

[R. A. TODD]

PAULINE PRIVILEGE, the principle by which the Church permits divorce and remarriage on condition that both partners were unbaptized when married, that one is now baptized, and that the unbaptized spouse refuses to live peacefully with the other. The privilege is based on Paul's practical guidelines to the Corinthians (1 Cor 7.12–16). Paul did not advocate remarriage, and most probably would have advised against it as in 1 Cor 7.8–11, but the Church has always permitted it. BIBLIOGRAPHY: P. Dulau, "The Pauline Privilege, Is It Promulgated in the First Epistle to the Corinthians?" CBQ (1951) 13:146–152.

[E. CABEY]

PAULINUS, OF AQUILEIA, ST. (c.750–802), patriarch. Born near Friuli, P. made himself a noted grammarian and scholar. In 776 Charlemagne appointed him first a master in the Palace School, where he became closely associated with *Alcuin, and then in 787 patriarch of Aquileia. One of P.'s main concerns was the teaching of *Elipandus of Toledo and *Felix of Urgel. At councils in Aachen (789), Regensburg (792), and Frankfurt (794), and in the Synod of Cividale for his own diocese, he joined in condemning these Christological errors. P. also composed three books against Felix, the *Libellus sacrosyllabus* against Elipandus (794), and many hymns, poems, and letters (PL 99:9–683). BIBLIOGRAPHY: Butler 1:188; I. Daniele, BiblSanct 10:144–148.

[R. B. ENO]

PAULINUS OF BITERRAE, the first bp. of Béziers, S France (in ancient Gaul:Biterrae), whose existence is not legendary. He is known to have been living c.410, to have been bp. c.418 or 419, and to have authored a circular letter (no longer extant) depicting terrifying portents occurring in that city about that time. BIBLIOGRAPHY: M. H. Laurent, DHGE 8:1352–56; S. A. Bennett, DCB 4:246.

[E. J. DILLON]

PAULINUS OF MILAN (d. c.420), biographer of St. *Ambrose. At an early age he entered the presbyterium founded by Ambrose in 375 to provide community life for certain clerics. He became secretary to Ambrose c.395, and after Ambrose' death (397) went as a deacon to Africa. In Carthage he encountered Coelestius, the companion of Pelagius, whose heretical doctrine he brought to the attention of Aurelius, Bp. of Carthage. After being condemned by a synod in Carthage, Coelestius appealed to Pope *Zosimus, who summoned P. to Rome. Instead of appearing in person, P. sent a letter *Libellus adversus Coelestium Zosimo Papae oblatus* (PL 20:711–716). P. wrote his *Vita S. Ambrosii* (PL 14:24–46) at the request of St. Augustine. Sulpicius Severus was his model for hagiography and his purpose was more to edify than to recount historical detail. BIBLIOGRAPHY: S. M. S. Kaniecka, *Vita S. Ambrosii* (introd. and tr., 1928).

[M. F. McNAMARA]

PAULINUS OF NOLA, ST. (Pontius Meropius Anicius Paulinus; 353–431), bp. from 409, poet and man of letters. Born of a prominent and wealthy family of Bordeaux, and a cousin of the two SS. Melania, P. was well educated under the care of the poet *Ausonius and began a career of public life. In part through the influence of his wife, a Spanish woman named Therasia, he was baptized in Bordeaux in 390. At the death of their only child he and Therasia decided to undertake a quasi-monastic life, and for this purpose withdrew to Spain (390) where, in Barcelona c.394 he was ordained priest at the insistence of the people. The following year P. and his wife settled in Nola to live in their chosen way of life near the tomb of St. *Felix to whom P. was singularly devoted. He is noted for the construction of an aqueduct, for the building of churches, and for his generosity toward the poor, to some of whom he gave lodging in his own home. He corresponded with many of the leading churchmen of his day, including, among others, SS. *Sulpicius (Severus), *Augustine, *Martin of Tours, *Delphinus, and *Victricius of Rouen. His surviving letters number 51 and his poems 35. Of the latter, 14 are concerned with St. Felix, for it was P.'s custom to write a poem each year for the celebration of that saint's feast. As a poet no one in Christian antiquity has been held in greater esteem except only *Prudentius. Works: PL 61; (crit. ed. W. Hartel, CSEL 29 and 30, 1894); tr. Letters 1–22 (ed. P. Walsh, ACW 35, 1966). BIBLIOGRAPHY: Altaner 482–483.

[R. B. ENO]

PAULINUS OF PELLA (376–c.460), Christian poet. Probably a grandson of the poet *Ausonius, P. was born in Pella in Macedonia, lived as a child in Carthage, and then returned to the family seat in Bordeaux. At the close of his long life he wrote an autobiography in verse. Its style and versification are indifferent in quality, but it is valued for its account of life in the period and places in which the poet lived. BIBLIOGRAPHY: Altaner 485; LexAW 2234.

[R. B. ENO]

PAULINUS OF PÉRIGUEUX (fl. 460), Christian poet. P. composed an epic of 3,622 lines, *De vita S. Martini episcopi* (CSEL 16, 1:190). He also composed two lesser poems about the saint, along with a covering letter to Bp. Perpetuus, whose account of Martin's miracles underlies the first book of the epic. BIBLIOGRAPHY: K. Krüger, EncRelKnow 8:420–421.

[M. J. SUELZER]

PAULINUS OF VENICE (c.1274–1344), Franciscan bp., diplomat, historian. P. served as chaplain, apostolic penitentiary, and inquisitor (1321–26) under John XXII at Avignon. In 1322 John XXII sent him as a diplomat to Venice to persuade the republic to cease hostilities against Rimini, and then to Ferrara which was in rebellion against the Holy See. He was used also by Venice as diplomat to Robert of Naples whose friend and advisor he became. In 1324 he was named bp. of Pozzuoli. Several unimportant histories were attributed to him, but his most significant contribution is the *Provinciale ordinis fratrum minorum*, a catalogue of Franciscan provinces, custodies, and convents (ed. P. C. Eubel, 1892); an appendix in *Bullarium Franciscanum* 5 (1898) 579–602. Between 1313 and 1315 he composed *De regimine rectoris* in Venetian dialect. Its three parts discuss government of self, family, and republic (ed. A. Mussafia, 1868). BIBLIOGRAPHY: A. Ghinato, *Fr. Paolino da Venezia* (1951); J. J. Smith, NCE 11:29.

[J. J. SMITH]

PAULINUS OF YORK, ST. (d. 644), bp. of York and Rochester. A monk of St. Andrew's, Rome, P. was sent (601) to assist St. Augustine. As St. Ethelburga's chaplain-bishop he converted her Northumbrian husband, King Edwin (627). York became his see. In the persecution after 632 he fled S to become bp. of Rochester. BIBLIOGRAPHY: Bede, *Historica ecclesiastica gentis Anglorum;* Butler 4:80–81; H. Farmer, BiblSanct 10:163–164.

[J. DRUSE]

PAULISTS (CSP), a clerical missionary *society of common life, the first community in America to have as its apostolate the conversion of non-Catholic Americans. The institute, officially the Society of Missionary Priests of St. Paul the Apostle, was founded in 1858 in New York City by Rev. Isaac Thomas *Hecker. With three other Redemptorists, also American convert-priests, Fr. hecker believed that the U.S. missions would progress more and vocations increase if their work was not limited to the then Redemptorist apostolate in the U.S., the care of German immigrants. After Hecker experienced many misunderstandings and obstacles from his Redemptorist superiors in Rome, his plans were finally presented in 1858 to Pope Pius IX, who suggested he begin a new community. The constitutions of the institute were granted final approval in 1940 by the Holy See. The members take solemn promises to practice the evangelical counsels and to live a communal life. To advance the convert movement, the Society has depended greatly on the press to disseminate information. In 1865, the founder began the publication of the magazine, the *Catholic World,* and in 1946 the society published another magazine, *Information.* By 1940, the Paulist Press, formerly the Catholic Publication Society (1866), was the largest distributor of Catholic pamphlets throughout the world. Five information centers have been established in the U.S. and Canada since the first opened in New York City in 1943. The Paulist Institute for Religious Research was also founded in the same city in 1960. Paulists have been continuously active in campus ministry at secular universities. Today the society maintains about 39 houses and has a total of 309 members of whom 235 are priests. A president who presides over the Paulists lives in Scarsdale, N.Y., and the procurator-general in Rome.

[R. A. TODD]

PAULITES (Ordo fratrum S. Paul Eremitae: OSPPE), originally monks of St. Paul, the first hermit, belonging to a one-time important community founded in 1215 in Hungary by Bl. Eusebius of Gran. The congregation received papal approval in 1308 and the final approbation of its constitutions in 1930. The members lead a contemplative-active life and engage in pastoral activities in their own churches. They also maintain the shrine of Our Lady of Czestochowa in Poland. The Paulites established a foundation in the U.S. in 1955 with headquarters at Doylestown, Pennsylvania. Today the order has about 20 houses and 127 priests with a total of 229 members. The prior-generalate is in Czestochowa, Poland, and the procurator general resides in Rome.

[R. A. TODD]

PAULSEN, FRIEDRICH (1846–1908), German philosopher and educational theorist. After receiving his degree from the Univ. of Berlin in 1870, P. remained there as student and teacher, holding the rank of ordinary professor of philosophy and pedagogy from 1894 until his death. He was more generally accepted as a writer than as a pure philosopher. P.'s objective was to make philosophy more relevant to contemporary man. He had no particular interest in any system as such but thought that the individual should be free and independent in his thinking. He strove to reform secondary schools and succeeded in creating a new system by which a person could be admitted into the departments of the universities without going through the classical Gymnasium. He insisted upon an improved method of instruction that would develop the initiative of students and better prepare them for full participation in university life. BIBLIOGRAPHY: See his autobiography (tr. T. Lorenz, 1938); R. Lehmann, ''Friedrich Paulsen,'' *Educational Review* 37 (1909) 188–196.

[M. A. WATHEN]

PAULUS EUERGETINOS (d. 1054), Byzantine monk and ascetical writer who founded a monastery near Constantinople. His *Synagoge* was intended to provide an ascetical education for his monks. Far from being original, it is an anthology of a cross-section of the ascetical writings of the early Church.

[E. J. DILLON]

PAULUS SILENTIARIUS (fl. under Justinian I), a high official and poet, the author of 82 extant epigrams, and two longer poems the *Ekphrasis* (Description) of the Church of the Holy Wisdom, and the *Ekphrasis* of its ambo. Both were composed for the dedication of the great church, probably in 563. He draws heavily on Nonnus (4th or 5th cent.) for his treatment of subject matter and verse technique. The poems are of the greatest value for the architectural history of the Hagia Sophia. BIBLIOGRAPHY: P. Friedländer, *Johannes von Gaza und Paulus Silentiarius. Kunstbeschreibungen justinianischer Zeit* (1912); G. Downey, s.v. Ekphrasis, RAC 4:921–944, esp. 940–944.

[M. R. P. MCGUIRE]

PAULUS, NIKOLAUS (1853–1930), German historian of the Reformation period. After a short stint as parish priest (1878–83) sandwiched between his theological studies at Strassburg and Munich, P. devoted his life from 1896 on to the thorough investigation of the German Reformation. He was particularly interested in the Catholic polemicists who had done verbal battle against Martin Luther, many of whom were subsequently lost to sight. Scrupulously fair in his handling of the German Reformer and guided always by the principle of absolute truthfulness, P. made it possible for Catholics to view the Reformation in a new light. His works include *Luthers Lebensende* (1898), *Johann Tetzel, der Ablassprediger* (1899), *Hexenwahn und Hexenprozess in 16. Jh.* (1910), *Protestantismus und Toleranz in 16. Jh.* (1911), and his chef d'oeuvre the *Geschichte des Ablasses im Mittelalter* (3 v., 1922–23).

[E. M. GATES]

PAVELIĆ, MILAN (1878–1939), Croatian poet and translator. Of peasant stock, P. was ordained in 1902 but devoted much of his life to poetry and journalism, working either in his native Senj or in the Croatian cultural capital, Zagreb. He became a Jesuit in 1924. A member of the Catholic-inspired Circle of Croatian Writers, he was best known for his contemplative nature poems and for his mystically tinged ballads and elegies. Collections of his poetry appeared regularly from 1902 to 1940, the last, a posthumous publication, entitled *Pod okom Gospodnjim* (Under the Eye of God). Pavelić also won recognition for his translations of the French poets Verlaine, Péguy, and Claudel.

[E. M. GATES]

PAVIA, BATTLE OF, decisive Imperial victory Feb. 24, 1525, over the French in the Habsburg-Valois Wars in Italy. Encouraged by a successful defense of France against the Imperials and the English, Francis I decided to repeat his earlier triumph at the Battle of Marignano by another invasion of Italy. In Oct. 1524 he drove the Imperial forces out of Milan, but later encountered resistance at the city of Pavia. A siege began, but Imperial troops marched to Pavia's relief. After a hard fought battle the Imperials won an overwhelming success. Not only was the French army defeated, but Francis I and several leading French nobles were also captured. This battle had important religious as well as political implications. The *Parlement* of Paris used the king's imprisonment in Madrid as an opportunity to attack the Meaux circle of Reformers in March 1525. Previously, these men had enjoyed Francis's personal protection. BIBLIOGRAPHY: J. Giono, *Battle of Pavia* (tr. A. E. Murch, 1965).

[C. T. EBY]

PAVIA, UNIVERSITY OF, an institution of higher learning at Pavia in N Italy. It developed from a school of arts founded in 825, which in the 11th cent. became an important center for the study of law. In 1361 it was established as a *studium generale* by Emperor Charles IV and approved as such by Boniface VIII in 1391. Under the favor of Gian Galeazzo Visconti, Duke of Milan, who issued the statutes in 1395, and of the Sforza family, the institution prospered and by the mid-15th cent. was distinguished among Italian *studia* as a center of humanistic culture. In the 16th cent. two colleges for poor students—Borromeo (1564) and Gislieri (1569)—were founded respectively by SS. Charles Borromeo and Pius V. The 17th cent. brought a reorganization of faculties, and the 18th the closing of the faculty of theology. Despite political fluctuations, the university maintained its high academic standing, esp. in scientific research. In its present organization, the university, now under state control, comprises faculties of jurisprudence, political sciences, letters and philosophy, medicine, science, and pharmacy. The teaching staff averages about 355 and student enrollment, 6,345. The library has 381,000 v. and 1,828 MSS. BIBLIOGRAPHY: H. Rashdall, *Universities of Europe in the Middle Ages* (ed. F. M. Powicke and A. B. Emden, 3 v. 1936).

[M. B. MURPHY]

PAVILLON, NICOLAS (1597–1677), bp. of Alet in Languedoc from 1637. He was recommended for the see by St. *Vincent de Paul, whose coworker he had been. The ascetical teachings of *Jansenism appealed to P., and he followed A. *Arnaud's distinction between *droit* and *fait* in refusing to sign the 1665 formulary of Alexander VII condemning the five Jansenist propositions (see D 2020). P. later (1668) accepted the compromise formula of Clement IX. He refused in 1673 to accept Louis XIV's claim to the right of the *régale* (revenues from vacant sees). P. was the author of theological treatises and of the *Rituel d'Alet* (1667), all of his writing reflecting his Jansenist leanings.

[T. C. O'BRIEN]

PAVLA, see PAPAL VOLUNTEERS FOR LATIN AMERICA.

PAVLOV, IVAN PETROVICH (1849–1936), Russian physiologist. P. is best known for his theory of conditioned reflexes. Working on a dog, he noted that the secretions from the salivary glands could be controlled by learning as well as by direct physiological and biochemical means. The dog reacts to the sight of food (the unconditioned stimulus) with a flow of saliva. P. presented a light stimulus just before giving the dog food. After several repetitions of this sequence, a flow of saliva followed the light stimulus when presented alone. The light became a condition for the reflex: the conditioned reflex. Most important in this experiment was the fact that P. used a method that could lead to a scientific and objective psychology. BIBLIOGRAPHY: I. P. Pavlov, *Conditioned Reflexes* (tr. G. V. Anrep, 1927, repr. 1957).

[B. A. NACHBAHR]

PAX. (1) The *kiss of peace in the Eucharistic Liturgy, the Latin word meaning peace. (2) See *INSTRUMENTUM PACIS.

PAX CHRISTI, an international Catholic federation with national centers in various countries of Europe, reestablished in 1950 at Fribourg, Switzerland. The purpose of Pax Christi is the promotion of unity and peace in the world by furthering a new international order founded on natural law and on the justice and charity of Christ. The organization began in 1945 in Lourdes, France, with a small group of French and German Catholics seeking reconciliation among themselves in order to heal the wounds of World War II. The exchange of prayers for peace soon spread to Poland and Italy and the movement became international when it joined the English Pax. The American foundation, Pax Christi-U.S.A. (1973) has its headquarters at Manhattan College, Riverdale, N.Y. The program of the federation is very broad in scope and while it covers every possible phase of a universal peace movement, it esp. seeks to unite Catholics of different political persuasions. The general secretariat is located at The Hague, Netherlands.

[R. A. TODD]

PAX ROMANA, the "Roman peace," the great achievement of the ancient world that brought a long period of relative tranquillity and unprecedented prosperity, as may be seen in the impressive ruins of the 1st, 2d, and 3d cent. in Europe, N Africa, and the Near East. The ideal of a "common peace" arose in Greece during the 4th cent. B.C. and was partially attained in the East under Alexander and his successors. Under Augustus, Rome after centuries of foreign conflicts finally achieved an almost universal peace. Though Horace and Vergil foresaw Rome's destiny as the preserver of order, the expression *pax Romana* does not appear as a fixed formula until the time of Seneca (*De providentia* 4.14). This peace was appreciated by non-Romans (Aelius Aristides, *Ruling Power* 70–71) and by Christians, who saw in it a providential means for the spreading of the gospel (Melito of Sardis, quoted in Eusebius, *Hist. eccl.* 4.26; Origen, *Contra Celsum* 2.30; Ambrose, *Exp. Ps. XLV* 21; Augustine, *Enarr. in Ps. XXXII* 2.10).

[M. J. COSTELLOE]

PAYNE, PETER (*c.*1380–1455), English-born follower of Wycliffe and Hus. He was a graduate of Oxford (1406) and principal of St. Edmund's College (1411–13) when he converted to Wycliffe's teachings. He subsequently wrote to John Hus, praising Wycliffe and attaching the university's seal to his letter. On a point of privilege, the university defended P. against the investigations initiated by Abp. Thomas Arundel, but requested the oath of orthodoxy from P. who fled to Prague. Here he took part in religious conflicts for 40 years until his death at the Hussite monastery of Emmaus in Prague where he was rector. BIBLIOGRA-PHY: K. B. McFarlane, *John Wycliffe and the Beginnings of English Nonconformity* (1953).

[M. E. DUFFY]

PAZBAN (East Arm., bazpan), one of the pair of cuffs worn by the Armenian celebrant over the sleeves of the *shapik*; made of the same material as the *shourtchar*.

[A. CODY]

PÁZMÁNY, PÉTER (1570–1637), preacher and author, leader of Catholic reform, cardinal primate of Hungary (1629–37). Of ancient Hungarian noble family, the Protestant P. became a Catholic at 13 and a Jesuit at 17. He studied and taught at foreign universities; then returning to his native country, converted the heads of about 30 of Hungary's leading families to Catholicism, who in turn led their dependents with them. Through personal contact, pulpit sermons, and his forceful written style, he succeeded in making Hungary a predominantly Catholic country once more. As a by-product, he made the Hungarian language into a pliable instrument of modern literary expression. A prolific author in Hungarian and Latin, he published about 40 books on religious subjects, which are still admired for their powerful style. His most lasting contributions are the numerous educational institutions founded by him, particularly the Pazmaneum in Vienna (1623) and the Univ. of Budapest (1635) which until recently also bore his name. P.'s *Collected Works* are available in Latin, German, and Hungarian. BIBLIOGRAPHY: J. Kornis, *Le Cardinal Pázmány* (1937); S. Sik, *Pázmány* (1939); N. Öry, *Doctrina Petri Cardinalis Pázmány de notis ecclesiae* (1952); D. Sinor, *History of Hungary* (1959). *HUNGARY.

[D. H. BRUNAUER]

PAZZI, a family of Florentine merchants and bankers (*fl.* 12th–17th cent.). Their bank was second in size only to that of their competitors, the Medici family. Political conflict with the Medici led the Pazzi into an unsuccessful attempt to overthrow them (1378). BIBLIOGRAPHY: R. de Roover, *Rise and Decline of the Medici Bank* (1953).

[J. MULDOON]

PAZZI, MARY MAGDALENE DE, ST. (1566–1607), mystic. An Italian Carmelite who professed her vows at the point of expected death in 1584, P. led a life filled with mystical experiences. At the direction of her confessor her visions and observations were written down by sisters of her convent in Florence. They constitute five volumes covering the period of 1584 to 1586. A book of her spiritual instructions (*Avvertimenti et avvisi . . .* 1669) was published. Beginning in 1960 a multivolume collection of her writings, a critical edition, was published. P. was canonized in 1669. BIBLIOGRAPHY: E. Ancilli, BiblSanct 8:1107–31; Butler 2:416–419.

PAZZI CHAPEL, FLORENCE, a gem of early Florentine Renaissance architecture begun by Brunelleschi (1429–30), with interior relating to the Old Sacristy of S.

Lorenzo. The exterior presents problems. In 1451 still incomplete, the inconsistent portico (added 1461) and roofing were perhaps designed by Guiliano da Maiano, the cupola probably according to Brunelleschi's plans. Pilasters and arches in gray *pietra serena* accent the rhythmic proportions of the interior. A frieze and medallions of Apostles and Evangelists in glazed terra cotta mark participation of Luca della Robbia, Donatello, and Desiderio da Settignano. BIBLIOGRAPHY: P. Sanpaolesi, *Brunelleschi* (1962).

[M. J. DALY]

PAZZI CONSPIRACY, a plot to eliminate Lorenzo the Magnificent and Medician rule in Florence. The Pazzi, an old Florentine banking family and rivals to the Medici, were the chief instigators of the plan. Francesco Pazzi, with the aid of Girolamo Riario and Francesco Salviati, abp. of Pisa, planned to murder Lorenzo and his brother Guiliano, while they attended Mass at the cathedral of Santa Maria del Fiore on April 26, 1478. The signal agreed upon for the assassinations was to be the elevation of the host, and at that moment Francesco and his cutthroats leaped upon their victims. Guiliano was stabbed to death, but Lorenzo was able to escape by taking refuge in the sacristy. The conspirators had misinterpreted Florentine sentiment, which they supposed to be anti-Medician, and were astounded when the people demanded their lives after the failure of the plot. They and most of their accomplices were captured and hanged by a bloodthirsty populace. BIBLIOGRAPHY: F. Schevill, *Medici* (1949).

[D. G. NUGENT]

PEABODY, FRANCIS GREENWOOD (1847–1936), American Unitarian theologian. P. taught homiletics and social ethics at Harvard Divinity School, which he tried to establish along the lines of German faculties and which he served until his retirement in 1913. With Walter Rauschenbusch he was a leading exponent of the Social Gospel. Among his works were *Jesus Christ and the Social Message* (1900; 6th ed., 1915) and *Approach to the Social Question* (1909). BIBLIOGRAPHY: A. C. Piepkorn, RGG 5:201–202.

[M. J. SUELZER]

PEACE, the harmonious union of affections and desires brought about by *charity. In this meaning it is first of all the inner tranquility of one who loves God above all; in consequence it is the peace of concord among those who, united in loving God, are united in loving one another as well. Because charity means a preferential love of God as the Father to be loved above all, it is a union of wills with him, and thus the exclusion of any conflicting wish or desire. Charity thus brings all interests, all desires, and all values into their proper place under the rule of its totality of love for the Father. The intent of charity, then, is the principle of harmony, the restraint of any conflicting appetite. The tranquility can be perfect only when the process of salvation

is complete, union in love with God made full and unbreakable through the *beatific vision. The process of salvation is a process of growth in the reign of charity, which diminishes but never, until it is completed, totally suppresses the resistance of "flesh against spirit." As love of God begets love of neighbor, there is a fundamental concord among those who are co-sharers in love of and for the Father. They are agreed in that overriding consideration; that in turn makes possible control of conflict in lesser matters, and, positively, the mutual willingness to be in accord. The peace that comes from charity in both its meanings is the *pax Christi*. For it is a peace of reconciliation brought about through Christ's sacrifice (ThAq ST a, 48.3). The union of love for the Father as his children is sustained and perfected only through the constantly redeeming effect of Christ's Passion. That, in turn, is the basis for the reconciliation and genuine concord that unite the Father's children to one another. Thus the greeting of Christ after his Resurrection, "Peace be to you." That is the grounds for unity and peace being particularly the fruit of the Eucharist. The significance and source of true Christian peace, then, underlies the link between grace and peace that appears so often in St. Paul's salutation, "Grace be to you and peace from God our Father, and from Our Lord Jesus Christ" (Rom 1.7; 1 Cor 1.3; 2 Cor 1.2; Gal 1.3; Eph 1.2; Phil 1.2; Col 1.2). This theological meaning of peace throws light on the connection between peace and *justice. Justice is a particularly human need: it restrains the self-interest of one person from infringing on the legitimate rights of another, thus a condition for human concord (ThAq ST 2a2ae, 29.3 ad 3). But justice is not friendship; it is impersonal, an impartial respect for the external media of human relations. Aristotle remarks, "If men are friends, there is no need of justice between them" (*Ethics* VIII, 1.1155a29). Charity alone has the effective power to make a person a friend to all. The peacemakers are indeed the children of God (Mt 5.9).

[T. C. O'BRIEN]

PEACE (IN THE BIBLE), term for a developing, multifaceted idea.

Old Testament. The Hebrew word *šalom* is derived from a root which in its Sumerian and Akkadian forms means "to be whole, healthy, undamaged." This is the primary significance of the Hebrew word too. It signifies a state of ordered and harmonious well-being, whether this applies to an individual, a social group or nation, or even an inanimate entity such as a tract of land or an abstract one such as the undertaking of a project. This state of well-being is the outcome of all the organic parts of a given entity or group working together harmoniously so as to fulfill the potentiality of the whole to the fullest possible extent. This harmony or order is established by God's blessing or, in matters of human decision, by the right ordering of man's will as expressed in conformity to the covenant laws. Hence peace is constantly associated with righteousness, which is, in essence, moral harmony or right order. In human terms peace means physical health (Is 57.18; Jer 6.14), freedom from fear of any kind, and the absence of any threat from enemies, wild beasts, etc. It also means rain, plentiful crops, power to pursue and conquer enemies, and security and prosperity in all spheres of life (Lev 26.3–13). But above all it means the protecting presence of the covenant God in the midst of his people. Peace is the immediate outcome of blessing, and under God the king is the fount of *šalom* and *ṣedaka,* peace and righteousness, for all people. And it embraces the whole span of human life. It is used in greetings (cf. Gen 29.6; 43.57; 1 Sam 16.4, etc.). One "walks" in peace (Gen 26.29; Ex 18.23); "seeks the peace of another" (Dt 23.7); "sleeps in peace" (Ps 4.9); "is buried in peace" (Gen 15–15; 2 Kg 22.20).

It is important too to recognize that in the earlier traditions peace is not the opposite of war. Victory over an enemy and the taking of booty from him can actually be included in peace (Jg 8.7–9; 2 Sam 19.25, 31; 1 Kg 22.28). At a time when war is actively being waged David can actually ask after "the peace of Joab and the peace of the people and the peace of the war" (2 Sam 11.7), i.e., whether it is prospering as it should under Joab's leadership. The idea of peace as the opposite of war is introduced later by the Prophets, and notably by Isaiah (Is 2.4; 9.4); and here too the link between peace and rightousness is even more emphasized (Is 32.16–20; Ps 72.3,7; 85.11). The Prophets also have to fight against the proclamation of a false peace (Jer 6.14; 14.13; 28; Ezek 13.16), and to insist that peace will never come but only disaster so long as the people refuse to honor their covenant obligations (Is 26.12; 45:7).

A further development is the idea of peace as the object of eschatological hopes. Here peace tends to be envisaged as a state of paradisal harmony embracing beasts as well as men and bringing miraculous fertility (Is 11.6–8; 35.9; Ezek 40.7, etc.). It also involves peace among the nations of the world (Is 2.2–4; 19.23–25; Zech 8.23, etc.). This eschatological peace will be even more directly and manifestly the effect of Yahweh's presence to his covenant people. To a lesser extent it will also be the outcome of the purging away of their sins.

New Testament. Perhaps the most significant indication of the extension and further development of the concept of peace in the NT is the frequency with which it is associated with grace (*charis*), esp. in the introductory greetings of the Pauline Epistles (1 Cor 1.3; 2 Cor 1.2; Gal 1.3; Eph 1.2; Phil 1.2; Col 1.2; 1 Tim 1.2;2 Tim 1.2; Tit 1.4; Philem 3). In Mt 10.13 and Lk 10.5 the Disciples are directed to let their opening words be "Peace be to this house." Peace is now the immediate outcome of union with God the Father in and through Christ for "he is the peace between us" (Jew and gentile, Eph 2.14). The peace he brings is the defining characteristic of the messianic age of salvation he has ushered in, the sign that it has dawned (Lk 1.79; 2.14; Mk 5.34). It is a peace that God creates through his Son (Acts 10.36; Phil 1.2; Col 1.20), becoming the "God of peace" (Rom 15.33; 16.20; 1 Cor 14.33), a peace that Jesus himself gives and bequeathes to his own, and that the world is incapable of giving (Jn 14.27; cf. 16.33). It is a peace as elemental as life itself (Rom 8.6), and is in fact co-extensive with the newness of life that is the condition of one who has been incorporated into the kingdom of God (Rom 14.17; 1 Cor 7.15; Eph 4.3, etc.). And as the gospel is the further projection of Christ's salvific work, so it too bestows this divine and other-worldly peace; it is the "gospel of peace" (Eph 6.15). Christians must strive to deepen and to disseminate this peace (1 Pet 3.11), eagerly awaiting the fullness of it in the parousia and in heaven. BIBLIOGRAPHY: A. Bea, "L'idea della pace nel Vecchio Testamento", *XXXV Congreso Eucaristico International, Barcelona* (1952) 49–59; H. Gross, *Die Idee des ewigen und allgemeinen Friedens im Alten Orient und im Alten Testament* (1956); J. J. Stamm and H. Bietenhard, *Der Weltfriede im Alten und Neuen Testament* (1959).

[D. J. BOURKE]

PEACE, LETTERS OF, see LIBELLI PACES.

PEACE CORPS, a U.S. Department of State agency open on a voluntary basis to American citizens over 18—single or married (without dependents). It was temporarily established by executive order of President John F. Kennedy on March 2, 1961 and given permanent status with the passage of the Peace Corps Act of Sept. 22, 1961, under R. Sargent Shriver as director. Its purpose is to supply trained manpower where needed to underdeveloped nations; to establish mutual understanding; to make young Americans aware of living conditions in underdeveloped countries by personal experience, and to share this knowledge with their fellow Americans. The normal tour of duty, including training, is 2 years and is renewable for the same country. Projects include education, agriculture, health, and community development. They receive a living allowance based on the host country standard, but no salary. On terminating their tour, they receive $75 for each month of satisfactory service. Although the Peace Corps is not a religious agency in any sense, its objectives have been warmly endorsed by religious leaders of many faiths. BIBLIOGRAPHY: R. Hoopes, *Complete Peace Corps Guide* (1965).

[M. B. MURPHY]

PEACE OF AUGSBURG, see AUGSBURG, RELIGIOUS PEACE OF.

PEACE OF GOD, collective name for various ecclesiastical efforts, beginning in the 10th cent., to control feudal warfare, violence, and depredation of ecclesiastical and lay property. The efforts in France were supported by the Capetians and elsewhere in N Europe by other secular rulers. Pope Urban II inaugurated the peace of God in Italy in 1089. The "Truce of God", first mentioned *c.* 1027, was an armistice decreed first on Sundays, then extended to last in some places from Wednesday through Monday, and to major seasons of the liturgical year.

PEACE OF THE CHURCH, a phrase that may refer to: (1) the era after the Edict of Milan (313), which had put an end to persecution of Christians; (2) a compromise achieved in the conflicts over *Jansenism, under Pope Clement IX in 1669; also called the Clementine Peace (*Paix de Clément*). The Pope agreed to a qualified acceptance of the bull *Regiminis apostolici* by four bps. who had hitherto flatly rejected it. The decade of comparative suspension of doctrinal and political controversy that ensued is called the Peace of the Church.

[T. C. O'BRIEN]

PEACE OF WESTPHALIA, see WESTPHALIA, PEACE OF.

PEACE OFFERING, in Hebrew *shelamin,* one of the two forms of sacrifices in which only a small part of the animal was consumed by fire on the altar. A small part of what remained was given to the priests and the rest to the donor to eat with friends and relatives to "rejoice before the Lord" (Dt 12.18), and thus enter into loving communion with him. On the supposition that the term *shelamim* is derived from *shalom* (peace), these sacrifices would express a state of well-being between God and men and a desire to confirm this state by the sacrifice. BIBLIOGRAPHY: R. De Vaux, *Studies in Old Testament Sacrifice* (1964). G. B. Gray, *Sacrifice in the Old Testament* (1970).

[A. J. TKACIK]

PEACOCK, in Christian art a symbol of the immortality of the soul. It had other connotations as well: the vigilant Church; heavenly glory; the grace of sacraments (the peacock feeding on grapes symbolizes the Eucharist; with an olive leaf or branch, the Church bringing peace). It is sometimes associated in hagiography with St. Barbara. In other uses it indicated luxurious and regal beauty, other-worldly glory, and this-worldly pride. For Bosch, in his *Ars symbolica,* the peacock tail in its blending together of all colors symbolized totality. For the Romans the peacock on a coin signified the apotheosis of a princess. In Hinduism, the eye pattern of the wings represented the stars. It stood for dusk in some astrological horologies. The common presentation of two peacocks symmetrically placed on either side of a tree, suggesting the duality of the human psyche, came to the West through Islamic Spain, and to Islam from Persia. BIBLIOGRAPHY: F. E. Hulme, *History, Principles and Practice of Symbolism in Christian Art* (1891, repr. 1969).

[R. J. LITZ]

PEARL, THE, a uniquely beautiful poem of the 14th cent. Middle-English alliterative revival; it is preserved in the same MS as *Sir Gawain, Purity, Patience,* and on grounds of dialect, etc., is usually judged to be by the same unknown author. Made up of 101 elaborately rhymed, alliterated 12-line stanzas, the poem tells of a man who on a harvest feast in August loses a "pearl of price" and who in a dream-vision finds himself in an earthly paradise where, on the opposite bank of a river he sees his Pearl transformed and transfigured. She instructs him in sacred theology and shows him a vision of heaven. It has been variously interpreted as an elegy of a child (E. V. Gordon, 1953; and A. C. Cawley, 1962); as a symbol of purity (W. H. Schofield, 1909); as Eucharist (R. M. Garrett, 1918); as spiritual dryness (Sr. M. Madeleva *Wolff, 1925; Sr. Vincent Hillman, 1959). Its ambiguities are a part of the poem's charm. BIBLIOGRAPHY: *Pearl* (ed. E. V. Gordon, 1953); *Pearl* (tr. and ed. S. de Ford, 1967).

[M. N. MALTMAN]

PEARL MOSQUE, AGRA, mosque built (1647–54) by Shah Jahan (1628–58), one of the most beautiful buildings in the Indian capital at Agra on the River Jumna, of marble inlaid with precious stones in Persian floral motifs, the arches supporting three white domes, and floor inlaid with yellow marble. Lattices of marble screen the ladies' section, and a beautiful pool centers the court.

[M. J. DALY]

PEARSE, PADRAIC HENRY (1879–1916), Irish poet and patriot. An early advocate of the return to Gaelic, P. edited the Gaelic League's official organ. He published a collection of poetry and prose in Gaelic under the title *Iosagán.* He founded a bilingual school in Dublin, St. Enda's, where he was joined by T. *Mac Donough. In the ill-fated Easter uprising of 1916, P. was commander-in-chief of the rebels and president of the Provisional Republic. When the failure of other forces to join in the rebellion left P. and his group hopelessly isolated in the General Post Office in Dublin, he had to surrender. He was executed by a British firing squad. After his death *Collected Works* (1917) and *Poems* (1918) were published.

[J. R. AHERNE]

PEARSON, JOHN (1613–86), Anglican bp. of Chester (from 1673). P. was the English Church's ablest scholar in the 17th century. His classical *Exposition of the Creed* (1659) was in origin a series of lectures given in secret at St. Clement's, Cheapside. His defense (1672) of the authenticity of the letters of St. Ignatius of Antioch against the attacks of Jean Daillé (1666) is confirmed by present–day research. BIBLIOGRAPHY: C. Schöll, EncRelKnow 8:431–432.

[M. J. SUELZER]

PEASANTS' WAR (Ger. *Bauernkrieg*), armed rebellion (1524–25), against the feudal overlords which spread through S Germany, Austria, Alsace, and the provinces of the Lower Rhine. There were precedents of peasant militancy against encroachments on their traditional rights; the

Peasants' War was connected with the Reformation in that the rule of the gospel was interpreted in support of social demands, esp. by the establishment of an evangelical kingdom that would overthrow existing authority. This is apparent in the extreme teachings of T. *Münzer, one of the leaders, and in the *Twelve Articles of 1525 setting forth peasants' demands. Luther, at first seeking to mediate between princes and peasants, replied to the Twelve Articles, cautioning the peasants against violence; then, unheeded and disturbed by the depradations perpetrated in the name of the gospel, he wrote *Against the Murderous and Thieving Bands* (1525), a pamphlet urging the princes to a course of extermination. This has always been considered a stain on Luther's name, for the Lutheran princes mercilessly put down the revolt; more than 5,000 rebels were slaughtered at Frankenhausen, May 15, 1525. A few remnant forces survived for another year; many survivors joined the Anabaptists. The War solidified the power of the princes and esp. the *territorial church organization that continued in Germany into the 20th century. BIBLIOGRAPHY: G. Franz, *Der deutsche Bauernkrieg* (2 v., 5th ed., 1958); H. Kirchner, *Luther and the Peasants' War* (tr. D. Jodeck, pa. 1972); F. Engels, *German Revolutions: The Peasant War in Germany* (1967).

[P. DAMBORIENA]

PEĆ, seat of the Serbian abps. and patriarchs, now a city of the Kosovo-Metohija Region of the Serbian Federal Republic of Yugoslavia. In 1253 Abp. Arsenije I, successor of St. Sava, the founder of the independent Serbian archiepiscopate, transferred his residence from the monastery of Zica to the Ascension Monastery in Peć. It remained the nominal and sometimes actual residence of the patriarchs till the abolition of the second Serbian patriarchate (1766). The title was reassumed by the head of the third Serbian patriarchate (1920), who styles himself "Abp. of Peć, Metropolitan of Beograd and Karlovci, Serbian Patriarch." Because the region around Peć is today inhabited nearly exclusively by Islamic Albanians, Peć is not an episcopal see.

[V. J. POSPISHIL]

PECHERSKY LAURA (Monastery of the Caves), one of the most influential monasteries in Kievan Russia, located on the outskirts of Kiev where the original monks dug caves out of the limestone hills. St. Theodosius (d. 1074), considered the founder of Russian monasticism and this monastery, led the hermits from the underground to build a church and new cells above the old caves. He introduced the Studite rule which was adopted by many other Russian religious communities. Theodosius, who practiced kenosis, established a hospice nearby for the sick and poor. Nestor the Chronicler, a contemporary of Theodosius, was a member of the community. The monastery became a center of learning, and over the centuries it has been the center of countless pilgrimages. BIBLIOGRAPHY: G. P. Fedotov, *Russian Religious Mind* (1946) 110–157.

[D. DIRSCHERL]

PECHSTEIN, MAX

PECOCK, REGINALD (Peacock; Lat., *Pavo; c.*1393–1461), bp. of Chichester, theologian. P., a Welshman, was deposed from his bishopric in 1457 on a charge of heresy; he had rejected the authenticity of the Apostles' Creed and exalted the light of reason as a rule of faith. His troubles were due in part to his support of the House of York against Lancaster. P.'s *The Repressor of Overmuch Wijting (Blaming) of the Clergy* (1455; ed., 2 v. 1860) was a critical summation and rebuttal of *Lollard teaching, as well as a landmark in English literature. BIBLIOGRAPHY: V. H. H. Green, *Bishop Reginald Pecock* (1941); E. F. Jacob, *Fifteenth Century (1389–1480)* (1961).

[T. C. O'BRIEN]

PECTORAL CROSS, a cross usually containing a relic of the true Cross, worn over the breast by popes, bps., and certain other prelates. In the West it was adopted by the pope in the 13th century. It can be traced back to the early Christian *encolpia* (lockets hung around the neck containing relics, scripture texts, etc.). It came into general use in the 16th century. In the East it is sometimes worn by bps., although in various Eastern Churches it is either replaced by the medallion called the encolpion, or worn together with the encolpion. In the Byzantine Church today, the pectoral cross has come to designate its bearer as an archimandrite, while the right to wear an encolpion is the specific prerogative of a bishop.

PECTORIUS, EPITAPH OF, an inscription preserved in seven fragments found in 1830 in an ancient cemetery not far from Autun, S France. The form and style of the lettering point to a late 4th–cent. origin. The phraseology, however, is exactly that of the late 2d–cent. inscription of Abercius. The first seven verses are a poem of Christian faith addressed to the reader. The last four begin with a prayer of one Pectorius for his mother's eternal rest, and then there follows a prayer to his deceased father to join with his mother and deceased brothers in remembering Pectorius ("your Pectorius"). The inscription is evidently an epitaph that Pectorius provided for the tomb of his mother. There are echoes of the *disciplina arcani* (discipline of the secret), with cryptic references to Christ as the Fish, to baptism as the immortal fountain of divine water; to the Eucharist as food as sweet as honey, of which the faithful joyfully partake, holding the Fish in their hands. BIBLIOGRAPHY: Quasten 1:173–175.

[E. J. DILLON]

PECULIUM, a small sum allowed by the superior to a religious for personal use. The arrangement of this kind of allowance is for practical convenience and does not mean giving the religious the right of ownership renounced by the vow of *poverty.

[T. C. O'BRIEN]

PEDALION (Gr., steering paddle), a compilation of the canons of the Greek Orthodox Church in use in the patriarchate of Constantinople. The work of 10 Greek monks, it was first published in 1800 and again in 1831. It contains, besides the canonical writings of the Fathers, the Nomocanon of John the Faster, patriarch of Constantinople (582–595), the penitential book attributed to him, and two additional series of canons. The latter are attributed to St. Nicephorus, patriarch of Constantinople (806–815). They are of doubtful authenticity, esp. the canons dealing with marriage of bigamists and the power of the abbot to ordain. The Pedalion was accepted by the Orthodox patriarchate of Bulgaria, and the latter transmitted it to the Russian patriarchate. BIBLIOGRAPHY: A. Coussa, *Epitome praelectionum de iure ecclesiastico orientali* (1948) 1:86–131, 157.

[E. EL-HAYEK]

PEDRELL, FILIPE (1841–1922), self-taught Spanish composer and musical historian who revitalized the Spanish nationalist movement of composition. P. taught music history and aesthetics at the Madrid Conservatory (1874–1894); his students included Gerhard, de Falla, and Granados. He composed operas, *El Último Abencerraje* (1871), *Los Pirineos* (1894) and others, Masses, a *Te Deum* for chorus, orchestra, organ and harps, cantatas, and a Requiem for four-part chorus. His scholarly works include periodicals and volumes devoted to Spanish music, the Gregorian chant, the editing of the complete works of Victoria, and a collection of ancient Spanish church music. Two periodicals, which P. founded and edited, *Salterio Sacro-Hispano* and *Música Religiosa* contemporized Spanish church music and urged Spanish liturgical reform.

[R. J. LITZ]

PEDRO II (Dom Pedro de Alcantara; 1825–91), emperor of Brazil from 1840–89. Perhaps the most enlightened head of state in Latin American history, a man of cultural, scientific, and intellectual interests, P. ruled Brazil for nearly 50 years. Succeeding to the throne at the age of 5, he was declared full-fledged emperor at 14 (1840), putting an end to the troubled period of regency. Highly educated and politically prepared, P. was the dominant force in Brazil at age 17. As emperor, he was forward looking, socially sensitive, and pursued sound policies of economic growth. In politics he skillfully used Liberals and Conservatives in the ministries, although his frequent changes earned the hostility of both. A democratic person, P. encouraged a free press, constitutional guarantees, and was responsible for the abolition of slavery in Brazil. He encouraged the formation of the Republican Party after 1870. On the other hand P. was at times arbitrary. He had to contend with revolts at various times from 1835 to 1850. He fought two major wars against neighboring countries. In 1872 and thereafter the Emperor engaged in a bitter controversy with the bishop of Olinda over Freemasonry, which became a national dispute. Alienation of the army led to his ultimate downfall, which occurred in 1889 but was essentially a revolt against the Liberal ministry of Visconde Ouro Prêto. P. died in exile in Paris. BIBLIOGRAPHY: M. W. Williams, *Dom Pedro the Magnanimous, Second Emperor of Brazil* (1937).

[J. R. AHERNE]

PEERS, EDGAR ALLISON (1891–1952), British Hispanic scholar. Educated at Christ's College, Cambridge, he taught Spanish at the Univ. of Liverpool for 32 years and was the founder of the Institute of Hispanic Studies. He is best known for his authoritative translations of the writings of St. Teresa of Ávila and St. John of the Cross as well as for his further investigations into Spanish mysticism.

[E. M. GATES]

PEETERS, FLOR (1903–), composer and organist, one of the most influential Catholic church musicians of the 20th century. His church compositions include Masses, motets, and cantatas as well as numerous organ works. Among the latter are some fine hymn preludes and pieces on Gregorian themes as well as larger forms. His style, firmly grounded in classical technique, utilizes traditional materials and forms in a refreshingly modern but not extreme idiom; it has proved to be a most palatable step into 20th–cent. musical style in church. P. has also written much secular music and is a prominent recitalist and teacher. BIBLIOGRAPHY: A. Corbet, MGG 10:966–997.

[A. DOHERTY]

PEETERS, PAUL (1870–1950), French Jesuit, hagiographer and Orientalist. In 1905 he joined the Bollandists, with whom he was associated for the rest of his life, succeeding H. Delahaye as president (1941). P. pioneered in Oriental hagiography and its relation to the Byzantine. He also wrote on the political factors affecting church councils and schisms, and he produced a history of the Bollandists. BIBLIOGRAPHY: P. Devos, LTK 8:243.

[M. J. SUELZER]

PÉGUES, THOMAS (1866–1936), French Dominican theologian, whose most renowned work is his *Commentaire français littéral de la Somme théologique de Saint Thomas d'Aquin* (21 v., 1907–32). The work relies on St. Thomas's other writings to elucidate the text of the *Summa*. P. also published as a companion-aid, *Dictionnaire de la Somme théologique de Saint Thomas d'Aquin et du commentaire français litéral* (2 v., 1935).

[T. C. O'BRIEN]

PÉGUY, CHARLES PIERRE (1873–1914), French poet and essayist. Proud of his Orléans peasant heritage, P. was considered provincial in Paris, partly because he chose to remain poor. At once generous and stubborn, he made friends, but later alienated most of them. Opposed to both socialist or intellectual "parties," he nevertheless was both a socialist and an intellectual in his own way. Social concern and high patriotism are reflected in his *Jeanne d'Arc* (1897; as a play, 1910). As a volunteer officer in 1914, he was killed at the Battle of the Marne. Little is known of the process of P.'s conversion (after early loss of faith), but he had something of the mystic in his character and was inspired by every aspect of Joan of Arc. By 1908 he was fervently and openly Catholic, but family circumstances that he considered insurmountable, hence to be accepted, prevented a return to the sacraments. His wife and three of his children were baptized after his death. He was influenced by the philosopher H. *Bergson, to whom he paid homage. Combining reforming zeal, literary interest, and financial need, he founded the *Cahiers de la Quinzaine (Fortnightly Notebooks)* in 1900, publishing contributions from friends and most of his own works. P. was a "prophetic thinker" in every sense: witness, interpreter, seer of ideals. He spoke of a future "Harmonious City" in which there would be no injustice. In slow-moving biblical-verse style, he has God speak in some works, such as the medieval-type *Mystery of the Porch of the Second Virtue* (1911), almost in French peasant language, which he found nearer to the people and to the heart of France. His last long work, *Eve* (1913), presents Christianity as an inevitable development since man's beginning. P. became popular during World War II. Works: *Oeuvres complètes* (15 v., 1916–42). BIBLIOGRAPHY: Y. Servais, *Charles Péguy: the Pursuit of Salvation* (1953); J. Viard, *Proust et Péguy: des affines méconnues* (1972).

[L. TINSLEY]

PEIRCE, CHARLES SANDERS (1839–1914), American philosopher, physicist, mathematician, founder of pragmatism. Son of Harvard astronomer Benjamin Peirce, he was educated by his father in logic, mathematics, and natural science and at Harvard where in 1859 he took master's degrees in mathematics and chemistry. After graduating from the Lawrence Scientific School (1863), he lectured in logic at Harvard (1864–65), spent 3 years in its astronomical observatory, and taught logic at Johns Hopkins Univ. (1879–84), where one of his students was his continuator in pragmatism, John *Dewey. P. was associated with the U.S. Coast and Geodetic Survey (1861–91) as a physicist, winning acclaim for his research in geodesy, pendulum movement, astronomy, and optics. In 1903, he gave a series of lectures on pragmatism at Harvard, and another on logic at Lowell Institute in Boston (1903–04). His greatest contributions were in logic and scientific method, but he wrote in many fields such as psychophysics, philology, astronomy, metaphysics, and optics.

P. is widely known as the originator of the philosophic view termed pragmatism or pragmaticism, which is basically a system for clarifying ideas or a method of logic for ascertaining the meaning of concepts. Unlike his contemporary, William *James, who sought to confirm religious and moral concepts with pragmatism, P. was averse to such a procedure. Apart from pragmatism, however, P. tried to create a philosophical system including the methods and results of science but compatible with Christianity. Although deeply opposed to dogmatic theology, he was con-

vinced that science is not atheistic and contradictory to religion. Holding that the scientific method is the only way of acquiring true knowledge, he contended that metaphysics had to be made into an exact discipline by using that method. In the end, P. felt that his own metaphysical theories were in accord with Christian teachings, that his cosmology of evolving perfection was consistent with the Gospels, and that man has empirical evidence for God's existence. BIBLIOGRAPHY: *Collected Papers of C.S. Peirce* (ed. C. Hartshorne and P. Weiss, 6 v., 1931–35, with two subsequent v. ed. by A. Burks, 1958); M. Thompson, *Pragmatic Philosophy of C. S. Peirce* (1953, repr. 1974); F. E. Reilly, *Charles Peirce's Theory of Scientific Method.* W. P. Haas, *Conception of Law and the Unity of Peirce's Philosophy* (1964).

[J. T. HICKEY]

PEKAH (PHACEE), KING OF ISRAEL. Described in 2 Kg 15.25–37; 16.5; 2 Chr 28.6–15; and in Is 7.1–9 with some variations, Pekah perhaps a shortened form of Pekahiah, his predecessor, is also mentioned in the annals of Tiglath-Pileser III, *c*.745–728. He was the son of Remaliah (of no particular fame) and reigned over the Northern Kingdom (Israel) from 737 to 732 B.C. (conjectural chronology, but the 20 years assigned him in 2 Kg 15.27 is not possible). He served as a royal officer for Pekahiah whom he caused to be assassinated. He, in turn, was killed by Hoshea, who became the last of the Northern kings. Not only was Pekah the next to last king of the North, but he allied himself to Syria in a last-ditch effort to attack Judah and to resist the Assyrians who had been summoned by Judah. The four sources of information mentioned above agree only in a general way regarding Pekah. The statement in 2 Chr 28.6 (otherwise unverified) that he slew 120,000 warriors in Judah in one day is incredibly hyperbolic. BIBLIOGRAPHY: J. Bright, *History of Israel* (1959) 256–257; B. McGrath, NCE 11:250.

[I. HUNT]

PELAGIA, ST., the name of six saints mentioned in the Roman Martyrology, and three saints contained in Butler's *Lives of the Saints*. Of these only the existence of one can be verified with any shred of serious historical data: that of Pelagia, virgin and martyr of Antioch, whose martyrdom probably occurred *c*.311. She was only 15 years old when the Roman soldiers surrounded her house. Rather than suffer sexual assault, which was typically in store for young women before superstitious Roman soldiers would feel free to put them to death, P. threw herself from the top of the house. Her choice of preserving her chastity at the cost of her life was praised by both Ambrose and Chrysostom. BIBLIOGRAPHY: Butler 2:510–511.

[E. J. DILLON]

PELAGIANISM AND SEMI-PELAGIANISM, teachings on grace, named from Pelagius. His original name is conjectured to have been Morgan (man of the sea); he was a

British monk, and little is known about his early life. A harbinger of those remarkable bands who carried back to the Continent the religion and culture they had received from the Celtic coasts, he became an esteemed teacher in Rome, well versed in Scripture and classical literature; his followers were few yet influential. He set himself to fight immorality, excused by the plea of human weakness, by showing that the responsibility was man's own and should not be ascribed to God or the absence of divine grace. His favorite maxim was, "If I ought, I can." With his disciple Celestius, a bolder man and more apt to draw opponents' fire, he crossed to Africa before the sack of Rome by Alaric the Goth (410) and met Augustine, who was to speak of him as a holy man. Shortly afterward he sailed for Palestine, where he found a more congenial religious climate and made his home, at least until 418, when he disappeared from history. In 415 Orosius, a Spanish priest, came from Augustine to warn Jerome about Pelagius's teachings. A synod was convoked at Lydda, a miserable affair, said Jerome—who also was to ridicule Pelagius as "stuffed with Scots porridge"—and the upshot was an acquittal. The fact was resented by the African Church, which appealed to Pope Innocent I. His successor, Pope Zosimus, ratified the Acts of the Council of Carthage (see D 222–231), and, though at first hesitant, drew up a circular inviting all bps. to subscribe to a condemnation of Pelagian opinions. Julian, bp. of Eclanum, a man of birth and sanctity, refused and became the leader of the party and the target for four works of Augustine, *De nuptiis et concupiscentiis, Contra duas epistolas Pelagianorum,* and the two tractates, one incomplete, *Contra Julianum.* Soon Julian and Celestius were disgraced and discredited, and with the condemnation by the Council of Ephesus (431) and with East and West united against it, the cause became hopeless.

Pelagianism can be reconstructed from authentic writings. It was a teaching about divine grace, and it hinged on two principles. First, grace comes from man's own choice, since human free will requires an equipoise before right and wrong, and it is by an act of his own that man takes the initiative in salvation. Second, *infant baptism is useless, since Adam's sin was personal and therefore does not damn others. The massive attack launched by Augustine was directed against the denial of original sin and the gratuitousness of divine grace; the controversy was cleanly conducted without vituperation.

Semi-Pelagianism was an attempt to hold a middle course between the extremes of doctrines that virtually abolished man's intrinsic need for grace and man's freedom. The term Semi-Pelagianism dates from the early 17th cent., and was applied by opponents to *Molinism, a usage forbidden after the *Congregatio de auxiliis. Semi-Pelagianism refers properly to a movement that began in the last years of Augustine's life; it is the subject of his *De gratia et libero arbitrio, De correptione et gratia, De praedestinatione sanctorum,* and *De dono perseverantiae.* Augustine's opposition was continued by Prosper of Aquitaine; Rome from the first favored this opposition but reserved its official endorsement of a predestinarian system. Semi-Pelagianism grew almost as a reaction of Provence to the harsher shores of Africa across the Mediterranean. Men such as John Cassian and Vincent of Lérins disavowed Pelagianism, as well as any doctrine that destroyed human freedom and responsibility. Provoked by the savage damnationism of the priest Lucidus, the learned and holy abbot of Lérins, Faustus of Riez, held that a man takes the first step toward salvation, for which grace is indeed necessary, but which is a recompense for his merits. Under the influence of Caesarius of Arles, abp. there in 503, Rome hardened, and the Semi-Pelagians, called Massilians (from Marseilles), were condemned at the Council of Orange II (529); the condemnation, which was cited at Trent, was given ecumenical authority by the approval of Pope Boniface II (531), and the movement died out.

Pelagianism and Semi-Pelagianism are not, however, simply episodes in Christian history. They represent a perennial human response in the search to express the place of human cooperation with grace. In the controversies of the Reformation, as well as within Protestantism and Roman Catholicism, those who have defended human cooperation have been called Pelagians by their adversaries. In preaching, devotional literature, and in the thought of the ordinary Christian, the naturalness of a Pelagian mentality manifests itself. Those who defend the transcendence and gratuitousness of divine grace regard as a practical Pelagianism the reduction of the gospel of grace and the Christian life to the level of good behavior benignly regarded and vaguely assisted by God. BIBLIOGRAPHY: J. Ferguson, *Pelagius, a Historical and Theological Study* (1957); L. Duchesne, *L'Église au VIe siècle* (1925); G. Bonner, *Augustine and Modern Research on Pelagianism* (1972).

[T. GILBY]

PELAGIUS I (d. 561), **POPE** from 556. As papal apocrisiarius in Constantinople P. opposed the condemnation of the *Three Chapters and wrote a treatise in their defense (*In defensione trium capitulorum*) c.554. Before becoming pope, however, he changed his position and supported the submission of *Vigilius to the demands of Justinian, holding the question to be one of policy and expediency rather than of religion. Much of his effort during his pontificate was directed toward overcoming the opposition to the condemnation of the Three Chapters in Africa, Gaul, and N Italy, but he was notably successful only in Gaul. BIBLIOGRAPHY: Altaner 555–556.

[R. B. ENO]

PELAGIUS II (d. 590), **POPE** from 579. He was son of a Goth, the second pope of German blood, and was elected on the death of Benedict I (579), while Rome was under siege by the invading Lombards. He succeeded in negotiating a 3-year truce with the barbarians, but his attempt to obtain assistance for Italy from the Emperor Maurice, even with the aid of his able representative at Constantinople, Gregory the Great, came to nothing. P.'s entire reign was overshadowed by the growing disorder brought on by the Lombards and, in effect, he became the sole ruler of Rome and its environs. He was unsuccessful in his attempt to heal the schism separating Aquileia from Rome in consequence of the acceptance by Pope *Vigilius of the condemnation of the *Three Chapters. P. made an issue of the application of the title ecumenical (or universal) patriarch to the patriarch of Constantinople, and Gregory continued to oppose the legitimacy of the title, which became an important bone of contention between East and West. P. accomplished some reconstruction in the sanctuary of St. Peter's and is credited with the restoration of the basilica of St. Lawrence Outside the Walls where his portrait appears. He died in a plague that followed a flooding of the Tiber and is buried in the portico of St. Peter's. Six of his letters may be found in PL 72:703–760. BIBLIOGRAPHY: J. Chapin, NCE 11:56–58; T. G. Jalland, *Church and the Papacy* (1944).

[P. F. MULHERN]

PELAGIUS (354?–418?), monk for whom *Pelagianism is named. His birthplace is variously given as Britain, Ireland, or the East. At Rome *c*.400 he was known as a man of upright life and good education. After the fall of the city (410) he went to Carthage with his disciple *Celestius. He later traveled to Palestine, where Jerome showed antagonism to him because of the warning sent (414) by Augustine's emissary, the priest Orosius. Jerome coined the term Pelagianism for the doctrines P. developed as an answer to Manichaeism. Only some of P.'s treatises survive: *Expositiones XIII epistularum Pauli, Libellus fidei ad Innocentiam I,* and *Epistola ad Demetriadem.* His teaching is fully known from the works of his adversaries, particularly Augustine. In 415 P. was acquitted by the synods of Jerusalem and Diospolis in Caesarea. In 417, however, he and Celestius were both excommunicated by Innocent I, whose successor, Pope Zosimus, was at first favorable to P.; but renewed investigation and the condemnations by the Council of *Carthage XVI (418; see D 222–230) caused him to ratify the council's decrees and to renew his predecessor's excommunication of P. and Celestius in his *Epistola tractoria,* of which fragments survive (see D 231). P.'s history after 418 is unknown. BIBLIOGRAPHY: S. J. McKenna, NCE 11:58–60.

[M. J. SUELZER]

PELAYO OF OVIEDO (PELAGIUS OVETENSIS; d. 1153), bishop. Details of his life are lacking. He became bp. of Oviedo in 1101, resigned his see in 1129, but reoccupied it in the years 1142–1143. His several historical writings are in ill repute, for he was not above falsifying documents in his attempt to obtain metropolitan status for Oviedo. BIBLIOGRAPHY: M. C. Díaz y Díaz, *Index scriptorum Latinorum medii aevi Hispanorum* (1958) 1:117, 425, 900; D. Mansilla, LTK 8:252.

[W. A. JURGENS]

PELAYO, ALVARO, see ALVARO PELAYO.

PELICAN, a large waterfowl with long beak. In disgorging food to feed its young, the pelican so presses beak against breast that the bill appears to be piercing the breast. This action, together with the reddish breast plumage and beak-edge, gave rise to the folk notion that the bird draws blood from its own breast to revivify the obstreperous young it has killed. A 2d-cent. bestiary recounts the story as a type of the Redemption. In the Middle Ages the death of the young no longer figures in the tale; instead, the pelican is employed frequently in both literature and art as a sign of the Eucharist. Renaissance and baroque designers use it often on altar appurtenances. The pelican in Ps 101.7 is construed as a symbol of Christ solitary on Olivet, or of Hermits. BIBLIOGRAPHY: G. G. Sill, *Primer of Symbols in Christian Art* (1975); F. E. Hulme, *History, Principles and Practice of Symbolism in Christian Art* (1891, repr. 1969).

[M. J. SUELZER]

PELLA, a town of Transjordan about 3 miles across the Jordan River from Scythopolis. Founded during the Hellenistic period, it remained one of the cities of the Decapolis and was not involved in Jewish life. After the Jewish War of 70 A.D., Jewish Christian refugees, under the leadership of James' brother Simeon, fled there to escape Roman and Jewish persecution. Tombs and inscriptions found there indicate a flourishing Christianity. After the second Jewish revolt (135 A.D.), part of this community reestablished itself on Mt. Sion under the gentile bishop Mark.

[S. MUSHOLT]

PELLICANUS, KONRAD (Kürschner; Pellikan; 1478–1556), Alsatian Reformer, author of the first Hebrew grammar by a Christian, *De modo legendi et intelligendi Hebraeum* (1504). He was a Franciscan from 1493, who turned to the teachings of Luther and Zwingli, accepted the post of professor of Scripture at Zurich, and became a Protestant in 1526. He was a collaborator in Bible translations, published his own *Commentaria Bibliorum (7 v., 1532–37),* and helped in the formulation of the *Helvetic Confession of 1536.

[T. C. O'BRIEN]

PELLIPARIO, NICOLA (NICOLA'DA URBINO); (*c*.1480–1547), very great Italian Renaissance majolica painter, father of Guido Durantino and grandfather of Orazio and Camillo Fontana. P.'s *istoriato* style, based on Italian engravings and illustrations, influenced painters in Venice, Pesaro, and Urbino. P. executed *Apollo and Daphne* for Isabella d'Este (British Museum) and worked at Fabriano (1527) and at Urbino (1528) where work with his son Guido is documented by the signed plate, *The Martyrdom of St. Cecilia.*

[M. J. DALY]

PELLISSON-FONTANIER, PAUL (1624–93), French apologete. Reared as a Protestant, he became a lawyer and member of the royal court, but fell into disfavor and was imprisoned for 5 years (1661–67). On release he became a convert to Catholicism (1670), a priest, and an apostle to his former coreligionists. His religious works include *Reflexions sur les différends en matière de religion* (4 v., 1686) and *Traité de l' Eucharistie* (1694).

[T. C. O'BRIEN]

PELOQUIN, C. ALEXANDER (1918–), Catholic composer of church music, conductor and choir master. P. was born into a musical family and was involved, from childhood, in the music of his parish church in Millbury, Massachusetts. He made his concert debut at 18 and, a year later, won first place in the Rhode Island competition of the American Guild of Organists. P. studied with Jesus Maria Sanroma and Isidor Phillip and for two summers on a scholarship at the Berkshire Music Center. A long-time conductor of the Boston Univ. and Peloquin Chorales, he is presently composer-in-residence at Boston College and music director at the cathedral of SS. Peter and Paul, Providence, Rhode Island. He has lectured, taught, and conducted workshops throughout the U.S., and in Canada, and in Europe, has made recordings and had several television and radio performances. His numerous published works, which include Masses, hymns, and other liturgical settings, have been performed across the U.S. and Canada, as well as abroad. Convinced that 20th-cent. man must bring his creative energies to the liturgy, P. is an advocate of freshness in liturgical settings and of using art to add grandeur and excitement to the prayers of the people. Popular among his recent publications are: *Mass for Joy* (1968), *Mass of the Bells* (1972), and *Lyric Liturgy* (1974). BIBLIOGRAPHY: "Alexander Peloquin on Prayer and Music," *Pastoral Music* 1 (1977) 44–45; C. A. Peloquin, "A New Song for a New Liturgy," *Liturgical Arts* 39 (1970) 7–9; L. J. Lind, "Honey from the Rock," *Columbia* 46 (1966), 16–19; *idem*, "Liturgical Pied Piper," *The Catholic Choirmaster* 50 (1964) 137–139; "Laborer in the Vineyard" *Caecilia* 82 (1955) 91–92.

[M. T. LEGGE]

PELZER, AUGUST (1876–1958), medieval scholar. P. studied at Liège, and obtained a doctorate at Louvain. Ordained a priest in 1901, he was sent (1907) by Card. Mercier to Rome to foster medieval studies at the Vatican Library. In 1910, P. was named "Scrittore aggiunto" at the Vatican Library, and in 1915, "Scrittore onorario." He remained attached to the Vatican Library for 50 years, even after being named emeritus in 1949. P. edited the catalog *Codices Vaticani latini, 679–1134* (2 v., 1931–33), with Addenda (1947), and went on to produce 85 other works. He utilized the scientific techniques he learned from Alfred Cauchie, founder of the *Revue d'histoire ecclésiastique*. He also collaborated in the critical editions of the *Quodlibeta* of Godfrey of Fontaines and was a member of the Royal Academy of Belgium. BIBLIOGRAPHY: *Mélanges Auguste Pelzer* (1947) 17–21.

[N. F. GAUGHAN]

PEMBROKE, PRIORY OF, a monastic house in Pembrokeshire, Wales, founded in 1098 as a cell of St. Martin's Abbey, Séez, Normandy, by Arnulf Montgomery, lord of Pembroke. It was confiscated by Richard II (1378); restored by Henry IV (1399); confiscated again and granted to the abbey of St. Albans (1443); and dissolved by Henry VIII (1539). It continues as an Anglican church. BIBLIOGRAPHY: W. Dugdale et al., *Monasticon Anglicanum* (1846); Knowles-Hadcock.

[C. MCGRATH]

PENAL POWER OF THE CHURCH, the capability and right existing in the Church to level penalties on those violating its laws, a corollary to the power to legislate and command. To exercise authority in the Church has always been understood as to teach, to sanctify, to rule. The meaning of these functions depends on the meaning of the Church itself. Accordingly, the coercive or penal power as an element of ruling is in process of reevaluation in view of Vatican Council II's teachings on the Church itself. An earlier age explained the penal power as a logical consequence of the Church's status as a perfect society, juridically possessing all the resources needed to regulate its societal life; there was an emphasis on analogies with the sanctioning powers legitimate to a civil government. The Council's strong affirmations on the Church as unique, with an evangelical, salvific mission, and specifically on the theme of authority as service (VatII ConstChurch, nn. 8, 18–19) have led to a view of penal power at once more pastoral and more faithful to the Church's unique and specific character. The reassessment is in process, but there are some generalities already well established. In principle the penal law of the Church reflects the need to defend both the individual and the community when one member speaks or acts contrary to the one life in truth and in grace that communion with Christ and witness to his presence mean. That defense of the Church's mission is most clearly exercised by the punishment of *excommunication. Yet the primary concern and aim ever remain a community obedience motivated by love and correction of failings by interior conversion. Thus punishment is a step of last resort and in extreme cases. Such is the broad context for evaluating the penal power of the Church that clearly influences the draft revision of the penal code of the Church issued in 1973 by the Pontifical Commission for the Revision of the CIC (*Schema documenti quo disciplina sanctionum seu poenarum in Ecclesia Latina denuo ordinatur*). The document is but a draft, does not suspend present legislation, and has not been received with unmixed approval. It does, however, clearly embody a new and more pastoral conception of coercive power; this is evident from its Preliminaries (*praenotanda*), from the draft *motu proprio (Humanum consortium)* for promulgation of a new penal code; and from the draft of the canons themselves. In explicit fidelity to Vatican II, the preliminaries express the intent that the exercise of penal power be marked by mercy and be regarded as a last resort. The *motu proprio* stresses the priority of moral conversion over coercive correction. Describing authorities in the Church as pastors, not enforcers (*pastores, non percussores*), it recalls the themes of gentleness and pastoral charity, decries multiplication of penalties, and proposes obedience from love as the ideal for the community. Penalties should be reduced, restricted to the external forum, and reservation should be kept to a minimum. The draft of penal canons reduces the number from the 220 of the CIC to 26. Rather than classifying penalties as medicinal or remedial (see CENSURES), and vindicative (see INFAMY) the draft (c. 3) describes them as remedial and expiatory. The new approach is also evident in restrictions on *latae sententiae* penalties, in the dropping of infamy as a penalty, and of the distinction among excommunicates of the *vitandi* and the *tolerati*. Such indications mark a new direction that undoubtedly will modify the final revision of the penal code and the general understanding in the Church of its penal power. BIBLIOGRAPHY: *Canon Law Society of America: Proceedings of the Thirty-Sixth Annual Convention* (1974) 130–139.

[T. C. O'BRIEN]

PENAL REMEDIES (CANON LAW), disciplinary measures established by law to prevent canonical crimes: admonition (*monitio*), rebuke (*correctio*), precept (*praeceptum*), surveillance (*vigilantia*) (CIC, c. 2306). There is a gradation in severity among these corrective measures; the application of each may be public or private; secret records must be taken of the steps taken; the application of the remedies must be marked by care both to protect the good name of the one disciplined, and to invoke the measures appropriate to serve their purpose. In recent history and in current discussion of the revision of canon law, a relevant theme emphasized is the right of the person to due process. It has been felt that in past use of penal remedies neither that right nor the principle of presumptive innocence has always been scrupulously observed. BIBLIOGRAPHY: *Canon Law Society of America Proceedings of the Thirty-Sixth Annual Convention* (1974) 132–133.

[T. C. O'BRIEN]

PENANCE, a series of external actions that accompany conversion and are indicative of internal repentance. Penance is associated with, but should never be identified with, the central biblical and prophetic concepts of conversion (from the Heb. *shuv,* to turn, to turn back) and repentance (from the Gr. *metanoia,* change of heart). Each of these latter concepts is meant to include the whole movement that the two of them together clearly denote. One comes from Hebrew language and culture, the other from Greek, and each has a different emphasis. Conversion, to turn back,

involves action: a concrete change to a new way of life; a turning in one's tracks and going in a new direction. Repentance, change of mind, involves a feeling of regret or remorse which leads to a trusting obedience to God. Unfortunately, it was once considered acceptable to translate one or the other of these concepts by the phrase "do penance," which is hopelessly inadequate. There is in fact no biblical word for penance which comes from the Latin *poena,* which means pain or punishment. The reality of this Latin concept can be found in Scripture, however. In the confession of sin and the penitential prayer that accompanied conversion or repentance, it was normal to fast, to keep a long vigil of prayer, to wear sackcloth and ashes, to weep and rend one's garments, to sleep on the ground, to pluck hairs from the head and beard, to offer sacrifice for sin, and to give alms. This was a normal concomitant of the remorse that accompanies repentance and leads to conversion.

[E. J. DILLON]

PENANCE, NEW RITE OF, for the new *Roman Ritual* three forms for celebrating the sacrament of *penance, approved by Paul VI and promulgated in its Lat. version by the Sacred Congregation for Divine Worship (Dec. 2, 1973). Use in the various regions of the Church begins when an appropriate vernacular version has been readied by the episcopal conferences and approved by the Holy See. The new rite was developed in response to the directive of Vatican Council II (Vat II SacLit 72). In its Introduction the decree of promulgation indicates the conformity of the new rite with the norms laid down by the Congregation for the Doctrine of the Faith (*Normae pastorales circa absolutionem sacramentalem generali modo impertiendam,* June 16, 1972). The general inspiration of the new rite is an intent that it should express the pastoral (rather than the juridic) and reconciliatory meaning of the sacrament of penance. The particular new emphasis it gives is on the ecclesial aspects of sin and repentance: separation from God by sin is also a diminution of the inner unity of the Church community, since this rests on the union in charity of each member with Christ and thereby with one another. The rite of reconciliation with God should also express reconciliation and healing within the body of Christ. The three forms of the rite approved consist in: Form I, the reconciliation of the individual penitent by the priest-confessor, and the communitary Forms II, III; Form II culminating in individual confession and absolution; Form III in a generalized confession and general absolution. The rite of individual reconciliation should include the greeting of the penitent by the confessor, appropriate readings and prayers, before confession and absolution; and the whole rite should make clear the ecclesial aspect by underlining that it is the ministry of the ecclesial community that is being exercised. Forms II and III are more explicitly communal. In both the preparatory parts are carried out by the community together. Preparation consists in hymns and readings of the word of God, followed by a homily, all stressing the themes of mercy, reconciliation with God and one another, and true repentance. The preparation ends with the community expression of contrition, a litany, a generic confession, e.g., as in the Confiteor, and finally with the recitation of the Lord's Prayer, which is never to be omitted. Form II continues with each penitent approaching a confessor, making a specific confession of sins (see CONFESSION, SACRAMENTAL), and receiving absolution individually. Form III includes only the generic confession of sins, the other prayers, ending with the Our Father, then general absolution by the priest. The decree of promulgation also commends nonsacramental *penitential services as fostering a spirit of repentance in the community (see ABSOLUTION, GENERAL). The right to employ Form III of the rite, i.e., with general absolution, belongs to the ruling bp., apart from exceptional conditions (see COMMUNAL PENANCE). The choice of prayers and readings to implement the outline of the new rite, as well as adaptations to regional needs, customs, and practices, is left to the national conferences of bishops. In the U.S. appropriate adaptation of the new rite and instruction in its use preceeded its introduction into the parishes between Advent, 1976 and, at the latest, Lent, 1977. In England and Wales the new rite, introduced at Easter, 1976, became obligatory by Easter, 1977. Special attention, with a degree of wariness, is being given to Form III of the new rite. Efforts are being made (e.g., by the Federation of Diocesan Liturgical Commissions, 1307 S. Wabash, Chicago, Ill.) to formulate guidelines for the use of general absolution that will derive the benefit intended in the promulgation of the new rite while observing the required caution. Where prior permission of the bp. has not been obtained, general absolution may only be given when three conditions are present all at once: a large number of penitents; an insufficient number of confessors to hear individual confessions properly; the resulting disadvantage that many would be deprived of the grace of the Eucharist unless general absolution be given. Recipients must intend individual confession at an opportune time. BIBLIOGRAPHY: U.S. Catholic Conference, *Rite of Penance* (1975); *idem, Pastoral Norms concerning the Administration of General Sacramental Absolution* (1972); Federation of Diocesan Liturgical Commissions, *New Rite of Penance* (1974).

[T. C. O'BRIEN]

PENANCE, PRACTICES OF. Penance, as understood in Judaic and Christian religions, consists most essentially in an interior consciousness of sin and a change of heart in which the sinner regrets and turns from his sinful deeds and is converted to God. There is frequently, but less essentially, some external manifestation of the inner change of heart. This commonly takes the form of a confession of guilt and the performance of certain difficult or humiliating works which (1) testify to the depth and sincerity of the interior conversion of heart and (2) are a voluntary assumption, at least in symbolic form, of the punishment the sinner acknowledges himself to have merited by his violations of

God's law. Practices of penance are works undertaken in this spirit. In popular usage the term also embraces works of the same kind performed less by way of penalty than for ascetical purposes (i.e., to establish mastery over the disorderly inclinations of sinful nature) or out of a motive of love that wishes to share in the sufferings of Jesus. Among the commoner forms the practice of penance has taken are: fasting, abstinence, abstemiousness, continence, poverty, isolation, privation of sleep, manual labor, and the infliction upon self of discomfort and pain. The penitential spirit has existed in the Church from the earliest times, but at some periods it has been more strongly emphasized than at others, and cultural or other historical circumstances account for considerable differences in the forms in which it has expressed itself. In the contemporary Church there has been a great reduction in the number of obligatory penances. The need of penance was strongly reaffirmed by Vatican Council II (e.g., Vat II SacLit 12, 105, 109) and by Pope Paul VI in his apostolic constitution *Poenitemini* (1966), but the selection of ways of practicing it has been left more to the conscience of the individual Catholic. BIBLIOGRAPHY: M. Viller and M. Olphe-Galliard, DSAM 1:959–977; J. de Guibert, *ibid*. 1:977–990.

[P. K. MEAGHER]

PENANCE SACRAMENT OF, a true sacrament of the new law, instituted by Christ, for the purpose of reconciling the sinner to God as often as he falls into sin after baptism, (cf. Council of Trent, Session 24; D 911). The rite of penance is made up of the three acts of the penitent—contrition, confession, and satisfaction (the quasi-matter)—and the words of the priest "I absolve you, etc." (the form). Basic to Catholic teaching on the sacrament of penance is the belief that the ministry of divine pardon was first exercised by Christ in his sacred humanity (cf. Mt 9.1–8; Mk 2.3–12; Lk 5.18–26), and that it was entrusted by Christ to his Apostles and their successors in the priesthood.

New Testament. Christian tradition appeals to the Gospels of Matthew and John to found the belief that Christ conferred on his Apostles the power of forgiving sins. To Peter, Christ promised the power of the keys: "And I will give thee the keys of the kingdom of heaven; and whatever thou shalt bind on earth should be bound in heaven; and whatever thou shalt loose on earth shall be loosed in heaven" (Mt 16.19). To the Twelve along with Peter Christ again promised the power of binding and loosing, but in the context of a sinner who refuses to hear the Church and who is to be regarded as a heathen and a publican (Mt 18.18). The Fathers of the Church will interpret the power of binding as the power of excommunicating the sinner, the first step in the discipline of penance, and the power of loosing as the power of reconciling the sinner to the community, an interpretation which is contextually sound. Thus, whom the Church binds by excommunicating, God binds; whom the Church looses by reconciling, God looses, or reconciles, to himself. Reconciliation with the community is a sign of reconciliation with God. The power promised in Matthew is conferred in John: "As the Father has sent me, I also send you . . . . Receive the Holy Spirit; whose sins you shall forgive, they are forgiven them; and whose sins you shall retain, they are retained" (Jn 20.22–23). Thus the apostolic ministry of forgiveness is regarded as the continuation of Christ's own ministry. Whom the Church in the person of its representatives forgives God forgives—granted, of course, the proper dispositions on the part of the sinner.

Early Discipline. The procedure of penance was normally public; it followed the practice of St. Paul in excommunicating the sinner and ultimately reconciling him (cf. 1 Cor 5.5; 2 Cor 2.10). The first step in the discipline was confession, either to the bishop or in more populous churches to the priest-penitentiary. Although penance was public, the confession of sins was usually private. After confession, the sinner was enrolled in the order of penitents, an order corresponding to that of the catechumens. During the period of penance, the penitents were excluded from the Prayer of the Faithful and from the Eucharistic Sacrifice that followed. In private, penitents were obliged to fast, to multiply their prayers, and to contribute alms to the poor. In the Roman Church penitents were reconciled in a solemn ceremony on Holy Thursday. In the East those guilty of more serious crimes usually spent a number of years as mourners, hearers, penitents, and bystanders before qualifying as participants in the Eucharistic Sacrifice. The practice of private penance and of devotional confession for venial sins was probably introduced by the Irish monks and English missionary scholars of the 6th and 7th centuries. On the Continent, however, public penance for those guilty of more public crimes lasted well into the 12th century.

Theological Reflections. The Montanist and Novatianist schisms of the 3d cent. offer indirect proof that Catholics at the time believed that the Church had the power on earth of ministering divine pardon. Again, the sacramental aspect of penance is evidenced by the parallel repeatedly drawn between baptism and penance. Thus, the author of the *Syriac Didascalia* (*c*.250) likens the final imposition of the hand on the penitents to the effect of baptism: "For whether by the imposition of the hand or by baptism they receive the communication of the Holy Spirit (2.41.2). The sacramental nature of the priest's reconciliation as well as its necessity is given eloquent expression by St. Augustine in an exhortation to his clergy to remain at their posts during the Vandal invasion: "How great a crowd of both sexes and all ages is accustomed to gather in the church, some demanding baptism, others reconciliation, others the discipline of penance itself, all seeking consolation and the administration of the sacraments. But if ministers are lacking, how great will be the destruction that follows those who leave this life either unregenerate or bound?" (*Serm. 329.3*). This early emphasis on the importance of the priest's reconciliation was obscured by early scholastic teaching on the necessity of sorrow motivated by love as the operative element in the sacrament of penance. The absolution of the priest came to be regarded as a simple declaration that the sinner was al-ready reconciled by God through perfect contrition, or as the remission of the temporal punishment due to sin. Thus Peter Abélard and Peter Lombard had great influence on later scholastic doctors. SS. Bonaventure and Thomas Aquinas also stressed the need of sorrow elicited by the virtue of charity, but they integrated the acts of the penitent and the absolving action of the priest by insisting that the reconciliation of the priest informed and elevated the acts of the penitent as part of the one sacramental sign of penance. Against Luther and the reformers of the 16th cent., the Council of Trent confirmed the true sacramentality of penance as well as the necessity by divine law of confessing all serious sins committed after baptism.

Recent Trends and Development. Penance is regarded as a sacrament of the new law by the Greek and Russian Orthodox Churches and since the time of the Oxford Movement by Anglo-Catholics and some Episcopalians. A growing number of Lutherans, particularly in Germany, are reviving the early Lutheran practice of private confession to the minister, or pastor, followed by absolution. In Southern France the community of Taizé (a Calvinist foundation) has not only introduced the practice of private confession and absolution, but many of the members regard penance as a sacrament. Among Catholics there is a growing awareness that sin is not only an offense against God but also against the Church and that reconciliation with God ordinarily presupposes reconciliation with the Church. Liturgical expression of this awareness is to be found in the growing practice of introducing some of the more communal and public features of the ancient liturgy of penance. BIBLIOGRAPHY: P. Palmer, *Sacraments and Forgiveness (Sources of Christian Theology* 2, 1960); B. Poschmann, *Penance and the Anointing of the Sick* (tr. F. Courtney, 1964); P. Anciaux, *Sacrament of Penance* (1962); *PENANCE, NEW RITES OF.

[P. F. PALMER]

PENANCE, SACRAMENTAL, part of the sacrament known as *satisfaction, prayer or deed imposed by the confessor and accepted by the penitent as a sign of repentance and renewal of life and as remedy for his weakness—the "penance." (see PENANCE, VIRTUE OF.)

In ancient times there was a period of rehabilitation, living out conversion, in a communal and liturgical context prior to reconciliation; penitential practices expressed sincerity and depth of conversion, externalizing the penitent's effort to center his life on God rather than creatures. In medieval practice, largely because of Celtic and Anglo-Saxon secular law, the penance became more punitive than medicinal and the relationship to life, liturgy, and community was gradually lost. Theology, reflecting medieval practice, came to see the sacramental penance as reparation, expiation, or satisfaction; a punitive debt or fine ("tariff") owed to God for having offended him. Interaction with medieval commutations, redemptions, and indulgences, and the postponement of the penance until after absolution made it more and more symbolic (e.g., the assignment of prayers) and individualistic, with acceptance (intention to perform it) required for sacramental integrity. Contemporary theology and practice suggest instead a work of charity to express and complete conversion, following from a new realization of the social and ecclesial effects of sin and sacrament, the reconciliatory nature of the sacrament, and its expression in everyday life. The 1973 *Rite of Penance* incorporates this emphasis. BIBLIOGRAPHY: P. J. Schellens, *De satisfactione sacramentali* (1964). *PENANCE, NEW RITE OF.

[J. DALLEN]

PENANCE, VIRTUE OF, a supernatural, infused virtue empowering a person for acts of Christian repentance with a view to forgiveness of sins (see REMISSION OF SINS). St. Thomas Aquinas significantly does not consider this virtue in the course of dealing with the moral *virtues, but in the discussion of the sacrament of penance (ThAq ST 3a,85). For the discourse on the moral virtues he draws on the ideas and vocabulary of Aristotle; but the meaning of penance is intimately bound up with the Christian concept of mortal *sin. A natural ethic can conceive of sin as a serious moral disorder, even as an offense against an order of divine justice. But sin in a merely ethical framework is a disorder not incompatible with a habitually settled life of moral uprightness; its disorder can be rectified by a counter, virtuous act. The mystery of grace, however, means that sin can be mortal: it can create a separation from the Father's loving communion of grace, and so destroy the spiritual life of the soul and any inner resource of rectification. Mortal sin is not corrected by simple retraction, nor, on God's part, by a mere remittal of guilt. Mortal sin is rectified only by a positive reconciliation that is made possible and actual by the grace of the Father who takes back the sinner by his grace of pardon. Christian repentance is the approach to that reconciliation. The virtue of penance is the gift that gives the sinner the willingness to be reconciled, the willingness to renounce sin out of a contrite, restored love. The virtue is infused fully at the moment the process of *justification reaches its term. The primary act of the virtue is *contrition, motivated by a faith in the saving power of Christ and by love for the Father. That penitential act includes an attitude of expiation, of submission to whatever God calls for in recompense as the condition for reconciliation; it thus includes the intention of receiving the sacrament of penance. The virtue of penance, however, does not only enter into the process of justification. Prompted by charity it is a constant willingness to reject sin because that means estrangement from the Father, and to imitate Christ in accepting the sufferings of life as expiation or even by voluntary acts of mortification as a share in his atoning suffering. BIBLIOGRAPHY: ThAq ST Lat-Eng (v. 60, *Penance* ed. R. Masterson and T. C. O'Brien) appendices.

[T. C. O'BRIEN]

PENATES, Roman household gods whose images were kept with those of *lares* in the *lararium* (shrine) and to whom sacrifices were offered.

PENDA, KING OF MERCIA, (*c*.600–654). He won independence for Mercia from Northumbria. In 653 he allowed Christian missionaries to operate for the first time in the Midlands of England. Of his three sons and two daughters, Ethelred, Cyneburg, and Cyneswitha were venerated as saints in the Middle Ages. BIBLIOGRAPHY: Bede, *Historia ecclesiastica* 2:20; 3:7; F. M. Stenton, *Anglo-Saxon England* (3d ed., 1970) *passim*.

[L. E. BOYLE]

PENINGTON, ISAAC (Pennington; 1616–79), prominent early Quaker. P. was the son of the lord mayor of London, Sir Isaac Penington (*c*.1590–1661). First an ardent Puritan, P. became a Seeker, but after meeting G. *Fox, publicly joined the Friends (1658). His prestige, his noble character, and his able writings contributed to the growth of the new movement. After 1661 he suffered loss of property and long imprisonments. His son, Edward Penington (1667–1711), established the family in Pennsylvania. P.'s collected writings were published posthumously in two parts, 1680 and 1681. BIBLIOGRAPHY: W. C. Braithwaite, *Beginnings of Quakerism* (2d ed., 1955) 13–15; 501–507.

[T. C. O'BRIEN]

PENITENTIAL CONTROVERSY, a dispute about the nature and practice of sacramental penance in the early Church, one of the most difficult and subtle problems in the history of dogma. The NT frequently portrays Christ as forgiving sins, e.g., in the case of the paralytic (Mk 2.3–12) and of the penitent woman (Lk 7.36–50). He promised this same power first to Peter (Mt 16.15–19) and then to the rest of the Apostles (Mt 18.15–18) under the metaphor of "binding and loosing," and conferred it upon them the evening of his Resurrection with the words: "Whose sins you shall forgive, they are forgiven them" (Jn 20.23). Through the Apostles this same power has been conferred upon their successors (Council of Trent, D 1670).

Clement of Rome (*c*.96), the author of the *Didache* (*c*.100), Ignatius of Antioch (*c*.110), Polycarp (*c*.110), the author of the *Second Epistle of Clement* (*c*.150), and other early Christian writers refer to repentance and/or confession and the forgiveness of sins, but they are vague as to how this reconciliation with God and the Church was effected. Hermas, the author of the *Shepherd* (*c*.100–140), states that it was brought about through the "shepherd," which probably is to be here taken as the "bishop." But he also writes as if there were but one penance for serious sins committed after baptism (*Commandment,* 4.3), an opinion later held by Clement of Alexandria (*Miscellanies,* 2.13) and Tertullian in his still Catholic days (*De paenitentia,* 7). Later, however, as a Montanist, Tertullian roundly condemned a bp. for issuing an edict promising pardon for adultery and fornication after the performance of penance (*De pudicitia,* 1).

During the persecution of Decius (250–251) there were numerous defections and the problem arose as to what should be done with those who wished to be reconciled. Novatian, writing for the clergy of Rome, informed Cyprian that there they were only being readmitted when in danger of death and that in the meantime others were being deferred until a new bp., who would decide what further should be done, could be elected (Cyprian, *Ep.*, 30.8). When the persecution had passed, Cyprian had to complain about those who were "doing violence to the Body and Blood of the Lord," that is, receiving communion "before their crimes are expiated, before their confession is made, before their consciences are cleansed by sacrifice and the hand of the priest [bishop]" (*De lapsis*, 16). After the election of Pope Cornelius (251–253), Novatian left the Church, adopted a more rigorous attitude, and maintained that apostates could never be absolved.

In 314 the Council of Ancyra made provision for the penance and absolution of those who had fallen during the Great Persecution (c. 6), and in 325 the Council of Nicaea offered pardon to the Novatianists through the imposition of hands and the apparent completion of a fixed penance (c. 11; D 127).

From this and other data that could be adduced, a number of different conclusions have been drawn with respect to the practice of penance in the early Church. Many non-Catholics have been of the opinion that the Christians of the first centuries were a community of "saints" who had been cleansed once and for all in the waters of baptism. The Church therefore excluded from its assemblies all those guilty of more serious crimes, esp. the three capital sins of adultery, apostasy, and murder, since it did not have the power to forgive them. With the passage of time and the practical experience of the frailty of human nature, this rigorous attitude was gradually mitigated, first with respect to adultery, then apostasy, and finally murder, which was explicitly provided for by the Council of Ancyra. (c. 23).

A number of Catholic scholars, following the lead of the 17th-cent Petavius, have held that for practical purposes the Church actually did refuse to grant absolution for the three capital sins and that the subsequent relaxation was of a disciplinary rather than doctrinal character. Other Catholic theologians deny even the possibility of such a state of affairs. It may well be, however, that prior to Nicaea individual bishops adopted a policy of refusing absolution to adulterers and other grave sinners; but after Nicaea, such a course of action would have been an error in doctrine rather than in judgment since it would have been an implicit denial of the Church's competence in this regard.

Whatever may have been the advantages of the rigorous penitential attitude of the early Church, it had the serious disadvantage of causing many to put off baptism out of a fear of falling into sin and not being strong enough to perform the penance that would be enjoined. Two of the most famous examples of deferred baptism are St. Augustine, who pleaded for the sacrament as a boy when he was seriously ill but failed to receive it (*Confess. 1.11*), and Constantine, who was baptized only on his deathbed. This difficulty was eventually obviated by the introduction of private and more frequent confession in the 7th cent. largely through the activities of Celtic monks. BIBLIOGRAPHY: P. F. Palmer, *Sacraments and Forgiveness* (1959) 1–71; É. Amann, DTC 12.1:749–845.

[M. J. COSTELLOE]

PENITENTIAL PSALMS, seven psalms that have traditionally accompanied confession of sin in penitential liturgies and seasons. In the Hebrew numbering they are: Psalms 6;32;38;51;102;130;143. Six of these can be classified as Individual Laments, and the remaining one (Ps 32) is actually a Wisdom Psalm giving instruction on how to act when sickness comes. Individual Laments are numerous in the Psalter and are simply cries for deliverance from sickness, affliction, the taunts of enemies, persecution, and death. A penitential theme involving deliverance from sin can sometimes enter the plea. Thus, among the seven traditional penitential psalms, Ps 6 is the cry of a sick man for deliverance; Ps 102 is an appeal to God for help against sickness and the taunts of enemies; Ps 143 is basically a cry for deliverance from deadly persecution. The penitential note comes through in Ps 38 with is frank confession of sin and its absence of rancor toward enemies. Ps 51 (the *Miserere*), however, is the classic penitential prayer of the psalter, the sufferer cries out for deliverance from the agony of soul felt by the sinner conscious of being cut off from God by the sin always before him. His expiation is his broken and contrite heart; his plea is for God to create a pure heart within him, and to give him a new and steadfast spirit. Ps 130 is the prayer of penitential hope of the sinner in deep distress as he waits patiently for relief from the Lord for his burden of unforgiven sin.

[E. J. DILLON]

PENITENTIAL SERVICE, the extra-sacramental gathering of the People of God to hear God's Word proclaimed on the theme of repentance and to respond in true contrition. The practice received impetus from Vatican Council II's emphases on the liturgy of the Word and on the communal aspects of sin and repentance (see PENANCE, NEW RITE OF). Both in parishes and in other more specialized communities penitential services were celebrated with Bible readings, homily, and prayers of sorrow for sin. The Congregation for Divine Worship, taking into account the value of such services and following the pastoral norms laid down (1972) by the Congregation for the Doctrine of Faith, in promulgating the new rite of penance (1973) also approved and encouraged the extra-sacramental penitential service. The general format outlined recommends songs or prayers of greeting and introduction, readings from Scripture as well as from the Fathers or other writers, a homily—all devoted to the theme of sin, repentance, forgiveness; then the community response in litanies or other penitential prayers, the recitation of the Lord's Prayer, dismissal. The penitential service does not include general *absolution. The advantages intended are: the quickening of the penitential spirit of the community; preparation for the sacrament of penance to be received in due time; instruction of children, and the *ascesis* of the catechumenate for adult converts. The celebration is particularly commended as part of the observance of Lent, or where confessors are not readily available. The Congregation notably underlines as a possible effect the forgiveness of sin by reason of the desire for the sacrament of penance included in the genuine contrition aroused through the penitential service. BIBLIOGRAPHY: U.S. Catholic Conference, *Rite of Penance: Study Edition* (1974).

[T. C. O'BRIEN]

PENITENTIALS, manuals of directions for confessors containing prayers, questions to be asked, lists of sins together with appropriate penance to be allotted. They originated from the Celtic Church in Wales and Ireland in the 5th cent. and spread over Europe with the Irish and Anglo-Saxon missions. They were not decreed by episcopal synods, but were the work of monks, and possessed no authority other than the compiler's reputation for wisdom and holiness. They were useful when private confession began to supersede public confession and the canonical penances of the Church. The Anglo-Saxon penitentials are in the tradition received from Iona. St. Columbanus brought the penitential system—if that is not too strong a word—into Frankish Europe. The resulting compilations were criticized by the Carolingian reform for their lack of canonical authority and for discrepancies, also for likely abuses consequent on the substitution of alms for fasting. New penitentials were composed more in accord with Roman discipline. Later penitentials from the 11th cent. onwards offer informed guidance rather than uniform rules and set tariffs. BIBLIOGRAPHY: T. P. Oakley, "Celtic Penance: Its Sources, Affiliation, and Influence," IER 52 (1938) 147–164, 581–601; G. Le Bras, DTC 12.1:1160–79. J. T. McNeill and H. M. Gamer, *Medieval Handbooks of Penance* (1965).

[T. GILBY]

PENITENTIARY, CANON, an official of a chapter of canons at a cathedral, which canon law requires to have a canon theologian and a canon penitentiary (CIC, c. 398). The canon theologian is a kind of official theologian for a diocese, charged with teaching doctrine in the cathedral church or as a seminary professor. The canon penitentiary is charged with moral and canonical teaching and with cases of conscience (the internal forum). By law he has power to absolve from sins and censures reserved to the bishop (c. 401); at stated times he should be present in the cathedral confessional for the benefit of penitents (*ibid*. §2); during his tenure he may not be deputed to any other office to which is attached jurisdiction in the external forum (obviously to avoid a "conflict of interest" with his care of consciences) (c. 399 §3). There are no cathedral chapters of canons in the United States.

PENITENTIARY, MAJOR, the cardinal prefect of the Sacred Penitentiary, one of the tribunals of the Curia Romana (CIC, c. 258).

PENITENTIARY, SACRED APOSTOLIC. The Sacred Apostolic Penitentiary is, in addition to the Rota and the Apostolic Signatura or Seal, one of the three Roman tribunals provided for in the CIC, c. 258. Its specific province is the penitential life of the Church, i.e., the internal forum. The office can be traced back to the early 13th cent. when the duties of the pope's own personal confessor were expanded also to the review of penitential problems referred to the Holy See. As it now exists, the Sacred Penitentiary has two major functions: judgments in the internal forum and the bestowing of faculties to grant indulgences. Functions in the internal forum include the absolution of sins, including those reserved to the papacy and those committed by Catholics of the Oriental rites, dispensations from vows, oaths, and hidden matrimonial impediments, and the convalidation of marriages and religious professions. The Sacred Penitentiary also administers the case of a priest who, having attempted marriage, continues to live with his consort.

The *motu proprio* of Paul VI, *Pastorale munus* (1963), diminished the exclusive importance of the Sacred Penitentiary in the administration of indulgences by extending to all bps. the power to bless devotional articles with the sign of the cross, to bless crucifixes to be used to gain indulgences by those unable to make the Way of the Cross, and to annex indulgences conceded by the papacy.

[R. A. ARONSTAM]

PENMON, CELTIC MONASTERY OF, a monastic establishment in Anglesey, Wales, founded in the 6th cent. and refounded in 1221 (probably for Black Canons). It was at first a dependent hermit settlement of Puffin Island (or Ynys Seiriol), but became eventually the main settlement with a more regular form of monasticism. Both places were dissolved in 1536. BIBLIOGRAPHY: Knowles-Hadcock; A. W. Wade-Evans, *Welsh Christian Origins* (1934); J. E. Lloyd, *History of Wales* (2 v., 1948).

[C. MCGRATH]

PENN, WILLIAM (1644–1718), Quaker, founder of Pennsylvania. Son of Admiral Sir William Penn (1621–70), at the age of 11 he had an experience of communion with God that gave a religious direction to his whole life. His father tried to discourage the interest in Quakerism that began while P. was at Oxford (1660–61) by sending him to France, but in Ireland in 1665, P. definitively embraced Quaker belief. From 1667 onward he was an approved minister and at London engaged in preaching, controversy, and writing. Twice he was imprisoned (1668 and 1670), the first time for his work *The Sandy Foundation Shaken*, against belief in the Trinity and Christ's atonement. By a grant of Charles II, in payment of a debt due to his father, P. became proprietary governor of Pennsylvania (1680); he formulated a constitution for the new colony, his "holy experiment," and called it the Frame of Government. This incorporated the most enlightened liberal ideas, including religious and political equality even for Catholics. P. resided in Pa. from 1682 to 1684 and again from 1699 to 1701, when he secured final approval of the revised Frame of Government. His life became difficult as political and financial crises multiplied for his colony. He died in England, having suffered a paralyzing stroke in 1712. He wrote many treatises during his Quaker life; *No Cross No Crown* (1669) is a treasured Quaker classic, and his *Fruits of Solitude* (1692) is an esteemed collection of religious reflections. His works were collected and edited after his death by J. Besse (1726). BIBLIOGRAPHY: E. B. Bronner, *William Penn's Holy Experiment* (1962); W. W. Comfort, *William Penn 1644–1718, a Tercentenary Estimate* (1944); *Witness of William Penn* (eds. F. B. Tolles and E. G. Alderfer, 1957) with selections from P.'s writings; H. E. Wildes, *William Penn: A Biography* (1974); H. Fantel, *William Penn: Apostle of Dissent* (1974).

[T. C. O'BRIEN]

PENNI, GIOVAN FRANCESCO (''Il Fattore''; 1488?–1528), Italian painter, with Giulio Romano, Raphael's closest pupil and inheritor of Raphael's drawings. P. finished many of Raphael's paintings both before and after the master's death (*Madonna dell' Impannata; Visitation*). P. is distinguished from Raphael by ''fatty'' hands and faces, and overblown drapery.

[M. J. DALY]

PENNINGS, BERNARD HENRY (1861–1955), abbot, missionary. A Dutch Premonstratensian, ordained in 1866, P. volunteered for the Wisconsin missions to work among Belgian immigrants. In 1898 P. became superior of the first house of his order in North America at DePere, Wis., and in 1925 first abbot. During his tenure the monastery established five secondary schools and St. Norbert's College, operated television and radio stations, and served in parishes of eight dioceses.

[J. R. AHERNE]

PENNSYLVANIA, a Middle Atlantic state, second of the original thirteen states admitted to the Union. It was founded by William Penn, a Quaker, in 1681. Although he began the colony as a ''holy experiment'' in political and religious pluralism, his ideal was not fully achieved. After the Revolutionary War, the Quaker ranks diminished rapidly, while a tide of German immigration produced a sharp increase in other denominations, esp. the Lutheran.

Afforded considerable liberty by colonial Pennsylvania, some 6,000 Catholics had settled there by 1765. In 1808, Philadelphia became one of four suffragan sees in the U.S., with Michael *Egan as its first bishop. By 1875 it had attained archdiocesan status as the metropolitan see for Pennsylvania. Its suffragan sees, now seven in number, are the Dioceses of Pittsburgh (established 1843), Erie (1853), Harrisburg (1869), Scranton (1869), Altoona–Johnstown (1901), Greensburg (1951), and Allentown (1961).

Prior to the Civil War, the Catholic Church had to deal with nativist opposition, which provoked riots in Philadel-

phia in 1844, and with lay trusteeism, which led to a schism condemned by Pius VII in 1822. Heavy immigration between 1830 and World War I caused an enormous increase in church membership, creating a need for schools, churches, and other facilities that were constructed under Bp. Francis P. *Kenrick and his successor, St. John *Neumann. Building programs remained a primary concern during the subsequent episcopates of Patrick J. *Ryan, Edmond F. *Prendergast, Dennis *Dougherty, John F. *O'Hara, and John J. Krol, the present cardinal-archbishop.

Pennsylvania's population of 11,908,156 over 70% urban, makes it the third most populous state in the Union. In 1976 Catholics numbered 3,722,247 or 31.2% of the total state population. This represents more than a 5% increase since 1952, a year when Protestant sects made up 28.2% of the population. The United Lutheran Church in America, with 6.8% of the state's population, and the Methodist Church, with 6.2%, were the largest denominations. The Jewish population (1968) was 443,595 or 3.7% of the total.

Since the founding of St. Mary's parochial school in Philadelphia (1782), Catholic education has grown phenomenally in Pennsylvania, most notably in the Philadelphia archdiocese during the last half century. Of the 97,393 students enrolled in the state's Catholic secondary schools, 55.4% attend one of the 50 archdiocesan high schools. Similarly, the 139,087 students enrolled in the archdiocese's 299 elementary schools acount for almost half (47.7%) of the state's 815 Catholic elementary school pupils. Catholic institutions also account for one-fifth of the college enrollment in the state. There are 25 Catholic colleges among the Commonwealth's 130 institutions of higher learning, which also include 16 Commonwealth campuses and 25 other church-related colleges. BIBLIOGRAPHY: W. F. Dunaway, *History of Pennsylvania* (2d ed., 1948); S. K. Stevens, *Pennsylvania, Birthplace of a Nation* (1964); J. T. Ellis, *Catholicism in Colonial America* (1964); *History of the Archdiocese of Philadelphia* (ed. J. F. Connelly, 1976); *Records ACHS,* Index 1–31, 355–356.

[J. L. MORRISON; R. M. PRESTON]

PENOLOGY, the study of *punishment for crimes: the sentencing process; the meaning, kinds, and purpose of punishment; the conditions of prisons; the custody of prisoners. The study belongs properly to jurisprudence and sociology; moral theology offers only extrinsic, ethical norms pertaining to moral *justice. In its proper and direct meaning punishment is retributive or vindicative. An act that deviates from what is required by justice creates a *debt to undergo punishment; because such an act violates subjection to the exigencies of the order belonging to justice, it is against other persons—whether individuals or moral persons—and so is deserving of retribution. The one who has unduly indulged in wilfulness must suffer a consequence that goes against his will; that is punishment (ThAq ST 1a,48.5; 1a2ae,21.3 & 4). The public authorities imposing or carrying out a punitive sentence are exercising an act of *legal justice, a concern for the public good. That concern includes respect for the persons who make up the public, including even the criminal, who is to be punished justly, not vengefully or cruelly. The quality of punishment must, then, be in accord with community standards of humaneness (*ibid.* 2a2ae,108.3). Concern for the public good gives punishment also a preventive or rehabilitative meaning; it becomes medicinal or remedial. It has a preventive function in society as a deterrent from imitating the crime punished. It may also be rehabilitative, where the interests of the public good are served by returning the criminal to society as a good citizen. That relationship to legal justice is the moral justification of the penologist's concern for the quality of life in prison. Rehabilitative considerations, however, do not negate the intrinsic relationship between the commission of a crime and the objective liability to undergo punishment. BIBLIOGRAPHY: ST ThAq (Lat-Eng, v. 27, ed, T. C. O'Brien) app. 1.

[T. C. O'BRIEN]

PENQÎTO (Syriac; Arab., *fanqît*), West Syrian liturgical book. In modern use it refers to the volumes containing the propers of the Divine Office for Sundays and feasts, or at least the choral parts of those propers; formerly the name was given to a codex containing liturgical texts to be said by a priest on various occasions.

[A. CODY]

PENTAGRAM (pentangle, pentacle), five-pointed star with varying symbolic usages: in Christian art, a symbol of Christ's five wounds; a sign of the cross for Greek Christians; among Jews, a lucky-mark by association with the legendary key of Solomon and linked to the shield of David. Other connotations include eternity, perfection, wealth. In occultism it has been used as a generator (as opposed to an intermediary) in spells and invocations, or as a charm or hex against devils and witches. In the Tarot it signifies money and possessions.

[R. J. LITZ]

PENTAPOLIS, an alliance of five cities; any five-city league or confederation. This Greek word—from *pente,* (five) and *polis* (city)—is similar in usage to that of *decapolis* for a 10-city confederation. Thus, in Gen 14, the cities of the plain which banded together in a common struggle are a pentapolis: Sodom, Gomorrah, Adamah, Zeboim, and Bela. The Philistine league of cities was also a pentapolis: Gaza, Ashdod, Ashkelon, Gath, and Ekron.

[E. J. DILLON]

PENTARCHY (Gr., rule by five), a theory of ecclesiastical organization which holds that the Church is governed by the five major patriarchates. To the three ancient sees of Rome, Alexandria, and Antioch, whose authority was recognized by the Council of Nicaea (325), there was soon added Constantinople as an important ecclesiastical center when Constantine the Great transferred the seat of government to that city and, under the designation of New Rome, made it equal to Old Rome. This is reflected in c. 3 of the Council of Constantinople (381), stating that "the bishop of Constantinople shall have the primacy of honor after the bishop of Rome, because it is New Rome." The Council of Chalcedon (451) established Jerusalem as an independent ecclesiastical center and patriarchate. While references to a pentarchy are found as early as Justinian (527–565), later centuries considered these five patriarchates as established by God (e.g., Theodore of Studius in explaining Mt. 16.18), like the five senses of the mystical body of Christ (Peter of Antioch, 11th cent.). The Council of Constantinople in 869 established their preeminence and called them the five "heads," "master builders," "great lights" of the Church. The entire earth was conceived as divided among them, excepting the independent archiepiscopate of Cyprus (431). They rank in this order: Rome, Constantinople, Alexandria, Antioch, Jerusalem. While the Roman pontiff was recognized as enjoying a special preeminence, a juridical primacy and doctrinal infallibility were always rejected by the Eastern Orthodox patriarchates. The idea of the pentarchy was opposed to the claim of the Roman pontiffs for supremacy over the entire Church, esp. in the schism of Caerularius (1054). The emergence of other patriarchates (Bulgarian 1235, Serbian 1346), the final liquidation of the Byzantine Empire by the Turks (1453), and the appearance of Moscow as the Third Rome (patriarchate 1589) made the idea of a pentarchy obsolete.

[V. J. POSPISHIL]

PENTATEUCH, the name (from the Gr. meaning "five-roll") is given to the first five books of the OT. Collections of laws form the greater part of the last four books, whence the Jewish title of "Torah" or "Law" (cf. 2 Chr 23.18; Neh 8.1–2). But these are worked into a narrative framework relating the story of Israel's exodus from Egypt, convenant of Sinai and the wandering through the wilderness to the land of Canaan. The arrangement reflects Israel's conviction that all Law, whenever formulated, is an emergent of God's saving activity at the beginning of Israel's history. Because of Moses' predominant role in that history, the Pentateuch is called the "Law of Moses." The first book, Genesis, relating the religious history of mankind from Creation to Abraham (1–11) and the story of the patriarchs (12–50), introduces the history of Israel. The Pentateuch is a composite work, consisting of four principal traditions, Yahwist, Elohist, Priestly, and Deuteronomist. The literary formation took place over a long period between the 10th and the 5th cent. B.C. BIBLIOGRAPHY: M. Noth, *History of Pentateuch Traditions* (tr. B. W. Anderson, 1972).

[E. H. MALY]

PENTECOST, second of the three main Hebrew festivals (Ex 23.14–17; Lev 23; Num 28.26–31; Dt 16); it was also known as the Day of First Fruits, Feast of Weeks (Shabuoth), and Feast of Harvest. The Greek name Pentecost, meaning 50th, derives from its celebration on the 50th day following the Feast of *Unleavened Bread. Originally a festival (perhaps derived from the Canaanites) marking the end of the grain harvest, it became in later Judaism a commemoration of the giving of the Law at Sinai. Following the presentation of the sheaf to end the season of unleavened bread, the new grain could be used as food; after Pentecost, it could be used for ritual offerings. This feast took on much greater importance in the NT, because, from Acts ch. 2, the outpouring of the Spirit gave birth to the Church and the manifestation of the Christian community living and proclaiming the Gospel. *WEEKS, FEAST OF.

[T. EARLY]

PENTECOST, HEBREW FEAST OF, see WEEKS, FEAST OF.

PENTECOST CYCLE (from the Gr. *pentēkostē,* meaning 50th, day being understood), a festival period of the ecclesiastical year which was allotted to the celebration of Pentecost with its vigil and its octave. It was not liturgically distinct from, but was rather the conclusion of, the Easter cycle. The Sundays after Pentecost, numbered according to their succession from that feast, did not pertain in any proper sense to the Pentecost cycle, for they had no intrinsic relationship to Pentecost or to one another. Presently the weeks and Sundays after Pentecost are called weeks and Sundays in ordinary time. Pentecost (or Whitsunday) is the celebration of the Holy Spirit's gift of the new law and of his formation of the new people. It is celebrated 50 days after Easter. The Jewish pentecost, also celebrated 50 days after the Passover, marked the completion of the wheat harvest and commemorated the reception of the Law by Moses. First evidence of the Christian feast comes from the mid-2d cent., and from the 4th cent. there are indications of the beginnings of a Pentecost cycle. The Ascension broke from its original unity with Pentecost and became the feast of the 40th day after Easter. At the same time Pentecost became, in the West, a feast of the Holy Spirit. Its vigil had been celebrated from the 4th cent., and on that occasion baptism was administered to those prepared for it who had not been baptized at the Easter vigil. Although there is some indication of an octave of Pentecost in the 4th cent., it was only in the 7th that the octave was unified under one theme, i.e., that of recalling the first Pentecost and celebrating the Spirit's continuing work among Christians. The Ember Days of Pentecost, which originally had no connection with the feast, were given a pentecostal theme at this time. The observance of Trinity Sunday on the octave day of Pentecost began in N Europe in the Middle Ages, and after some resistance was finally extended to the universal Church by John XXII in 1334. Before this the octave day simply continued the theme of Pentecost, or was observed as the feast of *All Saints. BIBLIOGRAPHY: R. Cabie, *La Pentecôte: l'évolution de la cinquantaine paschale au cours des cinq premières siècles* (1965); N. M. Dénis-Boulet, *Christian Calendar* (tr. P. J. Hepburne-Scott, 1960); T. Maertens,

Feast in Honor of Yahweh (1965); A. A. McArthur, *Christian Year and Lectionary Reform* (1958).

[N. KOLLAR]

PENTECOSTAL WORLD CONFERENCE, a triennial worldwide meeting of Pentecostals. There is an advisory committee to prepare for these conferences, but the conference itself does not have a formal membership or constitution. The distrust of Pentecostals toward ecclesiastical organization was partially overcome in the 1920s and 1930s by a desire for some external expression of unity, and several international meetings of fellowship were held. The most significant was a conference on unity in Stockholm (1939). After World War II efforts were renewed, and the first Pentecostal World Conference was held in Zurich in 1947. The basis for a more effective association of Pentecostals, however, was achieved at the Paris world conference of 1949. Decisions included a triennial meeting and a secretary with advisory committee to serve between conferences; the principle of autonomy of the local churches and Pentecostal bodies was affirmed; fellowship and cooperation of Pentecostals were set as the objectives of the conferences. Subsequent meetings have been held in London (1952), Stockholm (1955), Toronto (1958), Jerusalem (1961), Helsinki (1964), Rio de Janeiro (1967), Dallas (1970), Seoul (1973), and Jerusalem (1976). The meetings have been assemblies for worship and preaching rather than for practical decision making.

PENTECOSTALISM, that form of Christianity teaching the "Pentecostal experience," namely, that *baptism with the Holy Spirit is accompanied and manifested by *glossolalia (tongues speaking) and *divine healing and that the charismatic gifts of the early Church, a continuing Pentecost, should be ordinary occurrences in Christian life (Nichol, xi). Many of the typical elements in Pentecostalism were taught by the 19th-cent. *Catholic Apostolic Church. The actual Pentecostal movement, however, began in the U.S. in the early 1900s, as an outgrowth of the *Holiness movement. Prominent at the origins of 20th-cent. Pentecostalism were the Apostolic Faith movement (1901) of C. P. *Parham in Kans., Mo., and Tex., and the *Azusa Street Revival (1906). Some groups in the East originated as break-offs, over tongues speaking, from the Christian and Missionary Alliance. The intense spirit of evangelism, in the form of *faith mission, spread the movement. There has been traditionally little formal organization in the Pentecostal bodies, and this has often led to internal disputes and divisions. In recent years, however, larger Pentecostal bodies have adopted some set form of church government. The early deliberate downgrading of education has also changed among the larger Pentecostal groups. There are Pentecostal Churches, or, as they are often called, "Assemblies," in all of the states of the U.S. (see major bodies under proper names). Many smaller units of less than a few hundred members exist throughout the country. Certain more extravagant *cults in the South, e.g., *snake-handlers, use the Pentecostal name but are disowned by official Pentecostal bodies. The *Neo-Pentecostalism of recent years refers to the search for the Pentecostal experience by small groups within other Christian Churches; it has no formal connection with Pentecostalism.

Membership. The total number of Pentecostals throughout the world is estimated at more than 20 million. The movement was spread from the U.S. to Europe, by way of Scandinavia, by T. B. Barratt; to S.A. (Brazil and Chile) by W. C. Hoover, L. Francescon, and G. Vingren; and to Asia and Africa by missionaries of the particular Pentecostal bodies. Pentecostalism is widely referred to as a ''Third Force'' in Christianity alongside the historic Protestant and Catholic Churches. The title has its principal significance because of the missionary impact of the distinctive Pentecostal message; there are Pentecostal missionaries laboring on all continents. The 20th-cent. expansion of Pentecostalism in S.A. is one of the most remarkable phenomena in modern Christianity. The highest concentrations of Pentecostals are in Brazil (more than 3 million) and Chile (more than 700,000); there are also large, well-established bodies in Argentina and Colombia. In Africa Pentecostalism in some form is found in all of the sub-Saharan countries, but esp. in S Africa; adherents in Africa number far more than 1 million (see AFRICAN INDEPENDENT CHURCH MOVEMENT). To a great extent Pentecostal missionary efforts have been aimed not at winning converts from paganism but at bringing over active or nominal members from other Christian Churches. This is considered to be not proselytizing but leading Christians to the acceptance of baptism with the Holy Spirit, without which they cannot be saved. In its missionary endeavor Pentecostalism has to a certain extent achieved what remains a desideratum for other Churches, namely, that members become true apostles to their brethren in the world at large.

Doctrine. Pentecostals agree in their distinctive doctrines, the Pentecostal experience and divine healing and in their *fundamentalism; in other matters there is wide diversity. At times some Pentecostals are accused of diminishing belief in the Trinity (see PENTECOSTAL ASSEMBLIES OF THE WORLD), and of misunderstanding the doctrine of justification by faith. In keeping with their Holiness origins they are *Arminian. Pentecostal *dispensationalism means that these last days are a period for the preaching of charismatic gifts to a morally depraved generation. Baptism and the Lord's Supper are recognized as *ordinances; but the first (water baptism) is seen only as a pledge of regeneration already obtained (see BELIEVER'S BAPTISM), and the second, as a purely symbolic rite. Many Pentecostal groups reject *infant baptism (while practicing at times the dedication of children to the Lord); some observe *footwashing. Pentecostals forbid smoking, drinking, dancing, gambling, and frivolous entertainment. This type of puritanism has been effectively applied against the abuse of alcohol—a widespread vice in more than one nominally Catholic nation—

and to cure drug addicts, and has become one of the secrets of their missionary penetration. Ecclesiologically Pentecostals are heirs to the concept of *Pietism, *ecclesiola in ecclesia;* the Church is not an instrument of sanctification but rather a holy club in which the members help one another and thereby sanctify the community itself. They have admirably developed the sense of *koinōnia,* mutual brotherhood and friendship. Congregationalism, emphasis on the autonomy of the *local church, has been a traditional ideal for church polity. In practice, with the increase of organization, the governing of many denominations has become more centralized through the adoption of elements from Presbyterian or Methodist polity. Pentecostal authorities often have the power to act in a stern way to enforce church discipline.

Practice. Pentecostals shun elaborate liturgies in order to adhere to the simplicity of the primitive Church. Their religious services are spontaneous, at times even disorderly; the central element is the sermon, long and often delivered in a stylized monotone; it may turn into a dialogue between the preacher and members of the congregation. The topics are biblical, and the emphasis is not on punishment but on the love of God for mankind, provided men follow the right path willed by the lord. Preaching is enthusiastic and geared to create in the listeners a fervent desire for the charismatic gifts of the Spirit. The service may also include testimonies of those who have been healed or have become beneficiaries of divine favors. There are religious services intended almost exclusively to provoke among specially prepared listeners the reception of baptism with the Holy Spirit. In certain European and middle-class American Pentecostal communities, the worship services are losing some of their primitive and spontaneous flavor and becoming more set and sober.

Pentecostals have had little interest in the ecumenical movement; many Pentecostal groups live in utter isolationism. Those that are more open have joined such organizations as the *National Association of Evangelicals, which openly opposes the World Council of Churches. Pentecostalism is trying to achieve greater internal unity, and from 1948 the *Pentecostal World Conference has held conventions on different continents. The admission of two Chilean Pentecostal bodies to the World Council of Churches in 1961 did not end the theological opposition of most Pentecostals to full cooperation with other Christian Churches. Many, however, are establishing useful contacts with other Christian bodies and are tending to establish closer friendship with other followers of Christ. BIBLIOGRA- PHY: N. Bloch-Hoell, *Pentecostal Movement* (1962); P. Damboriena, *Tongues As of Fire* (1969); J. T. Nichol, *Pentecostalism* (1966).

[P. DAMBORIENA]

PENTECOSTALISM AMONG CATHOLICS, see NEO -PENTECOSTALISM IN THE ROMAN CATHOLIC CHURCH.

PENTECOSTARION (Gr., regarding Pentecost; in Slavic, *tzvyetnaya triod*, i.e., flowery triodion), the Byzantine liturgical book that contains the proper Offices for the period from Easter Sunday to the first Sunday after Pentecost (Sunday of all Saints) inclusively. The contents seem to be mainly the work of the Studite monks, Theodore and Joseph, or perhaps of their disciples. The term also designates the period itself from Easter to the first Sunday after Pentecost.

[R. K. GOLINI]

PEOPLE OF GOD, an image or metaphor to describe the Church. The phrase was given new prominence by its central use in the *Constitution on the Church* of Vatican Council II. The document refers to the OT passage Jer 31.31–34, and esp. to 1 Pet. 2.9–10, "You who in times past were not a people, but are now the people of God." The description of the Church as the people of God epitomizes the view of the Church common to many Christians. The Church is the People of God because it is a community through which God reveals himself as savior. For this purpose he chooses, calls, and gathers his people by his grace (see ECCLESIA). The reference that the phrase has to the OT implies the continuity of the divine plan of salvation beginning with the chosen people, the Jews, then taking a new form through Christ. The image also suggests the biblical themes of God's constituting a community of salvation, not saving men simply as individuals; thus it is connected with the Pauline image of the Church as the body of Christ. People of God does not mean only the laity, but all the members of the Church, through baptism sharing in the priesthood of Christ. The whole People of God as called and gathered are one, holy people; thus the image serves to bring out holiness and unity, essential attributes of the Church as unified and sanctified by Christ. BIBLIOGRAPHY: Vorgrimler 1:153–168; Kittel TD 4:29–57; Y. Congar, *Concilium* I (1965) 7–19.

[T. C. O'BRIEN]

PEP PILLS, also known as "speed," belong to the amphetamines, which stimulate the nervous system. They are used medically for the relief of mild depressions, for neurological illnesses, and as appetite regulators for those dieting. Used occasionally, they produce euphoria, exhilaration, and increased capacity for thought, but they are dangerous when taken in excess. The intoxication signs include severe insomnia and agitation, irrational and aggressive behavior that may lead to violence, hallucinations, and even psychosis. Some deaths have also been reported from overdose. Pep-pill addicts are accident prone both because of the stimulation to their bodies and because of the excessive fatigue that may break through at the wrong time. Only under medical supervision does their use seem morally justifiable. BIBLIOGRAPHY: J. Cashman, *LSD Story* (1966) ch. 9; R. S. DeRopp, *Drugs and the Mind* (1961).

[P. SMITH]

PEPIN III (d. 768), **KING OF THE FRANKS** from 751. Son of Charles Martel, he and his brother succeeded as mayors of the palace (741) until Carloman retired (747). Deposing, with papal consent, the last Mervingian king and securing election (751) of himself to the kingship, he was anointed in 752 by St. Boniface and in 754 by Stephen II. His donation to the pope of lands conquered from the Lombards laid the foundation for the Papal States. His achievements prepared the way for his illustrious son Charlemagne. BIBLIOGRAPHY: Hauck 1:479–552; 2:3–70.

[A. CABANISS]

PEPUZIANS, an alternative designation for the *Montanists. The name is derived from Pepuza, a no longer identifiable site in Phrygia, which was the center of Montanism, and where it was believed that Christ would soon come in the parousia to inaugurate his millennial rule.

[M. J. COSTELLOE]

PER SALTUM (Lat., by a leap), without intermediate stages; as in *per saltum* evolution, with reference to the biological phenomenon of mutation by which new life forms come into existence. The latter phenomenon is a storm center of controversy both within the natural sciences and in the philosophy and theology of creation. The term is applied when something is attained at a single bound or without intermediate stages, e.g., a high office in the Church.

[E. J. DILLON]

PERCEVAL, see PARZIVAL.

PERCY, JOHN (al. John Fisher or Fairfax; 1569–1641), English Jesuit controversialist. P. converted to Catholicism in 1583, became a Jesuit *c.* 1593, and after his ordination in Rome returned to England (1595) where he was immediately imprisoned. Escaping after 7 months, he labored in Yorkshire (1596–98) and later elsewhere in England. He was instrumental in the conversion of W. *Chillingworth. P. was arrested in 1610 and condemned to death; but after a year in prison his sentence was commuted, through the influence of the Spanish ambassador, to banishment from England. For a time he was professor of Scripture at St. John's, Louvain, but returned to England and was again imprisoned, this time for 3 years. During this period he engaged in a controversy with W. *Laud, then bp. of St. Davids. He received a free pardon through the French ambassador in 1625, but was apprehended again in 1634 and kept in prison until 1635, when he was released through the intercession of the Queen.

[J. P. WHALEN]

PERCY, THOMAS, BL. (1528–82), seventh earl of Northumberland. Son of Sir Thomas Percy who was executed as a leader of the Pilgrimage of Grace, he was allowed by Queen Mary to succeed to the earldom, and was made high marshal of the army in the north. With the accession of Elizabeth, his staunch Catholicism made him suspect, but he avoided trouble until the flight of Mary Queen of Scots (1568). A natural leader in a then still-Catholic section, he espoused the cause of her liberation and joined the northern rebellion (1569). Defeated by royal forces, T. fled to Scotland, was captured, and given over to Elizabeth (1572). He refused freedom at the price of his faith and was executed. BIBLIOGRAPHY: N. Del Re, BiblSanct 10:485–487; Butler 3:407–409; Gillow BDEC 5:265–267.

[V. SAMPSON]

PERDITION, originally in the OT, merely death, descent into Sheol or Abaddon, a place of darkness, dust, and weakness, in which all activity, pleasure, participation in and knowledge of what goes on on earth cease, and also all praise of God (Job 17.13–16; Is 14.9–11; Ps 6.6); but there is no differentiation of the just and the wicked. Differentiation begins to appear in Ezek 32.17–32 (esp. 27), Is 24.22, and Sir 21.10. This concept merged with the Post-Exilic concept of Gehenna, an eschatological place of eternal punishment for the wicked. Gehenna was first a valley below Jerusalem where the wrath of God would punish the sins of Juda (Jer 32.26; 7.30–8.3; 19.6). In Is 66.22–24 (which omits the name Gehenna, but alludes to Jer 7.30–33), Gehenna becomes a place of eschatological ruin, outside the walls of Jerusalem. In the NT the concepts of Sheol, Abaddon, and Gehenna are combined in a concept of everlasting ruin in fire, darkness, and gnawing worms, where there is weeping and gnashing of teeth (Mt 3.12; Mk 9.43; Mt 8.12).

[W. G. MOST]

PEREA, the land beyond the Jordan; Transjordania; the E side of the Jordan. The NT does not refer to it by a name, but uses the phrase "beyond the Jordan." Rabbinical literature refers to "the land beyond Jordan." The Greek preposition *peran* (beyond) must be the origin of the word Josephus uses to describe this region: *Peraia* (Perea). It extends from the banks of the Yarmuk in the N to those of the Arnon in the S; from the steep banks of the Jordan in the W to the desert in the E. Within these natural boundaries, roughly corresponding to modern Jordan, lies a land checkered with mighty watercourses, picturesque ravines, oak forests, pasturelands, grape vineyards, olive orchards, and perennial springs. It corresponds to the land that, under Joshua, was allotted to Reuben and Gad and included Gilead. It is doubtful that the Israelites in these lands were ever assimilated to Canaanite ways as their brothers W of Jordan were. From E of Jordan came such an arch-conservative as the Thesbite, the Gileadite, Elijah—the great foe of syncretism. The Assyrian conquest resulted in repopulation of these lands with gentiles, and so they remained for centuries. Even in the time of the Maccabees the Jews living beyond Jordan were

considered to be living in diaspora, among a gentile majority. Through the efforts of Hyrcanus and Alexander Jannaeus this region was gradually Judaized, so that the Mishna could include it along with Judea and Galilee as part of Israel. So it was at the time of Jesus. By going through Perea, Jews from Galilee could go up in pilgrimage to Jerusalem without passing through gentile territory (Samaria) W of the Jordan.

[E. J. DILLON]

PEREGRINATIO AETHERIAE, a pilgrim diary kept by an early 5th-cent. noblewoman named Aetheria, of Latin culture, perhaps from Gaul or Spain. An 11th-cent. MS of the text was discovered at Arezzo in 1884 and first published in 1887. The text is incomplete and somewhat mutilated. The first half deals with her journey to Sinai, Transjordan, Mesopotamia, Asia Minor, and finally Jerusalem. The second half is a detailed description of the liturgy in Jerusalem, and is of major importance for historical studies in liturgy. The liturgy she describes must be the original model of the West Syrian, Armenian, and Byzantine rites. The major feasts were Epiphany and Easter, each with its octave. The Ascension and Pentecost were linked, and Lent had a special liturgy ending with the "Greater Week." She describes various churches associated with events and sites in the Gospels. She is the first to witness to the existence of a developed daily Office of liturgical prayer. Although no exact date is available, her journey must have taken place *c.*400.

[E. J. DILLON]

PEREGRINI, a medieval liturgical play performed at Vespers on one of the days of the Easter octave; its title refers to the travelers whom the risen Christ encountered on the road to Emmaus. Easter Vespers was an unusually elaborate ceremony in the high Middle Ages, involving a procession through the church, at some point of which this play was staged. The most spectacular feature was the travelers' recognition of the Lord as he broke bread with them at the inn, after he had reproved them for their lack of faith.

[E. C. DUNN]

PEREGRINUS (CANON LAW), a person traveling in a territory other than that where he is resident, i.e., has *domicile (CIC c. 91). The classification comes into question with regard to the binding force of church laws proper to a particular place. One traveling outside the place of his residence is not obliged to laws proper to that place unless they be personal, not territorial laws, or unless his nonobservance would be detrimental to the interests of the place of his residence (*ibid.* c. 14 §1). Nor is the peregrinus obliged to observe laws proper to the place where he is visiting, except where *public order is clearly at issue, or some formal, legal act that must be recordable (*ibid.* §2).

[T. C. O'BRIEN]

PEREGRINUS PROTEUS, (2d-cent. A.D.), wandering philosopher. In *The Passing of Peregrinus* Lucian portrays P.'s public self-immolation at the Olympic games of 165 as a signal example of his thirst for notoriety; but P. himself seems to have conceived it as an imitation of Heracles and a fitting capstone for his career. For a time he held a position of importance in a Christian community and, once expelled from it for failing to observe dietary regulations, he became a popular Cynic teacher. Lucian thought him a charlatan who duped Christians and pagans alike and charges that he left home only to avoid retribution for the murder of his father. BIBLIOGRAPHY: M. Caster, *Lucien et la pensée religieuse de son temps* (1937).

[E. V. GALLAGHER]

PEREIRA Y CASTELLÓN, SIMEÓN (1863–1922), Nicaraguan bishop. Member of a prestigious family, he entered the Jesuits and was ordained in 1894. In 1896 he was consecrated auxiliary bp. of León with the right of succession. Known as the ''martyr bishop'' because of the political harassment he endured, he suffered both imprisonment and exile for his forceful objections to the anti-Catholic climate of the day. But he eventually returned to Nicaragua in triumph.

[M. A. MCFADDEN]

PERELLA, GAETANO MARIA (1890–1946), Italian exegete, priest (from 1917) of the Congregation of the Missions. P. served as professor at Collegio Alberoni in Piacenza (1920–41) until he became superior of St. Sylvester's in Rome. His researches centered on three themes: biblical theology, the doctrine of inspiration, and the Holy Places. BIBLIOGRAPHY: J. J. Twomey, LTK 8:271.

[M. J. SUELZER]

PEREYRA, BENITO (*c.*1535–1610), Jesuit biblical commentator. P. taught at Rome, and wrote treatises on philosophy, theology, and biblical exegesis for which he is best known. His writings demonstrate great erudition, but often lack balanced judgment.

[T. M. MCFADDEN]

PEREYRA, CARLOS (1871–1942), Mexican journalist and historian. Although in his earlier life he was actively engaged in politics and held diplomatic positions under P. Díaz and V. Huerta, his most important work was done in the fields of literature and history. His eight-volume *Historia de la America Española* is a thorough, well-documented, highly readable account of Spanish American history. He had a high regard for Spain's contribution to South America, and in his earlier writings was often inspired by a deep distrust of the expansionist policies of the U. S. BIBLIOGRAPHY: M. Quirarte, *Carlos Pereyra: caballero andante de la historia* (1942).

[P. DAMBORIENA]

PÉREZ, ESTEBAN (1854–1934), Spanish-born Discalced Franciscan missionary who served in Peru. An eloquent preacher, P. traveled about giving missions in Peru, Chile, Bolivia, Ecuador, and even California. He and his fellow missionaries were active at a time when the political climate in South America was quite sectarian and antireligious propaganda was persuasive.

[M. A. MCFADDEN]

PÉREZ, JUAN (d. *c.*1515), Franciscan, patron of Columbus. Of noble Spanish family, he was an accountant in Queen Isabella's service, then became a Franciscan and, for a time, the queen's confessor. While guardian of La Rábida friary in Andalusia (1491), he became Columbus' friend and court advocate, helped prepare the voyage, signed Columbus' contract, and confessed and blessed the crew. P. accompanied the second voyage, celebrating the first Mass in the new world (Haiti, 1493), and remained as guardian at Santo Domingo. P. has been confused with Antonio de Marchena, guardian at La Rábida in 1485, who likewise sheltered and encouraged Columbus.

[R. I. BURNS]

PÉREZ DE RIVAS, ANDRÉS (1575–1655), Spanish-born Jesuit missionary and historian. He entered the Jesuits in 1602 and while still a novice was sent to complete his novitate in Pueblo, Mexico. He became fluent in several Indian languages and later helped to establish several mission stations in the areas of Sinaloa and Sonora, Mexico. Poor health ended his missionary activities, and he spent the remainder of his life as an administrator and historian for the order.

[M. A. MCFADDEN]

PERFECTI (the perfect, the pure), those who strictly observed the teaching of the *Cathari and who were their preachers. They were Cathari (Gr. *katharoi,* the pure) par excellence, as distinguished from the ordinary believers or hearers. Initiation into the circle of *perfecti* was through the ceremony called *consolamentum.* Their austere asceticism in contrast to the luxury of many ecclesiastics was one cause of the spread of such Cathari groups as the *Albigenses. A distinction between *perfecti* and believers was also used among the medieval *Waldenses.

[T. C. O'BRIEN]

PERFECTIBILISTS (Ger. *Perfektibilisten*), the original name of the Illuminati founded by Johann Weishaupt (1748–1830) in 18th-cent. Bavaria. The name alludes to the belief that by a process of initiation the members were to progress to perfection. *ILLUMINATI, ORDER OF.

[T. C. O'BRIEN]

PERFECTION, CHRISTIAN. The Lat. *perficere* and the NT Gr. *teleioō* (bring to completion) have to be held in the notion of the perfection here considered; it is that of an "end in" rather than of an "end to" a living process, otherwise it loses its leap and becomes rather statuesque, or indeed, as in too many books about the spiritual life, somewhat flat and dull in a mannered sort of way. The objective end for human beings is God, the subjective end is their sharing in his life. This they do not only as effects participating in his creative casualty, but also as persons open to him in their knowing and loving. "Not servants, but friends" (Jn 15.15), they are called to dwell in the society of the three blessed Persons, now in faith, hereafter in vision, but always in friendship. This is called charity (*caritas, agapē*): "he who abides in charity abides in God" (1 Jn 4.16). Hence the solid agreement of theologians that Christian perfection consists in charity, which is the "bond of perfection" (Col 3.14).

Now this is a matter of command, not exactly as this might be juridically understood, but according to the gospel imperative of loving God with our whole heart and our neighbor as ourself: "on these two commandments hang all the law and the prophets" (Mt 22.40). Hence, too, the solid agreement of theologians in identifying Christian perfection with keeping these two precepts. The moral virtues and the evangelical counsels are instruments to this end, which lies beyond them. Though vowed poverty, chastity, and obedience may constitute what is called "a state of perfection," the term "state" in this context expresses a canonical or Roman Law concept, and does not mean being or becoming perfect in the theological sense. The distinction, which is most important, has been sometimes overlooked, with the result that members of religious orders have been regarded, and what is worse, have sometimes regarded themselves, as constituting an elite.

So then, first, Christian perfection is a present condition, not just one in the future to which we may aspire, for "Lo! the kingdom of God is within you" (Lk 17.21); and second, the call to it is addressed to all, not reserved to the few and those charismatically endowed: "Be ye perfect, as also your heavenly father is perfect" (Mt 5.48). Clearly it has to be treated as an analogical term, i.e., one admitting different degrees of meaning, if we are to respect its Christian usage, which has rejected Gnostic and Manichaean readings of it as an achieved condition of sinlessness and invulnerability. The degrees of perfection correspond to those of charity. We may rule out at once any question of loving God as much as he is lovable. Such comprehension is beyond any creature; it is for God alone, in the Holy Ghost who is subsistent love, and in Son and Word who is subsistent knowledge. The measure refers to our capacity, to our loving as much as we can.

Here the threefold division is classical, ever active, often active, never actively opposed. To look at these more closely: all are modes of being in love with God, and we shall do well to resent any suggestion of spiritual snobbishness which looks down on what may be called the working masses in the business of salvation, in fact we shall be blessed if by divine mercy we manage to be numbered among them.

For our loving to be always active is possible only in heaven. As it is not desirable that we should always be attending to our breathing, neither is it that we should be always conceptually and explicitly formulating God's presence to ourselves, despite the examples of high multiplication of ejaculatory prayer in some people. Nobody becomes a nervous wreck by aiming at Christian perfection: *perfectionism is another matter. The substance of charity, as St. Augustine saw, is being in friendship with God, and this is a steady and settled endowment (*habitus*), which, like all friendship, can speak with silence, and in it resolve or intention is more decisive than attention. Of course acts are required, but which great master in the spiritual life lays down a rule about how frequent they should be?

God places us in this life with its many occupations. He is our friend above all, not our taskmaster. And he should be in all our loving, a loving that should be free and not stilted, and certainly not requiring a dutiful religious tag on it as a guarantee of its genuineness. In the welter of human activity a double emphasis can be discerned, to cleave to God and "the things of God," and to avoid being separated from him. These should not be regarded as separate sorts of act, but more like the diastolic and systolic rhythm of the pulse. The distinction is sufficient, however, to enable us to classify a way of life mainly engaged in the search for God and in what the somewhat prim cliché calls "the practice of virtue," and a way of life mainly concerned with not losing him by grave sin. Anybody with much experience of life will know how much more generous this last is in fact than it may look on paper: contrition lies at the heart of Christian perfection. Any spiritual volume which affects a sort of lordly patronage for the least in the kingdom of God deserves to be closed at once.

Intercalated with the above divisions of charity are the states of perfection variously entitled "for beginners, for those getting on, and for the advanced," or "the purgative, illuminative, and unitive ways," or even, though unfelicitously, "the moral, the ascetical, and the mystical." They do not refer to separate zones, but describe by synecdoche different phases in the single and continuous process that begins at baptism and ends in heaven, to the threshold of which the highest forms of contemplative prayer approach.

A final warning, or perhaps a reassurance. The works devoted *ex professo* to Christian perfection tend to be somewhat labored productions, without lilt or grace of style. The authors often write an officialese quite their own, and not rarely fall into the occupational hazards of being mean-spirited about God's creation and of overcharging the significance of religious vapors. The classics are comparatively few, but they are outstanding. For the rest, the sources are the Scriptures, the liturgy, and the theologians who are more interested in God than in themselves.

[T. GILBY]

PERFECTION, CHRISTIAN (WESLEYAN), a Methodist doctrine, first taught by John *Wesley. He defined it as "loving God with all our heart, mind, soul and strength. This implies no wrong temper, none contrary to love remains in the soul; and that all thoughts, words and actions are governed by pure love" (*A Plain Account of Christian Perfection,* 1777). He stated that Christian perfection is not perfect knowledge, or freedom from certain mistakes, or freedom from infirmities ("inward and outward imperfections that are not of a moral nature"), or freedom from temptation. Rather, he felt it is freedom from known outward sin, since "whosoever is born of God sinneth not," as well as from such inward sins as evil thoughts and tempers. It is inward and outward purity arising from a new, clean heart that completely loves God. The attainment of perfection is by an act of God's grace distinct from and following upon conversion of justification, whereby a believer, by faith, was filled with the Spirit of God and empowered to overcome all sin. In short, whereas justification is a change in man's condition whereby God, through an act of pardon, forgives man his sins, restoring him to divine fellowship. Christian perfection is a change in man's very nature; God "extirpates man's sinful nature," empowering him to overcome all sin and to live a life of perfect love.

The doctrine created a great deal of trouble in many of Wesley's *societies, esp. in London, where T. *Maxfield encouraged Methodists who, claiming such a grace themselves, felt that only those with a similar experience were sufficiently informed spiritually to teach them. Eventually, led by Maxfield, these people split from Wesley, forming independent congregations. The result was that many of the Methodist preachers ceased teaching Christian perfection, fearing a dispute similar to that in London. Wesley himself never claimed to possess "perfect love"; several times he discussed with his brother Charles the advisability of omitting the doctrine from Methodist teaching. He decided against this action, however, continuing to proclaim it and urging his preachers to do the same. He felt that in Christian perfection God had given the Methodists an important doctrine to propagate. Wesley's doctrine was taken up and elaborated in *revivalism, and esp. the *Holiness movement. The interpretation of the Holiness Churches was not accepted by most Methodist bodies (see ENTIRE SANCTIFICATION).

Contemporary Methodists explain Christian perfection as a gradual growth in grace whereby a believer is enabled to live a victorious Christian life. They stress the "going on" to perfection rather than the "attainment" of it, and they use modern terminology, referring to Christian maturity, a personality integrated in God or spiritual wholeness. BIBLIOGRAPHY: C. W. Williams, *John Wesley's Theology Today* (1960), with bibliog.; C. E. Jones, *Perfectionist Persuasion: The Holiness Movement and American Methodism, 1867–1936* (1974). *PERFECTIONISM; *CONCUPISCENCE.

[T. GILBY]

PERFECTIONISM. That human perfection can be attained is commonly held by all systems that do not postulate a never-ending evolutionary process, or by cynicisms more or less benign, content to leave men and women just as they find them. The abstract term "perfectionism" was not, however, applied originally to secular movements toward moral, social, or political betterment, but to religious belief in the possibility of perfection in the present life, often negatively described as a condition of sinlessness, and to the consequent methods to bring this about. It appeared in the mid-19th cent.; "perfectionist" a hundred years earlier had been applied to the Methodists, sometimes as a term of disparagement: they are, writes Samuel Richardson in *Clarissa,* "enough to make a better man than myself either run into madness or despair." The evangelical command "Be ye perfect" (Mt 5.48; the word used in Gr. is *teleisi,* end-achievers) was consistently maintained from the beginning by the Christian Church; efforts to restrict membership to the righteous or elect were as consistently resisted (see MONTANISTS). Charity was the bond of perfection (Col 3.14). Yet this friendship with God and men was a positive and analogical value, which admitted of degrees and growth in intensity. The universal call to holiness finds a classical theological articulation in Thomas Aquinas; nevertheless in practice the note grew uncertain when perfection became specialized to religious life under the vows, the "canonical state of perfection."

Against such professionalism Luther protested. The full Christian has an utter trust in God and confidently asks for what is necessary in his trials and tribulations; he is a justified sinner, yet is still subject to the curse of evil. No more did Calvin's ideal of the man obedient to God's will agree with the Anabaptist picture of the completely blameless man or the *antinomianism that anticipated in this world the perfect state of the blessed requiring no preaching of the law (see LAW AND GOSPEL). Henceforward, it may be noted, Hellenic conceptions of Christian perfection become overcast with the cloud of Reformation and Counter-Reformation writings and their preoccupation with guilt. *Wesley's ideal of the perfect man is the subject of a special article (see PERFECTION, CHRISTIAN [WESLEYAN]). He was influenced by the Moravians and also by his father's *Arminianism and by William *Law; the correspondences run deeply between Wesley's insistence on the experience of the great work wrought in us by God in renewing our fallen nature and the teaching of much Catholic spirituality. His own conversion seems to have been "mystical" rather than "evangelical," and he never claimed perfection for himself or the assurance that he was completely free from sin. Methodism has justly been compared with Franciscanism, and the grand division in it between Perfectionists and anti-Perfectionists to that between the *Spirituals and the Conventuals.

A rhetoric at once simpler and more metaphorical, and which preaches *entire sanctification and cleansing from sin, is characteristic of the various *Holiness Churches and of *Pentecostalism. So too the Salvation Army strives that we may be found unblamable and unreprovable before God. The word "perfectionism" was antonomastically applied to the *Oneida Community. All the examples so far indicated agree in committing themselves completely to God in a spirit that is quite non-Pelagian. In our own days, however, "perfectionism," though sometimes used half-admiringly, has come to be recognized almost as a clinical entity in psychological and pastoral treatment, as when we make for ourselves a "pseudo-person" and set up for ourselves a false image of what we think we ought to be, instead of being open and "abandoned" to God. The central tradition in Christianity is wise in looking rather beadily at claims to invulnerability or the preaching of an innocence that may have been once upon a time but never is at present this side of heaven. In pastoral psychology, the term refers to a sort of *Pelagianism without sunniness and with anxiety, a compulsion to achieve a success beyond criticism and by one's own effort.

Some qualifications are obviously necessary. It will be convenient to follow the Aristotelean distinction between man as an artist making a work (*opus*) and man as a moral agent doing a deed (*agibile*). As to the first it is right that a professional artist should strive even at a taxing cost to produce a flawless work or performance (e.g., a concert pianist). Though even here, as art critics have noticed, the effect may well be asymmetrical and should keep the tang of its material, the rasp of the strings, the split blare of the brass, the feel of the stone, and so forth. A denatured effect is not particularly admirable, and a great artist will not work without attention to the limitations of his medium. With amateur art we can be altogether more easy-going. There a perfectionist can be a bore both to himself and to his friends if he makes a cult of success, whether he is fingering at the well-tempered clavichord, or playing vicarage tennis, or sitting down to a rubber of bridge. This is not a defense of sloppiness, but a recognition of what G. K. Chesterton meant when he said that if a thing is worth doing, it is worth doing badly: the tests to be applied are those of personal recreation without spoiling the social amenities of others. Winning ought not to be the main object of the game.

It is in the sphere of moral practice that perfectionism becomes most threatening to human health and happiness. Here it appears rooted in an insecurity that feels one is not accepted unless one is a flawless success. This not uncommon illusion is sometimes fostered by faulty education. Its application to acceptance by God involves a basic misconstruction of Christian teaching. God gives of his pure mercy and loves the contrite of heart. Who are we to make bargains with him, as though he could be bound to render what is due to us because of our goodness? Not only human vice but bogus virtue also can keep us away from God. The theme constantly reappears in the Bible and is dwelt on in the theology of devotion. Such merits as we have are consequences, not conditions, of divine mercy; and like the Galatians, we shall need to be told that although regenerated by baptism and justified by faith, "you cannot do the things that you would" (Gal 5.17). BIBLIOGRAPHY: M. Piette, *John Wesley in the Evolution of Protestantism* (tr. J. B. Howard, 1937); Knox Enth.

[T. GILBY]

PERGAMUM, a city in Asia Minor; a great and famous city of Mysia. After its victory against the Galatians in 240 B.C., it symbolized the triumph of Hellenic culture against barbarism. Its acropolis contained an agora, a gymnasium, a Greek theatre, temples of Dionysos and Athena, and a great altar of Zeus. Eventually, its most popular deity was Asclepius, the healing savior whose cult was native to Epidaurus in Greece. Under Roman rule Pergamum became the capital of W Asia Minor, called the province of Asia. As such it became the locus for the imperial cult. At one time there were three temples in Pergamum for the cult of the emperor, each with its separate priesthood and staff of attendant ministers. Those who refused to perform the traditional ritual of worship of the emperor would be tried and executed in the provincial capital. This explains the reference to Pergamum in Rev (2.13) as "the place where Satan has his throne," and the reference to "Antipas, my faithful witness [martyr], [who] was killed in your city, the home of Satan." The letter to the angel of the Church at Pergamum warns against conforming to idolatrous custom in order to survive and promises: "To him who is victorious . . . I will give . . . a white stone, and on the stone will be written a new name, known to none but him that receives it" (2.17). Pergamum gave its name to "parchment"—*charta Pergamena*—the durable writing material manufactured there. The baptismal name given in secrecy in time of persecution is written even more durably than if it were written on the famous parchment of that city.

[E. J. DILLON]

PERGOLESI, GIOVANNI BATTISTA (1710–36), Italian composer of the late Baroque. P., in conjunction with Leonardo *Leo, another Neapolitan composer, worked out the classic formula for comic opera or *opera buffa*. Enormously prolific, P. is esp. known for his operas, most notably, *La serva padrona*, although he worked in other genres, the trio-sonata for example. P. was essentially a miniaturist, employing a style characterized by lightness and delicacy rather than grandeur and power. He composed a large quantity of sacred music, most of it clearly showing the influence of his teacher *Durante. His *Stabat Mater* is his best known religious work. BIBLIOGRAPHY: F. Walker, Grove DMM 6:626–634.

[P. DOHERTY]

PERICHORESIS, CHRISTOLOGICAL (Lat., *circumincessio christologica*), the mutual indwelling of the divine and human in Christ, based on the oneness of person (excluding every species of Nestorianism) in two distinct, inseparable, unconfused natures (excluding every form of

Monophysitism). From another viewpoint it may be considered as the subsistent indwelling of the divine Logos in the human nature of Jesus, all the more perfectly human for its intimate actuation by the divine. An understanding of Christological perichoresis makes the communication of idioms rich and meaningful. We cannot think of God in Christ without thinking also that he is man, nor of man in Christ without thinking that he is God also. For the theologian such an understanding safeguards and implies the ancient faith of Chalcedon, and suggests the study of the kerygmatic Christ, who is the Jesus of history, sign and sacrament of the Christ action in the whole work of Redemption. By the grace of union the human nature is sanctified, sinless, priestly, God's presence among men in history—the divine way in human acts, the human way in the divine—until the second coming and the eternal reign of the glorified Kyrios. BIBLIOGRAPHY: M. Schmaus, LTK 8:274–276.

[E. G. KAISER]

PERICOPES (Gr., meaning excerpts), passages from the Scriptures appointed to be read in the liturgy, esp. at Mass and in the Divine Office, on determined occasions. At certain seasons the readings on successive days are arranged to provide a continuous presentation of the books of the Bible and in their proper sequence. In other cases particular readings have been selected because of their appropriateness to feast or season.

[N. KOLLAR]

PÉRIGORD, CHURCHES OF, Romanesqe French churches of strong Byzantine influence, in Périgord (Aquitaine), their façades embroidered with sculpture, the bell towers detached, and multiple domes capped by cone-shaped turrets. Aisleless, with galleries, bays covered with domes on pendentives (Byzantine), the interiors are plain, eschewing sculptural decoration, though capitals are at times enhanced (Angoulême, Périgueux, Aulnay).

[M. J. DALY]

PÉRIGUEUX, SAINT-FRONT, CATHEDRAL OF, one of the most renowned Romanesque cathedrals in Europe of domed Greek-cross plan (1120–60) vaulted by five domes on pendentives uniquely Aquitanian with prototypes in Constantinople, Sardinia, and Cahors, mutilated in 1557, restored 1852–1901. Six columns of the earlier church of Frothaire (976–1047) support the steeple. The façade, a precious example of architectural sculpture of the early 11th cent., was restored in the 19th. BIBLIOGRAPHY: M. Aubert, ''Notice sur Saint-Front,'' *Congrès archéologique de Périgueux* (1927); H. Saalman, *Medieval Architecture* (1962).

[M. J. DALY]

PÉRIN, HENRI CHARLES XAVIER (1815–1905), first to hold the chair of economics at the Univ. of Louvain (1844–91), leading Catholic economist. He organized the Maline Congresses of 1863, 1864, 1867; he was an opponent of the 19th-cent. economic theory that free enterprise and the dynamics of the marketplace would generate social justice; he was equally opposed to the welfare state concept. P. resigned from Louvain because his position on civic freedom was reproved by Leo XIII. The ideal that his works sought to advance was social betterment as the result of the free cooperative association of people and an enlightened beneficence on the part of the upper classes. He published: *Les économistes, les socialistes et le Christianisme* (1849); *De la richesse dans les sociétés chrétiennes* (1861); *Le socialisme chrétien* (1879); *Économie politique d'après Rerum novarum* (1891); *Premiers principes d'économie politique* (1896).

[T. C. O'BRIEN]

PERIODIC ABSTINENCE, see RHYTHM.

PERITUS, Lat., expert, one learned in the sacred sciences who acts as a consultant to a bishop (council father) at a church council. The *periti,* as at Trent and Vatican Council II e.g., exercise a great influence, but the conciliar decisions are made by, and have their authority from, the council fathers.

PERJURY, falsely swearing (*jurare*) an *oath; i.e., formally attesting to a falsehood. The moral meaning of the term includes more than the civil or legal crime of perjury, i.e., giving false court testimony under oath. Morally, perjury offends against the virtue of *religion; it is an irreverent contempt for God's knowledge and truthfulness; the falsehood of what is sworn makes the oath itself an offense against God's honor. Even if the falsehood be about a trivial matter, the swearing is perjury and, in fact, shows greater contempt for God (see SWEARING). The moral disorder of perjury in a judicial procedure is increased by being also a sin against *legal justice (see FALSE WITNESS).

[T. C. O'BRIEN]

PERMANENT SYNOD (Gr. *synodos endemousa*), the council of Orthodox bps. resident in the Turkish Republic who assist the ecumenical patriarch in the administration of the Great Church, i.e., the Church of Istanbul (Constantinople) and in other matters pertaining to the Orthodox Churches over which the patriarch and his synod have jurisdiction. These matters, however, are not always definite and clear, and this has occasionally been a source of controversy with other patriarchates within the Orthodox communion.

Since the Orthodox Church prides itself on being a conciliar Church (*Sobornaja* among the Russians), the ecumenical patriarch has always been assisted in his government by a synod. However, its composition has not always been the same. During the days of the Empire, it was composed of neighboring bps. together with what other bps. happened to be in the capital. The president has always been the ecumenical patriarch. In the 18th cent. some laymen came to occupy positions in church administration and even occupied seats on the synod. This is no longer the case. At present, the synod consists of 12 bps. half of whom retire each year to make room for new bishops. Since there are only four dioceses in the patriarchate, all of which have metropolitan status, some of the bps. have to be consecrated with titular sees. The exact powers of the synod cannot be enumerated, but the patriarch would venture to do nothing of importance without consulting it and abiding by its decision.

The term permanent synod is also applied to analogous conciliar bodies in other national or autocephalous Churches, e.g., Bulgaria, Rumania, Greece.

[A. WALKER]

PERNET, ÉTIENNE CLAUDE (1824–99), French Assumptionist, with Marie Fage (1824–83), cofounder of the *Little Sisters of the Assumption, at Nîmes in 1865, a congregation devoted to care of the sick poor. P.'s cause for beatification was introduced in 1931, advanced in 1956.

[T. C. O'BRIEN]

PERPENDICULAR STYLE, English Gothic style of architecture (14th–16th cent.) showing dominant verticality and reserved horizontality. As in all English Gothic, roofs and arches are lower denying the soaring quality of French style.

PERPETUA AND FELICITY, SS. (d. 202), martyrs at Carthage along with four others: Revocatus, Saturninus, Secundulus, and Saturus. All with the exception of Saturus were catechumens at the time of their arrest and were voluntarily joined in prison by Saturus, who had instructed them in the faith. The account of their trial, experiences in prison, visions, and execution is contained in the *Passion of Perpetua and Felicitas,* written in Latin but later translated into Greek. The largest portion of this work was written by Perpetua herself, who was about 22 years old, ''well-born, liberally educated, honorably married,'' and with an infant son at her breast. Her account was continued by the catechist Saturus, and the whole work was edited with an introduction, a description of the martyrs' deaths, and a conclusion by a skilled writer who may have been Tertullian. The passion, which is one of the most beautiful pieces of early Christian literature, is an important record of 3d-cent.-- Christian eschatology. Perpetua and Felicity are mentioned in the Roman calendar of 354 and in the Roman Canon of the Mass. BIBLIOGRAPHY: Quasten 1:181–182; E. C. E. Owen, *Some Authentic Acts of the Early Martyrs* (1927) 74–92; C. J. M. J. van Beek, *Passio SS. Perpetuae et Felicitatis* (1936, 2d ed., 1956); Butler 1:493–498; A. Quacquarelli, BiblSanct 10:493–501.

[M. J. COSTELLOE]

PERPETUAL ADORATION, in the RC Church, the practice of maintaining uninterrupted adoration of the Blessed Sacrament, preferably with the Sacrament exposed on the altar. The adoration of Christ present in the Sacrament may be seen as a reminder of his continuing presence in his community body, the Church. Historically the practice of perpetual adoration is closely connected with the Forty Hours devotion, although it was pioneered by such medieval lay groups as the Beguines of Liège (12th cent.) and confraternities of the Blessed Sacrament (13th century). The religious Congregation of the Blessed Sacrament, founded for men by St. Pierre Julien Eymard (Paris, 1856), and the People's Eucharistic League, which he established for lay men and women (Marseilles, 1859), have been closely associated with the devotion, as have the Congregation of Perpetual Adorers (1872), and other cloistered and noncloistered communities. Some parish churches maintain the devotion, although nocturnal adoration would be more common on the parish level. Regulations of the revised Roman Ritual (1973) recommend that the practice be patterned after the spirit of the liturgy and permit a member of such a group, lay or religious, appointed by the bp., to expose the Sacrament for adoration.

[J. DALLEN]

PERPETUAL ADORATION, SISTER SERVANTS OF THE HOLY GHOST OF, cloistered religious community commonly called the Pink Sisters, founded in 1896 at Steyl, Netherlands, by Fr. Arnold *Janssen, SVD, and Mother Mary Michael Tönnies. The purpose of the institute is primarily the propagation of the faith and the sanctification of the priesthood. In 1950, the rule was granted final approval by Rome. Rose and white habits worn by the sisters symbolize their great devotion to the Holy Spirit. Their life includes, not only perpetual adoration of the Blessed Sacrament, but also choral Office, manual work, and literary activities. The work of the Pink Sisters has extended from Europe to Argentina, the Philippines, and 3 U.S. cities: Philadelphia, Austin, Tex., and St. Louis, where perpetual adoration centers have been established. The general motherhouse is located at Steyl, Holland. In 1975, the community maintained 13 houses and had a membership of 313 sisters.

[R. A. TODD]

PERPETUAL ADORATION OF THE BLESSED SACRAMENT, NUNS OF THE (AP), an order of cloistered religious who engage in constant prayer before the exposed Blessed Sacrament. The nuns take solemn vows and dedicate themselves to the Divine Office, prayer, and other sacrifice. The papally approved community was founded in 1807 at Rome, Italy, by Mother Mary Magdalene of the Incarnation (Caterina Sordini Movizzo; 1770–1824). By 1964, the order had established independent houses throughout Europe and the Americas. U.S. foundations (1925) are located in El Paso, Texas, and San Francisco, California.

[R. A. TODD]

PERPETUAL ADORATION OF THE BLESSED SACRAMENT, SISTERS OF (ISA), a congregation of religious closely associated, in their early history, with the Sacramentine Sisters (1882) of Bergamo. Fr. Francesco Spinelli (1853–1911) founded the community in 1889 at Rivolta d'Adda (Diocese of Cremona), Italy. Definitive papal approval was given in 1932. The sisters take simple, perpetual vows and are dedicated to perpetual adoration of the Blessed Sacrament and charitable works—they conduct kindergartens, homes for the aged, hospitals, and orphanages. The motherhouse is in Cremona, Italy. The congregation has a membership (1976) of 1,028 sisters and maintains 118 houses.

[R. A. TODD]

PERPETUAL VIRGINITY OF MARY, the belief that Mary of Nazareth, the mother of Jesus Christ, was ever a virgin, i.e., that she conceived her Son through the power of God and not by a human father; that in bringing forth her Son she preserved her bodily integrity intact; and that after the birth of Jesus she had no intercourse or other voluntary use of her generative faculties. The Christian belief differs fundamentally from Greek and Oriental myths and did not originate with them. It is already found in apostolic tradition, in the independent infancy sections of the Gospels (Mt 1.18–25; Lk 1.26–38).

Virginal Conception. Belief in Mary's virginal conception was explicit and unchallenged in the primitive catechesis of the Church, in the teaching of the Church Fathers, and in the Creeds (Apostles', Nicene, Athanasian). Tradition at an early date linked the Virgin Birth with preexistence of the Son of God. The doctrine is clear in Scripture. Matthew 1.18–25 speaks of Mary's being with child through the Holy Spirit, unknown to Joseph her betrothed. Angelic revelation makes the facts known to Joseph, who then accepts Mary as wife and establishes the legal paternity of Christ as a son of David. The Evangelist himself sees in this miraculous conception (and birth) a fulfillment of the prophecy in Is 7.14. Luke 1.26–38, in tones reflecting OT ideas and terminology, records an angelic annunciation made to Mary (not Joseph) that she was to conceive and bear the Messiah, Son of the Most High. When Mary asks how this would agree with the resolve (or vow) she had made to remain a virgin, the answer is given: the conception would be effected by God and his Spirit. And Mary acquiesced. Some modern scholars see further verification of the virginal conception (and birth) in an important variant reading of Jn 1.13—who was "born not out of human stock or urge of the flesh or will of man but of God himself."

Virginal Birth. The belief that Mary gave birth to Christ miraculously, in a virginal way, although found earlier in apocryphal works and in some of the Fathers, became the universal and unanimous teaching of the Church Fathers from c.400 on. It was accepted at the Council of Chalcedon (451) and is found in both Eastern and Western liturgies and the major catechisms of the faith. The NT offers no explicit text concerning Mary's virginity in childbirth; some claim the truth is implicit in the fact that Mary herself wrapped her newborn baby in swaddling clothes (Lk 2.7). Others see the miraculous birth as a literal, or a typical, or a fuller verification of Isaiah's prophecy (7.14; cf. Mt 1.22–23). Church Fathers seem to regard the virginal childbirth as a privilege primarily of Christ, which looks ahead to his Resurrection. Mary is the new Eve. When discussing how Mary preserved virginal integrity in parturition, the Fathers compare her unopened womb to the "garden enclosed" and the "sealed fountain" of S of S 4.12 and to the closed sanctuary gate reserved for the passage of God in Ezek 44.1. Further comparison is made between Christ's emergence from the womb and his emergence from the closed sepulcher, or his entrance into the Upper Room through closed doors (Jn 20.19). Some attempts have been made (Durandus, 14th cent.; A. Mitterer, 20th cent.) to explain the Virgin Birth as Christ's passage through the normal birth channel, since this would seem more consonant with the idea of true maternity.

Virginity after the Birth of Christ. The belief that Mary remained a virgin in mind and body after the birth of Christ is found even earlier in the Church Fathers than belief in the virginal parturition, and from c.350 the expressive term "ever virgin" was used more and more. The Council of Chalcedon accepted this belief (451) and the Lateran Council (649) included it in the definition of the divine maternity of Mary. From early times some attacked the doctrine as conflicting with what we read in the New Testament. Critics pointed to the term "brethren" of the Lord (Mt 12.46–50; 13.55–56) as proof that Mary must have had other children besides Jesus. Church Fathers as early as Origen explained the phrase as referring to children of Joseph by a former marriage. Modern scholars suggest that the evangelist refers not to blood-brothers of Christ but to more distant relatives, perhaps cousins, since this could well be the meaning of the Hebrew/Aramaic word underlying the Greek word for brethren. Another objection has been based on the designation of Christ as Mary's "firstborn" Son (Lk 2.7), which would seem to indicate that he was first of a number of children. But modern scholars point out that firstborn was a special term for the first male child opening his mother's womb, because of certain privileges and obligations (cf. Ex 13.2), with no necessary reference to any further children. Again, critics cite Mt 1.25 (Joseph did not know Mary [by intercourse] "*till* she brought forth her firstborn son") as evidence that regardless of Christ's virginal birth, other children subsequently were born of the normal union of Joseph and Mary. However, modern scholars insist that the Greek text says nothing pro or con the subsequent relationship between Joseph and Mary. On the other hand, there are some who point to Mary's resolve (vow) to remain virgin, and to the absence of children beneath the Cross, as indirect confirmation of her perpetual virginity. BIBLIOGRAPHY: L. G. Owens, NCE 14:692–697; E. Pax, LTK 5:1210–12; A. Vögtle, "Mt 1.25 und die Virginitas B. M. Virginis post

Partum'' ThQ 146 (1967) 28–39; Carol Mariol v. 1; R. Brown, *Virginal Conception and Bodily Resurrection of Jesus*. (pa. 1973).

[E. MAY]

PERPIGNAN, UNIVERSITY OF, a medieval institution in the Spanish kingdom of Majorca, now the French province of Roussillon. An initial attempt to establish a university at Perpignan was made by the Spanish king, Peter IV of Aragon, who, in 1350 issued a decree declaring the erection of a *studium generale* with all faculties (including canon and civil law) except theology. The institution, however, did not take root, and a more permanent foundation was laid in 1379 by the Avignon pope, Clement VII, who issued a bull establishing all faculties except theology. The latter was later sanctioned by Nicholas V in 1447 but confirmed by statute only in 1459. The university, whose statutes were based on those of Lérida and Toulouse, was governed by a ten-member council. It ceased to exist in 1793.

[M. B. MURPHY]

PERRAUD, ADOLPHE LOUIS (1828–1906), French ecclesiastic and writer. Ordained in 1855, he was successively professor of church history at the Sorbonne (1865–74), bp. of Autun (1874), superior general of the Oratory in France (1884–1902), and cardinal (1893). Known for his eloquent preaching style, he also produced several biographies—on Richelieu, Lavigerie, and his friend Auguste Gratry—and a two-volume work, *Études sur l' Irlande contemporaine* (1862). He became a member of the Académie Française in 1882.

[E. M. GATES]

PERRAULT, CHARLES (1628–1703), French writer. A Parisian lawyer at the start of his career, he was subsequently appointed to head the Public Works Department by the powerful Controller General of Finance, Jean Baptiste Colbert. For this P. was elected to the Académie Française in 1671. In his own day he was best known for having sparked the so-called Quarrel of the Ancients and Moderns, a cultural controversy which lasted many years in France and was eventually also taken up in England. It began in 1687 with the presentation before the Academy of his poem *Le Siècle de Louis le Grand,* in which he argued for the superiority of the modernists over the classicists owing to their greater maturity and reasonableness. This elicited a violent rebuttal from the critic Boileau, after which all the intelligentsia were drawn into the dispute. P. restated his position in two additional works: *Les Parallèles des anciens et des modernes* (1688–1697) and *Les Hommes illustres qui ont paru en France pendant le XVIIe siècle* (1697–1701). The idea of progress clearly articulated in these volumes was to become a touchstone of 18th-cent. Enlightenment thinking. Later centuries remember P. chiefly for the charming collection of fairy tales he published in 1697. Subtitled *Contes de ma mère l' Oye* (Tales from Mother Goose), this contained such famous stories as "Cinderella," "Red Riding Hood," "Sleeping Beauty," and "Puss in Boots."

[E. M. GATES]

PERRET, family name of French architects, **Auguste** (1874–1954) and **Gustave** (1876–1952) working together in Paris. Auguste, the more renowned, designed the Municipal Casino at St. Malo (1899), its 54 ft. reinforced concrete slab floor an early use of ferro-concrete in his boldly simple style. After 1905 he exposed the concrete in structures of classic simplicity (Théâtre des Champs Elysées, Paris, 1911–13). Most famous is his avant-garde church of Notre Dame du Raincy (1922–23) supported on thin shafts, the exterior wall a screen of pierced precast concrete units. Though revolutionary in structure he adhered to 19th-cent. classical forms.

[M. J. DALY]

PERREYVE, HENRI (1831–65), French priest, writer, and from 1861 professor of church history at the Sorbonne. He was the friend and the publisher of the correspondence of H. *Lacordaire: *Lettres du P. Lacordaire à des jeunes gens* (1862). P.'s own works, written on a popular level, include: *De la critique des Évangiles* (1859); *Méditations sur le chemin de la croix* (1859); *Une station à la Sorbonne* (1864); and the posthumous *Études historiques* (1875) and *Lettres à un ami d' enfance* (1879).

[T. C. O'BRIEN]

PERRONE, GIOVANNI (1794–1876), Italian Jesuit theologian. He taught theology at Orvieto and at the Collegium Romanum except for a period (1830–34) when he served as rector in Ferrara and another (1848–51) which he spent in exile in England. He played an important part on the commissions that prepared for the definition of the Immaculate Conception, was a strong opponent of Hermesianism, and in general contributed notably to the revival of ecclesiastical studies. His writings, esp. his *Praelectiones theologicae* (9 v., 1835–42), went through many editions. BIBLIOGRAPHY: Sommervogel 6:558–571; C. Boyer, DTC 12.1:1255–56.

[M. J. SUELZER]

PERSECUTIONS (IN THE BIBLE). It is often difficult to disentangle the motives upon which the harassment and violence practiced against individuals or groups is based. Religious persecution is therefore not always clearly distinguishable from persecution based on political, cultural, social, or racial grounds. Thus, e.g., the oppression of the Israelites by Pharoah may have been largely a reaction against the earlier ascendancy of the Israelites under Joseph in collaboration with the occupation of Egypt by the Hyksos (Gen 46.34). The first clear case of religious persecution recorded in the Bible seems to be that of the Prophets by the decadent kings of Israel. Jezebel, the Tyrian wife of Ahab, introduced the worship of the god Melkarth and persecuted the Prophets of Yahweh (1 Kg 18.4; 18.13; 19.10), a measure followed by retaliation on the part of Elijah (1 Kg 18.40) and then of Jehu (2 Kg 10.18–28). Jeremiah was persecuted by the nobles and narrowly escaped death (Jer 38.4–6), but another prophet did not (Jer 26.21). A persecution of Israel for its faith but allied to political and cultural motives was that by Antiochus IV (1 Macc 1.44–61) in his attempt to Hellenize his empire.

The NT provides its greatest example of persecution in the harassment of Jesus by the religious authorities (Lk 4.30) and the government (Lk 13.31) and his final execution. After this the persecution of Jesus' followers was quickly taken up by the religious arm of the nation (Acts 5.40), though the slaying of Stephen (Acts 7.54–60) appears to have been a local action and was perhaps simply an example of mob violence. Nevertheless, a general persecution by authorities followed.

[A. J. TKACIK]

PERSECUTIONS (EARLY CHURCH.) The history of the early persecutions of Christianity lacks adequate documentation. Contemporary Christian testimony is largely apologetic in tone and therefore suspect; and the loss of many early documents (e.g., the passions of martyrs and letters to Churches) gave rise in a later age to replacements often embellished with legend. Ulpian's collection of anti-Christian measures has not survived. As a result, investigators cannot determine the exact nature of the legal charges lodged against Christians and the penalties incurred. It is, however, abundantly clear that extremes of cruelty were practiced at some times and in some places. Another difficulty for the historian stems from the fact that early writers presented persecution merely as the conflict of certain emperors with a new sect. Hence comes the tradition that the early persecutions were 10 in number, though the reality is far more complex. Until Decius (249–51), the extent of persecution was determined more by local feeling than by the policy of any emperor. Likewise, the problem of ascertaining the number of Christians who underwent punishment is knotty. One modern scholar asserts that the total did not exceed 3,000. Other writers present figures that range up to 100,000.

The earliest account of Christians harassed or put to death for their belief in Christ are to be found in the Acts of the Apostles: Stephen's martyrdom (6–8); the imprisonment of St. Peter and his companions (12.1–5); the scourging of St. Paul and Silas at Philippi (16.19–24). In the eyes of the first Christians, persecution was looked upon as the fulfillment of Christ's prophecy (Mt 10.17–23) and a continuation of the penalties meted out to the Apostles (1 Th 2.2; Phil 1.29). At first the chief enemies were the Jews, whereas the Roman State tolerated Christians as it did most other sects as long as they did not interfere with the official cult or with public security. As a matter of fact, in the first decades of the Church, Rome seems not to have differentiated between Christians and Jews. Thus, when the latter were expelled

from the city c.49, the Christians were probably exiled also. The first direct imperial attack upon the Christians occurred as aftermath to a fire that had destroyed more than half of Rome. Nero, in an attempt to quell the rumor that he himself had started the conflagration to clear space for the enlarging of his palace, accused the Christians of arson. Tacitus (*Ann.* 15.44) states than an *ingens multitudo* was then put to death, the specific charge being "hatred of mankind." (It is understandable that the Christians' withdrawal from public life, their social aloofness, and the secrecy with which they surrounded their doctrine and their worship left them open to such charges as incest and child-murder.) The victims of Nero's persecution were limited to the city of Rome, SS. Peter and Paul probably being among them. Though the condemnation of the Christians had been on charges other than the holding of a particular creed, Nero's action nonetheless set a precedent for treating Christians generally as criminals. Severe oppression was renewed under Domitian (81–96), who in his attempt to revivify paganism, condemned Christians for atheism. The most prominent of those who suffered in his reign, however, seem to have been exiled or killed for personal and political reasons. The policy of Trajan (98–117) towards the Christians is known from the rescript he sent Pliny the Younger, governor of Bithynia, c.112. The latter had asked the emperor's advice about treating those who had been accused before him as Christians. Trajan answered that anonymous accusations must never be entertained; that Christians were not to be hunted out, although any accused must be tried; that only those who remained obdurate in refusing to sacrifice to the gods and to offer incense to the emperor's statue were to be punished. Tertullian was the first to point out the inconsistencies in Trajan's practice, an indication that Rome had by no means resolved the problem the new religion posed. Hadrian (117–138) is said to have added the requirement that a specific charge be made other than that of being Christian before a suspect could be arraigned; yet there are trustworthy records of the execution of innocent Christians during his reign. In the public disasters that marked the years of Marcus Aurelius' principate (131–168), the superstitious populace turned against the Christians and they became once again scapegoats of the common misfortune. Marcus Aurelius himself in his *Meditations* (11.3) branded the Christian contempt of death "obstinate and theatrical." Septimius Severus (192–211) forbade converts to both Judaism and Christianity because he feared an increase in the number of adherents. In 235 Maximinus Thrax directed his attack against the highest leaders, exiling the reigning pope.

Although the name of Decius (249–251) is seventh in the list of imperial persecutors handed down by Orosius, his persecution may be classified as the first truly general attack upon Christianity. At his command Christians were everywhere ferreted out and forced to prove their conformity with the state religion before a specially established commission, under pain of death. The courage of many failed (*lapsi*). Some Christians purchased false affidavits (*libelli*) stating that they had complied with the emperor's order. Yet the years of this persecution and those of Diocletian's 50 years later are universally regarded as the heroic age of the Church. In 257 the emperor Valerian, reversing his own earlier favorable attitude, ordered all ranks of the clergy to sacrifice to idols. He also forbade visits to cemeteries and assemblies for worship. In the following year he increased his opposition by demanding the execution of all high-ranking Christians. His successor Gallienus (260–268) published the first decree of tolerance ever issued by Roman authorities. The respite was, however, short-lived, for Diocletian (284–305) in 303 inaugurated what proved to be the last and greatest of the persecutions by ordering the destruction of all churches and the burning of the Scriptures; and in 304 he decreed the death penalty for all Christians. After his resignation persecution continued until 311, when Galerius published an edict of toleration. Shortly thereafter the Convention of Milan gave complete religious liberty to the Empire. The last official attempt to revive paganism was made unsuccessfully by Julian the Apostate (361–363). The Church, however, was not destined to enjoy freedom from harassment. The Persians, who had begun their opposition to Christianity in 337, continued to trouble Christians until the 7th century. BIBLIOG - RAPHY: H. Leclercq, "Droit persécuteur" DACL 4.2:1565–1648; M. J. Costelloe, NCE 11:146–149, with bibliog; T. R. Glover, *Conflicts of Religion in the Early Roman Empire* (1909, repr. 1975); *Conflict between Paganism and Christianity in the Fourth Century* (ed. A Momigliano, 1963).

[M. J. SUELZER]

PERSEVERANCE, the virtue, a part of fortitude or courage, of sticking to a task despite the difficulties of its protractedness; it also embraces constancy, a persistency despite difficulties set up from outside, and goes with patience, the endurance of pain and opposition. By deficiency it is opposed by softness (Lat. *mollities,* Gr. *malakotēs*), by excessiveness, by obstinacy (*pertinacia*), and also by what Aristotle calls a headlong rush (*propeteia*). The above headings, indicated by the *Nicomachean Ethics,* were treated by the Latin Stoics and patristic moralists as general conditions of all virtue or vice, but were later analyzed by St. Thomas Aquinas into specific dispositions. See ThAq ST 2a2ae, 137–138 (esp. in Lat-Eng ed., v. 42, ed. A. Ross and T. Walsh).

[P. F. MULHERN]

PERSEVERANCE, FINAL, as an idea is made up of two distinct but necessarily connected concepts: continuance in the state of grace, and death in that state. While the notion of *confirmation in grace stresses the first element to the extent of envisioning a real and lasting immunity from sin, the notion of final perseverance emphasizes the second, for that precisely ties it in with predestination and makes it the great gift about which the Council of Trent spoke (D 1566). In sanctifying grace itself every just person receives at least the remote power to persevere in good. But whether he actually will or not depends upon his use of that power. Because of the present labile human condition, theologians commonly teach that even the righteous need God's special help to actualize that potentiality. This special help is always at hand and easily obtainable, esp. through prayer. Actual perseverance in the state of grace then is a gift of God not necessarily included in the gift of justification itself. But even beyond this special gift of actual perseverance lies the circumstance of death in the state of grace. Here one is directly confronted with the mystery of divine predestination, for one is saved precisely by dying in the state of grace. This circumstance can be understood only in the light of God's special providence exercised over the elect. While the gift of final perseverance cannot be merited, theologians often say it will be infallibly given to those who sincerely seek it through assiduous prayer. BIBLIOGRA - PHY: A. Michel, DTC 12:1293–1302.

[C. R. MEYER]

PERSIA, MARTYRS OF, 120 martyrs believed to have been put to death the same day in the year 304 at Seleucia-Ctesiphon under the persian King Sapor II. No names have been preserved, but nine were thought to have been consecrated virgins, with the rest being priests, deacons, or monks. Their story is told in the Adiabene cycle of martyr-acts, a source that is by no means uniformly trustworthy. According to this source they refused to worship the sun, were imprisoned in a squalid dungeon for 6 months, and then decapitated. A wealthy woman gave them honorable burial nearby. BIBLIOGRAPHY: Butler 2:39–40; J. M. Sauget, BiblSanct 10:504–505.

[E. J. DILLON]

PERSIAN RELIGION, ANCIENT, the religion or religions of Persia to the triumph of Islam in the 7th and 8th cent. A.D. The chief ancient sources are the *Avesta preserved in part from the Sassanid edition; the *Dēnkart, a religious encyclopedia in Pahlavi or Middle Persian, which quotes or summarizes ancient material now lost; the *Būndahishn (Cosmology), and several related works, all likewise in Middle Persian. The *Avesta* includes the *Gāthās,* the oldest part of the collection and the part that reflects most faithfully the teachings of Zoroaster.

At the time of their settlement on the plateau of Iran the Persians worshipped *Mithra as a supreme god and *Anahita* as his consort, the great goddess or *Magna Mater.* This was really the cult of the Bull-god and of the Mother as dispenser of all life. Certain spirits presided over waters and flocks, sacrifices of goats and oxen were offered, and the *haoma ritual was a special feature. The *Magi, apparently, were the traditional priests. This popular current in Persian religion may be characterized as a form of nature worship. It stressed fertility and made the cult of fire of central importance. Side by side with this popular religion, however, the existence of a higher form of religion is to be noted. It stressed a supreme sky god, imposed moral precepts, and the concept of *Rta,* the eternal order of nature, but likewise good conduct—a high moral order based on right and truth.

Ahura-mazda is the supreme god of the Achaemenid kings, the creator and benefactor of the world. However, it is clear that the more popular polytheistic religion continued to flourish beside the lofty cult of *Ahura-Mazda.* Xerxes (486–465 B.C.), the successor of Darius I (541–486 B.C.) made the worship of *Ahura-Mazda* and *Rta* official, but the last kings of the dynasty in the 4th cent. mention also the old divinities in their inscriptions. Furthermore, the *Magi,* despite their revolt under Darius, gradually acquired a monopoly in the field of religion and eventually adopted in large part the religion of Zoroaster.

*Zoroaster (in Persian, *Zarathusthra*) is one of the great figures in the history of religion, a prophet and a reformer rather than an innovator in the strict sense. He carried on his work in NE Iran in the early 6th century. His doctrine spread westward more slowly than was once thought, making its greatest progress under the Parthian Arsacids (249 B.C.–226 A.D.) and the Sassanids. The Sassanid kings (226–651 A.D.) organized Zoroastrianism into a state religion and adopted a stern policy against other religions or "heresies." Zoroaster made *Ahura-Mazda* the supreme god, the Good Power, the Holy, the Unique. His principle role is to combat Evil Power, *Angra Manyu (Ahriman).* His system is dualistic only in a limited sense, because at the end of the world the Good Power will triumph completely and the Evil Power will be annihilated. Zoroaster, however, justified holy war, admitted certain magical practices, and exaggerated the importance of the ox, dog, and fire. Room was found not only for a whole series of benevolent higher beings but also for a corresponding list of demons, werewolves, and evil fairies. Much emphasis was placed on purification, which is accomplished best by water, fire, and *gomez,* the urine of the bull. Fire, after *Ormazd,* was the first of all beings to be worshipped, as it is fundamental for daily life, religious sacrifices, and purification. Festivals were seasonal and essentially agricultural. Man must make a choice between Ormazd (Ahura Mazda) and Ahriman. He must worship with his heart as well as with his tongue. He must hate evil and do good, that is, what is in accord with *Rta,* good order deified. The Mazdean believes in the survival of the soul after death, but he must provide for the total decomposition of the body by exposure to birds and beasts of prey on a structure above the ground ("tower of silence"). The skeleton only is to be reduced to dust and buried in the earth. The soul of the just man must pass the trial of the *Cinvat* (separation) Bridge for entry into happy eternity. The evil man will fall from the bridge into hell. However, at the end of time all evil will be destroyed. Persian religion, at least in its Zoroastrian form, is one of the highest religions of paganism, with a central emphasis on ethical content and conduct.

Exhaustive investigation has shown that Persian religion did not exercise any major influences on either Judaism or Christianity. On the other hand, through its emphasis on the conflict between Good and Evil, and its cosmological speculations, it had a far-reaching influence on Gnosticism and Manichaeanism. BIBLIOGRAPHY: J. Duchesne-Guillemin, *La Religion de l' Iran ancien* (1962); F. König, *Zarathustras Jenseitsvorstellung und das Alte Testament* (1964); M. N. Dhalla, *Zoroastrian Theology from the Earliest Times to the Present Day* (1914, repr. 1970); A. V. Jackson, *Zoroastrian Studies: Iranian Religion and Various Monographs* (1928, repr. AMS).

[M. R. P. MCGUIRE]

PERSICO, IGNATIUS (1823–95), missionary bp., envoy, cardinal. An Italian Capuchin ordained in 1846, P. volunteered for the missions in India and served in Patna and Bombay. In 1850 he became the first editor of the Bombay *Catholic Examiner.* P. was instrumental in preventing the Goan Christians from schismatic break with Rome. On a mission to London he obtained a guarantee of Catholic mission rights in India. He became coadjutor-bp. of Bombay in 1854 and vicar apostolic of Agra in 1856. Illness forced him to resign in 1860. He went to Charleston, S.C. in 1867 and participated in 1869 in the Tenth Provincial Council of Baltimore. He attended Vatican Council I, where he was named bp. of Savannah, Georgia. Again ill health forced his resignation. In 1874 Rome sent P. on a secret mission to Canada, and in 1877 helped prepare for the initiation of a hierarchy in India. Appointed bp. of Aquino, Italy, again he had to resign for health reasons. In 1887 he was sent to Ireland as papal envoy. Returning to Rome he became secretary of Propaganda Fide. Pope Leo XIII created P. cardinal in 1893.

[J. R. AHERNE]

PERSON (PHILOSOPHY), a term with special significance in Christian philosophy and scholasticism because of its importance in theological discussions of the Incarnation and the Trinity. According to the former doctrine, Christ is one divine person who subsists in two distinct natures, human and divine. The orthodox doctrine of the Trinity is that there are three divine persons subsisting in the one divine nature. In the Latin tradition of Christian philosophy the classic definition of person designed to fit these two dogmas was devised by Boethius: "an individual substance of a rational nature." Centuries later this definition was accepted by Aquinas, but made to mean: "a complete substance, subsistent by itself, separated from others, of a rational nature" (ThAq ST 1a, 29.1).

[E. J. DILLON]

PERSON (THEOLOGY), a key concept in Christian dogma. The early councils used it and made it one of the basic tools by which the two fundamental dogmas of the Christian message, that of the Triune God and of Christ, are expressed: God is three Persons in one nature; Christ is one

Person in two natures. The Christian faith has also its own concept of the human person: man's dignity lies in this, that in Christ he is called to enter into personal relations with God.

From a psychological standpoint personhood emerges through self-consciousness; this, however, does not mean that consciousness constitutes its formal element. For faith tells men that there are three Persons in God but one consciousness only; Christ on the contrary is one Person, self-conscious on two different planes, the divine and the human. Metaphysically, a person is the existential center to which the experience of consciousness is referred. It is constituted as an ego, self-contained and subsistent, insofar as it is ontologically complete and integrated. Thus the Divine Persons are three, because Father, Son, and Spirit find within the same divine nature their ontological completeness and subsistence. Christ's human nature, on the contrary, is not closed on itself; it attains integration through, and receives subsistence from, its union with the Son of God. As to the human person, it is in itself an ontologically self-possessed subject but is taken up by Christ into the sphere of God's personal life.

The mystery of God completes the notion of person. In human experience a person is self-contained and ontologically integrated prior to, and in view of, communicating with others. The possibility of communicating presupposes the ontological constitution of the person. In God however, each Person is related to the others not accidentally but by a substantial relationship. Here each is personally self-possessed through total communication; complete self-giving coincides with personal integration. This intrinsic law of the divine life constitutes the last foundation of Christian morality. Man becomes himself by giving himself; "he who loses his life for my sake, will find it" (Mt 10.39). Disinterested charity is the way to self-realization. While the notion of person remains underdeveloped outside Christianity, every man open to God and to his fellowmen becomes a person in the Christian sense. BIBLIOGRAPHY: B. Lonergan, *De Deo Trino II*, Pars Systematica (1964) 152.

[J. DUPUIS]

PERSON, DIVINE, see DIVINE PERSON.

PERSON, JURIDICAL, a technical term in the canon law of the Latin Church denoting status before the law. A juridical person is an entity possessing rights and obligations in its own name which the law recognizes and secures; the subject of rights and obligations. This would include individual persons, groups of persons, corporations, churches, monasteries, municipalities, and other entities that become the subject of rights and obligations.

[E. J. DILLON]

PERSONALISM, a philosophic interpretation of reality which has had great impact on Christian theology in recent years. Personalism, which originated as a significant movement in the 19th cent., has undergone some changes. The unifying thread is the root position that human persons are much more important than any materialistic considerations and/or all-inclusive system of thought or reality that tends to subsume persons to the system.

Personalism in the 19th cent. developed as a reaction to the various "-isms" of the day: materialism, evolutionism, idealism, scientism. These theories of reality all stress, in various ways, that man is so much a part of the chemical-biological-physical aggregate called nature that he differs from raw nature only quantitatively. The phenomenal growth of scientific knowledge in the 18th and 19th cent. convinced many leading thinkers that man's origin is due, not to the personal fiat of an omnipotent Creator, but to a purely natural process. If this be so, then it was only a short step to saying that this process, whatever its name, is more important in the last analysis than one of its products (perhaps even an accidental product) such as man. These conclusions took their inspiration from the thought of men like: Newton, whose clear-cut formulations of the laws of inanimate nature encouraged others to attempt to formulate like laws for human beings; Darwin, whose studies led many to the notion that the highly organized biological complex called Homo sapiens can be totally reduced to the comparatively simple cellular organism; and Hegel, whose dialectical upward movement is evolving toward an absolute collectivity of the future. In these conclusions lay the seeds of destruction of two formerly held attributes of human existence: sacredness (untouchability or unmanipulability) and uniqueness.

The 20th cent. has added further stimulus to the growth of personalism. Two major world wars in which many millions of people were killed in the name of ideologies and efficient military tactics exemplified the extent to which the individual human person's worth had decreased. The specter of atomic mass destruction is ever lurking in the background of one's plans for the future. Also, the rapid population growth throughout the world has necessitated a proportionate increase in the drive toward organizational planning and efficiency—with the corresponding decrease in the amount of influence that a single individual has in many decisions that affect his life. The phenomenal growth of automation and cybernetics, which replace human effort and computation, further intensifies the general feeling of individual inferiority. The so-called alienated man of today, much heralded in contemporary literature and art, is the most likely convert to personalism.

American personalists such as B. P. Browne (1814–1910), A. C. Knudson (1873–1954), and E. S. Brightman (1884–1953) base their positions on a theistic premise: since God is a person, then all moral and ethical truth derives from the absolute value of the person. They sought to distinguish their brand of personalism from other interpretations which they called individualism. This individualism does not imply a clear-cut distinction between God and man as opposed to the rest of nature. Some forms of personalism do not seem to harmonize with scriptural revelation, e.g., that God is growing, evolving, and not fully omnipotent and omniscient (E. S. Brightman, *The Problem of God*, 1930).

Some recent Catholic literature stresses the value of the person from the viewpoint of the doctrine of the Trinity. The reasoning is that since it is the interpersonal relationships within the Trinity which constitute the highest form of activity and existence, so the highest form of human activity should also be interpersonal relationships. Hence everything Christian should be put in the service of more effective personal relationships. The same goal, however, is being advocated by many Western thinkers who disavow or deliberately ignore any reference to the God of the Judeo-Christian tradition. These latter thinkers generally maintain that the human person is the highest level of evolution yet attained and that the cultivation of the individual person, not institutions or machines, will lead to the next advancement in the evolutionary process.

Personalism in its most basic, simplistic form—that persons count, not things—is one antidote to the mounting impersonalism of the latter half of the 20th century. Yet it is valuable and wholesome only insofar as it is in tension with its opposite pole. It is unrealistic to hope that personalism is the complete answer to human problems. There will always be inanimate things and other free human beings that the individual human person will never have at his own beck and call. In addition, most of the life conditions that encouraged personalism in reaction, e.g., war, poverty, and unwieldy bureaucracy, are capable of being nullified and/or solved by persevering human intelligence and determination. Personalism, if it is to harmonize with the Christian ideal of maximizing the potential of the human person made in the image of God, must include the social dimension of the human person, as exemplified in the incarnational principle of God's dealings with men as well as the individual dimension. BIBLIOGRAPHY: A. C. Knudson, *Philosophy of Personalism: A Study in the Metaphysics of Religion* (1927, repr. 1968); A. Ligneul, *Teilhard and Personalism* (1968).

[C. NEELY]

PERSONALITY. (1) In dogmatic or systematic theology, the term refers to the ontological constitutive of person as such. The meaning of "person" was developed in the centuries of Trinitarian and Christological controversy; Latin theology in discussing both the unity with distinctness of the three divine persons and the *hypostatic union used the term *persona* and also *subsistentia* (in spite of its abstract verbal form) as equivalent to the Greek, concrete term, *hypostasis*. Later *subsistentia* and *personalitas* were used as abstract terms for the quality that makes an individual substance *subsistent* and an intelligent, individual substance, a *person*. Particularly with regard to Christ the problem faced was the individuality of his human nature's being complete, yet not having its own personality, there being one hypostasis or person subsisting in divine and human nature. Thus it became necessary to distinguish between the individuality of a particular nature and its subsistence (and in the case of a particular human nature, its personality); the philosophical attempts to formulate such a distinction were both complex

and not transparently successful. (2) In moral theology personality (and the rather unappealing term "personhood") may be accepted as referring to both the proper dignity that founds the rights and equality of every human person, and the complex of individual character traits, endowments, and temperament forming part of the uniqueness of each human being. It is one of the limiting principles of a sound moral theology that its findings and determinations are generalities; particular moral judgments are the work of *prudence.

[T. C. O'BRIEN]

PERSONALITY DISORDERS, in the broadest sense, include the mental, emotional, and behavioral difficulties which the psychiatric branch of medicine treats when they become serious enough to warrant professional handling, with the exception of disorders which are demonstrably based on organic damage, e.g., mental incapacity based on brain-damaging accidents, infectious diseases, use of drugs, senility, genetic factors, etc. Thus personality disorders include the psychoses and neuroses, psychosomatic illnesses, sexual deviations, and psychopathic personalities as well as disruptions of interpersonal relations based on chronic or acute anger, hostility, bitterness, envy, jealousy and prejudice, and individual problems of excessive tension, anxiety, fear, hopelessness, and grief. The most serious of these disorders are the psychoses, which involve major disorganization of mental processes, emotional control, interpersonal relations, and productive activity. The four major classes of psychoses are: the involutional psychoses, which involve intense agitation and depression and usually occur in later middle age; the schizophrenias, which involve withdrawal from reality and inability to organize thought and feeling constructively; the manic-depressive reactions, which involve disturbing shifts of mood from exhilaration to deep depression; and paranoid reactions, which involve elaborate systems of delusion. The neuroses involve anxieties, dissociations of memory and feeling, hysterias, phobias, obsessive-compulsive behavior, and depressions. Psychosomatic illnesses comprise the ulcers, asthmas, neuralgias, insomnias, diarrheas, palpitations, etc., caused by psychological stresses. Sexual deviations include the compulsive urges toward socially unacceptable forms of sexual activity. The psychopathic personality is characterized by behavior that grossly violates social and moral codes without generating feelings of guilt or repentance. The remainder of the personality problems which disrupt interpersonal relations or cause individual distress may be classified as emotional reactions which have formed persistent and extreme emotional habit patterns beyond the person's own capacity to alter.

The relationships between personality disorders and religion fall under two general headings: the practical roles of the clergy in handling these problems and the more theoretical question of the import of personality disorders in spiritual development. As a practical matter, the clergy are often the first to know of personality problems, as their parishioners and penitents present themselves for advice and help. In fact, clergymen are credited with giving help in more cases than psychiatrists. This is partly because people respond more spontaneously to clergymen with the attitude of trust that makes therapeutic assistance effective, and partly because psychiatrists receive the incurable cases. Besides giving direct assistance to people, the clergy also play an important role in referring severe cases of disorder for appropriate professional treatment, in overcoming the false fears and shames which people feel towards psychiatry, and in supplying moral support to people undergoing treatment. There was often misunderstanding between clergy and psychiatrists in the past which prevented effective cooperation, but this is rapidly disappearing in favor of constructive collaboration. On the question of personality disorders and spiritual growth, some authors believe that spiritual growth is virtually impossible unless disorders are cured, since the disorders distort or inhibit normal human responses. Others believe that many disorders represent the breakup of behavior patterns that are preventing spiritual growth, and that the suffering entailed in all personality disorders can be invested with spiritual meaning. BIBLIOGRAPHY: F. J. Braceland and M. Stock, *Modern Psychiatry: A Handbook for Believers* (1963); O. Q. Hyder, *Christian's Handbook of Psychiatry* (1971).

[M. E. STOCK]

PERSONS, ROBERT (Parsons; 1546–1610), English Jesuit. Educated at Oxford, he was converted to Catholicism, probably at Louvain, and became a Jesuit (1575). With St. Edmund *Campion, he returned to England (1580) and worked with remarkable success as a missionary until forced to flee after Campion's arrest. He then resided chiefly at Rouen where he wrote works of controversy and organized priests for the English mission. He also participated in futile plans to engage Philip II in an invasion to depose Elizabeth (1582–83), and helped William Allen become cardinal. Sent by the order to Spain, he founded English seminaries at Valladolid and Seville, and developed his theory of the claims of the Spanish infanta as successor to Elizabeth. As rector of the English College in Rome after 1597, he restored order to that seminary, supported the Archpriest George Blackwell, and continued to promote Jesuit ascendancy in the affairs of the English Church. BIBLIOGRAPHY: L. Hicks, NCE 11:183–184, bibliog.

[J. C. WILLKE]

PERTH PRIORY, the only Carthusian monastery ever built in Scotland. The "Vale of Virtue" Charterhouse near Perth was founded in 1426 by King James I, who was later buried there with his queen. It was sacked by the Reformers under John Knox in 1559 and then suppressed. BIBLIOGRAPHY: D. E. Easson, *Medieval Religious Houses: Scotland* (1957) 73.

[L. J. MACFARLANE]

PERU, predominantly Catholic republic of South America, on the Pacific just below Ecuador; capital, Lima. About half the population is Indian, another third mestizo, and most of the remainder white. The Incas had established the center of their empire in Peru in the century before Pizarro arrived in 1532 to conquer the region for Spain, executing the Inca ruler Atahualpa for refusal to accept Spanish sovereignty and Christianity. Priests accompanying the conquerors began the work of conversion, and dioceses were established at Cuzco (1537) and Lima (1541, raised to archdiocese 1546). In 1542 Spain created the viceroyalty of Lima as its principal governing arm in South America. Although the Spaniards were troubled in the early years by wars among themselves and Indian revolts, including one led by Tupac Amaru, who would remain a symbol of resistance, Spain was able to consolidate its conquest. Indians were forced to labor in mines and on lands held by Spaniards under the *encomienda system. During the colonial period Indians were excluded from the clergy, and mestizos discouraged. Because of the presence of the viceroyalty, Peru remained loyal to Spain when the independence movement of the early 19th cent. began. But Peru achieved independence in 1821 through the efforts of outsiders, principally San Martin and Bolívar. After a period of turmoil in Peru, it was brought into a confederation by the Bolivian ruler Santa Cruz in 1836. But Chile intervened, and the federation was dissolved in 1839. The rest of the century was marked by political and economic turmoil, including the 1879–83 War of the Pacific in which Peru lost part of its territory to Chile. During this period the Catholic Church lost much of its wealth, and the number of men entering the clergy sharply declined. There is a high concentration of U.S. Catholic missionaries in Peru (over 400 in 1977), both from religious communities and from the Society of St. James, diocesan priests from Boston.

[T. EARLY]

PERUGINO (Pietro di Cristoforo Vannucci; *c.*1450–1523), important Umbrian master and teacher of Raphael, noted for his clearly articulated compositions and restrained, somewhat sentimental types with invariably oval faces gazing heavenward. Assistant to Piero della Francesca in Arezzo and cohelper of Leonardo da Vinci, according to Vasari, P. was assisted by Pinturicchio while painting murals in the Sistine Chapel (1481). Though some were destroyed, the most significant of all P.'s works remains the *Christ Giving the Keys to St. Peter* (1481–82). P.'s finest works belong to this earlier period—the utterly serene *Crucifixion* (1493–96), and the *Sposalizio* (1504). The decoration of the Collegio del Cambio (*c.*1500), the culmination of P.'s career, indicated his decline, though he painted innumerable works later: *Adoration of the Magi, Martyrdom of St. Sebastian, Descent from the Cross, Adoration of the Shepherds,* and, with assistants, many panels, scattered throughout the world. The work of this foremost Umbrian painter of the 15th cent. is characterized by symmetry and serenity, though at times affected in pose. BIBLIOGRAPHY: F. Canuti, *Il Perugino* (1931); E. Camesasca, *Tutta la pittura del Perugino* (1959).

[L. A. LEITE]

PERUZZI, BALDASSARRE (1481–1536), Italian painter and architect, from the shop of Pinturicchio. P. assisted in the decoration of S. Onofrio, Rome (1503). He probably designed the Farnesina Palace, aiding in its frescoes (1509–11), planned the coronations of Popes Leo X (1513) and Clement VII (1524), decorated the chapel in Sta. Maria della Pace (1516–17), and assisted in work on St. Peter's (1520–35). In 1532 he began work on his most important building, the Palazzo Massimo alle Colonne, completed after his death.

[M. J. DALY]

PES (also **PODATUS**), a neume in *Gregorian chant notation signifying a succession of two notes, the second higher in pitch than the first.

[A. DOHERTY]

PESCH, CHRISTIAN (1835–1925), Jesuit professor of theology at Valkenburg, Holland, from 1895; opponent of *Modernism; author of *Praelectiones dogmaticae* (9 v., 1894–97), a long-lived seminary text in theology.

[T. C. O'BRIEN]

PESCH, HEINRICH (1854–1926), German Jesuit, economist. Born in Cologne, P. entered the Society of Jesus in 1876 after having studied at the Univ. of Bonn. His personal observations of the problems of the working class in England and Belgium turned his attention to the field of economics. He studied privately for many years while publishing his earliest volumes. From 1901 to 1903 he attended the Univ. of Berlin and thereafter produced his major work, *Lehrbuch der nationale : Ökonomie* (5 v., 1905–23). P. sought alternatives to economic liberalism and socialism. His social philosophy is sometimes designated as Christian solidarism. BIBLIOGRAPHY: L. Koch, *Jesuiten-Lexikon* (2 v., 1962) 2:1406–07.

[R. H. SCHMANDT]

PESCH, TILMANN (1836–99), German Jesuit, contributor of noteworthy volumes to the series *Philosophia lacensis* (named for the Abbey Maria Laach, then in Jesuit hands) and thus to the 19th-cent. revival of Thomism: *Institutiones philosophiae naturalis* (2 v., 1880); *Institutiones logicales* (3 v., 1888–90); *Institutiones psychologicae* (3 v., 1896–98).

[T. C. O'BRIEN]

PESHITTA, the best-known Syriac version of the Bible, and the one still used by Christians whose liturgy is in this language. The name signifies "simple," and connotes either, like the word Vulgate, that this was the text in common use, or that it was the version most readily understood. Parts of the OT text go back to 1st– or 2d–cent. translations from Hebrew; but in the course of the centuries the whole OT was modified in accord with the Septuagint, and also the *deuterocanonical books were incorporated. The NT is probably from the first half of the 5th cent.; the text does not include 2 Pt, 2 and 3 Jn, Jude, or Revelation. The whole translation is manifestly the work of many hands; traditional attribution to Rabbula, bp. of Edessa is unfounded. The earliest MS dates from 464; the most important is the 6th– or 7th–cent. Codex Ambrosianus. BIBLIOGRAPHY: P. Kahle, *Cairo Geniza* (2d ed., 1959) 265–313; M. H. Goshen-Gottstein, "Prolegomena to a Critical Edition of the Peshitta," *Text and Language in Bible and Qumran* (1960) 163–204.

[T. C. O'BRIEN]

PESSIMISM, the philosophical or theological conviction that evil dominates over good. Systematically this characterizes the philosophies of A. *Schopenhauer, E. von *Hartmann, and of certain atheistic existentialists (see J.P. *SARTRE). Theologically the various forms of Manichaean *dualism are pessimistic, as is the teaching of *total depravity proposed by some Reformers; *Jansenism is pessimistic in some of its tenets. On a practical level, pessimism can be a form of inordinate depression over the reality of evil in oneself or in the world, unchecked by the positiveness of theological *hope or the joy consequent upon the reality of charity.

[T. C. O'BRIEN]

PESTALOZZI, JOHANN HEINRICH (1746–1827), Swiss social and educational reformer whose ideals and ideas have exercised a wide influence on educational theory and practice in Europe and America. Educated at Zurich Univ., he studied theology and later law, but abandoning both, turned to education as a means of bettering the masses. His religious background was Calvinist but he lost interest in dogmatic Christianity, although he stressed the importance of faith in God and a sound ethical education based on love. BIBLIOGRAPHY: H. M. Pollard, *Pioneers of Popular Education* (1957, repr. 1974); K. Silber, *Pestalozzi: The Man and His Work* (1973).

[M. B. MURPHY]

PESTIVIEN (PESTINIEN, PRESTINIEN), JEHANDE (1380–1463), French miniaturist, painter, and bookbinder. Related to J. Daret in style, and executed for Philip the Good in Dijon, P's Franco-Flemish work derives from the 15th-cent. Flemish school.

[M. J. DALY]

PÉTAIN, HENRI PHILIPPE BENONI (1856–1951), the hero of Verdun in World War I and the disgraced head of Vichy France in World War II. After the collapse of France in 1940 he set up a form of authoritarian and antidemocratic state in which the influence of the Catholic Church was strongly felt in family, youth, and educational matters. P.'s popularity decreased as he yielded to harsh German demands, gaining little in return. After 1942 he appears to have been merely a figurehead in the Vichy government. Taken to Germany during the invasion of France (1944), he returned voluntarily in 1945 to face treason charges. P. was sentenced to death; the sentence was later commuted to life imprisonment. BIBLIOGRAPHY: S. Huddleston, *Pétain: Patriot or Traitor* (1951); D. Thomson, *Two Frenchmen: Pierre Laval and Charles de Gaulle* (1951, repr. 1975).

[J. P. REID]

PETASTHE, in *Byzantine chant notation, one of the somata, or signs indicating a note one scale step higher than the previous note. Petasthe gives a warning of a coming descending note. It is rarely used.

[A. DOHERTY]

PETAU, DENIS (1583–1652), Jesuit classical scholar and theologian. His early proficiency in the classical languages enabled him to correspond with I. Casaubon in Greek. At the age of 19 he taught philosophy at the Univ. of Bourges. He became a Jesuit in 1605, was ordained in 1610, and his most important assignment was to the Collège de Clermont in Paris where he taught positive theology (1621–44). *Dogmata theologica,* planned for 10 volumes, was his most important work, but 20 years of scholarly labor resulted in the completion of only four of the planned volumes. BIBLIOGRAPHY: P. Galtier, DTC 12.1:1313–37; C. Baumgartner, LTK 8:314.

[H. DRESSLER]

PETER, ST., APOSTLE, head of the Apostles. Simon, surnamed Peter by the Lord, was a fisherman, originally of Bethsaida in Galilee (Mt 4.18–22; Mk 1.16–20; Lk 5.1–11; Jn 1.40–42), but later, apparently, living at Capernaum (Mt. 8.14). Together with his brother Andrew, he was one of the first Apostles to be called by Christ. The fact that he figures so prominently in the Gospels, and that his name comes first in the lists of the Twelve (Mt 10.2; Mk 3.16; Lk 6.14; Acts 1.13) plainly implies that he occupied a special position among the Apostles as the representative and spokesman of them all. He plays a major role in the following episodes in the Gospels:

The healing of his mother-in-law (Mt 8.14); his attempt to walk on the water (Mt 14.18–31); his request for an explanation of Jesus' sayings (Mt 15.15; Lk 12.41); the rebuke he incurs for objecting to Jesus' prediction of the Passion (Mt 16.22–28); his presence at the Transfiguration (Mt 17.1; Mk 9.2; Lk 9.28) and at the raising of Jairus' daughter (Mk 5.37; Lk 8.51) and at the agony of Gethsemane (Mt 26.37; Mk 14.33), where he is reproached by Jesus for having fallen asleep together with the rest (Mt 26.40; Mk 14.37); the temple tax paid by Jesus for both

himself and Peter (Mt 17.24–27); the preparations for the Passover (Lk 22.8); his question about forgiveness (Mt 18.21) and about the Disciples' reward (Mt 19.27; Lk 18.28); his denial that he will ever take scandal or deny Jesus (Mt 26.33–35; Mk 14.29–31; Lk 22.33–34; Jn 13.36–38); his questions about the fig-tree (Mk 11.21) and (together with James, John, and Andrew) about the second coming (Mk 13.3); the Disciples' pursuit of Jesus into the desert (Mk 1.36); the healing of the hemorrhagic woman (Lk 8.45); the washing of the Disciples' feet (Jn 13.6–9); the Last Supper, where it is Peter who asks who will betray Jesus (Jn 13.24); the cutting off of Malchus' ear (Jn 18.10); the news of the Resurrection (Mk 16.7); the arrival at the empty tomb (Jn 20.2–10).

The supremely important gospel texts bearing upon Peter's authority in the early Church are Mt 16.16–18 and Jn 21.15–19. With regard to the first, it is disputed whether the "rock" on which the Church is to be built is Peter himself or the faith in virtue of which he has just acknowledged Jesus as Christ and Son of God. But it is more natural, in view of the personal name Peter, a masculine form of the word meaning rock, to regard Peter himself as the foundation. At the same time the authority symbolized by "the keys of the kingdom of heaven" is conferred, and also the power of "binding and loosing," i.e., of imposing decisions in God's name, though the precise nature and extent of this authority is unspecified. What is clear is that Peter is set apart from the rest as having some kind of supreme authority which they do not share, and on which the future stability and endurance of the Church as a whole depends to an extent not yet defined. The significance of Jesus' commission to Peter in Jn 21.15–19 is rather clearer. Jesus is handing on his own office of shepherd (cf. Jn 10.11) to Peter. Henceforward he is to care for the faithful and "feed" them, doing for them what the Good Shepherd has already done, up to and including the laying down of his life (Jn 21.18–19).

The references in Acts 1–12 bear unambiguous witness to the fact that Peter was the leader of the first Christian community. He presides over the election of Judas' successor among the Twelve (1.15–26); appears as the spokesman and leader of the community at Pentecost (Acts 2), before the Jews (Acts 3, 4, 5.29), in the episode of Ananias and Sapphira (5.1–11), and in rejecting Simon Magus (8.14–24). He also appears to exercise a decisive influence in the decisions of the Council of Jerusalem (15.7–11). Paul too refers to him in a manner that attests his importance as leader (1 Cor 1.12; 3.22; 15.5). The fact remains that in the Council of Jerusalem (Acts ch. 15) and at Antioch (Gal 2.11–14) a degree of authority is ascribed to James which seems, in effect, to make him the leader of the Church at Jerusalem. It may be, therefore, that with the expansion of the early Church, and possibly with the departure of Peter himself to Rome, James assumed the leadership of the Church at Jerusalem while Peter retained the overall primacy based on the commission he had received from Jesus. The tradition that he ended his life as a martyr at Rome and was buried there is so strong, so early, and so well supported by archeological evidence that only the most skeptical or the most prejudiced can still reject it. The tradition that Peter died a martyr's death is adumbrated in Jn 21.18–19, but neither the NT nor any well-grounded tradition tells us anything of the manner in which he died. BIBLIOGRAPHY: O. Cullmann, *Peter, Disciple, Apostle and Martyr* (tr. F. V. Filson, 2d ed., 1962); A. Rimoldi, *L'apostolo S. Pietro, fondamento della chiesa . . . nella chiesa primitiva dalle origini al concilio di Calcedonia* (1958); P. Benoit, "La Primauté de S. Pierre selon le Nouveau Testament" and "S. Pierre d'après O. Cullmann," *Exégèse et Théologie* 2 (1961) 250–308; A. Penna et al., BiblSanct 10:588–650; D. W. O'Connor, *Peter in Rome: The Literary, Liturgical and Archeological Evidence* (1969).

[D. J. BOURKE]

PETER III (1240–86), **KING OF ARAGON** from 1276, Peter II of Catalonia. He continued James I's expansionism. Troubadour, art patron, Crusader in Spain and N Africa, he conquered Sicily (beginning the 20-year Sicilian Vespers War), dominated the W Mediterranean, and destroyed France's Crusade into Aragon. BIBLIOGRAPHY: R. I. Burns, NCE 11:205, bibliog.

[R. I. BURNS]

PETER THE GREAT (1672–1725), **CZAR OF RUSSIA** from 1682. He is identified with the wholesale cultural and technological reforms made during his reign and for changing Russia into a modern state. He strove for Europeanization, and his open door policy to the West included the promotion of education, importation of Western technicians, introduction of scientific textbooks, reforms in the army, formation of a navy, the development of an industrial and trade base, and the complete reorganization of government service. These efforts were largely bound up with his desire for a strong and efficient State and to strengthen Russia for the successful prosecution of its war with Sweden. Though the move for modernization and piecemeal borrowing from the West had an almost century-long tradition, the ruthlessness of the Czar's enforcement of his policies precipitated a reaction from the masses, esp. the peasants who resented Western wearing apparel and the order to shave off their beards. The abolishment of the patriarchate and gradual secularization of the Orthodox Church also met with resistance. BIBLIOGRAPHY: V. Klyuchevsky, *Peter the Great* (tr. L. Archibald, 1958); J. Cracraft, *Church Reform of Peter the Great* (1971).

[D. DIRSCHERL]

PETER ACONTATO, BL. (1115–80), a noble Venetian who became a Benedictine monk at S. Giorgio, Venice, after the death of his wife. His life was marked by great charity and devotion; his cultus was approved by Clement VIII. Since the early 19th cent., P.'s relics have been preserved in the church of S. Trovaso, Venice. BIBLIOGRAPHY: AS Sept. 6:651–655.

PETER OF AILLY (De Alliaco; 1350–1420), French theologian, churchman, a leading figure in the Great Western Schism. As a student at Paris his mind was formed esp. by the writings of *William of Ockham and *Roger Bacon. He became master of arts in 1368, doctor in theology in 1381, and chancellor of the university in 1389. His influential commentary on the *Sentences* of Peter Lombard was developed from his lectures. Jean *Gerson was his disciple and friend. Beginning in 1379, P. was active in the political and ecclesiastical aspects of the Great Western Schism, including the question of French obedience to the various rival claimants to the papacy. He also became wealthy through a plurality of benefices conferred by Charles VI of France, whom he served as chaplain and confessor. Benedict XIII appointed him bp. of Le Puy in 1395, then abp. of Cambrai in 1397. The antipope John XXIII in 1412 made him a cardinal, as well as administrator of the dioceses of Limoges and Orange. After the Council of Constance, Martin V appointed him legate to Avignon.

P.'s philosophical and theological writings were highly regarded by the leading nominalists of the 15th and 16th cent.; some of his positions were favorably cited by 18th-cent. rationalists. A copy of his treatise *Imago mundi*, which discussed the possibility of the earth's being spherical, was possessed by Christopher Columbus. P.'s principal treatise, however, was the *Tractatus de reformatione ecclesiae*, written in 1403 as part of a larger work, *De materia concilii generalis*, but not published until 1416. The work reflects his incessant activity to achieve ecclesiastical unity through moderation and compromise. As a temporizing means to heal the Western Schism he strongly advocated the superiority of a general council over the pope. His conciliarist thought was dominant at the Council of Constance, in which he took a leading part; it also made him a prime authority for Gallicanists, and a favorite author of Martin Luther. Yet some of the disciplinary measures P. proposed in the treatise on the reformation of the Church were incorporated into the reform decrees of the Council of Trent. BIBLIOGRAPHY: A. Emmen, NCE 11:208, bibliog.

[T. C. O'BRIEN]

PETER OF ALCÁNTARA, ST. (1499–1562), Spanish mystic and reformer. After joining the Franciscans of the Strict Observance, he was ordained a priest and was promoted to various offices in his province and order. He fostered the strictest reform of the order, whose adherents, known as Alcantarines, continued to exist as one of the four branches of the Observants until all were united in 1897. A man of the greatest austerity and mortification, he was a renowned mission preacher, confessor and spiritual director of St. Teresa of Avila, whom he advised, encouraged, and supported in her reform of the Carmelites. He wrote a treatise on prayer and meditation (*Tratado de la Oración y Meditación*) that became very popular and greatly influenced St. Francis de Sales. Canonized in 1669, he is the patron saint of Brazil. BIBLIOGRAPHY: E. A. Peers, *Studies of the Spanish Mystics* (v. 2, 1930).

[D. A. MCGUCKIN]

PETER OF ALEXANDRIA, ST. (d. *c*.311), bp., martyr. P., who had been director of the catechetical school of Alexandria, was made bp. (*c*.300) in succession to *Theonas just before the outbreak of the persecution of Diocletian. He followed a policy of leniency with regard to the lapsed, i.e., those who apostatized during the persecution. During the second phase of the persecution, while P. was in hiding, Bp. Meletius of Lycopolis, who favored a more stringent policy toward the lapsed, came to Alexandria and usurped the rights of P. by ordaining and otherwise assuming authority as bp. of Alexandria. Meletius was deposed, but his followers persisted for centuries as a ''Church of the Martyrs.'' After a final brief respite in the persecution, P. was seized and martyred under Maximinus Daia. In his festal letter of 306, P. outlined his policy on the lapsed in 14 canons. A number of doctrinal treatises are mentioned by ancient authors, but of these only fragments have survived. Works: PG 18:449–522. BIBLIOGRAPHY: Butler 4:423–424; Quasten 2:113–118.

[R. B. ENO]

PETER OF ANAGNI, ST. (1030 or 1035–1105), bp. and crusader. A Benedictine from Salerno, he became a papal chaplain, and in 1062 Pope Alexander II made him bp. of Anagni. In 1071 he was sent as the papal representative to the Byzantine Emperor Michael Ducas. He interrupted the reconstruction of his cathedral of Anagni to take part in the First Crusade as a member of the expedition led by Bohemund I. After the capture of Jerusalem he retired to Salerno and died there. His remains were later translated to Anagni. He was canonized in 1110. BIBLIOGRAPHY: Baudot-Chaussin 8:59–60; Zimmermann 2:530; V. Fenicchia, BiblSanct 10:663–665.

[M. R. P. MCGUIRE]

PETER OF APAMEA (6th cent.), Monophysite bp. of Apamea in Syria. A disciple of Severus of Antioch, he was made a metropolitan of Apamea, but was deposed in 518. In 535 he accompanied Severus to Constantinople at the invitation of the Empress Theodora. However, both were condemned in the synod held the following year by the Patriarch Mennas. In a letter from the Emperor Justinian to Mennas, Peter along with Anthimus, the deposed patriarch of Constantinople, Severus of Antioch, and the monk Zooras were all anathematized and banished from the capital and all major cities of the Empire. Nothing more is known about him. BIBLIOGRAPHY: P. Roche, NCE 11:209–210; Martin 4:427, 452.

[M. R. P. MCGUIRE]

PETER OF AQUILA (1275–1361), Franciscan theologian and bishop. P. earned a degree in theology at Paris, served as teacher, provincial, and bishop. He is best known, however, for the summary he wrote of the major work of Duns Scotus in which he calls himself *Scotellus*. BIBLIOGRAPHY: A. Teetaert, DTC 14.2:1730–33; V. Heynck, LTK 8:347–348.

[H. DRESSLER]

PETER OF ARAGON, BL. (1305–81), Franciscan visionary, the son of James II of Aragon and Blanche, the sister of Charles II of Naples. In 1331 he married Joan of Foix. Four sons and a daughter were born of this union. Peter held a number of important offices in the Kingdom of Aragon before his wife's death in 1358. He then entered the Franciscan Order. In a vision Christ instructed him to urge Urban V to return from Avignon to Rome. The Pope made this move in 1370, but it is not known how much Peter's admonitions influenced his decision to do so. Immediately after his death, Peter became the object of popular veneration. BIBLIOGRAPHY: A. M. de Barcelona, ''El Infante Frey Pedro de Aragón,'' *Estudios Franciscanos* 11 (1913) 132–136; 12 (1914), 129–141, 434–438; 13 (1914) 204–215; 14 (1915) 205–218; 15 (1915) 58–65; G. M. Pou y Martí, *Visionarios, beguinos y fraticelos catalanes* (1930) 308–397; Sbaralea 2 (1921) 323.

[C. J. LYNCH]

PETER ARBUÉS, ST. (1440–85), Augustinian canon, inquisitor. He studied theology and law at Bologna and became a Canon Regular of St. Augustine at Saragossa in 1474. At the request of Ferdinand VII he was made first inquisitor for Aragon (1484) in the newly established Spanish Inquisition. His zeal in carrying out his duties and the executions that followed soon occasioned his assassination. BIBLIOGRAPHY: H. Platelle, BiblSanct 10:665–666.

[R. I. BURNS]

PETER ARMENGOL, BL. (1238?–1304?), Mercedarian with a wide cult in Catalonia, prayed to for cures and rain. Questionable 17th-cent. sources for his vita describe him as a descendant of the family of the counts of Urgel, who gave up banditry to join the Mercedarians (1258) and ransom captives in North Africa, where the Blessed Virgin miraculously saved him from death by hanging. His immemorial cult was confirmed in 1686. BIBLIOGRAPHY: Butler 2:174–175.

[E. P. COLBERT]

PETER AUREOLI (*c*.1280–1322), French Franciscan theologian, known as *Doctor facundus* and *Doctor in-*

geniosus. He taught at Bologna, 1312–14; at Toulouse, 1314–16; at Paris, 1316–18. He was elected provincial of the Franciscans of Aquitaine in 1320, was consecrated abp. of Aix-en-Provence in 1321. P.'s chief works included an important treatise defending the Immaculate Conception, composed in 1314 (modern ed., 1904), and a commentary on the *Sentences* of Peter Lombard, first written in 1316–18, and revised in 1318–19. He was a thinker of great subtlety, independent and critical toward other scholastics, and skeptical about the power of human reason. BIBLIOGRAPHY: *Peter Aureoli: Scriptum super primum Sententiarum* (ed. E. M. Buytaert, 2 v., 1953).

[T. C. O'BRIEN]

PETER OF AUVERGNE (Alvernia; *c.*1245–1304), secular master at the Univ. of Paris, bp. of Clermont from 1302. P. is regarded as one of the early admirers of the writings of St. Thomas Aquinas, whose unfinished commentaries on Aristotle's *Politics, Meteora,* and *De coelo et mundo,* he completed. Many points in his own philosophical positions, however, were at variance with the thought of St. Thomas. BIBLIOGRAPHY: A. P. Monahan, NCE 11:211–212.

[T. C. O'BRIEN]

PETER OF BAVARIA, BL. (Peter of Clairvaux; d. 1154), Cistercian monk and hermit. Son of Duke Henry the Black of Bavaria, P. became a Cistercian in 1125 at Morimond and was later at Clairvaux under Bernard. In 1143 he received permission to go to the Holy Land and settle there as a hermit. When the Islamic peril increased with the unhappy outcome of the Second Crusade, he went to Italy, intending to return to Clairvaux, but he died in Apulia. He was chiefly venerated in S Italy; his relics are in the cathedral of Molfetta. BIBLIOGRAPHY: A. Dietrich, "Der Selige Konrad von Bayern," serial in *Cistercienser-Chronik,* 26 (1914); Butler 1:337–338; B. Bedini, BiblSanct 4:200–201.

PETER OF BERGAMO (d. 1482), Dominican theologian, compiler of the *Tabula aurea* (1475), a three–part index of the writings of St. Thomas Aquinas. P. was a professor of theology at Bologna. The *Tabula aurea* comprises an index to the principal terms in St. Thomas's writings, a concordance of apparently antithetical passages, and an index to biblical texts cited. The *Tabula aurea* as published in the Piana edition (1570) of Aquinas's works was reprinted in 1960.

[T. C. O'BRIEN]

PETER OF BLOIS (*c.*1135–*c.*1212), English humanist and political thinker. He studied at Tours, Bologna, and Paris, served as tutor to King William II of Sicily, then returned to France, and finally moved to England to serve under Henry II. He was appointed archdeacon at Bath in 1175, and in 1202 he was made archdeacon of London, served as chancellor or secretary to two abps. of Canterbury, as well as counselor and special ambassador for Henry II and later (1191–95) as secretary to Queen Eleanor. He was a pupil and friend of John of Salisbury and wrote poems, sermons, satires, political tracts, and numerous letters. Works: *Opera omnia* (ed. J. A. Giles, 1847). BIBLIOGRAPHY: E. J. Kealery, NCE 11:212 bibliog.

[V. BULLOUGH]

PETER OF BRUYS (d. between 1126 and 1133), priest, founder of the sect of Petrobrusians. A zealous preacher of gospel poverty, P. was burned by a French mob at St. Gilles in Languedoc for his desecration of the cross, an object he held unworthy of veneration. P. also allegedly attacked the church hierarchy and the efficacy of the sacraments, spurned the clergy, and believed that only the Gospels should be included in the Bible. He disapproved of all ceremonies and outward forms, even the building of churches, rejected art, and ridiculed hymns. Upon his death many of his followers joined Henry of Lausanne. BIBLIOGRAPHY: E. W. McDonnell, NCE 11:212.

[V. BULLOUGH]

PETER OF CANDIA, see ALEXANDER V, ANTIPOPE.

PETER CANTOR (d. 1197), theologian at the cathedral school of Paris and from 1184 cantor of the cathedral. His works included treatises on dogmatic, moral, and canonical subjects, as well as biblical glosses. Only one work was published, *Verbum abbreviatum* called also *Summa de virtutibus* (1693). He was also a renowned preacher.

[T. C. O'BRIEN]

PETER OF CASTELNAU, BL. (d. 1208), legate, martyr. He became a Cistercian at Fontfroide abbey in 1202. Innocent III appointed him papal legate to Languedoc (1199) to deal with the Albigensian problem. He was responsible for the recanting of heresy by Raymond VI of Toulouse who later lapsed, was excommunicated by P. and then submitted. On Jan. 15 a henchman of Raymond's assassinated Peter. This led to Simon de Montfort's Crusade against the Albigensians. BIBLIOGRAPHY: AS March 1:409–415.

[J. J. SMITH]

PETER OF CELLE (*c.*1115–83), abbot, bp. of Chartres (1181). He introduced the Cluniac reform as abbot at Moutier-la-Celle (near Troyes, NW France) and at Reims. His letters and other writings were treasured for their literary style and their teaching on the ideals of Christian spirituality. BIBLIOGRAPHY: J. Leclercq, *La Spiritualité de Pierre de Celle 1115–1183* (1946).

PETER OF CHELCIĆ (*c.*1390–*c.*1460), Czech writer and religious leader whose ideas inspired those *Hussites who were dissatisfied with the *Utraquists to found the *Unitas Fratrum in 1457. Though of only limited academic training, P. read *Wycliffe and *Hus and went beyond them in rejecting the authority of the Church, substituting for it the NT, esp. the Sermon on the Mount. He proposed as an ideal a Church divorced from all temporalities. He anticipated the Anabaptists in his pacifism, *nonresistance, and rejection of oaths. The most complete summary of his thought is *Net of Faith,* written in 1440 and first printed in 1520. BIBLIOGRAPHY: P. Brock, *Unity of Czech Brethren* (1957).

[J. R. WEINLICK]

PETER CHRYSOLOGUS, ST. (*c.*400–*c.*450), bp. of Ravenna, then the imperial capital of the West, from *c.*431. A native of Imola (Italy), he was, during his ecclesiastical career, a close friend of Popes *Sixtus III and *Leo the Great, and of Germanus of Auxerre. He also enjoyed the favor of the Emperor Valentinian III and of Galla Placidia who aided him materially in his building program. There exists a collection of 183 homilies attributed to him. P. was primarily a preacher concerned more with matters of a practical and moral nature, and the theological depth of his homilies is not great. They are, however, a valuable source of information on the daily life of the people and of the survival of pagan customs in N Italy at that time. P.'s support was sought by *Theodoret of Cyr and *Eutyches. In his response to the latter, P. insisted upon the necessity of adhering to the teaching of the bp. of Rome. The title Chrysologus was first applied to P. in the 7th cent. in an infelicitous attempt to make him the Western equivalent of *John Chrysostom. He was proclaimed a Doctor of the Church by Benedict XIII in 1729. BIBLIOGRAPHY: Butler 4:485–486; G. Lucchesi, EncCatt 9:1433–35; A. Olivar, BiblSanct 10:685–691.

[R. B. ENO]

PETER OF CLAIRVAUX, SEE PETER OF BAVARIA, BL.

PETER CLAVER, ST., SEE CLAVER, PETER, ST.

PETER COMESTOR (*c.*1100–*c.*1180), author of *Historia scholastica,* a work that became the accepted bible history for the Middle Ages. P. was chancellor of the cathedral school of Paris, where he also lectured in theology; he became a canon regular at the abbey of St. Victor in 1169. His other writings included scriptural commentaries and a treatise on the sacraments.

[T. C. O'BRIEN]

PETER CRISCI OF FOLIGNO, BL. (d. 1323), Franciscan tertiary. The son of wealthy parents, after a worldly youthful career, he became at 30 a hermit at Pesaro where he built the church of Sta. Maria di Montegranaro. As a tertiary he spent his days in the active apostolate in the environs of Foligno, in whose cathedral church he is buried.

His cult was approved by Urban VI in 1385. BIBLIOGRAPHY: M. F. Pulignani, AnalBoll 8:358–369; M. Sensi, BiblSanct 10:821–823.

[J. J. SMITH]

PETER DAMIAN, ST. (1007–72), monk, cardinal, leading forerunner of the Hildebrandine reform, Doctor of the Church. Educated at Ravenna, Parma, Modena, and Faenza, P. taught at Ravenna and was ordained priest before entering the monastic hermitage at Fonte Avellana (1035). As prior of that community he reorganized its life with regulations embodying the ideals of both SS. Benedict and Romuald. As cardinal bishop of Ostia (from 1057) he served the Church for a quarter of a century in synodal work, diplomatic missions, and with his writings, achieving a great renown for his learning, zeal, and integrity. He fought vigorously against the evils of the day, upholding clerical celibacy and struggling against simony (although his *Liber gratissimus* defended the validity of orders conferred gratis by simonists, and as legate to Milan he reinstated erring priests who undertook to live continently). His *Liber gomorrhianus,* excoriating the clergy of evil life, made him many enemies. He upheld the primacy of Rome at Milan (1059–60) in the conflict between the abp. and the Patarines, and during the schism of the antipope Honorius II he defended the interests of Alexander II in his *Disceptatio synodalis*. He was one of the greatest medieval Latin stylists; his prolific writings include letters, sermons, vitae, treatises, and minor works in prose and verse. He was a man of great vehemence, quick to attempt the heroic himself and capable of inspiring others to follow his example. His zeal for asceticism makes him appear an austere and stern figure. He sometimes went to extremes in fasting and vigils, as he himself recognized. His *De laude flagellorum* encouraging the use of the discipline was much read during the Middle Ages and exerted a great influence on ascetical practice for many centuries, although its authority, great because of P.'s reputation, was sometimes abused in later times to support practices of questionable value. Works: PL 144, 145. BIBLIOGRAPHY: O. J. Blum, *St. Peter Damian: His Teaching on the Spiritual Life* (1947).

[M. S. TANEY]

PETER THE DEACON OF MONTE CASSINO (*c.*1107–52), librarian, chronicler, and forger. According to the autobiographical sections of his chronicle of Monte Cassino, P went to the abbey as a 5-year-old oblate and remained there until exiled by Abbot Seniorectus in 1128. Recalled two years later, he was appointed librarian and placed in charge of compiling the chartulary of the monastery, the *Registrum Petri Diaconi*. A few years later he was assigned to defend the position of the monastery during the schism (it had favored the antipope, Anacletus II) before the Emperor Lothair III, an adherent of Innocent II. P.'s extant writings are of two main types: hagiographical writings telling the story of great Benedictines, particularly those of

Monte Cassino, and a chronicle of Monte Cassino. Even today it is difficult to separate the true from the false in the work of this consummate forger who interpolated his own inventions into the works of older writers or ascribed them to well-known authorities. BIBLIOGRAPHY: E. Caspar, *Petrus Diaconus und die Monte Cassineser Fälschungen* (1909), H. Bloch, NCE 11:215–216.

[M. A. WINKELMANN]

PETER THE DEACON OF ROME, BL. (d. *c.*605), friend and fellow student of Pope Gregory I. After entering Gregory's monastery of St. Andrew's in Rome, he traveled to Sicily at the Pope's request. As Gregory's subdeacon he was charged with the temporalities of the Roman Church. Created cardinal deacon, he appears in the *Dialogues* as the Pope's constant companion. Peter is cited as attesting to various marvels that occurred during Gregory's life, but the accounts are late and legendary. Since 1480 his remains have rested in Salussola, Italy. BIBLIOGRAPHY: O. J. Blum, NCE 11:216.

[O. J. BLUM]

PETER OF DIEBURG (*c.*1420–1494), chronicler. P. was a pious man who observed the rule of the Brethren of the Common Life at Hildesheim. He wrote the Latin chronicles of the Brethren, a dependable account which begins with the year of their foundation, 1440, at Hildesheim. After joining the Brethren, he helped in the kitchen, then became a copyist, priest, and finally, rector. This office he held until his death, administering the rule in strict discipline. During his term he founded a *domus scolarium* for the moral training of candidates for the Brethren as well as other students, all of whom continued their studies away from the *domus*. He also established new houses of the Brethren at Lüchtenhof, Magdeburg (1482), and Berlicum (1483). BIBLIOGRAPHY: W. J. Alberts, NCE 11:216.

[M. E. DUFFY]

PETER OF FOSSOMBRONE, see ANGELUS CLARENUS.

PETER THE FULLER (d. 488), *Monophysite, usurper of the patriarchate of Antioch. P. is alleged to have joined the monastery of Acoemetae at Constantinople, exercising the trade from which he took his name. He was expelled for his tenacious Monophysite views and opposition to *Chalcedon. Aligning himself with the *Apollinarians at Antioch, through the patronage of the Emperor Zeno the Isaurian, P. had himself consecrated bp. and installed over the rightful patriarch of Antioch, Martyrius (470). Almost immediately deposed, P. regained the patriarchate in 475; ousted again in 477, he recaptured it once more in 482 after signing the *Henoticon of Zeno and retained power to his death. P.'s chief renown lies in the liturgical innovations he introduced to further the Monophysite cause. He inserted into the *Trisagion, the phrase "he was crucified for us"; it became a war cry of all anti-Chalcedonians, for despite its

innocent sound, it was intended to express one nature in Christ. *Theodore the Lector, the only historical source on P., also states that P. introduced the singing of the *Nicean Creed at the Eucharistic Liturgy (as a proclamation of Monophysite adherence to Nicea), the blessing of the *chrism, and the commemoration of the *Theotokos at every service. BIBLIOGRAPHY: Theodore Lector, PG 86 1:175–178; G. Fritz, DTC 12:1933–35.

[T. C. O'BRIEN]

PETER GEREMIA, BL. (1381–1452), Italian-born Dominican preacher and theologian. After receiving a doctor of law degree from Bologna, he joined the Dominicans. An outstanding preacher, he was a leader in reform movements of the day. He attended the Council of Florence in 1439 and was appointed apostolic visitor to Sicily by Pope Eugene IV.

[M. A. MCFADDEN]

PETER GONZÁLEZ, BL. (before 1190–1246), Spanish Dominican. A worldly noble and canon of Palencia, he became a celebrated Dominican preacher, chaplain to King Ferdinand III of Castile, Crusade-enthusiast, and missioner, esp. in Galicia and along the coast. Patron of sailors, he is sometimes called St. Elmo through confusion with St. Erasmus. NCE errs in listing P. as a saint and in giving 1741 as the date of canonization; in that year Benedict XIV confirmed his cult as a *beatus* (it dated from a 1254 approval). BIBLIOGRAPHY: Butler 2:94–95; A. Silli, BiblSanct 7:108–109.

[R. I. BURNS]

PETER GROSSOLANO (d. 1117), theologian and bp. of Savona, afterwards of Milan. His attempts at effecting reunion between the Churches of Rome and Byzantium were ill-fated, perhaps because of his somewhat tactless approach to the divisive questions of the *filioque* and of the use of unleavened bread in the Liturgy. In 1116 he was obliged by the Council of the Lateran to resign the See of Milan because of his uncanonical transfer from Savona. He refused to return to Savona and retired to the monastery of St. Sabas in Rome. BIBLIOGRAPHY: PL 162:1005–15; PL 173:1447–56; PG 127:909–919; V. Grumel, DTC (1939) 12:2.

[W. A. JURGENS]

PETER THE HERMIT (Peter the Little; *c.*1050–1115), preacher of the First Crusade. Born probably near Amiens, he was known by his contemporaries as "Little Peter," the surname hermit came because of the hermit's cape he wore. Before the Council of Clermont (1095), he tried to make the pilgrimage to Jerusalem but was maltreated by the Turks and turned back. After Clermont, he preached, journeying from Berry to Cologne, and gathered 15,000 followers. His success was due in part to his preaching, though social and economic insecurity and apocalyptic teaching were factors. P. led the "People's Crusade" from Cologne with 20,000 in 1096. At Civetot most were killed by Turks while P. had gone to Constantinople for help. P. gathered the survivors and joined Godfrey of Bouillon's army. During the siege of Antioch in 1098, he made an unsuccessful attempt to escape. He survived this dishonor and later became prior of the Augustine monastery at Neufmoutier (Huy) which he helped to found. BIBLIOGRAPHY: H. Hagenmeyer, *Peter der Eremite* (1879); Y. Le Febvre *Pierre l' Ermite et la croisade* (1946).

[N. F. GAUGHAN]

PETER IGNEUS, BL. (d. 1089), cardinal bishop of Albano. A member of the Vallombrosan Order, P. was given the name Igneus in 1068 because he passed unharmed through fire in order to prove Pietro di Pavia, bp. of Florence, guilty of simony. He was made cardinal bishop of suburbicarian Albano in 1074. His cult was approved in 1673. BIBLIOGRAPHY: AS July 3 (1867) 297–298, 330–331.

[W. A. JURGENS]

PETER OF IRELAND (*c.*1200–after 1260), Irish philosopher. P. taught philosophy at Naples, where Thomas Aquinas was one of his pupils. He is the author of unpublished commentaries on works of Aristotle and on Porphyry's *Isagoge*. His one published work suggests that he was influenced by Averroës. BIBLIOGRAPHY: M. B. Crowe, *Studies* 45 (1956) 443–456.

[L. E. BOYLE]

PETER OF JERUSALEM, patriarch of Jerusalem (524–552). His career illustrates the difficulty encountered even by those who tried to avoid both heresy and quarrels, in surviving the ecclesiastical storms of the times. Through legates he confirmed (536) the deposing of Anthimus as patriarch of Constantinople. He was part of the synod of Gaza (539) which deposed the patriarch Paul of Alexandria. He welcomed the Roman deacon and future pope Pelagius to Jerusalem and supplied him with information leading to the condemnation of Origen by the Emperor Justinian (543). Later P. was forced to sign the Emperor's edict against the *Three Chapters (544). During his last years, the Origenist monks of Palestine seem to have gained the upper hand over him despite his best efforts.

[E. J. DILLON]

PETER JOHN OLIVI (1248–98), Franciscan philosopher and theologian, a leader of the *Spirituals. P. was born at Sérignan in Languedoc. Soon after his entrance into the Friars Minor he became associated with the rigorist party within the order. He studied at Paris from 1267 until 1273 when he was appointed lector at Montpellier. About 1275 he became intellectual leader of the Spirituals of Provence and involved himself in that party's struggle with the *Communitas*. In 1279 he was requested to submit a memorandum on Franciscan poverty for the guidance of a papal commission. While his views on this subject were much less extreme than those of the Italian Spirituals, his polemical writings on the *usus pauper* still led to his being accused of heresy at the general chapter of the order in 1282. The theological commission appointed to examine his writings found 34 propositions worthy of censure, and the minister general ordered his works withdrawn from circulation. But at the chapter of 1287 P.'s orthodoxy was vindicated, and the new general, Matthew of Aquasparta, appointed him lector at Santa Croce in Florence. He was transferred to Montpellier in 1289, where he occupied the same post until 1292, when he was called to the general chapter at Paris to explain his doctrine of the *usus pauper*. He escaped censure by tactical evasion. His last years were spent at Narbonne. P.'s writings played a part in the *poverty controversy even after his death. The Council of Vienne condemned three of his opinions in 1311. The Franciscan general chapter of 1319 forbade circulation of his writings, and in 1326 John XXII condemned his commentary on the Apocalypse. BIBLIOGRAPHY: D. Douie, *Nature and Effects of the Heresy of the Fraticelli* (1932); G. Gál, NCE 11:219–220, esp. for bibliog.; M. Lambert, *Franciscan Poverty. The Doctrine of the Absolute Poverty of Christ and the Apostles in the Franciscan Order, 1210–1323* (1961); C. Parte, "Peter John Olivi: Historical and Doctrinal Study," Franciscan Studies 20 (1960) 215–296.

[C. J. LYNCH]

PETER OF JULLY, BL. (d. 1136), Cistercian monk of Molesme. Although English by birth and descent, P. is always associated with Jully in Champagne where his last years were spent. He made a pilgrimage to Rome with St. Stephen Harding. On the return journey as they passed through Burgundy they stayed at the Cistercian abbey of Molesme, and Stephen remained; later P. received the habit there and perhaps holy orders. Bl. Humbelina, St. Bernard's sister, requested P. to be chaplain for the convent at Jully-les-Nonnains, which office he held until death. BIBLIOGRAPHY: V. Gellhaus, NCE 11:220; Butler 2:622; G. Mathon, BiblSanct 10:704.

[M. C. BRADLEY]

PETER OF LAODICEA (7th or 8th cent.), a Greek author supposed to have commented upon the Gospels. Practically nothing is known of him. In an 11th-cent. MS of gospel catenae, P. is credited with a commentary on the Gospel of Matthew. In several MSS of the 12th and 14th cent., passages of comments on all four Gospels are attributed to him, but falsely, since the comments in question are drawn from other authors. The one surviving work known with certainty to be P.'s is an explanation of the Lord's Prayer (PG 86.2:3321–36). BIBLIOGRAPHY: Altaner 626; ODCC 1054; J. Reuss, LTK 8:367.

[R. B. ENO]

PETER OF LA PALU (Paludanus; *c.*1277–1342), French Dominican theologian and churchman. Successor of

*Durandus of Saint-Pourçain at Paris (1309), P. in 1313 served on the Dominican commission to censure his works. He also defended the rights of mendicants against John of Pouilly (1318–21), participated in the examination of *Peter John Olivi's doctrine, and of John XXII's teaching on the beatific vision (1333). He served the papacy in many diplomatic missions, and as patriarch of Jerusalem (1329) sought to negotiate the return of the holy places by the Sultan of Egypt. He wrote works on ecclesiology, on moral questions, and a biblical commentary. He ardently defended Thomism, but was not well acquainted with St. Thomas Aquinas's works. BIBLIOGRAPHY: J. A. Weisheipl, NCE 11:220–221.

[T. C. O'BRIEN]

PETER LOMBARD (c.1095–1160), author of the *Book of Sentences,* the standard medieval theological text; the ''Master of the Sentences.'' A native of Lombardy in Italy, hence his name, he visited Paris c.1134, heard the lectures of Hugh of St. Victor, and remained as master at the cathedral school at Notre Dame. By 1143 he was a theologian of renown. His glosses on the Psalter and on the Letters of St. Paul, both of which served to prepare for his major work, date from his earlier years in Paris. The *Sentences,* developed in connection with his teaching, took final form c.1157–58. P., who had been a canon of Notre Dame since 1144, was elected bp. of Paris in 1159, a year before his death. The *Libri IV Sententiarum* received immediate and widespread acceptance; it satisfied the desire for a systematic summary of all theology that presented a comparative study and analysis of scriptural and patristic authorities, and that made a restrained use of dialectic. The orthodoxy of the *Sentences* on the Trinity was affirmed by the Council of the Lateran IV in 1215 (D 803–804). The *Sentences* became a standard text in the academic curriculum after 1222 when Alexander of Hales adopted it for his own course at the Univ. of Paris. Most of the major theologians of the next 3 cent. wrote commentaries on the *Sentences.* P. based his division of theology on a text of St. Augustine's *De doctrina christiana.* The fundamental division of subject matter is into *res* (realities) and *signa* (signs). The *res* are God in his unity and Trinity (Book 1); the Creation, esp. man and sin (Book 2); the Redemption by the Word Incarnate (Book 3); the *signa* are the sacraments, in connection with which death, judgment, heaven, and hell are considered (Book 4). The prologue declares P.'s intention to set out an orderly compilation of theological tradition; the contents rely heavily on St. Augustine, but other late Fathers and St. John Damascene are also included, as are some contemporaries, esp. Hugh of St. Victor. Although opposed to an exclusive reliance on dialectics, P. made excellent use of the methodological principles of *Abelard. While P.'s teaching was superficial in some areas and was rejected on specific points by other theologians, the *Sentences* set a high standard for the organization and method of theology. Two volumes of a modern critical edition were issued at Quarac-

chi, Italy, in 1970; two more are in preparation. BIBLIOGRA-PHY: P. Delhaye, *Pierre Lombard, sa vie, ses oeuvres, sa morale* (1961); I. Brady, NCE 11:221–222; *idem,* EncPhil 6:124–125, bibliog.

[T. C. O'BRIEN]

PETER OF LUXEMBURG, BL. (1369–87), ecclesiastic. Sixth son of Guy of Luxemburg, Count of Ligny, P. was orphaned at 4 and sent at 10 to Paris for studies. Here he became friends with Peter d'Ailly, his teacher at the College of Navarre. The antipope, Clement VII of Avignon, tried to win favor with P.'s powerful relatives by naming him canon at Notre Dame at 15, Bp. of Metz in 1384, and two years later, cardinal deacon. Despite ill health, P. practiced great austerities, and in 1387 after renouncing his offices, he retired to Villeneuve, near Avignon, where he died at the age of 18. BIBLIOGRAPHY: H. Francois, *La Vie du B. Pierre de Luxembourg* (1927); K. Kunze, BiblSanct 10:705–706.

[N. F. GAUGHAN]

PETER OF MARICOURT (Peregrinus; fl. 1261–69), French teacher and writer on scientific experimentation, esp. on magnetism. He had a strong influence on Roger Bacon, and by reason of his descriptions of scientific method of inductive experiment is considered to be a forerunner of modern science.

[T. C. O'BRIEN]

PETER MARTYR, ST. (c.1205–52), also known as St. Peter of Verona, Veronese Dominican inquisitor, assassinated by the Cathari near Milan, canonized in 1253. He was a Dominican from 1221, devoted his energies to antiheretical preaching. He gave counsel and assistance to the founders of the Order of Servites of Mary at Florence (1241–44).

PETER MARTYR D'ANGHIERA (1457–1526), Italian priest and historian. As a member of the Council of the Indies and royal chronicler under Charles V of Spain, he described Spanish discoveries in the New World.

[P. J. HENNESSEY]

PETER MARTYR VERMIGLI (1500–62), Italian prominent in the English Reformation. P. joined the Augustinians at Fiesole in 1516 and was a superior in Spoleto and Naples as well as a professor. He was influenced by writings of M. *Bucer and H. *Zwingli and accepted Reform teachings. He had to flee from Italy and became professor of OT at Strassburg (1542), where he also married. Invited by T. *Cranmer, he went to England with B. *Ochino and became regius professor of theology at Oxford (1548). The 1552 revision of the *Book of Common Prayer reflects his Zwinglian views on the Holy Eucharist; he also collaborated in the reorganization of English canon law. With the accession of Mary Tudor, he was forced to return to Strassburg (1554), and 2 years later he became professor of Hebrew at Zurich.

By his correspondence P. continued to influence the English Reformation. His writings included commentaries on Sacred Scripture, on the Nicomachean Ethics, and a *Tractatus de sacramento eucharistiae* (1549); they evidence his power of synthesis and his attempt to reconcile Lutheran and Calvinist teachings. BIBLIOGRAPHY: F. C. Church, *Italian Reformers* (1932); J. C. McLelland, *Visible Words of God, an Exposition of the Sacramental Theory of Peter Martyr Vermigli* (1957), with bibliog.

[T. C. O'BRIEN]

PETER OF MOGLIANO, BL. (Peter Corradini; d. 1440), Franciscan preacher. Born in Mogliano, Italy, he studied law at Perugia, but soon joined the Franciscans, became a popular preacher and missionary, and served four terms as vicar provincial in Rome and Ancona. Bl. Baptista Varano, his penitent, described his holy death in Camerino. BIBLIOGRAPHY: Butler 3:217–218; F. A. Ferretti, BiblSanct 4:197–198.

[L. J. LEKAI]

PETER MONGUS (d. 489), Monophysite patriarch of Alexandria from 477. He gained power by political opportunism, became a *persona non grata* to Emperor Zeno and a fugitive. He achieved restoration in 482 by accepting the *Henoticon of Zeno, but was repudiated by the monks of Alexandria because the Henoticon did not satisfy their extreme Monophysitism.

[T. C. O'BRIEN]

PETER MONOCULUS, BL. (d. 1186), Cistercian abbot. Born of high French nobility, possibly related on his mother's side to King Louis VII (who held him in great esteem), P. joined the Cistercians in his youth and became abbot successively at Valroy (1164), Igny (1169), and Clairvaux (1179). At Valroy he lost one of his eyes (hence Monoculus; French, *le borgne*), either as a result of disease, according to his vita, or by weeping too copiously for his sins, as some pious authors have preferred to believe. Noted for piety and wisdom, he advised popes and kings. His vita can be found in AS Oct. 8:53–90. BIBLIOGRAPHY: A. A. King, *Cîteaux and Her Elder Daughters* (1954); M. A. Dimier, BiblSanct 10:710–712.

PETER OF THE MOTHER OF GOD (Bertius; 1610–83), Dutch Carmelite. P. became a Catholic and entered the Carmelites in Paris (1627). In 1654 he founded a mission station in Leyden and wrote numerous works to further conversions there. BIBLIOGRAPHY: O. Merl, LTK 8:370.

[M. J. SUELZER]

PETER NIGRI (Schwarz; 1434–83), Bohemian Dominican theologian and Hebrew scholar. He became a defender of Thomism against nominalism, esp. in his *Clypeus Thomistarum* (1481). He published a Hebrew grammar, the

first in Europe by a Christian, and engaged in theological debates with the Jews. His *Der Stern des Messiah* (1477) is the product of these debates.

[T. C. O'BRIEN]

PETER NOLASCO, ST. (*c.*1182–1249 or 1256), founder of the *Mercedarians (Order of Our Lady of Ransom). The place of his birth (Barcelona, Languedoc, or Liguria) and the details of his early life have been the object of much controversy and what the facts were cannot be determined with certainty. Many of the things told of him had their basis in documents too opportunely "discovered" when the cause of his canonization needed support and are now admitted to have been forgeries. Nevertheless, it is sufficiently established that he had great compassion for the poor, esp. for the plight of the Christian slaves of Muslim masters. With the help of King James of Aragon and *Raymond Peñafort he established a fellowship in the form of a military order dedicated to the ransoming of captives. The order was approved by Pope Gregory IX in 1235, and P. became its first master general. BIBLIOGRAPHY: Butler 1:185–187; V. Ignelzi, BiblSanct 10:844–852.

[R. I. BURNS]

PETER OF ONESTI, (Peter de Honestis; mid-11th cent.–1118 or 1119). He was the founder and superior of an order of canons regular at the church of Sta. Maria in Portu on the Isle of Isola, opposite Ravenna. The question of the authenticity of the rule attributed to him is still unsettled. BIBLIOGRAPHY: E. Amort, *Vetus disciplina canonicorum* (2 v., 1747) 1:339 ff.; PL 163:703–748 (text of the rule); G. Mercati, "Pietro Peccatore," *Studi e documenti di storia e diritto* 16 (1895) 3–47; N. Widloecher, EncCatt 9:1443.

[W. A. JURGENS]

PETER ORSEOLO, ST. (928–987), doge of Venice, Benedictine recluse. Married young, P. had a son and thereafter lived with his wife in continence. He was elected doge after the murder of Peter IV Candiano (976). In this office he promoted peace and advanced social works. Impressed by a sermon on Lk 14.26, he became a Benedictine. His secular affairs were consigned to his son Otto. Later, some claimed his motive for entering religion was reparation for political crimes, but his chaplain defended his motives. After his death, P. became the center of a cult which was finally approved for all Benedictines and Camaldolese. BIBLIOGRAPHY: C. M. Aherne, NCE 11:226.

[F. G. O'BRIEN]

PETER THE PAINTER (fl. *c.*1100), poet. Peter was canon of the cathedral of St. Omer, the probable place of his education. He was an excellent practitioner of the literary genre known as the *carmina,* the short and often satiric poems produced in cathedral and monastic schools of the 12th century. His work dealt with the ignorance and abuses of the clergy. BIBLIOGRAPHY: E. R. Curtius, *European Literature and the Latin Middle Ages* (tr. W. R. Trask, 1953), 472.

[B. F. SCHERER]

PETER PAPPACARBONE, ST. (Peter of Cava; *c.*1038–1123), abbot. He became a monk at La Cava and later went to Cluny. He was named bp. of Policastro, but soon resigned in favor of monastic life. Again at La Cava, he succeeded Leo I as abbot (1079) and introduced the Cluniac reforms which brought new prosperity to La Cava. BIBLIOGRAPHY: F. Russo, BiblSanct 10:680–682; Butler 1:481.

[G. E. CONWAY]

PETER PASCUAL, ST. (1227?–1300), Mercedarian bp. of Jaén (1296) who was captured by the Moors (1298) and died imprisoned in Granada; his cult was approved in 1670. The relics are in Baeza, seat of the diocese before the reconquest of Jaén in 1246. He taught theology in Paris and Barcelona and then administered the See of Toledo (1266–75). Religious works in Catalan and Castilian include a gloss on the Our Father against Judaism and Islam.

[E. P. COLBERT]

PETER OF PISA (d. before 799), deacon, grammarian, and poet at Charlemagne's court. A close bond existed between P. and the Emperor whom he instructed and with whom he read the Latin authors. He wrote letters in verse for Charlemagne to Paul the Deacon, another member of the learned court circle. While most of these poems are intact, at least one is lost. When writing his grammar, he borrowed from Latin authors; his work is very much like the anonymous author of MS Bern 207, fol. 112a–127b. It is believed there may have been a common source for both. P. preceded his work by a dedicatory preface written in elegiac verse, stating it to be a work of love for his lord the emperor. He praises Charles as a conqueror, builder of churches, converter of heathens, and punisher of evil. BIBLIOGRAPHY: C. M. Aherne, NCE 11:227.

[F. G. O'BRIEN]

PETER OF POITIERS (*c.*1130–1205), the chancellor under whom the cathedral school at Notre Dame developed into the Univ. of Paris (1193–1205). By his teaching and his most important work, *Sententiarum libri quinque,* he contributed to the perfecting of the scholastic method by the use of dialectics and to the expansion of moral theology. He is credited with being the first to use the theological terms *ex opere operato, ex opere operantis,* and *synderesis.* BIBLIOGRAPHY: P. S. Moore, NCE 11:227–228.

[T. C. O'BRIEN]

PETER RIGA (*c.*1140–1209), poet, canon of Notre Dame and St. Denis, who wrote *Aurora,* a metrical paraphrase of most of the books of the Bible, with allegorical interpreta-

tions and moral applications. BIBLIOGRAPHY: *Aurora Petri Rigae biblia versificata* (ed. P. Beichner, 2 v., 1965); M. I. J. Rousseau, NCE 11:228, bibliog.

[V. BULLOUGH]

PETER DES ROCHES (d. 1238), Poitevin ecclesiastic, statesman, soldier, and diplomat; bp. of Winchester (1205); justiciar of England (1213–15). He served Richard I and supported John against both Innocent III and the English rebels. He discharged John's duties in his absence and conducted French negotiations for him and for Henry III. As Henry's guardian, he raised the French siege of Lincoln (1217) and shared in government until dismissed (1227). He accompanied Frederick II's Crusade to Jerusalem (1229) and mediated between Frederick and Gregory IX. He regained Henry's favor (1231) but lost it through misusing authority (1234). Before returning to Winchester, he rendered distinguished military service to the Pope. An efficient ecclesiastical administrator, he founded and patronized many churches and religious houses. BIBLIOGRAPHY: C. Duggan, NCE 11:228.

[R. W. HAYS]

PETER OF RUFFIA, BL. (*c.*1320–65), Piedmontese Dominican inquisitor (from 1351), assassinated by Waldensians, beatified in 1856.

PETER OF SAMPSON (fl. mid-13th cent.), French canonist at Bologna and Avignon. The synodal decrees he prepared for the diocese of Nîmes in 1252 and his glosses on the Decretals of Gregory IX are valuable sources for the history of canon law.

[T. C. O'BRIEN]

PETER OF SPAIN (fl. late 12th cent.), canonist at Bologna and Padua, whose glosses on canon law became the source of later commentaries. He is to be distinguished from a 13th–cent. canonist of the same name. Before becoming pope, *John XXI, a learned philosopher, was also known as Peter of Spain.

[T. C. O'BRIEN]

PETER OF TARENTAISE, ST. (1102–74), Cistercian archbishop. Of peasant origin, P. joined the Cistercians at Bonnevaux (1122), became abbot of Tamié (1132), and abp. of Tarentaise (1141). He reformed his diocese and mediated successfully between Alexander III and Frederick Barbarossa, and between Henry II of England and Louis VII of France. BIBLIOGRAPHY: Butler 2:253–255; M. A. Dimier, *St. Pierre de Tarentaise* (1935); *idem,* BiblSanct 10:781–787, bibliog.

[L. J. LEKAI]

PETER THOMAE (*c.*1280–*c.*1340), Spanish Franciscan theologian, a leader in the development of the Scotist school, and one of the first to seek to present a scriptural basis for the doctrine of Mary's Immaculate Conception. BIBLIOGRAPHY: J. C. Brady, NCE 11:229, bibliog.

[T. C. O'BRIEN]

PETER THOMASIUS, see HOOGSTREATEN, JACOB VAN.

PETER (CAPUCCI) OF TIFERNO, BL. (1390–1445), Dominican preacher, mystic, and miracle worker. After receiving the Dominican habit (1405) and making profession (1406) at Tiferno, he was assigned to St. Dominic's Priory at Cortona. There he was ordained, probably in 1413, together with St. *Antoninus. From this same convent he launched his preaching mission in which his apostolic labors were attended by many miracles. BIBLIOGRAPHY: S. M. Bertucci, BiblSanct 3:774–775.

[J. A. WEISHEIPL]

PETER OF TREVI, ST. (d. 1052). After receiving the tonsure from his patron, Gregory, bp. of Tibur, P. spent 2 years as an itinerant preacher in the region between Subiaco and Trevi. Persecuted during life, he was canonized in 1215 and is now honored as patron of Subiaco and Trevi. He is invoked for protection against wolves. BIBLIOGRAPHY: AS Aug 6:634–647; F. Caraffa, BiblSanct 10:735–737.

[M. A. WINKELMANN]

PETER OF VAUX-DE-CERNAY (d. after 1218), a Cistercian who took part in the Fourth Crusade and in the war against the Albigensians. His *Hystoria Albigensis,* covering events between 1212 and 1218 (ed. P. Guébin and E. Lyon, 3 v., 1926–39), favors Simon de Montfort and is very informative. BIBLIOGRAPHY: *Histoire littéraire de la France* 17:246–254; A. Borst, *Die Katharer* (1953); É. Brouette, NCE 11:230.

[L. J. LEKAI]

PETER THE VENERABLE (*c.*1094–1156), 9th abbot of Cluny, saintly foil to, and dear enemy of St. *Bernard of Clairvaux, protector of *Abelard who was attacked by Bernard. Born in the Auvergne, prior of Vézelay, P. was elected by acclamation to rule his abbey of 300–400 monks, with 2,000 dependent houses. Humane and balanced as an administrator and theological controversialist, as in his criticism of *Peter de Bruys, he held that the study of humane letters was a part of monastic discipline and, for apostolic reasons, promoted the first translation of the Koran into Latin (1143). His writings, limpid in style, manifest a knowledge deeper of the Scriptures than of the Fathers, and he preferred the literal sense to allegorical speculations. Though his fame is eclipsed by St. Bernard's, he was a more formative influence for the 13th century. BIBLIOGRAPHY: D. Knowles, *Bulletin John Rylands Library* 39 (1956) 132–145.

[T. GILBY]

PETER OF VIENNA (d. 1183), French scholastic, disciple of Gilbert of Poitiers, who taught at Vienna *c.*1155 and engaged in controversy about the distinction of person and nature in Christ.

[T. C. O'BRIEN]

PETER OF VINEA (*c.*1190–1249), lawyer, imperial official. P. served Emperor Frederick II (d. 1250) as a legal advisor and in Frederick's conflict with the Church wrote pamphlets defending the imperial position. BIBLIOGRAPHY: E. Kantorowicz, *Frederick the Second, 1194–1250* (tr. E. O. Lorimer, 1931, repr. 1957).

[J. MULDOON]

PETER WALDO, see WALDO.

PETER, ACTS OF, see APOCRYPHA (NT), 44.

PETER, APOCALYPSE OF, see APOCRYPHA (NT), 45.

PETER, GOSPEL OF, see APOCRYPHA (NT), 46.

PETER, LETTERS OF, two NT *Epistles traditionally ascribed to St. Peter. First Peter seems to have been written from Rome (the "Babylon" of 5.13), and it seems probable that the Christian scribe Silvanus (5.12) played a major part in its composition. This might account for the inclusion of numerous Pauline ideas and turns of phrase, as well as for the polished Greek and the familiarity with the Septuagint that it displays. With this important reservation the traditional ascription to Peter is difficult but not impossible to accept. The Epistle seems to have been written to encourage Christians in a number of local communities who were suffering persecution and hostility. It reminds them of the grace of Christ's redeeming death and Resurrection, which have been made theirs through baptism, and exhorts them to be true to the baptismal grace they have received, sustaining themselves with the expectation of the *parousia. Through this grace they have been made heirs to the glorious promises of the OT, which provides types and prefigurings of what has taken place in them, and this thought should enable them to live charitable, sober, humble, and virtuous lives in the midst of a hostile and pagan environment. A special point of interest is the reference to Christ's descent into hell in 3.19–4.6. The allusions to baptism in this Epistle are important, and it has been argued plausibly that it may in large measure be based on the liturgy and creedal profession associated with baptism in the early Church. This, if correct, would tell decisively against Petrine authorship.

Second Peter differs radically from 1 Pet alike in contents and manner of presentation and raises quite different problems. The author's primary purpose is to reassure Christians who have been disappointed by the delay of the parousia, and to warn them against false teachers. The references to the first generation of Christians as the "fathers" already deceased, and to the Apostles as heroes of the past (3.2), as well as the reference to the letters of Paul as Scripture

(3.15), show fairly conclusively that 2 Pet was written much later than 1 Pet—perhaps as late as *c.*100 A.D.—and by a different hand. Moreover in the sections dealing with false teachers this author draws very heavily on *Jude (cf. 2 Pet 2.1–3.3 with Jude 4–18). The central point of interest for the author is the parousia and the final judgment, which he depicts in vividly apocalyptic tones. He may have thought of himself as a disciple of Peter reproducing some of the Apostle's ideas. In any case the fictional ascription to Peter is a matter of literary convention and would not have been intended as a serious assertion of historical fact. The canonicity of 2 Pet has been much disputed; it was accepted by Origen, but in the Western Church only from *c.*400 onward. BIBLIOGRAPHY: F. W. Beare, *First Epistle of St. Peter* (1958); C. E. B. Cranfield, *First Epistle of Peter* (1958); B. Reicke, *Epistles of James, Peter and Jude,* (Anchor Bible, 1964); E. G. Selwyn, *First Epistle of St. Peter* (1958).

[D. J. BOURKE]

PETER, PASSION OF, see APOCRYPHA (NT), 47.

PETER, PREACHING OF, see APOCRYPHA (NT), 48.

PETER, SLAVONIC ACTS OF, see APOCRYPHA (NT), 49.

PETER AND ANDREW, ACTS OF, see APOCRYPHA (NT), 50.

PETER AND MARCELLINUS CATACOMB, ROME, 3d-cent. Christian catacomb on the Via Labicana, named for two Christians martyred under Diocletian. It is probably the most completely painted of all catacombs; 30 to 40 martyrs are buried here.

[M. J. DALY]

PETER AND PAUL, ACTS OF, see APOCRYPHA (NT), 51.

PETER AND PAUL, PASSION OF, see APOCRYPHA (NT), 52.

PETER AND THE TWELVE APOSTLES, ACTS OF, see APOCRYPHA (NT), 53.

PETERBOROUGH, ABBEY OF, former Benedictine monastery in Peterborough, Northamptonshire, England. The original monastery was established *c.*655, but was plundered by the Danes in 870. It was rebuilt *c.*970, and dedicated to St. Peter; thus the name of the village. It was a wealthy and important abbey; however, in 1534 the monks accepted the supremacy of the king, and Peterborough's last abbot, John Chambers, became the first Anglican bp. under Henry VIII. Hence in 1541 the celebrated abbey church was made the cathedral church of the new Anglican Diocese of Peterborough. Its church is one of the most celebrated of English cathedrals for its architecture. Catherine of Aragon's tomb is in the church. Some ruins of the monastery buildings remain, other parts are incorporated into the diocesan offices and the boys' school.

[M. A. MCFADDEN]

PETERS, NORBERT (1863–1938), biblical scholar. P. taught OT at Paderborn from 1892. He was a careful and prolific scholar who published 27 books and 54 articles for scholarly periodicals. He wrote commentaries on several OT books, made valuable contributions to OT textual criticism, and consistently addressed himself to the central scriptural problem of his time—the relationship between the Bible and science. P. insisted upon the distinction between inspiration and revelation, the necessity of determining literary genres, and a complete openness to both science and religious truth. BIBLIOGRAPHY: O. Schilling, DBSuppl 7:883–886.

[T. M. MCFADDEN]

PETER'S CHAIR, see CHAIR OF PETER.

PETER'S PENCE: (1) any collection taken up for the pope; in some areas there was a Peter's Pence collection annually, e.g., around the time of the feast of SS. Peter and Paul (June 29); (2) in English history a levy of one pence per annum on every household; it began in the 8th cent., was gradually formalized, constantly contested, and finally abolished in Henry VIII's reform.

PETERSEN, JOHANN WILHELM (1649–1727), German Lutheran theologian and author. His numerous treatises on *millenarianism, *universalism, and the person of Christ were popular in Pietist circles less because of their originality than because of their effective presentation of thoughts common to *Boehme, Weigel, and Jane *Leade. His efforts to combine universalism with covenant theology bore fruit in 19th– and 20th–cent. evangelical thought. BIBLIOGRAPHY: C. Berthau, EncRelKnow 8:499–500.

[M. J. SUELZER]

PETERSHAUSEN, ABBEY OF, former Benedictine monastery on the Rhine near Constance. It was founded in the late 10th cent. by Bp. Gebhard II of Constance. The beautifully ornamented abbey church contained the head of Pope Gregory I the Great. The Hirsau reform was introduced, but the monks were forced to leave the monastery during the Reformation. The stones from the various buildings were used to build a bridge across the Rhine. However, under Pope Gregory XIII, Petershausen had a revival and in 1769 it was made an independent imperial abbey. It was suppressed in 1802; the abbey church was demolished in 1832, but its Romanesque portal has been preserved. The abbey library is at Heidelberg University.

[M. A. MCFADDEN]

PETERSON, ERIK (1890–1960), German biblical and church scholar. Originally a Protestant, he taught church history and NT studies at Göttingen and Bonn from 1920 to 1928, but was converted to Catholicism in 1929. From then on, he lived in Rome, teaching at the Pontifical Institute of Christian Archeology after 1934. His chief interest lay in exploring the theological nature of primitive Christianity through the archeological and epigraphical evidence that could be amassed. His publications included *Der Monotheismus als polit. Problem* (1935); *Das Buch von den Engeln* (1935); *Zeuge der Wahrheit* (1937); *Theol. Traktate* (1953); and *Frühkirche, Judentum u. Gnosis* (1959).

[E. M. GATES]

PETERSON, JOHN BERTRAM (1871–1944), bp. of Manchester, N.H., educator. Ordained for the archdiocese of Boston in 1899, he taught at St. John's Seminary in Boston for 25 years and was its rector from 1911 to 1926. He was named auxiliary bp. of Boston in 1927, and bp. of Manchester in 1932. He wielded considerable influence in dealing with industrial problems. P. was a founder of the National Catholic Educational Association in 1904. In 1930 he was named to a presidential commission investigating national educational issues. P. served also as episcopal chairman of the Education Department of the National Catholic Welfare Conference.

[J. R. AHERNE]

PETGŌMŌ, in West Syrian liturgical usage, a hemistych, used: 1) of the psalm-fragments remaining before the intercalated strophes of a *qōlō;* 2) of the introductory hemistych of a psalm or other Biblical canticle.

[A. CODY]

PETIOT, HENRI JULES, see DANIEL-ROPS, HENRI.

PETIT, LOUIS (1868–1927), French Assumptionist, Oriental scholar, archbishop. He was the founder of the review, *Échos d'Orient* (1897), a leader in the establishment of the Pontifical Oriental Institute (1917) and of the Congregation for the Oriental Churches. In 1901 and 1905 he was a collaborator in the exploration of Mt. Athos and contributed to the publication of findings there in *Recueil des inscriptions chrétiennes de l'Athos* (1904). To the reprinting and editing of G. *Mansi's *Sacrorum conciliorum collectio* he contributed 12 volumes, 3 on Vatican Council I. From 1912 he was apostolic delegate and Latin abp. in Athens; he resigned in 1926.

[T. C. O'BRIEN]

PETIT-DIDIER, MATTHIEU (1659–1728), Benedictine abbot of St. Léopold, Nancy (1705) and of Senones (1715), author of *Traité théologique pour l'autorité et l'infaillibilité du pape* (1724), and of a study of the participants and teaching of the Council of Constance on *conciliarism.

[T. C. O'BRIEN]

PETITE ÉGLISE, the "Little Church" of those French and Belgian Catholics who refused to accept the Concordat of 1801 between France and the papacy. That agreement completely abolished the existing dioceses, and the Pope requested all bps. to resign. In 1801 in London 14 of them, motivated in part by *Gallicanism, but also by their own fidelity during the Napoleonic persecutions of the Church, publicly refused the papal request; 2 years later in London 38 bps. in exile formally protested the Concordat. The exiles had clerical and lay followers in France who comprised the Petite Église. The groups suffered persecution under Napoleon I and the Bourbon Restoration. By 1817 the exiled bps. had been reconciled with Pius VII, except for Bp. de Thémines of Blois; he remained primate of the Petite Église until his death (1829). At its height there were more than 40,000 members of this Church, but it did not proselytize, expecting the imminent collapse of the Concordat. No new bp. was consecrated, nor was any priest ordained. The last priest, Ozouf, died in 1847. In 1869 the two largest congregations petitioned Vatican Council I for recognition of pre-Concordat bishops as the basis for reconciliation, but Rome refused. In the early 20th cent. a French Old Catholic priest and an Anglican clergyman tried unsuccessfully to unite the Petite Église with the Old Catholics. Papal efforts at reconciliation have so far failed, although since 1949 neither retraction nor abjuration of errors is required of any who wish to return. There are nearly 4,000 adherents, most of them peasants. The largest number is in Vendée, where members are called Illuminés; they are known as Louisets in Brittany, Clémentins in Rouergue, Filochois in Toulouse, and Blancs, Burs, Elus, and Fidèles elsewhere in France. In Belgium there are some 400, called Stevenists after the Vicar Capitular C. Stevens of Namur, who led the local opposition to the Concordat of 1801. The Church is not a unit, but the independent congregations have similar practices. A member selected by the community administers baptism, the only sacrament, and officiates at marriages, funerals, and Sunday service. In Vendée divine service is in Latin according to the ancient Paris Breviary; at Lyons it is in French following the ancient Lyons liturgy. Parents teach children the ancient diocesan catechism and prepare them for first (spiritual) communion. The members, pious, austere, and closely knit, observe the festivals abolished by the Concordat. BIBLIOGRAPHY: I. de la Thibauderie, *Églises et évêques Catholiques non Romains* (1962); H. C. Chéry, *L'Offensive des sectes* (1959) 472–473.

[E. E. BEAUREGARD]

PETRA, an ancient city, called Sela in biblical times, *c.* 100 miles S of the Dead Sea in Jordan. The brilliant hues and the fantastic eroded shapes of its native Nubian sandstone make Petra a city of considerable interest. For many centuries the center of the caravan trade, Petra declined with the rise of Palmyra and Bosra. Most of its architectural remains (in some cases simply façades) come from the Roman occupation that began in 106 A.D. The approach to Petra is through the Siq, a mile-long dark winding pass. Water from the nearby Spring of Moses sometimes flows along the pass. Occupation began in prehistoric times and was continued by the Edomites, Nabataeans, Romans, Christians, Muslims, and Crusaders. Petra was rediscovered in 1812 by the Swiss traveler, John Lewis Burckhardt. Since 1958 the excavations of the British School of Archaeology in Jerusalem and the American Schools of Oriental Research have added considerably to our knowledge of Petra. BIBLIOGRAPHY: N. Glueck, *Deities and Dolphins* (1965); F. Cumont, CAH 11:630–632; W. F. Albright, *Archeology of Palestine* (pa. 1969) 160–165.

[M. F. MCNAMARA]

PETRARCH, FRANCESCO (1304–74), Italian poet and scholar and one of the first and greatest of the Renaissance humanists. Born in Arezzo, P. was educated at Montpellier and Bologna in law, but his true interest lay in the world of literature and the study of the classics. From 1327 he was deeply affected by his love for a woman called Laura, and neither his assumption of clerical status (1330), nor the fact that his passion was unreciprocated, nor Laura's death (1348) could purge his fantasy of this preoccupation. He wrote poems about her in life and death (*Rime in vita; Rime in morte*). These, together with his other sonnets and *canzoni,* profoundly influenced literary trends throughout Europe. He himself thought less of his vernacular than of his Latin compositions. One of his major Latin works, the *Secretum,* gives an insight into his spiritual life. Besides manifesting the tension Renaissance writers felt between active and contemplative lives, it is an acknowledgement of folly, a recognition of misery, a declaration of repentance, and an expression of hope that he might find God. P.'s Latin writings include collections of letters, a collection of Roman biographies (*De viris illustribus*), and a great epic (*Africa*) on the subject of the war between Rome and Carthage. P.'s humanism (*humanitas*) was a reaction against the cultural sterility of late scholasticism. It stands in contrast not to religious or God-centered values but to the arid subtleties and abstractions with which the schools were then occupied. Far from turning from God and religion, P. proposed rather to seek God in the pursuit of values that can be most effectively set forth concretely and in the round in the manner of the classics. BIBLIOGRAPHY: E. H. Wilkins, *Life of Petrarch* (1961); *idem, Making of the ''Canzoniere'' and Other Petrarchan Studies* (1951, repr. 1973); A. S. Bernardo, *Petrarch, Laura and the ''Triumphs''* (1974).

[D. G. NUGENT]

PETRE, recusant family of wealth and prominence, which substantially contributed to the preservation of the Catholic faith in England. (1) William (*c.*1505–72) established the family seat in Essex and the family fortune largely through political connections as secretary of state during the reigns of Henry VIII, Edward VI, and Mary. (2) William (1602–

77), second Lord Petre, begot numerous progeny and translated into English the *Flos sanctorum* of Pedro de Ribadeneira. (3) William (1627–84), fourth Lord Petre, died in the Tower of London after being unjustly accused in the Oates plot. (4) Edward (1631–99), a Jesuit, became confessor to James II, privy councilor, and fled to the Continent in 1688. (5) Benjamin (1672–1758) was coadjutor bp. of the London district (1721) and then vicar apostolic (1734). (6) Francis (1692–1775) became coadjutor of the northern district (1750) and succeeded to the vicariate. (7) Robert Edward (1742–1801), ninth Lord Petre, was a leader of the Catholic Committee and was instrumental in the passage of the first Catholic Relief act (1778). BIBLIOGRAPHY: Gillow BDEC 5:288–300; T. Cooper et al., DNB 15:976–983.

[J. C. WILLKE]

PETRI, OLAUS (Olaf, Olavus; *c.*1493–1552), establisher of the Lutheran Reformation in Sweden. After returning (1518) from studies at Wittenberg, where he had witnessed the beginning of Luther's revolt, P. devoted himself to preaching, writing, and political persuasion to spread Reform teaching, which already had gained some acceptance in Sweden. He was ordained a deacon in 1520, but did not receive final ordination until 1539. In 1524 the King, Gustavus Vasa, gave him the cathedral pulpit in Stockholm to preach the Reformation. P. married in 1526. In 1527 the Diet of Västerås officially broke with Rome. In 1531 P. became chancellor to the King; he fell into disfavor for his defense of church freedom, was sentenced to death, but then let off with a heavy fine. In 1543 he became pastor of the cathedral and remained in that office until his death. In the Reformation cause he provided Swedish translations for the liturgy and catechetical instruction; with his brother Lorenz he published a Swedish translation of the Bible in 1541; he also came to be called the ''father of Swedish hymnody'' because of his musical compositions.

[T. C. O'BRIEN]

PETRICCA, ANGELO (d. 1673), Franciscan theologian and polemicist. P. was invited in 1631 to go to Persia to treat with the Shah about the safety of Christians, but circumstances prevented the journey. He was then made provincial in Hungary, prefect apostolic in Moldavia and Walachia, and patriarchal vicar in Constantinople. There he successfully opposed the union of Greeks and Calvinists fostered by *Cyril Lucaris. On his return to Rome he taught theology and served as procurator general of his order. He also wrote copiously in defense of the Church. BIBLIOGRAPHY: G. Odoardi, EncCatt 9:1300–01.

[M. J. SUELZER]

PETRINE TEXTS, the name given to those NT (and esp. gospel) passages that to Catholics at least afford the biblical basis for the claim that Christ established in Peter as chief of the Apostles a perpetual office of guiding and teaching the Church as its supreme pastor. Generally it is to three passages that appeal is made: Mt 16.17–19; Jn 21.15–17; Lk 22.31–32.

Of these perhaps the most telling is the passage in Matthew, since the metaphor of the bedrock (which naturally endures as long as the structure raised upon it) and the explicit promise of indefectibility for the Church (which intimates that Our Lord is making provision for an indefinite future and not just for one lifetime) argue for the establishment of a permanent constitutional arrangement in the Church. In recent times non-Catholic exegetes, while frequently conceding that Our Lord is presented in this passage as promising to erect the Church on the person Peter (and not upon his faith or confession) have generally refused to grant that the passage suggests a permanent function (in which others in later generations would succeed to Peter's role) or in keeping with the tenets of form-criticism have questioned whether the words of the promise do more than evince and legitimize the conviction of the primitive Christian communities on the role of Simon Peter.

The passages in John and Luke clearly designate Peter as one singled out to shepherd (Gr. verb *poimainein*) the flock of Christ and as the one who, when he and his fellow Apostles are being tested and threatened by the powers of evil, is to confirm and bolster them; but they do not as clearly as the passage in Matthew envisage an enduring office in the Church. BIBLIOGRAPHY: J. Jeremias, Kittel TD 3:744–753; O. Cullmann, *Peter, Disciple, Apostle, Martyr* (tr. F. V. Filson, 2d rev. ed., 1962).

[S. E. DONLON]

PETROBRUSIANS, a sect named for its founder, Peter of Bruys. A suspended priest, he gained a large following in Languedoc and Provence in the first third of the 12th century. He aroused the people against the clergy and encouraged monks to marry. In matters of doctrine he rejected *infant baptism, the use of church buildings, prayers for the dead, veneration of the cross, hymn singing, the Mass, ecclesiastical authority, and the Bible except for the Gospels. The Council of Toulouse (1119) and Lateran Council II (1139) condemned these teachings. Sometime *c.*1130 the populace of St. Gilles near Nîmes became so enraged when on Good Friday Peter attempted to cook meat over a pile of burning crosses that they put him to death. Many of his followers joined *Henry of Lausanne. Peter the Venerable was active in combating the Petrobrusians. BIBLIOGRAPHY: L. Cristiani, *Heresies and Heretics* (1959) 59; S. Runciman, *Medieval Manichee* (pa., 1961) 118–119.

[C. J. LYNCH]

PETROCK, ST. (6th cent.), in all probability, a Welsh-born saint who went to Cornwall. In the ancient Latin life of St. Cadoo he was of the royal family of Gwent (Southeast Wales). His body was stolen from Cornwall in the late 12th cent. and brought to Brittany, where a cult sprang up. From Brittany comes the Latin *Vita Petroci*. BIBLIOGRAPHY: Butler 2:475–476; G. Stephan, BiblSanct 10:509–510.

[R. T. MEYER]

PETRONILLA, ST. (3d cent.?), martyr. The *Roman Martyrology* on the basis, it seems, of the unreliable *passio* of *Nereus and Achilleus declares that P. was the daughter of St. Peter the Apostle, and states that she died a natural death after 3 days of prayer and fasting while she deliberated upon a proposed marriage. The legend of Gnostic origin that Peter had a daughter is unworthy of serious attention. Petronilla appears rather to have been an authentic Roman martyr. A fresco, dating from the 4th cent., in the cemetery of Domitilla, depicting her as a martyr, has been discovered in modern times. A basilica was erected over her tomb during the pontificate of Pope Siricius (384–399). BIBLIOGRAPHY: W. Wehr, EncCatt 9:1302–03; Butler 2:434.

[R. B. ENO]

PETRONIUS, ST., bp. of Bologna *c.*432–445. His father may have been prefect of the praetorium in Gaul. P. himself may have held civil office before assuming ecclesiastical office. He repaired the churches of Bologna that had been reduced to ruins by the devastations of the Goths. Churches he built in apparent imitation of holy places in Palestine were themselves destroyed in the 10th cent. by later waves of marauding barbarians. BIBLIOGRAPHY: Butler 4:33–34.

[E. J. DILLON]

PETRUCCI, OTTAVIANO DEI (1466–1539), first printer of polyphonic music who held patents for the printing of tablature and measured music in Venice (1498–1511) and in Rome (1513–16). His editions, of unsurpassed excellence in the printing art, were eventually replaced with the simplification of printing techniques. He issued collections of sacred and secular music, chansons, Masses and motets.

[R. J. LITZ]

PETRUCCI, PIER MATTEO (1636–1701), Oratorian ascetical and mystical theologian, who with M. Molinos, was a leader of the Quietist movement. P. became a cardinal in the Roman Curia, but on Dec. 17, 1687 he was required by the Holy Office to retract 54 propositions taken from his writings on the spiritual life.

[P. J. HENNESSEY]

PETRUS COLLIVACCINUS (Beneventanus; d. 1219 or 1220), cardinal and canonist. He first studied and taught at Bologna, was in Rome in the papal curia by 1205; became card. bp. of Sabina by 1217. P. is the author of *Compilatio III antiqua*, a collection commissioned by Innocent III in 1210 of decretals belonging to his pontificate, from 1198.

[T. C. O'BRIEN]

PETRUS PIERLEONI, see ANACLETUS II, ANTIPOPE.

PETTAZZONI, RAFFAELE (1883–1959), Italian historian of religions. He was a professor at Bologna (1914–23) and Rome (1923–53); cofounder and first president (1950–59) of the Association Internationale pour l'Histoire des Religions; founder of the journals, *Studi e Materiali di Storia delle Religioni* and *Numen*. His major work, on the concept of a high god as a common religious phenomenon, *L'Omniscienza di Dio* (1955), appeared in English as *The All-Knowing God* (tr. H. J. Rose, 1956). The influential study, *Saggi di storia delle religioni . . .* (1946) appeared as *Essays on the History of Religion* (tr. H. J. Rose, 1954). Another important work is P.'s *La confessione dei peccati* (3 v., 1929–36).

[T. C. O'BRIEN]

PEUTINGER, CONRAD (1465–1547), German humanist, antiquarian, and diplomat. His interest in antiquity was aroused during a stay in Italy. He was syndic in his native city, Augsburg, and imperial councilor; under Charles V he represented his city at the Diets of Worms (1521) and Augsburg (1530). Though at first sympathetic to Luther's cause, he refused to break with the Church. When in 1534 religious changes were proposed without regard for the wishes of the Catholics, he resigned under protest from all public office and devoted himself entirely to his studies. He published a collection of Roman inscriptions and histories of Jordanis and Paul the Deacon. BIBLIOGRAPHY: P. Pfeiffer, "Peutinger und die humanistischen Welt" *Augusta 955–1555* (1955); H. Lutz, *Conrad Peutinger* (1958).

[S. A. SCHULZ]

PEW, a fixed bench with a back, rows of which are usually arranged to face the main altars of churches in Northern Europe and North America. The custom appears to have had its origin in the stone benches sometimes put against the walls of churches or attached to nave piers to accommodate the infirm. Their use became common about the 13th century. Large pews with high enclosures were common in English churches of the 18th and early 19th centuries. Like choir stalls, the backs and ends of pews were sometimes ornamented with carvings.

[P. K. MEAGHER]

PEW RENT, sometimes called bench rent, the charge levied upon an individual or a family for the reservation or use of special pew space at religious services. From the 16th cent. the renting of *pews in parish churches was a common practice, with the rent payable at designated intervals. In the Catholic Church it is not forbidden by canon law so long as sufficient provision is made to allow the poor and those without established residence to assist at Sunday Mass. In the U.S., pew rent at one time was a common form of church revenue. However, when the circumstances of urban life gave greater mobility to the faithful and Masses in most

churches became more numerous, the system became impractical. It was generally abandoned in the first half of the 20th cent. in favor of the seat collection, which differs from pew rent only in the circumstance that space is not reserved and the rental is paid at each single use of the facilities.

[P. K. MEAGHER]

PEYOTE, a small cactus found mainly in Mexico, a natural hallucinogen which for centuries was an integral part of the religion of various Indian tribes. Today it is still used in the ritual of the predominantly Indian, Native American Church, and in this capacity its use is entirely legal. The Indians believe that peyote contains "God's flesh" in some way and it was given to them by Jesus in a time of need. Its use offers some analogy to the Christian Eucharist. It is also the sole mediator between the church member and God, so the Church has no need for ministers. The bitter-tasting, dried buttons of peyote are either chewed or chopped up and brewed as tea. There have been rare cases of psychotic reactions to peyote, but in the intermittent way that it is used in religious services there is no evidence of adverse long-range effects. Because peyote has an obnoxious taste and produces nausea and because other drugs give better results without the unpleasant side effects, its use is generally limited to the Indian Church and presents no significant moral problem except for those whose use of it in ritual would amount to an objectionable form of *communicatio in sacris*. BIBLIOGRAPHY: N. Taylor, *Narcotics, Nature's Dangerous Gifts.* (1966) ch. 6.

[P. SMITH]

PEYTO, WILLIAM (Peto; 1477–1558), English Observant Franciscan, cardinal. He served as Mary Tudor's girlhood confessor. In 1532, he preached an Easter sermon in Henry VIII's presence, strenuously condemning the King's proposed marriage to Anne Boleyn. After release from prison (1533), P. fled to Antwerp and for the next 20 years worked with the Continental Counter Reformation. He returned to England after Mary's accession. In spite of his age, P. was appointed cardinal legate in 1557 by Paul IV to succeed Card. R. *Pole.

[R. J. LITZ]

PEZ, BERNARDUS (1683–1735) and **HIERONYMUS** (1685–1762), Austrian brothers, both of them Benedictines, librarians, and historians. Bernardus, librarian at the Abbey of Melk from 1713, was one of the foremost archivists of his day, in touch with all the leading men in his field and consulted even by the Emperor. Together with his brother, he surveyed the archival resources of monasteries throughout Austria and southern Germany. As a historian, he cast aside the allegorical approach typical of the baroque era. He was succeeded in the library post by Hieronymus, who by his researches made possible a more scholarly approach to Austrian history.

[E. M. GATES]

PFÄFERS, ABBEY OF, former Benedictine monastery in Switzerland, near the spa of Ragaz. It was founded *c.* 750 and enjoyed the protection of the Carolingian ruler Lothair I. Abbot Johann Jakob Russinger (1517–49) followed Zwingli for a brief time but returned to Catholicism. Because of economic and disciplinary problems, the abbey was suppressed in 1838. In 1845 it became a mental institution, but the abbey church continues to serve a parish.

[M. A. MCFADDEN]

PFAFF, CHRISTOPH MATTHÄUS (1686–1760), Lutheran theologian with leanings to Pietism. A child prodigy, P. began his studies at the Univ. of Tübingen at the age of 13. He developed a special interest in Oriental languages and church history. Among the valuable MSS he discovered in the library of Turin was an epitome of Lactantius. The four fragments he discovered of letters of Irenaeus, however, were proved by Harnack to be forgeries. BIBLIOGRAPHY: M. Schmidt, RGG 5:265–266; P. Meinhold, LTK 8:393–394.

[H. DRESSLER]

PFANNER, FRANZ (1825–1909), Austrian Trappist, abbot, founder of the *Mariannhill Missionaries in Natal, South Africa. A diocesan priest from 1850, after a pilgrimage to Rome he became a Trappist in 1863 at Marienwald, diocese of Aachen. In 1869 he founded the priory of Mariastern, Banajaluka in Bosnia, a Muslim region. His work in South Africa for the evangelization of the Zulus began when with 31 Trappists he established a priory (1880) in Dunbrody, then transferred it to Pinetown, celebrating the first Mass in the priory of Mariannhill (Dec. 27, 1882). Mariannhill became an abbey in 1885 with P. as abbot; there he established both the Congregation of Mariannhill Missionaries and the Missionary Sisters of the Precious Blood. He devoted his own full efforts to missionary work and died at Emmaus, one of the 11 stations he had established.

[T. C. O'BRIEN]

PFEFFERKORN, JOHANNES (1469–1524), German Jewish RC convert and polemicist. P. was baptized at Cologne (*c.* 1505). He published violently anti-Jewish works, among them *Osternbuch* (1508) and *Judenfeind* (1509), both translated into Latin by Ortwin *Gratius. P.'s most notorious work, however, was his *Handspiegel,* circulated in 1511 against Johannes *Reuchlin. In the interest of learning, the latter opposed the proposal of P., who knew no Hebrew, that all Hebrew books be burned. P. was supported by the inquisitor Jacob *Hoogstraeten; a long and bitter controversy ensued, during which the *Epistolae obscurorum virorum* appeared, discrediting the supporters of P. before the intelligentsia of Europe. BIBLIOGRAPHY: F. G. Stokes, *Epistolae Obscurorum Virorum: The Latin Text with an English Rendering, Notes and an Historical Intro-* duction (1909); R. Coulon, DTC 7:11–17; F. Zoepfl, LTK 8:416.

[T. C. O'BRIEN]

PFLEIDERER, OTTO (1838–1908), German Protestant theologian, professor of theology at Jena and later at Berlin. P. argued vigorously for the nonmiraculous origin of Christianity. He was esp. influential in England, where he delivered the Hibbert lectures (1885) and the Gifford (1892–94), and was looked upon as the leader of German liberal theology. BIBLIOGRAPHY: EncRelKnow 9:6–7.

[M. J. SUELZER]

PFORR, FRANZ (1788–1812), German romantic painter, student of Tischbein. P., with Overbeck in Vienna, founded (1810) the Brotherhood of S. Isidoro (Nazarenes) in Italy. *NAZARENES.

[M. J. DALY]

PFORTA, ABBEY OF, a monastery near Naumburg, Germany, founded in 1127 for Benedictines. It became Cistercian in 1132. The community flourished under imperial protection and soon established the daughter abbeys of Leubus, Altzelle, and Dünamünde. Through their agricultural activity the monks contributed to the economic development of medieval Thuringia. In 1540 the abbey was secularized. Since 1543 the buildings have accommodated a secondary school of nationwide reputation. The impressive Gothic church was restored in the 19th century. BIBLIOGRAPHY: R. Pahncke, *Schulpforte* (1956).

[L. J. LEKAI]

PHACEE, KING OF ISRAEL, see PEKAH, KING OF ISRAEL.

PHAINŌ (E Syrian, *painā*), outer garment, sometimes also called *shaddōyō,* worn by W Syrian and Chaldean celebrants for the Eucharist, and by a bp. for his singing of the Gospel in solemn morning and evening Offices. In form it is much like a Latin cope. Among the Maronites it has been replaced by the Latin chasuble (*badlah*), although Maronite bps. still wear the *phainō* (for which they use an Arab. word, *guffârah*) at the beginning and end of Mass. The Nestorian equivalent of the *phainō* is called *ma'aprā.*

[A. CODY]

PHALÈSE, PIERRE (Petrus, Phalesius; 1510–73 or 74), Flemish music publisher and founder of the Phalèse music publishing house (1545). It was the leading house in the Netherlands until the death of the last family member in 1674. Of note are the printer's marks used by the Phalèse house, which include the figures of David, St. Peter, Melpomene, and the Blessed Virgin with Child.

[R. J. LITZ]

PHANAR, the Greek quarter of Istanbul under Ottoman rule; the residence of the privileged Greek families called

Phanariots, who came into prominence in the late 17th century. The higher Orthodox clergy, the governors of Moldavia and Walachia, and the minister of foreign affairs were ordinarily chosen from their ranks. They dominated commercial life, and were hated by their Christian subjects, even other Greeks. Their knowledge of foreign languages gave them a hold over Ottoman diplomacy. They played an important part in Greek politics in the 19th century.

[E. J. DILLON]

PHANTASM, in scholastic philosophy of knowledge, a term taken from Plato and Aristotle and meaning the object presented by the imagination (*phantasia*) to the mind. In its scholastic use it covers the images of the internal senses (imagination, the common sense, memory, the cogitative power); the internal senses, for various purposes, form an image from the distinct sense impressions in the "external" senses (sight, hearing etc.). From the phantasm the mind, by the process called "abstraction," forms its ideas and in process of thinking must always revert to the phantasm. BIBLIOGRAPHY: ThAq ST 1a, 78.3; 84.7; 85.1 & 2.

PHARAN, DESERT OF, see PARAN, DESERT OF.

PHARAOH (Heb. *par'ō*), as found in the Bible, not a proper name but a title of Egyptian rulers. The word in Egyptian probably means large[st] house, and was already used in the Early Kingdom (2800–2200 B.C.). The oldest-known use of the term in Egyptian texts as referring to the ruler, and not to his palace building, dates from the time of Ikhnaton (14th cent. B.C.). The pharaoh in fact had five titles. By preference Egyptians tended to use the fourth title, while the Bible uses the fifth, often without any further identification, thus giving rise to problems of identification, esp. in connection with Joseph (Gen 37.36; 50.7) and with the Exodus (Ex 1.8–10). In the OT five pharaohs are named: Hophra (Apries, *c.*588–568 B.C.), mentioned in Jer 44.30; Necho (Nksw, *c.*609–594 B.C.), referred to in 2 Kg 23.29–35; 2 Chr 35.20–24; and Jer 46.2; Shishak (Shoshenk, *c.*935–914 B.C.), mentioned in 1 Kg 11.40; 14.25–26; 2 Chr 12.2–9; so (perhaps, Sib'e) is mentioned in 2 Kg 17.4 as king of Egypt, but may have been only a high-ranking military authority; and Tirhakah (king of Ethiopia, who became ruler of Egypt, *c.*690–664 B.C.), mentioned in 2 Kg 19.9 and Is 37.9. Six other Egyptian kings are spoken of without further identification.

[I. HUNT]

PHARHAT, see APHRAATES.

PHARISEES, from the Gr., *pharisaioi,* the Aram. being *perishayya* and the Heb. *perushim.* They were a party within Judaism in NT times composed mostly of laymen, in contrast to the sacerdotal Sadducees. Calling themselves *haberim,* "comrades," they were organized into societies called *haburoth,* "brotherhoods," that were pledged to maintain strict ritual purity in accordance with the Torah and to keep separate from anyone who would not take similar vows; hence the meaning of their name in Hebrew: "separated" or the "set apart," or the "separators." They seem to have evolved out of a conservative protest movement against the Hellenizing efforts of the Seleucid rulers in the early years of the 2d cent. B.C. The movement was known as the *hasidim* (pious ones) and Pharisees was a name given to a group who broke from the original movement in opposition to the purely secularistic policies of its later leaders, the priest-princes of the Hasmonean dynasty, Jonathan (161–143 B.C.), and esp. Hyrcanus (135–104 B.C.).

Going under the names of scribes, rabbis, teachers, lawyers in the Gospels, most of the lawyers, moralists, and theologians belonged to the Pharisaic societies. Schools of disciples formed around them, in the time of Jesus the chief being that of Shammai, the more conservative, and Hillel, the more liberal.

Theologically, the Pharisees were progressive in as much as they accepted the oral traditions of the elders (Mt 15.2; Mk 7.5), taught the resurrection from the dead, accepted angels as divine messengers (Acts 23.7–8), maintained God's governance of history, and stressed the value of prayer and works of love and mercy. They are mentioned quite frequently in the NT, most often as hostile to Jesus but not invariably so, since he ate in their houses (Lk 7.36) and at least one of them became his disciple (Jn 3.1). Another aspect that is manifest in the NT as well as in the rabbinical writings is the Pharisees' tendency to hair-splitting definitions and refinements of the Law, mainly, it should be said, from a desire to eliminate confusion about prescriptions and to make them practicable. Further, an attitude of spiritual superiority and of condescension toward all who were not enrolled in their societies is evident. BIBLIOGRAPHY: L. Finkelstein, *Pharisees and the Men of the Great Synagogue* (1950); C. Barrett, *New Testament Background: Selected Documents* (1957) 124–127.

[A. J. TKACIK]

PHELAN, DAVID SAMUEL (1841–1915), priest-journalist. Born in Nova Scotia but at an early age brought to St. Louis, Mo., P. was ordained in 1863. As parish priest at Edina, Mo., he founded the *Missouri Watchman* (later called the *Western Watchman*). He was a vigorous and courageous, if at times imprudent editor. Criticism of the clergy abounded in his writing, more esp. of bps., whom he often denounced as overbearing. His own bp., P. R. *Kenrick, regarded P.'s writing as dangerous. P. was a zealous pastor and builder but a passionate controversialist. Admired by Abp. Ireland, he was censured by Abp. Keane and in conflict with Bp. Schrembs. P. is credited with having disrupted the American Protective Association in St. Louis by his exposure of some of its members. In spite of his difficulties, he was a great influence in the West.

[J. R. AHERNE]

PHELAN, GERALD BERNARD (1892–1965), Canadian philosopher, psychologist, and educator. A native of Halifax, Nova Scotia, P. was ordained a diocesan priest of Halifax (1914), and later studied at The Catholic University of America, St. Francis Xavier University, Nova Scotia, and the University of Louvain. At the beginning of his priesthood, he was engaged in parochial work in Nova Scotia and Bermuda. He lectured (1917–22) in philosophy at St. Mary's College, Halifax, and in 1925 was appointed professor of psychology at St. Michael's College, the University of Toronto. He served (1926–46) as professor of philosophy at St. Michael's and became librarian of the Pontifical Institute of Medieval Studies at the University of Toronto, and with É. Gilson, was codirector of the Institute, and was its president (1937–46). In 1946, he undertook the founding and directorship of the Medieval Institute at the University of Notre Dame, continuing in that capacity until 1952, and serving as chairman of the philosophy department during this same period. P. returned to St. Michael's College as professor of philosophy (1952–62), and served in the same capacity in The Pontifical Institute (1958–62), retiring in the latter year. His works include: *Collected Essays* (1966); *Jacques Maritain* (1937); *St. Thomas and Analogy* (1941); *The Wisdom of St. Anselm* (1960); *On The Governance of Rulers,* tr. of St. Thomas's *De regimine principum* (1939); *Some Illustrations of St. Thomas's Development of the Wisdom of Saint Augustine* (1946).

[J. T. HICKEY]

PHELAN, MARIE GERARD, MOTHER (1872–1960), superior general, educator. Born in Ireland, P. joined the Religious of the Sacred Heart of Mary and came to the U.S. in 1907 to aid in the establishment of Marymount School in Tarrytown, New York. She became dean and then president of Marymount College in the same city. Provincial of the North American province of the Congregation, she was elected superior general in 1946 and again in 1952. In her term of office the institute founded 28 schools and colleges in 11 countries.

[J. R. AHERNE]

PHELONION (Lat. *paenula,* traveling cloak; Sl. *phelon*), the large outer vestment proper to priests in the Byzantine liturgy. Until the 16th cent. it was also worn by bps. but has since been replaced by the *sakkos. The phelonion is a very ample, conically-cut vestment, closed in front, with an opening in the center to admit the head. Its ancient form reached to the ground on all sides and was gathered up by the arms in front, producing an extremely graceful and noble effect. Unfortunately, as with the Western chasuble, a clipping process has destroyed the fullness of the garment. It has been cut to allow freer movement of the arms, in Russia up to the height of the elbows in front, but with the Greeks never above the height of the knee. The back part of the phelonion retains its ancient length. The Greek form has a close-fitting, flat-lying neck cut, while the Russian form has preserved the ancient "top of the cone" neck shape, but unfortunately the soft collar-like effect has been stiffened with cardboard and embroidery so that it stands up high in the neck of the wearer almost hiding his head. This is said to have been done to keep the customary long hair of the Russian priests from soiling the back of the vestment. The phelonion is usually ornamented with a Greek cross on the back and the Russians invariably add the eight-pointed star, symbol of the Resurrection, near the rear hemline. In addition, galloons are often used to outline the shape of the garment. The phelonion is worn during the Liturgy over the sticharion or alb but it is also used in many non-eucharistic services where it is worn with the *epitrachelion* (stole) directly over the *rason.* The vestments of most of the other Eastern Churches have been developed from the ancient form of the Byzantine phelonion and therefore still somewhat resemble it. Both the Western chasuble and the Byzantine phelonion derive from the same early Christian traveling cloak or *paenula.*

[A. J. JACOPIN]

PHEME (Gr., proclamation), the acclamation which announces the name and titles of a hierarch or patriarch at a solemn Divine Liturgy celebrated by him. It is usually chanted by a deacon or archpriest in a loud and clear voice immediately before the epistle. It concludes with the acclamation "for many years," during which the hierarch blesses the chanter and the congregation.

[A. J. JACOPIN]

PHENOMENA, a Kantian concept, referring to the world of sensually perceived facts, appearances as opposed to realities. The distinction between noumena, the things-in-themselves of intelligible reality, and phenomena dates to Kant's *1770 Dissertation* where he argued that since phenomena are present to us within a spatio-temporal framework and that since time and space are forms of human sensibility not aspects of independent reality, then phenomena, being dependent on the senses, are not features of independent reality. Scientific knowledge, he maintained in his *Critique of Pure Reason,* is concerned with the phenomenal realm where natural laws of causality are in effect. When humans act freely as moral agents, they function in the noumenal realm, but humans, as perceived by others, are, like the world, phenomena. *KANT, I.

[R. J. LITZ]

PHENOMENOLOGY, a philosophical term having a variety of meanings prior to the 20th cent., but in present usage referring principally to a philosophical movement or method the purpose of which is the examination and description of phenomena present to human consciousness. In its origins, the word phenomenology is traceable to a probable first usage by the Swiss-German philosopher, Johann Lambert (1728–77), in his *Neues Organon* (1764). He defined it as "the theory of illusion" and applied it to that aspect of his epistemology which seeks to distinguish truth from error. L.'s contemporary, Immanuel *Kant, gave rise to a new context for the term in contrasting phenomena, or things as they appear to man, with noumena, or things as they are in themselves. But the German thinker, Georg *Hegel, reacted against Kant in his *Phänomenologie des Geistes* (1807), again causing a new interpretation of the word in his description of the evolutionary process through which Mind or Spirit finally becomes aware of itself as noumenon. By mid-19th cent. the expression had become a generic one, having reference to a descriptive investigation of any factual area, as for instance, in the meaning of the American philosopher, C. S. *Peirce, a study and enumeration of all possible categories of being, real and mental.

Phenomenology in modern contexts, however, is usually understood as the philosophic formulation of Edmund *Husserl, professor of philosophy at Göttingen and Freiburg. From the early 1900s phenomenology has been presented as the approach to philosophy that employs Husserl's phenomenological method. In its broadest terms, it was gradually conceived as a science descriptive of phenomena through direct awareness, and was intended to provide a new basis for both natural science and philosophy, making of the latter a rigorous discipline probing the fundamental structures of reality. Yet it was not viewed as describing empirically observed matters of fact, for it was to be a nonempirical, intuitive and a priori science. In his *Logische Untersuchungen* (1900–01), Husserl sets forth the goal of defining the essence of all conscious data, with particular stress upon intentionality or the relation of consciousness to objects of knowledge, and upon intuition as the cause of the content of cognition. It is the effort of this school to penetrate human subjective experience to the point of arriving at a so-called "pure consciousness," remaining after the superficial accumulation of usual daily conscious states has been removed. At this juncture, certain elemental structures or essences are intuited, emphasizing the existence of something prior to and independent of experience. For Husserl and his disciples, this intuitive method probes the very vitals of existence, and hence, is the only acceptable approach for philosophic investigation. Martin *Heidegger, a student of Husserl, applies the phenomenological method to the problem of being, particularly the being of man. In his *Sein und Zeit* (1927), he points to the tragic role of man, a being who without his own consent emerges from nothingness and throughout life faces the inevitability of returning to it in death. Thus, the whole of human existence is riddled with anxiety or anguish, fear, and guilt, confronting always the annihilation of death. The basic metaphysical question becomes one of why there is something rather than nothing at all. But still, the individual is not confined within himself but is capable of achieving a self-transcendence—however one which does not imply an approach to God, but rather a relation to the world, a rapport with other humans, and finally an ability to overcome momentary existence and its preoccupation with death.

Jean Paul *Sartre, the French existentialist, follows to some extent in the tradition of both Husserl and Heidegger, setting forth a "phenomenological ontology" which portrays human existence as the one thing man really knows. There is no hidden reality or essence behind the screen of our experiences, for existence is prior to essence. Developing existentialism as a philosophical system in his *Being and Nothingness* (1956), he combines it with phenomenology and sees it thus as an attempt to draw all of the consequences from an atheistic point of view. Man is not a finished product in the beginning but rather has to make himself. He is what he wills himself to be. And there is no external support forcing man to fall back on his initiative to cope with an existence having no meaning or purpose apart from what his freedom creates. Since there is no God, that freedom is not restricted by any concept such as that of a universal moral law. Despite this, however, man still has responsibility for the ideals which he freely chooses and the effect these have on other humans. BIBLIOGRAPHY: *Husserliana* (ed. by H. van Breda, 1950); Husserl's *Ideen zu einer reinen Phänomenologie* (1913); the periodical *Philosophy and Phenomenological Research* (ed. M. Farber, 1940–); M. Farber's *Foundation of Phenomenology* (1943); M. Scheler's *Formalismus in der Ethik,* (1916); Heidegger's *Was ist Metaphysik?* (1929); Sartre's *Existentialism* (tr. B. Frechtman, 1947).

[J. T. HICKEY]

PHIDIAS (PHEIDIAS; fl. *c.*470–425 B.C.), greatest Greek sculptor of the Periclean age, genius of the Classical style which reached an apotheosis in P.'s Parthenon marbles (*Elgin Marbles)—the *Panathenaic procession frieze, heroic figures of the pediments (*Three Fates, Dionysus*) and the metopes, (some figures, no doubt, by assistants following P.'s designs), the gold and ivory (chryselephantine) colossal cult statue of the Athena Parthenos (40 ft high), described by Pausanias and Pliny and preserved in copies on coins, and the beautiful Lemnian Athena, the "thoughtful Athena with the delicate cheek" (of attribution sometimes questioned), and the chryselephantine Zeus for the temple at Olympia (*c.*430), considered the greatest religious statue of Greece, of which Quintilian says "its beauty can be said to have added something to traditional religion." (*Inst. oratoriarum* 12,10,9). BIBLIOGRAPHY: G. M. A. Richter, *Sculpture and Sculptors of the Greeks* (1957).

[M. J. DALY]

PHILADELPHIA CONFESSION, a Baptist *confession of faith. The Philadelphia Baptist Association, organized in 1707, adopted the *Second London Confession of 1689 as its standard. The date of adoption is uncertain; in 1742, the association voted that a new edition be printed, but the minutes of 1724 refer to "the Confession of Faith, set forth by the elders and brethren met in London, 1689, and owned by us." No changes were made in the original text, but two new articles were added. One declared that singing praise to God is of divine institution and enjoined churches to sing psalms, hymns, and spiritual songs in their services. The other affirmed that the ''laying on of hands (with prayer) upon every baptized believer . . . is an ordinance of Christ.'' It was the most widely used Baptist confession in America until supplanted by the *New Hampshire Confession. BIBLIOGRAPHY: *Baptist Confessions of Faith* (ed. W. L. Lumpkin, 1959).

[N. H. MARING]

PHILADELPHIA YEARLY MEETING OF THE RELIGIOUS SOCIETY OF FRIENDS, a group of the Society of Friends comprising since 1955 the former Arch Street Yearly Meeting (Orthodox) and the Race Street Yearly Meeting (Hicksite). It is affiliated with the Friends General Conference.

[J. C. WILLKE]

PHILADELPHIANS, a sect of religious mystics that developed from followers of J. *Boehme who gathered about J. Pordage (1607–81), rector of Bradfield in Berkshire. The most influential of the group was Mrs. Jane Lead (Leade; 1623–1704), who had been a visionary from her youth and who recorded many of her mystical experiences and prophecies in books published between 1681 and 1704. The group was organized in 1670 as the Philadelphia Society for the Advancement of Piety and Divine Philosophy. Although membership in the society was not intended at first to supplant or interfere with existing church affiliation or creedal commitment, the society did eventually put forth its own confession of faith (1703). Its doctrine was inclined to natural pantheism and mystical extravagance as well as to *chiliasm. The translation of one of Mrs. Lead's books into Dutch in 1693 brought her to prominence; through this work and through the influence of F. Lee, a former Oxonian and then a medical student at Leiden, the society gained some Dutch and a few German adherents, whose teachings had some effect upon certain leaders of *Pietism. After Mrs. Lead's death repressive measures taken by the government caused the society in England to dwindle into extinction.

[P. K. MEAGHER]

PHILAE, granite island in the Nile, site of the Ptolemaic temple to Isis, with columned porticoes added by Augustus, a pilgrimage center with the shrine of the tomb of Osiris (W of Philae). The Hathoric capitals are typical of Ptolemaic architecture.

[M. J. DALY]

PHILARET DROZDOV, see FILARET.

PHILARET (Filaret; Theodore Nikitich Romanov c. 1554–1633), patriarch of Moscow and coruler in the reign of Tsar Michael Romanov. When Boris Godunov assumed power, Theodore, a rival claimant, came under suspicion. In 1601 Godunov forced him into a monastery and sent his son, Michael, into exile. When Theodore, now Philaret, entered the religious life, he lost his rights to the throne, but

his political career was not ended. He became an important figure during the Time of Troubles and later was taken to Poland as a hostage. His ineffective son, Michael, was tsar for 6 years before P. returned in 1619. From that date until his death P. was the true ruler of Russia. Not only did he control domestic and foreign politics, but also, as head of the Russian Church, religious life. In religious matters he was conservative and anti-Latin. In other areas, such as finance, administration and the military, P. instituted changes that foreshadowed the later reforms of Tsar Peter the Great. He encouraged, for example, the use of foreigners in the army. His aggressive foreign policy was motivated by his hatred of Poland. BIBLIOGRAPHY: G. Vernadsky, *Tsardom of Moscow, 1547–1682* (*History of Russia* 5, 1969); J. H. Billington, *Icon and the Axe: An Interpretive History of Russian Culture* (1966).

[C. T. EBY]

PHILASTER (PHILASTRIUS), see FILASTER.

PHILEAS OF THMUIS, ST. (d. 304), bp. in Lower Egypt. P. was elected bp. after his conversion to Christianity, but was seized during the persecution of Diocletian and taken to Alexandria for trial before Culcianus, governor of Egypt. Because he was a man of position and wealth, more care than usual was taken at his trial and he was defended by able lawyers. The account of his trial and martyrdom is held by some to be based on court documents. T. *Ruinart thought well of it, but the opinion of H. *Delehaye was less favorable. A letter from P. to his flock, written from prison, is cited by Eusebius. BIBLIOGRAPHY: Butler 1:248–249.

[R. B. ENO]

PHILELEUTHERUS LIPSIENSIS, PSEUD., see BENTLEY, RICHARD.

PHILEMON, LETTER TO, Pauline *Epistle, almost certainly sent with the Letter to the Colossians, probably from Rome in A.D. 60–63, and normally grouped with the *Captivity Epistles. The only purely private and personal letter among Paul's Epistles, it concerns a slave, Onesimus, who, having fled from his Christian master, Philemon, met Paul, and became a Christian. Paul now writes to Philemon asking him to forgive Onesimus and to receive him kindly as a brother rather than a slave when he returns. Paul also alludes to services rendered to himself by Onesimus. BIBLIOGRAPHY: G. H. P. Thompson, *Letters of Paul to the Ephesians, Colossians and Philemon* (1967).

[D. J. BOURKE]

PHILIBERT OF REBAIS, ST. (d. 685), abbot. He became a monk c. 636 at the monastery of Rebais, founded by his friend St. Ouen, and was elected abbot c. 650. P.'s administration proved unsuccessful and he left Rebais to study monastic observances elsewhere, esp. at Bobbio and Luxeuil. In 654 he founded a monastery in the forests of Jumièges. For denouncing Ebroin, mayor of the palace, P.

was removed and temporarily imprisoned. He later founded the monastery of Noirmoutier off the coast of Poitou. BIB-LIOGRAPHY: P. Rouillard, BiblSanct 5:702–704; Butler 3:367.

[G. M. COOK]

PHILIP, ST., APOSTLE, one of the Twelve. Philip is just a name on a list in each of the lists of the Apostles found in the Gospels of Matthew, Mark, and Luke, and again in the opening chapter of Acts. In the fourth Gospel, however, P. figures in four different episodes which reveal the outlines, at least, of a real person. He comes from the same town (Bethsaida) as Andrew and Simon, and like them he came to Jesus through the testimony of the Baptist. P. brought Nathaniel to Jesus with the words: "We have met the man spoken of by Moses in the Law, and by the prophets . . ." (Jn 1.45). Jesus already knew Nathaniel to be "an Israelite worthy of the name" with nothing false in him, and added: "I saw you under the fig tree before Philip spoke to you." (Jn 1.47–49). In chapter six of this Gospel, it is to P. that Jesus said: "Where are we to buy bread to feed these people?" to which P. gives the kind of reply you might expect from someone used to seeing to the daily provisioning of the Rabbi and his disciples: "Two hundred denarii (60 dollars) would not buy enough bread for every one of them to have a little" (vv. 5–7). Again in ch. 12 P. is approached as someone familiar with the day-to-day workings of the band of disciples. Some Greeks (Jews of Greek culture and language on festival pilgrimage to Jerusalem) came to him with the request to see Jesus. P. went and told Andrew, and the two of them went to tell Jesus (vv. 20–22). It was probably natural for the two disciples with Greek names to act as cultural intermediaries in this way. P. was the one accessible to outsiders, and he needed Andrew to gain for them access to Jesus. According to John's narrative of the Last Supper events, P. made an impetuous request which triggered a profound "Joannine" discourse. But the actual request also fits very well into the traditional Passover observance. Indeed it is still traditional to proclaim the events of the first Passover by the recurring formula: "If He had delivered us from Egyptian bondage, and not led us through the desert, . . . it would have been enough for us;" "If He had led us through the desert and not brought us into the land of promise, . . . it would have been enough for us." Such a traditional litany with recurring refrain provides a natural background for P.'s exclamation: "Lord, show us the Father, and it is enough for us" (14:8). Jesus' response, colored in the telling no doubt by Joannine insight, was simply: "Have I been all this time with you, Philip, and you still do not know me? Anyone who has seen me has seen the Father" (14:9). These episodes, containing historical reminiscences, present a rather coherent outline of a definite person: a person quick to believe, and quick to act on his belief; a disciple first of John and then of Jesus; the humble provisioner, neither too important nor too busy to share with others his access to the Rabbi; a man whose simplicity helped him get to the heart of things without necessarily understanding at once the full implications of what he heard and saw.

[E. J. DILLON]

PHILIP I (1052–1108), **KING OF FRANCE** from 1060. Son of Henry I and Anne of Kiev, he added Gâtinais, Corbie, Vexin, and Bourges to the royal domain, the first Capetian king to extend his territorial claims. He came into conflict with the Church when he repudiated his wife, Bertha of Holland, the mother of his heir, Louis (VI), to marry in 1094 Bertrada of Anjou, wife of Count Fulk. Though he was excommunicated and put under papal interdict for his action, his bishops tolerated his adultery. Both Urban II and Paschal II were handicapped in dealing with him because of their struggle with the Emperor. Philip agreed to renounce Bertrada in 1104, but it is not certain that he did. BIBLIOGRAPHY: A. Fliche, *Le Règne de Philippe I*er, *Roi de France* (1912); D. J. A. Matthew, NCE 11:269–270.

[V. BULLOUGH]

PHILIP II (1165–1223), **AUGUSTUS, KING OF FRANCE** (from 1180), one of the greatest of medieval French kings; founder of a centralized state subject to uniform royal administration; son of Louis VII and Adèle of Champagne. The title Augustus was coined by his chaplain, but was popularized only by later historians. He set out on the Third Crusade (1190) but quarreled with Richard I of England and returned to France in order to conspire against him. He separated Normandy from England in 1204 and 10 years later defeated Emperor Otto IV at the Battle of Bouvines. His repudiation of Ingeborg, his second wife, brought him into violent conflict with Pope Innocent III. Philip Augustus found a new source of support for monarchy in the rich bourgeoisie of the towns. BIBLIOGRAPHY: CMedH 6:285–330 for bibliog; R. Fawtier, *Capetian Kings of France* (tr. L. Butler and R. J. Adam, 1960).

[J. E. WRIGLEY]

PHILIP III (1245–85), **KING OF FRANCE** from 1270, son of St. Louis, father of Philip the Fair. Through the marriage of his son, Navarre and Champagne were added to the royal domain, while he simply annexed Languedoc and Poitou. An attempt to encroach upon Aragon failed and cost him his life. The Second Council of Lyons (1273–74) was held under his protection. BIBLIOGRAPHY: R. Fawtier, *Capetian Kings of France* (tr. L. Butler and R. J. Adam, 1960).

[J. E. WRIGLEY]

PHILIP IV (1268–1314) the Fair, **KING OF FRANCE** from 1285. Although several new aspects of the French monarchy became quite clear during P.'s dramatic reign, his character remains an enigma. Some scholars assert that a group of clever civil lawyers (Flotte, Nogaret, Marigny) deserve both the credit and the blame for his policies. Whether Philip dominated his unscrupulous servants, or they him, may never be known. He imposed the first general tax in French history and wanted to tax the clergy without papal consent. His quarrel with Pope Boniface VIII centered about his need for money and his firm determination to achieve sovereign independence for the French crown. He accused the Knights Templar of heresy, probably because he coveted their wealth. His direct influence on the establishment of the papacy in Avignon has been seriously questioned. He no doubt used Clement V to destroy the Templars, but that he made of the pope a tool of France is now generally rejected. From 1295 on he steadily debased the royal currency. In 1302 he summoned his vassals together with representatives from the towns to consult with him regarding his conflict with Boniface VIII. This has been called the first meeting of the States-General. In 1306 he drove the Jews out of France and in 1311 expelled the Italian bankers—in both cases, because he owed them large sums of money. The tendency toward control of specialized administrative functions by laymen instead of clerics grew rapidly during his reign. New financial and administrative arrangements indicate the rapidly widening gap between the king as a private person and the king as the embodiment of the secular state. Although P.'s administrative structure endured, his unsavory methods severely damaged royal prestige. BIBLIOGRAPHY: J. R. Strayer, ''Philip the Fair: A 'Constitutional' King,'' *American Historical Review,* 62 (1956–57) 18–32; *idem,* NCE 11:271–272.

[J. E. WRIGLEY]

PHILIP II (1527–1598), King of Spain from 1556. In 1556 his father, Charles V, gave him Spain, the Netherlands, the Italian territories and the New World as an inheritance. P. proved to be completely different from his father. Religiously scrupulous to the point of fanaticism, P. was constantly trying to impose his will upon Europe. He possessed a deep sense of his kingship and its sacred obligations. In political affairs he distrusted his ministers and took upon himself the burden of governmental details; he valued his own judgments alone. Unlike Charles V, he attempted to ignore the institutions and traditions of his scattered holdings and to impose centralization and uniformity based upon the Spanish model, as exampled in his treatment of the Netherlands. In his reliance upon Spain, esp. Castile, P. isolated himself from the rest of his empire. He possessed an overwhelming fear of heresy and attacked it vigorously wherever found. Yet he was usually at friction with the papacy over such issues as the Tridentine reforms and the control of the Spanish bishoprics. At times P. may have believed that he was more capable than the pope in achieving religious reform. Historically, it is difficult to be neutral about P.'s reign. From one viewpoint he was a stubborn, arrogant, unreasonable tyrant while from another he was a devout Catholic motivated by the best interests of Church and State. BIBLIOGRAPHY: H. G. Koenigsberger, *Habsburgs*

and Europe 1516–1660 (1971); *Character of Philip II* (ed. J. C. Rule and J. J. TePaske, 1963).

[C. T. EBY]

PHILIP THE ARABIAN (Marcus Julius Philippus; *c.*204–249), **ROMAN EMPEROR** from 244. P. was a native of Bostra in Arabia Trachonitis. Rising through the ranks to become praetorian prefect, he connived in the assassination of the youthful Gordian III near Zaitha in 244 and was himself proclaimed emperor. In 247 he gained a significant victory over the Carpi and the following year celebrated the thousandth anniversary of Rome with great magnificence. He and his son were slain in battle near Verona by the soldiers of Decius, whom he had sent to command the troops in Moesia and Pannonia. A very unlikely tradition preserved in Eusebius, Jerome, Orosius, and other Christian writers that Philip was the first Christian emperor is best explained by his benevolent tolerance, his curiosity in religious matters, and his death fighting against Decius, whom the Christians came to regard as an archfiend. BIBLIOGRAPHY: E. Stein, PW 10:755–770; CAH 12:87–95.

[M. J. COSTELLOE]

PHILIP BENIZI, ST. (1223–85), fifth superior general of the Servites. Originally trained as a physician at Paris and at Padua, he practiced medicine until joining the Servites (1254), eventually being elected superior general (1267). BIBLIOGRAPHY: Butler 3:385–388; A. M. Serra, BiblSanct 5:736–752.

[J. MULDOON]

PHILIP THE CHANCELLOR (d. 1236), theologian at the Univ. of Paris. During his administration as chancellor (from *c.*1218) he was involved in the conflicts that were settled by Gregory IX in 1231 in the statutes *Parens scientiarum* that became the definitive charter of the University. P. was one of the principal theologians of the transitional era before high scholasticism. His unedited *Summa de bono* combines Neoplatonic ideas with an impressive knowledge of Aristotle's writings. Many of P.'s ideas on virtue, grace, and sin had special influence on 13th-cent. theology. Until the 20th cent. P. was mistakenly identified with *Philip of Grève.

[T. C. O'BRIEN]

PHILIP THE DEACON, also known as Philip the evangelist (Acts 21.8). Chosen as one of the seven to serve the Hellenistic Christian community (6.5), he preached and baptized in Samaria (8.4–13) and from Azotus to Caesarea (8.26–40).

[M. A. MCNAMARA]

PHILIP OF GORTYNA, 2d-cent. bp. of Gortyna in Crete, known only through the references to him in Eusebius (*Hist. eccl.* 4, 21.23.25). He is mentioned as bp. in a letter addressed by Dionysius of Corinth to the Church of Gortyna. Dionysius commends P. for the manifestations of fortitude displayed by the Church under his care. Dionysius also warns him about the perversions of the heretics. Eusebius himself notes that P. had written a very elaborate refutation of Marcion.

[E. J. DILLON]

PHILIP OF GRÈVE (d. *c.*1220–22), canon and master at Notre Dame, Paris. Henri Meylan (1927) discredited the long-accepted identification of P. with his more famous contemporary, Philip the Chancellor, theologian and chancellor of the Univ. of Paris and outstanding poet of his time. Philip of Grève was a canon of Notre Dame from 1182, master from 1194, and taught canon law there (*c.*1200). He died as dean of the cathedral chapter of Sens. BIBLIOGRAPHY: G. M. Cook, NCE 11:275.

[G. M. COOK]

PHILIP OF HARVENGT (d. 1183), Premonstratensian abbot at Bonne-Espérance from 1158. His *De institutione clericorum* is a spiritual guide for monastic formation; he also wrote works of philosophy and theology, scriptural commentaries (allegorical), and a life of St. Augustine (P.'s works are contained in PL 203). Early in his monastic life he became embroiled in controversy with St. Bernard of Clairvaux and was actually exiled from Bonne-Espérance in 1149, until his reinstatement in 1151.

[T. C. O'BRIEN]

PHILIP OF HESSE (1504–67), Landgrave of Hesse from 1519, promoter of the Reformation. With little formal education, but skilled in politics, he soon established a model government in Hesse. He met Martin Luther at the Diet of *Worms (1521), put down the Peasants' Revolt (1526), and beginning in 1526 established the Reformation in his territory. He founded a university at Marburg (1527) for Protestant theologians. In an attempt, which proved unsuccessful, to reconcile Luther and Zwingli in regard to eucharistic teaching, he called (1529) the Marburg Colloquy (see MAR- BURG ARTICLES). He also organized the Protestant princes in the Schmalkaldic League (1530), sharing leadership with the Elector of Saxony. The League was hampered by rivalries and by P.'s own alliances with the Emperor, Charles V. His need to placate Charles arose in part from a bigamous marriage (1540), secretly countenanced by Luther. P. did, however, raise an army for the Schmalkalden War (1546–57) against the Emperor; he was captured, imprisoned for 5 years, and upon his release lost interest in politics, but worked for religious reunion. BIBLIOGRAPHY: U. Heinemeger, RGG 5:332–333.

[T. C. O'BRIEN]

PHILIP OF MOSCOW, ST. (1507–69), bp. and martyr. A wealthy nobleman, Feodor Kolyshov, at the age of 30 became a monk at Solovetsk, taking the name Philip. Ten years later he was chosen abbot and devoted himself both to the spiritual and physical direction of the monastery. In 1567 he was elected metropolitan of Moscow in a time of great trouble, for the Tsar was Ivan IV, called the Terrible. A massacre of political suspects including many innocent persons led Philip to rebuke him publicly during the liturgy in the Moscow cathedral. Not long afterwards Ivan had him deposed, dragged about in chains, and finally strangled.

[G. T. DENNIS]

PHILIP NERI, ST. (1515–95), called the "Apostle of Rome," founder of the Oratorians. As a Florentine he was attracted to the memory of *Savonarola (executed 1498) and to the Dominicans of San Marco, who were his schoolmasters. He showed no interest in becoming a notary like his father, Francesco, nor in holding a clerkship in the offices of his cousin, a successful merchant at San Germano. Instead he came to Rome (1533), where he lived as a solitary for 2 years. After courses in philosophy at the Sapienza and in theology at Sant' Agostino (1535–38), he sold his books and commenced a social apostolate during which he spent his days in works of charity and his nights in prayer. In the Catacomb of S. Sebastiano on Whitsunday, 1544, he experienced an ecstasy; afterwards his heart was discovered to have become miraculously enlarged. In 1548 he organized the *Confraternita di SS. Trinit*à, a group of laymen who cared for pilgrims and convalescents. He accepted ordination to the priesthood in 1551 and lived with other priests in the church of S. Girolamo della Carità. His confessional became popular, and his afternoon instructions to men and boys in a room over the church revealed his great affability and his talent for imparting wisdom with wit. P. also led pilgrimages to the seven churches, but in 1559 all his activities were temporarily suspended by *Paul IV, who feared they encouraged a plot against himself. From 1564 Philip lived with some priests, in community but without vows, at the Church of S. Giovanni dei Fiorentini where prayers, informal talks in theology and Church history, and musical settings prepared by his friend Palestrina, formed the pattern of the future Oratory. In 1567 *Pius V was strongly inclined to suppress the group, which he had been told was a band of heretics; the timely intervention of St. *Charles Borromeo saved the community. In 1575 the Congregation of the Oratory was officially approved by Gregory XIII. A new church, called still *Chiesa Nuova,* was built and became the center of the new congregation; P. was first superior, and was succeeded by C. *Baronius. Revered as a saint during his lifetime, P. was beatified in 1615, and canonized in 1622. He received the title "Apostle of Rome" because of his success in converting many high ecclesiastics to strive for personal holiness. His cheerfulness and warm personal devotion to Christ have made P. a particularly attractive saint. BIBLIOGRAPHY: L. Bouyer, *Roman Socrates* (tr. M. Day, 1958); M. Jouandeau, *St. Philip Neri* (tr. G. Lamb, 1960); L. Ponnelle and L. Bordet, *St. Philip Neri and the Roman Society of His Times* (tr. R. F. Kerr, 1933).

[E. D. MCSHANE]

PHILIP SIDETES (5th cent.), Church historian. A native of Side in Pamphylia, P. was ordained deacon by St. John Chrysostom. In the years that followed his ordination to the priesthood he wrote his *Christian History* in 36 books taking as his subject the whole history of the world down to his own time. Of this work only fragments remain; an apology against *Julian the Apostate is lost. BIBLIOGRAPHY: Quasten 3:528–530.

[R. B. ENO]

PHILIP THE TETRARCH, son of Herod the Great and Cleopatra of Jerusalem and husband of Salome. He ruled the territory N and E of the Lake of Galilee from 4 B.C. to 34 A.D.

[M. A. MCNAMARA]

PHILIP, ACTS OF, see APOCRYPHA (NT), 54.

PHILIP, GOSPEL OF, see APOCRYPHA (NT), 55.

PHILIPPA MARERI, BL. (b. betw. 1190 and 1200; d. 1236), Poor Clare abbess. Wishing to avoid the quarrels between her brother, a powerful local baron, and Frederick II, she refused all marriage proposals and withdrew with a few friends to a grotto near Mareri to lead a life of prayer and penance. She later built a convent for her purposes that is today the oldest Poor Clare convent in Sicily. She was recognized for her administrative ability, humility, austerity, and charity. BIBLIOGRAPHY: Léon de Clary, *Lives of the Saints* (1885–87) 1:257–260; L. Ziliani, *La baronessa santa* (1935); R. T. d'Arenzano, BiblSanct 8:754–756.

[O. J. BLUM]

PHILIPPE, CHARLES LOUIS (1874–1909), French writer. P. completed his bachelor's degrees, but after being refused admission to L'École Polytechnique, served in minor Parisian municipal posts. His realistic novels, frequently drawn from autobiographical sources, portray accurately but sympathetically the sufferings of the rural poor and urban social outcasts. Representative works include his masterpiece, *Bubu de Montparnasse* (1901), *Le Père Perdrix* (1903), *Marie Donadieu* (1904), and *Charles Blanchard* (published 1913). P. had ceased practicing Catholicism, but evangelical themes and a quasi-religious nostalgia for pristine naturalness inspired his works. Contact with Catholic writers, particularly Paul Claudel, who consciously tried to convert him, had apparently brought him close to accepting Catholicism anew at the time of his death. BIBLIOGRAPHY: E. Guillaumin, *Mon compatriote Charles-Louis Philippe* (1942); L. Lanoizelée, *Charles-Louis Philippe, l'homme et l'écrivain* (1953).

[G. E. GINGRAS]

PHILIPPIANS, LETTER TO THE, 15th book in the NT canon, written by St. Paul to the community he established at Philippi on his second missionary journey (Acts 16.11–40). According to Acts 20.1–2,6, Paul twice visited this community before his imprisonment at Caesarea (Acts 23.23–24) and Rome (Acts 28.16). The Epistle seems to have been written before these visits, since Phil 4.15–16 suggests that the communication between Paul and the community has been only by way of their contributions to him. Some modern scholars have doubted, therefore, that this letter was written during Paul's first Roman imprisonment, as early Christian tradition held. They suggest that it was written from Ephesus during the apostle's third missionary journey, and prior to his visits to Philippi, when he underwent an imprisonment at Ephesus that Luke does not record in Acts 19.1–20.1 (cf. 1 Cor 15.32). Mention in Phil 1.13 and 4.22 of the praetorium and of Caesar's household does not require the conclusion that Paul writes from Rome, since these terms refer to the administrative staff of the emperor, the presence of which in Ephesus and elsewhere throughout the empire is attested by inscriptions. The position of a few scholars that the Epistle was composed during Paul's Caesarean imprisonment encounters the same difficulty as the view that it was written at Rome (see above). On the plausible hypothesis that the letter originated in Ephesus, its date of composition ranges from about A.D. 54 to 58. The chatty quality of this Epistle that permits it to pass from one topic to another without consistency of development has induced some scholars to see it as a compilation of several letters to the Philippians. As a possibility this theory remains open, but the explanation of the disunity may also lie in the historical circumstances under which Paul composed it. The letter reflects Paul's affection for this community and aims to conserve and deepen his relationship with it. The Apostle expresses satisfaction over the Philippians' spiritual state (1.3–11), offers news about his personal circumstances and feelings (1.12–26), and encourages them to stand firm in the faith (1.27–30) through the imitation of Jesus' humility (2.1–11). He recommends patience and unity within the community (2.12–18). He reveals his plan to send Timothy to them and informs them of the condition and future of their emissary, Epaphroditus (2.19–30). He warns them against the Judaizers (3.2–21) and concludes with an appeal for the resolution of personal conflicts and with personal reminiscences (4.1–23). Philippians, with Colossians, Ephesians, Philemon, is traditionally listed among the "captivity Epistles." Its passage (2.5–11) on the *kenosis of Christ, probably borrowed from the liturgy, provides valuable insight into the early Christian conception of the humanity and divinity of Christ. BIBLIOGRAPHY: D. Guthrie, *New Testament Introduction* (1961); Wikenhauser NTI; P. Feine, et al., *Einleitung in das Neue Testament* (1964).

[C. P. CEROKE]

PHILIPPINE INDEPENDENT CHURCH (Iglesia Católica Filipina Independiente; IFI), a body that separated from the RC Church in 1902; popularly it is known as the Aglipayan Church. Native insurrection about the time of the

Spanish-American War included an attack against the friar-bishops, who were identified with Spanish policy. After the failure of political resistance in 1901, the IFI was proclaimed by the nationalist leader, Isabelo de los Reyes, Sr. (1864–1938), and Gregorio *Aglipay (1860–1940), a native secular priest, was acknowledged as supreme bishop. Nationalist feeling initially drew large numbers into the new Church, but the Aglipayans diminished to about 5% of the population in 1966. RC church buildings and property that had been seized earlier were ordered restored by judicial decision in 1906. Initially *apostolic succession was ignored. Doctrinal disputes and strong factionalism developed. One group allied with American Unitarians and split into various parties; another, a trinitarian group, moved toward the Protestant Episcopal Church, from which they received orders in 1948 and with which they were formally united in 1961. The legally recognized IFI is the episcopal and trinitarian body. At the Old Catholic Congress of 1965 the IFI was received as a full member of the *Union of Utrecht. The Church is also in full communion with 12 Churches of the Anglican Communion, and its bp. participated at the Lambeth Conference of 1968. Its supreme bp. is elected by a general assembly for a 4-year term. BIBLIOGRA-PHY: P. S. de Achútegui and M. A. Bernad, *Religious Revolution in the Philippines: The Life and Church of Gregorio Aglipay, 1860–1940* (2 v., 1960–66).

[J. C. WILLKE]

PHILIPPINES, island republic of the S Pacific (115,707 sq mi; pop. [1975] 42,760,000). The original inhabitants were probably Negritos, later replaced in part by Malays, Moros, and Chinese. Official languages are English, Tagalog, Visaya, and Ilocano. The islands were taken by Spain in the 16th cent. and by the U.S. in 1898. P. achieved independence in 1946. The Filipinos have the distinction of being the only modern Asian country to enter the Church in large numbers. The Augustinian Urdaneta began evangelization in 1560. Then others entered the field: Franciscans (1578), Jesuits (1581), Dominicans (1578), and Augustinian Recollects (1606). Christianization advanced rapidly: the archipelago became a province in 1595 with Manila as its head and Cebu, Cáceres, and Nueva Segovia as suffragan sees. The Church was active in building the nation: missions laid out townships and villages, constructed bridges and canals, improved farming, fostered education, and provided medical care. The 600,000 Catholics of 1591 increased to 2,000,000 by 1670. The Philippines also served as a base for mission work in Taiwan, China, Japan, Annam, and Cambodia. Decadence set in after 1850, and the U.S. occupation in 1898 brought further trouble. More than a thousand missioners were expelled. Government positions were filled by Protestants and Freemasons openly hostile to the RC Church. In 1902 the Aglipayan schism gave rise to the *Iglesia Filipina Independiente,* which still claims 1,500,000 adherents. The *Iglesia ni Krsto,* a Protestant splinter group, has almost 2,000,000 members. Despite

difficulties the Church has continued to expand. Native clergy are being prepared; 13 archdioceses, 33 dioceses, 11 prelatures, and 4 vicariates constitute the hierarchy. In 1977 Catholics numbered 35,505,954, cared for by 4,455 priests, 3,763 men religious, and 6,797 women religious. There are three Catholic universities and many high schools and colleges. Some effort has been expended on badly needed social work. A powerful Catholic radio station serves many nations of SE Asia. In Manila the East Asian Pastoral Institute is attended also by students from neighboring countries. Christianity has become an integral part of life in the Philippines. The masses are deeply religious. Under the martial-law regime of Ferdinand Marcos, began in 1972, those in the Church pursuing the cause of human rights have been persecuted, missionaries have been deported, and church activists harassed. Amnesty International, International Commission of Jurists, and other observers have documented the denial or curtailment of human rights. The Association of Major Religious Superiors has been particularly active in the ministry of social justice.

Protestantism was introduced in 1898. Episcopalians, Methodists, Presbyterians, Baptists, and the Christian and Missionary Alliance are represented. Silliman Univ. and Central Philippines College are denominational schools. In 1970 the number of Protestants was 785,399. BIBLIOGRA-PHY: Latourette CRA v. 3, 5.

[P. DAMBORIENA]

PHILIPPISM, a designation for theological views of Philipp *Melanchthon, is contrasted with pure or *Gnesiolutheranism. Melanchthon's teachings were involved in many of the bitter controversies that beset Lutheranism after Martin Luther's death (see ADIAPHORISTS; INTERIMS; CRYPTO-CALVINISM; SYNERGISM; MAJORISTIC CONTROVERSY) and that are reflected in the *Formula of Concord (1577). An important feature in Philippism is *irenicism toward both Calvinist and RC teaching.

[T. C. O'BRIEN]

PHILIPS, DIRK AND OBBE (Philipsz), sons of a Catholic priest, early leaders of the Anabaptists in the Netherlands. **Dirk** (1504–68) had been a Franciscan before joining the Anabaptists in 1533. An associate of *Menno Simons, by his writing and preaching he strengthened the persecuted Mennonites; he eventually left the Netherlands and became founder of the congregation at Danzig. The most learned of the Mennonites of the period, D. wrote an *Enchiridion* (1564) that exerted considerable influence for several centuries, being translated from Dutch into German and English. He stressed the need for the visible Church to be pure, without stain; his strong advocacy of the *ban earned him special regard among Old Order Amish. See MennEnc 2:65–66. **Obbe** (*c.* 1500–68) first turned away from the Catholic religion to embrace *Sacramentarian views, then became an Anabaptist (1533). His prominence was such that the early Dutch Anabaptists were often called

Obbites or Obbenites. He baptized and ordained Menno Simons. His posthumous *Confession* (1584), written in Germany *c.*1560, indicates that he left the Anabaptists, unsure that any visible Church could be the true Church of God. See MennEnc 1:268.

[T. C. O'BRIEN]

PHILISTINES (Heb., *Pelishtim*), the non-Semitic people who ironically gave their name to Palestine (Heb., *Pelĕshĕt*). Ethnically Indo-Germanic, they were one of the "peoples of the sea" who came originally from a region, not precisely known, N of the Aegean. They migrated southward, perhaps settling for a time in Crete, the possible Caphtor of Dt 2.23, Jer 47.4, and Amos 9.7. It is impossible to determine this migration in detail as regards specific causes, possible splinter-groups, and lengths of sojourn, but foreign invasions must have been involved. The Philistines were one of the peoples of the sea who attempted an invasion of Egypt during the reign of Ramses II (*c.*1196–1165 B.C.). They were turned back in a battle fought on both land and sea, recorded in words and reliefs at Medinet Habu. After this they settled on the lower coastal region of Canaan, gaining a strong foothold. If this settlement was initially made through conquest, nothing is known of it. It has been suggested that a settlement was made through agreement with the Egyptians, who at that time probably controlled parts of Canaan. The Philistines entered Canaan at approximately the same time as the Israelites; and conflict was inevitable.

The remark in Gen 10.14 is geographic, with remote historical value, since it brings in "descent" from the Egyptians, and relates the Philistines to the Caphtorim. Many OT references to the Philistines are anachronistic, e.g. Gen 21.32,34 and 26.1,8.

The Philistines produced a specific type of pottery which was found in Canaan from early 12th cent. levels on. It is similar to Mycenean, Cypriot, and Rhodian ware. The importation of iron was one of the great cultural contributions of the Philistines to Canaan, and they retained a certain monopoly on its use for some time (1 Sam 18.19–22). They had their own religion, alluded to in the OT, with the gods Dagon (Jg 16.23; 1 Sam 5.2–5), Astarte (1 Sam 31.10) and Baal-zebul (2 Kg 1.2–6) being mentioned. There were probably others, in keeping with Canaanite and ancient Near Eastern polytheistic practices. The Philistines were a powerful people, and their confederated cities of Ashdod, Ashkelon, Ekron, Gath, and Gaza were closely knit, forming a Pentapolis that constituted a continual threat to the Israelite settlement in Canaan.

The Philistines were referred to disdainfully as the "uncircumcised" (e.g., 1 Sam 14.6; 31.4), even though other groups did not practice this rite, and other nations besides Israel did practice it.

The accounts in 1 and 2 Sam, 1 and 2 Kg, and Chr esp. are frequently concerned with the Philistines. At times they made territorial gains, even inflicting the serious humilia-

tion upon Israel of capturing the ark of the covenant (1 Sam 5–6). David's relationship with the Philistines was probably much closer than openly stated in the OT, yet it was he who broke their power. Mention of them becomes increasingly rare after David's time, although they continued to exist down into the 2d cent. B.C. (cf. Sir 50.26). There is some reference to them in the Assyrian records. BIBLIOGRAPHY: B. Mazar, *Philistines and the Rise of Israel and Tyre* (1964).

[I. HUNT]

PHILLIMORE, JOHN S. (1873–1926), English classicist. Educated at Christ Church, Oxford, where he taught briefly, he spent most of his life as professor of classical literature at the Univ. of Glasgow. An authority on the works of Propertius and Statius, he also translated Philostratus and produced two volumes of his own poetry, *Poems* (1902) and *Things New and Old* (1918). He converted to Catholicism in 1906.

[E. M. GATES]

PHILLIP, ROBERT (d. 1647), Oratorian and court chaplain. He was ordained at Scots College, Rome (1612), was arrested as a seminary priest in Edinburgh (1613), and was sentenced to exile. In France he joined the Oratory and in 1628 was chosen by Card. de Bérulle to become confessor to Queen Henrietta Marie. When P. acted for the queen to obtain from Rome financial support for Charles I in 1640, parliamentary leaders charged him with being a papal spy. He was imprisoned, released, and left England with the queen (1642), for whom he continued as chaplain until his death. BIBLIOGRAPHY: Gillow BDEC 3:304–305; M. J. Havran, *Catholics in Caroline England* (1962).

[V. SAMPSON]

PHILLIPS, GEORGE (1804–1872), German canonical scholar and legal historian. The son of Anglo-Scottish parents who had settled in East Prussia, P. devoted most of his life to the teaching of history and law at Berlin (1827–28), Munich (1834–47), and Vienna (1851–72) universities. Converted to Catholicism in 1828, he participated actively in the revival of Catholic culture in the German-speaking countries, contributing particularly to the widespread acceptance of the ultramontanist positions on papal primacy and papal infallibility which ultimately carried the day at Vatican Council I (1869–70).

[E. M. GATES]

PHILLIPPS MANUSCRIPTS. Sir Thomas Phillipps (1792–1872) began his famous MS collection buying the Meerman collection in 1824. Then he added to this other important purchases, original materials for Irish, Welsh, Dutch history. A famous MS of Dioscorides, a Greek medical writer, various biblical MSS, etc., helped swell the library, which was housed at Cheltenham, England. After P.'s death it was sold. Important materials on Irish history were transferred to the National Library of Ireland.

[R. T. MEYER]

PHILO OF ALEXANDRIA, see PHILO JUDAEUS.

PHILO OF BYBLOS (fl. *c.* 100 A.D.), Phoenician scholar, author of a history of ancient Phoenicia (*Ta Phoinika*) that is important to biblical studies. The theogonic and cosmogonic myths he records provide knowledge of the religious milieu surrounding early Israel. P.'s work purports to be a Greek translation of a Phoenician history by Sanchuniaton, dated by some *c.* 1400 B.C., by others *c.* 700 B.C. Some of the myths recorded have been substantiated by the discovery of certain Ugaritic and Hittite texts at *Ugarit.

[T. C. O'BRIEN]

PHILO OF CARPASIA (fl. A.D. 5th cent.), bp. of Carpasia on Cyprus, author of a commentary on the Song of Solomon that was erroneously attributed to St. Epiphanius. (see PG 40:27–154).

[T. C. O'BRIEN]

PHILO JUDAEUS (*c.* 13 B.C.–betw 45 and 50 A.D.), Jewish philosopher and theologian. He was thoroughly trained in Greek literature and learning, including the various philosophies flourishing in his time, and likewise in the study of the Hebrew Scriptures and rabbinical interpretation. As a representative of the Jewish community of Alexandria, he was sent on a mission to the Emperor Gaius Germanicus (Caligula) at Rome to obtain exemption from the imperial cult for the Jews and to obtain confirmation of their earlier special privileges. As a philosopher and theologian, he wished to establish a harmony between Platonic philosophy, esp., and the Pentateuch. He was convinced that Plato and other Greek philosophers were actually indebted to the Scriptures for some of their basic teachings, and this point of view gave a greater impetus to his harmonizing process. In his exegesis of Scripture he made constant—and sometimes extreme—use of allegorical interpretation. However, he did not reject the historical value of Scripture and insisted on the literal sense in particular in its ritual prescriptions. He stresses throughout the transcendence of God. Because of God's perfection, any immediate contact of God with the world is excluded. His relations with the world are to be found in the results of his activity only, and not in the presence of his own being. The insistence on the transcendence of God and his elevation above all material things led Philo to conceive of intermediary beings to bridge the gulf between God and the material cosmos. His highest intermediary being is the *Logos*, "the firstborn of God," but this *Logos* is inferior to God and is not to be identified with the Christian concept of the *Logos*. Philo places the Platonic Ideas in the *Logos*, making the *Logos* the place (*topos*) in which the ideal world is located. There is a parallel between this aspect of the *Logos* and the *Nous* of *Neo-Pythagoreanism, and it seems very probable that the Neo-Pythagorean *Numenius was influenced by Philo on this point. In addition to his *Logos*, Philo recognizes other Powers (*dunamies*) or intermediary beings. If his *Logos* is regarded as an aspect of God, the Powers may be taken as qualities or ideas of God. But if his *Logos* is regarded as a relatively independent being, yet subordinate to God, the Powers may be taken as minor subordinate beings or forces.

Under the influence of Platonism Philo emphasizes the duality of soul and body and the necessity for man to free himself from the sensual element. Virtue is the only true good, and man's task is to attain the greatest possible likeness to God. While he speaks of apathy in regard to the passions, using Cynic and Stoic terminology, he maintains that man must put his trust in God, and not in himself. Public life is to be avoided because of its distracting influence on the soul, and science is to be valued in direct relation to the help it can render to the soul's interior life. One must strive, by ascent of the soul, to attain heavenly wisdom or the immediate intuition of the ineffable Godhead. The passive state of ecstasy is the highest stage that the life of the soul can attain on earth.

The *Logos* doctrine of P. is peculiar, the *Logos* being a kind of intermediary between men and God, yet less than God, and an all-pervasive force and unity. Few today regard it as the source of the Johannine Logos doctrine, though all relationship need not be rejected. John's doctrine is more likely drawn from older Jewish sources, but it may easily have been intended as a corrective to other current *Logos* doctrines, including that of P.

Philo, strictly speaking, is rather an exegete of Scripture and a theologian than a philosopher in the formal sense. While he is familiar with Hellenistic philosophy and employs Greek terminology freely, his thought is basically Jewish and is within the confines of Jewish orthodoxy. His influence on ancient Judaism was relatively minor. On the other hand, he exercised a major influence on Clement of Alexandria, Origen, St. Gregory of Nyssa, St. Ambrose, and others. He was primarily responsible for the wide use of allegorical interpretation in the Christian exegesis of Scripture. The extant works of Philo are easily accessible in Greek and English, with accompanying notes, in the *Loeb Classical Library* (12 vols.). BIBLIOGRAPHY: R. Arnaldez, NCE 11:287–291; Copleston 1:457–462; CHGMP 137–157; H. Thyen, LexAW 2301–02; C. Mondésert, LTK 8:470–471; C. Colpe, RGG 5:341–346; E. R. Goodenough, *Introduction to Philo Judaeus* (2d ed., 1963).

[M. R. P. MCGUIRE]

PHILO OF LARISSA, head of the so-called Fourth Academy (110–88 B.C.). At the outbreak of the Mithridatic War in 88 he sought refuge in Rome, where, among others, he had Cicero as an auditor. The latter held him in high esteem throughout his life. Philo admitted that there could be apprehension (*Katālepsis*) of objects—but not in the Stoic sense, and that certain truths were knowable, even if not understood and established in a strictly scientific way. He thus moved away from the epistemological probabilism of Carneades in the direction of the teaching of his pupil and opponent Antiochus of Ascalon. BIBLIOGRAPHY: OCD 684; LexAW 2304; Ueberweg 1:465, 469–470.

[M. R. P. MCGUIRE]

PHILOKALIA (Gr., love of spiritual beauty), the title of an anthology of writings by ascetical and mystical Fathers of the Eastern Church, Sinaite, Syrian, and Greek, which deals mainly with the Hesychast method of prayer, contemplation, and interior warfare against passions. This anthology in its most complete edition includes no less than 30 authors ranging from the 4th to the 14th cent., among whom are found, sometimes pseudonymously, Anthony of Egypt, Mark the Ascetic, Evagrius Ponticus, Hesychius of Jerusalem, Nilus of Sinai, Maximus the Confessor, John Climacus, Isaac of Syria, John Damascene, Simeon the New Theologian, Gregory of Sinai, Gregory Palamas, Callistos and Ignatius of Xanthopoulos, and, of more recent times, Macarius of Corinth and Nicodemus of the Holy Mountain, who in 1782 published the first edition of the *Philokalia* in Venice. The only Latin included in the list of writings is John Cassian. In 1792, Paissy Velichkovsky, the Moldavian *starets who was the originator of a spiritual renaissance among the Orthodox Slavs, made a Slavonic translation of the *Philokalia,* and a greatly expanded Russian version was published (1876–90) in 5 volumes in the Russian monastery of St. Panteleimon on Mt. Athos. This was the work of Bp. Theophan Govorov, called after his monastic retirement by the title "the Recluse." He gave his work the Russian title, *Dobrotolyubiye.* A number of modern Greek editions of the *Philokalia* are available; there is a critical edition in Rumanian (1946), and selections mostly from Theophan's Russian version, have been translated into several European languages.

The *Philokalia* has played a great role in the spiritual revival of the Orthodox world since the 19th century. Its influence has been strongly apparent not merely in the cloister, but even among Christians living in the world. The popularity of the Jesus Prayer, its virtual domination of the prayer-life of Orthodox monasticism, and its extended use among the common Orthodox faithful owes much to the existence and the availability of the *Philokalia,* which has been called the *summa* on the Jesus Prayer. Together with the Holy Scriptures, the *Philokalia,* despite its severely monastic, Hesychastic style and content, continues to be almost the only source of spiritual direction for those Orthodox who wish to cultivate the interior life of the spirit. In recent times the *Philokalia* has become known in the West, and has even entered the world of American religion and literature. BIBLIOGRAPHY: *Writings from the Philokalia on Prayer of the Heart* (tr. E. Kadloubovsky and G. Palmer, 1951); *Unseen Warfare* (1952); *Early Fathers from the Philokalia* (1954).

[T. HOPKO]

PHILOLOGY, a term derived from the Gr. *philologia* (from *philos,* a lover of, and *logos,* word, speech, language, reason) and understood in both ancient and modern times as a love of, or interest in, literature and learning. The Alexandrian philologists of the early Hellenistic Age were largely concerned with problems of textual criticism as they attempted to rid the earlier Greek epics and dramas from errors of transmission. Crates of Mallos brought the art from Greece to Rome *c.*168 B.C. (Suetonius, *Gram.* 2), where it was used to purify the texts of Plautus, Terence, and other playwrights of changes made by their producers. Later philologists such as Porphyrion, Servius, and Donatus produced critical commentaries on Horace and Virgil. Christian writers, particularly Origen and St. Jerome, used philological techniques to establish and interpret the texts of Scripture. In later cent. the tradition was carried on by Isidore of Seville, Cassiodorus, and Alcuin, and during the Middle Ages by the translators of Greek and Arabic philosophical texts. The Renaissance brought with it a whole new interest in ancient letters. The invention of the printing press and the theological controversies of the Reformation required a reexamination and reevaluation of the texts of the Old and New Testaments and of the Fathers of the Church. During the 18th cent. the discovery of the relationship existing among the Indo-European languages, the newly created interest in classical art and archeology, and the intellectual stimulus of the Enlightenment provided a new impetus to philological studies, which now came to embrace Romance, Germanic, and Slavic works along with those of classical antiquity. Today philology in its most comprehensive sense is practically synonymous with "humanities," taking as its field of interest not only the prose and poetry of many different nations of both ancient and more recent times but also their art and archeology, their religion and ethics, their public and private lives, their history and philosophy, and whatever else is significant to an understanding of their total culture. BIBLIOGRAPHY: U. von Wilamowitz-Möllendorff, *Geschichte der Philologie* (3d ed., 1959); G. Funaioli, Enc-Catt 5:1337–42. M. Platnauer, *Fifty Years of Classical Scholarship* (1956).

[M. J. COSTELLOE]

PHILOMENA, LEGEND OF ST., imaginary figure formerly accepted as a saint by the Church but since 1961 relegated to the ranks of the legendary. The discovery in 1802, within an ancient catacomb near Rome, of some relics (including bones, a phial believed to contain blood, and tomb tiles inscribed with the words "Lumena—Paxte—Cum—Fi," which, transposed, could be taken to read "Pax Tecum Filumena") was responsible for the rise of a cult based on the belief that P. was a martyred Christian virgin of the 3d century. In 1805 the relics were translated to Mugnano del Cardinale (near Naples), where the parish priest wrote a colorful but totally ahistorical account of her life. Miracles connected with her name together with the popularity of the cult led to approbation of a liturgical office for P. by the Congregation of Rites in 1855. This was withdrawn a century later for lack of either scientific or hagiographical evidence.

[E. M. GATES]

PHILOSOPHER'S STONE, a marvelous substance alchemists supposed to exist. They sought it as a means of transmuting baser metals into gold but believed it efficacious also in restoring health and youth. The comparable liquid form was known as elixir. The concept perhaps originated in Alexandria.

PHILOSOPHIC SIN, see SIN, PHILOSOPHIC.

PHILOSOPHICAL CRITICISM, see CRITICISM, PHILOSOPHICAL.

PHILOSOPHY, originating with the Greeks (6th cent. B.C.), came to be regarded as love of wisdom or excellence of the mind (in contrast with other forms of excellence). Its origins currently are regarded as deriving from mythical and religious symbols, as well as from a progressive acclimatization of man within nature. Philosophy reached a high form of excellence among the Greeks, primarily in and through the triumvirate, Socrates, Plato, and Aristotle, although a great variety of other philosophers and philosophical options both precede and follow them. In this, its nascent period, philosophy was regarded both as a theoretical and structured outlook on the world (e.g., as in Plato's dialogues, and Aristotle's treatises, *Physics, Metaphysics, On the Soul),* and as offering models for human activity (e.g., Aristotle's *Ethics, Rhetoric, Politics).*

A second period of philosophical affluence arose in the Middle Ages (A.D. 9th to 16th cent.), partly due to such thinkers as Boethius (a transmitter of some of the Greek philosophical heritage), St. Augustine of Hippo (who synthesized a form of Platonism with his Christian faith), and Arabic and Jewish thinkers who served as intermediaries by making Aristotle's complete works available to Western culture. Through philosophical giants such as St. Albert the Great, St. Thomas Aquinas, St. Bonaventure, Duns Scotus and William of Ockham, medieval philosophy achieved its own identity, which was generally termed scholasticism, or the philosophy of the schoolmen. This movement generally is characterized by its attempts at coordinating Christian faith with philosophy, its emphasis on and contributions to logic and methodology, and as leading, indirectly at least, to the rise of the sciences in the 16th and 17th centuries. Within a Christian perspective, in addition to the Augustinian-Platonic current, the Middle Ages gave birth to a Thomistic-Aristotelian synthesis, and, towards their close, to the so-called *via moderna* of William of Ockham and others.

A third period is characterized by its partial success in challenging both the Greek and Christian approaches to philosophy. Influenced by the Renaissance movement and the rise of the new sciences (among other factors), notables such as Francis Bacon, René Descartes, Leibniz, Hume, Kant, and Hegel still regard philosophy, in the Greek and medieval sense, as the search for ultimate essences. However, in practice, they either adulate or outrightly model their philosophies on the picture of the world arising from the new sciences, or, at the least, they adapt the methodology of these sciences to philosophy.

If one can (somewhat inaccurately) characterize philosophy prior to the 19th cent. as essence-seeking and as adapting itself successively to the models of myths, of religion, or of the sciences, then many contemporary movements can be regarded as the search for new ways of philosophizing. Søren Kierkegaard, Friedrich Nietzsche, and Karl Marx are outstanding examples of 19th-cent. philosophers who attempted to free themselves from the presuppositions of classical philosophy and by so doing, opened the way towards current philosophical trends (Phenomenology and Existentialism). Edmund Husserl, the founder of Phenomenology, and his somewhat errant disciples, the more prominent of whom are Max Scheler, Martin Heidegger, and Jean Paul Sartre, have employed phenomenological techniques and insights that also fall within the growing Existentialist emphasis. Another orientation, coming from the 19th-cent. Logical Positivist filiation with the sciences and the new symbolic logic, accounts for what is now termed Linguistic Philosophy. The confrontation of the Western with the Eastern philosophers is another movement of philosophical and ecumenical significance. All three options—Existentialist, Linguistic, and Eastern—are exercising increasing influence on the Christian and the other faiths and theologies. Present-day philosophers still exercise a variety of ancient, medieval, and modern, as well as contemporary, options on the nature of philosophy, its relationships with the arts, the sciences, and religious faith, and with practical life. BIBLIOGRAPHY: E. A. Maziarz, NCE 11:294–299; J. Passmore, EncPhil 6:61–64.

[E. A. MAZIARZ]

PHILOSOPHY OF NATURE, also called "natural philosophy" (see COSMOLOGY), that part of philosophy concerned with material reality as subject to all the forms of change; thus with "nature" (Gr. *physis).* According to Aristotle there is a general inquiry that, once having established the principles common to all things subject to change, can reach necessary conclusions about the universal properties of such beings. Thus he developed his *Physics,* then his other physical treatises on specific kinds of changeable beings. From his *Physics* he established the need that there be an unchangeable first mover; thus his philosophy went further in his "Post Physics," i.e., the *Metaphysics;* the study of beings as changeable did not exhaust the intelligibility of being as being. The Aristotelian physical treatises became throughout the Middle Ages the basic vehicle of study of the nature of the physical universe. With the development of a new scientific methodology from the 16th cent. on, the experimental physical sciences grew, and with them the split between philosophy and science. There have always been those, however, who see as the ideal the complementarity of the philosophical and the empirical in the study of nature.

[T. C. O'BRIEN]

PHILOSOPHY OF RELIGION, reasoned reflection on religious belief, in itself, in its claims, in its expressions. The term, prominent in academic curricula, receives interpretations as varied as the understandings of its components, "philosophy" and "religion." The description given, however, allows two generalizations. (1) Taken theoretically and in isolation the term may stand for any philosophy that, on reasoned grounds, raises, for acceptance or rejection, issues commonly associated with religious belief (the existence of a provident deity, revelation, the soul, afterlife, the basis of morality). That merges into the meaning and handling of the philosophy of religion a good deal of the history of philosophy itself (see, e.g., H. D. Lewis, "Philosophy of Religion, History of," EncPhil 6:276–285). It would seem also to incorporate such specific disciplines as *natural theology, *apologetics, particularly on the possibility of revelation, and even *philosophical theology as it is commonly understood. This generalization also implies the aim of a philosophy of religion: the critical evaluation of religious claims. It is normative and as such distinct, at least abstractly, from the comparative study of religion, an expository presentation, through appropriate investigative methods (anthropological, archeological, historical, etc.) of the structures and content of mankind's religions. These findings philosophy of religion may incorporate into its critique of religious claims; its range may also encompass analysis of religious language, the psychological and sociological dimensions of religion, human nature or culture and religion. (2) Taken concretely and in its historical background, philosophy of religion has had one founding presupposition: religion as the human spirit's outreach or intentionality towards the transcendent makes objectively unverifiable claims. That presupposition reflects I. *Kant's critique: an intellectual discipline concerned with affirmations about the transcendent has no critically verifiable referent. Yet religion, and in the milieu of Kant's revolution, the Christian religion, is a fact; the only "philosophical" alternative to absolute *agnosticism is a critical study of religion as a subjective phenomenon of the human spirit. The philosophy of religion is that search. The acknowledged philosophers of religion (see, e.g., F. *Schleiermacher; G. *Hegel; R. *Otto; W. *James) have developed normative positions on what religion is or should be. Courses in the philosophy of religion frequently have such evaluations as their core. A notable and influential reaction to what "religion" means in such an understanding of the philosophy of religion is the *crisis or dialectical theology of K. *Barth. Indeed, any Christian theology linked with its own tradition must join in opposition to "religion." A

theology resting on faith as assent to God himself and the transcendent truths he attests stands at variance with the treatment of religion as a wholly subjective phenomenon and the a priori determinant of what either God or his revelation can mean.

[T. C. O'BRIEN]

PHILOSTORGIUS (c.386–c.439), Arian Church historian. A native of Borissus in Cappadocia Secunda, P. spent most of his life in Constantinople where he wrote his history of the Church. He was a follower of *Eunomius, and his history purported to be a continuation of *Eusebius. It is an important source of information about the Arian controversy because P. had access to documents of Arian origin no longer available. Most of the history has been lost although *Photius has summarized the book and commented on it unfavorably. The work is biased and inaccurate. Text: PG 65:459–624; GCS 21 (ed. J. Bidez, 1913). BIBLIOGRAPHY: Quasten 3:530–532.

[R. B. ENO]

PHILOTHEUS COCCINUS, (c.1300–79), **PATRIARCH OF CONSTANTINOPLE** during the mid-14th cent., well-known Byzantine theologian and defender of the Hesychastic (illuminationist) theory of Gregory *Palamas. Born in Thessalonica of a Jewish mother, he became a monk on Sinai and was later abbot on Mt. Athos. He entered theological controversy in defense of Gregory Palamas in 1340, was named abp. of Heraclea in Thrace in 1347, patriarch of Constantinople in 1353. He was deposed and imprisoned in 1354, but eventually permitted to return to his original see in Heraclea. In 1363 he was officially rehabilitated and in 1364 reappointed patriarch. He asserted the patriarch's independence from Rome, in spite of pressure to seek Latin Christianity's help in the face of Ottoman advances. He canonized Gregory Palamas and declared him a doctor of the Church. In 1376 P. resigned because of ill health. His writings cover liturgical, biblical, spiritual, speculative, and homiletic topics. But of special importance are his works on Hesychasm, e.g., his *Antirhetica* and his *Hagiorite Tome*. From his monastic years date his *Précis of the Divine Liturgy* and *Order of Service for the Diaconia*.

[E. J. DILLON]

PHILOXENUS (Arkenaia; d. 523), bp. of Mabbugh in Syria, Monophysite theologian. Excommunicated about 499 because he refused to accept the definitions of Chalcedon, P. became involved in intrigues against orthodox bps., and succeeded in having several deposed. But he himself was exiled by Emperor *Justin I in 519. His writings are considered classics in Syrian literature and he is also honored as a doctor of the Church by the *Jacobites. A creative and original thinker, P. composed a large number of exegetical, dogmatic, ascetical, and liturgical works. His Monophysitism is probably only verbal, since he adheres to pre-Chalcedonian terminology. BIBLIOGRAPHY: A. de Halleux, *Philoxenus de Mabbugh, sa vie, ses récits, sa théologie* (1963).

PHILPOT, JOHN (1516–55), English Reformer. After a fellowship at New College, Oxford (1534–41), P. was won over to Reformation doctrine while traveling abroad. Under Edward VI he was made archdeacon of Winchester, but early in the reign of Mary Tudor he was imprisoned for publicly attacking the doctrine of *transubstantiation and was burned at the stake in Dec. 1555. He was the author of numerous works of controversy.

[R. B. ENO]

PHINEHAS (PHINEES), two men of considerable importance bear this name, the Hebrew meaning of which is uncertain, in the Old Testament. The first is a son of Elezar and grandson of Aaron (cf. genealogies and information in Ex 6.25; 1 Chr 5.30 and 6.35). Ezra was among his descendants (Ezr 7.5), as was the priest Gershom, associate of Ezra (Ezra 8.2). According to Num 25.7–11 an Israelite and a Midianite woman were having sexual relations in a tent at Shittim in keeping with fertility practices honoring the god Baal-Peor. According to the account the woman had been openly brought to the tent in clear defiance of Yahweh. In a moment of violent zeal, Phinehas pierced them simultaneously through their reproductive organs with his spear. His action became a classic of loyalty to Yahweh (Ps 106.30), and he was promised an everlasting priesthood (Num 25.13) as a reward. The incident served to support the claims of the house of Phinehas. This same Phinehas had a leading part in a war avenging Israel against Midian, described in Num 31.6. He also headed a legation of cis-Jordanian Israelite tribes in a controversy with the trans-Jordanian tribes over an altar (Jos 22.13,30–32). In the later life he settled in Gibeah (Jos 24.33) and was acknowledged as a leader of a group of Levites (1 Chr 9.17–20).

The second Phinehas was the son of Eli and the brother of Hophni (1 Sam 1.3). The two brothers were classics of priestly worthlessness (1 Sam 2.12–36) and both were killed in the battle of Aphek when the ark was captured (1 Sam 4.4,11,17). Hearing the news of Phinehas's death, his wife gave birth, somewhat prematurely, to Ichabod (whose name means ''Where [has] the glory [gone]?''). Ahijah, a priest in the time of Saul, was the grandson of this Phinehas (1 Sam 14.3). The priestly line of Phinehas continued on actively until Abiathar, its representative, was deposed by Solomon in favor of Zadok (1 Kg 2.35).

[I. HUNT]

PHOBIA, from Gr. *phobos,* fear, flight, a neurotic, nonrational type of *fear with regard to certain situations or objects. Actions done under phobic compulsion are not morally imputable.

[T. C. O'BRIEN]

PHOCAS, SS, the name of several saints believed to be martyrs of the early Church, Phocas the Gardener is com-

memorated September 22, and believed to have been martyred at some unknown date. Phocas of Antioch is mentioned on March 5 in the Roman Martyrology and is thought to have been martyred at Antioch. Phocas, bp. of Sinope, commemorated in the Roman Martyrology on July 14, is thought to have been martyred under Trajan. All three probably derive from the same Phocas who was the subject of a fanciful panegyric composed by St. Asterius, bp. of Amasea *c.*400. Despite the abundance of legends about the saint's hospitality, his delight in gardening, his generosity to the poor, and the many miracles worked through his powerful intercession, all that is known for certain about his life is that he lived, was martyred at some unknown date, and was widely venerated. His relics are claimed by many places. BIBLIOGRAPHY: Butler 1:485, 3:617–619; J. M. Sauget, BiblSanct 5:948–950.

[E. J. DILLON]

PHOCIS, CHURCHES OF ST. LUKE OF STIRIS, two early 12th-cent., connected Greek churches of mid-Byzantine quincunx plan. The N church is older; the S church, Constantinopolitan in type, though less delicately proportioned, is noted for ''classical mid-Byzantine'' mosaic cycles (destroyed but replaced by frescoes in the original style), depicting the Ascension, Resurrection, Virgin and Child, in the celestial vaults, earthly beings in lower zones. The churches are important for the study of Byzantine art and architecture. BIBLIOGRAPHY: O. Demus, *Byzantine Mosaic Decoration* (1955).

[M. J. DALY]

PHOEBADIUS, ST. (d. *c.*395), bp. of Agennum (Agen) in S France. P. wrote a circular letter *c.*357 to the bps. of Gaul denouncing the second Sirmian formula (see SIRMIUM) as Arian. A Gallican synod under his leadership condemned the formula the following year. The other writings of P. have perished. Text: PL 20:13–30. BIBLIOGRAPHY: Altaner 430.

[R. B. ENO]

PHOENICIA, a coastal strip of land between the E shore of the Mediterranean and the Lebanon mountains. Its name derives from the Greek term for reddish purple, the color of the dye for which the region was famous. The strip has a delightful climate, the soil is rich, and the coast has a number of natural harbors. The inhabitants were a Semitic people who became famous for sea trade and commerce in the Mediterranean world. Through them the alphabet extended to the Greek world. Their religion was the same as the Canaanites of the Old Testament. Jesus journeyed in the S sections of Phoenicia where at first he refused to help a woman because she was not a Jew (Mk 7.24–30). Christianity arrived with fugitives after Stephen's stoning (Acts 11.19).

[S. MUSHOLT]

PHOENICIANS, an ancient Semitic people, the greatest merchants and navigators of antiquity. As early as the 4th millennium B.C. they inhabited the narrow strip of land between the E Mediterranean and the Lebanon mountains northward from Carmel for about 150 miles. They named their land Canaan, perhaps from a word meaning "Murex," the shellfish from whose secretion they made purple dye by a process now lost. The Greeks called them "Phoenicians," from *phoinix*, "crimson-purple," either because of their complexions or again because of the dyestuff so valued by the ancients. By convention some modern scholars refer to the land as Canaan before 1200 B.C.; after that date, as Phoenicia. Situated at the crossroads between Egypt and Mesopotamia, the Phoenicians were the slow but constant agents of a transmission of ideas throughout the Mediterranean world. Apart from periods of anarchy they were ruled in turn by Egyptians, Hittites, Hurrians, Israelites, and Philistines. In the middle of the 2d millennium B.C. they began to accumulate wealth through trade and their city-states became independent *c.* 1200 B.C. Acre, Byblos, Tyre, Sidon, Beirut, and other towns founded colonies in Cyprus, Sicily, Sardinia, Africa, and Spain. Their aim was not territorial expansion but the establishment of emporiums and "factories" for their far-flung commerce. Such were Carthage, Gaddir (Cadiz), Malaga, Tartessus (Tarshish), Tingis (Tangiers), Utica, and other provisioning posts. Phoenician trade in purple dye, cedarwood, building stone, metals, cloth, and slaves remained unparalleled for 3 centuries. In 842 B.C., Assyria conquered Phoenicia, renaming it Syria. With some change of boundaries the land became successively the possession of Babylonia, Persia, and Macedonia; but commerce did not cease. After the Macedonian conquest in 333 B.C. the trade center of the Phoenicians shifted to Carthage and survived until 146 B.C. when the Romans razed the city. Meanwhile Syria itself had fallen to the Seleucids and then to the Ptolemies. Rome made it a province in 64 B.C.

Excavations at many Phoenician sites have been very productive. The literary texts found at Ugarit (modern Ras Shamra), for instance, are the most important materials ever unearthed for OT studies. They document the influence exerted on the Israelites by the common Canaanite literary heritage. Several books of the OT show in their lyrical and aphoristic passages marked similarity to Canaanite texts, particularly in prosody, imagery, and liveliness of nature descriptions; and Proverbs contains direct borrowings. Phoenician religion was akin to Assyrio-Babylonian. Along with the chief gods the divinities of trees, waters, rocks, and high places were also worshiped. Fertility rites were prominent. Sacred prostitution of both sexes was practiced; and sacrifice of the first-born persisted in some degree until the coming of Christianity. The Greeks credited the Phoenicians with numerous discoveries besides their precious purple dye; but their main contribution to civilization was the invention, before 1500 B.C., of the linear alphabet from which Hebrew, Syriac, Arabic, and other scripts derive. In the early 8th cent. B.C. the Greeks borrowed this alphabet, which Phoenician traders had already made common to the Mediterranean area, and started it on its path through the West. BIBLIOGRAPHY: W. F. Albright, "Role of the Canaanites in the History of Civilization," *Bible and the Ancient Near East* (ed. G. E. Wright, 1961) 328–362; J. Gray, *Legacy of Canaan* (1957) and *Canaanites* (1964).

[M. J. SUELZER]

PHOENIX, a mythical bird which, according to Greek transformations of the original Egyptian story of Bird-Bennu, could raise itself from its own ashes after each 500-year cycle of its life. This beautiful and mysterious creature appears in Old Sanskrit poetry, in Egyptian texts, and after Hesiod, in Greek and Roman literature, particularly Herodotus where it is said that immediately after its birth in Arabia, Phoenix flew to Heliopolis to bury his father. At Heliopolis, Egyptians worshipped Bennu as the soul of Osiris; figuring in the Egyptian cult of the daily return of the sun, he was associated with Ra. For Romans, Phoenix represented the apotheosis of emperors. In Christian appropriation, the phoenix became a common symbol for Christ, one who could raise himself from the dead. This symbol appears throughout the Latin and vernacular literature and in iconography of the patristic and medieval periods.

[R. J. LITZ]

PHŌS HILARON, the famous ancient hymn of the Byzantine liturgy. Its Greek name means "gladdening light," and it was known as the Candlelight Hymn. In the ancient Church it was sung as the lamps were being lighted. It is the heart of the Byzantine rite of *Hesperinos,* the equivalent of Vespers or Evensong. In the Byzantine Office this hymn of thanksgiving follows after the invitatory, the litanies and the psalms, and provides the focus towards which all the other prayers converge. Its authorship probably cannot be established with certainty. Attributed by St. Basil to St. Athenogenes the Martyr, in modern Greek liturgical books its author is given as Sophronius. There are dozens of English hymns inspired by it and purporting to be translations of it. In one such translation the hymn has found a place in Anglican Evensong.

[E. J. DILLON]

PHOTIAN SYNOD OF 879–880. The Council of Constantinople IV, considered by Western canonists as the eighth ecumenical council, sitting October 5, 869, to Feb. 28, 870, is also called the Ignatian Council, since its purpose was to reinstate the Patriarch Ignatius and to condemn Photius as a usurper of the patriarchal throne. Because this Council created animosities, Ignatius had difficulties in his administration. The situation was cleared when the emperor Basil I brought Photius back from an exile and entrusted him with the education of his sons. Then both Ignatius and Photius were reconciled. Another council was subsequently planned in order to effect the reconciliation of followers of both men and to end the internal schism in the Byzantine Church. Unfortunately, before papal legates reached Constantinople, Ignatius died; Photius was validly reinstated as patriarch. This Council was convened in Nov., 879 and ended in March 880. Photius was confirmed by many conciliar fathers with the assent of the papal legates and the representatives of other patriarchs. This Council is called the Photian Synod. The previous Ignatian Council of 869–870 which had condemned Photius was hereby abrogated. This explains why the Greek original of the Acts of this Council was not preserved, but only a Latin translation, provided by the papal librarian Anastasius, who took part in the Council as envoy of the Emperor Louis II. There exists only a Greek extract of the Acts compiled by an opponent of Photius, who had refused to accept him as patriarch even after Photius' reconciliation with Ignatius and his restoration by the Council of 879–880, which was confirmed also by Pope John VIII. This extract was later incorporated into an anti-Photian collection by one zealot and became one of the sources of the anti-Photian propaganda.

The Photian Council was convoked by the Emperor Basil I and representatives of all five patriarchs were present together with 300 bishops. The conciliar fathers were thus entitled to designate this Council as a "holy and ecumenical synod." And in the Acts of this Council it is called "a holy Synod convoked under the most holy and ecumenical Patriarch Photius for the union of the Holy and Apostolic Church of God." In view of the fact that Ignatian Council of 869–870 was held ecumenical by the West and the Photian Council of 879–880 by the Orthodox, question of the ecumenicity of both became controversial. The problem is reducible to the question whether Pope John VII by making use of his supreme power, actually annulled the Acts of the Ignatian Council of 869, thus depriving it of its ecumenical status. The answer is affirmative if the Greek text of the last two sessions of the Photian Synod of 879–880 are considered authentic, as Dvornik or Amann attest. On the other hand, the answer could be negative if reference is had to other documents, esp. to the letter (885) of Pope Stephen V to Emperor Basil I, as Grumel attests. This letter reveals that Photius was still trying to have the Ignatian Council annulled, a step that would be inexplicable if prior to this time Pope John VIII had annulled it. Dvornik was successful in explaining why the Ignatian Council of 869–870 had been added in the West to the list as the Eighth Ecumenical. This happened during the reign of Pope Gregory VII; he had opened the Lateran archives to his canonists, who were looking for new arguments for the papal primacy. They needed a strongly worded document which they could use in their fight against the investiture. They found such a document in canon 22 voted by the Ignatian Council, which forbade laymen to influence the appointment of prelates. All canonists and reformers of the Gregorian period utilized this canon as their most powerful weapon in their struggle for the freedom of the Church in the election of prelates. To give more weight to this argument they promoted the Ignatian Council to one of the most important ecumenical synods, overlooking the Acts of the Photian Council of 879–880 which had cancelled the Council of 869–870, although the Acts of this Council were also kept in the Lateran

archives. The Ignatian was designated by canonists in their collections as the eighth ecumenical council. But previously, as is clear from declarations by the Popes Marinus II and Leo IX, or of St. Peter Damian or Card. Humbertus, the Romans, like the Greeks, numbered only seven ecumenical councils.

Only Card. Deusdedit copied a part of the synod of 861 and that of the Photian Council of 879–880. He was followed by another canonist, Ivo of Chartres, who in his prologue to his collection of canon law, quoted a long passage of the letter of Pope John VIII to Emperor Basil I concerning the restoration of Photius in the "doctored" version read at the Council. It must be kept in mind also that the controversy between Latins and Greeks concerning the number of ecumenical councils was really begun very late, only in the 15th cent., during the Council of Ferrara-Florence. The Greeks continued to count only seven ecumenical councils and in the Council's definitions every reference to the eighth council was intentionally omitted. After the Eastern Schism (1054) the Western Church kept the count of their councils, having no concern for the Eastern, and as a result the controversy lost its force. While both Churches are going their separate ways, the question of which are ecumenical councils is still waiting for permanent and final solution, although modern research favors Dvornik's views in stressing rather the ecumenicity of the Photian Council of 879–880, which is described frequently however by the West as "pseudo-synod." BIBLIOGRAPHY: Hefele-Leclercq 4:481–546; M. Jugie DTC 3:1273–1307; É. Amann, ibid., 12:1549–82; 16:666–667; Fliche-Martin 6:493–497; F. Dvornik, *Photian Schism, History and Legend* (1948); idem, *Patriarch Photius in the Light of Recent Research* (1958); idem, *Ecumenical Councils* (1961); L. Nemec, "Photius—Saint or Schismatic?" JES 3 (1966) 277–313; K. Baus, LTK 6:496–497, with recent literature, J. M. A. Salles-Dabadie, *Les Conciles oecuméniques dans l'histoire* (1962). On ecumenicity: (1) favoring the thesis of abrogation by John, F. Dvornik, "L'Oecuménicité du VIIIe concile (869–870) dans la tradition occidentale du moyen-âge," *Bulletin de l'Académie Royal de Belgique, Section des Lettres* 24 (1938) 445–487, a study included also in the *Photian Schism* (see above); idem, "Which Councils are Ecumenical?" JES 3 (1966) 314–328; idem, "Mélanges Eugène Tisserant" *Studi e testi* 2, no. 232 (1964) 93–101; (2) favoring nonabrogation and hence ecumenicity, V. Grumel, or La Lettre du Pape Étienne V à l'empéreur Basile I," *Revue des études latines* 11 (1953) 129–155; "New Light on the Photian Schism," *Unitas* 5 (1953) 140–148; M. Jugie, DTC 3:1304–07. Texts of canons are in Mansi 16:160–178. V. Peri "Il numero dei concili ecumenici nella tradizione cattolica moderna," *Aevum* 37 (1963) 472–500.

[L. NEMEC]

PHOTINIANS, followers of *Photinus, bp. of Sirmium, also known as Homuncionistae since they held that Christ, though endowed with miraculous powers and the adopted Son of God, was in reality no more than a mere man. They were condemned by Pope St. Damasus in the synod of Rome in 375 and again at the Council of Constantinople in 381. Never very numerous, they may have survived among the followers of Bonosus in the Danubian provinces. BIBLIOGRAPHY: B. Kotter, LTK 8:483–484; A. Mayer, EncCatt 5:1553–54; J. Chapman, CE 12:43.

[M. J. COSTELLOE]

PHOTINUS (PHOTINIANUS), 4th cent. bp. and heretic. A disciple and friend of *Marcellus of Ancyra, P. became bp. of Sirmium c.343, not long before he and Marcellus were condemned by the Council of Antioch (345). Though condemned again by a council convened in Sirmium in 347, he was not deposed until 351 when another council held in the same city convicted him of error. He was recalled to his see briefly by Julian in 364. His writings have perished but his doctrines as described by others seem to involve a type of *Sabellianism or dynamic *Monarchianism similar to that of *Paul of Samosata, according to which Christ was only a man, although endowed with miraculous powers. Certain of his adherents became known as Photinians. BIBLIOGRAPHY: G. Bardy, DTC 12:1532–36.

[R. B. ENO]

PHOTIUS (c.821–891), **PATRIARCH OF CONSTANTINOPLE** 858–867 and 878–886. He gave up the idea of becoming a monk and chose a secular career during which he taught philosophy at the Univ. of Constantinople and held various state positions. Because of a Church-State conflict the reigning patriarch, *Ignatius, resigned and the synod elected the layman Photius in the hope that he would be acceptable to the conservative and moderate factions of the Byzantine Church. (See PHOTIAN SYNOD OF 879.) He was one of the leading figures in the intellectual renaissance of the 9th cent. and, during his patriarchate, extended Christianity to the Slavs. He died in the monastery of Armeniakon c.891 and is venerated as a saint by the Orthodox Churches. BIBLIOGRAPHY: F. Dvornik, *Photian Schism* (1948); *idem*, NCE 11:326–329.

[G. T. DENNIS]

PHREAS, JOANNES, see FREE, JOHN.

PHRENOLOGY. (1) In the history of medicine, the study invented by the German anatomist Franz Josef Gall (1758–1828) that located specific human faculties in 37 organic parts of the brain, and proposed to determine dominant qualities of intelligence and personality through the distinctive contours of a person's skull as indicators of the relative development of the various faculty-organs of the brain. The schema of faculties was derived from the *Scottish School of Common Sense. The pseudoscience had a great vogue in Europe and in the U.S. before it was definitively discredited (c.1880). But the principle of cerebral localization did lead

to sounder studies of the brain and its functions. (2) As a form of charlatanry, phrenology survives as a companion to palmistry or spiritualism, pretending to analyze character and predict the course of a person's life by the protuberances and depressions of the skull. Consultation of a phrenologist in a serious way would amount to the sin of *divination. BIBLIOGRAPHY: G. Lanteri-Laura, *Histoire de la phrénologie* (1970).

[T. C. O'BRIEN]

PHRYGIAN (MUSIC) also *tertius tonus,* third mode, the *mode or scale beginning on E. Its plagal form is termed hypophrygian (*quartus tonus,* fourth mode).

[A. DOHERTY]

PHRYGIANS, see CATAPHRYGIANS.

PHYLACTERIES, derived from the Gr. *phylactērion,* literally a fort, hence a means of protection, so called either because the objects to which the name was applied served as a reminder to preserve the memory of the Law, or because they were considered by some to be a means of warding off demons. This latter interpretation has led to their being wrongly understood as amulets. The Aramaic term for them was *tepillia,* possibly associated with the Heb. *tephillah* (prayer). The philacteries were two small leather cases, one containing four hollow spaces into which were put tiny scrolls containing the following passages of the Torah: Ex 13.1–10; 13.11–16; Dt 6.4–9; 11.13–21. This was worn on the forehead. The other contained the same four passages on one tiny scroll and was fastened to the upper left arm by straps. They were originally supposed to be worn always but in later times at any rate were actually worn only during prayer. The practice was a rigidly literal carrying out of the prescription of Ex 13.9 and Dt 6.8 and 11.18 that the Torah be "as a sign on your hands and as a memorial between your eyes." BIBLIOGRAPHY: JE 10:21–28; EDB 1853–54.

[A. J. TKACIK]

PHYLETISM, from the Gr. *phylē* (tribe or nation), a term applied to the ecclesiastical nationalism that appeared in the newly restored Bulgarian Church and was condemned by a Greek Orthodox synod held in Constantinople in 1872. The condemnation came as a result of the conflict during the years 1860–72 between the Bulgarian Orthodox and the Phanar, i.e., the Greek Orthodox see of Constantinople. Encouraged by the promise of more freedom contained in the sultan's imperial decree *hatti-humayum* of Feb. 1856, the Bulgarians started a strong campaign against the Greek element in their lands and set about expelling Greek prelates from their sees throughout the Bulgarian territory. Several joint councils and minimal concessions on the part of the Greeks failed to satisfy the demands of the Bulgarians, who gradually took dissident steps, cutting one after another their links with the Phanar. In the pontifical liturgy for Easter 1860, celebrated by the Bulgarians in the Galata section of

Constantinople, the commemoration of the patriarch was omitted, a step regarded by the Orthodox as a serious breach of inter-Church relations. Fearing a pro-Catholic movement among the Bulgarians and the growing interest of Russia, both the Phanar and the Turkish government showed a sudden willingness to do something for the Bulgarians. In Mar. 1861 the Bulgarians presented a list of minimal demands to the Turkish government. These included: Bulgarian prelates in all districts inhabited by Bulgarians; election of prelates in mixed population districts; the limitation of their ecclesiastical relations with the patriarch of Constantinople to the strictly religious sphere; a Bulgarian abp. who would reside in Constantinople; a Bulgarian clerical and lay council in Constantinople to care for Bulgarian interests before the Turkish government. The patriarch was willing to accept Bulgarian prelates for Bulgaria itself, but rejected the other demands. The impasse of a mixed Bulgarian and Greek commission (1869–70) was resolved only by a firman of the sultan (Feb. 28, 1870). The document established an ecclesiastical province for the Bulgarian Orthodox of the Empire, with an exarch at its head, who would reside in Constantinople and hold jurisdiction in a number of predominantly Bulgarian dioceses. Notwithstanding a strong protest of the patriarch, the Bulgarians on Mar. 23, 1872, elected their first exarch, the Metropolitan Antim of Vidin. The patriarch then convoked a pan-Orthodox synod, actually attended only by representatives of the Greek Churches. The Bulgarian secession was condemned as opposed to Orthodox ecclesiology and canon law and for pretending to establish an autonomous Church on purely national grounds, i.e., for phyletism. An autonomous, autocephalous Church would have been perfectly possible on political grounds according to the traditional interpretation of canon 28 of Chalcedon. Whatever may be the theological and canonical reasoning behind the condemnation, the modern scholar is disposed to regard it as historically false and ecclesiastically unjust. The Bulgarian claim to a national Church was not a novelty in the Orthodox Church, where ecclesiastical nationalism has been common for many cent., at least since Tsar Simeon of Bulgaria asked for and obtained his own patriarch in the 10th century. Within the boundaries of the Turkish Empire there already existed several national Churches, all in communion with the see of Constantinople. The only fault of the Bulgarians seems to have consisted in choosing Constantinople, the see of the ecumenical patriarch, as the see of their own exarch. However, this did not come from the Bulgarians, who would have preferred one of their ancient capitals (Trnovo or Ohrid), but from the Turkish authorities, with a view to keeping better control of the new church organization. The Phanar seems to have been concerned with protecting Greek interests over a large portion of non-Greek Orthodox Christians. In fact, most Orthodox communities are organized along national lines, with several bps. in the same metropolitan see. As a result of its condemnation in 1872, the Bulgarian Church was considered outside the Orthodox communion only by the Greek Churches, while other Orthodox Churches, notably the Russian, maintained a *de facto* communion with it. The anathema was lifted in 1945, apparently through the mediation of the Russian Church and by a small symbolic reparation on the part of the Bulgarian Church. BIBLIOGRAPHY: S. Vailhé, DTC 2.1:1206–12.

[G. ELDAROV]

PHYSIOLOGICAL PSYCHOLOGY, the branch of psychology that investigates the physiological structures and processes which underlie or accompany cognition, emotion, drive, and behavior in men and animals. Historically it antedates *experimental psychology (for which it provided impetus) and claims among famous names, Helmholtz, J. Müller, Fechner and Weber. The differentiations of the nervous system and its interconnections, the electrochemical nature of nerve impulses, the neurological correlates of acquired behavior patterns, the biochemical bases of mental and emotional dysfunction, the neural basis of general bodily function control are examples of areas in which research is active. The major question in physiological psychology, i.e., the nature of the relation between a psychic and a physiological event, is still under investigation.

[M. E. STOCK]

PHYSIOLOGUS, 2d-cent. early Christian work composed in or near Egypt, the most widely known animal book during the Middle Ages. Describing actual and legendary animals, with a moral commentary on their nature and habits, and with quotations from the Bible, it was one of the main sources for bestiaries. *BESTIARY.

PHYSIS, a Gr. term, the equivalent of the Lat. *natura* (Eng., nature), used in Aristotelian and scholastic philosophy to denote the intrinsic principle of growth or change in self-subsisting beings. Theologically the concept of *physis,* or nature, played a significant part in the Trinitarian and Christological controversies. It was used to explain the single principle of operation *ad extra* in the Trinity and the double principle of operation (the human and divine natures) in the one person of Christ.

PIANO (It. from *piano abito*-plain dress), the dress of prelates: black cassock with red piping and sash worn by cardinals; purple worn by bishops and lesser prelates.

PIARISTS, a congregation of religious men dedicated to the Christian education of youth. Officially, it is called the Order of Poor Clerics Regular of the Mother of God of the Pious Schools (Sch.P.) and was founded in 1617 in Rome by St. *Joseph Calasanctius. During various political revolutions in the 19th and 20th cent., the Piarists lost many provinces and schools as well as priests. The order, however, has grown and its work continues both in Europe and the Americas. It has a total membership of 1,861 residing in about 177 houses. The generalate is located in Rome. The alumni of the Piarist schools include such notables as Pius IX and St. John Nepomucene Neumann. The Piarists of the U.S. work in Washington, D.C., Philadelphia, Pa., Buffalo, N.Y., Miami, Fla., New York, N.Y., and Los Angeles, California.

[R. A. TODD]

PIAZZETTA, GIOVANNI BATTISTA (1683–1754), Italian painter, in Venice with A. Molinari, and with Crespi in Bologna, becoming a leading painter in Venice. Opposed to his rival Tiepolo, P.'s early works are dark in earth colors and dramatically angular in composition. His *Susanna and the Elders* (1715) and *St. James Led to Martyrdom* (1721) show intense mystical passion. He lightened his palette in the *Madonna Appearing to St. Filippo Neri* (1725–27), vitalizing the quiet composition by his distinctive diagonals. A *St. Francis* and *St. Dominic* introduce the rococo style of Ricci and Tiepolo, seen again in P.'s delicate and elegant *Assumption of the Virgin* (1735). His profound 17th-cent. approach to form and subject provided an organic basis for the lighter 18th-cent. rococo style.

[M. J. DALY]

PICA, see PIE.

PICARD, MAX (1888–1965), essayist and philosopher who was part of the Catholic intellectual revival in Switzerland and had great influence on Swiss thought.

[J. R. AHERNE]

PICARDIANS (Picards), a sect of late medieval origin. Interpreting the notion of personal union with God in a pantheistic sense, the Picardians felt themselves free to indulge in community of wives and other immoral practices. They rejected the Bible as revelation, the sacraments, and the hierarchical structure of the Church. They existed from *c.*1406 in parts of France and Belgium. In 1418 some of them, fleeing the Inquisition, went to Bohemia, where they were received among the *Taborites. Soon, however, their ideas were judged pernicious, and many of them were slain. Some Picardians survived in Moravia and Bohemia down to the 19th century.

[T. C. O'BRIEN]

PICCOLOMINI, a noble family of Siena, originally of Rome, but resident in Siena as early as 1098. Engaged in commerce quite early, by the 13th cent. the Piccolominis controlled several banks in Italy, France, and England. Their title of counts palatine was granted in 1458 by Emperor Frederick III. Among the more illustrious members of the family were Pius II; Pius III; Card. Jacopo Ammanati de'Piccolomini; Bl. Ambrogio (d. 1348) a founder of the Olivetan Benedictines; Alessandro (d. 1578) humanist, philosopher, theologian, and bp.; Francesco (d. 1651) gen-

eral of the Jesuits; Celio (d. 1681) cardinal and abp. of Siena; Octavio (d. 1656) a military commander during the Thirty Years' War. The family still exists in its several branches. BIBLIOGRAPHY: A. Lisini and A. Liberati, *Genealogia dei Piccolomini di Siena* (1900); F. V. Cerreta, *Alessandro Piccolomini* (1960).

[W. A. JURGENS]

PICHARDO, JOSÉ ANTONIO (d. 1812), Oratorian of Mexico, then part of New Spain. P. was a teacher of philosophy and expert in languages. His great work was *Vida y martirio del protomartir mexicano San Felipe de Jesús de las Casas*, an accurate picture of life in New Spain (published only in 1934). At the behest of Viceroy Garibay, P. studied the boundaries of Texas and Louisiana, at the time a matter of controversy, and prepared a voluminous report, the greatest extant gathering of sources on Texas under the Spanish.

[J. R. AHERNE]

PICHL, WENZEL (Vaclav Pichel; 1741–1804), violinist and composer of Czech descent. He studied counterpoint with Seeger in Prague. He worked as violinist and vice director of music (with director Ditters von Dittersdorf) to Bp. Patachich in Hungary (1763–1769); conducted in Prague (1769–71); was a member of Vienna's National Theatre Orchestra (1771); served as music director and chamber composer to Archduke Ferdinand in Milan (1775–96). As both violinist and composer, he was well regarded by contemporaries. Some 700 works include Masses and other church music, operas, symphonies, concertos, pieces for voice.

[R. J. LITZ]

PICHLER, ADOLF (full name, Adolf Pichler, Ritter von Rautenkar; 1819–1900), Austrian poet, novelist, one of the most prominent 19th-cent. poets of his native Tyrol, best known for his realistic verse epos (*Fra Serafico; Der Hexenmeister*). Son of a customs official, P. studied at Innsbruck and Vienna and became professor of earth sciences at the Univ. of Innsbruck (1867).

[B. F. STEINBRUCKNER]

PICHLER, JOHANN (1860–1924) and **WILHELM** (1862–1938), Austrian brothers known for their contributions to catechetics and pastoral theology. In Vienna after 1903, they jointly pioneered the so-called Viennese catechetical method: this eschewed the formalized approach to religious instruction characteristic of the 19th cent. in favor of a new curriculum which combined Scripture, doctrine, and liturgy. They stressed the importance of basing religious instruction on firm biblical foundations. Their innovations were most influential on the teaching of young children.

[E. M. GATES]

PICKETING. The moral evaluation of picketing must look to its purpose and to its own nature. Picketing as a means to dramatize a cause or to enforce a strike more effectively is legitimate where the cause it serves is just; where civil law is respected as to the place and manner of picketing; where it does not involve violence, i.e., it does not include physical constraint to prevent crossing the picket line, but only moral suasion to respect it. With regard to picketing as part of a strike, it is a just act when the strike is not in violation of an existing contract, and is intended to correct a just grievance.

[T. C. O'BRIEN]

PICO DELLA MIRANDOLA, GIOVANNI (1463–94), Italian humanist. Born to the ruling family of Mirandola, a small duchy near Modena, he received the title Count of Concordia. He began study of canon law at Bologna in 1477 and 2 years later went to Florence, where he became associated with M. *Ficino and the Platonic Academy. He studied Aristotle at Padua (1480–82), and became one of the first Europeans of the Renaissance to study Hebrew and Arabic. After some time in Mirandola and other places, he returned to Florence in 1484, but in 1485 went to Paris for study in scholastic philosophy and theology. Returning to Florence in 1486, he drew up the *Conclusiones,* 900 theses, many taken from other writers, in philosophy, theology, and science, which he proposed to defend at Rome against all challengers. Innocent VIII found some of the theses heretical, however, and cancelled the disputation. P. fled to France the following year to escape arrest, but was imprisoned there for a short time. After his release he went to Florence, where he was under the protection of the Medici. He wrote *Heptaplus* (1489), a commentary on the six days of creation; *De ente et uno,* an attempt to reconcile Plato and Aristotle; and *Disputationes contra astrologiam,* the latter two published posthumously. His most famous work was his *Oratio,* preface to his proposed disputation. In it he celebrated man's freedom and dignity in exalted Renaissance fashion. Toward the end of his life, eager for reform, he became a follower of Savonarola. BIBLIOGRAPHY: A. Dulles, *Princeps Concordiae* (1941).

[T. EARLY]

PICPUS FATHERS, see SACRED HEARTS, FATHERS OF THE.

PICPUS SISTERS, religious members of a congregation officially named Sisters of the Sacred Hearts and of the Perpetual Adoration of the Blessed Sacrament (SS.CC.). It was cofounded by Joseph Coudrin and Henriette Aymer de la Chevalerie at Poitiers, France, in 1797. The members take simple, perpetual vows, observe an adaptation of the Benedictine rule and lead contemplative-active lives. Although their apostolate is mostly educational work, the Picpus Sisters are esp. dedicated to the spread of devotion to the Sacred Hearts of Jesus and Mary and also to perpetual adoration in reparation for irreligious acts against God. The motherhouse, formerly on Rue Picpus in Paris, is now located in Rome. In 1975 the congregation had 1,333 members and maintained 97 houses throughout Europe and North and South America.

[R. A. TODD]

PIE, LOUIS FRANÇOIS DÉSIRÉ (1815–80), bp. of Poitiers from 1849, cardinal in 1879. Ordained from Saint-Sulpice in 1839, he was attached to the cathedral of Chartres and became vicar general of that diocese in 1844. As bp. he was a strong ultramontanist and infallibilist, opposing the views of Bp. *Dupanloup. At Vatican Council I, P. was a member of the commission on faith, and a leader in the Council's opposition to rationalism and liberalism. In politics, as well, he was a conservative, attached to the restoration of the monarchy in France; under Leo XIII, however, he acted as intermediary in relations with the French Republic. In his diocese P. promoted theological studies, church discipline, religious and parochial life; he also restored use of the Roman liturgy in 1856. He was a renowned orator; his sermons, addresses, essays, and letters were published in various collections, one in nine volumes, 1887.

[T. C. O'BRIEN]

PIE (Pica), a name given in medieval England to the rubrical section of liturgical books, specifically in the 15th-cent. book of direction (*Ordinale; Directorium*) for conducting a religious service and coordinating the elements of the liturgy appropriate to the given feast day, resolving such questions as which Collect to use if two feast days fall on the same day. The Name Pie refers to the red and black ink used for these rubrical directions.

[R. J. LITZ]

PIEDRA, ABBEY OF, former Cistercian monastery in the Saragossa province of Spain. It was founded in 1194 on lands donated by Alfonso II of Aragon. The 15th-cent. Cistercian reformer, Martin de Vargas, was from Piedra. Suppressed in 1835, it was eventually turned into a public tourist accommodation since it is located near the beautiful cascades of the Piedra River.

[M. A. MCFADDEN]

PIEMONTANUS, see BUTZBACH, JOHANNES.

PIERIUS, ST. (d. *c.*309), head of the catechetical school of Alexandria during the episcopate of Theonas (281–300). Although later authors such as *Photius list him as a martyr, St. *Jerome reported that he survived the persecution of Diocletian and died peacefully at Rome. In his theology P. seems to have closely followed the teaching of Origen even in its deviation into error. A few sermons and fragments are all of his writings that survived (PG 10:241FF). BIBLIOGRAPHY: L. B. Bradford, *Three Teachers of Alexandria* (1908).

[R. B. ENO]

PIERLEONI, a leading medieval Roman family. The first known member was Baruch, a converted Roman Jew. His son, Leo, who consistently favored Hildebrand (Gregory VII), was succeeded by his own son, Petrus Leonis (d. c.1128), from whom the family took its name. He, too, remained a staunch supporter of the popes. His son, also known as Petrus Leonis, a monk at Cluny, was named cardinal by Pope Paschal II before 1113. After the death of Honorius II (1130), the college of cardinals, fearing schism, chose eight of their number as an electoral committee which selected Gregorio Parareschi (Innocent II). In a few hours the remainder of the cardinals (21) elected as pope the above-mentioned Card. Pierleoni (Anacletus II), who, although he was accepted in Rome and Italy, was considered an antipope. Innocent II, aided by Bernard of Clairvaux, reigned until his death in 1143. This serious schism was ended by Lateran Council II in 1139. The Pierleoni family, on the whole, continued to support the papacy and to have members among the hierarchy. BIBLIOGRAPHY: H. Bloch, "Schism of Anacletus II and the Glanfeuil Forgeries," *Traditio* 8 (1952) 159–262.

[G. E. CONWAY]

PIERLING, PAUL (1840–1922), historian. Born in St. Petersburg, P. joined the Society of Jesus in Austria and studied in Rome, but he spent most of his life after 1876 in Paris and Brussels. The chief area of his historical interest was the 16th-cent. diplomatic relations between Russia and the Holy See; *La Russie et le Saint Siège* (5 v., Paris, 1896–1912) and numerous related studies are devoted to the False Dmitri, Polish-Russian conflicts, and A. *Possevino's mission. P.'s work rests on thorough research in major European archives and is marked by an effort to achieve objectivity.

[R. H. SCHMANDT]

PIERO DI COSIMO (1462–1521), Italian painter in the shop of C. Rosselli (1480), but influenced by Filippino Lippi, Leonardo, and Botticelli. The *Visitation* (Washington, D.C.), an *Immaculate Conception* and *Madonna and Saints* (both in Florence) suggesting Flemish influence in enamel-like color and crisp outlines, a *Madonna Enthroned with Saints* (St. Louis) bearing the arms of the Pugliese family, *Adoration of the Child* and *Mary Magdalen* (Rome) belong to the period 1485–1500. P. introduced bizarre features after the death of Rosselli (1507), his strange creature in wild landscapes forming a compositional X which strongly influenced Andrea del Sarto and Franciabigio.

[M. J. DALY]

PIERO DELLA FRANCESCA (de' Franceschi; c.1420–92), Italian painter of the Florentine School. Although one of the greatest painters of the *Quattrocento*, certainly the most rigorously intellectual, he preferred living in his provincial hometown of Borgo San Sepulcro rather than in Florence. Having a total mastery of L. Alberti's perspective, he creates sober, dignified compositions populated by sharply defined, sculpturesque figures, which are in many ways a kind of ultimate statement of the ideals of the Early Renaissance. Already present in his superb monumental fresco cycle depicting *The Legend of the True Cross* (c.1453–55; Church of San Francesco, Arezzo) are P.'s characteristic reduction of form to its basic geometric substructure, his interests in a classicizing modeling of anatomy and in light-filled landscape. P.'s silent figures fixed in clear, limpid space dominate his *Baptism of Christ, Madonna della Misericordia* (Borgo San Sepolcro), *Flagellation*, the impressive fresco *Resurrection* (c.1463) and the *S. Agostino Altarpiece* (1454) of Urbino (P.'s patrons), the *Sinigallia Madonna* (c.1470), the unfinished *Nativity* (1472–75) and his last painting—the *S. Bernardino Altarpiece* for the funerary chapel of Baptista Sforza (Duchess of Urbino). An increasing preoccupation with mathematical relationships as the source of harmony in the universe as in art led him to abandon painting for theoretical treatises during his last 20 years. BIBLIOGRAPHY: E. Battisti, *Piero della Francesca* (1972); L. Venturi, *Piero della Francesca: Biographical and Critical Study* (1959).

[S. CONWAY]

PIEROZZI, ANTONIO, see ANTONINUS, ST.

PIERRE D'ANGICOURT, French Gothic master-architect residing in Cyprus in the period following the Crusades. Cyprus under the Lusignans of Poitou was a main link between East and West, a meeting-place of Christian and Muslim merchants. Here P. built for princes who donated money for religious buildings by French architects. Models for the Cathedral of Sta. Sophia, Nicosia, were Notre Dame of Paris and of Mantes. At Famagusto, richest port in the Mediterranean in the 14th cent., St. Nicolas, with a French inscription indicating the work under Bp. Baldwin Lambert, has towers and portals from Reims, and apse a replica of St. Urbain, Troyes.

[M. J. DALY]

PIERS PLOWMAN, a Middle English allegory, generally attributed to William Langland; full title, *The Vision of William Concerning Piers the Plowman*. Its subject is the plight of mankind. The poet first invites the reader to see the world as it is. Entering his vision, one sees fine ladies glutting themselves while others are in woeful hovels. Flattery, Liar, and Guile are there and witness a marriage between Lady Meed and Falsehood and watch a friar absolve her "in return for a stained glass window." It is a world in which the poor are neglected and their credulity exploited by a Catholicism that has gone bad and become a religion of amulets, pardons, and bulls. Holy Church has betrayed the trust of men "who would not have held her role lightly" had she practiced what she preached. The poet then takes the reader off in search of Saint Truth, i.e., of the world as it ought to be. Advice is sought from everyone encountered: from Knowledge, Thought, Study, Clergy, and others until, at long last, Piers Plowman "puts forth his head" and offers to be guide whether one's vocation here is that of Do well (the active life), Do better (the contemplative), or Do best (the episcopal). In the end one comes to Christ on his cross and witnesses in a famous passage his majestic descent into hell to liberate his own.

It is easy to respond to the poet's compassion for the poor, his irony, and even his severity expressed in a language full of tang; less easy to grasp is his overall plan. Modern critics insist that he has one and that the work is neither quaint social history nor Wycliffite propaganda but a great religious poem by a poet whom some compare to Dante. There are three versions, the A, B, and C texts, in all of which are references to "Long Will." In 1906 J. M. Manly of Chicago queried their validity and suggested five authors. Modern criticism favors single authorship. Text in translation, J. F. Goodridge, *Piers the Plowman Translated into Modern English with an Introduction* (1959); D. and R. Attwater, *Piers Plowman* (1957). BIBLIOGRAPHY: N. Coghill, *Langland's Piers Plowman* (1964); *idem*, "The Character of Piers Plowman," *Medium Aevum* 2 (1933) 108; H. W. Wells, *Construction of Piers Plowman* (Publications of the Modern Language Association of America 44.1, 1929); G. Kane, *Piers Plowman: The Evidence of Authorship* (1965).

[M. O'CONNOR]

PIERZ, FRANCIS XAVIER (Franz; 1785–1880), missionary. He was born in what is now Yugoslavia and ordained in 1813. He was a parish priest and the author of a celebrated book on horticulture, *Krajinski vertnar*, based on his own experiments and published in 1830. Volunteering for the missions, he moved to the U.S. in 1835. He worked first among the Indians of Michigan where he taught the natives farming skills; at the age of 67 he undertook work among the Chippewa of the upper Mississippi. His reports to Europe succeeded in attracting much financial support. In the Sioux uprising of 1862, P. was instrumental in keeping the Chippewa from joining the war. He did much to colonize Minnesota with German and Slovene immigrants through letters and the book *Die Indiäner in Nord Amerika* (1855). He returned to his homeland in 1873.

[J. R. AHERNE]

PIETISM, "the new Reformation" during the 17th and following centuries, which protested against the moral laxity and religious indifference that had befallen the Protestant Churches. In its original inspiration, associated with the names of Philipp Jakob *Spener (1635–1705) and August Hermann *Francke (1663–1727), Pietism claimed to remain loyal to the Lutheran *confessions of faith. It was not the doctrinal substance of the *Book of Concord but the dead orthodoxy based upon it that was a danger to true Christianity. Inevitably, however, the Pietist attack affected the content of orthodox Lutheranism, not only its theological form; and the insistence of the Pietists on deep and genuine conversion came to imply a disparagement both of the conventional Christianity of the Church and of the usual means of grace, baptism, the Eucharist, and the preaching of the word of God.

Pietism was responsible for the development of a number of separate denominations, notably the *Herrnhuters, or Moravians (see MORAVIAN CHURCH), who, under the leadership of Count Nikolaus Ludwig von *Zinzendorf (1700–60), took up the episcopal succession of the Hussite *Unitas Fratrum. Through the Moravians Pietism affected John *Wesley and *Methodism, but the primary importance for church history of the Pietist movement lay in its impact upon the older Protestant communions, the Lutheran and the *Reformed. After the conflicts between Pietism and orthodoxy had subsided, many elements of both combined forces in opposition to *rationalism and the *Enlightenment. Accepting the validity of the Pietist critique but lamenting the emotionalism into which Pietistic religion had often fallen, the defenders of Lutheran confessional orthodoxy during the 19th cent. all showed the effects of the reformation it had wrought.

Perhaps the most visible effect of Pietism within the Churches was the revival of a zeal for the missions. Neither Luther nor the high Lutheran orthodoxy of the 17th cent. had succeeded in organizing a missionary movement—partly because of the paralysis caused by the abolition of the religious orders, partly because of political reasons, but also partly because of failure to accept the demands of the missionary imperative. Pietism corrected this lack in Lutheranism, fostering the formation of missionary societies in the various Lutheran lands and territories. It also took up the task of eliciting vocations to the missions among theological students and clergy. As a result, the evangelical Christianity exported by these missionaries and planted in pagan cultures bore (and often still bears) marks of its Pietist origins: a moral seriousness, a concern for individual conversion, and a stress upon the use of the Bible, esp. upon its private study; but also a tendency to underemphasize the presence and power of God within the structures of nature and of human culture.

From this historical development within Protestantism, specifically Lutheranism, the term pietism has acquired a more generic sense. It is often used for a great variety of phenomena within Western Christianity, including Roman Catholicism. Although it is usually meant pejoratively, it does designate certain emphases, particularly in the moral and the devotional spheres, which show analogies to the original Pietist demand for personal religion and good works. Thus total abstinence from alcohol, prayer meetings, opposition to the social mission of the Church, and novenas have all been labeled "pietistic." This usage tends to obscure the original historical meaning of the term and the historical importance of the movement, which is still a factor that one must consider in order to understand Protestant Christianity. BIBLIOGRAPHY: P. J. Spener, *Pia Desideria* (Eng. tr. T. G. Tappert, 1964, repr. 1974); F. E. Stoeffler, *Rise of Evangelical Pietism* (1965); D. Carpenter, *Radical Pietists* (1975).

[J. PELIKAN]

PIETY. English usage originally kept the strength of Lat. *pietas,* and the term signified dutiful and affectionate observance with respect to God, country, and parents, also "compassion" and "pity." Now, however, it can carry an air of faint disparagement and suggest an addiction to religiosity and works of edification. The earlier and more proper sense of the term is Roman rather than Greek, and in treating of it the moralists quote Cicero instead of Aristotle. St. Thomas Aquinas very exactly and delicately defines its place in the field of justice. In the service we owe to those above us the note of equality and contractual obligation is absent; thus our service of God, *religio,* and of legitimate superiors, *obedientia.* Likewise with the duties of respect and honor we owe our parents and "our own." Here there are values too warm and close for the detachment of cool justice, quasi-instinctive forces without which the strictly rational virtues will run out of juice. So there is a *pietas* in loyalty to our kin, and it extends to patriotism toward our country, deeper than being a good citizen in the State, and more than being tractable under the government, and still more than serving a party. Yet it can include the mystique of limited though benign partisanship, thus attachment to Texas, the Packers, the Jesuits. All such are the objects of proper, though restrained, Christian virtue. BIBLIOGRAPHY: ThAq ST 2a2ae, 101, esp. Lat-Eng ed., v. 41, ed. T. C. O'Brien.

[T. GILBY]

PIETY, GIFT OF, a gift of the Holy Spirit. The Septuagint and Vulgate double one of the six charismata of Is 11.2 into the fear of the Lord and piety (Gr. *eusebeia,* Lat. *pietas*). Though identical in the Scripture text, a theological tradition has—somewhat forcedly yet not unprofitably—treated them as distinct gifts. *Pietas* has a deeper ring than the English "piety." It is a reverence with undertones of loyalty, patriotism, even partisanship and commitment to family, people, and country, more prejudiced (in no bad sense) and less deliberate than obedience to superior and general justice to the State. The virtue of *piety covers factors of social cohesion basic to political and contractual engagements, both civil and ecclesiastical. It enters into religion and is there enhanced by this special gift, which communicates a certain instinctive mode of operation and a familial devotion, so that God is worshipped not just as a Creator but as Father, and creatures are served as his children. By a schematic treatment of the virtues and gifts it is fitted into the place provided for justice. St. Augustine pregnantly relates it to the second Beatitude, "Blessed are the meek, for they shall inherit the earth." BIBLIOGRAPHY: ThAq ST 2a2ae, 101 and 102.

[T. GILBY]

PIFFL, FRIEDRICH GUSTAV (1864–1932), card. and abp. of Vienna (1913–32). Having joined the Canons Regular of Augustine at Klosterneuburg (1883), P. was ordained in 1888. Made cardinal in 1914, he served as abp. of Vienna and later as apostolic administrator of Innsbruck (1922). Supporting the Austrian monarchy during World War I, after the war he urged popular support of the new Republic. His concern with current social issues gained him the appelation "people's bishop." He was the target of ineffectual accusations of Modernism by the so-called integralists (see INTEGRALISM).

[R. J. LITZ]

PIGHIUS, ALBERT (Pigge; *c.*1490–1542), Dutch theologian whose teachings were much discussed at the Council of Trent. After studies at Louvain P. served in Rome under Adrian VI, his former teacher, then became dean at the church of St. John, Utrecht. His teaching that original sin is not an inherent fault but an extrinsic imputation was included in a list of 13 statements labeled "heresies" and distributed during deliberations on original sin; its rejection is reflected in the 3d canon of the final decree (D 1513). In the debates on justification G. *Seripando proposed his *double justice teaching, which the Council also rejected; P. was among the theologians who had defended what Seripando proposed. P.'s ideas on these two points are explained in part by his efforts to achieve a degree of understanding with the Reformers in discussions at Worms (1540) and Ratisbon (Regensburg; 1541). But P. earned respect for his overall theological work, and was frequently cited by contemporary authors. He also demonstrated criticial acumen as an historical theologian, particularly in his *Hierarchiae ecclesiasticae assertio* (1538), a forceful, documented examination of papal primacy.

[T. C. O'BRIEN]

PIGNATELLI, JOSEPH MARY, ST. (1737–1811), Jesuit who led the exiled Jesuits in Italy after the Society's expulsion from Spain following the Cloak and Sombrero Riots in Saragossa and Madrid (1767). Of noble Calabrian descent, he was born in Spain, entered the novitiate at Tarragona in 1753, and was ordained in 1762. At Saragossa he was chaplain to the prison and teacher. During the exile, he went to Bologna when Clement XIV suppressed the entire order (1773). Unable to join the Jesuit remnant in White Russia because of ill health, he worked to establish a vice province in Parma. He reentered the Society in 1797. Pius VI, whom P. aided in 1798, gave him permission to admit novices at Parma. His general in St. Petersburg named him provincial of Italy in 1803. Through P.'s efforts, the Society's full restoration in 1814 was facilitated. He was canonized in 1954 by Pius V.

[R. J. LITZ]

PIKE, JAMES ALBERT (1913–69), Episcopal bishop. Born in Oklahoma City, P. was reared as a Catholic, but became an agnostic and studied law (J.S.D., Yale, 1938). After service with the Securities Exchange Commission and the Navy, he entered the Episcopal Church and received ordination in 1946. He served as a parish rector in Poughkeepsie, N.Y. (1947–49), chaplain and chairman of the religion department at Columbia Univ. (1949–52), and dean of the cathedral of St. John the Divine, New York (1952–58). Chosen bp. of California (San Francisco area) in 1958, he continued his espousal of liberal social causes and became increasingly controversial for his attacks on orthodox doctrine. Charged with heresy, he was censured by his fellow bps. in Oct. 1966. Earlier that year he resigned his bishopric and joined the Center for the Study of Democratic Institutions, remaining there until June 1969. He died after becoming lost in the desert while on a visit to Israel. BIBLIOGRAPHY: W. Stringfellow and A. Towne, *Death and Life of Bishop Pike* (1976).

[T. EARLY]

PILAR, RICARDO DE (d. 1700), Brazilian Benedictine, painter in São Bento monastery, creating in seclusion paintings of visionary quality for the walls and chapels.

PÎLĀSĀ, the ordinary East Syrian word for the paten.

[A. CODY]

PILATE, PONTIUS, Roman procurator of Judea (26–34 A.D.) who presided at the trial and condemnation of Jesus. The gospel accounts reflect a growing tendency in the early Church to contrast the reticence of P. with the demands of the Jewish leaders and the crowd. Philo and Josephus describe him as a cruel and inflexible governor. The mention of P. in the early Christian creed historically roots the death of Christ. Eusebius speaks of his exile and suicide in Gaul. Legends concerning him include the *Acta Pilati* and the *Paradosis Pilati.* Because of the latter account the Abyssinian Church venerates P. and his wife as saints. The Greek Church honors his wife as a saint. In 1961 a Latin inscription containing the words *Pontius Pilatus praefectus Judaeae* was discovered at Caesarea in Palestine.

[M. A. MCNAMARA]

PILATE, ACTS OF, see APOCRYPHA (NT), 56.

PILGRAM, ANTON (1460–1515), German architect and sculptor of the transitional period from late Gothic to Renaissance. P.'s pulpit (*c.*1510) in St. Stephen's Cathedral, Vienna, carries a sculptured self-portrait.

[M. J. DALY]

PILGRAM, FRIEDRICH (1819–90), German lay ecclesiologist, esp. in his *Physiologie der Kirche* (1860), a study of the communion and community of charity as the formally constitutive element in the Church.

PILGRIM OF BORDEAUX, otherwise nameless pilgrim who in 333–334 made a pilgrimage from Bordeaux to the Holy Land. The significance of the pilgrimage lies in the fact that he stopped at every city or town mentioned in the Bible. He also wrote a lengthy description of the journey, *Itinerarium Burdigalense,* the oldest extant pilgrim's account; his description of Jerusalem contains information of great value concerning the topography of the city. *PILGRIMAGES.

[J. R. RIVELLO]

PILGRIM OF PASSAU (d. 991), bp. of Passau, restorer of the churches and monasteries destroyed by Hungarian invasions. He undertook the conversion of Hungary, sending missionaries and going there himself to evangelize, thus preparing the way for the general conversion that came about under King Stephen. P. also sought to establish that Passau was an archdiocese, with jurisdiction therefore over Hungary, by counterfeiting documents, the *Forgeries of Lorch.* He is also thought to have been the Latin translator of the *Niebelungenlied.*

[T. C. O'BRIEN]

PILGRIM CHURCH, the People of God viewed as a community of wayfarers walking in faith toward a goal not yet attained; an image reflecting a dramatic change in the self-understanding of the Church. The document *Lumen gentium* on the Church resulting from the discussions of Vatican Council II used the phrases "pilgrim Church" and "pilgrim People" and presented the Church as a mystery in the process of being revealed in history (VatII ConstChurch 48). The pastoral document *Gaudium et spes,* on the Church in the modern world reinforced the image. Postconciliar theological movements have elaborated the image, in opposition to the more entrenched traditional image of the Church as a perfect society, a Rock in the turbulent sea of human history. The image of a pilgrim People is less triumphalistic, presenting a Church that learns as well as teaches; is healed as well as heals; seeks dialogue and collaboration with those of other religious traditions and with agnostics and atheists who sincerely seek justice and truth. The pilgrim Church is always in need of reform and renewal, and shows itself as needy as well as richly endowed. Like all wayfarers the pilgrim People must look for God's presence in the signs of the times and in the voices of the age. The new self-understanding has already begun to affect the character of catechesis, the style of ministry and service, and the tradition of liturgy, prayer, and ascesis.

[E. J. DILLON]

PILGRIMAGE (IN THE BIBLE), solemn and festive journey and visit to a sacred place, made holy by a unique manifestation of divine activity, by its link with sacred tradition and solemn covenant, or for recurring cultic assembly. As Israel gained control of the land of Canaan, the Israelites gradually gained control also of the Canaanite cult sites, reinterpreted the cultic traditions, and incorporated the Canaanite forms of festival and pilgrimage into the Israelite view of history. This was the common fate of such biblical cult centers as Bethel, Gilgal, Beersheba, and Zion (Jerusalem). It was Canaanite tradition to go on pilgrimage to the nearest cult center for the recurring agricultural festivals: at the beginning and end of the grain season, and for the olive and grape harvest. The Israelites combined the beginning of the grain season with their own pastoral tradition of Passover involving sacrifice of the firstborn of herd and flock, into a festive commemoration of the event of liberation from bondage. Secondly, the grain harvest (Pentecost) festival became commemorative of the giving of the Law at Sinai. The most joyous feast—the grape harvest festival (Tabernacles)—came to commemorate the desert wanderings when Israel lived in tents. The pilgrimage festival was a time and place for grand markets and fairs; for hearing legal processes; for celebration among kin. The joy of pilgrimage was the greatest joy. The Prophets inveighed against such cultic festivals where the celebrants were oblivious to injustice and oppression (Amos 4.4–5;5.5–6,21ff); where the hands outstretched in prayer were covered with blood (Is 1.15–17); where the house of prayer was really a gathering place for thieves (Jer. 7.11). Under King Josiah and the Deuteronomic reformers, a concerted attempt was made to have Jerusalem the only legitimate place of pilgrimage, and the covenant law more integral to the celebration. From the days of the Exile to Babylon, throughout the centuries of the dispersion, the dream of festive pilgrimage to Zion was paramount. Luke recounts the pilgrimage of Jesus and his parents to Jerusalem for Passover (Luke 2.41ff).

[E. J. DILLON]

PILGRIMAGE OF GRACE, an uprising in the North of England in 1536 led by Robert *Aske, a Yorkshireman. It was a stand for the old order in religion and a protest against the suppression of the monasteries and other measures taken by T. *Cromwell. In mid-October 1536 Aske moved on York at the head of 9000 men, the marchers wearing crosses marked with the five wounds of Christ. The movement gained such wide support that Henry VIII sent the Duke of Norfolk and the Earl of Shrewsbury to negotiate with the pilgrims at Doncaster. By this time their number had quadrupled. Aske was promised that the grievances would be remedied and that a parliament would soon meet at York. With this assurance he dismissed his followers, but when it began to be apparent that the government had no intention of carrying out its promises, new disturbances broke out in the North. Although Aske had no part in these, he and certain others prominent in the pilgrimage were arrested. On the same indictment for treason Aske and 15 others were

tried, found guilty, and executed. BIBLIOGRAPHY: M. H. and R. Dodds, *Pilgrimage of Grace 1536–37* (2 v., 1915); Hughes RE 1:303–319.

[R. B. ENO]

PILGRIMAGE ROADS, ART OF THE, an important school of shared Romanesque architectural and sculptural features in the 11th and 12th cent. developed along the four major pilgrimage routes through France to the shrine of Santiago de Compostela, Spain, under the aegis of Cluny. Important pilgrimage churches sheltering the relics of local saints were: Ste. Foy (Congues), St. Sernin (Toulouse), St. Pierre (Moissac), St. Trophime (Arles), at Souillac and Vézelay and numerous other abbey churches boasting magnificent cloisters, impressive tympana, and portal carvings, and interiors with galleries, radiating chapels, and ambulatories to permit circulation around the relics, all evidencing a stylistic unity through craftsmen moving along the routes. In baroque Germany, also, the pilgrimage churches show similar unification (Vierzehnheiligen Church, Franconia). BIBLIOGRAPHY: K. J. Conant, *Carolingian and Romanesque Architecture* (1959); A. K. Porter, *Romanesque Sculpture of the Pilgrimage Roads* (10 v., 1923; repr. 3 v., 1969).

[R. C. MARKS]

PILGRIMAGES, journeys made out of such religious motives as entreaty, repentance, or thanksgiving, to a shrine or sanctuary as a place of the presence of the sacred or holy (see HIEROPHANY). The pilgrimage is a widespread phenomenon in the history of religions, including Greek and Roman religion, and remains so in Judaism, Christianity, Islam, and Hindu religion. The pilgrimage is part of OT history (see PILGRIMAGE [IN THE BIBLE].)

Early Christian Pilgrimages. Christians of the first 7 cent. journeyed to sites sanctified by the life and death of Christ and his saints out of a spirit of devotion, in fulfillment of a vow, or as an act of repentance, and esp. to Rome and to Jerusalem. During the centuries of persecution it was difficult for the faithful to engage in this practice to any great extent, but there are records of pilgrim journeys to Rome by, e.g., Polycarp of Smyrna (c.150), Origen (c.212), and Abercius of Hierapolis (c.216); and to Jerusalem by, e.g., Melito of Sardes (c.160) and Alexander of Cappodocia (c.216). After the Peace of the Church (313) and the erection of basilicas by Constantine over the tombs of SS. Peter and Paul in Rome, and over the cave at Bethlehem and the Holy Sepulcher at Jerusalem, the number of Christian pilgrims greatly increased. St. Jerome has described the large numbers of pilgrims who came from the East and West to the Holy Land in the later 4th cent. (*Ep.* 46.10). Among the more interesting accounts of pilgrimages to Jerusalem is that of the *Pilgrim of Bordeaux who went there in 333 and of the nun Etheria who was present for the Holy Week liturgy in Jerusalem in 395. The favorite places of pilgrimage in Rome were the tombs of the

Apostles and of the Roman martyrs. Numerous graffiti and the various "itineraries" or pilgrims' guides from the 7th to the 9th cent. indicate the great popularity of this type of devotion. Other sites were also visited, e.g., the birthplace of the martyr Menas SW of Lake Mareotis in Egypt and the pillar of St. Simeon Stylites at Qa'al Sem'an in N Syria.

Medieval and Modern Pilgrimages. Throughout the Middle Ages and up to the Renaissance and Reformation the passion for pilgrimages was a prominent part of European Christianity. The Crusades themselves, from 1095, were ostensibly undertaken to keep the Holy Land open to Christians. Rome in 1300, during the first Holy Year proclaimed by Boniface VIII, had a population of 200,000 in excess of the normal. But equally a feature of medieval piety were the pilgrimages to local shrines; there was hardly a region that did not have its center of miracles. Among the most frequented were the shrines of *Santiago de Compostella; St. Martin of Tours; St. Thomas à Becket at Canterbury; of Our Lady at Glastonbury and Walsingham. In France there was Chartres and Mont St. Michel; in Switzerland, Einsiedeln; in Italy, Bolsena and *Loreto. With the Renaissance came humanist ridicule of medieval piety (thus Erasmus in his *Religious Pilgrimage*); *Zwingli was appalled by the abuses at Einsiedeln in 1516; the Reformers generally condemned pilgrimages, their shrines and their relics, even the veneration of saints, as blasphemous and superstitious, and many shrines were ransacked and torn down. The Wars of Religion, then the French Revolution made European pilgrimages all but impossible; the Enlightenment heaped further scorn on them as being unworthy of a man of reason. Yet from the 17th cent. on, older pilgrimages were revived, new shrines emerged—even in the New World, as at Guadalupe in Mexico; the ardor for pilgrimages became more sober, but it has remained a part of Catholic piety. The most frequented shrines have become those of the Blessed Virgin Mary, and esp. where apparitions have occurred: La Salette (1846), Lourdes (1858); Fatima (1917). In North America the shrines of Cap de Madeleine, Ste. Anne de Beaupré, and St. Joseph's Oratory in the Province of Quebec; and the shrine of the North American Martyrs, Auriesville, N.Y., are thronged by the devout. A special form of pilgrimage in the 20th cent. was begun by students, walking from Paris to Chartres, and has been taken up by Anglican and Catholic students going on foot to Walsingham and to Glastonbury. In Poland, the 14th-cent. shrine of Our Lady of Częstochowa, always a symbol of Polish Catholicism and patriotism, has become even more so under the Communist regime. The 20th cent. has also seen a succession of great pilgrimages to Rome during the Holy Years, 1933, 1950, 1975, and the Marian Year, 1954.

Theological Evaluation. The practice, so ancient and so constant, must be seen as an expression of the "sense of the faithful"; it stands as one expression of faith, of prayer, of penance, and of devotion; official ecclesiastical approval has been given to many specific pilgrimages—to Rome, to the Holy Land, to shrines of Mary and of local saints. While there have been exaggerations, even hysterical claims, carefully documented miracles are a fact, and the *miracles by definition are a sign of divine approval. The theological category that best fits the pilgrimage is that of the *sacramental: an outward expression of inner faith that is not, like a sacrament, an effective sign and cause of grace given, but that provides the opportunity for inner acts of the theological virtues and of prayer in all its aspects—impetration, expiation, thanksgiving, adoration. As an act of the virtue of religion the pilgrimage has as its meaning, also, that to honor those near to God is to honor God himself who brought them near and made them holy. The history of pilgrimages bears out that such considerations all enter into their intended meaning. The garb of the medieval pilgrim had a penitential aspect; the beginning of the pilgrimage was marked by a special liturgical blessing; the pilgrim on his way received hospitality given as an act of piety in recognition that, for the moment, the pilgrim was one set apart on a devout mission. The satire against pilgrimages, as well as the rage of the Reformers, are sign enough that the pilgrimage often became a lark, its theological meaning disfigured by superstitious practices. Yet in modern pilgrimages the intense prayer, the penitential practice of ascending stairs on one's knees, fasts, all-night vigils, solemn processions are age-old rituals that attest to the survival of the essential. Criticism has had its purifying effect; the boisterous revelry suggested by the *Canterbury Tales* would hardly be expected at Lourdes or Fatima. Most importantly, the center of every place of pilgrimage is more than ever the confessional and the eucharistic table; the miracle most often sought and most often attested is an increased faith and trust in God.

[M. J. COSTELLOE; T. C. O'BRIEN]

PILGRIM'S PROGRESS, the great epic of Puritanism written by John *Bunyan, probably in 1676, and published in 1678. "Strait is the gate and narrow is the way that leadeth into life" (Mt 7.13) is the text upon which the work is built. It describes the lonely journey of Christian, "a man clothed in rags, a heavy burden on his back," who turns away in anguish from the half-life he has been leading and goes forth to find the road to his salvation. When, with the help of Evangelist, he finds it, it is narrow indeed, and as he presses forward, temptations assail him the form of monsters with whom he does battle. Violent battles give way to conversations with other pilgrims: with friends such as Hopeful and Faithful; with hypocrites such as Talkative and Worldly Wiseman, subtle tempters who would accommodate religion to a life of cultured ease. These are natural, flowing conversations, in a language homely and racy, with frequent echoes of the Bible. When Christian comes to the cross of Christ, his burden falls from his back but many are the trials he has yet to endure before he is welcomed to the sound of trumpets into the Celestial City. In Part II, Christian's wife and her friend Mercy set out on a much tamer journey.

Pilgrim's Progress went into innumerable editions, was translated into most languages, and influenced the religious thought of three generations of Englishmen. In the 20th cent., however, the work is seldom read. The modern reader recoils from a religion that permits a man to sin himself completely out of God's mercy and from what seems to be a rejection of the whole secular world as a Vanity Fair. Closer study may convince him that the world rejected by Christian is not "the world whom God so loved as to send his son" but all those forces of the world that, when banded together, conspire to keep him at a lower level and prevent him from becoming his true self. The book has its detractors, those who think that its stern Calvinist theology has done harm to religion, but most critics place it among the classic expressions of Christian imagination. It is more a myth than an allegory. BIBLIOGRAPHY: O. E. Winslow, *John Bunyan* (1961); H. Talon, *John Bunyan: The Man and His Works* (tr. B. Wall, 1951); U. M. Kaufmann, *Pilgrim's Progress and Traditions in Puritan Meditation* (1966); J. Kelman, *Road: A Study of John Bunyan's Pilgrim's Progress* (2 v., 1973).

[M. O'CONNOR]

PILLAR, a consecrated stone that served a cultic purpose. It is twice recorded in the OT (Gen 28.18; 35.14) that Jacob erected such a pillar (*masseba*). But because the Çanaanites erected pillars as symbols of idolatrous fertility cults, the Israelites were ordered to destroy them (Ex 23.24; Dt 7.5) and were forbidden to erect any themselves (Lv 26.1; Dt 16.22). But the practice was never fully eradicated (1 Kg 14.23; Hos 3.4). The purpose of the two pillars of bronze in front of Solomon's Temple is not known (1 Kg 7.15–22).

[A. J. TKACIK]

PILLAR SAINT, see STYLITE.

PILON (*Philon*), cloak worn by Armenian priests and bishops in choir or in the sanctuary when their function does not require hieratic vestments. It has the shape of the *shourtchar* but is black, although bishops wear a violet *pilon* on Sundays and feasts. Permission to wear a *pilon* of flowered pattern that is not black is given to certain priests as a mark of honor.

[A. CODY]

PILON, GERMAIN (*c.*1530–90), French sculptor in Paris and Fontainbleau (1550) receiving payment for eight sculptures (lost) for the monument to Francis I (1558), carving three Graces on the monument of Henry II (1560) for the mannerist Francesco Primaticcio, with whom P. further collaborated on the tomb-complex for Henry II and Catherine de Médicis, St. Denis (1563–70), combining the mannerism of Primaticcio with the classicism of P. Bontemps. In 1570–80 he carved portrait busts and a series of medals in the Italian manner with great virtuosity. P.'s mature, dramatic style (1580s) marked carvings for the Valois chapel (*Re-*

surrection, Virgin of Pity, St. Francis in Ecstasy) and for the Birague chapel (a bronze kneeling figure, massive and restrained, and a *gisant* [recumbent effigy] of Gothic poetic, fluid style).

[M. J. DALY]

PIMENTA, SILVERIO GOMES (1840–1922), bishop. Son of black parents in Brazil, P. was educated in the seminary of the Diocese of Mariana at the expense of Bp. Viçoso and ordained in 1862. From 1871 to 1888 he taught Latin in the seminary, acquiring masterly proficiency. After working as a journalist for 4 years, he became vicar capitular, then vicar general of Mariana (1877). In spite of difficulties because he was a black, he was named auxiliary bp. of Mariana in 1890 and bp. in 1896. P. displayed great zeal in leading his diocese and became its first abp. when Mariana was raised to metropolitan status in 1906. He was elected in 1920 to the Brazilian Academy of Letters, the first cleric so honored.

[J. R. AHERNE]

PINARD DE LA BOULLAYE, HENRI (1874–1958), French Jesuit, theologian, scholar of comparative religion, apologetics, and philosophy. Entering the Society (1893) after completing studies at Reims, he served as professor of fundamental theology at a Jesuit theologate in Enghien (1910–1927), then, in Rome at the Gregorian Univ. (1927–1934) where he taught history of religion. His major work, *L'étude comparée des religions* (2 v., 1922, 1925), demanded his attention for years in new subsequent editions. From 1940 to 1956, he wrote extensively on St. Ignatius's *Spiritual Exercises*. P.'s works are distinguished by their defense of the reasonableness of belief. He maintained that religious experience and belief followed on a logical deduction, a rational conclusion that God exists.

[R. J. LITZ]

PINEDA, JUAN DE (1558–1637), Spanish Jesuit biblicist at Seville and Madrid, author of commentaries and historical studies marked by his thorough knowledge of biblical languages. He also edited, with P. Daza, the *Index* (1612–14) of the Spanish Inquisition.

[T. C. O'BRIEN]

PINELLI, LUCA (1542–1607), Italian Jesuit philosopher and theologian. Born in the Kingdom of Naples, he entered the Society at the age of 20; taught philosophy and theology for several years before being sent to Germany to combat Protestantism. He taught at Ingolstadt for 2 years, then, at the request of the duke of Lorraine, at Pont-à-Mousson for 3 years. He introduced the use of the *Summa* of St. Thomas Aquinas as a textbook. Upon returning to Italy, he was rector in Florence and Perugia, then Jesuit superior in Palermo. He composed several ascetical works, containing meditations on various Christian mysteries. A complete edition of his works was published in four volumes in Italian (1604–1609), and in three volumes in Latin (1608–14).

[E. J. DILLON]

PINKŌ, Syriac name commonly used by the West Syrians for the paten. It is also called $k^e p\bar{o}p\bar{o}$, piyallō, pilasō.

[A. CODY]

PINNACLE, in architecture, small spire-like member, elaborate and ornamental, actually adding weight to strengthen the buttress in counteracting the thrust of the vault.

PINOT, NOËL, BL. (1747–94), martyr. A French cleric ordained in 1771, P. was a hospital chaplain and later pastor at Louroux-Béconnais. Exiled because he refused to take the oath required by the Civil Constitution of the Clergy in 1790 he continued his ministry in secret. He was arrested in 1794, tried and guillotined in full vestments, his last words being *Introibo ad altare Dei.* P. was beatified in 1926.

[J. R. AHERNE]

PINSK, JOHANNES (1891–1957), German secular priest, liturgist, and spiritual leader who contributed notably to the liturgical movement in Germany. Besides editing *Liturgische Zeitschrift* (1929–33) and *Liturgisches Leben* (1934–38), he wrote a number of books and contributed many articles to various periodicals.

[N. KOLLAR]

PINTORICCHIO (Bernardino di Betto di Biagio, *c*.1454–1513), an Umbrian painter, famous for his murals. His work shows the influence of Perugino but it is more decorative and elegantly festive. His principal works are the frescoes in the Piccolomini Library, Siena, which show scenes from the life of Pius II, and those in the Borgia apartments in the Vatican. BIBLIOGRAPHY: E. Carli, *Il Pintoricchio* (1960).

[P. P. FEHL]

PINY, ALEXANDER (1640–1709), French Dominican writer in spiritual theology. Some of his works were marked by language that had affinities with *Quietism, but he was not under Quietist influence. He did, however, cease writing and devoted his last years to pastoral work. P. also was the author of highly valued works on the philosophy of St. Thomas Aquinas.

[P. HENNESSEY]

PINYTUS OF KNOSSOS, bp. of Knossus in Crete, sometime between 161 and 180. He is mentioned in passing in Eusebius's discussion (*Hist. eccles.* 4.23) of the letters of Dionysius, bp. of Corinth. Apparently the latter viewed P. as something of a rigorist and urged him not to impose too heavy a burden of chastity on his brethren, but to consider the weakness of the many. Eusebius commends P. for his care for his flock, his orthodoxy, and his learning, and notes that his reply to Dionysius contained a warning not to feed his brethren with milk only, but to give them solid food, i.e., advanced instruction, and to make more demands on them lest they grow old under a discipline calculated for children.

[E. J. DILLON]

PIO, PADRE (Francesco Forgione; 1887–1968), Capuchin mystic and reputed stigmatic. Ordained in 1910, he was noted as a spiritual adviser who became world-famous in 1918 when what appeared to be *stigmata marked him. Hundreds of thousands from all over the world visited him each year. His followers ascribed extraordinary powers to him but the Church has never rendered judgment on their validity. BIBLIOGRAPHY: D. Gaudiose, *Prophet of the People: A Biography of Padre Pio* (1974).

[J. R. AHERNE]

PIOMBO, SEBASTIANO DEL, see SEBASTIANO DEL PIOMBO.

[M. J. DALY]

PIONA, ABBEY OF, a Benedictine and later a Cistercian monastery in Italy, situated on a mountainous site where the Adda River and Lake Como merge. It was founded in the early 12th cent. by Cluniacs, but because of its remote location, the community never gained many members. In the late 15th cent. the monks left the abbey. In 1937 it was given to a Cistercian congregation, and today houses Italian Cistercians. The abbey church is regarded as an outstanding example of 12th-cent. Lombard Romanesque architecture. BIBLIOGRAPHY: Cottineau 2:2286.

[M. A. MCFADDEN]

PIONIUS, ST. (d. *c*.250), martyr who died for the faith in Smyrna in the Decian Persecution, or, according to Eusebius, in the persecution under Marcus Aurelius. His martyrdom was allegedly recorded by eyewitnesses in *acta* whose claim to authenticity was regarded by H. *Delehaye as impressive (see *Les passions des martyrs,* 1921, 27–59). P. is not to be identified with the author of the legendary life of Polycarp (*c*.400), but he may well be the Pionius whose name occurs at the end of the *Martyrdom of Polycarp.* BIBLIOGRAPHY: Butler 1:224–225. The *Acta* can be found in *Decian Persecution* (Eng. tr. J. A. F. Gregg, 1897) 249–261.

PIOUS BELIEF, a theological note or qualification used in systematic (dogmatic) theology to describe a proposition that lacks a firm explicit or even implicit basis in public revelation, but yet contains nothing contrary to it and does, in fact, reflect a wholesome and sound spiritual outlook. Pious beliefs are sometimes based on private revelation; sometimes they are no more than conjectures of the devout that reach beyond the certain truths of faith, with which, however, they retain a harmony and consonance. Many pious beliefs are encouraged by local or more general ecclesiastical authority.

[E. A. WEIS]

PIOUS CAUSE. A religious purpose or work for which alms are collected; "pious" translates *pius* from *pietas* as devotedness to God and the things of God. The term "pious cause" is used equivalently in CIC regarding the regulation of religious mendicants or others seeking to raise funds for religious reasons (CIC cc. 621–624;1503).

PIOUS CONGREGATION OF ST. JOSEPH (TUR-IN), priests and brothers, known also as Giuseppini, members of a papally approved society founded in 1873 in Turin, Italy, by Bl. Leonardo Murialdo. The purpose of the institute is the Christian education of youth in schools and in other institutions, priestly and parochial ministry, and foreign missions. Besides schools, the members also conduct reformatories, orphanages, and agricultural settlements in Europe, Africa, and North and South America. The general motherhouse is in Rome and the U.S. headquarters is in Avon, Ohio. In 1975, the Society had 98 houses and a total membership of 765. BIBLIOGRAPHY: E. Reffo, *Il fine della Pia Società di S. Giuseppe* (1961).

[R. A. TODD]

PIOUS DISCIPLES OF THE DIVINE MASTER (PDDM), a congregation of women religious founded by Don Giacomo Alberione at Alba (Cuneo), Italy, in 1924. It was granted papal approbation in 1960, and is one of eight congregations Alberione founded, known together as Famiglia Paolina. The sisters take simple, perpetual vows and their apostolate engages them in perpetual adoration, domestic duties in the houses of the Famiglia Paolina, care of sick, needy priests, and various liturgical work. The Pious Disciples publish a monthly liturgical periodical in Italian, French, and English *(Life in Christ and in the Church)*. In 1975 the congregation had 1,274 members and 118 houses located in about 20 countries on all of the continents. Rome is the site of the motherhouse, and the U.S. headquarters is located in Boston, Mass.

[R. A. TODD]

PIOUS FOUNDATION a fund or property given or bequeathed to a church, diocese, religious house or other legal ecclesiastical entity . the income of which is to be applied to the celebration of Masses, to other devotional exercises, or to works of charity. Usually the establishment of a foundation covers a long-term period; but in modern times is less frequently made in perpetuity. The acceptance, stipulations, administration, alteration or abrogation of pious foundations are strictly determined by canon law, much as endowments are in civil law. Records for so-called foundation Masses must be strictly kept.

[T. C. O'BRIEN]

PIOUS FUND (Pious Fund of the Californias) gifts of money and land made to the missions used as capital, the interest on which supported the missions. It originated with the Jesuit missionaries in Lower California at the end of the 17th century. Later the Spanish Crown directed the Fund, supporting the Dominicans in Lower California and the Franciscans in what is now the state of California. When Mexico broke away from Spain, the new government administered the fund to support a bp. in California. In 1842 Mexico appropriated the Fund but paid annual interest to religious projects. When California became a state of the U.S., payment closed. In 1875 the California bps. protested the lack of payment and an arbiter ordered back interest paid. The Mexican government paid the accrued interest to 1875 but refused to continue. In 1902 The Hague Tribunal ordered Mexico to pay the U.S. back interest and a perpetual annuity for use of the Church in California. After 1913 Mexico refused to comply.

[J. R. AHERNE]

PIOUS UNION is the status that a religious foundation has before becoming a fully religious institute.

PIOUS UNION OF THE BENEDICTINES OF STILL RIVER, a community at Still River, Mass., formally constituted as a pious union Nov. 19, 1976, by Bp. Bernard J. Flanagan of Worcester. The community residing at St. Thérèse House, part of Fr. L. Feeney's St. Benedict's Center, comprised at the time 26 men and 19 women; there were also extern members sharing in some of the community's life. That life is Benedictine in its main lines, devoted to prayer, study, and manual labor. The pious union was constituted as a step towards St. Thérèse House's becoming a full-fledged Benedictine priory; two of its members were ordained priests in 1976. The community's history traces back to Fr. Feeney's original foundation, the Slaves of the Immaculate Heart of Mary, the group which in turn developed out of St. Benedict's Center, the Catholic Student Center near Harvard Square in Cambridge in the 1940s. The 1953 excommunication of Fr. Feeney, because of his teaching on salvation outside the Church (see D 3866-73),was lifted on Nov. 22, 1972. Twenty-nine members of his community at Still River made a simple profession of faith before Bp. Flanagan on March 4, 1974. The 18 nonreconciled members form the community of St. Anne House also at Still River.

[T. C. O'BRIEN]

PIRANDELLO, LUIGI (1867–1936), Italian dramatist, and novelist. P. was educated at the Univ. of Palermo, Rome, and Bonn, after which he became a professor of Italian literature at the Normal College for Women in Rome (1897). In the 1890s he began to write short stories which eventually totaled about 300. The trials of his early life—a domineering father, lack of public recognition, the failure of his father's mining business, and the mental illness of his wife—may have contributed to the pessimism in his works. He wrote six novels, the most celebrated being *The Late Mattia Pascal* (1905). P.'s fame, however, was due primarily to his intellectual and grotesquely humorous plays, which clearly reveal his despairing outlook on life. He began writing them during World War I and up to the time of his death had produced more than 40. The most widely known are *Right You Are If You Think You Are* (1917), *The Pleasure of Honesty* (1917), *Six Characters in Search of an Author* (1921), his most important and most famous one: *Henry IV* (1922), and *As You Desire Me* (1931). His principal themes are the necessity and vanity of illusion, the many appearances, all unreal, of what is presumed to be truth. His plays quickly proved successful in Italy and abroad and were translated into many languages. P. was one of the outstanding figures in 20th-cent. European drama. His works had a great influence on authors of different countries and were models for later existentialism. He stated his artistic creed in two volumes entitled *Arte e scienza*. He received the Nobel Prize in 1934.

[S. A. HEENEY]

PIRANESI, GIOVANNI BATTISTA (1720–78), Italian graphic artist and architect. After unsuccessfully publishing works on architecture in Rome (1740), P. returned to Venice executing important and distinctive *Carceri* (Prisons) and *Grotesques,* to this day considered remarkable. In 1747 he executed 47 views of Rome, and began his lifelong interest in ancient Rome, publishing his *Antichità romane dei tempi della Repubblica e de'primi Imperatori* (1748). P. redesigned Sta. Maria Aventina with sculptural enrichment. From his prolific copper plates, now steel-faced, P.'s designs, half-archeological, half-visionary, and further dramatized by his knowledge of stage design, continue to be admired.

[M. J. DALY]

PIRE, DOMINIQUE (1910–69), Belgian Dominican patriot, practical philanthropist who was ardently devoted to the building of bridges instead of walls between peoples. P. studied at the Angelicum in Rome (1932–36), was ordained in 1934, and taught at Huy, Belgium. When Belgium was overrun by the Nazis in World War II, he participated in the underground movement and played an important role in setting up an escape route for downed Allied airmen. After the war, moved by the plight of the hardcore of refugees and displaced persons to whom sufficient help could not be brought through the regular agencies for relief and rehabilitation, he organized them into "European villages" near cities in Belgium, France, Austria, and West Germany, gathered funds for their aid, and inspired them to hope and work toward rehabilitation. In 1958 he received the Nobel Peace Award. The following year he established the Open Heart to the World Organization, which set up a University of Peace at Huy where seminars were held to find means of promoting peace and fraternity among mankind. In the

1960s P.'s humanitarian efforts reached beyond Europe. A "peace island" was founded in East Pakistan to help educate its 40,000 inhabitants, improve their agricultural methods, and bring them medical help. A similar island was later set up in India.

[P. K. MEAGHER]

PIRENNE, HENRI (1862–1935), Belgian historian. He attended the Lycée at Verviers, then went on to Liège, Paris, Leipzig, and Berlin for further education. P. used the German academic method of scientific historical study at the Univ. of Ghent, where his seminar in diplomatics, paleography, and history was recognized as outstanding. He received the professorship at 23 and remained at Ghent from 1886 to 1930. As Card. Mercier represented Louvain and the intellectual tradition of Catholic Belgium, P. represented the secular universities. In addition to his monumental seven-volume *History of Belgium* (1900–32), he produced 29 books, 275 articles, and over 100 reviews. He became a specialist in social and economic history, writing with great clarity and precision, often for a general audience. His outstanding contribution may have been his thesis on the origins and nature of the medieval city (*Medieval Cities,* 1925). BIBLIOGRAPHY: B. Lyon, "L'Oeuvre de Henri Pirenne après vingt-cinq ans," *Le Moyen-âge* 4 (1960) 437–93; F. Ganshof, *Henri Pirenne, le maître, l'historien* (1936).

[N. F. GAUGHAN]

PIRKE AVOTH (chapters of the fathers), a tractate of the Mishnah, consisting of wise sayings and religious moral doctrine of rabbis who lived during the 2 cent. before 200 A.D. Used for readings in Jewish liturgy, it continues to offer its ancient wisdom to Judaism.

[J. F. FALLON]

PIRKHEIMER, CHARITAS AND WILLIBALD, sister and brother of some prominence in the early days of the Reformation in Nuremberg. **Charitas** (1466–1532), abbess of the Poor Clares in Nuremberg. She was widely read in the classics and the Fathers; through her brother she was acquainted with many of the prominent German humanists of the time. Firmly anti-Lutheran, she and her community were subjected to harassment and persecution. Her diary of events during this time, discovered in 1852, is a valuable source of information. **Willibald** (1470–1530), humanist scholar and historian. He favored Luther at the beginning of the Reformation, wrote an attack upon Johann Eck, was excommunicated in 1520, but after renouncing his support of Luther was absolved the following year.

[J. R. SCHULZ]

PIRMIN, ST. (d. 753), abbot and bishop. A Visigothic refugee from Aquitaine or Spain during Moorish invasions, he became a Benedictine missionary around the Upper Rhine. Bishop (not of Meaux) near Hornbach, he founded monasteries important to the area's conversion and imperial assimilation—Hornbach, Gengenbach, Schwarzach, famed Reichenau (c.724), and in Alsace as a political exile, Murbach (726). He also reformed Schuttern and Maursmünster. Patron of the Rhine Palatinate, Alsace, and Innsbruck, he is noted for his missionary catechetical manual, *Dicta Pirminii,* widely used in the Carolingian empire. His earliest biography, jejune but our main source, dates from 830. BIBLIOGRAPHY: J. E. Gugumus and M. C. Celletii, BiblSanct 10:927–932; Butler 4:248–249.

[R. I. BURNS]

PIRROTTI, POMPILIUS, ST. (1710–66), teacher, preacher. A Neapolitan, P. joined the Order of the Pious Schools in 1727 to pursue a life of teaching. Devoted to the poor, he was an early advocate of devotion to the Sacred Heart. P. encouraged daily communion, an advocacy almost unknown in his age.

[J. R. AHERNE]

PIRSTINGER, BERTHOLD, see BERTHOLD OF CHIEMSEE.

PISA, CATHEDRAL COMPLEX (1063–1272), cathedral baptistery, campanile and *campo santo* (cemetery) in Pisa, ancient Roman city and powerful maritime republic (11th to the 14th century). The cathedral, begun in 1063 after the design of Buschetus (Boschetto), consecrated in 1118, was finally completed in 1272. In Tuscan-Romanesque style of impressive majesty, the basilica, distinguished by elaborate, lace-like marble exterior, is five-aisled, with galleries, and transepts terminating in apses. The vaulted crossing supports a dome in Eastern style. The alternation of green and cream marble in the vaulted aisles is distinctively Tuscan-Romanesque. The bronze W doors (1180) are by Bonnanus of Pisa, the pulpit (1302–11) by master G. Pisano. The circular baptistery designed by Diotisalvi echoes the cathedral in blind arcades on the ground floor, open arcading of two stories (remodeled in Gothic style), with a pulpit of N. Pisano (1255–59). The cylindrical Romanesque campanile of Bonnanus of Pisa, begun in 1174 (settling has caused a leaning) repeats the architectural details of the other units of the group. Spared from destruction in World War II, the Pisa complex with the adjacent *camposanto* is one of the handsomest ensembles in the history of architecture. BIBLIOGRAPHY: H. Leisinger, *Romanesque Bronzes* (1957); C. Ricci, *Romanesque Architecture in Italy* (1925).

[M. J. DALY]

PISA, COUNCIL OF, a RC *general council that marked an important phase in the conciliar movement. The council was convened in 1409, when Europe had been divided for 30 years over the claims of rival popes in Avignon and Rome. Instead of healing the *Great Western Schism, the council elected a third claimant to the papal office. At the time of his election in 1394 the Avignonese pope, Benedict XIII, took an oath to do everything in his power to heal the schism. A similar oath was taken by the Roman Gregory XII at his election in 1406. In 1408, when it seemed Gregory would hold on to his disputed office at all costs, his cardinals deserted him. Together with cardinals from Avignon they summoned a council to meet in Pisa the following year. Despite threats of excommunication from both Benedict and Gregory, the meeting was well attended. In the 23 sessions held March 25–August 7, 1409, the council examined the issues; constituted itself a general council representing the universal Church; declared Benedict and Gregory deposed; and elected Alexander V (1409–10). While Pisa did not succeed in ending the schism, it helped nurture the conciliar ideas that were to bear fruit at the Council of *Constance five years later. BIBLIOGRAPHY: E. F. Jacobs, *Essays in the Conciliar Epoch* (rev. ed., 1963); Hughes HC 3:270–282; L. E. Boyle, NCE 11:384–385. *CONCILIARISM.

[B. L. MARTHALER]

PISAN POPES, the two antipopes during the Great Western Schism who owed their election to the Council of *Pisa. Disillusioned at the unwillingness of Benedict XIII and Gregory XII to heal the schism, cardinals from both allegiances convened at Pisa in 1409. Asserting the superiority of an ecumenical council, which they claimed to be over the papacy in this emergency situation, they declared deposed the Roman and Avignon Popes and elected *Peter of Candia, Abp. of Milan, as Alexander V. When he died in 1410, many of the same group elected Baldassare Cossa, cardinal legate of Bologna, as John XXIII. He reigned until his deposition by the Council of Constance on May 29, 1415. BIBLIOGRAPHY: Hughes HC 3:270–290; *Das Konzil von Konstanz* (ed. A. Franzen and W. Müller, 1964).

[R. H. SCHMANDT]

PISANELLO, ANTONIO (Pisano; 1359?–1455), Italian painter and medallist. Finest of the late International Style artists active in N Italy, P. studied and worked with Gentile da Fabriano until the master's death. The close observation of nature and fascination with opulent costume which characterize P.'s style are combined with a new Renaissance realism as seen in the detail of two hanged men in the *St. George and the Princess* fresco (c.1433, Museo Civico, Verona). An extraordinary draftsman, P. exhibits in hundreds of surviving drawings a truly Renaissance spirit of experimentation. His heightened sensitivity to the quality of contour and silhouette (*Portrait of a Princess of the House of Este*) may partially account for his invention of the new style of Renaissance portrait medal, seen in the series cast not struck, from 1438–49 depicting John VIII Paleologus, Lionello d'Este, Alfonso of Naples (1448), and others. BIBLIOGRAPHY: E. Sindona, *Pisanello* (1961).

[S. CONWAY]

PISANO, ANDREA (*c.* 1270–1348), goldsmith, architect, and the greatest Tuscan sculptor of the second quarter of the *trecento,* whose fame rests on two major works: the first gilt-bronze doors (1330–36) of the baptistery, Florence with 28 quatrefoil panels portraying the life of St. John the Baptist (now the S doors), and marble reliefs (1343) for Giotto's campanile in Florence, with scenes from Genesis and the Labors of Man. A.'s late Gothic style is skilled in composition and eloquence of narrative, the plasticity of forms in shallow space pointing to his great contemporary, Giotto. BIBLIOGRAPHY: J. Pope-Hennessy, *Italian Gothic Sculpture* (1955).

[L. A. LEITE]

PISANO, GIUNTA (1202?–58), most important Italian painter of the early 13th cent. in the school of Pisa. Painting a cross for the Basilica of S. Francesco, Assisi (1236), and three later signed crosses for Assisi, Pisa, and Bologna, he established a new iconographic type of the 13th and 14th cent. which abolished Passion scenes and figures of the Virgin and St. John at extremities of the arms of the cross and so emphasized the dead Christ. G's expressionistic form and stylized features combine a Byzantine style with Franciscan emotionalism, adding pathos.

[M. J. DALY]

PISAREV, DMITRI IVANOVICH (1840–68), radical Russian journalist, political thinker, and literary critic, leading representative of Russian Nihilism. Under the influence of Büchner's *Kraft und Stoff,* he applied the criteria of practical utility and social purpose indiscriminately in the evaluation of morality, art, and politics, as well as of the social institutions of family, Church, and State. BIBLIOGRAPHY: E. Lampert, *Sons Against Fathers* (1965) 272–338.

[M. F. MCCARTHY]

PISCETTA, LUIGI (1858–1925), Italian Salesian, professor of moral theology at the Turin seminary from 1880 until his death, author of *Elementa theologiae moralis* (1898), a work that went through many editions, the last, under A. Gennaro, in 1923.

[T. C. O'BRIEN]

PISCINA (Lat., a basin), a drain *(sacrarium)* connected with the earth for the disposal of water, etc., which has been used for a sacred purpose. The opening is usually in the wall on the epistle side of the altar with a shelf directly underneath for the Mass cruets. Sometimes the piscina is replaced by a credence table if the *sacrarium* is in the sacristy.

[R. C. CLIGGETT]

PISE, CHARLES CONSTANTINE (1801–66), writer. A native of Maryland who entered the Jesuits and then transferred to the Diocese of Baltimore, P. was ordained in 1825. He contributed the most appreciable literary work by an American writer in *History of the Church from Its Estab-* *lishment to the Present Century* (5 v., 1827–1830). Nominated by Henry Clay as chaplain of the U.S. Senate he was elected in 1832, the first priest to be so honored. While in Ireland to collect funds for an orphanage he became a disciple of Father Matthew, the temperance leader. In 1841 P. founded the *Catholic Expositor and Literary Review.* A noted lecturer and kindly controversialist, P. wrote many works, among them *Aletheia or Letters on the Truth of Catholic Doctrine* (1843), *Saint Ignatius and His First Companions* (1845); and *Zenosius or the Pilgrim Convert* (1845).

[J. R. AHERNE]

PISTIS SOPHIA, see APOCRYPHA (NT), 57.

PISTOIA, SYNOD OF, a RC synod held in seven sessions Sept. 18–28, 1786, under Scipione de' Ricci (1741–1810), Bishop of Pistoia-Prato, Italy, to enact specified Gallican-Jansenist diocesan reforms (see GALLICANISM; JANSENISM). It comprised 171 pastors, 14 chaplains, 14 canons, 13 selected religious priests, and 22 others. To stimulate unanimity Ricci excluded his opponents and imported Jansenist consultants. His collaborator, Grand Duke Leopold of Tuscany, had sent 57 articles to Tuscany's 18 bps. for consideration, recommending changes in clerical and liturgical usages, revision of Missal and Breviary, removal of images and side altars, and imposition of Jansenist catechesis. Ricci had earlier assailed popular devotions, relics, and confraternities, had published a journal and pamphlets promoting Jansenism. Now at his synod he secured acceptance of Leopold's 57 articles through force, fear, favor, and the failure of pastors to comprehend the subtleties to which they subscribed; retractations later were numerous. Extolled by Jansenists abroad, Pistoia's synod was regarded by many Tuscans as farce.

Because "enlightened" priests were few, Ricci urged intense indoctrination prior to any national council, but the compliance at Pistoia persuaded Leopold to convoke all Tuscan bps. at the Pitti Palace to review his 57 articles, plus six propositions summarizing the favorable action at Pistoia. But this meeting at Florence, April 23 to June 5, 1787, strongly opposed Pistoia. Only three bps. approved Leopold's Gallican ideas; the majority made minor concessions but rejected basic changes. Reluctantly Leopold relinquished hopes of a national council; in October 1788 he approved publication of the Acts of Pistoia "as discipline, not doctrine." These were widely read, esp. among the French clergy, and engendered much controversy. His people, however, opposed Ricci. At Prato on May 20, 1787, defending a traditional shrine against threatened removal, crowds burned Ricci's throne and Jansenist books. In 1790 an uprising drove Ricci to his native Florence and abolished his reforms. He resigned as bp. on June 3, 1791. The constitutional French clergy, with whom he corresponded, made the Acts of Pistoia a basis for the *Civil Constitution of the Clergy.

Pius VI appointed a commission to examine the Acts; Ricci was invited to defend them, but declined. In *Auctorem fidei* Aug. 28, 1794, Pius specifically condemned seven propositions quoted from Pistoia as heretical, 78 others—allegedly reflecting early church practice—as variously pernicious (cf. D 2600–2700). Ricci submitted in 1805, though with Jansenist afterthoughts. *Auctorem fidei* dealt a deadly blow to Gallican Jansenism. Modern ecclesiastical historians, however, have come to recognize positive and genuine liturgical and pastoral insights in the Acts of this synod and in the works of Ricci himself. BIBLIOGRAPHY: J. Carreyre, DTC 12:2134–2230; Pastor 39:125–156; A. Jemolo, *Il giansenismo in Italia* (1928); B. Matteucci, NCE 11:388–390.

[W. DAVISH]

PITHOM (PHITHOM), one of the two "store-cities" in Egypt built, according to the narrative of Exodus (1.11), by the forced labor of the Hebrews for the Pharaoh of the oppression. Store-cities were simply the sites of storehouses, i.e., warehouses for the storage of government supplies of various kinds. Although Egypt was well known for this kind of arrangement, it was not unknown elsewhere. David had such stores in various villages and towns of Palestine, as did Solomon, Hezekiah, and Jehosaphat, kings of Judah. Archeological finds tend to confirm the existence of Pithom and Rameses. There is evidence of a town called Pi-Tum ("the house of the God Tum") which existed in Ramesside times in the Wâdī Tûmilât, a district corresponding to the biblical land of Goshen. The name occurs in a papyrus dating from the reign of Seti II (*c.* 1205 B.C.). The site of Pithom was formerly thought to be Tell el-Maskhûteh; now it is identified with Tell er-Retâbeh.

[E. J. DILLON]

PITHOU, FRANÇOIS (1543–1621), French jurist, brother of the more renowned P. *Pithou. He rejected Calvinism and became a Catholic in 1578. His work includes collaboration with his brother on *Observationes ad Codicem* and an edition of the *Corpus Juris Canonici; and his own edition (1587) of the Lex Salica.

[T. C. O'BRIEN]

PITHOU, PIERRE (1539–96), French lawyer and Gallican theorist. He shared an interest with his two brothers in legal codification and theory. P. became a member of the Parlement of Paris in 1560, but lived for a time in Sedan and Basel because he was a Huguenot. He became a Catholic *c.* 1573 and gained a position in the French legal bureaucracy. From about 1579 he supported Henry IV and rose in his service. During the controversy over Henry IV's accession to the throne, P. formulated in 83 articles a basic statement of *Gallicanism, *Les Libertés de l'église gallicane* (1594), which in 1682 constituted the basis for the Four *Gallican Articles. After his retirement he edited several volumes of civil and canonical legal codes.

[J. M. HAYDEN]

PITRA, JEAN BAPTISTE (1812–89), French Benedictine patrologist, cardinal, and bishop. Ordained to the diocesan priesthood in 1836, P. joined the Benedictines of Solesmes in 1841. He first gained scholarly acclaim by publishing in 1839 a study of the epitaph of *Pectorius, found (1830) at Autun. During his travels in search of financial help for Solesmes, he found MSS which he published in his *Spicilegium Solesmense* (4 v. 1852–58). At the request of the pope he undertook research into Oriental ecclesiastical law. He was made a cardinal in 1861 and Vatican librarian in 1869, and was consecrated bp. in 1879. During these years he published important studies of Eastern canon law and hymnography as well as eight more volumes of texts for the *Spicilegium Solesmense*. BIBLIOGRAPHY: C. Vogel, Enc Catt 9:1584–85.

[R. B. ENO]

PITTS, JOHN (1559–1616), English Catholic biographer and historian. An exile on the Continent, he was ordained in Rome (1588) and worked in both academic and ecclesiastical positions in France. In his major work, *Relationum historicarum de rebus Angliae,* his aim was to offset the anti-Catholic bias of the history of English writers by John Bale (1495–1563), bp. of Ossory. Only volume one of P.s work was published (posthumously, 1619). Without resources for research, P. could not deal effectively with the medieval period, but on contemporary Catholic authors he provided valuable information.

[R. J. LITZ]

PITZIUS, ALBERT, see GOTTHELF, JEREMIAS.

PIUS I, ST. (d. 155), **POPE** from 140. According to the *Liber Pontificalis* P. was a native of Aquileia, but the *Muratorian fragment states that he was a brother of Hermas, author of the *Shepherd. During his pontificate the Gnostics Valentine and Cerdo were active in his community. There is no early evidence to support the belief that he died a martyr. BIBLIOGRAPHY: Butler 3:70–71.

[R. B. ENO]

PIUS II (Aeneas Sylvius Piccolomini; 1405–64), **POPE** from 1458. Humanist and statesman, P. was one of the most attractive figures of the Renaissance, and indeed in the history of the popes. Until his middle years he led an elegant and dissolute life, though not unresponsive to the calls of the Spirit: during a diplomatic mission to Scotland he made a pilgrimage to Our Lady of Whitekirk through snow and ice, and contracted frostbite, from the effects of which he never recovered. At first a supporter of *Conciliarism, he was reconciled to Eugenius IV, and a reformed rake but still agreeable, he was made bp. of Trieste, of Siena, and cardinal, and elected pope. His famous words, "Reject Aeneas, but accept Pius," now ran through his policy of securing the independence of the Holy See from the princes of Europe and their nominees. Above all, shocked by the fall of Constantinople, he bent his energies to the defense of Christendom against the Turks. He proposed to lead the Crusade himself, and despite ill-health, struggled to Ancona, the port of embarkation, but died there, bereft of all but meagre support from the powers. BIBLIOGRAPHY: R. J. Mitchell. *The Laurels and the Tiara: Pope Pius II, 1458–1464* (1963).

[T. GILBY]

PIUS III (Francesco Todeschini Piccolomini; *c.* 1440–1503), **POPE** for less than a month in 1503. A nephew of Pius II, he was born in Siena, was made abp. of Siena when he was still a deacon, and became a cardinal in 1460. In papal service under four pontiffs he distinguished himself for his upright life, learning, and statesmanship as legate in Germany. He succeeded Alexander VI; the conclave that elected him was held at the Minerva and was defended by the Roman populace against the Borgia troops who occupied the Vatican. His short reign marked the beginning of the collapse of Borgia power in Italy.

PIUS IV (Giovanni Angelo de'Medici; 1499–1565), **POPE** from 1559, instrumental in the final calling of the Council of Trent on January 18, 1563. Although he had a similar name, P. was not related to the famous Florentine Medicis. His talents lay not in theological speculation, but in administration. Under his capable leadership the Council of Trent completed its work. Such reform measures as the Index of Forbidden Books, the requirement of residency for bps., and the establishment of seminaries were settled. He was also responsible for the appointment of the important Tridentine figure, Girolamo *Seripando. Yet like his fellow Renaissance popes P. followed the practice of nepotism. His selection of his nephew, Charles Borromeo, however, proved fortunate for the Counter Reformation Church. Borromeo's urgings were influential in convincing P. to finish the necessary work of reform. BIBLIOGRAPHY: M. O'Connell, *Counter Reformation* (1974).

[C. T. EBY]

PIUS V, ST. (Michele Ghislieri; 1504–72), **POPE** from 1566, first of the Counter Reformation popes. He became a Dominican in 1520; was ordained in 1528; and taught theology in the order's studium in Pavia until 1550. He then began a career in the Inquisition that led to his becoming a cardinal in 1557 and Roman grand inquisitor in 1558. He took notable measures against heresy and immorality and for his severity fell out of favor with Pius IV. With the backing of St. Charles Borromeo, however, P. was elected Pius IV's successor. From the outset of his pontificate, P., a vigorous opponent of heresy and church abuses, made it clear that such Tridentine reforms as the residence of bps. and discipline of the clergy were to be strictly enforced, particularly in the Roman Curia. He had decreed publication of the Latin edition of the Catechism of the Council of Trent (1566), a reformed Roman Breviary (1568), and Roman Missal (1570). He also saw to the publication of the first

printed edition of the works of St. Thomas Aquinas, the so-called Piana edition (17 v., 1570) and proclaimed St. Thomas a Doctor of the Church (1568). P. also had an active political career. Supporting the cause of Mary, Queen of Scots, P. encouraged a Spanish invasion of England and in 1570 issued his famous excommunication of Elizabeth I, *Regnans in excelsis*. Finally, he was successful in forming an alliance between Spain and Venice against the Ottoman Turks which ended in the victory at the Battle of Lepanto in Oct., 1571. He was canonized by Clement XI in 1712. BIBLIOGRAPHY: Pastor 5:17–18; A. Iszak, BiblSanct 10:883–897.

[T. C. O'BRIEN]

PIUS VI (Giovanni Angelo Braschi, 1717–99), **POPE** from 1775. He served in the Curia Romana as a canonist and financial officer; became a priest only in 1758; was created cardinal in 1771. He reigned at a time of virulent anticlericalism, secularism, and state absolutism. He lacked the balanced judgment and strength to deal effectively with any of the problems he faced. He antagonized Ferdinand II of Prussia and Catherine II of Russia by trying to have them enforce the suppression of the Jesuits in their lands. He faced, and dealt ineptly with, *Febronianism in Germany and *Josephinism in Austria (he even visited Joseph II personally in 1782 at Vienna, but without success). In Italy he did act effectively against the Jansenist-inspired Synod of *Pistoia (1786) by the apostolic constitution *Auctorem fidei* (1794). The French Revolution brought the greatest disasters; P. not only condemned the *Civil Constitution of the Clergy in 1791, but also roundly denounced the Declaration of the Rights of Man and all the libertarian political ideals that inspired the Revolution. Napoleon *Bonaparte invaded Italy in 1796, but it was General Louis Berthier who invaded the Papal States, took Rome itself (1798), routed the Pope and his Curia from Rome. P. was driven from city to city out of Italy until he finally died a prisoner at Valence, SE France.

[R. H. SCHMANDT]

PIUS VII (Barnaba Chiaramonti; 1742–1823), **POPE** from 1800. Born at Cesena in the Papal States, P. entered the Benedictines (1756) among whom he was known as Dom Gregorio; he became bp. of Tivoli in 1783, was transferred to Imola and made cardinal in 1785. He was elected pope at a conclave held at Venice. Owing to troubles arising from the French Revolutionary invasion of Italy and the establishment of the Cisalpine Republic, the previous Pope had left instructions that the conclave should take place where the greatest number of cardinals was gathered. The business was protracted for several months, and Chiaramonti emerged as a compromise choice, acceptable even to electors devoted to the *ancien régime*. He was to prove firm on principle, but extremely conciliatory in his dealings with Napoleon, with whom he concluded a concordat (1801), Napoleon being then First Consul. P. assisted at the imperial coronation (1804). Gentle as he was, Napoleon found him not compliant enough, and imprisoned him, first at Savona (1809), afterwards at Fontainebleau (1812); during this period, which included the Emperor's divorce from Josephine and remarriage to Marie Louise, effective papal government lapsed. Following the French defeats in Russia and Germany, he was released (1841) and he returned to Rome. His resistance had roused the sympathy of the powers who had been fighting revolutionary and Napoleonic governments, notably of Protestant Great Britain, which had never wavered from the beginning, and this lent great strength to the papal policies, ably conducted by Card. Ercole *Consalvi, the constant and faithful secretary of state to P., at the Congress of Vienna. The restoration of the Society of Jesus was among the more notable acts of this Pope, who, though kindly and peaceful, could yet be very courageous when it came to the point. BIBLIOGRAPHY: E. E. Y. Hales, *Revolution and Papacy 1769–1846* (1960).

[T. GILBY]

PIUS VIII (Francesco Saverio Castiglioni; 1761–1830) **POPE** from 1829. Born in the Marches of Ancona, P. was a man of virtuous life and enjoyed a reputation for learning in canon law, numismatics, and biblical literature. He had the support of the conservatives at his election; his chronic ill-health soon brought his reign to a close. Its chief events of religious interest were Catholic Emancipation in Great Britain and the independence of Belgium. His own contribution is seen in the proscription of secret societies and the acceptance of the revolution of 1830, which ended Bourbon rule and brought bourgeois monarchy to France. BIBLIOGRAPHY: E. E. Y. Hales, *Revolution and Papacy 1769–1846* (1960).

[T. GILBY]

PIUS IX (Giovanni Maria Mastai-Ferretti; 1792–1878), **POPE** from 1846. He was born in the Marches of Ancona, of a family belonging to the petty nobility. The liberal tendencies he inherited lasted until his late middle age; with him they seemed to be more a matter of sentiment than of conviction. As a member of a papal mission to Chile and Peru he had helped in the accommodation to regimes that succeeded the break-up of the Spanish Empire; as an Italian bishop he had shown his sympathy with the cause of Italian nationalism and composed factional strife with his mildness; as a cardinal he had disapproved of the reactionary policies of Gregory XVI, his predecessor, and his election, in the teeth of conservative and Austrian opposition, was applauded as representing the alliance of religion and liberty.

His pontificate was important both for its ecclesiastical policies and for its influence on theology; both were intimately connected and, it seems, overcentered on his personality. His liberal programs as temporal ruler of the Papal States were more palliative than curative, more concerned to remedy abuses than to reform structures, and when his prime minister, Pellegrino Rossi was assassinated (1848)

and Giuseppe Mazzini proclaimed the Roman Republic, his disenchantment with political liberalism spilled over into his theology, or at least his ecclesiology; when he returned from exile at Gaeta, supported by the diplomacy of the European powers and the bayonets of the French, it was to inaugurate a reign of kindly, though unimaginative and ineffective, repression. Despite the adroit rearguard action fought by his secretary of state, Card. Giacomo *Antonelli, who, whatever the shortcomings of his private character, at least had the virtue of faithfulness and was not given to political illusions, the Romagna and the Marches were lost after the Franco-Austrian War, to be followed by the Patrimony of Peter when the Piedmontese, taking advantage of the Franco-Prussian War (1870) occupied Rome, and P. became "the prisoner in the Vatican."

With the political failure of the temporal power of the papacy, however, went a great increase in its spiritual power, a true blessing in some respects but not an unmitigated one in others. The tighter centralization of the Church was providential for the foreign missions and beneficial in countries where its vitality had been weakened by the regalian tradition, but was regretted and resented, not only in the Eastern Churches in communion with Rome, but also elsewhere in countries where the advantages of pluralism were appreciated. The situation was embarrassed by an unprecedented phenomenon, the devotion of the Catholic masses to the person, not merely the office, of the Pope; this continued throughout what was to prove the longest pontificate in history. It was a response to his warmth, charm, and simple piety; it was all the keener because of his misfortunes.

His own wanting to be loved and sensitiveness to the Italian dignity of his office contributed to his deficiencies in political understanding, and prompted some very personal interventions at the *Vatican Council I (1869). This and the definition of the Immaculate Conception (1854) were the chief doctrinal events of his reign, but he maintained a steady pressure, punctuated by condemnations, against traditionalism and ontologism, and above all against the *romanticismus, rationalismus,* and *liberalismus* which he saw as the backwash of the Enlightenment and French Revolution. They are all summed up in the famous *Syllabus of Errors* (1864) which, in religious history, is like the contemporary charge of the Light Brigade in the history of war. He quenched Catholic liberalism for a time, and his, personally, was an ultramontanism barely satisfied by the cautious conciliar definition of papal infallibility. Except for Antonelli, he was badly served by his entourage, which contained some exalted and mystical amateurs addicted to chimerical schemes; they could evoke the ideals of chivalry, but on occasion were quite capable of sharp practice. As has often happened in the history of the papacy, his failures in a sense of proportion were corrected by his successor. BIBLIOGRAPHY: E. E. Y. Hales, *Pio Nono* (1954); R. Aubert, *Le Pontificat de Pie IX* (2d. ed., 1964).

[T. GILBY]

PIUS X, ST. (Giuseppe Melchiorre Sarto; 1835–1912), **POPE** from 1903. He was born of humble parents in the province of Treviso in the region of Venezia, where he became a devoted parish priest and diocesan official. When bp. of Mantua, he was created patriarch of Venice and cardinal (1893). To his own anguish he was elected pope after the Austrian veto on the leading candidate, Card. Mariano Rampolla. This imperial prerogative was abolished soon afterwards. He chose the name Pius in tribute to Pius IX; the gesture was not merely nominal, for his pontificate was marked by a return to the offensive in defense of the Church's authority and the simple pieties which contrasted with the more relaxed and confident policies of Leo XIII. His conception of his office was warmly pastoral. He was ably served by his secretary of state, Card. Raphael Merry del Val who was of one mind with him, though from a different and hidalgo background, and whose holiness, English training, and diplomatic courtesy did not render him quick to discern the shades between black and white.

Relations with the central powers were cordial, but not at all subservient; with anticlerical France, not surprisingly, they were somewhat frozen. Liberalism among French Catholics was snubbed. In the domestic life of the Church the practice of frequent communion and of early communion for children extinguished the last embers of Jansenistic devotion. In this the Pope showed the solicitude of the Church's parish priest, as he did when he cut out the florid ornaments and restored plainsong as the exemplar of the music of worship. Doctrinally the main issue was that of *Modernism. The papal response was forthright and without ambiguity. The decree *Lamentabili* condemned 65 propositions (taken largely from Alfred *Loisy) and the encyclical *Pascendi*, followed this up in the same year (1907) with a full and clear exposition of the reasons why. The Pope's intervention was strong, decisive, and providential. Conformity was enforced under oath. For the authentic expression of the Church's consciousness of the historic truth and enduring values of its dogmas, future generations have had cause to be grateful. There was, however, a rather shady fringe to the anti-Modernist movement, which was not disavowed during the pontificate and which practically succeeded in making itself the official party-line. Under the name of *Integralism, and clustering round such organizations as the *Sodalitium pianum*, the "League of St. Pius V," it conducted what amounted to intellectual witch-hunts, without the bonfires indeed, but with the accompanying whispering campaigns and secret delations. P. himself was no narrow-minded obscurantist, but he must bear some of the responsibility for what was at best a somewhat administrative regard for truth as a utility or a holy fear of scholarship on the part of an ultrazealous faction. He died heartbroken when the lamps were going out and the old Europe was breaking up in World War I. He was canonized in 1954. BIBLIOGRAPHY: G. Dal Gal, *Pius X, the Life Story of the Beatus* (tr. and ed. T. F. Murray, 1954); E. Poulat, *Histoire, dogme et critique dans la crise moderniste* (1962); N. Vian, BiblSanct 10:907–919, bibliog.

[T. GILBY]

PIUS XI (Ambrogio Damiano Achille Ratti; 1857–1939), **POPE** from 1922. Born near Milan of a family in modest circumstances, P. became a seminary professor, paleographer, and scholarly editor, prefect of the Ambrosian and Vatican Libraries. He was appointed apostolic visitor and nuncio to Poland, then emerging after World War I from the ruins of the three empires that had partitioned it: the country and people held his affections for the rest of his life. He was named cardinal and abp. of Milan in 1921. On his election as pope his blessing to the world from the outside loggia of St. Peter's presaged the outgoing policies of his pontificate.

He was a man with a clear grasp of ideas, a steady and strenuous worker, a lover of mountains, and an expert Alpinist, sturdy in physique and temperament, unafraid of coming to decisions and tough in holding to them, and unconcerned with personal popularity. His own utterances were free of any trace of whimpering, even sublimated. In some ways his style was not unlike that of the buildings he put up in Vatican City, somewhat massy and without instant charm. He was loved by his many friends to whom he was intensely loyal, but he brooked no opposition, though it was not from vanity.

He must be reckoned one of the most considerable of the Post-Reformation popes. His great achievement was to lay foundations that support, and often are concealed by, later developments. He settled the Roman Question with the *Lateran Pact. His attempts at striking some measure of coexistence having failed, he denounced the persecutions conducted by Mexican anticlericalism and Bolshevik communism, and when the time came was similarly unequivocal about German Nazism. He was criticized abroad for not intervening against Fascism in Italy and Spain, but the threat there to the human decencies was never so portentous, though bad enough for Christian Liberalism; all the same there were warning growls to show that he was prepared to repeat what he had done with the *Action Française and be quite rough with a pagan political philosophy which claimed to speak for Christianity. He was the originator of *Catholic Action, though in those days it promised more than it performed in the encouragement of proper lay freedom from clerical tutelage. He instituted the feast of Christ the King; both the theological depths and the literary slabbing are characteristic. He promoted the arts and sciences, more esp. the latter. Two of his encyclicals, *Casti connubii* (1930) on Christian marriage, and *Quadragesimo anno* (1931), which extended the social teaching of Leo XIII, are landmarks in moral theology. He laid solid foundations for the Church's work in foreign missions; his prescience about the need for native episcopates, his solicitude for the customs and rites of the Eastern Churches, which are now bearing fruit, were all the more impressive for coming from so European and indeed Latin a type. BIBLIOGRAPHY: P. Hughes, *Pope Pius XI* (1937); R. Fontenelle, *His Holiness Pope Pius XI* (tr. M. E. Fowler, 1938).

[T. GILBY]

PIUS XII (Eugenio Maria Giuseppe Pacelli; 1876–1958), **POPE** from 1939. Son of a lawyer in the service of the Vatican, P. specialized, after his ecclesiastical training, in canon law and diplomatics, which gave a concordat cast to his mind. Nuncio to Bavaria during World War I, afterward to Germany, he was named cardinal secretary of state for the second half of the pontificate of his predecessor, so that his quick election 6 months before the outbreak of World War II caused no abrupt deviation from the aims of inherited papal policies. The changes came from the general catastrophe in the world around, and the pervasive influence of his personality in the impact, sacred and profane, of the Vatican. Tall and thin, refined and ceremonious, he was a contrast to Pius XI. He was not hesitant about displaying the warmth of his piety, nor embarrassed by the adulation which not rarely distorted what was for millions a genuine affection for his person. His charisms were to prove a weakness toward the end of his reign: to push, if only tacitly, one's own style in religious mentality and feeling produces after a time an effect many find strained and artificial, and no less uncongenial when also admitted to be august. Moreover, to reserve public relations and ordinary working decisions to oneself and to deny subordinates the proper play of responsibility is not a pattern for successful government, not even for a centralized regime.

His position when faced with a temporarily triumphant Nazism has been both defended and, with more feeling, attacked. Temperamentally he was more alert to the evils of a persecuting Communism, which were older and were to prove more lasting. The fact that he had a particular affection for Germans did not color his neutrality. On the contrary he protested against their successive aggressions. The reasons for his detachment may be readily appreciated. Protesting, like punishing, is better reserved for occasions when it will do some good, otherwise it can lapse into a mere relief of feeling. His somewhat reserved attitude was understandable enough at the time; a blunt and total condemnation would have made matters worse for the actual sufferers and brought in fresh victims. In a sense he had less freedom of action than Michael *Faulhaber and Clemens von *Galen, his cardinals of Munich and Münster, and even they, staunch Christian warriors though they were, had to walk rather warily for the sake of others. Now, however, that the enormity of the horrors that were perpetrated, and often by men acquiescing to their subservience to events, and allowing themselves to believe what they are told by their rulers, has come into the open, it seems that anything would have been better than the papal reticence.

Yet if his public protests fell rather thin and proved ineffective to remedy the tragic and wicked situation, the Pope's own more personal initiatives were imaginative and widespreading. Despite the obstructions of governments, his charity reached out to hundreds of thousands of families with news of their missing ones. Orders went out for special solicitude to be shown for the Jews under the terror; many found a safe harbor in the Vatican itself and in religious houses in Italy. This cloak work without the dagger went on after the Nazis had been destroyed, for there were new repressions and new displacements of populations. With the resultant wrongs the Pope attempted to cope as best he could. But the main importance of the postwar years of his pontificate lies in the more specifically religious field. His thought was rich and generous, and he set himself to the statement of Catholic faith and morals in relation to modern problems. It was sometimes an overstatement because he was extremely fluent, and his oral allocutions, sometimes at great length, numbered over a thousand. Stripped of their encrustations, however, they stand revealed as well-engineered expositions of authentic theological thought. The doctrine of our Lady's Assumption was officially proclaimed (1950). The encyclicals *Divino afflante Spiritu* and *Humani generis* offered more freedom to scholars and a guarded welcome to some advances in the biblical and anthropological sciences. *Mystici corporis* expounded revealed doctrine on the Church; *Mediator Dei* gave a systematic treatment of liturgical theology. A controversy was settled about the essential form of priestly ordination, and some changes on points of discipline made the sacraments more accessible to Christ's faithful.

After World War II his desire to keep the world informed of the RC position with regard to contemporary socio-moral problems led to an unprecedented multiplication of pronouncements, some of which, it has been charged, anticipated full theological discussion and the accumulation of relevant information. BIBLIOGRAPHY: *Mind of Pius XII* (ed. R. C. Potlock, 1955); R. Leiber, NCE 11:414–418; J. S. Conway, "The Silence of Pope Pius XII," *Review of Politics* 27 (1965) 105–131; *Wartime Correspondence between President Roosevelt and Pope Pius XII* (ed. M. Taylor, 1975).

[T. GILBY]

PIUS AFFECTUS CREDULITATIS, a term used in the theology of faith. St. Paul speaks about "the obedience of faith" (Rom 1.5; 16.26), an obedience implicit in faith. The "devout will to believe" recalls this saying of his. It consists in a religious attitude of openness toward God, who speaks and acts as the first witness of his revelation. St. Augustine says, "God acts with suasions that we may will and believe. What is more, God himself brings about in a man the very will to believe" (*Spir. et litt.* 34.60). The will to believe was originally a Semipelagian phrase that did not imply the influence of grace. The Council of Orange II (529) borrowed it from Semipelagian writings but gave it a new twist of meaning. Rather than have it designate the command of the will to believe, the Council referred it to a faith animated by the love of the will. Modern theology sees in it the idea of the will disposing the intellect to an assent consequent upon the acts of credibility and credendity. BIBLIOGRAPHY: R. Aubert, *Le Problème de l'acte du foi* (3d ed., 1958).

[J. FICHTNER]

PIYYUTIM, in Jewish liturgiology, lyric poems for festivals and special days, many of which have become part of synagogue worship, esp. those of the 8th-cent. poet Eleazar Kalir. The word (here given in the plural) derives from the Aramaic word for "poet." BIBLIOGRAPHY: A. Z. Idelsohn, *Jewish Liturgy and Its Development* (1967) 34–46.

[J. DALLEN]

PLACE, JOSUÉ DE LA (Lat. Placeus; 1596–1655 or 1656), Calvinist theologian. A professor at the theological academy of Saumur from 1633, P. rejected current orthodox Calvinist theory that original sin was imputed to each man as a share in Adam's sinful action. He maintained that Calvin himself recognized only an imputation by reason of the inherited depraved nature. P. published his views in *Disputatio de imputatione primi peccati Adami* (1655). The *Helvetic Consensus Formula repudiated P.'s teaching.

[T. C. O'BRIEN]

PLACES, SACRED, those areas of the world which bear a particular significance for the basic orientation of man. Since life is realized within time and space, there is always need for temporal and spatial distinction and value. Consequently, for every man space is not homogeneous and for religious man space may be differentiated on the basis of its relationship with the holy. Thus the character of holiness that adheres to sacred places can be of different origins and varying intensity. Though properly belonging in the context of religion, sacred places are not restricted to it and can be found in all modes of behavior. Four basic types of sacred places can be distinguished. There are those places that are particularly significant to the psycho-social nature of man: the house, the threshold, the hearth, the grave, and in their transformative extension, the village, the city, the fatherland. The second type of sacred places such as mountains (the center of the earth, the dwelling place of the godhead), stones, caves, trees, sylvan glades, rivers, etc., appears primarily in the context of mythologies. A third type relates to revelatory events, hierophanies, or important decisions that took place at a particular site, rendering it holy. Mt. Sinai, where Moses received the Jewish law, and Lourdes would be examples of this. A fourth type of sacred place originates by human declarations of sacrality, although the motivational background for such a declaration has to be sought in the previous types. Instances for this type are temples, churches, or even cities such as Jerusalem, Rome, and Mecca. By declaring a site apt for a temple, this site is not only cut out of the chaotic profane world but becomes the true center of the universe, the navel of the world according to which everything else has to be oriented. Symbols, laws (asylum, sanctuary), taboos, myths, ideologies, etc., carry on the meaning of holy places throughout life and society. BIBLIOGRAPHY: W. Bogaras, "Ideas of Space and Time in the Conception of Primitive Religion," *American Anthropologist* 27 (1925) 205–266; H. Rust, *Heilige Stätten* (1933); M. Eliade, *Sacred and the Profane* (tr. W. R. Trask, 1961); G. van der Leeuw, *Religion in Essence and Manifestation* (tr. J. E. Turner, 1963). *SACRED AND PROFANE; *SYMBOL.

[W. DUPRÉ]

PLACET, see EXEQUATUR AND PLACET.

PLAGIARISM, in its strict legal sense, the infringement of copyright laws; morally any unjust appropriation of another's written work and use of it as though original. It is a sin against commutative justice, the expropriation of another's property, it may also offend against distributive justice if the plagiarized material fraudulently deprives another of a reward or honor due. It is also a sin against the virtue of truthfulness, since plagiarism involves a lie. The legal sense of plagiarism is as modern as copyright laws; in the history of medieval and even later theology authors frequently incorporated the work of others without citation; the practice rested not on fraud, but on the customary attitude of considering the literature on theological topics to be a common patrimony.

[T. C. O'BRIEN]

PLAGUES OF EGYPT, ten disasters brought upon Egypt through Moses and Aaron because of the Pharaoh's refusal to let the Israelites leave. The plagues consisted of water turning to blood; frogs; gnats; flies; murrain, a plague on cattle; boils; hail; locusts; darkness; the death of all firstborn of Egypt, people and cattle (Ex 7.14–12.30).

The plagues were later cited as the signs and wonders of Yahweh, who used them to give deliverance to his people (Ps 78.43–54; 105.26–36; Jer 32.21). Biblical students have debated the historicity of the plagues without coming to any generally accepted conclusion. The first nine plagues have been seen as accentuations of natural disasters sometimes experienced in Egypt, with their severity, concentration, and timeliness being attributed to divine intervention. At the height of its inundation, for example, it is said that the Nile becomes a blood red color, and that such a phenomenon was perhaps the basis of the first plague. Extraordinary locust plagues have also been known in Egypt, even in recent years. Scholars analyzing the biblical account from the standpoint of the *documentary theory conclude that the Yahwist (J) had only seven plagues (cf Rev 15.1); the Elohist (E) added darkness; and the Priestly (P) added gnats and boils. The accounts of plagues were designed to show Yahweh's power to deliver his people and to manifest Yahweh's judgment against their enemies. In Rom 9.14–

18, a passage often debated in theological discussions of the doctrine of election, Paul cited Pharaoh to illustrate God's way of dealing with man.

[T. EARLY]

PLAINCHANT, see GREGORIAN CHANT.

PLAINSONG, see GREGORIAN CHANT.

PLAINTIFF, a person who brings his case to court to seek remedy for an injury to his rights. According to moralists, he should press only those claims whose justice and provability are at least probable. He should not use unjust means to establish a just claim and should avoid evil motivation in pursuing it. He should also consider the rights of his adversary, witnesses, his own attorney, court, and society at large. Fraternal charity demands that he consider the needs of his adversary as weighed against his own. He owes his attorney honest candor, an understanding of the attorney's conscience, and a just fee. He should be considerate of his witnesses and their due convenience and certainly should not induce them to lie on his behalf. In court he is bound to tell the truth and is further bound to restitution for any real injustice he causes. In 1 Cor 6.1–7, St. Paul teaches it is better to suffer injustice than to enter into contention, but prudence will reconcile the urgency of this counsel with the responsibilities of the Christian to possible higher duties and the protection of society itself from the unscrupulous.

Before presenting claims for personal damages the plaintiff must have at least the probable opinion that his adversary is in the wrong. The amount of damages demanded should represent what the plaintiff deserves plus the fees for the attorney rather than the sum he can recover without respect for justice. If his opponent refuses to negotiate a fair settlement, the plaintiff's claim may be increased to compensate for the delay, inconvenience, and expenses of court litigation. A validly drawn will should remain uncontested unless the plaintiff has at least the probable opinion that it erroneously represents the decedent's intentions in his regard, or is the result of undue influence on the testator by others. BIBLIOGRAPHY: R. H. Dailey, NCE 11:424.

[R. H. DAILEY]

PLAN OF UNION, an agreement made in 1801 for cooperation between Presbyterians and Congregationalists. Evangelical fervor and expansion of settlement into western N.Y. and Ohio led these Churches to cooperate in home missionary work to eliminate unfortunate competition. The Plan of Union made it possible for congregations to be connected with both denominations and to be served by pastors of either. Presbyterian churches might be represented in Congregational associations by elders, while Congregational churches could be represented in presbyteries by committeemen. For a while the Plan worked so well that Presbyterians invited Congregational associations to become integral parts of Presbyterian synods, and Congregationalists formed no separate organizations for clergymen in the West. Unhappiness over ''presbygationalists'' developed, particularly among Presbyterians who saw a threat to Presbyterian doctrine and church order and who gained enough power to abrogate the Plan in the General Assembly of 1838 and to cut off certain synods that were overly influenced by Congregationalism. BIBLIOGRAPHY: R. H. Nichols, *Presbyterianism in New York State* (1963).

[J. H. SMYLIE]

PLANCTUS, a medieval lyric poem or song of lamentation. The genre originated in Latin poetry and was imitated in the vernaculars. Many of the poems are religious, like the celebrated *Planctus Mariae,* lamentations of Mary at the foot of the Cross, in which some historians see the origin of the Passion Plays.

[E. C. DUNN]

PLANETA an alternative name for the chasuble, found as early as the Council of Toledo IV (633). It is perhaps derived from the Greek for ''wanderer''; the garment was a cloak worn while traveling.

[J. DALLEN]

PLANNED PARENTHOOD, full title the Planned Parenthood Federation of America, adopted in 1942 by the organization formed by Margaret Sanger as the National (later American) Birth Control League. The original purpose of the organization may be classified as a type of women's liberation, particularly from prostitution and unwanted pregnancies, and as a concern for family life. Advocacy of artificial methods of contraception was a primary means for achieving these social objectives and also of eliminating abortion. An anti-abortion campaign was a prominent feature of the early history of Planned Parenthood. The organization depended on private contributions to maintain and spread its programs. These programs gradually won recognition for their medical, educative, and counselling excellence in the whole area of sexual behavior, family planning, and responsible parenthood. Catholic opposition, remaining firm after most Protestant bodies turned from early opposition to positive support, was directed against the advocacy of artificial contraception, not against most of the objectives of Planned Parenthood.

More recently, however, Catholic objection has been directed against Planned Parenthood's new definition of its function and objectives. In this opposition the Catholic League for Religious and Civil Rights has been one prominent arm of Catholic opposition. Planned Parenthood is now, in fact, largely subsidized by federal funds, therefore, by tax dollars; grants received have amounted to over $250 million. The organization's general definition of purpose, formulated in its ''Five Year Plan'' of 1975, is the fostering of social change. That involves the acceptance and dissemination of the tenets of the so-called sexual revolution. Sexuality is to be seen as divorced from its reference to familial life. Programs in schools and communities implemented by Planned Parenthood literature and audio-visual aids are directed toward guidance for full, but safe enjoyment of absolute sexual freedom. The second, more specific objective is the protection of the absolute right of women, even minors, to elective abortion, as is evident from the decision of the U.S. Supreme Court in Planned Parenthood vs Danforth (1973). Clinics under Planned Parenthood auspices accounted for 35,000 abortions in 1975. The organization is a powerful abortion lobby and has access and influence on many federal agencies. Thus there has emerged a direct confrontation between Planned Parenthood and Catholic pro-life advocacy. For the ''Five-Year Plan'' see M. C. Schwartz, ''. . . Planned Parenthood Five Year Plan'' in *Our Sunday Visitor* 138 (Feb. 18, 1978) 114–116.

[T. C. O'BRIEN]

PLANTAGENET—from Lat, *planta genista,* the shrub called broom, which was their emblem —family name of the Angevin rulers of England from Henry II who succeeded to the crown in 1154. The direct line died out with Richard II in 1400. Called by their enemies ''the Devil's brood,'' and rather respected for this by the people, they produced able administrators in Henry II, the friend and enemy of St. Thomas Becket, and Edward I. Most were good soldiers, and those who were not were great patrons of the arts and of the Dominicans. Their wives could be highly redoubtable, thus Eleanor of Aquitaine and Isabella, the she-wolf of France. The collateral line of Lancaster was succeeded by that of York. The last of the Plantagenets was Richard III, Crouchback. The first *Tudors, who had little of the blood, managed to dispose of those who had more, on pretexts of treason or of failure to conform to the royal supremacy.

[T. GILBY]

PLANTIER, CLAUDE HENRI (1813–75), bp. of Nîmes, in France, champion of the papacy. Before being named bp. in 1855 he had been Lent and Advent preacher at Notre Dame de Paris. As bp. he was a forceful apologist, attacking *Renan's *Vie de Jésus,* the Reformed Church of France, and liberalism. He was an *ultramontanist and at Vatican Council I a strong infalliblist. He wrote in defense of Pius IX and that Pope's *Syllabus of Errors; he strongly condemned any questioning of papal temporal sovereignty and sought to bring about the return of the Papal States.

[R. J. LITZ]

PLANTIN, CHRISTOPHE (*c.*1520–89), French printer who settled in Antwerp in 1549 as a bookbinder and later turned to printing. Among his numerous works, noted for both accuracy and beauty, the most famous was his eight-volume *polyglot Bible (1569–73) with Hebrew, Aramaic, Greek, Syriac, and Latin texts. His original building with its equipment is preserved as the Plantin-Moretus Museum.

[T. EARLY]

PLANTIN BIBLES, editions printed by C. *Plantin of Antwerp. The most noted is his *Biblia regia,* an eight-volume *polyglot (1569–73) with Hebrew, Aramaic, Greek, Syriac, and Latin texts. Plantin's Bibles are esteemed for their accurate and beautiful typography.

[T. EARLY]

PLANUDES, MAXIMUS (*c.*1260–*c.*1310), Byzantine humanist and theologian. Born in Nicomedia, he entered a monastery in 1283 and despite the opposition of the patriarch he founded a monastery for laymen in Constantinople and a school close to the Emperor's palace, with access to the imperial library. He had an excellent grasp of Latin, defended the orthodoxy of Western theology, and favored rapprochement with the Roman Church. He translated parts of Augustine, Boethius, Cicero, Ovid, and Caesar into Greek.

[E. J. DILLON]

PLASDEN, POLYDORE, ST. (1563–91), English martyr. A student at the English College in Reims, P. was ordained in 1586. Returning to the English mission in 1588 he labored in Sussex and later in London, where he was arrested and convicted of treason. He was hanged at London in 1591. P. was canonized in 1970.

[J. R. AHERNE]

PLASSMAN, THOMAS BERNARD (1879–1959), biblical scholar and educator. Except for a 3-year period as Franciscan provincial, P. was associated with St. Bonaventure College and Seminary as a professor of Scripture, college president, or seminary rector from 1910 until his death. He wrote many scriptural articles for scholarly publications and published several books fostering a biblically centered spirituality. P. also founded and was president (1919–47) of the Franciscan Educational Conference.

[T. M. MCFADDEN]

PLASSMANN, HERMANN ERNST (1817–64), one of an eminent group of German Catholic Thomists. His work on Thomistic philosophy *Die Schule des hl. Thomas* (5 v, 1858–61) was influential in the Thomistic revival. BIBLIOG-RAPHY: J. Höfer, LTK 8:549–550.

[J. R. AHERNE]

PLATER, CHARLES DOMINIC (1875–1921), English Jesuit activist in the Catholic social movement of the early 20th century. He entered the Society in 1894 after his education at Stonyhurst. A paper (1906) proposing retreats for workingmen as a means of furthering social justice resulted in the establishment of a number of retreat houses. He is best known for founding the Catholic Social Guild. The Catholic Workers College at Oxford, founded after his death, grew out of P.'s dedication to the education of workers in social problems. Nearly all of his written work was concerned with current issues.

[R. J. LITZ]

PLATERESQUE STYLE, term meaning "Silversmith style," relating to the elaborate and fine detail of silver work originally coined in 16th-cent. Spain to describe decoration on the Gothic cathedral at Léon. Later it came to apply to a style of architectural ornament, current in 16th-cent. Spain and her S American possessions, in which highly elaborate, intricate low relief was concentrated about doors and windows. Early Plateresque style changed the Gothic structure of arches and buttressing to the hall church of flat roof. The second phase (1540–70) showed a concentrated and heavier ornament in Italian High Renaissance style (portal of the Royal Hospital, Santiago de Compostela). BIBLIOGRAPHY: G. Kubler and M. Soria, *Art and Architecture in Spain and Portugal and Their South American Dominions, 1500–1800* (1959).

[S. D. MURRAY]

PLATINA, BARTOLOMEO (1421–1481), Italian humanist whose works include a history of the popes (1474–79), valuable for its treatment of contemporary events but which he used to gratify his dislike of Paul II.

[R. J. LITZ]

PLATINA (PIADENA), GIOVANNI MARIA (d. 1500), Italian master of intarsia, who worked on the choir stalls (cathedrals of Mantua, 1482, and Cremona, 1484) and screens at Cremona cathedral and the Churches of S. Antonio and S. Abbondio.

[M. J. DALY]

PLATO (*c*.428–347 B.C.), Greek philosopher and stylist. An Athenian by birth and follower of Socrates, P. was perhaps impelled by his master's trial and execution to compose the works which in the first instance defend and memorialize Socrates' character and teaching. Among P.'s certainly authentic works all but the *Apology* (Socrates' speeches at his trial) are in dialogue form. Of the 40 or more attributed to him, 28 are certainly or probably genuine. Their chronological order of composition was unknown until stylistic analysis in the 19th cent. permitted an approximate arrangement. Of 13 letters attributed to him few are defended as genuine. He was perhaps the creator of the dialogue form, which he used with such lifelike effects of language and characterization and occasionally with such inventive force that it complicates the task of analyzing his meaning. The most disputed question about P.'s works is the extent to which they may merely reproduce Socrates' thought or may represent his own original developments. A compromise position holds that earlier "aporistic" dialogues are more representative of Socrates, those near the *Phaedo* and later are increasingly independent, as Socrates becomes a less prominent figure in them or disappears entirely.

Underlying all P.'s work is the question of what we really know of the world around us and how we know it. In earlier dialogues it is a matter of simple definition: how to define bravery (*Laches*) or piety (*Euthyphro*) or temperance (*Charmides*) or friendship (*Lysis*) or justice (*Republic* I); obvious definitions are found on examination to be inconsistent or incomplete, ending in an impasse (*aporia*). A related problem is whether virtues are teachable (*Protagoras*), a question which is itself intimately connected with the nature of the learning process (*Meno*). These discussions of knowledge and definition lead in a direction which suggests that a part of the human makeup called "soul" (*psychē*) had a preexistence and continuing life (*Phaedo*) through which it could gain knowledge of the only really unchanging and therefore really knowable elements of experience, a set of ideal definitions called "ideas" or "forms," of which all particular things are only imperfect instances. This "theory of ideas" (*idea, eidos*), which appears in earlier dialogues and undergoes continuing redefinition in the *Phaedo, Symposium, Republic*, and *Parmenides*, is never explicitly abandoned, but is later replaced or modified by other theories and methods of definition. The dialectic of this earlier period proceeds characteristically by tentative assumption (*hypothesis*) and critical testing (*elenchos*). Speculation about the immortality and separate life of the soul leads not only to a strongly emphasized contrast with the body and material things, but also to a series of remarkable "myths" about the fate and judgment of the soul after death or about its visions of the intellectual realm—at the end of the *Apology*, of the *Phaedo*, of the *Gorgias*, of the *Republic*, and in the *Symposium* and *Phaedrus*. The *Republic* (10 books) combines all these interests and speculations in its attempt to define justice and the just man by defining a perfect state and investigating more fully the theory of ideas and the relationship of various levels of reality. These levels are crowned by "the idea of the good" as the source of being and value.

On more than one occasion (esp. in the *Gorgias* and *Republic*) P. showed his dislike of radical democracy and his contempt for the politicians who had built the power of Athens in the preceding century. His own political interests took a practical form in his ill-fated advisory visits to the court of Dionysius at Syracuse (recorded in the *Letters*). Perhaps he hoped to put into effect his ideal of a "philosopher-king," and perhaps his passionate rejection of political life in favor of pure speculation and philosophy in the *Theaetetus* was the result of his disappointment. In his last work, the *Laws* (12 books), he returns to political questions in a far more detailed and dogmatic form than earlier. Religious features are paramount, and discussion of the concept of soul and its relationship to a divine and universal order continues on one hand the detailed cosmology of the *Timaeus* and on the other hand the complex questions of epistemology, definition, and value judgment which had been pursued in the *Theaetetus, Sophist, Politicus*, and *Philebus*. In the three latter dialogues and the *Phaedrus* he had developed the method of "division" (*diaeresis*) and the identification of "class" (*genos*) as a way of arriving at definition and truth. P.'s oral teaching included material not found in his written works and preserved most prominently in the discussions of his pupil, Aristotle. A late lecture *On the Good* appears to have concentrated on the mathematical formulations of reality (e.g., *the one* and *the indeterminate dyad*) which characterized P.'s school at the time of his death and immediately after. This Pythagoreanizing development, and its analogue in astral theology, is found also in the doubtfully genuine *Epinomis*.

P.'s importance in the history of thought is twofold: first, he brought to a critical summation the philosophical trends seen in previous Greek thinkers; and second, his discussions provide the groundwork for most subsequent developments in Western philosophy. Except for a time during the Hellenistic period his writings have been studied in every age and variously interpreted or criticized. He dealt with every realm of human activity and thought—aesthetics and education, language and logic, theology, epistemology, and mathematics, along with ethics, politics, religion, psychology, and natural science. His discussions dealt in rich complexity with such fundamental problems as necessity and free will, nature and convention, providence, teleology, the meaning of god, and, by implication, the possibility of dualism. "Platonism" has therefore designated a multitude of interests with varying emphases in different ages. An eclectic form of Platonism was the dominant philosophical tendency among pagan thinkers during the early centuries of Christianity, which therefore developed its theology largely within this framework. BIBLIOGRAPHY: P. Shorey, *What Plato Said* (1933); G. M. A. Grube, *Plato's Thought* (1935); P. Friedländer, *Plato* (tr. H. Meyerhoff, 3 v. 1958–69); A. E. Taylor, *Plato, the Man and his Works* (7th ed. 1960); a comprehensive and critical bibliographical survey by H. Cherniss in *Lustrum* 4 (1959) and 5 (1960); W. K. Guthrie, *Plato: The Man and His Dialogues* (*History of Greek Philosophy 4*, 1975).

[Z. STEWART]

PLATONIC LOVE, the spiritual intimacy and emotional communion of friends based in a shared love of God or some higher principle or being, as opposed to carnal love which is said to blind lovers to higher principles in their passion for one another. The distinction between Platonic and "vulgar" love was originally presented by Marsilio *Ficino, Italian philosopher of the Florentine Medici court and leader of the Platonic Academy, in his *De amore* (1469), a commentary on Plato's *Symposium*. Ficino interchangeably referred to this unsensual philosophic attraction and affection of one man for another as either Platonic or Socratic love; he did not extend the term to women, modelling the concept on the behavior of Socrates at the Symposium. Throughout the Renaissance, Ficino's theory of love was widely accepted and acknowledged, particularly by poets who shifted the notion of Platonic love to a heterosexual base, celebrating the revised concept in their love lyrics and sonnets. Other writers wove the concept into longer works, philosophic treatises and poems. In Italy, the Platonic love theme appears in works by Lorenzo de'Medici, Pietro Bembo, Michelangelo, and others; in France, it is found in the works of Scève and the *Pléiade; and in England, Spenser, Sydney, Raleigh, Shakespeare and others all incorporated the theme into their works. Though less pronounced after the Renaissance, the idea of Platonic love retains a definite and recurrent place in the amorous literature of the West.

[R. J. LITZ]

PLATONISM, the term used in the strict sense to designate the philosophy of Plato himself. In a broader sense it is employed to designate the teachings of philosophers who modified in many ways the doctrines of Plato and who incorporated into their philosophy elements borrowed from Aristotelianism, Stoicism, Neopythagoreanism, and Oriental mysticism. One may distinguish the following stages in the development of Platonism: the *Old Academy, the *Middle Academy, the *New Academy, *Middle Platonism, and *Neoplatonism. *GREEK PHILOSOPHY 2 bc; 3 d; 4 c; 5.

[M. R. P. MCGUIRE]

PLATONISM AND NEOPLATONISM, ANCIENT CHRISTIAN. The spread of Christianity in the Greco-Roman world took place at a time when the leading schools of Greek philosophy (see GREEK PHILOSOPHY) were becoming more and more eclectic and more and more preoccupied with religion and theology. The early Christian writers, whether converts to Christianity or born Christians, were all trained in the pagan schools of rhetoric and philosophy and were intimately familiar with the philosophical tenets and tendencies of their age. They were faced with the twofold task of explaining Christianity to, or defending it against, contemporary pagan intellectuals and of developing a Christian theology in a strict sense. They found much in Greek philosophy which they had to refute, but also much that could be put to good use in the development of Christian doctrine. Philo had helped to bridge the gap between Greek philosophy and Judaism by maintaining that the Greek philosophers, including Plato, had borrowed their leading ideas from the Old Testament. Furthermore, Scripture furnished Christian writers with the examples of Moses and Daniel who had been wise in the learning of Egypt and Babylonia and put this learning to good use in the service of the true God. In the first 2 cent. and early 3d cent. of the Christian era, the leading Greek philosophies were Stoicism and Platonism. Both Middle and Late Stoicism were definitely eclectic, and Middle Platonism was even more so. Accordingly, when one speaks of the Stoicism or Platonism of the early Christian writers before the rise of Neoplatonism, it should be kept in mind that one is dealing with the eclectic forms of Stoicism and Platonism mentioned. Justin Martyr, Clement, and Origen make full use of Middle Platonism in their apologetic and exposition of Christian teachings, while Tertullian, on the other hand, leans heavily on Stoicism, esp. in his treatment of the nature of the soul.

But the Platonism that had the greatest influence on Christianity was that of Plotinus, the last great ancient Greek philosopher. His own system, and the modifications and elaborations made by his successors, have justified modern scholars in calling this form of Platonism Neoplatonism. As developed by *Porphyry, *Iamblichus, and *Proclus, Neoplatonism became a very complicated body of doctrine in which the theurgic element assumed a central role. The pagan Neoplatonists, on philosophical and cultural grounds, were hostile to Christianity to the end, esp. at Athens. Yet despite this hostility and the many elements in Neoplatonism repugnant to Christians, Neoplatonic tenets like the absolute transcendence of God, and the necessity for the soul, by stages of contemplation, to seek to attain union with God, made a special appeal to Christian thinkers. In the East the influence of Iamblichus was dominant in Neoplatonic thought, while in the West Plotinus and Porphyry were long the sole sources of Neoplatonism. Among the Christian fathers or writers profoundly influenced by Neoplatonism in the West were *Marius Victorinus, St. *Ambrose, St. *Augustine, *Calcidius, and Claudius Mamertus; in the East, St. Basil of Caesarea, St. *Gregory of Nyssa, *Nemesius of Emesa, *Synesius of Cyrene, and, above all, *Pseudo-Dionysius, who owes so much to *Proclus. *Boethius was trained at the schools of Athens and Alexandria and reflects the influence of both. It should be noted that at Alexandria, with its emphasis on scholarship, pagan and Christian Neoplatonists tended to work together in amicable fashion. A number of the later Neoplatonic scholars at Alexandria were Christians. BIBLIOGRAPHY: P. Hadot, NCE 10:334–336; Copleston 2:13–103; CHGMP 331–555 (excellent); F. Bonnard, DTC 12.2:2258–2392.

[M. R. P. MCGUIRE]

PLAY, from the root notion of an operation performed with ease and freedom, a word that has come to mean an activity in the form of recreation, diversion, sport, or game. It is connected with the notions of fun, delight, and enjoyment. All these have their place in theology. Well aware that all work and no play makes Jack a dull boy, and that the amenities, to say the least, of human fellowship require a certain wit and light humor, the moralists recognize a special virtue, a part of temperance and social fairness, in playfulness, *eutrapelia,* lying in the mean between buffoonery and boorishness, whereby the individual relaxes and exchanges pleasantries with his neighbor. Though, of course, they are professionally inclined to frown more on too much than on too little of it, Aquinas agrees with Seneca in seeing the need for occasional ridiculousness. Even so, this is regarded as being useful, rather than valuable in itself. It is like playing a game for the sake of health, not just because you enjoy it. However, the word takes on a nobler and less dutiful meaning when it moves from moral to more contemplative and mystical theology. There it is connected with the Augustinian teaching of *frui* in contrast to *uti,* and the psychology of sheer play, where nothing is to be gained and everything is to be delighted in. A high tradition relates this

to the Vulgate version of Wisdom playing before God all the time, playing round the globe, delighting in the sons of men (Pr 8.30,31). BIBLIOGRAPHY: Aristotle, *Nicomachean Ethics,* 4.8; ThAq ST 1a2ae, 11, 16; 2a2ae, 158, (esp. in Lat-Eng ed., v. 17, ed. T. Gilby).

[T. GILBY]

PLAYFORD, JOHN (1623–86 or 87), London music publisher of virtually all the music published in the second half of the 17th century. He was also composer of many psalm tunes, and author of a work on music theory, *Introduction to the Skill of Musick,* a text used for a century.

[R. J. LITZ]

PLEASURE, the experience of delight (Lat. *delectatio;* Gr. *hēdonē*). As the equivalent of the Latin *voluptas,* it usually refers to sensuous responses. As *quies* (rest), *fruitio* (enjoyment), and *gaudium* (joy), it is the final phase of activity, the satisfaction of appetite in a good present and possessed. It is an analogical term applied by common likeness to cases quite simply diverse (a dog with a bone, a man with a woman, an angel with God, and God with Himself) and to differing human situations, as when one speaks of seeking pleasure from, finding pleasure in, taking pleasure with, or just pleasuring.

This article is concerned with the place of pleasure in moral theory. This depends on, though it is not to be resolved into, its wider place in psychology; for morality is confined to the field of *human acts which is occupied with deliberations and choice, and as pleasure is an object of these, it is more or less obscure, whereas, as it is realized in fact, it is more or less vivid. Pleasures as experienced are postscripts to the morality of an act which has been already decided for good or for ill.

Since pleasure is the normal complement of healthy activity, the moralists might have been expected to start with a prejudice in its favor. Such has not proved to be the case, historically; except for the exponents of frank *hedonism and more delicate *Epicureanism, they have tended to look at pleasure askance, partly on ascetical grounds, and partly because of the deep vein of puritanism that seems to run through human nature. Then, too, the Latin Stoics were the prevailing ethical influence on the Christian homilists for many centuries, and a distrust for what is of the soil still endures despite St. Thomas Aquinas, who showed that some moral virtue lived in the medium of pleasure-toned affects and that in those matters unfeelingness (*insensibilitas, anaesthesia*) was a vice.

His analysis continued the thought of the *Philebus, Timaeus,* and *Nicomachean Ethics.* Pleasure itself is morally neutral. Morality hinges on what the pleasure is about; it is this, the shaping object of action, that is the crucial point. Pleasure is not this object, but a consequence of its being possessed. Pleasure is because of this object; this object is not because of the pleasure. But here one is speaking of efficient or formal causes, not of final causes, for pleasure is an ultimate and not sought on account of anything else, or because it serves a purpose; it is this quality of pure release that tempts people to think that they are hedonists when in fact they are not. Another thing contributing to the same confusion is the alternative of duty or pleasure forced on some by ethical formalism. St. Thomas draws a distinction between two phases in happiness, the holding of the good, and the enjoying of it, but he warns against splitting the singleness of the drive towards both together. And Aristotle remarks how absurd it is to ask someone why he wishes to enjoy himself.

At this point the classical tripartite division of good used by St. Ambrose may be recalled, namely, worthy (*bonum honestum*), the delightful (*delectabile*), and the useful (*utile*); it will help to correct the impression, which renders some religious thinking somewhat stilted, that pleasures are attached to some necessary operations in order that we should perform them; a parallel argument considers the beneficence of pain, since otherwise we should never have an angry appendix removed. On the supposition that the world is designed, the reflection is true enough, but only for the level of purely sensory experience; it seems a fair presumption that animals would not eat or breed unless there were pleasures in the appropriate functions. But pleasure as such is not to be judged from types relatively low in the scale; in which, moreover, there is no appreciation of the good aimed at (*ratio boni, ratio finis*), and no value judgments relating the useful and the pleasurable to what is good for its own sake, but merely a series of particular attractions. Whereas on the human level there is a recognition that the *delectabile* is a quality of an end, and therefore too good to be treated as a means, expressed by St. Augustine's observation that we should not use what should be enjoyed: indeed his distinction between *uti* and *frui* opens out into the theology of the fruits of the Spirit, against which there is no law (Gal 5.23) and the esthetics of sheer play.

Theology, then, regards pleasure as more than a bodily thrill and a kind of feeling, but as one aspect in a larger conscious complex, and takes it into the life of the spirit and even the divinity itself. It draws a working distinction between bodily and spiritual pleasures, though, significantly, St. Thomas includes among the latter those of the imagination. Bodily pleasures are presumed to be innocent until they are proved guilty; all the same their disturbing or distracting role in reasonable living is well recognized, and abstinence from them, even when they convey no threat of sin, is a practice common to most religious traditions. Nor do they constitute safe guides to moral conduct. Spiritual pleasure, however, is a sign that the action that produces it is right. The *Summa theologiae* has no use for the principle that the more an action is against the grain, the better it is, or that we should aspire to the "pure love" of God without thought of enjoying Him. He has made us, in the deepest sense, creatures built for comfort rather than for speed. Yet happiness is to pleasure as health is to feeling healthy; preoccupation with pleasure defeats its own end and produces a kind of inverted hypochondria. If one takes care of

the *honestum*, the *delectabile* will take care of itself. BIBLIOGRAPHY: ThAq ST 1a, questions 5 and 6; 1a2ae, question 2; 6.1–2; questions 31–34; 70; 2a2ae, questions 141–143.

[T. GILBY]

PLEASURE PRINCIPLE, in psychoanalytic theory, the basic law of mental operation. The constant internal arousal of instinctual drives causes constantly rising internal tension which is felt as pain or unpleasure. Activities gratifying these sexual or aggressive drives lower this tension, and this is pleasure. Many critics accept this principle as a partial explanation of behavior dynamics, but to take it as the total explanation, as Freud tended to do, reduces all human behavior to the instinctual level.

[M. E. STOCK]

PLEDGE, a statement of resolve to follow or to refrain from some course of action. If a pledge is understood as a solemn *promise, then it means giving one's word to another person and its fulfillment becomes a matter of *justice or of *truthfulness, as this virtue means fidelity. But the more usual sense of "pledge" is a declaration of intent, sometimes made publicly or in connection with some movement or campaign. Thus one may pledge a certain amount of money in a fund-raising drive; this is not, however, a formal *contract and failure to make good cannot be a sin against justice. A pledge is also part of moral campaigns against pornographic films or literature, or for the *Pro-Life movement. Violation of such pledges does not constitute a distinct moral wrong; the matter which the violation involves, however, may. "Taking the pledge" was a practice preached in the cause of *total abstinence from alcoholic drink by Theobald *Mathew among the Irish, and by others. For pastoral and psychological reasons the practice is now regarded as simplistic and unwise in the case of the problem drinker.

[T. C. O'BRIEN]

PLEDGE (IN THE BIBLE). In the OT the term was used either of some object given by a borrower as a token of his intent to pay a loan (see e.g., Dt 24.12–13; Ex 22.25–26); or for a person, i. e., a friend who was, as it were, a co-signer for another's loan (Sir 29.14–15). In the NT Jesus is called such a friend, as the guarantor of God's covenant and promises (Heb 7.22). The Holy Spirit is called the guarantee given by God (the pledge of our inheritance; see 2 Cor 1.22;5.5; Eph 1.14) in the sense that as a gift already given, he is the assurance of the full sharing in what God promises.

[T. C. O'BRIEN]

PLEGMUND OF CANTERBURY (d. 914), a Mercian-born hermit who became tutor and adviser to Alfred the Great and participated in the literary revival. Appointed abp. of Canterbury (890), he crowned Edward the Elder (901), consecrated the New Minster, Winchester (c.903), and helped subdivide the West Saxon dioceses (c.909). BIBLIOGRAPHY: W. A. Chaney, NCE 11:440.

[W. A. CHANEY]

PLÉIADE, LA, the name given to a group of seven French poets of the 16th cent. who, inspired considerably by Neoplatonism, sought to enrich French language and literature by imitating and borrowing from the classics and the Italians, esp. Petrarch. Headed by *Ronsard, it included *Du Bellay, J. A. de Baïf, R. Belleau, P. de Thiard, E. Jodelle, and Dorat. The group's name, taken from the constellation, had already been applied to a group of Alexandrian tragic poets (285–246 B.C.). BIBLIOGRAPHY: R. J. Clements, *Critical Theory and Practice of the Pléiade* (1969).

[R. N. NICOLICH]

PLEKHANOV, GEORGI VALENTINOVICH (1856–1918), known as the theoretician of Russian Marxism and, for founding the émigré Marxist group called the Liberation of Labor, as the "father of Russian social democracy." From 1900 to 1903, with V. I. Lenin (1870–1924), he published the first party newspaper *Iskra (The Spark),* but his belief in historical determinism led to an eventual break with Lenin, whom he accused of forcing Russia prematurely into socialism. His writings include both philosophical and aesthetic works. BIBLIOGRAPHY: G. V. Plekhanov, *Selected Philosophical Works* (5 v., tr. R. Dixon et al., 1960–); S. H. Baron, *Plekhanov, The Father of Russian Marxism* (1963).

[M. F. MCCARTHY]

PLENARY INDULGENCE, see INDULGENCES.

PLEROMA, a Gr. word meaning fullness, used in the NT to indicate the fullness and perfection of all things as realized in God. Although this idea appears in Greek and Gnostic thought, its roots are more conspicuous in the OT recognition of God's all-pervasive activity in nature (Gen 1–2.3; Ps 24.1–22; 50.10–12; 89.8–12; 104) and in history (Ex; Jer 1.10; Ps 105–107). From this last–mentioned conviction flows the realization that God acted most fully in history in Jesus who, therefore, has the fullness of the divinity (Col 1.19; 2.9; Eph 1.19–20).

From the fullness of the deity in Christ flows the fullness of Christ's presence in the Church which he fills with his life-giving activity, like the head in relation to the body (Eph 1.23). From one point of view it can appear that it is the Church which completes Christ, like the complement of men and cargo completes a ship (Col 1.24). But more important is the thought that Christ fills the Church, because he has the fullness of the deity and himself fills all things, esp. that reality which is most closely united to him, the Church. He is thus able to "reconcile all things to himself" (Col 1.20) and "in him all things hold together" (Col 1.17).

The *pleroma,* the fullness of God in Christ, manifests itself in history also as the completion and fullness of God's plan in its chronological dimension (Gal 4.4; Eph 1.10); in its eschatological decisiveness (Mk 1.15); in the fullness of means available to man (Jn 1.16; Rom 15.29; Eph 3.19; Col 2.2–3); in the measure of growth possible to a person (Eph 4.3–16); in the measure of the fullness of growth and perfection possible to the human race (Rom 11.12). BIBLIOGRAPHY: J. B. Lightfoot, *Saint Paul's Epistle to the Colossians and Philemon* (1892) 254–271; InterDB.

[A. J. TKACIK]

PLESSINGTON, JOHN, ST. (c.1637–79), English martyr. Of an old Catholic family, P. attended the English College at Valladolid, Spain, and was ordained in 1662. Returning to England, P. ministered at Holywell, the shrine of St. Winifride, then as a tutor and missionary in the Massey household at Puddington. His opposition to the marriage of a prominent Catholic to a Protestant caused his arrest and attempted to link him with the Titus Oates conspiracy. He was executed at Chester in 1679. His canonization occurred in 1970.

[J. R. AHERNE]

PLESSIS, JOSEPH OCTAVE (1763–1825), bp. of Quebec. After studies at the Quebec seminary and service as Bp. Briand's amanuensis, he was ordained in 1786. He became coadjutor bp. of Quebec (1801) and later bp. (1806). P. was a tireless traveler, visiting every part of his diocese from Nova Scotia to Ontario at regular intervals. He devoted much effort to education and in 1824 secured government support for confessional schools. BIBLIOGRAPHY: J. B. A. Ferland, *Mgr. Joseph Octave Plessis. . .* (1878); H. Têtu, *Les Évêques de Québec* (1889).

[R. K. MacMASTER]

PLETHON, GEORGE GEMISTOS (d. 1452), Byzantine philosopher and humanist who founded a school of philosophy and religion in Mistra. He addressed treatises to the emperors on social reform of the Peloponnesus and was one of the Greek theologians at the Council of *Florence (1439). He signed the act of union at the council but later wrote a treatise against it. While at Florence, P. strongly influenced the Italian humanists with Platonic philosophy and may have been responsible for encouraging Cosimo de 'Medici to found the Platonic Academy of Florence. In his chief work, *Nomōn Syngraphē,* P. proposed a sort of political utopia based on an idealized paganism derived largely from Neoplatonic philosophy. He also sought to create a new religion whose liturgy is contained in his three books on the *Laws.* In spite of his wide influence, P. had no real successors and was later opposed by *Bessarion, a former pupil, and his *Laws* were burned by *George Scholarios when he became patriarch of Constantinople. BIBLIOGRAPHY: Beck 754–755; E. Stepanou, DTC 12.2:2393–2404; A. A. Vasiliev, *History of the Byzantine Empire* (1964) 2:699–670.

[G. T. DENNIS]

PLINY THE YOUNGER (*c*.61–before 114), Roman jurist and writer. Upon adoption by his celebrated uncle, Pliny the Elder, Publius Caecilius Secundus changed his name to Gaius Plinius Caecilius Secundus. He became *consul suffectus* in 100 and imperial legate to Bithynia in 112. His extant writings are 10 books of letters and a panegyric honoring Trajan. The 10th book of letters contains correspondence between Pliny and Trajan concerned mainly with administration in Bithynia. Two of the letters are of prime importance for church history. The first, in which Pliny asks Trajan for advice about treating those accused before him of being Christians, describes their beliefs and mores. The second contains Trajan's illogical response.

[M. J. SUELZER]

PLINY'S LETTER TO TRAJAN (*Ep*. 10.96) written from Bithynia when he was a *legatus Augusti* about A.D.111 and the Emperor's reply (*Ep*. 10.97) constitute the most complete and accurate account of the official pagan Roman attitude towards the Christians during the 1st cent. of their existence. After noting that he had never been present at the trials of Christians, Pliny asks if any consideration is to be given for age or repentance, and if Christianity as such or rather the crimes associated with it are the objects of repression. He then describes the procedure which he had followed in the case of Christians brought before him, including the torture of two Christian deaconesses. In conclusion he states that the severity he had employed has brought about a change of attitude in many and that more will amend their ways if given a chance to repent. His interrogation of the Christians brings out some interesting details with respect to their liturgical practices, i.e., the first non-Christian reference to the agape. In his reply Trajan approves Pliny's manner of acting and gives some practical norms that seem to have been largely followed during the 2d. cent.: Christians should not be sought out; if delated they should be given a chance to renounce their errors by offering sacrifice to the gods; no unsigned accusations should be accepted, for that would set a bad precedent and be quite out of accord with the spirit of his principate. BIBLIOGRAPHY: A. N. Sherwin-White, *Letters of Pliny: A Historical and Social Commentary* (1966) 691–712; B. H. Streeter, CAH 11:253–256.

[M. J. COSTELLOE]

PLOTINUS (204 or 205–269 or 270), Greek philosopher. Having studied in Alexandria with Ammonius Saccas, P. moved to Rome (244) and remained there as an influential teacher until the year before his death. At age 50 he started to write down his lecture-essays, which were collected by his student, Porphyry, arranged in six groups of nine (*Enneads*), and published with a prefatory *Life* (301–305). The founder of Neoplatonism, he reinterpreted the thought of Plato in an original system that organically included certain Aristotelian and Stoic traits. His work thus brought to culmination philosophical tendencies loosely designated as Middle Platonism. He conceived all modes of being and value as originating in an overflow or procession from a single ineffable power, the first hypostasis, which he identified with the One of the *Parmenides* or the Good of the *Republic*. Three descending grades of reality—world-mind (*nous*), world-soul (*psychē*), and nature (*physis*), a lower level of world-soul—are marked by diminishing unity and increasing individuation. *Nous*, the second hypostasis, resembles Aristotle's unmoved mover in its timeless self-thinking, and within it lie the Platonic Forms as differentiating forces; *psychē*, the third hypostasis, with its weaker unity creates time and space by its mental activity, but transcends its creation; *physis*, corresponding to the Stoic world-soul, projects the physical world as its dim consciousness of a now-distant perfection. Matter (*hylē*) exists only as a logical or ideal boundary of reality at its furthest remove from the source. Man contains within himself the potentialities of all these creative principles, and can choose in his life to make the ascent (*anagōgē*) from normal discursive reasoning to intuitive intelligence and even, with great effort, to moments of personal union (*henosis*) with the ultimate which lies beyond being, thought, and goodness. Every branch of philosophy except politics is treated by P., who attempted with strict symmetry to relate concepts of ethics and psychology to his view of the intelligible universe and of natural phenomena. Thus arises his notion of intelligible matter and thus his explanation of evil (to which he devoted several discussions) as the boundary or limiting cause of good. Rejecting Plato's denigration of art as mere imitation of natural objects, he described it as imposing a structure in accordance with archetypal Forms.

Despite attempts to derive P.'s thought from Oriental sources or relate it to Near Eastern religions, most scholars find nothing in his works that is not a natural development of purely Greek speculation, particularly of Platonism. He dealt systematically with the thorniest problems debated by his predecessors, the relation of transcendence to immanence, perfection to imperfection, fate to free will. His own rationality shows nothing of the mystification and theurgy practiced by his successors. BIBLIOGRAPHY: CHGMP 195–268 and bibliog.; S. MacKenna, *Plotinus: the Enneads* (4th ed. rev. B. S. Page, introd. P. Henry, 1969); J. N. Deek, *Nature, Contemplation, and the One: A Study in the Philosophy of Plotinus* (1967).

[Z. STEWART]

PLOWDEN, CHARLES (1743–1821), English Jesuit. A member of the Society from 1759, he was ordained at Rome in 1770. At Bruges, where he was teaching, he was briefly imprisoned in 1773 at the time of the suppression of the Jesuits. After his release he taught for a time at Liège with other former Jesuits, then in 1784 became chaplain to Thomas Weld at Lulworth Castle in Dorset. The two founded Stonyhurst College in 1790, and with the formal restoration of the Society in 1817 P. became rector of the college and provincial of the English Jesuits. He was a friend and correspondent of Bp. J. *Carroll, his colleague at Bruges. P. also published several polemical works.

[J. R. AHERNE]

PLOWDEN, EDMUND (1518–1585), English jurist. Regarded by contemporaries as one of the most gifted lawyers of his age, P. was a staunch and courageous Catholic who refused the position of lord chancellor offered him by Queen Elizabeth because the price was renunciation of the old faith. He studied at Cambridge and the Middle Temple (and probably also at Oxford) and was admitted to the bar in 1538. A contemporary historian asserts that he was also licensed to practice medicine by Oxford. P. served as a member of Parliament throughout the reign of Queen Mary and into the reign of Queen Elizabeth. His career as a lawyer brought him frequently into opposition with the government, and he was regarded with suspicion by the Privy Council; he was often defense counsel for prominent Catholics. No one dared, however, press serious charges against him though he was a known defender of the old religion. Among his unpublished MSS is a defense of the title of Mary Queen of Scots to the throne of England.

[J. R. AHERNE]

PLOWDEN, FRANCIS (1749–1829), English jurist, brother of Charles. He was enrolled in the Jesuit seminary in Bruges, but was released from first vows by the suppression of the Order in 1773 and returned to England. P. studied law at the Middle Temple and was awarded an honorary degree by Oxford on his publication of the work *Jura Anglorum*. He wrote extensively on legal and political matters, his best work being *An Historical Review of the State of Ireland* (1803). A libel action decided against him forced P. to flee to France to avoid paying a heavy fine; he died in exile.

[J. R. AHERNE]

PLUMMER, ALFRED (1841–1926), Anglican theologian, scripture scholar, and historian. Born near Gateshead in Durham, England, he studied at Oxford where he graduated in 1863; he was successively fellow of Trinity College (1865–75) and master of University College, Durham (1874–1902). Although ordained deacon in 1866, he never sought priesthood. He wrote commentaries on Scripture, studies in English church history, and a handbook on the Church of the early Fathers. He also translated many works of Ignaz von *Döllinger.

[J. A. WEISHEIPL]

PLUMMER, CHARLES (1851–1927), deacon in the C of E, fellow and chaplain of Corpus Christi College, Oxford, Celtic scholar. He edited Bede's *Ecclesiastical History* (2 v., 1896), wrote the *Life and Times of Alfred the Great* (1902), and edited Latin and vernacular lives of the Irish saints. BIBLIOGRAPHY: R. T. Meyer, NCE 11:445.

[R. T. MEYER]

PLUMPE, JOSEPH CONRAD (1901–57), editor, patristic scholar. A native of Ohio ordained in 1908, P. did classical studies in Germany at Münster and Berlin. He taught classics at the Josephinum in Ohio from 1932 to 1941, and ecclesiastical Latin and NT Greek at The Catholic Univ. of America (1954–57). P. was with Quasten first editor of the *Ancient Christian Writers* series. His chief individual work was *Mater ecclesia: An Inquiry into the Concept of the Church as Mother in Early Christianity* (1943).

[J. R. AHERNE]

PLUNKET, OLIVER, ST. (1625–1681), primate of Ireland, martyr. He studied for the priesthood at the Irish College in Rome and was ordained in 1654. For 15 years he acted as the agent of the Irish bps. in Rome. In 1669 he was named abp. of Armagh and primate of Ireland. In the brief years of religious peace in Ireland he demonstrated great energy in the pastoral care of his long-neglected people. A new persecution of Catholics broke out in 1673. P. was obliged to hide in woods and thatched huts but still circulated widely to attend his scattered flock. He was arrested by the British representative in Ireland and his trial in Dublin was such a farce that the proceedings were transferred to London. The infamous trial with its perjured witnesses and openly hostile Chief Justice Pemberton has long been branded a mockery. P. was accused of planning an invasion of England and conspiring in the "Popish Plot." Condemned to death, he was the last martyr of Tyburn. Immediately after his death Lord Shaftesbury and Titus Oates, who had invented the Catholic Conspiracy, were arrested and imprisoned. In 1886 P. was among those approved by Leo XIII for beatification; he was canonized in 1975. BIBLIOGRAPHY: A. Curtayne, *Trial of Oliver Plunket* (1953); Butler 3:73–77; N. Del Re, BiblSanct 10 :971–974.

[J. R. AHERNE]

PLUNKETT, CHRISTOPHER (d. 1649), Irish rebel. A member of the Irish parliament and Earl of Fingall, P. was a noble of the Pale, the English establishment in Ireland. In the Ulster rebellion of 1641 he assumed a position of neutrality, but his conduct aroused the suspicion of the government and he was declared an outlaw. He joined the northern uprising and was taken prisoner at the battle of Rathmines where he died shortly afterwards under sentence of high treason.

[J. R. AHERNE]

PLUNKETT, JOSEPH MARY (1887–1916), Irish poet and patriot. Descendant of the famous Catholic branch of Plunketts, one of whom was St. *Oliver Plunket, P. was a frail, scholarly man with the same combination of poetic bent and fierce patriotism as his teacher, T. *MacDonough. His small literary output is deeply religious and sometimes mystical. Only one book, *The Circle and the Sword*, was published in his lifetime (1911). P. was editor of the *Irish Review* and associated with the Irish Theater. Joining the

Irish Volunteers in 1913 he became a member of the Executive. He joined *Pearce and MacDonough in the Easter Rebellion and was executed with them.

[J. R. AHERNE]

PLURALISM (religious), existence of several religious groups in one society on a relatively equal basis. The term is frequently used to characterize the current situation in the U.S. where Jews, Catholics, numerous Protestant and Orthodox Churches, and several other religious bodies maintain distinctive patterns of life with no one able to dominate the culture. Pluralism is distinguished from societies where one religion is given a dominant position by the State, or where one religious group is able to dominate through its possession of a numerical majority or in some other way. It is also distinguished from a homogenous secular culture. Pluralism has been achieved only recently in American life. Prior to the Revolution several colonies had established Protestant Churches, and Protestant influence generally prevailed until recent years. Prohibition was primarily a Protestant standard enforced on the total population, and the desire of some Protestants to keep the nation's highest office in Protestant hands was maintained until 1961. The growing strength of the Catholic and Jewish communities, together with secular forces reducing the influence of religion generally, has forced American society to acknowledge the right of all groups to play a more equal role. It is now widely held that such a development is not only a practical necessity and demanded by the American commitment to religious freedom, but also the way to a more desirable society because of the richness provided by each group's making its distinctive contribution.

Latterly much has been heard from some liberal theologians of a religious pluralism, not only within the same civil community or cultural society, but within the RC Church itself. In a sense, of course, various kinds of pluralism are not new phenomena in the Church, for a considerable variety of life-style, convention, devotional and liturgical practice, art-forms, theological opinion, canonical observances, and the like has coexisted with the unity of faith among Catholics with no apparent detriment to their unity of faith. The guiding rule has been the Augustinian dictum: in necessary matters, unity; in matters left to choice, liberty; in all things, charity. The Church has never demanded monolithic uniformity in everything. If a really new type of pluralism is called for, this seems to involve an allegedly permissible diversity in what has heretofore been regarded as necessary to the unity of faith itself, and the freedom to deny or question its defined dogmas. *PLURALISM, THEOLOGICAL.

[T. EARLY; P. K. MEAGHER]

PLURALISM, THEOLOGICAL, the development of theology according to diverse conceptual systems and categories. There is an obvious theological pluralism among the Churches. The term has, however, special, historical force as it refers to theological diversity within the RC Church esp. since Vatican Council II. There has never in fact been a monolithic system of RC theology. There was no single medieval or scholastic theology (see SCHOLASTICISM: THOMISM) or a single Tridentine theology or one Neo-Scholastic theology. There was, however, in the late 19th and early 20th cent., following on Leo XIII's *Aeterni Patris* (1879), its further implementation by Pius X, and the legislation of the CIC (1917) an official endorsement, even a prescription, that seminary professors treat both philosophy and theology in conformity with the view, the doctrine, and the principles of St. Thomas Aquinas (CIC, c. 1366.2). That gave to theology courses and texts a certain similarity of approach, order, and terminology. That also created the general impression to outsiders that RC theology was identical with "Thomism" or Thomistic theology; the impression was enforced by the frequent papal citation of Aquinas in encyclicals. The similarity was in fact verbal at most; the impression taken was mistaken. Conformity to Aquinas was officially and frequently given a broad interpretation. There was a spectrum of schools and conceptual differences among courses and texts. There was little similarity between the theological manuals, invariably subtitled as *ad mentem D. Thomae,* and the genuine spirit, theological viewpoint, or gospel inspiration of the *Summa theologiae.* So little were these qualities perceived that the *Summa*'s champions could glory in and its attackers be revolted by its "rigid rationalism." Vatican Council II's reendorsement of St. Thomas Aquinas (Vat II PriestForm 16), against the background of the debates preceding it, has been taken as a *pro forma* tip of the mitre that in fact has liberated and liberalized theological studies. Theological pluralism does have one point of near unanimity: anti-Thomism (whatever Thomism may mean to its quondam exponents). Positively, the conciliar document cited pointed to three resources for the development of theological inquiry and study: biblical, patristic, philosophical. The Bible and its study can provide theology with categories of thought in the meaning that they had in a Judaic and early-Christian cultural context; through biblical categories a de-Hellenized theology can be developed. The Bible as the presentation of the mystery and history of salvation, therefore centrally of Christ, can found a Christocentric and soteriological order and viewpoint for theology that can be further enriched and itself enrich the liturgical celebration of the mysteries of salvation. The patristic resource particularly stressed by the Council is the Fathers—the theology founded on their writings—of the Eastern Church. This resource can foster a theology that is de-Westernized, more ecumenical, employing categories of greater mystical and symbolic meaning; this is a particular enrichment for the theology of grace. The philosophic resource pointed out is particularly contemporary philosophy, or better, contemporary philosophies. These can found a theology that is descholasticized and deessentialized; contemporary philosophies make possible theologies that express and develop the mysteries of faith in categories consistent with contemporary cultures and personalist views of man and his world. The most significant of the philosophies various RC theologians appropriate are existentialism, phenomenology, and process philosophy (see PROCESS THEOLOGY). The contemporary diversity within RC theology is not one of "schools" as formerly; rather it is a diversity explained by an emphasis on one of the resources indicated or on a combination of them, and the diversity is almost as varied as the number of theologians or theology texts. Theological pluralism is grounded on and justified by a simple consideration: theology is concerned with divine truths, the subject matter of revelation itself; there is no single conceptual system that gives exclusive or adequate expression to the divine mysteries; thus diverse conceptualizations can be complementary, each making up for the inadequacies of the others. There are, however, also two limitations on this diversity. Theology is a *sacra doctrina* which has its right to exist, as well as its reason for existing, because it is in continuity with divine revelation, and divine revelation is the authentication of its message as true. Any Catholic theology must respect that; a legitimate pluralism cannot mean relativism. Further, even as is the case with the divine truths it considers, theology exists in continuity with the understanding of the historical believing community; theological pluralism cannot mean a chosen amnesia towards that understanding of the teachings of faith. Such limitations seem obvious; they raise the question of whether the much maligned Pius XII was altogether wrong in declaring that not every philosophical truth changes from day to day; that not every philosophical system is compatible with Catholic dogma (*Humani generis,* 1950).

[T. C. O'BRIEN]

PLUS, RAOUL (1882–1958), French Jesuit, author of widely read works on the spiritual life. He was a Jesuit from 1899, a chaplain during World War I, and afterwards taught at the Université Catholique, Lille. Among his translated works are: *God within Us* (1924); *Ideal of Reparation* (1922); *Mary in Our Soul Life* (1940). Central in his teaching is the theme of union with Christ in the mystical body.

[T. C. O'BRIEN]

PLUTARCH OF ATHENS (*c.*350–433), Neoplatonic philosopher. He was the teacher of *Syrianus and *Proclus and the first member of the Platonic Academy at Athens to reflect directly the influence of Plotinus. According to Proclus, he maintained that the first five hypotheses of Plato's *Parmenides* could be considered expositions of the five Plotinian hypostases (One, Intellect, Soul, Sensation, and Matter). He regarded Aristotle's active intellect only as a part of the soul, and divine, but not God. BIBLIOGRAPHY: P. Merlan, LexAW 2384; CHGMP 302–303.

[M. R. P. MCGUIRE]

PLUTARCH OF CHAERONEA (*c.*46–after 120 A.D.), Middle Platonist, biographer, and encyclopedic writer, esp. well known through his biographies of Greek and Roman soldiers and statesmen, usually arranged in pairs. While he follows pretty much the Peripatetic scheme of biography, he is primarily concerned with furnishing examples of political and moral virtues. Owing to the nature of the sources available to him, his biographies vary much in respect to historical value. P. however, is much more important for the wealth of information which he contains on many aspects of antiquity and in particular for his philosophical and religious ideas. Under the traditional title of *Moralia,* we have extant some 80 works of an ethical, religious, physical, political, and literary character, presented in the form of dialogues or diatribes. P. reveals himself to be a typical Middle Platonist in his eclecticism. He combines Platonic teaching with elements borrowed from Aristotelianism, Middle Stoicism, and Neopythagoreanism, and he exhibits a marked admiration for Oriental (Egyptian) wisdom and mysticism. In striving to attain a purer conception of God, he had to face the problem of evil in the world. His solution was to absolve God of authorship of evil, and to make the World-Soul the divinized principle of evil. A dualism was thus established between the good God and the evil World-Soul. Perhaps influenced by Xenocrates and Poseidonius, he maintains the existence of astral divinities and a whole series of good and bad *daimones* as connecting links between God and man. The good "demons" are the instruments of Providence, while the evil "demons," being affected for the worse by the evil of the lower world, are harmful to man and are worshiped by barbarous and obscene rites. He reflects the tendency towards religious syncretism common in his age in declaring that all peoples worship the same God under different names and by his wide use of allegory to explain religious beliefs and practices. In his *De Iside et Osiride,* for example, he interprets Osiris as the good principle, Tryphon as the evil principle, and Isis as matter, but a matter naturally disposed to love the Good. In his psychology, he teaches that the *nous* is superior to the *psychē.* He believes in immortality and a happy existence for the soul in the other world. In his ethics he combines Aristotelian and Stoic doctrines. He is definitely Stoic in permitting suicide. BIBLIOGRAPHY: F. W. Walbank, OCD 706–707; P. Merlan, LexAW 2381–84; CHGMP 56–64; Copleston 1:452–455.

[M. R. P. MCGUIRE]

PLUVIAL, from Lat. *pluvia,* rain, another name for the *cope, the origin of which derives from the Roman rain covering.

PLYMOUTH BRETHREN, a religious body, begun in England and Ireland in the 19th cent., that seeks to imitate the simple Christianity of the apostolic age. The first members called themselves simply Brethren, Christians, or Saints; they were also popularly called *Darbyites (see DARBY, JOHN NELSON); the present name, not an officially adopted title, was given because the largest early center was in Plymouth, England. Dissatisfied both with the formalism of the C of E and with divisions among *Nonconformists, early members joined together in small groups, united in prayer and in the expectation of Christ's second coming as well as in separation from all non-Brethren. Small assemblies of Brethren were founded in many countries of Europe, in North America, Australia, and New Zealand; they have never had any formal ecclesiastical organization, church buildings, or international unifying agency. In doctrine the Plymouth Brethren adhere to *fundamentalism and *premillenarianism, and in general to the contents of the Apostles' Creed, although rejecting any creedal formula. Their doctrine of salvation is strictly Calvinistic; true believers have *assurance of salvation. The charismatic ministry enjoyed by all believers does away with the need of ordained or salaried ministers. Worship, conducted in a home or small hall, is austere, with the Sunday celebration of the Lord's Supper central; during the week prayer meetings and Bible study are also conducted. Against the division of Christians into sects or denominations, they interpret the Church as the visible congregation of all true believers. This doctrine, however, has been the main source of the many divisions among the Brethren. In 1848 the question of whether to associate with other Christians resulted in the split between Exclusive Brethren and Open Brethren. In the U. S. there are eight distinct divisions, which, because they do not use denominational names, are simply designated by the Roman numerals I through VIII. These groups differ mainly on the points of exclusiveness vs. openness, minor doctrinal emphases, or polity. The eight branches in 1971 numbered about 63,268 members in 682 congregations; Plymouth II was the largest, with a membership of 15,000 BIBLIOGRAPHY: Mayer RB 394–396, bibliog.

PNEUMATICS (Gk. *pneuma,* spirit), the study or doctrine of spirits. The term is used particularly for the branch of theology dealing with the Holy Spirit, but also considers spiritual beings such as angels. The study is also known as pneumatology and was considered a separate branch of philosophy in the 17th cent., dealing with the natural knowledge of God, angels, and the human soul.

[T. EARLY]

PNEUMATOMACHIANS (From the Gr. for "fighting against the Spirit"), a 4th-cent. sect that denied the divinity of the Holy Spirit. They were also called Macedonians, because the origin of their doctrine was wrongly attributed to Macedonius, bp. of Constantinople. They affirmed that the Holy Spirit is never represented in Scripture acting as a divine person. Some supposed that he was a being intermediate between God and creatures, not consubsantial with the Son but "like him in substance." The sect was condemned at the First Council of Constantinople (381).

[P. FOSCOLOS]

POAU, see PROTESTANTS AND OTHER AMERICANS UNITED FOR SEPARATION OF CHURCH AND STATE.

POBEDONOSTSEV, KONSTANTIN PETROVICH (1827–1907), Russian civil servant, jurist, and political philosopher. He received his legal training at St. Petersburg, entering civil service in 1846, serving as tutor to the children of Tsar Alexander II, advisor to Tsars Alexander III and Nicholas II, senator (1868), member of the Council of State (1872) and lay head of the *Holy Synod (1880). Known as the "Grand Inquisitor," P. proposed a reactionary political philosophy, dedicated to expunging Western influences in Russian life; he became the advocate of repressive measures in matters concerning minority groups and peoples, religion, censorship, and education. P.'s essays, *Moskovskii sbornik* (1896), demonstrate his dedicated opposition to religious liberty, public education, trial by jury, constitutional government, and freedom of expression.

[R. J. LITZ]

PODATUS, see PES.

PODEBRAD, GEORGE OF, see GEORGE OF PODEBRAD.

PODECHARD, EMMANUEL (1866–1951), OT scholar. P. taught Scripture at the seminary and Faculté Catholique in Lyons from 1892 until retirement. His main scholarly achievement was his commentary on the Psalms, published in two parts in 1949 and posthumously in 1954.

[T. M. MCFADDEN]

PODIUM (platform), a portable platform on which the pope is carried in processions of the Blessed Sacrament. It includes a faldstool where he sits or kneels before the monstrance.

[J. R. AHERNE]

POEPPELMANN, MATTHAEUS DANIEL (1662–1736), German Baroque architect, responsible for the rebuilding of Dresden under Augustus the Strong. His buildings are imaginatively ornamented in the rococo manner, but their basic forms are disposed in a sumptuous, heavy magnificence characteristic of German Baroque sensibility. P. is most famous for very ornate Zwinger Palace in Dresden (1711). BIBLIOGRAPHY: B. Doering, *Matthes Daniel Poeppelmann* (1930).

[P. P. FEHL]

POETA SAXO (fl. last quarter of the 9th cent.), a medieval Latin poet and monk of Corvey known only under the name, "the Saxon poet." About 888, he composed an historical poem on Charlemagne. Books 1–4 are entitled *Annales de gestis Caroli magni imperatoris* and book 5, *De vita et obitu eiusdem.* The work is based essentially on the *Annales Einharti,* Einhard's *Life of Charlemagne,* and similar earlier sources. His prosody is fairly correct, but his poetry is mediocre. BIBLIOGRAPHY: M. R. P. McGuire, NCE 11:455; Raby SLP 1:260; Manitius 1:583–584.

[M. R. P. MCGUIRE]

POETRY OF THE OLD TESTAMENT. The English term poetry derives from the Greek *poiēsis,* meaning something made [in a special way]. That this applies to Hebrew poetry may be shown from Ps 45.2 where the writer speaks of *ma'asai,* my work or composition. Poetry attempts to follow artistic patterns. As far as Hebrew poetry is concerned Sir 44.5 shows that there were certain rules and norms, and the poetic sections of the Bible bear out this fact, even though the writers, allowing for editing, came from different ages and background. They used a large number of special terms and ancient word forms, often rendering their composition most difficult for later translators. Even when one has allowed for such factors as variant Hebrew MSS (from which translations were made), improper vocalization by the Masoretes, and a faulty division of the "continual script" into individual words, the fact remains that Hebrew poetry is obscure in itself and often baffled translators, even the most ancient.

The most obvious feature of Hebrew poetry is its parallelism, the two or even threefold repetition of the same basic idea in successive lines. This feature was known to the poetry of Assyria, Egypt, and Phoenicia-Ugarit, but was not brought to the perfection found in the OT. Each line of poetry is called a *stich* or a *colon,* and poetic units may involve two lines (distich), three lines (tristich), but seldom more than this. Hebrew poetry involves many stylistic differences in the use of parallels. Thus we may find synonymous parallels, in which the second line simply repeats over in different terms what was said in the first line, e.g., Ps 2.4: "He who sits in the heavens will laugh / Adonai will deride them." This is by far the most frequent type of parallel structure and, as can readily be seen, an obscure word in one stich may be cleared up by a well known word in the other stich of the synonymous distich. The antithetic parallel presents a contrast in the second stich to what was stated in the first stich. Thus Ps 1.6: "For Yahweh knows the path of the righteous/but the path of the wicked fails." Synthetic parallel structure is characterized by one, two or three stichs that complete, bring out, or clarify what was said in the first stich. There are many varieties of such parallels. Psalm 1.1 offers an example: "O the blessings of the man who has not followed the counsel of the wicked / who has not stood in the path that sinners follow / nor sat in the chair of scoffers." These forms take on many variations and there can often be valid doubt as to how a parallel structure should be classified. The climactic or stepladder type of parallel is highly effective in bringing out a point. In Am 1.3,6,9,13 the first three deeds are not mentioned. Only the fourth and most abominable deed of each nation is brought out. This form may however be used in a fuller form, as in Prov 30.18–20. It is important to realize that these categories often overlap.

In Hebrew poetry, unlike that to which many moderns are accustomed, rhyme and assonance have almost no part to play. Whatever small resemblance might be found usually has to do with noun suffixes (e.g., Ps 2.3); or with clever alliterations (Is 5.2), in the Hebrew text, of course. Rhythmic and metric structure of Hebrew poetry is a most difficult matter, but the singing of parts of OT poetry to musical accompaniment is already an indication that there was such a structure. The meter was even marked in some Akkadian texts. However, the fact that Hebrew texts are at times corrupt, improperly vocalized by the Masoretes, and the primitive pronunciation uncertain, have all contributed to the difficulty in working out a viable metric structure. Certainly in this matter the word-accent and the number of syllables serve as a good starting point. This yields various combinations, e.g., each stich of a distich may have three accents or stresses. However the various systems that have been advanced by scholars have met with only limited acceptance and still present enormous problems.

Hebrew poetry is often collective in nature, even when an individual seems to be speaking. This has even been suggested by Reventlow for the so-called confessions of Jeremiah (11.18–12.6; 15.10–21; 17.12–18; 18.18–23; 20.7–18), though his suggestion may be incorrect.

The poetry of the OT was adapted to many usages. Among them are: allegories (e.g., Ezek 19.2–4); parables (e.g., 2 Sam 12.1–4); oracles of various kinds (e.g. Gen 25.23; Ps 2.7–12; Num 23–24 *passim*); many types of song, including the Song of Songs, most of the Psalms, songs of sorrow (Lam); didactic usages (e.g., Proverbs, Qoheleth, and Job); riddles (e.g., Jg 14.12–18); and summations of sacred history (e.g., Ps 105), to mention only some forms.

Poetry in the OT abounds, constituting altogether about one half of the entire Hebrew Bible. The differences between poetry and the higher types of prose are not so pronounced in the Hebrew OT, and it is probable that many could speak in poetic forms on more solemn occasions. BIBLIOGRAPHY: S. Gevirtz, *Patterns in the Early Poetry of Israel* (1963); S. C. Yoder, *Poetry of the Old Testament (pa. 1949).*

[I. HUNT]

POGGIO BRACCIOLINI, GIOVANNI FRANCESCO (1380–1459), Italian humanist. Born near Arezzo, P. later moved to Florence, where he studied Latin under Giovanni da Ravenna and became proficient in Latin epistolography. He entered the service of the papal chancery under Pope Boniface IX in 1404. In this capacity, he was able to rediscover the works of many Latin authors, a task with which his name will always be associated. Most of these treasures were found in the monastic libraries. An author himself, P. is best known for his *Letters* and *Liber facetiarum,* collections of humorous, satirical tales often directed at the clergy, although he himself, a father of 14 illegitimate children, was no model of virtue. He also wrote a *History of Florence,* which is useful but distorted.

[D. G. NUGENT]

POHL, ALFRED (1890–1961), Jesuit Orientalist and editor. P. was professor of Assyriology and ancient Oriental history at the Pontifical *Biblical Institute and, in 1945, dean of the Oriental faculty there. He published original editions of several Babylonian and Sumerian economic texts, and was eminently successful as editor of *Orientalia* and *Analecta Orientalia*. He contributed toward a Sumerian lexicon, and founded the *Keilschriftbibliographie,* an annual bibliography of Mesopotamian studies. BIBLIOGRAPHY: S. Moscati, *Orientalia* 31 (1962) 1–6.

[T. M. MCFADDEN]

POHLE, JOSEPH (1852–1922), German professor of apologetics at The Catholic Univ. of America, 1889–94. He was professor of philosophy at Fulda when invited to the United States. He became involved on the side of the German-American Catholics in the dispute over their right to have national parishes and their own schools (see CAHENSLY, P.). He returned to Germany in 1894 to teach dogmatics at Münster, then, from 1897, at Breslau. He published *Lehrbuch der Dogmatik* (1902–05), as well as other scholarly works, and was a major contributor to the *Catholic Encyclopedia*.

[T. C. O'BRIEN]

POIDEBARD, ANTOINE (1878–1955), Jesuit archeologist. P. served as a missionary in Armenia, organized relief services for Armenian refugees in 1924, and was commissioned in the French air force reserve (1925). He pioneered the now accepted use of aerial photography for archeological research. This method enabled him to publish several important studies on the history of Upper Syria, an undiscovered Mediterranean seaport, and Port Said.

[T. M. MCFADDEN]

POIMANDRES, the semi-divine being that figures in the first of the 18 treatises that make up the *Corpus Hermeticum*. His name is sometimes given to the entire corpus. It is only in the first and most ancient treatise, however, that P. plays the mediating role which in the others is performed by Hermes Trismegistus (thrice-great). Egypt was the country of origin of the so-called Hermetic literature, and when the themes were taken up by the greater Hellenistic world, the Greek god Hermes replaced the Egyptian Thoth, god of writing, of learning, and of occult knowledge. Hermes was sometimes represented as a shepherd and the Greek word Poimandres could easily be taken as a clipped form of phrase meaning "shepherd of men"; but is also remarkably close to the Coptic p-eime-n-rē (meaning "the knowledge of the Sun-god") and may therefore be an earlier attempt to translate the emerging Gnostic motifs into Greek. At any rate, all the essential elements of the later Gnosis are present in the treatise on Poimandres: the fall of the human soul into the world of matter because of a fault committed in the higher realm; the possibility of a return to the higher realm by means of illumination; salvation through understanding,

esp. self-understanding. *Poimandres* may have influenced the Christian Gnosticism of Valentinian; it has similarities with the central theme of the fourth Gospel. BIBLIOGRAPHY: H. Schwabl, LTK 5:257–258; G. W. MacRae, NCE 6:1076–77; F. M. Braun, "Jean le théologien et son évangile dans l'église ancienne," *Études bibliques* (1959) 122–130.

[E. J. DILLON]

POINCARÉ, RAYMOND (1860–1934), French premier (1912–13, 1922–24, 1926–29) and president (1913–20) who sought to strengthen France by fostering alliances with Russia and England and by advocating military preparedness. Although a believer in individual religious liberty, P. denied any special rights to religious bodies, claiming that state sovereignty was without rival. He approved the complete separation of Church and State, but despite his anticlerical bias, favored reopening of diplomatic relations with the Vatican and a *détente* in Church-State relations. Works: *Memoirs of Raymond Poincaré* (tr. G. Arthur, 4 v. 1926, repr. 1975). BIBLIOGRAPHY: S. Huddleston, *Poincaré* (1924); G. Wright, *Poincaré and the French Presidency* (1942); J. Chastenet, *Raymond Poincaré* (1948).

[J. P. REID]

POIRET, PIERRE (1646–1719), French Protestant writer on mysticism. A spiritual crisis in 1674, while he was pastor for the French settled in the Palatinate, brought P. to distrust philosophical reasoning and to equate Christianity with mysticism. He lived in Amsterdam with Anne *Bourignon from 1676 until her death in 1680. His *L'Économie divine* (7 v., 1687) presented her ideas; he also edited her writings (19 v., 1679–84). Through his biographies and editions of Mme. Guyon, J. Olier, P. Bérulle and other earlier writers, P. influenced Gottfried Arnold and Gerhard Tersteegen, and through them, German *Pietism. His masterwork was *Bibliotheca mysticorum selecta* (1708), an extensive collection of authors on mysticism. BIBLIOGRAPHY: Knox Enth 352, 355, 390, 398.

POISSY, CONFERENCE OF (Disputatio Pussicena), a meeting held in 1561 at Poissy near Paris, between French RC bps. and representatives of French Calvinists. Among the latter were T. *Beza and *Peter Martyr Vermigli. The Conference was summoned by the regent, Queen Catherine de Médicis, in the hope of achieving religious peace. With little communication between the two sides, the meeting had no real success.

POITEVIN STYLE, distinctive style of French Romanesque churches of Poitou, their façades flanked by clustered piers surmounted by cone-shaped helmets or pinnacles covered by overlapping stone scale patterns, and surpassingly rich in carving, their "sculptured screens" teeming with monumental, disarming, crude and fantastic figures, and Oriental designs in incredible variety (Notre-Dame-la-

Grande). The crossing tower may echo the conical pinnacles of the façade but frequently is low and square. A single, broad gable roof on the hall church spans the nave and side aisles, eliminating the clerestory and rendering the interior dark. Handsome frescoes often decorated the apses and vaults of the nave. The finest surviving cycle of Romanesque wall painting is that of the nave vault at St. Savin-sur-Gartempe (early 12th cent.)—intensely dramatic and expressive.

[M. J. DALY]

POITIER DE COURCY, HENRI, see DE COURCY, HENRY.

POITIERS, NOTRE-DAME-LA-GRANDE, French church from the early 12th cent., finest example of *Poitevin Romanesque, though small, called "la Grande" to distinguish it from other churches of Our Lady. It boasts a sculptured façade of overwhelming richness: a frieze of Adam and Eve, the Prophets, Tree of Jesse, and scenes from the life of Christ, surmounted by Apostles about a central window. An almond-shaped aureole niche frames the figure of Christ with Evangelists. Portal carving in Poitevin style cuts each voussoir individually, alternating a Roman soldier and a child to illustrate the massacre of the Holy Innocents. The exterior shows the Poitevin cone-shaped turrets covered with overlapping "fish-scale" design. The simple gable roof—spanning nave and groined-vaulted side aisles—carries a handsome crossing (bell) tower. There are three apsidal chapels, important 12th-cent. frescoes of Christ and the Virgin (both in majesty), and a crypt with frescoes antedating those in the upper church.
BIBLIOGRAPHY: Y. Labande-Mailfert, *Poitou roman* (1957); K. J. Conant, *Carolingian and Romanesque Architecture, 800–1200* (1959).

[M. J. DALY]

POLAND, people's republic in E central Europe, bounded on the N by the Baltic Sea and the Soviet Union, on the E by the Soviet Union, on the S by Czechoslovakia, and on the W by East Germany (present area, 120,633 square miles; pop. cen. 1970 32,589,000). Although the people are principally Latin rite Catholics, Eastern rites, Orthodox and Catholic, are represented by a significant number of adherents.

Latin rite. Poland was evangelized chiefly from the West. In 966 Mieszko I (d. 992) ruler of Poznań (Posen) was baptized and this opened the way to missionaries from Germany and Bohemia. A missionary bp. operated from Poznań from 668, and in 1000, when Gniezno was made an archbishopric, Poland became independent of the German hierarchy. It took more than 2 centuries of missionary effort to establish the faith generally throughout the land. By the close of the 13th cent. Poland had a numerous clergy, flourishing religious houses, and excellent schools serving the development of its culture. Under King Casimir III (d.

1370) Galicia (Halicz) and Volhynia were incorporated into Poland, bringing with them substantial numbers of Orthodox believers. The Galician metropolitanate was restored and the Armenian bp. of Lvov was recognized. For many years the Orthodox and Latin Churches existed side by side, not without occasional tensions, but on the whole as peaceably as could be expected. The Union of Brest-Litovsk put the Ruthenian Orthodox into communion with the Holy See, but they retained their Slavic liturgy. Churches of the Armenian rite were also united to Rome (see below).

The Reformation made some headway in Poland during the 16th cent., but the Counter Reformation, working with strong papal and royal support, and the need for national unity against the threat of attack from without overcame the drift toward Protestantism, but not without the use of repressive measures. These gave the King of Prussia cause to see himself as the champion and protector of the Protestant minority in Poland. On the other side the Russians assumed a similar attitude toward the Polish Orthodox when antagonism grew up between them and adherents of the Union.

In the 17th and 18th cent. the Polish government weakened, a situation to which defeats suffered at the hands of Tatars, Turks, Swedes, and Russians contributed. Three partitions of Polish territory (1772, 1793, 1795) wiped Poland from the map, most of the country going to Russia, with smaller shares to Prussia and Austria. Under Russian control Catholics suffered persecution, although this fell more heavily on Ruthenian than upon Latin Catholics. There was much confiscation of church property and the clergy were subjected to many restraints. Catholics under German rule fared better, although the government's policy of promoting German culture and institutions led to conflict and some repression. The Catholics under Austrian rule were least affected, although there was some tension in the early 19th cent. in consequence of the government's Josephinist policies.

With the establishment of Polish independence in 1918 began a period of religious peace in which the Catholic Church made great progress. The clergy, diocesan and religious, increased in number, new dioceses and parishes were founded, and the spiritual, educational, and charitable works of the Church were multiplied. This interval of peaceful development ended with the Nazi invasion in 1939, as a result of which substantial portions of the country were incorporated into Germany, a strip to the E was taken over by the Russians, and the remainder, organized under the administration of the puppet Government General, was used by the Nazis as a labor pool. Everywhere the Church became an object of merciless persecution. When the Nazis were driven out by the advancing Russians in 1944, the Polish Committee for National Liberation held out the promise of freedom of conscience and respect for the rights of the Church, but the Communist-controlled government restricted the freedom of Catholics, dissolved Catholic associations, expropriated church property, and imposed censorship on Catholic publications. In the years 1952–55 the conflict was at its height, but with the coming of W. Gomułka to power in 1956 there was a relaxation of some of the tensions, and despite the many obstacles still put in the way of its work, the Church has made remarkable gains.

Eastern rites. In the E portion of Poland there is a large minority of White Russians and Ukrainians of the Byzantine-Slavonic rite, both Orthodox and Catholic. The Catholics among these people are descendants of forebears who resumed communion with the Latin Church at the time of the Union of Brest-Litovsk in 1596. At that time, the metropolitan of Kiev, Michael Ragosa, together with the bps. of Vladimir, Lutsk, Polotsk, Vitebsk, and Chelm adhered to the Union, which meant that all the West Russian lands forming part of the Duchy of Lithuania in the Polish Kingdom came into communion with the Roman See. The union was resisted by Constantine (George) of Ostrog and the bps. of Lvov and Przemysl, together with the lay brotherhoods of those and other West Russian cities. With the partitions of Poland, all the above-mentioned eparchies passed under the rule of Moscow, a regime, whether political or ecclesiastical, their forefathers had never known. This aggregation of Byzantine-Slavonic rite Catholics to the Moscow patriarchate was accomplished by two major persecutions, one under Catherine II, the other in 1831. When freedom of conscience was allowed in Russia after 1905, some 200,000 White Russians returned to the Catholic Church, adopting the Latin rite, since the Byzantine-Slavonic rite was still unlawful in Russia.

The Polish Orthodox faithful at present number about 500,000. Their vernacular is Polish, but they employ church Slavonic in the liturgy. They are grouped into four dioceses under the metropolitan of Warsaw and all Poland. The suffragan bps. are at Bialystok, Lodz, and Wroclaw.

In the past, all the eparchies of the present Polish Orthodox Church were under the jurisdiction of the Moscow patriarchate, or the Holy Governing Synod. When Poland was reconstituted as a republic after World War I, those eparchies falling within its boundaries withdrew from their Russian ecclesiastical alignment and sought to place themselves under the ecumenical patriarchate with the status of an autocephalous Church. The ecumenical patriarchate granted the request and the Polish Church has retained its autocephalous status ever since. In 1949, after the Red Army had occupied Poland, the Ukrainian Catholic Church of Galicia was liquidated, becoming a part of the metropolitan province of Kiev under the Moscow patriarchate. Patriarch Alexi reconfirmed the autocephalous status of the Polish Church, however, and he rewarded Markary Osaniuk with the see of Warsaw for his work in the liquidation of the Galician Catholic Church.

The Orthodox Church of *Poland is divided into about 200 parishes in its four eparchies; these are served by about approximately the same number of priests. A monastery for men is located in the Biala Podlaska region and one for women in Grabarka in the Siemiatycze district. There are

faculties of Orthodox theology at the Christian Theological Academy of Kielce and at the seminary in Warsaw, both of which are reported to have several scores of students. A periodical, *The Church Messenger,* is published in Russian, Ukrainian, and Lemkovian (a West Slavic dialect).

In 1969 the bps. issued a list of grievances against the government (restricted freedom to conduct pastoral work, censorship of Catholic newspapers, etc.) which led toward improvement in Church-State relations. A pastoral letter, urging resistance to the official atheism imposed by the government was issued in 1973.

[A. WALKER]

POLDING, JOHN BEDE (1794–1877), English-born Benedictine, first bp. of Australia. Joining the order (1811), ordained (1819), he served as a tutor at St. Gregory College, Downside, England. Consecrated vicar apostolic of New Holland and Australia (1834), he arrived at Sydney the following year. At Rome he was named metropolitan of Australia and abp. of Sydney in 1842. His efforts encouraged the growth and organization of the Church in Australia, and improved Catholic education including the establishment of St. John's College at the Univ. of Sydney.

[R. J. LITZ]

POLE, MARGARET, BL. (1473–1541), martyr. Of royal blood, daughter of the Duke of Clarence, Countess of Salisbury and mother of Card. Reginald Pole, P. was a member of the court of Henry VIII and governess for Princess (later Queen) Mary. Because of Reginald Pole's attack on Henry's divorce and assumption of authority as head of the English Church P. was imprisoned in the Tower on legal pretext in 1539 and was beheaded 2 years later. She was beatified in 1886.

[J. R. AHERNE]

POLE, REGINALD (1500–58), cardinal and last abp. of Canterbury in communion with Rome. His father was related to the Tudors by marriage; his mother was daughter of George, Duke of Clarence. The cousinship of his family to the ruling house was later to prompt Henry VIII to try to exterminate it: his brother Lord Montague, and his mother, Bl. Margaret, Countess of Salisbury, were in fact beheaded, and he himself, though out of the realm, was scarcely safe from bravoes hired by the royal spleen to kill him. Yet at first all went well, and it was by Henry's munificence that Pole went from Magdalen, Oxford, to continue his studies, mostly at Padua, where he became a member of the reforming circle of devout humanists largely responsible for the Council of Trent. His work *Pro ecclesiasticae unitatis defensione,* which attacked the royal supremacy, completed the breach with Henry. Created cardinal by Paul III in the same year (1536), he was used in two unsuccessful missions to rally the Catholic princes, and was happier in his court at Viterbo as governor of the *Patrimony of Peter, the oldest of the papal States. He was one of the three who presided over the Council of Trent at its opening (1545) and, supported by Charles V, would have been elected pope in 1550 had he not hesitated and awaited late comers to the conclave. He was appointed papal legate to England after the accession of Mary Tudor. He formally absolved the realm and received it back into unity. On Cranmer's deposition he was consecrated abp. of Canterbury, having been ordained 2 days before. After the departure of Philip of Spain, the Queen relied more and more on his counsel. Though personally lenient, he exerted no restraint on the religious persecution that marked her reign. He fell into disgrace with Paul IV for obstructing the anti-Spanish policies of that fiery and severe Caraffa and was deprived of his legatine authority. He died at Lambeth Palace 12 hours after Mary and was buried near the site of St. Thomas Becket's shrine at Canterbury. BIBLIOGRAPHY: W. Schenk, *Reginald Pole* (1950); D. Fenlon, *Heresy and Obedience in Tridentine Italy: Cardinal Pole and the Counter Reformation* (1973).

[T. GILBY]

POLEMICAL THEOLOGY, theology developed in conscious opposition to doctrinal systems of other Churches. Every theology is to some extent polemical, defending its approach in contrast to others, but polemical theology implies a special interest in defending the tradition of a particular Church and attacking the teachings of other Churches. In the denominational conflicts of past centuries theologians of each Church have been concerned to prove the correctness of their Church's distinctive dogma and the errors of other Churches. As was to some extent the case in the mid-1960s, theologians were considered to be representatives of particular denominations and to have as a part of their professional responsibility defense of their Church's teaching against competing Churches. With the development of the *ecumenical movement in the 20th cent. it has come to be widely felt that greater progress can be made through *interfaith dialogue than through polemics, and agencies such as the *World Council of Churches are designed in large measure to facilitate such dialogue. *FAITH AND ORDER.

[T. EARLY]

POLIGNAC, MELCHIOR DE (1661–1742), French cardinal, ambassador to Poland for Louis XIV, author of an epic poem, *Anti-Lucretius, sive de Deo et natura libri novem,* written as an apologetic against materialism, ancient and contemporary.

[R. J. LITZ]

POLING, DANIEL ALFRED (1884–1968), American Protestant minister who, as editor of the *Christian Herald* (1925–65) was the prominent spokesman of conservative causes, political and theological. He was the author of many popular works of devotion and counsel. He was the father of Clark V. Poling, one of four heroic chaplains who sacrificed their lives on the transport *Dorchester* Feb. 3, 1943.

[T. C. O'BRIEN]

POLISH NATIONAL CATHOLIC CHURCH OF AMERICA, an autonomous American foundation, maintaining *intercommunion with the Old Catholic Churches and the Anglican Communion. The Polish National Catholic Church is the largest and most successful secession from the RC Church in the U.S.; separation came as part of a broader upsurge of Polish national sentiment against the power of the predominantly Irish and German RC hierarchy over church property after the Third Plenary Council of Baltimore (1884). A clash occurred (1897–1900) at Scranton, Pa., which culminated in the repudiation of RC organization, doctrine, and worship forms by the parishioners of St. Stanislaus Church, led by the pastor, F. *Hodur. By 1905 he was able to give formal organization to the new Church, which had a membership of about 20,000; 2 years later he received episcopal consecration from the Little Church of Utrecht; in 1909 his Church entered communion with the *Union of Utrecht. Two similar Polish separatist bodies joined the Polish National Catholic Church: one from Chicago, Ill. (1907); another from Buffalo, N.Y. (1914). From 1923 a mission, later a separate diocese, was established in Poland. It has suffered both Nazi and Communist persecution; its bp. died in prison (1951), and relations with the Church in the U.S. were severed (1953–59), though some contact has since been resumed. The Lithuanian National Catholic Church, which Bp. Hodur helped found in 1914, became independent in 1923 but merged with the Polish Church in 1964. Latest available figures for the Church (1960) show a membership of about 280,000 in the United States.

The Confession of Faith dates from 1913. Although the Church subscribes to the Declaration of *Utrecht, it does not conform to Old Catholic teaching on all points. Through a theory of *restorationism, it rejects eternal punishment for sin; faith is deemed helpful but not necessary to salvation; confirmation and baptism are parts of the one sacrament, but seven sacraments are kept, since the word of God as preached and heard is a sacrament. Liturgy has been from the beginning in Polish, but English is permissible and is increasingly used. Confession is individual for children, general for adults; clergy may marry. The supreme authority in the Church is the quadrennial General Synod, made up of the bps. and of elected priests and laymen. The bp. of Scranton is prime bp., and with a general council carries on the regular affairs of the Church. BIBLIOGRAPHY: T. Andrews, *Polish National Catholic Church in America and Poland* (1953).

[E. E. BEAUREGARD]

POLITENESS, the courtesy and good manners that have bearing on several virtues. Politeness is a form of indebtedness to others, owed, not in exact justice, but out of a sense for the virtuous, the humanely decorous and civil (see DEBT). The virtue of *truthfulness or candor includes an aspect of politeness in its care for what is appropriate to human conversation. Thus "people who exaggerate about themselves are bores, . . . people who are reticent about themselves, agreeable'' (ThAq ST 2a2ae, 109.4; cf. 169.1 ad 3). The virtue of friendliness or affability observes the decencies (as distinct from more intimate signs of friendship) in word and act towards all (*ibid.* 114.1 & ad 2). This virtue, as well, keeps the distinction between politeness and fawning or *flattery; avoids quarrelsome rudeness and disagreeableness. There is, further, a virtue specifically concerned with good manners, proper comportment and dress; the virtue called in Lat. *modestia* attends, without affectation or ostentation, to what is of good grace and taste, simply because these are in accord with being human (*ibid* 168.1). The meaning of *charity reinforces such values; because it rests in God's love it transforms all human relationships into the mutual regard of those who together are children of God.

[T. C. O'BRIEN]

POLITICAL CATHOLICISM, term used in Germany and later elsewhere, to characterize Catholic political involvement as distinguished from educational or charitable activity. Liberal anticlericals employed it critically often, implying undesirable Vatican influence. But increasingly after 1850 parties like the German *Zentrum* understood it in the context of statements by Leo XIII: the Church would remain aloof from civil politics, would express no preference for any form of government, would seek to defend the rights of the Church to freedom for its religious, educational, and charitable mission. Priests and prelates, Rome later urged, would enter politics only because of special competence. Political Catholicism at its best tried to function in this Leonine spirit. Critics sometimes thought it too patriotic and prone to favor compromises in national policy in order to assure church rights. In most North-European countries, this program was effective, but could not be fostered in Italy because of the Roman Question. It was evolutionary in character, and, in general, differed from some later Christian Social movements in that it was conciliatory rather than revolutionary. BIBLIOGRAPHY: *Church and Society* (ed. J. N. Moody, 1953) ch. 5.

[G. N. SHUSTER]

POLITICAL THEOLOGY, orientation of Christian theology toward a critique and change of social structures, normally from a Marxist or generally leftwing perspective. Advocates distinguish their position from ontological theologies such as Thomism, which they charge with upholding the political *status quo,* and from existentialist theologies focusing on individual, inner concerns. This approach has been largely a phenomenon of German theology, though it closely resembles the various forms of *liberation theology developed elsewhere and, more loosely, the American *Social Gospel. Earlier, political theology had been a term used to designate theologies supporting a particular political order, and in that sense became the subject of debate in the 1930s. J. B. Metz, a Catholic theologian at

Münster, revived the term from a different perspective in the late 1960s, making it denote a theology of revolutionary change in the political order. He contended that emphasis on the individual as in existentialism or the I-thou relationship brought a ''privatizing'' tendency into Christian thought, and he called for a ''deprivatizing'' program to extend the demythologizing of R. *Bultmann. In similar vein, the German Protestant theologian, J. Moltmann, like Metz associated with the theology of hope, has advocated ''a political hermeneutic of the Gospel.'' Political theology stresses the eschatological dimension, contends for the unity of knowledge and action, and proceeds in the spirit of Marx's aphorism that the need is not to interpret the world but to change it. The program of political activity is not drawn in its details from the NT and the example of Jesus, but from what exponents of political theology see as the basic thrust of the Gospel toward liberation. BIBLIOGRAPHY: J. B. Metz, *Theology of the World* (tr. W. Glen-Doepel, 1969); D. Soelle, *Political Theology* (tr. J. Shelley, 1974).

[T. EARLY]

POLITICS, from Gr. *polis,* city or state, the art and science of taking part in a civilized community: the word has no association, etymologically and often otherwise, with polite (from Lat. *polire,* to polish). It will be useful to simplify the Western history of the notion in three stages, classical, medieval, and modern.

(1) For the Greeks it was the most developed part of morals: man's full perfection was not achieved by living alone in a *monastērion,* but in intercourse with fellow-citizens in a *politeia* and, preferably, involved in the business of government (*politeuma*). Thus Aristotle's political doctrine is introduced in the *Nicomachean Ethics* and unabruptly carried over into the *Politics.* Nonpolitical virtue was a contradiction in terms, and so was nonethical politics. Likewise for the Romans the notion of being part of the *populus* was essentially a matter of justice, just as civics were a matter of religion. The theme runs through St. Augustine, even though, at once proud of the empire and somber about its origins, his views were ambiguous about governmental authority; it was divinely instituted yet only because of our wickedness (*propter peccatum*), and to keep that well policed. Moreover he set the City of God over against the earthly city. He was to prove a dominant influence in Christian political sentiment which, without withholding due obedience, has often taken a somewhat dusty look at political power; even Erastian Protestantism may treat the State as no more than an interim value.

(2) The second stage began to emerge with the rise of the nation-states as the 13th cent. drew to a close. Well before the Church had appeared as a completely equipped political society, governing itself according to its own canon law and protected by ecclesiastical and customary laws which were juridically established and universally acknowledged. Nor were the means lacking for their enforcement. The only power that might have competed with it, the Holy Roman

Empire, lived in its shadow; the Hohenstaufens had tried, and they had failed. Midway through the century it seemed likely that the canonists would bring about a papal hegemony over Europe which, it has been maintained, would not have been undeserved in virtue of their superior culture and more advanced instruments of civilization. Fortunately for the Church, they did not succeed; a clerical theocracy has its merits, but the benefit of religion is not among them.

As the State organized itself to meet its proper lay interests with their appropriate techniques, so it began to separate slowly from the Church; relations were to remain intimate, and normally might even be cordial, yet by the end of the Middle Ages each could be seen as composing a distinct political body. Matters secular and sacred, or temporal and spiritual, or clerical or lay (the doublets are not synonymous), were afterwards to dichotomize the political field. There was, however, another split, scarcely less important, though here it can be only roughly touched on. The rise of a professional class inevitably meant rule by experts for better and bureaucrats for worse. Hence the multiplication of statutory laws in addition to, and sometimes to the detriment of custom. It had happened in the Church, where the canalization of religion had not been to the mind of theologians who looked to earlier and more hallowed sources. So too, in what was becoming the ''lay'' side of life a difference was hardening between what the nation did, and had immemorially done, according to natural justice and custom, and what the governing powers now required it to do for their own good and official reasons. The notion of duty to the group now became divided. Already St. Thomas Aquinas (d. 1274), who recovered a political Hellenism unclouded by Augustinianism and unaffected by the nostalgia of Latin Stoics for a Golden Age, had required two words, social and political, *animal sociale et politicum,* to render Aristotle's simple *zoön politikon.* Just as positive law was coming to be developed apart from natural law, so too was political art and science beginning to stir with a life of its own apart from the plain social duties incumbent on each individual. The two processes were parallel, or rather they coincided. However it was still generally agreed that observance of positive law and political obedience were binding in conscience—a category of personal morality.

(3) The name of Machiavelli may serve to introduce the further narrowing of the notion of politics that began with the Renaissance and Reformation. ''What scoundrels we should be,'' exclaimed Cavour, ''if we did for ourselves what we do for our country.'' Though frequently, if unfairly—for the exceptions are neither rare nor inconspicuous—politics are regarded as a dirty business, that is because of the personalities engaged and the opportunities for evil provided, not because it is thought that morals come into them one way or another. The prevalent view has been, at least in English-speaking countries, esp. in those where party politics were pursued on a basis of common social agreement, that they are concerned with ways and means, rather than ends, and decide on the more practicable of two alternatives both of which can be countenanced. ''Politics,'' said Vincent McNabb succinctly, ''the social art of the morally permissible.'' Consequently it was generally held, and by many Christians, not too happy about St. Thomas Becket, that religion—and priests emphatically—should stay out of politics. Look at the defects of a Christian party in a modern democratic state: did it not commit the Church on such questions as methods of public sanitation, muzzles for dogs, the rate of income tax, and so forth?

Such an isolation of pure politics as ethically neutral was understandable in a relatively secure society, confident that ideals of freedom and reform could be put into practice without destroying the existing social structure, and living on the capital of its Christian past, a heritage often forgotten or taken for granted. Most of the indications at present are that this condition of affairs belongs to the past. The values of human nature itself, as well as of Christianity which is committed to them, are now threatened by political action, and have to be defended by equivalent means, the same in kind if not in degree. This is not a plea for Catholic Action, but for energetic and effective activity by Catholics and all Christians in the realm of politics. Gandhi himself, the supreme exponent of nonviolence and of other-worldly values in our day, was a redoubtable politician. And in fact the present stress in theology is not laid on world-renouncing, or even on contemplating God's truth, but on directly acting socially and politically, or even on revolutionizing our institutions. BIBLIOGRAPHY: T. Gilby, *Between Community and Society* (1953); M. P. Fogarty, *Christian Democracy in Western Europe, 1820–1953* (1957); B. Crick, *American Science of Politics* (1959); T. M. Parker, *Christianity and the State in the Light of History* (1955); J. C. Murray, *We Hold these Truths* (1960); John XXIII, Encyclicals *Mater et magistra* (1961), *Pacem in terris* (1963).

[T. GILBY]

POLITUS, AMBROSIUS CATHARINUS, see AMBROSIUS CATHARINUS.

POLITY, in ecclesiastical usage, the form of government of a Church; sometimes extended to refer even to the doctrinal and liturgical position of a Church. In his debate with the Puritans, Richard *Hooker published *Of the Laws of Ecclesiastical Polity* (1593–1597); he preferred to speak of church polity rather than church government, because it ''includeth both government and whatsoever besides belongeth to the ordering of the church in public'' (bk. 3.2, 13). A term that includes the laws, offices, nature of authority, and even forms and ceremonies is thus susceptible of a wide variety of combinations. It is often asserted that there are three types of polity: episcopal, synodal (presbyterian), and congregational. Such a classification, however, is of limited value, for not all episcopal systems are alike, and many *church orders combine elements of all three types.

For example, one may characterize the RC, Anglican, Orthodox, and Methodist Churches as episcopal in polity, but the authority, functions, and interpretations of the office of bishop are vastly different in these different communions. Even within a single tradition, there may exist different types of government. In the U.S. most denominations have been influenced to some extent by congregational emphases, favoring the influence of each particular congregation in decision-making and a share by the laity in governing the Church. The C of E considers episcopacy essential to the Church, while American Methodists deny *apostolic succession and regard episcopacy only as one possible convenient form of organization. The source of authority and its theological rationale, the offices and their functions, the liturgical practices, and the processes by which decisions are made and implemented all are necessary for determining the precise polity of any particular Church.

[N. H. MARING]

POLLAIUOLO (POLLAIOLO), family name of brothers, Italian painters and sculptors of the Florentine School. **Antonio di Jacopo Benci** (c.1431–98), who in his study of the human figure in violent action (bronze *Hercules and Antaeus*) added a new dimension to early Renaissance art. Exploring this theme in a variety of media, he revealed an advanced knowledge of anatomy in the executioners of the painting *The Martyrdom of St. Sebastian* (1475; National Gallery, London) and figures in the engraving *Battle of the Ten Nudes* (1465). He painted a *David* (1470), the heroic *Hercules and Antaeus* (1475), and the *S. Miniato Altarpiece*. **Piero di Jacopo Benci** (c.1441–96), the less able brother, collaborated on the *Labors of Hercules* (1464), *Tobias the Archangel,* a *St. Michael Archangel* and the major series of *Virtues* (1470). Antonio appears to rely more on Piero in his last works, the bronze tombs of Pope Sixtus IV (1484–93) and Pope Innocent VIII (1493–96). BIBLIOGRAPHY: J. Pope-Hennessy, *Italian Renaissance Sculpture* (1958); C. Seymour, *Sculpture in Italy, 1400–1500* (1966).

[S. CONWAY]

POLLIEN, FRANÇOIS DE SALES (1853–1936), French Carthusian spiritual writer. Ordained at Annecy (1877), he entered La Grande Chartreuse in 1884. Serving in a number of charterhouses, he served as prior of Mougères (1901), Pleterjé (1911), before retiring to the house of St. Bruno in Calabria. His written meditations were circulated in MS, edited and published by others. His most notable work, which influenced a revival of interest in asceticism and mysticism in the early 20th cent., was edited by J. Tissot, *La Vie intérieure simplifiée et ramenée à son fondement* (1894), and was followed by the lengthy *La Plante de Dieu,* on mystical union.

[R. J. LITZ]

POLLUTION, see EMISSION.

POLLUTION, ENVIRONMENTAL. The immorality, corresponding in degree to the damage done, of wanton exploitation of the resources of nature is clear from the many positive moral values that human beings are called on to respect in regard to God's creation. The virtue of *religion, as the acknowledgment of God's supreme lordship, has as its implication man's stewardship over the goods of the earth, he is to cultivate them, he does not have complete sovereignty over them; the message is clear from Gen 1.28–30. The virtue of *piety means a respect for the created sources of human existence and betterment; it honors parents and country; but the "country" of mankind is the material universe, and mankind's unity in dependence upon its resources forbids exploitation by any individual or single nation. There is, as well, in the meaning of piety an honor due to a heritage, derived from the past and owed to posterity. This respect includes preservation and transmittal of shared resources. The theological meaning of *private property includes an obligation in justice towards others: natural resources are the common patrimony of all mankind; ownership includes the obligation to make such resources serve the common well-being. No consideration of profit or individual rights can neutralize that obligation, or justify the destruction of forests, water resources, land, or the ecological balance. At the same time the moral obligation towards the environment does not mean, as some environmentalists seem to intend, that nature must be left untouched by any human use. The use must be reasonable and a husbanding of natural resources, but that use remains part of the meaning of natural resources: their subordination to genuine human need; conservation is not an absolute goal unto itself.

[T. C. O'BRIEN]

POLTERGEIST, a "force" responsible for certain sets of unexplained, undesirable, and bothersome events. The word, derived from two German words meaning "noisy ghost," reflects a popular belief in preternatural beings that mischievously and unpredictably disturb human lives. Whatever their cause, poltergeist activities display certain common characteristics. They are completely spontaneous; there are no known series of conditions conducive to their origin. Poltergeist occurrences are of relatively short duration; for this reason it is difficult for scientists to study such events on the scene at first hand. They have an ephemeral character; there is no recognizable human "medium" calling for or directing these happenings. Lastly, poltergeist activities are completely purposeless and thus mischievous; in this they are unlike the strange but intended occurrences reported in seances. Because of their peculiar properties, it is most difficult to make a proper study of such occurrences. A few conclusions have been tentatively offered for discussion among *parapsychologists on the basis of what research has been done. In those cases in which deception and fraud can definitely be ruled out, there does seem to be something active; apparently there is an agent unobservably at work. These occurrences have most often taken place in households in which children and adolescents live. These observations have led to the suggestion that the agent in poltergeist activities is not a mischievous ghost but an adolescent desirous of attention or notoriety. The events, under this hypothesis, are actually examples of *psychokinesis: mind over matter. Whether or not this hypothesis can stand scientific criticism, its proposal reflects a change of viewpoint. Poltergeists are no longer given a preternatural but a natural explanation. BIBLIOGRAPHY: H. Thurston, *Ghosts & Poltergeists* (ed. J. H. Crehan, 1954); C. P. Svoboda, NCE 11: 534.

[C. P. SVOBODA]

POLTON, THOMAS (d. 1433), English curialist; bp. of Hereford (1420), Chichester (1421), Worcester (1426)—all by papal provision. Papal envoy to England (1413), royal proctor at Rome (1414), delegate to the Councils of Constance, Siena, and Basel, he devoted his life to the combined service of Church and State. BIBLIOGRAPHY: Emden Ox 3:1494–95; R. L. Storey, NCE 11:535.

[R. W. HAYS]

POLYANDRY, a form of *polygamy in which the one woman has two or more husbands simultaneously. The instances of institutionalized polyandry are rare in history. Where practiced it is usually because of a sexual disproportion in the population; and usually one of the men has chief domestic responsibility. The moral objection to polyandry is its threat to the right upbringing of children and to harmonious family life.

[T. C. O'BRIEN]

POLYCARP OF SMYRNA, ST. (c.69–156), *Apostolic Father. Unlike the other Apostolic Fathers, P. actually sat at the feet of an Apostle (John), who later made him bp. of Smyrna. *Ignatius of Antioch addressed a letter to P. urging him to bring the far-flung early Christian communities in touch with one another through an exchange of official letters. He is the author of a *Letter to the Philippians* enjoining obedience to the presbyters and deacons, without allusion to the presence of any bp. at Philippi. The *Martyrdom of Polycarp,* attributed to a certain Marcion, the earliest extant account of the death of a martyr, essentially reliable, compares P.'s death to Christ's Passion and reports his courageous words and the actions of the executioners in some detail. BIBLIOGRAPHY: Quasten 1:76–82; G. Bosio, BiblSanct 10:985–988.

[R. R. BARR]

POLYCARP, MARTYRDOM OF ST., an account of eyewitnesses of the arrest, trial, and execution of St. *Polycarp, bp. of Smyrna, composed by a certain Marcion and written down by a scribe Evarestus in the name of the Church of Smyrna and addressed to the Christians at Philomelium and "to all the communities of the holy Catholic Church." To this letter are added three supplements, a chronological appendix, a commendatory postscript, and an account of the transmission of the document. The Martyrdom, which has come down in five Greek MSS and Latin, Armenian, Syriac, and Coptic versions, gives a remarkably moving account of the death of the aged bishop. It also provides our earliest evidence for the veneration of the relics of martyrs. BIBLIOGRAPHY: J. A. Kleist, ACW 6 (1948), 85–102; J. A. Fischer, LTK 8:597–598.

[M. J. COSTELLOE]

POLYCHRONIUS (d. c.430), bp. of Apamea, brother of *Theodore of Mopsuestia. Theodoret in his history lauded P. as the "best of shepherds." An advocate of the exegetical traditions of Antioch, P. wrote commentaries on Job, Daniel, and Ezeckiel, of which only fragments are to be found in various catenae. Commentaries on other books of the Bible have been assigned to him but the attribution is uncertain. He strongly condemned the Alexandrian tradition but seems to have died before the decisions of the Council of *Ephesus. Works: PG 93:13–468. BIBLIOGRAPHY: A. Vaccari, EncCatt 9:1673; Quasten 3:423–424.

[R. B. ENO]

POLYGAMY, literally plural marriage; the practice of having more than one marital partner; primarily connotes polygyny, the marriage of one man to several wives concurrently; *polyandry is the opposite, less common form of polygamy. In pagan antiquity polygamy was a common practice, but the Greeks and Romans were monogamous as far as the social and legal institution of marriage was concerned. In the OT polygamy was accepted, usually because of fear of childlessness (see POLYGAMY [IN THE BIBLE]). In Islam, polygamy is sanctioned by law, but a man may not have more than four wives concurrently, and the choice of wives is restricted by rules concerning their consanguinity. Polygamy is also permitted by Hindu law. Plural marriage was a practice among *Mormons that was bound up with their fundamental conception of God; it is probable, however, that no more than ten percent actually carried out the practice. Because of conflict with U.S. law and punitive measures against them, the Mormons declared plural marriage a suppressed doctrine in 1892; that was also a condition for Utah's admission to the Union (1896). The argument of moral theology against polygamy is not that it is altogether incompatible with the purposes of marriage (see GOODS OF MARRIAGE), but that it makes their attainment more difficult, esp. the proper upbringing of children and true family harmony. The precise Christian rejection of polygamy is based on the nature of marriage as a sacrament symbolizing the singleness of union between Christ and his spouse, the Church (Eph 5.32). Where polygamy has been an established, domestic institution, there still have been controls amounting to what some anthropologists have called "multiple monogamy." Thus the first wife is often conceded a primacy of honor; a man must have sufficient means to see to the upkeep of the household and the rearing of the children.

[T. C. O'BRIEN]

POLYGAMY (IN THE BIBLE), the practice of having many spouses concurrentty. In biblical tradition polygamy is always polygyny, whereby a man has several wives. Polyandry, a woman having several husbands, is unheard of in patriarchal cultures. The closest thing to polyandry in biblical narrative is the custom of *Levirate marriage, in which a man is obligated to raise offspring by his dead brother's widow, and thus ensure continuity of family and tribal inheritance. With the decline of the seminomadic way of life, and Israel's assimilation to the settled life and culture of Canaan, polygyny devolved to, at best, bigamy, until finally monogamy became the norm. In both seminomadic and agricultural life, a large working force of sons was considered necessary, whether to tend flocks or fields. Sons were essential to the basic economic strength of family, clan, tribe, and nation. This basic economic reality reinforced the natural desire for sons. So powerful as a cultural value was the craving of a man for a son of his own conception, that a wife was virtually defined as the means of securing that result. During the patriarchal period, if the first and cherished wife failed, taking a second or secondary wives was in order (Sara and Hagar [Gen 16.1–10]; Rachel, Leah, and their handmaids [Gen ch. 29 and 30]). The era of David and Solomon marks the end of the seminomadic and the beginning of the settled phase of Israel. David and his wives illustrate the transitory liaisons of the guerilla warrior. Solomon's prodigious achievement (700 wives and 300 concubines) presents polygyny in the role of service to the national security through strategic alliance. The conflict and dissension endemic to a polygamous ménage are readily apparent in the sagas of the Patriarchs. The rivalry among David's sons for succession to the throne provides the connecting thread of the great historical narrative in 2 Sam 9–20, culminating in Solomon's bloody accession to the throne. When polygamy gave way before the monogamous ideal, the value of sons was still paramount. When a wife bore no son, divorce and a second marriage became the demanded remedy.

[E. J. DILLON]

POLYGENISM, the theory that mankind has descended from many progenitors, not from a single pair. Polygenism may be either monophyletic or polyphyletic, according to whether one or many prehuman species are held to have achieved human status. The eventual proof for or against polygenism is properly a question for biologists, bound up with the evidence for the evolution of man. The theologian is indirectly involved, however, since the answer must be reconciled with the doctrine of original sin and the unity of the human race. Pius XII's encyclical *Humani generis (1950) affirmed the right of a Catholic to hold the theory of evolution as a scientific opinion. Although one is not bound

to the biological presuppositions of the inspired writers, Pius declared, ''Christ's faithful cannot embrace that opinion which maintains either that after Adam there existed on this earth true men who did not take their origin through natural generation from him as from the first parent of all, or that Adam represents a certain number of first parents; since it is in no way apparent how such opinion can be reconciled with what the sources of revealed truth and the documents of the teaching authority of the Church propose with regard to original sin, which proceeds from a sin actually committed by an individual Adam and which through generation is passed on to all and is in everyone as his own.'' The cautious wording of the encyclical indicates that the apparent impossibility of reconciling polygenesis with the doctrine of original sin is not necessarily final. Some contemporary theologians are seeking a more evident distinction between monogenesis and the nucleus of Church teaching on original sin. Cosmic polygenism and the relationship that may exist among the different races of intelligent beings who may be scattered throughout the universe has only recently been recognized as a possible theological issue. BIBLIOGRAPHY: P. De Rosa, *Christ and Original Sin* (1967); J. Dubarle, *Biblical Doctrine of Original Sin* (1965); P. Schoonenberg, *God's World in the Making* (1965); K. Rahner, ''Theological Reflections on Monogenism,'' Rahner ThInvest 1 (1961). *MONOGENISM.

[O. W. GARRIGAN]

POLYGLOT BIBLES, editions containing the text in several languages, arranged in parallel columns for purpose of comparison. In a sense Origen's *Hexapla was the first polyglot, but the term is generally applied to printed Bibles. The first and perhaps best-known of those is the Complutensian, which contained the first printed Greek NT. Published in six volumes (c. 1522), it had the OT in Hebrew, Aramaic, Greek and Latin, and the NT in Greek and Latin. Another major polyglot was the *Biblia regia,* published in Antwerp by C. *Plantin in eight volumes (1569–73). The best of the polyglots is considered to be the Londinensis or Waltoniana (1657) published under the patronage of Oliver Cromwell and edited by B. Walton (c. 1600–61). In six volumes it contained Hebrew, Samaritan, Aramaic, Greek, Latin, Ethiopic, Syriac, Arabic, and Persian.

Though some have included modern translations, the polyglots are basically designed to present the oldest versions for side by side comparison for the purpose of determining the most reliable text. Polyglots are not considered of special importance to textual criticism, however. BIBLIOGRAPHY: *Cambridge History of the Bible: The West from the Reformation to the Present Day* (ed. S. Greenslade, 1963).

[T. EARLY]

POLYGYNY, see POLYGAMY.

POLYNESIA, one of the three main divisions of *Oceania. Included are the islands of *Hawaii, *Samoa, *Tonga, Tokelau, Tubuäi, Tuamotu, Society (*Tahiti), *Marquesas, Cook, Wake, Midway, Johnston, Kingman, Palmyra, Howland, Baker, Jarvis, Canton, Enderbury, Austral, Wallis, Futuna, Fanning, Malden, Christmas, Starbuck, Rotuma, Easter, Rapa, Gambier, Union, Niue, Kermadec, and others. Their combined area is about 10,000 square miles.

[P. DAMBORIENA]

POLYPTYCH, altar retable of more than three panels, whose wings are movable in N Europe but in Italy are usually fixed.

POLYTHEISM, the acknowledgment of a plurality of deities. The Genesis account of the beginnings of mankind indicates that acceptance of the one God was part of the primitive human condition. The biblical emphasis on the continued struggle to keep Israel monotheistic, faithful to the one God, implies that polytheism is sinful and is the effect of sin. The position of anthropology, on the other hand, is that polytheism is not a primitive religious attitude and even a less sophisticated preliminary to monotheism. But in many religious systems the numerous gods are often forms or concretizations of one high god, who is behind the origins of all things, but remains aloof. In Greece and Rome it was the philosophers, secular and separated in their theories from popular polytheistic religion, who suggested that there can be but one supreme divinity. Christian theology, reflecting on the affirmation *Credo in unum Deum,* has developed the argument that the oneness of God also means uniqueness, unicity. The absolute, divine being can have no limitation, and limiting differences would be necessary for there to be many deities. The mystery of the Trinity, and its problem for theological articulation, is that the divine unity and identity includes the three distinct persons.

[T. C. O'BRIEN]

POLYTHEISM (IN THE BIBLE), the belief in and worship of many gods. Polytheism—from the Greek *poly* ("many") and *theoi* ("gods")—is usually contrasted with monotheism—from the Greek *monos* ("sole," "alone"). Monotheism is the belief that there is only one God. Such a belief is late in biblical tradition, emerging clearly for the first time perhaps as late as the Babylonian Exile, in the refrain of Second Isaiah: "I am God, and there is no other." The real rivalry in Israelite tradition was between polytheism and henotheism (from the Greek *hen,* "one"). Henotheism is the service of one god. A henotheist presumes there are many gods, and individual gods have chosen various peoples to serve them, through whom these gods manifest their Name and their Glory. The various peoples bind themselves to serve their god much as a vassal pledges fealty to a more powerful lord; but it is the lord who initiates the relationship. A classic expression of henotheism is the first Commandment: "I am . . . your God; you shall not have foreign gods before Me." The god of henotheists is a jealous god. The faith of henotheists is shaken when his people are conquered by another people,

showing the foreign god to be more powerful. Monotheism should be a more serene thing. The ancestors of Abraham worshiped many gods. The Israelites were attracted to both Canaanite and Phoenician polytheism. Settled peoples preferred a full pantheon. Seminomadic peoples preferred one warrior god. Jewish, and later Muslim and even Christian, monotheism is a development from Israelite henotheism, and reflects the limitations of the latter. There is no room for the female element in the godhead—as there was in the pantheons of the settled cultures of the Mediterranean. There is the intolerance toward, and even fear of, foreign cultures and religions. Not until the influence of Persian dualism is there a tradition of wisdom dealing with Evil (with the capital "E"). Only in apocalyptic Judaism and esp. in the Christian Gospels is there an assimilation of some of the symbolism of demonology to explain and highlight the real power of evil in the universe.

[E. J. DILLON]

POMBAL, SEBASTIÃO, MARQUIS DE (1699–1782), Portuguese statesman who has been called the Bismarck of the 18th cent., which is rather unfair to the Iron Chancellor who was more moderate and successful about his political objectives and would have paled before using like terrorism. He came to power at the age of 51, and his ascendancy was confirmed by the exemplary courage and energy he displayed at the great Lisbon earthquake (1755). He reorganized education, the public finances, industry, agriculture, the colonies, and the armed services. Partly in consequence of his policies with respect to the *Paraguay Reductions, he became the implacable enemy of the Jesuits. Their property was sequestered and they were deported from the Portuguese dominions. Working in concert with the Catholic courts, he prevailed on a rather craven Pope to have them suppressed everywhere. He believed in keeping the Church tamed and domesticated. His ideals were those of the Age of Enlightenment; his methods, however, were not, for he proceeded ruthlessly alike against nobles and common folk with fire, the garotte, the rack, the axe, and death by neglect in solitary confinement. He died of leprosy and in disgrace, but to the end he had many admirers among the clergy. BIBLIOGRAPHY: M. Cheke, *Dictator of Portugal: A Life of the Marquis of Pombal, 1699–1782* (1938).

[T. GILBY]

POMBEIRO, ABBEY OF, former Benedictine monastery in Lugo province, Spain. Queen Goto of Galicia was its foundress in 964. In the 11th cent. it came under Cluniac control. Attached to a nearby abbey, it became part of the Benedictine Congregation of Valladolid in the 16th century. The monastery was suppressed during the early 19th cent., and today the abbey church serves a parish.

[M. A. MCFADDEN]

POMERIUS, JULIANUS (d. after 498), ascetical writer. P. migrated from his native North Africa to Gaul, opened a school of rhetoric at Arles, and became a priest. His treatise

De vita contemplativa, on combining contemplation and action, long ascribed to Prosper of Aquitaine, enjoyed great popularity in the Middle Ages. P. also wrote *De virginibus instituendis, De contemptu mundi,* and *De anima et qualitate eius.* These works are not extant but a summary of the last-named is to be found in Pseudo-Gennadius (*Vir. ill.* 99) and Isidore of Seville (*Vir. ill.* 25). BIBLIOGRAPHY: G. Fritz, DTC 12:2537–43.

[M. J. SUELZER]

POMMEREL, CELESTINE, MOTHER (1813–57), religious superior. A Frenchwoman, P. became a Sister of St. Joseph in Lyons. At the age of 24 she was sent by Mother St. John Fontbonne to Carondelet, Mo., where the motherhouse and novitiate of the Sisters of St. Joseph were located. She taught in the first RC school for the deaf (1837) in the U.S.; as superior of the American missions (from 1839), P. founded seven elementary schools, an Indian mission, three hospitals, and novitiates in Philadelphia, Pa.; Wheeling, W. Va.; St. Paul, Minn.; Buffalo, N.Y.; and in Toronto, Canada. *FOURNIER, ST. JOHN, MOTHER.

[J. R. AHERNE]

POMPALLIER, JEAN BAPTISTE FRANÇOIS (1801–71), French missionary and bp. of Oceania. Ordained (1829), appointed vicar apostolic to Western Oceania (1836), he was among the first Marists to take a mission to the South Pacific. His successful mission in New Zealand was well established by the time he went to Rome in 1846. He returned to the South Pacific in 1850 as bp. of Auckland, but soon had to go back to Europe to recruit more priests. During the 1860s difficulty in retaining priests, economic depression, the Maori wars, and lack of European support for his endeavors discouraged him. Returning to France, he resigned his see in 1869.

[R. J. LITZ]

POMPIGNAN, JEAN JACQUES LEFRANC DE (1709–84), French poet. Failing as dramatist, P. turned to poetry. He is remembered mainly for his *Ode sur la mort de Jean Baptiste Rousseau,* but there are also verses of high merit in his *Poésies sacrées* (2 v., 1751 and 1755). Having attacked the philosophes when he was received into the French Academy, he incurred their disfavor and became one of the victims of Voltaire's satire. BIBLIOGRAPHY: R. Finch, *Sixth Sense: Individualism in French Poetry 1686–1760* (1966).

[A. S. CRISAFULLI]

POMPONAZZI, PIETRO (1462–1525), controversial Italian Aristotelian philosopher at Padua from 1488 and at Bologna from 1512. P.'s most discussed and interpreted work is *De immortalitate animae* (1516), to which he added an *Apologia* (1518) in response to G. *Contarini, and a *Defensorium* (1519) in response to A. *Nifo. Two other of P.'s works were published posthumously: *De incan-*

tationibus (1556), on the natural causes of phenomena attributed commonly to demonic or angelic intervention; and his longest work, *De fato . . .* (1567), on the philosophical and theological aspects of determinism, providence, and free will. Many other works, both of his own composition and *reportationes* of his lectures on Aristotle, remain in MS only. There has been much modern interest in P. in connection esp. with the history and philosophy of science and scientific method. But his name continues to evoke primarily the *De immortalitate animae,* an annotated English translation of which is to be found in *Renaissance Philosophy of Man* (ed. E. Cassirer, P. Kristaller, and J. Randall, 1948). In it P. examines St. Thomas Aquinas's argument for the immortality of the soul (ThAq ST 1a, 75.6) and three other types of argument, Platonic and Avicennian, for the same position: he concludes that no purely reasoned proof is an apodictic demonstration that the soul is immortal. P. has sometimes been described as an exponent of a *double truth theory (that a position could be false philosophically yet held by faith); or even as a freethinker, a secret precursor of the *Enlightenment. But the *De immortalitate animae* is not a denial of immortality; it questions the demonstrability of the truth, even as does Thomas de Vio Cajetan in his commentary on the *Summa theologiae.* There is no evidence to warrant questioning the honesty of P.'s profession of faith, or categorizing it as outward conformity for fear of reprisal. BIBLIOGRAPHY: G. Di Napoli, *L'Immortalità dell'anima nel Rinascimento* (1961); J. H. Randall, *School of Padua and the Emergence of Modern Science* (1961).

[T. C. O'BRIEN]

POMPONIUS LAETUS (*c.*1425–97), Italian humanist. The illegitimate son of Giovanni di Sanseverino, P. came to Rome and studied under Lorenzo Valla. With fellow enthusiasts for classical antiquity he formed the Accademia Romana which for a time came into ill repute because of its pagan propensities and anticlericalism. Recent scholarship is inclined to show more interest in this humanist's work on grammar entitled *Ars grammatica.* He shows the many facets of his genius in his writings on classical authors, archeology, history, and topography, and in his activities in producing plays by Plautus and Terence and directing George Lauer's press. Among P.'s other works are: *De antiquitate urbis Romanae; Romanae historiae compendium;* commentaries on the writings of Vergil and other Latin authors. BIBLIOGRAPHY: Cosenza 4:2906–14; 5:1458–60; H. Dressler, NCE 11:546.

[H. DRESSLER]

POMPOSA, ABBEY OF, former Benedictine abbey near Codigoro, Italy. Its origins go back to the 7th century. Pomposa was an influential and wealthy abbey with large land holdings. It had been made a royal abbey under Emperor Otto III. A cultural center, the abbey was visited by musicians and poets, including even Dante. Earthquakes and harsh weather which threatened the area in the 16th cent. prompted the monks to move to Ferrara. It was turned into a private farm after the suppression in the 18th cent., but in recent years its beautifully decorated buildings have undergone restoration.

[M. A. MCFADDEN]

PONCE, ALONSO (dates unknown), Spanish Franciscan superior. In 1584 he was sent to New Spain as commissary general of his order. In the succeeding 8 years his journeys took him to the Franciscan missions in Mexico, Guatemala, Costa Rica, Honduras, San Salvador, Nicaragua, and Granada. The valuable chronicle, *Relación breve y verdadera de . . ., P. Fray Alonso Ponce en las provincias de Nueva España . . . ,* was probably written by two of his Franciscan companions.

[J. R. AHERNE]

PONCE DE LEÓN, JUAN (1460–1521), Spanish explorer and adventurer who voyaged throughout the Caribbean, discovered Florida on Easter Sunday, 1513, and near Tampa Bay began a settlement which was soon routed by native Americans. Legend has it that Ponce de León discovered Florida while searching for the fountain of youth but neither the royal patent for his expedition nor reports of the voyage mention the fabled fountain.

[R. J. LITZ]

PONTANUS ROMANUS, LUDOVICUS (1409–39), Italian canonist, author of a valued set of decisions on legal problems, his *Singularia,* as well as of commentaries on the *Corpus Iuris Canonici and other juridical collections.

[T. C. O'BRIEN]

PONTAS, JEAN (1638–1728), French moral theologian, author of a many-times edited and translated *Dictionnaire des cas de conscience* (2 v., 1715; 3 v. supplement, 1718). His solutions favor a strictness that runs counter to the more popular *probabilism of the time.

[T. C. O'BRIEN]

PONTIAN, ST. (d. 235), **POPE** (230–235). During his reign a Roman synod approved the condemnation of Origen by local synods held under Bp. Demetrius of Alexandria (231–232). No doctrinal issues were clearly involved in the Alexandrian condemnations, however. Demetrius disapproved of Origen's preaching as a layman and felt outraged by his ordination without proper permission. P. was one of the first victims of the persecution of Maximinus Thrax. He was sent to work in the mines of Sardinia where he had as a fellow prisoner Hippolytus, the anti-pope. In order to facilitate the government of the Roman Church P. resigned and *Anterus was elected in his place. Within a month of his resignation he died, probably in consequence of his harsh treatment. Pope Fabian had his remains brought to Rome and they were probably the first to be laid in the papal crypt

of the catacomb of Callistus. His tomb was discovered and identified in 1909. BIBLIOGRAPHY: E. G. Weltin, NCE 11:548–549; J. P. Kirsch, CE 12:229–230; Butler 4:391.

[P. F. MULHERN]

PONTIFEX MAXIMUS, the head of the pontifical college at Rome. Originally 3, the pontiffs increased in number until they reached 16 under Caesar. As guardians of the state religion their influence extended over public and private rites and ceremonies, including marriages, adoptions, and funerals. As experts in divine law, they could issue edicts and give answers on religious problems. The pontifex maximus was at first appointed, but later elected, for life. He could punish delinquent vestals and members of the pontifical college who neglected their duty. In 12 B.C., after the death of Lepidus, Augustus assumed the role of pontifex maximus, thus reuniting the sacred and secular authorities as they had earlier been under the kings. The title continued to be used by succeeding emperors until it was renounced by Gratian A.D. *c.*378. Since the pontificate of Pope St. Leo the Great (440–461), it has been used as an honorary title of the popes. BIBLIOGRAPHY: C. D'Onofrio, EncCatt 9:1742–44.

[M. J. COSTELLOE]

PONTIFICAL, ROMAN (*Pontificale Romanum*), a liturgical book containing the prayers and ceremonies reserved to the bishop for all liturgical acts apart from the Mass. In the early Church there was no special book for the bishop; liturgical books simply assumed that the bishop was officiant. In those services in which the place of the bishop was sometimes taken by a simple priest, he adapted his procedure to that of the bishop in the manner prescribed by local tradition. The modern *Roman Pontifical* has its remote roots in two sources: the *Hadrianum,* the sacramentary sent by Hadrian I to Charlemagne, whose ecclesiastics supplemented it with Gallican material, and the *Ordines,* or manuals of ceremonial. The *Pontifical* reached its present form toward the end of the 13th cent. through the work of Bp. Durandus of Mende. Durandus' book attempted to portray the Roman usage but actually was an amalgam of Roman, Gallican, and Germanic practices. This book was generally accepted in Rome in the 15th century. It was first published in 1485 as the typical Roman Pontifical. Recommended by the Council of Trent, it was made obligatory for the whole RC Church by Clement VIII (1596). It is in process of revision.

[N. KOLLAR]

PONTIFICAL ACADEMIES, learned societies founded by the Holy See to foster the arts and sciences, including: the Artists of the Pantheon (1542); the Arcadian (literary) Society (1690); the Theological Academy (1718); the Academy of Liturgy, and the Academy of Archeology, both founded by Benedict XIV; the Academy of the Catholic Religion, founded by Pius VII in 1801; and the Academy of St. Thomas Aquinas, founded by Leo XIII in 1879. The most important and prestigious is the Pontifical Academy of the Sciences, called Academia Linceorum from its emblem, a lynx. It was refounded by Pius IX in 1847 and has its offices in the Vatican Gardens. Mathematicians and scientists from all parts of the world, regardless of religion, are invited by the popes to membership.

[E. J. DILLON]

PONTIFICAL ASSOCIATION OF THE HOLY CHILDHOOD, see MISSIONARY CHILDHOOD.

PONTIFICAL BIBLICAL COMMISSION, see BIBLICAL COMMISSION.

PONTIFICAL BIBLICAL INSTITUTE, see BIBLICAL INSTITUTE, PONTIFICAL.

PONTIFICAL CHAPEL (*Cappella pontificia*), the members of the papal household who serve in assistance to the pope at sacred functions, esp. on certain designated feast days; it includes the sacred college of cardinals and other prelates; it is distinct in the composition of the papal household from the ''pontifical family,'' which serves in capacities and functions other than the liturgical. The papal household was reorganized to achieve greater simplicity by Paul VI's motu proprio, *Pontificalis domus,* March 28, 1968.

PONTIFICAL COMMISSION FOR LATIN AMERICA, a branch of the bureaucracy of the Roman Curia, instituted by Pius XII in 1958, to respond in a unified way to the complex problems confronting the Church in Latin America; to monitor the activities of the Council of Latin American Bishops (CELAM); as well as the various national conferences of bishops. Since 1969 it has come under the jurisdiction of the Curia's Sacred Congregation for the Bishops.

[E. J. DILLON]

PONTIFICAL ECCLESIASTICAL ACADEMY, formerly called the Pontifical Academy of Noble Ecclesiastics, a school in Rome, Piazza Minerva, training clerics for work in the papal diplomatic service. Those accepted must first have gained a doctorate in canon law. The Academy was established by Clement XI in 1701. The papal secretary of state is cardinal protector of the institution.

PONTIFICAL INSTITUTE OF MEDIAEVAL STUDIES, an autonomous institution in Toronto, Canada, for advanced studies and research. It was founded in 1929 by Étienne Gilson, Henry Carr, CSB, Gerald Phelan, and the administrators of St. Michael's College. In virtue of a pontifical charter (1939), the Institute grants the licentiate and doctorate in mediaeval studies. The first president was Henry Carr (1929–37).

[J. A. WEISHEIPL]

PONTIFICAL INSTITUTE OF ORIENTAL STUDIES, a foundation for promoting studies in the history, theology, liturgy, spirituality, and jurisprudence of the various Eastern Churches, established in Rome by Pope Benedict XV in 1917. The Institute began functioning in 1918 with a faculty drawn from religious orders, secular clergy and the laity, but the initial problems of faculty recruitment and cooperation led Pius XI to entrust the Jesuits with entire responsibility for the Institute in 1922. In 1928 it was affiliated with the Gregorian University. To the original faculty of Oriental ecclesiastical studies a second faculty, of Oriental canon law, was added in 1963. Each faculty has a 3-year program leading to a doctorate when a thesis has been successfully written and defended, with a licentiate conferred after the examinations terminating the second year. In the original faculty students specialize in either theology and patristics, or history of the Christian Orient, or Oriental liturgies. The institute is responsible for the journal, *Orientalia Christiana Periodica,* and a monograph series, *Orientalia Christiana Analecta,* as well as critical editions of Syriac *anaphoras and of documents from the Council of Florence. BIBLIOGRAPHY: A. Raes, ''Pour les cinquante premières années de l'Institut Pontifical Oriental,'' *Orientalia Christiana Periodica* 33 (1967) 303–330, with bibliog.

[A. CODY]

PONTIFICAL INSTITUTE OF SACRED MUSIC, an institute suggested by Angelo de *Santi, and founded by Pius X in 1911. Its first name was the Scuola Superiore di Musica Sacra; its present name dates from 1931. Its object is to train clerical and lay students from all parts of the world in sacred music according to the spirit of the *motu proprio* of Pius X. Its present concern is the provisions made for the revision of the liturgy in Vatican Council II. The institute has schools affiliated with it throughout the world.

[R. C. CLIGGETT]

PONTIFICAL MASS, a *solemn Mass celebrated either: (1) at the throne with full ceremonial by a bishop (ordinary) in his own diocese (in another's, by permission), or by an abbot in his own abbey; or (2) at the *faldstool with less ceremonial by a bishop in a diocese other than his own, by an abbot outside his own abbey, by a titular bishop, or by a prelate of certain rank. Vatican Council II, however, declared it fitting that the use of pontificals be reserved to persons of episcopal rank or who possess some particular jurisdiction (Vat II SacLit 130).

[R. B. ENO]

PONTIFICAL MISSION FOR PALESTINE, an organization, having headquarters in New York, dedicated to the care of Palestinian refugees in Syrian Lebanon, Jordan, and the Gaza Strip. It was founded in 1949 by Pius XII after the war between Israel and the Arab states.

PONTIFICAL UNIVERSITIES, ROMAN. Institutions of higher learning (classified in the *Annuario pontificio* as *Instituzioni culturali*) having pontifical charters come under the general grouping, *atenei*. Until the pontificate of John XXIII only the Gregorianum enjoyed the formal rank and title of university. Pope John, however, conferred this rank and title on the following *atenei*: the Lateran (1959); Propaganda (1962; it became the Pontificia Università Urbaniana); the Angelicum (1963; it became the Pontificia Università San Tommaso d'Aquino). Three, the Gregorian, Lateran, and St. Thomas Aquinas, have faculties of theology, philosophy, and canon law. The Urban Univ. has faculties of theology, philosophy, and missiology. To the Gregorian are also annexed the Pontifical Biblical Institute and the Pontifical Institute for Oriental Studies. The pontifical universities are empowered to confer pontifical academic degrees in all their faculties. Other *atenei* of pontifical rank are: San Anselmo, a Benedictine institution founded in 1687, which has faculties of theology, philosophy, and canon law, as well as a special institute for monastic and liturgical studies and is empowered to grant degrees in all these areas. The Franciscan Antonianum, erected in 1933, was made pontifical in 1938; it also confers degrees in the three principal ecclesiastical disciplines. The Salesianum was established in 1940 with faculties in theology, canon law, and philosophy (1956), and institutes of pedagogy and Latinity (1964). Other pontifical institutes of higher learning are the Pontifical Institute of Sacred Music (1914) and of Christian Archeology (1925). The Pontifical Theological Faculty, San Bonaventura (1935) for Friars Minor Conventual dates from 1587. The Pontifical Theological Faculty of St. Teresa of Jesus and St. John of the Cross was established as the Teresianum in 1935; it received pontifical rank in 1963; it is the seat of the Pontifical Institute of Spirituality, established in 1964, and conferring degrees in spiritual theology. The Theological Faculty Marianum, a Servite foundation with origins dating from 1398, has its present charter and title since 1955, and pontifical rank since 1971; it confers degrees in Mariology. The Pontifical Institute for Arabic Studies was formed originally as the Institut Pontifical des Études Orientales in 1926 and located in Tunisia. Its present title and transferral to Rome date from 1964. It is under the care of the White Fathers, and its specialties are Arabic languages and Islamic studies.

PONTIFICAL UNIVERSITIES AND FACULTIES. Besides those in Rome there are institutions of higher learning through the world empowered to give pontifical, or at least canonically authorized, degrees. The *Annuario pontificio* classifies such institutes into "Catholic universities"; "faculties of ecclesiastical studies"; theological faculties within State universities." Among Catholic universities, i.e., those canonically established with an ecclesiastical charter, some also have formally the title and rank of "Pontifical University." Among the institutions of this title are: the Javeriana in Bogotá (Colombia), S. Maria, Buenos Aires; Santo Tomás (Manila); Salamanca; São Paolo (Brazil). Within several of the institutes classified as "Catholic" there are faculties of theology, canon law, and philosophy empowered to give canonical degrees (as well as those for which they have a civil charter). This is the case with the faculties indicated at The Catholic University of America, the Catholic University of Louvain, of Lublin (Poland), St. Patrick's Maynooth (Republic of Ireland), Laval in Quebec City. Among faculties of ecclesiastical studies there are: St. Mary's Seminary, Baltimore; St. Mary of the Lake, Mundelein, Ill.; Heythrop in England; the Pontifical Institute of Medieval Studies, at the Univ. of Toronto. Theological faculties within state universities (because of the arrangement of state support for higher education) are found in many countries of Europe (Fribourg, Switzerland; Innsbruck, and Salzburg, Austria; Munich and Tübingen, Germany; Strassburg in France); also at the Univ. of Montreal. Another type of pontifical faculty, whether of philosophy or theology, is one canonically established in the house of studies or seminary of a religious order and authorized to grant degrees only to members of the order.

PONTFICALS (*pontificalia*), the liturgical vestments and other insignia that are reserved for the bishops. These include *crozier, miter, *pectoral cross, ring, pallium, and the throne (*cathedra*) with a canopy. Reserved to the pope are the *falda, *fanon, *subcinctorium, and tiara.

[N. KOLLAR]

PONTIGNY, ABBEY OF (*Pontiniacum*), former Cistercian abbey, the second daughter of Cîteaux, founded in 1114 by Hugh of Mâcon in the diocese of Auxerre (now Sens). The monastery is noted for having given refuge to three abps. of Canterbury: Thomas Becket, Stephen Langton, and Edmund of Abingdon whose tomb is there. During the French Revolution the buildings of the abbey were sold. In 1910 Desjardins restored them for his Union. They now serve as a seminary for the Mission de France. BIBLIOGRAPHY: Cottineau 2:2331–32; A. A. King, *Cîteaux and Her Elder Daughters* (1954).

[J. DAOUST]

PONTIUS, ST. (d. *c.*260) deacon who volunteered to accompany St. Cyprian during the latter's banishment to Curubis. Through St. Jerome he is also known to be the author of the panegyric *Life of St. Cyprian*. When Cyprian was condemned to death, P. was spared, probably because he was considered of little importance. It is not known where and how he died. He is commemorated on March 8, and is not to be confused with the dubious martyr Pontius commemorated on May 14. BIBLIOGRAPHY: G. D. Gordini, BiblSanct 10:1020–21.

[E. J. DILLON]

PONTIUS OF BALMEY, BL. (d. 1140), Carthusian, bp. of Belley. Of noble lineage, P. became a canon and schoolman at Lyons. In 1116 he founded the charterhouse of Meyriat, financing the project from his own funds. He joined the Carthusians, making his profession at La Grande Chartreuse. Two years later he became prior at Meyriat and in 1121 was elected bp. of Belley. About 1134 he resigned his see to spend his last days in solitude. BIBLIOGRAPHY: BHL 2:6895; L. Le Vasseur, *Ephemerides ordinis cartusiensis* 4 (1892), 492–496; J. Marilier, BiblSanct 10:1018–20.

[O. J. BLUM]

PONTIUS OF FAUCIGNY, BL. (fl. *c.* 12 cent.), abbot. Born in Savoy, he became, at 20, a canon regular at Abbey of Abondance (Augustinian) in Chablais. He revised the constitutions of the house, founded in 1144 a new monastery at Sixt, and became its first abbot. After 26 years he was recalled to Abondance as abbot, but relinquished the office soon after. He died a holy death at Sixt. Pope Leo XIII confirmed his cult in 1896. BIBLIOGRAPHY: R. Van Doren, BiblSanct 10:1017–18.

[N. F. GAUGHAN]

PONTORMO, JACOPO DA, (Jacopo Carucci, 1494–1557), gifted Florentine mannerist painter famous for his sensitive draftsmanship. Though influenced by Andrea del Sarto, Fra Bartolommeo, Dürer, and Michaelangelo, P. introduced an increasingly emotional, tortured quality peculiarly his own. He executed altarpieces and many frescoes stressing the ornamental beauty of figures rather than their volume, stating weightless, elongated forms in a pastel translucence. His last great undertaking was the *Genesis* fresco cycle at S. Lorenzo, Florence (*c.* 1547–57) which, though covered over in 1742, is known through grandeur of drawings in the Uffizi. BIBLIOGRAPHY: S. J. Freedberg, *Painting of the High Renaissance in Rome and Florence* (1961) v.i.

[L. A. LEITE]

POOLE, REGINALD LANE (1857–1939), British scholar and historian. The son of an Arabic scholar, he was reared and educated by his grandmother in the home of a great-uncle, Edward Lane, renowned Orientalist. He entered Oxford in 1874. In 1876 he went to Leyden to study Hebrew. At Balliol he studied modern history under William Stubbs. Among his contributions to scholarly fields are *Sebastian Bach,* articles in Grove DMM, numerous articles in the DNB, and in the EHR which he edited from 1901–20. BIBLIOGRAPHY: T. C. Crowley, NCE 11:565–566; EHR (1940) 55:1–7.

[F. D. LAZENBY]

POOR BOX, receptacle for alms to assist the needy; it is usually found near the entrance of a church.

POOR CATHOLICS, *Waldenses, led by Durand of Huesca, who were reunited to the Church by Innocent III in 1208. They were suppressed by Gregory IX in 1237. BIBLIOGRAPHY: H. C. Lea, *History of the Inquisition of the Middle Ages* (1888, repr. 1958) 1:246–248.

[C. J. LYNCH]

POOR CHILD JESUS, SISTERS OF THE (PCJ), an institute of women religious founded for the support and education of spiritually endangered and socially underprivileged children and young people. The congregation was established in 1844, at Aachen, Germany by Mother Clara *Fey with the assistance of her brother, André Fey, Wilhelm Sartorius, her spiritual advisor and author of the first rule, and Bp. Laurent. Their constitutions, founded on the Rule of St. Augustine, received papal approval in 1888. During the *Kulturkampf, the sisters were evicted from Germany. It was not until the 20th cent. that the congregation began to expand. New foundations were made in countries of Europe, Asia, and North and South America. In 1975, the Sisters maintained 65 houses and had a total membership of 1,515. The general motherhouse is in Simpelveld, Holland. The sisters assist in staff work for the Pontifical Association of the Holy Childhood, a mission society.

[R. A. TODD]

POOR CLARE NUNS, the Franciscan Second Order of contemplative and cloistered women, including: the Poor Clares (PC); the Order of St. Clare (OSC); the Colettines or Poor Clares of St. Colette (PCC); the Poor Clares of Perpetual Adoration (PCPA). There is also an active order engaged in the Mexican Apostolate, the Poor Clare Missionary Sisters (*Misionaras Clarisas;* MC), with its novitiate in Garden Grove, California. The common origin of the contemplatives is the Convent of S. Damiano near Assisi, established by St. Clare under St. Francis' direction. In 1212 she received the Franciscan habit from him and a simple "formula of life" that, through gospel texts, was meant as a model for a life of contemplation and absolute poverty. Card. Hugolino, later *Gregory IX, turned the formula into a rule of life; this "Constitution of Hugolino" was unsatisfactory to St. Clare because it allowed common ownership of property and freed the sisters from a complete dependence on the Friars Minor. She composed another rule, patterned on that of the Friars; designated the *Primitive Rule,* it was finally approved in 1253. This rule was modified by Urban IV, 1261–64, and the nuns following this version—a majority—became known as the Urbanists, while the remainder were called Primitivists. The Colettines have their origin in the work of St. Colette, who, beginning in 1408, restored the *Primitive Rule* in Urbanist monasteries in France and Belgium and established 20 new foundations. There are 24 autonomous American Poor Clare cloisters, with daughter houses in 19 other countries; all observe the *Primitive Rule.* The Poor Clares (PC) originate from the monastery of Newry in Ireland, which established a daughter house in Chula Vista, California. The Colettines (PCC) of Omaha, Neb., are of Italian origin; the Colettines of Cleveland, Ohio (with two other foundations in Ohio and one in Washington, D.C.) came from a Colettine house in Holland in 1877. The Poor Clares of Perpetual Adoration (PCPA), founded in Paris in 1854, came to the U.S. in 1921.

The contemplative Poor Clares live a life of primitive monastic observance, including abstinence from meat, celebrate the choral Liturgy of the Hours, live on their labors and on alms, and seek to grow in contemplative union with God. BIBLIOGRAPHY: S. Cita-Malard, *Religious Orders of Women* (tr. G. J. Robinson, 1964) 16–17; 47–48; T. V. McCarthy, *Challenge for Now* (pa. 1974), with bibliog.

POOR HANDMAIDS OF JESUS CHRIST (Ancilla Domini Sisters), a religious congregation of women dedicated to teaching and home nursing, founded in 1851 by Mother Maria (Katharina Kasper; 1820–98) at Dernbach, Germany, where the general motherhouse is located today. The rules and constitutions, an adaptation of those of St. Vincent de Paul, were granted final approval by Leo XIII. In their apostolic work, the sisters conduct schools, orphanages, and homes for the aged in Germany, Holland, England, and America. The U.S. motherhouse and novitiate are in Donaldson, Indiana. In 1975 total membership of the congregation was 2,254 sisters residing in 146 foundations.

[R. A. TODD]

POOR INFIRMARIANS, see OBREGONIANS.

POOR MEN OF LOMBARDY, a sect of *Waldenses that separated from the *Poor Men of Lyons in 1205. Members were divided into three classes: missionaries, women under vows, and married persons. In 1210 some of them sought reunion with the Church, and Innocent III organized them into an order known as Reconciled Lombards. This group, under their leader, Bernard Prim, rendered useful service in combating the Waldenses and *Cathari, until the mendicant orders were established.

[C. J. LYNCH]

POOR MEN OF LYONS, early name for the Waldenses, members of a movement for evangelical poverty founded *c.*1175 at Lyons by the merchant *Waldo. Under this name (Paupères de Lugduno) they were condemned by the Council of Verona (1184) under Pope Lucius III. *WALDENSES.

[T. C. O'BRIEN]

POOR SERVANTS OF THE MOTHER OF GOD (SMG), a congregation of sisters whose members staff schools, instruct catechetical and convert groups, conduct orphanages, hospitals, homes for the chronically ill, the aged, the mentally retarded, and manage hostels for students and working girls. The institute was founded in London in 1869 by Mother Magdalen (Frances Margaret Taylor, 1832–1900), with the assistance of Lady Georgiana Fullerton (1812–85). The sisters take simple, perpetual vows and observe a rule modeled after that of the Jesuits. In 1975 they had a total membership of 490 sisters and maintained 42 houses located in England, Scotland, Ireland, France, Italy, and the U.S. The superior general resides at Maryfield, Roehampton, London.

[R. A. TODD]

POOR SISTERS OF JESUS CRUCIFIED AND THE SORROWFUL MOTHER (CJC), religious members of a congregation of diocesan origin founded in 1924 by the Passionist Fr. Alphonsus Maria, (1884–1949) in Scranton, Pa. The first three sisters received their religious training with the Sisters, Servants of the Immaculate Heart of Mary. SS. Paul of the Cross and Gabriel Possenti were chosen as patrons. With an increase of members and new houses, the congregation spread to other dioceses in Connecticut, Massachusetts, New York, and Pennsylvania. Brockton, Mass., has been the location of the motherhouse since 1945, when Abp. Richard J. Cushing invited the sisters to the Archdiocese of Boston. They are engaged in educational and social work, and conduct several schools, nursing homes, and centers for catechetical instruction.

[R. A. TODD]

POOR SISTERS OF NAZARETH (PSN), a congregation of religious, originating under the patronage of Card. Wiseman (1802–65) and founded in 1851 by Mother St. Basil (Victoire Larmenier, 1827–78) in London. The members take simple, perpetual vows and observe the rule of St. Augustine. In 1899 the community was approved by Rome, and a revision of the constitutions received approbation in 1962. Besides the care of the aged, the sisters engage in the education of children and the care of underprivileged infants. Their work has spread from the British Isles to South Africa, Australia, and the U.S. in 1975 the congregation had 762 members in 66 houses. The generalate is located at Hammersmith, London.

[R. A. TODD]

POOR SOULS, see ALL SOULS' DAY.

POORE, RICHARD (d. 1237), bishop. P., the son of the bp. of Winchester, required a dispensation to hold his numerous ecclesiastical offices. An able, holy, and learned man, he became bp. of Chichester in 1214. When he was translated to Salisbury (1217), he moved the see from Old Sarum and established the present well-planned town of Salisbury with its famous cathedral. Since he had become deeply interested in reform at the Lateran Council (1215), he drew up for Salisbury diocesan statutes which admirably expressed the church reform movement of the time. These decrees express also his concern for his flock. P. became bp. of Durham (1228–37), and he is said by some to have written here the *Ancren Riwle*.

[A. WARDLE]

POPE, one of the titles most commonly used in English by Catholics and non-Catholics to designate the visible head of the RC Church. The word itself is derived from a Greek word (*pappas*), a child's colloquial equivalent for the more formal term father. It is therefore basically close to the title Holy Father, a term very commonly used by Catholics to designate the same person. Though earlier applied to all bps., the title pope has been from about the 6th cent. reserved in the West to the bp. of Rome.

Other titles, however, better or more clearly express the exact nature of the office of the head of the Church. It is because he is "successor of St. Peter," whom Our Lord constituted the enduring bedrock on which his Church rests, to whom he committed the keys of the kingdom (Mt 16.16–18), whom he set over his flock (Jn 21.15) that the pope as general "vicar of Christ" and pastor of the whole Church "has in regard to the Church full, supreme and universal power, which he is always able to exercise fully" (Vat II ConstChurch 22). This succession to the primacy of Peter he receives through his canonical election as bp. of Rome, for in that see so closely associated with Peter's labors and martyrdom the Church has always recognized the succession to carry with it the special position that Peter held as head and chief of the apostolic college.

That the pope is "primate of Italy" and "patriarch of the West" is due to the geographical location of Rome and to the fact that no other important Church in the West was so clearly of apostolic origin in the time when the patriarchal divisions of the Church and the special rights accruing to patriarchs were recognized and canonized (4th and 5th centuries).

Finally, that the pope is "sovereign of the State of Vatican City" arises out of a complexus of historical and political events by which Vatican City is recognized as a sovereign state with the pope as its temporal ruler. Several patriarchates exist in the West besides that of Rome—Venice, Lisbon, and Goa—but these are nominal and honorary, and carry with them no jurisdictional right or prerogative, except for the right of precedence over primates.

The title of pope is still preserved in the Eastern Church, Catholic and Orthodox, for the patriarch of Alexandria, who is called "The Most Blessed and Holy Pope and Patriarch of the Great City of Alexandria and of all Egypt, the Pentapolis and Pelousia, Lybia and Ethiopia; Ecumenical Judge." It is also used for ordinary priests among the Greeks (*pappas*) and the Slavs (*pop*). BIBLIOGRAPHY: H. Leclercq, DACL 13.1:1097–1111; A. P. Frutaz, EncCatt 9:752–767.

[S. E. DONLON]

POPE, ALEXANDER (1688–1744), English poet, outstanding satirist, Catholic and thus barred from a university degree, friend of Gay, Swift, Arbuthnot, and Bolingbroke. He won attention by his *Essay on Criticism* (1711) and his brilliant social satire *Rape of the Lock* (1712 and enlarged 1714). Verse translations of the *Iliad* (1715–20) and the *Odyssey* (1725–26) brought fame and financial security. Devoted to poetic art he attacked with moral indignation pedantry, ignorance, and dullness in poor writing. An *Essay on Man* (1733–34) and four *Moral Essays* (1731–35) on false taste, avarice, characters of men and women, reveal pity mingled with scorn in his views on corrupt finance and politics under Walpole. Preeminently the poet of his age, his sensitive use of the heroic couplet is unsurpassed by any writer. BIBLIOGRAPHY: G. W. Sherburn, *Early Career of Alexander Pope* (1934); B. Dobree, *Alexander Pope* (1951).

[M. M. BARRY]

POPE, HUGH (1869–1946), English Dominican biblical scholar and preacher. Educated at the Oratory School under Card. Newman and at Louvain, P. had a sound classical training and became an expert Hebraist. He took his doctorate in Scripture at Rome in 1909 and served for a time as professor of Scripture at the Angelico (as it was then called). After returning to England he was a pioneer in open-air preaching and was one of the founders of the Catholic Evidence Guild; quite fearless, his improvisations contributed greatly to the rough-and-tumble of debate. As regent of studies for his province (1920–32) he applied the regulations he received from Rome with robust discrimination. P. was an unflagging student and writer; though his own work was too directed to *ad hoc* communication for scholarly detachment, his encouragement and enthusiasm did much to enlarge the prestige of his province in the next generation. In character he was a foil at every point, except in a common dedication, to his contemporary, Vincent *McNabb. The two, even in their eccentricities, are still cherished legends among their brethren. He was trim, straight, old-fashioned in dress; his imaginative sympathies and devastating candor led him on occasion to be mistaken for a Modernist or a bolshevik, but fundamentally he was a man of the right though independent of the tradition. Among his writings he was esp. well known for his *Catholic Students' Aids to the Bible* (5 v., 1913; rev. ed 1936). BIBLIOGRAPHY: K. Mulvey, *Hugh Pope of the Order of Preachers* (1954).

[T. GILBY]

POPERY, commonly a derisive term for the RC religion, connoting esp. beliefs and practices rejected by the English and Scottish Reformers. Doctrine and ritual that W. *Laud, Abp. of Canterbury, sought to preserve, were impugned by Puritans in England and *Covenanters in Scotland as popery. The term, however, is also used more soberly simply to refer to the polity of the RC Church, in which the pope is the supreme head.

[T. C. O'BRIEN]

POPES, LIST OF. The most accurate list available, i.e., that of the *Annuario pontificio* (1975), follows. The first date given is the date of election; the last date, that of death, deposition, or resignation; the middle date, that of coronation. For further information on individual popes, see separate article under each pope's name. The names appearing within brackets are those of antipopes.

St. Peter, . . . 67
St. Linus, 67–76
St. Anacletus (Cletus), 76–88
St. Clement I, 88–97
St. Evaristus, 97–105
St. Alexander I, 105–115
St. Sixtus I, 115–125
St. Telesphorus, 125–136
St. Hyginus, 136–140
St. Pius I, 140–155
St. Anicetus, 155–166
St. Soter, 166–175
St. Eleutherius, 175–189
St. Victor I, 189–199
St. Zephyrinus, 199–217
St. Callistus I, 217–222
   [St. Hippolytus, 217–235]
St. Urban I, 222–230
St. Pontianus, July 21, 230–Sept. 28, 235
St. Anterus, Nov. 21, 235–Jan. 3, 236
St. Fabian, Jan. 10, 236–Jan. 20, 250
St. Cornelius, March 251–June 253
   [Novatian, 251]
St. Lucius I, June 25, 253–March 5, 254
St. Stephen I, May 12, 254–Aug. 2, 257
St. Sixtus II, Aug. 30, 257–Aug. 6, 258
St. Dionysius, July 22, 259–Dec. 26, 268
St. Felix I, Jan 5, 269–Dec. 30, 274
St. Eutychian, Jan. 4, 275–Dec. 7, 283
St. Gaius (Caius), Dec. 17, 283–April 22, 296
St. Marcellinus, June 30, 296–Oct. 25, 304
St. Marcellus I, May 27, 308–Jan. 16, 309
St. Eusebius, April 18, 309–Aug. 17, 309
St. Miltiades, July 2, 311–Jan. 11, 314
St. Silvester I, Jan. 31, 314–Dec. 31, 335
St. Mark, Jan. 18, 336–Oct. 7, 336
St. Julius I, Feb. 6, 337–April 12, 352
Liberius, May 17, 352–Sept. 24, 366
   [Felix II, . . . 355–Nov. 22, 365]
St. Damasus I, Oct. 1, 366–Dec. 11, 384
   [Ursinus, 366–367]
St. Siricius, Dec. 15, 22, or 29, 384–Nov. 26, 399
St. Anastasius I, Nov. 27, 399–Dec. 19, 401
St. Innocent I, Dec. 22, 401–March 12, 417
St. Zosimus, March 18, 417–Dec. 26, 418
St. Boniface I, Dec. 28 or 29, 418–Sept. 4, 422
   [Eulalius, Dec. 27 or 29, 418–419]
St. Celestine I, Sept. 10, 422–July 27, 432
St. Sixtus III, July 31, 432–Aug. 19, 440

St. Leo I, Sept. 29, 440–Nov. 10, 461
St. Hilary, Nov. 19, 461–Feb. 29, 468
St. Simplicius, March 3, 468–March 10, 483
St. Felix III (II), March 13, 483–March 1, 492
St. Gelasius I, March 1, 492–Nov. 21, 496
Anastasius II, Nov. 24, 496–Nov. 19, 498
St. Symmachus, Nov. 22, 498–July 19, 514
   [Lawrence, 498; 501–505]
St. Hormisdas, July 20, 514–Aug. 6, 523
St. John I, Aug. 13, 523–May 18, 526
St. Felix IV (III), July 12, 526–Sept. 22, 530
Boniface II, Sept. 22, 530–Oct. 17, 532
   [Dioscorus, Sept. 22, 530–Oct. 14, 530]
John II, Jan. 2, 533–May 8, 535
St. Agapitus I, May 13, 535–April 22, 536
St. Silverius, June 1, 536–Nov. 11, 537
Vigilius, March 29, 537–June 7, 555
Pelagius I, April 16, 556–March 4, 561
John III, July 17, 561–July 13, 574
Benedict I, June 2, 575–July 30, 579
Pelagius II, Nov. 26, 579–Feb. 7, 590
St. Gregory I, Sept. 3, 590–March 12, 604
Sabinian, Sept. 13, 604–Feb. 22, 606
Boniface III, Feb. 19, 607–Nov. 12, 607
St. Boniface IV, Aug. 25, 608–May 8, 615
St. Deusdedit I, Oct. 19, 615–Nov. 8, 618
Boniface V, Dec. 23, 619–Oct. 25, 625
Honorius I, Oct. 27, 625–Oct. 12, 638
Severinus, May 28, 640–Aug. 2, 640
John IV, Dec. 24, 640–Oct. 12, 642
Theodore I, Nov. 24, 642–May 14, 649
St. Martin I, . . . July 649–Sept. 16, 655
St. Eugene I, Aug. 10, 654–June 2, 657
St. Vitalian, July 30, 657–Jan. 27, 672
Deusdedit II, April 11, 672–June 17, 676
Donus, Nov. 2, 676–April 11, 678
St. Agatho, June 27, 678–Jan. 10, 681
St. Leo II, Aug. 17, 682–July 3, 683
St. Benedict II, June 26, 684–May 8, 685
John V, July 23, 685–Aug. 2, 686
Conon, Oct. 21, 686–Sept. 21, 687
   [Theodore, . . . 687]
   [Paschal, . . . 687]
St. Sergius I, Dec. 15, 687–Sept. 8, 701
John VI, Oct. 30, 701–Jan. 11, 705
John VII, March 1, 705–Oct. 18, 707
Sisinnius, Jan. 15, 708–Feb. 4, 708
Constantine, March 25, 708–April 9, 715
St. Gregory II, May 19, 715–Feb. 11, 731
St. Gregory III, March 18, 731–Nov. 741
St. Zachary, Dec. 10, 741–March 22, 752
Stephen, March 22(23?)–26(25?), 752
Stephen II (III), March 26, 752–April 26, 757
St. Paul I, . . . April, May 29, 757–June 28, 767
   [Constantine, June 28, July 5, 767–769]
   [Philip, July 31, 768]

Stephen III (IV), Aug. 1, Aug. 7, 768–Jan. 24, 772
Adrian I, Feb. 1, Feb. 9, 772–Dec. 25, 795
St. Leo III, Dec. 26, Dec. 27, 795–June 12, 816
Stephen IV (V), June 22, 816–Jan. 24, 817
St. Paschal I, Jan. 25, 817–Feb. 11, 824
Eugene II, . . . Feb.–May 824– . . . Aug. 827
Valentine, . . . Aug. 827– . . . Sept. 827
Gregory IV, . . . 827– . . . Jan. 844
   [John, . . . Jan. 844]
Sergius II, . . . Jan. 844–Jan. 27, 847
St. Leo IV, . . . Jan., April 10, 847–July 17, 855
Benedict III, . . . July, Sept. 29, 855–April 17, 858
   [Anastasius, . . . Aug. 855– . . . Sept. 855]
St. Nicholas I, April 24, 858–Nov. 13, 867
Adrian II, Dec. 14, 867–Dec. 14, 872
John VIII, Dec. 14, 872–Dec. 16, 882
Marinus I, Dec. 16, 882–May 15, 884
St. Adrian III, May 17, 884– . . . Sept. 885
Stephen V (VI), . . . Sept. 885–Sept. 14, 891
Formosus, Oct. 6, 891–April 4, 896
Boniface VI, . . . April 896– . . . April 896
Stephen VI (VII), . . . May 896– . . . Aug. 897
Romanus, . . . Aug. 897– . . . Nov. 897
Theodore II, . . . Dec. 897– . . . Dec. 897
John IX, . . . Jan. 898– . . . Jan. 900
Benedict IV, . . . Jan. or Feb. 900– . . . July 903
Leo V, . . . July 903– . . . Sept. 903
   [Christopher, . . . July or . . . Sept. 903– . . . Jan. 904]
Sergius III, Jan. 29, 904–April 14, 911
Anastasius III, . . . April 911– . . . June 913
Lando, . . . July 913– . . . Feb. 914
John X, . . . March 914– . . . May 928
Leo VI, . . . May 928– . . . Dec. 928
Stephen VII (VIII), . . . Dec. 928– . . . Feb. 931
John XI, . . . Feb. or March 931– . . . Dec. 935
Leo VII, Jan. 3, 936–July 13, 939
Stephen VIII (IX), July 14, 939– . . . Oct. 942
Marinus II, Oct. 30, 942–. . . May 946
Agapetus II, May 10, 946–. . . Dec. 955
John XII, Dec. 16, 955–May 14, 964
Leo VIII, Dec. 4, Dec. 6, 963–March 1, 965
Benedict V, May 22, 964–July 4, 966
John XIII, Oct. 1, 965–Sept. 6, 972
Benedict VI, Jan. 19, 973– . . . June 974
   [Boniface VII, . . . June 974–July 974; then Aug. 984–July 985]
Benedict VII, . . . Oct. 974–July 10, 983
John XIV, . . . Dec. 983–Aug. 20, 984
John XV, . . . Aug. 985– . . . March 996
Gregory V, May 3, 996–Feb. 18, 999
   [John XVI, . . . April 997– . . . Feb. 998]
Silvester II, April 2, 999–May 12, 1003
John XVII, . . . June 1003– . . . Dec. 1003
John XVIII, . . . Jan. 1004– . . . July 1009
Sergius IV, July 31, 1009–May 12, 1012
Benedict VIII, May 18, 1012–April 9, 1024
   [Gregory, . . . 1012]

John XIX, . . . April or May 1024– . . . 1032
Benedict IX, . . . 1032– . . . 1044
Silvester III, Jan. 20, 1045–Feb. 10, 1045
Benedict IX, April 10, 1045–May 1, 1045
Gregory VI, May 5, 1045–Dec. 20, 1046
Clement II, Dec. 24, Dec. 25, 1046–Oct. 9, 1047
Benedict IX, Nov. 8, 1047–July 17, 1048
Damasus II, July 17, 1048–Aug. 9, 1048
St. Leo IX, Feb. 12, 1049–April 19, 1054
Victor II, April 16, 1055–July 28, 1057
Stephen IX (X), Aug. 3, 1057–March 29, 1058
   [Benedict X, April 5, 1058–Jan. 24, 1059]
Nicholas II, Jan. 24, 1059–July 27, 1061
Alexander II, Oct. 1, 1061–April 21, 1073
   [Honorius II, Oct. 28, 1061– . . . 1072]
St. Gregory VII, April 22, June 30, 1073–May 25, 1085
   [Clement III, June 25, 1080; March 24, 1084–Sept. 8, 1100]
Bl. Victor III, May 24, 1086–Sept. 16, 1087
Bl. Urban II, March 12, 1088–July 29, 1099
Paschal II, Aug. 13, Aug. 14, 1099–Jan. 21, 1118
   [Theodoric, . . . 1100]
   [Albert, . . . 1102]
   [Silvester IV, Nov. 18, 1105– . . . 1111]
Gelasius II, Jan. 24, March 10, 1118–Jan. 28, 1119
   [Gregory VIII, March 8, 1118– . . . 1121]
Callistus II, Feb. 2, Feb. 9, 1119–Dec. 13, 1124
Honorius II, Dec. 15, Dec. 21, 1124–Feb. 13, 1130
   [Celestine II, . . . Dec. 1124]
Innocent II, Feb. 14, Feb. 23, 1130–Sept. 24, 1143
   [Anacletus II, Feb. 14, Feb. 23, 1130–Jan. 25, 1138]
   [Victor IV, . . . March 1138–May 29, 1138]
Celestine II, Sept. 26, Oct. 3, 1143–March 8, 1144
Lucius II, March 12, 1144–Feb. 15, 1145
Bl. Eugene III, Feb. 15, Feb. 18, 1145–July 8, 1153
Anastasius IV, July 12, 1153–Dec. 3, 1154
Adrian IV, Dec. 4, Dec. 5, 1154–Sept. 1, 1159
Alexander III, Sept. 7, Sept. 20, 1159–Aug. 30, 1181
   [Victor IV, Sept. 7, Oct. 4, 1159–April 20, 1164]
   [Paschal III, April 22, April 26, 1164–Sept. 20, 1168]
   [Callistus III, . . . Sept. 1168–Aug. 29, 1178]
   [Innocent III, Sept. 29, 1179– . . . 1180]
Lucius III, Sept. 1, Sept. 6, 1181–Sept. 25, 1185
Urban III, Nov. 25, Dec. 1, 1185–Oct. 20, 1187
Gregory VIII, Oct. 21, Oct. 25, 1187–Dec. 17, 1187
Clement III, Dec. 19, Dec. 20, 1187– . . . March 1191
Celestine III, March 30, April 14, 1191–Jan. 8, 1198
Innocent III, Jan. 8, Feb. 22, 1198–July 16, 1216
Honorius III, July 18, July 24, 1216–March 18, 1227
Gregory IX, March 19, March 21, 1227–Aug. 22, 1241
Celestine IV, Oct. 25, Oct. 28, 1241–Nov. 10, 1241
Innocent IV, June 25, June 28, 1243–Dec. 7, 1254
Alexander IV, Dec. 12, Dec. 20, 1254–May 25, 1261
Urban IV, Aug. 29, Sept. 4, 1261–Oct. 2, 1264
Clement IV, Feb. 5, Feb. 15, 1265–Nov. 29, 1268
Bl. Gregory X, Sept. 1, 1271, March 27, 1272–Jan. 10, 1276

Bl. Innocent V, Jan. 21, Feb. 22, 1276–June 22, 1276
Adrian V, July 11, 1276–Aug. 18, 1276
John XXI, Sept. 8, Sept. 20, 1276–May 20, 1277
Nicholas III, Nov. 25, Dec. 26, 1277–Aug. 22, 1280
Martin IV, Feb. 22, March 23, 1281–March 28, 1285
Honorius IV, April 2, May 20, 1285–April 3, 1287
Nicholas IV, Feb. 22, 1288–April 4, 1292
St. Celestine V, July 5, Aug. 29, 1294–Dec. 13, 1294
Boniface VIII, Dec. 24, 1294, Jan. 23, 1295–Oct. 11, 1303
Bl. Benedict XI, Oct. 22, Oct. 27, 1303–July 7, 1304
Clement V, June 5, Nov. 14, 1305–April 20, 1314
John XXII, Aug. 7, Sept. 5, 1316–Dec. 4, 1334
    [Nicholas V, May 12, May 22, 1328–Aug. 25, 1330]
Benedict XII, Dec. 20, 1334, Jan. 8, 1335–April 25, 1342
Clement VI, May 7, May 19, 1342–Dec. 6, 1352
Innocent VI, Dec. 18, Dec. 30, 1352–Sept. 12, 1362
Bl. Urban V, Sept. 28, Nov. 6, 1362–Dec. 19, 1370
Gregory XI, Dec. 30, 1370, Jan. 5, 1371–March 26, 1378
Urban VI, April 8, April 18, 1378–Oct. 15, 1389
Boniface IX, Nov. 2, Nov. 9, 1389–Oct. 1, 1404
Innocent VII, Oct. 17, Nov. 11, 1404–Nov. 6, 1406
Gregory XII, Nov. 30, Dec. 19, 1406–July 4, 1415
    [Clement VII, Sept. 20, Oct. 31, 1378–Sept. 16, 1394]
    [Benedict XIII, Sept. 28, Oct. 11, 1394–May 23, 1423]
    [Alexander V, June 26, July 7, 1409–May 3, 1410]
    [John XXIII, May 17, May 25, 1410–May 29, 1415]
Martin V, Nov. 11, Nov. 21, 1417–Feb. 20, 1431
Eugene IV, March 3, March 11, 1431–Feb. 23, 1447
    [Felix V, Nov. 5, 1439, July 24, 1440–April 7, 1449]
Nicholas V, March 6, March 19, 1447–March 24, 1455
Callistus III, April 8, April 20, 1455–Aug. 6, 1458
Pius II, Aug. 19, Sept. 3, 1458–Aug. 15, 1464
Paul II, Aug. 30, Sept. 16, 1464–July 26, 1471
Sixtus IV, Aug. 9, Aug. 25, 1471–Aug. 12, 1484
Innocent VIII, Aug. 29, Sept. 12, 1484–July 25, 1492
Alexander VI, Aug. 11, Aug. 26, 1492–Aug. 18, 1503
Pius III, Sept. 22, Oct. 1, Oct. 8, 1503–Oct. 18, 1503
Julius II, Oct. 31, Nov. 26, 1503–Feb. 21, 1513
Leo X, March 9, March 19, 1513–Dec. 1, 1521
Adrian VI, Jan. 9, Aug. 31, 1522–Sept. 14, 1523
Clement VII, Nov. 19, Nov. 26, 1523–Sept. 25, 1534
Paul III, Oct. 13, Nov. 3, 1534–Nov. 10, 1549
Julius III, Feb. 7, Feb. 22, 1550–March 23, 1555
Marcellus II, April 9, April 10, 1555–May 1, 1555
Paul IV, May 23, May 26, 1555–Aug. 18, 1559
Pius IV, Dec. 25, 1559, Jan. 6, 1560–Dec. 9, 1565
St. Pius V, Jan. 7, Jan. 17, 1566–May 1, 1572
Gregory XIII, May 13, May 25, 1572–April 10, 1585
Sixtus V, April 24, May 1, 1585–Aug. 27, 1590
Urban VII, Sept. 15, 1590–Sept. 27, 1590
Gregory XIV, Dec. 5, Dec. 8, 1590–Oct. 16, 1591
Innocent IX, Oct. 29, Nov. 3, 1591–Dec. 30, 1591
Clement VIII, Jan. 30, Feb. 9, 1592–March 3, 1605
Leo XI, April 1, April 10, 1605–April 27, 1605
Paul V, May 16, May 29, 1605–Jan. 28, 1621
Gregory XV, Feb. 9, Feb. 14, 1621–July 8, 1623
Urban VIII, Aug. 6, Sept. 29, 1623–July 29, 1644

Innocent X, Sept. 15, Oct. 4, 1644–Jan. 7, 1655
Alexander VII, April 7, April 18, 1655–May 22, 1667
Clement IX, June 20, June 26, 1667–Dec. 9, 1669
Clement X, April 29, May 11, 1670–July 22, 1676
Bl. Innocent XI, Sept. 21, Oct. 4, 1676–Aug. 12, 1689
Alexander VIII, Oct. 6, Oct. 16, 1689–Feb. 1, 1691
Innocent XII, July 12, July 15, 1691–Sept. 27, 1700
Clement XI, Nov. 23, Nov. 30, Dec. 8, 1700–March 19, 1721
Innocent XIII, May 8, May 18, 1721–March 7, 1724
Benedict XIII, May 29, June 4, 1724–Feb. 21, 1730
Clement XII, July 12, July 16, 1730–Feb. 6, 1740
Benedict XIV, Aug. 17, Aug. 22, 1740–May 3, 1758
Clement XIII, July 6, July 16, 1758–Feb. 2, 1769
Clement XIV, May 19, May 28, June 4, 1769–Sept. 22, 1774
Pius VI, Feb. 15, Feb. 22, 1775–Aug. 29, 1799
Pius VII, March 14, March 21, 1800–Aug. 20, 1823
Leo XII, Sept. 28, Oct. 5, 1823–Feb. 10, 1829
Pius VIII, March 31, April 5, 1829–Nov. 30, 1830
Gregory XVI, Feb. 2, Feb. 6, 1831–June 1, 1846
Pius IX, June 16, June 21, 1846–Feb. 7, 1878
Leo XIII, Feb. 20, March 3, 1878–July 20, 1903
St. Pius X, Aug. 4, Aug. 9, 1903–Aug. 20, 1914
Benedict XV, Sept. 3, Sept. 6, 1914–Jan. 22, 1922
Pius XI, Feb. 6, Feb. 12, 1922–Feb. 10, 1939
Pius XII, March 2, March 12, 1939–Oct. 9, 1958
John XXIII, Oct. 28, Nov. 4, 1958–June 3, 1963
Paul VI, June 21, June 30, 1963–Aug. 6, 1978
John Paul I, Aug. 26, Sept. 3, 1978–Sept. 28, 1978
John Paul II, Oct. 16, Oct. 22, 1978–

POPES, NAMES OF. In the first 900 years of the history of the papacy, those elected pope seem to have used their given name, adding a distinguishing number, e.g., John XII. So far as is known the first to take a new name on assuming the papacy was Peter Canepanova in the year 983, who became John XIV. The most frequently chosen names thereafter and the number of popes choosing them from 985 to the present were John (9), Gregory (12), Benedict (8), Clement (13), Leo (5), Alexander (7), Innocent (12), Urban (7), Paul (5), and Pius (11). Peter of Pavia, out of reverence for the first pope, took the name of John. Motives for the choice of a papal name are several: the desire to assume a Roman name, admiration for or special knowledge of a predecessor bearing the name, in the 11th cent. the wish to be associated with popes preceding them in early centuries of the Church.

POPES, PALACE OF THE, AVIGNON (1335–65), French Gothic papal palace, combining the austere Old Palace of Benedict XII (1334–42) and the richly ornamented ogive-vaulted New Palace of Clement VI (1342–52), much damaged in the 19th cent., now in the course of restoration. Of huge dimensions the vast Gothic-vaulted rooms—though missing their paintings—are impressive. The remaining frescoes of the 14th cent. by M. Giovanetti, important chapel frescoes suggesting S. Martini, and hunting and fishing murals pointing to Italian artists (*c.* 1350) have considerable value. BIBLIOGRAPHY: L. H. Labande, *Le Palais des papes et les monuments d'Avignon au XIV*e *siècle* (2 v., 1925).

[M. J. DALY]

POPISH PLOT, see OATES PLOT.

POPPO OF STAVELOT, ST. (978–1048), abbot, reformer. In 1008, P. entered the Benedictine Order at the abbey of St. Thierry after time spent in the army and in pilgrimages to the Holy Land. Transferred to the abbey of Verdun-sur-Meuse, he began work as reformer of abbeys in Flanders and was appointed to the abbatial See of Stavelot-Malmédy in 1020. He was aided and encouraged by successive emperors to reform abbeys in Lorraine and Flanders. A type of medieval imperial abbot and great monastic reformer, P. acted as negotiator between the Empire and France. BIBLIOGRAPHY: H. Roeder, *Saints and Their Attributes* (1955); Butler 1:166–167; R. Van Doren, BiblSanct 10:1029–34.

[M. E. DUFFY]

POPULAR FRONT, governing coalition in France, 1936–37. The Popular Front consisted of the Radical, Socialist, and Communist parties. The agreement of these parties stemmed from their common opposition to deflationary economic policies and concern over the danger of fascism both in France and abroad. This agreement had been symbolized when the leaders of the three parties marched side by side on Bastille Day, 1935. It was formalized in the Popular Front Program of January 11, 1936. The program promised defense of freedom through suppression of the Fascist leagues and upholding civil liberties, defense of peace through support for the League of Nations, economic recovery through increased purchasing power and agricultural reform, and "financial purification" through reform of the tax system and security markets. Campaigning on this program the parties of the Popular Front won a decisive victory in the elections of 1936, and the Socialist leader Léon Blum headed the new government. Blum's first task as premier was to mediate a sit-down strike which had spread throughout France in the wake of the Popular Front victory which had excited the workers and frightened the bourgeoisie. The Popular Front aroused the concern of French Catholics by promising to insure the nonreligious character of education and by voicing support for the anticlerical government of the Spanish Republic. The Blum government, however, declared a policy of nonintervention in the Spanish Civil War, and its educational reforms were generally nonprovocative. Although a law of August 7, 1936, raised the age for compulsory schooling to 14, other reforms were administrative steps undertaken by the minister of education, Jean Zay, with the intention of equalizing education in the primary and secondary schools. While many Catholics feared a "monopoly of education," other Catholics favored these democratic reforms. The real obstacle to Zay's program was the inability of the Popular Front to solve the economic crisis and to provide the financial resources to implement social reform. BIBLIOGRAPHY: J. E. Talbott, *Politics of Educational Reform in France, 1918–1940* (1969).

[R. J. GIBBONS]

POPULATION CONTROL. The current context of the term is the problem of overpopulation. Statistics of demographers and findings of ecologists have long been a warning that the earth's resources cannot for long sustain the rate of increase in the earth's population. Zero-population growth is the ideal dictated by such warnings. The problem of overpopulation has its actual and most pressing urgency in the developing nations. Development understood as a process towards a point where a nation's people enjoy a subsistence level that at least approximates a human and humane existence is negated by population growth that cancels out any economic gains made.

Population control is related to the problem of overpopulation as the immediate remedy. The control has taken the form, e.g., of compulsory sterilization in India; in other countries, of fines imposed for unauthorized pregnancies. The chief form of the campaign for population control, however, is the dissemination of information and devices for artificial contraception and nontherapeutic abortion. The Catholic position on the issue is complex. Vatican Council II affirmed the goals of decent human existence for all people and particularly espoused the cause of betterment for the peoples of the Third World (Vat II ChurchModWorld 5,87). The Council even takes a more positive view of research and practice with regard to family planning (*ibid.* 87) than did John XXIII in *Mater et magistra* (185–194). Paul VI's *Humanae vitae* (17, 23) and *Populorum progressio* (37) and the 1971 Synod of Bishops' *Justice in the World* (ch. 3) all face the issue of overpopulation as an admitted problem. What the Catholic Church does not accept, however, is the violation of human rights and the thesis that population control by artificial contraception, compulsory sterilization, or elective abortion is the only or the right solution to overpopulation.

The Church applies to the social and economic problem of overpopulation the same norms regarding contraception, sterilization, and direct abortion as it does at the level of individual morality. But on the level of "social engineering" there is another reason for opposition. Compulsory forms of population control imposed by governments are a violation of the dignity of the human person. In regard to the inner relationships and rights of marriage the State has no right to interfere; in this area there is no subordination to any human authority (ThAq ST 2a2ae, 104.5). A secondary, yet germane consideration in the human rights area is that those affected by compulsory measures are the poor and the de facto disenfranchised. Also relevant to the Church's opposition is the fact that there is by no means a ''secular'' or scientific agreement that that artificial and/or compulsory measure to control population are the unique solution to overpopulation. One reason for recourse to it is relatively simple and immediate. The imbalance between the ''First World'' and the Third World, it can be urged, is rectifiable by the genuine possibilities of the ''Green Revolution'' as established by the Nobel laureate agronomist, Norman Berlang. But an approach that is more human, because it requires the most human of all virtues—justice, is the positive espousal of economic justice. That would involve—as it already does involve in the case of the thorny issue of the UN's ''New International Economic Order''—a formidable and complex task, a readjustment of economics, the distribution of wealth, the ''profit principle,'' the relation of the First World to the Third World. Because such matters are the products of human art and invention, they also admit of human adjustment. The artificiality, however, the self-interest, and the level of life in developed nations make any concerted effort at readjustment merely a utopian proposal. Population control will, therefore, continue to be the one avenue advocated and followed, the exploitation of peoples and resources not created by man will continue to be preferred to readjustment of the exploitive system that man did create.

[T. C. O'BRIEN]

POPULORUM PROGRESSIO (Development of Peoples), encyclical issued by Pope Paul VI on March 26, 1967. It deals with ''development of those peoples who are striving to escape from hunger, misery, endemic disease, and ignorance; of those who are looking for a wider share in the benefits of civilization and a more active improvement of their human qualities; of those who are aiming purposefully at their complete fulfillment.'' It has received wide attention for its expression of the social conscience of the Church in regard to poverty and wealth. It draws on the Vatican Council II's *Pastoral Constitution of the Church in the Modern World,* and follows in the tradition of such encyclicals as *Rerum novarum* (Leo XIII, 1891), *Quadragesimo anno (Pius XI, 1931), and *Pacem in terris* (John XXIII, 1963). Denouncing ''the scandal of glaring inequalities not merely in the enjoyment of possessions, but even more in the exercise of power,'' it declares that ''the superfluous wealth of rich countries should be placed at the service of poor nations.'' While warning against revolution, it calls for ''urgent reforms . . . without delay.'' It opposes nationalism and racism and defines the goal as ''complete humanism.'' Included in its analysis are several specific recommendations, such as ''rectification of inequitable trade relations.'' It gives a guarded approval of some birth control programs. Often quoted is its statement that ''the new name for peace is development.'' BIBLIOGRAPHY: P. Riga, *Church of the Poor* (1968).

[T. EARLY]

PORCARO, STEFANO (d. 1453), Italian revolutionary. Born of a wealthy family, well-educated, and a capable administrator, P. nevertheless nurtured an obsession for liberating Rome from ''papal slavery'' and making it a republic. Apprehended in an attempt to carry out his design P. was hanged in Castel Sant' Angelo. BIBLIOGRAPHY: H. Schmidinger, LTK 8:618; H. Dressler, NCE 11:592–593.

[H. DRESSLER]

PORDAGE, JOHN (1607–81), English astrologer who expounded the writings of J. *Boehme and introduced Jane *Leade to them. In his hands Boehme's metaphysics were simplified and extended according to his own ideas. P.'s numerous visions won him a circle of followers, who were called Behmenists. He was deprived of his ministerial office in 1655 but reinstated in 1660. BIBLIOGRAPHY: N. Thune, *Behmenists and the Philadelphians* (1948).

[M. J. SUELZER]

PORDENONE (GIOVANNI ANTONIO DE' SACCHI; 1483–1538), N Italian master, the only Venetian High Renaissance painter in fresco. P.'s early works are linear in the manner of Mantegna. After a visit to Rome, influenced by Michelangelo, P. developed force and heavy movement in broad strokes, moving from *Madonna of Mercy* (Pordenone cathedral), frescoes in Treviso cathedral (1520–22), to a violent *Passion of Christ* (Cremona, 1521). Work in Venice (1529) at the Scuola di S. Rocco, Cortemaggiore, and at Piacenza (1531) in an early Baroque style were of value to artists from Titian to Rubens.

[M. J. DALY]

PORNOGRAPHY, from Gr. *pornē*, prostitute, *graphein,* to write, the portrayal of sexual actions, in words or pictures, with a pandering intent. The publicized perplexity about enforcing laws of *obscenity, as well as the pervasive, open purveyance and display of pornographic books and films can obscure moral evaluation. Permissiveness neither legitimates pornography morally, nor changes its meaning. That the pornographic exists, in distinction from the genuine and integral portrayal of the sexual as part of human experience, is a fact acknowledged, not by moralists alone, but by its creators, purveyors, and exhibitors. Defense and purveyance of pornography are not simply concerned with a general freedom of speech or expression, but with the specific content defended and peddled. To the protagonists of pornography pandering is something perfectly acceptable: to provide any and every kind of source for sexual arousal and orgasm is right because sexual gratification is always right, no matter how or by whom it is achieved. It is an absolute personal freedom. To regard pandering as reprehensible is to deny any such absolute right. For moral theology the proscription of pornography rests on the recognition that there is a virtue of *chastity that is to guide and control sexual activity as part of an integrally human life; that there can be a serious violation of chastity even in purely internal thoughts and *desires. Literature, live or filmed portrayals that are pornographic, i.e., pandering to sexual arousal alone, are thus immoral. Because of that the production, purveyance, or exhibition of pornography are sins. Moral evaluation also includes a special concern for the young, since the availability of pornography is a scandal, a threat to their moral development. Such moral judgments take into account the more exacting and demanding standards of sexual morality that are part of the Christian understanding of the Gospel (see Mt 5.27–28; 1 Cor 6.15–20). That understanding does not depend on the mores of society nor on legal decisions. Christian conscience needs to be clear about its own standards; they are wholesome, and the proliferation of pornography truly symptomatic of a social disease.

[T. C. O'BRIEN]

POROURAR (*Phorourar*), Armenian sacerdotal stole, the equivalent in form and use of the Byzantine *epitrachelion*. Armenian Catholics often call it an *ourar,* like the diaconal stole.

[A. CODY]

PORPHYRY OF GAZA, ST. (c. 347–420), bp. of Gaza from 395. He had been a monk before being ordained (392). As bp. he won many converts and succeeded, with imperial help, in repressing the anti-Christian pagans in his territory.

PORPHYRY OF TYRE (232–after 301), Neoplatonic philosopher, biographer and editor of Plotinus. Though a devoted pupil of Plotinus and a conscientious expounder of his teachings, he assumed an independent position on some important points. He emphasized the use of the categories of Aristotle, commented upon them, and gave them an essential place in Neoplatonism. P.'s *Tree,* a classification of predicables based on Aristotle, was destined to have an enormous influence in the history of logic. A man of wide scholarly interests, he commented upon Homer and several other Greek writers or works. Unlike Plotinus, he recognized the theurgic element in philosophy and religion, being esp. impressed by the teachings of the *Chaldaean Oracles.* At times, however, his position seems ambivalent. He warns against divination and superstition, yet was a firm believer in demonology. He promoted pagan cults and attempted to give a kind of systematic theology to paganism by interpreting the pagan myths as allegorical representations of philosophical truth. He advocated various ascetic practices and the exemplification of piety in works as well as in prayer and sacrifice. P., along with *Celsus, was the ablest of the ancient intellectual opponents to Christianity. His work *Against the Christians* in 15 books was burnt by the Emperors Valentinian III and Theodosius II in 448 A.D., but its contents can be largely reconstructed from fragments and references to and refutations of his arguments in Eusebius and other Christian writers. His opposition, like that of Celsus, was based on his conviction that Christianity

posed a grave threat to Hellenic tradition. Doctrines, like the divinity of Christ, he regarded as philosophically absurd. He showed an unusual knowledge of the Old and New Testaments and anticipated modern Higher Criticism in his treatment of the Book of Daniel and the Mosaic authorship of the Pentateuch. BIBLIOGRAPHY: E. R. Dodds, OCD 719–720; P. Lerlan, LexAW 2415–16; Copleston 1:473–475; CHGMP 283–297; P. De Labrille, *La Réaction païenne* (6th ed., 1942), 223–296.

[M. R. P. MCGUIRE]

PORPORA, NICCOLÒ ANTONIO (1686–1768), Italian opera composer and singing-master. He studied with Greco, Giordano, and Campanile in Naples, where his first opera, *Agrippina* (1708) was performed. He served as *maestro di cappella* and singing teacher in Naples and in Venice. An unmatched singing teacher, he instructed the famous Uberti, Farinelli, Caffarelli, Salimbeni, and Hasse. Hadyn served as his pupil and valet in Vienna. P.'s operas rivaled those of Handel in London and of Hasse in Dresden. His numerous works include 50 operas, oratorios, sacred and secular cantatas, 6 Masses, motets, and some instrumental music.

[R. J. LITZ]

PORRAS, Y AILLYÓN, RAFAELA, ST. (1850–1925), foundress. A member of the Society of Mary Reparatrix, she was directed by her adviser to remain in Córdoba, when the community moved to Seville, to found a new society Sisters of Reparation of the Sacred Heart (later named Handmaids of the Sacred Heart of Jesus.) The community engaged in perpetual adoration, teaching, and catechetics. In 1886 the society was approved by Rome, and P. became first superior general. She was beatified in 1952 and canonized in 1977. BIBLIOGRAPHY: R. Bidagor, BiblSanct 10:1370-73.

[J. R. AHERNE]

PORRECTUS, a neum in *Gregorian chant notation signifying a succession of three notes, the second lower in pitch than the other two.

[A. DOHERTY]

PORRES, MARTÍN DE, ST. (1579–1639), Dominican. A mulatto of Peru, P. joined the Dominicans of Lima as a lay brother in 1603. He became a symbol of heroic charity toward the poor for whom he built a hospital. A mystic, he was a celebrated figure in Lima. Beatified in 1837, P. is the center of veneration in Latin America, esp. among blacks. He was canonized in 1962. BIBLIOGRAPHY: G. Cavallini, *St. Martin de Porres: Apostle of Charity* (tr. C. C. Holland, 1963);

[J. R. AHERNE]

PORT-ROYAL, the Cistercian abbey of nuns founded in 1204, and in the 17th cent. the main center of *Jansenism. The original monastery, about 17 miles from Paris, near

Versailles, came to be called Port-Royal des Champs after 1625; in that year the community was transferred to Paris, to a new monastery, Port-Royal de Paris, in the Faubourg Saint-Jacques. In 1665 most of the nuns, having refused to sign a formulary condemning the five Jansenist propositions, were transferred back to Port-Royal des Champs, where they were virtually prisoners for 4 years. With the *Peace of the Church (1669) they enjoyed a decade of quiet. Their continued loyalty to the Jansenist cause, however, was viewed as opposition to his royal power by Louis XIV; in 1679 Port-Royal des Champs was forbidden to receive novices, and its temporalities were severely diminished. In 1706 the aging nuns refused to accept yet another papal condemnation of Jansenism, *Vineam Domini;* 3 years later the abbey was suppressed and the nuns sent to various convents. In 1710 the buildings of Port-Royal des Champs were razed; even the bones in the cemetery were transferred.

The name Port-Royal connotes a whole circle of leading figures in the Jansenist movement. Mère Angélique *Arnauld, named abbess at Port-Royal des Champs at the age of 7, and its reformer at the age of 18, effected the transfer of her flourishing community to Paris. Through her director after 1633, the Abbé de *Saint-Cyran, Port-Royal acquired its spirit of moral rigorism and its loyalty to his friend, Cornelius *Jansen, author of *Augustinus.* Saint-Cyran's disciples, priests and laymen, became Les Messieurs de Port-Royal; solitaries devoted to the spiritual life and scholarship, they lived first near Port-Royal de Paris, then after Saint-Cyran's arrest in 1638, at Port-Royal des Champs. There they established Les Petites-Écoles, important in the history of pedagogy, esp. for the inculcation of moral training and the emphasis on French and Italian letters rather than on Jesuit classical tradition. Among Les Messieurs was Antoine *Arnauld, brother of Mère Angélique. His *De la fréquente communion* (1643) intensified the Saint-Cyranian moral rigorism and shaped the liturgical life of Port-Royal. The Port-Royalists also tenaciously used Arnauld's distinction between the Pope's right (*droit*) to condemn the heresy in the five Jansenist propositions, and the fact (*fait*) that the propositions were present in Jansen's *Augustinus.* The name of Blaise *Pascal, author of the Provincial Letters, was also associated with Port-Royal, and his sister Jacqueline was a nun there. BIBLIOGRAPHY: Knox Enth; L. Cognet, NCE 11:597–598, bibliog.

[T. C. O'BRIEN]

PORTA, COSTANZO (*c.*1530–1601), Italian monk, composer, master contrapuntist, and madrigalist. He studied at Venice with Adriaen Willaert. P. served as choirmaster at Osimo (1552–64), at Padua (1564), at Ravenna (1567), at Loreto (1575), and again at the Basilica of St. Antony of Padua (1595–1601). P.'s first works were published at the same time as those of Lassus and Palestrina. His compositions include Masses, motets, canons, madrigals, psalms, hymns and other sacred music.

[R. J. LITZ]

PORTA, GUGLIELMO DELLA (Fra Guglielmo del Piombo; 1490–1577), Italian sculptor and architect, Cistercian lay brother at Fossanova. In Rome (1537) P. was influenced by Michelangelo, working (1546) under A. da Sangallo on the Scala Regia of the Vatican. He executed 16 *Prophet* reliefs, 14 of the *Life of Christ,* and stuccoes for the Massini Chapel, Trinità de' Monti (1537–38). P.'s monument for Pope Paul III is considered his greatest work.

[M. J. DALY]

PORTABLE ALTAR, see ALTAR.

PORTAL, ÉTIENNE FERNAND (1855–1926), French Vincentian priest and pioneer ecumenist. A chance meeting with the Anglican second Viscount *Halifax in Madeira in Dec. 1889 led to a lifelong friendship and to P.'s principal work: the *rapprochement* of the Churches of Canterbury and Rome. The campaign for Anglo-Roman reunion launched in 1894 by P.'s *Les Ordinations anglicanes* (under the pseudonym of F. Dalbus) and skillfully promoted by Halifax in England led to surprising initial success, but then to the condemnation of *Anglican orders by Leo XIII in the bull *Apostolicae curae* (1896). Despite this defeat P. retained both his faith in the cause of *ecumenism and the confidence of his superiors. He broadened his ecumenical interests to include Eastern and esp. Russian Orthodoxy. A scholarly man, P. insisted on history as the necessary basis for dogmatic studies; his principal literary remains are in his pioneering ecumenical periodicals: *Revue Anglo-Romaine* (3 v., 1895–96) and *Revue des Églises* (6 v., 1904–09). Possessed of a charismatic gift for friendship, P. was able to bring together those with the most varied backgrounds, to communicate his ecumenical enthusiasm to others, and to inspire them to scholarly research, personal contact with Christians of other Churches, and prayer for reunion. P.'s most tangible ecumenical success was the *Malines Conversations (1921–25), which were originated and sustained through his and Lord Halifax's tireless efforts. BIBLIOGRAPHY: lives by H. Hemmer et al. (1947) and A. T. Macmillan (1961); A. Gratieux, *L'Amitié au service de réunion* (1952); J. J. Hughes, *Absolutely Null and Utterly Void* (1968).

[J. J. HUGHES]

PORTALIÉ, EUGÈNE (1852–1909), Jesuit theologian. After teaching theology for 11 years at various Jesuit scholasticates, P. was appointed professor of positive theology at the Institut Catholique de Toulouse in 1899. His chief professional interests centered around the history of the development of dogma and St. Augustine's teaching on grace. He took vigorous part in the controversy occasioned by the writings of Loisy and Tyrell, and contributed scholarly articles to the *Bulletin de littérature ecclésiastique* and the *Dictionnaire de théologie catholique.* BIBLIOGRAPHY: F. Cavallera, DTC 12.2:2590–93; R. Metz. LTK 8:624.

[H. DRESSLER]

PORTALIS, JEAN ÉTIENNE MARIE (1746–1807), French lawyer and statesman. Leaving Aix during the Revolution (1792), he was imprisoned during the Terror. After release he served on the Council of Elders. Banished after Fructidor (Aug. 18 to Sept. 21), he returned to Paris in 1800. He helped establish the Civil Code then continued to serve the government as an officer in charge of religious matters (1801), until he became minister of cults (1804). He conceived the Gallican *Organic Articles* and presented them to the legislature. He later defended these Articles against Pius VII's opposition. He was instrumental in the ecclesiastical reorganization of France under Napoleon. He was supremely loyal to Napoleon, but not hostile to the interests of the Church.

[R. J. LITZ]

PORTER, ARTHUR KINGSLEY (1883–1933), American art historian, professor at Harvard Univ. (1920–33), he was the first scholar to challenge seriously French theories on Romanesque art, in his definitive, exhaustive study *Romanesque Sculpture of the Pilgrimage Roads* (10 v., 1923) and *Spanish Romanesque Sculpture* (1928; repr. 2 v. in 1, 1969). P. further published *Lombard Architecture* (4 v., 1915–17) which remains a standard text, and *Crosses and Culture of Ireland* (1931).

[R. C. MARKS]

PORTER, FRANCIS (1632–1702), Irish-born Franciscan professor, historian, and controversialist. Professed in the order (1654), he studied in Rome for the priesthood and after ordination taught philosophy and theology at the College of St. Isidore at Rome where he lived for the rest of his life. His most noted controversial work, *Securis evangelica* (1674), is based on Bossuet's *Exposition de la foi,* and Porter's *Compendium annalium ecclesiasticorum regni Hiberniae* (1690) is a derivative historical work on the early Irish kings and the island's conversion to Christianity. Appointed in 1690, he served as theologian and historian to exiled King James II of England.

[R. J. LITZ]

PORTER, see DOORKEEPER.

PORTICO DE LA GLORIA (1168–83), carved doorway at the cathedral of Santiago de Compostela, Spain, a Romanesque masterpiece (1075–1211), modeled after St. Sernin, Toulouse. An inscription dates the three portals and their column figures to 1188 identifying Maestro Mateo as architect-sculptor. He combined French early-Gothic elements with the emotional intensity of Spanish Romanesque carving, creating a sculptural ensemble of forceful originality. Full-length human figures radiate from the Christ in the tympanum effecting a dynamic decorative pattern. Whereas early French Gothic figures are definitely subsidiary to the architectural rhythms, Spanish figures remain quite vital—their master carvers gently, even amorously, fitting them

with innocent intent—so that these Spanish portal figures appear poignantly human and disarmingly guileless. BIBLIOGRAPHY: G. Gaillard, "Le Porche de la Gloire à S. Jacques de Compostelle," *Cahiers de civilisations médiévales,* 1 (1958), 465–473.

[R. C. MARKS]

PORTIER, MICHAEL (1795–1859), bp., missionary. Of French origin. P. was ordained in New Orleans in 1818. A devoted missionary, he distinguished himself during the yellow fever epidemic. He became vicar general of New Orleans before being named vicar apostolic of the Floridas and Alabama in 1825. A zealous pastor and the sole priest in the area, he made great progress with settlers, Indians, and also Spanish colonists. His vicariate became the Diocese of Mobile, Ala., which under his administration made considerable progress: in 1830 Spring Hill College was founded; the Visitation nuns opened a school in Mobile in 1833; orphanages were opened by the Sisters of Charity of Emmitsburg and the Brothers of the Sacred Heart; many churches were built.

[J. R. AHERNE]

PORTINARI, CÂNDIDO (1903–62), Brazilian mural painter whose massive forms in romantically nativist works are powerful and decorative. Important historic frescoes in the Hispanic wing, Library of Congress (1941, Washington, D.C.), treat of the *Discovery of the Land,* Franciscan missions, and the Gold Rush.

[M. J. DALY]

PORTINARI ALTARPIECE (Uffizi Gallery, Florence), a large triptych painted in Flanders *c.*1475 by Hugo van der Goes (*c.*1440–82). The altarpiece, whose central panel depicts the *Adoration of the Shepherds,* was commissioned by Tommaso Portinari, a representative of the Medici in Bruges. Portinari shipped it to Florence, where it changed the conventions of Italian painting, causing D. Ghirlandaio to adopt the Flemish forthright realism, introducing the ordinary man of vulgar mien in his *Adoration of the Shepherds* (1485). BIBLIOGRAPHY: E. Panofsky, *Early Netherlandish Painting, Its Origins and Character* (1953); M. J. Friedländer, *Early Netherlandish Painting* (tr. H. Norden, 1967); C. D. Cuttler, *Northern Painting* (1968). *GOES, HUGO VAN DER.

[R. E. FLEISCHER]

PORTIUNCULA, meaning a little portion, is the name of the chapel of St. Mary of the Angels, situated a short distance below the town of Assisi in Italy, and also the name of an indulgence associated with it. The little chapel, whose origin is obscure, belonged to the Benedictine monks of Mt. Subasio. It had fallen into ruin but was restored in 1207 by St. Francis in answer to a heavenly command to rebuild the Church of Christ. There he realized his vocation, founded his order, and received St. *Clare into the Franciscan life.

Given the use of the chapel by the Benedictines in exchange for an annual payment of a basket of fish, Francis made it the center of his activities, gathered his friars there in general chapters and in 1226 died in one of the small cells which he and his friars had built nearby. Designated as the mother church of the Franciscan Order, this small stone chapel, measuring 22 by 13½ feet, and the death cell of St. Francis, were enclosed in 1578 under the cupola of a magnificent triple naved basilica which has become one of the important Marian shrines of Europe. The Portiuncula indulgence, known also as "The Pardon of Assisi," is a plenary indulgence which may be gained by the faithful for visiting the parish church on Aug. 2 (or on the following Sunday with the permission of the bp. of the place), receiving the sacraments of penance and the Eucharist, and reciting prayers for the intentions of the pope. The origin of the indulgence, long a matter of dispute by historians, is commonly attributed to Pope Honorius III, who, in 1216, granted it at the request of St. Francis after the latter was directed in a vision by Christ and the Blessed Virgin Mary to seek ratification of it from the Pope. At first restricted to the Portiuncula itself, it was extended by later popes to all Franciscan churches and finally today to all parish churches. BIBLIOGRAPHY: R. Huber, *Portiuncula Indulgence, from Honorius III to Pius XI* (1938); R. Brown, NCE 11:601–602.

[D. A. MCGUCKIN]

PORTSMOUTH ABBEY, monastery, raised to the status of an abbey in 1969, for the Benedictines of the English Congregation. It is situated on Naragansett Bay, 8 miles from Newport, Rhode Island; its official title is Abbey of St. Gregory the Great. In 1976, the community consisted of an abbot, 24 priests, 2 scholastics, and 1 brother. A boarding school for approximately 240 boys (Portsmouth Abbey School) from grades 8–12 is conducted by the abbey.

[T. M. MCFADDEN]

PORTUGAL, predominantly Catholic republic of the SW Iberian peninsula, with capital at Lisbon. The area, known as Lusitania during the Roman period, was conquered by Julius Caesar and Augustus. Christianity was probably introduced at an early date, and was well established in the 4th century. But further missionary work was required after the tribal invasions. Christianity continued to exist following the Arab conquest (711), though its history in this period is obscure. Modern Portugal was created during the Christian reconquest. First the northern part, a county, was freed from Muslim rule and in 1139 Alfonso Henriques, son of Henry of Burgundy, began calling himself King Alfonso I of Portugal. Spain recognized Portugal's independence in 1143. Alfonso III completed the consolidation of modern Portugal in 1249. The country's golden age came with the 15th cent. as Portuguese explorers and colonists, accompanied by missionaries, built an empire that included possessions in South America, Africa and Asia. However, internal weaknesses

led to takeover by Philip II of Spain in 1580. Although Portugal regained independence in 1640, it was never again a great power. Portugal had a strong Jewish community in the 15th cent. and accepted many Jews expelled from Spain, but Portuguese Jews who refused to convert were expelled in the 16th cent, and those accused of converting insincerely were subjected to the Inquisition. When Napoleon invaded Portugal in 1807, the royal family moved to Brazil, which subsequently became independent under Pedro I. The monarchy ended in 1910 with a republican revolution, and the Church was disestablished in 1911. Fatima, in central Portugal, became a renowned pilgrimage center after three children reported visions there in 1917. A coup in 1926 led to the dictatorship of A. Salazar (1932–68) and M. Caetano (1968–74). Army officers dissatisfied with Portugal's African policy overthrew the government in April 1974, and independence was subsequently granted to Guinea-Bissau, Angola, and Mozambique. Elections in 1975 brought a government led by democratic socialists. With Goa lost in 1961 and Timor in 1976, only Macao was left of Portugal's empire. BIBLIOGRAPHY: H. V. Livermore, *Portugal* (1966).

[T. EARLY]

POSADA, JOSÉ GUADALUPE (1851–1913), Mexican printmaker, accomplished and famous by 1887, who produced the well-known *Calavera* (skeleton) series and the sensational *corridos* (penny sheets) on all themes of popular interest, influencing the master painters Orozco and Diego Rivera, and many artists in the graphics field.

[M. J. DALY]

POSADA Y GORDUÑO, MANUEL (1780–1846), Mexican archbishop. P. became vicar general of Puebla and was senator from Puebla in Mexico City in 1824 when appointed to a church there. In 1839 he was named abp. of Mexico. He was a staunch defender of the clerical position against the government. In 1824 P. returned to the senate but was sent into exile 9 years later. He returned to his see in 1834 but thereafter his influence in politics and on his diocese was slight.

[J. R. AHERNE]

POSADAS, FRANCISCO DE, BL. (1644–1713), Dominican preacher and confessor in Córdoba, Spain. He wrote biographies, among them a life of St. Dominic (1691–1701), and a treatise against Molinos (1698) that were published before his sudden death; his confessor published other writings which included sermons and treatises on ascetical topics (5 v., 1736–39). Combining religious erudition and logic, he urged moral reformation and the good use of time. He was beatified in 1818. BIBLIOGRAPHY: Butler 3:608–609; J. F. Alonso, BiblSanct 10:1052–53.

[E. P. COLBERT]

POSIDONIUS OF APAMEA (c.135–51 B.C.), with Panaetius of Rhodes (c.185–109 B.C.) the founder of Middle Stoicism. He is called by E. Zeller, the historian of Greek philosophy, "the most universal mind that Greece had seen since the time of Aristotle." *STOICISM.

[M. R. P. MCGUIRE]

POSITIVE THEOLOGY, the type of theology, characterized by its historical and philological methods, which attempts scientifically, a posteriori, and in the light of faith to discover the exact data of the divine revelation from its positive sources (i.e., original and historical: Scriptures, tradition, and esp. the Church's magisterium or teaching authority); to interpret it as accurately and methodically as possible, and, by the study of historical development, to explain the relation between the contemporary dogmatic-theological context and its sources in revelation. Thus positive theology (including exegesis, biblical theology, and dogmatics) by methodical and scientific study of its auxiliary sciences raises the simple hearing of the revealed truth of the faithful (*auditus fidei*) to a scientific level. It applies the strict rules of historical and philological methods but evaluates its findings in the light of faith and the Church's teaching authority, which is its starting point and the formal proximate rule of faith. Its primary task is to discover and explain the contemporary theological context and to further the investigation of the dialectical element in the true and false development of the understanding of the Christian faith. Its ultimate task is the discovery of the absolute, transcendent, objective, immutable, eternal, salvational, and divinely revealed truth, which as an unconditional affirmation of being was uttered in a particular historical context but which transcends it and must be uttered in any context. Positive theology also investigates the thematization of the truth found in the deposit of faith, i.e., its passing from one type of apprehension and expression to another type, bringing new knowledge and clarification or obscuring of the same. Positive theology, therefore, may not project anything upon the relevant historical witness, which does not contain it explicitly, and also must stand in a close relationship to speculative theology. Otherwise it would become lifeless in its positivism. BIBLIOGRAPHY: G. F. Van Ackeren, NCE 14:39–49; J. B. Metz, LTK 10:62–71; Y. M. J. Congar, *La Foi et la théologie* (1962); M. Schmaus, *Katholische Dogmatik* (6th ed., 1960) 1:46–51; *Exegese und Dogmatik* (ed. H. Vorgrimler, 1962).

[P. B. T. BILANIUK]

POSITIVISM, a term that embraces a set of philosophical positions usually associated with the name of Auguste Comte, the 19th-cent. father of sociology and founder of the "Religion of Humanity." There are, today, several versions of the positivist doctrine, the most important being the logical, the empirical, and the scientific. Positivism appeared to offer a metaphysics congenial to many empirical scientists during the 18th and 19th centuries. As an outlook it insists on restricting the scope of intellectual inquiry to what is verifiable in present sense experience and in recognizing

as valid only the hypothetico-deductive method of the modern physical sciences. The task of philosophy is then reduced to the analysis and classification of the findings of these empirical sciences, the result being the most radical antimetaphysical bias. Comte thought that, eventually, the science of man in society, which he named sociology, would achieve the rightful status of supreme arbiter and coordinator of all the disciplines and provide a panoramic view of man and his world.

The antecedents of positivism are a dogmatic *empiricism, sensationalistic and easily tending to *materialism, and a scientism that would impose on all lines of inquiry, speculative and practical, the method and perspective of the physico-mathematical sciences. Logical positivism develops on the pattern of mathematics, complete with elements, definitions, theorems, and forms of inference. In a broader, and perhaps improper, sense, an approach to, or conception of, inquiry is said to be positivist when it sticks so closely to the collecting and analyzing of natural or historical facts as to eschew in principle large-scale theoretical construction. BIBLIOGRAPHY: W. M. Simon, *European Positivism in the Nineteenth Century* (1963); F. Harrison, *Positive Evolution of Religion: Its Moral and Social Reaction* (1913); R. von Mises, *Positivism: A Study in Human Understanding* (1951).

[J. P. REID]

POSSESSION, DIABOLICAL, see DIABOLICAL POSSESSION.

POSSESSOR IN GOOD, BAD OR DOUBTFUL FAITH. Moral theology takes "possessor" in this phrase as one having something of value that by right belongs to another; the possessor is not the rightful owner. Since unjust possession is a sin against commutative *justice, kinds of possessors are classified in order to determine moral obligations. In every case a possessor who is or becomes aware of the rightful owner of an object is bound to return it. A possessor in good faith, i.e., one who becomes aware for the first time of the true ownership, must return the property; but he has no obligation if it has ceased to exist. He is obliged to return any natural or contractual yields from the property (e.g., animal offspring; rents); he may retain benefits deriving because of his own labors, and deduct expenditures for maintenance. In some cases *prescription may give such a possessor rightful ownership. A possessor in bad faith, knowing all along the rightful owner, must restore the property and compensate the owner for any loss incurred; but may retain the fruits of his own labor, and has a right to compensation for expenditures of maintenance. A possessor in doubtful faith, if the doubt cannot be solved, may retain possession; if he does, or culpably does not, resolve the doubt, retention makes him a possessor in bad faith.

[T. C. O'BRIEN]

POSSEVINO, ANTONIO (1534–1611), Italian Jesuit, papal envoy to Sweden and Russia. After a period of successful preaching against Protestantism in Savoy and France, P. was appointed by Gregory XIII to negotiate with John III of Sweden. He arrived in Stockholm in Dec. 1577 and in the following May John became reconciled with the Church. Conditions for the return of his country to Catholicism (marriage of the clergy, communion under both species) were unacceptable to the Pope, however, and the matter died. In 1581 P. met with the Czar Ivan the Terrible in Moscow and arranged a peace between Russia and Poland; he also opened reunion negotiations with Ivan, but the issue did not prosper. Thereafter P. spent several years as nuncio to Poland, then returned to Italy, where he taught (1587–91) at the Univ. of Padua, and published *Apparatus sacer ad Scripturam Veteris et Novi Testamenti* (1603–06). BIBLIOGRAPHY: W. Delius, *Antonio Possevino S.J. und Ivan Grosnyj* (1962); O. Gerstein, *Rome and the Counter Reformation in Scandinavia* (1963).

[R. H. SCHMANDT]

POSSIDIUS, ST. (d. after 437), bp. of Calama in Numidia and first biographer of St. Augustine. Before his elevation to the episcopate P. was one of the clergy of Augustine's monastery at Hippo. He maintained a lifelong friendship with Augustine and, having sought refuge during the Siege of Calama by barbarians, was present at his death in Hippo (430). In his early years as a bp. he was subjected to danger and violence in the turbulence stirred up by the *Donatists and pagans in his diocese. At the Council of Milevis (416) he was active against the *Pelagians. Driven from his see by the Arian Genseric, he died in exile, probably in Italy. His biography of St. Augustine can be found in PL 32:31–66, or in Eng. tr. in F. Hoare, ed. *Western Fathers* (1965) 191–246. BIBLIOGRAPHY: Altaner 488; Butler 2:327.

POSTCOMMUNION, the prayer after communion, the last variable presidential prayer of the Roman Mass. Like the other two such prayers (the opening prayer or Collect, the prayer over the gifts or Secret), this follows a procession (which is accompanied by singing) and silent congregational prayer. It is a prayer of thanksgiving for communion, given by the priest in the name of the assembled congregation and like the other presidential prayers addressed to the Father through Christ. The Postcommunion prayers provide a rich source for the Church's understanding of the benefits and effects of communion, which they generally ask to be continued in daily life. BIBLIOGRAPHY: J. A. Jungmann, *The Mass of the Roman Rite* (tr. F. A. Brunner, 2 v., 1951–55) 2:419–425; T. Krosnicki, *Ancient Patterns in Modern Prayer* (1974).

[J. DALLEN]

POSTEL, MARIE MADELINE, ST. (1756–1846), French religious foundress. Opening a school for poor children, she maintained religious instruction for her charges throughout the French Revolution. In 1807 she and three others took vows in a new community, Sisters of the Christian Schools of Mercy, an institute for the education of girls, which, from 1837, adopted the rule of the Brothers of the Christian Schools. The congregation grew steadily under her leadership. She was an imaginative educator who improved the curriculum of the times. She was canonized in 1925.

[J. R. AHERNE]

POSTILLA (postil, apostil), homiletical glosses or notes on the biblical text developed in medieval times. The term is perhaps from the Lat., *post illa verba textus,* "after the words of the text." It was applied to homilies on the Gospel or Epistle of the day and to books of homilies. The *Postillae* of *Hugh of Saint-Cher (*c.*1200–63) is a classic example. BIBLIOGRAPHY: B. Smalley, *Study of the Bible in the Middle Ages* (2d ed., 1952).

[T. EARLY]

POSTIMPRESSIONISM, 20th-cent. school of artists reacting against the limitations of Impressionism, moving away from naturalism to a new dynamic visual order (Cézanne), considering the picture an evocative symbol with spiritual values (Gauguin), advancing toward Fauvism with an emphasis on the emotive power of color and line (Matisse, Rouault) and the intellectual structures of Cubism.

[M. J. DALY]

POSTLAPSARIANISM, equivalent alternative for infralapsarianism, or sublapsarianism, the interpretation in Calvinist teaching that God predestined men to heaven or hell only after the Fall. *SUPRALAPSARIANISM.

[T. C. O'BRIEN]

POSTMILLENARIANISM (*Postmillennialism*), the doctrine that a millennium of righteousness is to come upon earth through the operation of Christian agencies, which will gradually overcome the forces of evil opposed to the gospel until at length its spirit pervades and dominates the entire world. This condition will last 1,000 years, at the close of which there will be a brief apostasy of some, and a final conflict between the saints and the forces of evil. Then Christ will come, the dead will rise to judgment, and the world will be destroyed by fire. Postmillenarianism differs from premillenarianism in holding that the visible advent of Christ follows rather than precedes the millennium. *MILLENARIANISM.

[P. K. MEAGHER]

POSTQUAM APOSTOLICIS LITTERIS, a *motu proprio* of Pope Pius XII promulgated on Feb. 9, 1952. It deals with the laws regarding religious (cc. 1–231), with the temporal property of the Church (cc. 232–301), and defines certain legal terms (cc. 302–324). This legislation gave

Eastern rite religious institutes the opportunity to decide whether to retain the Western canonical organization which they had acquired through the centuries or to return to the original form of the monastic institute of the East. BIBLIOG - RAPHY: V. J. Pospishil, NCE 10:763–766 s.v. "Oriental Codes (Canon Law)."

[E. EL -HAYEK]

POSTULANCY, the period, now more commonly referred to as the prenovitiate, of preparation for reception of the religious habit and admission into the novitiate of a religious community. The duration varies with different religious constitutions.

POSTULANT, a term, becoming obsolete, for a candidate seeking or preparing for admission to a novitiate.

POSTULATION (CANON LAW), in the law of elections, a power given to voters to petition by their vote a candidate whom some impediment excludes from being elected. The impediment must be of a kind from which the competent superior can and ordinarily does dispense. Postulation requires a simple majority, except when in the same elective process a nonimpeded candidate has received votes; then postulation requires a two-thirds vote. The superior need not grant the postulation; only when he does, does the postulated person acquire right of office. Where a postulation is denied, the right to elect reverts to the elective body, unless it has knowingly made a postulation impossible to grant; in such a case the superior has the right of appointment to the office in question. (CIC. c. 179–182.)

[T. C. O'BRIEN]

POSTULATOR OF CAUSES, title of the one charged with representing a diocese or order at Rome in the case for the beatification or canonization of a person deemed worthy of consideration by the Congregation for the Causes of Saints.

POTAMIUS (d. after 357), first known bp. of Lisbon, Portugal. Colorful and assertive language mark four short orthodox works (PL 8:1411–18; Suppl. 1:202–216); one on the Triune substance is of special interest because P. was said to have helped compose the second formula of Sirmium (357). The Luciferian *Liber precum* accuses him of betraying his faith for gain, only to die before he could enjoy it.

[E. P. COLBERT]

POTENCY AND ACT, a term in common use in scholastic philosophy and theology. In the special sense in which it is there employed it does not mean the quality or state of being strong or powerful, but rather the possibility or capacity of development or exchange. To be in potency to a perfection describes the condition of a thing prior to its achieving or receiving that perfection. A potency may be active or passive according as it is a principle by which a thing may act or be acted upon. One's faculties (e.g. mind, will, senses) are examples of active potencies. One's ability to be changed or perfected is a passive potency. *Act is the correlative of potency taken in the passive sense. Potency is essentially postulated by the scholastic notion of change. A thing can change only if it is in potency to some form of actuation other than it presently enjoys. In other words, in everything subject to change there must be two elements: (1) the act or perfection or being what it is; and (2) the passive potency of acquiring a form of act or perfection it does not yet possess. The development from potentiality to actuality is brought about through the activity of an efficient cause. Thus in all finite being, which is essentially subject to change, there is a composition of act and potency. But the infinite being which is God is pure actuality without admixture of potency of any kind; no cause makes Him what He is, nor can He be other than He is.

Men (and angels) are fitted by nature to attain only the perfection that is connatural to them, i.e. that to which they have a natural potency. Yet, in fact, man's actual destiny is supernatural. He could not be destined to this, however, unless he were in some sort of potency to it. Theologians describe this potency as obediential. It is man's capacity for a perfection completely beyond his natural potentialities and one that can be realized only by the power of God. BIBLIOG - RAPHY: W. N. Clarke, NCE 11:633–635; W. H. Principe, NCE 10:606–607; H. de Lubac, *Surnaturel: Études historiques* (1946); *Le Mystère du surnaturel* (1965).

[B. FORSHAW]

POTHIER, JOSEPH (1835–1923), French Benedictine scholar of Gregorian Chant. He entered the abbey of Solesmes in 1858. He served as subprior, prior, and abbot at other houses of the order, notably St. Wandrille. Collaborating with P. Jausions, P. wrote *Mélodies grégoriennes* (1881), an important early work of chant scholarship influenced by A. Gontier. P. advocated the "oratorical" theory which maintains that the rhythm of a chant is based on the metrics and rhythm of the Latin phrases. His book of graduals (1883, 1895) and antiphonal chants (1891) prepared him for his leading role in preparation of the Vatican editions of the *Graduale* (1908) and *Antiphonale* (1912). He was editor of *Revue du chant grégorien* for 23 years.

[R. J. LITZ]

POTHINUS, ST. (c. A.D. 87–177), bp. and martyr. He was the first bp. of Lyons, having been sent to Gaul by St. *Polycarp about the middle of the 2d cent. At the age of 90 he was taken in the persecution under Marcus Aurelius and died in prison after being beaten, kicked, and stoned. BIB - LIOGRAPHY: Butler 2:454–458. *LYONS AND VIENNE, MARTYRS OF.

POTTER, MARY (1847–1913), English foundress of the women's charitable order, the Little Company of Mary, in 1877 at Hyson Green, England. The Little Company is dedicated to the comfort of the sick and dying.

[R. J. LITZ]

POTTHAST, AUGUST (1824–98), German historian, librarian, and editor. Custodian of the Berlin Royal library (1868), he later served the German legislative assembly as librarian (1874–94). Contributing to the *Monumenta Germaniae Historica* (MGH), his most important works were a *Regesta* of popes from 1197 to 1304 and his *Bibliotheca historica medii aevi* . . . (1862; 2d ed., 1896), still used in medieval studies as a convenient compilation of original sources, titles, editions, and translations; a modern revision of the *Bibliotheca* has been in progress since 1965.

[R. J. LITZ]

POTURI, Yugoslavian Bogomils, who, after a superficial conversion to Catholicism, went over to Islam during the 16th and 17th centuries.

[G. ELDAROV]

POUGET, FRANÇOIS AIMÉ (1666–1723), French Oratorian catechist whose popular but controversial Montpellier Catechism was condemned and placed on the Index for its Jansenist doctrines. The catechism itself, both in its longer and shorter (children's) editions, was organized into three parts on: the origin and development of religion from creation to the judgment; prerequisite behavior to enter the kingdom of heaven; a practical direction for Christian living. Appearing under the patronage of Abps. de Noailles of Paris and Colbert of Montpellier, the work had 30 French editions from 1702 to 1710, including editions in other European languages. The French version was put on the Index in 1721, the English version in 1725.

[R. J. LITZ]

POUGHKEEPSIE PLAN, an arrangement approved by Abp. (later Cardinal) John McCloskey and school authorities, designed to satisfy Catholic educational aims in a public school setting. Inaugurated in 1873 when St. Peter's Catholic School, in Poughkeepsie, N.Y., was leased to public school authorities for an annual fee of $1.00, the plan provided that the local public school board exercise complete control over the school during the legal school day, and religious instruction be given after regular school hours. No child was obliged to attend religious instruction without parental consent, and non-Catholics were free to send their children to St. Peter's. Catholic teachers, including religious, if equally competent as those elected by the local board, would be on the staff. The plan was publicly well-accepted and officially approved until 1887 when Andrew S. Draper, N.Y. Superintendent of Public Instruction, declared illegal the employment of teachers wearing a distinctive religious garb. The plan later became involved in the Bouquillon controversy and in 1899 was terminated by Charles R. Skinner as "unwise as a matter of school policy and a violation of the letter and spirit of the Constitution." BIBLIOGRAPHY: E. M. Connors, *Church-State Relationships in Education in the State of New York* (1951).

[M. B. MURPHY]

POULAIN, AUGUSTIN (1836–1919), French Jesuit, author on the ascetical and mystical life. A Jesuit from 1858, he was a professor at the Catholic Faculty of Angers, 1881–97, then spent the rest of his years in Paris as a spiritual director and retreat master. His greatest work is *Des Graces d'oraison* (1901: *The Graces of Interior Prayer,* ed. L. Bainvel, 1950); he published in addition, *La Mystique de St. Jean de la Croix* (1893); *Lucie Christine: Journal intime* (1910). P. was regarded as a mystic himself; his writings are prized for their practical direction and concrete, psychological analysis of the phenomena of the mystical life.

[T. C. O'BRIEN]

POULENC, FRANCIS (1899–1963), major French composer. He was a member of the antiromantic "Les Six" associated with Jean Cocteau. P.'s greatest work was in his choral compositions, including his *Mass* (1937), *Exultate Deo* (1941), and *Salve Regina* (1941). These and other works were composed under the influence of his rediscovery of Roman Catholicism in 1935, his enthusiasm for which never waned. A semi-sacred work for which he is known is the *Dialogues des Carmélites* (1953–56). He also composed songs, ballets, chamber music, and orchestral music.

[P. HENNESSEY]

POUND, EZRA (1885–1972), American poet. Controversial in outlook, experimental and innovative in style and subject. P. is considered enormously important in the shaping of 20th-cent. poetry. During the 1920s he lived in Paris, associated with Gertrude Stein, Hemingway, and other expatriates. Translation, attempts at epic, critical and literary essays poured from his pen. He remains esp. known through his *Pisan Cantas,* a fascinating and frightening poetic work. He translated Sophocles' *Women of Trachis.*

[R. M. FUNCHION]

POUNDE, THOMAS (1539–1615), English *recusant. A lawyer and a courtier under Elizabeth I, and outwardly a Protestant, he retired from court after 1569, professed his Catholicism, and began to live a devout life. He was arrested for the first time in 1574 and during the rest of his life was imprisoned 15 times, and fined heavily. While in the Tower of London (1579) he received a letter affiliating him officially into the Society of Jesus. He obtained a final release from prison under James I in 1604. P. circulated among Catholics his MS treatise attacking the Protestant *sola scriptura* principle.

[R. J. LITZ]

POURRAT, PIERRE (1871–1957), theologian. A French cleric ordained a Sulpician in 1896, P. was teacher of dogma at the major seminary of Lyons, rector, and vicar general of the archdiocese. From 1926 to 1945 he served as superior of the Solitude, formation house of Saint-Sulpice. His masterpiece is the four-volume *La Spiritualité chrétienne,* a history of spirituality beginning in biblical times.

[J. R. AHERNE]

POUSSIN, NICOLAS (1593 or 1594–1665), French painter of religious and mythological subjects, and of classical landscapes. Profoundly significant for the history of French painting as the founder of French Neoclassicism, P. was deeply influenced by classical antiquities and the styles of Raphael, Giulio Romano, and the Carracci. After early experiments in mannerist OT scenes (1624–26), a Baroque *Madonna del Pilar,* and the Venetian *Mystic Marriage of St. Catherine* and *Martyrdom of St. Erasmus* (1628–29) for St. Peter's, P. became a *cognoscente* of the antique which he studied in great detail, living as he did in Rome from 1624 until he died, making only one brief return to Paris, 1640–42. Throughout his career P. sought an idealized beauty in rational, classicizing settings populated by sharply delineated, sculpturesque figures. Prior to 1640 he was greatly interested in sizeable compositions filled with physically and frequently emotionally agitated figures, e.g., *The Rape of the Sabines* (*c.*1636, The Metropolitan Museum, New York). After 1640 P.'s mature style increasingly favored quieter compositions of impressive, almost severe monumentality as in the idealized, perfectly ordered landscape of *The Burial of Phocion,* (1648, The Louvre, Paris), eloquently evocative of the stoic philosopher whose corpse is being transported from the insistently geometric city in the middle distance. This period produced solemn religious works: two sets of the *Seven Sacraments* (1642–48), *The Eucharist* (1647), *Holy Family on the Steps* (1648). In his last years P. moved toward a more extreme simplification—even a cubistic abstraction (*Rest on the Flight into Egypt,* 1655–57). BIBLIOGRAPHY: A. Blunt, *Nicolas Poussin* (2 v., 1967).

[S. CONWAY]

POVERTY. In a Christian view of human existence poverty as voluntary is a Gospel ideal; poverty as involuntary deprivation is an object of the ministry of social justice.

Poverty, Evangelical Ideal. As a voluntary detachment from temporal possessions poverty is counselled by Christ in the beatitudes and as a condition for following him and of expressing confidence in the Father's providence; it is exemplified in his own life and characteristic of the first Christian community that held all things in common. Vatican Council II, recalling the capital biblical NT texts on the matter (Mt 6.5,20,25;8.20; 2 Cor 8.9), repeats the Christian tradition that vowed poverty in the religious or consecrated life is a form of witness in the Church made by religious both individually and corporately (VatII RenReILife 13). But the Council reminds Christians universally, whatever their state in life, that luxury, wealth, accumulation of possessions (ibid.) are contrary to the spirit of the Gospel and Christ's predilection for the poor (see VatII ChModWorld 72). Priests are thus encouraged to live a life of voluntary poverty and to avoid anything in their manner of life that would offend (scandalize) the poor (VatII MinLifePriests 17). The Council commends to all the laity a life free of enslavement to wealth (VatII ApostLaity). The witness of poverty is one of affirming transcendence, that blessedness is not achieved by accumulating possessions; the element of renunciation is a safeguard against absorption in the temporal to the exclusion of charity's orientation towards God above all. The witness of poverty is also an affirmation to the poor: a continuing assurance to the poor that Christ is one of them. The necessity of evangelical poverty has been shown by the dark history of abuses of wealth in the Church (see POVERTY AND REFORM). Religious make this witness by vow (solemn vow in this matter means renunciation of the right of ownership; a simple vow, the surrender of the power to dispose of and to acquire materialities). But the witness of poverty can also become a matter of obligation to all Christians, not simple as detachment of heart but as the effective expression of this in sacrifice for those in dire need. The love of neighbor can only be respected in such cases by real poverty, that is by releasing possessions for someone in need. There can be no true fidelity to the Gospel for anyone who holds back of what is not needed when someone else lacks the necessities of life. The obligation to give of what is not strictly needed is serious and to fail in this is not to fail to do a kindness, but to fail to do a duty.

Poverty and Social Justice. The affirmation of the spirit of voluntary poverty is not an indifference towards the poverty of destitution. Vatican II suggests that there is a motivation in the spirit of evangelical poverty to perfect "the work of justice under the inspiration of charity" (VatII ChModWorld 72). Destitution, as it means a subhuman level of subsistence—hunger, lack of housing, lack of the possibility of attending to any human, higher value or aspiration—is an evil. It is usually in some measure the effect of sins against justice, "social sins." "With regard to wealth, one person cannot have an overabundance without another's having too little" (ThAq ST 2a2ae, 118.1 ad 2). Poverty as it exists in the contemporary world is in large measure artificial, i.e. a by-product of the art of economics systems that determine the value and availability of material goods. The poverty of those nations that make up the Third World is in some degree caused by their inability to participate in the economic order as it is controlled by the First World. This is the reason of the UN's New International Economic Order, which, however, has so far had little effect on redressing the economic imbalance. Poverty within societies is also caused by the unequal distribution of wealth. This is particularly evident in agricultural areas or societies, where the land is controlled by a very small minority. Vatican II, therefore, calls for reform that will bring fruitful use of and equitable sharing in the land so that it will benefit the many, not just the few (VatII ChModWorld 71). The Council also reminds all that the right to private property or ownership is not absolute; radically the earth's goods and resources are for the well-being of all mankind; the institution of private property is justified to guarantee more effective use for the benefit of all (ibid.). But in the actual working of the economic systems the norms of economics, not of social justice, are decisive. Thus it is determined that a certain percentage of unemployment is ''tolerable'' as a protection against inflation. Migrant farm workers are left completely outside the scope of normal law as to minimum wage or child labor; the laws or labor contracts that protect women from working excessive hours or that guarantee decent working conditions for all, are disregarded in favor of corporations whose profits depend on cheap labor.

Since Vatican II's *Gaudium et spes* there has been a marked advance in advocacy and action in the area of social justice. Thus the *Medellin Documents (1968), the 1971 Synod of Bishops, *Justice in the World,* the pastoral letter of the bishops of Appalachia, *This Land Is Home to Me* (1975), the Detroit Call to Action papers (1976), esp. on work and on humankind all have been forceful statements against the degradation and crushing weight of poverty. The reason for these statements comes down basically to this: ''Now a man can scarcely arrive at the needed sense of responsibility unless his living conditions allow him to become conscious of his dignity and to rise to his destiny by spending himself for God and for others. But human freedom is often crippled when a man falls into extreme poverty . . .'' (VatII ChModWorld 31). There has never been a point in human history where there has been no poverty; misfortune and human failure are causes that never will disappear. But the ministry of justice seeks to eradicate causes that create poverty as a social condition. The Council rightly suggests that justice is not simply the absence of infringement or exploitation; it requires the inner and constant willingness to give to every person what is due. The positive espousal of justice has not yet been integrated into the art of economics. That integration is the first objective of the ministry of justice.

[T. C. O'BRIEN]

POVERTY AND REFORM. Preoccupation with wealth is detrimental to the life of the spirit. Reasonable simplicity, on the other hand, enhances that life. It is therefore not surprising to find that religious reformers invariably oppose materialism in the Church, both corporate and individual. One of the earliest reactions against the growing wealth of the Church was monasticism. From the 5th to the 11th cent. the monks kept alive the gospel ideals of renunciation and simplicity of life. With the passing of time, however, many monasteries departed from their original fervor. The reform movements which began in the High Middle Ages were in large part a protest against the excessive wealth of the Church and its ministers. The reformers were usually laymen who expressed their demand for the revival of the apostolic life in anticlerical and antisacramental terms. The most radical stand was taken by the *Cathari, whose condemnation of material possessions was a corollary to the Manichean dualism they had adopted from the *Bogomils. Sects like the *Waldenses, *Petrobrusians, *Humiliati, and *Apostolici pushed renunciation to the point of frustration, while the *Spirituals, *Michaelists, and *Fraticelli adopted the apocalyptic phantasies of *Joachim of Fiore.

In the 13th cent. the founders of the mendicant orders furnished an example of evangelical poverty and invited the laity to share their life in the third orders. Eventually though, the friars fell victim to success. Wealth was almost forced upon them, always with good intentions.

During the 14th and 15th cent., *Wycliffe and *Hus launched a violent attack against ecclesiastical wealth and papal exactions. The most radical of the sects proposed a program of total reform, including abolition of private property and class distinctions together with a forcible overthrow of the existing social order. The Reformation was the climax of the protests against clerical cupidity and the fiscal obsessions of the Roman Curia. Soon left-wing Protestants like the *Anabaptists proposed an egalitarian society based on common ownership.

The Industrial Revolution and the rise of capitalism militated against the gospel attitude towards poverty. (Corporate enterprise produced vast wealth, only a small share of which accrued to the workers.) Poverty lost supernatural significance and came to be looked upon as the deserved lot of the shiftless or as a social problem which technology would soon solve.

The tardy Catholic reaction against 19th-cent. materialism manifested itself in a number of unrelated efforts. *Lacordaire preached against the evils of *laissez-faire* *capitalism. Bp. Von *Ketteler applied gospel principles to social morality. Organizations for the relief of the poor were launched by *Ozanam and *Kolping. *Montalembert and *Windthorst sponsored factory laws: De Mun and *La Tour du Pin promoted workers' study groups. Cardinals *Manning and *Gibbons supported the labor movement; and the social encyclicals of the popes presented a comprehensive outline of reform which if followed would have relieved many ills.

During the early part of the 20th cent. a group of prominent British Catholics including *Belloc, *Chesterton, and Eric *Gill, proposed *distributism as the most effective means of counteracting the evils associated with large concentrations of wealth and the dehumanizing factory system. Human freedom and dignity, they maintained, could be safeguarded only by a wider diffusion of personal ownership. They hoped to accomplish this by a return to family farming, by establishing small industrial units, and fostering personal craftsmanship. In the U.S. the Catholic Worker Movement, founded by Peter Maurin and Dorothy Day, adopted the distributist program but also stressed private practice of the works of mercy as demonstrated by the houses of hospitality.

Vatican Council II challenged Christians to rediscover poverty as an existential value beyond the morally justified use of material possessions. The poverty suited to the present age must transcend moralism, find its motivation in love, and express itself in service, responsibility, and witness. Such poverty derives directly from evangelical conversion, by which one becomes vitally aware of dependence on God and of universal brotherhood. Christian poverty today imposes three obligations: relief of urgent and immediate misery; provision for self-help to those living in want; and reform of those structures that cause or exploit human misery. In line with these policies, agitation for the liquidation of the assets of the Church is gathering force. BIBLIOGRAPHY: Y. Congar, *Power and Poverty in the Church* (tr. J. Nicholson, 1965); B. Ward, *Rich Nations and the Poor Nations* (1962).

POVERTY CONTROVERSY, a theoretical debate on the nature of evangelical poverty that grew out of a dispute over the practice of poverty in the Franciscan Order. Soon after the death of St. Francis his order requested from the Holy See an official interpretation of certain disputed portions of the rule. Four bulls on this subject were issued between 1230 and 1312. To a group of rigorists known as *Spirituals these pronouncements constituted a betrayal of the founder's ideal of poverty. They sought to separate themselves from the order so that they might live the rule in its primitive severity. Their efforts were stubbornly resisted by the majority party, known as the Communitas, and both Boniface VIII and John XXII took severe measures against them. In 1321 a Dominican inquisitor declared heretical the doctrine of the *paupertas altissima,* according to which Christ and his Apostles owned nothing either personally or in common. This attack on what was considered a basic Franciscan tenet temporarily united the Spirituals and the Communitas. The general chapter of 1322 unanimously affirmed that the doctrine of the *paupertas altissima* was sound Catholic teaching. John XXII answered this challenge by revoking the legal fiction by which the Holy See held proprietorship over the goods used by the Franciscans (*Ad conditorem canonum,* 1322), and by declaring the doctrine of the *paupertas altissima* heretical (*Cum inter nonnullos,* 1323). Many leading Spirituals and a number of prominent members of the Communitas followed the minister general, Michael of Cesena, into schism and sought the protection of Emperor Louis of Bavaria. By 1329 most of these *Michaelists had returned to the order and submitted to the Church. BIBLIOGRAPHY: D. Douie, *Nature and Effects of the Heresy of the Fraticelli* (1932); M. Lambert, *Franciscan Poverty. The Doctrine of the Absolute Poverty of Christ and his Apostles in the Franciscan Order, 1210–1323* (1961).

[C. J. LYNCH]

POWDERLY, TERENCE VINCENT (1849–1924), American labor leader whose influence, somewhat ironically in the event, both prevented a papal ban on membership in the *Knights of Labor and helped prepare the way for Leo XIII's encyclical *Rerum novarum* (see Browne, pp. 355–356). P., the son of Irish Catholic immigrants, began work as a railroad laborer at age 13, became a local union organizer in 1869, mayor of Scranton, Pa. as a labor candidate (1878–84), and in 1879 master workman (president) of the Knights of Labor. The second phase of his career began

with his passing the bar in 1894, the culmination of his continued self-education; from 1897 he held a succession of posts in federal government in Washington, with interruptions based on political conflicts; his last position was as head of the Division of Information in the Dept. of Immigration. During this second period of his career he abandoned the Church; his posthumously published memoirs (*The Path I Trod,* H. J. Carman *et al* ed., 1940) reflect embitterment against church authorities. P. began to experience ecclesiastical hostility because of his labor activities even as a young man—and a faithful communicant—in Scranton. Yet his own actions in lessening the secret-society side of the Knights of Labor by playing down ritual and the oath with its theological implications, his patient explanations of the need of trade unions in the face of reactionary opposition from the hierarchy, and his cooperation with Card. *Gibbons saved the Catholic working man from having to choose between the cause of social justice and allegiance to the Church. The affair of the Knights of Labor was part of the process towards the revolutionary turnabout in *Rerum novarum* and its positive recognition of the rights of workers. P. was not an advocate of violence or even of strikes, but of labor's solidarity as the means towards the ideal of an equitable share in the profits the working man helped to create. He was also a proponent of land reform, temperance, and the single tax program of H. *George—another point of conflict with some ecclesiastics. He published *Thirty Years of Labor* (1899) as well as frequent journal articles. BIBLIOGRAPHY: H. J. Browne, *Catholic Church and the Knights of Labor* (1949), which makes use of the collection of P.'s papers and letters at the Mullen Library, The Catholic University of America.

[T. C. O'BRIEN]

POWELL, EDWARD, BL. (d. 1540), English martyr. A secular priest and headmaster of Eton College, P. was at the time of his death vicar of St. Mary Redcliffe, Bristol.

POWER, EDMOND (1878–1953), Jesuit biblical scholar. After studies in Oriental languages at Beirut, P. taught Arabic and Syriac at the *Pontifical Biblical Institute (1914–38) and Scripture at Milltown Park, Dublin (1938–53). He wrote articles for several scholarly periodicals, and was editor of *Biblica* (1926–31). BIBLIOGRAPHY: E. Vogt and P. Nober, *Biblica* 35 (1954) 122–126.

[T. M. MCFADDEN]

POWER, EMILY, MOTHER (1844–1909), mother general of the Sinsinawa (Wis.) Dominican sisters. Born in Ireland, she was brought to the U.S. as a child. She entered her community at Benton, Wis. in 1861 and was elected mother general in 1867. It was she who moved the motherhouse back to its original foundation site at Sinsinawa. In the history of the community she is credited with planning its educational apostolate that includes schools at every level, including two colleges and centers for European studies at Fribourg, Switzerland and Florence, Italy. During the violent labor strife of the late 19th cent., P. championed the cause of miners in Minnesota and Montana, and of the stockyard workers in Chicago, and brought them assistance in their poverty.

[T. C. O'BRIEN]

POWER, JOHN (1792–1849), missionary. A native of Ireland, P. came to the U.S. as a priest in 1819. A great preacher, he served as pastor of St. Peter's in New York. He was nominated (1825) as bp. of New York, where he was vicar general but was not chosen. He was a consultant at the Second Provincial Council of Baltimore in 1833 and a recognized apologist; he also compiled *True Piety* (1832), a prayer book. He was a promoter of the Irish Emigrant Society. In 1837 when he was again passed over as coadjutor of New York, he accepted his situation and worked zealously as vicar general to Bp. Hughes. Besides his work in New York, P. also traveled to New Jersey and Connecticut to minister to Catholics there. The last days of his life were saddened by the problem of *trusteeism and St. Peter's having to be auctioned to pay its debts.

[J. R. AHERNE]

POWER, LIONEL (*c*.1375–1445), English composer of church music, colleague of *Dunstable, influential on Continental music of the period. He left a treatise on descant, music for the liturgy, motets honoring the Virgin Mary. He spent the latter part of his life at Canterbury's Christ Church.

[T. C. O'BRIEN]

POWER (HISTORY OF RELIGIONS), the energy of being (or of whatever ontological presence has meaning to the subject), which manifests itself in such a way as to produce a heightened sense of awe-inspired fear, respect, and proximity to the sacred in the witnessing subject. The term as it is used in religious discourse, liturgy, prayer, and the scientific study of religion is inevitably culturally specific in its many definitions. What "power" means to a Mayan priest, a Plains shamann, a Catholic priest, Christian believer, Hassidic Jew, or Muslim pilgrim to Mecca, differs according to the cultural context of the person's religious disposition. Yet there are certain common features in most human experiences of sacred power, a power that cannot be tapped, stored, savored, or diverted for uses other than religious experience and worship. Sacred power cannot be manipulated by humans. It is too great and radically "other," too different from the normal to be turned to practical use. A naturalist analogy might be that a volcanic eruption could be sacred while the geo-thermal energy used to drive steam turbines, perhaps "powerful" and "awesome" in itself, could not. Sacred power is what characterizes the most important aspects and elements of the cosmos available to the witnessing subject. These aspects, when charged with being (ontological presence) define the

whole of the witness's world in terms of the power, not the power in terms of his world. A revelation having sacred power as its chief characteristic of course must be interpreted, but if it is reduced to meanings that lie completely within the familiar parameters of a culture's common knowledge, it ceases to be sacred, it loses its mystery, its fundamental incomprehensibility, hence also its power. Power must be experienced, witnessed, felt to be sacred; it cannot be procured, imagined, or described by humans nor can it be presumed to exist in mere potentiality. Power must be actual, at least occasionally; the effect of its actuality must be memorable. Impotent power is a contradiction in terms. Power that cannot be experienced has been desacralized. Inadequately treated in language, power divests itself of some of its strangeness, its otherness, in hierophanies, manifestations of the sacred or holy which point to and suggest the inexpressible and unknown depths of the sacred.

[R. J. LITZ]

POWER AND WISDOM OF GOD (IN THE BIBLE), two attributes of God manifested in conjunction. His works of power in creation and in history manifest his wisdom; and wisdom was with him from the beginning ordering all things mightily. By the time of Jesus, however, the influence of Jewish apocalyptic had subverted conventional wisdom, and both the power and the wisdom of God were viewed as mysteries revealed only to chosen ones. This gave play to paradox, such as: blessed are the poor, but woe to you rich; more numerous are the children of the barren, than of her who is with child; and esp. Jesus' hymn of jubilation (Mt. 11:25ff), in which he praises God for hiding his greatest works from the wise and prudent ones, and revealing them to the little ones. And for Paul (1 Cor 1:18–2:5), Greek philosophers, men of letters and rhetoricians, along with Jewish wise men, scribes, and rabbis belong to the wisdom of this age. Paul's message was the word of the Cross, a scandal to Jews, and folly to the Greeks. Paul was convinced that God reveals his mysteries to the weak and foolish to confound the wise and the powerful. The foolishness of God is stronger than men; the weakness of God is wiser than men. True wisdom comes from the power of the Holy Spirit, the gift of God to those who believe the message of the Cross.

[E. J. DILLON]

POWER OF THE KEYS, see KEYS, POWER OF.

POWERS in postbiblical writings, one of the *choirs of angels. In the NT they are regularly joined with Principalities and are sometimes spiritual beings and sometimes civil authorities. BIBLIOGRAPHY: W. Foerster, Kittel TD 2:562–574.

[E. A. WEIS]

POWICKE, FREDERICK MAURICE (1879–1963), English historian. Professor at Queen's University, Belfast

(1909–19), Manchester (1919–28), and Oxford (1928–47); P.'s primary interest lay originally in political, subsequently in ecclesiastical and intellectual history. His works include *The Loss of Normandy* (1913); *Bismarck and the Origin of the German Empire* (1914); *Ailred of Rievaulx* (1922); *Stephen Langton* (1928); *The Medieval Books of Merton College* (1931); *Medieval England* (1931); *The Christian Life in the Middle Ages* (1935); revision, with A. B. Emden, of Hastings Rashdall's *Universities of Europe in the Middle Ages* (3 v. 1936); *History, Freedom, and Religion* (1938); *The Reformation in England* (1941); *King Henry III and the Lord Edward* (2 v. 1947); *Modern Historians and the Study of History* (1948); *Ways of Medieval Life and Thought* (1950); *The Thirteenth Century* (1953, rev. 1961); and, with C. R. Cheney, *Councils and Synods with Other Documents Relating to the English Church* (v. 2, 1964). BIBLIOGRAPHY: R. W. Hays, NCE 11:656.

[R. W. HAYS]

POYNTER, WILLIAM (1762–1827), bishop. Ordained in 1786 at the English College at Douai, P. served there as prefect of studies until imprisoned during the French Revolution. President of the College of St. Edmund in England from 1801 to 1813 he became vicar apostolic. A moderate in the controversy with Protestants, P. was the leader of the Catholic group opposed to the position of the bps. on the Relief Act of 1791.

[J. R. AHERNE]

POZZO, ANDREA (1642–1709), Jesuit lay brother, baroque fresco painter, renowned for illusionistic architectural perspectives, chiefly active in North Italy, Rome, and Vienna. His masterpiece the *Triumph of St. Ignatius* in S. Ignazio in Rome is the last of the great baroque ceiling decorations. Completed in 1694, it is the culmination of complicated painted architecture developed by the Bolognese School. To the viewer who stands in the correct position in the nave of S. Ignazio the heavens appear to be opened and a multitude of figures swirl in swift and dramatic patterns ecstatically connecting this world with that above. P. wrote a book on perspective *Tractatus perspectivae pictorum et architectorum* (1693) which was translated into many languages. This writing influenced decoration in Germany and Austria, where P. finally settled (Vienna, 1704). BIBLIOGRAPHY: R. Marini, *Andrea Pozzo Pittore* (1959).

[P. P. FEHL]

PRABHUTARATNA (To-pao), central figure in the Buddhist Lotus Sūtra. P., one of the Buddhas from a previous cycle, long in nirvana, returns to hear the preaching of the Buddha Sākyamuni. P. appears seated on a throne discoursing with Sākyamuni, in Chinese bronzes at the rock-cut sanctuaries of Yün-Kang, Lung-mên and elsewhere.

[M. J. DALY]

PRACTICAL APOLOGETICS, see APOLOGETICS, PRACTICAL.

PRACTICAL REASON, the mind described in its function of guiding and regulating action, as distinct from its purely cognitive function. The mind or reason as "speculative" or theoretical has *truth as its concern. But since to act humanly is to act under the direction of knowledge, the mind serves, as it were, the whole nature, in directing human activities that fall under the general headings of producing outward effects or artifacts, and of reacting inwardly to moral objectives or situations. The mind's right direction of productive activity involves the arts, liberal or mechanical; the direction of moral action involves *synderesis, moral science, and *prudence. Moral theology, presupposing the function of practical reason in moral choices, takes into account the psychological difference between the mind as practical and the mind as purely cognitive. Truth or falsity in moral judgment is not directly the conformity to or aberration from the structure of the real; rather it is conformity to or departure from rightness of *appetite. That implies that in the formulation of effective moral decisions (as distinct from pure moral theory) evaluation of what is good and to be pursued or evil and to be avoided, corresponds to and reflects the bent of appetite—will or emotion. That, not the purely mental weighing of pros and cons, explains the effective, moral imperative; it explains also the need for integration between the moral virtues and prudence. BIBLIOGRAPHY: Aristotle, *Ethics* 3, 5.1114a32; ThAq ST 1a2ae.57,5 ad 3;58, 2, 3, 4 ad 3,5.

[T. C. O'BRIEN]

PRACTICAL THEOLOGY, that division of study, esp. in Protestant seminaries, that relates to carrying out the activities of the Church, as distinguished from such studies as Scripture, church history, dogmatic theology, and philosophy of religion. "When we turn to the fields of homiletics, religious education, and church administration, as well as to liturgy and church music, we come to studies which are often designated 'practical' in contrast to 'theoretical.' . . . What distinguishes these fields is that they have to do with the meaning of Christian faith as it bears upon specific functions of the minister or other religious worker so that work in these fields involves practice as well as instruction" (H. R. Niebuhr, D. D. Williams, and J. M. Gustafson, *The Advancement of Theological Education* [1957], 102). Pastoral counseling, with its programs of classroom and clinical training, is also included in the practical field. Courses in practical theology have become increasingly numerous in seminary curricula in recent decades. Although critics sometimes assert that too much emphasis is thereby placed upon technique in the training of ministers, the increased role of practical theology seems fairly well established.

[T. EARLY]

PRACTICE OF RELIGION, in an abstract sense, the respect for the indebtedness towards God as source and end of human existence that engages the virtue of *religion. That respect includes the obligation to *worship, i.e., to externalize in an appropriate manner an inner *reverence due to God. The practice becomes more particularized through the commandment of the Decalogue to "keep holy the Sabbath," and the church precept enjoining assistance at Mass on Sundays and holydays of obligation. This church law is intended to ensure a regular expression of the worship owed to God. In RC understanding a *"practicing Catholic" is one who observes the commandment and precept, and also other connected observances, such as the law of Easter duty and of fast and abstinence. Other Christian bodies generally hold in principle for the obligation to worship God regularly; *church attendance, however, is not always strictly enjoined or taken as a sure indicator of membership in the Church.

[T. C. O'BRIEN]

PRACTICING CATHOLIC, a term generally understood to mean a Catholic who, generally speaking, lives in substantial accordance with his baptismal commitment. It represents a judgment based upon objectively discernible data rather than upon the interior fact of grace, except when an individual uses it in application to himself. A person could not rightly be classified as a practicing Catholic who is habitually involved in serious injustice or lives over an extended period of time in a state of unrepented sin, or if he is regularly unfaithful in the performance of his important religious obligations (e.g., his Easter duty, his participation in the liturgy at required times, his duty to train his children in the knowledge and practice of the faith.) The term, obviously, can be more or less perfectly applicable to individuals.

[P. K. MEAGHER]

PRADO, JERÓNIMO DE (1547–1595), Jesuit exegete. P. taught Scripture at Córdoba and is noted for his commentary on Ezechiel (3 v., 1596–1605), the last two volumes of which were completed by J. B. Villalpando. The work had continuing value for its thorough study of Jewish coins, weights, and measures although its description of Jerusalem has proven to be generally erroneous. BIBLIOGRAPHY: W. Drum, CE 12:332; L. F. Hartman, NCE 11:659.

[T. M. MCFADDEN]

PRADO, JOHN OF, BL. (1563–1631), missionary, martyr. A Spanish Franciscan, P. founded (1620) the Andalusian province of his order and became its provincial. Named prefect apostolic of the Franciscan mission in Morocco in 1630, when he went there a hostile sultan imprisoned him and his companions. Called before the sultan, P. urged him to accept Christ. The sultan's response was to

stab him to death. P. was declared blessed in 1728. BIBLIOGRAPHY: I. da Villapadierna, BiblSanct 10:870–871.

[J. R. AHERNE]

PRADT, DOMINIQUE DUFOUR DE (1759–1837), better known as Abbé de Pradt, French political figure, ecclesiastic, and prolific writer, esp. on topics concerned with international politics and Church-State relations. He opposed the Revolution, but later became Bonaparte's chaplain, bp. of Poitiers, abp. of Malines (an appointment unconfirmed by the Holy See), and ambassador to Poland. A close friend of Talleyrand, P. was mundane in his life, a staunch Gallican in theology, and an interested observer of political developments in South America. His writings, esp. his *Des colonies et de la révolution actuelle de l'Amérique* (1817) exerted a strong influence on the independence movement in Latin American countries. BIBLIOGRAPHY: M. Aguirre Elorriaga, *El Abate de Pradt en la emancipación hispanoamericana, 1800–1830* (1946).

[P. DAMBORIENA]

PRAEDESTINATUS, a 5th-cent. anonymous treatise written in Italy, possibly at Rome. The title was given by J. Sirmond, who edited the text in 1643. There are three books; the first is a reproduction of St. Augustine's *De haeresibus,* with fanciful additions; the second presents arguments in favor of an extreme theory of predestination, which it falsely attributes to Augustine; the third is a Pelagian refutation of the arguments. BIBLIOGRAPHY: É. Amann, DTC 12:2775–80.

[T. C. O'BRIEN]

PRAEMUNIRE (Lat., to fortify; confused in medieval Lat. with *praemonere,* to forewarn), a term variously applied in English law: (1) to statutes, 23d Edward III (1353), and 16th Richard II (1393); (2) to the appropriate writs that charged a sheriff, *praemunire facias,* to summon a person accused of prosecuting in a foreign court a suit cognizable by the law of England; (3) to the offense itself; and (4) to the penalty incurred of forfeiture, outlawry, and imprisonment at the king's pleasure. The measures go back to the legislation of Edward I (1206) against papal provisions of benefices, dignities, and their revenues, impositions increasingly resented during the Hundred Years' War and regarded, particularly when the popes were at Avignon, as operating for the comfort of the French enemy. They were not, however, steadily applied until Henry VIII invoked them against asserting or maintaining papal jurisdiction, most famously in his proceedings against Cardinal Wolsey and in his coercion of the clergy to acknowledge the royal supremacy over the Church.

[T. GILBY]

PRAENESTE (PALESTRINA), SANCTUARY OF, from ancient times the oracle of the goddess Fortuna

Primigenia, oldest daughter of Zeus, in the ancient city Praeneste, on the slopes of the Apennines. The Sanctuary (2d–1st cent. B.C.) is built on terraces, with a monumental *propylaea* (entrance), two large basilicas, two halls paved with magnificent mosaics, a rectangular portico above, and, on top, the circular temple (*tholos*) for the cult statue. Constructed of tufa, limestone, and concrete, its plan of axial symmetry marks a turning point in Roman architecture. Excavated after World War II, the sanctuary yielded the important *Mosaic of the Nile* (1st cent. B.C.–3d cent. A.D.) with crocodiles, hippopotamuses, and late Roman Republican biremes with soldiers. Bronze reliefs of Amazonomachia and gigantomachia were also found. BIBLIOGRAPHY: G. Jacopi, *Santuario della Fortuna Primigenia . . .* (1959).

[M. J. DALY]

PRAEPOSITINUS OF CREMONA (Prévostin; *c.*1150–*c.*1210), scholastic chancellor of the Univ. of Paris from 1206. He studied law at Bologna and theology at Paris. As master at the Mainz cathedral he was involved in opposition to the papal legate over the nomination of the diocesan bp., and had to make submission to Pope Innocent III, but this Pope did appoint him to the chancellorship at Paris. P.'s *Summa theologica,* which follows the order of Peter Lombard's *Sentences,* is an important example of theological thought in the era preceding the introduction of Aristotle's full philosophical corpus to the West. P. also wrote: *Summa de poenitentia injungenda; Summa de officiis,* a popular liturgical handbook; *Summa super psalterium;* a *Summa contra haereticos* is of doubtful authenticity.

[T. C. O'BRIEN]

PRAETEXTATUS, an unknown person after whom one of the oldest and most interesting catacombs in Rome was named; located along the Via Appia Pignatelli; abounding in Christian and pre-Christian decor and motifs. BIBLIOGRAPHY: U. M. Fasola, LTK 8:700.

[E. J. DILLON]

PRAETEXTATUS OF ROUEN, ST. (d. 586), bp. of Rouen. P. incurred the hatred of Chilperic and his wife Fredegund by permitting and perhaps officiating at the marriage of Meroveus, son of Chilperic by his first wife, with his aunt-by-affinity, Brunhilda, widow of Sigebert, brother and rival of Chilperic, who was murdered (at the instigation of Fredegund?) in 575. Chilperic had P. appear at a synod in Paris (577) and charged him with abetting the treason of his son and with violating canon law by permitting an incestuous marriage. The intervention of *Gregory of Tours restrained the synod from deposing P., but it did condemn him. P. was imprisoned and after attempting to escape was sent into exile on the Island of Jersey. After Chilperic's death, P. was exonerated and restored to his see, but was fatally stabbed by an agent of Fredegund while at Matins in his cathedral. P.'s name appeared in no martyrology before

the 16th cent. when J. Molanus inserted it in his edition of the martyrology of Usuard (1568). This influenced Baronius to include it in the Roman Martyrology. BIBLIOGRAPHY: Butler 1:411–412; J. Marilier, BiblSanct 10:1094–96.

[P. K. MEAGHER]

PRAETEXTATUS, VETTIUS AGORIUS (*c.*320–384), Roman statesman and scholar, and champion of paganism. He translated Aristotle's *Analytics* and reflected pretty much the philosophical outlook of Neoplatonism. With Q. Aurelius *Symmachus and others, he tried to restore paganism in public and private life. He himself held numerous pagan priesthoods and had been initiated into Mithraism and other mystery cults. He represents the marked syncretistic character of late Greco-Roman paganism. BIBLIOGRAPHY: PW 22.2:1575–79; T. W. Nicolaas, *Praetextatus* (1940).

[M. R. P. McGUIRE]

PRAETORIAN GUARD, translation of *praetorion* in Phil 1.13. If the Epistle was written in Rome, Paul is speaking of the imperial guard or of people attached to it. In another city it would be the bodyguard of the household of the Roman governor. *PRAETORIUM.

[A. VIARD]

PRAETORIUM, originally the praetor's tent in a Roman camp; later, a Roman governor's residence or the part of it, accessible to all, where he gave judicial sentences. When in Jerusalem, the praetor or procurator usually resided in the palace of Herod, near the Jaffa gate. He may also have sometimes stayed in the Antonia fortress in the NW corner of the Temple in order to watch over it. BIBLIOGRAPHY: EDB 1888–92.

[A. VIARD]

PRAETORIUS, MICHAEL (Michael Hieronymus Schultheiss; 1571–1621), German composer, organist, author of *Syntagma musicum* (3 v., 1615–19), a treatise, in Latin and German, on all known instruments and on sacred and secular music. He served as *Kapellmeister* at Lünenburg and beginning in 1604 as organist, then *Kapellmeister* to the Duke of Brunswick. His compositions include sacred and secular settings of German and Latin works for several voices. Included are settings of the Kyrie, Gloria, and Magnificat; *the Megalynodia Sionia* (1611); a few organ settings, *Musae Sioniae* (1605–10), and many other elaborate choral works.

[R. J. LITZ]

PRAGMATIC SANCTION, a royal decree establishing fundamental law of State or Church. In France, the most important was the Pragmatic Sanction of Bourges (1438), issued by Charles VII, which proclaimed Gallican "liberties" and limited papal rights. French electors were to fill ecclesiastical vacancies, strengthening the king's role, with papal power of nomination recognized only if an occupant died in Rome. The Bourges Sanction also approved the conciliar decrees of Basel, limited papal financial and judicial privileges, and reformed ecclesiastical abuses. The papacy opposed its restrictions and its strengthening of the conciliar movement. Louis XI revoked the Pragmatic Sanction temporarily (1461), hoping for papal assistance, and Popes Julius II and Leo X condemned it, but it was superseded only by the Concordat of Bologna (1516). Even then its principles survived in Gallicanism. In Austria, the Pragmatic Sanction of 1713 was Charles VI's attempt to assure the undivided realm to his oldest daughter, if no sons survived. However, it failed to prevent the War of the Austrian Succession (1740–48). The Spanish Pragmatic Sanction (1830) permitted female succession to the throne, giving Ferdinand VII's later daughter precedence over Don Carlos, his brother. BIBLIOGRAPHY: Hefele-Leclercq 7.2:1053–61; L. Buisson, *Potestas und Caritas* (1958).

[W. A. CHANEY]

PRAGMATISM, originally and essentially an epistemological theory originated by Charles S. Peirce and adopted by William James and John Dewey. As originally formulated by Peirce in an essay entitled "How to Make Our Ideas Clear," the basic principle of pragmatism is: ". . . consider what effects, which might conceivably have practical bearing, we conceive the object of our conception to have. Then, our conception of these effects is the whole of our conception of the object." (*Collected Papers* [1935] 5.402). In other words, Peirce is arguing that the meaning of an idea or concept is precisely and totally summed up in the bearings which the idea or concept has on the conduct of life. This notion of truth comes from Peirce's suggestion that the sole function of thought is to fix belief, so that the thinker is confident enough in his thought to act. It is a matter of complete indifference whether or not the idea arrived at is true, in some manner independent of the thinker having the thought. There is, Peirce suggests, no such thing as a false belief from the point of view of the believer at the moment that he believes. Pragmatism states, then, that the total meaning of an idea believed is the sum total of conceivable actions that the believer would be willing to undertake based upon his belief.

This definition of truth is appropriated by William James, and put forth in popular fashion in a book called *Pragmatism*. James here suggests that the method of pragmatism revolves around the "cash-value" of an idea, i.e., its practical consequences. He says: "There can be no difference anywhere that doesn't make a difference elsewhere—no difference in abstract truth that doesn't express itself in a difference in concrete fact . . ." (*The Writings of William James* ([1968] 379). On the basis of this definition of pragmatism, James suggests that truth is an "action word"; truth is something that is produced, engendered upon reality, as opposed to being something which conforms itself to an already present reality. This enables James to combine pragmatism as a theory of truth with his metaphysics of

radical empiricism which states that man carves his facts out of an undifferentiated world of pure experience, and that the world therefore "is waiting to receive its final touches at our hands."

The basic difference between James and Peirce was that James saw the task of creating meaning and truth as a profoundly personal task, while Peirce maintained that it was a community function. For Peirce "the opinion which is fated to be ultimately agreed to by all who investigate is what we mean by truth, and the object represented in this opinion is the real." (*Collected Papers,* 5.407)

The third great pragmatist is John Dewey, whose theory of truth parallels Peirce's notion that the function of thought is to fix belief. Dewey, in a theory of truth which he labels "instrumentalism," sets down the position that the function of thought is primarily not to settle abstract intellectual problems, but to effect something beyond itself. Thought, then, is important only insofar as it is instrumental to the production of something other than the thought itself. With James, Dewey believes that truth is created. Ideas become true insofar as the future confirms and supports our belief in them. The ultimate criterion of truth for Dewey is whether or not thought is instrumental to both immediate satisfaction and the establishment of a more satisfactory working relationship with the environment. BIBLIOGRAPHY: *Pragmatic Philosophy* (ed. A. Rorty, 1966).

[F. J. CUNNINGHAM]

PRAGUE, DEFENESTRATION OF, see DEFENESTRATION OF PRAGUE.

PRAISES, DIVINE, see DIVINE PRAISES.

PRAJAPATI, Sanskrit for "Lord of Creatures," called also "generator of the earth"; more a title than a name, used (esp. in Rig-Veda 10.121) to refer to the creator and source of the universe in early (Vedic) Indian religious thought. Prajapati is both transcendent creator-god and an immanent, pervasive spirit sustaining all living things. The functional title seems to represent a stage in Indian thought in which the plurality of gods became an embarrassment to the philosophically minded and in which there is manifest a quest for the unifying principle of the universe. The term is also used as a title for the creator-god *Brahma. BIBLIOGRAPHY: R. C. Zaehner, *Hinduism* (1966) 39–42; W. D. O'Flaherty, *Hindu Myths* (1975) 25–55.

[D. P. EFROYMSON]

PRAKṚTI, Sanskrit: *pra* "before," *kṛti* "creation," in the Samkhya system of Indian philosophy (later appropriated and developed in the *Yoga system), the dynamic and creative force or principle of "nature" or "matter," from which the entire physical universe evolves. It is composed of three "strands" (*gunas*) or constituents, which, in varying degrees of opposition and harmony, account for change, movement, and development in the universe: *rajas:* activity or energy; *tamas:* resistance, static inertia, "darkness"; *sattva:* order, being, "luminosity." In Samkhya, *prakṛti* is a principle explaining "the way things are"; Yoga goes further by recommending a discipline for extricating or isolating (*kaivalya*) the human soul or "self" (*purusha*) from its involvement in *prakṛti.* BIBLIOGRAPHY: M. Éliade, *Yoga* (1970) 3–41; A. B. Keith, *Samkhya System* (1924); S. N. Dasgupta, *Yoga as Philosophy and Religion* (1924) 1–91.

[D. P. EFROYMSON]

PRANDTAUER, JAKOB (1660–1726), Austrian architect. One of the great masters of late baroque style, he applied his art chiefly to monastic projects, notably the rebuilding of the famous abbeys of Melk (1702) and St. Florian (near Linz, 1745), a masterpiece of baroque style. The famous shrine of the Holy Trinity at Sonntagberg with its baroque church (1706–29) belonging to the abbey of Seitenstetten is the work of P. Though rich and complex in their organization these buildings are yet distinguished by the graceful reticence of classical baroque, and truly Benedictine in their harmony with the culture of their time.

[P. P. FEHL]

PRĀSĀ, a word that originally meant the skin of an ass. Christ's ride upon an ass gave the ass's skin a symbolic value and it came to be spread on Nestorian altars in place of the *ṭeŵîlaitā.* Today the skin has itself been replaced by a corporal, but the corporal retains the name *prāsā.*

[A. CODY]

PRAT, FERDINAND (1857–1938), French biblical scholar. A Jesuit, he was ordained in 1886. He studied Oriental languages at Beirut and Paris and exegesis in Rome and England. He taught in France, Belgium, and Lebanon, and from 1902 to 1907 was in Rome as one of the first consultors to the Pontifical *Biblical Commission. P. also assisted in planning the Pontifical *Biblical Institute. During World War I he served as a chaplain and received the *Croix de la Légion d'honneur.* From time to time he was on the editorial staff of the journal *Études,* publishing over 100 articles in it and other periodicals. He was also the author of several books, including *Origène* (1907), *Theology of St. Paul* (2 v., 1908–12; Eng. tr., 1926–27), and *Jésus-Christ* (1933; Eng. tr., 1950).

[T. EARLY]

PRATENSIS, FELIX (*c.*1495–1558), Jewish convert, Augustinian, who edited the first of the Hebrew Bibles published by D. *Bomberg. *RABBINICAL BIBLES.

[T. C. O'BRIEN]

PRATENSIS, JODOCUS, see DESPREZ, JOSQUIN.

PRAXEAS (fl. late 2d and early 3d cent.), anti-Montanist, accused by Tertullian, to whom we are indebted for the little

that is known of him, of *Monarchianism. According to Tertullian P. persuaded Pope Zephyrinus to quash a letter the Pope had prepared acknowledging the prophetic gifts of Montanus, Prisca, and Maximilla. BIBLIOGRAPHY: Tertullian's *Treatise against Praxeas* (ed. E. Evans, 1948); J. Chapman, CE 12:344.

PRAXEDES, ST. Virgin, and in some accounts, martyr. The *Acta* giving an account of her and St. *Pudentiana are known to be spurious and nothing is known of her beyond the probable fact that her remains were transferred from the catacombs to the church of St. Praxedes by Pope Paschal I (817–824). Legend, however, has made her the daughter of *Pudens and the sister of Pudentiana, and tells that she sheltered, protected, and otherwise sustained her fellow Christians during the persecution of Marcus Aurelius. BIBLIOGRAPHY: Butler 3:157.

PRAXITELES (fl. *c.*370–330 B.C.), Greek sculptor in Athens, epitomizing the graceful, delicate style of the disillusioned Hellenistic world. P.'s finest work, *Hermes Holding the Infant Dionysus* is characterized by softly modulated planes and the languid stance of the period. His famous *Aphrodite of Cnidus* and a Roman copy of his *Apollo Sauroctonus* ("lizard slayer") are sensuous, sinuous, and dreamy conceptions contrasting strongly with the noble, ideal vision of the gods by 5th-cent. masters, *Phidias and others.

[M. J. DALY]

PRAY, GYÖRGY (1723–1801), historian, philologist. Ordained in the Society of Jesus in 1745, P. taught at the Theresianum in Vienna and later at Budapest. After the suppression of the Jesuits in 1773, he was appointed royal historiographer by Maria Theresa. As librarian of the Univ. of Budapest he pursued a vigorous career in writing. He demonstrated the philological significance of the 12th-cent. Magyar *Oratio funebris.* A member of the Hungarian Diet, P. was created abbot in 1801. Among his writings were *Annales regum Hungariae 997–1564* (1763–70) and *Specimen hierarchiae Hungaricae* (1779).

[J. R. AHERNE]

PRAYER, in its root meaning (Lat., *precari, preces;* Gr., *euchomai*) and in the strictest sense, humble religious petition, the free approach of man to God to seek the divine benevolence and the benefits he needs for life, both temporal and eternal. Thus, it involves a request (silent or uttered), a loving (in some sense) attention to the presence of God (it is contemplative), and a self-offering in some way (devotion, commitment) (Nedoncelle, 5). In a broader sense all devout elevation of the spirit to God in faith is termed prayer: praise, thanksgiving, worship, all loving conversation with God (SS. Teresa of Avila, Thérèse of Lisieux). In a third and broadest sense, prayer is seen to lie at the heart of all communion with God, in every loving response to divine initiatives of nature and grace. The unity latent in these three senses is appreciated in recognizing that all petition, acknowledging the divine goodness, ultimately seeks union with God; and that all loving attention to or communion with God, given the divine transcendence and man's indigence, must in truth rest in dispositions of petition.

Historically, prayer is a religious phenomenon common in all ages and cultures, in natural (primitive prayer) or revealed religion (Jewish, Christian, Muslim) where there is faith in a personal God. Theologians recognize that the prayer of the Old and New Covenants is unique in that it is a response to the word of God: moved by a historical intervention of God and guided by the divine revelation. Christian prayer, further, is different from all other in that it is rooted and centered in the Incarnate Word, Jesus Christ, the sole mediator between God and man, in whom divine revelation and communication reached its fulness and from, through, and with whom all communion with God is realized. The prayer of the Church (liturgical prayer) and of each member (personal prayer) prolongs the earthly prayer of Jesus and is both an extension and an instrument of his eternal priestly intercession. Christ's earthly prayer was an integral element of his redemptive mission, and Christian prayer has an analogous function in Christian life; this explains the necessity of prayer, the scope of intention of liturgical prayer, the apostolate of prayer, the intent of contemplative religious life.

Theologically, then, prayer is a personal communion with the Father in the Son (Incarnate) through the Holy Spirit, a functioning in man of his participation in divine life. And while it is, psychologically, essentially of the mind (the practical intellect), in the full context of faith it is moved by love (the desires of charity) and is a direct and explicit expression of hope (ThAq ST 2a2ae, 83). It has been treated by theologians chiefly (with *sacrifice, *adoration, *devotion) as an act of the virtue of religion; yet it is realized in some way in all exercise of the theological virtues (Suarez). As a distinct "exercise" in religious life, prayer is a simple and unique activity; yet it is intimately involved in the totality of the spiritual life. It has been called the "central phenomenon of religion" (Heiler) or "the spiritual life itself as a conscious tending to God" (K. V. Truhlar, *Structura theologica vitae spiritualis* [1960] 169). Indeed, all conscious functioning of faith implies prayer which is (as the interior life) the essential vein or core of the religious life of man; it is the area of openness and response to God, of communion and communication with him; it is the animating force or soul of liturgical participation; it gives meaning to sacrifice, vows, religious consecration; it has been termed the "soul of the apostolate" (Chautard) and is the principal object or area of spiritual direction.

While all prayer belongs to the domain of the vocative (Nedoncelle, 3) and all prayer, as such, is (in the literal sense) mental, commonly prayer is termed vocal where there is a fixed formula of approach to God; it is termed mental where the approach is a free, spontaneous (yet prop-

erly discerning) expression of the desires (J. De Guibert). The types of prayer commonly distinguished (discursive, affective, contemplative) represent the forms that prayer takes according to the growth or stages of the spiritual life (as a life of prayer). Thus, discursive prayer (*meditation) is usually that of one entering seriously upon a life of prayer; affective prayer develops with the loving understanding gained through familiarity with divine realities in meditation; *contemplation (a simple, loving intuition or attention) characterizes the prayer of one who has deepened in union with God in love. The life of prayer develops not in isolation, but as an integral element of the spiritual life and involves the necessary renouncement of self interest and sincere commitment to the divine will. Prayer thus tends to pervade all activities and circumstances of life.

Objections raised against the prayer of petition, where they do not rise from prejudice against faith (e.g., atheism, materialism), are usually to be ascribed to a misunderstanding of the content of the faith or of the intent of the one praying. Prayer supposes faith in the providence of a personal God upon whose wisdom and will and on whose power all things depend. And one prays not to alter immutable decrees or to change the will of God, but rather to dispose oneself (with the aid of grace) to be able to receive what God wills to be effected through and in response to prayer. Finally, granted the common nature of all Christian prayer, modalities of doctrine or practice will be appreciated by considering the vocation and spirituality of an individual or group. BIBLIOGRAPHY: F. Heiler, *Prayer* (tr. and ed. S. McComb, 1950); J. DeGuibert, *Theology of the Spiritual Life*, (tr. P. Barrett, 1953); M. Nedoncelle, *Nature and Use of Prayer* (tr. A. Manson, 1964); C. Bernard, *La Prière chrétienne* (1967).

[W. J. READ]

PRAYER, AFFECTIVE, see AFFECTIVE PRAYER.

PRAYER, BIDDING, see BIDDING PRAYER.

PRAYER, DISCURSIVE, often referred to as *meditation, a reasoned kind of prayer in which one applies the mind to some truth of faith and, through that application, comes to embrace the truth more firmly and relate it to daily life. The purpose of discursive prayer is twofold, to develop in oneself clearer and firmer convictions about some truth and, as a result, to turn to God and the things of God with an ever stronger love and devotion. In the concrete, the combination of reasoned and affective action influences the one praying to make his prayer practical by resolving on some course of action which is seen to be needed. The subject, the matter meditated on, may be anything which has an appeal to the reason, e.g., the fatherliness of God, an event from the life of Jesus, as his acceptance of the cross, his compassion for sinners, etc. The choice of the subject matter is to be indicated by one's needs and one's capacities; hence, beginners are advised to accentuate what will have an imaginative appeal, as scenes from the life of the Savior, esp. those susceptible of a moral application to self, e.g., a virtue to practice or a vice to avoid. All agree that the heart of discursive prayer, which is the usual type of prayer for those who are in the early stages of the spiritual life, is the so-called "affective acts," i.e., acts having a volitional content, such as sorrow for sin, or gratitude to God. Otherwise the prayer easily becomes a purely intellectual exercise in which one thinks about a sacred subject. The purpose of the thinking or reasoning is not achieved until the affections begin to be produced, that is, when the will, aided by the emotions, turns toward God. While method is never primary in prayer, but only a means by which one can overcome the natural obstacles to be found in every human being, some method is generally found to be useful. With practice—whatever the method a person uses—each one tends to adjust the method to his particular temperament and spiritual attraction; in effect, as he advances, each individual will elaborate his own method. There are, however, several methods of discursive prayer which may be called classical. For example, the Ignatian, the method of St. Francis de Sales, the Sulpician and the Carmelite methods. All of these and other methods of meditation can be reduced to a basic outline or framework: thought about some supernatural truth or a truth with supernatural applications; a movement of the heart, that is, the will towards God; and, finally, a resolution to do something about it in one's daily life. In these elements, the various methods agree; they differ only in the nonessentials, like the names of the various acts and the different ways in which to begin or end the exercise. Meditation, or discursive prayer, is seen by all recognized authorities on the spiritual life to be an indispensable exercise for growth in spiritual perfection. With practice, imperceptibly, discursive prayer develops into a simpler kind of prayer, but even advanced souls are advised to begin their mental prayer as if they were exercising discursive prayer. BIBLIOGRAPHY: A. Toyo and J. Aumann, *Theology of Christian Perfection* (1952) 514–521; G. Lercaro, *Methods of Mental Prayer*, (tr. T. F. Lindsay, 1957).

[P. F. MULHERN]

PRAYER, FAMILY, see FAMILY PRAYER.

PRAYER, POSTURE AT, a thing that may be regarded as an external or outward manifestation of interior sentiment (determined by culture or liturgical custom to be proper for prayer), or as a position helpful to the conduct of prayer (according to the needs or dispositions of the one praying). In different cultures, standing, kneeling, prostration, arms outstretched or hands joined, have been considered appropriate for prayer. Standing (with some exceptions) was the normal posture of prayer in the OT and in the NT (Lk 18.11,13; Mk 11.25; Mt 6.5) and the early *Orantes* in catacomb art are depicted standing with arms outstretched and eyes upraised (catechumens with eyes lowered). The Council of Nicaea, 325 A.D., decreed that for the sake of

uniformity the faithful should stand for prayer on Sundays and during the Pentecost season. But in more recent times kneeling, standing, sitting (even prostration) all have place in liturgical participation, and kneeling is common in private prayer, although any posture that enables one to pray well, with due regard to the reverence required, is suitable and proper for prayer.

[W. J. READ]

PRAYER BOOK, AMERICAN, see AMERICAN PRAYER BOOK.

PRAYER BOOKS, books distinguished according to common usage from official liturgical (or service) books (such as the *Breviary* and the *Missal*), and which serve as manuals or collections of prayers, hymns, devotional practices and the like intended for private (nonliturgical) devotions. Exceptions are the C of E prayer book (*Book of Common Prayer*) which contains the official C of E liturgy, and the Jewish prayer book (*siddur* or *seder tepillah*) containing the liturgy for both synagogue and home use. Actually, many Catholic Missals intended for general liturgical use by the faithful include abundant instruction and prayers for personal devotions, and recent prayer books contain substantial portions or paraphrases of liturgical texts and prayers; thus, it is sometimes difficult to distinguish the categories clearly.

There are some early collections of prayers of the Church Fathers (and some of anonymous prayers), but the prayer book, as we understand it today, is derived from the early and widespread use of the Psalter for private as well as for liturgical devotion. From the 9th and 10th cent. on, elaborate MSS, often ornate and richly embossed, of the *Psalter* and of the *Book of Hours* (which developed, as did the *Divine Office with and from the Psalter) offer valuable insight into the devotional practice as well as into the art and iconography of the Church. And the *Book of Hours*, perhaps, varying slightly yet with a basic content in different exemplars, should be called the prayer book of the Middle Ages. It would contain, typically: the Little Office of the Blessed Virgin, the liturgical calendar, the Gradual and penitential Psalms, passages of the Gospel, the Office of the Dead, and various forms of prayer or devotion. This it was that (as the *prymer* or *primer*) was the first prayer book printed in England in the late 15th century.

With the advent of printing, the prayer book (Jewish as well as Catholic) came into wide popular use, the vernacular first appearing with and then replacing the Latin. With the religious struggles and the Counter Reformation they became, during the 16th and 17th cent., a frequent and favored instrument for popular religious instruction (St. Peter Canisius added prayers to his catechisms). With the growth and spread of sodalities and confraternities common manuals of devotion or prayer books increased greatly. In the space here available it is impossible to distinguish types or select titles of the prayer books of the past 200 years (some of which have had immeasurable influence on religious piety), but an example might be cited, the *Garden of the Soul,* of R. *Challoner (revised through a 7th edition by the author after the first printing in 1740, and reissued in countless editions, with many changes). It was the first RC prayer book printed in the U.S. (1770 or 1774), and it was reissued as late as 1945. We should not, however, overlook the value and the influence of the prayer book not only in the development of religious piety and the practice of devotion, but also as an instrument of religious instruction and of spiritual direction. BIBLIOGRAPHY: F. J. Witty, NCE 11:678–684; H. Thurston, CE 12:350–354. *IMITATION OF CHRIST.

[W. J. READ]

PRAYER OF MANASSEH, a penitential psalm of great beauty and devotion, composed in the 1st or 2nd cent. by a Jewish author writing in Greek. The Prayer is printed in Protestant Bibles among the *apocrypha. While not recognized as canonical by the Council of Trent, the Prayer in a late Latin translation is printed as an appendix in the Sixto-Clementine Vulgate. The Prayer purports to be that addressed to God in repentance for idolatry by King Manasseh (687–642), according to 2 Chr 33.11–13.

[T. C. O'BRIEN]

PRAYER OF QUIET, a technical expression for a form of contemplation that rests content with God without much interior speech, imagination, cogitation, and affective effort. A stage is reached when a person is more acted upon by God than acting for himself; it follows the prayer of recollection, which is more centered on cognitive attention, and should be the aspiration of the practice of discursive prayer. This last should be like Martha; its solicitude should not be encouraged to hinder the simple and silent enjoyment of the presence of God, which leaves the soul refreshed, not exhausted.

[P. F. MULHERN]

PRAYER OF SIMPLICITY, that act of communion with God which is characterized by its uncomplicated gaze, loving and intellectual, on him or on one of his mysteries. Ordinarily it is the fruit of previous efforts at *meditation, but differs from meditation in this, that the many considerations yield to a prolonged and loving look, and that the formerly numerous expressions of diverse affections are unified into a single act of love. Bossuet was the first to use the expression (*Manière courte*) but other authors describe the same reality as simple gaze, presence of God, or simple vision of faith. St. Teresa calls it the prayer of acquired recollection, and describes it in brilliant detail (*Way of Perfection,* ch.28–29; *Interior Castle,* Fourth Mansions, ch.3). In her view, it is the transition point between ascetical, acquired prayer and the later infused, mystical contemplation. BIBLIOGRAPHY: A. Royo, *Theology of Christian Perfection* (tr. J. Aumann, 1962) 524–527; P. Marie-Eugène, *I Want to See God* (tr. M. Verda Clare, 1953) 198–213.

PRAYER OF THE FAITHFUL, called general intercessions, consisting of litany-type prayers of petition said, after the homily, by priest and people for the Church, civil authorities, those in need, for all men, and for the salvation of the world. This ancient prayer was restored by Vatican Council II (Vat II SacLit 53).

The prayer can be found in the earliest liturgical documents (e.g., 150 A.D., St. Justin's *First Apology to Anthony the Pious*). The liturgical books of the Roman Rite retain it until the 6th cent. after which the only traces of it were in the Wednesday and Friday of Holy Week. The general intercessions still form a part of the Liturgy of Good Friday. Up until the 6th cent. these prayers had the form of solemn intercessory prayers. First there was a proclamation of the intention by the deacon, then a silent prayer by all followed by a prayer proclaimed by the celebrant in the name of all, to which the people replied, "Amen." In the East a different form of prayer of the faithful was developed and is still retained today: the deacon proclaims the intentions and the people reply "Lord, Have mercy on us," or some similar response. At the end of the litany the celebrant pronounces a prayer to which the faithful reply, "Amen."

The last evidence of the prayer of the faithful in its traditional place after the homily is found in a letter of Felix II (478). At about the same time (492–496) the *Kyrie* was introduced into the Roman liturgy and probably influenced the gradual demise of the prayer. Various remnants of the prayer are found in the English *Bidding Prayer, and the French *Prière du Prône.* In the modern liturgical development both the ancient Roman and Oriental forms of this prayer are in use. The contents of the prayer have remained the same. BIBLIOGRAPHY: J. Jungmann, *Mass of the Roman Rite* (tr. F. Brunner, 2 v., 1951) 1:485–490; T. Maeder, "Towards a Theology of Prayer," *Worship* 40 (1966) 218–230; A. Nocent, "Prayer of the Faithful," *The Liturgy of Vatican II* (ed. J. Lang, 2 v., 1966) 2:83–106. *PRONE.

[N. KOLLAR]

PRAYER OF UNION, a way, degree, or stage, of prayer proper to the unitive life. Hence the fruition of growth in a life of prayer that is characterized by the union of all the powers or faculties of the soul or spirit with or in God. Terminology differs among spiritual authors, that of St. Teresa of Jesus' *Interior Castle* usually being followed, but it is for all a contemplative prayer, infused and supposing recollection and tranquillity. The prayer of union itself is seen to admit degrees that are termed: simple (or ordinary) union (of the interior faculties); ecstatic (or conforming) union (a "captivity" of the external senses); and transforming union (or spiritual marriage, seen as the fullest union with God in prayer). BIBLIOGRAPHY: A. Royo and J. Aumann, *Theology of Christian Perfection* (1962) 528–545 "Contemplative Prayer," 546–561 "Highest Stages of Prayer"; J. G. Arintero, *Stages in Prayer* (1958). *CONTEMPLATION; *PRAYER.

[W. J. READ]

PRAYERS FOR THE DEAD, see DEAD, PRAYERS FOR THE.

PRAYING BOY, bronze statue, a Roman copy of the Greek 4th-cent. B.C. original. By Boidas, son of Lysippus, the *adorans* (worshiper) is mentioned by Pliny (*Natural History,* 34, 73). Standing with (restored) arms in prayer, the statue evidences Lysippean proportions.

[M. J. DALY]

PREACHER APOSTOLIC, the preacher of the pontifical household (It., *predicatore della casa pontificia*). A member of the ecclesiastical pontifical family he is by tradition a Capuchin friar and charged with preaching to the papal entourage in Lent, Advent, and on special feast days.

PREACHING, in its primary Christian meaning, the act of proclaiming God's saving word. The term also denotes the art of pulpit oratory, which has its own history, not considered here. In the first sense, the English term preaching stands for several NT terms: *kērussein,* to herald, proclaim (noun form *kērugma,* proclamation); *euangelizesthai,* to announce the good news (noun form *euangelion,* the good news, the gospel), *marturein,* to witness, is used in the Johannine writings. These are central in the dynamics of Christianity: by preaching Christianity had its beginnings, its growth, and its continuation, whatever the forms it has taken. The fact should not be obscured by exaggerating a contrast between preaching in the RC Church and in the Churches of the Reformation. The Reformation does, however, remain a useful point of division in the history of Christian preaching.

From the NT to the Reformation. NT literature indicates that the one who preaches announces his message with authority; he is commissioned, sent. John the Baptist, for example, was herald for Jesus, proclaiming the good tidings of the Redemption (Mk 1.38; Lk 4.18). Preaching describes the whole ministry of Jesus and the Apostles (Mk 1.2; 3.14; Jn 1.23; Acts 6.2–4; 1 Cor 1.17; 9.16). When Jesus preached in towns and villages "with him went the twelve" (Lk 8.2), and he commissioned them to proclaim "to the whole world" what he had told them (Mt 24.14; Lk 24.46). They did this, announcing "in season and out of season" (2 Tim 4.2) the word of God received from Jesus (Tit 1.3). No complete record of apostolic sermons remains, but Acts gives many reports of preaching in which the Apostles' proclamation of the kingdom is revealed (Acts 2.14–40; 3.12–26; 10.28–43). St. Paul preached in connection with the celebration of the Eucharist (Acts 20.7). Preaching is presented as the saving act of God (Mk 1.15; Lk 4.16–21), and its subject matter is the whole work of salvation through Christ (see, e.g., 1 Cor, ch. 1 and 2).

In postapostolic times Justin Martyr mentioned (*c.* 150) preaching as part of the regular liturgical service (*Apol.* 1.67). The discourses of Polycarp (d. *c.* 116) to his people of Smyrna are referred to by Tertullian (d. *c.* 220) and also by Irenaeus (d. *c.* 202), whose own sermons, collected in the 4th cent. by Eusebius (*Eccl. hist.* 5.20.6), are no longer extant. Among the earliest surviving preached sermons is a prolix homily on wealth by Clement of Alexandria (d. *c.* 210), based on Mk 10.17–31. By the 4th cent. preaching had become an integral part of Christian worship, as the collected sermons of the great preachers attest. Preachers of East and West were trained rhetoricians, particularly proficient at the exegetical sermon, a running commentary on the Sacred Scripture used in the day's liturgy. Famed in the East were the Cappadocians, SS. Gregory of Nazianzus (d. *c.* 390) and Basil the Great (d. 379), together with St. John Chrysostom (d. 407); and in the West SS. Ambrose (d. 397) and Augustine (d. 430). The latter often preached several times a day and composed a work on preaching, Book IV of his *De doctrina christiana.* Gregory the Great (Pope Gregory I, d. 604) wrote series of homilies that were widely read in the following centuries and gave directions for preaching in his *Liber regulae pastoralis,* a guide for parish priests. In the Dark Ages after the barbarian invasions preaching fell into disuse, and the sermon was almost restricted to monastery churches, where homiliaries, collections of patristic sermons, like that of Paul the Deacon (*c.* 720–*c.* 800), were employed. The Carolingian reforms of the 9th cent. improved both clerical education and preaching, notably by collections of sermons made by Alcuin and Rabanus Maurus, and church councils (at Tours and at Reims, 813; at Mainz, 847) decreed that bishops preach homilies, and in the new vernacular languages. While preaching spread, its quality declined quickly with the invasions of the Muslims and Northmen.

The 12th cent. is marked by the mystical and scriptural preaching of St. Bernard of Clairvaux (1090–1153), which had lasting influence; the era also saw the development, connected with the rise of the universities, of the scholastic sermon. Based on the scholastic method of exposition, this type of sermon was preached at all the university centers by the medieval schoolmen. A desire to fill a need for popular preaching (Lateran Council IV in 1215 complained of the near-illiteracy of most parish priests) led to lay preaching in such reform movements as the *Humiliati and *Waldenses; doctrinal vagaries led to ecclesiastical condemnation. With the coming of the friars in the 13th cent., principally the Dominicans and Franciscans, to whom freedom to preach everywhere was granted (e.g., by the Council of Vienne, 1312), a great rebirth of popular preaching took place throughout the West. Great crowds gathered to hear the friars, and outdoor sermons became a regular practice.

Popular preaching during the centuries preceding the Reformation had several developments. One was the spread of the mystical sermon by Meister Eckhart (1260–1327), Johannes Tauler (*c.* 1266–1367), Henry Suso (*c.* 1295–1366), Jean Gerson (*c.* 1363–1429), and others. Another was the sermon similar to the later parish mission or revival sermon, urging repentance, frequently in apocalyptic terms; SS. Vincent Ferrer (*c.* 1350–1419), Bernardine of Siena

(1380–1444), and John Capistran (1386–1456) preached in this style. Preaching was also used as a powerful weapon of reform by John Wycliffe (*c.*1329–84), who sent out his Lollards and Poor Preachers in England; by Jan Hus (*c.*1369–1416); and by Girolamo Savonarola (1452–98). The many sermon aids, preachers' manuals, and collections of sermons published throughout these centuries attest to the frequency of preaching; but the strictures of Lateran Council V (1516) indicate that much of it had become devoted to superstition instead of the gospel.

Preaching in the Churches of the Reformation. Protesting against a special sacrificing priesthood, *sacramentalism, and papal teaching authority, the Reformers asserted the primacy of the word of God as present in Scripture, sermon, and sacraments. Early Reformers designated themselves simply ''the preachers.'' Both the *Augsburg Confession (Art. 7) and the *Thirty-Nine Articles (Art. 19) defined the Church as existing where the gospel is rightly preached and the sacraments rightly administered. The preaching of the word was proposed as the instrument through which justification comes about and the Holy Spirit is given (*Formula of Concord, Art. 12; *Westminster Confession, ch. 14). The *Reformed tradition esp. extolled preaching as the primary function of the ministry (Zwingli's Sixty-Seven Articles, Art. 14, 62; First *Helvetic Confession, Art. 20; Second *Helvetic Confession, ch. 14, 18). While Anabaptists—the radicals of the Reformation—and later the Quakers rejected any special ministry, the influence of preaching nevertheless had a paramount influence on their history.

The high value set on preaching as characteristic of the Reformation was exemplified by Luther, Zwingli, and Calvin. A close alliance between the biblical and the preached word was observed through the expository sermon, closely following the scriptural text. The original esteem for preaching the word has never been lost in Protestantism. Conviction that the living word of God is present in the act of preaching inspired the Puritans of England and New England, the evangelists John *Wesley and George *Whitfield, and preachers of *revivalism. Almost every Protestant Church has had its beginning with a great preacher; throughout Protestant history the major figures and the most significant movements are closely connected with preaching.

The content and quality of preaching has naturally reflected theological trends. The original Reformation zeal for the living word of God has sometimes stiffened into a letter-bound *biblicism. Within the century after the Reformation, both Lutheran and Reformed pulpits became platforms for a scholastic orthodoxy, in which emphasis was placed upon correct formulation of doctrine. In reaction, *Pietism developed themes and styles inculcating an individualistic experience of salvation, an emphasis carried on in Wesleyan and revivalistic preaching. The impact of the *Enlightenment and of rationalism turned sermon emphasis away from distinctive Christian dogma in favor of

ethical and naturalistic explanations of the gospel. This trend was continued and compounded in the 19th cent. by *liberal theology; preachers sought to present an enlightened view of biblical themes accommodated to evolutionary theory, and stressed the subjective appeal of religious truths. In the *Social Gospel movement the pulpit became a forum for addressing all social questions and for a humanitarian Christianity. Protestants described as *evangelicals resisted both liberals and ritualists (see RITUALISM), and emphasized preaching, relying on a literal understanding of the Bible and minimizing sacraments and ritual (see FUNDAMENTALISM; NEW EVANGELICALISM). In the 20th cent. the rejection of liberal theology in favor of a return to Reformation orthodoxy was led by Karl *Barth, who asserted the primacy of the word of God: the original Word in Christ, the record of that word in the Bible, and the word made present in preaching that depends on the biblical word about Christ. For many Rudolf Bultmann has renewed concern for the preached word; he has sought to show the relevance of the NT to contemporary man by his thesis that the demythologized and dehistoricized kerygma is God's present revelation calling for authentic faith (see BULTMANN SCHOOL). There has also been a return in many Protestant Churches to the relation between word and sacrament, esp. the Lord's Supper, and a strong trend to keep the two together, as conjoined expressions of God's saving action and presence.

RC Preaching since the Reformation. One RC reaction to the Reformation was a strong reaffirmation of church doctrine on the sacraments and the Mass. The Council of Trent also sought to remedy the failure of bishops and priests to preach properly. Early in the Council (Session V, June 17, 1546) preaching was made the topic of a special decree, urging it as the principal function of bishops, legislating that all priests having the care of souls preach on Sundays and great feast days. A reform decree in session 23 (Nov. 11, 1563) reiterated (can. 4) the earlier legislation, recommended special sermons during Advent and Lent, and advised bps. to remind the faithful of the obligation to hear the word of God in their own parishes. The legislation on seminaries earlier in session 23 (July 15, 1563) also was a reform measure that led to a better preparation for preachers. The *Catechism of the Council of Trent* was designed as a doctrinal guide, esp. for preaching. Since Trent there has been a conscientious fulfillment of the preaching ministry, at the parish Sunday Masses, in special sermons, particularly during Lent, and in the development of the parish mission, novenas, and retreats. In these centuries there also have been throughout the Church powerful preachers, sometimes brilliant pulpit orators.

The most significant factor in RC preaching since the reforms of Trent, however, has been a new, or newly stated, evaluation of preaching. The formulation of a RC theology of the word was slow to come. There has been a sense of the obligation to preach; the sermon has been used for doctrinal instruction, moral exhortation, and for polemical or apologetic purposes. Vatican Council II in the *Decree on the Liturgy* recognized the evangelizing, instructional, and exhortatory functions of preaching (Vat II SacLit 9). But the Council described preaching in its fullest significance as "a proclamation of God's wonderful works in the history of salvation, that is, the mystery of Christ, which is ever made present and active within us, especially in the celebration of the liturgy" (35). The one liturgy comprises the "liturgy of the word and the Eucharistic liturgy" (56). The Council recognized the presence of the saving Christ esp. in the liturgy, that Christ is present in sacrifice and sacraments; "he is present as well in his word since it is he himself who speaks when the holy Scriptures are read in the church" (7; see also Vat II MinLifePriests 4). These teachings have led to a richer theology of preaching, to an appreciation of the union between word and sacrament and of preaching as essentially the present celebration of the mystery of salvation. BIBLIOGRAPHY: E. C. Dargan, *History of Preaching* (2 v., 1954); H. Dressler et al., NCE 11:684–700, with bibliog.; P. Hitz, *To Preach the Gospel* (tr. R. Sheed, 1963); J. Murphy-O'Connor, *Paul on Preaching* (1964); O. Semmelroth, *Preaching Word* (tr. J. J. Hughes, 1965).

[P. F. MULHERN]

PREACHING (IN THE BIBLE). In the OT there is nothing that can be completely identified with the concept of preaching as understood in Christian times. The two activities that resemble it most closely are (1) the giving of the Torah by the priests, i.e., the teaching, which included the narration of God's saving action of the past in behalf of Israel, the explanation of the law of the covenant, and the passing of judgment in concrete cases; and (2) the proclamations of the Prophets, who felt themselves directly called by Yahweh to speak his word and to make his will known to the people, esp. in announcing God's judgment for the infidelities against the covenant and in exhorting to repentance (Is 5.1–30).

Likewise in the NT nothing can be found to correspond perfectly to the sermon or the homily of later times. The first and most common term used by the NT for preaching is the verb *kērussein,* i.e., to herald, proclaim, announce, or preach, with the noun *kērux,* i.e., the herald or preacher, and *kērugma,* i.e., the proclamation or preaching. Another common term is *euangelizōmai,* i.e., to announce the good news, with the cognate nominal forms *euangelion,* i.e., the announcement of good news, and *euangelistēs,* i.e., the evangelist or announcer of the good news. In Johannine writings the verb used is *marturein,* i.e., to give witness or to testify.

In the NT the object of preaching is the coming of the kingdom of God (Mk 1.15; Lk 4.43–44; Acts 20.25). John the Baptist preaches the kingdom of God as at hand and somehow present in Jesus (Mk 1.15; Lk 16.16). Jesus preaches the good news of the kingdom himself (Mt 4.17; 19.35; Lk 9.2); he instructs the Disciples to do so (Mt 10.7; Mk 16.15; Lk 9.2). The generation that follows Jesus also preaches the kingdom and associates or identifies it with Jesus (Acts 10.37–38; 17.3; 1 Cor 1.23). The object of the preaching of the good news is sometimes given under the figure of speech of metonymy, e.g., repentance (Mk 6.12; Lk 24.47); the word (2 Tim 4.2); the word of faith (Rom 10.8); the word of God or the Lord (Acts 13.5; 15.36); the way of salvation (Acts 16.17); the riches of Christ (Eph 3.8); peace (Eph 2.17); the resurrection from the dead in Jesus (Acts 4.2); the faith (Gal 1.23).

The *kērugma* or preaching contains three elements: (1) The announcement of the working of God in Jesus through signs performed by him, and esp. the greatest sign, namely, God's raising him from the dead (Acts 2.22–24; 3.13). (2) The argument, namely, the evidence from the OT that Jesus is the expected one in whom the promises have been fulfilled (Acts 2.25–36; 3.18). (3) The appeal to listeners to open themselves to the activity of God (Acts 2.37–39; 3.18–21). This same format is followed when the good news has to be presented to the pagans in their frame of reference. For example, in Paul's preaching at Athens there is: the announcement (Acts 17.22–23); the argument, drawn in this case from reason (*ibid.* 23–29); and the appeal (*ibid.* 30–31).

From the NT it can be said in general that Christian preaching is a ministry of the creative and the saving word of God (1 Th 2.13) which somehow makes present the Word of God Incarnate, the Christ event (1 Cor 4.1). Preaching is faith at work (1 Cor 2.4–5; Rom 1.15–17; Gal 1.23). It is therefore, God's saving act both for those who listen (Mt 11.5; Lk 4.18,21) as well as for him who preaches (1 Cor 9.16–23). BIBLIOGRAPHY: C. H. Dodd, *Apostolic Preaching and its Development* (1960).

[A. J. TKACIK]

PREADAMITES, human beings who allegedly lived before the time of Adam. The appellation was given by the Huguenot Isaac de la Peyrère in his *Praeadamitae* (1655) to the progenitors of the gentile peoples, Adam being the parent of the Jews and their kindred only. The theory was originally designed to account for reports that people of the New World and Far East had histories dating earlier than the date ascribed to Adam according to J. *Ussher's computation (*Annales Veteris Testamenti,* 1650); it has since been held on other grounds. The encyclical *Humani generis* (1950) warns the faithful against embracing the opinion that after Adam, men existed on this earth who were not descended from him, (see MONOGENISM: POLYGENISM). The doctrine involved is the common unity of mankind in original sin and salvation by Christ. The appellation is not given to hominids, antediluvians, the gods and heroes of mythology, or intelligent beings elsewhere than on this planet.

[T. EARLY]

PREAMBLES OF FAITH, the body of metaphysical and moral truths within the grasp of human reason that are presupposed to the act of faith. These include the mind's ability to know truth, the existence of God, the value and necessity of worship, and the existence of the human soul. The term has also been applied to the *motives of credibility, such as miracles and the holiness of the Church, as adduced to show that it is not unreasonable to accept the fact of Christian revelation and the truth of its content. Without the acceptance of the preambles of faith, the act of faith would not be fully human and consonant with the dignity of man as an intellectual being, because the denial of these truths logically implies the denial of the revealed doctrines that constitute the object of faith. This does not mean, however, that the acceptance of these truths must be prior to the act of faith in point of time; logical priority suffices and is perhaps more generally the case. Nor is it necessary that assent to the preambulary truths be explicit. These truths are also relative in the sense that a satisfactory basis for one person's judgment may not be convincing for another. Recent *apologetics has emphasized this last characteristic, pointing out that faith is not the conclusion of a syllogistic argument but a human commitment to which a variety of personal religious experiences may contribute. Assent to the preambulary truths does not constitute the act of faith itself; it simply enables a person to make a speculative judgment of credibility and a practical judgment that he should believe. The help of supernatural grace, empowering a man to perform an act beyond his natural potentialities, is necessary for the final commitment of faith. BIBLIOGRAPHY: M. C. D'Arcy, *Nature of Belief* (rev. ed., 1958); J. Alfaro, Sac-Mund 2:324–326; J. P. Whalen, NCE 11:702–703. *FAITH.

[T. M. MCFADDEN]

PREBEND (Lat. *praebenda,* a living, or pension), a type of *benefice, specifically a canon's individual share in the income from church property set aside for the support of the cathedral chapter (see MENSAL FUND). The usage dates from the 9th cent., when, rather than living in common from the one general fund, the canons singly received a designated income attached to their office; they thus came to be called prebendaries. In modern times the terminology no longer reflects the much altered forms of clergy support; a prebend may designate a stipend or other income, and prebendary is an honorary title.

[T. C. O'BRIEN]

PREBOSTE, FRANCESCO (1554–1607), Italian servant of El Greco who accompanied the master to Spain, assisted him, and completed commissions on the master's death.

PRECEDENCE (CANON LAW), the right of superior rank or place given by law, over and above the hierarchic rank deriving from holy orders. Precedence in canon law belongs to the consideration, CIC Book II, of the classification and qualities of persons in the Church. Since a person is either an individual (physical person) or an organized, juridic group of persons (moral person), precedence belongs both to physical and to moral persons. The law of precedence among individuals applies mainly to the clergy. Canon 106 gives general norms for determining precedence; some of the main details on precedence among physical persons (most observable in seating or processions at liturgical ceremonies) are these: a resident bp. in his own territory has precedence over all other bps. and abps., but not over a cardinal or papal legate; a patriarch outranks a primate; a primate, an abp.; an abp., a bp. (CIC cc. 280, 347); where individuals are of equal rank, precedence is determined on such secondary grounds as date of ordination or tenure in office. Precedence among moral persons has its most obvious instance in the ranking between secular clergy and religious institutes, and the ranking among the religious institutes themselves. Thus: the body of secular clergy has precedence over all religious, outside the churches of the religious who are clerics; a cathedral chapter has precedence even in churches of religious. Precedence among religious institutes is: clerical over nonclerical; orders of canons regular over monastic orders; monastic over nonmonastic orders of regulars; regular orders over religious congregations; pontifical over diocesan congregations (*ibid.* c. 491).

[T. C. O'BRIEN]

PRECENSORSHIP, in RC canon law *praevia librorum censura,* the examination and licensing by ecclesiastical authority required before certain classes of religious books may be published for general circulation; this is censorship in the strict sense (see BOOKS, PROHIBITION OF). The law of precensorship was introduced first in Germany in the 15th cent. after the invention of printing; it became universal law at the Council of the Lateran V under Leo X (1515), and extended to all books, even the purely secular. Leo XIII (*Officiorum ac munerum,* 1897) limited censorship to religious works. The classes of works regulated by current law are: Bibles and biblical commentaries; works on the Scriptures, theology, church history, natural theology, or ethics; also devotional, ascetical or mystical works, and prayer books; printed religious pictures or holy cards come under this law (CIC c.1385.1, nn. 1–3). For such publications the competent authority is the bp. of the diocese where the work was written, or will be printed or published. (The Holy See reserves to itself the right to approve certain works, e.g., collections of indulgenced prayers, c. 1391). In each diocese censors are appointed, who must be competent, judge works objectively and not by personal opinion, and submit their judgment in writing. The censor's favorable judgment, the *nihil obstat,* indicates that the book contains nothing contrary or dangerous to faith or morals. The bishop's permission to publish, the imprimatur, must appear in the work approved (c. 1394.1).

While this legislation remains in force, it undoubtedly will be revised. Since the era of Vatican Council II there has been strong opposition to prior censorship, as unduly protective of the faithful, and an infringement on the freedom and professional integrity of authors. In practice censorship is interpreted broadly; the imprimatur frequently is not sought, or if obtained is not printed.

In European Judaism religious books that were in accord with Jewish doctrine and morality often carried the approbation of an eminent rabbi. To forestall Christian confiscation of Hebrew books, the rabbis also exercised a precautionary censorship over anything that might be considered offensive to Christianity. In England after the Reformation censorship was rigidly enforced by the Crown until the revocation of the Licensing Act (1695). On the Continent in Protestant territories censorship by the State was a normal part of establishment: with the secularization of the State purely religious censorship all but ceased. There is no church censorship in Protestantism as formalized as that of the RC Church; in some denominations works published under church sponsorship require previous approval by theologians. BIBLIOGRAPHY: G. H. Putnam, *Censorship of the Church of Rome* (2 v. 1966); Bouscaren-Ellis-Korth 775–784.

[T. C. O'BRIEN]

PRECEPT, (1) a command that obliges but is distinct from law. This distinction made by moral theology is sometimes clear, sometimes not. One distinguishing feature traditionally assigned is that law is enacted as permanent; a precept of its nature regards a temporary situation. A precept that is strictly particular, given to an individual person, or to a special group, is distinct from law, which is enacted directly for a whole community and directly orders it towards the common good. A superior's precept, as particular, is the objective to which the virtue of obedience responds. Canonists further distinguish precepts as being personal while laws are territorial. In practice, laws in the full sense are often referred to as precepts; this is true both of the Decalogue and the commandments of the Church. (2) Precept in theology also designates the commandments of God, whose observance is necessary for salvation. Such precepts are distinguished from the evangelical counsels, gospel ideals recommended for intensifying the life of charity, but not imposed. *COUNSELS, EVANGELICAL.

[T. C. O'BRIEN]

PRECEPTS OF THE CHURCH, see COMMANDMENTS OF THE CHURCH.

PRÉCIOSITÉ (preciosity), a movement originating in 17th-cent. France as a reaction against vulgarity, and a general desire for distinction and refinement. The term is now identified with the salon circles of Mme. de Rambouillet and esp. Mlle. de Scudéry, where the cultivation of politeness and elegance reached *précieux* extremes in the refinement of dress, conversation, language, literature, and feelings. Historically, however, the term itself seems to have come into use only after 1650, and is identified with a feminist protest against the subjection of the woman in prearranged marriages, and an attempt to develop a refined,

idealized concept of love free from social constraint. Préciosité is thus not merely a linguistic but a moral phenomenon seen as developing out of the aristocratic and secular ethical teaching of the Neo-Stoic moralists. BIBLIOGRAPHY: R. Bray, *La Préciosité et les précieux de Thibaut de Champagne à Jean Giraudoux* (1960).

[R. N. NICOLICH]

PRECIOUS BLOOD, the object of a theology and a devotion centering in the divine mystery of Redemption through the blood of Jesus. The theology aims to organize and formulate the body of revealed truths (with conclusions and applications) on this basic theme; it seeks to sum up and synthesize these truths (with conclusions and applications) in the sign-symbol of blood as they are found in the sources of Bible and tradition. It lays the foundations for the devotion, justifies its use, establishes its boundaries, and orients it to the kerygma, the cult, and the spiritual life of the Christian. Hence it must be both conceptual and existential. The theology proclaims the devotion as loving and grateful worship of the Blood, the price of Redemption. It singles out the blood because of its singular meaning in the real and mystical bloodshedding. Theology also underscores the dynamic import of the blood in its shedding. As such it not only reflects the words and acts of Calvary and Last Supper, but also is their divinely chosen real-symbol (metonymy). The blood stands as such symbol (and also in our profound intent) for the final summation of the salvific work of Christ on Calvary, and is therefore symbol of the total synthesis of Christ's supreme redemptive work with its utter submission to the Father, its merit, its satisfaction, its Redemption, its sacrifice, its efficacy. Adequately, the devotion comprises (and the theology explains) the three great stages of Christ's redemptive act through blood: the earthly reality, the mystic presence and action in the sacramental Church with its anticipation of the ultimate priestly fulfillment in glory. Both theology and devotion embrace the two specific Precious Blood symbols, the Lamb and the Cross, which mutually explain and enrich the devotion with profound reference to the background of Scripture and tradition. As every other special theology (and devotion) so this one also offers a striking synthesis of the whole body of revealed truth, casting light esp. on the motive of Incarnation (often treated superficially), the meritorious (and instrumental) cause of grace, the relation of Christ to the entire race of man and angels, the meaning of sin, and Christocentrism in general. BIBLIOGRAPHY: R. T. Siebeneck, et al., NCE 11:705–708; John XXIII, "Inde a primis" (Apostolic Letter, June 30, 1960) [AAS 52 1960] 545–550; *Precious Blood Study Week, Proceedings of the First and Second* (1957, 1960).

[E. G. KAISER]

PRECIOUS BLOOD, SOCIETY OF THE (CPPS), an institute of priests and brothers organized under the influence of Fr. Francis Albertini, whose work in the Confraternity of the Precious Blood inspired St. Gaspare del

Bufalo (1786–1837) to found the Society of the Precious Blood in 1815 at Giano in Umbria, Italy. They observe the rule of their founder, which was approved by the Pope in 1841 and after revision was reapproved in 1946. The members follow a common life, make a promise of fidelity, and are bound by charity, not religious vows. Formerly, the scope of the Society was officially restricted to such work as giving missions, novenas, and retreats, but since 1946 it has included all ecclesiastical work and now engages in spreading devotion to the Precious Blood, preaching, parochial ministry, education of youth, and foreign mission work. The Society is divided into provinces with 267 houses in countries of Europe, South America, and the U.S., and has a total membership of 788 of which 629 are priests. The moderator general resides in Rome, Italy. BIBLIOGRAPHY: P. J. Knapke, *History of the American Province of the Society of the Precious Blood* (1958); V. Sardi, *Herald of the Precious Blood: Gaspare del Bufalo* (1954).

[R. A. TODD]

PRECIOUS BLOOD SISTERS, religious women of several congregations of this title, founded by or under the patronage of St. Gaspare del Bufalo.

(1) The Sisters Adorers of the Most Precious Blood (ADPPS), founded by Bl. Maria De Mattias in 1834 in Acuto, Italy, according to the plan of St. Gaspare, are dedicated to the education of the poor. They conduct schools and hospitals in countries of Europe, Asia, Africa, South America, and the U.S. The life of the sisters centers around the devotion of Redemption through the Precious Blood and they spend an hour in daily adoration honoring this mystery. In 1975 the congregation supported 389 foundations and had a total membership of 2,842 sisters. The motherhouse is in Rome.

(2) The Sisters of the Most Precious Blood of O'Fallon, Mo. (CPPS), originally founded in 1845 at Steinerburg, Switzerland, by Rev. Karl Rolfus (1819–1907) and Mother Teresa (Magdalena Weber) for the purpose of honoring the Precious Blood in convents of perpetual adoration. Gradually their apostolate grew more active and by 1860, the congregation became associated with the Sisters Adorers of the Most Precious Blood. Responding to a need for teachers in America, most of the sisters left the European congregation and established a new community at O'Fallon, Mo., in 1874 with the assistance of Abp. Peter Kenrick of St. Louis. Papal approval was granted them in 1938. The sisters conduct schools in 10 states and also engage in foreign mission work in Finland, Bolivia, and Peru. They have 55 houses and a total membership of 500.

(3) Sisters of the Precious Blood (CPPS), religious members of a congregation founded at Castle Loewenberg, Switzerland, in 1834 by Mother Maria Anna Brunner, widowed mother of six children. During the Holy Year pilgrimage to Rome in 1833, Mother Maria became acquainted with the Society of the Precious Blood and its saintly founder, Gaspare del Bufalo, who inspired her to establish a community

honoring the Precious Blood. Devotion to the mystery was accomplished by perpetual adoration of the Blessed Sacrament, while the active life of the sisters involved them in the training of orphans and educating the young. In 1844 the community was transferred to the U.S.—7 years after the death of its foundress, whose son, Fr. Francis de Sales Brunner, CPPS, acted as guide and was responsible for the move. As the apostolate grew, the type of work varied and soon the sisters were engaged in caring for the sick and aged, serving the clergy in seminaries and episcopal residences, supporting lay-retreats and promoting liturgical arts. In 1946, the U.S. community received approval from Rome. There are 72 houses and 564 members missioned in 11 states and Santiago, Chile. The general motherhouse is in Dayton, Ohio. BIBLIOGRAPHY: *Not with Silver or Gold: A History of the Sisters of the Congregation of the Precious Blood, 1834–1944.* (1945).

[R. A. TODD]

PRECISIANS, a name used briefly for *Puritans, because of their exactness in religious matters. In a broader sense the term is applied to anyone with similar religious attitudes.

[T. C. O'BRIEN]

PRECONIZATION, from Lat. *praeco,* a herald (cf. It. *preconizzare*), a nonce word for the public announcement by the pope of appointments to bishoprics or other offices.

[T. C. O'BRIEN]

PRECURSOR, one who goes before another to prepare the way. The term was linked to the apocalyptic hope that God would come at the end of the age to establish his reign upon earth and restore the earth to obedience, justice, and peace. The restored Israel was to be an instrument of this reign, and often some individual was seen as a precursor to usher in the reign. This precursor was sometimes viewed as a prophet like Moses who would teach the Law; or as a prophet like Elijah who would restore true worship and perform wonders; or as a king like David who would rule with justice. The term "anointed one" ("Messiah") was sometimes used, and could refer to prophet, priest, or king, but was most often used in reference to the restoration of a kingdom like David's. When John came baptizing with a call to repentance, he also spoke of "one who is to come," whose judgment would be exacting, who would look for fruit worthy of repentance. Since John was of a priestly family, it was natural for his expectation of God's reign to center on restoration of true worship, and to be colored by the imagery of the Prophet Malachy. In Malachy, who looks for the cleansing of the Temple, the messenger who is sent before the Lord to prepare his way, is identified as Elijah, who is to return before God comes in judgment (Mal 3.1–4; 4.5). When John's disciples ask Jesus: "Are you the one who is to come, or should we look for another?" (Mt 11.2–5), it is the imagery of Malachy that is implied. Indeed there is abundant evidence that Jesus was viewed as that Elijah who was to come. The same wonders are ascribed to him as to Elijah (and Elisha) in the Book of Kings: a miraculous feeding of disciples; the raising to life of a widow's dead son; the curing of lepers. In Luke the journey to Jerusalem is introduced by the solemn phrase reminiscent of Elijah: "as the time approached for him to be taken up into heaven . . ." (9.51). When they were not welcomed by a Samaritan village his disciples wanted to call down fire from heaven—Elijah fashion—but he rebuked them (Lk 9.54). The Elijah hope may be the source of the Joannine expression about the Son of Man being lifted up; and easily supplies a precedent for the outpouring of the spirit after the Ascension into heaven. In John's Gospel, shortly after being pointed out by the Baptist as the one coming after him, Jesus cleanses the Temple in Jerusalem (Jn 2.12–22), which would easily have been understood as the fulfillment of the Elijah role in Malachy. In fact, when asked (according to the Synoptics) by what authority he did this, he asked them what authority they recognized in the activity of the Baptist (Mk 11.28–33). Despite all this, and despite the fact that (according to Jn 1.21) when the Baptist was asked: "Are you Elijah?" he replied: "No," the Christian tradition has come to view John as Elijah, the Precursor of Jesus, the Messiah. In Luke (1.17) John's birth is foretold as that of the Precursor, possessed by the spirit and power of Elijah. And Jesus is depicted telling his Disciples that— "for any who can accept it"—John is Elijah, the messenger of Malachy's prophecy (Mt 11.10,15). And then, finally, the words that all the Gospels use to introduce John: "the voice of one crying in the wilderness: 'Prepare the way of the Lord' " no longer refer to the way of the Lord God coming to reign; but to the way of the Lord Jesus, the Messiah. John was finally understood as the Messiah's Precursor. BIBLIOGRAPHY: J. A. T. Robinson, "Elijah, John, and Jesus," *Twelve New Testament Studies* (1962).

[E. J. DILLON]

PREDESTINARIANISM, a term to designate any teaching that interprets predestination as the election of some to eternal life and the absolute condemnation of all others to sin and punishment. *PREDESTINATION.

[T. C. O'BRIEN]

PREDESTINATION (Gr. *proorizo,* decide on in advance), a word that does not occur in the OT and is seldom used in the NT. The chief NT passages (Rom 8.29; Eph 1.5) refer to the divine plan choosing people for a favored position in the external economy of salvation: the chosen people of the OT, the Christians of the NT. This choice is intended to bring them to eschatological salvation; it bears indirectly on it, however, in that men so favored can cast aside the means if they so will, and those not so favored can still be saved (Rom 2.14–16). Nowhere in Scripture is "predestine" used to mean an infrustrable divine arrangement sending a man to eternal happiness (the opposite, reprobation: an infrustrable advance decision sending men to perdition).

Still less does Scripture know of such a reprobation decided before consideration of a man's deserts. Rather, it implicitly excludes such meaning in saying (1 Tim 2.4) that God wills all men to be saved. He could not honestly decide this while simultaneously deciding on the perdition of some without even considering their deserts. Nor could he bind himself in the covenant at an infinite price (1 Cor 11.25; 6.20) to offer all graces (Rom 8.32) in favor of each individual man (Gal 2.20) and yet reprobate even Christians without considering their deserts. Rather, he has promised to offer even the critical grace of final perseverance (1 Cor 1.5–8; 1 Th 5.23–24) to all. If an answer to the riddle is implied in Scripture anywhere, it is likely to be in the basic revelation that God is our Father. On the one hand, a father can indeed cast a son out of his house permanently, but not without grave, persistent cause. On the other hand, the basic reason why a father does give his love and care to those who do not rebel is due basically to his goodness, not to any merit on the part of his children.

Early Theology of Predestination. The history of the doctrine of predestination in the Western Church begins properly with St. Augustine, who coined the word *praedestinatio* from the verb *praedestinavit* in the Latin text of Rom 8.29. For Augustine and the whole theological tradition that he inaugurated, the text of Romans dictated the formulation of a doctrine of predestination, even though modern exegesis finds scant support in Scripture for these theological elaborations. Augustine's understanding of predestination evolved from his teaching on the necessity and gratuitousness of grace against *Pelagianism. The Pelagians were intent on defending the reality of free will against the Manichaeans, and in explaining the relationship between free man and God they explained freedom as a total independence, or emancipation, from God and his causal activity. Consequently, by the use of man's free will and his naturally endowed capacities, and without the added aid of God's supernatural grace, man is self-sufficent for the beginning, the process, and the attainment of eternal salvation. The Pelagians did, however, recognize a form of predestination, i.e., God's foreknowledge wherein he knows which men will reach salvation through their own efforts.

Augustine's definition became classic in Western theology; predestination is "the foreknowledge and preparation of those gifts of God whereby they who are liberated are most certainly liberated" (*Persev.* 14.35, PL 45:1014). Both in pre-Pelagian and in anti-Pelagian works he developed this idea that predestination is infallibly effective of itself, anterior to and unconditioned by any foreknowledge of man's actions. The plan to save some men is based on an utterly benevolent or gratuitous divine choice. Concomitantly there is an antecedent reprobation of those to whom mercy will not be shown; they will be justly left in the "mass of perdition," the condition of original sin. He does not suggest that a divine decree was the cause of the Fall; Augustine's doctrine presupposes the Fall: men are sinners, God freely chooses to save some, the rest are justly left to damnation. As to the working out of the plan of predestination, Augustine describes grace as irresistible, i.e., it necessarily and infallibly accomplishes the salvation of the elect, overcoming the obstacles in the will, bringing about conversion, growth, recovery from sin, perseverance. The irresistible quality of grace is an expression of the gratuitious benevolence of predestination. Some of Augustine's contemporaries and others of the 5th cent. thought Augustine's fundamental principle that the ultimate reason for the salvation of the elect was God's gratuitious pre-election negated the will to save all men. Their teaching, called since the 17th cent. *Semi-Pelagianism, affirmed the need of divine aid for fallen man to be justified, for with his natural capacities alone he is unable to achieve justification, act meritoriously, and so attain eternal glory. Nevertheless, in many cases at least, it does lie in man's power to make the initial step in seeking God and believing in him. Moreover, since God desires the salvation of all, he does not antecedently to his foreknowledge of men's sins determine their reprobation.

Church teaching gave a measured approval to Augustine's doctrines on the need for grace and on the gratuitousness of grace, but not on irresistible grace. There was, as well, a continued affirmation of human freedom and rejection of predestination to evil. The Council of *Carthage (418) condemned the Pelagian teaching that man could keep the commandments without grace (D 227). Council of *Orange II (529) maintained, against the Semi-Pelagians, the need for grace for the beginning of faith and for final perseverance (D 374–395). With regard to predestination, the conclusion of the council document, by Caesarius of Arles, states that all the baptized having the will to strive faithfully with Christ's help can and must fulfill what pertains to their salvation. The conclusion anathematizes the teaching proposed by Lucidus, a priest of Gaul, that some are predestined to evil (D 397). During the 9th cent. a short-lived predestinarian movement arose under the leadership of the Saxon monk *Gottschalk of Orbais. Claiming a basis in Augustine, he proposed a double predestination, whereby God chooses some for eternal bliss and reprobates others to eternal misery. At the urging of Hincmar of Reims (d. 882), Gottschalk's teaching was condemned at the Councils of Quiercy-sur-Oise (853) and of Valence (855). Both clearly asserted God's will to save all without exception, affirmed predestination to life, and denied predestination to evil (D 621–623; 626–629). Valence declared that God has eternally decreed to punish those whose sins and final impenitence he foresees; their sins are permitted but in no way caused by him (D 626–627).

Medieval Teaching. Thomas Aquinas formulated a definition of predestination as ''the plan existing in the divine mind whereby some persons would be directed to eternal salvation'' (ThAq ST 1a, 23.2). Predestination is thus distinguished from God's general providence both for all creation and for mankind. In the same context, St. Thomas indicated the elements that became fundamental in later RC

theology. Predestination may be considered in its total scope as including the whole series of graces, from conversion through final perseverance, by which men are saved; or in its partial aspect as the plan to confer one or another of these graces. Predestination is affirmed simultaneously with the truth of God's eternal will to save all men. There is no reprobation of some to sin and punishment anterior to the foreknowledge of actual culpability. Predestination in its total scope, however, is antecedent to the prevision of human merit or worthiness; it is not conditioned by man's good actions. Man cannot in any way merit predestination; nor can he positively prepare himself for salvation. The only positive causality is absolutely and entirely rooted in God's benevolence. In the working out of the divine plan, grace so touches the will that man freely responds to the divine initiative.

In the 14th cent. the English theologian Thomas Bradwardine (d. 1349) sought to defend the sovereignty of the divine will against the part in the salvation process attributed to the human will by theologians he called ''modern Pelagians.'' Bradwardine has been classified, perhaps unjustly, by some historians as a determinist, proposing the irresistibility of grace and implying a double predestination. He did have an influence on John *Wycliffe, the Oxford scholar who adopted his theological determinism and espoused Augustinian predestinarianism, developing it in his *Trialogus*. This work influenced not only Jan *Hus, whose predestination teaching was similar to that of Wycliffe, but perhaps Martin Luther as well. The writings of Hus certainly contributed directly to Luther's thought.

The Reformation Era. Luther's position on predestination was explained in his *De servo arbitrio* (1525), a reply to the *De libero arbitrio* of Erasmus, who accepted man's dependence upon God but defended some participation of man's will in the process of salvation. Luther responded with a rigid predestinarianism. From eternity, God chose (prior to any foreknowledge) those whom he would lead to eternal beatitude, and he carries out his will by working everything in them, including their decision to believe and their faith. This is a double predestination, but Luther did not claim that God himself willed and caused the Fall of man and sin itself. Though his teaching is not strictly a form of *supralapsarianism, Luther does use deterministic lines of thought that could easily be construed as supralapsarian if carried to their logical conclusions. His prime concern was to safeguard salvation as due exclusively to the election and grace of God. Later Lutheranism mitigated Luther's teaching with significant limitations. The *Augsburg Confession (1530) does not mention predestination, and Article II of the *Formula of Concord (1577) states that predestination is concerned ''only with the pious children of God.'' It rejects any and all cooperation of the human will in the salvation process and rejects a predestination to damnation. God wills to save all men, so that if anyone is saved, it is exclusively through God's grace; if anyone is lost, he is lost through his own fault.

*Zwingli taught a double predestination in his *Sermo de providentia Dei* (1530). Although predestination holds an eminent place in John Calvin's theology, it is not to be regarded as the cornerstone of his thought. It was his successor in Geneva, Theodore *Beza, who made predestination the basic principle of Calvinist dogmatics. In Calvin's *Institutes of the Christian Religion* (1536) predestination is defined as "God's eternal decree, by which he compacted with himself what he wills to become of each man . . . eternal life is foreordained for some, eternal damnation for others. Therefore, as any man has been created to one or the other of these ends, we speak of him as predestined to life or to death" (3.21.5). God not only freely wills, but through his irresistible grace he effectually leads the elect to faith, perseverance, and glory. Conversely, God not only wills the damnation of the non-elect, but their very sins have been divinely ordained, just as he had ordained the Fall. While the reprobate are predestined to sin, Calvin claims they still fall by their own fault (3.23.8), and in their predestination to destruction they give glory to God (3.23.6). Predestination and reprobation are God's will, and man ought not inquire into the divine mystery. After Calvin's death, some of his followers adopted a rigid and some a somewhat more flexible understanding of predestination: (1) The supralapsarians, following Calvin, held that divine predestination to glory and reprobation to punishment were antecedent to God's prevision of the Fall; consequently, God did not efficaciously desire the salvation of all men, and Christ's sacrificial death on the cross was a limited atonement. (2) The infralapsarians maintained that the decree of predestination and reprobation came after the prevision of the Fall. In both cases, a double predestination is maintained. Reformed confessional writings generally reproduce Calvin's predestinarianism, but in the infralapsarian style (e.g., Second *Helvetic Confession, c. 10; *Belgic Confession, Art. 16; *Scots Confession, Art. 8). The *Heidelberg Catechism (1563) makes no mention of it. Article 17 of the Anglican *Thirty-Nine Articles is usually regarded as in the Reformed tradition. The Council of Trent, in addressing itself to the doctrine of the Reformers on justification, implicitly touched on predestination in the following points: (1) According to Scripture Christ died for all men (D 1523). (2) God's grace is needed for every salutary act; grace is utterly gratuitous. (3) God offers grace even to sinners, but it can be rejected (D 1543). (4) All will not receive the benefits of Christ's death (D 1523). (5) There is no predestination to evil (D 1567). (6) No one can have absolute assurance that he is justified (D 1534) unless he receives a special revelation that he is numbered among the predestined.

Post-Tridentine RC Developments. Not long after Trent the RC Church condemned (1567) an attempt by Michel de Bay (see BAIUS, M.; BAIANISM) to revive rigid Augustinian teaching on grace (D 1901–80). The attempt to reconcile the gratuitousness and efficacy of grace with the freedom of man's will led to the disputes that occasioned the *Congregatio de auxiliis (1598–1607). The theological positions involved, *Báñezianism, and *Molinism, included distinctive explanations of predestination. Báñezians taught a predestination antecedent to any foreknowledge of man's use of grace and based on God's election, and a negative reprobation of the non-elect. Molinists taught a predestination consequent on God's "middle knowledge" (*scientia media*) of how man could cooperate with graces offered. Reprobation is also consequent to the prevision of sin. Other RC explanations were related to one or another of these explanations (see AUGUSTINIANISM). The last important RC decision on predestination was connected with the Jansenist controversies. Cornelius *Jansen, in his *Augustinus*, revived Augustine's doctrine on the irresistibility of grace and taught that Christ died only for the predestined. Both points were contained in the Jansenist propositions condemned in Innocent X's *Cum occasione* (1653; D 2001–07).

Post-Reformation Protestant Developments. Among the Calvinists of Holland, Jacobus *Arminius inaugurated a movement against Calvin's predestinarianism. Arminius and his followers, called Remonstrants, set forth their views in five articles, termed Remonstrances; they championed God's universal salvific will; rejected a limited atonement; admitted that the good deeds of the regenerate are to be ascribed to God but declared that God's grace is not irresistible; and allowed a predestination conditioned by man's free will. At the Synod of *Dort (1618–19) the Reformed Church rejected these articles and excluded the Remonstrants from the Reformed parishes. The Canons of Dort are reflected in Ch. 3 and Ch. 11 of the *Westminster Confession (1648). Arminianism spread with astonishing rapidity. It gave background to the teaching of the *Cambridge Platonists, who sought a proper and truer understanding of human freedom; it found expression in Methodism's emphasis on the moral responsibility of man, and in the whole course of *revivalism; it is discernible in the *New England theology of the late 18th century. In the 19th cent. C. *Hodge and the *Princeton theology sought to reassert the Calvinist orthodoxy of Dort. Revivalism and *liberal theology, however, pushed predestinarian doctrine into practical oblivion. In the 20th cent., the theology of Karl *Barth (d. 1968) has had its admirers and critics. Basically a Calvinist, and responsible for the modern renewal of interest in Calvin, Barth opposed the Reformer's doctrine of double predestination. Man's election to grace can be ascertained only in Christ, in and through whom the Father has elected and predestined man to eternal glory. Christ alone had been chosen for rejection, i.e., through the cross. Barth does not abolish the contingency that some men may be eschatologically rejected by their own doing. His critics, however, seem to find in him a tendency toward universalism, the restoration of all men in Christ. BIBLIOGRAPHY: J. Farrelly, *Predestination, Grace and Free Will* (1964); H. Buis, *Historic Protestantism and Predestination* (1958).

[J. TYLENDA]

PREDETERMINATION, a term descriptive of the effectiveness of actual grace, developed in the Thomist-Molinist debates that culminated in the *Congregatio de auxiliis* (1598–1607). The Thomists (called by their opponents Báñezians, after D. *Báñez) stood by the expression that actual grace physically predetermines the act of the will (see PREMOTION, PHYSICAL). On a broader scale the same term applies to the divine *concurrence in all created activity. The acceptability of the term, much of whose connotation is polemical, rests on St. Thomas Aquinas's teaching on divine causality. The priority of that causality explains the prefix, "pre-." The priority means that the divine causality itself is eternal, prior to all created effects and activity; it means also the order between cause and effect, wherein causality is always prior in being and meaning to what it effects, and every created phenomenon stands as an effect of divine causality, as well as of its proximate, created cause. The greater difficulty with the term predetermination rests on its meaning as a composite word: a causality determining its effect "ahead of time" seems incompatible with the meaning of free will. The determinateness of the divine causality is in opposition to an indeterminateness. For St. Thomas the second is simply incompatible with the divine causality. Because divine, that causality is infallible: from the point of view of the divine knowledge in which all created realities are eternally present, known not by acquisition but through the divine being itself; from the point of view of the divine will and providence as they are the first cause by which every created cause exercises its causality, and not a co-related cause completed by created action. The divine causality brings about the working of the created cause in keeping with the connatural way in which the created cause activates itself. In the case of the human will the divine causality enables the will to bring itself to a concrete choice of good. The strands of meaning in the relationship of the created cause to the divine cannot be put into a single unity in which the concordance of grace or divine concurrence with human freedom becomes clear. The force of "predetermination" in its complexity resists *Molinism at every point, esp. on *scientia media* and a merely simultaneous divine concurrence. As to actual grace, the term means that its inner effectiveness consists in its being the effect of God's special providence, given as the principle for the will's choice and consent to a salutary good. It may be added that the controversy the term reflects has become of merely antiquarian interest. Theology has moved into more biblically grounded categories and discusses grace in ways less confident of or tied to causal categories. BIBLIOGRAPHY: T. C. O'Brien, NCE 11:722–723.

[T. C. O'BRIEN]

PREDIS, DA, family of 15th-cent. Milanese painters and miniaturists. **Ambrogio** (1472–1508), the most important, was court painter to the Duke of Milan (1482) and medal designer for the imperial mint. In 1483 he collaborated with Leonardo da Vinci on the *Virgin of the Rocks,* probably doing one of the angels. **Evangelista** and **Bernardino** assisted in Ambrogio's workshop; only **Cristoforo** independently executed miniatures in a northern decorative style, producing MSS *Officium,* and *Life of SS. Joachim and Anna* (1476) related to T. Crivelli and V. Foppa in large ornamental borders with candelabra and *putti* in architectural and landscape settings.

[M. J. DALY]

PREESTABLISHED HARMONY, a principle in the thought of Gottfried von Leibniz (1646–1716), German philosopher, seeking to reconcile teleology with mechanism or to show that God's intended purposes in the universe are carried out by natural laws. In this view, all reality is comprised of simple psychic substances termed *monads, each of which develops and changes in accord with its own unique inner law preestablished by God. While each monad is simple, it manifests a manifoldness in the multiplicity of its modifications, as a microcosm mirroring the macrocosm in its own singular manner. All progress in the universe is thus a harmony of movements by separate autonomous entities acting concurrently but with no interaction. Like precisely synchronized clocks, numberless monads produce a concert of independent activities, in keeping with the foreordained inner law pertaining to each, but perfectly coordinated and related to form a consonant whole, thereby resulting in the kind of universe God intends.

[J. T. HICKEY]

PREEVANGELIZATION, a term that, broadly speaking, refers to every means of preparing someone for Christianity or, within Christianity, for Catholicism. But more properly it means the process or method of predisposing people to receive the gospel. The term is most commonly applied to those who live in a professedly non-Christian, but religious, culture like Islam or Hinduism and to those in nominally Christian lands where the culture (or the persons themselves) have become indifferent or alien to genuine religious values. The form of preevangelization differs in the two situations.

Among religious believers who are not Christian, preevangelization means especially the preparation of mind necessary to make the Christian faith intelligible to a people totally unfamiliar with Christian modes of thought and behavior. It also seeks first to discover the valid principles of belief and ritual inherent in the prospective converts and then to build on this established foundation. Thus the Muslim belief in monotheism and Buddhist hope of deliverance from suffering can serve as bases for the Christian doctrine of God's transcendence and man's salvation through Jesus Christ.

In societies where people once Christian have lost perhaps even their firm belief in God, preevangelization means above all the predisposing of the will for ready submission to Christian standards of conduct. Here the task is enlightenment, too, but only secondary to making the affections favorable, or at least not hostile, to the ethical demands of the gospel. Accordingly, every improvement in cultural patterns, increase in respect for spiritual values, encouragement in the practice of basic natural virtues, use of educational and communications media to raise people's religious literacy are effective means of preevangelizing those who are hindered by inordinate fears and desires from accepting the moral imperatives of Christ. BIBLIOGRAPHY: J. P. LaBelle, NCE 11:725; A. M. Nebreda, *Distinguishing the Different Stages in Missionary Preaching* (1962).

[J. A. HARDON]

PREEXISTENCE, a term that in theology has relevance to the question of the origin of the human soul, and of Christ's assuming human nature. The preexistence of the human soul was a teaching of *Origen, tied in with his theory of universal restoration (see *APOCATASTASIS). In its preexistence the soul was a spiritual being (*nous*) that sinned and therefore became a soul (*psychē,* a term Origen traces to the Gr. verb for becoming cold); the qualities diversifying souls correspond to the kinds of sins they committed; they retain the power of self-restoration during life. (see his *Peri Archē* 2,9,3; D 404). The *Priscillianists had a similar teaching (see D 201,285,455,456); it was also a part of Neoplatonism (Plato himself in his theory of knowledge and reminiscence refers to a preexistence in which the soul contemplated the Ideas; see *Phaedo* 72 E, *Meno* 81 D). St. Thomas Aquinas rejects any possibility of a preexistent soul on the grounds that it can only exist as the substantial *form of the body (see ThAq ST 1a, 75. 2,4;118.3). With less certainty, to Origen is ascribed also, the position that Christ's soul preexisted the union with his body in the Incarnation (see D 404). Such a preexistence, however, would be contrary to the genuineness of Christ's humanity, and particularly of the manner of his conception by the Blessed Virgin Mary.

[T. C. O'BRIEN]

PREFACE, originally a term applied to any prayer that accompanied a liturgical action and was solemnly pronounced by the presiding celebrant before the congregation. In present usage, however, the term is restricted to the hymn of praise introducing the Eucharistic Prayer or Canon, sung or said by the priest following responses by the people. The principal theme is praise and thanksgiving for the salvific acts of God in history. Nearly all Prefaces begin with the phrase, "It is truly right and just . . . " and end with the "Holy, holy, holy." There are fixed Prefaces in the Eastern liturgies presenting an overall and unchanging view of the process of salvation; in the Western liturgies there are a variety of Prefaces for use on different occasions with themes commemorating events in God's plan of salvation,

the life of Christ and the saints, or in the lives of God's people such as marriages and Christian burial.

[C. J. NOONE]

PREFECT (Lat. *praefectus,* one in charge); (1) used as part of a formal ecclesiastical title for the cardinal heading a congregation of the *Curia Romana, for the head of the prefecture of the papal household, for the head of an ecclesiastical territory, the prefect apostolic; (2) in ecclesiastical establishments a supervisory functionary, a term now obsolescent.

PREFECT APOSTOLIC, according to CIC cc.293–311, the prelate in charge of a prefecture apostolic, i.e., a mission territory in that stage of its development antecedent to becoming a *vicariate apostolic and eventually a diocese. The prefect apostolic usually does not receive episcopal consecration, but in his prefecture has jurisdiction and obligations equivalent to those of a diocesan bishop. A primary function is care for the development of a native clergy.

[T. C. O'BRIEN]

PREGIZERIANS, Lutheran communities in Württemberg, Germany, named after Christian Gottlieb Pregizer (1751–1824), from 1795 pastor of Haiterbach. He tried to influence local pietistic-enthusiastic groups of separatist tendency to remain within the Lutheran Church. Since they did not become a separate religious body, it is hard to define their teaching or to determine their number. They did place extreme emphasis on the effects of justification by faith without works; baptism and the Eucharist put man in a state of bliss and happiness in which he is impervious to sin and sorrow. Because of their joyfulness and the singing of lively songs at their meetings, they sometimes were called Hurrah Christians, or the Merry Ones; because they shook their heads in dissent during sermons in the established Church they were also called Shakers. *Antinomianism apparently was accepted by some extremists. BIBLIOGRAPHY: G. Müller, RGG 5:539–540; C. Kolb, EncRelKnow 9:198–199.

[J. R. FANG]

PREGNANCY, ECTOPIC, see ECTOPIC PREGNANCY.

PREJUDICE, judgment (opinion) coupled with an emotional attitude, favorable or unfavorable to some person or group of persons, formed without reasonable examination and consideration of evidence. Used without qualification the term generally is understood to mean an adverse judgment and/or attitude. In its cognitive component, i.e., as opinion or judgment, prejudices are faulty generalizations that lead to illogical categorizations and the establishment of preposterous stereotypes. Prejudice differs from a simple error in generalization because, unlike error, it is emotionally toned and is characterized by a certain inflexibility. The clear refutation of the "evidence" alleged in justification of a prejudiced view does not commonly shake the prejudiced individual's adherence to his position, though it may cause him to shift to other arguments to support his convictions. Prejudice is generally the result of a strong emotional commitment to certain values and interests, or to the concern to safeguard one's social status, prestige, or economic and other advantages. Religion, being concerned for values of profound importance to the believer, is a matter about which strong prejudices tend to develop.

The effects of prejudice are baneful to the individual who harbors it, to the persons and groups that are its victims, and to society in general. The prejudiced individual lives to some extent in an unreal world; his judgments about the people and things touched by his prejudice are distorted; he invites against himself the retaliation of counterprejudice; he keeps alive within himself disquieting feelings of ill will and hostility; and he damages himself spiritually by his neglect of the demands of charity and justice. The harm done to the individuals and groups who are victims of prejudice may be small or great, depending on circumstances, but it is always an injustice, a moral injury in the strict sense, and hence, from the ethical point of view, something intolerable. The social evil that comes of prejudice, esp. in a pluralistic society, is also evident. Prejudice is a divisive force, a constant threat to domestic and international harmony, and sometimes potentially the source of massive injustice, as was the anti-Semitism of the Nazi regime, and the widespread denial to racial groups of fundamental human rights.

Prejudices are often acquired through cultural and social influences and apparently cannot be overcome on a broad scale without cultural change of a kind that usually comes about slowly. For individuals, however, the prognosis is more hopeful. A good education generally enables a person to recognize and uproot some of his more obvious prejudices, but complete liberation is probably an unattainable ideal.

The objective evil there is in prejudice is sufficiently evident, but the subjective morality of individual instances of prejudice is difficult to assess. Prejudice is easier to recognize in another than in oneself. The prejudiced person, esp. if he is unskilled in the evaluation of evidence, is likely to look upon his prejudiced view and attitude as soundly based. He is subjectively at fault only to the extent that his views are culpably erroneous—i.e., only to the extent that he could and should know better. In some cases a prejudiced person could not perhaps be expected to know better, but on the other hand there may often be a measure of subjective responsibility, because even a relatively unsophisticated person should be alert to the possibility of illusion and self-deception, esp. in matters that concern the welfare of his neighbor. A person with any sensitivity of conscience, esp. a Christian who believes in the unity of the children of God, should see himself as bound to question views and attitudes on his part that could be injurious to others.

From a moral point of view, prejudice is a form of *rash judgment. The principles relevant to its moral appraisal are generally discussed by moral theologians under that heading. BIBLIOGRAPHY: G. W. Allport, *Nature of Prejudice* (1954), the best study from a psychological point of view; E. Hoffer, *True Believer* (1951); statement of the American bishops, *Discrimination and the Christian Conscience* (1958); J. P. Fitzpatrick, NCE 11:728–734.

[P. F. MULHERN]

PRELATE, an ecclesiastical official of superior rank. In the RC Church the term is applied to a cleric, whether secular or regular, who has authority over others as determined by law (CIC c. 110). Those having episcopal authority are called major prelates; those who have a quasi-episcopal authority (e.g., abbots, vicars general, vicars and prefects apostolic, and major superiors of exempt religious orders) are called minor prelates. Honorary prelates have no authority; they are either members of the Roman Curia, or clerics receiving the honorary title from the pope. In the C of E bishops alone are designated as prelates. The term prelacy was used disparagingly from Puritan times of an episcopal polity in the Church, e.g., in the rejection of episcopacy by the *Solemn League and Covenant (1643).

[T. C. O'BRIEN]

PRELATE NULLIUS, short for *nullius dioecesis,* of no diocese, and the equivalent in power to an *abbot *nullius;* a prelate in charge of a territory, usually in the missions, that is not part of an existing diocese. The prelate *nullius* has jurisdiction equal to that of diocesan bps., can consecrate churches and altars, use episcopal insignia in his territory, and elsewhere, can continue to wear ring and pectoral cross.

[T. C. O'BRIEN]

PRELATES, HONORARY, apostolic *prothonotaries, honorary prelates of His Holiness, chaplains of His Holiness. These are the only honorary prelatial titles retained by the *motu proprio* reforming the papal household, *Pontificatus domus,* March 28, 1968.

PRE-LENTEN SEASON, the interval formerly observed between Septuagesima Sunday and Ash Wednesday which served in the Church's liturgical cycle as an introductory period to Lent. The period embraced Septuagesima, Sexagesima, and Quinquagesima Sundays. It was penitential in character, but fasting, although highly recommended, was never prescribed for it in the West. As a preparatory period for Lent it may have been suggested by the longer fast of the Byzantine Church, but its introduction into the liturgical cycle was more immediately occasioned by the numerous public calamities of the 6th century. The liturgy during these days reflected the spirit of the season: penance, devotion, and atonement. Liturgical celebrations were marked by the omission of the *Alleluia* and by purple vestments. BIBLIOGRAPHY: F. X. Weiser, *Handbook of Christian Feasts and Customs* (1952, 1958) 154–168.

[B. ROSENDALL]

PREMILLENARIANISM (Premillennialism), the belief in a period—a millennium, though not understood by all as a period of 1,000 years—when righteousness will generally prevail throughout the world. This period will be introduced by the visible return of Jesus Christ, who will reign with his saints. Premillenarianism differs from postmillenarianism in its insistence that the millennium is to be ushered in, not terminated, by the visible coming of Christ. *MILLENARIANISM; *ADVENTISM.

[P. K. MEAGHER]

PREMONITION, an awareness of some future event in which the perceptor need not be a participant. It is thought by some to be a type of extrasensory perception. Because this phenomenon is often experienced in dreams—nocturnal or daydreams—premonition is difficult to study under scientific controls. Parapsychologists have devised few tests that satisfactorily detect premonitional powers. J. B. Rhine of Duke Univ. has proposed and conducted a test that measures a testee's calls of the sequence of cards in packs not yet shuffled but to be employed during that particular trial. Parapsychologists feel that such tests have produced statistical evidence which proves the existence of some type of premonition. The data obtained from experiments seem to indicate that a subject enjoying premonition is not greatly affected by his distance from the event perceived. However, the efficiency of his ability does deteriorate over an extended test-period. No psychologist has yet offered a theory which adequately explains the function or characteristics of premonition. BIBLIOGRAPHY: C. P. Svoboda, NCE 11:736.

[C. P. SVOBODA]

PREMONSTRATENSIAN RITE, the manner of celebrating the Catholic liturgy proper to the Premonstratensian Order. It is an adaptation of the Rhenish liturgical tradition, which is itself an expression of the Western tradition of liturgy originating in Rome and assimilated by the early medieval monastic centers along the Rhine: Sankt Gallen, Reichenau, Mainz, and Cologne. This Romano-Germanic tradition was taken over by the order founded by St. Norbert in 1120 called Premonstratensians after their place of origin, the valley of Prémontré in N France. The rite underwent Cistercian influence and reflects the early 12th-cent. liturgical renewal. It was the key to the order's life and continuity. It was gradually altered and virtually abolished by persistent pressure from the Congregation of Rites to conform to the Roman rite. It survived as a hybrid from 1628 to 1949. As a result of the liturgical renewal of the 20th cent., it has recently been restored. It is notable for its stress on the Paschal mystery; it has retained rites of the *Ordo Romanus antiquus* (*c*.950); rites for the dying and for burial dating from Carolingian times; and a chant that has not suffered

alterations to the extent that is true of Gregorian chant. BIBLIOGRAPHY: A. A. King, *Liturgies of the Religious Orders* (1955) 157–234, with bibliog.

[E. J. DILLON]

PREMONSTRATENSIANS (Canons Regular of Prémontré, White Canons, Norbertines), a semi-monastic Order founded in 1120 at Prémontré, France, by St. Norbert. The community combined the contemplative and active orientations. At first a loosely organized group, St. Norbert's followers adopted the Rule of St. Augustine, formed communities, and wore a white habit. It was originally planned as a decentralized community, but in a short time the various houses were united in a federation under the abbot-general at Prémontré, assembled annually in a general chapter of abbots, and followed Cistercian practices. The 12th and 13th cent. brought rapid growth to the Norbertines, with abbeys and priories in France, the Low Countries, Germany, Austria, Hungary, Poland, Spain, Greece, England, Scotland, and Portugal. With the aid of Premonstratensian nuns, a network of hospices was established. The Norbertines staffed numerous parishes surrounding their abbeys, and established training schools for clerics. The first cent. of the Order produced a number of saints and scholars. Among them were St. Godfrey of Cappenberg, St. Gilbert of Neuffontaines, St. Evermode, and St. Herman Joseph. Scholars included Gervase of Chichester, Adam Scotus, and Philip of Harvengt.

As with many Orders, the 14th cent. was an era of decline in spirituality for the Norbertines. The Reformation and the wars of religion in the 16th cent. decimated the Order. The houses in England, Ireland, and Scotland were lost, as well as those in N Germany, Hungary, and Scandinavia. With the Counter Reformation, a revival began in S Europe with a series of reforms. The Council of Trent led the way to new statutes for the community. The French Revolution and the harassment of Emperor Joseph II of Austria, in addition to the Spanish revolution of 1831 practically destroyed the Norbertines. A slow revival occurred in the late 19th cent. but the days of ascendancy never returned. Today the order has foundations in Belgium, Holland, France, Austria, the U.S., several mission territories in Africa and Latin America, and dependent houses in Canada and Denmark. The Norbertines came to the U.S. from Switzerland in 1893 and settled in Wisconsin. In 1898 St. Norbert's Abbey was established in De Pere, Wis., as a priory, abbatial status being conferred in 1925. In the U.S. the Norbertines operate a college (St. Norbert's), a number of secondary schools, and serve in many parishes.

The Order is organized in semi-autonomous abbeys with an elected abbot general (with lifetime tenure) residing in Rome. The life of the Order is dominated by the liturgy of Mass and Office. Penitential practice is an ancient tradition. Norbertines are active in promotion of the liturgy, in education, and in parochial ministry. The houses in France and Belgium particularly are mission-oriented. In 1975 there were 1,384 Premonstratensians (of whom 1,121 are priests) living in 51 houses; the generalate is in Rome. BIBLIOGRAPHY: F. Petit, *The Order of Canons Regular of Prémontré* (tr. and rev. B. Mackin, 1961).

[J. R. AHERNE]

PRÉMONTRÉ, MONASTERY OF, a former Premonstratensian abbey near Laon in France founded by St. Norbert of Xanten in 1120. In the beginning it was a double monastery. There the general chapters of the Premonstratensian Order were celebrated, and its abbots were at the same time generals of the order except during the years 1535–72 and 1635–42 when there were commendatory abbots. Splendid new buildings were constructed in the first half of the 18th century. The monastery was suppressed in 1790, the community numbering 80 canons at the time. The church and chapterhouse were torn down. Abortive efforts were made by Belgian Premonstratensians to rebuild the monastery (1843 and 1855–56). The property was sold by the bp. of Soissons and was put to use as an asylum. BIBLIOGRAPHY: Backmund 2:521–530.

[N. BACKMUND]

PREMOTION, PHYSICAL, a term developed in the era of the *Congregatio de auxiliis (1598–1607) to describe the inner effectiveness (efficacy) of actual grace. The controversies between Thomists and Molinists are of little contemporary interest and their terminology is eschewed in favor of a more biblical language. Accepting the pleonastic term reluctantly, the Thomists saw in it an expression of the priority of God's causality over every exercise of created causality, and the designation of divine causality as *motio* since it conferred *motus,* the movement of the created cause from potentiality to actual exercise. It was seen not as an anticipation of created action, but as making such action possible. The qualification "physical" was accepted in reference to the human will to mean that the causality of divine grace in the actual exercise of choice is not limited to a "moral" motion, i.e., to the attraction to the good through the mind's proposal, but extends directly to the will itself, giving it the completion necessary for it to exercise its choice. *PREDETERMINATION.

[T. C. O'BRIEN]

PREPARATION DAY. the law of Moses prescribed that on the 14th day of Nisan, the Passover eve, a year-old lamb be slaughtered in liturgical assembly (Ex, ch. 12). This Passover eve is called the Preparation Day or *Parasceve. The blood of the lamb was put on the doorposts and lintels in commemoration of and to begin the celebration of the Passover (Ex 12.6; Lv 23.5, etc.). The term occurs in the Gospels in Mk 15.42; Lk 23.54; Mt 27.62; Jn 19.14, 31, 42, and presents a chronological problem. According to Jn 19.31, Jesus died on the Parasceve. According to the Synoptics, Jesus died on the Passover itself. Recent attempts according to which John followed a calendar similar to that of the Qumran sect and the Synoptics followed the official Jewish reckoning of dates help toward a solution but occasion other difficulties. Today, the Passover ceremony is begun on the Parasceve with prayers and a symbolic searching the house for any leavened foods which must be removed before the Passover. BIBLIOGRAPHY: *Passover Haggadah* (tr. by S. Maximon [no date]); T. H. Gaster, *Passover, Its History and Traditions* (1964); R. E. Brown, "Date of the Last Supper," *Bible Today,* 11 (1964) 727–733.

[W. E. LYNCH]

PRE-RAPHAELITES, or the Pre-Raphaelite Brotherhood, a band of artists, originally D. G. Rossetti, Holman Hunt, and J. E. Millais, later joined by W. Rossetti, W. Morris and others, who adopted (1848) a stand against "classical" art as presented by Reynolds in favor of simplicity and clarity of Italian primitives. *The Germ* (1850), which lasted only four issues, advocated painting and writing with "reality" as a standard. Strong criticism against the Brotherhood climaxed in Buchanan's "Fleshly School of Poetry," in *Contemporary Review* (1871). In painting Pre-Raphaelite interest in details early developed into neo-medieval decorative style. In poetry love of colors, exact numbers, and diction of vague emotive power replaced clarity of meaning. The Pre-Raphaelites favored a romantic world far from 19th-cent. life and problems. Their Religion of Beauty derives from the great Romantics and Tennyson and leads to the Aesthetic Movement of the 1890s. BIBLIOGRAPHY: W. Gaunt, *Pre-Raphaelite Tragedy* (1942); the chapter on the Pre-Raphaelite Brotherhood in F. E. Faverty, ed., *Victorian Poets,* by H. M. Jones (1956); S. St. M. McCreavy, *Centenary of the Pre-Raphaelite Movement* (Villanova Univ., 1948).

[M. M. BARRY]

PRESANCTIFIED, LITURGY OF THE (BYZANTINE), a liturgy sometimes called "of St. Gregory Dialogos" (Pope St. *Gregory I) used on the weekdays of Lent and composed of *Hesperinos with a Communion service attached. According to legend, while Gregory was papal *apocrisiarius* at the imperial court in Constantinople, he saw the faithful of the Byzantine rite going without Communion during most of the days of Lent and in order to remedy this situation he arranged the Liturgy of the Presanctified or preconsecrated gifts. However, this account is almost certainly without historical foundation. The remote origin of the Liturgy of the Presanctified and its use are traceable to the Council of Laodicea (c.370) which forbade the celebration of the Divine Liturgy during Lent without specifying what was to take its place. The present liturgy is most probably a composition of St. *Epiphanius of Constantia (310–403). It seems first to have been used in Syria in the 6th cent., Constantinople taking it up the following cent. with subsequent revisions. Both Orthodox and Catholics of the Byzantine rite use the Liturgy of the Presanctified on every Wednesday and Friday of Lent, after Cheesefare Sunday, as well as on the first 3 days of Holy Week. It is not celebrated on Good Friday as might be expected from the corresponding Western practice (see PRESANCTIFIED, MASS OF). The faithful communicate or not at this liturgy in accordance with local custom. Other Eastern Churches (except the Armenian, Coptic, and Ethiopian) have Liturgies of the Presanctified during Lent, but the Maronites and Malabarese use theirs only on Good Friday. BIBLIOGRAPHY: A. A. King, *Rites of Eastern Christendom* (1948), 2:234–246.

[A. WALKER]

PRESANCTIFIED, MASS OF THE, a medieval development of the Communion service of Good Friday. In the West Good Friday has always been an *aliturgical day, i.e., a day on which Mass is not celebrated. Neither was it the custom, before the 7th cent. at the earliest, to distribute communion on this day. The practice of communicating on this occasion declined after its introduction, along with the general decline of frequent communion, until finally only the celebrant was permitted to communicate. The celebrant's communion developed during the Middle Ages into a service that had much of the external appearance of a Mass and came in fact to be called the Mass of the Presanctified, i.e. a "Mass" at which the eucharistic species is previously consecrated (at the Mass of Holy Thursday). This came to be the principal liturgical observance of the day and about it centered the other ritual proper to the occasion, i.e., readings, prayers, and the *adoration of the cross. With the restoration of the Holy Week Ordinal in 1955 the Mass of the Presanctified was suppressed and the Communion service was restored to its earlier form. For bibliography, see *GOOD FRIDAY.

[P. K. MEAGHER]

PRESBYTER (Elder), a word whose rootmeaning in Greek is "elder," but which was also used simply to refer to an old man. In the NT the word is also used collectively and as a plural to indicate leadership. Collectively, the NT usage flows from descriptions of the Sanhedrin, a member of which was designated as belonging to the *presbyteron* (Lk 22.66; Acts 22.5). The plural derives from both Jewish and Gentile designation for leaders and is used of the leaders of the Christian community (e.g., Acts 11.30; 14.23; 15.2; 20.17; 1 Tim 5.17,19). The distinction between *presbyteroi* and *episkopoi* (root-meaning, "overseers") seems small: the former emphasizes dignity; the latter stresses the office itself. In the earliest traditions of the NT, these terms referred to a group who were to "watch over" the flock of Christians in a local community (Acts 20.17, 28). The later tradition of the NT, in the Pastoral Letters, uses the term *episkopos* as a model or type for the *episkopoi,* although there seems to be some indication that an individual was becoming the overseer of a local congregation (1 Tim 3.15; 5.22; Tit 1.5; Rev 1–3). Assuredly by the time of the early

Fathers of the Church the leadership involved in the terms *presbyteros* and *episkopos* was resident in a single person in local communities.

The leadership, which the presbyter was to undertake, was found in conserving the apostolic teachings and ruling with apostolic authority in faith and under charity (see esp. Acts 20.17–35). The personal apostolic privileges were, of course, not passed on with the office; it was the office itself and its responsibilities that were transmitted. BIBLIOGRAPHY: H. W. Beyer, Kittel TD 2:608–622, s.v. "*episkopos*"; J. McKenzie, *Authority in the Church* (1966); J. H. Newman, *Essay on the Development of Christian Doctrine* (1845). *ELDER; *BISHOP; *MINISTRY.

[W. E. LYNCH]

PRESBYTERIAN, related to the form of church polity in which authority is exercised by the church courts. *Presbyterianism is named from its adherence to this polity, but other Christian bodies also have adopted it. A presbyterian polity is distinguished from both episcopal and congregational forms of church government.

[T. C. O'BRIEN]

PRESBYTERIAN CHURCH IN THE U.S., a Presbyterian denomination that came into separate existence in 1861. The Civil War was the original cause of disruption and separation from the Presbyterian Church in the U.S.A. (see UNITED PRESBYTERIAN CHURCH IN THE U.S.A.), while continued bitterness and an attempt to contribute a particular emphasis to American Presbyterianism has perpetuated the denomination. It accepts the *Westminster Confession of Faith and Catechisms as doctrinal standards and organizes itself under a series of courts, the Session of the local congregation, the Presbytery, the Synod, and the General Assembly. It recognizes two Sacraments—the Lord's Supper and Baptism, including the Baptism of infants. After the Civil War the work of the denomination between annual meetings of Assemblies and other judicatories has been carried on by committees. These have become Boards of Education, World Mission, National Missions, and Pensions. Executives of these judicatories and boards have functional not sacerdotal status. The denomination has four theological seminaries as well as other institutions of higher education. Its official periodical is *The Presbyterian Survey,* although its members support several other journals. Among its most influential leaders are James Henley Thornwell (1812–62), Robert Lewis Dabney (1820–98), and Ernest Trice Thompson (1894–). Although the denomination is broadly ecumenical (a member of the National Council of Churches, World Presbyterian Alliance and the World Council of Churches), it refused to reunite with the parent body in 1954. In recent years members have questioned its distinctive doctrine of the "spirituality of the Church" which was developed during the days of slavery, and the denomination has been more and more progressive in the development of its programs. In 1974 the denomination numbered 4,284 congregations, 951,788 communing members, and approximately 3,000 clergy. BIBLIOGRAPHY: E. T. Thompson, *Presbyterians in the South,* v. 1 (1963); T. W. Street, *The Story of Southern Presbyterians* (1960).

[J. H. SMYLIE]

PRESBYTERIANISM (Gr. *presbuteros,* elder), a form of church government found in the Reformed Churches, i.e., those following John *Calvin in matters of doctrine, worship, polity, and discipline. The name particularly designates Reformed Churches in the British Isles and North America. Calvin's insistence on the divine authority of the Church came to produce a distinctively "presbyterian" type of ministry and congregational life in which preaching, the sacraments, Christian instruction, and pastoral care are integral parts. Though Presbyterian history has at times been darkened by controversy and dogmatism, a characteristic zeal for the glory of God has also given Presbyterianism its passionate theocentrism; its uncompromising criticism of political absolutism; its antipathy toward *popery, prelacy, and *Erastianism; and its desire to regulate the whole of life in accordance with the divine will.

History and Polity. Convinced that the RC Church of the 16th cent. had deformed what John *Knox called "the reverend face of the primitive and apostolic Kirk," the Genevan and Scottish Reformers sought to return to the faith and practice of the early Church. Calvin had returned to Geneva in 1541, and, having secured the collaboration of the city magistrates, he set himself to the task of reordering the life and worship of the Genevan Church. Out of this reordering Presbyterianism arose. In the Reformed understanding the Church is *semper reformanda,* i.e., always to be renewed and reformed by the word of God and through obedience to the Holy Spirit. The Church, therefore, can have no final or perfect form. This does not mean that the true Church of God cannot be ascertained, though in the Reformed understanding it certainly cannot be identified exclusively with particular communions or denominations. The *Ecclesiastical Ordinances* (1541) of Geneva and Calvin's *Institutes of the Christian Religion* (1st ed., 1536) both speak of the Church as the community of believers, known by certain signs: the preaching of the gospel of Christ, the administration of the sacraments according to his command, and the exercise of godly discipline. They further teach that the ministry is ordained by God and consists of four offices: pastor, or bishop (who alone may preach and administer the sacraments); doctor, or teacher; *presbyter, or *elder (who is associated with the minister in the exercise of discipline); and *deacon. In Geneva the pastors and elders formed the Consistory, the principal organ of disciplinary oversight and fraternal correction, and the ministers were further required to attend a quarterly assembly called the Venerable Company for mutual admonition and correction. In these two bodies the earliest expressions of Presbyterian polity can be found. The *Scots Confession (1560) and Knox's *Book of Discipline generally follow Calvin's teaching on Church and ministry, though it is only in the second Book of Discipline, written by A. *Melville and officially adopted in 1581, that the developed form of Scottish Presbyterianism appears (see CHURCH OF SCOTLAND).

Presbyterianism has always affirmed the supremacy of the State on secular matters and the independence of the Church in its own affairs. Only in Scotland, however, is the *national Church Presbyterian; yet even there the fundamental principle of spiritual independence has been strongly asserted. Though some Presbyterians have held that Presbyterian polity is *jure divino,* most have taught simply that it is "agreeable to the Word of God," and all have found its origins in the NT itself. Several views of the presbyter or elder have been held within Presbyterianism. The general view is that the NT teaches one order of presbyters, differentiated into ministers of the word and sacraments, and (ruling) elders, assisting in the administration of sacraments, pastoral care, and church government. Occupying an intermediate position between *episcopacy and *Congregationalism, Presbyterianism, though not in the strict sense democratic, provides in its system of graded courts broadly representative assemblies that legislate on matters of doctrine, government, discipline, and polity. The church session (in Scotland, kirk session), consisting of the minister(s) of a local congregation, together with certain ruling elders, usually elected by the congregation, is charged with maintaining the spiritual government of that church. The presbytery consists of all the ministers and normally one elder from each of the churches within a particular district. The synod consists of a number of presbyteries in a particular region. The highest court in Presbyterianism is the general assembly, which meets at least annually and consists of delegates or commissioners (usually equal numbers of ministers and elders) from every presbytery.

Doctrine. In doctrine the Presbyterian Churches have mainly followed Calvin in holding the word of God given in the OT and NT to be the supreme rule of faith and life. In addition, the creeds of the ancient Church and the confessions of faith and catechisms of the Reformed Churches, tested by the apostolic preaching and teaching, are the important subordinate doctrinal standards. The First *Helvetic (1536), *Gallican (1559), Scots (1560), *Belgic (1561), and *Hungarian (1562) Confessions and *Heidelberg Catechism (1563) have been widely honored and used in the Reformed Churches, though since 1645 almost all English-speaking Presbyterians have adhered to the *Westminster Confession as the chief subordinate standard. This Confession, however, has been substantially modified by some Churches (see DECLARATORY ACTS), and the adoption by the United Presbyterian Church in the U.S.A. of the *Confession of 1967 and of revised formulas for ordination represents a major departure from earlier *confessionalism. In the view of many the Confession of 1967, the fruit of modern biblical and theological studies, is an important restatement of the doctrines held by Presbyterians. While the Calvinism of the *Institutes* has been preserved more or less intact among Presbyterians to the present, certain teachings, notably on predestination, have since been modified, and in the modern period Karl *Barth, who did more than any in his age to illuminate and reinterpret the issues of the Reformation, stated in his preface to the *Church Dogmatics* (II/2) that, though he would have preferred to follow Calvin in his doctrine of *election, he could not do so. Others have also felt themselves driven to reconstruction of other parts of Calvinism.

Worship. In worship the Reformed Churches have never been tied to a fixed liturgy, and though service books have been used, e.g., the Book of Common Order (1940) in the Church of Scotland and the Book of Common Worship, Provisional Services (1966) in the United Presbyterian Church in the U.S.A., their use has been recommended, not mandatory. Worship in the Presbyterian tradition is characterized by an austere simplicity. The sermon occupies a central place, and wide freedom is allowed in the conduct of worship. Though Calvin permitted only metrical psalms to be sung in worship, the use of hymns is now general. Recent liturgical renewal has also encouraged Presbyterian Churches to enter more fully into the liturgical heritage of the whole Church. In the Reformed tradition baptism is the sacrament of incorporation into Christ and initiation into the Christian fellowship. Infant baptism is normal practice, though adult baptism is not uncommon. The Lord's Supper is the supreme act of worship, setting forth the sufficiency of Christ's perfect sacrifice and mediating the mercies of God. From the time of the Reformation it has normally been administered quarterly. In the past this service was preceded by a day of fast and followed by a day of thanksgiving. Today more frequent celebrations are found; Calvin himself advocated a weekly communion. The celebration of the sacrament is a ministerial act, and the bread and wine are usually distributed to the communicants, who remain seated in the pews, though the older custom of approaching the table to communicate standing or seated around it is also found. The bread and the cup are passed from one communicant to another, after being received from the hands of the elders.

Ecumenical Cooperation. In the 20th cent. Presbyterian Churches have participated actively in ecumenical discussions, and there have been several important unions. "No other family of churches has been more consistently favorable to ecumenical cooperation and unity," Dr. John T. McNeill states, and in South India, South Africa, Australia, Canada, England, and Scotland Presbyterians have taken a leading part in movements toward unity, at times across denominational boundaries. In 1958 the United Presbyterian Church of North America and the Presbyterian Church in the U.S.A. united to form the United Presbyterian Church in the U.S.A. (1977 membership, 3.3 million); since 1963 this Church has participated in the *Consultation on Church Union. The Presbyterian Church in the U.S. (the "southern" Presbyterian Church; 1977 membership, 900,000) is also a participant. The *Alliance of Reformed Churches has

prepared with the International Congregational Council proposals, principles, and a draft constitution that, if approved by the respective member Churches, will unite these two confessional bodies. The existence since 1938 of the *Iona Community, an experimental group in the service of the Church of Scotland, may be regarded as a symbol of a widespread desire among Presbyterian Churches to fulfill their missionary obligations in new and at times radical ways. BIBLIOGRAPHY: J. T. McNeill, *History and Character of Calvinism* (repr., 1968, with rev. bibliog.); G. D. Henderson, *Presbyterianism* (repr., 1956); L. J. Trinterud, *Forming of an American Tradition* (1949). *CALVINISM.

PRESBYTERY, in Presbyterianism, a legislative, executive, and judicial court, presided over by a *moderator, who is elected annually. Quarterly meetings are customary, though the Presbytery may meet as specially called. The Presbytery consists of all the ministers and usually one ruling *elder from each church within a certain district, over which it corporately exercises authority (see CHURCH SESSION). The equal representation of ministers and elders exhibits the parity of presbyters, who share jointly in the government and supervision of the churches they represent. Ministers must hold membership within the Presbytery in which they work, though in some cases (e.g., chaplaincy) permission is given to work beyond the geographical boundaries of the Presbytery. This court is empowered to receive under its care candidates for the ministry, to sanction and approve the call issued by a congregation to a minister, to ordain and install him in his office, and to receive, dismiss, judge, or remove ministers. In this way it exercises a kind of corporate *episcopacy. The Presbytery alone can organize, dissolve, unite, or divide churches. Presbyteries in a particular region constitute the *synod, the next higher court in Presbyterianism.

[J. A. R. MACKENZIE]

PRESCHOOL EDUCATION, the development and formation of the child in social behavior before beginning formal schooling, usually between 2 and 6 years of age, although strictly speaking, education begins at birth. It includes the nursery school, for children between 2 and 4; and the kindergarten, for those between 4 and 6. Both are designed to meet the social, emotional, and physical needs of the young child in an environment capable of fostering growth, encouraging creativity, and stimulating intellectual curiosity through play, games, and wholesome personal experiences. The nursery school, a 19th-cent. European development, also offers a safe place for working mothers to leave their children. The kindergarten was inspired by J. A. Comenius (1592–1670) and developed by Friedrich Fröbel (1782–1852), who gave it its name. An outstanding Catholic educator, proponent of preprimary education, was M. Montessori, whose method has been acclaimed in the U.S. and abroad. The National Catholic Kindergarten Association was established in the U.S. in 1941. BIBLIOGRA -

PHY: National Catholic Kindergarten Association, *This We Believe about the Kindergarten* (1956).

[M. B. MURPHY]

PRESCOTT, WILLIAM HICKLING (1796–1859), writer in the grand manner on Spanish history, notably in America. His important works include *Ferdinand and Isabella* (1837), *Conquest of Mexico* (1843), *Conquest of Peru* (1847), and *Philip the Second* (1855–58). His narrative is clear and vivid, and his materials are well composed in books that remain very readable. But to later research and appreciation there are more glories and humanities in the Spanish Empire than were discoverable by his Bostonian approach.

[T. EARLY]

PRESCRIPTION, THEOLOGICAL USE OF. (1) In moral theology prescription that is in conformity to law is one of the titles to *ownership. Its acceptance as such a title takes into account a rule of law, e.g., in the common law tradition of England and the U.S., that a long, unchallenged possession or use of property confers ownership. Prescription is a morally right title if the possessor is one in good faith and if the duration of possession or use meets the stipulations of civil law. The meaning of prescription is also transferred to include a way in which an uncollected debt may cease, or an exercised right be acquired. The same condition of good faith must prevail in both instances: the debtor has not evaded payment or the one exercising a right has not been in defiance of law. (2) In dogmatic theology the juridical concept of prescription is transferred to mean an indirect way of authenticating a doctrinal teaching. The force of an argument based on prescription can be seen by regarding the Church as the sole, legitimate guardian and possessor of the deposit of faith (see D 3018). The fact of a constancy in teaching on some point of belief proves a long-time possession of such a truth. Since to be the guardian of the deposit of faith means to be the preserver of what authentically belongs to God's revelation, by prescription the truth at issue is guaranteed to be an object of faith. This method of arguing derives from *Tertullian, who defended the continuity of church teaching with the apostolic witness (*De praescriptione haereticorum*, esp. 38.PL 2:50). The presupposition is that revelation is communicated in Scripture and apostolic tradition. To show that a given truth rests on tradition, however, is not a matter of chronological documentation back to the Apostles, even were that possible. The true force of tradition is that the living understanding of the Church, its possession of truth in that sense, is authentication of its teaching. The value of prescription as an argument is enhanced by the clarification made on the relationship between Scripture and tradition in the Church by Vatican Council II (see VatII ConstChurch 7–10). *MIND OF THE CHURCH.

[T. C. O'BRIEN]

PRESENCE OF GOD. The idea that the God of Israel renders himself present in a unique manner to his covenant people raised a basic problem for Israelite thinkers: how to reconcile the idea of his *immanence* upon earth with that of his *transcendence* in heaven.

In the earliest traditions Yahweh is represented as descending from heaven at specific points in history to "visit" the denizens of earth (cf. e.g., Gen 11.5, 7; 18.21; Ex 3.8, etc.). In the case of the covenant people Yahweh descends upon a particular place chosen and designated by himself, and in one relatively early tradition this is the "tent of meeting." In this tradition he is thought of as making himself present not directly and in person but through the medium of his *kabod* or "glory," the fiery cloud of radiant brightness which constitutes the visible manifestation of his presence (cf. Ex 16.10; 29.43; Num 14.10; 16.19; 17.7; 20.6). In this sense, therefore, his "glory" can be present on earth even while he remains transcendent actually in heaven. An extension of this idea is that Yahweh "goes with" his people, leading them and making himself present to them through the medium of the pillar of fire and cloud in the wilderness wanderings. Thus in Ex 33.14 Yahweh declares: "My presence (lit. 'face') will go with you." The emphasis here is upon the fact that his presence to his covenant people is direct, personal, and continuous. It is on this alone that the people rely for help, and it is this "going with" the people that makes them unique among the nations (cf. Ex 33.16). Other traditions, however, sensing the problem that this entails for the idea of Yahweh's transcendent presence in heaven, have interposed a different kind of medium in and through which Yahweh makes himself present in this sense, namely an "angel." The Elohist tradition in particular avoids the idea of Yahweh appearing directly to his people and represents him as speaking to them through the medium of angels (cf. Gen 22.15; Ex 14.19; 23.20, etc.) though Moses is an exception to this, being favored with more direct visitations from Yahweh (Num 12.7–8).

In the Priestly tradition the idea of Yahweh's presence through his radiant fiery cloud seems to have predominated; and the tabernacle and subsequently the Temple become the shrine where his "glory" takes up its more or less permanent abode. In this tradition too the ark seems to have been thought of primarily as a throne on which the *kabod* or glory comes down and rests. According to von Rad and other scholars, in the Priestly tradition and the "David-Zion" tradition a whole theology is developed round this distinctive conception of how Yahweh makes himself present to Israel. It is known as *kabod* theology.

In the Deuteronomist theology, on the other hand, the medium in and through which Yahweh renders himself present is first and foremost his *word*. All the emphasis here is upon the divine voice and the divine word as the supreme expression of the numinous, and here too a whole theology grows up of worshiping Yahweh by hearing and obeying his word, cherishing it in one's heart, etc.

In the NT Christ in effect *becomes* this medium and so

renders God present. He *is* the Word (Jn 1.14) and becomes the center and source of the *glory (cf. Mt 17.2 par; Mk 8.38; 2 Cor 4.6), and in him the light of the glory and the power of the Word penetrate to the innermost hearts of believers. BIBLIOGRAPHY: G. von Rad, *Studies in Deuteronomy* (Eng. tr. 1961) 37–44; R. E. Clements, *God and the Temple. The Idea of the Divine Presence in Ancient Israel* (1965).

[D. J. BOURKE]

PRESENCE OF GOD, PRACTICE OF THE a moment of prayer or recollection in which the person adverts to the truth of God's nearness and providence with the purpose of making explicit charity's intent to direct all life and activity towards loving God. The practice is praiseworthy and recommended as a check on mindless activism. But the meaning of the practice needs to be evaluated. The presence of God means, par excellence, the uninterrupted union in beatific vision and love with Father, Son and Holy Spirit. The earthly beginning of, the incomplete but real share in that final union is the indwelling of the divine persons. The experience of that presence through grace consists in the vitality of the theological virtues and the gifts of the Holy Spirit. These are not "practices" but the essence of the life of grace. The full, and esp. the relatively continuous awareness of the divine persons' presence is not something one "does." Rather it is given and in its intense form marks the higher stages of Christian perfection. The truth that God as omnipotent cause is omnipresent, omniscient, and provident is subordinate and ultimately a facet of the grace-presence of the Trinity. The "practice" of the presence of God, then, has its value, like all ascetical practices, when measured as a disposition, a preparation, for what in itself is the sublime ideal and gift that grace promises. *TRANSCENDENCE AND IMMANENCE, GOD'S.

PRESENTATION, DAUGHTERS OF ST. MARY OF THE (FSM), a congregation instituted for the purpose of teaching, nursing, and other apostolic works. It was founded in 1828 in Broons, Côtes-du-Nord, France, by Rev. Joachim Fleury in cooperation with Mère Sainte-Louise (Louise Le Marchand) and Mère Saint-André. In 1902, when the anticlerical government in France began suppressing religious communities and confiscating their property, the Daughters of St. Mary established their houses in other parts of Europe and North America. They built a novitiate in the U.S. in 1903 at Spring Valley, Illinois. Papal approval was granted the community in 1959. The superior general resides in Broons, France. Statistics show the congregation has 65 houses and a total membership of 1,515 sisters.

[R. A. TODD]

PRESENTATION, RIGHT OF, the right to propose to church authorities a candidate for appointment to a benefice. Part of the right of patronage, this right is traceable to the 12th cent. and it provided for founders or builders of a church some oversight over the incumbency. From the 16th cent. it became a part of concordats with Catholic governments; but that practice has been abrogated since the time of the CIC. Where right of presentation exists it must be exercised, under pain of forfeiture, in respect for the authority having right of confirmation (CIC, c. 2393). Since the CIC legislated against the establishment of the right of patronage and sought to induce surrender of existing rights, the right of presentation is no longer conferred and exists only as tolerated (CIC, c. 1450 and 1451). Vatican Council II in affirming the freedom of the Church with respect to the appointment of bps. expressed the desire that the right of presentation of bps. not be granted to any civil government and that any possessing such a right voluntarily renounce it. (Vat II BpPastOff 20). In the U.S. the Second Plenary Council of Baltimore excluded any right of patronage from the American Church.

[T. C. O'BRIEN]

PRESENTATION BROTHERS, religious members of a congregation officially called the Brothers of the Presentation of the Blessed Virgin Mary (FPCP), founded by Brother Edmund Ignatius Rice (1762–1844) at Waterford, Ireland, in 1802. The primary apostolate of the community is the instruction and Christian formation of youth. Simple perpetual vows are taken by the brothers, who in 1809 adopted the constitutions of the Sisters of the Presentation of Mary and were thus called Presentation Brothers. The *Irish Christian Brothers originated from this congregation when Rice adopted the rule of the Brothers of the Christian Schools, and other Presentation Brothers under the leadership of Brother Michael Riordan remained with the original rule. Final approval was received by the Presentation Brothers from the Holy See in 1899. They conduct schools in Ireland, England, Canada, and the West Indies; they maintain 33 houses and have a total membership of 251. The generalate is located in Cork, Ireland.

[R. A. TODD]

PRESENTATION OF JESUS, the dedication of Jesus to Yahweh in the Temple. The incident is recorded only in Lk 2.22–24, where it is presented as the fulfillment of God's command to Moses, "Consecrate to me all the first-born; whatever is the first to open the womb among the people of Israel, both of man and of beast, is mine" (Ex 13.1–2). The episode indicates not only Jesus' conformity to the prescriptions of the Mosaic Law, but also recalls the dedication of Samuel who as a great prophet is a type of Jesus (Acts 3.22). There is no mention of Jesus' being bought back or redeemed by his parents from this total dedication, as would have been the custom, and the ceremony ritually effects Jesus' consecration of himself to the service of his Father. BIBLIOGRAPHY: JBC 125. *PURIFICATION OF MARY.

[T. M. MCFADDEN]

PRESENTATION OF MARY, the offering of Our Lady, when she was a girl, to service in the Temple by her parents. There is no historical basis for the tradition, but there are accounts of the presentation in the NT apocrypha. Since the Mosaic Law requires that the first-born male be dedicated to God (Ex 13.12.), a private, pious practice of dedicating a first-born female to the Lord may have arisen. In this spirit, the NT apocrypha narrate that Anne and Joachim had taken a vow to give their daughter over to the service of the Temple and they fulfilled that vow when Mary was 3 years old. The Gospel of Pseudo-Matthew speaks of Mary running up the steps of the Temple on the day of her presentation, never looking back. Once in the Temple she devoted her life to the study of sacred Scripture, prayer, and to the few other works permissible to a young girl in the Temple. In Christian tradition, Mary's presentation has often been seen as a symbol of religious dedication to God's service. BIBLIOGRAPHY: Carol Mariol 1.156–184; H. French, NCE 11:758–759.

[T. R. HEATH]

PRESENTATION OF MARY, SISTERS OF THE (PM), a papally approved community founded in 1796 in France by Mère Anne Marie Rivier (1768–1838) as a counteraction to the effort of de-Christianizing France following the French Revolution. Besides teaching in countries of Europe, Africa, Asia, and North America, the Sisters conducted catechetical and retreat centers, nurseries, hostels, and homes for the young and aged. Rivier College in Nashua, N.H. was established by the Sisters in 1933 but is now independent. In 1975 the congregation had 256 foundations and a total membership of 2,924 sisters. The general motherhouse is in Rome.

[R. A. TODD]

PRESENTATION OF THE BLESSED VIRGIN MARY, SISTERS OF THE (PBVM), an institute of women religious originating at the time of the Penal Laws in Ireland, when Christian education of youth was forbidden. Devoted to the cause of educating poor children, Nano (Honoria) Nagle (Mother Mary of St. John of God, 1728–84) founded the congregation in 1775 at Cork. It was then named Sisters of Charitable Instruction of the Sacred Heart of Jesus. A rule by a curé of St. Sulpice was kept until after the death of the foundress, when constitutions based on the Rule of St. Augustine were formulated. These were approved in 1793 and received final approbation by Rome in 1805. It was about this time that the community received its present title. Besides conducting schools for the Christian education of the young, the sisters also minister to the sick and aged in hospitals and homes. Their apostolate extends to missions in England, Asia, Africa, and North America. The first establishment and filiation from the motherhouse in Cork was at Kerry, and following that was the second affiliated foundation at Dublin. In 1975 the congregation in the diocese of Kerry had 13 houses and a total membership of 260 sisters, while in Dublin they had 20 foundations and 144 sisters. In 1953 all the houses of the sisters in the U. S. were amalgamated to form a Conference of Presentation Sisters. BIBLIOGRAPHY: T. J. Walsh, *Nano Nagle and the Presentation Sisters* (1959).

[R. A. TODD]

PRESIDING BISHOP, the head of the Protestant Episcopal Church. He is elected by the *General Convention when the office becomes vacant, and remains in office until the retirement age, set at 68.

[T. C. O'BRIEN]

PRESLAV, a capital city of the First Bulgarian Empire (681–1018) and a center of church life and Slavic letters in the 9th and 10th centuries. It came into prominence when the Great Bulgarian Assembly of 893 made it the capital of the state. During the reign of Czar Simeon I (893–927) it became celebrated throughout the Slavic world for its wealth, culture, and power. It was the site of a famous school of Slavic letters founded in the nearby monastery of St. Pantaleimon (Patleina) by St. Naum, a disciple of St. Methodius, and counted among its early scholars Konstantin Prezviter, Ioan Eksarkh, and Chernorizets Hrabr. For a short time Preslav was also the see of the newly erected patriarchate of Bulgaria (926–927). The city began to decline as a result of its occupation by the Russians (969) and by the Byzantines (971–976; 1001–1185). Nothing remains of the ancient splendor of the city but the foundations of the city walls and of a few impressive buildings and churches, including an interesting round church. Today Preslav is a joint metropolitan see (with Varna) of the Bulgarian Orthodox Church.

[G. ELDAROV]

PRESOCRATICS, a term frequently employed to characterize the representatives of Greek philosophy from *c*.600 to *c*.400 B.C. In general, the Greek philosophers or scientists—for a sharp distinction was not made and was as yet hardly possible—in this period were preoccupied almost exclusively with cosmology and related problems—the One and the Many, Being and Becoming, the Origin of the Cosmos—i.e., with the external world. *Heraclitus and *Anaxagoras were great pioneers with their concepts of *Logos* and *Nous* (Mind) respectively, but it was too early for them to apply their speculation in any systematic, concrete way to the microcosm, man. By the time of Socrates, it was evident that these thinkers as a group had failed to find satisfactory solutions for the cosmological problems with which they had been so deeply concerned. However, when one considers that the Presocratics were the creators of both philosophy and science in the strict sense, their achievement in the short period of 200 years is an amazing one. Furthermore, they laid the solid foundations for the further investigation and solution of the questions they raised by Plato and Aristotle. It is a mistake, furthermore, to think that failure to solve their problems was the primary reason for the new interest in man and his concerns in the Greek city-state. Athens and other Greek city-states developed rapidly in the 6th and 5th centuries, and their complicated political, social, and intellectual and religious life occasioned a new and necessary interest in education, political life in theory and practice, and in human conduct. It was precisely as educators, and not as philosophers, that the Sophists entered upon the scene to meet the new needs. Cosmological investigation was no longer the major center of intellectual interest, but it continued without interruption. It should be noted that *Democritus of Abdera, for example, was active during the whole life-time of Socrates and for a generation after his death. BIBLIOGRAPHY: Copleston 1:76–80; W. K. C. Guthrie, EncPhil 6:441–446.

[M. R. P. McGUIRE]

PRESS ASSOCIATIONS AND SERVICES, CATHOLIC. The apostolate of the Catholic Press and its numerous services provides a means of communicating news and knowledge of the Church to the world, and of news and comments on religion and Christian life of the world to the Church. Its activities are conducted in the light of Christian principles and it has become most effective through its world and national organizations. Most significant is the International Catholic Union of the Press (ICUP) founded in 1935. This confederation has six specialized branches: the International Federations of Catholic Journalists (1927), Dailies and Periodicals (1928), Press Agencies (1950), Schools of Journalism (1965), the International Catholic Association of Teachers and Scientific or Technical Research Workers on Information (1968), and the Federation of Church Press Associations (1974). The ICUP endeavors to have worldwide extension and organization of the Catholic press and aims to join all Catholics who are influential in forming public opinion through the press and mass media. A bimonthly *Catholic Journalists* is published in four languages by the Union, which has its headquarters in Geneva, Switzerland. Since the organization was founded, triennial congresses have convened in cities of Europe and America. The interests of the Catholic Press on a national level were inaugurated when the Catholic Press Association of U. S. and Canada (CPA) was established in 1911. Statistics of the Catholic Press are reported annually in its chief publication, *The Catholic Press Directory.* In 1976 there were 439 Catholic newspapers and magazines in the U. S., Canada, and the West Indies with a circulation of 26,888,753. *The Catholic Herald Citizen* of Milwaukee has the largest circulation (149,333) of any diocesan newspaper in the country, and the magazine with the largest circulation (1,162,212) is *Columbia,* the official organ of the Knights of Columbus. CPA has its headquarters in Rockville Centre, New York. A U.S. press service established in 1920 is the National Catholic News Service (NC), a branch of the U. S. Catholic Conference. It provides daily news around the world through radio, television, editorial, pictorial, and other specialized services. The NC News Service has headquarters in Washington, D. C.

[R. A. TODD]

PRESSURE, MORAL, threats or promises aimed at inducing a person to do or omit some action. It usually connotes inducement to wrongdoing; it is called ''moral'' both to distinguish it from *force, and to suggest that no external influence on the will can be more than persuasive. One exerting pressure may be guilty of *scandal, the attempt to lead another into sin; of injustice by seeking to injure the rights, the liberty or moral integrity of another person; or of *cooperation in the specific kind of sin towards which the pressure is directed. As to the victim, an action done under pressure cannot be completely involuntary, unless the influence completely overwhelms the power of self-control; otherwise the victim's submission and its consequences are voluntary, but, as with *fear, the degree of voluntariness may be lessened because of moral pressure.

[T. C. O'BRIEN]

PRESTER JOHN (Presbyter Johannes; Priest, Priester, etc.), subject of a legend accepted as history from the 12th to the 17th century. He was reputed to be the Christian priest-king of a remote region of Asia (esp. of India) or of Ethiopia. The name was frequently connected with the Crusades, as of one who would, it was hoped, aid in the recovery of the holy places by attacking the Arabs. Even letters purporting to be from him circulated throughout Europe, and Marco Polo mentions him in the account of his journeys.

PRESTON, THOMAS (ROGER WIDDRINGTON; d. 1640). Benedictine monk of Monte Cassino (1590). Arrested on a mission to England (1602), he spent most of his later life in the Clink prison, London, though in comparative comfort because of his friendship with the Anglican abp. of Canterbury. A champion of the condemned oath of allegiance against the pope's deposing power, he wrote several works on that subject. BIBLIOGRAPHY: DNB 71:180–182; T. H. Clancy, NCE 11:761.

[C. D. ROSS]

PRESTON, THOMAS SCOTT (1824–91), diocesan official, and polemicist. P. became an Anglican priest in 1847 and adhered to the High Church position. A convert to Catholicism in 1849, he was ordained to the Catholic priesthood in 1850. P. served the Archdiocese of New York for almost 40 years under Card. McCloskey and Abp. M. Corrigan, as bp.'s secretary, chancellor (1855–91) and vicar general from 1873 to his death. A conservative and severe disciplinarian, he was uncompromising and sometimes harsh. In the single tax controversy, P. was partially responsible for the excommunication of E. *McGlynn in 1887. Among P.'s writings are: *Life of St. Vincent de Paul* (1866); *Lectures on Christian Unity* (1867); *The Catholic View of the Public School System* (1870); *Protestantism and the Church* (1882).

[J. R. AHERNE]

PRESUMPTION, a term applied in the general sense of overconfidence by traditional RC moral theology to two vices, one contrary to the theological virtue of hope and the other to the moral virtue of *magnanimity.

As contrary to hope, presumption is antipodal to despair. Hope sees eternal life as attainable by relying upon the help God has promised; despair sees it as unattainable; presumption sees it as attainable but by means through which it cannot be reached (as when one expects to be saved by one's own powers or without repenting for one's sins—*praesumptio contra spem*), or by means of extraordinary help that God could, but has not promised, to give (as when one expects an opportunity for conversion at the end of life—*praesumptio praeter spem*). The former type of presumption is a radical perversion of hope and is always seriously sinful. The latter type is more or less seriously sinful to the extent in which it involves neglect of the ordinary means of salvation. To sin with the intention of confessing the sin afterwards and receiving absolution involves an element of presumption and perhaps some abuse of the mercy of God. But on the other hand it may also indicate a will less firmly fixed upon evil purpose than that of one who is prepared to sin with no regard whatever to future consequences.

The presumption opposed to magnanimity is the rash confidence of one who aspires to something which, though humanly possible, ought to be seen as beyond the limits of reasonable ambition on any honest appraisal of one's capacities. Presumption of this kind is not considered a serious sin unless the rash expectation introduces notable disorder into one's life or may be the occasion of loss or damage to others (as when one assumes serious responsibilities he ought to see himself as ill-qualified to meet). BIBLIOGRAPHY: ThAq ST 2a2ae,21; 130–133; P. K. Meagher, NCE 11:762.

[P. K. MEAGHER]

PRESUMPTION (CANON LAW), a term used in canon law for a conjecture applicable in certain types of case in which direct evidence of fact is not available. Presumptions are inferences drawn from what is generally true in certain kinds of situation or from probable indications of fact that may exist in a particular situation. Some, known as legal presumptions (*praesumptiones iuris*), are established by the law itself; others, called personal presumptions (*praesumptiones hominis*), are those formulated by an ecclesiastical judge, not arbitrarily and by way of personal opinion, but by inference from certain specific types of fact.

The effect of a presumption is to put the burden of proof on the party who would challenge it.

[P. K. MEAGHER]

PRETERNATURAL GIFTS, endowments given to a person that are over and above (*praeter*) the natural, but are not supernatural in the proper sense. The term supernatural properly qualifies the gifts of grace as these mean a direct and immediate relationship to God in his own life of knowing and loving. Preternatural gifts may have a connection with the level of grace, as dispositive or manifestive, but are not in themselves resources for living the grace life. Theologians have described the essence of *original justice as grace properly so-called; the other endowments of spirit and body in the first man as preternatural (St. Thomas Aquinas, however, maintains that all the primordial gifts were inextricably linked to grace; ThAq ST 1a,100.1). Taken in isolation some gifts classified in the NT as charismatic are of the same quality, e.g., the gift of certain kinds of miracle or of some infused knowledge: but in the actual economy of salvation the charisms function for the building up of the life of grace in the Church. A further generalized norm for typing the preternatural is that while the properly supernatural exceeds any created, or even creatable, nature's capacities, the preternatural is relatively above nature, i.e., beyond some, e.g., freedom from death is natural to angelic being, preternatural for the first man.

[T. C. O'BRIEN]

PRETI, MATTIA (1613–99), Italian painter, as a wandering student influenced by artists in Rome, Parma, Bologna, and Venice. His Caravaggesque *Concert* was followed by a Classical *St. Charles Borromeo Giving Alms* (1642), and frescoes in Rome and Modena. In 1656–60 a mature *Belshazzar's Feast* and *Raising of Lazarus* evidence a new baroque style. Climactic frescoes at Valmontone (1661) are the high point of his career and mark a revolution in 17th-cent. ceiling decoration extended by Pozzo and others.

[M. J. DALY]

PREUSS, ARTHUR (1871–1934), journalist, author, theological editor, and translator. He was baptized a Lutheran but his parents became converts and reared him as a Catholic. After receiving an M.A. from St. Francis College, Quincy, Ill., P. became in 1892 editor of several German-language publications, then began his own magazine (eventually named the *Fortnightly Review*) which he transferred to St. Louis in 1896. His chief journalistic interests centered on controversial issues involving German Catholics, esp. the issue of education (see CAHENSLY, PETER). P.'s most permanent contributions to theological literature were accomplished during his 40 years as editor for B. Herder Book Co. The most widely circulated of his translations from German were the so-called Pohle-Preusse volumes on systematic theology, *Dogmatic Theology* (12 v.) and his edition of Hartmann Grisar's *Martin Luther* (1935). He also translated Brunsmann's *Fundamental Theology* (4 v., 1928–32), A. Koch's *Moral Theology* (5 v., 3d ed., 1918). He was author of *Fundamental Fallacy of Socialism* (1908) and *Dictionary of Secret and Other Societies* (1924).

[T. C. O'BRIEN]

PREVITALI (CORDELIAGHI; CORDELLA), ANDREA (fl. 1502–28), Italian painter whose early works in Venice (1502–10) signed "Andrea of Bergamo" and "pupil of Giovanni Bellini" are intense in color and sharp in planes. Later works from Bergamo show Carpaccio's rigid frontal figures. Among many religious works his masterpiece is the *Madonna with the Casotti Family* (Bergamo). BIBLIOGRAPHY: B. Berenson, *Italian Paintings of the Renaissance: Venetian School* (1957).

[M. J. DALY]

PRÉVOST, ABBÉ ANTOINE-FRANÇOIS (called Prévost d'Exilés; 1697–1763), French novelist and man of letters. He was successively Jesuit, soldier, Benedictine before fleeing to Holland and England where he spent several years. A voluminous writer, he is best remembered for the novel *Manon Lescaut* which appeared as the seventh volume of his *Mémoires d'un homme de qualité* (1728–1731). Reflecting P.'s own experience, this story of passion portrays a type of Romantic youth, the Chevalier des Grieux, who remains faithful to Manon in spite of her infidelities. BIBLIOGRAPHY: Frederick C. Green, *Minuet: A Critical Survey of French and English Literary Ideas in the Eighteenth Century* (1935, repr. 1971).

[A. S. CRISAFULLI]

PREYSING, KONRAD VON (1880–1950), bp. of Berlin and cardinal. Of Bavarian origin, P. studied law and began a career in the Bavarian diplomatic service before entering the seminary at Innsbruck. Ordained in 1912, he became secretary to Card. Bettinger of Munich and worked closely with Eugenio Pacelli (Pius XII), papal nuncio in that city. Between 1928 and 1935 P. held the See of Eichstätt and then became bp. of Berlin. He consistently opposed National Socialism, without, however, associating with the active resistance movement. After 1945 he had to deal with the Soviet authorities, since most of his ruined diocese lay within their occupation zone. In 1946 Pope Pius XII named him cardinal. BIBLIOGRAPHY: W. Adolph, *Kardinal Preysing und zwei Diktatüre* (1971); G. Lewy, *Catholic Church and Nazi Germany* (1964).

[R. H. SCHMANDT]

PREZ, JOSQUIN DES, see DESPREZ, JOSQUIN.

PRICE, RICHARD (1723–91), population analyst. A writer on life expectancy, P. entered the controversy in England over population analysis with his book *An Essay on the Population of England, from the Revolution to the Present Time* (1780).

PRICE, THOMAS FREDERICK (1860–1919), editor, missionary. The first native of North Carolina to become a priest, P. was ordained in 1886. He worked in North Carolina, built five churches and chapels, preached on street corners, and was beloved esp. by the blacks for whose conversion he labored. P. founded the magazine *Truth,* for the purpose of apologetics and edited it for 25 years. By establishing a group of priests to train others for the missions he laid the foundation of an apostolate later developed by the Paulists. With James Francis Walsh he set about founding an American Catholic foreign mission society. The society, to be known later as Maryknoll Missioners, established itself near Ossining, N.Y. P. also established a seminary near Scranton, Pa. (1916) and a procuratorship in San Francisco (1917). In 1918 P. joined the group going to Yeunkong Mission in China, despite his age, and died in Hong Kong a year later. BIBLIOGRAPHY: P. Byrne, *Father Price of Maryknoll* (1923).

[J. R. AHERNE]

PRICE, JUST, see JUST PRICE.

PRICE CONTROL, governmental regulation, whereby either a maximum price is set in order to protect consumers against high prices, or fixing a minimum price in order to protect producers against low prices. Usually, the term "price control" is restricted to the former whereas the latter is referred to as "price support." Price control is frequently associated with war-time when the difficulties of supply could otherwise lead to exceptionally large increases in prices. Price control was used in many countries during both World Wars, and in the U.S. also during the Korean War. Such a price control means that prices are kept below the equilibrium, and at such a level that the quantity of the commodity demanded will exceed the available supply. Under such conditions, some form of rationing becomes necessary, either officially and justly by the State or unofficially, and possibly unjustly, by producers and sellers. Price controls were used in the U.S. during the period 1971–74 when there were serious economic problems. There is a marked divergence of opinion among economists as to the benefit and propriety of utilizing price controls in order to stabilize the economy.

[F. T. RYAN]

PRIDE. In the Christian theological tradition the sin both of Lucifer and Adam is pride, as an absolute reliance on personal gifts and powers and a refusal to bow before God (ThAq ST 1a, 63.2–3; 2a2ae, 163.1–2). This points to its being, rather than an isolated act, a radically disordered attitude: the refusal to accept the creaturely, dependent condition before God. In this sense it is a far more likely attitude than direct opposition to charity by hatred of God. Pride in its full sense is a peculiarly "intellectual" or "spiritual" sin: a distorted evaluation of the gifts one has as though they were self-created or a preference of one's own goals to the disposition of destiny by the Father through Christ. Such an attitude in its full-blown expression is, perhaps, rare. Yet the surrendering of self to the Father and his disposition of each person's life is the crisis that every man faces; it is the crisis of salvation itself. Ultimate pride is ultimate rejection of the share in Christ's "Thy will be done." There are pale shadows of pride in day-to-day attitudes of arrogance, willfulness, snobbishness, silly vanity. Such virtuous attitudes as candor, simplicity, humility are meant to check them. The true estimate of self and of the challenges of excellence in life are expressed by theological hope and by magnanimity. All of these involve ultimately finding "justification" not in self, but in the grace and the ways of the Father through Christ.

[T. C. O'BRIEN]

PRIEST AND PRIESTHOOD. Christian denominations generally recognize the priesthood of Christ and the common *priesthood of all believers, but not all accept the ordained or ministerial priesthood. All generally hold, in various senses, the threefold function of the priesthood-prophetic, royal, and sacrificial; but they differ greatly in their understanding of the ministerial priesthood, esp. in relation to the Eucharist, the sacrificial character of which is affirmed by Roman Catholics but generally denied by Protestants. Protestants are generally agreed about the priesthood of Christ, who once for all by the sacrifice of the cross brought about man's reconciliation and redemption. Christ is the high priest whose unique and all-sufficient sacrifice has made all other sacrifices superfluous. Protestants also stress the common priesthood of the faithful, who are a royal priesthood meant to offer spiritual sacrifices and to proclaim God's marvelous deeds (see 1 Pet 2.5–9). Luther held that all Christians are truly of the priestly order and that there is no distinction between them except regarding functions. For good order's sake the community entrusts some priestly functions to certain persons. The denial of a ministerial priesthood in Protestantism followed mainly upon the denial of the sacrificial character of the Lord's Supper, or the Eucharist. The pastor or minister has no other priestly functions than such as are common to all believers. The pastoral function of the ordained minister is reduced to preaching and administering baptism and the Lord's Supper; Luther, Calvin, and Zwingli agreed on the nonsacrificial character of the Eucharist. Consequently the clergy are, in their teaching, not priests but ministers or pastors.

In Anglicanism, despite the *Reformed or Calvinistic sense in which eucharistic doctrine is set forth in the BCP and in the Thirty-Nine Articles (a sense always insistently defended by many Anglican divines), there have always been some, and since the *Oxford movement there have been many, who have favored a stronger interpretation of the Lord's Supper that would leave some room for the notion of sacrifice. This divergence of view has been reflected in a difference of position with regard to the priesthood. Those whose eucharistic thought is in the Reformed tradi-

tion see no doctrinal necessity for an ordained priesthood, and they even tend to deny that the common priesthood of the faithful is exercised in the Lord's Supper, which they do not conceive to be an offering in any sense. Their opponents see a place for both the common and the ordained priesthood in the celebration of the Eucharist. For the common priesthood, they see the Eucharist as an offering in which all share, an offering symbolic of the will of the participants to render to God the worship of their whole lives. For the ordained priesthood, because although Christ is the unseen celebrant of every Eucharist, the single mediator between God and man through whom the worship and prayer ascends to the heavenly altar, the observance still requires a visible minister not only to preside at the liturgy on behalf of all but also to act in the name of Christ, esp. in repeating the words and acts of the Lord's Supper. Absolving, blessing, and the eucharistic consecration are seen by these Anglicans as priestly functions, by which the Anglican ministry differs essentially from the Protestant ministry.

RC understanding of priest and priesthood esp. as proposed by Vatican Council II in the constitutions on the Church and the liturgy and in the decree on priestly ministry and life, gives full recognition to Christ's high priesthood. Once for all he offered the one sacrifice of the new and everlasting covenant, the sacrifice of Calvary, which worked man's redemption. The council describes the Church as the new People of God, commissioned to continue Christ's saving work, not only through the ministry of the hierarchy, but also through the sharing in the Church's ministry by all the faithful. Therefore, Christ's priesthood and mediatorship are shared, and this in two ways. The common priesthood of the faithful enables them not only to offer spiritual sacrifices but also to be co-offerers of the Eucharistic Sacrifice, in which the sacrifice of Calvary is re-presented. The ministerial priesthood is exercised by the ordained priest, who acts in the person of Christ, and through whom the Church offers this re-presentation of the one sacrifice of Christ. Thus in RC teaching the ordained priesthood supposes the sacrificial character of the Eucharist, and the offering of the Eucharistic Sacrifice is the summit of the ordained minister's priestly functions. In this way in the constitutions on the Church and the liturgy Vatican Council II organically unites the priesthood of Christ, that of the faithful, and that of the ordained priest.

As ministry has become a central theme for the Christian Churches actively participating in ecumenical, bilateral consultation, they come closer together in the understanding of ordained ministry as priestly. BIBLIOGRAPHY: P. F. Palmer, NCE 11:768–772; J. Haekel et al., LTK 8:735–748, 756–758; B. Lohse, RGG 5:578–581; K. E. Kirk, *Apostolic Ministry* (1947); B. Lambert, *Ecumenism* (1967).

[P. DELETTER]

PRIEST AND PRIESTHOOD, ISRAELITE. Prior to the building of the Temple (and in many cases long after this also) Israelite worship was conducted at local shrines throughout the land by local families of priests. Whether all these hereditary dynasties of priests belonged to the tribe of Levi in a racial sense is extremely doubtful. The process by which priesthood in Israel was restricted to this tribe alone was largely an artificial one, many non-Levite families being "adopted" into this tribe. Even under David and Solomon, with the new centralized organization of the cultic personnel that they introduced, considerable rivalry must have continued between the various priestly families. Thus it is clear that the houses of Zadok and Abiathar were rivals, and it has even been suggested that the house of Zadok would have been of Canaanite or Jebusite origin and that priests from this family would have ministered at Jerusalem long before David's capture of the city. According to this theory David would have retained Zadok and his family in their priestly office, merely redirecting their worship to Yahweh the God of Israel and causing them to be adopted into the Israelite priesthood (cf. the artificial genealogy of 1 Chr 5.34). It is much more probable that the priests appointed by Jeroboam I at the shrines of Bethel and Dan (1 Kg 12.31) were of genuinely Aaronite descent. However this may be, under Solomon the Zadokites became supreme, displacing their rivals of the house of Abiathar (cf. 1 Kg 2:26—) and retaining the priesthood of Jerusalem in their hands right down to the time of Josiah.

The function of the priest in Israelite society is basically threefold. He gives oracles (cf. Dt 33.7–11; Jg 18.5; 1 Sam 14.41; 28.6), instructs in the law (Dt 33.10), and officiates at sacrifices (Dt 33.10). In all these areas he is, as W. Eichrodt remarks, "the indispensable mediator for entrance into the sphere of the divine." There are grounds for believing that in early Israelite society the function of oracle-giving was primary, the tasks of instructing and offering sacrifices being performed, in many cases, by the father of the family or the head of the clan, tribe, or ethnic group. It may also be the case that whereas in the northern kingdom no distinction was drawn between Levites and priests, in the Jerusalem Temple the principal role in sacrifices was confined to the Aaronic priesthood, while the Levites exercised subordinate roles. In post-Exilic times these functions were still more diversified, and probably particular families specialized in particular functions.

By NT times the high priesthood had become a largely political office retained in the hands of a few priestly families, the heads of which are referred to in the NT as the "chief priests." These aristocrats of the priestly class are seen to have been most hostile of all to Jesus, and most active in securing his condemnation and death. BIBLIOGRAPHY: De Vaux AncIsr 345–405.

[D. J. BOURKE]

PRIESTCRAFT, skill in exercising priestly functions. The term is now used in a pejorative sense to signify the craftiness of priests in imposing themselves on the multitude to further their own interests. The abuse of ecclesiastical power may batten on the credulity of simple folk, and commonly is not to be remedied by its inversion, antipriestcraft, which uses the same tricks under other names.

[T. EARLY]

PRIESTHOOD OF ALL BELIEVERS, the doctrine that by virtue of their union with Jesus Christ, the High Priest, all Christians, through their baptism, participate in his priestly mediation to other believers and to the world. In the NT the word "priest" (Gr. *hiereus*) is never used to refer to the ordained ministers of the Church. It refers either to the Jewish priests, who repeatedly appear in the Gospels, or to the person of Christ himself (esp. in the Epistle to the Hebrews, which is the only NT writing to apply the word "priest" to him), or to believers in Christ. This does not imply, however, that there is any necessary contradiction between the priesthood of all believers and the ordained priesthood of those who have specially set aside for the service of Christ and of his Church; on the contrary, the two concepts of priesthood are mutually supportive and interdependent, just as both of them are in turn dependent upon their source in the priestly ministration of Christ as "the one mediator between God and men" (1 Tim 2.5).

Nevertheless, the ordained priesthood and the priesthood of all believers were set into opposition during some of the controversies of the Reformation and Counter-Reformation. Martin *Luther, who stressed the universal priesthood of believers, also insisted upon the ministry of word and sacrament. Other Protestant theologians, however, placed the two into disjunction, ascribing to all the members of the Church all the rights and the authority of the priesthood. This position received its ultimate expression in the teaching of the Society of Friends and some other groups of the radical Reformation that have no ordained ministry at all. In opposition not only to this extreme form of doctrine but also to its more moderate statement in Luther and Calvin, many theologians of the RC Counter-Reformation dismissed the idea of the priesthood of all believers or subordinated it so drastically to the emphasis upon the ordained priesthood as to render it meaningless. Thus the word "priest" in RC usage still tends to refer only to the clergy. The Constitution on the Church and the Constitution on the Liturgy of Vatican Council II may be interpreted as an effort to go beyond this false antithesis to a more balanced and a more scriptural view (Vat II ConstChurch 9–11).

The key text in the NT for the doctrine of the priesthood of all believers is 1 Pet 2.9: "You are a chosen race, a royal priesthood, a holy nation, God's own people, that you may declare the wonderful deeds of him who called you out of darkness into his marvelous light." These words are addressed to all the members of the Church, who, both in their life and in their worship, mediate the wondrous deeds of God to others, an authentically priestly function. Therefore the prayers of the congregation in the liturgy and the work of believers in the world are an extension of the priesthood of Christ. Yet the believers have been constituted as priests by being "called out of darkness." This calling has taken place through baptism and through the teaching of the word of God, which have been mediated to them through the ordained priesthood.

The doctrine of the priesthood of all believers requires, for its full explication and application, a doctrine of vocation by which the life of the Christian in his community, his family, and his daily work is interpreted as a calling from God, where the priest exercises his mediating function in relation to others. It also requires a strong emphasis upon baptism, which is then to be seen as the ''ordination'' to the universal priesthood of believers. BIBLIOGRAPHY: T. F. Torrance, *Royal Priesthood* (1955); J. E. Rea, *Common Priesthood of the Members of the Mystical Body* (1947).

[J. PELIKAN]

PRIESTHOOD OF CHRIST. A priest (Gr. *hiereus,* from *hieros,* meaning removed from profane use and consecrated to God; Lat. *sacerdos,* from *sacer,* the Lat. equivalent of *hieros*) is a man, who, by virtue of a sacral office, acts on men's behalf in their relationship with God. He is *pontifex,* a bridge-builder. This term describes best the priestly functions: a priest is men's go-between with God.

In the complex reality of his divine-human Person, the Word Incarnate unites both Godhead and mankind. He is the bridge between God and men; not an intermediary being, but the only mediator (cf. 1 Tim 2.5). In Christ mediation and priesthood are identified. Christ is priest essentially and absolutely for he is priest by his ontological makeup, not by any added quality. His priesthood extends to the various aspects of his mediation: his revealing, redeeming, and kingly functions.

Of Christ's three functions the revelatory is best brought out in St. John's Gospel, the kingly in the Synoptics, the sacrificial in the Epistle to the Hebrews. The kingly function is referred to an unction of Christ's humanity in his Resurrection (Acts 2.36); the prophetic, to one received by Christ in his baptism (Lk 4.18); of a priestly unction of Christ's humanity by the Incarnation itself the NT does not speak. The Fathers of the Church, however, do affirm that the sacred humanity has been anointed by the very Incarnation of the Word. Thus the three functions of Christ are rooted in three unctions. Christ unites in a striking manner the three functions of prophets, priests, and kings of the old dispensation.

Jesus himself never claims the title of priest. The reason for this abstention seems to be that in his environment the title referred to the Levitic priesthood, which he transcended. The Epistle to the Hebrews, however, calls Christ priest (*hiereus*) and high priest (*archiereus*). Its central theme is the uniqueness and transcendence of the priesthood of Christ (4.14): not only does it surpass the Levitic priesthood, it abolishes it (7.11). The letter opposes the transitory character of the old priesthood to the inadmissible, unchanging, eternal character of the new (7.23–25). Perfectly identified with men (2.17), having been tested in every way (4.15), Christ is sinless (4.15), undefiled (7.26). Hence,

unlike the high priests of old who offered sacrifices for their own sins as well as for the people (7.26–28; 5.1–3), he offers only for others. While all sacrifices offered before him had been powerless (10.2–3; 9.9), his is efficacious; this is why Christ offers once for all (7.27).

The high priesthood of Christ is dynamic. It is real from the beginning, being rooted in Christ's makeup as Son Incarnate, at once true man (2.10–18) and true Son of God (1.1–13). It is nonetheless progressively realized and actualized through the paschal mystery (2.10; 5.9–10), and reaches its perfection in Christ's glorification (6.20). It is a heavenly priesthood (8.1–2). To the priesthood of the glorified Christ the Church's priestly mediation lends visible presence in the world. BIBLIOGRAPHY: A. George, DBT 406–411; C. Dillenschneider, *Christ the One Priest and We His Priests* (tr. Sr. M. Renelle, 2 v., 1964–65) 2:17; O. Cullmann, *Christology of the New Testament* (tr. S. C. Guthrie and C. A. M. Hall, 1959) 83.

[J. DUPUIS]

PRIESTLEY, JOSEPH (1733–1804), English Unitarian. Born at Fieldhead, Yorkshire, P. studied at an academy of *Dissenters at Daventry, where his views changed from a moderate Calvinism and belief in the freedom of the will to Arianism and determinism. After serving pastorates at Needham Market in Suffolk and at Nantwich in Cheshire, he became a tutor at Warrington Academy, where he found the congenial company of other Arians and determinists. He then became pastor of the Mill Hill congregation at Leeds. An acquaintance with Theophilus *Lindsey encouraged his adherence to Unitarianism. The Royal Society awarded Priestley its highest honor, the Copley Medal, for his scientific researches. His discovery of oxygen (1774) and of other gases made him a founder of chemistry. His many theological works include *Institutes of Natural and Revealed Religion* (1772–73), a basic statement of the liberal Dissenters' faith, *Disquisitions Relating to Matter and Spirit* (1777), *A Harmony of the Evangelists* (1777), *History of the Corruptions of Christianity* (1782), and *History of Early Opinions Concerning Jesus Christ* (1786). His ministry at the New Meeting Society in Birmingham, where he preached Unitarianism, ended when a mob burned his church and home because of his defense of the French Revolution, but he escaped to London, where he became pastor of the Gravel Pit Meeting at Hackney. In 1794, he immigrated to America, where he settled in Northumberland, Pennsylvania. Works: J. T. Rutt, ed., *Theological and Miscellaneous Works* (25v., 1817–31). BIBLIOGRAPHY: T. E. Thorpe, *Joseph Priestley* (1906); A. Holt, *Life of Joseph Priestley* (1931); E. M. Wilbur, *History of Unitarianism* (2v., repr., 1965); J. G. Gillam, *Crucible* (1954).

[J. C. GODBEY]

PRIESTLY CITIES, cities set aside for the exclusive use of the sons of Aaron. During the apportionment of the land under Joshua (Josh 21.1–42; 1 Chr 6.54–81), 48 cities with their surrounding pastureland were set aside as dwelling places for the tribe of Levi. This was their lot in Palestine (cf. Num 35.1–5). Thirteen of these cities were for the exclusive use of the sons of Aaron and were the inalienable allotment of priests. Any lands within these cities that would have been sold might be redeemed at any time, but had to be released to the original owners in the Year of Jubilee (Lev 25.32–34). The six cities of refuge for those who had committed homicide were among the levitical cities. It is conjectured that this complex of legislation reflects a tradition, going back to the time of David and Solomon, of attempting to assimilate Canaanite holy places with their cult centers, priesthood, and ministers into the Israelite scheme of things. The tradition also served to keep alive the ancient Israelite idea that all land belongs to God, and every Israelite has a share in it.

[E. J. DILLON]

PRIESTLY COURSES, in the OT, the division of lesser functions in the Temple to various members of the priestly families. This division undeniably had a long history. The post-Exilic books (1 Chr ch. 24 and Neh ch. 10–12) attribute such an apportionment to David. Different lists mention 24 or 22 or 20 families. Each family had a weekly turn, further subdivided into the customary daily actions. Zachary in Lk 1.5 belonged to a family named Abia. As he carried out the duties of his division at the altar of incense, the birth of a son, John the Baptist, was foretold to him.

[L. A. BUSHINSKI]

PRIESTLY SPIRITUALITY. As a spirituality (the way or modality of the spiritual life proper to individual persons or groups) is determined principally by the vocation of the individual in his life situation (with all that this implies of nature and grace), priestly spirituality must be seen in the light of the nature of the priesthood and the function of the priest. All priesthood in the Church is a participation in the priesthood of Christ, who continues his priestly function in and through the Church in her liturgy. And while there is a priesthood in the Church common to all "of the faithful" or "of the laity" (that of the member of the Church as such, had through baptismal consecration), we are concerned here primarily with the spirituality of the ministerial priesthood (that possessed by virtue of the sacrament of orders) realized in the "priest" (diocesan or regular) and, in its fullness in the bishop.

Through their episcopal consecration bps. are made "sharers in Christ's consecration and mission," and priests are "coworkers in the . . . fulfillment of this apostolic mission," participating thus in the "office of the Apostles" (VatII MinLife Priests) and continuing instrumentally the threefold office of Christ (Prophet, Priest, and King) in the task of the proclamation of the gospel, the ministry of the sacraments (centered upon the Eucharist, sacrifice and sacrament), and in the pastoral guidance of the people of God. Sharing the common vocation to sanctity of all of God's people (Vat II ConstChurch, ch. 5), the priest is called to

holiness by the special title of his priestly ordination (*Sacerdotalia primordia,* July 31, 1959), a sanctity to be achieved through service (of word, sacrament, and pastoral care) "in the midst of men." Configured thus to Christ the Priest (through the sacrament of orders) to act in his person, and taken from among men (Heb 5.1) to act on their behalf, the spirituality of the priest, as a mediator in the one Mediator, will be characterized, by his unique relationship to Christ the Priest, his priestly participation in and service through the Paschal mystery of the people of God (and of all men), his ministry being directed to this work and perfected in it (VatII MinLifePriests). It is an apostolic spirituality of priestly sanctity in and through service in the midst of men.

The spirituality of the bp. will be determined further through his episcopal ordination, that of the diocesan priest by his diocesan state of life (in his union with the bp.), and that of the religious priest will be qualified further by the circumstances of his priestly ministry (monastic or missionary) and the characteristics of the spirituality of his particular religious family. The best approach to priestly spirituality will be had through the pertinent documents of Vatican Council II (which have precluded the discussions of the early 20th cent. on the relative nature of the spirituality of the diocesan and religious priest)—*On the Ministry and Life of Priests* (1965), *On Priestly Formation* (1965), *On the Sacred Liturgy* (1963), *On the Bishop's Pastoral Office in the Church* (1965), together with the *Dogmatic Constitution on the Church* (1964) and the *Pastoral Constitution on the Church in the Modern World* (1965), with the *Decree on the Apostolate of the Laity* (1965) and the pertinent portions of the Constitution on the Church serving to delineate the priestly spirituality of "all the faithful." A priestly spirituality was thoroughly developed by the Oratory (Card. Bérulle, Condren, Olier) in the 17th cent. centered upon union with and apostolic dedication in Christ, the one High Priest.
BIBLIOGRAPHY: C. Marmion, *Christ, the Ideal of the Priest* (1952); E. Suhard, *Priests among Men* (repr. 1960); A. M. Charue, *Diocesan Clergy* (tr. M. J. Wrenn, 1963); *Spiritual Renewal of the American Priesthood* (ed. E. E. Larkin and G. T. Broccolo, 1972). *PERFECTION, CHRISTIAN.

[W. J. READ]

PRIESTLY TRADITION, a documentary source of the Pentateuch; those anonymous writers responsible for the final edition of the Torah and the insertion of parts which have a special interest in priests and matters in Jerusalem pertaining to the cult life of Israel. Though their additions are extensive they do not present a complete account of history as do the other three Pentateuchal traditions. Their hand is noticeable in places where the origin of a feast or religious practice or a genealogical listing is to be discerned. Holiness was ever the objective of this reediting and insertion of new material (cf. Lev ch. 17–26). It is commonly accepted that these writers did their work between the 6th and 4th cent. B.C. *DOCUMENTARY THEORY.

[L. A. BUSHINSKI]

PRIEUR, BARTHÉLEMY (1545–1611), French sculptor. Pupil of G. Pilon, P. was sculptor to the King (1594), worked on the inner façade of the S wing of the Louvre, and executed bronze dogs for the Fountain of Diana (1602). His masterpieces are *Peace, Abundance,* and *Justice* for the monument of Anne de Montmorency (Louvre), formerly in the church of St. Martin de Montmorency. He and P. Biard are the most important sculptors in the time of Henry IV.

[M. J. DALY]

PRIMACY OF CHRIST, an attribute of Christ as man whereby he is said to occupy the first place in the divine creative plan and in the universe brought into being in accord with that plan. The term primacy is traced to Col 1.18 where *proteuon,* applied to Christ, means literally "one who holds the first place." Equivalent scriptural affirmations are contained, e.g., in Eph 1.10 (Christ sums up all things in Himself), Heb 1.13 (Christ is seated at the Father's right hand), and Rev 22.13 (Christ is the beginning and the end, alpha and omega).

Patristic development of the notion of Christ's primacy was implicit, the most striking testimony being that embodied in St. Irenaeus' view of the "recapitulation of all things in Christ." The medieval theologians, beginning with Rupert of Deutz (d. 1135), debated the hypothetical question, whether God would have become man if Adam had not sinned. St. Thomas, e.g., agreed with St. Augustine that a sinless world would need no redeemer and hence no Incarnation (ST 3a, 1.3). John Duns Scotus answered the same question affirmatively, but his answer is not confined to the hypothetical order: as God's masterpiece, Christ as man could not depend for his existence on sin (*In 3 sent.* 7.3, Vives ed., v. 14:354–355). Louis Molina sought to reconcile the two views by theorizing that Christ's own glory and man's Redemption were "equally first" in God's plan (*Concordia* [1876] 477–490).

Modern development of the question dates from the publication of Hilary of Paris' dissertation *Cur Deus Homo* (1867). Important contributions were made by such prominent theologians as R. Garrigou-Lagrange, G. M. Roschini, and Ugo Lattanzi, but the most elaborate development was that of J. F. Bonnefoy, who explained Christ's primacy in the categories of Greek metaphysics. From the revealed datum that Christ as man "holds the first place" among creatures, Bonnefoy deduced the logical priority of Christ's predestination, and His threefold secondary causal relationship toward the rest of creation. As meritorious efficient cause, Christ earned the existence of other creatures; as final cause He is their proximate goal or reason for being; and as exemplary cause He is the model whose perfections have been reproduced to a lesser degree throughout creation.

Current doubts about the validity (at least necessity) of Greek metaphysical concepts are leading to a reevaluation of traditional expressions of Christ's primacy. Conciliar theology seems to indicate the direction of this trend by stressing the central role of Christ as primordial sacrament ever active in the world to lead all things to the Father (Vat II ChurchModWorld 43). BIBLIOGRAPHY: J. F. Bonnefoy, *Christ and the Cosmos* (1965) which contains full bibliog.; M. D. Meilach, *From Order to Omega* (1966) is a broader treatment incorporating some Teilhardian features.

[M. D. MEILACH]

PRIMACY OF THE POPE, in RC teaching, a priority among bps. accorded to the pope as bp. of Rome and successor of St. Peter. The pope's primacy is no mere priority in dignity or right to the honor of precedence before other bps. of the Church. He is not simply *primus inter pares* (the first among equals), a prerogative that some who are not Roman Catholic would allow. His primacy means more than a right to impede, as by some sort of veto, the actions or decisions of the episcopal college. Though Vatican Council II emphasized the collegial character of authority in the Church and that the episcopate, which "succeeds the college of the Apostles in the office of teaching and in pastoral direction," is also a "subject of supreme and full power over the universal Church," it also teaches that the college is vested with such power "together with its head, the Roman pontiff, and never without the head"; that this power "cannot be exercised except with the consent of the Roman pontiff," for this college "does not have authority unless it is thought of in union with the Roman pontiff as its head" (Vat II ConstCh 22). In the same section the Council declares that the pope has in the Church "by reason of his office, namely, that of vicar of Christ and pastor of the whole Church, full, supreme, and universal power over the Church, which he can always freely exercise."

The council had already made clear (*ibid.,* 18) that in keeping with the teaching of Vatican I it too held that to secure the unity of the episcopate, Christ "set Peter over the other Apostles and in him instituted a perpetual visible principle and basis for unity of faith and communion," and that it again proposed to the faithful as matter of belief the doctrine enunciated by Vatican I concerning the establishment, perpetuity, nature, and meaning of the primacy and the infallible teaching authority of the Roman pontiff" (see D 3050–75 for the teaching of Vatican I).

If then the authority of the pope is an authority that he shares with the rest of the college of bishops and one that he can exercise in full collegial collaboration with his fellow bps., as occurs most clearly in ecumenical councils, still the pope can so concentrate that authority in himself as head of the college that he can exercise it fully without invoking their actual positive collaboration or consent. As the explanatory note 3-4 (from the acts of the Council, AAS 57 [1965], 74–75) indicates: "It is within the competence of the Pope, to whom the care of the whole flock of Christ has been committed, to decide according to the needs of the Church in what manner this care is to be exercised: by personal action or by collegial action. The Roman pontiff proceeds according to his own discretion and in view of the welfare of the Church in arranging, promoting and approving any exercise of collegiality." Hence "as supreme pastor the Pope can always exercise his authority as he chooses. While the College always exists, it does not for that reason permanently operate through strictly collegial action, as the tradition of the Church shows. In other words it is not always 'in full act'; indeed it operates through collegial action only at intervals, and only with the consent of its head.''

In the Catholic mind the difficulties that may be found in the existence of a college and a collegial power that are in some ways unique will be resolved in large measure in the practical order by the unifying Spirit within the whole Church and by living contact and communion among all pastors in the Church. The pope, recognizing that by Christ's will he is the head of a college that shares in his pastorate, will be sensitive and alert to the views, attitudes, and feelings of those who share with him the daily concern for the whole People of God. It was to ensure such constant reciprocal action between the head and the members of the college that the council, in Vat II BpPastOff 5, stated that ''bishops from various parts of the world, chosen through procedures established or to be established by the Roman pontiff, will render especially helpful assistance to the supreme pastor of the Church in a council to be known by the name of Synod of Bishops. Since it will be acting in the name of the entire Catholic episcopate, it will at the same time demonstrate that all the bishops in hierarchical communion share in the responsibility for the universal Church.'' Postconciliar ecclesiology more and more refers to the pope's role in the Church as the ''Petrine service'' or ministry. The meaning of primacy has been fruitfully discussed in Lutheran-RC dialogue. BIBLIOGRAPHY: F. A. Sullivan, NCE 11:779–780; G. Glez, DTC 13.1:247–344; K. Rahner, LTK 8:44–48; K. Rahner and J. Ratzinger, *Episcopate and the Primacy* (tr. K. Barker et al., 1962); Lutheran-Catholic Dialogue; ''Joint Statement on Papal Primacy,'' *Origins* 3 (1974) 585–600.

[S. E. DONLON]

PRIMASIUS, 6th-cent. bp. of Adrumetum, or Justinianopolis, in the Byzacene province of North Africa. In 551 he was summoned to Constantinople by Justinian. Because of his association with the teachings of Theodore of Mopsuestia, P. was embroiled in the controversy surrounding the *Three Chapters. He took no part in the 5th general council held at Constantinople, and was one of the 16 bps. who sided with Pope Vigilius (553). When Vigilius later accepted the decrees of the council, so did Primasius.

[E. J. DILLON]

PRIMATE, a title given to certain bps. and abps. in the West. In early usage it was accorded to bps. and abps. with whose sees the office of vicar of the Holy See was annexed; in those times the dignity carried with it certain jurisdictional rights and privileges. The title is retained in modern times, but it is properly accorded only to bps. and abps. of those sees whose occupants were formerly ex officio papal vicars, e.g., Armagh in Ireland and Arles in France. Primates in this modern sense enjoy a precedence of honor but ordinarily no special jurisdiction by reason of their primacy (see CIC c. 271). Sometimes the title is applied in a looser sense to bps. or abps. whose sees are the oldest or most prominent in a particular territory or country. Thus the abp. of Baltimore in the U.S. and the abp. of Westminster in England are sometimes referred to as primates. The *Anglican Communion defines the primate as the first among equals. The abp. of Canterbury is the primate of the entire Anglican Communion. The head of each of the autonomous Churches in the Anglican Communion bears the same title of honor. The Protestant Episcopal Church does not use the title; it elects a *presiding bishop to head the House of Bishops. The title primate is also used in some Old Catholic and other hierarchical Churches. In the East the title was not in use until the recognition of the independence of the Church of Romania (1881). The metropolitan of Bucharest chose not to take the title of patriarch but that of primate, which he bore until the establishment of the Romanian patriarchate in 1925. Pope Innocent III had offered the title of primate to Basil, the chief bp. of the Bulgarian Church, in reply to the request of King Kalojan that he be granted the patriarchal dignity (1204). The two Armenian bishops of New York and Los Angeles are styled primates.

[V. J. POSPISHIL]

PRIMATICCIO, FRANCESCO (1504–70), Italian painter, decorator, and architect, principal disseminator of Italian mannerism in France, and founder of the School of Fontainebleau. In complete charge of all projects at the Palace of Fontainebleau from 1540 until his death, P., influenced by Raphael and Parmigianino, planned galleries of stucco ''conceits'' of elegant, elongated figures in the affected and sinuously graceful poses of a sophisticated mannerism. P. counted, among many assistants, the distinguished French sculptor G. Pilon and the architect P. de l'Orme. The School of Fontainebleau dissolved 2 years after his death. BIBLIOGRAPHY: L. Dimier, *Le Primatice, peintre, sculpteur, et architecte des rois de France* (1900); L. Dimier, *Le Primatice* (1928).

[L. A. LEITE]

PRIMER, the English name for the ordinary prayer book used by the literate laity from the 13th to the 16th cent. Primers varied in content, but almost without exception they included the Little Office of the Blessed Virgin, the Office of the Dead, the gradual and penitential Psalms, and the Litany of the Saints. To these common elements various private devotions were added, sometimes in the vernacular. For an account of the origin and variety of Primers, see H. Thurston, CE 12:425–427. *PRAYER BOOKS.

[P. K. MEAGHER]

PRIMEVAL AGE (IN THE BIBLE), the first age; the beginnings of things. This is a concept meaningful to the ancient world and to the biblical writers (cf. Gen ch. 1–11). The primeval age includes the beginnings of the universe; of the earth and the heavenly bodies; of living things upon earth; and of humankind. The concept usually includes the origins of tribes, peoples, customs, and tongues. It only gives way to history in areas where tribal memory begins.

[E. J. DILLON]

PRIMEVAL HISTORY, the panorama of events contained in the first 11 chapters of Genesis. These chapters serve as an introduction to the patriarchal history (Gen ch. 12–50). Together they comprise the introduction to the Mosaic events that give Israel its identity (Ex and Num) and lead to the conquest of the Promised Land (Joshua). Primeval history is not history or even prehistory in any modern sense; nor does it compete with the modern sciences of geology, biology, or anthropology. It is a statement of faith: teaching that the origins of the universe and of the human family derive their ultimate meaning from the experienced history of Israel, and set the stage for that history. During the Solomonic Renaissance of the 10th cent. B.C., an author known to us as the Yahwist composed the national epic of Israel, which remains the nucleus of the Pentateuch as we have it today. During this high-water time of national achievement, when Israel felt itself to be the equal of the great kingdoms of the world, this author brought together all the various patriarchal legends into interconnected sagas, all the legends concerning the beginnings of things into a primeval history, and wove them into the basic story of Israel's deliverance from bondage in Egypt, covenant with Yahweh at Sinai, and conquest of the Promised Land. A later tradition, the Priestly tradition, has added its own genealogies, its own version of the Flood story, other minor details, and esp. the tour de force of the Priestly tradition: the serene monotheism of the first creation story with which Genesis opens. To the Yahwist, however, belongs the rest. It was left to him to make utterly real the tragic dimension of human life: the dynamic of rebellion against God; the disorder and violence among men; the diversities of peoples, customs, and languages; the pain of childbirth; the attraction and conflict between the sexes; the necessity of sweat-labor; and the inevitability of death. The origin of evil is attributed to the sinful rebellion of man. Evil gains momentum until it engulfs man himself in the devastation of the Flood. After the Flood, the story of the disrespect of Noah's sons and the story of the Tower of Babel portray man's disorder, but the scene is set for the call of Abraham.

[E. J. DILLON]

PRIMIANISTS, followers of Primian, who succeeded Parmenian as Donatist bp. of Carthage in 391 or 392. He antagonized the more solid members of the community by excommunicating the deacon Maximian, readmitting the Claudianists to communion, and indulging in acts of capricious violence. He was deposed by a council of some 50 bps. held at Cebarsussa in June 393 but was vindicated at a

more general council held at Bagai in April 394. He took part in the great conference of Carthage held under the presidency of the imperial commissioner Marcellinus in June 411 which brought about the ultimate condemnation of the Donatist schism. BIBLIOGRAPHY: W. H. C. Frend, *Donatist Church* (1952) 213–226. *DONATISTS.

[M. J. COSTELLOE]

PRIMICERIUS. (1) An administrative office of the RC Church, ranked with the archdeacon and treasurer, who managed the activities of the lesser clergy in liturgical matters, choir, and often served as head of the cathedral school in many dioceses. The office was universal in the West during the 6th and 7th centuries. With Pope St. Gregory I the Great (590–604), the primicerius at Rome was placed in charge of the college of notaries responsible for papal documents. An important official during the 7th and 8th cent. the *primicerius notariorum* with the archdeacon and archpresbyter ruled during a papal vacancy and was head of the *judices palatini,* the judges at the papal palace. The office gave way to that of papal chancellor. (2) The name given to the superior or subsuperior of some chapters of canons. It is a functional synonym, if not a mild epithet; derived from the Latin, *primus in cera* "first on the wax," referring to one whose name is first on a wax tablet. It came to apply to any first name on a list, a likely position for the superior's name.

PRIMITIVE BAPTISTS, a Baptist denomination that originated in 1835, when the Chemung Association, straddling the border of N. Y. and Pa., demanded a separation from all *associations that participated in missionary activity. The concept of mission appeared to be contrary to a tenet of rigid Calvinism, namely that God elected his own people in Christ before the world was formed. Mission activity, then, is useless at best and could be viewed as contrary to the will of God. Evangelistic preaching is supported as a means of edifying the elect. Support for *Bible societies, church schools, state conventions, colleges, and theological seminaries is totally withheld. Most of the clergy have little or no formal training, the *call being all-important. In the South large numbers of Scotch-Irish immigrants who brought a Calvinistic theological inheritance with them became Primitive Baptists. The 1844 membership of 121,000 in 3,000 churches has decreased to about 69,000. *ANTIMISSION BAPTISTS; *ANTIMISSIONARY MOVEMENT.

[R. A. MACOSKEY]

PRIMOGENITURE. Various ideas, ritual practices, and superstitions, often invested with religious significance, have centered about the firstborn, not only among primitive peoples but also among many of more developed cultures. With the Jews first fruits belonged in a special way to God, and as a particularization of this general principle, a firstborn son had to be consecrated to the Lord. Among Christians no special importance has been generally attached to the circumstance that a child is the first of a family to be born, although in different Christian countries law, custom, or usage has decreed that the eldest son (or eldest child) should succeed to leadership or title upon the death of his father, or to the undivided possession of the family's landed property. This last practice was introduced into England at the Norman Conquest. It is contrasted with "gavelkind," where property is divided among all the sons, or with "Irish gavelkind," where property is thrown into the common stock and redivided among members of the sept, and with "borough English," a custom in the south of England whereby the youngest son inherited all the land. Like the right of succession to a title, this was simply a pragmatic feudal arrangement and had no special religious significance. The exclusion of women from succession to landed property, which was fought by the Church, was dictated by the connection between inheriting land and the duty of bearing arms.

PRÍMOLI, JUAN BAUTISTA (1673–1747), missionary and architect. An Italian who joined the Jesuits in 1716, P. went to Buenos Aires. He and a fellow Jesuit, Brother Andrés Blanqui were professional architects and they worked together in La Plata building the cathedrals of Buenos Aires and Córdoba, many churches in Argentina and the *Reductions of Paraguay, as well as private homes. They followed the simple lines of architecture in Argentina.

[J. R. AHERNE]

PRIMUS, in the *Episcopal Church in Scotland, the presiding bishop. The office and its designation date from 1731. The primus does not have the rank of metropolitan; he is elected by his fellow bps. and may be from any of the seven dioceses of the Church.

[T. C. O'BRIEN]

PRIMUS INTER PARES, first among equals, a phrase applied to a chairman of a board, the president of a group, the senior bp. of a bench, or wherever some primacy of honor or function of leadership is accorded for the joint action of members with identical powers. Thus it is used with reference to metropolitans, patriarchs, and other hierarchical officials who have no sacramentally higher status than that of other bishops. Some Anglican and Orthodox theologians have suggested that such a conception of the bp. of Rome would be acceptable. Some talk on episcopal collegiality also moves in that direction. Primacy of honor is commonly contrasted with primacy of jurisdiction.

[T. EARLY]

PRINCE BISHOP, an ecclesiastic who possessed both spiritual and regal-temporal sovereignty. Characteristic of the Holy Roman Empire but also found in England, prince bishops were independent territorial rulers subject only to emperor or king.

Bishops were often the natural leaders when centralized authority collapsed, and with the need of rulers for educated churchmen in government, the fusion of secular and religious tasks caused episcopal and abbatial civil authority—rights of justice, minting, taxation, etc.—to be granted by secular rulers in the early Middle Ages. The episcopal feudalism of Emperor *Otto I (d. 973) undercut the stem dukes by utilizing bps. as imperial counts, with secular powers and lands. The concomitant imperial and royal appointment and investiture of bps. and abbots conflicted with the *Gregorian reform (11th–12th cent.), an *investiture struggle compromised in the Concordat of Worms (1122). The sovereign territorial jurisdiction of the imperial prince bps. —esp. the Rhineland abps. of Mainz (archchancellors after 965), Cologne, and Trier, who became ecclesiastical electors of the Empire—made them influential as *principes imperii*. Other important prince bishoprics included Liège, Salzburg, Utrecht, and Würzburg. Many prince bishoprics in central and northern Germany were secularized in the Reformation. Under Napoleon, all prince bishoprics in the Empire (excluding Regensburg, which continued briefly) were abolished in 1803.

In England, the prince bp. of Durham both defended the northern frontier against the Scots and exercised customarily royal prerogatives—e.g., making judicial appointments, pardoning treason and felony, holding chancery and exchequer courts and parliament-like councils, minting coins—so that it was said the king's writ did not run between Tyne and Tees. The palatinate of Durham, abolished under the Commonwealth but restored under Charles II, was transferred to the Crown, its powers diminished with time, in 1836. BIBLIOGRAPHY: H. Tüchle, NCE 11:786–787 (bibliog.); G. Lapsley, *County Palatine of Durham* (1924).

[W. A. CHANEY]

PRINCE OF THE CHURCH, a common designation for a member of the College of Cardinals. The title is derived from the protocol regulations which rank him immediately after princes of reigning houses of kings.

[T. M. MCFADDEN]

PRINCETON THEOLOGY, a conservative theological system in the Calvinist tradition, which developed in the 19th cent. at Princeton Theological Seminary. When A. *Alexander became Princeton's first professor of didactic and polemic theology in 1812, he built up a system based solidly on the *Westminster Standards and other *Reformed confessions and the writings of the 17th-cent. Calvinist scholastics, esp. F. *Turretini, who interpreted them. Intelligible explanation, rather than innovation, became the hallmark of Princeton. Alexander's pupil, C. *Hodge, succeeded him in 1840 and further developed a theological tradition characterized by dogmatic rigor and confessional loyalty, fairly meeting the challenges posed by the innovations of N. *Taylor, H. *Bushnell, and the New England liberals. Hodge's *Systematic Theology* (1871–72) was a reasoned, logical approach to traditional Christian doctrine. B. B. *Warfield, who had studied under Hodge, followed him as professor of systematic theology in 1879 and continued until 1921, in the same tradition of loyalty to the historic confessions of the Reformed faith. Hodge, along with Alexander, also developed a clearer understanding of scriptural inerrancy and inspiration to meet the new challenges of modern biblical criticism. Warfield's tradition was broken with the reorganization of Princeton Seminary (1927) and the founding by J. G. *Machen of Westminster Theological Seminary (1929). It has more recently inspired a new generation of *evangelicals at Princeton and elsewhere. BIBLIOGRAPHY: H. T. Kerr, *Sons of the Prophets* (1963); L. Loetscher, *Broadening Church* (1957); Smith-Jamison 1:260–266.

[R. K. MacMASTER]

PRINCIPAL CAUSE, an *efficient cause proportionate in kind and in power to an effect produced; thus principal in distinction from an *instrumental cause. In the consideration of divine *causality, the distinction is made between God as first cause, and created causes as secondary causes. Created causes are true and principal causes, but have their efficacy in subordination to the indispensable primacy and influence of God's causality. BIBLIOGRAPHY: ThAq ST 1a, 104. 1;105. 5 (Lat-Eng v. 14, ed. T. C. O'Brien) app. 1 ''*Esse,* the Proper Effect of God Alone.''

[T. C. O'BRIEN]

PRINCIPALITIES (*archē*). In Rom 8.38; 1 Cor 15.24; Eph 1.21; 3.10; 6.12; Col 1.16; 2.10,15, St. Paul speaks of Principalities as of angelic, or spiritual, beings. Regularly in these places the word is used in conjunction with Powers (*exousia*). Later thought about the angels identified the Principalities as one of the *choirs of angels. However, the same two Greek words are used in Lk 12.11; Tit 3.1 to signify those wielding civil authority. BIBLIOGRAPHY: Lampe 111–112.

[E. A. WEIS]

PRINCIPLE (Lat., beginning), in scholastic philosophy and theology, that from which anything flows in any manner whatsoever. Thus a point is the beginning or principle of a line, a unit is a principle of arithmetic number, and a parent is the beginning or principle of a child. All *causes are principles but all principles are not causes, since a cause is a principle from which something proceeds with dependence in being. According to St. Thomas, principles have two characteristics: everything in the order under consideration is derived from them, and they are underived within the order in question. BIBLIOGRAPHY: ThAq ST 1a, 33.1.

[F. T. RYAN]

PRINKNASH ABBEY, Benedictine abbey near Gloucester, England. It was founded by a group of Anglican Benedictine monks and nuns, who under the leadership of Aelred Carlyle (d. 1956), settled on Caldey Island (1906 and 1913), and converted to Catholicism in 1913. Financial problems followed and they were forced to sell Caldey—now a Trappist abbey—and move to donated property at Prinknash Park.

[M. A. McFADDEN]

PRIOR, title used in monastic orders and in some of the later religious orders, e.g., the Dominicans, usually to designate the person in charge of a *priory, charterhouse, or local community. In an *abbey it is used to designate the second in authority or the person who replaces the abbot in his absence. Although *St. Benedict did not favor this latter office lest it give occasion to rivalry and create factions in the community, it has been almost a constant in Western monasticism since his time. In this latter case, as the Benedictine Rule required, the prior is almost always chosen by the abbot himself after consultation. When it is a matter of designating the second in authority, however, the prior is more often elected by the community, although he is sometimes named by the general chapter (esp. among the Carthusians and the Camaldolese).

[M. B. PENNINGTON]

PRIOR, CLAUSTRAL, the second in authority in an *abbey. He is to be appointed by the abbot himself and not by those who elected the abbot, and he is to remain wholly subjected to the abbot (Rule of St. Benedict 65). In the absence of the abbot he presides over the community and in many monastic congregations has the responsibility of assuming the government of the community upon the death of the abbot until a new abbot can be elected.

[M. B. PENNINGTON]

PRIOR, CONVENTUAL, among Benedictines and Cistercians, the superior of an independent house that does not enjoy the status of an abbey. He is elected either for life or for a defined term of office according to the custom of the congregation. He is a prelate with all the prerogatives of a major superior, but unlike an abbot does not receive a solemn blessing, nor may he use pontificals or confer minor orders. Among the Carthusians and later orders such as the Dominicans, the conventual prior is the superior, elected or appointed, of a monastery of conventual status but subject to higher authority, e.g., that of a provincial or general superior.

PRIOR GENERAL, the supreme moderator or head of some monastic orders and congregations which do not have abbots (e.g., the Camaldolese) and of some of the later mendicant orders (e.g., the Brothers of St. John of God). They are usually elected by the general chapter and are major superiors whose powers are carefully defined by the constitutions of the respective orders or congregations. Their term of office varies with the different congregations. *CONSTITUTIONS, RELIGIOUS.

[M. B. PENNINGTON]

PRIOR MARRIAGE, see IMPEDIMENTS TO MARRIAGE.

PRIOR PROVINCIAL, a title used in contradistinction to claustral or conventual prior. When some of the mendicant orders such as the Brothers of St. John of God or the Carmelites grew to international proportions and divided into provinces, the title of prior was given to the religious who had charge of the houses in the specified region called a province. He usually has the responsibility of visitation and presides at provincial chapters. His rights and duties are defined by the constitutions of his order.

[M. B. PENNINGTON]

PRIORESS, the nun who holds within a monastery or convent the position equivalent to that of a *prior among monks or friars. Like a prior, she may be at the head of an autonomous house and therefore be a major superior (but unlike some priors, a prioress never has lifetime tenure), or she may be the subalternate of an abbess.

[M. B. PENNINGTON]

PRIORY, a name used by most monastic orders, some of the later mendicant orders, and some modern congregations that base themselves on the Rule of St. Benedict, to designate a house that has a *prior or *prioress for its superior. However, the term is not universally employed; e.g., the Carthusians call their houses, even though ruled by a prior, charterhouses, and in other orders, as among the Dominicans, the term "convent" is often used. A priory may be an autonomous house, which, although it enjoys the right to elect its own superior, does not yet have sufficient size or stability to qualify for the status of an *abbey; or it may belong to a monastic order that does not have abbots. In the Benedictine tradition more often than not it is a nonautonomous house, dependent upon an abbey, whose abbot nominates the prior.

PRIORY, ALIEN, a small community of monks of a kind established in England after the Norman conquest, which retained ties with a mother abbey in France and served its interests, esp. economic, in England. Some were completely dependent, the prior being named by the foreign abbot; others elected their own prior but were subject to foreign visitors and paid annual tribute. After a century of harassment by the English kings, they were finally suppressed by Henry V in 1414.

[M. B. PENNINGTON]

PRISCA VERSIO, canonical collection of Roman provenance dating from the second half of the 5th century. Known also as the *Itala* it contains versions of canons from the Councils of Ancyra, Neocaesarea, Gangra, Antioch, Carthage, Chalcedon and Constantinople. Canons from the Councils of Nicaea and Sardica (joined under one heading as Nicene) are also represented in the MSS which best preserve the collection, but there is reason to believe they did not form part of the original. The MSS in question are the Chieti (Cod. Vat. Reg. 1997) and the Justel (Bodleian, Mus. 100–102). Although not an official collection, the *Prisca* is an important witness to canonical development between the *Hispana* and the *Dionysiana* collections. BIBLIOGRAPHY: C. H. Turner, "Chapters in the History of Latin MSS of Canons: The Version Called Prisca," JTS 30:337–346; 31:9–20; A. Van Hove, *Commentarium Lovaniense in Codicem iuris canonici*, 1:497.

[J. E. BIECHLER]

PRISCIAN (fl. late 5th-early 6th cent.), Latin grammarian whose *Institutiones grammaticae* became a standard text (*auctoritas*) in the medieval trivium and therefore had influence on the evolution of medieval philosophy and theology because of the importance of grammar in this development.

PRISCILLA, see AQUILA AND PRISCILLA.

PRISCILLA THE MONTANIST (Prisca; fl. 2d cent.), with Maximilla, prophetess-companion of Montanus in Phrygia (see MONTANISTS). The three were seized with raptures in which they spoke in tongues and professed to be uttering revelations from the Holy Spirit. Tertullian (*Adversus Praxeam* 1) claims that the prophetic gifts were approved by the bp. of Rome; he also quotes P. on the merits of continence (*De exhortatione castitatis* 10). Jerome quotes Apollonius, an enemy of Tertullian as Montanist, to the effect that "Montanus and his mad prophetesses" died of hanging, and that Priscilla and Maximilla were given to worldliness and licentiousness. BIBLIOGRAPHY: Knox Enth 25–49.

[T. C. O'BRIEN]

PRISCILLA, CATACOMB OF, ROME, with that of Domitilla, one of the first early Christian *catacombs from the 1st or early 2d cent., on the Via Salaria Nuova, containing the oldest-known image of the Virgin and Child.

[M. J. DALY]

PRISCILLIAN (*c.*340–386), learned Spanish nobleman after whom *Priscillianists were named. Born in Spain, he was executed for heresy at Trier, the first heretic to receive capital punishment. He joined a lay community of wandering ascetics and preachers who roused the suspicion of the Spanish bps. to the point that the latter banned participation of women with men in religious gatherings. The Council of Saragossa (380) issued decrees against laymen's teaching. Nevertheless P. was elected bp. of Ávila, although unable to take possession of the see because of the opposition of civil authority and his ecclesiastical enemies. As an exile in Italy he was unable to gain the support of Pope St. Damasus I or St. Ambrose. After being reinstated by civil authorities, P. was again deposed by a council at Bordeaux (384–85).

At this point he appealed to the Roman Emperor Maximus at Trier, only to be condemned and executed.

[E. J. DILLON]

PRISCILLIANISTS, a Christian reform group of the 4th and 5th cents. given to asceticism and called Gnostics and Manichaeans by fellow Christians. They flourished on the Atlantic littoral from Portugal to Aquitaine. Priscillian, a rich and eloquent lay noble, c. 375 attracted well-educated people, including women and two bps. to the esoteric movement in Betica, Lusitania, and Galicia. Secret assemblies in out-of-the-way spots; preaching by laymen and women; fasts, abstentions, and contempt of the world beyond Christian custom; unauthorized monastic practices by secular clergy; veiling of virgins before 40 years of age; private handling of the Eucharist; recourse to apocrypha; abuse of the title doctor; communion with excommunicates; and claims to special illumination and prophecy aroused opposition among the bishops. The Council of Saragossa I (380) condemned some Priscillianist practices, if not Priscillian himself; in 382 Emperor Gratian decreed exile for "Manichaeans," as Priscillianists were called, and seized their churches. Priscillian, then bp. of Ávila, moved to Aquitaine and proselytized with success, only to be expelled by Bp. Delphinius of Bordeaux. Failing to get a hearing from either Pope Damasus (a Spaniard) or Ambrose, Priscillian turned to imperial officials, who had the decree annulled. He returned to Spain in triumph. When Emperor Maximus (a Spaniard) replaced Gratian, he recalled the case to Bordeaux (384–385). Priscillian, however, appealed to Maximus, who beheaded him and six followers in Trier for immorality and magic (385).

Priscillian was probably the first Christian to die by the secular arm as a heretic; the decision of the Council of Bordeaux and his own testimony in Trier provided the evidence for his conviction. Martin of Tours, Ambrose, and Pope Siricius were scandalized at the execution, as were some pagans; the reaction in Spain cost Priscillian's enemies their sees as the Priscillianists formed a schismatic Church. Priscillian's relics were returned to Galicia c. 396, and he was venerated as a martyr. There is no sure extant textual basis on which to convict Priscillian of heresy. But the general Christian attitude toward him, the refusal of Damasus and Ambrose to receive him, definitely Manichaean developments in Spain a few years later with the barbarian invasions, and the testimony of Sulpicius Severus, Orosius, Augustine, Jerome, and Pope Leo I indicate that Priscillian was hardly a mirror of orthodox asceticism or the victim of an episcopacy that evidently did need reform. Priscillianism, which was contemporary with the rigorist Gregory of Elvira, was put down at the Council of Toledo I in 400; Emperor Honorius condemned Priscillianists by rescript (408–409); the Council of Braga I (561 or 563) condemned 17 errors attributed to Priscillianism, forbidding the use of any hymns but those of the NT. Priscillianist works also contained Trinitarian doctrines that de-

nied the distinctness of the three divine Persons. BIBLIOGRAPHY: J. N. Hillgarth, NCE 11:790–791, with bibliog.

[E. P. COLBERT]

PRISONERS, ESCAPE OF, see ESCAPE OF PRISONERS.

PRIVACY, from Latin *privatus,* withdrawn from public life, affecting a person or group apart from the general community, not open to common view. In morals privacy implies the right of persons or associations of persons to live without intrusion by state officials, together without interference, and to decide for themselves when, how, and to what extent information about themselves is to be divulged and published. It serves several functions. Without privacy neither individuals nor social groups can be sufficiently free from manipulation or domination by others, and thus sufficiently autonomous for real growth. Neither should be constantly supervised, neither should lack the assurance that their exchanges are privileged and will not be revealed or used without appropriate consent. Moreover, there are human interests too intimate to be made into common property, and their general exposure should be discouraged as a socially dangerous form of exhibitionism. Even worse is an invasive prying into and prurience about the thoughts and feelings of others exemplified in the television interviewing of parents who have just received word of the tragic death of a child. The surveillance of the activities of persons and associations by outside bodies is governed by ethical considerations already indicated and by the State's right to protect itself against subversive conspiracy. These are complemented by the laws upholding constitutional rights, that limit governmental interference and the civil liberties that limit the scope of corporations, unions, and suchlike agencies.

The methods of violating privacy have become highly complex. Technological sophistication makes available many kinds of listening and watching devices, which afford new techniques of physical surveillance. The growth in the physiological and psychological sciences provides a variety of ways of probing thoughts and feelings, conscious and unconscious, thus providing new tools for control. So does the revolution in collecting information and processing data. BIBLIOGRAPHY: A. F. Westin, *Privacy and Freedom* (1967).

[E. F. FALTEISEK]

PRIVATE JUDGMENT, a phrase suggesting that the believer's understanding of God's word is the rule of faith. The phrase has been used by both historians and polemicists to contrast the Protestant and RC positions on the rule of faith: that through the Reformation principle *sola scriptura* the Protestant believes what his own conscience declares the Bible to mean, not, as in the case of the Catholic, what the Church declares the Bible to mean. Thus Protestantism extols private judgment; Catholicism decries it. The contrast is an oversimplification.

For all Christians the Bible expresses God's word, the

content of faith. For Christian theology generally faith is personal, the acceptance and trust in God's word. Faith is first a trusting assent to God himself, and therefore to what his word contains. The essential assent of faith is grace-inspired; the Christian believes only because the Holy Spirit prompts and aids him. And because the assent of faith is Spirit-guided it is to the right things, to the true meaning of God's word (see ThAq ST 2a2ae, 1.3). The true RC understanding of the teaching authority of the Church does not and cannot view the Church as supplanting the personal, Spirit-guided assent of faith. Rather it presupposes that the same Spirit which guarantees the assent of the believer also guides the community of believers as a whole and gives special assistance to the church *magisterium, or teaching office. The Reformation was a protest against the teaching Church, authoritatively declaring and proposing the meaning of God's word. The accepted Protestant understanding of the Reformation protest did not mean an arbitrary, purely human interpretation of the Bible. The presupposition is that the one Spirit inspires all believers together to a common understanding of the word of God, to which each believer responds in a personal decision. The principal Protestant traditions, Lutheran and Reformed, regarded that understanding to be the understanding of the biblical word; the confessions of faith were subordinate rules of faith, as expressions of the true, community understanding of the biblical word. The Anabaptist, Mennonite, and Quaker tradition regarded private judgment to mean the acceptance and understanding of God's word directly experienced; the experience, though consonant with the Bible, was not mediated through the Bible. There have been, throughout Christian history, manifestations of *enthusiasm and *subjectivism, but these are phenomena apart from the main RC and Protestant traditions and from the overdrawn distinction connoted by the phrase private judgment. BIBLIOGRAPHY: R. McAfee Brown, *Spirit of Protestantism* (1965) 8–11.

[T. C. O'BRIEN]

PRIVATE MASS, strictly speaking because of the ecclesial nature of the Eucharistic prayer there is no such thing as a private Mass. However, the term has traditionally been applied to a *Low Mass celebrated out of devotion rather than out of pastoral necessity.

[R. B. ENO]

PRIVATION, the lack (not mere absence, i.e., Negation) of an element that could or should be present in a subject. In scholastic philosophy, it is one of the three first principles of changeable (material) being, matter and form being the other two. Privation and form also constitute two contrary principles in relation to a common subject. In every change, whether it be substantial or accidental, there is a common subject which remains the same before and after the change occurs; the subject is called matter. Thus, at the end of motion or change, the subject which receives a new form did not have that form before the change occurred. If it

already had the form, the subject or matter could not receive the form through motion and consequently no motion would have taken place. The lack of the form to be acquired in a change or motion is privation. Hence, the green apple that is to become red lacks redness before it ripens. In this case, the lack of redness is a privation in the apple. Privation, then is required to explain physical motion, for if there were no initial lack of a form which is to occur as a result of a motion the subject or matter would already possess, at the beginning of the motion, the form which it is to receive at the completion of the motion which is a contradiction. This is why mobile or material being requires a subject and two contraries as principles. In moral theology, sin is interpreted as a privation of a due order which should be present in a human act.

[F. T. RYAN]

PRIVILEGED ALTAR, see ALTAR, PRIVILEGED.

PRIVILEGED COMMUNICATION, confidential information between lawyer and client, physician and patient, or clergyman and penitent (or the equivalent). Since the 16th cent. common law has regarded the communication between a lawyer and his client in a question of the client's rights or obligations as beyond disclosure by the lawyer. It covers both confidential statements to the lawyer and advice to the client by the attorney. The client may waive this privilege, in which event the lawyer could be compelled to reveal what he received in confidence. In the case of physician-patient relationship, common law does not provide privilege but statutes in the U.S. have been widely adopted, rendering the communication between physician and patient privileged, unless the patient consents to the disclosure in judicial proceedings. (This applies also to psychologist or counselor and client.) In England before the Reformation the seal of the confessional was recognized by judges, except where the crime was high treason. After the Reformation disclosures made to a clergyman have usually not been regarded as privileged, though in a few cases the privileged character of such revelations has been recognized. In the U.S. there has been a growing disposition to acknowledge communications between clergymen and penitents as privileged but this has occurred as a matter of specific legislation rather than court interpretation. Public opinion in favor of acknowledging privilege in cases where a penitent consults a priest or minister has brought about legislation in 41 states and in the District of Columbia safeguarding the privilege. A basic provision of such legislation is that the statement made to a clergyman be an admission of wrongdoing, made in confidence, and in a situation where spiritual advice is sought. A further requirement in most states is that the revelation be made in the course of the discipline of the denomination. This is easy to establish in the case of a Catholic in confession but causes some confusion in the case of extraconfessional communications either of Catholics or of members of other religious bodies.

While there is no federal statute on the question of privilege for clergyman-penitent, the Supreme Court has upheld the confidentiality of such communication. The armed forces also provide that in courts-martial such communication is privileged. BIBLIOGRAPHY: V. Allred, ''The Confessor in Court,'' *Jurist* 13 (1953) 2–32.

[J. R. AHERNE]

PRIVILEGIUM FORI, see BENEFIT OF CLERGY.

PRIZEFIGHTING, as a theological topic, differs markedly from many other sports in which there exists a danger of suffering physical injury, in that its rules not only allow but even encourage the deliberate causing of harm to one's opponent by giving extra points for more damaging blows and even awarding victory for knocking the opponent unconscious. In sports in which there is question only of the accidental suffering of damage, the morality of a sport may be judged by application of the principle of the indirect voluntary (*double effect): whether such a risk is moral or not depends on whether there is a reasonable proportion between the risk and the good achieved by participation in the sport.

Prizefighting adds the question: is it in accord with Christian morality intentionally to deliver blows which cause permanent injury to the brain? Moral theologians who have discussed the question in print since publication in recent years of medical studies showing the permanent brain damage caused by blows to the head are unanimous in judging it immoral. The magisterium of the Church has not pronounced on the question. If it is immoral to deliver such blows intentionally for mere sport, entertainment, or money, it is also immoral deliberately to encourage or approve such actions.

Further objections arise from the often shady business dealings associated with prizefighting as well as the effect of arousing a sort of blood lust in the spectators. This latter it shares with professional wrestling, cock-fighting, and bull-fighting. Amateur boxing avoids some of these objections but still poses the same basic questions. BIBLIOGRAPHY: G. C. Bernard, *Morality of Prizefighting* (1952); J. J. Farraher, ''Notes on Moral Theology,'' ThSt 24 (1963) 64–69; R. J. McCormick, ''Is Professional Boxing Immoral?'' *Sports Illustrated* 17 (Nov. 5, 1962) 71–82; idem, NCE 11:812–13.

[J. J. FARRAHER]

PRO ARMENIS DECREE, the formula of reunion with Rome, *Exsultate Deo,* 22 Nov. 1439, for the American patriarchate, subscribed by its two representatives at the Council of *Florence. The section on the sacraments, largely incorporating the *De articulis fidei et ecclesiae sacramentis* of St. Thomas Aquinas, has an importance in itself as a church document on their number and nature (D 1310–28). Whether it has dogmatic standing is disputed, esp. with regard to the teaching that the ''handing down of the in-

struments,'' e.g., the chalice, belongs to the essence of the sacrament of holy orders (D 1326); that was not part of the rite prior to the 9th cent. The constitution of Pius XII, *Sacramentum ordinis,* Nov. 30, 1947, declared that the laying on of hands alone made up the matter of the sacrament.

[T. C. O'BRIEN]

PRO CIVITATE CHRISTIANA, canonically approved lay organization founded in Assisi, Italy, in 1939 by Fr. Giovanni Rossi, for the purpose of making Jesus Christ known, esp. in influential circles of nonbelievers. In 1959 it was approved as a primary association by the Holy See. Its members are men and women who renounce families and professions and abstain from matrimony in order totally to dedicate themselves to the apostolate. Prerequisites for membership are completion of university studies and a 3-year course of theology. The work of the association is conducted through the press, art, conferences, and many other cultural forms. Periodically, they give courses in Christian studies and hold art exhibits at *Cittadella cristiana* (Christian Citadel), the headquarters at Assisi. Among its members are a number of priests who give spiritual assistance, particularly when, at the request of the bps., missions are preached in cities throughout Italy. Friends and associates called ''radials'' conduct meetings in local *Domus Christianae* throughout Italy, and in this way assist in the apostolic effort of the members. Of special interest is *Osservatorio cristiano,* a documentary and study center that collects Christological literature, thought, art, cinema, and music from all eras and nations. Along with books and records, the association publishes *Rocca,* a biweekly review. BIBLIOGRAPHY: G. Rossi, ''For a Christian Civilization in Art,'' *Liturgical Arts* 30.1 (1961) 21–22; J. Karlin, ''Contemporary Art and the Church in Italy,'' *ibid.* 26–38.

[R. A. TODD]

PRO ECCLESIA ET PONTIFICE, see PAPAL MEDALS.

PRO JUÁREZ, MIGUEL (1891–1927), Mexican Jesuit of saintly life. P. became a Jesuit in 1911, studied in Mexico, California, and Spain, and took advanced social studies in Belgium. Back in Mexico in 1926, he served the Catholics of Mexico City as best he could at a time when public worship was suspended because of the persecution under President Calles. He was arrested in 1927 and executed with his brother Humberto on the fabricated charge of complicity in a plot against the government. The news of the event aroused a storm of protest throughout the world. The cause for his beatification was introduced in 1952 and the decree on the validity of the acts of the process was issued in 1961. BIBLIOGRAPHY: F. Royer, *Padre Pro* (1954).

[P. DAMBORIENA]

PROBABILIORISM, the moral system opposed to *probabilism and veering towards *tutiorism; it holds that, in conscientious doubt about the morality of a particular action, it is lawful to favor liberty only when that opinion is more likely (more probable) than the opinion favoring the existence or application of law. It was held as a *reflex principle, esp. by many Dominicans in the post-Tridentine period of *moral theology, in opposition to general Jesuit espousal of probabilism. While probabilorism received some official approval, and indeed had some intrinsic merit opposed to certain excesses of probabilism, it can only be tangentially Thomistic, since it does not give the important role St. Thomas himself accorded to *prudence. Indeed, the context of the question is legalist (see LEGALISM), and the response slavish with its obvious lack of personal spontaneity, creativity, and originality in living Christian life. Even though it continued to be defended after St. Alphonsus' pastoral abandonment of it in favor of *equiprobabilism, contemporary consensus, refusing to place such a question, understands the principle in a different sense and restricts its application. BIBLIOGRAPHY: D. Prümmer, *Handbook of Moral Theology* (1957) no. 152, p. 65; Davis MorPastTh 1.

[C. WILLIAMS]

PROBABILISM, the moral system opposed to *probabiliorism by inclining in favor of freedom; it holds that in conscientious doubt about the morality of a particular action, one may lawfully follow a likely (probable) opinion about the existence or application of law. It is based on the principle that a dubious law does not bind, and as a common-sense intuition has a long history. Its precise formulation however was the work of Dominican Bartolomé de *Medina in 1577: "if an opinion is probable, it is permissible to follow it, even if the opposite opinion is more probable." But it was the Jesuits who, despite some initial opposition, came to be identified with the system, and at times to be severely castigated for its use in the interests of *laxism. Probabilism is important to understand for it is the one moral system to which all the others are in some way related, and because it ultimately triumphed, even though its meaning and use were somewhat modified. Still, a real grasp of the meaning of this reflex principle is very difficult apart from its historical context. While something similar to probabilism was long used in the application of positive law, both civil and ecclesiastical, its use in moral theology developed at the end of the 16th cent. when the principal emphasis of that discipline fell on the relation of law to the freedom of conscience. Thus a predominantly legal interest was transferred, albeit unwittingly, to the level of moral involvement. A great deal of the probability was extrinsic, i.e., based on the authority, say, of five or six contemporary theologians or one outstanding doctor such as St. Thomas Aquinas and later St. Alphonsus. At times the intrinsic probability, that founded on reasons taken from the nature of the case, was slighted as was the important place of personal responsibility in prudence. Moreover, the degrees of probability—certainly so, doubtfully so, or even only

slightly so—required an assessment of a skilled professional to determine with mathematical exactness all the niceties. In contest with other moral systems such as probabiliorism and *equiprobabilism, and with pendulum swings from Jansenist rigorism to libertine laxism, probabilism eventually emerged in quite chastened form, not only modified in itself, but with several important restrictions, notably that it should not be used where there was a question of the validity of a sacrament or where there was a question of a certainly existing obligation towards a neighbor's rights or one's own ultimate salvation. The rather strong antipathy towards law in contemporary moral-study and developing personalism make probabilism and indeed *casuistry seem outmoded but both have perennial value despite their past abuses. BIBLIOGRAPHY: Davis MorPastTh 1; T. Deman, DTC 13:417–619.

[C. WILLIAMS]

PROBABILITY, in moral theology, the quality of that kind of moral knowledge classified as *opinion. As in all forms of intellectual judgment the perfect kind of moral judgment is an assent or adherence to one alternative as true, to the reasonably firm exclusion of its opposite. The quality such a judgment has is moral *certitude, the highest degree of certainty possible and sufficient for moral choice. The other extreme is a suspension of judgment in the face of alternatives (see DOUBT), because no decisive basis for adherence to either side is seen. Assent to one alternative as true, without clear exclusion of the opposite possibility is opinion; probability is the quality of such a judgment. Doubt can never be the basis of right moral choice, because this means a positive evaluation and intention of the good chosen. But probability can be such a basis; because moral issues are so variable, not even moral certitude can always be achieved. Probability may be intrinsic, based, that is, on evaluation of the issue at hand in terms of general moral principles. The value of extrinsic probability is more controverted; it derives from and is based on the opinions of received moral authorities. *MORALITY, SYSTEMS OF: *PROBABILISM.

[T. C. O'BRIEN]

PROBABLE, a term used in theology to qualify a doctrine based on evidence strong enough to establish presumption but not full proof of validity. The object of probable teaching may be any aspect of the Christian religion that concerns faith or morals.

The evidence for probability may be either intrinsic to the doctrine or drawn from ecclesiastical (or theological) authority. When the evidence is intrinsic, it may arise from interpretation of known revealed truth. More often it depends on the premises of a theological system. Thus the probability of *scientia media* in Molinism and of physical predetermination in Bañezianism is tied in with the respective systematic theories. Basing probability on the extrinsic evidence of authority is valid provided certain norms are observed: the authority must have competence in the matter and deal with the precise question at issue. It is also understood, of course, that the Church's magisterium has not already resolved the matter by declarative judgment.

Probable doctrines are sometimes referred to as "open questions" in speculative theology. They are most common in the many explanatory theories dealing with the refinements of Christian belief, where "faith seeks understanding." BIBLIOGRAPHY: E. J. Fortman, NCE 10:523–524.

[J. A. HARDON]

PROBATIONER, a person awaiting ecclesiastical acceptance. For a long time Methodists, following John *Wesley, required a period of probation for a person to prove himself worthy of membership in a *society. Many Methodist bodies refer commonly to one who has been ordained a deacon and plans to become a fully ordained minister as a probationer. In the Church of Scotland, and until modern times among Presbyterians in the U.S., the term was used as a synonym for a candidate for the ministry. Some RC religious communities apply the term to postulants or novices.

[N. H. MARING]

PROBST, FERDINAND (1816–99), German historian of the liturgy. He was professor at the Univ. of Breslau from 1864, rector, 1889–90, and dean of the cathedral from 1896. His works, concentrating on liturgical development during the early centuries, are rich in research, but P.'s interpretations of the material are regarded as frequently fanciful. Among his publications are: *Liturgie der drei ersten christlichen Jahrhunderte* (1870); *Sakramente . . . in den drei ersten christlichen Jahrhunderten* (1873); *Kirchliche Disciplinen in den drei ersten christlichen Jahrhunderten* (1873); *Die abendländische Messe vom V. bis zum VIII. Jahrhundert* (1896).

[T. C. O'BRIEN]

PRO-CATHEDRAL, a church used by a bishop as a cathedral provisorily, until an edifice in keeping with cathedral rank can be built.

PROCESS THEOLOGY, a contemporary approach to a systematic understanding of Christian revelation based on a positive evaluation of the categories of becoming (process) and relation. Process theology has emerged from the insights of several 20th-cent. philosophers: William James, John Dewey, Henri Bergson, and esp. Alfred North Whitehead and his disciple Charles Hartshorne. In theology, its main protagonists have been John Cobb, Shubert Ogden, Daniel Day Williams, W. Norman Pittenger and, in some ways, Pierre Teilhard de Chardin. Because of its emphasis on the dynamic nature of reality, process theology has been readily compatible with contemporary scientific views, esp. within the U. S. and England where its influence continues to be extensive. The central conviction of process thought is that scientific insistence on evolution,

on the universe as an energy-event which is constantly coming to be through interaction with other limited realities, must be taken into full account. Existence should not be conceived as composed of things but of events, not inert substances but dynamic processes. Whitehead points out, however, that we come to this recognition of change as basic not by an "objective" recognition of the external world, but by a "reformed subjectivist principle," i.e., that we can talk about any reality only by generalizing elements disclosed in the personal experience of human beings. Basically, this being-of-the-self that is the pattern of reality is relatedness: my coming to be through interaction with my body, my freedom, and the interlocked, temporal community of other realities-in-process. The subjectivist principle shows me that the positive perfections of existence are becoming (change or process) and mutual interaction (that through and on account of which change takes place). These perfections are seen as opposed to the Aristotelian/Thomistic system, which places positive value on being and aseity.

This radical switch from classical philosophical categories has its most significant repercussions in the theological doctrines of God and Christ. If the positive perfections of existence are seen as becoming and relation, then Absolute Existence or God must also be involved in process and mutuality. In contrast to classical theism, which enshrines a static, fully realized God who is thereby incapable of being related to the world in any way that would truly affect him, process theology insists upon a God who is the unique and perfect instance of creative becoming, eminently social and temporal. God is related to everything through an immediate sympathetic participation (panentheism). But although God is change, He is not pure change. In one respect He is unchanging, viz., insofar as he always fully knows and loves the world (God's primordial nature or pole). But precisely because this relatedness is the unchanging reality of God's abstract identity, the content of God's experience (his consequent nature) is itself changing and sensitive to temporal affairs. Thus God's perfection entails not his completeness but the immeasurable fullness of his love. Process theologians maintain that the classical two natures/one person doctrine of God's relationship to Jesus is unworkable insofar as it inevitably leads to a loss of humanity. They base their Christology on a new manner of expressing how God may be present to limited realities. Just as one human event can be present and effectively related to another event without losing its own identity, so God is related and effectively present to human beings in a way that does not displace their "moment of immediacy," or actual existence. But this relationship need not be equally effective or real in all persons. There can be a uniquely effective prehension of God in Jesus, which would be a fulfillment of God's loving relationship to human beings and also a completely harmonious realization of Jesus' humanity in and through this action of God. BIBLIOGRAPHY: C. Hartshorne, *Natural Theology for Our Time* (1967); S. Ogden, *Reality of God* (1966); J. Cobb, *God and the World* (1969); *Process Philosophy and Christian Thought* (ed. D. Brown et al., 1971); W. N. Pittenger, *Christology Reconsidered* (1970).

[T. M. McFADDEN]

PROCESSION OF THE HOLY SPIRIT, see FILIOQUE.

PROCESSIONS, RELIGIOUS, ritual actions in which people go solemnly from one place to another. Such ceremonies were fairly common in pagan religions and have a resemblance to the more secular parade; in fact their universality gives rise to a suspicion that there is something natural in them as more or less conscious community expressions of the *pilgrimage of life. The Christian Church adopted them by purifying them, insofar as possible, from licentiousness and other improprieties and changing their significance for other purposes. The Christian procession uses prayers and hymns and the accompaniment of the clergy to remind the people that prayer itself is "walking with God." The procession is indeed a striking image of the people of God on the pilgrimage of life. Some processions recall particular events such as the Passover, the deliverance from Egypt with Yahweh's accompanying presence in the cloud by day and the pillar of fire by night. More prominent in the Christian consciousness is the NT Passover, the Palm Sunday triumph and the *Way of the Cross. According to RC church law (CIC cc. 1290–1295) some liturgical processions are classified as ordinary, i.e., they take place at specified times of the year such as anniversaries of events; others are extraordinary and are held for certain specific occasions or needs. Some processions originally extraordinary, e.g., the rogation procession, became ordinary for regularly recurrent needs such as the harvest. Still other processions are functional, e.g., funeral and Offertory processions, or simply the entrance and recession of the clergy and faithful at Mass. BIBLIOGRAPHY: B. Mullahy, NCE 11:819–820.

[P. F. MULHERN]

PROCESSIONS, TRINITARIAN, the immanent operations of the *Trinity which give rise to the distinction of persons in God. These internal processions (*ad intra*) are distinguishable from the creative activity of God (processions *ad extra*) whereby all things came to be. This concept of the divine processions is based upon the scriptural testimony of the three distinct persons in God and, more specifically, upon Jn 8.42 for the procession of the Son from the Father, "For I [Jesus] proceeded and came forth from God," and upon Jn 15.26 for the procession of the Spirit from both Father and Son, "When the Counselor comes, whom I [Jesus] shall send to you from the Father, the Spirit of Truth who proceeds from the Father, he will bear witness to me." The immanent procession of the Son from the Father was constantly defended in Christian tradition by all who acknowledged the Son's divinity, but was denied by the *Sabellianists who did not acknowledge the Son or Spirit as persons distinct from the Father, and by the Arians who thought the Word to be a creature. The procession of the Spirit from the Father and the Son was the object of a prolonged dispute among Western and Eastern theologians (see FILIOQUE). The Eastern Fathers preferred to say that the Spirit proceeded from the Father through the Son, thus intending to preserve the doctrine that the Father is the ultimate source of the Godhead; the Western Church inserted the *filioque* into the Nicaean Creed to express the double procession of the Spirit. Contemporary theology continues to employ the analogy of intellectual and volitional emanations to explain the processions, reasoning that the intrinsic activities of God must be spiritual; that the Father, in an eternal and perfect act of self-understanding, speaks forth the Word as the sublime expression of himself; and that the Father and Son, in an act of mutual love, breathe forth the Spirit who is that love substantiated. BIBLIOGRAPHY: B. Lonergan, *Conceptio analogica divinarum personarum* (1959); L. J. McGovern, NCE 11:821–823.

[T. M. McFADDEN]

PROCLAMATION (West Syrian, *kōrûzûṯō*; East Syrian, *kārôzûṯā*; Armenian, *qaroz*), a series of short petitions, or, at times, laudatory declarations, formulated as invitations to prayer and sung traditionally by the deacon, to each of which the congregation responds, usually with "Lord have mercy."

[A. CODY]

PROCLUS, ST. (d. 446), theologian, bp. of Cyzicus, patriarch of Constantinople, 434–446. When first named bp., he was unable to take possession of his see (426) because of popular opposition. During the Christmas season of 428 he delivered a homily on the Theotokos in the presence of the then patriarch Nestorius. This may have triggered the Nestorian crisis. The Emperor Theodosius II was instrumental in having him replace Maximianus as patriarch (434), only 3 years after the latter had replaced the deposed Nestorius. P. intervened in Armenian disputes concerning the teaching of Theodore of Mopsuestia. He may be the one who introduced the Trisagion into the liturgy. Of his 35 homilies preserved, many reflect the contemporary bias against Jewish beliefs and morals. An expression in one of his letters about the Passion of Christ became the issue in the 6th cent. *Theopaschite controversy.

[E. J. DILLON]

PROCLUS (*c.*411–485), Neoplatonic philosopher, the greatest and most influential of the later Neoplatonists. He was scholarch of the Platonic Academy at Athens for many years. He combined a wide knowledge of Plato and Aristotle and of his Neoplatonic predecessors, and in particular of Plotinus, Porphyry, and Iamblichus, with an equal knowledge of, and belief in, all forms of theurgy and magical practices. He maintained that the primary One is the original principle of the whole principle of development, and that development itself has a triadic character. After the primary One and before the Intelligibles he places the Units (*henades*), which he regards as divinities, and between the Intelligible and the Intellectual he introduces the Intelligible-Intellectual. Soul occupies a sphere below that of *nous,* and the sphere of soul is subdivided into three sub-spheres, divine souls, "demonic" souls, and *psychai* (human souls). The Greek gods appear in the sphere of divine souls, and gods and "demons" are assigned an hierarchical order in terms of their functions. The soul of man possesses an ethical element composed of light, and is imperishable. With the eyes of the ethereal element it can perceive theophanies, and it can ascend through different stages of virtue to ecstatic union with the primary One. There are three stages in the soul's ascent: Eros, Truth, and Faith. Faith is defined as the mystical silence before the Incomprehensible and Ineffable. Among his works, his *Elements of Theology* was esp. important and influential. In the elaborate system of Proclus the philosophical and the religious are treated side by side in harmony, but it is the religious interest that dominates his thought. BIBLIOGRAPHY: P. Merlan, LexAW 2441–42; Copleston 1:478–481; CHGMP 302–314; Ueberweg 1:621–624 and 625–631.

[M. R. P. MCGUIRE]

PROCOPIUS OF CAESAREA (*c.*490–*c.*562), Byzantine historian whose anecdotal wit and realism rank him in the same class with Herodotus, Thucydides, and Polybius among Greek historians. Born in Caesarea in Palestine, he became associated with the Emperor Justinian's general, Belisarius, as the latter's legal adviser and private secretary. He accompanied Belisarius in various campaigns in Persia, North Africa, and Italy. He wrote three important works: one dealing with the wars of Justinian and the general history of his reign; a second (published posthumously) detailing, and likely exaggerating, the scandalous private lives of both Justinian and his Empress, Theodosia, and of Belisarius and his wife, Antonina; a third in praise of Justinian's accomplishments in building construction. An English translation of P.'s works by H. B. Dewing is included in the Loeb Classical Library.

[E. J. DILLON]

PROCOPIUS OF GAZA (*c.*475–*c.*528), Bible commentator. P. belonged to a leading school of Christian rhetoric at Gaza, but little of his rhetorical writings survives. He is more noted for his commentary on the Octateuch and other OT books. These commentaries form a continuous explanation of the biblical text by indicating any exegetical opinion common to the early Church Fathers or, where there is a variety of interpretations, presenting each of them separately. The corpus of works attributed to P. is contained in PG 87:19–2842.

[T. M. MCFADDEN]

PROCREATION, one of the *goods of marriage, the begetting and rearing of children. The term, however, has a precise connotation. Creation is an act proper to God alone (ThAq ST 1a, 45.5). In the case of the human being theology speaks of the creation and of the *infusion of the human soul; because the soul is spiritual, it cannot be the effect of the physical process of conception (*ibid.* 118.2). But the term of that process is the whole person, even as it is of God's creative causality. God causes the soul to exist in causing the person to exist. In subordination to divine causality, the act of begetting is dispositive, preparatory to the divine act of infusing the soul. The parents are thus procreators, participating in the divine creative causality.

[T. C. O'BRIEN]

PROCTOR, a contracted form of the Latin *procurator,* the title of an official in some universities. In modern times at Oxford and Cambridge the proctor has certain duties in connection with meetings, boards, examinations, the conferment of degrees, and the maintenance of discipline among the students. In the C of E the term is applied to elected representatives of the clergy in the lower house of convocations.

[M. B. MURPHY]

PRODICUS OF CEOS (fl. 2d half of 5th cent. B.C.), one of the most famous of the ancient Sophists. He may have been a pupil of Protagoras and he is mentioned often by Xenophon and Plato. The latter considered his work on *Synonyms* as of special importance. His *On Nature* included both cosmology and anthropology and his *Hours* seems to have had an ethical content. His famous myth on the choice of Hercules apparently comes from the latter work. It was often quoted, and as late as the 4th cent. A.D. St. Basil makes apt use of it in his *Address to Young Men on the Study of Greek Literature.* In the field of religion, he taught that primitive mankind honored the necessities of life— water, fire, cereals, and wine—as gods. BIBLIOGRAPHY: OCD 733; LexAW 2439–40; Copleston 1:91–92; M. Untersteiner, *Sophists* (tr. K. Freeman, 1954) 209–227.

[M. R. P. MCGUIRE]

PRODIGALITY, from the Lat. *prodigus* (wasteful), the fault of being recklessly extravagant or spendthrift, and precisely against the virtue allied to justice called liberality, the free-giving generosity that it caricatures by its excessiveness. The dead opposite of stinginess or meanness (*avaritia*), it is, if foolish, not so ignoble as its countertype, for at least it gives and is more easily curable by discipline, and, Aristotle adds, by old age and poverty. Yet it often is associated with dishonesty or unscrupulosity in acquiring the means with which to be lavish. BIBLIOGRAPHY: Aristotle, *Nicomachean Ethics,* 4.1; ThAq ST 2a2ae, 119 (esp. in ed. Lat-Eng v. 41, ed. T. C. O'Brien, 1970).

[T. GILBY]

PROFANATION, from Lat. *profanus*, literally "outside the temple," the action, a subspecies of *sacrilege, of violating sacred things either by turning them without just cause to common or vulgar use, or by desecrating them by sinful use. In both cases there is some sort of degradation, but whereas the latter is always wrong and a defilement, e.g., shooting hostages in the village church, burlesquing in the vestments, or robbing the offertory, the former is to be judged according to the laws and customary and enlightened notions of propriety. Turning a church into a casualty station is clearly right, so also melting down the plate to relieve the needy. So-called secular performances are now accepted: a stately gavotte might be tolerable, more vulgar performances however, probably not. Civil law often supports church law in respecting sacred places and things, e.g., cemeteries, and punishes their violation: this last may call for reconsecration (cf. CIC cc. 1154, 1173). The classical protest against profanation is Our Lord's driving the traffickers out of the Temple. BIBLIOGRAPHY: ThAq ST 2a2ae, 99.3 (esp. in ed. Lat-Eng, v. 40, ed. T. A. O'Meara).

[T. GILBY]

PROFANITY, as understood here, the irreverent use of the names of God, or irreverent reference to holy persons or to things held in esteem because of their relationship to God. From the Latin *pro* and *fanum*, it designates in its broadest sense what is before (i.e., outside) the temple or holy place; in other words, something nonholy (as when one distinguishes between sacred and profane music), or something directly unholy, as in the case of profane speech. If an expression is not wanting in due reverence to what is holy, either because its meaning is quite unconnected with what is holy, or because popular usage has obliterated such a connection, it cannot properly be termed profane, though its use may be unconventional or in bad taste.

Profanity is also to be distinguished from blasphemy. Blasphemy is any word, sign, or gesture that is insulting to the goodness of God. The same expression may be either profane or blasphemous, depending upon the intention of the speaker and the presence or absence of the note of contempt or insult. Although blasphemy is usually considered gravely sinful, profanity rarely is so. Whatever moral fault may lie in it consists simply in showing less than due reverence to holy things and the act, unmalicious in intent, of itself rarely involves more than minor moral disorder, although this may be aggravated in some cases by the scandal or offense it gives to others. Some use of profanity in literature in drama may be fully justified. BIBLIOGRAPHY: P. K. Meagher, NCE 11.828; B. Häring, *Law of Christ* 1:206–207.

[C. NEELY]

PROFESSION, RELIGIOUS, the act by which one publicly embraces the religious state, vowing poverty, chastity, and obedience. In the primitive Church, there were virgins who were recognized as consecrated to the service of God. Not until the time of St. Pachomius, however, was there a ceremony of profession. With him, entry to the monastery was recognized as the expression of an intention to persevere in the service of God. St. Benedict was the first to introduce the more formal element of a written promise embodying a commitment to seek God in the monastery for a lifetime. The actual ceremony of profession varies from one community to another, and many ceremonies were laden with symbols indicating sacrifice, as the carrying of a cross, the wearing of a crown, etc.

Vatican Council II in its *Constitution on the Sacred Liturgy* (80) called for a drawing up of a rite for religious profession in order to achieve greater unity, sobriety, and dignity, and it expressed the desire that religious profession should be made during Mass. The Latin text of the revised rite was issued in 1970; the final English text in 1974. BIBLIOGRAPHY: C. Peifer, *Monastic Spirituality* (1966).

[P. F. MULHERN]

PROFESSION OF FAITH, see FAITH, PROFESSION OF.

PROFIT. In accounting, it is the difference between total revenue and explicit costs, these being payments to suppliers who are not owners of the firm. In economics, it is the difference between income and both explicit and implicit costs, i.e., labor, material, rents, and all expenses together with the interest on the capital employed. This is also the concept of pure profit. In a free-enterprise system, profit functions as an incentive for the businessman to organize the factors of production and also serves to allocate resources among various lines of production. The morality of the profit motive is indifferent in itself, i.e., its end or purpose determines whether it is morally good or not. The amount of profit justly realized is measurable by the moral standards for the just price (see BUYING AND SELLING).

[F. T. RYAN]

PROFIT SHARING, an agreement, freely entered into, by which the employee in a business enterprise receives, in addition to wages, a share, fixed in advance, of the profits of the enterprise, profits being understood as the net balance of financial gain realized by the business over a given period of time. Today three types of profit-sharing plans are in use: (1) the cash or current payment plan that provides for payment in cash to the employee of his share, usually on an annual basis; (2) the deferred plan that provides for payment of the share into an employee trust which is invested and held for distribution to the employee at some later date (e.g., death, severance, or retirement); (3) the combination plan that blends elements of both other types, permitting part of the share to be paid in cash and part deferred until some later date.

In economics profit sharing has been advocated as a solution to the dilemma raised by the theory of the subsistence wage, as a method of increasing productivity, and as a means of improving labor-management relations. Some sociologists see in it a superior method of organizing industrial groups to achieve high standards of performance through cooperation. Social psychologists have favored it as a means of attaining a high level of ego involvement. Approval and encouragement of profit sharing has been expressed in the constitutions and laws of various countries, esp. in Latin America. In the Soviet Union, sharing profits with employees is incorporated in the "new economics" (Libermanism).

Anthropological studies reveal a widespread use of sharing systems among primitive peoples as well as the association of such systems with their religious concepts. In Judaism, systems of sharing have been advocated from early history to modern times. The first profit-sharing group in the U.S., formed in 1890, was organized largely by Protestant clergymen and educators in the eastern United States. Beginning with Leo XIII, the popes have issued a series of social encyclicals, each of which has contained some mention of the urgency of incorporating systems of sharing into any modern economy. BIBLIOGRAPHY: J. J. Jehring, NCE 11:832–833; B. L. Metzger, *Profit Sharing in Perspective* (1964).

[J. J. JEHRING]

PROJECTION, a mental phenomenon by which a person attributes his own undesirable impulses, wishes, and attitudes to other people. It is common for people to believe that other people think and feel as they themselves do; moreover, when people are accused, esp. children, it is common to blame someone else for the fault. In psychoanalysis it has been discovered that in cases of severe mental stress, people unconsciously attribute great parts of their own hostility, meanness, sexual impulses, etc., to others, to the point of delusion, as in paranoia. Moralists, spiritual directors, counsellors, etc., must consider projection insofar as it distorts self-knowledge and relations with others.

[M. E. STOCK]

PROKOPOVICH, FEOFAN (1681–1736), Russian churchman and theologian. He studied at the Academy of Kiev, became a Roman Catholic, and a Basilian monk. After studies in Rome he returned to Kiev and to Orthodoxy, was professor at the academy from 1704, rector 1711–16; became bp. of Pskov (1720), then abp. of Novgorod (1785). As collaborator with Peter the Great's suppression of the patriarchate of Moscow and formation of the Holy Synod in Russia, P. was the theoretician of the complete subjection to the tsar that thereafter marked the life of the Russian Church. P. also Protestantized Russian theology, in reaction against the RC scholasticism dominant since Peter *Mogila. Through his own and his disciples' writings, and through the seminary he founded at St. Petersburg on the model of Halle, P. injected into Russian theology Lutheran ideas on the Church, Scripture, and jus-

tification. His own writings, written in Latin, were based on Lutheran theologians, esp. J. *Gerhard. P. was the first Russian theologian to reject the deuterocanonical books of the Bible as found in the Septuagint. The Prokopovian trend dominated Russian theology until 1836, when a return to Orthodox traditions was inaugurated by Count N. A. Protasov (1798–1855), procurator of the Holy Synod.

[T. C. O'BRIEN]

PRO-LIFE MOVEMENT IN THE U.S., THE. As an organized movement, Pro-Life groups are a phenomenon that appeared slowly in the early 1970s, growing as multiple, scattered small groups until the stimulus of the U.S. Supreme Court decisions on abortion of January 22, 1973. Subsequently, rapid, progressive, and increasingly effective organizational growth and activity took place throughout the United States. In 1970, there were fewer than 50 groups; by 1973 there were 300; by 1976, more than 1500. In attempting to list the different groups and speak briefly of their composition and activity, one is aware that often any individual pro-life activist would belong to several groups. For example, one person would most likely belong to the local Right to Life group, but perhaps also to one associated with a Church, or with his professional status, while possibly also contributing to yet another national or local group. To understand the groups, however, we have to list them in general categories.

Broad Based Citizen's Action Groups. Larger by many multiples than all other groups combined, these are usually called *Right to Life,* although names vary in different states, e.g., Tennessee Volunteers for Life. By the mid-1970s, almost every city or area in the nation had a Right to Life group. These typically have broad general membership of citizens cutting across all lines of age, religious denomination, race, profession, etc. In most large cities, the group typically consists of a number of chapters, will have a representative board of directors, be incorporated, operate under a constitution, publish a newsletter, etc. In most states, such groups affiliate as members of their state Right to Life society. The State Right to Life society will typically have a board of directors elected to represent the various state regions as well as at-large members; it will be an incorporated activist group responding to the needs of the various state chapters, and often will hold an annual state Right to Life convention. This representative organization will also elect a delegate to represent it on the board of the National Right to Life Committee (NRLC). The NRLC thus has a national board of over 50 delegates. It also holds a national convention, has regular meetings, and operates as a central national organization hopefully coordinating a national pro-life effort. In the first years of its existence (organized June 1973), this national office had serious growing pains. Its attempt to coordinate the efforts of all the states was hampered by the problems of a new national organization, i.e., lack of coordinated leadership, personality conflicts, serious financial difficulties, etc. Slowly, however, if not because of it and perhaps even at times in spite of it, the state and city units of the Right to Life movement continued to grow apace in organization, in size, in strength, and in educational and political sophistication; e.g., in the spring of 1976, there were 52 city and regional Right to Life groups making up Michigan Citizens for Life and 64 such groups making up the Ohio Right to Life Society. It would seem that time alone, plus the universally felt need, will bring to this national office the hoped-for expertise needed by the movement. One of its greatest national contributions has been the excellent monthly newspaper, the *National Right to Life News*.

Religious Affiliated Groups. The grandfather of these was the original National Right to Life Committee set up in the late 1960s and a de facto part of the American Bishops Conference. When it became apparent that the movement needed to have a major citizens action group totally divorced from any religious affiliation, this name was adopted by the newly formed NRLC above. The NCCB continued to maintain an office, the Committee for Population and Pro-Life Activities, to coordinate the pro-life activities of the Catholic dioceses of the United States.

The National Committee for a Human Life Amendment was also created by the Catholic bps., funded and specifically delegated to work toward obtaining a Human Life Amendment to the U. S. Constitution. As contrasted with the pastoral and educative activity of the group within the NCCB, this committee was chartered specifically as a lobbying organization to obtain the amendment.

During the years 1974–75, a major group of fundamentalist Protestant church people came together and founded the *Christian Action Council*. This broad-based, pro-life group included among its sponsors Dr. H. Preuss, President of Missouri Synod Lutheran Church; Ruth Graham Bell, wife of Rev. Billy Graham; Rev. Robert Holbrook, President of Baptists for Life; Rev. Harold Brown, editor of *Christianity Today;* and a lengthy list of other prestigious sponsors. Its stated purpose for existence is the education of Christian groups to the value of human life and its need for protection by law.

Among the sectarian pro-life groups, probably the most effective has been Baptists for Life, which has attempted to galvanize the entire Baptist community for the pro-life cause. Episcopalians for Human Life is one more example of an increasing number of other denominational groups of varying sizes with similar purposes.

Americans against Abortion, a Christian fundamentalist group in Tulsa affiliated with Rev. Billy James Hargis, for a time conducted a very extensive mailing campaign against abortion while at the same time appealing for funds to continue the campaign. It also prepared and showed on TV and radio across the nation certain pro-life movies and programs.

National Youth Group. While most groups cut across all age differences in their membership, it is important to note a vigorously growing group, the National Youth Pro-Life Coalition. This group limits its membership to young people. It seeks to bring together youth into a single pro-life group nationally. In certain areas, it has stimulated the growth of large and effective youth groups. In other areas, such movements do not yet exist.

Other National Groups. No other groups have the broad based membership typical of the Right to Life groups. They are many and varied, however. Probably the one with the broadest support is the Coalition for Human Life based in Export, Pennsylvania. This group has concentrated more than others on the population issues and has been most effective as a watchdog in Congress. Supported by donations nationally, it has a limited nuclear leadership and membership but has exercised an influence far beyond this small number of people.

The Ad Hoc Committee in Defense of Life consists of a very small group of people but again has had an influence far beyond its numbers. As publisher of the excellent *Life Letters* and of the scholarly, quarterly journal *Human Life Review,* this group has served to help coordinate the political activity of the entire pro-life movement. It has no national membership.

The Committee of Ten Million, actually a single person in California, has also operated independently. It has produced certain pro-life educational materials including reprinting *The First Days of Life* by G. Flanagan and has mailed them to very large numbers of people nationally, particularly within the Catholic community.

American Citizens Concerned for Life, organized in the fall of 1974 by a small group of people who had left the National Right to Life Committee, has tried to obtain membership nationally with limited success. It has prepared a number of useful pro-life materials and is particularly known for its success in sponsoring the National Prayer Breakfast for Life preceding the Washington Marches on January 22.

The Washington March Committee is an organization created specifically to sponsor and coordinate the annual major March for Life in Washington, commemorating the U. S. Supreme Court decision, every January 22. It invites to this march all pro-life people in the United States.

Another similar organization is the annually created National Right to Life Convention Committee, whose sole purpose is the creation, sponsoring, and carrying out of the one major pro-life convention held in the U. S. annually.

Professional Groups. As might be expected in a slowly burgeoning national movement, individual professional groups have also been founded and find themselves growing apace. The most important of these include Nurses Concerned for Life, the American Association of Pro-Life Obstetricians and Gynecologists, and a small but active and effective Feminists for Life. In addition to these, there are Pediatricians for Life, Scientists for Life, Stewardesses for Life, and others including Women Exploited, which limits

its membership to women who have had an abortion, who are deeply distressed by that fact, and who are active in counseling others not to have an abortion.

Human Life Foundations. Tax structures being what they are, it has been found advantageous to erect, alongside of the broad-based Right to Life groups, tax free human life foundations. These groups, with their unique tax deductible status, can accept major contributions. This support is typically channeled into purely educative aspects of the pro-life movement. One national group, Americans United for Life, has been responsible for publishing the excellent book *Abortion and Social Justice,* and has attempted to maintain a national information service. The Human Life and Natural Family Planning Foundation functions under RC auspices. All other pro-life foundations are regional in their base and typically tend to supplement the more activist role of the Right to Life groups.

Crises Pregnancy Counseling Groups. The original organization of this kind, Birthright, was founded in Toronto. The idea was picked up nationally and then internationally. Somewhat later, an international coordinating group was founded, based in Toledo, Alternatives to Abortion International. These are service groups. They offer help to the distressed pregnant woman who does not want to abort her child. These constitute a parallel service movement to the Right to Life (educational and political) groups above.

The list would not be complete without mentioning several commercial and private companies and individuals who because of their publishing and writing have made contributions to the pro-life movement, whose value is beyond estimation. In addition to the literature mentioned above, these groups have provided the ammunition, the books, brochures, and teaching materials needed for the movement. The most important of these has been Hiltz & Hayes Publishing Co., Inc., Cincinnati, publishers of Dr. and Mrs. J. C. Willke's *Handbook on Abortion* (1975), *How to Teach the Pro-Life Story* (1973), *Life or Death, U.S. Supreme Court Ruled,* and *Abortion, How It Is;* Dr. D. De-Marco's *Abortion in Perspective* (pa. 1974), and Rev. D. Shoemaker's *Abortion, the Bible and the Christian* (c. 1976). Dr. R. Sassone, operating through a private publishing house, has written *Handbook on Population* (1973; originally published as *Report to the California Legislature on Population*) and *Handbook on Euthanasia* (1975). He has also published C. Clark's *Population Growth: The Advantages* (1972) and the translation of the original German book largely responsible for the German euthanasia program of the 40s, *The Release of Destruction of Life Devoid of Value.* Liturgical Press has published Professor P. Marx's pioneering *Death Peddlers, War on the Unborn* (c.1971) as well as his *Death Without Dignity: Killing for Mercy* (1975).

Other important pro-life books issued during this time, in a more religious context, include D. Granfield's *The Abortion Decision* (1969, pa. 1971); K. D. Whitehead's *Re-*

spectable Killing (1972); C. E. Bajema's *Abortion and the Meaning of Personhood* (1974); G. G. Grisez's *Abortion—The Myth, the Reality and the Argument* (1970); M. R. Joyce's *Let Us Be Born* (1970); S. Ernst's *Man the Greatest of Miracles* (tr. M. Nathe and M. R. Joyce, 1976).

[J. C. and B. WILLKE]

PROMISE. Throughout the Bible, the word and idea of "promise" is used in the sense of declaring an intention to do or refrain from doing something. However, this general idea frequently refers to a technical notion of a divine declaration of some intent. The OT has no single word which means "promise." Words which signify "to say" or "to speak" are used in a context which means God's promise of something. God's most important promises in the OT were to Abraham, to the people of Israel, and to David. The prophets exhorted that the people keep their own promises to God.

The notion of "promise" in the OT is bound to that of "election" and "covenant." God chose certain people over others, his "election" of Abraham out of all the peoples of the world, his "election" of Jacob over Esau, etc. With those whom he elected, he covenanted. When God freely made an agreement with someone, he also made promises.

Thus, he chose to covenant with Abraham. He bound himself to make a great people of Abraham and to bless his descendants (Gen 12.1–3,15; 17.1–14). The most important covenant of the OT was that at Sinai. There, God bound himself to the Hebrews who were to form the theocratic community called Israel. He promised a homeland, protection, and to make them a holy nation (Ex 19; all of Dt). Israel, in turn, promised to be faithful, to serve God as a son serves a father, and to love their God, Yahweh (*ibid.*). Israel's promises were capsulized in the Decalogue.

Another important covenant was God's to David. In this pact, God promised an eternal Davidic dynasty. With this promise many later messianic notions were coupled. The prophetic literature appeals to God's promises, frequently as threats if the people do not keep what they had bound themselves to keep. But, most of the prophetic literature also contains hope for the future. If God be bound to chastise Israel, the punishment will be medicinal. Some place, some time, God would abundantly bless—at least a remnant of Israelites.

Prior to NT times, in extrabiblical rabbinic literature, words from the root *epangellomai* (in Heb. *baṭăh*) became technical expressions for God's promises with strongly eschatological overtones. The future hope was founded on God's promises. The NT took up this expression. Almost exclusively, words rooted in *epangellomai* refer to divine promises. The words themselves do not occur in Mt, Mk, or Jn. The idea that the promises to Abraham, to Israel, and to David along with a hope for the future is found in their teachings concerning salvation in Jesus the Messiah.

Luke has ideas similar to the other Evangelists. But, he

uses the root *epangellomai*, esp. in an eschatological sense, which is pregnant with meaning. God's promise is the spirit, i.e., God's power to spread Christ's salvation to the ends of the world. Thus, the word occurs in the last chapter of Lk and eight times in Acts (Lk 24.49; Acts 1.4; 2.33, etc.). Paul makes extensive use of the technical meaning of the word (e.g., Rom 4.13–16; 9.9; Gal 3.17; 2 Cor 7.1).

The promises to Abraham are fulfilled in his descendant who is Christ (Gal 3.16–19). The risen Christ is David's son who fulfills the good news promised in the Prophets (Rom 1.1–7). In Christ, all men become heirs of the promise not by keeping the OT's Law but simply as a freely given gift from God (Gal 3.29; Rom 3.21–4.25). The promise for Paul includes the spirit, and also justification and an inheritance based on divine sonship and life. Thus, the promise also looks to the future since in Christ, life is assured.

The Epistle to Hebrews uses the term frequently and with much of the Pauline meaning. God's promise, fulfilled in the new covenant, underlies the author's appeal to the decisiveness of "today," as well as the guarantee for the future "rest." Thus, the pilgrim Christianity lives in priestly and sacrificial tension between the importance of their present activity and the assurance of future happiness (4; 6.12–20, 9; 11.1–12.4, etc.).

In the rest of the NT, promise has various stresses, but includes the notions of present messianic salvation which is a guarantee to those who persevere. In 1 Jn, God's promise has brought the Son and Father to dwell in the Christian and will continue in the life to come (2.24–28; 1.1–4). In James, those who love God receive the crown of life which is God's promise (1.12; 2.5). In 2 Pet, God's promise that the parousia will come should suffice to silence all who scoff at its delay.

"Promise" then in the Bible refers to God's binding himself to help now and in the future those whom He chooses. Conversely, it refers to the promises those He has chosen make to Him.

BIBLIOGRAPHY: W. Eichrodt, *Theology of the Old Testament* (tr. J. A. Baker, 1961–67); P. van Imschott, *Theology of the Old Testament* (tr. K. Sullivan and F. Buck, 1965); W. Kummel, *Promise and Fulfillment* (1958); J. and F. Schniewind, in Kittel TD s.v. *epangellomai*.

[W. E. LYNCH]

PROMISE, BREACH OF, see BREACH OF PROMISE.

PROMOTER OF JUSTICE, an official in a diocesan *curia, appointed by the bp. to take charge of trials for crimes against church law and of other judicial litigations in the diocese (CIC, c. 1586). The bp. may appoint a promoter of justice for a specific case (ibid. c. 1588 §2). The appointee must be a qualified priest-canonist, of mature age and prudence (*ibid*. c. 1589 §1).

[T. C. O'BRIEN]

PRONE, a relic of the Prayer of the Faithful originating in medieval France and surviving until the 20th cent. in France and some parts of Canada and the U.S. It is an extesion of the word service. Its variable structure has the following elements: (1) prayers for the state, church, public and private necessities, the sick, and the dead; (2) announcements regarding parish affairs; (3) an instruction dealing with the fundamentals of the faith. The term prone has sometimes been used loosely for the third of these elements alone, i.e., the instruction or homily. Before Vatican Council II the remnant of this practice in the U.S. was found in the custom of reciting an Our Father, and Hail Mary, for the sick and the dead after the sermon. Since Vatican Council II the Prayer of the Faithful has been reintroduced after the homily in the Eucharistic Liturgy.

[N. KOLLAR]

PROOEMION (Syriac *prûmiyôn*), in West Syrian and Maronite Liturgies, an invitatory doxology, usually addressed to the Son, preceding a *seḍrō, with which it today forms the ensemble called a *ḥûssōyō*. BIBLIOGRAPHY: J. Mateos, "Trois recueils anciens de Prooemia syriens," *Orientalia Christiana poetica* 33 (1967) 457–82.

[A. CODY]

PROOF, in logic, the reasoning process or evidential means of determining the truth of a proposition. Inductive proof, of which statistical proof and mathematical induction are special cases, proceeds from the less universal to the more universal proposition, while deductive proof proceeds to the equally or less universal proposition. Deduction is either dialectical, satisfied with establishing probability, or demonstrative, achieving scientific certitude. Modern metamathematics, or Hilbert's proof theory, provides the use of a logicist system as an objective test of probability and proofs within a deductive theory.

[R. E. HENNESSEY]

PROPAGANDA. (1) In RC parlance the term is sometimes short for the Congregation for the Evangelization of Peoples or Propagation of the Faith or for the Urbanianum, the College of the Propaganda (founded by that Congregation), now formally having the title Pontificia Universitas Urbaniana (see PONTIFICAL UNIVERSITIES, ROMAN). In that usage the term refers to the task of propagating, i.e., disseminating the gospel. (2) Propaganda in a more general usage is the spread of an ideology, system of thought, life style, product, etc. It connotes the use of half-truths or falsehood (the Big Lie in Nazi Germany, e.g.,) by pressure tactics, hard-sell or "programming" of its victims. Whether for political, religious, or commercial purposes propaganda is an offense against truthfulness, often against justice as fraud, and is a violation of the dignity of the human person. The fact of its use is one reason for the Church's concern about the exploitation of the media of social communication.

PROPAGATION OF THE FAITH, CONGREGATION FOR THE, see EVANGELIZATION OF PEOPLES, CONGREGATION FOR THE.

PROPAGATION OF THE FAITH, PONTIFICAL SOCIETY FOR THE, an organization which acts as the central agency, with headquarters in Rome, for distributing aid to Catholic missions. The idea of such a society was conceived by Pauline *Jaricot, who saw the need for one agency to support the missions by prayer and alms, rather than a variety of societies in competition. In Lyons, France, Jaricot laid the foundations of a society, highly organized, and serving all missions. Bitter opposition was encountered at first but by 1822 a group of laymen active in charitable works in France adopted the plan and the name, Society for the Propagation of the Faith. Sanctioned by Pope Pius VII in 1823 the Society enjoyed rapid growth and attracted support from bps. and clergy. By 1840 the Society had branches throughout Europe, in the U.S. and Latin America. U.S. missions were the principal beneficiaries of financial aid. By 1896 there was a national organization of the Society in the U.S. There was some dissatisfaction at the centralization of the work in France and in 1922 Pope Pius XI issued the *motu proprio, Romanorum Pontificum* making the Society pontifical with headquarters in Rome and subject to the Congregation for the Propagation of the Faith. A later document, Pius XI's encyclical *Rerum ecclesiae* (1926) made the Society the principal organization for support of the missions.

The Society is governed by a superior council whose members are designated by the pope and are representative of all nations which contribute to the missions. The secretary-general of the Congregation for the Evangelization of Peoples presides over the council. There is a national director, named by the Congregation, and diocesan directors appointed by the bishop of the diocese. The Superior Council alone makes distribution of alms donated for the missions. BIBLIOGRAPHY: F. J. Sheen, NCE 11:844–846.

[J. R. AHERNE]

PROPASSIONS OF CHRIST, the concupiscible and irrascible appetites in Jesus. Christian thought could not reconcile its conception of a sinless human nature in Jesus with the possession of the passions of ordinary men with proneness to sin and rebellion against the higher power of reason. Hence from the time of SS. Jerome and John Damascene on Catholic writers have called the concupiscible and irrascible appetites in Jesus propassions instead of passions. If one follows St. Thomas Aquinas in looking upon the passions as essential to human nature and possessed by Christ without their imperfection, one may hold that he possessed all the animal or psychological passions—rightly understood—in the most eminent fashion. Always subordinate to right reason and directed in obedience to God's will, they steered clear of any imperfection of excess in object, principle, or effect and were the most perfect instrument of his loving affection for God and man and of sympathy for sinners. They were truly responsive to every grace. Many passages in the NT depict Christ as having passions in this sense. Notable surely are his love or liking (Jn 11.3, 5, 33, 38), his joy (Jn 11.15), his profound sorrow and sadness (Mt 26.37–38), his agony (Lk 22.44). To deny the reality of his passions would be equivalent to denial of the perfection of his human nature and the redemptive action upon man's passion. Theological perplexity arises not so much from the existence of passions in the Savior but from the attempt to reconcile such passion as sadness or agony with his possession of the intuitive vision of God. The passions in Christ never attained morbid independence but existed in true and perfect unity and balance. They are never negative. BIBLIOGRAPHY: I. Solano, STS BAC 3.1:361–369.

[E. G. KAISER]

PROPERTIES, in Trinitarian theology, those attributes of the three divine persons in the *Trinity which, according to some authors, constitute them as distinct persons or, according to others, render the divine persons distinct from each other. Those theologians who maintain that the divine properties are constitutive enumerate three of them: *paternity, *filiation, and passive *spiration. Those who hold that the properties are only distinctive add unoriginatedness as a fourth attribute. A further distinction is also common: a Trinitarian "notion" is identical with a property except that it may be common to more than one person. Active *spiration is the only example of a notion that is not a property since it is a relation to the Spirit common to both the Father and the Son. Thus the designation of Trinitarian properties is an attempt to specify, by an abstract term, those attributes by which the divine persons may be distinguished. As such, the designation appears fairly frequently in early conciliar documents, e.g., the Lateran Council IV (1215) states that, "The Trinity is one according to a common essence, but distinct according to personal properties" (D 800). BIBLIOGRAPHY: ThAq ST 1a, 33.3; B. Lonergan, *De Deo Trino* (1964).

[T. M. MCFADDEN]

PROPERTY, institutionally structured relationships of privileges and duties between an individual, group, or society and a thing. It involves the right to possess, use, and dispose of a thing within generally specified constraints. The thing may be tangible, such as "real property" (land and all things permanently attached thereto) and "personal property" (a physical thing capable of being moved over space), or intangible, such as a patent or similar claim that is capable of being enforced (a "chose in action"). Property may be: (a) productive or consumptive (depending upon whether or not the thing involved is primarily used to produce other goods or services); (b) public, social, corporate, or private. The rights to public property are invested in the State; to social property, in the society with the judiciary usually exercising specific decision-making (e.g., water or air); to corporate property, in managers who are not the *de jure* owners; and to private property, in an individual or group who possess both ownership and control. The central issues with which all theories of property must deal concern the manner in which different systems of rights over things affect the efficiency of resource use, the conservation of resources, the equitableness of the distribution of production, and human freedom.

In the OT property is viewed as created by and thus ultimately owned by God. Man administers property as the steward of God and consequently is not entitled to use property for selfish advantage but only to achieve social justice and the common good. Christian thought carries forth these ideas by placing emphasis on the public as well as the private character of property. The Fathers saw private property as something that would violate justice and goodness in a completely pure world but as a necessary creation of the state in this world in order to minimize the disorder that accompanies greed, avarice, and the general weaknesses of fallen man. St. Thomas Aquinas followed in this tradition. Although he described the perfect state as one in which no property existed, he recognized the inability of man to attain such a state in this life and thus defended the division of possessions into mine and thine as an exercise of human reason for the benefit of human life. He judged private property to be beneficial because it makes man more careful of things, which in turn conserves things; because it makes affairs more orderly; and because it provides for a more peaceful state (ThAq ST 2a2ae, 66.1 ad 2).

With the increase in economic activity in the late Middle Ages, new theories of property began to be developed. Emphasis came to be placed on acquiring property for its own sake and on the rights of the individual rather than the society. One such line of thought was based on arguments from natural law; another on utilitarian criteria. The former, developed most thoroughly by John Locke, proceeds from the position God gave land and other natural resources to all men, but the labor expended by a particular man on removing such things out of nature gives to the laborer a property right to the thing. The right once established can be freely transferred to other men either through exchange or as an outright gift. In utilitarian thought the basis of property is the expectation to an individual of the usefulness a thing possesses. This leads people to frame and obey legal conventions concerning private property in order to enhance the welfare of each and thereby maximize the common welfare of all. Although both theories defend private property, the utilitarians place much greater emphasis on civil laws as the authority over property. Both theories were incorporated into the economic liberalism of the 19th cent. and it was against this thought that Socialists and Catholic moralists reacted, although for vastly different reasons.

For Socialists the basis of property is the labor expended on production, but production is a social act and consequently property should be possessed by the State in the name of society, not by the individual. When possessed by the individual "property is theft" (Proudhon) and it results in "exploitation" (Marx). In *Rerum novarum* Pope Leo XIII condemned these ideas, as he did those of economic liberalism. He returned to the emphasis in Christian thought on the right to private property while forcefully indicating that the social nature of property means the private right is never an absolute one.

The rapid developments of the 20th cent. have raised new questions concerning property. The separation of ownership and control in the modern corporation has been particularly cited as a reason for rethinking property rights. The current contribution of labor skills to the distribution as well as the production of goods and services has led to the argument that property rights exist in an individual's education and employment. Pope John XXIII acknowledged the validity of this argument but concluded it in no way diminishes the right to private ownership of goods, including productive goods, because private ownership "is part of the natural law" (*Mater et magistra,* 109). Such ecological problems as air pollution, noise, and urban congestion have also required the rethinking of property connotations. In general all of these new problems have focused attention on the constraints within which private property rights can be exercised rather than on the legitimacy *per se* of private property. BIBLIOGRAPHY: A. A. Berle and G. Means, *Modern Corporation and Private Property* (rev. ed., 1968). R. Schlatter, *Private Property: The History of an Idea* (1951, repr. 1973).

[J. J. MURPHY]

PROPHECY OF ST. MALACHY, SEE MALACHY, ST.

PROPHET AND PROPHECY, Hebrew *nābî,* from an Akkadian word meaning "one sent" or "one made to speak," translated both in the LXX and the NT by Greek *prophetēs*. Though the biblical tradition traces the origins of Israelite prophecy to Moses (Num 11.24–30; 12.2–8), not much is heard of prophets until the late period of the judges and the early monarchy, when they are mentioned in connection with the Philistine wars as stimulating religious and patriotic fervor. The prophets of this period were ecstatic prophets living and traveling in groups (cf. 1 Sm 10.6–8, 10–13). Such prophets are given the name "sons of the prophets" *(benê hannebî îm)* indicative of their communal existence (cf. 1 Kg 20.35; 2 Kg 2.3–20; 5.22; 6.1). The ecstatic experience during which they prophesied was often induced by mutual excitation through dance and music. These prophets often served as disciples or apprentices under some noted prophet, but could also live apart as private individuals (2 Kg 4.1–4). In either capacity, they can often be found attached to sanctuaries as "cult prophets" (1

Kg 14.1–17; 2 Kg 22.14–17; Am 7.10–17) or serving the king as "court prophets" (2 Sam 7.1–3; 12.1–15; 24.11; 1 Kg 1.8; 22.6–24). Apparently they wore a distinctive garb of haircloth (2 Kg 1.8; Zech 13.4) and often bore other distinguishing marks (cf. 1 Kg 20.38, 41). Ecstaticism continued to some degree throughout the entire history of Israelite prophecy, for Samuel is represented on one occasion as leading a band in ecstatic prophecy (1 Sam 19.20–24) and both Elijah and Elisha are habitually associated with the "sons of the prophets." Jer 29.26 shows that ecstatic prophecy was common in Jeremiah's time and Ezekiel certainly received many of his prophecies in ecstatic trance.

By "classical prophecy" is meant the prophecy of those whom the OT regards as exemplifying what is distinctive about the Israelite prophets, that is, the prophecies of Amos, Hosea, Micah, Isaiah, Nahum, Zephaniah, Habakkuk, Jeremiah and Ezekiel. The basic sources of what constitutes a prophet are found in the accounts of the call of the major prophets (Is 6.1–13; Jer 1.4–19; Ezek 1.1–3.21; Am 3.7–8; 7.14–16). These accounts with other passages reveal: that the prophet is delegated to speak on behalf of Yahweh (Is 6.8–9; Jer 1.9); that the prophetic vocation is compelling even though the prophet be reluctant or untalented (Am 3.7–8; Jer 1.7–8); that God communicates His word to the prophet (Is 6.9; Jer 1.7–9; Ezek 2.8–3.3); that this communication involves visual and auditory experiences.

While Jeremiah and Ezekiel at the beginning of the exile and Second Isaiah at the end of the exile provided a new vision of the divine plan to inspire the people, the post-exilic prophets lack much of the vigor and spontaneity of the pre-exilic prophets. The diversity of Third Isaiah, Haggai, Zechariah (1–8), Malachi, Obadiah, Joel, the prophet of Zech 9–11, 12–14, is mainly one of styles which are often frankly derivative and lacking in the freshness of the earlier prophetic oracles. The themes are fairly common, typical of a people living in a Judaism where Temple and Torah had become the enduring realities that would ensure unity. Prophecy itself helped ensure the conditions under which the people of God could survive for many generations. It did so by responding to the needs that Jeremiah and Ezechiel had already forseen before the exile, by insisting on individual responsibility and fidelity to the Law. The prophets often opposed the priesthood for its neglect of the precepts of the moral law, but opposition was not a matter of jealous rivalry, for at its best the priesthood did the same work or part of the same work as the prophets, namely, transmitting the moral will of the God of Israel. Priesthood did so by the traditions of the religious law preserved in the sanctuaries; prophecy accomplished the task by the communication of the living word, which was always consistent with the Law even if expressed in its own way. Similarly, despite some strong statements against abuses in the Israelite sacrificial system (Am 5.21–27; Hos 6.6; Jer 7.21–23; Is 1.2–17), it cannot be maintained that the prophets were against either religious ritual or sacrifice in principle. In terms of time span, Israelite prophecy and the monarchy coincided almost exactly. Paradoxically, prophecy was instrumental in establishing this institution for which prophetic enthusiasm was at best lukewarm. Nonetheless, the prophets never initiated any countermovement to replace the monarchy with another form of government. While the monarchy existed, the prophets insisted upon a return to the old covenant precepts which had been relegated to the realm of private morality by regal legislation and the changes in the structure of the society that accompanied the monarchy. Yet the prophets did accept the prophetic oracle given to the house of David (2 Sam 7.14–17) as a revelation of God, and however reluctantly did include the king as the elect of God in their hopes for a better future (Is 7.13–17; 9.5–6; 11.1–5; Ezek 37.25; Jer 23.5–6). Enthusiasm for royal messianism waxed and waned in post-exilic prophecy, and it must be said that while the prophets never denied the relevance of messianism in the divine plan, it was generally never one of their overriding themes.

The prophetic theology centered itself in the one God who had chosen the people of Israel and had communicated his will to this people in the Law. It was in the light of this election that the prophets foretold judgment and salvation for the people, criticized empty forms of worship, and called the people to their social responsibilities. While it is difficult to confine Jesus to the category of prophet, the NT bears witness to the fact that there were prophets in the early Christian communities (Acts 11.27; 21.10–11; 13.1–3; 1 Cor 13.2; 14.3–5; Eph 3.5; 1 Tim 1.18; 4.14; Rev 22.6–8). The Christians were particularly conscious that the spirit of prophecy had returned to them as a community, which they claimed as evidence that they were indeed God's elect and chosen community. Negatively, the importance of prophecy in the communities can be demonstrated by Mt 7.22–23, the warning against false prophets and exorcists; 23.8–10, the warning not to acknowledge any leadership except that of Christ. While prophets were among the charismatic leaders of early Christianity (Rom 12.6; 1 Cor 12.10; Eph 2.20), prophecy itself was submerged in the development of the hierarchical offices at the close of the first century. BIBLIOGRAPHY: B. Vawter, JBC 12 (223–237); J. Lindblom, *Prophecy in Ancient Israel* (1962); R. B. Y. Scott, *Relevance of the Prophets* (1968).

[T. J. RYAN]

PROPHET PLAYS, dramatizations of a lesson from the Office of Matins at Christmas. The lesson itself was an excerpt from an early medieval sermon erroneously attributed to St. Augustine, in which an interlocutor summoned a number of OT prophets to come forward and deliver their testimony to the Messiah and his redemptive mission. The prophet plays came to serve as prologues to nativity dramas and later to link OT and NT scenes in the great vernacular mystery cycles.

[E. C. DUNN]

PROPHETESS, a woman with the gift of prophecy, who performs the role of prophet. Miriam, the sister of Aaron, is given this title (Ex 15.20), perhaps because of the ascription to her of the ancient victory song (Song of Miriam) preserved in that text: "Sing to the Lord, for He has risen up in triumph; the horse and his rider He has hurled into the sea." Deborah, a judge in Israel, is given the added title "prophetess" in Jg 4.4. This also could be due to the ascription to her of another victory song—the Song of Deborah—preserved in ch. 5 of Judges. In 2 Kg 22.14 the prophetess Huldah is mentioned as a contemporary of Jeremiah whose message confirmed his. In Nehemiah 6.14 the prophetess Noadiah is mentioned as one of many prophets who were adversaries of Nehemiah. In Luke 2.36 Anna is called a prophetess. She never left the temple area, and at the presentation of the child Jesus at the Temple "she talked about the child to all who were looking for the liberation of Jerusalem." In Rev 2.20, in the letter to the angel of the church at Thyatira, mention is made of "that Jezebel, the woman who claims to be a prophetess, who by her teaching lures my servants into fornication and into eating food sacrificed to idols." These texts would seem to indicate that throughout biblical history neither true nor false prophecy was the exclusive domain of males.

[E. J. DILLON]

PROPHETIC BOOKS OF THE OLD TESTAMENT.

The Hebrew Bible is divided into three parts: the *Torah; the Prophets; and the Writings. By far the longest of the three sections is the Prophets. The formation of all the sections was gradual and seemingly unplanned. This section of the Hebrew Bible was completed and closed sometime between 400 and 132 B.C., for, on the one hand the Samaritans who separated themselves from their Jerusalem brethren shortly after 400 B.C. accepted only the Torah (i.e., Pentateuch), and on the other hand the grandson of Ben Sira, who translated the book into Greek in 132 B.C. and wrote a Prologue to it, was already aware of the Prophetical section of the Hebrew Bible. Completion of a section of the Bible is one thing, but its gradual formation is quite another, and scholars hold that the literary history of nearly all of the books of the OT was gradual, with a general passage from the oral tradition to the written document.

The Prophetic section is divided into the Earlier Prophets and the Later Prophets. The Earlier Prophets include the books of Jos, Jg, 1–2 Sam, 1–2 Kg, often described by Christian scholars as historical books. However, aside from the fact that these books had to be distinguished from the Torah, they record the lives of numerous men (and some women) who were called to deliver the Word of God to Israel. Hence, under this conception of prophet, based on Akkadian philology, there is no good reason why these books should not be styled prophetic. Nice categorizing of the biblical books was hardly an objective of those who gathered the books together, for Hebrew literature seldom falls easily into one class. The books that comprise the

Earlier Prophets are not historical in the modern sense of the word, and they are geared almost totally to the workings of God through men whom he used to speak and to act for him, with greater or less success. The Later Prophets include Is, Jer, Ezek, but not Dan, the four of whom are often referred to as Major Prophets; and the twelve Minor Prophets. Daniel apart from being more of an apocalyptic than a prophetic type of writing, was simply too late to find its place in the Prophetic section of the Hebrew Bible. The distinction between Major Prophet and Minor Prophet is largely based on length of the books rather than importance, and it might even be suggested that certain nonliterary Prophets, such as Elijah and Elisha, had far greater influence on popular Hebrew thinking than at least many of the literary Prophets. One may also ask, in the light of evidence within the book, whether Jon does not belong rather to the didactic and sapiential books than to the Prophets. For the book seems to be fictional, attributed artificially to a Prophet by the name of Jonah (2 Kg 14.25), but who serves to put across the point of an unknown author of a much later age. The book is primarily a criticism of Jewish nationalism and an unwillingness to share the riches of Judaism with others. Jonah represents this attitude. As far as authorship is concerned, something similar might be said of Dan, and even Mal may not have been the name of a prophet in the usual sense, but rather a fictitious name ("my prophet") of someone who wished to improve the cultic deficiencies of the Jewish people. Most of the Prophetic books were edited to some degree, and it is hardly daring to suggest that those Prophets whose oral messages were committed to writing said much more than has been preserved in their books. The last books of the Hebrew Bible, 1–2 Chr, go over approximately the same ground that was covered in 1–2 Sam and 1–2 Kg. However the work was done later, and with different preoccupations, e.g., the exaltation of the Davidic dynasty, but it was esp. the chronological reason that caused these books to be placed the very last in the Hebrew Bible rather than in the Prophetic section.

Generally speaking, the longer the Prophetic book, the more literary complications does it present. Isaiah esp., but also Jer and Ezek abound in them. So does Zechariah.

Despite these literary complications the Prophetic books of the OT present a marvellous testimony to the fact that numerous men, and a few women, felt called to express themselves on behalf of God to his people, and they did it in such a way that their message has a ring of authenticity about it even today. BIBLIOGRAPHY: B. Vawter, *Conscience of Israel* (1961); E. Maly, *Prophets of Salvation* (1967).

[I. HUNT]

PROPHETS, EARLY CHRISTIAN, members of the primitive Church endowed with a free, charismatic gift of the Holy Spirit that enabled them to discern unbelievers (1 Cor 14.24–25), know divine mysteries (1 Cor 13.2), foretell the future (Acts 11.28), encourage the brethren (Acts 15.32), and edify the Church (1 Cor 14.5, 12). Because of their special gift, the prophets of the NT were taken as a proof that "the last days" had come and that God had poured forth his "Spirit upon all flesh" (Acts 2.17). They were ranked in honor after the Apostles but before teachers, workers of miracles, administrators, and those who spoke with tongues (1 Cor 12.28); and with the Apostles they were the foundation of the Church (Eph 2.20). Local churches had their prophets as well as teachers (Acts 13.1), but they could also travel from place to place (Acts 11.27). The recipients of visions and auditions, they could give practical advice where needed, as when the prophets of Antioch sent Paul and Barnabas to work among the gentiles (Acts 13.1–3). There was, of course, a danger from false prophets, who could be detected by their fruits (Mt 7.15–23) and through an appeal to the analogy of faith (Rom 12.6). Prophetism continued within the Church in post-Apostolic times. Both the *Didache* (ch. 11–13) and the *Shepherd of Hermas* (Mand. 11) give rules for discerning true and false prophets. It disappeared in the latter part of the 2d cent. because of the exaggerated emphasis that the heretical Montanists placed upon prophetic gifts, but also because private inspiration of this kind was not always amenable to ecclesiastical discipline. BIBLIOGRAPHY: D. J. McCarthy, NCE 11:872; M. H. Shepherd, Jr., InterDB 3:919–920.

[M. J. COSTELLOE]

PROPITIATION, an action one takes to restore himself to favor with another after having incurred his displeasure. In biblical language, the notion is used of one human to another, or even of a human being with respect to God. This is expressed in the OT by *KPR* (to atone) or one of its forms, usually in relationship to *kapporet* (propitiatory place or thing), the mercy seat where Yahweh was thought to accept propitiatory actions. It is disputed whether the principal emphasis is on propitiation or on expiation. If on propitiation, God would be influenced to change his attitude towards people by sacrifice alone. Several Prophets vehemently opposed excesses in this direction. If the emphasis is on expiation, then the action was directly on the offense. The NT usages of the concept are to be read in this light. *ATONEMENT.

[L. A. BUSHINSKI]

PROPOSITION, CONDEMNED, see CENSURES, THEOLOGICAL.

PROPRIETARY CHURCHES, in the Middle Ages those over which a lay lord had rights of ownership and of appointment of the ecclesiastical *locum tenens*. The rights led to abuses, became part of the issue over *lay investiture, and were supplanted gradually by the right of *patronage.

PROPYLAEUM, in Greek architecture the main gate to the sacred enclosure. If there are many passageways the term *propylaea* is used (Acropolis, Athens; Eleusis).

PROSELYTE (Gr. attached to another community). Many Greeks were disenchanted with their religion, and philosophy made them tend towards religions promising more moral character. Many in various parts of the Roman Empire embraced Judaism. A ritual was prescribed, effecting a "new birth" which affected all previous relationships. Some embraced Judaism in its totality (proselytes); others, only partially ("God-fearers"). The rabbis continued to distrust them and concretized their opposition by the year 100 A.D. In the NT proselytism became an imperative with "Go, therefore and make disciples of all nations" (Mt 28.19).

[L. A. BUSHINSKI]

PROSELYTIZING (Gr. *proselutos,* one who has come to a place), in a religious reference, the making of converts to a religious belief or ecclesiastical adherence. In the NT "proselyte" is used in the sense of a full-fledged (Acts 2.11) or partial (Acts 10.2) convert to Judaism. Historically in Buddhism, Judaism, Christianity, and Islam proselytizing has been practiced, although to an extent and by methods that have varied considerably by reason of cultural and political influences as well as theological interpretations. Proselytizing is intense where, from a well-defined body of revelation and a strongly developed systematic theology, the conviction arises that the believer has a personal mission to bring to the unbeliever the special redemption, grace, or benefits of the religious message. For Christians the term in itself may simply connote fulfillment of the sense of mission that seems inherent in acceptance of the gospel and is acknowledged by most of the Churches. Proselytizing, however, has often evoked disfavor (Mt 23.15) and is currently used mostly in a pejorative sense to imply unscrupulous methods of persuasion or a divisive competition among the Churches. BIBLIOGRAPHY: *Church for Others* (World Council of Churches Publications, 1967).

[T. C. O'BRIEN]

PROSKE, KARL (1794–1861), music publisher. As *Kapellmeister* of Ratisbon Cathedral, he developed a great collection of church music and published many MSS which were unknown until that time.

[P. HENNESSEY]

PROSKOMIDE, known also as the *prothesis,* liturgical preparation of the gifts of bread and wine as an integrating part preceding the liturgy of the Catechumens and of the Faithful. In the Holy Liturgy of St. Basil and of St. John Chrysostom of the Eastern Byzantine rite, the Proskomide takes place at the table known as the *prothesis.*

[L. PEANO]

PROSŌPON, Gr. term for "person"; like the Lat. *persona,* its first meaning, a mask or stage identity. In later Greek patristic literature the term became acceptable. Earlier, however, it was often rejected, and the term *hypostasis* insisted on as the orthodox expression describing the Divine Persons, both in the Trinity and in the hypostatic union. Sabellius admitted the use of *prosōpon* as expressing the mode of manifestation denoted by the names Father, Son, and Holy Spirit; but not that each *prosōpon* existed in a real *hypostasis* (SABELLIANISTS). *Nestorius also referred to Christ as the *prosōpon* of union, but maintained that in Christ there is a human and a divine person (see D 250).

[T. C. O'BRIEN]

PROSPER OF AQUITAINE, ST. (d. *c*.465), theologian and defender of the Augustinian doctrine of Grace. A native of Aquitaine, P. was living at Marseilles, probably as a monk (though not a priest) when *c*.426 the semi-Pelagian controversy broke out. In 428 he wrote to Augustine to inform him of the opposition to his teachings on grace and predestination which was arising in the monasteries of Southern Gaul. In reply, Augustine wrote the treatises *De praedestinatione sanctorum* and *De dono perseverantiae*. In 431, after Augustine's death, P. went to Rome to seek the condemnation of Augustine's opponents. During the next few years P. gradually tempered his enthusiasm for strict Augustinianism, rejecting predestination to damnation and stressing the universal call to salvation. In the last part of his life, he served as secretary to Pope *Leo the Great. The bulk of his writings are concerned with the problem of grace and the defense of St. Augustine. In his first Roman period he wrote against *Vincent of Lérins and *Cassian. P. published an explanation of the Psalms based on Augustine's *Enarrationes* (only Ps 100–150 are extant). During his second Roman sojourn, most of P.'s works were compilations. His *Chronicle* is useful for the history of his own times. Works: PL 51:1–868; *Call of All Nations* (ACW 14 Eng. tr. ed. P. de Letter, 1952); *Defence of St. Augustine* (ACW 32, assorted shorter wks., 1963). BIBLIOGRAPHY: Altaner 535–537; LexAW 2456.

[R. B. ENO]

PROSPHORA, (Gr. for oblation; Sl. *prosfora*), the altar bread used in the Byzantine liturgy. Round in shape, leavened, it is about five inches in diameter and two inches thick. The center of the loaf is stamped with a Greek cross, the squares formed by the arms of the cross containing the letters IC XC NI KA (see IC XC NIKA). This principal portion is the first one cut during the *proskomide*. Sometimes the stamp is more elaborate and in addition to the seal, to the left is found a triangle commemorating the Mother of God, and on the right side nine smaller triangles for the commemoration of the angels and saints. Although often cut from only one loaf, as in Greek usage, the various particles may be detached from five different loaves, the unused remnants of which are distributed to the faithful after the Liturgy as the *antidoron*.

[A. J. JACOPIN]

PROSTITUTION, the act or practice of giving oneself to sexual activity with another for a price. The term prostitute is usually applied to women, but it is also used of men who perform comparable services for hire by women or by other males. The practice of prostitution has existed everywhere and in all recorded history. Among the Israelites of OT times we find no specific ban against its practice, except in cases involving *adultery or cultic worship as this was practiced among Israel's idolatrous neighbors. Some stigma may have attached to ordinary prostitution, however, for Israel's infidelity to Yahweh was referred to as adultery and fornication. In the NT the practice was reprobated, esp. by St. Paul, who cautioned the Corinthians: "You know surely that your bodies are members making up the body of Christ; do you think I can take parts of Christ's body and join them to the body of a prostitute? Never! As you know, a man who goes with a prostitute is one body with her, since *the two* as it is said, *become one flesh*." (1 Cor 6.15–16). Since that time all Christian moralists have condemned prostitution. However, not all moralists have urged the suppression of the vice by force of civil law. Some, like St. Augustine and St. Thomas Aquinas, have advocated its toleration by civil law as the lesser of two evils. Others, like St. Alphonsus, have argued that toleration of the vice by civil authority amounts to complicity. By the end of the 15th cent. fear of venereal diseases led to stronger attempts by police regulation to control or suppress the vice. Nowhere, however, have these attempts enjoyed complete success, and the charge is sometimes made that by driving the vice underground, the danger of venereal infection is increased. In a report submitted to the Wolfenden Committee (1956) seven Catholic priests and laymen argued against penalties enacted by the State in the effort to prevent sins against sexual morality committed in private by responsible adults. Latterly activists in the Women's Liberation Movement have expressed dissatisfaction with the existent penalties in the U.S. because, at least as enforced, they unfairly penalize the woman and let the man go free in an offense in which they equally share.

As mentioned above, ritualistic prostitution was practiced in the Near East; it was also found in Greece, Egypt, and India. BIBLIOGRAPHY: Hastings, ERE 6:672–676.

[P. K. MEAGHER]

PROSTITUTION, SACRED, prostitution officially provided for at a sanctuary, known to have been practiced in Mesopotamia (at least after the arrival of the Semites), in Canaan, in the Greek cult of Aphrodite, the cults of the Magna Mater and of Attis in Asia Minor, and elsewhere in the Middle and Far East. Its sense and purpose entailed genuinely religious elements along with those magical and merely sensual, for it did, at best, celebrate human sexuality as a religious thing and a divine gift, although in practice it was little more than an excuse for immorality. Often it aimed at assuring by sympathetic magic the continuing fertility of nature as a whole; related to it in this respect, but distinct from it, was the rite of sacred marriage, in which two persons, at least one of them representing a divine being (Dumuzi, represented by the king, in Mesopotamia, Adonis in Phoenicia, Dionysus in Athens) united in a sexual rite. Cultic prostitutes were on the regular staffs of temples, and male prostitutes were not unknown. In addition, a woman might offer her virginity as a sacrifice by playing such a role once at the time of her marriage (cf. Jer 2.20,25; Hos 4.13). BIBLIOGRAPHY: W. von Soden, RGG 5:642–643; M.R.P. McGuire, NCE 11:881.

[A. CODY]

PROTAGORAS OF ABDERA (c.480–c.410 B.C.), one of the first and most famous of the Sophists, who as a thinker as well as a teacher exercised a marked influence on Democritus, Plato, and Antisthenes. He claimed that he could teach "virtue" (aretē), in the sense of efficient conduct of life in its various aspects. He is esp. important for his doctrine that "Man is the measure of all things, of those that are that they are, of those that are not that they are not" (Frg. 1), and for thus introducing the notion of the relativity of knowledge. In his work On the Gods he declared: "With regard to the gods, I cannot feel sure either that they are or that they are not, nor what they are like in figure; for there are many things that hinder such knowledge, the obscurity of the subject and the shortness of human life." However, as presented by Plato in his dialogue, Protagoras, he does not seem to have been as sceptical in religion as this statement would lead one to assume. In his Antilogiai, he contributed to the development of dialectic, and he was a pioneer in the classification of grammatical categories. On the basis of the extant evidence, there is no trace of relativism in his outlook on morality and moral conduct. He seems to have taught in practice, at least, conformity to the traditional morality of the Greek city-state. He was so highly respected that he was asked to draw up a code of laws for the new Athenian colony of Thurii in 444. BIBLIOGRAPHY: G. C. Field, OCD 740–741; LexAW 2457; Copleston 1:87–91; M. Untersteiner, Sophists (tr. K. Freeman, 1954) 1–91.

[M. R. P. MCGUIRE]

PROTASE, ST., see GERVASE AND PROTASE, SS.

PROTERIUS, ST. (d. 457), **PATRIARCH OF ALEXANDRIA** from 451, anti-Monophysite. He was an archpriest when he was appointed by the nobiles civitatis to replace *Dioscorus, who had been deposed from the patriarchal See of Alexandria by the Council of Chalcedon (451). P. had to face the opposition esp. of Egyptian monks who favored Dioscorus. After futile attempts to reconcile the parties, in 456, he exiled the monastic leaders Timothy Aelurus and Peter Mongus from the city. Upon the death of Emperor Marcian, Jan. 457, Proterius was left unprotected against the attacks of his opponents. The Monophysite party declared Aerulus patriarch and assassinated Proterius.

[L. PEANO]

PROTESTANT EPISCOPAL CHURCH (Episcopal Church), that American denomination whose heritage derives from the reformed Church of England established by law in 1559 during the reign of Elizabeth I. The C of E contributed significantly to the political, religious, and economic plans of the Virginia Company in the founding of Jamestown in 1607. The Church, transplanted with the colonists, reflected the fluid religious situation in the mother country at the time. Largely Puritan in cast, the earliest Church in Virginia was represented by a variety of opinion within that movement. Stricter conformity to Anglican practice after the colony reverted to the crown in 1624 was thwarted by the inability of Charles I and Abp. W. *Laud to send a bp. to America on the eve of the English Civil War (1638). Virginia Anglicans adapted to this lack, and with the Vestry Act of 1641 the Church became lay-controlled and Congregationalist in fact. In the period of the *Restoration the bp. of London sought to exercise control of the Church through a system of commissaries, who contributed to further changes in the colonial Church, ultimately rejecting complete reliance on the State. Commissary James *Blair of Virginia, writing to John Locke in the late 1690s, sharply criticized royal gubernatorial despotism, and Commissary Thomas *Bray of Maryland turned to voluntary means of extending the Church's influence by founding (1701) the *Society for the Propagation of the Gospel in Foreign Parts (SPG). Bray's parochial libraries increased knowledge of the *historic episcopate in the early Church, thereby serving to enhance Anglican assurance and aggressiveness as the Church spread to the Middle Colonies and to the Congregational North. There, converts from Puritanism, such as Samuel *Johnson of Conn., pleaded unsuccessfully for bps. for America. Successive abps. of Canterbury were rendered ineffective on this issue by the powerful Puritan lobby in Parliament. Nevertheless, increased numbers of SPG missionaries, the founding of colleges (William and Mary, 1693; the Univ. of Pennsylvania, 1740), influential churches (e.g., King's Chapel, Boston, 1689; Trinity Church, New York, 1689; Christ Church, Philadelphia, 1695) indicated new strength. This was largely offset by formal ties with the increasingly unpopular British government, by the fact that ministerial candidates had to cross the Atlantic for ordination, by suspicion in New England, by well-organized competition (Lutherans, Presbyterians, Quakers) in the Middle Colonies and by the Church's inability to move beyond aristocratic tidewater areas in the South. Moreover, high churchmen refused to join the triumphant progress of Puritan Calvinism that reached its climax in the *Great Awakening under the aegis of George *Whitefield. Isolation from this first popular movement of the American people resulted in later rejection of such Anglican revivalists as Devereux *Jarratt and John *Wesley's "Methodist" missionaries. After the "Bishops' Controversy" (1760–66), Anglican pamphleteers Charles Inglis, Thomas Bradbury Chandler, Samuel *Seabury, and others sought to justify their Church's needs to an unresponsive Parliament and their "rights" to a religious majority that increasingly chorused for disestablishment in the South.

After the Revolution, remaining Episcopalians were forced to accept denominational *voluntaryism. William

*White's *Case of the Episcopal Churches in the United States Considered* (1782) argued for immediate Episcopalian unity, a titular episcopate if necessary, and lay rights by representation. White's Whig constitutionalism and "parochialism" were challenged by high churchmen who, in Conn., elected Samuel Seabury bp., judging that only a "regular" episcopate could serve as initiator of Episcopalian unity. Believing in a nonpolitical episcopate as most nearly reflecting the apostolic Church, Seabury sought consecration abroad. Unable to take the C of E's loyalty oath to the crown, he traveled to Scotland in 1784 to be consecrated by nonjuring bishops (see NONJURORS). Meanwhile White and William Smith of Md. moved ahead on their own, forming local and interstate conventions. These bore fruit; by 1786 White and William Provoost of N.Y. were elected to the episcopate. A special enabling act dispensed with the loyalty oath to the crown, and the two were consecrated at Lambeth in 1787. By 1789 the question of the validity of Seabury's orders (a political issue arising from his loyalist sympathies) was settled by the *General Convention. Unity with Conn. high churchmen assured, the convention went on to adopt a constitution that allowed lay participation in a *House of Deputies. Seabury's request for a separate House of Bishops was granted. Adoption of canons and a *Book of Common Prayer completed organization (see AMERICAN PRAYER BOOK).

Throughout the 19th cent. Episcopalians debated the nature of their Church vis-à-vis the C of E on the one hand and American *revivalism on the other. Pre-Tractarian high churchmen John Henry *Hobart and Benjamin Moore, along with the faculty of the General Theological Seminary (1817), anticipated the arrival of the *Oxford movement. As a result of the latter, 30 clergy and one bp. (L. S. Ives of N.C.) entered the RC Church. Tractarianism led also to heresy trials within the Church and to debates with similar *high-church movements in other denominations (e.g., Arthur Cleveland Coxe vs. John Williamson Nevin). In the 1870s older high churchmen joined *evangelicals in attempting to suppress the newer Anglo-Catholic movement led first by James DeKoven and later by "Nashotah House" (1841) in Wisconsin (see KEMPER, JACKSON). Despite the "Ritual Canon" of 1873, more elaborate ceremonial and monasticism were accepted, though not before some evangelicals broke from the Church and founded the *Reformed Episcopal Church (1873). Early evangelicals, whose model for their denomination was neither subapostolic nor medieval but late 17th-cent. Calvinistic, were led by Bps. William Meade and Charles McIlvaine and the faculty of the Virginia Theological Seminary (1823). With the abandonment of forensic and penal views of the atonement, evangelicals, some of whom had participated in the *Second Great Awakening, merged into liberalism (see LIBERAL THEOLOGY). Derived from a variety of sources, the so-called broad-church movement reflected diverse interests. The *Social Gospel, begun in the denomination by Caleb Sprague Henry (1840s), gained momentum with F.

D. Huntington's Church Association for the Advancement of the Interests of Labor and the "institutional churches" of Henry C. Potter and William Rainsford; it moved into academic circles with economist Richard T. Ely, socialist W. D. P. Bliss's *New Encyclopedia of Social Reform* (1908), and George Hodges's leadership of the Episcopal Theological School (1867). *Anglo-Catholicism, sanctioned by J. H. Hopkins's *Law of Ritualism* (1866), joined the Social Gospel with James O. S. Huntington and Vida D. Scudder, merging into F. D. Roosevelt's "New Deal" in the persons of Frances Perkins and Henry A. Wallace. Clearly the new Episcopalian social concern marked a dramatic change, for before the Civil War the issue of slavery was never mentioned in the Church, and the "Protestant Episcopal Church in the Confederate States . . . " appeared (1861) and merged again (1865) with the larger body without the slightest difficulty. Liberals related church doctrine to theories of evolution in the writings of Elisha Mulford and William P. *DuBose of the University of the South (1868).

Church unity became an increasingly pressing concern after William A. *Muhlenberg's "Memorial" of 1858. Liberal William Reed Huntington's *Chicago-Lambeth quadrilateral (1886, 1889) was succeeded by Anglo-Catholic Charles Henry *Brent's efforts in arranging for the Faith and Order Conference at Lausanne, Switzerland (1927). The period prior to World War I, when Episcopalians judged their denomination to be suited for national leadership, came to a gradual close beginning with the debate in the General Convention of 1907 over whether to extend the Social Gospel into the arena of race relations; from this the denomination drew back, the subsequent efforts of such men as William Scarlett and Walter Russell Bowie notwithstanding. Since that time the Episcopal Church has tended to revert to the various types of theological traditionalism seen in the Neo-Anglicanism of Francis Hall and John Macquarrie, Walter Lowrie's introduction of the thought of Søren Kierkegaard to North America, and Norman Pittenger's and A. T. Mollegen's "Anglicized" *neo-orthodoxy. Since 1919 the Church has had a National Council, whose activities have grown while its authority has remained advisory.

Bishops and priests constitute the ministry, with the order of deacons peripheral and temporary. Organization and authority are maintained in parishes, dioceses, and the General Convention. The denomination maintains that the Holy Scriptures are the ultimate rule of faith. The symbols of doctrine are the Apostles' and Nicene Creed; baptism and the Lord's Supper are considered to be the two sacraments necessary for salvation. Episcopalians use exclusively the Book of Common Prayer (1928) and the Hymnal (1940) in worship. The 1970s have seen full development of steps toward organic union with the RC Church (see ANGLICAN-ROMAN CATHOLIC CONSULTATION, U.S.), but also a rending of the internal unity of the Church. The split involves the proposed Prayer Book, whose revision was approved in

1976, but cannot be ratified until 1979 (see BOOK OF COMMON PRAYER). The most severe split, however, involves ordination of women to the priesthood. The issue came to a head with the ordination of 11 women on July 29, 1974, at the Church of the Advocate in Philadelphia by Bps. Daniel Corrigan, Antonio Ramos, Edward Wills, and Robert Dewitt. The General Convention of 1976 voted in favor of women's ordination. This has led Episcopalians deeply opposed to women priests into separate jurisdictions. In 1978 there is the sad prospect of permanent schism and a disruption of ecumenical progress. BIBLIOGRAPHY: J. F. Woolverton, "Histories of the Episcopal Church in America: A Survey and Evaluation," *Historical Magazine* (March 1965); W. W. Manross, *History of the American Episcopal Church* (1935); E. Clowes Chorley, *Men and Movements in the American Episcopal Church* (1946).

[J. F. WOOLVERTON]

PROTESTANT ETHIC, a term given currency esp. through the writings of M. Weber (1864–1920) to indicate the assertedly characteristic Protestant view that diligence and material success are significantly related to Christian virtue. Weber contended that the rise of industrial *capitalism owed much to the typically Calvinist and Puritan estimation of the values connected with hard work, asceticism, and frugality. BIBLIOGRAPHY: M. Weber, *Protestant Ethic and the Spirit of Capitalism* (1958).

[T. M. MCFADDEN]

PROTESTANT PRINCIPLE, the primary Protestant concept of justification by faith, sometimes called the material principle of Protestantism in distinction from the formal principle, the sole and sufficient authority of the Bible. In contemporary theology the concept is associated particularly with P. *Tillich (1886–1965), for whom it made all religious forms relative and therefore subject to criticism in the light of the ultimate. It thus became a principle of protest against idolatries, against absolutizing anything in the human sphere—social, intellectual, or religious. In the light of the Protestant principle no church structure or system of dogma could be considered final. The principle allowed Tillich to accept historical criticism of the Bible and gave him a base for criticizing forms of society that had been traditionally supported by the Churches. Tillich identified the principle with OT prophetism, but not with Protestantism as a historical movement. "The Protestant principle (which is a manifestation of the prophetic Spirit) is not restricted to the churches of the Reformation or to any other church" (*Systematic Theology,* III, 245). According to Tillich the principle is both found in every Church and betrayed by every Church. He correlated the Protestant principle with what he called the Catholic substance, "the concrete embodiment of the Spiritual Presence," and held that both were necessary. BIBLIOGRAPHY: P. Tillich, *Protestant Era* (1948).

[T. EARLY]

PROTESTANTISM, an expression of Christianity emerging from the 16th-cent. Reformation. It has become so diverse that it is difficult to delimit its boundaries or distill its essence. Chillingworth's oft-quoted statement, "The Bible and the Bible only is the religion of the Protestants," is very misleading. Also, the view that "the basic difference" between Catholics and Protestants is "the right of private judgment" (A. C. Knudson, *Protestantism: A Symposium* [ed. W. K. Anderson, 1944] 126) is far wide of the mark. The name "Protestant" originated with the Second Diet of Speyer (1529), when several princes and cities drew up a *protestatio,* objecting to the reversal of a previous decision to allow each prince (or city) to decide between Catholicism and Lutheranism. In support of their stand they affirmed: "In matters which concern the honor of God and the salvation of our souls, every individual must stand alone before God and give his account." The sense of "to protest" is not only negative; it also means "to witness." This positive note can better be seen by reviewing the origins of Protestantism than by surveying its present heterogeneity.

Origins. Although the Reformation has been interpreted in economic, political, psychological, and social terms, there is a growing reaffirmation among Catholic and Protestant scholars that it was primarily a religious movement. The development of Lutheranism was complex, but Luther's personal quest was for a "gracious God," and his insight into the meaning of justification by grace through faith was pivotal for subsequent developments. Misled partly by *nominalism and by exaggerated emphases upon the wrath of God, he found no assurance of divine forgiveness by the usual means. Through study of the Bible, he came to the insight and experience of God's free grace. The Scriptures pointed him to Jesus Christ, in whom God's grace was manifested. Tending to use hyperbole for emphasis, Luther spoke of *sola fide, sola gratia, sola scriptura,* and *solus Christus;* but for him each of these terms symbolized the same pattern in which a gracious God was central. The Scriptures were "the cradle in which Christ lay," Christ was the fullest disclosure of God's mercy, and the gospel was the good news of free pardon apart from any worthiness of the recipient. One could do nothing to merit salvation but could only repent and trust in God's mercy.

That these concepts were at the heart of Luther's concern is attested not only by Protestant but also by many modern RC scholars (Tavard, Lortz, Küng, Rahner, Adam, Bouyer, and others), who grant that these were part of sound Catholic doctrine (at least as far as they went). Many Catholics are in virtual agreement with the assertion of J. Pelikan that the Reformation was a "tragic necessity" caused by "loyalty of the Reformers to the best and highest in Roman Catholic Christianity" in the face of theological confusion and indifferent leaders (*The Riddle of Roman Catholicism* [1959] 46). J. Lortz wonders whether there would have been a Reformation "if not only Luther and his coreligionists, but all men of the time, had been fully and accurately aware that the doctrines we have mentioned are articles of the Catholic faith'' (*The Reformation: A Problem for Today* [1964] 220). There were, of course, other traditions besides the Lutheran that spread over much of Germany and the Scandinavian countries. The *Reformed Churches, stemming from Zwingli, Calvin, and others, became predominant in Switzerland, the Netherlands, and Scotland; and the Puritans were influential in England and in New England. The C of E was another Reformation Church that spread to all subsequent British colonies, although some Anglicans do not wish to be classified as Protestants. A fourth category was that of the Anabaptists, a sect that began at Zurich, and from which Mennonites, Amish, Hutterites, and other groups derived. Finally there was a miscellaneous group of mystics and rationalists, who are sometimes grouped with the Anabaptists as the left-wing of the Reformation. Most of these groups are classified as Protestant, although there are those on the fringes (e.g., mystics and Unitarians on one hand, Anglo-Catholics on the other) whose classification is problematic.

Common Heritage. In spite of many differences, the four main traditions shared Luther's basic convictions about sin, God's grace, the authority of the Bible, the lordship of Jesus Christ over the Church, justification by faith, and the priesthood of all believers. It was not the intention of Luther to found a new Church; all of the Reformers believed that they were simply recovering the pristine gospel that had become obscured by the institutionalism of the RC Church. Nevertheless, in defending his basic insights, Luther progressively questioned the abuse of indulgences, then indulgences themselves, and finally the entire sacrament of penance. Appealing to the pope, he was disappointed and called for a general council; finally he concluded that both popes and councils were subject to error. When the hierarchy seemed indifferent to reforms, he appealed to the German nobility to initiate necessary reforms, contending that they belonged to the priesthood by virtue of their baptism. Ultimately Luther rejected the concept of the Church as a divinely ordained juridical and sacramental institution, headed by a pope who claimed fullness of power over the Church and supremacy over temporal rulers on the basis of a primacy transmitted from Peter through the line of Roman bishops. He defined the Church as the ''communion of saints,'' the congregation of the faithful; and although denying that the Church was invisible, he held that it was hidden except to the eyes of faith. In no sense was the Church a worldwide organization, subject to a single head and having a magisterium that alone could rightly interpret the Bible. The number of sacraments was reduced from seven to two, and these were reinterpreted. Although he retained as much of the older service of the Mass as possible, Luther revised it to eliminate all suggestions of a sacrificial interpretation. He also rejected purgatory, images, veneration of saints, relics, monasticism, etc. Thus, beginning with his understanding of ''the just shall live by faith,'' he had felt impelled to raise one critical question after another until the Church could scarcely avoid excommunicating him.

Protestant Unity. Tensions within original Protestantism have remained difficult to keep in balance: the objective action of God vs. the individual's response to God's grace; the worthlessness of human works vs. recognition of the importance of ethics; the significance of the corporate Christian community vs. the individual conscience; unity vs. diversity; freedom vs. order. These polarizations are already present in the NT, and they opened the way to endless divisions and doctrinal divergence. One must note, however, that nearly 90% of Protestants belong to about six family groups (Lutheran, Reformed and Presbyterian, Anglican, Methodist, Baptist and Disciples, Congregationalist); the 20th cent. has seen a Protestant interest in unity manifested in mergers and in such conciliar movements as the World Council of Churches (WCC) and local and regional church councils. Also, despite differences, the essential characteristics of original Protestantism still constitute a common denominator. While interpretations of the nature of the Bible and its authority vary, there is general recognition that Scripture is the unique witness to God's revelation and that it bears the tradition by which all traditions must be judged. Protestants share Luther's concern for the gospel, although they may not all understand it in the same way. This is the fundamental emphasis of conservative Protestants, of the *Bultmann School's demythologizing and stress on kerygma, of Karl *Barth's stress on Christology as the center of theology, and of P. *Tillich's interest in alienation, ultimate concern, and the new being in Christ. The desire to acknowledge the centrality of Jesus Christ is still prominent in Protestantism, shared by fundamentalists, Christocentric liberals, neo-orthodox, and even exponents of the so-called *radical theology. Thus, despite differences among Protestants, there are still signs of preoccupation with the original interests of the Reformation.

Protestantism and Roman Catholicism. These interests are not foreign to Catholic concerns, although not all Protestant formulations of problems or their answers are acceptable to Catholics. After centuries of hostility, Protestants and Catholics have moved toward a greater degree of understanding, marked by the presence of Protestant observers at Vatican Council II, the appointment of nine Catholics as members of the Faith and Order Commission of the WCC at Uppsala in 1968, and the sharing of classes by many Protestant and Catholic seminarians in the United States. Several factors have contributed to breaking down the barriers between Protestants and Catholics; among these are Catholic recognition of the legitimacy of Luther's original concerns and insights; the conviction that the Protestant doctrine of justification by faith is not essentially different from that of the Council of Trent; Catholic clarification of the Tridentine statement regarding Scripture and tradition and growing Protestant awareness of the importance of tradition; the subordination of juridical to pastoral concerns; and greater attention to the idea of development in interpreting both doctrine and canon law.

When this greater understanding and mutual appreciation

have been gratefully acknowledged, there still remains a question as to whether there is still an insoluble difference that will indefinitely separate Catholics from Protestants. There seems to be an impasse that is related to the doctrine of the Church as a movement and as an institution, and the related points of ministry and Sacraments. It is reflected by G. Tavard when he writes that Luther was interested not only in "purifying his faith . . . , but wished to purge the faith of the church itself" (*Protestantism* [1959] 21). H. Küng says something similar when asserting that "Catholic reform cannot take place in the sphere of the absolute, the essence of Catholicism; it occurs in that of the relative, the working out at the historical level" (*The Council, Reform, and Reunion* [1961] 53). For the Protestant no institution can be exempted from judgment, and the Church itself stands in constant need of correction and reformation. This is what P. Tillich has called the *Protestant principle, i.e., that "every religious and cultural reality, including the religion and culture which calls itself 'Protestant,'" must come under judgment (*The Protestant Era* [1948] 163). Every institution (organizational forms, worship patterns, ethical systems, and doctrinal formulations) that has a human element is subject to the limitations of partial perspectives and self-assertive pride. Of course, God, Christ, and the gospel are not under man's judgment, but human apprehension of revelation develops and changes, and men revise their formulations accordingly.

Hence Protestants generally refuse to accept the possibility of any Church on earth as being exclusively "the" Church of Jesus Christ. They reject the concept of a magisterium that can speak the last irreformable word on any doctrinal question, or a pope (even with the aid of a council) who in speaking *ex cathedra* in faith and morals stands above contradiction or correction. Related to this point is the denial of a special priesthood that receives by ordination special status and power to perform the miracle of *transubstantiation. Indeed, most Protestants regard transubstantiation as alien to the meaning of the Lord's Supper, although some would concede that in the 13th cent. (with its philosophical presuppositions) it might have been an allowable way of stating the reality of Christ's presence in the Eucharist. Protestants understand that the ministry was given by Christ to the whole people of God, but that orderliness requires some specialized ministries representative of the Church as a whole. The specialized minister needs special education, but he differs from the rest of the members only as to function. In case of necessity, an unordained person might do anything that the ordained minister could do. It is difficult to be certain whether an essentially Protestant point of view is irreconcilably opposed to the Catholic meaning of such terms as "irreformable" and "infallible." Perhaps here, as in so many other instances, the difference will ultimately prove to be largely semantic. At present however, Protestant and Catholic conceptions of Church, ministry, and sacraments seem really opposed. BIBLIOGRA-PHY: L. Bouyer, *Spirit and the Forms of Protestantism*

(1957); R. M. Brown, *Spirit of Protestantism* (1965); *Christianity Divided: Protestant and Roman Catholic Theological Issues* (eds. D. Callahan et al., 1961); G. W. Forell, *Protestant Faith* (1960); O. Piper, *Protestantism in an Ecumenical Age: Its Roots, Its Rights, Its Task* (1965); W. Pauck, *Heritage of the Reformation* (rev. ed., 1961); G. H. Tavard, *Catholic Approach to Protestantism* (1955); S. J. Whale, *Protestant Tradition: An Essay in Interpretation* (1955). *CHURCH HISTORY (U.S.).

[N. H. MARING]

PROTESTANTISM, U.S., see CHURCH (U.S. HISTORY).

PROTESTANTS AND OTHER AMERICANS UNITED FOR SEPARATION OF CHURCH AND STATE (POAU), a nonprofit organization formed in 1947 with the stated purpose of maintaining "the separation of Church and State" in accord with the intention of the First Amendment of the U.S. Constitution. The organization also uses officially the shortened title, Americans United for Separation of Church and State. Headquarters are in Washington, D.C., with local chapters in each state; support is derived from a wide variety of sources. POAU informs people regarding alleged violations of the First Amendment through its monthly *Church and State*, pamphlets, films, and speakers. It sends spokesmen to congressional hearings, seeks the support of members of Congress, and finances litigation in specific cases. The RC Church has been the main target of the POAU. BIBLIOGRAPHY: L. P. Creedon and W. D. Falcon, *United For Separation: An Analysis of POAU Assaults on Catholicism* (1959); S. C. Lowell, *Embattled Wall—Americans United: An Idea and a Man* (1966). *CHURCH AND STATE.

[N. H. MARING]

PROTHESIS (Gr. for antedeposition; Sl. *zhertvennik*), a word with three interrelated uses. (1) It signifies the altarlike table, located on the north (left) side of the sanctuary of a Byzantine Church. Upon this table bread and wine for the liturgy are prepared (*proskomide*) and remain until they are borne through the church to the altar in solemn procession at the great entrance. After the communion of the faithful the remnants of the holy gifts are transferred back to the prothesis to be consumed at the end of the liturgy. The prothesis table is covered by a cloth of white linen or any other colored or brocaded fabric and it has one and sometimes two lighted candles on it when the ordinary bread and wine or the holy sacrament are present. In some churches the *artophorion* (tabernacle) is placed on it. Above the prothesis an icon of the nativity of Christ is traditionally placed. A matching table on the south side of the sanctuary is called the *diaconicon*. (2) Prothesis is also another name for the *proskomide* or preparation rite. (3) The name is sometimes given to the whole side chapel apse in which the prothesis table is located.

[A. J. JACOPIN]

PROTHONOTARY APOSTOLIC, an ancient title given originally only to the seven men responsible for registering the acts of the martyrs. Their modern successors (apostolic prothonotaries *de numero*) witness the signing of papal bulls and perform ceremonial duties in Rome. Also bearing the title (supernumerary) are certain canons of famous basilicas in Rome and elsewhere. Clerics anywhere may be named such by papal brief. By reason of their office, all vicars-general of dioceses carry the title. There are ceremonial privileges attached to the title.

[E. J. DILLON]

PROTO-EVANGELIUM, a term used in reference to Gen 3.15, "I will put enmity between you and the woman, between your seed and her seed; he shall crush your head, and you shall lie in wait for his heel."

Verbal Criticism of the Text. "He shall crush your head and you shall lie in wait for his heel." The Vulgate's translation of "she" for the "he" of this text cannot be justified. The "he" could be translated by "it" which would then refer to a collectivity. "He" is to be preferred because of poetical parallelism whereby "he" is parallel to "you" which is certainly an individual, namely, the snake. In practice, however, Hebrew thinking makes little distinction between an individual and a group and thus there is little point in quibbling, since either and both would have been understood by the author and his audience. "Shall crush" and "lie in wait" translate exactly the same verb-root in the Hebrew text. The root means something like "bruise" or "strike at," but, since the object of the verb limits the meaning of it, the CCD translation cited above is a good interpretation of the text.

Explanation of the Literary Form and Style. In general, Gen 2 and 3 are of the literary form of myth by which is not meant stories about gods but an explanation of the present world through some primeval action. Thus, in general, Gen 2 and 3 through the literary form of myth teach that mankind is ever sinful, even though God is not responsible for evil, since he had made all things very good, as Gen 1.31 had already taught.

The immediate context of Gen 3.15 is the pericope of Gen 3.14–19 whose literary form is etiology. In general, the Bible uses etiologies to set down popular causes of some evident phenomenon in order to teach some religious truth. Neither the phenomena nor the popular causes are taught. Thus, in Gen 3.14–19 the etiologies are the divine curse causing snakes to crawl, childbirth to be painful, and work to be burdensome. These things are not taught. What is taught is that mankind is cursed by temptation and that sin is punished.

Too, it is important to note that the style of Gen 2 and 3 is very anthropomorphic, e.g. God is a potter, He walks and talks, etc. Thus, in summary, the religious teaching of Gen 3.15 can be learned only after the etiology and the anthropomorphic picture of Gen 3.15 are uncovered.

Exegesis. Who are the serpent and the woman in the picture, i.e. in the anthropomorphic statement of the teaching? The serpent, for the ancients, was a figure of a magic power for cunning, sensuality, and healing. In other words, the serpent is a figure of intellectual and physical life. The woman is the same woman of all Gen 2 and 3; namely, womankind, just as Adam is mankind, a collectivity, not an individual.

In Gen 3.14–15, the serpent is cursed by being made to grovel, although in Gen 3.1 he was described as the proudest of all the beasts of the field. God makes him the traditional enemy of man in a struggle of the species in which each inflicts wounds.

With this picture in mind, the religious teaching of Gen 3.15, the Proto-evangelium, is very simple: temptation to find life away from God is a continuous curse for woman's offspring, i.e. mankind, who nevertheless has God's promise of help to find life in Him.

Messianic and Mariological Interpretations. So far discussion has centered only on the literal sense of Gen 3.15, i.e., the sense meant by both God and man. Now consideration will be given to a fuller sense or an accommodation. By fuller sense is meant a sense God intended whether known or unknown to the human author. By an accommodation is meant a pious application of the text to some later truth.

Although there has never been complete agreement on a Mariological interpretation of this text, many have seen Mary in the Vulgate's "She shall crush your head." Others have also argued for Mary's being the woman of Gen 3.15 since only she was sinless among women and thus the general application of the law of talion followed in Gen 3.14–19 would find its specification in the sinless woman. Pius XII referred to Gen 3.15 in the declaration of the dogma of the Assumption. Whether Mary is in Gen 3.15 in a fuller sense or merely an accommodation is a point of dispute. She is not present in the literal sense.

Pius IX in his bull *Ineffabilis Deus* capsulized the teaching of many writers that "the merciful Redeemer of the human race is clearly and openly foretold" in Gen 3.15. There is no difficulty in seeing the Messiah in this text once the full light of Christian revelation had been given. This light would reveal the darkness contained in Gen 3.14–15's declaration of war on the serpent. This war is against an enemy so malicious that its guilt is questionless. It will end in the complete, total degradation and humiliation of God's mortal enemy, Satan. It will deprive him for all time of the power to spoil God's work, though Satan will "lie in wait" to wound the heel of the conqueror. But, this understanding is in the fuller sense or is merely an accommodation; the author of Gen did not tell that he knew it and certainly taught nothing about a personal Messiah.

In summary then, Gen 3.15 is called the proto-evangelium. By this is meant that this is the earliest occurrence in the books of the Bible as now arranged of God's promise of help in the midst of sinfulness—and this promise finds its ultimate understanding in Christ our Savior.

BIBLIOGRAPHY: L. Hartman, "Sin in Paradise" CBQ, 20 (1958) 26–40; C. Hauret, *Beginnings: Genesis and Modern*

Science (1964); J. McKenzie, *Myths and Realities* (1963); "Archaeology and Genesis 1—11", *The Bible Today* 16 (1965) 1035–41; G. von Rad, *Genesis* (tr. J. H. Marks, 1961).

[W. E. LYNCH]

PROTOIEREUS (Gr., first priest), diocesan priest of higher rank, originally superior of cathedral clergy or rural dean. Nowadays the title is mostly honorary, and its holder is sometimes called protopope. *ARCHPRIEST; *PROTOPRESBYTER.

[F. WILCOCK]

PROTOMARTYR, first martyr, the term is applied particularly to Stephen, the first martyr recorded in the NT (Acts 7.60). It is also used for the first martyr to the Christian faith in a particular country or persecution, e.g., St. *Alban, called the protomartyr of England.

[T. EARLY]

PROTOPOPE, see PROTOIEREUS.

PROTOPRESBYTER (Gr. first elder or priest), a title reserved in Russia for the *protoierei* of the cathedrals of the Assumption and Annunciation in Moscow, the head of the military and navy chaplains, and the court chaplain.

[F. WILCOCK]

PROTOS OF MT. ATHOS, title given to the superior general of Mount Athos, elected by the abbots of its monasteries. Formerly the *protos* had to be confirmed by the Byzantine emperor. The first to be known under this title was the monk Andreas, confirmed by Emperor Leo VI (886–912). The *protos* defended Mount Athos from the growing influence of Great Monasteries as well as from the ambitions of territorial bps. of Hierissos. In 1312 Andronikos II placed the *protos* under the direct jurisdiction of the patriarch of Constantinople.

[L. PEANO]

PROTUS AND HYACINTH, SS. (date unknown), Roman martyrs buried in the cemetery of Bassilla (St. Hermes) on the Via Salaria. Beyond those basic facts nothing certain is known of them. An epitaph of Pope Damasus I mentions them as brothers. According to the late and fanciful legend they were eunuch brothers, slaves of Eugenia, Christian daughter of the prefect of Egypt, who took them with her when she fled from her father's house. After various adventures, in the course of which they converted many to the faith, the three were beheaded in the persecution of Valerian. In 1845 in the cemetery of Bassilla the remains of H. were found in a niche, the cover of which was inscribed with his name and the day of the month on which he was buried. The charred state of the remains suggested cremation or possibly death by fire. The tomb of P. was discovered nearby, but it was empty, the remains having been removed (it is thought) in the mid-9th cent. by

Pope Leo IV. BIBLIOGRAPHY: Butler 3:537–538; A. Amore, EncCatt 10:200; B. Kotter, LTK 8:838.

[R. B. ENO]

PROUDHON, PIERRE JOSEPH (1809–65), French author, journalist, and philosophical theorist in areas of social, economic, and political reform, called the "Father of Anarchy" because of movements attributed to his teachings. Born at Besançon, he attended the local college but was largely self-educated. Although he had far-flung scholarly interests, including such subjects as theology, philology, Hebrew and Greek, his principal concerns were economics and politics as witnessed by his first important treatise, *What Is Property* (1840), in which he described property as theft. However, this was not a condemnation of private property so much as of its abuses, as when economic power is so concentrated as to permit the exploitation of labor, e.g., in absentee landlordism. In P.'s view, whenever property appropriates the value produced through the labor of others, whether in rent or in interest or in profit, it is to be condemned, and so is the State insofar as it protects it and the inequitable institutions that flow from its unjust use.

Neither a Socialist nor a Communist, P. was the first to set forth the tenets of philosophic anarchism. Though usually considered to advocate the overthrow of governmental forms, anarchism for P. was itself a form of government that seeks to achieve social order, not by authoritarian imposition but by economic structures and functions freely adopted. Drawing upon the works of Kant, Comte, Feuerbach, and Hegel, in whatever measure he found these acceptable, P. formulated a dialectic against the abuses of both private property and Communism, offering a state of social liberty in which producers organize themselves in mutual interest through free contracts so that formal government becomes unnecessary. In this theory of "mutualism" under which workers over the entire world unite on an economic rather than a political basis, a rule by free association rather than by law, P. sought a perfect social order based upon an ideal of moral progress in which man himself exercises control of self among free and equal fellows. Works: *Oeuvres complètes de P. J. Proudhon* (26 v., 1867–70; Eng. tr. B. Tucker, *What Is Property?* 1876). BIBLIOGRAPHY: J. B. Robinson, *General Idea of Revolution in the Nineteenth Century* (1923).

[J. T. HICKEY]

PROVENCE, CHURCHES OF, S French Romanesque architectural school inspired by the Roman remains of the region, evident in style and detail of portal sculpture (St. Trophîme, Arles; St. Gilles-du-Gard).

[M. J. DALY]

PROVENCHER, JOSEPH NORBERT (1787–1853), Canadian missionary. He was ordained in 1811 and began his missionary labors in 1818 at the Red River Settlement in modern Manitoba, serving the settlers, as well as the nomadic Métis and the neighboring Cree Indians. In 1822

he was consecrated vicar apostolic, later bp., of St. Boniface, and entrusted with the care of the Catholics in present-day Saskatchewan and Manitoba. He established churches and brought the Oblates of Mary Immaculate to the diocese, devoting his own efforts to the Indians. BIBLIOGRAPHY: D. Frémont. *Mgr. Provencher et son temps* (1935).

[R. K. MACMASTER]

PROVERBIOS, LOS, see GOYA.

PROVERBS, BOOK OF. This compilation consists of the following seven easily recognizable collections: (1) 1.1–9.18: The "Proverbs of Solomon, son of David": prolonged admonitions of a fatherly nature, idealizing wisdom and recommending it as the most desirable of all gifts, intimately connected with God himself in his creative activity. (2) 10.1–22.16: the "Proverbs of Solomon": a collection of 375 sayings setting forth the rules of good conduct in practical, everyday living. This probably includes the earliest material in the book, some of which may well go back to the time of Solomon. (3) 22.17–24.22: "Words of the Wise": further rules for right living (probably pre-Exilic), particularly emphasizing duties to one's neighbor and the benefits of temperance and self-restraint. This section in particular exhibits points of contact with Egyptian wisdom literature. (4) 24.23–34: A further pre-Exilic collection of "Words of the Wise," praising diligence and condemning sloth. (5) ch. 25–29: A further group entitled "Proverbs of Solomon," said to have been copied by scribes of Hezekiah. It shows a special interest in religion and the law. (6) ch. 30: The "Words of Agar." (7) ch. 31: "The Words of King Lemuel," including the final acrostic poem in praise of the virtuous woman.

Insofar as one can point to a single message of Proverbs it is that man can be admitted to a share in that divine wisdom that is the supreme point in Yahweh's creative power and plan for nature and history alike. Having been so admitted, man can turn back to human living in all its aspects and apply this wisdom to it in such a way as to live wisely, moderately, and harmoniously with his fellows, and so achieve the greatest possible happiness. BIBLIOGRAPHY: D. Kidner, *Proverbs* (1964); E. Jones, *Proverbs and Ecclesiastes* (1962); W. O. E. Oesterly, *Wisdom of Egypt and the Old Testament* (1927); R. N. Whybray, *Wisdom in Proverbs* (1965); O. S. Rankin, *Israel's Wisdom Literature* (2d ed. 1954); K. V. H. Ringgren, *Word and Wisdom* (1947); A. D. Power, *Proverbs of Solomon* (1949); H. Gese, *Lehre und Wirklichkeit in der alten Weisheit* (1958).

[D. J. BOURKE]

PROVIDA MATER ECCLESIA, apostolic constitution of Pius XII, Feb. 2, 1947, giving official status to *secular institutes as a genuine form of religious life in the Church.

[T. C. O'BRIEN]

PROVIDENCE OF GOD, the divine knowledge and government of the world as the object of his love. A notion of providence is evident in man's earliest philosophical efforts and occurs in various forms within classical Greek thought. Plato condemns the opinion that the gods are not interested in human affairs; the Stoics taught God's care of the universe, even though their abstract notion of God sometimes led them to equate providence with *fate; and Aristotle firmly maintained that God cares for all things, if not in their individuality at least insofar as they are members of a species. In the OT, an awareness of providence as God's sovereignty over nature, individuals, and history is pervasive. God is the creator to whom all things are subject (Gen 8.22; Job 38.33; Ps 148.6); he has dominion over man's will (Jer 18.6; Prov 21.1); and determines the course of history, esp. that of his chosen people through whom he brings about his salvific plan (Is 7.18; Amos 9.7). The NT continues this perspective: Christ taught that God provides for all his children who must trust in him (Mt 6.25–33). Yet man's will is free, and it is through this free human cooperation that God accomplishes his eternal designs (Rom 8.14–16). This freedom explains sin in the world, even though nothing can thwart the comprehensive plan of God who works for good in everything (Rom 8.28).

Patristic reflection is typified by Augustine who explained the apparent historical evils of his time by recourse to a supernatural rather than a natural providence according to which history has purpose and meaning only insofar as it is the vehicle for man's redemption. The question of moral evil, raised esp. by the *Manichaeans, was answered through the Neoplatonic notion of evil as the privation of good and not as something positive which would be caused by the all-holy God. Scholastic theology often concerned itself with providence, linking it with the principle of finality or the order of all things toward their full realization as directed by the mind of God (ThAq ST 1a, 22.1). In regard to intelligent creatures, God's governing action follows according to the creature's natural freedom. Thus God is the primary cause of a man's free acts, but man as a secondary cause is truly capable of self-determination (*ibid.* 1a, 103.7; 83.1 ad 3). BIBLIOGRAPHY: EDB 1951–54; Augustine, *Divine Providence and the Problem of Evil* (ed. and tr. R. Russell, 1942); Thomas Aquinas, *Providence and Predestination* (tr. R. W. Mulligan, 1961); R. Hazelton, *Providence* (1958).

[T. M. MCFADDEN]

PROVIDENTISSIMUS DEUS, an encyclical letter of Leo XIII (Nov. 18, 1893) urging a deeper study of Sacred Scripture in view of attacks by natural scientists and rationalists. The Pope insists that since the entire Bible has God for its principal author there can be no real contradiction in the Bible itself and no real conflict between the theologian and the natural scientist if each remains in his proper field. He also gives the directives for the interpretation and defense of the Bible. BIBLIOGRAPHY: ASS 26 (1893–94) 269–292; D 3280–94; *Rome and the Study of Scripture* (Eng. tr., 1962).

[J. H. ROHLING]

PROVINCE, ECCLESIASTICAL, a territory made up of several dioceses and erected by the Holy See, i.e., constituted as a province and given its boundaries (CIC, c. 215, §1). The structure consists of a metropolitan see (usually an archdiocese) and one or more suffragan sees. The metropolitan does not have direct power over the suffragan sees, but does have oversight and can intervene, with permission of the Holy See, where there is neglect; he receives appeals from judicial sentences and is a judge in controversies. The province holds a provincial council at least every 20 years; the bps. meet every 5 years to further the spiritual life in the dioceses and to make administrative decisions. Vatican Council II strongly supported the place of ecclesiastical provinces and their synods in discussing interregional cooperation among bps., recommended that where necessary territorial boundaries of provinces be revised for efficiency, and that every diocese not already incorporated into a province be so incorporated. The conciliar consideration of this matter is bound with its determinations concerning *episcopal conferences (see VatII BpPastOff, nn. 39–41). One of the standing committees of the National Conference of Catholic Bishops is responsible for determining boundaries of dioceses and provinces.

[T. C. O'BRIEN]

PROVINCE, RELIGIOUS, a juridic and usually geographical division of a religious institute formed by grouping or uniting a number of religious houses under one major superior, the provincial. Provinces are generally established when the institute grows and spreads too much to be governed by one general superior; regional administration and government are in the hands of provincials. Pontifically approved religious institutes obtain the right to divide into provinces through the Holy See.

[R. A. TODD]

PROVINCIAL, in a religious institute, the major superior over a region or province, which must consist of at least three canonically erected houses (CIC, c. 488, n.6). In clerical institutes enjoying *exemption he has power of *jurisdiction in the external *forum. Requirements for holding the office of provincial include being at least 30 years old, being professed for at least 10 years (*ibid.*, c. 504). The provincial must reside in the provincial residence (*ibid.*, c. 508), make periodic canonical visitation of the province (*ibid.*, c. 511), exercise a supervisory care over the *économe's administration of finances.

[T. C. O'BRIEN]

PROVINCIAL LETTERS (Les Provinciales), full title: *Lettres écrites par Louis de Montalte à un Provincial;* a series of 18 letters written in 1656–57 by Blaise *Pascal, probably with the cooperation of Antoine *Arnauld and Pierre Nicole. Meant as a defense of Arnauld, then on trial before the theological faculty of the Sorbonne for his Jansenist views, they satirically attack the Jesuits, characterizing their ideas on moral questions as lax and essentially casuistic (i.e., applying general precepts to a diversity of cases). Letters 5–9 bear the burden of Pascal's ironic attack on Jesuit moral theology; letters 1–3 defend Arnauld; and letters 15–16 protest as unjust the persecution of the Jansenist center at *Port-Royal. The letters were successful from the first because of their topical nature, but they are also a classic of French literature because of the brilliance of Pascal's style and his passionate advocacy of a cause in which he firmly believed. His own deep spirituality was repelled by what he considered mere toying with the divine. The letters were placed on the Index by Roman authorities soon after their publication. BIBLIOGRAPHY: Eng. tr. by A. G. Krailsheimer (pa., 1968); J. Mesnard, *Pascal: His Life and Works* (tr. G. S. Fraser, 1952).

[L. TINSLEY]

PROVISION, the concession of an ecclesiastical office made in legal form by the appropriate ecclesiastical authority. Historically, it denotes the right of the papacy to dispose of or "provide to" all benefices. The oldest form (1137) of "provision" was a simple request by the pope to give a benefice to a certain cleric. By the middle of the 13th cent. these requests had turned into mandates; by the middle of the 14th cent., a thorough, profitable system had been established, chiefly through legislation of John XXII. BIBLIOGRAPHY: The standard monograph in English is G. Barraclough, *Papal Provisions* (1935).

[L. E. BOYLE]

PROVISORS, STATUTE OF. Papal provisions, i.e., appointments, often of nonresident aliens, by the pope to English ecclesiastical offices, provoked opposition as financial and political encroachments, esp. after the Avignonese Papacy (1309–77) was identified with France. Although often used for deserving candidates, provisions caused the first Statute of Provisors (1351). This asserted the right of English electors and patrons to fill ecclesiastical vacancies, with imprisonment for papal provisors (appointees) until they paid compensation and refused appeal. The king could appoint directly if the papacy intervened. The second Statute of Provisors (1390) penalized clerics accepting papal favors and banned retaliatory pronouncements. BIBLIOGRAPHY: G. Barraclough, *Papal Provisions* (1935).

[W. A. CHANEY]

PROVOST (PREVOST), JAN (1465–1529), Flemish painter working in Antwerp and Bruges (1493–94). Competing with H. Memling of the "old school," P. strove to inject the "new" spirit of Antwerp—a hybrid mannerism—into Bruges. His *Adoration of the Kings,* and two *Pietàs* (Zurich and Prado) suggest the mellow, soft, later style. A *Last Judgment, Madonna with Angels*, and *St. Catherine Disputing*, distinguished by light color, youthful figures, soft forms, and flowing drapery, recall Metsys. P.'s works, through stylistic affinities, have been attributed to Metsys and to Memling. BIBLIOGRAPHY: M. J. Friedländer, *Early Netherlandish Painting* (tr. H. Norden, 1967); C. D. Cuttler, *Northern Painting* (1968).

[M. J. DALY]

PROVOST, a title derived from the Latin *praepositus,* used in some countries in different vernacular adaptations. In its earliest Christian usage *praepositus* was the title given to the chief executive official, under the abbot, in a monastery. Later it was used as the title of the head of a cathedral or collegiate chapter. It is the proper title for the head of certain colleges in England, and in some U.S. colleges and universities it designates a high official, the nature of whose duties varies from institution to institution. In its Latin form the term is used as the title, or part of the title (e.g. *praepositus generalis*) of the head of certain orders or congregations, but this is not commonly translated into English as provost.

[P. K. MEAGHER]

PRUDENCE (Lat. *prudentia;* Gr. *phronēsis*), practical wisdom, the intellectual and moral virtue of choosing and pursuing the right means to right ends. Its name, like that of charity, has come down in the world, and now suggests a contriving and accommodating, even a mean-spirited quality, which, if defensible, is scarcely admirable. For Aristotle, however, it holds the key to good moral practice; for St. Thomas Aquinas it represents the energetic, and on occasion heroic, descent of grace into the dusty arena of human deeds, so much so that the real tussle is seen as less one between conscience and law than as one between truth in the concrete and conformity to an abstract ideal. For the real world is largely, though not entirely, intractable by pure reason, and the human actions performed in it cannot be wholly resolved into the generalizations that form the stock-in-trade of philosophical and theological science, even as regards their moral teachings. These are essential, indeed without them the good life would be little more than a series of disconnected improvisations to situations as they arise, animated by a highly personalist love; nevertheless we are not meant to be hide-bound by them, but to go out from them and mingle with incidents, contingencies, and individuals, and stand or fall by the attitudes we take up and the decisions we make. For this man's native powers of intelligence are not enough, not even when instructed by theory; he must be schooled by experience and, moreover, have the will of doing the right things.

These two are supplied by the good "habit" or settled "training" of prudence, first, namely, the wit to see what should be done, and second, the readiness to do it. By the first it is an intellectual *virtue, sufficiently informed about the principles and conclusions or credal formularies in faith and morals, yet which recognizes that their application to a given case is not a straight inference drawn as a conclusion from them, but rather a determinative construction of them. By the second it is a moral virtue, affectively disposed to be fair to others, brave in the face of frightening circumstances, and tempered about pleasures. Prudence does not work in a vacuum; one cannot be prudently prudent, but only prudently obedient, patient, and so forth. Thus prudence is a virtue in human acts directed to ends not its own. It is an *orthos logos,* a *recta ratio agibilium,* a right reason in the doing of things. What this means will appear in the delineation of its features.

The parts of a virtue are classified into three groups (see VIRTUE), (1) its component elements or integral parts, (2) its kinds or species, and (3) its close allies or virtual parts. Arranged according to this classification the parts of prudence are as follows:

(1) The Latin Stoics—and they were followed here by the patristic and ascetical authors—considered prudence less as a special virtue than as a general condition of all moral virtue, that is to say, as the sagacious side of living according to reason, and they were detailed and acute in their description. Thus it required memory for lessons of the past, insight into situations, getting the hang of a thing, a quick response to the unexpected, a readiness to learn, foresight, wariness, and an appreciation of circumstances.

(2) The specific types are personal prudence (*prudentia monastica*) in the direction of one's own life, and social prudence, which, after Aristotle, is divided into statesmanship (*prudentia regnativa*), political good sense in citizens (*prudentia politica*), and household management (*prudentia oeconomica*). To these the medievals, who saw a special virtue in the defense of one's country, which they were not content to leave to the art of war, added good generalship (*prudentia militaris*).

(3) The character of prudence as a special virtue is best apparent in the consideration of the prudential virtues that cluster around it. These are the qualities of being well-advised or of good counsel (*eubulia*), of coming to right decisions from sound judgment (*synesis*), which in the exceptional case in which ordinary rules do not fit and recourse must be had to higher principles is called *gnōmē*. This last operates in cases of *epikeia*. These three parts of prudence direct one's deliberations and choices of what he intends to do. The executive command (*imperium*) of reason needed to put the choices into effect (*usus*) is the special function of prudence itself, which therefore can be defined as the virtue that translates right choices into practice.

The vices against prudence follow the pattern of those against the other moral virtues, and they err either by excess or defect. The first include worldly prudence (*prudentia carnis*), being over-solicitous about temporal matters, low cunning (*astutia*) expressed in guile and fraud. The second, generally called imprudence, includes scorning advice, being negligent, precipitate, and fickle.

Technically *conscience is an act, not a moral sense, a practical judgment that this should be done or that avoided, and therefore when right belongs to *synesis*. It commands respect whenever it is sincere, and then to disobey it is always wrong. Yet it may be mistaken or doubtful, and therefore is not always a safe guide for conduct. Moreover a person may have a good conscience, yet, as when he sins, may choose to go against it. Whereas prudence, as has been indicated, goes beyond the judgment about what is to be done, and effectively carries the act into execution. Sure and unerring, it does not expect the certitude of the theoretic sciences nor undue verification by or reassurance from a system of laws (though this was attempted in the heyday of casuistry), but, fair-spirited, robust, and honorable it carries friendship with God into the business of living. BIBLIOGRA-PHY: ThAq ST (Lat-Eng v. 23; T. Gilby, NCE 11:925–928.

[T. GILBY]

PRUDENTIUS, AURELIUS CLEMENS (348–after 405), the most esteemed of the Christian Latin poets. A native of Spain, P. turned to poetry after a career in law and public office. Adopting an ascetical way of life, he sought to make amends for his past life, and esp. the wantonness of his youth by singing the praises of God. He brought freshness and originality to the classic forms, in which he was profoundly versed, by skillfully adapting them to Christian themes and habits of thought. His poetry is less suitable for the liturgy than the Ambrosian hymn. His thought unfolds itself at too slow a pace and he does not confine its expression within the narrow metrical and symmetrical limits of the liturgical hymn. Nevertheless, excerpts from his poems, esp. from the *Cathemerinon,* have been incorporated into the Latin liturgy (see M. Britt, *Hymns of the Breviary and Missal* [rev. ed. 1948]). The *Cathemerinon* is a collection of poems for the hours of the day. Among his other better known works are *Peristephanon,* which contains hymns celebrating various martyrs, a work inspired by his visiting the tombs of the Apostles while on a pilgrimage to Rome in 403; *Apotheosis,* on the divinity of Christ; *Hamartigenia,* on the origin of sin; and *Contra Symmachum,* a poem written against the resurgent pagan party in Rome. His *Psychomachia,* an allegory of the battle within the soul between the virtues and the vices, though not his greatest poem, was widely read during the Middle Ages and exercised a broad influence upon both literature and art. Works: PL 59 and 60; CSEL 61 (crit. text ed. J. Bergman, 1926); Loeb 387, 398 (text and tr. ed. N. J. Thomson, 1949). BIBLIOGRAPHY: F. J. E. Raby, *History of Christian Latin Poetry* (1927) 44–71; Altaner 478–481; G. Bardy, DTC 13:1076–79; Lex AW 2464, bibliog.

[R. B. ENO]

PRUDENTIUS OF TROYES (d. 861), native of Spain, bp. of Troyes (NW France), defender of the predestinarian teaching of *Gottschalk of Orbais. P. wrote a *De praedestinatione contra Joannem Scotum* (Erigena) and an *Epistola*

ad Hincmarum (Hincmar of Reims, opponent of Gottschalk). P.'s position in his *Epistola tractoria* is more in conformity with St. Augustine's than the teaching his earlier works defended.

PRÜM, ABBEY OF, a monastery in the Rhineland, N of Trier. One of the most famous Benedictine abbeys of Germany, it was founded in 721 by a noblewoman, Bertrada, with the aid of St. Willibrord, then abbot of Echternach. Prüm became the "family monastery" of the Carolingians; Emperor Lothar I died and was buried there 855. The annals of Abbot Regino (until 906) are among the most valuable sources of empire history of that age. With the 13th cent. decay set in. In 1222, 32 nobles and knights were its vassals. The immense riches of the abbey excited the jealousy of the neighboring abps. of Trier. Finally in 1576, the abbey with its independent principality was united to the archbishopric. The community was suppressed in 1802. The buildings (18th cent.) are used now as parish church, schools, and offices. BIBLIOGRAPHY: *Handbuch der Historischen Stätten Deutschlands* 5:294–297; J. Semmler, LTK 8:848–850, with full bibliog.

[N. BACKMUND]

PRÜMMER, DOMINIKUS (1866–1931), German Dominican, canonist and moral theologian. A Dominican from 1884, after receiving his doctorate in canon law at Rome in 1908, he spent the rest of his life as professor at the Univ. of Fribourg, Switzerland. His *Manuale theologiae moralis secundum principia S. Thomae Aquinatis* (3 v., 1914; 10th ed. 1946) is characterized by conciseness in its summaries of Aquinas's moral teaching; its defense of the moral system termed *compensationalism; its incorporation of pertinent material from the CIC. P. also published *Manuale juris ecclesiastici* (2 v. 1907–09), and edited *Fontes vitae S. Thomae Aquinatis . . .* (1911–37).

[T. C. O'BRIEN]

PRUNER, JOHANN EVANGELIST (1827–1907), moral theologian at the seminary of Eichstätt, Germany, rector from 1862, author of the pastorally oriented *Katholische Moraltheologie* (2 v., 1875–77) and *Lehrbuch der Pastoraltheologie* (2 v., 1900).

[T. C. O'BRIEN]

PRUS, BOLESLAW (1847–1920), pseud. of Alexander Glowacki, novelist and short story writer. A young romantic, P. took part in the unfortunate Polish uprising against Russian domination in 1863, which brought him a term in prison. The experience disillusioned him and P. became a realist, looking for the betterment of Poland through a realistic approach, hard work, and improvement of social and economic conditions. Out of journalistic work on *Warsaw Courier* came the short stories and later the novels that made him famous. In the short stories he achieved an international reputation as one of the few Slavic masters of that genre. P. was particularly able in delineating peasant life in Poland, as is evident in his first novel, *The Outpost* (1885). The most famous of the novels was *The Pharaoh and the Priests* (1895–1896), in which he used an ancient setting to illustrate modern problems. P. is regarded as a founder of the modern novel and has often been compared to Charles Dickens.

[J. R. AHERNE]

PRYNNE, WILLIAM (1600–69), Puritan polemicist and pamphleteer. After Oxford and Lincoln's Inn (1621) he became a lawyer. Beginning with his *Histriomastix* of 1632 he suffered, in the cause of publishing his views, imprisonments, disbarment, heavy fines, physical disfigurement. In over 200 pamphlets and monographs, he throughout his life published attacks on the royal family of Charles I, Anglican ritual and episcopal polity, the Independents, the Levellers, the Quakers, the papists; he strongly defended Presbyterianism and subjection of Church to State. He won a seat in Parliament in 1648 and again in 1660, and towards the end of his life found favor with Charles II, who made him Keeper of the Tower Records. P.'s major work of historical interest is *Brevia Parliamentaria rediviva* (1162).

[T. C. O'BRIEN]

PSALMODY, the singing or recitation of the psalms in worship. The early Church took over the practice from Jewish worship, and it has been an important part of Christian liturgy through the centuries. Recited in plainsong (Gregorian chant), the Psalms became a major part of the monastic Divine Office. *Reformed, Lutheran, and Anglican Churches all maintained the use of psalms in worship. Reformed churches have been esp. noted for their emphasis on the singing of psalms, which they sang from metrical Psalters. Considerable controversy raged over the question of composing new texts not taken directly from the Bible. The hymnals of C. *Wesley (1707–88) and I. Watts (1674–1748) included both metrical psalms and new texts, and served as a bridge toward the current situation in which Protestant hymnody makes only slight use of psalmody. BIBLIOGRAPHY: J. A. Lamb, *Psalms in Christian Worship* (1962).

[T. EARLY]

PSALMS, BOOK OF. This compilation of 150 rhythmic prayer poems of a type peculiar to the ancient Near East was assembled over a period extending from the early monarchy to late post-Exilic times, the First and Second Temples probably providing the chief seed-beds for psalm composition. In the compilation as it now exists the enumeration of the Septuagint and derived versions differs from that of the Masoretic text and derived versions in that Ps 9,113 in the Septuagint correspond respectively to Ps 9–10 and 114–15 in the Hebrew, while Ps 146–147 in the Septuagint corresponds to 147 in the Hebrew, with the effect that the enumeration of the Hebrew and its derivatives is one in advance of the enumeration of the Septuagint and its derivatives for most of the Psalter.

The titles of the psalms do not provide a sound basis for classification. Instead the psalm categories evolved by H. Gunkel have been almost universally adopted nowadays with only minor modifications. Gunkel held that the "setting in life" in which particular types of psalm were characteristically composed could be reconstructed, and on this basis he divided the psalms into the following categories:

Hymns. An introductory "summons to praise" is addressed to the Israelite people, to Zion, to the priests or even to heaven and earth and their inhabitants. This is followed by the main part of the hymn, the "grounds for praise," in which Yahweh's wisdom, power, and goodness as manifested in nature and history are extolled. Finally the conclusion of the hymn often resumes and reiterates the introductory motifs.

Royal Psalms. Often quasi-prophetic in character, these magnify the power, wisdom, or warrior strength that Yahweh bestows upon the Davidic king either at his enthronement or in the course of his reign.

The Communal Laments. These were probably composed for some regularly recurring occasion of mourning, a fastday, or day of penance, or else on the occasion of some isolated calamity in the life of the people.

Individual Laments. These constitute far the largest category in the Psalter. The introduction usually consists of an urgent entreaty for help, in which Yahweh is often addressed by his covenant name and in the imperative. This is followed by a section setting forth the reasons why Yahweh should respond: chiefly his own honor as covenant God, his attributes of mercy, justice, chivalry to the poor, etc., the psalmist's own sufferings and the malice and wickedness of his enemies. Then follows an expression of trust in which the psalmist often changes to a mood of triumph, as though anticipating the answer to his prayer. Finally this type characteristically concludes with a "vow to offer praise" in return for the help which the psalmist is confident of receiving.

Thanksgivings. In these the psalmist summons his fellows to praise Yahweh for intervening favorably in his own personal life. He also usually dedicates his future life to praising Yahweh.

Wisdom Psalms. In these the wonders of divine wisdom are extolled, esp. as manifested in the Law; and the happiness accruing to those who follow this wisdom is described. Other minor categories are the Psalms of Trust, Prophetic Psalms and Pilgrimage Psalms. The distinctive characteristic of the psalms is a deep awareness of Yahweh's *responsiveness* as covenant God to his people's words. BIBLIOGRAPHY: H. J. Kraus, *Psalmen* I–II (1961); H. Lamparter, *Das Buch der Psalmen* I–II (1959); C. S. Rodd, *Psalms 1–72* (1963), Psalms 73–150 (1964); R. Tournay and M. Schwab, *Les Psaumes* (3d ed. rev. by A. Gelineau et al. 1964); B. Gemser et al., *Studies on Psalms* (1963); G. S. Gunn, *God in the Psalms* (1956); R. de Langhe, *Le*

Psautier, ses origines, ses problèmes littéraires, son influence (1963); S. Mowinckel, *Psalms in Israel's Worship* I–II (1962); H. Ringgren, *Faith of the Psalmists* (1963); L. Sabourin, *Un classement littéraire des Psaumes* (1964); A. Weiser, *The Psalms* (1962).

[D. J. BOURKE]

PSALTER (Gr. *Psalterion,* stringed instrument for accompaniment of the psalms), term used in two senses: (1) in the Middle Ages, a book containing the psalms used in the Divine Office (*psalterium*), and later that part of the Breviary containing the psalms; (2) the Book of *Psalms itself. The Psalter, in this second sense, was formed by the liturgical use in the Jewish Temple; it became the hymnal of the Second Temple. The Psalter is usually considered to have five distinct parts or ''books,'' possibly after the model of the Pentateuch. These divisions are indicated in the text itself at Ps 41.14, 72.19; 89.52, 106.48 and 150.6—the group of psalms before each of these doxologies forming a unit. The enumeration of the 150 psalms forming the Psalter differs in Bible versions based on the Hebrew Bible and those based on the Greek or Vulgate versions. Psalms 10–148 are numbered one ahead in the Hebrew Bible, because the Greek and Vulgate joins Ps 9–10 and 114–115, then divide Ps 116 and 147 into two. The Hebrew enumeration is followed by the AV, RSV, Chicago Bible, Jerusalem Bible; the Greek and Vulgate by the Douay and Confraternity Versions.

[T. EARLY]

PSALTER, GALLICAN, popular name for St. Jerome's second Latin version of the *Psalter, also known as the Vatican Vulgate edition. This version, based on the *Hexapla* of Origen, was undertaken at the request of SS. Paula and Eustochium between 387 and 391. By the 6th cent. it was in general use in Gaul, hence the Gallican designation. Eventually it came to replace the Roman Psalter (St. Jerome's first revision) in liturgical use and in 1568 was incorporated into the Breviary of Pius V. Because of this association with the Breviary until 1945, when the option was given to use a new version, it was the best known of the Psalters. It is not without some difficulties, containing occasionally incomprehensible verses because of faulty translation or a disregard for biblical thought forms. BIBLIOGRAPHY: H. Leclercq, DACL 14.2:1951–1952.

[B. C. ROSENDALL]

PSALTER, ROMAN, Latin version of the psalms, used esp. in Italy until the pontificate of Pius V (1566–72), when it was replaced, except at St. Peter's Basilica in Rome, by the Gallican Psalter. The claim that it is Jerome's first translation of the psalms, a correction of the *Old Latin version produced *c.* 384, has been questioned. The Roman Missal and Breviary retained some elements based on the Roman Psalter.

[T. EARLY]

PSALTERIUM JUXTA HEBRAEOS (Psalter from the Hebrews) a Latin translation of the psalms made by St. Jerome from the Hebrew text. This version never was widely used in the Church, although Jerome preferred it to his translation that became the Gallican Psalter. A modern edition by H. de Ste. Marie from the few surviving MSS appeared in 1954.

[T. C. O'BRIEN]

PSALTERIUM PIANUM, a designation for the *Liber psalmorum cum canticis* published by authority of Pius XII in 1945 for use in the Roman Breviary, and referred to in English as the New Latin Psalter. The translation, made by professors of the Pontifical Biblical Institute, was from the Hebrew text into a stiff and school-exercise type of classical Latin. The translation was meant to correct the inadequacies of the Gallican Psalter. Praised for its clarity, the *Psalterium pianum* has also been criticized as unsuited for liturgical chant.

[T. C. O'BRIEN]

PSALTERS, METRICAL, paraphrase translations of the psalms into metered verse in the vernacular. Protestants, wishing to have the entire congregation join in singing, prepared metrical Psalters that would be more suitable for the purpose than Latin versions chanted by choir monks. Calvin issued his first metrical Psalter in 1539, and other influential versions included the French Psalter of Marot and Beza, with music by Bourgeois (1562), and the English Psalter of Sternhold and Hopkins (1562). *Reformed Churches were distinguished from the Lutheran by insistence on closer fidelity to the biblical text in congregational singing, whereas Lutheran chorales employed poetic and religious sentiment not strictly in biblical wording. English and Scottish Protestants in Geneva produced the Anglo-Genevan Psalter of 1561 and the Scottish Psalter of 1564. The Church of Scotland has been particularly noted for its use of psalmody. Though Sternhold and Hopkins included some freely composed hymns, the work of I. Watts (1674–1748) and C. *Wesley (1707–88) was decisive in freeing English-speaking Protestants from rigid adherence to biblical texts and for the supplanting of psalms with hymns in congregational worship. BIBLIOGRAPHY: M. Patrick, *Four Centuries of Scottish Psalmody* (1949).

[T. EARLY]

PSEAUME, NICOLAS (1518–75), Premonstratensian abbot of St. Paul, Verdun, from 1540; bp. of Verdun from 1548. He represented his order at the Council of Trent in 1551 and as bp. of Verdun took part in the final sessions in 1562. He contributed notably to the formation of the Council's disciplinary decrees and edited the conciliar acta. In his own diocese he built up its religious institutions, brought in the Jesuits to further education, and both preached and wrote in defense of Catholic teaching against the Reformers.

[T. C. O'BRIEN]

PSELLUS, MICHAEL (1018–*c.*1078), Byzantine scholar and statesman. A prolific writer in history, theology, and philosophy. P. was the first professor of philosophy at the Univ. of Constantinople. He was noted for stressing the ancient classics, esp. Plato, which led him to be suspected by the Church. P. was imperial secretary (1041–42) and later secretary of state (1042–45), but his involvement in court intrigues led to his dismissal. His writing includes commentaries on Plato, Aristotle, and the Bible, and his *Chronography* remains an important historical source for the years 976–1077. BIBLIOGRAPHY: Beck 538–542; J. M. Hussey, *Church and Learning in the Byzantine Empire* (1937) 867–1185.

[G. T. DENNIS]

PSEUDO-CLEMENTINES, the following early Christian writings erroneously attributed to or linked with Clement of Rome: (1) Two *Epistles to Virgins,* written probably in Palestine during the 3d cent., which describe the ideals of celibate life and the dangers that threaten it. (2) *Homilies,* written between 325 and 380, a series of 20 sermons supposedly preached by St. Peter. Two letters (one from Peter, the other from Clement) to James, bp. of Jerusalem, serve as a preface to the discourses. (3) *Recognitions,* dating from the second half of the 4th cent., a minute account of the manner in which Clement and members of his family, separated by unusual events, meet and recognize one another through the good offices of Peter. (4) *Epitomes* which contain two excerpts from the *Homilies,* the supposed letter of Clement, and the *Martyrdom of Clement.* BIBLIOGRAPHY: H. Baus, LTK 6:334–335; H. Dressler, NCE 11:942–943.

[H. DRESSLER]

PSEUDO-DIONYSIUS (late 5th or early 6th cent.), author of mystical treatises of great importance and influence. The writer, who assumed as a pseudonym the name of St. Paul's Athenian convert Dionysius the Areopagite (Acts 17.34), is first mentioned by *Severus Patriarch of Antioch in 533 A.D. Severus quotes him as an authority and indicates that his writings must have been in circulation for some time before. The writings were almost universally regarded as those of the 1st-cent. Dionysius and, before the Renaissance, enjoyed an authority only little short of Scripture itself. In the East they were commented on by Maximus the Confessor and were cited as an authority by St. *John Damascene. In the West Pope Martin I appealed to their authority in the First Lateran Council in 649, and in 858 *John Scotus Erigena, at the request of Charles the Bald, translated them into Latin and commented upon them. These treatises played an enormous role in the history of medieval and early modern theology, and in particular, in the development of mystical theology. Elaborate commentaries were written upon them, e.g., by *Hugh of St. Victor, *Albert the Great, *Thomas Aquinas, Meister *Eckhart, J. Tauler, J. van *Ruysbroeck, and *John of the Cross. While questioning voices began to be raised from the early 16th

cent. about the authorship of Dionysius the Areopagite and a 1st-cent. date for the content of the treatises, it remained for two scholars working independently, J. Stiglmayr and H. Koch, to solve the problem in 1895 by a penetrating use of higher criticism. They demonstrated that the author was a Christian Neoplatonist and that he could not be earlier than *Proclus who was one of his sources. Further research has confirmed their pioneer contribution. The treatises were composed about 500 A.D., but the identity of the writer is still unknown.

The treatises are: "On the Divine Names" (*De divinis nominibus*), "On Mystical Theology" (*De mystica theologia*), "On the Celestial Hierarchy" (*De caelesti hierarchia*), and "On the Ecclesiastical Hierarchy" (*De ecclesiastica hierarchia*). The *Corpus Dionysiacum* includes also 11 letters written, among others, to "John the theologian, apostle, and evangelist, exiled on the island of Patmos," and to "Titus," the disciple of St. Paul. Letters I (On the knowledge of God), V (On the divine darkness) and IX (On wisdom and on affirmative and negative theology) are esp. important, as they shed light on the author's mysticism. He reflects Neoplatonic philosophy and theology as it had developed from *Plotinus through *Proclus, the emphasis on the latter's triads being repeatedly in evidence. "On the Divine Names" is the basic theological work of Dionysius. It comprises 13 chapters, the three first forming an introduction and stressing Scripture as the means for attaining a knowledge of God. Chapters 4–13 deal with the names given to God in Scripture and explain them in such a way as to give a pure, intellectual, and spiritual idea of God, one removed as far as possible from the senses and imagination. His "Mystical Theology" in 5 chapters teaches and commends another approach to the knowledge of God which is "secret," mystical, and higher than the first described. This knowledge comes from God himself, who reveals himself in the superluminous darkness and in silence that initiates into the mysteries. Preparation is made for this silence of the mind, not so much by affirming the special perfections of God as by denying to him all created perfection, beginning with the lowest. When the soul has arrived at the highest of the perfections denied, it will be completely speechless (*aphōnos*) and will be fully united with the Ineffable. The latter part of the work explains the absolute transcendence of God. The treatises "On the Celestial Hierarchy," and "On the Ecclesiastical Hierarchy," are complementary and are dominated by a mystical theory of the author on santification, which he calls a deification (*theōsis*). This deification comprises three successive operations: purification, illumination, and perfection (*catharsis, phōtismos, teleiōsis*). God does not perform this triple action on us directly, but makes use of intermediaries that are subordinate to each other and thus constitute a hierarchy. The purpose of this hierarchy is to achieve union with God, but it must keep its eyes constantly fixed on God, the guide of all knowledge and action. There is a twofold hierarchy, the celestial or angelic, and the terrestrial, or ecclesiastical.

The treatise "On the Celestial Hierarchy" comprises 15 chapters. The angels are divided into three hierarchies, each having three orders. The first hierarchy (Seraphim, Cherubim, Thrones), receives directly from God purity, light, and perfection, and transmits these to the second (*Dominations, Virtues,* and *Powers*); the second hierarchy transmits the same in turn to the third hierarchy (Principalities, Archangels, and Powers). The second hierarchy watches over the good of all creation, while the third, which is nearest to men, has the task of helping humanity *in toto* and individually. All angels are spiritual beings, simple, intelligible, and intelligent. "On the Ecclesiastical Hierarchy" in 7 chapters is a kind of mystical and symbolic treatise on the liturgy, in which the ecclesiastical hierarchy exercises functions analagous to those of the celestial hierarchy. Contemplation plays a central role throughout the treatises, and Scripture is stressed as the foundation of all contemplation and knowledge of God. The author deliberately makes wide use of allegory, and probably more in the tradition of the Alexandrians than directly on the model of *Porphyry and *Proclus. His teaching is esp. rich on the divine attributes, on angels, and on the Sacraments. Despite his lack of emphasis on Christ, and the charge that he was a Monophysite, a careful analysis of his theology indicates that he was orthodox in his Trinitarian teaching. BIBLIOGRAPHY: Texts: PG 3:119–1122; T. Campbell, *Dionysius the Pseudo-Areopagite: The Ecclesiastical Hierarchy* (1955); *Dionysiaca, Receuil donnant l' ensemble des traductiones latines des ouvrages attribués au Denys de l' Aréopage* (ed. P. Chevalier, 2 v., 1937; 1950). Studies: D. Rutledge, *Cosmic Theology* (1964); G. Théry, *Études Dionysiennes* (2 v., 1937; 1950); H. F. Dondaine, *Le Corps Dionysien de l' Université de Paris an XIIIᵉ siècle* (1953).

[M. R. P. MCGUIRE]

PSEUDO-MATTHEW, GOSPEL OF, see APOCRYPHA (NT), 58.

PSICHARI, ERNEST (1883–1914), French writer and soldier. The grandson of Renan, P. was baptized in the Greek Orthodox rite but received no formal religious training. After taking a licentiate in philosophy, P., disillusioned with the prevalent intellectual atmosphere, joined the colonial artillery (1903) and thereafter led a soldier's life, principally in North Africa. Several influences were operative in his spiritual development culminating in conversion to Catholicism (1913): Bergson's critique of rationalism, Péguy's mystique of France, the quest for order reflected in army, Church, and religious communities, and the experience of faith afforded by contact with Islam. A Dominican tertiary, P. contemplated becoming a Dominican before his death in battle (Aug. 1914). His novels—*L'Appel des armes* (1913) and *Le Voyage du centurion* (published 1915, Eng. tr. *A Soldier's Pilgrimage*)—embody a major theme of the Catholic Revival, viz., the spiritualization of patriotism

crystallized in the army as a matrix of Christian heroism and in the figure of the soldier-saint. Insights into his religious thought will be found in selected correspondence published as *Lettres du centurion: l'adolescent, le voyageur, le croyant* (1947) and in *Terres de soleil et de sommeil* (1908). BIBLIOGRAPHY: W. Fowlie, *Ernest Psichari. A Study in Religious Conversion* (1939); H. Daniel-Rops, *Psichari* (1947); and A. M. Goichon, *Ernest Psichari* (1953).

[G. E. GINGRAS]

PSYCHIANA, an American religious cult, promoted in the popular press and by direct mail advertising, without any ecclesiastical organization. It was begun in 1929 by Frank B. Robinson of Moscow, Idaho, the son of an English Baptist preacher, who had studied at the Bible Training School in Toronto, Canada. Robinson had very strong prejudices against the Christian Churches and the Christian message itself. He developed a religious system that began with absolute monotheism and totally rejected traditional Christian teachings. Robinson's God was impersonal, being simply Power or Life. The aim of the Psychiana lessons, which Robinson sold to those who answered his advertisements, was to enable every individual to achieve a relationship to or an understanding of the nature of God, which would make the power of God freely available to the individual for his own uses. These lessons consisted primarily of a series of exercises in mental concentration aimed at enabling the reader to correct his own thought processes and to experience the power of God. Robinson regarded himself as a prophet and included dogmatic assertions about the future and rather inane "miracle" stories in his many published writings. As Psychiana was essentially a mail order publishing house, no accurate count of members could be made, but nearly one million sets of lessons were sold between 1929 and 1949. *NEW THOUGHT.

[R. K. MACMASTER]

PSYCHIATRISTS, GUILD OF CATHOLIC, see NATIONAL GUILD OF CATHOLIC PSYCHIATRISTS.

PSYCHIATRY, a special branch of medicine that diagnoses and treats deficiencies and sicknesses of the psyche, whether these arise from congenital or accidental defects of brain tissues or from psychological conflicts not associated with structural changes in the brain. Thus psychiatry treats the acute brain disorders caused by diseases like encephalitis, meningitis and acute rheumatic fever, or by different intoxicants and poisons, or by head injuries or brain tumors, insofar as all of these impair intellectual function, orientation, memory, and emotional stability. Psychiatry also treats chronic brain disorders arising from congenital cranial defects, as in Mongolism, or from irreversible brain damage caused by diseases like syphilis or pellagra; it treats mental retardation in children and the psychoses associated with senile decay in the aged.

Among the disorders of psychogenic origin, the most

severe are the psychoses: the schizophrenias, paranoias, and manic-depressive and involutional reactions. (The tendency in psychiatry today is to avoid hard and fast categories of mental illness in favor of diagnoses which emphasize the particular clusters of symptoms that characterize each individual's illness.) Psychiatry also treats the neuroses, which are primarily emotional disorders, involving anxieties, phobias, obsessions, compulsions, hysterias, amnesias and other dissociative patterns of behavior, psychogenic paralyses, and other conversion reactions, depressions, etc. And finally psychiatry addresses itself to psychosomatic disorders, e.g., ulcers, asthma, colitis, etc., arising from emotional conflict, and personality disorders such as psychopathy, alcoholism, and sexual deviation, as well as transient disorders occurring in stress situations, such as battle fatigue.

In treating these many illnesses, psychiatrists employ any means that work (see PSYCHOTHERAPY). Psychotherapy includes all methods of treatment based on communication with the patient, whether verbal or non-verbal. Reparative psychotherapy does not involve a deep analysis of the origins of the patient's sickness, but intends rather to reinforce his existing assets, strengthen his existing defences and lessen the intensity of his troublesome symptoms, using the knowledge of human psychodynamics and the medical skills gained by psychiatric study and experience. The therapist may use techniques of authoritative assurance, suggestion, persuasion, guidance and moral support, along with recommendations on changing environmental situations, depending on the illness in question, the age and temperament of the patient, etc.

Reconstructive psychotherapy, of which *psychoanalysis is the major representative, aims at achieving deeper personality changes and adjustments through insights into the origins of the problems and of methods the patient has been using to cope with them. Other important forms of reconstructive analysis are the distributive analysis pioneered by Adolf Meyer, Jungian and Adlerian psychotherapy, and the therapies emphasizing social and cultural relationships as propounded by Karen Horney, Harry Stack Sullivan, Erich Fromm, etc. Viktor Frankl's logotherapy is a recent contribution in the field. Variations in the simple therapist-patient relationship include the use of drugs or hypnosis to reach the patient's unconscious complexes more quickly, group therapy and psychodrama which bring more complex interpersonal relationships into play.

Besides psychotherapeutic techniques, psychiatrists use different forms of somatic treatment, methods of rehabilitation, and drugs. Somatic treatment includes shock (usually insulin or electro-) treatments which are regarded with varying degrees of approval by different psychiatrists, although they have had good results in some cases, esp. in severe depressions, and psychosurgery, in particular the operation called prefrontal lobotomy, i.e., the severance of connections between the thalamus and the frontal lobes of the brain, which is admittedly drastic. Methods of rehabilitation

are employed to assist the chronically disabled to make the best possible life out of the resources still available. Since one of the major problems of the chronically disabled is emotional acceptance of the situation, psychiatry can make a major contribution. The greatest recent advance in psychiatry is in the discovery of new drugs more powerful than the bromides and barbiturates already in use and free of some of their disadvantageous side-effects. These drugs are in general of two classes, the tranquilizers like chlorpromazine and reserpine which calm agitation, and the antidepressants.

In the 20th cent., psychiatry is a hopeful branch of medicine. Today, the number of patients in mental hospitals is lessening, cases long thought hopeless are returning to active, productive life, the public is more aware of the needs of mental health. The three major causes of these changes are (1) Freud's discoveries of some basic dynamics of emotional and mental operations and the subsequent insights and refinement of a host of researchers stimulated by Freud's work; (2) the new concepts of mental health institutions, i.e., small, more homelike, open-door mental hospitals with as much use of out-patient clinics as possible; and (3) the discovery of helpful drugs.

Once a branch of medicine often reduced to mere custodial care of hopeless cases (in institutions often badly run), psychiatry now considers itself as capable as any branch of medicine of returning its patients to productive life. Nevertheless there is much to be done to present an undistorted image of the new psychiatry to the public, and it is here that the cooperation of psychiatry and religion has become important. For many years there was some hostility between the two, mainly because many features of Freudian psychoanalysis were unacceptable to religious people. Freud described God as a projected father-image and religion as an obsessional neurosis, seemed to reduce human motivation to sexual drive, to deny objective morality and to counsel license in gratifying instinctual drives. In recent decades, unacceptable implications have been winnowed out and the sound truths of psychoanalysis have been accepted by clergy and religious people, to the mutual advantage of psychiatry and religion. Psychiatry throws light on the psychological dynamics involved in many religious, moral and spiritual problems, for example, sexual incontinence, alcoholism, and drug addiction, scruples and *anxieties, hostilities, adolescent rebellions, prejudices, etc. It also throws light on the faulty and immature ways in which many people conceive of God, religion, prayer, rituals, etc. It illumines the dynamics of religious conversion and loss of faith, vocations and their loss, etc. It provides insight into the attitudes and defenses people adopt which prevent full moral growth, e.g., dependency attitudes, passive aggressiveness, repressions, projections, reaction formations, etc. On the other hand, religion and the clergy have much to offer psychiatry. Generally the clergy first meet the people needing psychiatric attention, and can resolve the simpler problems, esp. if they are psychiatrically knowledgeable.

Surveys show that people feel they receive more help in mental and emotional problems from clergymen than from any other group, including psychiatrists. The clergy can also refer the more difficult problems to those professionally trained. In referral, their influence is important in overcoming the reluctance people have about seeing psychiatrists and the fears and prejudices they entertain about admitting to themselves that they have mental or emotional problems. The clergyman can also do much to reassure the patient's family, and in general to dispel false apprehensions and misinformation about the psychiatric profession. For people receiving psychiatric help, the clergy can contribute greatly by religious counseling. It seems clear that many psychiatric problems are alleviated by gaining sound spiritual and religious insights and attitudes. The mutual advantages of cooperation between religion and psychiatry are being promoted nowadays by fostering working arrangements between clergymen and psychiatrists and by the formation of organizations to integrate religion and mental health programs. BIBLIOGRAPHY: F. J. Braceland and M. Stock, *Modern Psychiatry: A Handbook For Believers* (1963).

[M. E. STOCK]

PSYCHIATRY, FORENSIC, see FORENSIC PSYCHIATRY.

PSYCHICS, (1) In church history the term is associated with *Tertullian. After he became a Montanist he used it to condemn Catholics for their unspiritual laxity, calling them *psychikoi,* ''natural,'' as distinct from *pneumatikoi,* ''spiritual'' (*De pudicitia* 1.10; cf. 1 Cor 2.14). (2) In early Gnostic sects the term means material-minded. (3) In Spiritualism and in current usage, those alleged to have special receptivity to communications from the spirit world regarding the occult or the future (see MEDIUM). To consult psychics seriously involves *superstition and *divination, contrary to the virtue of *religion.

[T. C. O'BRIEN]

PSYCHOANALYSIS, a system comprising: (1) an investigative technique, (2) a method of *psychotherapy, (3) a body of psychological doctrine, and (4) an approach to the interpretation of cultural phenomena. All derive from the original discoveries of *Freud and have been elaborated by numerous contributions from many disciples.

(1) As a technique for the investigation of mental and emotional behavior, psychoanalysis uses *free association in the analytic session and manipulation of *transference. The patient relaxes, often on a couch, and without effort at voluntary control, reports to the analyst everything that comes into his mind. The starting point is often a dream the patient had, for the theory is that dreams express unconscious strivings. Transference is a reaction by which the patient unconsciously attaches emotional significance to the analyst from attitudes formed in infancy towards parents and other important love-objects. By listening to the free associations which tend towards repressed yearnings, hostilities, fears, etc.,

and by analyzing the transference-reactions, the analyst can come to an understanding of the patient's unconscious attitudes and conflicts, and thus help the patient to understand himself.

(2) As a psychotherapeutic method, psychoanalysis operates on the assumption that mental and emotional problems are caused by repressed drives. The two basic drives, *libido and *aggression, are repressed when their expression in overt behavior, or even fantasy, is prevented by an unconscious mental reflex which guards the mind from intolerable, threatening thoughts. This *repression is triggered by *anxiety which is rooted in the memory of severe punishment or even its threat, e.g., withdrawal of parents' love or the menace of mutilation (fancied or real) particularly genital, accompanying the expression of these drives in early life, especially in the Oedipal period. Once repressed, these drives continually strive for satisfaction, and thus the internal pressures generated cause psychiatric problems. If the repressions can be removed and drives allowed an acceptable expression, the patient could be cured. Both the psychoanalytic treatment in general and the method of free association in particular have been criticized and even condemned by some ecclesiastical authorities because they involve the revival and expression of sexual and hostile fantasies and feelings. However, Pope Pius XII in several allocutions between 1953 and 1958 sanctioned the use of psychoanalysis in cases of urgency under carefully controlled conditions. In 1961 the Holy See made permission of the appropriate authority a condition for psychoanalysis by clerics and religious. It should be noted that the purpose of psychoanalysis is not the removal of inhibitions for the sake of licentious behavior, but rather to replace repressive mechanisms, which are infantile and irrational, with mature and deliberate self-control.

(3) As a body of psychological doctrine, psychoanalysis posits three major components or structures in the human psyche, the *id, *ego, and *superego. The id comprises the instinctual drives and the connected unconscious fantasies continually striving for gratification. Ego concerns itself with the reality-oriented aspects of the psyche, organized, logical thinking, and the control of motor behavior. Finally superego contains mostly unconscious ''moral'' norms and ideals, attitudes and aims incorporated by identification with parental figures. While the id is governed by the pleasure principle, i.e., its strivings are always in the direction of maximizing pleasure by the reduction of tension caused by unsatisfied instinctual drives, the ego is ruled by the reality principle, i.e., pleasure is found and pain avoided by adaptation to reality. But the superego functions by the generation of guilt feelings when its prescriptions are violated. The life of the person therefore is an effort to find modes of gratifying instinctual drives under the conditions imposed by the circumstances of real life and within limits prescribed by superego restrictions.

The instinctual drives go through developmental stages marked off by different preferences in the mode of erotic gratification. In the first (oral) stage, they are gratified by sucking, in the next (anal) stage, by defecation, and in the phallic stage, by masturbation. A major crisis occurs in life when the person enters the *Oedipal situation at the age of four to six. Then there is the experience of passionate yearning for the love of one parent, jealous resentment against the other, and fear of punishment because of this hostility. This conflict is frequently resolved wholly or partly by a repression which is the model and cause of later repressions. After a period when libidinal drives are latent, puberty brings on a fresh arousal of sexuality. If these impulses are handled by massive repression, there will ensue an inability to arrive successfully at mature psychosexual development, which consists in satisfying heterosexual relations with a chosen partner.

It is evident that psychoanalysis emphasizes the unconscious thoughts, attitudes, and motivations of human life. One of its greatest contributions to psychology is its analysis of the ways in which people operate under the influence of unconscious factors, and of the many *defense mechanisms unconsciously employed to handle the instinctual drives. As a psychology, it has been criticized for being materialistic and for reducing human life to instincts, especially the sexual. In the last three decades, it has broadened its basic concepts, aligning them more closely with traditional ideas of human nature, for instance, allowing for independent ego-functioning. Many students find that it offers insights into human psychology which are not necessarily incompatible with a spiritual conception of man.

(4) As an approach to the interpretation of cultural phenomena the concepts of psychoanalysis have been used to explain the arts, social institutions, religion, and even the idea of God. The basic themes of explanation are *repression and *sublimation. The first theory accounts for cultural phenomena as desexualized expressions of repressed instinctual drives. Freud never attempted to prove, but rather assumed that God did not exist and that religion is an illusion. He attempted to explain the universality of belief in God and the practice of religion in psychoanalytic terms, that is, that the idea of God was a projected father-image and religion, a universal neurosis. Although few would agree that he succeeded in accomplishing his precise aim, many accept his theories as useful interpretations of the superstitious ways God has actually been conceived and religion practiced. Although psychoanalysis is still controversial in many of its aspects, there is widespread agreement that it is the major psychological development of the 20th century. BIBLIOGRAPHY: C. Brenner, *Elementary Textbook of Psychoanalysis* (1957); S. Freud, *New Introductory Lectures on Psychoanalysis* (1933).

[M. E. STOCK]

PSYCHOKINESIS, a species of psi-phenomena, abbreviated PK, that manifests "the power of mind over matter" by operating on physical objects directly without intervening instruments. It was formerly considered identical with certain "supernatural" powers claimed by mediums and other practitioners of the occult, a view not confirmed by recent scientific investigation. Laboratory studies are at present restricted to such actions as the direct determination of a selected face on a trial throwing of dice. Most parapsychologists feel that the results of such tests positively indicate the existence of psychokinesis. It seems that the power is not seriously affected by differences in size, shape, or weight of various test materials. However, a fatigue effect is detected after protracted trials. Serious study of PK and other psi-phenomena is relatively recent and limited. As yet, no acceptable theory has been proposed which explains its existence, function, or nature.

[C. P. SVOBODA]

PSYCHOLOGICAL UNITY OF CHRIST, a mystery that is among the most challenging aspects of the mystery of Christ; today it occupies a prominent place in the field of Christological thinking. How far can theology probe into the human consciousness of the Word Incarnate? How is psychological unity achieved in a Person in whom there is both divine and human consciousness? With these questions the theology of the hypostatic union passes from the ontological to the psychological level. Three main problems arise. (1) Does the Word Incarnate possess a human psychological ego? (2) Is his human nature autonomous in its conscious states and volitional acts? (3) How does Christ the man know that he is God, the Son Incarnate? The encyclical *Sempiternus Rex* (1951) has warned that no complete autonomy can be attributed to the man Jesus such as would contradict the unity of his Person (cf. D 3905).

Christ possesses a true—and most perfect—human personality, understood as psychological makeup: he is a man of character and determination, all intent on fulfilling his messianic mission. There seems, however, to be no room in him for a human psychological ego; the center of reference of his human experiences is none other than the ontological ego, subject of attribution. Christ's human acts are elicited, specified, and determined by his human nature; in this precise sense his humanity is fully autonomous. If, however, autonomy is understood as implying attribution and responsibility, this belongs exclusively to the Divine Person of the Word. To reduce Christ's human awareness of his divinity to an objective knowledge derived from the beatific vision hardly seems satisfactory. It is necessary to postulate in him a subjective consciousness of his divine personhood. Two enunciations of this mystery are proposed, one upward, the other downward. Either the man Jesus is subjectively conscious of his divinity through his awareness of the hypostatic union; or—and probably better—the Word of God becomes selfconscious in the human nature that he assumes and in which he exercises his spiritual activity. Whatever the enunciation, Christ's human consciousness of his divinity extends to the psychological level the hypostatic union of his human nature with the Word of God. BIBLIOGRAPHY: Rahner ThInvest 5:193; B. Lonergan, *De constitutione*

Christi ontologica et psychologica (1964) 83; J. Galot, ''La Psychologie du Christ,'' NRT 80 (1958) 337; *idem, ''Science et conscience de Jesus,'' ibid.* 82 (1960) 113–131.

[J. DUPUIS]

PSYCHOLOGY, variously defined as the science of life, the study of the mind, and the science of behavior, particularly human behavior. At present, general psychology deals with external sensations (sight, hearing, taste, smell, and the various categories of touch, including temperature, resistance, pain and pleasure, etc.), with perception, and with the internal, image-making functions of fantasy and memory, with emotions such as love, desire, joy, sorrow, hatred, anger, fear, anxiety, courage, etc., and with drives or needs like hunger, thirst, sex, etc. It studies intelligence in its various operations, as organizing, adaptive, creative, problem-solving, etc., and with the phenomena connected with willing, voluntary control, and decision making. Physiological psychology studies the structural and functional operations of the organs connected with these activities, esp. the senses, brain, nervous system, and endocrine glands. Psychometrics studies the quantitative relations of stimulus and response, reaction times, retention patterns, etc. Social psychology studies interpersonal reactions, i.e., the formation of human relations, or people in groups. Animal psychology explores behavior in lower species which is similar or analogous to human behavior for the comparisons it affords. Developmental psychology, one of the most active branches today, studies the maturation of the organism and the acquisition of experience, esp. the learning process, i.e., the acquisition of knowledge, skills, and other patterns of behavior. Developmental psychology is also concerned with the formations of deeper attitudes and patterns of emotional response, esp. as they exhibit phases of growth. Differential psychology investigates the ranges of human capacities and behavior, and the variations due to sex, temperament, race, etc. Abnormal psychology deals with personality disorders and the aberrant reactions characteristic of mental and emotional sicknesses, neuroses, and psychoses. Philosophical psychology explores the meaning and significance of these human phenomena and of human existence itself.

Historically psychological phenomena were first studied intensively by the Greeks, Plato and Aristotle (4th cent. B.C.). Plato speculated on the nature of mind and ideas, love and immortality, education and political structure; Aristotle approached the phenomena of life more empirically, collecting, organizing, and speculating on the movements and natures of plants and animals, investigating sensation, memory, intelligence, feeling, health and sickness, sleep and dreams, and other functions in man, and summing up his researches in a speculative treatise on the principle of life in living things, the soul. Between these early Greeks and the scholastic philosophers of the Middle Ages, the greatest contributions to psychological lore were from the Stoic and Epicurean philosophers who enlarged on the affective and voluntary sides of human nature, the Greek and Roman physicians (e.g., Hippocrates, Galen) who contributed psychological data and physiological theory from their medical observations, the Christian Fathers of the Church (Tertullian, Augustine, Gregory the Great, Chrysostom) who wove psychological speculation, often profound, into their extensive moral treatises, the Arabian philosophers (Averroës, Avicenna) commenting on the Greek treatises, and the Arabian physicians.

The revival of learning in the Middle Ages, spurred on by the influx in Europe of classical and Arabian philosophies, resulted in the re-organization and restatement of much of the ancient psychological science with many refinements but without extensive increase in data. Psychological matters were still a part of natural philosophy, more speculative than empirical, and presented generally in treatises on the nature of the soul or in connection with moral or ethical studies. The word psychology had not yet been coined, (it was first used by Goclenius in the 16th cent.) and the unifying concept for all the psychological data studied and taught was the concept of life rather than mind or behavior. Beginning in the 17th cent., biology and physiology began to be studied as empirical disciplines separate from the philosophical speculations on living processes, and psychology began to be restricted to psychic functions such as perception, imagination, emotion, intelligence, and voluntary action. These were still treated speculatively and contributions to psychological lore were made by Descartes, Locke, Berkely, Hume, Leibniz, Kant, Herbart, and Lotze. It was not until the 19th cent. that psychological phenomena first began to be subjected to study according to the canons of modern scientific investigation. Johannes Müller, E. H. Weber, G. T. Fechner, and H. L. F. von Helmholtz were pioneer investigators in empirical psychology, primarily from a physiological or psychophysical point of view, but the honor of establishing the first experimental laboratory (in 1879 at Leipzig) and influencing the first generation of scientific psychologists belongs to W. Wundt.

After Wundt, psychology exploded in a dozen directions. Famous names include Carl Stumpf, who was influenced by F. Brentano's Aristotelian-Thomistic act psychology and in turn influenced the Gestaltist school (M. Wertheimer, K. Koffka, W. Köhler), H. Ebbinghaus who pioneered memory studies, G. Müller, E. Hering, and O. Külpe in Germany. In England, the great names are F. Galton, the student of genius and eugenics; W. McDougall in physiological and social psychology; and C. Spearman, in factorial analyses. In France, A. Binet the inventor of intelligence testing, is the most famous name; Belgium produced E. A. Michotte; Italy, A. Gemelli; and Russia, I. P. Pavlov whose experiments on conditioned reflexes in animals founded reflexive psychology. In the U.S., E. B. Titchener was influential in propounding the structuralist theory of psychology; J. Dewey led the functionalist revolt against it. W. James, S. Hall, and J. Cattell were leaders in teaching psychology and stimulating research; J. B. Watson produced behaviorism as an attempt to put psychology on a strictly objective or scientific basis.

The most significant new movements of the 20th cent. are psychoanalysis, pioneered by S. Freud, and the other depth psychologies propounded by men like C. Jung and A. Adler; the phenomenological psychologies stemming from the work of E. Husserl, which have contributed rich descriptions of and deep insights into complex human experiences, and the existential psychologies which focus mainly on the significance of human life. In developmental psychology, the most noted recent advances come from J. Piaget in the area of phases of mental growth and E. H. Erikson on identity and stages of psychosocial development. In comparative psychology, L. Morgan instituted extensive systematic research on lower animals; R. M. Yerkes achieved prominence for his work on the higher primates. The study of temperamental differences, given impetus by the researches of E. Kretschmer in Germany and A. de Giovanni in Italy, was re-worked by W. H. Sheldon in America, but to date has not yielded conclusive results. Personality psychology which emphasizes the whole individual and/or his social relations, and variations and development, is the central theme in the work of men like H. S. Sullivan, G. W. Allport, K. Lewin, C. Rogers, A. H. Maslow, G. Murphy, etc. The principal contribution to more rigidly scientific psychology is the operant conditioning experimentation of B. F. Skinner in America.

Besides the many schools and branches of psychology proper, many disciplines in the area of specialized or applied psychology have developed. W. James first treated religious psychology as a special field, and after a period of halting growth, this discipline is beginning to gain momentum. The refinement and expansion of techniques for psychological testing not only in the areas of intelligence and skills, but also in the spheres of attitudes, interests, and motives, and in personality disorders (e.g., Rorschach, TAT) and in overall personality assessment (e.g., Minnesota Multiphasic Personality Inventory) have provided tools for many uses in education, industry, counseling, and psychiatry. Schools at all levels as well as public and private agencies are now prepared to administer tests to help people decide on the most suitable vocations, and to detect personality problems and offer psychological counseling services. Industry and the armed services use tests extensively for rough screening of masses of applicants and recruits. There is a growing interest in testing aspirants to the clergy and religious life, although this field has special problems. Industrial psychology is an applied branch of the science that deals with problems of ideal working conditions, worker motivation, effects of fatigue and boredom, etc. Another contribution to economic activities comes from motivational research which supplies data for effective marketing of products and successful advertising.

The same kind of research coupled with techniques for sampling attitudes, beliefs, and opinions, and discovering how they are formed and altered provide tools for guiding political action and for successful propaganda. The application of the psychology of mental stress and breakdown represents a more extreme and sinister use of the techniques of propaganda and mind control, e.g., in brain washing.

Other areas in which psychology finds application are law and criminology (e.g., determination of legal insanity, rehabilitation of convicts), in resolving family and domestic problems (e.g., marriage counseling, adolescent rebellion) and in social reform (e.g., analysis of subculture mentalities, their causes and remedies).

Psychology, like all other disciplines in the 20th cent., aspires to the status of a rigorous science. Unlike other disciplines, however, psychology has materials to handle which cannot be measured nor described exactly nor organized effectively, namely, the rich experience of inner life available to introspection. If psychology limits its data to external behavior which can be observed objectively and measured, it misses the greatest part of life as experienced. Even when psychology deals with this inner life, if it restricts itself to statements which can be supported with hard facts, it finds that in some way the essence and heart of the phenomenon which is man has slipped through its techniques untouched. Ecstasy and anguish, love and sacrifice, religious conversion, heroic courage, nobleness of spirit, simple delights, common sense, and most of what makes human life peculiarly human escapes the methodology of psychology. At present the artists, philosophers, poets, dramatists, and novelists say more about these things than the psychologists, and this may always be the case. BIBLIOGRAPHY: C. E. Spearman, *Psychology down the Ages* (2 v., 1937); A. A. Robach, *History of American Psychology* (rev. ed., 1964); R. S. Peters, ed. *Brett's History of Psychology* (rev. ed., 1962); J. C. Flügel, "A Hundred Years of Psychology (1833–1963)" (Enl. ed., 1964).

[M. E. STOCK]

PSYCHOMACHIA, the most influential of the poems of *Prudentius, which depicts the epic struggle of Christianity with paganism under the allegory of a battle between the Christian virtues and the pagan vices in the soul. It was among the most widely read books of the Middle Ages, and in addition to setting a style in the use of allegory, it provided art with a moral iconography. For bibliog. see PRUDENTIUS.

[P. K. MEAGHER]

PSYCHOPATHIC PERSONALITY, the name given personality disorder of one who, though not classifiable as psychotic as that term is currently understood, is characterized by a notable lack of guilt feeling for acts held by ordinary persons to be wrong (e.g., violations of the rights of others or of the laws of society), and is apparently unable to grow in moral judgment through experience. Fundamentally the psychopathic person is one who has never developed the sense of attachment to others, on the basis of which his offenses could be felt as wrong. The inevitable conflicts with other people and with the law are explained away and no personal blame is accepted. Therapy for psychopaths involves building up some kind of relationship of trust and affection for the therapist and then extending it to others. Counselors and clergymen can also help psychopaths if they can evoke this relationship. Probably the real moral guilt of a psychopathic person for his characteristic offenses is greatly diminished because the retardation of his development makes it difficult or impossible for him to form sound moral judgments. His responsibility in the matter of contractual obligations is open to serious question. This may pose special problems in adjudicating the validity of his assumption of the obligations of marriage or of holy orders—problems aggravated by the fact that the nature of the affliction is not clearly understood and the verification of the type in particular instances is difficult to establish beyond doubt. BIBLIOGRAPHY: H. Cleckley, *Mask of Sanity* (5th ed., 1976); R. D. Hare, *Psychopathy: Theory and Research* (1970). *SOCIOPATH.

[M. E. STOCK]

PSYCHOPHYSICS, the branch of psychology that studies the relationships between physical stimuli impinging on sentient subjects and the sentient reactions of these subjects. The physical stimuli are measured as exactly as possible with the aid of refined instruments, to determine their qualities, intensity, duration, and location. The responses of the subjects are determined by a variety of methods, e.g., ability to reproduce the stimuli, and to detect minimal quantities or changes in quantity as reported, subjective ranking of stimuli in some order, etc. The greatest difficulties in establishing exact conclusions come from the uncontrollable variables in the sentient subject, e.g., in terms of attention, fatigue, motivation, etc.

[M. E. STOCK]

PSYCHOPNEUMONES, those who claimed that the souls of the wicked are changed, in accord with their sins, into demons or animals. Filaster mentions them (*Haer*. 124) and Augustine repeats him (*Haer*. 78). In his index to Augustine's work, Danaeus calls them *Tertulli* (PL 12:1249). The name Psychopneumones comes from the **Praedestinatus* (1:78).

[L. G. MÜLLER]

PSYCHOSIS. The term psychosis refers to a variety of mental states and is used by both professionals and laymen in a variety of ways. It is often mistakenly considered synonymous with schizophrenia, although the schizophrenic may be nonpsychotic for long periods of time or may be floridly psychotic at other times. Psychosis is generally considered a behaviorally descriptive term referring to a process in which disorganization of the individual occurs in many spheres of function: thoughts may be flighty and tangential or unrelated; hallucinations, delusions or ideas of reference may appear; emotional lability is increased. Un-

realistic behavior, often as an attempt to adapt to this confused internal state, is the outward manifestation of psychosis.

There are many forms of psychosis: manic-depressive, paranoid, schizophrenic, organic—including senile, arteriosclerotic, alcoholic, toxic drug reaction—infectious, and traumatic psychosis. Many factors contribute to their development. Among them are biologic and genetic factors. Studies of twins have demonstrated the genetic heritability of certain of these traits. In addition patterns of child rearing, life stresses, or socioeconomic conditions, may contribute to a web of predisposing factors that may increase the vulnerability of a given individual to psychosis. As might be guessed, when a set of behavioral reactions seem to result from biological internal assault, as in brain trauma or toxic drug reactions, as well as from psychological assault in extreme emotional deprivation, there are most likely several distinct disorders being lumped together in the term psychosis. Recent evidence suggests that this is the case and that the term psychosis should be used only as a behavioral descriptor of generalized personal disorganization, rather than as a diagnostic category.

Antipsychotic medication can often be helpful in normalizing the behavior of the person who is experiencing a chaotic inner state. However, many supportive services may also be necessary to help this person adapt to and compensate for his rather idiosyncratic perceptual world. This support and reeducation can come from psychotherapy or from family or from a community of people who can gently guide and assist in making what may seem to the psychotic person a strange and inexplicable world into the familiar, comfortable, livable world which most of us perceive. BIBLIOGRAPHY: A. M. Freedman et al., *Comprehensive Textbook of Psychiatry* (1976) 851–1059.

[P. B. AMAR]

PSYCHOSOMATIC ILLNESS. The ancient term psychosomatic illness stems from the Greek *psychē* (mind) and *sōma* (body) and illustrates the interrelatedness of mind and body. A more current formulation using the term psychophysiological illness points to the physiological processes through which mind and body interact. Such illness represents a maladaptive response to ordinary stress followed by a natural physiological sequence. When an individual encounters stress, the body responds with a normal arousal pattern which the physiologist, Cannon, termed the "fight or flight" response. The human organism, like all others, responds to emergency with an alarm pattern in which pupils dilate, heart rate increases, respiration increases, blood vessels constrict, brain electrical activity speeds up, sweating occurs, etc. These set patterns of arousal permit a rapid survival response. After the emergency has passed, the rate of response quickly returns to normal. All of these response patterns are built in and mediated by the two branches of the autonomic nervous system, the sympathetic and parasympathetic.

When an individual perceives danger and responds accordingly, the response is an adaptive survival response. However, when an individual perceives neutral, non-threatening events as emergencies and responds accordingly, that response is a maladaptive response which when repeated often becomes a habitual pattern, or is called psychophysiological illness. It is not clearly understood why some individuals respond to minor stresses with full-strength "fight or flight" responses or why each individual appears to have a particular vulnerability to stress in a particular system. There is a growing body of data to suggest that such vulnerabilities run in families; it is not uncommon to find first and second degree relatives of migraine patients who also suffer migraine headaches. Hypertension patients often have family histories of hypertension. Such response specificity suggests that genetic factors or very early learning are involved in susceptibility to stress disorders.

Although it has been popularly assumed that psychosomatic illness is unreal or "all in the head," it is indeed a real physiologic response producing real biological changes but precipitated by perception of a nonemergency as if it were a full-blown danger. Thus a psychophysiologic disorder could be compared to the situation in which the whole fire department has been called out with sirens blaring to quench a one-bucket blaze. There are many forms of psychophysiologic disorders, ranging from generalized anxiety or hyperarousal in which the individual sweats profusely or experiences shortness of breath, heart palpitations, dizziness and feelings of panic, to very specific response patterns such as asthma, migraine headache, hypertension, insomnia, peptic ulcer, ulcerative colitis, tics and muscle spasm, and dysmenorrhea. Many forms of sexual dysfunction are also classified as psychophysiological illness.

The most important first step in treatment of the psychophysiologic disorders is a thorough medical examination and whatever immediate medical procedures are necessary to control the physiologic process and prevent a medical emergency from occurring. The second step may involve a psychotherapy approach aimed at reduction of the stress reaction by helping the individual to alter his perception of danger or by aiding the person to understand the symbolic meaning of his perception of danger. A more recent and promising form of treatment involves biofeedback training in which the individual is taught, through the use of electronic monitoring devices to "listen" to the actual signals of his body and modify them by making small, gradual, self-imposed changes. For example, the person with a muscle spasm will observe that muscle by monitoring the electrical activity of the muscle, listening to it and relaxing it, long before the muscle goes into spasm or contracts in a tic. The peptic ulcer patient may learn to monitor the amount of gastric secretion and relax, thus reducing acid formation and allowing the gut to heal. The heart patient with premature ventricular contractions listens to his heartbeat and learns to even them out. Biofeedback applications are only beginning, but promise to become an important part of treatment of psychophysiologic disorders, as more specific information accumulates demonstrating what biofeedback can and cannot do. BIBLIOGRAPHY: F. Alexander, *Psychosomatic Medicine: Its Principles and Applications* (1950). P. B. Amar, "Biofeedback: Myth or Method," *Medical Communications* 4, No. 3 (1976); R. B. Malmo, "Activation: A Neuropsychological Dimension," *Psychological Review* 66 (1959) 367; H. Selye, *The Physiology and Pathology of Exposure to Stress, Acta* (1970).

[P. B. AMAR]

PSYCHOSURGERY, brain surgery performed for the purpose of altering certain behaviors or relieving specific psychiatric symptoms. Actually this term lumps together a vast array of neurosurgical interventions in an equally diverse array of psychiatric conditions. Prior to the development of the major tranquilizers in the 1950s, psychosurgery was frequently performed in an attempt to relieve intractable symptoms. Since that time, there has been a movement away from the use of such dramatic and irreversible procedures primarily for moral and ethical reasons. It is difficult to justify a treatment that destroys tissue permanently, when the available follow-up research has been equivocal in finding much of permanent benefit. It is possible, however, as neurosurgeons refine their skills and more becomes known about the working of the brain, that this form of treatment could increase. Its use would remain as a last resort however, since once brain tissue is destroyed, it can never be replaced. BIBLIOGRAPHY: W. Freeman and J. W. Watts, *Psychosurgery* (1950); L. V. Laitenen and K. E. Livingston, *Surgical Approaches to Psychiatry* (1973); P. London, *Behavior Control* (1969).

[P. B. AMAR]

PSYCHOTHERAPY, the treatment of mental and emotional disorders which operates on the basis of interpersonal communication between the therapist and the person receiving the therapy, as distinguished from physical treatments based on the use of drugs, surgery, shock, etc. In the broadest sense, every situation in which an emotionally troubled person seeks relief by talking to and listening to a confidant, guide, or director is a kind of psychological therapy. More strictly, psychotherapy is the treatment of more serious emotional and mental problems by trained psychologists and psychiatrists, and in its most intensive forms, psychotherapy is a part of the medical discipline of *psychiatry. The heart of psychotherapy is the relationship between therapist and patient, which is based on the experience of transference. Transference is a strong emotional rapport, or trust and dependency, which reflects emotional attachments the patient formed early in life for important persons (esp. parents) and which are "transferred" unconsciously to the therapist. Fortified by this rapport, and by the feeling that the therapist is a person with specialized knowledge and healing power, the patient is enabled to express himself more openly, overcome inhibitions, recognize and acknowledge weakness, and learn more effective ways of coping with his problems. The respect of the therapist for the patient as a person, and his understanding, accepting, and reassuring manner are essential for the establishment of a good rapport.

Psychotherapy can be divided roughly into reparative therapy, which seeks to relieve symptoms and overcome problems of which the patient is to some extent cognizant, and reconstructive therapy, which seeks to alter deeper patterns of faulty thought and attitude of which the patient is unconscious. Reparative therapy uses techniques of authoritative direction, reassurance, suggestion, support, and guidance; reconstructive therapy uses explorative analysis, like *psychoanalysis, with or without methods of psychological conditioning. Reparative therapy does not attack deep underlying psychological problems, but attempts instead to strengthen a patient's ego defences, remove unnecessary inhibitions when possible, and teach the patient how to handle residual weaknesses. By persuasion, reasoned argument, and the influence of his authority the therapist encourages the patient to handle his problems more adequately; by subtle and indirect suggestion he induces the patient to believe that his symptoms can be cured and in fact are being cured; and by supportive techniques such as permissive attitude, explanations, advice, exhortation, and manipulation of the environment he shores up the positive and healthy defences of the patient so that he can relinquish the unhealthy ones. These techniques are often effective but since the root of the problem is not attacked, the symptoms can return in new stress situations.

Reconstructive therapy attempts to go more deeply into a patient's repressed, unconscious mental life to analyze the deep defences that have been set up against the expression of instinctual drives, release the repressed urges, and reorganize the patient's deep personality patterns for more effective living. Psychoanalysis analyzes repressed sexual and aggressive drives, esp. in the light of the Oedipal conflict. Distributive analysis, pioneered by A. Meyer, analyzes the patient in terms of a thorough life history study, balances his personal assets and liabilities, and tries to construct a viable pattern of life on the basis of the patient's present situation. Alfred Adler's individual psychology explores the patient's life for signs of inferiority complexes and the overcompensations by which the feelings of inferiority are being denied. This is often useful for adolescents' problems. The *analytic psychology of Carl Jung attends mainly to the imbalances in the development of the many aspects of personality, and seeks to help the patient achieve a full sense of self in which all urges and needs find appropriate satisfaction; this approach has been esp. useful with middle-aged people.

Other schools of analysis emphasize cultural and interpersonal relationships and the resolution of the anxieties and defences against anxieties that occur in social contact; Karen Horney, Harry Stack Sullivan and Erich Fromm represent this approach. Group psychotherapy and the psychodrama developed by J. L. Moreno make use of the therapeutic values of more complex modes of interpersonal reaction. Some psychotherapists use inhibition-releasing drugs or hypnosis as adjuncts to the interpersonal therapy to enable the patient to come to repressed materials more quickly.

More recent developments in analytic psychotherapy include existential analysis and logotherapy. Existential analysis while not denying the importance of instinctual drives and interpersonal conflicts in patients, holds that more fundamental problems arise on the level of personal existence and the unfolding of the meaning of life. A reflective person seeking his authentic reality as a being and a being-in-the world, encounters existential anxiety as the threat of non-being. The existential analyst helps him master this. Viktor Frankl, the originator of logotherapy, similarly believes that many patient's problems stem from the fact that their lives are meaningless, devoid of spiritual values which give hope and courage. Logotherapy is a curative search for value and meaning in life.

One of the most recent developments in psychotherapy is the application of the principles of psychological conditioning. After several decades of application of analytic therapies, it became clear that simple insight into the origins of psychic conflicts does not automatically afford a cure. On the theory that patients had become conditioned to their symptoms, some therapists have been applying deconditioning techniques, based on the operant conditioning psychology of B. F. Skinner, who showed how appropriate patterns of reward and punishment establish firm behavior patterns. Some therapists use deconditioning as an adjunct to analysis while others believe it can replace analysis.

Psychotherapy in its milder and reparative forms has been traditionally a part of the clergyman's role, as counselor, adviser, spiritual guide, and confessor. Nowadays some clergymen are trained for deeper, reconstructive psychotherapy, including psychoanalysis. This represents a change of attitude because, for many decades after Freud introduced it, the clergy in general viewed psychoanalysis with suspicion. However, Pope Pius XII in a series of allocutions (1952–58), while condemning pansexual views, and encouraging ego-supportive forms of therapy, allowed for the usefulness and legitimacy of psychoanalysis. The principal moral problem in psychoanalysis is allowing sexual and aggressive fantasy free access to consciousness, particularly when the phenomenon of *abreaction may occur. This phenomenon is a strong and sudden emotional outburst representing long repressed passions, and the patient generally cannot control it. Some moralists argue that these fantasies and passions violate mental purity. It seems likely however that since fantasies and emotions elicited in therapeutic sessions are not directly aroused for immoral purposes, they are not *per se* morally objectionable. The purposes of the session are therapeutic and the patient is often in serious need; moreover the atmosphere of the analytic session tends to preclude morally objectionable intentions. Hence the lawfulness of permitting sexual and aggressive fantasy and feeling can be argued on the principle of double effect. It should always be remembered however that deep analysis is a serious undertaking, as painful and disrupting as major surgery. The norms of the Church today require priests and religious to obtain the permission of their ordinary superiors before undertaking psychoanalysis. BIBLIOGRAPHY: F. J. Braceland and M. Stock, *Modern Psychiatry: A Handbook for Believers* (1963).

[M. E. STOCK]

PTAH, the local deity of Memphis in the religion of ancient Egypt; the creator God, patron of craftsmen, esp. of sculptors. The Greco-Roman world identified Ptah with Hephaestus/Vulcan, the divine blacksmith. Originally Ptah was associated with his consort Sekhmet, and their son Nefertum. Since Memphis was the capital of the Old Kingdom (2686–2160) his cult spread throughout Egypt, and in Rameside times Ptah was part of the Memphite Triad, including Ptah, Re, and Amun. The sophistication of the priests of Memphis is illustrated by their description of the act of creation through the power of Ptah's heart and speech. He shaped the concept of things in his heart and brought them into existence through divine speech. The craftsmen of the Third and Fourth (Memphite) Dynasties (c. 2686–2494), who revered Ptah as their patron, produced in the decorations of the necropolises outside Memphis a perfection of beauty, serenity, and order never surpassed in Egypt. They rival the wonder of their counterparts, the great pyramids and the Sphinx. Both the excellence of art and craft declined, along with the religion of Ptah, during the time of ascendancy of the sun cult centered at Heliopolis. Ptah is always represented in purely human form, often swathed in a winding sheet. The sacred bull Apis had his stall in the great temple of Ptah in Memphis.

[E. J. DILLON]

PTOLEMAIC SYSTEM, pre-Copernican theory attempting to explain movements of the heavenly bodies. It was set forth by Ptolemy (Claudius Ptolemaeus), who worked in Alexandria in the 2d century. In his *Almagest* (Arabic title of a work later known as *Mathematical Collection*), he summarized the work of Greek astronomers in a form that remained the standard authority until N. *Copernicus (1473–1543). According to the Ptolemaic system, the earth (a sphere) is stationary, and the sun and planets revolve around it. The system used the theory of epicycles and eccentric circles to explain certain observed motions of the celestial bodies.

[T. EARLY]

PTOLEMAIS, former name of Acre, Israel (in Jg 1.31, Acco). Known as early as the *Amarna Letters, the town was named Ptolemais perhaps for Ptolemy II Philadelphus (285–246 B.C.). Paul visited there (Acts 21.7; see also 1 Macc 11.23–24; 12.45–48), and Aeneas of Ptolemais was at the Council of Nicaea (325). Captured by Muslims in 638, it

was taken in 1104 by Crusaders under Baldwin I of Jerusalem (c. 1058–1118). Saladin captured it in 1187, and Richard the Lion-Hearted regained it in 1191. As Saint-Jean-d'Acre, it became the center for the Knights of St. John until its surrender to the Saracens in 1291.

[T. EARLY]

PTOLEMIES, the Graeco-Egyptian ruling family of Egypt from 323 to 31 B.C., founded by Ptolemy, son of Lagus, one of Alexander's generals. Octavian (later Emperor Augustus) in 31 B.C. ended the dynasty by ordering the death of Ptolemy XIV (Caesarion). The Ptolemaic Empire in the first 100 years acquired and rather permanently added Cyprus, Syria, Cyrene, Phoenicia, and Palestine to Egypt. The early Ptolemies relied on Greek and Macedonian soldiers and businessmen to reorganize the empire economically and to maintain a strong army and navy, but did not succeed in Hellenizing the Egyptian religion. Immigrant Syrians, Anatolians, and Jews plus the Egyptians, Macedonians, and Greeks produced a very cosmopolitan population. Their capitol, Alexandria, the city founded by Alexander in the Nile Delta in 331 B.C., was not a true city-state under the Ptolemies because it was not autonomous. Rather, it was the largest city in an absolute monarchy whose law was the will of the ruling Ptolemy.

For the 1st century of rule the Ptolemies used their considerable revenues to encourage architecture, arts, and industries. Some of their noteworthy buildings were the Library, the Museum, the Mausoleum, and the Lighthouse of Pharos. They invited from all over the ancient world the best poets, scholars, scientists, and philosophers. Among these learned men they included the geometrician Euclid and the astronomers Aristarchus and Eratosthenes.

In the 2d century of their rule the earlier cosmopolitan outlook of the Ptolemies became narrowly nationalistic. In 198 B.C. they lost Palestine and Phoenicia to the Seleucids and started to cultivate Rome. At that time they increased the estates and the privileges of the priests, put Egyptians rather than Greeks in control of policy-making, and replaced Greek soldiers with native Egyptians. The Ptolemaic Empire became a protectorate of Rome in 168 B.C. and a province of Rome in 31 B.C.. BIBLIOGRAPHY: M. Rostovtzeff, ''Ptolemaic Egypt'', *CAH* 7:75–154; F. M. Heichelheim, OCD 745–746.

[M. F. MCNAMARA]

PTOLEMY (c. 100–c. 165), astronomer. Little is known of P.'s life except that he lived in Alexandria, Egypt. Although he wrote treatises in mathematics, geography, and philosophy, he is well known for his *Almagest*—the standard work of astronomy until the Copernican revolution in the 16th century. The *Almagest* is a comprehensive presentation of a geocentric astrology. P. begins by indicating the mathematical basis for his study and setting down his basic presuppositions. The earth is a sphere in a state of rest at the center of the universe which is bounded by a multitude of fixed stars and planets. The apparent movement of these bodies is explained by a complicated system of epicycles and eccentric circles. P.'s theories were regarded as accurate during the early Christian era and the Middle Ages and were frequently cited by the major scholastic writers. BIBLIOGRAPHY: E. H. Warmington, OCD 746–747; S. Sambursky, NCE 11:996–997.

[T. M. McFADDEN]

PTOLEMY THE GNOSTIC (d. *c*.180), disciple of *Valentinus. He was the author of a *Letter to Flora* on the Pentateuch. He taught that Moses made adaptations of God's laws, while the oldest laws are of human content; God's laws are partly absolute (Decalogue), partly vindictive, partly typical and symbolic (ritual laws). Christ abolished the law of talion and transformed it into precepts of spiritual offerings (Eucharist, love of neighbor). Irenaeus makes reference to P.'s teaching.

[L. PEANO]

PTOLEMY OF LUCCA (Bartholomew of Lucca; *c*.1236–1327), Dominican theologian, historian, and bishop. Born Tolomeo Fiadoni, P. came from a middle class (merchant) family. He joined the Dominicans in Lucca and became, after 1261–1268, a close friend of Thomas Aquinas. From 1285 to 1302 he was prior at various Dominican houses. P. was representative of Pope Benedict XII in a quarrel with the clergy of Lucca in 1303 and was at Avignon from 1309 to 1318. He came as bp. to Torcello (near Venice) in 1318, was imprisoned briefly by the patriarch of Grado, and released by Pope John XXII. P. wrote a tract limiting imperial power, *Historia ecclesiastica,* a church history to 1314 in 24 books (books 22 and 23 are sources for the life of Aquinas). He was reputed to have written the second part of Aquinas' "De regimine principum," but this is lately contested. BIBLIOGRAPHY: A. D'Amato, EncCatt 2:923–924.

[N. F. GAUGHAN]

PUBLIC AFFAIRS OF THE CHURCH, COUNCIL FOR, since 1908, the first section of the Vatican Secretariat of State, formerly (since 1827) the Congregation for Extraordinary Ecclesiastical Affairs. It receives its commissions, which generally concern questions relating to civil governments, directly from the pope. The prefect is the card., secretary of state, whose office is responsible for the execution of the Council's determinations. The origins of this curial agency are traced to the 18th-cent. Congregation for the Ecclesiastical Affairs of the Kingdom of France. The present name dates from the reorganization of the *Curia Romana* as set forth in Paul VI's apostolic constitution *Regiminis ecclesiae universae* (1967). During the 19th cent. the Council was formally distinct from the Secretariat of State and normally administered ecclesiastical territories now entrusted to the Congregation for Bishops (former Consistorial Congregation) and the Congregation for the Evangelization of Peoples (former Congregation for the Propagation of the Faith).

[R. A. ARONSTAM]

PUBLIC OPINION. Polls have become a prominent feature of contemporary life and the subject of sociological studies and political analysis. Vatican Council II noted the massive force and authority exerted by public opinion on the public and private life of every class of citizen (Vat II Soc-Comm 8). For moral theology the issue is not the fact of that influence of public opinion, but the validity of its authority in issues of moral right and wrong. Purely philosophical moral thinking has its noblest expression in Socrates, Plato, and Aristotle. The last notes that the meaning of the what is just is that which men of good will think to be right (*Ethics* 2,6.1105b28). In fact a purely reasoned ethics has no other clear basis for determining what the morally good and the morally good life are than the consensus of society on what makes for community well-being. In the American system of law public opinion is also the arbiter of what is just and of what are good laws. Thus public opinion does not mean the will of the masses in a chaotic or libertine sense; the presumption for the civilized existence of a society is that a consensus emerges that will establish and adapt ethical norms conducive to the public good and the personal well-being of the members.

Moral theology begins, however, not with the moral opinions of men of good will, but with a "given": salvation as the final moral good and, consequently, a scale of human goods valuated by their relation to the final good. In the pluralistic pattern now generally the environment of the Church's existence in the modern world there are obvious conflicts between public opinion and church teaching on moral issues. To speak only of the American Church, the policy statements of the National Conference of Catholic Bishops (NCCB) on public issues are evidence that the NCCB regards it as the right of the Church and of the Catholic as a citizen to enter into the formation of public opinion. Such policy statements invoke a right to influence the moral climate and the political process on issues of public, social morality. These are issues of justice, not of purely supernatural, religious, or sectarian provenance. Issues directly involving human rights are not matters of private morality; the effort to mold public opinion by any citizen is not the imposition of private religious beliefs on others, but participation in the political process.

At the level of individual conscience the authority conceded at many levels to public opinion has another implication. Public opinion influences style of life and dress, manners and morals. In many instances that influence is a legitimate norm even morally, e.g., what modesty of dress means in any era or society. But the Christian conscience is also formed by the general principle of moral theology (now admittedly under attack within the Church) that there are moral*absolutes. When public opinion runs counter to a conscience so formed then it loses its moral authority for the Christian, who cannot accept or follow the consensus of society.

[T. C. O'BRIEN]

PUBLIC ORDER (CANON LAW), a particular norm for determining the obligation of a traveler (*peregrinus*) to observe the particular, local ecclesiastical laws in the place he is visiting. The general rule that such a person is not obliged to local laws is stated in the CIC. c. 14, § 1,n.2. But an exception is made where a law involves "public order." Such a law is one laid down as necessary for the common good, the peace, and the stability of the whole community; it must be obeyed.

[T. C. O'BRIEN]

PUBLIC PROPRIETY, see IMPEDIMENTS TO MARRIAGE.

PUBLIC RELATIONS, as here understood, the occupation of trained specialists employed by business, government, churches, educational establishments, and other institutions: (1) to give the institutions employing them counsel on policies or practices likely to create favorable or unfavorable impressions on the public; and (2) to interpret the institution, its objectives, and activities to the public in such a way as to secure a favorable attitude. As a special profession offering organized and well–planned services, public relations began in the 1920s, and its function has grown more significant with the modern development of the media of communication. The concentration of such effort on the shaping of public opinion is obviously a matter of grave social and hence moral concern. If an institution is acting against the public interest, or if it is less than honest in its communications, public relations can use its skill to abet the injustice. Fortunately this is recognized by men of conscience in the profession. The Public Relations Society of America has adopted a code of ethics for the profession, which is designed to insure that its members conduct themselves in accordance with the public welfare and are guided by generally accepted standards of truth, accuracy, and good taste.

PUBLIC SCHOOLS, RELIGIOUS GARB IN. Controversy has arisen in the U.S. particularly over nuns employed as public school teachers. Many non-Catholics have objected that the practice gives a sectarian atmosphere to a public institution. In some cases courts have sustained the objections, but in other cases have declared that the religious freedom of public school teachers includes the wearing of religious dress if they so choose. In some states the wearing of religious garb in public schools has been prohibited by legislation.

[T. EARLY]

PUBLIC SCHOOLS, RELIGIOUS PRACTICES IN. Though the earliest schools in the American colonies were explicitly religious, and a religious atmosphere pervaded many public schools until recent years, activities to promote any one religious belief have gradually been excluded from public schools under the pressure of secular forces in the name of liberty. Protests by religious groups, however, have also played a part. Catholics opposed reading from Protestant versions of the Bible and other Protestant-oriented practices. Jews objected to public schools promulgating Christian doctrines, and other religious minorities have created other obstacles to a generally acceptable religious expression. A number of recent Supreme Court decisions have led to the virtual elimination of all religious practices from public schools. Considerable public opposition to those decisions has been expressed, with proposals for a constitutional amendment to allow nonsectarian activities. BIBLIOGRAPHY: A. P. Stokes, *Church and State* (3 v., 1950).

[T. EARLY]

PUBLIC WORSHIP REGULATION ACT, law passed by Parliament (1874) against *ritualism in the Church of England. The measure, drafted by A. C. Tait, abp. of Canterbury, was hostile to Anglo-Catholics and was amended in Parliament by Lord Shaftesbury, a fervent evangelical who was both a humanitarian and an Erastian. It provided for a special civil judge to try cases involving ritual, allowed for right of appeal to the Privy Council, and at the instance of the primate, for an episcopal veto on proceedings. The imprisonment for contumacy of four respected clergymen brought it into discredit a few years afterward; since then it has remained a dead letter.

[T. GILBY]

PUBLICANS, the tax collectors who figure somewhat prominently in the Gospels. There the term refers to the agents of the imperial procurator of Judaea, whose job it was to collect the customs dues on exports. Some Jews apparently were willing to serve the Roman State in this capacity. The term originally referred to a member of one of the great Roman financial companies who had bought at an auction the exclusive right to farm the taxes of a particular province of the Empire in the name of the Roman State. This transaction no doubt freed the Roman State of an expensive and irksome burden, but it led to corruption and oppression. It was not unknown for provincial governors to be slack in supervision and to wink at extortion. There was no guarantee that the taxes would not be collected more than once. The Jewish people viewed as a traitor and held in deepest contempt any fellow Jew who would become an agent of such a system. The Jewish publican was the quintessential sinner. It is necessary to have this in mind to appreciate the impact of the parable in Luke 18.9–14, in which Jesus portrays this apostate traitor (the Publican) more "justified," because of his overwhelming awareness of his need for mercy, than an enlightened teacher of righteousness (the Pharisee) who sensed no such need.

[E. J. DILLON]

PUCELLE, JEAN (fl. *c*.1300–50), innovative French miniaturist of the Parisian School between Master Honoré and the brothers Limbourg (15th cent.), advancing the greater naturalism of the former in a French-Gothic elegance enriched (1320's) by Italian spatial concepts recalling Duccio in the *Belleville Breviary* (*c*.1325), *The Hours of Jeanne d' Évreux* (*c*.1325–28) and the *Bible of Robert de Billyng* (1327). P.'s non-Italian innovations are in calendar pages showing not the medieval labors of the months but pure landscapes of bare trees in January, the rains of February. His contributions are *drôleries,* enrichment of imagery, a rhythmic freedom and tactile form. The "dragon-fly" (a pun on the name Pucelle) appears in borders as P.'s signature. BIBLIOGRAPHY: K. Morand, *Jean Pucelle* (1962).

[M. J. DALY]

PUDENS AND PUDENTIANA, SS. There is mention in 2 Tim 4.21 of a Pudens in Rome who joined with others in sending greetings. Legend later identified this man with St. Peter's host in Rome, conferred senatorial rank upon him, and gave him two daughters, Pudentiana and *Praxedes. His home on the Viminal, according to the legend, was the first Christian oratory in Rome and *c*.150 was made a church by Pope Pius I under the title of Pudens (*titulus Pudentis,* or *ecclesia pudentiana*). It seems altogether probable that the *ecclesia pudentiana* does trace back to the gift of a house or plot of ground made by someone named Pudens, but the daughter Pudentiana is probably no more than a popular misinterpretation of the adjective in the title. The *acta* of SS. Pudentiana and Praxedes date back no further than the 8th cent. and are acknowledged to be spurious. There is no evidence to identify the Pudens of 2 Tim 4.21 with the man whose name is associated with the church. The association of Praxedes and Pudentiana is probably due to the fact that their names were joined on the list of the virgins whose remains were transferred from the catacombs to the Church of St. Praxedes by Pope Paschal I (817–824). BIBLIOGRAPHY: Butler 2:347–348; H. Delehaye, AS Nov. 2:263.

[P. K. MEAGHER]

PUERTA DE LAS PLATERIAS, see SANTIAGO DE COMPOSTELA CATHEDRAL.

PUERTO, NICOLÁS DEL (d. 1681), vicar general, bishop. A Mexican Indian, P. was ordained as a diocesan priest, working for a time in his native Oaxaca but leaving when he felt discriminated against in promotion. He became a teacher, and later rector and chancellor of the Colegio Mayor de Santos in Mexico City. In 1657 P. was named commissioner general of the Cruzada. He became consultant to the Inquisition and vicar general of Mexico City. In 1679 P. was appointed bp. of Oaxaca.

[J. R. AHERNE]

PUERTO RICO, an island of the Greater Antilles (3,423 sq. mi.; pop [1976] 2,874,412. Columbus discovered it on his second voyage (1493); Ponce de León began its conquest and colonization. Harsh treatment and disease depleted the native population, and as early as 1513 Negroes began to be imported as slaves to work the plantations of the conquerors. The island served as a stopping place on the voyages back and forth between Spain and the more important centers in the New World. Neglected for other purposes, the island was exposed to the incursions of buccaneers. Although there was unrest in Puerto Rico at the time other Spanish American nations were winning their independence, no effective uprising took place. During the Spanish American War, Puerto Rico was occupied by U.S. troops, and in the Treaty of Paris (1898) Spain ceded it to the U.S. After a period of military rule, an administration was set up (1900) with an appointed governor and executive council and an elected house of delegates. In successive stages the government became more independent and in 1952 Puerto Rico achieved the status of a self-governing commonwealth in voluntary association with the U.S. The illiteracy rate has been reduced from 77% in 1898 to about 15%, and considerable gains, esp. during the last 25 years, have been made in the development of agriculture and industry. Among the early missionaries were Dominicans, Mercedarians, Hieronymites, and secular priests. The evangelization of the natives was more thorough than on the other islands. In 1511 Puerto Rico was made an episcopal see suffragan to Seville. In the unsettled conditions that prevailed in the 19th cent., the state of the Church deteriorated; much of its property was confiscated and many religious communities were disbanded. The situation did not improve greatly during the first three decades of the 20th century. There was a great shortage of priests, and although religious came from outside to help, there was friction with the Spanish-speaking clergy, and there was too little adaptation in the methods employed by the missioners. The general secularization of life, and esp. of education, under U.S. rule created a new obstacle to religious development for a people culturally unprepared for it. Slow but steady progress has been made in the past 40 years. In 1977 the Catholic population numbered 2,622,685; the number of priests has increased to 743, 500 of whom are religious and 243 diocesan. There are 276 parishes, 617 men religious and 1,581 women religious. Notable advances have been made in education on all levels. In 1948 the Catholic Univ. of Puerto Rico was established in Ponce and a minor seminary in Aibonito in 1956. The socioreligious problems of Puerto Ricans have not yet been solved, but conditions are beginning to improve. There are a fair number of vocations from the island itself for the various sisterhoods, but far too few for the priesthood. Many of the people are deeply religious, but there is also much superstition among the masses. Lay activities and movements (Cursillos, Movement for a Better World, the Legion of Mary, Catholic Action, the Christian Family Movement) have taken good root. Actual attendance at Sunday Mass was found in a study conducted (1956) at the Catholic Univ. of Puerto Rico to be the practice of 8.6% of the Catholics in the Ponce Diocese and of 9.7% in that of San Juan. The greatest needs of the Catholic Church are held to be religious instruction, the Christianization of homes, and island vocations. In 1924 the Diocese of Ponce was erected, in 1960 that of Arecibo; in 1964 that of Caguas. San Juan was elevated to the status of an archbishopric in 1960; in 1973 Abp. Luis Aponte Martinez was made first native Puerto Rican cardinal by Paul VI. Protestant Churches (Presbyterians, Methodists, Episcopalians) began to be active in Puerto Rico when the island came under U.S. control. Other denominations arrived later. The Protestant bodies have made a great effort in the field of education. Their total community amounts to about half a million or 10% of the population.

[P. DAMBORIENA]

PUFENDORF, SAMUEL (1632–94), German historian and jurist. Born in Saxony, son of a Lutheran pastor, he studied at Leipzig and Jena, where he came to know the works of T. *Hobbes and H. *Grotius. In his career he was professor at Heidelberg (1661) and Lund (1670); historiographer of the King of Sweden (1677); and at the court of Frederick William, the Elector of Brandenburg, in Berlin (1686). P.'s historical work included *De statu imperii Germanici* (1667), on the Holy Roman Empire which asserted the need for a strong imperial power. His philosophy of law combined both empiricism and rationalism. Largely derived from Grotius, his natural law theory in *De jure naturae et gentium* (8 v. 1672) sharply separated natural law from the moral law of revelation, and made it the basis and criterion of positive law. The ground of natural law is the social nature of man, expressed in the dictates of reason. Natural law has its origin in the divine will to create man's social nature, not in the eternal law reflective of God's essence. Grotius' work gave great impetus to the study of philosophy of law and its development in a rationalistic manner. He also expounded the theory of *collegialism that came to regulate Church-State relations in Germany. BIBLIOGRAPHY: L. Krieger. *Politics of Discretion: Pufendorf and the Acceptance of Natural Law* (1965).

[T. EARLY]

PUGET, PIERRE (1620–94), French sculptor, painter, architect. In Florence (1640) and in Rome (1641) pupil of Pietro da Cortona, P., in 1652 painter to the city and urban planner in Marseilles was called by Louis XIV to Toulon to supervise the decorative wood carving of ships (1668–79). Among P.'s sculptured classical allegorical masterpieces are the *Gallic Hercules* and the remarkable *Milo of Crotona* (1671–82). He painted scenes from the life of Mary, a *Sta. Cecilia* (1650), *Baptism of Constantine and Chlodwig,* and in Genoa after 1661 *St. Sebastian* and *St. Ambrose in Ecstasy* for the Church of Sta. Maria di Carignano. In his intensive baroque-pathos P. was a "Provençal Michelangelo" at odds with the official French art of his day. BIBLIOGRAPHY: E. Baumann, *Pierre Puget: Sculpteur,*

1620–1694 (1949). P. Rotondi, "Sculptures inconnues à Génes attribuèes à Pierre Puget," *Gazette des Beaux-Arts* 51 (1958).

[L. P. SIGER]

PUGIN, AUGUSTUS WELBY (1812–52), English architect, son of an architectural draughtsman in whose office he worked making measured drawings of Gothic buildings in England. He became a Roman Catholic *c.* 1833 and eventually the leader of the English Gothic revival, working out details for the new Houses of Parliament at Westminster. He was constantly frustrated in that economic needs of parishes caused changes in his plans and proportions and substitutions of sham materials. Only one of the 30 churches he designed followed his complete design, and this he paid for himself, St. Augustine's, Ramsgate. In 1836 he published *Contrasts: A Parallel between the Architecture of the 15th and 19th Centuries,* which Hitchcock (*Early Victorian Architecture in Britain,* 1954) says marked the end of the Georgian age of architecture. BIBLIOGRAPHY: Gillow BDEC 5:379–381.

[M. M. BARRY]

PŪJĀ, ceremonial worship in Hinduism, in which the image of the deity is accorded the honor suited to a royal guest. The ceremonies range from brief daily rites in the home to elaborate temple ritual, and differ from sect to sect, in accord with the needs of the worshiper. The various attentions (upacāras) accorded the deity manifested in his image, can include rousing him from sleep, serving him meals, offering him a seat, water for ablutions, perfume, flowers and incense, food and entertainment, putting him to bed, and solemn leave-taking. The ringing of a bell or the blowing of a conch shell indicates the termination of each separate part of a *pūjā.* Private, home *pūjās* end with the saying of a *mantra;* temple *pūjās* conclude with the temporary closing of the doors of the inner sanctuary by the priest. BIBLIOGRAPHY: *Religion of the Hindus* (ed. K. W. Morgan, 1953).

[E. J. DILLON]

PULASKI, CASIMIR (1748–1779), Polish patriot and American Revolutionary War officer. The son of Count Pulaski whom he joined in 1768 in rebellion against the foreign powers occupying Poland, he enjoyed initial success but was finally defeated and fled to Turkey. After fruitless efforts to involve Turkey in a war with Russia, he volunteered, through Benjamin Franklin in Paris, to aid the American Revolutionists. He met Washington who recommended to the Continental Congress that Pulaski be placed in command of the newly added cavalry. P. participated in the battles of Brandywine and Germantown. He quarreled with General Wayne and his own subordinates and finally resigned his command. His subsequent history is largely a series of disastrous defeats. In the siege of Savannah P. made a heroic but ill-timed charge on the British forces and was fatally wounded. A quixotic character of great personal bravery, his service to the Revolution was devoted but not effective.

[J. R. AHERNE]

PULCHERIA, ST. (399–453), **BYZANTINE EMPRESS.** Noted for her strong attachment to the Church and to the orthodox faith, P. was forced to lead a secluded life away from the imperial court. On the sudden death of her brother, Theodosius II, in 450, she assumed power, married the elderly senator, Marcian, and brought about better relations with Pope *Leo I. She convoked the Council of *Chalcedon in which she took an active interest.

PULPIT, derived from the Latin for ''platform,'' an elevated stand for preachers. It came into use in the late Middle Ages (bishops earlier had preached from the cathedra). Made of wood or marble, pulpits became quite elaborate, particularly in the Baroque period. The pulpit is usually placed on the north (''gospel'') side of the nave.

[J. DALLEN]

PUNCH, JOHN (1599–1661), Irish-born Franciscan, philosopher, and theologian whose dedicated study and presentation of the philosophy of John *Duns Scotus earned him the respect of contemporary scholars, including opponents. He taught at St. Isidore's in Rome. He avoided the often futile scholarly task of reconciling Thomas Aquinas and Scotus. He taught and wrote Scotist philosophy and theology rather than following the traditional approach of commenting upon the *Sentences* of Peter Lombard. P. was the collaborator of L. *Wadding in the editing of Scotus's *Omnia opera*. P.'s own chief work was his *Commentarii theologici* (1661).

[R. J. LITZ]

PUNCTUM, in *Gregorian chant notation, one of the two signs for a single note. Probably derived from the acute accent, it generally took the form of a dot or short horizontal line in early MSS, later assuming the square shape without a stem still used in modern printed chant books. It originally signified a note relatively low in pitch, while the *virga indicated a relatively high note. This distinction has been suppressed in the modern editions, where the punctum is used for all single notes.

[A. DOHERTY]

PUNIET DE PARRY, PIERRE DE (1877–1941), French Benedictine liturgical scholar, best known for his research on the Gellone Sacramentary and the Roman Pontifical.

[N. KOLLAR]

PUNISHMENT, a word derived from the Lat. *poena* and the Gr. *poinē,* and etymologically associated also with the Eng. pain, the incurring or infliction in requital for a mis-

deed of an evil, i.e., an evil in the sense of a deprivation against the will of the one who suffers it. As unwilled it is enforced (*violentum; biaion*) and so differs from *satisfaction. As incurred, it supposes an internal nexus between fault and penalty; as inflicted, an external nexus formed by the intervention of a judge.

In traditional Western thought, evil, the privation of due good, covers both a defective doing (moral evil, the evil of fault, *malum culpae*) and the defective condition which is its after-effect (*malum poenae*), which is a type of what is sometimes called physical evil. The connection between the two is as interior and inevitable as that between any cause and effect; punishment is the rebound, the counterpoise, so to speak, that maintains the balance of justice inherent in creation. Seek ''the self and non-God'' and you will find it; and if the effort is serious and protracted enough, the result, but for divine mercy, will be *hell—the supreme example of vindictive or retributive punishment.

In this sense punishment is said to be retrospective. The effect is there simply by reason of its cause. On last analysis it neither seeks moral justification nor the reverse, for it is as little a moral matter as getting burned if you put your hand in the fire. Moral and religious questions arise when we ask about the rights involved when one human being punishes another.

''Vengeance is mine; I will repay, saith the Lord'' (Rom 12.19), but whether retribution as such should be imposed by human authority is a matter of debate. While allowing for the dangers of vindication lapsing into pure vindictiveness, the venting of spleen and revengeful feelings, an eye for an eye and a tooth for a tooth, Lord Devlin has argued in a celebrated lecture that the avenging reaction of the community's sense of outrage is well founded in the historical etiology of law and in social theory. For it is a fact that the overtones, though not the etymologies, of to punish and to punch back are common. Moral indignation, however, is a bad guide to civilized practice, and poetic justice is not for institutions; the more general and utilitarian view is that punishment inflicted by human authority can be justified only as prospective, that is, as seeking a good from the penalty it exacts. Fight for the laws as you would for the city-walls, said the old Greek, for they are the defenses of freedom. Free-men, then, are called upon to be forcible, and, as will appear, their practice can be stern enough without appealing to retribution. Their punishing, however, has to be selective; their public office is not to punish all wrong-doing, but that which directly harms or menaces the community: St. Thomas Aquinas would not put virtue as such under police patronage.

The good sought in the evil of punishment may be of three sorts. First, it may be the very health and safety of the body politic which can be ensured only by the excision of a diseased and dangerous member, whether by death, banishment, or safe detention. This side of the argument for prospective punishment, which of course applies only when guilt is established, tends to be overlooked; abolitionists of capital punishment notably succeed in presenting their opponents as entrenched on the "kill-and-you-will-be-killed" position, whereas in point of fact the line they take is surgical, and even not unmerciful when the facts of penal servitude, for everybody concerned, are appreciated.

Second, the welfare of the wrongdoer is to be considered. The remedial value of punishment is well recognized in a good household, and in larger groups, but he would be very ill-informed who claimed that the modern State had yet succeeded, despite the patient, devoted, and skilled ministrations of its social workers and guardians, in this reformative part of penology.

Third, the role of deterrence in the prevention of crime is evident, but the scales adopted as standard should always be open to revision, particularly in the light of field work conducted by expert criminologists.

The effort always should be to make punishment fit the crime. Yet here public justice can rarely hope to be more than extrinsic, arbitrary, and pragmatic: fines and imprisonments do not exactly correspond to the wrong which has been done. The virtue that rules the power of punishing is called vindication, the upholding of justice; over-harshness or over-leniency both offend against it. Punishment for punishment's sake is a perversion. Anger, cruelty, terrorism, and savagery are treated as opposed to the clemency that should temper the severity of justice. A gap not yet filled in humanitarian theory and criminal law in modern states is concern for the victim by making the aggressor himself repair the damage as far as possible. His punishment might then take on another and more Christian meaning. BIBLIOGRAPHY: ThAq ST 1a2ae, 87, 95 and 96 (esp. in ed. Lat-Eng, v. 27, ed. T. C. O'Brien 1974; v. 28, ed. T. Gilby, 1967); 2a2ae, 61.4; 64.2; 65.3; 67.4; 108, 157, 158, 159; W. Temple, *Ethics of Penal Action* (1934); P. Devlin, *Enforcement of Morals* (1965); H. L. A. Hart, *Morality of the Criminal Law* (1965).

[T. GILBY]

PURANAS, a class of non-Vedic Sanskrit writings dealing with ancient material, though actual compilation dates from the 6th to the 16th cent. A.D. These pantheistic verse dialogues between a rishi (sage) and one or more gods have, or, by precept should have, five characteristics: an account of creation; genealogy of rishis and gods; a description of the aeons ruled by the Manus (patriarchs); the universe's destruction and re-creation, including a history of mankind; and legends of the dynasties of Sun and Moon. The 18 puranas, which have been called the popular Veda or Veda of the common folk, differ in length and content. Six of them are dedicated to Vishnu and the theme of purity; six to Siva and gloom; and a final third to Brahma and the passions. The six puranas of the Vishnu group are the most important, and the *Vishnu Purana* in particular is the best known and most influential of all. Besides these there are as many as 88 minor works or lesser puranas called the *Upa-Puranas*.

[R. J. LITZ]

PURCELL, EDWARD (1808–81), lawyer, brother of Abp. J. B. Purcell. Born in Ireland, P. came to the U.S., studied law, and began a law practice. But he decided to study theology and was ordained in 1838. P. became vicar general of Cincinnati, editor of the *Catholic Telegraph,* the diocesan weekly, and was entrusted with the finances of the diocese. In Cincinnati as in other areas, immigrants entrusted their savings to the Church rather than to banks, which often failed. P.'s unwise handling of money resulted in a failure of the fund, and he with his brother signed over personal property to meet creditors' demands. When the creditors claimed all church property as personal to the abp., the Ohio Supreme Court ruled that archdiocesan holdings were not personal property.

[J. R. AHERNE]

PURCELL, HAROLD (1881–1952), editor, missionary. Born in the anthracite country of Pennsylvania, P. became a Passionist and was ordained in 1904. After 15 years as a preacher of missions, he founded *The Sign* magazine and was its editor for 13 years, which saw the periodical grow and achieve a high reputation for quality. When P. left the Passionists to work in the Southern missions with blacks, the *Literary Digest* offered him a position as editor-in-chief. P. went to Montgomery, Ala., where he built The City of St. Jude, a $5 million project, containing a clinic, hospital, schools, churches, and social centers that were open to all but largely for blacks.

[J. R. AHERNE]

PURCELL, HENRY (c.1659–95), English composer. He was for a time chorister of the Chapel Royal where he was taught by Henry Cooke and then Pelham Humfrey. Later he studied under the composer John Blow, whom he succeeded (1679) as organist at Westminster Abbey. From 1682 he was, in addition, appointed to the post of organist to the Chapel Royal. As "composer in ordinary to the king" he composed an ode or anthem for each public event. He wrote vocal and instrumental chamber music, the opera *Dido and Aeneas,* five semi-operas, and incidental music for plays. Of the latter category, the best known music is that which he wrote for Congreve's comedy *The Double Dealer* and for S. Behn's *Abdelazar.* Of his more than 500 compositions, *Dido and Aeneas* is best known and most admired. His sacred music consisted of canticles and anthems for church services and the massive choral works *Te Deum, Magnificat, Nunc Dimittis,* and the *Jubilate* for St. Cecilia's Day (1694). He was influential in reshaping sacred music after the "reform" of the earlier Puritan revolt. He injected secular elements into church music by introducing forms from the theater such as verse anthems and ritornellos for strings. BIBLIOGRAPHY: D. D. Arundell, *Henry Purcell* (1927, repr. 1971); J. R. Westrup, *Purcell* (1949, repr. 1962).

PURCELL, JOHN BAPTIST (1800–83), second bp. of Cincinnati, Ohio. Among U.S. bps. few have had such a combination of great success and heartbreaking failure. Born in Ireland he came to the U.S. in 1818, and taught briefly in Queen Anne's County, Maryland. He entered Mount Saint Mary's College, Emmittsburg, Md., and was ordained in Paris in 1826. He became professor and in 1829 rector of Mount Saint Mary's and obtained for it a state charter. Named bp. of Cincinnati, P. proved himself a tolerant and able administrator. He was esp. considerate of the Germans who were numerous in his diocese, and treated German clerics the same as Irish priests, an unusual procedure for Irish bps. in his day. An ardent advocate of parochial schools and charitable institutions, he brought to Cincinnati Sisters of Notre Dame de Namur, Ursulines, Sisters of Charity, Sisters of Mercy, Sisters of the Good Shepherd, and Little Sisters of the Poor. In addition, P. introduced into his diocese the Jesuits (whom he helped in founding St. Francis Xavier College), the Passionists, and the Fathers of the Precious Blood, who established a seminary and college. Hospitals, orphanages, and asylums rose under his direction. A skillful controversialist, P. engaged in a 2-day debate in 1836 with Alexander *Campbell, and succeeded in lessening nativist hostility. Among the most influential bps. of the U.S., P, was instrumental in the selection of bps. for American sees. Named abp. in 1850, P. voted against the definition of infallibility at Vatican I, but freely accepted the decree. At his golden jubilee in 1876 P. had become a powerful figure in U.S. Catholic life. Misfortune occurred a year later. Distrustful of banks, Catholics in 1837 and thereafter placed their money with the diocese, in a fund administered by the bishop's brother, E. *Purcell, who proved to be an incompetent financial manager. In 1877 there was a run on the fund and it went into bankruptcy. Although both Purcells turned over their personal property to creditors, the abp. was heartbroken. His administration was assumed by Bp. W. *Elder as coadjutor and P. retired to an Ursuline Convent.

[J. R. AHERNE]

PURE, MICHEL DE (1620–80), French man of letters, priest. Appointed almoner to the king (1647) and historiographer of France (1653), he wrote numerous works, among them a tragedy, a biography of Richelieu's older brother, Alphonse Louis du Pléssis, cardinal abp. of Lyon (1653), and a novel, *La Prétieuse ou le mystère de la ruelle* (1656), an interesting document on 17th-cent. salon life. BIBLIOGRAPHY: *La Prétieuse* (ed. E. Magne, 1938), introduction.

[R. N. NICOLICH]

PURE ACT, God's unlimited and full realization of existence. According to scholastic philosophy, act is opposed to potentiality as realization is opposed to a mere capacity for change. Since God is a total perfection, he is fully in act. God is pure act insofar as he possesses no potentiality; the one act of his subsisting existence is the highest and absolute reality. This scholastic teaching has its roots in the Aristotelian division of being into the potential and the actual, although for Aristotle pure act was linked to indeter-

minacy and thus excluded change but not limitation. Some nonscholastic philosophers (notably G. Hegel, G. Gentile, and M. Blondel) have used pure act to refer to divine perfection. BIBLIOGRAPHY: ThAq ST 1a, 3, 4 and 7.

[T. M. MCFADDEN]

PURE AND IMPURE, clean *(ṭāhēr)* and unclean *(ṭāmē')* in biblical law. No exact definition is possible. People became unclean for various reasons: by eating certain foods, leprosy, contact with a corpse, genital emissions. All these were unleashed or were connected with dangerous forces somehow connected with the holy. The "unsuitability" was of the physical, not the moral order. Particular classes, like priests, were subject to even stricter rules because of their functions. In the NT Jesus had serious disputes on this issue with Pharisees (Mk 7. 1–23), who had so strictly defined fitness for an Israelite that they had gone far toward formalism and magic. Jesus "made all things clear." It must be admitted, however, that the transformation of long standing beliefs of primitive people into religious concepts did much to preserve the monotheism of the Israelites through the centuries.

[L. A. BUSHINSKI]

PURE LOVE, THE PROBLEM OF, see DISIN-TERESTED LOVE.

PURE NATURE, STATE OF, that condition human nature would be in if it were not called to grace but destined purely to attain its connatural end. Human nature, as one knows it, is human nature called to grace, fallen, and redeemed. The theological tradition received from the scholastics tended to regard grace as perfecting nature in such a way that without grace, which elevates a human being in himself and in his activity, human nature would have been recognizably the same as it is now. Today, however, many theologians, considering the fact that all human nature actually created by God is oriented to a supernatural destiny, will not concede that one is capable of envisaging what human nature would have been like had God not given it a supernatural destiny. We have, they insist, no knowledge of human nature apart from its supernatural as well as its sinful condition. That God could create human beings without orienting them to the beatific vision and calling them to it was affirmed by Pius XII (*Humani generis;* D 3891); in thus asserting the gratuitousness of the supernatural order, Pius XII was asserting the possibility of the state of pure nature, for denying which M. Baius was condemned in 1567 (D 1901–80); Baius is however judged less harshly by some theologians today. BIBLIOGRAPHY: H. de Lubac, *Surnaturel: Études historiques* (1946); *idem, Le Mystère du surnaturel* (1965); Rahner ThInvest v. 1.

[B. FORSHAW]

PURGATORY, in RC belief, the state of purification to which the soul of the just is subjected immediately after death if either unremitted venial sin or temporal punishment for sin is still to be atoned for. The only pertinent scriptural passage to support this belief is 2 Macc 12.39–45: after a battle against Gorgias, Judas found that, contrary to the prescriptions of the law (Dt 7.25), some of the slain Jewish soldiers were wearing amulets. Concluding that their death was a divine punishment, Judas made a collection among the survivors in order to have expiatory sacrifices offered for the dead, that they might be freed from their sins. The inspired author approves of Judas's belief, which embraces both his faith in the resurrection (see, e.g., 2 Macc 7.9, 11, 14) and his conviction that the dead can be helped by the prayers (2 Macc 12.42) and the sacrifices (12.43) of the living. The fallen soldiers are not damned since they expect the final resurrection (12.45), but they still stand in need of purification. This intermediary state is substantially purgatory.

In the NT, I Cor 3.10–15 is inconclusive: the fire in question (13, 15) is not purifying but eschatological (13), and, besides, the entire context points in the direction of testing the worthiness of the apostolic work. Other texts sometimes quoted (2 Tm 1.18; Mt 12.32) being equally inconclusive, one may assert that the scriptural testimony is meager. Nevertheless, this tiny scriptural seed gradually developed through the analysis of faith, the Church's liturgical practice, and a hesitant patristic interpretation, not always free from error. Origen is the first explicit witness to this tradition, but his testimony is a blend of light and darkness. According to him the soul is stained by its union with the body, hence there is a general need for final purification affecting all men. They must all be purified "from the lead that weighs them down and which must be dissolved by fire" (Hom. in Ex. 6; PG 12:334). This purification will take place not immediately after death but at the general judgment by means of real fire (see Cels. 4.13; PG 11:236). St. Augustine wrote that the final purification does not affect all men (Civ. 20.26.1); it takes place immediately after death (Civ. 21.13); purgatorial fire is probably metaphorical, not real (Civ. 21.4).

Both East and West were joint heirs to this common tradition up to the 13th cent., but at this time the two Churches began to develop distinct though mutually complementary tendencies. In the West, Peter Lombard's distinction between guilt and its temporal punishment is immediately applied to the doctrine of purgatory, and as a consequence the juridical aspect of satisfaction prevails. The sinner has to pay off the debt contracted; his personal guilt is to be fully expiated. The Eastern conception is less juridical and more mystical: purgatory is not a place but a state of "maturation and perfection" (Irenaeus), a final stage of spiritual growth where God's image, blurred by sin, is fully restored. "These two traditions are compatible within the unity of the same ecclesial communion" (Congar). Against this theological background the Council of Florence (1439–45) expounded the doctrine in an eclectic manner. Purgatory is a means of both satisfaction and purification (Latin and Greek conceptions combined); there is

no mention of purgatorial fire, but rather of "purgatorial sufferings"; there is no mention of purgatory as a place (see D 1304). This fundamental agreement of the Churches was shaken in 1524 by Luther, who openly rejected purgatory: apart from the lack of scriptural support (he holds even 2 Macc to be a noncanonical book), this "popish" doctrine goes counter to the very core of Lutheran soteriology, in which man is saved exclusively by God alone and therefore any medium of purification after death should be rejected as sheer Pelagianism. The doctrine of purgatory was rejected in the *Reformed tradition (e.g., Art. 57 of Zwingli's Sixty-Seven Articles; Second *Helvetic Confession, ch. 26; *Westminster Confession, c. 32) and in Anglicanism (*Thirty-Nine Articles, c. 32). The Council of Trent in 1563 restated the traditional doctrine but in a very sober manner, which contrasts with certain popular, but only dubiously valuable, descriptions of purgatory. The Council teaches only the existence of purgatory and the possibility of helping souls therein by means of suffrages (see D 1820).

There is a marked tendency among some theologians (P. Fransen, Y. Congar, and L. Boros) to "demythologize" and spiritualize the doctrine: purgatorial fire need not be taken literally as real fire, for the dying person is possessed by the Holy Spirit, who is often associated with fire (Mt 3.11; Lk 3.16; Acts 2.3–4). God's image, which had been imprinted on the soul by the Spirit and obscured by sin, is now restored to its pristine splendor by the same Spirit who "burns" from within. The strange coexistence of joy and suffering in purgatory affects only the psychological level but is rooted in the deeper, ontological coexistence of the Spirit and *concupiscence. The soul rejoices because it possesses the Spirit forever, and yet it suffers on account of its unextinguished concupiscence. Its joy will be unalloyed, without any mixture of suffering, only when it is totally possessed by the Spirit without any trace of concupiscence. The Spirit draws man into himself, scorching and purifying him down to the deepest layers of his personality and making him ready for the vision of God. Purgatory is possibly a momentary occurrence, linked to the quality of the decision made at the moment of death. Consequently the duration of purgatory should be measured by the various degrees in the intensity of purifying suffering. The degree to which that "fire" of the Spirit cleanses the soul one tends to express in terms of temporal duration, which would be only an anthropomorphism. This purification is an active, loving acceptance of a suffering imposed by Love, before the soul "enters into the joy of the Lord" (Mt 25.21). BIBLIOGRAPHY: Y. Congar, "Le Purgatoire," Le Mystère de la mort et sa célébration (Lex Orandi 12; 1956) 279–336; P. Fransen, "Doctrine of Purgatory," ECQ 13 (1959) 99–112.

[A. M. BERMEJO]

PURIFICATION (IN THE BIBLE). Behind the elaborate rituals of purification described in such detail in the Priestly sections of the OT, lies a basic conception of the holy and the profane as two sharply differentiated spheres which must be kept separate. Man stands, so to say, midway between these spheres, and can be "infected" by physical contact with that which fully belongs to either, and which is imbued, as it were, with the invisible force associated with it. Thus contact with corpses, with bodies disfigured with leprosy, with beasts deemed to be unclean (because associated with idolatry, etc.), or with sexual effluvia—all render man alien to the holy and disqualify him from entering its sphere. Similarly contact with the sacred cult objects or with sacrificial offerings, etc., renders him "holy" and before returning to the profane sphere of normal everyday life he has to free himself from the physical force of holiness by which he has thereby become "infected." The rites of purification, therefore, are designed to rid man of the "infection" of uncleanness considered as a physical force, and so to enable him to resume his due place in the "holy sphere" created by the presence of Yahweh dwelling in the midst of the people and in their land. Basically these rites of purification consist of sacrifices, ablutions, and aspersions with specially prepared water.

Purification is achieved by: (a) *Sacrifices*. Sin offerings, and holocausts are prescribed after childbirth (Lev 12.1–8), after sexual discharges (Lev 15.14–15; 29–30), after recovery from leprosy (Lev 14.10–32), and by a *Nazarite who has come in contact with a corpse (Num 6.9–12). The purpose of these sacrifices seems to be to induce Yahweh to restore the Israelite to his presence and to the sphere of his holiness, from which the latter's contact with uncleanness has temporarily debarred him. (b) *Ablutions*. The basic conception that uncleanness is incurred through physical contact with that which is alien and offensive to Yahweh makes the idea of ritual washing to remove all trace of such contacts readily comprehensible to us. The priest washes himself before entering the sphere of the holy or engaging in his cultic functions (cf. Ex 29:4; 30:17–21, etc.). Vessels or garments used in the cult must likewise be washed before being used (Lev 11.24–25, 28, 32, 40; 15 *passim*; 22.6). But they must also be washed, or even ritually broken, afterwards, because it is equally important to remove all traces of contact with the holy before they are withdrawn once more into the relatively profane sphere (cf. Lev 6.26–28). For the same reason the high priest has to wash himself and change his garments both before and after entering the Holy of Holies on the Day of Atonement (cf. Lev 16:4, 23–24). In later times scribes washed their hands both before and after writing the sacred name YHWH. (c) *Aspersions*. A third method of purification by aspersion was also used; a special "water for impurity" was prepared for this from running water into which the ashes of a red heifer, burned according to a prescribed ritual, were mingled together with hyssop, cedarwood, and scarlet stuff (cf. Num 19.1–10). It is clear that an ancient nomadic ritual, originally with a strong element of magic, has here been taken over by Yahwism and radically modified. Its purpose is to counter and ward off the positive force of that kind of uncleanness that is incurred through contact with the dead.

(d) *Purification after Leprosy* (cf. Lev 13–14). A special rite is used here, in which two birds are employed. One is sacrificed over fresh water while the other is dipped into the water mingled with the blood of the first, together with hyssop, cedar, and scarlet stuff and then allowed to fly away. The sufferer is then sprinkled with the water and blood. The bird which flies away here is considered to carry the contamination with it. These were the main types of purification employed in Hebrew society. BIBLIOGRAPHY: W. H. Gipsen, "Clean and Unclean," *Oudtestamentische Studien* V (1948) 190–196; P. Reymond, "L'eau, sa vie et sa signification dans l'Ancien Testament," VT Suppl 6 (1958); De Vaux AncIsr 462–465.

[D. J. BOURKE]

PURIFICATION OF MARY, the ceremony whereby Mary, 40 days after Christ's birth, complied with the Mosaic Law precept (Num 18.15) to present and redeem her firstborn at the Temple and be purified (Lev 12.2–8; Lk 2.22–24). According to Jewish tradition, the mother of a male child was unclean for 7 days and was to remain secluded for an additional 33 days. After this period, she was to bring a lamb to the Temple as a holocaust of thanksgiving and a young pigeon or turtledove as a sin offering. In case of poverty, two turtledoves or pigeons would suffice. Upon the priest's prayer, she would be cleansed. In addition, if the male child was the firstborn and thereby dedicated to the Lord, a payment of five shekels was made to have a *Levite assume the child's direct service to the Lord. Mary fulfilled all of these regulations: she awaited the 40 days of her seclusion; presented Jesus at the Temple; offered the turtledoves; and was blessed by the priest Simeon. The liturgical celebration of the event originated in Jerusalem in the 4th cent., spread throughout the East, and finally (7th cent.) to Rome. In the revised general calendar (Feb. 2) major emphasis in the feast is given to the presentation of Jesus. BIBLIOGRAPHY: S. Garofalo, *Mary in the Bible* (tr. T. J. Tobin, 1961); EDB 1966–67; P. J. Gaffney, NCE 11:1042–1043. *CANDLEMAS.

[T. M. MCFADDEN]

PURIFICATOR, a folded piece of white linen used in the Roman Mass to wipe the lip of the chalice after receiving communion from it and to dry the chalice after it is washed ("purified") near the end of or after Mass. It serves the purpose of a napkin or small towel. It is not mentioned in liturgical books until the late 13th and early 14th centuries.

[J. DALLEN]

PURIM, FEAST OF, Jewish festival celebrating the deliverance of the Jews from Hamaan's plot as recorded in the Book of Esther. Celebrated on Adar 14–15 (generally Feb.–March), the observance is more nationalistic than religious. The principal religious observance is the reading of the Book of Esther on the evening and morning of Adar 14. Traditionally the celebration has been characterized by something of a carnival spirit, with production of Purim plays since the 17th century. An oft-quoted rabbinic injunction says that at the festive meal on the evening of Adar 14 one should drink until he can no longer distinguish "Cursed be Hamaan" from "Blessed be Mordecai." It is also a time for distributing gifts of food to neighbors and for almsgiving.

Modern scholars, who generally consider the Book of Esther legendary, disagree as to the historical origins of the festival; the Persian feast of the dead, Farwardigan, and the Persian New Year's festival are among the suggestions. It was possibly brought to Palestine by Diaspora Jews, later crowding out Nicanor Day (see 2 Macc 15.36 where Purim is called Mordecai's day). BIBLIOGRAPHY: T. H. Gaster, *Purim and Hanukkah in Custom and Tradition* (1950).

[T. EARLY]

PURITANISM, a quality of mind and spirit conspicuous among the *Puritans, from whom it takes its name, but by no means confined to them, for it transcends confessional lines and in analogous form may be found even among people without religious faith. Its prominence in England in the 17th cent. was due largely to its systematization and organization under Calvinist inspiration, a movement to which powerful economic, social, and political forces, in addition to influences of a religious nature, contributed greatly. Elsewhere, even in France and the Low Countries where it was organized and influential for a time in the form of Jansenism, it never achieved stable predominance. Its spirit is complex and paradoxical. Haunted by a consciousness of sin, it honors hard work and thrift, and lays great stress upon a discipline of plain and godly living, reproducing some of the severity and decorum of the Latin Stoics. It tends to find the OT more to its liking than the New (hence its severe Sabbatarian preoccupation), takes much of its inspiration from the consideration of God's wrath, has little sympathy for human frailty, and is overly distrustful of human pleasure. The tendency toward Puritanism has probably always been present in the Christian Church, but generally it has been tempered by the coexistence of an opposing tendency, so that the two forces exercise a mutually mitigating influence upon each other. In certain times and places, however, circumstances cause them to polarize, and purer types of both Puritanism and its counter-movement emerge to take structured shape in opposing religious or philosophical sects (as, e.g., in the Stoic-Epicurean polarity in ancient philosophy). Both tendencies have contributed much to human culture; and both, when they exist in isolation, appear morbid. The roots of the tendency to Puritanism probably lie deep in human nature, in the suspicion and distrust men have of their creaturely ambivalence as this is aggravated by sinfulness, innate or acquired. In some of its manifestations in individuals it represents a clinical entity for medical or pastoral psychology. BIBLIOGRAPHY: W. Haller, *Rise of Puritanism* (1938); A. Simpson, *Puritanism in Old and New England* (1955); Knox Enth.

[T. GILBY]

PURITANS. (1) In England as a proper name the term referred in the 16th and 17th cent. to those accepting episcopacy, but wanting to rid the C of E of ritual; to those favoring a Presbyterian *polity (see WESTMINSTER ASSEMBLY); or to the Separatists favoring *congregationalism and complete independence from the Established Church (see INDEPENDENTS). After the *Restoration of Charles II in 1660 the term was no longer used; those rejecting the C of E were called Dissenters or Nonconformists. (2) In the American colonies the term applies mainly to the settlers of the Plymouth Colony, who were Separatists, and to those of the Massachusetts Bay Colony; the church polity in Massachusetts was congregationalist. Puritans from England also colonized Virginia and the Carolinas.

[T. C. O'BRIEN]

PURITY is the state of cleanliness *(tāhēr)* or freedom from contact and/or mixture with what is relatively base (see IMPURITY). The primitive idea of the pure was neither exclusively physical (hygienic) nor moral, though related to both. Purity is more closely connected with *holiness for which it is the prerequisite condition. The OT (esp. Lev) prescriptions for purity, while fostering monotheism and morality, were often the occasion of formalism. The Prophets protest against this formalism, and the Wisdom-writers, especially the Psalmists, celebrate moral purity. Jesus, continuing and completing the prophetic tradition, teaches that moral purity is the important consideration (Mk 7.15); nevertheless, the early Christian community had the problem of formalism in regard to ritually forbidden foods (cf. Acts 10.15; Rom 14.14). At the same time that OT concepts of ritual purity were being abandoned, the apostolic authority had to warn against the sexual impurity of the pagan world. The motive presented for sexual purity was the indwelling of the Holy Spirit who had cleansed the Christian from sin (1 Cor 6.11). Later Christian authors sometimes put undue emphasis on this, thus giving some occasion to the unfortunate inference that sex itself is impure. St. Thomas Aquinas saw *chastity rather in terms of control and discipline, and purity in a sense wider than chastity, as a raising of the spirit toward God (ThAq ST 2a2ae 7.2; 81.8). The earliest English meaning of the term purity was chastity (OED 8:1022), and this usage continues, although it is sometimes avoided for the sake of theological preciseness. BIBLIOGRAPHY: J. Lachowski, NCE 11:1031–32; P. Van Imschoot, EDB 1962–64.

[U. VOLL]

PURITY OF INTENTION, *simplicity or singleness of purpose toward achieving the virtuous good. Virtuous acts do not just happen; they mean intending the true moral good. The very meaning of the virtues is the possibility of that *intention, which gives any act its dominant moral quality. Purity of intention, however, does imply the possibility of *mixed motives, even of conflicting impulses copresent with the primary motivation in any action. That does not negate the primary intention, but is a sign of the need for healing grace in the continuing process of salvation. The primary intention in the Christian life is the direction given to the will by *charity. Purity of intention is the totality expressed in the great commandment of loving God above all. That totality will be fully achieved only with the beatific vision of God. But it is minimally preserved where mortal sin is avoided. In between there is open a greater and greater growth of the reign of charity. Striving for purity of intention is the continuing process of growth in charity; it will be marked by both active, ascetical purification and by the passive purification worked by the Holy Spirit.

[T. C. O'BRIEN]

PURPOSE OF AMENDMENT, the intention, esp. that formulated in connection with the sacrament of penance, of avoiding in the future the type of sin into which one has fallen in the past. It is implicit in all true *contrition and *attrition, but its distinct formulation is generally recommended. It is not be confused with an emotional sense of loathing for the type of sin with which it is concerned, for that may well be beyond the capacity of the penitent, who may be quite unable to avoid feeling the attraction of what he has found pleasant in the past. Neither should it be confused with a certainty of mind that one will be successful in the effort to avoid the sins in question. It is simply a resolution of the will which is here and now determined to make an earnest effort, using whatever effective measures seem necessary, to avoid relapse into the same sinful acts.

[P. F. MULHERN]

PÜRSTINGER, BERTHOLD, see BERTHOLD OF CHIEMSEE.

PURUSHA (Sanskrit, man, person, self), a term used in two completely distinct contexts. (1) In the *purusha-sukta* of early India (Rig Veda 10.90), *purusha* is the primeval, cosmic "man" or "person" who is sacrificed and dismembered in the act which constitutes the creation of the universe. (2) In the Samkhya system of Indian philosophy (later appropriated in the Yoga system), *purusha* is the "soul," or "spirit," the autonomous, transcendent, and impassive principle of self-consciousness. The point of Yoga discipline is to achieve that level of interiority (*Samadhi*) and lucid self-awareness possible only through the isolation (*kaivalya*) or extrication of *purusha* from the fragmenting "embrace" of *prakrti* (nature, matter), with which *purusha* erroneously tends to identify itself. BIBLIOGRAPHY: R. C. Zaehner, *Hinduism* (1966) 43–52; 67–74; M. Éliade, *Yoga* (1970) 3-41; A. B. Keith, *Samkhya System* (1924).

[D. P. EFROYMSON]

PURVEY, JOHN (1353?–after 1407), dedicated companion of J. *Wycliffe, presumed to be the translator, revisor, and popularizer of Wycliffe's works among English *Lollards. In 1387, the bp. of Worcester condemned P.'s sermons, in Bristol, then banned him from preaching. Lollard

writings including P.'s were confiscated (1388), and later, anyone possessing his works was arrested. P. himself was arrested, then released when he publicly recanted (1401).

[R. J. LITZ]

PUSEY, EDWARD BOUVERIE (1800–82), theologian, Oriental scholar, religious leader, canon of Christ Church, Oxford, and regius professor of Hebrew. He was a Berkshire man, and as a fellow of Oriel was brought into intimacy with Keble and Newman, and set on a course he followed with great courage and steadfastness through "a succession of insulated efforts, bearing indeed upon one great end—the growth of catholic truth and piety among us." Aware that "dead orthodoxy" was not enough, he spent years in Germany preparing for the defense of revealed religion against *rationalism and *latitudinarianism. His students were taught Hebrew in order "to enter more fully into the meaning of God's word, without the dryness of the lower criticism and the precarious assertions of the higher." But it is as leader of the *Oxford Movement, after Newman had departed, that he is famous and revered, and still, like Mr. Gladstone, given his prefix, Dr. Pusey, as though he were alive. His books, and above all his sermons—he preached wherever he was asked to go—based on the Fathers and the Anglican divines of the 17th cent., maintained his ideals through many troubles, with the confidence of deep learning and the tranquillity of a life of prayer. For 2 years he was forbidden the university pulpit for his defense of the Real Presence. Suspected of Romanism because he declined to make assertions against the Church of Rome, his first *Eirenicon* was followed by two more; they argued that official doctrines were less the bar to union than unofficial devotions; they were not always received with common courtesy by the authorities to whom they were sent. Himself not given to ceremonies, he formed a rallying-point for the ritualists, or "Puseyites." He is the virtual founder of all Anglican sisterhoods.

[T. GILBY]

PUSEYISM, a contemptuous name, now out of date, for the *Oxford Movement, after E. B. *Pusey became the first of the authors of *Tracts for the Times* to make his identity known.

[T. C. O'BRIEN]

PUSHKIN, ALEXANDER SERGEYEVICH (1799–1837), most influential poet of Russia's golden age and creator of her literary language. P. was twice exiled: in 1820, for the early epigrams and poems that expressed his sympathy with the revolutionary ideas of the Decembrists (though he was prevented by his second exile from participating in their uprising of 1825), and again in 1824 for the atheistic sentiments contained in a letter intercepted by the censor (cf. also the mock-epic Gavriliada [1821]). His later works (e.g., The Bronze Horseman [1833]) reflect his growing conviction that reforms in Russia must emanate from the Tsar, hence his glorification of Peter the Great. His numerous works, which provided future generations of Russian writers with models of nearly every European genre as well as with a vast reservoir of types and plots, include *Ruslan and Lyudmila* (1820), a fairy tale in the light vein of French and Russian classicism; *The Prisoner of the Caucasus* (1820–21), a romantic tale in which the influence of Byron is clearly evident; his greatest work, *Eugene Onegin* (1823–31), in which, in a masterly combination of romantic subject matter, classical style, and realistic treatment, he creates the type of the ''superfluous man'' and its counterpart, the morally strong heroine, Tatyana; *Boris Godunov* (1824–25), a historical drama modeled on Shakespeare; the ''little tragedies,'' esp. *Mozart and Salieri* (1830), with their cogent analyses of human vices; and the prose works, *The Tales of Belkin* (1830), *The Queen of Spades* (1834), and *The Captain's Daughter* (1836), his only completed novel. BIBLIOGRAPHY: D. Magarshack, *Pushkin* (1969); D. Mirsky, *Pushkin* (1963).

[M. F. MCCARTHY]

PUSILLANIMITY, smallness of soul, *micropsuchia,* more opposed by defect to magnanimity (which is a part of *courage) than is vanity by excess, being, says Aristotle, both more prevalent and worse. Yet, he observes with a lordly disdain Aquinas repeats, petty-spirited men are not thought to be actually vicious, since they do no harm: a classical instance of damning with faint praise. They are compared to the man in the parable who did not use his talent. Their fault of fearing by a sort of inverted pride to stretch out to the good things they could deserve, is not to be identified with a modest and retiring temperament. BIBLIOG-RAPHY: *Nicomachean Ethics* 4.3; ThAq ST 2a2ae, 133.

[P. F. MULHERN]

PUSOKSA TEMPLE, Buddhist temple, the oldest wooden structure in Korea (rebuilt 1350). Panel paintings on wood of Vairocana and a Bodhisattva—rare relics from the Koryo period (918–1392)—and a gilded wooden statue of Amitabha (surviving from the 10th cent.) are treasures.

[M. J. DALY]

PUTTI, nude, winged cupid-like child-figures appearing in Roman wall paintings, such as the gay *Cupid Riding a Crab* (House of the Vetii, Pompeii) in an amazing ''impressionist'' technique full of action, or at times playfully personifying man (*Cupids Making Wine,* House of the Vetii, Pompeii), and again seen in Christian art: *Making Wine* in the early Christian mosaic (4th cent. A.D., Sta. Costanza, Rome), on the sarcophagi of Roman Christians, and in Coptic textiles of the 4th and 5th centuries. *Putti* were reintroduced in the Renaissance period with the original ancient identity (*Putto with Dolphin,* A. del Verrocchio, 1470) and in mythological and religious subjects (Sistine Ceiling, Michelangelo; *Galatea,* Raphael; *The Garden of Love,* Rubens; *Triumph of St. Ignatius,* A. Pozzo). BIBLIOGRAPHY: A. de Franciscis, *I Tesori, Pompei* (1966).

[M. J. DALY]

PUTZER, JOSEPH (1836–1904), Redemptorist canonist and theologian. A native of the Austrian Tyrol, P. entered the Redemptorists and was ordained in 1859. After years as home missioner in Austria he came to the U.S. and engaged in pastoral work, 1876–87, then began his teaching career in the Redemptorist Seminary at Ilchester, Maryland. A clear and accurate writer on canonical questions, he published *Commentarium in facultates apostolicas* (1893), a revision of an earlier work by a confrere, Anthony Konings, that was substantially a new and highly regarded treatise. He also published *Instructio de confessariis.*

[J. R. AHERNE]

PUVIS DE CHAVANNES, PIERRE (1824–98), French painter-muralist, student with T. Couture, admiring Delacroix and T. Chassériau, noted for murals *Ludus pro patria* (1863), the famous *Life of St. Genevieve* (1874–78) in the Panthéon, Paris; cycles in the Sorbonne (1887) and in the Boston Public Library (1895–98). In allegorical, mythical, and religious works, P. retained the two-dimensionality of the wall in cool, neutral hues and flattened forms, attaining a serene repose. Approaching the abstract and influencing the symbolist-synthesists Seurat, Gauguin, M. Denis, and Maillol, P. was acclaimed by rebels and conservatives.

[M. J. DALY]

PYRRUS I (d. 655), **PATRIARCH OF CONSTANTINOPLE** (639–649). Upon succeeding to Sergius I, in 639, he confirmed the *Ekthesis* of Emperor Heracleius. He was deposed by Constans II and went to Northern Africa, where he had a disputation with Maximus the Confessor. Having disavowed Monothelitism P. was accepted in Rome; later on he changed his viewpoint and was deposed by the Lateran Synod of 649. He was reappointed patriarch of Constantinople for a short time before he died. Of P.'s writings little survives.

[L. PEANO]

PYTHAGORAS OF SAMOS (570/560, at Croton from *c.*531 B.C.) and **OLD PYTHAGOREANISM.** The life and work of Pythagoras is very poorly known and is further obscured by the growth of legend about him and by the tendency of his followers to assign later developments in Pythagoreanism to the master. It seems certain that he founded a religious brotherhood whose chief aim was perfection of the soul, that he taught the doctrine of metempsychosis, and that he discovered that the musical intervals between the notes on the lyre may be expressed in numerical ratios. It is possible that he also worked out in some form the so-called Pythagorean theorem attributed to him by Euclid. From the time of P. to the disappearance of the Old Pythagorean Society or School in the late 4th cent. B.C., the basic religious and scientific ideas of P. were greatly elaborated. Numbers came to be regarded as living entities and were employed to explain the composition of the universe and the harmony of the spheres. They symbolized their basic teaching in the geometrical figure made by dots, which, when connected, form an isosceles triangle:

. The figure is called the Four (tetractys), and the dots are the sum for the four integers. They maintained that the universe was produced by the First Unit, and that all things, even abstract qualities like justice, are numbers. By the early 5th cent. they rejected geocentrism and held that the earth was spherical, and that the earth, the sun, and other celestial bodies circled around a central fire. Pythagoreanism is of primary importance because it is the first Greek philosophy that is strictly a way of life and concerned with salvation. The Pythagorean doctrine of metempsychosis and theory of numbers was destined to exercise a profound influence on Plato. BIBLIOGRAPHY: Copleston 1:29–37; Guthrie 1.146–340.

[M. R. P. McGUIRE]

PYTHAGOREAN SCHOOL, a school or society of philosophers founded by Pythagoras *c*.550 B.C. at Crotona in S Italy. It had its own characteristic ascetical and religious elements besides an intense scientific spirit. Adherents of the doctrine suffered persecution (*c*.440 B.C.) but exerted an influence as late as the first half of the 4th cent.

B.C. and perhaps later. Its peculiar doctrines (apart from dietary prohibitions and religious rules) were transmigration of soul, the superiority of soul over body and its tripartite nature (said to have influenced Plato), the belief that number is the basic element of reality (things *are* numbers), the application of number ratios to music, a naive numerology that describes and determines events, and the belief that the earth is spherical and with other planets and the sun revolves around a central cosmic fire called number one. See Copleston v. 1

PYTHON, GEORGE (1856–1927), director of public education and state councilor for Fribourg, Switzerland. By his advocacy of an institution of Catholic higher education for his canton, he was the main force in the setting up of a financial fund and a legal basis for the Univ. of Fribourg, founded in 1889. P. was urged in his efforts by J. Schonderet of the Catholic Press Apostolate in Switzerland.

[R. J. LITZ]

PYX, a watch-shaped vessel used in carrying the Eucharist to the sick. It came into use for this particular purpose around the 5th century.

Q

Q. from the German *Quelle,* source, designation for a hypothetical written source consisting largely of eschatological discourse material, emanating from earliest Palestinian apocalyptically oriented Christianity, common to Mt and Lk but not found in Mk. Q. constitutes the second major document of the two-source hypothesis of gospel composition, the other being Mk. There is widespread acceptance among scholars of Q. as a working hypothesis, with these features: it was originally arranged topically rather than chronologically; it is represented by the non-Markan discourse material common to one third of Mt and one fourth of Lk; it contained little narrative and no Passion account; it was composed largely of detached sayings either originating with Jesus or attributed to him by Christian prophets; Luke edited the Q material to a lesser extent than Matthew. The basic message of the Q material is the presence of the reign of God among men in the person and words of Jesus, and the anticipated fulfillment shortly of this reign with the coming of the Son of Man. Jesus is portrayed in the Q material as God's eschatological prophet and wisdom teacher bringing salvation to men with the rule of God, and as the one through whom the prophetic and wisdom traditions of the past are moving rapidly toward their divine consummation, when Jesus as Son of Man will be revealed as God's eschatological Redeemer. At least the following material formed the Q source: the healing of the centurion's slave (Lk 7.2, 6b–10); some exhortatory or admonitory material (Lk 16.13; 11.34–36; 17.3b–4, 6); eschatological warnings (Lk 3.7–9, 16–17; 6.37–42; 10.13–15; 11.39–52; 12.49–53, 54–56, 57–58; 13.24–29; 34–35; 17.24, 26–27, 33–37); sayings of eschatological conflict (Lk 4.2–12; 11.14–22, 23–26); statements of eschatological promise (Lk 6.20b–23, 27–36; 11.2–4, 9–13; 12.22–31, 33–34; 22. 28–30); discipleship statements (Lk 9.57–60; 10.2–12; 12.2–12; 14.26–27); eschatological parables (Lk 12.39–40, 42–46; 13.20–21; 14.16–23; 15.4–7; 19.11–27; 6.47–49); sayings which portray Jesus as eschatological messenger and salvation bringer (Lk 7.18–23; 24–35; 16.16–17; 10.16; 11.29b–32; 14.15; 22.28–30; 13.34–35; 19.41–44). BIB- LIOGRAPHY: R. Edwards, *Sign of Jonah in the Theology of the Evangelists and Q* (1971); *idem, Theology of Q* (1976); J. Jeremias, *Parables of Jesus* (1963); H. C. Kee, *Jesus in History* (1970) 62–103; N. Perrin, *Rediscovering the Teaching of Jesus* (1967); H. E. Todt, *Son of Man in the Synoptic Tradition* (1965).

[T. J. RYAN]

QA'AL SEM'AN (Fortress of Simeon), the ruins of the famous church and monastery erected in the last quarter of the 5th cent. around the pillar of St. *Simeon the Stylite above Deir Sem'an, 19 mi NW of Aleppo in Syria. The still extant base of Simeon's column is surrounded by an octagonal hall 92 feet in diameter giving access to four triple-naved basilical style halls. The whole complex forms a Greek cross measuring 289 feet north and south and 328 feet east and west. It is ''the most beautiful and important existing monument of architecture between the buildings of the Roman period of the second century and the great church of Sta. Sophia of Justinian's time'' (H. C. Butler). BIBLIOGRA- PHY: G. Tchalenko, *Villages antiques de la Syrie du Nord* I (1953) 223–276; H. C. Butler, *Early Churches in Syria* (1929) 97–105.

[M. J. COSTELLOE]

QAHANA (Qahanay), generic word for priest in Armenian (*yeretz*); derived from Syriac *kah^ená.*

[A. CODY]

QALTĀ, in East Syrian liturgy: (1) a pair (or pairs) of verses introducing psalmody; (2) a group of psalms sung with intercalated halleluyah after the *hûllālē* of the night office for Sunday.

[A. CODY]

QAWMŌ (station), a nocturn of the night office among the West Syrians (who have three called such in the night office) and the Maronites (who have four); also called *teshmeshtō* or *'eddōnō*.

[A. CODY]

QEṢŌYŌ (E Syr., *qᵉṣāyā*), the rite of fraction in both W Syrian and E Syrian Eucharistic Liturgies.

[A. CODY]

QESṬRÔMÔ (Syr., from Gr. *kastrōma*), in W Syrian churches, the space for the choir between the nave and the sanctuary.

[A. CODY]

QŌHELETH (Koheleth), Hebrew title of the OT book called Ecclesiastes in English and other versions of the Bible. Qoheleth is the pen name of the author (12.9–10), and means "leader of the assembly," i.e., preacher or teacher. *ECCLESIASTES, BOOK OF.

[T. C. O'BRIEN]

QŌLŌ (E Syrian, *qālā*, voice, tune), as a technical term: (1) West Syrian and Maronite: a series of basically four strophes sung to a set melody, their originally intercalatory nature being revealed by the psalm-hemistychs (*petgōmē*) preceding the first two and the halves of the doxology preceding the last two; often expanded far beyond this to make up the bulk of the West Syrian office today; (2) Maronite: a set of *'enyōnē;* (3) East Syrian: various uses, always as part of a compound term, for a series of strophes or for parts of offices, e.g., *qālē d-shahrā*, the latter part of the present night office for Sundays and feasts, derived probably from the ancient cathedral vigil.

[A. CODY]

QŌNÛNŌ (E Syrian, *qānônā*, from Gr., kanōn): (1) East Syrian: a refrain inserted after the first or second hemistych of a psalm; the ensemble of a psalm with such a refrain; the ecphonetic conclusion to a *gᵉhāntā* in the Eucharistic Liturgy; (2) West Syrian "Greek canon," a series of poetic refrains translated from Greek, intercalated after each verse of an OT canticle or portion thereof.

[A. CODY]

QUADRAGESIMO ANNO, 1931 encyclical of Pope Pius XI "On the Reconstruction of the Social Order," commemorating Leo XIII's encyclical, *Rerum novarum,* and amplifying its principles. While reaffirming the right of private property and the condemnation of socialism, the encyclical recognized that "the right of private property is not absolute" and pointed out the necessity of some state control of the means of production, since "certain forms of property carry with them an opportunity of domination too great to be left to private individuals." Socialism, Pius acknowledged, contains an element of truth, and its social programs "often strikingly approach the just demands of Christian social reformers." The encyclical's severest stric-

tures were reserved for capitalist abuses: the "immense power and despotic economic domination . . . concentrated in the hands of a few" and the "economic dictatorship" that makes economic life "hard, cruel, and relentless." Unions were to be promoted, and it was desirable that the wage contract "should, when possible, be modified somewhat by a contract of partnership so that workers . . . become sharers in ownership or management or participate in some way in the profits." Without explicitly mentioning contemporary fascist social theories, Pius nevertheless drew a pointed distinction between laudable union activity and the form of corporative or syndical order that was "serving particular political aims rather than contributing to the restoration of social order." Text: AAS 23 (1931) 177–228.

[D. CODDINGTON]

QUADRATUS, ST. (2d cent.), a native of Asia Minor, generally considered the first of the Christian apologists. H. addressed *c.*124 an apology for Christianity to the Emperor Hadrian while the latter was visiting the East. Except for a fragment in Eusebius (*Eccl. Hist.* 4.3), this treatise is lost, and attempts by various scholars to identify the work or parts of it in later writings have proved failures. Q. is often mentioned by early writers as a disciple of the Apostles. He is not to be identified with a bp. of Athens of the same name who lived during the time of Marcus Aurelius. BIBLIOGRA-PHY: Quasten 1:190–191; F. X. Murphy, NCE 12:1–2; Butler 2:399–400.

[R. B. ENO]

QUADRUPANI, CARLO GIUSEPPI (1740–1806), celebrated Barnabite preacher and spiritual writer. From 1771 until his death, Q. preached, esp. during Lent, in the principal cities throughout Italy, conducted retreats for the clergy, and spent much time hearing confessions and ministering to the sick. His spiritual writings were immensely popular, the most significant of which were published as *Documenti di vita spirituale.*

[T. M. MCFADDEN]

QUAESTIONES DISPUTATAE, first a scholastic method of debate in the medieval universities; then the written publication of the debate. The disputation from the 12th cent. was a regular, even daily, exercise in the schools. By the 13th cent. the disputed question came to be differentiated from the special disputations held in Advent and Lent, and called *quaestiones de quolibet* or *quodlibetales.* The disputation embodied and refined the *sic et non* method, i.e., two sets of arguments were prepared, one for each side of a given question. A bachelor first argued in favor of one side, then replied to the opposite arguments. The master then gave his own solution, the *determinatio,* and refined the replies to the opposite positions. Seven works of St. Thomas Aquinas are collected under the title *Quaestiones disputatae,* the *De veritate* and the *De potentia* being the best known. BIBLIOGRAPHY: M. D. Chenu, *Towards Un-*

derstanding St. Thomas (tr. A. M. Landry and D. Hughes, 1964) 58–69, 77–99.

[T. C. O'BRIEN]

QUAESTOR, Roman official who in early republican times assisted the consuls and exercised judicial powers; later he was concerned mainly with finance. There were originally two quaestors, later four, but their number was fixed at twenty by Sulla, who also admitted them to the Senate. The most important were the two *quaestores urbani* who administered the state treasury (*aerarium*), the repository not only of money reserves but also of public documents. Other quaestors were assigned to the staffs of generals and provincial governors, while two were connected with the fleet and one with the corn supply. The office was the first step in the *cursus honorum*. BIBLIOGRAPHY: G. Stevenson, OCD 753.

[F. J. MURPHY]

QUAKERS, members of the *Religious Society of Friends. G. *Fox states in his *Journal* that the name, which had been used earlier for a small sect in England, was applied to him in scorn by a judge in court. Some associate the name with the tremblings of the early Friends at their meetings. No longer is it used derisively, nor is it offensive to Friends themselves. BIBLIOGRAPHY: OED 8:15.

[T. C. O'BRIEN]

QUALIFICATIONS, THEOLOGICAL, the carefully distinguished levels of certitude connected with various teachings in the Catholic Church. In a corresponding way they are related to the obligation to believe. The origin of theological qualifications may be traced to the Scriptures, church discipline, and academic speculation among scholars.

St. Paul used the word anathema (Gal 1.8–9) to denote separation from the Christian community, imposed for sins such as preaching a gospel different from the one received from Christ. Along with Paul, Peter and John made it clear that certain truths had been received from the Savior. Anyone who denied them was a false teacher (2 Pet 2.1). In the early Church it became a regular procedure to declare that a doctrine was apostolic and to disqualify those who denied it as heretics. The term apostolic was equivalent to the later terms revealed and of faith.

As dogmatic problems increased in number and complexity, church authority sometimes taught that a given doctrine was binding on the faithful but would not state either that this was a matter of revelation or that anyone who denied it was cut off from the Church. The Church's intention was to insure doctrinal unity by appealing to the virtue of obedience—and not precisely faith—among the people of God. Different censures were used—e.g., temerarious, offensive—to identify the contrary positions.

In modern times a wide spectrum of qualifications has been coined by scholars either to designate their own certitude about some teaching or to declare that the point at issue is an open question to be discussed freely among theologians. On this level, the virtue involved is prudence and calls for a wise appraisal of the evidence before accepting or dismissing a proposition. Prudential judgment is required to determine soundness of theological insight and consistency with the apostolic faith.

Theological qualification has been recently applied to what Vatican Council II called a "hierarchy" of Catholic truths, "since they vary in their relationship to the foundations of the Christian faith" (Vat II Ecum 11). Thus, the closer a doctrine is to the central mysteries of revelation, the higher it ranks in the doctrinal hierarchy, e.g., the divinity of Christ before the bodily Assumption of the Blessed Virgin Mary. BIBLIOGRAPHY: H. Quilliet, DTC 2:2101–13; S. Cartechini, *De valore notarum theologicarum* (1951); R. Latourelle, *Theology of Revelation* (1966) 249–314.

[J. A. HARDON]

QUAM OBLATIONEM, the first words of the fifth paragraph of the First Eucharistic Prayer (Roman Canon). This paragraph repeats the prayers of the *Te igitur and *Hanc igitur for the acceptance and blessing of the offering. The English text begins, "Bless and approve this offering . . . ." This prayer fits well with the characteristic of oblation that should be found in every anaphora as a link between the thanksgiving narrative (Preface) and the institution narrative. The prayer may be the remnant of an *epiclesis*. The meaning of the first three of the accumulation of five adjectives in the Latin text (*benedictam, adscriptam, ratam, rationabilem, acceptabilem*) is expressed in the verbs "bless" and "approve" in the English. *Rationabilem* is translated as spiritual, which the translators understood in this context to mean sincerely and inwardly intended. This prayer dates in substance from the 4th cent. and is found in the Roman Canon by the end of the 5th century.

[N. KOLLAR]

QUAM SINGULARI, the title of a decree issued (1910) by the Congregation of the Sacraments during the pontificate of Pius X, regulating the age for receiving first communion. From the 17th through the 19th cent., the practice developed in the Latin rite of administering first communion sometime between the 10th and 14th years. Taking note of this trend, *Quam singulari* recalled the teaching of Lateran Council IV and the Council of Trent that the faithful were to receive first communion upon attaining the use of reason. This decree reestablished this ancient practice and enjoined bps. to suppress the more recent trend to delay the reception of the Eucharist. The more important stipulations of *Quam singulari* are: (1) the age for first confession and first communion is the age of reason, usually calculated at 7 years; (2) complete knowledge of Christian doctrine is not required in children approaching these sacraments for the first time; (3) the recipient of first communion must have some knowledge of those elements of Catholic faith that are necessary for salvation, and he must be able to distinguish Eucharistic Bread from ordinary bread. BIBLIOGRAPHY: M. M. Crotty, *Recipient of First Communion* (1947); J. T. McNicholas, CE 12:590–591. *COMMUNION, FIRST.

[J. J. FLOOD]

QUANTA CURA, an encyclical letter of Pius IX (Dec. 8, 1864), which condemns some of the political tendencies of rationalism and liberalism, forcefully insisting that the authority of the Church is supreme because it is received from Christ and therefore completely independent of the authority of the State. It rejects the view that the power of the Church is not distinct from and independent of the civil power, and that the legislation of the Church does not bind in conscience unless promulgated by the civil authority. BIBLIOGRAPHY: D 2890–96; J. F. Clarkson et al., *Church Teaches* (1955) 85–86.

[J. H. ROHLING]

QUARACCHI, informal designation of the Franciscan center of historical research, formerly at the Collegio S. Bonaventura, Quaracchi, near Florence, Italy. The center was established in 1871 to edit the works of St. Bonaventure, an edition that appeared in 10 volumes (1882–1902). From Quaracchi also issued two editions of Peter Lombard's *Sentences;* the *Summa* attributed to Alexander of Hales (4 v., 1924–48); the *Bibliotheca Franciscana scholastica* (1903–––); the *Bibliotheca Franciscana ascetica* (1904–––); the *Analecta Franciscana* (10 v., 1893–1941); and the quarterly, *Archivium Franciscano-Historicum.* The center and its work continue at Grottaferrata, near Rome, in facilities shared with the Dominican Leonine Commission, for the critical edition of the *Opera omnia* of St. Thomas Aquinas.

[T. C. O'BRIEN]

QUARANTINE, in indulgence formulas, a period of 40 days (It., *quaranta,* forty), meaning that the indulgence granted corresponded to the effect of 40 days of penitential practices, a term of penance common in the early Church.

QUARESIMO, FRANCESCO (1583–1650 or 1656), Orientalist and historian of the Holy Land. Q. held various posts of importance in the Franciscan province of Mantua and in the East where he traveled extensively as a missionary and papal commissary. His *Elucidatio terrae sanctae* (2 v., 1634–39; 2d ed., 1880–81) is a classic contribution to the history, geography, and archeology of the Holy Land. In his *Jerosolymae afflictae . . .* (1631), Q. appealed to *Philip IV to organize another crusade. BIBLIOGRAPHY: A. Teetaert, DTC 13.2:1442–44; G. Golubovich, CE 12:593.

[T. M. MCFADDEN]

QUARLES, FRANCIS (1592–1644), English poet, who took the royalist side in the Civil War, in reprisal for which the Parliamentarians ransacked his house and destroyed his papers. He published religious poems: *Divine Fancies* (1632), *Emblems* (1635), *Hieroglyphics of the Life of Man* (1638), in which he shows his zealous and sober outlook, presenting man as restless and uncertain before the power and glory of God. He combines Puritan and Catholic attitudes. *Emblems,* best known of his works, consists of sets of symbolic pictures, each accompanied by verses. Each emblem is made up of a paraphrase from Scripture written in ornate and metaphysical style, followed by a passage from the Christian Fathers, and ending with a four-line epigram. His plates were taken from two Jesuit emblem books. He influenced the imagery of Donne, Herbert, and Crashaw. BIBLIOGRAPHY: DNB 47:96; R. Freeman, *English Emblem Books* (1948).

[M. M. BARRY]

QUARR ABBEY, a Benedictine abbey near Ryde, Isle of Wight. Originally an important Cistercian house, it was founded by Baldwin de Redvers in 1132. It was suppressed during the reign of Henry VIII. The buildings were demolished and the stones used to build military fortifications. Eventually rebuilt in the early 20th cent. by exiled Benedictine monks from Solesmes, Quarr was made an abbey in 1937. A small part of the medieval structure remains. Quarr has become an important center for liturgical studies.

[M. A. MCFADDEN]

QUARREL, an angry exchange of words and/or signs between private persons resulting in severed, or at least strained, relations. Actually, since friendship and even mere courtesy represent harmonies of hearts rather than minds, differences of opinion need not be material for such irascible altercation. However, St. Paul (Gal 5.20–21) lists quarrels with feuds, wranglings, dissensions, and factions as results of self-indulgence, the flesh as opposed to the spirit; and human experience shows that touchiness and temper are hard to avoid in the expression of dissension. Since *anger is the most frequent source and accompaniment of quarreling (ThAq ST 1a2ae, 41.2), much of the morality of a quarrel can be gleaned from the justifiability and moderation of this underlying resentment. Justice, or perhaps charity itself, may dictate open, even firm disagreement with a false position, or a policy perilous to some real good, esp. if it is the common good. Jesus spoke of the danger of the sword (Mt 26.52–53) but he also brought a sword (Mt 10.34). He did not refuse to unsheathe this sword of the word in the lifelong quarrel which those who perverted God's word for their purposes provoked. He displayed holy anger against those befouling his Father's house (Jn 2.13–18). Probably most quarrels are without such noble justification and unhappily continue even when the trifling cause is forgotten. But even if justifiable cause exists, not only is moderation a demand of human maturity, but the Christian vocation to the peace of charity (Rom 12.18) calls for every effort to bring about harmony with all with whom it is possible.

[P. F. MULHERN]

QUARTERLY CONFERENCE (Methodist), the governing body of the local church. *CONFERENCE (METHODIST).

[T. C. O'BRIEN]

QUARTIER-LA-TENTE, AUGUSTE (1848–1936), Protestant mystic. Born at Cartigny in the canton of Geneva and orphaned at an early age, he overcame his economic difficulties by a successful trade as a baker. At the age of 18 he underwent a profound religious crisis. Thereafter his life was marked by three great passions: Christ, charity to the poor, and the quest for perfection. His *Journal intime,* simple yet poetically profound, expresses his spirit of fraternal charity, his yearning for union with Christ, and his total abandonment to God. E. Christen, *Je riposte par l' amour* (1939).

[I. M. KASHUBA]

QUARTODECIMANS (Lat. *quartodecimum,* fourteenth), those Christians who followed a Jewish tradition of dating and celebrating the Passover on the 14th of the month Nisan. The term is most frequently used in reference to the Churches in Asia Minor which Bp. Victor of Rome (*c.* 190 A.D.) tried to excommunicate, on the strength of the newer and growing Christian custom of celebrating the Christian Passover, Easter, on the following Sunday, the day commemorating the Resurrection of Jesus (the observance of the Churches of Rome, Alexandria, and probably Caesarea). The sources, however, (esp. Eusebius, *Hist. Eccl.* 4.26.3; 5.23–25; *Epistle of the Apostles* 15; *Chronicon Paschale;* Hippolytus *Ref. Haer.* 8,18), suggest that there were at least two disputes (one in the 160s in Asia Minor; the other *c.* 190 between Asia Minor and Rome), concerning, not simply one issue (the date of Easter), but several: a newer tradition emphasizing the Resurrection of Jesus vs. an apparently older tradition emphasizing Jesus' Passion and death and looking forward to his return; fasting vs. feasting; the chronology of the Synoptic Gospels (Passover—Last Supper) vs. that of John (Passover—Jesus' death the next day); maintenance of an ancient (Jewish) heritage vs. a conscious attempt to separate Christianity from Judaism. BIBLIOGRAPHY: C. C. Richardson, JTS 24 (1973) 74–84.

[D. P. EFROYMSON]

QUAS PRIMAS, encyclical of Pius XI, Dec. 11, 1925. Liberal use of citations from Scripture and the Fathers "vindicate for the Christ-Man both the name and power of a king in the full and literal meaning of that term" (D 3675). Devotion to the *kingship of Christ is closely linked to veneration for the Eucharist and the Sacred Heart. The liturgical feast of Christ the King is instituted to foster recognition of Christ's royal rights over men's minds, wills, and hearts and thus effectively to meet the challenge of modern secularism and atheism. Text: AAS 17 (1925) 593–610; *Encyclicals of Pius XI* (tr. J. H. Ryan, 1927).

[M. D. MEILACH]

QUASI-DOMICILE, a designation in canon law for a place of residence, less permanent than a *domicile, which has certain juridical effects. It may be acquired by staying in a place with the intention of remaining more than 6 months, or by actually staying in a place for more than 6 months (CIC c. 92.2). A person in his place of quasi-domicile is known in canon law as an *advena* (CIC c. 91). BIBLIOGRAPHY: W. Thompson, *Quasi-domicile* (1956).

[L. M. KNOX]

QÛBBŌLŌ, a term sometimes used for a four-strophe *qōlō* in the West Syrian festive office; Maronite prayer for the acceptance of incense.

[A. CODY]

QUEBEC, UNIVERSITY OF, see LAVAL UNIVERSITY.

QUEBEC ACT, title given to a bill of the British Parliament which received the royal assent in 1774. It extended the bounds of Canada toward the Ohio and Mississippi and granted liberty to profess "the religion of the Church of Rome." On both counts it angered the American colonists and contributed to the Revolution. At the same time it helped to keep the Canadians from joining it. BIBLIOGRAPHY: C. H. Metzger, *Quebec Act* (1936).

QUEDLINBURG, CONVENT OF, both a former Benedictine and Lutheran convent in Saxony. It was originally founded in 936 by Matilda, widow of Emperor Henry I, as an imperial Benedictine convent for nobility. The convent was richly endowed and had political power: its abbess held the title of imperial princess. It became a Lutheran convent (1539) during the Reformation period under Anna II and was secularized in 1803. BIBLIOGRAPHY: R. Joppen, LTK 8:931.

[M. A. MCFADDEN]

QUEEN ANNE'S BOUNTY, a fund formed by Queen Anne of England in 1704 to administer for the benefit of the Church *annates and other revenues confiscated by Henry VIII in 1534. BIBLIOGRAPHY: A. Savidge, *Foundation and Early Years of Queen Anne's Bounty* (1955).

[T. EARLY]

QUEEN OF HEAVEN, goddess whose worship by Jews of Judah and Egypt (refugees) was condemned by Jeremiah (7.18; 44.15–28). She was worshipped particularly by women, who made cakes, possibly figurines, for her. She is perhaps the Mesopotamian Ishtar, goddess of love and fertility. In Christian tradition the title has been applied to the Virgin Mary.

[T. EARLY]

QUEEN'S DAUGHTERS, an association otherwise called The Daughters of the Queen of Heaven, founded at St. Louis in 1889. It is composed of laywomen who supplement the charitable works of the Society of St. Vincent de Paul. This group also works in collaboration with various religious orders and has branches in many parts of the U.S.A.

[R. C. CLIGGETT]

QUELEN, HYACINTHE LOUIS DE (1778–1839), abp. of Paris. Q. was from a noble family in Brittany and studied at St. Sulpice before his ordination to the priesthood (1807). As coadjutor with the right of succession, he became abp. of Paris upon Card. *Talleyrand-Périgord's death in 1821. Q. was an able and pastorally committed ecclesiastic and warned against the teachings of F. de *Lamennais. His opposition to the Revolution of July 1830 and the subsequent rule of Louis Philippe were perduring obstacles to the normalization of relations between the Holy See and France. Q. established the conferences at Notre Dame de Paris under the charge of H. D. *Lacordaire.

[T. M. MCFADDEN]

QUENSTEDT, JOHANN ANDREAS (1617–88), Lutheran theologian. Q. taught at the Univ. of Wittenberg and is famous for his *Theologia didactico-polemica sive systema theologicum* (Wittenberg 1685; Leipzig 1715). The significance of this work consists, not in its originality, but in its systematic and stylized (statement of a thesis, its proof, discussion of difficulties, and disputed corollaries) presentation of Lutheran orthodoxy. BIBLIOGRAPHY: C. J. Berschneider, NCE 12:19.

[T. M. MCFADDEN]

QUENTIN, HENRI (1872–1935), Benedictine textual critic and Vulgate scholar. Q. was a member of the Commission for the Revision of the Vulgate; produced photographic copies of the important Vulgate MSS, although his textual and historical evaluation of them met with considerable opposition; and served on the Commission as editor-in-chief (1926–36) for the Pentateuch. He was a member of the Pontifical Roman Academy of Archeology and of the Congregation of Rites, and became (1933) the first abbot of S. Girolamo. BIBLIOGRAPHY: H. Rumpler, NCE 12:19–20.

[T. M. MCFADDEN]

QUERCIA, JACOPO DELLA (*c.*1374–1438), greatest Sienese sculptor of the late 14th and early 15th cent. whose style shows a transition from the Gothic to the early Renaissance (tomb of Ilaria del Carrette, Lucca Cathedral, 1406). Q. moved from the calm lyricism of the early tomb and the Ferrara *Madonna*, through deeply cut, agitated forms of the *Fonte Gaia* influenced by Donatello, to the suppressed relief of concentrated energy anticipating Michelangelo in the *Porta della Mandorla* (S. Petronius, Bologna; 1425–38). His brother **Priamo** (fl. 1438–67), painting frescoes in Siena and Volterra, introduced a Renaissance architectural framework: *Blessed Augustine Investing the Director of the Hospital* (1442), a *St. Anthony* triptych, and other works.

BIBLIOGRAPHY: A. C. Hanson, *Jacopo della Quercia's Fonte Gaia* (1965).

[L. A. LEITE]

QUERCITANUS, ANDREAS, see DUCHESNE, ANDRÉ.

QUESNEL, PASQUIER (1634–1719), an Oratorian priest and scholar, who became a Jansenist. He published in 1671 a popular little book, later entitled *Le Nouveau Testament . . . avec des réflexions morales*. Suspected of *Jansenism, he left the Oratory, joined his friend Antoine *Arnauld in exile in Brussels in 1685, and succeeded him as Jansenist leader. By 1693 *Réflexions* was four large volumes; it was denounced to the Sorbonne and the Holy Office as a summary of Jansenism. Bossuet recommended corrections that Q. rejected. After much controversy, in 1703 Louis XIV, mistrusting Jansenists, obtained Q.'s arrest; but Q. escaped and won support with his violent pamphleteering. Having read Q.'s confiscated papers, Louis asked Clement XI to condemn the Jansenists and their tracts. The Pope complied with *Vineam Domini,* which was accepted by Parlement and the bps. but not by the nuns of *Port-Royal, who consequently were dispersed. After long examination, *Réflexions* was condemned in 1708; Q. protested and republished it. Upon further study, Clement in 1713 issued the famous bull *Unigenitus,* censuring 101 Quesnellian propositions (see D 2400–2502), esp. for being a repetition of previously condemned Jansenist propositions. The issue at stake in the condemnation and its aftermath was as much *Gallicanism as theological orthodoxy. Eight French bishops objected, 112 fully assented, and a few temporized. In 1717, Q. joined the appeal of four bishops from *Unigenitus* to an ecumenical council (see APPELLANTS). Jansenism, which he developed into a political party including freethinkers in its ranks, gradually deteriorated after Q.'s death. He also published theological and devotional works, notably *Prières chrétiennes* (1687), and an edition of the works of Leo the Great. BIBLIOGRAPHY: J. Carreyre, DTC 13:1460–1535; *Le Jansénisme durant la régence* (1932); J. Tans, *Pasquier Quesnel et les pays-bas* (1960); Pastor 33:192–313.

[W. DAVISH]

QUEST, begging for alms. It is a privilege of the various branches of the Franciscan friars and Poor Clares. In more recent times it has been granted to other communities such as the Little Sisters of the Poor.

[J. R. AHERNE]

QUÉTIF, JACQUES (1618–98), Dominican historian. After some years in the ministry, Q. spent his life from 1652 as librarian at the priory of the Annunciation, Paris. He began the compilation of the monumental history of Dominican writers, the *Scriptores ordinis praedicatorum,* which is still an indispensable tool of Dominican research. He completed 800 entries and had gathered data for about

2,000 others before his death. Jacques Échard continued, amplified, and published the work. It appeared during the years 1719–21. Q. also edited the canons of the Council of Trent and wrote or edited various other historical and theological works. BIBLIOGRAPHY: R. Creytens, "L'Oeuvre bibliographique d'Échard: Ses sources et leur valeur," *Archivum Fratrum Praedicatorum* 14 (1944) 43–71; M. Gasnier, *Les Dominicains de St. Honoré* (1950).

[W. A. HINNEBUSCH]

QUEVEDO, JUAN DE (?–1519), Spanish Franciscan, first bp. on the New World mainland. In 1513 he was appointed to the see at Darien, Panama, by Leo X at King Ferdinand's urging. Q. was a constant critic of Pedrarias Davila, a particularly cruel conqueror of the people of Darien. When recalled to Spain he engaged in a debate with B. de *Las Casas over Spanish policies in the Americas.

[R. J. LITZ]

QUI PLURIBUS, an encyclical letter of Pius IX, Nov. 9, 1846. It defends the proper relation between faith and reason against the inroads of rationalism and liberalism in philosophical and theological thought, upholding the capacity of reason, but also pointing out its limitations. It stresses the teaching authority of Peter and his successors and the obligation of heeding the teaching of Peter's See. It condemns certain secret societies and is the first papal document to mention and condemn communism. BIBLIOGRAPHY: D 2775–86; *Church Teaches* (Eng. tr. J. F. Clarkson et al., 1955) 13–16.

[J. H. ROHLING]

QUICK, OLIVER CHASE (1885–1944), Anglican theologian. Educated at Oxford, ordained an Anglican priest in 1912, Q. was regius professor of divinity at Oxford and canon of Christ Church for the last 5 years of his life. His popular expositions of Christian doctrine are able and effective.

[R. B. ENO]

QUICUMQUE (*Quicumque vult*), a name for the *Athanasian Creed, a creed composed in Latin and beginning with the words *Quicumque vult salvus esse* (whoever wishes to be saved).

QUIERCY, COUNCILS OF. A residence of the Frankish kings located at Quiercy near Noyon, France, was the location for several notable meetings. In 754 Pope Stephen II met with Pepin III to arrange an alliance and to receive a promise of territory. In 849 Gottschalk was disciplined there for his heretical teachings on predestination. At least four other councils were held at Quiercy in the 9th century.

[B. L. MARTHALER]

QUIET, PRAYER OF, see PRAYER OF QUIET.

QUIETISM, derived from "quiet," a form of contemplative prayer, a term with two uses. (2) Taken in a general sense, it refers to a recurring phenomenon in the history of the Church. The principles that underly manifestations of quietism down through the ages might be thus summarized: there exist in man two rival tendencies, sensual and spiritual; perfection implies the annihilation (in the moral sense) of the sensual for the benefit of the spiritual; the best means to obtain this is not through the struggle of asceticism but through a total passivity on the sense and intellectual level; only this quiet passivity leads to direct contact with God; in this passivity one is not morally responsible for sensual movements. Typical forms of this quietist passivity are found in certain Manichaean and Gnostic manifestations, in some tendencies of the *Cathari and *Fraticelli, among the *Brethren of the Free Spirit, the *Beghards, the *Beguines, and the *Alumbrados. In a faintly analogous sense, Quaker historians refer to the second generation of Quaker history as the quietist period because of Quaker withdrawal from society.

(2) In its second and more specific sense, Quietism refers to a spiritual movement at a particular time (late 17th cent.) and in a particular environment (Italy and France). In this movement the old principles were applied again. This period of Quietism has been divided by historians into Pre-Quietism, Quietism, and Semi-Quietism, to which they then add Anti-Quietist reaction. Modern investigation has shown that practically none of the Pre-Quietist authors condemned at the moment of the Quietist crisis had presented dangerous innovations in their writings. The Quietist movement in Italy was more popular and widespread; in France it was more confined and aristocratic. The most famous of those accused of spreading Quietism in Italy was Miguel de *Molinos. The worst feature of the Quietist doctrine condemned by the bull *Caelestis pastor* (D 2001–69) is that those in the interior way would disturb their quiet by trying to resist temptation, and that God allows the devil to make some perfect souls do evil. The movement in France may be reduced practically to the events surrounding P. LaCombe and Madame *Guyon. In their writings and activities there was more eccentricity and lack of discipline than real error. Rather than on "quiet," they insisted upon "extreme abandon." Late 17th-cent. Quietism was a movement of small proportions, very localized with little effect on the Christian people. The Anti-Quietists, the many writers who attacked Quietism when it was nothing but an unhappy memory, sowed distrust of mysticism. These writers frightened more than one generous spirit when the danger no longer existed. BIBLIOGRAPHY: L. Cognet, *Post-Reformation Spirituality* (tr. P. Hepburne Scott, 1959).

[K. KAVANAUGH]

QUIGLEY, MARTIN JOSEPH (1890–1964), publisher. A native of Ohio, Q. early became interested in trade publications for the motion picture industry. He combined several journals into the *Motion Picture Herald* and in 1931 assumed publication of *Motion Picture Daily*. In 1930, collaborating with Daniel A. Lord, S.J., he drafted the Motion Picture Production Code, applying moral principles to the production of films, and the Code was accepted by the Motion Picture Producers and Distributors of America. Q. was author of *Decency in Motion Pictures* (1937).

[J. R. AHERNE]

QUIGNON BREVIARY, a revision of the Divine Office made in the 16th cent. by Card. *Quiñones at the request of Clement VII. Intended for private recitation, the Quignon Breviary abolished all antiphons, hymns, and versicles. Readings from the lives of the saints were reduced, and the whole of the Psalter was to be said during the week, and most of the Bible read during the year. While authorized by Paul III in 1535, it was suppressed as too radical by Paul IV in 1558. T. *Cranmer made use of the Quignon Breviary in his work on the Book of Common Prayer. BIBLIOGRAPHY: Hughes RE 2:112–113; J. Meseguer Fernandez, NCE 12:30–31.

[R. B. ENO]

QUILISMA, in Byzantine chant an indication of a rolling and rotating of the voice.

QUIMBY, PHINEAS PARKHURST (1802–66), pioneer in mental healing. He was born in Lebanon, N. H., but lived most of his life in Belfast, Maine. He had little formal schooling and became a clockmaker. In 1838 he began to practice hypnosis as a way of healing but by 1847 developed the idea of healing simply by changing mental attitudes of patients. Essential in his theory was the denial of the reality of matter. He rejected established forms of Christianity but claimed to have gained the secret of Jesus' way of healing. The "Quimby Manuscripts" expressed his theories, which were developed by followers as the basis of *New Thought. Mary Baker *Eddy was his patient but denied that she owed her theories to him.

[T. C. O'BRIEN]

QUIMPERLÉ, ABBEY OF (called also the Abbey of the Holy Cross; *Keinperlegia*), a monastery founded *c*.500 at the junction of the Ellé and the Isole (Diocese of Quimper, Finistère, France), by St. Gunthiern, with the help of Grallon of Brittany. In 1029 Alain Canihart, count of Cornuailles, entrusted this monastery to the Benedictines. It was amalgamated with the Congregation of St. Maur in 1665 but was suppressed at the time of the Revolution. The cloisters of the monastery are now used as a town hall. BIBLIOGRAPHY: Cottineau 2:2390–91.

[J. DAOUST]

QUINCTIAN OF CLERMONT, ST. (Quintian, d. 525 or 526), bishop. Fleeing to Gaul from Africa to escape the Arian Vandal persecution, Q. became bp. of Rodez in succession to Amantius, taking part in the Synods of Adge

(506) and Orléans (511). Troubles with the local Arian Visigoths drove him from his diocese, and he took refuge with St. Euphrasius at Clermont where he became bp. 3 years later. Q. was famed for his concern for the poor and for his miracles. BIBLIOGRAPHY: G. M. Cook, NCE 12:28; G. Dordini, LTK 8:841–942.

[R. B. ENO]

QUINET, EDGAR (1803–75), French historian, literary and political figure. Q. became a professor of Romance literature at the Collège de France in 1842, but was suspended in 1846 because of his harsh criticism of the Jesuits and a papally centralized Catholicism (see ULTRAMONTANISM). He was forced to Belgium in exile and later to Switzerland because of his support for the 1848 revolutions. With the fall of Napoleon III, Q. returned to Paris where he was elected to the National Assembly. Throughout his life, Q. was ardently democratic and liberal, anticlerical yet deeply religious. His literary works, several of which were placed on the Index, were mainly concerned with contemporary political movements in France, Germany, and Italy, and the philosophical forces that motivated these movements. His complete works were published posthumously (30 v., 1877–82).

[T. M. McFADDEN]

QUINISEXT SYNOD, known also as the Trullan Synod (or *in Trullo*), held in 692 by the Eastern bishops. Its purpose was to complete the results of the Fifth (553) and Sixth (680) Councils (hence its name "Quinisext" or Fifth-Sixth) by passing disciplinary canons. The synod was held in the domed room (*trullus*) of the Emperor Justinian II's palace at Constantinople. The pope rejected its disciplinary decrees. Later they were only partially observed by the Eastern Church; yet they served to enhance the growing split between the Western and the Eastern Church.

Some of the subjects advanced for legislation included clerical marriage, ecclesiastical dress, the age of ordination, and impediments to matrimony. Sometimes it is wrongly stated that the Sixth Ecumenical Council passed the decrees, which then seemed to have received some sort of recognition by the pope. Surviving from the synod is only an allocution to the emperor and the 102 Canons with the signatures of the participants.

[L. PEANO]

QUINN, EDEL (1907–44), Irish lay apostle. Q. was a tireless worker among the sick, poor, and aged of Dublin as a member of the Legion of Mary. In 1936, she went to Africa as a delegate of the Legion where she continued her charitable work until her death in Kenya. BIBLIOGRAPHY: L. J. Suenens, *Edel Quinn: A Heroine of the Apostolate, 1907–1944* (1954).

[T. M. McFADDEN]

QUINÓNES, FRANCISCO DE (1480–1540), Spanish Observant Franciscan, cardinal, church reformer. As Fray

Francisco de los Angeles he was minister general from 1523 until 1528 and promoted both studies and religious discipline. It was as general that he sent to Mexico the early Franciscan missionaries, the so-called Twelve Apostles. While still general he was named a cardinal and was employed by Clement VII on papal missions. He also represented the cause of Catherine of Aragon against Henry VIII's divorce petition. He became bp. of Coria in 1531 but served that see only for two years. The rest of his life he spent in Rome, devoted to the causes of both humanism and church reform. Q. is perhaps most known because of the Quignon Breviary, a 1535 revision of the Roman Breviary suppressed by the Council of Trent. BIBLIOGRAPHY: J. F. White, "Traditions of Protestant Worship," *Worship* 49 (1975) 272–277; P. Salmon, *Breviary through the Centuries* (tr. D. Mary, 1962).

[T. C. O'BRIEN]

QUINQUAGESIMA, the Latin name for the Sunday preceding Ash Wednesday, literally meaning the fiftieth days before Easter. Quinquagesima, Sexagesima (60th) and Septuagesima (70th) Sundays - gave their name to a kind of pre-Lent or preparation for the 40 days of Lent (whose Latin name is Quadragesima). The liturgical reform following on Vatican Council II has eliminated the names of these Sundays and the observance of this pre-Lent as an unnecessary elaboration of the penitential season that detracted from Lent's essential role as preparation for the Paschal mystery. As late as the 5th and 6th cent. in the West outside Rome, there was no consensus concerning the pre-Lent observance. But by the time of Pope Gregory the Great, Rome had three such Sundays of preparation for Lent, and this became the Western tradition for over 1400 years. Far from being inappropriate as preparation for Lent or for Easter was the epistle selection read on Quinquagesima Sunday all through those centuries: St. Paul's canticle, 1 Cor 13, in praise of love (charity) as the greatest gift of the Spirit.

[E. J. DILLON]

QUINQUARTICULAR (Lat. *quinque,* five; *articulus,* article, point), related to the five articles or points summarizing *Arminianism. The disputes culminating in the Synod of *Dort are referred to as the Quinquarticular Controversies. The term is applied to advocates of Arminianism, as quinquarticular theologians. BIBLIOGRAPHY: OED 8:66; Schaff Creeds 1:516–519.

[T. C. O'BRIEN]

QUINQUE COMPILATIONES ANTIQUAE, five collections of decretals important to the history of canon law. They are compilations of legislation for the period following general acceptance of Gratian's *Decretum* (*c.*1150), up to the *Decretals of Gregory IX* (1234). The five were not the only such collections made but were the most widely used; two were promulgated by papal bull; the third, by Innocent III in 1210; the fifth, by Honorius III in 1226. *Raymond of

Peñafort followed the plan of Bernard of Pavia's *compilatio prima* (1187–91), and incorporated most of the five collections in drawing up the *Decretals of Gregory IX*.

[T. C. O'BRIEN]

QUINQUECENTENNIAL CONSENSUS, see CONSENSUS QUINQUESAECULARIS.

QUINTILIAN (Quintilianus, Marcus Fabius; *c.*35–*c.*97 A.D.), Roman rhetorician and educator. Q. was born in Calagurris in Spain but studied in Rome under Remmius Palaemon and Domitius Afer. Under the Emperor Galba he earned a reputation as a lawyer and teacher of eloquence. Appointed the first public professor of rhetoric by Vespasian, he taught with great success for 20 years, having as pupils Pliny the Younger and the future Emperor Hadrian. Q.'s only extant work is his *Institutio oratoria,* published in 12 books *c.*94 A.D. Though it is primarily directed at the teaching of oratory, it covers the whole range of ancient education. The work everywhere manifests its author's good sense, high ideals, and sound literary judgment. In contrast with the prevailing fashion, Q. proposes Cicero as the ideal orator. He himself writes in a clear and natural style that is not lacking in grace and delicacy. His treatise is the most complete and practical work on education that has come down to us from antiquity. BIBLIOGRAPHY: J. W. Duff, *Literary History of Rome in the Silver Age* (3d ed., 1964) 311–337.

[M. J. COSTELLOE]

QUIRINAL, the most northerly and the highest of the traditional seven hills of Rome that contained traces of primitive settlements from the 9th cent. B.C. and was later settled by the Sabines. Its name comes from an old sanctuary to Quirinus, a major Roman deity ranking close to Jupiter and Mars. Many wealthy Romans such as Atticus, Narcissus, and Martial had homes on the Quirinal. Cemeteries and Julius Caesar's gardens, which became the *Horti Sallustiani,* bordered its northern edge. Constantine built baths there. In 1574 Pope Gregory XIII began on the Quirinal the erection of the summer papal palace. This building, which was completed in 1730, became known as the Quirinal Palace. King Victor Emmanuel II in 1870 and Italian monarchs after him had the Quirinal Palace as their residence. In 1946 with the establishment of the republic, the Quirinal became the palace of Italy's president. BIBLIOGRAPHY: D. R. Dudley, *Urbs Roma* (1967); S. B. Platner, *Topographical Dictionary of Ancient Rome* (1965).

[M. F. MCNAMARA]

QUIRINUS, according to Lk 2.2, governor of Syria when the census that brought Joseph and Mary to Bethlehem took place. He is definitely known to have been legate to Syria twice, once in 10–8 B.C., and again in 6–9 A.D. Luke's text *hautē apographē prōtē* may be understood as referring to a census taken up before the one Quirinus made as governor of Syria, i.e., in A.D. 6. Luke probably refers to the census begun by Q. in 10–8 B.C., and carried out by his successor, Saturninus (8–6 B.C.). Jesus was certainly born before the death of Herod, that is, before 4 B.C. BIBLIOGRAPHY: E. Seraphin, "Edict of Caesar Augustus," CBQ 7 (1945) 91–96.

[R. T. A. MURPHY]

QUIROGA, VASCO DE (1470s–1565), Spanish defenders of the Indians in Mexico, bp. from 1536 of the Mexican province of Michoacán. Through his efforts as a member of the five-man governing *audiencia* of New Spain, Spanish relations with the native inhabitants were tempered with legal justice and charity. In Indian slavery cases, Q. actively promoted the interests of the slaves and often judged in their favor. He established two hospital towns named Santa Fe, patterned after the social plan of More's *Utopia*, where care for the sick and instruction in the Catholic faith could be provided. In order to train priests who were proficient in the native languages, he founded the Colegio de San Nicolás, the first New World institution of its kind.

[R. J. LITZ]

QUIRÓS, PEDRO FERNANDEZ DE (*c*.1565–*c*.1615), Portuguese navigator. Q. founded Espiritu Santo in the New Hebrides, mistaking the land for fabled Australia. An opponent of colonialism, he hoped to build a Christian utopia. To this end he established the Knights of the Holy Spirit and the New Jerusalem, but a storm destroyed his flotilla and his foundation. BIBLIOGRAPHY: O. Kubler, RGG 5:739.

[M. J. SUELZER]

QUITO, SCHOOL OF, one of the most important Spanish colonial schools of painting in Ecuador. It was founded in the mid-16th cent. at the Franciscan monastery in Quito, evidencing a European style (Spain, Flanders) through imported artists and works. Baroque 18th-cent. Quito art is distinguished (with the Cuzco school) by a new creativity in beautiful works of mestizo painters, who introduced holy figures of dark Indian complexion, in garments decorated with Indian fabric patterns in gold. Quito exported such holy pictures to Colombia, Bolivia, and Chile. BIBLIOGRAPHY: P. Damaz, *Art in Latin Architecture* (1963).

[M. J. DALY]

QUMRAN, KHIRBET. Prior to the initial discoveries of the *Dead Sea Scrolls in 1947, Khirbet (meaning "ruins of") Qumran was generally thought to be the buried remains of a fortress built by the Roman army. It had not been excavated, and there was no provocation for doing so prior to the discoveries of the MSS. The cemetery nearby, which was (and still is) quite obvious, had caused some speculation, for the graves did not match the customary Arab-Muslim style. Since the caves that had yielded the Scrolls called for clarification, an excavation of the ruins was un-

dertaken by G. L. Harding, then head of Jordan Antiquities, and Roland de Vaux, OP, then director of the École Biblique et Archéologique Française at Jerusalem. Five campaigns took place between 1951 and 1956. The results were rewarding, since the complex structure that was discovered revealed three principal periods of occupation (discounting the foundations of an Israelite fort of the 6th cent. B.C.). The first two periods of habitation were by the *Qumran Community between *c*.134 and 31 B.C. (the year of a great earthquake) and from *c*.4 B.C. to 68 A.D. Violent destruction seems to have occurred at this latter date, and there is evidence that the buildings were destroyed during the Jewish rebellion against Rome (A.D. 66–70). The final occupation period marked its use as a Roman garrison from 68 to late in the 2d Christian century. After that time the site was abandoned.

The region abounds in caves, and some of them served as dwellings (overcrowded conditions at the monastery?), as the oil lamps testify. The Scrolls were very likely placed in some caves as an emergency measure prior to the destruction in 68 A.D., with the hope of recovering them later. Other suggested explanations have not won great favor.

The Qumran ruins were roughly a large square. Surrounded by a heavy wall and equipped with a defense tower at the NW corner, there are many rooms within, one which served as a scriptorium. It was not so much the tables that proved this, but the inkwells in which there was found dried ink. There were also a chapter-room, dining room, pantry, and numerous water-storage rooms, for the group did a greal deal of ritual bathing. The water system, easily traceable, led from the Wadi Qumran by means of a long duct to the dwelling. The water was then stored in great cisterns within the building. The cemetery contains some 1,100 graves, many as yet unopened. The bodies were buried with the head toward the South. Some female skeletons have been found, suggesting that nonresidents were associated with the monastic group and given burial there. The site is located on a plateau promontory overlooking the Dead Sea, with huge, cave-pocked cliffs behind it. There was a nearby farming area with the fresh water spring known as 'Ain Feshkha. BIBLIOGRAPHY: F. M. Cross, *Ancient Library of Qumran* (1958); G. Vermès, *Discovery in the Judean Desert* (1956).

[I. HUNT]

QUMRAN COMMUNITY, the ascetical community that dwelt near *Qumran *c*.150 B.C.–70 A.D. Its members, called Covenanters and Sons of Light, were probably *Essenes. Information about the community comes from: (1) the *Dead Sea Scrolls, esp. the *Manual of Discipline,* the *Rule of the Community,* the *War Scroll*, the *Damascus Document* (the *Zadokite Fragment*), and the peculiar commentaries on the Bible with heavy sectarian flavor, e.g., the "Pesher" on Hab 1–2. (2) the thorough excavation and archeological evaluation of their monastic dwelling and its surroundings (1951–56); (3) the descriptions of the Essenes found in Josephus, Pliny the Elder, and Philo Judaeus. The strongly reactionary community at Qumran was made up of priests and laity. The priests were called sons of Aaron and sons of Zadok. They had legislative and judicial powers. The *Manual of Discipline* has the community governed by 12 laymen and 3 priests, with 1 elected member servng as *mebagger,* or overseer. New members were received by vote, and only after 2 years of probation was one admitted to full membership. Punishment for various transgressions was officially administered, and property was held in common. Community life was strict, and the common meal was reserved to full members. This meal, of bread and wine, seems to have had an eschatological significance, with such a text as Is 25.6 in mind (cf. Mk 14.25; Lk 22.14–19). Isaiah was one of the most widely cultivated books at Qumran, judged by its heavy representation in the MS finds. One member was supposed to be studying the law at all times. There were also nocturnal vigils in common that consumed one-third of the night; during these, study, reading, prayer, and blessings were the principal activities. During the daytime there was manual labor. Despite the proximity of the Dead Sea there is a considerable section of arable land south of the Khirbeh. The solar calendar used at Qumran called for different festal dates from those commonly observed in Jerusalem. It is not certain that animal sacrifices were offered at Qumran, and ritual bathing may have replaced them.

The community regarded itself as the authentic Israel, and for that reason thought that it could not be overcome in the trials that were expected. It was not enough to be Jewish by birth; one had to make a free choice to become a Son of Light. A strong dualism runs through their doctrine on all levels. Heavy emphasis on the Covenant made such OT passages as Jer 31.31–34 and Ezek 36.22–28 favorites. Despite the constant influence upon man of the spirits of light and darkness, the community emphasized predestination for themselves.

There was a strong messianic expectancy at Qumran, not only of one, but of two Messiahs, one of whom was to be a descendant of Aaron (priestly), while the other was to be Davidic (kingly). The founder of the group was called the Teacher of Righteousness, a priest who felt authorized to interpret the Law. This title may have become the name of an office that was passed on. That he was somehow linked to their messianic expectation is dubious. The texts are obscure on the point, and their theology also was probably obscure. They could hardly qualify as professional theologians. The archopponent of the Teacher is the "wicked high-priest" who seems to be one of the Hasmoneans, Jonathan or Simon being good possibilities.

The group is not to gain the sympathies of most men. There is a certain fanaticism about their doctrine. The emphasis is on the apocalyptic, the eschatological, with wars being, or about to be, carried on in heavenly as well as earthly spheres. There is no explicit belief in bodily resurrection, yet they looked for a new heaven and a new earth with the redeemed somehow attaining purification from all sinfulness and being granted everlasting happiness.

Matching the doctrine found in the Scrolls with what was said about the Essenes brings out the fact that although there are certain discrepancies, there are many more points of agreement geographically, regarding the type of life, and doctrinally. From Qumran sources it is hard to establish that the sectarians were committed to celibacy for life, although this is found in descriptions of the Essenes. Josephus, however, states that one community of Essenes did not practice celibacy. Nearly all scholars today tend to identify Essenes and Qumranites.

Almost from the beginning of the Scroll publications there have been various suggestions regarding the influence of Qumran on the NT. It has been suggested, e.g., that John the Baptist came under their influence. This is not impossible, since he went out into the Judean desert (Lk 1.80) and he stressed Isaian teaching. However, that Jesus found inspiration from Qumran in working out his life and mission is without foundation. Texts once adduced to show such dependence, esp. those regarding an alleged death and resurrection of the Teacher of Righteousness, have since been better understood and the suggestions once made have been largely withdrawn by those who made them. There are points of contact between Qumran doctrine and Christianity, which might also point to some similarities in organization. By far the greatest concentration of similar material is to be found in the Fourth Gospel. A number of common phrases have been listed by F. M. Cross. Parallels between the *mebagger* and the Christian *episkopos* (overseer) are only partially valid. The primitive Christian community in Jerusalem stressed common ownership of property (Acts 4.32), as did Qumran. All things considered, it is important to study the similarities and differences between Qumran and Christianity, but any fears on the part of Christians that there was some sort of essential takeover of Qumran doctrine and practice are groundless. BIBLIOGRAPHY: T. H. Gaster, *Dead Sea Scriptures* (2d ed., 1964); E. F. Sutcliffe, *Monks of Qumran* (1960).

[I. HUNT]

QUMRAN SCROLLS, see DEAD SEA SCROLLS.

QUO VADIS. According to the apocryphal *Acts of Peter* (*c.*200 A.D.), Peter was fleeing Rome during the persecution of Nero at the urging of the Christians when a short distance from the gates he was met by Christ traveling toward the city. Peter cried out in amazement, "Lord, where are you going?" (*"Domine, quo vadis?"*). When Christ replied reproachfully, "I am going to Rome to be crucified for a second time," Peter immediately turned back. The small church of Domine, Quo Vadis on the Via Appia at Via Ardeatina, which contains a copy of the footprint said to have been left by Christ himself, marks the traditional meeting-place. BIBLIOGRAPHY: Quasten 1:133–135.

[F. J. MURPHY]

QUODVULTDEUS, ST. (d. 454), deacon of Carthage from at least 427, bp. of that city in 437. He was a pupil and friend of Augustine, to whom he suggested *c*. 428 the composition of the *De haeresibus*. After the Vandals under Genseric had conquered Carthage, Q. refused to embrace Arianism; as a result he and a great number of his clergy were exiled. Being warmly received by the bp. of Naples, he helped to refute the preaching of the Pelagian bp. Florus. A number of discourses on the Creed and against various heresies are most probably to be ascribed to him. BIBLIOG - RAPHY: D. Ambrasi, BiblSanct 10:1335–38.

[F. J. MURPHY]

QÛRBŌNŌ (East Syrian, *qûrbānā;* Arab. *qurbân;* oblation). It may signify the Eucharistic Sacrifice, more often called *qûrrōbō* by West Syrians, or the Maronite unleavened host, also called (Arab.) *bûrshânah*.

[A. CODY]

QÛRRŌBŌ (Offering), common Syriac word for the Eucharistic Sacrifice among the West Syrians.

[A. CODY]

R

RA (RE), ancient Egyptian sun-god, particularly associated with Heliopolis. Myths recount that after emerging from Nun, the primeval water, Ra created the world and several other gods; he thus conquered chaos, assumed domination of the world, and instituted *maat,* eternally prevailing order. Other tales depict Ra's daily journey across the sky in the barque of the sun and his nightly trip through the underworld. The daily rising of the sun was thought to reaffirm the power of the sun-god over death. At times the rising (Khepri) and setting (Atum) suns were distinguished from Ra, but the texts insist on the essential unity of the three phases. Though Horus was the earliest royal god, later pharaohs were explicitly identified as "sons of Ra." The ritual ascent of each new pharaoh to the throne echoes Ra's fashioning of the primordial hill, his subjugation of chaos, and establishment of order. Similarly, several features of the myths about Ra (hill, waters, barque) were often reproduced in or near the solar temples. From the fifth dynasty on, Ra became a national god, but Amenhotep IV (*c.*1364–47) failed to establish solar monotheism as the national religion. Worship of Ra was often combined with that of other gods, including the supreme god Amon and many local deities. At Heliopolis he became Ra-Harakhti: "Ra-Horus of the Horizon." In hieroglyphics Ra is represented by a sun-disk; and pyramids, obelisks (Ra's cult symbol), and sphinxes also symbolized the sun-god. BIBLIOGRAPHY: S. Morenz, *Egyptian Religion* (1973); C. J. Bleeker, "Religion of Ancient Egypt," in *Historia Religionum I* (1969) 40–114; A. Scharff, *Ägyptische Sonnenlieder* (1922).

[E. V. GALLAGHER]

RAAMSES, see RAMESES, CITY OF.

RABANUS MAURUS, BL. (Hrabanus Magnentius Maurus; 776–856), Benedictine abbot of Fulda, abp. of Mainz. H. studied at Tours under Alcuin and from 803, as director of the monastic school at Fulda, achieved such fame as a teacher, writer, and scholar as to earn him the title

Praeceptor Germaniae. He was abbot of Fulda from 822 to 842 when, as a supporter of Lothair I in his unsuccessful struggle with Louis the German, he resigned. In 847 he was elected abp. of Mainz and in this office distinguished himself as a reformer and defender of doctrine, esp. in the synods of Mainz (847, 848, 852 [or 851]) and in his extensive correspondence and consultations. He played a leading role in the celebrated controversy surrounding the theological opinions of Gottschalk of Orbais. Though not known for originality of thought or expression, R. was a prolific writer and wide-ranging in his interests. His numerous scriptural works are important as examples of early medieval exegesis, and his *De institutione clericorum libri tres* is a summary of ecclesiastical life. *De rerum naturis* (or *De universo*), heavily dependent upon Isidore of Seville's *Etymologiae,* is a mystically informed catalogue of creation. Treatises on grammar and philosophy, poems, penitentials, homilies, and letters are extant. Some have attributed to him the authorship of the hymn Veni Creator Spiritus. Works: PL 107–112; MGH *Epistolae* 5:379–533; *ibid. Poetae lat.* 2:154–258; BIBLIOGRAPHY: H. Peltier, DTC 13.2:1601–20; J. E. Gugumus, BiblSanct 10:1339.

[J. E. BIECHLER]

RABAT, vest, waistcoat, or shirtfront, generally black, worn with Roman collar and suit as part of clerical garb where it is not customary to wear the cassock.

[J. DALLEN]

RABATÀ, ALOYSIUS, BL. (d. 1490), Sicilian Carmelite. He entered the Carmelite Order at Trapani (Sicily) and eventually became prior at Randazzo. Notable for humility, patience, and asceticism, he was a zealous confessor. When dying from a blow on the head he refused to identify his assailant. BIBLIOGRAPHY: Butler 2:275–276; P. Simonelli, BiblSanct 10:1339–40.

[N. G. WOLF]

RABBAH (Rabba), capital of Ammon; the site of the modern Ammān, Jordan. Destroyed in the 6th cent. B.C., it was rebuilt in Hellenistic times and named Philadelphia (for Ptolemy Philadelphus 285–246 B.C.). The famous bed (sarcophagus?) of Og was there (Dt 3.11). In the Bible Rabbah is mentioned most prominently in connection with David's battles against the Ammonites (2 Sam ch. 11–12; see also Am 1.14; Jer 49.2–3; Ezek 21.25). There was another city of this name in Judah (Jos 15.60).

[T. EARLY]

RABBI (also Rabboni, "my great one"), an expert in *Torah. Though its origins are obscure and it is not in the OT, it was a title frequently used in the time of Jesus. In the NT it is used almost exclusively in addressing Jesus. For non-Jewish readers (cf. Lk) various substitutes like "master" and "teacher" were used. The striking prohibition by Jesus for the use of the title (Mt 23.7–8) may have been due to some unknown scribal practice of absolute respect that Jesus did not consider part of the Christian spirit. The Jewish scholars mentioned in the *Mishna, particularly the editor *Judah ben Nasi were given this honorific title. In later times the emphasis was placed on the aspect of "teacher." It exists in variant spellings. In modern times the word is used of a man trained and ordained to exercise the office of leadership for a Jewish congregation.

[L. A. BUSHINSKI]

RABBINICAL BIBLES, printed editions of the Hebrew Bible with targums in parallel columns and surrounded by commentaries of celebrated rabbis; also called *miqrā-ôt g' dōlôt,* large editions. The first rabbinical Bible was published at Venice in 1516–17 by D. Bomberg (c. 1470–1549), a Christian, and edited by F. Pratensis (c. 1500–58), a Jewish convert. In the period 1524–25 Bomberg published another edition, this one edited by the Jewish scholar Jacob ben Ḥayyim (Chayim), who sought to establish a better text and added Masoretic notes (see 1968 ed., *Introduction to the Rabbinic Bible of 1525,* with notes by C. D. Ginsburg). The Bible text in Bomberg's Bibles was based on 14th- and 15th-cent. MSS, basically the *Ben Asher text but influenced by the *Ben Neftali. Though not reflecting the oldest or most reliable MSS, it remained the standard text until it was supplanted by the 3d ed. of R. *Kittel's *Biblia Hebraica* (1930–37). Another rabbinical Bible (*Q'hillôt Mōšeh*) was published in Amsterdam (1724–27) by Moses ben Simeon Frankfurter, and A. B. Lebensohn published one in Warsaw in 1860–68.

[T. EARLY]

RABBULA (c. 350–435), appointed bp. of Edessa from 412, leading figure in the Syrian Church. He opposed Nestorianism and attacked the writings of Theodore of Mopsuestia. To defend orthodoxy more efficiently, he compiled the Peshitta text of the NT, superseding Tatian's Diatessaron. He translated into Syriac St. Cyril of Alexandria's *De recta fide;* he also wrote many letters, hymns, and a sermon against Nestorius.

[L. PEANO]

RABELAIS, FRANÇOIS (1483, 1490, or 1494–1553), French Renaissance writer. Probably already a Franciscan novice (c. 1511), R. entered the monastery of the Observantine Friars Minor at Fontenay-le-Comte (c. 1521). Granted an indult by Clement VII to join the more scholarly Benedictines (c. 1524 or 1525), R. became secretary to Geoffroi d'Estissac, abbot and bp. of the monastery-cathedral of Maillezais. During a period of travel and a stay in Paris (c. 1528–30) where, by an unknown woman, he fathered two children later legitimized by Paul III (1540), he put off his monk's habit without permission, entered the Montpellier medical faculty (1530) as a secular priest, and received his bachelor's degree. In Lyons (1532), where he was physician at the Hôtel Dieu, the first book of *Pantagruel* (now Bk. 2) was published (1532) under the anagrammatic pseudonym Alcofrylas Nasier, followed by *Gargantua, Père de Pantagruel* (1534; now Bk. 1). After the Sorbonne's condemnation of *Pantagruel* as obscene (1533), R. accompanied Jean du Bellay to Rome (Feb.-April, 1534), as personal physician. During the repercussions following the *Affaire des Placards* (Oct. 1534), R. prudently disappeared from Lyons, again accompanying the now Card. du Bellay to Rome (1535–36). Here he received a papal bull of absolution freeing him from ecclesiastical censure, and he entered the cardinal's own Benedictine monastery at Saint-Maure-les-Fossés shortly before the abbey was secularized. He thereupon again undertook, in secular habit, his medical activity in various French cities, except for trips to Italy and a stay at Metz (1546–1547) where he sought refuge after the publication of *Le Tiers livre* (1546), which was condemned, as was *Le Quart livre* (11 ch., 1548; rev. and enl., 1552). Shortly before his death, R. was appointed curé at Saint-Martin-de-Meudon (1551), but never resided, and only after his death did *Le Cinquième livre* appear (16 ch., 1562; complete, 1564), of questionable authenticity since it is suspected that an unknown Protestant had a hand in it. R.'s ideas represent the discoveries and humanistic spirit of the Renaissance, while his style is still very medieval. Through his giants, symbols of the new faith in the moral and physical powers of man, he attacks traditional institutions. He satirizes scholastic learning and monasticism, offers his Abbey of Thélème as the ideal Renaissance model of the civilized community, and advocates the study of law, medicine, classical languages, and thought. Influenced by *Lefèvre d'Etaples, Erasmus, and Luther, he ridicules both Catholics and Protestants, defends liberal humanism and Gallicanism, and denies the validity of ecclesiastical marriage law. Much of his work is a voyage of discovery, symbolically undertaken to find the Oracle of the Divine Bottle which concludes by advising, "Trink" (Bk.

5), Thus expressng R.'s own intoxication with life and learning. His orthodoxy is still questioned. BIBLIOGRAPHY: L. Febvre, *Le Problème de l'incroyance au XVIe siècle: La Religion de Rabelais* (1947); A. Krailsheimer, *Rabelais and the Franciscans* (1963).

[R. N. NICOLICH]

RABULA GOSPELS, four 6th-cent. Syriac Gospels, examples of illuminated Eastern Christian MSS, distinguished by figural narrative cycles neither Alexandrian nor Hellenistic, evidencing the unique Byzantine realism preserved entirely in these Gospels of the Cappadocian monk Rabula. Christ in a mandorla with four Evangelists and four-wheeled chariot (from the vision in Ezek ch. 10) in a Rabula miniature (586 A.D.) is indicative of the epiphanies of the Lord in the narrative cycles of these Syriac MSS.

[M. J. DALY]

RACA, opprobrious term of uncertain meaning. It was often used by rabbis for students who could not grasp their teaching. It occurs only in Mt 5.22.

[L. A. BUSHINSKI]

RACAN, HONORAT DE BUEIL DE (1589–1670), French poet. Court page of Henry IV, R. served in the army, probably in campaigns against the Protestants, before retiring early (beginning *c.*1625) to his estates in Touraine where he devoted himself to writing poetry, esp. (after 1639) religious poetry. R. is known esp. for his *Stances sur la retraite* (1618), and for his pastoral drama, *Les Bergeries* (1625), commended by the Jesuit theologian Garasse (Garassus) for the role ascribed to Divine Providence. R.'s religious poetry includes: highly sensitive verse translations and paraphrases of the psalms as *Odes sacrées* (1661); *Les Psaumes de la pénitence* (1631); hymns to the Virgin and *Cantiques*. BIBLIOGRAPHY: L. Arnould, *Racan, histoire anecdotique et critique de sa vie et de ses oeuvres* (1896).

[R. N. NICOLICH]

RACCOLTA (It., collection), collection of prayers and other religious acts for which papal indulgences are granted, together with general regulations concerning them. The first such collection was published in 1807 by T. Galli, a consultor of the Congregation of Indulgences, which published its official version in 1877.

[T. EARLY]

RACE RELATIONS, see RACISM; DISCRIMINATION.

RACHEL, younger of Laban's two daughters, second wife of Jacob, and mother of Joseph and Benjamin. When Isaac sent Jacob to Paddan-aram to find a wife, Jacob met R. and agreed to work for Laban 7 years to have her as his wife (Gen ch. 29). Laban tricked Jacob, however, giving him R.'s sister Leah, so Jacob then worked another 7 years for

Rachel. For the first years of her marriage she was barren, whereas Leah had six sons and a daughter (Gen ch. 30). R. gave Jacob her maid Bilhah, who had two sons. Later "God remembered Rachel" and she bore Joseph. When Jacob took the family to Palestine, she stole her father's household gods and took them with her (Gen 31.19,34–35). She died giving birth to Benjamin (Gen 35.16–20) on the journey from Bethel to Ephrath. She was buried "on the way to Ephrath," which is identified with Bethlehem (Gen 35.19; 48.7; cf. Ru 4.11; Mic 5.2; but see 1 Sam 10.2 and Jer 31.15 for another tradition). A monument has marked the traditional burying-place near Bethlehem from at least the 4th cent. A.D.; the present building was built by the Crusaders. The significance of the R. stories, according to some scholars, is that they were intended to assert the claim to preeminence of the Joseph tribes, particularly Ephraim (see Gen 48; Is 11.13). R. is mentioned in Mt 2.16, 18 in a metaphorical sense.

[T. EARLY]

RACHIS (d. after 757), successor to Liutprand as king of the Lombards. Because he favored papal interests and a policy of peace with the papacy, many Lombard nobles opposed him and allied themselves with his brother Aistulf. Deposed, he retired to the abbey of Monte Cassino. On the death of Aistulf (756) he regained the throne for a brief period, 756–757.

[G. M. COOK]

RACIAL JUSTICE. In moral theology *justice pure and simple includes racial justice, since the rightness that justice respects is *equality, whether a natural equality based on the community of human nature, or an equality before the law. Legal or general justice, whether in the civil authorities or in the members of society, seeks the public good, which allows for the maximum benefit of all in the community. *Distributive justice regards the rights of each person in proportion to service to, or even dependence on, the community. Considerations of race are not a determinant of what rightfully belongs to the recipient of justice. Thus *discrimination is contrary to justice in all its forms. Where denial of rights has been institutionalized in any society, it has had as its basis the denial of the natural, therefore political, equality of all human beings. The attempt to justify such discrimination by the "separate but equal" principle that gave all in the community the same kind of advantages while preserving segregation or apartheid, has been recognized as unjust; its defendants are characterized as racists. Such an understanding of what racial justice requires is a development of the meaning of "fraternity" in the triplet, "liberty, equality, fraternity"; a common association and share in all public advantages is the only true form of justice in a society's life. Equality before the law *de facto* requires recognition of the natural equality of all races. The members of society have an obligation in legal justice to observe the laws that promote and enforce the concept of equality before the law. One means of achieving such equality is racial integration. There can, however, be a moral dilemma about the means of achieving integration. Thus parents may perceive court-ordered busing as in conflict with their rights to see to their children's upbringing, education, and safety. Further, observance of justice is first of all a matter of the externals of human concourse and interaction; that is why civil law has its powers over matters of justice. But the ultimate assurance that justice will be done is the internalizing of true friendship among men. It can be questioned whether simply being human is the basis of a universal brotherhood. For the Christian the true and effective realization of such brotherhood is the work of *charity, which makes possible acceptance of every person as one's *neighbor.

[T. C. O'BRIEN]

RACINE, JEAN BAPTISTE (1639–99), French dramatist. Educated in schools that were strongly Jansenistic in spirit, e.g., the Collège de Beauvais (1654–55), he was greatly influenced by their thinking. In Paris (1658), at the Jansenist-connected Collège d'Harcourt, R. began his literary contacts. At Uzès in Languedoc (1661), R. briefly studied theology before returning to Paris. His first-performed tragedy, *La Thébaïde* (1664), was presented by *Molière's troupe. This was followed by *Alexandre* (1665). He now engaged in open controversy with his former Port-Royal masters who condemned his theatrical career. His ultimate reply came in the seven tragedies in the classical tradition, almost all of Greek and Roman background, which followed: *Andromaque* (1667); *Britannicus* (1669); *Bérénice* (1670); *Bajazet* (1672); *Mithridate* (1673); *Iphigénie* (1674); and *Phèdre* (1677). In the preface to *Phèdre* he maintains that tragedy can be, as it had been for the Greeks, a school of virtue. R.'s originality lay in his ability to present passion, no longer in the context of the heroic drama of *Corneille, but as a truly tragic, blinding, uncontrollable, destructive force associated with hatred in the desire to possess the beloved. This view of passion is in conformity with a pessimistic Jansenist outlook, as is the tragic view of the human condition. Among the several reasons given for Racine's silence after *Phèdre* are: his reconciliation with Port-Royal, his appointment along with *Boileau as royal historiographer (1677), and his marriage (1677). At the request of Mme. de Maintenon he returned to the drama with *Esther* (1689) and *Athalie* (1691), biblical plays written for the religious edification of the students at Saint-Cyr. His last works included four *Cantiques spirituels* (1694), also of biblical inspiration, and his secretly composed *Abrégé de l'Histoire de Port-Royal* (pub. 1742–67), which reveals his fidelity to the Jansenists in later years and caused his loss of some court favor. His last 2 years were spent in scrupulous Jansenist austerity, and his remains, buried in the cemetery at Port-Royal-des-Champs, were removed to Paris after the destruction of the abbey (1710).

BIBLIOGRAPHY: L. Goldmann, *Hidden God; A Study of Tragic Vision in the Pensées of Pascal and the Tragedies of Racine* (1964).

[R. N. NICOLICH]

RACINE, LOUIS (1692–1763), French writer on religious themes, an adversary of the philosophes. Born in Paris, he was the seventh and last son of Jean Baptiste Racine, who died when R. was only seven. R. studied at the Collège de Beauvais, became a lawyer, and, after a 3-year retreat at the Oratory of Notre-Dame-des-Vertus, began his religious writing. At the age of 26 he was a member of the Academy of Inscriptions. He authored collections of memoirs such as *Réflexions sur la poésie* (1747) and *Mémoire sur la vie de Jean Racine*. He wrote poetry and translated into French *Paradise Lost* (1755). In 1750 he became a member of the French Academy. A six-volume edition of his complete works appeared in French in 1808. His biography was written in 1852 by A. de la Roque.

[E. J. DILLON]

RACISM, an attitude of prejudice against members of a race, or perhaps against members of all races other than one's own, coupled with a readiness to discriminate against them socially, economically, or in the matter of human, political, and social rights, and to withhold from them the honor, esteem, and perhaps even the fair treatment due to human beings. Racism does not appear from a moral point of view to differ essentially from prejudice and discrimination based on considerations other than that of race, e.g., national origin, religion, or social status. Practically, however, it is more difficult to overcome, for its color basis, where intermarriage is unacceptable, is an enduring fact, and inequalities in education and cultural tradition tend to perpetuate the antipathies, which, unfortunately, are often mutual. Ill will naturally begets ill will with the consequence that an initial prejudice can be aggravated as conflict and tensions continue. Economic and political developments in modern times have created a situation in which there are in many countries substantial minorities of people who differ racially from a majority of the population. In these circumstances racism can, and frequently does, constitute a major threat to social and political order.

Racism obviously is opposed to the spirit of Christianity. Christ insisted on love for all fellowmen, even for those from whom no return can be expected (Mt 5:43–47), and for those who belong to categories held in popular contempt (Lk 10:25–37). St. Paul repeatedly taught that there should be no distinction between Jew or Greek, slave or free, since all are children of the same God (e.g., Rom 10:12; Gal 3:28). This equality of all within the kingdom has always been the teaching of the Church, even from the time when slavery was an accepted social institution, down to the present time when the antiracist position of Christianity was restated by Vatican Council II: ''The Church rejects as foreign to the mind of Christ any discrimination against men or harassment of them because of their race, color, condition of life or religion.'' (Vat II NonChrRel 5). No doubt in many instances feelings of antipathy, being deeply rooted in the emotions, cannot be easily and quickly overcome. To the extent that they are involuntary they are not sinful. But it should be within the power of a rational agent to control his actions and to refrain from the wrongs against justice and charity that are done by discriminating against anyone on grounds of race in matters in which fundamental human values and social rights are concerned. This applies esp. to public areas of contact, such as serving the public in lodging and eating places, in any public buying and selling, in employment, or in doing business. In private affairs and dealings, an individual may be free to choose according to personal preference those with whom he wishes to associate, but even in these matters, the exclusion of anyone simply because of race seems to indicate a mean and unfair xenophobia. BIBLIOGRAPHY: Bishops of the U.S., *Discrimination and the Christian Conscience* (1958); J. T. Leonard, *Theology and Race Relations* (1963).

[J. J. FARRAHER]

RACLOT, MATHILDE (1814–1911), missionary. R. was born in Surauville (Vosges) and entered (1832) the Institute of the Sisters of the Holy Infant Jesus or Ladies of St. Maur. She worked as a teacher, and founded orphanages and schools in Bagnoles, Bergier, Malaysia, and finally Japan where she established religious houses in Tokyo and Shizuoka.

[T. M. MCFADDEN]

RACONIS, ABRA DE, see ABRA DE RACONIS, CHARLES FRANCOIS D'.

RACOVIAN CATECHISM, *confession of faith for *Socinianism. On the basis of a draft prepared by F. Sozzini (see SOCINUS), this catechism was written by George Schomann in 1574; it was published in Polish by Valentin Schmalz in 1605 at Raców, and there were versions in German, 1608, and Latin, 1609. In England in 1614 the Latin version and in 1652 an English version by J. *Biddle were burned. The distribution of the contents of the Catechism corresponds to Christ's triple role as prophet, priest, and king. During the 17th cent. it was widely read by rationalist Protestants. An English edition with a historical introduction was published in 1818 by Thomas Rees. BIBLIOGRAPHY: P. Wrzecionko, ''Die Theologie des Rakower Katechismus,'' *Kirche im Osten* 6 (1963) 73–116; bibliog. for Socinianism.

[T. C. O'BRIEN]

RAD, GERHARD VON (1901–71), Lutheran theologian and OT scholar. He was for many years professor of OT at Heidelberg, after serving in the same position at the Univ. of Jena and Göttingen. Among his important works translated into English are: *Old Testament Theology* (2 v.,

1962–65); *Genesis* (rev. ed., 1972); *Deuteronomy: A Commentary* (1966); *Studies in Deuteronomy* (1953); *Wisdom in Israel* (1971).

[T. J. RYAN]

RADBOD OF UTRECHT, ST. (*c.*850–917), bp., monk. R. was born of Frankish parents in Namur, Belgium; his great-grandfather was the last pagan king of the Frisians. R. received his first schooling under Gunther, bp. of Cologne, his maternal uncle. A monk at 30 and teacher of the famous Abbot Hugo, in 900 R. was chosen bp. of Utrecht. He was renowned for charity and pastoral rule, trying to remove the traces of Frisian paganism. He wrote hymns, an office of St. Martin, poems, a sermon on St. Lebwin, and a hymn to St. Swithbert. Under a Danish invasion, he moved the see to Deventer, where he died. BIBLIOGRAPHY: MGH 15:569–571; N. Del Re, BiblSanct 10:1345–46; Butler 4:446.

[N. F. GAUGHAN]

RADEGUNDA, ST., QUEEN OF THE FRANKS (518–587). She was born in Erfurt. She was seized as part of the reward of invasion by Theoderic, King of Austrasia, and Clothar I, King of Nuestria. Then 12 years of age, she lived for 6 years at Athies, devoted to prayer and religious practice, until she was told to become the wife of Clothar. The years that followed the marriage were disturbing ones. Clothar lived a dissolute life and the more involved he was in the pursuit of pleasure, the more devoted to service and prayer she was. This continued even when R. left him *c.*555 to live in a monastery at Saix, and then at Poitiers. There she had erected the monastery of St. Mary, later called the monastery of the Holy Cross and lived as a member of the large community she attracted to monastic life. It is related that she cured a blind man who was at her funeral. Her cultus began from that time and continues. BIBLIOGRAPHY: Butler 3:318–320; N. Del Re, BiblSanct 10:1348–52.

[J. R. RIVELLO]

RADEWIJNS, FLORENTIUS, see FLORENTIUS RADEWIJNS.

RADHAKRISHNAN, SARVEPALLI (1888–1975), Indian philosopher, translator, lecturer and statesman. He is most important as an interpreter of the Indian view of life to the West. R. began his philosophical career in 1908 with the publication of his M.A. thesis, *The Ethics of Vedānta;* was professor of philosophy and chancellor of various Indian universities; professor of comparative religion, Manchester College, Oxford (1929). In public life he was president of the Executive Board, UNESCO, Paris (1949); Indian ambassador to the U.S.S.R. (1949); vice president (1952–61), and president (1962–67) of India.

R. received international recognition as a philosopher in 1920 with the publication of *The Reign of Religion in Contemporary Philosophy,* and his *Indian Philosophy* (2 v.,

1923, 1927) established both R. and Indian philosophy as a serious subject for Western philosophers. In his most systematic and best-known work, *An Idealist View of Life* (Hibbert Lectures, 1929), R. attempted to synthesize Western idealism with the Indian or Vedantic idealist tradition. Similarly, in his *Eastern Religions and Western Thought* (1939) R. compared Hindu mysticism and ethics with Greco-Roman and Christian values. Following in the tradition of *Shankara, *Ramanuja, Madhva and other major Indian thinkers, R. has written lengthy commentaries on the three great Hindu scriptures: *Bhagavad Gita* (1948), *Principal Upanishads* (1953), and *Brahma Sutra* (1960).

As a philosopher, religious thinker, and statesman, R. has consistently emphasized the need for greater understanding between the East, primarily India, and the West. Perhaps more than any figure of the first half of the 20th cent., R. helped to create what he believed to be an emerging world community "based on the truths of spirit and the unity of mankind." BIBLIOGRAPHY: *Philosophy of S. Radhakrishnan* (ed. P. A. Schilpp, 1952) for excellent articles on R. and for his replies to interpreters.

[R. A. MCDERMOTT]

RADICAL THEOLOGY, a recent trend in theology characterized by a rejection of transcendence and traditional structures—intellectual, ethical, and ecclesiastical. Exemplified notably by the *death of God theologians, radical theology attempts to develop an expression of Christian faith that is not religious in traditional terms. Influenced by linguistic philosophy, the movement rejects supernaturalism and metaphysical language about God. It calls for a *new morality of love, as opposed to law, with Jesus as an example, and generally supports a radical social ethic. It is critical of traditional forms of church life and seeks fundamental restructuring or abandonment of the *institutional Church. Associating itself with the prison writings of D. *Bonhoeffer (1906–45), it speaks of a world come of age and sees the contemporary period as one whose secularity makes traditional piety and religious language impossible. To some extent it is reflected in such popular works as Bp. J. Robinson's *Honest to God* (1963), based upon P. Tillich (1886–1965), R. Bultmann, and Bonhoeffer, and H. Cox's *Secular City* (1965). Radical theology may be taken as an extension of various liberal tendencies found in theology since the *Enlightenment (see LIBERAL THEOLOGY). But whereas liberalism has sought to conserve basic aspects of the Christian tradition while making such adjustments as modern thought seemed to demand, radical theology has minimized any conservative interest, emphasizing relevance to the present and openness to the future. BIBLIOGRAPHY: W. Miller, *New Christianity* (1967).

[T. EARLY]

RADIN, PAUL (1884–1959), anthropologist. A long career in univ. teaching that included the Univ. of California, Kenyon College, and Cambridge Univ. culminated in R.'s appointment as head of the department of anthropology at Brandeis Univ., Waltham, Massachusetts. He was an authority on the American Indian, with special interest in primitive religion. Among his 17 published volumes were *Primitive Man as Philosopher* (pa. 1927), *Story of the American Indian* (rev. 1944), and *Primitive Religion: Its Nature and Origin* (pa. 1937).

[J. R. AHERNE]

RADIO AND TELEVISION, NATIONAL CATHOLIC OFFICE FOR, see FILM AND BROADCASTING, OFFICE FOR.

RADIOCARBON DATING, method of establishing absolute chronology of organic samples found in archeological excavations. The process of radioactive carbon dating was developed by Willard F. Libby at the Univ. of Chicago in 1948. It is based on the fact that upon the death of an organism the radiocarbon begins to decay at a rate in time that is known. The activity of radioactive carbon (carbon-14) present in bones, wood, or ash is measured and compared to carbon-14 activity in presently living organic matter. Radiocarbon years are not precisely equal to astronomic years, but the time scale can be corrected for at least the last eight millennia. Despite some uncertainties in applying it, it is the most versatile method for establishing absolute chronology going back at least 40,000 years. Comparative chronology, as based, for example, on pottery styles, gives much more hesitant and limited results, and can hardly be applied to prehistoric archeology.

[E. J. DILLON]

RADLA-ASTERICUS, see ANASTASIUS OF HUNGARY, ST.

RADULFUS ARDENS (Raoul Ardent; late 12th cent.), dialectical theologian, one of the Porretani, followers of Gilbert de la Porrée (Porretanus); author of *Speculum universale* (*c.*1200), early example of the medieval philosophico-theological compendium.

RAEYMAEKER, LOUIS DE (1895–1970), distinguished Belgian philosopher. R. earned doctorates in theology and philosophy while studying for his ordination, and taught Thomistic Scholasticism at Malines Seminary. He wrote many scholarly articles and books, among them *Introduction to Philosophy,* 1938, *Philosophy of Being: Essay of Metaphysical Synthesis,* 1946. Following a professorship at Louvain Univ. and a 12-year presidency at the Leo XIII Seminary, he was appointed (1948) president of the Institut Supérieur de Philosophie at Louvain Univ., which also entailed being president of the Philosophic Society of Louvain and director of its *Revue philosophique.* He established the Cardinal Mercier Chair at the Univ. to carry on the Neo-Scholastic movement begun by Mercier. He also lectured all over the world, and was a founder of Lovanium Univ., now the National Univ. of Zaire, Kinshasa Campus. R.'s chief significance lies in his contribution to the spread of Thomistic philosophy in the 20th century. BIBLIOGRAPHY: G. Van Riet, "In memoriam Monseigneur Louis de Raeymaeker," *Revue Philosophique de Louvain* 68 (1970) 5–10.

[J. MORGAN]

RAFFAEL, see RAPHAEL SANZIO.

RAFFAELLINO DEL GARBO (Raffaello de'Carli; Raphael de Florentia *c.*1466–1527), Italian painter whose varied names have caused confusion. Vasari identifies R. del Garbo as assistant to Filippino Lippi. *The Resurrection* (1496–1505) in the Capponi Chapel, and *S. Bartolomeo,* Monte Oliveto, determined as R.'s are Peruginesque.

[M. J. DALY]

RAFFEINER, JOHN STEPHEN (1785–1861), missionary. A native of the Austrian Tyrol, R. left the field of medicine to study for the priesthood and was ordained in 1825. As a volunteer for the U.S. missions he came to New York in 1833 and was given the charge of establishing German churches and centers throughout New York State. He became vicar-general for the Germans of New York and founded parishes in New York City, on Long Island as well as Boston and in New Jersey. Later in N.Y. he helped establish missions in Albany, Rochester, Buffalo, Utica, and Syracuse. Much revered, he was regarded as the apostle of the Germans.

[J. R. AHERNE]

RAFIDITES (Arab., *rawâfid,* sing., *râfidî*) a term used often to designate the *Shiites. The word is taken from the participle *râfid,* "rejector" and refers specifically to the Shiites' rejection of the validity of the election of the first three *caliphs.

[R. M. FRANK]

RAGES (Ragae, Rhagae), ancient city *c.*5 miles SE of modern Teheran, Iran. Possessing a strategic location, it was the capital of Media before Ecbatana. It was a Zoroastrian stronghold before being taken over by the Muslims. Tobit entrusted ten talents of silver to Gabael, who lived there (Tob 1.14; 4.1,20; 5.5; 6. 12; 9.2). Judith referred to Ragae as the general region (1.5,15), asserting that Nebuchadnezzar defeated Arphaxad there.

[T. EARLY]

RAGGI, ERCOLE ANTONIO (1624–86), Italian sculptor, Bernini's best pupil, executing works of agitated style. His masterwork is the stucco decoration of the Gesù (Rome, 1670–85), one of the largest sculptural commissions of the period.

RAGUSA, JOHN OF (John Stojkovic; *c.*1390–1443), Dominican theologian. Having joined the Dominicans at Ragusa, R. studied at Paris, becoming a doctor of theology

in 1420. In 1423 he was the envoy of the Univ. of Paris to the Council of Pavia; in 1429 he served as procurator-general of the Dominicans at Rome. The chief interest in John is his role at the Council of Basel. He delivered the opening address there in 1431; in 1433 he was one of the Council's theologians who negotiated with the Hussites; in 1435 and 1437 he went on behalf of the Council to Constantinople, persuading the Greeks to send a delegation to the Council. In 1438, he went over to the conciliarist party, and was made a cardinal by the antipope Felix V. Among his writings the most important is the treatise *De cognoscibilitate ecclesiae* (ed. B. Duden, 1958).

[L. E. BOYLE]

RAHAB, a biblical name. (1) R. was the harlot of Jericho who sheltered two men Joshua sent as spies (Jos ch. 2). When Jericho was destroyed, she and her family were saved in return for her kindness (Jos 6.22–25). She may be the R. listed in the genealogy of Jesus as the wife of Salmon and father of Boaz (Mt 1.5). In the NT she is listed among those who prevailed through faith (Heb 11.31), and included among those justified by works (Jas 2.25). (2) The mythological sea dragon killed by Yahweh in a primordial conflict is named Rahab (Job 26.12; Ps 89.10; Is 51.9). This conflict is similar to a myth found in various forms throughout the ancient Near East.

[T. EARLY]

RAHEWIN OF FREISING (d. between 1170 and 1177), historian. R. served as assistant, chaplain, and notary, *c.*1144 to Bp. Otto of Freising. He is remembered for his continuation of Otto's *Gesta Frederici imperatoris,* adding books 3 and 4 and bringing the account up to 1160. He was also the author of *Dialogus de pontificatu sancte Romane ecclesie* and of the poems *Theophilus* and *De Deo et angelis.* BIBLIOGRAPHY: Manitius 3:388–392; F. J. Schmale, *Deutsches Archiv für Erforschung des Mittelalters* (1950–) 19:168–214.

[O. J. BLUM]

RAHLFS, ALFRED (1865–1935), German Lutheran scriptural scholar. R. spent almost all of his academic career at the Univ. of Göttingen, both as a student of P. A. de Lagarde and as an OT professor. His life's work was editing a critical text of the LXX, identifying each codex according to its recensional family. Only three volumes appeared: *Ruth* (1922), *Genesis* (1926), and *Psalmis cum Odis* (1931). A students' edition in two volumes of the whole Septuagint was published in 1935 using only the three basic codices.

[T. M. MCFADDEN]

RAHMANI, IGNATIUS EPHRAEM (Ephrain II), patriarch of Antioch (526–545). Upon his election to the patriarchate he started fighting against the Monophysites who were the followers of his rival Severus of Antioch. His writings manifest that he represented the new current of Chalcedonism and that he was familiar with the heritage of Cyril of Alexandria. Photius professed admiration for R.'s writings. R. on many occasions took position against Origenism, but after long indecision he endorsed Justinian's Edict against the Three Chapters.

[L. PEANO]

RAHNER, HUGO (1900–68), Jesuit theologian. Born in Pfullendorf, Germany, the older brother of Karl Rahner, R. entered the Jesuits in 1919, was ordained in 1929, and made his final vows in 1936. He was professor of church history and patrology at the Univ. of Innsbruck, where he taught from 1937 until his death. He also held the position of rector magnificus there. Some of his works are: *Theology of Proclamation* (1968); *Parish, from Theology to Practice* (1958); *Our Lady and the Church* (1961); *Man at Play* (1967); *Letters of St. Ignatius Loyola to Women* (1960); *Ignatius, the Theologian* (1968); *Greek Myths and Christian Mystery* (1963); *Church and Readings in Theology* (1963, Rahner et al.).

[J. R. RIVELLO]

RAHNER, KARL (1904–), German Jesuit theologian. Ordained in 1932, R. studied under M. Heidegger at the Univ. of Freiburg and received his doctorate from the Univ. of Innsbruck. After teaching on the Jesuit faculty there, R. became professor of dogma at the Univ. of Münster in 1967. Though once controversial, R. was a major influence at Vatican II. His writings are all characterized by the transcendental Thomistic method, an existential Christian anthropology that grounds his innovative reinterpretation of dogma. Man, as incarnate spirit, can come explicitly to accept Christ, since he is necessarily open to the presence of God, which he implicitly discovers in his acts of knowing, willing and loving. All men are anonymously Christian in so far as they experience the reality of grace through selfless affirmation of the world already objectively redeemed by Christ. The Church is the community which has made thematic that which even those outside its boundaries can intensely realize. R. places dogmatic statements into the broader framework of man's inherent supernatural ability to respond to God's self-communication in history. BIBLIOGRAPHY: K. Rahner, *Spirit in the World* (tr. 1968); *Hearers of the Word* (tr. 1969); *Theological Investigations* (14 v., 1961–76); L. Roberts, *Achievement of Karl Rahner* (1967).

[P. J. ROSATO]

RAIKES, ROBERT (1735–1811), a founder of the Sunday school system in England. R. was the publisher of the *Gloucester Journal,* and generally interested in social service. When he became aware of the lack of any religious training for poor children, he was instrumental in establishing (1780) a Sunday school in his own parish. R.'s idea quickly caught on, and a Society for the Establishment of Sunday Schools was established in London in 1785. R. has come to be regarded as the founder of Sunday schools, although his main contribution seems to have been the propagation of awareness concerning the need for religious training and a workable plan for meeting that need. BIBLIOGRAPHY: L. Stephen, DNB 16:611–613.

[T. M. MCFADDEN]

RAIMONDI, LUIGI (1912–75), cardinal theologian, canonist, apostolic delegate to the United States. Born at Acqui-Lussito, N Italy, R. entered the Acqui diocesan seminary in 1924. He was ordained in 1936 and studied at Rome, receiving doctorates in theology and canon law. He was nuncio to Guatemala (1938–42); auditor of the Washington apostolic delegation (1942–49); consultor and chargé d'affaires of the internunciature of New Delhi, India (1949–53); titular bp. of Tarsus and nuncio to Haiti (1954–56); apostolic delegate to Mexico (1957–67). R. served in the U.S. in the same role (1967–73) and was made cardinal in 1973 when he returned to Rome. There he became cardinal prefect of the Congregation for the Causes of Saints. Unfortunately he did not live to accomplish the 7 beatifications and 6 canonizations he had scheduled for the Holy Year.

[M. R. BROWN]

RAIMONDI, MARCANTONIO (*c.*1480–*c.*1534), master Italian engraver of revolutionary technique. Early works in the style of Francia, his teacher, show rigid strokes flattening figures. In Venice (1506), R. engraved 17 plates of Dürer's woodcuts of the *Life of the Virgin* and the *Dream of Raphael* after a painting by Giorgione introducing curved strokes effecting plasticity of form. The influence of Lucas van Leyden is seen in 1508 in *The Climbers* (from Michelangelo's *Battle of Cascina*) which shows remarkable gradations. In Rome (1510) R. studied antiquities, and in 1513 began his renowned work with Raphael, translating the master's ideal beauty of form, and through his prints introducing the Renaissance to N Europe. R. continued to interpret designs from the school of Raphael after the master's death.

[M. J. DALY]

RAIN (PRIMITIVE RELIGION). Rain is the object of particular concern in agricultural societies and in places where there is abnormal rainfall. As rain is one part of the larger complex of symbols of fertility, ritual actions and myths are not concerned with it in general but with rain at the propitious time. Specialists in rain-making are usually well aware of the seasonal variations in precipitation and of the limits of their own influence. A particularly elaborate system of beliefs and observances regarding rain is found among the Louedu, a Bantu tribe of South Africa. The queen is thought to have general care and control of seasonal regularity; she is much more a rain-maker than a ruler. Her intervention is not confined to drought situations; cultic prescriptions must be kept throughout the year. Only with the consent of her ancestors and predecessors in office can the queen control the rain. Her methods and medicines are shrouded in secrecy and are transferred only from one queen to the next. The rain-queen always works with a specialist who has inherited the art of rain-making from his father and who may also be consulted by neighbouring tribes. Breach of taboos, witchcraft, and angry ancestors can prevent rainfall, and appropriate ritual steps must be taken in each instance to rectify the situation. In societies where rain-making is a more peripheral activity, it is still found in the hands of specialists who inherit sacred knowledge, and the activity itself is hedged round with ritual observances. BIB-LIOGRAPHY: E. O. James, in Hastings, ERE 10:561–565; M. Eliade, *Patterns in Comparative Religion* (tr. R. Sheed, 1958); E. J. and J. D. Krige, *Realm of a Rain-Queen* (1943).

[E. V. GALLAGHER]

RAINALD OF BAR, BL. (d. 1150), abbot of Cîteaux. A member of the family of the counts of Bar-sur-Seine, he was nominated abbot of Cîteaux by St. Bernard. He is credited with writing part of the statutes, *Instituta generalis capituli*, which were published by his successor. BIBLIOGRAPHY: M.-A. Dimier, BiblSanct 11:29–30.

[V. BULLOUGH]

RAINALD OF DASSEL (*c.*1118–67), imperial chancellor and abp. of Cologne. An ardent supporter of imperial power, particularly of Frederick I Barbarossa in his struggles against the pope, Rainald was excommunicated for his imperial partisanship. He died on a campaign in Italy. BIB-LIOGRAPHY: J. Gilchrist, NCE 12:66 (bibliog.).

[V. BULLOUGH]

RAINALD OF RAVENNA, BL. (Rainald of Concorezzo; 1250–1321), archbishop. Of the prominent Milanese family Da Concoregio, R. received appointments of increasing importance from Boniface VIII: bp. of Vicenza in 1296; legate on a peace mission to England and France in 1299; director of spiritual affairs in the Romagna, and abp. of Ravenna in 1302. In 1308 he was appointed to preside over a commission of bps. chosen to investigate the affairs of the *Knights Templars in central and N Italy. The bps. found the Templars were substantially innocent of the charges brought against them. Rainald refused to give heed to confessions extracted by torture. He also took an active part in the Council of Vienne concerning the question of the Templars and though Clement V yielded to the pressures exerted by the King of France and suppressed the knights; he was obliged to acknowledge that none of the charges had been proved. BIBLIOGRAPHY: L. Samarati, BiblSanct 11:192–198.

[N. G. WOLF]

RAINALDI, Italian architects of the Baroque period. **Girolamo** (1570–1655) mannerist worked in High Baroque style in Bologna, Parma, Modena, and Rome; his most important work is the Pamphili Palace in the Piazza Navona. His son **Carlo** (1611–91) the greater architect, created the brilliant Baroque church, Sta. Maria in Campitelli (1663–67), noted for its innovative spatial and light effects, the façade of Sant 'Andrea della Valle, and the twin churches at the Piazza del Popolo which served as the monumental N gateway to Rome. In 1673 Carlo became head of the Guild of St. Luke. BIBLIOGRAPHY: F. Fasolo, *L'Opera di Hieronimo e Carlo Rainaldi* (1960; R. Wittkower, *Art and Architecture in Italy, 1600–1750* (1958).

[L. P. SIGER]

RAINALDO DEI CONTI DI SEGNI, see ALEXANDER IV, POPE.

RAINBOW, in Gen 9.12–17, from the *Priestly tradition, a new creation, a symbol of Yahweh's promise to Noah after the Flood, that he would not repeat that kind of punishment for sin. Among primitive peoples the rainbow has been regarded as a portent of various significance.

[T. C. O'BRIEN]

RAISED OFFERING, Douay version translation for the Hebrew *teruma* (to be high or raised), used in connection with some Israelite sacrifices. Apparently a ritual motion up and down (contrast *wave offering), it signifies something lifted from a larger object. The priests' portion of a sacrificial animal was lifted (Ex 29.27 RSV; cf. AV). The AV used the translation, heave offering (Lev 7.14; Num 6.20; Dt 12.6). It was not a special type of offering, however, and the RSV omits the terms, raised and heave.

[T. EARLY]

RAISON, ANDRÉ (*c.*1650–1719), French composer and organist of the Paris churches of Ste. Geneviève and of the Jacobins. An eminent organist and composer, R. composed two books of organ works (1687 and 1714) containing Masses and *Magnificats*. A theme from R.'s first book, a *passacaglia* in G minor, was used by J. S. Bach in an organ work.

[R. J. LITZ]

RAJPUT PAINTING, two groups of Hindu schools of painting in the Rajput courts: Rajasthani in Rajputana and Central India (with local subdivisions in Bundelkhand, Udaipur, Jodhpur), and Pahari in the Punjab Himalayas (with local schools at Jammu, Kangra, Garhwal). The Gujarati school of 12th- to 16th-cent. palm-leaf MSS is probably the source of Rajput painting. Illustrations from the Gujarati *Uttaradhyāna Sūtra* (1591) and the *Gita Govinda* (Song of the Cowherd), dedicated to Krishna, are important.

Rajput painting deals with mythology and epics, esp. the symbolic love story of the god Krishna seeking Rādha (the soul), a Hindu counterpart of the *Hound of Heaven*. Rajasthani paintings relating to 36 *rāgas* and *rāginis* or musical modes (Boston, New York, and Washington, D.C.) are bright in color. Mughal court painting under the emperors Akbar and Jahangir was influenced by the Rajput school. The popular Rasikapriyā (1591) shows varied influences; examples in New York and Boston are characterized by the cool colors of Mughal style.

Pahāri 18th-cent. centers, after the decline of the Mughal Empire, in powerful Himalayan hill states at Kangra and Garhwal illustrated the Krishna and Rādha theme in romantic, graceful rhythms and beautiful female forms. The distinctive Basohli style of rich color and great elegance (1695) continues the vigorous 18th-cent. *Gita Govinda* (1730, India) by the painter Marnaku. A. K. Coomaraswamy first analyzed and publicized these works. BIBLIOGRAPHY: A. K. Coomaraswamy, *Rajput Painting* (2 v., 1916); B. Gray, *Rajput Painting* (1949); G. Archer, *Indian Painting in the Punjab Hills* (1952).

[M. J. DALY]

RAJPUTANA TEMPLES. The Rajputana area of NW India (now Rajasthan). In the 8th to the 11th cent. it was a region of magnificent Brahmanic and Jain temples of a northern ''Indo-Aryan'' style remarkable for beauty of columned halls, later destroyed by Muslim invaders.

[M. J. DALY]

RÂLE, SEBASTIEN (*c.*1657–1724), missionary. Born and educated in France, R. joined the Jesuits in 1675. Ordained, he volunteered for the Quebec missions and became an expert in the Huron and Abnaki languages. He worked among the Ottawas (1691–93) and left an accurate record of their customs. From 1693 his work was with the Abnaki Indians in what became the state of Maine. A popular and highly successful missioner, R. compiled an Abnaki dictionary still preserved at Harvard University's library. The dispute between the French and British over territorial rights to Maine, and above all the policy of the French to use the Indians to raid British settlements, and the French missionaries to act as political agents led to R.'s murder by British soldiers in a raid at Norridgewock, Aug. 23, 1724. His influence on the Indians was powerful and continues today in the use of his collection of prayers by the Indians of Maine. BIBLIOGRAPHY: J. Baxter, *Pioneers of New France in New England* (1894).

[J. R. AHERNE]

RALL, HARRIS FRANKLIN (1870–1964), American Methodist theologian who was educated at the Univ. of Iowa, Yale Divinity School, the Univ. of Berlin and of Halle-Wittenberg where he received the doctorate degree. In 1910 he became President of Iliff School of Theology, Denver, Colo., but his greatest work was as professor of systematic theology at Garrett Biblical Institute (now Garrett Evangelical Theological Seminary) where he served from 1915 to 1945. Author of 14 full-length books, he also wrote numerous articles for learned journals. In 1940 his work *Christianity; An Inquiry into Its Nature and Truth* won the $15,000 Bross Prize Award over 200 other entries. Active in the Methodist Federation for Social Service, his social concerns deeply infiltrated his theology. He was active in various international ecumenical conferences. BIBLIOGRAPHY: Encyclopedia of World Methodism (1974).

[F. E. MASER]

RALLIEMENT, the policy of Leo XIII, calling for French Catholics to rally to the support of the existing government. The Third Republic (1870–1914) was hostile to the Church and carried out policies and legislated against its activities and institutions. But in his encyclical of 16 Feb. 1892 (*Au milieu des sollicitudes*) Leo XIII, seeking to achieve a modus vivendi, urged Catholics, the most loyal of whom were monarchists, to support the actual government as the legitimate civil power. The papal nuncio at Paris, D. *Ferrata, was given the task of implementing this policy. For many Catholics, however, *Ralliement* seemed a scandal and an unwarranted papal dictation in political matters. Whatever success it achieved, the policy became pointless for a considerable time after the *Dreyfus affair: religious orders were expelled, diplomatic relations with the Holy See were broken off; strict separation of Church and State was legislated. Under Pius X *Ralliement* was formally negated. But after World War I, and esp. under Pius XI, relations between the French government and the Church were bettered through a kind of renewed *Ralliement*. BIBLIOGRAPHY: A. Sedgwick, *Ralliement in French Politics, 1890–1898* (1965); A. Dansette, *Religious History of Modern France* (2 v., 1961).

[T. C. O'BRIEN]

RALPH OF CAEN (1080–*c.*1131), historian of the first Crusade. Best known for his individualistic and lively *Gesta Tancredi,* an account of the Norman contributions to the Crusades, he wrote a mixture of prose and verse, and was influenced by Virgil, Horace, Caesar, and Cicero. BIBLIOGRAPHY: P. B. Corbett, NCE 12:70 (bibliog.).

[V. BULLOUGH]

RALPH OF COGGESHALL (d. after 1227), Cistercian abbot (1207–18) at Coggeshall (Essex), chronicler. His contribution to the *Chronicon anglicanum* (ed. J. Stevenson, 1875) covers the years 1187–1224; it is a valuable source for Richard I and John. BIBLIOGRAPHY: M. F. Laughlin, NCE 12:70; C. H. Lawrence, LTK 8:967.

[L. J. LEKAI]

RALPH OF DICETO (*c.*1125–1202), historian and chronicler. Possibly of French origin, R. was made archdeacon of London (1152) and dean of St. Paul's (1180). He studied at Paris as a youth and again after 1152. He was one of the outstanding personalities of the late 12th century.

Works: *Opera Historica* (ed. W. Stubbs, 2 v., Rolls Series 68; 1876). BIBLIOGRAPHY: M. M. Chibnall, NCE 12:70–71.

[J. A. WEISHEIPL]

RALPH HIGDEN (var. Ranulf; *c.*1280–1364), English Benedictine chronicler. A monk of St. Werburgh's Abbey, Chester, from 1299, he compiled the *Polychronicon* (ed. C. Babington and J. R. Lumby, 9 v., 1865–86), a highly popular compendium of medieval knowledge of history, geography, and science. C. L. Kingsford, DNB 9:816–817, lists R.'s other writings. BIBLIOGRAPHY: F. D. Blackley, NCE 12:71.

[R. W. HAYS]

RALPH STRODE (fl. late 14th cent.), English philosopher and logician. R. was a contemporary of John *Wycliffe at Oxford. Only two works have survived, viz, *Consequentiae* and *Obligationes,* which were used as textbooks on the Continent and eventually printed at Padua and Venice. BIBLIOGRAPHY: Emden Ox. 3:1807–08; F. D. Blackley, NCE 12:71.

[J. A. WEISHEIPL]

RALPH TORTARIUS (*c.*1063–after 1117), author of poetry and prose, a monk at Saint-Benoît-sur-Loire, a noted center of intellectual activity. His writings reflect the interest in classical literature that flowered in the 12th century. BIBLIOGRAPHY: C. H. Haskins, *Renaissance of the Twelfth Century* (1927; repr. 1957).

[J. MULDOON]

RAMADAN (Arab., *Ramaḍân*), the 9th month of the year in the Islamic calendar. According to Muslim tradition, it was in the latter part of Ramadan that the *Koran was revealed to *Mohammed. The fast of Ramadan is one of the "five pillars" (i.e., basic religious obligations) of Islam; every Muslim who is physically able must refrain from all food and drink from dawn to dusk throughout the month which, because of the strictly lunar calendar, may fall at any season of the year. Travelers are excused from the fast but must make up the days omitted at the end of their journey. BIBLIOGRAPHY: S. D. Goitein, *Studies in Islamic History and Institutions* (1966) 90–110.*ISLAM.

[R. M. FRANK]

RAMAH (Rama), name of six sites in the Bible: (1) border town in the territory of Asher (Jos 19.29); (2) town of Naphtali (Jos 19.36); (3) town of Benjamin (Jos 18.25), where one tradition placed Rachel's tomb (Jer 31.15); (4) town in the hill country of Ephraim and home of Samuel (1 Sam 1.19; 7.17; 25.1); also called Ramathaim-zophim (1 Sam 1.1), it may be the NT Arimathea (Mt 27.57); (5) town in the territory of Simeon (Jos 19.8); (6) alternate name for Ramoth-Gilead (2 Kg 8.28–29).

[T. EARLY]

RAMAKRISHNA (1836–86), also called Sri Ramakrsna Parahamsa, a Bengali brahman saint who inspired the religious movement that bears his name. After succeeding his brother as chief priest at the temple of Kali in Dakshineshwar near Calcutta, while engaging in strenuous meditative practices, he began having visions of Kali, the dialectically destructive-creative goddess consort of *Siva. A mendicant nun, Yogeswari or Brahmani, introduced him to both *Vaishnavism and *Tantrism. Then with the guidance of Tota Puri, an Advaitin monk, be began to interpret his visions in a way consistent with nondualistic or Advaita *Hinduism. In contrast to medieval Advaita, in which the world was considered maya, or illusion, and only the Absolute was believed real, R. held both the world and Brahman to be equally real. For him the two great spiritual obstacles throughout life are lust and money. He refused to touch money and actually suffered adverse reactions to contact with gold. Though he married early in life, he purportedly never had sexual relations with his wife. He dedicated himself to personal exploration of different religious paths. He practised both Christianity and Islam, concluding after having personally experienced Christ and Allah, that a universal truth persists in all religions. When asked what was the true path to God, he answered that there were so many paths to reach one and the same goal. He transcended religious discriminations and passed beyond what he came to recognize as the evil Hindu caste system. Though he wrote nothing, his teachings in parables and similes have been preserved, mainly through the movement which was organized by his most notable disciple, Vivekananda (1863–1902). Vivekananda and other disciples gathered in a monastery after R.'s death, making missionary excursions throughout India. Vivekananda went to the World Parliament of Religions in Chicago, 1893, where his impact led to lecture tours through America and England. In his teachings, based upon Ramakrishna, he advocated religious humanism, the unity of all religions—distinct traditions being mere secondary characteristics of their more fundamental unity—and meditative practises which help realize the divinity which is already in every human being. The movement was formally organized in 1897 as the Ramakrishna Mission. *VEDANTA SOCIETY.

[R. J. LITZ]

RAMANUJA (d. ?1137), Vaishnavite Tamil philosopher whose teachings on the human soul and commentaries on the *Brahma Sutra,* the *Bhagavad Gita,* and especially his *Sribhashya,* a long commentary on the Vedanta, deeply influenced subsequent Hindu thought. His *Sribhashya* continues to be the classic text for Vaishnavism. He greatly reduced the rigors of the caste system, and sought reforms against priestly greed, licentiousness in religion, and popular ignorance. R. advocated the social and religious equality of men and women, encouraging female education. He taught that a spiritual principle, the eternally perfect Deity, is the basis of all nature and that this principle is reality, not

illusion. The individual human soul (jiva) is an utterly dependent fragment (amsa) of the Supreme Deity, yet it is a
fragment retaining its own individual consciousness, even
when reunited with the Deity. By making the soul distinct
from, yet subordinate to, the Deity, his philosophy became
known as qualified nondualism (vishishtadvaita). Love of
God or faith (bhakti), not knowledge (jnana), is the means
of salvation (moksha). Some of Ramanuja's more
Christian-like ideas are thought to be influenced by Nestorian Christianity. BIBLIOGRAPHY: J. B. Carman, Theology of
Rāmānuja (1974).

[R. J. LITZ]

RAMBERT OF BOLOGNA (c. 1250–1308), early
Dominican defender of St. Thomas Aquinas's teaching, bp.
of Castello, near Venice, from 1303. He was a student at
Saint-Jacques, Paris, during St. Thomas's second tenure at
the Univ. of Paris (1269–72). R. himself taught there,
1290–95. His Apologeticum veritatis contra corruptorium
(c. 1293; ed. J. Müller, 1943) was a response to *William de
la Mare's Correctorium fratris Thomae (1278), and is
noteworthy as evidence of early Dominican allegiance to
Aquinas's teaching. It corrects misrepresentations of St.
Thomas's genuine positions and replies to many contemporary critics. R.'s only other known works are a lost commentary on the Sentences and one surviving sermon. BIB-
LIOGRAPHY: Gilson HCP, 414–416.

[T. C. O'BRIEN]

RAMBLER, THE, a review which was started as a
weekly by John Moore Capes, a convert from Anglicanism,
in January 1848. It had a series of editors but a fairly consistent editorial policy; its motto was "In necessariis unitas, in
dubiis libertas, in omnibus, caritas," and it represented the
liberal Catholic point of view in contrast to the ultramontane
Dublin Review. John Henry *Newman was involved in it
from the beginning and served for a brief period in 1859 as
the editor. One of his articles, "On consulting the Laity in
Matters of Doctrine," was handed over to Rome and he was
obliged to resign. Lord *Acton then became editor and increased the "liberal" orientation of the journal. Its theological and philosophical speculations were denounced by representatives of the "old Catholics" in England and by the
Roman Congregations. In 1862 The Rambler became The
Home and Foreign Review, a quarterly which Acton hoped
could concern itself with serious articles on contemporary
movements. By the change of name and format, Acton
hoped to circumvent the censure already pronounced against
The Rambler. But his treatment of the question of papal
temporal power cost him even Newman's friendship, for the
latter thought he had gone too far in his position. The Review's support of the Malines Congress in 1863 and its
denunciation of the Munich Brief (published in March
1864), which had condemned the teaching of J. *Döllinger
on the question of scholarly freedom, led to its downfall.
Acton held that the Brief made it impossible for him " . . .

to carry on the Review as hitherto with a good conscience."
He announced the cessation of the Review in April 1864.
BIBLIOGRAPHY: G. Himmelfarb, Lord Acton (1952); G. A.
Beck, English Catholics (1950); H. A. MacDougall,
Acton-Newman Relations (1962); J. L. Altholz, Liberal
Catholic Movement in England (1962).

[G. RUPPEL]

RAMEAU, JEAN PHILIPPE (1683–1764), French musical theorist and composer. As a theorist, R. sought to systematize musical techniques and to demonstrate scientifically the principles governing the progressive style of the
Enlightenment period. His major theoretical work is Traité
d'harmonie (1722). R. wrote numerous harpsichord pieces
as well as several motets, composed while he occupied various posts as a church organist. Later in life he began to
compose operas, and it is upon works such as Les Indes
galantes (1735) and Castor and Pollux (1737) that his reputation as one of the great European composers rests. BIB-
LIOGRAPHY: Grove DMM 7:31–40.

[T. MCFADDEN]

RAMESES (RAAMSES), CITY OF, under Ramses II
(c. 1290–1224 B.C.) of Egypt, the N and chief capital of
Egypt. Although Rameses was filled with portentous constructions, Ramses II called it his "house," the etymological meaning of Rameses. It is certainly to be located in the
NE delta of the Nile, but its precise site is disputed. Archeological support can be found for both modern San el-
Hagar (formerly Tanis; Avaris) which lies 10 miles S of
Lake Menzaleh; and Qantir (formerly Zoan), 20 miles S of
San el-Hagar. Rameses' biblical import is that it is one of
the cities of Hebrew forced labor referred to in Ex 1.11. As
such, the date and starting point of the Exodus could be
determined. It was destroyed by Pharaoh Amosis I (1570–
46 B.C.) and probably not reoccupied before the end of the
14th century. The mention of the "land of Rameses" in
Gen 47.11 is an anachronism. BIBLIOGRAPHY: G. E.
Wright, Biblical Archaeology (1957); P. J. King, "When
Israel Was a Child . . ," Bible Today 5 (1963) 287–293.

[W. E. LYNCH]

RAMIÈRE, HENRI (1821–84), French Jesuit, professor
of theology at the Institut Catholique, Toulouse, credited
with the spread of the *Apostleship of Prayer, esp. through
his L'Apostolat de la prière (1859) and his establishment of
the Messenger of the Sacred Heart. R. was also theologian
for the abp. of Beauvais at Vatican Council I, and published
a bulletin on its theological discussions.

[T. C. O'BRIEN]

RAMIREZ, SANTIAGO (1891–1967), Spanish Dominican, held by some to be the premier modern Thomist, but
whose work had little influence in English-speaking circles.
R.'s teaching career was passed mainly at the Univ. of
Fribourg, Switzerland (1921–45) and Salamanca (1945–

66). He was a man of immense erudition, but also of profound powers for analysis and synthesis. The first quality is marked by the monumental research evidenced in his works; the second, by their tightly ordered structure and their unity. Part of the reason for his relative lack of influence was a reluctance to publish; he regarded the subject matter always to be in need of further polishing. Thus his celebrated *De hominis beatitudine,* a massive study of the fundaments of moral theology, appeared rather late (1940). His doctoral work, *De ipsa philosophia in universum,* was published first in *Ciencia tomista* in 1922; in book form it did not come to publication until 1968, posthumously. It literally covers every major philosopher and philosophical system, including ethical thought, and its organizing principle for critique and resolution of the nature and division of philosophy is St. Thomas's explanation of the three degrees of abstraction. A work which R. perfected by a lifetime of study and teaching was his *De analogia,* also published posthumously (1970); in dealing with analogy he is recognized as the peer of Cajetan, whom he corrects. Other published works include: *De certitudine spei christianae* (1936); *De ordine* (1963); *El concepto de filosofia* (1955). Though a consummate scholastic, R. was also deeply involved in contemporary philosophy and wrote a renowned work on Ortega y Gasset, *La Filosofia de Ortega y Gasset* (1958). His last great service to the Church and to theology was as a *peritus* at Vatican II, during which he wrote *De episcopatu* (1968), on the bishops' place in the Church and on collegiality.

[T. C. O'BRIEN]

RAMOTH-GILEAD, city in northern Gilead, perhaps the modern Tell Ramit. Assigned to Gad, it was a refuge and Levitical city (Dt 4.43; Jos 21.38). There Ahab was fatally wounded (1 Kg 22.29–36). Ahab's grandson Joram was wounded (2 Kg 8.28), and Elisha's servant anointed Jehu king of Israel (2 Kg 9.1–13).

[T. EARLY]

RAMPOLLA DEL TINDARO, MARIANO (1843–1913), church diplomat and Vatican secretary of state under Leo XIII. Subsequent to his ordination in Rome and studies in both civil and ecclesiastical law, R. began a lifelong career in the Vatican diplomatic corps. From 1875 to 1887, he held a variety of important posts—most notably as nuncio to Spain. Leo XIII named him secretary of state, a post R. retained until Leo's death in 1903. His attitudes apparently coincided with Leo's on the two major diplomatic issues at the time: the *Roman Question and the need to overcome the Vatican's political isolation by alliances with France and Russia rather than with the Central Powers (Germany, Austria, and Italy). This latter policy led to Austria's use of its veto power against R. in the papal conclave of 1903. BIBLIOGRAPHY: *Leo XIII and the Modern World* (ed. E. T. Gargan, 1961), with extensive bibliog.

[T. M. MCFADDEN]

RAMSES (RAMESES) II, Egyptian pharaoh of the 19th Dynasty (1290–24 B.C.), almost certainly the one who "knew not Joseph" and forced the Hebrew people, to build *Pithom and Rameses, the "store-cities," for him in the delta region (Ex 1). The 19th Dynasty was attached to Egypt's northern tradition, and to the worship of the sun god, Ra of On (Heliopolis). In fact the name Ramses means "(the sun god); Ra is the one who begot him." Since the dynasty moved the capital to the NE delta, there would have been need for new "store-cities." Because R.'s reign was so long, and because so many monuments in Egypt have his name on them, including some that were actually built by his predecessors, his name evoked memories of imperial grandeur to Egyptians for a thousand years. His reputation probably outstripped his accomplishments. He did build temples and colossi in Karnak, Thebes, and Memphis, as well as in Nubia and Asia, yet he notably lacked the military acumen and administrative skill of his 15th cent. predecessor, Thutmose III, who had established the Asian empire on a firm foundation. R. was fortunate to escape ambush in his one bold sortie into Syria. His campaigns to Palestine were less than decisive; the Hittites had replaced Egypt as the dominant force in N Syria. R. had eventually to sign a peace treaty with them to have them as a future ally in the event of Assyrian expansion. It is likely that some of the people later to become part of the confederation of Israel were part of the slave labor force that built Pithom and Rameses. It is also likely that the other tribes experienced vassalage to R., the common lot of SW Asian peoples in Palestine and the other lands in the vicinity of Egypt. The last 40 years of R.'s reign were marked by peace and prosperity; he was succeeded by his son Merneptah.

[E. J. DILLON]

RAMSEY, ARTHUR MICHAEL (1904–), abp. of Canterbury (1961–74). Born in Cambridge, he attended Magdalen College, where his father taught mathematics, and then Cuddesdon College, Oxford. He was ordained deacon in 1928, priest in 1929, and served from 1928 to 1930 as curate of Liverpool Parish Church. He was later subwarden of Lincoln Theological College (1930–36), lecturer of Boston Parish Church (1936–38), vicar of St. Benet's Church, Cambridge (1939–40), professor of divinity at Durham Univ., canon of Durham Cathedral (1940–50), and Regius Professor of Divinity at Cambridge (1950–52). He was consecrated bp. of Durham in 1952 and translated to York 4 years later. In 1961 he became the 100th abp. of Canterbury, succeeding *Geoffrey Fisher, who had been his headmaster at Repton School. R. was active in ecumenical affairs and served as a president of the World Council of Churches from 1961 to 1968. Visiting Rome in 1966, he exchanged the kiss of peace with Paul VI. He also supported the unsuccessful merger attempt of the C of E and the British Methodist Church. He retired in 1974. R. published numerous theological works, including *The Gospel and the Catholic Church* (1936), *The Resurrection of Christ* (1944),

Glory of God and the Transfiguration of Christ (1949), and *God, Christ and the World* (1969). BIBLIOGRAPHY: J. B. Simpson, *Hundredth Archbishop of Canterbury* (1962).

[T. EARLY]

RAMSEY, ABBEY OF, former Benedictine monastery in Ramsey, England. It was referred to as "Ramsey the Rich" because of its wealth, which was largely received from its founder, Aylwin, Duke of East Anglia, who founded the monastery *c*.970. In 1143 the monks were forced from the monastery by Geoffrey de Mandeville, who turned the monastery into a fort during the Barons' War. After its restoration in the 12th cent., the monks became involved in expensive lawsuits over their land holdings and fell into debt. The abbey was dissolved under Henry VIII in 1539 and only the gateway remains standing.

[M. A. MCFADDEN]

RAMUS, PETRUS (1515–72), the Latinized form of Pierre de la Ramée, French humanist, mathematician, logician, and philosopher. Born at Cuts or Cuth (Oise) near Soissons in Picardy, he was educated there and at the Collège de Navarre in Paris, receiving the master's degree in arts in 1536, on which occasion he is said to have defended the dissertation *Quaecumque ab Aristotele dicta sunt commentitia sunt.* Until recently, scholarship has interpreted this to mean that all Aristotle said is false; however, more modern views tend to see R. as one who tried to simplify and reorganize the Aristotelian corpus rather than question its authority, though his two principal works are forthright attacks on A.'s logical treatises. These, both appearing in 1543, are *Dialecticae partitiones (On the Structure of Dialectic)* and *Aristotelicae animadversiones (Remarks on Aristotle),* the first being a criticism of the old logic and the second a textbook of the new logic proposed by himself. Teaching his innovations at the Collège du Maine in Paris, and later at the Collège de l'Ave Maria where he collaborated with Omer Talon in writing philosophical tractates, R. finally aroused the ire of orthodox Aristotelians at the Univ. of Paris and led to the suppression and burning of his books by Francis I in 1544. With the aid of Cardinal de Lorraine, the ban against his teaching logic on the grounds of undermining philosophy and religion was lifted by Henry II in 1547, after which the king appointed him Regius Professor of Philosophy and Rhetoric at the Collège de France. In 1562 R. became a Calvinist, subsequently fleeing Paris and then France, only to return in time to die in the massacre of St. Bartholomew's Day.

The range of his works includes some 60 titles on subjects such as logic, rhetoric, physics, mathematics, grammar, and metaphysics. A brilliant and effective writer, R. enjoyed a wide celebrity throughout Europe in the 16th and 17th cent. in his advocacy of a closer union between the arts of exposition and argumentation or rhetoric and logic, and in his urging of a theory of method for analyzing reality and

thought. BIBLIOGRAPHY: W. J. Ong, *Ramus and Talon Inventory* (1958) and *Ramus: Method and the Decay of Dialogue* (complete bibliog., 1958).

[J. T. HICKEY]

RAMUZ, CHARLES FERDINAND (1878–1947), novelist. Of Swiss origin, R. spent some years writing in Paris but wisely decided that his native Switzerland was a more appropriate milieu for his work. Of philosophical and mystical bent, he wrote realistically of the simple Swiss villagers. Among highly successful novels were *The Reign of the Evil One* (1917), *Great Fear in the Mountain* (1926), and *When the Mountain Fell* (1935), the last named being most widely read by English-speaking readers. In 1945 R. was considered for the Nobel Prize in Literature.

[J. R. AHERNE]

RANCÉ, ARMAND JEAN LE BOUTHILLIER DE (1626–1700), reforming abbot of the Cistercian monastery of Notre Dame de la Trappe. R. was directed to a Church career by his father in order to preserve the family's numerous benefices (two priories and three abbeys, one of which was La Trappe). After his ecclesiastical studies, which he completed brilliantly, and ordination, R. indulged in a rather dissipated life, from which he emerged in 1657 upon the death of his close friend, the Duchess of Montbayon. He disposed of all his benefices except La Trappe, became abbot there, and devoted himself to its reform. R. unsuccessfully sought the independence from Cîteaux of the *Cistercians of the Strict Observance. He was extremely severe in the regimen of the monastery, and advanced an ascetical ideal out of touch with true monastic traditions. Nevertheless, his reforms spread and laid the foundation for the ideals later espoused by the Trappists. BIBLIOGRAPHY: H. Bremond, *Thundering Abbot* (1930).

[T. M. MCFADDEN]

RANKE, LEOPOLD VON (1795–1886), German historian. A Lutheran and an eminent figure in 19th-cent. German historiography, R. set a pattern for the critical study of primary sources and archival material. He did not accept the theory of history as progress toward a future age of brilliance; to him each age was equally important. Although he wrote extensively on modern Germany and other states of Europe, he also produced works of a more general nature, *History of the Popes during the Sixteenth and Seventeenth Centuries* (placed on the Index in 1841) and *History of the World to 1453*, written after his 80th birthday. R. was not only a writer but his career includes many years of teaching at the Gymnasium of Frankfurt and as professor of history in Berlin (1825–71). BIBLIOGRAPHY: F. Schevill, *Six Historians* (1956) 125–155; G. P. Gooch, *History and Historians of the Nineteenth Century* (1952) 72–121; T. H. Laue, *Leopold Ranke, The Formative Years* (1950).

[M. A. WATHAN]

RANSOM (Gr. *lutrov*), a payment by which a person is liberated from bondage, an image used in the NT to explain the death of Jesus (Mk 10.45). Its Greek cognate, *lutrōsis*, redemption (a buying back), designates the work accomplished by Christ on Calvary (Rom 3.24; Col 1.14; Eph 1.7) and its consummation in the Parousia (see, e.g.,Lk 21.28; Rom 8.23; Eph 1.14). Borrowed from the OT (Ex 6.6–7; Is 62.11–12; Ps 129 [130].7–8), it includes two notions: a deliverance at the cost of a heroic work; an acquiring or taking possession by Him who ransoms. Through the paschal mystery Christ ransoms: he delivers men from sin at the cost of his death, and he acquires them as God's possession through his Resurrection. He is himself the ransom (1 Cor 6.20; 1 Pet 1.18). There is no question of a creditor to whom the price is paid in the biblical image, though at times patristic and medieval piety did speak of the ''rights of the devil.'' BIBLIOGRAPHY: J. M. Carmody, NCE 12:81; DBT; M. Van Caster, *Redemption–A Personalist View* (1965).

[C. REGAN]

RANULF HIGDEN, see RALPH HIGDEN.

RAPHAEL (God has healed), the *angel of the Lord who has a main role in the deuterocanonical book of Tobit, as the companion of young Tobias, counselor and guard against the evils of Asmodeus. It has been proposed that there is nothing conclusive in the text against R.'s being God himself as healer. He is mentioned nowhere else in canonical literature. However, R. does play an important part in the apocryphal Book of Enoch, wherein he appears as one of the archangels, with Michael, Gabriel, and Uriel. The cult of the Archangel Raphael only became widespread in the 17th cent. He is sometimes depicted as a patron of travelers.

[L. A. BUSHINSKI]

RAPHAEL SANZIO (SANTI; 1483–1520), Italian painter and architect of the Umbrian School. R. first studied with his father, Giovanni Santi, and was apprenticed to Perugino with whom he identifies in early composition and models (*The Marriage of the Virgin*, 1504; *Madonna del Granduca*). Moving to Florence in 1505, R. quickly absorbed influences from Leonardo and Michelangelo. Rarely an innovator, Raphael's great accomplishment was to synthesize the inventions of others in such a way as to make a new, personal statement. Arriving in Rome (date uncertain), he was commissioned by Pope Julius II to paint fresco decorations for the Vatican Stanze. Here he painted with Sodoma in the Stanza della Segnatura, the *Disputa* (1509) and the *School of Athens* (1510–11); which are visual definitions of the High Renaissance ideals of solid, classicizing figures set within convincing three-dimensional space arranged in stable, orderly compositions, usually based on geometric configurations. R., enjoying increased papal patronage after the accession of Leo X, was appointed architect

to St. Peter's in 1514 upon the death of Bramante, and superintendent of antiquities. R. employed an enormous workshop to deal with the ever-increasing demand for portraits, frescoes, easel paintings, and tapestry designs. From his Roman period date the well-known *Alba Madonna, Sistine Madonna, Transfiguration,* and portraits of *Donna Velato, Baldassare Castiglione,* and *Leo X with Cardinals Guiliano de Medici* and *Ludovico de' Rossi.* As architect, R. designed the Villa Madama in Rome (1515–21), attempting to unify interior space with the exterior setting. He died prematurely at age 36. BIBLIOGRAPHY: J. Beck, *Raphael* (1977); A. P. Oppé, *Raphael* (1970).

[S. CONWAY]

RAPIN, RENÉ (1621–87), French Jesuit theologian and man of letters. Entering the Society of Jesus at 18, R. took a strong stand against Jansenism despite his otherwise gentle personality. His *Eclogae sacrae* (1659) began his widespread literary reputation during his lifetime. The quality of his poem on gardens, *Hortorum libri IV* (1665), is considered so far above the rest of his work that his authorship has been doubted. His literary criticism, of great European influence, includes *Observations on Horace and Virgil* (1669) and *Reflections on Aristotle's Poetics* (1674). At present, however, he seems to remain interesting as a historian of Jansenism with his *Histoire du Jansénisme,* thought lost and not published until 1861, and *Mémoires sur l' Église, la société, la cour, la ville et le Jansénisme* (3 v., 1865). These works are important for the abundance of information they provide regarding the early phase of the Jansenist crisis in France. He wrote several other works on religion and Latin poetry, including a devotional heroic verse poem, *Christus patiens.* BIBLIOGRAPHY: *Renati Rapini, Hortorum Libri IV* (ed. I. T. McDonald, 1937) Introduction.

[R. N. NICOLICH]

RAPTURE, or ecstasy, an effect of intense mystical union of the soul with God, which causes the suspension of the use of the external senses, and the normal signs of consciousness. Often the result of the body's inability to withstand the impact of divine communications sometimes given in the highest kind of prayer, it is neither foreseen nor willed; as in the case of St. Teresa of Avila, it can overcome a person, in spite of determined efforts to head it off. It may pass with advance in the spiritual, and be recollected, as by St. Paul (2 Cor 12.2) if not in tranquility, in the midst of intense activity. BIBLIOGRAPHY: A. Royo and J. Aumann, *Theology of Christian Perfection* (1962) 551–556; ThAq ST 2a2ae, 175 (esp. in ed. Lat-Eng, v. 45, ed. R. Potter, 1970).

[P. F. MULHERN]

RAS SHAMRA, mound in Syria, site of *Ugarit, city of the 2d millenium B.C., excavated 1931. An extensive literature discovered there has significantly influenced modern biblical scholarship concerning Canaanite religious mythology and cultic practices that influenced Israel.

[T. EARLY]

RASH JUDGMENT, an assurance one adopts about another's character, usually to his discredit, not founded on enough evidence. It is more assertive than suspicious. It is an interior bumptiousness that is a form of imprudence called precipitateness by Gregory the Great and temerity by Thomas Aquinas (ThAq ST 2a2ae, 53.3), a preliminary to the injustice of detraction (*op. cit.,* 73). It is a sin against charity, serious when it concerns more than trifles, about which Jesus is ominous: "Judge not and you will not be judged . . ." (Lk 6.37). How little one knows about one's own virtue is often a tonic reflection, and all can say with St. Philip Neri looking at the felons, "But for the grace of God, there go I."

RASHDALL, HASTINGS (1858–1924), English historian, philosopher, and theologian. His reputation as a historian was established by his celebrated work, *Universities of Europe in the Middle Ages* (3 v., 1895). His philosophical interests were primarily ethical, and his most important contribution in that field was his *Theory of Good and Evil* (2 v., 1907). He described his position as ideal utilitarianism, ranking himself with the utilitarians in rejecting an intuitionism that would define morality independently of consequences, but qualifying his utilitarianism by admitting pleasure as only one of the determinants of the ideally good pattern of life. In theology he was a leader among the liberal Anglicans. In his Bampton Lectures of 1915, *The Idea of Atonement in Christian Theology* (1919), he defended the exemplarist or moral theory of atonement. BIBLIOGRAPHY: P. E. Matheson, *Life of Hastings Rashdall* (1928); A. K. Stout, EncPhil 7:68.

[R. B. ENO]

RASHI (1041–1105), at Troyes (NW France), one of the foremost Jewish commentators on the Bible and the Talmud. Rashi abbreviates, by the use of initial letters, his full name: Rabbi Shelomoh ben Isaac. He commented on nearly all the books of the Jewish canon as well as on most parts of the Talmud. His works for centuries were the accepted introduction of young Jewish students into the teachings of Bible and Talmud; their influence remains important to the history of Jewish thought and culture. The first known and dated Hebrew work in print was the Bible with R.'s commentaries (1475). The "Rashi script" is the hand in which these commentaries were printed, surrounding the text. His commentaries were esp. acceptable because of their clarity, conciseness, and practicality. Christian studies of his commentaries had their influence on Luther's translation of the Bible. BIBLIOGRAPHY: *Rashi, His Teachings and Personality* (ed. S. Tederbusch, 1958); H. Hallperin, *Rashi and the Christian Scholars* (1963).

[T. C. O'BRIEN]

RASKOLNIKS (schismatics), term used by Russian Orthodox Church for members who refused to accept liturgical changes ordered by Patriarch Nikon in 1653. *OLD BELIEVERS.

[T. EARLY]

RASON (Gr. *exorason*; Sl., *ryasa*; Arab., *jibba*). The outer mantle worn by Byzantine clerics over the *anterion. It is the ordinary outer dress of monks and secular clergy alike. The rason reaches to the ankles, laps from right to left as the anterion does, and among the Greeks is full cut and flowing with wide round sleeves. The Russians have narrower sleeves and a tighter cut. For monks and Greek secular clergy the color is invariably black, but Russian secular clergy sometimes use other colors. The rason closes at the collar with a button or hook, but is left open from that point down so that it is free-flowing. It is never girded in any way. The Russian form closes at the side with a button. In church at the offices or administration of sacraments the sacred vestments are worn directly over the rason.

[A. J. JACOPIN]

RASPUTIN, GRIGORIĬ EFIMOVICH (*c.*1871–1916), Russian religious enthusiast, advisor to the court of Tsar Nicholas II. R. came from a peasant family (surname, Novykh), married, and had four children, whom he left in order to adopt the role of a religious pilgrim. He joined the Khlysty sect, which combined mystical pantheism, ascetical extremities, and sexual license. The name Rasputin (debauched) began to be applied to him at this time, although he also came to be regarded as a faith healer. He was introduced to the royal family and seemed at first to be able to cure the hemophilia of the tsarevitch, Alexis. The empress Alexandra regarded him as a friend and savior of the royal family, and his influence in court grew to be extensive. But R.'s political capabilities were nil; he followed the advice of reactionary elements, and helped widen the breach between the royal family and the people. A group of nobles assassinated him in an effort to save the monarchy. BIBLIOGRAPHY: C. Wilson, *Rasputin and the Fall of the Romanovs* (1967).

[T. M. MCFADDEN]

RASSLER, CHRISTOPH (1654–1723), Jesuit moral theologian. R. taught at Ingolstadt and Dillingen from 1685 to 1716, when he was sent to Rome as revisor general of the Jesuits. He adopted a moderate position in the controversy over the rectitude of following a merely probable moral opinion, and is acknowledged as one of the earliest proponents of *equiprobabilism. His principal work is *Norma recti* (1713). BIBLIOGRAPHY: Sommervogel 6:1461–64.

[T. M. MCFADDEN]

RASTELL, John (1475–1536), English printer, brother-in-law of St. Thomas More. Under John Frith's influence he adopted Lutheran ideas, and campaigned against tithes. He died in prison. **William** (1508–65), English judge, printer, like his father, John. He published the controversial works of St. Thomas More. Exiled during the reign of Edward VI, he returned at Mary Tudor's accession, was made a judge of the Queen's bench (1558), and published More's *English Works* (1557). Exiled again under Elizabeth, at Louvain, he wrote a biography and published the Latin works of More.

[R. J. LITZ]

RASTISLAV (846–869), Moravian prince who succeeded Mojmir, the founder of Great Moravia. To counteract Frankish influence Rastislav sent an embassy to Constantinople in 862 requesting Byzantine missionaries for Moravia. Emperor Michael III dispatched SS. Cyril and Methodius who established Christianity first in Moravia and then among other Slavic peoples. BIBLIOGRAPHY: Z. R. Dittrich, *Christianity in Great Moravia* (1962).

[L. NEMEC]

RATHERIUS OF VERONA (c.890–974), Benedictine monk, theologian; bp. of Verona 931–968, of Liège 953–956. Although a scholar, reformer, and monk of Lobbes, Ratherius lacked the tact, patience, and humility that mark the true reformer. He managed to antagonize his fellow monks while receiving help from those in power. Accompanying his rejected abbot, Hilduin, to Verona, he succeeded him there as bp. but then lost the favor of Hugh of Provence, king of Italy, who had him imprisoned in Pavia and exiled (936–939) to Como. From there he returned to Lobbes, was recalled to Verona, and was again forced to flee (948). After campaigning with the sons of Emperor Otto I, he was made bp. of Liège by Abbot Bruno of Cologne, Otto's brother. Driven from Liège, he acted as abbot of Aulne-sur-Sambre (956), was recalled to Verona, finally giving up his see there (968) after more difficulties with his priests. He returned to Aulne and died on a visit to the count of Namur. As writer and theologian, his most important work is *Praeloquia*, a guide to right living. BIBLIOGRAPHY: J. N. Garvin, NCE 12:88–89.

[M. E. DUFFY]

RATIO FIDE ILLUSTRATA, literally, reason illumined by faith. This and similar expressions (e.g., *ratio fide informata;* see ThAq ST 1a2ae, 104.1 ad 3) are generally regarded as mottoes or principles of Augustinian and/or Thomistic inspiration. The term seems to designate (1) a greater vigor, finer insight, and thus a perfecting of human reason as graced by faith in contrast with reason in a nonbeliever; and/or (2) that unified complex of reason and faith enabling a believing person to be aided in his processes of reasoning both about matters of faith and reason by divine illumination (as in Augustine of Hippo), or by divine *concursus* (as in Thomas Aquinas). Basically, the expression seems to be metaphorical, expressing insights about the composite of faith and reason in terms of light (*lux*), or form (*forma*) of the hylomorphic theory. The phrase has a notable use in Vatican Council I's description of theological think-

ing (D 3016). BIBLIOGRAPHY: R. P. Russell, NCE 1:1063–71; J. A. Weisheipl, *ibid.* 14:126–135.

[E. A. MAZIARZ]

RATIO STUDIORUM, the abbr. title of the Jesuit educational manual (*Ratio atque Institutio Studiorum Societatis Jesu*) comprising a collection of practical educational guidelines for teachers, students, and administrators, in three curricular areas: letters (humanities, grammar, and rhetoric); arts (philosophy, science, mathematics); and theology. The Fourth Part of the Jesuit *Constitutions,* written by St. Ignatius himself and dealing with the training of Jesuits and with their schools, called for the eventual publication of such a work. After much experience and discussion a tentative version of the work was published in 1591 under the direction of Claudius Acquaviva, fifth general of the Society. A final and more polished version was issued in 1599. A revised edition of the *Ratio* appeared in 1832. It is at present undergoing intensive study and revision with a view to adapting it to contemporary needs. BIBLIOGRAPHY: St. Ignatuis and the Ratio Studiorum (ed. E. A. Fitzpatrick, 1933).

[M. B. MURPHY]

RATIONALISM, a trend or system that overstresses the role of reason, either in relation to sense observation (philosophical rationalism, opposed to empiricism and positivism), or in relation to faith. Rationalism in this latter sense exalts reason and its autonomy or sufficiency and gives it primacy in religious matters. As a trend rationalism has been confined to no particular period; as a system it is a phenomenon of modern times. Philosophical rationalism manifested itself in the systems of R. Descartes, B. Spinoza, and G. Leibniz in the 17th and 18th centuries. Religious rationalism as a trend underlies systems that reject the spiritual and religious, most conspicuously materialism and naturalism. In patristic times it appeared as one strand in the doctrine of *Pelagianism. In the Middle Ages it was present in Abelard's trinitarian teaching, and later was an element in the theology of *nominalism. Modern rationalistic systems strongly affirm the autonomy of reason and reject revelation and faith, or at least neutralize these by reducing them to the level of human thought. The way was opened to an overt relationship by the Renaissance, which introduced new modes of thinking and living. The movement toward the emancipation of reason that arose in 15thcent. Italy spread to other European countries. Rationalists, in fact, were the *libertins* of France who drew the fire of B. *Pascal. In England systematic rationalism took the name and form of *deism, which rejected faith as opposed to the supremacy it attributed to reason. T. Hobbes, M. Tindal, J. Locke, and D. Hume in the 18th cent. advocated a "natural" religion, freed from revelation and incompatible with belief in, worship of, or devotion to the God of faith. In Germany rationalism came to the fore in the *Enlightenment (*Aufklärung*), and Lessing, Goethe, and Schiller were at its service after Reimarus (d. 1768) attacked the whole of revelation. It culminated in Kant's *Religion within the Limits of Reason* (1793).

Among Roman Catholics the same trend led to the rise of the Order of *Illuminati in Bavaria (1776). To meet the onslaught of rationalism, RC theologians G. Hermes (d. 1831) and A. Günther (d. 1863) undertook to show that Christian dogmas known from revelation are open to rational proof, an effort later condemned as *semirationalism (D 2738, 2829, 3035–56). In France the leaders of rationalism were Voltaire (d. 1778) and J. J. Rousseau (d. 1778) and the men of the *Encyclopédie,* whose ideas also exercised a strong influence in Germany. In the 20th cent. rationalism was one of the diverse elements discernible in the heterogeneous body of thought in RC *modernism; it has also been an active force in Protestant modernism and *liberal theology. In the second half of the 20th cent. the current rationalism has little use for a "natural religion." At the root of atheistic, existentialist and materialist systems is a debased rationalism in which reason not only refuses to leave room for faith but also denies its own powers to construct a valid metaphysics. Thus the only option left is simply between God and no God. In the rethinking of dogma and the life of the Church after Vatican Council II there is a noticeable rationalistic trend on the part of some Roman Catholics in the sense of a denial of the supernatural and the mysterious. This appears to be associated with a general trend toward secularism. BIBLIOGRAPHY: A. W. Benn, *History of English Rationalism in the Nineteenth Century* (2 v., 1962); J. D. Collins, *God in Modern Philosophy* (1959); E. Cassirer, *Philosophy of the Enlightenment* (tr F. Koelln and J. Pettegrove, 1951).

[P. DeLETTER]

RATISBON, CONFERENCE OF, see REGENSBURG, CONFERENCE OF.

RATISBONNE, family name of two brothers, Jewish converts from Alsace, cofounders of the Congregation of Sion and the Fathers of Sion. The elder, **Marie Théodore** (1802–84), was converted to Catholicism after his study of the Bible and of church history. After ordination he established, with his brother, the two religious congregations for the work of converting Jews. Among his principal writings are: *Histoire de Saint Bernard et de son siècle* (2 v., 1840); *Nouvelle manuel de la mère chrétienne* (22d ed., 1926); *La question juive* (1868). **Marie Alphonse** (1812–84) was strongly anti-Catholic before his conversion at Rome, 1842, after a vision of the Blessed Virgin. Having founded the two religious congregations he carried on his convert apostolate in Palestine from 1855; there he established a convent and two orphanages.

[T. M. McFADDEN]

RATRAMNUS OF CORBIE (d. after 868), Benedictine of the abbey of Corbie, near Somme, France; theologian

whose Eucharistic teaching has been controverted. He was a pupil of *Paschasius Radbertus and a friend of *Gottschalk of Orbais. Of R.'s works (PL 121.9–346) three are esp. noteworthy. His *De praedestinatione* (850), written at the request of Charles the Bald, was against *Hincmar of Reims and follows Gottschalk in proposing a double predestination, but denies that God is the cause of evil. R.'s *Contra Graecorum opposita* (c.867), written at the request of Pope Nicholas I at the time of *Photius' revolt, contains an explanation of the *filioque, affirms the need for unity of faith along with diversity in usages and traditions between Greeks and Latins, defends clerical celibacy and the primacy of the pope. But R.'s most discussed work is *De corpore et sanguine Christi* (c.850), also written at the request of Charles the Bald. Against Paschasius' more realist explanation of the Eucharistic change and presence, R. proposed a spiritualized and more symbolic interpretation. The work, falsely ascribed to *John Scotus Erigena, and defended by *Berengarius of Tours, was condemned at a council at Vercelli in 1050; from the time of the Reformation until 1900 it was on the Index of Prohibited Books. During the Reformation controversies the work was edited by *Oecolampadius, and frequently translated, in support of the view that transubstantiation was an alien doctrine. Modern RC scholarship vindicates R.'s orthodoxy; he does affirm that there is a true change in the Eucharistic consecration, and the reality of Christ's Eucharistic presence. Impreciseness in language, as well as R.'s dialectic subtleties, however, make interpretation difficult.

[T. C. O'BRIEN]

RATTNER, ABRAHAM (1895–   ), American painter student in the U.S. and France (1920), influenced by G. Rouault whose intensity R. adopted. Returning to the U.S. R. expressed his outrage at the desolation of war in *The Emperor* (1940); in expressionist, jewel-like mysterious colors rooted in Romanesque, Byzantine, and Greek iconic designs reflecting a search for spiritual values (*Moses,* 1957). In 1956 R. designed tapestries and mosaics for Temple Tifereth Israel, Cleveland.

[M. J. DALY]

RATUM, NON CONSUMMATUM, sometimes expressed simply as *ratum,* designation of a valid marriage between two baptized persons, and as such sacramental, but in which marital intercourse has not occurred. "Marital intercourse" means complete, unimpeded intercourse subsequent to the marriage. The importance of the designation concerns the indissolubility of marriage. A *ratum* (i.e., sacramental) marriage that has been consummated can never be dissolved (CIC, c. 1118); a *ratum non consummatum* marriage is dissolved by law with the taking of solemn religious vows (the person making such vows would have had to receive permission of the Holy See to enter religious life), or by the dispensing power of the pope (*ibid.,* 1119). Cohabitation after marriage establishes the presumption of consummation; claim to nonconsummation requires a strong proof. As far as the point of dissolution is concerned, what holds for marriage between the baptized, holds also for marriage in which only one partner is baptized.

[T. C. O'BRIEN]

RAUS, JEAN-BAPTISTE (1881–1943), Redemptorist scholar. Born in Aspelt in the grand-duchy of Luxembourg, he was professed in 1901, ordained priest in 1906, and taught canon law, sociology, and history of philosophy at the scholasticate in Echternach. From 1924 until his death he was general archivist of his congregation in Rome. Of his 26 listed works, most are topical articles, more than a few of which concern various aspects of the religious vow of obedience. He edited the highly regarded manual of moral theology entitled *Institutiones morales alphonsianae,* written by his fellow Redemptorist, Clément Marc. The Raus version is exemplified in the 19th edition of the work published in Paris (2 v., 1934–35).

[E. J. DILLON]

RAUSCHEN, GERHARD (1854–1917), German patrologist and church historian. After studying at the Univ. of Bonn and Freiburg, R. became professor of church history at Bonn (1902). There he published a manual of patrology, which went through many editions, and produced studies on the Eucharist and penance in the early Church (1908). In 1904 he founded the series of patristic texts, *Florilegium patristicum,* for which he edited 11 works. BIBLIOGRAPHY: J. Quasten, NCE 12:94; H. Erharter, LTK 8:1017.

[R. B. ENO]

RAUSCHENBUSCH, WALTER (1861–1918), American Baptist theologian and architect of the *Social Gospel. He came from a family of German clergymen and prepared for the Baptist ministry at Rochester Theological Seminary, after studies in Germany and at the Univ. of Rochester. As a pastor in New York City (1886–97) he became deeply concerned with urban problems and joined with Christian Socialists and social reformers. R. accepted a call to the faculty of Rochester Theological Seminary in 1897 and taught there until his death. The publication of *Christianity and the Social Crisis* in 1907 established him as the recognized leader of the Social Gospel movement. Deeply and sincerely religious in its tone, the book pointed out the interest of the Hebrew prophets in the social and political life of their nation and the condition of the poor and oppressed. He saw Jesus as the founder of a new society embracing all human needs, powers, and relations and contrasted the social impotence of the contemporary Church with the social power of Christianity in the apostolic age. *Christianizing the Social Order* (1912) insisted upon social justice and economic democracy as minimum requirements for building a Christian social order. More than 20,000 copies of his short manual, *The Social Principles of Jesus,* were distributed by the YMCA alone during 1916. His lec-

tures at Yale Divinity School, *A Theology for the Social Gospel* (1917), discussed the social implications of sin and salvation and had the kingdom of God as its central theme. He saw the kingdom as a collective conception involving the whole social life of man. The solidarity of human society, whose progressive perfection would realize the divine kingdom of righteousness, was predicated on the indwelling of God in his world. The process of Christianizing society required the strengthening of its fraternal and cooperative elements and the rejection of its unchristian elements, e.g., competition, monopoly, the concentration of economic power, and the profit motive. BIBLIOGRAPHY: C. H. Hopkins, *Rise of the Social Gospel in American Protestantism* (1967).

[R. K. MacMASTER]

RAUSCHER, JOSEPH OTHMAR VON (1797–1875), prince abp. of Vienna from 1853, cardinal from 1855. Ordained in 1823, he taught philosophy at Salzburg from 1825. As religious adviser to the Austrian government from 1832 he negotiated the terms of the Jesuit ministry in Austria-Hungary. As bp. of Seckau (1849) he participated in the agreement abolishing *Josephinism and in drawing up the concordat of 1855. R. was against both the opportuneness and the doctrine itself of papal infallibility at Vatican Council I and was among the conciliar fathers who left Rome before the final vote on the decree. He did, however, in 1870 allow its publication in his diocese.

[T. C. O'BRIEN]

RAUTENSTRAUCH, FRANZ STEPHAN (1734–85), Benedictine theologian who contributed directly to the effectiveness of *Josephinism in the Austrian empire. He was a favorite of Maria Teresa, who forced the abp. of Prague to accept R.'s *Prolegomena in jus ecclesiasticum* (1769), a work the abp. had already condemned for its teaching that Church was subordinate to State. The empress also imposed (1776) as a syllabus for all Austrian ecclesiastical faculties R.'s *Synopsis juris ecclesiastici publici et privati* (1769), a work that suppressed principal points of church teaching, notably on the papal primacy.

[T. C. O'BRIEN]

RAVALLI, ANTONIO (1811–84), missionary, ranked second only to Pierre Jean De Smet as a missionary of the Northwest. R. was born and educated in Italy, entered the Society of Jesus, and was ordained in 1843. Volunteering for the U.S. missions, he reached Vancouver, Canada in 1844 and worked in the Kalispel Indian territory of what is now Montana and then among the Coeur d'Alènes of Idaho. Here he built a flour mill, sawmill and adorned the church he built with his own artistic wood carvings. R. had considerable skill in medicine and used it to advantage among the Indians. After 3 years as master of novices at Santa Clara College in California, he returned to Montana in 1863, where his ministry included Indians and whites of the newly developing mining towns and ranches. Even in old age, R. continued his arduous journeys and ministrations in an unsettled land.

[J. R. AHERNE]

RAVASCHIERI, BALTHASAR, BL. (1419–92), Franciscan. R. served as superior and vicar provincial of the Franciscans in Chiavari, except for many years as professor at Santa Maria del Campo Seminary in Binasco where he was known as a model religious and a good theologian. In 1478 he became acquainted with Bernardine of Feltre whose friend and associate in his missions he became until his activities were cut short by a crippling case of gout. In this condition he continued to perform works of the apostolate whenever he could. His exemplary life so attracted the attention of his associates that a cult developed after his death. In 1805 his relics were transferred to Pavia and in 1812 to the basilica. On Jan. 7, 1930 his cult was confirmed for the Franciscans and for the Diocese of Pavia and Genoa. BIBLIOGRAPHY: B. da Carasco, *Il beato Baldassare Ravaschieri* (1930); J. Cambell, NCE 12:96.

[J. J. SMITH]

RAVENNA, an ancient city in Emilia-Romagna in NE Italy highly important for its history and its art. Except for the fact that its name is certainly Etruscan, practically nothing is known of its origins. During the Late Roman Republic it became a *civitas foederata* and subsequently acquired the status of a *municipium* in 89 or 49 B.C.. Under Augustus it became the station for the Roman fleet on the Adriatic. In 402, because of its strong position between the sea on the E and marshes to the W, it was chosen by Honorius II as the capital of the West. In 540 it was captured by Belisarius and made the seat of the Byzantine exarchate until its capture by the Lombards in 751. In 1276 it was given by Rudolph I of Habsburg to the Holy See, and it remained a part of the Papal States with the exception of a few short intervals until 1859, when it was incorporated into the Kingdom of Italy. From the middle of the 2d to the beginning of the 5th cent., the episcopal see was at Classe, the harbor of the city, and was a suffragan of Milan. In 430 under St. *Peter Chrysologus, Ravenna itself became a metropolitan with jurisdiction over Forli, Faenza, Imola, Bologna, and Modena. Among the many treasures of early Christian art in Ravenna is the so-called Mausoleum of Galla Placidia (440–450). It is in the form of a Greek cross with vaulted ceilings and a dome at the center. The interior is decorated with magnificent mosaics, the most famous of which is that of Christ as the Good Shepherd. Another famous structure is the Baptistery, a converted Roman bath (449–452), with a mosaic portraying the baptism of Christ by St. John in the dome. The most famous churches are San Apollinare Nuovo, originally the Arian cathedral (c. 500), the octagonal church of San Vitale (547), and San Apollinare in Classe (549), near the ancient harbor. The art and architecture of Ravenna represent a fine blend of early Christian art with Eastern influences, and both in quantity and quality the city possesses a unique position in the world. BIBLIOGRAPHY: N. Tobias and A. Jacopin, NCE 12:96–102; B. S. Myers, *Ravenna Mosaics* (1962); W. L. MacDonald, *Early Christian and Byzantine Architecture* (1962).

[M. J. COSTELLOE]

RAVIGNAN, GUSTAVE FRANÇOIS XAVIER DE (1795–1858), Jesuit successor, from 1836, of H. D. *Lacordaire as preacher at Notre Dame de Paris. R. was a successful lawyer when he entered, first, the seminary at Issy, then the Society of Jesus in 1822. Ordained in 1828 he won a reputation for eloquent preaching both at Amiens and Paris. At Notre Dame he attracted immense congregations by his oratory and imposing presence, and won many converts from the intelligentsia of Paris. Besides his Lenten conferences, he also conducted Easter retreats and was much sought after as a spiritual guide. The *Conférences du R. P. Ravignan,* posthumously published in 1860, were notes taken during his conferences that he himself had edited. He also wrote in defense of the Society, *De l'existence et de l'institut des Jésuites* (1844), and, on the process that led to suppression by Clement XIV, studies bringing out strong evidence of anti-Jesuit machinations.

[T. C. O'BRIEN]

RAVOUX, AUGUSTIN (1815–1906), missionary. Born in France, as a student for the priesthood there he volunteered in 1838 for the missionary area of the upper Mississippi, directed by Bp. J. *Loras of Dubuque. Ordained at Dubuque in 1840, R. was sent in 1841 to explore the chances of a mission among the Sioux of the upper Mississippi. From 1841 to 1844 he worked among the Indians and half-breeds along the Minnesota River. Learning the language of the Dakotas, he published in 1843 a devotional work in their language, *The Path to the House of God.* From 1844 to 1851 R. was pastor of the extensive territory at the headwaters of the Mississippi. Two wide-ranging trips in the mid-1840s brought R. to the whites and Indians on the Missouri River. He also later ministered to the Sioux in Minnesota after the uprising of 1862. His influence led to the establishment of the diocese of St. Paul in 1851. He did much to build up the new diocese and was its vicar general under two bishops. R. published *Reminiscences, Memoirs and Lectures of Monsignor A. Ravoux* (1890) and the *Labors of Mgsr. A. Ravoux Among the Sioux or Dakota Indians . . .* (1897).

[J. R. AHERNE]

RAVY, JEAN (fl. 14th cent.), French sculptor, working on Notre-Dame, Paris (1318–46). Follower of Pierre de Chelles, R. finished the N portal, choir cornice and pillars, and cabinet reliefs.

[M. J. DALY]

RAYMOND OF AGILES (or Aguilers; fl. late 11th cent.), historian of the First Crusade. Author of the *Historia Francorum qui ceperunt Jerusalem,* a major source on the First Crusade, in which he was a participant, R. concentrates on the role of the count of Toulouse. The work has come under some questioning because of R.'s uncritical acceptance of the events surrounding the discovery of the Holy Lance. BIBLIOGRAPHY: S. Runciman, *History of the Crusades* (3 v., 1951–54) v. 1; M. W. Baldwin, NCE 12:103.

[V. BULLOUGH]

RAYMOND OF CAPUA, BL. (*c.* 1330–99), Dominican master general from 1380, spiritual director of St. *Catherine of Siena from 1374, religious reformer. R. worked with Catherine at Avignon in 1376 to bring about the return of Gregory XI to Rome and end the Avignon papacy. His *Legenda,* first published in 1477, was important to studies on St. Catherine's life and spirituality; he also wrote a biography of St. *Agnes of Montepulciano, a nun of the convent where he was spiritual director in 1363. As master general he instituted in 1390, after 10 years spent in visitation of the order, a return to primitive observance. R. was beatified in 1899.

[T. C. O'BRIEN]

RAYMOND OF FITERO, ST. (d. *c.* 1163), Cistercian abbot. Known in Spain as Raimondo Serra, he entered the newly founded (1137) Cistercian monastery of l'Escale-Dieu (France), but soon participated in the foundation (1140) of Fitero (Navarre), where he became abbot. With the aid of King Sancho III of Castile he founded (1158) the order of the Knights of Calatrava. BIBLIOGRAPHY: Butler 1:265; A. Romero, BiblSanct 11:11–12.

[L. J. LEKAI]

RAYMOND JOURDAIN IDIOTA (d. *c.* 1381), Canon Regular of St. Augustine and abbot of Selles-sur-Cher (Bourges). He wrote mystical works under the pseudonym Raymundus Idiota; identification of R. with Raymundus Idiota was made by T. Raynaud, SJ, who edited R.'s works. Previously their author was thought to be a 9th- or 10th-cent. writer. The works are *Contemplationes de miserabili cursu vitae praesentis* and *Contemplationes de amore divino;* they were first edited in 1569.

[T. C. O'BRIEN]

RAYMOND MARTINI (*c.* 1220–85), Dominican theologian. Professor in the Dominican Schools of Hebrew Studies, Barcelona, and of Arabic Studies, Tunis, R.'s best-known work is the apologetic work *Pugio fidei,* written in 1278 (Paris 1642, 1651; Leipzig 1687). The fullest account of him is A. Berthier in *Archivum Fratrum Praedicatorum* 6 (1936) 267–311.

[L. E. BOYLE]

RAYMOND NONNATUS, ST. (*c.* 1200–40), ransomer of Christian captives. His surname refers to his reputed birth by Caesarean section after his mother's death. He became a Mercedarian (*c.* 1224) and is credited with noteworthy activity in ransoming Christian captives in Moorish North Africa and Spain. The biographical details of his life are not well authenticated; the earliest extant *vita* was written long after his death. He is the patron of midwives, expectant mothers, and of the innocent charged with crime. BIBLIOGRAPHY: N. Del Re, BiblSanct 11:12–16; Butler 3:449–450.

[O. J. BLUM]

RAYMOND OF PEÑAFORT, ST. (*c.* 1180–1275), Dominican, canonist. A Catalan, R. studied and then taught law at Bologna before joining the Dominicans in Spain in 1222. After completing his most influential book, *Summa de casibus,* a systematic treatment of doctrinal and canonical questions for the guidance of confessors, R. was summoned to Rome. He held various curial offices until Pope Gregory IX directed him to prepare an authoritative collection of papal decretals, promulgated as the *Decretals of Gregorii IX.* From 1238 to 1240 R. was master general of the Dominicans. He spent most of his later years in Spain writing, preaching, and working against heresy and Islam.

[R. H. SCHMANDT]

RAYMOND OF RODA-BARBASTRO, ST. (d. 1126). He was prior of the monastery of St. Saturninus in Toulouse and then made bp. of Roda and Barbastro. In the political turmoil of the time he was driven from his see and, despite the intervention of Pope Paschal II, it was not restored to him. R. accompanied Alfonso I of Castile on his Cutanda campaign and his expedition to Malaga. He died at Huesca. His body was later transferred to Roda, and Barbastro was again placed under the jurisdiction of Roda. BIBLIOGRAPHY: M. R. P. McGuire, NCE 12:105–106; BHL 2:7074–78.

[M. R. P. McGUIRE]

RAYMOND OF SABUNDE (Sibiude, Sebond; d. 1436), Spanish theologian, author of *Theologia naturalis,* also called *Liber creaturarum,* a work of Neoplatonic inspiration, following *Raymond Lull. The Council of Trent put the prologue of the work on the Index because it obliterated the distinction between knowledge within reason's range and knowledge attainable solely through revelation. The skeptic Montaigne made a translation of R.'s work and wrote an *Apologie de R. R. Sebond.*

[T. C. O'BRIEN]

RAYMOND OF TOULOUSE, ST. (d. 1118), patron saint of Toulouse. After the early death of his wife, he devoted himself to charitable work and eventually became a regular canon at Saint-Sernin. He was noted for his generosity to the poor, for his establishment of a home for poor clerics, and esp. for rebuilding of the church of Saint-

Sernin, a famous place of pilgrimage during the Middle Ages. BIBLIOGRAPHY: P. Rouillard, BiblSanct 11:25–26; Butler 3:43.

[V. BULLOUGH]

RAYMOND OF TOULOUSE, name of several of the family of rulers of the countship of Toulouse.

Raymond IV (c. 1043–1105), founder of the Latin County of Tripoli in the Holy Land. In 1066 R. was marquis of Provence and in 1093 count of Toulouse. In 1096, R. set out for the Holy Land. After Antioch was captured (1098), he tried to gain control of that city for the Byzantine Emperor, Alexius I Comnenus, but was prevented by *Bohemund I. When the Crusaders took Jerusalem, R. was unable to establish himself there. Later he was allied with the Byzantines and escaped general massacre of the unsuccessful Crusade of 1101 and returned to Syria. There he took Tortosa, dying before the capture of Tripoli (1109).

Raymond of VI Toulouse (1156–1222), defender of Provence against the Albigensian Crusade. Early in his reign he settled a war begun by his father with Richard I, king of England. R. was excommunicated by Innocent III in 1207 for protecting the Albigenses or Cathari. After the assassination of a papal delegate, Peter de Castelnau, by one of R.'s officers, both the Albigenses and R. as their protector were attacked by a Crusade (1208). After the calamitous battle of Muret, R. went into exile. He tried to clear his name at Lateran Council IV but lost his lands, part of which he recovered later.

Raymond VII (1197–1249), last count of Toulouse, assisted his father in reconquest of his estates. New bands of Crusaders began to plunder the county of Toulouse, and soon R. lost all his strongholds. After the conference of Meaux (1229) he returned to Paris and there kept his promise to give his daughter, Jeanne, in marriage to Alphonsus of Poitiers, brother of King Louis IX, thus assuring that his remaining estates would be under the control of the French monarchy. BIBLIOGRAPHY: J. A. Brundage, NCE 12:106–107.

[M. C. BRADLEY]

RAYNAUD, THÉOPHILE (1583?–1663), French Jesuit, theologian. A Jesuit from 1602, ordained in 1613, he became professor of philosophy for 6 years and of theology for 8 at the Lyons Collège de la Trinité. In 1631 he was in Paris as confessor to Prince Maurice of Savoy, but displeased Card. Richelieu and returned to Lyons. There, except for a brief teaching assignment in Rome, he spent the remainder of his life, mostly in writing and editing his own works. These are marked by wide erudition, but with resources rather randomly quoted; by intemperate, biting language; by prolixity and digressions. Many of R.'s opuscula and short treatises contained in the posthumous *Opera omnia* (ed. J. Bertel, 19 v., 1665; v. 20, anonymously edited, 1669), were put on the Index at the time of their original publica-

tion, R. waged a constant literary war with the Inquisition, the system of prohibiting books, and violently attacked the Dominicans, who were in the majority in the Inquisition. He also was a violent opponent of the Dominicans in regard to the doctrine of grace. An anti-Dominican diatribe, published pseudonymously in 1662, caused the Jesuit general, J. P. Oliva, to disown the work; it was put on the Index and was publicly burned at Aix and Toulouse.

[T. C. O'BRIEN]

RAYONNANT STYLE, mid-13th- to early 14th-cent. decorative change of great refinement in Gothic style, evidenced in an increased window-area, delicate "radiating" tracery, a filigree as insubstantial as lace and openwork gables over portals (Reims, Amiens, Bourges). A handsome example is the Sainte-Chapelle, Paris (1243–48) with emphasis upon slenderness, extreme reduction of supports and dissolution of wall into stained-glass, an architecture of line and light.

[M. J. DALY]

RAZNOCHINTSY, literally, men of different classes. The term designates the new Russian intelligentsia of the 1860s and later, i.e., educated members of the middle and lower classes. The *raznochintsy* were radical nihilists, who opposed existing institutions; rationalists, who put their faith in science and enlightenment; socialists, who clamored for agrarian reforms. BIBLIOGRAPHY: E. Lampert, *Sons against Fathers* (1965) 85–93.

[M. F. MCCARTHY]

REACTION FORMATION, a psychological *defense mechanism first detected by *psychoanalysis by which a person represses (renders unconscious) one aspect of an ambivalent (love-hate) relationship and expresses usually in an exaggerated way the other aspect. Like all defense mechanisms, reaction formation operates unconsciously, as the *ego defends itself from acknowledging an unacceptable aspect of instinctual urges. Thus a person may develop attitudes of tenderness and affection to check and keep unconscious cruel and hostile impulses, or, conversely, develop attitudes of hostility to ward off affectionate impulses. Although morally neutral, because unconscious, the repressed aspects and the overcompensations of reaction formations represent immature attitudes and defects in self-knowledge.

[M. E. STOCK]

READ, HERBERT (1893–1968), English writer and art critic. Assistant at the Victoria and Albert Museums (1922–31), R. wrote about English stained glass, edited (1933–38) the world-circulated *Burlington Magazine*. A champion of modern art, relating it to society, R. philosophically evolved the theory of instinctual organic art, defending an autonomous, intuitive knowledge extending the area of consciousness. R.'s works include: *Meaning of*

Art (1931); *Philosophy of Modern Art* (1952) and monographs on H. Moore (1944), P. Klee (1948), and J. Arp (1968).

[M. J. DALY]

READER, a lay minister who assists at the liturgy by proclaiming the Scriptures and also by instructing the faithful in the meaning of the day's liturgy. With the office of acolyte, this is one of the two lay ministries universal in the Church since Paul VI's *motu proprio, Ministeria quaedam* (1972). A person becomes a reader not by ordination, as was the case prior to *Ministeria quaedam* when the office of reader was a minor order, but by a rite of "institution." Persons may exercise the function of reader without formal institution, but such institution is desirable so as to give proper expression to the permanence of this ministry in the life of the Church. *Ministeria quaedam* excludes women from institution as readers, but not from exercising the ministry.

READING, ABBEY OF, a reformed Benedictine monastery in Berkshire, England. Founded by Henry I in 1121, it became one of the richest and most important abbeys in England. Its first abbot was Hugh of Amiens, who was made abp. of Rouen in 1130. Reading had strong ties with Cluny, although it was not a member house; one of its abbots, Hugh II (1186–99) became abbot of Cluny. Known for its relics, i.e., the head of St. Philip, the abbey was the setting for many important marriages and meetings. The last abbot, Hugh Cook Faringdon, was executed for not accepting royal supremacy; the abbey was dissolved in 1539 and is now a ruin.

[M. A. MCFADDEN]

READING, SPIRITUAL, the nourishment of the mind and heart with material calculated to protect and increase the life of faith. Although the recent past thought of it as private, somewhat in the way Shakespeare's plays became "closet drama," present reform in the Church tends to return to the primitive practice of public performance by professional lectors for the benefit of listeners. The Church inherited from the synagogue a fundamental pattern of reading and prayer which was adapted for the Mass, other Sacraments, and the Office (Lk 4.16–22; Acts 13.27). Mental prayer as distinct from liturgy followed almost the same procedure beginning with *lectio divina* ("divine" reading) which was designed to provide material for the rumination of meditation. This arrangement is not merely fortuitous nor arbitrary; in fact, it answers the demands of sound psychology. But more than that, the primacy of reading corresponds to the very nature of the economy of salvation. God is the author of salvation; we receive his revelation when we hear or read his word. The psychology of belief, which is necessarily of unseen truths, requires as a practical corollary frequent, even daily, perusal of the divine message, esp. those ideas and ideals which are relevant to our present situation.

As preparation, if not proximate at least remote, for common celebration of the mystery of salvation as well as for the union of personal prayer, spiritual reading is essential.

The Bible of course keeps its pride of place as spiritual reading par excellence. Christ himself "starting with Moses and going through all the Prophets, explained to them the passages throughout the Scriptures that were about himself" so that "they said to each other, 'Did not our hearts burn within us as he talked to us on the road and explained the Scriptures to us?' " (Lk 24.27, 31). While the Church has never stopped reading and defending the OT, the Christian community was also assiduous in reading "the teaching of the Apostles" (Acts 2.42) esp. the words and deeds of Jesus in the Gospel. Still, reading the Bible from Genesis to Revelation is likely to be spiritually arid for long stretches unless there is some planned route to the centrality of the mystery of Christ. (cf. ThAq ST 2a2ae, 82.3 ad 2). Moreover what is best in itself may not even be good for this person in this situation; the material needs tailoring to the shape of the individual.

Thus the experience of the Church through the ages added even to the liturgy itself the homilies of the Fathers; their devout exegesis is preserved in *florilegia* and works such as Aquinas's *Catena aurea* which illumines each gospel verse with relevant patristic texts. Hagiography's preoccupation with the marvelous has made it less fruitful; brilliant exceptions such as the *Life* of Teresa of Ávila or Thérèse of Lisieux's *History of a Soul* show that the writings of saints are better than their legend. An entire genre of spiritual readings for beginners developed in the course of Church history; some like the *Imitation of Christ* have enjoyed a popularity second only to the Bible.

Since the Christian life is a business of constant conversion the dialogue between the Church and her Spouse, the Christian individual and Christ must ever reopen with a hearing of the Word (which implies reading) so that the Spirit may lead to complete truth (Jn 16.13–15). BIBLIOG - RAPHY: J. Leclercq, *Love of Learning and the Desire for God* (1961); P. Journel, "Bible in the Liturgy," *Liturgy and the Word of God* (ed. Martimort *et al.,* 1959); P. Philippe, "Mental Prayer in the Catholic Tradition," *Mental Prayer and Modern Life* (tr. F. C. Lehner, 1950).

[U. VOLL]

READING OF HEARTS, when authentic, a *charismatic gift of knowing the spiritual condition of another person or the secrets of hearts. It is a supernatural gift since only God has the power to know the mind and will of a person. This gift of spiritual clairvoyance is attributed to such saints as St. Catherine of Siena and St. John Vianney.

[T. C. O'BRIEN]

REAL PRESENCE, expression denoting an actual and literally true presence of Christ's body and blood in the bread and wine of the Eucharist or Lord's Supper. The RC

Council of Trent asserts that Christ's body and blood are really, truly, and substantially contained in the sacrament, and rejects a merely symbolic presence (see ZWINGLIANISM) or the *virtualism of John Calvin (D 883). The *Augsburg Confession (Art. X) of Lutheranism teaches that the body and blood of Christ are truly present and communicated to the recipients; the *Formula of Concord rejects the *Sacramentarians' interpretation of true presence as that of the spirit or power of the absent body of Christ, and affirms a "true and substantial presence" (Art. VII). Article XXVIII of the *Thirty-Nine Articles has received in the C of E and the *Anglican Communion both a symbolic and a realist interpretation. Not only the *Reformed Churches but all other non-Lutheran Protestant bodies reject the Real Presence. Those that recognize the Lord's Supper affirm a sacramental presence of Christ that is true, but either virtual or in some way figurative. The opposition to other teaching underlined by the word "real", then, is between the presence of the natural body of Christ and the presence of what is effected or symbolized by his body; or between a presence in and under the bread and wine of the sacrament and a presence evoked in the believer through faith and the sacramental symbolism.

The manner in which Christ's body and blood become really present is called in RC teaching *transubstantiation; this implies an abiding Real Presence (see TRANSIGNIFICA- TION). Lutherans, rejecting transubstantiation, assign the sacramental union itself as the reason for the Real Presence; and this presence is verified only in the actual celebration of the Lord's Supper (see CONSUBSTANTIATION). One Anglican form of expressing the manner of the Real Presence is called *receptionism.

REALISM, the philosophical position that the mind knows reality, not simply its own ideas or mental images. The term classifies a variety of epistemologies in the history of philosophy. The thought of Plato on the possibility of knowing truth may be viewed as an extreme realism. In order to establish a basis for certitude and truth, which the deceptiveness of the senses could not do, Plato postulated a world of separated Ideas: these are the real, subsistent prototypes of both the existents of experience and the ideas in the human mind. Aristotle parted with Plato on this point, preferring to affirm the power of thought to attain certitude by its grasp of the natures of existent material beings. In the medieval problem of *universals, those who affirmed that the universal as such has real existence opposed the opposite extreme position of the early nominalists, that the universal is simply a mental collective, with no counterpart in the actual world. St. Thomas Aquinas and other "high scholastics" adopted a moderate realism, i.e., that the universal as such exists only in thought, but that its foundation is in the real nature of sensible beings. The later medieval nominalists (conceptualists or terminists) rejected this stand, and kept "contact" with the real by asserting an

intellectual intuition of the singular as such (see WILLIAM OCKHAM).

In modern philosophy, beginning with Descartes, the general starting point of epistemology has been that the object of intellectual knowledge is the idea; the insoluble problem then becomes a vindication of the reference of the idea to the real. Realism, an epistemological view that the referent of knowledge is the real existent, not a mental image or affect, is a minority position. See *EPISTEMOLOGY; *IDEALISM.

[T. C. O'BRIEN]

REALISM, AMERICAN. Realism developed as a movement in America in the early 20th cent. as a reaction against the idealism of Josiah Royce. It initially involved a group of six American philosophers: R. B. Perry, W. P. Montague, E. B. Holt, W. B. Pitkin, E. G. Spaulding, and W. T. Marvin. In 1910, these men published "The Program and First Platform of Six Realists" in *The Journal of Philosophy* (7, no. 15 [1910] 393–401), which was intended as a general statement of their position and the beginning of a realistic trend in American philosophy. The six men agreed on about five points. (1) That which is known is not dependent upon its being known for its existence. (2) The alteration of a relation existing among things does not necessarily imply the alteration of other existing relations. Thus, the ignorance or discovery of some relations does not invalidate a limited knowledge of relations. (3) Subjects and objects belong to the same order of nature and therefore there is nothing transcendental about cognition. The difference between subjects and objects is one of function and not one of substance. (4) The scope and extent of consciousness within nature is a matter for empirical observation and not logical deduction. (5) Some real things are apprehended directly by consciousness, rather than through representational copies.

In order to further their cause, these six coauthored a collection of essays entitled *The New Realism* (1912). The book was not well received; the group published nothing more cooperatively, and the movement dissolved shortly thereafter.

It was followed by a movement toward "critical realism," led by R. W. Sellars, who authored *Critical Realism* (1916). Sellars' position differed substantially from that of the new realists only insofar as he denied the possibility of immediate knowledge of things and substituted the notion of the knowledge of a percept which is causally related to a thing. He maintained that there was no strictly defined line between perception and conception. BIBLIOG- RAPHY: H. W. Schneider, *Sources of Contemporary Philosophical Realism in America* (1964).

[F. J. CUNNINGHAM]

REALSCHULE, a general term indicating the modern German secondary school in which science, mathematics, and modern languages are emphasized in lieu of the classical studies of the *Gymnasium*. The term was first used in 1739 by Christopher Semler, a professor at Halle University. The terrain for the *Realschulen* was prepared by the pietist, August Francke (1663–1727) who established secondary schools in which both modern sciences were taught together with religious and humanistic studies. It was one of Francke's students, Julius Hecker, who in 1747 founded the first *Realschule*. BIBLIOGRAPHY: W. K. Medlin, *History of Educational Ideas in the West* (1964).

[M. B. MURPHY]

REASON, AGE OF, the time of life at which a person is capable of discerning between moral right and wrong. (1) In canon law at the age of reason or "discretion" the faithful incur the obligation of receiving the Eucharist during the paschal season (c. 859, §1), and consequently of preparation, in the case of grave sin, through reception of the sacrament of penance (c. 906). It is a general norm of law, as well, that no ecclesiastical obligation binds before the age of 7 years (c. 12). The canonical and pastoral determinations concerning the time of first reception of the Eucharist have received special recent attention (see FIRST COMMUNION). (2) In moral theology the more general issue of moral *responsibility governs the meaning of the age of reason (see REASON, USE OF).

[T. C. O'BRIEN]

REASON, CULT OF THE GODDESS OF, a fanatical attempt to substitute a revolutionary "religion" for traditional Christianity during the French Revolution. As part of the de-Christianization movement some of the deputies including Fouché, Chaumette, procurator of the Paris commune, and the radical Hébert converted churches into "temples of reason," persecuted clergy, and demonstrated against Christianity, esp. Catholicism. The movement culminated in the festival of Liberty at Notre Dame Cathedral Nov. 10, 1793, celebrating the victory of Philosophy over Religion. Integrated with the patriotic cult of the martyrs of Liberty (Marat, Lepeletier, Chalier), the undefined deistic (perhaps atheistic) "religion of reason" found many partisans. The executive Committee of Public Safety, fearing the cult and the consequent opposition from the bourgeoisie and Catholics, reacted promptly. On Nov. 21 Robespierre espoused religious liberty; Chaumette and the Commune followed. On Dec. 8 the National Convention adopted a policy of religion. In May 1794, after the purge of the radical Hébertists, Robespierre introduced his short-lived cult of the Supreme Being, also a deistic belief; religious freedom was not again spelled out until Sept. 29, 1795. BIBLIOGRAPHY: F.V.A. Aulard, *Christianity and the French Revolution* (1966); A. Soboul, "Religious Sentiment and Popular Cults during the Revolution: Patriot Saints and Martyrs of Liberty," *New Perspectives on the French Revolution:*

Readings in Historical Sociology (ed. J. Kaplow, 1965) 338–350.

[R. J. MARAS]

REASON, USE OF, in moral theology the capability of discerning between moral right and wrong; the power to apply this discernment in a particular moral choice. (1) The point at which the use of reason begins is the point at which moral life begins. That need not coincide with the norm of canon law that only at the age of 7 years do ecclesiastical laws bind. The morally good act is a positive choice of a moral good; its objective is the "good-as-meant," and the objective of the wrong moral choice, the "lack-of-good-as-meant" (see T. Gilby). Moral discernment is the power to recognize and intend the moral good; only where that is present can there be a choice that falls short of a good that could and should have been chosen. St. Thomas Aquinas (ST 1a2ae, 89.6) offers an abstract outline of an initial act of moral discernment. The act is a concrete choice of some good, perceived in its value to the natural bent of the will upon the human good. Discernment is involved because the evaluation means a recognition of self in comparison to what is truly perfective; a good choice requires a consciousness of self as not absolute but as related to perfective goals, and of self as human, not simply as a bodily being. That consciousness sets the possibility of meaning the good or failing to do so. The manner and degree in which moral discernment dawns necessarily vary with each individual; it obviously presupposes a process of maturing. The only generalization possible is that moral discernment must begin at some point, or else the human being never becomes a responsible moral agent. (2) The same kind of moral discernment is required in every truly moral choice. The use of reason is one indicator of responsibility; diminution lessens responsibility (see FEAR; FORCE; IGNORANCE; VOLUNTARINESS). BIBLIOGRAPHY: ThAq ST Lat-Eng (v. 18, ed. T. Gilby) app. 10, "The Form of Moral Good"; (v. 27, ed. T.C. O'Brien) app. 4, "Question 89.6: a Commentary."

[T. C. O'BRIEN]

REASONING, THEOLOGICAL, the endeavor to define the truths of revelation and to analyze their content. Though human reason could not itself discover these mysteries of faith, it can progressively expound the Church's understanding of them as revealed. Vatican Council I teaches that reason "enlightened by faith . . . attains by a gift from God some understanding, and that very fruitful, of mysteries; partly from the analogy of those things which it naturally knows, partly from the relations the mysteries bear to one another" (D 3016). Scripture speaks in concrete rather than general terms, and it is theology's task to proceed, for instance, from the revelation that Christians are to believe that Jesus is the Son of God to inquiries concerning the nature of belief and the mystery of divine sonship. Further, theology aided by philosophy can organize articles of faith into an orderly system. This work advances from basic definitions to analysis, classification, and distinction, so as to bring order into the body of revelation and into the Christian life built upon it. Philosophical concepts must be adapted to the special uses of theology, e.g., the notions of substance and accident as applied to explain the Eucharist, and the notions of person and nature as applied to the Incarnation and the Trinity. Theological reasoning has as a norm the analogy of faith, i.e., the harmony of revealed truths with one another so that specific interpretations may not be contradictory but in agreement with the whole deposit of revealed truth (D 3887). BIBLIOGRAPHY: M. D. Chenu, *Is Theology a Science?* (tr. A. H. N. Green-Armytage, 1959).

[W. DAVISH]

REBAPTISM, the practice of repeating baptism; the subject of controversy (255–257) between St. Cyprian of Carthage and Pope Stephen I and again in the Reformation era. Cyprian's view, endorsed by three synods of African bps., was that heretics or schismatics could not validly administer the sacraments of the Church. Accordingly, those who had received Novatianist baptism had to be rebaptized in order to be received into the Church. The Pope insisted that the practice of the Roman Church recognized baptism by heretics or schismatics as valid (see D 110). Cyprian accused Stephen of subverting church unity. The actual controversy remained unresolved, but the Roman view prevailed in practice and became universal. The controversy has often been an issue in discussions of the primacy of the pope. Rebaptism also is connected with the view of the *Anabaptists (rebaptizers). They did not consider *believer's baptism to be a repetition, however. Their view was that infant baptism is meaningless; baptism can only be received by one who has personally experienced faith and conversion; the baptism is simply and exclusively the outward profession of the inner experience. They were called rebaptizers because those who became Anabaptists and received believer's baptism had already received "water baptism."

In RC practice, the administration of the sacrament of baptism to someone who has been previously validly baptized, even though the baptism was conferred by a heretic or unbeliever, is not permitted. If, however, the invalidity of the earlier baptism is certain, rebaptism is necessary. In cases of doubt concerning the validity of the earlier baptism, baptism should be administered conditionally. Ecumenical considerations, and other reasons also, militate against conditional rebaptism in cases in which investigation shows that baptism has been validly administered. The sacrament imprints a character on the soul; this is the theological basis for its being deemed unrepeatable, a fact defined by the Council of Trent (D 1609). Before Trent and since, the Church has in its official declarations emphasized the same point (e.g., D 110, CIC c. 732). Vatican II gives this teaching a more positive meaning, the recognition of the ecclesial realities in other Christian Churches (Vat II ConstChurch 14); this in turn is reflected in the simple rite of receiving baptized Christians into full communion with the Catholic Church.

[T. C. O'BRIEN]

REBEKAH (Rebecca), wife of Isaac and mother of Esau and Jacob (Gen 25.20–26). She was the daughter of Bethuel, Abraham's nephew (Gen 22.20–23). Her courtesy at the well won the attention of Abraham's servant, who had been sent to find a wife for Isaac (Gen 24). She was instrumental in Jacob's supplanting his elder brother Esau (Gen 25.28; 27).

[T. EARLY]

REBELLION, active resistance to authority, either of a people against a political regime, or of private person against superiors. (1) Political rebellion can be considered with respect both to civil obedience and to charity. The term "rebellion" in its political meaning usually connotes forceful resistance to an usurped or tyrannically exercised ruling power ("revolution" has the further implication of effecting change in a social and economic system). Since civil obedience is owed only to just laws and to legitimately constituted and exercised authority, rebellion is morally justified in itself (ThAq ST 42.2 ad 3); in concrete circumstances, however, it may not be morally right. Where odds against overthrowing a tyrannical regime are hopeless, rebellion would be rash, against *prudence. Where the good of most citizens, i.e., the public or common good, would not be served by rebellion, violent resistance would be contrary to *legal justice. Since charity has peace as its effect, rebellion to be right must also serve the end of charity towards neighbor. It can do so by creating conditions of justice, without which conflict arises among men; in rightly pursuing such an aim, however, rebellion must truly contribute to the total good of the community, temporal and spiritual; where it would cause harm greater than the evils it seeks to remedy, it would be a wrong course. From these considerations, rebellion manifestly differs from *sedition—a purely political coup, promoting the self-interest of a faction against a legitimate government at the expense of social unity and peace. (2) Rebellion has come also to describe the private, personal resistance of youth against authority in the home, Church, school, and against social convention and tradition. In an abstract evaluation such resistance seems to be *disobedience in its strongest sense as contempt for persons in authority and for what they command or commend. Concretely, however, youthful rebellion of this kind may not be fully culpable. Permissiveness is often given as its cause. But permissiveness itself has a deeper cause, a lack of conviction and nerve with respect to the values the exercise of authority is meant to serve and to foster. That in turn indicates a further moral impoverishment, a lack of *piety as this means loyalty not only to a bloodline, but to a heritage, intellectual, spiritual, social, political, and humane. For those in authority, piety is not subservience to the past as such, but a recognition of what the past positively contributes to the present level and meaning of life. It implies a willingness of elders to act as elders, to accept their position, no matter their feelings of personal inadequacy, as transmitters of values. They stand for such values *ex officio;* they need the conviction that the values are not formalisms, but were developed out of the experience of need to enhance human life. That antidote to permissiveness may lead the young to recognize their own identity to be that of heirs, rather than of destructive rebels.

[T. C. O'BRIEN]

REBIRTH, being born again to life in Christ. Nothing is more certain for man than death. Yet his thirst for immortality has always been the mainspring of his religious thought and activity. Among the ancients cosmogonic myth as well as the interpretation of natural phenomena like the waxing and waning of the seasons, lunar phases, and animal oestrous cycles, fanned the spark of hope in an afterlife. The earth became a sacrament and its seasonal changes the archetypes of primitive ritual. Man sought identification with his gods by dramatizing the never-ending Paschal cycle of their rising and falling in nature. So he tried to solve the mystery of his own existence and to secure for himself an immortality like that of the gods. Baal myth from the Ras Shamra texts as well as carbon-cycle theory point to the same fact: life feeds upon death. Rebirth is possible only for those who have died.

Christian belief in rebirth is founded upon the Gospel: No one can see the kingdom of God without being begotten from above (Jn 3.3). Life from above is described as emanating from water and the Spirit of God. To the peoples of the ancient Middle East water was a ritual symbol of both life and death. Swimming was uncommon. A person immersed in water was as good as dead. Yet in the ubiquitous arid regions water brought new life both to man and the crops that sustained him. By being immersed in water and rising from it, by acting them out in typical Hebrew fashion, the Christian initiate symbolized both his own future as well as Christ's past death and Resurrection. Acting out the Paschal mystery brought death to his old self and made him an image of the God-Man. The ritual assured identity with the immortal one. In the Eucharistic Meal this identity was once again proclaimed. The gifts of the community, representing its very life, sustained as it was by food and drink, were converted into the body and blood of the dead and risen Christ. When the sacred elements were introjected at communion time the believer was reminded that he was flesh of Christ's flesh and blood of His blood. The Paschal mystery in which he had been reborn was renewed in the here and now.

Catacombs abound in references to Christian belief in rebirth. The Fathers of the Church also bear vibrant witness to the Paschal mystery. Cyril of Jerusalem tells Christians: "At the same identical moment you died and were born. The saving water was both your grave and your mother. For you . . . the time to die was the time to be reborn. Your

birth went hand in hand with your death" (*Catech. Myst.* 2.4; PG 33:1080–81). BIBLIOGRAPHY: M. Eliade, *Rites and Symbols of Initiation: the Mysteries of Birth and Rebirth* (tr. W. Trask, 1958); C. Davis, *Making of a Christian* (1964).

[C. R. MEYER]

RECAPITULATION, a theological term. In general the word means to go over again concisely; to give the headings of what has already been treated; to sum up. The notion of recapitulation is verified not only in logic and in human utterance but also in divine things. The idea is found in the sources or revelation and is developed in theology. In Christology and a soteriology not completely distinguished from it, recapitulation (*anakephalaiōsis*) is a theme first enunciated by St. Paul in Eph 1.10: "And this his good pleasure he purposed in him to be dispensed in the fullness of the times: to reestablish [recapitulate] all things in Christ, both those in the heavens and those on earth." The use of recapitulate in this sense is rare in English, but it means "to bring together again; to sum up or unite in one" (OED 8:228). The meaning of Rom 13.9, the only other place the word is used in the NT, has some relation to the above, but the sense of Rom 13.9 is in reference to the logic of including particular commands in those more general. Ephesians 1.10 may anticipate a mention in 1.22 of Christ as head.

St. Irenaeus (d. 202) took up this theme and explains that as all creation fell in Adam, so all creation is taken up again, restored, renewed, and reorganized in Christ, in whom time reaches its high point. What had fallen, and not something else, was saved by Christ, man's new and spiritual head. Recapitulation as taught by Irenaeus had both its moral and physical aspects, as this distinction is made in soteriological theory. That is, Christ recapitulated both by what he was and what he did, by his being and by his acts. To understand such recapitulation one must recognize how Irenaeus based it on the solidarity of the human race both with Adam and Christ. As Adam in a sense summed up the whole human race, so did Christ, as in a closed unit, human flesh fell, and Human Flesh redeemed. That flesh in Adam came from the virgin soil; in Christ it came from the Virgin Mother. Christ by obeying offset Adam, who disobeyed; Christ by resisting temptation offset Adam, who yielded; Christ by dying on the 6th day of the week offset Adam, who sinned on the 6th day of Creation; and so on. Adam was the head; Christ was the new head, the recapitulator, and the unifying antithesis of Adam in many particulars. Not only that: by shedding his blood Christ recapitulated the shedding of the blood of all the righteous. Finally, as Christ the head arose from the grave, so will all the members of his body. However, since Christ existed before the world and since in him all things were created, there is a sense in which he was head of all creation, animate and inanimate, before he ever entered it. Recapitulation being a keystone of Irenaeus' theology, it is likewise reflected in his Mariology. Justin rather than Irenaeus was the first to draw the parallelism between Eve and Mary, but Irenaeus extended it. Mary by doing the will of God and performing in her life acts that counterbalanced those of Eve, becomes the new Mother of mankind. Eve, still a virgin, disobeyed, and was the cause of the death of herself and all her children; Mary, still a virgin, obeyed and thus became a cause of salvation for herself and all mankind. The key role Irenaeus gives to Mary in salvation history is a dramatic, early, and long step forward in the development of Mariology.

In some patristic Trinitarian theology recapitulation (here *synkephalaiōsis*) is the description of that aspect of the unity in the Holy Trinity whereby what the Father has is communicated to the Son and with him to the Holy Spirit without substantial division. Son and Spirit are consubstantial with the Father, who, thus, as the *First* Person and source of the other two, recapitulates the whole Trinity. There is a sense in which the Son and Spirit are in the Father and summed up in him; as the Second and Third Person come from him, so they can in a sense be reduced to him, i.e., recapitulated in him. So, at least, one finds in Dionysius of Alexandria: ''. . . and [so] again we recapitulate the Trinity, which cannot be diminished, in the unity [the Father]'' (cited by Athanasius, *Dion.* 16–17; PG 25:504–505, cf. 477–478; ed. H. G. Opitz 2.1:58). Other early ecclesiastical writers also explored or touched on the theology of recapitulation, e.g., Hippolytus, Ambrose, and Augustine; but since once suggested it naturally lends itself to development, it is found in a great deal of the patristic soteriology: oddly enough, the notion was not widely developed among the scholastics. In modern times the thought of Pierre Teilhard de Chardin has found a resonance in the concept of recapitulation—in his speculations stimulated and fed by his interest in evolution. The Omega Point toward which man moves is in fact Jesus Christ, in whom all creation, material and spiritual, finds a unity. BIBLIOGRAPHY: H. Schlier, Kittel TD 3:673–682; Lampe 1:1060; J. I. Hochban, ThSt 7 (1946) 525–557.

[E. A. WEIS]

RECCARED (Recared; d. 601), Visigothic **KING OF SPAIN** from 586. Brought up with his brother *Hermenegild in Arianism, R. succeeded his father Leovigild as king because death had removed Hermenegild from the scene in 585. In the first year of his reign R. was converted to the Catholic faith, and through the efforts of *Leander, abp. of Seville, a great number of the Arian clergy, nobles, and people followed his example. He called the third Council of Toledo (589) which, together with the series of local councils that followed, helped establish and solidify the Catholic ascendancy in Spain. BIBLIOGRAPHY: Bihlmeyer-Tüchle 1:225.

[R. B. ENO]

RECCESWINTH, VOTIVE CROWN OF, devotional crown of pierced goldwork and large gems, with jewelled letters hanging from the lower rim to form the words *Rec-*

ceswinthus Rex offert. Recceswinth (649–672) was one of the most important Visigothic kings of Spain. This crown and that of King Swintila (621–31) belong to the famous treasure of Guarazzar (near Toledo) found in 1858. The technique is Byzantine but they are barbarian in form and in stones cut *en cabochon* and filigree *cloisons*. The treasure is now in the Madrid Archeological Museum. BIBLIOGRAPHY: *Dark Ages* (ed. D. Talbot-Rice, 1965).

[R. C. MARKS]

RECEPTIONISM, a term invented for the theory of certain 19th-cent. Anglican theologians that in the Holy Eucharist the communicant really receives the body and blood of the Lord along with the bread and wine, which remain unchanged. The teaching of M. *Bucer in the 16th cent., an attempt to mediate between Lutheran and Zwinglian doctrine, was similar. *REAL PRESENCE; *TRANSUBSTANTIATION.

[T. C. O'BRIEN]

RECHABITES, group commended by Jeremiah for loyalty to their traditions in contrast to the disloyalty of the people of Judah to Yahweh (Jer ch. 35). For religious reasons, presumably in protest against the Canaanites' settled way of life, they were nomads, lived in tents, and had no vineyards or fields (see NAZIRITES). Their origin is obscure. Hammath is listed as father of the house of Rechab (1 Chr 2.55). The Rechabites associated with Jeremiah had come to Jerusalem out of fear of Nebuchadnezzar. Jehonadab, son of Rechab, supported Jehu (2 Kg 10.15). Existence of Rechabites has been reported up to modern times.

[T. EARLY]

RECIDIVISM, in Catholic theology, the state of a penitent who has the same sin to confess again and again, when the repetition can be explained only as a consequence of an insincere or substantially defective *purpose of amendment. The recidivist is not the same as a habitual sinner, though both repeatedly commit the same sin. What distinguishes them is that the habitual sinner has, at the time he makes his confession, a sincere intention to mend his ways, while the recidivist lacks such an intention. Repeated lapses may cause the confessor to suspect the penitent may be a recidivist, but he will recognize the possibility that other factors, such as youth, frailty, unavoidable temptations, human inconstancy, rather than the want of a sincere purpose of amendment, may account for the repetition of the sin. It is inadvisable to deny absolution unless it is beyond doubt that the penitent has no real intention to make an effort to avoid his sin. BIBLIOGRAPHY: N. Halligan, *Administration of the Sacraments* (1963); P. F. Mulhern, NCE 12:127–128.

[P. K. MEAGHER]

RECIPROCITY, in connection with ecumenism, signifies generally a mutual and equal exchange between two parties and has taken on a specialized meaning in the contemporary ecumenical movement as a principle governing the give and take of dialogue, common prayer, and sacramental sharing between ecclesial groups. The following documents illustrate the growth of understanding among Roman Catholics and the current use of the term. Vatican Council II's *Decree on Ecumenism* (n. 9) urged that a mutual knowledge among those separated be pursued through dialogues "where each can deal with the other on an equal footing (*par cum pari*)." The *Interim Guidelines,* established by the U.S. Bishops Commission for Ecumenical Affairs in 1965, appealed to reciprocity as a principle that should guide those preparing and conducting common prayer services. To offer an invitation implies a readiness to accept one; to accept an invitation implies a willingness to extend one. Joint action is discouraged unless there can be reciprocity.

The *Directory* (1967) of the Secretariat for Promoting Christian Unity appealed to this principle as necessary to the growth of mutual goodwill, charity and harmony among Christians (n. 27). Reciprocity was also interpreted (n. 43) as a norm of limiting mutual sacramental activity, e.g., Catholics were not allowed to read scriptural lessons or preach at the official services of other Churches since other church members or ministers were not to be allowed to preach in Catholic liturgical services.

The basis for the principle of reciprocity may be interpreted superficially as a kind of civil and church etiquette. Its more substantial foundation lies in an ecumenical theology of mutual recognition of churchliness, of members and ministers. The degree of reciprocity possible in ecumenical action indicates practically the degree to which any two or more ecclesial groups are able theologically to recognize the equality and mutuality between them. Practical norms of reciprocity then are relative and changeable according to the degree of growth in mutual recognition and sacramental fellowship between Churches.

At a meeting of NCCB, Nov. 15–19, 1971, the proposal of pulpit exchange was voted down, 152 to 81. This resolution to ask for restudy of a general prohibition *v.* pulpit exchanges by priests and ministers at full liturgical celebrations such as Mass and Protestant Eucharistic services was vetoed; but the veto does not preclude permission already granted for bishops to permit pulpit exchanges in particular cases, esp. in less formal prayer services.

[L. B. GUILLOT]

RECOLLECTION, a concentration of one's powers on God or things pertaining to him so that one is able to live constantly in his presence. Recollection is one of the interior means of striving for perfection, according to the scriptural injunction: "Walk in my presence and be perfect" (Gen 17.1). It requires, first, that one eliminate all voluntary distractions from the awareness of God's presence and that one use supernatural motivation and virtual intention to preserve recollection even when full attention must be given to other affairs, such as duties of one's state, association with others or the needs of life. Secondly, although no one can give

continual attention to God and the things of God, the practice of recollection enables one to see God in all things. The reason for this is that God is actually present to all creatures by his causal presence of immensity, since he creates, conserves, and activates them, and all things are present to his knowledge and power. Moreover, God is present in a special and supernatural way through sanctifying grace, which is a participation in the divine life and nature; therefore, the souls of the just can use interior recollection in order to intensify their union with God, who dwells in them through grace (The kingdom of heaven is within you). St. Francis de Sales teaches that interior recollection, accompanied by devout ejaculations, can supply for any pious practice, but its absence cannot be remedied by any other (cf. *Introduction to the Devout Life,* 2.13). The value of the practice of recollection is evident from its consequences in the spiritual life: it removes us from numerous occasions of sin and temptation; it prompts us to avoid even light sins; it is an incentive to do all things with the greatest possible perfection; it cultivates Christian modesty of deportment; it disposes for the devotion necessary for prayer; it prevents many failings in charity against our neighbor; it nourishes the supernatural motive, which is necessary for meritorious good works. BIBLIOGRAPHY: St. Teresa of Avila, *Way of Perfection; Interior Castle* (tr. E. A. Peers, 1946); A. Royo, *Theology of Christian Perfection* (tr. and ed. J. Aumann, 1962); G. Lercaro, *Methods of Mental Prayer* (tr. T. F. Lindsay, 1957).

[J. AUMANN]

RECOLLECTION, DAY OF, see DAY OF RECOLLECTION.

RECOLLECTS (AUGUSTINIAN), see AUGUSTINIAN RECOLLECTS.

RECONCILIATION (Gr. *katallagē, katallāssein*), the image used particularly in the Pauline writings of the NT to describe the restoration of man and the world from a state of estrangement to the status of friendship with God and his fellowman through the death of Jesus Christ. In secular usage reconciliation denotes a change of relationship between individual persons or groups of persons, a change from anger, hatred, or hostility to love, friendship, intimacy (cf. Jg 19.2–3; Mt 5.23–24; 1 Cor 7.11). While reconciliation in the theology of St. Paul may be understood as atonement (at-one-ment), it should not be confused with expiation, the wiping away of man's sins by Christ who is the new mercy seat (Rom 3.25) and has, practically speaking, nothing to do with propitiation, the appeasing of an angry God by rites and sacrifices. In the OT God revealed himself as the initiator of forgiveness for his errant people (Ex 34.6–7), as the one who restrains his anger (Ps 85.4; 103.8–12) and speaks of peace to his people (Ps 85.9–10), and who through the Prophets promises a new and eternal covenant (Jer 31.31–34; Ezek 36.26–33). In NT reconciliation God is always the subject, and man or the world the object (cf. 2 Macc 1.5; 7.33; 8.29). God has brought about the definitive reconciliation of mankind through the Passion, Death, and Resurrection of his Son Jesus Christ. Man has objectively been restored to a state of peace and union with the Father after a period of estrangement and rebellion through sin and transgression (Rom 1.18–3.20; 5.10). Paul tends to associate the figure of reconciliation with the death of Christ (Rom 5.10) or sometimes more specifically with the blood of Christ (Col 1.19–20; Eph 2.13). By the gratuitous action of Christ Jesus the sinner once again has access to the presence of God, is introduced once again into the royal court of God himself (Rom 5.2). Christ has become our "peace" (Eph 2.14), because he has broken down the wall of separation between Jews and Greeks and abolished the Law's commandments. He has made "one new man" from both and has reconciled them to God in one body (Eph 2.15–16). Through his cross hostility has come to an end, and Christ has brought "peace" to men (Rom 5.1; 2 Th 3.16; Gal 5.22; Phil 4.7; 1 Cor 7.15; Rom 14.17; Col 3.15). Moreover this reconciliation is cosmic (2 Cor 5.19) embracing "all things whether on earth or in heaven" (Col 1.20–21). Individual persons participate in the reconciling work of Christ through accepting the gift of faith and baptism and sharing in the life of the Church, whose mission to the world may be described as a "ministry of reconciliation" (2 Cor 5.18). BIBLIOGRAPHY: J. Dupont, *La réconciliation dans la théologie de Saint Paul* (1951); J. Fitzmyer, *Pauline Theology* (1966) 43–44; *idem,* "Reconciliation in Pauline Theology," *No Famine in the Land* (ed. J. Flanagan, 1975) 155–177; V. Taylor, *Forgiveness and Reconciliation* (1948) 70–108; D. E. H. Whiteley, *Theology of St. Paul* (1964) 130–154.

[T. J. RYAN]

RECONCILIATION, RITES OF, see PENANCE, NEW RITE OF.

RECREATION, a term used in opposition to work. It is diversion from toil and often involves activity of a pleasurable kind that has no end other than amusement or enjoyment. Recreation is necessary for relaxation, refreshment, and the renewal of human energies, spiritual as well as physical. Need for it varies from individual to individual according to differences in their psychological makeup, susceptibility to tension, and the nature of the work in which they commonly engage. This diversion is governed according to Aristotle and St. Thomas Aquinas by the moral virtue of *eutrapelia.* BIBLIOGRAPHY: ThAq ST 1a2ae (esp. in Lat-Eng. ed., v. 17, ed. T. Gilby). *PLAY; *LEISURE.

RECTOR (Lat. *regere,* to rule), applied in the Middle Ages to a priest appointed head of a church or university. It is used today in the C of E and the Protestant Episcopal Church to designate the chief pastor, who is responsible for control of worship and spiritual jurisdiction of the parish and has authority over any curate or other person on the parish staff. In continental Europe it is still a common title for the heads of universities, but in England only two colleges at Oxford have rectors. In Scottish universities rectors are elected officials. In RC usage the term refers to priests in charge of nonparochial churches, the heads of seminaries and of some universities, and the heads of the houses of certain orders, e.g., the Society of Jesus. In the U.S., a priest who actually administers a cathedral church, which is properly the bp.'s church, is often called the rector.

[N. H. MARING]

RECTOR MAGNIFICUS, in the Roman pontifical universities and *atenei* the title of the actual administrative head; the higher official title is chancellor, held by a cardinal or the general superior of the religious order to which the institution belongs. The title *rector magnificus* will probably be deflated into simply *rector.*

RECUSANT POETS, the large group of English Catholic poets and dramatists of the 16th to the 18th cent., who made permanent contributions to English literature in an age when to profess Catholicism was to draw down disapproval of society and in many instances persecution, exile, or death. Many of the recusants were converts to the old faith, a few lapsed under grinding persecution, but all shared a flowering made possible by their Catholicism. The most celebrated of the recusants was St. Thomas More, but writers like James Shirley, Richard Crashaw, John Dryden, and Alexander Pope illustrate the high achievement of the group. Ben Jonson is representative of the few who lapsed. BIBLIOGRAPHY: L. I. Guiney, *Recusant Poets* (1939).

[J. R. AHERNE]

RECUSANTS ("refusers"), a term that in its principal use in English law was applied to those, esp. but not exclusively papists, who refused to attend divine worship in the established Church. Recusancy laws were in effect from the reign of Elizabeth I until that of George III. Their frankly terroristic intent was to force the people to embrace the English Church, and to reduce to beggary, or drive from the country, or kill those who would not. Their effectiveness was enhanced by a ruling of a committee of theologians at the Council of Trent, among whom was D. Lainez, condemning the casuistry used at first by many Catholics to justify attendance. The harsh penalties for nonattendance included a fine ruinous to all but the very wealthy, various disabilities, and a prohibition of travel beyond 5 miles from one's home. One convicted had either to submit and renounce belief in papal supremacy or, if required by judges, to abjure the realm, i.e., to swear to leave the country and never return without permission of the Crown. To fail to depart or to return without leave was a capital felony. The recusancy laws were not always and everywhere enforced with equal rigor. The number of recusants was greater in the N of England, especially in Lancashire, and in certain parts of Wales. BIBLIOGRAPHY: J. R. Roberts, *Critical Anthology of English Recusant Devotional Prose* (1966); J. A. Williams, NCE 12:135.

[P. K. MEAGHER]

RED HAT, the flat-crowned, broad-brimmed hat, with two clusters each of 15 tassels conferred upon cardinals. It was originally shaped like a pilgrim's headgear, but now has been distorted to fill a purely symbolic function. It is chief among the insignia of a cardinal, first used by cardinal legates, granted to others in 1245, and extended to all members of the sacred college including those from religious orders in 1591. Its conveyance is the sign of a cardinal's creation. It hangs above his tomb and, taking the place of a crested helm above the shield, is displayed among his armorial bearings. It is to be distinguished from the scarlet biretta.

[T. EARLY]

RED MASS, a votive mass in honor of the Holy Spirit in the appropriate liturgical color celebrated at the opening of councils, deliberative assemblies, and similar occasions, to invoke guidance, and also the Mass attended by judges and other court officials at the beginning of a judicial year. The custom began in England under Edward I.

[T. EARLY]

RED SEA, body of water between Africa and Arabia, extending from the Gulf of Aden north to Sinai, where it divides into the Gulfs of Aqabah and Suez. It is a continuation of the rift valley of the Jordan River and Dead Sea, and is over 7,000 feet deep. Following the LXX, English translations of the Exodus story call the water crossed by the Israelites the Red Sea (Ex 13.18). The Hebrew term is Sea of Reeds, however, and probably refers to some area of sweet-water marshes N of the Gulf of Suez. Solomon and Hiram of Tyre carried on trade with Ophir from Ezion-geber at the head of the Gulf of Aqabah, i.e., the Red Sea (1 Kg 9.26–28).

[T. EARLY]

REDACTION CRITICISM (Ger. *Redaktionsgeschichte*), a post-Bultmannian method of NT criticism that seeks to interpret the Gospels by a study of the editing or redaction done by the Evangelists. The Gospel is seen not simply as a written collection of data, but as the product of the Evangelist's own theological reflection and interpretation. The theory was a reaction to a principle of form criticism that the Evangelists were simply compilers. BIBLIOGRAPHY: G. Bornkamm et al., *Tradition and Interpretation in Matthew* (Eng. tr. 1963); H. Conzelmann, *Theology of St. Luke* (tr. G. Buswell, 1960).

[T. C. O'BRIEN]

REDDITIO SYMBOLI, the catechumens' recitation of a *creed (symbolum)* in the rites preliminary to baptism at the Easter Vigil. In the *traditio symboli* during Lent candidates received the credal formula to be learned as part of the catechumenate.

[T. C. O'BRIEN]

REDEEMER (IN THE BIBLE), a biblical name or title for God to express his saving activity toward his people. To redeem is to buy back; when applied to persons it refers to the purchase of freedom for bonded servants. When applied to a whole people or nation, it means their rescue from the control of an alien power. The Hebrew term *padha* has cognates of related meaning in other Semitic languages. It denotes the act of paying a price, and it implies nothing about the status of the person who is paying, or his obligation to do so. A second Hebrew word *gaal,* without cognates in other languages, is closely bound up with the conception of the solidarity of family, clan, tribe, and people. It refers to the action of the next of kin to recover the forfeited property of his kinsman, or to purchase his freedom if he has fallen into slavery. The next of kin is privileged and obligated to do this, if he has the means. The active participle *goel* can mean either "redeemer" or "next of kin." In Exodus, Deuteronomy, and the Psalms, the Lord's deliverance of his people from bondage in Egypt is expressed by both Hebrew words, without the metaphor's being pressed to include paying a price to someone. It was simply a deliverance. In Second Isaiah the title *Goel* is used exclusively to refer to God in his forthcoming deliverance of his people from a second captivity in Babylon. *Goel* has connotations of kinship and responsibility. God must do it for his name's sake, because he has adopted them for his own. God's redeeming activity in the biblical tradition relates to troubles of all kinds, whether of individuals or of the nation, esp. sickness, death, and bondage. Only in the NT, esp. in Paul, does it include sin. The price that is paid comes into prominence in Paul and in the one Synoptic verse: "The Son of Man (came) to give his life as a ransom for many" (Mk 10.45). Nowhere is the symbolism pushed to the point of speculating on the one to whom such a price is to be paid. The heart of the metaphor remains the act of deliverance. Theological speculation on what price is paid or to whom easily leads away from the mainstream of biblical tradition concerning God's dealings with his people.

[E. J. DILLON]

REDEMPTION, a biblical and theological term, from the Latin (*redimere,* meaning to buy back, or reacquire at a cost), used figuratively to describe the renewal of man's condition through the liberating and reconciling effect of God, forgiveness of sin, and justification by grace through the death and Resurrection of his Son, Jesus Christ.

Man's need for reconciliation arises from the realization of his solidarity with the progenitor of the human race in the latter's culpable rejection of God and his own personal ratification of this spiritual alienation from God by personal sin. St. Paul describes this condition of sinfulness (Rom

7.15–23), which the law of the OT made clear to men in order that they might look for justification through Christ, the promised Messiah (Rom 7.24–25).

This deliverance from sin and this recovery of man's lost relationship of community with God and his fellowmen are two aspects of the one redemptive experience of mankind. The deliverance by God for the sake of acquisition is the consistent theme that runs through the whole of salvation history. Through a series of divinely initiated liberations terminating in sacrificial acts of worship God unfolds his redemptive plan to be merciful and to bring mankind back into relationship with himself. The liberation is the first phase of the redemptive event; it is completed by the second phase, the covenant of loving worship that transforms man's life relationship with God.

In Christ, the human embodiment of God's complete self-communication to mankind, the types and figures of the OT redemption become fully realized. God himself in the person of his Son becomes fully man by being born into the human race. In his human nature the Son of God freely accepts the death of a sinner, although sinless, in an act of love for his Father and all mankind, in view of which the Father loves the human race as a whole. The Father's acceptance of the divine act of loving worship offered by his Son, is shown by Jesus' Resurrection and his sending of the Holy Spirit. For this reason the glory that belongs to the man Jesus, whom the Father has raised bodily from the dead because of his worshipful act of love as man, is offered to all mankind. Through the gift of the Holy Spirit, whom Christ as risen Lord is now empowered to send all men who put their faith and hope in Jesus, men are definitively redeemed and receive incorporation into the redemptive life and love of Christ.

Redemption is, then, a liberation to become sons of God in Jesus Christ, the risen Lord; it is a deliverance from sin by Christ for the sake of the justification that comes by grace from God; it is mercy extended to sinful man for a renewed life lived in a spirit of love; it is the incorporation of mankind as a whole into the events of Christ's death and Resurrection, which unite all men mysteriously yet really with the risen humanity of Christ. This union remains hidden in faith and sacramental symbol until the return of Christ in glory, when Redemption will be revealed as salvation, the total victory of God over sin, death, and Satan manifested in the fullness of eternal Glory. BIBLIOGRAPHY: R. Brown, *Jesus, God and Man* (1967); Y. Congar, "Christ in the Economy of Salvation and in Our Dogmatic Tracts," *Who Is Jesus of Nazareth?* (*Concilium* v. 11, 1966); K. Rahner, *On the Theology of Death* (tr. C. Henkey, 1961).

[J. C. MURRAY]

REDEMPTORISTINES, a contemplative order of nuns founded in 1731 in Scale, Italy, by Ven. Celeste Crostarosa with the help of St. Alphonsus Ligouri, who believed in her revelations and composed a rule based on them. The rule was approved in 1750. According to this rule each month is dedicated to growth in a particular virtue exemplified by Christ. The Redemptoristines are cloistered, take solemn vows, and recite the Liturgy of the Hours in choir. They have expanded from Italy to Japan and Africa. In 1957 a community came to Esopus, N.Y., and in 1960 another to Missouri. In 1976 the order had 37 monasteries and 795 nuns.

[R. C. CLIGGETT]

REDEMPTORISTS (The Congregation of the Most Holy Redeemer, CSSR), a community of priests and lay brothers spread throughout the world, bound by simple vows together with a vow and oath of perseverance in the congregation. They were founded by St. Alphonsus Ligouri (1732) to spread the Word of God through missions, retreats, and novenas. He also sought to instill an asceticism into his priests, brothers, and students, by proposing that they imitate one of the 12 virtues of the Redeemer each month. The congregation began in Naples but only after some houses were opened in the Papal States were the rule and constitutions approved by Benedict XIV in 1749. By the middle of the 19th cent. the conflict between the Kingdom of Naples and the Papal States brought about a division of the order. However in 1869 all Redemptorists throughout the world were united under one superior general in Rome. St. Clement Hofbauer, who became a Redemptorist in the Papal States established a branch in Vienna, then in Poland and again in N Italy, where his work was destroyed by the legions of Napoleon. After many hardships one group of his missionaries settled in Switzerland and another in Bulgaria. From here they were to expand through northern Europe and in North America. After the foundation in Pittsburgh, Pa. in 1839 the order increased rapidly in the U.S. In 1976 they had 807 houses, 5,376 priests and 1,143 brothers.

[R. C. CLIGGETT]

REDING, AUGUSTINE (1625–92), Benedictine abbot, theologian. R. entered the monastery of Einsiedeln, Switzerland, in 1641. He studied philosophy and theology at the Univ. of Freiburg-im-Breisgau, taught at Salzburg, became prior (1659) and later (1670) abbot of Einsiedeln. The monastery prospered under R.'s direction: the number of monks doubled, an extensive building program was completed, and strong commitment was given to intellectual pursuits. R. himself was a distinguished theologian; his principal work *Theologia scholastica universa* (1687) is a 13-volume commentary on the *Summa theologiae* of St. Thomas Aquinas.

[T. M. MCFADDEN]

REDON, ODILON (1840–1916), French painter and lithographer using a personal symbolism in a period when exterior reality was popular. R. emphasizing interior reality, feelings and dreams was appreciated by M. Denis, Bernard, and others. At first a lithographer using dramatic chiaroscuro from deepest black to blinding white, R. turned to painting and pastels in lyrical evocations of exquisite color.

[M. J. DALY]

REDON, ABBEY OF, a former Benedictine monastery located in the department of Ille-et-Vilaine, France, founded *c.* 830 by St. Convoyon, who was its first abbot. In 869 it was destroyed by the Normans. Rebuilt in the 10th cent., it became involved in Breton political wars and was pillaged. For a brief time in the 15th cent., Redon was an episcopal see and favored by Louis XI. In 1628 Card. Richelieu established the Maurists at Redon. The abbey was suppressed in 1790, and the church with its outstanding Romanesque tower now serves a parish. A school is also conducted at Redon by the Eudists. BIBLIOGRAPHY: Cottineau 2:2422–23.

[M. A. MCFADDEN]

REDUCTIONS OF PARAGUAY, a system of mission communes eatablished and managed by the Jesuits in Rio de la Plata in the 17th cent. and in the 18th up to the time of the expulsion of the Jesuits from Latin America (1768.) The Guarani Indians comprised the population of these missions, a people of considerable culture and civilization. At the beginning of the 17th cent. the first groups of Jesuits established missions in Paraguay. The chain of missions in time extended through what are now S Brazil, Paraguay, Uraguay, and N Argentina. Because of the disputed claims to territory on the part of Spain and Portugal, the reductions had a disturbed history. Through the first half of the 17th cent. the notorious Paulistas of Brazil sent raiding parties to bring back slaves from the reductions and destroyed several. The Treaty of Limits of 1750 forced the removal of a number of reductions to Spanish territory but the Indians rebelled against the move. The expulsion of the Jesuits in 1768 and the turning over of the communes to a civil administrator and secular priest marked the beginning of the decline of reductions. The achievement of the Jesuits was to give the Indians pride of ownership and the security of free men whom no one could enslave.

The reductions were communes but provided for some individual ownership. Each mission was a self-contained economic, social, and political entity. Physically the buildings surrounded a central plaza. The church, priest-house, Indian dwellings, a home for widows and orphans, offices and storehouses, and a cemetery constituted a great quadrangle. The village was located in the midst of fertile farmland near a river. Only one official, the chief magistrate, was appointed by the governor. The pastor was really the administrator of the commune. The Indians elected to the *cabildo* or council for a year, then elected their successors. The Jesuits taught Christian doctrine, reading, writing, and singing. The graphic arts were encouraged. All aspects of living were integrated in the religious orientation of the reduction. In spite of some criticism, the reductions and their Jesuit creators were a profound civilizing influence recognized today by all historians.

[J. R. AHERNE]

REFECTORY (from the Lat. *re-ficere,* to restore or refresh), the name monks gave to their dining room. This designation was frequently adopted by later religious orders and congregations. In the traditional abbey, the refectory was a distinct building on the S side of the monastic quadrangle opposite the church and connected with the other monastic buildings by the cloister walk.

[M. B. PENNINGTON]

REFICE, LICINIO (1883–1954), Italian priest, composer, and conductor. In Rome he was professor of church music at the Scuola Pontificia (1910) and *maestro di cappella* at the Church of Santa Maria Maggiore. In 1947 he conducted the Roman Singers of Sacred Music on a U.S. tour. His compositions include many Masses, motets, two oratorios, hymns, sacred cantatas, a Requiem, a *Stabat Mater,* operas, and symphonic poems for chorus. Of the operas, *Sta. Cecilia* and *Sta. Margherita da Cortona* are best known. Pope Pius XII paid tribute to his contributions to church music upon his retirement.

[R. J. LITZ]

REFLEX PRINCIPLES, in RC moral theology, certain general norms that may be applied by a person in reaching a moral judgment concerning the rightness or wrongness of a particular course of action when such weighty considerations favor either position that he cannot be certain of the rightness of his choice between them. The legitimate application of these principles supposes: (1) that there be a case of true, solidly based, practical doubt; (2) that the doubt cannot be dispelled by a reasonable investigation of the problem itself; (3) that reliable external guidance is not available to help clarify one's mind.

Moral theologians differ in their listings of reflex principles, but among those most commonly cited are the following: (1) a doubtful law does not bind. Although moralists differ in their interpretation of the kind and degree of doubt needed to excuse one from the obligation of a doubtful law, the general principle is in some sense admitted by all. Its basis is the assumption that the God of mercy and goodness does not require an individual to satisfy a moral obligation when there is solidly probable reason to think that the obligation in question does not exist (see MORALITY, SYSTEMS OF). There are, however, certain exceptions, namely, when the doubt concerns the validity of the sacraments, or when it concerns something absolutely necessary to salvation, or when it concerns the certain and established rights of another person. (2) When a legitimate presumption favors one side or the other, that presumption cannot be set aside by anything less than morally certain argument. (3) In doubt a presumption favors the one in actual possession of what is under dispute as against the claim of one not in possession. BIBLIOGRAPHY: F. J. Connell, NCE 12:169. *DOUBT, MORAL; *EQUIPROBABILISM; PROBABILISM; *PROBABILIORISM.

[T. M. MCFADDEN]

REFORM AND THE CHURCH. Both historically and from the nature of the Church the process of betterment and of renewal is a fact of church life. Reform, the taking of a new form, refers to the past, regaining the pristine form of life in the apostolic Church; it refers also to the future, to the eschatological ideal placed always before the Church: the building up of the body of Christ to perfect manhood, to the mature fullness of Christ (see Eph 4.13). Both ideals have motivated the many efforts at reform in church history. The desire to recreate the Church of the NT or to come close to the perfect sanctity that is the goal of the Church have been primary factors in the emergence of almost all new church bodies in the history of Christianity. For example, a return to apostolic simplicity was the motivation not only of the monastic and mendicant orders but also of many lay evangelical movements of the Middle Ages. One of the key themes of the *Humiliati, *Waldenses, and *Lollards was that of evangelical poverty. The spectacle of wealth in the Church, the unworthiness of rich churchmen, was decried as perverting the true image of the Church, betraying the apostolic tradition, and stifling the gospel. Most often the lay evangelical movements led to an attack upon the institutional Church of worldly clerics, and the priesthood and sacraments came to be regarded as part of the institution. An eschatological motivation has usually characterized the apocalyptic or millenarian movements that have proclaimed the millennium, a kingdom of the just that with Christ as leader would prevail over all institutions of the wicked, including the institutional Church.

Reform in the Church. Both the lay evangelical and the apocalyptic types of reform have largely existed on the fringes of the RC and the Protestant Churches. In the major historical Churches there has been a belief that there is something in the essential being of the Church that cannot be reformed. The Church is holy, it is the spouse of Christ "without spot or wrinkle or any such thing" (Eph 5.27). Defects that exist arise from the weakness and sinfulness of members. Thus part of the process of renewal throughout church history has been understood as disciplinary reform, i.e., the correction of abuses by laws on church discipline, and by use of excommunication. Novatianists and the Donatists attempted to keep the Church holy by disciplinary rigorism. The centralization of authority and the codification of law in the medieval Church were reforms of ecclesiastical abuses. The first reaction to the evils in the Renaissance Church was also to seek disciplinary reform. The Council of *Trent gave much of its attention to the reform decrees concerning ecclesiastical discipline. In the Churches of the Reformation and in their confessional documents church discipline was held out as one of the signs of the true, reformed Church (e.g., Belgic Confession, Art. 29; Scots Confession, Art. 18).

Reform of the Church. Disciplinary reform is described as reform *in* the Church, needed because of the weakness of the faithful. Reform *of* the Church, a purging, a remaking of its very being, is said to be the *Protestant principle, inadmissible in RC theology. *Ecclesia reformata, sed semper reformanda* (the Church reformed, but always in need of reform) has been regarded as central to the Protestant, but alien to the RC teaching on the Church. The reason for the opposition of views is that the Reformation regarded the holiness of the Church to be the holiness of Christ its head; the Church as an institution, like the justified man, remained sinful; its forms, or visible structures, do not share intrinsically in the holiness of Christ; they are always reformable. RC teaching, however, regards many of the visible elements of the Church as essentials, as unalterable, and not in need of reform. Such essentials are viewed as instituted by Christ; the power to teach, to sanctify, and to govern in the Church are part of the communication by which he makes the Church inherently holy. These elements are not subject to reform.

Theological reflection in the 20th cent. has regarded this opposition as oversimplified. A deepened Protestant appreciation for the mystery of the Church has led to a sense of the need that the Church be faithful to its past. There are new evaluations of ministry, of tradition, of sacraments and liturgy, which recognize that these are essentials in the Church; that the holy Church is not exclusively the invisible Church. From the documents of Vatican II it is clear that there is no longer a refusal of Roman Catholics to speak of reform of the Church: "Christ summons the Church, as she goes her pilgrim way, to that continual reformation of which she always has need, insofar as she is an institution of men here on earth. Therefore, if the influence of events or of the times has led to deficiencies in conduct, in Church discipline, or even in the formulation of doctrine (which must be carefully distinguished from the deposit itself of faith), these should be rectified at the proper moment" (Vat II Ecum 6). The council speaks of renewal in every phase of the Church's life as having ecumenical importance. Protestants and Catholics share in a sense of the simultaneous holiness and sinfulness of the Church. They agree in the urgency of reform whereby the Church adapts itself as a servant Church to the needs of a world to be saved. The diversity of Protestant and Catholic belief in the nature of the Church does mean different acceptance of reform. But the shared desire for church unity is itself a part of Church renewal, of a desire to regain the ideal of the Church in its original design, and so to press on toward an ideal of holiness to be reached. BIBLIOGRAPHY: Y. Congar, *Vraie et fausse réforme dans l'Église* (1950). H. Küng, *Council, Reform and Reunion* (tr. C. Hastings, 1963); R. E. McNally, *Reform of the Church* (1962); *Renewal of the Church* (3 v.; ed. W. B. Blakemore, 1963).

[T. C. O'BRIEN]

REFORMATIO LEGUM ECCLESIASTICARUM (*Reform of the Ecclesiastical Laws*), a book first published by J. Foxe in 1571, containing a system of order and discipline projected for the C of E to replace Roman canon law. An act of 1549 had empowered Edward VI to appoint a wide commission to compile a corpus; the work was taken in hand by a cabal, and presented to Parliament in 1553 a few months before the death of the King. In view of its Calvinism the assertion that it would have been sanctioned but for the accession of Mary Tudor is open to question.

[T. GILBY]

REFORMATION, the religious changes occurring in the 16th and 17th cent. on the Continent and in the British Isles. The term itself did not come into general acceptance until the 19th cent.; the Reformers preferred to consider their efforts a renewal or restoration of the primitive purity of Christianity.

CONTINENTAL REFORMATION

The beginning of the Protestant Reformation is usually dated from 1517, with Martin Luther's *Ninety-Five Theses. Basically a religious movement, it was reinforced by complex cultural currents. Long before Luther, there had been persistent demands for reform to deal with incompetence and worldliness of clergy, pluralism of benefices, and a multiplicity of financial abuses. J. *Hus and J. *Wycliffe had criticized the Church, questioned papal claims, and challenged commonly accepted doctrine on the sacraments and other theological issues, but their influence was localized and limited. By the 16th cent. new factors were present that were favorable to protest and reform: (1) the rise of national states; (2) a weakening of papal authority by the *Babylonian Captivity at Avignon, the *Great Western Schism, and the conciliar movement (see CONCILIARISM); (3) German resentment of domination by Pope and Emperor; (4)*humanism, which ridiculed *scholasticism and superstition, stressed biblical study in the original language, encouraged Bible translation into the vernacular, and accented NT standards of ethics; (5) the presence of a piety in Germany fostered by practical Christian mystics and such movements as *Devotio moderna; and (6) the invention of the printing press.

Martin Luther. Luther had no desire to divide the Church and at first had no quarrel with fundamental RC teachings. Conferences with papal representatives, written exchanges, the *Disputation of Leipzig, and threats of excommunication pushed him to further examination of the implications of his understanding of the gospel. By 1521, his views had changed radically. He asserted that both popes and councils had erred. He reinterpreted the sacraments, limiting them to two (or possibly three), denying that the Mass was a sacrifice, and disagreeing with the doctrine of *transubstantiation. He affirmed that every Christian is made a priest at baptism, and that the minister has no special power or status that sets him apart from the laity (see PRIESTHOOD OF ALL BELIEVERS). Basic to all of his conclusions was the concept of *justification by faith alone, which came by preaching the gospel of Jesus Christ; the Holy Scriptures that witnessed to Christ were for him the final authority in matters of doctrine. At the Diet of Worms (1521) he refused to recant any of his writings, and therefore was placed under the ban of the Empire and then excommunicated from the Church. Excluded from the RC Church, Luther believed that he and his followers still stood in continuity with the Catholic Church, which had been corrupted in the Middle Ages and was now being reformed. In reforming the liturgy, Luther retained much from the past; but the central elements of the Mass were omitted, and prominent place was given to reading Scriptures, preaching, and congregational singing. Catechisms were prepared for instructing children and adults, and public education was encouraged to enable people to read the Bible. Without the former episcopal structure, he had to devise an administrative system for the churches. Apostolic succession was rejected, and ministers were ordained without the aid of bishops. The ''godly prince,'' as a member of the Church, was considered a suitable leader in reform, and the concept of the prince as *summus episcopus* became general, being reinforced by the principle *cuius regio, eius religio,* firmly established by the Peace of Augsburg (1555). Luther's attitude in the Peasant's War, his dispute with *Erasmus, and his loss of support from the German knights alienated many former sympathizers. Lutheranism spread, however, to Finland and the Scandinavian countries; and Luther's teachings permeated other lands (see LUTHERANISM).

Ulrich Zwingli. The Reformation in Switzerland began with Ulrich *Zwingli at Zurich. In Jan. 1519, he began his ministry there. Stricken by plague in 1520, he had a long period of convalescence, during which he committed himself more fully to emphasize justification by faith and the authority of the Scriptures. Gradually these emphases led him to oppose many Catholic practices, papal authority, the sacerdotal ministry, and finally the Mass as a sacrifice. After two public disputations in 1523, the magistrates voted that Zurich should be an evangelical city, images should be removed from churches, and the Mass should be abolished. Although Zwingli denied any dependence, he was familiar with Luther's writings, and his evangelical development probably owed something to them. At many points he differed from Luther, as in his interpretation of the Lord's Supper, his attitude toward the use of music in worship, and his view of the Church's role in society. Zwingli's work was continued by Henry *Bullinger, and their followers eventually merged with the other Reformed Churches of Switzerland.

John Calvin. The Reformer who did most to give form and substance to the *Reformed Church tradition was John *Calvin. At Basel, he published the first edition of the *Institutes of the Christian Religion* (1536), the monumental exposition of his distinctive teaching on predestination and election (see CALVINISM). Invited by Farel to assist in reforming Geneva, Calvin soon won recognition by his learning and ability, and took the lead in drafting plans for a new *church order, agreeing with Luther regarding the authority of Scriptures and the doctrine of justification by faith, as well as many other points. Calvin, perhaps because of his humanistic training, was more rationalistic and more systematic in formulating his theology and his conception of worship. A significant difference from Luther is his understanding of the Church's active role in ordering and changing society. Calvin sought to establish Geneva as a city where everyone assented to orthodox doctrine and observed Christian ethical standards, and where civil magistrates governed in conformity with the word of God. Calvin's views on worship were similar to those of Zwingli; unlike Luther, he did not regard liturgical forms as subject to human opinions. Where Luther held that absence of specific biblical instruction left a question to be decided by the Churches, Calvin held that only what the Bible directly commanded was permissible in the service of worship. His order of service included reading of the Scriptures, prayers, singing, and a lengthy sermon. Instrumental music and pictures were eschewed as distractions, and singing was restricted to Psalms or other biblical passages. Great emphasis was placed upon learned ministers having command of the Greek and Hebrew tongues so that they could expound the Scriptures. Public education was provided, and children were thoroughly instructed in the catechism and in direct teaching from Scripture. The Reformed Church in Switzerland was consolidated when Geneva and Zurich resolved differences over the Lord's Supper, stating their agreement in the *Zurich Consensus (Consensus Tigurinus) in 1549. The influence of Calvin was probably more widespread than that of Luther, partly because of his systematized theology in the *Institutes,* which went through five revisions and were translated into French, Latin, and English. His advice was sought by Protestants in many other countries, and he directly influenced the establishment of Reformed Churches in France, the Netherlands, and Scotland and the rise of the Puritans in England.

The Anabaptists. A third branch of Protestantism was the Anabaptist movement. This term has often been used to include all of the religious parties and individuals who could not be classified as Reformed, Lutheran, or Anglican. Only in recent years has careful research sorted out the tangled skeins of miscellaneous religious dissidents in the movement. There were such mystics as Caspar *Schwenkfeld; rationalistic anti-Trinitarians like Servetus and the Sozzini; and the Anabaptists proper, who called themselves Swiss Brethren. Originating at Zurich, these people believed that Luther, Zwingli, and Calvin had stopped the Reformation at a halfway point. Their early leaders, *Grebel, *Manz, *Blaurock, and others, were university-educated and friends of Zwingli. They parted company with him over two points, *believer's baptism and freedom of the Church from control by civil magistrates. The essential emphasis of the Swiss Brethren was upon Churches made up only of baptized believers, freedom of the Church from the State, and an ethic of love. Believing *infant baptism not to be a genuine baptism, they baptized only those who had reached a responsible age; and only such belonged to the Church. Following literally the commands of Scripture, they refused to take oaths. Believing that the Bible forbade killing, they would not undertake military service. Since they believed

that the duties of a civil official might require him to act contrary to Christian principles, they opposed office-holding in civil government. Considered a threat to public order, these people were fiercely persecuted; thousands of them died by drowning, burning, and hanging. Despite opposition, their numbers increased, and they found refuge in Poland, Moravia, and a few other localities. Today their ideas survive with the Mennonites and Hutterites. BIBLIOG - RAPHY: H. J. Grimm, *Reformation Era* (1954); T. Lindsay, *History of the Reformation* (2 v., 1906–07); J. T. McNeill, *History and Character of Calvinism* (1954); E. G. Schwiebert, *Luther and His Times* (1950); G. H. Williams, *Radical Reformation* (1962).

In the British Isles

At its inception, the English Reformation was prompted more by personal than by religious considerations, but other factors combined to produce genuine religious reforms. Most of the forces that contributed to a desire for reform on the Continent were present in England. Besides abuses that needed correction, there were the influence of such Christian humanists as John *Colet and Thomas More, renewed study of the Greek NT, vestiges of the *Lollard movement, and acquaintance with Luther's writings. It was Henry VIII's desire for an annulment of his marriage, however, that precipitated the break with Rome. Supported by the laity in Parliament, Henry proceeded to reduce the clergy to submission. In 1531, Convocations acknowledged that he was "as far as the law of Christ allows, even the supreme head" of the Church in England. One year later, the clergy agreed not to approve any more canons without his consent. Thomas *Cranmer was consecrated abp. of Canterbury in 1533, and a few months later he declared Henry's marriage null and void. In 1534, Parliament passed the Act of Uniformity, declaring Henry the "supreme head on earth of the Church of England." Denying that this step broke the continuity of Christ's Church, Henry maintained that he was simply restoring an original power of jurisdiction that had been usurped by the papacy. No alterations in doctrine or ceremonies were contemplated, but he suppressed monasteries and confiscated their properties, encouraged Bible reading, and sought to eliminate superstitious practices. Most of the clergy acquiesced in his renunciation of papal authority, but John Fisher, bp. of Rochester, was put to death for denying the King's supremacy, as were some Carthusians and Thomas More. Among the bps. were Cranmer and Hugh *Latimer who had been influenced by Lutheran teachings and wished to inaugurate further reforms; but few of the clergy favored doctrinal innovations. To secure unity of religious belief, several doctrinal statements were issued during Henry's reign. The *Ten Articles (1536) dealt with three sacraments (baptism, penance, and the Eucharist), teaching the doctrine of the Real Presence, but not mentioning transubstantiation; emphasized the need to teach the Bible and the creeds to the people; declared that justification is by faith, confession, absolution, and amendment of life; and, while not disapproving Masses for the dead, invocation of saints, and the use of images, warned against excesses in these matters. One year later, the *Institution of a Christian Man* (*Bishops' Book) was issued as a handbook on Christian Faith for the ordinary man. Containing an exposition of the Apostles' Creed, the seven sacraments, the Ten Commandments, and the Lord's Prayer, it incorporated a statement on justification by faith and another that denied purgatory. In 1543 this work was revised and published as *A Necessary Doctrine and Erudition for Any Christian Man* (*King's Book). It explicitly affirmed transubstantiation and strongly emphasized celibacy of the clergy. An English translation of the Bible was authorized by the King, and a copy was ordered (1536) to be placed in every church. Thinking that he might need an alliance with the Schmalkaldic League, Henry briefly allowed a theological conference of English and Lutheran divines; but he abruptly ended their proceedings in 1539 by the *Six Articles Act. This ''whip of six strings'' asserted belief in transubstantiation, imposing a death penalty for denying it. Other articles forbade clerical marriage, denied the necessity of communion in both kinds for the laity, and approved the binding power of vows of chastity, auricular confession, and private Masses.

Impetus to additional reforms came during the reign of Edward VI. He was too young to assume personal rule, but the regencies of Somerset and Northumberland advocated Protestant doctrines. The presence of refugees from the Continent, such as Martin *Bucer, *Peter Martyr Vermigli, and Bernardino *Ochino, had considerable influence during this period. The major developments between 1547 and 1553 were: permission of clerical marriage, issuance of the Book of Common Prayer, and publication of the *Forty-Two Articles. The Prayer Book was largely the work of Cranmer. The first Prayer Book (1549) changed the Mass into the Lord's Supper, allowed communion in both kinds, and was in the vernacular. Some phrases were ambiguous, making possible an interpretation of transubstantiation. This book was unsatisfactory to many, and a revision appeared in 1552. By this time, Cranmer had rejected the doctrine of the Real Presence, and everything suggesting it was omitted. The communicant received bread and wine with the words, ''eat [drink] this in remembrance.'' References to purgatory and prayers for the dead were also left out, as was the rubric requiring the minister to wear alb and cope. The threefold ministry was retained, including apostolic succession, but the term ''minister'' replaced ''priest'' in many places. The altar was called a ''table'' and was placed in the body of the church.

In 1553, Mary Tudor succeeded Edward. Daughter of Catherine of Aragon, she was a staunch Roman Catholic and resented all Reformers. At her instigation, Parliament revoked all laws by which religious changes had been instituted, except that monastic properties could not be retrieved. The Act of Supremacy was revoked, the BCP discontinued, and the Mass restored. Card. Pole was put in charge of restoring the former order; other exiled priests were recalled; papal supremacy was again recognized; and old laws against heresy were revived. Abp. Cranmer and Bps. Latimer, Ridley, and Hooper were among the nearly 300 persons executed during Mary's reign. Many ministers fled to the Continent, where they became more thoroughly imbued with Reformed doctrines. Although her subjects accepted the restoration of Catholicism, many became alienated by her burning so many enemies. Moreover, her marriage to Philip II was unpopular, and her joining him in a war against France resulted in the loss of Calais, England's last possession on the Continent.

Elizabeth I sought a religious settlement acceptable to most of her subjects. A new Act of Supremacy was passed in 1559, declaring Elizabeth the ''supreme governor of the realm'' in both ecclesiastical and temporal affairs. At the same time, an Act of Uniformity adopted the Prayer Book of 1552, with some modifications. Most of the Marian bps. were replaced by new ones, but only about 200 of the lower clergy refused to comply with the new requirements. The *Thirty-Nine Articles were published in 1563, and subscription by the clergy was required by an act of 1571. With this act the direction of Elizabeth's settlement was clear. She wished a Church that was clearly Protestant in its main tenets, but which retained as much of the ritual as possible and allowed some breadth of interpretation.

Elizabeth's policies were a blow to Catholic hopes, and they also disappointed many Protestants. Catholics continued to seek restoration of England to their faith, hoping for aid from France and Spain. Elizabeth was excommunicated by Pius V in 1570, a series of anti-Catholic laws was passed, and intrigues formed around the imprisoned Mary Stuart until exposure of the Babington Plot led to her execution in 1587. The defeat of Philip's Armada in 1588 brought an end to the fear of invasion, but strong anti-Catholic feelings had been engendered that were to become a legacy of Anglo-Saxon Protestantism for generations. Still, many Protestants considered the Elizabethan settlement a compromise. Opposition flared up c.1565–66 in the Vestiarian Controversy, as Abp. Parker tried to enforce the wearing of clerical vestments in public worship. Those who opposed wearing of alb and cope also objected to making the sign of the cross on a child's head at baptism and kneeling during communion. Many objected to the BCP in its entirety. This party, made up largely of Marian exiles enamored of the doctrine and practice of the Reformed Churches, was variously dubbed ''Precisians,'' ''Disciplinarians,'' and ''Puritans.'' By 1570, some Puritans tried to make the national Church Presbyterian, sending two ''Admonitions'' to Parliament in 1572, objecting to the existing system, and giving reasons why their proposal was in accord with the Word of God. Although they were unsuccessful in obtaining their desire, a quasi-Presbyterian system was carried on within the C of E in the next few years. By 1580, a Separatist wing of Puritanism had emerged, adopting the *gathered-church idea and forming congregations independent of the C of E.

Robert *Browne and Robert Harrison were early leaders in this movement, and it was continued by others to become the Independents or Congregationalists. The Baptists were an offshoot from them in 1609.

In Scotland, the Reformation took a different course. Similar factors contributing to the English Reformation were present, but it was complicated by pro-French and pro-English parties and by political rivalries among the Scottish nobility. Lutheran writings had been disseminated there in the 1520s, and the first martyr was Patrick *Hamilton in 1528. Efforts to stamp out heresy were unavailing, however, and a strong Protestant party developed. After George Wishart, its leading spirit, was burned at the stake in 1546, his friends retaliated by murdering Card. Beaton, Abp. of St. Andrews. Wishart's mantle fell upon John *Knox, who was taken prisoner by the French and served 19 months as a galley slave. Released in 1549, he went to England, but fled to the Continent at the accession of Mary and was greatly influenced during his exile by Calvin and Bullinger. Back in Scotland for a few months in 1555 and 1556, he won support for reform, which resulted in the covenanting of some nobles to establish a Church in accord with the Word of God. At the invitation of these "Lords of the Congregation," he returned to Scotland in 1559 and assumed leadership of the Reformation. With military aid from England, French control of Scotland was broken. In 1660, the Scottish Parliament adopted the Scottish Confession prepared by Knox, and proceeded to reject the authority of the pope, outlaw the Mass, and revoke all laws not consonant with the new Confession. The first Book of *Discipline outlined a plan of church government generally patterned after Calvin's system, but providing for superintendents who had many former functions of bps. and of lay readers. The *Geneva Catechism was ordered to be used for instructing children. A *Book of Common Order was adopted in 1564, which showed the influence of Calvin and was approved by him. Mary Stuart returned to Scotland in 1561, after the death of her husband, Francis II of France. Refusing to assent to the new laws, she was determined to restore the RC faith. Marrying her cousin Darnley, she was suspected of complicity in his murder and was forced to renounce the throne. Escaping from prison, she fled to England, where Elizabeth held her prisoner until her execution in 1587. The work of Knox was continued by Andrew *Melville, who was instrumental in formulating the second Book of Discipline and the subsequent transfer of administrative powers of superintendents to presbyteries (see PRESBYTERY), thereby giving finished form to Scottish Presbyterianism. Scottish worship followed the Reformed pattern, with singing being confined to paraphrases of the Psalms; the first Psalter was issued in 1564.

In Wales, the course of the Reformation largely followed that in England; but attempts to impose the doctrines and ceremonies of the C of E upon Ireland were unsuccessful except around Dublin and in N Ireland, where Scottish colonization was undertaken by James I. BIBLIOGRAPHY:

Hughes RE: G. Donaldson, *Scottish Reformation* (1960); A. G. Dickens, *English Reformation* (1964).

[N. H. MARING]

REFORMED, as a proper adjective, Protestant in the Calvinist tradition, distinct esp. from Protestant in the Lutheran tradition. Within the Calvinist tradition itself, the term Reformed suggests continental origins, while the term Presbyterian denotes origins in England and Scotland. Reformed also connotes a designation on the basis of doctrine; Presbyterian, on the basis of polity. As a common adjective, reformed may simply refer to Churches originating in the Reformation. *REFORMED CHURCHES.

[T. C. O'BRIEN]

REFORMED CHURCH IN AMERICA, the oldest Protestant denomination with a continuous history in the United States. The probable date of organization is April 10, 1628, at New Amsterdam (Manhattan Island), under the direction of Jonas *Michaelius. The Dutch Reformed churches of New York, Pennsylvania, and New Jersey remained under the ecclesiastical control of the Reformed Church of the Netherlands throughout the colonial period. Until 1763 the Dutch language alone was used. When autonomy was granted in 1772, the denomination had 100 churches and 40 clergymen. The first church constitution was adopted in 1792, an adaptation of the articles on *church order of the Synod of *Dort (1618–19). The liturgy framed by the same synod, one derived from earlier sources in the Reformation, was also adopted, with the Nicene and Athanasian Creeds appended. The forms for the sacraments were required to be used; other forms were given optional usage. The *Heidelberg Catechism, the *Belgic Confession, and the Canons of the Synod of Dort were made authoritative *doctrinal standards.

Although the Reformed Church in America did not share in the large growth experienced by the Protestant denominations that moved with the American frontier in the 19th cent., significant growth came in mid-century with a new Dutch immigration to the Midwest. The 20th cent. found a somewhat even balance between the eastern and western branches of the Church. While a gradual growth in number of churches came in a few southern states, the Reformed Church remains for the most part a northern Church. The larger number of its churches are located in rural and semirural areas. Domestic missions are carried on among Indians in the West, among Negroes in Alabama and in inner-city efforts, in schools and churches in Kentucky, and in a province of Mexico. Dutch immigration to Canada in the past quarter-century added 30 new churches. Foreign missions begun early in the 19th cent. are continuing in a number of countries. The Church has operated or been associated with four colleges, including Rutgers, founded under Reformed Church auspices in 1766. Two theological seminaries, in New Brunswick, N.J., and in Holland, Mich., are operated by the denomination. The *Church*

Herald is the official periodical. In 1975 the Reformed Church numbered 923 churches, with an inclusive membership of 366,381.

Theology remains that of a moderate Calvinism. Extreme points of view are avoided. In eucharistic teaching, and in the stronger emphasis given preaching than the sacrament, the Church holds positions closer to those of *Zwingli than of Calvin. In polity the model of *presbyterian government is followed. The denomination has participated freely in the ecumenical movement since its inception. Attempts at merger to begin in 1970 with the Presbyterian Church in the U.S., however, were defeated in 1969 because of grass-roots opposition in the Reformed Church itself. BIBLIOGRAPHY: E. Eenigenburg, *Brief History of the Reformed Church in America* (1958).

[E. EENIGENBURG]

REFORMED CHURCH IN THE UNITED STATES, a title used by two *Reformed denominations: (1) a body organized in Philadelphia in 1747, which adopted the name German Reformed Church in 1793 and from 1863 used the title Reformed Church in the United States. The Church joined in the merger forming the *Evangelical and Reformed Church in 1934, which since 1959 has been part of the *United Church of Christ. (2) The former Eureka Classis of the original Reformed Church in the U.S., organized in South Dakota in 1910, which remained out of the 1934 merger. It continues to use the name Reformed Church in the U.S. The Church follows the doctrine of the *Heidelberg Catechism and is governed by an annual *classis meeting. In 1975 membership was 4,008, in 24 congregations.

REFORMED CHURCHES, those bodies that share a religious and theological heritage derived mainly from the circle of Protestant Reformers having John *Calvin (1509–64) as its chief spokesman; they include both Reformed and Presbyterian denominations. The term "Reformed" was used in an informal and unofficial way in the 16th cent. by the various branches of the Protestant movement. The tense controversy on the Eucharist between the successors of Luther and Calvin near the end of that century did much to compel the upholders of the *Formula of Concord (1577) to adopt the title "Lutheran" in a symbolical and official sense. Calvin's followers became known as "Reformed." The distinction slowly became accepted in various countries in which the Reformation movement was strong. Followers of Ulrich *Zwingli (1484–1531) also had a claim upon the name "Reformed," but they became attached finally to the developing Calvinistic Church, which, unlike the Zwinglian movement, became international. The Reformed Churches spread in the Reformation period from Calvin's Geneva to France (see HUGUENOTS), the Netherlands, Germany, Eastern Europe (Poland, Bohemia, Hungary, Transylvania), Scotland (see CHURCH OF SCOTLAND), England, Ireland, and North America. In some instances, as in the Netherlands and Scotland, the Reformation functioned as the religious phase of movements for political independence and imparted much of the power of these movements; political and religious motivations were thoroughly intermingled. English and American Puritanism, often mistakenly regarded as rather pure forms of Calvinism, and hence Reformed, represent instead an admixture of various Reformation sources, among which the Reformed component is significant but not controlling. Most American Puritans adopted a congregational polity. The complete Reformed tradition was maintained in N.A. by the Presbyterian Churches of English and Scottish origin and by the Reformed Churches established by Dutch immigrants. Contemporary Reformed Churches are associated internationally in the *Alliance of the Reformed Churches; the Alliance includes most of the Presbyterian and Reformed denominations.

The Reformed theological tradition is characterized by a considerable number of variations on theological themes originally proposed by Calvin (see CALVINISM). Rather than unanimity on the meaning of such topics as God's sovereignty, divine *predestination, the manner of Christ's presence in the Eucharist (see REAL PRESENCE), and the ethical task of the Christian man, there is a kind of general agreement as to the proper accent and point of view. In one manner or another the Reformed Churches have been distinguished by their emphasis upon the duty of Christians to do the will of a sovereign God at all costs. Every area of human experience, personal and social, is included in the field of effort. Religious activism has thus typified many of the Reformed Churches and their members. There have also been advocates of mystical piety, which frequently has provided the inspiration and direction for church action. The old Reformed accent upon God's choice of certain persons for salvation, and his repudiation of others (divine election and reprobation), is scarcely heard in any of the Reformed Churches today, though in earlier centuries various views on the subject were a main topic of debate and conversation (see ARMINIANISM; DORT, SYNOD OF). Most Reformed Churches today appear to be more Zwinglian than Calvinistic in their understanding of how Christ is present in the sacrament of the Eucharist. Calvin himself held to the Real Presence "in a spiritual manner." Today most observances lean toward the notion of Zwingli, that the Eucharist is simply a memorial of what Christ did for us long ago in his death. For the most part the Reformed tradition has placed emphasis upon the past, present, and future aspects of the Eucharist.

The Reformed Churches follow a middle-of-the-road attitude in worship procedures. Avoiding, on the one hand, the highly liturgical emphases of RC, Anglican, and other Churches, and, on the other, the casual, informal worship practices of some Protestant bodies, most Reformed Churches have been semiliturgical. Liturgical forms are used in moderation, mainly in connection with the celebration of the sacraments. Free prayers esp. have marked Reformed worship services. The Reformed Churches employ the presbyterian form of church government, the main principles of which are the following: (1) the Church of Christ is a living communion of the one people of God with the one Christ as their head; (2) Jesus Christ is the only head of his Church; (3) all authority in the Church is received from Christ; (4) representative governing bodies, called *courts, function on several levels; (5) the Church is governed by *elders (clergymen and elected laymen); and (6) the local churches, clergymen, elders, and deacons all on their own level are equal. BIBLIOGRAPHY: J. T. McNeill, *History and Character of Calvinism* (1954).

[E. EENIGENBURG]

REFORMED CHURCHES, ALLIANCE OF, see ALLIANCE OF THE REFORMED CHURCHES.

REFORMED EPISCOPAL CHURCH, a Church founded in New York City in 1873 by Bp. G. D. *Cummins, and a small group of other members of the Protestant Episcopal Church who felt that tendencies toward Catholic doctrine and ritual were too strong to be resisted within the Anglican communion. Their movement had gained cohesion from the formation of the Society to Promote Evangelical Religion in 1868 and from the organization of an American branch of the *Evangelical Alliance the previous year. Bp. Cummins's wholehearted participation in the meeting of the Evangelical Alliance at New York in 1873 and his demand for *intercommunion and exchange of pulpits between the Protestant Episcopal Church and evangelical Protestant Churches occasioned the split. No exodus of low churchmen materialized, however, and Cummins's group remained essentially a minority faction. By the consecration of Bp. C. E. Cheney in 1873, the new Church secured episcopal succession. Bp. Cheney was followed as presiding bp. by Bp. Samuel Fallows in 1889. The Reformed Episcopal Church then had 15 clergymen, and about 1,200 members and had itself been torn by dissension and schism. Bp. Fallows brought about a reunion with the Reformed Church of England (Canada) in 1894 and commenced the foreign mission work of the Church with a station in India in 1899. In Puerto Rico shortly afterward the Reformed Episcopal Church supported Manuel Ferrando and raised him to the episcopate of an independent Church of Jesus. Additional overseas missions were developed in the 20th cent. in S Africa and the Sudan. In 1927 the Church united with the Free Church of England. In 1974 there were 66 churches and some 6,727 members of the Reformed Episcopal Church.

As a conservative protest against the influence of the *Oxford movement, the Church adopted a revision of the *Thirty-Nine Articles and the American BCP of 1785 as doctrinal standards. This provisional version of the Prayer Book differed in some details from that adopted in 1789, which, with revisions, has remained the standard of the parent Church. (See AMERICAN PRAYER BOOK.) Both the ordination ritual and the communion service in the 1785

version are so worded as to rule out any interpretation of the ministry as a sacramental priesthood or of the holy communion as anything but a symbolic sharing in the Lord's Supper. In its polity, the Reformed Episcopal Church has been equally conservative, keeping the forms of the Protestant Episcopal Church, but with a virtual autonomy for local congregations. *Episcopacy is retained, not as being of divine right, but simply as an ancient, desirable form of polity.

[R. K. MacMASTER]

REFORMKATHOLIZISMUS, a term first used in 1898 by Joseph Müller (1855–1942), a German priest-editor and literary critic, to describe the work of prominent Catholic intellectuals trying to reform and renew the Church. These intellectuals came from several countries but were preponderantly German; and while some were still active after World War I or even after World War II, their collective achievement was greatest in the two decades before 1914. The so-called Reform Catholics did not constitute a group of even loosely united personalities with the same specific aims; at most they were agreed on trying to make Catholicism more contemporary and effective spiritually and intellectually. Among them were Franz Xavier Krause, noted art historian and long an opponent of Catholic political activity; Herman Schell, professor of apologetics at Würzburg, who wrote against Catholic exclusiveness and in favor of understanding with other communions; Albert Ehrhard, professor of church history at Freiburg, who stressed the Catholic need to accept science; and Carl Muth, publisher of *Hochland,* who called for a Catholic acceptance of realism and of the secular contribution in German literature. Still other less well known Catholic scholars attempted to organize an anti-Index movement (1907). In the heated debates that occurred among different Catholic groups just before World War I, ''Reform Catholics'' were often erroneously identified as Modernists. BIBLIOGRAPHY: W. Spael, *Das katholische Deutschland im 20. Jahrhundert* (1964).

[J. K. ZEENDER]

REFRIGERIUM, a Latin word meaning refreshment, the equivalent of the Greek *ánápsuxis.* By the pagans *refrigeratio* and *refrigerare* were used to indicate any kind of physical relief or relaxation (Cicero, *De senectute* 46, 57), but among the Christians *refrigerium* acquired the special connotations of a relief from punishment and of the eternal happiness of heaven (Tertullian, *De monogamia* 10: *spe aeterni refrigerii*). In a more particular sense the term was used to designate the practice common to pagans, Jews, and Christians of holding a commemorative repast at the tomb of a relative or friend on the day of burial or anniversary. The custom was extended to the tombs of the martyrs and was a particular devotion of St. Monica (Augustine, *Confessions* 6.2). Pious Christians on such occasions would share their food and drink with the poor, but it led to numerous abuses in Rome, Milan, and elsewhere and was gradually suppressed by ecclesiastical authorities (Augustine, *Ep.* 20.10). BIBLIOGRAPHY: E. Josi, EncCatt 10:627–631; H. Leclercq, DACL 14.2:2179–90. *BURIAL.

[M. J. COSTELLOE]

REGALIA (Lat. *regale*; Fr. *régale*) royal possessions in general, and esp. the right of secular rulers to the patronage of bishoprics and abbacies and the revenues thereof during vacancies. It arose in feudal times with the conception that bishoprics and imperial abbeys, with all their temporalities and privileges, were royal estates given as fiefs to the bps. and abbots, and subject to the feudal laws of the time. At first the right was claimed only during actual vacancies, but was abused later by deliberately keeping the see vacant or extending the collection of revenue even after the vacancy had been filled. It first appeared in France at the end of the 10th cent. where it continued to be exercised, not only by the king but also by powerful lay lords, throughout the Middle Ages. In England it appeared in the 11th cent. and spread rapidly. In Germany it was a major issue in the *investiture controversy and died out only in the mid-13th century. Regalian rights were consistently opposed by the popes. In the 17th cent. the practice was gradually revived in France; it was an issue in the Gallican controversy, and it continued to be exercised until the Revolution. BIBLIOGRA-PHY: L. Boyle, NCE 12:199.

[J. C. WILLKE]

REGALISM, the political doctrine or practice of the supremacy of the political sovereign, usually a monarch, in ecclesiastical matters. It overlaps with *Erastianism. The term does not seem to be applied to Caesarism, either in Byzantium or in great medieval conflicts between the Holy Roman Empire and the papacy, but only since the distinction between Church and State began to open out at the beginning of the 14th century. The claims of Philippe le Beau, however, were mild compared to the pretentions of the Reformation princes. Even Catholic rulers in France, the Iberian and Italian peninsulas, and the Germanies in varying degrees established control over *iura sacra*, often with the acquiescence or support of churchmen. (See *GALLICANISM; *FEBRONIANISM; *JOSEPHINISM; *LEOPOLDISM; *PISTOIA, SYNOD OF.) They asserted a supremacy, not in spiritual or even purely canonical, but in ecclesiastical matters, that is, those touching the interests of the state, e.g., the accumulation or disposal of property, the age of consent for marriage, or the taking of religious vows. Frederick the Great of Prussia hit the point when he referred disparagingly to the Emperor Joseph II as ''My brother, the sacristan.'' BIBLIOGRA-PHY: V. Del Giudice, *Corso di diritto ecclesiastico* (8th ed., 1950) bibliog.

[T. GILBY]

RÉGAMEY, PIE RAYMOND (1900–   ), French Dominican priest, monk, artist, author, and worldwide authority on Christian sacred art, thoroughly aware of 20th cent. dramatic tensions between faith, canon law, progress, individualism, ''piety,'' decrying the ''scandal'' of mediocrity of cheap mass production, indignant (though patient) with the incompetence of ''parish councils'' examines all in his seminal *Summa* of sacred art, *L'Art sacré au XXe Siècle* (1955; Eng. tr. *Religious Art in the Twentieth Century,* (1963).

[M. J. DALY]

REGAN, AGNES GERTRUDE (1869–1943), pioneer in social work who gave special attention to causes concerning women. R. was born and educated in San Francisco, Cal., taught in public elementary schools there for 13 years, was a principal for 14 years, and a member of the board of education (1914–1919). In 1920 she participated in the formation of the National Council of Catholic Women in Washington, D.C., became its executive secretary, and moved to Washington. Her influence nationally on the solution of social problems was significant. She played a major role in education for social work with the organization at The Catholic Univ. of America of the National Catholic Service School for Women in 1921 (later the National Catholic School of Social Service). From 1922 she served as instructor at the school and from 1925 to 1943 as its assistant director. Her prestige as a national figure in social work was acknowledged in the many organizations she served in an advisory capacity.

[J. R. AHERNE]

REGENERATION (Gr. *paliggenesia*), a term that explicitly occurs in Mt 19.28 in reference to the Jewish idea of the renewal of the cosmos in the age to come; and in Titus 3.5, in reference to the rebirth of the individual through Christian baptism. While the concept of a new birth or rebirth of the individual was a commonplace in the philosophical and religious literature of the Greco-Roman world (e.g., Apuleius, *Met.* 11.21), it is absent from Jewish writing prior to *Philo, since such ideas had polytheistic and idolatrous associations (Jer 2.27). The OT itself never speaks of a new birth for the individual, since by his natural birth an Israelite possessed all the rights pertaining to the people of God. However, in a broadly understood moral sense the choice of the people as a whole is often represented in the OT as a divine generation. Israel is the ''first born'' of God (Ex 4.22; Wis 18.13). God begot her in the Exodus-Sinai experience (Deut 32.6, 18–19); life in the wilderness was like the infancy of the people (Deut 1.31; 13.10; Hos 11.1). The new era spoken of by the Prophets is described as a new creation (Is 65.17–18; 66.22–23), when men's hearts would be renewed by God's Spirit (Ezek 36.26–28) and be engraved with the knowledge of the law (Jer 31.31–34; Deut 30.10–14). This new era was later given a futurist eschatological setting and associated with the eternal age to come in both apocryphal literature (Enoch 72.1; 91.16–17; Jubilees 1.29; 2 Baruch 32.6) and in the Qumran writings (1QS 4.25; 1 QH 13.11–12), but these events are not described as a new birth. In the NT the Synoptic Gospels do not report Jesus' speaking of a new birth.; they do speak of his comparing the word to a seed planted in man's heart (cf. Jas 1.18–21) there to become the principle of a new way of life (Mt 13.18–23), and of his teaching the necessity of becoming as children to enter the kingdom of heaven (Mt 18.3). It is in the Johannine literature that a concept of rebirth is explicitly found. Belief in Jesus is described as a being born of God (Jn 1.13; 1 Jn 2.29; 3.9; 4.7; 5.1,4,18). St. Paul avoids the rebirth concept but does speak of conversion as the work of a new Creation in which the old creature has disappeared (2 Cor 5.17; Gal 6.15). The baptized are to put on the new man (Col 3.10; Eph 4.22–24) and live the new life (Rom 6.4) that is both a continuing work of the Spirit (Rom 7.6; 8.1–16; Gal 5.16–25) and the restoration of mankind in the image of the Creator (Rom 13.14; Col 3.10). Through the believer the work of renewal must extend itself to the entire universe, since Christ has reconciled all creation with God (Rom 8. 19–23; Col. 1.20; Eph 1.10). The Pauline tone is continued in 1 Peter where Christians are described as newborn babes, ever to be nourished by the milk of the word (1 Pet 2.2) that has effected their new birth (*anagennaō*) both objectively (1 Pet 1.3) and personally (1.23). Where found in the NT, regeneration or new birth attempts to describe a profound reality. Recreated by Word and Spirit, man has become a new being (Tit 3.5) whose life and conduct is to be radically transformed (1 Pet 1.4;22–25; 1 Jn 3.9–10). The ethical difference alone is sufficient to distinguish the Christian reality from all pagan analogates. BIBLIOGRAPHY: J. Dey, *Paliggenesia* (1937); J. Fitzmyer, *Pauline Theology* (1966); E. Sjoberg, *Studia theologica* 4(1950) 44–85; 9(1955) 131–136.

[T. J. RYAN]

REGENSBURG (RATISBON), CATHEDRAL OF. Built upon an earlier basilica (1000) the Romanesque structure, from which remain important murals in All Saints Chapel (1155–64), was destroyed by fire in 1273. The Gothic structure, completed in 1400, boasts a sculptured *Annunciation* by the 13th-cent. Master of Erminold and external sculptures (1300–1400) by the noted Parler family. The spires were added 1860–72.

[M. J. DALY]

REGENSBURG, CONFERENCE OF, the meeting on reunion in 1541 between German Protestants and Catholics. It was the high point in attempts at reconciliation sponsored by the Emperor Charles V. The earlier Conference of *Hagenau (June 1540) and the Disputation of *Worms (Nov. 1540–Jan. 1541) had not succeeded but had created an atmosphere of dialogue. In spite of suspicion at the imperial attempts, Pope Paul III sent Card. Gasparo Contarini (1483–1542) as his legate to Regensburg. The Conference opened on April 5, 1541. The Protestant spokesmen were: P. *Melanchthon, M. *Bucer, Pistorius (d. 1583), and Cas-

par Cruciger (Creutzinger; 1504–48). John *Calvin was also present. The Catholics were J. *Eck, Julius von Pflug (1499–1564), and Johann Gropper (1503–59). The basis of discussion was a 23-article statement drawn up mainly by Bucer and Gropper, and later called the *Regensburg Book*. By May 2, 1541, the discussions had reached a statement of agreement not only on *original sin and *total depravity but also on the crucial issue of justification. The influence on Contarini of G. *Seripando's *double-justice theory seems to have helped the Catholic party accept a formula on justification agreeable to the Protestants, while they in turn agreed to the place of good works. The Conference came to an impasse, however, on the subject of the nature of the Church, the teaching authority of the pope, and the Eucharist. In addition there was suspicion on the part of both Rome and Martin Luther that the essential doctrinal opposition did not admit of compromise or concession. The Emperor ended the Conference July 29, 1541, with the Interim of Regensburg, pending a general council. When at Trent in 1547 the Regensburg formula on justification was examined, it was rejected. BIBLIOGRAPHY: Jedin Trent I:377–389; Léonard HistProt I:242–245.

[T. C. O'BRIEN]

REGGIO, ISAACO SAMUEL (IaShaR; 1784–1855), Italian rabbi, author, and scholar, who helped found the Collegio Rabbinico Italiano in Padua. He translated the Pentateuch into Italian, with Hebrew commentary (1821), produced the Book of Isaiah in poetic Italian (1831), wrote a scholarly introduction to the Scroll of Esther (1841), and translated Joshua, Ruth, and Lamentations. His Hebrew works were both exegetical and philosophical. He sought to prove the divine authority of the Torah in his *Ma'anar Torah min ha-Shamayim* (The Torah as Divinely Revealed, 1818). In his *Ha-Torah ve-ha-Filosfyah* (1827) he demonstrated the compatibility of philosophy, reason, and the Torah. His claim that the ancient laws no longer applied to Jews provoked controversy with other rabbis, including his own father.

[R. J. LITZ]

REGIMINI ECCLESIAE UNIVERSALIS, apostolic constitution of Paul VI, Aug. 15, 1967, reorganizing the Roman Curia, on the basis of the work of the commission appointed for this purpose after Vatican Council II. *CURIA, ROMANA.

REGIMINI MILITANTIS ECCLESIAE, the bull of Paul III, Sept. 27, 1540, canonically approving St. *Ignatius of Loyola's plan for the formation of the Society of Jesus, and implementation of the plan by means of a constitution to regulate Jesuit religious life.

REGIMINIS APOSTOLICI, a bull of Alexander VII dated Feb. 15, 1665, which imposed on four recalcitrant French bps.—Caulet, Buzenval, Pavillon, and Henri

Arnauld—the admission that five propositions previously condemned were heretical and were in fact taught by Cornelius *Jansen in his work *Augustinus. The bps. demurred: the Church can censure but cannot impute authorship infallibly (Antoine *Arnauld's famous distinction between *droit* and *fait*). The bps. bade their people accept the formulary "as to law but not fact." Alexander VII condemned this directive and planned a trial but died in 1667. Clement IX proved conciliatory and accepted from the bps a modified formulary (see PEACE OF THE CHURCH). His nuncio Bargellini remarked, quite prematurely, "Jansenism is dead." BIBLIOGRAPHY: F. Mourret, *History of the Catholic Church* (tr. N. Thompson) 6:412–415; DTC I:728.

[W. DAVISH]

REGINA MUNDI, see PONTIFICAL UNIVERSITIES, ROMAN.

REGINALD OF CANTERBURY (c. 1040–c. 1109), Latin poet and Benedictine monk of Saint Augustine's, Canterbury. R. wrote a great amount of verse in rhyming hexameter and was complimented for his work by the famous scholar, Hildebert, bp. of Le Mans. His longest poem is in six books (about 3,390 lines), and is the life of St. Malchus, a Syrian hermit. R.'s *Ad Fagiam castellum* (a poem of 27 stanzas) is very pleasing. He wrote with grammatical accuracy, much spirit, and taste. R. shows acquaintance with some Latin poets of classical times, and he combines the language of paganism with Christian sentiment. BIBLIOGRAPHY: W. Hunt, DNB 16:863–864.

[M. C. BRADLEY]

REGINALD OF PIPERNO (d. 1290), Italian Dominican theologian, from 1259 friend, confessor, and secretary to St. Thomas Aquinas. To complete the unfinished *Summa theologiae* he added the Supplement, mainly from St. Thomas' commentary on the book of the *Sentences;* he also completed the commentaries on St. Paul's Epistle, St. John's Gospel, and Aristotle's *De anima.*

[T. C. O'BRIEN]

REGINALD OF SAINT-GILLES, BL. (of Orleans; 1183–1220), early, important disciple of St. Dominic and his collaborator during the days of the founding of the Dominican Order. He was born at Saint-Gilles, Languedoc, not far from Arles. He taught canon law in the Univ. of Paris, (1206–1211); was appointed dean of the collegiate chapter of Saint-Aignan at Orleans (1212); and met St. Dominic while at Rome on pilgrimage in 1218. Shortly after becoming Dominic's disciple, R. became vicar for the rapidly expanding order while Dominic was absent in Spain. He was involved in Dominican foundations in Bologna and Paris during his short Dominican life. He was buried in Notre-Dame-des-Champs. From the beginning his tomb was venerated as that of a saint. His cultus was officially confirmed in 1875. In Dominican legend, Mary in a vision showed R. that the scapular was to be made part of

the Dominican habit. BIBLIOGRAPHY: A. Ferrua, BiblSanct 11:74–75; Butler 1:359.

[E. J. DILLON]

REGINALD, VALERIUS (Regnault, Raynauld; c. 1545–1623), French Jesuit, moral theologian, whose works were highly regarded by SS. Charles Borromeo, Francis de Sales, and Alphonsus Liguori. R.'s major work, *Praxis fori poenitentialis* (2 v., 1616), belongs to the period of casuistry's dominance in moral theology,

[T. C. O'BRIEN]

REGIUM DONUM (royal gift), an annual grant of money to *Nonconformist ministers in England, Scotland, and Ireland. The custom was started by Charles II, who, after the *Declaration of Indulgence of 1672, ordered 600 pounds distributed among Presbyterian ministers throughout Ulster; from 1690 to 1869 Presbyterian ministers in Ireland received financial aid. In England and Scotland the custom was not firmly established until 1723, when George I provided an allowance for needy widows of Nonconformist clergymen. By 1827 the gift had been extended to include Presbyterians, Baptists, and Congregationalists; but in 1851 it was discontinued, in part because of the wishes of the recipients themselves.

[F. E. MASER]

REGNANS IN EXCELSIS, the bull of Pius V, issued Feb. 25, 1570, excommunicating Queen *Elizabeth I of England. The document refers to her as the "servant of iniquity," the "pretended queen of England." It blames her for claiming "the place of the supreme head of the Church throughout all England," and lists her heresies and changes of Catholic doctrine and practice. She is therefore formally declared a heretic, and is excommunicated; her claim to the throne is nullified, and her subjects absolved of all allegiance and loyalty. The bull resulted from a formal trial held in Rome against Elizabeth. Its issuance marked the final severance of England from Rome and the beginning of harsher penal laws against Catholic *recusants. BIBLIOGRAPHY: Hughes RE 3:418–420.

[T. C. O'BRIEN]

REGNIER, NICOLAS (Niccolò Renieri), 1590–1667, baroque painter. R. studied with A. Janssens (Antwerp) and painted with B. Manfredi in Rome c. 1615. Active in Venice (1626–41), he was strongly influenced by Caravaggio and his early work was often attributed to that master. Later Bolognese influence points to G. Reni. Though R. was a portrait painter signing few of his works, H. Voss attributes to him the religious works, *Annunciation, Baptism of Christ, St. Teresa,* and *St. Philip Neri* (all in the Accademia, Venice). A *St. Jerome* (Berlin) and *John the Baptist* (Dresden) of false attribution have been established as R.'s works by H. Voss.

[M. J. DALY]

REGRESSION, a psychological phenomenon first investigated extensively by psychoanalysts. Freud observed that psychological development, by which he meant psychosexual or libidinal development, does not proceed as an undifferentiated process of growth, i.e., by a steady and gradual increase in capacities, but rather by a succession of phases or stages which are qualitatively distinct. At different stages, the libido attaches itself to different objects and seeks different modes of expression. Growth to maturity involves relinquishing each attachment successively and forming new attachments, the progress being from oral, anal, and phallic phases, to attachment to other persons (the parents) in the Oedipal phase, to adolescent and finally adult sexual attachments. Other psychologists (e.g., Erikson) have found analogous phase development in psychosocial attitudes (trust, independence, initiative, etc.), and in intellectual development (e.g., Gesell, Piaget). Regression involves a retreat from or relinquishing of a more advanced phase of sexual, social, or mental development and a return to a more immature phase. It is provoked by difficulties or conflicts encountered in adjusting to the advanced stage, or in maintaining an adjustment. When, e.g., a baby is born in a family that has an older child who has already begun to speak fairly well, and to care for himself in dressing, eating, use of toilet, etc., this child may retreat to baby talk and helplessness to regain the undivided attention he enjoyed before there was a rival. Again, an adolescent failing in good peer relations may retreat to the family circle. In sickness, many people crave the care and comfort they received when children. Regression is a common feature of neuroses (in which case it may serve a purpose, as a chance to recover strength by a temporary retreat). Clinically, regression is often indistinguishable from fixation, an attachment to some aspect of an immature phase persisting uninterrupted to adulthood.

[M. E. STOCK]

REGUERA, EMMANUEL DE LA (1668–1747), Jesuit mystical theologian. R. taught philosophy and theology at Valladolid for 24 years, and served in Rome for 9 years as revisor general of the Jesuits. His *Praxis theologiae mysticae* translated into Latin Michael Godinez's *Práctica de la teología mistica,* but added a great deal of commentary and theological substantiation. The *Praxis* became known as one of the best 18th-cent. works on mystical theology after it was revised and rearranged by Dominikus Schramm in his *Institutiones theologiae mysticae,* first published in 1774. BIBLIOGRAPHY: J. de Guibert, *Jesuits: Their Spiritual Doctrine and Practice* (ed. G. E. Ganss, tr. W. J. Young, 1964).

[T. M. MCFADDEN]

REGULA, ST., see FELIX, REGULA, AND EXSUPERANTIUS.

REGULA INCLUSARUM, see ANCRENE RIWLE.

REGULA MAGISTRI, a collection of maxims and rules for monastic life, dating probably from the 5th cent., and having much content and probably a source in common with the *Rule of St. Benedict; also showing the influence of Eastern monasticism and of *John Cassian in particular.

[T. C. O'BRIEN]

REGULAR BAPTISTS, a name that distinguished Particular from Separate Baptists during the *Great Awakening. The term had its chief significance in the South, where Shubael *Stearns and Daniel *Marshall, Separate Baptists from New England, labored as revivalists. The Separates were characterized by emotional preaching, prejudice against educated ministers, and reluctance to accept the *Philadelphia Confession. The Separates and Regulars united in North Carolina (1777) and Virginia (1787). A group called Regular Baptists exists today and claims continuity with the original English Baptists. This body is not listed in the *Yearbook of American Churches.* BIBLIOGRAPHY: W. L. Lumpkin, *Baptist Foundations in the South* (1961). *BAPTISTS.

REGULAR CLERGY (REGULARS), a term that refers to priests who are professed members of a religious order or institute, having solemn vows. In a broader sense, the term distinguishes any clerics who are bound by vows and live in community according to a religious rule, from the diocesan or secular clergy.

[R. C. CLIGGETT]

REICHENAU, ABBEY OF, a former German Benedictine monastery. The origins of the abbey date back to 724 when Charles Martel founded a Benedictine abbey on the Island of Reichenau in Lake Constance. It was known for its important relics of St. Mark and St. George and had an outstanding library and school. Reichenau was also known for its distinctive illumination work, characterized by strong, intense color and animation. Poor administration, however, brought about a decline in the 11th century. The abbey was brought under the Diocese of Constance in 1535, and secularized in 1802. Many of its buildings stand today. BIBLIOGRAPHY: Cottineau 2:2427–30.

[M. A. MCFADDEN]

REICHENAU, SCHOOL OF. The abbey of Reichenau, on an island on Lake Constance, was a great centre of civilization in the early Middle Ages. Until recently the finest Ottonian illuminated MSS were thought to have been produced there, but this is now disputed. Nevertheless, the nave frescoes of St. George at Oberzell (before 997) reveal the high quality of artistic production on the island. BIBLIOGRAPHY: C. R. Dodwell and D. H. Turner, *Reichenau Reconsidered* (1965); A. Grabar and C. Nordenfalk, *Early Medieval Painting* (1957).

[R. C. MARKS]

REICHENSPERGER, AUGUST AND PETER FRANCIS. August (1808–95), German jurist and politician, brother of Peter R. Reflecting the sentiment of his native Rhineland, he became a champion of Catholicism and an opponent of Prussianism. His political experience included tenure in the Frankfort Parliament, the Prussian National Assembly, the Erfurt Parliament, the Prussian Landtag, and the German Reichstag. He organized Catholic members of the Landtag into a faction that became the nucleus of the imperial Center Party in 1870, with the aim of protecting the freedom of the Church from State encroachment. The Kulturkampf was his greatest political struggle. Interested in art and architecture, he was also instrumental in the completion of the Cologne cathedral. **Peter Francis** (1810–92), German jurist and politician. His career closely paralleled that of his brother August. Educated in law and involved in contemporary political activity, he held judicial positions culminating in an appointment in Berlin in 1859. He was one of the founders of the Center Party and opposed Bismarck's *Kulturkampf. On strictly political and economic matters he developed independent views. His many writings include the autobiographical volumes *Reden der Gebrüder August und Peter Franz Reichensperger* (1858) and *Erlebnisse eines alten Parlamentariers im Revolutionsjahre 1848* (1882), plus technical volumes on the agrarian question and jurisprudence.

[R. H. SCHMANDT]

REICHERSBERG, MONASTERY OF, Augustinian monastery located on the Inn River near Linz, Austria. It was founded in 1084 by Werner of Reichersberg. After being pillaged, it was restored by Abp. Conrad I of Salzburg in the early 12th century. The work of Gerhoh and his brother Arno, who were active in the Gregorian reform, are associated with Reichersberg. Although suppressed in the early 19th cent., the monastery came under the control of the Augustinian Canons in 1907. BIBLIOGRAPHY: W. Jungschaffer, LTK 8:1109.

[M. A. MCFADDEN]

REICHLE (REICHEL, REUCHLIN), HANS (1570–1642), German Baroque sculptor and architect. R., after study (1588) with G. Bologna, carried the master's expressive style to the North, executing a *Magdalen* (1595), *St. Michael* (1603–06), the decoration of the palace of Card. Andreas, Austria, and tombs of Card. Philip von Regensburg (1611) and Prince-Bishop Conrad von Gemmingen (1612) in Einstatt.

[M. J. DALY]

REID, RICHARD (1896–1961), journalist. A native of Massachusetts, R. worked in Augusta, Ga., as a newspaperman. In 1921 he became executive secretary of the Catholic Laymen's Association of Georgia and editor of the *Bulletin,* a Catholic weekly. Continuing as a journalist, he was admitted to the bar and practiced law from 1930 to 1940. R. was president of the Catholic Press Association (1932–34). From 1940 until his death he was the editor of *The Catholic News,* diocesan weekly of New York, gaining wide recognition for his forceful promotion of racial equality and his attacks on totalitarianism.

[J. R. AHERNE]

REIGN OF TERROR, a term that describes the extreme efforts of the revolutionary government in France from March 1793 to Aug. 1794 to impose order and establish security at a time when conditions threatened national anarchy and foreign invasion. Internal factional strife, esp. in the National Convention, inaugurated the Terror. Political clubs—bourgeois Girondins, democratic Jacobins, and leftist Hébertists—competed for ascendancy. Meanwhile a war had to be won, and an epochal revolution resolved. Thus Terror ''legislation'' resembled martial law: the Law of Suspects, Sept. 17, 1793 made vague and arbitrary definitions of ''suspected persons'' to be arrested; the law of Dec. 4 served as the Terror's constitution; laws of Feb. and March 1794 (Ventôse Laws) approved land redistribution, and the Law of June 10 (22nd Prairial) defined enemies, legal procedure, and penalties; the Parisian Revolutionary Tribunal had the duty of imposing the death penalty for offenses under its jurisdiction. Estimates of the number of victims of the ''Terror'' have run to 40,000. Court records disclose that between March 1793 and Aug. 1794 there were 16,594 victims. The Great Terror of Paris (June-July 1794) numbered 1,515 victims. Terror machinery included central governmental committees, representatives on mission, and local watch committees. Unfortunately the Terror continued even after the military victory at Fleurus (June 24, 1794) had secured the E frontier and the Robespierrists had been purged in July (Thermidor). Many historians justify the Terror for its success in defending the Republic and defeating the enemy abroad. BIBLIOGRAPHY: D. Greer, *Incidence of the Terror during the French Revolution: A Statistical Interpretation* (1935); J. H. Stewart, *Documentary Survey of the French Revolution* (1951). *COMPIÈGNE, MARTYRS OF.

[R. J. MARAS]

REILLY, WENDELL (1875–1950), biblical scholar. R. was the first American to be granted a doctorate in Scripture by the *Pontifical Biblical Commission. He taught Scripture at St. Mary's Seminary, Baltimore (1911–47); translated and commented upon St. John's Gospel for the Westminster Bible; and was editor of the Confraternity of Christian Doctrine NT version, to which he contributed a translation of Ephesians. He helped found the Catholic Biblical Association and the CBQ, of which he was the first editor-in-chief (1939–47).

[T. M. MCFADDEN]

REIMARUS, HERMANN SAMUEL (1694–1768), German exegete; exponent of *deism. For a time (1723–27), R. was a Lutheran pastor but his career was spent mainly as professor of Oriental languages at the Johanneum Gymnasium, Hamburg. His *Apologie oder Schutzschrift für die vernünftigen Verehrer Gottes* (Apology for or Defense of the Rational Worshipers of God) was 20 years in the writing, but R. withheld it from publication. G. *Lessing published portions as anonymous writings (*Fragmente eines Wolfenbüttelschen Ungennanten*, 1774–78; sometimes referred to as the Wolfenbüttel Fragments). R.'s principal intent was to show reason as the basis of religion, the world as the adequate revelation of God, other revelations and miracles as mere human inventions. Controversy followed Lessing's publication, esp. because of R.'s attack on the historical character of the Gospels. D. F. *Strauss published a work on R. (1862) and an exposition of the whole of the Apology; R.'s work also influenced A. *Schweitzer's *Quest of the Historical Jesus* (1910). BIBLIOGRAPHY: P. Gay, *Enlightenment: The Rise of Modern Paganism* (1966) 61–62, 351, 381–382.

[J. P. REID]

REIMS (RHEIMS) CATHEDRAL OF, E of Paris, the traditional church of the coronation of the French monarchs, building continuously from Roman times until after World War 1 (1918–37), when mosaics, thermae with baptistery superstructure, and 5th-cent. apse were discovered, with the Crypt of St. Remi dating from the time of Abp. Hervé (c., 900–922). The Carolingion edifice, with westwork similar to St. Riquier, begun by Abp. Ebbo, was completed by Abp. Hincmar (845), consecrated in 862, with 10th-cent. additions by Abp. Adalberon (1140–60), a façade by Abp. Samson in 1152, and a Romanesque *chevet* with fine sculptured capitals of astonishing variety. After destruction by fire (1210), the Gothic cathedral was built with nave vaults 124′9″ and aisles 54′. The sketchbook (c.1232) of Villard de Honnecourt carries these drawings. A labyrinth (destroyed 1779) carried inscriptions determining the four architects—Jean d'Orbais (working 1210–31), Jean Le Loup who completed the transept portals, W front, and towers (1231–47), Gaucher de Reims (1247–55), and Bernard de Soissons who completed the nave and aisles (1255–1290). A large central figure is likely that of Aubri de Humbert who laid the first stone (1211). Robert de Coucy directed construction from 1290 to 1311. Sculptural work at Reims, more renowned than the architecture, is famous for the *Smiling Angel* and the magnificent *Beau Dieu* (a perfect synthesis of Christian thought and Gothic style). Important are (1) the antique *Visitation* group, (2) *Virgin of the Annunciation* in idealized Amiens style, (3) most original works in the style of the Joseph Master called *le style rémois*. The influence of Reims on late European medieval art was enormous. (The Bamberg *Visitation* is a paraphrase of Reims). The work of the Joseph Master led to the elegant sculpture of the 14th cent. which culminated in the Interna-tional Gothic style. BIBLIOGRAPHY: H. Reinhardt, *La Cathédrale de Reims* (1963).

[M. J. DALY]

REIMS, SCHOOL OF, 9th-cent. Continental MS school of which the *Utrecht Psalter (c.820) and the *Gospels of Bp. Ebbo of Reims (816–33), Epernay, are leading examples. The lively pen-drawn narrative scenes of animated outline (developments from Late Antique prototypes) characteristic of the Reims School, are considered a chief source of the Anglo-Saxon Winchester School.

[R. L. S. BRUCE-MITFORD]

REINACH, SALOMON (1858–1932), French archeologist, and author of over 70 books on art, religion, and philosophy. R. was long associated with the Musée d'Antiquités Nationales at St.-Germain-en-Laye, was a member of the Académie des Inscriptions from 1896, and a joint editor of the *Revue archéologique*. His works include *Manuel de philologie classique* (1884), *Répertoire de la statuaire grecque et romaine* (3 v., 1897–98), *Répertoire de peinture du moyen âge et de la Renaissance, 1280–1580* (1922); and his best-known book, *Orpheus, histoire générale des religions* (1909, with many subsequent editions; second English edition by F. Simmonds in 1942). R. was quite critical of Christianity and religion in general, once defining religion as "an ensemble of scruples that raises obstacles to the free exercise of our faculties." BIBLIOGRAPHY: E. Pottier, "Salomon Reinach," *Revue archéologique* (1932) 137–154.

[T. M. MCFADDEN]

REINCARNATION, see TRANSMIGRATION OF SOULS.

REISACH, KARL AUGUST VON (1800–69), German ecclesiastic. R. studied at the German College in Rome and after ordination was appointed prefect of studies at Propaganda College there (1830). He became bp. of Eichstätt (1836), then abp. of Munich-Freising (1846). He fought against the anti-Catholic sentiments of the time, upheld the Church's freedom from state interference, and was mainly responsible for the settlement of the *Cologne mixed marriage dispute. His strong stand moved King Maximillian II to request his transfer; Pius IX called R. to Rome where he became Cardinal Prefect of the Sacred Congregation of Studies and president of the commission for Church-State questions in the preparations for Vatican Council I. BIBLIOGRAPHY: H. Rall, LTK 8:1151–52.

[T. M. MCFADDEN]

REISCH, GREGOR (c.1467–1525), German Carthusian humanist. His major work was *Margarita philosophica* (1503), a textbook covering 12 branches of the arts and sciences. He was dedicated to the defeat of Lutheranism.

[P. J. HENNESSEY]

REITZENSTEIN, RICHARD (1861–1931), professor of the history of religions at the Univ. of Strassburg (1893–1911) and Göttingen (1914–31), specializing in Hellenistic religions. His major work, *Die hellenistischen Mysterienreligionen* (1910) is regarded to have exaggerated the influence of Greek mystery religions on the development of Christianity.

[T. C. O'BRIEN]

RELAND, HADRIAN (1676–1718), Orientalist. R. is noted for his studies on the history and geography of the Holy Land, *Antiquitates sacrae veterum Hebraeorum* (1708) and *Palaestina ex monumentis veteribus illustrata* (1714). These are classical studies, of use even today, gathered from a vast variety of ancient sources. R. also wrote a treatise on Hebrew coins and a description of the Islamic faith.

[T. M. MCFADDEN]

RELATIONS, TRINITARIAN, the references in the Trinity of one Divine Person to another that have been used since patristic times to express and illustrate their distinction from one another despite the unity of the divine nature. The three Persons constitute the divine essence, and the distinctive mode of being of each consists in its relationship to the other two (D 1330). This mutual interdirectedness of persons supposes four modes of relationship in God: *paternity, *filiation, active spiration, and passive spiration. The relationships connect the persons related (e.g., Father and Son) without joining them in a composite, personal unity. The terms of the relationship remain as concrete existents, and they are united only insofar as they remain distinct but ordered to each other. Thus Father, Son, and Holy Spirit are distinct and really existing persons, but they exist only in terms of their relatedness. Christian tradition holds that these relations are real and not merely mental—i.e., the relations truly exist between the Persons independently of our thought. The relations are also held to be subsistent, i.e., they are not an accidental quality but constitute God's nature. That is to say, it is of the very nature of the God made known in Christian revelation to be relational. BIBLIOGRAPHY: ThAq ST 1a, 39 and 40; B. Lonergan, *De Deo Trino* (1964) 2:201–204; J. Splett, SacMund 5:240–242; L. J. McGovern, NCE 12:219–220. *PROCESSIONS.

[T. M. MCFADDEN]

RELATIVES, those bound to each other by blood or marriage, and morally by an indebtedness in both *piety and *charity. Filial piety is concerned with honoring those who are sources of one's being and betterment (ThAq ST 2a2ae, 101. 1); in its direct expression it presupposes the beneficent influence of parents on offspring, and, remotely, of a person's ancestry on who and what he is. Loyal honor and devotion toward family are the descendants' rightful response to that indebtedness. The marks of respecting this duty vary in degree according to the degree of relationship

and so of beneficence received. Special circumstance may also require a reversal: that filial piety towards parents or other relatives include beneficence on the part of the younger towards the elder. Thus when parents or relatives (even brothers or sisters as forming part of the family lineage) are in need, the duty of piety includes coming to their aid. The amount and kind of assistance demanded is proportionate to the degree of relationship, to the need in question, and, of course, to the means available to the one obliged (*ibid*. 2). Charity towards neighbor also includes a special esteem for relatives. The order of charity—God, self, others—in regard to neighbor includes a preferential intensity between those bound together by family ties. The natural stability of this bond is the basis for that intensity, and for the special obligation to assist relatives in need (*ibid*. 26, 8).

[T. C. O'BRIEN]

RELATIVISM, as an ism, a classification—made esp. by those who accept absolutes as given—of any body of knowledge in which the criterion of validity or worth is relatedness to a knowing subject, or to a culture, a historical period, or other variable measure. Epistemological relativism is a classification applicable to any system of thought affirming the sheer relativity of human knowledge and denying the possibility of true, certain, and defensible knowledge of reality as it is. Thus skepticism, pure empiricism, pure idealism, are forms of epistemological relativism. Pure historicism, the reckoning of sociology of knowledge to be its sum total are other forms; pure positivism rests on a presupposed epistemological relativism. Ethical relativism is a classification of any theory about morals that denies moral *absolutes or that there is an objectively determinable moral good or evil, right or wrong, and consequently, any universally applicable norms of morality. Thus an unqualified personalism or pure situationalism, pragmatism, or utilitarianism are expressions of ethical relativism.

Epistemological relativism has bearing on theology with regard to the issue of religious language and the thought of which, presumably, language is the expression. The classical treatise "On the Divine Names" inspired in the West by the work of that title of Pseudo-Dionysius, in fact represented an effort to deal at once with the divine *transcendence, therefore incomprehensibility and ineffability, and the truth-value of human statements about God. St. Thomas Aquinas refused to accept that all predicates (divine names) applied to God were pure equivocations or even that all were purely relational names, expressing the creaturely dependence of the perfection they signified on God's causality, but saying nothing of the divine perfections themselves (ThAq ST 1a, 13. 2, 3, 4). He also acknowledged the limitation of the mode of signifying inherent in human language but still affirmed that in content the language expressed something positive and true about the divine reality. In this position Aquinas was guided by two principles: one that intelligence as such has bearing on being as such "whatever can be, can be understood" (*quidquid esse potest intelligi potest* 2 CG, 98); the second, is that since God has drawn man into a relationship with himself in human terms, human language cannot be utterly irrelevant to the divine truth ("this is not what people want to say when they talk about God" i.e., to make statements only meaning human relations to God ST 1a.13, 2). A second, allied bearing of epistemological relativism on theology is the issue of the value of dogmatic formulas or any propositional statement of the object of faith. Again St. Thomas touches on this issue in a celebrated text "the act of the believer terminates, not in a proposition but in a reality" i.e., in the divine reality expressed propositionally (ST 2a2ae,1, 2 ad 2). The point of this statement is that the assent of belief is to the divine reality itself; the psychological condition in which that assent is made includes the mediation of the "articles of faith" in which the reality is present to the mind and outwardly expressed in words. Theology deals with these statements, e.g. the articles of the Creed, other scriptural statements, dogmatic formulas of the ecumenical councils. What is the value of such propositions in respect to the reality to which they are supposed to point? In the recent history of Catholic theology, in this matching what has earlier occurred in Protestant theology, varying degrees of epistemological relativism have appeared. One form was condemned as *Modernism, which was accused of reducing dogmatic formulas or the truths of faith to being simply the expressions of the aspirations of the believing community at any given time. More recently other forms of reductionism have won acceptance by some Catholic theologians: the demythologizing of R. Bultmann; the dehellenizing of dogma advocated, e.g., by L. Dewart, i.e. ridding the biblical message of the Greek philosophical categories uncongenially imposed on it. Historicism and a form of the sociology of knowledge have also had their influence, namely in the reduction of the value of dogmatic formulas to the historical, cultural, and social conditions in which they were enunciated. Hans Küng's denial of the possibility of an infallibility in the Church with regard to propositional "truths" reflects such a line of thought. An advance in theological vision has been opened by Vatican Council II's recognition of a hierarchy of truths—that some are more basic and of the essence of the Gospel message than others. Yet there is a fundamental issue that probably will more and more divide Catholic theologians. It comes down to the acceptance or the rejection (perhaps disregard is the more exact word) of intelligence and intelligibility. This amounts to the acceptance or the disregard of intelligence as connaturally ordered to being and of intelligibility as the openness and coherence of being. In God intelligence and inelligibility are one. Acceptance of the mind's assent to truth and of the coherence of being ultimately affirms that unity of mind and being in God. Confidence in intelligence and intelligibility will not admit that the mediation of ideas and propositions in human knowledge of God makes that knowledge purely relative or in fact irrelevant. To oppose sheer relativism is to insist that, however deficient, dogmatic formulas possess an irreducible intelligibility that cannot be without counterpart in the pure being and intelligibility of God himself.

The meaning and application of ethical relativism to moral theology cannot be better presented than in the present work, the article by Thomas Gilby on moral *absolutes.

[T. C. O'BRIEN]

RELEASED TIME, a plan allowing public school pupils, on written parental request, to be excused for part of one afternoon each week to attend off-campus religious instruction given at no public expense by a representative of the pupils' religious faith. The movement is believed to have begun in the late 19th cent. following the establishment of public schools, when Protestant religious leaders, concerned with increasing juvenile delinquency and religious indifference, sought to promote various religious educational programs outside school hours. Although some Catholic leaders endorsed attempts to establish released-time programs, most Catholics at the time were more concerned with their own expanding parochial and Sunday school systems. The idea received considerable publicity in 1913 with the Gary, Ind. program, which was widely adopted. Because of alleged conflict with the First Amendment to the Constitution, released time gave rise to several court decisions, notably, the 1948 *McCollum v. Bd. of Education* (333 U.S. 203) case, which declared the Champlain, Ill. plan unconstitutional; and the *Zorach v. Clauson* (343 U.S. 306) 1952 case, which upheld the New York City released-time program. BIBLIOGRAPHY: R. F. Drinan, *Religion, the Courts and Public Policy* (1963).

[M. B. MURPHY]

RELICS, bodies or portions of the bodies of the saints after death, clothing or articles they used in life, or articles (e.g., bits of cloth) that have touched their remains or tombs. That the bodies of the great should be held in honor and articles associated with them treasured is too common a human phenomenon to require apology. That something of the same sort should appear in religious practice is therefore not surprising, but what has given offense to some is that relics of the saints have been made the object of religious veneration and that wonders have been attributed to them. Yet this was not a late development in Christian history. The bones of the martyred St. Ignatius (d. 108 A.D.) were carefully gathered in linen and were held to be a priceless treasure left to the Church. The bones of the body of St. Polycarp (d. 155?), held to be more precious than precious stones and finer than gold, were taken up by the Christians and put where it was meet (*Martyrdom of Polycarp,* 18). Towels and napkins were put out to catch up the blood of Cyprian when he was about to be beheaded (258). That such practices were common in the days of persecution, and that the Eucharist was celebrated at the tombs of the martyrs are facts too well-known to be denied. The common belief that graces could be obtained through the relics was testified to by the Fathers of the Church, esp. those of the 4th and 5th centuries. Cyril of Jerusalem justified the belief by reference to the dead man whose life was restored by touching the bones of Elisha (2 Kgs 13.21) and by the wonders wrought with the handkerchiefs and aprons carried from Paul's body to the sick (Acts 19.11). The practice was widespread in both East and West. It was approved by the Council of Nicaea II (787) and by that of Constantinople (1084). Constantinople was once the greatest repository of relics in the Christian world and attracted large numbers of pilgrims from both East and West. The cult gained greatly in popularity in the West during the time of the Crusades, when many notable relics (many spurious) were brought to Europe. Devotion to relics thereupon became even more popular in the West than it had been in the East, where it was perhaps somewhat overshadowed by the role played by icons in Eastern spirituality. In the West splendid reliquaries were built, and shrines possessing distinguished relics became centers of pilgrimage. There were abuses enough in the form of trafficking, the exhibition of inauthentic or doubtful relics, dubious claims made by competing shrines, and general superstitious practice, to provide some basis for the repudiation of the cult of relics by the Reformers. The Council of Trent renewed the measures already taken by Lateran Council IV to put a stop to the sale of relics and to provide proper authentication for relics exposed for public veneration, but it affirmed the lawfulness and utility of the veneration of relics (D 1822), basing the practice as the Fathers had done, on the fact that the bodies of the saints were, while on earth, temples of the Holy Spirit and they themselves were living members of Christ. Present regulations governing the veneration of relics are contained in CIC cc. 1281–89. BIBLIOGRAPHY: F. Chiavaro, NCE 12:234–240.

[P. F. MULHERN]

RELIGION (IN PRIMITIVE CULTURES). From the evolutionary theories of Spencer, Tylor, and Frazer and the quests for the origins of religion (e.g., by Durkheim and Freud), through the functionalist emphasis of Malinowski and Radcliffe-Brown on religion as a type of "social glue," to the recent concern with meaning (e.g., V. Turner) and with classification and communication (e.g., Lévi-Strauss), the study of primitive religions has revealed as much about the cultural ideologies of those who pursued it as about the subject itself. That situation can be traced partly to the ideological freight which the term "primitive" has carried. As E. E. Evans-Pritchard observes, "explanations of primitive religions were often couched at the same time both in terms of historical origins and of psychological origins, which made for great confusion, especially as the logical and chronological senses of 'primitive' and 'origin' were also seldom kept distinct" (*Neuer Religion*, 312). In what sense, then, can the welter of religious systems usually clas-

sified as primitive be seen as belonging together, particularly since many of the classical examples have either disappeared completely or changed dramatically in the course of recent history? Many attempts at a unified interpretation have relied on untenable theoretical presuppositions; W. Schmidt's idea of "primitive monotheism," Tylor's "animism," and Freud's totemic horde are cases in point. More promising is the observation that particular types of religious belief are associated with particular modes of subsistence. A. Jensen, for example, links the "high god" with cattle-breeders and cereal growers; the "dema deity" with root-crop cultivators; and the "master of the animals" with hunting cultures. Though such constructs remain abstract, they provide more solid ground for comparison and generalization than the various theories of origin and evolution. Unfortunately Jensen's own typology is part of a broader view of cultural history that contrasts the primal creative process with its later degeneration, a strategy tending to a denial of the autonomous interest of contemporary "primitives."

It has become increasingly clear, however, that individual primitive societies have long and complex cultural and religious histories. Changes in the natural environment and a people's relation to it, patterns of migration, technological innovations, the growth and diminution of local populations, and many other factors form the background of any contemporary society. The essential task of rethinking, adapting, and renewing traditional beliefs in the face of those challenges has been constant. The contemporary confrontation with representatives of Western European culture (which has prompted a variety of "readjustment movements") only highlights the dynamic relationship, long a part of primitive religions, between the past and the present, tradition and innovation. The contrast between the approaches to primitive religions as static reflections of origins and as dynamic historical movements can be summed up in a few remarks on the myth of Hainuwele from the Wemale of the island of Ceram. The myth relates the story of a young maiden who was formed from the blood of her father and the sap of a palm tree and who grew to maturity in 3 days. She had the extraordinary ability to produce such valuable objects as porcelain dishes, copper boxes, metal knives, and golden earrings in her excrement. Her father profited from that activity, but the rest of the tribe viewed her with increasing jealousy and hostility. They killed her; her father dismembered the corpse and buried pieces of it throughout the area. Tuberous plants, the principal Wemale foodstuff, grew from Hainuwele's remains. Jensen established the dominant interpretation of the myth as a tale of the origins of death, sexuality, and cultivated food plants. He stressed its archaic characteristics and the importance of the murder for the present order of Wemale society. For Jensen, and those who have accepted his view, the myth is important evidence for the archaic world-view of tuber-cultivators. In a brilliant dissent from that consensus, J. Z. Smith (in *History of Religions* 16 [1976]) has

3006 RELIGION, COMPARATIVE STUDY OF

noted that the opening lines of the myth presume rather than explain the origins of sexuality and death. Consequently, Jensen's views are groundless from the outset. In contrast, Smith takes his cue from Hainuwele's incongruous mode of production. She produces, without labor, manufactures goods that render reciprocal exchange between her and other Wemale impossible. The presence of those goods in the myth dates it to the recent period of contact with European civilization and suggests that the myth as it stands is an attempt to come to grips with a vastly superior material culture. The myth is intelligible only as a product of recent Wemale history, not of some dimly perceived and remembered ancestral period.

The task of assessing the interrelations of myth and history, or tradition and innovation, in primitive religions is particularly urgent for native populations and scholars alike. If the confrontation of primitive societies with contemporary western cultures throws into stark relief the social, cultural, and religious mechanisms which govern their life, perhaps it may also foster a new understanding of their past and the role of religion in it. BIBLIOGRAPHY: E. E. Evans-Pritchard, *Theories of Primitive Religion* (1965); *Anthropological Approaches to the Study of Religion* (ed. M. Bantan, 1966); A. E. Jensen, *Myth and Cult among Primitive Peoples* (tr. M. T. Choldin and W. Weisleder, 1963); M. Eliade, *Myths, Dreams and Mysteries* (tr. P. Mairet, 1960); B. Ray, *African Religions* (1976); *Gods, Ghosts, and Men in Melanesia* (ed. P. Lawrence and M. J. Meggitt, 1965); *Seeing with a Native Eye: Essays on Native American Religion* (ed. W. H. Capps, 1976); V. Turner, *Ritual Process* (1969); M. Douglas, *Purity and Danger* (1966); C. Lévi-Strauss, *Structural Anthropology* (tr. C. Jacobsen and B. G. Schoepf, 1963).

[E. V. GALLAGHER]

RELIGION, COMPARATIVE STUDY OF.

Comparative religion, a term more or less homologous with history of religion(s), is the scientific study of religious phenomena. In this sense the study of comparative religion can be described as the English equivalent of the German *Religionswissenschaft* (science of religion).

Origin. Comparative religion is a relatively young discipline which gained scientific status in the 19th cent. when the discovery of Indo-European languages and the ancient civilizations of the Near East shed new light upon the history of mankind and consequently modified the historical consciousness of the age. The universal humanism that characterized the romantic movement gave particular importance to the growing accumulation of data concerning newly discovered peoples and their religions. Since men first began to record their experiences in contact with people of cultures other than their own, some information of this kind had always been available; and this was greatly augmented by the Age of Discovery. What was new was the attitude toward such data. In principle at least the data came no

longer to be considered from a primarily monocultural point of view, as was the case when theology treated them within the framework of apologetics, or when the secularized theology of the philosophy of Enlightenment and its successive ideologies used them as instances to corroborate the thesis of natural religion, or even of atheism. Even though these and similar monocultural and ideologically biased approaches did not cease during the 19th cent., the objective of comparative religion was clearly set: a comprehensive understanding of religion as a phenomenon of man. This is the goal toward which the comparative study of religion is directed.

Scope. Because it is concerned with human behavior, attitudes, and ideas, comparative religion is necessarily historical. Religion is not a matter of *a priori* deduction, but of the empirically given, and this must be both confirmed and deciphered (interpreted) in its overall significance. This involves:

(1) The development of the history of religion(s) as an accurate and reflective account of regional and cross-cultural phenomena. The synchronical confirmation of religious data is completed by deciphering them in accordance with their diachronical genesis.

(2) The systematic analysis of specific religions as well as the empirical whole formed by them. In this, one confronts the question of the significance and the function of religion for and in the development of man. This in turn makes it necessary to get at the meaning and structure of religion, its "elementary forms" (Durkheim), and its many syntheses with the process of culture.

(3) The employment of the many disciplines presupposed to, or implied by, comparative religion as here described. Because man is a cultural being, a multitude of facets must be taken into consideration—psychological, social, political, and gnoseological. Texts and documents must be confirmed and interpreted. The psychology, sociology, and philosophy of religion must be explored. The problem of a standpoint, as a predicament as well as a necessary precondition of understanding, confronts comparative religion with theology and ideology. The methods of history and hermeneutics are shared with those of the study of culture in general.

An Independent Discipline? Certainly comparative religion is not self-sufficient. Yet none of the disciplines mentioned so far exhausts the object of a comprehensive understanding of religion, unless one denies religion itself—i.e., that there exists something like a cluster of cultural phenomena which is formed and qualified by the awareness of and the attempt to realize the meaning of ultimate symbols. Theology, for instance, may assimilate the religious data of mankind in many ways. But, as the expression of the consciousness of a community of believers, it necessarily precedes the comprehensive analysis of religious data to which comparative religion aspires. Theology of its nature is already committed to an interpretation of man that has to be seen at the root of the religious process. This holds true even among scholars of comparative religion as appears when they become involved, e.g., in the formation of the World Parliament of Religions or of a new universal synthetic religion, etc. Though activities such as these might be desirable from the viewpoint of human understanding, their rationale is by no means that of a comprehensive interpretation of religious phenomena.

A reduction of religious phenomena to the soul and/or society (psychology of religion, sociology of religion) is, from the viewpoint of culture, an ideological speculation rather than an interpretation of the empirically given. There always remains something more which can neither be swallowed by reductionist omnivorousness nor, for this reason, be removed from the scenery of man's search for an understanding of cultural reality. At the same time this situation of interdependence shows that it is neither desirable nor possible to establish a valueless interpretation of religious phenomena. Religion is simply too deeply integrated into the whole of culture to be isolated from it, without altering its phenomenality in basic ways.

Standpoint and Method. The scientific inquiry made by comparative religion stretches by inner necessity toward the ultimate horizon of humanity, for it is only by this relation that the subject matter is initially constituted. This explains why comparative religion came into being the moment such a horizon was reflectively envisaged. It also explains why the accumulation of data is not, nor ever will be completed, and why comparative religion cannot disregard the metaphysical problem of primitive and ultimate religion. To describe and to understand religious phenomena presupposes the theoretical anticipation of this relation. Both description and understanding will therefore be modified in accordance with the particular situation of those who study the complex reality of religions. As a cross-cultural comparison such a study presupposes the basic similarity of man. It will be successful to the extent that it succeeds in remembering the principles that constitute this similarity, while describing and systematizing the phenomena in their historical and functional context. In this sense we may also say that the methodological outlook of comparative religion is basically a phenomenological one, presupposing that phenomenology is meant as an imperative rather than as a well established philosophical method and system, an imperative which, in the context of empirical necessity and transcendental freedom, refers us to "things themselves."

BIBLIOGRAPHY: L. H. Jordan, *Comparative Religion, Its Genesis and Growth* (1905); W. Schmidt, *Handbuch der vergleichenden Religionsgeschichte* (1930); J. Wach, *Comparative Study of Religion* (1958); R. C. Zaehner, *Comparison of Religion* (1958); G. van der Leeuw, *Religion in Essence and Manifestation* (tr. J. E. Turner, 2 v., 1963); J. H. Randall, *Meaning of Religion for Man* (1968); *Phenomenology of Religion* (ed. J. D. Bettis, 1965); M. Eliade, *Patterns in Comparative Religion* (tr. R. Sheed, 1965).

[W. DUPRÉ]

RELIGION, PHILOSOPHY OF, see PHILOSOPHY OF RELIGION.

RELIGION, PSYCHOLOGY OF, a field of psychological inquiry concerned with the phenomena of religious belief and practice. As a special discipline it has taken several forms that differ from one another in the sources of data and in methods of investigation. Theological psychology of religion seeks to resolve theological data into terms meaningful from the viewpoint of psychology; philosophical psychology of religion aims at the philosophical analysis of the operations of the psyche involved in religious belief and practice; and analytical, or psychoanalytical, psychology of religion begins with clinical data and speculates on the role and function of religion in the integration of the human psyche. More esp. the name is given to the discipline that employs the methods of a positive science to study the manifestations of religion in individuals and groups. This discipline collects, arranges, and classifies its observations; it seeks to determine the causal factors operative in the arousal and development of religious attitudes, convictions, and forms of behavior. As understood in this sense, it appeared as a special discipline only in the latter part of the 19th century. It is not yet fully organized as a science; nor has it completely shaken itself free of a preoccupation with extraordinary events and psychopathological manifestations, a focusing of attention that has retarded its development. Important advances have been made, however, and the valuable research being conducted in the field is reflected in the number and quality of the reviews and periodicals devoted to the subject. The discipline is closely associated with the study of comparative religion, the sociology of religion, and cultural anthropology. The competence of the discipline does not extend to the evaluation of religious experience in terms of objective validity, a judgment that belongs properly to theology, although the theologian finds the psychology of religion a valuable ancillary discipline in reaching his conclusions. In the field of pastoral theology particularly, in matters such as counseling, vocational guidance, catechetics, the formation of moral judgment, preaching, and liturgical activity, studies undertaken by the psychology of religion have proved most useful. For an excellent select bibliography of the field, see A. Godin, NCE 12:258–261.

[P. K. MEAGHER]

RELIGION, SOCIOLOGY OF, the study of religions in their sociocultural context. This point of view regards religion either as an institution emerging with other institutions from the conditions of the larger society or as a unique subculture or set of subcultures interacting with other subcultures in cooperation or conflict. The discipline has gone through several stages. First some classical social theorists in the early 20th cent. took religion as one major institution to be integrated into their great social schemes. Max Weber (1864–1920) first coined the name and is often referred to as its founder. His interest in the sociological analysis of religion was shared by Émile Durkheim (1858–1917), as well as by his friend and collaborator Ernst *Troeltsch (1865–1923). After World War II, esp. in the U.S., the sociology of religion entered another stage in which it received increasing academic interest. This revival developed two distinct approaches: one can be considered a technical branch of academic sociology; the other, of broader scope, stems from what is called *Religionswissenschaft,* a term that has acquired a meaning equivalent to "history of religions."

Academic Sociology of Religion. The first is represented by Thomas O'Dea who treats substantive issues under two heads: functionalist and developmental theories. The functionalist treatment, leaning heavily on Durkheim, looks at religion as having an important role in the maintenance of general society or culture—most often that of providing meaning in the face of life's uncertainties and the inevitabilities of sickness and death. Developmental theory, stemming from Weber and popularized in the U.S. by Talcott Parsons, concentrates on aspects otherwise neglected: the role of religion in social change, its conflict with other elements in the social system, and typical developmental sequences in the growth of particular religions. This approach lists types of generalizations arrived at through the empirical study of religion: the likely sequence of development, the functional significance of religion to social stability, the role of religion in innovation and change, the relationship between historical developments and religious ideas, and the possible options open to religious movements and their probable consequences. Ordinarily these generalizations, although based on historical and other empirical findings, belong to theoretical sociology. Increasingly, however, such generalizations are either supported or challenged by strictly empirical surveys and studies. The two outstanding research centers are at the Univ. of Chicago and the Univ. of California at Berkeley.

Religionswissenschaft Approach. Under the influence of Joachim Wach (1898–1955), whose *Sociology of Religion* (1947) is already something of a classic in the field, the principal center for this approach became the Univ. of Chicago. Max Müller first used *Religionswissenschaft* in 1867 to describe the search for the "universal essence" of religion, but the "history of religions" approach has become much broader. Mircea Eliade suggested that the attempt to grasp the essence of the phenomena of religion by physiology, psychology, sociology, economics, linguistics, art, or any other study is false if it misses the unique and irreducible element in it—the element of the sacred. Nevertheless, assuming such irreducibility of religious phenomena, the approach does make use of all disciplines in conjunction with detailed historical studies of particular religions. One of Eliade's collaborators, Joseph Kitagawa, divides this approach into historical and systematic subdivisions. Under the first come the general history of religion and the histories of specific religions; under the second come phenomenological, comparative, sociological, and psychological studies of religion. Kitagawa suggests that

the crucial problem is the development of coordination and cooperation with historians who are competent in auxiliary disciplines as well as scholars in related subjects.

Relation to Other Disciplines. An accurate historical account of the cultural conditions and development of particular religions is obviously presupposed in the *Religionswissenschaft* approach; it is also the groundwork for such theoretical systems as those of Durkheim and Weber. Disciplines whose relationships need to be clarified include the philosophy and the psychology of religion, as well as academic sociology and *Religionswissenschaft* themselves. To clarify them, the three elements common to most religions should be distinguished: the conceptual-philosophical, the personal-mystical, and the sociohistorical. The purpose of the philosophy of religion should be the philosophical analysis of the conceptual element in given religions; that it is not always such is partly a lack of clarity about the nature of the discipline throughout the history of the philosophy of religion. Psychology of religion, a study of the personal-mystical elements, should be considered with psychological studies of religious men, whether contemporary or historical; in fact, much contemporary psychology of religion concerns itself with conversion, atheism, and myths, and with the relation between religion and psychiatry. In the relationship of *Religionswissenschaft* to general history and sociology, the latter can be taken as an attempt to study man in society, to investigate the conditions and consequences of living in one or another type of society. Sociology thus views religion either as a function of society or as related to the conditions of society. *Religionswissenschaft,* however, while its point of view is generally social as well as historical, insists on treating religious phenomena as irreducible even while relating them to psychological or sociological factors. It may also be worthwhile to relate the sociology of religion to the sociology of knowledge, an important but relatively uncultivated field that goes back to Karl Mannheim's *Ideology and Utopia* (1929). Sociology of knowledge turns the instruments of social analysis inward, reflecting on the work of communities of knowers. This has been done mostly with respect to sciences other than social, but a number of social scientists recognize the need for subjecting their own community to this analysis. What this suggests for the sociology of religion is that its practitioners should subject their work to critical self-evaluation.

Importance for Theology. The sociology of religion supplies material for theological, conceptual analysis, which in turn supplies criteria for evaluating religious experience. Beyond this obvious relationship sociology of religion can supply for theology: (1) a cultural background against which theological statements become meaningful in a way they often are not in the abstract; (2) the related possibility of understanding historical dogmatic statements when external controls are not available (as with the literary genre approach in biblical studies); (3) a ground for the comparison of theologies in an ecumenical spirit; and (4) concrete, dynamic details on how religion is actually lived—something that can safeguard theological conceptualization from excessive idealism. BIBLIOGRAPHY: E. Durkheim, *Elementary Forms of the Religious Life: A Study in Religious Sociology* (Fr. original, 1912; Eng. tr. J. Swain, 1947); M. Weber, *Sociology of Religion* (Ger. original, 1922; Eng. tr. E. Fischoff, 1963); *History of Religions: Essays in Methodology* (ed. M. Eliade and J. Kitagawa, 1959); M. Berkowitz and J. Johnson, *Social Scientific Studies of Religion: A Bibliography* (1967); R. McDermott, "Religion as an Academic Discipline," *Cross Currents* 18 (1968), 11–33.

[P. T. DURBIN]

RELIGION, TEACHER OF.

Vatican Council II reaffirmed the Church's own title as educator, "because she has the responsibility of announcing the way of salvation to all men, of communicating the life of Christ to those who believe, and of assisting them with ceaseless concern so that they may grow into the fulness of the same life," and because as a mother she has the mission of giving her children the kind of education through which their entire lives can be penetrated with the spirit of Christ" (VatII ChrEduc 3). Of the particular means proper to the Church "catechetical training is foremost. Such instruction gives clarity and vigor to faith, nourishes a life lived according to the spirit of Christ, leads to a knowing and active participation in the liturgical mystery, and inspires apostolic action" (*ibid.* 4). These statements stand as the motives and functions of the teacher of religion in the Church. The Council identifies as the first teachers the parents (*ibid.* 6), describes the vocation of those who teach in schools as an assistance to enable parents to fulfill their task (*ibid.* 5), and characterizes teachers as witnesses to the presence of the Church, exercising a true apostolic ministry (*ibid.* 8; cf. VatII ApostLaity 12,16). As an apostolate connected with the education mission of the Church itself, the teaching of religion is in the service of the hierarchic ministries in the Church of teaching, governing, sanctifying, and is a genuine form of service to these ministries. A model of the teaching of religion can be seen in the renewal of the adult catechumenate in the new rite of baptism. Through the centuries the teaching of religion has been a continuation of the catechesis in the Early Church. In the decree introducing the catechumenate the new ritual describes the ministries of bp., presbyter, and deacon, then that of catechists: "The office of catechists is important for the progress of the catechumens and for the growth of the community. As often as possible they should have an active part in the rites. When they are teaching, they should see that their instruction is filled with the spirit of the Gospel, adapted to the liturgical signs and the course of the Church year, and enriched by local traditions as far as possible" (48). The new rite also envisions a post-baptismal catechesis (mystagogia) for deepening Christian experience. The sentiments and objectives of the whole catechesis are really continuous in the work of the teacher of religion. The primary objective is the formation of a Christian spirit, character, and way of living; the knowledge imparted and the way in which it is imparted are directed toward the will as much as to the mind. This formal character of the teacher of religion can be brought out in distinction from the role of the theologian. Theology is, in purpose, a science of salvation; but it seeks, at least in some of its forms, to achieve that purpose by the profundity, coherence, clarity of its address to the mind. Content, method, effective communication are part of the religion teacher's responsibility. But primarily and formally the aim is to lead to the beginning and development of religious attitudes and decisions. That makes a primary characteristic of the religion teacher, commitment to that aim and emphasizes the task of communicating conviction through that commitment and through example. On that basis the professionally trained teacher of religion should be able to count on participation in the work by parents and by volunteers. There is in fact in the Church a spread of the ideal of the catechesis in parents' becoming involved in the learning process as they help prepare their children for first communion. Parish study programs for both school-age members and for adults are being developed with the participation of volunteers. If both parents and volunteer assistants surround the trained teacher of religion, there is a communal share in the spirit of the Church's own educative mission, a true ministry, and a true presence of Christian witness.

[T. C. O'BRIEN]

RELIGION, VIRTUE OF.

Cicero derived the Latin word *religio* from *relegere,* to read again, to deepen one's knowledge of. Lactantius and Augustine derived it from *religare,* to connect, to join. It is this latter etymology that has prevailed in Christian theology. The word has come to mean the relationship between God and man, a very wide and indeterminate concept. This article discusses only part of this concept: its use in Christian moral theology.

The Bible. The word "religion" is seldom used in Scripture. The biblical expressions corresponding to what theologians call religion are fear and piety (*pietas*).

Fear. Man's immediate reaction to the Godhead is one of anguish. The sacral is acknowledged first as *tremendum* (Ex 20.18). God is the all powerful and all holy, and man is utterly unable to face him (Is 6.5). Man is impressed by the awesomeness of God. The acknowledgment through faith of the fact that this almighty God loves us introduces a new situation inviting respect and devotion and is the NT concept of the fear of God (Acts 10.35).

Pietas. In the Sapiential Books the fear of the Lord is identified with *pietas* (Sir 1.11–20), a much wider concept in biblical language than in ours. The word originally denoted the bond among family, friends, and servants (e.g., filial piety). According to the Covenant it is used to express the relationships between God and his people. Piety then finds its expression in worship, but also in obedience and dutifulness, in justice and righteousness. Piety toward God is inseparable from a correct relationship with our fellowmen (Is 1.10–17). Christ is its perfect expression (Acts 2.27; I Tim 3.16) because he gives perfect worship (Heb 10.5–10) and fulfills his Father's will (Jn 8.29). The new man who practices Christ's meekness and takes part in God's worship practices the true religion (Heb 12.28), which is pleasing to God.

Moral Theology. The word "religion" is used in modern theology almost without exception in a psychological, sociological, or religio-historical sense. Modern moral theology is concerned either with the idea of the divine common to all religions or with the psychological factors that characterize man's relationship to God, but hardly at all with religion as a moral virtue. Medieval scholasticism, however, systematized biblical teaching in making it precise but also in limiting it. Thomas Aquinas treats of religion in the second part of the *Summa theologiae* on morals, and makes it a subdivision of justice (ThAq ST 2a2ae, 81–100). Even though religion has God's worship as an object, it does not come under the theological virtues since it belongs to all men and is not specifically Christian. And as God is other than man, religion comes under justice, the cardinal virtue that regulates man's relations with others. What is the right relationship between two people who are unequal—one of whom is unable to give as much as he receives from the other? This unequal relationship—parent to child, government to citizen—brings with it the double duty of respect and service from the side of the inferior. The same is true for man's relationship with God: both in his inner life and in public. St. Thomas limits religion to the direct God to man relationship: respect is expressed through worship, and service, through the liturgy. But the NT notion of service is a much wider one (Jas 1.27); Jesus' words on the two equal commandments (Mt 27.39) widen the field of religion very considerably. On this point the Thomist synthesis belongs more to moral philosophy than to NT theology.

This classical moral theology was the basis for the spirituality of Card. de Bérulle (1575–1629). It was a theocentric reaction to the anthropocentric character acquired by Western Catholic spirituality through the *Devotio moderna*. Bérulle insisted that worship is the chief duty of man, and that Jesus is the religious man par excellence since he is first and foremost the Father's worshiper.

Protestant theology has not regarded religion as a virtue. The Romantics, F. *Schleiermacher (1768–1824) in particular (who defined religion as the feeling of absolute dependence), used religion as an apologetic; but modern Protestant theology, under the influence of Karl *Barth, has definitely dissociated itself from any form of combination of the gospel and religion, regarding them as two quite different elements.

A standpoint such as that adopted by Thomistic theology will, incidentally, be entirely foreign to a Protestant theology for which the human side of God's relationship is subordinate. One notices less intransigence where religion is concerned, among those Protestant theologians who are occupied more with pastoral than dogmatic problems, but this has very little to do with the virtue of religion in the ordinary RC use of the term. BIBLIOGRAPHY: A. I. Mennessier, "Virtue of Religion," TL 4:393–444; A. Vonier, *New and Eternal Covenant* (1930); C. M. Magsam, *Inner Life of Worship* (1958).

[V. DUCLOS]

RELIGIOSITY, a term with different meanings in popular usage, anthropology, and Hegelian philosophy. (1) In the pejorative sense in which the word is popularly understood, it signifies an exaggerated, inappropriate, or affected concern about, or preoccupation with, matters of religion. (2) In anthropology, it signifies man's capacity to enter into communion with God and things or persons that are sacred. History testifies that man is a relational being, that he cannot find ultimate fulfillment in himself. He craves communication with an Absolute. (3) G. W. F. *Hegel uses the term to signify the continual human effort to move beyond selfish or merely bodily interests, to participate in cultural achievements, and to grow into a community of spiritually concerned people. Religiosity becomes a saving bridge between total objectivism, recalling men to themselves lest they live entirely for things, and total subjectivism, rejecting exclusive self-concern in order to achieve community service and an ordered search for truth. BIBLIOGRAPHY: A. Van Kaam, *Religion and Personality* (1964); J. D. Collins, *Emergence of Philosophy of Religion* (1967) 289–292, 302–310.

[T. M. MCFADDEN]

RELIGIOUS, CONSTITUTIONS OF, see CONSTITUTIONS, RELIGIOUS OR MONASTIC.

RELIGIOUS, DISMISSAL OF, see DISMISSAL OF RELIGIOUS.

RELIGIOUS ABSTRACT ART, nonfigurative art intentionally made to serve religion. Three pioneers of abstract art wrote of spiritual content as a primary concern in their art: W. Kandinsky, *Concerning the Spiritual in Art* (1912); K. Malevich, *The Non-Objective World* (1927); and P. Mondrian, *Plastic Art and Pure Plastic Art* (1937). Their thesis that nonfigurative work transcended the materialistic in a spiritual extension of man, formed a basis for later acceptance of spiritual values in abstract art. Controversy arose concerning the religious value of abstract art which offers no image or figurative subject. The Christian experience of art had been dominantly one of image and representation, e.g., devotional picture, biblical illustration. Some ecclesiastics questioned whether abstract art, having no subject to distinguish it from the profane, could be properly considered religious. Resistance to the use of nonfigurative art in Catholic and Protestant churches lessened after World War II. By the late 1950s leading abstract artists were represented in new and significant churches: J. Albers and H. Bertoia in the U.S.; A. Manessier and R. Ubac in France; G. Meistermann in Germany; M. Subirachs in Spain; and

M. Goeritz in Mexico. In the U.S. Roman Verostko was the first to clarify the religious values of abstract art in the church; these values became an important concern of the First International Congress on Religion, Architecture, and the Visual Arts held in New York, 1967. BIBLIOGRAPHY: R. J. Verostko, NCE 1:44–54; *Journal of the First International Congress on Religion, Architecture, and Visual Arts* (National Council of Churches, N.Y., 1969); W. Wilson, *Modern Christian Art* (1965) 72–74 and *passim*.

[R. J. VEROSTKO]

RELIGIOUS COMMUNITIES, ANGLICAN. Religious orders were reintroduced into the Church of England in connection with the *Oxford Movement. This development followed three centuries in which they were virtually absent from Anglican life. All monastic establishments in England were suppressed by Henry VIII and though some were briefly revived under Mary, they were not allowed to continue under Elizabeth. Later years saw occasional attempts to establish communal religious life, but these were sporadic and transitory. One of the best known is Little Gidding, a manor in Huntingdonshire where N. Ferrar, a deacon, led a group of about 40 people, all related to him. It was established in 1625, and continued until Cromwell's soldiers dispersed the group in 1646. For a long period after the Reformation, Anglicans generally exhibited a strong antagonism to the idea of monasticism, considering it a principal evil of the religion they had rejected. But the Gothic revival and other influences of the 19th cent. gradually brought new attitudes, though the "Anglo-Catholic" trends were stoutly resisted by "Protestant" Anglicans. Early in the century, poet Robert Southey was asking why the Church of England produced no Sisters of Charity. Then after the Oxford Movement's beginning, usually dated from 1833, its leaders discussed the idea. In 1841 E. B. *Pusey took the vows of Marian Rebecca Hughes, the first woman to make vows in the Church of England since the Reformation. In 1849 she became mother superior of the Society of the Holy and Undivided Trinity. But meanwhile other orders had been formed. The first was the Sisterhood of the Holy Cross, founded by Pusey in London in 1845. Since then more than 100 women's communities have been established, a majority devoted to serving the poor and other active ministries but some following the contemplative life. Some ceased to exist but several others have emerged in the 20th century. At Littlemore, J. H. *Newman while still Anglican lived with a small community of men without vows. But the first regular order for men was the Society of St. John the Evangelist, founded in 1865 by R. M. Benson. Other important men's orders, all still in existence, included the Community of the Resurrection, founded 1892 by C. Gore; Society of the Sacred Mission, founded 1891 by H. H. Kelly; English Order of St. Benedict, founded 1914 at Nashdom Abbey after a Benedictine community at Caldey turned to Rome; and Order of St. Francis, founded 1921. Religious communities gained official standing in the Church of England in 1935 when an Advisory Council on Religious Communities was established. Some English orders have branches in the U.S. and other countries. U.S. orders were also formed independently, beginning about the same period as in England and several survive. Among the more influential is the Society of the Holy Cross, West Park, N.Y., founded in 1881 for men. BIBLIOGRAPHY: P. F. Anson, *Call of the Cloister* (rev. ed. 1964).

[T. EARLY]

RELIGIOUS COMMUNITIES AND PROTESTANTISM. A reaction against monasticism constituted a principal emphasis of the Reformation, exemplified in Luther's own experience. Almost all religious orders were suppressed in the regions where Protestantism became dominant. Exceptions included such minor survivals as the Mollenbeck Augustinians, near Rinteln, Germany, who accepted Lutheranism and survived until the Thirty Years War. The impulse toward religious community emerged in other forms, however. Anabaptist groups such as *Hutterites established patterns of communal religious life, and similar influences came from *Pietism, as at *Herrnhut. In the 19th cent. liturgical, "high church" movements in Lutheranism led to reestablishment of religious orders in the traditional sense. Orders of deaconesses were founded, with some resemblance to religious orders. Several 20th-cent. theologians, including D. *Bonhoeffer, have directed attention to religious life in community. The most influential of several modern Protestant monasteries has been *Taizé, a men's order founded in 1940; in origin Reformed, it has a special commitment to Christian unity. Among the more influential women's orders has been the Evangelical Sisterhood of Mary, founded in 1947 in Germany. In the U.S. a variety of communities have arisen under Protestant influence. Examples range from *Shakers to *Koinonia Farm in Americus, Ga. BIBLIOGRAPHY: F. Biot, *Rise of Protestant Monasticism* (tr. 1963); D. Bloesch, *Wellsprings of Renewal* (1974). *RELIGIOUS ORDERS ANGLICAN; *IONA COMMUNITY.

[T. EARLY]

RELIGIOUS DANCING, see DANCING, RELIGIOUS.

RELIGIOUS EDUCATION, a term and concept developed in the 20th cent. and having three referents, one or all of which sometimes overlap. 1) education directed in general to the inculcation of religious values and morals; 2) education in the specific tradition, tenets, doctrines and/or ceremonies of any religious sect or denomination; 3) education about religion, about different religious bodies (sometimes described as comparative religion), or religious literature (Bible, Torah, Koran), etc.

Scholars in psychology and sociology are credited with bringing together religion and education to form the sense religious education now has. The social sciences delineated elements religion has in common with educational theory and practice so that religious education is seen as a dimension of socialization into a particular religious tradition or denomination. The works of Émile Durkheim (1858–1917), H. Paul Douglass (1871–1953), Joachim Wach (1898–1955), Max Weber (1864–1920), and other sociologists pointed out the interrelationship of religion and culture. Taken generically, according to those scholars, religious experience and factors integral to it are derived from and are characteristic of all religious faiths. The works of George Albert Coe (1862–1951), John Dewey (1859–1952), William James (1842–1910), Lewis J. Sherrill (1892–1957), and others demonstrated that the believer's genuine religious experiences involved both her/his discernment of truth and value along with the integrating behavioral response consequent upon it. In many countries religious education is viewed as a shared responsibility of the home, the Church and the State. In some areas, in the Muslim world for example, religion and education are interwoven. Because Jewish education is a matter of transmitting a particular culture at the heart of which is a covenantal commitment, the home and synagogue (or temple) are intimate collaborators.

Religious education, as a descriptive term, is used primarily in English-speaking countries, with Great Britain claiming its longest use. Though worship and religious instruction had had a place in the curriculum of most British schools for centuries the Education Act of 1870 assured the continuance of the tradition. However, it was the 1944 Education Act that made religious education and collective worship obligatory in both county and voluntary schools. The Act includes a qualifying statement specifying that this be implemented "in accordance with an agreed syllabus." No other item of the curriculum is so specifically detailed in the Act. Two troublesome issues have surfaced in the implementation of that legislation: the relationship between religious education and moral education; the distinction between teaching religion and teaching *about* religion. Linked to both is a third matter. Non-Christian adherents maintained that their beliefs, values, emphases, and practices found little hospitality or understanding in a country predominately Christian. They have urged a phenomenological approach toward the study of religion as well as a more scientific concentration on the religious development of children.

The widespread use of the term religious education in the U.S. is linked to the founding of the Religious Education Association and that association's organ, *Religious Education,* which began circulating in 1906. The association came into existence to counter the inadequacies experienced by the Christian-nurture philosophy and by the regular Sunday School. The REA is an interdenominational body whose purpose, as its constitution states, "shall be to promote religious and moral education." The Association described its broader objectives in this way: "To inspire the religious forces of our country with the educational ideal; to inspire the educational forces with the religious ideal; to keep before the public the ideal of religious education and the sense of its needs and value." To realize its objectives is no small task in a nation where Church and State are constitutionally separate.

D. Campbell Wyckoff of Princeton noted a discomfort with the amorphous aspect of the term religious education. He observed that after 1940 Protestant groups increasingly employed "Christian education" in their reference to church-sponsored education, while the three main branches of Judaism (Orthodox, Conservative, and Reformed) used "Jewish education." Roman Catholics, with their mushrooming parochial school systems in the 1940s and 50s referred to their educational theories and practices as "Catholic education." The latter make a distinction between education as specifically school centered and an education that is directly religious and as such is both more comprehensive and ongoing in its incorporation of the whole of life.

The term religious education first appeared in U.S. Catholic periodical literature in 1911. Gradually the term permeated the Roman Catholic vocabulary so that by 1970 religious education had, in general usage, become almost synonymous with or used interchangeably with "teaching catechism," "teaching religion," "religious instruction," and "CCD classes (Confraternity of Christian Doctrine classes)." With the promulgation of the *General Catechetical Directory* in 1971, however, there was a distinctive turn about, and the term catechesis and its derivatives began to reappear with greater frequency. Catechesis, an ancient term, is considered indigenous to Christianity. In the verb form *(katēcheō)* it occurs eight times in the NT and was subsequently adopted by early Christian writers. Its current popularity stems from its identification with an ecclesial activity instead of a school-based subject. It encompasses all aspects of the Church's educational ministry: prebaptismal instruction, postsacramental experiences, shared understandings of the faith, Bible reading, total community responsibility, and life-long explorations into the meaning of being a committed Christian. BIBLIOGRAPHY: G. A. Coe, *Social Theory of Religious Education* (1969); Durham Report on Religious Education, *The Fourth R* (SPCK, 1970); G. Durka and J. Smith, *Emerging Issues in Religious Education* (1976); D. Huebner, "Education in the Church," *Andover Newton Quarterly* 12 (1972) 122–129; D. Konstant, "Religion in Public Education: The English Experience," *Living Light* 10 (1973) 455–467; *Studies in Religious Education* (ed. P. H. Lotz and L. W. Crawford, 1931); B. L. Marthaler, *Catechetics in Context* (1973); C. F. Melchert, "Does the Church Really Want Religious Education?" *Religious Education* 69 (1974) 12–22; "Religious Education in a Pluralistic Society," *Religious Education* 68 (ed. H. L. Puxley, 1973); W. R. Rood, *Understanding Christian Education* (1970); R. M. Rummery, *Catechesis and Religious Education in a Pluralist Society* (1975); J. H. Westerhoff, *Will Our Children Have Faith?*

(1976); D. Campbell Wyckoff, ''Religious Education'' *Encyclopedia Americana* 23 (1975) 348–354.

[M. C. BRYCE]

RELIGIOUS EDUCATION AND PUBLIC SCHOOLS.

On the contemporary scene two prominent issues emerge: the practice of released time and religion in general education. Both surfaced in the wake of the 1940 White House Conference on Children in Democracy. Concern over religious illiteracy and disquieting waves of juvenile delinquency confronted educators, parents, and civic leaders and their search for solutions directed them to the schools. The White House Conference recommended that a comprehensive study be made of ways to make available to children the resources of religion through public education in cooperation with the Churches.

Released time is the practice of excusing during school hours those students in public schools who wish to attend religion classes in church institutions of their choice. Only those students who request, or whose parents have requested, regular release are excused during the academic session. It is a practice that existed unofficially in some parts of the U.S. during the 19th century. The main thrust of litigation and judicial decisions on this matter (*McCollum* v. *Bd. of Education* [Champlain, Ill] 333, U.S. 203 at 225 [1948]; *Zorach* v. *Clauson* [New York] 343, U.S. 306 [1952]) has been to define the permissibility of specific applications rather than to obstruct the expansion of the movement. Released time programs are operating successfully in some areas of the nation at the present time.

A second issue to come to the fore with new vigor after the White House Conference of 1940 was that of including the study of religion in public school curricula. For many years certain educational leaders favored including the objective teaching about religion in the public schools, as a necessity for a complete secular education. In 1952 (*Zorach* v. *Clauson* above) the Supreme Court indicated that such a possibility was not in conflict with the constitution as long as such classes were elective, not compulsory, and did not advocate denominational points of view. Studies of the ways and means of incorporating religion classes into the general curricula of public schools were made by numerous groups, particularly the American Association of School Administrators and the Religious Education Association, along with universities that could prepare religious education faculty. In 1971 the National Council on Religion and Public Education was founded to encourage the movement. The NCRPE is not a membership organization but a forum for facilitating cooperation among persons and groups interested in the cause.

Strictly speaking, the programs which include religion in the general education curricula more legitimately bear the title ''religious education'' than do many others by the same name. One British educator, writing in 1973 out of years of experience, cautioned his U.S. peers about too great an optimism on this matter. ''The provision of religious education in state schools does not necessarily solve the problem of the Churches in this field.''

[M. C. BRYCE]

RELIGIOUS EXPERIENCE, see EXPERIENCE, RELIGIOUS.

RELIGIOUS FORMATION CONFERENCE,

successor to the Sister Formation Conference, constituted by the Conference of Major Superiors of Men and the Leadership Conference of Women Religious in 1976. The purpose of the Religious Formation Conference is to support and promote the work of those charged with the spiritual formation of men and women religious, and also to assist religious communities in renewal, self-understanding, and the identification of their specific ministry. The Conference defines religious formation as ''the process by which the Holy Spirit forms the Christian through consecration to an evangelical way of life within the Church to work more effectively to build up the Kingdom of Christ.'' Formation is taken to mean a never-ending process for personal vocation affirmation and community sense of mission. The Conference exists in its present form because of Vatican Council II's *Perfectae caritatis,* the Decree on the Appropriate Renewal of Religious Life, and more proximately because of the implementation of that decree by the 1969 Instruction of the Congregation of Religious and Secular Institutes, *Renovationis causam.* The conference serves religious communities, secular institutes, and the new form of conserated life called ''noncanonical communities.''

Deepening of the awareness that religious formation needed to be rethought and restructured was at the origins of the Sister Formation Movement. As a self-conscious movement it is of fairly recent origin, though little by little, in the U.S. at least, efforts grew in the direction of educational formation for sisters. A doctoral thesis by Sister Bertrande Myers, DC in 1941, *The Education of Sisters,* underlined the necessity to integrate spiritual, intellectual, social, and apostolic formation in a way which earlier training had not done. In 1947 a nationally known college president, Sister Madeleva *Wolff, CSC, gave impetus to the new notion in a paper read at the convention of the National Catholic Educational Association. A world-wide meeting in Rome held in 1950 issued a year later in a call by Pope Pius XII for better training for sisters. In 1953 the first Congress of major superiors discussed how to improve sister training. Out of these and other meetings came the Sister Formation Movement, made a permanent organization in 1957. Sisters from other continents came to the U.S. for the kind of training provided by Sister Formation. The Movement established a center in Peru for Latin American communities. By the advent of Vatican II the aims of the Movement had been substantially realized. BIBLIOGRAPHY: B. Meyers, *Sisters for the 21st Century* (1965).

[J. R. AHERNE]

RELIGIOUS FREEDOM, the human right to accept, reject, or change beliefs, to worship, and to live in accordance with beliefs without external constraint or coercion. As a right, it calls for positive recognition, not mere toleration.

History. Early Christians experienced persecution because of their claim that they alone worshiped the only true God. With the Edict of Milan (313), Christianity was legally tolerated. The Church soon began to receive special privileges, and by the end of the 4th cent. was the only religion allowed. Having become the state religion, Christianity became intolerant. Gratian and Theodosius (380) forbade pagan worship and took strong measures against heretics. Even Augustine, who inclined toward toleration, finally decided that coercion was necessary to deal with the *Donatists. Throughout the Middle Ages, the concept of *Christendom prevailed in western Europe, and heretics were severely treated, while Jews were discriminated against but permitted to exist. The Reformation brought little change in the situation, for religious uniformity supported by civil government was a general presupposition of Lutherans, Calvinists, and Anglicans. Only the Anabaptists raised their voices in defense of freedom of conscience. The Thirty Years' War brought widespread revulsion against religious intolerance, and conciliatory figures (e.g., G. Calixt, H. Grotius, J. Comenius) proposed bases for mutual acceptance among Protestants. In France, the *Edict of Nantes (1598) granted considerable freedom to the *Huguenots, but it was revoked in 1685. English Baptists (J. Smyth, T. Helwys) appealed for complete freedom of conscience, and during the Civil Wars (1642–49) Milton's *Areopagitica* and Roger Williams' *Bloody Tenet* were published. Williams contended that God wills ''a permission of the most Paganish, Jewish, Turkish, or anti-Christian consciences and worships, be granted to all men in all nations and countries; and they are only to be fought against with . . . the Sword of God's Spirit.'' The English struggle to enforce religious uniformity during the Restoration (1660–88) ended with the *Toleration Act (1689), granting freedom to Protestant *Dissenters. Not until the 19th cent., however, did complete religious freedom even for Roman Catholics come in England.

The U.S. has been the land of the first complete experiment in religious freedom; notwithstanding religious restrictions in early state constitutions, there was a general separation of functions of *Church and State.

Current Status. Progressively the U.S. has achieved a degree of religious freedom that has pointed the way for others. On the Continent, religious liberty had been extended considerably by the 20th cent., but its achievement was due to economic, political, and religious changes that made tolerance more conducive to the public weal. Where communism prevails, religious freedom seldom amounts to more than a toleration of worship. Italy, Spain, and Latin America have been slow to acknowledge the rights of religious dissenters, but the degree of toleration varies greatly in those lands. In non-Christian countries also there are discriminatory religious laws (e.g., in Burma, Israel, and Muslim countries in the Near East). The United Nations, in its Universal Declaration of Human Rights (1948), proclaimed ''the right to freedom of thought, conscience, and religion;'' and a special subcommission drew up a more specific ''Code on Religious Liberty'' in 1960, but not all nations have subscribed to it. The World Council of Churches (WCC) issued a Declaration on Religious Liberty at Amsterdam (1948) and another at New Delhi (1961). RC Church theologians also have effected a change in the historic attitude of their Church, with John C. *Murray making a great contribution to this development in the United States. Of historic significance was the promulgation (1965) by Vatican Council II of the Decree on Religious Freedom (*Dignitatis humanae*). Declaring that human beings, as individuals or groups, have the right to freedom of conscience, it acknowledged that a man is not to be forced to act contrary to his conscience or restrained from acting in accord with conscience in religious matters. Although some at the Council wished further clarification of ambiguities, the document has met with general approval by Protestants. The Commission on Religious Liberty of the WCC drew up a list of the ''fundamental agreements'' between the conciliar decree and the WCC declarations on the subject and drafted a project of common Christian insights concerning religious liberty. Thus, although in large areas of the world religious liberty, or even toleration, is minimal, considerable progress has been made in recent years. Significant agreements in principle have been reached, although interpretations of such matters as *proselytism, care of children's religious nurture, and the protection of society remain thorny questions in some nations. BIBLIOGRAPHY: M. Searle-Bates, *Religious Liberty: An Enquiry* (1945); *Religious Freedom* (*Concilium*, v. 18, ed. N. Edelby and T. Jiménez-Urresti, 1966); S. Meade, *Lively Experiment* (1963); *Religious Liberty: An End and a Beginning* (ed. J. C. Murray, 1966).

RELIGIOUS GENUINITY, see GENUINITY, RELIGIOUS.

RELIGIOUS HABIT, see HABIT, RELIGIOUS.

RELIGIOUS HOSPITALLERS OF ST. JOSEPH, a religious nursing order of women founded at Laflèche, France, in 1636 by Marie de la Ferre under the direction of the bp. of Angers. Convents were established at Laval, Bauge, and Beaufort. At first the religious took simple vows but Laval inaugurated the custom of solemn vows in 1663. Alexander VII approved the congregation in 1666 and the Parliament of Paris recognized it in 1667. In 1685 the constitutions were revised by the bp. of Angers. The sisters were bound by a fourth vow to serve the poor. Mlle. Mance after caring for the sick for 17 years at the Hôtel-Dieu brought the hospitaller nuns to Montreal. From its motherhouse in Montreal the order expanded in Canada and northern U.S. In 1975 it numbered 74 houses and 881 members.

[R. C. CLIGGETT]

RELIGIOUS INSTITUTE, called in CIC *religio,* an ecclesiastically authorized society of members living a common life and striving for Christian perfection by following the proper rule of the institute and by keeping the three public vows of poverty, chastity, and obedience (CIC c. 488). The term religious institute embraces, therefore: orders, in which vows are solemn; congregations, in which vows are simple; institutes of pontifical rank, i.e., that have received at least the initial approval (called a decree of praise) from the Holy See; institutes of diocesan rank, i.e., that have been established by a local ordinary in his territory; clerical institutes, in which the majority of members are priests; lay institutes, in which the members are brothers or sisters; exempt and nonexempt institutes, i.e. subject or not in their internal life to diocesan authority. The authority competent to establish a religious institute of diocesan rank is the diocesan bp., with the approval of the Congregation for Religious and Secular Institutes. Application for such a foundation must include the identity and objectives of the leader of the proposed institute, the title, the work to be undertaken, description of the garb to be worn, indication of means of support, justification of the need for the institute. Only in mission territories are new establishments encouraged by the Holy See. An order or institute of pontifical rank can be authorized only by the Holy See. Since a religious institute is a state of perfection in the canonical sense (CIC, c. 487), it has its distinctive stability by reason of the members' profession of public vows, perpetual or periodically renewable. The rule or constitution proper to the institute is approved both as to its conformity with canon law and as to its being an authentic expression of evangelical ideals of perfection. The rule becomes the measure of the member's fidelity to the fundamental commitment of religious life, the striving for the perfection of charity. *SECULAR INSTITUTE. *SOCIETY OF COMMON LIFE.

[T. C. O'BRIEN]

RELIGIOUS LIFE, as understood in the RC Church today, the institutionalized form, sanctioned by the authority of the Church, of the life of the evangelical counsels of poverty, chastity, and obedience. Three canonical types of this life are recognized: religious life properly so-called (entailing the three vows plus community life); societies of common life (entailing no public vows); and secular institutes (entailing no common life). The teaching and decrees of Vatican Council II have made it clear that, although Christ, from whom the evangelical counsels stem, did not establish religious institutes for living a life according to the counsels, such institutes are nevertheless necessary to the life of the Church in its present situation. They are an expression of its charismatic life, each institute taking its origin in a charism given to its founder. Religious life is thus a divine gift to the Church itself, and not simply a grace given to certain of its members.

In history, the first steps toward religious life were the practice and recognition of a special way of life followed by virgins and widows (2d cent.). The 3d cent. saw the beginning of a life of special asceticism practiced by fathers of the desert in Egypt and Syria; groups of anchorites gathered around a master, such as St. Anthony. St. Pachomius developed this into cenobitism, and St. Basil promoted this form of life. In the West St. Augustine drew up his rule for the common life of clerics. St. Benedict organized monastic life for both clerics and laymen, men and women. Medieval reform movements, such as those of Cluny and Cîteaux, reinvigorated Benedictine monasticism, and new forms of it sprang up with the Carthusians and the Orders of Canons Regular and the Premonstratensians. The 13th cent. saw the rise of the mendicant orders—first the Franciscans and Dominicans, who were freed from the monastic obligation of stable residence in the interest of apostolic activity—and later the Carmelites and others. About the time of the Council of Trent a new development appeared with orders of clerics regular, who were freed from the obligation of choral office. Among these were the Jesuits and Theatines. Further evolution came with the appearance of congregations whose members took simple rather than solemn vows, and of congregations whose members took no vows, for educational, nursing, and missionary purposes. In the 17th cent. St. John Baptist de la Salle initiated the nonclerical congregations of teaching brothers. Secular institutes began in the 19th cent. and were sanctioned as a canonical form of the life of the counsels by Pope Pius XII in 1947. The same Pope fostered and centralized the movement for renewal and modernization of religious life. Vatican Council II recognized the vitality of the various forms of the religious life, active and contemplative, monastic and conventual, and the secular institutes, and while it encouraged renewal and adaptation to the circumstances of contemporary life, it also urged a continuous return to the sources of Christian life and to the original inspiration that brought them into being (Vat II RenRelLife 2).

The revival of religious life in Protestantism is a phenomenon worthy of attention. Despite the opposition of Luther and Calvin to monastic vows, and despite the rejection of monasticism by the Reformers generally, there have been survivals and revivals of something like organized religious life in Protestantism from its early years; e.g., the Moravian Brethren (18th cent.), the diaconies of Germany, Switzerland, and France (19th cent.), the Protestant Sisters of Charity. The recent cenobitic revival in the *Taizé community is well known, and there are many other witnesses to the vitality of the ideal represented by this way of life. An ecumenical orientation marks several of the new communities. In the C of E the religious orders were suppressed, but within a cent. there were attempts at restoring some form of religious life and these continued in the 17th and 18th centuries. Since 1845 communities of men and women have been growing in number. In 1935 an Advisory Council was established to look after the welfare of Anglican religious communities. At the present time there are in the British Isles 11 communities of men, the oldest of which, the Cowley Fathers, dates from 1866; for women there are some 60 communities. The U.S. and Canada also have similar religious communities for those who wish to take up this mode of life within the Anglican communion. BIBLIOGRAPHY: R. F. Smith, NCE 12:287–294; S. Mayer et al., LTK 7:1192–1204; F. Biot, *Communautés protestantes* (1960); P. Anson, *Call of the Cloister* (1955).

RELIGIOUS OF JESUS AND MARY, a community of religious women founded in Lyons, France, by Claudine Thévenet (Mother Mary St. Ignatius) in 1818. Its work is principally education and the missions. Its constitutions, approved in 1847, are based on the Rule of St. Ignatius of Loyola. The community has houses in Spain, England, Canada, Switzerland, Ireland, Argentina, Mexico, Germany, Cuba, and India. It came to the U.S. in 1877 where foundations were made in Massachusetts, New York, New Hampshire, Maryland, California, and New Mexico. In 1975 the community numbered 2,331 sisters in 156 houses; the motherhouse is in Rome.

[R. C. CLIGGETT]

RELIGIOUS OF THE HOLY UNION OF THE SACRED HEARTS, a congregation of sisters founded by Fr. Jean Baptiste Debrabant in Douai, France, in 1826 in order to provide religious instruction in the period following the French Revolution. The congregation received canonical approbation in 1843. The French government confiscated their convents and schools between 1902 and 1904, and the motherhouse was transferred to Tournai, Belgium. From there the community spread to England, Ireland, Argentina, Spain, Africa, and in 1886 to the U.S. In 1975 the congregation numbered 1,039 members in 95 houses; the generalate is in Rome.

[R. C. CLIGGETT]

RELIGIOUS PROFESSION, RITUAL OF, the rite whereby individuals dedicate themselves by vow or promise as members of a religious community, whether order, congregation, or secular institute approved by the Church. Various ceremonies for the consecration of virgins and profession of monks have existed in the history of the Church, with a great deal of variation from one group to another. Many have been modelled on the sacramental rites of initiation. The present rite for religious profession, part of the Roman Ritual, was issued in 1970 and is to be adapted by particular religious communities to their spirit and needs. Reform was called for by Vatican Council II's Constitution on the Liturgy, 80 to provide for greater uniformity, simplicity, and dignity. The rite is ordinarily to take place within Mass and consists basically of the candidate's declaration of intention, proclamation of vows, and the acceptance of the vows by an official representative of the Church and/or of the religious community.

Rites are provided for initiation into the religious life (formerly often known as "reception of the habit" and "entrance into the novitiate" and "reception of novices"), temporary profession, perpetual profession, and renewal of vows. BIBLIOGRAPHY: *Ordo professionis religiosae* (1970; English translation available from Bishops' Committee on the Liturgy, USCC publ. 1975).

[J. DALLEN]

RELIGIOUS SOCIETY OF FRIENDS, often called Quakers, the corporate title for those whose distinctive belief is the *Inner Light as preached by G. *Fox. Turning against the "steeple houses" and "hireling ministry" of the organized Churches, Fox began to preach the doctrine of the Inner Light: that the source of all religious truth and life is the voice of God experienced within each person. In the north and midlands of England, he attracted Familists, Seekers, and others dissatisfied with the C of E and the *Nonconformist Churches. He and his followers called themselves the "Children of Light," "Friends of Truth," and later the Society of Friends; by 1652 he had given them a sound plan of organization. Their resistance to laws of religion, military service, oaths, and certain marks of civil deference made them the target of ferocious legal and popular oppression until the *Toleration Act (1689). Many migrated to the American colonies; Pennsylvania was established as a refuge under William *Penn, but elsewhere they suffered. The post-persecution era is called the "quietist" phase in Quaker history; they became a "peculiar people," separated, plain in dress, using biblical forms of speech, avoiding all worldly frivolity.

The source of the beliefs and norms for living characteristic of the Friends is the Inner Light. Hence they have a traditional unwillingness to adopt an ecclesiastical structure, creeds, a liturgical or sacramental system, or a teaching authority residing either in Church or Scriptures. All such elements presuppose a mediate revelation of doctrine or a mediate bestowal of sanctity. The immediacy of the Inner Light has led to preoccupation with mysticism and meditation, as well as a high regard for the individual person. Since all men can or do share equally in the Inner Light, in the name of this human equality and dignity Quakers have promoted education, prison reform, and social equality, and they have opposed slavery, warfare, and conscription.

Fox and the other early Friends preached the Inner Light within a setting of traditional Christianity. But as the immediacy of the God-man relationship through the Inner Light was stressed, some came to question dependence upon the historical Jesus as Redeemer. Such a line taken by Elias *Hicks (1748–1830) occasioned a schism in American Quakerism; during 1827–28, the meetings in Philadelphia and elsewhere split into "Hicksites" and "Orthodox," i.e., adherents of orthodox Protestant tenets; the schism continued until 1955. In the mid-19th cent. a further schism occurred within the Orthodox group because of the preaching of Joseph J. *Gurney (1788–1846), which stressed traditional evangelical themes and combined the Inner Light doctrine with the teaching that Jesus is the one mediator between God and man. The Gurneyites, who continued to call themselves Orthodox, were resisted by the Wilburites (John *Wilbur, 1774–1856), who were "Conservatives," standing for the sole sufficiency of the Inner Light. The Gurneyite and Wilburite groups in New England terminated this schism in 1945. In the rest of the eastern U.S. most of the Quakers are Hicksites or Wilburites. In the middle and far West, Quakers are mostly Gurneyites.

Forms of worship reflect varying interpretations of the Inner Light in relationship to the person of Jesus. Those in the Gurneyite line have tended to develop a mode of worship similar to that of the Baptists or Congregationalists. The minister is usually a person who has had theological training; meetings are marked by programmed worship (sermon, organ music, singing, etc.). Quakers of the Wilburite line have emphasized the silent unprogrammed meeting, in which each is free to speak as the Inner Light prompts.

Since Fox's own times, the basic organization of the Friends has been the meeting. The "monthly" meeting is the local unit, gathering weekly for worship, and monthly for business; "quarterly" and "yearly" meetings embrace wider geographical regions. In the U.S., where 60% of the Friends' worldwide membership (approx. 200,000) is found, the various yearly meetings are either unaffiliated or affiliated to the Friends United Meeting, the Friends General Conference, the Evangelical Friends Alliance, or the Conservative Friends. There has been continuing effort toward greater unity among Friends; the *Friends World Committee for Consultation seeks to promote the interests and association of Friends throughout the world. The American Friends Service Committee operates as an effective agency for the betterment of society and for peace in the world. BIBLIOGRAPHY: W. C. Braithwaite, *Beginnings of Quakerism* (2d ed., 1955); R. M. Jones, *Later Periods of Quakerism* (2v., 1921); *American Quakers Today* (ed. E. B. Bronner, 1966).

[J. J. FLOOD]

RELIGIOUS TEACHERS FILIPPINI, a pontifical institute of religious women founded by St. Lucy Philippini in Montefiascone, Italy, in 1692. Clement XI asked St. Lucy to establish schools in Rome. In 1910 Pius X asked the community to go to the U.S., where they made a foundation in Morristown, New Jersey. In 1975 the community numbered 1,225 members in 148 houses.

[R. C. CLIGGETT]

RELIGIOUS TEST FOR PUBLIC OFFICE, a requirement that office holders swear belief in certain religious doctrines or engage in certain religious practices. Where the Church has been legally established, the State has frequently made some restriction of public office to members of the established Church. In England, for example, the Test Act of 1673 required office holders to take communion according to the usage of the C of E; it remained in force until Catholic Emancipation, 1829. Though such restric-

tions have generally been eliminated in modern times, they have not been totally erased. In Argentina, for example, the president must be RC and in Great Britain the sovereign cannot be. In the American colonies the Church was established and office holders required to meet various religious tests, except in Rhode Island for a period. Religious tests in England and the colonies were opposed both by papists and dissenters, and later by secularists and deists. The U.S. Constitution ruled that "no religious test shall ever be required as a qualification to any office or public trust under the United States." Some states continued to require that office holders affirm their belief in God or take an oath of office that included a reference to God. In 1961, however, the U.S. Supreme Court ruled unconstitutional the Maryland requirement that office holders affirm a belief in the existence of God. (The strength of voter prejudice in making a religious test was greatly reduced by the election of President J. F. Kennedy).

[T. EARLY]

RELIQUARIES, containers for religious relics. The caskets or boxes, made of costly materials (precious metals), richly ornamented with gems, enamels, and paintings, were designed from the 4th century. Figural reliquaries followed, at times in the shape of the relic encased (e.g., an arm). In 12th-cent. Germany and the Low Countries shapes of churches prevailed. Examples are Nicholas of Verdun's *Drëikonigenschrein*, Cologne Cathedral; *St. Ursula Shrine* by Memling (1489); *Sebaldsgrab* by P. Vischer.

[M. J. DALY]

REMARQUE, ERICH MARIA (1898–1970), German writer. He served in the German army in World War I. His antiwar novel, *Im Westen nichts Neues* (1929, Eng. tr. *All Quiet on the Western Front*, 1929), was widely read and translated into many languages. It contributed greatly to the development of pacifist sentiment. R. became a U.S. citizen in 1947 and produced other successful books.

[I. MERKEL]

REMARRIAGE, a term that can be understood as (1) equivalent to what the CIC calls *bigamia* (CIC c. 984, n. 4), i.e., a second or third valid marriage successively contracted that, according to ancient discipline, is an *irregularity with respect to reception of holy orders; (2) simply a valid marriage contracted after a previously valid marriage, e.g., by a widow; (3) a second marriage entered into by a Catholic after civil divorce terminated a prior marriage. The third meaning involves the issues of the indissolubility of *marriage and of the pastoral care, much discussed at present, for remarried Catholics. Some canonists and theologians have urged that such Catholics be permitted in certain circumstances to receive the sacraments. There is, however, no official change in church discipline that bars those living in an invalid marriage from the sacraments, except in the case where the couple in such a marriage live as brother and sister. *DIVORCED CATHOLICS.

[T. C. O'BRIEN]

REMBERT OF BREMEN-HAMBURG, ST. (Rimbert; d. 888), second bp. of Bremen and Hamburg. He had been a monk in Flanders, then the companion of the first bp., St. Ansgar, whom he succeeded and whose biography he wrote. R. is reported also to have visited and evangelized some parts of Scandinavia, but that detail of his life is doubtful.

REMBRANDT HARMENSZ VAN RIJN (Rhyn, Ryn; 1606–69), Dutch painter and master etcher, one of the greatest artists the world has known, comparable to Michelangelo, Titian, and Rubens, treating biblical, historical, portrait, and genre subjects. After working under various minor instructors, R. as an independent master produced in an early Leyden period (1625–32) works of Italianate composition, bright color, strong light and dark (*Money Changer*, 1627) and relates to Caravaggio and Honthorst in artificial light (*Supper at Emmaus*, 1628–30; *Presentation in the Temple*, 1631). These paintings are spiritual interpretations in human terms, a refinement of Baroque lighting expressing psychic and emotional states through finer and finer nuances of light and dark. In Amsterdam (1632–40) *Dr. Tulp's Anatomy Class* established R. as master of portraiture. He married Saskia, model for many of his paintings (1634), executing *Self-Portrait with Saskia* followed by five paintings of *Christ's Passion* and the famous *Descent from the Cross*, which though related to Rubens shows R.'s significant and unique lighting. *The Night Watch* (1642) or *The Company of Captain Franz Banning Cocq* shows R. at an apogee of Baroque expression and golden tonality. Saskia having died (1642), R. married Hendrickje Stoeffels (who died in 1663). In 1648 he produced *Christ at Emmaus,* and in the 1650s, impoverished, produced in virtuoso technique works immediately claimed by his creditors. He probed character in the *Syndics of the Cloth Hall* (1661) and the *Denial of St. Peter* (1660) with its dramatic light.

R.'s 60-odd *Self-Portraits* of deep penetration record the decline of the successful, affluent citizen (1629) to the poverty of old age, spent by election in the Jewish ghetto (1658). Works of sensuous beauty from the middle years gave way to statements of simple dignity of the poor (*Christ Preaching,* 1652; *Return of the Prodigal, c.*1665). R.'s greatest etchings of amazing velvety depth, surpassing those of all other masters of the technique are: *The Three Trees, The Hundred Guilder Print* or *Christ Healing the Sick, The Three Crosses* and *Christ Preaching.* R., painting the soul of man in the piercing light of his humane concern and the physical penetration of his painted environments, was as Michelangelo and Titian in their respective schools, genius,

and timeless force in European art. BIBLIOGRAPHY: S. Slive and E. H. ter Kuile, *Dutch Art and Architecture, 1600–1800* (1966).

[M. J. DALY]

REMESAL, ANTONIO DE (d. 1627), Spanish chronicler of the Dominican missions in Mexico and Central America. R. came to America in 1613, and settled in Guatemala and Mexico. He wrote *Historia de la Provincia de San Vincente de Chiapa y Guatemala,* a valuable and precise description of missionary activity beginning with the conquest of Mexico and Central America. In Spain (1619) to procure royal permission to publish, R. was imprisoned for a time because of objections to his work. He was vindicated by the Inquisition, however; his book was published and he returned to the missions for the remainder of his life.

[T. M. MCFADDEN]

REMIGIUS OF AUXERRE (Remi; *c.*841–before 908), Benedictine monk and teacher at the abbey of St. Germain, Auxerre, at Reims (*c.*862), and at Paris, where Odo of Cluny was his pupil. R.'s importance to the evolution of scholasticism rests on his glosses on texts that were standards in the medieval educational program: he was the glossator of the grammarians Priscian and Donatus, of such authors as Cato, Terence, Vergil, Juvenal, Bede, and Martianus Capella. He also commented on Boethius's theological works and the *De consolatione philosophiae,* as well as on Genesis and Psalms. R.'s contribution was as conservator of the learning revived during the Carolingian renaissance.

[T. C. O'BRIEN]

REMIGIUS OF LYONS, ST. (d. 875), bp. of Lyons from 852. R. succeeded Amulo (840–852) in the See of Lyons in the midst of the predestination controversy. Although he disapproved of the views of Gottschalk of Orbais, he was no partisan of Gottschalk's adversary, Hincmar of Reims; and presiding at the Council of Valence (855), he condemned four propositions formulated by Hincmar in 853. In addition to his active participation in the Councils of Langres (859) and Toucy (860), R. is also known for his efforts to regain confiscated church property. Florus of Lyons probably was the author of the works attributed to R. in Migne's *Patrologia Latina.* BIBLIOGRAPHY: G. Mathon, BiblSanct 11:103–104.

[H. DRESSLER]

REMIGIUS OF REIMS, ST. (Lat. Remedius; Fr. Remi, Remy; *c.*436–*c.*533). Two ancient lives of this saint have survived, one long erroneously attributed to Fortunatus, the other written by Hincmar of Reims; neither is reliable. R. was the son of an influential family; he received a good education and became bp. of Reims *c.*458. His episcopal activity appears to have extended over a period of more than

70 years. On Christmas Day 498 or 499, he baptized Clovis, King of the Franks. He is known also for his missionary work and for founding the bishoprics of Arras, Laon, Therouanne, Cambrai, and Tournai. Four of his letters and a testament of dubious authenticity are extant. BIBLIOGRAPHY: H. Platelle and M. C. Celletti, BiblSanct 11:104–113; G. Tessier, *La Baptême de Clovis* (1964).

[H. DRESSLER]

REMIGIUS OF ROUEN, ST. (Remedius; d. *c.*772), illegitimate son of Charles Martel and brother of Pepin III. Educated at the royal court, he became abp. of Rouen in 755. While in Rome in 760 on a mission to Pope Paul I and Desiderius, King of the Lombards, R. was deeply impressed by the chant of the monks. He was instrumental in introducing this chant (that it was Gregorian chant is doubtful) and Roman liturgical uses in the Frankish kingdom. R. was one of the 25 bps. present at the Council of Attigny in 765. BIBLIOGRAPHY: É. Brouette, LTK 8:1227; H. Platelle, BiblSanct 11:113–114.

[H. DRESSLER]

REMIREMONT, ABBEY OF (Saint-Mont, Romarieberg, *Habendse, Mons S. Romarici*), former double monastery founded *c.*620 on Mt. Abend in the present diocese of Saint-Dié, France, by two disciples of St. Columban. In 1623 the regular canons who had become established there at the end of the 11th cent. ceded the abbey to the Benedictines of the congregation of St. Vanne. The convent for women, rebuilt in 910 after the Hungarian devastation, in time received only those of noble blood, and its abbess became a princess of the realm, answerable only to the pope. The abbey was suppressed in 1792. BIBLIOGRAPHY: Cottineau 2:2442–43.

[J. DAOUST]

REMISS ACTS, acts, whether interior or outward, motivated by charity, but with a *fervor less intense than a person's capabilities. Quantitative concepts are transferred to express the idea that grace and charity have an essential direction towards growth, since they are the sources of progress toward the goal of eternal life. Thus theological tradition speaks of degrees of charity, and of the generalized levels proper to the beginner, the advanced, and the perfect (ThAq ST 2a2ae, 24.4,5,9). The degree of charity means the intensity of the power it gives to the will to love God with one's whole mind and heart and strength. The charity present in a remiss act is less intense than that degree. But a remiss act is not only not sinful, it is an act of charity, and so both good and meritorious, even of an increase in charity itself. The positive value of such an act, however, will have its result only at the point where another act of intense fervor becomes the immediate disposition for God's increasing charity in proportion to all antecedent acts (*ibid.* 6). The negative aspects of remiss acts is not in the acts themselves

but in the fact that they might indicate the beginnings of *acedia, or incipient failures to control other appetitive movements that retard spiritual progress.

[T. C. O'BRIEN]

REMISSION OF SINS, part of the process of *justification; the negative side, as it were, of what saving grace brings about. One reason for the prominence of the term is its occurrence in the Nicene Creed under the third major section on the Holy Spirit: "one baptism for the remission of sins." In itself the term has the juridic connotation of a release from the debt of guilt that sin incurs. But the reality the term refers to is the mystery of forgiveness and pardon through the grace of Christ. The repentance that leads to the justification of the sinner does not mean simply the redress of offended justice; it is a conversion leading to reconciliation, the restoration of love between the sinner and God (ThAq ST 3a, 90.3). "Sin" in the expression means sin in its full and primary sense, mortal *sin (although baptism is also a remission of *original sin and, in the case of an adult, of all personal sin). The mortality of sin is its cutting off the communication of grace that makes the recipient God's friend and child. Justification as reconciliation means the removal of that obstacle to divine love. The only source of that removal is God's forgiving grace. His gift converts, turns the sinner away from the sin-obstacle back toward the Father again. Thus the remission of sins is not a forensic cancelling of guilt; it is the bestowal again of the gift of grace that makes the prodigal again a beloved son, puts an end to estrangement. The remission of sin is coming back to life through the infusion of grace. It is forgiveness and pardon because the sinner was indeed guilty, but the pardon is through a positive restoration not a merely negative remittance of guilt. The ordinary way in which this pardon for mortal sin is received is the sacrament of penance; but it may well happen that reception of the sacrament simply ratifies and finishes the process of conversion and forgiveness already accomplished. In the case of venial *sin there is no break from God's love; pardon comes with a greater fervor of charity that reaffirms love for God and turns away from that lapse in intensity which venial sin primarily means. BIBLIOGRAPHY: ThAq ST 1a2ae, 113.6; (Lat-Eng v. 27, ed. T. C. O'Brien) app. 2, "Mortal Sin"; app. 3, "Venial Sin."

[T. C. O'BRIEN]

REMIZOV, ALEXEY MIKHAYLOVICH (1877–1957), Russian émigré writer, humorist, and leading Ornamentalist. His works often show man at the mercy of fate. Though realistic, even naturalistic, in content, they are, as a result of R.'s experimentation with archaic and dialectical elements, intricate and mannered in style. In his religious legends and fairy tales, grotesquerie and whimsicality reign side by side. His *Lay on the Destruction of the Russian land* (1918) states his belief that Russia's spiritual destiny is not to be identified with that of Western Europe. BIBLIOGRAPHY: D. S. Mirsky, *Contemporary Russian Literature* (1926) 281–291; M. Slonim, *From Chekhov to the Revolution* (1962) 229–233.

[M. F. MCCARTHY]

REMNANT OF ISRAEL, portion of the nation surviving after God's judgment (Is 10.20; Jer 31.7; Mic 2.12). The concept, related to the doctrine of *election, has considerable importance in biblical theology. God's chosen people are unfaithful and therefore suffer punishment; but God fulfills his promise to preserve them, using the surviving remnant. The themes of judgment and mercy are thus interwoven. The remnant is subject to judgment also, however (Jer 8.3). It is scattered but will be gathered to the land of Israel (Is 11.11) and triumph over its enemies (Zeph 2.7, 9). It is only by God's mercy that the remnant survives (Is 1.9); at the same time, it is those who are faithful who survive (Zeph 2.3). The idea of the surviving remnant has antecedents in the story of Noah (Gen 6.7–8). Paul used the concept in his discussion of the Jews' rejection of the Gospel (Rom ch. 9–11). The concept of the Church as the "Chosen People of God" directly involves the biblical theology of the remnant.

[T. EARLY]

REMONSTRANTS, the name given after 1610 to the followers of J. *Arminius. The name comes from the *Remonstrance,* a five-point statement of *Arminianism drawn up after the death of Arminius by S. *Episcopius and H. Grotius, and addressed to the states of Holland and W. Friesland. The opponents of the Remonstrants, sometimes called Contra-Remonstrants, were led by F. Gomarus. The controversy was on *predestination but also involved political issues. At the Synod of *Dort (1618–19), the Remonstrants were condemned, and many were persecuted or banished. After the death of Prince Maurice of Nassau (1625), protector of the Gomarites, the Remonstrants were allowed to return and in 1633 were granted religious freedom. The Society of Remonstrants in Holland (Remonstrantse Broederschap) in 1967 had 27 congregations, with about 20,000 members. They have a congregational polity, the synod having no authority over the local church. In the last cent. the Remonstrants embraced Modernism. BIBLIOGRAPHY: Schaff Creeds 1:516–519; W. H. van de Pol, *World Protestantism* (1964) 269–271; bibliog. for Arminianism.

[T. C. O'BRIEN]

REMORSE, derived through Low Latin from *remordere* (to bite again), a feeling of distress for a wrong one has committed. Instinctively healthy, these pangs of conscience, as they are called, can masquerade as the will's sorrow for having offended God, whereas they are sometimes psychological guilt feelings preoccupied with real or imagined faults and centered upon their effect upon oneself, e.g., their stain or the reproach they incur. When luxuriated in, they can be morbid and may require treatment by medical psychology if not firmly kept in place by a non-scrupulous and confident out-going love of God.

[P. F. MULHERN]

REMY, ARTHUR FRANK JOSEPH (1871–1954), philologist. Born in Germany and educated in the U.S., R. joined the faculty of Columbia Univ. in 1899 as a teacher of Germanic philology and remained there for 42 years. He served a term as president of the United States Catholic Historical Society. He was the author of *The Influence of India and Persia on the Poetry of Germany.*

[J. R. AHERNE]

RENAISSANCE, the complex era of transition between medieval and modern times. It enjoys no fixed dates. Some have preferred to speak of it as the 15th cent., plus several decades at either end. A more recent view is to enlarge its chronological frontiers to 1300–1600. The problem is compounded by the necessity of differentiating between Italy and the transalpine countries. The Italian Renaissance can be said to have begun 1300–50; the northern Renaissance, c. 1450. Most scholars would see the Renaissance as superseded by the Reformation in the 3d or 4th decade of the 16th century.

Personalities and Spirit. Among the key personalities of the Renaissance are Dante (1265–1321), whose *Divine Comedy* is a lyrical synthesis of the Middle Ages, but who in some respects points to the Renaissance; Francesco Petrarch (1304–74), sometimes called the father of Renaissance *humanism, whose attitudes comprise something of the Renaissance in miniature; Giovanni Boccaccio (1313–75), whose *Decameron* and life suggest the moral ambivalence of humanism; Vittorino da Feltre (1378–1446), an educator who played a role in transforming humanism from an enthusiasm to a program; Lorenzo Valla (1405–57), who shows the philological or scientific side of humanism; Marsiglio Ficino (1433–99), Neoplatonist philosopher and theologian of the Platonic Academy of Florence; Giovanni Pico della Mirandola (1463–94), the great eclecticist and boundless spirit of this Academy; and Niccolò Machiavelli (1469–1527), whose controversial work *The Prince* suggests a climax of the Italian Renaissance. In the North the key figures are Erasmus of Rotterdam (1469?–1536), prince of Christian humanists, who represents a conjunction of the older *Devotio moderna* and Italian humanism; Jacques Lefèvre d'Étaples (1455?–1536), the great French proponent of a moderate religious reform; Thomas More (1478–1535), English humanist, statesman, martyr, and saint; Ximénez de Cisneros (1436–1517), Spanish cardinal, biblical humanist, educational patron, and religious reformer; and Johann Reuchlin (1455–1522), celebrated Hebraist.

As an era of transition the Renaissance possesses no single character or spirit. It was a highly unstable period between two relatively stable and definable world orders. It contains both medieval and modern features and is a rather ambiguous period of history. C. S. Lewis wrote of it as "a complex of heterogeneous events." This view qualifies or counters the 19th cent. formulation of the Renaissance by the French historian J. Michelet and the Swiss German historian J. Burckhardt. Their view, which became tradition, stressed the revolutionary character of the Renaissance as "the discovery of the world and of man," with a corresponding depreciation of the Middle Ages. Though the Michelet-Burckhardt thesis still has popular adherents, few scholars hold it today without qualification. If one stresses the this-worldly rationality of the period, it can be pointed out that it was a great period of the occult, on the one hand, and a golden age of mysticism, on the other. If it be stated simplistically that the Renaissance was a revival of ancient learning, it can be replied that Aristotle was revived in the 13th cent. with scholasticism and the universities. And if it be urged that the Renaissance was an age of neopaganism, it can be pointed out that it produced such great saints as Catherine of Siena and Thomas More, and it is today acknowledged an open question whether Machiavelli was more characteristic of the age than More.

Yet there are positive generalizations that can be made about the period. It emerged out of the late Middle Ages, first in Italy and then across the Alps. Its culture was less clerical and feudal than the Middle Ages, more laic and urban. Humanism set the dominant cultural tone. This was not so much a revival of learning pure and simple as it was a continuation of an earlier revival of learning, now accelerated and transferred to the field of arts and letters, with a stress upon the ancient languages, and particularly upon fine Latinity. To contrast it with the Middle Ages, the trend was from philosophy to philology, and within philosophy, from metaphysics to moral philosophy, logic to literature, and to some extent, from the more scientific Aristotle to the more poetic Plato. Finally, the Renaissance was a great period of productivity in the fine arts. The arts have been seen as the form of the Renaissance and the artist as the model of the period. This "cultural explosion," as E. Garin has styled it, was probably related to medieval and Byzantine precedents, to the revival of antiquity, and perhaps to a peculiar Italian genius of the time. One might say that the arts were to the Renaissance what philosophy was to the Middle Ages. And both were more often than not in the service of religion.

The Renaissance and Religion. While humanism fostered a certain eclecticism, breadth, tolerance, and indulgence, it is almost uniformly held today that Renaissance society was basically Christian. There was very little theoretical paganism and virtually no atheism. Morals are another thing, and there probably was a decline in morality, and certainly a decline in the moral authority of the institutional Church. In the late Middle Ages the papacy suffered a long chain of severe shocks that left it in a condition of disequilibrium and disarray, more reactive than dynamic. The medieval papacy probably reached its height under In-

nocent III (1198–1216), overextended itself in the subsequent wars with Emperor Frederick II (1215–50) and his children, and suffered retribution under Boniface VIII (1294–1303). His struggle with Philip IV of France (1285–1314) issued in humiliation and abuse at Anagni in 1302, the first shock to the late medieval papacy. There followed the Avignonese papacy (1309–77), which compromised the international prestige of the popes. The disputed papal election of 1378 led to the chaos of the *Great Western Schism (1378–1417). This led in turn to *conciliarism, which thereafter ruled discussion of institutional reform and which the popes resisted as a cure worse than the illness. Moreover, the foregoing dislocations seem to have created a defense psychology in the Roman curia, the cardinals regarding a solidified Papal State as the indispensable guarantor of papal independence, and accordingly electing popes on the basis not of spiritual qualities but of political and financial expertise. This new attitude helps account for the election of the scandalous Alexander VI (1492–1503), the martial Julius II (1503–13), and the statesman and patron Leo X (1513–21). With the election of this last son of Lorenzo the Magnificent, the center of Renaissance humanism was effectively transferred from Florence to Rome. The consequent inattention to spiritual affairs was hardly justified by the lavish patronage of the arts by the papacy. The classics, which involve attitudes like individualism, a lust for fame and glory, and a relaxed attitude toward sexuality, may have had a corrosive effect upon morality in general. The effects of the spectacle in Rome were various. Its example could be paralleled elsewhere. Simony, nepotism, pluralism, absenteeism, and concubinage were widespread. Such conditions engendered the reformist but orthodox protest of the tragic Savonarola (1452–98). In would-be-Catholic countries, it inspired or reinforced anticlericalism and antipapalism. Elsewhere it compromised the very credibility of the papacy, underscoring a Protestant thesis that the papacy was a mere historical growth lacking biblical foundation.

Yet the redeeming and salutary aspects of the Renaissance were felt in the subsequent RC reform movement, as well as in the Protestant Reformation. First, humanism from its origins had a strong didactic and reformist strain. Petrarch sought to wed Christianity with eloquence, in contradistinction to the earlier synthesis of reason and revelation. Second, humanist education, while not theological in the scholastic sense, fostered religious training. Vittorino da Feltre, a model of Renaissance educators, was a saintly man. Third, the philological side of humanism could and did turn from the pagan classics to the Christian classic, the Bible, beginning with Lorenzo *Valla's *Annotations on the New Testament*. A more accurate text of the Scriptures was to be a major goal of later humanism. Fourth, reform was a major interest of the Platonic Academy of Florence. The *Theologica platonica* of Ficino breathes much of the same spirit as the *Imitation of Christ* of Thomas à Kempis, and Ficino's influence upon Renaissance religion and art is incalculable. But *Erasmus was probably the foremost influence in Renaissance religion. Some earlier studies of the man have been a caricature of him. He was neither a coward nor a forerunner of Voltaire; and it is now acknowledged that he was a deeply committed and dedicated Christian. He spent the greater part of his life in biblical studies, patristics, ethical concerns, and in trying to effect a system of education that would remedy the evils of his times. His *Philosophia Christi,* with its Christocentric, biblical, personalist, and pacifist stress, had a momentous effect in the 16th century. There were similar humanist figures all over Europe. It was no accident that RC reform began with the Christian humanists and later, under the pontificate of Paul III (1534–49), infiltrated the papacy. Thus, if humanism had some role in the deterioration of the Church, it made its recompense.

The Protestant relation to the Renaissance also reveals ambivalence. In some respects the Reformation continued the Renaissance, as can be seen in the Renaissance revival of the study of Paul and Augustine. It is apparent also in the Renaissance return to the Bible and in a certain though not uniform penchant for an exegesis that was philological and grammatical rather than philosophical and allegorical. The continuity is present in the Reformers' common disdain for the subtleties of late scholasticism, their critique of clerical immorality and ignorance, their pronounced ethical bent, and their indifference or aversion to the fossilized formalism of late medieval piety. Likewise, Protestant educators like Philipp Melanchthon (1497–1560) continued the humanist curriculum, which became traditional.

In some other respects the Renaissance contrasts sharply with the Reformation. The two inclined to represent different assessments of human potentialities. The stress of classical Protestantism upon *total depravity was incompatible with the humanist emphasis upon the dignity of man. The great confrontation of these principles was the polemic between Luther and Erasmus on free will (1524–25). It is pertinent that so many of the Italian Reformers, who were almost all of a humanist cast, side-stepped or modified the doctrine of *double predestination. Again, the Protestant reading of the Decalogue's proscription of images made the Reformation generally uncongenial to the arts. Finally, the Christian humanists of the Renaissance envisioned a reform within the context of the Church; they generally considered Christendom inviolable. This judgment is reinforced by the correspondence between humanism and ecumenism throughout the 16th century. In general, both the Reformation and the Counter Reformation preserved the form of Renaissance humanism but repudiated much of its spirit. It was truly a question of the letter and the spirit. BIBLIOGRAPHY: W. K. Ferguson, *Renaissance in Historical Thought* (1948), with review of bibliog. from the Renaissance to present; *idem, Europe in Transition: 1300–1520* (1962); M. P. Gilmore, *World of Humanism* (1952), excellent bibliog.; D. Bush, *Renaissance and English Humanism* (1939); M.

Bataillon, *Erasme et l' Espagne* (1937); L. W. Spitz, *Religious Renaissance of the German Humanists* (1963); Pastor v.1–7.

[D. G. NUGENT]

RENAISSANCE COURT SCHOOLS, schools, largely inspired by Quintilian's *Institutes of Oratory,* connected with the courts of the Italian city-states, whose rules sponsored them to provide a polished education for the sons of the nobility. In contrast to the medieval guild school, which was narrowly technical, preparing its students for one type of service, trade, or profession, the Renaissance court school stressed the liberal and cultural arts and sought to produce a well-rounded individual by combining the new humanistic studies with the best religious ideals and practices of the old chivalric education, dedicated to loyalty to God and country, and to the development of honor and virtue. Two outstanding teachers were closely allied with the development of the court school: Vitterino da Feltre, whose famous school at Mantua (1423–46) served as a prototype, and Guardino da Verona, who conducted a successful school at Ferrara (1429–60). In both schools, boys— sons of noblemen and promising poor boys—were received at 9 or 10 years of age and kept until they were 20 or 21. In some instances, exceptionally gifted girls were admitted, e.g., Cecilia Gonzaga, a student of Da Feltre, who became one of the most cultured women of her time. The curriculum emphasized Latin and Greek, allowed for physical activities, and gave careful attention to courtly manners and moral formation. Outstanding scholars and some of the most distinguished leaders of Church and State received their education in the court schools. BIBLIOGRAPHY: W. H. Woodward, *Studies in Education in the Age of the Renaissance* (1924).

[M. B. MURPHY]

RENAISSANCE PHILOSOPHY, European philosophy of the period from the 14th to the 16th centuries. Like the Renaissance as a whole, its philosophy defies simple characterization but is especially marked by its opposition to the scholasticism of the medieval universities. Aristotelico-scholasticism remained powerful during the Renaissance. Thomist, Scotist, and Ockhamist Aristotelians continued to dominate the universities, and this was the period of the great commentaries on St. Thomas, culminating in the work of the Dominicans, Thomas de Vio, Cajetanus (1469–1534) and Francis Sylvester Ferrariensis (1474–1528). Even within Aristotelianism, however, the scholastic integration of faith and reason could be lost. Thus Cajetanus and Pietro Pomponazzi (1462–1525) denied the scholastic thesis that the immortality of the soul could be proved by reason alone. But the Renaissance was clearly a period of ''rebirth'' for the study of the humanities, including grammar, rhetoric, poetry, history, and moral philosophy, to the detriment of logic, metaphysics, and natural science. The best in Renaissance humanism is seen in Francesco Petrarch (1304–74) and Desiderius Erasmus (1466–1536). The work of the former contains virtually all the ideas and ideals of the entire epoch. At first for aesthetic and then for moral and religious reasons, he substituted the beauty of classical literature for the syllogisms of scholastic dialectics, the aim of *litterae humanae* being no less than the perfection of human virtue and the restoration of religious values. While having but little taste for philosophy, Erasmus, the greatest representative of the northern Renaissance, was an outstanding classical, biblical, and patristic scholar. The attack of his *Discourse on Free Will* on Luther's denial of free will and his caustic attitude towards the religious and moral practices of his day were very influential.

In the Renaissance context, it was natural that the new resources in classical studies should lead to the cultivation of interest in the ancient alternatives to Aristotelian philosophy. Of primary importance was Platonism. Card. Nicholas of Cusa (1401–64), ecclesiastical politician, mathematical amateur, anti-Aristotelian philosopher, and mystical theologian, unified the Christian and Pythagorean strands of Neoplatonism with a disdain for Aristotelian principles to form a world view based on the paradoxes of the infinite. Thus for him the universe was an infinite sphere, the circumference of which is nowhere and the center of which is everywhere, while in the infinity of God was to be found the *coincidentia oppositorum*, the unification of all opposed perfections.

But the effective foundation of Renaissance Platonism was laid by Marsilio Ficino (1433–99), who was led to Platonism from his early scholasticism by the reading of St. Augustine. His immense contributions included his translation from Greek to Latin of Hermes Trismegistus, the Platonic *Dialogues*, and some writings of Porphyry, Proclus, Pseudo-Dionysius, and Plotinus, as well as his own syncretism of Christian and Platonic wisdom; his theories of the immortality of the soul and of friendship and Platonic love were esp. important. Renaissance Platonism admitted more than Platonic elements. Thus Count Giovanni Pico della Mirandola (1463–94), connected with Ficino and his Platonic Academy and likely the first Renaissance figure to study Hebrew and Latin, attempted to unify Platonism not only with Aristotelianism but with Arabian philosophy and the Jewish Cabala as well. Still less orthodox, unhappily for him, was the thought of Giordano Bruno (1548–1600), executed by the Inquisition for heresy. Bruno's perspective combined Cusa's Neoplatonism and the Hermetic tradition with the new astronomy of Copernicus; from this resulted the conception of an infinite and organic cosmos, pantheistically formed and unified by divinity.

Other than Platonism, Ciceronian, Stoic, and skeptical influences were at work. The Ciceronian was particularly strong in the Renaissance subordination of logic and dialectics to rhetoric; Rodolphus Agricola (1444–85), the Petrarch of German humanism, and Petrus Ramus (1515–72) were the major forces behind this subordination. Stoic influences were ubiquitous, but the most noted Stoic of the period was Justus Lipsius (1547–1606), who produced editions of Tacitus and Seneca and whose *De constantia* presented virtue as the sole good. Michel Eyquem de Montaigne (1553–92) introduced a perspective at once humanistic in its preoccupation with man, Stoic in its acceptance of limitations, and Pyrrhonian in its skeptical disdain of physics and metaphysics. Political philosophy, too, saw the breakdown of the scholastic synthesis. Most notable, of course, is the work of Niccolò Machiavelli (1469–1527). His *Il Principe* put avowedly amoral techniques of gaining and retaining power in the service of nationalism. But Jean Bodin (1530–96) maintained that sovereign power, necessary indeed as the ultimate source of authority in society, was subject to moral law. By the end of the Renaissance, European civilization had clearly undergone significant departure from medieval ideas and institutions. The stage had been set for modern philosophy. BIBLIOGRAPHY: J. H. Randall, *Career of Philosophy from the Middle Ages to the Enlightenment* (1962).

[R. E. HENNESSEY]

RENAN, JOSEPH ERNEST (1823–92), Orientalist and philosopher; born in Tréguier (Brittany), France; professor of Hebrew and Chaldaic at the Collège de France (1870); administrator of the Collège from 1884 to his death in Paris. He received training in Scripture and Semitic languages at the major seminary of St. Sulpice, Paris. In 1845 he decided not to accept ordination to the priesthood and embarked upon university studies. His first work, *Histoire des langues sémitiques* (1848), won him a reputation in the field of Semitic languages. In 1859 he was nominated for a professorship at the Collège de France. While he awaited the official confirmation of the government, he went to Phoenicia on an archeological expedition, accompanied by his sister, Henriette, and later joined by his wife, Cornélie. At the urging of his sister he began to write a life of Jesus. In 1862 his professorship was confirmed, but his inaugural lecture, which spoke of Jesus as "an incomparable man," caused so much stir that the professorship was suspended until 1870. In 1863 his *Vie de Jésus* was published and became the most renowned of R.'s writings. It was written in the fashion of 19th-cent. "Lives of Jesus," and was esp. noteworthy for its characterization of Jesus as a romantic revolutionary. Although R. followed the life with six other works on the origin of Christianity under the general title *L'Histoire des origines du christianisme,* he failed to achieve scholarly stature in this field. His enduring contributions to scholarship appeared esp. in his *Corpus inscriptionum Semiticarum,* wherein he published Phoenician inscriptions. BIBLIOGRAPHY: L. F. Mott, *Ernest Renan* (1921); M. J. Lagrange, *Christ and Renan: A Commentary on Ernest Renan's "Life of Jesus"* (tr. M. Ward, 1928).

[C. P. CEROKE]

RENAUDOT, EUSÈBE (1648–1720), a leading French Oriental scholar and historian of the liturgy. R. was editor of *Gazette de France* from 1680 and a member of the French Academy from 1689. He had withdrawn from the Oratorians as a cleric in minor orders but retained a lifelong interest in theology, liturgy, and church history, which his familiarity with Oriental languages enabled him to direct toward the Eastern Churches. He published a large collection of Oriental liturgical texts in Latin translation, *Liturgiarum orientalium collectio* (2 v., 1715–16). Notable also are his history of the Jacobite patriarchs of Alexandria (1713) and the two volumes he contributed to the *Perpétuité de la foi catholique de l' Église* (between 1708 and 1713) in defense of the antiquity of the Eucharistic faith of the Oriental Churches. BIBLIOGRAPHY: P. W. Skehan, NCE 12:375–376; A. Raes, EncCatt 10:771–772.

[R. B. ENO]

RENGEOIN, Japanese Buddhist temple in Kyoto, also called Sanjusangendō (Hall of Thirty-three Bays) built (1164), destroyed by fire (1249), rebuilt in 1266, with repairs 1649–51. The huge hall (198 feet) houses 1,001 statues of the thousand-armed Kannon created by the master sculptors Unkei and Tankei with other carvers.

[M. J. DALY]

RENI, GUIDO (1575–1642), Italian painter. Working in the Carracci Academy (1594), he actually surpassed his master Ludovico Carracci in a competition (1598). R. painted a *Madonna of the Rosary* (c.1595–98), a *Crucifixion of St. Peter* (c.1603) evidencing the naturalism of Caravaggio, and *Job* (1622–36) discovered in Notre Dame, Paris, all displaying the graceful contours of Classicism *(St. Sebastian, Archangel Michael Overcoming Satan)*. In the *Aurora* ceiling fresco (1613–14; Rome, Casino Rospigliosi) R. treats forms as in an easel picture eschewing the tradition of illusionism *di sotto in su* (painting of figures as if seen from below). Despite a degree of affectation, R. achieved a certain poetry in his creations. After Carracci's death, R. became the leading artist in the Bolognese school. His influence produced in lesser artists a sentimental Classicism.

[M. J. DALY]

RENIER OF HUY (fl. *c*.1110), Mosan sculptor and goldsmith (earliest known sculptor of the Meuse River region, Flanders) noted for the magnificent inscribed baptismal font of St. Barthélemy, Liège, originally commissioned by Bp. Hellinus for the Church of Notre Dame aux Forts. The font—a bronze cylinder supported by 12 oxen, is decorated with 4 relief panels of biblical scenes of baptism, showing the influence of Ottonian and Byzantine art in a strikingly free style.

[M. J. DALY]

RENOUVIER, CHARLES BERNARD (1815–1903), French critical philosopher. R. studied at the École Polytechnique under A. *Comte. His general philosophical position is called neocriticism insofar as he utilized Kant's critical phenomenology, although R. came to significantly different conclusions. He asserted that there are no things-in-themselves (noumena) and no Kantian antinomies. Human beings are free and rational, and there is a finite, personal God whose worship is compatible with Protestantism but not with Catholicism. He influenced Octave Hamelin and, to a lesser extent, William James. BIBLIOGRAPHY: G. Boas, EncPhil 7:180–182.

[T. M. McFADDEN]

RENUNCIATION OF SATAN, part of the rite of baptism. Satan has been de-emphasized in the reformed rituals of Paul VI. Although the new 1972 *Rite for Christian Initiation of Adults* retains the threefold renunciation of Satan, it is a far less impressive ritual moment than in times past when the adult catechumen, newly anointed for combat with the devil, would turn to the west, the abode of darkness and satanic power, and vehemently spit at Satan. Now in the restored ritual the renunciation of Satan is separated from the scrutinies (exorcisms) and given a new place, forming one rite with the catechumen's profession of faith in the Savior and in the mystery of the Trinity. Clearly, emphasis in the new ritual is with Christ who has "conquered that spirit" of evil. There are two formulas for the renunciation. For a society that finds it easier to acknowledge the reality of sin, the second formula seems more appropriate, since it begins with the renunciation of evil and leaves Satan to make his appearance last on the list. Commitment to Christ is far from being a passive event in the ritual of baptism. The threefold renunciation of evil reflects the active dimension to any profession of faith. Episcopal conferences are encouraged by the ritual to adapt these formulas to specific evils in the world that the catechumen is called upon to renounce. As in Christian antiquity so in modern worship ritual words and gestures should reflect the cultural horizons of people. The renunciation is renewed by those participating in the Easter Vigil. BIBLIOGRAPHY: *The Rites of the Catholic Church* (1976) 98–99; 145, 146; 221–222; 245.

[D. J. FINNERTY]

RENWICK, JAMES (1818–95), American architect, noted designer of churches: Grace Church, N.Y. (1843–46), 14th-cent. English Gothic, St. Patrick's Cathedral, N.Y. (1859–79), French Gothic, Smithsonian Institute, Wash. D.C. (1848–49), Romanesque revival, Corcoran Art Gallery (1859) and Vassar College, N.Y. (1860) French Second Empire derivatives. Later buildings show added ornamental richness and loss of clarity of detail.

[M. J. DALY]

REORDINATION, a repetition of the ceremony conferring orders because of doubts concerning the validity of the first conferral. The First Council of Arles (314) recognized the validity of ordination by a bp. who might have been a betrayer (*traditor*) of the Sacred Books. Against Donatists, who continued the African practice of rebaptizing and reordaining those of the Catholic party, St. Augustine stated the principle that neither orthodox faith nor probity of life is required for the valid administration of the Sacraments. The Council of Trent (1547) reaffirmed the principle that "a minister who is in mortal sin" may confer the Sacraments (D 1611). Despite this clear teaching of the Church of the West, individual popes of the unenlightened period from the 8th to the 12th cent. insisted on the reordination of clerics who had been ordained by bps. accused of simony and other irregularities. It has been suggested that in some cases the original ordinations were regarded as illicit (*irritae*) and that they were repeated for canonical and not strictly theological reasons. BIBLIOGRAPHY: J. Gilchrist, NCE 12:378–379; L. Saltet, *Les Réordinations* (1907).

[P. F. PALMER]

REPARATION, a notion that lies close to that of *restitution, of *satisfaction, of compensation, of *redemption, of *merit, of *sacrifice, of expiation, and of restoration. All should be freed from that of undergoing *punishment, though they entail pain in the providential order of things. The last two express the negative and positive sides respectively of reparation as it appears in theological and devotional writings. Literally a "repairing," in Chaucer a reconciliation, reparation is the renewal of something to its proper state after it has decayed or gone wrong. Between persons it means to make amends, to make at one—the original sense of atonement, vigorous yet peaceful, has sometimes been obscured by the livid clouds of a religious rhetoric about appeasing God's wrath. Theologically its purpose is to be restored to his friendship, yet it is involved in the whole story of human dereliction and rescue by Christ, in whose life and death we must share if we are to come to his Resurrection (Rom 6. 3–4; 1 Pet 1.18–2.20). Its explanation requires an analysis of *sin, which is not just a turning away from God but a turning to something else, and in which the elements of guilt, penalty, stain, and perhaps other psychological *sequelae,* have to be discerned and remedied. Without sin himself, Christ took on the whole burden of our sins, (Is 53.6; Jn 1.29; 1 Pet 1.19; Acts 8.32–35), yet invites all to help shoulder the cross. Reparation, then, is for all. The term, however, has a special intonation for those persons or groups who dedicate themselves explicitly to the work, traditionally associated with devotion to the Sacred Heart. It is not the suffering itself which is a value, but the love of God and others which is ready to embrace it or even to go out and seek it. Yet a cool appraisal in terms of disalienation, even were it done in the temper of an Anselm, can be made to look rather patronizing and impertinent before the holiness which thrives on metaphors with which the Scriptures abound, and which is quick to pay the price for the insult sin offers to God's majesty and honor. BIBLIOGRAPHY: Philippe de la Trinité, *What is Redemption?* (tr. A. Armstrong, 1961).

[T. GILBY]

REPENTANCE, a term that does not render the full sense of the Gr. *metanoia,* nor, though it is nearer, that of the Lat. *poenitentia,* to which it adds the "backwards" inflection of the suffix re-. The first means the turning or conversion to God of mind and heart; the second, often joined with some form of *agere,* to do, adds the notion of shouldering the penalties incurred by sin. The Douay Version renders it as doing penance, and the Latin tradition tends to fix on sorrow for sin as central both in the virtue of penitence and in the reception of sacramental forgiveness. Protestant tradition has kept the Greek sense of losing "God-forsakedness" and opening out on to a new life without looking back, like Lot's wife, on the past. The senses are not contrary, yet differences of language can sometimes induce differences of religious psychology. The call to repentance rings throughout the Bible (e.g., Jer 4.8, Mt 18.23; Mk 1.15, Acts 2.38).*PENANCE.

[C. NEELY]

REPHAIM, a Hebrew word with two apparently distinct usages in the Hebrew Scriptures: (1) the community of the dead; the inhabitants of Sheol; (2) the "giants" who were among the pre-Israelite peoples of Palestine. The origin of each of these meanings is obscure. Any relation or link between the two meanings is even more obscure. Rephaim as the shades of the dead, weak and shadowy continuations of the living who have lost vitality and strength, could come from the Hebrew *raphah:* "to sink down" (to Sheol, to powerlessness); or from *rapha:* "bound together" (in the common lot of the dead). The Ugaritic Ras Shamra texts (13th cent.) provide the most numerous and the earliest references to the Rephaim. One text refers to them as the gods of the underworld whom the Supreme God El invites to a feast. This is somewhat akin to the reference in Isaiah to the Rephaim as an aristocracy among the dead, who greet the king of Babylon who comes to join their company. This usage in turn is similar to that of a warning inscription on a 4th-cent. Phoenician sarcophagus, imparting to all who would disturb or rob the tomb a curse depriving them of a resting place among the Rephaim. "Rephaim," as an ethnic term for the pre-Israelite giant people of Palestine, may also have a Ugaritic origin, since in Ugaritic texts it is commonly used in parallelism with heroes of manly vigor and vitality. Whatever the origin, it is questionable how much experience Israel actually had with any such giants. Og, king of Bashan, was considered the last of them, and his massive iron bedstead is mentioned with suitable awe (Deut 3.11). Whether there actually were people who were as tall as the Anakim, who used huge weapons, whom the Moabites called Emim, and the Ammonites called Zamzummim; or whether they were invented and attributed to Transjordania because of the megalithic remains of the Neolithic period still found there, is open to conjecture. A link between the two usages of *Rephaim* might be found in the fact of the Ugaritic use of the same word for mighty heroes and for the gods of the underworld. But that is more conjecture.

[E. J. DILLON]

REPIN, ILYA EFIMOVICH (1844–1930), Russian painter. After work in an icon shop, R. won a traveling scholarship (1864) for an academic *Resurrection of the Daughter of Jairus.* Later, breaking away from the academy, R. painted grim, socially realistic works (*Religious Procession of Kursk,* 1880–83). From somber portraits of Tolstoy and Mussorgski R. moved in bold strokes of bright color to the heroic beauty of Andreyev (1905). In Finland, after the October Revolution, R. painted scenes of the Passion in an Expressionistic vein.

[M. J. DALY]

REPINGTON, PHILIP (Repyngdon; d. 1424), bp. of Lincoln, cardinal. An Augustinian canon at Oxford, R. was suspended and excommunicated in 1382 for preaching the doctrines of John *Wycliffe. He recanted his heretical views, however, and after a few years his earlier deviation from orthodoxy proved no obstacle to ecclesiastical preferment. He was made abbot of St. Mary-de-Pré (1394), chancellor of Oxford (1397), bp. of Lincoln (1404), and cardinal (1408). He was reinstated in the latter office by the Council of Constance (1415) because the Council of Pisa had deposed and annulled the acts of Gregory XII (1409) who had appointed him. He resigned his bishopric in 1419, probably for political reasons. BIBLIOGRAPHY: K. B. McFarlane, *John Wycliffe and the Beginnings of English Nonconformity* (1953).

[R. B. ENO]

REPOSE, ALTAR OF, the altar at which the Eucharist is reserved following the Evening Mass of the Lord's Supper on Holy Thursday until the Mass of the Easter Vigil. The rubrics of the 1970 Roman Missal call for it to be in a chapel suitably decorated. It should, therefore, be outside the main body of the church and not elaborately decorated. Adoration before the Sacrament is to continue until midnight, but there is to be no solemn adoration after this hour.

Historically, this ancient custom gave rise to the Forty Hours devotion. Presumably, following the general rule that ancient customs are preserved for more solemn occasions, this custom originated before the practice of reserving the Sacrament on the main altar came into vogue.

The term is sometimes applied to the altar at which the Sacrament is reserved, as distinguished from the altar where Mass is celebrated, which is then termed the altar of sacrifice. The term altar, however, should be used only for that on which Mass is celebrated. The General Instruction of the Missal (#267) recommends that minor altars should be in separate chapels and that the reserved Sacrament should be kept in a prominent and properly decorated place, though this is not necessarily an altar (#276).

[J. DALLEN]

REPPLIER, AGNES (1855–1950), American essayist and biographer. At 16 R. began to submit short stories and sketches for publication in Philadelphia papers. In 1881 she published a story in the *Catholic World* and was advised by the editor, Isaac *Hecker, to concentrate on writing essays. Among her distinguished collections are *Books and Men* (1888), *Points of View* (1891), *A Happy Half-Century* (1908), *To Think of Tea!* (1932), *Eight Decades* (1937), and *In Pursuit of Laughter* (1936). Her essays are scholarly, witty, and stimulating, covering a wide variety of subjects. With the personal and literary pieces she achieved greater success than with political and social themes. Her essays plus her three excellent biographies—*Père Marquette* (1929), *Mère Marie of the Ursulines* (1931), and *Junípero Serra* (1933)—have earned for her a lasting place in American literature. BIBLIOGRAPHY: G. S. Stokes, *Agnes Repplier: Lady of Letters* (1949); E. Witmer, *Agnes Repplier: A Memoir* (1957).

[S. A. HEENEY]

REPRESSION, in psychoanalytic literature the mental process by which threatening and unwelcome thoughts, usually of obscene or brutally cruel nature, are unconsciously prevented from entering conscious awareness by a kind of spontaneous act of repulsion. It is then a mechanism by which the mind defends itself from the intrusion of frightening and shameful thoughts prompted by the instinctual drives. Its purpose is to relieve the need to admit and articulate the instinctual impulses of which one is unbearably terrified or ashamed. Repression is triggered by a "signal anxiety" which warns of the threatening intrusion of these impulses and ideas. Its effect is to render them unconscious, but not inactive, because they tend to continue to intrude themselves into consciousness. After one thought has been dealt with, other thoughts tending to recall it by the process of association will likewise be repressed. In this way a person can become virtually incapable of reflecting on large areas of his own internal life, esp. those of sexuality and aggressiveness. This tends to impede development into a spiritually and morally mature personality, for maturity demands the acceptance of the real self, the understanding of the nature and force of the instinctual drives, and their rational and voluntary (as opposed to repressive) control. BIBLIOGRAPHY: M. Oraison, *Love or Constraint* (1961).

[M. E. STOCK]

REPRISAL (medieval Lat., *repraesalia*), literally a taking back. Moral theology can look at it under two aspects, as an indemnification and as a retaliation. As to the first: the seizure of the persons or goods belonging to another group as compensation for loss or injury suffered from that group, originally from a personal initiative to settle by force a question of right incapable of settlement by peaceable agreement, and given a juridical standing by medieval polity, was a concept that lay behind the maritime practice of privateering under letters of mark. This, which was not abolished until the international Convention of Paris (1852) and did not of itself produce a state of war, had been tempered, and not only in theory, by a common code of decency as well as by the healthy acquisitiveness which sought gain, not destruction, by fighting. Henceforth reprisal was reserved to the public forces of the State; the outcome was not altogether to human advantage, for not rarely the mass-will shows itself much more savage, splenetic, and uncontrollable than individual wills.

This brings us to the second aspect, of reprisal less as reparation than as *punishment, a getting your own back which loses its literal sense and gets charged with feelings of *revenge, of repaying a hurt with a hurt. Now there is a case for draconian measures as deterrents or even as pieces of social surgery, less certainly as vindications by human authority of outraged law. There is none for the answering of cruelty by cruelty, which develops by an insane logic of its own into an ever mounting series, such as has produced the monumental crimes against humanity of which this century has been guilty. If reprisals are to be allowed at all, then it is only on condition that they are utilitarian and seek a good effect. They should be preceded by a public declaration calling on the enemy to stop their occasion, and should be discontinued as soon as he does; they should not fall on neutrals and innocents. The last point suffers from the tragic, old, and still-unresolved problem of discriminating between the opposed community as people (*ut singuli*) and as a whole (*ut universitas*).

[T. GILBY]

REPROBATION, the divine plan and decree regarding those who do not attain salvation; the opposite of *predestination. Theologians have classified reprobation as positive and negative; antecedent and consequent. Positive reprobation means the divine decree to condemn or inflict punishment; negative reprobation means a divine decree of nonelection to glory, or exclusion from glory. Antecedent reprobation precedes the foreknowledge of an individual's sinfulness; consequent reprobation is subsequent to such foreknowledge. Classical Calvinism included the teaching of a positive antecedent reprobation (see DOUBLE PREDESTINATION). The Council of Trent repeated earlier conciliar rejections of this teaching. *Arminianism also mitigated the Calvinist doctrine. The only positive reprobation accepted in RC theology is consequent. *Báñezianism proposed a negative reprobation that was antecedent; *Molinism, one that was consequent.

[J. TYLENDA]

REPUTATION. "A good name is to be chosen rather than great riches" (Pr 22.1); Aristotle considered *timē*, called *honor* by the Romans, which we may render as esteem, the greatest of all external goods. Christian morals do not reserve this to the particularly magnanimous man, for it is everybody's right if human society is to be conducted with decency and respect. Hence the denigration of another's good name (Lat., *fama*; Gr., *doxa*), is the grave sin of *detraction, to which listeners must not even tacitly consent (ThAq 2a2ae, 73). In a positive sense a man's good reputation is conditional upon his deserts; in a negative sense it should always be presumed unless you are certain it is baseless. Even when you know that another is undeserving of the good name generally attributed to him, it is held you may not divulge hidden information to his discredit except when that is necessary for the protection of others or for the public good.

[T. GILBY]

REQUIEM (MUSIC), a Mass sung on occasions honoring the dead to promote the repose of the soul of the departed. Among the outstanding Requiems are those composed by Palestrina, Verdi, and Berlioz.

[P. HENNESSEY]

REQUIEM MASSES (LITURGY). In the Roman Catholic Church, Masses offered for the dead, so named from the first words of the entrance antiphon (introit): *Requiem aeternam dona eis, Domine, et lux perpetua luceat eis* (Give them eternal rest, O Lord, and may perpetual light shine on them; cf. 4 Ezra 2:34–35). The antiquity of the text can be seen from its use of an apocryphal book often regarded as canonical prior to the late 5th century. Other texts used in the Mass until recently were introduced in the 6th and 7th centuries. The antiquity of the offertory antiphon can be seen from its ambiguity regarding the situation of the dead (i.e., wandering, searching for heaven). Evidence of Masses for the dead is found as early as the 2nd cent., particularly on certain days after death and burial (3d day and anniversary in all rites; 7th and 30th days in the West and 9th and 40th days in the East). Funeral Masses appear to have begun in Rome in the 4th cent. and to have become common in the early Middle Ages, except in the East. The practice is theologically based on the belief that the living can assist by their prayers those who have died (see PURGATORY) because of the *Communion of Saints. Recent liturgical reforms have attempted to replace the mood of sorrow and fear of judgment with an atmosphere of Christian hope, based on Christ's rising from the dead and the Christian's entrance at baptism into eternal life. In the New Missale Romanum of 1970 the *Requiem aeternam* is one of the entrance antiphons of the three alternative texts for funeral Masses outside paschal time; it is also the second of the three for All Souls Day. Other texts of Scripture are used for funeral Masses in paschal time and for the various forms of memorial Masses for the dead throughout the year.

[J. DALLEN]

REQUIESCA(N)T IN PACE, Latin for "may he/she (they) rest in peace," a prayer for the dead; also a burial inscription.

RERUM NOVARUM, the first of the great social encyclicals of modern times, issued by Leo XIII in 1891. Appearing at a time of socialist unrest in all of Europe, it strongly condemned socialism and affirmed the inviolability of private property—going on, however, to assert the right of the worker to a family wage that would enable him, too, to become a property owner. The encyclical opposed to economic liberalism the right and duty of the State to intervene in the economic sphere, to protect the workers' right to reasonable hours of work, healthful working conditions, and just wages; and it pointed out that the "free-contract" system of hiring labor, while theoretically acceptable, was often, in practice, not free on the part of the worker: "If through necessity or fear . . . the worker accepts harder conditions because an employer or contractor will give him no better, he is the victim of force and injustice." The encyclical appealed to the conscience of the well-to-do on behalf of the underprivileged, quoting the words of St. Thomas Aquinas: "Man should not consider his possessions as his own but as common to all, so as to share them when others are in need." Perhaps the most revolutionary aspect of the encyclical was its espousal of the right of workers to form associations for the prosperity and well-being of the members—associations which were not to be forbidden, and in fact should be protected, by the State. BIBLIOGRAPHY: *Acta Leonis XIII* 4 (1894) 177–209.

[D. CODDINGTON]

RERUM ORIENTALIUM, encyclical of Pius XI (Sept. 8, 1928), an important modern initiative towards reunion of the Roman and the Eastern Churches.

[T. C. O'BRIEN]

RESCRIPT, in canon law (CIC c.36–62), a written reply (Lat. *rescriptus,* written back) from the Holy See to a petition for a favor, dispensation, information, or interpretation. Two basic types are the rescript in a judicial matter and the rescript conceding a favor. The second may be one communicated directly to the petitioner and is effective at the time of its writing or one communicated to the petitioner through an executor or agent (e.g., through the bp. or a confessor) and is effective when communicated. All members of the Church may request rescripts except those under explicit excommunication or interdict and suspended clerics. Granting of a rescript always presupposes that the petition is grounded on truth (c. 40). The degree of truth essential for validity, however, is that the reason or motive for the petition be true or that at least one of several reasons be true. Falsification (obreption) or suppression (subreption) in the narrative portion of the petition need not, then, nullify a rescript (c. 42). A rescript must also conform to legal precedent, i.e., to usual curial practice. A rescript granted by one ecclesiastical authority without knowledge of a prior denial of the favor is invalid. Errors of fact in the rescript do not nullify it as long as the meaning is clear from the nature of the case. Interpretation of a favor granted must be strict and exclusive to the case involved. Where the rescript sent to the petitioner stipulates or where public order or some other reason is at issue, it must be presented to the bp. or other competent authority. Where a rescript involves an executor, the execution must take place at the time and according to the other conditions required by the document. Execution cannot be withheld except for some grave reason obvious to the prudent judgment of the executor. When the external forum is involved, execution must be in written form. An error or alteration contrary to what is required for execution may invalidate the execution, but does not invalidate the rescript itself; the execution alone must be regularized.

[T. C. O'BRIEN]

RESERVATION OF THE BLESSED SACRAMENT, see EUCHARIST (WORSHIP AND CUSTODY).

RESERVED SINS, those which normally can be absolved only by a confessor with special faculties from his ecclesiastical superior. The power to reserve sins resides in the diocesan bp. and in the Holy See, but no bishop may reserve to himself cases already reserved to the Holy See. The purpose of reservation is to protect the community from serious and public violations of Christian discipline, and to correct individuals guilty of particularly heinous sins. The current tendency within the Church is to limit severely the number of reserved sins (See PENAL POWER OF THE CHURCH). In missionary lands and on retreats, in premarital confessions, in cases where the penitent is physically or psychologically unable to leave his home, and preëminently when the penitent is in danger of death, no sin is considered to be reserved, and all sins may be validly and lawfully absolved by the confessor.

[R. A. ARONSTAM]

RESIGNATION (medieval Lat. *resignatio,* adaptation from *resignare,* to unseal, cancel, give up), in religious literature, as in the *Imitation of Christ,* a giving up of oneself to God, or in particular at the end rendering your life back to him. It implies one's compliance with the divine will, but this conformity, as shown by Our Lord's example at Gethsemani (Lk 22. 42), "Not my will, but thine," and the careful analysis of St. Thomas Aquinas (ThAq ST 1a2ae, 19.10) does not entail the extinction of your own desires. The adverb "resignedly" sometimes suggests reluctant acquiescence.

[T. GILBY]

RESPECT, see OBSERVANCE.

RESPECT OF PERSONS, see DISCRIMINATION.

RESPIGHI, OTTORINO (1879–1936), Italian composer. He began violin and viola studies in Bologna (1891–99), became first violist in the St. Petersburg Opera orchestra (1900) where he met and studied composition and orchestration with Rimsky-Korsakov, and was a pupil of Max Bruch in Berlin (1902), also studying composition. R. taught composition at the Conservatorio di Santa Cecilia in Rome (1913) and became director of Rome's Conservatorio Regio (1925), where he taught till his death. His works include symphonic works, *The Fountains of Rome* (1917) and *The Pines of Rome* (1924), operas, including *Maria Egiziaca* (1931), ballets, choral works, chamber music, and church music. The Gregorian chant certainly influenced his modal music after 1920. His compositions are noted for their lyrical quality and their subtleties and reflect his interest in the Italian masters of the 17th–18th centuries.

[R. J. LITZ]

RESPONSA, JEWISH. Throughout the Levant prominent Rabbis began in the 9th cent. to solicit practical and theoretical questions in order that by answering them they might gain revenues for their schools. The practice continued in the Middle Ages down to the present time in Rabbinical centers of scholarship. The Responsa were short, mainly practical, in the earliest Gaonic period, but became dissertations and monographs in the Rishonim period (Early Rabbis–to the 14th cent.) and the Aharonim period (Latter Rabbis–to the present). The vast amount of literature accumulated over the centuries has never been completely published, but in the state of Israel it is now in process of being computerized and indexed. The Responsa are of inestimable value for the study of Jewish lore and history.

[J. F. FALLON]

RESPONSA AD BULGAROS (Lat., Replies to the Bulgarians), a series of 106 replies of Pope *Nicholas I to questions about Christianity sent him by the Bulgarian Khan *Boris in 866. The questions vividly reflect the concerns and the customs of the Bulgarians at the time of their conversion. The papal reply is not an ordered treatise, but primarily pastoral in intent. Text: PL 119:978–1016. BIBLIOGRAPHY: G. Dennis, "Anti-Greek Character of the *Responsa ad Bulgaros* of Nicholas I," *Orientalia Christiana Periodica* 24 (1958) 165–174.

[G. T. DENNIS]

RESPONSIBILITY, (1) the accountability or, literally, the answerability of a moral agent for his voluntary acts. It is not the mere fact of psychological freedom that imposes responsibility; but that the exercise of freedom is a choice expressing the inner finality of an action towards the true human good (see FINALITY). The moral agent is one who, like any being, has a natural orientation toward his integral perfection. Unlike lesser agents, however, he is capable of apprehending the value or meaning of the good, and so of

acting for the good as meant (see Gilby). Because the full human good is one to be attained, its true value is a measure exacting an act matching what attainment requires. The good to be achieved is a measure to which the moral agent is subject; it is a rule according to which his concrete choices are right or wrong: right when the choice is of the true good-as-meant; wrong when the choice is vitiated by a lack-of-good-as-meant. The basic accountability of the moral agent, then, is not to a merely imposed, external law, but to the inner law of his own being. For moral theology that inner finality proper to the human being is a reflection of and participation in God's eternal law (ThAq ST 1a2ae, 91.2). But that way of sharing becomes active and actual through the judgment of personal *conscience; that is the immediate measure to which the moral agent answers. True moral responsibility is highly personal (which is not to say purely subjective); it requires honest fidelity to conscience and the confident willingness to invest the self in moral choices inwardly prompted, not merely exteriorly dictated (see CONSCIENCE, EDUCATION OF). Charity, of course, transforms the abstract structure of morality; Christian responsibility becomes responsiveness of the child of God to the Father. The finality of the new being of grace is the intention to love God wholly, answering the Father's love by a return of love, that is, a willingness to choose only in comformity with the bond of love. The meaning of grace as a law of love is its interiority and willing disposition toward what is consonant with the new identity given through grace (see ThAq ST 1a2ae, 107.1; 108.2 & ad 2). Built on the presupposition of the inwardness of moral responsibility, there are also specific forms of it that correspond to the fact that positive law is also a moral norm. The moral agent is answerable to divine and human law, and to the second in both its civil and canonical forms. Both civil and canon law recognize the possibility of diminished responsibility (see FEAR: FORCE: FORENSIC PSYCHIATRY: IGNORANCE: PASSION: VOLUNTARINESS). Pastoral theology also recognizes that it is not possible to decide subjective responsibility in every instance. But it is no solution to exempt a whole range of human experience (e.g., sexuality) from the possibility of control; a denial of responsibility is a denial of the capacity for good and for personal maturity. Trust in personal conscience and honest decision means also trust in God's respecting them, who "has left man in the hand of his own counsel" (Sir 15.14 - Vulg). (2) A consequent meaning, the reliability of a person in regard to the requirements of the Christian life and of his particular station in life. Responsibility in this sense directly engages the virtue of *prudence, which is the right disposition towards the deliberation and counsel needed for right and effective moral choices. Responsibility means, as well, the avoidance of *negligence in regard to the due knowledge and care required for fulfilling the duties of one's state and in regard to attentiveness in carrying them out. BIBLIOGRAPHY: ThAq ST (Lat-Eng v.18, ed. T. Gilby) app. 1–6; 10–11.

[T. C. O'BRIEN]

RESPONSIBILITY, COLLECTIVE, the accountability of a group for sin or crime. Theology can consider its possibility in several areas. (1) Traditional teaching on *original sin reflects on it, at least implicitly, as a possible way of expressing the mystery. The culpability of original sin is a problem, since sin means a voluntary fault, and original sin is a "sin of the nature," without personal voluntariness. One classical solution is the theory of Adam's moral headship, based on an implicit pact between God and Adam (see AMBROSIUS CATHARINUS), which stipulates that he would act vicariously for all and that his acts would be imputable to all. Such a theory equivalently involves collective responsibility. St. Thomas Aquinas expresses the meaning of original sin more simply; it is the presence in a person of a human nature voluntarily deprived (by the act of Adam alone) of its rightful relationship to God. Responsibility means voluntariness; original sin involves no collective will, is minimally voluntary, and has no personal punishment attached to it. (2) In the OT dispensation involving a pact or covenant with the whole people, Israel, collective responsibility and punishment exacted of the whole people seem to be the rule. In dealing with Abraham, Moses, and the kings, God was dealing with the whole people. "The collapse of the Israelite political society in the time of Jeremiah and Ezekiel left no relationship of the individual to Yahweh" (McKenzie, 73). But the two mentioned and later Prophets introduced—without replacing the old—a new personal accent on moral responsibility. The newness of the NT includes its inner, personal emphasis; St. Thomas Aquinas indicates that the first bestowal of grace on each person was through the nature (in Adam)—one might add on the Israelite through Israel—but that "grace does not come to us through human nature [or the 'people of God'] but only through the personal action of Christ" (ST 3a, 8.5 ad 1); "Christ . . . first restores what belongs to the person, and later, all at once in all men, he will restore what belongs to human nature" (*ibid*. 69.3 ad 3). (3) Collective responsibility can also be compared to the meaning of cooperation in *sin. In a general sense, the two are distinct, since the meaning and degree of cooperation are determined according to one person's individual voluntary, therefore culpable, participation in another's sin. One form of cooperation in sin touches on specific, historical instances of holding a whole people responsible for the action of its leaders, namely silence, taken as tacit agreement in a crime. The reparation exacted after World Wars I and II, even the trials for war crimes, seemed to hold the vanquished peoples collectively responsible. Moral justification for that would seem to invoke the concept of cooperation by silence. (4) Collective responsibility in a more positive sense may be referred to the meaning of *legal justice. Every member of a community has a responsibility to the public or common good; it is collective as meaning each member's proportionate contribution to the life and well-being of the whole community. Some of the specifically emerging aspects of such responsibility are: concern for the earth's ecology; the issue of actuating the potential of technology or science, i.e., whether the scientific community should do whatever it has the technique and power to do or should exercise self-limitation for the well-being of mankind. BIBLIOGRAPHY: J. L. McKenzie, "Aspects of OT Thought," JBC (1968) 77.70–73 (pp. 748–749); Th Aq ST (Lat-Eng v. 26, ed. T. C. O'Brien) app. 7, "Sin Caused by Origin."

[T. C. O'BRIEN]

RESPONSORIAL PSALM, selected verses of a psalm, together with a recurring refrain, used as a response to the first scripture reading of the Roman Mass. Basically a meditation song for cantor or psalmist and congregation (to which belongs the refrain), it echoes the central theme of the reading. While intended to be sung, it is recited when that is not possible. Prior to the 1969 Lectionary of the Roman Missal, this chant existed only in a truncated form in the *Gradual of the Mass. BIBLIOGRAPHY: J. A. Jungmann, *Mass of the Roman Rite* (tr. F. A. Brunner, 2 v., 1951–1955) 1:421–442.

[J. DALLEN]

REST, a biblical theme that denotes fulfillment of activity (See Gen 2.1–3). Various biblical words are used to denote repose, beginning with the objective of the Exodus (Ps 94(95).11) and ending with the thought of heaven. The Sabbath is a perpetual reminder of this. What man attains only by succession of time and hard labor now, exists already with God in a purified and endless way.

[L. A. BUSHINSKI]

RESTENNETH PRIORY, an Augustinian house in Angus Scotland, founded by King Malcolm IV *c*.1153, which evidently incorporated an earlier church on the site, since the tower still extant at the W end of the ruined nave is Saxo-Norman. It was suppressed at the Reformation in 1560. BIBLIOGRAPHY: D. E. Easson, *Medieval Religious Houses: Scotland* (1957) 81; W. D. Simpson, "Early Romanesque Tower at Restenneth Priory, Angus," *Antiquaries Journal* 13 (1963).

[L. J. MacFARLANE]

RESTITUTION, restoration of the equality upset by a violation of *justice. The term connotes the moral obligation to rectify the consequences of sins of injustice. Such consequences are of two kinds: deprival of what by right belongs to the offended person (including a "moral person" a social unit); the injury done to the offended person. The binding force of the obligation is as serious as the offense committed; the degree of obligation corresponds to the offender's share in the offense.

The meaning and obligation of restitution is in strict correlation with the meaning of justice. Once justice is violated the violator can never be exonerated until the objective wrong is righted. As far as the sacrament of penance is concerned, repentance or contrition for an injustice must include the intention to make restitution; absolution and forgiveness require that intention. The offender who in fact culpably fails to carry out that intention perpetuates the injustice and is again guilty. Justice and its demands are unrelenting; the contrary wrongs never just "go away"; there are no moral "statutes of limitation." The only way that the obligation to restitution ceases is by the victim's completely waiving repayment or redress. A complete inability to make restitution may excuse for as long as the inability lasts; even in such a case, however, the obligation is suspended, not abolished.

The sin of taking another's possessions by theft, fraud, and the like, or the fact of becoming an unjust possessor require restitution of the object taken or its equivalent and according to an exact value. Sins of unjust injury—whether as a consequence of theft and the like or direct infliction of harm—require reparation of the damage done to others in terms of monetary loss, bodily injury, loss of reputation, of opportunity, or advantage due. Fringe considerations—e.g., the offender's expenses necessary for maintenance of unjustly acquired goods—are taken into account in computing restitution. Cooperation in sins of injustice can be more or less direct and effective so that gradation of guilt also comes into the issue of restitution. Sometimes such considerations make the topic seem complicated. There is, however, nothing complicated about the central fact. Ill-gotten goods "cry out for their rightful owner"; that cry never ceases. Unjust injuries "cry out" for rightful redress; that cry never ceases, no matter how long the perpetration of injury is perpetuated by either an individual or a "system." Justice is the most typically human virtue, i.e., the most rational; its demands, therefore, have also been quite readily rationalized. Catholic moral theology has always been clear about the objective norms and unyielding requirements of justice; Catholic practice, at the personal and the political level—civil or ecclesiastical—has not always been conspicuously sensitive to the inexorability of justice and its consequences. *COOPERATION IN SIN; *POSSESSORS IN GOOD, BAD, DOUBTFUL FAITH.

[T. C. O'BRIEN]

RESTITUTION, EDICT OF, see EDICT OF RESTITUTION.

RESTORATION, the term used in English history for the reestablishment of the monarchy with the accession of Charles II (1660) after the collapse of the Protectorate government. In religion the Restoration brought victory to the C of E over the Puritans and made secure the episcopal, as opposed to the presbyterian, form of church government.

[R. B. ENO]

RESTORATION MOVEMENT, a term applied to groups originating in early 19th-cent. U.S. that committed themselves to the dual goals of Christian unity and the reestablishment of simple NT Christianity. Specifically, it refers

to the Disciples of Christ led by Thomas and Alexander *Campbell, and to the "Christian" movements that arose in New England, Virginia, and Kentucky at about the same time. Most of the followers of Barton *Stone who called themselves simply "Christians," merged with the Disciples, but the others continued separately and merged with the Congregational Churches in 1931 (see UNITED CHURCH OF CHRIST). The idea of reforming or purifying the Church by restoring the early Church has been a recurrent theme in church history. Distinctive of the American groups was the combination of concern for restoration with an equally strong concern for Christian unity. Adherents of the movement rejected creeds and ecclesiastical organization, calling their Churches simply "Christian Churches." They believed that Christians had become separated into denominations as a result of creedal, organizational, and sacramental developments that occurred after the first cent., and that unity could be realized by a return to pristine faith and practices. Yet this movement aiming to unify Christians has itself experienced division; the Churches of Christ gradually separated from the Disciples of Christ, claiming to be truer to the original intent of restoration than the Disciples. *CHRISTIAN CHURCHES, *CHRISTIAN CHURCHES (DISCIPLES OF CHRIST), INTERNATIONAL CONVENTION.

[P. J. BOCK]

RESTORATIONISM, a term denoting the subject of a controversy in American Universalism that arose about 1817. In opposition to the beliefs of Hosea *Ballou (1771–1852), some Universalists believed in a future state of punishment that would precede the final restoration of all sinners to a state of holiness and happiness. In 1831 the "Massachusetts Association of Universal Restorationists" seceded from the Universalist General Conventions; in 1841 the separatist organization was dissolved. The Universalist ministers of Boston issued a statement in 1878 that signalized the end of the controversy. BIBLIOGRAPHY: R. Eddy, *Universalism in America* (2 v., 1884–86). *UNIVERSALISM.

[J. C. GODBEY]

RESTOUT, JEAN, THE YOUNGER (1692–1768), French religious and history painter. In a broad, soft manner R. executed large decorative paintings on the ceiling of the library of the Abbey of Ste.-Geneviève, Paris, in churches of Paris and at Versailles and also designed for Gobelins' tapestries. His *Essai sur les principes de la peinture* (1755) was a standard art work in 18th-cent. France. *Christ at the Pool of Bethesda* and *St. Paul at the House of Ananias* (1709) in French lighting and composition, mark R.'s most successful work.

[M. J. DALY]

RESTREPO, JOSÉ MANUEL (1781–1863), Colombian statesman and historian. R. supported the independence movement, helped to write the first constitution of Colombia, served as deputy to the first congress, and represented

Antioquia for the triumvirate of 1815. During the brief Spanish restoration, he took refuge in the United States. On various occasions he represented Colombia in its boundary disputes with Ecuador and Venezuela. His main literary work was: *Historia de la revolución de Colombia* (10 v., 1827).

[P. DAMBORIENA]

RESURRECTION, GRECO-ORIENTAL, prominent motif in Iranian texts. Both a personal judgment after death and an eschatological judgment are mentioned. The soul is thought to hover near the dead body for 3 days before it is judged on the 4th on the "Bridge of the Requiter." Good souls gain heaven, evil ones hell. Some texts mention a "place of the mixed," which receives those whose good deeds equal their evil ones. Ohrmazd, the power of light and good, rules heaven, Ahriman, the power of darkness and evil, rules hell. Since history is conceived as a continual struggle between Ohrmazd and Ahriman, the final resurrection coincides with Ohrmazd's definitive triumph, which is more a rehabilitation of the cosmos than a final judgment. The savior Saoshyans raises bodies from the elements and reunites them with their souls. After enduring a 3-day ordeal in molten metal, all drink the elixir of immortal life (Haoma), which Saoshyans prepares from the fat of a sacrificed bull. Despite many parallels, direct Iranian influence on Christian thought is generally doubted. Less convincing are purported parallels with Ancient Near Eastern "dying-and-rising gods." Antecedents of Christian beliefs are best sought in the Jewish tradition, which evinces by the 2d cent. B.C. belief in resurrection. (2 Macc 12.40 ff.; Dan 12.1–2).
BIBLIOGRAPHY: A. T. Nikolainen, *Auferstehungsglauben in der Bibel und ihrer Umwelt* (2 v., 1944–46); R. C. Zaehner, *Teachings of the Magi* (1956) 131–50; S. G. F. Brandon, *Judgment of the Dead* (1967).

[E. V. GALLAGHER]

RESURRECTION OF JESUS, the act of God proclaimed by the Twelve, St. Paul, and other witnesses (Acts 2.14–36; 3.12–26; 4.8–12; 5.29–32; 10.34–43; 13.16–41; 1 Cor 15.1–8) by which Jesus of Nazareth, crucified, dead, and buried was raised from the dead on the third day after burial to be declared the Lord and Savior of all mankind (Acts 2.36). The Resurrection of Jesus is the central datum of NT Christianity; its proclamation by the Twelve originated the Christian community in Jerusalem (Acts 1.15; 2.41), whence it spread elsewhere in Palestine and throughout the Roman world, and ultimately produced the literature of the New Testament.

According to the NT the Resurrection of Jesus was an event that occurred within history, i.e., within the experience in time and place of chosen witnesses (Acts 10.40–41), yet is not a historical fact, i.e., an occurrence within history that was open to the perception of the ordinary human observer, as was, for example, the crucifixion of Jesus. It is a matter of irrelevance to the thought of the NT that there were not witnesses to the actual moment of Jesus' Resurrection from the tomb. For his restoration to life from the dead and the transformation of his being that accompanied it (1 Cor 15.42–45) would not have been perceptible to observers at his tomb as an act of God, apart from prophetic illumination, but only as a phenomenon susceptible of divergent explanations. That God raised Jesus to proclaim him living Lord and Savior of men is an explanation of the cause and meaning of the Resurrection that by its own definition lies beyond the purview of human reason.

The NT proclamation of the Resurrection continues the tradition of prophetic testimony established in OT times. As with the OT prophets, the Twelve testified to a personal and unique experience of God, in this instance, of God manifesting himself to them through their experience of the risen Jesus. The fact of their proclamation, its manner, and the nature of their testimony are subject to critical evaluation, both historical and theological; but the object of their proclamation, the Resurrection of Jesus as an act of God, lies beyond the scope and methodology both of historical inquiry and of theological expectation that would reason to the event from the general principle of the likelihood of the resurrection of the dead.

In situating the Resurrection of Jesus in the singularly exclusive experience of divinely chosen witnesses, the NT does not deny historical and theological dimensions to the event. It acknowledges that the very testimony of the prophetic witnesses to "God raising Jesus" (Acts 2.32; 3.15; 4.10; 5.30; 10.40; 13.30) has such dimensions. The material in the kerygmatic speeches of Peter and Paul in Acts (cf. the listing above) and of the Resurrection narratives at the conclusion of each Gospel reflects the preoccupation of early Christianity with the theological and historical questions that naturally arise from the proclamation of the Resurrection. The kerygmatic speeches in Acts are mainly preoccupied with the theological implications of the Resurrection. Outside of the sheer appeal to the Twelve as witnesses, the speeches are not concerned with the historical aspects of the Resurrection-event. They include no data on the empty tomb or on the disciples' experience of the risen Jesus. Their theological concern is to validate the crucifixion and death of Jesus as well as his Resurrection by appeal to the prophetic quality in the literature of the OT

This use of OT texts, however, is in itself a prophetic reinterpretation of them in the light of the actuality of Jesus' Resurrection (cf. Lk 24.44–46). The principal OT texts that came into traditional use were Is 52.13, the concept of the suffering servant (Acts 3.13, 26; cf. 8.32–33), an explanation of the crucifixion; Ps 16.8–11 (Acts 2.25–28; 13.35), a prophecy concerning the Davidic Messiah seen fulfilled in the Resurrection; Ps 110.1 (Acts 2.34); likewise a prophecy concerning the Davidic Messiah seen fulfilled in Jesus' departure to his Father (the Ascension); and Ps 2.7, a declaration of the unique sonship pertaining to the Davidic line (Acts 13.33; cf. 9.20), esp. appearing in the person of Jesus.

The historical dimension of the Resurrection-event derives from the tradition of the apostolic *didachē*, i.e., teaching (Acts 2.42), that elucidated and supported the kerygma. Two natural objections against the prophetic testimony to the resurrection were that the body of Jesus was stolen from the tomb and that the witnesses were the victims of subjective delusion concerning Jesus' appearances to them. The first objection was customarily met by recounting the experience of the first visitors to the tomb from among Jesus' own followers. These persons were not his male disciples but a number of women who initially discovered and reported the tomb open and empty (Mk 16.1–5; Lk 24.1–3; Mt 28.1–2; Jn 20.1). To this testimony Mt 27.62–66 adds an account of the guarding of the tomb authorized by Pilate, the strongest possible affirmation that Jesus' followers did not in fact remove his body from the tomb. The suggestion that the Disciples were in some way hallucinated is responded to in terms that endeavor to express their psychological recognition of the risen Jesus as identical with the person of the Jesus of the ministry familiarly known to them. Thus Peter, one of Jesus' closest and most fervent Disciples who repudiated him during the trial, acknowledged the reality of the Resurrection-appearances (Lk 24.34). The witnesses were in the company of the risen Jesus for the duration of meals (Lk 24.42–43; cf. Acts 1.4; Jn 21.9–12), and had opportunity to receive instruction from him that they perceived accorded in manner and content with his teaching during the ministry (Lk 24.44–46; Jn 21.15–17; cf. Mk 14.29). Through these experiences the witnesses became convinced of their personal contact with the actual reality of the living person of the risen Jesus (cf. also the independent testimony of Paul, 1 Cor 9.1). This conviction embraced more than the fact that God had raised Jesus; it included also a beginning recognition of the religious significance of his person: God "glorified" Jesus (Acts 3.13), i.e., endowed him with a trans-human existence and with the divine prerogatives of religious authority and power (Mt 28.18).

Under the impact of the Resurrection-event Christian understanding of the religious significance of the risen Jesus grew apace through experience and reflection: Jesus was "Lord and Christ" (Acts 2.36), i.e., the religious ruler of Israel and the world, established as such by divine power; he was Son of God in the messianic sense of Ps 2.7 (Acts 13.33); he was "the Lord" in the sense of the more absolute prerogatives of divinity (1 Cor 12.3; Rom 10.9), a concept probably emphasized in worship, that soon elevated the understanding of his messianic sonship to the divine plane (Mt 11.25–27) and led ultimately to the formulation of Jn 1.1–14, wherein under the concept of the *logos* his full equality with God is most clearly and forcefully enunciated.

Thus the apostolic proclamation of the Resurrection made Jesus the center of Christian life and thought. The "breaking of the bread" (Acts 2.42) was both a commemoration of his voluntary death upon the cross for the Redemption of men (1 Cor 11.23–26) and an anticipation of his parousia

(Acts 1.11; cf. Jn 6.62) when the whole Church would be gathered to him (1 Thes 4.17). The ministry of Jesus—his sayings, his miracles, his Passion itself—took on a new and normative meaning, more deeply penetrated in the light of the significance of his Resurrection. BIBLIOGRAPHY: A. M. Ramsey, *Resurrection of Christ* (1945); F. Morison, *Who Moved the Stone?* (1930); R. Russell, "Modern Exegesis and the Fact of the Resurrection," DownRev 76 (1958) 251–264; 329–343.

[C. P. CEROKE]

RESURRECTION OF THE DEAD (IN THE BIBLE), the restoration to personal existence, by divine power, of deceased human beings. In the history of OT thought, belief in the resurrection of the individual was a slow development. Throughout the prophetic period from the 8th to the 6th cent. the concept of human immortality was entertained, but not the concept of individual resurrection. At death the life principle, or spirit, of man was thought to be consigned to a nether (lower) world, variously termed the Pit, the nether world, or Sheol. This state was not a truly human existence, since in the Hebrew concept of man the separation of the life principle from the body destroyed the unity of the person (Is 38.17; 51.14; Ezek 26.20; 32.21). The OT prophetic texts that speak of resurrection (Hos 6.1–2; Is 26.19; 53.11; Ezek 37.1–14) are, in the opinion of the majority of OT scholars, a reflection on the future national restoration of Israel as a people that would be faithful to Yahweh. The book of Job, composed after the completion of Israel's main prophetic tradition (sometime after 600 B.C., perhaps as late as 300 B.C.), does not envision individual resurrection as a solution to the inequities of reward and punishment its author observes as an anomaly of human life (cf. Job 3.16; 7.9; 10.21; 14.7–22; 38.15); hence the author of Job is not aware of an Israelite tradition of individual resurrection.

It is first in the book of Dan, written *c*. 164 B.C., that there appears in the OT a categorical declaration of individual resurrection (Dan 12.1–3, 13). The author's horizon, however, is not one of universal resurrection, but only of a limited number of just and unjust, who will rise to everlasting life or punishment. This conviction seems to have arisen in the context of the Seleucid persecution of Judaism under Antiochus IV Epiphanes, when many Jews suffered martyrdom rather than repudiate their religious laws (cf. also 2 Macc 7.9, 11, 14, 23).

By the 1st cent. B.C. belief in individual resurrection was generally current in Judaism, although it is not clear that all Jewish sects accepted it. The evidence of the Dead Sea Scrolls leaves the attitude of the Qumran sectaries uncertain. If they followed Essene doctrine as described by Josephus, they believed in the immortality of the human spirit, but not in individual resurrection. The Sadducees are known to have been strong opponents of resurrection (Acts 23.8; 26.8), while the Pharisees, whose teaching dominated popular belief, were equally strong adherents of the doctrine. The Gospels reveal that Jesus not only accepted the current belief in individual resurrection, but declared it to be a doctrine necessitated by the promises of God to the Patriarchs, which could be fulfilled for them and their descendants only by resurrection (Mk 12.18–27).

The NT doctrine of individual resurrection was the result of the belief of Judaism, the teaching of Jesus, and the event of his own Resurrection as an act of God brought about for man's salvation (Acts 4.12). Baptism incorporates the believer into the existence of Jesus and sets in motion first a moral resurrection (Rom 6.1–4; Ephes 5.14) that is to culminate in the glorious resurrection of the just (1 Thes 4.13–16; Rom 6.5–11). The objection that the disintegration of the human body makes individual resurrection impossible is answered by Paul in terms of God's creative power, which produces a ''spiritual body'' for a new kind of existence in a resurrected life (1 Cor 15.35–44; cf. Mk 12.24–25). According to Jn 5.28–29 the unjust also rise through the power of Christ as the divinely appointed judge of all men (cf. Acts 10.42; 17.31). BIBLIOGRAPHY: E. F. Sutcliffe, *Old Testament and the Future Life* (1947); F. X. Durrwell, *Resurrection: A Biblical Study* (1960).

[C. P. CEROKE]

RESURRECTIONISTS, religious congregation of priests and brothers whose first members pronounced their vows in 1842 on the feast of the Resurrection in the catacombs in Rome. The founders were three young Poles, Bogden Janski, Peter Semenenko, and Jerome Kajsiewicz, who, inspired by the French Catholic lay movement to return to the faith, tried to help their Polish compatriots in Paris. In 1863 they began leading a common life under the direction of Janski, who was never ordained and who died before Semenenko became the first superior general. Despite many difficulties the congregation began to work in Italy, France, Canada, Turkey, Bulgaria, the U. S., Poland, and Austria. In 1902 final approval of the constitutions was granted. The Resurrectionists established missions later in Bermuda, Bolivia, and Brazil. Their motherhouse is in Rome. In 1976 the congregation had 44 houses, 343 priests, and 158 brothers.

[R. C. CLIGGETT]

RETABLE (RETABLO: ALTAR BACK), panel of stone, metal or wood, at the rear edge of the altar table, or supported immediately behind the altar. At first simply sculptured, in the Gothic and Renaissance periods painting and sculpture were often combined in elaborate many-winged masterpieces (Van Eyck, *Mystic Lamb;* M. Grünewald, **Isenheim Altarpiece,* polyptych).

[M. J. DALY]

RETICIUS OF AUTUN, ST., bp. of Autun, France, at the beginning of the 4th cent. and the first bp. of that diocese whose tenure is documented. According to St. *Gregory of Tours, R. married a woman as virtuous as he, with whom he lived many years. After her death he was called to govern the Church at Autun. He was among the bps. of Gaul whom Constantine called to sit in judgment on the Donatists at a synod in Rome (313). R. also took part in, and signed the anti-Donatist acts of a synod at Arles (314). Jerome mentions also his writings against the Novatianists.

[E. J. DILLON]

RETREAT, CONGREGATION OF THE, a union (1966) of three congregations: the Retreat of the Sacred Heart, Society of Mary, of Angers; the Retreat of the Sacred Heart of Bruges; and the Daughters of the Holy Virgin, of the Retreat of Vannes. The union was made following a regrouping of houses which had been founded separately in the second half of the 17th cent. at Vannes by Catherine de Franchville and at Quimper by Claude-Thérèse de Kerméno, and then in different cities of France. These houses were centers of deep spirituality, following the Exercises of St. Ignatius, under the impetus of Père Vincent Huby. The work, interrupted by the French Revolution, later came to include works of education in order to respond to the needs of the times. Today, answering the call of the Church through *Evangelii nuntiandi* and different synodal declarations, the congregation has taken on new apostolic works. In doing this it remains faithful to the original charism and to the Ignatian spirituality, while keeping its first objective: education in the faith and response to the spiritual needs of the time. The Congregation numbers (1977) 617 sisters and 53 houses, 27 of which are in France. The motherhouse is in Versailles. The sisters labor also in Germany, Belgium, Italy, Ireland, Chile, Cameroun, and the Low Countries.

[H. P. ANNAS]

RETREATS, times set apart for more intense spiritual exercises, ordinarily in a situation removed from the regular setting of daily life. Jesus gave an example of such special times of recollection by his 40 days in *solitude (Mt 4.1–2) and by going ''off to some place where he could be alone and pray'' (Mt 14.23). He also admonished the Apostles of their need, at a time when they were busy, to go ''away to some lonely place . . . and rest for a while'' (Mk 6.31). The Apostles carried out this admonition after the Ascension when ''they joined in continuous prayer'' in the upper room (Acts 1.12–14), and Paul after his conversion spent 3 days in fast and solitude (Acts 9.9.) Following this tradition, the Fathers of the Church from earliest times emphasized the need of some solitude for the achievement of sanctity. As a result, the practice grew of making *Lent a period of retreat for all. Great bishops such as Ambrose and Augustine, retired to monasteries for *silence in which to find energy for their busy lives. From such examples grew the custom of bps., and later priests, preparing for the reception of orders with a retreat. Great impetus was given to the retreat movement after the Reformation by the **Spiritual Exercises* of St. Ignatius and the writings of St. Francis de Sales, esp. *Introduction to a Devout Life*. In current church law, secular priests are obliged to make a retreat every 3 years (CIC c. 126) and all religious, every year (CIC c. 595). Retreats for laymen have grown in popularity because of national retreat leagues encouraged by the popes. In the U.S., a National Catholic Laymen's Retreat Conference (founded 1928) and the National Laywomen's Retreat Novement (founded 1936) have done much to interest the Catholic laity in weekend retreats made in local retreat houses. Pope Paul VI, in 1966, in a message to the National Catholic Laymen's Retreat Conference, noted the relevance of retreats to the spirit of renewal fostered by Vatican II, emphasizing the value to souls of an opportunity ''to be alone with God.'' BIBLIOGRAPHY: T. DuBay, NCE 12:428–429.

[P. F. MULHERN]

RETRIBUTION, reward or punishment as the consequences of a morally good or bad action, the punitive meaning being more usual (see also MERIT). An abstract moral consideration can see every human action as deserving of either reward or punishment. For human actions have a relationship to God, to self, to other people, which any given action may respect or violate, and so become either well– or ill–deserving (ThAq St 1a2ae, 21.3). In its usual, punitive sense retribution is due to a deviant human action (sin), which violates the requirements of justice: the inner subordination of man's powers to the full, true human good; the submission to God's rightful dominion; or the respect owed the rights of other persons. ''One who by acting against a divine commandment [or other due order] has indulged his own will beyond what is right, should, according to the order of divine [or other] justice either voluntarily or by constraint undergo something not to his liking'' (ibid. 87.6). Because of the meaning of charity and of union with Christ in the Christian life, the meaning of punishment as purely afflictive is transformed into atoning or expiatory punishment, accepted in imitation of Christ. Sin is not purely a matter of justice; it is a rupture of love. Repentance is not sheer endurance of retribution; it is reconciliation through Christ, and includes the willingness to accept suffering in atonement conjoined to Christ's Passion.

[T. C. O'BRIEN]

RETTENBACHER, SIMON (1634–1706), Benedictine Christian humanist, scholar, poet, chief representative of Benedictine school drama. As director (pater comicus) of the Salzburg school theater, R. wrote many plays in Latin (Selecta dramata, 1683). His voluminous writings, for the most part still unprinted, also include homiletic works in German, some 6,000 poems in Latin, a Hebrew grammar, and several translations from French and Spanish. BIBLIOGRAPHY: W. Kosch, Deutsches Literatur-Lexikon (1963) 334; H. de Boor and R. Newald, Geschichte der deutschen Literatur 5 (1951) 428–435.

[M. F. MCCARTHY]

RETZ, JEAN FRANÇOIS PAUL DE GONDI, DE (1613–79), card. and politician. R. was well-educated and directed to the clergy by his family. He became (1643) coadjutor to his uncle, abp. of Paris, and aligned himself with the Paris Parliament and the revolt, the so-called Fronde, of the French princes against the court. He thus became an erstwhile opponent to Card. *Mazarin and supporter of Prince Louis II de Condé, leader of the Fronde. Upon Mazarin's return to power in 1652, R. was imprisoned but automatically became abp. of Paris upon the death of his predecessor. R. escaped to Rome in 1654 where he received the support of Pope Innocent X and continued to try to influence French politics. Louis XIV allowed him to return after Mazarin's death, but only after R. resigned as abp. of Paris. He received a large benefice, served Louis XIV well in his relations with the papacy, and underwent a spiritual conversion toward the end of his life.

[T. M. MCFADDEN]

REUCHLIN, JOHANNES (1455–1522), German philologist and humanist. By extensive study and travel, esp. in Italy, R. perfected himself in the classical languages, Hebrew, and the literature of the Cabala. He published many works reflecting these interests; his De rudimentis hebraicis (1506) was an epoch-making introduction of the use of Hebrew in Christian scriptural exegesis. *Erasmus held R. in the highest esteem and wrote an Apotheosis at his death. In the last decade of his life, R. opposed the Jewish convert J. Pfefferkorn, who sought to have all Hebrew books burned as a danger to Christian faith. Pfefferkorn circulated his violent Handspiegel (1511) against R., who replied in kind with Augenspiegel (1511). This work was publicly burned (1514) by the inquisitor J. Hoogstraeten. The controversy was marked by the *Epistolae obscurorum virorum, written against R.'s enemies. In 1519 R. won an initial victory, being vindicated by the abp. of Spire, but ultimately the Augenspiegel was condemned by Leo X (1520), and R. was made to pay the costs of the litigations. He remained a loyal Catholic to the last and even endeavored to win back his nephew Philipp *Melanchthon. BIBLIOGRAPHY: L. Geiger, Johannes Reuchlin (1871); K. Hannemann, LTK 8:1260–61, with extensive bibliog.; F. G. Stokes, Epistolae obscurorum virorum: The Latin Text with an English Rendering, Notes and an Historical Introduction (1909).

[T. C. O'BRIEN]

RÉUNION, French overseas department, an island in the Indian Ocean (969 sq mi; pop. est. [1972] 470,000). R. was discovered in 1513 by the Portuguese and occupied in 1642 by the French, who called it Bourbon. In 1715 it had only 1,200 inhabitants but slave traffic and the rise of coffee plantations brought in many settlers. During the island's occupation by the British (1802–15) its name was changed to Réunion. Systematic mission work began at the end of the 18th cent. under Lazarists. In 1850 Réunion was made a prefecture apostolic depending on Bordeaux, and in 1916 it became a diocese in the care of Holy Ghost missioners. In

1970 Catholics numbered 420,000, cared for by 93 priests and 461 sisters, most of them native. Protestants totaled 2,500. *Bilan du Monde* 2:733–735.

[P. DAMBORIENA]

REUNION OF THE CHURCHES. The basic rationale of the reunion of Christian Churches is stated by the *Decree on Ecumenism of Vatican Council II. Christ founded one Church, but many Christian communions present themselves to man as the true inheritors of Jesus Christ. Such division "openly contradicts the will of Christ, scandalizes the world, and damages that most holy cause, the preaching of the Gospel to every creature" (Vat II Ecum 1). However, in recent times Christians have been inspired with remorse over their divisions. Many Churches and ecclesial communities that invoke the triune God and confess Jesus as Lord and Savior strive, in an ecumenical movement fostered by the Holy Spirit, for the restoration of unity among all Christians. Their goal is "the one visible church of God, a church truly universal and sent forth to the whole world that the world may be converted to the Gospel and so be saved, to the glory of God" (Vat II ConstCh 1).

Church union negotiations and mergers among Protestant and Anglican Churches have taken place in increasing numbers as the ecumenical movement has grown in strength. In April 1967, the *Faith and Order Commission organized the Consultation on Church Union Negotiations at Bossey, Switzerland. Forty-five participants from 26 countries, representing 27 different union conversations in 8 confessional families, exchanged information, heard about new approaches, and received recommendations for the formation of covenants to make *intercommunion possible and for programs of education for union. A survey of church union negotiations has been regularly carried in the *Ecumenical Review* beginning in 1954 and intensifying since Vatican II's impetus to ecumenism. In the various schemes of union under development, a general agreement is emerging that an episcopally ordered ministry in continuity with the *historic episcopate is to be sought in the united Churches, an element echoing the distinctive feature of the *Lambeth Quadrilateral (1888). Other factors also emerging are a common desire for flexibility in church structure, a view that the Church should truly serve in the world as a reconciling force, and a concern over the tension between the necessarily local nature of the Church and its universality. Among the unions already consummated, the *Church of South India and the *United Church of Christ in the U. S., because they involve different concepts of *polity and different traditions of ministry, are most significant. Among those pending, the union of the C of E and the Methodist Church, and the *Consultation on Church Union involving nine denominations in the U.S. are of major importance. Vatican Council II, by its doctrine of *collegiality, its acceptance of limited worship in common (*communicatio in sacris;* see Vat II EastCathCh 26–29), and its praise of authentic theological traditions in the Eastern Church, together with Pope Paul VI's visits with Patriarch Athenagoras and other friendly gestures, has done much to prepare for eventual reunion of the Orthodox and RC Churches.

No complete theology of church reunion exists, but as developed by the World Council of Churches (WCC) several points are pivotal. The *Amsterdam Assembly (1948) of the WCC declared that although the Christian Churches are divided as Churches, they are one in Jesus Christ, acknowledging him as Lord and Savior. The relationship of the member Churches with one another and with the WCC was not made clear, however. To clarify these relationships, the Central Committee of the WCC received a report at its Toronto meeting (1950) on the *Ecclesiological Significance of the WCC*. The statement declared that the WCC cannot be based on any one particular concept of the Church, nor does membership in the WCC imply that a Church treats its own conception of the Church as relative or that a specific doctrine about the nature of church unity has to be accepted. The meaning of the unity was further refined at the *New Delhi Assembly (1961).

The *Constitution on the Church* and the *Decree on Ecumenism* of Vatican II present RC theology on reunion. The Church is Christ's presence through his Spirit among the People of God. As such, the Church of Christ "subsists" in the RC Church while transcending it (Vat II ConstCh 8). Other Christians are incorporated in the Church of Christ, and Christian Churches are institutions whose ecclesial gifts and sacred actions are capable of admitting their members into the life of grace and the community of salvation. In the teaching of the Council, only the RC Church perfectly embodies the Church of Christ, but this does not prevent the partial realization of the Church of Christ elsewhere. The reunion of Christian Churches is the goal of the movement to which Protestant and Orthodox members of the WCC are committed. Since Vatican Council II, the RC Church has also been committed to the ecumenical movement and is cooperating more and more with the WCC and with other Christian Churches in common action. Yet, as Paul VI stated to the WCC at Geneva (June 10, 1969), many obstacles—theological, pastoral, cultural, and educational—remain. BIBLIOGRAPHY: *History of the Ecumenical Movement 1517–1948* (eds. R. Rouse and S. C. Neill, 1954); Official Reports of the WCC Assemblies; *Documentary History of the Faith and Order Movement 1927–1963* (ed. L. Vischer, 1963); A. Bea, *Unity of Christians* (ed. B. Leeming, 1963).

[R. MATZERATH]

REUSCH, FRANZ HEINRICH (1825–1900), ecclesiastical historian and leader of German *Old Catholics. Born in Westphalia, R. attended Bonn, Tübingen, and Munich Univ., and became a RC priest in 1849. At Bonn (1854), he taught and wrote on OT exegesis. Excommunication (1872) followed his condemnation of papal infallibility. Active in international Old Catholic congresses, he ran second in an episcopal election (1873) and became vicar general and a parish priest in Bonn. He was prominent in the *Bonn Reunion Conferences (1874–75). Although conducting occasional services, R. resigned church offices because of Old Catholic abolition of clerical celibacy (1878). Among his works were a magisterial study on the Index of Forbidden Books (*Index der verbotenen Bücher,* 2 v., 1883–85) and a historical treatise on the varying schools in RC moral theology, written with I. *Döllinger (*Geschichte der Moralstreitigkeiten in der römisch-katholischen Kirche seit dem 16. Jahrhundert,* 2 v., 1889).

[E. E. BEAUREGARD]

REUSS, ÉDOUARD GUILLAUME (1804–91), OT biblical scholar and forerunner of J. *Wellhausen. R. was a highly influential professor of Scripture at Strasbourg whose main contribution was to the historical composition of the Pentateuch. He denied the unity of Pentateuch authorship; maintained that Israel's cultic law was composed after the desert wanderings; and proposed a documentary or source theory of composition that was perfected by J. Wellhausen.

[T. M. MCFADDEN]

REVELATION, the self-disclosure of God and the communication of the truth about his nature and will. Because so much of the Christian doctrine of revelation has been formulated in discussions of its relation to other themes and issues, an examination of several of these relationships may serve as a useful basis for a definition and description of the doctrine itself.

Revelation and Event. At the center of the biblical view of revelation, both in the OT and in the NT, is the conviction that God makes himself known through happenings. Above all, it was in the Exodus from Egypt that the OT believer saw a special manifestation of God's relation to the people of Israel. Here it was that the covenant between the Lord and Israel had been established; the Law had been given to Moses; and the promises sworn to Abraham about the land had been fulfilled. In the NT the revelation of God reached its consummation and climax when "the Word became flesh and dwelt among us, full of grace and truth; we have beheld his glory, glory as of the only Son from the Father" (Jn 1.14). The biblical theology of the 19th and 20th cents., both Protestant and Roman Catholic, has rediscovered this emphasis upon the deeds of God in human history as the bearers of his communication of himself to men. When God speaks, he speaks by his mighty acts.

Revelation and Truth. Earlier generations of theologians often tended to define revelation in the category of truth rather than in the category of event. Revelation is the disclosure of what is supernaturally true about God. For the very events that serve as bearers of revelation become this by virtue of the word of God that is spoken in them and to them. Other nations have emigrated from the captivity of their oppressors; what made the Exodus of Israel from Egypt a revelation was the truth about God that was spoken by him through his servant Moses in the Torah. The revela-

tion in Christ was not simply an event, but "grace and truth came through Jesus Christ" (Jn 1.17). Because this truth has taken the form of doctrines, revelation has often been interpreted as the delivery of accurate and reliable information, stated in the propositions and dogmas of faith.

Revelation and Scripture. Whether as event or as truth, the revelation of God is recorded in the Bible; on this all Christians agree. Where they disagree is on the question whether all revelation is contained in Scripture. Protestants have generally maintained that Scripture, and Scripture alone, records the word and will of God for men. Roman Catholics have assigned to the tradition of the Church a role in the proper interpretation of divine revelation; some have asserted that all revelation is contained in Scripture, at least implicitly, and needs tradition to give it authoritative expression; others have treated tradition as in fact a "second source" of revelation. In practice, these differences have often been less sharp than they are in theory; for Protestant theology has continued to confess such dogmas as the Trinity, which are not stated in so many words in the Bible; and Roman Catholics have striven to find biblical warrant even for such dogmas as the Immaculate Conception and the Assumption, despite the acknowledgment that Scripture does not teach them in so many words. (See TRADITION.)

Revelation and Religion. From the earliest days of the Church, the Christian claim to be in possession of divine revelation has had to take account of the rival claims of other faiths. Although some theologians have found it possible to dismiss the problem by denying to other religions any true knowledge of God, most interpreters of the question have distinguished between those truths that have been known outside the historical revelation of God—be it through remnants of primitive revelation or through reason or through other means—and those that can be known only through the supernatural act of God's self-disclosure. In its missionary work, too, the Church has proceeded on the assumption that the grasp of the divine already present among non-Christians did not need to be unlearned, but needed to be corrected and completed by the Christian message.

Revelation and Reason. A related question is the relation of revelation to what can be discovered by the unaided human reason. Theologians and Christian philosophers have debated the scope and the limits of the truth to which reason can attain. A special case in this debate has been the demonstrability of the existence of God. Most Christian theologians have taught that reason can prove that God is, but *what* God is, they have taught, is largely the exclusive concern of revelation (see NATURAL THEOLOGY). Much of the work of traditional apologetics has dealt with such issues. Sometimes this has resulted in a theory of revelation that saw it as different from reason only quantitatively, but as similar to it in the way of knowing. But the consensus of theological thought would be that revelation is distinctive not only in its content but also in its form. BIBLIOGRAPHY: J. Baillie, *Idea of Revelation* (1956); *idem* et al., *Revelation*

(1927); É. Gilson, *Reason and Revelation in the Middle Ages* (1938); H. R. Niebuhr, *Meaning of Revelation* (1946); R. Latourelle, *Theology of Revelation* (1968); G. Moran, *Present Revelation* (1972); J. H. Walgrave, *Unfolding Revelation* (1966). *REVELATION, SOURCES OF.

[J. PELIKAN]

REVELATION, BOOK OF, the 27th and last book in the NT canon; it was written probably in the last years of the reign of the Roman Emperor Domitian (A.D. 90–95) to encourage the Christians of Asia Minor suffering from persecution or the threat of it. To deliver his message of hope and liberation, the author chose the literary method of apocalyptic as his chief vehicle. This literary *genre* has OT antecedents in Is 24–27 and Dan, and was utilized for such Jewish apocryphal works as the Book of Enoch and the Apocalypse of Baruch. Revelation, however, differs from the apocalypses of late Judaism in several significant respects: it provides the name of its author, John (1.1, 4, 9; 22.8), obviously not the pseudonym customary in apocalyptic works; it is addressed to the Christian community at large, not to a select group; and it presents a theological conception of history that revolves around the living person of the risen, ascended Christ as the Lord and judge of history, thus having at the center of its thought, not a subjective mythical idea, but a divine reality to be ultimately experienced by all mankind. Although the author uses symbolic numbers and the lavish imagery peculiar to apocalyptic writing, he is conscious that his work is prophecy (1.3; 19.10; 22.7, 10, 18–19) and understands himself as a prophet in the OT tradition (10.7; 22.6, 9).

The main divisions of Rev are clear: the introduction (1.1–20) designating the work as an apocalypse and prophecy, indicating its author, the place of its composition (Patmos) and its audience (the Christians of Asia Minor), and relating the circumstances of its composition (a visionary experience). Individual letters follow to seven churches (a symbolic number for completeness) that evaluate the spiritual condition of each (2–3). The main portion of Rev (4–22) is a series of visions allowing the author to witness through symbolic signs the blessedness of those faithful to Christ, the condemnation of their persecutors, and the final triumph of Christ over anti-Christ. Scholars of Rev are not agreed upon the literary structure of ch. 4–22. Certain sections are clearly identifiable as literary units (e.g., the seals, 4.1–8.1; the trumpets, 8.2–11.19; and the bowls, 15.1–16.21); but other sections do not have as clear an indication of literary unity.

The author of Rev intends to show that the life-experiences of Christians are known to God, that He takes note of their fidelity and infidelity, and that he will reward and punish the just and the unjust, esp. in view of the redemptive death and Resurrection of Christ. Although Rev was almost certainly occasioned by the persecution of Christians who refused to practice emperor-worship, its thought rises far above these concrete historical circumstances to stamp the Christian mystery of salvation through Christ upon the entire course of human history that is to be consummated in the parousia of Christ (22.20–21). The book is not, therefore, a prophecy of church history, but a proclamation of the gospel message of the divine judgment in Christ.

In the judgment of modern NT scholars the literary author of Rev is not the Apostle John but a disciple of John the Apostle. Having learned the Apostle's teaching, he was moved to record it in Rev at the appropriate time for the instruction of the Church. BIBLIOGRAPHY: A. Feuillet, *Apocalypse* (1964); W. J. Harrington, *Understanding the Apocalypse* (1969); P. S. Minear, *I Saw a New Earth* (1968).

[C. P. CEROKE]

REVELATION, PRIMITIVE. (1) "Primitive" being taken to mean "original" in a historical sense, the expression means the knowledge of supernatural truths given to the first man at his creation; or the knowledge of all necessary truths given by God's revelation, then passed down to all as the object of the "common sense," i.e., consensus of all mankind. The first meaning was included in the common theological understanding of the endowments of the first man (see *ORIGINAL JUSTICE); the second meaning is associated with *Traditionalism. In this usage there is also the connotation of a progressive loss of originally possessed knowledge. (2) "Primitive" being taken to mean "rudimentary" by comparison to the explicit revelation that is the object of Christian belief, the expression means God's self-manifestation implicit in the right moral and religious conceptions of those lacking knowledge of Christian revelation. Such a primitive revelation is a necessary postulate, on the grounds of the biblical account of God's dealings with men before the call to Israel; and of the truth that God makes possible to every human being a grace-relationship with himself. Whatever the explicit, conscious terms in which one not a believer in the Christian sense, relates to or turns away from God, those terms are the manner in which God presents himself as the object of a salvific choice.

[T. C. O'BRIEN]

REVELATION, SOURCES OF, in RC teaching, Scripture and apostolic tradition. Prior to the era of Vatican Council II this teaching was designated the "two-source" understanding of the way divine revelation is communicated. Against the Reformers' teaching, *sola scriptura,* the Council of Trent declared that the revealed truth and manner of life are contained "in written books and in the unwritten traditions" handed down, as it were, from the Apostles and preserved in the Church (D 1501). Vatican Council I in its dogmatic constitution on faith quoted the Tridentine teaching (D 3006). Vatican Council II in its dogmatic constitution *Dei Verbum* on revelation expressed a more unified understanding of how revelation is communicated. The document continues to speak of both sacred Scripture and sacred tradition (VatIIDivRev 9), but also states, "flowing from the same wellspring, in a certain way they merge into a unity and tend towards the same end" (*ibid*.), and that they "form one sacred deposit of the word of God, which is committed to the Church" (*ibid*. 10). Theological reflection on the theme of Scripture and tradition is esp. guided by the Council's more dynamic understanding of tradition; that understanding is reflected in this statement: "The Church in her teaching, life, and worship perpetuates and hands down (*tradit*) to all generations all that she is, all that she herself believes. This tradition which comes from the Apostles develops in the Church with the help of the Holy Spirit. For there is a growth in the understanding of the realities and the words which have been handed down"(*ibid*. 8). That growth is accomplished, the document continues through the contemplation and study of believers, through their own intimate understanding of what they experience, through the preaching of those who have received from episcopal succession the sure gift of truth (*ibid*.). One of the drawbacks that is overcome by this line of thought is an undue emphasis on a propositional concept of revelation. The two sources were often understood as two containers of objective revelation, i.e., of some propositions handed down as written in Scripture and of some handed down from the Apostles and from age to age repeated. There is, however, a prior and more vital meaning to both revelation and its reception. In its first, active sense revelation is God's communicating himself to be believed. In that sense revelation is a continuously present reality, to which the faith of the believer and therefore of the whole community of believers adheres; the immediate, primary, and distinctive object of faith is God revealing. In consequence of that acceptance of God himself by faith, the believing community believes that God's word authenticates the community's own being and own understanding. It believes, therefore, to be part of the content that God communicates the mission of Christ and of the Apostles, and the community's own continuity with that single, Christ-inspired mission. The individual's and the community's adherence to God revealing is a belief in the Church's own understanding and faithful transmission of what God attests to. That continuous understanding and transmittal are tradition. Faith-rooted tradition is the reason for regarding the Bible as the mirror by which the Church judges herself; the Bible is not the rule of faith as a written document, but as its meaning is itself understood and proclaimed in the community of belief. Because faith is the ever-present acceptance of God's ever-present word, there is a growth in understanding of the words and realities he communicates. BIBLIOGRAPHY: ThAq ST (Lat–Eng, v. 31, *Faith,* ed. T. C. O'Brien, 1974) 186–194.

[T. C. O'BRIEN]

REVELATION, VIRTUAL, in an objective and narrow sense, a truth necessarily connected with, and logically deducible from, an actually and formally revealed truth. In this restricted sense what is virtually revealed is equivalent to what technically is a theological conclusion: thus, Christ is true God and true man; because will belongs to divine and to human nature, Christ has two wills. Within the same framework of deducibility, a truth can be counted as virtually revealed if it has a link with revealed truth, not of necessity but of appropriateness; thus from Duns Scotus on theologians developed arguments of fittingness for Mary's Immaculate Conception. The discussion of the virtually revealed belongs in the context of ecclesiology and the issue of the Church's faithful preservation and proposal of the deposit of faith, and of what are secondary, but infallibly definable matters for the Church's magisterium. Other truths that come under this heading are: dogmatic facts (e.g., the legitimacy of the Council of Trent, a fact necessary to the authentication of its dogmatic definitions); necessary presuppositions to revealed truth, the preambles of faith (e.g., that man has intelligence); certain disciplinary decrees (e.g., of canonization, which attests to authentic Christian holiness). The terminology has become less settled with the current development of the theology of revelation and in ecclesiology.

[T. C. O'BRIEN]

REVELATION THEOLOGY, a name sometimes given to the effort of certain modern theologians to build up a theology of revelation that sees in it more than the information about himself in the form of propositions that God has made to man. It must be understood in contrast to the view of revelation that dominated much of RC apologetical literature of the 19th and early 20th cent., according to which the possibility and fact of revelation are capable of philosophical demonstration. Against this position modern revelation theology holds that for revelation to be in fact God's communication of himself to man requires a vital transformation of the recipient's manner of apprehension and life, without which neither the possibility nor the fact of revelation can be satisfactorily established. BIBLIOGRAPHY: W. Bulst, *Revelation* (1965); A. Dulles, *Revelation Theology* (1969); H. Fries, *Revelation* (1969); K. Rahner, *Spirit in the World* (1968); *idem,* SacMund 5:348–353.

[P. K. MEAGHER]

REVELATIONS, PRIVATE, divine disclosures of or insights into truths or wonderful facts of particular Providence inaccessible to human effort whether ordinarily or in the given situation. They are meant for the benefit less of the individual recipient than of the community of the faithful who already believe the saving truths taught by Christ in his Church, the so-called "public" revelation which was completed with the Apostles. They are no integral part, neither explicit nor implicit of the Church's *deposit of faith, are para-ministerial in respect to its commissioned teaching, and consequently cannot be declared *de fide. They have featured prominently in hagiographical and devotional literature in the past, nevertheless they usually belong to the world of the miraculous and preternatural, of the rare and accessory charismatical gifts (cf 1 Cor 12) that are to be approached in a critical, pragmatic, noncredulous temper, which starts with respect and is prepared to be grateful. Frauds and delusions are not unknown, and even genuine phenomena may be mixed and rendered with unconscious self-deception, particularly when they are projected very pictorially: the highly theological ''seers'' usually are quite ordinary in their manner, and are extraordinary mainly in the depth of the wisdom that is given to them by the Spirit. The Church has been wary about esoteric *illuminism from the beginning; and its authorities usually, but not always, have shown themselves more hesitant than approving of marvelous apparitions, visions, and locutions.

[T. GILBY]

REVENGE, see VENGEANCE.

REVERENCE, in its theological meaning, an attitude of fear, awe, respect, high regard, connected with both *justice and *charity. (1) The indebtedness in justice (see DEBT) to which reverence is the virtuous response is towards those who, because they are sources of the debtor's well-being and betterment, stand in a position of superiority and eminence. In its most general sense, reverence is the motive and purpose of the honor to be shown towards such persons (ThAq ST 2a2ae, 103.1 ad 1); and it stands for the moral attitude proper to all the virtues of veneration: *religion, filial piety, respectful service (see DULIA), *obedience, *gratitude. The degree and kind of reverence, therefore of honor, shown match the beneficence of the one revered, and the debtor's consequent indebtedness. At the level of moral virtue, reverence has as its highest form an expression of indebtedness towards God as the source of all being and goodness; it is the reverence belonging to the virtue of religion (see LATRIA). This is the acknowledgment of God's transcendence and majesty, and the creature's comparative littleness; of the divine lordship, justice, and sovereign claims. Such reverence expresses awe before the absolutely holy, as well as a deference and submission based on a sense of complete dependence. The meaning of religious reverence is the scale set for the descending degrees of respect towards those persons who, in the orderly pattern of divine *government, share in God's beneficent causality (ibid. 101.1; 102.1). (2) Reverence in a higher theological sense is connected with charity as filial love for the Father. To love the Father as Father means to love in a way corresponding to the divine fatherhood and grace-given sonship. Two gifts of the *Holy Spirit are supportive and expressive of that love. The gift of *fear of the Lord has reverence as its primary act; it is a filial fear, the dread of separation from the Father by sin, and a positive submissiveness, the willingness to be a faithful child. The gift indicates that charity itself includes a sense of awe for the Father's majesty, and acknowledgment of the disproportion, the sheer goodness and condescension in the Father's love; includes the refusal to find any glorification in self for

the divine love that need not have been shown. The *beatitude expressing such reverence is that of the poor in spirit (ibid. 19.11–12). The gift of piety that transforms all the relationships of justice also expresses the filial reverence included in charity towards the Father and its brotherly attitude toward all men (ibid. 121). Piety particularly corresponds to the spirit of adoption of sons whereby we cry ''Abba, Father'' (Rom 8.15). That spirit surpasses a reverence simply towards the Lord and Creator. It begets, as well, honor and esteem toward all whose beneficence is a reflection of the divine fatherhood, who, as it were, are the elders in the Father's family.

[T. C. O'BRIEN]

REVEREND, a word used adjectivally in formally addressing or identifying a clergyman. From the Lat. reverendus (worthy of reverence), it is used as a mark of respect. Custom in some places and religious communities gives the title to some who are not clergymen, e.g., Reverend Brother, or Reverend Mother for certain superiors. In hierarchically ordered Churches, the varying degrees in which respect is due are indicated by adding ''very'', ''right'', or ''most''. Although properly an adjective, the word is sometimes used colloquially, more often among Protestants than Roman Catholics, as a noun for clergyman.

REVERSURUS EX HOC MUNDO, Pius IX's bull (1867) directed to the Armenian Catholic Church, providing for greater papal authority over Armenian ecclesiastical affairs. The bull fixed the Armenian patriarch's residence at Constantinople, excluded the laity from episcopal elections, and stipulated that the pope would have the sole authority to appoint bps. and the patriarch. The bull was regarded as a violation of the traditional rights of the Armenian Church, and a schism took place that lasted until 1887.

[T. M. MCFADDEN]

REVISED PRAYER BOOK (1928), full title *Book of Common Prayer with the Additions and Deviations Proposed in 1928*, the result of an unsuccessful effort to revise the official liturgy of the Book of Common Prayer (BCP) of 1662. Its background lay in controversies and litigation over ritual and ceremonial deviations developing in the latter half of the 19th century. A Royal Commission Report of 1906 recommended a ''reasonable elasticity'' in public worship to enforce obedience to the BCP by all parties in the Church. The first stage of this revision was done by Convocations (1906–20), which was then broadened to include the *Church Assembly, established in 1919, with lay participation. Intense discussion marked the years 1920–27, with publication of several unofficial proposals of revision (''The Green Book,'' ''The Grey Book,'' ''The Orange Book''). A final draft (''The Deposited Book'') was approved by Convocations and the Church Assembly in 1927 by large majorities. But the House of Commons rejected it (238 to 205) in Dec. 1927, and again (in a revised form) in June

1928 (266 to 220). The failure of this revision to receive legal sanction was due to partisan strife—neither Evangelicals nor Anglo-Catholics liked the Book; to the attempt to tie disciplinary aims to the law of public worship; and to the prejudice of many members of Parliament to "Catholic" additions to a "Protestant" liturgy—notably the provisions for reservation of the Sacrament. The 1928 Book has, however, been widely used, and has greatly influenced other revisions of the BCP in the *Anglican Communion—notably in Scotland, South Africa, and the United States. BIBLIOGRAPHY: W. K. Lowther Clarke, *Prayer Book of 1928 Reconsidered* (1943); R. Currie, "Power and Principle: The Anglican Prayer Book Controversy, 1927–1930," *Church History* 33 (1964) 192–205. *BOOK OF COMMON PRAYER.

[M. H. SHEPHERD]

REVISED STANDARD VERSION (RSV),

English translation of the Bible produced by American Protestants and published in 1946 (NT), 1952 (OT), and 1957 (Apocrypha). It was not an altogether new translation but a revision of the 1901 American Standard Version (ASV), itself a variant of the 1881 English Revised Version, which in turn was a revision of the Authorized or King James Version. The International Council of Religious Education secured possession of the ASV copyright and in 1937 authorized the revision. It directed that the RSV should "embody the best results of modern scholarship as to the meaning of the Scriptures, and express this meaning in English diction which is designed for use in public and private worship and preserves those qualities which have given to the King James Version a supreme place in English literature." The two requirements reflected criticisms that had been made of the ASV. L. A. Weigle, Yale Univ. professor, headed the 32-member committee that made the revision. Since 1950 the National Council of Churches has held copyright to the RSV and authorized its publication. Though some fundamentalists have charged that the RSV shows a liberal theological bias, it is generally regarded as the best revision of the Authorized Version. For Roman Catholics, the RSV as it appears in the 1966 ed. of the *Oxford Annotated Bible* received the approval of Card. Cushing of Boston; an RSV Catholic edition, i.e., with notes and some NT textual alterations, was published in 1965–66 with the imprimaturs of a Scottish and of an American bishop.

[T. EARLY]

REVISED VERSION (RV),

English translation of the Bible authorized in 1870 by the Church of England. The NT was published in 1881; the OT in 1884, the *Apocrypha in 1895. The RV, prepared by Anglican and free church scholars, was a revision of the Authorized Version that, while employing the resources of textual scholarship, by intent sought as much as possible to preserve the language of the AV. The RV met with much criticism, literary and traditionalist; scholars acknowledge its worthiness, but it

has never been widely used in liturgy or for private reading. *AMERICAN STANDARD VERSION; *REVISED STANDARD VERSION.

[T. C. O'BRIEN]

REVIVALISM, a form of evangelism intensely emotional in style, with sin and salvation as its dominant themes and a dramatic conversion-experience as its aim. While applicable to any strongly emotional movement for Christian renewal, the term revivalism has a specific historical connotation, particularly in American Protestantism. A primary cause in its development was *Pietism, with its emphasis on experience religion (see EXPERIENCE, RELIGION OF). Historical revivalism began with Methodist evangelizing, led by John *Wesley, in 18th-cent. England, Ireland, and Wales. Revivalism in the U.S. had its most significant impact on the shaping of Protestantism between *c*.1725 and the Civil War. The revivalistic history of that era includes the *Great Awakening (see FRELINGHUYSEN, T.; TENNENT, G.; WHITEFIELD, G.; EDWARDS, J.); the *Second Great Awakening (see DWIGHT, T.; STONE, B.) after the Revolution, when the *camp meeting evolved on the frontier; and beginning *c*.1825 the "new measures" of Charles G. *Finney (see OBERLIN THEOLOGY). After the Civil War, Dwight L. *Moody set the pattern of the so-called professional revivalist, with business-like organization and skillful use of music and theatrical techniques in the campaigns. Most famous of the numberless evangelists continuing the tradition into the 20th cent. were Billy *Sunday and Billy *Graham. But revivals are a part of the regular church life of many denominationsn and the practice of an annual revivalistic renewal begun in the 19th cent. continues; revivalism is at the origin and remains an essential part of the life of the Holiness and Pentecostal Churches. While essentially a Protestant phenomenon, the revival was paralleled by the parish mission in RC churches during the 19th and early 20th centuries.

The emotional extremes of preachers and the physical extravagances of the converted (paroxysms, the "jerks," barking, tremors) form but part of the picture of revivalism. It also achieved a moral and social betterment of the populace. Its value as genuine evangelism, however, has always been questioned (see CHAUNCY, C.), particularly with regard to the once-for-all conversion experience and neglect of *Christian nurture (see BUSHNELL, H.). Theologically, emphasis on a personal, felt conversion replaced Calvinism by an almost universal *Arminianism stressing free cooperation in salvation. The revivalist approach to doctrine has been simplistic, suited to the audience and the objective; *confessions of faith and doctrinal orthodoxy have been minimized. Revivalism is a nonintellectual approach to faith, and its prevalence impoverished American Protestant theology; some of the most serious orthodox theological efforts in the 19th cent. were reactions (see PRINCETON THEOLOGY; MERCERSBURG THEOLOGY). Yet revivalism was a key element in the survival and growth of the

Churches in the American denominational pattern. At the time of colonial revivals, 90% of the population were not church members. The campaign against "infidelity," i. e., *deism and *rationalism, succeeded as a recruitment program for the Churches. The diminution of doctrinal differences created an atmosphere favorable to the experiment of religious freedom in the context of separation of Church and State. Revivalism proved that *voluntaryism works, that without an established Church and the coercion of law, persuasion could create church membership. BIBLIOGRAPHY: W. W. Sweet, *Revivalism in America* (1949); W. G. McLoughlin, *Modern Revivalism* (1959); S. E. Mead, *Lively Experiment* (1963) 120–127; Smith-Jamison 1:322–368.

[F. E. MASER]

REVIVISCENCE OF MERIT, literally, the revival of merit, the RC theological doctrine concerning the restoration of lost merit to the repentant sinner. When a person who has grown in the life of grace through the merit of good works happens to lose sanctifying grace by mortal sin, his merits die. When through repentance he is restored to the state of grace, his merits revive. This common theological doctrine is based on what has been revealed about the real remission of sins (see Lk 15.11–32—the parable of the Prodigal Son; cf. D 1528, which is concerned with the forgiveness of sin in justification). Ontologically it means that a repentant sinner is restored to the degree of grace he was in before his sin. There are various ways of conceiving this reviviscence of merit. According to one, grace is restored actually in proportion to the degree of the individual's repentance; i.e., it is partly restored, if repentance is imperfect; fully, only when repentance is perfect (see ThAq ST 3a, 89.5). Another conception sees grace restored fully at once (F. Suárez). A third holds that grace is restored at once in the degree of the penitent's disposition and fully at the moment of death (D. Scotus). BIBLIOGRAPHY: F. L. Sheerin, NCE 12:449–450; S. González, STS 3.3:347–352.

[P. DeLETTER]

REVIVISCENCE OF SACRAMENTS, the theological position that a valid but unfruitful sacrament achieves its grace-effect once the *obex* or obstacle in the recipient (i. e., impenitence) is removed. Explanations vary according to theories of sacramental causality, but all presuppose a real effect other than grace. The position derives from the early practice of not repeating valid but unworthily received baptism and orders. Augustine, e.g., insists that these become salvific once the individual repents. Medieval sacramentology distinguished external rite (*sacramentum tantum*), symbolic reality (*res et sacramentum*), and the grace of the sacrament (*res sacramenti*); the symbolic reality came to be seen as the basis for revival since it is effected on whether grace follows or not. Theologians, however, have disagreed whether the symbolic reality causes or disposes for grace and whether it is an impression in the faculties of the soul or modification of the baptismal character. The symbolic reality of baptism, confirmation, and orders (not repeatable) is the *character; in marriage it is the interior sacramental bond; and in anointing, the consecration of the sick to God's mercy in a particular illness. There is general agreement that these may revive but not the Eucharist or penance, which are easily repeated. The symbolic reality is now generally seen as an ecclesial effect, a definitive union with the Church-Body of Christ. If the unrepeatable sacraments did not revive, the individual, even if he repented, would be deprived of the graced state implied by the definitive ecclesial relationship. With growing consensus that the symbolic reality of penance is reconciliation with the Church rather than interior penitence, it would seem to follow that this sacrament, too, can revive once the obstacle of impenitence is removed. BIBLIOGRAPHY: B. Leeming, *Principles of Sacramental Theology* (1960). *PENANCE, NEW RITE OF.

[J. DALLEN]

REVOLUTION, a radical change in which one order of things is displaced by another. A coherent, well-articulated theological appraisal of revolution has not yet been worked out, although the materials seem abundantly at hand in almost 2 cent. of experience of very diverse kinds. The concept of revolution still bears political overtones but has been extended to the undertaking of measures aimed at spelling the definite end of an old order and bringing about the birth of a new. The elements of novelty, beginning, and violence are all more or less intimately connected with what has become the current understanding of revolution, but these factors are realized in various ways and degrees in different instances. Revolution is spoken of in some circles when any radical reform is in question, provided the effort called for may encounter massive resistance and require drastic measures. The upheaval of poor and oppressed peoples in many places on earth has a genuine revolutionary character and poses serious moral and theological questions which are only just beginning to be faced.

Revolution is authentic and must be dealt with in terms of its significance for Christian understanding and its relevance to man's life as citizen of two worlds. Problems are raised in three areas: (1) science and technology, (2) ethics and moral conduct, and (3) the struggle of emerging and underdeveloped peoples and nations to achieve political independence and stability and a decent standard of living. Christians are required to match Marxists and others with a viable theory of revolution, one which relates this phenomenon to man's vocation to renew all things in Christ. BIBLIOGRAPHY: H. Arendt, *On Revolution* (1963); M. Harrington, *Accidental Century* (1965); *Vatican II/Church in the Modern World* (eds. G. Baum and D. R. Campion, 1966).

[J. P. REID]

REVOLUTION OF 1688, the "Glorious Revolution," which settled fundamental issues of government and religion in England. With the *Restoration, the constitutional struggle between Parliament and the early Stuarts, Charles II (1660–85) avoided open conflict with Parliament but worked secretly to reestablish unlimited prerogatives of the monarch. James II (1685–88), less sensitive to the temper of the times, made a host of enemies by arbitrary exercise of power in defiance of Parliament. His religious policies contributed largely to his downfall. Decreeing freedom of worship to all subjects and ignoring the *Test Act, he appointed Catholics to prominent posts. When he ordered his second *Declaration of Indulgence to be read in all churches, the abp. of Canterbury and six other bps. refused to obey and were tried for seditious libel. In 1688, when the birth of a male heir made likely the succession of other Catholic sovereigns, Whig and Tory representatives invited William of Orange to bring troops to England. Deserted by former supporters, James fled from England; Parliament offered the vacant throne to William and Mary. By a bloodless revolution, Parliament had deposed a king and appointed his successor, settling once for all the principle of limited monarchy. The rights of Englishmen were guaranteed by a *Declaration of Rights in 1689, and the *Toleration Act published the same year granted freedom of worship to dissenting Protestants but denied the same to Catholics. BIBLIOGRAPHY: M. Ashley, *Glorious Revolution of 1688* (1967).

REWARD, in moral theology the correlative of *merit. Abstractly considered the human or moral act has an essential quality that it is deserving either of reward or punishment, the positive quality then of meritoriousness or the privative quality of a lack of meritoriousness. This abstract evaluation is based on the presupposition that moral action has a relationship to persons and particularly to God, who will reward the good act and punish the evil (ThAq ST 1a2ae, 21.3 & 4). More concretely the Christian meaning of reward involves the understanding of the gratuitousness of grace. God has freely called man to share in his own divine life and blessedness. No simply natural act could attain that goal; but grace as given is a resource whereby man enters responsively and responsibly into a filial relationship with God. Instead (as is conceivable) of beatifying man outright, God invites him to enter through grace into the process of seeking salvation. Grace is a principle of merit because its purposiveness is the direction of man's life to blessedness. The attainment of that blessedness becomes a reward, i.e., not something exacted like a wage, but a gift given by God to the child he loves in view of a life lived in love for God. The failure to live such a life brings punishment, i.e., the loss of God's love forever; the separation from God of one intended to be eternally united to him. Most concretely the characteristics of the reward of a Christian life are set out in Christ's beatitudes. BIBLIOGRAPHY: ThAq ST (v. 27, Effects of Sin, ed. T. C. O'Brien, 1974) 105–109.

[T. C. O'BRIEN]

REXISM, originally a movement of young Catholics inspired by Pius XI's proclamation of the feast of Christ the King (1925) and by the ideal of a corporate authoritarian state, which gathered to itself the regional pride of the French-speaking half of Belgium and the protest against both communism and liberal capitalism. Under the leadership of Léon Degrelle, the Rexists gained an important parliamentary victory at the elections in the mid-30s and struck a temporary bargain with the extreme Flemings, but, becoming more and more Fascist in aims and manners, they declined in influence before the war. A rump collaborated with the Nazis during the occupation from 1940, and the division *Wallonie* was formed to fight on the Russian front, where Degrelle distinguished himself as a capital soldier. The movement was proscribed after the war; he, condemned as a traitor, managed an adventurous escape through Spain to South America.

[T. GILBY]

REY, ANTHONY (1807–1847), educator, army chaplain. A French Jesuit who entered the Society in 1827, he taught in France and coming to the U.S. in 1840, became professor of philosophy at Georgetown College, Washington, D.C., and vice-president in 1845. During the Mexican War he served as an army chaplain at the siege of Monterey; embarking on a mission to Matamoras, Mexico, he was ambushed and slain.

[J. R. AHERNE]

REYNOLD, FRÉDÉRIC GONZAGUE DE (1880–   ), French-Swiss historian and critic. Of aristocratic Catholic parentage, R. studied in France at the Institut Catholique, received a Sorbonne doctorate in letters for his *Histoire littéraire de la Suisse au XVIII siècle: I. Le Doyen Bridel et les origines de la littérature suisse-romande* (1909); *II. Bodmer et l'école suisse* (1912), and held successive professorships at Geneva (1910), Bern (1915), and Fribourg (1931) universities. He served on diplomatic missions including one to the Vatican (1923) and with the League of Nations Committee on Intellectual Cooperation (1922–38). Specifically Catholic functions have included memberships on the International Committee for Eucharistic Congresses (1925) and presidency of the Catholic Union for International Studies (1926). His writings reflect three major interdependent themes: expounding the individuality and uniqueness of the Swiss nation and its literature; developing an European-orientated philosophy of history; and evolving a Christian-centered theology of the historical process. In his chief work, *La Formation d'Europe* (7 v., 1941–59), he maintained that the concept of European unity derives from a Christian ideal. R. has written studies on *Charles Baudelaire* (1920) as a Catholic-minded poet; on a Renaissance Swiss churchman, *Le Cardinal Schiner* (1923); and on *Le XVIIe siècle: le classique et le baroque* (1944). BIBLIOGRAPHY: *Hommage à Gonzague de Reynold* (ed. W. Egloff; 1941).

[G. E. GINGRAS]

REYNOLDS, RICHARD, ST. (*c.*1487–1535), English martyr. A fellow of Corpus Christi College, Cambridge, R. was appointed university preacher in 1513. Becoming a Bridgettine monk in 1513, he achieved prominence at Syon Abbey as preacher and spiritual adviser. Henry VIII sought the support of Syon Abbey and failed. Soon thereafter R. was arrested and in the Tower stoutly disputed the King's claim to head the English Church. Condemned for treason, R. was executed at Tyburn. He was canonized in 1970.

[J. R. AHERNE]

REZIN (RASIN), King of Damascus (d. 732 B.C.). R. figures prominently in the biblical narrative of the last days of Israel before the Assyrian conquest of both Syria and Israel (2 Kg ch. 15 and 16). He also figures in Is 7 where both he and Pekah, king of Israel, are referred to by Isaiah as "two smoldering stumps of firebrands" whose waning power Isaiah correctly assessed. When R. and Pekah could not persuade Ahaz to join them in an allied attack against Assyria, the two jointly attacked Juda with the hope of placing an Aramean on the throne of Juda. Ahaz then sent temple treasures to bribe the Assyrian king to help him against these two. Assyria, already receiving tribute from both Syria and Israel, did indeed attack. In the face of this attack, according to Assyrian annals, R. "fled like an antelope" to Damascus where he was besieged "like a caged bird." Hundreds of towns near Damascus were destroyed, including Bit-Hadara, Rezin's birth-place. The gardens and parks around Damascus were destroyed. In 732 B.C. Damascus was captured, R. was executed, the inhabitants were exiled, and the kingdom of Damascus lost its independence entirely. It became part of an Assyrian province and remained a province of one empire after another for centuries.

[E. J. DILLON]

RHABDOMANCY, a type of *divination by examining the direction of a rod or wand (Gr. *rhabdos*), or the chance pointing of an arrow.

RHAZES (RAZES; *c.*865–*c.*925), Islamic physician, scientist, and philosopher. R. is the Latin form of the ethnic designation al-Rāzī, which is the Arabic word for someone from the city of Rayy (once called Rages/Rhagae), important in the Eastern caliphate, near modern Teheran. His complete name was Abū Bakr Muḥammad ibn Zakarîya al-Rāzī. After an early interest in music and alchemy, he turned to medicine and headed first a hospital in Rayy, and then one in Baghdad. He is the author of more than 100 works, including three medical texts in wide use in the Latin Middle Ages. He stressed the importance of diet in maintaining health and preferred simple medicines to the complex. Until recently he was known to the Arab world mostly as a physician. Lately his importance as a philosopher has come more to the fore. Philosophy, to him, was God's gift that liberates the soul from the body. It is the supreme way

of life, in contrast to sectarian religion. The philosopher, like God, is able to treat human beings with justice and kindness. He commended the full life, avoiding excess; pleasure is as normal to man as health. BIBLIOGRAPHY: G. Makdisi, NCE 12:456–457.

[E. J. DILLON]

RHEIMS-DOUAY BIBLE, see DOUAY BIBLE.

RHEINBERGER, JOSEPH (GABRIEL VON, 1839–1901), Liechtenstein-born organist, composer, and renowned teacher. A gifted child, he was appointed church organist at Vaduz at age 7. He was a pupil of Schmutzer in Feldkirch (1848–50), of Herzog, Leonhard, and Maier at the Munich Conservatory (1851–54), and also studied with Lachner in Munich. R. was appointed professor of pianoforte (1859), then professor of composition at the Munich Conservatory. He conducted the Munich Court Opera (1865–67), was Royal Professor at the reorganized conservatory (1867), and later became director of the court church music (1877). His ecclesiastical works include Masses, hymns, cantatas, motets and requiems. His secular compositions include operas, orchestral works, organ concertos, sonatas, choral works, and pieces for piano and organ.

[R. J. LITZ]

RHENANUS, BEATUS (1485–1547), humanist. After studying at Paris R. worked as an editor of classical texts, most notably for John Froben at Basel (1511–27) where Erasmus was also employed. After Erasmus' death, R. helped gather the great humanist's writings and letters for publication. In his own right, R. was a noted historian, perhaps the most critical writer of his generation in Germany. At the outbreak of the Reformation he supported Luther's attacks on ecclesiastical abuses but refused to break with the Church. BIBLIOGRAPHY: P. Allen, *Age of Erasmus* (1914; repr. 1963); P. Smith, *Erasmus* (1923; repr. 1962).

[J. MULDOON]

RHETORIANS, followers of Rhetorius, who, according to Filaster (*Haer.* 91), taught that all heretics are right and speak the truth. In a note on Filaster (*Haer.* 91, PL 12:1202), Fabricius suggests that it is not a proper name, but a reference to the rhetor Themistius (317–388), who taught that a variety of religious opinions was pleasing rather than offensive to the Deity. The teaching was probably Gnostic. BIBLIOGRAPHY: É. Amann, DTC 13:2654–55.

[L. G. MÜLLER]

RHETORIC, a term derived from the Greek *rhētōr*, a public speaker, or later, a teacher of eloquence. In a narrow sense it may be defined as the ability to discover the possible means of persuasion with respect to any particular subject

(Aristotle, *Rhetoric* 1.2.1). But since the art of persuasion presupposes a study of oratorical works, of style, and of the techniques of composition, it is frequently understood in a broader sense as ''the art of adapting discourse, in harmony with its subject and occasion, to the requirements of a reader or hearer.''

In some form or other, rhetoric is as natural to man as speech itself and is an essential element in political and social life. It was highly esteemed in classical antiquity, and the speeches which Homer placed in the mouths of Nestor, Odysseus, and Achilles won for him the title of Father of Oratory. The birthplace of rhetoric as a conscious art was, according to Aristotle, Sicily (cf. Cicero, *Brutus* 46), where Corax and Tisias drew up sets of rules that could be taught to citizens wishing to plead their cases in the courts after the expulsion of the tyrants (467 B.C.). The art was brought to Greece proper by Gorgias of Leontini, who came to Athens as an ambassador (427) and later made it his headquarters as an itinerant teacher of philosophy and eloquence. It was further perfected by the Sophists. Among the most prominent of these was Protagoras of Abdera, who was the first to make a scientific study of language and was the author of a treatise on accuracy of style. Taking advantage of the previous treatises on rhetoric and of the abundance of finely wrought orations of Attic orators of the 5th and 4th cent., and chagrined by the success of Isocrates (Quintilian, *Institutio oratoria* 3.1.14), Aristotle set forth the results of his own study of the theory and practice of oratory in his *Rhetoric,* probably the most complete and penetrating treatment of the subject ever written. His division of the art is as follows: deliberative, forensic (or judicial), and epideictic; he also discusses the qualities required in a speaker: practical wisdom, virtue, and good will; and describes different types of argumentation, style, and arrangement.

Though Greek rhetoricians were regarded with suspicion by the Romans of the Republic and on occasion even banished from the city, the art of rhetoric came to be practiced with great effect by such orators as Hortensius, Julius Caesar, Mark Antony, and above all by Cicero. The latter is not only one of the most eloquent speakers of all time but he also wrote a number of important treatises on rhetoric, e.g., *De oratore, Brutus, Orator.* Towards the end of the 1st cent. A.D., Quintilian, a great admirer of Cicero, wrote his *Institutio oratoria,* the best treatise on education, largely rhetorical, that has come down from antiquity.

During the Middle Ages, rhetoric together with grammar and logic made up the *trivium,* the basic program for those pursuing a course in the liberal arts. Rhetorical theory was the object of considerable attention during the Renaissance on the part of Dante, Ascham, Sidney, and others; and the interest was continued during the neo-classical period of the 17th and 18th cent. by Dryden, Pope, Johnson, and numerous French and Italian critics. Rhetorical and literary criticism flourished in the 19th cent. in the works of Coleridge, Hazlitt, and Arnold. In the 20th cent. with the developments in psychology, linguistic analysis, and the growth of the communication arts of radio and television, the older arts and techniques of rhetoric have taken on a new appearance and significance. BIBLIOGRAPHY: J. F. D'Alton, *Roman Literary Theory and Criticism* (1931); E. P. Corbett, *Classical Rhetoric* (1965); H. M. McLuhan, *Medium is the Message* (1967).

[M. J. COSTELLOE]

RHIPIDION (Gr. for fan; Sl. *ripidi*), a metal fan usually circular in shape with a short handle and bearing the image of a six-winged seraph (*hexapterygon*). In the Byzantine Church it is traditionally associated with the deacon and is presented to him by the bp. at the ordination ceremony to be used in fanning the holy gifts during the anaphora. Designed to ward off insects, the rhipidion is regarded as symbolically representing the vibration of the wings of the seraph hovering over the throne of God, the holy altar. It is now usually replaced by the waving of the *aër*. Rhipidia with longer handles are used as processional standards and are carried by servers at the Little Entrance and again at the Great Entrance of the Liturgy. This usage resembles the flabellum of ostrich feathers carried before the pope on solemn occasions. When the processional rhipidia are not in use, they are placed directly behind the altar on either side of the cross. Embroidered veils are sometimes attached to the staff. The use of these ceremonial fans is also found in the Coptic, Maronite, Armenian, and Syrian Churches. The Western rite proper to the Carmelites still mentions them in the rubrics of the Missal but they are no longer in actual use.

[R. K. GOLINI]

RHO, GIACOMO (1592–1638), Jesuit mathematician and missionary in China from 1624. He sought converts through science and religious writings in Chinese. He worked with J. *Schall von Bell at the Imperial Bureau of Astronomy in Peking on reform of the Chinese calendar.

[R. J. LITZ]

RHODE ISLAND, a New England state, admitted to the Union (1790) as the last of the original Thirteen States. The colony's history began with the arrival in 1636 of Roger *Williams, who had been forced to leave Massachusetts by his quarrel with the Puritan oligarchy. Rhode Island's charter put into effect Williams' ideas of toleration and separation of Church and State. In 1639 the Baptists founded their first American church in Providence, while Congregationalists arrived in 1643, Quakers in 1657, and Jews in 1658.

Despite Rhode Island's religious freedom, Catholicism did not flourish there during the colonial period. Not until 1828 did Bp. B. J. *Fenwick of Boston assign the first resident priest, Robert Woodley, to Pawtucket and Newport. In 1843 Rhode Island was placed under the jurisdiction of the newly created Diocese of Hartford, Conn., and the first three bishops of Hartford resided in Providence. The

Diocese of Providence itself was established in 1872 and T. F. Hendricken appointed as its first bishop. He was succeeded by M. Harkins (1887), W. A. Hickey (1912), Francis P. *Keough (1934), Russell J. McVinney (1948), and Louis E. Gelineau (1972–).

In 1976 Catholics numbered 602,467, or 64.9 percent of the total state population. The major Protestant denominations are the Episcopal Church, with 4.6 percent of the total population in 1971, and the American Baptist Convention, with 2.8 percent. Other Protestant denominations comprised 5 percent of the population. The Jewish population was 27,700, or 3.2 percent. There are 2 Catholic colleges in Rhode Island, with a total enrollment of 5,093 students. Over 6,000 students attend the state's 15 Catholic high schools, and 16,106 pupils attend 58 Catholic elementary schools. BIBLIOGRAPHY: T. F. Cullen, *Catholic Church in Rhode Island* (1936).

[J. L. MORRISON; R. M. PRESTON]

RHODES, ALEXANDRE DE (1591–1660), French Jesuit missionary to Asia. R. worked in Goa, Cochin (China), and founded the Church in Vietnam (1627). After persecution and exile, he returned to Europe in order to recruit missionaries for central Asia. R. supported a native clergy and accommodation to local customs in the liturgy. He died in Persia, where he had spent 5 successful years as a missionary.

[T. M. MCFADDEN]

RHODES, a Greek island (with a city of the same name) that lies off the SW coast of Asia Minor. After Crete it is the largest island in the Aegean Sea. It is referred to in 1 Macc 15.23; Acts 21.1; and possibly in Ezek 27.15. The island, noted for its beauty and fine harbors, easily lent itself to settlement, crafts, culture, and trade, but also to the tragedies that befall a site of such strategic importance. BIBLIOGRAPHY: M. J. Mellink, InterDB 4:77–78.

[I. HUNT]

RHOMAIOS (Gr. Roman), a subject of the Byzantine Empire, which considered itself the Roman Empire; its ruler bore the title Emperor of the Romans (*tōn rhomaiōn*). From the Turkish conquest in 1453 until independence in the 19th cent., a Greek was still called *rhomaios* (or *rhomiós*), and because of his religion the term came to designate an Orthodox Christian and is still occasionally used in this sense.

[G. T. DENNIS]

RHYTHM, a term here used by autonomasia for the alternation of sterile and fertile periods in the menstrual cycle of human females, and, by application, to the method of restricting intercourse to certain periods in order to avoid conception. The medical findings began to be publicized in the early 1930s from the studies of K. Ogino, a Japanese, and H. Knauss, an Austrian, which had been conducted independently. They hinged on the time of ovulation, roughly 14 days before the onset of the next menstruation. For rather less than a week about this time conception is possible; at other times a so-called safe period could be assumed. The findings displaced other customary and contrary computations and old wives' tales. Calculation, however, is difficult because in a large minority of cases there is no regular 28-day cycle; the adoption of the method has sometimes resulted in the conception of children who in the event have gladdened their parents' hearts. Medical research has arrived at supplementary rules to determine the fertile period; it seems that the rhythm method is generally effective given intelligent observance of the known biological tests.

The moral issue has been thrashed out in religious journals, scientific and otherwise: its underlying principle was clear in *Casti connubii*. The following points are enough. First, no one pretends that it offers a panacea to modern problems of sexuality in marriage. Second, it is certainly not a contraceptive type of act, and as such, therefore, it is not inherently defective. The Church advocates birth control as an end; what it condemns are certain means, and this method is not one of them. Third, its morality, then, will depend on circumstances and personal intentions, and will be decided by whether or not the loving responsibilities undertaken in marriage are being promoted or denied. Fourth, the discipline required is not so stilted as some critics have maintained; with the integral wholeness of their sacramental relationship as persons, the sexual lovingness of a couple is expressed in reticence as well as in release. BIBLIOGRAPHY: J. C. Ford and G. Kelly, *Marriage Questions* (*Contemporary Moral Theology* 2, 1963).

[T. GILBY]

RIBADENEYRA, PEDRO DE (1526–1611), Spanish Jesuit. A Toledo nobleman and page to Cardinal Farnese, R. entered the newly formed Jesuits (1540), and studied at Padua, Paris, and Louvain. Ordained in 1533, he acted for the Jesuit generals throughout the Netherlands (1556–60) and Italy. He returned to Spain for his health (1573) and entered upon a brilliant literary-historical career. BIBLIOGRAPHY: Sommervogel 6:1724–58.

[R. I. BURNS]

RIBALTA, FRANCISCO (1555–1628), Spanish painter. An early *Nailing to the Cross* (1582) is manneristic, showing erratic lighting. From a successful studio in Valencia, R. executed for the Archbishop Juan de Ribera eclectic works combining the ecstatic poses of El Greco, and Juan de Juanes' effulgent mildness. After 1616 in *St. Bernard* and *Portacoeli Retable* R. achieved the realism and monumentality of Velásquez, Zurbarán and Ribera. Juan Ribalta, son of F. R. painted complicated compositions in *tenebroso* style.

[M. J. DALY]

RIBBON STYLE, a 6th-8th cent. Anglo-Saxon modification of Germanic animal ornament. Animal bodies and limbs are elongated, twisted into the shape of S's and knots, and interlaced in intricate but coherent designs. A spectacular example of polychromed jewelry with ribbon style animals was found in 1939 at Sutton Hoo in a royal ship burial. Ribbon style characterizes decoration of Celtic MSS (e.g., the Book of Lindisfarne). Themes develop in later phases of Hiberno-Saxon and Germanic art and finally influence medieval art.

[R. L. S. BRUCE-MITFORD]

RIBERA, FRANCISCO DE (1537–91), Jesuit exegete and biographer of St. *Teresa of Ávila. R. taught at Salamanca, and wrote scriptural commentaries notable for their use of patristic sources and attention to the literal sense. He was confessor to St. Teresa, and his biography of her went through many editions.

[T. M. MCFADDEN]

RIBERA, JUSEPE DE (Lo Spagnoletto; 1591–1652), Spanish painter, whose work suggests Caravaggio in chiaroscuro, and in composition reflects the Carracci and Bolognese painters. Violence and dramatic intensity mark R.'s early baroque saints and grotesques (1621–24), an extreme *tenebroso* in sweeping brush strokes characterized *St. Jerome, Martyrdom of St. Andrew* (1628) and *St. Bartholomew* (1630) with dramatic foreshortening and isolation against a dark ground in *St. Mary of Egypt* and *St. John the Baptist* (1630's). A more spiritualized expression appears in the *Immaculate Conception* (1635) and *Trinity* (1636). *Jacob's Dream* is a masterpiece of interlace between the figure and landscape. R.'s last works are gentle interpretations of the old, frail and suffering in transparent colors (*Escape of St. Januarius*, 1646; *St. James the Great* and *St. Roch*, 1651).

[M. J. DALY]

RIBET, JÉRÔME (1837–1909), Sulpician mystical theologian. R. taught philosophy and theology at several French seminaries, then left the Sulpicians to become (1885) secretary to the bp. of Châlons, and pastor of the parish church at Saman. His principal work is *La Mystique divine distinguée des contrefaçons diaboliques et des analogies humaines* (3 v., 1879–83), in which he distinguishes mystical stages and contrasts them with totally natural phenomena.

[T. M. MCFADDEN]

RICCARDI, NICOLÒ (1585–1639), Dominican, Master of the Sacred Palace (1629) under Urban VIII. R. was a professor of theology and regent of the Collegio San Tomasso at the Minerva, Rome, and a renowned preacher. He published *Historiae Concilii Tridentini emaculatae synopsis* (1627), as well as scholastic and biblical commentaries.

[T. C. O'BRIEN]

RICCARDI, PLACIDO, BL. (1844–1915), Benedictine priest, spiritual director. R. was attached to the Benedictine Abbey of St. Paul-Outside-the-Walls in Rome. He held several positions at the Abbey and came to be revered as a confessor and spiritual director for nuns and clergy. In 1895, he was designated rector of the basilica at Farfa, where his pastoral care led to his being called the apostle of the Sabine region. He was beatified in 1954. BIBLIOGRAPHY: P. Granfield, "Blessed Placid Riccardi," ABR 5 (1954) 299–305.

[T. M. MCFADDEN]

RICCI, LORENZO (1703–75), 18th general of the Society of Jesus, in office at the time of its suppression. He had been secretary to his predecessor, Aloysius Centurione, when elected (May 25, 1758) and earlier had been professor of theology at the Collegio Romano from 1736 and spiritual director (1751–55). He was a man of learning and deep spirituality. To the Jesuits, already under assault in Bourbon lands, R. conveyed Clement XIII's counsel of silence, patience, prayer, and hope. Clement himself refused to yield to the Jesuits' enemies; but the Society was expelled from Portugal, France, Spain, and the Kingdom of Naples, and Clement is thought to have died from the pressures put upon him for suppression. His successor, Clement XIV, whose election was probably dependent on his acceptability to the Bourbons, sent to R. on Aug. 10, 1773 the bull of suppression, *Dominus ac Redemptor*. From the beginning of his generalate R. had been victimized by the forging of letters in his name and by tales spread in evidence of Jesuit treachery and wealth. With suppression came his final ordeal, close confinement in the prison of Castel Sant' Angelo and subjection to incessant grilling and hearings. He died after 2 years of this, before the next pope, Pius VI, could release him. R. was given a funeral of honor at the Church of the Gesù and buried there with his predecessors.

[T. C. O'BRIEN]

RICCI, MATTEO (1552–1610), Jesuit missionary and scholar who inaugurated an important attempt to convert the Chinese nation to Christianity. Under the direction of Alessandro Valignano, the Jesuit visitator to the Orient, who was seeking a method to break through the cultural isolation of the Chinese Middle Kingdom, R. began (1583) his missionary endeavors at Chao-ch'ing; moved to the S capital of Nanking; and finally settled (1601) in Peking, the imperial city and residence of the Ming court. R.'s plan was to convert the Chinese masses through the aristocrats and intellectuals of their country. Accordingly, he completely mastered the Chinese language and culture, demonstrated his extensive knowledge of astronomy, cartography, and mathematics, and introduced some rudimentary scientific equipment, which he had brought with him from Europe. His wide scientific knowledge, cultural awareness, and openness to Chinese traditions earned him a reputation as a learned man. R. and his fellow Jesuit missionaries published books in Chinese on literature, mathematics, and religion, acclaimed by Chinese intellectuals as true masterpieces of art and wisdom. R. also published a catechism which presented the basic truths of the Christian faith, refuted some Chinese practices such as idol worship and the belief in the transmigration of souls, but accepted many of the religious insights contained in ancient Chinese books. R. adopted the terms T'ien (heaven) and Shang-ti (Sovereign Lord) as acceptable names for God, although later missionaries maintained that they referred to a material heaven. The practice of paying special homage to Confucius and honoring ancestors by prostrations and sacrifices was approved by the earliest Jesuit missioners under R.'s direction, and became an issue of acrimonious controversy for the next century (see CHINESE RITES CONTROVERSY). Although the number of Chinese converts to Christianity during R.'s lifetime was small, his contribution toward the predisposition of the Chinese toward accepting Christianity was invaluable. BIBLIOGRAPHY: N. Trigault, *China in the 16th Century* (tr. L. J. Gallagher, 1953), the Eng. version of a 17th-cent. Latin translation of R.'s memoirs and correspondence; G. H. Dunne, *Generation of Giants* (1962) 23–108; J. Brucker, CE 13:34–40. *ADAPTATION, MISSIONARY.

[T. M. MCFADDEN]

RICCI, SCIPIONE DE' (1741–1809), bp. of Pistoia, responsible for the Synod of *Pistoia (1786), condemned for its Jansenist and Gallican decrees by Pius VI's *Auctorem fidei* (1794). R. had developed his extreme views of church reform as a student at the Univ. of Pisa, and by association with defenders of *Jansenism and *Gallicanism. From 1775 he had been vicar general of the Florence archdiocese before becoming bp. of Pistoia, a preferment he owed to his friendship with Leopold I, Grand Duke of Tuscany. With the assistance of the theologians V. Palmieri and P. *Tamburini, R. prepared the final form of the decrees for the Synod of Pistoia (see D 2600–2700). They represented aberrant changes in ecclesiology, church discipline, seminary studies (e.g., introduction of Jansenist texts for all courses), and liturgy. A year after the synod, the national assembly of the bps. of Tuscany repudiated R.'s attempt to establish a schismatic body. He was forced to flee from his see in 1791. After *Auctorem fidei* he became a semifugitive, was captured and imprisoned in 1799 at Passignano, then (1801) at San Marco in Florence, and finally at Rignana, near Florence. During his confinement he studied the Fathers and Jansenist authors, composed his own *Memorie*. Pressured by family and friends, as well as by the abp. of Florence, R. made a verbal submission to Pius VII at Florence in 1805. Oddly, many of R.'s proposals anticipated 20th-cent. changes in the Church; but his were based on a subversion of the structure of the Church and defiance of authority.

[T. C. O'BRIEN]

RICCI, VITTORIO (1621–85), Italian Dominican, missionary to China and the Philippines. As a student in Rome he was attracted by J. B. *Morales to mission work, and

began his apostolate in 1648. He labored in Parian (P.I.), Fukien and Formosa, China, and was vicar provincial for China and prefect apostolic for Formosa and S China. His *Istoria della missione de' FF. Predicatori nel regno di Cina* is an account of Dominican missions, esp. of the Province of the Holy Rosary of the Philippines.

[T. C. O'BRIEN]

RICE, EDMUND IGNATIUS (1762–1844), founder of the *Irish Christian Brothers and the *Presentation Brothers. After the death of his wife in 1789, R. devoted himself to the education of poor boys in Ireland. With several followers he formed a religious society modeled after the rule of the Presentation Sisters, and opened (1803) a school in Waterford. When this type of rule proved impractical for them, Pius VII permitted adoption of the constitutions of the Christian Brothers. R. became the first superior general of the Irish Christian Brothers in 1821. BIBLIOGRAPHY: J. D. Fitzpatrick, *Edmund Rice* (1945).

[T. M. MCFADDEN]

RICE, LUTHER (1783–1836), promoter of Baptist missions. Born in Northborough, Mass., he was one of the first seven appointees of the American Board of Commissioners for Foreign Missions and in 1812 was sent to India. Rice, like Adoniram and Anne *Judson, became a Baptist soon after his arrival, and he felt obliged to return to America to arouse Baptist interest in supporting foreign missionaries. He remained in the U.S. to promote the foreign missions. To provide an educated ministry, he was the main founder of Columbian College (now George Washington Univ.) in Washington, D.C. His travels, preaching, and writing helped bind Baptist churches together, but he encountered opposition from Baptists who were suspicious of educated ministers and missionary organizations. BIBLIOGRAPHY: E. W. Thompson, *Luther Rice, Believer in Tomorrow* (1967).

[N. H. MARING]

RICH, EDMUND, see EDMUND OF ABINGDON, ST.

RICH, RICHARD (1496–1567), lord chancellor of England. Trained as a lawyer, R. became solicitor general (1533) and provided the evidence that secured the conviction for treason of SS. John *Fisher and Thomas *More. More accused him of perjury. R. had a hand in the ruin of other leading men, notably T. Cromwell. Some had been his friends and benefactors. Appointed to administer the revenues of the dissolved monasteries he amassed a fortune, some of which he used to found Felsted Grammar School. Created baron and lord chancellor 1548, R. became, under Mary Tudor, a persecutor of heretics. BIBLIOGRAPHY: P. S. McGarry, NCE 12:474–475.

[J. OGDEN]

RICHARD I (Coeur de Lion; 1157–99), **KING OF ENGLAND** from 1189. Duke of Aquitaine, R. rebelled against his father Henry II, whom he succeeded. He was the greatest warrior in Europe and sold offices and privileges to finance the Third Crusade. On his way, he stormed Messina, conquered Cyprus, and married Berengaria of Navarre. In Palestine, he won military success, quarreled with Philip Augustus, and made a 3-year truce with Saladin. Shipwrecked and captured by Leopold of Austria, R. paid ransom and did homage to Emperor Henry VI. His last 5 years were spent in intermittent warfare against Philip. BIBLIOGRAPHY: P. Henderson, *Richard Coeur de Lion* (1959).

[W. A. CHANEY]

RICHARD II (1367–1400), **KING OF ENGLAND** (1377–99). Grandson of Edward II and son of Edward the Black Prince, R. inherited a kingdom suffering from war with France and from a decadent and privileged nobility, against whom he adopted exalted views of royal rights. He married (1382) Anne, sister of Wenceslaus IV of Bohemia, and after her death (1394), married (1396) Isabella, daughter of Charles VI of France. England had theretofore supported the Roman pope in the Western Schism, but R. now favored Charles's plan to depose both popes, and Boniface IX was forced to grant various privileges and concessions in order to detach R. from France. R. subdued Ireland (1394) and after a long struggle with the English nobles seized control of government (1397); but his cousin overthrew him (1399) to become Henry IV, and he died a prisoner. His character and ability are variously estimated. BIBLIOGRAPHY: A. Steel, *Richard II* (1941; repr. 1963).

[R. W. HAYS]

RICHARD III (1452–85) **KING OF ENGLAND** from 1483. Duke of Gloucester (1461–83) and loyal servant of his brother Edward IV, R. was virtual ruler of the North (1471–83). Though not the unnatural monster of Tudor tradition, he ruthlessly usurped the throne in 1483 and probably murdered his nephews, Edward V and Richard of York, the "Princes in the Tower." Had he lived, he might have proved an able and efficient king, but his ruthlessness cost him support. He survived a dangerous rebellion in 1483 only to be defeated by Henry Tudor and killed at Bosworth. BIBLIOGRAPHY: J. Gairdner, *Richard III* (1898); P. M. Kendall, *Richard III* (1955).

[C. D. ROSS]

RICHARD OF BURY (Richard Aungerville; 1287–1345), English ecclesiastic, statesman, diplomat, and book-collector, bp. of Durham from 1333; chancellor of England (1335). Able, generous, patron of learning and friend of Petrarch, R. used his many official positions to build the great library described in his *Philobiblon* (ed. A. Taylor, 1948). He also compiled *Liber epistolarum* (ed. N. Denholm-Young, 1950); Emden Ox 1:323–326.

[R. W. HAYS]

RICHARD OF CAMPSALL (*c.*1285–*c.*1350), regent master at Oxford from 1322, opponent of *William of Ock-

ham's nominalism, esp. in *Logica Campsale valde utilis et realis contra Ocham.* R. also wrote *Quaestiones super librum Priorum Analyticorum* and a set of *Dicta* on divine foreknowledge. BIBLIOGRAPHY: *Nine Medieval Thinkers: A Collection of Hitherto Unedited Texts* (ed. J. R. O'Donnell, 1955).

[T. C. O'BRIEN]

RICHARD OF CANTERBURY (d. 1184), Benedictine, abp. of Canterbury. R. succeeded to Canterbury after the death of Thomas *Becket. Educated at Christ Church, Canterbury, he became a monk there and later chaplain to Abp. *Theobald of Canterbury. After being prior of St. Martin's Abbey in Dover, he was duly elected to the primatial see, even though his election was contested. Particularly known for his contribution to medieval canon law, he presided over one of the earliest provincial councils in English ecclesiastical history. BIBLIOGRAPHY: M. Chibnall, NCE 12:477–478; W. Hunt, DNB 16:1077–80.

[J. A. WEISHEIPL]

RICHARD OF CHICHESTER, ST. (Richard de Wyche; *c.*1197–1253), English ecclesiastic, bp. of Chichester from 1245. He studied at Oxford, where he became chancellor, and at Paris, Bologna, and Orléans. As chancellor of Canterbury, he served both Edmund of Abingdon, whose memory he helped to preserve, and Boniface of Savoy. Elected bp. over Henry III's candidate, Robert Passelew, R. was consecrated by Innocent IV, but after long exclusion from his temporalities, found his resources wasted by royal officials. Humble and ascetic, as bp. he reformed clerical discipline, encouraged lay religious observance, patronized Dominicans, and preached Crusades. Urban IV canonized him (1262). BIBLIOGRAPHY: H. Farmer, BiblSanct 11:165–168; Butler 2:22–25.

[R. W. HAYS]

RICHARD OF CONINGTON (d. 1330), English Franciscan theologian, the 16th provincial minister of the English province of Franciscans (1310–16). Involved in the poverty debate, R. wrote the *Beatus qui intelligit* and *Responsiones ad conclusiones domini papae,* a dialogue between a friar and the pope relative to problems on the papal bull *Ad conditorem canonum.* There is a lost commentary on the *Sentences* attributed to him, eight *Quaestiones disputatae,* and two *Quodlibeta.* His doctrine is characterized by Augustinian and Aristotelian features. His tomb is at Cambridge. BIBLIOGRAPHY: A. Heysse, "Fr. Ricardi de Conington, OFM. *Tractatus de paupertate fratrum minorum,*" AFH (1930) 57–105, 340–360; J. R. H. Moorman, *Grey Friars of Cambridge, 1225–1538* (1952).

[J. J. SMITH]

RICHARD OF DEVIZES (fl. *c.*1192), English chronicler; Benedictine monk of St. Swithun's, Winchester. His historically valuable *Chronicon de rebus gestis Ricardi* *primi* (ed. J. T. Appleby, 1963), covering the Third Crusade (1189–92), contains originality, learning, wit, and mordant criticism of regulars and seculars. He probably also wrote *Annales monasterii de Wintonia* (ed. H. R. Laurd, 1865). BIBLIOGRAPHY: W. Hunt, DNB 16:1083–84; J. T. Appleby, *Journal of the Institute of Historical Research 36* (1963) 70–77.

[R. W. HAYS]

RICHARD FISHACRE (d. 1248), first Dominican to study theology at Oxford University. He belonged to the Augustinian school, but sought to incorporate the writings of Aristotle into his theology, sometimes forcing the texts to do so. He was the author of the first commentary at Oxford on the *Sentences* of Peter Lombard and of other theological and scriptural writings. BIBLIOGRAPHY: D. A. Callus, NCE 12:479.

[T. C. O'BRIEN]

RICHARD FITZRALPH (d. 1360), archbishop. A doctor of theology of Oxford (1331), R. held benefices in various English dioceses before becoming abp. of Armagh, Ireland (1346). He wrote many treatises against the mendicant orders, notably *De pauperie Salvatoris* and *Defensorium curatorum.* Unsuccessful attempts were made in the late 14th cent. to obtain his canonization. BIBLIOGRAPHY: Emden Ox 2:692–694; G. Leff, *Richard Fitzralph* (1964).

[L. E. BOYLE]

RICHARD GRANT OF CANTERBURY (var. Le-Grand or Wethershed; 1231) abp. of Canterbury (1229–31). He had been chancellor of Lincoln (1221–29). As abp., he engaged in jurisdictional disputes with Henry III and Hubert de Burgh, the justiciar. After journeying to Rome to plead his case there, he died in Italy.

[R. W. HAYS]

RICHARD OF GRAVESEND, name of two 13th-cent. English bishops. (1) a churchman (d. 1279) who held the See of Lincoln from 1258. He assisted Simon de Montfort in negotiations for Anglo-French peace (1258), supported the provisions of Oxford, sided with De Montfort against, and represented him in dealings with, Henry III. Suspended but soon reinstated (1266), he devoted his remaining years to strict and competent administration of his diocese. (2) nephew of the foregoing (d. 1303), bp. of London from 1280. He opposed Abp. Peckham's metropolitical claims, created the office of subdean of St. Paul's, required that the chancellor should lecture on theology, and served Edward I on missions to France. His extensive library is listed in the earliest known priced book catalogue.

[R. W. HAYS]

RICHARD OF KILVINGTON (d. before 1362), English theologian. R. had received his master's degree in theology

by 1350. He held many benefices, among them the deanship of St. Paul's, London. He was a strong supporter of *Richard Fitzralph in the antimendicant controversy. BIBLIOGRAPHY: Emden Ox 2:1050–51; C. L. Kingsford, DNB 11:353; T. P. Dunning, NCE 12:480.

[J. A. WEISHEIPL]

RICHARD KNAPWELL (Clapwell, etc.; d. *c.*1288), Dominican master of theology at Oxford, who defended the orthodoxy of St. Thomas Aquinas, specifically on the unicity of substantial forms. R.'s own position was condemned (1286) by *John Peckham, abp. of Canterbury; after trying to vindicate himself in Rome, R. died at Bologna. BIBLIOGRAPHY: D. A. Callus, *Condemnation of St. Thomas at Oxford* (2d ed., 1955).

[T. C. O'BRIEN]

RICHARD OF MIDDLETON (Mediavilla; *c.*1249–1302), Franciscan theologian at Paris. Whether he was of English or French birth is uncertain. His principal work, a commentary on Peter Lombard's *Sentences,* is in the Augustinian tradition, but on some points concerning cognition, he seems to have accepted the position of St. Thomas Aquinas. BIBLIOGRAPHY: Gilson HCP 347–350.

[T. C. O'BRIEN]

RICHARD DE MORES (Ricardus Anglicus; d.1242), Augustinian prior and annalist of Dunstable from 1202; earlier (*c.*1195) the first English canonist to teach at Bologna. During his teaching years R. composed several works important to the history of canon law: *Summa quaestionum; Summa brevis; Distinctiones decretorum; Summa de ordine judiciario; Casus decretalium; Apparatus decretalium.*

[T. C. O'BRIEN]

RICHARD OF SAINT-VICTOR (d.1173), mystical theologian. Born in Scotland, he came early in life to the abbey of St. Victor in Paris. He became subprior in 1159, prior in 1162, and died in office. Noted as the first writer to systematize mystical theology, he continued the line of his predecessor *Hugh of Saint-Victor. He combined traditional methods with the new scholastic emphasis on reason. His mystical thought is found particularly in the *Benjamin Minor* and *Benjamin Major;* his systematic thoughts in his *De Trinitate.* His teaching on the six stages of contemplation became influential through St. Bonaventure and the Franciscan school. BIBLIOGRAPHY: *Richard of Saint Victor,* a collection of his writings with tr. and introd. by C. Kirchberger (1955).

[T. EARLY]

RICHARD DE LA VERGNE, FRANÇOIS MARIE (1819–1908), abp. of Paris from 1886, cardinal in 1889. He had been vicar general of Nantes (1850–69), bp. of Belley (1872–75), where he instituted the petition for the beatification of the Curé d'Ars, and coadjutor bp. of Paris from 1875 before succeeding to that see. As abp., R. was faced with the hostility of the Third Republic toward the Church; strongly conservative, he rejected Leo XIII's policy of Catholic cooperation in civil matters (see RALLIEMENT). With the law abrogating the concordat with the Holy See and separating Church and State in 1905, R. was expelled from his see because he supported Pius X's rejection of the status given the Church in France. Among R.'s episcopal acts were his resistance to A. *Loisy and to *Modernism, his contributions to the ideas in the anti-Modernist decree *Lamentabili (1907), and his support for the formation of the Institut Catholique of Paris.

[T. C. O'BRIEN]

RICHARD OF WALLINGFORD (c.1292–1336), English Benedictine; abbot of St. Albans (c.1328). Educated at Oxford and, despite affliction with leprosy, a conscientious administrator, he wrote on mathematics, astronomy, and the general statutes of the Benedictines, and invented a great astronomical clock, "Albion." BIBLIOGRAPHY: L. Thorndike and P. Kibre, Catalogue of Incipits of Medieval Scientific Writings in Latin (1963).

[R. W. HAYS]

RICHARD DE WYCHE, see RICHARD OF CHICHESTER, ST.

RICHARD, GABRIEL (1767–1832), missionary, member of U.S. Congress. A native of France and ordained as a Sulpician in 1791, R. fled the French Revolution for Baltimore, Md. in 1792. In 1798 he went to Detroit, then a trading post, to work among the Indians, becoming pastor of St. Anne's church and vicar general of the region. Serving the Indians of Sault Ste. Marie, Mackinac, and other fur-trade posts, R. became a famous figure. In 1805 when Detroit was destroyed by fire, he led the relief work. He rebuilt St. Anne's, founded six elementary schools and two academies. In 1809 he established the first printing press in Detroit, which published among other things a Bible for Indians and the laws of Michigan. Imprisoned during the War of 1812 by the British, he was released through the efforts of the Indian, Chief Tecumseh. A cofounder and vice-president of the Univ. of Michigan in 1817, R. was elected to the U.S. Congress in 1822—the only priest to serve up until that time—and served with great vigor. Returning to Detroit when defeated for a second term in 1824, he resumed his work with the missions, rebuilt St. Anne's, and took a prominent part in civic affairs. His death occurred as a result of his ministering to victims in a cholera epidemic.

[J. R. AHERNE]

RICHARDSON, CYRIL CHARLES (1909–76), church historian and theologian. Born in London, he attended college in Canada and received the Th.D. from Union Theological Seminary, New York, in 1934. The same year he was ordained an Episcopal priest and began teaching at Union,

where he remained for the rest of his life, continuing to teach there even after his formal retirement in 1974. From 1954 to 1974 he also served as dean of graduate studies. R. specialized in the history of the early Church, and also taught a highly regarded course on the history of worship. In addition to historical works, he published a critique of orthodox trinitarian dogma, The Doctrine of the Trinity (1958).

[T. EARLY]

RICHARDSON, HENRY HOBSON (1838–86), American architect who worked with T. Labrouste in Paris, returning to the U.S. in 1865. R.'s forms, though derivative, are unique in ensemble. Grace Episcopal Church (Medford, Mass. 1867–68), Brattle Square Church (Cambridge, 1870–72), and the famous Trinity Church (Boston, 1872–77) in Romanesque style, exemplify R.'s eclectic "revivalistic" structures showing power, and form related to function. Pittsburgh Jail (1874–76) and R.'s railway stations (1881) confirm his creative manipulation of traditional styles. BIBLIOGRAPHY: H. R. Hitchcock, Architecture of H. H. Richardson and His Times (1966).

[M. J. DALY]

RICHELIEU, ARMAND JEAN DU PLESSIS (1585–1642), card. and chief minister of Louis XIII. R. came from a family with a tradition of service to the French monarchy. Originally he was not destined for a religious career, but when his brother left the family bishopric of Luçon, R. took over. When his patron, Marie de Médicis, fell from power in 1617, he spent several years of agonized waiting. On August 24, 1624, however, he was appointed the king's minister and from that date until 1642 he dominated French political life. Events such as the crushing of the Huguenot Revolt in 1628 and the French participation in the Thirty Years' War occurred during his ministry. At his death, R. had achieved his political aims, namely, the establishment of the French absolutist state and the rise of France as the leading European power. He is often criticized for being a purely Machiavellian politician. It is true that he often resorted to political expedients when no other alternatives were open. On the other hand, he was a man of his age, and the 17th cent. was a time of rising religious fervor and piety. Recent scholars argue that R. did not separate politics from religion. Moreover, he possessed sincere religious convictions. In fact during his early years as bp. of Luçon, from 1608 to 1623, he actively cared for the spiritual welfare of his diocese. The French historian, V. L. Tapié, notes "as was his duty as a statesman, Richelieu the king's minister subordinated everything to 'the conservation of the Crown'; but he never sacrificed Catholic doctrine or the Catholic faith." BIBLIOGRAPHY: V.-L. Tapié, France in the Age of Louis XIII and Richelieu (tr and ed. D. McN. Lockie, 1975); W. F. Church, Richelieu and Reason of State (1972).

[C. T. EBY]

RICHER, EDMOND (1559–1631), French cleric, canonist, and theorist of *Gallicanism. Son of a poor peasant, he became a doctor of the Sorbonne in 1592, rector of the Collège du Cardinal Lemoine in 1595, and syndic of the Sorbonne in 1602. In this latter position he was called upon to defend the Sorbonne against the religious orders, its traditional enemies, who competed with it for students and jurisdiction. The free education of the Jesuits was the greatest problem, and his attacks on them led R. to develop a radical statement of Gallicanism in opposition to their ultramontanism in his work *De ecclesiastica et politica potestate* (1611; Fr. tr., 1612). This book was condemned through the intervention of the papal nuncio, Card. Ubaldini, and the ultramontanist abp. of Sens, Card. du Perron; and R. lost his position as syndic in 1612. He continued to defend himself through a number of pamphlets until forced by Card. Richelieu to issue a partial retraction in 1629. R. supported the superiority of a general council over the pope, the competence of all the faithful to preserve divine revelation, episcopal freedom from papal jurisdiction, and the absolute independence of a king within his own domain. His ideas were adopted in a modified form by adherents of *Jansenism in the 18th cent. and had an influence on the lower clergy in the second half of that century. BIBLIOGRAPHY: E. Puyol, *Edmond Richer* (2v., 1876); Pastor v.26.

[J. M. HAYDEN]

RICHTER, ADRIAN LUDWIG (1803–84), leading German romantic painter and draftsman, important for book illustrations, associated (1823–26) with the Nazarenes in Italy.

[M. J. DALY]

RICHTER, FRANZ XAVER (1709–1789), Moravian composer, conductor, singer, and violinist. He served as *Kapellmeister* at the Abbey of Kempten (1740–50) and was a singer, violinist, and composer at the Mannheim court (1747–1769). He was appointed *Kapellmeister* at the Strassburg Cathedral (1769), where he remained till his death. R. and other composers of the Mannheim orchestra contributed much to early symphonic history. His sacred music reflects both the symphonic influence of the Bohemian-Mannheim school and of the traditional Viennese baroque church music. Religious works include over 40 Masses, 2 Passions, 2 Requiems, motets, psalms, and other church music. Secular compositions include 70 symphonies, chamber music, concertos, and sonatas. He also authored a textbook on harmony.

[R. J. LITZ]

RICKABY, JOSEPH (1845–1932), English Jesuit, professor of philosophy at Stonyhurst (1879–96) and of theology at Campion Hall, Oxford (1899–1924). His chief work was an annotated translation of St. Thomas Aquinas's *Summa contra gentiles*, entitled *God and His Creatures* (1905); but R. also wrote more than 30 other works that contributed significantly to the neoscholastic revival. His translation (1929) of A. Rodríguez' *Ejercicio de perfección y de virtudes cristianas* under the title, *Practice of Perfection and Christian Virtues*, appeared in 3 volumes and was his last work.

[T. C. O'BRIEN]

RICOEUR, PAUL (1913–), French philosopher, university professor, teacher of the history of philosophy, member of the team of *Esprit*, listener to the Christian message. R. is also considered the most knowledgeable French historian of phenomenology and has translated Husserl's *Ideen zu einer reinen Phänomenologie und phänomenologischen Philosophie* and written detailed, analytical commentaries on Husserl's works. R. received his *docteur dès lettres* at the Univ. of Paris (1950) as well as several honorary degrees. He has been professor of philosophy at the Univ. of Strasbourg, the Univ. of Paris, and the Univ. of Chicago. Of a Protestant family of Provence, in his studies R. was first exposed to Barthian theology, which he rejected. While R. is a recognized interpreter of Husserl, the first major influence on his own philosophy was that of Gabriel *Marcel. In his *Philosophy of the Will* (1950–), R. states that "meditation on the work of Gabriel Marcel is in fact at the root of the analyses in this work"; but R. also wished to put Marcel's thought to the test of problems posed by classical psychology. Thus, his systematic project was "to put himself at the intersection of two exigencies: that of a thought nurtured by the mystery of the body, and that of a thought concerned for the distinctions inherited from the Husserlian method of description." R. considers Marcel's epistemology imperfect, and indicates that Husserl's work can broaden the narrow conception of the intellect which Marcel forcefully criticizes. Along with Husserl and Marcel, R. was influenced by the thought of Jaspers, Scheler, Hartmann, Heidegger, von Hildebrand, as well as by Emmanuel Mounier, the founder of a new Christian personalism.

R.'s phenomenology is descriptive and eidetic in the sense of Husserl's view of the older German movement. As to the "reduction," R. adopts a modified version with its function of enabling man to focus on the appearances of things as distinct from things appearing. The "phenomenological constitution" consists in determining the manner in which phenomena received establish themselves in man's subjective consciousness. Phenomenological idealism in the Husserlian sense, however, is unacceptable to R., who regards phenomenology as the beginning of philosophy rather than as its end.

In a collection of self-revealing essays entitled *History and Truth* (1955) R. infers that philosophy and phenomenology are probably subsidiary to his own main concerns—the philosophical strengthening of a Christian synthesis with a program of social and international action. R. rejects the Sartrian notion that freedom is essentially negation while maintaining that philosophy and freedom are essentially affirmations. Throughout his writings R. maintains a central motif of reconciliation, that is, a reconciliation of man within himself, his body, the world and even a reconciliation with ontology. Such a reconciliation is required because R. maintains that the basic philosophical experience is that man is a broken unity: man's existential condition can be described in terms of fallibility, finiteness, culpability or "fault" in the geological sense—thus man's proneness to become divided against himself and thereby to become the "flawed" creature. Only in transcendence can a final reunification be hoped for.

R. is most known for his monumental work *Philosophy of the Will*, a systematic phenomenology of the human will. The project is divided into three parts or moments. The first stage, *The Voluntary and the Involuntary* (1950) is called an "Eidetics" of the will which employs the descriptive method to bear on the reciprocity of the voluntary and involuntary aspects of man. Through abstraction or "reduction" from the symbolic, empirical and poetic dimensions, R. hopes to show man's fundamental possibilities in the "eidetic" dimension. This "reduction," however, omits two important factors from the descriptive analyses, "fault" and "transcendence." These two factors are treated, respectively, in the second and third volumes of *Philosophy of the Will*. It is in *The Voluntary and the Involuntary* that one finds an interplay between Marcel's motion of the "mystery of the body" and Husserl's "eidetic reduction." *Finitude and Guilt* (1960), the second volume of *Philosophy of the Will*, marks the first phase of passage from the "Eidetics" to the "Empirics" of the will. In fact, the first two books of the second volume, *Fallible Man* (1960), and *The Symbolics of Evil* (1960), serve as a preparation for the empirical study of the will which constitutes the third volume. *Fallible Man* is not so much concerned with concrete manifestations of fault as with that which permits faults to arise: man's fallibility. *The Symbolics of Evil*, the second volume of *Finitude and Guilt*, marks the transition from fallibility to fault. Moving from a method of pure reflection, R. commences with the fullness of language and moves on to a hermeneutics of symbols and myths. The third volume of *Finitude and Guilt* starts out from the evocative power of the symbol and formulates a true philosophical anthropology, and truly empirical study of the will. Based on the original program of *Philosophy of the Will*, the ultimate goal of the third volume is to arrive at the "poetics" of the will and thereby to explicate the factor of man's "transcendence" as a longing for a beyond. Works: *Gabriel Marcel et Karl Jaspers; Philosophie du mystère et philosophie du paradoxe* (1948); *Husserl: An Analysis of His Phenomenology* (tr. E. G. Ballard and L. E. Embree, 1967); *History and Truth* (tr. C. A. Kelbey, 1965); *The Voluntary and the Involuntary* (tr. E. Kohak, 1966); *Fallible Man* (tr. C. A. Kelbey, 1965); *Symbolism of Evil* (tr. E. Buchanan, 1967); *Freud and Philosophy* (tr. D. Savage, 1970); *Conflict of Interpretation: Essays in Hermeneutics* (1974). BIBLIOGRAPHY: H. Spiegelberg, *Phenomenological Movement* (v. 2, 1965) 563–579; D. Ihde, *Hermeneutic Phenomenology, The Philosophy of Paul Ricoeur* (1971).

[F. T. RYAN]

RICOLDUS DE MONTE CROCE (*c.* 1243–1320), Dominican writer, missionary. Entering the Florentine Dominicans at Sta. Maria Novella in 1267, R. taught at Pisa, Prato, and Florence (1272–88). In 1288 he set out on a journey to the East, returning *c.* 1301. The *Itinerarium* which he wrote as a result is of some historical and geographical value (ed. J. C. M. Laurent, *Peregrinationes medii aevi quattuor*, 1864). The fall of Acre in 1291 occasioned an *Epistola ad ecclesiam triumphantem*. On his return to Florence he composed an *Impugnatio Alcorani*, a useful work of apology against Islam, which was printed many times in the 15th and 16th cent., and recently by U. M. de Villard, *Il libro della peregrinazione di frate Ricoldo da Montecroce* (1948).

[L. E. BOYLE]

RIDDER, CHARLES H. (1888–1964), journalist. A native of New York City, R. joined the staff of *The Catholic News*, privately owned weekly of the archdiocese of New York, in 1910 when his father was publisher. In 1936 he became the publisher. President of the Catholic Press Association in 1938, R. was also a president of the U.S. Catholic Historical Association. In 1933 he headed the American committee for the Vatican press exhibit. He was honored for his work as an outstanding Catholic layman by Popes Pius XII and John XXIII.

[J. R. AHERNE]

RIDLEY, NICHOLAS (*c.* 1500–55), Reformation bp. of Rochester (1547), then of London (1550) under Edward VI, burned at the stake as a heretic in the reign of Mary Tudor. R. was one of the most influential Protestantizing theologians and churchmen of the period; as Master of Pembroke Hall (1540), he helped turn Cambridge Protestant. As bp. of London he assisted in the preparation of the 1549 BCP, rejected the doctrine of transubstantiation, and had all altars replaced by plain tables in the churches of the diocese.

[T. C. O'BRIEN]

RIDOLFI, ROBERTO DI (1531–1612), conspirator. A Florentine banker resident in London, he had been party to earlier plots against Elizabeth, but in 1571 he devised his own scheme wherein, with the support of Pope Pius V, Philip II of Spain would undertake an invasion to overthrow Elizabeth and place on the throne Mary Queen of Scots, who would marry the Catholic Duke of York, Thomas Howard. Though R. traveled to Brussels, Rome, and Madrid, his plot had little serious support and was quickly uncovered by the English government. BIBLIOGRAPHY: Hughes RE 3:277–280; DNB 16:1176–78.

[V. SAMPSON]

RIEMANN, HUGO (Karl Wilhelm Julius; 1849–1919), German musicologist and educator. He studied at the Leipzig Conservatory, where he began his treatises and books on musical history and theory. He held academic posts at universities and conservatories throughout Germany after 1878. His treatment of harmony served as a foundation for musical theory. His literary works covered all branches of musical knowledge; *Musiklexikon* (1882), which has had more than 10 editions, is his best known work. R. edited collections of ancient music, music notation, and theory. *Geschichte der Musiktheorie* (1898), a history of music from the 9th to the 19th cent., includes important references to ecclesiastical musical works.

[R. J. LITZ]

RIENZO, COLA DI, see COLA DI RIENZI.

RIEVAULX, ABBEY OF, one of the earliest Cistercian foundations in England, located 3 miles north of Helmesley in the Archdiocese of York. It was founded in 1131 and settled by monks who had been sent by St. Bernard from Clairvaux. A large and influential abbey, it soon established other foundations in Scotland and England, Melrose being among them. The works of Aelred are associated with Rievaulx. Its influence waned in the 14th cent. and it was eventually destroyed by the Scots. At the time of the Dissolution there were only 23 religious besides the abbot. The abbey is now in ruins, but a good part of the early English cruciform church remains.

[M. A. MCFADDEN]

RIGAUD, HYACINTHE (1659–1743), French painter of distinguished portraits and religious subjects. R. won the Prix de Rome (1682) but remained in Paris on the advice of Charles Le Brun. He painted an *Adoration of the Shepherds* (1687; lost), *Christ on the Cross* (1696), and *Presentation in the Temple* (1743). His *Portrait of Bossuet* (1699) and the famous painting of *Louis XIV* (1701) rooted in Titian, A. van Dyck, and the sober P. de Champaigne, unite master draftsmanship with brilliant color. His sitters included 5 kings, many European princes and the most distinguished persons of his age. BIBLIOGRAPHY: G. V. Gallenkamp, "Rigaud's Portrait Group at Ottawa," *Journal of the Warburg and Courtauld Institutes*, 23 (1960).

[M. J. DALY]

RIGBY, JOHN ST. (*c*.1570–1600), English martyr. A servant in a Catholic household, R. became a firm Catholic after having lapsed for several years. Sent to the Old Bailey to plead the case of his master's daughter, under questioning he openly professed his own Catholicism. He was imprisoned and later sentenced to death. He was canonized in 1970.

[J. R. AHERNE]

RIGGS, THOMAS LAWRASON (1888–1943), univ. chaplain, writer. A native of Connecticut and product of Yale and Harvard, R. taught at Yale for several years before serving as an officer in France during World War I. Upon his return to the U.S. he entered the seminary and was ordained for the diocese of Hartford, Conn., in 1922. His career from that year until his death was that of RC chaplain at Yale where he built the striking St. Thomas More Chapel. R. was a founder of the Calvert Associates, member of the editorial board of the *Commonweal*, and a frequent contributor to periodicals. Among his books were *Saving Angel* (1943) and translations, including *The Social Principles of the Gospel* by Alphonse Lugan (1928).

[J. R. AHERNE]

RIGHT AND RIGHTS. The term right (Lat. *jus*; also *debitum*) describes an objective reality or a way of action that is due to a person; the term rights describes that person's corresponding entitlement or claim to retain or to receive what is due. Justice is the correlative virtue that respects such a claim through the medium of the "what is right," "what is due"; the norm it observes is *equality, the rendering of what is right in the precise measure of the other person's entitlement to it. Because a reasonably recognized and achieved equality exists only between persons, as this term includes moral persons, beings that are less than human do not have rights. There is a consensus that issues of justice and so of rights should be objectively and impartially evaluated and dealt with; there is no consensus about the basis of such objectivity and impartiality. In St. Thomas Aquinas's moral theology "right" first means the *justum*, that which is right, adjusted as it were; it is something a person can call his own (*suum*); equally objectively "right" means a *debitum*, something a just person respects as belonging to another (*alienum*; ThAq ST 2a2ae, 57.1). He also basically divides these into the naturally right or due and the legally right or due. The naturally right rests on the very nature of things, particularly on the meaning of human nature; the legally right or due is what *positive law establishes. The division is based on Aristotle, who speaks of these as the concern of political justice "found among men who share their life with a view to self-sufficiency, men who are free and either arithmetically or proportionately equal" (*Ethics* 5,6.1134a26; see JUSTICE). Aristotle is speaking of justice in the *polis*, the Greek city-state, in which only free men, citizens, had rights and among whom alone the equality of justice prevailed. The *Ethics* has as its basic force of argument the consensus of right-thinking people, not a theoretical evaluation of human nature. Christian theology, however, rests the meaning of natural rights on the objective reality of a God-given nature in which all human beings are equals. Natural rights are those that correspond to this equal share in humanity; legal rights correspond to the determinations of positive law (presupposing that the positive law is in keeping with what is of nature). Even as the objectivity and impartiality of justice itself are recognized, so too, there is a consensus in moral theories that legal rights mean equality before the law that is their source and that enforces them. Natural rights are recognized as well; but there are necessarily as many theories on their source and their meaning as there are on the meaning of morality and of human nature itself (see ETHICS, HISTORY OF). In the terms of U.S. law, "civil rights" in meaning correspond to that of legal rights; their source and guarantee is the Constitution, which aims at equality before the law. But positive law is not the source of natural human rights. BIBLIOGRAPHY: ThAq ST (Lat-Eng, v. 41, ed. T. C. O'Brien, *Virtues of Justice*) 316–320.

[T. C. O'BRIEN]

RIGHT REVEREND, term of respect used for certain ecclesiastical officials. It is used for bps., abbots, as well as for moderators of the Church of Scotland. In the U.S. Catholic bps. are called Most Reverend. The former "Right Reverend" and "Very Reverend" as titles for a RC monsignor have been dropped. *REVEREND.

[T. EARLY]

RIGHT TO LIFE MOVEMENT, see PRO-LIFE MOVE-MENT IN THE U.S.

RIGHT TO WORK LAWS. To require of an employee that he become a member of a labor union as a condition of employment has been a heated economic, political, and moral issue in the U.S. since the turn of the century. Its more recent expression is found in campaigns to enact or repeal right-to-work laws.

Under federal law, a majority of employees can democratically elect a union to represent them in collective bargaining, but that union must then represent all the workers in the bargaining unit. Thus the union ordinarily seeks to persuade the employer to agree to a union-shop contract whereby all employees must become members within a specified time, usually 30 days.

State right-to-work laws prohibit the union shop and similar arrangements. Their authority is derived from Section 14(b) of the Labor-management Relations Act of 1947, popularly known as the Taft-Hartley Act, framed as an exception to the right to establish a union shop under specified conditions. Allegedly introduced as a protection of employee freedom, a correction of excessive union power, or a step to industrial peace, some form of right-to-work bill has come before the legislatures of most of the states but enacted in fewer than half of them.

The economic effects of this legislation are almost impossible to measure. The laws have found acceptance mainly in states where unions are weakest and agriculture strongest. At the same time, the concentration of economic power in the corporation has clearly not declined elsewhere since the emergence of strong unions. Nor is the union shop an isolated factor in determining the power a union holds when negotiating with the employer.

The right-to-work law is a poorly designed instrument for some of the purposes that many of its proponents want to achieve, such as the correction of unfair or undemocratic union practices. Under the law, members can withdraw and withhold financial support and thereby weaken the union but lessen the advantages they gain from collective bargaining. Stronger unions, even if tainted with corruption, have little to fear from this law; while weaker ones, esp. in hostile political climates, are more likely to be hurt by the freedom of members to come and go.

Protection of the rights and freedom of employees must exist in and out of unions, but it is questionable whether the right-to-work law is a reasonable means to achieve it. Many safeguards have already been provided by law and through the courts. Compulsory union membership under the Taft-Hartley Act, for example, has a very restricted meaning according to judicial interpretation. The courts have ruled that no employee can be discharged for failure to belong to a union under a union-shop contract if membership was denied or terminated for any reason other than his failure to tender reasonable initiation fees, dues, and assessments to the union legally certified to represent him.

The most important fact in making a moral judgment about this issue is to recognize that the right-to-work law has become a symbol of beliefs and feelings that lie much deeper than the requirement of membership. The real issue is whether unions should exist. Brought into the political arena, the right-to-work question tends to become explosive more for its symbolic than its practical meaning.

A moral evaluation of the right-to-work law rests, therefore, on whether strong, effective, and responsible labor unions are necessary in the present stage of economic life in the U.S. and whether the union shop is a reasonable arrangement for achieving that end.

The necessity of unions is widely accepted today, mainly because collective bargaining is thought to be the best method so far devised for preventing chaotic labor conditions and government control of the economic order. While strong, effective unions are a restraint on the economic freedom and unilateral authority of employers, responsible business leaders recognize that some curb on their bargaining power is necessary and that employees will justly benefit by uniting in an organization which has some control over a firm's labor supply.

Joining an organization to achieve certain goals that are impossible by oneself will also put some restriction on absolute individual freedom. Certifying a union to represent employees will take away the right of individual bargaining. The very existence of collective bargaining implies, however, that the individual employee must forego the privilege of unrestrained freedom in return for the greater job security and ordered liberty he hopes group action will bring. The federal government long ago decided that collective bargaining is a legitimate purpose in national economic and social policy.

The right-to-work laws do not seem to have been an exercise of prudent public policy. Despite some good effects on occasion, these statutes favor employees who are unconcerned about the needs of people they work with and restrict those who urge more social cooperation to satisfy their needs. The considerable support given the laws suggests the need of additional safeguards for employees who may be denied their rights. On the other hand, the right-to-work controversy has brought to light numerous cases which show the fairness of organized labor's claim to more effective security for unions. The effects of the laws, which have generally been insignificant, indicate that the legislation is not worth the effort required to enact it.

The right to work itself—apart from the concrete or contemplated U.S. laws—it should be noted is a natural human right. As John XXIII wrote: "It is clear that man has a right by the natural law not only to work but also to go about his work without coercion." (*Mater et magistra* 18). Opponents of right-to-work laws hold that such laws work against the natural right; advocates hold that the unions' position contravenes the right to work.

[W. J. LEE]

RIGHTEOUSNESS, the translation of the AV and RSV for the Gr. word *dikaiosúnē* (Lat. *justitia*), translated as "justice" in the Douay and Confraternity versions of the Bible. It is a keyword in the doctrine on justification, i.e., that man becomes just or right through the justice or righteousness of God. The biblical connotations, esp. that of St. Paul in Romans, are not the legal senses of the word justice. The term "righteousness" has the advantage of avoiding such connotations. The emphasis on God's saving justice was one aspect of Luther's insight into the gospel of grace. The doctrine of justification means that, through the righteousness by which God himself is absolutely holy, he saves man, making him right or just before God. The righteousness of man, his justice, is not an ethical or legal purity, but the rightness given to him by God in Christ. In English use righteousness has long had a Protestant association; a better Protestant-Catholic understanding of each other's doctrine of justification has taken away some of the reason for this exclusive association. *JUSTIFICATION.

[T. C. O'BRIEN]

RIGHTEOUSNESS OF GOD, God's justice, which consists primarily in his always doing the proper thing and keeping the right order in his actions relating to creatures. This propriety, or rightness, is what St. Anselm called *condecentia divinae bonitatis*, what benefits the divine goodness, namely, that all things should be according to the disposition of his divine wisdom and goodness. In doing so, God is no debtor to creatures but only to himself. The righteousness of God also includes, but is not limited to, his retributive justice, by which he rewards good works and punishes evil deeds, if not in this world at any rate in the life to come—a retribution that is perfectly just, for God is all-powerful and all-knowing and no accepter of persons.

God's fidelity to himself and to the disposition of his wisdom and goodness is seen in both testaments of the Bible as fidelity to the covenant he made with his chosen people, the old and the new Israel, and by extension with the whole of mankind, in the Noah covenant or the covenant included

in creation itself. Here God's righteousness appears as saving justice, by which he leads his people to salvation. In St. Paul this is proposed mainly in the justification of sinners. This divine saving righteousness is one with his mercy and love. Belief in the righteousness of God is not only biblical but a common witness of all religions. By his sense of justice, man is convinced that human affairs and the whole of creation are governed by a righteous Lord, who sees to it that the right order prevails. BIBLIOGRAPHY: D. M. Crossen and P. De Letter, NCE 8:73–75.

[P. DeLETTER]

RIGHTEOUSNESS OF MAN, man's being and doing what he ought to be and ought to do; in other words, man's keeping the right order with regard to God, to other people, and to himself. (It includes the justice of giving individual persons and the community of which one is a member their due). This inclusive concept appears at two different moments in the history of salvation. Before the Fall, in the state of original justice as this was traditionally conceived, righteousness included, besides grace, a preternatural harmony in man's composite being called the gift of integrity. After the Fall and the Redemption by Christ, sinners can be made righteous again, as St. Paul teaches in Romans, by justification through faith in Christ, in which they are made just. This Christian righteousness does not imply perfect harmony in man's nature. Concupiscence, a disorder, remains. Despite this, man can through grace be in right order toward God, his neighbor, and himself, or be without grave sin. Protestants consider this disorder as sinfulness and say forgiven sinners are both righteous and sinners. Perhaps the difference between Catholic and Protestant positions is to a large extent more verbal than real. However, this righteousness is ever unstable, and open to progress.

The teaching of Scripture and the Church on man's righteousness through grace, in the face of the sin of the world, is a realistic optimism, equally distant from Manichaean pessimism and naive naturalism. BIBLIOGRAPHY: D. M. Crossan and P. De Letter, NCE 8:75–77.

[P. DeLETTER]

RIGORD OF SAINT-DENIS (*c.* 1150–1208), chronicler, physician, royal chaplain, and later monk of St. Denis. In a work dedicated to Philip II, the *Gesta Philippi Augusti,* he introduced the laudatory title Augustus. After the king's divorce and his appropriation of ecclesiastical property, R. became severely critical of Philip's reign.

[J. E. WRIGLEY]

RIGORISM, see TUTIORISM.

RIG-VEDA, the most ancient of the four Vedas, sacred texts of the Hindus. Veda means "knowledge, wisdom," and the Vedas are collections of ancient revelations of eternal truth written in human language (Sanskrit) by gifted men inspired by the gods. The Upanishads are philosophical discourses flowing from the Vedas. All systems of knowledge thus based on the Vedas, no matter how diverse, are considered orthodox by Hindus; all others, unorthodox. Rigveda (or Ṛgveda) is a collection of more than 1,000 hymns grouped into 10 books or cycles (mandālas), and is as voluminous as the three other Vedas combined (Sāma, Yajur, and Atharva). The hymns of Rigveda came down originally by word of mouth, and comprise the earliest collection of such hymns, attaining their present form c.900 B.C. They are divided according to the author families and are subdivided according to the gods invoked and other such principles. Somewhat reminiscent of the poems of Homer in Greek religion, they are addressed to various gods who represent different powers of nature: the sun-god; the fire-god; the god of thunder; and the goddess of dawn. They are considered guides to the soul of man, to lift his spirit to sing the Song of Humanity. Later hymns, e.g., in the 10th book, involve speculation on the nature of god and the universe, notably, the "Hymn of the Person," which is one of the latest. A special form of chant is used in India to recite the hymns.

[E. J. DILLON]

RILKE, RAINER MARIA (1879–1926), Austrian lyric poet. After an unhappy youth and without completing his formal education, R. became a free-lance writer. He moved much from place to place, traveling in Italy, Russia, France, Africa, and Spain. In Paris he came under the influence of the sculptor A. Rodin and studied French impressionistic poetry. He was intensely dedicated to his mission as a poet and became one of the most influential modern lyricists. His work is a peculiar blend of impressionism and mysticism. He made extensive use of religious ideas and symbolism, but his religious views are individualistic and unorthodox. Much of his work has been translated into English: Poems (1934), Requiem (1935), Later Poems (1938), and Selected Poems (1944) by J. B. Leishman; and other selections by M. D. H. Norton (1939), C. F. MacIntyre (1941), and J. Lamont (1943). BIBLIOGRAPHY: E. M. Butler, Rainer Maria Rilke (1946); E. Buddeberg, Rainer Maria Rilke (1955).

[I. MERKEL]

RIMBAUD, ARTHUR (1854–91), French poet and adventurer who embarked at the age of 16 on a meteoric literary career marked by rebellion against authority and bourgeois mores, and by revolutionary innovations in the concept, themes, and forms of modern French poetry. While leading (1870–75) a turbulent life that ended with a stormy affair involving Paul Verlaine, he composed his three groups of works: poems in verse form like Voyelles, Bateau ivre, Poètes de sept ans; the metaphysical autobiography, Une Saison en enfer; and the prose poems of Illuminations. Thereafter he ceased writing and lived an adventurer's and explorer's life in the Orient, Arabia, and East Africa. His sister Isabelle, an eyewitness, testified that R.

was converted on his deathbed. Catholic critics like Claudel, for whom a reading of Illuminations was a revelation of the supernatural and a catalyst in his conversion, interpreted his poetry as translating a religious experience of Being. However, R. more nearly resembles the later surrealists in believing that the poet should become a voyant or seer "through a long, profound and logical derangement of the senses" (Letter to Paul Demény, May 15, 1871), becoming finally "the Supreme Knower—for he would have reached the Unknown" (ibid.). Religious references abound in his poetry, but they translate not a vision of salvation but the struggle of a new Prometheus to wrest truth from experience. BIBLIOGRAPHY: M. Étiemble, Le Mythe de Rimbaud (4v., 1954–61); E. Starkie, Arthur Rimbaud (1961); W. M. Frohock, Rimbaud's Poetic Practice (1963).

[G. E. GINGRAS]

RIMINI, SAN FRANCESCO, originally a 13th-cent. Gothic structure, redesigned in Renaissance style (1447–50) by Leon Battista Alberti. Commissioned by Sigismondo Malatesta, lord of Rimini, Alberti designed a Roman triumphal arch as entrance. His original plan to place the sarcophagi of his two patrons under the side arches was aborted. He sheathed the interior of the old medieval church with marble from S. Apollinare in Classe, Ravenna. In accordance with his theory that "temples" be raised above the level of the common world S. Francesco rises from a high base that effects gravity and detachment. A's further plan for a second story is known only from the medal of Matteo de'Pasti (1450). The piers and Roman arch construction, with columns become the principal ornaments in a Roman aesthetic which used Greek functional members as decoration. BIBLIOGRAPHY: R. Wittkower, Architectural Principles in the Age of Humanism (1952).

[M. J. DALY]

RIMINI (ARIMINUM) AND SELEUCIA, SYNODS OF, two councils held in 359 to which the bps. of the West and East were respectively summoned by the Emperor Constantius in an attempt to bring an end to the Arian controversies. His original plan had been for a single council to be held at Nicaea, but the creed associated with this site prompted the Semi-Arian Basil of Ancyra to suggest a change to Nicomedia. When this city was destroyed by an earthquake, the Anomoeans, radical Arians, who held that the Son was "unlike" the Father, took advantage of the subsequent confusion. Fearing that in a single council the Semi-Arians (Homoeousians) might join forces with the Catholics (Homoousians) to condemn them, they persuaded the Emperor that it would be less expensive to hold two councils, one at Rimini in Italy and one at Seleucia in Isauria. More than 400 bps. from the West assembled at Rimini in May 359. The vast majority were orthodox in their beliefs, but they had to contend with some 80 Arian bishops. When the assembly was asked to sign the famous Dated Creed, (Fourth Formulary of Sirmium) which had been drawn up a short time before at Sirmium by Homoeans and by Homoeousians, it refused to do so and, instead, excommunicated the Arian leaders. Deputations were then sent both by the Catholics and by the Arians to the Emperor. Worn out by delays and deceived by the ambiguities of their adversaries, the Catholic deputies from Rimini eventually signed a new version of the Dated Creed at Nice in Thrace on October 10, 359. The council fathers themselves, after initial resistance and some specific qualifications, eventually accepted this creed which rejected the term *ousia* (''substance'') as being unscriptural and declared that the Son was *homoios* (similar) to the Father. In the meantime, some 160 bps. had assembled at Seleucia, the majority being Semi-Arian (Homoeousian) in their views. The first session of the council was held on September 27, 359, and on the following day a creed that had been drawn up in Antioch in 341 was accepted. When disputes between the Anomoeans, and the Semi-Arians resulted, *Acacius introduced the Creed of Nice and the Emperor demanded its acceptance. The signing of this Arianizing formula by both councils representing the bps. of the East and the West occasioned St. Jerome's famous observation: ''The whole world groaned and was surprised to find itself Arian'' (*Ingemuit totus orbis et Arianum se esse miratus est.* Jerome, *Dial. adv. Luciferianos* 19). Worthy of note is that Pope Liberius was neither present nor represented by anyone at these councils. BIBLIOGRAPHY: C. J. Hefele, *History of the Councils of the Church* (tr. W. R. Clark, 1876) 2:246–271; G. Bardy, Fliche-Martin 3:163–167.

[M. J. COSTELLOE]

RINALDI, ODORICO (Raynaldus; 1594–1671), church historian. R. twice served as superior general of the Oratorians, the congregation in which he was ordained. He succeeded Card. *Baronius as director of the *Annales ecclesiastici*, extending that defense of Roman Catholicism and the papacy from 1198 to 1565 (v. 13–22, 1646–77). R.'s work was distinguished by its use of original sources and inchoate critical historiography, even though later scholarship pointed out its historical inaccuracies and numerous chronological errors. BIBLIOGRAPHY: K. Oehler, RGG 5:807.

[T. M. MCFADDEN]

RING, THOMAS FRANCIS (1841–98), Catholic lay leader. A Bostonian, R. founded the first central council of the St. Vincent de Paul Society. He was a member of the Boston Board of Overseers from 1886 to 1895, vice-president of the Associated Charities from 1893, and an officer of the National Conference of Charities and Corrections. He spoke as a Catholic layman at the Chicago World's Fair in 1893 and was selected by the American bps. to address the Columbian Congress.

[J. R. AHERNE]

RINGATU, a religious group of the Maoris, the Polynesian natives of New Zealand. Little is known about them except that they broke off from the C of E in New Zealand.

[J. R. FANG]

RINGEISEN, DOMINIKUS (1834–1904), German priest who erected in the Diocese of Augsburg model establishments for the mentally and physically handicapped. To assure the permanence of his work, he founded the Congregation of St. Joseph in 1897. He was in advance of his time in using gentle care and occupational therapy to make his charges, as he said, ''good and happy.'' BIBLIOGRAPHY: F. X. Kerer, *Dominikus Ringeisen von Ursberg* (1927).

[M. J. SUELZER]

RINGS, ECCLESIASTICAL USE OF. The giving or exchange of ring(s) by husband and wife as pledge of fidelity and union has been customary among Christians since Roman times and is provided for in the rituals of most Churches. In the RC Church, the wearing of a ring by bps. (including pope and cardinals) probably began in a practical way, through its use as a seal, and is mentioned as early as the 4th cent.; it eventually became symbolic of the bp.'s marriage to his diocese. Apart from prelates (including abbots), members of some religious orders, and those with pontifical doctoral degrees, clerics are forbidden by canon law to wear rings, although contrary custom has recently developed. At least since the 14th cent., most professed nuns and sisters have worn rings as a sign of their dedication to Christ; St. Ambrose speaks of their right to do so.*FISHERMAN'S RING.

[J. DALLEN]

RINSER, LUISE (1911–   ), German Catholic writer. R. has worked as a teacher and writer in Germany since 1935. She was imprisoned by the Nazis from 1944–45. From 1953–59 she was married to the musical composer, Karl Orff. Her psychological novels often present the horrible and extraordinary, as well as the development of female personality structures. Among her major works are *Mitte des Lebens* (1950), and *Ich bin Tobias* (1966).

[T. M. MCFADDEN]

RIO, MARTIN ANTOINE DEL, see DEL RIO, MARTIN ANTOINE.

RIORDAN, PATRICK WILLIAM (1841–1914), second abp. of San Francisco. Born in New Brunswick, Canada and coming to the U.S. as a child, R. was ordained for Chicago in 1865. As pastor he exhibited administrative ability; the great fire of Chicago brought him to the fore collecting for rebuilding diocesan institutions. In 1883 R. was named coadjutor to Abp. Alemany of San Francisco and succeeded him the same year. R. built a cathedral, seminary, hospitals, and other charitable institutions, and founded the parochial school system of San Francisco. He helped the Christian Brothers establish St. Mary's College, Oakland, and the normal school at San José. R. was a leader in the successful effort to exempt churches from taxation in 1900. He was a delegate before the international arbitration court at The Hague and was instrumental in settling the Pious Fund case against Mexico. When earthquake and fire devastated the archdiocese in 1906, R., with help from all over the U.S., rebuilt church institutions. His prudent administration left his archdiocese in admirable condition.

[J. R. AHERNE]

RIOT, in early sense wanton or loose behavior, thence the disturbance arising from this, a breach of the peace, public violence, or an outbreak of active lawlessness by an assembly of three or more (the earliest Riot Act, 1715, specified 12 or more). As a sin it is against the peace which is an effect of Christian charity (ThAq ST 2a2ae, 42), an incipient *sedition, condemned by St. Paul (2 Cor 12.20), often leading to grave violations of commutative and general justice. It has often happened that governments were more to blame than the rioters; nevertheless, the duty must be insisted on of maintaining the people against a mob. BIBLIOG - RAPHY: *Report of the National Advisory Commission on Civil Disorders* pts. 1 and 2.

[G. A. VANDERHAAR]

RIPA, CESARE (fl. 16th cent.), Italian iconologist whose book *Iconologia,* published in Rome (1593), illustrated edition (1603), translated into many languages, is a source of meaningful imagery for artists and writers. BIBLIOGRAPHY: E. Mâle, *L'Art religieux après le Concile de Trente* (1932); M. Praz, *Studies in Seventeenth Century Imagery* (1947).

[M. J. DALY]

RIPA, MATTEO (1682–1746), missionary to China and educator. R. was born in Salerno, Italy, was ordained in 1705, and was sent to China as part of a papal legation. He worked from 1711 as a court painter during the reign of Emperor K'ang-hi, whose favor permitted R. to do missionary work. Upon K'ang-hi's death, R. returned to Italy (1723), opened a school in Naples for the education of missionaries (the so-called Chinese College), and founded a congregation of secular priests for the missionary apostolate. R. wrote an extensive description of his work in his *Storia della fondazione dalle Congregazione e del Collegio de' Cinese* (3 v.; 1832).

[T. M. MCFADDEN]

RIPALDA, JUAN MARTÍNEZ DE (1594–1648), Jesuit theologian. Most of his professional career was spent at the Univ. of Salamanca. His principal work is *De ente supernatuali* (3 v. 1634–48). His thought is marked by penetrating analysis, clarity, and comprehensive detail; he adopted distinctive positions on grace and faith.

[T. C. O'BRIEN]

RIPIDION, see RHIPIDION.

RIPOLL, ABBEY OF, a former Benedictine monastery in Ripoll, Catalonia. The abbey was founded and richly endowed by Count Wilfrid I of Barcelona (c.880). It was given papal protection in 951 and full exemption some 60 years later. Ripoll reached the height of its importance in the 11th cent., but because of community disagreements with its benefactor, Count Bernard II of Besalù, it went into a period of decline. The monastery was destroyed during the 19th-cent. Carlist wars, but the abbey church with its ornate Romanesque portal was rebuilt to serve as a parish church. BIBLIOGRAPHY: J. J. Bauer, LTK 8:1319–20.

[M. A. MCFADDEN]

RIPON, ABBEY OF, early monastic foundation located near York, England. It was settled by Celtic monks from Melrose Abbey c.651. Because of disputes concerning Roman practices, the Celtic monks left some 10 years later. The Benedictine Rule was soon established at Ripon by Wilfrid of York, who later became bp. of York. Destroyed (c.948) during King Edred's war with the Danes, the abbey was eventually rebuilt. The monastery was dissolved under Henry VIII; the abbey church became the cathedral church of the Anglican Diocese of Ripon in 1836. BIBLIOGRAPHY: ODCC 1167.

[M. A. MCFADDEN]

RISK, see LIFE, RISK TO.

RISORGIMENTO (Ital., resurrection), the period and movement for the liberation, reform, and unification of Italy from about 1789 to 1870. The 14 years of Napoleonic rule in Italy awakened a dormant patriotism that the political arrangements of the Congress of Vienna only served to stimulate. During the first period of the Risorgimento (1815–48), the literary conspiracy against Austrian rule enlisted the allegiance of intellectuals and created an atmosphere conducive to liberalism and nationalism. Militarily, this phase of the Risorgimento was a failure, for Austria defeated Piedmont in the First War of Independence. The sole triumph for Italian liberals and nationalists was the retention of the Albertine constitution of 1848. During the second period of the Risorgimento (1848–70), two wars with Austria saw the expulsion of that country from the greater part of the Italian peninsula. The same years saw the absorption of the Papal States and the Kingdom of the Two Sicilies into the Kingdom of Italy. The chief architects of Italian unity were Giuseppe Mazzini, Count Camillo di Cavour, and King Victor Emmanuel II. BIBLIOGRAPHY: G. F. H. and J. Berkeley, *Italy in the Making* (3 v., 1932–40).

[E. A. CARRILLO]

RIST, VALERIUS (1696–1737), Bavarian Franciscan missionary. After ordination in Rome, R. worked as a missionary in Indochina esp. in Cambodia, Vietnam, and Cochin China. In 1730, he became pro-vicar of Cambodia and Laos, and a titular bishop. His missionary activities were extremely successful. He wrote an unfinished catechism in Cambodian and a valuable itinerary of his years in Indochina. BIBLIOGRAPHY: B. H. Willeke, LTK 8:1321–22.

[T. M. MCFADDEN]

RISTORI, GIOVANNI ALBERTO (1692–1753), Italian organist and composer primarily of operas and church music. He went to Dresden with his father, an Italian theater company director, in 1715. He became composer of the Royal Italian Opera and director of the Polish Chapel (1717). He was court organist (1733) and was later appointed vice-*Kapellmeister* (1750). His works include some 20 operas, 16 cantatas, 3 oratorios, 15 Masses, motets, Requiems, and other church music.

[R. J. LITZ]

RITA OF CASCIA, ST. (*c.*1380–1447), Augustinian stigmatic, wonder-worker. In obedience to the wishes of her parents R. married a young man who, as it later proved, had a brutal and violent nature. She endured maltreatment at his hands with patience, and gradually he was won to better ways. When, after 18 years of marriage, he was slain by enemies, R. prayed earnestly that her two sons be kept from the revenge they were plotting. As if in answer to her prayer the youths were taken ill and died. R. then entered the convent of S. Maria Maddalena in Cascia, where she lived a life of heroic penance that won the admiration of all. Devoted esp. to the Passion of Christ, she experienced a painful wound, as though made by a thorn, on her forehead. She became celebrated as a patron of those in desperate straits. She was canonized in 1900, and her cult was very popular in the early years of the 20th century. BIBLIOGRAPHY: N. Del Re, BiblSanct 11:212–221.

[P. K. MEAGHER]

RITE, in the Catholic Church, a family or grouping of Churches with some autonomy (canonically indicated by its own hierarchy) and characterized by distinctive liturgical forms, canonical organization and discipline, customs, traditions, and spiritual and theological heritage, though in full communion with one another and with the pope. The origins of the various rites lie largely in the geographic, cultural, and political diversity that accompanied the spread and development of the Church. The early Church contained a great variety of liturgical forms and disciplinary organization. The division of the Roman Empire into East and West (395) influenced the development of rites as ecclesiastical organization modeled itself on the political. Subsequent heresies and the later schism between East and West contributed. Centralizing tendencies (particularly the association of smaller Churches under the leadership of the bishop of the chief city of the area) led gradually to the adoption of similar forms in an area and eventual canonical regulation.

The interrelations of the various rites may be seen through their derivation from such various centers.

The rites are no longer confined to specific territories but are rather intermixed. Seventeen Eastern rites are canonically recognized. With the exception of the Maronites, each of these is or has been paralleled by an Orthodox Church differentiated by little other than non-communion with Rome. While many of these Eastern rites in communion with Rome have been heavily influenced by Latin customs, Vatican II in particular urged the preservation of the traditional rites (Vat II EastCath n. 1–6). Only one major center, Rome, developed in the West; consequently, although diversity of forms has existed (esp. Gallican) and to some extent still exists (Ambrosian or Milanese and Mozarabic liturgies; some primatial sees and religious orders), there has been no real canonical autonomy in the modern sense nor, therefore, distinctive canonical rites.

By Church law baptism initiates not only into the Church but also into a specific rite. Acquisition of rite is thus normally determined by the baptism ceremonial, provided it is conducted according to the norms of canon law, which prescribe that children are to be baptized in the rite of the parents or, if the parents belong to different rites, in the rite of the father. Baptized non-Catholics already have their rite prior to joining the Catholic Church and ordinarily must retain that rite. The non-baptized may choose their rite on joining the Church. Transfer from one rite to another generally involves the permission of the Holy See, except that in an interritual marriage the wife may transfer to the husband's rite and children under the age of puberty change rites with their father. Catholics are permitted to receive the sacraments in any Catholic rite, although marriage and ordination are to be in one's own rite. Priests are ordinarily forbidden to celebrate the sacraments in a rite other than their own, although biritual faculties are sometimes given.

[J. DALLEN]

RITE, WESTERN, see WESTERN RITE.

RITES, CONGREGATION OF, see SACRAMENTS AND DIVINE WORSHIP, SACRED CONGREGATION FOR THE.

RITES, EASTERN, see EASTERN RITES.

RITES, ENGLISH MEDIEVAL, local variants on the Roman rite in several medieval English dioceses. The rites, called in English "uses," primarily reflect adaptations from those of N France. Sheppard (see bibliog.) indicates as principal the Uses of Sarum (Salisbury), of York, Hereford, and Bangor in Wales. The last-named is unknown in its details, but Cranmer mentioned it in his introduction to the 1549 Book of Common Prayer. There were, however, many other local adaptations of the Roman rite or variants of the Uses of Sarum and York. The Sarum rite is best known and researched and is typical of the variants in liturgical colors, order of Mass, and in the texts composed for Mass and

Divine Office. Sheppard finds little in the English medieval rites that is of great aesthetic or liturgical value. Minor details have survived in, e.g., the formula of the marriage rite in England. BIBLIOGRAPHY: L. C. Sheppard, NCE 12:519–522 with bibliog.

RITSCHL, ALBRECHT (1822–89), German theologian. R. studied at Bonn, Halle, Heidelberg and Tübingen, then taught (1846) NT and patristics at Bonn. The major part of his career was as professor of theology at Göttingen, beginning in 1864. R.'s theology, which centered on the primacy of moral value, had a broad influence that extended into the 20th century. His position sought a middle ground between an ontological or metaphysical articulation of Christian truths, and a theology conformed merely with a subjective piety. Significantly he was the first major theologian to rely on the critical philosophy of Kant. Part of the appeal of R.'s thought was its liberation of theology from a reliance on metaphysics or from any relation to empirical scientific studies. At the same time he sought a theological synthesis that derived its objectivity and consistency from its assertion of the primacy of moral value in revelation. Jesus Christ is the revelation that God intends man's moral perfection. The kingdom of God is temporal, and consists in the social diffusion of moral perfection. Justification is not juridic nor merely the taking away of sin, but a true reconciliation, a reestablished harmony of the sinner with God. The community of the justified manifests the kingdom of God by their acts of love for one another. The community has priority in R.'s thought. The Church is the expression of the community's striving for ethical redemption. R.'s influence was such that a Ritschlian school of theology developed. But more extensively his socio-ethical and historical view of theology was a main element in liberal theology's estimate of the nature of theology, its interpretation of revelation and gospel, and the growth of the *Social Gospel movement. In particular A. von Harnack, E. Troeltsch, K. Barth and R. Bultmann were all in some way conditioned by R.'s theology. His main works were *Die christliche Lehre von der Rechtfertigung und Verschnung* (3 v., 1870–74; Eng. tr. *Critical History of the Christian Doctrine of Justification and Reconciliation*, 3v., 1872–1900); and a history of Pietism (*Geschichte des Pietismus*, 1880–86). BIBLIOGRA-PHY: D. Ritschl, NCE 12:523; R. Anchor, EncPhil 7:202–203; K. Barth, *Protestant Thought: From Rousseau to Ritschl* (tr. B. Cozens, 1959) 390–399.

RITUAL (Methodist), the fixed forms and offices of worship prescribed by the *General Conference. Included are: baptism, confirmation, and reception into the Church; holy communion; marriage; burial service; ordination of deacons and of elders; and consecration of bishops. These rituals are set forth in the *Discipline. Additional, optional offices for other occasions are found in the Book of Worship. The Ritual is not one of the doctrinal standards of the Church and may be altered by the General Conference. The first Ritual for American Methodism (since revised) was provided in 1784 by John *Wesley, who abridged the *Book of Common Prayer. BIBLIOGRAPHY: N. B. Harmon, *Rites and Ritual of Episcopal Methodism* (1926); R. J. Cooke, *Ritual of the Methodist Episcopal Church* (1900).

[F. E. MASER]

RITUAL, ROMAN, a liturgical book of the Roman rite containing the sacramental and extrasacramental rites performed by the priest. The evolution of the Roman *Pontifical for the use of bishops, was supplemented by a parallel development of manuals of ritual for the use of priests. From the 11th cent. on, collections of ritual formulas were gathered by monks. Most formulas were composed with a view to the monastic rather than the pastoral ministry and for that reason tended to be long. After the 12th cent. books of ritual were in common use among the clergy, and with the invention of printing they became indispensable guides in the administration of the sacraments and the execution of the priest's pastoral duties. The rituals of Castellani (1523) and Samarino (1579), both very popular during the 16th cent., provided a basis for the Roman Ritual promulgated by Paul V (1614). That ritual was strongly recommended to bishops and parish priests but it was never obligatory. Its promulgation did not preclude the use of other rituals, and in many dioceses and religious orders special rituals have been approved and employed, esp. for particular formulas. Some of these formulas have been incorporated into the Roman Ritual in an appendix. The Roman Ritual has been revised often; the last pre-Vatican II edition was in 1952. An English translation with introductions and commentary was prepared by P. T. Weller and published in 1965. It incorporated the significant additions and revisions made by the Sacred Congregation of Rites since the last typical edition, as well as the changes introduced by the *Instruction* of Sept. 26, 1964, published by the Consilium on the Liturgy. A complete revision of the Ritual, in process since Vatican II, has covered all rites except the section on blessings. For the rites revised to date see *Liturgical Books (Roman Rite). The new rites are notable for their theological and pastoral instruction.

RITUAL MURDER, the taking of a human life during a religious and/or magical ceremony. As such it is part of the general complex of *human sacrifice, *cannibalism, and headhunting. Ritual murder is usually identified with ceremonial killing inasmuch as it is enacted to provide materials for cultic purposes, e.g., blood or fat, which are occasionally needed by secret societies for their rituals. In Western history the accusation of ritual murder was at times an effective means to defame religious communities. It served as an argument against the Christians whose eucharistic practices were distorted by Roman officials. In the 11th cent. and esp. during the Third Crusade the accusation was leveled against the Jews. Their alleged murdering of Christian children in order to obtain blood for the Passover was an excuse for pogroms and the reinforcement of anti-Jewish laws (see ANTI-SEMITISM). BIBLIOGRAPHY: M. Eliade, *Patterns in Comparative Religion* (tr. R. Sheed, 1963); H. L. Strack, *Jew and Human Sacrifice* (1909); J. Trachtenberg, *Devil and the Jews. Medieval Conception of the Jew and Its Relation to Modern Anti-Semitism* (1945). *SIMON OF TRENT; *WILLIAM OF NORWICH.

[W. DUPRÉ]

RITUALISM, an advocacy or practice of liturgical ceremony regarded as excessive; a word much used in the second half of the 19th cent., and often in disparagement. ''Ritualist'' originally meant one versed in liturgical rites and ceremonies; then afterward, one who advocated or performed them to an extent regarded as excessive. Together with the more hissing phrase ''ritualistic practices,'' it was applied not to the participants of the *Oxford movement but to the Romanizers in worship and discipline of the high-church party. In the C of E the implementation of the *Six Points—altar lights, eucharistic vestments, eastward position of the priest at the altar, wafer bread, the mixing in the chalice, and incense—meant falling foul of the average Anglican bishop of the day, the chance of prosecution in the courts, brawls in church, and the jibes of Punch. The matter, featured in Victorian literature, e.g., Ouida's character ''who was very religious and strongly ritualistic,'' was the subject for a Royal Commission set up in 1867; its hostile recommendations proved a dead letter. The ritualists succeeded the earlier evangelicals in promoting the social gospel of the Church; it was not a question of dressing up for the sake of it, but of bringing light and color to the slums. They were better symbolized by the East End parson than by the Pale Curate with a penchant for frills. ''I am told,'' wrote an observer, ''they give short and practical sermons.'' Ritualism has now settled down to respectability in the Church of England. The post-Edwardian style, if less romantic and daring, is more stately and sumptuous than the Victorian. When it comes to pageantry Lambeth can hold its own with anything that can be put on by the Earl Marshal, the Brigade of Guards, or the Papal Master of Ceremonies. *PUBLIC WORSHIP REGULATION ACT.

[T. GILBY]

RIVA AGÜERO, JOSÉ DE LA (1895–1944), Peruvian historian and politician. After completing his studies at S. Marcos Univ., R. became one of its youngest and most brilliant teachers. He headed the democratic party, served as mayor of Lima and minister of state, and traveled widely in Europe. He gave up his political activities in his disgust at the passage of a law permitting divorce. Thereafter he devoted his time to historical research and to the defense of the Church to which he had returned after a period of religious skepticism. Among his writings are: *La historia del Perú* (1910); *El carácter de la literatura del Perú independiente* (1910). BIBLIOGRAPHY: R. Porras Barrenechea, *Fuentes históricas peruanas* (1954).

[P. DAMBORIENA]

RIVADAVIA, BERNARDINO (1780–1845), Argentinian politician. He joined the revolution in 1810, served as secretary of war, performed several diplomatic missions in Europe, was minister of government and foreign affairs for the province of Buenos Aires, and in 1826–27 was president of the republic. He died in exile in Cádiz, Spain. His promotion of various administrative and educational reforms gives him a place among the founders of modern Argentina. In an effort to bring about reform in the Argentinian Church, he sought to subject the Church to the State, suppressed monasteries and confiscated their properties, and led the country to the brink of schismatic separation from Rome. BIBLIOGRAPHY: G. Gallardo, *La Política religiosa de Rivadavia* (1962).

[P. DAMBORIENA]

RIVAROL, PSEUD., see DAUDET, LÉON.

RIVER BRETHREN. The group takes its name from a meeting place by the Susquehanna River in Eastern Pennsylvania and is an offshoot of a group formed in the 18th cent. with substantial similarities to the Mennonites or Dunkers. Pietist in tradition, the River Brethren emphasize inward sense of salvation, adult baptism by immersion, simplicity and plain dress, and a strong pacifism. In 1843 a small group, the Yorker brethren, concentrated in York, Pa., seceded from the River Brethren. The Yorkers repudiate churches, worshiping in homes or barns, and follow an even stricter regime than the parent body.

[J. R. AHERNE]

RIVERO, MARIANO EDUARDO DE (1798–1857), Peruvian scientist and educator. He studied in Europe and achieved distinction in the sciences; after his return to his native continent he was active in fostering scientific studies in Latin America. He wrote in collaboration with J. J. Tschudi *Antiqüedades peruanas,* an important study of pre-colonial Peru.

[P. DAMBORIENA]

RIVIÈRE, JACQUES (1886–1925), French essayist, associated with the *Nouvelle revue française,* of which he became secretary and editor. Born in Bordeaux, he returned to Catholicism under the influence of Paul Claudel, though the timbre of his theological thought is variously echoed by later critics.

[T. GILBY]

RIVIÈRE, JEAN (1878–1946), theologian. R. studied at the Albi seminary and the theologate at Toulouse. After ordination, he taught dogma at Albi (1903–19), but was removed when the Holy Office censured his teaching on Christ's knowledge. R. then occupied the chair of fundamental theology at the Univ. of Strasbourg (1919–46). His principal concern was the history of the dogma of the Redemption. BIBLIOGRAPHY: M. Bécamel, NCE 12:527–528, with bibliog.

[T. M. MCFADDEN]

ROBBERY, the unjust taking from another of what belongs to him when this is accomplished by actual or threatened violence. Common parlance sometimes identifies robbery with theft, but from the moral point of view robbery is a more serious wrong because it adds to the evil of stealing a violent affront to the person of the victim. Like theft, moralists consider robbery a sin because it is opposed to the virtues of justice and charity, and it offends against the same two virtues on the added count of violence. Both theft and robbery are considered grave sins in themselves, yet theft may in some cases be a slight sin because of the relative triviality of what is taken, whereas robbery, even when something of little value is stolen, remains a grave sin because of the outrage against the person of the victim. BIB-LIOGRAPHY: A. Doolan, NCE 12:258; ThAq ST 2a2ae, 66.8–9.

[P. F. MULHERN]

ROBBIA, DELLA, see DELLA ROBBIA.

ROBERT II (*c.*950–1031) **KING OF FRANCE** from 996, second of the Capetian line. R. spent much time in winning the Duchy of Burgundy and in settling the troubles caused by Constance of Arles, his third wife. He was banned by Gregory V in 998 until he renounced his second wife, Bertha of Burgundy. R. was the first king to claim thaumaturgic powers; he believed in primogeniture in royal succession and sponsored the *"Peace of God."* R. received the surname Pious as he enjoyed singing hymns in the company of clerks and advocated monastic reform.

[M. C. BRADLEY]

ROBERT OF ARBRISSEL, BL. (*c.*1047–1117), itinerant preacher, founder of the Order of Fontevrault, and arch-priest of the diocese of Rennes where he suppressed simony, lay investiture, clerical concubinage, irregular marriages, and was sought to heal feuds. Later R. left his lectures at Angers to become an anchorite in the forest of Craon, and there the many imitators who followed him he formed into a community of canons regular. He was called by Urban II to become an itinerant public preacher, and opened a house of prayer for those who could not take part in the Crusade. R. built the first house at Fontevrault (*c.*1100), which was a double monastery. BIBLIOGRAPHY: B. Hamilton, NCE 12:528–529; H. Platelle, BiblSanct 11:228–231.

[M. C. BRADLEY]

ROBERT BACON (after 1150–1248), Dominican theologian. The first Dominican master of theology at Oxford, R. was trained at Paris, where he became a master of theology in 1219. He joined the Dominicans in 1234. He is known to have written a number of works of theology, but only a few fragments survive. BIBLIOGRAPHY: Emden Ox 1:87.

[L. E. BOYLE]

ROBERT DE BALDOK (d. 1327), English churchman and chancellor of England (1323–26). B., a man of great ability, was the first important keeper of the privy seal (1320–23). Though he was three times recommended for bishoprics by Edward II, he failed to win appointment. Captured with the King (1326), to whom he remained loyal, B. died of wounds inflicted by a London mob. BIBLIOGRAPHY: T. F. Tout, *Chapters in the Administrative History of Mediaeval England* (6 v. 1920–33); Emden Ox 1:96–98.

ROBERT OF BRUGES, BL. (d. 1157), abbot. Born at Bruges of the noble family of Gruthuysen, R. was called to the monastic life (with 29 companions) by Bernard of Clairvaux and entered Clairvaux in 1131. He was installed as first Cistercian abbot in April, 1139, at Our Lady of Dunes Abbey in Flanders (founded 1107 by Léger) which became in 1120 a Savigny foundation and was later attached to Clairvaux. R. succeeded Bl. Idesbald as the second abbot of the monastery. There he became renowned for his wisdom, prudence, and piety. He is reported to have been named successor by Bernard and did in fact succeed him in 1153 as second abbot of Clairvaux. BIBLIOGRAPHY: *Biographie nationale de Belgique* 19:416–422; M. A. Dimier, BiblSanct 11:232–233.

[N. F. GAUGHAN]

ROBERT OF COURÇON (*c.*1160–1219), English scholastic, cardinal in 1212, papal legate to France from 1213. He taught at Paris, 1204–10; wrote a *Summa theologica* (*c.*1204), mainly on moral matters and sacraments; and a now-lost commentary on Peter Lombard's *Sentences*. R. is chiefly remembered for promulgating, under mandate of Innocent III, the statutes of the *Universitas magistrorum et scholarium Parisiis studentium*, regarded as the charter of the Univ. of Paris. The document determined the texts and curriculum for the Paris masters; it continued the 1210 prohibition of the study of the texts of Aristotle's philosophical works in the Faculty of Arts, a point of significance in the history of scholasticism. R. fell from papal favor and died in Egypt while accompanying the Crusades, not as papal legate, but as preacher.

[T. C. O'BRIEN]

ROBERT COWTON (COTTON, CONTON; fl. *c.*1300), English Franciscan theologian. He lived in the Franciscan friary at Oxford in 1300; studied theology there under Philip of Bridlington and Adam of Howden, and was incepted at the Univ. of Oxford *c.*1313. He was a disciple and successor of Scotus as lecturer on the *Sentences* at Oxford. R. wrote a very popular commentary on the *Sentences* which has been shown to have been strongly influenced by the Master. Greatly attached to Scotus' philosophy, R. wrote a strong criticism of Henry of Ghent. The Dominican Thomas Sutton devoted three books of his questions on the *Sentences*, defending St. Thomas against Cowton. There is an abbreviated edition of R.'s commentary extant (1400), but the original remains unedited. BIBLIOGRAPHY: A. Emmen, LTK 8:1337–38.

[J. J. SMITH]

ROBERT DE CRICHLADE (Cricklade; also called Canutus; d. *c.*1174), English Augustinian Canon, prior of St. Frideswide's, Oxford (1141). He wrote a life of Becket, known through the anonymous Icelandic *Thómas Saga*. His *Flores*, an abridgment of Pliny's *Natural History*, was dedicated to Henry III. R. knew Hebrew and wrote scriptural commentaries. BIBLIOGRAPHY: Emden Ox 1:513–514.

ROBERT OF FLAMBOROUGH (betw. 1135 and 1181–betw. 1219 and 1233), canon penitentiary at the abbey of St. Victor, Paris. He was author of a *Liber poenitentialis*, which became a prototype for subsequent manuals of moral theology. This book of instructions for confessors was based on canonically obsolete penitential discipline and resulted in excessive legalism in moral guidance. BIBLIOGRAPHY: F. Firth, "*Poenitentiale* of Robert of Flamborough," *Traditio* 16 (1960) 541–556; *idem*, NCE 12:530.

[J. E. WRIGLEY]

ROBERT OF GENEVA, see CLEMENT VII, ANTIPOPE.

ROBERT GROSSETESTE (*c.*1175–1253), English bp., scholar, and ecclesiastical reformer. One of the most learned men of the 13th cent., R. studied at Paris and Oxford where he later became chancellor. He had received many benefices but failing health forced him to renounce them (1232) and devote himself entirely to the Diocese of Lincoln. As a scholar, R. was committed to investigations from the original sources and thus commented on the Greek texts of the NT, translated Aristotle from the original, and edited many early Christian writings. In addition to his philosophical and theological works, R. had wide scientific and mathematical knowledge, which he substantiated by a strict experimental method. As an ecclesiastical administrator R. was zealous but perhaps overly rigoristic. He was a firm supporter of the English Franciscans but became involved in several controversies with local monasteries concerning parochial authority and administration. He severely criticized many practices of the Roman Curia, esp. the appointment of Italian prelates to wealthy English benefices, but did not (as many Reformation historians sought to establish) deny the doctrine of papal supremacy. BIBLIOGRAPHY: *Robert Grosseteste: Scholar and Bishop* (ed. D. A. Callus, 1955); F. F. Urquhart, CE 7:37–39.

[T. M. MCFADDEN]

ROBERT GUISCARD (1016–85), Norman conqueror of S Italy. He began his career, aided by his brothers, by helping the Lombards against the Byzantine Empire in S Italy. From 1052 to 1059 he systematically conquered S Italy and was then recognized by Nicholas II as Duke of Apulia, Calabria, and Sicily. He became a dubious helper of Gregory VII against Emperor Henry IV in 1084. He died in an expedition against the Byzantine Empire and was succeeded by his less competent son, Roger. BIBLIOGRAPHY: C. H. Haskins, *Normans in European History* (1915; repr. 1959).

[J. J. SMITH]

ROBERT HOLCOT (Holkot; d. 1349), English Dominican, exegete, preacher, and theologian. He studied and taught at both Oxford and Cambridge. He was under the patronage of Richard of Bury, bp. of Durham (d. 1345), whose *Philobiblion* he edited (Eng. tr. 1832 and 1861). The authenticity and dates of many of the 26 surviving writings attributed to R. are problematical. His commentaries on Sacred Scripture and a collection of *exempla, his Moralitates*, were held in high regard (see B. Smalley). As a theologian, H. professed himself a Thomist, but there were *Nominalist elements in his teaching. He rejected the power of reason to attain any knowledge of God's existence or attributes; set the logic of faith against the logic of reason; and emphasized the absolute power of God (*potentia Dei absoluta*) to the point of obliterating the need of grace. BIBLIOGRAPHY: Gilson HCP 500–502, 793–794; Glorieux L 2:258–261; Knowles ROE 2:80–82; B. Smalley, AFP 24 (1956) 9–97. *THOMAS BRADWARDINE.

[T. C. O'BRIEN]

ROBERT OF JUMIÈGES (d. *c.*1055), abp. of Canterbury. R., a Norman monk, was prior of St. Ouen, Rouen, and later abbot of the Benedictine abbey of Jumièges. During this period he became the friend of Edward (later to become Edward the Confessor), who was in exile in Normandy. Two years after Edward's accession to the throne, R. was appointed bp. of London (1044). He became Edward's leading adviser, head of the Norman party, and abp. of Canterbury (1051–52). Influential in the banishment of the Earl of Godwin (1051), R. was deposed upon the return to power of Godwin in 1052. Outlawed himself, R. returned to Jumièges where he directed the production of a missal which typifies the liturgy before 1066. BIBLIOGRAPHY: W. Hunt, DNB 16:1244–45; F. Cabrol, DACL 11.2:1451–52; A. Manser, LTK 8:1340.

[R. A. FOULK]

ROBERT KILWARDBY (*c.* 1200–79), abp. of Canterbury and later cardinal-bishop of Porto. A native of England, R. achieved some distinction as a lecturer in theology at Oxford and a master in logic and grammar at Paris. He joined the Dominican Order in the 1240s and was provincial of its English province (1261–72). R. was appointed abp. of Canterbury in 1272, the first member of a mendicant order to be advanced to a high post in the English Church. As abp. he carefully avoided politics, called frequent synods, was assiduous in visitating his diocese, insisted upon monastic discipline, and promoted charitable works among the poor. He is remembered for his condemnation of certain doctrines, among which was the teaching of St. Thomas Aquinas regarding the unicity of substantial form, which he conceived to be, in its implications, opposed to faith. His principal work, *De ortu scientiarum*, is preserved in MS in the Bibliothèque Nationale in Paris. BIBLIOGRAPHY: W. F. Hook, *Lives of the Archbishops of Canterbury* (v. 3, 1865); E. M. F. Sommer-Sickendorff, *Studies in the Life of Robert Kilwardby* (1937).

[J. T. HICKEY]

ROBERT OF MELUN (*c*. 1100–67), English scholastic at Melun, bp. of Hereford from 1163. At Paris he studied under both Abelard and Hugh of St. Victor before going to Melun, where John of Salisbury was one of his students. R.'s *Liber sententiarum* (1152–60) was important in the evolution of the medieval theological *summa*. The work reflected both the dialectical method of Abelard and the organization of the material of theology found in Hugh of St. Victor's *De sacramentis;* it is also a step towards conciseness and coherence in handling theological debate.

[T. C. O'BRIEN]

ROBERT OF MOLESME, ST. (*c*. 1027–1110), founder of the famous monastery at Cîteaux. While serving as prior at Molesme, R. and 21 other monks were permitted to secede and to organize a new monastery at Cîteaux based on the strict interpretation of the Benedictine rule. About 18 months later he was ordered to return to Molesme and assume the leadership of his original monastery. Cîteaux, however, continued to grow under Alberic, *Stephen Harding, and St. *Bernard. The Cistercian movement led a new wave of reform. BIBLIOGRAPHY: G. Battista, BiblSanct 11:238–245; Butler 2:189–191.

[V. BULLOUGH]

ROBERT OF NEWMINSTER, ST. (d. 1159), Cistercian abbot. A native of Yorkshire, R. was educated in Paris, became a secular priest, and later a Benedictine monk at Whitby. In 1132 he was one of a group of monks attempting to revive strict Benedictine observance and with them had part in the establishment of Fountains Abbey, which affiliated itself with the Cistercian reform. R. became founder and first abbot of Newminster (Northumberland). BIBLIOGRAPHY: Butler 2:496–497; M. A. Dimier, BiblSanct 11:245–247.

[L. J. LEKAI]

ROBERT OF ORFORD (De Colletorto; fl. late 13th cent.), English Dominican at Oxford, defender of Thomism against *Henry of Ghent, *Giles of Rome, and *William de la Mare.

[T. C. O'BRIEN]

ROBERT PULLEN (Pullus, Pollanus, Pulein; *c*. 1080–1146), scholastic, first English cardinal. From the period of his teaching at Oxford, beginning in 1133, R. left a *Sententiarum libri VIII*. He taught also at Paris *c*. 1142. He was called to Rome by Lucius II, who created him cardinal in **1444 or 1445**.

[T. C. O'BRIEN]

ROBERT OF REIMS (*fl*. early 12th cent.), monk, chronicler of the First *Crusade, probably identified with Robert of St. Remi. He visited the Holy Land at the beginning of the 12th cent. and on his return wrote a popular account, *Hierosolymitana expeditio*, which is primarily an enlargement of the *Anonymi gesta Francorum*.

[V. BULLOUGH]

ROBERT OF SOLETO, BL. (Robert of Salla; 1273–1341), Celestine monk received into the order by Peter of Morrone (later Pope Celestine V) in 1289. He became prior and then general procurator of his order, but refused Pope Celestine's offer to make him a cardinal (1294). He was revered for his spirit of penance, his devotion to meditation on the Sacred Passion, and his care of the sick and orphans. BIBLIOGRAPHY: F. da Mareto, BiblSanct 11:247–248.

[N. G. WOLF]

ROBERT DE SORBON (1201–74), theologian, preacher, and founder of the Sorbonne, theological college of the Univ. of Paris. Ordained *c*. 1226, R. became a canon at Cambrai (*c*. 1250) and taught at the Univ. of Paris from 1254 to his death, a period of intensive academic activity and religious discussion. Through the influence of the Comte d'Artois, he was appointed in 1258 to Notre Dame de Paris as chaplain to King Louis IX, who had encouraged and aided him in his project of founding a theological college for needy lay students, opened in 1257 and later known as the Sorbonne.

[M. B. MURPHY]

ROBERT STRATFORD (d. 1362), English ecclesiastic and administrator; bp. of Chichester from 1337. Educated at Oxford, where he became chancellor (1335), he held many church and state offices, including the chancellorship of England (1337–38; 1340). Honest but undistinguished, he owed his advancement to his brother John, in whose fortunes he shared.

[R. W. HAYS]

ROBERT OF TORIGNY (Robertus de Monte; d. 1186), Benedictine abbot and chronicler important for Anglo-French history. A member of the abbey of Bec (prior in 1154), he was later the most celebrated abbot of Mont-Saint-Michel, where he promoted discipline, learning, and physical expansion. He revised the *Gesta Normannorum ducum* of William of Jumièges, continued the chronicles of Sigebert of Gembloux, translated the works of Aristotle, and drew up an important catalog of the episcopal sees of France. BIBLIOGRAPHY: O. J. Blum, NCE 12:535–536.

[O. J. BLUM]

ROBERT WALDBY OF YORK (d. 1398), Augustinian friar, bp. of Aire in Aquitaine (1386); abp. of Dublin (1390–95); bp. of Chichester (1395–96); abp. of York (1396–98); chancellor of Ireland in 1392. He served the Black Prince and Richard II. R. was active in the condemnation of Wycliffe and was buried in Westminster Abbey. BIBLIOGRAPHY: Emden Ox 3:1959.

[C. D. ROSS]

ROBERT OF WINCHELSEA (d. 1313), English ecclesiastic and statesman; abp. of Canterbury from 1294. After serving as rector at the Univ. of Paris (1263), he received a doctorate in theology at Oxford and became chancellor there. As abp., he upheld Boniface VIII's bull *Clericis laicos* and resisted Edwards I's encroachments, opposing Edward's treasurer, Walter Langton. At Edward's behest, Clement V suspended R. (1305), but he resumed his see on Edward II's accession (1307). Against Edward II, he favored Gaveston's banishment (1308) and dominated the lords ordainers (1310–13). Ascetic, generous, able, and energetic despite ill-health, R. upheld his prerogatives against ecclesiastical as well as royal encroachment.

[R. W. HAYS]

ROBERT, ANDRÉ (1883–1955), OT scholar. R. taught at the seminary in Issy-les-Mouleneaux and at the Institut Catholique in Paris. In addition to publishing numerous articles on the OT, R. was director of the *Supplément au dictionnaire de la Bible,* associate editor of the *Bible de Jerusalem* and the *Initiation biblique*.

[T. M. MCFADDEN]

ROBERTS, JOHN, ST. (1576–1610), English martyr. A Welsh Protestant, R. became a Catholic in Paris in 1598. He was ordained a Benedictine in Spain in 1602 and returned to England. In 1603 he was arrested and exiled. Returning the same year he labored on the English mission for 7 years, was arrested four times and banished twice. In 1610 he was brought to trial in London, condemned and executed at Tyburn. He was canonized in 1970.

[J. R. AHERNE]

ROBERTS, ORAL (1918–   ), evangelist and healer. Born in Pontococ Co., Okla., R. was for many years an ordained minister of the Pentecostal Holiness Church; in 1968 he received Methodist ordination. He is second in fame and influence as an evangelist only to Billy *Graham. His evangelistic campaigns, which began in 1947 in Tulsa, Okla., have become worldwide. The organizational center is the Oral Roberts Evangelistic Association, Tulsa, where Oral Roberts Univ. was established with the goal of sending into his crusades 1,000 trained ministers each year. R. preaches the essential message of *Pentecostalism: *baptism with the Holy Spirit, *glossolalia, and *divine healing. He is most popularly known as a healer, and many cures are claimed during each crusade.

[T. C. O'BRIEN]

ROBERTS, THOMAS D'ESTERRE (1893–1976), Jesuit archbishop. Known as the "rogue bishop" for his nonconformist views on contraception, nuclear war, and Catholic marriage laws, R. was abp. of Bombay, India, from 1937 to 1950. He traveled and lectured widely, often in support of such causes as ban-the-bomb.

[M. A. MCFADDEN]

ROBERTSON, JAMES (1839–1902), Canadian Presbyterian ecclesiastic. R. was born in Scotland, but emigrated to Canada in 1855. He studied at the Univ. of Toronto, Princeton, and Union Theological Seminary. He was ordained a minister of the Presbyterian Church in Canada, became a highly effective superintendent of the Presbyterian missions in W Canada (1881), and moderator of the Presbyterian Church in Canada (1895). A lecture series in his honor is given each year in the theologates of the United Church of Canada. BIBLIOGRAPHY: J. T. McNeill, *Presbyterian Church in Canada, 1875–1925* (1925).

[T. M. MCFADDEN]

ROBESPIERRE, MAXIMILIEN FRANÇOIS DE (1758–1794), leader in the French Revolution. Having acquired a reputation as a champion of the people in his native Arras, R. was elected to the Estates General and National Assembly (1789–91). Through his newspaper, *Défenseur de la constitution,* and his Jacobin party contacts he won election to the Convention in 1792. He dominated the Committee of Public Safety during the Reign of Terror. R.'s intellectual indebtedness to J. J. *Rousseau manifested itself in his conduct. He denounced anti-Christan radicals, aimed to establish the reign of natural virtue, and persuaded the government to proclaim the deistic cult of the Supreme Being, whose festival in Paris (8 June 1794) he organized. This cult ended with his execution on July 10. BIBLIOGRAPHY: J. M. Thompson, *Robespierre* (2 v., 1935).

[R. H. SCHMANDT]

ROBINSON, EDWARD (1794–1863), biblical scholar and Palestinian geographer. R. taught Scripture at Andover Seminary, Mass., and Union Theological Seminary, New York. He traveled in the Holy Land (1837–39), fixing more Palestinian archeological sites than had been discovered since Eusebius. His findings were published in the highly significant *Biblical Researches in Palestine, Mount Sinai, and Arabia Petraea* (1841; rev. ed., 1856). BIBLIOGRAPHY: JBL 58 (1939) 355–387.

[T. M. MCFADDEN]

ROBINSON, HENRY WHEELER (1872–1945), OT scholar. R. was educated in Edinburgh and Mansfield College, Oxford. He was a tutor at Rawdon Baptist College (1906–20), where he established his reputation as an OT scholar. In 1920, he was appointed principal of Regent's Park College and was mainly responsible for moving the college, in spite of the hesitation of his fellow Baptists, from London to Oxford. Among his major works are

Deuteronomy and Joshua (1907); *Christian Doctrine of Man* (1911); *Religious Ideas of the Old Testament* (1913); and *Christian Experience of the Holy Spirit* (1928).

[T. M. MCFADDEN]

ROBINSON, JOHN (1576?–1625), pastor of the Pilgrim fathers. Born in England, probably a student at Cambridge, R. became a minister and early separated from the established Church to join a small band of Congregationalists. In 1608, with some members of the separatist group, R. migrated to Amsterdam; they removed to Leyden a year later. R. wrote a number of pamphlets from 1610 to 1624, largely controversial but showing him to be a man of some culture. After 3 years in preparation, a plan, which included a declaration of fealty to the British crown and the Anglican bps., was drawn up to establish a colony along the Hudson River for members of the small congregation. Two vessels started out but only the *Mayflower* finally made the voyage, leaving Leyden on July 22, 1620. R. remained behind but was acknowledged as pastor of the Pilgrims who landed at Plymouth Rock, on Nov. 11, 1620. In his last years at Leyden R. published a volume of essays, *Observations Divine and Morall, . . .* (1625).

[J. R. AHERNE]

ROBINSON, JOSEPH ARMITAGE (1858–1933), early church scholar, dean of Westminster Abbey and Wells Cathedral. R. was a fellow at Christ's College, Cambridge (1881–99). His chief scholarly interest was in NT and early patristic thought, and he began and edited a series at Cambridge called *Texts and Studies*. He edited the *Passion of Perpetua* and Origen's *Philocalia* for that series. He became dean of Westminster in 1902 and of Wells Cathedral in 1911. He did much to restore the cathedral of Wells and wrote a history of the Saxon bps. of that see.

[T. M. MCFADDEN]

ROBINSON, PASCHAL (Charles; 1870–1948), papal diplomat, scholar. Born in Ireland, he came to the U.S., became a journalist, and was associate editor of the *North American Review* from 1892 to 1895. Entering the Franciscan Order in New York State, he was ordained in 1901. Called to Europe to take part in the work of the Franciscan institute of historical research at Quaracchi, near Florence, Italy, he became associate editor of *Archivum Franciscanum historicum* in 1907. From 1913 to 1919 R. was professor of medieval history at The Catholic Univ. of America. He served on the American delegation to the Paris Peace Conference in 1919. He was sent by the Holy See as apostolic visitor to Palestine (1920–1921) and to the Latin and Uniate Churches in Palestine, Transjordan, and Cyprus (1925–1928). Created a titular abp. in 1927, R. served as apostolic delegate to Malta and from 1930 until his death as the first papal nuncio to Ireland since the time of Cromwell. His writings included numerous journal articles, and *The Writings of St. Francis of Assisi* (1906) and *A Short Introduction to Franciscan Literature* (1907).

[J. R. AHERNE]

ROBOAM (REHOBOAM)—the first spelling is from the LXX, the second from the Hebrew—king of Judah from *c.*922 to 915 B.C., son and successor of Solomon. His rule is described in 1 Kg 11.43–14.31; 1 Chr 3.10; and 2 Chr 9.31–12.16. On the advice of youthful counselors, he began his rule with the threat to be more severe than Solomon. This led to the secession of all the tribes except Judah and Benjamin and to the formation of the kingdoms of Judah (South) and Israel (North). After the ambassador he sent to the northern tribes was killed, he received a divine command to make no further attempts to unite the two kingdoms (1 Kg 12.17–24). His reign was marked by: an initial influx of priests and levites from the North; his personal sinfulness which was divinely punished by a plundering invasion by Shishak of Egypt; and a fortifying of the southern boundaries of Judah. BIBLIOGRAPHY: J. Gray, *I and II Kings, a Commentary* (1963); M. Noth, *History of Israel* (tr. S. Godman, 1958).

[C. J. LYNCH]

ROBOT, ISIDORE (1837–87), missionary, bishop. A French Benedictine, R. was ordained in 1862. At the invitation of Abp. Perché of New Orleans he volunteered for the missions, coming to New Orleans in 1871. He founded a Benedictine monastery of primitive observance at Sacred Heart, Oklahoma. Under his direction, the Benedictines became the first resident priests of the Indian Territory, ministering to the Potawatomi and Chocktaw Indians. In 1876 R. became prefect of the newly established prefecture of Indian Territory. When the monastery was raised to abbatial status in 1877, R. became first abbot. He was a vigorous administrator of the territory, building schools and training centers for the Indians. As a member of the Third Plenary Council of Baltimore in 1884, he pleaded for the cause of Indian missions. He retired in 1886.

[J. R. AHERNE]

ROBUSTI, JACOPO, see TINTORETTO.

ROCAFUERTE, VICENTE (1783–1847), Ecuadoran revolutionary and politician. After a varied experience in diplomatic missions, R. became involved in the domestic political struggle in Ecuador and in 1835 became president of the republic. He was an upright man, liberal in his views, and an excellent administrator. He was, however, dictatorial in his methods and assumed a control over ecclesiastical as well as civil matters. BIBLIOGRAPHY: J. M. Velasco Ibarra, *Teorías políticas de Rocafuerte* (1921).

[P. DAMBORIENA]

ROCCA, ANGELO (1545–1620), Italian Augustinian, titular bp. from 1605, humanist who wrote numerous historical, liturgical, and ascetical works. As editor of the Vatican Press, he edited and published the Vulgate, patristic works, and conciliar documents. He later edited works by fellow Augustinians as well as two volumes on Augustine's teaching. His private book collection became the core of the Biblioteca Angelica, Rome's first public library, named for him.

[R. J. LITZ]

ROCCO DA CESINALE (1830–1900), Italian Capuchin, apostolic delegate to Santo Domingo, Haiti, and Venezuela (1874–83); abp. of Otranto, then (1887) of Chieti, both in Italy. Before his mission assignment R. was procurator at Rome for the missions of his order and also served as a theologian at Vatican Council I. In Santo Domingo (1877) he discovered and authenticated the remains of Christopher Columbus in the cathedral there. He left an important history of Capuchin missions, his *Storia delle missioni* (v. 1 1867; v. 2–3 1872–73); it covers the period up to 1700.

[T. C. O'BRIEN]

ROCH, ST. (c.1350–c.78), miracle worker. Little is known of R.'s life except that he was born in Montpellier, France; that his father seems to have been a wealthy merchant, and that as a young man he entered upon a life of pilgrimage and performance of charitable works. His reputation as a miracle worker sprang from his having cured a brother of Pope Urban V. His cult first appeared in Montpellier (1410) and spread to Italy where the ending of a plague (1439) was attributed to his intercession. Most of the later writings dealing with his life and career were based on popular legends and are of doubtful historical value. BIBLIOGRAPHY: Butler 3:338; A. Vauchez, BiblSanct 11:264–273.

[J. MULDOON]

ROCHAMBEAU, COMTE DE (JEAN BAPTISTE DONATIEN DE VIMEUR, 1725–1807), commander of French forces during the American Revolution. Though his fame rested on the exploits of a military commander, R. was a highly educated man of thought whose knowledge of men, diplomacy, and gentlemanly arts served him as well as his military skill. Educated in France by the celebrated Père Houbigant and later by the Jesuits at Blois, he was studying for the priesthood, but the death of his older brother recalled him to secular life. In Paris he met some of the brilliant minds of the century. He served with distinction in the War of the Austrian Succession. After a period of retirement to his estate, he returned to the wars and through skill and ability to handle troops rose to the rank of brigadier-general. When France decided to aid the American revolutionaries, R. was placed in command and came to Rhode Island in 1780. Despite the imprudent insistence of Lafayette, R. resisted the suggestion that his force move against New York, recognizing that a naval force would also be needed. In 1781 Admiral de Grasse brought a French fleet to the West Indies to aid the Americans. R. persuaded Washington to avoid New York and march against Cornwallis in Virginia. The secret movement of the French and American forces bypassing New York and emerging in Virginia, to-

gether with the movement of de Grasse's fleet to Chesapeake Bay bringing 4,000 troops to join Lafayette, was a brilliant maneuver. Harassed by Lafayette, attacked by Washington and R. and the French fleet, Cornwallis at Yorktown was forced to surrender on October 19, 1781, effectively ending the War of the Revolution. R. returned to France, and in 1791 was named a marshall of France. He barely escaped the guillotine in the Reign of Terror. His last days were spent at his chateau.

[J. R. AHERNE]

ROCHET, a knee-length, white linen lace garment of prelates worn under outer vestments. It seems to have developed during the Middle Ages from a kind of coat worn for protection against the cold.

[N. KOLLAR]

ROCK, DANIEL (1799–1871), Engish RC ecclesiologist. R., ordained in 1824, is best known as a scholarly defender of the Church. His chief works are *The Church of Our Fathers* (1849–53; pub. in 4 v. in 1903–04 with introductory life of R.), in which he examines medieval English ritual, and *Hierurgia, or the Holy Sacrifice of the Mass* (2 v., 1833). He was one of the first canons of Southwark Cathedral.

[T. M. MCFADDEN]

ROCK, a name of God, dating from the pre-Mosaic era of biblical tradition, found often in the Psalms, and used down to the present day in both Jewish and Christian worship. The Rock (Zur) was part of the imagery associated with El Shaddai, God the Almighty, the title for God used by the Patriarchs. This sacred name evoked imagery similar to that associated with mountain deities and the great storm god known as Baal among Canaanites. Yahweh's name remained linked with a sacred mountain, so that he could be called the Rock who begot Israel at Sinai in the desert (Dt 32.18); and those who went on joyous pilgrimage to the Lord's hill in Jerusalem (Zion) went to be gladdened by the Rock of Israel (Is 30.29). Yahweh is the Rock of our salvation (Ps 95.1); my Rock where I find safety (Ps 18.2). In the blessing of Joseph (Gen 49.24), Joseph's enemies are shattered by God the Almighty, the God of the fathers, whose name is paralleled with the titles: the Eternal, the Strong One of Jacob, and the Shepherd Rock of Israel. In the Song of Moses (Dt 32), Jacob (called also Jeshurun) is chided for growing fat and forsaking God, dishonoring the Rock of his salvation (v. 15); no enemy could have hurt Jacob had not his Rock sold him to his enemies in punishment, for the enemy have no Rock like Israel's (vv. 30–31). Yahweh is an everlasting Rock (Is 26.4) and therefore to be trusted as a stable refuge. A rabbinic *haggadah elaborated on this imagery and represented God as the Rock who followed the people during their wilderness wanderings. This would shed some light on Paul's statement that the Rock that accompanied Israel was Christ (I Cor 10.4).

[E. J. DILLON]

ROCK-CUT TEMPLES, structures formed by cutting directly into a mass of rock: Temple of Abu Simbel, Egypt with 4 colossal seated gods over 65 feet high; Indian chaitya halls at Kārli, rock-cut caves in Ajantā with sculptured façades, Chinese Buddhist caves at Yün-Kang and Lungmén, Viharas (monasteries) were cut into rock, the rock treated as a façade. Egyptian tombs of the 11th and 12th dynasties, the ancient Persian tomb of Darius at Naqsh-i-Rustam and the Nabataean tombs of Petra (c.750) are also rock cut forms.

[M. J. DALY]

ROD, DIVINING, see DIVINING ROD.

RODAT, ÉMILIE DE, ST. (1787–1852), educator, foundress of the Sisters of the *Holy Family of Villefranche. R. was concerned with the needs of the poor early in her life. After trying her vocation at various religious congregations, she opened a school for poor girls in Villefranche and eventually founded, with Abbé Antoine Marty, a congregation of nuns devoted to educational and charitable work among the poor; they pronounced their vows in 1820. R. as first superior guided the community's rapid growth. Her own sanctification included severe experiences of desolation. She was canonized in 1950. BIBLIOGRAPHY: G. Bernoville, *La Sainte de Rouergue: Émilie de Rodat* (1959).

[T. M. MCFADDEN]

RODIN, AUGUSTE (1840–1917), French sculptor, painter, and draftsman of supreme talent, first sculptor of genius after Michelangelo and Bernini; innovator who restored sculpture to its traditional eminence as a powerfully expressive medium through dramatization of surface and most powerful dispositions of bodily gesture. R.'s revolutionary *Man with a Broken Nose* (1864) was finally accepted by the Academy as *Portrait of a Roman*. R. cast the *Age of Bronze* (1877), a work of power equal to that of Michelangelo and Donatello. After examining French Gothic cathedrals (1877) R. executed *John the Baptist* (1880) and in the same year, inspired by Ghiberti's *Gates of Paradise,* began his famous *Gates of Hell,* producing the *Thinker* (reminiscent of Michelangelo's Jeremiah and Lorenzo de' Medici), *Crouching Woman,* and many other renowned forms later recast as single statues. The eloquent, heroically tragic *Burghers of Calais* (1886) was followed by portrait busts of *Beaudelaire* (1898) and the provocative *Balzac* (1892–97), a dramatic interpretation of R.'s technique of agitated, "molten" surface, expressing the dilemma of man in the modern world. A rebel in society and in art, R. exerted an extraordinary force upon contemporary sculpture. BIBLIOGRAPHY: A. E. Elsen, *Rodin* (1963).

[M. J. DALY]

RODOLPHUS OF GLABER (c.985–c.1047), Cluniac *oblate at St. Germaine-d'Auxerre, chronicler—

Historiarum liber quinque—and biographer of the abbot of St. Germain, St. William. R.'s work provides not otherwise extant evidence on the details and spirit of the Cluniac reform.

RODRIGUES, FERREIRA, ALEXANDRE (1756–1815), Brazilian naturalist. He studied divinity at Bahia, law at Coimbra, but did not proceed to take major orders. He led an expedition to N Brazil, which lasted 10 years, and explored the natural and human resources of Amazonia.

[H. JACK]

RODRÍGUEZ, ALFONSO (1538–1616), Spanish Jesuit, writer in ascetical theology. A Jesuit from 1557, after studies at Salamanca, R. filled the post of novice master for most of his life. The work for which he is renowned collects the spiritual conferences given to novices on acquiring and practicing the virtues: *Ejercicio de perfección* (1609; Eng. tr., J. Rickaby, *Practice of Perfection and Christian Virtues,* 3 v., 1929).

[T. C. O'BRIEN]

RODRÍGUEZ, CAYETANO JOSÉ (1761–1823), Franciscan Argentine patriot, poet, leader against the English occupation of Buenos Aires (1806–07) and in the struggle for Argentina's independence. As a member of the first national assembly (1812), R. was an active opponent of anti-Catholic and Masonic influences in the government, and to aid in this struggle he founded two newspapers, *El centinela,* and *El oficial del Día.* BIBLIOGRAPHY: V. O. Cutolo, NCE 12:548.

[P. K. MEAGHER]

RODRÍGUEZ, LORENZO (1704–74), Spanish-Mexican designer and architect. Andalusian 18th-cent. design and Mexican (1730) formed his style. From 1740 R., the leading Mexican architect, popularized the *estípite* (a mannerist columnar form introduced by Balbás) and a Mexican retable façade of widespread influence. Many works are being studied because of conflicting stylistic evidences in attributions.

[M. J. DALY]

RODRÍGUEZ JUÁREZ, JUAN (1675–1728), Mexican painter, with his brother Nicolás a pupil of his father Antonio. One of the major baroque painters in Mexico City, R. painted the *Adoration of the Kings* and an *Assumption* in the cathedral, Mexico City.

[M. J. DALY]

RODRÍGUEZ DE MENDOZA, TORIBIO (1750–1825), Peruvian priest and educator. A doctor in theology at the Universidad de San Marcos, Lima, in 1770, he became in 1771 professor of theology and philosophy at the Collegio Mayor de S. Carlos, Lima. Ordained in 1778, he worked first in pastoral ministry among the Indians at Marcaval. In 1785 he was named vice-rector and a year later rector of the Convictorio de San Carlos in Lima. He held office for 30 years and made the institution an effective educational center.

[T. C. O'BRIEN]

RODRIGUEZ TÇUZU, JOÃO (1562–1633), Portuguese Jesuit missionary in Japan and China from 1613; author and interpreter at the Japanese court. He was considered the highest European authority on Japanese language and culture in the 16th and 17th centuries. He wrote a history of the Church of Japan. His philological investigations of the ancient Chinese name for God laid the groundwork for the subsequent *Chinese rites controversy. He also produced a Portuguese-Japanese dictionary and grammar.

[R. J. LITZ]

RODRÍGUEZ ZORRILLA, JOSÉ SANTIAGO (1775–1832), Chilean bp. and political figure. R. taught at the Univ. of San Felipe and was twice its rector. He refused to recognize the junta of independence and to endorse certain passages of the constitution of 1812. He became bp. during the Spanish restoration but was exiled by the patriots in 1821. He regained his see in the following year, but it was taken over by the government in 1825. R. was deprived of his income and was obliged to take refuge in Spain. BIBLIOGRAPHY: C. Silva Cotapos, *Don José Santiago Rodriguez Zorrilla* (1915).

[P. DAMBORIENA]

ROE, ALBAN ST. (1583–1642), English martyr. An English Protestant, R. became a convert to Catholicism, was admitted to the English College at Douai in 1608. Dismissed for insubordination, he applied to the Benedictines at Dieulouard, was accepted and ordained in 1615. R. went on the English mission, was arrested, and imprisoned in 1618. After 5 years in prison he was banished. Returning from France a second time he was imprisoned. In 1642 he was condemned to death and executed at Tyburn. R. was beatified in 1929 and canonized in 1970.

[J. R. AHERNE]

ROEMER, THEODORE (1889–1953), educator, historian. A native of Wisconsin and ordained in the Capuchin Order in 1913, R. taught at St. Lawrence College, Wis., for most of his career. His specialty in historical research and writing was the field of mission-aid. Among works in this area are *The Ludwig–Missionsverein and the Church in the United States* (1838–1918) and *Ten Decades of Alms* (1942). For seminaries he published *The Catholic Church in the United States* (1950), a textbook for church history. R. was prominent in the fields of Franciscan education and Franciscan history.

[J. R. AHERNE]

ROGATION DAYS, in the Roman rite, special days of penitential prayer like the ember days; formerly called the "Litanies" because the Litany of the Saints was sung during the processions central to the observance. The "Major Litany" (so called since the time of St. Gregory the Great) was on the feast of St. Mark (25 April); those in procession prayed for the protection of the growing crops and supplanted a similar pagan rite at Rome. The "Minor Litanies" on the 3 days preceding Ascension Thursday were begun by the bp. of Vienne, France, c.470 to pray that the earthquake that had devastated the city would not recur; this custom spread throughout France and in the 9th cent. to Rome. These dates are no longer observed universally. Since the 1969 reform of the Roman calendar, days of thanksgiving and of petition (esp. for the productivity of the earth and for human labor) are to be established by national episcopal conferences. In the U.S. these presently vary according to diocese.

[J. DALLEN]

ROGATION OF NINEVEH, also called Lent of the Ninevites, the fast observed in all Syrian churches on the first 3 days of the 3d week before the Great Lent.

[G. T. DENNIS]

ROGATISTS, members of an obscure and conservative sect of *Donatists founded by Rogatus, bp. of Cartenna in Mauretania Caesariensis c.365. He and nine colleagues broke away from the main body of Donatists and established a community based on the principle of nonviolence and specifically opposed to the drunken orgies and cruelty of the *Circumcellions. BIBLIOGRAPHY: Augustine, *Ep.* 93.11, 21, 49; W. H. C. Frend, *Donatist Church* (1952), 197–199.

[M. J. COSTELLOE]

ROGER BACON (c.1220–c.1292), English Franciscan philosopher and scientist, called "Doctor Admirabilis." R. was well educated in the classics at Oxford and Paris and taught in the arts faculties of both. His interests appear to have been those of a typical university master until the mid-1240s when he began to devote his complete attention to scientific investigation and experiment, spending great sums in acquiring books and apparatus in an effort to become wholly versed in the technical data of his day. Under the influence of the new disciplines appearing at Oxford such as optics, astronomy, and alchemy, he had ambitious plans for using science in the service of religion. He joined the Franciscans c.1252 and though he was permitted to carry on his researches, he was openly scornful of the academic methods of his time, and this attitude eventually brought upon him the severe censure of his superiors. About 1266, he secretly appealed to Pope Clement IV, proposing a vast scheme for the reform of Christian education through the use of science, and encouraged by some evidence of papal interest, R. undertook the composition of his *Opus majus, Opus minus,* and *Opus tertium,* outlining his plans for probing nature through the experimental method and the use of languages and mathematics. However, the Pope died in November 1268, thus ending R.'s projected enterprise.

R.'s uniqueness lies not so much in his contribution to the sum of knowledge as in his foresight and insight into the practical uses of science, and his insistence upon research and experiment to that end. His writings represent an encyclopedia of medieval learning, esp. his *Communia naturalium, Communia mathematica* (both 1268), and *Compendium philosophiae* (1272).

In philosophy, R. followed Aristotle, whom he understood, however, with the help of Neoplatonist interpretation. Many of his main ideas are found in *Opus majus,* as for instance: All wisdom flows from God through three channels of divine revelation—Scripture, nature, and the interior illumination of the soul. These three may be deciphered only through an understanding of languages, a thorough grasp of mathematics, and the practice of the moral and spiritual disciplines. But all knowledge is verified by experimental science which involves the application of the theoretical to the practical needs of human material existence, and likewise to the moral and spiritual aspects of man's life, leading to eternal beatitude. Crowning the entire edifice of R.'s thought is the emphasis he places upon the importance of moral philosophy as guiding and directing the uses of scientific knowledge once acquired.

Between 1277 and 1279, R. was condemned to prison by his superiors, probably because of his bitter attacks upon theologians and scholars. He is thought to have been released before his death. BIBLIOGRAPHY: A. G. Little, *Roger Bacon Commemoration Essays* (full bibliog. of R.'s works; 1914); S. Easton, *Roger Bacon and His Search for a Universal Science* (1952); T. Crowley, *Roger Bacon: The Problem of the Soul in His Philosophical Commentaries* (1950).

[J. T. HICKEY]

ROGER OF ÉLAN, BL. (d. after 1162), Cistercian abbot. R., a native of England, joined the Cistercians at Loroy (France); he became the founder (1148) and first abbot of Élan (Champagne). His vita, probably written by one of his monks (AS Jan. 1:182–185), is unreliable. BIBLIOGRAPHY: P. Rouillard, BiblSanct 11:493–494.

[L. J. LEKAI]

ROGER LE FORT, BL. (d. 1367 or 1368), bp. and confessor. He was professor of canon and civil law at Orléans; became bp. of Orléans (1321) and then of Limoges (1343); established a hospital at Bourges and founded the Celestine priory at Ternes. His austerity of life, dedication to the apostolate, and personal charity caused him to be venerated during his life; his tomb became a popular place for pilgrimage. BIBLIOGRAPHY: AS March, 1:119–122; P. Rouillard, BiblSanct 11:494.

[J. J. SMITH]

ROGER (RUGERUS) VON HELMARSHAUSEN (fl. *c.*1100), German goldsmith at one time identified with Theophilus Presbyter, author of *De diversis artibus.* A brother in the Benedictine abbey at Helmarshausen, and master of the portable altar in the cathedral treasury,

Paderborn, R. worked in gold and bronze in the Byzantine style of the Lower Rhine.

[M. J. DALY]

ROGER OF HOVEDEN (Howden; d. after 1201), English chronicler. Yorkshireman, priest, and king's clerk, he represented Henry II in Scotland (1174) and acted as itinerant justice of the forest for him and for Richard I, whose Crusade, the Third, he also joined (1191). He wrote a chronicle covering the period 649–1201 (ed. W. Stubbs, 4 v., 1868–71); and another, formerly attributed to Benedict of Peterborough (ed. W. Stubbs, 2 v., 1867).

[R. W. HAYS]

ROGER MARSTON (*c.*1245–*c.*1303), English Franciscan theologian. Present at the Paris disputation of *c.*1270 between St. Thomas Aquinas and John Peckham, he became a relentless opponent of Thomist departures from traditional Augustinianism. His own writings are also important in the development of Scotism.

[T. C. O'BRIEN]

ROGER OF NOTTINGHAM (*fl.* 1343–58), Franciscan theologian and graduate of Oxford. His only extant works are an *Insolubilia* and an *Introitus* to the *Sentences.* He seems to have been a faithful follower of the older Franciscan tradition in theology. BIBLIOGRAPHY: Emden Ox 2:1377; J. A. Weisheipl, NCE 12:554–555.

[J. A. WEISHEIPL]

ROGER DE PONT L'ÉVÊQUE (d. 1181), abp. of York (1154), opponent of *Becket. He pressed the rights of his primacy over Scotland and was suspended for crowning the young Henry (1170), but was absolved from blame in Becket's death. BIBLIOGRAPHY: D. Knowles, *Episcopal Colleagues of Archbishop Thomas Becket* (1951).

[F. D. BLACKLEY]

ROGER OF SALISBURY (d. 1139), chancellor of England (1101–02), and shortly after, bp. of Salisbury, and justiciar (1102–39). A priest of Caen, he attracted the attention of Henry I by his astute financial administration. He remodeled Salisbury cathedral and built many castles. As chief minister, he was probably regent during royal absences abroad (1110–35). He reorganized the English exchequer, pledged to support Matilda (1126), backed Stephen (1135), and obtained the chancellorship for his son, Roger le Poer, and the treasurership for his nephew, Nigel. Too powerful, he was arrested and dismissed by King Stephen (1139). BIBLIOGRAPHY: F. West, *Justiciarship in England* (1966).

[F. D. BLACKLEY]

ROGER I OF SICILY (1031–1101), Great Count of Sicily and Calabria from 1072. Youngest son of the Norman Tancred, with his brother Robert Guiscard he systematically brought about the overthrow of the Muslims and Byzantine

3072   ROGER OF SWYNESHED

elements in Sicily and granted religious tolerance to both groups. His conquest and rule of Sicily played a decisive part in the decline of the Saracens in the Western Mediterranean. **Roger II** (1093–1154), King of Sicily and successor of Roger I. He conquered Apulia and Salerno and was crowned King of Sicily by the antipope Anacletus II. Later he won the recognition of Innocent II. He gave his realm a firm, just government and is sometimes called the first modern ruler.

[M. A. WINKELMANN]

ROGER OF SWYNESHED (d. 1365), English Benedictine logician and natural philosopher, master of theology presumably from Oxford. He wrote treatises on logic, *De obligationibus et insolubilibus,* used as textbooks at some Continental universities, and a treatise on physics, *De motibus naturalibus,* in part concerned with "the possible proportions of velocities in moving bodies," not yet fully appreciated. BIBLIOGRAPHY: J. A. Weisheipl, "R. Swyneshed, O. S.B., Logician," in *Oxford Studies Presented to Daniel Callus* (1964) 231–252.

[F. D. BLACKLEY]

ROGER OF TODI, BL. (d. 1237), Franciscan. In 1216 he was received into the Order by Francis himself, who characterized him as an exemplar of charity (*Speculum perfectionis,* ch. 85). He exercised the apostolate in Spain and Italy, esp. at Rieti where he was director of the Convent of Poor Clares. Gregory IX, his friend, approved his cult for the city of Todi where he is buried. Sixteen miracles are ascribed to him by Thomas of Pavia in his *Dialogus.* His feast, approved by Benedict IV, is celebrated only by the Franciscans of the Province of Todi. BIBLIOGRAPHY: AS March 1:415–417; J. J. Smith, NCE 12:556.

[J. J. SMITH]

ROGER OF WENDOVER (d. 1236), English chronicler; Benedictine monk of St. Albans, and prior of the dependent house of Belvoir. His *Chronica sive Flores historiarum* is derived largely from other writers but is an original source for English history from 1201 to 1235, and a useful compilation of facts. BIBLIOGRAPHY: M. M. Chibnall, NCE 12:556, bibliog.

[R. W. HAYS]

ROGER OF WORCESTER (*c.*1133–79), English canonist, bp. of Worcester (1164–79). The grandson of Henry I, R. studied at Bristol and Paris. He was a friend of Abp. Thomas Becket, yet he managed to retain some favor with his cousin, Henry II. R. shared Becket's exile from 1167 but was absent from England when Becket was murdered (1170). As a judge-delegate his importance is seen in the decretal collections of the mid-1170s. Gerald of Wales considered him one of the outstanding and exemplary English prelates of the time, as did Pope Alexander III. BIBLIOGRAPHY: D. Knowles, *Episcopal Colleagues of Arch-*

bishop Thomas Becket (1951); C. Duggan, *Twelfth-Century Decretal Collections and Their Importance in English History* (1963).

[F. D. BLACKLEY]

ROGERS, JOHN (*c.*1500–55), first Protestant martyr of the Marian persecution. R. graduated at Pembroke Hall, Cambridge, and became chaplain to the English merchants at Antwerp. There he became the associate of William Tyndale, turned to Protestantism, and was married. Under the alias "Thomas Matthew" he prepared Matthew's Bible, and his valuable marginal notes constituted the first scriptural commentary in English. He returned to London, where his patron was Bp. Ridley, and to his credit he denounced the greed of the chief courtiers around Edward VI. Arrested in 1554 under Mary Tudor, he and other prisoners drew up a confession of faith that includes extreme Calvinistic doctrines. He endured ill-treatment with great cheerfulness; "there was never a little fellow," remarked Hooper, "that would better stick to a man than he." Before the faggots were kindled at Smithfield, he refused a pardon conditional on recantation. "He died," said Noailles, the ambassador of France, "in a manner as if he had been led to a wedding." BIBLIOGRAPHY: life by J. L. Chester (1861).

[T. GILBY]

ROGERS, MARY JOSEPH (1883–1955), foundress of the Maryknoll Sisters. A native of Massachusetts, R. began her career as a biology teacher at Smith College. Her interest in the missions brought her into contact with Fr. (later Bp.) James A. Walsh in Boston. She assisted him in early efforts to establish the Catholic Foreign Mission Society of America (Maryknoll) and was instrumental in acquiring the first headquarters property at Maryknoll, N.Y. In 1912 R. with five other women established the Maryknoll Sisters, a congregation she headed for 35 years. She saw a phenomenal growth in the new society, which by the 1950s had over 1,000 members and staffed more than 80 missions in Latin America and elsewhere. The genius conveyed to the community was a strictly American spirit. In 1954 the group was recognized by Rome as a congregation of pontifical right.

[J. R. AHERNE]

ROGIER VAN DER WEYDEN, see WEYDEN, ROGIER VAN DER.

ROGUE, PIERRE RENÉ, BL. (1758–96), martyr. R. was a Vincentian priest who taught at the seminary in Vannes. He refused to subscribe to the *Civil Constitution of the Clergy during the French Revolution and continued to exercise his priestly functions in Vannes. After his arrest, he carried out his spiritual ministry among his fellow-prisoners until he was guillotined. He was beatified in 1934.

[T. M. MCFADDEN]

ROHLFS, CHRISTIAN (1849–1938), German Expressionist painter and graphic artist, student and teacher at the Weimar Art School. Influenced by E. Munch, and criticized for modernist leanings, R. met E. Nolde (1906) in the medieval town of Soest where he began his woodcuts. Recipient of several honorary degrees, R. was denounced and expelled by the Nazis, 400 of his works disappearing. After a restrained impressionism and pointillism (1910) R. painted medieval towns with heavy dark lines and bright colors intermingled for vibration in an expressionist manner. His woodcuts are dramatic and forceful (*Death and a Child,* 1912–13). As R. requested a Barlach statue marks his grave. BIBLIOGRAPHY: M. L. Keiler, "Christian Rohlfs, Pioneer of German Expressionism," *College Art Journal* 18, 3 (1959).

[M. J. DALY]

ROHRBACHER, RENÉ FRANÇOIS (1789–1856), church historian. After ordination and several pastoral assignments, R. began (1826) an association with Hugues Félicité de *Lamennais that culminated in R.'s joining and becoming director of novices for the Congregation of St. Peter, a community of priests that Lamennais founded. R. also was a contributor to *L'Avenir.* Upon Lamennais's condemnation by Rome and his refusal to submit, R. split with him and began to teach church history at the seminary in Nancy. He wrote two principal works: *Catéchisme du sens commun* (1825), and the monumental *Histoire universelle de l'Église catholique* (28 v., 1842–49), in which R. proposed a progressive history of the Church and emphasized the contributions of the papacy. He was dismissed from the seminary in 1849 because of his anti-*Gallicanism and *ultramontanism. His works are not highly regarded. BIBLIOGRAPHY: L. Marchal, DTC 13:2767–74.

[T. M. MCFADDEN]

ROJAS, JOSÉ RAMÓN (1775–1839), Guatemalan Franciscan missionary. He became a Franciscan in 1794, was ordained in 1798, spent most of the years 1798–1820 in mission work in Costa Rica and Nicaragua. He established several stations that later became thriving centers of Christian life. During the independence movement he served as consultor to the abp. of Guatemala and the bp. of León. In this capacity he strongly opposed the attempts of civil authorities to assume control of the Church. He was once condemned to death and twice sent into exile. He took refuge in Peru in 1831 where his solicitude for the poor and apostolic zeal at Callao and Ica earned him the name Padre Guatemala. BIBLIOGRAPHY: E. D. Tovar y Ramírez, *El apóstol de Ica, fray José Ramón Rojas, el Padre Guatemala* (1943).

[P. DAMBORIENA]

ROLAND OF CREMONA (d. 1259), early Dominican master at the Univ. of Paris. He was a master in the arts faculty at Bologna when he became a Friar Preacher in 1219. In Paris he became a doctor in 1228, and in 1229, during a strike of the secular masters, the first friar to hold a chair of theology there. R. returned to Italy in 1233, was a preacher and inquisitor, and in his last years again taught at Bologna. He is important in the development of the Dominicans' devotion to sacred learning that provided the setting for the emergence of St. Thomas Aquinas. R.'s *Summa theologica* and a commentary on Job survive in MS form; they evidence R.'s encyclopedic turn of mind, familiarity with Aristotle exceptional at the time and with traditional theological authorities.

[T. C. O'BRIEN]

ROLANDO BANDINELLI, see ALEXANDER III, POPE.

ROLDUC, MONASTERY OF, former abbey of Canons Regular of St. Augustine in Rolduc, the Netherlands. It was founded in 1104 by Ailbert D'Antoing, who was its first abbot. In 1136 the abbey came under the protection of the counts of Limburg. It avoided suppression but was secularized in 1797. Known from medieval times for its school and extensive library, it was turned into a minor seminary in the mid-19th century. BIBLIOGRAPHY: A. F. Manning, LTK 6:350–351.

[M. A. MCFADDEN]

ROLENDIS, ST. (Rollandis; fl. 7th or 8th cent.), virgin. Details of R.'s life are unknown. A 13th-cent. (?) vita, which describes her as a daughter of the Lombard king Desiderius, relates how, to avoid marriage, R. fled to the convent of St. Ursula but died in Villers-Poterie, Belgium, before reaching Cologne. BIBLIOGRAPHY: M. De Somer, BiblSanct 11:306–307.

[M. F. MCCARTHY]

ROLEVINCK, WERNER (1425–1502), Carthusian theologian and historiographer. Very erudite, R. wrote more than 50 exegetical, ascetic, and theological works, many still unpublished. His best-known work, *Fasciculus temporum* (1472), a universal history, went through many editions. R. died at Cologne while assisting others during a plague. BIBLIOGRAPHY: S. Autore, DTC 13.2.2763–66.

[F. D. LAZENBY]

ROLL AND CODEX, book formats used prior to the development of printed books. The roll (*scroll) was made from sheets of papyrus, leather, or parchment joined together in a strip *c.* 30 feet long for a standard book. Rolled for storage, it was unrolled a little at a time for reading (Jer 36.2, 23). The codex, which had replaced the scroll by the 3d cent. A.D. and is the form in which the most important existing biblical MSS were made, consists of several leaves laid on one another.

[T. EARLY]

ROLLAND, ROMAIN (1866–1944), French writer, music historian, and humanitarian socialist. Born a

Catholic, R. experienced a spiritual crisis (1883–87), losing his faith but remaining a theist whose religious views were expressed in an unpublished *Credo quia verum* (1887). His spiritual outlook was a blend of Spinoza's pantheism, Tolstoy's mystical humanitarianism, Péguy's mystique of socialism, French Republican idealism, and a Romantic utopianism crystallized in a fervor for justice. He fought for Dreyfus, allied himself with the working class's struggle, and advocated Franco-German solidarity. A pacifist, he gained renown during World War I through his appeals for peace, like *Au-Dessus de la mêlée* (1915), issued from Switzerland, where he had gone at the outset of hostilities. With his faith in the moral power of Christianity and the traditional socialist parties weakened by the war, R. sought new idealisms in messianic communism and Indian religious thought. In *Par la Révolution, la paix* (1935) and *Comment empêcher la guerre* (1936), he defended the Russian Revolution as a force for peace, while his attraction to India's blend of mysticism, political action, and nonviolence is reflected in works like *Aux peuples assassinés* (1917), *Mahatma Gandhi* (1924), his *Vie de Ramakrishna* (1929), whom he called the Indian St. Francis of Assisi, and his study of the "St. Paul of India," *La vie de Vivekananda et l'Evangile Universel* (1930). After vigorously opposing Hitler and Fascism, he spent his last years in silence at Vézelay. His chief work remains *Jean-Christophe* (1904–1912), a 10-v. *roman-fleuve* or saga novel embodying the pre-World War I generation's idealized quests in a literary form whose structure resembles a spiritual ascent. Only a few of his publications can be cited here: novels like *Colas Breugnon* (1919) and *L'Ame enchantée* (7 v., 1922–33); plays like *Les Loups* (1898) on the Dreyfus case, and the trilogy of *Saint-Louis* (1897), *Aërt* (1898), and *Le Triomphe de la raison* (1899), tragedies of faith glorifying three spiritual stages of the French people, Catholicism, nationalism, and rationalism; biographies of *Michel-Ange* (1905), *Tolstoï* (1911), and *Péguy* (1944), the latter his friend, publisher, and collaborator; and musicology, *Béethoven. les grandes époques créatrices* (1928–1949). His partially published diaries and memoirs and the *Cahiers Romain Rolland,* issued by a society dedicated to exploring his work, offer valuable insights into his thought and religious development. BIBLIOGRAPHY: M. Doisy, *Romain Rolland* (1945); A. Aronson, *Romain Rolland* (1946); W. T. Starr, *Romain Rolland and a World at War* (1956) and J. Robichez, *Romain Rolland: L'Homme et l'oeuvre* (1961).

[G. E. GINGRAS]

ROLLE OF HAMPOLE, RICHARD (*c.*1300–49), late Middle-English mystical writer and hermit. Born at Thornton Dale, near York, R. left Oxford for religious reasons; settled for a time on estate of the Dalton family where he composed some of his early works; lived for a time in Richmondshire; finally settled at Hampole; died probably of the plague. He was never formally canonized,

but his life seems to have been given almost wholly to meditation, prayer, writing, and the spiritual comfort of others. He was by far the most widely read English mystical writer of his time: his many works in poetry and prose have survived in some 400 manuscripts. His more important mystical writings are in Latin, notably *Incendium amoris, Emendatio vitae,* and *Melos amoris* (first published in 1957, ed. E. J. F. Arnoule). R. acquired disciples and, despite an antifeminist bias in his writings, became the spiritual adviser to certain holy women—a nun of Yedingham, one of Hampole, and a recluse, Margaret Kirkby. For them he wrote three English epistles on the love of God and its attainment through contemplation—*Ego dormio, Commandment of the Love of God,* and *Form of Living,* the latter being of the three, the most mature expression of his views. *The Prick of Conscience,* long attributed to him, is not his. At the center of Rolle's mysticism is "joy in the life of Jesus." According to David Knowles (*The English Mystical Tradition* 1961; 1964), R.'s doctrine, though sound, can be seriously misleading to the general reader if it is taken as a description of an advanced state of contemplative prayer. His works were frequently copied and imitated. BIBLIOGRAPHY: R. Rolle, *English Writings* (ed. H. E. Allen, 1931); E. Colledge, NCE 12:561.

[N. MALTMAN]

ROMAGNÉ, JAMES RENÉ (1762–1836), missionary. A French priest, R. refused to take the French Revolutionary oath decreed by the Civil Constitution of the Clergy and fled to England in 1792. Coming to the U. S. in 1799 he worked for many years among the Indians of Maine. R. acted as agent for the Indians of Passamaquoddy Bay in 1801, securing for them a land grant. *The Indian Prayer Book* (1834) was composed by R. in 1804 for the Passamaquoddy and Penobscot tribes. He taught the women spinning and weaving and the men agriculture. He also ministered to the white settlers in Maine.

[J. R. AHERNE]

ROMAIN, LE, see MIGNARD, PIERRE.

ROMAINMÔTIER, ABBEY OF, former Benedictine abbey near Lausanne, Switzerland. The monastery was founded *c.*450 by SS. Romanus and Lupicinus. In 753 the abbey church was dedicated to SS. Peter and Paul by Pope Stephen II, who also placed the abbey under the Holy See. It became a royal abbey of the Kingdom of Burgundy in 888 and eventually came under the jurisdiction of Cluny. After its suppression in 1536, it was used by Calvinists, but a small community of monks tried to maintain their community life at the Franche-Comté until the French Revolution. BIBLIOGRAPHY: Cottineau 2:2497–98.

[M. A. MCFADDEN]

ROMAN BREVIARY, see BREVIARY, ROMAN.

ROMAN CATECHISM, the *Catechism of the Council of Trent,* published at Rome in 1566 under the auspices of Pius V, commonly referred to as the *Catechismus Romanus.*

[T. C. O'BRIEN]

ROMAN CATHOLIC, a term used as an adjective to indicate the association of something with the Church whose visible head is the pope, and as a noun for a member of that Church. The term is not much used by Roman Catholics themselves, for whom "Catholic" needs no qualification to indicate the sense in which they understand it. Often, however, esp. in ecumenical discussion, the qualification is a useful means of obviating possible ambiguity. The term first appeared in the 16th cent. and was used disparagingly by Anglican divines who took offense at the way in which those who remained in communion with Rome appropriated to themselves the description of Catholic. Later the term was useful to those who propounded a *branch theory of the Catholic Church, for its apparent suggestion that "Roman" was a specific form of the genus "Catholic," other forms being Eastern Orthodox and Anglican. The odious connotation of the original use has been forgotten. Even the originally more invidious "Romish," "popish," or "papist" are now likely to sound quaintly humorous rather than acrimonious. The designation is now generally accepted as a noncontroversial and sometimes useful mode of identification. BIBLIOGRAPHY: H. Thurston, CE 13:121–123.

[P. K. MEAGHER]

ROMAN CATHOLICISM, the teaching and practice of the Roman Catholic Church. Distinctive of the Church in relation to other Churches of the West is its understanding of itself and of its teaching authority. The Church teaches that its visible structure and the invisible spiritual life of the community of believers are two aspects of the one reality. That one reality is the Church, in historical and doctrinal continuity with the Church as Christ founded it. Full historical and doctrinal continuity is guaranteed for members of the Church through communion with the bishop of Rome as successor of Peter (see MEMBERSHIP IN THE CHURCH). The primacy of the pope is the main connotation of the term Roman in the title of the Church. As to its teaching authority, the Church maintains that the *rule of faith is divine revelation as contained in Scripture; the authentic understanding and the declaration of that revelation belong to the church *magisterium. In this context the meaning of *tradition as a rule of faith is to be understood in RC teaching. Tradition is not understood as an addition (as opposed to *sola scriptura), rather it is the living understanding of what God's revelation does in fact contain. The acceptance or recognition of Scripture itself is safeguarded or authenticated by the living understanding of the magisterium. Nor is the teaching authority or tradition opposed to the personal direction of the Holy Spirit in the individual

Christian. The Church does believe that this guidance for the community is guaranteed in a special way to the community as a whole. That guarantee of corporate fidelity to God's word is given to those who are the ordained teachers and pastors in the Church. Vatican Council II stressed this in its declaration on the *collegiality of the bishops. At the head of the college of bishops is the bishop of Rome. He is the supreme teacher (see PRIMACY). The doctrine of papal *infallibility fits in with this pattern of belief in the teaching authority of the Church as the rule of faith.

RC belief affirms the Trinity and Unity of God, and the redemptive incarnation of the Son of God, Jesus Christ. The special veneration of Mary rests on the belief that she is the mother of Jesus Christ, the Son of God, and for that reason was immaculately conceived and perpetually a virgin. Sacraments are accepted as signs of Christ's continually present, saving grace, and as therefore having the power to produce grace in recipients who believe in Christ. The sacraments are seven: baptism, confirmation, the Eucharist, penance, anointing of the sick, holy orders, and matrimony. Baptism, the sacrament of Christian rebirth, is administered to infants on the basis of the faith of the Christian community, and in the belief that original sin, besetting every human being, must be removed. The Eucharist is celebrated as a sign of Christian love, and of the continuous presence of Christ's sacrificial death in the Church. Penance, the sacrament of reconciliation, includes the need of auricular confession. The celebration of the sacraments combined with the proclamation of the word of God constitutes the liturgy of the Church. Grace is believed to transform man inwardly, empowering him to work out the way of salvation, in dependence on the freely given promise of grace in his life. Those whose lives have reflected in a heroic degree the working of Christ's grace are venerated as saints; their prayers and intercession as friends of God are sought. Those whose charity is defective in minor degree at the time of death are believed to have need of purgation before being admitted to heaven; their purification can be hastened by the prayers of their living brethren in Christ. Belief is maintained in hell as an everlasting state of punishment for the impenitent sinner.

The polity of the RC Church basically depends on the belief that the teaching and pastoral authority in the Church is a sacred power. The structure is hierarchical. The supreme authority is that of the pope as head of the college of bishops. Through holy orders the bishops are teachers and pastors in the Church. (See COLLEGIALITY) This, the Church believes, is in accord with Christ's institution.

[T. C. O'BRIEN]

ROMAN CHURCH, THE (1) In a sense more common in preecumenical times, the term, like Roman Catholic, was used to put the Catholic Church in its place, countering its claim to be the universal Church by classifying it as, at most, one among equals. (2) In a simple geographical sense, the term may mean the Church at Rome, even as early Christian literature speaks of "the Church at Corinth" or "at Jerusalem"; it could also mean the Diocese of Rome; or the Catholic Church as having Rome at the center of its structure and the Roman rite as its liturgy. (3) In a more dogmatic, ecclesiological sense, the term appears in Vatican Council I's profession of faith, which begins "*Sancta catholica apostolica Romana ecclesia credit et docet . . .*" (D 3001; note the absence of commas). The formula was much discussed at the Council. Certainly it reflects the sentiment of some ultramontanists that *romana,* was on a par with "one, holy, catholic, and apostolic," of the Creed. The geographic sense becomes part of the dogmatic sense.

The Catholic Church is Roman in the sense that it is Petrine: the successor of St. Peter enjoys primacy among the bps. of the church. Historically the successor is the bp. of Rome as Rome was the See of Peter. The geographical is, however, not the essential; the succession is. That succession is authenticated by the Church's election of the pope. Since Catholic faith accepts the primacy of the pope, the mode of election as the election *by the Church* is presumably the mode determined to be legitimate by a pope with regard to subsequent elections; thus Paul VI revised the manner of papal election by his 1975 apostolic constitution *Romano pontifici eligendo* (AAS 67[1975]609–645).

One aspect of papal primacy by which theologians have moderated extreme views connected with the deliberations of Vatican Council I is the way in the early centuries the Church of Peter, i.e., of Rome, was regarded as a norm of faith. The meaning was not that the bp. of Rome made continual pronouncements. Rather the faith as in fact understood and practiced at Rome was taken to be a lived guide and norm. Since Vatican II there have been two features of ecclesiology that recover this earlier understanding of the place of the Church of Rome. One is *collegiality, which recognized that episcopacy itself, i.e., ordination, constitutes the bp. as teacher and pastor, and the body of bps. as responsible for the faith of the whole Church. The other important development is the theology of the local Church, so that the universal Church is, as it were, embodied in the Church of each diocese; the Church at Rome is central in the *communio* of local Churches.

[T. C. O'BRIEN]

ROMAN COLLAR, a stiff clerical collar, white, solid in front and fastened at the back of the neck. It is worn either with cassock or a suit and rabat. As religious brothers have begun wearing the collar, it has become customary for a vertical black line to be added to distinguish them from priests.

[J. DALLEN]

ROMAN COLLEGE, see GREGORIAN UNIVERSITY, THE PONTIFICAL.

ROMAN CREED, the ancient creed used at Rome, basis for the *Apostles' Creed in its present form. In the early Church, creedal formulas were committed orally to catechumens, to be repeated at their baptism, as Hippolytus (*c.*170–*c.*236) attests in his *Apostolic Tradition* with regard to the Roman Creed. In substance this was formulated before 190, and from the 4th cent. was referred to as *Symbolum Apostolorum*. The text is found substantially in Hippolytus's work; a Greek version presented at a synod in Rome (340) by Marcellus of Ancyra closely conforms to the Latin text in *Commentary on the Apostles Creed*, written, 404, by Rufinus of Aquileia. BIBLIOGRAPHY: D 10–36.

[T. C. O'BRIEN]

ROMAN CURIA, see CURIA, ROMAN.

ROMAN DE FAUVEL, French satirical poem written by Gervais du Bus (1310–14), critical of church abuses. The poem's subject, a fawn-colored stallion, symbolizes the vices. The name *Fauvel* is formed with the first letter of each vice, i.e., *Flatterie, Avarice, Vilenie, Vanité,* and *Lâcheté*. One of the MSS in the Bibliothèque Nationale in Paris, includes motets, plainsong, and other musical pieces inserted by Chaillou de Pesstain (1316).

[R. J. LITZ]

ROMAN DE LA ROSE, one of the undeniable classics of medieval literature. This work's beginning, by Guillaume de Lorris presents a jewel-like allegory of courtly love; its conclusion, by Jean de Meung (Meun), is a realistic encyclopedia of lay knowledge and interests. This unique and paradoxical combination thus blended two mainstreams of 13th-cent. thought. The work remained popular and controversial through the Renaissance. Its influence on Dante, Chaucer (who translated parts), Cervantes, Villon, Boccaccio, Spencer, and Shakespeare is inestimable.

[J. P. WILLIMAN]

ROMAN EMPIRE. The complex of political, social, economic, military, and cultural forces that prevailed throughout the Mediterranean world and much of Western Europe for more than five centuries and which, because of a change in the character of its rule, is usually divided into the Principate (27 B.C.– A.D. 285) and the Dominate (A.D. 285–476). Since the Roman Empire saw the ultimate unification of Greek culture with the Roman genius for law and administration and the rise and spread of Christianity, it is rightly considered to be one of the most significant periods in world history.

Augustus and the Julio-Claudian Line (27 B.C.– A.D. 68). The founder of the Roman Empire was Octavian, the grandnephew and heir of Julius Caesar. In 43 B.C. as a member of the Second Triumvirate with Mark Antony and Lepidus, he had received extraordinary powers for reestablishing the state. Though these, after a renewal, had expired in 33 B.C., Octavian continued to exercise them, as he later claimed, "by popular consent." In 31 B.C. he defeated the combined forces of Antony and Cleopatra at Actium. Two years later he celebrated a triple triumph in Rome. In 27 B.C. he ostensibly restored the Republic without actually giving up the authority which he had to rule the state. The old forms of the Republican constitution were revived, but Octavian himself received two new titles, that of *princeps* and that of *Augustus*. The former was a mark of courtesy that had been used in earlier times and indicated a certain precedence over one's fellow-citizens. The latter was a new and quasi-religious designation that added dignity to his person. In 23 B.C. he relinquished the consulship which he had held from 31 B.C. and received instead a proconsular *maius imperium* that was renewed for periods of 5 and 10 years. This gave him a supreme command of the military in the provinces, while his authority in Rome itself was secured by his reception of the annually renewed *tribunicia potestas*, or power of a tribune. In 12 B.C., upon the death of Lepidus, he became *pontifex maximus*, thus reuniting in his own person the sacral and secular powers of the early Roman kings. In 2 B.C. he was further honored with the title of *Pater Patriae* (Father of his Country). As a means of unifying the empire, he permitted the worship of his genius together with that of the goddess Roma in the Eastern provinces, and from there it spread to Gaul and Spain. Augustus was a practical statesman with a high sense of duty. He tried to check the spread of immorality by introducing laws to check adultery and to encourage the aristocracy to have more children. He promoted extensive works of repair and new construction in Rome and elsewhere, and his various efforts at reform were ably seconded by the classical writers of the Augustan Age, particularly Vergil, Horace, and Livy.

As founded by Augustus, the Roman Empire may be described as a constitutional magistracy, but as such it had two serious defects: no adequate checks on the authority of the princeps and no real provisions for succession. Since the princeps, who only later came to be known as emperor, had complete control over the military, there was nothing to prevent his absorbing all the civil powers in the state as well; and this is what eventually happened. But since a magistrate is at least theoretically appointed by the people, there was no direct means for the princeps to name his own successor. He could build up by honors and commands one who would then be qualified to take over the office, or he could adopt one whom he wished to succeed him, but the actual choice fell upon the senate and all too soon upon the armies.

When Augustus died he was succeeded by his stepson Tiberius (A.D. 14–37), whom he had adopted 10 years before. An able general and administrator, Tiberius was of a morose and suspicious temperament. His reign was marred by numerous trials in the senate for treason. He spent the last 10 years of his life at his villa on the island of Capri. Tiberius was succeeded by his grandnephew Gaius Ger-

manicus (37–41), better known by his nickname of Caligula ("Little Boots"). After a wild and tyrannical career of only 4 years, he was assassinated by a tribune of the Praetorian Guard. His successor was his uncle Claudius (41–54), who, despite his numerous idiosyncrasies and physical disabilities, proved to be quite a capable ruler. After his death, allegedly at the hands of his fourth wife, Agrippina, Claudius was succeeded by the latter's 16-year-old son Nero (54–68). Under the tutelage of the Praetorian Prefect Burrus and the philosopher Seneca, Nero ruled well for 5 years. Then throwing off their restraints and giving free vent to both his lusts and his artistic inclinations, he went to every excess. After killing his wife and his mother, he instigated a persecution of the Christians, whom he made the scapegoats for the fire that destroyed much of Rome in July, 64 A.D. Revolts of the armies in Britain, Judea, Gaul, and Spain led to Nero's deposition by the Senate and his ultimate suicide with the words "What an artist is being destroyed!"— *Qualis artifex pereo!* (Suetonius, *Nero* 49).

The Flavian Emperors (69–96). The death of Nero occasioned a power struggle among several generals for the imperial office. This ended with the victory of Vespasian, commander of the legions in the East, and his acceptance by the Senate as princeps. Vespasian (69–79), the son of a tax collector who had risen in the ranks, favored the employment of men of equestrian rank rather than of freedmen in the important administrative posts. His son and successor Titus finished the siege of Jerusalem, which he had begun, and the rest of Britain was brought under Roman control at his command. Besides enlarging the franchise and reorganizing the army, Vespasian undertook many important public works, the most famous being the Flavian Amphitheater, or Colosseum, at Rome. The short reign of Titus (79–81), "the delight and darling of the human race" (Suetonius, *Titus* 1), was marred by the eruption of Vesuvius and the consequent destruction of Pompeii and Herculaneum. He was succeeded by his brother Domitian (81–96), an able administrator but of a proud and somber intelligence. His attempts to restore the old standards of Roman morality were in odd contrast with his own dissolute life. His reaction to senatorial opposition led him to convert the last years of his life into a reign of terror. Among those accused of treason at this time were the ex-consuls Flavius Clemens and Marcus Acilius Glabrio. It has been conjectured that they were in reality converts to Christianity. That there was a persecution of the Christians at this time seems quite evident from the testimony of Clement of Rome and the Apocalypse of St. John. Though Domitian's career ended with his assassination, the rule of the Flavians was on the whole beneficent, being marked by a strengthening of the defenses of the empire and a real increase of prosperity in the provinces.

The Five "Good Emperors" (96–180). Nerva (96–98), Domitian's successor, was an aged senator without capacity to command or administrative ability. He wisely adopted

Trajan to assist him in ruling. With his death, the role of princeps fell to his adopted son. Trajan (98–117), born at Italica, advanced in the army to become a popular and able general. His administration was economical but progressive. Among his many magnificent public works was his building of the *Forum Traiani,* the most striking element of which is the still-standing column recording his numerous military campaigns. A born leader, he rightly earned the title of *Optimus Princeps,* "Best Prince," which was officially conferred upon him in 114, though it had been unofficially applied to him much earlier than this.

Hadrian (117–138), Trajan's adopted son and heir to the empire, was probably also born in Italica. He was of a very curious mind and traveled throughout the empire. In the last years of his life he erected a huge villa below Tivoli with buildings recalling many of the places he had visited. A revolt of the Jews during his reign led to the destruction of Jerusalem in 135. His foreign policy was, however, more defensive than offensive. He withdrew from Mesopotamia, conquered by his predecessor, and built the wall across northern Britain that still bears his name. Before his death, Hadrian adopted a member of his *consilium,* Titus Aurelius Antoninus. The Senate approved him and added to his name the title of "Pius." Antoninus Pius (138–161) continued the process of centralizing the government. His reign on the whole was one of peace and great material prosperity. After his death he was succeeded by the coemperors Lucius Verus (161–169) and Marcus Aurelius (161–180), both of whom he had earlier adopted at Hadrian's request. Marcus Aurelius aspired to put into effect Plato's ideal of the philosopher-king. Unfortunately, his reign was plagued with almost continual wars. He himself died while fighting the Marcomanni in Pannonia. He is perhaps best remembered for his Stoic reflections (*Meditations*) and for a few severe persecutions of the Christians during his reign, particularly at Lyons in France.

One of Marcus' greatest mistakes was the choice of his dissolute and profligate son Commodus (180–192) as his successor. Commodus' assassination marked the end of the Pax Romana and the beginning of anarchy and civil wars throughout the Roman world.

Military Monarchy and Military Anarchy (192–285). The Senate chose Publius Helvius Pertinax as emperor, but he ruled for only a few months and was then slain by the Praetorian Guard. Rival candidates rose up in Britain, Syria, and Pannonia, with the victory going to the governor of the latter province, Lucius Septimius Severus (193–211). A native of Leptis Magna in North Africa, Severus was an excellent soldier who gave a definite military cast to his regime. The Senate lost whatever influence it still retained, and the empire became in effect a military monarchy. On his deathbed at York in England, Severus is said to have advised his sons and heirs Geta (211–212) and Marcus Aurelius Antoninus, better known as "Caracalla" (211–217), to live in peace, enrich the soldiers, and despise the rest of the world. Caracalla was a cruel and dissolute ruler, who

murdered his brother, Geta. He was fond of display, e.g., the baths which he built in Rome; and his edict, the *Constitutio Antoniniana,* which granted Roman citizenship to all free subjects in the Empire. He was murdered by the Praetorian Prefect Macrinus while campaigning against the Parthians. Macrinus, after a brief reign, was defeated by the Parthians and succeeded by a dissolute youth and priest of the Syrian sun god Elagabal. Aurelianus Antoninus (218–222), better known as "Heliogabalus," was a weak and depraved ruler who was eventually murdered by the Praetorians. He was succeeded by the 14-year-old Marcus Aurelianus Alexander, who added the title of Severus to his name. Honest, but a poor administrator and general, Alexander Severus (222–235) was murdered by Maximinus at Mainz. The next 50 years were a period of military anarchy during the course of which 26 individuals were officially recognized as Augusti, but only one of whom died a natural death. The Empire was assailed on the frontiers and for 15 years afflicted with a devastating plague. Among the more capable rulers of this period were Decius (249–251), who instigated the first general persecution of the Christians throughout the Empire; Valerian (253–260), under whom Pope St. Sixtus II and St. Cyprian were put to death; Gallienus (253–267), who granted an amnesty to Christians and even allowed them to recover their churches and cemeteries after the death of his coregent Valerian (Eusebius, *Eccl. Hist*. 7.13.1); and Aurelian (270–275).

The Dominate (284-476). From the Accession of Diocletian to the Death of Theodosius (395) and the Separation of the Empire. In the struggle for power after the death of Carus (282–283), the veteran general Diocles, later known as Diocletian was proclaimed emperor by his troops, a title which was officially conferred upon him after the murder of Carinus (283–285). The reign of Diocletian (285–305) was marked by a thorough reorganization of the state. The Empire was divided into two parts, East and West, each with a separate ruler with the title of Augustus. Diocletian chose for himself the East and selected as his colleague Maximian for the West. A further division of power was made by the appointment of two assistants or "Caesars" for the two Augusti, Constantius Chlorus for the West and Galerius for the East. Among the many reforms effected by Diocletian was a revision of the system of taxation, a reorganization of the army, the establishment of a new system of civil service, and an attempt to halt inflation by the issuance of an elaborate edict setting down a maximum of prices for services and goods. He also introduced the trappings of oriental despotism to enhance the dignity and prestige of the imperial office. On May 1, 305, he abdicated, forcing Maximiam to do the same. But the subsequent quarrels that were effected by this made it necessary for him to reestablish order at a conference held at Carnuntum in 308. Besides being the refounder of the Empire, Diocletian has the dubious honor of being the author of "the Great Persecution," which was only ended with the defeat of Maxentius by Constantine at the Milvian Bridge in

312 and the issuance of the so-called Edict of Milan in 313, granting tolerance to Christianity throughout the Empire.

The reforms that had been introduced by Diocletian were carried on by his successor Constantine (312–337), who rightly bears the title of "the Great." An outstanding general, an administrator and legislator of great ability, and a man of high integrity, he became deeply interested in Christianity, though deferring his own baptism until he was on his deathbed. He recognized the importance of Christianity for the future of Rome and personally, or through his mother Helena, erected numerous churches in Rome and Palestine. He used his energies to bring about a unity within the Church itself, divided as it was by the Donatists in Africa and the Arians in the East.

Constantine was succeeded by his Arian son Constantius II (337–361), a cruel and inefficient ruler who died at Tarsus on his way to meet his cousin Julian, who had been hailed as a rival emperor by his troops at Paris. Becoming emperor by default, Julian the Apostate (361–363) undertook a disastrous expedition against the Persians and was slain on his retreat from Ctesiphon. Though he was a great soldier, Julian is better known for his vigorous and varied writings and his hostility to the Christianity which he had accepted in his youth. Julian's successors were all Christians, though not always orthodox in their beliefs. Valentinian I (364–375) again divided the Empire, taking the West for himself and assigning the East to his brother Valens (364–378). It was reunited under Theodosius I, the Great (379–395), who suppressed paganism and proclaimed Christianity as the official religion of the state. In 390 he submitted to the public penance imposed upon him by St. Ambrose for the massacre at Thessalonica, which he had ordered in one of his fits of temper. Before his death he divided the Empire between his two sons, Arcadius (395–408), who was given the East, and Honorius (395–423), who received the West.

The 5th cent. was a period of great difficulty for the Western Roman Empire because of the barbarian invasions and the consequent political and economic chaos. In 410 Rome itself was sacked by Alaric. In 415 the Visigoths crossed the Pyrenees into Spain, and in 429 the Vandals landed in North Africa. In 455 Rome was again sacked by the Vandals under Genseric. The emperors of this period were largely under the control of barbarian chiefs who commanded the imperial armies. The series of ineffective rulers was brought to an end with the deposition of Romulus Augustulus by the king of the Heruli, Odoacer, in 476. In the general confusion of the times, this was an event that was not particularly noted and can hardly be compared with the fall of the Eastern Roman Empire and the capture of Constantinople by the Turks in 1453.

Though nearly 1500 years have passed since the fall of the Roman Empire, its remains are still most impressive—in the Romance languages, in countless ruins all through the Mediterranean world, in Romanesque architecture, in Continental law, but perhaps most of all in the sense of solidarity that Roman civilization gave to the West and in its adop-

tion and spread of Christianity. Modestinus, one of the great classical lawyers of the early 3d cent., well expressed the sentiments of his contemporaries and their descendants when he observed that "Rome is our common fatherland," *Roma communis nostra patria est* (*Dig.* [50.1] 33). The providential character of the Roman Empire was deeply appreciated by the Fathers of the Church: "In order that the effect of this ineffable grace might be spread throughout the whole world, the Divine Providence prepared the rule of Rome."—*Ut autem huius inenarrabilis gratiae per totum mundum diffunderetur effectus, Romanum regnum divina providentia praeparavit* (St. Leo, *Serm.* 82.2; cf. Origen, *Contra Celsum* 2.30; St. Ambrose, *Expl. Ps. XLV 21;* St. Augustine, *Enarr. in Ps. XXXII 2.10;* Prosper of Aquitaine, *De vocatione omnium gentium* 2.16.

[M. J. COSTELLOE]

ROMAN LAW, the law of ancient Rome from the time of the traditional founding of the city in 753 B.C. to that of the publication of the Justinian Code in 534 A.D.. It continued, however, to have a dominating influence in the East, where it is known as "Byzantine law" down to the fall of Constantinople in 1453; and in the West, where it is known as "Romanistic law" down to the time of the revival of interest in classical law in the 11th and 12th cent., particularly in Bologna.

A number of useful distinctions for the understanding of Roman law are made in the first book of the Institutes, a part of the Justinian Code: The natural law (*ius naturale*) is that which nature teaches all animals (including men). International law (*ius gentium*) is that which is common to all peoples. National law (*ius civile*, in one of its varied meanings) is that which pertains to particular states. Roman law (*ius Romanum*, or *ius Quiritium*) is that which is proper to the Romans themselves. This latter law may be written (*ius scriptum*) or not written (*ius non scriptum*), that is, custom (*quod usus comprobavit*). The sources of this written law are statutes (*leges*), plebiscites (*plebiscita*), decrees of the Senate (*senatus consulta*), imperial constitutions (*principum placita* or *constitutiones*), edicts of magistrates (*magistratuum edicta*), and the replies of jurists (*responsa prudentium*). This description of the sources of Roman law was in a sense anachronistic at the time of its publication since the emperor had been the sole source of new law for some 3 centuries. Nevertheless, it is of great historical and even practical interest since it stresses the continuity of Roman law and the Roman conviction that all law is binding in perpetuity until abrogated by newer legislation.

According to these same Institutes, "a statute (*lex*) is a law which has been passed by a vote of the Roman people at the request of a magistrate of senatorial rank, such as a consul." The earliest known example of a law of this type is that of the only partially extant Twelve Tables, a codification of previously existing customary law drawn up by a special board of ten men in 451 and 450 B.C. and approved by the *comitia centuriata*. "A plebiscite (*plebiscitum*) is a law which has been passed by a vote of the plebeians at the request of a plebeian magistrate such as a tribune." Originally the decisions of the *consilium plebis* were binding only upon the plebeians and not upon the patricians, but they were given equal authority with the *leges,* that is, made applicable to all Roman citizens, through a centuriate law, the Lex Hortensia of 286 B.C. "A decree of the senate (*senatus consultum*) is that which the Senate orders and decides." During the Republic the decrees of the senate were, at least theoretically, only advice to the various magistrates, which they could follow or not at their own discretion. Under the empire, however, they acquired the force of law. Similarly, "whatever seems good to the emperor (*quod principi placuit*) has the force of law." Accordingly, "whatever the emperor has established by letter, deliberately decreed, or commanded by edict is a law." A distinction, however, should be drawn in that "some of these constitutions (*constitutiones*) are of a personal nature and should not be taken as an example to be followed (*ad exempla*), . . . but others are general and binding on all." "The edicts of the praetors have no slight authority in law." This refers particularly to the edicts that the Roman praetors would issue at their entrance into office, giving the norms they would follow in handling lawsuits. Usually a praetor would simply adopt the edict of his predecessor, modifying it slightly where this seemed necessary. The gradual perfecting of the praetorian edict, which was finally codified under Hadrian as the *edictum perpetuum,* gave rise to what was known as the praetorian law (*ius praetorium,* or, more commonly, *ius honorarium*). "The replies of jurists (*responsa prudentium*) are the opinions and decisions of those granted permission 'to establish laws' (*iura condere*)." Under the empire, a judge was obliged to follow the opinion of an official jurist whom he had consulted on a particular case. All of these various types of law are concerned with persons (*personae*), things (*res*), or actions (*actiones*), as the Institutes note at the end of this description of the law (*Institutiones* 1.2.1–12).

The Roman law of persons was concerned with such matters as liberty and servitude, citizenship, the authority of the head of a household (*paterfamilias*), marriage, divorce, and guardianship. The law of things covered such matters as ownership, inheritance, contracts, and delicts, that is, offenses against individuals that were not punished by the state but that could be the subject of a private suit. The law of actions was concerned with matters of procedure. In civil suits during the Republic and first centuries of the Empire, the procedure was divided into two stages, one before the praetor (*in iure*), during which the plaintiff and defendant had to agree upon the points at issue. The matter was then given to a private, nonsalaried citizen to examine (*apud iudicem*) and give a decision (*sententia*). A modification of this procedure known as the "formulary procedure" became popular at the end of the Republic, but in the late 3d cent. A.D. private suits were settled by a single official in what was known as a *cognitio extra ordinem*; but there was always the possibility of an appeal to a higher official and eventually to the emperor himself.

Roman penal law never reached the high state of perfection of Roman civil law. In the early Republic, Roman citizens gained the right to appeal a capital sentence to the *comitia centuriata*. In the last century of the Republic, special jury courts known as *quaestiones perpetuae* were erected to try specific crimes such as extortion and adultery. During the early Empire the Senate acted as a court of criminal prosecution, but soon all criminal jurisdiction was absorbed by the emperor and his legates in the *cognitiones extraordinariae,* where the judges were really not bound by the earlier laws of the Republic.

Without doubt Roman law, the principles of which are still operative in almost all European continental codes, was one of the greatest achievements of the ancient world. Even more than Roman administration and Roman architecture it shows the Roman genius for learning by practical experience and for adopting suitable means for desired ends. BIB - LIOGRAPHY: H. J. Wolff, *Roman Law* (1951); F. Schulz, *Principles of Roman Law* (1936); *idem, Classical Roman Law* (1951); *idem, History of Roman Legal Science* (1946); V. Arangio-Ruiz, *Storia del diritto romano* (1947).

[M. J. COSTELLOE]

ROMAN MISSAL, see MISSAL, ROMAN.

ROMAN QUESTION, a term used in reference to the Church-State quarrel in Italy which resulted from the unification of that country at the territorial expense of the papacy. Pius IX, during whose pontificate the Papal States were absorbed by Italy, refused to recognize the existence of the Kingdom of Italy and ordered Catholics not to vote in parliamentary elections. The Law of Guarantees, a unilateral settlement carried through by the Italian parliament, did not heal the breach, for the papacy refused to recognize its validity. Gradually, however, a *modus vivendi* was worked out, since bishops had to be acceptable to the monarchy before they could take possession of their sees. On the surface, however, the Vatican's attitude was one of intransigent opposition to the Italian State.

By the beginning of the 20th cent., the Roman Question was becoming secondary to the Social Question, particularly in view of the fact that all hope of intervention by some Catholic power or powers to restore the Papal States had been abandoned. Encouragement and support was now given to a militant Italian Catholicism. The Roman Question, as a juridical question, was not formally revived until the Mussolini era. In an effort to make Catholicism a prop of his new order, Mussolini courted the Church. Negotiations begun in 1926 culminated in the Lateran Pacts of 1929 which resolved the Roman Question.

[E. A. CARRILLO]

ROMAN RELIGION, a religion that had its origins in prehistoric times in a fusion of the beliefs and religious practices of Indo-European invaders into the Italian peninsula with those of earlier indigenous peoples. Through a natural process of evolution and a continual assimilation of foreign deities and modes of worship, it developed into a diffuse and complicated system but without losing its essential features.

Because of the nature of our sources—ancient calendars, data furnished by poets, historians, and encyclopedists of the Late Republic and Early Empire, and the deductions of comparative linguistics and religion—knowledge of the beliefs of the early Romans is limited and ambiguous. From the Indo-Europeans the Romans obtained their knowledge of a great sky- and weather-god Jupiter, etymologically connected with the Greek ''Zeus'' and the Sanskrit ''Dyaus,'' and their practice of offering bloody sacrifices and of celebrating special rites for the dead. From the earlier inhabitants of Italy, the Romans came to know the gods of the Lower World and how to propitiate them with offerings of flowers and milk and of the first fruits of the land.

In comparison with the polytheistic anthropomorphism of the early Greeks, the religion of the early Romans was of a ''primitive'' character. The gods they worshiped had definite functions to perform but were themselves poorly defined and practically devoid of any legends. They were little more than the unseen forces behind the varied phenomena of nature, which had to be honored or placated with suitable prayers, offerings, and sacrifices to secure the well-being of individuals, families, and the state itself. This is evident from the frequent use of the word *numen* in connection with the gods. The word may be variously translated as ''life,'' ''spirit,'' ''will,'' or ''power'' and may be compared with the Melanesian ''mana,'' which has similar animistic connotations. Only in later centuries, after the Romans had come into contact with the Greeks of S Italy, did their gods acquire a definite personality and mythology. Through a process known as the *interpretatio Romana,* they came to identify their own gods with those of Greece and to assimilate the myths of the Greeks.

At the head of the early Roman pantheon was a triad of three gods, who had even in historical times their own priests or *flamines*. The first of these was Jupiter. The second was Mars, originally a god of agriculture but later of war. The third, of Sabine origin, was probably at first the god of the popular assembly, but he later became identified with Romulus, the founder of Rome. Allied with these major powers were others such as Vulcan (god of fire), Neptune (god of water), and Janus (god of the outer door and of beginnings), and a host of lesser deities or spirits whose names were largely derived from the objects or activities with which they were connected. Faunus and Silvanus were guardians of the woods, Terminus of the boundary stones; the Lares were deities of the farm who were later introduced into the house; the Penates were the gods of the storeroom, and Vesta the goddess of the hearth. Robigus was responsible for the rust on wheat and could be placated with the sacrifice of a red-haired dog. Pomona watched over the ripening fruit and Messor, the harvest. Cunina tended a child in its cradle and Statulinus helped it to stand. In addition to a countless number of spirits of this sort, it was quite commonly believed that every man had his guiding *Genius* and every woman a corresponding *Juno* (Pliny, *Nat. hist.* 2.16).

During the Etruscan domination of Rome, the original triad of Jupiter, Mars, and Quirinus was replaced by that of Jupiter, Juno, and Minerva; and a great temple was erected to them upon the Capitoline hill. Juno was an old Italian goddess of women and Minerva another Italian goddess of arts and crafts whom the Etruscans had adopted for themselves. From the Greeks the Romans received Castor, Pollux, and Apollo, and an identification of Venus with Aphrodite, Neptune with Poseidon and Ceres with Demeter. Imitating Greek customs, they deified Romulus, the founder of their city in the 4th cent. B.C. and later their living rulers, the emperors. In an attempt to secure the assistance of more potent deities, the Romans also turned to the East. The first official import of this kind was occasioned by the disasters of the Second Punic War. In order to rid Italy of Hannibal, upon the advice of a Sibylline oracle, they brought the black stone of the goddess Cybele from Pessinus to Rome in 204–205 B.C. Later they added to their religious observances the worship of the Egyptian Isis and Osiris, the Syrian Astarte and Adonis, and the Iranian Mithras, who became extremely popular with the soldiers throughout the empire.

Just as the worship of the Roman family was primarily the concern of the head of the household, the *paterfamilias,* so the worship of the state was primarily the duty of the rulers, whether these were kings, as in the first centuries, or consuls during the Republic, or emperors during the Principate. But they were assisted in this by a large number and variety of priests. In the 1st cent. B.C. there were, e.g., four priestly colleges and a number of sodalities, most of which went back to early times. The college of pontiffs consisted of a *rex sacrorum,* 12 *flamines,* 6 Vestal Virgins who tended the fire at the state hearth, and 15 pontiffs properly so called, who were the experts in sacral law. The other three colleges consisted of the augurs, 15 experts in reading the auspices; the *quindecimviri sacris faciundis,* who were consulted on the introduction of foreign cults; and the *septemviri epulones,* who supervised a feast of Jupiter celebrated on the Capitoline. Of lesser rank or more occasional service were the sodalities, which included the *Salii,* the *fratres Arvales,* the *Fetiales,* the *Titii,* and the *Luperci.*

The gods were honored in various ways, with prayers, vows, dances, races, games, and above all, with sacrifices, which could be simple or very elaborate. Male animals were offered to the gods and female to the goddesses. Light-colored animals were sacrificed to the celestial deities, and black to the infernal. The sacrifices were regularly offered by the magistrates but with the assistance of priests who recited the proper verbal formulas for them to follow.

Despite the fact that the Romans in their official dealings

with their gods adopted a legalistic attitude and expected a *quid pro quo,* they were on the whole deeply convinced of the need of keeping the *pax deorum* through the exact performance of their official cult acts. In the 2d cent. B.C., the Greek historian Polybius praised the Romans for their religious convictions and declared that it was their fear of the gods which maintained the unity of the Roman state (Polybius 6.56.6–7). Fear of offending foreign gods was a partial cause of their general toleration of the beliefs of conquered nations, but they were at the same time convinced that "those who do not worship the religion of Rome should recognize the ceremonies of Rome" (*Acta Cypriani* 1.1). Failure on the part of the early Christians to do so led to frequent persecutions and eventually to the collapse of Roman religion itself. BIBLIOGRAPHY: W. Warde Fowler, *Religious Experience of the Roman People* (1911); K. Latte, *Römische Religionsgeschichte* (1960).

[M. J. COSTELLOE]

ROMAN RITE. Originally the rite of Rome and vicinity, and particularly that used by the pope, the Roman rite has become the dominant rite of Western Catholicism and the one most widely used throughout Christianity. Its origins, though obscure, are undoubtedly local. The oldest source, Hippolytus's *Apostolic Tradition* (*c.*215), is consonant with later development, even though questions have been raised concerning its Roman character. The developed Roman rite is closely related to the Ambrosian rite of N Italy in the West and to the Alexandrian rite of N Africa among the Eastern rites. The new public character of Christianity after its legalization in the early 4th cent. made possible the expansion and development of the earlier simple structure. Despite the adoption of insignia and ceremonial from civil society and of more dramatic elements from various Eastern rites, the Roman rite maintained a basic simplicity and terseness (undoubtedly related to the original domestic setting of the Roman liturgy). The simple outline of its primitive structure remained evident, even though it was being complicated. Early in this period the language of the Roman liturgy became Latin rather than Greek, a change completed by the late 4th century.

An earlier period of improvisation gradually gives way to the use of fixed texts, and the rite was fairly well established by the early 7th century. By the beginning of the 7th cent. for example, the characteristic Roman Canon—the only one in use until 1969— was fixed in form. In the late 8th cent. the Roman rite was introduced into the areas now known as France and Germany, and in the early 9th cent. Charlemagne, seeking to unify his dominions, obtained a copy of the Gregorian Sacramentary from Pope Adrian and called for its use in place of the various Gallican liturgies then current. This papal liturgy needed adaptation, however, before it was usable in parishes. Alcuin and Amalarius are associated with this process of adaptation which ended in a "Gallicanization" of the Roman rite. This hybrid, a Roman structure with numerous Gallican additions and decorations,

returned to Rome in the late 10th cent. and was adopted there. Its organization through use by the papal curia led to its adoption and spread by the Franciscans in the 13th century. Medieval liturgical variety—local uses and those of religious orders, all basically variants of the Roman rite— was ended by the Tridentine call for the preparation of a uniform liturgy for use in the West. Rome then issued the service books that remained largely unchanged until the 20th cent.: the Breviary (1568), Missal (1570), Pontifical (1598), *Caeremoniale episcoporum* (1600), and Ritual (1614).

The liturgical movement of the late 19th cent. took a pastoral orientation under 20th-cent. popes, beginning with Pius X. The reforms called for by Vatican II's Constitution on the Liturgy (1963) have led to the use of the vernacular, the restoration of the more original Roman structures without medieval accretions and distortions, and, presently, to the cultural adaptation of the Roman liturgy to fit the needs of various modern cultures and societies. Throughout its history the Roman rite has remained basically clear, simple, direct, practical, and efficient, in contrast to other sometimes florid and verbose, poetic, and dramatic rites. It has, however, been strongly influenced by these other rites, since the Roman genius—characterized by E. Bishop as "soberness and sense"—has never shown much imagination or originality, confining itself generally to borrowing rather than innovating. BIBLIOGRAPHY: J. A. Jungmann, *Mass* (1976); *idem, Mass of the Roman Rite* (2 v; 1951–55); A. A. King, *Liturgy of the Roman Church* (1957); T. Klauser, *Short History of the Western Liturgy* (1969); S. J. P. van Dijk and J. Hazelden Walker, *Origins of the Modern Roman Liturgy* (1960).

[J. DALLEN]

ROMAN RITUAL, see RITUAL, ROMAN.

ROMAN SEMINARY, see COLLEGES AND SEMINARIES, ROMAN.

ROMAN SYNOD, a pastoral synod convoked by Pope John XXIII in 1960 for the Diocese of Rome. It was the first such synod held in Rome for at least 300 years and entailed widespread participation not only by the diocesan clergy but also by cardinals, high-ranking Roman prelates, seminary rectors and professors, and chaplains. Extensive surveys of the attitudes and wishes of both the Roman clergy and laity were conducted prior to the synod, and 755 synodal statutes were proclaimed dealing with the total life of the diocese at that time. The Synod presaged the pastoral focus characteristic of Vatican II.

[T. M. MCFADDEN]

ROMANCES, a term that originally designated any vernacular (*romanz*) work, as opposed to Latin works. Expanded to infer fiction, folklore, adventure, and fantasy, the term seems in the 13th cent. to have achieved genre status: a vernacular composition, usually amatory and often allegorical, to be heard over several sittings. Often elaborating the legends of Arthurian or pagan heroes, their composition is episodic and rhetorical, relying on stock situations and formulaic diction. Rhymed in octosyllabic couplets for ease of memorization, the romance has only a subdued lyric content. The romance differs from the *lai* in that its story is sustained and fairly complex; some authors, as *Chrétien drew on Ovid, Virgil, Statius, and Lucan for such narrative art. "Ancient romances" used Alexander, Troy, and Thebes as subjects; "Byzantine" or adventure romances told of Eracles, Cligés, Floris, and Blancheflor, and Apollonius of Tyre; the Celtic or Britannic romances developed from Arthurian legend: Lancelot, Tristan, Gawain, and the Grail are familiar topics.

[J. P. WILLIMAN]

ROMANESQUE BAPTISTERY, see FLORENCE, CATHEDRAL OF.

ROMANIA. The Romanian people, as descendants of the veterans of Trajan sent to colonize the Danubian basin and delta (Dacia) some 2 cent. after Christ, are basically a Latin people. Christianity was probably introduced to them by Latin missionaries, but of this liturgy, undoubtedly in Latin, nothing has survived. In time, the Romanians were subjected to Bulgarian domination and they began to write their language in the Cyrillic alphabet of their conquerors. As the Bulgarians became more Slavonized, the Romanians began to adopt Slavic words into their language. From Bulgarian tutelage the Romanians passed to Serbian domination, where the same process continued. Ecclesiastically, the Romanian seemed to have been subjected first to the Bulgarian see of Trnovo then, with the Turkish conquest, they formed a part of the jurisdiction of the Serbian patriarchate of Ochrid. Along with the Serbs, the Bulgarians, and their brother Valchs of Macedonia, the Romanians underwent a period of Hellenization after the Turkish conquest.

In time three metropolitanates were established in Moldavia, Walachia, and in Ungro-Walachia. Turkish rule in these principalities was less strict and direct than S of the Danube. In 1712, the era of the Phanariotes began. Wealthy Greek merchant families began to acquire land and property in the principalities where they took over all authority politically and ecclesiastically. Greek became the liturgical language in the larger monasteries, cathedrals, and churches, and many bishoprics and abbacies were filled by Greeks. This time of Greek domination came to an end with the treaty of Adrianople in 1829, when Moldavia and Walachia were granted internal autonomy. Complete independence came in 1864, and with political independence came a thirst for ecclesiastical independence. Shortly after 1864, the Romanian Church declared itself autonomous of Constantinople, but their autocephalous status was not recognized by the Phanar, which had protested their earlier move for autonomy, until 1885. The Romanians, both Orthodox and Catholic, had already begun to use the vernacular in the liturgy.

With the end of World War II, the Orthodox Church had to reorganize itself completely. The Patriarch, "His Beatitude the Patriarch of Romania, Deputy of Caesarea in Cappadocia, Metropolitan of Ungro-Valachia and Archbishop of Bucharest," is president of the Holy Synod and consecrates the holy chrism for his jurisdiction. Under him there are five metropolitans and apparently five other bishoprics. There are three theological faculties—in Bucharest, Sibiu, and in Cernauti—for the formation of the clergy. Next to the Russian Church, the Romanian Church is the largest in Orthodoxy with 14 million faithful and publishes some four or five theological journals, which recently have contained work of high quality.

Like her sister Church in Russia, the Romanian Church knows the problems of living under a Communist regime. The patriarch, Justin Marina, was elected to his post with the help of the present regime and assisted in the "reform" of the Romanian Church, which deposed bishops, suppressed monasteries, and imprisoned and exiled many religious and laity. He also assisted in the destruction of the Catholic Byzantine-rite Church of Transylvania, much as his Russian counterparts did in the case of the Ukrainian Catholic Church of Galacia. BIBLIOGRAPHY: M. Lačko, NCE 12:714–717, with bibliog.

[A. WALKER]

ROMANIAN CATHOLICS OF AMERICA, ASSOCIATION OF, founded in 1948 by the clergy and laity of the Romanian Catholic Church of the Byzantine rite in the U.S. to preserve and promote the Catholic culture and traditions of Romania in America. In the same year as the establishment of this association, the Church in Romania was dismembered by the Communist government. On Sept. 5, 1948, 7,000 Romanian Catholic immigrants to the U.S. met at Youngstown, Ohio, to adopt a constitution for their association. This organization publishes a monthly review, *Union,* a yearly almanac-directory, and some devotional and liturgical books. A branch organization was formed in 1960, the Federation of Romanian Catholic Women of America.

[R. C. CLIGGETT]

ROMANIAN RITE, one of the 18 Eastern Catholic rites. Christianity was first brought to Romania by Latin missionaries; however, in the 4th cent. Romania was transferred to the jurisdiction of the Eastern Empire and hence fell under the influence of Byzantine bps., who proceeded to introduce the Byzantine rite. Eventually, Romania followed Constantinople into separation from Rome. A union attempt was made at *Lateran Council IV (1215) when it was decreed that the Romanians of Ardeal (Transylvania) were to be given vicars of their own rite after their defeat by the Magyars. This decree, however, fell into abeyance and as a result many faithful were lost. In the 14th cent., Romanians overthrew the yoke of Turkish and Polish domination, and separate jurisdictions were created for the principalities of Valachia and Moldavia. Damian, the metropolitan of Moldavia, signed the Act of Union at the Council of *Florence (1439), but because of its lack of acceptance, he and his successor were forced to take refuge in Rome. After Leopold I expelled the Turks in 1687, conditions favoring union with Rome finally prevailed. The inroads made by the Huguenots in Romania also made union advisable. In 1698, the metropolitan of Alba Julia, Theoplilus Szeremy, signed an Act of Union under the terms of the Council of Florence, accepting papal primacy, the *filioque,* purgatory, and the validity of unleavened bread for the Eucharist. Owing to political intrigues, this was not confirmed until 1700 by his successor, Athanasius Popa. Despite the opposition of both Orthodox and Calvinists, the union continued. The Romanian Church enjoyed great prosperity under its fourth bp. Petru Paul Aron (1752–64). New sees were created in 1777 and 1853. Surprisingly enough, because of the specific terms of the formula of union, the Romanian rite was allowed to grant full divorces, with the right of remarriage even until the mid-19th century. With the establishment of the kingdom in 1919, the Church was given official status as a minority national religion. Eventually, the Romanian Catholic Church came to constitute the second largest body of Orientals in union with Rome, numbering 1,500,000. With the takeover of Romania by the Communists, the Romanian Catholic Church was suppressed and its property given to the Orthodox Church in 1948. All bps. were arrested, and there followed a general persecution in which many priests were executed. Many Orthodox, including Mircea Eliade, protested this action, and some Orthodox priests preferred jail to new parishes, formerly in union with Rome. The Romanian liturgy has maintained the normal Byzantine usage with few variations. On an official level the Romanian rite continues to exist overseas. There are 5,000 faithful in 18 parishes in the U.S., served by 16 priests and under the jurisdiction of local bishops. In 1972 the Holy See appointed Msgr. Octavian Barlea as an apostolic visitor to Romanians in the U.S. Most Americans of Romanian ancestry live on the shores of Lakes Erie and Michigan. There is also one parish in Montreal, a center in Paris, and scattered groups in Austria, Germany, Spain, Argentina, Brazil, and England. An ordaining prelate was consecrated in 1960. There is now a Pontifical Romanian College in Rome. BIBLIOGRAPHY: Attwater CCE 1:98–104; C. Kormos, *Romania* (1945); OrientCatt 273–287.

[P. MCGHEE]

ROMANO OF ROME (d. *c.*1273), member of the Orsini family, Dominican who studied under St. Thomas Aquinas and succeeded him as master at Paris in 1272. In doctrine he was not a continuator of St. Thomas.

[T. C. O'BRIEN]

ROMANO, GIULIO (1499–1546), Italian painter and architect of the Roman school. In his teens R. had already

become the most important assistant in Raphael's workshop, helping in the execution of frescoes in the Vatican Stanza (*The Battle of Ostia* and *The Fire in the Borgo*) and completing *The Transfiguration* (1520, Vatican Museum) left unfinished at Raphael's death. After enjoying success in Rome as joint heir with Gianfrancesco Penni to Raphael's workshop, R. moved to Mantua (1524) establishing a workshop largely in the service of the Duke Federigo Gonzaga. His most important work in Mantua was the design of the Palazzo del Tè (1527–34) together with fresco decorations (esp. the Sala dei Giganti, 1530–32). In architecture and painting R. demonstrated his basically classicizing style which was increasingly invaded by the ambiguities and distortions of the Mannerist period. BIBLIOGRAPHY: F. Hartt, *Giulio Romano* (2 v., 1958).

[S. CONWAY]

ROMANOS PONTIFICES, an apostolic constitution issued by Leo XIII in 1881 dealing with relations between local ordinaries and the regular (nondiocesan) clergy. The constitution deals with the exemption of regulars from episcopal jurisdiction and their ministry and possessions in a diocese. The Third Plenary Council of Baltimore (1884) applied the constitution to the United States.

[T. M. MCFADDEN]

ROMANOS SCHOOL, Byzantine ivories of the imperial court in Constantinople produced from the late 9th through the 10th cent. distinguished by elongation of figures, delicate elegance, and finesse of technique. Their decorative line and frontality mark the Macedonian revival. *The Harbeville Triptych* (10th cent.), *Christ Crowning Constantine VII* (944), and *Crowning of Romanos and Eudoxia* (*c.*950) are most renowned.

[M. J. DALY]

ROMANS, LETTER TO THE, the 6th book of the NT canon. Paul remarks in Rom 15.19 that he had preached the gospel "from Jerusalem to Illyricum" and in Rom 15.25–26 that he was about to journey to Jerusalem to bring there the collection taken up in the gentile Churches. A comparison of these data in the epistle with Acts 19–20 and 2 Cor 8–9 leads to the conclusion that Rom was written toward the close of Paul's third missionary journey, A.D. 57–58. According to Acts 20.3, Paul spent 3 months in Greece, probably in the area of Corinth, before setting out for Jerusalem, and it was probably during this period that he wrote Romans.

The Apostle planned to evangelize Spain (Rom 15.24) and to visit the Christian community at Rome en route (Rom 1.10; 15.24). Since he was unknown to most of the Christians of Rome, he wrote the epistle by way of introducing himself to them. As his principal theme he chose justification by faith (Rom 1.17), a doctrine that his missionary experience with those who demanded the adherence of Christians to the law and ritual of the OT caused him to develop (cf. Gal). For Paul the gratuitousness of salvation by faith in Christ clearly opened up this way of salvation to gentile as well as to Jew (Rom 1.16). The epistle is the best planned of all the Pauline writings. It consists of an introduction (1.1–15), a doctrinal section (1.16–11.36) that reflects on the justification and salvation announced in Christ, a moral section (12.1–15.13) providing exhortations for Christian conduct, and a conclusion (15.14–33). Many scholars of Rom have questioned if the 16th chapter of the epistle was an original part of it. Some think Rom 16.1–23 was originally a separate letter of the Apostle later appended to Romans. The doxology with which the epistle concludes (16.25–27) may be from a hand other than Paul's; scholars remain divided over its Pauline authenticity. Because of its lengthy and profound theological treatment of its theme, Rom has consistently attracted the study and reflection of the greatest minds in Christendom from Augustine through Thomas Aquinas, Luther, and Barth. BIBLIOGRAPHY: C. K. Barrett, *Commentary on the Epistle to the Romans* (1957); F. W. Beare, InterDB 112–122; J. Fitzmyer, JBC (1968) 291–331.

[C. P. CEROKE]

ROMANTICISM, a movement, esp. in literature and the fine arts, but one that also affected religious, social, political, and economic values and goals, that arose in opposition to the rules, confines, and restraints imposed by classicism. In literature this belief in self-expression placed a higher value on the imagination than on reason, saw nature as a mirror reflecting the human being who looks at it, and valued the expression of the artist's unique personality in the art object rather than the object apart from the artist's personality. In English literature the Romantic period (early 19th cent.) followed the neo-classical, and its writers stressed various aspects of the general tendency toward person interest and self–expression. Among the characteristics of Romantic literature are sensibility, which values emotions in themselves and sees them as indicating moral values; primitivism, which sees the uncivilized man as having moral values which civilization destroys rather than perfects; love of nature in its uncultivated aspects as revealing divinity or moral qualities; interest in the past and particularly in medieval civilization because it seems colorful and free; mysticism, which finds harmony between man and divinity through nature, or in a visionary or dream world; stress on the ego and the imagination, which strain against the social bond and the control of reason. The great Romantic writers are devoted to large ideas such as brotherhood, liberty, love, and beauty, but see these as checked by human society and themselves as frustrated. They consider that man has infinite potentialities not actualized in human living. One important result of the Romantic movement has been an expansion of areas of human interest in literature, an imaginative awareness of many experiences in life which reveal man's nature to himself and his relation to what lies outside himself. BIBLIOGRAPHY: H. N. Fairchild, *Romantic Faith* (*Religious Trends in English Poetry* 3, 1949); H. M.

Schueller, "Romanticism Reconsidered," *Journal of Aesthetics and Art Criticism* 20 (1962).

[M. M. BARRY]

ROMANTICISM (RELIGIOUS ASPECTS), an interpretation of the universe that made man's interests central in the cosmos. Reality is symbolized as "God," "Providence," some "friend who cares," behind appearances. Man's ideals are safe because the Power behind Nature, never precisely defined, is also devoted to them. For the great majority, during the Romantic reaction to *En-lightenment, the failure of "rational religion" was reflected in the revivals of traditional religious faiths. This meant German Pietism, English evangelicalism, and a great resurgence of Catholicism on the Continent. Some Romantics were mere apologists for these faiths, men such as J. G. Hamann (1730–88) and F. Jacobi (1743–1819) or the French traditionalists J. de Maistre (1753–1821) and L. de Bonald (1754–1840). But many were not satisfied to turn to the past for inspiration, and even the prophets of the older faiths were influenced in countless ways by specifically Romantic values and attitudes. Their new interpretations of religion excluded identifying it with a set of pseudoscientific propositions that could not be maintained in the light of scientific reason. Religion was not to be identified with knowledge of what religion is. The influence of J. J. Rousseau (1712–78) on both the traditionalists and the reconstructors in Romanticism was of paramount importance. Rousseau emphasized intuition rather than analytic or discursive reasoning; he stimulated the urge to subjectivity and introspection, encouraged *emotionalism, and strengthened *individualism. His "Confession of Faith of a Savoyard Vicar," from *Émile* (1762), illustrates each of these perspectives on religion.

The Romantics offered three major interpretations of the nature and function of religion. First, religion is a form of knowledge, a philosophical explanation of the universe that uses symbols, whereas pure philosophy uses only concepts. The content and aim of both religion and pure philosophy are therefore equivalent. This view is best presented by G. Hegel (1770–1831) and his followers, but Hegelian idealism is least typical of Romantic concepts of religion. A second interpretation is that religion is not a form of knowledge but a form of art and aesthetic experience. It is a certain organized life of the feelings, a matter of emotion, and not, or only secondarily, of explanation or understanding. Theology furnishes symbols, not for the explanatory concepts of science and philosophy, but for the evocation and expression of man's deepest feelings. This view was worked out by J. Herder (1744–1803) and, more fully, by F. *Schleiermacher (1768–1834). A third interpretation is that religion is a form neither of knowledge nor of feeling but rather a form of action, of man's behavior. The religious life is a moral striving, to realize human and social goals. Matthew Arnold spoke of "morality touched with emotion," making "the will of God prevail." Its greatest 19th-cent. formulator was A. *Ritschl (1822–89), and it had a profound influence even into the 20th cent., through the *Social Gospel movement. BIBLIOGRAPHY: P. E. More, *Drift of Romanticism* (1955); M. Peckham, *Beyond the Tragic Vision* (1962); A. O. Lovejoy, "On the Discrimination of Romanticism," in *Essays in the History of Ideas* (pa., 1960).

[J. P. REID]

ROMANUS, SS., name of a number of saints, particularly as objects of local cult, but for whose lives there is little historical information. Among them are martyrs: Romanus of Rome, (d. 258); Romanus of Caesarea, martyred under Diocletian; Romanus of Antioch (d. *c.*303). Confessors include: Romanus of Blaye, a hermit (d. 380); Romanus of Cilicia, a thaumaturge; Romanus, monk of Condat (d. 463). Among holy bps. of this name are: Romanus of Reims (d. 535); of Auxerre (d. *c.*550); and of Rouen (d. *c.*640).

ROMANUS (d. 897), **POPE** for 4 months in 897. He was cardinal priest of St.-Peter-in-Chains when elected to replace the murdered *Stephen VI in the summer of 897. Nothing is known of the circumstances of his election and little more of his short reign. Rome was divided by the dispute about *Formosus, and it is thought that R. belonged to the Formosan party. During his reign the remains of the degraded pope were rescued from the Tiber and were given decent burial. BIBLIOGRAPHY: L. Duchesne, *Beginning of the Temporal Sovereignty of the Popes, A.D. 754–1073* (tr. A. Mathew, 1908); Mann 4:86–87; P. Mullins, NCE 12:641.

[P. F. MULHERN]

ROMANUS I LECAPENUS (*c.*870–945), **BYZANTINE EMPEROR** 920–944. While Patriarch Nicholas Mysticus lived, R. did not interfere in domestic ecclesiastical affairs, but after 925 he adhered to caesaropapist policies. He appointed three successive patriarchs: Stephen of Amasea (d. 928), Tryphon of Opsicium (removed in 930), and then his own unworthy 13–year–old son Theophylact. At R.'s request papal legates in 933 consecrated Theophylact. For diplomatic reasons R. strove to maintain friendly relations with Rome. No doctrinal controversies marred his reign. He was deposed by Constantine VII, and died an exile on the island of Prote. BIBLIOGRAPHY: S. Runciman, *Emperor Romanus Lecapenus and His Reign* (1963).

[R. H. SCHMANDT]

ROMANUS MELODUS, ST. (d. *c.*560), greatest religious poet of the Byzantine Church, probable author of the *Akathist Hymn* and scores of other liturgical hymns, of which about 80 are extant. Born in Syria, probably of Jewish extraction, R. came to Constantinople as a deacon near the beginning of the 6th century. His *Akathist Hymn*, 24 alphabetically arranged, highly picturesque stanzas in praise of the Virgin Mary, is still one of the most widely known and best-loved liturgical texts of the Byzantine Church. BIBLIOGRAPHY: *Romanos le Mélode* (ed. J. Grosdidier de Matons, 13 v., SC 1964–65); Beck 425–428.

[R. R. BARR]

ROME, a city on the Tiber in central Italy 17 miles from the sea, the former capital of the Roman Empire, the Papal States, the Kingdom of Italy, and now of the Italian Republic, known also as "the City on the Seven Hills" and "the Eternal City." The legendary date for the founding of the city is 753 B.C., though there is archeological evidence for occupation of the site from the 10th cent. B.C. The early kingdom was changed into a republic after the expulsion of the Etruscans in 510 B.C., and the latter into an empire through the reforms of Julius Caesar (49–44 B.C.) and his successor Octavian, Princeps and Augustus (27 B.C.–14 A.D.). The empire in the West survived under various forms, principate, military monarchy, and dominate until the capture of Rome in 476 by Odoacer, the king of the Heruli. During the succeeding centuries, because of the continuous attempts of the Goths, the Lombards, the Byzantine emperors, and the Germans to gain control of Italy, the papacy became a center of unity for much of the country. The prolonged rivalries among the leading Roman families to control the papacy led to a great deal of anarchy during the Dark Ages and to the eventual withdrawal of the popes to Avignon from 1309 to 1377. In 1527 the city was sacked by the soldiers of Charles V. In 1809 Pius VII was taken prisoner by Napoleon but was able to return to Rome in 1814. On September 20, 1870, Rome was captured by the forces of Garibaldi, and the popes withdrew to the Vatican as a means of protest. On Feb. 11, 1929, a concordat was finally signed between the Holy See and the Fascist government recognizing the Vatican as an independent state and granting it partial indemnification for its lost territories.

The archeological remains and artistic treasures of Rome are quite in keeping with its position as the capital of the ancient world and the center of Christendom. In comparison with the numerous monuments that have survived from imperial times, those of the republic are relatively few. Among the more significant of these are the *Cloaca Maxima,* the ancient drain for the Roman Forum, still functioning today; the *Tullianum,* or state prison; the *Tabularium,* (archives) where the state records were kept; the Tomb of the Scipios; the *Pons Mulvius* (Milvian Bridge) and the *Pons Fabricius* (Fabrician Bridge), and the remains of a number of roads and aqueducts leading into the city. Among the more important monuments of the Empire may be mentioned the *Ara Pacis* (Altar of Peace); the Mausolea of Augustus and Hadrian; the Flavian Amphitheater, or Colosseum; the Arches of Titus, Septimius Severus, and Constantine; the Columns of Trajan and Marcus Aurelius; the Basilica of Maxentius; the Baths of Caracalla; the Aurelian Wall; and the obelisk of Thutmose III, which was brought from Egypt and placed on the spina of the Circus Maximus but is now standing in the Piazza di San Giovanni in Laterano.

Among the many foreigners whom Rome attracted were a large number of Jews. The first historical reference to these immigrants, the founders of the oldest continually existing community of Jews in the world, is that of their expulsion from the city in 139 B.C. by the praetor Gnaeus Cornelius Hispanus (Valerius Maximus 1.3.3). Six Jewish catacombs from the first cent. of Christianity have been discovered, though not all of these are still extant. From inscriptions found in them, the names of at least 11 ancient synagogues are known.

St. Peter may possibly have come to Rome by the year 42 A.D. Be this as it may, by the time of St. Paul's arrival c.59 A.D., there was a flourishing Christian community in the city. During the last years of Nero's reign (64–68), both SS. Peter and Paul were executed at Rome, the former being buried on the Vatican Hill and the latter on the Ostian Way. Despite intermittent persecutions, the Church flourished in Rome, and Pope St. Cornelius (251–253) could write to Fabius, bp. of Antioch, that there were in Rome "46 presbyters, 7 deacons, 7 subdeacons, 42 acolytes, 52 exorcists, readers, and doorkeepers, more than 1,500 widows and people in distress, all of whom are supported by the grace and loving-kindness of the Master" (Eusebius, *Eccl. Hist.* 6.43.11), data which would seem to indicate a total of some 40,000 Christians within the city. At first the Christians met in the homes of private individuals to celebrate the Eucharist (cf. Justin, I *Apology* 65) and buried their dead in graves beneath the surface of the ground. In the mid-2d cent., however, they began to bury them in catacombs, subterranean corridors with connecting chambers excavated in the soft rock, or tuff, lying beneath the soil outside the city walls. During the next 3 cent. these cemeteries were greatly expanded, and they are still today among the most remarkable remains of ancient Rome.

Archeological evidence such as that found beneath the churches of St. Clement and SS. John and Paul and the tradition of Roman title churches (*tituli*) indicate that by the end of the 2d cent. there were a number of buildings specifically set aside for Christian worship. After the granting of freedom of religion throughout the empire by the Edict of Milan (313), the Christians were able to begin a golden age of church construction. Among the numerous churches from the 4th, 5th, and 6th cent., though many have been modified in later times, are Sta. Pudenziana with its wonderful mosaic in the apse, dating from c.385 A.D.; S. Prassede (rebuilt in the 9th cent.); S. Sabina with its carved cypress doors from c.425 A.D.; and Sta. Maria Maggiore, also of the 5th cent., with its well-preserved mosaics. During these same centuries many of the ancient buildings of Rome were also converted into churches. In 609 the Pantheon was consecrated by Boniface IV to Sta. Maria dei Martiri, and much later the tepidarium of the Baths of Diocletian was transformed into the church of Sta. Maria degli Angeli from plans drawn by Michelangelo.

Though new churches continued to be built in Rome during the Middle Ages, the Gothic style, so popular in northern Europe and also in other parts of Italy, never took hold in Rome. The only church of this type is that of the Dominicans near the Pantheon, Sta. Maria sopra Minerva. In Rome

the Renaissance ushered in an extraordinarily productive period in painting and sculpture, but esp. in architecture. Among the notable palaces erected at this time are the Palazzo Venezia, begun in 1455, and the Palazzo della Cancelleria, ascribed to Bramante (1444–1514). The most remarkable achievement of this age was the erection of St. Peter's basilica (1506–1626) to replace the earlier church erected by Constantine over the tomb of the Apostle. Among those who labored on it were Bramante, Raphael, Antonio da Sangallo, Michelangelo, Giacomo della Porta, and Carlo Maderna. The colonnade in front of the basilica is a later addition by Bernini. Among numerous other churches of the Renaissance are the Gesù, the principal church of the Jesuits, and Sant' Agnese in Agone by Rainaldi and Borromini.

As patrons of the arts, the popes laid the foundations of a number of great museums, and others have been created by the state in more recent times. Among the more famous museums of Rome are the Vatican, Lateran, Capitoline, Borghese, Villa Giulia, and Terme, the latter being located within the Baths of Diocletian. Among the many fountains that grace the city, the most famous is the Fontana di Trevi, of the 18th century.

Rome possesses a number of important foreign institutes such as the American, French, and German academies. It also has native academies, colleges, and universities, both secular and ecclesiastical. The Univ. of Rome was founded in 1303; and the Accademia di S. Luca, its beginnings traceable to c.1460, is considered the oldest in the world dedicated to the fine arts. Among the most famous ecclesiastical institutions are the Gregorian Univ., which had its origins in the Roman College founded by St. Ignatius Loyola in 1551; the Angelicum (renamed the Univ. of St. Thomas Aquinas), a pontifical university under the direction of the Dominicans, begun in 1577; the Lateran Univ. founded in 1773 by Pope Clement XIV; and the Pontifical Biblical Institute and the Pontifical Oriental Institute, which were affiliated with the Gregorian Univ. in 1928.

As the transmitter of Hellenic culture and the source of much of the linguistic, legal, and political structures of the West, Rome has had an incomparable place in the history of the world. If there is any truth to the saying that "all roads lead to Rome," it is due to the fact that it has been for the people of Europe and their cultural heirs "our common fatherland" (*Roma communis nostra patria est;* Modestinus, *Dig.* 50.1.33). BIBLIOGRAPHY: M. Cary, *History of Rome down to the Reign of Constantine* (1954); Pio Paschini, *Dal mondo romano al mondo cristiano* (1964); Bihlmeyer-Tüchle v. 1–3; F. X. Murphy, NCE 12:643–657. *PAPACY; *CHURCH OF ROME; *VATICAN.

[M. J. COSTELLOE]

ROME, EASTERN CHURCHES IN. In Christian Rome's first millennium, the presence of Eastern Churches and esp. of Greek monks in the city is well known, although precise locations are often difficult to determine. Apart from the Italo-Greek Byzantine abbey at Grottaferrata, S of

Rome, which has enjoyed uninterrupted, though often precarious, existence since 1004, the history of modern establishments of Eastern Churches in Rome begins with the union of Eastern groups with the Holy See in the last few centuries. Except for the Greek and Russian Orthodox churches opened in the present century, all Oriental establishments in Rome belong to the Catholic Eastern Churches. The Copts, Chaldeans, and Syro-Malankarese have no churches or institutions in the city. The Syro-Malabars have a small chapel for the use of their students in the College of St. Josaphat. The Syrian Catholics have the use of the church of Sta. Maria in Campo Marzio, where their Roman procurator lives. In 1883 the church of S. Nicola da Tolentino was given to the Armenians, who opened the Pontifical Armenian College nearby; they also retain possession of the church of S. Biagio, which they rarely use. Since 1859 the mother house and novitiate of the Armenian Sisters of the Immaculate Conception has been in Rome, where the Mekhitarists of Venice, too, have a procuracy and house for students. The Maronite College, closed after 2 cent. of existence in 1808, was opened in another location in 1891 with the church of S. Marone; the college was closed again in 1939, but the church remains that of the Maronite patriarchal procurator. Three Maronite communities of men have houses of studies in Rome. The church and hospice of S. Stefano in the Vatican Gardens, given to the Ethiopians in 1481 but later abandoned by them, were reopened in 1919 as the Ethiopian College and moved to another place in the Gardens in 1930. Attached to the Church of Sant' Atanasio, of Greek Byzantine rite since its foundation in 1580, is the Pontifical Greek College, now directed by Belgian Benedictines, which receives students from the Byzantine communities of S Italy and those of both Latin and Byzantine rites from Greece itself. The Russian Byzantine rite is represented since 1929 in the church of Sant' Antonio Abate and the adjacent Russian College, both under Jesuit direction, as well as in a number of small house chapels. The Romanian Byzantines still have the church of the Santissimo Salvatore, but in 1950 their college with its public chapel was given to the interritual Institute of St. John Damascene. The Ukrainian Byzantines have no churches other than the chapels of their Pontifical College of St. Josaphat (founded in 1897, directed by the Ukrainian Basilians since 1904, moved to its present location in 1932), of their Minor Seminary of St. Josaphat (founded in 1952, directed by Salesians), and of the procuracies of three religious communities. A small community of Ukrainian Studite monks has been established south of Rome. BIBLIOGRA-PHY: OrientCatt (1962) 476–495; 795–797.

[A. CODY]

ROME, PATRIARCHATE OF, the ecclesiastical jurisdiction of the bp. (patriarch) of Rome, as it took shape and was finally defined by law within the Roman Empire. The title of patriarch, borrowed from the OT, first appeared in the 4th cent. and was used to designate prominent bishops. Each civil province of the empire was headed by a met-

ropolitan, bp. of the civil capital. A larger administrative unit comprising many provinces was called a diocese, presided over by an exarch. The latter title was gradually replaced by that of patriarch. Some patriarchs extended their authority over several dioceses: Rome over the Western empire; Alexandria over Egypt, Libya, and Pentapolis; and Constantinople over Pontus, Asia, and Thrace. After the Council of Nicaea, as the Church settled into its role as the imperial religion, church structure was patterned more and more on the administrative divisions of the empire. The Emperor Diocletian (293) had divided the empire into four prefectures—Gaul, Italy, Illyricum, and the Orient. The prefectures of Gaul and Italy constituted the Western empire after Theodosius (395). When Justinian defined in law the jurisdictions of the five patriarchs (the Pentarchy), the patriarchate of Rome was given primacy of honor and comprised basically the Western empire. The prefecture of Gaul included three dioceses—Spain, Gaul, and Britain. That of Italy also comprised three dioceses—Africa, Western Illyricum (now, Yugoslavia), and Italy. The diocese of Spain contained seven provinces; Gaul had seventeen; Britain five. The diocese of Africa had seven provinces, Illyricum seven, Italy seventeen. Italy's provinces were divided into two subgroups—seven of the north under the vicar of Italy, the other ten administered by the vicar of Rome. The latter group was further subdivided and administered by the prefect of the city (Rome) and the prefect of the suburban areas. These were all originally civil administrative divisions. Each patriarchate imposed its patriarchal rights according to the peculiar history and conditions of its area. The bp. of Rome was not able to impose any effective rule over his far-flung patriarchate. He neither chose nor consecrated the bps. of Gaul, Spain, and Africa, nor called synods in those areas. Latin Africa was centered in Carthage. Spain and Gaul were virtually autonomous. The Emperor Valentinian III did help Pope St. Leo I the Great exercise some control over the Italian provinces, but the major advance in jurisdictional influence stems from papal initiative in missionary activity in Germany, the Frankish Empire, and England. The Muslim invasions of Egypt and Syria (638–640) left only Rome and Constantinople with any considerable power. With the eventual conversion of the Slavic peoples came five new Orthodox patriarchates, independent Churches in communion with the patriarch of Constantinople: Moscow, Georgia, Serbia, Romania, and Bulgaria. The patriarchate of Rome gained uncontested primacy over the emerging Latin Christian nations and in later centuries over the countries of the Western European diaspora, North, Central, and South America, as well as African, Asian, and Pacific lands colonized by Europeans. In the years since Vatican Council II there have been some tentative steps within the Latin Church to acknowledge the dignity and autonomy of the Eastern patriarchates and even to step back a bit from the distinctly Roman tradition of ecclesiastical centralization. BIBLIOGRAPHY: G. A. Maloney, NCE 12:658–659.

[E. J. DILLON]

ROME, UNIVERSITY OF, an institution of medieval origin, now a secular university in Rome. A *studium curiae* or *sacri palatii*, or university of the papal court, was established by Innocent IV *c.*1244. Boniface VIII founded a *studium urbis* in 1303, with all faculties except theology. The latter institution closed *c.*1370 because of the disorders of the Great Schism; it reopened in 1406 under Innocent VII and was reorganized in 1431 by Eugene IV. In the pontificate of Leo X (1513–21) the *studium curiae* and the *studium urbis* merged, and the Pope pressed forward with the construction of the larger facilities begun by Alexander VI. The building came to be known as the Sapienza and this became the commonly used name of the university itself from the mid-16th until the end of the 19th cent. when the institution came under the control of the Italian government. Some claim that the Sapienza was designed by Michelangelo; it was completed by Giacomo della Porta during the pontificate of Gregory XIII (1572–85). The university became famous for its medical school and it was an important center of humanistic studies. Student attendance, however, was never large, and during the 17th and 18th cent. its academic glories waned. Leo XII in 1824 undertook a restoration, and under Pius IX (1846–78) it was on the way toward a new era of prosperity. The Alexandrine Library, founded in 1661, houses 900,000 volumes. Enrollment at the present university is about 130,000; the teaching staff, about 7,000. BIBLIOGRAPHY: H. Rashdall, *Universities of Europe in the Middle Ages* (ed. F. M. Powicke and A. B. Emden, 3 v., 1936).

[M. B. MURPHY]

ROMERO, JUAN (1559–1630), Spanish Jesuit theologian and missionary in South America, appointed superior of the Argentina mission and later (1625) first vice-provincial of Chile. He organized missions and schools among the Indians and wrote a two-volume work on predestination.

[R. J. LITZ]

ROMMEN, HEINRICH (1897–1967), jurist and political scientist. German born, he came to the U.S. in 1938 because of his opposition to Nazism (he had been arrested and imprisoned for 6 months in 1933 for his anti-Nazi stand). After several earlier teaching posts, his academic career from 1953 was spent at the Georgetown Univ. School of Foreign Service. His work, *Natural Law*, was first published (1936) in German; the Eng. tr. by T. P. Hanley, 1947. This historical and philosophical presentation endures as an esteemed work on its theme and the applications to political theory. H.'s *The State in Catholic Thought* (1945) is also a substantive study of lasting value.

[T. C. O'BRIEN]

ROMUALD, ST. (*c.*952–1027), founder of the Camaldolese monks. Son of the nobleman Sergius, R. entered (*c.*972) the monastery of S. Apollinare in Classe in reparation for his father's murder of a kinsman. Searching for a more austere life, he left (*c.*974) to join the hermit Marinus near Venice (*c.*978), attaching himself to the abbey of Cuxa in the Pyrenees as a hermit for 10 years. He returned to Italy, continuing as a solitary until Emperor Otto III named him (998) abbot of S. Apollinare in Classe; but he returned after a year to eremitical life and founded eremitical monasteries, the most important of which was the one he established *c.*1023 at Camaldoli near Arezzo. BIBLIOGRAPHY: E. S. Duckett, *Death and Life in the Tenth Century* (1967) 187–188; Butler 1:266–268; G. Tabacco and P. Cannata, BiblSanct 11:365–384.

[G. E. CONWAY]

ROMUALD II OF SALERNO (d.1182 or 1183), archbishop. A member of the Guarna family of Salerno, R. is renowned as churchman, scholar, and politician. Elected to the archiepiscopal See of Salerno in 1153, he was at the same time councilor and intimate friend of King William I of Sicily, serving as regent to the latter's son, King William II, during the son's minority. R. was much esteemed likewise in Rome and was entrusted with arranging the treaty of peace between Pope Alexander III and Emperor Frederick I Barbarossa. He is the author of a *Chronicon universale*, a history of the world from Creation until his own time. BIBLIOGRAPHY: For the *Chronicon*, see L. A. Muratori, *Rerum italicarum scriptorum* 5:7–244 (or 2d ed., v. 7); MGHS 19:398–461; G. Crisci and A. Campagna, *Salerno sacra* (1962) 76–78.

[W. A. JURGENS]

RONAN, ST. (Rumon), 7th-cent. bp. venerated in Brittany. That he was an Irish missionary is uncertain; several saints with the name Ronan are venerated in Ireland: e.g. SS. Ronan of Lough Derg, of Lismore, of Co. Down, of Co. Louth, of Co. Meath.

RONCHAMP, NOTRE-DAME-DU-HAUT (1950–55), French pilgrimage church designed and built by Le Corbusier in the Vosges mountain village of Ronchamp. Constructed of old stone from the earlier chapel destroyed in World War II, and set high on its mountain elevation, the curvilinear structure, with towers, boasts a provocative billowing concrete-shell roof rising to a point at the E, and draining through a concrete spout (gargoyle) into a free-form pool. The processional main door, pivoting at the middle, is brilliantly enhanced by enameled steel designs. The dramatic lighting of the interior through deeply splayed, scattered and varied rectangles of colored glass, is a principal aesthetic component. The worshipper moves around, within and about this multidimensional, emotionally conceived work determined by the rationale of Le Corbusier's controlled proportions. The church, a powerful "sculptured architecture," is one of the most expressive and uniquely beautiful works of the 20th century. BIBLIOGRAPHY: Le Corbusier, *Chapel at Ronchamp* (1957).

[M. J. DALY]

RONGE, JOHANN (1813–87), founder of the German Catholic movement (*Deutschkatholizismus). As a Breslau priest he was in repeated difficulties with church authorities, and was suspended and later degraded from the priesthood in 1844 after writing a public letter severely attacking Bp. Wilhelm Arnoldi of Trier for fostering veneration of the relic of the Holy Coat. He thereafter organized a schismatic Church, which shortly abandoned its Catholic foundations, veering toward the contemporary rationalism that R. favored. He was more an agitator than a religious reformer. After a few years of notoriety, he spent the remainder of his life in oblivion.

[J. C. WILLKE]

RONSARD, PIERRE DE (1524–1585), French humanist poet. A court page, R. renounced a military career because of early deafness, devoted himself to letters, studied classics under Jean Dorat, and along with Joachim du Bellay headed the new school of French Renaissance poetry, the *Pléiade (1556). His works, including *Odes* (1550–55), *Amours* (1552), *Mélanges* and *Le Bocage* (1554), *La Continuation des amours* (1555–56), *Hymnes* (1555–56), and *Les Amours d'Hélène* (1578), reveal first the inspiration of Pindar, then of Horace, the *Greek Anthology*, Homer, Virgil, the neo-Latins, and Petrarch. Although only in minor orders (1543), he held various ecclesiastical benefices, receiving for his *Eglogues* and *La Bergerie* (1559–65), the abbey of Bellozane (1563), then the priory of St.-Cosme-en-l'Isle. Becoming court poet (1559), he was appointed counselor and almoner in ordinary to the King (Charles IX). His polemical *Discours* (1558–63) deals with politics and religion. During the French religious wars he sided with the Crown despite his early evangelical tendencies, condemned the Huguenots (*Remonstrance au peuple de France*, 1563), was hostile to Théodore de Bèze, but dedicated works to Elizabeth I of England while remaining sympathetic to Mary Queen of Scots. He was accused of paganism by the Calvinists, yet his *Hercule chrétien* reveals a fusion of classicism with Christianity and attests to his later orthodoxy. BIBLIOGRAPHY: H. Chamard, *Histoire de la Pléiade* (new ed., 5 v., 1960–64); P. de Nolhac, *Ronsard et l'humanisme* (1921); P. Perdrizet, *Ronsard et la réforme* (1902).

[R. N. NICOLICH]

ROOD, a crucifix mounted on a beam above the entrance to the *chancel of a church, often with figures of the Virgin Mary and the Apostle John on either side. It became almost universal in 14th- and 15th-cent. Gothic churches. Sometimes it rested on a platform used for an organ and choir gallery.

[T. EARLY]

ROOTHAAN, JOHANN PHILIPP (1785–1853), 21st Jesuit superior general. R. was born in Amsterdam but joined the Jesuits in Dvinsk, Russia, in 1804, where the Society survived during the suppression. After studies and ordination he escaped Russia when the Jesuits were banned there (1820) and assisted the Jesuit vice-provincial in Switzerland. He served as superior general from 1829 to 1853 and contributed significantly to the reemergence of the Jesuits after the restoration of 1814. The Jesuit contribution to the Church in the U.S. was a concern to him: he encouraged European Jesuits to work in the U.S., built up the Maryland province, formed the St. Louis province, and provided for the founding of Marquette University. BIBLIOGRAPHY: R. North, *General Who Rebuilt the Jesuits* (1944).

[T. M. MCFADDEN]

ROPER, WILLIAM (*c.*1495–1578), friend and son-in-law of Thomas More. A Lutheran for a time, he returned to the Catholic faith while continuing to live in England throughout the religious troubles. He is known to have given generous financial support to Catholics in England and to have helped those in exile by contributing to the publication of books in defense of the faith, and by aiding in the foundation of the English College at Douai. R. is chiefly famous for his charming and sympathetic account of his father-in-law, St. Thomas More, written after the latter's execution, with its vivid picture also of his wife, Margaret More. This book, circulated at first in MS, was printed in 1526 and is the chief source of information regarding More's personal life.

[M. J. BARRY]

RORE, CYPRIANO DE (Cyprien de; Van Rore; 1516–1565), Flemish composer and madrigalist. He was a pupil of Willaert in Venice before 1546. R. was appointed to the court of Ferrara as *maestro di cappella* (1547), to Parma (1560), then to St. Mark's, Venice (1563–64) after Willaert's death. His liturgical works include traditional Masses, motets, a St. John Passion, and other church music. He published books of five-part and four-part madrigals, fantasies, and *ricercari* (1549) with Willaert. Well-regarded by contemporaries, R.'s compositions and madrigals were both experimental and innovative. R. influenced Monte, Lasso, Palestrina and even Monteverdi.

[R. J. LITZ]

RORICIUS, see RURICIUS.

ROSA, ENRICO (1870–1938), director of the periodical *Civiltà cattolica*. R. entered the Jesuits in 1886 and was ordained in 1900. He joined the staff of *Civiltà cattolica* in 1905 and was its director from 1915 to 1931. He was a strong defender of the Holy See, an opponent of political and philosophical liberalism, and of *Modernism. BIBLIOGRAPHY: C. Testore, EncCatt 10:1338.

[T. M. MCFADDEN]

ROSA, MARIA CROCIFISSA DI, ST., see DI ROSA, MARIA CROCIFISSA, ST.

ROSA, SALVATOR (1615–73), Italian painter, etcher, musician, poet, actor. Travelling to Rome, Viterbo, and Naples 1635–37, R. returned to Rome in 1639, becoming court painter to Prince Gian Carlo de' Medici, Florence (1640). Evidencing versatility in the sophisticated "Accademia dei Percossi" R.'s landscape-history paintings of classical organization are peopled with mythological and biblical characters (*Cain and Abel*). He was most successful in quasi-romantic panels of landscape and *capricci*.

[M. J. DALY]

ROSA Y FIGUEROA, FRANCISCO DE LA (1697–*c*.1780), archivist and historian of Mexico. After 7 years as a secular priest he entered the Franciscan Order in 1724 and held a variety of pastoral and administrative posts within the Franciscan province of the Holy Evangelist in New Spain. As provincial archivist, he uncovered and published several important documents relating to the early Spanish presence in the area. He supported the native Indian languages against the decree of King Charles III that only Spanish be spoken in New Spain.

[T. M. MCFADDEN]

ROSALIA, ST. (d. 1160?), recluse, thought to have been a Benedictine or more probably a Basilian nun, patroness of Palermo. Information concerning her life and cult cannot be traced back beyond the 17th cent., although there appear to have been churches in Sicily dedicated to a St. Rosalia in the 13th century. A vision, said to have been granted to one stricken by a plague that raged in Palermo in 1624, led to a search for R.'s remains, which were found encased in stalactitic deposit in a cave on Monte Pellegrino. They were brought to Palermo in a procession and the plague abated. Forty days after the translation of the bones, a supposedly autographic inscription was found on the walls of the cave in which her relics had been discovered. It identified her and stated that she chose to dwell in the cave for the love of Jesus Christ. In 1630 Pope Urban VIII added her name to the Roman Martyrology. Her cult, widely diffused in Italy and Sicily, has been carried overseas by Sicilian emigrants. BIBLIOGRAPHY: M. R. P. McGuire, NCE 12:667; Zimmermann 3:15; G. Bronzini, EncCatt 10:1346–50; Butler 3:486–487.

[M. R. P. MCGUIRE]

ROSARY, known also as the Dominican rosary, is a Marian prayer that leads through Mary to Jesus, the source of all grace. It offers 15 scriptural mysteries as subjects of mental prayer, the primary focus of the devotion. Divided into three sets of five mysteries, i.e., meditations: joyful, sorrowful, and glorious, the rosary centers around the Incarnation, sufferings, and glorification of Christ. Each mystery is accompanied by the recitation of an Our Father, ten Hail Marys, and a Glory Be. Mental prayer on the mystery may also precede or follow the vocal prayer. It may take a general form, consider a distinct point of the mystery, or move from point to point in the same mystery as the Aves are recited. Various introductory and concluding prayers (notably the Hail, Holy Queen and the prayer of the rosary feast) are attached to, but are not parts of, the rosary. Historical proof is lacking for the pious tradition (which first appeared and gained acceptance after 1470 and is traceable to *Alan de la Roche) that St. Dominic received the rosary from Mary. Papal bulls and encyclicals, issued to foster the rosary as a prayer, did not claim to settle the question of origin.

The rosary developed as various Christological and Marian devotions coalesced during a complicated, detailed, and 5-cent.-long (12th to 16th) history. A profuse variety of combinations of Paters, Aves, and mysteries dealing with Christ and his Mother, which drew their inspiration from biblical and liturgical themes, led slowly to the present rosary. During the 12th cent. the recitation of 150 Paters by the illiterate substituted for the 150 psalms. The Paters were often divided, as the psalter, into 3 sets of 50 each. Strings of beads (paternosters) were a convenient method of counting. Concurrently liturgical antiphons were used to celebrate Mary's joys. Her clients multiplied Gabriel's Ave, believing that she relived her Annunciation joy when they did so. Chaplets of 50 or psalters of 150 standardized these recitations. Later the psalters of Paters and of Aves were combined, an Ave following each Pater. Other joys experienced by Mary in her life with Christ were gradually added to the Annunciation joy until chains of 50, 100, or 150 phrases describing her joys were composed. A set of 50 was styled a *rosarium,* rose garden, because the rose, a symbol of joy, was applied to Mary. When her dolors were added in the 14th cent., they were interspersed between sets of her joys on earth and those in heaven.

Contributing to this development were psalters that applied the psalms to Jesus or Mary or both by attaching to each psalm a statement, often rhymed, that developed some Christological or Marian reference. When later the psalms were omitted, the phrases were strung together in loose concatenations or lines. These phrases reinforced the custom of reflecting on Mary's joys. Thus the rosarian mysteries arose as meditation points.

The rosary as we know it became recognizable once mental prayer on the joys and sorrows was coupled with the recitation of the Aves. Either one joy was meditated upon during each set of 50 Aves or a separate mystery was attached to each Ave. In the latter case, a book of phrases or pictures was used when praying. *Dominic of Prussia, a Carthusian, popularized this method about 1409. Before him, his confrere the Carthusian Henry Kalkar (d. 1408), bracketed the Aves into decades by inserting a Pater between each ten. About 1480 the method of attaching one mystery only to each decade was developed. At times this mystery, joined to the Pater, was divided into ten subsidiary mysteries, one for each Ave. The simpler form of one mystery for each decade prevailed during the 16th cent. and the 15 mysteries were gradually standardized. During the same cent., the second half of the Hail Mary: "Holy Mary, etc." and the Glory Be were added to the vocal prayers of the rosary.

Once the rosary reached full development, Dominicans made it a popular prayer by their preaching, writing of rosary books, and promotion of the Rosary Confraternity, whose members undertook to use this prayer. Saints and members of other orders also became rosary advocates. By presenting the mysteries as an essential part of the rosary, a rosary bull of Pius V (1569) helped to establish the double thrust of the devotion as vocal and mental prayer. Since Leo XIII, the popes have fostered the rosary as a traditional, popular, and highly efficacious prayer. It seems to be among the devotions that were "warmly commended" by Vatican II. Its mysteries "accord with the sacred liturgy, are in some fashion derived from it, and lead the people to it" (Vat II SacLit 13). BIBLIOGRAPHY: F. William, *Rosary, its History and Meaning* (1953); J. G. Shaw, *Story of the Rosary* (1954); M. Ward, *Splendor of the Rosary* (1945).

[W. A. HINNEBUSCH]

ROSARY ALTAR SOCIETY, a spiritual association also called the Confraternity of the Most Holy Rosary. It was founded by Alan de la Roche, a Dominican friar in the last quarter of the 15th cent. in France, Saxony, and the Low Countries. Its members say 15 mysteries of the rosary each week. The word altar is popularly used in its title because some altar of the church must be designated as the altar of the Confraternity. In 1898 Leo XIII issued the apostolic constitution on the Most Holy Rosary (*Ubi primum*) containing the laws, rights, and privileges of the confraternity. It has spread throughout the world including the U.S., where membership is restricted to women.

[R. C. CLIGGETT]

ROSAS, JUAN MANUEL (1793–1877), Argentinian dictator. Of a wealthy family but with no formal education beyond the elementary level, R. was a big-scale rancher and head of a large meat packing business. He was popular among the gauchos whom he organized into an informal army for use against marauding Indians but which he also employed in support of conservatism and federalism. He was governor of the province of Buenos Aires from 1829 to 1832 and again from 1835 to 1852. During his latter term of office he extended his dictatorial power over the other provinces of Argentina. Imperialistic ambitions led him into war with Uruguay (1841–51) and brought on blockades by the French and English fleets. During his regime there were constant uprisings which he suppressed by means of terror, ruthlessly using his Mazorca gangs to stifle all opposition. In 1852 he was overthrown by J. J. de Urquiza, and the remainder of his life was spent in exile in England. BIBLIOGRAPHY: A. Delpiane, *Rosas* (1951).

[P. DAMBORIENA]

ROSATI, JOSEPH (1789–1843), abp. of St. Louis, Missouri, teacher. An Italian who joined the Congregation of the Mission and was ordained in 1811, R. early volunteered for the U.S. missions. Arriving in Baltimore in 1816, he proceeded to Bardstown, Ky., where he taught theology at St. Thomas Seminary. He next went to Perryville, Mo., in 1818 to open St. Mary's Seminary ("The Barrens"). This institution, the first of its kind W of the Mississippi, became under R.'s leadership a primary source of missionaries for the West. He was named superior of American Vincentians in 1820, and vicar apostolic of Mississippi and Alabama, but this appointment was changed (upon his and other's plea that the jurisdiction was premature) to coadjutor of Louisiana, a post R. was forbidden to decline. He was consecrated a bp. in 1824. Louisiana was divided into two dioceses in 1826, St. Louis and New Orleans. R. requested St. Louis and was approved for that jurisdiction, although obliged to administer Louisiana for 4 more years until a new bp. was named. R. brought the Religious of the Sacred Heart of Jesus to St. Louis, built St. Mary's College at "The Barrens," opened St. Louis Hospital with the Sisters of Charity of Emmitsburg, Md., and fostered the Jesuit St. Louis College (now University). A cathedral and many churches attest his administrative vigor. In 1840 R. was sent as apostolic delegate to Haiti and successfully negotiated an agreement with Rome; returning to Rome, he died there. BIBLIOGRAPHY: J. G. Shea, *Hierarchy of the Catholic Church in the U.S.* (1886).

[J. R. AHERNE]

ROSCELIN OF COMPIÉGNE (c.1050–1125), French dialectician and philosopher. Usually regarded as the founder of medieval nominalism, R. left no writings that have survived. His doctrine is known only through others' reports, including those of his pupil, Abelard, who was critical of him, and those of his adversary, St. Anselm. R. seems to have been an extreme antirealist who held that universals have no objective reality except a verbal one. It is possible, however, that R. accepted some form of conceptual universal. His dialectics brought him under suspicion of teaching tritheism. BIBLIOGRAPHY: M. M. C. de Wulf, *History of Medieval Philosophy* (tr. E. C. Messenger, 1935–38) v. 1; T. Gilby, EncPhil 7:211.

[V. BULLOUGH]

ROSCREA, ABBEY OF, a monastery in County Tipperary, Ireland, founded by St. Crónán (d. c.665). It was given in commendation to a lay abbot in the 9th century. Some of its abbots also held office in Clonmacnois. In 1152 Roscrea became a diocesan seat but was reduced in the 12th cent. to the status of a deanery. From its scriptorium came the *Book of Dimma* (8th cent.), *Annals of Roscrea*, and *Rule of Échtgus Úa Cúanáin* (12th century). BIBLIOGRAPHY: A. Gwynn and D. F. Gleeson, *History of the Diocese of Killaloe* (1962); D. F. Gleeson, *Roscrea* (1947).

[C. MCGRATH]

ROSE OF LIMA, ST. (1586–1617), Dominican tertiary, the first saint of the New World to be canonized (1671).

Born in Lima, Peru, she was baptized Isabel de Flores but was called Rose from infancy because of the beauty of her face, and under that name she was confirmed at 14 by Toribio Alfonso de *Mogrovejo, abp. of Lima, who was himself to be canonized 60 years after Rose. She began in childhood to live a life of remarkable austerity and penance. At the age of 20 she became a Dominican tertiary and modeled her life on that of St. Catherine of Siena. When not ministering to destitute children and elderly persons in an infirmary that was set up in her family home, she would withdraw to a small hermitage in the garden and give herself to prayer. She was named patron of Peru, the Americas, the Indies, and the Philippines. BIBLIOGRAPHY: F. P. Keyes, *Rose and the Lily* (1961); S. Kaye-Smith, *Quartet in Heaven* (1952); Butler 3:444–446; V. Vargas Ugarte, *Vida de Santa Rosa de Santa María* (1951).

[P. DAMBORIENA]

ROSE OF VITERBO, ST. (1235–52), Third Order Franciscan. She joined the Third Order Secular of Francis of Assisi and championed the Pope's cause against Emperor Frederick II. For 4 years she spoke in the streets and environs of Viterbo. She retired at 15 to live in solitude, dying at 17. After 7 cent. her body is incorrupt. Callistus III canonized her in 1457. BIBLIOGRAPHY: M. A. Habig, *Franciscan Book of Saints* (1959) 633–636; F. Casolini, BiblSanct 11:413–425; Butler 3:487–488.

[O. J. BLUM]

ROSE WINDOW, a name given to the large stone-traceried, stained glass window of a medieval church. It is usually placed either over the west façade or on at least one of the transept ends. When fully developed, esp. in France, it appeared in practically every important Gothic cathedral. It gets its name from the design of an open rose, which the tracery suggests.

[S. A. HEENEY]

ROSEGGER, PETER (1843–1918), Austrian novelist from Styria, whose popular narratives, often didactic, describe with realism and humor the simple life of the peasantry and reveal a love of nature and a liberal humanism. Lacking strength to earn his livelihood at farming, he was apprenticed to a tailor. He attended high school (1865–69) in Graz, where he wrote little stories for the *Volkskalender.* Later he edited his own periodicals (*Fröliche Stunde; Heimgarten,* from 1876). Among his works were the novels *Schriften des Waldschulmeisters* (1875) and *Jakob der Letzte* (1875).

[B. F. STEINBRUCHNER]

ROSELINE, ST. (1263–1329), prioress. A member of a noble family, she joined the Carthusians where she acquired a reputation for great austerity of life and eventually (c.1300) became prioress of the convent at Celle-Roubaud. BIBLIOGRAPHY: Butler 1:112–113; P. Rouillard, BiblSanct 11:435–436.

[J. MULDOON]

ROSENBERG, ALFRED (1893–1946), Nazi Party leader and philosopher. He was born in Reval, capital of the Russian province of Estonia, where his ancestors had migrated from Germany. Although his father never went to church, R. was confirmed in the Protestant Church in 1909, but the event stirred contradictory sentiments in his mind. After taking a degree in architecture from the Technical School in Riga (1918), he left revolutionary Russia for Germany. In Munich he joined the infant Nazi party and wrote for its newspaper, the *Völkischer Beobachter;* he became the chief editor of the newspaper in March 1923. During Adolf Hitler's brief imprisonment following the abortive Putsch of November 1923, R. also served as acting party leader. His main interest, however, was in racial philosophy. Influenced by the writings of Houston Stewart Chamberlain and by the infamous forgery, *The Protocols of the Elders of Zion,* of which he edited a new edition, R. provided the most elaborate argument for Nazi theories of anti-Semitism and German racial superiority in his book, *The Myth of the Twentieth Century.* Although sometimes described as the basic treatise of Nazi ideology, it was a rambling unorganized diatribe. It espoused a ''Germanic religion,'' which Rosenberg claimed had been subverted by the universalism of Christianity. After the Nazis had taken control of the German government and given R. responsibility for indoctrination and education, the book was placed on the Index. Ironically, as Minister for Occupied Eastern Territories after 1941, R. became an unsuccessful advocate of toleration for the Orthodox Church in Russia, but his political activities in Germany attempted to undermine all influence of religion. BIBLIOGRAPHY: R. Cecil, *Myth of the Master Race* (1972).

[R. J. GIBBONS]

ROSENIUS, CARL OLOF (1816–68), Swedish Lutheran lay preacher. He worked within the established Church, and by his preaching, writings as editor of the *Pietist,* his hymns, and mission work, he was a leader of the spiritual revival in the 19th century. Many Swedish Lutheran immigrants to the U.S. brought with them his *Pietist* as teachings on spiritual regeneration and righteous living.

[T. C. O'BRIEN]

ROSER, ISABEL (d. 1554), Spanish patroness of St. Ignatius of Loyola. In 1541 she tried with some of her friends to form a congregation attached to the Jesuits. She gained formal approval from the Pope in 1545, but Ignatius arranged the cancellation of her vows. After she had sued him unsuccessfully, she became reconciled with him and entered the Franciscan Order. BIBLIOGRAPHY: H. Rahner, *Ignatius von Loyola, Briefwechsel mit Frauen* (1956) 301, 604.

[M. J. SUELZER]

ROSES, BLESSING OF THE: (1) papal blessing of the Golden Rose, a symbol of the pope's recognition of outstanding service to the Church, on Laetare Sunday; an ancient tradition, the first record of which is in 1049; (2) a blessing given in Dominican and other churches on the feast of the Holy Rosary.

[J. DALLEN]

ROSETTA STONE, a 3′9″ by 2′4½″ black basalt stone, discovered by a captain in the French army in 1799 in Egypt about 30 miles from Alexandria near the town of Rosetta. The stone bears an inscription in Egyptian and Greek honoring the accession of Ptolemy V Epiphanes of Egypt in 196 B.C. The portion of the inscription in Egyptian is written in two scripts, hieroglyphic and demotic, the popular form of hieroglyphic. Working from the proper names on the stone, Thomas Young and J. F. Champollion undertook to decipher the hieroglyphic inscription and succeeded in establishing how the hieroglyphic signs were to be read and what their Greek equivalents were. Thus the stone, now in the British Museum, afforded the basis for the translation of Egyptian hieroglyphic. BIBLIOGRAPHY: E. A. W. Budge, *Rosetta Stone in the British Museum* (1929).

[C. P. CEROKE]

ROSH HA-SHANAH, Jewish New Year (the head of the year), a very important 2-day holiday at the beginning of the month *Tishri* (Sept.-Oct.). It is followed by a solemn period of repentance, the High Holidays, ending on the 10th of *Tishri*, the Day of Atonement. There is almost complete silence as to the origin and nature of this feast in the Bible, but the Mishnah bears witness that it was celebrated as early as the 2d Christian cent. with solemn acclamations in voice and horn (*shofar*) to God's kingship and his loving kindness for his people.

[J. F. FALLON]

ROSICRUCIANS, a name adopted by certain societies or fraternities claiming hidden knowledge. The symbolism of the rose and cross, from which the word is derived, is uncertain. Rosicrucianism has had two periods of florescence. Its origins in its earlier form are obscure, allegedly because of deliberate efforts to veil the history from outsiders. Stories of obviously fabulous character have been advanced to substantiate claims to antiquity. Some Rosicrucians have held that their order can be traced back to the time of Pharaoh Thutmose III. Others claim that the movement began with the foundation of the Society of the Rose and Cross by Christian Rosencreuz, a German scholar, in 1413 in order to share with others the advanced knowledge of medicine, philosophy, and science he had gathered from Muslim sages on his extensive travels in the East. Authorship of a book that appeared in the 17th cent., an allegorical work of occult science called *Die Chymische Hochzeit,* was attributed to Rosencreuz. However, the earliest appearance of Rosicrucianism of which we can be reasonably sure was in the circle of Paracelsus (d. 1541), the Swiss alchemist and physician. Possibly it was founded by Paracelsus himself, or if not, by one of his disciples. Johann Valentine Andreä published the *Fama fraternitatis* in 1614–15; in 1616 the

Die Chymische Hochzeit appeared. Andreä gave out the story of Rosencreuz in great detail, claiming that his writings had been buried with him and had only recently been discovered in his tomb. Later, however, Andreä declared that his account of the early history and of the documents supposedly left by Rosencreuz had been a hoax. After Andreä's *Fama fraternitatis* had aroused interest, other treatises on Rosicrucianism appeared in swift succession. The English Rosicrucian Henry Fludd (d. 1637) published two treatises on the subject on the Continent; the manuscript of a third, addressed to King James I, was found among his papers. Like many 17th-cent. philosophers, Fludd was steeped in Neoplatonism and his thought was markedly pantheistic. Extant correspondence between Continental Rosicrucians and Fludd indicates that groups of scholars in Germany and elsewhere were organized as members of the Fraternity of the Rosy Cross and that they rejected both Catholic and Lutheran teachings in their pursuit of wisdom. Little is known of the nature of this movement and still less of its formal organization. Its members made use of the language of alchemy, medicine, and the occult to transmit their philosophic speculations.

Kenelm Digby (d. 1665) is thought to have been a Rosicrucian. Thomas Ashmole (d. 1692) is said to have organized a lodge of the fraternity at London in 1646. A translation of *Die Chymische Hochzeit* was published in English in 1690 under the title *The Chemical Wedding*. The later history of both Continental and English Rosicrucianism is as obscure as its origins. It does not seem to have survived the 18th cent. in any recognizable form, except for possible influences on Freemasonry.

A modern Rosicrucian revival began in 1868 with the publication of *The General Statutes of the Order of Knights of the Rose Cross* by R. W. Little. As reorganized by Little, this form of the movement was a branch of Freemasonry. William Wynn Westcott succeeded Little as leader of the *Societas Rosicruciana in Anglia* and published a history of the Rosicrucians in 1885. Little's society was primarily a fraternal organization closely allied to Freemasonry. Local units (colleges) were established in various parts of the English-speaking world and elsewhere after 1875. An American branch was established with headquarters in New York City (*Societas Rosicruciana in America*), and a Rosicrucian Brotherhood was founded at Quakertown, Pa.; Reuben Swinburne Clymer, a prolific writer on religious and occult subjects, reorganized this brotherhood in 1902. The Ancient Mystical Order Rosae Crucis (AMORC) was founded by H. Spencer Lewis in 1915 with headquarters at San José, California. AMORC is strongly missionary, advertises extensively, and distributes more than 6 million pieces of literature a year. Both the Rosicrucian Brotherhood and AMORC can be classified as religious movements, although AMORC insists that it is simply a fraternal organization. Both promise their members the power to utilize cosmic forces by discovering the secret wisdom of the ages. Clymer's theology is a mystical Gnosticism based on a progressive divinization of the initiate. Man is created with a spark of the divine in him and, by recognizing and bringing it to consciousness through the secret laws of nature known to the initiated, it becomes an inexhaustible source of wisdom and power. This theme is at the heart of religious Rosicrucianism and can be found in the AMORC literature as well. A fourth branch of the movement, the Rosicrucian Fellowship, founded by Max Heindel at Oceanside, Calif., is also religious in its orientation, with considerable emphasis on astrology. BIBLIOGRAPHY: R. K. MacMaster, NCE 12:676–677; A. C. Jones, Hastings ERE 10:856–858.

[R. K. MacMASTER]

ROSMINI-SERBATI, ANTONIO (1797–1855), founder of the Institute of Charity (see ROSMINIANS), papal counselor, philosopher and theologian. Ordained in 1821, R. founded the Institute of Charity in 1828 at Calvarie, Piedmont, as a clerical congregation and guided it throughout his life. He was devoted to the papacy, to the unification of Italy under the presidency of the pope (see NEO-GUELFISM), and to freedom from Austrian domination in Italy. He was close to Pius IX during that pontiff's period of liberal, constitutional sympathies, and was with the Pope in the flight from Rome to Gaeta in 1848. In the conservative reaction against the Italian nationalists, R. lost papal favor. Two of his politico-ecclesiastical works, *Of the Five Wounds of the Holy Church* (1840) and *A Constitution Based on Social Justice* (1848), were summarily put on the Index in 1848; R. submitted obediently and accepted the condemnation. His renown rests above all on his stature as a speculative thinker. His thought and writings were motivated by a Christian apologetic aim; they constitute a highly personal synthesis grounded on an epistemology of the idea of being that is applied to speculative and moral philosophy, theology, and educational theory. R. was deeply imbued with the psychological and ontological thought both of Augustine and Aquinas; he wished to develop out of their thought an objective and unifying base for all human knowledge and action that would counteract the subjectivism developed by Kant in the face of skeptical empiricism. He found that base in the primordial concept of being, which he insisted is neither an a priori category of mind nor the idea of God. Nevertheless, because of his original and complex language and system, R. was early accused of heterodoxy and in particular of *ontologism and of errors on original sin, the Trinity, the Incarnation, and the Eucharist. In 1854 because of such attacks, a papal commission, in which Pius IX himself participated, examined all of R.'s works, the commission's verdict, *dimittantur* (let them be dismissed) led to controversy after R.'s death. The Jesuit magazine *Civiltà cattolica* obtained from the Congregation of the Index in 1881 a response that the *dimittantur* was neither an approbation nor a declaration that R.'s works were free from error, neither did it rule out charging them with error (see D 3154s). In 1887 a series of propositions extracted from R.'s

various works was censured by the Holy Office, as repudiated, condemned, proscribed (D 3201–41). Interest in R.'s thought, however, has never lagged, esp. in Italy. (Pope John Paul I wrote his doctoral thesis on Rosmini.) There can be no doubt of the genuineness and profundity of his insights into Augustine and Aquinas that were not appreciated by the more letter-bound curialist and scholastic critics of the 19th century. Among R.'s works in translation are: *Origin of Ideas* (3 v., 1883–84); *Psychology* (3 v., 1884–88); *Of the Five Wounds of the Holy Church* (1883); *Letters, Chiefly on Religious Subjects* (1901); *Theodicy* (3 v., 1912); *Counsels to Religious Superiors* (1961); *Maxims of Christian Perfection* (1889; repr. 1963). BIBLIOGRAPHY: A. R. Caponigri, EncPhil 7:213–216.

[T. C O'BRIEN]

ROSMINIANS, the Institute of Charity, a clerical congregation founded at Calvarie, Piedmont, in 1828 by A. *Rosmini-Serbati, approved by Gregory XVI in 1839. Rosmini was encouraged to found the Institute by Bl. Maddalena Canossa. After 1832 the Sisters of Providence in Italy became associated with the Rosminians. In 1835 the Institute was established in England, spread to Ireland, and has exercised considerable influence on the devotional life of the Church in both countries. The Irish-American province has parishes in the dioceses of Peoria, Ill., Jefferson City, Mo., and St. Augustine, Florida. The religious spirit of the Rosminians reflects the founder's *Maxims of Spiritual Perfection* (1830; Eng. tr. repr. 1963). Members make profession of the three vows of religion, wear a simple cassock, in their life are devoted to prayer and study and to the acceptance of whatever apostolate may be required by the needs of the Church. In 1976 they numbered 313 priests and 117 brothers.

[T. C. O'BRIEN]

ROSSANO GOSPELS, 6th-cent. illuminated MS from the *Codex purpureus* in the monumental tradition of Asiatico-Eastern art with rich and elegant ornamentation, scenes disposed in the manner of great mosaics of the period, of the same tradition as the narrative cycles of the Gospels (586 A.D.) of the monk Rabula.

[M. J. DALY]

ROSSELLI, COSIMO (1439–1507), Italian painter, teacher of Andrea del Sarto, Fra Bartolommeo and Piero di Cosimo. Student of Neri di Bicci (1453) and Benozzo Gozzoli, R. assisted in the decoration of the Sistine Chapel (1482) painting a highly derivative fresco of the *Last Supper* with references to A. del Castagno, Bellini and Mantegna. A *St. Barbara* (1475) combines the decorative style of B. Gozzoli and the fixed figures of N. di Bicci in Cosimo's Renaissance composition. *S. Filippo Benizzi* (1476), *Holy Sacrament* (1485), *Madonna and Saints* (1492) and *Coronation of the Virgin* (1505) are his greatest works.

[M. J. DALY]

ROSSELLINO, family name of brothers, Italian sculptors, **Antonio** (1427–79), trained by his elder brother Bernardo, executed a signed work (1456) and the commissioned tomb of the Cardinal of Portugal (1461) in S. Miniato al Monte, Florence, and carved many important altars, pulpit reliefs, and other tombs. Following the tradition of his brother Bernardo and that of Desiderio da Settignano, Antonio's style shows subtle planes, soft modeling, and penetration of character. **Bernardo** (1409–64), architect as well as sculptor, built the Cathedral and Piccolomini Palace for Pope Pius II at Pienza (1460–63). A decorative sculptor influenced by Michelozzo and Della Robbia, Bernardo's tomb of Leonard Bruni (1444) in Sta. Croce, Florence, in its harmonious relation of sculpture to architecture, was one of the most influential Florentine tombs of the 15th century. BIBLIOGRAPHY: A. Markham, "Desiderio da Settignano and the Workshop of Bernardo Rossellino," *Art Bulletin* 45, 3 (1963).

[M. J. DALY]

ROSSELLO, MARIA GIUSEPPA, ST. (1811–80), foundress of the Daughters of *Our Lady of Mercy. R. first worked among the poor in Savoy, Italy, as a Franciscan tertiary, and then founded the Daughters to care for abandoned girls in 1837. She was elected superior general of her congregation in 1840, expanded its mission to the education of girls and the care of the sick, and directed its rapid growth until her death. She was canonized in 1949. BIBLIOGRAPHY: K. Burton, *Wheat for This Planting* (1960).

[T. M. MCFADDEN]

ROSSETTI, CARLO (1614–81), Italian cardinal; from 1639 papal agent to the English court where he worked on behalf of English Catholics and sought to convert Charles I. When he attempted to negotiate a loan to assist Charles in his struggle with the Parliamentarians, R. gained the enmity of the Puritans; he fled to Flanders in 1641. In 1643 he was appointed bishop of Faenza, and later cardinal.

[R. J. LITZ]

ROSSETTI, CHRISTINA (1830–94), poet, sister of Dante Gabriel Rossetti. She did not marry, took an active part in the Pre-Raphaelite group, and was acknowledged a fine poet. Her poems can be classified as fantasy, love poems, and religious poems. *Goblin Market* (1862) is original in fantasy and has great technical dexterity. Her sonnet sequence *Monna innominata* (Lady Nameless) presents the theme of blighted love. Much of her poetry is religious and puts her in comparison with Crashaw. Her language is austere and depends often upon the King James Bible for its cadences. She is a careful metrist and achieves a simplicity which the other Pre-Raphaelites failed to reach. She is held by many to be the finest English woman poet. BIBLIOGRAPHY: L. M. Packer, *Christina Rossetti* (1963); M. Bell, *Christina Rossetti* (1898, repr. 1973).

[M. M. BARRY]

ROSSETTI, DANTE GABRIEL (1828–82), poet and painter, son of an Italian poet and political refugee who married and settled in England. In the Royal Academy, with Millais and Hunt, R. formed the Pre-Raphaelite Brotherhood, extolling the purity and simplicity of the Italian primitives and urging naturalistic accuracy of detail. The austere religious intensity of his early painting, e.g., *The Annunciation* (Ecce Ancillae Domini!), gave way to a later mannered sensuousness. He married Elizabeth Siddal, favorite model of the Brotherhood. In poetry he stresses decorative details, which are often irrelevant and imprecise, cultivates the archaic, and uses religious language without religious meaning. His general mood is one of listlessness, decay, and desolation. His works include *The Early Italian Poets* (tr. mostly from Dante), *Poems*, and a sonnet sequence, *The House of Life*. His love poetry alternates between Romantic idealization, strong passion, inevitable weariness and disappointment. His interest was in the Middle Ages as opposed to 19th-cent. industrialism but the Middle Ages without religious ideals. BIBLIOGRAPHY: M. Beerbohm, *Rossetti and His Circle* (1922); E. Wood, *Dante Rossetti and the Pre-Raphaelite Movement* (1894, repr. 1972).

[M. M. BARRY]

ROSSI, GIOVANNI BATTISTA DE (1822–94), premier archeologist of Christian Rome. While a law student R. became interested in the exploration of ancient catacombs, and in 1848 was appointed to work in the Vatican Library. He had the insight to use ancient documentary indications as a guide for his explorations. These led to discoveries that enabled him to map out and to interpret the inscriptions in the catacombs. His work became the foundation for all subsequent Christian archeology. His masterwork is *Roma sotteranea cristiana* (3 v., 1864–77). He founded and directed the *Bollettino di archeologia cristiana* (1864); he also edited the first two volumes of *Inscriptiones christianae urbis Romae* (1861, 1868); was a voluminous contributor to archeological journals and a collaborator for the *Corpus inscriptionum latinarum*.

[T. C. O'BRIEN]

ROSSI, JOHN BAPTIST, ST. (1698–1764), apostle of the poor. Of sickly constitution, R. was an Italian ordained by dispensation in 1721. His life was a continuous service to the poor, spiritually and in physical aid. R. founded a refuge for homeless children and a hospital for the poor. His own income he devoted to the support of these institutions. R. was canonized in 1881. BIBLIOGRAPHY: Butler 2:379–381; G. B. Proja, BiblSanct 6:959–963.

[J. R. AHERNE]

ROSSI, SALAMONE DE' (Salomone; 1570–1630), composer and violinist of Italian-Jewish heritage. R. served at the court of Mantua (1587–1628), a Jewish musician to a gentile court. He probably fled Mantua after 1630 when Austrian troops conquered the city. Musicologically, R. is important for his contributions in form and technique in instrumental variation. His works include Hebrew psalms, the most important being his "Shirim Asher Li'Shlomoh", canzonets, madrigals, and instrumental music.

[R. J. LITZ]

ROSSIGNOLI, BERNARDINO (1547–1613), Italian Jesuit, writer on the spiritual life. A Jesuit from 1563, he taught philosophy and theology in Milan and became provincial of the Roman and Milanese provinces. His works of note are: *De disciplina christianae perfectionis* . . . (1600); *De virtutibus* (1603). The first follows the pattern of the traditional three stages of the life of perfection; both works are richly documented from patristic sources.

[T. C. O'BRIEN]

ROSSIGNOLI, GIOVANNI PIETRO (1851–1909), Italian social philosopher. After training for a career in medicine, R. entered the seminary and was ordained in 1878. As professor at the seminary of Novara, he published a Neoscholastic *Corso di filosofia*. His devotion to social questions was expressed by his establishing a chair of sociology at the seminary, frequent articles in the journal *Scuola cattolica*, and in his major publications, *Il determinismo nella sociologia positiva* (1893) and *Concetto dell' autorità politica nella sociologia cristiana* (1903).

[T. C. O'BRIEN]

ROSSO FIORENTINO (Il Rosso; Giovanni Battista di Jacopo di Gaspare; 1495–1540), Italian painter, one of the originators of Florentine Mannerism, and source of its diffusion in the art of northern Europe. In Rome (1523) R. probably knew G. Romano and Parmigianino. Tortured during the sack of Rome (1527) he fled first to Perugia, worked in Florence, Rome, Venice, and was finally called to the court of Francis I of France, decorating at Fontainebleau. Early Florentine works (*Assumption of the Virgin*, 1517, *Madonna Enthroned with Four Saints*, 1518) established R. as a major artist. *A Descent from the Cross* (1521) in harsh color relates to Pontorno, but in spatial ambiguities evidences R.'s innovations in Mannerism. Elongated figures and textural effects (*Marriage of the Virgin*, 1523) further realize his goals. *Moses Defending the Daughters of Jethro* (1523) is a major statement in tensions and distortions.

The refined elegance of R.'s Roman period reaches its apogee in works at the French court (1530), particularly in *Galérie François I* (1534–37, at Fontainebleau), a syntax of Mannerist vocabulary in female figures of Parmigianino elegance, shifting scale and ambiguity of texture (stucco-like marble, leather, etc.). R. helped create Florentine Mannerism and determined native French Mannerism of the School of Fontainebleau. His *Pietà* (1537–40) sums up R.'s power and elegance. BIBLIOGRAPHY: P. Barocci, *Il Rosso Fiorentino* (1950).

[M. J. DALY]

ROSTAND, EDMOND (1868–1918), French dramatist, member of the French Academy. His *Cyrano de Bergerac*, a romantic play in verse which it is said made every man who viewed it one foot taller, is his chief claim to fame. His gentle satire on Romanticism called *Les Romanesques* is attractive, and several of his plays were made important by the presence of the immortal French actress, Sarah Bernhardt. R. was fortunate in the actors who portrayed Cyrano, particularly Coquelia and Richard Mansfield, as well as Bernhardt in other works. His election to the French Academy in 1902 was a culminating award to a journeyman of the theater. BIBLIOGRAPHY: E. E. Hale, *Edmond Rostand* (1911); E. Harth, *Cyrano de Bergerac and the Polemics of Modernity* (1970).

[J. R. AHERNE]

ROSTOCK, SEBASTIAN VON (1607–71), bp. of Breslau. R. was ordained in 1633, engaged in pastoral work in Niesse for 16 years, and then became vicar general and later bp. of Breslau. The *Thirty Years' War had just ended (1648), and over 600 churches in the Breslau Diocese were restored to Catholicism. R.'s principal work was to provide spiritually for these parishes and to staff them with priests.

[T. M. MCFADDEN]

ROSWEYDE, HERIBERT (Rosweydus; 1569–1629), Belgian Jesuit hagiographer and writer. Ordained in 1598, he taught rhetoric, philosophy, and controversial theology at Brussels intermittently from 1592 to 1607. R. conceived and initiated the composition of the *Acta sanctorum*, a work intended to eliminate legendary and apocryphal material from the lives of the saints. His treatise, *Fastes des saints* (1607), stated his plan to examine the facts of saints' lives as recorded in MSS in Belgian libraries. His edition of the texts and lives of the Desert Fathers, *Vitae Patrum* (1615), instituted the larger 67–volume *Acta* which his successor, Jean van Bolland, continued. In two treatises, *Vindiciae Kempenses* (1617) and *Certissima testimonia* . . . , R. defended Thomas à Kempis' authorship of the *Imitation of Christ*. *BOLLANDISTS.

[R. J. LITZ]

ROSWITHA (Hrotsvitha, Hrosvitha, Hrosvit; c.935–c.1000), canoness of Gandersheim abbey in Saxony, poet. She was exceptionally well read for her time in classical as well as in Christian literature. Her works include metrical legends, dramas, and historical poems. Her poetry on historical themes is of some value as a source for German history, but she is better known for her plays. In these she modeled her work on Terence but sought to illustrate Christian virtue rather than human frailty as Terence had done. There is no evidence that her work was much read in the Middle Ages; it was discovered and first printed in 1501, and there has been some revival of interest in it in modern times. Works: PL 137:941–1168; Eng. tr. of dramas, H. J. W. Tillyard (1923) and C. St. John (1923); nondramatic works, M. G. Wiegand (1936); *Liber tertius,* M. B. Bergman (1943). BIBLIOGRAPHY: Raby SLP 1:277–278.

[M. S. TANEY]

ROTARY INTERNATIONAL, service organization made up of local Rotary Clubs, founded in the U.S. by Paul Harris in Chicago, Feb. 23, 1905. Forming a federation of clubs in 1910, the group became the National Association of Rotary Clubs; the movement became Rotary International in 1922. Like all service clubs, Rotary draws its membership from business and professional ranks, one executive from each being admitted to the local club. The goals of Rotary include pursuit of service to others, maintenance of ethical standards, community service, and promotion of international good will. There are clubs in the U.S. and Canada, Latin America, Europe, Asia, and Africa as well as other areas. Although Rotary is not a religious or secret society, there was a period when it was frowned on by the Holy See, which in 1951 forbade priests to join. Bp. Noll of Fort Wayne, Ind., long a Rotarian, opposed the ban. In 1965 Pope Paul VI received a group of 1,500 Italian Rotarians and praised the work of the organization as a service force and international influence for good.

[J. R. AHERNE]

ROTHKO, MARK (1903–1970), American painter, coming to the U.S. from Latvia (1913), studying at Yale Univ., and at the Art Students League with Max Weber. R. advanced through Realism and Surrealism to the increasingly abstract and distinctive rectangular blurred shapes of the 1940s, his Exhibitions—creating "chapel-like, contemplation rooms" (1958–59), finally culminating in the ecumenical chapel (1971) of the Institute of Religion and Human Development at the RC St. Thomas Univ., Houston, Texas, the building under community patronage, co-designed with the paintings acquired through Mr. and Mrs. John de Ménil. Intensely religious, R. created for the utterly stark interior, 14 awesome "color-field" canvases (3 triptychs and 5 single works) of symbolic light and darkness, in exquisite textures of restricted colors (renunciation) of blood and wine to be experienced rather than viewed. The dedication was attended by Vatican representative Card. Jan Willebrands, and Greek, Jewish and Islamic delegations in true ecumenical witness. The Rothko chapel, with which intuitive free-spirits have full empathy, takes its place in this century with the famed Matisse Chapel at Vence. R. having taken his life (1970) did not see his works in position. BIBLIOGRAPHY: P. Selz, *Mark Rothko* (1961); L. Alloway, "Art: Mark Rothko," *Nation* (1971).

[M. J. DALY]

ROTHMANN, BERNHARDT (Bernt; b. *c.*1495), Anabaptist leader at Münster. While parish priest at St. Mauritz in Münster, R. first began to preach Lutheranism (1531), but soon embraced the teaching of M. *Hofmann. When the Anabaptists captured Münster in 1534, R. joined them; in the Münster kingdom, he was court preacher and shared in the practice of polygamy by taking nine wives. He published a manifesto of Anabaptist teaching, *Von rechter und gesunder christlicher Lehre, Glauben und Leben* (1533–35; ed. R. Stupperich, 1964). At the fall of the Münster kingdom, R. probably escaped; the date of his death is unknown. BIBLIOGRAPHY: H. Börsting, LTK 9:67–68; R. Stupperich, *Die Schreiben der Münster: Täufer und ihrer Gegner* (v.1, 1964); bibliog. for Anabaptists.

[T. C. O'BRIEN]

ROTROU, JEAN DE (1609–50), French dramatist, who along with Pierre *Corneille, is considered one of the founders of French classical drama. Noteworthy among his 35 extant plays, mostly tragi-comedies, are *Venceslas* (1647), *Cosroès* (1648), and *Saint Genest* (1646), this last being a Christian tragedy on the martyrdom under Diocletian of the actor Genest who, while playing the role of the martyr *Adrien,* is himself converted. BIBLIOGRAPHY: J. Morel, *Jean Rotrou, dramaturge de l'ambiguité* (1968); J. Rotrou, *Saint-Genest* (ed. R. W. Ladborough, 1954).

[R. N. NICOLICH]

ROTULUS, rolled or scroll manuscript. Egyptian papyrus rotuli are known from the 12th dynasty (*c.*2000 B.C.). Though ideally suited for narrative illustration, rotuli without illustrations became the traditional form of the Hebrew Torah. The Christian rotulus was an Eastern form, the West using the codex (book) form. However the West adapted the illustrative narrative technique of the rotuli for certain codices. One of the most famous of extant rotuli is the *Joshua Roll,* a Byzantine work of the Macedonian Renaissance (9th-10th cent.) now in the Vatican Library.

[M. J. DALY]

ROUAULT, GEORGES (1871–1958), major 20th-cent. French Catholic painter and printmaker, apprentice in stained glass (1885–90), student of G. Moreau, with Matisse and others associated with the Fauves (1903–1907), though always a distinctively unique Expressionist, engaged as a 20th-cent. Daumier in social commentary, using corrupt judges, sad clowns and prostitutes as interpretative of the vices of his age, though tempering all with a truly Christian mercy and gentleness. R. took prizes for religious and mythological works hung in official salons (1895–1901), became director of the Moreau "museum" (1898), and held a one-man show (1910). In 1916 A. Vollard persuaded him to engage in printmaking. R. developed thickly encrusted, luminous, richly colored images, vibrant as Byzantine enamels, and stained glass bound as cloisons within thick black lines—expressive contours. Internationally famous after 1930, R. designed tapestry and stained glass. Among countless important works are: *The Child Jesus among the Doctors* (1893), *Head of a Clown* (1908), *Three Judges* (1913), *The Old King* (1936), *Twilight* (1952). R., a most distinguished printmaker in lithography, etching, and wood engraving, executed the famous *Miserere* series (60 etchings and aquatints published 1948), *Fleurs du mal* (1930), and *Les Réincarnations du Père Ubri* (1928, 82 wood engravings and 7 color etchings). Though relating to Nolde and Die Brucke, R.'s Expressionism, completely free of the violence and anger of the German school, is full of mercy and compassion. BIBLIOGRAPHY: L. Venturi, *Rouault* (1959); P. Courthion, *Georges Rouault* (1962).

[M. J. DALY]

ROUGEMONT, FRANÇOIS (1624–76), Belgian Jesuit, missionary to China. He arrived there in 1659 after a 3-year journey, including a trek through India on foot. His work was centered around Shanghai; he was, however, exiled and imprisoned in Canton (1665–71). During this period he wrote his *Historia Tartaro-Sinica nova* (1672), important as a record of the persecution of missionaries. For his converts, he also wrote catechetical and apologetic works in Chinese. He contributed to the history of missiology by a memorial (1667) to the Jesuit general urging the need of a native clergy and the use of Chinese as a liturgical language. He also collaborated on a Chinese-Latin edition of a biography of Confucius, published in 1663, along with an examination of Confucianism; the work introduced Confucian ethical theories to the West.

[T. C. O'BRIEN]

ROUGEMONT, ABBEY OF, former Benedictine convent near Dijon, France. It was founded in the 11th cent. (the exact decade unknown), and because of financial difficulties was transferred to the Augustinians in the 15th century. A lawsuit over this action followed and Pope Callistus III had the convent returned to Benedictine rule. During a reform period, the convent was joined to a nearby priory. This community was called Abbaye de Notre Dame et de S. Julien de Rougemont; it was transferred to Dijon in 1673; a new convent, St. Julien de Rougemont, was built. BIBLIOGRAPHY: Cottineau 2:2551.

[M. A. MCFADDEN]

ROULEAU, FÉLIX RAYMOND MARIE (1866–1931), abp. of Quebec, cardinal. A native of Quebec, R. entered the Dominicans and was ordained in 1892. A teacher in the Dominican seminary for many years, he became provincial of his order in 1919. He was named bp. of Valleyfield, P.Q., in 1923 and was appointed to Quebec in 1926; he was created cardinal in 1927. Known as a mystic and theologian, R. was involved with the establishment of the Canadian Academy of St. Thomas Aquinas at Laval University.

[J. R. AHERNE]

ROUQUETTE, ADRIEN EMMANUEL (1813–87), missionary, writer. Born in New Orleans, R. was dominated by lifelong fascination with the Choctaw Indians of Louisiana. A solitary by nature, he preferred the uncivilized to New Orleans society. After publication of his poetic essay *Les Savannes* in 1842, he became editor of *Le Propagateur Catholique* of Louisiana. In 1845 R. was ordained for New Orleans. A famous preacher revered for his sanctity, he left his work in 1859 to live and work among the Choctaws for the rest of his life. Among his works were *La Nouvelle Attila* (1879) and *Wild Flowers* (1848).

[J. R. AHERNE]

ROURE, LUCIEN (1857–1945), Jesuit theologian. R. was long associated with the periodical *Études*, to which he contributed articles dealing with spiritualism and the occult. His principal works are *Le Spiritisme d'aujourd'hui et d'hier* (1923) and *Au pays de l'occultisme* (1926).

[T. M. MCFADDEN]

ROUSSEAU, JEAN JACQUES (1712–78), French Swiss writer and philosopher. Born in Geneva of Protestant parents, R. lost his mother in infancy and was educated by his father, who apprenticed him to an engraver. At 16, he fled to Annecy, France, and accepted the protection and the Catholic religion of Mme. de Warens. She encouraged in him a love of nature as well as his musical and literary bents. In 1742 R. went to Paris with a system of musical notation which he had invented. He was rejected by the Academy of Sciences but made friends among the philosophers, esp. Diderot and D'Alembert, who invited him to write articles for the *Encyclopédie*. He took an ignorant servant girl as common-law wife and put their five children in a foundling home, a not unusual practice at the time, which he thought justified. In 1749 R. wrote a prize-winning essay (known as his *First Discourse*) on the subject of whether the sciences and arts have contributed to improve or to corrupt public morality. He argued on the side of corruption, and in 1754 he wrote his *Second Discourse*, in another contest, on the origin of inequality among men. Returning to Geneva, he resumed Protestantism and took the title "Citizen of Geneva," but continued to move back and forth until his death at Ermenonville, France. Besides physical ills, Rousseau suffered increasing persecution mania, alienating all his friends and becoming a brooding solitary. His *Confessions* (begun in 1765), although indispensable documents, are often inaccurate and show the warped thought of his later life. R.'s influence has been felt esp. in three areas: (1) literature, through the introduction into France of Romanticism with his novel *La Nouvelle Héloïse* (1761); (2) education, with the novel *Émile* (1762); (3) political and social philosophy, through the two *Discourses* and the *Social Contract* (1762).

In education, he initiated the theory that a child should merely be assisted in the development of his natural qualities and finally led towards a natural religion, without dogma. The last idea is elaborated in the famous discourse of the vicar of Savoy. R. had come to believe that religion was necessary and that all religions were good, except the Catholic, as this involved a foreign sovereign.

Politically and socially, he thought that virtue is to be found only in closeness to nature, that inequality among men results from the establishment of organized society, that laws are created to protect private property, and that magistrates are appointed to enforce laws. All this has given rise to despotism and class divisions. But since man cannot return to nature, R. proposes positive remedies for the ills of society, and he favors a republican government. He castigated the theater (*Letter to D'Alembert*, 1758) as a particularly pernicious expression of social corruption. BIBLIOGRA-PHY: E. H. Wright, *Meaning of Rousseau* (1929); J. H. Broome, *Rousseau: A Study of His Thought* (1963); A. Schinz, *La Pensée religieuse de J.-J. Rousseau et ses récents interprètes* (1927).

[L. TINSLEY]

ROVENIUS, PHILIPPUS (1575–1651), first vicar apostolic for Holland (from 1619); titular abp. of Philippi (1620). He ministered to the spiritual needs of Dutch Catholics during the anti-Catholic period of revolution against Spain, and from 1630 had to live in hiding to escape punishment. He was in fact sentenced *in absentia* to exile in 1640; but he was never captured. R. was in dispute with the religious orders because of their refusal to accept his jurisdiction. He left a *Tractatus de missionibus . . .* (1624).

[T. C. O' BRIEN]

ROVETTA, GIOVANNI (d. 1668), Italian priest, composer, and bass singer. He began his musical career as a choir boy at St. Mark's, Venice. He was appointed vice-*Maestro di cappella* there (1627), and *maestro* after Monteverdi's death (1644). R.'s church music includes Masses, motets, and psalms; secular works include madrigals and operas.

[R. J. LITZ]

ROYAL DECLARATION, a solemn affirmation concerning religion made by every monarch of England from William III (1689) to Edward VII (1901). The declaration was imposed by Parliament in 1689 to secure Protestant succession to the throne (see DECLARATION OF RIGHTS). At coronation or at the opening of his first Parliament, the king was required to declare his rejection of *transubstantiation, the Mass, and invocation of Mary or the saints. By the end of the 19th cent., long after Catholic emancipation (1829), a movement began to soften the language, which was offensively anti-Roman. Under George V, such a modification was passed by Parliament and approved by the King (1910). The new monarch simply professes that he is a Protestant and will uphold the law of Protestant succession to the throne.

[T. C. O'BRIEN]

ROYCE, JOSIAH (1855–1916), the most important of the American idealist philosophers, with an essentially religious view of reality. The son of English born "forty-niners," he was born and raised in California, and studied engineering at the Univ. of California at Berkeley, (1871–1875). There, decisively influenced by his teachers, the Darwinian geologist J. Le Conte, and the poet E. R. Sill, and by the reading of Herbert Spencer and J. S. Mill, he developed his characteristic empiricism. R. then pursued graduate study in philosophy at Leipzig and Göttingen, under W. Wundt, W. Windelband, and R. H. Lotze. His reading centered on Kant, the primary determinant of his thought, on Fichte, with whose help he tried to circumvent the Kantian obstacles to metaphysics, and on Schopenhauer, who was behind R.'s theory of the role of the will in knowledge and thus in reality. In 1876, R. accepted a fellowship at Johns Hopkins Univ. and received his doctorate in 1878. There he met William James, whose *Will To Believe*, despite its pragmatism, gave much to R.'s "absolute voluntarism." Subsequently, after having taught English for 4 years at the Univ. of California, R. was invited to Harvard, through the influence of James and G. H. Palmer. From that time until his death, he was one of the pillars of the philosophy department, debating with James, falling under the influence of C. S. Peirce's theories of signs, relations and community, and supervising the doctoral work of G. Santayana. To this day, some aspects of R.'s thought are influential at Harvard, through their continuation in the epistemology of C. I. Lewis and the metaphysics of W. E. Hocking. R.'s efforts in such diverse areas as mathematical logic, psychology, literary criticism, and history, as well as in ethics and metaphysics, did much to elevate both the level of philosophical discussion and, despite the growing strength of pragmatism, the reputation of European idealism in the United States. His later conception of God as an Interpreter, joining distinct selves in a spiritual unity of love, is a unique approach to the much–neglected Third Person of the Trinity. Among his major works are *Religious Aspect of Philosophy* (1885), *World and the Individual* (1900–01), *Philosophy of Loyalty* (1908), and *Problem of Christianity* (1913).

[R. E. HENNESSEY]

ROZANOV, VASILI VASILIEVICH (1856–1919), Russian philosopher, writer, critic. Though a Christian, R. rejected the Christian attitude toward sex as too ascetic and sought to establish a naturalistic cult with procreation as its central rite. His best essays and aphorisms are collected under the titles *Solitaria* (1912) and *Fallen Leaves* (2 v., 1913, 1915). He is also the author of some excellent studies of Dostoyevsky. BIBLIOGRAPHY: *Russian Philosophy* (eds. J. M. Edie et al., 1965) 2:281–304; N. O. Lossky, *History of Russian Philosophy* (1951) 342–344.

[M. F. MCCARTHY]

ROZO (East Syrian, *rāzā*; Syriac word for mystery), a term that may signify one of the eucharistic species, even before consecration, or the Syro-Malabar Solemn Mass.

[A. CODY]

RTA (Sanskrit, the course of things), early Indian conception of the ''law,'' both cosmic/natural and cultural/moral, that is the principle both of the regularity of natural phenomena and of the rightness of the social order (though here it was believed to be less manifest). It is usually described as sovereign, i.e., not so much the creation of the gods as ''guarded'' by them, esp. by Varuna, who punishes the law's transgressors. The term is the predecessor of the later, more inclusive term *dharma* (that which upholds or maintains the order of the universe and of society). BIBLIOGRAPHY: S. Radhakrishnan and C. A. Moore, *Source Book in Indian Philosophy* (1957) 25–31; R. C. Zaehner, *Hinduism* (1966) 14–35.

[D. P. EFROYMSON]

RUBEIS, LEONARDO DE (Rossi; d. after March 17, 1407), Franciscan minister general, theologian. R. was elected minister general of the Franciscans in 1373, but was deposed by Urban VI at the beginning of the Great Western Schism. At Avignon he was inquisitor for the writings of the Dominican John of Monzon and was also involved in the controversy on the condemnation of Raymond Lull. Clement VII (Avignon) made him a cardinal (Dec. 16, 1378). His most important theological contributions are the unedited commentary on the *Canticle of Canticles*, a soliloquy written in prison, two works on the Schism, and a commentary on the *Four Books of Sentences*. BIBLIOGRAPHY: E. Longpré, DTC, 9.1:396–397; J. J. Smith, NCE 12:695.

[J. J. SMITH]

RUBEN (REUBEN), the first named in all the lists of the 12 tribes of Israel, whose eponymous hero was the firstborn of Jacob. This must mean that the tribe of Ruben had at one time a preeminence. It would be difficult otherwise to explain the reference to Ruben, in Jacob's final words to his sons, as ''my firstborn, my strength and the first-fruit of my vigor, excelling in pride, excelling in might . . .'' (Gen 49.3). Ruben is also presented as the leader of the 12 sons in the Joseph story. By the time of David and Solomon, however, the remnants of Ruben lived in cities E of Jordan within the territory assigned to Gad (Jos 13; Num 32). It is speculated that the four Leah tribes, Ruben, Simeon, Levi, and Juda, attempted an incursion into Canaan from the S considerably before the more successful invasion of the Rachel tribes from E of Jordan under Joshua. In this earlier invasion, only Judah gained a foothold and maintained its strength and separate identity. It could be that the decline of Ruben is linked to some tragic impetuousness to which veiled reference is made in Gen 35.22. This incident figures also in Jacob's final words to Ruben, ''turbulent as a flood, you shall not excel; because you climbed into your father's bed; then you defiled his concubine's couch'' (Gen 49.4). In the narrative, this incident is localized at Migdal-eder—''the tower of Eder''—which would place Ruben in the Judean hillsides W of Jordan in the days of his strength. By the time of the Song of Deborah (Jg 5), which celebrates the later victory of the Rachel tribes joined by the later Leah tribes of Issachar and Zebulun, Ruben is singled out for rebuke for remaining among the cattlepens in Gilead, E of Jordan.

[E. J. DILLON]

RUBENS, PETER PAUL 1577–1640), brilliant Flemish Catholic painter and engraver of religious, mythological, historical, and genre scenes, portraits and landscapes; the apotheosis of Flemish expression as were Michelangelo, Titian, and Rembrandt in their respective schools; true man of the Renaissance, scholar of classical learning, associate and diplomat of princes (King of Spain, Charles I of England, Marie de Médicis of France). First in Venice (1600), then in the court of Vincenzo I Gonzaga, Duke of Mantua, R. executed mannerist works (*St. Helena, Christ Crowned with Thorns*) related to the Carracci and Caravaggio, and the famous *Elevation of the Cross* (1610) for the Antwerp Cathedral, evidencing influences of Michelangelo and Tintoretto. R. was in the service of the Gonzaga court at Mantua and there he painted the *Twelve Apostles* series and altarpieces for the Jesuits (*Baptism of Christ, Transfiguration,* 1604–05). Painter to the archduke in Antwerp, married to Isabella Brandt (1609), R. built his great house (1618) with studio executing his innumerable commissions with the aid of many assistants. Held in highest esteem, he was eminently successful in an early system of mass production, assigning specialties to master-assistants, retouching areas of helpers, while reserving for himself preliminary sketches and major figures (*Prometheus Bound* with vulture by Snyders, master of birds). In 1620–30 R. produced his ''great'' series in splashes of Venetian color in unctuous pigment (*Cycle of Life of Marie de Médicis* and of Henry IV, unfinished). In Spain (1628) he painted the royal family and met Velasquez, was in England 9 months painting the King and Queen, and the ceiling of the Banqueting Hall, London. The period 1630–40 marks his marriage to Helena Fourment—and an age of full maturity in R.'s complete mastery of color and technique (*Ildefenso Altarpiece* of rare perfection). He then bought a new estate (Steen) to which he retired often to paint joyous, dynamic landscapes of universal significance. A final style of impressionistic touch marks the last works of his crippled hands. R. died in 1640, mourned by all Europe. For him was named the school of colorists (''Reubenists'' or modernists) in late 17th-cent. French art. BIBLIOGRAPHY: L. van Puyvelde, *Rubens* (1952); J. Held, *Rubens, Selected Drawings* (1959).

[M. J. DALY]

RUBINO, ANTONIO (1578–1643), Italian Jesuit, missionary, prominent in the *Chinese Rites controversy. The field of his apostolate from 1602 until 1638 was India; there he composed a seven-volume *Catena evangelica* as a guide for preachers. As visitator to the missions of China and Japan he was seized in Japan in 1643 and died in prison at Nagasaki. R.'s views on missionary *adaptation in China were published while he was visitator; the Italian translation from Portuguese, *Metodo della dottrina che i padri della Compagnia di Gesù insegnano ai neofiti nelle missioni della Cina . . .* (1641, but not published till 1665) was placed on the Index in 1680. Another work, falsely attributed to R. and advocating that the use of crucifixes be abolished in China, was in fact written by a Jansenist of the Sorbonne; it contains references to dates and events posterior to R.'s own death.

[T. C. O'BRIEN]

RUBRICS (printed in red), directions for performance of the liturgy. Canon law prescribes observance of these directions.

[J. R. AHERNE]

RUCH, CHARLES (1873–1945), bp. of Strasbourg. R. held several positions in the diocese of Nancy: seminary professor (1897–1907), vicar general, co-adjutor, and finally (1918) bishop. His term as bp. of Strasbourg (1919–45) was marked by two controversies: his defense against French lay laws of the Church's privileges, granted in the 1801 Concordat with France, concerning religious instruction in primary schools; his support of the French position on Alsace-Lorraine. These questions caused a split among the Catholics of his diocese, but R. refused to resign and spent the war years (1940–44) in Dordogne, after which he returned to Strasbourg.

[T. M. MCFADDEN]

RÜD, VALERIUS, see ANSHELM, VALERIUS.

RUDIGIER, FRANZ JOSEF, VEN. (1811–84), bp. of Linz. R. held a variety of church posts before becoming a bp.: seminary professor in Brixen; director of an institute for advanced ecclesiastical studies; court chaplain and tutor to Franz Josef and Maximilian. As bp. of Linz (1852–84), he was distinguished by his pastoral commitment and strenuous defense of the Church's rights against state regulations and the political liberalism characteristic of the time in Europe. His cause for beatification was introduced in 1905.

[T. M. MCFADDEN]

RUDOLPH I, GERMAN KING (1218–91), Swabian count and head of the Habsburg house, elected king in 1273 after a long interregnum. Since King Ottocar II of Bohemia refused to acknowledge the election, R. in 1276 laid siege to Vienna. Ottocar was forced to surrender all his estates in the empire except for Bohemia and Moravia. In Germany this battle marks the shift of power to the East. Vienna was to become the seat of Habsburg control for the next 650 years. In 1278 Ottocar united the neighboring Polish and Silesian princes in a racial war against the Germans. With the help of the Hungarians, traditional enemies of the Slavs, R. crushed the Slavic empire. R. was ready to sacrifice imperial pretensions and to maintain friendly relations with France in order to obtain the principle of a hereditary monarchy. After the

next king proved to be a disastrous choice, R.'s son Albert resumed Habsburg control. BIBLIOGRAPHY: J. Wodka, LTK 9:87–88.

[J. E. LYNCH]

RUDRA, god of Vedic India who is depicted as powerful, unpredictable, and separate from other gods. He is frequently malevolent, or at least wrathful, and terrifying ("The god that kills": Atharva Veda 1.19.3); the human reaction to him is wariness and appeasement ("Do not slaughter our father or our mother": Rig Veda 1.114.7). He is sometimes accompanied by the Maruts (minor storm-gods) or by the Rudras (his sons). Many of his attributes are absorbed into the figure of the later and more important god *Siva (who is sometimes called Rudra: the "red" one; just as Rudra is sometimes called Siva: "the auspicious"). BIBLIOGRAPHY: W. D. O'Flaherty, *Hindu Myths* (1975) 116–140; A. Daniélou, *Hindu Polytheism* (1964) 192–206.

[D. P. EFROYMSON]

RUE, PIERRE DE LA, see LA RUE, PIERRE DE.

RUFFO, FABRIZIO (1744–1827), cardinal and advisor to the Bourbon kings of Naples. R. worked within the Roman Curia, most notably as treasurer general where he incurred aristocratic opposition to the economic reforms that he recommended for the *States of the Church. He then attached himself to the Bourbon court of the Kingdom of Naples, and fled to Palermo with the royal family when Naples was attacked by the French army. With the authorization of King Ferdinand IV, R. organized an army (the *Sanfedists) from among the people of Calabria and regained Naples for the Bourbons by promising easy peace terms to the French and Italian Jacobin forces. When these terms were repudiated by the restored Bourbons, R. returned to Rome where he acquiesced to the changes of the Napoleonic period and filled various posts under Pius VII. BIBLIOGRAPHY: H. M. Acton, *Bourbons of Naples 1734–1825* (1958).

[T. M. MCFADDEN]

RUFFO, VINCENZO (1510–87), Italian composer and church musician. He was born to a noble Veronese family. He served as *maestro di capella* at Verona (1554), at Milan (1563), at Pistoia (1574–79), then again at Milan (1580). Card. Abp. Charles Borromeo, to implement Reforms of the Council of Trent, urged R. to revise and clarify his musical style; the change is evident in Masses published after 1570. R.'s liturgical works include numerous Masses, motets, settings of the Magnificat, and psalms. He is better known for his madrigals, which are stylistically varied though not profoundly expressive.

[R. J. LITZ]

RUFINA, SS., two different saints, revered as virgin martyrs, whose cultus goes back to the ancient Church. The first is commemorated with St. Secunda on July 10. Nothing is known for certain about Rufina and Secunda beyond their martyrdom and their early cultus. The second Rufina is commemorated with St. Justa on July 19. This pair was greatly venerated in Spain and probably martyred in Seville. Nothing else can be known with certainty.

[E. J. DILLON]

RUFINUS (d.*c*.1192), canonist, theologian, writer, bp. of Assisi before 1179, abp. of Sorrento. His chief writings are a *Summa decretorum*, completed in 1160, and a *De bono pacis* (1174–80). The influential *Summa*, using techniques borrowed from civil law writers, introduced for the first time a systematic exposition of Gratian's *Decretum*. The *De bono pacis*, in effect an exposition of Augustine's *De civitate Dei*, follows Pope Gelasius and Gratian in asserting that the spiritual and temporal orders are, each in its own sphere, independent of each other. The most recent discussion of his works is R. L. Benson, *Bishop-Elect* (1969).

[L. E. BOYLE]

RUFINUS OF AQUILEIA (345–410), ecclesiastical writer who became a close friend of St. Jerome while studying at Rome. R. visited Egypt in the company of Melania the Elder (371), and after a 6-year stay there, finally settled in Jerusalem on the Mount of Olives where he built cells for his fellow monks and pursued an ascetic life and literary career. During the initial stages of his monastic life, R. maintained a frequent and friendly association with St. Jerome, who had founded a monastery in nearby Bethlehem. But the Origenist controversy occasioned a serious disagreement between the two monasteries. Reconciled temporarily with St. Jerome through the efforts of Bp. John of Jerusalem (397), R. returned to Italy and renewed what was to become a permanent breach in the friendship by mentioning St. Jerome's alleged admiration for Origen in the preface of his translation of the Alexandrian's writings. A series of angry letters continued between the two men until 402 when R. refused to answer the final letter of St. Jerome. Driven from Aquileia by the Visigoth invasion (407), R. took up residence in Messina where he died (410).

His personal writings include: two books of *Historia ecclesiastica*, an addition to his translation of Eusebius in which he records the events from 324 to the death of Theodosius (395), the first history in the West; *Commentarius in symbolum Apostolorum* (Commentary on the Symbol of the Apostles) which quotes the first Latin text of the baptismal creed (404); two apologies, one to Pope Anastasius (400) in defence of his own orthodoxy and his translation of the works of Origen; and one to St. Jerome in which he attacks his position and several letters which have not survived (PL 21). His better-known translations include the *On the Principles of Origen* (398), and the complete *Historia ecclesiastica* of Eusebius (403). BIBLIOGRAPHY: J. Brochet, *Saint Jerome et ses ennemis* (1905); F. de Lab-

riolle, *Latin Christianity* (1925); F. Wright, *Fathers of the Church* (1928).

[F. H. BRIGHAM]

RUINART, THIERRY (1657–1709), Benedictine scholar of the Congregation of Saint–Maur. He entered the abbey of Saint–Remi in 1674. As favorite pupil of Mabillon at Saint-Germain-des-Prés, R. wrote the *Acta primorum martyrum sincera* (1689). Although possessing many merits and often reprinted, the work does not meet modern historical standards. Among his other works is the *Historia persecutionis Vandalicae* (PL 58). With Mabillon he published the *Acta sanctorum ordinis S. Benedicti*. His polemical works are the *Apologie de la mission de saint Maur en France* (1702) and *Ecclesia Parisiensis vindicata* (1706). He also wrote a life of Mabillon and other biographical works. His journal was written during the period of disputes between the Jesuits and the Maurists. The correspondence of Dom Ruinart is in the Bibliothèque Nationale of Paris. BIBLIOGRAPHY: J. Daoust, NCE 12:704–705.

[M. J. FINNEGAN]

RUIZ, PETER OF THE VISITATION (d. 1601), Spanish priest and liturgist, who attained fame in his day for his unparalleled mastery of the rubrics of the various ecclesiastical ceremonies and was dubbed "prince of the rubricists." Born in Toledo, he took part in Rome in the thoroughgoing reform of the Roman Calendar under Gregory XIII; and the reform of the Breviary and Roman Missal under Clement VIII. He worked 26 years on the work entitled *De ceremoniis ecclesiasticis*, only to have it ignored by the Congregation of Rites because of the petty intrigue of a curial cardinal. He wrote extensively on every aspect of rubrics and ceremonies.

[E. J. DILLON]

RUÍZ BLANCO, MATÍAS (1645–*c*.1708), Spanish missionary. A Franciscan, he spent more than half his life at the Piritú missions in Venezuela and was outstanding in promoting the welfare of the Indians. He also was the author of grammars and dictionaries of the Indian Cumanagoto language and of accounts of his mission experiences.

[P. J. HENNESSEY]

RUÍZ DE MONTOYA, ANTONIO (1585–1652), Peruvian Jesuit and pioneer of the Paraguayan Reductions. He studied and was ordained at Córdoba, Argentina; was mission superior (1623–37); founded a number of stations; and was a staunch defender of the rights of the Indians against the attacks of the Paulistas or in Spain before the Council of the Indies. His *Tesoro de la lengua guaraní* (1639) and *Arte y vocabulario de la lengua guaraní* (1640) are works of notable linguistic value. BIBLIOGRAPHY: G. Furlong, *Antonio Ruíz de Montoya y su carta a Comental* (1964).

[P. DAMBORIENA]

RUIZ LOZANO, FRANCISCO (1607–77), astronomer. A native of Peru, R. studied astronomy under the Jesuits. A friend of the viceroy of Peru, R. was responsible for the establishment of an academy for navigators, in which he taught mathematics. His observations on certain planets anticipated those of European scientists.

[J. R. AHERNE]

RUÍZ Y FLORES, LEOPOLDO (1865–1941), Mexican abp. and apostolic delegate. He was ordained in Rome and then taught for a time in the diocesan seminary in Mexico City. He was named bp. of León in 1900, abp. of Linares-Monterrey in 1907 and of Morelia in 1912, a position he held until his death. R. was a zealous promoter of Catholic schools and catechetical instruction, founding in all eight schools within his various bishoprics. Sensitive to the needs of the social apostolate, he directed his efforts to industrial and agricultural workers. Loyal to Pres. Porfirio Diaz, R. was exiled in 1914. Again in 1925, during the Mexican persecution of the Church, R. was exiled and lived in the U.S. Named apostolic delegate to Mexico, he achieved a *modus vivendi* with Pres. Portés Gil and the churches were reopened. Once more, when the Holy See condemned violations of the agreement he had concluded, he was exiled. In 1937 he returned to Morelia.

[J. R. AHERNE]

RULE, as here understood, a plan or pattern of life intended to organize an individual's use of time and energy in such a way as to assure a maximum of spiritual profit. The utility of such a rule has been recognized from early Christian times as a protection against the inconstancy and haphazardness that fritter away much spiritual effort. In the 3d cent., St. Cyprian drew up regulations for the daily life of virgins. In the 4th cent., when the experience of the solitaries in the desert proved the need of a more organized and communal way of life, St. Pachomius composed a rule for those who came to him for instruction in the ways of perfection. Among later monastic rules were those of SS. Basil, Benedict, Augustine, and Columbanus. A rule of life for individuals living outside religious communities came into general use among tertiaries and oblates affiliated with religious orders; generally these were patterned after the rules of the orders with which they were associated. Later it became common for rules to be drawn up by individuals, with the guidance of their spiritual directors, for their own personal use. To be truly helpful and an aid to spiritual development, a rule should be definite and firm to support the will; it should also have a calculated elasticity adaptable to the demands of charity and prudence. BIBLIOGRAPHY: P. Pourrat, *Christian Spirituality* (tr. W. H. Mitchell et al., v. 1 1922, repr. 1953) 36–164; P. F. Mulhern, NCE 12:710.

[P. F. MULHERN]

RULE OF FAITH, the criterion or norm that guarantees the truth of what is believed. Christian theology regards faith as an immediate contact with God; the word of God revealing is the motive for the believer's acceptance; and it is the primary guarantee that what is believed is true. But theology has used the phrase "rule of faith" in a more determinate sense. The object or content of faith is a body of truths, the content of God's word. The rule of faith is a norm by which the believer has assurance that what he believes is indeed conformed to what God reveals. Christians generally have agreed that such a rule of faith is the Bible. The Bible is accepted as containing God's revelation, and therefore the believer's understanding must be conformed to the Bible (see BIBLE, AUTHORITY OF). Exceptions throughout Christian history, however, have been the various manifestations of *enthusiasm, religious *illuminism, or *subjectivism, which have replaced the Bible with some direct intuition or experience as the rule of faith.

Sola scriptura, the Bible alone, is a phrase intended to express the division between Roman Catholics and Protestants over the rule of faith since the Reformation. RC teaching was reasserted, but also significantly clarified, by Vatican Council II: "The office of authentically interpreting the word of God, whether written or handed down, has been entrusted exclusively to the living teaching office of the Church, whose authority is exercised in the name of Jesus Christ." However, this "teaching office is not above the word of God but ministers to it, teaching only what has been handed on . . . it draws on the deposit of faith everything it proposes for belief as divinely revealed" (Vat II DivRev 10). The rule of faith according to RC teaching is the Bible as the written word of God; tradition, apostolic or ecclesial, i.e., the living understanding and transmission in the Church of God's revelation (which includes and is not extraneous to the Bible); and the teaching authority, or *magisterium. These three "are so linked together that one cannot stand without the others" (*ibid.*). *Sola scriptura* has an exclusive sense: the rejection of both tradition and the mediation of the magisterium as rules of faith. But the exclusiveness can be oversimplified. Protestant appeal to the sole sufficiency of Scripture has not in fact been only to a book or to the written word. Reliance is upon the Scripture become the living word through the Holy Spirit evoking the response of the believer. In the left-wing Reformation and in the Quaker doctrine of *Inner Light this experience was made more central than the Bible itself. Nor did the Bible exclude the formulation of confessions of faith as subordinate rules of faith (see NORMA NORMATA). The many anti-creedal movements in Protestantism are a negative indication that such formulations assumed a major significance for determining orthodoxy. The major 20th cent. theological trends in Protestantism have been a search to reaffirm the meaning of Scripture as rule of faith, to reassert the primacy of God's word.

A real and substantive difference separates Christians in their explanation of the rule of faith. The root of the difference is in diverse concepts of the Church. Yet the mutual enrichment and dialogue of RC and Protestant theologians on the meaning of the mission of the Church, tradition, and the primacy of Scriptures are hopeful signs of progress toward unity.

[P. De LETTER]

RULE OF LIFE, or plan of life, an horarium or daily schedule providing a set pattern for the fulfillment of obligations for times of prayer, recreation, and rest. Such a plan is analogous to the rule of religious and has a similar purpose: it is recommended to those striving for a closer union with God in order to create a setting of constancy of purpose and of disciplined, orderly living. It is also recommended that the rule of life adopted be submitted to a confessor or spiritual director for approval. The daily schedule is meant to create a setting that is a safeguard against frenetic activity and the dissipation of energies, and assists concentration on the goal of prayerful union with God. As a means, not an end in itself, the rule of life yields to the dictates of charity, esp. toward a neighbor in need.

[T. C. O'BRIEN]

RULE OF ST. ANTHONY, see ANTHONY, RULE OF ST.

RULER-CULT, the rendering of divine honors or actual worship to living or dead rulers or other prominent individuals because of their achievements or position. Ruler-cult in a variety of forms is fairly common among polytheistic peoples, who have no clear concept of the divine transcendence, and is intimately connected with the world-wide conviction that a king or ruler is in some way sacred.

From the very beginning the Egyptian pharaohs were thought to be gods. The earliest inscriptions identify them with Horus, but from the Fifth Dynasty on they were rather regarded as sons of Ra. In Babylonia down to the time of Hammurabi the name of a ruler could be written with the determinatives used for gods and objects of worship. He could also receive shares of the temple offerings. But such prerogatives were not an actual deification. The king of Persia was thought to be the representative of Ahura Mazda and was honored with the rite of prostration (*proskynesis*), which at least some Greeks (erroneously) thought to be a sign of his divinity.

In early Greece kings and warriors could be compared with gods or even honored as gods by the people, as they are in Homer; but actual worship was reserved for deceased oecists, or city-founders, who received a kind of posthumous deification by being enrolled among the heroes. Religious crises brought about through the constant wars and philosophical speculations led to the eventual deification in Greece of living men. The first example of this was the divinization of Lysander at Samos in 405 B.C. It reached a developed form under Alexander the Great, who was proclaimed the son of Amon-Zeus by the oracle of Siwah in 331, and who asked the Greek cities of the League of Corinth to render him divine honors in 324. These same honors were freely given by the Greeks to his successors and their descendants and were manifested in dedications, the erection of statues, and the enrolling of the rulers among the official divinities of various localities.

Ruler-worship in Rome had a native foundation in the sacrifices offered to the ghosts of the dead (*manes*) and to the *genii*, particularly those of the head of a household, semi-independent spirits watching over living persons. Influenced by Greek practice, the Romans in the 4th cent. deified their founder Romulus. From the time of conquest of Syracuse by Marcus Claudius Marcellus in 211 B.C., Roman generals and officials such as Publius Scipio Africanus and Titus Quinctius Flamininus, the "liberator" of Greece, received divine honors from the Greeks. Similar honors were given to the dictator Caesar (45–44) by the Romans themselves, and after his death he was deified by the Senate (42).

Augustus was keenly aware of the advantages to be obtained from ruler-worship as a cohesive bond for the State. In Italy he ordered the worship of his predecessor Divus Iulius, and in the East he permitted the worship of himself in conjunction with the goddess Roma, a cult that soon spread also to the cities and provinces of the West. After his death his cult was officially established on the Palatine. Augustus' successor, Tiberius, rejected divine honors officially offered him, but his successor Gaius Caligula exacted them. During the 2d cent., the good emperors continued to be honored after their deaths by the apotheoses of the Senate. During the 3d cent., however, the emperor came to be regarded as a being divinely protected rather than as a god himself. This was a concept that was maintained under the Christian emperors and eventually developed into the theory of the divine right of kings.

Ruler-cult may be interpreted in various ways. It could be mere flattery, as in the case of the Augustan poets who raised the emperor to the ranks of the gods; it could be a sincere token of gratitude for the benefits of peace and prosperity that came from Greek and Roman rule; and, finally, it could be a form of actual worship. To the pagans such worship made little difference, merely the addition of another to an already long list of deities, though some, like Cicero, were opposed to it (*I Phil*. 13). To Jews and Christians it was an abomination. The former, as members of a *religio licita*, were specifically exempted from the obligations of rendering divine honors to the emperors, a privilege to which the Christians could make no claim. An oath by the genius of the emperor and the offering of sacrifice to his image along with that of the other gods of the State came to be tests of loyalty to the State and the occasion of martyrdom for those who refused. BIBLIOGRAPHY: L. Cerfaux and J. Tondriau, *Un Concurrent du christianisme, le culte des souverains dans la civilisation gréco-romaine* (1957)

[M. J. COSTELLOE]

RULES OF LAW (*Regulae juris*), norms of canonical jurisprudence that the CIC frequently cites. The *Regulae juris* were codified and edited by the canonist Dino Rosoni of Mugello in the 13th cent., in conjunction with the *Liber* *sextus*, under the mandate of Boniface VIII. The main source of these rules is the Code of Justinian, but some derive from the *decretists and the *decretalists. BIBLIOGRAPHY: V. Bartocetti, NCE 12:713–714.

[T. C. O'BRIEN]

RUM MILLET (Turkish, Roman nation), the name given to the Christian Church under Turkish rule. In the Ottoman Empire, as in other Muslim countries, each non-Muslim religious body formed a *millet* or nation under the jurisdiction of their religious head. The Orthodox Church, having been the Church of the Byzantine, or Roman, Empire, was known as the Roman nation and was under the ecclesiastical and civil jurisdiction of the patriarch of Constantinople, who held the title *ethnarch or *millet-bashi*.

[G. T. DENNIS]

RUMANIA, see ROMANIA.

RUMMEL, JOSEPH FRANCIS (1876–1964), abp. of New Orleans, promoter of racial integration. Born in Germany and coming to the U.S. as a child, R. was ordained for New York and served in Harlem, where he observed the racial problem. In 1928 he was named bp. of Omaha, and in 1935 abp. of New Orleans. His vigorous leadership resulted in great growth for the archdiocese. R. came to national prominence beginning in 1949 when he refused to sanction an outdoor celebration because city officials ruled that whites and blacks could not participate together. In 1953 he decreed that blacks would no longer be required to receive holy communion after whites, and that they were to be admitted to parish organizations. Bitter opposition by clergy and laity built up. At the age of 80 he ordered the racial integration of all parochial schools. State and city officials, many of them Catholics, mounted a campaign of opposition, harassed R., and appealed to Rome against him, but Rome supported his policy. Integration was delayed, but it was achieved in 1962. R. also threatened with excommunication any Catholic legislator who worked for segregation. When parishioners outside New Orleans refused to accept a black priest sent to the parish, R. closed the church. By his courageous policy of integration, R. led the way for a new era in Catholic practice in the South.

[J. R. AHERNE]

RUNCARII, the name by which members of one group of *Cathari were known in Germany during the 13th century. Derivation of the term is uncertain, but it was probably a geographic reference. BIBLIOGRAPHY: S. Runciman, *Medieval Manichee* (pa., 1961) 185; H. C. Lea, *History of the Inquisition of the Middle Ages*. (1888; repr., 1958) 1:88.

[C. J. LYNCH]

RUPERT OF DEUTZ (*c.*1075–1129), Benedictine abbot *c.*1120 of St. Eriberto, at Deutz near Cologne, theologian.

He was a strong supporter of the *Gregorian reform and a critic of simoniacal bishops. His name came into prominence during the Reformation: he was cited as a proponent of *impanation rather than of transubstantiation in the Eucharist. "The Word, who became flesh, now becomes bread, not as though changed into bread, but by taking up bread and bringing it into a unity with his person" (*In Joann*. 6. PL 169, 181). R. was a prolific writer in the monastic tradition of biblical and patristic inspiration, in opposition to the use of dialectics in theology, esp. against Anselm of Laon and William of Champeaux. He wrote on the liturgy of the church year *De divinis officiis*, a highly allegorical and symbolic work; *De voluntate Dei* and *De omnipotentia Dei* were polemics against Anselm of Laon, whom R. accused of making God the cause of evil. He wrote apologetics against the Jews: *Annulus seu dialogus christiani et judaei* and *De glorificatione Trinitatis*, a tracing of the mystery in the OT. His highly allegorical scriptural works include *De sanctissima Trinitate et eius operibus* and the most complete exegetical work, *De victoria Verbi Dei*. He left also a valuable personal reflection on monastic life, *Super quaedam capita Regulae S. Benedicti abbatis*.

[T. C. O'BRIEN]

RUPERT OF OTTOBEUREN, BL. (d.1145), Benedictine abbot. R. became abbot of the monastery of Ottobeuren, Germany, in 1102, where he introduced the Cluniac reforms and helped to advance the cause of ecclesiastical reform in Germany. He was the object of great popular devotion. BIBLIOGRAPHY: Zimmerman 2:572–574; O. Scheib, BiblSanct 11:505–506.

[B. F. SCHERER]

RUPERT OF SALZBURG, ST. (d. *c.*718), founder and first bp. of Salzburg. R. seems to have been bp. of Worms before undertaking missionary work in Bavaria. There, on land received from Duke Theodo (695–718), he founded the oldest monastery in Austria, Sankt Peter (*c.*700), on the site of the ancient Roman Juvavum, and erected the convent of Nonnberg, of which his niece Erentrude became the first abbess. With his companions, Vitalis, Chuniald, and Gislar, he evangelized the country around Salzburg, built churches, and civilized the people. He is credited with having developed the salt mines and given Juvavum its modern name of Salzburg. BIBLIOGRAPHY: J. Baur, BiblSanct 11:506–508; Butler 1:700–701.

[M. F. MCCARTHY]

RUPRECHT-KARL-UNIVERSITÄT, see HEIDELBERG, UNIVERSITY OF.

RURAL BISHOPS, see CHORBISHOP.

RURAL CHAPTER, see CHAPTER, RURAL.

RURAL DEAN, see DEAN, RURAL.

RURICIUS, SS., two bps. of Limoges, France, of whom the earlier one is the uncle of the later one. The early Ruricius was of a noble family and married a wealthy patrician named Iberia. One of their sons became a priest, and R. himself, when he was older (*c*.485), was elected bp. of Limoges, a see which had remained vacant for ten years after the devastation of the Visigoths. He favored the eremitic life and wrote countless pastoral letters, often citing the Latin Fathers. He apparently did not attend the provincial councils of his area at the turn of the century, and sometime before the council at Clermont in 535 he was succeeded by his nephew. The latter was a disciple of Saint Junianus. As bp. he attended the councils of Clermont and of Orleans IV and V. He must have died *c*.550. Uncle and nephew are buried in the Church of St. Junianus, which the second Ruricius had built over the sarcophagus of that saint. Venantius Fortunatus inscribed a common epitaph for the two bishops. BIBLIOGRAPHY: P. Viard, BiblSanct 11:508–510.

[E. J. DILLON]

RUS', early name (9th and 10th cent.) of the Scandinavians, also known as Varangians, who established their rule over the East Slavic lands; it was also applied to the Slavic inhabitants themselves as well as to all the land under the domination of the Rus' who resided in Kiev (*Russkaya zemlya*, the Russian land). Although the origin of these rulers and the name has been fiercely debated, particularly by the "anti-Normannist" school of Russian historians, there is little doubt as to their Scandinavian origin. The term derives from the Old Swedish *rōther,* largely as found in compound forms such as *rōths-karlar,* rowers or seafarers. Attempts to connect the name with the Syrian *Ḥros* or the Alanic *Rukh-As* have received little acceptance. From the 9th cent., Byzantine sources consistently used the indeclinable *hoi Rhōs* in referring to the rulers and the people of Kievan Russia. While the Scandinavian, mainly Swedish, origin of the Rus' is now beyond serious question, the debate, often clouded by extrahistorical considerations, regarding their role in the foundation of Russia still continues. But it is generally admitted today that while the social and economic foundations of the Kievan state were laid by the Slavs along the Dnieper, it was the Scandinavian invaders in the second half of the 9th cent., led by the Viking chief Rurik according to sources which may be more legendary than historical, who united under their rule the Slavic tribes into one state based on the Baltic-Black Sea waterway and to which they left their "Russian" name. BIBLIOGRAPHY: G. Vernadsky, *Kievan Russia* (1948); *Constantine Porphyrogenitus, De administrando imperio, II Commentary* (ed. R. J. H. Jenkins, 1962) 16–23.

[D. DIRSCHERL]

RÛSHMŌ (East Syrian, *rûshmā*), in Syrian Eucharistic rites, the consignation of one consecrated species with the other.

[A. CODY]

RUSINS (Rusini), hence Ruthenian (Latin), Slavic peoples of the old Czechoslovak province of Pod Karpatska Rus, or Ruthenia, presently incorporated in the Zarkarpatska oblast of the Ukrainian Soviet Socialist Republic. The Rusins are cousins to the Galicians N of the Carpathians and speak a Slavic dialect akin to that of the Galicians and the Ukrainians. The original apostles of the Rusins are not known, but the Rusins embraced Christianity in its Byzantine form. They were divided into dioceses in Mucachevo, Uzhorod, and Hajduderog with one diocese in Eastern Slovakia at Preshov for the Slovaks of the Byzantine rite. Along with their faith they imbibed from their Byzantine teachers a suspicion and dislike for Latin Christianity. Metropolitan Isidore of Kiev, who journeyed through their regions in the 15th cent. on his way back to Moscow from the Council of Florence, would have proclaimed the reunion of the Eastern and Western Churches to them.

The real work of reunion in this area was begun by Galician monks who visited those parts preaching reunion. From early times, the bp. of Przemysl had jurisdiction in Ruthenia, and some of the early bps. of Mucachevo were Galician Ukrainians. Under Bp. Hryhorovych and his successor Bp. Basil Tarasevitch in the See of Muchachevo, Catholic Byzantine monks and clerics were given a free hand to promote resumption of communion with Rome. Finally, on April 24, 1646, some 63 Ruthenian priests adhered to the Union at Uzhorod, and the reunion movement slowly spread. Most of them retained church Slavonic as their liturgical language, except in the Diocese of Hajduderog, where Magyar was widely used. Rusin church music is esp. beautiful and the Rusins have preserved the Byzantine rite in greater purity than have their Galician cousins.

[A. WALKER]

RUSKIN, JOHN (1819–1900), English art critic and writer on social and economic problems. His reputation as an art critic and literary stylist was established by his *Modern Painters* (4 v., 1843–60), *The Seven Lamps of Architecture* (1849), and *The Stones of Venice* (1851–53). He lectured and published extensively, developing his view that art is the expression of man's rational and disciplined delight in the forms and laws of the creation of which he forms a part, and is esp. the expression of his religion and morality. To produce art that reveals truth, beauty, and significance, man must have skill plus an integrated personality. R.'s view of art and morality was the object of some ridicule, but basically he was attacking vulgarity and the sensational in art. After 1860 he wrote much on social and economic matters and was actively engaged in the establishment of guilds and agricultural and industrial settlements. His interest in the Middle Ages and his friendship with Cardinal Manning caused some to expect his conversion to Roman Catholicism, but this never came about. In his religious views he had little sympathy for the emphasis commonly put upon dogma. He originally professed a simple sort of evangelistic piety, and in the latter years of his life appeared to be unassociated with any organized religious body. BIBLIOG- RAPHY: G. Hough, *Last Romantics* (1949); J. Evans, *John Ruskin* (1954).

[M. M. BARRY]

RUSSELL, BERTRAND, 3rd Earl (1872–1970), English logician, philosopher, writer on social questions, Nobel laureate (Literature, 1950) and holder of the Order of Merit. A pupil of *Whitehead at Trinity College, Cambridge, he later wrote with him *Principia mathematica,* perhaps the most influential theoretical work of the 20th century. R.'s voluminous writings and correspondence are marked by penetrating insight, rigor (in his theoretical writings), and supple, lucid prose. A Platonist in his early life, he then shifted to an empirical realism not unlike Hume's. For R., philosophy must be constructed on the analogy of science; indeed it is *prescientific* in that it treats of questions not yet settled by positive science. Inclined to materialism (mental phenomena, e.g., are wholly dependent on the nervous system), R. nevertheless cannot accept the whole materialistic doctrine. His social thought is based on the axiom that the good life is one of tender love guided by knowledge; it is neither hedonistic nor libertarian. The doctrine of immortality is nonsense, as is that of God as First Cause. R. has variously described himself as agnostic or atheist. He was no maker of systems; his thought remained in constant flux. BIBLIOGRAPHY: Autobiography (3 v., 1967–69); *Philosophy of Bertrand Russell* (ed. P. Schlipp, 1944); A. Wood, *Bertrand Russell: Passionate Skeptic* (1956).

[W. B. MAHONEY]

RUSSELL, CHARLES TAZE (1852–1916), founder of the Watch Tower Bible and Tract Society (see JEHOVAH'S WITNESSES). As a young haberdasher in Allegheny, Pa., R. undertook a study of the Bible and was much influenced by Adventist doctrines. He founded a religious organization (1872) whose members were called Russellites, Earnest Bible Students, Watch Tower People, or Millennial Dawnists until J. F. *Rutherford gave them the name Jehovah's Witnesses in 1931. R. denied the existence of hell, preached that the final battle of Armageddon and Christ's second coming were imminent, and rejected the orthodox doctrine of the Trinity. Pastor Russell, as he called himself, organized Bible study groups throughout the U.S. and began publication of the *Watch Tower and Herald of Christ's Presence* in 1879. He completed a 6-volume Bible commentary called *Studies in the Scriptures,* or *Millennial Dawn* (v. 6, 1886–1904). R.'s wife sought a legal separation in 1903, and he was involved in several suits over support payments. In 1908 he moved the headquarters of his movement from Pittsburgh, Pa., to Brooklyn, New York. His marital difficulties and unfulfilled prediction that the world would end in 1914 lost him some followers in his last years.

[W. J. WHALEN]

RUSSELL, GEORGE W. (pseud. AE; 1867–1935), Irish writer and amateur painter, theosophist. Educated at Rathmines school, Dublin, he entered an accountant's office, but in 1897 joined the Irish Agricultural Organization and became an organizer of agricultural societies and a practical worker for agricultural reform in Ireland. During the years 1904 to 1923 he was editor of *The Irish Homestead,* the organ of the agricultural cooperative movement. In 1923 he became editor of *The Irish Statesman.* His poems reveal an Oriental quietism plus a devotion to the earth as expressed in *Homeward: Songs by the Way* (1894), *The Earth Breath and Other Poems* (1897), and in several later volumes of poetry. His unfinished autobiography, *The Candle of Vision* (1918), is concerned with the one and eternal truth, hints of which were the outcome of his mystical experiences. His poetry is noted for its exquisite delicacy and melody.

[S. A. HEENEY]

RUSSELL JOHN (d. 1494), bp. of Rochester (1476–80), of Lincoln (1480–94). A trusted councilor of Edward IV, he was keeper of the privy seal (1474–83) and Richard III's chancellor. He amassed a considerable library, and St. Thomas More praised him as "a wyse manne and a good . . . one of the best learned menne undoubtedlye" of his time. BIBLIOGRAPHY: Emden Ox 3:1609–11.

[C. D. ROSS]

RUSSELL, MARY BAPTIST, MOTHER (1829–98), foundress of the Sisters of Mercy in California. Professed in her native Ireland as a Sister of Mercy in 1851, R. engaged in the two areas of service which would be her life work, education and nursing. When her community was invited to establish a foundation in San Francisco, Cal. by Abp. J. Alemany, R. was sent as superior of the group and thus established the Sisters of Mercy in California. The city was in a wretched situation for social welfare in 1854, and the sisters had to provide what care there was. In the cholera epidemic of 1855, they were given charge of the county hospital. R. turned the institution into St. Mary's Hospital in 1857, the first Catholic hospital on the West coast. Other charitable foundations followed in San Francisco, Sacramento, and Grass Valley. From 1871 to 1892, R. established five schools in the archdiocese.

[J. R. AHERNE]

RUSSELL, RICHARD (1630–93), bp. in Portugal and member of the English Chapter. R. was born in Berkshire but as a young man worked at the English College in Lisbon, then began studies for the priesthood. After ordination (1655), he served as procurator of the college, secretary to Queen Luisa, and chaplain to the Portuguese ambassador to England. While in England, he was made a canon of the English Chapter (1661). After becoming bp. of Portalegre, Portugal, in 1671, the Chapter sought to have R. resign his see and, as a validly ordained bp. with jurisdiction in England, exercise his episcopal powers in England. R. refused, regarding the plan as schismatic. He later became bp. of Vizeu, Portugal. BIBLIOGRAPHY: Gillow BDEC 5:455–457.

[T. M. MCFADDEN]

RUSSELL, WILLIAM THOMAS (1863–1927), bp. of Charleston, South Carolina. A native of Maryland, R. was ordained for the Archdiocese of Baltimore in 1889. He was appointed secretary to Card. Gibbons in 1894 and became pastor of St. Patrick's in Washington, D.C., where he inaugurated the annual Pan-American Mass, and the Field Mass offered annually on the grounds of the Washington Monument. He served as the representative of Gibbons in Washington; in 1916 R. was appointed bp. of Charleston. His administration of the diocese was a fruitful one. One of four bps. to administer the National Catholic War Council during World War I, he continued to serve on the executive board of its successor, The National Catholic Welfare Council. R. contributed to *Maryland, the Land of Sanctuary* (1908), and wrote articles for *The Catholic Encyclopedia*.

[J. R. AHERNE]

RUSSIA, formerly an empire of Eastern Europe and since 1917 the principal republic of the *Union of Soviet Socialist Republics. The modern history of Russia dates from the 9th cent. and the arrival of the Eastern Slavs and Varangians (Scandinavians). The name ''Rus'' perhaps designated the latter originally, but was then applied to both. According to tradition, the Varangian Rurik established a dynasty at Novgorod (*c.*862), and his successor transferred his seat to Kiev. Vladimir I (980–1015) made Christianity (Byzantine rite) the state religion. In 1237–40 the Mongols, known in Russia as Ta(r)tars, invaded and established the empire of the Golden Horde in S and E Russia, maintaining their hold until 1480. Under Ivan I (1328–41), Moscow began assuming dominance over other cities in the Vladimir duchy, though still subject to the Tatars. Rulers of the duchy later took the title grand dukes of Moscow, or Muscovy. Ivan III (1462–1505) initiated a period of expansion, including conquest of Novgorod, an independent state (1136–1478). He ended tribute to the Tatars, married the niece of the last Byzantine emperor, and considered himself heir to the Byzantine Empire. Beginning with Ivan IV (The Terrible) in 1547, Russian rulers were crowned as czars (tsars), Slavic word for Caesar. Ivan IV expanded the area of Russian control and prepared the way for annexation of Siberia, while tightening autocracy at home. After the Time of Troubles, Michael Romanov was chosen czar in 1613, and his dynasty ruled until 1917. In the 17th and 18th cent., Russia pushed westward, taking the Ukraine and much of Poland. Peter the Great (1696–1725) sought to Westernize Russian society, which had lagged behind the rest of Europe economically and culturally. He gained territory on the Gulf

of Finland and established St. Petersburg (now Leningrad) in 1703, making it the capital in 1712. Over the next 2 centuries, Russo-Turkish wars resulted in further Russian expansion into Ottoman lands. Under Catherine the Great (1762–96) Russia became the chief power of Continental Europe. In 1812 Napoleon took Moscow, but had to withdraw. Russia and Austria then headed the *Holy Alliance. During the 19th cent., expansion continued in Asia, reaching to Vladivostok. But though reforms such as emancipation of serfs were effected (1864), internal discontent grew, and World War I reverses led to overthrow of the czar. For subsequent Russian history see *Union of Soviet Socialist Republics.

[T. EARLY]

RUSSIA, CHURCH IN. The conversion of Russia to Christianity began just as the modern state of *Russia was being formed in the 9th and 10th centuries. Christians for several centuries had evangelized and established Churches on the N shore of the Black Sea and other areas later incorporate in Russia. Olga, regent of Kiev, accepted Christianity *c.*955. But it did not become the state religion until Vladimir was baptized *c.*988. The Church was established in Russia under the auspices of Byzantine clergy and with the Byzantine conception of Church-State relations. It received the Bible and liturgy in the translation of SS. *Cyril and Methodius, a South Slav dialect (Old or Church Slavonic) that became the liturgical language of the Russian Church. Metropolitans of Kiev, who held jurisdiction over the entire Russian Church from *c.*1037, were appointed by Constantinople. Russian monasticism, a primary religious influence in ''Holy Russia,'' began when Anthony, a monk of Mt. *Athos, founded the Kiev Crypt (or caves) Monastery in 1051, and Theodosius introduced the Basilian Order there in 1072. It reached its peak with Sergius of Radonezh (*c.*1314–92). Russia was allied with the Eastern Churches after the schism of 1054. Though the area was under Ta(r)tar domination (1240–1480), generally the Church was able to operate unhindered. In 1441, after the Council of Florence, Metropolitan Isidore proclaimed reunion with Rome, and was deposed by Grand Duke Basil. Early in the 14th cent. the metropolitan see had moved from Kiev to Moscow. The Russian Church now assumed autocephalous status by appointing its own metropolitan, Jonas (1448–61), who changed the see title to Moscow. From 1386 Lithuania and Poland, both Catholic, had been allied, and their rule extended over the Kiev region. Rome began appointing metropolitans to Kiev after the prelates in Moscow gave up the title. After the fall of Constantinople (1453) and the Balkans to the Turks, Russia became the only independent Orthodox power, and Russians began thinking of Moscow as the Third Rome, though they never formally claimed to supplant the ecumenical patriarchate. In 1589, Job was consecrated by Jeremias II of Constantinople as the first Moscow patriarch. From 1321 a bp. for Latin rite Catholics was in Kiev, and from 1798 the Archdiocese of Mogilev (White Russia) held jurisdiction over all Latin Catholics, though the last holder of the see was exiled in 1932. In 1596 much of the Eastern rite Church in the Kiev region, controlled by Catholic Poland, accepted union with Rome in the union of *Brest-Litovsk, and the question of Ukrainian ties with Rome became a matter of perpetual discord. As Russia subsequently gained dominance over the Ukraine, some Uniates returned to Orthodoxy, and at various times state authorities acted to suppress Uniate dioceses, most recently in 1946. However, reports indicate that an underground Uniate Church survives. Another division in the Russian Church developed through the schism of *Old Believers in the 17th century. In the 18th cent. Peter the Great abolished the patriarchate to make the Church subordinate to the State in the manner of Western Protestant countries. He set up a Holy Synod (1721), whose deliberations were always to take place with a lay representative of the czar present. This procurator gradually became the chief administrative officer of the Church. The patriarchate was not reestablished until the 1917 Revolution, and after the first patriarch, Tikon, died in 1925, the office remained vacant until *Stalin made concessions to the Church in 1943. After a period of imprisonment, Metropolitan Sergius, locum tenens of the patriarchate, issued a declaration in 1927 calling on Orthodox believers to give the Soviet government full support, and demanding that Russian Orthodox clergy outside the Soviet Union give a written promise of their loyalty. The demand on clergy outside the USSR was widely disregarded, but the declaration established the policy that subsequently guided Orthodox authorities in Russia. For a time after the Revolution, Orthodox Christians welcoming the new government formed a ''Living Church,'' but it failed to develop popular support. From 1918, when the Soviet government declared separation of Church and State, the Russian Orthodox Church has been constitutionally independent, though like all other aspects of Soviet life it has in fact been tightly controlled by government authorities. During Stalin's lifetime, Russian church leaders were able to take only a minor role in international church life, aside from attending certain peace conferences that supported Soviet political positions in the Cold War. But later this situation changed, and in 1961 the Russian Orthodox Church entered the World Council of Churches. Though reliable statistics are unavailable, estimates generally place the number of Orthodox believers in Russia at 30 million–50 million. Theological seminaries and monasteries are allowed to function, church services often draw large crowds and, despite heavy atheistic propaganda by the government, the Church in recent years has had some success in attracting the interest of intellectuals and youth.

In addition to the Orthodox, Russian Christians include a considerable Baptist community dating to the 19th cent. and smaller numbers of other groups. With influence from the German Baptist movement led by J. G. Oncken (1800–84), Baptists in Russia began to grow rapidly and formed the Russian Baptist Union in 1884. Another group of similar orientation formed the Union of Evangelical Christians in 1908. They merged in 1944 to form the All-Union Council of Evangelical Christians-Baptists. It participates in the Baptist World Alliance. Baptists gained in membership after the 1917 Revolution, but later suffered under the repressions of Stalin. Currently they are estimated to number *c*.500,000. A dissident Baptist group of uncertain size has refused cooperation with the main body because of its acquiescence in state control of the Churches.

[T. EARLY]

RUSSIAN CANON LAW. Since Christianity came to Russia primarily from the Byzantine Church, Russian canon law has received its chief influence from that tradition. The Orthodox Churches did not develop anything comparable to the comprehensive and systematized canon law of the Roman Church, worked out in detail by a specialized corps of jurists. Rather, Orthodox Churches were guided in a general way by decisions of councils, synods, and hierarchical authorities, while their history resulted in more of their governance coming from secular rulers. Byzantine bps. going to Russia took the Church and imperial documents they had been using, some partly translated into Slavonic before they left and others translated in Russia. Canon law specifically designed for the Russian situation began with acts of Kiev synods in 1051, 1147, and 1160, and rulings of individual authorities. After the Russian Church became autonomous, various synods were called to order ecclesiastical affairs, and by 1700 a virtually perpetual synod had come into existence. From the time of Peter the Great, the Church functioned as a department of State in the pattern of Protestant national Churches, and church legislation was set forth by imperial authority. A council of 1917–18 reestablished the patriarchate and enacted various decrees. The Church received formal independence by the decree of Church-State separation in 1918, though in practical terms it remained under strict government control. A 1945 council of the Russian Orthodox Church approved a new statute for its governance. BIBLIOGRAPHY: *Russian Orthodox Church: Organization, Situation, Activity* (1958), an official publication of the Moscow Patriarchate.

[T. EARLY]

RUSSIAN LITURGICAL BOOKS. In the Russian Orthodox Church the Office for a given day contains readings from several books. Those described below are the most essential for daily use but constitute only a selection of those available. *Sluzhebnik* (Service Book): contains the fixed portions of the Liturgies of St. Basil the Great (celebrated only 10 times a year), St. John Chrysostom, and the Lenten Liturgy of the Presanctified. *Chasoslov* (*horologion*): contains the fixed portions of the canonical Hours, with a selection of hymns for different occasions. *Chinovnik*: the *Sluzhebnik* of episcopal usage, containing the order of service for conferring major and minor orders, episcopal consecration, and such other rites as the consecration of the antimension. *Oktoich* (*Book of Eight Tones*): eight sets of changeable prayers for the Divine Liturgy and the canonical Hours, the tones or melodies being used for a week at a time in rotation during the time between Pentecost and Lent. *Mineja*: 12 monthly volumes containing the changeable prayers of the sanctoral cycle. *Anthologion* or *Prazdnichnaja Mineja* (*Festival Mineja*): contains the order of service for the 12 major feasts. *Triod*: in two parts, the Lenten (*Postnaja*) and Paschaltide (*Tsvetnaja*) Triods contain the changeable prayers of the Divine Liturgy and the canonical Hours peculiar to these two seasons. *Irmologion*: contains hymns sung at various liturgical services, from the Divine Liturgy to short services in honor of the Blessed Virgin, St. Nicholas, and others. *Tipikon* or *Ustav* (Rule): contains the rubrics concerning the prayers to be used on every occasion; a guide to the use of the *Sluzhebnik*, the *Chasoslov*, the *Oktoich*, the *Minejas* and the *Triodions*, and instruction on how the several cycles are to be combined. *Trebnik* (*Book of Needs*): contains the order of service for all the sacraments other than the Eucharist and ordination, as well as numerous other public and private services, from funerals to the blessing of a new dwelling. *Apostol*: contains the Acts of the Apostles, the Pauline and other Epistles, and often the Apocalypse, as well as Graduals, Introits, and anthems for particular feasts. *Evangelie*: the four Gospels. *Psaltir*: the Psalms; often printed together with the *Chasoslov*, as well as other readings and minor services.

[R. H. MARSHALL]

RUSSIAN LITURGY.

The lands of Rus received the Christian faith in the 9th cent., principally from missionaries from Byzantium who brought with them the liturgy in use in the imperial capital. Most probably the early Greek missionaries to Russia used their own rite in Greek, but at an early date they must have decided to use the Slavonic version of the same liturgy initiated by SS. Cyril and Methodius and completed by St. Clement of Ochrid and his disciples in Serbia and Bulgaria. This is the origin of the Church-Slavonic version of the Byzantine liturgy.

The Russian usage of the Byzantine rite is, in all principal points, identical with the same rite as it is celebrated by the Greeks, Syrians, Romanians, and other Orthodox peoples; however, the practiced observer can notice some peculiarities in the Russian way of celebrating the Eucharistic Liturgy: the third antiphon is almost always the "Beatitudes," whereas among the Greeks, these are used only at funerals; at the Creed, the veil or *aër* is held differently by the Russian celebrant from the Greek or Ukrainian usage; the Creed and the Lord's Prayer are always sung solemnly by the Russians, whereas among the Greeks they may be recited by an individual, often a child; and within the anaphora the Russians recite the troparion for Pentecost three times during the epiclesis of the Holy Spirit. There are other minor differences, but they often escape the casual observer.

The greatest difference one detects in the Russian liturgy, however, is the chant. Very soon after their conversion, the Russians began to adapt the old, pagan Slavonic chants to the hymns, antiphons, and troparia of the liturgy. The work was taken up esp. by the monasteries so that today there is a chant proper to the Kievo-Petcherskaya Laura (the oldest one on Russian soil), a chant of Pochayev in Volhynia, a chant of Solovetskiye in the Arctic Ocean, a chant of Valaam, and others. Much of the most ancient chant exists only among the Old Believers today, as do the old translations of the liturgical texts in use in the Russian Church before the reforms of Patriarch Nikon in the 17th century. With the coming of the Renaissance ethos to Russia through Italians who came to the capital in the employment of the czars, harmonized chant began to be widely used. With their musical genius, the Russians took naturally to this new mode of rendering the chants of the liturgy and soon reached a high degree of perfection. Some Russian harmonized chant is very florid and operatic, while some is very simple but exquisitely beautiful. Of all church music in the world, that of the Russian Church is among the most beautiful.

In the calendar, the Russians have their own saints as do other Orthodox countries. However, there is a peculiarity in that the Russians have a class of saints, "fools for Christ's sake" or "yorodivy" that do not appear in other Orthodox calendars. Several miraculous icons of the Mother of God found only in Russia and venerated only by Russians are commemorated on different days of the year.

[A. WALKER]

RUSSIAN METROPOLIA (U.S.A.),

the common name for the E Russian Orthodox Greek Catholic Church of America, the largest of the three Russian Orthodox jurisdictions in America. In 1970 it took the name *Orthodox Church in America.

RUSSIAN ORTHODOX CHURCH,

see RUSSIA, CHURCH IN.

RUSSIAN ORTHODOX CHURCH IN THE U.S.A., PATRIARCHAL PARISHES,

parishes that have chosen to remain under the jurisdiction of the Moscow patriarchate. Following the Russian Revolution of 1917, the question of what relationship Russian Orthodox communities outside the country should maintain with the patriarchate became highly controversial. In the U.S., Russian Orthodoxy has become divided among three groups. The largest is the *Orthodox Church in America, which acknowledged patriarchal authority but exercised de facto independence until granted autocephaly in 1970. A small amount of support has gone to the *Russian Orthodox Church Outside Russia, which renounced all relationships with Moscow pending a change in Church–State relations there. Then, there were some parishes that accepted the jurisdiction of bps. appointed by the Moscow patriarchate. Through court action, the group loyal to Moscow secured the New York Cathedral of St. Nicholas in 1925. Formally the patriarchate claimed the canonical right of jurisdiction over all Russian Orthodox parishes in America until the 1970 grant of autocephaly to the Orthodox Church in America. According to 1974 statistics, there were 41 patriarchal parishes with 51,500 members.

[T. EARLY]

RUSSIAN ORTHODOX CHURCH OUTSIDE RUSSIA (formerly, ROC Abroad), body organized after the Russian Revolution to unite emigré Russian Orthodox independently of the Moscow patriarchate. It contends that the patriarchate is under Communist domination and should not be recognized until it is able to act freely. In 1920 Russian bps. who had gone to Istanbul established the Supreme Russian Church Administration Abroad. The following year a *sobor* was held at Sremski Karlovci, Serbia. Passage of a resolution there calling for restoration of the Romanovs, together with later developments, led the Church to be widely viewed as a voice of political reaction. Its bps. formed a Temporary Holy Episcopal Synod of the Russian Orthodox Church Abroad, and it was sometimes called the Synodal Church. Headquarters remained in Sremski Karlovci until after World War II. Then, following a period in Munich, it moved to New York in 1950. It proved unable to unite emigré Russians and dwindled to minority status. Some parishes preferred to maintain ties with the newly formed Moscow patriarchate (see ROC IN THE USA, PATRIARCHAL PARISHES). One group based in Paris affiliated with the ecumenical patriarch of Constantinople (Istanbul). And the main Russian body of the U.S. continued to recognize Moscow while exercising practical independence (see ORTHODOX CHURCH IN AMERICA). The ROC Outside Russia has continued to espouse a strongly conservative position in both theology and politics, and maintains almost no ties with other Churches.

[T. EARLY]

RUSSIAN ORTHODOX THEOLOGY. The coming of Christianity to Russia from Byzantium in the 10th cent. resulted in the Russian Church's taking over *Eastern Orthodox theology as it had been formed by the patristic writers and the ecumenical councils. The Eastern tradition remained dominant, though in later cent. Russian theology was heavily influenced by Western movements, both Catholic and Protestant. Its distinctive quality emerged from the way these diverse influences were appropriated. The circumstances of Russian history were not conducive to the development of strong theological schools producing original work, and Russian theology has no great figures comparable to Aquinas, Calvin, and Schleiermacher. Perhaps the most creative period of Russian theology came following the 1917 Revolution when exiles such as N. *Berdyaev (1874–1948), S. Bulgakov (1871–1944), and G. Florovski (1893–   ) found themselves in situations where they could work with intellectual freedom and in creative dialogue with Western thinkers.

Russian theology began with missionaries translating into Slavic the works of Chrysostom, Damascene, and other Greek Fathers. The continuing alliance of Russia with Constantinople after 1054 meant that Russian theology was characterized by such Eastern features as rejection of papal primacy and the *filioque* clause. Later, the works of Gregory *Palamas were translated. After the fall of Constantinople in 1453, the concept of Moscow as the third and last Rome became important in Russian thought. The subsequent inability of Constantinople to exercise its customary influence in Russia opened the way for increased Western influence. After the Union of Brest-Litovsk (1596), Catholic patterns of theology were introduced in the Kiev region, then under Catholic Poland. The school of P. Moghila (1596–1646) in Kiev opposed Catholicism but operated on Latin and Jesuit models, making the distinction between Orthodoxy and Catholicism primarily one of ecclesiastical jurisdiction. These Western influences were later transmitted to the theological academies of Moscow and other cities. In the Russian Church, liturgical practice was also a key test of Orthodoxy, and the schism of the *Old Believers occurred over the decision to make Russian liturgy conform more exactly to Greek. From the time of Peter the Great (1672–1725), Protestant thought became more important, particularly among the official leadership. F. Prokopovich (1681–1736) served as the principal ecclesiastical adviser to Peter. A reaction against this trend and a return to older Russian Orthodox tradition began in 1836 under the influence of the lay procurator of the Holy Synod, N. A. Protasov (1799–1856). Metropolitan Filaret Drozdov (1782–1867) of Moscow, though influenced by Protestantism, became a noted exponent of Orthodoxy. The most important theologian of this period was A. S. Khomiakov (1804–60), a Slavophile who developed the ecclesiological concept known as *sobernost*. In his view it combined the unity emphasized by Catholics with the liberty stressed by Protestants. Also important was the lay philosopher-theologian, V. Solovyev (1853–1900), who advocated a synthesis of Eastern and Western Christianity. Khomiakov and Solovyev provided the basis for the theological system developed in the U.S.S.R. by P. *Florenski.

More important than particular schools or individuals in Russian theology have been the underlying, pervasive aspects of Russian spirituality. To a considerable extent Russian religious life has moved at two levels. At the level of the top officials, it has been generally in subjection—to Constantinople, to Mongols (Tatars), to czars and since 1917 to Communist authorities. But at a lower level, the bulk of the church membership has maintained a continuing pattern of Orthodox worship and devotion. From the initial conversion of Russia to Christianity, a liturgy of beauty and splendor has held central importance for Russian believers. Icons have held an honored place both in the churches and in home worship centers. Several noted icons at particular churches and monasteries have become centers of pilgrimage. Also important to Russian spirituality have been the monasteries, closely related to Byzantine monasticism and particularly Mt. *Athos. Russian believers have looked to monks for luminous examples of Christian personality. The ideal found a place in world literature through depictions by Dostoyevsky. Russian spirituality has also been fused with a deep patriotic sense. Russian believers have been emotionally attached to their land and to their national existence, and have held strong convictions about the spiritual destiny of the Russian people.

[T. EARLY]

RUSSIAN RITE, see RUSSIAN LITURGY.

RUSSICUM, the short name of the ecclesiastical college located on the Esquiline hill in Rome on the Via Carlo Cattaneo, the Pontifical Russian College of St. Theresa of the Child Jesus. It was founded on August 15, 1929, by Pius XI and entrusted to the Jesuits. Its students are trained for priestly apostolate among Russians of the Byzantine rite. The college comes under the jurisdiction of the Congregation for the Oriental Churches.

[E. J. DILLON]

RUSTEBUEF, see RUTEBEUF.

RUSTICUS, a 6th-cent. Roman deacon, an ardent defender of the *Three Chapters. He accompanied his uncle Pope *Vigilius to Constantinople when the latter was summoned by Justinian (548). After resisting the extreme Alexandrian position favored by Justinian, Vigilius finally issued his *Judicatum*, a mitigated condemnation of the Three Chapters, upholding the decisions of Chalcedon. R. left to promulgate the document at Rome and became convinced by its opponents in the West that Vigilius had betrayed Chalcedon. Vigilius in 550 excommunicated and deposed his nephew. When the Council of Constantinople II (553) went further and anathematized the Three Chapters, R., in league with the African Abbot Felix, published a polemic against the conciliar decisions. Justinian exiled the two of them to the Thebaïd. Around this time R. wrote an important work, *Contra Acephalos disputatio* against the Monophysites: the adversaries of both Chalcedon and the Three Chapters. After the death of Justinian (565), R. returned to Constantinople, to a monastery faithful to Chalcedon, whose library was rich in documentation of the controversies of the preceding cent. and a half. Here he produced an improved Latin translation of the Acts of Ephesus and Chalcedon. His writings shed valuable, and mostly favorable, light on the Nestorian side of the controversies.

[E. J. DILLON]

RUTEBEUF (fl. 1250–80), lyric poet of intense personal involvement. Influenced by the *Roman de la rose* of Guillaume de Lorris, he surely influenced that of Jean de Meun whose tone and vigor he shares. Antimendicant, prouniversity, R. attacked the Crusades though enjoying the epics. His varied and large work includes *fabliaux*, prayers, complaints, ditties, visions, *Renart* material, the famous *Miracle de Théophile* satires, invective, and allegory.

[J. P. WILLIMAN]

RUTFORD, ABBEY OF, English Cistercian abbey in Nottingham, founded between 1146–48. It was established by the monks of *Rievaulx. At the time of the Dissolution in the 16th cent. the monks of Rievaulx refused to elect a successor when the royal commissioners removed their abbot, Edward Kirby. As a result Richard Blyton of Rutford was imposed.

[M. A. MCFADDEN]

RUTH, GEORGE HERMAN (BABE; 1895–1948), American baseball player; in 1969 voted by the baseball writers of America, "Greatest Player in the History of Baseball." He was the eldest of eight children born to a Baltimore saloon-keeper and his wife. When he was 7, his parents committed him to St. Mary's Industrial School for Boys, a combination orphanage and reform school run by the Xaverian Brothers, a Catholic order. (His parents were Lutherans.) At St. Mary's he adopted Catholicism, learned the tailoring trade, and took up baseball. In 1914 he was signed by the Baltimore Orioles, a minor league baseball club, and a few months later was sold to the Boston Red Sox. From 1914 to 1919 he was one of the best pitchers in baseball. In 1919, because of his phenomenal hitting ability, he was shifted to the outfield, and a year later was traded to the New York Yankees. His ability to hit home runs revolutionized the game, and he led the American League in home runs 12 times. His popularity with the public during his years with the Yankees (1920–34) literally saved baseball from the infamous "Black Sox" scandal of 1919. In 1930 and again in 1931 his salary was $80,000, a staggering figure in those years. He was known for his flamboyant lifestyle but was always available for charitable works: visiting children in hospitals and participating in fundraising activities. In 1936, a year after his retirement, he was voted into the Baseball Hall of Fame. BIBLIOGRAPHY: R. W. Creamer, *Babe* (1974).

[G. J. JONAS]

RUTH, BOOK OF. This post-Exilic story, which is largely if not entirely fictitious, relates an episode of the period of the judges. Naomi, an Israelite mother, loses her husband and both her sons while living in Moab, and returns home to Bethlehem with one of her widowed daughters-in-law, Ruth, who in spite of being a Moabitess shows heroic loyalty and devotion to her. In Bethlehem a rich farmer, Boaz, decides to marry her and buys the right to do so from a nearer kinsman according to the law of the levirate. Subsequently Ruth bears Obed, the grandfather of David (this particular detail is probably historical). The message underlying this story is that Yahweh, protector of widows and the unfortunate, causes virtue to triumph over misfortune even in an alien, and makes her the ancestor of his anointed king. BIBLIOGRAPHY: J. M. Myers, *Linguistic and Literary Form* *of the Book of Ruth* (1955); G. S. Glanzman, "Origin and Date of the Book of Ruth," CBQ 21 (1959) 201–207; O. Loretz, "Theme of the Ruth Story," CBQ 22 (1960) 391–399.

[D. J. BOURKE]

RUTHENIAN RITE. All Eastern Slavs of the Byzantine rite in the former kingdoms of Poland and Hungary were called Ruthenians, or Rusins. This usage lasted in Galicia and Bukovina until 1918; in Subcarpathia and Czechoslovakia until 1945. Today (1977) those people are called with their national names: (1) White Russians (*Bielorusi*), (2) Ukrainians, (3) Slovaks. Only Ruthenians who emigrated to Backa (today in Yugoslavia) and Ruthenians in the U.S. preserve the original name. The Ruthenian rite in the large sense, i.e., comprising the liturgical ceremonies and all ecclesiastical discipline is the rite of the Ruthenians. This designation was kept by the Holy See in Rome until 1961. From that year the modern names have been used except for the Ruthenians in the U.S.

Ruthenian Rite until 1961. Basically it was the Byzantine-Slavonic rite (comprising also the ecclesiastical discipline) of the Metropolis of Kiev in the former Kingdom of Poland, esp. after the Union of Brest-Litovsk (1595–96); and of the Bishopric of Mukacevo in the Kingdom of Hungary, esp. after the Union of Uzhorod (1646). These two units, although they have many features in common, canonically did not follow the same legislation. The Metropolis of Kiev established its discipline in the Synods of Zamostja (Zamosc) in 1720 and in the Synod of Lviv (Lvov) in 1891. The bishopric of Mukacevo celebrated (together with Romanians and Croatians in Hungary) one synod only, in 1773. In all these synods some Latin elements were admitted into Ruthenian rite (in liturgical texts, liturgical ceremonies, discipline, clerical garb, ecclesiastical customs, etc.). All the Ruthenian hierarchy met together only once, in 1929 in Rome, to discuss and approve the common liturgical books (the *Liturgikon* appeared in 1930). This Ruthenian rite is thus followed basically by all Catholic Ruthenians, who since 1961 adopted their modern national names: White Russians, Ukrainians in Ukraine, Ukrainians in the U.S., Slovaks, Hungarians, Croatians. They do not constitute a common hierarchical unit and for several decades have been forming their special discipline or rite. For example, the Hungarians celebrate in Hungarian, and Slovaks in the Slovak language. Consequently for them now there is no common Ruthenian rite.

Ruthenian Rite in the Strict Sense after 1961. This is the rite of the Ruthenian Metropolitan Province in the U.S. It comprises the Archdiocese of Munhall, Pa., and the Dioceses of Passaic, N.J., and Parma, Ohio. In 1972 the number of the faithful was 287,758. Besides the Ruthenians in the proper sense, it comprises some minorities of Slovaks, Hungarians, and Croatians. The basic discipline of this metropolitan province is that of the Sees of Mukecevo in Subcarpathia and of Presov in Czechoslovakia, the places

of origin of the faithful who immigrated to the U.S. At first their clergy practically transplanted the rite of their homeland to the U.S. This was the reason why the common Apostolic Exarchy, established in the U.S. in 1913, split *de facto* in 1916 and *de jure* in 1924 into two exarchies and later into two metropolitan provinces: Munhall for Ruthenians, and Philadelphia for Ukrainians. Ruthenians in the U.S. have not celebrated any synod. However, besides the English language in the liturgy, they have adopted several other changes: in the liturgy; in the ecclesiastical calendar; in the law of fast; in mandating clerical celibacy. All these changes are slowly creating a special Ruthenian rite of the Ruthenians in the U.S. BIBLIOGRAPHY: V. J. Pospishil, *Interritual Canon Law Problems in the United States and Canada,* (1955); W. Warzeski, *Byzantine Rite Rusins in Carpatho-Ruthenia and America* (1971); A. B. Pekar, *Our Past and Present: Historical Outlines of the Byzantine Ruthenian Metropolitan Province* (1974).

[M. LACKO]

RUTHERFORD, JOSEPH FRANKLIN (1869–1942), second president of the Watch Tower Bible and Tract Society, now known as *Jehovah's Witnesses. After the death of Charles Taze *Russell in 1916, R. was elected president of the society. Once a small-town lawyer in Missouri, he had become the society's legal adviser. During World War I he served a year in Atlanta penitentiary for excessive defense of conscientious objection. Known to his followers as Judge Rutherford, he supervised the growth of the organization for 25 years. During this time, the membership grew from a few thousand to 106,000, and societies were established in many foreign countries. He wrote a book almost every year, as well as many tracts, pamphlets, and articles; *Harp of God* (1921) summarized his teachings. R. was particularly critical of Catholicism, although he opposed all organized religion. In 1931 he chose the name Jehovah's Witnesses to identify those who supported the Watch Tower Society.

[W. J. WHALEN]

RUTHWELL CROSS, a large stone cross of the 8th cent. found at Ruthwell on the Scottish border among Northumbrian remains. Some of the runic inscriptions have been effaced, but others refer to the events sculptured on the two main parts of the Cross, the washing of Christ's feet by Mary Magdalen and the Crucifixion of Christ. The runic verses relating to the second event are similar to some in *The Dream of the Rood.* Whether the Ruthwell inscription is a condensation of an early Anglian poem or whether the MS poem in the Vercelli Book is an expansion of the inscription on the Cross is not known.

[M. M. BARRY]

RUTILIUS NAMATIANUS, see NAMATIANUS, RUTILIUS CLAUDIUS.

RUTTEN, CESLAUS (1875–1951), Belgian Dominican sociologist and political figure. He was among the first in

Belgium who sought to put *Rerum novarum* into practical effect. He promoted Christian trade-unionism and professional organization, was active in the Belgian Semaines Sociales, had part in the foundation of a school to train leaders in the struggle for social reform, and from 1921 was an influential member of the Belgian senate. He wrote a number of books on social questions and produced many articles for French and Flemish journals.

[M. J. SUELZER]

RUWET, JEAN (1876–1956), secretary of the Pontifical Biblical Institute in Rome. R. studied at Louvain and the Pontifical Biblical Institute in Rome, and after ordination taught Scripture at Louvain. In 1923, he returned to Rome where he served as secretary to the editor of *Gregorianum*, general secretary of the Gregorian Univ., and secretary of the Pontifical Biblical Institute (1935–52). He wrote numerous articles in *Biblica* and *Verbum Domini* on the canon of Scripture and on inspiration. BIBLIOGRAPHY: *Biblica* 37 (1956) 384–385.

[T. M. MCFADDEN]

RUYSBROECK, JAN VAN, BL. (Rusbroek, Ruisbroeck, Russbroec; 1293–1381), Flemish mystic. R. was reared by a saintly uncle, a canon of St. Gudule's in Brussels. After ordination in 1317 he continued to live with his uncle and another canon, F. van Coudenberg. In 1343, the three men withdrew to a hermitage at Groenendael, where they were soon joined by disciples. The group adopted the rule of the Canons of Saint-Victor in 1349, with Van Coudenberg as provost and R. as prior. The society they formed appears to be a link between the *Friends of God and the *Brethren of the Common Life. R. was influenced by Meister Eckhart and was in touch with Gerard Groote and Johann Tauler. He corrected the error and excess into which the attempts of simple persons to become like God had fallen: that God asks of exalted souls that they become indistinguishable from him. R. preached a true *deificatio*: that the self is not fused in God but preserves its identity, rising to Christian perfection by three stages: the active life, the inward life, and the contemplative life. This he expounded in his earliest extant work, which is also his masterpiece: *The Spiritual Espousals* (*c.*1330). Other treatises among the 13 ascribed to him are *The Kingdom of Lovers* and *The Tabernacle*. When a copy of the latter was pirated and given to the Carthusians at Herne, they asked R. for an explanation of parts that disturbed them. Their request gave rise to his *Little Book of Enlightenment,* the best defense against the charges, esp. of quietism, that have been made against him. R. has been represented as an untutored man, miraculously inspired; but his writings show that he was a master of theology. BIBLIOGRAPHY: L. Reypens, LTK 9:127–128; RGG 3:529–530; R. Wautier d'Aygalliers, *Ruysbroeck the Admirable* (1969).

[M. J. SUELZER]

RYAN, ABRAM (1839–86), Vincentian priest, poet of the Confederacy. Ordained just prior to the Civil War, R. was a chaplain in the Confederate Army for the duration. His poignant poem ''The Conquered Banner'' became the lament of the entire South over its defeat. After the Civil War R. served in Louisiana, Georgia, and Alabama. He edited two weekly newspapers in the South and was much admired as an orator. Most of his poetry is devoted to patriotic subjects and a variety of religious themes. His book *Poems Patriotic, Religious and Miscellaneous,* had a long printing history.

[J. R. AHERNE]

RYAN, JAMES HUGH (1886–1947), abp. of Omaha, Nebraska, educator. A native of Indiana ordained in 1909, R. taught psychology at St. Mary-of-the-Woods College, Indiana, 1911–21. He served 1920–28, as executive secretary of the National Catholic Welfare Conference. He was a professor of philosophy at The Catholic Univ. of America from 1922 to 1928, and was rector from 1928 to 1935. Named titular bp. in 1933, he was appointed to the See of Omaha, Neb., in 1935 (abp. in 1945). R. was a member of the special bishop's committee, Pius XII's Peace Points, and the administrative board of NCWC. R. was recognized as an authority on the Vatican in international relations. An inveterate foe of Naziism he incurred the anger of Joseph Goebbels. Among his books were *Introduction to Philosophy* (1924) and the *Peace Points of Pope Pius XII* (1942).

[J. R. AHERNE]

RYAN, JOHN AUGUSTINE (1869–1945), American Catholic social philosopher. The gradual awakening of American Catholics to the realities of the social order, clearly defined by Leo XIII in the encyclical *Rerum novarum*, was preeminently R.'s work. A midwesterner by birth and education, he was ordained for St. Paul, Minn., in 1898. He taught at the seminary in St. Paul for 13 years. He gained the doctorate in moral theology from The Catholic Univ. of America in 1906; his doctoral thesis *A Living Wage: Its Ethical and Economic Aspects* became a classic exposition. Widely invited as a lecturer, he wrote much, his article in the *Catholic Encyclopedia* on the moral aspect of labor unions being regarded as definitive. *Socialism: Promise or Menace* (1914) again constituted a classic expression of Catholic social thought. As a member of the theology faculty at The Catholic Univ., he taught political science and moral theology, serving several terms as dean of the School of Sacred Theology. In 1916 appeared *Distributive Justice*, which became the standard work on the subject and R.'s most important contribution to social thought. He founded the review *Catholic Charities* in 1917 and was its editor for 4 years. He wrote the original version of the ''Bishops' Program for Social Reconstruction'' in 1919. The document proposed social reforms now part of the American scene. In 1920 he became director of the Social

Action Department of the National Catholic Welfare Conference and continued in that post the rest of his life. With the presidency of Franklin D. Roosevelt, R. became a consistent supporter of the New Deal and a prized adviser of the President. In spite of controversy created in 1928 by his work, *The State and the Church* (publ. in 1923) and his acrimonious controversy with the "radio priest," Charles E. Coughlin, R.'s lifelong and positive impact was the most significant Catholic influence on the social order in America. BIBLIOGRAPHY: F. Broderick: *Right Reverend New Dealer: John A. Ryan* (1963).

[J. R. AHERNE]

RYAN, PATRICK JOHN (1831–1911), abp. of Philadelphia. He was born and educated in Ireland, migrated to St. Louis, Mo., in 1852, and was ordained there in 1853. A noted orator, R. preached at the Second Plenary Council of Baltimore in 1866, which he attended as Bp. Peter Kenrick's theologian. Pope Pius IX invited him to preach the English Lenten sermons in Rome in 1868. R. was consecrated coadjutor bp. of St. Louis in 1872. He took an active part in the preparation at Rome of the work of the Third Plenary Council of Baltimore and in the council itself (1884). That same year he was named abp. of Philadelphia. His celebrity as an orator at church and civic functions throughout the U.S. increased as he spoke, among many other occasions, at the centennial of the Archdiocese of Baltimore and the Republican national convention in 1900. Pres. Theodore Roosevelt appointed him to the U.S. Board of Indian Commission. It was, however, as an able administrator of Philadelphia that he made his greatest contribution. He gave the parochial school system of the archdiocese its forward movement. The number of schools increased from 59 to 141 during his tenure. R. was responsible for the founding of the first free Catholic secondary school in America, Roman Catholic High School for Boys (1890); three high school centers for girls; St. Francis de Sales Industrial School (1888); the Protectory for Boys (1898); as well as other charitable institutions. The number of churches grew during his regime from 127 to 297, many of them being national churches. From 1890 to his death, R. was editor of the *American Catholic Quarterly Review*. An amiable and witty man, R. displayed simplicity and democracy in his manner, encouraged higher education at Catholic colleges, and enjoyed the esteem of the entire city. BIBLIOGRAPHY: J. L. J. Kirlin, *Life of the Most Rev. P. Ryan* (1903); M. C. Duffy, "The Church of Philadelphia (1884–1918)," *History of the Archdiocese of Philadelphia* (ed. J. F. Connelly, 1976) 271–338.

[J. R. AHERNE]

RYD, VALERIUS ANSELMUS, see ANSELM, VALERIUS.

RYDER, ALBERT PINKHAM (1847–1917), American romantic, visionary, and eccentric artist who spent most of his solitary life in New York painting mystical interpretations of religious, literary, and marine subjects. With little formal training, he developed an individual style employing a dark rich palette of encrusted colors and abbreviated forms which resulted in unique, poetic visions. In *Jonah, Death on a Pale Horse, Toilers of the Sea*, R. records nature not merely as background but as an embodiment of the human condition. BIBLIOGRAPHY: L. Goodrich, *Albert P. Ryder* (1959).

[F. S. GRUBAR]

RYGGE, ROBERT (d. *c.*1410), a supporter of Wycliffite ideas at Oxford; chancellor of Oxford Univ. (1380–88). Initially R. encouraged Wycliffe's supporters, but under pressure, eventually condemned them and was on a commission to eradicate Wycliffism from Oxford (Nov. 1382). He advised Richard II on the schism (1399). In 1400 R. became chancellor of Exeter Cathedral and bequeathed books to Exeter College. BIBLIOGRAPHY: Emden Ox 3:1616–17.

[C. D. ROSS]

RYKEN, FRANCIS XAVIER (1797–1871), founder of the Xaverian Brothers. Born in Holland, R. in 1823 joined the group of the convert-editor Joachim Le Sage ten Broeck. In 1827 he sought approbation in Rome for a community of brothers devoted to education but was unsuccessful. After a brief period as a Trappist brother, R. came to the U.S., joining a missioner among the Potawatomi Indians of Michigan. Eager to establish a community to work among the Indians R. returned to Belgium where he received encouragement from Bp. Francis Boussen of Bruges. Returning to America, R. was urged by Bp. J. *Rosati of St. Louis to undertake educational work. Supported by the approval of seven U.S. bps., he established in 1839 at Bruges the Brothers of St. Francis Xavier (Xaverians). Many problems attended the early years of the foundation but ultimately it served schools in Belgium, England, and the United States, where the first Xaverian school was opened in 1845 at Louisville, Kentucky. Forced to resign as superior general, R. led a quiet and humble life.

[J. R. AHERNE]

RYLE, GILBERT (1900–76), a founder and major figure of the "ordinary language" school of linguistic analysis. Ryle was born in Brighton, England. He read classics at Oxford, then went on to the School of Philosophy, Politics, and Economics at Queen's College. He became a lecturer at Christ Church, Oxford, in 1924, remaining there as student and tutor until his appointment, after World War II, as Waynefleet professor of metaphysical philosophy in the university. R. was the editor of *Mind* from 1947 to 1971. He was an orthodox participant in the reaction at Oxford, begun by G. E. Moore and Bertrand Russell, against the metaphysical excesses of the idealism of the previous century. Philosophy was not restricted to being linguistic analysis, but was the activity of dissipating conceptual confusion arising from the misuse of language. R.'s own preoccupation was less the analysis of the "formal language" of logic and mathematics than that of "ordinary language." From his position as editor of *Mind*, he was able to exercise great influence in the direction of philosophical discussion in his day. But further, the publication of his book, *The Concept of Mind*, was a major event of postwar Anglo-American philosophy. Featuring, in addition to the method of linguistic analysis used to analyze talk about mind and soul, a requirement that all references to the mental be understood in terms of observable activities, *The Concept of Mind* showed the content of R.'s philosophy to be indistinguishable from behaviorism.

[R. E. HENNESSEY]

RYLLO, MAXIMILIAN (1802–48), Jesuit missionary. R. fled from Russia at the age of 17, entered the Society of Jesus in Rome, went to Mesopotamia and then to Syria, where he founded an interritual seminary that later became the Catholic Univ. of St. Joseph of Beirut. In 1844 he was appointed rector of the College of the Propagation of the Faith in Rome, but the following year was designated provicar apostolic to open a mission in Upper Egypt. BIBLIOGRAPHY: B. Reynaldi, DE 3:634.

[M. J. SUELZER]

S

SA, MANOEL (c.1530–1596), Portuguese Jesuit, theologian and exegete. Having gained a reputation as a scholar and teacher, he was appointed by Pius V to join a commission to revise the Vulgate, and later by Gregory XIII to publish an authorized edition of the Septuagint. His clear exegetical works focused on the literal meaning of Scripture. He also published a guide for confessors, *Aphorismi confessariorum* (1595), that was on the Index from 1602 until a corrected version was published in 1900.

[R. J. LITZ]

SA' ADIA BEN JOSEPH, GAON (882–942), scholar, writer, leader of Babylonian Jewry. A scholar of Torah and science from Egypt, after 921 he represented the Babylonian Jews in their struggle with the Jerusalem Academy under Gaon Aaron Ben Meir over the right of that Academy to alter the religious calendar, a dispute that generated a deep schism from which the Babylonian leaders emerged dominant. With a literary reputation for opposing heretics and *Karaism, S. was called by exilarch, David b. Zakkai, to head the Sura Academy (928). Disagreement over an inheritance became a public struggle between S. and the exilarch. Zakkai deposed S. S. named a new exilarch. When the caliphate changed hands (932), S.'s position eroded and he relinquished the Gaonate. Free of duties, he wrote his major philosophical work in Arabic, *Kitâb al-Amanât wa-al-I 'tiqadât* (Hebrew tr. Judah ibn Tibbon, 1186, 1562; Arab. Text ed. S. Landauer, 1880; Eng. tr. S. Rosenblatt, *Book of Beliefs and Opinions*, 1948; tr. and abridged by A. Altmann, *Three Jewish Philosophers*, 1965). S.'s work sought to evince rational proof for teachings of the Law. He influenced later Jewish Neoplatonists, and his work was used by opponents of Moses Maimonides's antirationalist *Guide of the Perplexed*. Particularly important was S.'s epistemological analysis of doubt and the approach to truth through speculation aided by revelation, which he held never contradicts reason. His four proofs for creation rely on Aristotle and the Islamic tradition of *Kalâm* and lead to a conception of God who is living, powerful, and wise, creator and incorporeal cause of a corporeal world. His anthropology holds man to have three faculties: appetite, reason, and spirit. Human actions are freely willed, not caused by divine foreknowledge; happiness is attained through performance of the Law. His defense of divine justice is a balance of punishments and rewards in this world and the next. S. made the first translation of the Bible from Hebrew into Arabic and incorporated rational commentary directly into the translated text.

[R. J. LITZ]

SAAR, FERDINAND VON (1833–1906), Austrian writer whose work was concerned with the growing signs of decadence that appeared in Austria in the latter part of the 19th cent. when the Habsburg monarchy was slowly disintegrating. He came of a distinguished family and was a member of the Austrian parliament. He wrote psychological short stories tinged with melancholy (*Novellen aus Österreich*, 1881; *Herbstreigen*, 1897); some dramas (*Kaiser Heinrich*, 1865–67); and impressionistic lyrics (*Wiener Elegien*).

[B. F. STEINBRUCHNER]

SABA (SHEBA), the geographical name in biblical usage for the SW corner of the Arabian peninsula, corresponding roughly to modern Yemen. The wealth and commerce of this region were legendary in the ancient world (Ps 72.10,15). The Romans referred to it as Arabia Felix— Happy Arabia. The Sabeans dominated the major caravan route on land to the North. Frankincense, myrrh, and other exotic products from Africa passed that way. By sea came gold and precious stones from India and the Far East. The Sabeans were engaged in trade and commerce from early times. Their sphere of influence expanded and contracted with the shifting political scene. The exotic nature of the goods that passed through their hands combined with the fact of their relative isolation in S Arabia at a safe distance from the great empires, to make people uncertain as to just where this magic land was located. The biblical genealogies reflect this uncertainty. At one time they are listed as descendants of Ham through Cush—therefore Nubian and African. Another time they are listed as descendants of Sem and as kin to the northern people of the fertile crescent.

[E. J. DILLON]

SABA (SHEBA), QUEEN OF, royal visitor to King Solomon (1Kg 10.1–13). The heir to David's throne had extended the boundaries of Israel, had brought such prosperity to the kingdom, and had personally attained such wealth and wisdom that his renown had reached the distant legendary land of Saba (Sheba), SW Arabia. The Queen of Saba then journeyed to Solomon's court, according to the biblical account, "to test him with hard questions." She came with gifts of gold, spices, and precious stones and received gifts in return. This high-level "gift-giving" is meant to epitomize the economic wisdom of Solomon. The recounting of riddles and stories is part of the cultured conversation Arabs associated with commerce among the wise. The Queen returned with her retinue to her own land convinced that Solomon's wisdom and prosperity surpassed the report she had heard. From Assyrian sources there is record of Tiglath-Pileser IV (732–731 B.C.) receiving tribute from an Arabian Queen. There is an Arabic legend of a marriage of an Arabian Queen to King Solomon. The Abyssinian royal line claims descent from this union.

[E. J. DILLON]

SABAOTH, Hebrew term meaning hosts (armies). It is used in the frequent biblical phrase Yahweh of Hosts (1 Sam 17.45). In the King James and Douay Versions it was transliterated in two places (Rom 9.29 and Jas 5.4). The word also appears in the Sanctus of the Latin Mass.

[T. EARLY]

SABAS, ST., see SAVA, ST.

SABAS THE YOUNGER, ST. (d. 990). With his brother Macarius the Younger, S. left Sicily during the Arab advances and the famine of 940–941, visiting N Calabria and Lucania and erecting churches and monasteries in the monastic eparchies of Mercurion and Latinianon. His intervention led to the freeing of hostages of Otto II. BIBLIOGRA - PHY: M. Petta, NCE 12:776; G. Mongelli, BiblSanct 11:531.

[M. A. WINKELMANN]

SABATIER, AUGUSTE (1839–1901), Protestant theologian, leader of the "Paris School" in the 19th century. Professor at the Paris Protestant faculty of theology from 1877, S. based his thought esp. on that of F. *Schleiermacher (see LIBERAL THEOLOGY). He regarded the essence of religion as the feeling of dependence experienced by the soul in distress from consciousness of its lofty aspirations

and inability to achieve them. Revelation is the progressive presence of God to the soul and the soul to God through this conscious and willed feeling of dependence. All dogma is simply the expression, the objectification as symbol, of subjective religious experience. It is essentially and interminably evolving, to match the feelings it represents. The thought of S., called *symbolofideism, or critical symbolism, influenced the development of *Modernism. S.'s works included *Apostle Paul* (1891), *Outlines of a Philosophy of Religion* (1897), and the posthumous *Religion of Authority and Religion of the Spirit* (1904).

[T. C. O'BRIEN]

SABATIER, PAUL (1858–1928), French Protestant minister and historian. Forced by poor health to retire from the ministry, he devoted more than 40 years to the discovery, study, interpretation, and publication of Franciscan sources. His popular, but biased and liberal, *Vie de Saint Françoise d'Assisi,* published in 1894 and promptly placed on the Index, aroused a storm of bitter criticism and controversy. However, his theories and interpretations, proven false in many cases and rejected today, served to spark a new interest and enthusiasm for the study of St. Francis and Franciscan literature among Protestant as well as Catholic scholars. S. founded the International Society of Franciscan Studies at Assisi and the British Society of Franciscan Studies at London and directed two series of publications in Franciscan research. Many regard him as "The Father of Franciscan Studies." BIBLIOGRAPHY: A. G. Little, "Paul Sabatier, Historian of St. Francis," *Franciscan Papers, Lists and Documents* (1943).

[D. A. MCGUCKIN]

SABATIER, PIERRE (1682–1742), biblical scholar. S. devoted most of his life to the reconstruction of a Latin version of the Bible predating Jerome's. Accordingly, he gathered Scripture quotations from Church Fathers, ancient missals, lectionaries, and Acts of the Martyrs. His labors appeared as the monumental *Bibliorum sacrorum Latinae versiones antiquae* (3 v., 1743–51; the last 2 v. were published posthumously). His work is still of value, although modern scholarship has generally gone beyond it.

[T. M. MCFADDEN]

SABBATAI, ZEVI, see SHABBATAI SEVI.

SABBATARIANS, a name applied either to those who keep Saturday as the Lord's Day, or to those who are rigid in their interpretation of Sunday observance. (1) Those Jews who are strict in keeping the OT Sabbath are called Sabbatarians. The term is also a classification applicable to those Christian bodies that adopted the OT observance. These include: a group of Anabaptists, followers of Oswald Glait, in Silesia, *c.*1528, against whose practice Luther protested; an adventist body in 16th-cent. Finland; certain Unitarians in Transylvania who by the 19th cent. had converted to

Judaism; a sect in Russia suppressed in 1825; the Southcottians in 19th-cent. England; Seventh-day Adventists; and Seventh Day Baptists. (2) Those who adhere to Sabbatarianism teaching that Sunday observance means abstention from all work, recreation, and amusement (see SUNDAY OBSERVANCE). The insistence upon these prohibitions has been a distinctive feature of post-Reformation Churches of England, Scotland, and Wales. The rigid Sabbatarianism of the Puritans was expressed in Nicholas Bound's *True Doctrine of the Sabbath* (1595); during the *Commonwealth, severe Sabbatarian laws were passed. Every form of recreation, even walking for pleasure, was forbidden. Even more stringent were the laws enforced by the Scottish Presbyterians. Strict Sunday observance was part of life in the New England colonies, and the Blue Laws remaining in some places are vestiges of this stringency. In the 18th and 19th cent., both in England and in North America, Baptists, Methodists, and Presbyterians were zealous Sabbatarians. While there were no RC ecclesiastical laws curtailing Sunday recreation, some Catholics, esp. in the eastern U.S., shared in Sabbatarian attitudes. The secularism of the 20th cent. has not completely overcome Sabbatarian influence in regard to surviving laws or legal decisions concerning Sunday observance. In England there is a Lord's Day Observance Society, and in the U.S., a Lord's Day Alliance, both promoting Sabbatarian objectives.

[T. C. O'BRIEN]

SABBATH, the seventh day; the day of rest; the day sacred to the Lord. The origins of the Israelite Sabbath are obscure. There are connections in Babylonian writings, as well as in the prophetic writings, between the new moon and the Sabbath. The Canaanite culture, being settled and agrarian, is likely to have had a recurring day of rest. The Israelites, while seminomads, may well have had taboo days, when certain activities could not be performed. Such days may have corresponded to phases of the moon. The days of taboo, of moon phases, and of rest eventually combined to become the Sabbath sacred to the Lord. Starting with the reforms of Josiah, the Sabbath gradually became the supreme observance of Judaism, the day of rest and of worship. It was the day of the Lord, made for man. The Jesus logion: ''The Sabbath is made for man'' is enlightened Judaism. In a striking departure from Judaism, the observance of the Sabbath became optional in Pauline gentile communities, but eventually the first day of the week became the Day of the Lord (the risen Christ) for Christians, to replace the Jewish Sabbath (cf. Rev 1.10).

[E. J. DILLON]

SABBATH YEAR, every 7th year, a rest for the land. To let the land lie fallow is a common agricultural practice, and the 7–year cycle was until recently still followed in Syria. The custom took on religious significance in Israel. The land is to participate in the Sabbath rest, during which time the fruit of the land that ripens without man's labor belongs

to the poor (Ex 23.10–11; Lev 25.1ff). The concept expanded to include remission or at least suspension of debts (Deut 15.1–3) and the freeing of Israelite slaves every 7th year (Ex 21.2–6). It is doubtful these laws were ever commonly observed. In fact 2 Chr 36.21 attributes the 70 years of exile in Babylon and the desolation of the land to the unobserved Sabbaths. Isaiah and Micah denounced land-grabbing. The impact of these Sabbath-year laws, as well as the law of Jubilee (7 times 7 = every 50th year) proclaiming freedom for all slaves at the blowing of the trumpet on the Day of Atonement (Lev 25), was largely psychological: to discourage slave-owning, usury, and land-grabbing. The oracle in Is 61.1–3 proclaiming a visionary Jubilee Year is the oracle chosen by Jesus to announce the beginning of his prophetic ministry (Luke 4.18ff). The Isaiahan oracle includes the key phrases: ''to evangelize the poor . . . to proclaim liberty to captives . . . to proclaim a Jubilee Year of the Lord.''

[E. J. DILLON]

SABBATIANS, a group of *Novatianists at Constantinople founded by the Jewish convert, and later bp., Sabbatios (d. *c.*410), who celebrated Easter according to the Jewish calendar and advocated an even greater rigorism than the rest of the Novatianist community. Sabbatios was exiled for life to the Island of Rhodes as punishment for having been consecrated a Novatian bishop. His grave was venerated by his followers; the group disappeared by the 6th century.

[J. R. FANG]

SABBATINE PRIVILEGE, the favor of special intercession of the Blessed Virgin Mary believed to be granted to those who have in their life constantly observed chastity and regularly practiced devotions in her honor, particularly the wearing of the brown *scapular and daily recitation of the Little Office of the BVM. The name comes from *Sabbatum*, Lat. for Saturday, a day set aside esp. to honor Mary. Some versions of the privilege have it that the devotee will be delivered from purgatory by Mary's intercession on the first Saturday after death. The pious belief has had a long-standing acceptance; but an alleged papal bull by John XXII confirming it is inauthentic.

[T. C. O'BRIEN]

SABELLIANISTS, followers of the heretical doctrine of Sabellius (fl. *c.*220) who regarded the Godhead as a monad, trinitarian only insofar as God could be regarded as Father in creation, as Son in the Redemption, and as Spirit in the bestowal of grace. The heresy is a sophisticated modalism, first formulated by Sabellius who came to Rome (*c.*217), was attacked by Hippolytus, and eventually excommunicated by Pope Callistus (217–222). *MODALISM; *MONARCHIANISM.

[T. M. MCFADDEN]

SABETTI, LUIGI (1839–98), Italian Jesuit, professor of moral theology at the Jesuit theologate, Woodstock, Md., from 1871 until his death. He published *Compendium theologiae moralis* (1884), an adaptation of the probabilist moral works of H. *Busenbaum, J. *Gury, and A. *Ballerini; a 28th edition of S.'s work, edited by T. Barrett, appeared in 1928. S. was a counsellor esteemed by Card. Gibbons and theologian at the Third Plenary Council of Baltimore (1884). He was also a teacher beloved by American Jesuits.

[T. C. O'BRIEN]

SABIGOTONA, ST., see AURELIUS AND SABIGOTONA, AND COMPANIONS, SS.

SABINA OF ROME, ST., supposedly, a martyr of that name commemorated on August 29. However, the actual existence of such a martyr can be doubted. The earliest account of the martyr's ordeal (*passio*) goes back no further than the 6th century. There is early mention of the *titulus Sabinae,* referring to the church on the Aventine, built by a noble person named Sabina. Perhaps, as often happened, the titular of the church was mistakenly assumed to be the saint under whose invocation the church had been built. The 5th cent. Church of Santa Sabina on the Aventine remains one of the finest Romanesque basilicas in Rome. BIBLIOGRAPHY: Butler 11:540–542.

[E. J. DILLON]

SABINIAN (d. 606), **POPE** from 604. A Tuscan, S. represented the Holy See at Constantinople in the reign of *Gregory the Great and was charged esp. to curb the presumption of Patriarch John IV who had taken the title of ecumenical or universal patriarch. Gregory became dissatisfied with S.'s conciliatory attitude and recalled him to Rome in 597. He was elected to the papacy after Gregory's death in 604 but he waited 6 months for the Emperor's approval before being consecrated. His short pontificate was disturbed by marauding Lombards and great famine in central Italy. He has been accused of profiteering from the sale of corn during the famine, but this seems a defamation arising from his control of the sale in order to take care of the most needy. BIBLIOGRAPHY: P. Brezzi, *Papacy* (1958).

[P. F. MULHERN]

SABINUS OF HERACLEA, mid-4th-cent. bp. of Heraclea in Thrace. He is responsible for the comprehensive collection of the acts of the various Eastern synods, beginning with that of Nicea until at least 373. Although now lost, the work was copiously used by later Byzantine historians, such as Socrates and Sozomenos.

[E. J. DILLON]

SABIO, EL, see ALFONSO X, KING OF CASTILE.

SABOTAGE, in its most specific sense, covert action to cause damage disruptive of an enemy's forces in time of war; then more generally, any similar action by a person or group against an "enemy." In its full scope sabotage involves inflicting property damage, bodily injury—even death, or destruction of reputation: all matters safeguarded by *justice. The only moral defense for any form of sabotage, therefore, is a higher right, esp. the right of self-defense against an unjust aggressor by means proportionate to repel the aggression. Sabotage in time of war seems to be commonly accepted as a means fitting the conditions that justify waging war; yet the aggression it opposes must be of such a nature as to warrant disregard, by the use of stealth, of the international convention that combatants be distinguishable from civilians. Even if sabotage in time of war is justifiable, the more extended sense of the term raises different moral questions. The conditions for just war cannot be invoked to justify indiscriminate terrorism by revolutionaries against the general population. Sabotage in labor disputes seems never to be justifiable, since in the actual conditions existing between labor and management unjust aggression is seldom clearly establishable, and damage to factory or equipment is a means disproportionate to the issues. Acts of sabotage against a rival in business or against an opponent in a political campaign are totally immoral both in intent and in the malicious damage they inflict.

[T. C. O'BRIEN]

SABRAN, LOUIS DE (1652–1732), Jesuit preacher. Of a noble French father and English mother, S. joined the English Jesuits, became chaplain to James II, and fled England in 1688. His appointment as an anti-Jansenist rector at the seminary of Liège was so strongly opposed that troops accompanied his installation. He was instrumental in committing the papers of Pasquier Quesnel to Louis XIV. S. also held influential positions in the order and was rector at St. Omer's (1712–15). BIBLIOGRAPHY: Sommervogel 7:359.

[V. SAMPSON]

SACERDOTALISM (Lat. *sacerdos,* priest), a term usually used disparagingly of the claim to special power or its exercise by the clergy. (1) In its specific sense sacerdotalism refers unfavorably to the system of a special priesthood, in which the ordained priest is regarded as possessing sacred power to offer sacrifice, to consecrate, to absolve from sin, to bless. The term sacerdotalism disparages such a system as being opposed to the *priesthood of all believers and as an intrusion of human mediation between the believer and God's communication of grace through Christ. (2) The term is used more generally to connote domination of church life by clergy to the exclusion or downgrading of the laity. *SACRAMENTALISM; *ECCLESIASTICISM, *CLERICALISM.

[T. C. O'BRIEN]

SACHER-MASOCH, LEOPOLD VON (1836–95), Austrian short story writer. After a brief teaching career, he turned to writing and for some years to journalism as editor of several periodicals and a newspaper. His delineation of character resembles that of Turgenev. Though S. produced a number of novels, the collections of short stories, *Das Vermächtnis Kains* (4 v., 1874) and *Galizische Geschichten* (1876) on his native Galicia are his highest achievements. S. has the dubious distinction of giving his name, through his portrayals of it, to the sexual perversion called masochism.

[J. R. AHERNE]

SACHS, HANS (1494–1576) popular poet and *Meistersinger* of Nuremberg, Germany. A cobbler by trade, S. was an early supporter of Luther (e.g., "The Nightingale of Wittenberg," 1523). He produced about 4,000 mastersongs, 1,800 gnomic and lyrical poems, and more than 200 dramas and Shrovetide plays. Hampered by the pedantic traditions of the *Meistersang,* he composed artificial, often clumsy songs. Although some of his scenes are suggestive and crude, his works typify the bourgeois virtues of thrift, piety, and forthrightness. The following generations ignored S. completely, until Goethe wrote on Sachs' poetical mission; Richard Wagner glorified him in the music drama *Die Meistersinger von Nürnberg.* BIBLIOGRAPHY: E. Geiger, *Der Meistergesang des Hans Sachs* (1956).

[S. A. SCHULZ]

SACK, FRIARS OF THE, a mendicant order established in Provence, France, approved by Innocent IV in 1251, but at the Council of Lyons II (1274) forbidden to receive any more novices or to make new foundations. The council was motivated by the desire of diminishing disputes between the bps. and the burgeoning mendicant orders. The Friars of the Sack had a constitution modelled on that of the Dominicans. By 1274 they had more than 100 foundations in France and in other Western European countries, including England. The order's foundations gradually passed into the hands of the other mendicants, and the order ceased to exist c.1315.

[R. C. CLIGGETT]

SACKCLOTH (Heb. *Saḳ*; Gr. *sakkos*), material of goat or camel hair often worn as a sign of mourning (2 Sam 3.31), penitence (1 Kg 21.27), and supplication (Dan 9.3). Some scholars suggest it was made in the shape of a grain bag with holes for the head and arms. Others think it may have been just a loincloth. Jacob put sackcloth on his loins when he was grieving for Joseph (Gen 37.34). King Hezekiah, however, covered himself with sackcloth when Jerusalem was under siege by the Assyrians (2 Kgs 19.1). It was dark in color (Rev 6.12). There is no evidence that it produced physical discomfort, but it was a sign of mental anguish. It could be worn under regular clothing (2 Kgs 6.30), presumably to be seen by God alone. The wearing of sackcloth was not regulated by the Law, but it appears to have been a general custom from Israel's earliest days. It is mentioned also in the NT as a symbol of repentance (Mt 11.21). The origin of sackcloth is unknown, but it is presumed to go back to primitive times when it may have been the common

garment. It is associated with fasting (Ps 35.13), ashes (Jer 6.26), and shaving the head (Is 22.12). The garments worn by Elijah (2 Kg 1.8) and John the Baptist (Mt 3.4) were probably not sackcloth.

[T. EARLY]

SACRA CONVERSAZIONE, "holy conversation," arrangement or composition in paintings of the Madonna and Child in 15th- and 16th-cent. Italian painting, showing the Virgin surrounded by saints who appear to dialogue or converse among themselves concerning the Madonna. The *St. Lucy Altarpiece,* by D. Veneziano, c.1445, Florence is an example.

[M. J. DALY]

SACRA VIRGINITAS, an encyclical letter of Pius XII (March 25, 1954), which sets forth the nature and excellence of consecrated virginity, indicates errors of contemporary thought on the matter, and recalls what is spiritually requisite for living the commitment to perpetual virginity. Proposing scriptural and patristic teaching on the excellence of virginity and pointing out its fruitfulness for both the apostolic and the contemplative life, the encyclical rejects the errors of the day which would depreciate it. Basic to the errors is the assumption that such a lifelong consecration impedes growth and maturity and renders difficult the development of the personality and understanding of others. This assumption insists that the "mutual assistance" of marriage is better than the "loneliness of heart" of the virgin or celibate. The encyclical emphasizes that virginal consecration when properly lived frees the person for a more generous dedication to the "things of the Lord" and thus for personal and spiritual growth and a more universal dedication to others. Divine grace more than supplies what is lacking of the mutual assistance of marriage. (Vat II RenRelLife 12,15). The encyclical indicates that the life of perpetual chastity is nourished and sustained by vigilance, prayer, and a life of devotion, concluding with an exhortation to encourage vocations to the priestly and religious life. BIBLIOGRAPHY: AAS 46 (1954) 161–191; English text in G. Courtois, *States of Perfection* (tr. J. A. O'Flynn, 1961) 220–253 (no. 482–552). *VIRGINITY, *CELIBACY.

[W. J. READ]

SACRAMENT, as defined by St. Thomas Aquinas, "a sign of a sacred reality insofar as this reality sanctifies men." Sacraments are sacred actions used in the Church and authorized by the institution of Christ in which physical, external means are made to serve both as signs and as channels of sanctifying grace. This notion is the result of centuries of theological evolution. The word "sacrament" and its Greek equivalent "mystery" have been used in many different ways and for many different actions, some of which do not qualify as sacraments under the current definition. Since any such definition is, in the last analysis, arbitrary, it is necessary in reading any author to ascertain how he uses the word and not to draw conclusions from any such usage about the correctness of his theology. Even in the sacramental system, moreover, some elements in the definition as given apply more easily to some of the sacraments than to others; thus, for example, most theologians today would agree that it is difficult or impossible to find biblical evidence for the direct institution of confirmation by Jesus Christ.

The component elements of the definition should be specified with some care, for each serves to clarify and to limit the meaning of the others. Sacraments must be not only signs of grace but also channels of grace. The use of the sign of the cross, whose ancient provenance in Christian practice may be evidence for an origin in apostolic times and therefore for "institution" by Christ, is not ordinarily interpreted by Christian theologians as a channel of grace. The external, physical means required for an action to be a sacrament would seem to rule out the preaching of the gospel from the category of sacrament, even though it may claim institution by Christ himself and is "the power of God for salvation" (Rom 1.16). Recent RC theologians, however, have been careful to make clear that "institution by Christ" does not necessarily mean an explicit act of the historical person, Jesus Christ, establishing and commanding a sacramental action. As the one who founded his Church and who built it "upon the foundation of the apostles and prophets, Christ Jesus himself being the cornerstone" (Eph 2.20), Jesus also provided it with the instruments by which it would be able to carry out its saving mission. In the development of the sacramental life of the Church, therefore, the risen Christ has continued to exercise his lordship and in this sense to "institute" those actions by which the Church has faithfully carried out its mission.

Above all, then, the sacraments are means and channels of the grace of God. In this understanding of their function and nature, two historic misunderstandings must be avoided. The communication of divine grace through the sacraments is not to be thought of in a mechanical or an automatic sense, as though grace were a measure of sacred stuff distributed in so many doses through sacraments. As the gift and favor of a personal God, grace cannot be reduced to magic or to material; nor can the connection between sacrament and grace be made arbitrary or accidental, as though the recipient of the sacrament could not depend upon the presence of grace in it, but had to wonder each time whether it was in fact being proffered there. The scholastic formula "God is bound by the sacraments but not to the sacraments" seeks to ensure both that the personal relationship to God is not degraded into magic and that the objective availability of divine grace in the sacrament is not jeopardized. As means and channels of grace, the sacraments convey to those who rightly receive them the benefits of the death and Resurrection of Christ, uniting them to his work. Although it is more explicit in the case of baptism than in that of other sacraments, this union with the saving work of Christ in his death and Resurrection characterizes

the sacraments: "We were buried therefore with him by baptism into death, so that as Christ was raised from the dead by the glory of the Father, we too might walk in newness of life" (Rom 6.4).

As means of grace, the sacraments are more than symbols or signs, but they are never less. Their very nature as actions that point beyond their intrinsic meaning to an ultimate significance is bound up with their being "signs." The laying on of hands that takes place in confirmation or in holy orders is an ancient rite by no means confined to Christianity; in Gen 48.14 it was part of the patriarchal blessing. But within the context of the Christian sacraments this ceremony becomes a sign of the grace being conferred in and through the sacramental transaction. Similarly, there have been ceremonial washings and sacred meals in many religions, so that Christian baptism and the Christian Eucharist may attach themselves to a widespread, if not indeed universal, phenomenon of religious experience. Yet they are special "signs" because they point not only to some timeless truth about the cosmos but to the events in the life of Jesus by which the salvation of the human race was achieved. Locked as he is into a world of sense-experience, man cannot look beyond this world without signposts that, appearing within the empirical realm, nevertheless show the way to another realm. The sacraments have a special role among such signposts, and the rituals surrounding their celebration have sought to enhance their importance as signs, their *significance*.

It belongs to the nature of sacraments that they are properly carried on within the Church. As the body of Christ, who is himself the fundamental mystery (or sacrament) of salvation, the Church participates in his sacramental character and dispenses his sacramental gifts. Thus there have been many writers, both in the scholastic period and again in the modern, who have not hesitated to designate both Christ and the Church as "sacraments." Without becoming involved in dogmatic nomenclature, one may nevertheless see in this a recognition that the sacraments, to be effective, are simultaneously grounded in the person and work of Christ and set into the context of the Church. This emphasis protects them from an individualistic (and often magical) distortion. *Infant baptism, for example, is not a magical incantation over an individual child but the responsible action of the Christian community and of the parents of the child, assuming the responsibilities of *Christian nurture of which baptism is the first and most important step. As the dispenser of the sacraments, the Church through them invites and welcomes men to participation in the life of God himself; as the "sign" of the Incarnation and of the Redemption, the Church employs the other "signs" instituted by its Lord.

The sacraments are also, in the pregnant phrase of St. Augustine, "the visible words of God." In many definitions of what constitutes a sacrament, the word of God is identified as an indispensable factor. "Let the word come to the elements, and a sacrament comes to be," was St. Augustine's formula. Therefore it is also necessary to consider the sacraments in their relation to the spoken and the written word of God. St. Paul says of the Eucharist: "As often as you eat this bread and drink this cup, you proclaim the Lord's death until he comes" (1 Cor 11.26). Sharing in the sacramental action is evidently a form of that proclamation which is normally carried on by word of mouth. In some forms of Protestant theology, this function of the sacraments as "visible words" has tended to predominate, to such an extent that the sacraments have been thought to confer nothing other than is conferred by the word. But even where this extreme subordination of sacrament to word has not been present, it has been recognized that a coordination of the two is beneficial to an understanding of both; and it is no exaggeration when some theologians, esp. within Protestantism but also within Roman Catholicism, have spoken of "the sacramentality of the word" as a corollary of the idea that the sacraments are the visible words of God.

From what has already been said it will be evident that the question of the specific number of the sacraments, about which so much of the polemic between Protestant and RC theology has argued, is not the central issue it has sometimes appeared to be. Theologians of impeccable orthodoxy have maintained, on the basis of a particular definition, that there are more than seven (e.g., fourteen) or fewer than seven (e.g., two or three) sacraments. The seven traditionally identified as sacraments are: baptism, confirmation, the Eucharist, penance, the sacrament of the sick (formerly called extreme unction), holy orders, and matrimony. Protestants have usually restricted the number to baptism and the Eucharist; Luther was willing to call absolution a sacrament as well. Both the problem of a proper definition and the question of a biblically validated institution by Christ have played a part in the debates about the number of the sacraments. BIBLIOGRAPHY: O. C. Quick, *Christian Sacraments* (1917); B. Leeming, *Principles of Sacramental Theology* (1956); J. de Ghellinck, *Pour l'histoire du mot "Sacramentum"* (1924).

[J. PELIKAN]

SACRAMENT HOUSE, in medieval times a container, frequently of metal or ivory, in the shape of a building or tower, used for the reservation of the Eucharist; a forerunner of the tabernacle.

[J. DALLEN]

SACRAMENTAL CHARACTER, while customarily defined in terms of the effect it has upon the recipient, that is, as imprinting an indelible mark or seal on the soul, is perhaps better viewed today from the aspect of what it actually is, a spiritual power to receive or produce something sacred. The word itself is of Greek origin and originally meant a distinctive sign or mark, e.g., of ownership, or a quality of a thing by which it can be distinguished from others. The Council of Trent affirmed the existence of the character relative to three sacraments, baptism, confirma-

tion, and holy orders (D 1609), but left the precise nature of the character open for theological discussion.

Sacred Scripture does not explicitly speak of the sacramental character, but a foundation for the doctrine can be found in the NT references to the "seal" (*sphragis*) of God with which the elect are marked (2 Cor 1.22; Rev 7.2–8). Further development of the doctrine came about through the Church's reflection upon the doctrinal implications of certain sacraments. The firm tradition that baptism could not be repeated, heightened by the baptismal controversy of the 3d cent., eventually evolved under the guidance of Augustine into a systematic doctrine of the character. Augustine made clear the distinction between the character as a permanent reality and grace, and emphasized that the character is a sign of one's consecration to Christ and a sacramental setting apart for the service of Christian worship.

Medieval scholastic theology determined that the character was an effect of the external sacramental rite, distinct from the effect of grace, yet in some way disposing the soul for grace. At this time it was also concluded which sacraments confer the character, a conclusion which was later confirmed by the Council of Trent. With this settlement regarding the existence of the character, attention then turned to its nature and effect. Basic solutions relative to both were provided by the Scholastics. As to its nature, it was commonly agreed that it was a quality of the soul, but whether a habit, power, or relation could not be decided upon. Thomas Aquinas, who produced a lasting synthesis of the theology of character, regarded it as an instrumental power of the spiritual order. Regarding the effect of the character, it was suggested that it accomplishes a spiritual transformation or configuration to Christ. Thomas Aquinas describes this effect as a participation in the priesthood of Christ, deputing and enabling the recipient to participate in the public worship of the Church.

Modern theology seeks a refinement of these solutions, esp. how the character configures one to Christ and orients one to the Christian cult. The configuration is to Christ as the head of the Church which makes the Christian capable of association with Christ's own priestly action in the Church, the sacraments. It is seen as necessary today, then, to stress the ecclesial nature of the character, the fact that it is a special power needed to take part in the official sacramental or cult activity of the Church. BIBLIOGRAPHY: P. L. Hanley, NCE 12:786–789; T. Marsh, "The Sacramental Character," *Sacraments, The Gestures of Christ* (ed. D. O'Callaghan 1964) 109–138.

[B. ROSENDALL]

SACRAMENTAL CONFESSOR, the priest who has received from a bp. the jurisdiction permitting him validly to absolve sins in the sacrament of penance. The role of the priest as sacramental confessor derives from the role in Christian antiquity of the bp. who directed the liturgical rite of reconciliation of sinners. The bp. was informed of serious sins of Christians. When such Christians presented themselves for public penance, the bp. would assign the satisfactory works whose nature and duration were determined by the seriousness of the sin. Reconcilation by the bp. followed completion of the satisfactory works. In the 7th cent. the Celtic missionary monks introduced into Europe a penitential rite less severe and more private than the ancient rites. In Celtic penance, the penitent confessed his sins privately to a priest who then reconciled the penitent to God and to the community. The privacy of Celtic penance and the gradual disuse of severe satisfactory works accentuated both the role of the priest confessor and the auricular nature of confession. The priest as confessor occupies the bp.'s position in the penitential rites of Christian antiquity because his priesthood is a sharing in the full priesthood of the bp., and his faculties to hear confessions in a particular locality are received from the local bishop. BIBLIOGRAPHY: P. Anciaux, *Sacrament of Penance* (1962); B. Poschmann, *Penance and Anointing of the Sick* (tr. F. Courtney, 1964). *PENANCE, SACRAMENT OF.

[J. J. FLOOD]

SACRAMENTAL PENANCE, see PENANCE, SACRAMENTAL.

SACRAMENTAL THEOLOGY, HISTORY OF. The sacraments, because of the central place they occupy in a Christian understanding of the plan of salvation, have been an object of interest and reflection from the beginnings of Christianity. This reflection, at first eclectic, gradually evolved into a systematic study of the sacraments using the data and methods of the science of theology. In the beginning, concern for the sacraments arose spontaneously out of the need to clarify a particular point of belief or to provide an answer to some particular situation; later, attempts were made to evolve principles applicable to all the sacraments and to explain the nature and function of each of the sacraments individually. This systematic consideration of the sacraments concerned itself with a variety of questions relative to the sacraments: their nature and place in the plan of salvation, their nature and value as signs, the way in which they work, and the effect which they accomplish. While it is, indeed, this latter type of investigation which is true sacramental theology, the earlier spontaneous reflection cannot be overlooked in a history of sacramental theology.

The thoughts and activities of the first Christian community, recorded in the NT, provide the first data about the sacraments. This amounts to mention, at least, of all the rites and states which afterwards were to be called sacraments, with the greatest attention given, however, to baptism and the Eucharist. The first Christian writers after the Apostolic period, such as Justin and Irenaeus, were not remiss in writing about the sacraments, but they do not present us with any type of developed doctrine. For this one must wait until the 3d cent. in which, stimulated by the controversy on rebaptism, a number of writers undertook to present lengthy treatises about that sacrament. In the following century, the catechetical works of Gregory of Nyssa and

Ambrose touch upon the sacraments, again esp. the Eucharist and baptism, but there is still no lengthy systematic treatment. Augustine (354–430), who is considered the father of sacramental theology, had occasion in his controversy with the Donatists to deal with a number of sacramental questions not yet considered, notably the concept of a sacrament and the idea of character.

The next moment of significance in sacramental theology did not come until quite some time after Augustine. In the 11th cent. the Eucharistic controversies involving Paschasius Radbertus, Ratramnus, Berengar, and Lanfranc opened the question of sacramental symbolism, and interest in the sacraments was revived. The 12th cent. witnessed to important advances in sacramental theology and the first attempts at a synthesis; it was an era of important names in sacramental investigation, among them Hugh of Saint-Victor and Peter Lombard. But the real peak of sacramental theology was reached in the 13th cent. to which are attached the names of Thomas Aquinas, Bonaventure, Albert, and Duns Scotus. With these great Scholastic theologians we have a systematic presentation of the sacraments and a thorough integration of them into the overall plan of salvation as conceived by Christianity. The work of this century relative to the sacraments was truly monumental, and much of later sacramental theology has been little more than an attempt to elaborate upon and clarify certain aspects of the thought of these men. The councils of the Church noted for their attention to the sacraments, those of Florence (1438–45) and Trent (1545–63), did nothing more than affirm the teaching of the Scholastic theologians.

A new focus was given to sacramental theology upon the occasion of the Reformation in the 16th century. Sacramental investigation became largely defensive, an attempt on the part of RC theologians at least to preserve and defend both the doctrine and practice of the Church as it had evolved up to that time. Attention was directed in large part to the number of the sacraments, to their mode of efficacy, and to their liturgical rites. As a result, subsequent centuries until comparatively recent times witnessed what was largely a polemical presentation of the sacraments by both Catholics and Protestants. In the 17th cent. a less polemical and more scientific approach to the sacraments was undertaken by Spanish theologians, and in the 18th cent. there was some revival of interest in historical investigation relative to the sacraments. But it was not really until the 20th cent. that an entirely new attitude to sacramental investigation emerged. Under the influence of the ecumenical movement and of revived liturgical and biblical study, a new era of sacramental theology, which views the sacraments as acts of Christ demanding a faith response, has opened up. BIBLIOGRAPHY: J. R. Quinn, NCE 12:789–790; B. Leeming, *Principles of Sacramental Theology* (1956), 38–58.

[B. ROSENDALL]

SACRAMENTALISM, emphasis on the sacraments as central to the Christian life; often a pejorative term applied to a value allegedly set on sacraments as external acts apart from faith and inward appreciation of their meaning (see SACRAMENTS). The term is particularly used to discredit the theory that sacraments confer grace *ex opere operato,* and suggests that this implies a devotion to sacraments that neglects God, who acts through them, and turns from faith in Christ himself to dependence on the performance of the signs of his action. Those who affirm the objective effectiveness of sacraments, however, mean that it is God's action that causes this effectiveness, and that the sacraments bring Christ's presence; they agree that actual reception of this effectiveness and presence is in proportion to the faith of the recipient.

[T. EARLY]

SACRAMENTALS, sacred signs instituted by the Church according to Vatican Council's II's *Constitution on the Sacred Liturgy* ''. . . which bear a resemblance to the sacraments: they signify effects, particularly of a spiritual kind which are obtained through the Church's intercession. By them men are disposed to receive the chief effects of the sacraments and various occasions in life are rendered holy'' (60). Examples include those related to baptism: the blessing of holy water, the blessing of baptismal water at the Easter Vigil, the ceremony of baptism (invocations, exorcisms, serving of white garment and candle); those related to holy orders, the ministries below diaconate; marriage (the nuptial blessing, the blessing of the home, and blessing of women); anointing of the sick, blessing of sick, burial rites, etc., the various blessings associated with the Mass. Objects associated with the cult of Mary or the saints are also classified as sacramentals. The similarity with sacraments is their being tangible signs or symbols of realities related to sanctification; the effectiveness toward actual sanctification of the sacramentals, however, totally depends on the faith, devotion, and love of the user, whereas sacraments are objectively authenticated channels of grace. BIBLIOGRAPHY: J. R. Quinn, NCE 12: 790–792; A. Michel, DTC 14:1:465–482; J. H. Miller, *Signs of Transformation in Christ* (1963).

[F. H. BRIGHAM]

SACRAMENTARIANS, a term used in two senses. (1) The primary use was that originated by Martin Luther, opposing the eucharistic teaching of *Zwingli, *Oecolampadius, and others who understood the sacramental presence of Christ in the Eucharist to mean a metaphorical presence, as opposed to a *Real Presence (see *Formula of Concord, Art. VII). Throughout the 16th cent. the term became a designation for anyone denying the Real Presence. (See MARBURG ARTICLES; UBIQUITARIANISM.) (2) Less commonly, those who teach the objective power of the sacraments to confer grace have been disparagingly called sacramentarians.

[T. C. O'BRIEN]

SACRAMENTARY, the book used at the altar by the celebrant at Mass and at rites associated with the Mass. It contains only the things said by the celebrant. The early sacramentaries were the fruit of the first 7 cent. of liturgical evolution. The use of a sacramentary, as distinct from a complete Missal, and a *lectionary, has been revived in the liturgical reform of Vatican II.

For the first 3 cent. the officiant's prayer was largely extemporaneous, though in its general lines it was governed by the tradition of the local church. The 3d and 4th cent. saw the appearance of model eucharistic formulae such as that of Hippolytus. These were written down in booklet form (*libelli missarum*) to serve as memory aids, perhaps at first with only one Mass in a single booklet. From the 5th to the 7th cent. collections of these *libelli* were gathered together, the great collections of which were known as sacramentaries. The two largest families of sacramentaries are the Franco–Gallican and the Roman–Italian. Of these the most famous are the Roman-Italian group, which are the Leonine, Gelasian, and Gregorian Sacramentaries.

The Leonine Sacramentary (6th cent.), now called the *Sacramentarium Veronense,* is more a collection of *libelli* than a proper sacramentary. Along with this appeared the Old Gelasian (6th cent.), which gives evidence of the non–episcopal parish liturgy in the Roman titular churches. The new Gelasian (8th cent.) is the Old Gelasian after it was influenced by the Frankish liturgies. The Gregorian Sacramentary is an official Roman book containing the papal feast day and stational liturgies. A development of this, known as the Hadrian Sacramentary (*Hadrianum*) was sent to Charlemagne by Adrian I in 785. Augmented with a supplement adapting it to fit the needs of the Frankish clergy, this was officially adopted in Charlemagne's empire. It was a major source from which the Missal developed in the 10th century. BIBLIOGRAPHY: G. Every, *Basic Liturgy* (1961); A. Hamman, *Early Christian Prayers* (tr. W. Mitchell, 1961).

[N. KOLLAR]

SACRAMENTINE NUNS, a cloistered, contemplative order whose members take solemn vows; official name, Religious of the Order of the Blessed Sacrament and Our Lady. It was founded in France in 1639 by Ven. Antoine Le Quieu, O.P., canonically established in 1659, and given papal approval in 1693 by Innocent XII. The constitutions were approved again in modern times in 1935. The nuns recite the Divine Office in the vernacular and each monastery is autonomous. This is probably the first order founded specifically for perpetual adoration of the Blessed Sacrament. Some of the Sacramentines were guillotined during the French Revolution and later the anticlerical laws of 1901 forced the nuns to leave their monastery at Bernay, France. Some went to Belgium, others to the U.S. where they founded a monastery in Yonkers, N.Y. (1912), and later in Conway, Mich. (1951). In 1977 they numbered about 144 sisters in Europe and in the U.S.

[R. C. CLIGGETT]

SACRAMENTINE SISTERS OF BERGAMO, a congregation which has as its special purpose perpetual adoration of the Blessed Sacrament and the education of youth; its official name is Institute of the Sisters of the Blessed Sacrament. It was founded at Bergamo, Italy, in 1882 by Caterina Comensoli and later received papal approbation; the foundress became known in religion as Mother Gertrude of the Blessed Sacrament. She and her companions received the habit in 1884 and began their work at Bergamo. They then moved to Lodi, Italy, where they received episcopal approbation in 1891. The process of the beatification of the foundress began in 1928. In 1975 the sisters numbered 1,403 in 162 houses, in Italy, Switzerland, and Brazil.

[R. C. CLIGGETT]

SACRAMENTS (SIGNS OF FAITH). The sacraments are so designated insofar as they embody and express the realization of the Christian community that they are the present activity of Christ in the Church, and insofar as they effect for the community and the individual, entry into the divine plan of salvation which is accomplished through faith. Several aspects are involved here: the sacraments as signs of the faith of the Church in their presentation of the object of faith to the community; and the sacraments as signs of faith of the Church and the individual in being the response in faith of both to the mysteries of God. Each of these aspects will have to be treated separately, although they are obviously connected since the faith of the individual derives from the faith of the Christian community.

Faith is our total response to the self-presentation of God in the historical economy of salvation. This self–presentation of God, accomplished through the Person of Christ insofar as Christ is the visible intervention of God in time and history by means of his humanity, is the object of our response, and consequently the object of our faith. The mystery of God is symbolized and made present for us in the sacramental acts of the Church which are in reality the gestures of Christ himself being re-presented in symbolic form. The sacraments relate to us the mystery of God in Christ, identifying this as our object of faith, and in this sense they are signs of faith.

But God's offer of himself in the sacramental mysteries seeks a response on the part of man which is also provided for by the sacraments. The answer of man is first a corporate answer, the prayer or confession of faith of the whole Christian community, expressed in the sacramental rite. The response, then, is first an expression in faith from the part of the Church; and this is evidenced from the fact that the Church determines the real meaning of the sacramental symbols by developing a suitable matrix for the sacramental act and by determining more precisely by words, the meaning of these religious symbols. In this sense, the sacraments are signs of the faith of the Church.

But the sacraments also make provision for more than this communal response to the mystery of God; in them, by looking beyond the rite, the individual Christian expresses his faith and consequent commitment to God's offer of grace. This is the sacramental encounter, the total surrender of self to Christ, present and active in the sacramental experience, which amounts to a total response to God in the present economy of salvation. To make this kind of response, the Christian must approach the sacraments in faith and have this faith strengthened and transformed by means of the sacramental encounter. In this way, the sacraments are signs of personal faith, both that which the individual brings with him to the sacrament and that which he takes away from the sacrament.

There is a good deal of scriptural evidence for this view of the sacraments, implied in the total revelation of the mystery of God, brought out more explicitly in the Acts of the Apostles (2.41, 8.12) and in the writings of St. Paul (Rom 6.4–8), where the relationship between faith and baptism is frequently alluded to. The Fathers are also profuse in their testimony to this doctrine, and certain elements were distinctly elaborated by St. Augustine who stated that grace was received in the sacraments in proportion to the personal faith of the recipient.

Among the scholastic theologians of the Middle Ages, Thomas Aquinas elaborated an important synthesis of this doctrine, referring to the sacraments as ''of faith'' and ''of the Church,'' and emphasizing how the sacraments in the context of the Church provide for the external and social confession of faith necessary for salvation. He also stressed the absolute necessity of personal faith for the effective reception of grace in the sacraments. The Reformation and post-Reformation eras, however, saw unfortunate distortions of this doctrine resulting from the individualistic and subjectivistic framework given the sacraments by the Reformers, and from the neglect of post-Reformation RC theologians for the role of personal faith relative to sacramental efficacy. Contemporary theology, however, has acted to restore this imbalance both in theology and in liturgical practice. Vatican Council II provides the following summary statement of this doctrine: ''[The sacraments] not only presuppose faith, but by words and objects they also nourish, strengthen, and express it; that is why they are called 'sacraments of faith.''' (Vat II SacLit 59). BIBLIOGRAPHY: L. Villette, NCE 12:813–816; C. Ernst, ''Acts of Christ: Signs of Faith,'' *Sacraments, The Gestures of Christ* (1964, ed D. O'Callaghan) 56–75.

[B. ROSENDALL]

SACRAMENTS, CONDITIONAL ADMINISTRATION OF, a practice that provides, even on occasion obliges, that a sacrament be performed in a conditional manner, generally by adding a condition to the verbal form of the sacrament, in cases where some doubt occurs relative to the necessary prerequisites on the part of the recipient for an absolute reception of it. The practice is intended not just to safeguard the sacrament, which since it is an act of God, might otherwise be subjected to irreverence, but even more so, to safeguard the recipient who, if conditional administration were not allowed, might otherwise be deprived of the sacramental action. Underlying the practice is the thought that the sacraments are the acts of Christ and the Church, and that the minister is but conforming his intention to that of the Church. The practice occurs most frequently relative to the sacraments of baptism, penance and anointing.

[B. ROSENDALL]

SACRAMENTS, THEOLOGY OF.

In the 12th cent. the word sacrament was defined with sufficient precision to distinguish seven and only seven rites as sacraments of the New Law. In the following cent. at the reunion Council of Lyons II, a profession of faith expressing belief in the seven sacraments was accepted by the Greek Emperor Palaeologos and the Patriarch Bekkos (D 860). Unlike the mysteries of the Trinity and the Incarnation, the sacraments had been regarded more as mysteries to be celebrated than as truths to be contemplated and formulated. Thus, there is no mention of sacraments in the early Christian creeds. True, Augustine in his numerous writings on baptism, directed against the Donatist practice of rebaptizing and reordaining, stressed the objective efficacy of baptism as the sacrament of Christ; identified the permanence of three sacraments—baptism, confirmation, and orders—with the sacramental character; distinguished between a valid and a fruitful sacrament, and gave the theological basis for the doctrine of reviviscence. But the systematic treatment of the sacraments began with the scholastics. The composition of the rite, the sacramental reality, and the grace of the sacraments were explored; the minister and the recipient of the rites were defined; and various theories of sacramental causality were proposed. Against the Reformers of the 16th cent. the Council of Trent stated that the sacraments confer the grace that they signify, and this in virtue of the rite itself (*ex opere operato*) and not solely because of the faith or trust of the recipient (D 1606, 1608). Today, theologians are more interested in exploring the sign value, or signification, of the sacraments. Finally, there is more emphasis on the faith response of the adult recipient, since the sacraments as signs of faith imply an encounter or dialogue with God in Christ and in his Church. BIBLIOGRAPHY: P. Palmer, *Sacraments and Worship* (*Sources of Christian Theology* 1, 1955); E. Schillebeeckx, *Christ the Sacrament of the Encounter with God* (1963).

[P. F. PALMER]

SACRARIUM,

a basin for washing altar linens, chalices, and the like, and for disposing of water from liturgical ablutions. It is generally in the church's sacristy and drains directly into the ground.

[J. DALLEN]

SACRÉ COEUR, PARIS

(1876–1910), pilgrimage church on Montmarte of imposing and beautifully domed silhouette commanding the skyline, erected through public funds from designs by Abadie, and finished by Lucien Magne. This outstanding structure combines elements of St.-Germigny-des-Près and St. Front-de-Périguex, though modified by a large portico, ambulatory and radiating chapels. An impressive example of Romanesque-Byzantine style, Sacré Coeur evidences the 19th-cent. monumentalization of the eclectic historical vocabulary.

[M. J. DALY]

SACRED AND THE PROFANE,

two modes of experience or of being in the world, conditional upon the presence of the *holy. The phrase is used frequently in the comparative study of religions (see RELIGION, COMPARATIVE STUDY OF), esp. since the writings of É. *Durkheim (1858–1917) who maintained that the distinction between the sacred and the profane is the fundamental characteristic of religion. But even though the phrase would be common to most students of religion, its meaning varies with their particular interpretation of the basis for sacrality; e.g., R. *Otto's idea of the sacred or holy as an a priori category of experience differs greatly from Durkheim's view of religion as a derivative of societal structures.

The notion of the sacred and profane is necessarily bound up with hierophanies. From earliest times, man has been aware of manifestations of the sacred in both spatial and temporal dimensions. These eruptions of the holy are the cause of any distinction between a profane world and a sacralized one. For the religious man space is not homogeneous; there are breaks in it, and some parts are qualitatively different from others. Thus Mecca can be called a holy city or Mount Sinai a holy mountain because, to the mind of the Mohammedan or Jew, God has been present to it in a special way, making it sacred. Time also can be regarded as numinous: primordial time when the absolute first came to be present in the chaos of mere existence is the holy time par excellence, but through ritual and a cycle of feasts this primordial time is again made actual. The primitive religious celebration of the new year is clear testimony of this drive to return to sacred time and to remain within it. Other experienced realities also serve man as a vehicle for the appearance of the sacred such as trees, mountains, animals, rivers, or even the wind. But characteristic of all these realities is that the sacred is discovered and not produced by man; that man must live in contact with the sacred or be condemned to a chaotic existence where there is no foundation for reality; and that the discovered sacrality of the world and of time must be extended by man through ritual, thanksgiving, and imprecation. BIBLIOGRAPHY: M. Éliade, *Sacred and the Profane* (tr. W. R. Trask, 1961); R. Otto, *Idea of the Holy* (tr. J. W. Harvey, 1958); É. Durkheim, *Elementary Forms of the Religious Life* (tr. J. W. Swain, 1961). *PLACES, SACRED; *SYMBOL.

[V. T. JOHNSON]

SACRED COLLEGE, see COLLEGE OF CARDINALS.

SACRED HARP,

a tune book, published in 1844. It was one of the more significant of several oblong tune books, collections of shaped-note hymns, which came out in

America in the first half of the 19th century. It is a compilation of psalms, hymn tunes, odes, and anthems put to old, unwritten secular melodies of the British Isles. BIBLIOGRAPHY: G. P. Jackson, *Story of the Sacred Harp 1844–1944* (1944).

[M. T. LEGGE]

SACRED HEART, the physical heart of Jesus as an object of devotion and symbol of the love which Christ has for mankind. The ultimate object of this devotion is the Incarnate Word, but particular attention is directed to Christ's heart insofar as it symbolizes his immense love, human and divine, for man. In the doctrine and practice of the Church, the Sacred Heart has also been recognized as an appeal to each individual to allow his own heart to be touched by the love God has manifested. The Sacred Heart can be adored with the cult of worship in the strict sense since Christ's heart is never to be thought of except in conjunction with his divine Person. It is the physical heart, not so much in a corporeal or physiological sense, but in its biblical sense as the center of affection, which is the most expressive symbol of Christ's inexhaustible love. The essence of devotion to the Sacred Heart also signifies the love by which the Father and the Holy Spirit love sinful humanity, since it is the charity of the Blessed Trinity which is the principle of human Redemption. The object of this love, therefore, is the whole of mankind, and devotion to the Sacred Heart, far from being a form of spiritual self-centeredness, must follow from the individual's situation within the Church and the world.

Within this context, there is a substantial scriptural basis for devotion to the Sacred Heart since the Bible presents the Redemption as a product of divine love. In the patristic era, the pierced heart of Christ upon the cross was interpreted as a fountain from which the Spirit was poured out upon men. But devotion expressly to the Sacred Heart began only in the Middle Ages and continued with great popularity through the *Devotio moderna* and the encouragement of St. *Francis de Sales, St. John Eudes, and the Visitation Order. In particular, the apparitions made to St. Margaret Mary *Alacoque (1647–90) did much to spread the devotion. The cult of the Sacred Heart has taken many forms: *First Friday devotions, nocturnal vigils of reparation, and enthronement of an image of the Sacred Heart (see SACRED HEART, EN-THRONEMENT OF). Among the encyclicals dedicated to the Sacred Heart are Leo XIII's *Annum sacrum,* dealing with the consecration of the world to the Sacred Heart; *Miserentissimus Redemptor* of Pius XI, concerned with reparation and expiation as an essential feature of this devotion; and *Haurietis aquas* of Pius XII, the most scientific theological statement of this devotion which he called "a duty of religion most conducive to Christian perfection." BIBLIOGRAPHY: A. Hamon, *Histoire de la dévotion au Sacré-Coeur* (5 v., 1923–1941); A. Hamon, DSAM 2.1:1023–46; A. Dachauer, *Sacred Heart* (1959); L. Verheylezoon, *Devotion to the Sacrd Heart* (1955).

[M. GRIFFIN]

SACRED HEART, ENTHRONEMENT OF, a special manifestation of devotion whereby the members of a family or any community place a picture or statue of the *Sacred Heart in a prominent place in the home as a sign of their acceptance of Christ's sovereignty. It is generally inaugurated by a ceremonial act of consecration to the Sacred Heart. The practice grew up as a result of the promise made by Christ to St. Margaret Mary *Alacoque in a series of apparitions, "I will bless every place where the image of my heart is singularly honored." The devotion has received the approbation of several recent popes. BIBLIOGRAPHY: F. Larkin, *Enthronement of the Sacred Heart* (1960).

[M. GRIFFIN]

SACRED HEART, SOCIETY DEVOTED TO THE, a religious congregation of women with simple vows founded in 1941 in Hungary and Czechoslovakia for the teaching apostolate. Sisters teach religion to public school students, operate clubs, sodalities, convert classes, train lay leaders and catechists. They transferred their motherhouse to Los Angeles, Cal. (1957) with Sister Ida Peterfy as superior general after escaping from behind the Iron Curtain. In the U.S. their numbers tripled. It was their custom to wear simple secular dress even before the changes in garb brought about by Vatican II.

[R. C. CLIGGETT]

SACRED HEART, SOCIETY OF THE, congregation of sisters, Religious of the Sacred Heart of Jesus (RSCJ), sometimes called Madames of the Sacred Heart, dedicated to the apostolate of teaching, but also engaged in retreat work and other forms of instruction. The need for a renewal of Christian education after the French Revolution prompted the Rev. Léonor de *Tournély to plan a congregation of sisters for this work. The actual foundress is St. Madeleine Sophie *Barat; at Paris in 1800 she and the first members consecrated themselves to the Sacred Heart. The first convent was established at Amiens, and Mother Barat was elected superior general in 1806. The rule, patterned on that of the Jesuits, was approved by the Holy See in 1826. Mother Barat governed the congregation until her death in 1865; in her lifetime she saw the establishment of 86 houses. The Religious of the Sacred Heart of Jesus are renowned for their educational program, followed, with adaptations, in all their schools. The American history of the society began with the work of Mother Rose Philippine *Duchesne; she made the first foundation at St. Charles, Mo., in 1818. Under Mother Aloysius *Hardy the congregation spread throughout the country. In 1975 there were 5,968 members in 441 houses throughout the world. The motherhouse is in Rome.

[R. C. CLIGGETT]

SACRED HEART BROTHERS, religious congregation devoted mainly to teaching boys in elementary and high schools. The institute was founded near Lyons, France, in 1821 by Rev. André Coindre; after his death, his brother,

Rev. Vincent Coindre, was superior. Since 1841, however, the superior general has always been one of the brothers; and the rule has been the one that was formulated by Bro. Polycarp, the first brother superior general. The work of the community in the U.S. began in 1847 at Mobile, Ala. Schools were opened in other cities of the South and from 1889, with a foundation in Manchester, N.H., also in the New England states. The greatest growth came in Canada, where the first school was established in 1872 and where the largest number of brothers and schools of the institute is concentrated. The brothers' work, however, has also extended to many countries of Africa, South America, and the South Seas of the Pacific. The generalate since 1950 has been in Rome. In 1976 there were 2,215 brothers in 268 houses of the congregation.

[R. C. CLIGGETT]

SACRED HEART MISSIONARIES (MSC), a religious congregation of priests and brothers, dedicated to the parochial, educational, and missionary apostolates. The founder, Rev. Jules *Chevalier, established the institute in 1854 to renew the faith of France by spreading devotion to the Sacred Heart; approval as an institute of pontifical rank was received in 1869. In the early decades it spread through the opening of schools in many European countries, and it began its mission apostolate in 1881, at the request of Leo XIII, in the Pacific missions of Micronesia and Melanesia. Missionary work extended throughout the S. Pacific, to Africa, South and Central America. In the U.S. from 1876 the Canadian province established houses in New England and New York State. The U.S. province covering the rest of the country, was formally established in 1939, having had its beginnings in 1910 when members of the German province established a house in Sparta, Wis., in the diocese of La Crosse. In 1976 the congregation numbered 1,986 priests and 715 brothers in 446 houses.

[R. C. CLIGGETT]

SACRED HEART OF JESUS, APOSTLES OF, formerly Missionary Zelatrices of the Sacred Heart, a congregation founded for the education of youth and the care of orphans by Mother Clelia Merloni in 1894 at Viareggio, Italy. Financial ruin threatened the community in its early years, and Bp. Giovanni Battista *Scalabrini became the sisters' friend and counselor. Under his guidance in 1900 they began foundations in the New World where many Italian immigrants had already settled. The U.S. province began with a hospital in Boston, Mass., in 1902, but the congregation soon moved to the Archdiocese of Hartford, Connecticut. In 1954 the provincial house and the novitiate were moved to Mount Sacred Heart, Hamden, Connecticut. In 1953 the sisters began to work with retarded children and by 1954 they had two institutions for exceptional children in Pennsylvania. They are engaged in education at all levels; they staff homes for retired women and for convalescents as well as residences for girls. In addition they do social work

and give catechetical instruction in parishes. In 1975 they numbered 1897 in 193 houses.

[R. C. CLIGGETT]

SACRED HEART OF JESUS, DAUGHTERS OF THE CHARITY OF THE, religious congregation that came into being in response to a need for religious teachers in the parish of La Salle-de-Vihiers in the Diocese of Angers, France, in the early 19th century. Jean Maurice Catroux, the pastor, founded a new congregation and invited one of his parishioners, Rose Giet, to become the first sister in 1823. Four sisters of the community came to the U.S. in 1905 when anticlerical laws forced religious schools to close. They opened a school in Newport, Vt., and later in Champlain, New York. Soon they extended their work into Canada. From 1935 the sisters have been engaged in African missions. The Holy See approved the community's being divided into five provinces; the American provincial house is in Littleton, New Hampshire. In 1975 the sisters numbered 1,830 in 274 houses.

[R. C. CLIGGETT]

SACRED HEART OF JESUS, PRIESTS OF THE, religious congregation of priests and brothers established in 1878 to preach devotion and reparation to the Sacred Heart. The founder was the Rev. L. G. *Dehon, canon at Soissons, France. Preliminary approbation was given by Leo XIII in 1898 and final approval by Pius X in 1906. The institute is devoted to the apostolate of preaching, education, pastoral ministry, and foreign missions. The first mission, to Ecuador, was accepted in 1898; since then the congregation has accepted missions in Finland, Africa, Indonesia, and elsewhere. The North American province, originating from the German province, was established in 1933, much of its work being devoted to black, Hispanic, and native Americans. In 1976 the congregation had 420 houses; the community numbered 2,788, of whom 1,970 were priests.

[R. C. CLIGGETT]

SACRED HEART OF JESUS, SOCIETY OF THE, religious congregation founded by Sulpicians François-Éléonor de Tournély and Prince Charles de Broglio to resume the life of the Society of Jesus, suppressed in 1773. The earliest priest members were French émigrés; they fled the French Revolution and nine of them took vows in Augsburg, Germany, in 1794. Three years later they established a house near Vienna and by 1799 had about 50 members. In that same year their merger with the *Paccanarists was accomplished at the instruction of Pius VI. Most of the members of the merged society, the Society of the Faith of Jesus, entered the Jesuits at the 1814 restoration.

[R. C. CLIGGETT]

SACRED HEART OF MARY, RELIGIOUS OF THE, an institute etablished for Catholic education and the service of the poor. It was founded in 1849 by Pierre Jean Gailhac and Appolonie Cure-Pélissier, who became Mother

St. Jean. The latter was a widow who desired to give herself to apostolic labors after years under Pierre Gailhac's spiritual direction. Together they drew up a rule based on that of St. Ignatius Loyola and gave it a Marian emphasis, as its motto "All for Jesus through Mary" testifies. While the first foundations in Ireland were being established, Mother St. Jean died (1869). Her successor then began to open schools in Portugal, England, and the U.S. The constitutions were approved by Pope Leo XIII. In 1905 foundations were established in Spain and Brazil. Under the leadership of Mother Marie Joseph Butler great expansion began in the U.S. in 1903. This was the beginning of the well-known Marymount Colleges, the first one opening in Tarrytown, New York. Similar institutions have been established on three continents. In 1975 there were 1,583 sisters in 170 houses.

[R. C. CLIGGETT]

SACRED HEARTS, FATHERS OF THE, a religious community of priests and brothers originating in the Congregation of the Sacred Hearts of Jesus and Mary, founded to make reparation to the Sacred Hearts of Jesus and Mary and to continue the religious work halted by the French Revolution. The founders were Rev. Pierre Marie Joseph Coudrin of the Diocese of Poitiers, France, and Countess Henriette de la Chevalerie who had been imprisoned, condemned to death, and released. Henriette joined a group of women who were secretly keeping up adoration of the Blessed Sacrament. In 1794 the priest and Countess established the Congregations of the Sacred Hearts of Jesus and Mary and of Perpetual Adoration of the Most Blessed Sacrament of the Altar. The men's community became known as the Picpus Fathers, since they came from the Rue de Picpus, Paris. The new congregation was approved by Pius VII in 1817. Missionaries were requested for Oceania by Leo XII in 1825, and in 1827 priests and brothers went to Hawaii, the Marquesas Islands, Tahiti (1833), Easter Island (1837), and Gambier and Tuomotu (1838). Expansion to S. America, Africa, the Far East, and Norway began in 1963.

In 1827 foundations were begun in the Far West, then they followed in the Midwest and Eastern United States.

Damien (Joseph de Veuster), Apostle of the Lepers, Father Edmund Dimillier, who wrote the first Catholic catechism and grammar in an Indian language, and Rev. Mateo Crawley-Boevey, founder of the Enthronement of the Sacred Heart and Night Adoration in the home, are among the most renowned members of the congregation. In 1975 the members numbered 1,728 brothers and 1,410 priests in 302 houses.

[R. C. CLIGGETT]

SACRED HEARTS OF JESUS AND MARY (BRENTWOOD), SISTERS OF THE, a congregation which stems from the Servantes du Sacré Coeur de Jésus, founded in France in 1866 by Fr. Victor Braun. The English community, which separated from France in 1903, received papal approbation in 1924. The motherhouse is situated at Chigwell, Essex, near London. The sisters are also known as the Chigwell nuns. They follow the Rule of St. Augustine. The work of the congregation includes teaching in elementary and high schools, schools for the mentally retarded, handicapped children, and unwed mothers. Missions were undertaken in Rhodesia and in the United States. In 1975 the sisters numbered 417 in 36 houses.

[R. C. CLIGGETT]

SACRED HUMANITY, DEVOTION TO THE. In the history of Christian devotion, worship has been extended not only to the eternal Word Incarnate in the person Jesus, but also to his human nature as the instrument of salvation. This worship is not extended to Jesus' humanity considered apart from its union with the Word, but only in its connection with the Word. Thus, as with all worship taken in the strict sense (latria), the formal object of devotion is God and the motive is divine reverence. These devotions have concentrated on the physical body of Jesus, especially the Sacred Heart and the Precious Blood. Historically, the early Church did not utilize this form of worship nor has it ever been developed in the Eastern Churches. But in the West, at the beginning of the Middle Ages, images of the suffering Christ came to be popular. St. Bernard (1090–1153) and St. Francis of Assisi (1182–1226) emphasized the details of Christ's life for the imitation of the faithful. Devotion to the Passion and wounds of Christ grew and came to be concentrated on the Sacred Heart—a devotion that was popularized esp. by St. John Eudes (1601–1680) and St. Margaret Mary Alacoque (1647–1690). These devotions continue into the present: Pius XII supported devotion to the Sacred Heart in the encyclical Haurietis aquas (1956), and Pierre Teilhard de Chardin, for instance, made this devotion central in his religious life. The particular value of this type of piety is that it focuses Christian worship on the historical and physical realities of the Redemption. BIBLIOGRAPHY: A. Williams, Sacred Heart in the Life of the Church (1957); P. Teilhard de Chardin, Divine Milieu (1959); K. Adam, Christ of Faith (1957).

[T. M. MCFADDEN]

SACRIFICATI, the most serious category of the lapsed (*lapsi*), Christians who had fallen away from the faith during the persecution of Decius (249–251). Sacrificati offered sacrifice to the pagan gods. They presented a problem to the Church because of their great number and because they sought reconciliation with the Church even while the persecution still raged. Various sections of the Church reacted differently. In Rome, *Novatian gave his name to the rigorist view that they be denied penance and reconciliation at least until after the persecution. In Carthage the various lapsi had recourse to the intercession of the faithful who remained steadfast in the face of great trial, by seeking *libelli pacis requesting bps. to admit the penitent back to communion. Cyprian of Carthage and Cornelius of Rome convened a synod to settle the issue. Accordingly, reconciliation was extended to the *sacrificati* who were in danger of death, if they had already begun to do public penance. *THURIFICATI.

[E. J. DILLON]

SACRIFICE, a term applied in Christian theology principally to (1) the Passion, death, and Resurrection of the Lord; (2) the symbolic, or sacramental, recalling (*anamnēsis*) of the Paschal mystery in the Eucharistic Liturgy, or Sacrifice, of Christians; and (3) the Last Supper, at which the Lord "offered to God the Father . . . His own body and blood. . . . This He did, that He might leave to His beloved spouse, the Church, a visible sacrifice, such as the nature of man demands, that by it the sacrifice in blood to be accomplished but once on the cross might be re–presented, that the memory thereof might remain to the end of the world, and its salutary effects might be applied to the remission of such sins as we daily commit" (Council of Trent Session 22, D 938).

The sacrificial and redemptive character of Christ's death is denied by no Christian. The basic theme of the Epistle to the Hebrews is the superiority of Christ's sacrifice over those of the Old Law. Since, however, the same Epistle insists that by one offering we have been justified once for all by Christ (Heb 10.14) and since Christ's sacrifice is distinctive in that it cannot and need not be repeated, Protestant theologians from the time of Luther, Calvin, and Cranmer have vigorously denied the sacrificial character of the Eucharist, or Lord's Supper.

Catholic theologians find the solution to the problem in the Synoptic account of the Last Supper (Mt ch. 26; Mk ch. 14; Lk ch. 22) and in Paul's elucidation of the narrative (1 Cor ch. 11). The body that is given *to* the disciples to eat is the body that is given *for* them; the blood that is given *to* them to drink is the blood that is even then being shed, though symbolically, *for* them. Again, reference to the "blood of the new covenant" irresistibly calls to mind the earlier covenant of Sinai, also sealed in blood (cf. Ex 19:24–24:8). Thus, according to Catholic teaching, Christ at the Last Supper instituted a true rite of sacrifice that would prefigure his death on the morrow, just as the same rite celebrated by Christians today represents and commemorates his death of yesterday. In stressing the symbolic, mystical, or sacramental nature of the Eucharistic Sacrifice and in eschewing all attempts to discover a real immolation in the Mass, Catholic theologians today have made it easier for their separated brethren to accept the sacrificial overtones of the Last Supper and to respond to the language of sacrifice that permeates the Eucharistic Liturgies of the East and the West from the beginning of the Christian era. BIBLIOGRAPHY: P. Palmer, *Sacraments and Worship* (*Sources of Christian Theology* 2, 1955); B. Cooke, NCE 12:837–840; F. Clark, *Eucharistic Sacrifice and the Reformation* (1960).

[P. F. PALMER]

SACRIFICE OF THE CROSS. The death of Jesus on the cross has been interpreted from earliest times as a sacrifice. This conception is at the heart of the human expression of the redemptive mystery.

To understand this one must seek the meaning sacrifice had in the Jewish religious experience. For the Jew, sacrifice was not a *do ut des* transaction for the purpose of manipulating the Deity and making him bend to the will of the people. Nor was there question properly of providing a ritual victim to substitute for the people and appease the vindictive justice of an injured God. Jewish sacrifice expressed a profound religious sentiment. It was a form of worship that graphically acknowledged the people's dependence on God and expressed their search for union with him. It was an act that was simultaneously ritual and personal. In the symbolic language of ritual every sacrifice transferred the victim into the presence and possession of God, and most sacrifices provided a way for the worshiper to share life with God through the now sacred victim. Ritual sacrifice was in the service of the person's interior sacrifice. The Prophets continually recalled the people to this essential element. It found its most perfect expression incarnate in the person of the suffering servant of Is 53, who offers his death as a sacrifice of expiation.

That Jesus saw his redemptive mission in sacrificial terms is evident in his acceptance of the role and title of the Servant: "The Son of Man himself did not come to be served but to serve, and to give his life as a ransom for many" (Mk 10.45). His death is set in the context of a new covenant sacrifice. "The night before he suffered" he proclaimed that the blood he would pour out in death is the sacrificial blood that seals the new covenant relationship with the Father, as sacrificial blood sealed the great covenant of Israel (Mk 14.24; cf. Ex 24.8). In the vocabulary of the NT, the sacrificial nature of Jesus' death on the cross is indicated by identifying him as the true Lamb of God (Jn 1.29; 19.33, 36) in the likeness of the paschal lamb, the annual immolation of which is the symbol of Israel's redemption (cf. 1 Cor 5.7; 1 Pet 1.18–20); by the frequent references to the redemptive blood of Christ (cf. Eph 1.7; Rom 3.25; 5.9; Col 1.20; 1 Jn 1.7); and by recognizing in his dying the element of free choice (Eph 5.2, 25; Gal 2.20) by which he accomplishes the Father's intention in delivering over his own Son (Rom 8.32). Finally, the Epistle to the Hebrews views the whole work of Christ's Redemption in the context of sacrifice: he is the eternal high priest who offers the unique and perfect sacrifice in the shedding of his blood, a sacrifice that finds its full consummation in his own humanity as he passes through death into the heavenly tabernacle where the identical sacrifice endures perpetually in the participated eternity given to his human priestly act of self-offering love and obedience.

While the whole life of Jesus was an act of worship in living testimony to the sovereignty of God, it is his death on the cross that is his sacrifice. This is the act that he designated as sacrifice, and such a determination is essential to the priestly act. It is his human act of dying that is the most perfect embodiment of his inner spirit of self-emptying adoration, obedience, and love. It is the act of dying on the cross that most perfectly reflects the ritual of covenant sacrifice: here the blood of the victim pours out on the flesh of Christ, which is simultaneously the altar (the place where the glory of God dwells), and on the people (who are totally recapitulated in the divinely constituted head of all mankind). And, most important of all, it is the act of dying that ushers the man Jesus from this world into the fullness of communion with his Father—a fullness that his Father proclaimed in raising him from the dead.

It is the belief of Christians that the Eucharist is this same once-for-all sacrifice of the cross made present in order that the Church may join its self-offering to that of Christ and may share the benefits of the paschal sacrifice by communing with its glorified Lord while awaiting the consummation of his sacrifice in itself. BIBLIOGRAPHY: A. P. Hennessy NCE 12:840–842; L. Richard, *Le Mystère de la rédemption* (1959); L. Sabourin, *Rédemption sacrificielle* (1961).

[C. REGAN]

SACRILEGE, a sin against the virtue of *religion by the abuse or desecration of a person, thing, or place set aside for the worship of God. Thus sacrilege may be personal, real (from *res*, thing), or local. To be properly sacrilegious, an action must be prompted by the intent of irreverence towards the sacred. The kinds and seriousness of the sin correspond to the nearness of the object profaned to the holiness of God. Thus sacrilege against a person consecrated to God is worse than sacrilegious treatment of a sacred vessel. Irreverence toward or desecration of the Eucharistic elements has a special malice. *DESECRATION.

[T. C. O'BRIEN]

SACRING BELL, bell rung at Mass to indicate key points in the liturgy. Dating from the 12th cent., it was an important aid when services were not in the vernacular or were held at a distance from the people. It is also known as the sanctus bell.

[T. EARLY]

SACRISTAN, a term sometimes used for the *sexton but more exactly applied to the person designated to care for altar utensils, vestments, and other such items kept in the *sacristy. Though sacristans are sometimes clergymen, esp. in large cathedrals, the office is normally held by a layman.

[T. EARLY]

SACRISTY, or vestry, an annex to a church where the ministers and assistants prepare themselves for divine worship and where such items as the vestments and altar furnishings are kept.

[T. EARLY]

SACRISTY, NEW, OF SAN LORENZO (Medici Chapel), Florence. Built by Michelangelo (1520–33) with mosaic floor by Vasari added in 1557, it follows the Old Sacristy plan with detail of dark *pietra serena,* and is renowned for the two magnificent tombs by Michelangelo. There is that of Lorenzo the Magnificent, with the famous portrait statue called *The Thinker* at the apex of the sarcophagus, which carries the poetic allegorical figures of Dawn and Evening. The companion group is crowned by the vigorous Giuliano, duke of Nemours, over similar, beautiful figures, of Night and Day. On a third wall facing the altar is Michelangelo's *Madonna and Child* flanked by *St. Cosmas* and *St. Damian* by A. Montorsoli and R. di Montelupo respectively. BIBLIOGRAPHY: C. de Tolnay, *Medici Chapel* (1948).

[M. J. DALY]

SACRISTY, OLD, OF SAN LORENZO, FLORENCE, gem of early Italian Renaissance architecture, erected (1420–29) by Brunelleschi adjacent to the Medici Church. The interior, a square room with apse, is of fine proportions emphasized by details in dark *pietra serena,* with colored stucco medallions from the life of St. John, lunettes of the Evangelists, a frieze of cherubim, and boasting bronze doors by the master sculptor Donatello, with sarcophagi of Giovanni and Piero de'Medici by Verrocchio (1472). BIBLIOGRAPHY: P. Sanpaolesi, *Brunellesco e Donatello nella Sacristia Vecchia* (1950).

[M. J. DALY]

SACY, LE MAISTRE DE, see LE MAISTRE, ANTOINE AND ISAAC LOUIS.

SADDUCEES, the priestly, aristocratic party in Judaism. The Sadducees arose sometime after the Maccabean rebellion. Josephus first mentions them at the time of John Hyrcanus I and his unsuccessful attempt to reestablish the monarchy. The Sadducees sustained heavy losses in the revolt against Rome (66–70 A.D.) and were no longer significant in Judaism after 70 A.D. It is important to note that all the sources for an understanding of the Sadducees are hostile to them. That includes the NT writings, Josephus, and the rabbinic writings. Judaism, after Jamnia, developed along Pharisaic lines. Josephus was from a Saducean family, which explains how he secured military rank in the Jewish war of independence against Rome. After he became a convert to Pharisaism, he exaggerated the importance of the Pharisees to the people and made the Sadducees appear subservient puppets of foreign tyrants. The truth may actually be that the Sadducees and Pharisees represented two divergent attempts to accomplish the same end: to maintain for the Jewish people whatever autonomy could be managed, and to protect them as much as possible from the cruelty and corruption first of the Syrian tyrants and then of Roman rule. The Sadducees' interests centered in the Temple, the priesthood, and the Torah, and they were apparently reluctant to encourage the apocalyptic hope in future rewards and punishments. But information on the real religious issues separating Sadducees and Pharisees may be irrecoverable.

[E. J. DILLON]

SADHANA, see TANTRISM.

SADISM, the psychological abnormality of deriving sexual gratification from inflicting pain and debasement on another; named from the degenerate and perverted life and writings of the Marquis de Sade (1740–1814). In its truly pathological form sadism is not morally imputable. When, however, sadistic practices are engaged in for sexual experimentation and variety, the deviance may be moral, not psychic (see SADOMASOCHISM). In a broader sense sadism sometimes describes the opposite of the virtue of clemency, which safeguards moderation in inflicting punishment. It seems the equivalent of savagery or ferocity, the taking of delight in inflicting harm. This is altogether against reason and is sheer brutishness. The moral enormity is increased in proportion to the harm inflicted on another's person or property (ThAq ST 2a2ae, 159).

[T. C. O'BRIEN]

SADNESS. In addition to the wider psychology of sorrow, which enters moral theology in such various manifestations as *contrition, response to the vanity of life, *acedia, and *envy, sadness is treated as a special *emotion of the desirous sensitive appetite, Aristotle's *epithumikon*, Aquinas's *concupiscibile*. Sadness (*tristitia*), the antithesis of pleasure (*delectatio*) is the psychosomatic reaction to a hateful object recognized as present, no longer avoidable or impending. Diffused and poignant, the affective response to the presence of an evil-for-us and to the loss of a good-for-us runs the gamut from top to bottom of human experience. Classical moral theology does not endorse the Stoic inculcation of *apatheia*; sadness is regarded as morally neutral. It may prove a wry blessing when integrated in harmonious living, a form of indulgence when luxuriated in. But, mindful of the Passion and death of his savior, a Christian's approach to sadness cannot be merely ethical (ThAq ST 1a2ae, 35–39).

[T. GILBY]

SADOC, see ZADOK.

SADOLETO, JACOPO (1477–1547), cardinal and bp. of Carpentras. Born in Modena and reared to become a public servant in Ferrara under the Este, he elected to pursue his studies of the classics and went to Rome in 1498. Upon completion of his education, he was recognized as a minor poet and fine Latinist. In 1511 he was ordained; in 1527 he became bp. of Carpentras and in 1536, cardinal. During those years he gained a reputation as a reformer. Although unwilling to compromise with the Protestants on religious doctrine, S. was in favor of implementing reform measures in the Church and participated in a famous reform commission under Paul III. During the years 1527–38 he produced

his chief works; the most famous are *De Laudibus philosophiae* (1538), a humanistic work, and *In Pauli epistolam ad Romanos commentariorum libri tres* (1535), a controversial theological work. S. was respected by Protestants, and in 1539 he addressed a letter to Geneva, attempting to win the city back to Catholicism. John Calvin's letter in reply (1539) is a famous *apologia* for the Reformation; the exchange is contained in J. Calvin and J. Sadoleto, *Reformation Debate* (ed. J. C. Olin, 1966). As both a humanist and an advocate of church reform, S. represented the trend from Renaissance to reform in the Roman Church.
BIBLIOGRAPHY: R. Douglas, *Jacobo Sadoleto (1477–1547), Humanist and Reformer* (1959).

SADOMASOCHISM, a sexual deviation combining *sadism and *masochism. Psychology designates each component as pathological; their interaction in the case of a complementarily abnormal couple is not inconceivable. But sadomasochism (S.M.) has become a form of sexual experimentation encouraged in the name of the sexual revolution, for the sake of variety in sexual gratification. It then means the interaction between partners in a "game," with one playing the part of the sadist, the other of the masochist. As a general moral norm actions accessory to marital intercourse (foreplay) are as right as is the act they prepare for and perhaps enhance. A further norm is that to intend and to bring about orgasm to the exclusion of intercourse is morally disordered. Such norms may apply to the practice in question. By a broader measure quasi-sadomasochistic practices seem morally indefensible. They involve inflicting or risking bodily injury without due cause; they involve real cruelty or ferocity. They deface the beauty and dignity of the human person; and the special love and trust proper to conjugal charity; they mock matrimony as the sacramental sign of Christ's cherishing his spouse, the Church. The disorder is the worse if one of the spouses imposes such practices on the other.

[T. C. O'BRIEN]

SAETA, a Spanish religious folksong, sung unaccompanied during the halt of processions or other outdoor devotions, particularly during Lent.

[M. T. LEGGE]

SAFAVIDS, a dynasty of shahs of Iran from 1502, when Isma'el Safāvi captured Tabriz and became shah, until 1736 when Sunnite Afghans under Nādir Qūli declared their independence from the Shiite Safavids, invaded Persia, captured Isfahan, and deposed the last Safavid shah. Ishma'el Shah had made *Shiism a state religion in order to unify Persians against the Ottoman Turks in the West and the Uzbeks in the North, both of whom were Sunnite Muslims. In the mid-16th cent., European powers sought a place in Safavid Iran as another front against the Ottoman Turks. The Dynasty declined but was restored by Shah 'Abbas I, the Great, who ruled from 1587 to 1628. At 'Abbas' request, Anthony and Robert Sherley from England helped organize the Safavid army. After 'Abbas' death. Safavid power and control in the region declined until 1736 when the dynasty ended.

[R. J. LITZ]

SAGHAVART (*Sal' avart*), a high bulbous crown of stiffened cloth, decorated with embroidery and ornamental stones, topped by a small cross, worn by Armenian priestly celebrants and at times by deacons, but not by bps., who wear a Latin–style miter.

[A. CODY]

SAHAG THE GREAT, ST., see ISAAC THE GREAT, ST.

SAHAGÚN, JOHN OF, ST., see JOHN OF SAHAGÚN, ST.

SAHAK, ST., see ISAAC THE GREAT, ST.

SAIFI, EUTHYMIOS (*c.*1648–1723), architect of reunion of the Melchites with Rome. A Syrian Orthodox ordained in 1666, S. was named in 1682 metropolitan of Tyre and Sidon. One year later he submitted to the authority of the Holy See. He founded a monastic order, the Salvatorians, following the Rule of St. Basil. He was named by Rome apostolic administrator of Melchites in the Near East (1701). His missionary endeavors brought him to Palestine, Lebanon, and Arabia. In his new capacity he was excommunicated by the patriarch of Constantinople and suffered imprisonment. S. wrote an important work in Arabic *Kitāb ad-dalāla al-lāmi 'a* justifying the doctrine of the Western Church.

[J. R. AHERNE]

SAIHOJI GARDEN, KYOTO (Kokedera Garden), Japanese garden of the Moss Temple, so-called because completely covered with a variety of mosses (*kokedara*), founded (710–784), converted into Zen monastery by Musō Soseki (1275–1351) with pond shaped as the Chinese character for heart as focal point. Only the small house for the tea ceremony (Shōnantei) remains.

[M. J. DALY]

SAILER, JOHANN MICHAEL (1751–1832), bp. of Regensburg from 1829, theologian and educator. He became a Jesuit in 1770, but because of the Society's suppression (1773) was ordained a diocesan priest in 1775. He taught at the Univ. of Ingolstadt (1780), Dillingen (1784–94), and Landshut (1800). During his career he was accused of unorthodoxy, esp. of rationalism, possibly because he ignored scholasticism and based his teaching on the Fathers and on thinkers of the 17th and 18th centuries. His nomination to the See of Augsburg in 1819 was rejected by Rome. He was finally vindicated in 1821, being appointed coadjutor with the right of succession to the See of Regensburg. In his teaching, writing (works: 41 v., 1830–45), and episcopal administration he is credited with trying to restore

Christian life and learning after the ravages of the Enlightenment, the Napoleonic Wars, and state attacks on church autonomy. S.'s works on catechetics and pastoral theology are of special merit. His contacts with Protestant leaders were remarkably friendly.

[T. C. O'BRIEN]

SAINT. (1) In the NT St. Paul esp. addresses his fellow Christians as "the saints" in the sense of those who are being or have been sanctified (see Acts 9.32; 1 Cor 6.11) by the gifts of grace and baptism. (2) In ecclesiastical usage the term is a title for one who has been canonized in any of the ways of *canonization. The cognate titles, indicating recognized sanctity of life (see HEROIC VIRTUE), are "blessed" and "venerable": the first indicates the completed process of beatification and the authorization of public cult; the second indicates that the cause of a "servant of God" has reached the point of acknowledgment of heroic virtue, but not of authorization of public cult.

[T. C. O'BRIEN]

ST. AGNES, SISTERS OF, a congregation founded by Casper Rehrl, an Austrian missionary who needed women to teach Christian doctrine to his already established parishes in Wisconsin during his absences. Pius IX gave his permission to begin the new community with a group of three young women. In 1864 Sister M. Agnes (Anna Mary Hazotte) was elected first superior at Barton. The congregation moved from Barton to Fond du Lac, Wis., in 1870 and in 1875 Rev. Francis Haas, wrote its rule and constitutions based on the Rule of St. Augustine. The work of the sisters continued to be education until 1896, when they opened St. Agnes Hospital in Fond du Lac; they later expanded their educational works to include institutions of higher education. The community also works in the missions of Central and South America. In 1975 the sisters numbered 722 in 68 houses.

[R. C. CLIGGETT]

ST. ALBANS, ABBEY OF, former Benedictine monastery located at present-day St. Albans in Hertfordshire, England, at the site of ancient Verulamium, about 20 miles NW of London. It is the reputed site of the martyrdom of St. Albanus, who suffered under Diocletian. In the time of St. Bede the Venerable, there was already a church at the site commemorating the martyr. The abbey was founded *c.*790 by King Offa of Mercia (d. 796) in expiation for his murder of King Ethelbert of East Anglia. It was refounded *c.*969, after the period of Viking devastation. In the 11th cent. the first Norman abbot, Paul of Caen, rebuilt the monastic building and the still extant abbey church. The English Pope Adrian IV gave it episcopal exemption and precedence over all other English abbeys. For three cent. it was an artistic and literary center of England, notable for its school of chroniclers, including Roger of Wendover, Matthew Paris, William Rishanger, and Thomas Walsingham, who provided a continuous account of the history of the abbey, its abbots, and, by reflection, all of England. One of its abbots was the early English humanist John Whethamstede (d. 1465). The abbey suffered during the War of the Roses, was given in commendation to Cardinal Wolsey in 1521, was suppressed by Henry VIII in 1539, and was surrendered by the abbot and 38 monks on December 5, 1540. The abbey church escaped destruction, served as a parish church and eventually became the cathedral church of the Anglican See of St. Albans.

[E. J. DILLON]

ST. ALEXANDER OF OROSH (OROSHI), ABBEY OF, a monastery located in the village of Orosh in the Mirdite Mountain region of N Albania. Originally a Basilian monastery dedicated to St. Alexander the Martyr, it was later given to the Benedictines. Following Turkish occupation in the 15th cent. the abbey was suppressed and its territory divided between the parishes of Orosh and St. Nicholas in the Diocese of Lesh. In 1888, Rome detached this territory, restoring it as an abbey *nullius* (independent from the diocese) and assigning certain parishes to the abbot's jurisdiction. The ordinary (bishop) holds the title of abbot and is elected both by members of the abbey and the Albanian secular clergy. The first bp. under this arrangement was J. Gjonali, and the last, Francis Gjini, who was murdered by the Albanian Communists in 1947. Since then, the monastery has been without an abbot. It is interesting to note that all the Catholics of this abbey-diocese belong to the Latin Rite. BIBLIOGRAPHY: F. Cordignano "Antichi monasteri benedettini in Albania, nella tradizione e nelle leggende popolari," CivCatt 80 (1929) 3:26–28; 4:507–515.

[L. NEMEC]

ST. AMAND-LES-EAUX, ABBEY OF (Elnonense, S. Amandus in Pabula), Benedictine abbey, on the Elnon in Pévèle, founded by St. Amandus, bp. of Maastricht (d.679). It was endowed by King Dagobert in 639. Many bps. came from this cloister, e.g., Abbot Agelfred, nephew of Charlemagne and bp. of Liège, Abbot Gozlin (d. c.887), bp. and defender of Paris. In 1014, Bl. Richard of St. Vanne restored monastic discipline at St.-Amand, and his successor, Abbot Malbode (d.1063) reformed many other abbeys. In 1505 the monastery was amalgamated with the Congregation of Bursfeld, and in 1608 with the exempt Benedictines under Abbot Nicholas du Bois. The abbey was suppressed during the Revolution; and only the palace, (now the town hall), the façade of the church, and its tower remain standing. The 17th-cent. tower, 295 feet high, is outstanding for its decoration inspired by the Spanish Renaissance.

[J. DAOUST]

SAINT-AMANT, MARC ANTOINE GIRARD, DE (1594–1661), French poet and one of the original members of the French Academy. Born a Huguenot, St.-A. was converted to Catholicism by the bishop of Nantes and spent much of his life traveling to America, Africa, and to various places in Europe. His stay in Italy inspired his satire, *La Rome ridicule* (1643), while the English were satirized in *L'Albion* (1644). His heroic idyll, *Moïse sauvé* (1653), a religious epic on the finding of Moses, possesses many of those individualistic and imaginative qualities found in much of his poetry, in which he takes a "preclassic" liberty in combining manneristically the most diverse elements. BIBLIOGRAPHY: F. Gourier, *Étude des oeuvres poétiques de Saint-Amant* (1961); R. A. Sayce, *French Biblical Epic in the Seventeenth Century* (1955) ch. 7.

[R. N. NICOLICH]

ST.-ANDRÉ-LEZ-BRUGES, ABBEY OF (S. Andreas de Zevenkerken prope Brugas, Brugense), Benedictine monastery founded as a priory (1098) by Robert le Frison (or, of Jerusalem), count of Flanders. It was placed under the rule of Affligem in 1105 and became an abbey in 1188 (diocese of Tournai; at present Bruges, Belgium). In 1516 it was amalgamated with the Congregation of Bursfeld and disappeared during the Revolution. In 1899 Gerard van Caloen, a monk of Maredsous, promoted to archabbot and bp. in Brazil, founded a procuratorship in the same spot, which was erected as an abbey in 1902. He restored the title of the former monastery of Zevenkerken, becoming its 43d abbot. His successor, Theodore Nève (1912–57), multiplied foundations all over the world including the mission of Katanga; Chinese priory of Si-shan, later Ch'eng-tu, at present transferred to California; the archabbey of Tyniec in Poland (1939); the monastery of Asirvanam in India (1950). The abbey has a world-wide liturgical influence through its publications. It recently established a foundation in Ottingnies, in the Walloon section of Brabant, near the future French language Univ. of Louvain. BIBLIOGRAPHY: Cottineau 2:2589.

[J. DAOUST]

ST. ANDREW, DAUGHTERS OF THE HOLY CROSS OF, a religious congregation founded in 1807 at Maillé in the Diocese of Poitiers by St. André Hubert Fournet and St. Jeanne Elizabeth Bichier des Anges. Its work is teaching in primary, secondary, and technical schools, helping the sick, the aged, and priests in parishes. The congregation also has missions in the Congo, Canada, Spain, Italy, Belgium, and Argentina. The Holy See approved it in 1867 and its motherhouse was established at La Puye, Vienne. In 1975 the sisters numbered 1,378 in 197 houses.

[R. C. CLIGGETT]

ST. ANDREWS, UNIVERSITY OF, the oldest university in Scotland, situated on the coast of Fife, near Edinburgh. It developed from an association of teachers and scholars who wanted to make available in Scotland the educational opportunities closed to Scottish students because of their exclusion from Oxford, Orléans, and Paris during the Great Schism. Chartered by Bp. Henry Wardlaw in 1411 and recognized as a *studium generale* by the antipope Benedict XIII in 1413, St. Andrews received a royal charter in 1532. Consisting by 1537 of three colleges—St. Salvator's, St. Leonard's, and St. Mary's—the university was confirmed and granted papal privileges by Nicholas V, Pius II, Paul II and Paul III. During the Reformation the university suffered reverses from which it did not recover until 1574 when a commission under the historian and scholar, George Buchanan, began a series of reforms that continued into the 17th century. In 1747 St. Salvator's and St. Leonard's were united, and in 1897 the University College, Dundee, a science center, became affiliated. In its present organization, St. Andrews comprises faculties of arts, science, social science, medicine, law, applied science, and divinity. The teaching staff averages about 534; enrollment, 3,620 men and women. The library houses approximately 660,000 volumes. Among its noted professors and students are Thomas Chalmers, Lewis Campbell, Bernard Bosanquet, and Herbert Jenning Rose. The playwright and novelist, James M. Barrie, the Norwegian explorer, Fridtjof Nansen, and the South African field marshal and prime minister, Jan Christian Smuts, were among its rectors. BIBLIOGRAPHY: H. Rashdall, *Universities of Europe in the Middle Ages* (ed. F. M. Powicke and A. B. Emden, 3 v., 1936).

[M. B. MURPHY]

ST. ANNE, DAUGHTERS OF (Associazione delle Figlie di Sant' Anna), a congregation founded by the widow Rose Gattorno in Piacenza, Italy, in 1866, as a result of her experience in helping Giuseppe Frassinetti to direct his pious associations. The works of the congregation are elementary education, hospitals, prisons, sanatoriums, homes for the blind, deaf, the poor, children, and boarding houses for young women. The motherhouse is in Rome; other houses are in France, Spain, the Near East, Africa, and Latin America. In 1975 the sisters numbered 2,952 in 287 houses.

[R. C. CLIGGETT]

ST. ANNE, SISTERS OF (Soeurs de Sainte Anne de Lachine), a congregation founded by Marie Esther Sureau-Blondin (Mother Mary Anne) at Vaudreuil, Québec, Canada, in 1850. Mother Anne established rural schools for the poor Canadian boys and girls, Protestant as well as Catholic. Later the Sisters also opened three liberal arts colleges. The rule, approved in 1903, was based on that of St. Ignatius and on the inspiration of gospel women in their service of the early Church. In 1858 the sisters journeyed to Vancouver Island in W Canada, where they opened hospitals, Indian residential schools, boarding schools, and sanatariums for the aged and destitute. In 1880 the community gradually took over Franco-American bilingual schools in N.Y., Mass., R.I., and Maine. They staff foreign missions in British Columbia, the Yukon Territory, Alaska, and Haiti; from 1934 to 1942 they were also in Japan. In 1975 the sisters numbered 1,747 in 148 houses.

[R. C. CLIGGETT]

ST. ANNE'S FUGUE, popular title given to Bach's organ fugue in E flat, so named because its theme is the same as that of the English hymn-tune, "St. Anne."

[M. T. LEGGE]

ST. ANSELM PRIORY, Tokyo, a monastery established in 1947 as a postwar foundation of the Benedictines from St. John Abbey, Collegeville, Minn., at the invitation of Bp. Peter Totsuo Doi. Father Hildebrand Yaiser, first prior, also served as pastor of the adjacent parish. In 1956, the church was consecrated. Later, school, library, and assembly hall were added to the completed priory. The American architect, Antonin Raymond planned the church as central to the rectory–priory and school buildings. In addition to its architectural design, St. Anselm's priory is a viable center for the culture and the faith it represents. The priory, located in busy downtown Tokyo, is a symbol of the need for understanding between Christians and non-Christians. Postwar in structure, the priory would seem to indicate that perhaps the most efficacious American–Japanese understanding will be permanently achieved on a religious basis. BIBLIOGRAPHY: J. Pichard, *Les Églises nouvelles à travers le monde* (1960); C. J. Barry, *Worship and Work* (1956) 319–320.

[L. NEMEC]

ST. ANSGAR'S SCANDINAVIAN CATHOLIC LEAGUE, association for the apostolate in Scandinavian countries, founded 1910. With headquarters in New York City, the League works by appeal, esp. to Catholics of Swedish, Danish, and Norwegian ancestry, for prayer and financial support. It publishes pamphlets and an annual magazine with a report on the Church in Scandinavia.

[T. C. O'BRIEN]

ST.-ANTOINE-DE-VIENNOIS, ABBEY OF, the former central house of the Hospital Brothers of St. Anthony, with numerous dependent commanderies throughout Europe, located in the department of Isère, France, in the Diocese of Grenoble, formerly the Archdiocese of Vienne. It originated as the Church of Saint-Antoine-de-la-Mothe, built to receive the relics of St. Anthony of Egypt brought back from Constantinople in the late 11th century. The church was entrusted to the Benedictines of Montmajour c.1083, was erected into a priory in 1101, and consecrated in 1119 by Pope Callixtus II, a former abp. of Vienne. From this religious center Gaston de Dauphiné founded the Antonine Hospitallers c.1095. Conflicts between the latter and the Benedictines led Boniface VIII in 1297 to detach a church from Montmajour and raise it to an abbey under the Antonines' Grand Master. It was a center of pilgrimage during the 14th and 15th cent., was pillaged five times by the Huguenots in the late 16th cent., declined despite reform attempts of Brunel de Grammont in the 17th cent., was joined to the Knights of Malta by Pius VI in the 18th cent., and was suppressed during the French Revolution. The abbey church now serves as a parish church. The cloister was recently occupied by a minor seminary, a distillery, and municipal offices.

[E. J. DILLON]

ST. ASSAPH MONASTERY (earlier Llanelwy), in Flintshire, Wales, a monastic foundation made reputedly by St. Kentigern c. 560, and named after one of his disciples. It had lost its monastic character by c. 1066 and became a diocesan seat. BIBLIOGRAPHY: Knowles-Hadcock; A. W. Wade-Evans, *Welsh Christian Origins* (1934).

[C. MCGRATH]

ST. AUGUSTINE, ABBEY OF, first–known monastery of the Anglo-Saxon Church, founded at Canterbury by King Ethelbert of Kent at the urging of St. Augustine of Canterbury, c. 598. The new conventual church was consecrated in 613 by Augustine's successor in the See of Canterbury, Lawrence, and dedicated to Saints Peter and Paul. The body of St. Augustine was reinterred in the North Porch. The first 10 abps. of Canterbury and several kings were buried there, until Abp. Cuthbert left contrary instructions for burial. The abbey attempted to be exempt from the authority of Canterbury and there were chronic enmity and litigation between the monks and the cathedral chapter. The abbey was probably not Benedictine at the beginning, and the Benedictine Rule might not have been introduced until the time of the Abbot Sigeric (c. 980). In 978 St. Dunstan rededicated the conventual church in honor of SS Peter and Paul and St. Augustine, since it was popularly named after its founder. The abbey was richly endowed from the beginning and was largely rebuilt in the 13th century. In 1051 Leo IX granted the abbots precedence over all others except the abbot of Monte Cassino. When Henry VIII dissolved it in 1538, there were 30 monks and a prior. In 1848 an Anglican missionary college was founded on the ruins of the abbey, now the site of St. Augustine's College, an Anglican theological college associated with King's College, London

[E. J. DILLON]

ST. AUGUSTINE, SISTERS OF CHARITY OF, a congregation founded in response to needs in the Diocese of Cleveland in 1851. Bp. Amadeus Rappe welcomed Mother M. Bernardine Cabaret and Sister M. Françoise Guillement, Augustinian Sisters of St. Louis Hospital, Boulogne-sur-Mer, France, to the U.S. They spent their first winter visiting the sick and the poor in their homes. The following year they opened Cleveland's first general hospital. Mother M. Ursula Bissonnette became the first native-born superior. In 1853 she established a small home for dependent boys which later became Parmadale. After the Civil War, St. Vincent's Charity Hospital was established to meet the needs of the wounded and today has greatly expanded to serve much of downtown Cleveland. St. Ann's Hospital and an infant home were opened the same year. In addition to hospitals and homes, the sisters are engaged in educational endeavors at all levels. The congregation follows the Rule of St. Augustine and has as its motto, "In all things charity." The motherhouse is located at West Richfield, about 20 miles south of Cleveland. In 1975 the sisters numbered 255 in 15 houses.

[R. C. CLIGGETT]

ST. BARTHOLOMEW'S DAY MASSACRE, the most widely known of several slaughters of the *Huguenots in France; it began in Paris, Aug. 24, 1572. It was probably not premeditated but an expedient adopted on the spur of the moment by Catherine de Médicis. After the third of the *Wars of Religion, Catherine, following her new policy of conciliation, allowed the Huguenot leader Gaspard de Coligny to hold an influential position at the court and to plan with King Charles IX a campaign against Spain in support of William of Orange. Coligny favored an all-out campaign; Catherine was against a major war. She decided to liquidate the Huguenot leader, whose increasing influence over the king displeased her. At her instigation an incident occurred on Aug. 22, in which Coligny was wounded by two shots from an arquebus. Fearing that the ensuing royal inquiry might reveal her own role in the event, Catherine extracted the king's consent to a mass slaughter as a countermeasure against an alleged Huguenot antiroyalist conspiracy. The massacre, in which Coligny was the first murdered, lasted several days and spread to the provinces. No reliable statistics of the number of victims are available; the figures quoted vary from 3,000 to 10,000. The immediate result of the massacre was the fourth of the Wars of Religion. BIBLIOGRAPHY: W. J. Stankiewicz, NCE 7:201–204 s.v. "Huguenots," with bibliog.; P. Erlanger, *St. Bartholomew's Night* (tr. P. O'Brian, 1962); H. Noguères, *Massacre of Saint Bartholomew* (tr. C. E. Engel, 1962).

[W. J. STANKIEWICZ]

ST. BASIL THE GREAT, ORDER OF, see BASILIANS.

ST.-BAVON OF GHENT, ABBEY OF, Benedictine monastery whose foundation is attributed to St. Amandus, probably c. 642, in Ghent, Belgium. The name derives from the famous hermit St. Bavon, who was converted from his worldly life by a sermon preached by St. Amandus. He lived as a recluse a short distance from the monastery. After his death his cult gradually developed, and he was made patron of the dioceses of Ghent and of Haarlem, Holland. The abbey was ravaged by fire in 813 but was rebuilt. Later, after its destruction by the Normans, it was restored by Arnauld, count of Flanders, and St.-Gérard de Brogne. Henceforth the monks followed the Rule of St. Benedict and the community flourished. Actively engaged in the development of uncultivated land, the abbey prospered, acquiring great wealth.

In 1536 the monastery was secularized, the monks continuing in residence. In 1540 it was demolished by Charles V. Some buildings of different eras remain, however. Its particular boast is the renowned *Ghent Altarpiece*, inscribed by Hubert and Jan Van Eyck and dated 1432. The panels were reassembled in 1920, though *The Just Judges*, stolen in 1934, was never recovered. *The Crucifixion* by Justus of Ghent, *Christ among the Doctors* of Pourbus, and Rubens' *Conversion of St. Bavon* are further treasures. BIBLIOGRAPHY: L. van Puyvelde, *Van Eyck, the Holy Lamb* (1947).

[S. A. HEENEY]

ST. BENEDICT, OBLATES OF, see OBLATES OF ST. BENEDICT.

ST. BENOÎT DU LAC, ABBEY OF, a Benedictine monastery in the Province of Quebec, Canada, founded in 1912 by Fontenelle of the Congregation of France (Solesmes). It became a center of the Gregorian chant revival; its theory and practice of chant were commonly adopted by schools throughout Canada. It attained the status of abbey in 1952. Its choir attained international reputation. In 1958 there were 78 monks, including 25 priests. BIBLIOGRAPHY: S. Hilpisch, *Benedictinism Through Changing Centuries* (tr. from German by L. J. Doyle; 1958) p.139 *passim*.

[E. J. DILLON]

ST.-BENOÎT-SUR-LOIRE, ABBEY OF, Benedictine abbey in the Diocese of Orléans, France, founded in the mid-7th cent. by Léodebold, abbot of St-Aignan d'Orléans with monks of Subiaco. The site may have been a Druid shrine at a bend in the Loire. Originally called Fleury-sur-Loire, the abbey gave up the patronage of St. Peter for that of St. Benedict when the latter's relics were translated there. The present church was begun by Abbot Gauzlin in 1026, augmented by Abbot Bartholomew in 1218. Saint-Benoît became one of the most powerful abbeys of the Middle Ages, reaching its peak from the 10th to the 13th cent., with learned abbots that included Theodulf, Abbo, and Hugh, an active scriptorium and a library containing Latin classics and works of the Latin Fathers. It was a center of Cluniac reform and from it St. Oswald of York (d. 992), a monk of Fleury, brought the reform to England. With Capetian support the abbots claimed primacy in Gaul. In 1562 the library was lost in the depredations of the Huguenots. In 1627, Richelieu, as commendatory abbot, introduced the Maurist reform. In 1790 the abbey was suppressed during the Revolution, the monastery destroyed and the church turned to parish use. In 1944, the abbot of Pierre-Qui-Vire was able to send a community of monks to restore Saint-Benoît to its Romanesque and Gothic splendor.

[E. J. DILLON]

ST. BERNARD, MONASTERY OF, see GREAT SAINT BERNARD, MONASTERY OF.

ST. BERNARD ABBEY, Benedictine monastery of the American Cassinese Congregation, founded in 1891 near Cullman, Alabama, 50 miles N of Birmingham. At that time it was the diocese of Mobile, but is now the diocese of Birmingham, Alabama. In 1975 there were 57 monks, including 42 priests. The abbey has a liberal arts college attached. BIBLIOGRAPHY: Cottineau 2:2615.

[E. J. DILLON]

ST. BERTIN, ABBEY OF S. Bertinus, Sithiense, Benedictine monastery established *c.*648, originally on a mountain near Ham, by St. Omer, bp. of Thérouanne. The foundation was put under the direction of monks of Luxeuil. Eight years later the monks moved to Sithiu, an island of the River Aa (at present Saint-Omer, Pas-de-Calais, France). There they founded an abbey with St. Bertin as first abbot. It was sacked by the Normans in 847 and 861, and it burned five times between the years 896 and 1152. However, it recovered from each of these disasters and reached the peak of its greatness in the 16th century. The abbey was a great cultural center and was renowned for its scriptorium. The names of many notable persons were associated with its history; e.g., Childibert III; Baudouin the Iron-Hand, count of Flanders; Thomas Becket; and St. Louis IX. Today only the ruins of the church remain, a vast Gothic edifice constructed between 1330 and 1520. Its tower collapsed in 1947. BIBLIOGRAPHY: Cottineau 2:2615–18.

[J. DAOUST]

ST. CALAIS, ABBEY OF, former Benedictine abbey in the diocese of Le Mans, Sarthe, France, first mentioned by Gregory of Tours (576), who called it Anninsola or Anille, and supposedly founded by Carileffus (hence, Calais) and his companions *c.*515–542. The remains of Carileffus reputedly rest there. The first–known abbots, Sigiramnus and St. Siviard (d. 683) obtained territorial rights from King Thierry III. Pope Nicholas I and a council at Verberie (863) upheld the abbey's autonomy vis à vis the bishopric of Le Mans. Abandoned and destroyed during the 9th-cent. Viking rampages, the abbey was rebuilt during the 10th and 11th cent., burned during the Hundred Years War, and pillaged by the Calvinists in 1562. It was taken over by the Maurists in 1659. Its greatest medieval abbot was Jean Tibergeau (d. 1415). When the abbey was suppressed during the Revolution, the abbey church was converted into a parish church, and the cloister into a municipal building.

[E. J. DILLON]

ST. CASIMIR, SISTERS OF, diocesan congregation founded in 1907 to instruct the children of Lithuanian immigrants. Rev. Anthony Staniukynas was delegated by Bp. John W. Shanahan of Harrisburg, Pa., and a group of his priests to establish the congregation, while Casimira Kaupas, a novice in Switzerland, was being trained to be its first superior. With two companions she came to the U.S. and studied under the Sisters of the Immaculate Heart of Mary at Mt. St. Mary's in Scranton, Pa. In 1907 these sisters opened their first convent at Mt. Carmel in the Harrisburg diocese. In 1911 the sisters were invited to work in Chicago, in 1920 they opened a branch of their community in the Republic of Lithuania, and in 1941 they opened missions in Argentina. By 1975 they numbered 402 sisters in 41 houses.

[R. C. CLIGGETT]

ST. CATHERINE, DEVOUT VIRGINS OF, or Sisters of St. Catherine of Alexandria, a congregation founded to teach young girls and to care for the sick in their homes and in hospitals. The foundress was Regina Protmann, and the congregation was established in Braunsberg, East Prussia, now Brauniewo, Poland. It follows the Rule of St. Augustine and was one of the first congregations of women with simple vows. Its rule was approved by the local bp., Martin Kromer, in 1582; the modern constitutions were approved by the Holy See in 1902. After the *Kulturkampf* the sisters' apostolates were more in the field of nursing, hospitals, care of orphans, and establishing homes for young women. The motherhouse is in Grottaferrata-Bivio in the Diocese of Frascati near Rome. In 1975 the sisters numbered 1,001 in 104 houses.

[R. C. CLIGGETT]

ST. CATHERINE, MONASTERY OF, a Greek Orthodox monastery located on the shady slope of Jebel Mûsā, traditional site of the burning bush in the Sinai Peninsula. Founded (527) by the Byzantine Emperor Justinian I, it became in the 7th cent. a refuge for the scattered Christians threatened by the rise of Islam. During the Middle Ages it was a pilgrimage center. Its independence was recognized by Constantinople (Istanbul) in 1575. Today its abbot is also abp. of Sinai, Paran, and Raithu; he is elected by the brotherhood and consecrated by the Greek Orthodox Patriarch of Jerusalem. The Muslim Bedouin Arabs who live nearby have always guarded the monastery and have been in turn supported by it. Because of its isolation, it has survived as a relic of an age long past. Some of its icons antedate the iconoclast controversy. Its library contains over 3,000 MSS, mostly Greek and Arabic, but also in Syriac, Georgian, Slavonic, and other tongues. The famous Codex Sinaiticus, 4th-cent. Greek biblical MS, was found there in 1844 by C. Tischendorf; it is now in the British Museum in London. The Codex Syriacus, a Syriac text of the Gospels (*c.*400), is still at St. Catherine's.

[E. J. DILLON]

ST. CLAUDE, ABBEY OF, former Benedictine monastery, motherhouse of Lauçonne, La Balme, and Romain-

môtier, forerunner of the present Diocese of Saint-Claude, suffragan of Besançon, in the Department of Jura, France. Founded as the Abbey of Condat (*c.*425–450) by SS. Romanus and Lupicinus, it was later known as Saint-Oyen-de-Joux after its third abbot (Eugendus Jurensis). In about 510 it developed its own rule, but subsequently adopted the Benedictine rule. It was renamed Saint-Claude (*c.*1213) when relics of its 12th abbot, Claudius of Condat, were interred there. From the 14th to the 16th cent. it was a pilgrimage center and an autonomous territory of the Holy Roman Empire until it became a part of France in 1674. Religious life suffered under such commendatory abbots as Cardinal d'Estrées (1681–1742). In 1742 Pope Benedict XIV erected the abbey into the See of Saint-Claude, suffragan of Lyon. The cathedral chapter held the abbey's dependencies until the French Revolution. The abbey was a prominent part of the controversy over mortmain, involving Voltaire. The Cathedral of St. Peter, built between the 14th and the 18th cent. still stands.

[E. J. DILLON]

SAINT-CYRAN, ABBÉ DE (Jean Duvergier de Hauranne; 1581–1643), theologian and spiritual adviser whose writings and activities were very influential in 17th-cent. France, esp. in connection with *Jansenism. Born in Bayonne of a rising merchant family, he studied theology at the Jesuit college in Louvain. There he met Cornelius *Jansen; in seclusion (1611–16) the two made a diligent study of the Scriptures and the Fathers, esp. St. Augustine. (There is no reason to suppose, however, that Saint-Cyran collaborated on Jansen's later *Augustinus.*) Ordained priest (1618), later made abbot *in commendam* of Saint-Cyran (1620), a title by which he was generally known, he lived in Paris, where he became an intimate friend of the founder of the Oratory, Bérulle. He gained fame under the name of Petrus Aurelius by defending the vicar apostolic of England, Richard Smith, against the Jesuits, thus giving wide publicity to Oratorian ideas on the priesthood and the superiority of the secular over the religious clergy. He made further enemies by defending the *Chapelet du Saint Sacrement* of Agnès *Arnauld (1627). But it was his open stand against Richelieu and the extreme position of some of his spiritual direction demanding perfect contrition for absolution that finally led to his imprisonment at Vincennes (1638). At the trial St. Vincent de Paul paid tribute to his zeal for souls and for the Church. During his nearly 5 years of imprisonment he maintained his influence as a spiritual director both by letter and by the visits of a circle of influential clients. His influence on the Jansenist movement was chiefly by his direction of the members of the Arnauld family, esp. Mère Angélique and Antoine, whom he encouraged to write *De la fréquente communion*. Saint-Cyran's spiritual doctrine, resembling that of St. Francis de Sales, reveals him as a devout man; some of his ideas on the priesthood, obedience to a spiritual director, and reliance on grace became standard themes in French devotional literature. Jansenist interpretation of predestination and the Jansenist penchant for intrigue are also suggested in his letters and spiritual treatises. His influence extended beyond the RC Church: John *Wesley translated many of his letters and was thoroughly familiar with his doctrine, although he naturally adapted it to his own audience. BIBLIOGRAPHY: J. Orcibal, *Saint-Cyran et le Jansénisme* (1961); bibliog. for Jansenism.

ST. DAVID'S MONASTERY (in Welsh, Mynyw or Tyddewi), in Pembrokeshire, Wales, a monastic foundation made by St. David some time after 530; became a center of extreme asceticism. To it belonged an extensive monastic parish of at least 53 churches. The historian Gildas was a monk here. It became the diocesan cathedral and chief seat of the British Church in Wales all through the Middle Ages, remaining monastic until the arrival of the first Norman bishop in 1115, when it was being occupied by a body of the "claswyr." BIBLIOGRAPHY: G. Williams, *Welsh Church from Conquest to Reformation* (1962); A. W. Wade-Evans, *Welsh Christian Origins* (1934); J. E. Lloyd, *History of Wales* (2 v., 1948).

[C. MCGRATH]

ST. DENIS, STYLE OF, style of illuminated MSS of latter half of 9th cent. associated with the emperor Charles the Bald (lay abbot of St. Denis), lavishly illuminated with gold, acanthus leaf, and jeweled borders in florid foliate forms and linear figural images, related to the Reims school in initials and figures. The *Psalter of Charles the Bald, Coronation Sacramentary, Codex aureus* of St. Emmeram are finest examples.

[M. J. DALY]

ST. DENIS-EN-FRANCE, ABBEY OF, ancient abbey near Paris closely associated with the French monarchy. According to tradition it is located at the site of burial of the 3d–cent. martyr bishop, St. Denys (Dionysius). King Dagobert I (d. 639) rebuilt the basilica and abbey as a repository for royal tombs. It remained linked to the monarchy through Carolingian and Capetian times. The Benedictines took over the abbey in 656. Charlemagne rebuilt it (775), and the abbot Hilduin (819), translator and biographer of *Pseudo-Dionysius, gave currency to the identity of St. Denys with the Areopagite. The abbey was reformed by Odilo of Cluny in 1008; in Capetian times it enjoyed enormous prestige under the Abbot Suger, a close collaborator of Louis VI and Louis VII. Suger (1152) rebuilt the basilica and collected and continued the abbey chronicles. Under the patronage of St. Louis and Queen Blanche, another renovation was begun in the time of Abbot Eudes (1231) and finished under Matthew of Vendôme (1281) in the Gothic style of the architect Pierre de Montereau. Its royal ties brought it continued pillaging and destruction during subsequent cent.: in the Hundred Years War, in the civil

and religious wars after the Reformation, and esp. in the Revolution. Becoming commendatory in 1528, it was the center of the new Congregation of the Exempts in 1607 and was given to the Maurists in 1633. It suffered further from ill-advised remodeling after the Revolution and from 19th– and 20th–cent. wars. BIBLIOGRAPHY: Cottineau 2:2650–57.

[E. J. DILLON]

SAINT DOMINIQUE, see HAITI.

ST. EDMUND, SOCIETY OF, originally known as Prêtres Auxiliaires, a congregation of priests and brothers founded to conduct missions and retreats to counteract Jansenism and to help overburdened priests. The society was founded by Ven. Jean Baptiste Muard in 1843 at Pontigny, France, under the patronage of St. Edmund Rich, abp. of Canterbury, who died in exile at Pontigny in 1240. At Mont-Saint-Michel a house was opened in 1867 to give public honor to Michael, patron of France. In 1879 the society began to direct its attention to education at the College of the Immaculate Conception, Laval, France, and in 1893 at the College of Chateau Gontier, Brittany. It founded St. Edmund's School at Sens in 1895.

In 1891 the fathers endeavored to open houses in Montreal but found their work in Vermont instead, finally establishing their scholasticate in Swanton in 1904 and building St. Michael's College for men in Winooski. They also worked among the Negroes and Indians in the United States. By 1963 the society staffed parishes in France, England, Canada, and the U.S., where it also founded a college, a hospital, and elementary schools. In 1975 the society had four houses and numbered 124, of whom 97 were priests.

[R. C. CLIGGETT]

ST. ELMO'S FIRE, bright blue flashes of light seen on mastheads before and after bad weather attributed to the intercession of St. Elmo or St. Erasmus by Neapolitan sailors who honored him as their patron. It is a phenomenon of nature caused by the presence of electrical power in the vicinity of an object such as a masthead, or, currently, the wing of an aircraft. BIBLIOGRAPHY: L. L. Rummel, NCE 12:879; Butler, 2:453–454.

[F. H. BRIGHAM]

SAINT-ÉVREMOND, CHARLES DE MARGUETEL DE SAINT–DENIS DE (*c*.1614–1703), French man of letters exiled in England (1661) as a result of his criticism of Mazarin's politics. One of his best works is his ironic *Conversation du maréchal d'Hocquincourt avec le P. Canaye* (1665), which satirizes religious fideism and reveals his skepticism influenced by the Epicurean freethinker, Gassendi. As a representative of the divorce of secular ethics from religion and as a deist and a believer in tolerance, St.-É. can be considered a forerunner of the Enlightenment. Among his other writings on religion and ethics, most of which were published after his death by his Huguenot friend, Des Maizeaux, are: *Conversation avec M. d'Aubigny* (1662); *Lettre au maréchal de Créqui, qui m'avait demandé en quelle situation était mon esprit . . . dans ma vieillesse* (1671); and *Sur la religion* (1680). St.-É. is buried in Westminster Abbey. BIBLIOGRAPHY: H. T. Barnwell, *Les idées morales et critiques de Saint-Évremond* (1957); A. M. Schmidt, *Saint-Évremond ou l'humaniste impur* (1932).

[R. N. NICOLICH]

ST.-ÉVROULT-D'OUCHE, ABBEY OF, former Benedictine abbey in the forest of Ouche, on the Charentonne, in Ferté-Fresnel, Orne, France, formerly in the Diocese of Lisieux, and now in Séez. Founded by St. Évroult (Lat., Ebrulphus), its first abbot (d. 596), a Merovingian courtier who led a group of hermits into the forest of Ouche (Lat., Utica), it was dedicated to Our Lady of the Forest and to St. Peter. It was destroyed by the Vikings in the 9th cent., was re-occupied in the mid-11th cent. by grant of William, son of Giroie, monk at Bec, and became an independent monastery that enjoyed first Norman and then royal patronage, prospering until the Hundred Years' War. It was here that the monk Ordericus Vitalis wrote his *Ecclesiastical History*, the most important single source for Norman monastic history up to the year 1141. In 1628 the Maurists undertook reform. During the Revolution (1790) the monks were dispersed and the buildings were destroyed.

[E. J. DILLON]

SAINT-EXUPÉRY, ANTOINE DE (1900–44), French novelist and essayist, who drew from his experiences as an aviator a philosophy of heroic humanism. St.-E. was commissioned a pilot by an air force conscript (1921), and despite ventures in industry and journalism, flying remained his career. An exile in the U.S. after the fall of France (1940), he returned to the war zone and died flying reconnaissance with a reconstituted French unit. A Catholic until age 18, he progressively lost his faith. Yet, because he defined his goal as a writer as restoring spiritual awareness to modern man (cf. his *Lettre au général X,* 1943), Catholic critics tend to regard his writing as Christian literature. An evolution in depth characterizes his work, from man acting (*Night Flight,* 1931), to man reasoning, to man contemplating (*The Little Prince,* 1943), and to the scriptural-like *summa* of the unfinished *Citadelle* (1948). As a humanist, he affirms the fraternity of man as the highest value and sees in science and technology, not necessarily the masters of man, but new elements potentially leading to greater solidarity and love among men. BIBLIOGRAPHY: M. Migeo, *Saint-Exupéry. A Biography* (tr. by H. Briffault, 1960); A. Devaux, *Teilhard et Saint-Exupéry* (1962); R. Zeller, *La Grande Quête d'Antoine de Saint-Exupéry* (1961); C. Borgal, *Saint-Exupéry, mystique sans la foi* (1964).

[G. E. GINGRAS]

ST.-FLORENT-LE-VIEIL, ABBEY OF, former Benedictine monastery located in the Diocese of Angers near Cholet, Maine et Loire, France. It grew up around the tomb (at Mont-Glonne) of Florentius, a disciple of Martin of Tours. The original anchorites were organized under Abbot Albaud (779–810) into a community of monks that became a model of reform for the abbeys of Aquitaine. It was enhanced by Charlemagne, burned by the Normans, pillaged by the Bretons, repaired by Charles II the Bald, and pillaged again by the Normans (905), causing the monks to flee, the greater part of them eventually founding Saint-Florent-lès-Saumur. In 1030 the original abbey was rebuilt by Guallo. It was reduced to priory status and dependent on the new foundation. Louis XIII gave the abbey to Charles Bouvard who introduced the Maurists (1637–39). During the Revolution the abbey was suppressed and destroyed.

[E. J. DILLON]

ST.-FLORENT-LÈS-SAUMUR, ABBEY OF, former Benedictine monastery near Saumur, Maine et Loire, France, in the Diocese of Angers. The monastery had endowments throughout W France, possessions in every part of the later Plantagenet empire, more than a dozen churches in Paris, and many priories. It was founded when the monks from nearby Saint-Florent-le-Vieil were forced to flee before the onslaught of Viking attacks. They wandered as far afield as Burgundy before being recalled to the Loire Valley by Theobald "Le Tricheur," Count of Blois, who installed them in the castle of Saumur. When the castle was taken by the Angevins (1025), the monks moved to the location nearby which came to be called Saint-Florent-lès-Saumur. The new abbey church was consecrated in 1041. In the 16th cent. it became commendatory. The Maurists attempted reform in 1637. It was dissolved in 1790. Only the 12th-cent. porch of the church remains. The abbey archives have survived, in part, at Angers.

[E. J. DILLON]

ST. FRANCIS, BROTHERS OF THE POOR OF, originally called the Poor Brothers of St. Francis Seraph, a congregation of lay brothers founded on Christmas Eve (1857) by Joannes Hoever at Aachen, Germany, for the care of underprivileged and neglected boys. In 1875 the brothers were expelled from Prussia and sought refuge in Bleyerheide, Holland. Several foundations were again made in Prussia when the brothers returned after 1888. St. Anthony Home for poor boys was opened in Cincinnati (1868), and a U.S. province was established (1871) with a motherhouse at Mt. Alverno on the Ohio River. The brothers were forced to close some foundations because of lack of funds and vocations, but the Protectory for Boys founded at Mt. Alverno remained open. The brothers maintain a boarding school for boys in Searcy, Ark., and teach at Assumption School in Emerson, New Jersey. In 1975 the brothers numbered 154 in 16 houses.

[R. C. CLIGGETT]

ST. FRANCIS DE SALES, DAUGHTERS OF, religious association or pious union founded in 1872 in Paris,

France, by Canon Henri Chaumont and Ven. Caroline Colchen-Carré-de Malberg to offer a deeper spiritual life and apostolic endeavor to women of all states of life. The spirituality of the association is based on that of St. *Francis de Sales. Although the association is neither a religious congregation nor a secular institute, it has a missionary branch, Salesian Missionaries of Mary Immaculate (1889), religious who wear a simple habit and take annual vows. Unlike this latter group, the Missionary Daughters of St. Francis de Sales wear no habit, take no vows, but live in community and work in the home missions. All three groups are ruled by the same constitution (approved in 1911) and recognize the same director general of the society. The central government is in Paris. In 1975 the Daughters of St. Francis de Sales numbered 3,669 in 130 houses.

[R. C. CLIGGETT]

SAINT-GAUDENS, AUGUSTUS (1848–1907), one of the most gifted Neoclassical sculptors in the United States. He carved an academic *Puritan,* the imagined portrait of deacon Samuel Chapin, and his greatest work, the *Adams Memorial* in Rock Creek Cemetery, Washington, D.C., a figure of *Grief* hooded, draped, and brooding, of poignant Gothic feeling.

[M. J. DALY]

ST. GENIS DES FONTAINES (c.819), Romanesque Benedictine monastery in Rousillon, French Catalonia, showing strong Carolingian influences, boasting a stone lintel of greatest importance to art history, evidencing in this remote village of the E Pyrenees the earliest return to figural sculpture (11th century). The lintel slab (6 ft 6 in by 2 ft 6 in) at St. Genis bears an authentic inscription dating the work (1019–21) in the time of King Robert II, the Pious, second of the Capetian dynasty: ANNO VIDESIMO QVARTO RENNATE RO'BERTO REGE VVILIELMVS GRA DEI ABA ISTA OPERA FIERI IVSSI' IN ONORE SCI' GENESII CENOBII CVE VOCANT FONTANAS. The lintel adorned with the figure of Christ in Majesty—in a mandorla supported by two angels imaginatively disposed with a keen grasp of the area to be filled, and flanked by six Apostles (?), their crudely cut figures marked by deeply channeled contours rounding the heads and bodies (perhaps too facilely identified with horseshoe arches), a convention repeated around the figure of Christ in deeply contoured upper mandorla (to the throne seat), supplemented by a half-circle mandorla outlining the lower area in a further evident adherence to the figure shape. These flat figures "drawn" (engraved, incised), keeping the plane of the stone slab, suggest earlier linear prototypes and altars of the Carolingian goldsmiths' art. St. Genis heralded the sculptural compositions of Romanesque portals with strong affinities at nearby St. André-de-Serrède (c.1030), which point to the same hand. The cloister, two portals, and bishop's throne of St. Genis, dismantled in 1925, were reassembled in the Philadelphia Museum of Art (1928). The cloister capitals in deep red stone indigenous to the Catalonian area are crudely cut with varied allegorical animal and vegetative motifs. The fountain from St. Genis is in the Metropolitan Museum of Art, N.Y. which owns the renowned cloister of Saint-Michel-de-Cuxa (c.1150), the fountain from which is in Philadelphia at the center of the St. Genis cloister. BIBLIOGRAPHY: H. Focillon, *Art of the West* (v. 1, 1963); A. K. Porter, *Romanesque Sculpture of the Pilgrimage Roads* (1969).

[M. J. DALY]

ST. GEORGE, ORDERS OF, organizations formed at various times during or since the Middle Ages by pope, emperor, or king having St. George (patron of all knights) as their own patron. Some were modeled on crusading military orders; others were companies; later there were orders of merit. Although its derivation is legendary, the Constantinian Order of St. George is the oldest and can be traced back to 1191 to Isaac II Angelus who survived the fall of the Byzantine Empire. Other orders honoring St. George were founded in the 18th or 19th cent.; one initiated by the Emperor Charles VII (1729) was suppressed by Hitler but exists today as a pious charitable corporation of Catholic noblemen.

[R. C. CLIGGETT]

ST. GEORGE'S UNITED METHODIST CHURCH, Philadelphia, Pa., the oldest Methodist meeting house in continuous use in America, a designated shrine of the United Methodist Church. The British Methodists have challenged its claim to be the world's oldest Methodist church edifice in continuous use. The St. George's Society was organized in 1767 by Captain Thomas *Webb who had assisted in the work of the John Street Methodist Society in New York City. On coming to Philadelphia he discovered a small group of converts of George *Whitefield meeting in a sail loft on Dock Creek (now Dock Street) at Front Street. The group had been meeting irregularly for twenty-six years when Webb organized them in 1767 as The Religious Society of Protestants called Methodists. Under Webb's leadership and forthright preaching, the Society grew and in 1768 purchased more commodious quarters at 8 Loxley Court on the N side of Arch Street. In 1769 John Wesley, at the request of the Methodist Society in New York, sent Richard Boardman and Joseph Pilmore to America as missionaries. They landed at Gloucester Point, N.J., walked to Philadelphia, and there met the leaders of the Methodist Society, which by then numbered about 100 persons. Boardman continued his journey to New York, but Pilmore remained in Philadelphia, where he prodded the "Methodies," as they were then called, to seek larger quarters. They secured their present structure in the following way. The shell of the building, consisting of four brick walls, a roof and a dirt floor, had been built by a splinter group of what was then the Dutch Reformed Church, now the United Church of

Christ, located at Fourth and Race Streets. This splinter group had overextended itself financially. Its trustees were arrested for the indebtedness on the building. To secure the release of the trustees, the group sold the edifice at public auction to the mentally deficient son of a William Branson Hockley. Hockley in turn sold the building in 1769 to the Methodists for 650 pounds. The splinter group who had erected the building had named it St. George's in a vain attempt to secure funds from the Anglicans. The Methodists continued the use of the name. The interior was eventually renovated as a typical colonial Anglican sanctuary. Francis *Asbury is purported to have termed the building "The Cathedral of Methodism." Although St. George's is not the oldest Methodist Society in America, its edifice is the oldest in continuous use, and its history is marked by a long list of distinctions. All the itinerants whom John Wesley sent to America preached their first sermons in the colonies at St. George's, Philadelphia being at that time the main port of entry into the New World. On August 31, 1770, John King, the first Wesleyan itinerant licensed to preach by an American Society was licensed by St. George's; and in 1784 Richard Allen, the first Negro, was licensed to preach by the Methodists in America. In 1789, under the leadership of John Dickins, then pastor, the Methodist Book Concern, now the Methodist Publishing House in Nashville, Tenn., was organized at St. George's. There also members of the Continental Congress attended services, the most distinguished being John Adams. The first three Conferences of American Methodism were held at St. George's in 1773, 1774, and 1775. For a short time during the Revolutionary War, the church was used by the British as a cavalry school. During its history the church is purported to have aided in organizing or preserving over one hundred Methodist churches along the eastern seaboard. In 1920 the church was threatened with destruction when plans called for an abutment of a bridge over the Delaware to be placed where the church now stands; the plans were altered through the influence of Bishop Thomas Neely. During the pastorate of Albert W. Cliffe (1951–57), guides were added to the staff, and under his successor, Frederick E. Maser, the endowment of the church was increased and group visitations were encouraged. Groups now come from all parts of the world. During this pastorate also, the St. George's Gold Medal Award was instituted. It is presented annually to at least one layperson and one Methodist preacher for "distinguished service to the Methodist Church." Under the leadership of Dr. John H. Barnes, the succeeding pastor, an additional award was instituted, The John Wesley Ecumenical Award. It commemorates both John Wesley's sermon, "The Catholic Spirit" and Vatican Council II. John Cardinal Krol of Philadelphia was one of the first recipients.

Directly adjoining the church is a historical center and museum. It houses and displays the possessions of the Historical Society of the Eastern Pennsylvania Conference of the United Methodist Church. These include nearly 10,000 volumes of Methodistica besides considerable memorabilia of early Methodism. Included are valuable letters of John Wesley, George Whitefield, Francis Asbury, Matthew Simpson, and other Methodist leaders. Under the present pastor, Dr. Robert L. Curry, the museum has been renovated and an air-conditioned vault built into the basement of the historical center. BIBLIOGRAPHY: A. W. Cliffe, *Our Methodist Heritage* (1957); F. H. Tees, *Ancient Landmark of American Methodism or Historic Old St. George's, Philadelphia,* (1951).

[F. E. MASER]

ST.-GERMAIN-DES-PRÉS, ABBEY OF, a former Benedictine monastery in Paris, France, founded under the Basilian Rule by King Childebert I (*c.*543) with St. Droctoveus from Autun. It was dedicated to the Holy Cross, St. Vincent, and St. Symphorianus and served as a burial place for Childebert I, Chilperic and their families, and St. Germain, an early bishop of Paris who died in 576. The Benedictine Rule was adopted in the 7th century. The name St. Germain was given the abbey in 754, when the Carolingian Pepin III exalted that saint's reliquary. In 815 there were 212 monks. The intensive literary activity of the ensuing years is illustrated by Abbo's *Parisian Wars*, the martyrology of Usuard, the *Liber miraculorum*, a famous obituary, several annals, and the *Polypticus* of Abbot Irmino. The Normans burned the abbey, and the dukes of Paris squandered its assets when they became its secular abbots. It revived under the Capetians and a regular abbot, William of Saint-Bénigne of Dijon (1025). The new Romanesque church (which still stands) was built and consecrated by Alexander III in 1163. Once again there was an active scriptorium. The abbey declined in the late Middle Ages along with monasticism in general and only revived under the Maurists (1630), when it became a center of studies, with Mabillon, E. Martène, U. Durand, and Ruinart working there. It was suppressed in the Revolution. The abbot general and 40 monks were massacred on September 2, 1792. BIBLIOGRAPHY: H. Leclercq, DACL 6.1:1102–50.

[E. J. DILLON]

ST.-GILDAS-DE-RHUYS, ABBEY OF (*S. Gildasius, Ruyense, S. Gustanus de Revisio*), a monastery founded *c.*538 by St. Gildas the Wise (d. 570 or 581), on the S shore of the peninsula of Rhuys, in the diocese of Vannes (Morbihan, France). It was destroyed by the Normans and restored (1008) by the monks of Fleury (Saint-Benoît-sur-Loire). In the 12th cent., the famous *Abelard was its superior. The Maurists reformed it in 1651, but it was closed at the time of the Revolution. The abbey-church and portions of the buildings are still standing.

[J. DAOUST]

ST. GILLES, former Benedictine abbey and famous pilgrimage center at the mouth of the Rhone River, in the diocese of Nîmes, France. Founded in the 9th century, it was dedicated to St. Giles, whose relics were venerated there, and located on a main pilgrimage route to Santiago de Campostela. The abbey was made exempt under Benedict VIII (1022–24) and entered the congregation of Cluny at the behest of Gregory VII (1066). It was visited in pilgrimage by several 11th- and 12th-cent. popes. Clement IV, monk of St.-Gilles, gave it privileges. It was caught in the Albigensian War involving its patrons, the Counts of Toulouse. It thrived after coming under the King of France (1226). The town of nine parishes that grew up around the abbey served as a prosperous port of embarkation for the Crusades. It became commendatory in 1472; was made collegiate in 1538; was looted and burned during war with the Huguenots; was occupied by the Protestants (1574–1622), who tore down the bell tower before leaving; and was suppressed and damaged during the Revolution. The abbey church still stands; its greatest glory is its triple portal, a masterpiece of 12th-cent. carving, evidencing, as does St. Trophime at Arles, the Roman classical heritage in S France: columns of Corinthian design supporting classical moldings and entablatures; narrative friezes; Provençal-Romanesque apostle figures of classic reserve within their niches clothed in the drapery of a Greco-Roman world; the tympanum Christ in a Roman "medallion" mandorla-framed in the unadorned, ever-varied Roman string courses, juxtaposed against animal-pedestals from Lombardy and reliefs in double-guilloche or lozenge frames showing camels from the East.

[E. J. DILLON]

ST.-GUILHEM-DU-DÉSERT, ABBEY OF (*S. Guillelmus de deserto, Gellonense*), Benedictine abbey founded in 806 at Gellone by William the Great, Count of Narbonne, a grandson of Charles Martel. In 793 he halted the Arabs at Villedaigne, conquered Barcelona in 801, and then retired to Gellone. There he founded a monastery whose first abbot was his friend, *Benedict of Aniane, and he himself became a monk. He is the hero of certain famous epic poems (*chansons de geste*) under the name of William of Orange, who was known also as William the Short-nosed. The abbey which he built was called from the 12th cent. on Saint-Guilhem-du-Désert. Sacked in the 16th cent. by Calvinists, it was reformed by the Maurists in 1626, but suppressed in 1781, when its property was given over to the bishopric of Lodève. The church and part of the cloister are still standing.

[J. DAOUST]

ST. HUBERT, ABBEY OF (*Andagium, S. Hubertus in Ardennis*), Benedictine monastery founded at Andage (Belgian Luxembourg) in 704 by St. Beregis, chaplain of Pepin II of Heristal. It was first entrusted to Augustinian canons, but the Benedictines soon replaced them under Valcand, bp. of Liège (810–836). He transferred here the relics of St. *Hubert (d. 727), bp. of Tongres, Maastricht, and Liège, for whom the abbey took its name. His stole, preserved by the monks, was thought to cure those afflicted by rabies. In the 11th cent., the monastery was under the rule of Bl.

Thierry of Leernes. It was reformed by the monks of Saint-Vanne in 1619 and suppressed in 1796. The former conventual buildings (1729), and the abbey church still remain, reconstructed (1526–64) in flamboyant Gothic style.

[J. DAOUST]

ST. JEAN, BAPTISTERY OF, POITIERS, 7th- or 8th-cent. French Merovingian Baptistery, the earliest of its kind preserved, therefore of great importance in the study of this period of Western Christian architecture. The square, unadorned, triapsidal, brick structure has been related to N African and Egyptian prototypes, ascribed to an influx of Eastern Syrian churchmen into France at this time. Enlarged after the fire of 1018 it was enriched by frescoes in the 12th and 14th cent. (*Constantine on Horseback*) and by fine paintings of *Christ in Majesty and the Apostles*. The Baptistery now houses a collection of Merovingian art.

[M. J. DALY]

ST. JOAN'S INTERNATIONAL ALLIANCE, an association which works for the recognition of the equality of the sexes and whose membership is open to men and women. It was founded in 1911 in London as the Catholic Women's Suffrage Society. When a French division was established in 1931 it became international. The alliance now has consultative status with the United Nations and special relations with the International Labor Organization and UNESCO. It gives attention, study, and active response to the traffic of persons, equality of opportunity in education and employment, the rights of married women to employment, and a single standard of wages or salaries.

[R. C. CLIGGETT]

ST. JOHN, DISCIPLES OF, a pagan, baptist, gnostic sect of Mandaeans, sometimes called Christians of St. John because of their devotion to St. John the Baptist. They follow a syncretistic religion which combines elements from a heretical Jewish sect, Gnosticism, and Christianity. Although their existence in the 4th or 5th cent. A.D. is fairly certain, merchants and missionaries revealed their existence to the West as late as the 16th and 17th cent. and a scientific study of the sect began only in the 19th century. Other names for the *Mandaeans, which means gnostic and is derived from the Aramaic (*maddā'*, knowledge), are: Sabaeans (baptizers) and Naṣoraens (observers). The latter name is reserved for priests.

[R. C. CLIGGETT]

ST. JOHN, HENRY (1891–1973), Dominican, pioneer in the RC ecumenical movement in England. Born Fleming St. John, the son of an Anglican clergyman, he was himself ordained an Anglican priest in 1913 after studies at Cambridge, Ely Theological College, and St. Stephen's House, Oxford. In 1917 he resigned his parish and, assisted by the counsel of Vincent *McNabb, entered the RC Church. St. J. immediately enlisted as a private in the British Army and served in the trenches in France. He became a Dominican in 1919 and was ordained a RC priest in 1927. The first phase of his career, remembered by all his "old boys," was at Laxton School, as teacher from 1929 and as headmaster from 1932. He served as provincial of England from 1958 until 1962. His last active years were spent as chaplain to the Dominican clositered nuns of Carisbrooke, Isle of Wight. By his own brethren he was regarded esp. as the apostle of community life, as friend and helper of the troubled, and as a man of prayer. In the English Church he was seen as the father of ecumenism, as Card. Heenan described him. He was devoted to Christian reunion from the days when, as a student, he attended the *Edinburgh Conference of 1910. Long before ecumenism became a formal cause in the Church, he fostered among Catholics a charity-motivated need to appreciate the Anglican point of view and from Anglicans he won a respect evoked by his clear honesty about RC theological positions. St. J. wrote journal articles on ecumenism throughout his life; his one book on the subject is *Essays in Christian Unity* (1955). His last formal service to the cause was as a member of the bishops' committee on ecumenism (1967–70). He died at Blackfriars, Cambridge.

[T. C. O'BRIEN]

ST. JOHN OF GOD, SISTERS OF, a diocesan congregation founded by Bp. Thomas Furlong in 1871 at Wexford, Ireland, to teach, nurse in hospitals, and visit the sick poor in their homes. In 1931 the congregation became a pontifical institute. In 1895 the sisters established missions in Australia, where they worked with the aborigines. By 1964 they had opened houses also in Africa and New Zealand and staffed 31 hospitals, 1 leprosarium, and several schools. The generalate is located at Wexford. In 1975 the sisters numbered 661 in 58 houses.

[R. C. CLIGGETT]

ST. JOHN'S ABBEY AND UNIVERSITY, oldest Catholic institution of higher education in Minnesota, with 2000 acres of land 80 mi N of Minneapolis. It was chartered in 1857, a year after the arrival of the Benedictine monks who at the invitation of Bp. Joseph Cretin to Abbot Boniface *Wimmer, OSB, St. Vincent Abbey, Latrobe, Pa., came to care for the German immigrants and Indians of the region. Shortly after their arrival in St. Paul, a small party moved on to St. Cloud. In 1857 a charter established St. John's Seminary to instruct "in science and . . . moral principles." In 1869 it was authorized to confer academic degrees and in 1883 became legally St. John's University. Originally it was known as the Abbey of St. Louis on the Lake in memory of King Ludwig I of Bavaria, patron of the 19th-cent. Benedictine revival and supporter of Abbot Wimmer's endeavors in America. Under Rupert Seidenbusch (1830–95) formerly prior of St. Vincent Abbey, the community grew, the school increased from 183 to 350 students, and 45 missions to 146. Division of opinions con-

cerning external activity dividing the group, there followed a concentration on monastic affairs (1848–94). In 1891 the monks undertook the Bahama Islands, established new abbeys in Canada (1892) and Washington (1895). A new era began under Abbot Alcuin Deutsch (1877–1951) in 1922 for the largest Benedictine religious house in the world. The liturgical movement, brought to America by Virgil Michel (1890–1938), developed at St. John's through publications of the Liturgical Press: *Orate Fratres (Worship), Sponsa Regis* for sisterhoods, *Bible Today,* and *The American Benedictine Review* and Collegeville became the center of the liturgical apostolate, of social action and rural life, with seminars and ecumenical dialogue. With a history of avant-garde culture through centuries of creative monastic building historically identified with the preservation and spread of civilization, St. John's began, under the leading contemporary architect Marcel Breuer, a centennial architectural program (1954). Seven buildings were erected by 1965, including the abbey and university church (consecrated 1961), characterized by visionary forms provocatively imaginative and inspiring. Abbot Baldwin Dworschak (1906–   ), sixth abbot, since 1951 directs 400 members, with new foundations in Japan, Mexico, and Puerto Rico. St. Maur's Priory, an interracial monastery, S Union, Ky., became independent in 1963. St. John's University has a graduate school of sacred studies, school of divinity, a college and college preparatory divisions, with 1,780 students (1977), a library of 267,000 volumes, 828 periodicals, and is fully accredited in National and State organizations.

In the early 1970s Fr. Paul Marx founded the Human Life Center at St. John's University. Its aims are to explore and clarify all dimensions of the human life issue through research, workshops, lifelong learning programs, publications, consultations, and the like. It is a nonprofit, international, education center that conducts long-range programs to help people of all faiths apply positive solutions to every problem of marriage and human life. On the positive side, they work in the areas of marriage preparation, marriage enrichment, Birthright counselling, parent effectiveness training, child abuse, death and dying, care of the aged and infirm, sexuality and love, breast-feeding, natural childbirth, and natural family planning (NFP).

[M. J. DALY]

ST. JOHN'S HOSPITAL, BRUGES, situated between Notre Dame, to which it was operationally attached, and the dwellings of the Béguines who provided lay care to the sick. The main buildings are Gothic (13th-cent. tympanum sculptures), the former chapter hall now houses H. Memlinc's works (*St. Ursula Reliquary Shrine* and *The Marriage of St. Catherine* with other triptychs). BIBLIOGRAPHY: M. H. Letts, *Bruges and Its Past* (1929); C. D. Cuttler, *Northern Painting* (1968).

[R. BERGMANN]

ST. JOSEPH, CONGREGATION OF THE SISTERS OF (CSJ, SSJ), an institute officially founded by John Peter Médaille, SJ, a relatively unknown French Jesuit, at Le Puy, Velay, France, on October 15, 1650. The congregation received canonical status during the ensuing year from Bp. Henry de Maupas of that city. A transitory foundation had been made by Fr. Médaille in approximately 1646, but remained "secret" in that it had neither civil nor ecclesiastical approval. Fr. Médaille, through his "Little Design," established the structure for and set in action a revolutionary idea: a religious congregation of women devoted to contemplation and apostolic service, a plan attempted earlier but abandoned by St. Francis de Sales for the Visitation nuns. Traditionally, to Bp. de Maupas is credited the Salesian influence evident in the Ignatian-Salesian spirituality basic to the congregation of the Sisters of St. Joseph. Sources indicate a close association between St. Francis de Sales and Bp. de Maupas, and later between Bp. de Maupas and Fr. Médaille.

Through the articulation of his vision in his "Little Design," Fr. Médaille established an ecclesiastically approved congregation of religious women who profess simple vows, and who dedicate themselves to the love of God as it manifests itself apostolically in the corporal and spiritual works of mercy. Original writings of Fr. Médaille that embody the charism of apostolic spirituality he desired for his sisters are the *Eucharistic Letter,* the *Règlements,* and the *Maxims of Perfection*, all written for the first foundation, and the *Constitutions for the Little Congregation of the Sisters of St. Joseph*. This primitive constitution of the Sisters of St. Joseph required so little modification to meet changing conditions of the apostolate that, after Vatican II, few significant changes had to be made to ensure its compliance with the decrees of *Perfectae caritatis*. Through the sponsorship of the Federation of the Sisters of St. Joseph, U.S.A., an inter-congregational research team under the guidance of Marius Nepper, a French Jesuit, has since 1969 made these primary sources available in English.

Early Development. The original group of six sisters attracted many and grew rapidly until, at the time of Father Médaille's death in 1669, unknown to him (since he had been removed from their spiritual direction by changes in his own apostolate), this "Little Design" was followed in approximately 12 dioceses throughout southern France. This rapid and continued growth of the congregation was brought to an end in 1789 by the French Revolution. Then, like other religious congregations in France, the Sisters of St. Joseph were disbanded, many of its members imprisoned, and at least five met death on the guillotine.

Restoration and Spread of the Congregation. Father Médaille's spiritual legacy, however, was preserved in the hearts of the sisters, especially in that of Sister St. John Fontbonne. With her sister Marie, Jeanne Fontbonne had been educated by the Sisters of St. Joseph in Le Puy, and later, in 1778, had entered the congregation where she received the name of Sister St. John. Imprisoned at Saint-Didier in 1793, she was released on the eve of her scheduled execution. Following 12 years of secularized life, Mother St. John, at the request of Card. Joseph Fesch of Lyon, began in 1807 the work of restoring the congregation. Le Puy and most of the other prerevolutionary convents were restored, and many new ones were founded so that by 1825 more than 100 houses existed in France. At the time of Mother St. John's death in 1844, she had established or reorganized 244 convents.

The first foundation at Le Puy had established a pattern in which every foundation was self-governing under the authority of the local bishop. In restoring the congregation, Mother St. John established a central novitiate and motherhouse from which smaller foundations were made and governed. Among the first foundations outside France were Turin, Italy, in 1821, and Carondelet, Missouri, U.S., in 1836. On the tercentenary of the death of Father Médaille in 1969, 46 such motherhouses throughout the five continents and Oceania claimed Father Médaille and his charism of contemplation and apostolic service as their own.

The French Family in North America. Five French motherhouses—Bourg, Chambéry, Le Puy, Lyon, and St. Vallier—are responsible for the establishment, either directly or through subsequent daughter foundations, of some 31 motherhouses in U.S. and six in Canada. As of 1978, two of these were still affiliated with their respective parent foundation in France: Hartford, Conn., 1885 (Chambéry) and Winslow, Me., 1906 (Lyon). New Orleans, La., 1854, Cincinnati, Ohio, 1892, Crookston, Minn., 1903 all founded from Bourg, have formed (1977) a new group, the Sisters of St. Joseph of Médaille. Carondelet, Mo. (Lyon) became independent in c.1849; St. Augustine, Fla. (Le Puy) in 1899; and Québec, Canada (St. Vallier) in 1953.

To the foundation made by Mother St. John at Carondelet in 1836, 20 motherhouses in the U.S. and 6 in Canada trace their existence. Established directly by Carondelet or from foundations established by Carondelet are: St. Louis, Mo., 1836 (Province of Carondelet, 1860); Philadelphia, Pa., 1847; St. Paul, Minn., 1851 (Province of Carondelet, 1860); Toronto, Canada, 1851; Hamilton, Canada, 1852; Wheeling, W. Va., 1853; Buffalo, N.Y., 1854; Brentwood, N.Y., 1856; Latham, N.Y. (Albany), 1858 (Province of Carondelet, 1860); Petersborough, Canada, 1858; Erie, Pa., 1860; Rochester, N.Y., 1864; London, Ontario, 1868; Baden, Pa. (Pittsburgh), 1869; Los Angeles, Calif., 1870 (Province of Carondelet, 1876); Cleveland, Ohio, 1872; Boston, Mass., 1873; Rutland, Vt., 1873; Springfield, Mass., 1880; Watertown, N.Y., 1880; Concordia, Kans., 1883; Tipton, Ind., 1888; Witchita, Kans., 1888; Nazareth, Mich., 1889; LaGrange, Ill., 1899; Superior, Wis., 1907; Pembroke, Canada, 1910; Orange, Calif., 1912; Sault Ste. Marie, 1937; Honolulu, Hawaii, 1938 (Vice-province of Carondelet, 1956).

From these 20 foundations, there were in existence in 1976, 1,357 houses in the U.S. including Hawaii, in addition to five motherhouses dependent on the U.S. foundations in the following countries: Africa, Australia, Central America, New Guinea, Japan, Puerto Rico, and South America. These foundations comprise a total of 15,560 Sisters of St. Joseph. In addition, the six motherhouses in Canada have established 140

The French Family in America

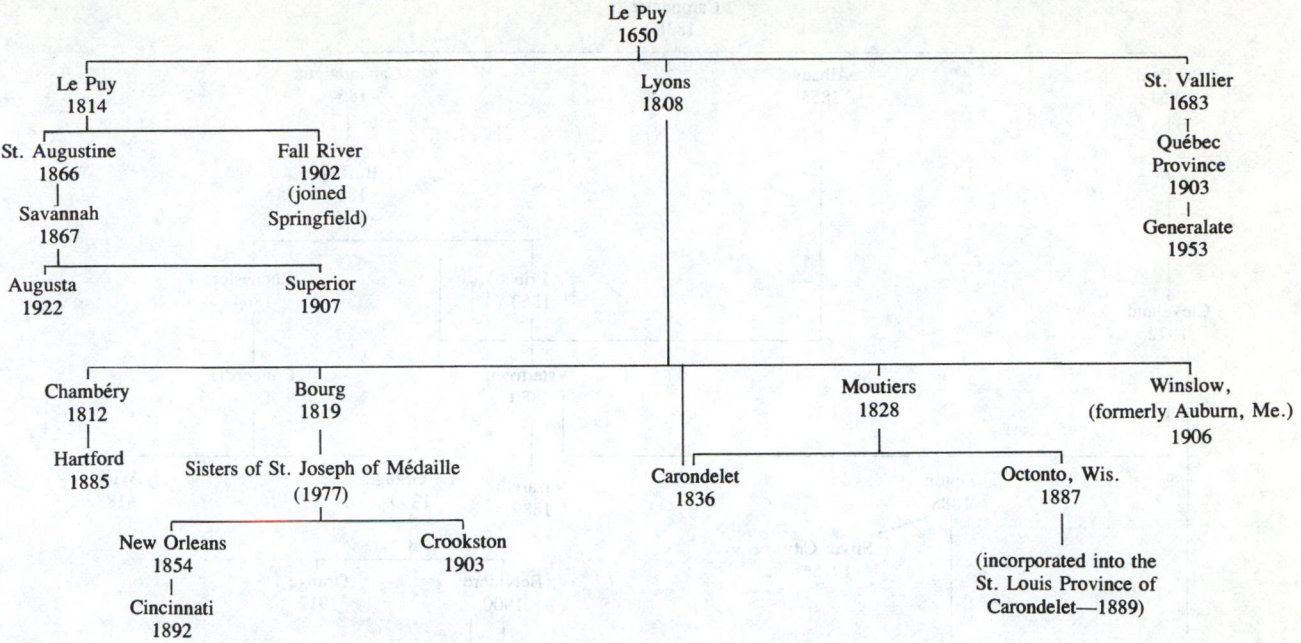

NOTES:

Hartford and Winslow are still provinces of their respective parent foundations.

Savannah became independent in 1871, Québec in 1953, Carondelet c. 1849, Chambéry in 1815, Bourg in 1823, Moutiers and St. Vallier (from foundation), and St. Augustine in 1899.

The Carondelet and Philadelphia Families

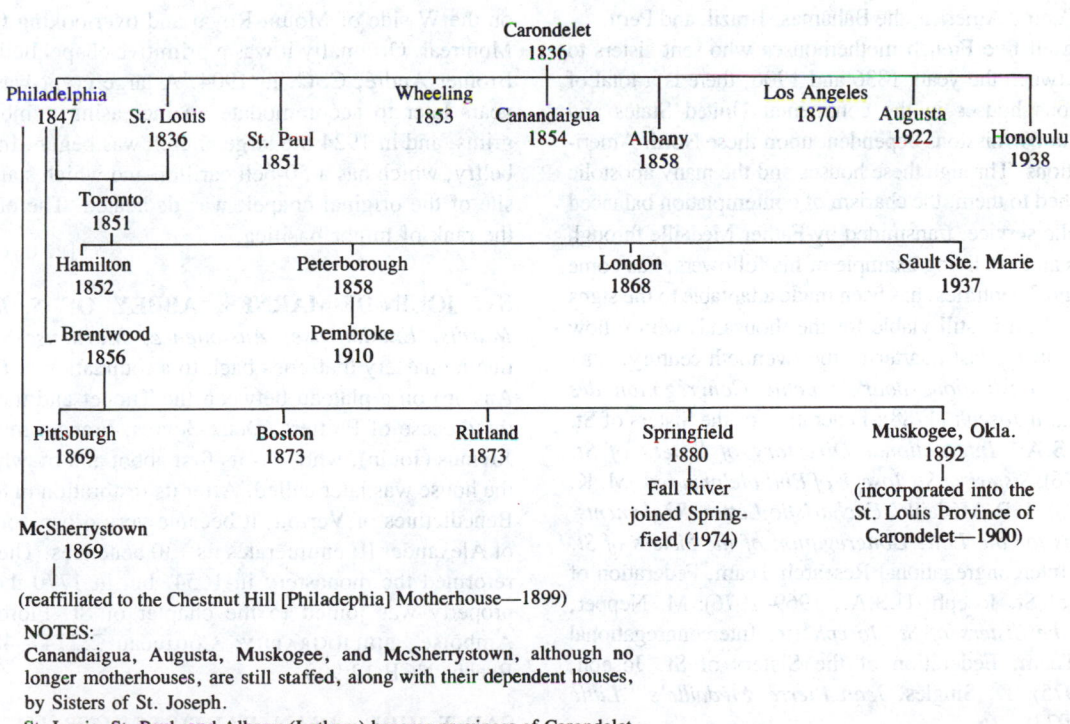

NOTES:

Canandaigua, Augusta, Muskogee, and McSherrystown, although no longer motherhouses, are still staffed, along with their dependent houses, by Sisters of St. Joseph.

St. Louis, St. Paul, and Albany (Latham) became provinces of Carondelet in 1860, Los Angeles in 1876, and Honolulu a vice-province in 1956.

The St. Paul-Canandaigua Family

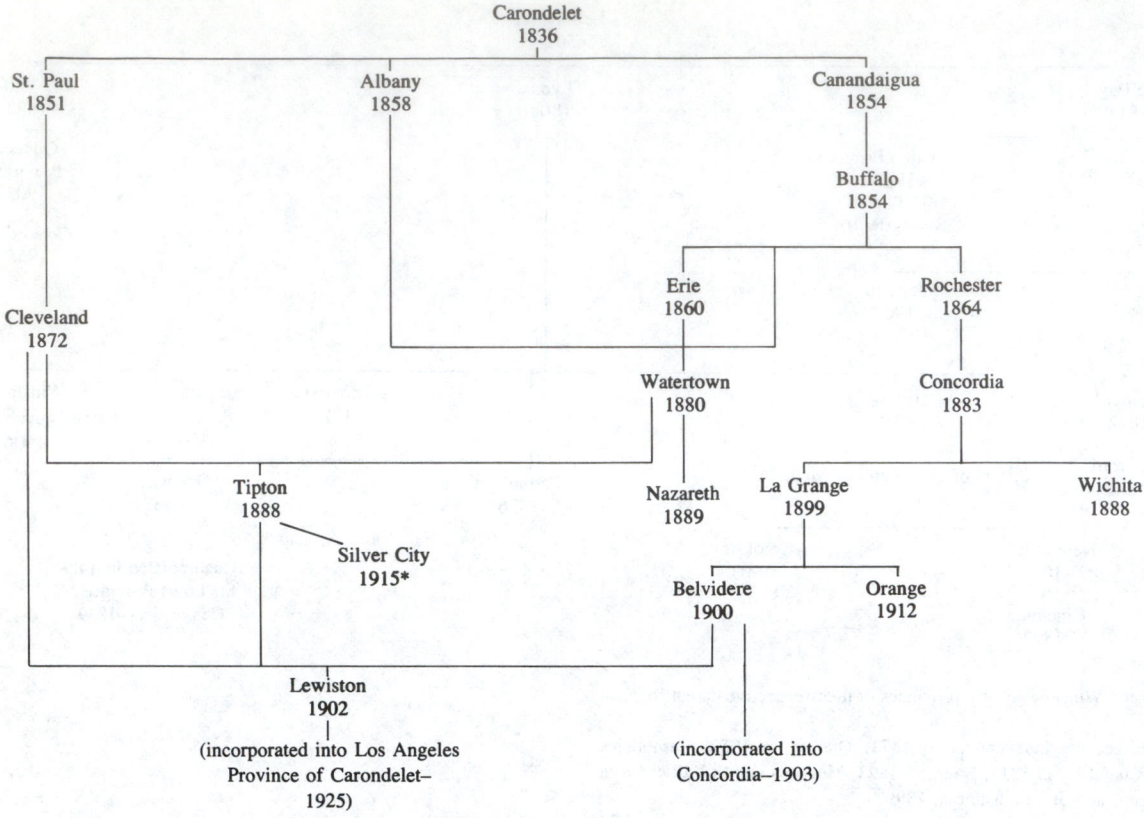

*(Silver City, New Mexico—incorporated into Concordia Motherhouse—1926)

[T. W. VON EIFF]

houses, with eight missions dependent on the Canadian foundations in Central America, the Bahamas, Brazil, and Peru.

Including all five French motherhouses who sent sisters to the U.S. between the years 1836 and 1906, there is a total of 1500 religious houses in the continental United States and Canada, with 59 missions dependent upon these North American foundations. Through these houses and the many apostolic works attached to them, the charism of contemplation balanced with apostolic service, transmitted by Father Médaille through his writings and the living example of his followers, has come down through 3 centuries, has been made adaptable to the signs of the times, and is still viable for the thousands who follow this charism in the last quarter of the twentieth century. BIB - LIOGRAPHY: *Constitutions pour la petite Congrégation des Soeurs de Saint Joseph* (1788); Federation of the Sisters of St. Joseph, U.S.A., *International Directory of Sisters of St. Joseph* (1976); *Sisters of St. Joseph of Philadelphia* (ed. M. K. Logue, 1950); J. P. Médaille, *Eucharistic Letter, Règlements, Constitutions for the Little Congregation of the Sisters of St. Joseph* (tr. Intercongregational Research Team, Federation of the Sisters of St. Joseph, U.S.A., 1969–1976); M. Nepper, *Origins of the Sisters of St. Joseph* (tr. Intercongregational Research Team, Federation of the Sisters of St. Joseph, U.S.A., 1975); D. Singles, *Jean Pierre Médaille's "Little Design"* (1973).

[B. F. LOUGHERY]

ST. JOSEPH'S ORATORY, an oratory basilica standing on the W side of Mount Royal and overlooking the city of Montreal. Originally it was a primitive chapel built there by Brother André, CSC, in 1904. A large crypt was built 11 years later to accommodate an increasing number of pilgrims, and in 1924 the large church was begun. In 1955 the belfry, which has a 50-bell carillon and which stands on the site of the original chapel, was dedicated. The oratory has the rank of minor basilica.

[R. C. CLIGGETT]

ST. JOUIN-DE-MARNES, ABBEY OF (*S. Jovinus de Marnis, Enixionense, Ansionense, Marnense*), Benedictine monastery that goes back to a foundation at Ension (or Ansion) on a plateau between the Thouet and the Dive, in the diocese of Poitiers (Deux-Sèvres, France) made by St. Jovinus (Jouin), who was its first abbot and by whose name the house was later called. After its restoration in 844 by the Benedictines of Vertou, it became very prosperous. A bull of Alexander III enumerates its 130 benefices. The Maurists reformed the monastery in 1654, but in 1770 the abbatial property was joined to the chapter of St. Florentinus of Amboise. BIBLIOGRAPHY: Cottineau 2:2747–48; G. T. Beech, NCE 12:905.

SAINT-JURE, JEAN BAPTISTE (1588–1657), French Jesuit writer, spiritual advisor to many mystics. A Jesuit from 1604, he became director for the cloistered Dominican nuns of Paris and is credited with saving them from the influence of *Jansenism. His written works influenced the piety of 17th-cent. France. They include meditative works on Christ and treatises dealing with spiritual practice and religious life. His biographical study of the mystic, the Baron of Renty, (1651) was immensely popular.

[R. J. LITZ]

ST. LAUMER OF BLOIS, ABBEY OF, former Benedictine abbey built in 924 near the castle of Count Thibault in Blois, central France. The monastic community had originally been founded near Chartres (c.575), by St. Laumer (d. c.590). The monks fled from there in an attempt to save themselves and their founder's relics in the face of Norman invasions (c.874). The new monastery's period of greatest vitality is represented by the wonderful 12th- and 13th-cent. church with its notable Romanesque architecture and sculpture. It became commendatory in the 16th cent., was pillaged by the Huguenots in 1568, joined the Maurists in 1627, had its revenue given to the new Diocese of Blois by Louis XIV in 1697, and was suppressed by the Revolution in 1791. The church became a parish church, and the other buildings were used as a hospital.

[E. J. DILLON]

ST. LAURENT OF LIÈGE, ABBEY OF, Benedictine monastery in Belgium. Founded by Bp. Heraclius (d. 971), the abbey began regular life only in 1026 under the first abbot, Stephen (d. 1060). The new church (consecrated in 1034), housed a relic of St. Lawrence after 1056. Two cent. of prosperity were followed by economic and spiritual decline. The house was destroyed during a siege (1568) but was soon rebuilt. The abbey was suppressed in 1796 during the French Revolution. BIBLIOGRAPHY: *Monasticon belge* 2 (1962) 32–57; Cottineau 1:1604–05.

[L. J. LEKAI]

ST. LAZARUS OF JERUSALEM, ORDER OF, knights hospitallers and nurses founded c.1120 in Jerusalem. It was established to operate hospitals, esp. for lepers, to spread the faith, and to assist pilgrims who visit the Holy Land. In 1253 the order established houses in France, Italy, England, Scotland, Hungary, Germany, and Switzerland. It fell into decay during the 14th and 15th cent., and Innocent VIII decreed that it be united with the Order of the Hospitallers of St. John of Jerusalem (Knights of Malta). This was opposed vigorously by the French knights of the Lazarite Order, who decided to live on as an independent order in France. Leo X restored the order's independence early in the 16th century. The autonomy as an order was threatened again when Gregory XIII commanded the members to unite with the Order of St. Maurice. Once again the Lazarites refused. However, both Italian and French branches of the order were suppressed during the French Revolution. There was a revival of the one in Italy in

1814 and of the other in France in 1830. At present the order is purely an honorific organization.

[R. C. CLIGGETT]

ST. LÉONARD LE NOBLAT, MONASTERY OF (*Nobiliacense*), Benedictine house established probably in the 6th cent. by the hermit of the Limousin, St. Leonard (d. 559), who was buried there and became its patron (Diocese of Limoges, Haute-Vienne, France). The abbey received financial aid from King Louis the Pious to construct the church above the tomb of the founder, venerated as the liberator of captives. Destroyed by the Normans, it was reestablished c.1060. In 1197, Richard the Lion-Hearted offered generous alms to the holy patron in thanksgiving for his deliverance from captivity. Later occupied by canons regular, it was disbanded at the time of the Revolution. The church is a beautiful 11th-12th–cent. Limousin structure frequently restored. BIBLIOGRAPHY: Cottineau 2:2764–65.

[J. DAOUST]

ST. LÔ, MONASTERY OF, former abbey of Canons Regular of St. Augustine, located on the Vire in Manche, France, in the diocese of Coutance. In 990 Hugh, bishop of Coutance, brought some canons from the priory of Saint-Lô at Rouen to restore the site that had been occupied by a college of canons before the Viking devastations. In 1132 Bishop Algar brought Augustinian canons from Sainte-Barbe-en-Auge. These canons, amply provided with endowments, served several parishes in the town of Saint-Lô and elsewhere in the diocese. In 1659 strict discipline was re-introduced by an uncle and nephew, both named André Merlet, who brought in canons from the Congregation of Sainte-Geneviève. The Revolution dispersed the canons (1790) and destroyed the abbey church.

[E. J. DILLON]

ST. LOUP-DE-NAUD, CHURCH OF, French church of Romanesque-Gothic type with unusual vaulting (barrel, groin, rib, and dome on squinches). The chevet, transept, and first 2 bays of the nave are dated 11th cent.; the remainder of the nave and the porch with magnificent portal sculpture, c.1170. The famous western portal depicts St. Loup on the *trumeau,* his life and angels on the voussoirs; a Christ in Glory with symbolic Evangelists; Apostles and Virgin in the tympanum and lintel; and Old and New Testament figures on the jambs. Related to the Royal Portal at Chartres, the Saint-Loup portal is the last and one of the most handsome sculptural assemblages of early Gothic style. BIBLIOGRAPHY: F. Salet, "Saint-Loup-de-Naud," *Bulletin monumental* 92 (1933).

[M. J. DALY]

ST. LOUIS, SISTERS OF, congregation with papal approbation founded in 1842 for the teaching apostolate. It was established by Fr. Louis Bautain at Juilly, France, but did not take root under his leadership. Instead it grew around the motherhouse founded in Ireland in 1859, and Mother Genevieve Beale opened a convent of the Sisters of St. Louis in Louisville, Co. Monaghan.

The community came to the U.S. in 1949 and established itself in California. By 1964 the sisters were teaching in 15 elementary schools and 3 high schools in the Archdiocese of Los Angeles and the Diocese of Sacramento. In Woodland Hills, Calif. the sisters established an American Louisville, a high school for girls. The novitiate is located in the same place. The sisters also have missions in Africa in Nigeria and Ghana. In 1975 there were 675 members in 55 houses.

[R. C. CLIGGETT]

ST. MAIXENT, ABBEY OF (*S. Maxentius, Pictaviense*), Benedictine monastery at Vauclair in the diocese of Poitiers, Fr., originally established (*c.*459) by Agapius and his companions and dedicated to St. Saturninus, a martyred bp. of Toulouse. St. Maixent succeeded Agapius as abbot, and the monastery later took his name. The abbey adopted the Benedictine rule, was sacked by the Normans and later restored, and in the 12th cent. enjoyed its period of greatest prosperity. In 1568 the Calvinists destroyed the church, which was rebuilt after 1670 by the Maurists, who took over the monastery in 1634. The conventual buildings, which date back to the 17th cent., have been transformed into a barracks. The former abbey-church (17th cent.) contains the ruins of the 12th–cent. church, one of the most important works of the Poitevin Romanesque school. BIBLIOGRAPHY: Cottineau 2:2775–77.

[J. DAOUST]

ST. MARK'S (SAN MARCO, VENICE), BASILICA OF, built *c.*830 to house the relics of St. Mark abducted from Alexandria, deriving its Greek cross-shaped plan with five glorious domes from Justinian's Apostoleion in Constantinople, which subsequently rebuilt, provided the inspiration for a new St. Mark's (core of the present structure), in 1063, with its domes mounted on high drums pierced by many windows. After the conquest of Constantinople (1204) a passion for decorative embellishment through booty and commissioned works, continued for 4 centuries. Notable are four gilded bronze horses (4th-3d cent. B.C.) and two pairs of porphyry tetrachs from Christian imperial workshops of the 4th century. There is a remarkable synthesis in the Byzantine and Romanesque mosaic cycles of the narthex (12th-14th centuries). Mosaics of the interior are less unified, e.g., some deriving from cartoons of great Venetian painters (e.g., Tintoretto and Veronese).

The *Pala d'oro (1105–1345) an altarpiece of hundreds of panels in enamel gold and silver work is extraordinarily sumptuous. A rich treasury boasts Byzantine MSS, reliquaries of precious materials, and objects in rock crystal (7th–12th centuries). Declared a cathedral in 1807, St. Mark's is uniquely important as a magnificent example of Veneto-Byzantine expression. BIBLIOGRAPHY: O. Demus,

Church of San Marco, Venice (1960); H. R. Hahnloser, *Il tesoro di San Marco* (1965).

[M. J. DALY]

ST. MARTHA, SISTERS OF, a diocesan congregation in Quebec founded in 1883 to perform domestic work in seminaries, clerical residences, and religious institutions. It was founded by Canon Jean Remi Ouellette and Éléanore Charron (Mother St. Martha) with the approval of Bp. Louis Z. Moreau of St. Hyacinthe. The motherhouse of the congregation is in St. Hyacinthe. In the U.S. the sisters manage the domestic departments of four institutions in New Hampshire and Massachusetts. In 1975 there were 146 sisters in 15 houses.

[R. C. CLIGGETT]

ST. MARTIAL OF LIMOGES, ABBEY OF, former Benedictine monastery named after the first bp. of Limoges (*c.*250), and located in that ancient city on the upper Vienne River in W central France. A church dedicated to the Holy Savior had been built over the tomb of St. Martial and attracted a monastic settlement sometime before 804, during the time of King Louis the Debonair. The Benedictines took over in 848. It came under Cluny in 1062 and at one time had more than 80 priories among its dependencies. Ruined during the Hundred Years' War and secularized and made collegiate in 1535, it went to the Augustinian Canons until the Revolution (1791). It was demolished soon afterwards. BIBLIOGRAPHY: Cottineau 1: 1618–19.

[E. J. DILLON]

SAINT-MARTIN, LOUIS CLAUDE DE (1743–1803), philosopher-mystic. A French aristocrat, S.-M. came under the influence of the Jewish mystic Pasqualis, who turned him to the promotion of mysticism. His book *Des Erreurs et de la vérité* (1775) was an appeal to interior illumination as an offset to the materialism of Condillac. The influence of Jakob Boehme gave his mysticism a new turn in 1788. Arrested by French Revolutionaries, S.-M. escaped death because of the fall of Robespierre. In 1796 he published *Considérations sur la révolution française,* proposing theocracy as model government. Other works were: *Le Nouvel homme* (1792) and *Le Ministère de l'homme-esprit* (1802).

[J. R. AHERNE]

ST. MARTIN, BASILICA OF, TOURS, early Romanesque church, replacing (1014) the early church (997) destroyed by fire. St. Martin probably initiated the pilgrimage-church plan of wide nave (four aisles), aisled transepts, and ambulatories about the apse with radiating chapels to accommodate great numbers of devotees. In 1050 influenced by Cluny the groin vault was replaced by a barrel vault. The fresco cycles are among the most notable of Romanesque paintings.

[M. J. DALY]

ST. MARTIN-IN-THE-FIELDS, LONDON (1721–26). Built by James Gibbs, St. Martin, which became the prototype for many churches, is rectangular in plan, with a giant Corinthian portico, the steeple rising through the roof inside the church, distinct from Wren's steeple which was an adjunct to the building. The interior is aisled and galleried. Gibbs accented the columns by individual entablatures and by placing the gallery behind them.

[M. J. DALY]

ST. MARTIN OF TOURNAI, ABBEY OF (*Tornacense*), Benedictine abbey founded *c*.652 probably by St. Elias of Noyon (d. 660), at Tournai, Belgium. The monastery first observed the rule of St. Columban but later adopted that of St. Benedict. Destroyed by the Normans (880), then occupied by canons regular, it was later restored by Odo of Orléans, director of the school of Tournai. Odo was responsible for imposing the customs of Cluny according to the observance of Anchin, as well as for having MSS of ancient classics copied by 12 scribes. Julius de' Medici (Clement VII) was one of its commendatory abbots. The monks were expelled in 1796. The former palace, designed by the architect Dewez in 1763, is at present the town hall. A part of the cloister (*c*.1500) and the Romanesque wine-cellars (12th cent.) still stand. Among its distinguished monks were: Alulfe, a cantor; Abbot Heriman, a 12th-cent. hagiographer; Dom Fievét, a canonist; Abbot Muevin, a chronicler; Abbot Li Muisis, a 14th-cent. poet and historian; Abbot de Maquais, 17th-cent. ascetical writer and theologian. BIBLIOGRAPHY: Cottineau 2:3187–88; A. d'Haenens, NCE 12:914.

[J. DAOUST]

ST. MARY, SISTERS OF, the Congregation of the Sisters of St. Mary of the Third Order of St. Francis, founded in 1872 in St. Louis, Mo., to nurse the sick. Mother Odilia, the foundress, was an immigrant from Germany because of the Kulturkampf. She came to St. Louis, with a few companions and under the direction of William Faerber, pastor of St. Mary's Church, the sisters dedicated themselves to a life of poverty and charity according to the Franciscan way of life. They then began to nurse the sick in their own homes. They were permitted to make public vows in 1880, and in 1932 the constitutions were approved by Rome. In its early days the community cared for unfortunate girls and neglected children, but later specialized in hospital nursing, nursing education, and care for the aged. Mother Mary Concordia, who was superior general from 1921–1958, was a leader in the Catholic Hospital Association and in securing better opportunities for black doctors and nurses. The sisters opened missions in Arequipa, Peru, and La Paz, Bolivia in the 1960s. In 1975 there were 394 sisters in 46 houses.

[R. C. CLIGGETT]

ST. MARY (LÜBECK), beautiful Low German brick Gothic church, built 1251–1310 by the burghers of Lübeck, unique among German churches in having its side aisles lower than the nave in the French Gothic clerestory style. The wall paintings are notable. BIBLIOGRAPHY: D. Ellger, *St. Marien zu Lübeck und seine Wandmalereien* (1951).

[M. J. DALY]

ST. MARY-LE-BOW, LONDON (1670–83), built by Sir Christopher Wren, based on the plan of the *Templum Pacis* of Serlio. The magnificent spire of circular and Greek-cross *tempietti*, crowned by an obelisk—Wren's first classical steeple—is unrivaled among his many London churches.

[M. J. DALY]

ST. MARY-LE-STRAND, LONDON (1714–17), first of 50 new churches built under the Act of 1711, and James Gibb's first important commission, evidencing his 16th-cent., Roman-mannerist style, its small scale unique among contemporary structures.

[M. J. DALY]

ST. MARY OF NAMUR, SISTERS OF, a pontifical institute of sisters founded for the purpose of teaching at Namur, Belgium in 1819. Nicholas Joseph Minsart, a Cistercian who was secularized during the French Revolution, opened sewing classes in St. Loup parish where he was dedicating his energies to the restoration of Christian family life. He was helped by Josephine Sana and Elizabeth Berger. Later in 1834 a group of Minsart's parishioners consecrated their lives to God through Mary by the vows of religion. In 1863 Pierre Jean de Smet cooperated with Bp. John Timon of Buffalo, N.Y., in establishing a convent of the sisters in that diocese. Mother Émilie opened a school in Lockport, N.Y. From there the sisters extended their work throughout the U.S. and Canada. The generalate is situated in Namur, Belgium, and governs the provinces of U.S., Canada, Scotland, England, and the missions in the Congo and Rwanda in Africa. In 1975 the sisters numbered 746 in 13 houses.

[R. C. CLIGGETT]

ST. MARY OF OREGON, SISTERS OF, a congregation founded for the education of youth in 1886 in Sublimity, Ore., by William H. Gross, archbishop of Portland. Pius XI approved the constitutions of the congregation in 1934. The sisters engage in catechetical work, staff elementary and secondary schools throughout the Northwest, instruct in colleges, and conduct a convalescent and nursing home. The motherhouse of the community was transferred from Sublimity to Beavertown, Oregon. In 1975 the sisters numbered 188 in 32 houses.

[R. C. CLIGGETT]

ST. MARY OF PROVIDENCE, DAUGHTERS OF, a religious institute established for the care of the aged and the instruction of young girls. In 1872 a group of young women in a small country parish of N Italy opened a hospice to care for the aged and to instruct young girls. They were organized as a formal religious community by Rev. Luigi Guanella in 1881 with Marcellina Bosatta as foundress and first superior general. Their rule was approved in 1917. In 1913 the Sisters came to Chicago to assist Italian immigrants and in 1925 opened a school for mentally retarded girls. They also opened schools for the mentally retarded in the Archdiocese of Philadelphia and homes for the aged in the Dioceses of Sioux Falls, S.D., and New Ulm, Minnesota. The generalate is in Como, Italy. In 1975, the Sisters numbered 1,073 in 64 houses.

[R. C. CLIGGETT]

ST.-MAUR-DES-FOSSÉS, ABBEY OF, former Benedictine monastery located in a suburb of Paris, in the canton of Saint-Maur-des-Fossés, Seine, France; founded in 638 under King Clovis II and Bishop Aubert, by Bildegisilus, archdeacon of Paris. Its first abbot was St. Babolinus. It was originally dedicated to Our Lady and SS. Peter and Paul; and then to St. Maurus of Subiaco when the latter's relics were translated there for safekeeping in 868, at the request of Charles the Bald. The abbey had already shown itself capable of withstanding Norman attacks in 861. It participated in the reform of Mayeul of Cluny (988); became a popular pilgrimage center in the Middle Ages and prospered accordingly; was secularized in 1534 by Pope Clement VII at the request of King Francis I; and was incorporated in 1749 into the chapter of Saint-Louis of the Louvre. On the eve of the Revolution (1786) scarcely any of the abbey buildings were still standing.

[E. J. DILLON]

ST.-MAUR-SUR-LOIRE, ABBEY OF, (*Glanfeuil, Glannafoliense, S. Maurus supra Ligerim*), Benedictine abbey, situated in the valley of the Loire in the diocese of Angers (Maine-et-Loire, France). According to a very uncertain tradition St. Maur, a disciple of Saint Benedict (d. 584), founded the monastery with the aid of King Theodebert I of Austrasia. It was restored *c.*840, destroyed by the Normans, then reestablished in the 11th century. Once again destroyed during the Hundred Years War and the Wars of Religion, it was reformed by the Maurists (1668), who lived there until the Revolution. (There were seven monks in 1768.) A 17th-cent. building and a 12th-cent. oratory still stand. BIBLIOGRAPHY: Cottineau 2:2802–03; J. de la C. Bouton, NCE 12:924.

[J. DAOUST]

ST. MAURICE, ABBEY OF, monastery of Canons Regular of St. Augustine with a colorful and checkered history dating back almost to the Roman times of St. Maurice and his companion martyrs of the Theban legion. The abbey survives as an abbey *nullius* with 6 parishes, over 300 religious, and about 4,000 laity in its 37–square–mile

jurisdiction. The abbey was founded in 515 by King Sigismund of Burgundy on the site of the basilica built in Valais by St. Theodore (380–391), the first bishop of Valais. The presence of the relics of St. Maurice and his companions, the abbey's location on the road over the Great St. Bernard Alpine pass, and its tradition of *laus perennis* (perpetual psalmody) conspired to make it a popular pilgrimage center. It was alternately endowed or dispossessed at the hands of the dukes of Burgundy and Savoy until a period of relative serenity (1150–1798) when the abbots were overlords of the surrounding wine-growing area. The king of Sardinia made the abbots counts in 1782. The Swiss government secularized the abbey after the Napoleonic invasion. Its treasures were restored to it when it reopened in 1814. In 1840 the abbot became titular bishop of Bethlehem; and the abbey has not ceased to be involved in on-going litigation, ecclesiastical and secular, in efforts to attain its present anomalous status.

[E. J. DILLON]

ST. MAXIMIN, ABBEY OF, originally a Benedictine priory, later a Dominican convent, situated N of the mountain of Saint-Baume, in the diocese of Aix (Var, France). A monastery that had existed on the spot from the 5th cent. disappeared during the Saracen invasions. The Benedictine priory was founded in 1038 as a dependency of the Abbey of Saint-Victor of Marseilles. In 1267 it was joined to the priory of Saint-Zacharie. Given by royal Angevin deed in 1295 to the Dominicans, it became an important center for their activity in S France until recently, when they were obliged by circumstances to give it up. Some of the conventual buildings date back to the 14th and 15th cent., the cloister to the 15th. The most outstanding monument is the basilica of Sainte-Madeleine, the most important Gothic edifice of Provence, constructed in various stages (1295–1532). It has been claimed that the crypt contains the tomb of Mary Magdalen, who, according to a legend traceable to the 12th cent., spent her last years at the nearby mountain of Saint-Baume. Vézelay also claims the honor of possessing the same remains. BIBLIOGRAPHY: Cottineau 2:2808–09.

[J. DAOUST]

ST. MAXIMIN, TRIER: CAROLINGIAN FRESCOES (*c.*882), among the few extant frescoes of Carolingian times, relating iconographically and stylistically to MS illumination of the Reims school in their expressive linear gesture.

[M. J. DALY]

ST. MEINRAD, ARCHABBEY, Benedictine abbey, located in Spencer County in the Archdiocese of Indianapolis, Indiana, founded by the abbey of Einsiedeln in Switzerland and dedicated to St. Meinrad, the hermit of Reichenau. From its modest origins in a log cabin in 1854, it has grown and founded 5 daughter monasteries in the U.S. and 1 in Peru and has had a leading role in the Swiss-American

Congregation. The monks labored first among the German settlers of their region, but under their first abbot, Martin Marty (1870–80), they also became missionaries to the Indians. The abbey has had a progressive impact on the education of priests at its seminary and upon the renewal of liturgical consciousness in the United States. At its centennial (1954) it was made an archabbey.

[E. J. DILLON]

ST. MICHAEL, HILDESHEIM,

German late-Ottonian structure (1001–15) showing Romanesque characteristics, founded and enriched by the famous Bp. Bernward. The basilica with three aisles, transept and apses E and W, the nave alternating two columns and a pier–in a Byzantine style (Hagios, Dimitrios, Thessalonika), seen also in the alternating white and colored masonry. Bays, arches, and capitals are cubic in module, the exterior a rational asymmetric balance. The famous bronze doors (1007–15) of Bp. Bernward, with scenes from Genesis and the life of Christ, stylistically related to earlier MSS and mosaics, and probably influenced by the wooden doors of S. Sabina, Rome, were executed in the Hildesheim workshop, setting a pattern for many subsequent church doors. BIBLIOGRAPHY: F. Tschan, *Saint Bernward of Hildesheim* (1942–52). *DOORS, CHURCH.

[M. J. DALY]

ST. MIHIEL, ABBEY OF,

a Benedictine monastery originally founded on Mount Castellion (Châtelet) in the diocese of Verdun (Meuse, France) in 709—according to an unreliable tradition, by a powerful noble named Vulfoad—and later (815) transferred to the banks of the Meuse by Abbot *Smaragdus. It lapsed from the flourishing state it had preserved through the Middle Ages when it became a commendatory abbey in the 15th cent.; later it was reformed by the religious of Saint-Vanne (1616) who occupied it until the Revolution. Its monks, like those of Saint-Vanne (see VERDUN-SUR-MEUSE, ABBEY OF), tended to support the cause of Jansenism. The superb 17th- and 18th-cent. buildings are still standing, as well as the abbey church of Saint-Michel (13th century). BIBLIOGRAPHY: Cottineau 2:2818–19.

[J. DAOUST]

ST. OMER, COLLEGE OF,

a Jesuit institution established in penal times for English laymen seeking abroad the education denied them in England. Founded in 1593 by Robert Parsons (Persons) SJ with the approval of Philip of Spain, in the ancient French province of Artois, then under Spanish rule, to counteract the stingent English laws against Catholic education, St. Omer's, despite early financial and political difficulties, soon became an academic center for English and American colonial youth. Twice destroyed by fire and rebuilt (1610 and 1725), for more than 150 years the college instructed youth in the rudiments of mathematics, grammar, poetry, rhetoric, Latin and Greek, counting among its students future martyrs for the faith and outstanding prelates and statesmen, among them: Bl. Thomas Garnet, St. Omer's protomartyr, Andrew White, apostle of Maryland, John Carroll, first bp. of Baltimore, and Charles Carroll of Carrollton, signer of the Declaration of Independence. Although in 1678 the province of Artois passed under French control, the college continued to prosper until 1762, when the French parliament decreed the expulsion of the Jesuits from France. Rather than give over the college to seculars, the Jesuits, with the students' cooperation, removed it to Bruges, Belgium, where it remained until 1773, when the Society was suppressed. The college then moved to Liège and there continued to function until 1794 when the Revolution drove students and masters from France to England where the college was reestablished at Stonyhurst through the generosity of an alumnus, Thomas Weld. BIBLIOGRAPHY: H. Chawick, *St. Omer to Stonyhurst* (1962); B. N. Ward, *Dawn of the Catholic Revival in England, 1781–1803* (2 v., 1909).

[M. B. MURPHY]

ST. OUEN, ABBEY OF,

former Benedictine monastery in Rouen, France, founded *c.*536 by grant of Clotaire I, with the zealous encouragement of his mother, St. Clotilde. At first dedicated to St. Peter by Bishop Filleul (533–542), it was later known as Saint Ouen after the saintly Abp. Ouen (640–683) who had been buried there. The abbey adopted the Benedictine Rule (*c.*610), but monastic life ceased after the Viking raids of 841. It revived in the 11th cent., and the abbey gradually became a center of Norman monasticism, a theological mecca, and its abbot mitred (1256) by decree of Alexander IV. Fire caused extensive damage in 1156, 1201, and 1248. The still extant abbey church is a Gothic masterpiece dating from the 14th and 15th centuries. The abbey became commendatory after 1462; it was pillaged by the Huguenots in 1562. Conventual life resumed under the Maurists in 1660. The renovations begun in 1753 were interrupted by the Revolution, when the abbey was suppressed (1790). The monks' quarters became the Town Hall of Rouen.

[E. J. DILLON]

ST. PATRICK'S COLLEGE (MAYNOOTH), see IRELAND, NATIONAL UNIVERSITY OF.

ST. PATRICK'S MISSIONARY SOCIETY,

officially known as the Society of St. Patrick for Foreign Missions, was founded with the specific object of preaching the gospel in mission countries. It was canonically established in 1932 with headquarters at Kiltegan, County Wicklow, Ireland. Msgr. P. J. Whitney was the founder and first superior general. The members take an oath of membership but no vows. For purposes of administration the society is divided into three parts: Ireland and America, East Africa, and West Africa governed by regional superiors appointed by the superior general. The society came into being as a result of a movement begun by the Irish diocesan clergy. An appeal had been made at Maynooth, the national seminary, for diocesan priests to volunteer for periods of time in the Nigerian missions. The response to this appeal made the need of a more permanent source of personnel for the missions felt acutely. In 1950 a mission was established in the U.S. at Camden, N.J., and in 1962 in São Paulo, Brazil. By 1975 there were 467 members of whom 376 were priests in 9 houses.

[R. C. CLIGGETT]

ST. PATRICK'S PURGATORY, a well known pilgrimage center on Station Island in Lock Derg, Co. Donegal, Ireland, probably dating back to the 12th century. It takes its name from the tradition that St. Patrick preached in the area and the less conclusive legend that he experienced a vision of the sufferings of Purgatory and the happiness of the saved, while fasting and praying in a cave there. A more recent legend attributes this experience to Owen, an Irish Knight (c. 1153). In 1790, the famous cave was replaced by a large church to minister to the increasing number of pilgrims. Presently, under the direction of the Bishop of Clogher, the three day exercise of prayer and penance, established in 1613, is observed by as many as 15,000 pilgrims from June 1st to August 1st each year.

[F. H. BRIGHAM]

ST. PAUL, PIOUS SOCIETY OF THE DAUGHTERS OF, a congregation founded in 1915 in Italy to spread the message of Christ through the media of social communication: press, motion pictures, radio, and TV. Rev. Giacomo Alberione, assisted by Teresa Merlo, later Mother Thecla, established the society at Alba, Italy. In 1953 it received papal approbation. The society expanded from a small group of women into an international community. The general motherhouse is located in Rome, Italy.

The sisters arrived in the U.S. in 1932 and established a provincial motherhouse, a novitiate, a juniorate, St. Paul High School and House of Studies in Boston, Mass. In 1975 the sisters numbered 2,700 in 210 houses.

[R. C. CLIGGETT]

ST. PAUL (CHARTRES), SISTERS OF, a congregation dedicated to works of charity and founded (1696) by Louis Chauvet, a parish priest of Levesville-la-Chenard, France. The community became a diocesan congregation when Paul Godet des Marais, bishop of Chartres, established the sisters in his diocese in 1708. In 1722 the sisters went to French Guiana. The community reconvened after the French Revolution and obtained the approval of Pius IX in 1861. The sisters were established in Vietnam, China, Japan, Korea, Thailand, Laos, the Philippines, Africa, France, Belgium, Switzerland, England, the West Indies, and Canada when they received final approbation in 1949. In 1963 they came to the U.S. and became active in the Diocese of Marquette, Michigan. The motherhouse is in Chartres; the

residence of the superior general, in Rome. In 1975 the sisters numbered 4,001 in 450 houses.

[R. C. CLIGGETT]

ST. PAUL-OUTSIDE-THE-WALLS, ABBEY OF, Benedictine abbey *nullius* next to the basilica of the same name, associated with the tomb of St. Paul the Apostle. Apparently already existing in the 6th cent., the monastic community was restored in 714 by Pope Gregory II. The Saracens destroyed both the monastery and the tomb of St. Paul in the 9th century. It was restored for nearly a cent. by the Cluniac reforms of St. Odo (942) and St. Majolus (994), and was rescued from the degradation of the 11th cent. by Hildebrand, the future Gregory VII. It retained its prestige as a strong feudal ecclesiastical domain until after the Avignon papacy. It was united to the Congregation of Monte Cassino by Martin V in 1425 and was saved from the prevailing monastic decay by the reform of Justina of Padua. It maintained itself by the revenue of a great landed estate from the 15th to the 18th century. Divested by Napoleonic and later Italian suppressions, it revived in the late 19th century. Following Vatican Council II, the abbey has attempted to relate to the dechristianized milieu of the largely working class neighborhoods surrounding it along the Via Ostiense in modern Rome.

[E. J. DILLON]

ST. PAUL'S CATHEDRAL (London; 1675–1708), designed by Sir Christopher Wren, leading architect of English Baroque, to replace the disintegrating medieval cathedral. Typical of Wren's eclecticism, the cruciform plan with domed crossing combines a Neoclassical style with elements derived from English Gothic architecture (nave equal in length to the choir), French Neoclassicism (paired columns of the façade) and Roman Baroque (curved porticoes of the transept façades). The majestic edifice with two-story façade, twin towers (West End) and dome rises 350 feet. Behind the façade is a domical vestibule with vaulted chapels. Interior, spatial divisions are likewise covered by grand domical vaults, the main dome formed of two shells, the interior one painted, the exterior one the most famous, imposing silhouette of London, a perfect tribute to Wren's genius in engineering and mathematics, and with St. Peter's, Rome and the Capitol, Washington, D.C., one of the three most magnificent Renaissance domes in the world. BIBLIOGRAPHY: J. N. Summerson, *Architecture in Britain, 1530–1830* (1963).

[S. CONWAY]

ST. PETER-IN-CHAINS, a famous basilica on the Esquiline hill in Rome, believed to house revered relics of the chains from which the Apostle Peter was freed by an angel, as described in Acts of the Apostles. The original basilica dates from the time of the Empress Eudoxia, wife of Valentinian III (442). In 680 an ancient mosaic of St. Sebastian as a bearded warrior was brought here from Constantinople.

Since the Renaissance, this "Eudoxian Basilica" is best known for the famed *Moses* of Michelangelo, designed as part of what should have been an immense monument to Julius II and planned for St. Peter's Basilica. There must have been monks attached to such a revered shrine from ancient times. The reforming monk Hildebrand was crowned pope here in 1073, taking the name Gregory VII. A settlement of Canons Regular of Bologna was formally assigned here in 1489. Today there is a monastery of Minims adjoining.

[E. J. DILLON]

ST. PETER OF MUENSTER, ABBEY OF, Benedictine abbey *nullius* carved out of the Diocese of Prince Albert in central Saskatchewan, Canada. It was founded in 1903 for the pastoral care of German- and English-speaking pioneer settlers of the region by American Benedictine monks from Cluny, Ill., and Collegeville, Minn., of the American Cassinian Congregation. The priory became an abbey in 1911 and an abbey *nullius* in 1921, with parishes, a high school, and (since 1926) a college.

[E. J. DILLON]

ST. PIERRE, CATHEDRAL OF, BEAUVAIS, great French Gothic triumph in extreme verticalism (choir 157 ft 6 in, aisles 69 ft 8 in), strengthened by double flying buttresses, and having such extensive surfaces of stained glass that the triforium and clerestory seem one continuous glazed area. The cathedral has a choir of three double bays with double aisles, an ambulatory with seven polygonal radiating chapels, a transept of three bays on each side of the crossing, and one nave-bay with double aisles on either side. Designed (1230–40) after the fire of 1225 had destroyed the Old Carolingian choir, the Cathedral called the "Haut Oeuvre" to replace *Notre-Dame "Basse Oeuvre"*, relates esp. to Amiens but also to Le Mans and the Abbey Church of St. Denis. Partial collapse of the buttresses (1284) caused a doubling of choir pillars and a change to sexpartite vaulting. Jean Vast and M. Chambiges constructed the transept and portals in magnificent Flamboyant Gothic, the S portal begun by Chambiges (1500) and finished (1548) by Michel de la Lalict, is the richer of the two and prototype for Senlis. The N portal begun by Chambiges (1510) was also completed by Lalict (1537). Over the loftiest crossing yet achieved, a 262-ft stone tower begun in 1561 under F. Mareschal was surmounted by a 96-ft wooden flèche (1564–67) by Jean Vast, son of the transept builder, attaining a total height from ground level of more than 502 ft. In 1573 the tower and spire fell (owing to inadequate foundations), ruining the crossing area. All vaults were repaired (1575), but due to an exhausted treasury and Wars of Religions the tower was not rebuilt. Later vaults of transept and crossing are of wood. BIBLIOGRAPHY: P. Frankl, *Gothic Architecture* (1962); M. Aubert and S. Goubet, *Gothic Cathedrals of France and Their Treasures* (1959).

[M. J. DALY]

ST. PIERRE OF GHENT, ABBEY OF, Benedictine monastery founded by St. Amandus (*c*.630–640), predating Saint-Bavon. Keen rivalry between them later created for scholars confusion about their early years, for 10th–cent. monks invented false records to make one outshine the other. Both were ravaged by the Normans (9th cent.) and restored by Count Arnould and St.-Gérard de Brogne. Saint-Pierre was destroyed by Calvinists (1578). Rebuilt in the 17th cent., the abbey prospered in the eighteenth. In 1796 the monks were dispersed by the French Revolution, but buildings were saved. Later, some were razed or put to public use. BIBLIOGRAPHY: E. Michel, *Abbayes et Monastères de Belgique* (1923) 124–128.

[S. A. HEENEY]

ST.-PIERRE-SUR-DIVES, ABBEY OF, former Benedictine monastery of Notre-Dame, located in what was Séez Diocese and is now the Diocese of Bayeux, France. Called Notre-Dame de l'Épinay (Beata Maria de Spineto), it was founded first for nuns and then for monks by Countess Lescelina of Eu, who recruited monks and the abbot Aynard from Saint-Trinité, Rouen (*c*.1046). The present abbey church, now a parish church, dates from the 13th and 14th centuries. The chapter house and some of the cloister have also survived. The monastery was fortified in the Middle Ages and escaped relatively unharmed from the Hundred Years' War. It was burned and pillaged by the Huguenots (1562), languished under commendatory abbots, and recovered under the Maurists after 1668. It was dissolved during the Revolution (1790).

[E. J. DILLON]

ST. PROCOPIUS ABBEY, Benedictine monastery of the American–Cassinese Congregation, founded in 1885 in Lisle, Illinois, in what is now the Diocese of Joliet, Illinois. In 1975, the abbey comprised 103 monks, including 73 priests, and helped staff Benet Academy and Illinois Benedictine College, two institutions in its care. It also has sponsored a Benedictine priory at Chiayi, Taiwan.

[E. J. DILLON]

ST. QUENTIN, MONASTERY OF, a monastery founded by St. Eligius (Eloi) of Noyon at Vermandois in the Diocese of Noyon (Aisne, France) *c*.650. The monastery was constructed next to a church built over the tomb of St. Quentin, a martyr of the 3d century. The monastery's first abbot was Ebertran, a monk from Luxeuil. The monks were replaced by canons regular *c*.900. The community was suppressed during the Revolution. Only the collegiate church, built in 1230, remains today. It was restored after being damaged by bombing in World War I. BIBLIOGRAPHY: Cottineau 2:2860–62.

[J. DAOUST]

ST. RAPHAEL'S SOCIETY, founded in 1871 at the Catholic Congress in Mainz, Germany, to advise prospective emigrants, to protect them while in transit, and to help them adjust when they arrived in the country to which they were destined. The society was founded by Peter Paul Cahensly, an outstanding Catholic layman, merchant, and member of the Prussian Diet. The society had representatives in every major port of Europe, North and South America, and Africa. It was criticized in the 1880s and 1890s for its alleged exclusive interest in German nationals. There was also strong opposition to its settling immigrants in colonies and securing pastors of the same nationality for them. In time the society broadened its base by organizing daughter societies, and its work shifted from countries of immigration to those of emigration. Its purpose in the mid-20th cent. was to be an effective instrument in the hands of the Church for carrying out papal suggestions concerning immigration.

[R. C. CLIGGETT]

ST. RÉMY SOUS ROCHEFORT, ABBEY OF, Cistercian abbey founded at the beginning of the 13th cent. in Mons, Namur, and dedicated to Our Lady of Perpetual Help. At first it was occupied by Cistercian nuns who were replaced in 1464 by monks of the same order. The abbey was secularized by Pope Pius VI (1792), and the monks were permitted to become canons. The French Revolution, however, caused the closing and then the sale of the monastery. Trappists have occupied it since 1887 and cultivate great fields in the environs. A great part of the abbey had been demolished, nothing remaining of the medieval church or cloisters. Some rebuilding was done in the late 19th century. Fortunately, the great entry was not altered much and enough remains—Gothic capitals of columns, the old abbatial palace with its grand windows, iron work and stone borders among them—to give graphic testimony to the activities and power of the monasteries of the Middle Ages. BIBLIOGRAPHY: E. Michel, *Abbayes et Monastères de Belgique* (1923) 254–255.

[S. A. HEENEY]

ST. RIQUIER, ABBEY OF (*Centulense*), Benedictine monastery located in a place once known as Centula in the Diocese of Amiens (Somme, France). It was already one of the most important abbeys in France in the 9th cent., when its community numbered more than 400; but the date and circumstances of its foundation are unknown. It was dedicated to St. Ricarius (Riquier, d. *c.*645), a hermit who died in the forest of Crécy. The monastery possessed his relics and regarded him as its founder, but available evidence does not support this claim, though Ricarius had served as a priest at Centula before retiring to his hermitage. Destroyed by the Normans, the monastery was rebuilt and reformed by Gérard de Brogne (d. 959). The abbey church, built in 13th cent., was destroyed by fire in 1487 and was almost entirely rebuilt in the 16th century. In 1659 the Maurists reformed the abbey and kept it until the Revolution, when

the community was dissolved. BIBLIOGRAPHY: Cottineau 2:2686–89.

[J. DAOUST]

ST.-ROBERT-DE-CORNILLON, PRIORY OF, a Benedictine house dependent on Chaise-Dieu, founded *c.*1075 by Count Guigo II the Fat and his son Guigo III in the diocese of Grenoble (Isère, France). It was reformed in 1657 by the Maurists; the community, which numbered only seven religious in 1768, ceased to exist in the Revolution. Very little remains of the 11th-cent. buildings. BIBLIOGRAPHY: Cottineau 2:2870.

[J. DAOUST]

ST. SABAS, MONASTERY OF, a renowned community of contemplative monks in the Judean desert near Jerusalem and the Dead Sea. Called the Great Laura monastery of St. Sabas, it was founded by St. Saba (d. 532) and served as a prototype for subsequent Eastern Orthodox monasticism. It was a standard-bearer of orthodoxy, combatting, like its founder, Origenism and Monophysitism and whatever belittled the reality of the humanity of Jesus. Saba came to Palestine from Cappadocia in 457 and then was given permission to withdraw from existing monasteries and live as a solitary. He settled in the Kidron gorge, near Jerusalem, NW of the Dead Sea. The number of his disciples grew until (*c.*483) he was constrained to construct a number of small cottages grouped about a chapel. From this modest beginning he went on to establish 14 monasteries and 4 hospices for pilgrims throughout southern Palestine. After the 7th cent., the Great Laura (meaning ''lanes of stone'' in reference to the structural pattern) became a center of ''kanon'' writers, the most elaborate of the poetic forms in Greek-Byzantine hymnody.

[E. J. DILLON]

SAINT-SAËNS, CAMILLE (1835–1921), French composer. A musical genius and a leading composer of France, he early demonstrated a versatile talent as pianist and organist, at the age of 11 making his concert debut. At the age of 17 his *Ode à Sainte Cécile* for voice and orchestra won the first prize of the Société Sainte-Cécile, and his first symphony was performed a year later. S. was the distinguished organist of the Church of the Madeleine (1858–77) and a founder of the Société Nationale de Musique (1871) to encourage French composers. He continued to appear as conductor and virtuoso until his death at 86. Among his ten operas the most successful was *Samson and Dalila* (1877). Among his more than 200 compositions are the three symphonies, the ever–popular *Carnival of the Animals* and *Danse Macabre*, an oratorio, *La Déluge,* five piano concertos, over 100 songs and 169 pieces for the piano. His music is distinguished for its sonorous orchestration, counterpoint, and full harmonic quality; he gave a depth to French music unknown before his time.

[J. R. AHERNE]

ST. SAUVEUR, AIX-EN-PROVENCE, cathedral in southeastern France, modified repeatedly from the 11th to the 18th cent. with the Provencal Romanesque portal of the original church on the right side of the west facade, which is historically precious though aesthetically unrelated to the Flamboyant Gothic central portal (16th century). Most exterior sculptures were destroyed in the Wars of Religion and the Revolution; only the Virgin and Child of the trumeau (1505) and St. Michael above the central window remaining. Adjoining are a Gothic bell-tower (14th-15th cent.) and a small, elegant Romanesque cloister. On the interior a 5th-cent. Baptistery, the sarcophagus of St. Mitre, the triptych of the *Burning Bush* by N. Froment, a 15th-cent. retable of the *Legend of St. Mitre* and 26 16th-cent. Brussels tapestries are treasures. BIBLIOGRAPHY: F. Benoit, "Cathédrale Saint-Sauveur," *Congrès Archéologique de France, 1932* (1933).

[M. J. DALY]

ST.-SAVIN-DE-BIGORRE, ABBEY OF, a Benedictine monastery founded by St. Savinus, a monk of Ligugé and a hermit in the Pyrenees (fl. 8th century). It was located in the diocese of Tarbes (Hautes-Pyrenees, France). Sacked by the Saracens, it was restored by the Benedictines at the time of Louis the Pious (d. 840), and again after the Norman invasions, by Raymond, count of Bigorre. In 1080 it came under the rule of Saint-Victor de Marseilles and in 1625 was reformed by the Maurists. The abbey church, a remarkable structure of Benedictine design (12th cent.), with a bell tower added in the 14th cent., still stands. BIBLIOGRAPHY: Cottineau 2:2882–83.

[J. DAOUST]

ST.-SAVIN-SUR-GARTEMPE, ABBEY OF, former Benedictine monastery founded (c.800) by Count Abbot Badilon of Marmoutier. It is located in the Department of Vienne, France, in the Diocese of Poitiers, and is named for the 5th-cent. martyr, St. Savinus, buried nearby. His relics were transferred to the abbey by Louis the Pious, who is also credited with enlarging the abbey and entrusting it to Benedict of Aniane. It was a center of Cluniac reform, whence Hugh of Anzy went to St-Martin-d'Autun (before 930) and Gombaud went to Charroux (1023). It declined during the Hundred Years' War, was pillaged during war with the Huguenots (1562–85), suffered under commendatory abbots until the introduction of the Maurists (1642–43), and was suppressed during the Revolution. The 11th-cent. church, renowned for its Romanesque frescoes, now serves as a parish church.

[E. J. DILLON]

ST. SERGIUS, THEOLOGICAL SCHOOL OF, the Orthodox Theological Institute of St. Sergius located in Paris, the major institution in the West for the study of Russian theology. The Institute is under the jurisdiction of the Russian Exarchate in Western Europe. Founded in 1925 as the Orthodox Theological Institute by Russian emigrés under the Metropolitan Eulogius-Georgievsky, it received its present name in 1940. Since 1931, it has been recognized by the Univ. of Paris. Most of the students are of non-Russian nationality, American, Bulgarian, Greek, Serbian; since 1958, both Russian and French have been the languages of instruction. Through S. *Bulgakov, N. Ajanassieff, G. Florovsky, A. Schmemann, J. Meyendorff, and many other outstanding theologians, St. Sergius has exerted a profound influence on Orthodox and other Christian theologians. The faculty have been leaders in orthodox participation in the ecumenical movement, and esp. in the *World Council of Churches. Many of the faculty of St. Vladimir's Orthodox Seminary in New York came from St. Sergius. BIBLIOGRAPHY: A. Lowrie, *Saint Sergius of Paris, The Orthodox Theological Institute* (1954).

[T. BIRD]

ST. SERNIN, TOULOUSE. One of the largest and most beautiful of Romanesque basilicas in S France, it is the final burial place of St. Saturnin, bp. and martyr of Toulouse, whose relics with the bodies of six apostles (gift of Charlemagne) made this a favorite pilgrimage church on the road to Santiago de Compostela. Begun in 1060 and completed c.1150, the very large church (377 ft, with transept 210 ft, the roof 69 ft) designed for the movement of large crowds of pilgrims, has double aisles, multiple naves, ambulatories, radiating chapels, and galleries. The interior, darkened by a tunnel vault with no clerestory, is enriched by fine carved capitals and seven bas-reliefs in the wall of the ambulatory depicting Christ in Majesty with angels and Apostles. A moving 12th-cent. Christ on the cross in copper-sheathed wood hangs at the N transept, and an upper and lower crypt contain reliquaries and liturgical objects. In the dominantly brick exterior the apse with five radiating chapels, the transepts with four, and a stone chevet are the oldest sections (1096). The octagonal tower rises with three Romanesque arcaded stories, two upper stories (13th cent.) and spire (14th century). The early 12th-cent. south portal, the Porte Miègeville, set a style for S France, with its Christ in the tympanum and Apostles gazing from the lintel below. "Restorations" by Viollet-le-Duc mar the exterior. The W front was not completed until 1929. BIBLIOGRAPHY: A. Auriol and R. Rey, *La Basilique Saint-Sernin de Toulouse* (1930); K. J. Conant, *Carolingian and Romanesque Architecture (800–1200)* 1959.

[M. J. DALY]

ST. SEVER, ABBEYS OF. Several abbeys shared this name. (1) Saint-Sever in Agde in S France, a monastery founded in the late 5th cent. by Severus, a Syrian monk. It was known also as Saint-André and was affiliated with Saint-Victor in Marseilles. (2) A monastery founded by St. Severus, a shepherd, in the diocese of Coutances in the 6th century. (3) Saint-Sever in Gascony (*S. Severus in capite Vasconiae*), a Benedictine abbey founded c.700? in the diocese of Aire (now Dax, Landes, France), and restored in the 10th cent. by Duke William Sanche. It owes its name, "Cap de Gascogne," to the fact that it is located at the border of this province, and the assemblies of the Novempopulanie (Gascons) were held here, convoked by the abbot of Saint-Sever. In the 11th cent. the famous illuminated MS called *Apocalypse of Beatus* was produced there. Sacked by Calvinists (1569), reformed by the Maurists (1646), the monastery survived until the French Revolution. The former monastic structures now belong to the municipality. The abbey church (c.1031–70), restored after the Hundred Years War and again in the 17th cent., is the most beautiful Romanesque structure in the area. (4) Saint-Sever-de-Rustan, a monastery in the Pyrenees, founded c.500, destroyed by the Saracens c.732, and refounded under the Benedictine rule in the 10th century. It came into the Maurist Congregation in the mid-17th cent. and was suppressed during the Revolution. The abbey-church, parts of which date back to the 11th cent., still stands and serves as a parish church. BIBLIOGRAPHY: Cottineau 2:2888–89.

SAINT-SIMON, CLAUDE HENRI DE ROUVROY, (1760–1825), social philosopher. A member of the French nobility, the Comte de Saint-Simon early revolted against the authority of Church and monarchy. He served with the rebels in the U.S. War of Independence. Abdicating his title during the French Revolution, he assumed it again under the restored monarchy. A man of grandiose plans for the unification of Europe, S.-S. published *La Réorganization de la société Européenne* in 1814. Basing his notion of politics on science, he called for a confederation of nationals with common industries, armies, currencies, and parliament. In 1821 he published *Système industriel,* which constitutes a primer of socialism. Like his follower Auguste Comte, he rejected Christianity in favor of positivism.

[J. R. AHERNE]

ST. SOPHIA, see HAGIA SOPHIA.

ST. SOPHIA, NOVGOROD: BRONZE DOORS OF, splendid Russian Romanesque doors (11 ft 8 in by 7 ft 9 in) probably executed by Saxon craftsmen (1152–54). They were—contrary to local tradition—originally for the Polish town of Plock, having Bp. Alexander of Plock depicted on one door, and Abp. Wichmann of Magdeburg on the other. The scenes are cast as separate panels and nailed to a wooden core, numbering 12 sq fields in each ½ door, topped by a broad rectangular field (26 in all), each with a Latin inscription, and Cyrillic inscriptions added at a later date, depicting OT and NT episodes, allegorical figures, and interesting portraits of the bronze founders Riquinus and Waismuth. Bronze tubular frames are perforated in decorative patterns, and two ferocious lions' heads as handles carry in their open mouths human heads which have been

too facilely interpreted as the damned. A similar deific, salvific motif (*t' ao t' ieh*) is ubiquitous on very early Chinese Shang ritualistic bronzes (1776 B.C.) and is echoed in Anteuil's sophisticated engravings of the Sun-King's head set within the open maw of a lion, all with beneficent, though varying interpretations. Christ, the Lion of Juda, truly the opener of the door of salvation, would seem a truer symbolic interpretation. Russian repairs added a centaur with bow and completed the excellent documentation by adding the portrait of the Russian bronze founder Abram. BIBLIOGRAPHY: A. Goldschmidt, *Die Bronzetüren von Nowgorod und Gnesen* (1932).

[M. J. DALY]

ST. STEPHEN'S CATHEDRAL (Stephansdom), Vienna, one of the largest medieval structures in central Europe, founded (1137) as a parish outside the city walls but now in the middle of the Inner City, with 14th-cent. reconstruction under Duke Rudolf IV. Damaged in World War II (1945), by 1952 the cathedral was fully restored. Its steeply pitched roof in patterned glazed tiles, and many pinnacled tower dominate the skyline. The late Romanesque west facade (1258), the oldest detail with its "Giant's Doorway," was pierced by the Gothic window (1422). Gothic construction of the elaborate net vaulting of Hanns Puchsbaum was completed (1304–1446). The tower (1359–1433) of Michael Chnab of Klosterneuburg rises 446 ft from the ground, a companion tower (discontinued) was topped (1579) by the cupola of Hans Saphoy. There are magnificent Gothic sculptures in the choir and St. Eligius' Chapel, and a famous Gothic pulpit (c.1510) by Anton Pilgram whose self-portrait is humbly placed at the foot of the steps beneath the four fathers of the church. The marble tomb (1467–1513) of Frederick III (d. 1493) is of interest. BIBLIOGRAPHY: R. K. Donin, *Der Wiener Stephansdom und seine Geschichte* (1946).

[M. J. DALY]

ST. SULPICE, the leading parish on the left bank of Paris. In the 17th cent., its pastor, J. J. *Olier, in order to carry out the wishes of the Council of Trent, founded a seminary in this parish. The *Sulpician Society grew out of this seminary, which remained near the church until the buildings were confiscated by the state in 1906, at which time it was moved to the Paris suburb of Issy-Les-Moulineaux. BIBLIOGRAPHY: C. Hamel, *Histoire de l'Église de St. Sulpice* (1900); C. Noonan, "Olier, Jean Jacques," NCE 10:679–680.

[R. B. ENO]

ST. THERESA OF JESUS, SOCIETY OF, otherwise known as Teresian Sisters, a congregation founded in Spain for the education of girls. Enrique de Ossó y Cervelló in 1876, a priest and seminary professor, established the society and definitive approval of its constitutions was given in 1908. The Teresians first came to the U.S. in 1910. The motherhouse is now in Rome. In 1974 the sisters numbered 2,094 in 116 houses.

[R. C. CLIGGETT]

ST. THOMAS AQUINAS, PONTIFICAL UNIVERSITY OF

since 1963 the name of the famous Dominican Univ. in Rome, formerly known as the Angelicum. The new title and rank were bestowed on it by John XXIII in his *motu proprio, Dominicanus Ordo*. This beloved univ. owes its origin to Gregory XIII who established the theological faculty in 1580 under the name "College of St. Thomas at Santa Maria sopra Minerva." It was for the exclusive use of students of the Order of Preachers. Benedict XIII, in 1727, extended the power to confer academic degrees to include non-Dominicans. In 1882 Leo XIII established the faculty of philosophy and in 1896 that of canon law. In 1909 it was moved to Via San Vitale; its name became Pontifical International Institute: the Angelicum. Its three faculties were confirmed by the Congregation of Seminaries and Universities, in accord with the Apostolic Constitution, *Deus scientiarum Dominus*. From 1932 its site has been the huge edifice built by St. Pius V as a monastery for Dominican nuns. In 1955, the Institute of Social Sciences was canonically established within the faculty of philosophy, with the power granted to confer relevant degrees. The name by which it is popularly known is still preserved in its address in Rome, on the Largo Angelicum.

[E. J. DILLON]

ST. THOMAS CHRISTIANS

the general name for the Christians of Malabar in the Indian state of Kerala who trace their Christianity to the Apostle Thomas, but are not necessarily in communion with one another. He is thought to have died as a martyr in Mylapore where his first grave still is shown at the cathedral of St. Thomas. The authenticity of this tradition cannot be proved, but it is known that there were Christians in Kerala before the 5th century. Possibly these were Persians who had fled persecution in their own land and settled here. These Malabar Christians, who were originally under the jurisdiction of the (Chaldean) patriarch of Seleucia-Ctesiphon, became virtually independent in their church life, a fact that kept them from involvement in the Nestorian controversies. With the coming of the Portuguese in the 15th cent., these Christians were at first considered loyal Catholics; but the new rulers, in an effort to eliminate—as they thought—all traces of Nestorianism, imposed on them Latin reforms and a Latin hierarchy (see MALABAR RITE; MALANKAR RITE). This resulted in a schism in 1653. Besides the two Catholic groups of the Malabar and the Malankar rites, the St. Thomas Christians include: a Syrian Jacobite Church under the patriarch of Antioch, with its own *catholicos; an independent (Protestant) Jacobite Church of Mar Thomas; an Evangelical Church of St. Thomas; and a small Nestorian Church, *Mellusians, under the Nestorian Chaldean patriarch. BIBLIOGRAPHY: L. Brown, *Indian Christians of St. Thomas* (1956); S. G. Pothan, *Syrian Christians of Kerala* (1963).

[J. MEIJER]

ST. THOMAS OF VILLANOVA, SISTERS OF

a congregation founded in 1661 by Pierre Le Proust, an Augustinian in Lumballe, Brittany, to aid in all forms of spiritual and material need. At first its members restored hospitals and worked for the sick in them. The congregation spread quickly throughout France but almost disappeared during the French Revolution. Napoleon I aided its renewal, and it received papal approval of its institute and constitutions in 1873. The motherhouse is in Neuilly-sur-Seine in the Archdiocese of Paris. The sisters are found also in Rome, Belgium, and Africa. In 1975 they numbered 425 in 56 houses.

[R. C. CLIGGETT]

ST. TROND, ABBEY OF

(Flemish, Sint-Truijen; Lat. *Sacrinium*), a monastery located at what is now Limburg, Belgium, founded *c*.662 at a site called Sacrinium by St. Trudo (d. *c*.693). It depended upon the bps. of Metz until 1223, when Hugh of Pierrepont, bp. of Liège, took it under his protection. It enjoyed a period of remarkable intellectual activity under Abbot Thierry (d. 1107). The monastery was amalgamated with the Congregation of Bursfeld in 1603 and was suppressed in 1796. A portal (1655), an entrance and buildings constructed during the 18th cent., and the church tower (11th-14th cent.) still stand. BIBLIOGRAPHY: Cottineau 2:2905–06.

[J. DAOUST]

ST. URSULA, SHRINE OF

four gilded, 3′ long Flemish reliquary casket in the form of a Gothic chapel, decorated (1489) with paintings of H. Memlinc for St. John's Hospital, Bruges. On the sides six arched panels depict the story of St. Ursula from the *Legenda Aurea*. In scenes 1, 5, and 6 Memlinc presents accurate, historic views of Cologne showing the Cathedral, St. Martin's Church, and the Church of St. Maria im Kapitol. The end panels show St. Ursula protecting her 11,000 companions, the Virgin with Child, and donors. Upon the roof are six painted medallions. Certain details suggest Memlinc's workshop. The reliquary of brilliant gilded Gothic tracery is a magnificent, worthy frame for masterpieces which make it famous. BIBLIOGRAPHY: C. D. Cuttler, *Northern Painting* (1968).

[R. BERGMANN]

ST. URSULA OF THE BLESSED VIRGIN, SISTERS OF

one of the first congregations of religious women to combine the contemplative life with an active life in the work of teaching. The congregation was founded in 1606 in Dôle, France, by Ven. Anne de Xainctonge. Its constitutions were based on the Rule of St. Ignatius of Loyola and were canonically approved in 1898 by Leo XIII.

By this time the society of St. Ursula was established in E France, Switzerland, and Germany. In 1901, however, the French government forced the religious to become exiles in Belgium, Italy, and America. By the year 1964 the sisters were conducting schools in France, Belgium, Italy, Switzerland, Germany, the U.S., the Congo, the Union of S. Africa, and India. In 1965 the Sacred Congregation of Religious joined the congregation at Tours, the motherhouse from which the sisters in the U.S. came, with the motherhouse at Dôle. The diocesan congregations in Fribourg, Brig, Freiburg im Brisgau of Villingen, and Sion were also joined to form the Federation of the Congregations of St. Ursula of Anne de Xainctonge. In 1977 there were 860 members in the federation, of whom 170 are in Tours; 70 in the U.S. conduct schools in New York and Rhode Island.

[R. C. CLIGGETT]

ST. VAAST (ARRAS), ABBEY OF, former Benedictine abbey in the town and Diocese of Arras, France, founded in 667 by Bp. Aubert de Cambrai to serve the funeral chapel of St. Vedastus, and richly endowed by King Thierry III, who made it exempt from episcopal jurisdiction. The monks fled to Beauvais during the Norman invasions, but the monastery was restored under Abbot Richard of Verdun (1009–20). It participated in the Cluniac reform under Abbot Leduin (1020–40); was devastated during the war between France and the Habsburgs (1479–92), was part of the Exempt Congregation of Flanders (1569–1768), and was suppressed during the Revolution. The abbey church, rebuilt between 1775 and 1883, is now the cathedral of Arras. The cloister houses a museum, a library, and the general treasury.

[E. J. DILLON]

ST.-VALÉRY-SUR-SOMME, ABBEY OF, a monastery founded in 611 at the mouth of the Somme River (Abbeville, Somme, France) by St. Valéry, a monk from Luxeuil, with the aid of Clovis III, King of Neustria. It was occupied by Benedictines from Saint-Lucien de Beauvais in the 10th cent. and was reformed by St. Godefroy (d. 1118), bp. of Amiens. William the Conqueror stayed here before embarking for England in 1066. Sacked during the Hundred Years War and the Wars of Religion, the abbey was restored and reformed by the Maurists in 1644. It was destroyed during the Revolution. Today only one 18th–cent. building and some poor ruins of an 18th–cent. church are standing. BIBLIOGRAPHY: Cottineau 2:2911–12.

[J. DAOUST]

SAINT-VALLIER, JEAN BAPTISTE DE LA CROIX CHEVRIÉRES DE (1653–1727), French-born bp. of Quebec. Ordained in 1675, S.-V. refused preferment and went instead to Canada (1685). In 1688 he succeeded Laval as bp. of Quebec. Although he established a general hospital, he allowed the seminary to decline in numbers and influence and in general lacked the decisiveness of his predecessor. He was away from his diocese (1700–13), 8 years of which time he spent in England after his ship was captured by a British privateer (1705). BIBLIOGRAPHY: H. Têtu, *Les évêques de Québec* (1889); A. Rambaud, "La Vie . . . de Mgr. de Saint-Vallier," *Revue de l' Université Laval* 9 (1959) 90–108.

[R. K. MacMASTER]

ST. VICTOR, MONASTERY OF, a house of Canons Regular and motherhouse of one of the four French Augustinian congregations built at Paris *c.*1113 through the generosity of King Louis VI the Fat. It was located near the walls of Paris, at the foot of Mont Sainte-Geneviève, in a place called *Cella Vetus* where the hermit Basilia lived. *William of Champeaux was the first abbot. After he had resigned his archdiaconate in Paris, he retired to this spot *c.*1100, to a hermitage dedicated to St. Victor, martyr of Marseilles. After William later accepted the see of Châlons-sur-Marne, his successor, Guildin developed the school, one of the foremost in medieval philosophy because of the famous "Victorines": Hugh, Adam, Richard of Saint-Victor, and Peter the Eater (12th cent.), Bernard of Clairvaux, Thomas Becket and Abelard spent some time in this monastery. Dependent upon Saint-Victor were 30 abbeys (among them Saint-Geneviève. Saint-Vincent of Senlis, St. Augustine of Bristol), 40 priories, and 80 benefices. The monastery was suppressed and entirely destroyed in 1790. BIBLIOGRAPHY: Cottineau 2:2221–22.

[J. DAOUST]

ST. VICTOR IN MARSEILLES, ABBEY OF, the monastery founded by John *Cassian, disciple of St. John Chrysostom, who settled in Marseilles (Bouches-du-Rhône, France) *c.*416. The monastery, originally dedicated to St. Peter, later took the name of St. Victor, a Roman soldier martyred in 290. In 1040 the Benedictines restored the monastery; in the 11th and 12th cent., a number of houses in S France and up into Rouergue were attached to it. Rebuilt 1200–09, the abbey was reformed in the 13th cent. by Abbots Maynier and Raymond Lourdet. It was enlarged in 1350 by Urban V, who had the high square towers built on it and was later buried there. Saint-Victor did not join the Maurist reform and was secularized in 1751. The church, which has a porch covered with one of the oldest ribbed vaults of Provence, is still standing. Its nave and side aisles (early 13th cent.) offer a curious compromise between Romanesque and Gothic styles. BIBLIOGRAPHY: Cottineau 2:1774–77.

ST. VINCENT ARCHABBEY, the first permanent Benedictine foundation in the U.S., at Latrobe, Pa., in 1846, by Boniface Wimmer, monk of St. Michael Abbey, Metten, Bavaria. He came with a small community to care for the pastoral needs of the German immigrants of Westmoreland Co. and its environs, making use of a chapel and farm donated by Bp. Michael O'Connor of Pittsburgh. The community attained the status of priory in 1852, of abbey in 1855, and by 1900 had founded 15 priories in various states. Abbot Wimmer guided the community 41 years, becoming the first president of the American Cassinese Congregation of the Benedictine Order (1855). Besides their involvement in parishes, the monks staff a major and minor seminary for diocesan and Benedictine priests, as well as a liberal arts college separate from the seminary. The Basilica, dedicated in 1905, of modified Romanesque structure includes a modern renovated crypt with stained glass by Emil Frei symbolizing Benedictine history. Fire destroyed most of the 19th cent. structure in 1963; a new six-story monastery with load-bearing walls and precast window units, designed by Tasso Katselas, dedicated in 1967, includes some 30 concrete castings of biblical messages designed by Roman J. Verostko.

[E. J. DILLON]

ST. VINCENT DE PAUL, SOCIETY OF, originally called the Conference of Charity, is an association of Catholic laymen who serve the poor through the spiritual and corporal works of mercy. Frédéric Ozanam and his associates formed the first conference at Paris in 1833. At first no ecclesiastical approbation was sought, but in 1845 Gregory XVI formally approved the lay character of the society.

In the U.S. the first conference was organized at St. Louis in 1845. There are now approximately 4,200 units of the society in this country with about 36,000 members. Those in this country in the past 50 years have distributed money and assistance to the poor amounting to approximately 195 million. Aid is also sent to poorer counterparts abroad to help them with information and financial assistance.

The society's regulations have been revised to admit women to membership. Stores and rehabilitation workshops are given increasing emphasis to help those with marginal incomes. The handicapped are employed in these endeavors. Joseph Rouast of Paris is president of the Council General, and membership numbers approximately 700,000.

[R. C. CLIGGETT]

ST. VITUS'S DANCE, popular term for the serious malfunctioning of the central nervous system known as chorea but in earlier times applied as well to epilepsy, hydrophobia, and other convulsive disorders. St. *Vitus, as one of the 14 auxiliary saints, or helpers in need, was traditionally invoked for protection against these scourges.

[E. M. GATES]

ST. VLADIMIR'S SEMINARY, Orthodox, under the jurisdiction of the *Russian Metropolia, is located in Crestwood, Tuckahoe, New York. It was founded in 1938 by Metropolitan Theophilus Pashkovsky, received a provisional charter in 1948 and an absolute charter in 1953, empowering it to grant the baccalaureate of divinity. In 1966 St. Vladimir's Seminary became the first Orthodox seminary with membership in the American Association of Theological Schools. St. Vladimir's offers both seminary and academy (graduate) programs of study and, in keeping with pre-revolutionary practice, it awards both the bachelor's and candidate's degrees in theology. Deans have included Metropolitan Makary, Abp. John Shakhovskoy, Georges Florovsky, and Alexander Schmemann.

[T. BIRD]

ST. WANDRILLE, ABBEY OF, see FONTENELLE, ABBEY OF.

STE. ANNE DE BEAUPRÉ, SHRINE OF, Canadian sanctuary near Québec City and dedicated to Saint Anne, the mother of the Virgin Mary and representing a transposition to the New World of a cult popular in 17th–cent. E France. In 1658 Étienne de Lessard donated a piece of land along the Beaupré on the St. Lawrence for such a shrine. Shortly thereafter three men whose small boat had capsized were cast ashore near the chapel and attributed their survival to the miraculous intervention of St. Anne. Since then pilgrims have been attracted to what became known as the Sailors' Chapel. By the mid-20th cent. the shrine was attracting about two million visitors and pilgrims annually.

[E. J. DILLON]

STE. CHAPELLE, PARIS (1246–48), jewel of French Gothic architecture in the courtyard of the former royal palace (now Palace of Justice), constructed by St. Louis as a reliquary chapel for the Sacred Crown of Thorns and a fragment of the True Cross. Small, beautifully proportioned, of two-stories, the lower chapel for the palace servants, dedicated to the Virgin, with winding staircase leads to the upper, single-naved royal chapel, completely surrounded by famous 13th-cent. stained glass, flooding the interior with light and color, and with a 15th-cent. rose in the wall above the two-storied porch. Under the windows pillars carry statues of the Apostles glowing with incrustations of gold and colored glass. The chapel, a reliquary of jewel-glass, is exquisitely light, with most slender buttresses between the high windows. The spire and gabled roof are 15th-cent. constructions. Defaced in the 17th and 18th cent., Sainte Chapelle was restored in the 19th century.

[M. J. DALY]

STE. CHRÉTIENNE, SISTERS OF, otherwise known as the Sisters of the Holy Childhood of Jesus and Mary of Ste. Chrétienne, a congregation founded for the education

3164 STE. FOY, RELIQUARY OF

of children and the care of the sick poor. It was founded in Metz, France, in 1807 by Anne Victoire de Mejanes, née Tailleur. The community was given papal approbation in 1899.

In 1903 the Sisters were forced into exile by the French government, and 15 of them came to the U.S. They founded a house at Salem, Mass., but later moved their provincial headquarters to Quebec, Canada. Houses were opened in the Archdiocese of Boston, Mass., and in the Diocese of Portland, Maine, and Providence, R.I. Missions were established in Mexico, Alberta, Canada, and French Somaliland, Africa. In 1975 the sisters numbered 552 in 69 houses.

[R. C. CLIGGETT]

STE. FOY, RELIQUARY OF (*Majesté de Sainte Foy*), Carolingian reliquary statue in the famous Romanesque pilgrimage church of Ste. Foy at Conques (1039–65), a remarkable example of repoussé metalwork and ornament in high relief—its wooden core covered with gold, silver-gilt, precious stones, and cameos. It is a composite piece of several dates, the head being probably 5th cent.; the gold-covered body added c.875–900; the whole receiving a new embellishment of gold plating and precious stones c.975–1000. BIBLIOGRAPHY: Musée des Arts Décoratifs, *Les Trésorés des Églises de France* (Exhibition Catalogue, 1965), 289–295.

[M. J. DALY]

STE.-GENEVIÈVE-DE-PARIS, MONASTERY OF, founded in 511 at the top of "the sacred hill of pagan Lutetia," by *Clovis and St. Clotilda, who were later buried there. In the 6th cent. the relics of St. Geneviève, patroness of Paris, were transferred to this monastery, and from the 13th cent. the institution bore her name. Sacked by the Normans in 857, the monastery was restored by Suger, abbot of Saint-Denis, who brought the Canons Regular of Saint-Victor to Sainte-Geneviève. The monastery enjoyed the right to exercise justice in major as well as minor matters, and the chancery of the Univ. of Paris was affiliated with it. Sainte-Geneviève was the motherhouse and the center of the French congregation known as the Génovéfains. François de La Rochefoucauld, its commendatory abbot, reestablished regular observance by installing canons from Saint-Vincent de Senlis under Charles Faure (1635). Many abbeys, priories, smaller houses, provostships, and benefices were affiliated with the monastery in its prime, though scholars disagree about their numbers. The basilica was reconstructed many times between the 12th and 17th centuries. Today only the tower (Clovis' Tower) remains. The conventual buildings that have survived have belonged to the Lycée Henri IV since 1802. BIBLIOGRAPHY: Cottineau 2:2206–07.

[J. DAOUST]

STE. RADEGONDE, POITIERS, 6th-cent. French abbey church first called St. Mary-outside the Walls, renamed Ste.-Radegonde for the illustrious Thuringian princess whose tomb is in the crypt. Burned (1083), reconstructed (1099), the present structure dating from the 12th cent. has a particularly beautiful octagonal bell tower, nave with Gothic vaulting (13th cent.), and main portal (15th century.) Fine sculptured Romanesque capitals around the ambulatory have been badly "restored." The sacristy with angevin Gothic vaulting supporting a cupola is unique. BIBLIOGRAPHY: R. Crozet, *Poitiers* (1948).

[M. J. DALY]

SAINTONGE, CHURCHES OF, architectural style of region S and W of Poitou, with distinct sculptural ornamentation characterized by magnificent undercutting, peculiarly beautiful treatment of angels, Vices and Virtues, and curious monsters—all attesting to Moorish influence, likely owing to regional leaders assisting in the reconquest of Spain. BIBLIOGRAPHY: É. Mâle, *L' Art religieux du XIIᵉ siècle en France* (1922).

[M. J. DALY]

SAINTS, CANONIZATION OF, see CANONIZATION AND BEATIFICATION (WESTERN CHURCH).

SAINTS, COMMUNION OF, see COMMUNION OF SAINTS.

SAINTS, DEVOTION TO, the ancient Christian practice of offering honor to those who are recognized as especially close to God. Both the Council of Trent (D 1821) and Vatican Council II (Vat II ConstChurch) stated the antiquity and rightness of this practice. Its dogmatic basis is the article of the Creed professing belief in the Holy Spirit as sanctifier, through whose action the holiness effected in some members serves the building up of others in the body of Christ (see EDIFICATION). Theologically, devotion is the concern of the virtues of both *religion and *charity. As it means a joyful readiness to honor and serve God, devotion includes honoring him in the reflection of his goodness through the saints. That prompts a *pietas* towards them as they are sources of spiritual good in the family of the Father (ThAq ST 2a2ae, 101.1; 102.1). Devotion also engages charity in that this means a union in love with God that loves as he loves; because their sanctity is a sign of a special divine love toward them, the saints are a particular object of charity as love of neighbor (*ibid.*, 25.1;26.6,7,12,13). The manifestation of piety and charity toward the saints includes reliance on their *intercession; but devotion toward them takes on also a particular meaning: a looking toward them as examples in the hope of imitating their reflection of the grace of Christ. This is particularly true of veneration for their founder by religious; and of devotion to patron saints for their particular way of reflecting Christ's holiness.

[T. C. O'BRIEN]

SAINTS, LEGENDS OF THE, accounts of the saints' lives or martyrdom, written for inspirational reading. The Lat. *legenda* means simply writings that "should be read," and does not in itself denote fanciful tales. In fact, however, the legend writer's concern was not history; and the legends contain many nonfactual elements and evince an easy transference to their subject of feats or data from other legends, since certain accomplishments were taken as ideals of saintliness. The works of the historian *Eusebius of Caesarea incorporated many pre-existent *Acta* of the martyrs; other famous early *legenda* are the *History of the Monks of Egypt,* beginning with St. *Athanasius's life of St. *Anthony; St. *Jerome's *De viris illustribus*. Devotional biographies increased throughout the Middle Ages; the most elaborate collection is Bl. *James of Voragine's *Golden Legend,* which he arranged according to the calendar year. From the time of the Renaissance, saints' biographies became more historical and critical; the *Bollandists' *Acta sanctorum* was intended to have such characteristics. In English hagiography the historical and critical work of H. Thurston is esp. noteworthy. See also the *Bibliotheca Sanctorum* (12 v., 1961–69), published by the John XXIII Institute of The Pontifical Lateran University.

[T. C. O'BRIEN]

SS. CYRIL AND METHODIUS, SISTERS OF, an American congregation of religious women founded to educate Slovak children for American citizenship while continuing to foster in them a love of their own native traditions. The founder was Matthew Yankola, a priest of the Diocese of Scranton, Pennsylvania. In 1903, he was instrumental in placing several young women with the Sisters of the Immaculate Heart of Mary for this mission. Six years later, the first group of sisters pronounced simple, temporary vows. The first school of the Sisters of SS. Cyril and Methodius was opened at Sacred Heart parish, Wilkes-Barre, Pa. in 1908, and in 1914 they took over the care of a new orphanage at Middletown, Pa., sponsored by the First Catholic Slovak Union. They established a temporary motherhouse here, also, but the permanent motherhouse was located five years later in Danville, Pennsylvania. An academy chartered as the First Catholic Slovak Girls High School (St. Cyril Academy) was opened at the motherhouse in 1922. The sisters' first home for the aged was opened in 1961. In 1975 the sisters numbered 381 in 34 houses.

[R. C. CLIGGETT]

SS. GIOVANNI E PAOLA, ROME (410), church on the Caelian hill said to be near the site of the martyrdom of SS. John and Paul, retains the walls of the 2d- and 3d-cent. foundation houses, with front portico and campanile of the 12th cent., and interior remodeled (1715–18). The two-storied Roman house beneath the church is decorated with pagan and Christian frescoes (2d–3d centuries.)

[M. J. DALY]

SAKKOS (Gr., a sack), the dalmatic-like outer vestment now proper to bishops in the Byzantine Church. It is related to the sticharion of the East and the dalmatic and tunicle of the West and was originally worn by the Byzantine emperor at Constantinople. With the fall of the imperial city to the Ottomans (1453), the patriarch assumed the imperial tunic and in time metropolitans and bishops did likewise. By the 16th cent. it had generally replaced the phelonion as the eucharistic vestment of the hierarchy. The sakkos is made of silk and is usually marked with a cross on the back. It should fall almost to the ground and has wide sleeves that come to the wrists. As with other liturgical vesture, time, bad taste, and a lack of awareness of the noble dimensions of the sakkos have reduced it somewhat and often covered it with poor 19th-cent. embroidery. The omophorion is worn on top of the sakkos and the epigonation is usually pulled out between the side openings of the vestment so as to be visible at the knee. The sleeves and sides of the sakkos are fastened by buttons, and sometimes small silver bells are attached at the bottom.

[A. J. JACOPIN]

SAKYAMUNI, STATUE OF, 8th-cent. granite statue of Gautama Buddha under the title Sākyamuni (Sage of the Sākya clan, in the Sokkulam cave, near Kyungju, Korea. Eleven-ft high, carved out of the solid rock in great simplicity, with shallow drapery, the *Ushnisha* tūrnā quite subtly rendered, Buddha's right hand touches the earth in the *bhūmisparśa* mudrā (calling the earth witness to his virtue), the left hand palm up on his lap signifying meditation.

[M. J. DALY]

SALADIN (Arab. Ṣalâḥ al-Dîn; d. 1193), a Muslim prince, *Sultan of Egypt and founder of the Ayyûbid dynasty. Of Kurdish origin, S. was sent to Egypt in 1169 by Nûr al-Dîn, the Seljuk ruler of Aleppe and Mawsul, at the request of the government of al-'Adid, the last *Fatimid ruler of Egypt, to aid in the war against the Crusaders. A devout *Sunnite, he suppressed the Fatimid Ismailism and rule in 1171 and returned Egypt to the fold of orthodox *Islam. At the death of Nûr al-Dîn, S. became commander of all the armies fighting the Crusaders and in this capacity succeeded in unifying Egypt, Syria, and large parts of Arabia and Mesopotamia under the banner of the *Caliph of Baghdad. He inflicted a total defeat upon the Crusaders at Hattin in 1187, retook Jerusalem, and in the following years under the most difficult circumstances, against the attacks of the Third Crusade, managed to retain almost all the territory that he had conquered. Though most renowned in East and West alike as a military leader against the Latins, S.'s foremost concern was the political and religious reunification of Islam under the orthodox caliphate and the moral reform of government and administration. He is unquestionably one of the most noble figures of the Middle Ages, a man of uncompromising integrity and profound religious devotion. BIBLIOGRAPHY: H. A. R. Gibb, "Achievement of Saladin," *Bulletin of the John Rylands Library* 35 (1952) 46–60; *idem, History of the Crusades* (ed. K. M. Seton, 1955) 1:563.

[R. M. FRANK]

SALAMANCA, OLD CATHEDRAL OF (*c.*1140), one of the least altered of Spanish Romanesque churches, with semi-domed triple apses beyond the transept and pointed barrel vault (1155) before the center apse. Probably Petrus Petriz (1163) completed the vaults over aisles and nave and designed the magnificent Torre del Gallo (1180–1200) derived from Angoulême and a model for Zamora. Extraordinary sculptured figural and vegetable capitals, and over-life-size sculpture-in-the-round at the spring of the rib vaults suggest the art of the pilgrimage roads and particularly Master Gundisalvas (1164). In the Chapel of St. Martin are murals by Antón Sánchez de Segovia (1262) and the painted tomb of Bp. Rodrigo Diaz (14th century). The great retable of the high altar in 11 tiers—the 53 painted panels of Christ and the Virgin attributed to Dello di Niccolo Delli (*c.*1440)—enshrines the *Virgen de la Vega* of gilded silver and jewels on a throne of Limoges enamels. The *Last Judgment* vault fresco is also by Dello (*c.*1445). The cloister (1162–78) damaged in an earthquake (1755) retains some fine sculptured capitals and tombs. The Chapel of Talavera (1180) with interlaced ribs supporting an octagonal dome relates to the vaults of Córdoba and the Torre del Gallo. BIBLIOGRAPHY: J. E. Cirlot, *Salamanca y su provincia* (1956).

[M. J. DALY]

SALAMANCA, UNIVERSITY OF, illustrious Spanish university, located in Salamanca in NW Spain; considered in medieval history as one of the four great universities of Europe (Paris, Bologna, Oxford, and Salamanca). It was founded by Alfonso IX of Leon *c.* 1227; was issued a charter by Ferdinand III of Castile in 1243; and was set on its course to greatness by Alfonso X, the Wise, when he issued his landmark code in 1263. He differentiated between school (*studium*) and university (*studium generale*). He recognized the community of scholars and teachers as an *universitas,* an autonomous organization empowered to elect its own rector. He also provided an endowment for teachers' salaries and other expenses, and for the first time introduced music into the curriculum of a European university. The 14th cent. saw a revival of medicine when professors at Salamanca translated the works of Avicenna and Averroës from Arabic. Salamanca's main claim to fame was its study of law, and probably reached its peak in the 16th century when it was a strong center of the Catholic Restoration. At that time there were 11 chairs in philosophy and logic; 17 in grammar and rhetoric; 10 in canon law; 7 in medicine and

theology, 4 in Greek, 2 in Hebrew and Chaldean, and 1 in music and astronomy. Francisco de Vitoria, leader of the Spanish "golden age" of Thomism, set forth in his lectures here (1526–46) some of the fundamental principles of international law. Among its alumni should be mentioned St. Ignatius of Loyola and later St. John of the Cross. In 1592 an Irish College was founded which was to train leaders of the Irish clergy through subsequent generations. In 1600 the Discalced Carmelites founded a school of philosophy here, whose number included the famous group known as the Salmanticenses, authors of the encyclopedic commentary on the *Summa* of St. Thomas. Enrollment declined steadily from the end of the 16th century until the 19th century, going from a high of 6,778 in 1584 to a low of 391 in 1875. It was greatly damaged by the Napoleonic occupation, was secularized in 1835, and its theology faculty was discontinued in 1868. The modern secular university is composed of four faculties: philosophy and letters, science, law, and medicine. Its most famous rector in recent times was the influential Miguel de Unamuno. In 1970 the university enrollment had again reached 5,700.

[E. J. DILLON]

SALAS, JUAN DE (1553–1612), Spanish Jesuit theologian. He taught in Spain and in Rome, where he was theologian for the Jesuit general during the **Congregatio de auxiliis*. S. was highly regarded in moral theology. His works include commentaries on Aquinas's *Summa theologiae* (1a2ae, 1–108), published during his lifetime (1607–11), and a set of questions on justice published posthumously (1717). A work *De gratia et auxiliis* was never published because of the ban on polemics in regard to grace with which the *Congregatio de auxiliis* was terminated.

[T. C. O'BRIEN]

SALAT, HANS (1490–1561), Swiss Catholic pamphleteer, poet, and historian. He fought in both Kappel Wars (1529, 1531) and as a result became a citizen of Lucerne, then that city's historian. His *Triumphus Herculis helvetici* (1532), a satire directed against Zwingli, compared the Reformation to a witches' sabbath. In other works he argued that the Reformation was a form of divine punishment. He was also the author of military histories.

[R. J. LITZ]

SALAZAR, ANTONIO DE OLIVEIRA (1889–1970), statesman. A Portuguese professor of economics, S. entered politics in 1926 when an Army coup overthrew the government. It was not until 1928, however, that he was given full authority as minister of finance. From 1928 to 1968 S. held various offices, but was in effect dictator of Portugal. A controversial figure, he was much influenced by Pope Leo XIII and the rightist Charles Maurras. He devised the Constitution of 1933, creating an authoritarian state with strong provision for social justice. S. achieved much for Portugal in public finance, modernization of railroads, and public works. He failed, however, to greatly improve the lot of the worker or to wipe out illiteracy. Under S., Portugal assumed a respected position in world affairs, despite its fascist character. S. himself was a devout Catholic who lived a simple frugal life totally dedicated to the welfare of Portugal. With the Concordat of 1940 he improved relations with the Holy See. BIBLIOGRAPHY: J. d'Assac, *Dictionnaire politique de Salazar* (1964).

[J. R. AHERNE]

SALAZAR, DOMINGO DE (1512–1594), Spanish Dominican missionary, first bp. of Manila. After missionary work in Mexico and Florida, he was nominated by Philip II of Spain to be the first bp. of Manila (1579). He struggled with cruel, greedy civil authorities, Gov. Ronquillo of Manila in particular, and over the *exemption of religious orders. He favored military action against China as a way in which Spain could Christianize the reluctant Chinese. Back in Spain (1591), S. reestablished the *audiencia,* successfully advocated the creation of new provincial bishoprics, and sought relief for natives in Spain's colonies. At his invitation the Dominicans opened missions in the Philippines, and the Province of the Holy Rosary of the Philippines began (1592).

[R. J. LITZ]

SALEM, locality where Melchizedek was priest-king (Gen 14.17–20). It is perhaps a shortening of the pre-Israelite name for Jerusalem, called *'urushalimma* (foundation of Shalem) in the Egyptian Execration Texts (*c.*1850 B.C.). Shalem, not to be confused with *shalom,* the Hebrew word for peace (Heb 7.1), was a deity mentioned in the *Ras Shamra Texts and apparently was the local deity of Jebusite Jerusalem. Salem was used as an equivalent for Zion in Ps 76.2. Other suggested sites, however, are the Salim near which John baptized (Jn 3.23), and the place where Jacob camped (in the LXX reading of Gen 33.18, which, however, is a mistranslation of the Hebrew).

[T. EARLY]

SALERNO, SCHOOL OF, earliest medical school in Europe; it flourished in Italy from the 11th to the 13th century. Its origin is obscure, although the town, a health resort or spa, was famous for its skilled physicians in the 10th cent., and as the school's renown spread, became known as the *Civitas Hippocratica.* There is little substantial proof that Salerno's medical skill developed from contact with the Saracens from Sicily or S Italy, or that the school later rose to prominence in the 11th cent. mainly through the Arabic writings introduced by Constantinus Africanus (1010–87), whose *Pantegni,* a Latin translation from the Arabic, established the canon of the *ars medicinae.* Gariopontus, one of the earliest and most noted physicians of Salerno, gives no evidence of Arabic influence in his writings (*c.*1040). In fact, Salerno's growing medical fame in the late 11th cent.

seems to have resulted from a merging of Greek, Latin, Arabic, and Hebrew influences derived from the writings of Hippocrates, Galen, and the Graeco-Roman medical classics. The school was first officially recognized in 1231 by Frederick II, King of Sicily, who forbade the teaching or practice of medicine without a royal license from Salerno; in 1280 it was recognized as a university (*studium generale*). Salerno seems to have been the first organized medical school; the first to call a physician "doctor" and the first to confer the degree *magister* or doctor (1359). As a medical school, Salerno reached its peak in the 13th century. It was finally dissolved under Napoleon: the medical school in 1811; the other departments in 1817. BIBLIOGRAPHY: P. O. Kristeller, "The School of Salerno: Its Development and Contribution to the History of Learning," *Studies in Renaissance Thought and Letters* (1956) 495–551.

[M. B. MURPHY]

SALES, CHARLES AUGUSTE DE (fl. early 17th cent.), French bp., writer. Son of Louis, brother of St. *Francis de Sales, S. was his student (1620–22) and "his first real biographer" (M. de la Bedoyere, *François de Sales* (1960). S. wrote in Latin which he later translated into French (1633). A two-volume, 6th edition of the work, *Histoire du bienheureux François de Sales . . .* appeared in 1857. The death of Francis (1622) disrupted plans for S. and J. J. *Olier to study theology with him at Talloires. S. was to succeed him and coadjutor Jean François de Sales in the See of Geneva.

[M. R. BROWN]

SALESIAN SISTERS, see MARY HELP OF CHRISTIANS, DAUGHTERS OF.

SALESIAN SPIRITUALITY, that form of the Christian life taught by St. *Francis de Sales, esp. in his *Introduction to the Devout Life* and *Treatise on the Love of God.* The author esp. proposed this form of Christian perfection as open to all devout Christians, not only to religious withdrawn from the world.

SALESIANS or the Society of St. Francis de Sales, otherwise known as the Salesians of Don Bosco (SDB), a religious congregation dedicated to the Christian education of youth. It was founded by St. John Bosco in 1859 and its members include priests, clerics, and lay coadjutors. Salesian youth work is centered around oratories.

At 26 years of age (1841), Don Bosco became the friend and teacher of a child who labored in the Church of St. Francis of Assisi in Turin, Italy. He established his first oratory five years later in a shed at Turin where the motherhouse now stands. His boys increased in number, and he decided to train some of them to assist him in his work. Thus he founded the Salesian Society in 1859, which received papal approbation in 1868, the constitutions were approved in 1874. Then the missionary expansion of the country began, and from Italy the Society moved into France, Latin America, and Spain. In 1875 the first missionaries left for Argentina.

The Institute of the Daughters of Mary Help of Christians, known as the Salesian Sisters, was also founded by Don Bosco. It has the same spiritual and educational ideals as the male congregation, which holds that education is based upon reason, religion, and amiability. The Cooperators, as Don Bosco's third Salesian family is called, is similar to the older third orders except that the Salesian Cooperators seek perfection principally through the exercise of charity toward needy youth. The principal Salesian missions, in addition to those mentioned above, are India, China, Thailand, and the Congo. The Society has also excelled in Communication Arts, and its publication of Catholic Readings, which began in 1863, still continues. Don Bosco was canonized in 1939. In 1975 his followers numbered 18,426 of whom 11,528 were priests in 1,524 houses.

[R. C. CLIGGETT]

SALIAN ART, major period of German Romanesque art under the four Salian emperors (1024–1125), following the Ottonian age. Important works are the Speyer Cathedral, the *Imad Madonna* (Paderborn), the portable altar of R. von Helmarshausen, and the Hitda Codex.

[M. J. DALY]

SALIC LAW (Lat. *lex salica*), pertaining to the Salian Franks, a tribe settled near the Zuider Zee, from which sprang the Merovingian dynasty. A compilation of property and criminal laws, it originally contained no trace of religious elements, though Christian enactments had already been introduced into it by pre-Carolingian times. One item was that a woman can have no portion in the inheritance of Salic land. It was later alleged to be a fundamental law of the French monarchy by which females were excluded from succession to the crown: in fact, however, it was by feudal law that possession of land reverted to the crown in default of a male heir, and the thin claims of Edward III of England which started the Hundred Years War were settled on grounds other than those of a famous but fictitious "Salic Law."

[T. GILBY]

SALICUS, in *Gregorian chant notation, a modified form of the *scandicus (a *neume signifiying three or more notes ascending in pitch). Its precise meaning is uncertain, but it may have had a rhythmic or melodic nuance different from the scandicus.

[A. DOHERTY]

SALIERI, ANTONIO (1750–1825), Italian composer. S. studied with various teachers in Venice and Vienna. He

composed both Italian and French operas and was Kapellmeister for some years at Vienna. There he enjoyed great renown as a teacher, having among his students Beethoven, Schubert, and Liszt. Besides operas, he wrote 6 Masses, 4 *Te Deums,* a requiem, and other church music.

[M. T. LEGGE]

SALIMBENE (BALIEN ADAM; 1221-after 1288), Italian chronicler. S. became a Franciscan in Parma in 1238. After studying in a number of places like Lucca, Siena (subdeacon), Pisa (deacon, 1246), Cremona, Parma (1247) and various places in France, he was ordained in Genoa (1248). He also lived in many of the friaries of his province. His *Chronicle* was written between 1283 and 1288 at Reggio and at a friary near Monte Falco. The *Chronicle* begins *c.*1262 (incompletely preserved MS Vat. lat. 7260). It is more of an autobiography than chronicle and is characterized by verbosity, lively and vivid description, lifelike portraits, and lucid language. The historian will find many of its details useful. BIBLIOGRAPHY: G. G. Coulton, *From St. Francis to Dante: A Translation of All That Is of Primary Interest in the Chronicle of the Franciscan Salimbene 1221–1288* (1906; 2d ed., 1907); J. Cambell, NCE 12:983–984.

[J. J. SMITH]

SALINAS, FRANCISCO DE (1513–1590), Spanish organist, musical theorist, and humanist. Although blind from age 10, he was organist at the Spanish court in Naples (1558–61), and at Léon (1563). He taught at the Univ. of Salamanca (1567–87). His *De musica libri septem* (1577), an important theoretical work, contains his formulation of a 24-note scale tuning system which allowed for performance of pure triads. A learned humanistic discussion of rhythm includes many examples from his collection of Spanish folk music, the earliest work on the subject.

[R. J. LITZ]

SALINAS Y CÓRDOVA, BUENAVENTURA DE (1592–1653), Peruvian Franciscan author and political advocate. His lengthy *Memorial de las historias del Nuevo Mundo* (1630), a panegyric on the virtuous achievements of Peruvians and an indictment of official abuse of power, originated as a foreword to his brother's biography of St. Francis de *Solano. When S. delivered a sermon in the same vein as his *Memorial* in 1635, Bp. Diego de Vera of Cuzco denounced him to the Spanish government and sent him to Spain for a hearing, where S. was cleared. While in Rome (1639–44), he acted on behalf of the abp. of Lima, the Franciscan province of Lima, and promoted the cause of Francis de Solano for beatification. He became deeply involved in the Portuguese and Catalan separatist movements. He later served with distinction as commissary general of New Spain (1646–53).

[R. J. LITZ]

SALISBURY CATHEDRAL, English cathedral built by Bp. Poore after removing the see from Old Sarum to the

Avon Valley (Wiltshire) in 1219, set in a perfect "cathedral-scape" of park or close of lawns and stately trees which distinguishes the English cathedral from continental churches. The overall plan was due to Elias of Dereham and master mason Nicholas of Ely. The Lady Chapel built by 1225, with grouped Purbeck marble shafts incredibly slender, elongated, and unattached—so that they seem to tether rather than support the floating vaults—sets the pattern from choir to screen front. Master Richard, mason (1267), added the magnificent cloister and chapter house (1263–84), unsurpassed in size and design, in a style that had changed from Early English to the Geometrical Decorated. Master Richard of Farleigh began the 404 ft tower with spire (1334), the supreme and crowning concept of the Cathedral (comparable to Ely), finished in 1380. The Cathedral was finally completed by the crossing vault (1479) of Henry Stevens. "Restorations" (1787–93) under J. Wyatt destroyed historic chapels and the great porches from Old Sarum Cathedral.

[M. J. DALY]

SALLUSTIUS (d. before 377 A.D.), Neoplatonic philosopher. He was a member of the Pergamene School and the author of *De diis et mundo,* a short work summarizing the basic tenets of Neoplatonism. BIBLIOGRAPHY: A. D. Nock, *Sallustius: Concerning the Gods and the Universe* (1926).

[M. R. P. McGUIRE]

SALMANASAR, see SHALMANESER.

SALMANTICENSES, Discalced Carmelites of Salamanca in Spain; editors of a renowned *Cursus theologicus* and also of a *Cursus theologiae moralis;* the name is also used to refer to the *cursus* themselves. The original 12 v. of the *Cursus theologicus,* following the plan of St. Thomas Aquinas's *Summa theologiae,* appeared between 1631 and 1712. The principal editors were Antonio de la Madre de Dios (1583–1637), Domingo de Santa Teresa (1604–60), and Juan de la Annunciación (1633–1701). The treatises, the product of lectures and discussions, are marked by close scholastic reasoning and by fidelity to the Thomistic school. A modern edition was published (1870–83) in 20 volumes. The *Cursus theologiae moralis* (6 v., 1665–1724) is on a more practical level, and inferior in quality to the *Cursus theologicus.* BIBLIOGRAPHY: R. A. Couture, NCE 12:987–988, with bibliog.

[T. C. O'BRIEN]

SALMASIUS, CLAUDIUS (Claude de Saumaise; 1588–1653), French Huguenot scholar. His early proficiency in Greek and Latin elicited the admiration of I. Casaubon. In classical studies Salmasius' most important contributions are an annotated edition of the *Historia Augusta* and a still useful explanation of excerpts from Pliny's *Natural History.* Of his many treatises, the *Defensio regia pro Carolo I,* vindicating the claims of absolute monarchy, is perhaps best known because of the fame of Milton's reply, *Pro populo anglicano defensio* of which "all Europe talks from side to side." BIBLIOGRAPHY: H. R. Guggisberg, RGG 5:1335–36; H. Dressler, NCE 12:988–989.

[H. DRESSLER]

SALOME, name of two women in the NT: (1) the first is the daughter of Herodias and Herod Philip. She is noted for receiving the head of John the Baptist as a reward for her dancing before Herod Antipas (Mk 6.14–29). Her name, not given in the Bible, was recorded by Josephus (*Antiquities,* 18.5.4). (2) the second is one of the women who followed Jesus in Galilee and was present at the Crucifixion (Mk 15.40–41; 16.1–8). Matthew listed the same women present at the Crucifixion except for Salome but added the mother of the sons of Zebedee (27.56). Presumably the two were the same and she was therefore the mother of James and John. The reference to "his mother's sister" in John's Gospel (19.25) may refer, not to Mary the wife of Clopas (presumably two sisters would not both be named Mary), but to Salome. If the references in all three Gospels are the same, Jesus was John's cousin, and it was therefore esp. appropriate that he asked John to care for his mother (Jn 19.26–27).

[T. EARLY]

SALSMANS, JOSEPH (1873–1944), Flemish Jesuit, professor of moral theology at Louvain; reviser, esp. after the promulgation of the CIC, of the 6th to the 15th edition of his uncle É. *Génicot's manual of moral theology.

[T. C. O'BRIEN]

SALT, whose uses as a preservative and a seasoning have been known from remotest antiquity, has had a place in the religious ritual of many peoples. It was employed in sacrifices by the Greeks and Romans, and to Semitic peoples its preservative effect made it a natural symbol of permanence, incorruptibility, and purity, and as such it was used in sacrifice among the Hebrews and in confirmation of contracts and friendship—hence the covenant between God and Israel was a covenant of salt (Num 18.19). Its preservative and seasoning properties explain Christ's calling his disciples the salt of the earth (Mt 5.13). In Col 4.6 salt has been understood to refer to wisdom. In the early Church in the West blessed salt was given to the catechumen, and this practice has survived in the baptismal liturgy. Possibly the practice was introduced under the influence of the pagan custom of putting salt on the lips of an infant a few days after his birth to dispel demons. In its use in the baptismal rite salt signified the grace of God, wisdom, and preservation from sin. Salt has also been used in the blessing of holy water from the 6th cent. BIBLIOGRAPHY: Kittel TD; E. J. Gratsch, NCE 12:989–990.

[P. K. MEAGHER]

SALTMARSH, JOHN (c. 1610–47), English religious writer. An M.A. from Magdalene College, Cambridge, he served as a rector of Heslerton, Yorkshire (1639). In close association with Sir John Hotham he became an ardent advocate of church reform and religious liberty. In a pamphlet (1643) he criticized a sermon by Thomas Fuller for leniency toward papists and attachment to ritual tradition. Refusing to accept tithes, he resigned his position and began preaching throughout Northhampton until 1645 when he settled in Kent. He continued to send out his pamphlets pleading for greater religious liberty. His *Smoke in the Temple* (1646) advocated complete freedom of the press and asserted the progressive nature of religious knowledge. His *Holy Discoveries* (1640) and *Sparkles of Glory* (1647) are his major spiritual works. Most of his other copious writing was polemical.

[R. J. LITZ]

SALUTARY ACTS, human actions performed under the influence of grace and conducive to salvation. In Catholic theology these acts are generally considered to be entitatively supernatural. There are two kinds of salutary acts: those that dispose man positively toward justification and those of the justified man by which he merits further grace and glory. Pelagians and Semi–Pelagians in the 5th and 6th cent. denied the need of grace for the performance of all or some of these acts. St. Augustine championed the Catholic views opposed to such doctrine. The Councils of Carthage (15th or 16th, 418) and Orange (2d, 529) defined the matter. In harmony with their view of fallen man, the Reformers denied him the possibility of performing truly salutary acts. Trent asserted the Catholic views in its decrees dealing with original sin and justification (sessions 5 and 6; 1546, 1547). BIBLIOGRAPHY: D 222–230; 370–397; 1510–16; 1520–83; H. Lennerz, *De gratia Redemptoris* (1940) 159, 272.

[R. J. TAPIA]

SALUTATI, COLUCCIO (1331–1406), humanist. A notary by training, S. served as chancellor of Florence (1375–1406). Under his leadership Florence became the recognized center of the humanist movement. BIBLIOGRAPHY: B. L. Ullman, *Humanism of Coluccio Salutati* (1963).

[J. MULDOON]

SALVADOR, VICENTE DO (Vicente Rodrigues Palha *c.*1564– before 1639), Brazilian Franciscan, historian. His *História do Brasil* up to 1627 (unpublished until the late 19th cent.) was the first history of that country. Born in Brazil, he studied at Coimbra, was ordained in his native land, and became canon and vicar general of Salvador before entering the Franciscans in 1599. He held office as Franciscan superior in Rio de Janeiro and Bahia. On returning there from a visit to Lisbon he was captured by the Dutch, who had occupied Bahia, and was kept prisoner aboard a ship for 6 months. He served subsequently as a missionary to the Indians in Parahiba.

[R. J. LITZ]

SALVADOR CARMONA, LUIS (1708–67), Spain's last inspired sculptor of images in late baroque style, working in stone and stucco for palaces, but famous for polychromed wood statues for churches. A Castilian working in the Seville style of Montañés and Pedro de Mena in intricately draped, active figures, S. combined his virtuosity, rococo grace, elegance, and deep humanity in the *Virgin of the Column* (1745–50) and the poignant *Christ of the Redemption* (1751), both in S. Maria del Rosario, La Granja.

[M. J. DALY]

SALVATIERRA, JUAN MARÍA DE (Gianmaria Salvaterra; 1648–1717), Italian Jesuit missioner. S. was sent to Mexico in 1675. He worked in the missions there, then went to Southern California in 1697, inspired by the celebrated missionary Father Kino. In California S. founded several missions. Provincial of the Jesuits in Mexico in 1704, he returned to the missions in 1707 and died in Guadalajara.

[J. R. AHERNE]

SALVATION, the deliverance of man from sin and death through the work of Jesus Christ. The term is variously employed in the Bible and in theological parlance; at least three of its meanings deserve to be noted.

Salvation means atonement. Jesus Christ is called Savior in Christian language because he achieved salvation by his life, death, and Resurrection. Western Christian theology has frequently defined this salvation in the language of vicarious satisfaction, as this was formulated in the *Cur deus homo* (c.1097) of St. Anselm. By his death on the cross Christ satisfied the injured justice of God and thus made atonement for human sin. In Greek theology the emphasis has been on the Resurrection of Christ as not only the declaration of salvation but its means as well. Christ triumphed over the spiritual enemies of man—sin, death, and the devil—and grants salvation as *Christus Victor*. These emphases are by no means mutually exclusive, but they do stress different aspects of the saving work of Christ. This definition of salvation underlies such biblical statements as Tit 2.11, 13–14: "The grace of God has appeared for the salvation of all men . . . our blessed hope, the appearing of the glory of our great God and Savior Jesus Christ, who gave himself for us to redeem us from all iniquity."

Salvation means conversion. Thus Christians of the evangelical traditions speak of "the day I was saved" as the day when, through an experience of repentance and conversion, they became Christian believers. The etymological meaning of salvation is "health," and in the NT, being saved means being restored to spiritual health and living a healthy life. In this sense, salvation is a state of being, brought about by the saving work of Christ and conferred upon the individual through the gifts of the Holy Spirit. As a new life in Christ, it is also a following in his steps. The joy and courage that are components of salvation in this sense of the word are described not only in the NT but also and esp. in the Old, as in Ps 27.1, 4: "The Lord is my light and my salvation; whom shall I fear? One thing have I asked of the Lord, that will I seek after; that I may dwell in the house of the Lord all the days of my life, to behold the beauty of the Lord, and to inquire in his temple'' (see CONVERSION; JUSTIFICATION; JUSTIFICATION BY FAITH).

Salvation means immortality. In some Christian traditions, this understanding of salvation as the life that will commence only after death has largely overshadowed the other meanings of the word, esp. the second. There is good NT warrant for interpreting salvation as immortality—though not for restricting it to this meaning. When St. Paul says that ''salvation is nearer to us now than when we first believed'' (Rom 13.11), salvation is being used for the eschatological hope of the return of Christ at the second coming and the beginning of life in heaven. But the same Apostle, quoting the Book of Isaiah, could declare: ''For he says, 'At the acceptable time I have listened to you, and helped you on the day of salvation.' Behold, now is the acceptable time; behold, now is the day of salvation'' (2 Cor 6.2). The solution to this apparent contradiction is to be found in the biblical use of such terms as ''eternal life,'' which refers to an existence that begins here and now within human history but reaches its consummation and perfection only at the end of history. For it is only there that the enemies of salvation are completely abolished and their power taken away. BIBLIOGRAPHY: G. Aulén, *Christus Victor* (tr. A. G. Herbert, rev. ed., 1969); A. Gelin et al., *Son and Savior* (tr. A. Wheaton, rev. ed., 1962).

[J. PELIKAN]

SALVATION (IN THEOLOGY). Salvation is a basic human hope expressed in many different religions. It is deliverance through religion from the perils of human existence. For primitive man these perils were encountered in his contest with nature, which threatened human survival in many ways, and only the appeasement of nature spirits or of various other divinities could keep a man from coming to harm.

Salvation constitutes the major theme of the Hebrew Old Testament. The God of the Hebrews was a saving God, and the history of Israel, a salvation history. Its great focal point was the exodus, the deliverance of the Hebrew people from the slavery of Egypt. This historical experience was above all else the foundation of the Israelites' conviction that Yahweh–Elohim was a saving God. Projected backward in time, it was the same God who delivered the patriarchs from earlier perils; projected forward into the future, the exodus event was a guarantee that Yahweh–Elohim would continue to save Israel from all the perils of social and political upheavals.

Gradually the conviction of God's salvific intervention in the history of Israel evolved into the themes of the Messianic end-time. This would be the final time of God's kingdom on earth established by his Messiah. It would be a time of peace and justice, not only for the people of Israel, but for all nations through Israel. The idea of salvation in the earlier stage of the OT was concerned with deliverance from immediate perils such as battles, famines, migrations, invasions, and captivities. Only gradually was the hope projected to a future and final salvific establishment of God's kingdom. The salvation hope of the Israelite centered in the main about the strength of his nation, his own happiness, and a long life. Salvation as a projection into the after-life was not a part of OT theology.

The NT theology of salvation focused on Jesus as the Messiah. Jesus proclaimed the immediacy of the kingdom of God. The end-time was begun through the prophetic agency of Jesus. Although NT salvation thought retains shades of national liberation from the Romans, a major shift had taken place. Jesus was preached, not as a national liberator, but as a deliverer from sin and death; and salvation was something to be finally and perfectly realized in the after-life. Jesus through his death-to-sin had established for all men the possibility of eternal life. The perils of human existence in this life were seen as the necessary consequence of human sinfulness. However, through faith in Jesus, human sinfulness could be overcome and death would resolve itself into a glorious after-life.

Later Christian theologies confirmed the association between salvation and resurrection. The Resurrection of Jesus was the sign that death and sin had been overcome. The forces of evil had been defeated. Sin and death would continue as part of human existence, but complete deliverance would finally come to those who believed in the redemptive power of Jesus. BIBLIOGRAPHY: W. G. Topmoeller, NCE 12:994–995, bibliog.

[W. J. DUGGAN]

SALVATION, ASSURANCE OF, see ASSURANCE OF SALVATION.

SALVATION, NECESSITY OF THE CHURCH FOR. In RC theology the Church is held to be necessary for salvation in two distinct but interrelated ways. The Church as Church is necessary for the salvation of mankind in God's saving plan. The one saving activity of Christ is made present in and through the Church, which is the visible continuation of the mission of Christ among men. The visible Church gives concreteness and corporeity, as it were, to the saving grace of Christ addressed to all members of the human family.

A continued Incarnation makes the Church a visible sacrament of sonship necessary for the human family if the call of grace and man's response to that call is to be fully human, i.e., expressed in manifest bodiliness. This the Church does through word and sacrament and through the bonds of communion. The Church makes present tangibly Christ's call to mankind to be indeed God's family. As such it is necessary for the salvation of man.

Distinct but related is the question of how necessary the Church is in the salvation of any individual person. That the Church is necessary in this sense and that outside of the

Church there is no salvation has been the constant teaching of the Church (e.g., D 469, 792).

It becomes clear immediately that in this aspect of the problem the term Church signifies a reality capable of different degrees of fulfillment or actualization.

Since the saving grace of the Lord calls out to every person, and this grace is rooted in the solidarity of Christ with mankind and in God's universal salvific will, the Church is operative, as presence of Christ's saving work among men, wherever the grace of the Lord is operative. The Church exists far more widely than the boundaries of the visible Church. It is an error to think that the Church in its fullest visible manifestation is so necessary that outside of it no one is saved (D 3866–73). Such a view is incompatible with the universality of God's saving will in Christ, when taken in relation to the experientially and historically proven limitation of effectiveness of the visible Church. The limitations of the visible sign cannot confine the power of the all-embracing grace of the Lord.

This does not mean, however, that the fullness of visible manifestation in the church community by way of unity of faith, unity in sacramental worship, and unity in divinely instituted ministry is insignificant or optional. Those who culpably refuse to be part of the fullest expression of the Church are indeed outside salvation as planned by God. To think otherwise is the error of indifferentism.

The saving grace of the Lord, active beyond the visible frontiers of the church community, forms the Church in incomplete expression among those who accept that grace and respond to it in faith and love. This is the anonymous Christian Church of those whose faith and love are in varying degrees implicitly Christian.

Since all saving grace is related to the visible event of paschal mystery and its presence in the visible church community, all saving grace that forms an anonymous Christianity tends at the same time to greater explicitness. The Church implicitly present in the acceptance of grace and manifest minimally is the very visible Church itself present by intrinsic tendency. The one Church, then, may be present in varying degrees of manifestation and explicitness. Its least manifest presence longs for and tends to its full manifestation and presence as efficacious sign of salvation offered to men.

It is the faith of the Catholic Church that the saving grace of Christ is concretely and tangibly present in sacramental manifestation in the Catholic Church. The saving grace of Christ is less fully manifest institutionally (which is distinct from the question of its personal manifestation) in other Christian bodies which share in many of the Church's signs of grace, such as Scripture, baptism, preaching, etc. And the grace of Christ is manifest at least to some degree in other religious rites and forms used by man beyond the frontiers of explicit Christianity. All such lesser and incomplete manifestations call for fullness of expression.

To share in the life of the full expression of Church is necessary because of the precept of the Lord. This precept binds only when awareness of the command and possibility of obeying it exists.

To share in the life of the full expression of Church is also necessary as means of salvation. But the graciousness of God, taking account of the built-in limitations of any visible sign and the humanness of the Church-sign, makes the Church necessary as means conditionally. For those who genuinely find in it the sign of salvation, it is necessary in its full reality. For those who through no fault of their own do not find the full sacramental manifestation of Church, its reality may be grasped implicitly (*in voto*), its presence realized implicitly in the free acceptance of the grace of the Lord in faith and love, however minimally explicit and manifest these are.

The question is complex. One seeks to proclaim both the role of the visible Church and the universality of God's saving grace in Christ in face of the human limitations of the presence of the visible Church. Understanding this complexity should lead one to avoid solutions of the problem of membership in the Church. One should also show a certain hesitance in applying to the Church the terms ordinary as opposed to the extraordinary, or normal as opposed to the unusual, means to salvation.

BIBLIOGRAPHY: Vat II ConstChurch 13–17; R. Hasseveldt, DTC Tables générales 1:118–19; E. Dublanchy, *ibid.* 4.2:2155–75; E. Suaras, SacMund 1:332–337; M. Eminyan, NCE 12:995–997; *idem, Theology of Salvation* (1960); P. Chirico, "One Church: What Does It Mean?" ThSt 28 (1967) 659–683; K. Rahner, "Membership in the Church," Rahner ThInvest 2:1–88; E. Schillebeeckx, "The Church and Mankind," *Concilium,* Dogma 1 (1964) 69–101; B. Willems, "Who Belongs to the Church?" *ibid.* 131–151.

[J. F. GALLAGHER]

SALVATION ARMY (SA), a religious body founded and organized on military lines by William *Booth at London in 1865. Booth had been a Methodist evangelist, but he organized the Christian Revival Association as a nondenominational Holiness mission to work exclusively in the slums of London. With slight modifications his organization became the Christian Mission, operating throughout the British Isles, and finally the worldwide Salvation Army. Booth made effective use of recent converts to evangelize others in a language familiar to them, and every enrolled Salvationist was licensed to preach. Booth retained control of every detail of the movement, and when the Christian Mission was reorganized as the SA, ownership of all its property and authority over all its members were vested in him. He issued the *Orders and Regulations for the Salvation Army* in October 1878, prescribing in minute detail the quasi-military organization, dress, and daily occupations of his followers. Expansion in Great Britain followed rapidly. While the Christian Mission operated 30 stations in 1878, the SA maintained 51 stations with 127 full-time evangelists by January 1879. Work began in the U.S. in 1880 and in

Canada in 1881. The SA's first station in India was established in 1882. Difficulties came with rapid growth, notably over efforts made by Thomas E. Moore to incorporate the SA as a religious body in the U.S. in 1884, which produced a division now represented by the *American Rescue Workers. A second effort to secure greater autonomy for American Salvationists led to the secession of Ballington Booth and the formation of the *Volunteers of America in 1896. The persistent problem of too much centralization was not solved until 1929, when the newly created High Council, composed of senior territorial officers, received power to elect and depose a commander-in-chief.

Early struggles to combat alcoholism and prostitution in English slums have expanded into the SA's respected and many-faceted social welfare program. In inspiration and purpose the SA is evangelistic, and while Booth did not intend to found another denomination, the SA is in fact a Church, with its own doctrinal and ritual systems. While accepting the primacy of the Bible, Salvationists also emphasize the immediacy of the Holy Spirit's inspiration of the believer. The central doctrines of sin and redemption are understood in an Arminian sense; *entire sanctification as a second blessing is a prominent theme. The traditional Christian sacraments of baptism and the Lord's Supper are disregarded; there is a ritual for the dedication of children and the Army's own military rituals are considered to be part of the process of salvation. There are about 300,000 Salvationists in the U.S., and about 30,000 officers in evangelizing work throughout the world. BIBLIOGRAPHY: H. A. Wisbey, Jr., *Soldiers without Swords: A History of the Salvation Army in the U.S.* (1956).

[R. K. MACMASTER]

SALVATION HISTORY, a general term for biblical history, used to describe the kind of history contained in the Old and New Testaments. Such history relates what God has done in the lives of men, for humanity as a whole, in order to fulfill in them the design of grace. It is a history, not in the sense that it relates an unbroken, causally connected chain of historical facts controllable and provable in their connection, but rather a history revealed by God in a completely incalculable selection of individual events. This history looks to only one end, or termination; it is the unfolding plan of God to bring man back to himself. In this plan all its events are explained and find their meaning. In the Judeo-Christian account of this saving will of God, it is viewed as a continuous attitude of his toward men that embraces the whole of human history where God's offer of salvation to all men is concretely and historically realized.

The history recorded in the Bible was written by men who came to know their God in a special way by what he did for them within the framework of their everyday lives. Through definite events, persons, and utterances, certain special experiences were recognized as embodiments of salvation and stood out in ever sharper relief from the general history as the gradually developing pattern of God's saving action. It is evident that this point of view distinguishes all biblical history from the notion of scientific history as we understand it today. The Bible narratives are concerned primarily with the divine pattern and significance in the events they relate rather than their political, economic, or scientific significance. Throughout the Old and New Testaments, what is being narrated as revelation of God comes in the framework of human history and is understood as conditioned and measured by its relation to man's salvation. In this sense God's self-revelation in history as savior is what is handed down as the testimony of the people who experience his salvation in their history; hence the name salvation history.

The importance of this question about whether or not the revelation of salvation found in Sacred Scripture is historical goes to the very roots of what Christianity is. Either Christianity is a salvation in history or it is no different from any other religion. The acceptance of the OT as revelation of God's saving activity in history by the first Christians and their insistence that the good news of salvation in the NT is in direct historical continuity as a divine salvation happening within a historical framework give support to this terminology.

Throughout its history Christianity has had to confront the denial of this uniqueness of its salvation in a variety of forms, and the unorthodox Gnostic and mystical notions that salvation is achieved through special knowledge or individual religious experience. The Gnostics of the 2d century attempted to dehistoricize salvation into a kind of religious experience of the divine reached by knowledge and asceticism. Christianity through Irenaeus emerged victorious over the Valentinian Gnostics, but only to fight the same battle again and again in different armor in each period of its history.

The biblical discussions over the historical Jesus and the demythologizing of his message in the NT are a revival of this same struggle. Those who would extend these critical approaches to biblical literature so far as to dehistoricize the event of man's salvation in Jesus Christ to the level of myth or merely moral example are again in danger of eliminating what is essential to Christian salvation, namely, its concrete embodiment in man's history.

Some of the existential approaches truncate and distort the message of the NT as a whole by making Christ's death as a saving event too dependent on the believer, thus reducing the Savior to a mere moral influence, who saves only by inspiring others to a similar selfcommitment in love.

The controversy between R. Bultmann and O. Cullmann over the use of the expression salvation history centers on this important truth. Bultmann argues that the term is unacceptable because it is not strictly biblical, that the essential features constituting history are absent, or that at least the word history in the phrase should be put in quotation marks to indicate its difference from authentic history. Cullmann in his book *Salvation in History* answers these objections by arguing that, although salvation history and history are not identical, there is an analogy between them that must be seen. First, salvation history is concerned with a connected series of events, even if the principle of connection is not arrived at historically. Second, within the divine plan, place is left for historical contingency, for human resistance, sin, and the mysterious detours taken because of this resistance and sin—in other words salvation history also includes a history of disaster. Third, the essential individual events constituting this series of events belong to history (that mythical elements are adduced to interpret the individual events does not change this fact). Salvation history actually comes to men in two stages: one inchoative and incomplete to God's chosen people in the OT; the other, definitive and complete through his only Son, Jesus Christ, to the Church in the NT. This kind of history, which we call salvation history, is the story of God's self-revelation and self-communication in the events of human history to save mankind. This history culminates in the eschatological event of salvation. BIBLIOGRAPHY: Y. Congar, "Christ in the Economy of Salvation and in Our Dogmatic Tracts," *Who Is Jesus of Nazareth?* (ed. E. H. Schillebeeckx, 1965); O. Cullmann, *Salvation in History* (1967); R. Schnackenburg, *New Testament Theology Today* (tr. D. Askew, 1963); J. Bourke, "Historical Jesus and the Kerygmatic Christ" (*Concilium* 11, 1966).

[J. C. MURRAY]

SALVATION OF THE UNBELIEVER, a theological issue connected with the two truths that God wills all men to be saved and that faith is necessary for salvation. The phrase is used to develop the theme that those who do not have knowledge of the gospel can yet be saved, but that one who culpably rejects the truth can not be saved. Vatican Council II teaches in principle that all men belong to the one People of God but in differing degrees (Vat II ConstChurch ch.2). As to "unbelievers" the Council sums up the Catholic tradition on the point: "Those also can attain to everlasting salvation who through no fault of their own do not know the gospel of Jesus Christ or His Church, yet sincerely seek God and, moved by grace, strive by their deeds to do His will as it is known to them through the dictates of conscience. Nor does divine Providence deny the help necessary for salvation to those who, without blame on their part, have not yet arrived at an explicit knowledge of God, but who strive to live a good life, thanks to His grace. Whatever goodness or truth is found among them is looked upon by the Church as a preparation for the gospel. She regards such qualities as given by Him who enlightens all men so that they may finally have life" (*ibid.* 16). St. Thomas Aquinas, in a celebrated article on which there has been some contemporary elaboration, offered a thought that illumines the Council's reference to the "dictates of conscience." He points out that the unbaptized (and one can understand also the unbeliever) at some point, whether suddenly or after a long process, will give his life a radical moral direction, either rightly or wrongly. If rightly, he will be acting under grace and will receive forgiveness, whatever the terms in which he consciously makes this radical choice. Even if the wrong choice is made, the opportunity is always present in the human being's power of moral judgment and decision, and so always the opportunity is present for acting under grace. Whenever the right radical self-determination is made and in whatever terms, it is under the influence of saving grace and brings forgiveness of sin (ThAq ST 1a2ae, 89.6). BIBLIOGRAPHY: ThAq St Lat-Eng v.27, ed. T. C. O'Brien, app. 4.

[T. C. O'BRIEN]

SALVATION OUTSIDE THE CHURCH, see EXTRA ECCLESIAM NULLA SALUS.

SALVATORIANS, THE SOCIETY OF THE DIVINE SAVIOR, congregation whose specific purpose is the preservation and the spread of the faith through the sacred ministry, the education of youth, retreats, and missionary work among non-Catholics. It was founded in 1881 by Father Franziskus Maria of the Cross Jordan. In addition to the vows of poverty, chastity, and obedience, the priests and coadjutor brothers make a fourth vow known as the "promise of the apostolate." They work under the special protection of the Blessed Virgin Mary and the Apostles. In 1889 the society sent its first missionaries to Assam, India, and after this mission was reduced in effectiveness by World War I, the missionaries went to China, which fell to the communists. The missionaries then went to Formosa and in 1955 opened two missions in Africa. Provinces were established in Switzerland, Germany, Italy, Czechoslovakia, England, Belgium, Colombia, Brazil, Austria, Romania, and Spain. The work of the society was centered in schools, parishes, and seminaries. The Salvatorians opened a mission in the U.S. in 1896 at St. Nazianz, Wisconsin. The principal work in the U.S. from New York to California is the education of youth in seminaries and high schools. The apostolate of the press was stressed from the beginning in the U.S., Germany, and Switzerland. In 1975 the members numbered 1,279, of whom 848 were priests in 136 houses.

[R. C. CLIGGETT]

SALVE REGINA (MUSIC), one of the four seasonal Marian antiphons, composed to be sung at the end of Compline. In addition to the very beautiful plain song version (*c.* 11th cent.), there are numerous polyphonic settings, particularly of the 15th and 16th cent. for voices and for organ.

[M. T. LEGGE]

SALVIAN, see INSTANTIUS AND SALVIAN.

SALVIAN OF MARSEILLES (*c.*400–*c.*480), ecclesiastical writer. A Gaul by birth, S. left his wife with her consent and went to Lérins to live as a monk (*c.*424). From *c.*439 he lived in Marseilles where he wrote his *De guber-*

natione Dei (On the Governance of God), a treatise in which, comparing the vices of the decadent Roman Christians with the virtues of the barbarian invaders, he depicted the invasions as a punishment inflicted by God on the Romans for their sins. Of his other writings, a treatise *Ad ecclesiam* on avarice and nine letters are extant. Works: PL 53:25–238; crit. ed. F. Pauly, CSEL 8 (1883); Eng. tr. J. O'Sullivan, FathCh 3 (1947). BIBLIOGRAPHY: G. Bardy, DTC 14:1056–58.

[R. B. ENO]

SALVIATI, FRANCESCO (Francesco or Cecchino de'Rossi; 1510–63), Italian painter, student of various Florentines. In Rome (1531) S. took the surname of Card. Giovanni Salviati, his patron. After visits to Florence, Bologna and Venice (1539), he painted the frescoes *Carita* and *Deposition from the Cross* (both in Florence), decorated for the Farnese family, went to the court of Francis I, and again in Rome, executed frescoes in the Sacchiti Palace and the Sala Regia in the Vatican. He helped diffuse the Roman-Florentine fresco style in the 1540s and 1550s using the figural vocabulary of Michelangelo and Raphael in historical and allegorical scenes. His *Visitation* fresco (1538) shows ceremonious movement and elaborate architecture, while his finest frescoes, replete with ancient Roman trappings, are mannered in movement, and ornamented as finely as goldsmith work. BIBLIOGRAPHY: M. Hirst, "Francesco Salviati's 'Visitation'," *The Burlington Magazine,* 103 (1961); L. H. Cheney, "Francesco Salviati's North Italian Journey," Art Bulletin, 45 (1963).

[M. J. DALY]

SALVIFIC WILL, a term used in theology to affirm God's willing salvation to all. The universality of that will is affirmed on the basis of 1 Tim 2, 4, the statement that God our savior "wills all men to be saved and to come to the knowledge of the truth." In the face of extremes of "predestinationism," the Church has always affirmed that even though in fact some men are not saved, the salvific will is not a mere fiction or an ineffective wish (velleity), as though a true willing of salvation only embraced the elect (D 623;626;1522;2304;2305;2429;3014). The term "salvific" is causal; it indicates against *Pelagianism that grace and salvation can come only from God as their first and free source. While constantly faithful to that truth, theology has developed complex attempts to assert the primacy and effectiveness of God's saving will together with the fact of human resistance and the outcome of that resistance. One element in the attempt is the distinction that antecedently and universally God wills all men to be saved; by a consequent will, in the actual situation of human resistance and sin, salvation is willed only to those who are faithful. But salvation remains a mystery and only some of its strands can be perceived by theology, while the totality remains obscure. The primary witness of the Gospels is that God addresses man as Father and Savior through Christ; that is

the message of hope, alongside which every man knows his own capacity to reject the divine invitation by sin.

[T. C. O'BRIEN]

SAMADHI, (Sanskrit, literally: trance, concentration), used (1) in the *Yoga system of India to refer to a state of consummate interiority which is at once inward stasis and transcendental self-consciousness. It constitutes the eighth and final stage of Yoga discipline, the goal of which is the liberation or isolation (*kaivalya*) of the "self" (*purusha*) or consciousness from its involvement in and identification with the distending and fragmenting force of nature or matter (*prakrti*). (2) In *Buddhism, the meaning is roughly similar, but as part of the eight-fold path (leading toward wisdom and *nirvana:* liberation; enlightenment). The emphasis is on tranquility, connected with the diminishing both of external (sense) stimuli and of discursive thought. BIBLIOGRAPHY: M. Eliade, *Yoga* (1970) 3–100; 162–199; E. Conze, *Buddhist Meditation* (1969), 7–41; 110–132.

[D. P. EFROYMSON]

SAMANTABHADRA, Bodhisattva of Univeral Kindness, most popular in Chinese Buddhism, represented with a blue lotus at the left shoulder, holding a *cintāmani* (magic jewel) in his left hand, his right hand in the mūdra of argument (*vitarka*), in Chinese sculpture often riding an elephant according to the Lotus Sūtra.

[M. J. DALY]

SAMARIA, the territory of Ephraim and the W part of Manasseh, of the fallen kingdom of Israel. It was called Samaria after its captured capital city. In 720 B.C. this region was made a province by the Mesopotamian king, Sargon II. Although most of the inhabitants had been carried off into exile, some remained behind and intermingled with the people Sargon imported from Babylon, Cuthah, Avva, Hamath, and Sepharvaim to form the new people. From that time on, these people were called Samaritans (2 Kg 17.24). Friendly relations existed between the Samaritans and the kingdom of Judah (cf. 2 Chr 30.1–11) until the Exile. When the Samaritans desired to assist the repatriated Jews in rebuilding the temple in Jerusalem, their offer was refused (Ezra 4.2–3). The Samaritans therefore built a temple of their own on Mt. Garizim. In the NT period S. was a larger territory, including the Plain of Sharon and part of the Plain of Esdraelon under the control of the Roman procurators. At this time the hostility between Jews and Samaritans resulted in the murder of some Jews at Ginaea in 54 A.D. Jesus' attitude toward the Samaritans was friendly, as appears, e.g., in his illustration of neighborly love by the good Samaritan (Lk 10.30–37). Some Samaritans believed in him (Jn 4.39–42), and he rebuked James and John for wanting to destroy a Samaritan village (Lk 9.51–56) which did not receive him. The deacon Philip's preaching was received in Samaria, and Peter and John conferred the Holy Spirit there (Acts 8.4–25). But some Samaritans persevered in their ancient faith and a few of these remain even at the present time. BIBLIOGRAPHY: H. Gaster, *Samaritans* (1925).

[S. MUSHOLT]

SAMARITAN PENTATEUCH, a Hebrew text of the first five books of the Bible in an ancient Palestinian reading that varies from the Masoretic text but often concurs with the LXX version. Assigned by some scholars to the 5th cent. B.C., by others to the 2d cent. B.C., the text has been known in the W only since 1616; the earliest extant MSS are medieval. BIBLIOGRAPHY: P. Skehan et al., JBC 2:566.

[T. C. O'BRIEN]

SAMARITANS, the people of *Samaria; they call themselves, not *Shomeronim*, inhabitants of Samaria, but *Shamerim*, the observant ones. To the Jews they were regarded as racially impure and syncretists in religion. The overtones of the name lend emphasis to several of the gospel narratives.

[T. C. O'BRIEN]

SAMA-VEDA, the third Veda, dating from 7th to 3rd cent. B.C. and incorporating the knowledge of chants and melodies into 1,549 metrical verses, nearly all of which can be traced to the Rig-Veda. The book served as a text for those who officiated at the rites of Soma, the Hindu god of moon, penance, and healing, at which the sacred soma plant was prepared, juiced, and ritually drunk by the priests. The mantras and invocations involved in the complicated preparations and sacrifices of this rite (performed no more than three times in a person's life and then usually only by kings and the wealthy, though witnessed by many) are gathered and preserved in this text.

[R. J. LITZ]

SAMGAR, see SHAMGAR.

SAMINSKY, LAZARE (1882–1959), Russian-born composer, conductor, and writer in the U.S. S. studied music under Nikolai Rimsky-Korsakov at the Petrograd Conservatory. He led an active life in music in Russia, spent some time in London and Paris, then came to the U.S. in 1920. He was a cofounder of the League of Composers, music director of the Temple Emanu-El in N.Y. (1924–58), director of the Three Choirs Festival of N.Y., and guest conductor with many symphony orchestras, American and European. S. was an important figure in the formation of a Jewish national school of composition. His liturgical works are an important contribution to synagogue music. In addition to composing operas, symphonies, ballets, songs, etc., S. wrote many books, among them *Music of Our Day* (1932); *Music of the Ghetto and the Bible* (1934).

[M. T. LEGGE]

SAMOA, formerly called Navigators' Archipelago, a part of *Polynesia. The E Samoan islands (76 sq. mi.; est. pop.

as of 1970, 27,159) were occupied by the U.S. in 1900. The W Samoans (1130 sq. mi.; est. pop. as of 1971, 146,000) belonged to Germany until 1915, when they were assigned to *New Zealand. Catholic missioners reached the Eastern Samoans in 1845. In 1850 the territory was annexed to the vicariate apostolic of *Oceania. More methodical evangelization began in 1865. In 1957 the vicariate became independent; and in 1966 the diocese of Apia was created. In 1977 Catholics totaled 34,472. Protestant missionaries have established strong Churches in the Samoans. British Congregationalists, Australian Methodists, Anglicans, and some other denominations are at work. The missions of the London Missionary Society are considered the finest in the Pacific. The Churches have sole care of education. Christians of Samoa have sent their own missioners to pioneer in the *Fijis, *New Hebrides, *Solomons, and New Guinea in advance of European and American missioners. In 1966 Protestant membership in the Samoans was 89,276. BIBLIOGRAPHY: *Bilan du Monde* 2:780–782.

[P. DAMBORIENA]

SAMOSATA, capital of the Seleucid kingdom of Commagene; annexed to the Roman province of Syria; home of satirist Lucian (mid-2d cent. A.D.) and of Paul, the controversial bp. elected in 260 and deposed for heresy in 268. It was the center of turmoil during the Arian controversies but gradually dwindled in importance in the Eastern Church until it was incorporated into the See of Amida in 879. It was conquered by Moslems in 1150 and is identical with the town of Samsat in modern Turkey.

[E. J. DILLON]

SAMSĀRA (Sanskrit: flow; course; passing through), Indian belief in each life as a rebirth, a reincarnation. Samsāra is the process of ''passing through'' a succession of lives or incarnations, though without the subjects' remembering previous existences. What determines that rebirth will occur, and esp. the kind of incarnation it will be (e.g., whether high or low caste, or an outcaste, or an animal: cf. *Chandogya Upanishad* 5. 10. 7) is *karma, one's actions, good or bad. The process is eternal and came to be perceived (*c*.500 B.C.?) as oppressive in its endlessness and apparent pointlessness; thus liberation (*moksha) from the process was believed both possible and desirable. In early Buddhism, samsāra became synonymous with conditioned human existence, with life itself experienced as empty and frustrating; release was sought in *nirvana. BIBLIOGRAPHY: R. C. Zaehner, *Hinduism* (1966) 57–67; T. Organ, *Hinduism* (1974).

[D. P. EFROYMSON]

SAMSON, SS. (1) **Samson of Constantinople,** priest, physician, and friend of the poor, who founded at his own expense a hospital for the poor in Constantinople. (2) **Samson of Dol** (*c*.485–*c*.565), important 6th-cent. British missionary, born of Welsh parents. He was a monk in Ireland, a missionary in Cornwall and Brittany, and perhaps bp. of Dol.

[E. J. DILLON]

SAMSON, son of Manoah of the tribe of Dan, judge during the premonarchial period of Israel (Jg ch. 13–16). The biblical story of his election before birth, his feats of physical strength and his weakness for women, is thought to be an extension of Yahwist (J) material. The Bible probably reflects folk stories concerning a giant of great strength, of towering anger and unchecked lusts, who became an Israelite hero during the Philistine oppression. The biblical account idealizes S. in order to teach that through him Yahweh chose to protect Israel. S. is cited in Heb 11.32 as an example of faith.

[T. C. O'BRIEN]

SAMSON OF BURY ST. EDMUNDS (c.1135–1212), English Benedictine abbot. Thomas Carlyle in *Past and Present* depicted him as the ideal medieval abbot, glorifying the portrait drawn in the *Chronicle* of Jocelin of Brakelond, one of Samson's monks. S. was, in fact, a representative abbot of his period. After attending the Univ. of Paris, he became monk, sacristan, prior and, from 1182, abbot of Bury St. Edmunds. A good administrator, an extensive builder, S. defended the rights of his abbey against successive kings, blocking William de Longchamp's attempt to curtail Benedictine privileges in England. BIBLIOGRAPHY: Knowles MOE.

[F. D. BLACKLEY]

SAMSON OF CÓRDOBA (d. 890), abbot and Latin author. In 864 he fled from Bp. Hostegesis of Malaga and Count Servandus of Córdoba, henchmen of the Moslem emir, and composed a lengthy *Apologeticus* defending his own faith and refuting his enemies. The treatise, which deals with the Trinity, the Incarnation, and the divine essence (substance), comes to grips with problems of anthropomorphism and pantheism. The unique MS (9th cent.) of the *Apologeticus* and of a similar treatise by Beatus of Liébana has an Arabic gloss.

[E. P. COLBERT]

SAMUEL, the powerful religious leader of 11th -cent. Israel. His career marked the end of the period of the judges, as he played the decisive role in bringing monarchy to Israel. The Book of Samuel, which reports his life and deeds, incorporates many traditions concerning S. and relies on diverse sources. It is difficult to see how one man could have fulfilled the many roles reported in that book. He is called a seer and at one point is associated with a prophetic guild, but his dominant prophetic role reminds one of the great 8th-cent. prophets, as he delivers the word of rebuke and of rejection to Eli the priest and to Saul the king. He can be compared to the greatest of the judges as he rallied Israel

against the Philistines so successfully that "they did not rise against Israel again in the days of Samuel" (1Sam 7.11–13). Later tradition referred to him as a powerful intercessor, second only to Moses (Ps 99.6; Jer 15.1). He is described as a circuit judge who made a yearly circuit of the cult centers Bethel, Gilgal, and Mizpah, and "judged Israel in all these places" (1 Sam 7.16). He was dedicated to the Lord from birth and grew up in the care of the priest Eli, under whose tutelage he ministered to the Lord at Shilo. Thoroughly conversant with priestly functions, he was the leading authority in his day in religious matters. His attitude toward monarchy and priesthood epitomizes well the one later associated with his tribe (Ephraim) and the northern tradition (Elohist). He considered monarchy an invitation to apostasy. When he reluctantly anointed first Saul and then David as king, it was probably because it seemed necessary to have such a stable authority structure against the constant Philistine threat. He did his best to make kingship the earthly vicegerency of the Lord's kingship, with the king owing absolute obedience to the word of God.

[E. J. DILLON]

SAMUEL, BOOKS OF. The fact that a single broad amalgam of traditions has been artificially divided into the two books of 1 and 2 Sam is due to purely material factors and does not affect the interpretation. The confusing practice of referring to these books as 1 and 2 Kg, as in the Vulgate and derived versions, has even less to recommend it from the aspect of content and is due to the influence of the Septuagint, where they are called 1 and 2 Kingdoms.

The saga as a whole begins with the story of Samuel's childhood (perhaps c.1040 B.C.) and is intended to culminate in the story of Solomon's accession in 1 Kg ch. 1–2 (c.970). It has as its central theme Yahweh's choosing of the house of David, and more specifically of Solomon and his heirs, to rule his people, and of Zion, the city of David as his home in the midst of that people. To develop this basic theme, four earlier and originally independent complexes of tradition have been subsumed and re-orientated.

The first of these is the ark stories (1 Sam 4–6 and 2 Sam 6), in which, because of the faithlessness of the former custodians of the ark at Shiloh in the north, it "allows" itself to be captured by the Philistines and subsequently forces them, entirely by Yahweh's miraculous power invested in it, to allow it to journey to a temporary resting-place in the south prior to being triumphantly conducted by David to its final and permanent home in Jerusalem.

The second tradition complex has as its theme the rise and fall of Saul. Units of tradition concerned wholly with praising Saul and his triumphs have been combined with others which explain his downfall as due to disobedience (1 Sam 13.8–15), yet which still retain a certain reverence for him and recognize his charismatic gifts.

The subject of the third tradition complex is the rise of David who, by his God-given warrior strength, cunning, and also "meekness," overcomes the most formidable obstacles and dangers, esp. persecution by Saul, to become king over all Israel. The climactic center of this complex is the oracle of Nathan (2 Sam 7). Yahweh's will to "choose" the house of David to rule forever is thus shown advancing inexorably and irresistibly toward its predestined fulfillment.

The fourth component (Sam 1–2) is not a complex of originally independent tradition units but a unified story that relates with marvellous skill how Solomon was chosen before his elder brothers as heir to David's throne even though his birth was the outcome of an originally sinful union.

Into the single broad amalgam of tradition woven out of these four complexes, later hands have inserted the story of Samuel's infancy and prophetic vocation (1 Sam ch. 1–3); the "anti-monarchist" account of Saul's election as king (1 Sam ch. 8 and 10.17–27), here interpreted as an act of faithlessness on the part of the people; two further accounts of the rejection of Saul (1 Sam ch. 15,28) and the anointing of David (1 Sam 16.1–13). In general, these additions reflect the conflict between prophet and king, which intensified after the division of the kingdoms. Samuel is represented, not merely as the seer who consecrates the king, but as prophet, judge, and priest, and even (1 Sam 7), as the conqueror of the Philistines. BIBLIOGRAPHY: H. W. Hertzberg, *1 and 2 Samuel* (1964); R. A. Carlson, *David the Chosen King: a Traditio-Historical Approach to II Samuel* (1964); A. Weiser, *Samuel, seine geschichtliche Aufgabe und religiöse Bedeutung* (1962); L. Rost, "Die Überlieferung von der Thronnachfolge Davids," *Das kleine Credo und andere Studien zum Alten Testament* (1965) 119–253.

[D. J. BOURKE]

SAMUEL HA-NAGID (993–1056), 11th-cent. Jewish scholar and statesman whose role as virtual caliph of Granada during the last two decades of his life marks the highest achievement of a Jew in medieval Muslim Spain. His full name was Abu Ibrahim Samuel ben Joseph Halevi ibn Nagdela. His family was from Merida; he was born in Córdoba. S. studied halakah under Ḥanokh ben Moses of Córdoba. After Córdoba was sacked in 1013 by Berbers, Samuel fled to Málaga, part of the Berber kingdom of Granada. His training in the Koran and his mastery of Arabic calligraphy prepared the way for his eventual appointment as vizier by Caliph Habbus, in which post he was in charge of diplomatic and military affairs. During the tenure of Habbus's son Bādis, Samuel was virtual caliph and proved his prowess in military strategy during the almost constant warfare (1038–56) throughout Andalusia against the allies of Seville. S.'s poetry, much of which is addressed to his son, recounts his military campaigns and may have introduced the poetry of war and battle into Hebrew literature. His triumphs were viewed by Jews as national victories and on one occasion celebrated by a special "Purim." His career as halakhist and Jewish communal leader culminated in his acceptance as chief (*nagid*) of

Granadan Jewry (1027), in which position he appointed judges and headed the Talmudic academy. He died on a campaign and his son Joseph succeeded him as vizier.

[E. J. DILLON]

SAN ALBERTO, JOSÉ ANTONIO DE (1727–1804), bishop. A Spanish Discalced Carmelite, he became a prominent bp. in Latin America, first in the see of Córdoba in Tucamán in 1778, then in the archdiocese of La Plata (Colombia) in 1786. His pastoral injunctions were published under the title of *Colección de instrucciones pastorales* (1786), letters which demanded inner religion and pastoral solicitude by laity and clergy. S. A. contributed to the improvement of the program at the Univ. of Córdoba. He was an influential voice, supporting the divine right of kings against any opposition by their subjects in the work *Catecismo real* (1786), which follows the doctrine of Bossuet.

[J. R. AHERNE]

SAN BAUDELIO DE BERLANGA, CHAPEL OF, Mozarabic chapel of the first half of the 11th cent., near the village of Casillas de Berlanga in the province of Sorio, Spain, with most important Romanesque frescoes of the mid-12th century. The unusual architecture consists of one room with a huge cylindrical pier from which spring eight horseshoe arches, with 10 small vaults forming a tribune connected to the central pillar by a *coro* (choir). The western side is built against a rock cliff with a rusticated hermitage under the tribune. Most important are the frescoes—one of the most complete series in existence, consisting of an uppermost zone in the principal room and unusual secular scenes on lower zones of the *coro,* together with figures of SS. Baudelio and Nicolas, and many varied decorative motifs (rosette, fret, checks). Three painters probably executed the frescoes: the Master of Maderuelo painting, the great Biblical themes on arches, vaults and apse (seen also at the Church of Holy Cross, Madrid, and the earlier world-famous frescoes in the main apse at Sta. Maria, *Tahull); a second Master of S. Baudelio executing hunts with animals (there is a hunting scene at Ebreuil, Allier) in Hispano-Arabic style distinct from the Italo-Byzantine mode of the Maderuelo master; a third style determined the *Epiphany* (nearly ruined) in the *coro.* The large religious frescoes of S. Baudelio, transferred to canvas, are now in The Cloisters, N.Y., the Museum of Fine arts, Boston, and the John Herron Art Institute, Indianapolis. BIBLIOGRAPHY: W. W. S. Cook, "Romanesque Spanish Mural Painting: San Baudelia de Berlanga," *Art Bulletin,* 12, 3 (1930).

[M. J. DALY]

SAN BENEDETTO DI POLIRONE, ABBEY OF, former Benedictine monastery, founded in 1003 by Theobald of Canossa at the junction of the Po and Lirone Rivers (hence, the name) in the Lombard Diocese of Mantua. St. Anselm of Lucca put the house under Cluny in

1077. It was later handsomely endowed by the Countess Matilda of Tuscany, sacked by the Emperor Henry IV for its allegiance to the papacy, and still later able to present itself as a model of collectivist agricultural economy. It declined during the Avignon papacy and was given in commendation to the Gonzagas of Mantua (1419), who affiliated it with the Congregation of St. Justina of Padua. Its subsequent history was marred by clashes with dependent farmers, struggles with the lords of Mantua, and looting by French, Spanish, and German armies. When the monastery was suppressed in 1797, its library was partially transferred to Mantua and Milan. Only the church, with its fragments of 12th-cent. mosaics, remains.

[E. J. DILLON]

SAN BENITO DE VALLADOLID, ABBEY OF,
former Benedictine monastery in Valladolid, León, Spain, founded c.1390 by the son of Henry II, Juan de Medina, who converted his fortified palace (Alcázar Real) into a monastery. It became the head of the Congregation of San Benito de Valladolid, one of the most illustrious of the Benedictine congregations of the 16th through 19th cent., reaching its apogee 1610–1749. After a decline it was suppressed in 1835. BIBLIOGRAPHY: Cottineau 2: 3278.

[E. J. DILLON]

SAN CARLO ALLE QUATTRO FONTANE (SAN CARLINO), ROME,
High Baroque church, masterpiece of F. Borromini, commissioned in 1634, built 1638–46, the façade added in 1667. The cloister built first with simple Tuscan columns is oblong in plan with concave corners. Interiorly the church is an irregular oval with concave-convex surfaces in undulating walls, the oval dome richly honeycombed with geometric coffering, all in subtle gray and white, only the altars richly colored. The façade is a most important example of High Roman Baroque, advancing and retreating sinuously under a rich overlay of varied architectural forms: dramatic columns, sculpture of intense light and shade, with imagination and unusual details of great beauty through harmony and the dramatic wholeness of its parts. San Carlo influenced late Baroque architecture in N Italy, S Germany, and Spain.

[M. J. DALY]

SAN CLEMENTE, BASILICA OF,
4th-cent. church retaining much of its Early Christian character despite rebuildings into the Baroque period—three aisled, with the apse raised on a bema under which are relics, the chancel separated from the nave by a low parapet. To the E is an area for choir, lectern, pulpit, and paschal candle, a timber roof, arcade between aisles and nave columns with Ionic capitals, all preceded by a propylaeum and atrium. Most interesting are the frescoes in the "lower" original structure, excavated in 1861, incoherent but historically precious because executed at different periods in varied styles. Most valuable for dating are the donors' portraits, a 9th-cent.

Harrowing of Hell, a *Deesis,* depicting the Slavic St. Cyril, a *Madonna,* and an expressive *Ascension* of later linear style, with the portrait of Pope Leo IV (847–855). Frescoes (before 1084) in the narthex and nave of the lower church depict the legend of San Clemente in decorative dark and light shapes, the elegantly lyrical, elongated forms lacking depth—witnessing to the varied styles of Roman painting of that era.

[M. J. DALY]

SAN CLEMENTE DE TAHULL, FRESCOES OF,
masterpieces of Romanesque painting. The frescoes are evidences of 12th-cent. monumental murals of great originality in regional styles of varying degrees of sophistication produced in artistic provinces. In Tahull, Catalonia, a "provincial" Byzantine style prevailed, less subtle and refined, yet with a strong directness peculiarly expressive, the figures and drapery rendered flat, stiff, and formal by subdivision into decorative segments characteristic of Ottonian painting. The bright colors and dramatic formalized facial expressions (apse fresco, *Pantocrator*) are characteristically Catalonian. They are now in the Catalan Museum, Barcelona. BIBLIOGRAPHY: A. Grabar and C. Nordenfalk, *Romanesque Painting* (1958); E. Junyent, *Catalogne Romane* (v. 1, 1960). *SANTA MARIA DE TAHULL, FRESCOES OF.

[R. C. MARKS]

SAN CUGAT DEL VALLES,
Benedictine abbey near Barcelona, the magnificent lower cloister (1190–1217), one of the most beautiful and complete of Catalan Romanesque style. The 144 extraordinary, rich capitals embrace Corinthian order: interlace, palmettes, human and animal forms, and histories. One depicting a mason cutting—carries the signature of Arnau Cadell, the earliest and finest sculptor working here. The capitals relate in style and iconography to cloisters in Gerona (1150). BIBLIOGRAPHY: J. Baltrusaitis, *Les Chapiteaux de Saint Cugat del Vallès* (1931).

[M. J. DALY]

SAN FRANCESCO, BASILICA OF, ASSISI,
first Franciscan church, built (1228–53) as a shrine for the body of St. Francis. It is two-storied to relate topographically to the hill site, with façade at the E end, together with a vast monastery on W and S. The dark lower church with two transepts connected by a nave and aisles divided into rectangular chapels, and with slightly domed cross-vaults is impressive for frescoes by Cimabue, P. Lorenzetti, and S. Martini completely covering the walls and vaults. The upper church of Italian Gothic style on a Latin cross plan, has an aisleless nave and four square bays with windows of stained glass, beneath which a gallery runs uninterruptedly around the church—historically precious with paintings of Giotto and Cimabue. The typically Italian basilica features a screen gable higher than the roof, pointed doorway, wheel-window, and beautifully proportioned and detailed Lom-

bard campanile. BIBLIOGRAPHY: B. Kleinschmidt, *Die Basilika S. Francesco in Assisi* (1928).

[M. J. DALY]

SAN FRUTTUOSO (CAPODIMONTE), ABBEY OF, former Benedictine monastery in the village of Capodimonte, near Camogli, in Liguria, Italy; Archdiocese of Genoa. Founded by charter of Oberto II (994), Count of Liguria, it was endowed by the Empress Adelaide. It flourished in the 13th cent. but was given in commendation by Julius II in 1550 to the Doria family, who held it until recent times. The abbey church is in pure Lombard style, with some Byzantine and Provençal influence. The church was partially damaged by a flood in 1928. The adjoining 13th-cent. palace was restored in 1934.

[E. J. DILLON]

SAN GALGANO, ABBEY OF, a Cistercian monastery near Siena, Italy, begun by Cistercians of Casamari at the tomb of the hermit St. Galgano (d. 1181). The monastery, however, was built and populated by monks from Clairvaux (1201). The abbey became the largest in Tuscany. It took over and reformed four other monasteries in the same province (S. Pantaleone, S. Salvatore, S. Michele near Pisa, and S. Michele a Quarto near Siena). The house declined under commendatory abbots after 1509 and was suppressed in 1783 by the government. Only ruins of the Gothic church survive. BIBLIOGRAPHY: B. G. Bedini, *Le Abazie Cistercensi d'Italia* (1964) 94–96; M. B. Morris, NCE 12:1030–31.

[L. J. LEKAI]

SAN GIMIGNANO, ART OF. In the Italian hill town of Gimignano near Siena (independent in the 12th cent.) under Florentine rule (1354) 48 notable house towers (fortifications against medieval fires) were built, 13 of which still extant inspired L. *Kahn in his 20th-cent. "utility" towers (Richards Medical Research Building. Phila., 1957–61), most imaginative and impressive of mid-20th-cent. architectural forms, with immediate impact in the U.S. and Europe. Frescoes by Taddeo di Bartolo and Bartolo di Fredi (14th cent.), B. Gozzoli (1465–66), works of Giuliano, and Benedetto da Maiano, D. Ghirlandaio, P. del Pallaiuolo's *Coronation of the Virgin with Saints* (1483), with master works of Fra Filippo Lippi and Il Pinturicchio are preserved in San Gimignano.

[M. J. DALY]

SAN GIORGIO, MAGGIORE, VENICE, Italian church on the island of San Giorgio, Venice, begun in 790, the present church designed by Palladio (1565), the façade completed by Scamozzi (1602–10) in a transitional Renaissance-Baroque style. Choir stalls (1594–98) by Albert van der Brulle, and paintings by Tintoretto, including his *Gathering of Manna* and *Last Supper* are noteworthy. The adjacent restored monastery—headquarters of the Giorgio

Cini Foundation—serves as an art-historical reference center. Remarkable are the cloister built by Palladio (1560), a superb staircase and library by Longhena (1645), and in the chapter house Carpaccio's *Four Legends of St. George* (1516).

[M. J. DALY]

SAN GIOVANNI DEGLI EREMITI, Sicilian church, founded by King Roger II in 1132, distinctively Norman in style, the rough domes and campanile juxtaposed against smooth surfaces, in Oriental mode. The structure, 16 ft by 50 ft is T-shaped, aisleless and triapsidal, with half-domes on squinches over the nave, choir, and transept, and a N tower with belfry pierced with windows. Remains of 12th-cent. frescoes on an earlier building (a mosque?) and a remarkable tropical garden within the cloister, retaining its Arab cistern, are provocative.

[M. J. DALY]

SAN GIOVANNI IN FIORE, ABBEY OF, former Florian monastery near Cosenza, the capital of Calabria, Italy, founded in 1189 by *Joachim of Fiore. It was approved by Celestine III in 1196 for the independent order of Florian monks, not affiliated with Cîteaux. It became commendatory in 1470, was united to the Cistercians in 1505, and was suppressed in 1806. Only a few ruins have survived.

[E. J. DILLON]

SAN GIROLAMO, ABBEY OF, Benedictine monastery founded in 1933 in the suburbs of Rome near Vatican City, in a building designed for the specialized mission given to it by Pius XI, that of carrying on the work of establishing the authentic text of the Vulgate, the version of the Bible which at that time enjoyed preeminence in the Latin Church and the Latin liturgy. The abbey and its mission replaced a pontifical commission established by Pius X and Benedict XV (1914) to bring to light, as nearly as could be done, the restored text in a critical edition. The abbey's Italian name could be rendered Pontifical Abbey of St. Jerome-for-the-Revision-and-Emendation-of-the-Vulgate. Its Latin name means Pontifical Abbey of St. Jerome-in-the-City (in Urbe). Its first abbot was Dom Henri Quentin.

[E. J. DILLON]

SAN ISIDORO, LEÓN, Spanish church in a great Christian kingdom of N Spain on the famous pilgrimage route to Santiago de Compostela, important in the development of the Spanish Romanesque style, consecrated (1063) upon reception of the relics of Isidore of Seville. An interesting Panteón de los Reyes (burial porch of the kings) in six vaulted compartments, renowned for magnificent carving of 32 capitals with vegetative, animal, human, and historiated subjects, indicating craftsmen of phenomenal skill in ivory carving, gold work, and illumination, evidencing Mozarabic and European influences (Rhineland and Gascony) are of a quality unparalleled in Europe at this time.

The frescoes of the vaults, lively and expressive (*Annunciation to the Shepherds, Last Supper,* 1175) are the most beautiful of the Spanish Romanesque period. A new three-aisled basilica added (1149) exists today, its capitals and sculptured S portals recalling work at Loarre, Jaca, and Santiago de Compostela. BIBLIOGRAPHY: D. M. Robb, "The Capitals of the Panteón de los Reyes, San Isidoro de León," *Art Bulletin 27* (1945).

[M. J. DALY]

SAN MARINO, predominantly Catholic republic of some 24 sq. mi. and 20,000 population, its capital also named San Marino. Located E of Florence, near the Adriatic, the mini-state is totally surrounded by Italy. It maintains close ties with Italy and Italian is the national language. According to an account dating to the 9th-10th cent., it was founded by St. Marinus, a Dalmatian Christian forced to work on the walls of Rimini during the Diocletian persecution. He reportedly became a hermit later on Mt. Titano, which today constitutes most of the mini-state. Its isolated mountain location has enabled it to escape much of the turbulence characterizing Italian history. Papal recognition of its independence in 1291 was solemnly reaffirmed by Urban VIII in 1631. Though it lay in the States of the Church region, it resisted incorporation; and Italy guaranteed its independence in 1862 (reaffirmed 1948). Ecclesiastically, San Marino falls under two Italian dioceses. After World War II it was governed by a Communist-Socialist coalition until 1957, when a more conservative government gained power.

[T. EARLY]

SAN MARTINO AL MONTE CIMINO, ABBEY OF, monastery in the Cimini mountains near Viterbo, Italy, which has given its name to the village that grew up around it. Benedictines from Farfa around 1045 rebuilt a dependent church of theirs dedicated to St. Martin and dating from at least 838. Eugene III assigned the monastery to the Cistercians of Saint-Sulpice near Belley (Savoy). In 1207 Innocent III transferred it to the Cistercians of Pontigny. There followed a period of splendor as an abbey *nullius,* during which the present church was built under Abbot Pietro. In its decline it was placed in commendation (1378) then given to the Olivetans in 1445 by Eugene IV, united to the chapter of St. Peter of the Vatican by Pius IV (1564), and given by Innocent X to the Pamphili family in 1645. The restorations of 1911–15 brought back to light the original structure. Since 1936 the bishop of Viterbo holds also the title of abbot of this monastery.

[E. J. DILLON]

SAN MINIATO AL MONTE (Florence; completed *c.*1062), timber-roofed basilican plan church built in the Tuscan Romanesque style. It is noted for the richness of the colored marble encrustations used to decorate the magnificent, geometrically patterned façade. The sanctuary rises over a groin-vaulted crypt containing the relics of S. Miniato.

[S. CONWAY]

SAN NICOLA, BARI, the Italian Romanesque basilica begun (1089) by Roger I, count of Sicily, completed (1139) under Roger II. It is timber-roofed, three-aisled, with two large staircases for pilgrims leading from the side aisles to the crypt under the transept. Tuscan and Lombard influences are evident in corbel tables and blind arcades of the exterior. Sculpture of the stone throne of Bp. Elias (*c.*1098)—the front supported by atlantes, the footrest by two crouching lions—relates to Guglielmo da Modena and to the style of S France. Christian sarcophagi (5th cent.) and a *Madonna with Saints* by B. Vivarini (1476) at San Nicola are noteworthy.

[M. J. DALY]

SAN NICOLA CATHEDRAL, TRANI, one of the finest structures in Italian Romanesque style in Apulia. Built by an architect known as Nicolaus Sacerdos, this cathedral dedicated to St. Nicholas the Pilgrim is a three-aisled basilica with triple apses, typical since the 5th century. It rises over a crypt retaining its fine Romanesque columns and capitals, and is crowned by a lofty, beautifully proportioned tower. The bronze doors by Barisano da Trani (1175) are treasures of S Italy.

[M. J. DALY]

SAN PAOLO FUORI LE MURA, see ST. PAUL OUTSIDE-THE-WALLS, ABBEY OF.

SAN PIETRO IN BREME, ABBEY OF, Benedictine monastery in Lombardy, located between the Po and the Ticino Rivers, in the diocese of Pavia, founded in 929 by dispersed refugees from Saracen destruction of the abbey of Novalesa. The monks were given refuge at Breme in Lomellina by Adalbert, Marquis of Ivrea. The abbey gained its independence from the surrounding principalities, ecclesiastical and secular in 1210 after years of struggle. In decline it was entrusted to the bp. of Vigevano in 1530; it was ceded to the Olivetan monks of Milan in 1543 and suppressed by Victor Emmanuel I in 1785. Under Napoleon I the church was destroyed and the other buildings expropriated.

[E. J. DILLON]

SAN PIETRO IN VINCOLI, see ST. PETER-IN-CHAINS.

SAN SALVATORE (MAGGIORE), ABBEY OF, former Benedictine monastery 35 miles north of Rome in the diocese of Rieti, founded in 735. Its time of greatest vitality came in the early 9th cent. when it was favored by Charlemagne and Pope Paschal I. The monks had their distinctive style of chant. The abbey was destroyed by the Saracens in 891 and rebuilt in 974. Its religious prestige was long past when it was made a *dioecesis nullius* by Urban IV

(1264). Its vassals revolted in the 14th century. In the 15th cent. it was placed in commendation to the Abbey of Farfa and was suppressed by Urban VIII in 1629. The Romanesque church with its cosmatesque décor survives as an impressive ruin.

[E. J. DILLON]

SAN SALVATORE DI MESSINA, MONASTERY, important center of Greek Christianity and the traditions of the Eastern Church, located in Messina, Sicily. Apparently there was already in the time of Roger I, Count of the Two Sicilies (1059), a monastery considered to be the head (mother) of all monasteries of the Greek rite. Then between 1122 and 1132 Roger II built a new one near the tip of the isthmus, co-founded by Bartholomew of Simeri and his disciple Luke, the important reform archimandrite who departed from Studite tradition and imposed his own rule on the confederation of 41 monasteries in nearby Sicily and Calabria that were under his exempt jurisdiction. Alexander III (1175) acknowledged the archimandrite's power to appoint abbots. Charles V demolished the monastery in the 16th cent. after its decline under Angevin rule had been checked by Card. Bessarion in the 15th century. A new monastery was built in nearby Messina. In the 17th and 18th cent. this became part of the Basilian Congregation of Italy. It was suppressed by the Italian government in 1883 and its territory incorporated into Messina.

[E. J. DILLON]

SAN VINCENZO AL VOLTURNO, ABBEY OF, Benedictine foundation near the source of the Volturno at Farfa in central Italy, in the former diocese of Isernia, Campania. Founded in 703 by three noblemen of Benevento it grew into a virtual monastic duchy whose autonomy was recognized by Charlemagne. In 882 it was devastated by the Saracens who massacred 900 monks. The survivors fled to Capua and built a new monastery of the same name. A few decades later the monks returned and rebuilt their former home. This was the place of origin of the important chronicle of the monk John, reflecting the history of central Italy down to c. 1070. At that point a decline set in from which the monastery never recovered. It was given by Innocent XII to Monte Cassino, to which it had always been linked, and was placed in commendation in the 15th century. A 9th-cent. frescoed crypt survives as a reminder of its days of splendor.

[E. J. DILLON]

SAN VITALE, RAVENNA (526–547), a most important and completely preserved Italian Byzantine church of Justinian foundation (dedicated by Bp. Maximian) in octagonal central-plan, closely related to the Constantinopolitan church of SS. Sergius and Bacchus. The subtle relation of the narthex, set at a 50-degree angle to the structure, creates an off-center axis to the church. Buttressed at each corner, the exterior triple subdivisions carry rhythmically through the ambulatory and gallery, the clerestory becoming a single statement. Within semicircular niches relating the nave and aisles, light from the low dome on pendentives—a Western construction of hollow amphorae, one within the other—dissolves into semi-darkness. The complex spatial concept of open areas versus screened arcades is emphasized by light and dark in the Eastern style of stone-undercut in basket-weave and interlace on capitals, and tendrils of the choir screen, the exploitation of marble graining, mother-of-pearl and magnificent glittering jewel mosaics in a coloristic overall green tonality about framed scenes of local color. The two monumental portrait mosaics of the imperial court of Justinian (with Maximian) and Theodora (d. 548), each with entourage, their tall, slim bodies ceremonial in gestures and robes, the huge eyes of remarkable address in the decorative medium, are supplemented by mosaics of sacrifice in figures of Abraham, Isaac, and Melchizedek, their naturalistic settings within flat floral and rinceau frames. San Vitale is Byzantine art at its height. BIBLIOGRAPHY: O. G. von Simson, *Sacred Fortress: Byzantine Art and Statecraft in Ravenna* (1948); G. Bovini, *Ravenna Mosaics* (1956).

[M. J. DALY]

SANABALLAT, see SANBALLAT.

SANABRIA MARTINEZ, VÍCTOR (1899–1952), Costa Rican abp., historian. S. was ordained in 1921 and in 1937 named bp. of Alajuela. Appointed abp. of San José in 1939, S. proved an enlightened administrator, supported the lay apostolate, founded the Confederación Rerum Novarum. A member of the Costa Rican Academy of History, he published widely read historical works, such as *Estudios de las aparaciones de la Santísima Virgen de los Angeles,* an important periodical essay "Continuación de los datos históricos para la historia de la Iglesia de Costa Rica," and *Genealogías de familias de Cartago.*

[J. R. AHERNE]

SANATIO IN RADICE (healing in the root), in canon law a radical convalidation, a means of effecting the validity of a previously contracted but invalid marriage. Its root is the preexisting consent of the partners, without which no marriage can be complete. In the *sanatio in radice,* a competent ecclesiastical superior may remove by dispensation either a diriment impediment that rendered the partners' consent invalid, or a legal obligation to renew formal consent to marriage, after the disappearance of a diriment impediment. A *sanatio in radice* may be granted retrospectively, even if one or both partners have since died. Through a legal fiction, such a *sanatio* would have the effect of legitimizing the children of the union in question, even though the marriage itself would not be considered to have been valid before the granting of the *sanatio.* A *sanatio a radice* can never be granted in cases where there is a lack or defect of consent in the mind of either partner, nor can it be granted if an impediment of natural or divine law invalidates the marriage. The power to grant a *sanatio in radice* is reserved to the Holy See, although this power is normally delegated to the local ordinaries. The term is used also for rectification of defects in other canonically regulated contracts, e.g., religious profession.

[R. A. ARONSTAM]

SANBALLAT (Sanaballat), opponent of Nehemiah's work to rebuild Jerusalem (Neh 2.10–19; 4.1–7; 6). S. appears in the Elephantine Papyri as a governor of Samaria. Nehemiah calls him a Horonite, perhaps an inhabitant of Upper or Lower Beth-Horon, towns of Ephraim. Nehemiah banished the grandson of Eliashib, the high priest, for marrying S.'s daughter (Neh 13.28).

[T. EARLY]

SANCES, GIOVANNI FELICE (*c*.1600–1679), Italian tenor and composer. S. was a singer, then vice-Kapellmeister and, later, Kapellmeister of the imperial chapel in Vienna. He wrote operas, oratorios, songs, motets, and other church music.

[M. T. LEGGE]

SÁNCHEZ, COELLO, ALONSO (1515–88), Spanish painter from Portugal. S., after study in Flanders, became court painter to Philip II. His many portraits of the dignified and reserved Spanish nobility are sober and precise. Among his religious works, Romanist mannerist in style, are *St. Catherine* (1578), *Trinity with Saints* (1582), and *St. Sebastian,* painted in the church of San Gerónimo, Madrid.

[M. J. DALY]

SÁNCHEZ, JUAN (d. 1624), a typical representative of laxism in 17th-cent. casuistry. S. was born at Ávila. His admired work, *Select and Practical Debates on Things Connected with the Administration of the Sacraments* was published in 1624, but put on the Index 18 years later until such time as its numerous, too easy-going opinions should be corrected.

[T. GILBY]

SÁNCHEZ, TOMÁS (1550–1610), Spanish Jesuit moralist. Ascetical, learned, acutely legal, his *magnum opus* on the sacrament of marriage (3 v., 1605) is regarded as a classic by canonists and as a great pioneering achievement by sexologists. It is a technical work for specialists, not for general reading, and though too deeply involved in casuistry to be in the high tradition of moral theology, it is certainly among the most noteworthy of its *marginalia*. Its preoccupation with detail incurred the charge of immodesty, which was not surprising if unjustified; its very kindness to human nature even in its oddities of behavior scandalized, of course, the Jansenists. Pascal's *Provinciales* were superb controversy, but one does not have to be either a Pelagian or a laxist to wonder whether the Jesuits there attacked may not

have been nearer to the pastoral realities after all. BIBLIOGRAPHY: Sommervogel 7:537–538.

[T. GILBY]

SÁNCHEZ COTAN, JUAN (1561–1627), Spanish lay brother, painter, student of Blas del Prado in Toledo. In his masterly, baroque, realistic still lifes, the isolated forms related within narrow confines of a ''window frame,'' are so concentrated that they attain a mystical intensity. Becoming a Carthusian lay brother (1603) S. in Granada (1612) created monumental religious works weakened by fantasy.

[M. J. DALY]

SÁNCHEZ DE ARÉVALO, RODRIGO, see ARÉVALO, RODRIGO SÁNCHEZ DE.

SANCHI, STUPAS OF. The best-preserved *stupas (Buddhist relic shrines) in India, are at Sanchi, Bhopal state (3d cent. B.C. to 11th cent. A.D.), the carved gateway of the impressive Great Stupa (2d cent. B.C.) boasting the finest early Buddhist relief sculpture. The Great Stupa, 120 ft in diameter and 54 ft high (excluding finials), rising over the brick stupa built earlier by Emperor Aśoka (*c*.3d cent. B.C.) is the usual solid rubble hemisphere, stone-encased, with a terrace, and balustrades evidencing wood prototypes surrounding processional areas. The four magnificent free-standing stone gateways (*torii;* 1st cent. B.C.) with most delicately carved surfaces, pointing to the ivory carvers of Vidiśā, depict figures and scenes from Hinayana Buddhist iconography. A smaller stupa (no. 3) has one such carved gateway. There are on the hill many smaller stupas, damaged Mauryan edict-pillars (some by Aśoka), temples and monasteries of the Gupta and post-Gupta periods. Another large stupa (no. 2) for teachers' relics and monastery—lower on the hill—are contemporary with the Great Stupa but lack gateways. BIBLIOGRAPHY: J. H. Marshall, *Guide to Sanchi* (1955); D. Mitra, *Sanchi* (1957).

[M. J. DALY]

SANCHUNIATHON, a Phoenician writer who lived in Berytus in the 7th or perhaps 6th cent. B.C., whose writings, now lost, were used by the Hellenistic writer, Philo of Byblos (*c*.100 A.D.), as a source of information on Canaanite mythology. Even at second hand, his data on Canaanite mythology accords reasonably well with what can now be found in the Ugaritic mythological texts of the second millennium B.C., found since 1929 at Ras Shamra in Syria. BIBLIOGRAPHY: O. Eissfeldt, *Ras Schamra und Sanchunjaton* (1939).

[A. CODY]

SANCIA, ST. (d. 1229), daughter of King Sancho I of Portugal. She promoted the coming of Franciscans and Dominicans to Portugal, founded the Cistercian monastery of Sta. Maria de Cellas, and entered its community in 1223. She was buried at the Cistercian convent of Lorvão, founded by her sister, St. Teresa. BIBLIOGRAPHY: AS June 4:385–435; L. J. Lekai, NCE 12:1042.

SANCTA SANCTIS (Lat.), holy things to the holy. This admonition to reverence for the Eucharist is proclaimed in many liturgies (not the Roman); it is also used as a general admonition to reverence for all that is sacred.

SANCTA SANCTORUM CHAPEL (Chapel of S. Lorenzo), a Roman chapel, originally part of the patriarchate, which survived the destruction of the patriarchate or pontifical palace by Sixtus V (1586). The chapel had been the private chapel of popes since the time of Constantine. It is reached by the *Scala Sancta. The chapel contains what are held to be relics of the Cross, Christ's sandals, and the *acheiropoieton* (not painted by human hands) portrait of Jesus.

[R. J. LITZ]

SANCTA SOPHIA, see HAGIA SOPHIA.

SANCTIFICATION, a second work of grace, distinct from *justification and bringing deliverance from sinfulness, or inbred sin. *ENTIRE SANCTIFICATION, *PERFECTIONISM.

[T. C. O'BRIEN]

SANCTION, the power of law and of a legislator for enforcement through reward or punishment; the reward or punishment itself. Almost universally, however, sanction is understood only as a punitive power or as a punishment. Law does not have its obligatory force from its power of coercing, but from its being enacted by competent authority and in a way consonant with the common good. Sanction has its most obvious and necessary instance in the case of human, positive law (see LAW, POSITIVE). Ideally such law, like all law, should be interiorized by those subject to it and followed as a guiding principle for just actions in the community; such interiorization is part of the meaning of *legal justice. By its nature, however, human law does not envision interior attitudes, but simply the observance of the law. Sanction becomes necessary because the human community is not a community of the virtuous or of the morally mature. For those who will not obey from an interior motivation, the threat of punishment becomes an adjunct necessary to achieve the purpose of law, the tranquil and orderly pursuit and sharing of the common good. The sanction as penalty is justly levied against violators of law because their violation infringes upon the order of justice; the violator, one who has wrongfully indulged in an act of self-will, rightly deserves or becomes liable to punishment, a deprival inflicted against the transgressor's will. The quality of sanctions in any society depends on the society's concept of man and of society. Since the infliction of punishment is, in a sense, a necessary evil, its exercise must be just, not exceeding the purposes and protection of the common good, and not inflicted out of sheer vengeance. *PENOLOGY.

[T. C. O'BRIEN]

SANCTION, DIVINE. Abstractly speaking, some idea of a divine reward or punishment seems called for as a final basis for a virtuous and just human life. Such an idea, however, did not form part of the ethical thought of classic Greek philosophy (e.g., of Epicurus, Socrates, Plato, Aristotle, the Stoics) nor of later systems of ethics in which, as in Kant, virtue is its own reward. The affirmation of divine sanctions involves an attempt to solve the problems of the unrighted injustices that mark human experience, the difficulties and abnegations required by virtue, and the immediate rewards of vice. Theology recognizes divine reward and punishment as attested to in revelation. But divine sanctions have a different function in the Old and in the New Law, the first being a law of fear and servitude, the second a law of love and freedom. The Old Law was explicitly based on the promise of reward and punishment for the people. ''The New Law, consisting primarily in spiritual grace itself implanted in men's hearts, is called the law of love; and it is said to contain spiritual and eternal promises, which are the objects of virtue, esp. charity. And so men are drawn to them from within, not as towards what is foreign to them, but as to what is their very own'' (ThAq ST 1a2ae.107, 1 ad 2). Under the Old Law there were those who by faith and grace belonged in spirit to the New Law; and under the New Law there are those who, lacking in that spirit, need to be coerced as though they were still under the Old Law (ibid.). This conception of the New Law does not abolish the recognition of divine justice, nor exclude a fear of punishment as the beginning of a process of conversion (see FEAR OF THE LORD). But the bond of charity means a relationship with the Father as his child and as his friend through Christ. The reward of eternal life is hoped for because it means completion of union with him; the fear of the child of the Father is fear of being separated from him. Even the ills and misfortunes of life, as well as death itself, are recognized as radically in punishment for sin. But by charity they cease to be purely penal; the one who loves the Father after the example of the suffering Christ undergoes these ills as atonement; they cease to be purely inflictive and punitive, and through charity's willingness are transformed into an expiatory imitation of Christ. BIBLIOGRAPHY: ThAq ST Lat-Eng (v. 27, T. C. O'Brien, ed., *Effects of Sin,* 1974) 99–109.

[T. C. O'BRIEN]

SANCTIS, DIONISIO DE (*c.*1507–77), Spanish Dominican bp. of Cartagena, New Granada (now Colombia), 1574–77, who compiled a catechism and a reading primer for the Indians in his diocese.

[R. J. LITZ]

SS. TRINITÀ, ABBEY OF, see LA CAVA, ABBEY OF.

SANCTITY, the quality of *holiness. In its strictest sense, sanctity belongs to God alone (the *Gloria* of the Mass addresses Christ, "You alone are holy.") However, it has come in a derived and participated sense to be used of those creatures which in some way belong to God. While this may have originally been used in a liturgical context to refer to *sacred furniture, vessels, and ministers, it is now generally used in reference to the spiritual condition of persons. The emphasis is on moral living, implying a purification from sin and a firmness in the service of God (ThAq ST 2a2ae, 81.8). However, the deeper, theological reference to those ontologically sanctified by God's action (ordinarily through the sacrament of baptism) should not be lost, for this divine initiative alone makes sanctity in any sense possible. While the term is now generally restricted to its heroic manifestation, St. Paul does not hesitate to apply the word to the entire Christian community.

[U. VOLL]

SANCTORAL CYCLE, the chronological arrangement of saints' feasts in the Church's liturgical calendar. It is contrasted with the temporal cycle which contains the events of Redemption, the feasts of Christ, and the Sundays and ferial days of the year. The two cycles, while distinct, run parallel and are intertwined. In the early centuries of Christianity, the cult of saints was local and was principally a veneration of the dead. The evolving of a universal sanctoral cycle began in the 5th and 6th cent. when the local Churches began to add saints of univeral interest to their calendars. In the Middle Ages, the emphasis changed from an honoring of the dead to reflection upon the contribution the saints had made to the life of the Church, and at this time numerous feasts were added to the cycle. Vat II SacLit, Appendix sought to restore a proper emphasis upon the mysteries of salvation itself and declared that only those saints who are of truly universal significance should be commemorated in the universal calendar. The General Roman Calendar of 1969 carried out the Council's decree and greatly reduced the number of saints given liturgical place during the year.

[B. ROSENDALL]

SANCTUARY, holy place. The term is frequently used for the worship area of a church, and in liturgical churches particularly, for the area around the altar. Until modern times criminals could often gain immunity at a sanctuary. Consequently, the term came to be used for the privilege of safe refuge.

[T. EARLY]

SANCTUS, the "Holy, holy, holy," a hymn of adoration and praise sung or said by the priest and people at Mass. It continues the Preface and links it with the rest of the anaphora. It is the participation of all in the sacrifice of praise continually being offered to the Father. It is divided into two parts, "Holy, holy, holy Lord God of hosts.

Heaven and earth are filled with your glory. Hosanna in the highest," and "Blessed is he who comes in the name of the Lord. Hosanna in the highest." The first part is based on Is 6.3 and Rev 4.8, and may have passed from the *kedushah* of the synagogue service by way of the Syrian liturgy to the rest of the Church. By the late 4th cent. it was a general feature of all the liturgies. The second part, "Blessed is he . . . ." entered the Western liturgy a short time after the "Holy, holy, holy," and was used by most of the Church by the 8th century.

With the passage of time the musical text of the *Sanctus* became so extensive and elaborate that the first part of it was sung before, and the rest after, the consecration. This practice disregarded the essential communal nature of the hymn and it is now forbidden. Indeed the celebrant should not proceed with the Canon until the singing or recitation has been completed.

[N. KOLLAR]

SANCTUS (MUSIC), hymn (Eng., Holy, Holy, Holy), based on Is 6.3 and Mt 21.9, sung at the beginning of the Canon of the Mass after the Preface. There are numerous plain song, polyphonic, part, and congregational settings of the text in Latin and in the vernacular.

[M. T. LEGGE]

SANCTUS BELL, in the Roman rite, a small handbell rung at the Sanctus of the Mass and at the elevation; also, in some places, at the *Hanc igitur* and at Communion. Its purpose was to inform the congregation of what part of the Mass was taking place, a necessity in large churches. Though no longer required, its use remains customary in some parishes.

[J. DALLEN]

SANCTUS CANDLE, in the Roman rite, a candle on the epistle side of the altar, fastened on the wall or placed on a candlestick on the altar step, lighted at Mass at the Sanctus and extinguished after Communion. Though rubrically called for, its use was never universally customary and is now obsolete.

[J. DALLEN]

SAND, GEORGE (pseudonym of Aurore Dupin; 1804–76), French novelist and humanitarian socialist, who at the age of 26 broke with family and class to pursue the romantic ideal of freedom in life and art. Educated at the convent school of the English nuns in Paris (1817–20), she experienced a period of religious fervor, was influenced by Chateaubriand's aesthetic apology for Christianity, and contemplated entering an order. Disillusioned in marriage with a country gentleman, she began in Paris (1830) a literary career during which she composed over 100 works falling into four periods. The first, one of tempestuous romanticism, included love affairs with Sandeau, Musset, and Chopin, and the novels *Indiana* (1832), *Lélia* (1833) and *Mauprat* (1837), embodying feminist ideals, exalting passion over social prejudices, and rejecting Catholicism's moral imperatives, e.g., clerical celibacy, as contrary to nature. Her establishment at Nohant (1839), coinciding with the publication of the theosophic novel *Spiridion* and the influence of Lamennais and Leroux, led to a period of socialist-inspired works (*Le Compagnon du tour de France,* 1841; *Le Meunier d'Angibault,* 1845) and the mystical novel *Consuelo* (1842), which expresses religious views akin to a liberal Protestant theism: belief in a Supreme Being guarantees human virtues like charity, pity, and justice; the Reformation gave man direct access to God; as Christ rebelled against insensitive religious structures, so updated Evangelical Christianity is a catalyst for social reform; and sacramental communion is a syncretic rite symbolic of romantic fraternity. Her finest works belong to the rustic period, when she objectified her idealism in novels glorifying the pastoral life like *La Mare au diable* (1846), *La Petite Fadette* (1848), and *Les Maîtres sonneurs* (1853). The society novels with which S. concluded her career (e.g., *Le Marquis de Villemer,* 1860) propound no social theses and romanticize middle class life. Her personal charity and concern for justice won her the appellation of ''The Good Lady of Nohant.'' BIBLIOGRAPHY: A. Maurois, *Lélia or the Life of George Sand* (Eng. tr. 1953); E. Thomas, *George Sand* (1959).

[G. E. GINGRAS]

SANDALS, footware for liturgical use, gradually reserved to bps. and abbots at Mass. Originally of various types corresponding to ordinary footware—*soleae* (sandals), *calcei* (shoes), *campagi* (an intermediate form)—by the 16th cent. They were generally ornamented slippers with the upper part of embroidered silk (velvet for the pope) following the usual color sequence. Their use is now optional. Sandals in their ordinary form, are worn by the *discalced religious.

[J. DALLEN]

SANDAY, WILLIAM (1843–1920), English NT scholar. He studied at Balliol and Corpus Christi Colleges, Oxford. After ordination in 1867, he was engaged in parish work until 1876, when he became principal of Hatfield Hall, Durham. In 1882, he returned to Oxford, serving as Dean Ireland's professor of exegesis. He wrote a number of scriptural studies and convinced many clergy of the value of critical NT studies. With A.C. *Headlam (1862–1947), he collaborated on a commentary on Romans (1895) that has been widely used.

[T. C. O'BRIEN]

SANDEMANIANS, designation for the *Glasites after R. Sandeman (1718–71) became their leader in 1739.

SANDER, NICHOLAS (Sanders; *c.*1530–81), English historian, controversialist, and Catholic agent. He left England after Elizabeth's accession (1559). After ordination in Rome he accompanied Card. *Hosius to the Council of Trent (1561). After serving on the theological faculty at the Univ. of Louvain (1565–72), he went to Spain (1573) and worked against the English crown until commissioned by the pope (1579) to go to Ireland and incite the Irish to rebel against England. The rebellion failed, S. fled, and probably died of exposure in the Irish hills. In MSS, his *De clave David* (1588) is a reply to criticism of his *De visibili monarchia ecclesiae* (1571), which attempts a comprehensive view of the Church in the vein of Augustine's *City of God,* defending the Church's monarchical government. *De monarchia* is also valuable for its list of penalized English *recusants. His unfinished *De origine ac progressu schismatis anglicani* (1585) served as a source for many Catholic accounts of the Reformation in England.

[R. J. LITZ]

SANDERS, HENRY ARTHUR (1868–1956), classicist and editor of the Freer Collection. For most of his life, S. taught classics at the Univ. of Michigan. His most important work was the editing of the ancient Greek MSS discovered (1906) in Egypt and purchased by Charles L. Freer. BIBLIOGRAPHY: R. L. Zell, NCE 12:1049.

[T. M. MCFADDEN]

SANDOMIERZ, CONSENSUS OF, see CONSENSUS OF SANDOMIERZ.

SANGALLO, DA, distinguished Florentine family of architects, sculptors, and engineers. **Giuliano** (*c.*1443–1516), the most versatile, like Bramante, was much influenced by classical antiquity and favored the central-plan church (Sta. Maria delle Carceri, Prato; 1485–92). He was also a sculptor (Sassetti tombs, Sta. Trinità, Florence, 1486) and military engineer (Arezzo fortress, 1502), in which capacity he fostered the development of polygonal bastions. He collaborated on the Medici Villa, and the Strozzi and Sforza palaces. **Antonio the Elder** (*c.*1453–1534), a brother, was primarily a military engineer (Città Castellana; 1494), executed the beautiful church of the Madonna di S. Biagio, Montepulciano (1518) and many palaces. **Antonio the Younger** (1482–1546), a nephew, is remembered chiefly for the Palazzo Farnese (1513) for his patron in Rome, and the Caprarola fortress (1515). BIBLIOGRAPHY: G. Marchini, *Giuliano da San Gallo* (1943).

[L. A. LEITE]

SANHEDRIN, a council or senate of Jewish leaders and elders, first attested to during the reign of Antiochus the Great (223–187 B.C.) as a kind of priestly senate. Much later, during the rule of Salome Alexandra (75–67) lay scribes were admitted also; under Hyrcanus II, both ethnarch and high priest, the technical term *synedrion* is first used (Josephus, *Antiquities of the Jews*, 20) to designate the council of priests and elders in charge of the administration of the state under the tutelage of the Roman authority. Seventy–one in number, presided over by the high priest, this council was the official guardian of the Law (Torah) and the traditions of the people. It sat as a court of justice in all matters which touched on the religious life of the nation, with authority in both civil and criminal cases, though its competence in regard to captial offenses is disputed. Outside Jerusalem the Sanhedrin seems to have exercised a kind of moral authority of prestige among the synagogues in Galilee and in the Diaspora. BIBLIOGRAPHY: S. B. Hoenig, *Great Sanhedrin* (1953).

[J. L. RONAN]

SANKEY, IRA DAVID (1840–1908), gospel singer and hymn writer. S. was born in Edinburgh, Pa., where he became choir master in a Methodist church. From 1870 his name was inseparable from that of Dwight L. *Moody, the great revivalist. For the campaigns they conducted in the U. S. and Great Britain, S. wrote the music for hymns and was soloist and leader of the congregational singing. His style set the musical standard for revivalist meetings. The collections of *Gospel Hymns* that he published beginning in 1875 sold millions of copies and provided funds for evangelistic education.

[T. C. O'BRIEN]

SANKT AEGIDIEN, ABBEY OF, former Benedictine monastery in Nuremberg, Germany, in the Diocese of Bamberg, Bavaria; founded in 1140 by Conrad III with Irish Benedictines. The abbey was taken over in 1418 by German Benedictines from Reichenbach; it became part of the Congregation of Bursfeld and was suppressed in 1528. BIBLIOG - RAPHY: Cottineau 2: 2111.

SANKT BLASIEN, ABBEY OF, former Benedictine monastery in the Black Forest, Baden, Germany, in the former Diocese of Constance. Its obscure origin may go back to 858 when a small community of monks centered around a reliquary of the popular St. Blaise. It became a center of Cluniac reform, founding the priories of Wiblingen and Ochsenhausen and reforming Muri (1082), Göttweig (1094), Garsten (1107), Seitenstetten (1112), Ensheim (1123), and Engelberg (1143). Later, in the 18th cent., Sankt Blasien revived through contact with the Maurists of France and became a scholarly center specializing in church history. In 1746 its abbot was made prince-abbot. In 1807 the abbey was dissolved by Baden and the monks resettled at Sankt Paul in Carinthia (1809).

[E. J. DILLON]

SANKT EMMERAM, ABBEY OF, former Benedictine monastery in Regensburg, Germany, first dedicated to the Holy Savior (697), then to St. Emmeram, its founder, who died *c.*715, and to St. Denis and St. Wolfgang. It became important through its link with the German Carolingians at Regensburg, was reformed by Abbot Ramwold (975–1000), who introduced the customs of Gorze throughout Bavaria. It was made a free imperial abbey soon after 1295, an exempt abbey in 1326, and joined the reform congregation of Kastl in 1451–52. Its abbot was made prince-abbot in 1732. Sankt Emmeram enjoyed an intellectual revival in the late 17th and 18th cent., was granted to Prince-Primate K. T. Dalberg in 1802, and was transferred to Bavaria in 1810, which dissolved it in 1812. The abbey church became a parish church, the remainder of the buildings were secularized.

[E. J. DILLON]

SANKT FLORIAN, MONASTERY OF, monastery of Augustinian canons at the site of the tomb of the martyr, St. Florian (d.304), in the Diocese of Linz, Austria. In Charlemagne's time there was already a community of Benedictine monks centered at the popular shrine. In 1071 St. Altman, bp. of Passau, granted the site to the Augustinian canons, who made it a center of the Gregorian reform. The still extant abbey church is a baroque masterpiece of the 17th and 18th cent., it was later graced by the organ music of Anton Bruckner (1845–55). The abbey's library with its hundreds of ancient MSS and impressive collections of medieval art was a center of scholarship in the 19th century.

[E. J. DILLON]

SANKT GALLEN, ABBEY OF, former Benedictine monastery in the city, canton, and diocese of the same name in Switzerland, south of Lake Constance, on the upper Steinach River. Founded (612–614) by the Irish hermit St. Gall, under the Rule of St. Columban, it was put under the control of the Alemanns by King Dagobert I (628–638), extending its holdings, under Abbot Othmar (720), from Swabia to north of the Danube into Breisgau. To the same abbot is credited construction of a hospital and a scriptorium and the introduction of the Benedictine Rule, all accomplished before he was imprisoned by the Franks until death. The abbey was granted immunity from the Diocese of Constance by Louis the Pious in 818 and made an imperial abbey. Sankt Gallen became famous for its illuminated MSS in the Irish tradition and its many poets and scholars whose works are still preserved in the monastery library and archives, a mine of medieval literature on theology, art, law, and medicine. The abbey suffered for its allegiance to the imperial party during the investiture struggle and revived under Prince-Abbot Ulric VIII in the 15th century. The abbey's domain became an associate state of the Swiss Confederation. The city became independent of the monastery in 1455 and joined the Protestant cause in 1525, which led to the destruction of the entire stock of the monastery's medieval sculptures and paintings. The monastery was suppressed in 1805.

[E. J. DILLON]

SANKT GEORGEN IM SCHWARZWALD, ABBEY OF, near Villingen, Germany, a Benedictine monastery founded in 1083 by certain knights named Hezelo, Hesso, and Konrad. It drew its monks from Hirsau and became wealthy and important. In the 16th cent. the monks resisted the attempts of the duke of Württemberg, in whose territory they were situated, to Protestantize the abbey and preferred to move to Villingen where they flourished until 1806. The monastery of St. Georgen was destroyed completely in 1633 but the buildings in Villingen still stand. BIBLIOGRAPHY: *Handbuch der Historischen Stätten Deutschlands* (1960) 6:578.

[N. BACKMUND]

SANKT LAMBRECHT, ABBEY OF, Benedictine foundation in the diocese of Graz-Seckau, Styria (Obersteiermark), Austria; founded between *c.*1066 and 1092 by Count Markward of Carinthia and his son, Duke Henry III and endowed with land to be administered jointly with the bishops of Regensburg. Placed under papal protection after 1109, the abbey was charged with missions in W Austria from 1652 to 1786 and conducted a famous philosophy and theology scholasticate from 1684 to 1783. The abbey was suppressed by Joseph II in 1786-87, was restored in 1802, and again suppressed under the Nazis (1939–47). Since the war the monks have rebuilt and are ministering in parishes.

[E. J. DILLON]

SANKT OTTILIEN, ABBEY OF, Benedictine abbey dedicated to the Sacred Heart of Jesus, located near Geltendorf, Türkheim, in Swabia, Diocese of Augsburg, Germany. It was founded for foreign missions in 1884, made a priory in 1896, an abbey in 1902. It serves as the motherhouse of the German Benedictine missionary effort, the Missionary Congregation of St. Ottilien. BIBLIOGRAPHY: Cottineau 2: 2830–31.

[E. J. DILLON]

SANKT PAUL, ABBEY OF (CARINTHIA), Benedictine monastery in Lavantal (Wolfsberg), Austria, in what was (until 1786) the jurisdiction of the prince-bishop of Salzburg. It was founded (1091) by Engelbert of Spanheim with monks from Hirsau. The Romanesque basilica, completed *c.*1200, is credited to the initiative of Abbots Peregrinus and Ulrich. There have been later Gothic and Baroque additions. The abbey was suppressed in 1782 by Joseph II and then given in 1809 to refugee monks from Sankt Blasien, who re-opened the school and later (1828) helped establish the gymnasium and philosophy scholasticate in the new abbey of St. Stephan in Augsburg. The monks still minister to local parishes.

[E. J. DILLON]

SANKT PETER, ABBEY OF, in Salzburg, the oldest Benedictine monastery north of the Alps, founded in the tradition of St. Columban by St. Rupert of Salzburg *c.*700. Round the abbey grew the town and diocese of Salzburg, which was governed by the abbot bp. of Sankt Peter until 987 when the abbey became separate from the archbishopric. The present collegiate church is 12th- and 13th-cent. Romanesque, now obscured by the rococo ornamentation of the interior. Famous for its active scriptorium in the 8th and 9th cent. and for its illuminated MSS of the 11th through the 13th cent., Sankt Peter helped found and provided scholars for the Benedictine Univ. of Salzburg (1622). It was made an archabbey in 1925, and was briefly suppressed during the Nazi era (1941–45).

[E. J. DILLON]

SANKT PETER AUF DEM SCHWARZWALD, ABBEY OF, former Benedictine monastery near Freiburg-im-Breisgau, Baden, in Württemberg. It was founded (1193) by Berthold II von Zähringen and then given by him to Abbot William of Hirsau, who brought over to St. Peter's the priory of Weilheim (founded in 1073). The abbey became part of the Swabian Congregation of St. Joseph in 1627 and was suppressed in 1806 by Count Karl Friedrich von Baden. BIBLIOGRAPHY: Cottineau 2: 2843–44.

[E. J. DILLON]

SANKT ULRICH VON AUGSBURG, ABBEY OF, former Benedictine monastery in Augsburg, Germany, founded 1012 by Bp. Bruno with monks from Tegernsee to replace a community of canons centered around the tomb of SS. Ulric and Afra. The abbey supported the papacy and the bp. supported the emperor during the investiture struggle. It was considered a model monastery in the 12th cent., was a center of the Melk Reform in Swabia after 1440, a center for humanist artists during the Renaissance, and a center of scholarship and art in the early 18th century. The monks were briefly banished during the Reformation (1537–48). The Abbot Bernard Hertfelder (1632–42) was considered the savior of Catholicism in Augsburg during the Thirty Years' War. The abbey was secularized in 1802, the abbey church becoming a parish church, and eventually (1937) a minor basilica.

[E. J. DILLON]

SANSEVERINO, GAETANO (1811–65), professor at the diocesan Liceo, Naples, from 1846, and pioneer in the revival of Thomism in the 19th century. He was himself a Cartesian in philosophy until he realized the need of a return to St. Thomas Aquinas for the preparation of students of theology. He founded in 1846 the Academy of St. Thomas Aquinas. Among his works are *Institutiones logicae* (1854) and *Philosophia christiana cum antiqua et nova comparata;* of the latter he published 5 of the 15 planned volumes in 1862. A summary of the whole work edited by N. Signorelli, appeared as *Elementa philosophiae christianae* (3 v., 1864).

[T. C. O'BRIEN]

SANSOVINO, ANDREA CONTUCCI (1460–1529), eminent Florentine sculptor, apprenticed to A. del Pollaiuolo. S.'s work is remarkable for restrained action, grace, and delicacy of carving and classical subordination of copious ornamental detail. Among his chief works are *St. John Baptizing Christ* (Baptistery, Florence), the tombs of the Card. Ascanio Sforza and Girolamo della Rovere (Sta. Maria del Popolo, Rome), marble screen reliefs, partially executed by students, around the Holy House at Loreto, and *St. Anne with the Virgin and Child* (S. Agostino, Rome, 1512).

[M. J. DALY]

SANSOVINO, JACOPO (Jacopo Tatti, 1486–1570), Florentine sculptor and architect, from 1518–27 active in Rome, after that in Venice. He studied with Andrea *Sansovino whose name he adopted. His art, always based on the study of classical precedent, combines an abundance of invention with grace and, in appropriate topics, majesty. Michelangelo aside, he was, perhaps, the greatest sculptor of his age. A famous example of his work is the *Madonna del Parto* (S. Agostino, Rome). The buildings he erected or redecorated in Venice contribute much to the effect the city makes to this day. His library of St. Mark, a building at once stately and joyous, surely is the most beautiful library in the world. BIBLIOGRAPHY: G. Lorenzetti, *Jacopo Sansovino* (1910).

[P. P. FEHL]

SANT'AGNESE FUORI LE MURA, ROME, early Christian basilica founded (337–341) by Constantina, daughter of Constantine the Great, rebuilt under Honorius I (625–638) with galleries and clerestory relating to San Lorenzo fuori le Mura in Rome, and with Byzantine measurements in nave and aisles. The apse mosaic from the time of Honorius I, one of the most magnificent examples of Byzantine art in Rome, depicts St. Agnes between Popes Symmachus and Honorius.

[M. J. DALY]

SANT'AMBROGIO, MILAN, most important Italian Lombard church, sole evidence of structural development in Italian Romanesque architecture. All other sporadic schools adhering to earlier basilica type engaged in decorative modifications: Tuscan doorways, wheel windows, Lombardy decorative bands, compound arches, and open lace-arcadings. At Sant'Ambrogio visionary ribbed vaulting, clustered pier, and pier-buttress (exterior) made possible future Gothic. The longitudinal, latitudinal and diagonal ribs of single bay, each supported by its specific pier in the nave cluster of piers, introduced the skeletal structural member which made possible the filling at ease and with airy lightness of nonstructural spaces. Transverse arches of the side aisles abut the nave-clustered piers, transferring the weight of domical vaults to exterior pier-buttresses, effecting a counterthrust. Here were inseminated the answers to all vaulting in centuries to come. Some fear of instability led to the single gable roof, eliminating the clerestory and rendering the interior dark. The church is preceded by an enclosed colonnaded atrium (*c*.1098) with two-storied porch (*c*.1095–96), enhanced by "Lombardy bands" and gallery, a feature which spread throughout Europe. Main portions of Sant'Ambrogio date from *c*.1128–86; the Monks' Tower, 10th cent., and handsome Canons' Tower, 12th century. The nave and aisles were remodeled in the 12th cent., the fourth bay opened into a lantern tower. Questions have arisen concerning vaulting at Durham (1104) and Sant'Ambrogio (1080). Norman-Lombard relationships are through William of Volpiano. Sant'Ambrogio relates to Speyer in square static bays, and Durham, related to the Normans at Caen, in bringing all ribs to the nave height is proto-Gothic. Sant'Ambrogio remains a key structure in Romanesque architecture. BIBLIOGRAPHY: A. K. Porter, *Lombard Architecture* (1915–17); F. Reggiori, *La basilica di Sant' Ambrogio a Milano* (1945).

[M. J. DALY]

SANT'AMBROGIO, MILAN, PALIOTTO OF. The golden altar of Milan is in the form of a casket 7 ft long with scenes from the life of Christ in framed compartments on the front (*paliotto*), and the life of St. Ambrose on the back. Donated by Abp. Angilbertus II (824–957), it was made (824–835) by "Wolvinus magister phaber," but its provenance remains uncertain. BIBLIOGRAPHY: V. H. Elbein, *Der Karolingische Goldaltar von Mailand* (1952).

[S. D. MURRAY]

SANT'ANDREA, MANTUA, a most important early Italian Renaissance church designed (1470) by L. B. *Alberti, its square left tower a remnant from the earlier Gothic church. Built by Luca Fancelli to the crossing (1472–94), the edifice was continued at the end of the 16th cent., A. M. Viani finishing the transept, the dome erected by F. Juvara (1732), and P. Pozzo completing the structure (end of 18th century). Alberti united ancient forms of the Roman temple and triumphal arch, in colossal pilasters pierced with triple openings in a Latin cross plan—the majestic coffered, barrel-vaulted nave repeating the pilasters and arches of the façade, the two side aisles under vaults and cupolas, the crossing bright under the dome of Juvara (18th century). There is much fine sculpture at Sant'Andrea. The great Mantuan painter A. Mantegna (1431–1506) is buried in the first chapel of the left aisle.

[M. J. DALY]

SANT'ANDREA AL QUIRINALE, ROME (1658–70), small oval church by Bernini commissioned by Card. Camillo Pamphili for the novices of the Jesuit Order, with transverse longer than the longitudinal axis, chapels flanking the entrance bay and the apse and pilasters closing off the bays of the transverse axis dramatizing the aedicule in front of the apse where the figure of St. Andrew rises heavenward from the broken pediment. Above walls of multicolored marble, angels on clouds and bearing garlands surmount the windows between ribs of the white and gold dome. A dramatic convex entrance portico with Roman string-coursed tympanum echoed in elegantly curved steps evidences constant invention in smaller treads spreading to wide expanses with delicate risers. Through this continual interplay of parts Bernini achieved integration and elicited the constant address and final ecstasy of the worshipper.

[M. J. DALY]

SANT'ANSELMO, see ANSELMIANUM.

SANT'ANTIMO, ABBEY OF, former Benedictine monastery in the Orcia valley near Siena in Tuscany, built by Charlemagne and his son Louis the Pious to house the relics of SS. Anthimus and Sebastian given to Charlemagne by Pope Adrian I. The abbey church is 12th cent. Italian Romanesque, and its crypt is an important 9th-cent. pre-Romanesque monument. With the rise of Siena the abbey lost its feudal jurisdiction, was given in 1291 by Nicholas IV to the Reform Augustinians, called Williamites, and suppressed by Pius II in 1462, its remaining holdings joined to the cathedral of Montalcino.

[E. J. DILLON]

SANT'ANTONIO, BASILICA OF, PADUA (1231–1307), Italian church in transitional Romanesque-Gothic style, with Byzantine tiered domes added in 1475. Important works are altar sculptures (1447–50) by Donatello, whose great equestrian statue (1444–47) of Erasmo da Narni ("Gattamelata") is in the basilica square; 14th-cent. frescoes by Altichiero and Avanzo; 16th-cent. reliefs of the tomb of St. Anthony; the sarcophagus of Card. Pietro Bembo (d. 1547), and reliquaries in goldsmith work of great excellence. The cloisters are dated from the 13th through the 16th centuries.

[M. J. DALY]

SANT'APOLLINARE IN CLASSE, RAVENNA (536–549), Italian basilican church in the old port city of Ravenna (Classe) where the body of St. Apollinaris, bp., martyred in Classe, rested until its removal in the 9th cent. by Theodoric to his palace church *St. Apollinare Nuova. Built under Julianus Argentarius, a wealthy Christian patron, Sant'Apollinare in Classe evidences the ascetic, unadorned exterior of the Christian church, contrasted with an extraordinarily rich interior of precious marble, and vast, brilliantly scintillating glass wall-mosaics, a Christian exploitation magnificently expressive of the spiritual in an immateriality of image and wall. The apse exterior built in the Constantinopolitan mode of narrow bricks with wide mortar beds is polygonal (Byzantine). The nave arcade rests on antique marble columns—their undercut foliate capitals prevalent in late 5th cent, but outmoded by 6th cent.—delicate Eastern lacework-basketweave capitals of Justinian

types. The mosaic portrait medallions in a band above the arcade are in 5th-cent. *retardataire* style of the construction period, the great Byzantine mosaic of the apse (7th cent.) signalling the degeneration of the Justinian tradition (at its peak 530–540). BIBLIOGRAPHY: G. Bovini, *Ravenna Mosaics* (1956).

[M. J. DALY]

SANT'APOLLINARE NUOVO, RAVENNA, built (490–510) by Theodoric, Arian king of the Ostrogoths. The wide-naved basilica with two aisles was transformed for Catholic worship under Abp. Agnellus c.527. The Arian mosaics (493–526) of Prophets and Apostles between the clerestory windows and NT themes above the windows, in Hellenistic illusionism show light and dark "sculptured" forms in spatial depth, their figures unrelated, establishing no rhythm. Most important are the Byzantine-Justinian mosaics (527–565), still extant on the nave walls above the arcading and below the clerestory, depicting saints, male (south) and female (north), linear and stylized, standing on their toes, in jeweled gowns and with golden haloes, each carrying a delicate palm branch of victory over death—all, in a magnificent decorative style devoid of classical illusionism, moving the eye rhythmically along the procession. Excellence of execution suggests Constantinopolitan craftsmen. BIBLIOGRAPHY: G. Bovini, *Ravenna Mosaics* (1956).

[M. J. DALY]

SANT'EUTIZIO DI NORCIA, ABBEY OF, former Benedictine monastery near the birthplace of St. Benedict, 6 mi from Norcia, in the Castorina valley, in the diocese of Spoleto, Umbria. According to tradition, there was originally a convent there, but after 536 the same Abbot Spes mentioned by St. Gregory in his *Dialogues* founded the Benedictine monastery. Then came the second abbot and cofounder, St. Eutychius, thought to have been a former hermit from Syria, a companion of St. Lawrence, founder of the nearby abbey of Farfa. The abbey reached its high point during the Cluniac reform, with its important scriptorium and library and extensive land holdings reaching to the Adriatic. The latter were taken from it by Innocent IV in 1257. It was placed under the Duke of Spoleto in 1327, joined to S. Benedetto di Norcia by Gregory XI in 1378, given to the Celestines, and then the Oratorians. It was commendatory after 1449, merged with the Diocese of Norcia by Pius VII in 1820. The Romanesque church survives, restored and reopened in 1956.

[E. J. DILLON]

SANTA COSTANZA, ROME, imposing early 4th-cent. round church almost certainly built by Constantine the Great, probably as his tomb. Rooted in Roman-vaulted style, the structure of two concentric circles shows a hgher inner cylinder lighted by a dome with a ring of windows; the lower, darker, surrounding ambulatory is surrounded by paired columns set radially from the center. Sta. Costanza marks an evolution from Roman imperial architecture (Pantheon) and is a link with the 6th-cent. masterpieces, S. Vitale, Ravenna, and SS. Sergius and Bacchus, Constantinople. Original mosaics in the vault of the circular ambulatory are not Bacchic, as sometimes stated, but evidence the early Christians' expression of a new iconography through Roman secular motifs, the grapes symbolic of the Eucharist, the vine a symbol of Christ. BIBLIOGRAPHY: H. Stern, "Les Mosaïques de l'église de Sainte-Constance à Rome," *Dumbarton Oaks Papers* 12 (1958).

[M. J. DALY]

SANTA CROCE, FLORENCE, Italian Gothic basilica-type church (begun 1295) by Arnolfo di Cambio (?), consecrated in 1442, the characteristically spacious but plain interior having many chapels oriented from a polygonal apse in a Franciscan architectural style. Important are the *Annunciation* relief of Donatello (*c.*1425–30) and frescoes by Giotto in the Bardi Chapel (1317) and the Peruzzi Chapel (1320), and the architecturally famous Pazzi Chapel (1430) by Brunelleschi. The W front dates from the 19th century. During restoration (1967) walls of the original 13th-cent. church and a fresco (*c.*1260) were discovered.

[M. J. DALY]

SANTA CROCE IN GERUSALEMME, a basilica in Rome containing relics of the Passion of Christ, including fragments of the wooden board gouged with the words of indictment and affixed to the tree of crucifixion; a favorite pilgrimage spot for Good Friday pilgrims, and the prototype of later European shrines. Called the Sessorian Basilica, it is built on the site once occupied by the gardens of Heliogabalus and afterwards by the Palatium Sessorianum, residence of the Empress Helena, mother of Constantine the Great. The latter, according to his biographer Eusebius, excavated the holy sepulchre in 327. His mother may have reserved a hall in her palace to house major relics unearthed in the excavations. Later Constantine added an apse and the relics were kept in a chamber behind the apse instead of beneath the altar in the customary manner. In the early 8th cent. the basilica was repaired by Gregory II. The monastery was added by Benedict VII *c.*975. The whole complex was rebuilt by Lucius II in 1144 and then completely modernized again in the 18th cent. by Benedict XIV, with only the tower of the 12th-cent. church left intact. When the clergy anticipated Visigothic raids *c.*455, they hid the relic bearing the inscription high above the main arch, where it was discovered in 1492 and later enclosed in glass by Innocent VIII.

[E. J. DILLON]

SANTA CRUZ, COIMBRA, MONASTERY OF, a monastic foundation made by Tello, a member of the Cathedral Chapter at Coimbra, Portugal, in 1131, as an independent abbey of the Canons Regular of St. Augustine

exempt from episcopal control. Theotonius (1132–52) was first prior. Under the patronage of Portugal's first king, Alfonso Henriques, it became a rich and famous institution. Through the centuries monastic discipline deteriorated. In 1527 under Blaise of Braga, reforms were effected through the promulgation of regulations and statutes restoring strict observance, and the monastery regained its influence as a center of piety and cultural revival, becoming the motherhouse of many religious foundations, including 19 monasteries. It was closed by the decree of secularization (1833) but stands today as a monument to the glories of medieval Portugal. BIBLIOGRAPHY: C. Erdmann, *Papsturkunden in Portugal* (1927); E. A. O'Malley, *Tello and Theotonio: The Twelfth-Century Founders of the Monastery of Santa Cruz in Coimbra* (1954).

[L. NEMEC]

SANTA CRUZ DE TLALTELOLCO, COLLEGE OF, a colonial college for Indians, the first secondary school for Indians in the New World. Founded in 1536 by Juan de Zumárraga, later first bp. and abp. of Mexico, aided by the viceroy, Antonio de Mendoza, Santa Cruz initially offered elementary and advanced studies, but later higher education only. Instruction was given in the Indian idiom, Nahuatl, by such eminent scholars as the linguist, Andrés de Olmos; the historian and ethnologist, Bernardine de Sahagún, and others, who saw the college as a means to train enlightened religious, social, and political leaders, build a native clergy, train native teachers, and spread the faith. The curriculum included theology, philosophy, Scripture, liberal arts, painting, and Indian herbal medicine. Despite its recognized academic success, opposition caused the institution to be reduced to an elementary school in 1576. BIBLIOGRAPHY: P. J. Barth, *Franciscan Education and the Social Order in Spanish North America 1502–1821* (1945); R. Becerra, NCE 14:182–183.

[M. B. MURPHY]

SANTA MARIA D'ARABONA, ABBEY OF, former Cistercian monastery near Chieti, Italy, founded in 1208 by monks of *Tre Fontane. The foundation prospered and in 1259 established the daughterhouse of S. Maria dello Sterpeto in the diocese of Trani. However, under commendatory abbots in the 15th cent., the monastery became impoverished and depopulated. It was finally given to the Franciscans in 1587 by Pope Sixtus V. Its recently (1951) restored church is a fine example of Burgundian Gothic. BIBLIOGRAPHY: B. G. Bedini, *Le Abazie cistercensi d'Italia* (1964); M. B. Morris, NCE 12:1066.

SANTA MARIA DE TAHULL, FRESCOES OF, masterpieces of Romanesque painting. The central apse figures (*Adoration of the Magi*) by an artist second only to the master of the San Clemente apse, evidence a like affinity to Ottonian painting in decorative segmented areas in figure and drapery, the formalized, dramatic, brightly colored murals having a rude, direct expressiveness peculiar to Catalonian frescoes. They are now in the Museum of Catalan art, Barcelona. BIBLIOGRAPHY: A. Grabar and C. Nordenfalk, *Romanesque Painting* (1958); E. Junyent, *Catalogne Romane* (v. 1, 1960). SAN CLEMENTE DE TAHULL, FRESCOES OF.

[R. C. MARKS]

SANTA MARIA DEI FRARI, VENICE, Italian church begun in 1340, completed *c.*1443, dedicated in 1469, of Latin-cross plan with transepts and three aisles, a façade in late Gothic style, and an impressive campanile. It contains the mausoleum of Venice's great master painter Titian, G. Bellini's *Madonna and Saints* (1488), Titian's celebrated *Assumption* (1519), Donatello's *St. John the Baptist,* and many other noted works.

[M. J. DALY]

SANTA MARIA DELLA PACE, ROME, domed octagon structure with short nave, built *c.*1480 under Pope Sixtus IV, probably by B. Pontelli. Frescoes of sibyls and prophets painted by Raphael and his shop (1514) above the chapel to the right of the nave were ordered by Agostino Chigi. Pietro da Cortona designed the new façade and piazza (1656–57) under Pope Alexander VII. The convex portico with concave wings projecting into the piazza is one of the earliest dramatic baroque concepts in urban planning.

[M. J. DALY]

SANTA MARIA DI FINALPIA, ABBEY OF, Benedictine monastery of the Olivetan Congregation, founded in 1477 by Marchese Biagio Galeotto del Carretto, located 16 mi from Savona, Liguria, along the Italian Riviera, near a famous shrine of Our Lady (Maria di Pia). Suppressed under Napoleon I (1799–1819), it was joined to the Benedictine Cassinese Congregation by Gregory XVI in 1844, was suppressed again by the Italian government in 1855–60, was restored by returning Benedictines from Subiaco in 1904–05, and became a center for liturgical renewal in Italy, esp. with its influential publication (after 1914), *Revista liturgica.* BIBLIOGRAPHY: Cottineau 1:1143.

[E. J. DILLON]

SANTA MARIA DI POLSI, ABBEY OF, Greek monastery on the Butrano River in the lofty solitude of the Calabrian Apennines in S Italy. Like so many remnants of Magna Graecia, it has been neglected by Latin–oriented ecclesiastical researchers and its origin and history are therefore still largely unknown. Dating perhaps from Roger I of the Two Sicilies in the late 11th cent., it was early settled by Basilian monks and was a popular pilgrimage center. In the 16th cent. the church was restored and the hostel for pilgrims built. The present church dates from the 19th century. The bp. of Gerace-Locri is its commendatory abbot.

[E. J. DILLON]

SANTA MARIA IN TRASTEVERE, ROME, church of the 3d or 4th cent., rebuilt by Pope Innocent II (1130–43) on the plan of 5th-cent. early Christian basilica churches, the nave colonnade trabeated rather than arcaded. The apse mosaics (1291) by P. *Cavallini are in early Christian-Byzantine style. BIBLIOGRAPHY: E. Mâle, *Early Churches of Rome* (1960).

[M. J. DALY]

SANTA MARIA MAGGIORE, ROME (St. Mary Major), one of the four primary or patriarchal basilicas. Called also the Liberian Basilica, representing the See of Antioch, rebuilt in 434 and consecrated to Our Lady in memory of the definition of the Council of Ephesus (431) declaring Mary the Mother of God, it is the church of the patriarch of Antioch. Best-preserved example of the Early Christian church despite remodeling—triple aisled, the clerestory with large windows, a triforium, and architrave carried on 44 antique marble columns of Ionic order, and semicircular apse—in light, open areas, exemplifies the impressive spatial effects of the Early Christian basilica. Reconstruction in the 12th-cent. under Eugenius III closed the lower semicircular apsidal section, and Sixtus V in 1587 reduced the majesty of the long architrave by two great chapels. Magnificent earliest extant mosaics, OT cycle in 28 compartments along the nave, in Roman "impressionistic" style, the cubes of large and varied shapes widely spaced in their bed, turned and twisted, are assigned to Pope Liberius (352–366) while those of the Triumphal arch of NT subject, Oriental, poetic, and idealized, are ascribed to Sixtus III (432–440) by dedicatory inscription (*Xystus Episcopus Plebi Dei*), their space-negating gold backgrounds portending the new Christian "nonnatural" iconographic symbolism further related to the Vatican Virgil and Quedlinburg Itala manuscripts. Later mosaics (13th and 14th cent.) produced by P. Cavallini and his assistant Jacopo Toritti are in Italo-Byzantine style. BIBLIOGRAPHY: C. Cecchelli, *I mosaici della basilica di S. Maria Maggiore* (1956); A. Grabar and C. Nordenfalk, *Early Medieval Painting . . .* (1957).

[M. J. DALY]

SANTA MARIA NOVELLA, FLORENCE, Italian Gothic, Dominican church on the Latin-cross plan and vaulted throughout, begun in 1278 and completed after 1350. Of four small chapels on two sides of the choir, the chapel of Filippo Strozzi is frescoed by Filippino *Lippi (1502); the choir frescoes are by Ghirlandajo (1485–90), the large Ruccelai chapel boasts Duccio's famous *Madonna* (1285) and the Strozzi Chapel decorations by Nardo di Cione (*c.*1357). In the nave is the famous *Trinity,* Masaccio's stupendous and earliest dated achievement (1425), depicting God the Father with the crucified Christ, the Virgin and St. John, with life-size donors of the Lenzi family (whose tomb was discovered recently beneath the mural), and a skeleton on a sarcophagus. In the cloisters are frescoes of Paolo Uccello (early 15th cent.) and of Andrea da Firenze

(1365–69). The unfinished Gothic façade completed by L.B. Alberti (1456–70) is proto-Renaissance in form.

[M. J. DALY]

SANTA PUDENZIANA, ROME, early Christian basilica-type church dating from the 4th cent., greatly altered, with bell tower of the 12th cent. and façade from the 19th century. Santa Pudenziana is famous for the earliest (4th-cent) extant Christian apsidal mosaic (though changed in size and "restored") depicting a majestic Christ at center on an ornate throne, and above him an immense jeweled cross, Apostles to right and left, and, before buildings signifying the cities of Jerusalem and Bethlehem, two female figures symbolizing the Jewish and gentile traditions (in the convention of *Mater Ecclesia* in early Christian iconography) hold wreaths over the heads of Peter and Paul, further confirming the symbolism through these Apostles of the Church of the Circumcision and that of the gentiles respectively. Symbols of the Evangelists frame the cross that together with the figure of Christ unites the upper and lower zones. This mosaic is important for the date which determines it as first evidence and prefiguration of Christian iconographic expression. BIBLIOGRAPHY: C. R. Morey, *Early Christian Art* (1953); W. F. Volbach, *Early Christian Art* (1962).

[M. J. DALY]

SANTA SOPHIA, see HAGIA SOPHIA.

SANTARELLI, ANTON (1569–1649), Italian Jesuit whose *Tractatus de haeresi . . .* (1625) caused controversy at the Sorbonne because of its claim, based on probabilism, that popes had power over kings. The controversy eventually involved Card. *Richelieu, but neither Urban VIII nor the Jesuit General, M. *Vitelleschi, would condemn the book.

[R. J. LITZ]

SANTAS CREUS, ABBEY OF, Cistercian monastery in Tarragona Province, Spain, founded c.1158 by William Raymond of Moncada with monks from Valladaura and put under papal jurisdiction by Alexander III. It is considered a Catalan version of El Escorial with its combination of abbey, royal residence, and burial place for the kings of Aragon; it reflects the close collaboration between the abbots and the kings during the high Middle Ages. Sacked and looted during the Napoleonic Wars and the Revolution of 1820, it was suppressed in 1834. Restoration and the return of the Cistercians date from 1884. It is less correctly sometimes referred to as Santa Cruz. BIBLIOGRAPHY: Cottineau 2:2644.

[E. J. DILLON]

SANTAYANA, GEORGE (1863–1952) American philosopher of a vast literary output (some 22 works in 29 volumes, besides papers and short monographs). Born in Madrid (he never gave up his Spanish nationality), he was brought to the U.S. at the age of 8. Educated at Boston Latin School and Harvard, he studied under W. *James and J. *Royce. After studies in Germany he joined the department of philosophy at Harvard where he taught (1884–1912). He retired to England and thence to Rome, continuing to write until his death. At his request he was buried "in neutral [unconsecrated] ground" in the Catholic cemetery of Rome.

S.'s fundamental philosophical position is one of critical realism. The subtlety of his thought and the rich beauty of his style have been at once the joy and the despair of his critics. Plato and Aristotle on the one hand and Indian philosophers on the other were early influences on his thought, but James and Royce marked it as well. His most productive years were spent in Europe and he always identified himself with Continental, even Mediterranean culture; but he must be classified as an American philosopher because of the character and influence of his writings, notable as they are for their pragmatism, materialism, and high regard for common sense. S.'s materialism has its own special accent. He speaks of "spirit," but it is epiphenomenal—matter alone is real.

For S., moral life is the life of reason, but not purely of reason. "The voice of nature" enters in, and S. would not rebuff those who identify the voice of nature with the divine. A professed agnostic, he sees religion as a myth, a symbolic truth that cannot be literally true. The instructions for his burial epitomize his life and thought: he saw himself always at the edge of the Church, at the church door, for he loved her external beauty and admired the internal logical consistency of her teaching. BIBLIOGRAPHY: *The Philosophy of George Santayana* (ed. P. A. Schilpp, 1949); R. Butler, *Mind of Santayana* (1955); D. Cory, *Santayana: The Later Years* (1962); F. A. Olafson, EncPhil 7:282–287.

[W. B. MAHONEY]

SANTEUL, CLAUDE AND JEAN BAPTISTE DE, humanists and Latin poets. **Claude** (1628–84). A cleric of the Oratorian Seminary of Saint-Magloire, Claude composed several hymns for the abp. of Paris and translated the letters of St. Paulinus of Nola. **Jean Baptiste** (1630–97), a subdeacon and canon regular of the monastery of Saint-Victor at Paris. A number of contemporaries described him as gifted and eccentric, but certainly one of the greatest Latin poets to appear in centuries. Like his brother, he composed breviary hymns for the abp. of Paris. BIBLIOGRAPHY: J. Carreyre, DTC 14.1:1103–04.

[B. F. SCHERER]

SANTI, family of Italian sculptors who with their pupils reinvigorated Venetian sculpture in the 14th century. **Andriolo di Pagani Santi** (d. 1370 ?), executed a crucifix (1328) in SS. Giovanni e Paolo, collaborated on the tomb of Jacopo da Carrara in S. Agostino (Padua, Eremitani) and probably on the companion grave of Albertino da Carrara

(1345). Masterpiece of **Giovanni de Santi** (d. 1392) is the tomb of Enrico Scrovegni in the famous Arena (Scrovegni) Chapel, Padua. *GIOTTO DI BONDONE.

[M. J. DALY]

SANTI, ANGELO DE (1847–1922), Italian Jesuit reformer of church music. In this field he began his service to the papacy by writing, at the bidding of Leo XIII, a series of articles in *La Civiltà Cattolica* (1887–92); they aroused intense controversy. S. prepared for Pius X both the *motu proprio, Tra le sollecitudine* (1903), laying down norms for emphasizing Gregorian Chant, and the Pope's letter on the same subject written to Card. Respighi (1903). From 1910 until his death, S. was director of the Roman school of sacred music, now named the Pontifical Institute of Sacred Music.

[J. R. AHERNE]

SANTI, GIOVANNI (d. 1494), Italian painter, father of Raphael, working at the courts of Urbino and Mantua, and author of a rhymed chronicle dedicated to the Duke Guidobaldo. His later dated works *The Madonna and Child with Saints* (1484) and an *Annunciation* in Senigallia, *Visitation* and *St. Jerome* (all signed), evidence the influences of Piero della Francesca, Melozzo da Forli, and Justus of Ghent, the Netherlandish master.

[M. J. DALY]

SANTIAGO, MIGUEL DE (1625–1706), Ecuadorian painter, major artist of the school of Quito, influenced by *Zurbarán and *Murillo, who painted 13 canvases of the life of St. Augustine (1656). His greatest work is *La Immaculada con la Santísima Trinidad* (c. 1680, Quito, S. Francisco).

[M. J. DALY]

SANTIAGO DE COMPOSTELA, city of Galicia, in NW Spain, famous since the 9th cent. as a pilgrimage center by virtue of its being the reputed burial place of the Apostle St. James the Greater. There are two main traditions concerning St. James: that he suffered martyrdom in Spain; and that, following his death in Jerusalem, disciples transported his body to Spain, the whereabouts of the tomb site subsequently being forgotten. In any event, it was there that Theodomir, bp. of Iria, discovered relics of the Apostle in the early 9th cent., after which St. James became the patron of the Christian and nationalist effort to wrest Spain away from its Moorish occupiers, while Compostela over the course of the next three centuries developed into the most popular pilgrimage shrine in W Europe. From across the Pyrenees came pilgrims and penitents, beggars and thieves, all converging on the road to Santiago along whose protected miles sprang up inns, hostels, and hospitals catering to the needs of the medieval pilgrims. In their ranks could be found such disparate figures as the hermit Simon of Armenia in the 10th cent., Count Raymond of Burgundy in the 11th, William of Aquitaine and Louis VII of France in the 12th, and St. Francis of Assisi and the Crusaders in the 13th. The original church, built over the saint's tomb by Alfonso II of Asturias in the 9th cent., was replaced by a larger one in 899, which, after its destruction in 997 by the Muslims, gave way in turn to a third in 1003. But it is the magnificent Romanesque cathedral, begun in 1075 and completed in 1211, that best illustrates the character of Santiago de Compostela during its heyday. Then its bps. (in 1120 Santiago was made a metropolitan see), ruling over nearly a dozen Portuguese and Spanish sees, vied with Toledo for religious primacy in Spain and, with their extensive lands and holdings, exercised great secular power as well. Though the church's main façade and two towers were given a Baroque appearance in the 16th and 17th cent., inside the original, Latin-cross architectural design is discernible; other features are the celebrated Portico de la Gloria by the 12th-cent. master sculptor and builder Maestro Mateo, the supposed tomb of the saint in a crypt beneath the principal altar, and, adjoining the cathedral, the Gothic cloister. Points of interest in Santiago include the palace of Abp. Diego Gelmírez (1100–40), the 12th-cent. churches of Santa Susana, Santa Salomé, and Santa Maria la Real de Sar, the Gran Hospital Real built by Ferdinand and Isabella to accommodate pilgrims, and buildings of the university, founded in 1501.

[E. M. GATES]

SANTILLANA, INIGO LÓPEZ DE MENDOZA (1398–1458), Spanish humanist and poet. He wrote a number of long Latinate imitative allegories, the most notable being the *Comedieta de Ponza* celebrating Alfonso V of Aragon's role in the naval battle at Ponza. Among his other works are a collection of 42 sonnets (the first Spanish imitation of the Italian sonnet), didactic and courtly poems, and a treatise on literary criticism and history.

[R. J. LITZ]

SANTO, religious figure or panel of cottonwood or pine carrying devotional images of the Spanish and Indian peoples of the American Southwest, made esp. in New Mexico (1750–1840). The pictorial panels *(retablos)* painted or in relief, and angular, jointed statues *(bultos)* were coated with gesso and painted. *Retablos* were executed on canvas, metal, leather, and paper also. *Santos* are a distinctive folk art in Spanish artistic tradition, expressing intense feeling in a moving primitive style. BIBLIOGRAPHY: W. Hougland, *Santos, A Primitive American Art* (1946).

[M. J. DALY]

SANTOS, JOÃO DOS (d. 1622), Portuguese Dominican missionary and writer who worked in Sofala (1586–90) and other parts of Mozambique before moving to India (1597) where he worked in Cochin and Goa. After study in Portugal (1606–17), he returned to India. His *Ethiopia oriental* describes the people, native customs, and fauna of East

Africa, and narrates the work of Dominican missionaries and the conquest of Africa by the Portuguese during the 16th century.

[R. J. LITZ]

SAÕ BENTO OF RIO DE JANEIRO, MONASTERY OF, a Benedictine *abbey nullius, dedicated to Our Lady of Montserrat and St. Benedict, located in Rio de Janeiro, Brazil, founded in 1590 restored in 1903. BIBLIOGRAPHY: Cottineau 2: 2469.

[E. J. DILLON]

SAPIENTI CONSILIO, apostolic constitution of Pius X (June 29, 1908) reorganizing the Roman Curia and defining its functions and competencies. Its directives were incorporated into Book II, part 1, ch. 4 of the CIC, promulgated in 1917, which regulated the Curia until Paul VI's reorganization, by the apostolic constitution *Regiminis ecclesiae universalis* (Aug. 15, 1970). *CURIA ROMANA.

[T. C. O'BRIEN]

SAPIENTIAL BOOKS, see WISDOM LITERATURE.

SAPIENZA, see ROME, UNIVERSITY OF.

SARABITES, a name of doubtful derivation given in early monasticism to a class of ascetics who lived, without regular superiors, either at home or in little communities near cities. St. Benedict in his Rule castigates them as "the third and most baneful kind [of monk]; whatever they think fit or choose to do, that they call holy, and what they like not, they consider unlawful." But Sarabite has come to mean generally a relaxed, bad monk. BIBLIOGRAPHY: F. A. Gasquet, *English Monastic Life* (1905).

[U. VOLL]

SARACENI, MAURUS (1540–88), Italian Conventual Franciscan, exegete, theologian, and missionary. He taught in colleges of the order at universities in Bologna, Florence, Milan, Naples, Padua, and Urbino before being elected procurator general (1578) and later visitator general of the order to Sicily and France. He held the chair of Hebrew at the Sorbonne (1583–86) until he went to Lithuania as a missionary and teacher. Ministering to the sick of Vilna during a plague he himself died.

[R. J. LITZ]

SARAH (Sara), wife of Abraham and mother of Isaac. She was originally named Sarai (Gen 17.15). Childless (Gen 11.29–30), she gave Abraham her maid Hagar, who became the mother of Ishmael (Gen 16). In accordance with God's promise, S. had a son Isaac in her old age, after which she made Abraham cast out Hagar and Ishmael (Gen 21.1–14). She died at Kiriath-arba at the age of 127, and Abraham bought the Cave of Mach-pelah as a burial place (Gen ch. 23). S. is mentioned several times in the NT (Rom 4.19;

9.9; Heb 11.11; 1 Pet 3.6; and Gal 4.21–31). S. figures in the allegory on the covenant of the Law and the covenant of the promise made to Abraham.

[T. EARLY]

SARAZU, ÁNGELES (Florencia; 1873–1921), abbess from 1904 of the cloistered monastery of the Purísima Concepción, Valladolid, mystic. She entered the cloister in 1891, taking the name María de los Ángeles. In works written out of obedience to her directors, she left highly prized descriptions of the mystical and contemplative union of the soul with God. Posthumous, they include: *La vida espiritual coronada por la triple manifestación de Jesucristo* (1924); *Autobiografía* (1929); *Exposición de varios pasajes de la Sagrada Escritura* (1926).

[T. C. O'BRIEN]

SARCOPHAGUS, a coffin made of stone, terra-cotta, lead, wood, or other material. These coffins hold whole corpses, and the name does not apply to the smaller chests that hold ashes of cremated bodies. The word comes from *lithos sarcophagos* (flesh-eating), a kind of stone found near Assos in the Troas that has the peculiar property of completely consuming corpses within 40 days after they are laid in it (Pliny, *Natural History* 2. 211). Usually coffins are only inlaid with this stone to hasten decomposition.

Earliest examples of sarcophagi come from Egypt. Typically their shapes are rectangular with heavy stone covers. However, the anthropoid type of sarcophagus, made in the shape of the mummy enclosed in it, is frequently found in Egypt, Cyprus, and Phoenicia. Terra-cotta sarcophagi in the shape of tubs and chests often come from Crete. The two most important examples of Cretan terra-cotta sarcophagi are from Palaikastro and Hierapetra. Another famous Cretan sarcophagus, made of painted limestone, comes from Hagia Triadha. While records reveal that the majority of sarcophagi were of wood, these only survive exceptionally. Examples of lead sarcophagi come mostly from Roman Syria.

Sarcophagi are *bisomus, trisomus,* or *quadrisomus* according as they have two, three, or four compartments. A *quadrisomus* in the Vatican Cemetery contains the bodies of the first four popes called Leo.

The East used sarcophagi extensively; but before the 6th cent. B.C., sarcophagi were relatively rare in Greece proper because of the widespread use of cremation. Most of the early examples of Greek sarcophagi come from the city of Clazomenae in the 7th and 6th centuries B.C.. Good examples of these painted terra-cotta sarcophagi are in the British Museum. These often depict scenes of war, of legend, and of games. In Hellenistic times the Greeks affirmed the imprint of architecture by including such elements as columns, architraves, and pediments. An outstanding example of this kind, carved and painted in imitation of a temple, is the sarcophagus of Alexander the Great found near Sidon and now in the Istanbul Museum. This sarcophagus, made by a

Greek for a Sidonian prince, is remarkable both for its marvelous preservation and for its admirable sculpture representing battles and hunting scenes of Alexander. In the same museum there are also other fine examples of Sidonian sarcophagi.

Etruscan sarcophagi, made of stone or terra-cotta, often have covers on which life-sized figures of the deceased recline. Some of them represent themes of the journey of the dead, the dead leaving relatives, and the dead being received at the entrance of Hades.

Roman sarcophagi are quadrangular and show the faces of the deceased in low relief. The earliest known Roman sarcophagus is that of the consul, Cn. Cornelius Scipio, of the 3d cent. B.C.. It is in the Vatican. By the 2d cent. A.D., as the rites of inhumation instead of urn burial spread, Rome began to export sarcophagi to the provinces of the West, Africa and Gaul. In the 4th cent. Constantine encouraged and inspired artists to develop this art form. Both pagans and Christians used sarcophagi adorned with bas reliefs down to the Byzantine period. These sarcophagi are the chief sources for the study of changing styles and composition in relief sculpture. In the Renaissance, tombs resembling sarcophagi are often cenotaphs or memorials erected above ground for bodies buried underground.

Themes differ in different countries at different times. On the painted sarcophagi at Crete, purely ornamental motifs such as papyrus, lotus, marine animals, and particularly, the spiral prevail. The limestone sarcophagus from Hagia Triadha shows ritualistic scenes of the sacrifice of the bull, the offering of fruit, and the offering of funerary gifts. Until the 4th cent. Christians adorned sarcophagi with themes such as the arrest of St. Peter, the miracle at Cana, the healing of the blind, and the raising of the dead. Many examples of these themes are in the Vatican Museum, the Lateran Museum, at Ravenna, in Arles, and in Spain.

Sarcophagi are frequently reused by later generations because of the ease with which they are adapted for baths, baptismal fonts, watering troughs, and dye vats. Wherever they have been found they have been widely perverted to such purposes. BIBLIOGRAPHY: EncWA; V. Ricci, NCE 12:1084–86; G. Rodenwaldt, CAH 11:792–805.

[M. F. MCNAMARA]

SARDICA, COUNCIL OF (343), convened by the Emperors Constantius and Constans to attempt a settlement of the Arian controversies. The Council affirmed that the three persons in the Trinity have one identical hypostasis or substance, that the Word was generated but never had a beginning (as the Arians held) nor will have an end. The Council invested the Roman bp. with certain prerogatives and jurisdiction over other sees and so provided a basis for further development of the concept of the Roman primacy. BIBLIOGRAPHY: Hefele-Leclercq 1.2:737–823; Fliche–Martin 6:107–120.

[P. FOSCOLOS]

SARDINHA, PEDRO FERNANDES (c.1496–1556), Portuguese clergyman who served in ecclesiastical positions at Madeira Island, Oporto, and Goa, before he was appointed first bp. of the Diocese of Salvador (Bahia) in Brazil in 1551. His love of pomp was strained by the poverty of his see. He ran into trouble with the governor and with the Jesuits over their approach to Christianizing Indians without "civilizing" them to European ways. Recalled in 1555, he was captured and killed by Caeté Indians when his ship was wrecked near Alagoas, Brazil.

[R. J. LITZ]

SARDIS, city of Asia Minor and capital of Lydia. A wealthy trading center, it was Croesus' capital and possibly the Sepharad where Jewish exiles were settled (Ob 20). One of the seven letters of Rev was to the Church of Sardis (3.1–6). The *Chester Beatty Papyri include a sermon by *Melito of Sardis. American archeological expeditions made excavations in 1910 and in 1958.

[T. EARLY]

SARGAVAK (East Armenian, *sarkavag*), Armenian deacon.

SARGON, name of three ancient rulers. (1) Sargon, founder of the Akkadian Empire (2360–2180 B.C.), is regarded as the first emperor in history. (2) Sargon I was king of Assyria, c.1850 B.C. (3) Sargon II (722–705 B.C.), king of Assyria, figures in Israelite history. During the year of his accession, succeeding Shalmeneser V, he conquered the N kingdom of Israel, making it part of an Assyrian province, and deported more than 25,000 Israelites (2 Kg 17.6; Is 20.1).

[T. C. O'BRIEN]

SARMIENTO, DOMINGO FAUSTINO (1811–88), Argentine educator, statesman, writer, president of the republic. A political opponent of Juan Manuel de Rosas, S., from 1831 until the ouster of Rosas in 1852, spent much of his time in exile in Chile. After 1852 he became successively provincial legislator, governor, minister to the U.S., and president (1868–74). During his administration, which was marked by material progress, he saw the end of the Paraguayan war and, inspired by U.S. and European models, reorganized the school system, reformed educational methods, and zealously promoted his ideas on education of the masses. His writings include *Facundo*, a political biography, and many works on educational topics. Works: *Sarmiento Anthology* (tr. and ed. S. E. Grummon and A. W. Bunkley, 1948, repr. 1971).

[M. B. MURPHY]

SARNATH, RUINS AT, near Benares, Uttar Pradesh, India, a site sacred to Buddhists (here Buddha preached in the Deer Park his first sermon after enlightenment) and religious center from the rise of Buddhism in the 5th cent. B.C. until the Muslim invasion of the 12th cent. A.D. Sacred to the Jain sect, also as site of the ascetic life and death of Sreyāmsanātha, the 11th *Tirthankara,* Sarnath evidences impressive shrines, temples, stupas (ruins) from Maurya through Gupta periods, and some of the finest sculpture in India, influencing the Buddhist missionary carving of Thailand, Cambodia and Java. Remaining are the foundations of Aśoka's Dharmarājikā stupa (destroyed in the 18th cent.), the Dhāmekh stupa elegantly carved in the Gupta period, a lion-pillar of Aśoka (its capital now the national emblem of India), and many other treasures now in the museums of Sarnath, Delhi, and Calcutta. BIBLIOGRAPHY: V. S. Agrawala, *Sarnath* (1957).

[M. J. DALY]

SARPI, PAOLO (1552–1623), Venetian Servite, antipapal historian of the Council of Trent. Ordained in 1575, he was 4 years later provincial of the Venetian Servites, then in Rome as procurator general (1585) and as vicar general of the order (1599–1604). During this Roman period he became hostile to both the Curia Romana and the Society of Jesus. As theologian and counsellor of the Republic of Venice from 1606, he participated in antipapal action and propaganda, denouncing as invalid the interdict laid against the city. When peace was restored (1607), Paul V ordered him to Rome to face the Inquisition, but S. refused to leave Venice, and was excommunicated. He spent the remainder of his life in Venice. He had close ties with the Anglicans of the British embassy there, but decisive in his project on Trent were the influence of Gallicanism and the Gallican attack on that council. The *Istoria del Concilio Tridentino* appeared first in 1619 at London, under the pseudonym Petrus Suavis Polanus, printed by the ex-Catholic abp., Marcantonio de Dominis; it was put on the Index (Nov. 22, 1619). The first of many English translations was done by N. Bent in London the following year. Obviously S. had limited access to true sources on the council. He himself thought his work neither Protestant nor anti-Catholic in spirit. Clearly, however, it sought to portray Trent as an exercise in papal and curial aggrandizement; it was long a favorite Protestant resource. S. himself came to be cited as an outstanding example of enlightened reason, seeing through obscurantist papistry. The long desired Catholic response to S. appeared only in 1656–57, the *Istoria del Concilio di Trento* of P. Sforza *Pallavicino. There is considerable doubt about S.'s Catholic orthodoxy; there is little about his astuteness in Venetian politics or about his broad learning, esp. in mathematics. An edition of his complete works, including his letters, appeared in 1677. BIBLIOGRAPHY: J. Lievsay, *Venetian Phoenix* (1973).

[T. C. O'BRIEN]

SARSFIELD, PATRICK, Earl of Lucan (c.1650–93), Irish Jacobite general and national hero. He served with the

English forces attached to the army of Louis XIV in France, during the reign of Charles II. He helped to suppress the rebellion of the Duke of Monmouth (1685), supported James II in 1688, and went with him into exile. He achieved some victories in Ireland as commander of James's forces; but in the Battle of the Boyne (1690), the armies of William III defeated those of James II, who fled to France. Permitted to go to France, S. took thousands of Irish soldiers with him into foreign service. Although he was not a great general, his countrymen esteemed him for his loyalty to Catholicism and to his king. BIBLIOGRAPHY: J. Todhunter, *Life of Patrick Sarsfield* (1901); R. H. Murray, *Revolutionary Ireland and Its Settlement* (1911).

[S. A. HEENEY]

SARTO, ANDREA DEL (1486–1530), Italian painter. Apprenticed to a goldsmith at 7 years, his drawing talent recognized at 10, S. studied under Piero di Cosimo, who, intensely interested in the innovations of Michelangelo and Leonardo, influenced his pupil. Until 1517, S. shared a workshop with Franciabigio and the sculptor Il Sansovino, numbering as pupils Pontormo and Rosso Fiorentino. S. at Fontainebleau (1518–19) executed the *Caritas,* returned to Florence and Rome, fled the plague (1523), and was again in Florence in 1524. His works are eclectic, with figures from Michelangelo and D. Ghirlandaio (*Life of S. Filippo Benizzi,* 1510). His frescoes in grisaille at the cloister of the Scalzo, more advanced in form and painterly in style, are considered his finest achievement. The well-known *Madonna of the Harpies,* the Virgin with Child attended by SS. Francis and John the Evangelist, though serene, is saccharine. A *Disputa* (1517–18) with many figures is bolder in form and texture, the *Madonna del Sacco* (1525) shows vivacity, while the *Madonna with Six Saints* (1527–28), pale in color and restrained in composition, suggests Fra Bartolommeo. Having established a vibrant, warm, classical style in 16th-cent. Florence, S. too often charming rather than noble, finally embraced mannerism. BIBLIOGRAPHY: J. Shearman, *Andrea del Sarto* (2 v., 1965).

[M. J. DALY]

SARTRE, JEAN PAUL (1905–   ), French existentialist philosopher and literary figure. Born in Paris, where he studied, S. later continued his education as research student at the Institut Français in Berlin and at the Univ. of Freiburg. He was co-founder of *Les Tempes modernes* (1945). S.'s philosophy is influenced by continental rationalism and idealism although he is clearly in opposition to the dualism of Cartesian thought. In assessing the influences that helped shape his thinking, one can trace those of *Descartes, *Kant, *Hegel, and of course *Husserl and *Heidegger, the latter representing the most consistent and thorough influence on Sartre. If, however, the first volume of *Critique of Dialectical Reason* (1960) points to anything, it brings to light a kind of philosophical *metanoia* taking place in S.'s thought; one that puts him squarely within the Marxist tradition. The content of S.'s works has several strands: the psychological and the ontological. In the former, S. makes a break with Husserl's position of consciousness; for S., the consciousness is the constituting one, aware and reflective; Husserl views the consciousness as rationally self-reflecting. Both, it appears, fail to describe it as consciousness of itself as subject rather than as object. The implications of seeing consciousness this way are manifold for establishing some connection between it and a system of ethics. On the other hand, S. does not subscribe to Heidegger's suppression of the consciousness in his philosophical thought. This is not to minimize Heidegger's influence on S., for his major work, *Being and Nothingness,* shows clear and decisive contributions from Heidegger. S. describes *Being and Nothingness* as a work of phenomenological ontology. Unlike other philosophers in the phenomenological school, he sees ontology as a purely descriptive philosophy. For him, it is the function of metaphysics to undertake the hermeneutics of human existence and experience. Obviously, holding such a view also frees him from having to deal with the concerns of the positivist and empirical schools. S. is, however, concerned with the moral exigencies of existence. In fact, the key to his moral philosophy is found in the consideration of existence—the traditional and philosophical conceptions of being are rejected by him. That rejection, along with his recognition of the validity of the philosophical quest expressed by the more traditional philosophies, yields the grounding for S.'s insistence that man is irrevocably circumscribed by contradictions and only when he recognizes that contradiction is he capable of being moral. S.'s works reveal other strands such as the ''being for itself, being in itself'' problem and the problem of other minds. With the completion of the *Critique of Dialectical Reason*, one may hope to find other and perhaps more clearly expressed strands. Besides his major work, *Being and Nothingness* (tr. H. E. Barnes, 1956), he authored several other works of philosophical importance and others of literary importance: *Transcendence of the Ego* (tr. F. Williams and R. Kirkpatrick, 1937); *Psychology of Imagination* (tr. B. Frechtman, 1948); *Nausea* (tr. L. Alexander, 1949); *No Exit* and *The Flies* (tr. S. Gilbert, 1947). He declined the Nobel Prize for Literature in 1964. BIBLIOGRAPHY: F. A. Olafson, EncPhil 7:287–293.

[J. R. RIVELLO]

SARUM CHANT, modifications and additions made to the Gregorian plain chant, originating at Salisbury (Lat. *Sarisburia*) and in use in England during the later Middle Ages. The English plain chant tradition had its roots in the Gregorian as introduced by St. *Augustine of Canterbury. Continental influences came with the Norman invasion; in the high Middle Ages the Sarum chant represented a combination of the two and a development of native variations in melody, esp. in its hymns. In the plainchant revival in the C of E, beginning from the *Oxford Movement, musicians have preferred the Sarum chants in creating liturgical settings.

[M. T. LEGGE]

SARUM RITE, a medieval variation of the Roman rite, in use at Salisbury, England. As a local variation it is more properly called the Use of Sarum. The tradition ascribing it to the 11th-cent. bp. St. Asmund is unfounded; it belongs to the early 13th century. Modeled on French usages, it contained elements of the Gallican liturgy; the Mass ritual resembled that used until recent years by the Dominicans and Carmelites. The ceremonial of the rite was elaborate and called for a great many officiants. By the time of the Reformation, the Use of Sarum was widespread in England and Wales, and was also found in Scotland and Ireland. It served as the basis for the 1549 Book of Common Prayer. The Marian RC priests continued to use it until the liturgical reforms of Pius V. In modern times Sarum customs have been introduced into some Anglican Churches. BIBLIOGRAPHY: W. H. Frere, *Use of Sarum* (2 v., 1898–1901); L. C. Sheppard, NCE 12:520–521.

[T. C. O'BRIEN]

SASSABASAR, see SHESHBAZZAR.

SASSETTA, STEFANO DI GIOVANNI (1392–1450), Italian painter, considered the greatest master of the Quattrocento in Siena. S. combines a knowledge of the new Renaissance interest in rationalized space and form being explored in Florence with a conservatism deeply influenced by the styles of Duccio and Simone Martini, masters of Trecento Sienese painting. The resulting highly decorative style is one in which the natural world is transformed into a lyrical, mystical vision with landscapes of convincing, but unscientific perspective, peopled by delicate ethereal beings as in *The Marriage of St. Francis to Lady Poverty* (c.1444, Musée, Condé, Chantilly). BIBLIOGRAPHY: J. Pope-Hennessy, *Sienese Quattrocento Painting* (1947).

[S. CONWAY]

SASSOFERRATO (GIOVANNI BATTISTA SALVI; 1609–85), Italian painter influenced by works of Raphael and the Carracci in Rome and associated with Domenichino. In Venice, Urbino, Perugia, and Rome, S. copying works of the masters was drawn esp. to the serene Perugino. S.'s consistently religious themes, Madonnas and ecclesiastical portraits, evidence a 16th-cent. archaism similar to the Pre-Raphaelites in smooth surface, and the sentimentality of late Baroque. His consistent style renders dating difficult, variations being of palette. *The Mystic Marriage of St. Catherine* (London) is warmer than other works; *The Madonna of the Rosary* (1643) is one of only four works known in churches, most of his commissions having been devotional paintings for private chapels. Many of S.'s drawings are in the Royal Library, Windsor Castle. BIB-

LIOGRAPHY: A. Blunt and H. L. Cooke, *Roman Drawings of the 17th and 18th Centuries in the Collection of Her Majesty the Queen at Windsor Castle* (1960).

SATAN, the one who tries to disrupt the relationship between God and man, and esp. between God and Israel. This definition, however, applies only to a later theology; the term went through a substantial evolution within biblical usage. The word satan originally had a juridical meaning in Israel: he was the accuser in a court of law (Zech 3.1), or a specific adversary who points out a person's guilt (1 Kg 11.9–26). According to the Book of Job, a similar function is carried out by a heavenly satan: he is the one who demonstrates man's sins in the court of heaven. As a kind of prosecuting attorney, this heavenly being questions man's goodness but only in the pursuit of justice. With God's approval he controls the means (sickness, isolation, natural disasters) of testing man. A further development can be seen in 1 Chr 21.1 where for the first time Satan is a proper name; he, rather than Yahweh, is the agent of temptation but always within the divine economy of salvation. In pre-NT Judaism, a variety of concepts about Satan emerged: he became the angel of death, one of the fallen angels, and the tempter who seeks man's separation from God. This view is carried over into the NT where two other distinctive aspects emerge: the absolute antithesis between God and Satan, and the destruction of Satan's dominion by the coming of God's kingdom in Christ. In the NT, the functions mentioned above coalesce within the power of a single, supernatural being—Satan (Lk 4.6; 2 Cor 4.4). But Christ puts an end to this dominion, casts Satan from heaven, and assumes judgment unto himself (Lk 10.18; Mt 12.29; Apoc 12.7–12). BIBLIOGRAPHY: G. von Rad and W. Foerster, Kittel TD 2:71–81; EDB 2134–37; W. F. Barnett, NCE 12:1093–94. *DEVIL; *DEMONS.

[T. M. MCFADDEN]

SATANISM, worship of the devil. Though reliable information about such a practice is difficult to obtain, it has apparently been conducted with some seriousness in circles hostile to orthodox religion. It is thought to date from the 12th cent., and to have enjoyed a revival in 17th-cent. France. It is associated with such features as the *black mass and the addressing of prayers to images of Satan. BIBLIOGRAPHY: H. T. F. Rhodes, *Satanic Mass* (1968). *DEVIL WORSHIP.

[T. EARLY]

SATIRE, MEDIEVAL LATIN. In contrast to earlier patterns, it focused on the weaknesses of certain classes or society in general rather than on the faults of individuals. Ecclesiastics, whether curialists or monks, were frequent targets of abuse. The beast epic of Reynard the Fox and Isengrim the Wolf offered a favorite vehicle. Nivardus of Ghent's *Ysengrimus* (c.1150) directs most of its criticism against the clergy. Rhythmic poetry was esp. suitable for

satire in the witty use of parody, allusion, and innuendo. The *Confession of Golias* by the unknown Archpoet (c.1150) defends a weakness for women, drink, and gambling. Gautier de Châtillon and Walter Map, author of *On Courtiers' Trifles*, are among the best satirists of the 12th century.

[J. E. LYNCH]

SATIRE MÉNIPPÉE (*Mennipean Satire,* 1594), the foremost 16th-cent. French literary and political satire, in prose and verse, directed against the Catholic political party, the Holy League. Originally known as *La Vertu du Catholicon d'Espagne,* it was conceived by P. Leroy, canon of Rouen, with the collaboration of J. Gillot, F. Chrétien, N. *Rapin, P. Pithou, J. Passerat, and G. Durand. A satire of the Estates General (1593), it ridicules the League's excesses through such characters as the papal legate, the abp. of Lyons and Cardinal Pellevé, contrasted with M. d'Aubray, representative of the third Estate, who speaks reasonably in his *Harangue*. Its name was inspired by Terentius Varro's prose-and-verse *Menippeae Saturae* (150 books) which, in turn, claimed its inspiration from the satires of Menippos, Greek poet and cynic philosopher (c.4th–3d cent. B.C.). BIBLIOGRAPHY: A. Bailly, *La Réforme en France jusqu'à l'Édit de Nantes* (1960) 473–484.

[R. N. NICOLICH]

SATIS COGNITUM, encyclical of Leo XIII (June 29, 1896) on Christ's foundation of the Church with a unity of teaching, sanctifying, and ruling power. The document had the concrete purpose of rejecting as erroneous the position of some in the Anglican communion that the unity of the Church can and does exist without the universal exercise of these powers by the one Roman Pontiff, and without unity of acceptance by particular Christian communions. On this score the encyclical was regarded as reactionary, esp. since it was followed shortly afterwards (Sept. 13, 1896) by *Apostolicae curae,* rejecting the validity of *Anglican orders. The broader significance of the document is its articulation of the constitution of the Church in its visible structure and its declarations on the *magisterium. Vatican Council II (Vat II, ConstCh n.8, Ecum, nn. 19–22), reiterated the basic position of *Satis cognitum,* but with a more positive emphasis on relationships with other Christian ecclesial communities.

[T. C. O'BRIEN]

SATISFACTION, from Lat. *satis-facere,* to do enough. Its meaning of fulfillment or gratification of desire comes into psychological and moral theology but may be here neglected for its earlier meaning of paying the price for wrongdoing, indeed the earliest in English refers to its part in the sacrament of penance, of which more later. Historically the notion, about which nothing has been defined *de fide,* has been so thoroughly tangled with that of punishment in a juridical frame of reference by sacramental and soteriological literature that it will be useful to ease it out. The essential idea is the making of amends for an offense committed. This entails not only the generous forgiveness of the one offended but also the loving effort of the one who has given the offense to put things completely right: such is the instinct in making, as we say, an ample apology. It is not essential that anybody should be hurt in the process, and both on this count and on that of its being freely rendered, and not just endured, it differs from being punished, most certainly from undergoing an ''inflicted'' punishment.

Penalty (*poena*) can be a wider term; in the order of things, not merely by judicial sentence, consequences can be incurred by wrongdoing that spell deprivation and cannot be remedied without tonic pain: sorrow is not enough to restore a drunkard; he must also toughen up by taking his cure. Satisfaction also differs from *compensation and *restitution, which mean returning a thing to its owner or making good the damage he has suffered from lacking it; these are matters of *commutative justice, whereas satisfaction, in its theological sense, is done for the complete restoration of friendship. It is the giving, says St. Thomas Aquinas, of what is dearer than the offense was hateful.

With these thoughts in mind we can address ourselves to the two places where the notion is prominent, in the theology, namely, of the sacrament of penance and of the Atonement. The first concerns our personal sins. The Catholic theory is that the grace of repentance springs wholly from God's mercy. We are forgiven, and we are God's friends again. But we still remain somewhat damaged goods. Can we just leave matters at that? Instead should we not rather, though still working under his grace, set ourselves to make reparation? It is not that God needs it, but that we do, out of the very honor of love which he himself instills in us. All this is highly satisfactory, and in every sense of the word. In particular, the sacrament of forgiveness comprises three elements on our side, namely, *confession, *contrition, and satisfaction (warrant for the use of the term in reference to a sinner's reparation for his sin by penitential acts goes as far back as Cyprian). In practice, the priest enjoins a ''penance'' or ''sacramental satisfaction,'' as it is called; it can be of varying stiffness, but is usually more of a token than an adequate counter to the sins forgiven. However, it is well understood that the act itself of going to confession exacts as much effort ''toward'' God as our previous lapses ''from'' him, and that the penitent will tackle difficulties as works of satisfaction he shares in union with Christ.

The devotion of offering satisfaction for others is encouraged; this may go to heroic lengths. Though its manifestation is sometimes embarrassing for its earthy and unpresuming beneficiaries, the idea is soundly based on the theology that includes in the kingdom the open-hearted humanity which says, ''Your friends are my friends.''

The doctrine of satisfaction has been popularized and at the same time somewhat coarsened by the picture of it as paying the debt of temporal punishment due to sin. Here again the underlying meaning is delicate and accurate; the metaphor is just within its limits and works out well for those who do not pursue it too literally. Others find it over-legalistic, and even metallic, and not unconnected with inflation of the currency in the matter of *indulgences. Its root, however, strikes deeper than the ecclesiastical abuses which prompted the Reformation, and taps depths where sin is seen, not only as a turning away from God, but also a turning toward something else, and where being with God is seen not only as standing right in his sight but also as being fit for his joy.

The doctrine of the satisfaction made by Christ on our account was developed by St. *Anselm, the first theologian to study the Atonement systematically. The argument of his famous *Cur Deus Homo* is based on the paradox that man must, but man *cannot,* pay his debt for sin to divine justice, and therefore only the God-Man could satisfy, is forensic and colored by Roman law conceptions. Still it was a great improvement on some previous savage ransom or sacrificial theories, according to which the devil's claim on us was bought out or the Father's anger was vented on a scapegoat for sin. It has inspired a wealth of devotion to our Lord's Passion and holds echoes from the Scriptures and tradition. It was never meant as a theological statement. A century and a half later it took its place in St. Thomas's *Summa* (3a,49), where the *merit, satisfaction, *sacrifice, *redemption, and effective causality of Christ's saving life are each distinguished, alongside other stumbling explanations of the mystery. In his mercy God forgives us; in his courtesy he does not let us go scot free. Our brother, one of us, makes atonement, and in that we too must share. ''And you, that were sometimes alienated, and enemies in your mind by wicked works, yet now hath he reconciled in the body of his flesh through death to present you holy and undefiled and irreproachable before him'' (Col 1.21–22). BIBLIOGRAPHY: J. McIntyre, *St. Anselm and His Critics, Reinterpretation of the Cur Deus homo* (1954); J. S. Whale, *Victor and Victim* (1960).

[T. GILBY]

SATISFACTION, VICARIOUS. The repairing of an injury done to another is satisfaction. It is a good work freely offered to the injured party and accepted by him in place of the punishment he should mete out. Ordinarily the one who performs the work is the guilty party, but in the concept of vicarious satisfaction the work is offered by another on behalf of the guilty party. Jesus Christ, offering in love his life to his heavenly Father for guilty mankind, effected man's salvation after the manner of vicarious satisfaction. Here the qualification ''after the manner'' is used to indicate that the human concept of vicarious satisfaction is not applied univocally to the redemptive work of Christ but only analogously. Some of the elements of the strict concept of vicarious satisfaction are verified in some way in the Redemption. BIBLIOGRAPHY: Philippe de la Trinité, *What Is Redemption?* (tr. A. Armstrong, 1961).

[E. A. WEIS]

SATISFACTION OF CHRIST. This consists in the love and obedience by which he accepted his Passion and death in order to compensate for sin's offense against the goodness and holiness of God. The concept came into general use in the theology of Redemption after the *Cur Deus homo* of St. Anselm of Canterbury. While the satisfaction of Christ is not a biblical expression, and while the satisfactory efficacy of Christ's acts has never been defined, that description of his work has been adopted by the teaching authority of the Church (D 1529, 3891). It expresses a facet of the biblical notions of expiation, sacrifice, cross, death for man's sins, and other such themes. The concept is valuable in forming a balanced theology especially of God's love and holiness; in preventing it from becoming merely sentimental. Sin is an offense against God, and he takes it seriously.

Satisfaction is made when the person offended is offered something that he values as much as or more than he detests the offense he has suffered (see ThAq ST 3a, 48.2). This is the principle underlying the theory. Christ's free acceptance of the cross is a moral act of infinite value—infinite because the moral value of an act before God derives, not only from the thing done, but esp. from the dignity of the person acting. In this case, the person is divine, and so the dignity of the love and obedience with which he accepts suffering and death (which are the consequences of the sinful human condition) is infinite and divine. If one considers this act as offered in behalf of all mankind, whose head he is, and as reparation for the offense of sin, then one can speak of Christ's Redemption as infinite satisfaction for all sin.

The satisfaction of Christ is a mystery of love, not of stoic endurance. Its consequence is the reconciliation of estranged persons. Jesus is not punished for man's sins; he is not a scapegoat (J. Calvin); he offers himself on sinful man's behalf, not in his place. Just as his death does not free man from the need of dying, and as he has not returned to the Father in place of his fellow man, so his satisfaction does not make that of his fellow man superfluous. Whatever value man's satisfaction has stems from Christ's and is an application of it. Only the dolorous aspect of the paschal mystery is said to be satisfactory. It is Christ's passage unto death, not his liberation from it, that is the human, moral act offered in compensation for sin's offense. BIBLIOGRAPHY: A. P. Hennessy, NCE 12:1095–98; Philippe de la Trinité, *What Is Redemption?* (tr. A. Armstrong, 1961); L. Richard, *Mystery of the Redemption* (tr. J. Horn, 1965).

[C. REGAN]

SATOLLI, FRANCESCO (1839–1910), Italian educator and churchman. Ordained in 1862, S., a neoscholastic and Thomist in the early days of the Thomistic revival, achieved some distinction in teaching and writing as well as in academic administration. He was made a titular abp. (1888) and was sent to the U.S. (1893) as the first to hold the post of apostolic delegate in the newly established permanent delegation. He had previously visited the U.S. twice (1889 and 1892) on missions for the Holy See. His coming as delegate was greeted with something less than enthusiasm in some quarters, not because of dissatisfaction with S. personally, but because many (including all the U.S. hierarchy with the exception of Abp. J. Ireland) had opposed the establishment of a permanent apostolic delegation in the U.S. S. was made cardinal (1895), recalled to Rome and made prefect of the Congregation of Studies (1896), and cardinal bishop of Frascati (1903). BIBLIOGRAPHY: J. T. Ellis, *Life of James Cardinal Gibbons* (2 v., 1952); R. Trisco, NCE 1:690–693. *APOSTOLIC DELEGATION IN THE U.S.

SATOR AREPO, a cryptogram consisting of five words,

```
S A T O R
A R E P O
T E N E T
O P E R A
R O T A S
```

arranged in the form of a square in such a way that the words can be read consecutively either horizontally or vertically. The device was once considered to be of Christian origin, since the central word "tenet" forms a cross, but with its discovery in the ruins of Pompeii (destroyed 79 A.D.) the probability of a non-Christian origin came to be recognized. It is likely, then, that it was a magical palindrome of pagan contrivance, later taken over by Christians and given a new interpretation without being completely purged of all of its superstitious associations. BIBLIOGRAPHY: V. Ricci, NCE 12:1098–99; J. Emminghaus, LTK 9:343–344.

[R. B. ENO]

SATORNILIANS, also called Saturninians, Gnostic heretics mentioned by Hegisippus, Justin Martyr, and St. Irenaeus. These took their name from Satornil or Saturninus, who taught in Antioch in the 3d century. According to Irenaeus, Satornil, following the general scheme of Gnostic teaching, taught that all things come from a Father who is utterly unknown and unknowable, who created the angels, of whom seven guard the planetary spheres, one of whom created man as a prostrate creature like a worm. Upon this pitiful being came the power of a higher angel making him stand erect. The God of the Jews, Yahweh, was also one of the seven angels, who deceived his followers. The Father took compassion upon man and sent a Savior with a phantom body to redeem man and to rescue him from involvement with the material world. Satornil taught an Encratite kind of morality—no marriage, no generation, and abstention from all kinds of animal foods, with a life of strict asceticism.

[A. WALKER]

SATTLER, MICHAEL (*c.* 1490–1527), early Anabaptist leader. Born at Freiburg, Ger., he became a Benedictine at the monastery of St. Peter, where for a time he held office as prior. Attracted to Reformation ideas as more in conformity to his study of St. Paul, he left the monastery, married, and went to Zurich. There in 1525 he joined the Anabaptist Swiss Brethren. In the same year he was expelled by the Zwinglian authorities and fled to Strassburg. He engaged in friendly discussion of their differing views with the Reformers M. *Bucer, and W. *Capito. He left the city, however, fearing that the authorities would prosecute him for his doctrine, and became a preacher around Rottenburg, where he won many followers. He presided at the conference at which the German and Swiss Anabaptists adopted the *Schleitheim Confession; he probably was its author. Shortly afterward, he and his wife were arrested. They were tried, condemned, and executed at Rottenburg (May 1527); he was burned; she was drowned. BIBLIOGRAPHY: MennEnc 4:427–434.

SATURDAY. (1) Liturgically, the vigil of Sunday was in the early Church ordinarily the time for the beginning of the celebration of the Lord's Day; the current "anticipated" Mass may be compared to the ancient Saturday liturgical observance. (2) Devotionally, Saturday is dedicated to Mary in various forms, among them the First Saturdays (analogous to First Friday) as part of the Fatima devotion. (3) Ascetically, Saturday was once prescribed as a day of fasting (e.g., the Ember Days) and has also been so observed as a day of voluntary penance.

SATURDAY ABSTINENCE, from the 4th cent. the Eastern Churches regarded Saturday as liturgically on a par with Sunday. The Roman Church, however, kept it as a fast day because of Christ's Passion. This was practiced until the 11th cent. when Gregory VII changed it to a day of abstinence. The Gallican rites do not seem to have observed this day of penance. The practice of Saturday abstinence was continued by some religious rules and also as part of Marian devotions. Until recent calendar reform, Saturday was also one of the *Ember Days and was also linked with Friday during Lent (CIC, c. 1252.2).

[J. DALLEN]

SATURNALIA, a Roman festival (Dec. 17–23) celebrated in honor of Saturn, who may have originally been an old Italic god of sowing or the Greek god Kronos imported into Rome by way of Etruria. The *Saturnalia,* which were a kind of ancient carnival and the merriest season of the year, marked the close of the year's labors. There was a cessation of public business, a sacrifice to Saturn at his temple near the Capitoline, public and private feasting, an exchange of gifts, and a general spirit of license and revelry. During this time slaves were permitted to do as they liked and could even exchange places with their masters. Though the early Christians frowned upon the excesses of the feast, some of its features passed over into their own celebration of the feast of Christmas. BIBLIOGRAPHY: H. J. Rose, OCD 797.

[M. J. COSTELLOE]

SATURNINUS OF ANTIOCH, 2d-cent. Syrian Gnostic, supposed to have taught at Antioch. His followers believed that the world and man were created by angels, who were themselves the creatures of the supreme, unknowable God. As first created, man could only crawl along the ground until the Supreme God, taking pity, gave him a divine spark to stand him on his feet. Christ's purpose in coming was to destroy both bad angels (among whom was the god of Jews) and bad men, and to save the good by releasing their sparks of divinity from the flesh created by the angels. They appear to have rejected marriage and the use of animal food. BIBLIOGRAPHY: Irenaeus, *Adv. haeres.* 1, 24; Hippolytus, *Philosophoumena* or *refutatio omnium haeresium* (EnchPatr 9, 397; Pseudo-Tertullian, *Advers. omn. haer.* 1; Epiphanius, *Haeres.,* 23 (ed. Hool) 1:247–256; Quasten 1:255, 289.

[R. B. ENO]

SATYRUS OF MILAN, ST. (d. *c.*379), elder brother of St. Ambrose. Born probably at Trier before 340, S. was educated at Rome with Ambrose after the death of their father in 354. He became a lawyer and held public office, but upon the election of Ambrose to the See of Milan he quit his post and went to Milan to help administer the episcopal temporalities. After his death at Milan, Ambrose on the occasion of his funeral preached a sermon that is considered a masterpiece of its kind. BIBLIOGRAPHY: CSEL 73:207–251; Butler 3:578.

[R. B. ENO]

SAUDI ARABIA, W Asian monarchy (925,000 sq mi; pop., 1973 est., 8,100,000). Until 1918 Saudi Arabia was part of the Ottoman Empire. Ten years later Ibn Saud proclaimed himself king. The constitution expressly forbids evangelization. There are about 10,000 Catholics, all foreigners. Saudi Arabia is part of the Vicariate Apostolic of Aden. Protestant mission work was begun in the latter part of the 19th century. The American Reformed Church, the Keith-Falconer Mission, Danish Lutherans, Presbyterians, and the Sudan Interior Mission are also represented, mainly by medical services. BIBLIOGRAPHY: *Bilan du Monde* 2:87–90.

[P. DAMBORIENA]

SAUDREAU, AUGUSTE (1859–1946), spiritual writer. A parish priest of France, S. wrote many ascetical works, among them *L'État mystique* (1903), *Manuel de spiritualité* (1917), *La Spiritualité moderne* (1940), and *Idéal de l'âme fervente* (1920).

[J. R. AHERNE]

SAUL, first king of Israel, r. *c.* 1020–1000 B.C. (1 Sam 9–31). Son of a wealthy Benjaminite named Kish (1 Chr 8.33), he was anointed king by the prophet Samuel to lead Israel against the Philistines (1 Sam 9.16; 10.19; 11.15). When he did not carry out Samuel's instructions regarding the Amalekites, however, Samuel announced that Yahweh had rejected him (1 Sam 15). At first attracted by David's gifts as a musician (1 Sam 16.23) and warrior (1 Sam 18.5),

S. later became jealous of David's popularity (1 Sam 18.7–9). To avoid being killed by the Philistines at Mt. Gilboa, he fell on his own sword (1 Sam 31). His son Ish-bosheth succeeded him for 2 years before David became king (2 Sam 2.10). Saul was also the Jewish name of St. *Paul (see Acts 7.58 and 13.9).

[T. EARLY]

SAUTER, BENEDIKT (Roman; 1835–1908), liturgist. A German ordained in 1858, S. served as court chaplain to the Duchess Katherine of Hohenzollern. In 1861 he joined the Benedictines, took the name Roman, studied at the Abbey of Solesmes where his teachers were Dom Guéranger and Dom Pothier, pioneers in the liturgical movement and the revival of Gregorian chant. In 1863 S. went to Beuron Abbey where he taught Gregorian chant. He was exiled from Beuron during the Kulturkampf. He was in 1885 named first reform abbot of Emaus, Prague; under his direction it became the center of the forces fighting the *Los-von-Rom movement. Among his published works were *Choir and Liturgy* (1865), *Holy Sacrifice of the Mass* (1894), and *Liturgical Choir* (1903).

[J. R. AHERNE]

SAUVÉ, CHARLES (1848–1925), Sulpician spiritual writer. Basing his work on Thomistic theologians and Scripture scholars, S. published numerous works of spirituality in the Sulpician tradition. His ascetical works are distinguished for theological precision and simplicity, if not for style. His approach was affective and warmly communicative. Typical of his outlook is the word "intimate," which carries through all the titles of his widely influential books, published between 1901 and 1924. Among his publications were: *Dieu intime: La Sainte Trinité; Jésus intime* (3 v.); *Marie intime; L'Eucharistie intime* (2 v.), and *Le religieux intime* (2 v.).

[J. R. AHERNE]

SAUVECANNE (SILVACANE), ABBEY OF, French Cistercian monastery near Aix, founded in 1147 by monks of Morimond. Its rapid growth facilitated the foundation of Valsainte near Apt (1188). The sack of Sauvecanne in 1358 destroyed its prosperity. In the 15th cent. it came under commendatory rule and its goods were transferred (1444) to the cathedral chapter of Aix. The remarkable Gothic church thenceforth served the local parish. BIBLIOGRAPHY: A. Dimier, *L'Art cistercien* (1962), 267–275; L. J. Lekai, NCE 12:1102

[L. J. LEKAI]

SAVA (SABAS) OF SERBIA, ST. (c.1174–1235), the organizer and patron of the Serbian Church. (See SERBIAN ORTHODOX CHURCH OR PATRIARCHATE.) Rastko, the son of the Serbian prince Stephen I Nemanja, became a monk on Mt. Athos, taking the name of Sava (Sabas). In 1195 his father abdicated, and the two of them founded the Serbian monastery of Chilandar on Mt. Athos. S.'s older brother,

*Stephen II Nemanja, received recognition as king from the pope. In 1208 S. returned to Serbia, later receiving from the Byzantine emperor and patriarch the approval to establish an autocephalous Church in Serbia, and was consecrated its first abp. (1219). After founding bishoprics, monasteries, and schools and placing the Church on a solid basis, Sava resigned in 1233 and died 3 years later. BIBLIOGRAPHY: J. Matl. LTK 9:350; Butler 1:86–87; I. Dujčev, BiblSanct 11:522–529.

[G. T. DENNIS]

SAVARIC OF BATH (d. 1205), bp. of Bath and Glastonbury. He obtained the bishopric of Bath, through Richard I's favor while on the Third Crusade (1192) with him. Afterward he negotiated with Emperor Henry VI for Richard's release from captivity (1193–94). Brutal and unscrupulous, he annexed Glastonbury Abbey to his bishopric over the monks' strong resistance. BIBLIOGRAPHY: F. Courtney, NCE 12:1103.

[R. W. HAYS]

SAVELLI, Roman noble family, one of the oldest and for 5 cent. one of the four most famous families in Rome. The last of the line was Giulio Savelli, who died in 1712. Some of the well-known members are Pope *Honorius III (1219–27) whose father Aimerico was the first known to bear the name; Pope Honorius IV (1285–87); seven cardinals, among whom are Silvio (1596–99), Giulio (1615–44), and Fabrizio (1647–59). Giacomo (1539–87), one of the most competent cardinals of his time, had wide experience in various dioceses and was instrumental in carrying out the reforms of the Council of Trent. In the Guelf-Ghibelline struggle, the Savelli were generally Ghibelline. In 1596 one of the Savelli villages, Castel Gandolfo, was sold to the papacy. The office of custodian of the conclave was assigned to the Savelli by Pope Paul III. BIBLIOGRAPHY: M. L. Shay, NCE 12:1103.

[G. E. CONWAY]

SAVIGNAC, MARIE RAPHAEL (1874–1951), French Dominican. S. spent a lifetime in biblical studies in Jerusalem; his principal work was *Mission archéologique en Arabie* (1914).

[J. R. AHERNE]

SAVIGNEY, FRIEDRICH KARL VON (1779–1861), historian of law. A native of Germany, S. was a pioneer in the history of Roman law. His work *Right of Property* (1803) provided a fresh approach to the subject; and in *Juridical Methodology* he presented the theory that jurisprudence is a natural science, unrelated to the concept of natural law. S. regarded law as springing from inner ethnic forces, not the notions of the legislator. He founded the journal *Zeitschrift für geschichtliche Rechtswissenschaft* in 1815, a new departure in legal journalism. The six-volume *History of Roman Law in the Middle Ages* (1815–31) became a classic. From 1840 to 1848 S. was minister for legislation of Prussia. He published in 1848 and 1849 *System of Present-Day Law* in eight volumes.

[J. R. AHERNE]

SAVIGNY, ABBEY OF, a monastery in the diocese of Avranches, France, started *c.* 1105 by the hermit Vitalis (d. 1122), a follower of Robert of Arbrissel. Within a few years the abbey adopted the Benedictine Rule, with Vitalis as abbot of the growing community. The foundation proved to be so successful that under the second abbot, Godfrey (1122–39), 32 other monasteries accepted the same regulations and placed themselves under the control of Savigny. Similarities between Savigny and Cîteaux were so close that in 1147 the third abbot, Serlo (1139–58), joined his congregation to the Cistercians. Savigny continued to flourish till it was sacked in the Hundred Years War. Reconstruction was hampered by commendatory abbots (after 1517) and the wars of the 16th century. In 1676 the abbey joined the Cistercian Strict Observance but was suppressed in 1791 in the Revolution. BIBLIOGRAPHY: L. J. Lekai, NCE 12:1104; B. Griesser, LTK 9:352.

[L. J. LEKAI]

SAVIO, DOMINIC, ST. (1842–57), an example of youthful sanctity. He was born in Riva di Chieri near Turin, one of the ten children of a blacksmith. For 3 years he was a pupil in the school founded by Don Bosco in Turin. S. was noted for his cheerful disposition, mature personality, and devotion to the Eucharist. Frail in health, he died at the age of 15. Don Bosco was greatly impressed by the boy's spirituality and wrote his biography. S. was canonized in 1954 by Pius XII. BIBLIOGRAPHY: J. Bosco, *Life of St. Dominic Savio* (tr. P. Aronica, 1955); E. Valentini, BiblSanct 4:741–743.

[E. A. CARRILLO]

SAVIOR, a biblical and religious title referring to the one true God, who manifested himself as Israel's deliverer and protector from all its enemies and to his Son, Jesus Christ, who became man to deliver mankind from sin and death. The title was also applied to the gods of paganism, especially the healing gods, and to Roman or Hellenistic emperors who were looked upon as divinities who brought both temporal protection against external enemies and spiritual favors from the gods who controlled the forces of nature.

As a Christian term, the title is applied esp. to Christ, whose name Jesus signifies that he is the one born to save mankind from its sins (Mt 1.21). Jesus Christ is the center and focus of the true God's intervention in man's history to bring man back to himself by being delivered up to death for the remission of sin and rising from the dead for man's justification and reconciliation with God (Rom 4.25).

Jesus Christ is eminently suited for this work as savior of mankind because he is a Divine Person. Possessing a visible human nature, he is Son of God. Jesus is God in a human way and man in a divine way, and therefore his human actions as actions of a Divine Person can be effective of man's salvation because they have divine saving value. They are the acts of the Son of God. Although every human act of Jesus Christ has divine saving power, mankind's salvation from sin and death is realized in a special way in the great mysteries of his life: his death, Resurrection, and Ascension, which taken together constitute the single mystery of salvation. St. Paul and St. John, each in his unique way, link these events together as the total saving act. They establish Christ as Lord and become the actual condition for Christ's sending the Holy Spirit (from the Father) into this world for the salvation of all men and the whole of creation as well.

Biblical witness brings to light the dynamic impact of the Resurrection and the Ascension as necessary and essential aspects of Christ's saving action. The scholarly work of F. X. Durrwell, L. Cerfaux, S. Lyonnet, and P. Benoit has put in relief the biblical message that Christ as Savior brings about a rebirth of mankind from the death of sin to a new life in Jesus Christ, the risen Savior. Jesus conquered Satan in his own Person (Jn 12.31–32), but the working out of that victory in time, the salvation of the world for Christ, is the work of the Church (Jn 17.15–18; Jn 15.4). This new life, given to men through the Spirit present now in the Church because of Christ's personal victory as man over sin and death, has become the motivating power moving men from within to acts of love and service for God and neighbor, with a hope for final victory firmly rooted in the risen glory of Christ's humanity. BIBLIOGRAPHY: L. Cerfaux, *Christ in the Theology of St. Paul* (tr. G. Webb and A. Walker, 1959); F. X. Durrwell, *Resurrection* (tr. R. Sheed, 1960); P. Benoit, "L'Ascension," RevBibl 56 (1949) 161–203; S. Lyonnet, "Redemption through Death and Resurrection," *Contemporary New Testament Studies* (ed. M. R. Ryan, 1965).

[J. C. MURRAY]

SAVIOR, DIALOGUE OF THE, see APOCRYPHA (NT), 59.

SAVOLDO, GIOVANNI GIROLAMO (1485–1548), Venetian painter from Brescia, whose hard shapes in light in the manner of Cima and Vivarini, are termed "Lombard" as distinct from the Giorgionesque atmospheric style. S.'s *Hermits* and *The Temptations of St. Anthony* show Flemish motifs while the *Shepherd* and *St. Jerome* (1520s) are more atmospheric as in Giorgione and Titian, the color giving form. In *St. George, Tobias and the Angel, Matthew and the Angel,* S. begins to exploit his distinctive nocturnal settings—the dark environment effecting a continuity of mass and void. S. painted many versions of *Mary Magdalene* and the *Nativity* but was unsuccessful in Venice because of the popularity of Titian's style. BIBLIOGRAPHY: A. Boschetto, *Giovanni Girolamo Savoldo* (1963).

[M. J. DALY]

SAVONAROLA, GIROLAMO (1452–98), priest, reformer. Born of a successful middle class family, S. was originally destined for a medical career. Without warning, however, he suddenly abandoned his studies and entered the Dominican convent at Bologna (1475). Some years later (1482) he was assigned to lecture in theology at the Dominican convent of San Marco in Florence where, except for a 4-year period (1486–90), he remained for the rest of his life. In 1490, because of the intervention of Lorenzo de' Medici, the ruler of Florence, S. was returned to Florence and began a series of sermons attacking the licentiousness and the corruption of life and morals there. The sermons won him a wide following among the people. His fellow Dominicans, equally impressed by S., elected him prior of San Marco in 1491. Implementation of the reforms which he demanded clearly required the use of force, and when Charles VIII of France invaded Italy (1494), S. saw in him the divinely ordained vehicle for the reform of the Church, esp. the papacy, and also of Florence. This position placed him in direct conflict with the Pope, Alexander VI, and with the Medici family. With the ouster of the Medici from Florence in the face of the French invasion, S. became virtual dictator of the city. For 4 years he headed the city, putting into practice the reforms which he had preached. His identification with the French placed him in an exposed position, however, and after their withdrawal from the city he came under ever-increasing attack, both from supporters of the Medici and from the papacy. Eventually, Alexander VI excommunicated him (May 13, 1497) for his attacks on the authority of the pope. With his power waning, Savonarola agreed to test the authenticity of his mission by undergoing an ordeal by fire. After several false starts and disagreements over the details of the ordeal, he refused to participate and thereby lost most of his remaining support. His enemies arranged for a public trial at which he was found guilty and condemned to death. Savonarola's career is difficult to evaluate. An austere preacher of reform and a Florentine patriot, S. desired the re-establishment of the Republic. On balance, however, he would seem to be a last burst of the medieval style of Church reform and not, as some have argued, the first stage of the Protestant Reformation. BIBLIOGRAPHY: Pastor 5,6; R. Ridolfi, *Life of Girolamo Savonarola* (tr. C. Grayson, 1959).

[J. MULDOON]

SAVOY DECLARATION, a *doctrinal standard and statement of *polity for Congregationalism. In 1658 an assembly was held at the Savoy Palace, London. Attending the meeting were 200 ministers and laymen representing 120 independent, or congregational, churches in England. The statement it prepared was accepted without dispute. The assembly expressed its joy in the fact that the churches, though separate and independent, had preserved through troubled times so close a uniformity of faith and practice. The doctrinal part—the Declaration of Faith in 32 articles—was almost word for word a reproduction of the *Westminster Confession of 1647. It was made plain, however, that it was not to be imposed upon any. Appended to the Declaration of Faith were 30 propositions: "Of the Institution of Churches and the Order appointed in them by Jesus Christ." This is a compact presentation of the principles of Congregationalism (see GATHERED CHURCH), agreed on after almost a century of experiment and experience. The principles were: the headship of Christ only; the constitution of the local Church by the union of believers; its complete autonomy; its right to choose and ordain the officers appointed by Christ; the necessity of a call from a Church to confer ministerial standing; the consent of the brethren as essential to all admissions and censures; and synods and councils for advice but without judicial authority. In England the Savoy Declaration, as it came to be called, was soon largely lost in events, but it was adopted in Mass. (1680) and in Conn. was incorporated into the *Saybrook Platform (1708). BIBLIOGRAPHY: A. G. Mathews, *Savoy Declaration of Faith and Order* (1959); Schaff Creeds 1:822–833; 3:707–729.

[R. F. G. CALDER]

SAXO GRAMMATICUS (mid-12th–early 13th cent.), a writer of a warrior family who composed the *Gesta Danorum* in 16 books at the suggestion of Absalon of Lund (1178–1201). Books 1–9 cover the period of 60 legendary Danish kings, his sources being Old Danish ballads. As he approaches his own time (books 14–16), it becomes a truly historical work. The importance of Saxo lies in the sagas which he tells about, which were lost in Iceland, and the differences between the Icelandic and Danish versions can be seen.

[R. T. MEYER]

SAXON CONFESSION, a Lutheran *confession of faith prepared by P. *Melanchthon in 1551. Melanchthon wrote it more to fulfill the Emperor's request for a document to be presented at the Council of *Trent than out of conviction that any rapprochement with Rome could be reached. The Saxon Confession was entitled in the original MS, *Repetitio confessionis Augustanae;* it did follow the plan of the *Augsburg Confession, but was more explicit in its rejection of Roman teaching. The delegation to Trent was fruitless. The Saxon Confession was not included in the *Book of Concord. BIBLIOGRAPHY: Schaff Creeds 1:340–343. *WÜRTTEMBERG CONFESSION.

[T. C. O'BRIEN]

SAXONS, a Germanic people distinguished from the other Germanic tribes by their long retention of paganism, their primitive customs, and their loose political federation. Ptolemy, in the 2nd cent. A.D., located them in an area perhaps to be identified with present-day Holstein. In the 4th and 5th cent. they moved west and southwest, gradually occupying the N coast of Gaul and the S coast of Britain, *litora Saxonica*, while at the same time extending their control of NW Germany from the Elbe to the Ems and southward to Hesse and Thuringia. Their history is marked by stubborn resistance to the Franks, who finally defeated them in a struggle initiated by Charlemagne in 772–776 and concluded in 803. Their introduction to Christianity, which belongs mainly to this period, inspired a major literary work, the Old Saxon *Heliand.* The relationship of these Old (continental) Saxons to the Saxons who invaded Britain (*c.*450) with the Angles and Jutes has not been determined. BIBLIOGRAPHY: J. W. Thompson, *Feudal Germany* (1928); F. S. Lear, NCE 12:1109.

[M. F. MCCARTHY]

SAYBROOK PLATFORM, a declaration of faith and polity approved by a synod of Congregationalists at Saybrook, Conn., in Sept. 1708. The document was approved by the general assembly of the colony in October and published in 1710. The confession of faith was the adaptation of the *Westminster Confession contained in the *Savoy Declaration (1658). Fifteen articles on polity created agencies to oversee the local Churches, a departure toward a presbyterian form of government.

[T. C. O'BRIEN]

SAYCE, ARCHIBALD HENRY (1845–1933), English Orientalist and archeologist. He was elected fellow of Queen's College, Oxford, in 1869, and was ordained in the Church of England in 1870. From 1891 he was a professor at Oxford; from 1898–1919 he was president of the Society of Biblical Archeology. S. shared in the preparation of the OT books for the Revised Standard Version of the Bible. From 1878 he was engaged in periodic archeological research in the Middle East. In 1882 he published a landmark work in the *Journal of the Royal Asiatic Society,* the deciphering of the ancient Armenian inscriptions at Van. In Egypt he helped found the Alexandria Museum. He played a major role in the excavations of Meroe, ancient capital of Ethiopia. His *Assyrian Grammar* (1872) and *Lectures on the Assyrian Language and Syllabary* (1877) facilitated study of that language. Other works include: *Principles of Comparative Philology* (1874–75); *Introduction to the Science of Language* (2v., 1880); *Higher Criticism and the Verdict of the Monuments (1894),* which defended Mosaic authorship of the Pentateuch.

[J. R. AHERNE]

SAYER, ROBERT GREGORY (Seare, Sayr, Saire, Sario, Sarius; 1560–1602), English-born Benedictine, moral theologian. He left Cambridge in 1582 when he was denied his degree because of papist leanings and went to the English colleges, first at Rheims and then at Rome. Ordained (1585), he became a Benedictine at Monte Cassino (1588) where he subsequently taught moral philosophy. In 1595 he was sent to Venice. His major theological works expounded moral principles through casuistry and earned him a reputation among contemporary moralists. They include: *De sacramentis in communi* (1599); *Thesaurus casuum conscientiae* (1601); and *Clavis regia sacerdotum casuum conscientiae* (1605).

[R. J. LITZ]

SAYERS, DOROTHY LEIGH (1893–1957), English writer. The daughter of an Anglican clergyman, she studied at Somerville College, Oxford, graduating in 1915. In 1926 she married Capt. Atherton Fleming (d. 1950). She established her reputation with a number of detective novels, but with the outbreak of World War II began to concentrate on religious themes. She published a translation of Dante's *Inferno* (1940) and a series of essays on him (1954). In 1941 she published *Mind of the Maker,* a study of the creative writing process as analogous to relationships within the Trinity. Especially popular was *The Man Born to Be King* (1943), a series of radio plays on the life of Christ. An Anglo-Catholic, she was generally identified with the circle that included C. S. Lewis and T. S. Eliot.

[T. EARLY]

SAYINGS OF JESUS, see LOGIA OF JESUS.

SBARAGLIA, GIOVANNI GIACINTO (SBARALEA 1687–1764), historian, Franciscan Conventual. His most important historical contribution was the 734-page *Supplementum* to Wadding's *Scriptores.* It lists 3,583 Franciscan authors as opposed to Wadding's list of 1,919 (3 v., 1806; 2d ed., 1908–36). Sbaraglia also edited the *Bullarium franciscanum* for the years 1218 to 1304 (4 v., 1759–68). He left many unpublished manuscripts. BIBLIOGRAPHY: H. Le May, "History of Franciscan Bibliography," *Franciscan Educational Conference* 16(1934) 149–174; A. Teetaert, DTC 14.1:1242–46; J. J. Smith, NCE 12:1110.

[J. J. SMITH]

SCALA SANCTA, in Rome across from the Lateran Palace, the holy stairs, a place of pilgrimage and of the penitential practice of ascending the 28 stairs on one's knees. They are of Tyrian marble, but covered with wood; there is a staircase on either side for the descent (legend has it that Martin Luther started the ascent but turned round and became the only one ever to walk down the Scala Sancta). The stairs lead to the former papal chapel of San Lorenzo. An 8th- or 9th-cent. legend identifies them as the stairs of Pilate's praetorium brought to Rome by St. Helena. They were the ceremonial staircase in the original Lateran Palace. *Pius IX made the ascent on his knees on Sept. 20, 1870, the night he lost Rome and retired to become the "prisoner of the Vatican."

[T. C. O'BRIEN]

SCALABRINI, GIOVANNI BATTISTA (1839–1905), religious founder. An Italian ordained in 1863, he served as rector of the seminary in Como from 1867 to 1870. S. was a forward-looking thinker on social and political matters and an authority on the *Roman Question. Named bp. of Piacenza in 1875, he reorganized catechetical instruction throughout Italy, establishing the first national Catechetical Congress. In 1887 S. founded the Pious Society of the Missionaries of St. Charles, popularly called the Scalabrini Fathers, to serve Italian immigrants throughout the world. He founded also the Missionary sisters of St. Charles Borromeo to do similar work.

[J. R. AHERNE]

SCALABRINIANS, or the Pious Society of the Missionaries of St. Charles as it is officially entitled. It has as its purpose, besides the personal sanctification of its members, the spiritual and social care of Italian immigrants. It was founded in 1887 by John Baptist Scalabrini, Bishop of Piacenza. The rule was approved in 1888 and the constitutions in 1948. Not only did Scalabrini found the society of the Missionaries of St. Charles but he established the Missionary Sisters of St. Charles and cofounded the Zelatrices of the Sacred Heart. His missions extended to the U.S., Brazil, Canada, Argentina, Chile, Venezuela, Uruguay, Belgium, France, Germany, Switzerland, Luxemburg, England, Australia, and Algiers, where parishes, schools, orphanages and homes for the aged were established. In 1975 the Scalabrinians numbered 752 of whom 598 were priests in 240 houses.

[R. C. CLIGGETT]

SCALIGER, JULIUS CAESAR AND JOSEPH JUSTUS. (1) **Julius Caesar** (1484–1558), classical scholar and natural scientist. He spent his early years in the service of Emperor Maximilian I and later studied medicine and natural science at Bologna (1514–19). As the personal physician to the bishop of Agen, he became a devoted humanist. His contributions to the literary world are in two completely different areas: science (botany and zoology) and letters (grammar and literary criticism). A pure Latinist, Scaliger attacked Erasmus and Lorenzo Valla for inferior style in *Oratio pro Cicerone contra Erasmum* (1531) and *De causis linguae latinae libri XIII* (1540). He also translated the *Natural History* of Aristotle into Latin and wrote a treatise on botany, *Animadversiones in IV libros de causis plantarum theophrasti* (1566).

(2) **Joseph Justus** (1540–1609), philologist and scholar, was the tenth child of Julius Caesar Scaliger. His education included the study of Latin, Greek, and Oriental languages and later the study of ancient history. Under the partronage of Louis Chastaigner de la Toche Pozay, he traveled widely and was converted to Protestantism. From 1593 until his death, he occupied the chair of history at the University of Leiden, the foremost Protestant seat of learning. His *Thesaurus temporum*, a reconstruction of the ancient system of chronology, established Scaliger as one of the founders of historical scholarship. BIBLIOGRAPHY: *Autobiography of Joseph Scaliger* (ed. and tr. G. W. Robinson, 1927).

[D. G. NUGENT]

SCAMNUM, the bench in the sanctuary for the seating of the presiding minister(s) at a liturgical rite (see SEDILIA). The more usual furnishing in the revised liturgy is a chair for the "president of the assembly," where he sits during the readings.

SCANDAL, (Gr. *skandalon,* stumbling block), the sin, contrary to *charity, of occasioning another person's spiritual harm or ruin. Sometimes the term also refers to the objective act or conduct involved in the sin; of any shocking way of acting; or of malicious gossip. The sin itself offends against the love of neighbor as this is bent on willing grace and goodness to others as God himself does. Scandal is the willful intent to cause or the culpable failure to prevent a word or external act that will lead to the complete opposite. Scandal is said to occasion another's downfall on the grounds that no human being can directly move the will of another to commit sin; but the occasioning is a strong inducement. Because of the supremacy of charity in Christian life, and because of the close interaction prevailing in human affairs, theology makes precisions about the meaning of scandal. Active scandal is the sin of the perpetrator; passive scandal is the reaction of the victim. To be a serious sin, active scandal must at least by intent be an inducement with regard to another's serious sin. Passive scandal, however, is not an automatic reaction: thus there can be scandal given without scandal being taken. Conversely, there can be scandal effected without true scandal being given. This implies that an act perfectly good in itself is maliciously misconstrued. That possibility is reckoned with through the distinction between the scandal of the Pharisees (Mt 15.12), and the scandal of the innocent. The first is a sin completely on the part of the one taking scandal: it is the hypocritical shock at and the evil misrepresentation of another's good action, prompted by hatred or envy of the person acting or by opposition to the good he does. The scandal of the innocent, on the other hand, is due to their naiveté, youth, lack of education, or of strongly developed moral judgment. The sensitivity of charity towards these "little ones" sometimes dictates omitting or delaying a word or an act that might have for them the semblance of wrong, or that they might wrongly interpret. This presupposes that the word or act can be put off without sin; if that is not the case, explanation or other steps should be undertaken out of concern for those who might misunderstand.

[T. C. O'BRIEN]

SCANDERBEG (GEORGE CASTRIOTA; 1403–68), Albanian prince and patriot. Given as hostage to the Turks, S. was reared in the Islamic faith in Constantinople. (*Iskander bej*, the Turkish original of "Scanderbeg," means "Prince Alexander.") In 1443, he escaped to Albania and declared himself Christian. For 24 years he opposed the Turks. When he died, his principate came under Turkish dominion. BIBLIOGRAPHY: J. Papin, NCE 12:1113; DE 3:735–736.

[F. D. LAZENBY]

SCANDICUS, a neume in Gregorian chant notation signifying a succession of three or more notes ascending in pitch. See also *SALICUS.

[A. DOHERTY]

SCANLAN, LAWRENCE (1843–1915), first bp. of Salt Lake City, missionary. A native of Ireland and ordained there in 1868, he came to San Francisco in that same year. S. labored in the city, in a mining camp at Pioche, Nev., and at Petaluma, California. Wherever he went, enduring great hardships on the rough frontier, he won the admiration of all for his integrity and compassion. He undertook mission work in Ogden and Salt Lake City, Utah, where his territory covered 85,000 square miles. His relations with the Mormons were cordial. Named vicar-apostolic of Utah and part of Nevada in 1887, he became first bp. of Salt Lake City in 1891. In his 24 years as head of the diocese he built more than 30 churches, including the cathedral, founded All Hallows College, 4 academies operated by the Holy Cross Sisters, 2 hospitals, an orphanage, and a house for aged and injured miners. He was active also in Utah and Western-state affairs.

[J. R. AHERNE]

SCAPEGOAT, term used in the King James and Douay Versions of the Bible for the goat sent into the wilderness to or for *Azazel on the Day of Atonement (Lev 16.8, 10, 26). One goat was killed and its blood sprinkled on the mercy seat as a sin offering (Lev 16.15). The high priest laid his hands on the head of the other goat, confessing the sins of the people, and sent it, accompanied by an attendant, into the wilderness (Lev 16.20–22). The Vulgate, which, following the LXX, had the term *caper emissarius,* emissary goat, accounts for the English escaping goat, or scapegoat.

[T. EARLY]

SCAPULAR, a length of cloth about shoulder width worn over the shoulder front and back as part of some religious habits. It originated as a sort of work apron worn by the monks. Sometimes made with two traverse pieces of cloth under the arms, it came to symbolize the cross or the yoke of Christ. By the 11th cent. it was beginning to be incorporated in the full monastic habit and eventually became part of the habit for those orders originating in the medieval period as well as for some later religious congregations. As third orders for the laity developed, the tertiaries were invested with some part of the habit, usually the scapular though reduced in size, as a mark of affiliation with the order. By the early 16th cent., a still smaller version (cloth pieces usually less than two or three inches square) came into use as a mark of membership in certain religious confraternities or of dedication to some special object of devotion. The small scapular normally bore an image of Our Lady or a particular saint, or some emblem of the devotion, e.g., the Sacred Heart or the Passion, to which the wearer was committed. A wide variety of small scapulars have since come into existence. Inasmuch as it is generally a manifestation of wholesome disposition of mind and heart and symbolizes a fellowship with others in dedication to a worthy cause, the wearing of the scapular has been a revered practice among the faithful in the RC Church. Perhaps the most popular is the Carmelite scapular. According to legend, Our Lady appeared to St. Simon Stock in 1251, giving him the scapular and promising salvation for those who wore it and liberation from purgatory on the first Saturday after death. The authenticity of the apparition is disputed and, if accepted, the promises are to be understood in terms of the right dispositions of soul to which the wearing of the scapular should attest. BIBLIOGRAPHY: F. Béringer, *Les Indulgences: Leur nature et leur usage* (tr. P. Mazayer, 2 v., 4th ed., 1925) bibliog. and list of small scapulars; C. Ceroke, "Credibility of the Scapular Promise," *Carmelus* 11 (1964) 81–123; P. Zammit, NCE 12:1114–16.

[J. C. WILLKE]

SCARAB (Latin *scarabaeus,* the Egyptian dung-beetle), a small representation of the Egyptian sacred beetle, usually of semi-precious stone, with an inscription on the flat side, sometimes used as a seal, but far more often as an amulet. Its form was determined by the ancient use of the dung-beetle as a symbol of the sun god, Re, because the young dung-beetles come forth, seemingly without generation, from a ball of dung, just as Re brought himself into being. BIBLIOGRAPHY: J. Pieper, PW 3A:447–459.

[A. CODY]

SCARAMELLI, GIOVANNI BATTISTA (1687–1752), Italian Jesuit spiritual writer. A member of the Society from 1706 and ordained in 1717, he taught philosophy briefly, but in 1722 began his real life's work, preaching parish missions and closed retreats throughout the Papal States. His biography of a nun-mystic published in 1750 was put on the Index in 1769 because of its unqualified claims to the sainthood of its subject. All S.'s other works were published posthumously. The most widely read of them is *Il direttorio ascetico* (2 v., 1754) on the ascetical life necessary to begin spiritual progress, esp. the life of the virtues. Its many editions and translations include eight in English. The most profound, as well as the most controversial, of his works is *Il direttorio mistico* (1754). The work is important for its descriptions of mystical contemplation and its counsels to spiritual directors in their guidance of those aspiring to mystical contemplation. Points of the work that have been challenged by other spiritual theologians are that only the ascetical life, not the life of either acquired or infused contemplation, is normal and ordinary for the Christian; the mystical life is de jure extraordinary; also that the distinction between acquired and infused contemplation is one only of degree of intensity.

[T. C. O'BRIEN]

SCARAMPI, PIER FRANCESCO (1596–1656), Italian Oratorian, papal envoy (1645–47) under Urban VIII to the

Catholic Confederacy of Ireland, whose aim was to secure from Charles I freedom for Catholics to practice their religion publicly. Under Innocent X he remained in Ireland as adviser to his successor G. B. Rinuccini. Then he returned to Rome (1647), frustrated at factionalism within the Confederacy and the compromising policies of Rinuccini. He brought back to Rome as a seminarian Oliver *Plunkett. S. was superior of the Roman Oratory when he succumbed in an epidemic while ministering to the victims.

[T. C. O'BRIEN]

SCARLATTI, ALESSANDRO (1660–1725), Italian composer. S. studied under G. *Carissimi in Rome in 1672 and probably under masters in N Italy. His first known opera *Gli equivoci nel semibiante* (produced in 1679) gained him the patronage of Queen Christina of Sweden, then in exile in Rome. From 1684 to 1702 he was musical director to the court of Naples where, except for periods of employment at Rome (*maestro di capella* at Sta. Maria Maggiore) and at Florence, he spent the greater part of his life. He composed more than 115 operas, of which *Mitridate Eupatore* (1707) is considered his finest, six Masses, sacred motets, and almost 700 chamber cantatas that represent his highest artistic achievement.

SCARLATTI, DOMENICO (1685–1757), composer and harpsichord virtuoso, son of Alessandro. He served as *maestro* to Queen Maria Casimera of Poland, later as *maestro di cappella* of the Vatican. In 1719 S. went to Lisbon as *maestro* of the royal chapel and teacher of Princess Maria Barbara, who in 1746 became Queen of Spain and appointed S. *maestro de cámara*. S. composed over 600 pieces for the harpsichord, a number of operas, cantatas, and sacred works. He introduced a new style to music for the harpsichord, based on keen study of the instrument and its special capabilities. S. is regarded as the founder of modern piano techniques.

[J. R. AHERNE]

SCAVINI, PIETRO (1791–1869), theologian. A canon of the cathedral of Novara, Italy, S. wrote a theological work widely used, *Theologia moralis universa ad mentem S. Alphonsi* (4 v., 1841), which took a position on *probabilism widely contested.

[J. R. AHERNE]

SCETE, the desolate SW section of the Nitrian desert, to the W of the Nile Delta. During the 4th and 5th cent., S. was a place where the most rigorous forms of Egyptian monasticism were practiced. Among famous monks who lived there are *Macarius the Egyptian and *Evagrius Ponticus.

[R. B. ENO]

SCÈVE, MAURICE (*c.*1510–*c.*60), French humanist poet. After reputedly discovering the tomb of Petrarch's

Laura at Avignon (1533), S. became a leader of the Lyonese school of Renaissance writers. His work reflects Italian, humanistic, and Petrarchan influences as well as vestiges of scholasticism and medieval rhetoric, so that he represents the transition of French poetry from Marot to the Pléiade. His *Délie, objet de plus haute vertu* (1544), is inspired by the contemporary Neoplatonic concept of love and "the ideal" (Délie is an anagram of "l'Idée"). His less-known epic, *Microcosme* (1562), optimistically praises human progress since Adam's fall. BIBLIOGRAPHY: J. P. Attal, *Maurice Scève* (1963).

[R. N. NICOLICH]

SCHADOW, WILHELM VON (1788–1862), German painter, son of sculptor Gottfried S. In Rome S. joined the Nazarenes (St. Luke Brotherhood, 1813) collaborating on frescoes. Returning to Berlin (1819) S. spread the romantic theories of the Nazarenes. See NAZARENES.

[M. J. DALY]

SCHAEPMAN, HERMAN (1844–1903), Dutch priest, poet, orator, statesman. Ordained in 1867, S. was cofounder of the periodical *De Wächter*. His fame as a poet was widespread, especially after publication of his great work *Aya Sofia* (1886). His prose writings were published under the title *Menschen en Boeken* (5 v., 1893–1902). As an orator S. had no equal in Holland. His political influence was great and exercised on behalf of Catholics, who were not given favorable treatment in 19th-cent. Holland. In 1883 he announced a campaign for Catholic emancipation but did not receive much support from fellow-Catholics. S. was the first priest to be elected to the States-General (parliament) and he was largely responsible for the reform of the school law. His major achievement was an alliance forged between Catholics and antirevolutionists, with consequent increased political strength for the Catholics.

[J. R. AHERNE]

SCHAFF, PHILIP (1819–93), *Reformed Church theologian and church historian. Born in poverty at Chur, Switzerland, S. won scholarships to finance his education. He studied a Tübingen, Halle, and Berlin and became a *Privatdocent* at the Univ. of Berlin in 1843. At Berlin, J. A. W. Neander influenced his theories of history and of the development of the Christian Church. S. became a professor at the Reformed Seminary, Mercersburg, Pa., in 1844, where with J. W. *Nevin he was instrumental in developing the *Mercersburg theology. In 1870 he became a professor at Union Theological Seminary, New York City. S. wrote widely on church history and ecumenical subjects; his *Creeds of Christendom* (3 v., first pub. 1877; repr., 1968) remains an important reference work. He organized the American Society of Church History and served as the editor of a series of denominational histories and of the *Schaff-Herzog Encyclopedia of Religious Knowledge* (1891), based on the German work *Realencyklopädie für* *protestantische Theologie und Kirche*. BIBLIOGRAPHY: D. S. Schaff, *Life of Philip Schaff* (1897); J. H. Nichols, *Romanticism in American Theology* (1961).

[R. K. MacMASTER]

SCHÄFTLARN, ABBEY OF, near Munich, Bavaria. Founded in 762 for Benedictines and abandoned in the 10th cent., it was refounded by Bp. Otto of Freising for Premonstratensians in 1140. Famous artists built its still admired church (1733–56). Suppressed in 1803, it became once more a Benedictine abbey (1866) whose monks conduct a college. BIBLIOGRAPHY: Hugo 2:765 ff.; Backmund 1:47–48.

[N. BACKMUND]

SCHALL VON BELL, JOHANN ADAM (1591–1666), German-born Jesuit astronomer and missionary to China. After Macao (1618–22), he went to Shen-si in China and then to Peking where he remained from 1630 until his death. In 1629, he and Giacomo Rho succeeded Johann Terrenz Schreck in the effort to reform the Chinese calendar on a scientific basis, a reform advocated by Hsü Kuangch'i. Their work was completed by 1635 but not applied until 1644 with the rise of the Ch'ing dynasty. S.'s personal influence in the Ch'ing court was extensive. Young Emperor Shun-chih called him "grandfather," and by 1658 S. had reached the top of the mandarin hierarchy. Some contemporaries considered him the most influential man in China. He is personally credited with some 100,000 converts. A fellow Jesuit, Gabriel de Magalhaes, complaining of misconduct, charged that S.'s imperial offices were in violation of his vows, but S. was eventually cleared at Rome. He was a multilingual, Renaissance man, his specialty was astronomy, yet he also planned and built the first Christian church in Peking (1650), planned the city's fortifications and manufactured cannons, wrote a treatise on mining and numerous astronomical subjects besides a history of the Chinese missions (1665). Through him, imperial permission to evangelize throughout China was obtained in 1657. After Emperor Shun-chih died in 1661, antiChristians removed Schall from the astronomical bureau, stripped him of all titles, and imprisoned him. His death sentence was commuted under pressure from S.'s protesting admirers.

[R. J. LITZ]

SCHANNAT, JOHANN FRIEDRICH (1683–1739), church historian. A German lawyer, S. studied for the priesthood and after ordination devoted himself to historical research. He wrote a history of the Diocese of Fulda, *(Diocesis Fuldensis* 1727), and of Worms, *(Historia episcopatus Wormatiensis* 2 v. 1734).

[J. R. AHERNE]

SCHANZ, PAUL (1841–1905), German theologian. Ordained in 1866, he taught at the Univ. of Tübingen. He applied the historico-critical approach to exegesis of the Gospels and the history of dogma. His principal works are *Die Lehre von der heiligen Sakramenten der katholischen Kirche* (1893) and *Apologie des Christentums* (3 v., 1887–88).

[J. R. AHERNE]

SCHAPER, EDZARD (1908–), German author and novelist. After eventful years (as a student, gardener, sailor, correspondent in Estonia, forest worker in Finland and Sweden, secretary) he settled down to writing in Switzerland. In 1951 he became a Roman Catholic. He had formerly belonged to the Orthodox Church whose sufferings under the Communists he movingly describes in *Die sterbende Kirche* (1935). Apart from translations of Scandinavian authors, S. writes deeply religious stories, in which the spiritual values (freedom, faith, conscience) are pitted against worldly powers.

[S. A. SCHULZ]

SCHATZGEYER, KASPAR (1463 or 1464–1527), Franciscan polemicist. In 1517 he became provincial of the Strassburg province and started his preaching and writing against Andreas *Osiander, Johann von *Staupitz, and Johann von Schwartzenberg. His many works on the Mass, the Sacraments, grace, and religious life were published by J. *Eck (1543). S. also wrote the *Status de observantia* (1517), an attempt to conciliate strong party positions taken among Franciscans on the interpretation of their rule. BIBLIOGRAPHY: E. Iserloh, LTK 9:371–372, bibliog.

[E. D. McSHANE]

SCHAUKAL, RICHARD VON (1874–1924), Austrian essayist, novelist, lyricist of the aristocratic Austrian tradition. His antipathy for the mass culture and poor taste of the new age increasingly isolated him from his contemporaries. Born in Brno, Moravia, the son of a merchant, he studied law in Vienna, and became a high official in the Austrian Department of Labor.

[B. F. STEINBRUCKNER]

SCHAUMANN, RUTH (1899–), a convert to Catholicism in 1924, a representative of modern German writers religiously oriented. In somewhat obscure poetry and prose she shows the place of faith and prayer in daily life. Her widely read *Amei* (1932) gives the account of her childhood.

[I. MERKEL]

SCHAUMBERGER, JOHANN BAPTIST (1885–1955), Orientalist and OT scholar. S. taught OT at the Redemptorist seminary in Gars, Germany, where he specialized in Babylonian astrology. He computed the various astrological systems of the ancient Babylonians, helped establish a definite chronology for the Maccabean period, and thus developed the work of J. *Epping and F. X. *Kugler. BIBLIOGRAPHY: B. Ebermann, NCE 12:1121.

[T. M. MCFADDEN]

SCHÄZLER, KONSTANTIN VON (1827–80), German theologian. S. was a convert to Catholicism in 1850. He entered the Society of Jesus and was ordained in 1856. A year later he left the Jesuits. From 1862 to 1873 he taught at Freiburg im Breisgau. As a theologian he attended Vatican I, remaining in Rome as consultor to various curial congregations. S. was one of the early representatives of neo-Scholasticism, his principal works being expositions of the teaching of St. Thomas Aquinas. Among his treatises were *Das dogma von der Menschwerdung Gottes im Geiste des hl. Thomas dargestellt* (1870); *Divus Thomas contra liberalismum invictus veritatis catholicae assertor* (1874); *Natur und Übernatur* (1865) and *Gnade und Glaube* (1867). In his last years S. returned to the Jesuits.

[J. R. AHERNE]

SCHEEBEN, MATTHIAS JOSEPH (1835–88), German theologian. S. studied at Rome and taught at the Cologne diocesan seminary from 1860 until his death. Early in his career, he gained a wide knowledge of patristic sources that appear frequently in his own speculative works. He was fundamentally a Thomistic theologian, although he also used Anselm and Bonaventure, and was strongly influenced by the contemporary theologians Passaglia, Franzelin, Möhler, and Wiseman. He was mainly concerned with the elucidation of the supernatural and the interconnection among the major Christian mysteries. His early work *Nature and Grace* (1861, tr. C. Vollert, 1954), is still read, as is his popular *Mysteries of Christianity* (1865, tr. C. Vollert, 1961). BIBLIOGRAPHY: Hocedez 3:377–384.

[T. M. MCFADDEN]

SCHEFFLER, JOHANNES, see *ANGELUS SILESIUS.

SCHEGG, PETER JOHANN (1815–85), Catholic scriptural scholar. S. taught Scripture at the German univ. of Freising (1843–68), Würzburg (1868–72), and Munich (1872–85). he was a prodigious scholar who published several volumes of commentary on both OT and NT books. Apart from a few unfounded original opinions, his exegesis is of the highest quality. BIBLIOGRAPHY: L. Fillion, DB 5.2:1528–29; L. F. Hartman, NCE 12:1122.

[T. M. MCFADDEN]

SCHEIL, VINCENT (1858–1940), Assyriologist. S. held the chair of Assyriology at the Hautes-Études in Paris (1895–1933). He was epigraphist of the excavations at *Susa, the winter residence of the Persian kings, and published his important *Mémoires de la Délégation en Perse* (16v., 1900–39). The Code of *Hammurabi, discovered at

Susa, was first published in the fourth volume of this series. BIBLIOGRAPHY: J. A. Brinkman, NCE 12:1122–23.

[T. M. MCFADDEN]

SCHELL, HERMANN (1850–1906), German theologian. Ordained in 1873, S. published his first work, *Die Einheit des Seelenlebens nach Aristoteles,* in 1873, a defense of Aristotle's doctrine on the unity of the soul. Though a defense of Aristotle, the thesis demonstrated that S. found Plato's metaphysics more adaptable to the defense of Christian concepts. Plato and St. Augustine influenced all his later writing. In *Das Wirken des dreieinigen Gottes,* S. drew on the Greek and Latin Fathers to expound the dogma of the Trinity, showing the simplicity of being and fullness of action to be both the expression of the divinity and the explanation of creation. In 1885 S. obtained the chair of apologetics at Würzburg. His *Katholische Dogmatik* (4v., 1889–93) carried his fundamental thesis further. Between 1895 and 1896, while rector of the Univ. of Würzburg, S. wrote a major work on apologetics, *Gott und Geist,* and published two essays: *Der Katholizismus als Prinzip des Fortschrittes* (1897; Catholicism As the Principle of Progress) and *Die neue Zeit und der alte Glaube* (1898; New Times and the Ancient Faith). These, his dogmatic theology text, and *Gott und Geist* were placed on the Index in 1898, suspected of Modernism. S. submitted completely to the judgment of the Church, and the orthodoxy of his thought has been vindicated.

[J. R. AHERNE]

SCHELLING, FRIEDRICH WILHELM JOSEPH VON (1775–1854), German philosopher of the Romantic school, a transcendental idealist. S.'s promise while still a Lutheran divinity student at Tübingen won him the favor of Goethe, Fichte, and other figures of the Romantic movement. His early philosophical writings show the strong influence of Fichte; his later ones, that of Spinoza and J. Boehme. S. moved from the subjective idealism of Fichte to his own philosophy of nature, to the "philosophy of identity," to "positive philosophy." The latter two stages are marked by a preoccupation with the Absolute, God. S.'s philosophy of identity has a pantheistic tone: Nature is inseparable from God, but distinguishable from him; God's essence is will and he can be apprehended only through the will, not rationally. In his last (and posthumous works), S. sees God as "eternal contrariety." God is the ground of being, but he is also the ungrounded, the eternal nothing. Man is the apex of creation and, as a being possessed of will, expresses his essence in his most profound activity of myth-making and religion. The contemporary interest in S.'s thought stems from the fact that he asked many of the same questions as today's existentialists: Why being rather than nothing? Whence comes man's anxiety? BIBLIOGRAPHY: Copleston 7:105–148, called by A. Margoshes the best account in English of S.'s philosophy (EncPhil 7:309).

[W. B. MAHONEY]

SCHELSTRATE, EMMANUEL VAN (1645–92), Belgian church historian, Vatican librarian. He served as canon precentor of the cathedral at Antwerp (1678–81), where he wrote and published works of topical scholarship on the antiquity of Roman primacy, defending papal supremacy over councils. From 1678 to 1683 he served at the Vatican library, first as guardian then as prefect; he was also a canon of St. Peter's and the Lateran. *Antiquitas Ecclesiae . . . illustrata* (1692–97) is his major work of ecclesiastical history.

[R. J. LITZ]

SCHERER, MARIA THERESIA (Anna Maria Katherina; 1825–88), foundress. A Swiss, in 1845 S. joined the Sisters of the Holy Cross, a teaching community. As superior of the congregation's first hospital, she was an early member of a new community formed for the ministry of nursing, the Sisters of Mercy of the Holy Cross, and was virtually cofounder with Theodosius Florentini. First superior general, S. was an admirable administrator for 31 years, and under her direction the congregation spread throughout Switzerland, Germany, and Austria-Hungary. Today the community is one of the largest in the Church and is located in several U.S. dioceses.

[J. R. AHERNE]

SCHERER, MARY JOSEPH, SISTER (1883–1967), member of the Sisters of Loretto at the Foot of the Cross, Nerinx, Ky. (1903). S. received her M.A. from Creighton Univ. (1921) and her Ph.D. from De Paul Univ. (1925). She taught English at Loretto academies (1905–17) and was librarian and professor of English at Webster College (1921–37). Her opposition to those who believed that "all good literature is dead literature" and her desire to make living Catholic authors better known resulted in the foundation of the Gallery of Living Catholic Authors. S. remained its directress until her death.

[C. KEENAN]

SCHERESCHEWSKY, SAMUEL ISAAC JOSEPH (1831–1906), missionary bp. and Bible translator. Born in Tauroggen, Lithuania, of Jewish parents, educated for the rabbinate, S. was converted to Christianity about the time of his immigration to America in 1854. After being ordained in the Protestant Episcopal Church, deacon in 1859, priest in 1860, he went as missionary to China and began an intensive, lifelong study of the Chinese language. The first edition of his translation of the OT into Mandarin was published in 1874. He was consecrated bp. of Shanghai (1877); his main achievement in that position was the founding of St. John's University in 1880. In 1881 he was partially incapacitated by a stroke and had to resign. He resumed his translation work, revising the Mandarin version and translating the whole Bible into modern, or "easy" Wenli, the prevailing literary language. BIBLIOGRAPHY: J. A. Muller, *Apostle of China* (1937).

[W. W. MANROSS]

SCHERVIER, FRÀNZISKA (1819–76), foundress. A native of Aachen, she was throughout her life dedicated to the care of the poor. After serving as a laywoman with the Trappistines, she, with four companions, founded a religious institute, the Sisters of the Poor of St. Francis (SPSF) under the rule of the Third Order Regular of St. Francis (1845). At the time of her death there were 31 foundations in Europe and 10 in the United States. S. was beatified on April 25, 1974 by Pope Paul VI. BIBLIOGRAPHY: T. Maynard, *Through My Gift: the Life of Frànziska Schervier* (1951); M. V. Schreiner, NCE 12:1127; *idem*, 6:63.

[G. RUPPEL]

SCHEYERN, ABBEY OF, Benedictine monastery in Bavaria, dedicated to St. Margaret, St. Martin, Our Lady, and the Holy Cross. It was founded *c.*1050 by hermits in Margaretenzell and then settled by monks from Hirsau Abbey *c.*1077 at the request of the widow (Haziga) of Count Otto II von Scheyern. The monks finally settled into the von Scheyern family castle, 1112–19. In 1452 came the introduction of the Melk reform; in 1684 the abbey joined the Bavarian Congregation. During the 17th cent. it supplied scholars to the Univ. of Salzburg. Secularized in 1803, it was restored by Benedictines from Metten in 1838. In modern times the monks have engaged in parish ministry and have staffed an institute for Byzantine studies. BIBLIOGRAPHY: Cottineau 2:2977–78.

[E. J. DILLON]

SCHIAVONE, ANDREA (ANDREA MELDOLLA; 1522–63), Venetian painter and etcher, whose career is obscure. He was active as an etcher (1547), executing numerous prints dominated by mythological themes and dainty figures in the manner of Parmigianino. S. was the dominant figure in the introduction of mannerism into Venice, together with Tintoretto giving it a Venetian character in elongated forms, atmosphere, rich color, and S.'s own fluid, swirling, winding patterns *(Philosophers, Adoration of the Magi),* and numerous works in Belluno (recently identified). Numerous works have been too readily attributed to S. because of his obscure and legendary career.

[M. J. DALY]

SCHIFFINI, SANTO (1841–1906), Italian Jesuit whose writings and esp. whose teaching at the Gregorian Univ. in Rome contributed to the 19th-cent. revival of Thomism in philosophy and theology.

[T. C. O'BRIEN]

SCHILLEBEECKX, EDWARD HENRY (1914–), Dominican theologian. Born in Antwerp, Belgium, entered the Flemish province of the Dominican Order in 1935. He was a student of M.-D. Chenu at the theological school of Le Saulchoir in Étiolles, France, where he received his doctorate. After teaching dogmatic theology at Louvain, S. became professor of dogmatic theology, history of theology, and Christian anthropology at the Catholic Univ. of Nijmegen, Netherlands, in 1958. Although not a *peritus,* he had enormous impact on the deliberations at Vatican Council II. He was a consultant to the Dutch bps. and a lecturer for many other episcopal conferences, thus becoming a major "unofficial force" keeping the Council proceedings sharp. During the Council, Abp. Helder Camara said that S. would say what the Council was still unable to say. In following years, moving beyond the horizon of Vatican II, his massive theological publications (*Christ the Sacrament of the Encounter with God, Eucharist, Marriage, Celibacy, Mary, Mother of the Redemption, Mission of the Church, etc.*) have solidly affirmed a Catholic heritage while attempting a transformation of the Church into a meaningful reality in the contemporary world. His projected eight volumes of *Theological Soundings* deal with basic hermeneutical problems, and draw together many and divergent views into a synthesis challenging the complacent and fostering a creative ferment in the theological community.

[D. J. FINNERTY]

SCHILLER, JOHANN CHRISTOPH FRIEDRICH VON (1759–1805), German dramatist, poet, historian, aesthetician. Important as his works were in the field of drama, poetry, and aesthetics, S. left no mark of consequence on the development of religious thought. He was idealistic and much interested in human and moral problems, but his classical, humanistic spirit was little concerned with Christian dogma and belief.

[I. MERKEL]

SCHINER, MATTHÄUS (Schinner; *c.*1465–1522), anti-French Swiss bp., card. from 1511, papal legate, and military leader. He became bp. of Sion, dean of the cathedral, and Lord of Valais (1499), then helped Ludovico Sforza regain Milan from the French (1500). In Rome (1510), S. worked to bring the Swiss into the Holy League. When Milan was surrendered to him in 1512, he released it to Maximilian Sforza, who in turn offered Locarno, Lugano, Medrisio, and Val Maggia to the Swiss. S. worked for alliances between the Swiss and Pope Leo X, whom he helped elect in 1513, and continued to oppose French military and political efforts for the rest of his life. An early friend of the Reformation, in 1519, he offered Luther support and a place of refuge. He associated briefly with Zwingli on behalf of reform, but his position shifted such that he opposed Luther at the Diet of Worms.

[R. J. LITZ]

SCHISM (Gr., split, crack), a division within the Christian community—local, national or universal—resulting in separated communities or Churches that generally profess the same faith but are not in communion with one another. The term was used by St. Paul to designate the factions in the Church at Corinth that threatened its unity (1 Cor 1.10; 11.18; 12.25). The Fathers speak of schism as any sinful splitting off of a group from the Catholic Church without the added element of heterodoxy. Yet most of them felt that error was somehow connected with schism, so they do not always clearly distinguish between schism and heresy. In arguing against the Donatists, St. Augustine held that some sort of error is at the root of schism. In the East St. Basil distinguished between (1) heretics, who have left the faith itself and are completely lost to the Church, (2) schismatics, who because of ecclesiastical causes or problems separate from one another in a way that does not preclude reunion, and (3) dissident groups, such as disgruntled clergy who refuse to obey the bishop without necessarily forming a rival Church (PG 32, 665). The malice of schism, according to the Fathers, consists in defying the one Spirit by leaving the one Body of Christ and setting up a rival altar and a rival Eucharist. St. Thomas Aquinas stressed schism as a violation of the fraternal grace by which the members of the Church are united (ST 2a2ae, 14.2 ad 4), and as the formation of a counter Church challenging the unique role of the RC Church (ThAq *In 4 sent.* 13.2.1). Schism was originally discussed in the context of a *local Church and was described as the separation from the bishop, the center of unity. In the medieval West, schism was seen more in the framework of the universal Church, with particular reference to the pope, and gradually came to be defined as disobedience to the Holy See, as it is in Latin canon law (CIC c. 1325.2). The Orthodox Churches, however, still generally look upon schism as internal to the local or national Church and tend to speak of Roman Catholics as heretics rather than as schismatics. Although surprisingly little theological reflection has been given to the nature of schism, it may perhaps best be defined as a breaking away from the unity of love that is symbolized and effected by the communal sharing of the Eucharist. Contemporary theology is correctly stressing the distinction between the sin of schism and the state of schism, which may or may not be culpable. BIBLIOGRAPHY: Y. Congar, DTC 14.2:1286–1312.

[G. T. DENNIS]

SCHISM, EAST-WEST, the breaking off of communion between the Eastern and the Western Churches, represented chiefly by the see of Constantinople and of Rome, and the resultant state of separation, or *schism, which still exists between the Orthodox and the RC Churches. Its extremely complex origins involve so many factors that one cannot assign a precise date to its beginning or fix upon any one cause, much less try to determine the blame for it. Perhaps more than any other event, this schism has caused the most serious harm to the Christian Church in both East and West.

In theory the disruption of ecclesiastical communion was signified by removing a prelate's name from the diptychs, but because of poor communications and other factors, several popes were not commemorated in Constantinople. By itself then, removing the name did not constitute schism. A more accurate criterion is the existence of rival patriarchs,

Greek and Latin, although this occurred at different times and under different circumstances in the various patriarchates. The schism really began only when the heads and members of both Churches believed that they were no longer in communion with one another. Religious and political conflicts had occasioned several schisms between Rome and Constantinople, but each time unity had been restored. In the 11th cent. political problems in S Italy apparently caused the removal of the pope's name from the diptychs of Constantinople. About the middle of that century the Byzantine patriarch Michael Cerularius tried to undermine a papal-imperial entente by launching an attack on Roman usages. This provoked the reform-minded Card. Humbert to retaliate with an equally absurd list of trivial accusations against the Greeks. The farce ended with Humbert dramatically excommunicating the Patriarch on July 16, 1054, and being himself excommunicated by a Byzantine synod shortly thereafter. Scarcely noticed by contemporaries, this unworthy episode was not the beginning of the schism as has usually been claimed. In 1089 Emperor Alexius I Comnenus insisted on the pope's name being replaced in the diptychs, since the Byzantine clergy did not know why it had been erased. Certainly at the time of the First Crusade schism did not exist. Early in the 12th cent., though, both Latin and Greek patriarchs laid claim to the Sees of Jerusalem and Antioch. Relations between the Latins in the East and the Greeks gradually deteriorated so that by the end of the century the Byzantine canon lawyer, Theodore Balsamon, asserted that the Western Church was clearly in schism. But it was popular animosity erupting in violence and culminating in the Latin capture of Constantinople in 1204 that made the rupture irreparable. Probably the establishment and papal recognition of a Latin patriarch in Constantinople marks the final step in the schism. The Greco-Latin council of Nymphaeum in 1234 was clearly a meeting between representatives of two separated Churches. In 1245 Pope Innocent IV spoke of the schism having occurred "in our own time, only a few years ago." About the same time the other Eastern Churches seem to have aligned themselves with the Byzantine Churches. Subsequent attempts at reunion have been unsuccessful or have been concerned only with small groups.

Differences in language, culture, liturgy, political circumstances, tradition, and customs facilitated the schism and have helped to maintain it, but they were not its causes. Divergence on such dogmas as the procession of the Holy Spirit and purgatory was not, as has sometimes been stated, the principal cause of the schism. Although filling volumes of controversy and polemics, the Eastern and Western viewpoints on these matters are certainly reconcilable. Studies on the schism have often hopelessly jumbled theological and nontheological factors, yet a basic theological issue underlies the whole situation. East and West gradually developed varying attitudes toward the nature and structure of the Church. Unfortunately this difference was never seriously discussed; in both East and West the study of *ecclesiology is a comparatively recent development. The Byzantine theology of the Church was merged in that of its union with the empire, and such matters as relations between bishops came to be regarded as mere administrative problems. As a result bishops seemed unaware of the dogmatic implications of the Roman primatial claims or else replied with ambiguous rhetoric. Eventually the Western concept of the primacy became more definite, universal and absolute, while the Byzantine Church thought only of its autonomy within the imperial framework. There developed, then, two decidedly different views of the structure of the Church. After the fall of Byzantium these attitudes remained fixed both in the West and in the several autocephalous Orthodox Churches in the East. That these two attitudes are not irreconcilable is evidenced by current endeavors to reexamine the notions of primacy and collegiality. Participation of many of the Eastern Churches in the World Council of Churches, dialogue with Rome and with the Anglican Communion have marked the path of progress toward unity between East and West. BIBLIOGRAPHY: S. Runciman, *Eastern Schism* (1955); Y. Congar, *After Nine Hundred Years* (1959); F. Dvornik, *Byzantium and the Roman Primacy* (tr. E. A. Quain, 1966); *idem, Photian Schism: History and Legend* (1947, repr. 1970).

[G. T. DENNIS]

SCHISM, GREAT WESTERN, see GREAT WESTERN SCHISM.

SCHISM OF UTRECHT, the separation of 1723–24 of the Church of Utrecht, Holland, from Rome. *LITTLE CHURCH OF UTRECHT.

SCHISMATIC, in a technical, ecclesiastical sense, separated from the one, catholic, apostolic Church. Since at least the 4th cent., a clear distinction is made between one who is schismatic (rejecting legitimate church authority and breaking unity without impairing faith or sacramental order) and one who is heretical (holding erroneous doctrine which itself separates from the Church). The CIC c.1325.2 defines a schismatic as a baptized person who refuses to submit to papal authority or to associate with those who do so submit; while in the Orthodox view he is one who rebels against his own bp. or, in the case of a bp., one taking a position incompatible with communion with the college of bishops. The Orthodox Church does not emphasize the distinction between schismatics and heretics in evaluating other Churches. In the Orthodox view, all non-Orthodox have deviated, though in different degrees, from orthodox faith and order. It is less easy to discover a clear official position of other Eastern Churches today on norms of schism or on the difference between a schismatic and a heretical position. BIBLIOGRAPHY: Y. Congar, DTC 14:1286–1312; F. X. Lawlor and F. X. Murphy, NCE 12:1130–32. *SCHISM; *SCHISMATIC CHURCH.

[A. CODY]

SCHISMATIC CHURCH, a body of Christians formally and wilfully separated from the universal Church, e.g., the *Novatianists and *Donatists in early Christianity. Roman Catholic theology regards those Churches that do not profess communion with the pope as schismatic or, if the cause of separation is doctrinal, heretical. Traditionally, the designation was applied by Roman Catholics to the Orthodox Churches, although the fact that Vatican Council II did not use the notion of schism in its documents suggests that it does not apply to any of the larger contemporary Churches, since the characteristic note of culpability is lost. Anglican and Protestant theologians use the term to refer to the various divisions within the Church, i.e., the Protestant, Catholic, Anglican, and Orthodox Communions. BIBLIOGRAPHY: Y. Congar, *After Nine Hundred Years* (1959); S. L. Greenslade, *Schism in the Early Church* (1953); H. Küng, *Structures of the Church* (tr. S. Attanasio, 1964) 262–341. *SCHISM; *SCHISMATIC.

[T. M. MCFADDEN]

SCHIZOPHRENIA (from Gr. *schizo* (split) and *phrēn* (mind), a term coined by Eugen Bleuler in 1911 to stand for a group of mental disturbances characterized by a fragmentation of the personality into independently functioning parts. It seems to be a generic term covering a multitude of syndromes. These, which have been increasingly studied and classified in recent years, include bizarre and disconnected processes of thought, an indifference, vacillation, and sometimes an unexpectedness of affectivity, and a withdrawal from normal contacts. The manifestations may be periodic; the condition, chronic. Its etiology is debated: the causes indicated include traumatic experiences, physical make-up, and endocrine dysfunctions. Treatment has included psychotherapy, electroconvulsive and insulin-coma therapy, and now, most promisingly, at least for short-range relief, chemotherapy with drugs. It is the most prevalent and severe of all the mental illnesses; more than half the population of mental hospitals are sufferers. BIBLIOGRAPHY: J. R. Cavanagh and J. B. McGoldrick, *Fundamental Psychiatry* (3d ed., 1964).

SCHLARMAN, JOSEPH HENRY (1879–1951), bp. of Peoria, Ill., (from 1930). Ordained (1904) for the diocese of Belleville, Ill., he obtained doctorates in philosophy and canon law, and was diocesan chancellor before being named to the See of Peoria. He was active in the National Catholic Rural Life Conference, framed its constitution, and served as president (1943–45). He also was a founder of Montezuma Seminary, New Mexico, for the training of Mexican clergy. Among his writings is *From Quebec to New Orleans* (1929), on French explorations in N America. In the year of his death he was given the personal rank of archbishop.

[T. C. O'BRIEN]

SCHLATTER, ADOLF (1852–1938), Swiss-born Protestant biblical scholar, mainly at the Univ. of Tübingen

(1898–1938). His studies on the NT were influential because of their emphasis on the need for knowledge of the intertestamentary period for an understanding of the NT. From 1897 he was an editor of the *Beiträge zur Förderung des christlichen Theologie*. His interest in social questions and his early opposition to national socialism are noteworthy. S.'s biblical studies include: *Geschichte Israels von Alexander den Grossen bis Hadrian* (1901); *Die Theologie des NT* (1909); *Die Theologie des NT und die Dogmatik* (1909); *Erläuterungen zum NT* (11 v., 1890–1911).

[T. C. O'BRIEN]

SCHLEGEL, KARL WILHELM FRIEDRICH VON (1772–1829), Romantic critic; Orientalist; joint publisher, with his brother August Wilhelm von Schlegel (1767–1845), of the *Athenaeum* (1798–1800), the organ of Early (Jena) Romanticism. His *Kritische Fragmente* (1797) contains the aesthetic doctrine of German Romanticism; his definition of Romantic poetry as "progressive Universalpoesie" and his theory of interpretative (as opposed to purely evaluative) criticism had a profound influence on literary criticism in his own and later generations. In Paris in 1802, S. studied Sanskrit and Persian; in 1808, he published *Über die Sprache und Weisheit der Inder,* thus laying the foundations of comparative philology. In 1808, he became a Roman Catholic. Two works, the *Philosophie des Lebens* (1827) and the *Philosophie der Geschichte* (1828), contain his attempts to present a philosophy of history in harmony with revelation. BIBLIOGRAPHY: I. G. Merkel, NCE 12:1135–36; for a bibliog., see W. Kosch, *Deutsches Literatur-Lexikon* (1963) 379–381.

[M. F. MCCARTHY]

SCHLEIERMACHER, FRIEDRICH DANIEL ERNST (1768–1834), German theologian. Son of a Lutheran minister who became a Moravian, S. in 1787 entered Halle, the most rationalistic university in Germany. He wrote later, "Religion remained with me when God and immortality vanished before my doubting eyes." In place of Kant's rigorous ethical rationalism, S. posed a certain ideal sense of life and declared that he sensed the divine presence more in Spinoza than in Kant. His fundamental problem was to find a world view that did justice to human personality without slighting the infinite universe to which man lies open. In Berlin Schlegel urged him to publish his *On Religion: Speeches Addressed to Its Cultured Despisers* (1799), which was followed by *Soliloquies* (1800). S. taught theology (1816–34) at the new Univ. of Berlin, of which he became the first head. He produced a most fully elaborated interpretation of religion as an organized life of the feelings and emotions, as primarily an aesthetic experience. Aesthetic openness to the universe *is* religion, a form of "cosmic consciousness." Its seat is the feelings, a sense of the All, a wholly individual matter. Religious experience is consciousness of man's oneness with the world. Religion is an independent sphere, neither that of morals nor that of dogma. The divine is wholly immanent so that the concept of the supernatural is meaningless. Central to S.'s doctrine is a monism and an emphasis on religion as feeling.

The *Soliloquies* were surpassed by *The Christian Faith* (1821), his greatest theological work, the first to make central the categories of religious and Christian "experience" rather than God. Theology is a description, not a speculative science; its data are chiefly men's feelings. The Bible and creeds are records of Christian experience and as such are valuable but have no universal or prescriptive validity. Rational demonstration is absolutely excluded from the sphere of religion. The traditional divine attributes do not represent God in himself but only in respect to men and the world. The sense of the power of Christian love and of the living Christ is what is specifically Christian in S.'s religion. From the works of Christ we conclude to his divinity, not the other way round, as in the 18th century. Christianity is the best religion because in it the religious consciousness is most highly developed. The Church is necessary to foster men's experience of oneness with nature and with one another and to enjoy fellowship in Christ. There are, however, varieties of religious experience, an irreducible plurality.

S.'s influence on subsequent Protestant theology was enormous, in particular his insistence that religion has its seat in the feelings and is the *Bewusstsein* (consciousness) of the All. Christian theology must be drawn from experience and not from authority or speculation. BIBLIOGRAPHY: G. Cross, *Theology of Schleiermacher* (1911); W. B. Selbie, *Schleiermacher: A Critical and Historical Study* (1913); R. R. Niebuhr, *Schleiermacher on Christ and Religion* (1964).

SCHLEITHEIM CONFESSION, a *confession of faith adopted by the Anabaptists at a conference in the Swiss canton of Schaffhausen in 1527. The principal author was Michael *Sattler. The seven articles dealt with baptism, the Lord's Supper, church discipline, the ministry, *nonresistance, and *nonconformity. BIBLIOGRAPHY: MennEnc 1:447–448 s.v. "Brüderliche Vereinigung"; 4:428–429.

[T. C. O'BRIEN]

SCHLÖGL, NIVARD (1864–1939), Austrian Cistercian scholar and teacher of Old Testament and Near Eastern languages. Born at Gaaden (near Vienna), he entered the Cistercians in 1884, was novice master (1890–1907), professor of exegesis in Heiligenkreuz from 1896, and at the Univ. of Vienna from 1908. His textual criticism was heavily influenced by his great interest in meter, which partly accounts for the fact that his conclusions never gained wide acceptance. BIBLIOGRAPHY: J. Gabriel, LTK 9:420; P. Nober, EncCatt 11:73–74.

[E. J. DILLON]

SCHMALKALDIC ARTICLES (*Articuli Smalcaldici*), a *confession of faith prepared by Martin Luther in Dec. 1536 and incorporated into the *Book of Concord (1580). The document was intended to present Reformation beliefs at the council summoned to meet at Mantua in May 1537; it was inspired by the desire to indicate to the council points both of unity and of unalterable opposition. The proposed council did not materialize until 1545 at Trent. The Articles received their name from the town of Schmalkalden in Thuringia, where the Schmalkaldic League met in Feb. 1537. The representatives at the gathering never did consider or approve the Articles, but most of the theologians present endorsed them, and they were quickly included in the *corpora doctrinae* of the various territorial Churches (see CORPUS DOCTRINAE). Philipp Melanchthon's *Treatise on the Power and Primacy of the Pope*, included in the Book of Concord with the Schmalkaldic Articles, for a long time was erroneously thought to be an appendix. The Articles are arranged in three sections. The first is on points of agreement: the Godhead, the Incarnation, and the Apostles' and Athanasian Creeds. The second section is on points on which the Reformers must remain unyielding: justifying faith and the rejection of the Mass, monasticism, and papacy. The last section includes articles on sin, repentance, baptism, the Lord's Supper, and other points open to discussion with *Reformed or RC theologians. BIBLIOGRAPHY: *Book of Concord: The Confessions of the Evangelical Lutheran Church* (ed. and tr. T. G. Tappart, 1959).

[J. PELIKAN]

SCHMALKALDIC LEAGUE, a politico-military alliance formed in Feb. 1531 by Protestant princes of north and central Germany at Schmalkalden in Thuringia. Led by Philip of Hesse and John Frederick I, Elector of Saxony, the League resisted the attempts of Charles V to control the political and religious situation in Germany. It blocked Protestant participation in the Council of Trent and strengthened the formation of *territorial Churches. The coalition dissolved after a military defeat by imperial forces at Mülhausen in 1547. BIBLIOGRAPHY: Jedin Trent I, index; Léonard HistProt 1:78–180.

[P. DAMBORIENA]

SCHMAUS, MICHAEL (1897–), German theologian. A member of the Roman Pontifical Theological Academy, S. has been professor of dogma at the Univ. of Münster and Munich. His lasting contribution to the development of Catholic dogmatic theology is the rediscovery of patristic insights which since Trent had been overlooked: the relational character of the Christian notion of being and of person; the inner connection between creation and redemption, the understanding of God's saving acts as temporal events in world history. At times S.'s scholastic approach to dogma seems too juridical or esoteric, as is evident when he favors the Scotist position that the Incarnation would have occurred even if man had not sinned. BIBLIOGRAPHY: M. Schmaus, *Katholische Dogmatik* (1954–59); *Essence of Christianity* (tr. 1961); *Preaching as Saving Encounter* (tr. 1966).

[P. J. ROSATO]

SCHMELZER, JOHANN HEINRICH (1623–80), Austrian composer. S. was a musician, *vize-Kapellmeister,* and *Kapellmeister* in the Court Chapel of Vienna. He wrote a *Missa nuptialis,* opera ballets, and other instrumental and vocal music.

[M. T. LEGGE]

SCHMID, CHRISTOPH VON (1768–1854), theologian, specialist in catechetics. A native of Germany, ordained in 1791, S. declined invitations to university teaching at Heidelberg and Tübingen, preferring pastoral work. In 1817 he was proposed as first bp. of Rottenburg. In 1837 he was made a nobleman. A man of simplicity and religious fervor, S. wrote a number of works of instruction, principally directed toward youth, and it was here he made his primary contribution. He applied the pedagogical theories of J. Sailer to cut through religious abstractions and present homely truths in a style immediately popular with young people. His many bible stories and fables and legends were translated for peoples as distant as Japan, China and the Near East. His *Reminiscences of My Life* (4 v., 1853–1857) contains much of his thought.

[J. R. AHERNE]

SCHMID, FRANZ (1844–1922), theologian. A native of the Austrian Tyrol, S. was ordained in 1872. For 36 years he served at the seminary in Brixen (now Bressanone, N Italy) as professor and for 8 years as rector. He was vicar general of the diocese (1916–18). The most notable of his works was *Die ausserordentlichen Heilswege für die gefallene Menschheit* (1899). Other writings included *Quaestiones selectae ex theologia dogmatica* (1891) and *Die Sakramentalien der katholischen Kirche* (1896).

[J. R. AHERNE]

SCHMIDLIN, JOSEPH (1876–1944), missiologist, historian. A German priest-professor, S. taught at Münster, where he established the first Catholic chair of missiology. S. established a periodical to promote mission science and was founder of the International Institute for Mission Science (1911). He was a collaborator of Ludwig von Pastor, whose work he continued. A foe of National Socialism, he suffered persecution and died in a concentration camp. Among his works are two seminal missiological studies translated into English: *Catholic Mission Theory* (tr. 1931) and *Catholic Mission History* (tr. 1933). His other main work on the subject was *Einführung in die Missionswissenschaft* (1917, 2d ed. 1925).

[J. R. AHERNE]

SCHMIDT, KARL WILHELM (1812–95), Protestant church historian, professor at the Univ. of Strassburg, who wrote numerous religious biographies and works on mysticism. He also produced a much esteemed literary history of Alsace (2 v., 1879).

[M. J. SUELZER]

SCHMIDT, WILHELM (1868–1954), Divine Word missionary and leading anthropologist of the influential culture-historical (Viennese) school of ethnology. Born in Hörde, Germany, he entered the Society of the Divine Word at Steyl, Holland, and was ordained in 1892. He studied linguistics in Berlin, taught ethnology and linguistics at his society's seminary at Mödling, near Vienna (1895–98), and at the Univ. of Vienna (1921–38). He escaped arrest by Nazi police in 1938, was welcomed in Switzerland, and taught at the Univ. of Fribourg (1939–1950). He was the first director of the papal ethnological museum at the Lateran (1927–39) and was instrumental in the founding of the similar museum in Vienna. He founded Anthropos Institute and the still-flourishing journal of the same name (1906), in which was reported Divine Word missionaries' ethnographic research, notably in New Guinea and Togo. He organized expeditions to Pygmy peoples, the Indians of Tierra del Fuego, African Bushmen, peoples of Brazil, India, Tibet, and New Guinea. As an expert in linguistics he discovered the "austric linguistic stock." His special concerns involved the evolution of the family, the relation of family type to subsistence patterns, the influence of individuals on community institutions, and the evolution of religion and the idea of God. He was influenced by such anthropologists as Franz Boas and Edward Westermarck, and most profoundly by Fritz Graebner's theory of cultural diffusion. S. opposed the prevailing evolutionary theory that portrayed man and civilization as products of a unilinear, step-by-step rise from the primitive state. S. depicted the existence, growth, and activity of primitive peoples as fully human types. In his main work, the 12-v. *Der Ursprung der Gottesidee* (1912–55), he maintained the essentially monotheistic nature of the religion of most primitive peoples.

[E. J. DILLON]

SCHMIDT-ROTTLUFF, KARL (1884–1976), German painter and engraver. Trained locally, S. met Kirchner (1904) who encouraged him in his woodcuts. After studying painting in Dresden (1905), S. joined *Die Brücke, juxtaposing boldest color in jarring dissonances. By 1910 his work became decorative in the style of Gauguin. S. produced 20 important woodcuts on NT themes (1917–19) of which the *Road to Emmaus* (1918) is famous. His work became more gentle after trips to Italy and Paris (1923–30) but was proscribed as decadent by the Nazis in World War II.

[M. J. DALY]

SCHMÖGER, KARL (1819–83), mystical writer. A German Redemptorist, S. was provincial of the North German Province of the Redemptorists during the Kulturkampf. His writings on the mystic Anne Catharine Emmerich were widely read in Europe. In 1881 he published *Great Synthesis of Biblical Visions.*

[J. R. AHERNE]

SCHMUCKER, SAMUEL SIMON (1799–1873), American Lutheran pastor and seminary professor. S.

served for 6 years as pastor in New Market, Va., and then persuaded the General Synod to establish a theological school at Gettysburg, Pa., the first Lutheran seminary in the U.S. (1826). He became its first professor and president, and he lectured on systematic theology until retiring in 1864. S. actively promoted an American Lutheranism that favored fellowship with other American Protestant Churches, but at the cost of departure from the *Augsburg Confession. The controversy over the issue led to a breakup of the General Synod in 1867, and to a reassertion of Lutheran confessional traditions in reaction to S.'s views.

SCHNEEMANN, GERHARD (1829–85), German Jesuit, church historian and theologian. S. was already a subdeacon when he entered the Society in Rome (1851). After a decade of teaching he was assigned to scholarly research at Maria Laach in Austria, then in Jesuit hands. S. wrote against Döllinger and in favor of papal infallibility in the period of Vatican Council I. He was a founder and editor of the theological journal *Stimmen aus Maria Laach* from 1879. His masterwork is *Acta et decreta sacrorum conciliorum recentiorum (Collectio Lacensis;* 7 v., 1870–90), on provincial councils held from 1862. Volume 7 on Vatican I was edited after S.'s death. He also edited *Sacri oecumenici et generalis Concilii Vaticani canones et decreta* (1871). He was a protagonist in the resurrected Jesuit-Dominican disputes over Molinism with his *Controversiarum de divinae gratiae liberique arbitrii concordia, initia, progressus* (1881), his Dominican respondent being F. A. M. Dummermuth.

[T. C. O'BRIEN]

SCHNEIDER, EMILY (Sister Emily of the Daughters of the Cross; 1820–59), subject of the 2-v. biography (including a collection of her letters) written by two Jesuits, K. Richstaetter and V. Couty, in which she is depicted as a modern German mystic. She was a schoolmistress in Lüttich and entered the Daughters of the Cross, a congregation of nursing sisters, there in 1845. She was novice-mistress in Appel in 1851 and in 1852 became the superior at Düsseldorf during a time of political turmoil in that city. BIBLIOGRAPHY: F. Baumann, LTK 9:440.

[E. J. DILLON]

SCHNEIDER, NICHOLAS (1884–1953), Sumerologist. S. taught Scripture at the Luxemburg seminary but is best noted for his painstaking scholarship on the cuneiform texts of the Third Dynasty of Ur (c.2070–1960 B.C.). The results of his studies, which supplied otherwise unobtainable information on this period, are published in ʾhe *Pontifical Biblical Institute's periodicals *Analecta Orientalia* and *Orientalia.* BIBLIOGRAPHY: L. F. Hartman, NCE 12:1140.

[T. M. MCFADDEN]

SCHNEIDER, REINHOLD (1903–58), German lyric poet and author (novels, dramas, essays, history, cultural

philosophy). The basic theme of his voluminous work, which includes more than 120 titles, is the antinomy between divine grace and secular power. After private studies, esp. in Spanish and Portuguese literature, he traveled throughout Europe. He was converted to Catholicism in 1938. His writings were condemned by the Nazi government during World War II but continued to circulate secretly. Most of his novels are historical and in them he traces the eternally recurring conflict between man's shortcomings and God's infinite grace. BIBLIOGRAPHY: S. A. Shulz, NCE 12:1140–41.

[S. A. SCHULZ]

SCHNITGER, ARP (1648–1718), German organ builder whose instruments rank among the finest examples of the German baroque period. His organs number about 80 and may be found in churches in Hamburg, Bremen, Magdeburg, etc. His two sons continued his work and founded a "school" of organ builders in N Germany.

[M. T. LEGGE]

SCHNITZER, JOSEF (1859–1939), Catholic church historian, professor in Dillingen and Munich. His main research centered on Savonarola. His criticism of the encyclical *Pascendi* caused him to be retired and he died under interdict, leaving incomplete a treatise in defense of Pelagius. BIBLIOGRAPHY: G. Maron, RGG 5:1468.

[M. J. SUELZER]

SCHOENBERG, ARNOLD (1874–1951), Austrian-born composer. S. learned violin and cello at the Realschule in Vienna and later studied composition with Alexander von Zemlinsky. S., who began composing as a youth, also taught in Berlin and Vienna, published text books on harmony and on composition, and became the master of such gifted students as Alban Berg (1885–1935), Egon Wellesz (1885–   ), and Anton Webern (1883–1945). Dismissed by the Nazi regime in 1933, S. emigrated to the U.S., settled in California, and taught at the Univ. of California at Los Angeles. S. wrote significant music for almost every medium. Though he began in the tradition of the great German romantic composers, he soon developed an expanded use of chromatic harmony that eventually led to atonality and to his system of composing with 12 notes. S.'s reconversion to Judaism, linked with political events of the day, inspired the composition of a body of religious music that includes tonal, atonal, and serial works. Some of the more important of these are *Kol Nidre* (1938), a cantata based on the Yom Kippur service, and *Moses and Aaron,* an unfinished opera, his longest work, written in the 12-tone technique.

[M. T. LEGGE]

SCHOENSTATT SISTERS OF MARY, a secular institute belonging to the Apostolic Movement of Schoenstatt, founded by Father Joseph Kentenich in Germany (1914).

Sharing with the entire movement the task of renewal of the individual and society, the Schoenstatt Sisters, founded in 1926, make up one of the nucleus communities of Schoenstatt. They were recognized in 1949 by Pius XII as one of the first secular institutes in the Church.

The Schoenstatt Sister of Mary is a woman in the world but not of the world. She centers her life on God according to the example of Mary. She may be engaged in almost any kind of apostolic activity in the Church or in society. She may live in a community or live alone; she may wear the common dress of the institute or regular street clothes, according to the demands of the apostolate and the needs of the time. Her mission is to renew the world in Christ through Mary. In 1977 there were 138 Sisters in the U.S. The entire institute numbers 2,784 who work on six continents: Europe, Asia, Australia, Africa, North and South America, in the U.S. and Mexico as well as in the Caribbean Islands of Puerto Rico and the Dominican Republic.

[R. C. CLIGGETT]

SCHOLA CANTORUM, a school for church singing. Of ancient origin, the first such Roman school dates probably from the 4th century. The Roman *schola cantorum* became the center from which instructors in chant were sent out to other churches and institutions and from which the singers for the solemn services in St. Peter's Basilica were drawn. In his reform *motu proprio* of 1903, *Tra le sollecitudini* Pius X recommended the founding of such choir schools wherever possible, in theological colleges and even in small churches. The present-day descendant of the Roman *schola cantorum,* the papal choir, is known as the *Sistine Choir.

[M. T. LEGGE]

SCHOLASTIC, literally, of or belonging to the theology and philosophy taught in the great schools of Western Europe from 1050 to 1300. More precisely, a new theological and philosophical method appearing at Paris, Oxford, Bologna, Toulouse, to deal with and to assimilate new philosophical and scientific materials being introduced, and to harmonize them with Revelation. The new materials were the old classic works of Greek and Roman philosophy, mainly Aristotle, which had been lost to the West but had survived in various Neoplatonic adaptations in the East. The Muslims in their conquests found them during the 7th and 8th cent., translated them into Syriac, then Arabic. These texts were used with great success at Baghdad and Córdoba, so that the Arabs moved ahead of the West in medicine, mathematics, and astronomy. Muslim philosophers as Avicenna (980–1037), Averroes (1126–78), and Jewish philosophers in Spain, as ibn-Gabirol (1020–70), and Moses Maimonides (1135–1204) made successful syntheses of Greek learning and Muslim culture. Arab translations of Aristotle came into the Christian West at Sicily, southern Italy, and Spain and sparked the scholastic revolution in ideas. The scholastic method consisted in a dialectic use of Aristotelian logic, Christian revelation, and the Platonic

ideas already assimilated through the current Augustine-influenced theology and philosophy. The task was to fuse these elements into an instrument to establish harmony between the new science and the Christian tradition and Revelation. Some prominent scholastics were Anselm (1033–1109), Peter Abelard (1079–1142), Thomas Aquinas (1223–74), Duns Scotus (1270–1308), and William of Ockham (*c.*1300–49). Scholastic learning in time degenerated into sterile word games and irrelevant discussions. Attempts were made to revive it under Pope Leo XIII, and Neo-Scholastic philosophy appeared in the early 20th cent. through the efforts of Cardinal Mercier of Belgium. BIBLIOGRAPHY: M. de Wulf, *Histoire de la philosophie médiévale* (6th ed., 1934, 1:15, n. 2); *idem,* ''Notion de la scholastique médiévale,'' *Revue Neó-scholastique de philosophie* 18 (1911) 177–196.

[N. F. GAUGHAN]

SCHOLASTIC METHOD, the technique of teaching and learning that was the single unifying characteristic of medieval scholasticism (it is inaccurate to speak of scholasticism as representing a single theological or philosophical system and content). The most obvious development of the method was in theology, but it was also adapted to the study of philosophy, law, medicine, and even to the trivium and quadrivium. The scholastic method had two components: the *lectio* or expounding (*expositio*) of a text; the *disputatio* or debate which grew out of and in a sense eventually overshadowed the *lectio.* The development and interaction of the two components marked the historical evolution of medieval learning. The *lectio* came first, because the roots of medieval learning were in the Carolingian renaissance with its retrieval and mastering of the writings of antiquity. From this veneration toward a prior, golden age of knowledge emerged the *auctoritates,* a term that designated, not so much the ancient authors themselves, as their texts, the academic patrimony. Each branch of learning had its *auctoritates,* certain received texts that were acknowledged as having a normative place in the discipline. As dialectics became more prominent, and dialecticians more skilled, the recourse to the texts became more conventional and formalistic; yet the *lectio* never was absent from the scholastic method. Even in the reading of a work so dialectic in style as Aquinas's *Summa theologiae,* the presence of the *lectio* cannot be forgotten; it is often a received text as governing a specific theological point that is implied in the language and direction of the discourse. Without such awareness, the plain sense of a medieval work can be missed and the argumentation misunderstood. The *disputatio* grew out of the *lectio* historically because many of the texts rediscovered were the logical works of Aristotle; they provided first of all dialectical tools. Epistemologically, there developed for the inquiring medieval mind the issue of conflict among received texts. Thus there emerged that phase of scholasticism marked most typically by Peter Abelard's *Sic et non,* the dialectical juxtaposition of texts and the attempt to reconcile them or to resolve the conflict in favor of one side. The finished form of the evolution was the *quaestio disputata of the 13th cent., where structure is embodied in Aquinas's *Summa theologiae*. In 19th- and 20th-cent. seminary study programs, the term scholastic method was used to describe the format of presenting theological theses; it was a technique quite removed from the medieval and consisted in: a definition of terms; recitation of opinions; patristic and biblical, ecclesiastical "proof-texting"; syllogistic argument for the position stated by the thesis; refutation of contrary arguments. It was quite often dull and sterile. BIBLIOGRA - PHY: M. D. Chenu, *Towards Understanding St. Thomas* (1964) 126–154; Y. M. Congar, *History of Theology* (1968) 69–84.

[T. C. O'BRIEN]

SCHOLASTIC PHILOSOPHY. (1) Historically, medieval philosophy as pursued through the *scholastic method, not any uniform content or system is properly the referent of this term. However, because of the dominance of literature in the scholastic method, the Neoplatonic and the Aristotelian are the two purely philosophic strains identifiable in the Middle Ages. The first is evident early in John Scotus Erigena and the school of Chartres, but because of the dominance of Augustine and of Neoplatonic influences on the Arabs, the Neoplatonic elements are constant throughout the medieval period. From the Arabs were added to Boethius's translations the rest of Aristotle's works. It was from use of Aristotle's Organon and *Porphyry's Isagoge in Boethius's translations that the dialecticians in the Middle Ages developed the long-dominant problem of *universals. It was from the full possession of Aristotelian works that philosophies of nature and of man developed. The fullest and richest philosophical discourse, as typified by St. Bonaventure and St. Thomas Aquinas, was, however, within medieval theology. "Pure philosophy" led to the crisis of Latin Averroism; reaction to that danger led to conservatism and philosophical skepticism, and to the decline of medieval philosophy. (2) Scholastic philosophy may also designate the philosophy program followed in Catholic seminaries (and adapted for some Catholic college courses) from the mid-19th to the mid-20th century. There was uniformity in a stereotyped Latin vocabulary, a set of typical "theses" or positions, a stylized method of expounding these theses, and the protestation of keeping the whole in conformity with "the mind of St. Thomas" (due allowance being made for the allegiance of nations or religious orders to their own masters). The program did not make philosophers; in some cases it prepared students for the study of a theology couched in the same vocabulary and expounded with a parallel methodology. The positive value of the "neoscholastic" period was almost a full century of scholarship that did retrieve and explore the genuine philosophic insights of the great medieval theologians. BIB - LIOGRAPHY: É. Gilson, *Spirit of Medieval Philosophy* (Eng. tr. 1936); D. Knowles, *Evolution of Medieval Thought* (1962).

[T. C. O'BRIEN]

SCHOLASTIC THEOLOGY, primarily, a methodology of applying human intelligence to revealed truth; secondarily, only a body or system of religious thought. Taking its inspiration from the *fides quaerens intellectum* of St. Augustine, Christian scholasticism has had three periods of prominent influence: the golden age of the 13th cent. with its principal exponents, St. Albert the Great, St. Thomas Aquinas, St. Bonaventure, and Duns Scotus; from the Reformation to the 18th cent. with Catholic and Protestant adherents; and the revival of the late 19th cent. to the present. Because theology moves in the experience of faith within the community of the Church, it preserves the contemplative or spiritual climate of monastic theology. It conceives its task to be more than to impose some organization upon the revealed data and so introduces the evidence of nonrevealed sciences to unfold meanings, show the inner relationships of Christian doctrines, draw out truths implicit in revelation, and defend revealed truths. Philosophy and logic become esp. important and in fact contribute to the formation of massive systems with their processes of definition, distinction, and argumentation, which critics have used to characterize *scholasticism. The methodology in its purity is one of discovery. The statement of the normative principles, as these are found in the Scriptures and ecclesiastical tradition, is confronted by a specific question or problem. Opposing arguments are presented, and the resulting discussion searches for a solution consistent with Christian faith, accepted authorities, factual evidence, and human reason. The nominalism of the 14th and 15th cent. reduced it to a kind of logical manipulation of theorems. The Renaissance saw it as a dialectic too restricted to do justice to biblical and patristic thought. Protestantism in the main could not accept its premises of the continuity of nature and grace and the unity of Bible and tradition. The epistemological inroads of the 18th cent. sapped the vitality it had from its openness to the investigations of the other sciences. Contemporary expressions of scholastic theology, e.g., Neothomism and transcendental Thomism, have addressed themselves to these objections. BIBLIOGRAPHY: Y. M. J. Congar, *History of Theology* (tr. H. Guthrie, 1968) 85–143; 154–162; 184–187.

[E. F. MALONE]

SCHOLASTICA, ST. (480–betw. 543–546), sister of St. *Benedict, and, according to Bede, his twin; foundress of women's branch of the Benedictine Order. Born in Nursia, Umbria, of an affluent family of lawyers, S. received a name (meaning "scholar") not rare in the locality. Her brother returned from study in Rome c.500, when presumably (esp. at the monastic school) she shared his learning. In girlhood she had been veiled as a virgin, which fact Gregory the Great related in his *Dialogues*, prime source of knowledge of her. S. lived a life of contemplation, for a time it seems in the family home, then as companions gathered about her, in a house established at Plombariola, not far from Monte Cassino. Her brother undertook the direction of what would indirectly form the second order of the community for which he wrote the Rule. Unique in the Church is the founding of the twin orders whose vitality has perdured through 14 centuries. Benedict allowed a meeting once a year, their last visit a classic story related in the *Dialogues* (bk. 2, ch. 33, 34; PL 66:194–196). Their meeting place, Capella del Colloquio at Cassino, was reconstructed in 1961. The vision of a dove made known to Benedict the death of his sister (memorialized in the Collect of her feast). Despite the ravages of war, the relics of the two are preserved at Monte Cassino. BIBLIOGRAPHY: Butler 1:292–293; A. Lantini, BiblSanct 11:742–750; M. C. Celletti, *ibid*. 2:1104–84; W. Goffart, "LeMans, St. Scholastica and the Literary Tradition of the Translation of St. Benedict," RevBén 77 (1967) 107ff; S. Hilspich, *History of Benedictine Nuns* (tr. M. J. Muggle, 1958).

[M. R. BROWN]

SCHOLASTICISM, originally used derogatorily by 16th-cent. humanists about their predecessors, the medieval schoolmen (*scholastici*); later a commodious term for a movement of thought that prevailed in the Christian West for 4 cent., lingered for another 4 and almost died, was revived under the aegis of Leo XIII (1879) and after an energetic and influential half-century of work, is no longer in vogue. Once again, "scholastic" tends to become a pejorative term; nevertheless it stands for a character as perennial as "rationalist" or "liberal," and it refuses to lie down. Drawing a distinction between scholasticism in theology and in philosophy will be convenient so long as it is not solidified into an exclusion, for the main interest of most of the schoolmen, even the most protractedly and, it must be confessed, boringly profane, was sacred theology. The first, which manifests a tighter unity than the second, seeks to implement the phrase, "faith seeking understanding" and to render the data of divine revelation into the communicable terms of human reasoning; the resulting meanings are developed, their harmonies displayed, and in various degrees of assurance and scepticism, according to the philosophy adopted, they are related to the data of secular experience. As such, scholasticism is generically the same as systematic theology, and so may be contrasted with biblical, positive, or historical theology. More specifically it is that systematic theology which works with the apparatus of Aristotle's *Posterior Analytics*.

In philosophy, scholasticism appears at once as more heterogeneous and difficult to fix, for it covers convictions as diverse as those of Neoplatonists, of Aristotelians, and of nominalists. Indeed the strains of illuminism from the Ideas, of abstractionism from empirical facts, of positivism in linguistic analysis persist throughout its history and remain largely unreconciled. All the same it is possible, despite the variety, to establish a certain community. This consists mainly in an agreement on the vocabulary and grammar of thought: technical terms abound, many coined to convey the precision of Greek in to Low Latin, which serve the purpose of keeping to the point without, however, sustaining the imagination; the terms are highly polished, but their total effect is gritty. Analytic exposition of a text followed by debate is the underlying method. All the parties lived in the same city of thought and conducted a civil conversation in the old sense of the phrase, for in controversy manners were often acrimonious and splenetic to the modern temper. An occupational disease was an arid verbalism within a system closed against historical learning and *litterae humaniores*.

By and large, then, philosophical scholasticism is to be identified less as a system of thought than as a heading in the history of thought. An outline of the movement may treat it in its medieval, middle, and modern periods. There were precursors during the Carolingian renaissance, yet its true originators were Anselm and Abelard in the 11th and 12th cent. and it flowered early in the humanism of the school of Chartres and the mystical science of the Victorines and Cistercians. Thenceforward its history is that of the rise of the European universities. Augustinian and Platonist, curious about this world though set on the next, a phase worthily represented by Alexander of Hales and Robert Kilwardby, it was convulsed by the reception of Aristotle in the West, at first in Arabic versions. The prospect opened out of a world of reason apparently independent of the world of faith. Following the debates on the "double-truth theory," the various schools emerged; the old Augustinianism was renewed by Bonaventure; Aristotelianism was incorporated by Albert and Thomas Aquinas; the stream of Averroism and Avicennism in Duns Scotus continued to run strong. The main metaphysical debate in the late medieval schools lay between Thomists and Scotists, yet high questions of philosophy were being displaced by formal and material logic, and a widespread *nominalism marks the end of medieval scholasticism. Yet modern research in the history of science has done much to upset the old picture of men who spent their time refining on their quiddities and droning in a vacuum.

The middle period was inaugurated in the 16th cent. by Sylvester Ferrariensis and Card. Cajetan, heirs of the Italian Renaissance and powerful philosophical thinkers; but the great names are those of the Spanish divines, Francisco de Vitoria, Domingo Báñez, Francisco de Suárez, and John of St. Thomas. Scholasticism drew aside from the main current of European thought, its glory was that of Spain, and so was its decline. However, it was not altogether remote; for it humanized policies in the Indies and so earned the noble tribute of Dr. Johnson to the Univ. of Salamanca; and mixed with elements from Descartes, Leibniz, and Wolff, it survived in the text books for theological training, even in Anglican and Protestant schools.

The modern Leonine revival—Neo-Scholasticism as it is called—began as a reaction against German philosophies of Romanticism and by the end of the 19th cent. had grown in a pre-Bergsonian climate into the official party-line for RC clerics; its juridical enforcement did not enhance it from a philosophical point of view. Yet a distinguished band of thinkers, notably at the Univ. of Louvain and later at Münster and Munich, and from the French Dominicans and Jesuits, have confidently taken its spirit into the social and philosophical sciences. BIBLIOGRAPHY: J. Pieper, *Scholasticism* (1960); É. Gilson, *History of Christian Philosophy in the Middle Ages* (1955); I. C. Brady et al., NCE 12:1153–70, with bibliog.

[T. GILBY]

SCHOLASTICUS (scholastic), in medieval times, the title of the canon of a cathedral chapter who served as headmaster of the cathedral grammar school; also the title of the master (*magister*) in charge of curriculum and discipline in a monastic school. In later times the word has often been used to designate a medieval philosopher or theologian, a schoolman, a representative of *scholasticism. Among the Jesuits and other religious a scholastic is a seminarian who has completed his novitiate and has not yet been ordained priest.

[M. B. MURPHY]

SCHOLIUM, an explanatory note written in the margin of an ancient manuscript. The Lat. *scholium* is from the Gr. *scholion*, plural *scholia*. The use of scholia (notes) was a regular practice in Greek schools of later classical antiquity and seems similar to the modern habit of footnotes. Scholia were apparently somewhat briefer and less distracting, since they were usually in the margin next to the word or phrase they elucidated. Christian scholars in such cosmopolitan and thoroughly hellenized cities as Alexandria probably appropriated this scholarly device in common use among their non-Christian colleagues and applied it to biblical and ecclesiastical manuscripts. Biblical scholia gave historical, geographical, grammatical, or theological information needed to understand an obscure text. A scholium is more elaborate than a gloss, which was often incorporated into the text by later copyists; and less elaborate and comprehensive than the later commentaries that gradually replaced them. Both the writer and the compiler of scholia are called scholiasts, and there are extant examples of biblical scholia from Origen, Clement of Alexandria, Jerome, and countless lesser lights. Since commentaries replaced scholia as the appropriate vehicle for elucidating texts, no corpus of ancient biblical scholia has yet been compiled.

[E. J. DILLON]

SCHOLLINER, HERMAN (1722–95), Benedictine historian and theologian. A Bavarian, S. became a monk in 1738. He served as director of the houses of study in Bavaria, professor of dogmatic theology at Salzburg and Ingolstadt, prior of the monastery at Welchenberg. In 1759 he was made a member of the Bavarian Academy of Sciences. S. was a prolific writer. He contributed volumes 11 and 12 for the Bavarian Academy's *Monumenta Boica;* other works were *De magistratuum ecclesiasticorum origine et creatione* (1757), *De hierarchia ecclesiae catholicae* (1757), and *Historia theologiae christianae saeculi primi* (1761).

[J. R. AHERNE]

SCHOLZ, JOHANN MARTIN (1794–1852), Orientalist and Scripture scholar. Prior to his career as Scripture professor at Bonn, S. traveled (1818–21) throughout Europe and the Near East, collecting ancient MSS of the Bible. He was thus enabled to publish a significant critical collection of these MSS in his *Novum Testamentum Graece* (2 v., 1830–36). His exegetical studies do not go beyond the conservative scholarship of his day. BIBLIOGRAPHY: F. E. Gigot, CE 13:553.

[T. M. MCFADDEN]

SCHÖNBORN, a prominent family which provided the Church from mid-17th to mid-18th cent. in the Germanies with ecclesiastics of such influence that the century has been called the Schönborn Era.

Johann Philipp (1605–73), named bp. of Würzburg in 1642, elector-abp. of Mainz in 1647, and bp. of Worms in 1663. He was a successful mediator in the peace negotiations to end the Thirty Years' War. As lord chancellor of Mainz he worked to free Germany from Spanish influence and to maintain peace between the Habsburgs and the Bourbons. A promoter of reform, he established the Mainz seminary, made extensive visitations, forbidding witchcraft trials, building churches, and regulating schools. J. brought Mainz to a high point as a spiritual center.

Lothar Franz (1655–1729), bp., statesman, a nephew of Johann Philipp, elected prince bp. of Bamberg in 1694. He became abp. of Mainz in 1695. As lord chancellor of Mainz he supported the imperial policy and guided his nephews to high ecclesiastical positions. As bp. he encouraged reforms, promoted parish missions, and defended the Imperial Church against Rome. L. was a sponsor of church architecture.

Johann Philip Franz (1673–1724), prince-bp., nephew of Lothar Franz. Provost of the cathedral in Würzburg and later in Mainz, official in Frankfurt and Mainz, J. became imperial ambassaor in the Netherlands, Paris, and Rome. In 1719 he was named prince bp. of Würzburg. Though an absolutist prince, he was an effective administrator of his diocese and a patron of the arts.

Friedrich Karl (1674–1746), bp., prince. A brother of Johann Philip Franz, F. was imperial vice-chancellor, through the influence of his uncle, Lothar Franz, and though opposed to policies of the Habsburgs, he remained loyal to the Austrian dynasty. In 1729 he was named bp. of Bamberg and later the same year became bp. of Würzburg. As bp. he was a strong pastoral influence on his diocese, improving the quality of the clergy, encouraging missions, and promoting piety.

Damian Hugo (1676–1743), cardinal bp., nephew of Lothar Franz. D. was imperial commissar in Hamburg, ambassador to Berlin, in 1715 made a cardinal, in 1719 named prince bp. of Speyer, and in 1740 prince bp. of Constance. He was an able administrator, both civil and ecclesiastical, and a man of humility and great piety.

Franz Georg (1682–1756), bp., statesman. Another

nephew of Lothar Franz, F. was cathedral provost of Trier. He was made elector and abp. of Trier in 1729 and also bp. of Worms in 1732. He sided with the party that labored to reduce the authority of the Roman Curia and of the papal nunciature in Cologne. A builder and patron of the Univ. of Trier, he was a zealous bp. and a capable elector. BIBLIOGRAPHY: H. Raab, LTK 9:451–453.

[J. R. AHERNE]

SCHONGAUER, MARTIN (called Martin Schön; betw. 1445 and 1450–91), German painter and engraver, son of a goldsmith in Colmar, which accounts for his excellent engravings. S. was probably a student under C. Isenmann. The influence of R. van der Weyden seen in *Christ in Glory* (1469), a copy of Weyden's altarpiece at Beaune, and the Schmerzensmann from Weyden's *Crucifixion Triptych* show that S. did not slavishly imitate but transformed the Flemish into a German style. S.'s *Virgin of the Rose Arbor* (1473) is a German masterpiece of late Gothic painting. Many of his works were destroyed, many assistants having imitated him closely—a *Nativity* and *Holy Family* are contested. His 115 engravings spread his influence throughout Europe. Signed by his initials separated by a cross and crescent (often imitated), S.'s early prints are in painterly terms, modeled with the burin strokes. Most famous is the Gothic, fantastic *Temptation of St. Anthony* (c.1475). The *Death of the Virgin, Flight into Egypt, Road to Calvary* (echoing Jan van Eyck and with a delicacy not equaled until Rembrandt's day), the *Large Crucifixion* and the set of 12 plates, *Passion of Christ,* are masterworks. Later prints are full of an exciting variety of delightful detail, perspective, and texture, the *Annunciation* or *Archangel Gabriel* (c.1480), expressing in dynamic fluidity of drapery an ecstatic lyricism), S.'s late style of ultimate refinement is simplified, delicate, ethereal, graceful (*St. Michael,* 1480–91) and profound in conception. The *Nativity* (c.1480–91) is the epitome of his religious works. A *Censer* from the same period, incredible in detail, is a model for goldsmith work. S.'s engravings influenced Dürer, Van der Goes, and Bosch. BIBLIOGRAPHY: A. Strange, *Deutsche Malerei der Gotik,* (v.7, 1955).

[M. J. DALY]

SCHÖNHERR, JOHANN HEINRICH (1770–1826), German pseudomystic who developed a form of theosophy, a philosophico-religious system that bore some resemblance to the thought of E. Swedenborg in its views of Scripture and the hereafter (though no direct influence can be traced) and some likeness also to early Gnosticism and Manichaeanism. S. did not seek to found a society, but he exercised a strong influence upon a circle of followers. BIBLIOGRAPHY: P. Meinhold, LTK 9:456–457.

[M. J. SUELZER]

SCHÖNHERR, KARL (1867–1943), Austrian Tyrolian dramatist, novelist, strongly influenced by German and French literary naturalism. The characters in his plays are men of passion who cannot escape their destination. The style of his short stories is reminiscent of P. *Rosegger. Son of a school teacher, S. studied medicine in Vienna and became a physician. Works: *Glaube und Heimat* (1910), drama; *Passionsspiel* (1933), drama.

[B. F. STEINBRUCKNER]

SCHOOL SISTERS OF NOTRE DAME, religious congregation dedicated to education. It was founded in Bavaria in 1833 by Bp. Georgs Michael Wittiman and Karolina Gerhardinger. The former, who was canon of the cathedral of Ratisbon, wished to establish a congregation of teaching sisters to continue the work of the suppressed Canonesses of St. Augustine de Notre Dame, the French community founded by Peter Fourier in 1597 and suppressed in 1809. In 1812 he began the work of establishing the new congregation with three young girls, one of whom was Karolina Gerhardinger. These young women attended a Bavarian normal school and taught for about ten years in public schools. Finally they began their community life in Neunburg vorm Wald, and the congregation commenced to grow very rapidly. Today the Sisters conduct schools on all levels, staff special schools, day nurseries, vocational schools, and orphanages located on four continents in 19 countries. The rule written by Mother Theresa of Jesus (Karolina Gerhardinger) was finally approved in 1865. The motherhouse is located in Rome. In 1975 the sisters numbered 9,706 in 911 houses.

[R. C. CLIGGETT]

SCHOOLS, DENOMINATIONAL, see DENOMINATIONAL SCHOOLS.

SCHOOLS OF NURSING, CONFERENCE OF CATHOLIC, a voluntary association formed to promote the interests of Catholic schools of nursing in the United States. It was formally established at a meeting preceding the convention of the Catholic Hospital Association (CHA), in Cleveland in 1948. It replaced the Council on Nursing Education and worked under the guidance of CHA but with relative autonomy. There was at that time a need for all types of Catholic schools of nursing—those connected with colleges and universities as well as those connected with hospitals or religious corporations—to work together to urge accreditation and to assist schools in achieving accreditation. The Conference was dissolved in 1972, its mission accomplished.

[E. J. DILLON]

SCHOOLS OF THEOLOGY, groups of theologians, who under a common local or personal influence, but within one Church and its one profession of faith, represent some more or less similar conceptions, orientations, trends, systems, or syntheses of theology or spirituality. Schools of theology have their origin in the history of dogmas (i.e., the history of the human knowledge of divine revelation and its theological explanation, and of its homogeneous evolution). It is legitimate, therefore, to speak of the one and objective divine revelation expressed in a definite historical setting and form and of its subjective, diversified but valid interpretations or schools. To constitute a healthy theological pluralism, these schools must keep within the limits of orthodoxy set by the teaching authority (*magisterium*) of the Church and avoid theological relativism and heresy. The teaching authority of the Church, therefore, has always distinguished between legitimate and illegitimate schools of theology. Some schools of theology are explicitly formed and sociologically and institutionally perpetuated by a religious order, a school, or a nation. Some are formed more implicitly through differentiation of method, of accentuation, and of philosophical foundation. As one reflects on the problems posed by the very existence of schools of theology, he can usefully keep the following in mind: "To wish to belong to no school would be the part of a proud and stupid man who imagines that here and now he can possess eternal truth outside historical time. To cling to a system as if it fully expressed the faith of the Church would be to deny the historicity of truth." BIBLIOGRAPHY: K. Rahner and H. Vorgrimler, *Theological Dictionary* (ed. C. Ernst, tr. R. Strachan, 1965) 428; K. Rahner, LTK 9:509–512; J. Ratzinger, RGG 6:754–779; Y. M. J. Congar, *La Foi et la théologie* (1962) 197–201; J. Daniélou, *Unité et pluralité en matière de théologie* (*Recherches et débats* 10, 1955), 11–21; J. H. Nicolas, "La Théologie et les théologies," VieS 103 (1960) 227–301.

[P. B. T. BILANIUK]

SCHOONENBERG, PIET (1911–   ), Dutch Jesuit theologian. Having studied at the Jesuit faculty in Maestricht, he was ordained in 1939 and received his doctorate in 1948. For years S. was professor of dogmatics at the Univ. of Nijmegen. His writings call for a reinterpretation of key dogmas. His innovative view that original sin is socially rather than biologically transmitted is widely accepted. His Christology, however, is disputed. Originally S. affirmed that the one person in Jesus was the human person. Now modified, his interpretation is that the Logos first became a mode of God's existence in the human person of Jesus. S.'s eucharistic doctrine emphasizes not the physical, but the personal and spiritual presence of the glorified Jesus. Though controversial, S. has been a gifted and sympathetic guide in developing the Catholic tradition. His works include: *God's Word in the Making* (1963); *Covenant and Creation* (1968); *Christ* (1970).

[P. J. ROSATO]

SCHOPENHAUER, ARTHUR (1788–1860), German philosopher, founder of philosophical pessimism. He was educated privately, then at Göttingen and Berlin. He was a voracious reader with a command of several modern and ancient languages. He taught briefly at Berlin, but Hegel

was at the height of his influence and the bitterly anti-Hegelian S. found few hearers. His philosophy is determinedly atheistic. Although his writings have a misanthropic and esp. misogynistic tone, he was regarded as a charming and witty companion with a perceptive taste in art, music, and the social graces. S. is a direct heir of Kant; indeed, he regarded himself as the only true defender of transcendentalism, while Fichte, Schelling, and Hegel were perverters of the tradition. His metaphysics is marked by Indian and Buddhist influences; his ethics to some extent, by Christian thinking. Distinguishing with Kant the *noumenon* and *phenomenon,* S. sees our knowledge as only phenomenal. He differs from Kant in that the unique thing-in-itself is cosmic will, a blind life-force. This cosmic Will begets the individual will or human consciousness, which in turn begets the phenomenal ideas. Desire for happiness follows on this consciousness; satisfaction of any desire increases consciousness and thus desire. The recognition that happiness is unattainable leads man inevitably to sorrow and suffering. Suffering is the natural state of man. This is the worst of all possible worlds. The only reasonable foundation for man's moral life is to destroy the individual will-to-live. But this cannot be achieved by violent or physical means. Art, by capturing the unique, impersonal idea of beauty, enables man to transcend, though only for a time, the malignant force of the will-to-live. Ultimate happiness is attainable only by the sort of contemplation seen in the mystics, Oriental and Western. When the personal consciousness thus knows and embraces the cosmic will, it is absorbed into it, much as the Buddhist attains Nirvana. S. is well regarded as a stylist. His critical insights, aesthetic and philosophical, surpass his efforts at systematic thought, while many of his reflections on the unconscious anticipate the views of recent and contemporary psychology. BIBLIOGRAPHY: F. C. Copleston, *Schopenhauer, Philosopher of Pessimism* (1946); P. Gardiner, EncPhil 7:325–332.

[W. B. MAHONEY]

SCHOTT, ANSELM (1843–96), German Benedictine, liturgist. He was ordained in 1867 and became a monk at Beuron the following year. Exiled to the abbey of Maredsous near Louvain during the Kulturkampf (1876–81), S. collaborated there in the editing of Benedictine liturgical books. This work led, on his return to Beuron, to his own *Das Messbuch der hl. Kirche* (1884), an immensely influential work in the German liturgical revival. In 1892 S. was assigned to the abbey of Maria Laach, newly restored to the Benedictines, and died there.

[T. C. O'BRIEN]

SCHOTTENKLÖSTER, medieval monasteries established or occupied by Celtic monks from Ireland or Scotland. The earliest were houses stemming from the 6th-7th cent. foundations of St. Columban and his disciples: at Luxeuil, Remiremont, Echternach, St. Gallen, Bobbio, and elsewhere. A later group sprang from Abbot Marianus's monastery of St. James in Regensburg (c.1090), including houses at Würzburg, Nuremberg, Constance, Vienna, etc. Popes Lucius III and Innocent III grouped these German houses into a single congregation under the abbot of Regensburg; they comprise the Schottenklöster in the strict sense. All came under the Benedictine rule, but Celtic customs prevailed, which, together with their Celtic ascetic and learned members, gave these monasteries a unique character. BIBLIOGRAPHY: P. Weissenberger, *Die schottenabtei St. Jakob zu Würzburg und die Fürstabtei St. Gallen-Schweiz* (1975).

[R. H. SCHMANDT]

SCHRADER, KLEMENS (1820–75), German Jesuit, dogmatic theologian at the Collegio Romano (1853–57), the Univ. of Vienna (1857–63), and the Catholic Univ. of Poitiers (1870–75). In 1867 he became a member of the theological commissions preparing for Vatican Council I. His published works include: *Theses theologicae* (1861–69, 1874); *De unitate romana* (2 v., 1862–68); *De Deo creante* (1875). Noteworthy also are his collaboration with his mentor, C. Passaglia in preparatory drafts for the Immaculate Conception dogmatic definition, and his contribution to *Der Papst und die modernen Ideen* (1864–67), a defense of Pius IX's *Syllabus of Errors.

[T. C. O'BRIEN]

SCHRAMM, DOMINIKUS (1722–97), Bavarian Benedictine of the abbey of Banz, Bamberg, professor of theology there (1757–82), renowned mainly for his *Institutiones theologiae mysticae ad usum directorum animarum* . . . (2 v., 1774), based chiefly on Jesuit sources. S. also published *Analysis operum SS. Patrum et scriptorum ecclesiasticorum* (18v., 1780–96), covering the period until St. Epiphanius, and a revision of B. *Carranza's *Summa conciliorum* (4 v., 1778).

[T. C. O'BRIEN]

SCHREMBS, JOSEPH (1866–1945), American archbishop. Born in Bavaria but coming to the U.S. as a child, S. was ordained in 1889 for the Diocese of Grand Rapids, Michigan. For 22 years he did pastoral work there and for eight of those years was diocesan vicar general; in 1911 he was named auxiliary bp. He was appointed later the same year first bp. of Toledo, Ohio, where his organizational skill achieved much in 10 years. Installed as bp. of Cleveland in 1921, he gave zealous administrative leadership to that see. Promoting education, charitable institutions, and social centers, S. made also notable contribution to the restoration of Gregorian chant and the reform of church music. S. was instrumental in securing Vatican approval for the National Catholic Welfare Conference (now USCC) and was the creator of its National Conference of Catholic Men and National Conference of Catholic Women. In 1939 he was made a personal archbishop.

[J. R. AHERNE]

SCHREMPF, CHRISTOPH (1860–1944), German theologian. He taught for a time at the Technical Univ. in Stuttgart, then left the Lutheran Church to form a society of his own in 1909. Under the influence of Kierkegaard he dismissed the dogmatic image of Christ and viewed him as an ethical revolutionary. S. espoused the ideal of a Christianity of simple humanity and truth, apart from Christian Churches. Among his writings were *Natural Christianity* (1892), *About the Open Secret of Life* (1920), and *Goethe's World View* (2 v., 1905–07).

[J. R. AHERNE]

SCHRIJVERS, JOSEPH (1876–1945), Belgian Redemptorist provincial, author of works on the spiritual life. A Redemptorist from 1894 and ordained in 1900, S. was a seminary professor from 1902 at Beauplateau, Belgium. He was assigned 1913–32 to the Ukraine, establishing (1913) at Uniw the first Redemptorist Ukrainian rite foundation and serving there as first vice-provincial in Galicia (formerly Poland, now USSR). S. was provincial of the Belgian province from 1932 until his appointment to Rome as general councillor for the congregation (1936–45). His published works were the fruit of his ministry to religious sisters in the Ukraine and as visitator to Canada, the U.S., and Brazil. As their titles indicate, his writings stress the theme of the Christian's submission to the loving will of the Father: *Les Principes de la vie spirituelle* (1913); *La Bonne volonté* (1913; *On Good Will*, 1917); *La Message de Jésus à son prêtre* (1933); *Le Don de soi* (1918; *The Gift of One's Self*, tr. a Carmelite of Bettendorf, 1934); *Le Divin ami* (1922; *Our Divine Friend*, 1922); *Les Âmes confiantes* (1930); *With the Divine Retreat Master* (tr. E. V. O'Hara, 1939); *Notre père qui êtes aux cieux* (1942). Many of his French works were translated into English and other languages: Flemish, German, Italian, Polish, Spanish, Portuguese, and Ukrainian. He wrote in Ukrainian the popular books: *Moja Nebesna Nenka* (My Heavenly Mother, 1925) and *Isuse, liubliu Tebe!* (Jesus, I Love You! 1930). BIBLIOGRAPHY: M. De Meulemeester *et al.*, *Bibliographie générale des écrivains rédemptoristes* 2 (1935) 391–395; 3 (1939) 383–384.

[T. C. O'BRIEN]

SCHROEDER, HERMANN (1843–1909), German musicologist and composer. S. studied at Magdeburg, taught at his own school and at the Royal Institute for Church Music in Berlin, composed orchestra and chamber music, and wrote a violin method as well as other books on music.

[M. T. LEGGE]

SCHROEDER, PETER JOSEPH (1849–1903), German professor of theology, member of the first faculty of The Catholic Univ. of America (1889–98). He had taught in Belgium (1875–87) and a year previous to his coming to the U.S. had been the successor of M. *Scheeben at Cologne. At CUA he became deeply involved on the German-

American Catholic side of controversies over national parishes and schools (see CAHENSLY, P.). S. resigned his post to join the theological faculty at Münster, where from 1903 he also served as rector.

[T. C. O'BRIEN]

SCHRÖRS, HEINRICH (1852–1928), Catholic church historian, professor at Bonn (1886–1916). He wrote on many contemporary questions and sought in particular to improve clerical education. Although he was looked upon as a liberal, his position was midway between reaction and reform. After his retirement he produced several works on the history of the Church in the early 19th century. BIBLIOGRAPHY: A. Franzen, LTK 9:497.

[M. J. SUELZER]

SCHUBERT, FRANZ (1797–1828), Austrian composer. Born into a modest but very musical family, S. was educated in the choir school of the Royal Chapel of Vienna where he was a student of A. *Salieri. Though he spent some time as a schoolmaster, S. early devoted himself totally to music. At 17 he wrote, among other things, his first Mass (in F), a work of beauty and promise, very well received. Though he was writing some operas at this time, it was the song in which he excelled. Perhaps his greatest song, *Gretchen am Spinnrade,* written at 17, marked what many hail as the birth of the German *Lied.* Innumerable others followed, along with symphonies, piano pieces, overtures, chamber music, cantatas, and other vocal music. Church music was not S.'s special bent; nevertheless, he composed 6 Masses (best known is the Mass in C), which evidence not only his talent but also his piety, a German Mass, settings of the Salve Regina, a Stabat Mater in 12 movements, and an unaccompanied choral setting on the Hebrew text of the 92nd Psalm. S. was a contemporary of Beethoven, whom he idolized and with whom he carried forward the classical school of Haydn and Mozart into the romantic period of music. The list of his works is very long and, although he was the least educated of the great German musicians, his keen musical sense and inexhaustible fund of melody greatly compensated. BIBLIOGRAPHY: Oscar Bie, *Schubert, The Man* (1928); *Music of Schubert* (ed. G. Abraham, 1969).

[M. T. LEGGE]

SCHUBIGER, ANSELM (1815–88), Swiss priest and church music authority. Among his publications are *Die Sangerschule St. Gallens* (1858) and a collection of essays on medieval music entitled *Musikalische Spicilegien . . .* (1876).

[M. T. LEGGE]

SCHULTE, JOHANN FRIEDRICH VON (1827–1914), historian of canon law, chief organizer of German *Old Catholics. A native of Westphalia, S., a layman, became professor of canon law at Prague (1854) and adviser to

the archbishop. Relinquishing these offices because of his opposition to Vatican Council I, he organized and chaired the first three Old Catholic congresses (1871–72) and obtained Bismarck's permission for an episcopal election. S. secured Old Catholic title to many RC churches in Germany and won Old Catholicism legal status in Austria. Professor at Bonn (1873–1906), he served in the Reichstag (1874–79), defending the *Kulturkampf. His historical studies are of high merit. BIBLIOGRAPHY: C. B. Moss, *Old Catholic Movement* (1966).

[E. E. BEAUREGARD]

SCHULTES, REGINALD (1873–1928), Swiss Dominican ecclesiologist; for most of his career professor at the Angelicum (now the Univ. of St. Thomas Aquinas), Rome. S.'s best known work is his *De ecclesia* (1925), a text that reflected the juridic viewpoint of the Church that has been largely replaced by post-Vatican II ecclesiology.

[T. C. O'BRIEN]

SCHUMANN, ROBERT (1810–1856), German composer. Son of a bookseller, S. received at Leipzig Univ. and Heidelberg a classical education aimed at a career in law. An early interest and talent in music led him, however, to apply himself seriously to music study under Wieck (whose talented daughter Clara he later married) and Dorn. An unfortunate accident cut off a promising career as a concert pianist, and S. turned entirely to composing and to literary works. As founder and editor of the periodical, *Neue Zeitschrift für Musik,* he exercised a great influence for good in the progress of music of the time. S. was one of the leaders, along with Chopin and Mendelssohn, of the romantic school. His works number mainly piano pieces and songs—his best works—but he also composed symphonies, piano concertos, chamber and choral music, etc. His output of religious music was limited: a setting of Psalm 60, a Mass, a requiem, and a few other compositions.

[M. T. LEGGE]

SCHUMANN-HEINK, ERNESTINE (1861–1936), one of the great prima donnas of the opera. Reared a Catholic in Austria, she endured poverty a good part of her life and found her way into opera only after many disappointments. Her first audition at the Court Opera in Vienna failed because of her appearance and poverty. She sang minor roles for four seasons in the Dresden Royal Opera, beginning in 1878. Dismissed because of her marriage to Ernest Heink, she concentrated on rearing the first four of her nine children. Heink deserted her and a divorce followed. A turning point in her career came in 1888 when she sang the role of Carmen in the Hamburg Opera. In 1898 she came to the Metropolitan Opera in New York, making her debut on November 7. She married Paul Schumann, by whom she had three children. S.-H. left the Metropolitan to sing in operatta in 1904; Schumann died and left her with seven children. She married again and had two more children. In

1905 she became an American citizen. S.-H. returned to the Metropolitan for Wagnerian roles. When the U.S. entered World War I, she spent much of her time singing for servicemen. Contemporaries remember her passionate pleas after World War I against the barbarism of war. Her farewell appearance at the Metropolitan came in 1932. Thereafter she made concert tours throughout the U.S. and sang extensively on radio.

[J. R. AHERNE]

SCHUPP, JOHANN BALTHASAR (1610–61), Protestant preacher, satirist, professor of history and rhetoric at Marburg (1634–46), pastor in Hamburg (1649–66). For his introduction of anecdotes and other humorous matter into his sermons, S. has often been compared with Abraham a Santa Clara. His writings (collected in 1663) are moral and didactic in purpose, satiric and popular in style (e.g., *Der Freund in der Not,* 1657; *Corinna,* 1660). BIBLIOGRAPHY: H. de Boor and R. Newald, *Geschichte der deutschen Literatur* (1951) 312–315.

[M. F. MCCARTHY]

SCHÜRER, EMIL, (1844–1910), NT scholar. S. taught Scripture at several German universities, and is best noted for his *Geschichte des jüdischen Volkes im Zeitalter Jesu Christi* (4 v., 4th ed., 1910–11), a scholarly history of the Jews at the time of Christ. S. published several NT studies, demonstrating the emphasis upon divine grace in Jesus' message and the continuity between that message and Paul's teaching. S. also founded and edited (1876–80; 1888–1910) the periodical *Theologische Literaturzeitung.* BIBLIOGRAPHY: G. F. Moore, HTR 14(1921) 237–241; O. Kaiser, NCE 12:1184.

[T. M. MCFADDEN]

SCHUSTER, ILDEFONSO (1880–1954), Benedictine liturgist and historian, abp. of Milan (from 1929) and card. (from 1929). Born of a Bavarian father and an Austrian mother in Rome, where his father worked as a tailor, S. grew up a Roman and made his profession as a monk (1899) at the Benedictine Abbey of St. Paul-outside-the-Walls. He served his order as novice master (1904–16), prior (1916–18), procurator general for the Cassinese congregation (1914–29), and abbot (1918–29). He was widely respected for his scholarship in the fields of monastic and liturgical history. His most important work, the *Liber sacramentorum,* (9 v., 1919–29) was translated into English under the title *The Sacramentary: Historical and Liturgical Notes on the Roman Missal* (tr. A. Levelis-Marke, 5 v. 1925–31), and his biography of St. Benedict appeared in English as *St. Benedict and His Times* (tr. G. J. Roettger, 1951). S. was a zealous abp. and was held in high esteem for his holiness of life. Nevertheless, he disappointed many of his admirers abroad by showing some favor to the Fascist regime, although he was strongly opposed to the racist trend that began under German influence and was felt in Italian Fas-

cism after 1938. BIBLIOGRAPHY: R. F. McNamara, NCE 12:1184–85.

[P. K. MEAGHER]

SCHÜTZ, HEINRICH (1585–1672), German composer. S. was a choir boy in the court chapel at Kassel. In 1609 he went to Venice where he studied under Gabrieli for 3 years. He returned to Kassel as court organist; then, in 1615, became court *Kapellmeister* at Dresden. He made frequent visits to Italy and to Copenhagen. S. was the composer of the first German opera, *Dafne,* now lost, and is considered of very great importance in the development of German music, standing, as he does, between Palestrina and Bach. S. not only succeeded in bridging the gap between the Italian and German, the Renaissance and Baroque, but produced a body of music of great beauty and masterful technique. S. is primarily a church music composer. His works include *Cantiones sacrae, Symphoniae sacrae,* psalms, motets, Passions, the "Resurrection" in oratorio, the "Seven Words from the Cross," and a Christmas oratorio. S. also wrote madrigals and arias. His works have had two complete printings in modern times.

[M. T. LEGGE]

SCHWABACH ARTICLES, a Lutheran statement of belief prepared in 1529; the basis for the for the first part (Art. 1–21) of the *Augsburg Confession. They were 17 in number, and were a revision of the *Marburg Articles made by Martin Luther assisted by P. Melanchthon, J. *Jonas, J. Brenz, and others. The articles took sharp issue with the eucharistic doctrine of *Zwingli. Presented at Schwabach, Oct. 16, 1529, they were intended as a statement of creedal unity by the Lutheran princes. BIBLIOGRAPHY: Schaff Creeds 1:228–229.

[P. DAMBORIENA]

SCHWANE, JOSEPH (1824–92), German theologian, historian of dogma, mainly at the theological faculty of Münster, where from 1881 he held the chair of dogmatics. His *Dogmengeschichte* (4 v., 1862–90) organizes the dogmatic themes of scholastic theology according to their historical development. He also published several dogmatic monographs, and two works in moral theology, *Spezielle Moraltheologie* (3 v., 1873–78) and *Allgemeine Moraltheologie* (1885).

[T. C. O'BRIEN]

SCHWARTZ, EDUARD (1858–1940), philologist, patristic scholar. A professor at a number of German universities, notably Strassburg and Munich, S. devoted his research to a series of studies of patristic writers. He published editions of Tatian, Athanasius, and Eusebius. His chief work was *Acta conciliorum oecumenicorum;* begun in 1914 and continued until his death, it was an edition of the Greek Councils based on his own research. This work presents the first critical edition of the acts of the Councils of

Ephesus and Chalcedon. Another significant contribution was his collection of papers on Athanasius in the *Göttingen Gesellschaft* (1904–11).

[J. R. AHERNE]

SCHWARTZ, RUDOLPH (1897–1961), German architect. Engaged in important secular works in postwar Cologne, and achieving also, through philosophical deductions, a spiritual significance in church building, he approached church design metaphysically, effecting a strength, directness, and overwhelming simplicity of sacred space embracing altar and congregation (Fronluchnamskirche, Aachen, 1930). In his famous book *Vom Bau der Kirche* (tr. *The Church Incarnate, The Sacred Function of Christian Architecture*), termed truly great by the visionary genius Mies van der Rohe, S. sought a "sacred inwardness" past materials, refuting the sterile, imitative eclecticism of a century. Following the disruption of wars S. designed in the 1960s finest buildings in the noble, strong, simple churches of Maria Königin Frechen (1954), St. Anna, Düren (1956), probably his greatest, and Maria Königin, Saarbrücken (1959).

[M. J. DALY]

SCHWARZENBERG, FRIEDRICH JOSEPH ZU (1809–85), prince abp. of Salzburg, abp. of Prague, cardinal. Making his ecclesiastical studies in Vienna, S. was influenced by Günther, who exercised a long influence over him and for whom S. interceded when Günther was condemned by Rome. Ordained in 1833, he became abp. at the age of 26 and at 33, a cardinal. A strongly pastoral bp., he convened the synod of 1848, the first to be held in Salzburg in 175 years. S. urged nonintervention in politics but counselled efforts to establish good relations with civil authority. The synod addressed the imperial parliament and asserted the rights of the Church as part of the current concern for civil rights. In 1849 under S.'s leadership, for the first time the Austrian bps. as a body met at Vienna. A series of decrees and memorials to the imperial government gave the Church's views on marriage, education, church property, ecclesiastical jurisdiction, monasticism, school and church funds, and ecclesiastical administration. Appointed abp. of Prague in 1850, S. continued his leadership, convening a meeting of bps. of the Empire at Vienna in 1856 to carry out the provisions of the recently approved concordat. The years following saw S. vainly striving to have the State observe the concordat, an ideal never realized. S. took part in Vatican I where he opposed the definition of papal infallibility. As a member of the House of Peers, he strove to stem anti-Church legislation. It was passed by parliament but not signed by the emperor. S. was a powerful figure in the conflict between Church and State in the 19th century. BIBLIOGRAPHY: C. Wolfsgruber, CE 13:595–597.

[J. R. AHERNE]

SCHWEITZER, ALBERT (1875–1965), German Protestant theologian, musicologist, and medical missionary, famed for his accomplishments in several fields but esp. for the hospital he founded in French Equatorial Africa. Born in Kaysersburg, Alsace (then part of Germany), the son of an Evangelical Lutheran pastor, he spent his earliest years in the village of Gunsbach and received his secondary education in Müllhausen. His prodigious intellectual development unfolded largely at the Univ. of Strasbourg, where he remained as a student or teacher from 1893 to 1913. He took a doctorate in philosophy in 1899, Kant being his special interest, and the next year received his licentiate in theology. His first book, *The Mystery of the Kingdom of God* (1901; tr. 1925), propounded what was to become the essential theme of his theological work: that Christ's life and teaching could only be interpreted in the light of his and his contemporaries' belief in the imminent end of the world—an eschatological approach ("consequent eschatology"; see ESCHATOLOGISM) that was developed still further in S.'s influential and controversial *The Quest of the Historical Jesus* (1906; tr. 1910) and was again to be applied in *Paul and His Interpreters* (1911; tr. 1912). Meanwhile, in 1902, S. had become lecturer and head of a theological college at Strasbourg. During the same period he was also acquiring a formidable reputation as a church and concert organist and as a leading authority on the composer Johann Sebastian Bach, of whom he published a highly regarded biography in 1905. Thus by the time he was 30, S. had established himself as a successful preacher and professor and achieved international recognition as a religious thinker, musical expert, and organ designer. It was at this point—in keeping with a vow to dedicate himself to the relief of mankind once he had reached that age—that he took up the study of medicine so as to prepare for a new career as a healer in Africa. In 1913, after receiving his medical degree, he and his wife, a nurse, left for Gabon in French Equatorial Africa, there to found the Schweitzer Hospital at Lambaréné on the Ogouwe River. There, amidst primitive tribesmen and far from the intellectual pleasures he had known, he was to minister to the sick for over four decades. His work was interrupted in 1917, when he was interned in France as an enemy alien; during this interlude he published *Civilization and Ethics* (1923), in which he set forth his "reverence for life" philosophy. He returned to Africa in 1924, thereafter travelling to Europe or America only to raise funds for his expanding hospital by means of lectures and organ recitals. His wide-ranging humanitarian achievements won for him the 1952 Nobel Prize for Peace.

[E. M. GATES]

SCHWENKFELD, CASPAR (Schwenkfeld von Ossig; 1489–1561), German reformer, exponent of a spiritualized Christianity. A Silesian nobleman, university educated, S. turned to Lutheran reform ideas *c.*1520. He had early misgivings, however, that Luther's teaching would be interpreted to make justification purely outward, without moral transformation of the Christian. S.'s own central idea was that salvation, a continuous inner experience, is deliverance from sin through Christ, the Divine Word made flesh, who communicates himself to the soul. The place of Bible, Church, and sacraments depends upon this primary inner spiritual experience. S. fell out with Luther in 1527 specifically over the interpretation of the Lord's Supper. He was denounced and persecuted by Lutherans; his doctrines were condemned in Art. 12 of the *Formula of Concord. The *Schwenkfelder Church descends from those "quiet spirituals" who treasured S.'s writings. The ideas of S. anticipated the *Inner Light doctrine of the Quakers and the emphasis on experience in Pietism and Methodism. An edition of his works has been published in the U.S. (v. 1–29, 1907–61). BIBLIOGRAPHY: R. M. Jones, *Spiritual Reformers in the 16th and 17th Centuries* (pa., 1959); P. I. Maier, *Caspar Schwenkfeld on the Person and Work of Christ* (1959).

SCHWENKFELDER CHURCH, a group inspired by the teachings of C. *Schwenkfeld, and owing its origins in the U.S. to a band of 184 religious exiles from Austrian Silesia who came to Pennsylvania, in 1734. Led by Christopher Schultz, these Schwenkfelders formed schools (1764) and a charity fund (1774) before formally organizing their Church in 1782 and did not erect a house of worship until 1790. Their five congregations, with about 2,300 members, are all in E Pennsylvania. The Schwenkfelder faith is built on experiential religion, like the later Pietism and Methodism, shunning the external for the internal. Faith is needed for a Christocentric life. External baptism cannot wash away sins. One who has heard or read the external word of the Bible without also hearing the inner word of Jesus Christ speaking to his heart has not heard the gospel of grace. Without faith one receives only the bread and wine and not the body and blood of Christ. Essentially a group of born-again Christians, Schwenkfelders have little formal organization, a congregational polity, and simple Protestant worship. To be baptized, members must profess Christ themselves. There is no proselytizing, although an extensive publication program of books by and about Schwenkfeld is supported, as well as missionary work in Angola and Rhodesia. BIBLIOGRAPHY: S. G. Schultz, *History of the Schwenkfelder Religious Movement* (1959).

SCHWETZ, JOHANN BAPTIST (1803–90), theologian. A citizen of the Austro-Hungarian Empire, S. taught theology at Olmütz and Vienna. In 1861 he published an erudite *Theologia dogmatica catholica,* which opposed Josephinism and the teachings of *Günther. Vatican Council I's statement against Günther had S. as author.

[J. R. AHERNE]

SCIENCE AND HEALTH, WITH A KEY TO THE SCRIPTURES, the principal work of Mary Baker *Eddy and the fundamental doctrinal statement of the *Church of Christ, Scientist. First published in 1875 as *Science and Health,* it was subsequently revised many times by the author. In 1883, the 6th ed., one of the most extensive revisions, added *A Key to the Scriptures* with much other new

material. The final revision was made in the 91st ed. in 1907. In all Christian Science services, readings from the Bible and from *Science and Health* alternate, and they are received as of equal weight, the latter interpreting the former.

[R. K. MacMASTER]

SCIENTIA MEDIA, literally, an intermediary kind of divine foreknowledge; an idea developed principally by L. *Molina and espoused by other Jesuit theologians. Molina conceived of three kinds of divine knowledge about creation: a necessary knowledge, the object of which is all possible being; a free knowledge, the object of which is all that God freely wills to create; a "middle" knowledge, the object of which are *futuribles. Like necessary knowledge, this knowledge is anterior to the causative decree of God's will. Like free knowledge it is not of the merely possible but of a kind of actual being: the futurible is an event or actuality that would come to be, given certain conditions. The specific futurible with which this kind of foreknowledge is connected is the consent of the human will to grace offered. Through this device Molina sought to solve the problem of the concordance of the divine, efficacious causality, and the freedom of the human will. Because the conditioned consent of the will is foreknown prior to any causative act of God's will, that consent is free on man's part, not brought about by divine causality. But because the grace given by reason of the foreseen favorable response of man involves God's choice actually to give his grace, in circumstances where it will be accepted, grace remains a free gift. This teaching led to acrid disputes between Dominicans and Jesuits and ultimately to the inconclusive *Congregatio de auxiliis.* The matters at issue are for contemporary theology of merely antiquarian interest.

[T. C. O'BRIEN]

SCIENTISM, the belief, of which positivism and behaviorism are contemporary examples, that the only valid knowledge is that derived from the mathematico-physical or empirical sciences. One basis of scientism is the obvious success of these sciences, esp. as contrasted with the supposed sterility of philosophical investigations. Forming the other basis are the specifically philosophical theses of mathematicism, influential through such thinkers as Pythagoras, Descartes, Russell, and Whitehead; and physicalism or materialism, as held by Democritus, Hobbes, and Carnap. Such philosophical theses, of course, cannot be established by scientific method. Because the method of physical science involves the observation and measurement of physical phenomena, i.e., of quantities of matter in motion, the reality permitted by scientism is an impoverished one; of its nature it leaves the non-measurable unknowable, thus eliminating the qualitative, the noumenal, love, the soul, and God, because these are beyond empirical methods.

[R. E. HENNESSEY]

SCILLITAN MARTYRS, a group of twelve Christians martyred in the Numidian town of Scillium (location unknown) on July 17, 180 at the beginning of the reign of Commodus. Their *acta,* authentic beyond doubt, besides being the earliest extant document of African church history, is also the earliest dated Christian document in Latin. It records the trial of seven men and five women at Carthage before the proconsul Saturninus and their condemnation and execution for refusing to give up their faith and to swear by the emperor. Their cult was widespread in Africa, and a large basilica was later built over their tomb. Text, *Passion of Perpetua with an Appendix on the Scillitan Martyrs,* Texts and Studies 1 (2) (ed. J. Armitage-Robinson, 1891) 104–121; *Some Authentic Acts of the Early Martyrs* (tr. and ed. E. Owen, 1927) 71–74. BIBLIOGRAPHY: H. Leclercq, DACL 15.1:1014–21; Butler 3:124–126.

[R. B. ENO]

SCIOPPIUS, KASPAR (Schoppe; 1576–1649), scholar and polemicst. His early work was in classical philology. He converted to Catholicism in 1598, recording the transformation in *De migratione sua ad Catholicos* (1599). In Rome, his avid anti-Protestant writings, particularly against James I of England, gained favor of the popes and Catholic princes. S. became the polemical protagonist of the Catholic side of the Thirty Years War, though he questioned the use of arms against heretics in *Classicum belli sacri* (1619). His hostility to the Jesuits escalated after 1632, and before his death he had written 17 antagonistic polemics against the Society.

[R. J. LITZ]

SCOFIELD REFERENCE BIBLE, an edition of the Bible edited by Cyrus I. Scofield (1841–1923), with a dispensational framework for interpreting the Scriptures (see DISPENSATIONALISM). A lawyer without theological training, converted in 1879, Scofield became a pastor and popular Bible Conference speaker. Drawing heavily upon the works of J. N. *Darby and other *Plymouth Brethren, he developed his Reference Bible with the aid of several consulting editors. First published in 1909 (rev., 1917), this Bible with its convenient divisions and explanatory introductions and footnotes offered a simplified and appealing system of Bible study. Adopted by many *Bible schools, the edition spread dispensational teachings across the northern states. In 1967 a revised edition was issued; the basic system was left unchanged, but some archaisms in the biblical text (the AV) were replaced. Ussher's chronology was abandoned, and some ambiguities were cleared up. BIBLIOGRAPHY: H. Lindsell, "Changes in the Scofield Bible," *Christianity Today* II (1967) 711–712; C. N. Kraus, *Dispensationalism in America: Its Rise and Development* (1958).

[N. H. MARING]

SCONE ABBEY, an abbey built by Augustinian canons adjoining the ancient church of Scone, Perthshire, once the capital of the Scoto-Pictish kingdom. The church was made over to the canons by Alexander I *c.*1120, and the abbey erected *c.*1163. It was destroyed by the reformers in 1559. BIBLIOGRAPHY: G. W. S. Barrow, "Scottish Rulers and the Religious Orders," *Transactions of the Royal Historical Society* 3 (1953) 77–100; D. E. Easson, *Medieval Religious Houses: Scotland* (1957) 83.

SCORN, a word of Teutonic origin, in morals a passionately and often indignantly toned contempt. A disdain for the squalid is part of the virtue of being finely tempered, *temperantia*; sometimes it is best expressed by silence. But despising is commonly a fault. It is against charity to hold our neighbor cheap, against justice to treat him as trash, and insult is added to injury when this is done with taunts (*contumelia*) and mockery (*derisio*). It incurs the obligation, in this case, difficult and delicate to fulfill, of making *restitution. BIBLIOGRAPHY: ThAq ST 2a2ae, 34.4; 37; 41.2; 72; 73; 75; 144; 145.

[T. GILBY]

SCORY, JOHN (d. 1585), successively bp. of Rochester (1551), Chichester (1552), and Hereford (1559). A Cambridge Dominican, S. became a secular priest upon the dissolution of the monasteries, a change of status that led to prosperity and advancement. He was one of the bps. who took part in the controversial consecration of M. *Parker as abp. of Canterbury. BIBLIOGRAPHY: W. A. J. Archbold, DNB 51:8–9.

[M. J. SUELZER]

SCOT, THOMAS (**Rotherham;** 1423–1500), chancellor of Cambridge Univ. (1469–71, 1473–79, 1483–85); master of Pembroke Hall (1480–88); bp. of Rochester (1468–72), of Lincoln (1472–80); bp. of York (1480–1500). He was chancellor of England (1474–83). A benefactor of Lincoln College, Oxford, he also left a large number of books to Cambridge University.

[C. D. ROSS]

SCOTISM, a major scholastic synthesis, Augustinian in its theological antecedents, Aristotelian in its philosophical ones. It derives from the development and application of the teachings of John Duns Scotus, the "Subtle Doctor." In his own lifetime (1265 or 1266–1308) he attempted to synthesize the traditional Augustinian theology of the Franciscans (as in Alexander of Hales and Bonaventure) with the emergent Aristotelianism of the schools. His followers were to do battle with those who preferred either the older way, or the new, nominalistic Aristotelianism of *William of Ockham. Scotism achieved the height of its influence in the 17th century. Identified chiefly with Franciscans, it also had a wide influence on thinkers of other orders and even on some outside the Roman Church, e.g., Christian Wolff, and C. S. Peirce. The philosophical positions of Scotism are different from those of *Thomism, some markedly so. The proper object of the human mind is the concept of being as being, not the essences of material things. Being is a unique metaphysical concept, and God and creatures are seen as two modes of being, infinite and finite. Metaphysics is presupposed to all particular sciences. In *natural theology, God's existence is provable from contingence and from his unique attribute of infinity. God's freedom and love are paramount. In moral philosophy, man's happiness and freedom derive from his love of God, for will is the superior power in man. Man knows the concrete singular directly and not by recourse to the internal sensible representation. In natural philosophy, primary matter is not purely potential but has an act of its own, a plurality of forms is asserted, and essence and existence are not really distinct. The most notable positions in theology are (1) God's love for man as the primary motive of the Incarnation; (2) the congruous merit accruing to natural human acts by reason of God's infinite love for man and the predestination of man for eternal happiness; (3) the doctrine of Mary's Immaculate Conception and her intimate role in man's salvation.

Duns Scotus died at age 42 with the synthesis he had envisioned unachieved, but his influence was immediate and began to spread. The new generation at Oxford accepted sympathetically his positions on grace and divine foreknowledge. A number of disciples appeared at Paris, where Francis of Meyronnes may be noted as the source of Scotism in its further development. Here two of the hallmarks, the univocal concept of being and the distinction "actual formal *a parte rei,*" received particular attention. John of Bassolis (d. 1347) expounded the chief points of Scotism, esp, the objective nature of genera and species. In the theological controversies of the cent., Peter of Aquila (d. 1361) was so faithful to the master that he acquired the nickname Scotellus. He published a compendium of Scotus's doctrine. The 15th cent. saw the publication of Scotistic commentaries on Peter Lombard's *Sentences,* works on the "formalities" of being, and many works on the Immaculate Conception. After 1500, several editions of Scotus's works were printed and commentaries on them proliferated. The Franciscans in Italy, esp. Maurice O'Fihely, Antonio Trombetta (the foe of Cajetan), and Francesco Licheto, spearheaded the new Scotism. Theological and philosophical lexicons and manuals multiplied. By 1593 Scotus's works had replaced the *Sentences* as the textbook in Franciscan houses of study. Interest was not confined to the Franciscans. At the close of the 16th and beginning of the 17th cent. Scotistic chairs were established at the Univ. of Salamanca, Alcalá, Coimbra, Rome, Padua, Paris, Louvain, Budapest, Cracow, and Kiev. The Franciscan general chapter of Toledo in 1633 made Scotism the official teaching of the order, directing that a philosophical manual be written and that a new edition of Scotus's works be printed. This was done by Luke Wadding, an Irish Franciscan. The directive gave new impetus; over the next 100 years many manuals and commentaries were published in Rome, Paris, Louvain, Spain, and Portugal. Other philosophers were influenced by this trend. The Scotistic concept of being and of the role of metaphysics in

philosophy can be noted in the work of Leibniz and Christian Wolff.

The 18th and the early 19th cent. brought the French Revolution, the supression of religious houses, the Napoleonic wars, and decline for all scholastic systems, Scotism not excepted. But historical studies in the later 19th cent., chiefly non-Franciscan, renewed interest in Scotus. He suffered in obscurity to some extent, for major work was centered on Thomas and Bonaventure, while every philosophical and theological error that had arisen since his time was laid at his door. Recent scholarship (from 1903) has corrected this imbalance. A critical edition of Scotus's works is in preparation and should make for an even more accurate judgment on his work. Scotism has generally been viewed in comparison with Thomism; they must be seen as two scholastic systems, both compatible with RC doctrine. From differing philosophical viewpoints (Avicenna for Scotus, Aristotle for Thomas), each strives for a deeper understanding of revelation BIBLIOGRAPHY: B. M. Bonansea, EncPhil 7:344–345; C. Balic and J. A. Weisheipl, NCE 12:1226–29.

[W. B. MAHONEY]

SCOTLAND. At the time when Christian missionary activity reached Scotland in the 5th cent., the country was composed of four tribal kingdoms, namely, going round clockwise from N to W, of the still-pagan Picts, about whom little is known; of the Angles, not yet converted to Christianity, pushing up from Northumbria; of the British, kin to the Welsh, among whom Christianity had persisted since Roman times; and of the Scots who had come from Ireland and brought their religion with them. The first missionary advance came from St. Ninian in the Southwest and he was followed up in the 6th cent. by St. Columba from Iona. By these efforts combined with the advance of the Benedictines from England, the Angles were Christianized; the Picts followed and were united to the Scots under the threat of the Norsemen who were raiding and eventually making settlements all round their coasts. By the 11th cent. a Celtic kingdom had been established, with a Celtic Church without diocesan organization and centered in the monks. A broad band of Picto-Scots stretched across the country between people of Scandinavian stock in the north and the Anglo-British to the south.

The cultural and religious pressures set up by the Norman conquest of England were too great to withstand. St. *Margaret, Queen of Scotland, an English princess, sought to apply the common Western discipline, and by the 12th cent. the administration, civil and ecclesiastical, of the country outside the W and N Highlands was of a piece with that of the rest of Europe. Politically, however, England became the hereditary enemy, and so remained even after the two crowns were united in 1603. "The auld alliance" with France was the cornerstone of foreign policy. We need not enter into the war, sometimes bloody conflicts between rival gangs rather than clashes of national interest, about which the great churchmen often showed themselves more solicitous than the nobles. Ecclesiastical freedom from the claims of Canterbury and York was won in the bull of Celestine III, which declared the Church in Scotland to be "the special daughter of the Holy See with mediation by none."

That there were many defects on the eve of the Reformation is undoubted; nevertheless, modern historians and a growing body of educated opinion no longer endorse the dour and godly interpretation of history prevalent for centuries. Mary Queen of Scots is seen as the last gesture, not only of Catholicism, but of a way of life more singing and sunny than that of Calvinism. By episcopal initiative and papal confirmation, the universities of St. Andrews (1412), Glasgow (1451), and Aberdeen (1495) had been founded—Edinburgh was post-Reformation—and the patronage of the arts and a belated renewal of discipline were features of clerical life. But lay control and the weakening of the parishes for the benefit of ecclesiastical and secular corporations left the Church without effective officers and a rank and file to fight the Reformers, most ably led by John Knox. In 1560 a parliament abolished papal supremacy; in the same year Knox's *Confession of Faith* was adopted, and in 1564 his *Book of Common Order*.

The Stuart kings were not successful in erecting an episcopal superstructure on presbyterian foundations, and the *Covenanters abolished the first attempt in 1638, while the second was brought to an end in 1690, when presbytery was re-established under William of Orange. In the following century both Catholics and Episcopalians continued to support the Stuart cause, but their hopes were extinguished with the failure of Prince Charles's uprising in 1745. The union of the English and Scottish parliaments and the creation of the United Kingdom formed one solidly Protestant power. Scottish law, however, was preserved, and its judicial procedures follow those of Roman law.

The Church of Scotland is the most powerful religious body in Scotland and represents the majority; it continues a high tradition in systematic theology and has developed a strong sense of social responsibility, and though still sensitive to popish and episcopal bogies, becomes increasingly appreciative of pre-Reformation Scottish Christianity. Catholicism, which survived in the Hebrides and Highland glens, has grown greatly through the Irish immigration concentrated on Clydeside and is now professed by about a third of the population. The RC hierarchy was restored by Leo XIII in 1878. The presence of the Irish was at first resented and still offers problems; but after all, they were but repeating a tribal movement of 1500 years earlier, which gave Scotland its name and, in fact, has produced a people with its own special identity.

The social importance of communicants of the Episcopalian Church is out of proportion to their numbers, about 60,000. Recognized denominational schools are supported by the State. Religious bigotry still lurks and crops up savagely on occasion.

[T. GILBY]

SCOTLAND, CHURCH OF, see CHURCH OF SCOTLAND.

SCOTS CONFESSION (Scottish Confession), the document presented to the Estates of Scotland in 1560 as a summary of the doctrines held by the new Reformed Kirk. It is sometimes known as the First, as distinguished from the Second Confession; the latter, sometimes called the Scottish National or Negative Covenant of 1581, being an anti-Roman appendix to the former. The 1560 confession, written in 4 days by John *Knox and five colleagues, was approved and engrossed in the register of Parliament on Aug. 17. Grounded on "God's holy Word," it contains 25 articles or chapters, 12 of which set forth the doctrines of the ancient creeds. The influence of Luther and Calvin is also evident in the teaching on justification and good works, preaching, and the sacraments. Article 16, "Of the Kirk," is of particular importance: the Kirk is defined as Catholic, "a company and multitude of men and women chosen of God," outside of which there is neither life nor eternal felicity. This visible Church is also ascertainable, and in Art. 18 the notes of the true Kirk are defined as neither "Antiquitie, Title usurpit, lineal Descence, Place appointed, nor multitude of men approving an error," but rather the true preaching of the word of God, the right administration of the sacraments, and ecclesiastical discipline uprightly ministered. The powers of the State (Art. 24) are ordained by God "for the singular profite and commoditie of mankind" magistrates are "Lieu-tennents of God" and have therefore both civic and religious powers. The Confession is marked by a freshness of expression, enthusiasm, and humility. In 1647 it was superseded by the *Westminister Confession, a creed of severer logic and theological exactness. BIBLIOGRAPHY: J. A. Duke, *History of the Church of Scotland to the Reformation* (1937) 247, 249–255; Schaff Creeds 1:680–685; 3:437–478.

[J. A. R. MACKENZIE]

SCOTT, JOSEPH (1867–1958), lawyer, lay leader. Born and educated in England, S. came to the U.S. in 1889. A prevailing force in the growth of Los Angeles for 65 years, he was at the same time a Catholic lay leader both in California and throughout the country. He became dean of law at Loyola Univ., Los Angeles, and well known across the U.S. As a defender of the Church, he founded the Los Angeles Chamber of Commerce, was a member of the school board and its president (1906–11). In 1932 at the Republican Convention, he nominated Herbert Hoover. He was active in promoting the Holy Name Society, the Society of St. Vincent de Paul, Society for Perpetual Adoration, and Catholic Big Brothers. He was honored by the Holy See and by many Catholic colleges.

[J. R. AHERNE]

SCOTT, RICHARD WILLIAM (1852–1913), political leader. A Canadian Catholic, S. studied law and served in the legislature of United Canada, 1857–63, and after Confederation as senator in that of Ontario, 1867–73. He was also secretary of state and registrar general for two terms. He was Liberal leader of the Senate from 1902 to 1908, sponsored the Separate School Law of 1863, in which provision was made for Catholic schools, and was a leader in the selection of Ottawa as the national capital.

[J. R. AHERNE]

SCOTT, WALTER (1796–1861), one of four pioneers of the Christian Church (Disciples of Christ). Born and educated in Scotland, he migrated to the U.S. in 1818. His chief contribution was in evangelism. He rejected emotional revivalism with its subjective ''signs'' of conversion and sought an objective pattern consistent with the rationalism of John Locke and Francis Bacon. This S. found in his analysis of ''the ancient gospel'' from Acts. It involved six steps: three for man (faith, repentance, and baptism by immersion) and three for God, assured on rational grounds and scriptural promise (remission of sins, gift of the Holy Spirit, and life eternal). By combining the last two steps into one, the five were graphically taught as a five-finger exercise and were widely used for three generations. Scott was the first president of Bacon College at Georgetown, Ky., the Disciples' first college. Chief of seven books S. wrote is *The Gospel Restored,* (1836). BIBLIOGRAPHY: lives by W. Baxter (1874) and D. E. Stevenson (1946).

[D. E. STEVENSON]

SCOTTISH NATIONAL COVENANT, a document of 1638, renewing the old Scottish custom of subscribing a band or covenant for mutual defense or in a religious cause. Petitioners against the ecclesiastical arrangements of Charles I appointed Alexander Henderson (*c.*1583–1646) and Archibald Johnston of Warriston (1611–63) to draw up a National Covenant. This incorporated the Negative Covenant (1581), or *King's Confession, that James VI himself had signed, a summary of Acts of Parliament condemning popery and favoring the Reformed Church, and a covenant to resist the evils threatening the *Reformed religion and to uphold the King's honor and the public peace. The Covenant was signed by thousands in Greyfriars Kirk, Feb. 28, 1638, with a zeal that aroused most of the country. The declaration in 1662 that the Covenant was unlawful and in 1685 that it was treasonable produced the trials of the later covenanting period. BIBLIOGRAPHY: Schaff Creeds 1:686–687. *COVENANTERS.

[J. A. R. MACKENZIE]

SCOTTISH SCHOOL OF COMMON SENSE, a philosophical system originating in the 18th cent. at the Univ. of Edinburgh, and affirming a body of truths grasped by reason anterior to philosophy or science. That body of truths immediately recognized constitutes common sense. The position was first of all an epistemological realism affirming primary intelligible truths in reaction against the subtleties of J. *Locke and the skepticism of D. *Hume. The exponents were particularly intent on establishing the foundations of morality in incontrovertibly recognizable moral truths that indicated moral duty. The originator was Thomas Reid (1710–96); other proponents were Dugald

Stewart (1753–1828); and W. Hamilton (1788–1856), editor of Reid's works. Through J. *Witherspoon (1722–94) and J. McCosh (1811–94), both at Princeton, common–sense teaching and moral education based on it became, and to a degree remain, a part of American ethical thought. Common sensism also had influence on the Continent, in particular on V. *Cousin, A. *Rosmini-Sabati, V. *Gioberti. BIBLIOGRAPHY: V. Bourke, *History of Ethics* (1968) 180–181.

[T. C. O'BRIEN]

SCRIBE, originally one who could read and write; in preexilic times, a clerk of legal documents or some other secular official such as a finance minister or a secretary of state; in postexilic Judaism, a member of the professional class of teachers and interpreters of the Law of Moses, the editors and compilers of sacred tradition. Judaism was a religion centered on the sacred writings, and the architects of this new era in biblical history were the scribes. Ezra typifies them in his pivotal role during the restoration. The men of the Great Synagogue were scribes drawn from the families of priests and Levites. They spearheaded the resistance to hellenization and prepared the ground for the Maccabean rebellion. They inspired the *Hasidaean movement and the Pharisaic movement, the latter being a kind of lay scribe movement interested in leading a popular, democratic party of political resistance. Then the scribes were a broader group including the lawyers and the learned class, and could be found in every village of Galilee, Judea, and in Jerusalem. Along with the chief priests and elders, they were members of the Sanhedrin. Most scribes remained in the Pharisaic party, although there may have been Sadducean scribes. The NT presents them as too concerned with the preservation of a traditional legal system, built on a too literal understanding of the Torah. Jesus' long polemic against the scribes and Pharisees in Mt 23 is easily understood as an expression of outrage against a ''lawyers' monopoly,'' an exclusive control of the Law that gave them power over the people. It is in the interest of such a clique to keep the law a dead and even archaic letter. The ideal was for the teacher of the Law to become a learner in the kingdom of heaven, so that he might bring forth from his treasure the new as well as the old (Mt 13.52).

[E. J. DILLON]

SCRIPTORES ECCLESTIASTICI DE MUSICA SACRA POTISSIMUM, usually designated *Gerbert Scriptores.* This is a publication (1784; fac. ed. 1931) in 3 v. of medieval treatises on 9th-11th cent. music. *HORNAU, G. VON.

[M. T. LEGGE]

SCRIPTORIUM designates a room or other place set aside for the copying of MSS in the medieval monastery. With the *Rule* of Benedict for a stimulus and the detailed instructions of Cassiodorus' *Institutiones* for a guide, monk copyists in the scriptoria were responsible for the major book production of the Middle Ages until the 13th cent. when lay scribes began to supplant them. The scriptorium was directly administered by the *armarius* (librarian) whose duties entailed both the discipline of the room's occupants and the maintenance of equipment and supplies. The copyists were usually trained monks or nuns of the institution, but visiting scribes were permitted to copy books deemed too precious to be lent. The general size and style for a book were determined in advance, and the text was ordinarily copied upon the loose parchment sheets exactly from the exemplar, then given to a corrector. Various kinds of decoration might be done by the scribe or by an independent artist. Most scribes remain anonymous, but the subscription of a MS might reveal the name and personal comments of its long-suffering scribe. BIBLIOGRAPHY: F. E. De Roover, "The Scriptorium," in *Medieval Library* (J. W. Thompson, 1939; repr. 1957); F. Milkau, *Handbuch der Bibliothekswissenschaft* (2d ed., G. Leyh, 1955) 3–1: 263–267.

[F. J. WITTY]

SCRIPTORUM DE MUSICA MEDII AEVI NOVA SERIES, the *Coussemaker Scriptores,* a publication in 4 v. (1864; fac. ed. 1963) of medieval treatises on 13th–14th cent. music.

SCRIPTURE, AUTHORITY OF. In both OT and NT the core-doctrines and essential events are associated with God's representatives, Moses and Christ respectively, each functioning differently, and being different—for Moses was never thought of as anything more than man, and his actions had, in themselves, no more than human value. In both cases their teaching was first and primarily transmitted orally and only later set in writing, with a consequent gradual growth of sacred writings that were judged as normative and inspired largely according to their conformity with the initial teaching. The growth of both Testaments was gradual and unplanned, and there were disputes over certain books that seem out of harmony with the initial core of faith. No final dogmatic statement by Jews for their books was ever made, though a "synod" at Jamnia often, quite wrongly and without support, is claimed to have had this function for the OT. For Catholic Christians this issue was definitively decided for both Testaments at the Council of Trent (see D 1501–04), but with the sacred books being set within the context of a living and continuing apostolic tradition and teaching authority.

Sacred Scripture for Catholics has a tremendous authority, but practically there has been, at various times in the history of the Church, little use made of Scripture, esp. by the faithful. Few texts have ever been defined by the Church, and certain sections of the Bible have limited practical value, e.g., the minute cult-regulations found in Lev, the genealogies—esp. those in 1–2 Chr, or various details found in the Apocalypse. The authority of the Bible rests ultimately on the authority of God, upon the inspiration granted to those who wrote the sacred books, and upon the

guarantee of the Church that they were written as inspired documents. BIBLIOGRAPHY: C. H. Dodd, *Authority of the Bible* (1950); H. H. Rowley, *Growth of the OT* (1950); C. F. D. Moule, *Birth of the NT* (1962); B. Vawter, *Bible in the Church* (1950).

[I. HUNT]

SCROLL, early form of book. Sheets of papyrus, leather, or parchment were joined together to form a strip several feet long. After the scroll was written on (normally only on the inner side), it could be rolled up for storage and unrolled again for reading. The scroll was in normal use until after NT times.

[T. EARLY]

SCROLL OF GUTHLAC (1196 A.D.), a vellum scroll containing tinted outline drawings in medallions of scenes from the life of St. Guthlac of Crowland, a Saxon anchorite (d. 714 A.D.). The drawings, in transitional Romanesque-Gothic style, may be a set of cartoons for stained glass or a record of Guthlac's translation in 1196. It is now in the British Museum.

[R. L. S. BRUCE-MITFORD]

SCROPE, RICHARD (*c.*1346–1405), English ecclesiastic and rebel. Of noble family, and doctor of both laws (Cambridge?) where he was chancellor (1378–79), he was elected bp. of Chichester (1385). Richard II quashed the election, but S. later became bp. of Coventry and Lichfield (1386) and abp. of York (1398). He joined other churchmen and nobles in deposing Richard II and enthroning Henry IV (1399). S. allied with the Percy family against Henry's tyranny, was captured by trickery, and summarily and unlawfully executed for treason. His reputed sanctity and martyrdom made his tomb at York into a shrine. BIBLIOGRAPHY: J. Tait, DNB 17:1082–85; Emden Camb 513–514; R. W. Hays, NCE 12:1253.

[R. W. HAYS]

SCROVEGNI CHAPEL (Padua; 1303–05). Also known as the Arena Chapel this small free-standing brick building was commissioned by Enrico Scrovegni as a private family chapel constructed adjacent to the Scrovegni Palace which faced a ruined ancient Roman arena. The chapel is known primarily for the innovative fresco cycles of the life of the Virgin and the life of Christ painted by Giotto (1305–10) which decorate the interior.

[S. CONWAY]

SCRUPULOSITY, an abnormal condition of a conscience obsessed by a sense of sin where there is no sin. *Conscience properly means an act of judgment about what is morally right or wrong in any given action. In its primary meaning it is a judgment antecedent to acting; in its secondary meaning, it is a reflection on an act already done. Scrupulosity may affect conscience in both senses. In an antecedent form scrupulosity prevents a person from making a balanced moral judgment out of fear of sinning, even when objectively a good or morally indifferent action is the issue. Scrupulosity in a consequent form is a pathological remorse—a fear or self-accusation that sin has been committed where there has been no sin. Since it is a complete disequilibrium and erroneous judgment, scrupulosity requires as one form of treatment surrender to the counsel and directives of a confessor. Having lost the power to judge, the scrupulous person must with trust and obedience substitute the confessor's directives as the norm of conscience. Often, in addition, because scrupulosity is pathological, it requires psychological therapy.

SCRUTINY, translates *scrutinium*, the Lat. term for balloting in an ecclesiastical election (CIC, c. 171). The tellers appointed are called "scrutators"; their obligation is to see to the secrecy and other legal requirements for balloting and to count the ballots (*ibid*. §§ 1–5).

[T. C. O'BRIEN]

SCUPOLI, LORENZO (*c*.1530–1610), Italian Theatine, author of *Spiritual Combat*, a celebrated work on Christian spirituality. S. became a Theatine only in 1569 and was ordained in 1577. For unknown reasons the general chapter of his order decreed in 1585 that he be reduced to the lay state; he lived out his life secluded in houses of his order. The *Spiritual Combat* appeared anonymously first, in 1589, and under S.'s name only posthumously.

[T. C. O'BRIEN]

SEABURY, SAMUEL (1729–96), first Protestant Episcopal bp. in the U.S., a native of Conn., and a graduate of Yale (1748). S. studied medicine in Edinburgh but changed to theology and was ordained (1753). After returning to the colonies, he served various churches in N.J. and N.Y. (1754–75). Loyal to the British during the Revolution, he wrote, under a pseudonym, a series of pamphlets for the British cause and was imprisoned for a time because his authorship was suspected. Released for lack of evidence, he escaped behind the British lines and served as military chaplain. He was chosen bp. by the Episcopalian clergy of Conn. (1783) and was sent to England for consecration. The English bps. refused to cooperate because S., now an American citizen, could not take the oath of allegiance. He reluctantly turned to the *nonjuror Episcopalian bps. of Scotland, who consecrated him in 1784. He served as bp. of Conn. until his death. BIBLIOGRAPHY: E. Pennington, *From Canterbury to Connecticut* (1941).

[R. B. ENO]

SEAL OF CONFESSION, the grave obligation to secrecy concerning information that one receives in sacramental confession when the disclosure of such information would reveal the penitent's identity. The purpose of the seal is to assure the penitent peace of mind, derived from knowing that the content of his confession is held in strict privacy. The basis for the confessional seal is both the natural law, since the penitent has a natural right to *secrecy concerning confessional matters, and divine positive law following from the very nature of sacramental penance as instituted by Christ. In the confessional the priest acts as the representative of Christ and has no personal dominion over the knowledge entrusted to him in that capacity. Because of the gradual development of private penance in the Church, it was not until the 9th cent. that any legislation concerning the confessional seal appeared. The first general ecclesiastical law concerning it was promulgated at the Fourth Lateran Council (1215). Today the obligations concerning the seal are clearly contained in canon law (CIC c. 889.1), which obliges the confessor not to violate the seal either by word, sign, or other means. Canon 889.2 obliges an interpreter and any other person who may obtain knowledge concerning the content of a confession also to observe the seal. The matter protected by the seal comprises all sins confessed, including public sins, and anything said for the better explanation of these sins (*e.g.*, number, circumstances) unless such information be known from a source other than confession; other information known only through confession, whose revelation would prove detrimental to the penitent. The seal is violated in two ways: directly, when information subject to the seal is revealed together with the penitent's identity without the latter's permission; indirectly, when confessional matter is disclosed in such circumstances that the possibility of another person's acquiring knowledge of what is protected by the seal arises. A confessor who presumes to violate the seal directly incurs an excommunication most specially reserved to the Holy See (CIC c. 2369.1), and a confessor who indirectly violates the seal is liable to the same penalities. Any other person who violates the seal may, by a condemnatory judgment, be subjected to proportionate penalties (CIC c. 2369.2). BIBLIOGRAPHY: B. Dolhagaray, DTC 3.1:960–974; H. Joné, *Moral Theology* (tr. U. Adelman, rev. ed. 1969); J. L. McCarthy, NCE 4:133–135.

[J. J. FLOOD]

SEALING, a ritual term with two usages. (1) In the Catholic Apostolic and New Apostolic Churches, it is a sacrament, also called baptism with fire, conferred by the laying on of hands to bestow the gifts of the Holy Spirit, citizenship in the heavenly Jerusalem, and a share in Christ's rule during the millennium. (2) Among the Latter-day Saints (Mormons), it is one of the temple ceremonies by which a temporal marriage may become a celestial marriage, or by which families are solemnly joined for eternal association.

[T. C. O'BRIEN]

SEALSFIELD, CHARLES (pseud. of Karl Anton Postl; 1793–1864), Austrian novelist chiefly remembered for his enthusiastic descriptions contained in his novels of the

American pioneer spirit of the early 19th century. Son of a village magistrate, he tried life in a religious community in Prague. Dissatisfied with the experiment, he left in 1823 and went to America, where he achieved some success as a speculator and became a citizen. However, he returned to Europe in 1832 and settled in Switzerland. Works: *Deutsch-amerikanische Wahlverwandtschaften* (1839–40); *Das Kajütenbuch* (1841).

[B. F. STEINBRUCKNER]

SÉANCE (Fr., a sitting), a meeting led by a *medium for the purpose of communication with the spirit world (see SPIRITUALISTS). The communication is purported to occur through such phenomena as rappings, movement or levitation of objects, the emission of luminous vapors. To take part in a séance seriously is contrary to the virtue of *religion by being a form of superstition. The practice may also take on the character of demonology (see DEMONS), trafficking with evil spirits.

[T. C. O'BRIEN]

SEARLE, GEORGE MARY (1839–1918), astronomer, Paulist superior general. Born in London, S. was educated in the United States. An astronomer, he worked at Dudley Observatory, Albany, N.Y., where he discovered the asteroid Pandora in 1858. He was a teacher of mathematics at the U.S. Naval Academy at Newport, R.I., and taught at the Harvard Observatory for two years. In 1862 he became a Catholic, in 1868 entered the Paulists, and was ordained in 1871. A teacher of science at the Paulist seminary, Washington, D.C., and of mathematics at The Catholic Univ. of America, S. was elected superior general in 1905. Among his works were *Elements of Geometry* (1877) and *Truth about Christian Science* (1916).

[J. R. AHERNE]

SEAT COLLECTION, an offering gathered from the faithful at Sunday Masses, distinct from the Offertory collection and conceived as a kind of rental for the use of the seating space and facilities. It is a development of the *pew rent of former times.

[P. K. MEAGHER]

SEAT OF WISDOM, a title of Mary honoring her as the source and sanctuary of wisdom insofar as Christ, who is perfect wisdom, dwelt in her and through her intercession comes to man. The title is also used in the *Litany of Loreto. It is first found in the writings of St. Anselm and St. Bernard of Clairvaux.

[T. M. MCFADDEN]

SEBALDUS, ST., patron of Nuremberg. S. is believed to have been a hermit and a preacher near that city. Pilgrimages to his tomb are attested from 1072, but neither the time (between the 8th and 11th cent.) nor the place of his origin

can be established. BIBLIOGRAPHY: K. Kunze, BiblSanct 11:754–767.

[M. J. SUELZER]

SE-BAPTISM (Lat. *se*, self), baptism of oneself, such as that performed by J. *Smyth when he established the first congregation of Baptists in Amsterdam in the 17th cent.; his followers were sometimes referred to as "Se-Baptists." The reason for Smyth's act was his acceptance of *believer's baptism.

SEBASTE, MARTYRS OF, forty Christian soldiers, claimed by legend to be members of the *Thundering Legion (famed on another account), martyred *c*.321 at Sebaste (the modern Sivas in Central Turkey) under the Emperor Licinius after he had broken with Constantine and repudiated the policy of toleration. The story told of them is that when they refused to sacrifice to idols they were put naked upon a frozen pond and died after 3 days and nights of exposure. Evidence of this event derives mainly from three sources: an ancient Greek *passio* from which various *acta* stem; panegyrics delivered within the century by SS. Basil, Gregory of Nyssa, Ephrem, John Chrysostom, and Gaudentius of Brescia; and a remarkable document known as the *Testament of the Holy Martyrs of Christ*, the authenticity of which has been established in modern times. The bodies of the martyrs were burned but portions of the charred remains were rescued and, passing to different persons and places, were greatly treasured. The cult of these martyrs was widespread in both East and West. An oratory in Sta. Maria Antiqua in Rome has frescoes dating from the 7th or 8th cent. depicting the martyrdom. BIBLIOGRAPHY: Butler 1:541–544; AnalBoll (1944) 113, index; P. F. de Cavalieri, "I quaranta martyri di Sebastia," *Note agiografiche 7* ST 49 (1928) 155–184.

[R. B. ENO]

SEBASTIAN, ST. (late 3d cent.), martyr. Despite the abundance of detail in later legends, little is known of S. for certain except that he was a Roman martyr, but probably connected also with Milan in some way, since he was venerated there from an early date. He was buried on the Via Appia, probably near the basilica later erected in his name. According to the most common version of the legend, he was an officer of the Praetorian Guard of the Emperor Diocletian. His position enabled him to be helpful to other martyrs and confessors until it was discovered that he, too, was a Christian. He was left for dead by archers appointed to take his life, but miraculously he recovered, only to be clubbed to death when he again came into the Emperor's presence. His cult as a patron of soldiers and protector against the plague was widespread during the Middle Ages. S. is usually portrayed as a young man pierced with arrows. BIBLIOGRAPHY: Butler 1:130–132; E. Hoade, NCE 13:18–19.

[R. B. ENO]

SEBASTIAN OF APPARIZIO, BL. see APARICIO, SEBASTIÁN DE, BL.

SEBASTIANO DEL PIOMBO (Sebastiano Luciani; 1485–1547), Venetian painter commanding Giorgione's poetic, idyllic mood and atmospheric form, though his figures are large and standardized. S.'s frescoes (1511) show Raphael's composition, while anatomical force in the *Raising of Lazarus* (1519), *Flagellation* (1516–24), and *Lamentation* show Michelangelo's influence. S. became a notable portrait painter experimenting with multiple portraits *(Card. Ferry Carondelet with His Secretaries)*. After 1520 he painted a truly Venetian *Birth of the Virgin,* excellent portraits of *Andrea Doria, Cardinal Salviati and His Servant, Clement VII* (1526) and a popular devotional *Christ Carrying the Cross.*

[M. J. DALY]

SECKAU, ABBEY OF, monastery near Knittelfeld in the present Diocese of Graz-Seckau in upper Styria, Austria. Founded with Augustinian canons from Salzburg cathedral in 1140, it became a bishopric in 1219 and had an adjoining women's cloister until *c.*1500. Suppressed by Joseph II in 1782, it was resettled in 1883 by Benedictines from Beuron, who rebuilt the church and abbey and made it a center of the modern liturgical movement. The Romanesque basilica dates from the 12th cent.; the abbey is 17th-cent. Renaissance. It was briefly suppressed during the Nazi era (1940–1945). BIBLIOGRAPHY: Cottineau 2: 2989–90.

[E. J. DILLON]

SECOND ADAM, a title for Christ as the new head of the human race, recapitulating mankind in himself so that the friendship with God destroyed by the first Adam might be restored. St. Paul employs this notion although he uses the term "last Adam" (1 Cor 15.45). It was a favorite theme among the early Christian Fathers, and was esp. significant in the thought of St. Irenaeus. BIBLIOGRAPHY: Quasten 1:294–297.

[T. M. MCFADDEN]

SECOND BAPTISM, a name sometimes used by Pentecostals for *baptism with the Holy Spirit.

SECOND BLESSING, a description of *entire sanctification. In the teaching of *Holiness Churches, the salvation brought by Christ is twofold: the first blessing is justification; the second blessing, sanctification, which is called a second definite work of grace, and brings deliverance of the believer from domination by sinful inclinations.

SECOND COMING, the visible return of Jesus Christ to earth. The term itself is not used in the NT, but the idea is expressed frequently. Three words often associated with the concept of a return of Christ in visible form are *parousia* (arrival, presence), *apocalypse* (revelation), and *epiphany*

(appearing). In Paul's statement of the tradition concerning the Lord's Supper, he said: "For as often as you eat this bread and drink this cup, you proclaim the Lord's death until he comes" (1 Cor 11.26). The Apostles' Creed affirms that "he will come again to judge the quick and the dead." Jesus spoke of the "Son of man coming in clouds with great power and glory" (Mk 13.26). At the Ascension, the disciples were told: "This Jesus, who was taken up from you into heaven, will come in the same way as you saw him go into heaven" (Acts 1.11). Many references in the NT indicate that the early Christian community expected such a second coming of Christ in glory. Belief in Christ's second coming is common to most Christians. The imminence of that coming, with supportive interpretations of the signs of the times, has given rise to the periodic manifestations of *apocalypticism and *millenarianism throughout history (see ADVENTISM; JEHOVAH'S WITNESSES). An emphasis on the literal truth of Christ's second coming is characteristic of fundamentalist Churches (see DISPENSATIONALISM).

[N. H. MARING]

SECOND CONFESSION OF BASEL, a name sometimes given to the first of the *Helvetic Confessions because it was composed at Basel in 1536.

SECOND GREAT AWAKENING, a nationwide revival (1797–1805) among the Churches in America, spreading also to the unchurched. It began in Connecticut among the Congregationalists, where Timothy *Dwight, the president of Yale, was its leading figure. Concerned over the impact of French *deism and naturalism on American life and a general religious torpor, he had countered with a theology and a preaching that grew into the Second Great Awakening. For the Methodists and the Baptists the Awakening centered in revivals in what was then the West—Kentucky, the Carolinas, and Tennessee. In New England and a large part of the country, among Congregationalists and Presbyterians the Second Great Awakening was unlike the earlier *Great Awakening, inasmuch as it was not accompanied by physical manifestations. Serious interest in the Churches and religion became universal, this time on a severely intellectual rather than an emotional basis. On the western frontier, however, the Second Great Awakening brought with it not only religious renewal but two phenomena, camp-meetings and the jerks.

Camp-meetings were tremendous outdoor gatherings where people came together for several weeks at a time, camping in the woods adjacent to the meeting places. Usually a large shed with benches was erected, sometimes for as many as 5,000 persons, with a large stand at one end for the preacher. The largest and most famous was the Cane Ridge Camp Meeting started by the Presbyterians (1801). According to reports, 25,000 persons gathered, and stands for preaching were strategically placed so that six or seven preachers could speak at one time. Francis *Asbury strongly favored camp-meetings and thought them divinely ordained to bring the gospel to the frontier and the backwoods. Methodists, Baptists, and Presbyterians often united for the services. Later, however, many Presbyterians turned against the revivalist movement. The revival at the frontier lacked the intellectual basis characteristic of the Second Great Awakening in New England and elsewhere and expressed itself in an emotionalism similar to the days of George *Whitefield. The jerks, a new physical phenomenon, was an uncontrollable and convulsive jerking that overcame a person, sometimes causing him to fall to the ground or to reach for a small tree to grasp as he sought to overcome the jerking of his body. Peter *Cartwright spoke of seeing at one meeting 500 persons with the jerks. Even persons of good education, recognized social standing, and keen intellect were seized by the inexplicable convulsions. Cartwright characteristically described the phenomenon as the judgment of God on sinners who, once they repented of their sins, were released. He also said that a person should not fight the seizure but should relax in prayer and singing and that the spasm would then abate.

The Second Great Awakening brought great good to the country. In spite of the extravagances that marked it on the frontier, the renewal manifested itself in greater church attendance, larger church membership, the beginning of home and foreign missionary work, and a renewed interest in theological education and religious journalism. BIBLIOGRAPHY: C. R. Keller, *Second Great Awakening in Connecticut* (1942); HistAmMeth 1:507–524; *Autobiography of Peter Cartwright* (ed. W. P. Strickland, 1857) ch.5; Olmstead 256–263.

[F. E. MASER]

SECOND HELVETIC CONFESSION, see HELVETIC CONFESSIONS.

SECOND LONDON CONFESSION, an early Baptist *confession of faith, drawn up in 1677 as a more detailed statement than the First London Confession of 1644. Anxious to manifest doctrinal unity with other *Dissenters during persecution, the *Particular Baptists issued this confession after the Restoration. Like the Independents' *Savoy Declaration (1658), it was an adaptation of the *Westminster Confession, repeating the themes of Calvinism verbatim but omitting chapters connected with Presbyterian polity and modifying the statements on the Church with Baptist teaching on *believer's baptism, the *gathered Church, the ministry, and Church-State relations. Adopted by the Philadelphia Baptist Association in 1707 (see PHILADELPHIA CONFESSION), the document was widely accepted as a doctrinal standard until superseded by the *New Hampshire Confession (1832). BIBLIOGRAPHY: *Baptist Confessions of Faith* (ed. W. L. Lumpkin, 1959).

[N. H. MARING]

SECOND ORDER, the nuns, usually cloistered, with solemn VOWS forming one branch of the mendicant orders, e.g., the Poor Clares, Dominican nuns; the original, men's order is considered the "first order." Theoretically, second-order communities or monasteries are under the jurisdiction of the general superior of the original order; in practice, notably in the U.S., they are under the local ordinary and receive only a fraternal interest from the first order. The "third-order" religious are usually noncloistered sisters engaged in the active apostolate, although there are some third-order, cloistered communities, the members having simple, not solemn vows.

SECOND WORK OF GRACE, a reference to Christian perfection or *entire sanctification as these are distinct from and subsequent to justification, which delivers the sinner from the guilt of personal sin; a second work of grace frees him from all tendency to sin.

SECONDA PRATTICA, as opposed to *prima prattica,* the polyphonic style of the late Renaissance, *seconda prattica* was a 17th-cent. Italian term that designated the monophonic-type singing of the recitative, the aria, etc.

[M. T. LEGGE]

SECONDARY EDUCATION, CATHOLIC. The development of Catholic secondary education (grades 7 to 12) in the U.S. traces its origin to the early Catholic academy, which preceded the parochial and diocesan high school by several decades. Despite severe penal restrictions, two Maryland academies, Newtown Manor in the 17th cent. and Bohemia Manor in the 18th cent., sought to provide, though somewhat clandestinely, some educational opportunity for Catholic colonial youth and to prepare them for study abroad. But it was in 1789, with the "Academy of Georgetown, Patowmack River, Maryland," that Catholic secondary and higher education for boys formally began. The Georgetown Visitation Academy for girls was opened in 1795, and by 1852, there were Catholic academies for boys and girls in almost all the then-existing states. The early 1900s, with its increasing demand for a broad, nonclassical curriculum, and the recognition by Catholic leaders for the need for religious training adapted to adolescent mentality, saw the development of the Catholic high school, where possible, as a central or diocesan institution serving several parishes, or a parochial or interparochial school. To achieve its objectives of developing enlightened, cultured, spiritually vigorous American citizens, the secondary school offers a 4-year program covering modern languages, science, social studies, mathematics, religion, and to some extent, vocational courses, besides curricular and cocurricular activities, in keeping with state and regional requirements. There are at present approximately 1,601 Catholic secondary schools in the U.S. serving 895,775 students. BIBLIOGRAPHY: A. M. Greeley and P. H. Rossi, *Education of Catholic Americans* (1966).

[M. B. MURPHY]

SECRET, DISCIPLINE OF THE, see DISCIPLINE OF THE SECRET.

SECRET PRAYER, see PRAYER OVER THE GIFTS.

SECRETARIAT FOR PROMOTING CHRISTIAN UNITY, see CHRISTIAN UNITY, SECRETARIAT FOR PROMOTING.

SECRETARIATE OF STATE (PAPAL), the ecclesiastical institution that is the most intimately associated with the pope in the conduct of the affairs of the Holy See. The cardinal secretary of state is often described as a sort of prime minister or minister of foreign affairs though the comparisons are only approximate. Historically the office originated in part from the institution of the cardinal nephew, a close relative and confidant of the pontiff, who supervised papal correspondence and had considerable influence. In the apostolic constitution *Regimini ecclesiae universae* (1967), Pope Paul VI reorganized the Roman Curia and the Secretariate of State. In the new arrangement, the secretariate is directed by a "substitute" under the cardinal secretary. Its broad function is to perform whatever duties are confided to it by the pope. Generally it handles current church matters that do not fall under the competence of the regularly constituted curial congregations. It receives reports from papal representatives abroad and deals directly with envoys of the civil powers accredited to the Holy See. It corresponds with bps. and private persons as occasion arises, and is responsible for the preparation and dispatch of papal letters and documents. The governor of the Vatican City State reports to the secretariate, which is also responsible for the Pontifical Commission for Social Communications. At the higher level, the cardinal secretary is empowered to call meetings of the cardinals heading the Roman Congregations, to coordinate their work, to communicate information, and to seek advice. In the pre-1967 organization, the Secretariate of State also included the Congregation for Extraordinary Ecclesiastical Affairs. This body is responsible for high policy in relations with civil governments, the preparation and execution of concordats and negotiations over problems of civil legislation affecting church matters. The new curial reform entirely separated this congregation from the Secretariate of State and renamed it the Council for the Public Affairs of the Church. It is directed by a secretary, but the Cardinal Secretary of State remains head of the Council as he is of the Secretariate. BIBLIOGRAPHY: H. Scharp, *How the Catholic Church Is Governed* (tr. A. Derrick, 1960); J. A. Abbo, NCE 13:28–29; R. A. Graham, *Vatican Diplomacy* (1959). *CURIA ROMANA.

[R. A. GRAHAM]

SECRETS, things not publicly disclosed, the knowledge of which belongs to a person by right and should not be sought, used, or revealed by other persons against the reasonable will of its original possessor. Secrets fall into three categories: natural, promised, and entrusted. If the very nature of a situation, independently of any special promise or contract, calls for secrecy, the secret is said to be a natural one. A promised secret is one that should be kept hidden because of a promise made by one who has come into possession of it. The entrusted or committed secret is one that is confided to another on the condition, either explicit or implicit, that it will be kept hidden. This type of secret may be entrusted either in friendly or in professional confidence. There are various kinds of professional secrecy. What a physician discovers about a patient in the course of examining him is a professional secret, but his obligation to secrecy differs somewhat from that of a counselor to whom a counselee reveals hidden things about himself, or from that of a priest to whom secret information is entrusted in sacramental confession.

Secure social living requires the recognition of the right to secrecy, not only because of an individual's need of it, but also because it is important to the community itself that there should be dependable advisors available to whom people in trouble and perplexity can go with a feeling of security.

One ought not, therefore, violate another's privacy, and if in some way an individual comes to know another's secret, he is bound not to disclose it, either directly or indirectly.

However, the obligation of keeping a natural and promised secret is limited because in some situations the failure to speak out would be unreasonable. The common view is that a natural secret may be justifiably used or revealed when keeping the secret would bring disproportionate harm upon the person it directly affects, on the person who shares it, on an innocent third party, or on the community. The same conditions govern a promised secret.

Even an entrusted secret, other than one of friendship, counseling, or of sacramental confession, is not exempt from the same conditions, although the importance of maintaining public confidence in professional integrity and the difficulty of estimating the harm that might follow its loss make disclosure rarely justifiable and still more rarely obligatory.

Entrusted secrets of friendship and of counseling may never be used or revealed without the free, informed consent of their original possessor, since here the social consequences of a breach would be more destructive than those of observance. The friend or counselor has the confidential knowledge only because the other person has freely chosen to share his inner life in the confidence it would not be manifested against his wishes. Such an assurance is an important force of social cohesion. This supposes, however, that the confider is *sui compos* (otherwise his permission might be presumed) or not engaged in a harmful project (otherwise he would have no right to load another with his secret).

The entrusted secrets of sacramental confession are so

utterly confidential that the minister may in no circumstances reveal them without the penitent's free, informed consent to do so (CIC cc. 889, 890). BIBLIOGRAPHY: R. E. Regan, *Moral Principles Governing Professional Secrecy with an Inquiry into Some of the More Important Professional Secrets* (1941).

[E. F. FALTEISEK]

SECT (Lat. *secta,* from the root *sequi,* to follow), meaning first a task, a mode of conduct, later a doctrine or those accepting a certain doctrine, and finally those separating themselves in doctrine from an established religious body. From the last sense, the etymology is sometimes traced to *secare,* to cut. The word has been used in a variety of senses in modern languages. Often it has been applied in a disparaging sense by Catholics to other religious bodies or by Protestants in an established or historical Church to newly emerging religious groups. The term has received more precise definition in the sociology of religion. To account for diverse patterns of religious expression, Ernst *Troeltsch developed a now classic typology: "church," "sect," and "mysticism." The sect-type is characterized by emphasis upon individual religious experience, voluntary membership, radical obedience to a Christian ethic, opposition to political interference in religion, suspicion of professional theologians, and appeal to the authority of the NT and the primitive Church. This contrasts with the church-type, which is more institutionalized, stresses the objective authority of ministry, creed, and sacrament, and seeks to dominate society by close relationship with the State. It differs also from mysticism, which is radically spiritual and individualistic, minimizes doctrine, and does not usually develop permanent organizations.

Although these classifications have been useful for sociological analysis, the dual categories of church and sect do not adequately take account of the variations of organized religion in the United States. J. M. Yinger uses a six-fold system of classification: the Universal Church, the Ecclesia, the Denomination, the Established Sect, the Sect, and the Cult. Denominations, according to this scheme, exhibit diversities but are predominantly conventional, middle-class in composition, and have compromised with their society, although not so extensively as have the "Churches." The sect is defined essentially in Troeltsch's terms, but it is further subdivided into those that: stress individual faith and moral standards without manifesting hostility to society; seek radical reform of society by means of the individual influence of Christians; or withdraw from the world, accepting the inequities of life and projecting their hopes into the hereafter. The established sect maintains its identity by retention of old emphases, but its members have moved into a more favorable socioeconomic position. Both of these are distinguished from the cult, which is more short-lived and more dependent upon a particular charismatic leader. Sects usually develop among "the disinherited," whose personal needs are not met by the more formal religious bodies, which they regard as compromises with the world. Today, sects flourish particularly among recent migrants to U.S. cities. The type of religious association that will appeal to under-privileged people is affected by the extent to which they feel an identity with the predominant culture and whether they are optimistic or pessimistic regarding their prospects of climbing up the socioeconomic ladder. There is a tendency for sects to become denominations as their adherents gain a better social status. Denominations and Churches, as well as sects and cults, are shaped in part by nontheological factors, and there are fairly clear correlations between the status of American denominations and their social, educational, and economic attainments. BIBLIOGRAPHY: J. M. Yinger, *Religion, Society, and the Individual* (1957); H. Richard Niebuhr, *Social Sources of Denominationalism* (1929); E. Troeltsch, *Social Teachings of the Christian Churches* (tr. O. Wyon, 2v., 1931).

[N. H. MARING]

SECT (CANON LAW), in the CIC a term designating a group or body of persons united in formal association and adhering to a doctrine or belief other than that of the Catholic Church. The term always appears with some modifier: non-Catholic (c. 542. 1; 1065. 1); heretical, schismatic, masonic (c. 1240. 1.1), proscribed (c. 693. 1), masonic (c. 2335). A person is considered a member of a sect only after formal enrollment.

[T. C. O'BRIEN]

SECTARIANISM, in ordinary usage either the narrow exclusiveness characteristic of a religious body classified as a *sect, or any excessive, even intolerant, attachment to a religious body and its teachings. The term may also be given more benign, historical meaning based on the 17th-cent. application of "sectarian" or "sectary" to Independents or Nonconformists in England; then sectarianism signifies simply *denominationalism.

[N. H. MARING]

SECTARY, in 17th-cent. England a term applied by Presbyterians to *Independents. With the proliferation of new movements during Cromwell's Protectorate (Levellers, Diggers, Quakers, Ranters, Familists, etc.), it came to mean an adherent of a schismatic or heretical sect. Today the word connotes a zealous, or even bigoted, member of any religious group.

[N. H. MARING]

SECULAR CLERGY, the diocesan clergy as distinct from religious or regular clergy. They are committed to pastoral ministry in parishes and in other capacities in a diocese under the direction of their bishop, to whom they are bound by a promise of obedience.

[R. C. CLIGGETT]

SECULAR INSTITUTES, one of the states of Christian perfection (see STATES OF PERFECTION), having its origins in the 18th cent., but formally recognized as such only in Pius XII's apostolic constitution, *Provida Mater Ecclesia,* Feb. 12, 1947. The members (who include laity and clergy) of a secular institute live and work "in the world" (*in saeculo*), do not live a community life or wear a distinctive garb, but by private vows or promises are dedicated to the evangelical counsels in striving for the perfection of charity. Vatican Council II recognizes secular institutes as one of the forms of seeking perfection to which, along with religious communities and *societies of common life, its decree on renewal of the religious life is directed (Vat II RenRelLife, n.1). The emphasis on presence in the world is endorsed by the Council as a leaven for strengthening and enlarging Christ's body (*ibid.*, n.11). In 1977 there were about 50,000 members of the Church living in secular institutes. There were 17 such institutes in the U.S.

[T. C. O'BRIEN]

SECULARISM, the view that holds the separation of God from his creation and denies his presence in the world, if not his existence. The secular city is the world of men and things moving on without him, doing without religion. This secularism as a world view and way of life denies the immanence of God or his existence and man's religious nature. Secularism denies as well the hidden presence and action of God or the cosmic role of Christ. This is a desacralization that denies two basic truths of the Christian faith: creation and Incarnation. BIBLIOGRAPHY: T. F. McMahon, NCE 13:36–38; J. Collins, "Marxist and Secular Humanism," *Social Order* 3 (1953) 207–232. *SECULARITY.

[P. DeLETTER]

SECULARITY, a mentality regarding the historical process of the secularization of human life as a source of many benefits for man and society. This outlook, characteristic of modern science and generally of this-worldly concerns, is almost universal in civilized countries. Religious secularity considers such an outlook to be compatible with faith in God, and Christian secularity finds it favorable to the message of the gospel. Since the theology of secularity is still developing, its terminology has not yet been settled. Nevertheless contemporary theologians generally use the term secularity as radically distinct from secularism, the ideology that looks upon religion as irrelevant to man's self-fulfillment in the world. Secularism of this type is opposed to religious and Christian secularity.

Secularization is "the historical process by which human culture, temporal society and its institutions, the arts and sciences, etc., have achieved a certain relative autonomy from religion, Christianity in its institutional form and sacral character, and have thereby attained a new and distinctive value in and for themselves" (Clarke). There are various opinions concerning the sources of this process within Western society. Some—Friedrich Gogarten, Arend van Leeuwen, and Harvey Cox—attribute its beginning to the biblical revelation and Christian faith itself. Others are more inclined to trace its real roots to the influence of Greco-Roman culture upon Christendom, and more esp. upon such medieval movements as the departure of St. Thomas Aquinas from *Augustinianism. Still others see the Gregorian Reform of the 11th cent. or the Renaissance and the Reformation as its origin. Whatever contribution these sources may have made to the process of secularization, the complete breakdown of the political and ecclesiastical unities within Christendom took place only with the *Enlightenment at the end of the religious wars between the confessional states. This set the historical stage for the French Revolution, probably the single most significant political event for the process of secularization.

A secularist state, inimical to religion, emerged from the Revolution. Unfortunately, from the viewpoint of secularity, secularization has come to be identified with the ideology of secularism. During the past 150 years Catholicism has been particularly on the defensive against the continually wider separation between the religious and the secular spheres. All too often modern political, social, and economic revolutions have meant the restriction or total suppression of religious freedom for Catholics; thus Catholics have traditionally seemed opposed to progress and human freedom because of their allegiance to religious values. Vatican Council II esp. directed the faithful to a more positive attitude toward the world: "If by the autonomy of earthly affairs we mean that created things and societies enjoy their own laws and values which must be gradually deciphered, put to use, and regulated by men, then it is entirely right to demand that autonomy. Such is not merely required by modern man, but harmonizes also with the will of the Creator" (Vat II ChModWorld 36).

Religious secularity sees the secular order as relatively autonomous, that is, having a meaning and value of its own. Unlike secularism, however, it does not consider temporal realities to be absolutely independent of God. Although the secular order prescinds from man's relationship to his creator, it by no means denies divine presence in the world. The inherent value of all that is directed toward the total welfare of man in this life should be enhanced by his religious convictions concerning the dignity and destiny of creation.

Christian secularity views the secularized society as most genuinely open to the message of the gospel. It favors a free, truly personal commitment of faith. In such a milieu a person's reasons for believing in Christ and the Church are not likely to be more sociopolitical than religious. Faith seems more easily purified of superstition; religious liberty is fostered in a society in which one set of ultimate values is not imposed upon the community, and a valid pluralism provides a culture of mutual enrichment for its members. The clearer differentiation between the religious and secular dimensions of human life contributes to forming Christianity into a world-wide Church. It helps to bring the realization that the cultural patterns of Western civilization are not essential to the message of salvation; there is a greater sense of mission and openness to other cultures and traditions in the work of religious renewal. In the ecumenical movement the religious and theological differences between the Churches can be identified with greater clarity when religion and the ambient culture are adequately distinguished. The effects of secularization may also help liberate the civilizations of Africa and the East from taboos that have blocked the path of progress.

Those who adopt the attitude of religious of Christian secularity are aware of some involved problems. The extremes of sacralism may be avoided only to fall into the pit of secularism. A suggestion pointing toward general solution may be in the vocation of the laity to sanctify without consecrating the secular, i.e., to bring the holiness of ultimate meaning to the world without distorting the world's own meaning. BIBLIOGRAPHY: T. E. Clarke, "What is Christian Secularity?" *Proceedings of the Catholic Theological Society of America*, 21 (1966) 201–221; J. Macquarrie, *God and Secularity* (1967), *Sacred and the Secular* (ed. M. J. Taylor, 1968).

[F. M. JELLY]

SECULARIZATION, the process by which religious influences on political and social institutions are replaced by a nonreligious orientation. Since the Peace of Westphalia (1648) the term has been used more specifically with reference to the seizure of church property by the State, as was done by many revolutionary governments of the 19th cent. following the pattern established by the French Revolution. It very often signified a radical *anticlericalism, but in some cases it was the only way to secure a more equitable distribution of wealth. BIBLIOGRAPHY: R. H. Potvin and D. Herlihy, NCE 13:38–43.

[P. DeLETTER]

SECULARIZATION OF CHURCH PROPERTY, the transfer of church possessions from ecclesiastical to civil ownership, by the State or laymen, an important problem in Church-State relations. The granting of property to the Church, under the Roman Empire and later, made it extremely wealthy: between one-fifth and one-third of the land of Europe was in ecclesiastical possession in the Middle Ages. Canonically, church property was largely inalienable due to its institutional, nonpersonal ownership, the sacrosanct nature of its use, and limitations imposed by its donors. The Council of Ancyra (314) made the first known prohibition of alienation of ecclesiastical property. Similar decrees—e.g., Pope Symmachus' limitations on such alienation in Rome (502)—followed. In imperial law, Emperor Leo I prohibited alienation of church property from the patriarchate of Constantinople (470), as did Justinian in the entire empire (535). Partial, private alienations were frequent in the late Empire when the Church, through *beneficia* or *precaria,* leased the usufruct while still vesting titular ownership in the Church.

In Merovingian Gaul, economic need brought extensive secularization of church lands by Charles Martel, Frankish mayor of the palace (714–741), who apparently utilized them to support new cavalry as defense against Muslim invaders, although sources for his policy are problem-ridden. The Carolingians, in contrast, rarely secularized ecclesiastical lands directly, but relied on the latter for support through taxation, lay administration, and military burdens (e.g., in Charlemagne's summons to Abbot Fulrad of St. Denis "with all your men well armed and prepared"). In the chaos of Carolingian collapse, feudal lords seized and secularized much ecclesiastical land. That trend was diminished by Otto the Great (936–973); his episcopal feudalism (see PRINCE-BISHOPS) undercut the secular dukes, increasing ecclesiastical holdings at the cost of combining temporal and ecclesiastical responsibilities in the episcopate. The Gregorian reform (11th–12th cent.) also helped to reassert the Church's material needs for its growing temporal role. Lateran Councils I (1123), II (1139), and III (1179) all condemned varying forms of lay ownership or control of church property. In the late Middle Ages, ecclesiastical ownership of property was attacked by heretical groups such as the Waldensians and Albigensians and by the Spiritual Franciscans, who emphasized the importance of apostolic poverty. Rome was criticized also (e.g., by the Minnesinger Walther von der Vogelweide) for draining financial resources from non-Italian peoples. These censures merged with the more philosophical attacks by Marsilius of Padua and Wycliffe, both of whom advocated state control of ecclesiastical property.

The great period of secularization occurred in the Reformation. Luther's emphasis on the interiorization of faith and his opposition to ecclesiastical worldliness and financial abuses influenced both the Knights' War (1522) against episcopal states and direct confiscations of ecclesiastical lands by cities and princes. In 1523–24, Bremen, Frankfurt-am-Main, Magdeburg, Nürnberg, Strassburg, Zürich (under Zwingli), and other towns seized church lands to utilize them largely for education and poor-relief under urban administration. German Protestant princes also secularized episcopal and monastic lands. The Teutonic Knights' possessions in East Prussia were secularized by the Order's grand master, Albrecht of Brandenburg, who became their temporal ruler under the Polish king (1525). The "ecclesiastical reservation" of the Peace of Augsburg (1555) forbade such transfer of ecclesiastical property by Catholic clerics who adopted the Reformed faith, but the Augsburg treaty acknowledged the new status of church territories confiscated before 1552. During the Thirty Years' War (1618–48), Emperor Ferdinand's Edict of Restitution (1629) ordered all ecclesiastical lands taken since Augsburg to be restored to the Catholic Church, but the Edict was revoked in the Peace of Westphalia (1648), which recognized all secularizations before 1624.

In England, limitations on expansion of church lands had

been made earlier (e.g., Statutes of Mortmain, 1279, 1391), but the Henrician Reformation witnessed the suppression of monasteries in two stages—the smaller ones in 1536, the larger in 1538–39—and confiscation of monastic lands. Pope Julius II recognized this alienation in his bull *Praeclara* (1555). Similar secularizations of church property occurred in Sweden and Denmark.

Gallicanism, mercantilism, and the philosophy of the Enlightenment all provided the background for 18th-cent. secularizations in Austria under Joseph II (1780–90), Poland, Russia under Catherine the Great (1762–96), and France during the Revolution, when all ecclesiastical possessions were confiscated (1789), an act confirmed by the Concordat of 1801. The suppression and secularization under Napoleon of the Rhineland ecclesiastical States were upheld by the Congress of Vienna (1814–15). Alienation continued in the 19th cent. when monastic lands were secularized in Portugal, Spain, and Switzerland, and Rome itself was seized (1870). The Russian Revolution secularized all ecclesiastical property in Russia (1917), and post-World War II Communist governments in Europe continued such alienations. The assumption by States of varying governmental philosophies of responsibility for social welfare and education, tasks formerly undertaken primarily by the Church, has changed both ecclesiastical and secular needs. BIBLIOGRAPHY: D. Herlihy, NCE 13:39–43 (with bibliog).

[W. A. CHANEY]

SEDECIA, see ZEDEKIAH.

SEDELLA, ANTÓNIO DE (Père Antoine; 1748–1829), missionary. A man of controversy all his life, A. was a Spanish Capuchin ordained in 1771 and came to Louisiana as a missionary in 1780. In 1785 the pastor of St. Louis parish in New Orleans, through storms of opposition he retained that position until his death. Bp. *Carroll mistrusted him and Bp. Cyril de Barcelona demanded that he return to Spain in 1890. The governor of the province attempted to give civil force to Cyril's demand, but S. produced a document wherein the Spanish King had appointed him supreme officer of the Holy Inquisition in Louisiana. In spite of this, he was deported in irons, was somewhere in Spain for 5 years, then returned to New Orleans, with a royal commission naming him honorary preacher to the King. In 1805 a dispute with the vicar general of Louisiana, Patrick Walsh, ended in S.'s suspension. The Catholics of New Orleans elected S. as pastor of St. Louis, claiming the church as their property. S.'s appeal to the King was supported by that monarch. In spite of lifelong conflict with his church superiors and colleagues, he was an extraordinary pastor of his parish, humble, dedicated, generous. In times of yellow fever he remained to minister to the sick. At his death, the entire city and public officials of Louisiana turned out to honor this most loved citizen of New Orleans.

[J. R. AHERNE]

SEDILIA, properly a bench in the sanctuary for the liturgical ministers, carved into the stone of the sanctuary wall or set into it. The term was also generally used for the bench of wood serving the same function and located in the sanctuary (see SCAMNUM).

SEDITION, the sin, also a crime in law, of insurrection against lawfully constituted civil government (see REBELLION). St. Thomas Aquinas includes in its moral meaning both the conspiratorial plotting of insurrection and its forceful execution (ST 2a2ae, 42.1); so understood, the sin of sedition also includes the meaning of treason. It is the sin of a faction, as its Lat. etymology suggests—a separation, a going apart; sedition treats the whole community as just another faction. Its malice consists in the attack upon the unity and peaceful good order of the community; it thus goes directly against the public or common good, the concern of *legal justice. Because it causes conflict and civil upheaval, it is also against the *peace that should reign among men, and so is against charity.

[T. C. O'BRIEN]

SEDRŌ, a type of extended prayer, preceded by a doxological prooemion, common in the W Syrian and Maronite liturgies. A *sedrō* is usually intercessory and characterized by a tendency to repeat an idea in different ways or to mention things in series. It is a development of the ancient Syrian prayers for imposing incense.

SEDUCTION, in medieval and even later moral theology, a specific sexual sin, consisting in the violation of a virgin. The term *stuprum* included both rape and sexual intercourse accomplished through guile and persuasion (ThAq ST 2a2ae, 154.6–7). The moral disorder, over and above that of extramarital sexual intercourse, consists in unjustly injuring the physical and moral integrity of the woman enticed, the rights of the parents to custody over her, and to the rightful expectation of her proper marriage; deprival of virginity violated all these rights. The narrower meaning and the moral deformities connoted have not changed; but seduction has also come to mean any enticement to immoral sexual acts, whatever the seducer's sex, and whether the seduction is to hetero- or homosexual acts. In addition to being a sexual sin, seduction is also a form of *scandal, worsened if it involves corruption of a minor. Where seduction leads to pregnancy the father has the moral obligation of paying for the costs of the birth and rearing of the child.

[T. C. O'BRIEN]

SEDULIUS, (fl. *c.*425–50), early Christian poet. Few facts are known about him: he was a priest, he studied secular subjects in Italy, he lived and probably wrote in Greece. *Paschale carmen*, his major work, consists of five books in hexameter verse. The first draws on the OT; the others detail wondrous events from the life of Christ, with S.'s allegorical, pious interpretations intertwined. The language and style are classical. The *Paschale opus* is a prose version written by himself. An abecedarian containing hymns and a collection of biblical stories from the OT and NT complete the list of his works. BIBLIOGRAPHY: P. de Labriolle, *History and Literature of Christianity from Tertullian to Boethius* (tr. H. Wilson, 1925).

[R. H. SCHMANDT]

SEDULIUS SCOTUS (fl. mid-9th cent.), grammarian, poet, commentator on the Scriptures. Probably a native of Ireland, S. went to Liège in 848 and there became the leading figure in an Irish cultural circle. His works show him well versed in the ancient classics and adept in the use of classical meters. Eager for patronage, he addressed many poems to wealthy and powerful individuals. In his *De rectoribus Christianis* (addressed to the Emperor), he set forth in prose and verse a somewhat extravagant view of royal authority. He is also credited with several scriptural commentaries. Works: Poems, MGHS Poetae 3.1:154–237. BIBLIOGRAPHY: Raby SLP 1:242–247; R. B. Palmer, NCE 13:46.

[M. S. TANEY]

SEE, the jurisdiction of a ruling bishop. The Lat. term is *sedes*, i.e., seat, as in the expression *Sancta sedes* or *Sedes apostolica*, the Holy See or the Apostolic See, since a symbol of the bp.'s authority is the episcopal throne or chair, the *cathedra*. Territorially the see is the local diocese.

[T. C. O'BRIEN]

SEEBERG, REINHOLD (1859–1935), Protestant theologian. A German, S. was successively professor in Dorpat, Estonia, and in Erlangen and Berlin. He was a historian of dogma and promoter of the concept that preaching the gospel must concern itself with social problems and national questions. He combined modern views with traditional ideas of German idealism and the Lutheran Reformation. S. directed the Institute for Social Ethics, was chairman of the Free-Church Social Conference in 1910, and president of the Central Committee for Inner Missions. Among his works were *History of Dogma* (4 v., 1895–98); *Church and the Social Question* (1897); *Church in Germany in the 19th Century* (1903); and *System of Ethics* (1911).

[J. R. AHERNE]

SEEGERT, JOSEPH FERDINAND (1716–1782), Bohemian organist and composer. Considered one of the greatest organists and teachers of his day, S. held appointments in various churches in Prague. He wrote Masses, choral works, and organ music, the best known of which is his "Eight (8) Toccatas and Fugues."

[M. T. LEGGE]

SEELOS, FRANCIS XAVIER (1819–67), missioner, spiritual director. German by birth, Seelos volunteered for the American missions and was ordained a Redemptorist in 1844 in the United States. In Pittsburgh he became a celebrated confessor. In 1860 S. became spiritual director at the Redemptorist seminary in Baltimore. He refused the bishopric of Pittsburgh when it was offered in 1860. S. returned to mission work in 1862. His cause for beatification has been introduced in Rome.

[J. R. AHERNE]

SEGARELLI, GERARD (Segalelli; d. 1300), founder of a medieval lay group known as the *Apostolici. He was uneducated, given to religious fantasy, and affected by *Joachimism. At Parma in 1260 he determined to embrace the evangelical life in a spirit of true gospel freedom. He and his followers dressed poorly, lived on alms, and preached penance without rule or vows. Their unstructured organization was loosely held together by what S. called interior, spiritual obedience. His harangues against the hierarchical Church, which he described as polluted and carnal, resulted in his temporary imprisonment by the bp. of Parma. His doctrines were condemned by Honorius IV and Nicholas IV; in 1300 he was retried as a relapsed heretic, found guilty, and delivered to the secular authorities for execution.

[C. J. LYNCH]

SEGESSER, PHILIPP (1687–1761), Swiss-born Jesuit missionary who served the expanding Pimería Alta mission shortly after he arrived in Mexico with other German Jesuits in 1731. Taken to an outpost near present-day Tucson by Captain Juan Bautista de Anza, he helped found the San Javier del Bac mission. His *Una relación* offers valuable descriptions of life in the Pimería where he eventually served as superior.

[R. J. LITZ]

SEGHERS, CHARLES JOHN (1839–86), bp. and missionary. A Belgian ordained in 1863, S. joined Bp. Modeste Demers on Vancouver Island, Canada. S. made several journeys into Alaska and established a permanent mission there. Named as coadjutor to Abp. Blanchet of Oregon City, S. succeeded to that see in 1880 and did missionary work in Idaho, Montana, and Oregon. At his own request he was reappointed to Vancouver Island in 1885. Intent upon opening missions in the Alaskan interior, with two Jesuits and a layman S. began an expedition to the Yukon in 1886. On the journey he was shot and killed by the layman, Francis Fuller, who was psychologically disturbed.

[J. R. AHERNE]

SEGNERI, PAOLO (1624–94), Italian Jesuit preacher and writer, whose flamboyant pulpit manner and oratorical style made him one of the most popular and influential preachers of his day. In his Lenten sermons (1661–92), 34 of which are collected in *Il Quaresimale* (1679, Eng. tr., J. Ford, 2 v., 1872), self-flagellation and processions of penitents accompanied the sermons. His other major sermonic collections are *Prediche* (1694) and *Panegirici sacri* (1664). Innocent XII brought him to Rome in 1692 as preacher and theologian of the Sacred Penitentiary. S. fought the publication of the antiprobabilist *Fundamentum theologiae moralis* by fellow Jesuit Tirso *González de Santalla and countered with his own defense of *probabilism, *Lettere sulla materia del probabile* (1732). His work against Quietism, *Concordia tra la fatica e la quiete nell' orazione* (1680) was condemned by the Inquisition, corrected, and republished in 1691.

[R. J. LITZ]

SEGNERI, PAOLO, THE YOUNGER (1673–1713), Italian Jesuit preacher, nephew of the elder Segneri, writer and translator of treatises on mission preaching and spiritual exercises. His most popular work was *Dell' amore di Dio e de' mezzi per acquistarlo* (1707). Throughout northern and central Italy his sermons effected numerous conversions.

[R. J. LITZ]

SEGNI, RAINALDO DEI CONTI DI, see ALEXANDER IV, POPE.

SEGOVIA, JOHN OF (d. after 1456), Spanish conciliarist, a canon of Toledo (1432), archdeacon, theology professor at Salamanca, and representative for university and king at the Council of Basel (1433), S. gained prominence as pamphleteer and negotiator for conciliarism (1434–36). Involved with the questions of Hussitism, Byzantine reunion, and the Immaculate Conception, he helped "depose" Eugene IV and elect Antipope Felix V, becoming Felix's cardinal and traveling apologist (1440–42). After the resolution of conciliarism, fortified with two French bishoprics and the Caesarea (titular) archbishopric, he withdrew to a Spanish monastery, writing his extensive history of the council and translating the Koran into Spanish and Latin. BIBLIOGRAPHY: É. Amann, DTC 8.1:816–819.

[R. I. BURNS]

SEGREGATION, the social separation of a group of people, usually according to their race. The term is applied in the U.S. to the condition in which Negroes are denied the opportunity to live in certain neighborhoods, hold certain jobs, or attend certain schools. It may extend to exclusion from certain places of social assembly and convenience, or reservation to special places there or in means of transport, these being of poorer quality than those used by whites. Wages also were lower for the performance of the same work. In the larger cities of the U.S. segregation combined with poverty in the black ghettos to breed a sense of failure, despair, and resentment, the seed-bed of crime, drug addiction, and dependency on welfare. The President's Advisory Commission on Civil Disorders reported in 1968 that "the corrosive and degrading effects of this condition (segregation) and the attitudes that underlie it are the sources of the deepest bitterness and at the center of the problems of racial disorder." *RACISM.

[G. A. VANDERHAAR]

SEGUR, LOUIS GASTON DE (1820–81), spiritual director and writer. Of French origin, S. studied law and became attaché to the ambassador to the Holy See. He studied for the priesthood and was ordained in 1847. His life was devoted to helping the unfortunate: children, workers, military prisoners. A community of priests founded to aid his work was short-lived. Auditor of the Rota for France, he lived in Rome from 1852 to 1856. Poor health forced his return to Paris and pastoral work. His complete works comprise 16 volumes and include *La Piété et la vie intérieure* in 8 volumes, placed on the Index in 1869 for suspected quietism and pantheism. S. obeyed the remonstrance, recalled the work, and reissued an emended version.

[J. R. AHERNE]

SEGURA Y SÁENZ, PEDRO (1880–1957), cardinal, primate of Spain. A foe of Protestantism, of Francisco Franco and the Falange, S. was a colorful figure, much revered by many Spaniards. He was a native of Burgos, ordained in 1906. He was a professor of canon law at Valladolid before becoming bp. of Coría Carceres in 1920. He became abp. of Burgos in 1927; later in that same year, a cardinal, abp. of Toledo and primate of Spain. When the Second Republic replaced King Alfonso XIII, S. did not conceal his opposition to the new government. He was exiled in 1931. Residing in Rome, he served in the Roman Curia. In 1937 he returned to Spain where he was with the Nationalist forces. In that same year he was appointed abp. of Seville, where he denounced modern dancing, freedom of thought, of religion, and of the press. Because of his pamphlet attacking the Vatican and Spanish officials over the concordat of 1953, the Holy See appointed an administrator for Seville, thus depriving him of power.

[J. R. AHERNE]

SEIPEL, IGNAZ (1876–1932), chancellor and foreign minister of Austria and leader of the Christian Socialist Party. Although born in humble circumstances in Vienna, S. demonstrated outstanding ability and dedication as a scholar, graduating from the Gymnasium with distinction. He studied for the priesthood at the Univ. of Vienna and was ordained in 1899. After receiving a doctorate in theology, he turned to a scholarly investigation of social ethics in the writings of the Church Fathers. He discovered that the Fathers neither condoned nor rejected property ownership, implying that the Church was not attached to any political or economic order, but should seek the order most nearly conforming to its principles. Thus S. became an advocate of reform of the Austro-Hungarian Empire, and after its collapse, he influenced the Christian Socialist Party toward support of the new Austrian Republic. He was elected to parliament in February 1919, and in May 1922 he became chancellor of the Republic, an office which he held twice more before his death in 1932. In the tense political atmosphere of this time, S. became an increasingly strident opponent of socialism and more receptive to authoritarian movements of the right. His outstanding accomplishments came in foreign policy, seeking a new order among Central European states and defending the rights of national minorities. In spite of the controversial nature of his political career, S. won universal respect as a statesman of unassailable integrity, dedication, and modesty. BIBLIOGRAPHY: K. von Klemperer, *Ignaz Seipel* (1972).

[R. J. GIBBONS]

SEISDEDOS Y SANZ, JERÓNIMO (1847–1923), Spanish theologian and apologist, with a special interest in the mystical writings of St. Theresa. He was already a priest and a professor in the seminary of Salamanca before entering the Society of Jesus in 1886. BIBLIOGRAPHY: A. del Portillo, EncCatt 11:266.

[E. J. DILLON]

SEITENSTETTEN, ABBEY OF, Benedictine monastery dedicated to the Blessed Virgin. Founded 1109 by Udalschalk of Stille and Heft for Augustinian Canons, it was given to Benedictines from Göttweig Abbey in 1112/6 and located in the Diocese of Passau, now in the Diocese of Sankt Pölten in lower Austria. The 13th-cent. Gothic church was rebuilt in the Baroque style in the 17th cent.; the present monastic buildings date from the 18th century. In 1964 the monks still labored in pastoral ministry in 14 parishes. BIBLIOGRAPHY: Cottineau 2:2995–96.

[E. J. DILLON]

SEIXAS, ROMUALDO ANTÔNIO DE (1787–1860), bp. and political leader. A native of Brazil, S. was ordained in 1810 and named bp. of Bahia in 1826, abp. and primate of Brazil in 1841. He was a leader in the General Assembly where his defense of the rights of the Church was persistent and highly influential. A moderate, he wrote numerous articles on religious questions of his day; the collection of these published in his lifetime runs to five volumes.

[J. R. AHERNE]

SEIYAS, FRANCISCO AGUIAR, see AGUIAR Y SEIYAS, FRANCISCO.

SELA, Edomite city taken by Amaziah and renamed Joktheel (2 Kg 14.7). It is generally identified with Umm el-Bayyârah, an imposing acropolis dominating the basin in which the Nabatean city of *Petra was built. On the W boundary of Edom, it lay about halfway between the Dead Sea and the Gulf of Aqabah. The Hebrew word for Sela is the same as for rock, so the city may be the intended reference in other passages (Is 42.11; Jer 49.16; Ob 3). According to an obscure reference in Isaiah (16.1), Moabites sent tribute to Jerusalem from Sela. Whether the same city was

meant is uncertain. The men of Seir may also have been thrown from the top of the rock at Sela (2 Chr 25.11–12).

[T. EARLY]

SELDEN, JOHN (1584–1654), English Jurist and Orientalist. In 1618 S. published *A History of Tithes*, in which he upheld their legal but not their divine right. The book was suppressed, and he was forbidden even to answer his opponents. He wrote other historical-legal works and a treatise, *De diis Syriis* (1617), which is still in repute. BIBLIOGRAPHY: A. Bertholet, RGG 5:1685.

[M. J. SUELZER]

SELEUCIA, SYNOD OF, see RIMINI AND SELEUCIA, SYNODS OF.

SELEUCIA-CTESIPHON. Seleucia on the Tigris was founded c.300 B.C. by Seleucus Nicator, one of Alexander the Great's generals and founder of the Seleucid dynasty of the diodoche. The city of Ctesiphon soon arose across the river, but the political capital of the Seleucids was moved to Antioch. The whole Mesopotamian region is thought to have been evangelized by Addai and Mari—perhaps Thaddeus and Thomas the Apostles. We do not know who the first bp. of Seleucia-Ctesiphon was, but the position soon became of such ecclesiastical importance that it was given the title catholicos by the patriarch of Antioch, with jurisdiction similar to that exercised by Thessalonica for Rome in Illyricum down to the 6th century.

With the condemnation of Nestorius at the Council of Ephesus (431), his partisans took refuge first in Edessa, then in Nisbis, whence they worked to ''Nestorianize'' the whole East Syrian or Mesopotamian Church. The two Nestorian champions were Ibas, bp. of Edessa, and Bar Sauma, bp. of Nisbis, who sought to gain control of the catholicate of Seleucia-Ctesiphon. With the death of Babai, the see was filled by Acacius (487), appointed by the Persian king, who immediately anathematized the Monophysites in a synod, upheld the abolition of celibacy, and issued a confession of faith which is definitely Nestorian. From 485 to 540, Seleucia-Ctesiphon remained the seat of the Nestorian catholicos, but after that the catholicos began to move about and the title of his see is almost forgotten. Some four synods in all were held in the city, at least three of which were Nestorian.

[A. WALKER]

SELEUCIANS (Hermians), Gnostics of the 2d and 3d centuries. Filaster (*Haer.* 55), and following him Augustine (*Haer.* 59, cf. 41), give a confused account of them. The truth seems to be that Seleucus was the master and Hermias his disciple. Their teachings were similar to those of the *Hermogeneans concerning the eternity of matter and the materiality of man's soul. In addition they taught that evil may have its source either in matter or in God; that there is no visible paradise; that baptism must not be with water;

that angels had created the human soul; that this world is the only hell; that the resurrection of the body means simply the procreation of children. BIBLIOGRAPHY: G. Bareille, DTC 6:2306, s.v. "Hermias."

[L. G. MÜLLER]

SELEUCID DYNASTY, the succession of kings of Greek language and culture, with their capital in Antioch of Syria, who attempted to carry on the imperial role of Alexander in the Asiatic provinces after his death (323 B.C.). The dynasty is named after one of Alexander's generals, Seleucus I Nicator. It began in the year of Alexander's death, and came to a definitive end in 65 B.C., when Pompey formally annexed the Syrian province into the Roman Imperium. The heart of the Seleucid empire lay near the mouth of the Orontes in N Syria near Cilicia, in four cities built by Seleucus, including the capital city Antioch, and the fortress city on the sea, Seleucia. The great rival of the Seleucids was the Ptolemaic dynasty, which ruled from Alexandria in Egypt, another new city and a center of Greek culture. For a century and a half the boundaries of one empire were expanded at the expense of the other, and the nations that lay geographically between them were caught in the power struggle. During this first century and a half after Alexander's death, it was Egypt that exercised at least nominal hegemony in Palestine; and although there was an inevitable imposition of Greek cultural values, the Ptolemies seem to have been notably tolerant of non-Greek ways. In the 2d cent. B.C. the picture changed dramatically when Antiochus III, the Great, of Antioch wrested control of Palestine from Egypt. The Seleucids then demonstrated cultural imperialism in its most arrogant and aggressive form. It assumed savage dimensions under Antiochus IV Epiphanes, whose name would suggest that he was the manifestation of Zeus. On his way back from Egypt, where he had been humiliated by a Roman ultimatum forcing his departure, he took his wrath out on the Jews in Jerusalem, devastating that city with the intent of creating a new Greek city. All Jewish worship ceased, and the "abomination of desolation" spoken of by Daniel was enshrined in the temple area. The Book of Daniel and the Books of the Maccabees give a picture of the Jewish resistance to the genocidal fury of the Seleucids. The rise of Jewish apocalyptic can only be understood against this background. The Jewish cry for liberation and the desire for the coming of the Messiah were a direct response to the Syrian tyranny. And when eventually the Roman emperor and his legates replaced the Seleucids, they came as the last of the Greek-speaking tyrants, whose contempt for provincial resistance to Hellenization was similar to that of the Seleucids. Rome's genocidal fury against Palestine, culminating in the destruction of Jerusalem, was in the tradition of Antiochus IV Epiphanes and his successors. The messianic fervor of Jesus' disciples and of the Palestinian Christian community was heir to the hopes and ideals of Daniel and the Maccabees. It was the Seleucid dynasty that beasts represented in apocalyptic literature, including the NT Book of Revelation, as the enemy of God's people.

[E. J. DILLON]

SELF-ABNEGATION, see SELF-DENIAL.

SELF-DEFENSE, the moral right to repel by proportionate means an unjust aggressor threatening bodily injury, death, or other grave damage. The classical adage theology followed—*vim vi licet repellere cum moderamine inculpatae tutelae*—was formulated by Lateran Council IV and incorporated into the Decretals of *Gregory IX. The primary moral issue is the right even to kill in defense of one's own life. The right is vindicated, first, on the grounds of the person's right to preserve his own existence; secondly, on the supposition that the steps taken in self-defense are truly necessary to meet the assailant, and his death is not the vengeful intent of the defense, but its unfortunate consequence (TH AQ ST 2a2ae, 64.7). The right of self-defense ceases when the aggression ceases, i.e., one cannot later kill the aggressor; only the public authority has the right to punish crimes (see VENGEANCE). The right of self-defense also implies the right to defend the life of another who is being unjustly assaulted, since by the bond of charity the *neighbor is another self. Where the aggression is not against life itself, the right of self-defense still exists, e.g., where grievous bodily harm that might cripple or maim is threatened, where the home is invaded, or where a great material loss is at stake; all of these touch on the substance and quality of life so closely that they can be legitimately defended. A woman threatened with rape also has the right to resist; but that is often more dangerous to herself. The right of self-defense cannot be invoked as grounds for abortion, since the unborn is not an unjust aggressor.

[T. C. O'BRIEN]

SELF-DENIAL, the practice of denying gratification to self in order to live in the unselfish manner of Christ. Inspired by the Savior's invitation, "If any man would come after me, let him deny himself. . . ." (Mt 16.24), it includes a refusal to cater to one's inclinations at given times, in determined matters, with the aim of achieving total unselfishness in action and outlook. The practice helps to nullify the effects of original sin and disposes the soul to the action of God's grace. Some degree of self-denial is necessary to obey the commandments, for the inclinations of fallen nature are not always in accord with God's law. This marks an indispensable minimum in the practice of self-denial. In addition to this, the denial to self of legitimate pleasures and satisfactions, whether for penitential purpose (see PENANCE, PRACTICES OF), or to establish mastery over self (see ASCETICISM), or to share in the sufferings of Christ, is recommended to individuals to a greater or lesser degree depending on a variety of prudential considerations applicable to different cases. Extremes of opinion—that of Molinos who counseled against the practice, and that of the Jansenists who exaggerated its role—have been condemned by the RC Church. BIBLIOGRAPHY: A. Royo, *Theology of Christian Perfection* (ed. and tr. J. Aumann, 1962).

[P. F. MULHERN]

SELF-INCRIMINATION, the revelation of one's own secret guilt of some crime or sin. Both civil and canon law afford a guilty person some protection against demands that he incriminate himself. Moralists are generally in agreement that an individual may rightfully avail himself of this protection, at least under ordinary circumstances, and that he is entitled in matters not covered by law to protect his own good name, and may indeed be obliged to do so, e.g., when his reputation is useful to him in the love and service of God and neighbor, or when the sacrifice of it would bring harm upon others, or even upon himself, if he sees this as likely to tax him beyond virtuous endurance. In a matter of the gravest concern to the common good, a man might be obliged in conscience to incriminate himself even when the law protects against the demand that he do so. To save another from conviction for a crime which he himself has committed, it would be laudable, but not necessarily obligatory, for him to confess his guilt. But if he has deliberately cast the suspicion on another that has led to conviction, he must acknowledge his own guilt if there is no other way to repair the injustice he has done. BIBLIOGRAPHY: B. Häring, *Law of Christ* (tr. E. Kaiser, 1966) 3:605–608.

[P. F. MULHERN]

SELF-INCRIMINATION, RIGHT AGAINST, IN THE U.S. Originating in the Fifth Amendment of the Bill of Rights, the right against self-incrimination is protected by the provision: "No person shall be compelled in any criminal case to be a witness against himself. . . ." In origin a federal protection, it did not bind individual states. The Fourteenth Amendment in 1868 with its insistence on due process and equal protection under the law has been held to require the states to offer the same guarantees required by the Bill of Rights. The position of the Supreme Court of the U.S. has been that only fundamental rights require observance by the states. The Court in 1908 (Twining *v.* New Jersey 211 U.S. 78 [1908]) asserted that the right against self-incrimination was not a fundamental one, but in 1964 the Supreme Court ruled that it was a fundamental right and therefore had to be acknowledged by the states. Since 1968 federal and state law are in agreement.

[J. R. AHERNE]

SELF-KNOWLEDGE, the understanding of self that is necessary to spiritual development. "Know thyself" has ever been the injunction of ascetical and spiritual writers, pagan and Christian alike. Critical reflection upon one's own character and conduct in the light of the standards one has accepted is taught by Scripture (Pr 20.27; 19.2; Ps 50.4–5; 118.10–11, 59; Mt 7.3–5; 6.22–23). Self-examination is enjoined before receiving holy communion (1 Cor 11.28), and it is an integral part of the sacrament of

penance. But differences are discernible in the intensity of the self-scrutiny recommended by different schools of spirituality. One, the older and, so to say, the more extraversive, lays greater emphasis upon the thought of God; the other, more psychologically exacting and, so to say, the more introversive, is analytic and more meticulously concerned with the purification of self. BIBLIOGRAPHY: ThAq ST 1a, 87 (esp. in Lat-Eng, ed. P. Durbin, 1968).

[P. K. MEAGHER]

SELF-LOVE, a term that usually implies an undue regard for oneself that tends to exclude other interests and affections; hence egoism, self-interest, contrasted with altruism, interest in others, as the spring of action; also egotism, an excessive use of the first person singular in conversation as a sign of self-assertion. These may be taken as forms of conceit, vainglory, or pride opposed to the virtue of modesty or humility, a central virtue for Christian adultness. But true self-love is a proper expression of living in friendship with God and our neighbor, and "pure" or "disinterested" love has been recommended as an ideal only by a fringe group of Christian teachers, with Jansenist or Quietist affiliations, at the end of the 17th century. Loving oneself in God is implicit in Lev 19.18 and reiterated by Christ: it is embraced in loving God, and is a tribute to our wanting him (cf. Gal 5.14; Jas 2.8; 1 Pet 3.10). This ordered love of ourselves, body and soul, is an essential element in friendship, which, after all, is more than a state of mutual benevolence: in Christian ethics, however, it allows for behavior of gallant self-sacrifice as well as a cooler temper of enlightened self-interest. BIBLIOGRAPHY: ThAq ST 2a2ae, 23.1; 25.4–5; 161.

[M. F. MORRY]

SELF-OBLATION, the offering or giving over of one's whole self to God in response to Christ's invitation to follow him (Mt 16.24; Mk 8.34; Lk 14.27). The phrase, which echoes the scriptural command to present ourselves as an oblation to God (1 Pet 2.4; Rom 12.1), is much used in the literature of the devout life and enters into the nomenclature of pious institutions, notably those of the period of explicit devotion to the Sacred Heart.

[T. GILBY]

SELF-REALIZATION FELLOWSHIP, a nonsectarian religion based on Hindu philosophy and Yoga. In 1920 its founder, Paramahansa Yogananda (1893–1952), visited the U.S. as a delegate to a conference on worldwide religious movements. He established himself in Boston and gathered a small following interested in his "muscle-will" system of physical perfection. Swami Yogananda taught the traditional raja-yoga discipline by which the initiate prepares himself for self-realization and union with the universal spirit through exercises of bodily and mental control. His published works stress the discipline, rather than the philosophic and theistic background of his teaching. In 1928 he set up his headquarters near Los Angeles, California. In 1932 he met James J. Lynn, a Kansas City millionaire, who became a convert to the movement and its principal benefactor. Lynn, or Rajasi Janakananda (1892–1955), succeeded Swami Yogananda as president of the Self-Realization Fellowship. Besides its center in California, the group has temples in the major American cities and claims some 2,500 adherents. Its temples and study centers are served by ordained monks from India, while the majority of the members are Americans.

[R. K. MacMASTER]

SELFISHNESS, a blanket term that covers a multitude of sins; like pride, an inturning on the self that flows through all sin, so much so that to denounce or admit to either selfishness or pride may serve as a substitute for more pointed and useful diagnosis. Self-interest may be enlightened, and one is bound by charity to love oneself, but selfishness is a self-seeking, easier perhaps to recognize than to define, clean contrary to the command to love God above all and our neighbour as ourself. The Gospels and morality apart, it is psychologically self-defeating: it never leads to human happiness, and that not merely in the long run. Seek only yourself and you will find only yourself, after a time, not very good company, either now or for eternity. BIBLIOGRAPHY: G. Gilleman, *Primacy of Charity in Moral Theology* (1961), 299–303; ThAq ST 2a2ae, 25.4; 162.2.

[T. GILBY]

SELJUKS, a Muslim Turkish tribe, named after its ruler, that entered W Asia in the early 11th century. Tughrul Beg (d. 1063), grandson of Seljuk, brought them into the Arab domains in Iran and Mesopotamia, and in 1055 into Baghdad. He cooperated with the caliph to uphold orthodox Islam. Alp Arslan (1063–72) and Malik Shah (1072–92) led the Seljuks against Byzantium and Egyptian Syria, which precipitated the Latin counterattack, the Crusades. Seljuk culture flourished, but political dissension disrupted the state, leaving the Seljuks a prey to the Mongols who established a protectorate over the Seljuk world at mid-13th century. The last Seljuk rulers disappeared early in the 14th century.

[R. H. SCHMANDT]

SELLIN, ERNEST (1867–1945), OT scholar and archeologist. S. taught OT at Vienna (1897–1908), Rostock (1908–13), Kiel (1913–21), and Berlin (1921–35); was editor of the series *Kommentar zum Alten Testament* and was one of the pioneer German archeologists in Palestine. He adhered to the History of Religions school of OT exegesis, subordinating biblical theology to a description of the historical evolution of Yahwism. BIBLIOGRAPHY: JBC 2:602.

[T. M. MCFADDEN]

SELLING, WILLIAM (d. 1494), Benedictine monk, classical scholar, bachelor of theology (Oxford), doctor of theology (Bologna), chancellor of Canterbury Cathedral priory (1470–72), prior (1474–94). Perhaps the foremost English classical scholar of his time, he studied (1464–68) at Padua and Bologna where he probably learned Greek, and was a chief promoter of Greek studies in England. BIBLIOGRAPHY: Emden Ox 3:1666–67.

[C. D. ROSS]

SELLING UNDER COST, see JUST PRICE.

SELLON, PRISCILLA LYDIA (*c.*1821–76), foundress of an Anglican religious community for women. In 1848 she responded to a public appeal made by Bp. Phillpotts of Exeter by volunteering to work among the destitute. With the assistance of E. B. Pusey she and some companions formed a society called the Sisters of Mercy of Devonport, erected schools and orphanages, and served heroically in the cholera epidemic. This community united with the Sisters of the Holy Cross (1856), and the combined sisterhood became known as the Society of the Most Holy Trinity, with present headquarters at Ascot Priory. BIBLIOGRAPHY: T. J. Williams, *Priscilla Lydia Sellon* (1950).

[M. J. SUELZER]

SEMAINES SOCIALES DE FRANCE, a lay institution, initiated in 1904 in Lyons, offering an annual week of courses on the social doctrine of the Church and current social realities. It functions as a "traveling university," providing, in a different place each year, courses by theologians, philosophers, jurists, trade-union leaders, economists, sociologists, and others. Although it is neither an action organization nor a movement, courses are guided by the slogan "Knowledge for Action," and its work has contributed to such 20th-cent. French social reforms as minimum wages, collective bargaining, family legislation, and social security. Annual weeks have focused on population growth, the land problem, family life, war and peace, education, class conflict, and rural life, among other subjects. BIBLIOGRAPHY: *Chronique Sociale de France* (1954) no. 3, and (1964) no. 6, *passim*.

[D. CODDINGTON]

SEMI-ARIANISM, an attempt in the 4th cent. to establish a compromise between the Catholic and Arian doctrines on the Incarnation. Catholics held that the Son is of the same nature, or consubstantial (*homoousios*), with the Father, while the Arians taught that he is not of the same nature or substance (*anomoios*, dissimilar). The Semi-Arians, chiefly Acacius of Caesarea and Basil of Ancyra, asserted that the Son was similar (*homoios*) to the Father, or of like substance (*homoiousios*), but still subordinated. BIBLIOGRAPHY: É. Amann, DTC 14.2:1790–96.

[P. FOSCOLOS]

SEMINAL REASONS (Lat. *rationes seminales*), the seed principles implanted by God during creation for all the varieties of material life that will develop. The term, which has a Stoic ancestry, was used by St. Augustine in his literal exposition of *Genesis*: the eternal reasons in the mind of God cause and conserve embryonic powers that act on the elements to produce distinctive characteristics through progressive changes. It should be treated rather as a symbol in the quasi-evolutionary sweep of his cosmogony than as a formal and literal meaning to be variously cast, as it was by the 13th-cent. scholastics, according to the categories of material, formal, and efficient causality. BIBLIOGRAPHY: ThAq ST la, 65–74 (Lat-Eng v. 10 ed. W. A. Wallace, *Cosmogony*).

[T. GILBY]

SEMINARIES, AND UNIVERSITIES, CONGREGATION FOR, see CATHOLIC EDUCATION, CONGREGATION FOR.

SEMINARY PRIESTS, in the history of the English Reformation, priests ordained at Douai, Rome, or elsewhere on the Continent, and sent on the English mission. Some have used the term to distinguish secular from Jesuit priests on the mission. Seminary priests were singled out by law from priests ordained in England during the reign of Mary Tudor (Marian priests); a law of 1585 made their coming to England an act of high treason.

[T. C. O'BRIEN]

SEMI-PELAGIANISM, name applied in the 17th cent. to an earlier teaching, mediating between predestinarianism and Pelagianism, condemned at the Council of *Orange II (520). *PELAGIANISM AND SEMI-PELAGIANISM.

[T. C. O'BRIEN]

SEMI-QUIETISM, a term used in reference to the 17th-cent. debate in France between Bossuet and Fénelon on pure love and contemplation. This debate resulted from their opposing positions at the Conferences of Issy (1694–95), in which the doctrine of Madame *Guyon was examined. The 34 Articles of Issy were due mainly to Bossuet, but since Fénelon was able to take part in the final deliberations, some concessions were made to mysticism. In 1695 Bossuet used the Articles of Issy to condemn Madame Guyon. Fénelon refused to do the same in his diocese, and in correspondence and writings imposed his own interpretation on them. In 1696 Fénelon wrote his *Explanations of the Maxims of the Saints on the Interior Life,* in which he declares his theory of mysticism built on the idea of pure love. He exaggerated the importance of the problem of indifference to salvation. Bossuet began to stir up opinion against Fénelon and a month after the appearance of the *Maxims* published his *Instruction on the States of Prayer*. In his work Bossuet confines the mystical life to a small number of miraculous cases. Fénelon, afraid of being condemned by the Assembly

of the Clergy in France, appealed to Rome. Moving his debate with Fénelon to the level of personalities. Bossuet wrote a pamphlet in 1698 entitled *Relation on Quietism*. He made use of confidences Madame Guyon wrote for her director under the seal of secrecy, and published a private letter to her from Fénelon. The pamphlet put both Madame Guyon and Fénelon in a bad light. Innocent XII was sympathetic toward Fénelon, who had been more favorable to the Holy See than Bossuet. The theologians of the commission charged with examining the *Maxims* were also divided. But the publication in Rome of Bossuet's *Relation on Quietism* hurt Fénelon's cause. The intervention of Louis XIV, favorable to Bossuet, put pressure on the Roman Curia and led the cardinals to pronounce against the *Maxims*. Innocent XII gave in, and with the brief *Cum alias*, March 12, 1699, condemned 23 propositions taken from the *Maxims* (D 2351–74). Fénelon submitted to this sentence. Later the Pope made Fénelon a cardinal.

The points of debate between Bossuet and Fénelon may be summarized as follows: Bossuet held that the passive state exists only during the time of prayer. Fénelon taught that it may exist both during the time of prayer and outside of it. Bossuet insisted that perfection is to be found in the practice of the virtues, since the passivity of the mystics is an extraordinary grace, and that the love that presides over the virtues cannot be pure love since such a love cannot be reached in this life. Fénelon held that perfection is found in the pure love that is attained in the passivity of the mystics. Bossuet taught that the ligature of the faculties is absolute; Fénelon, that it is relative, for it is freely accepted. Thus Bossuet was for the active way, Fénelon for the passive way. Each conceded to the other as little as possible. Fénelon overstressed the passive; Bossuet overstressed the active. In comparing the two, scholars today find Fénelon closer to the doctrine of recognized authorities on mysticism than Bossuet. The unfortunate aspect about the condemnation of the 23 propositions taken from the *Maxims* was that it amounted in popular opinion to a kind of attack on mysticism, and this opinion, as Innocent XII feared, was ultimately harmful to the Church. Deprived of the living source of inner experience, the literature of devotion gradually dried up and any mention of mysticism was made with the greatest caution and fear. BIBLIOGRAPHY: L. Cognet, *Post-Reformation Spirituality* (tr. P. Hepburne Scott, 1959). *QUIETISM.

[K. KAVANAUGH]

SEMIRATIONALISM, designation, esp. in RC theology, for certain 19th-cent. theories that gave rationalistic explanations of dogma. *Hermesianism, the theory developed by Georg Hermes (1775–1831), a German professor of theology, by proposing positive doubt as the basis for theological methodology, made human reason rather than faith the ultimate criterion and unique means for attaining knowledge of supernatural truths (see D 2738). *Guntherianism, named for Anton Günther (1783–1863), a priest in Vienna, was condemned for obscuring the distinction between faith and reason and for teachings opposed to the consubstantiality of the three Persons and God's freedom in creating (see D 2828–31). Jakob Frohschammer (1821–93) affirmed a supernatural order of truths and man's need for revelation, yet negated both by insisting that reason is absolutely free and that its probative power establishes the objective value of revelation (D 2852). Vatican Council I also condemned these theories (D 3015–20; 3041).

[T. C. O'BRIEN]

SEMITES, people speaking one of the Semitic languages. The term was first used in 1781 by A. L. Schlozer, who adopted it because the nations listed in the *Table of the Nations as descendants of Shem spoke related languages. To that time the languages had been called oriental. Semitic is therefore a classification of language rather than of race, though all Semites may have come from, or be mixed with, people of a common ethnic stock. The origin of the Semites is uncertain, but it is generally thought they were Bedouin, continually migrating from Arabia out into the surrounding areas. They were already present throughout the Fertile Crescent at the time of our earliest historical records. Some scholars postulate a Proto-Semitic language that developed into the later wide variety of Semitic tongues.

Semitic languages are sometimes divided into three groups: (1) Eastern: Akkadian (Babylonian-Assyrian); (2) Northwestern: Aramaic, Syrian, Samaritan, Palmyrene, Nabatean, Canaanite (Ugaritic), Phoenician, Moabite, Hebrew (Amorite); (3) Southern: Arabic, Sabean, Minean, Ethiopic (Amharic). Classifications vary, however. Semitic languages are characterized by emphasis on consonants, with vowel signs added late in their development. Verb roots are predominantly tri-consonantal, formed on the third person singular. Instead of past, present, and future tenses, they have complete and incomplete action. Together with Egyptian, Libyo-Berber, and Cushitic, with which they are related, they form the Hamito-Semitic language group.

Since the three major monotheistic religions—Judaism, Christianity, and Islam—have all arisen among Semites, the history of Semitic culture has been of special interest to students of comparative religions. BIBLIOGRAPHY: S. Moscati, *Semites in Ancient History* (1959).

[T. EARLY]

SEMLER, JOHANN SALOMO (1725–91), German church historian and biblicist. His early background was in *Pietism, but he adopted a rationalistic theological position that he referred to as *liberalis theologia*. His education and the major part of his professional career (1752–79) were at Halle. His main importance in church history is his study of the historical development of dogma, esp. in a 4-v. study of the biblical canon (1771–76). He evaluated dogma and theology as evolving, inadequate attempts to grasp religious truths. No confession or system should be considered definitive. He was a pioneer in the application of the historical and critical method to the study of the Bible. While maintaining the supremacy of reason and strictly personal character of religion, he also felt that public religious conformity should be secured by the State. BIBLIOGRAPHY: C. Mirbt, EncRelKnow 10:354–355.

[T. C. O'BRIEN]

SEMMELROTH, OTTO (1912–), German Jesuit theologian. Ordained in 1939, he received his doctorate in theology at the Univ. of Bonn in 1947. S. is rector and professor of dogma at the Jesuit theological college in Frankfurt. His writings center on ecclesiology, sacramentology, and Mariology. Since he understands the Church, not as an empty sign, but as representing the reality of grace both within and beyond itself, he is one of the first to regard the Church as the primordial sacrament through which is channeled the efficacy of the traditional seven. S. views Mary as the prototype of the Church and of humanity, which receives God's grace in faith. BIBLIOGRAPHY: O. Semmelroth, *Church as Primordial Sacrament* (1953); *Mary, Archetype of the Church* (1963).

[P. J. ROSATO]

SEMMES, RAPHAEL (1809–77), naval officer, writer. Of an old Catholic family of Maryland, S. was appointed a midshipman in the U.S. Navy in 1826. Much of his service in early years was in survey duty on the S coast and in the Gulf of Mexico. He served with distinction during the war with Mexico. In 1861 S. resigned, a commander, from the U.S. Navy and offered his services to the Confederacy before outbreak of hostilities. His career as a commander of the Confederate ships Sumter and Alabama was a brilliant one in which he carried the war against Union ship lanes. He is credited with having destroyed a man-of-war and captured 82 merchantmen. After the Civil War S. was persecuted by the North and driven from one position after another, including a one-year term as professor of moral philosophy and English literature at what is now Louisiana State University. His principal writings were *Service Afloat and Ashore during the Mexican War* (1851), and *Service, Afloat, during the War between the States* (1869).

[J. R. AHERNE]

SEMPITERNAL (Lat. *semper*, always, plus *aeternum*, everlasting). With the abstract term "sempiternity" it contrasts a never-ending duration with the eternity that is proper to God alone. The spiritual being of the angels is not subject properly either to time or the succession in change undergone by material beings, nor subject to mortality. The grace-given, endless possession of the beatific vision by the just is also of everlasting duration. The term "sempiternal" applies to such forms of duration.

[T. C. O'BRIEN]

SENAN, ST., 6th-cent, abbot and confessor, perhaps also a bp., credited with founding a series of monasteries centered on Scattery Island in the Shannon estuary in Ireland. S. is the most celebrated of the more than 20 saints that bore that name. The abundance of legend and miracle credited to him may indicate that he has acquired miracles originally attributed to one of the others. He came of Christian parents, was perhaps a friend of St. David's, and a disciple of a holy abbot named Cassidus.

[E. J. DILLON]

SENECA, LUCIUS ANNAEUS (c.5 B.C.– A.D. 65), Latin Stoic philosopher. Born in Cordova of an equestrian family, he was brought to Rome as a child and lived there or in Campania the rest of his life—apart from the years of his banishment to Corsica by Claudius (41–49). He received an excellent training in rhetoric and pursued philosophical studies as his major private interest. He soon acquired a reputation as an orator and writer. In 49 he was appointed as a tutor to Nero and in 50 he was made praetor. For 5 years, he exercised a good influence on Nero, who made him a *consul suffectus* in 55. From this time on, however, his relations with Nero deteriorated steadily. In 65 he was accused of being implicated in the Pisonian conspiracy and was permitted to take his own life.

It is acknowledged that S. lived in extremely dangerous times, yet his love of wealth and sumptuous living, his lack of fortitude in his exile, and, above all, his role in the murder of Agrippina and the letter he composed to exonerate Nero, exhibit a strange contrast between S. the moral philosopher and the unmasked S. as a person. It is very probable that he was a neurotic all his life, a circumstance that may explain in part at least the repulsive aspects of his conduct and personality. As a writer, he must be regarded as the master of a pointed and aphoristic prose style and as an effective exponent of the religious and moral teachings of Late Stoicism.

A number of his works are lost but the following are extant: (1) the so-called *Dialogues* (12 bks.), two of which are *consolations*; (2) *De clementia* (2 bks. out of 3 are extant); (3) *De beneficiis* (7 bks.); (4) *Epistles to Lucilius* (124 letters in 20 bks.); (5) *Naturales quaestiones* (a curious and superficial treatment of natural phenomena); (6) *Apocolocyntosis*, the "Pumpkinification of Claudius"; (7) 9 *Tragedies*, written to be read rather than acted, but destined to have a marked influence on European drama in the Renaissance and in the Baroque age. Most of these works are filled with Stoic aphorisms, moral counsels, and exhortations dealing with all aspects of life and conduct.

Philosophy is to be pursued purely as a means of acquiring virtue. God is regarded as transcending matter, and the treatment of the conflict between body and soul is more Platonic than Stoic. Despite the Stoic doctrine of determinism, every man is free to follow virtue, if he wills, and God will help. Every man must struggle constantly with himself wherever he may be. Daily examination of conscience is necessary to attain moral progress. One should love his fellow men and show this love in a practical way, and one should forgive his enemies. (See also STOICISM.)

The *Pseudo-Correspondence of *Seneca and St. Paul* indicates that he exercised some influence on early Christian writers, but this influence is really noteworthy chiefly on St. Cyprian, Lactantius, St. Jerome, and Martin of Braga. In the Middle Ages, however, he enjoyed wide popularity, in particular among the Cistercians. He was well known and used by a number of 12th-and 13th-cent. writers, and he occupied a central place in the Neostoicism of the Renaissance and of the 16th and 17th cent., esp. in France. BIBLIOGRAPHY: OCD 826–828; LexAW 2777–79; J. W. Duff, *Literary History of Rome in the Silver Age* (1960) 159–223; Copleston 1:429–431; M. Spanneut, NCE 13:80–81, esp. important for his influence on Christian writers.

[M. R. P. MCGUIRE]

SENECA AND ST. PAUL, CORRESPONDENCE OF. It consists of eight letters of Seneca to St. Paul and six of St. Paul to Seneca—all written in Latin. St. Jerome is the first writer to make mention of the collection, which he accepts as genuine (*De viris illustribus* 12), and St. Augustine does likewise (*Epist.* 153.14). Extant MSS date from the 9th cent., and for the period from 1200 to 1500 alone some 300 MSS are known. St. Jerome's acceptance of the collection gave it the stamp of authenticity, and this approval unquestionably contributed to the popularity and esteem which Seneca enjoyed throughout the Middle Ages and later. It was even believed that Seneca was a Christian. With the rise of historical criticism in the 17th cent., the authenticity of the work was challenged, and in the course of the 19th it was definitely established that the correspondence was a fabrication of the 4th century. It bears all the earmarks of a rhetorical exercise. The content is commonplace and the style is mediocre. BIBLIOGRAPHY: M. Spanneut, NCE 13:80–81; Bardenhewer 1:606–610; Altaner 140; Engl. tr. in James ApocNT 480–484.

[M. R. P. MCGUIRE]

SENESTREY, IGNAZ VON (1818–1906), bishop of Regensburg from 1858. A zealous prelate, S. encouraged liturgical renewal and worked to strengthen Catholic life in areas where the Church was not well represented. He was a strong advocate of the definition of papal infallibility at Vatican I, though most of his German confreres were opposed to the definition. S. was a strenuous opponent of Kulturkampf and a vigorous, if not always prudent, champion of the rights of the Church in Germany.

[J. R. AHERNE]

SENFL, LUDWIG (c.1492–c.1555), Swiss Renaissance composer, pupil of Heinrich Isaac. S. succeeded his teacher as Kapellmeister of the Court Chapel in Vienna. From there he went to Munich. He was esteemed as one of the great composers of his time. His works include Masses and motets as well as secular songs.

[M. T. LEGGE]

SENLIS, CATHEDRAL OF (1155–91), built under Thibaud, friend to Louis VII and Suger. Senlis is, after the choir of St. Denis, the first great example of Gothic style. In the Virgin portal (1185–91) of Senlis, masterfully balancing realism and idealism, the Gothic portal acquired its final form becoming the model for Braisne, Mantes, the Last Judgment, and two Virgin portals at Laon, and façades at Chartres, Paris, and Amiens. The 13th-cent. spire, flamboyant S façade, transept (redone in the 16th cent.) and chapel statues of St. Louis, Eloi, and the Virgin are noteworthy. BIBLIOGRAPHY: W. Sauerländer, ''Die Markenkrönungsportale von Senlis und Mantes,'' *Wallraf-Richartz Johrbuch* 20 (1958); H. Focillon, *Art of the West* (v. 1, 1963).

[M. J. DALY]

SENNACHERIB, KING OF ASSYRIA 705–681 B.C., son of Sargon II, father of Esarhaddon. His name in Akkadian means ''may (the Moon-deity) Sin replace the (lost) brothers.'' The dominant factor of his reign was the constant dissension, intrigue, and rebellion in Babylon against Assyrian hegemony. The main source of trouble was Merodach-baladan, the ruler of a powerful Chaldean tribe. He managed to keep S. distracted by successfully inciting the Arameans, the Elamites, the Arabs, the Phoenicians, the towns of Palestine, and even Hezekiah, King of Juda, to revolt against Assyrian rule. S. went on punitive campaigns into all these areas. The accounts in Isaiah and 2 Kings tell of S.'s army interrupting the siege of Jerusalem, backtracking to the Assyrian homeland because of a rumor. The biblical legend of the sudden death overnight of the large Assyrian army encamped near Jerusalem, although mentioned in Herodotus, has no corroboration from Assyrian, Babylonian, or other Near Eastern records. Probably S. realized the W and S troubles were largely diversionary tactics of his Chaldean nemesis; so he decided to concentrate his efforts on Babylon directly. Repeated insurrection and intermittent war finally culminated in the destruction of Babylon. According to S.'s own inscription, he tore down the walls, houses, palaces, temples, and even the legendary temple towers of Babylon, to their very foundations, including the earthern cores of the towers. His end is shrouded in mystery. According to the Babylonian Chronicle he was murdered in 681 by one of his sons; according to the biblical account in 2 Kg 19.37, he was worshiping one day in the temple of his god when two of his sons, Adrammelech and Sharezer, murdered him.

[E. J. DILLON]

SENS, COUNCILS OF. Some 24 councils were held at Sens in central France. The best known, in 1140, was the scene of the confrontation between St. Bernard and Abelard; it resulted in the latter's condemnation. BIBLIOGRAPHY: E. Josi, EncCatt 11:315–322; J. Rath, LTK 9:668–669 (for bibliog.).

[B. L. MARTHALER]

SENSES OF SCRIPTURE, the many meanings that can be attached to the words of the Bible. The literal sense is the meaning that the author intended to convey by his words, plain or figurative; Christians traditionally, however, have accepted the possibility of meanings beyond the literal. The books of the Bible are regarded as works, not only of human authorship, but of divine inspiration. God could have attached to the words of the Bible a meaning beyond that intended by the human author. The books of the Bible are taken as an expression of God's plan of salvation through Christ; the biblical persons, places, and events, therefore, may have a divinely intended reference beyond their immediate context in the biblical narrative. *Hermeneutics establishes rules for interpreting both the literal and other possible senses of Scripture; *exegesis applies such rules to actual texts.

The search for meanings beyond the literal is suggested in the OT itself, e.g., Deutero-Isaiah presents the return of the exiles from Babylon as a new exodus corresponding to, yet far more marvelous than the first exodus from Egypt. In the NT, and esp. in Heb, the figures of Moses, the high priest, and Melchizedek are all presented as types of Christ. The ritual Day of Atonement is a type of his redemptive sacrifice on the cross. Paul and the author of Heb show themselves aware of the unity of God's plan of salvation and of a consequent correspondence between the earlier stages of the plan and its culmination in Christ.

Origen, in the 3d cent., strongly affected the history of exegesis. He put forward the view (*Peri archon* 4.2–3) that there is a bodily or somatic sense available to simple believers, a deeper psychic sense which those more advanced in the faith can discern through and beyond the somatic sense, and finally a still deeper spiritual or pneumatic sense, which only the perfect can arrive at. This spiritual sense reveals the personages and events recorded in the OT as types or prefigurings of Christ and his redemptive work as presented in the NT. In their readings of the OT, therefore, the perfect can see beyond the immediate literal meaning which the inspired author would have had explicitly in mind when he wrote, and recognize the events, institutions, or persons he described as elements in the salvific plan of God culminating in Christ. Consequently these can also discern the correspondence and similarity between the type, which is provisional, transient, and imperfect; and the antitype, some aspect of Christ and his work which is perfect, final, and eternal. Subsequently modifications, variations, and developments, sometimes extravagant, were put forward, and in the 5th cent. the spiritual sense was subdivided (notably by the Egyptian Abbot Nesteros as recorded by John Cassian) into the allegorical or typological sense, the anagogical sense, and the tropological or moral sense. This fourfold division of the senses of Scripture guided medieval exegesis: (1) the literal sense, that explicitly intended by the human author and expressed in his actual words. Since this included metaphors, figures of speech, literary devices, etc., the word literal is used here in a specialized way; (2) the allegorical or typological sense embodied in the actual persons, events, and things referred to and described by the words; (3) the anagogical or eschatological sense, in which the events, institutions, and persons in Scripture were taken as types and foreshadowings of the future state of bliss awaiting the faithful; (4) the moral or tropological sense, in which Scripture was interpreted as a guide to right living. The whole is summed up in the adage of the Dominican Augustine of Dacia (d. 1282): *Littera gesta docet, quid credas allegoria; moralis quid agas, quid speres anagogia.*

Medieval emphasis on the spiritual sense neglected the literal sense. Occasionally the primacy of the literal sense was reasserted, e.g., by St. Thomas Aquinas who stated that nothing essential to faith is contained in the spiritual sense of Scripture that is not also set forth in the literal sense (ThAq ST la, 1.10 ad 1). Since the human authorship is inspired, neglect of the literal sense is a grave defect. Yet until the era of the Renaissance and Reformation, this neglect continued. Attention to the Greek and Hebrew text, the appeal to Scripture in the Reformation controversies focused attention on literal exegesis. But only in the 19th and 20th cent. with the development of biblical criticism, was the supremacy of the literal sense completely established.

Contemporary scholars are divided. Some insist that the only sense of Scripture admissible is the literal sense, and specifically that even a Christian reading of the OT is unwarranted. Others admit the possibility of senses over and above the literal. The *sensus plenior* (plenary or fuller sense) is a meaning not intended by the author, but by God who inspired them. Those who defend the *sensus plenior* maintain that the vagueness of some scriptural statements suggests that they contain by God's intention a fuller meaning to be perceived by the reader. The typical sense is a meaning to be derived from the realities portrayed in the Bible, in view of God's total plan of salvation and the consequent correspondence between type and antitype. Another important defense of meanings beyond the literal is present in the movement called the New Hermeneutic, which, on various bases, maintains that the actual understanding of the word of God here and now is a true meaning of Scripture, beyond the sense that can be discerned by historical and critical exegesis.

The consequent sense and the accommodated sense are not truly senses of Scripture. The first is a meaning derived by combining propositions contained in the Bible with other sources of human learning outside the Bible. Use of the consequent sense is a form of theological argumentation. The accommodated sense is a meaning given to the Scriptures by one who reads into the text some liturgical, literary, catechetical, or other application. Use of accommodation has characterized much patristic and medieval exegesis, as well as theological argumentation, and Christian preaching.

BIBLIOGRAPHY: C. Spicq, *Esquisse d'une histoire de l'exégèse latine au Moyen-Âge* (1944); H. de Lubac, *Histoire et esprit* (1950), particularly on Origen; *idem, Exégèse médiévale* (4 v., 1959–64); J. Daniélou, *Origen* (tr. W. Mitchell, 1955); R. E. Brown, *"Sensus plenior" of Sacred Scripture* (1954); *idem*, JBC 2:605–623; A. Fernandez, "Sentido plenior, literal, típico, espiritual," *Biblica* 34 (1953) 299–326.

[D. J. BOURKE]

SENSISM, a position in epistemology and psychology which seeks to reduce all cognitive and appetitive activities in man to the sensory level thereby denying, either explicitly or implicitly, the existence of the rational faculties of intellect and will. As an extreme view, it is opposed by a counter-extreme—idealism, which in Plato (427–347 B.C.) and René Descartes (1596–1650) deemphasizes the role of the senses in favor of exaggerated intellectualism. Sensism is often associated with materialism in philosophy and the natural sciences, though the two trends are not necessarily coextensive. For the sensist, concepts or ideas are usually regarded as mere images or phantasms, and hence, not as abstract, universal, and immaterial. Sensism likewise denies universals as the expression of real classes found in nature. Typical of the sensist view is the school of British empiricism as represented by John *Locke (1632–1704) and David *Hume (1711–76). According to the latter, not only does all human knowledge begin in the senses but it remains strictly a sensory function, and there is no necessity to introduce processes of a distinctly different character termed intellectual. Just as sensism offers no distinction between sensory and intellectual knowledge, it poses no distinction between bodily appetites and intellectual appetite or free will. This dual failure to differentiate between the sensory and the intellectual has important consequences for both theology and philosophy. It commonly leads to a denial of the substantiality and immortality of the human soul, the freedom of the human will, man's moral accountability, and the metaphysical bases for individual human rights and dignity. For typical examples of sensism, see Locke's *Essay Concerning Human Understanding* (1690) and Hume's *Enquiry Concerning Human Understanding* (1748).

[J. T. HICKEY]

SENSITIVITY TRAINING GROUPS, a term, often used interchangeably with encounter groups and T-groups, that refers to small group experience which is based on person-to-person encounter whose purpose is to make participants more aware of the present experience. In the late 60s there was a phenomenal proliferation of such small group experiences. During the years immediately preceding this, there emerged psychologists calling themselves humanists. Using many of the techniques of the psychodrama of Moreno, applying here-and-now existentialist emphasis, sensitivity training encounter groups moved from the therapeutic to diversified industrial and social areas. In industrial groups, which are intended to improve the management of their organizations, there are clearly defined objectives directed toward profitable dynamic interaction. However, most groups have no ultimate aims or ideology. The leaders encourage self-disclosure, expression of strong emotions, and interpersonal confrontations among the participants. The focus of the group is on reality of feelings; the morality of their expression is not adverted to. Because great numbers of people are seeking surcease from the alienation of the age, striving to establish relationships, to discover the meaning of life, to experience personal growth, there has evolved an emphasis on the emotional-sensuous life of the participants to the exclusion of the intellectual. The proponents of the movement (Rogers, et al.) are enthusiastic, zealous, and committed. They see great personal development in the areas of trust, openness, self-determination, and interdependence accomplished through self-revelation. The opponents (Koch, et al.) see in the techniques employed brain-washing, destruction of values and diminishment of personhood, leading by denial of ultimate goals to a cult of instantaneous sensual experience.

The encounter group experience, and hence its techniques, are found in almost every facet of society: industry, marriage, and education. The most developed educational format, called Human Development Program, is designed for pre-school through the elementary school. Its purpose is to stimulate and support emotional development. The Encounter Group culture has become a multi-million dollar business. BIBLIOGRAPHY: K. W. Back, *Beyond Words: The Story of Sensitivity Training and the Encounter Movement* (1972); *New Perspectives on Encounter Groups* (ed. L. N. Solomon and B. Berzon, 1972).

[A. WARDLE]

SENSUALITY (late Lat. *sensualitas, sensualis*), a term considered here in its affective, rather than in cognitive aspects. In scholastic philosophy and theology it signified that part of human nature which is the seat of the *emotions or passions, including both the instinctive and voluntary drives of animal appetite (ThAq ST la, 81. 1–2). As such it is quite innocent and possessed by Christ (*ibid*. 3a, 18. 2, 6). Under the attraction of scriptural references (e.g., 1 Cor 2.4; Jas 3.15) and Stoic patrology, it signified that part as a source of evil, the absorption of spirit by flesh, and so, according to most, but not all, Christian moralists, a vicious proclivity toward sense-pleasures. Milton apparently invented ''sensuous'' to avoid such associations to ''sensual,'' and from him it was adopted by Coleridge, and later extended in a favorable sense to feelings; though now even ''sensuousness'' has come down in the world and often carries a disparaging suggestion of self-indulgence.

[T. GILBY]

SENSUS ECCLESIAE, see MIND OF THE CHURCH.

SENTENCES AND SUMMAE, theological works, mainly of the 12th and 13th cent., whose purpose was the systematization of all Christian doctrine. The basic format of these treatises was to raise important theological questions, answer them first by quoting from *authority*, i.e., Scripture and the Fathers, and then apply various arguments from reason. Of the many *Books of Sentences*, *Peter Lombard's *Libri quatuor sententiarum* achieved the widest acclaim and became the usual textbook in medieval theological schools. By the 13th cent., however, more creative thinkers, commenting on the *Sentences*, but preferring not to limit themselves to the Lombard's format, developed new methods of organization and presentation which led to the theological *summae* properly so called. Many different versions appeared, among them the *Summa theologiae* of *Thomas Aquinas which by the 16th cent. became a textbook equal to the Lombard's *Sentences*. BIBLIOGRAPHY: P. Glorieux, DTC 14.2:1860–84; *idem*, NCE 13:94–96.

[J. MCGLYNN]

SENTIMENTALITY, the quality of exhibiting feeling or sensibility, its abundance, and perhaps even its prevalence. Its character will depend on a person's temperamental make-up, and the tough have their sentimental affectations as well as the tender, though usually the term refers to the softer passions. It now carries a suggestion of reproach, of being swayed by superficial feeling, not reason, which was absent when Sterne wrote the *Sentimental Journey*, when elevated and refined feelings were cultivated, and hard-fighting tars thought it no shame to shed tears of joy. Emotional fashions change. Now a prominent part of the field of sentimentality is held by an addictive indulgence in erotic fantasies, feelings, and prurience, not amounting to, and sometimes masking, the full function of sexuality. Those parts of chastity called *honestas*, a fine sense of honor (*pudicitia*), and a decent reserve (*modestas*), are tonic. BIBLIOGRAPHY: ThAq ST 2a2ae, 144; 145; 151.4; 160 (esp. in ed. Lat-Eng, v. 43, ed. T. Gilby, 1968).

[T. GILBY]

SENTIRE CUM ECCLESIA, see MIND OF THE CHURCH.

SEPARATE BAPTISTS, those who separated from the established Congregational Church in New England during the *Great Awakening and became Baptists. Shubael *Stearns formed an *association of Separate Baptists at Sandy Creek, N.C., in 1758; many other associations grew up in Va. and Kentucky. Most of these eventually united with the *Regular Baptists; those who did not, constitute the present-day Separate Baptists in Christ. BIBLIOGRAPHY: R. G. Torbet, *History of the Baptists* (1950).

[T. C. O'BRIEN]

SEPARATION, MATRIMONIAL. It has been the constant teaching of the Church that married people have the right and obligation to live together. This is the interpretation given to Gen 2.24, and it is clearly evident in the Pastoral Constitution on the Church (*Gaudium et spes* 47–52). The Church recognizes that this ideal of cohabitation cannot always be realized so it provides for separations but requires a hearing before the Church if one is to be final. Canon law for the Latin Church, as of this writing, provides for separation in CIC c.1128–32 and for the Oriental Church in the apostolic letter, *Crebrae allatae*, c. 117–121. Adultery is the sole cause for a permanent and perpetual separation, as long as the aggrieved party did not consent to it, condone it, or compensate for it. A temporary separation for a definite or indefinite period of time is the only separation permitted for causes other than adultery. The present CIC provides certain generic causes for temporary separation, but the Schema on the Sacraments, recently issued, provides that episcopal conferences shall determine the causes of separation, taking the customs of the people and local circumstances into account. The permission of the local ordinary is required even for temporary separations unless there is danger in delay; in this case the innocent party can depart without awaiting permission.

[J. P. KING]

SEPARATISTS, a term applied in England, esp. in the 16th and 17th cents., to those who separated themselves from the C of E, and first used with reference to the followers of Robert *Browne, who later developed into the Congregationalists or *Independents. *NONCONFORMISTS; *DIS-SENTERS.

[R. B. ENO]

SEPHARDIM, one of the three divisions of the post-Exilic Jewish people who lived in Spain and Portugal in the Middle Ages. After their expulsion from Spain in 1492 they spread to England, France, and the Low Countries as well as along the Mediterranean. They kept their own language, Ladino or Judeo-Spanish, as well as their customs. They are estimated to number about half a million people.

[R. T. MEYER]

SEPPELT, FRANZ XAVER (1883–1956), German historian of the papacy. He was ordained in 1906. His doctoral thesis demonstrated a bent for church history. In 1910 he published *Studien zum Pontifikat Cölestins V* (1910) and *Monumenta Coelestiniana* in 1921. A professor at the Univ. of Breslau, (1915–45), he wrote his masterwork *Geschichte des Papsttums bis 1789* (5 v., 1954–59), a work of brilliance which corrects the errors of previous writers, including Ludwig von Pastor. From 1946 to 1952 S was professor of church history at the Univ. of Munich.

[J. R. AHERNE]

SEPT-FONS (-FONDS), ABBEY OF, Cistercian monastery near Autun, France, founded in 1132 by monks of Fontenay. It was devastated by wars in the 14th-16th cent., but was restored by Abbot Eustache de Beaufort (1656–1700). In 1664, he introduced the Cistercian Strict Observance. During the 18th cent. the abbey was one of the most populous and respected in France. It was suppressed during the Revolution in 1791, but was restored by the Trappists in 1845. BIBLIOGRAPHY: K. Spahr, LTK 9:677; F. Lamy and E. Beaumont, *Histoire de N.-D. de Saint-Lieu Sept-Fons* (2 v. 1937–38).

[L. J. LEKAI]

SEPTEMBER, MARTYRS OF. More than 1,500 clerics and laymen were slain in France in the disturbances of late Aug. and early Sept., 1792. Of this number, 191 were beatified by Pius XI in 1926. A number or priests, loyalist soldiers, and other laymen were imprisoned in the Abbaye, a former monastery, which rioters attacked Sept. 2, 1792. The priests were put to death for refusing the oath to uphold the Civil Constitution of the Clergy (passed by the Constituent Assembly, 1790); the remaining prisoners were also massacred. Rioters then attacked the Carmelite church in Rue de Rennes, where more than 95 victims, known as the Martyrs des Carmes, included B1. John Mary du Lau, abp. of Arles; B1. Francis Joseph de La Rochefoucauld, bp. of Beauvais; and his brother, B1. Peter Louis, bp. of Saintes. On Sept. 3, a gang attacked the Lazarist seminary of St.-Fermin (also a prison), and 86 clerics were slaughtered for refusing the oath. BIBLIOGRAPHY: R. Wasselynck, BiblSanct 10:943–953; P. Caron, *Les Massacres de Septembre* (1935); Butler 3:472–474.

[P. K. MEAGHER]

SEPTUAGINT (LXX), chief Greek version of the OT, probably composed at various times and by various hands among the Alexandrian Jews, but none of it earlier than 250 B.C. The *Letter of *Aristeas to Philocrates* (2d cent. B.C.) gives an apocryphal and highly miraculous account of its composition by 72 Jews, 6 from each of the 12 tribes, specially commissioned by Ptolemy II Philadelphus (283–246 B.C.). The prologue of Sir (*c*.116 B.C.) refers to Greek translations of the Law, the Prophets, and the other books as already in existence by that date; and although this does not absolutely imply that these translations had all been assembled into a single Bible, it is difficult to believe that this was not the case since these are, in fact, the traditional divisions of the Jewish Bible. The quality of the translation throughout varies greatly, and it is clear that many of the translators had an inadequate knowledge of Hebrew and little skill in Greek composition. This quality ranges from an extreme fidelity to the original, amounting almost to servility as, for instance, in S of S and Ecc to mediocrity and inadequacy, as in Is, the Minor Prophets, Job, and Proverbs. The most successful part of the translation is the Pentateuch. Behind the extant LXX text lies a complex textual tradition; yet most scholars accept the evidence that this text ultimately derives from a single source.

The special importance of the LXX consists in its value as an independent witness to the Hebrew original; in its preponderant influence on the NT (the vast majority of the OT citations here are based upon it); in the fact that it was very widely accepted by the Greek and Latin Fathers and regarded by many as inspired; in the fact that it has preserved the deuterocanonical books or apocrypha, which are held by the RC Church to be of equal value with the other books as canonical and inspired; in its use through the centuries by Eastern Christians in liturgy, theology, and devotion. BIBLIOGRAPHY: H. B. Swete, *Introduction to the Old Testament in Greek* (ed., H. St. J. Thackeray, 1920; repr. 1968); H. St. J. Thackeray, *Septuagint and Jewish Worship* (2d ed. 1923); *idem, Some Aspects of the Greek Old Testament* (1927); P. Kahle, *Cairo Geniza* (2d ed., 1959) 209–264; F. G. Kenyon, *Recent Developments in the Textual Criticism of the Greek Bible* (1933); S. Jellicoe, *Septuagint and Mod-*

ern Study (1968); A. Rahlfs, *Septuaginta-Studien* I–III (2d ed., 1965); P. Skehan et al., JBC 2:569–570.

[D. J. BOURKE]

SEPULCHER, a sealed cave for burial of the dead. This was the common form of burial for the people of Canaan, and also for the Israelites who came to settle in that land. It remained the traditional form of burial for Jews into Roman times and was the form of burial given the body of Jesus. Other forms of burial existed, such as graves, trenches, and tombs; and eventually catacombs, where individual members of families and communities could be buried in separate niches (*loculi*) carved out of the walls of underground trenches, corridors, and chambers. But from early Canaanite days, the ordinary form of burial was in caves on the rocky slopes of hills on the outskirts of cities and villages, to prevent defiling contact with the dead. Jacob and the other patriarchs were buried in a cave at Machpelah, east of Mamre in Canaan (Gen 49.30). Prominent people might carve a suitable place for themselves out of soft stone in anticipation of their death and burial. By NT times it had become customary to mark such burial places by pouring over them whiting mixed with water to give warning of uncleanness. This would have prompted the unflattering reference of Jesus to the hypocrites as whitened sepulchers, that look well from the outside, but inside are full of dead men's bones and all kinds of filth (Mt 23.27). To be deprived of burial was a great calamity. It was an act of piety, and sometimes of courage, to protect the bodies of slain warriors or those killed during times of persecution, until they could be buried. It took courage for Joseph of Arimathea, a dissenting member of the Council that had sentenced Jesus, to approach Pilate and ask for the body for burial (Lk 23.50). The sepulcher of Jesus was probably typical of the rock-hewn chambers prepared by prominent Jews in the Roman period. It was a new one located in a garden (Jn 19.41), with a chamber large enough for Jesus' followers to enter (Lk 24.2–3), sealed with a large rolling stone, too heavy for the women who came to anoint the body to think of rolling it back themselves (Mk 16.3–4).

[E. J. DILLON]

SEPULCHRUM PLAY, a form of medieval liturgical drama in which the burial of Jesus was portrayed.

[M. T. LEGGE]

SEQUELA, a preexisting melody to which a sequence was set.

SEQUENCE, a liturgical poem, the text of which was set in syllable style to the final melismas of the Alleluia of the Mass. The origins of the sequence have been the subject of much discussion and research. Originally in free style, having a number of double-line stanzas preceded and followed by a single line, it developed in its intermediate stage into a poem in which the versification and meter became more regular and finally came to resemble a hymn, except that the music was not identical for each stanza. Sequences abounded in the Roman rite liturgy until the Council of Trent (1545–63) abolished all but four: Veni Sancte Spiritus, Lauda Sion, Dies Irae, and Victimae Paschali Laudes. In 1727 a fifth, the Stabat Mater, was added. The actual Sequences of the Roman Missal at present are Victimae Paschali (Easter), Veni Sancte Spiritus (Pentecost), Lauda Sion (Corpus Christi), Stabat Mater (Our Lady of Sorrows). Except on Easter Sunday and Pentecost, the Sequence is optional. The Dies Irae Sequence for All Souls' Day has been discontinued.

SEQUENCE (MUSIC), the repetition of a melodic figure (melodic sequence) or of a group of chords (harmonic sequence) at another pitch, usually one note above or below. If made without change of key, the sequence is called *diatonic*; if the intervals are preserved intact, it is called *real*. Most sequences are of a mixed type, called *modulatory*. The sequence is an important device very much and effectively used in musical composition.

SERAFINO DA FERMO (1496–1540), Italian Canon Regular of the Lateran, ascetical writer. In his preaching throughout N Italy and in his writings on spirituality, he drew largely from the thought of *Battista da Crema. His *Apologia di fra Battista da Crema* (1541) was placed on the Index in 1564, removed in 1900. S. emphasized ascetical self-renunciation, and mental prayer as the way to contemplation. BIBLIOGRAPHY: M. Gaspari, EncCatt 11:375.

SERAPHIM (Heb. *sārāp*, pl. *seraphim*), six-winged figures in Isaiah's temple vision (Is ch. 6, the only biblical reference). The statement that they covered their faces and feet (possibly a euphemism for genitals) suggests that they had a human form. Use of the same Hebrew term for the fiery serpents (Num 21.6) has led some scholars to trace their origin to cultic serpents. The seraphim have been regarded as angels, ranking first in the nine-choir grouping in traditional Christian angelology since Pseudo-Dionysius (*De caelesti hierarchia*, 7). In Isaiah's vision they hovered above Yahweh's throne, sang the *trisagion, and one touched Isaiah's mouth with an altar coal to take away his guilt.

SERAPHIM OF SAROV, ST. (1759–1833). Born Prokhor Moshnin, he took the name Seraphim on entering the monastery of Sarov in Russia. But much of his life was spent in solitude in the forest or on a high outcropping of rock. His reputation as a mystic spread widely, and he was consulted by many. Miracles and mystical phenomena were attributed to him. In his life he summed up the Russian ideal of the holy monk and spiritual father. BIBLIOGRAPHY: I. de Beausobre, *Flame in the Snow* (1945).

[G. T. DENNIS]

SERAPHINA SFORZA, BL. (baptismal name, Sueva; 1434–78), abbess. The daughter of Guidantonio di Mon-

tefeltro and Caterina Colonna, S. was orphaned at an early age and then bereaved successively by the deaths of the brother and the stepbrother who cared for her after the death of her parents. She then spent a year at the palace of her uncle, Card. Prospero Colonna, who arranged for her marriage to Alessandro Sforza, lord of Pesaro, at the age of 14. Unhappy at her husband's absences for military reasons and at his infidelities, S. may have been guilty of some indiscretion with an admirer. At any rate, she was accused by her husband not only of adultery but also of plotting against him. She was forced by Alessandro and his brother-in-law, the duke of Milan, to retire to a monastery of the Poor Clares, where, with a dispensation from Callistus III, she was permitted to make her profession in 1457, taking the name Seraphina. Thereafter she lived an exemplary life and was elected abbess of the community in 1475. Toward the end of his life Alessandro repented the injustice he had done to her. Her cult was confirmed by Benedict XIV in 1754.
BIBLIOGRAPHY: N. Del Re, BiblSanct 11:1010–12.

SERAPION OF ANTIOCH, ST. (d. *c*..211), bp. of Antioch from 199, known as a theologian of repute from brief mentions by Eusebius of Caesarea (*Hist. eccl.* 5, 19; 6, 12) and Jerome (*De viris illustr.* 31), and fragments of antiheretical writings.

SERAPION OF THMUIS, ST. (d. after 362), bp. of Thmuis in Lower Egypt (339–359). After studying and teaching in Alexandria, S. retired to the desert to live as a monk. He was one of the principal disciples of St. Anthony and, when made bishop, was the superior of a large monastic colony. *Athanasius, whose staunch defender he was at the synods of his day, addressed an important series of letters to him on the divinity of the Holy Spirit. S. seems to have been driven from his see in 359 by an Arian usurper. He wrote a treatise against the Manichaeans, and a *euchologion*, a collection of 30 prayers, 18 of which are eucharistic, is also attributed to him. Works: PG 40:895–942; crit. ed. R. P. Casey, *Serapion of Thmuis against the Manichees* (1931); *Bp. Serapion's Prayer Book* (tr. J. Wordsworth, 1899; 2d ed., 1923). BIBLIOGRAPHY: Quasten 3:80–85.

[R. B. ENO]

SERBIA, see YUGOSLAVIA.

SERBIAN CHANT. Serbian music was greatly influenced by the strong spiritual relationship that existed in the 12th and 13th cent. with the East. The line of this relationship was through the monasteries, particularly Chilandari of Mount Athos. Serbian melodies are marked by a scheme, discovered by A. Z. Idelsohn in the Arab melodies, and called the Maqam style: each melody consists of a number of short melodic formulas, continually repeated either exactly or with variations. Groups of these are united to form the equivalent of a "Hlas" or "mode." There are eight "Hlasy," which make up the "Oktoëchos," one mode of which is sung on each of eight successive weeks. The melodies of the hymns of the Serbian Church gave rise to the research on the relationship between the Church of Byzantium and the Churches of Russia and the Balkans.

[M. T. LEGGE]

SERBIAN ORTHODOX CHURCH OR PATRIARCHATE. The Serbs settled in the center of the Balkan provinces of the Roman Empire in the 6th century. Christian influences reached them in the 7th cent. only in areas close to the Adriatic coast. The missionary activity of SS. Cyril and Methodius and their disciples incorporated the Serbs into the cultural and religious orbit of the Byzantine Empire. The founder of an independent Serbian Church was St. Sava (Rastko), the younger son of Grand Župan Stephan Nemanja (St. Simeon), who later joined his son in their foundation, the Serbian monastery Chilandari on Mt. Athos. In 1219 Sava received from the emperor and the patriarch in Nicaea, while Constantinople was held by the Crusaders, independence for his Church, and was ordained its first archbishop. The archiepiscopate was elevated to a patriarchate when Stephan Dušan (1331–55) crowned himself "Emperor of the Serbs and Greeks" in Skopje (1346). The collapse of the Serbian states before the Turks led to the disappearance of the patriarchate (*c*.1500). Grand Vizier Mehmed Sokolović, a Serb converted to Islam, reestablished the Patriarchate at Peć (1557), with the expectation that it would unite all Slavs in the Turkish Empire and bring them under the control of the Sublime Porte. The wars of the Habsburgs against the decaying Ottoman Empire led to large migrations of Serbs (1690, 1730) into the area of the Danube, Sava, and Tisa, and the liquidation of the Patriarchate of Peć by the sultan (1766) at the instigation of the Greek patriarchs of Constantinople. The 19th cent. saw the development of several Serbian states and autocephalous churches: (1) The metropolia of the Kingdom of Serbia; (2) the archiepiscopate of Karlovci for the Hungarian half of the Austro-Hungarian monarchy with a titular patriarch as head; (3) the Serbian dioceses of the metropolia of Bukovina for the Austrian half; (4) the Dioceses of Bosnia-Herzegovina (occupied in 1878, annexed in 1908 by Austria); (5) the metropolia of the Kingdom of Montenegro; (6) the Dioceses of Macedonia (under the Patriarch of Constantinople). These Churches were united in 1920 in the reestablished Serbian Patriarchate of Yugoslavia. The incipiently close relationship between the State and the Church was totally severed with the coming of the Communist regime (1945). The Dioceses of the Macedonian Federative Republic of Yugoslavia proclaimed their autocephaly or independence in 1967, which was not recognized by the Serbian patriarchate. The Serbian Orthodox Church today has 28 dioceses, 21 in Yugoslavia and 7 abroad (3 in Europe, 3 in the U.S.A., and 1 in Australia), with 7.1 million faithful, 1,800 priests in 2,600 parishes, and 1,000 monks and nuns (1976). The Church is headed by "His Holiness, the Abp.

of Peć, Metropolitan of Beograd-Karlovci, and Serbian Patriarch'' (Constitution of 1947). He governs the Church with the assistance of the Holy Council of all bps. and with its permanent executive organ, the Holy Synod (4 menbers). The diocese *(eparhija)* is headed by the bp., assisted by a vicar general *(arhijerejski zamenik)*, and is divided into deaneries and parishes. Each parish has but one priest for 300 to 500 families, and several parishes sometimes share the same church. The Congregational Meeting (24–60 members) and its executive organn the Congregational Committee (6–12 members) permit the laity to administer the temporal affairs. At present, there is a great dearth of clergy. There are five seminaries at the junior college level (480 students) and a school of theology (graduate studies) in Belgrade (100 students). The Church follows in all respects the Byzantine rite as developed in Constantinople. The liturgical language is Church-Slavonic in the Ukrainian-Russian form, their own version *(Srbulj)* having been abandoned 2 cent. ago; the vernacular is being introduced slowly. The relationship of this Church with the Catholic Church in Yugoslavia has been disturbed by the fact that the members of both belong to nations (Serbs and Croats) which have long been in political conflict. The Orthodox Church has rejected the establishment of ecumenical contacts with Catholics (1975). It is represented on the North American continent by three dioceses, created by the patriarchate in 1963 by dividing the one diocese headed then by Bp. Dionisije (100,000 faithful; 60 priests). Since he refused to recognize this act of the Mother Church, he was deposed, but continued to exercise jurisdiction over some churches. This led to a fierce court battle between the parishes and the faithful who recognize the patriarchal jurisdiction and those who adhere to the autonomous diocese under Dionisije. BIBLIOGRAPHY: D. Slijepčević, *Istorija Srpske Pravoslavne Crkve* (2 v., 1962, 1966), a systematic survey of all previous histories; A. Hudal, *Die serbisch-orthodoxe National-kirche* (1922); V. J. Pospishil, *Der Patriarch in der Serbisch-Orthodoxen Kirche* (1965); L. Hadrovics, *Le peuple serbe et son église sous la domination turque* (1948); P. Popan and C. Drasković, *Orthodoxie heute in Rumänien und Jugoslawien* (1960).

[V. J. POSPISHIL]

SERGEANT, JOHN (1622–1707), RC controversialist. Educated at Cambridge, ordained in Lisbon (1650), S. became secretary to the chapter of English seculars (1655–67). In his writings, he attacked leading Protestants and quarreled with Catholics. He consistently worked against the Jesuits, supported the oath of allegiance, and enjoyed the protection and pay of the English government. BIBLIOGRA - PHY: Gillow BDEC 5:491–498.

[V. SAMPSON]

SERGIEV, IWAN IL'JITSCH, see JOHN OF KRONSTADT, ST.

SERGIUS I, ST. (d. 701), **POPE** from 687. At the election following the death of Pope Conon, the Archdeacon Paschal, supported by the exarch of Ravenna, whose favor had been won by the offer of a bribe, and the Archpriest Theodore, had substantial followings, and both claimed victory. But the better people of Rome rejected both claimants and chose S., a native of Sicily but of Syrian extraction. Theodore submitted but Paschal refused and was imprisoned. The exarch extorted from S. a sum equivalent to the bribe that had been offered by Paschal before giving his approval to the election. As Pope, S. disavowed the action of his legates in approving the acts of the *Quinisext Synod which were objectionable in the West because, if the synod were accepted as ecumenical, its disciplinary decrees would have forced Eastern customs upon the West. The Emperor Justinian II tried to have the Pope brought to Constantinople, but a show of force by the people of Rome, backed by troops from Ravenna, frustrated the attempts. S. took an active interest in the Church in France and Britain, and sent St. *Willibrord to Frisia. He is credited with having introduced the Agnus Dei into the Mass. BIBLIOGRAPHY: C. M. Aherne, NCE 13:112; Butler 3:509–511; Mann 1.2:77–104.

[P. F. MULHERN]

SERGIUS II (d. 847), **POPE** from 844. S., a Roman, of the noble family of *Eugene II and *Adrian II, was in the papal service from the reign of *Leo III. On the death of *Gregory IV he was the candidate favored by the Roman nobility, which overcame by force of arms an attempt of the opposition faction to install as pope a priest named John. In the haste to seat S. upon the papal throne, the Roman Constitution accepted by Eugene II in 826 was disregarded and the ceremony was performed without the consent of the Frankish Emperor, Lothair I. The Emperor's son, Louis II, led an army into Italy to vindicate his father's right, but after looking into the matter accepted S. as pope and received from him the crown of the Lombards, while the Romans swore to his father the oath of loyalty prescribed by the neglected Roman Constitution of 826. S. was old when elected and racked with gout and much of the administration was in the hands of his brother, Benedict. Charges of injustice, tyranny, simony, and the pillaging of monasteries have been repeated by historians, but whether the single ancient chronicle upon which these stories are based is adequate evidence of the truth of the charges has been doubted by some. Some building was done in S.'s reign, including the enlargement and renovation of the Lateran Basilica and the restoration of the Marcian aqueduct. But the defense of Rome against Muslim pirates was neglected, and St. Peter's and St. Paul's were sacked in 846 and many ancient treasures were carried away. BIBLIOGRAPHY: Mann 2:232–257; Hughes HC 2:184; C. Aherne, NCE 13:112.

[P. F. MULHERN]

SERGIUS III (d. 911), **POPE** from 904. A Roman of noble family, S. was consecrated bp. of Cere by Pope

*Formosus. In the papal election of 898, S., with a minority of the electors behind him, attempted to unseat the choice of the majority, *John IX (898–900); in this he failed and was banished from the papal court. But in 904, with the military aid of Alberic, Duke of Spoleto, he disposed of Christopher, the antipope who had seized the papacy in 903, and had himself accepted as pope. Evidence to justify the acceptance or rejection of his claim to that office is lacking, but he has been commonly numbered among the legitimate popes. In the disorder prevalent during his pontificate he needed and accepted the aid of *Theophylactus, whose family was to dominate the papacy for the next 50 years. Toward *Formosus, S. adopted the attitude of *Stephen VI, whose repudiation of that pope, reversed by several intervening pontiffs, he reinstated. He damaged the prestige of the Holy See in the eyes of the Eastern Church by approving a fourth marriage for the Emperor Leo VI. The story that S. fathered the future *John XI (931–936) through a liaison with *Marozia, daughter of Theophylactus, is derived from hostile sources and may be untrue, although it is credited by some scholars. BIBLIOGRAPHY: Mann 4:119–142; V. Gellhaus, NCE 13:112.

[P. F. MULHERN]

SERGIUS IV (Peter Buccaporci; d.1012), **POPE** from 1009. The bishop of Albano from 1004, he was promoted to the papacy under the tutelage of John Crescentius III. That he was responsible for touching off the Eastern Schism by inserting his belief in the *filioque* in his *Synodicon,* is a forgery of the 12th century. His call for a Crusade at the destruction of the church of the Holy Sepulcher in Jerusalem (1010) is probable. BIBLIOGRAPHY: A. Gieysztor, ''Genesis of the Crusades: the Encyclical of Sergius IV,'' *Mediaevalia et humanistica* 5 (1948) 3–23; 6 (1950) 3–34.

[O. J. BLUM]

SERGIUS I, PATRIARCH OF CONSTANTINOPLE (610–638), one of the ablest of the Byzantine patriarchs. He worked in close cooperation with the Emperor Heraclius. Appointed as regent when Heraclius was on campaign against the Persians (622–628), he repulsed the Avar attack on the imperial city (626). In religious affairs his main concern was to effect a reconciliation of orthodox (Chalcedonian) Christology and the Monophysite position. About 633, he published a formula that recognized two natures, but one energy, in Christ. This was temporarily tolerated by Pope Honorius I, but was soon strongly rejected by the Orthodox Sophronius, the new patriarch of Jerusalem (634). In his last years, Sergius worked out a compromise statement in which he attempted to meet the objections of Pope Honorius and Sophronius by deemphasizing the one energy, and declaring that Christ had two natures but one will. This statement of doctrine was incorporated into the *Ecthesis* of Heraclius (638). It was repudiated, however, by the Monophysites, by the new patriarch of Jerusalem, and by Rome. In 649, Sergius and his successors, the Monothelite

patriarchs Pyrrhus I and Paul II, were condemned by the Council of the Lateran, and later by both East and West in the General Council of Constantinople III (681). BIBLIOGRAPHY: Beck 292–295; Fliche-Martin 5:103–123, 131–134; Ostrogorsky 90–98.

[M. R. P. MCGUIRE]

SERGIUS II, PATRIARCH OF CONSTANTINOPLE (1001–19). He was a monk and *higoumen* (superior) of the monastery of Manuel before his election to the patriarchate. When he received a synodal letter from Pope Sergius IV (1009–12) on the occasion of that pope's election, he repudiated the term *filioque* in the Pope's letter, excommunicated him, and removed his name from the diptychs. This was a temporary measure, however, because c.1008 or 1009, the name of the reigning pope, John XVIII, was still inscribed on the diptychs of Constantinople. He banished Symeon the Younger Theologian on the ground that he had infringed upon the prerogative of the patriarch in attempting to organize a public cult in honor of his deceased master. S. supported the great landowners against the Emperor Basil II on the question of the responsibility for tax payments, but Basil succeeded in overcoming the opposition. In the course of this controversy and of Byzantine relations with the West, S. claimed that he had the right to the title of Ecumenical Patriarch. BIBLIOGRAPHY: F. Chiovaro, NCE 13:113–114; Ostrogorsky 272, 296; Fliche-Martin 7:134–135.

[M. R. P. MCGUIRE]

SERGIUS (IVAN NIKOLAIEVICH STRAGORODSKY; 1867–1944), PATRIARCH OF MOSCOW. A priest of the Russian Orthodox Church, S. became a monk in 1890 and served as a missionary in Japan for 3 years. Returning to Russia he headed the St. Petersburg Theological Academy and became successively bp. of Yamburg, abp. of Finland and Vyborg, and in 1917 metropolitan of Nizhni Novgorod. Although S. recanted his defense of the Orthodox party's supporting the Communist regime and even spent the years 1925–27 in exile, he returned to his original position as adherent of the regime and denied the fact of Soviet persecution of religion. His espousal of the Communist ruling party estranged the Russian Orthodox of Western Europe. In 1934 S. became metropolitan and in 1943 was illegally elected patriarch of Moscow.

[J. R. AHERNE]

SERGIUS OF RADONEZH, ST. (c.1314–92). At the age of 20 S. left the farm where he had been working at Radonezh, NE of Moscow, to live as a hermit in the neighboring forest. With others who came to join him he founded the monastery of the Holy Trinity, which became the model and motherhouse of N Russian monasticism. His reputation spread far, and he was influential in settling quarrels among the Russian rulers and is said to have prophesied the important victory of Prince Dmitry Donskoy over the

Tatars at Kulikovo in 1380. Of all Russian saints, S. is the most loved as a simple and gentle peasant saint who carried out in his own life the ideal that he preached, that a monk must be at the service of others. His shrine at Zagorsk is still a center of pilgrimage. BIBLIOGRAPHY: N. Zernov, *St. Sergius, Builder of Russia* (1939).

[G. T. DENNIS]

SERGIUS OF RESAINA, (d. 536), Syrian physician, priest, and translator. He translated into Syriac many Greek works of philosophy, medicine, and science, including the works of Pseudo-Dionysius the Areopagite and the *Gnostic Centuries* of Evagrius Ponticus. For this he is revered as one of the fathers of Syriac literature. From his studies in Alexandria he may have been a Monophysite in youth, but in 535 he was sent to Rome as a legate of the Patriarch Ephrem of Antioch to enlist the help of Pope Agapetus against the Monophysites. He died at Constantinople.

[E. J. DILLON]

SERIAL MUSIC, 20th-cent. compositions in which various new principles and rules replace the traditional rules and conventions governing tonality, harmony, rhythm, etc. A concept which sprang out of Anton Webern's Symphony, Op. 21 (1928), serialism has its basis in the 12-tone technique, a system of composition devised by Arnold *Schönberg. When this technique, which governs pitch only, is applied to rhythm, dynamics, and timbre, virtually total control dominates the process of composition. With the introduction of the electronic medium, the possibilities of combinations are extended almost limitlessly. Serialism developed almost simultaneously under Milton Babbitt (1916–) in the U.S. and Pierre Boulez (1925–) in France. Others who followed were K. Stockhausen (1928–) in Germany; H. Pousseur (1929–) in Belgium; O. Messiaen (1908–) in France; M. Kagel (1932–) in Argentina; and L. Berio (1925–) in Italy. The use of 12-tone and serial techniques in religious music has already been seen in works of Webern (1883–1945), Krenek (1900–), Messiaen, Stockhausen, and some others. It is not yet clear that such techniques will fit the idiom or prayerful purposes of religious and liturgical music. BIBLIOGRAPHY: E. Salzman, *Twentieth Century Music: An Introduction* (1974); J. Machlis, *Introduction to Modern Music* (1961). G. Perle, *Serial Composition and Atonality* (1968, 3rd rev. 1972).

[M. T. LEGGE]

SERIPANDO, GIROLAMO (1492–1563), Augustinian theologian, cardinal legate at the Council of Trent. Seripando entered the Augustinians in 1507, was named vicar general in 1538, and was elected general the following year. While general, he conducted extensive visitations in an effort to offset the Lutheran influence within the order, which he sought to reform by a program of spirituality based upon Sacred Scripture and the teachings of St. Augustine.

Challenges posed by the Lutheran theology, as well as by the evangelical and spiritualistic movements in Italy itself, occasioned an important change in Seripando's outlook. His earlier interest in humanism and in Renaissance Platonism began to wane, although he regarded Platonic philosophy as a natural preparation for the study of Pauline theology. Since he now viewed the new theology as a direct attack upon St. Augustine, he undertook an exhaustive study of the saint's writings, from which he elaborated his own theological positions against those advanced by Reformers. He attended the Council of Trent, where, successively as prior general, cardinal president, and papal legate, he espoused the teachings of his school on original sin and the nature of justification. Although these were not accepted by the Council, he nevertheless exercised an important constructive influence upon the final formulation of these doctrines. His advocacy of the *double-justice theory, the culminating point in his theology of justification, has its roots in the notion of concupiscence as understood by the Augustinian theologians of the period. For these, concupiscence remains in the baptized, not merely as the penal consequence of sin, but as a persistent and dynamic source of personal sin. And, because it hinders man's full observance of God's law, it is displeasing in God's sight and therefore somehow sinful. Consequently, unless the justice of Christ is also applied to the members of his mystical body, man's personal justice remains insufficient to merit eternal life. BIBLIOGRAPHY: H. Jedin, *Papal Legate at the Council of Trent: Cardinal Seripando* (tr. F. C. Eckhoff, 1947); A. Balducci, *Girolamo Seripando, Arcivescovo di Salerno* (1963).

[R. P. RUSSELL]

SERLO OF BAYEUX (c.1050–c.1122), Latin satirical poet, whose work was recovered by Dom M. J. J. Brial in 1820. His poems against worldly clerics include *Ad Odonem* (Odo of Bayeaux), *Invectio in Gislebertum abbatem Cadomensem* and *Ad Muriel sanctimonialem* (Abbot Gislibert of St. Stephen's cloister at Caen). S.'s most important work, giving account of the horrors of war, is the *De capta Baiocensium civitate*.

[M. C. BRADLEY]

SERLO OF WILTON (d. c.1181), poet, Cistercian abbot. Of English birth, S. taught in Paris and wrote secular, even erotic, poetry. First he joined the Cluniacs at Charité-sur-Loire, then the Cistercians at l'Aumóne near Chartres, and became abbot in 1171. After his conversion he wrote on Christian virtues. BIBLIOGRAPHY: Manitius 3:905–910; Raby CLP 340–342.

[L. J. LEKAI]

SERMON, any discourse or address delivered in conjunction with an ecclesiastical function. The term is usually employed as a general category which would include such discourses as a *homily (an explanation of a Scripture or liturgical text), an instruction (concerned with matters of

faith, morals, or liturgical practice), a panegyric (a talk on the life and virtues of a saint on his feast day), a eulogy (a funeral address extolling the life and virtues of the deceased), or an occasional sermon (given upon a special event such as a church dedication). The necessity of preaching the Good News was enunciated by Jesus (Mt 28.20), and is continued by the Church as part of her commitment to Christ's saving work (Rom 10.14–15). The style and content of preaching evolved with the growth in numbers and faith-reflection of the Church. Origen appears to be the first to distinguish the popular exegetical homily from the sermon or oration which tended to follow a classical arrangement, style, and delivery. More recent times have seen sermons classified into three basic categories: doctrinal, inspirational, and moral, although most sermons contain elements of all three. In the liturgical renewal emanating from Vatican Council II, there has been a tendency to identify the homily and sermon in concept and purpose. In Vat II SacLit 35, the sermon is viewed as part of the liturgical service and should be based mainly on liturgical and scriptural sources. It proclaims God's works in the history of salvation, made present and active esp. in the celebration of the liturgy.
BIBLIOGRAPHY: E. MacNutt, *Gauging Sermon Effectiveness* (1960); *Sunday Homily* (ed. J. Burke, 1966). *PREACHING.

[W. J. TOBIN]

SERMON ON THE MOUNT, the first of five discourses in ch. 5–7 of St. Matthew's Gospel; an impressive compendium of the teaching of Jesus; the *Torah of the New Testament. There is a much smaller version of this discourse in Luke 6.20–49, so there must have been such a compendium antedating both of these Gospels. To it Matthew added other material attributed to Jesus and deriving from Jewish-Christian catechetical tradition. Both in Matthew and Luke the discourse begins with the *beatitudes: ''Blessed are . . .'' This marks the proclamations of Jesus as gospel proclamations; they are ''good news.'' In Matthew they are good news to the poor in spirit, the meek, the sorrowful, those who hunger and thirst for justice, the merciful, the pure in heart, the peacemakers, and those persecuted for the cause of justice. The good news is the promise of God's kingdom, consolation, possession of the land, mercy, being satisfied with justice, seeing God, and being called the children of God. This ''gospel'' perspective is heavily indebted to the oracles of consolation of Second and Third Isaiah (Is 40–55; 56–66), and esp. to the oracle in Isaiah 61.1–3, which, according to Luke 4.18, Jesus proclaimed in synagogue at the very beginning of his ministry. Scholars speculate that the original emphasis of Jesus in the beatitudes was on God's reign, its character and purpose: to heal, to console, to redeem. The emphasis in Luke is to highlight who esp. are to be the beneficiaries of this saving reign: you poor, you who hunger now, you who weep now. The emphasis in Matthew is on the qualities of spirit necessary to receive the good news and the saving power: the poor in spirit, the meek, the merciful, the pure in heart. After the beatitudes

there follows a compendium of the religious and moral teachings of Jesus. It is intended as the essence of true religion and the fundamental demands of justice. The message, by its simplicity, sanity, and power, speaks for itself, and shows how much Jesus was in harmony with the ideals of the Pharisaic renaissance in Judaism. It was the burden and the achievement of the Pharisaic movement to simplify the complexities of religious tradition, and to make real for the common folk the heart of religion and the fundamental demands of the Torah. The following words of Jesus can be considered the finest flowering of this ideal: ''You have learned . . . 'Do not commit murder' . . . but what I tell you is this: Anyone who nurses anger against his brother must be brought to judgment. . . . Love your enemies and pray for those who persecute you. . . . There must be no limit to your goodness. . . . When you do an act of kindness, do not let your left hand know what your right is doing. . . . When you pray do not multiply words like the heathen, who imagine that the more they say the more likely they are to be heard . . . [And in words that echo the Jewish *Kaddish prayer] This is how you should pray: Our father in heaven, your Name be hallowed; your kingdom come, your will be done on earth as in heaven. . . . Set your mind on God's kingdom and His justice before everything else, and all the rest will come to you as well. . . . Pass no judgment, and you will not be judged. For as you judge others, so you will yourselves be judged, and whatever measure you deal out to others will be dealt back to you. . . . Always treat others as you would like them to treat you: that is the Law and the prophets.''

[E. J. DILLON]

SERPENT, BRONZE, the mysterious standard raised up by Moses during an incident in the desert wanderings. According to the biblical narrative in Num 21.4–9, the Israelite encampment left Mount Hor (Sinai) to march around the flank of Edom. There follows in typical sequence: the people murmuring in rebellion against the Lord and Moses for bringing them into the desert to die; the Lord's punishment in the form of poisonous snakes, which bite the Israelites so that many of them die; Moses then pleading to the Lord on behalf of the people; and the Lord's saving response. This last element in the sequence is as striking as it is bizarre. Moses was commanded to make a serpent of bronze and erect it as a standard, so that anyone who had been bitten could look at it and recover. Moses did as he was commanded, with the exact desired result. The use of Mount Hor for Sinai, and the presence of a miraculous cure link this narrative to the Elohist source. Perhaps this same source has linked a story about the ubiquitous menace of the wilderness, poisonous snakes, with a popular idol of healing power worshiped by Israel's neighbors in Canaan. In 2 Kg 18.4, King Hezekiah is praised for his destruction of idolatrous worship, including breaking up ''the bronze serpent that Moses had made; for up to that time the Israelites had been burning sacrifices to it; they called it Nehushtan.'' The words of Christ in the fourth Gospel represent a final attempt to view this bizarre phenomenon in a perspective of Christian faith: ''this Son of Man must be lifted up as the serpent was lifted up by Moses in the wilderness, so that everyone who has faith in him may in him possess eternal life'' (Jn 3.14–15).

[E. J. DILLON]

SERPENT IN PARADISE, the agent of man's temptation and fall in Gen 3. It is clear from the narrative that the Yahwist author, in confronting the mystery of man's sinfulness and nature's disorder, rejects the interpretation of a primordial conflict between good and evil deities: the serpent clearly belongs to the animal kingdom and is one of God's creatures (Gen 3.1). But the author mitigates the mystery of evil by demonstrating that the source of sin is not simply man but an ''outside'' agent, a power hostile to God which seeks to separate man from his Creator. Indeed, the curse which God levies upon the serpent, not only alters its own life (crawling on its belly and eating dust) but also its relationship with man: there is a perpetual enmity established between it and the offspring of the woman. An underlying force in creation, inimical to God, shall be a constant threat to mankind, continually tempting man to disobey. This notion led later Judaic thought to identify the snake and *Satan, and by a similar extension in the light of subsequent revelation, led Christian theology to recognize Christ, who vanquishes the reign of sin, as the one who crushes the serpent's head (Gen 3.15).

Although exegetes have differed in the past, the common interpretation today is that the serpent is symbolical rather than real, i.e., its usage in the narrative must be placed within the author's theological intent. Interpretations of why the snake symbolism was selected vary: the serpent could simply be a figure of evil, a mythological monster, dragon, or *Leviathan; it could be regarded, as in other OT passages (Ex 7.8–12), as having magical powers, hence its cunning and ability to speak; or it could be a fertility symbol, evoking the interpretation of the original sin as a sexual fault.
BIBLIOGRAPHY: O. Grether and J. Fichtner, Kittel TD 5:566–575; EDB 2174–79; I. Hunt, NCE 13:121–123.

[T. M. MCFADDEN]

SERPENT WORSHIP, the rendering to serpents of divine honor and reverence. The association of serpents with the numinous in the view of primitive man is facilitated by his reactions of fear and wonder in the presence of serpents. Poisonous serpents appear as incorporations of evil powers in many cultures. The observation of serpents creeping on the earth and living in holes has led to their association with chthonian gods (Egypt, Greece), while water snakes provide the basis for mythological dragons in the waters of chaos (the Ancient Near East, India, Teutonic Europe). The serpent as a phallic symbol is perhaps responsible for its association with the powers of fertility in many places. In the fetishistic or totemistic religions of certain peoples, one finds serpents looked upon as creatures actually incorporat-

ing numinous powers (Ahriman in Iran, Jinns in Arabia, Quetzalcoatl in Aztec Mexico); but elsewhere serpents appear rather as attributes or symbols of certain gods, or as creatures retaining a numinous aura from fetishistic or totemistic stages of religion without being looked upon as gods endowed with mythological personality. The latter case is, on the whole, that found in the religions of the Ancient Near East and the Mediterranean world; in these regions the actual worship of serpents as such seems to have been uncommon in historical times.

In ancient Egypt the association of serpents with certain gods was largely pictorial, part of the Egyptian tendency to depict gods in the form of animals or with the heads of animals whose behavior seemed to express some important characteristic of the god in question. Thus a serpent's yearly shedding of its old skin led to the portrayal in serpentine form of Nehebkaw, god of time, and of other time-gods, while the menace of poisonous serpents led to the serpentine form of Apophis, archenemy of the sun god Re. The association of water-snakes with the waters of chaos is found in Egypt too, for the four feminine members of the Hermopolitan ogdoad of primeval gods were sometimes represented as serpents. An Egyptian deity whose serpentine nature was not merely pictorial, however, was the dynastically important cobra goddess Edjo or Wadjet, originally the local goddess of Buto, then patron goddess of all Lower Egypt, whose cobra emblem (the uraeus) was placed on the royal diadem as a menacing sign of protection. In Mesopotamia a number of mythological serpents, representing daimonic forces, either became minor gods (among them a god of healing and a mythological temple doorkeeper), or were associated closely with a god, as in the case of Ningizida, god of the underworld and perhaps of fertility, represented with serpents rising from his shoulders or signified by the emblem of two intertwined serpents that appeared later as the Greek caduceus. The pre-Greek Minoan civilization knew a household snake goddess whose name is unknown to us. In classical Greek and Roman times serpents, still associated with household worship, figured in the cultic rites of Attis, Juno Sospita, and Asclepius (in the latter's cult as healing serpents); but serpents in Greek and Roman religion were not gods, and gods, apart from one or two known exceptions, were not represented as serpents.

In the OT the mythological idea of a serpent or dragon of the cosmic waters as adversary of a high god recurs in such passages as Job 26.13; Ps 89(88). 9–10; Is 51.9; and the biblical Leviathan is probably the seven-headed serpent Ltn (Lotan?) found in Canaanite mythological texts. The real significance of the bronze serpent destroyed as an idolatrous object in King Hezekiah's reform (2 Kg 18.4) is probably revealed by an earlier text, Num 21.6–8, indicating that the bronze serpent was essentially a healing serpent in fetishistic form. In early Christian times the gnostic group known as Ophites, in their opposition to the God of the OT, exalted his adversary, the serpent of Gen 3, as the illuminator of mankind. BIBLIOGRAPHY: for the data provided by general comparative religion, A. Schimmel, RGG 5:1914–20; K. Goldhammer, NCE 13:123–124, with their bibliogs.; H. H. Rowley, "Zadok and Nehushtan," JBL 58 (1939) 113–141; E. Dhorme, *Les Religions de Babylonie et d' Assyrie* (1945) 119–121; H. Bonnet, *Reallexikon der Ägyptischen Religionsgeschichte* (1952) 671–684; M. P. Nilsson and H. J. Rose, OCD (1949) 762–763, 830; J. A. MacCulloch and E. Welsford, Hastings ERE, 11: 399–423.

[A. CODY]

SERRA, JUNÍPERO (MIGUEL JOSÉ) (1713–84), luminary among the great missionaries of the New World. A Spanish Franciscan, S. arrived at the age of 37, with a small band of fellow religious in Mexico. Working first among the Indians of Sierra Gorda, Mexico, he later became *presidente* when the Franciscans took over the missions of the banished Jesuits in Lower California. As *presidente* with five Franciscans and the military force of Gaspar de Portola, he proceeded to Upper California and founded the first mission at San Diego in 1769, the first of 21 missions which would ultimately be established in California. Nine of these were his direct work: San Diego, San Carlos, San Antonio, San Gabriel, San Luis Obispo, San Francisco de Assisi, San Juan Capistrano, Santa Clara, and San Buenaventura. In addition to the conversion of thousands of Indians, the work of S. encompassed an amazing material progress. Agriculture, cattle raising, arts and crafts were vigorously pursued by the mission Indians. S. was a loved friend of the Indians, defender of their rights, the one man who held California for Spain, a source of inspiration to his brethren. A frail man with a persistent leg injury, he supervised an incredible network of missions. A statue of S. in the Capitol at Washington, D.C., erected in 1931 honors the foremost of missionaries in America. BIBLIOGRAPHY: *Francisco Palou's Life and Apostolic Labors of the Venerable Father Junipero Serra* (ed. G. Jamed, 1913).

[J. R. AHERNE]

SERRA INTERNATIONAL, an organization of Catholic men dedicated to promoting vocations to the priesthood. Taking its name from the great Franciscan missionary, Junipero *Serra, the society operates much like a secular service club, differing therefrom in its program of spirituality for members. Originating in Seattle, Wash., in 1935, the organization has had steady growth in numbers and service to bishops. In 1938 it became an international federation. Serra conducts an international annual conference, district conferences, and retreats. Both by prayer and financial assistance it supports priestly vocations. The group is associated with the Pontifical Work for Priestly Vocations. Its headquarters are in Chicago, Illinois.

[J. R. AHERNE]

SERRY, HYACINTHE (François Jacques; 1659–1738), French Dominican polemicist. He was a theologian and consultor of the Holy Office in Rome (1690–96); briefly professor at the Sorbonne; then from 1697 until his death, professor of theology at the Univ. of Padua. Throughout his life S. was an enemy of the Jesuits, as is apparent from his *Historia congregationum de auxiliis* (on the Dominican-Jesuit controversies on grace), which first appeared, preceded by a polemical exchange with Jesuits in French, in 1700, under the pseudonym Augustin Le Blanc. Answered by L. de Meyer, SJ, under the pseudonymn Theodorus Eleutherius, in 1705, S.'s work appeared in revised and definitive edition under his own name in 1709, with a supplement responding to de Meyer added. The tone of both authors is extremely partisan, revolting, and shocking, (e.g., marked by such endearing references to each other as *putridus litigator*). S. published other works against the Jesuits, was sympathetic to Jansenism in regard to the bull *Unigenitus,* and to *Gallicanism on the question of papal primacy.

[T. C. O'BRIEN]

SERTILLANGES, ANTONIN DALMACE (1863–1948), French Dominican philosopher and theologian. A man from the Auvergne, S. was a renowned preacher, very pastoral-minded in his approach to contemporary unbelief, and combined great expertise as a Thomist with an unpatronizing appreciation of questions raised by people in nonecclesiastical circles. The continuity between the sacred and the profane, without detriment to either, was as a constant theme throughout his numerous writings and conferences.

[T. GILBY]

SÉRUSIER, PAUL (1864–1927), French philosopher and post-Impressionist painter, academically trained (1886), who, after meeting Gauguin (1888), painted in the Gauguin manner a picture shown to Bonnard, Vuillard, Denis, and others who founded the Nabis or "prophets" a year later. S. stayed in Brittany with Gauguin (1889–90), and after meeting J. *Verkade (1891) became interested in theosophy. He traveled with M. Denis to Italy (1895), examining the art of Fra Angelico, Giotto, and the Sienese school. S. was influenced by religious symbolism (1897) and visited at Beuron, Verkade (the Benedictine Dom Wilibrord after 1894) and Father Desiderius *Lenz, founder of the *Beuron School of religious art. In *cloisonnisme* style of sharply defined contours and bright colors, S. interpreted contemplative Brittany peasants. His later works of mystical symbolism are weaker in design. BIBLIOGRAPHY: M. Denis, *Sérusier, sa vie, son oeuvre* (1943).

[M. J. DALY]

SERVANT OF THE LORD ORACLES, four poems in Deutero-Isaiah which appear to be distinct poems in their own right and have been inserted into the rest of Is 40–55 (perhaps by the same author or a member of his "school") when it was already complete. They are: Is 42.1–4; 49.1–6; 50.4–9; 52.13–53.12. The subject of them is a mysterious figure known as the "Servant of the Lord". In the first poem his mission is described. He is to bring forth or extend the "judgment" and "righteousness" of Yahweh, hitherto confined to the covenant people, to the whole earth, and he is to do this in a nonviolent manner, in the power and spirit of Yahweh the Creator of heaven and earth. In the second poem the Servant himself describes his mission and how he has been set apart and endowed with charisms for it right from his birth. Though faced with great initial difficulties and discouragements, he is to proceed from a salvific mission to restore and gather Israel, to one that brings light and salvation to the ends of the earth. In the third poem the opposition to the Servant has turned to active persecution; yet in spite of this he remains obedient to and confident in Yahweh, using his charism of the "wise word" to guide, sustain, and comfort those who are in need of it. In the fourth poem the Servant suffers an ignominious death, apparently at the hands of his persecutors; yet even this death and the sufferings leading up to it have a saving significance. They have a vicarious and atoning merit which redounds upon those who mock and persecute him. And he finds ultimate vindication and glory beyond death, when Yahweh bestows upon the victory he has won (solely by relying on the charisms he has been given) this ultimate glory as his reward.

The identity of the Servant is mysterious as is also his precise significance. Is he intended primarily as a prophet or priest, or even as a royal figure suffering vicariously on behalf of his people? Is he to be identified with some heroic figure of the past such as Moses, Jeremiah, or Zerubbabel? Is he, finally, a personification of Israel herself in her awareness of her mission in relation to the rest of the world? Arguments have been put forward for all of these views. It seems most probable that the Servant is intended as a prototype Israelite, combining in his own person the virtues of many different heroes of the past and uniquely endowed with divine charisms from the covenant God of them all. The idea that the persecution, suffering, and death which he suffers are themselves vicarious and atoning, and that they lead to an ultimate glory beyond the grave is an astonishing and unprecedented development in Hebrew thought. BIB-LIOGRAPHY: L. Lindblom, *Servant Songs in Deutero-Isaiah* (1951); C. R. North, *Suffering Servant* (2d ed., 1956).

[D. J. BOURKE]

SERVANTS OF MARY, a title given to various congregations of sisters who are members of the Servite Third Order. They are traditionally called Mantellate because of the long veil worn by some of them. They were founded by St. Juliana Falconieri in the 13th cent. in Florence, Italy. Juliana received the veil from St. Philip Benizi, Servite prior general who also composed a rule for her nuns in 1287. When Juliana was elected prioress in 1306 her first concern was to establish the sisters as members of the Servite Third Order Regular; until then they were secular tertiaries. During the century following it is difficult to distin-

guish the sisters of the Third Order from the monasteries of the nuns of the second order. By the middle of the twentieth century there were 24 congregations and 4 independent convents of Servite Sisters distributed throughout the world. Of these 11 were pontifical and 13 diocesan. At this time the sisters were established in 19 countries. The motherhouse is in Rome. In the U.S. 4 congregations of Servite Sisters were represented with motherhouses in Omaha, Neb., Ladysmith, Wis., Sublimity, Ore., and Blue Island, Illinois. In 1975 there were 963 sisters in 105 houses.

[R. C. CLIGGETT]

SERVANTS OF MARY, SISTERS, known also as the Handmaids of Mary or Siervas de Maria, ministres de enfermos, a religious congregation founded by Bl. Maria Soledad Torres Acosta in Madrid in 1851 to care for the sick in hospitals and private homes and, in exceptional cases, to teach. In its beginnings the congregation nearly foundered because of the large number of defections, difficulties over the rule, and serious slanders against the foundress. The rule was temporarily approved in 1867 and definitive approval came in 1896. The first foundation was established in the U.S. in 1914, and the motherhouse was established in Rome. In 1975 there were 531 sisters in 47 houses.

[R. C. CLIGGETT]

SERVANTS OF OUR LADY, QUEEN OF THE CLERGY, a diocesan congregation founded in 1929 at Salmon Lake, Matapédia Co., P.Q., Canada, by Fr. Alexandre Bouillon and Mother Mary of St. Joseph of the Eucharist to perform domestic work for the clergy. Papal approbation was granted in 1936, the year in which the sisters came to the U.S. They are represented in Massachusetts, Rhode Island, and New Hampshire. In 1977 they numbered 16 professed Sisters.

[R. C. CLIGGETT]

SERVER, the *acolyte at Mass.

SERVETUS, MICHAEL (1511–53), physician and anti-Trinitarian. Born in Villanueva, Spain, he studied at the Univ. of Toulouse. Biblical studies led him to oppose the doctrine of the Trinity, and in 1531 he published *De Trinitatis erroribus libri VII,* in which he distinguished between the eternal Word and the Son, who was not eternal; moreover, he denied that the Holy Spirit was a distinct being. Violent opposition to this work led him to publish *Dialogorum de Trinitate libri duo* (1532), a work that did not significantly change his position. He worked in Lyons as an editor, studied medicine a the Univ. of Paris, and discerned and wrote of the pulmonary circulation of the blood. His correspondence with John *Calvin disclosed serious theological differences. In 1553 he anonymously published his major work, *Christianismi restitutio.* The work continued earlier antitrinitarianism but also stressed an emanationist view of God and certain Anabaptist themes.

He was arrested by the Inquisition in Lyons and imprisoned, but escaped to Geneva. There Calvin also had him arrested; S. was tried and executed at the stake as a heretic, Oct. 27, 1553. BIBLIOGRAPHY: *Two Treatises of Servetus on the Trinity* (*Harvard Theological Studies* 16, tr. E. M. Wilbur, 1932); E. Wolf, "Deus Omniformis, Bemerkungen zur Christologie des Michael Servet," *Theologische Aufsätze, Karl Barth zum 50. Geburtstag* (1936); R. Bainton, *Hunted Heretic* (1953); *Autour de Michel Servet et de Sébastien Castellion* (ed. B. Becker, 1953); G. H. Williams, *Radical Reformation* (1962).

[J. C. GODBEY]

SERVICE. (1) As a liturgical term, the form or ritual for worship and its carrying out. Strictly used, the term indicates a distinction from holy communion and applies to choral Offices (Morning Prayer or Matins; Evensong or Vespers); the *Book of Common Prayer so employs the term. But in a more general sense it covers any form of divine worship or communal prayer. (2) In moral theology, one form of the homage that respects an indebtedness arising out of benefits received from another. The highest kind of such service is that owed to God as source and end of life, and that is the concern of the virtue of *religion (see DE-VOTION; LATRIA; REVERENCE). The term implies worship, obedience, and concern for God's honor. In proportion to varying degrees of the debtor's dependence, service is also owed out of filial *piety and patriotismn respect for superiors (see DULIA), and *gratitude.

[T. C. O'BRIEN]

SERVICE (MUSIC), in the Anglican communion the group of musical settings of the canticles and other parts of the Morning Prayer, Evening Prayer, or Communion Service as found in the Book of Common Prayer. The Morning Service consists of Venite, Te Deum, and Benedictus, with the alternatives Benedicite and Jubilate; the Evening Service, of Magnificat and Nunc Dimittis, with the alternatives Cantate Domino and Deus Misereatur; the Communion Service, of Kyrie, Gloria, Creed, Sanctus, Benedictus, and Agnus Dei. Although referred to by the Latin name, they are traditionally sung in English. A "full service" consists of all three groups, usually written in the same key. The terms "short service" and "great service" refer to the style of the setting: short and syllabic for the former, and contrapuntal and repetitious for the latter. The service has been the subject of compositions of most of the great English composers from Tye and Tallis down to Tippett and Britten.

[M. T. LEGGE]

SERVICE BOOK AND HYMNAL (LUTHERAN), the name given to a common liturgy and hymnal produced cooperatively by Lutherans of many diverse cultural and linguistic backgrounds in the U.S. and Canada. It was noted in the 1940s that one of the serious divisive factors among North American Lutherans was the diversity of liturgical practice and of hymnody. Many of the various linguistic groups were still conducting worship services in their own German or Scandinavian languages. It was recognized that a common liturgy and hymnal could serve as a unifying force. In 1944 a resolution was passed at the convention of the United Lutheran Church in America (ULCA), authorizing publication of a new revision of its own hymnal, and including a clause instructing the committee "to seek the fullest possible cooperation with other Lutheran bodies in the hope of producing, as nearly as proves feasible, a common Lutheran hymnal in America" (ULCA Minutes, 1944, 436). The Common Service Book Committee of the ULCA, under the leadership of its chairman, Dr. Luther D. Reed, began by extending invitations to the presidents of the various Lutheran Churches to join in the common venture. The Lutheran Church—Missouri Synod was excluded since that synod had recently produced its own new hymnal. The task was monumental in view of the number of individual synods involved, but through discussion and compromise difficulties were overcome, and the work was published in 1958. BIBLIOGRAPHY: L. D. Reed, *Lutheran Liturgy* (1959) 205–227.

[R. BEESE]

SERVICES AND PRAYERS, BOOK OF, see BOOK OF SERVICES AND PRAYERS.

SERVILE WORK. the kind of work forbidden by the commandment to "keep holy the Sabbath"; thus the kind of work forbidden as part of the Christian observance of *Sunday. The Sabbatarian precepts of the Jewish law did not become a part of general Christian observance, although there have been some rigid Christian Sabbatarians, e.g., the Puritans of England and New England, Seventh Day Adventists, Seventh Day Baptists. There was, however, a stricter recognition than now exists that the observance of Sunday and holydays of obligation included abstention from "servile work," i.e., the ordinary labors of the week. The simple fact of urbanization and the now usual 5-day work week make the literal prohibition all but obsolete. Those who do not have a "day off" on Sunday are obliged by the condition of their employment to work; for many, household tasks have to be done on weekends. The observance of holydays is practically impossible; most people can barely fit in attendance at Mass. The more important issue for Christians in a secularized society is to be attentive to the reformed liturgy's stress on Sunday as the day of the Lord and a kind of continual solemn celebration of the paschal mystery. Negatively, that could also well include refraining from shopping on Sunday as more and more shops do business on the Lord's Day.

[T. C. O'BRIEN]

SERVITES (the Order of Friars Servants of Mary), a religious family embracing a three-fold membership of friars: priests and brothers, contemplative nuns, and both conventuals and secular tertiaries. There is a Servite secular institute for unmarried women. The Servites founded in 1233 by St. Bonfilius and his companions, who were canonized in 1888 by Leo XIII, lead a monastic life in the tradition of the mendicant orders and undertake various apostolic works. In the beginning there was no intention of founding an order but simply a desire to live in the spirit of the primitive Church. They sought official recognition in order to avoid being joined to any already existing group of hermits or friars. In 1249 the papal legate in Tuscany, Raynerius Capocci, received the Servites under the protection of the Holy See and on March 23, 1256, Alexander IV solemnly approved them as an order of friars living in strict corporate poverty. In the definitive approval given by Benedict XI in 1304 there is no mention of strict mendicancy. The Servite Order underwent many reforms: in the 14th cent. under Peter of Todi; in the 15th cent. under Bl. Anthony of Siena at Monte Senario. In 1463 the observant friars entered the priory and shrine of St. Peregrine at Forlì which had formerly belonged to the conventuals. This became one of their chief centers, and the saint became their special patron. There was a gradual breaking away from the hermits of Monte Senario because the observant friars tended to undertake the works of the active ministry. The influence of the *Devotio moderna* is evident in their monastic spirit and apostolate. The Rule of St. Augustine was emphasized. However, in 1593 Clement VIII reestablished the hermitage of Monte Senario and decreed that the life there was to be according to the primitive observance. In 1503 the constitutions of the order were printed for the first time.

Disturbances during the Reformation caused the loss of many Servite convents in Germany. The 18th cent. witnessed the destruction of the province of Narbonne (1720) and the order was forbidden (1740) by the civil government to accept novices. The policies of Emperor Joseph II were responsible for the suppression of the Bohemian province. In the 19th cent. the order opened convents in England, and in the U. S. at Green Bay, Wis. (1870) and Chicago, Ill. (1874). By this time foundations had been opened in many countries within four continents. The motherhouse remained at Monte Senario and the generalate is at St. Marcellus, Rome. In 1976 the friars numbered 1,365, of whom 989 are priests in 236 houses.

[R. C. CLIGGETT]

SERVUS SERVURUM DEI, Servant of the Servants of God, a papal title first used by Pope St. Gregory the Great in the 6th cent. and continuously since. It is a title particularly suited to the Vatican II concept of hierarchy and ministry in the Church. BIBLIOGRAPHY: Vat II ConstChurch 5, 7, 8, BpPastOff 11, etc.).

[F. H. BRIGHAM, JR.]

SESAC I (Shishak), the biblical name for the Egyptian Sheshonk I, founding pharaoh of the 22d (Libyan) Dynasty of Egypt. He made his capital in the delta among the many independent Libyan chieftains living there, from whom he was descended. He is prominent in the narrative of 1 Kg, first for granting asylum to Solomon's antagonist Jeroboam, then for invading Palestine at the head of an Egyptian force including Libyan and Ethiopian scouts and mercenaries, in the reign of Solomon's successor Rehoboam. S. captured Jerusalem, looted the temple and palace of Solomon's treasures, and had them transferred to the temple of Amon at Thebes, where Shishak's son was established as high priest. An Egyptian triumphal stele at Megiddo refers to the Palestinian raid, and on the walls of the temple at Karnak are lists of the towns he captured. It is not known whether S. had anything to do with the division of the Davidic kingdom into Israel and Juda, but it is a fact that Jeroboam did return from exile as king of Israel. S.'s successors were not able to carry out their founder's dream of a renewed Egyptian empire in Palestine and Syria because of internal divisions in Egypt.

[E. J. DILLON]

SESSION, see CHURCH SESSION.

SESTO AL RÉGHENA, ABBEY OF, former Benedictine monastery called Sta. Maria in Sylvis (St. Mary-in-the-Woods). It was founded in 762 by Erfo and Marco near Concordia on the banks of the Réghena in Veneto, N Italy. Made exempt by Charlemagne in 775, it was destroyed during the upheavals of the late 9th cent. and rebuilt under Abbot Adolph (960–965). The monks reclaimed the marshy area fronting the Tagliamento River. Presented by Otto I (967) to the patriarch of Aquileia, who retained possession for two centuries, it gradually declined until made commendatory by Eugene IV in 1431, was placed under the control of the Republic of Venice, then abandoned by the Benedictines in 1440. Augustinians, Dominicans, and Franciscans made use of it until Paul V gave it to the Vallambrosans in 1612. It was suppressed in 1789–90. The 9th-cent. church survives. BIBLIOGRAPHY: Cottineau 2:3020.

[E. J. DILLON]

SETH, Egyptian god of power and force, and of "the desert" (which, for the Egyptians, included all foreign lands). Originally morally indifferent, though perhaps disorderly, he appears in Middle Kingdom popular tales as a crass, foolish rogue in conflict with a clever Horus. His secondary appearance in the cycle of Osirian myths as murderer of Osiris led to a version of the cycle in which he contests Horus' right to rule in Egypt after Osiris. In the Hyksos period (c.1674–1567 B.C.) he was identified with the national god of the foreign rulers (perhaps Baal), and in the New Kingdom (late 2d millennium) he was still appreciated. In the late period he fell completely out of favor, and by the Greco-Roman period he was the personification of all evil, resorted to in evil spells. BIBLIOGRAPHY: H. Bonnet, *Reallexikon der ägyptischen Religionsgeschichte* (1952) 702–715; H. te Velde, *Seth, God of Confusion* (*Probleme der Ägyptologie* 6, 1967).

[A. CODY]

SETHIANS, members of a Gnostic tradition or sect that must have flourished in Egypt and elsewhere between the 2d and the 4th cent. A.D. Until recently the main source of knowledge of this sect had been the writings of their ardent antagonists, Epiphanius of Salamis and Hippolytus of Rome. However, in 1945 or 1946 there was an archeological discovery of major importance at Chenoboskion in Egypt: a library of a Coptic Sethite Church dating from the 3d or 4th cent. A.D. There are 13 volumes (codices) of apocryphal writings containing extrabiblical revelations reflecting complex but well rationalized and harmonized mythologies. The biblical personage who is portrayed as the mediator of much of the revelation is Seth, the ancestor of Noah. This Seth seems to have taken on some of the symbolism associated with the Egyptian god Seth, including the symbol of the donkey's head.

[E. J. DILLON]

SETON, ELIZABETH ANN, ST. (1774–1821), Mother Seton, first native American saint, foundress of the Sisters of Charity of St. Joseph. She was born Elizabeth Ann Bayley into an Anglican family in New York City, where her father was first health inspector. As a young woman she was active in the Society for Destitute Women. She married (1794) William Magee Seton, a shipper associated with the Filicchi brothers of Livorno (Leghorn), Italy. They had five children, Anna Maria (1795), William (1796), Richard (1798), Catherine (1801), and Rebecca (1802). The couple went to Livorno in the hope of improving William's health, but he died there in 1803. Welcomed into the home of Antonio Filicchi and his wife Amabilia, S. there came to love their RC faith, and on returning to the U.S. was received into the Church by Rev. M. O'Brien, St. Peter's Church, New York City. Because she was an outcast in the eyes of her former friends, she could not establish herself in New York. Invited by Rev. W. Du Bourg, Sulpician superior, to Baltimore, in Paca Street, there she opened a school for girls. On March 25, feast of the Annunciation, she took religious vows. She received rules from Du Bourg to form aspirants to a sisterhood; with the first sisters and her children she moved (1809) to Emmitsburg, near to Mt. St. Mary's College. There in St. Joseph's Valley was established the motherhouse from which grew the present Daughters of Charity federation; her desire to be affiliated with St. Vincent de Paul's *Daughters of Charity was realized only in 1850 after her death. From her foundation grew seven separate religious congregations. Her labors began the American parochial school system.

Of her writing, poet L. Feeney in *An American Woman* (1938, repr. 1976) asks: "Who could . . . approach her in point of style, charm, literature?" Abp. Robert Seton edited his grandmother's *Memoir, Letters and Journal* (2v. 1869); S. wrote also of Vincent de Paul and Mlle. Le Gras (see B. Randolph, CE 13: 739–740) and translated ascetical works from French. C. I. White wrote the oft-revised and reprinted Life (1853); J. B. Code translated and adapted (1927) one

from the French, the 19th-cent. work of H. R. B. De Barberey (which C. M. O'Neill abridged 1940); Card. A. M. Melville's factual biography (1951) is based on archival research as is that of J. I. Dirvin (1962); J. Hindman (1976) wrote a life esp. for the young. Buried at Emmitsburg, S.'s body was exhumed (1962) in view of her beatification, with Card. L. Shehan presiding at its translation to St. Joseph's Provincial House chapel nearby. She was beatified in 1963 and canonized by Paul VI, Sept. 14, 1975.

[M. R. BROWN]

SETON, ROBERT (1839–1927), bp., scholar, diplomat. Cosmopolitan though passionately American, S. was a grandson of St. Elizabeth Seton, highly conscious of his aristocratic lineage. He was ordained in Rome in 1865. As a student at the Accadèmia dei nobili ecclesiastici he attracted the favorable attention of Pope Pius IX, who in 1866 made him a prothonotary apostolic, the first American to receive that honor. Briefly the American representative in Rome, he returned to the U.S. for over 25 years, in which time he was chaplain at St. Elizabeth's Convent, Convent Station, N.J., and later pastor in Jersey City. For many years he lectured at colleges and universities on Christian archeology. Returning to Rome in 1902, he served as unofficial representative of the American Church for 12 years. In 1903 he refused the appointment as abp. of Chicago, but accepted the titular archbishopric of Heliopolis. S. returned to the U.S., an impoverished man, and ended his days at St. Elizabeth's Convent. Among his writings were: *Essays on Various Subjects, Chiefly Roman* (1862); his editing of *Memoirs, Letters and Journal of Elizabeth Seton* (1869); and his own memoirs, *Memories of Many Years* (1923).

[J. R. AHERNE]

SETTIMO, ABBEY OF, Benedictine monastery of San Salvatore near Florence, Italy, founded after 998 by Lothar of Cadolo. Cluniac involvements attracted generous land grants in Emilia and Tuscany. In 1048 the abbot was made a count. The abbey enjoyed close association with the Vallambrosans from 1048–90. In 1236 it was given by Gregory IX to the Cistercians of San Galgano near Siena, was made commendatory under Eugene IV in 1435, and was suppressed in 1783. The buildings, partly restored in 1931, were damaged in air raids of World War II (1944). BIBLIOGRAPHY: Cottineau 2: 3021–22.

[E. J. DILLON]

SETTLEMENT, ACT OF IRISH, the law governing the ownership of land by Catholics in Ireland. The legislation passed in 1662 reduced the amount of land which could be owned by Catholics from the 61 percent held in 1641 to 22 percent in 1688 and 15 percent in 1704. No change occurred in the repressive action until the 1840s, as a result of Catholic Emancipation and the work of Daniel O'Connell. Essentially an outgrowth of Oliver Cromwell's adventure in Ireland, the dispossession rewarded his soldiers and supporters by assigning them Irish land grants. With the restoration of the Stuarts to the English throne some amelioration was attempted but did not succeed. The Act of Explanation in 1665 limited restoration to about 50 Catholics and forced the new Protestant owners to give up one-third of their lands. Various acts in the 1660s made certain restorations to individuals (e.g., the Earl of Ormand) "innocent papists" (i.e., who had not taken part in rebellion against the King in 1641), those Catholics who had been forced by Cromwell from their own lands and given property in Connaught and Clare, "innocent papists" of certain towns who received compensating land outside the towns, and Irish Catholics who had served the King's ensigns abroad. The complexity, if not arbitrariness, of the settlements was incredible. In spite of some attempts to deal justly with the dispossessed (such as the attempt in 1672 to reopen the matter, and the shortlived Irish Parliament's attempt under James II to repeal the Restoration acts) the effect was to deprive Catholics of their lands for 200 years. BIBLIOGRAPHY: W. Butler, *Confiscation in Irish History* (1917).

[J. R. AHERNE]

SEVEN APOSTLES OF SPAIN (*varones apostólicos*). Mozarabic calendars of the 11th cent. say that St. Peter sent them to Betica in A.D. 64–65: Torquatus to found the church in Guadix, Indalecius that in Urci, Ctesiphon in Verja, Euphrasius in Andújar, Cecilius in Granada, Hesychius in Carteya, and Secundus in Ávila. Braga claims as its first bp. Peter of Rates, disciple of St. James; Écija, St. Paul himself; Itálica, Gerontius; Pamplona, Honestus and Bp. Saturninus of Toulouse; Toledo, Eugene.

[E. P. COLBERT]

SEVEN CHURCHES, in Rome the Basilicas of St. John Lateran, St. Peter, St. Mary Major, St. Paul-outside-the-Walls, St. Lawrence-outside-the-Walls, St. Sebastian-outside-the-Walls, and of the Holy Cross-in-Jerusalem. These were the traditional pilgrimage churches from early times, and indulgences are still attached to the practice of visiting them for prayer. The Seven Churches in Asia mentioned in Rev 1.4 are the Christian communities of Ephesus, Smyrna, Pergamum, Thyatria, Sardis, Philadelphia, and Laodicea, addressed for praise or blame in ch. 2 and 3.

[T. C. O'BRIEN]

SEVEN COUNCILS, the first ecumenical councils: Nicaea I (325), Constantinople I (381); Ephesus (431); Chalcedon (451); Constantinople II (533); Constantinople III (680–681); Nicaea II (787). Since they antedate the schisms between East and West, as well as medieval teaching, they are regarded by many Christians as providing a particularly important basis for ecumenical agreement on a rule of faith (see also CONSENSUS QUINQUESAECULARIS).

[T. C. O'BRIEN]

SEVEN HEAVENS, the regions above the earth where God and the angels dwell. This is a commonplace of ancient cosmic theory. The earth was pictured as a flat disc near the abyss or great pit. Above the flat earth the concaved heavens were stretched, resting on pillars set at the distant horizons. The great pit was the abode of the dead, while God dwelt in the highest heaven. The plurality of the heavens was a commonplace of cultures as diverse as the Jewish, Arabic, Hindu, Siberian, Turkish, and Sumatran. There was great variation as to number. Seven was commonly accepted in rabbinic Judaism, but three was a popular alternative. The different levels were peopled by different sorts of superhuman beings. The second heaven was apparently reserved for evil spirits and angels awaiting punishment. Paul probably alludes to this region in his reference to the principalities and powers, the world rulers of this present darkness (Eph 6.12; 2.2). The elemental spirits of the universe were probably thought to be there, too (Gal 4.3). Paul refers to the third heaven as paradise (2 Cor 12.2), where the risen righteous live forever. Above that in the heaven of heavens is the throne of God.

[E. J. DILLON]

SEVEN HOLY FOUNDERS: SS. Bonfilius, John Bongiunta, Gerard Sostegni, Bartholomew Amidei, Benedict dell'Antélla, Ricoverus Uguccione, and Alexis Falconieri, Founders of the *Servites. They were canonized in 1888.

SEVEN LAST WORDS, the seven sayings of Christ that he uttered upon the cross. Three of these are peculiar to Lk; three others peculiar to Jn; and one common to Mt and Mark. They are commonly presented in the following order: (1) "Father, forgive them for they do not know what they are doing" (Lk 23.34). This plea for forgiveness was probably spoken as Jesus was being nailed to the cross. The ignorance of both the Romans and the Jews concerning Christ's identity mitigates their culpability. (2) "Amen I say to you, today you will be with me in paradise" (Lk 23.43). Christ promised salvation to the good thief, crucified on his right hand. Previously the thief had asked that Jesus remember him in that future day when He will come into power; Jesus corrects that future expectation with his "today." Paradise is association with Christ in his kingdom. (3) "Woman, behold your son . . . . Behold your mother" (Jn 19.25–27). These words, spoken to Mary and to the Disciple John, are variously interpreted. Some scholars see in them only an expression of filial devotion; others discern a reference to Mary as the new Eve who is proclaimed the spiritual mother of all Christ's followers, present in the person of John. (4) "My God, my God, why have you forsaken me?" (Mt 27.46; Mk 15.34). These are the first words of Ps 22, a prayer of constant confidence in God's presence and help. Jesus probably did not recite the psalm in its entirety since the Evangelists say that he uttered the words in a loud voice and with anguish. (5) "I thirst" (Jn 19.28). The soldiers then offer Christ vinegar or sour wine, and thus fulfill the messianic prophecy, "In my thirst they gave me vinegar to drink" (Ps 69.22). (6) "It is consummated'' (Jn 19.30). Said just before Christ's death in John's account, the saying means that the will of God as expressed in the Scriptures has been perfectly fulfilled. (7) ''Father, into your hands I commend my spirit'' (Lk 23.46). Jesus quotes Ps 31.6, confidently submitting himself at death into the loving care of the Father. BIBLIOGRAPHY: EDB 2182–84; W. J. Kenneally, ''Eli Eli, Lama Sabacthani: Mt. 27.46,'' CBQ 8(1946) 124–134.

[T. M. McFADDEN]

SEVEN LAST WORDS (MUSIC), the last utterances of Christ from the cross, as drawn from the Gospels. Composers, notably Schütz and Haydn, used them as the text for Passion music.

[M. T. LEGGE]

SEVEN SLEEPERS OF EPHESUS, seven Christian youths of Ephesus who according to an ancient legend took refuge in a cave during the persecution of Decius. The Emperor had the cave closed up so that they might die of hunger and thirst. For more than 200 years they slept until builders happened to remove the stones from the cave's entrance. They awoke and were amazed to find that their city was Christian. After they had made their story known to the Emperor Theodosius II, they died at the command of Christ and thereafter were venerated as saints. The legend, first recorded in the 6th cent. by *James of Sarug in the East and by *Gregory of Tours in the West, may be described as a Christian variation of a theme that appears in the folklore of most peoples. They have been invoked by those suffering from insomnia. BIBLIOGRAPHY: Butler 3:193–196, which gives much of William Caxton's translation of James of Voragine's version of the story; also AnalBoll 12:372–388 for the crit. ed. by B. Krusch of the version of Gregory of Tours; V. Saxer, BiblSanct 11:900–907.

[R. B. ENO]

SEVENTH-DAY ADVENTISTS, the largest of those Churches that have their origin in the *Adventism of W. *Miller. There are more than 1.5 million Seventh-day Adventists in the world. Among those who remained faithful even after Miller's prediction of Christ's second coming went unfulfilled were Joseph Bates, James White, and his wife, Ellen G. *White. On the basis of Miller's teaching and the observance of Saturday as the day of worship, they formed and organized the Seventh-day Adventists; the first conference of the Church was held at Battle Creek, Mich., in 1863. Mrs. White has always been considered a prophetess by this Church. Her views settled many points of doctrinal interpretation, and her writings are still standard doctrinal works, believed by the Church to be inspired. The Seventh-day Adventists follow a literalist *fundamentalism in accepting the Bible as the sole rule of faith; they also affirm the gift of prophecy not only of Mrs. White but as ever present in the Church. From her they received their primary doctrinal emphasis, the observance of the Sabbath law; it is the mark of those sealed by God and accepting his

salvation through Christ. Their attitude toward the Sabbath as strictly enjoined is the basis of their strict observance of OT tithing and dietary laws, their abstinence from all stimulants and from worldly dress or amusements, and their attacks on the pope and the Roman Church for introducing Sunday observance. The second main teaching of the Church is the second coming of Christ; they do not, however, attempt to set a time for this. In accord with a vision of Mrs. White, they believe that Christ began the cleansing of the sanctuary, i.e., a judgment on all men, in 1844; the judgment still goes on in preparation for his coming, which the Adventists are to proclaim. In the meantime souls are asleep. Adventists teach a *conditional immortality: man has a mortal soul and immortality is solely the gift of Christ to the just. At the second coming Christ's 1,000-year reign will begin (see PREMILLENARIANISM); he will take the just, both living and resurrected dead, into the heavens. After 1,000 years the wicked will be raised, judged, and after being led in a mighty battle by Satan, with him they will all be annihilated; there is no everlasting hell. The earth will be renewed and the just will reign upon it in glory. Adventists stress health and healing as adjuncts of the gospel teaching; dietary laws are strict, and many Adventists are vegetarians.

Local churches belong to state conferences, but each is autonomous, congregational in polity. The General Conference, which represents the whole Church, meets every 4 years. National headquarters were moved from Battle Creek to Takoma Park, Md., near Washington, D.C., in 1903. There are members or missionaries in 195 countries. The Church employs all mass media to win converts. One out of every 19 adult members is employed by the Church as a teacher, physician, pastor, missionary, dentist, nurse, printer, or administrator. Membership in the U.S. rose from 26,799 in 1906 to 449,188 in 1974. In keeping with their belief, Seventh-day Adventists have encouraged health reform and medical care; the Church operates a medical and dental school in Calif. and a network of hospitals, sanitariums, and clinics in the U.S. and around the world. Its parochial school system is 3d largest in the U.S.; worldwide, the Church supports 4,460 grade schools, as well as 570 high schools and 64 colleges. A large percentage of Adventists attends college. BIBLIOGRAPHY: E. T. Clark, *Small Sects in America* (1949) 25–45; L. E. Froom, *Prophetic Faith of Our Fathers* (4v., 1946–54); B. Herndon, *Seventh Day* (1960); A. W. Spalding, *Captains of the Host* (1949).

[W. J. WHALEN]

SEVENTY-FOUR TITLES, COLLECTION OF, designation for *Diversorum patrum sententiae*, a canonical collection made *c.*1175 that served as a model and possibly as a source of such later collections as that of *Ivo of Chartres and the *Decretum* of Gratian. Included are ordinances defending the Roman primacy and the independent rights of the Church over its property and revenues. The collection also served to circulate the *False Decretals.

[T. C. O'BRIEN]

SEVENTY WEEKS OF YEARS, 490-year period during which the Jews must suffer prior to the final consummation (Dan 9.24–27). Literally 70 weeks, the phrase reinterprets Jeremiah's prediction of a 70-year captivity (25.11–12; 29.10; compare Dan 9.2). It is uncertain whether any particular beginning point was intended.

[T. EARLY]

SEVERIAN (fl. *c*.400), bp. of Gabala, a leader among the enemies of St. *John Chrysostom. He was often in Constantinople, where he established a following as a preacher and made himself troublesome to Chrysostom. S. was favored and protected by Empress Eudoxia, who frustrated Chrysostom's efforts to keep him out of the capital. Thereafter S. conspired against Chrysostom and became his chief accuser as well as his judge at the Synod of the *Oak. After his success in bringing about Chrysostom's second and final exile, he returned to his own see. About 30 of his homilies survive in Greek or Oriental translations, many of them preserved, ironically, among the works of Chrysostom. He was completely committed to the Antiochene method of exegesis, and his scriptural interpretations are marked by an excessive literalism. Works: PG 56:429–516; 63:531–544. BIBLIOGRAPHY: Quasten 3:484–486; W. Kaegi, NCE 13:142–143.

[R. B. ENO]

SEVERIAN MONOPHYSITES, originally the adherents of the mitigated *Monophysitism of *Severus of Antioch (*c*.465–538), but by extension all the Monophysites since the 6th century. Their theology is characterized by a repudiation of both extreme Monophysitism, usually linked with *Eutyches, and the conclusions of the Council of *Chalcedon. The rejection of Chalcedon, however, seems to be based upon terminological rather than substantive differences: to admit two natures in Christ would be to deny the unity of the individual who was the incarnate Word.

[R. R. BARR]

SEVERIN, SS., the name of several saints commemorated in the Western Church, of which the most renowned are: (1) the famous *Boethius (d. 524), Christian philosopher and author of the *Consolation of Philosophy*, written while in prison awaiting death by order of Theodoric, Ostrogoth ruler of Italy. His full name was Anicius Manlius Severinus Boethius, and he was venerated as St. Severin. The cult was confirmed by Pope Leo XIII (1883); and his tomb is venerated at Pavia, and his feast is observed there as well as in the church of St. Mary in Portico, Rome. (2) **St. Severin of Noricum** (d. *c*.480), whose biography was written by his disciple Eugippius, may have belonged to a distinguished North African family, although he never alluded to his country of origin or to his family status. First he lived as an ascetic in the eastern deserts. Then he left to preach the gospel in Austria (Noricum). He held fast to his austere life-style, never eating until sunset (except on great feasts) and walking barefoot, even in winter. He was a father to the

poor, relieving the oppressed and redeeming captives, including one by personal intercession with the fierce Ostrogoth prince, Odoacer. Many towns wanted him as their bp., but he resisted, asserting that it was sufficient to preach and to tend to the afflicted. Although he founded monasteries, he never settled down in one. When he died, his relics were brought to Italy and finally came to rest in a Benedictine abbey named after him, in Naples. (3) **St. Severin of Bordeaux**, (d. *c*.420) is known only on the authority of Venantius Fortunatus. Before coming to Bordeaux, S. had apparently been bp. of Trier. (4) **St. Severin**, mid-6th cent. bp. of the town of Septempeda in the Italian province of Le Marche, which is now called San Severino in his honor. (5) **St. Severin** is venerated as the ancient protector of Cologne. (6) **St. Severin** (d. 507), abbot and confessor is credited with the miraculous cure of Clovis, King of the Franks. This may be the same Severin after whom the famous church in Paris is named.

[E. J. DILLON]

SEVERINUS (d. 640), **POPE** from 638. S. was a Roman of advanced age when he was elected to succeed Honorius I. His consecration was delayed a year and 7 months while the Emperor Heraclius attempted to extort an approval of the *Ecthesis*. The diplomacy of the papal legates at Constantinople finally won over the Emperor. It is not clear by what means the Emperor was persuaded to grant his approval; perhaps he had been led to believe that S. would accept his formulary. But after his consecration he did not do so he declared rather that as there are two natures in Christ, so there are in him two wills and two operations. BIBLIOGRAPHY: C. M. Aherne, NCE 13:143; Mann 1.1:346.

[P. F. MULHERN]

SEVERIOS, MAR (Joseph Valakuzhyil; 1894–1955), Indian Jacobite convert to Catholicism. S. studied at the Univ. of Calcutta under the future Mar Ivanios and was ordained a Jacobite priest in 1929. He was made bp. of Niranam in 1933, taking the name Mar Severios. When Mar Ivanios became a Catholic, S. replaced him as superintendent of the Jacobite Church; but in 1937 he, too, was converted. He was made administrator apostolic of Tiruvalla the same year and became its residential bp. in 1950. In 1953 he was given the personal title of archbishop. The flourishing state of the Church in the Syro-Malankar province is largely the result of his indefatigable labors. BIBLIOGRAPHY: E. G. Borghese, DE 3:834.

[M. J. SUELZER]

SEVEROLI, ANTONIO GABRIELE (1757–1824), cardinal, diplomat. Bishop of Fano from 1787 to 1801, Count Severoli then served (1801–16) in the difficult post of nuncio to Vienna, where he contended with the interference of Joseph II in church affairs. He was not liked by the Austrian government for his firmness in opposing Austrian influence in the Papal States. S. was made a cardinal in 1816 but was regarded unfavorably by Card. Consalvi, Secretary of State, and left the diplomatic service to become a zealous bp. of Viterbo (1817–1824). Austria's opposition vetoed his candidacy for the papacy in the conclave of 1823.

[J. R. AHERNE]

SEVERUS OF ANTIOCH (c.465–538), **PATRIARCH OF ANTIOCH** (512–518), leading theologian of *Monophysitism. After his baptism in 488, S. became a monk, then a hermit, and finally founded a monastery near Gaza where he soon accepted the Monophysite doctrine. He went to Constantinople (509) to defend his position, gained favor with the Emperor Anastasius I, came to accept the *Henoticon, and wrote against *Eutyches but also rejected Pope Leo's *Tome to Flavius* and the acts of the Council of *Chalcedon. He was consecrated patriarch of Antioch where his moderate position was criticized by both the extreme Monophysites and the adherents of Chalcedon. When Justin became emperor (518) and tried to reestablish religious accord, S. was forced to flee to Egypt where he organized the Monophysite opposition to the Emperor's policy. After Justin's death, S. returned to a position of prominence at Constantinople (535), but he had to flee again when, through the intervention of Pope Agapetus, his writings were condemned (536). He died in Egypt in 538. In the final analysis, S.'s theology is compatible with that of Chalcedon even though a divergent terminology gives an initial impression of opposition. BIBLIOGRAPHY: G. Bardy, DTC 14.2:1988–2000. *SEVERIAN MONOPHYSITES.

[T. M. MCFADDEN]

SEVERUS IBN AL-MUKAFFA', mid-10th–cent. Coptic author, the first Copt to write in Arabic. After holding civil office, he became a monk. In 987 he was named bp. in Upper Egypt. Among his works is an important history of the patriarchs of Alexandria, from the beginning (St. Mark) to S.'s contemporary Philotheus (976–979). He provided valuable information on the Church in Egypt, Nubia, and Ethiopia. His extant works include: *History of the Patriarchs; Book of the Councils; Second Book of the Councils*; and *Book of the Exposition* (theological treatises).

[E. J. DILLON]

SÉVIGNÉ, MARIE DE RABUTIN-CHANTAL, Marquise de (1626–96), French letter writer and granddaughter of St. Jane Frances de Chantal, foundress of the Order of the Visitation. Left a widow by Henri de Sévigné (1651), S. devoted herself to her two children: Charles (1648–1713) and Françoise Marguerite (1646–1705), assisted in the management of her affairs by the Abbé Christophe de Coulanges. The departure of her daughter (1671) after marriage (1669) to the Comte de Grignan (1629–1714), began the greatest part of S.'s literary production: letters to her daughter relating news of everyday reality, of society and the court, artistically written but perhaps without conscious literary intention. These letters contain controversial remarks concerning Jansenism, toward which S. was paradox-

ically inclined despite her temperament. While critics have seen her attitude as either orthodox or Jansenist, it can be said that her love for the heroic and for greatness attracted her to austere Jansenist virtue and to the concept of a Jansenistic baroque God of power, uncompromised by Jesuitical casuistry, asserting himself in the surprising workings of his providence. BIBLIOGRAPHY: H. R. Allentuch, *Madame de Sévigné: A Portrait in Letters* (1963); Y. Pirat, *Madame de Sévigné* (1959).

[R. N. NICOLICH]

SEWAL DE BOVILL (d. 1258), abp. of York (1256–58). Friend of Edmund of Abingdon, whose canonization he supported, and of Adam Marsh, he studied theology and became chancellor at Oxford (1245). He resisted papal provision of an Italian as his successor as dean of York, was excommunicated and suspended, but later restored (1257) BIBLIOGRAPHY: H. Mayr-Harting, NCE 13:147.

[R. W. HAYS]

SEX (IN THE BIBLE), the dynamic of human life which derives from the fact of gender; from the fact that "male and female he created them" (Gen 1.27). There are no words for "sex," "sexual," or "sexuality" in the Hebrew Scriptures, yet the reality of sex is pervasive, and its dynamic sufficiently apparent. The biblical writers and the various protagonists whose deeds they recount neither articulate a philosophy of sexuality nor reveal any preoccupation with the sexual dynamic in itself. Any related moral concern seems to have been centered in the social regulation of sexual behavior, the dominant concern being the impact on the welfare of the extended family, kinfolk, and the clan. The relatively ancient code of laws in Ex 20.14, 17 does not go much beyond the solemn injunction against adultery and coveting a neighbor's wife. The more extensive legislation in the Holiness Code of Leviticus (18.6–30), and the Deuteronomic Code (27.20–23) contains detailed prohibitions against various forms of incest within the extended family, together with denunciations of homosexuality and sexual relations with beasts. The death penalty is urged for all these and adultery as well. Legislation of lesser importance dealt with the state of uncleanness believed to have been incurred by such phenomena as male emission of semen, female menstruation, and even childbirth. The Wisdom literature, typified by the Book of Proverbs, viewed sexual morality as essentially a skill for living, a discipline fundamental to the good life and to long happiness. Like the biblical legislation it is largely male-oriented and never tires of urging a man to marry young and learn to find delight with the wife of his youth, and so to have deep roots in the land and live to see his children's children. Adultery and sexual adventure easily lead to violence and death. A woman who was unmarried or barren felt it as a curse and a reproach; her name became a by-word. Not until the era of Jewish apocalyptic were there any inroads against this dominant attitude. The hope in the resurrection of the just had the power of unsettling long-held traditions, even in sexual matters, as in the paradoxical affirmation in the Wisdom of Solomon that more numerous are the children of the barren than of her who has children; or Paul's reference to the children he has begotten by the Word of life received through his preaching.

[E. J. DILLON]

SEX BEFORE MARRIAGE, a phrase here understood to mean intimate sex relations, esp. between young people, before the parties are bound to one another by a formal marriage contract. One of the main traditional arguments condemning such intercourse was based on the illegitimate child's not having a home. In the past when little relationship was seen between intercourse and human love, and sexual pleasure was looked upon askance even within marriage, and procreation was commonly understood to be the only justification for marital sex, this argument was unchallenged. After Columbus' sailors introduced syphilis into Europe, a new major reason, that of preventing the spread of venereal disease, became important. Maintenance of a woman's virginity provided another natural argument. Theologically, Scripture was quite explicit in its condemnation of fornication, rounding out a fairly solid case for the maintenance of premarital chastity that remained relatively unquestioned in the Western world.

In recent years, a number of major developments have brought about a rather thorough reexamination of this traditional thinking. Negative arguments have been greatly weakened and new positive ones are being formulated. Pregnancy as a deterrent to premarital sex is much less a factor since the development of effective birth control methods. The fact that many young couples do not use, or use properly, the methods available does not change the fact that pregnancy need no longer be a common result of intercourse. It once seemed that venereal disease as a problem had found a quick and effective solution with antibiotics, yet the rise of resistant strains of these diseases, reluctance to seek treatment, ignorance, and other social factors have maintained it as a distinct threat, weaker, however, than it was a generation ago. Permanent adoption of illegitimate children into good homes plus a slowly increasing tolerance of illegitimacy itself have muted a classic objection.

Basic to some of the change in thinking has been the recognition in our day of a love relationship between husband and wife as crucial to the stability, harmony, and fulfillment of a marriage. We now see this bond of love as essential to their being able properly to rear and educate children. Young couples have, for the first time on large scale in human history, been given the freedom to choose their own partners in marriage, the criterion of this choice being that of mutual love. The physical aspects of sex in marriage, previously oriented toward procreation, are now universally recognized as being a crucial and integral part of the fostering and maintenance of love, harmony, and fulfillment in marriage. This enobling of the physical intimacies of marriage as an expression of love has not been lost on some young couples who, not yet married but deeply in love, are asking whether its full expression physically might not be justified prior to marriage.

Women's rise to new dignity, independence, and competency—educationally, socially, maritally, and sexually—with the partial elimination of the old double standard, is another fact of our time. Situational ethics, however interpreted at the moment by the individuals involved, introduces a theological dimension that has definitely tended further to weaken these objective norms, while the endless barrage of sexual stimulus and in-depth education by the public media, particularly television, has also been an immensely effective force for change.

In the light of the above, many are convinced that we live in a time of sexual revolution and that among young people "everybody is doing it." Contrary to the media's message, however, this is not yet true. Between 1930 and 1970, there has been almost no percentage of increase in the number of young people engaging in intercourse prior to marriage. Well-controlled studies such as Halleck's at the Univ. of Wisconsin testify to this (see bibliography). There has, however, been a substantial change in talking about it, particularly among women. It would seem that if the time-honored concept of premarital chastity is to retain its validity, we shall have to find new justification more relevant to our times. The dialectic in fact is now well underway; it is built upon our newly developing concepts of love and interpersonal relationships, the psychology of sexuality, and the need for intact secure family life.

It is evident that the family is the basic unit of society. A child needs both a mother and a father united by a bond of love with whose affectionate help he will grow and develop in security during his first 18 to 20 years. To the extent that one parent is absent by desertion, divorce, and much less so by death, or the bond of love that should unite them is missing, to that extent are the children issuing from this home less emotionally stable and more likely to recreate the broken and unstable home from which they have come. Families today stand alone, most being so-called nuclear families, unsupported by a ring of parents, aunts, siblings, etc., as in past years. Marriages today largely survive and bloom, or fail and end in divorce, because of the stability of the interpersonal relationship of husband and wife, which is more crucial in our time than at any time before in human history.

Sex in a marriage does not stand alone, but reflects the all-day-longness of the relationship of these two people with each other. A husband and wife who love and support each other all day long, will over the years develop with few exceptions a good sexual adjustment. A couple who have never really learned to support, communicate with, and love each other, but rather live out lives of individualistic exploitation of the other, soon find that the sex they share in bed reflects the nonlove of the day preceding and grows more and more destructive of love.

The experience of intimate sex prior to marriage, even with one's engaged partner, far from aiding in the creation of a stable happy marriage, in fact consistently renders its happiness and sometimes very continuance more and more precarious. True and total commitment, permanent and lifelong, of one person to another, cannot be practiced physically beforehand. If intimate sex at its best is an expression of love for one's married partner, then it is the job of parents and educators to convince young people that in order to form great marriages each must first become a great person whom another great person will want.

As more sociological studies are being made, most point to a fairly consistent conclusion in cultural areas in which a single lifetime marriage is a hoped-for ideal. Those groups of young people who have the most sexual experience before marriage consistently include the highest number of unstable persons, have the highest divorce and adultery rates, and ultimately rate themselves the least happy and the least sexually fulfilled. Those groups of young people who are virgins at marriage contain the highest percentage of stable persons and of intact marriages, the least adultery, and ultimately the greatest personal happiness and sexual fulfillment in marriage.

Presuming that continuing studies verify the above conclusions, we would suggest that Scripture's definitive teaching on premarital continence will remain not only good theology but good social and psychological truth as well. BIBLIOGRAPHY: S. Halleck, "Sex and Mental Health on Campus," *Journal of American Medical Association* (May 22, 1967).

[J. C. AND B. WILLKE]

SEX DIFFERENCES, male and female, the deepest in-born differences in human nature, representing greater fundamental diversity than that arising from temperament, race, or individual variation. These differences are manifested at biological, psychological, and behavioral levels, and at each level there are primary and secondary differences. In general, the relationship between male and female differences is one of complementarity, i.e., the differences are designed to unite man and woman in a complete functional unit. At the biological level, the primary differences are in the sexual or reproductive organs by means of which the male sperm is joined with the ovum in the uterus of the female to begin a new life. The secondary differences are the typical male characteristics, e.g., beard, deeper voice, heavier bone and muscle, etc., and the physical development, figure, voice, etc., characteristic of the female. These are caused by secretions of male and female hormones respectively and serve as signals for mutual attraction. At the psychological level, the primary differences are in the sexual urge itself. In men this tends to be aroused more quickly, to be more single-purposed, and to be less in evidence between arousals, whereas in women it rises more gradually, is more multi-purposed (i.e., including desires for affection, security, assurance of personal worth, etc.) and in the interims between arousals is not completely quiescent. Secondarily men are more openly aggressive, more concerned about achievement, more interested in impersonal reality, facts, and logic; women are more covertly aggressive, more concerned with personal relationships, feelings, and intuitions. These differences are not absolute but admit of considerable variation in individuals of both sexes and few generalizations not subject to many exceptions can be made. The differences correspond complementarily with man's role as provider and woman's role as care-giver. At the behavioral level, the primary differences stem from women's carrying, bearing, and nursing children; the many other differences are largely matters of cultural determination.

In interpersonal relations, the ability of men and women to understand the genuine differences of perspective and feeling is essential for marital harmony.

The differences between men and women, esp. in typical modes of thought and feeling, and the diversity of outlook caused by their respective roles in life, lead to discernible differences of emphasis in their distinctive approaches to God and in the moral values or disvalues to which each sex tends to attach peculiar importance. In cultural situations in which religion has become more exclusively a preoccupation of persons of one sex rather than the other, it is inevitable that the character of prevalent religious thought and observance will be somewhat over-influenced by the psychology of the sex from which the religion's practitioners are chiefly drawn. BIBLIOGRAPHY: *Development of Sex Differences* (ed. E. Maccoby, 1966); S. C. Callahan, *Illusion of Eve: Modern Woman's Quest for Identity* (1965).

[M. E. STOCK]

SEX EDUCATION—perhaps better, family life education—a program of teaching, the importance and proper function of which are best appreciated when it is understood in its broad concept. Although it provides instruction concerning the facts of human reproduction, this is only a small part of its total scope. It must be concerned with the whole person of the man or the woman. It must unfold the concepts of masculinity and femininity and show how a person lives out this total role in life and not just in its genital aspects. Its overall aim is to pass on to the next generation a set of attitudes and a system of values.

Four major educative influences contribute, for better or worse, to whatever sexual education children actually receive: parents, school, peer groups, and the public media.

Parents have always been the primary teachers in matters pertaining to sexuality and they remain so. Most of what children become and act out in adult life is what they have seen their parents do. Parental teaching is mostly nonverbal and consists quite simply of the example of the lives they lead in front of their children. From this the child learns unconsciously, but what he learns is acquired in depth and becomes a permanent part of his personality. Since Victorian times, parents have typically spoken little about the facts of life to their children. In the last decade there has been a concerted effort to overcome this prudish silence and to encourage parents not only to witness to, hopefully, a good marriage, but also to speak of sex and to discuss facts with their children openly, honestly, reverently, and much earlier than was done in past generations.

Peer groups have always accounted an important part of one's sex education; the child's contemporaries are the most vocal and outspoken of teachers. Opinion is divided as to whether peer group talk and pressure are prime motivating factors among young people. Probably they have little influence on those whose moral value systems have been firmly established by a good home, and probably also they are at least the precipitating cause for sexual activity among those whose background reflects less firm values and less stability.

School teachers have always been sex educators, but in the past commonly in the same nonverbal way as the parents. Though they provided some instruction in facts and values, they usually did so informally, responding to an apparent need of the moment. In many cases the school has been a remedial influence where parental example has been poor. What is new in the contemporary situation is the present strong movement to establish formal courses of sex education in schools at all grade levels.

The public media, most specifically the printed page and the television screen, have developed in the modern age into a profoundly effective educational influence. Graphic news reporting has introduced concepts of abortion, homosexuality, birth control, rape, etc., into the world of a child old enough to read, watch, or listen. Glorification of genital activity, particularly prior to and outside of marriage, ridicule of traditional roles of husband and wife, of fidelity and monogamy, are some of the negative aspects of this technicolor saturation course in human sexuality. To date, the good accomplished by public media in this matter has been substantially outweighed by the bad. What the effect of this imbalance will be upon the younger generation remains to be seen.

Peculiar to the last half of the 1960s has been the rise of a strong national movement calling for the development and introduction into all schools, from the kindergarten through the 12th grade, of definite courses in sex education and family life. For several years this aim met with growing support, but latterly a militant opposition developed spontaneously throughout the U.S., sparked by the excesses and reported abuses in some places in which sex education programs had been introduced. The opposition became organized through the efforts of several right-wing groups, but has been effective only in areas in which a large percentage of the parents became suspicious of the values they claimed were being taught to their children in school. In some of these places, bitter strife arose, the issue frequently becoming political, occasioning the defeat or resignation of school board members and superintendents, and in a number of instances culminating in resolutions and restrictive laws passed by state legislatures.

One or more of three major factors seem to have contributed to this backlash. Some parental misinformation and prudishness are likely to be present everywhere. Where programs were successful, these were usually dealt with by incorporating into the program a plan for familiarizing parents with its nature and purpose. Controversial programs neglected this and commonly all but wrote off the parents as having no right to information on the matter.

Second, where controversy arose, parents were generally convinced that bad values (by their judgment) were being taught their children. Exaggerations, rumors, and false reports were common, but actual happenings in sufficient number were well enough documented to arouse distrust on the part of many parents. In fact, common to most of the troubled areas was the teaching of a nonvalue system, highly biological, highly sociological, situationalist in its ethic, holding forth few objective norms of human conduct. This was true particularly of programs formed under the influence of the Sex Education and Information Council of the U.S. and similar groups. Concerned parents, anxious to have their children reproduce the stable families that had been their ideal, formed the bulk of those questioning many of the new school programs.

The third cause was the assumption by the professional educator of all but total responsibility for the development of this new curriculum, the selection of materials, and the teaching. In places in which a large and representative group of ordinary parents shared in the work, relatively little difficulty arose.

The solution to the controversy seems to lie in the recognition of the fact that the professional educator, though he may hold prime competence in teaching other disciplines of the curriculum, must have due regard for the prior competence and responsibility of the parent. Parents who have been successful in their own marriages and whose children reflect the love, stability, and security of their homes, should be the ones chosen to participate in the formation, teaching, and monitoring of school programs. When this has been done, parents have usually provided the common-sense balance that has produced programs containing facts and values acceptable to the community as well as being good for the children.

Parochial schools have not been altogether untouched by the controversy, but they were largely insulated with regard to the major point of conflict, i.e., that of the values being taught.

Pope Pius XI opposed public sex education programs in his encyclical *Christian Education of Youth*. This opposition was in essence reversed by Vatican Council II. In its *Declaration on Christian Education*, the Council stated: "As they [children and young people] advance in years they should be given positive and prudent sexual education" (Vat II ChrEduc 1).

The bps. of the U.S., elaborating on this in their 1968 pastoral letter, *Human Life in Our Day*, affirmed "the value and necessity of wisely planned education of children in human sexuality." They spoke of the grave obligation "to assist the family in its efforts to provide such training. This obligation can be met either by systematic provision of such education in the diocesan school curriculum, or by the inauguration of acceptable educational programs under other diocesan auspices . . .''

A heightened consciousness of the need for positive, prudent, and value-oriented sexual education will probably emerge from the above. Most programs under RC auspices will probably take the form of relatively informal, flexible, but structured programs from kindergarten up to the sixth or eighth grade, and a more formal course beyond. More parent participation is to be anticipated, including some actual teaching in high schools. Roman Catholics would welcome the inclusion of certain nonsectarian, family-preserving values in the public schools.

[J. C. AND B. WILLKE]

SEXTUS, late 2d- or early 3d-cent. Christian apologist, to whom fleeting reference is made in Eusebius's *Historia ecclesiastica* (5, 27), and in St. Jerome's *De viris illustribus* (50). Both name a certain Sextus as the author of a book *On the Resurrection*. Jerome places it in the time of the emperor Severus. Eusebius lists it among the monuments of virtuous industry written between 193–211 by orthodox ecclesiastical writers. He lists it along with works that deal with ''that question so much agitated among the heretics.'' Other of S.'s works are *On the Origin of Evil, On the Creation of Matter,* and *On the Six Days of Creation.* From these it is probable that S. was an antagonist of the Gnostic belief that matter was the source of evil for man. He must have insisted on the reality of the resurrection of the body as the ultimate refutation of that heresy.

[E. J. DILLON]

SEXTUS EMPIRICUS (fl. end of 2d cent. A.D.), Greek physician and the chief representative of later ancient Skepticism. The epithet *empiricus* indicates that he belonged to the Empirical School of medicine. He is esp. important because he is the only major extant source for our knowledge of ancient Skepticism in detail. Three of his works are preserved. His *Outlines of Pyrrhonism* covers basic skeptical terminology and method (bk 1), attacks dogmatic logic and theory of knowledge (bk 2), and likewise physics and ethics (bk 3). His criticism is presented in greater detail in his *Against the Dogmatists.* His third work, *Against the Schoolmasters* is directed against grammar, rhetoric, mathematics, astronomy, and music. BIBLIOGRAPHY: K. Brink, OCD 834; M. Soreth, LexAW 2791; Copleston 1:444–455.

[M. R. P. MCGUIRE]

SEXTUS, SENTENCES OF, a collection of ethical apothegms of pagan origin. A Christian revision of them appeared toward the end of the 2d century. Of these 451 were translated into Latin by *Rufinus under the erroneous impression that they were the work of Pope *Sixtus II (257–258), an attribution that St. *Jerome was quick to deny. The sentences reflect a Platonic background, stress the ideas of purification and illumination, and urge ascetical practice in matters of food and drink. Similarities to *Clement of Alexandria are plain. BIBLIOGRAPHY: *Sentences of Sextus* (ed. and Eng. tr. H. Chadwick, 1959); Quasten 1:170–171.

[R. B. ENO]

SEXUAL MORALITY, in its specific meaning within the consideration of morals, the goodness or badness inherent in the choice to experience the emotional and bodily gratification of genital activity. So to isolate the meaning conventionally given to the term is already a clarification in the present period of debate. Sexuality has become almost a vogue term. Current discussion emphasizes that it enters a human being's make-up as it is a constitutive element of the human person, even as are emotionality and rationality. Sexuality means maleness or femaleness and that is more than anatomy. Acting as a human person, it need scarcely be said, is acting as a man or as a woman. All human relationships are within or between sexes. Because sexuality in this broadest sense is part of humanness, it has personal and interpersonal potentialities and expressions; it is therefore measurable by a whole range of human, i.e. moral, values making for rightness or wrongness. But the widest range of human values for purposes of analysis and evaluation is coextensive with the possibilities of human virtue and vice. The merit of contemporary reflection on the full meaning of sexuality is that it opens the way to perceptions of ways in which the good of virtue, justice for the most obvious example, is nuanced positively because the many elements that make up the moral good include the positive identity of the human person as male or female.

However, to leave undistinguished the broadest connotations of the term ''sexuality'' from the specific human activity to which discussions of sexual morality have been directed, is to equivocate in moral discourse; to employ the equivocation for the sake of making a point is sophism. The topic of sexual morality is sex; the term itself implies that human sexual activity is open to being morally good or morally evil, because it is the activity of a human being. For the human being who is a Christian there is, as well, a Christian's sexual morality, since the Christian identity, it is theologically presupposed, suffuses and transforms every facet of a person's makeup and existence. In any rational discourse about morality, the morally right and the morally wrong are only such with reference to a standard. Many Christian Churches and many Christians are currently facing perplexity about the standards of Christian sexual morality. Roman Catholic teaching has one preeminent standard: the moral good in sexual activity is its positive value as intrinsic to and expressive of marital union; the lack of that positive value in any form of sexual activity makes that activity bad.

The questioning or the rejection in theory and the disregard in practice of what were once taken as clear norms have occurred in the RC Church as in other Christian bodies. Yet there can be no doubt about what is the official and therefore, in virtue of the very nature of the RC Church, authentic RC teaching. In the face of contemporary turmoil the Congregation for the Doctrine of the Faith on Dec. 29, 1975 issued its *Persona humana*, a *Declaration on Certain Questions concerning Sexual Ethics* (Eng. tr. with commentary, USCC Publications Office, 1977). The document affirms clearly that there are objective moral standards measuring human sexual activities and that on the basis of such standards premarital sex, homosexual acts, and masturbation are gravely wrong; the document also adds that, as has always been taught, many personal psychological factors and moral *circumstances may diminish culpability and lessen the seriousness of the actions in question. The document, in its address to particular questions, reflects the long-held, general church position that to be deliberately sexually active—even by internal affections provoking sexual excitement—except within the marital union is both morally wrong and a mortal sin. Contemporary dissent in the Church from that generalization is part of a wider contemporary search to establish personalist and more pliant standards of human sexual morality. The 1977 report received by the Catholic Theological Society of America and published, A. Kosnik et al. ed., as *Human Sexuality* (1977) proposes standards and pastoral directions to guide the person to express human sexuality in ways that are self-creating and integrating and communicative of good in interpersonal relationships. While many share its objectives, few have praised the intrinsic worth of the work.

In the traditional and still authentic RC teaching there are presupposed priorities. First in both the development of the teaching and in decisiveness for its validity is the Church's living understanding of the word of God: tradition in that sense, not merely in the sense of time-honored convention. That understanding of the force of Scripture underlies the recent Roman document's biblical quotations (esp. in nn. 11–12, USCC ed. pp. 12–14); the rightness of that understanding is not negated by an exegesis that restricts the meaning of the biblical word to its connotations in a past cultural milieu. Scripture as the rule of faith, and so of morals, is for the Catholic not a book; it is the word of God as living in the understanding of the Church, an understanding given in view of the mission of salvation. The first force of the Church's teaching that a particular way of human activity is evil, then, is that it is *mortally* evil: incompatible with the saving union of the Christian with the Father through Jesus Christ. To give this point theological formulation is to say that any particular action is sinful theologically, first because it is incompatible with the person's existing in grace and charity, i.e., with union with the Father. That implies a needed clarification. One stumbling block both for pastoral judgment and for Christian conscience has been the teaching that deliberate sexual sins are mortal sins. Particularly during the last century one emphasis in moral, as well as in systematic theology, has been on the consonance of theological teaching with sound reason, of the teaching on sexual morality with natural ethics or the natural

law or with a naturally good moral sense. The classifying of any action as objectively a mortal sin, however, cannot be based on ethical arguments or on an individual's reasoned reflection on what is morally good. Reason has nothing to say about sin as mortal, a concept strictly linked with the meaning of grace and charity. A mortal sin is one that blocks the communication in grace and love with the Father; its meaning is bound up with the mystery of grace revealed and is the obverse side of the mystery of grace that faith assents to. Virtue in Aristotelian ethics conditions a person to act for the morally right *ut in pluribus,* more often than not. Thus the ethical virtue of temperance in regard to human control of sexual appetites is not destroyed, nor the person's whole moral orientation reversed, by a single act from time to time contrary to virtue. The temperate man for ethics is one who has his passions under habituated control so that the over-all course of his living is directed toward the higher good; he does not abandon that direction because he is consumed by the preference for lesser goods. A necessary step in evaluating Catholic sexual morality, then, is to see its exacting ideal to be connected first, not with Aristotelian ethics or Stoic reasonableness, but with the measure of charity; the objective gravity (which is not the same simply as serious aberration) of sins against chastity rests on their objective incompatibility with love for the Father.

There is a second degree of priority in the RC understanding of sexual morality as it is evangelically inspired: it is the message of self-denial. The power of sex holds a threat to salvation because it holds the threat of mortal sin. Catholic sexual morality includes the wariness of the effects of original sin, of what classical theology called "concupiscence." Exaggeration, whether ascribed to Augustine or remembered from the Puritan or Jansenist brooding over total depravity, does not warrant as an alternative the complete discounting of the sinfulness that is part of the human condition. Psychology's mass of information that can assist an integrative maturing in a person's sexual development does not displace the fundamental law of Christian life: "If any one will come after me, let him deny himself." An essential concomitant of Christian charity is chastity's taming of the flesh. Chastity includes a repression of the potential for the disordered inversion of the positive values in all human capacities. Such repression is not the whole message, since the power of grace and charity includes the taking up of all human powers into their saving transformation of the person. But restraint is needed as a condition for the positive direction toward God of all the good in human nature, to deny that sexual conduct has its own particular need for restraint is absurd. The Christian view accepts the Father's providence that the combat against the power of sin is part of the way of salvation. That the combat and law of self-denial are Christian is a message reenforced by the virulence and degrading ill-effects of sexual permissiveness contaminating the media, even the city streets, all with the blessing of secular humanism and even civil law.

Subordinate to the primary norm—the word of God as

understood by the Church—the measure of a reasoned evaluation determines the identifiably Catholic teaching on sexual morality. At least since the Middle Ages it has been characteristic of the Catholic outlook to point to a consonance of religious teaching with genuinely human values. There is, accordingly, in the Church's moral teaching the presupposition of a moral order. Articulation of precepts of moral conduct rest on the existence of such a moral order. To speak of sexual morality is to imply that, like all human activity, sexual expression is not self-justifying; that its rightness or wrongness rests on its being in conformity or in conflict with a measure. That in fact is what is meant by an "objective morality." The expression is redundant if "objective morality" be taken to mean that the moral action or the person acting are subject to something other, that they are not a rule unto themselves. God is not a moral being; there is no divine morality precisely because God is identical with the good; there is no "other" good that is the measure of his goodness or of his action. The reason for that, in turn, is that God in his being or acting does not have to "reach out" to another, to a distinct good, in order to be bettered and so cannot be on the right track or the wrong. But the human being acts to achieve betterment and so can act in the right direction or can deviate. The recognition of morality means the recognition of a distinct, thus an objective, measure. If the person alone is the measure there can be no wrong, but neither can there be any right; nothing can be evil, but nothing can be good either. To speak of sexual morality at all, then, is to speak of an objective sexual morality, of a measure other than the person acting and other than the person's action itself. The problem, and the contemporary dissent, is over the acknowledgment of what the objective measure is. The teaching reiterated in the 1975 Roman document identifies that primary objective measure as the unitive and procreative, the love and life giving purpose of marriage. That in turn is the norm for affirming that the married state alone is the morally right setting for sexual activity and that conjugal sexual activity is right as it conforms to the twofold purposiveness of marriage. This line of thought has been judged to be lacking in cogency and to be a view of the conjugal act in isolation from the total context of human sexuality. As to lack of cogency, it may be conceded that the implications of the finality of the conjugal act or its consequent restriction to the married state are not primary and immediately clear dictates of nature. That impression has sometimes been given in presentations of Catholic teaching on sex and marriage; the insinuation is that any human being not assenting to that view is maliciously rejecting the immediate evidence of human moral sense. In fact, the rudimentary precept of natural law on the sexual life requires reflection and development before being concretized in the rightness of the institution of permanent, monogamous marriage as the way of fulfillment. The defense of marriage's finality, however, when subsumed under the sacramental theology of marriage has a strong

persuasive force. It also has at least as much empirical support as dissenting positions; the ideals of fidelity, familial piety, social order are well supported by this understanding of sex and marriage; it is not clear that any of these necessary human and humane values are supported by opposed views of the meaning of marriage. The stability of society has decreased as marriage has increasingly taken to be an exclusively personal issue.

As to Catholic teaching being an isolated view of the conjugal act, this charge is simply a gratuitous assertion. Both Vatican Council II and the more recent Roman document discuss the issues as sexuality is a facet of the whole human personality. The conjugal act becomes prominent in a discussion of marriage and morals because it is the symbol and concretization of the marital relationship between two persons. It can and does have all the resonances of their whole relationship; to discuss this act as unitive and procreative is to describe the whole relationship as unitive and procreative. The argument is with the second. But that moral evaluation does not center on the mere phenomenon of a physical transmission of seed that may fructify an ovum. Procreation is the action of two persons and it involves their whole nature and personality. They are not two potential breeders, but a potential father and mother. Implicit in the physical reality of the conjugal act are that human symbolism and natural sacramentality. The psychological and pharmaceutical separability of the procreative finality of the act does not warrant the conclusion that the procreative is separable in meaning and in theological evaluation. To draw such a conclusion is to make a distinction that separates person and nature to the point of giving the person the power to negate nature. The claim to such a power can be made; but the claim is in defiance of the fact that a fruitful conjugal act does not reproduce the self but begets another human being. The marital morality proposed as church teaching sees in marriage alone the proper condition for personal affirmation of the finality of the conjugal act; it sees also in every marriage union, whose symbol that act is, the possibility of an affirmation of the noblest values in human sexuality. The restriction of the conjugal act to married spouses affirms the uniqueness in that complete self-giving and unitive stability that is the ideal of the highest form of human love, of personal relationship, and of friendship. To maintain the inseparability of the procreative from the meaning of marital sexuality is to teach that even the hopelessly childless marriage is an affirmation of the institution of marriage and of family as the first and constant expression of the fruitfulness of human love, the originating and primordial setting of the communal sharing necessary for all human growth and development. Solitary, homosexual, premarital, extramarital sexual activity do not and cannot represent the choice to affirm the positive ideal and measure of sexual activity; that lack is their moral aberrancy. No noble personal purpose or motivation has the power to straighten these distortions. BIBLIOGRAPHY: *NCCB*

Committee on Doctrine Statement (USCC publication, 1977).

[T. C. O'BRIEN]

SEYCHELLES ISLANDS, an archipelago of 92 islands in the Indian Ocean (100 sq mi; est. pop. 1976, 59,000). First occupied by the French in 1742, the islands were captured by the English in 1794 and became a dependency of Mauritius in 1814. They have been independent since 1976. Priests from Réunion and the Maurice Islands served the colonists during the years of French occupation, but Catholicism declined sharply when the British took over. In 1850 the Capuchin Père Des Acanches renewed the mission. Seychelles became a prefecture in 1852, a vicariate in 1880, and a diocese in 1892. Twenty-three priests and 36 brothers serve 54,000 Catholics. Christian Brothers are in charge of education—a mission monopoly until 1954. Even now the brothers may veto the administration's appointments. Schools for girls and charitable institutions are staffed by sisters. Most other Christian are either Anglicans or Adventists. By a coup d'état on June 5, 1977 a communist regime took over and imposed a completely socialist system. There is a threat to the missionary schools and presence of foreign missioners. The situation of the Church is uncertain.

[P. DAMBORIENA]

SEYDELMANN, FRANZ (1748–1806), German composer. As a youth, S. became a member of the court orchestra in which his father played. He studied with Josef Schuster in Italy, and later the two became church music composers and conductors in the court of the Elector of Dresden. S. wrote operas, piano and chamber music, and numerous Masses, psalms, Offertories, and a requiem.

[M. T. LEGGE]

SFONDRATI, a prominent family of Milan which produced a number of churchmen in the 16th and 17th cent., including Nicoló, who became Pope *Gregory XIV.

Francesco (1493–1550) cardinal, diplomat. A senator of Milan and the father of the future Pope Gregory XIV, Francesco entered the priesthood after the death of his wife in 1538. Named a cardinal in 1544, he served as a member of the Inquisition in Rome. Papal legate to Emperor Charles V from 1544 to 1548, he became bp. of Capaccio and then bp. of Cremona in 1549.

Paolo Camillo (1561–1618) cardinal, nephew of Gregory XIV. Named a cardinal and secretary of state by his uncle, he proved a failure; he wielded great authority but showed little public concern. He was made bp. of Cremona.

Celestino (1644–96) cardinal, prince abbot. He entered the Benedictines at St. Gall, Switzerland, and became abbot in a few years. He taught canon law at Salzburg for 3 years and in 1686 he was made bp. of Novara. In 1687 Celestino became prince abbot of St. Gall and in 1695, cardinal.

Celestino was a capable monastic administrator and theologian. Among his works were *Gallia vindicata* (1688) and *Nodus praedestinationis ex sacris litteris, doctrinaque sanctorum Augustini et Thomae . . . . . dissolutus* (1697).

[J. R. AHERNE]

SFORZA, the ruling family of Milan for 85 years. It was founded by **Muzio Attendolo** (d. 1424), a shrewd mercenary soldier who made a fortune and was nicknamed *Sforza* (force). His son **Francesco** (1401–66) waxed widely through numerous children, legitimate and illegitimate. He gained power in Milan in 1450 through his marriage to Bianca Maria, the illegitimate daughter of Filippo Maria Visconti (d. 1447); he proved an outstanding statesman and a patron of humanists. Of his sons, **Galeazzo Maria** (1444–76) succeeded him as duke of Milan, and **Ascanio Maria** (1455–1505), worldly, magnificent, and learned, became a cardinal and a supporter of the Borgias. Francesco's daughter **Ippolita Maria** (1445–88), celebrated for her learning, married Alfonzo, duke of Calabria. Of the daughters of Galeazzo Maria, **Bianca Maria** (1472–1510) married the Emperor Maximilian I, and **Caterina** (illegitimate, *c.*1463–1509) first married a Riario and afterwards a Medici. **Gian Galeazzo** (1469–94), son and heir of Galeazzo Maria, was displaced by his uncle, **Ludovico il Moro** (1450–1508), who married Beatrice d'Este, kept a brilliant court, and patronized artists including Leonardo da Vinci. He made the fatal mistake of encouraging the French to enter into Italian politics. When they threatened his own position, he joined the league against them and ended in a French prison. He was succeeded by two sons, **Massimiliano** (1493–1530), and **Francesco II** (1495–1535). The death of the latter marked the extinction of the ducal line, and the duchy went to the Habsburgs. BIBLIOGRAPHY: L. Collison-Morley, *Story of the Sforzas* (1934).

[N. G. WOLF]

SGAMBATI, ANDREAS (*c.*1735–1805) theologian, major superior. A Neapolitan of the Order of Friars Minor Conventual, S. was rector of St. Lawrence College, Naples, in 1771 and held the chair of theology at the Univ. of Naples. His major work, *De theologicis institutis* (14 v., 1775–82) following the teaching of St. Bonaventure, became the textbook of his order's seminaries in Spain. A second well-received work was *De praecipuis theologiae locis* (2 v., 1785). As professor of theology in Rome after 1785, S. wrote vigorously against lotteries, which were very popular in his time, even including monastic participation. In 1805 he became procurator general of his order for the foreign missions.

[J. R. AHERNE]

SGHEMMA, GASPAR (*c.*1590–1657), theologian. A native of Sicily, S. entered the Order of Friars Minor Conventual in 1612. He taught theology for many years in Palermo,

Naples, and Catania. He was censor for the Inquisition in Sicily, visitator general of his order in Sicily, Calabria, and Naples, and provincial of the Sicilian province. As a writer S. was a devoted follower of Duns Scotus. Among his principal works were *Manuale scoticum in quatuor libros sententiarum* (1638) and *Opuscula scotica* (2 v., 1645–52). In the latter he followed the Scotist reasoning used later in support of the definition of the Immaculate Conception.

[J. R. AHERNE]

SHABBATAI ṢEVÏ, see SHABBATAIISM.

SHABBATAIISM, a Jewish messianic movement of the 17th and 18th centuries. It takes its name from one of the chief pseudo-Messiahs of this period. Shabbatai Ṣevi. The hope for a Messiah became esp. deep among the Jews as a result of the terrible sufferings they had endured and were enduring during the 15th, 16th, and 17th centuries. Moreover, these sufferings were regarded as the beginnings of the messianic age of Jewish tradition. A new theological foundation was given for the messianic movement by the revival of cabalism by Isaac Luria (1534–72) of Safed in Upper Galilee. He taught that Israel's exile is only one aspect of the cosmic fall of creation and that the whole cosmos is in dire need of salvation. The main task of mankind, and more specifically, of its elect group, Israel, is to participate actively in saving the world by leading a holy life, by mystical concentration, and by fulfilling the divine commandments. This renewal of religious fervor and practice was focused on the coming of the Messiah and the expectation of deliverance.

Shabbatai Ṣevi (1626–1676) grew up at Smyrna in this atmosphere of messianic longing and speculation. He attended the Talmudic school of Rabbi Joseph Escapa, but his main interest was in cabalistic studies and on the way of life taught by Luria and his successors at Safed. Shabbatai, who went through periods of mental depression and ecstatic exaltation, announced in 1648 to a small group of followers that he was the Messiah. The elders of the Jewish community of Smyrna condemned him and his followers, and he began a wandering life throughout the East, but without disciples and without promoting his messianic aspirations further. The year 1665 marks a new stage in his messianic career. In that year the cabalist Nathan of Gaza (1644–80) announced that the messianic age was to begin the following year and that Shabbatai was the Messiah. On New Year's Day, Shabbatai publicly proclaimed that he was the Messiah in the synagogue of Smyrna.

The news that the Messiah had come was sent to all the Jewish communities of Europe, Asia, and Africa, and aroused a religious enthusiasm that often exhibited extreme forms. It affected all classes of Jewish society, but esp. the masses. The Sultan, becoming alarmed at the new movement and its manifestations, arrested Shabbatai and imprisoned him at Abydos on the Gallipoli peninsula. He was finally given the choice of death or conversion to Islam and

His apostasy was explained away, esp. by Nathan of Gaza, and he continued to be regarded as the Messiah, with his life and work soon enveloped in legend. A minority of his followers joined Islam, but the majority continued to believe in him as the Messiah and constituted a heretical underground in European Judaism, eventually disappearing only in the early 19th century. Among the pseudo-Messiahs who claimed to be successors of Shabbatai it will suffice to mention Jacob *Frank of Galicia (1726–91), who at one stage of his career temporarily joined the Catholic Church. BIBLIOGRAPHY: M. J. Stiassny, NCE 13:154–156; G. G. Scholem, *Sabbatai Zevi and the Sabbatean Movement during His Lifetime* (1957); A. H. Silver, *History of Messianic Speculation in Israel: From the First through the Seventeenth Centuries* (1959).

[M. R. P. MCGUIRE]

SHADDAI (El Shaddai), name for God in the Israelite patriarchal period (Gen 17.1). Translated in the LXX as the Almighty (*pantokrator*), it probably meant "god of the mountains." In the time of Moses, El Shaddai was identified with Yahweh (Ex 6.2–3). *GOD, NAMES OF.

[T. EARLY]

SHADRACH, MESHACH, ABEDNEGO, the Chaldaean or Babylonian names given by the chief chamberlain of the Babylonian king to Hananiah, Misael, and Azariah the legendary companions of Daniel and models of Hebrew piety whose story is related in Daniel. In the first story (ch. 1), these nobly born Hebrew children grow fatter and healthier than the other children fed at the king's table in spite of their refusal to eat unclean food (1.12–16). They also prove wiser than all the magicians and sages of Babylon (1.17–21), pray for Daniel's success in interpreting the king's dream (2.17–18), are made administrators in the Babylonian empire (2.49), and miraculously survive the ordeal of the fiery furnace after their heroic refusal to worship the king's idol (ch. 3).

[D. J. BOURKE]

SHAFTESBURY, ANTHONY ASHLEY COOPER, FIRST EARL OF (1621–83), political leader. One of the most influential figures in British politics of the 17th cent., S. early entered public life as an adherent of King Charles I but soon deserted the Royalists for the Parliamentary faction, for whom he commanded a force in the Civil War then raging. S. enjoyed the favor of the Protector, Oliver Cromwell, during the latter's ascendancy and was a member of the so-called Barebones Parliament. He broke with Cromwell over the dictatorship but was elected to the Parliament of 1656. Cromwell blocked his seating for a time, but he was able to take his proper place in the Parliament of 1658, where he proceeded to oppose reinstatement of the House of Lords. As member of the Rump Parliament of 1659, S. had opposed the Protector and labored to strengthen the powers of Parliament. By 1660 S. was openly involved in securing the return of the King, Charles II. Under Charles, S. served as a capable chancellor of the exchequer. Throughout his career he was a proponent of tolerance to dissidents, except Roman Catholics. He supported the Duke of Monmouth, illegitimate son of Charles II, as possible successor. In 1672 S. was made Earl of Shaftesbury. In that same year he was named Lord Chancellor. In 1673 S. supported the Test Act which excluded Catholics from public office. Shortly thereafter he was dismissed from the chancellorship although Charles offered him a dukedom as recompense. In 1672 S. was committed to the Tower as enemy of both King and Parliament. Released after some months, he gave support to a supposed "papist plot" against the King. In the struggle to exclude the Catholic James, Duke of York, from succession, he continued to plot for the Duke of Monmouth and to urge clearing the court of all Catholics. Member of the Privy Council, he supported in Parliament the bill to exclude James from the succession. S. accepted the fable of an Irish Catholic uprising and was responsible for the execution of St. Oliver *Plunket. In 1681 he was arrested again and committed to the Tower for high treason, but a grand jury acquitted him. He next turned to a conspiracy to overthrow Charles and place Monmouth on the throne in 1682 but had to flee to Holland where he died in 1683. Though he was a leading political figure of his age, with some dedication to representative government, his sacrifice of consistency to expediency, his savage hostility to rivals and the constant enmity he showed Catholicism argue a man of less than admirable character. Dryden's ferocious caricature in his satire *Absolam and Achitophel* is not without foundation in fact.

[J. R. AHERNE]

SHAFTESBURY, ANTHONY ASHLEY COOPER, THIRD EARL OF (1671–1713), English moral philosopher. Educated under the supervision of Locke, S. nevertheless rejected Locke's view that all that is in man is impressed on him from without. He was chiefly concerned with the repudiation of Hobbes' selfish individualism as a basis for ethics. He found in human nature itself a foundation for virtue, a connatural affection for virtue, a "moral sense" that recognizes and prefers goodness. He was the first to speak of a moral sense and is regarded as the founder of the moral sense school. He accepted the present feeling of pleasure as the motive for virtuous action, but he understood the pleasure in question to include the superior pleasure of acting in accordance with the affections of his moral sense. He did not see religion as necessary to morality. Though theistic in his outlook, he defended no specific religious doctrines and advocated freedom in the discussion of religious matters and would not exclude the use of wit and ridicule in such discussion. His writings, collected in *Characteristicks of Men, Manners, Opinions and Times* (1711), had immense popularity and influence in the early

18th century. BIBLIOGRAPHY: F. M. G. E. Higham, *Lord Shaftesbury* (1945); E. Sprague, EncPhil 7:428–430; Copleston 5:172–178.

[M. M. BARRY]

SHAFTESBURY, ANTHONY ASHLEY COOPER, SEVENTH EARL OF (1801–85), social reformer. A member of Parliament who refused many high offices in order to pursue social reforms in Parliament, C. spread himself over an incredible number of philanthropic projects. He pioneered in reform of the dreadful treatment of the insane. A good part of his life was devoted to improving the lot of workers. In 1842 he secured passage of a law to end child labor and labor by women in the mines. Another great success came to him with the establishment of so-called Ragged Schools for the education of poor children. He is chiefly responsible for passage of the Lodging House Act to provide decent housing for the masses. C. also labored for the abolition of slavery. His efforts represented the highest achievement of 19th-cent. humanitarianism.

[J. R. AHERNE]

SHAHAN, THOMAS JOSEPH (1857–1932), bp., rector of The Catholic Univ. of America (1909–28), founder of the National Shrine of the Immaculate Conception. He was born in New Hampshire, received his early education in Massachusetts, and in 1872 entered the Sulpician College, Montreal. He completed his theological studies in Rome, receiving a doctorate at the Propaganda, and was ordained for the Diocese of Hartford in 1882. He served as secretary to the bp. until 1888 when he was invited to teach at The Catholic University. He prepared himself by further graduate study in history at Berlin and Paris. From 1891 he taught church history and patrology at the university and lived a life dedicated to research. To this period belong his scholarly publications: *The Blessed Virgin in the Catacombs* (1892), *Giovanni Battista de Rossi* (1900), the *Beginnings of Christianity* (1903), and other works on ancient and medieval church history; he also translated O. *Bardenhewer's *Patrologie* (1908). He was a principal editor and contributor to the *Catholic Encyclopedia* and throughout his life remained devoted to the cause of scholarship. As rector of The Catholic Univ. he was responsible for both its academic and physical growth, improving the faculty and building many new buildings, most notably its library. During his rectorship he was consecrated (1914) titular bp. of Germanicopolis. In the same year he received approval from Pius X for the erection of the National Shrine; he devoted himself to raising funds for its building, but in his lifetime only the crypt church was completed (1931). Fittingly, he is buried there. He spent the years from 1928 in retirement, graced by many academic honors. BIBLIOGRAPHY: M. F. Egan, *Song in Stone to Mary* (1952), 284–289; R. J. Deferrari, NCE 13:156–157; P. J. McCormick, "Bishop Shahan: American Catholic Educator," CathEdRev 30 (1932) 257–265.

[T. C. O'BRIEN]

SHAHN, BEN (1898–1969). Lithuanian-American painter of forceful political and social commentaries (*Miners' Wives*). S. first attracted attention (1931–32) by 23 gouaches on the Sacco-Vanzetti trial (*The Passion of Sacco and Vanzetti*) and again in 1933, a series on the Tom Mooney case, all in his peculiarly personal style of strongly primitivized, and often symbolic, images and economy of detail. S. assisted D. Rivera in Rockefeller Center, worked on Federal Arts Projects (1930s and 1940s) becoming increasingly imaginative and acid in color. He produced books of moving and almost brutalized images, coupled with an expressive calligraphy, again highly personalized and destructive of accepted conventions, for such themes as Hiroshima and Nov. 22, 1963 (J.F. Kennedy's assassination). He produced many works of wit and humor also (e.g., *Almost Everyone Reads the Bulletin*). With many retrospective shows at home and abroad, S. remains a major artist of social commentary in our day. BIBLIOGRAPHY: J. T. Soby, *Ben Shahn: Paintings* (1963); *idem, Ben Shahn: His Graphic Work* (1963).

[M. J. DALY]

SHAKER HYMNS, the first hymns of the United Society of Believers in Christ's Second Appearing, the *Shakers, wordless tunes, a kind of droning or babble. Solemn songs based on psalm-tunes were then used. In the western branch a new wave of song, similar to that of the Kentucky Revival, arose. The first collection of Shaker hymns, the *Millennial Praises*, appeared in 1813. They reveal a true folk art. Used to accompany their lively rituals, the hymns reflect the thought and yearning of the whole group as well as of the individual. In their songs and operations of worship, the Shakers found release for their human longings and spiritual aspirations. BIBLIOGRAPHY: E. D. Andrews, *Gift to Be Simple, Songs, Dances and Ritual of the American Shakers* (1940).

[M. T. LEGGE]

SHAKERS (United Society of Believers in Christ's Second Appearing; Millennial Church), largest and most permanent of the 19th-cent. religious communal movements in the U.S.; the name was used because Shakers regarded physical trembling as a manifestation of inner spiritual experience. The phenomenon, which arose among the *Camisards of 17th-cent. France, was carried to England, where Quaker converts were called Shaking Quakers, or simply Shakers. In 1774 eight Shakers under the spiritual guidance of Mother Ann *Lee immigrated to New York and established a community at Watervliet in 1776. Although Shaker dogma drew heavily on Pietist thought, i.e., it was millennial, spiritualistic, and literal in its interpretation of the Bible, Mother Ann's teaching led the sect to its distinctive practice of celibacy. She taught that God was of a sexual nature, that the masculine had become manifest in Christ, and that a feminine spirit would continue the work of Christ. Presumably she identified herself as this feminine savior,

but this view was later modified. Before the American Civil War, 18 Shaker communities had a total membership of about 6,000. Since Shaker law forbade marriage, enrollment was kept up both by conversion and by the adoption of orphans. The Shakers not only maintained economic autonomy but also developed many articles for commercial distribution. Their interior furnishings, simple of line, became famous, and have been widely copied. In 1968, in communities at Sabbathday Lake, Me., and Canterbury, N.H., there were 15 Shakers. The remnant has declared the end of the Shaker mission with their own demise. BIBLIOGRAPHY: E. D. Andrews, *People Called Shakers* (1958); C. E. Robertson, *Concise History of the United Society of Believers Called Shakers* (1893, repr. 1975).

[B. BLACKLAW]

SHAKESPEARE, JOHN HOWARD (1857–1928), English Baptist preacher and organizer. S. served as pastor at Norwich for 15 years. In 1898 he became secretary of the Baptist Union and was chiefly responsible for founding the Baptist World Alliance (1905) and the Federal Council of the Free Churches (1919). He also succeeded in having Baptist and Congregational chaplains appointed to the British army. He wrote *Churches at the Cross Roads* (1918), a compelling argument for the reunion of Christendom.

[M. J. SUELZER]

SHAKESPEARE, WILLIAM (1564–1616), poet, playwright, and actor. It is assumed that S. attended Stratford Grammar School in Stratford-on-Avon where he was born, and there acquired knowledge of Latin, classical mythology, and history. In 1582 he married Anne Hathaway; to the couple were born Susanna, and twins, Hamnet, (d. 1596) and Judith. By 1592 S. was an actor and playwright in London (as evidenced by Robert Greene's envious comments in *A Groatsworth of Wit*); and by 1594 a member of a company of players known as the Lord Chamberlain's Men (under King James, the King's Men), with which company he remained. In 1597 he was prosperous enough to buy New Place in Stratford; and by 1598 he was a well-known playwright (Francis Meres recorded 12 of his plays in *Palladis Tamia*), an actor (in Ben Jonson's *Every Man in His Humor*), and a shareholder in the Globe Theatre on the Bankside of the Thames. His last years were spent in Stratford-on-Avon, where he was part-collector of the tithes. He left a signed will (now in Somerset House, London), dated March 25, 1616. He was buried in the chancel of Trinity Church, Stratford. In 1623, John Heminge and Henry Condell, surviving actors of the Chamberlain's Company, published the *First Folio*, which contained 36 of the 38 plays. This volume, together with the Greene and Meres evidence, supplies proof of S.'s authorship. Influenced by Christopher Marlowe in the use of blank verse and the development of the tragic hero, and by Thomas Kyd in plot construction, S. brought English drama to its peak.

His great tragedies (*Hamlet, Othello, King Lear, Macbeth*), his romantic comedies (*As You Like It, Much Ado About Nothing, Twelfth Night*), his histories (*Richard II, Henry IV, Richard III*), his tragicomedies (*Measure for Measure, Cymbeline*), and his dramatic romances (*Winter's Tale, The Tempest*), as well as his narrative poems (*Venus and Adonis* and *The Rape of Lucrece*) and the *Sonnets*, reveal his outstanding ability in various forms. His genius is reflected in his portrayal of character, his powerful imagery, and his mellifluous verse. Particularly notable are his idealism and his strong ethical concepts. For continuing bibliography, see *The Year's Work in English Studies* (1919–) and the June Bibliography of *Publications of the Modern Language Association* (New York). Nothing can be said with certainty about S.'s religious convictions and affiliation. Some of his family ties are known to have been Catholic and he was commonly sympathetic in his portrayal of religious characters and practices associated with the old religion, but there is no direct evidence that he himself practiced that faith. Best biographies are J. Q. Adams, *Life of William Shakespeare* (1923); E. K. Chambers, *William Shakespeare, A Study of Facts and Problems* (2 v., 1930). Complete works edited by Neilson and Hill (1942) and by G. B. Harrison (1952); and individual plays in the new Arden series (1951–) are recommended.

[M. M. WILLS]

SHAKTISM, any cultic devotion to the female principle of the Hindu universe. Specific mention of Shakti (lit., energy) refers to the power of the consort of the god Siva. The sexual union of Shakti-Siva represents the ultimate union of Energy and Being, though Shakti herself represents the One in her person, combining both male and female principles, her female aspect subsuming the male. More generally, Shakti indicates the female consort of any god. The female power complements the male in the divine unity, and it is through the consort that the deity's power is expressed. The consort often takes a name that reflects the god with whom she is associated, such as Brahmani, consort of Brahma. The goddess Shakti has variants of the thousand names of Siva as well as many specifically her own. Certain Shakti cults, such as the Asapuri, Mekhapanthi, Nayaka, and Vilana, which antedate the Aryan arrival in India, worship the female deity as supreme. The literature of this devotion is called Tantras or *Shaktagamas*. Shaktism and Tantrism are frequently used synonymously. Shakti is worshipped diversely as wife, sexual partner, mother, the female in general, the feminine in all things, the energies of sexual desire and joy; as the deity of illicit sexual relations like incest and adultery; and also as the terrible goddess of gore, death, and destruction, personified as Durga, Kali, and Bhavani. For devotional purposes, Shakti is usually represented as a yoni, an image of the female vagina or some other representational substitute, such as the smooth inner chamber of a mollusk or conch shell, invaginated stones, carvings, drawings incorporated into mandalas, or, in certain rituals, a nude woman who sits in front of the worshippers with her legs spread.

[R. J. LITZ]

SHALMANESER (Salmanasar), name of five Assyrian kings, including S. III (858–824 B.C.), first Assyrian king to come into contact with a king of Israel. Ahab contributed troops to an alliance that fought S. at Qarqar (853 B.C.). Shalmaneser V (727–722 B.C.), son of Tiglath-pileser III, besieged Samaria, but its fall is usually dated in the first year of the reign of his brother Sargon II (2 Kg 17.1–6).

[T. EARLY]

SHAMAN, SHAMANISM, an ecstatic whose ability to leave the body at will enables him to undertake a wide variety of religious tasks. By virtue of ecstatic travel, the shaman occupies a pivotal position as the link between heaven, earth, and the underworld. Where disease is conceived as loss of the soul, shamans are thought to be able to recover the soul and effect a cure. They are also thought to conduct sacrifices to the heavens and to lead the souls of the dead to their appropriate abodes. One becomes a shaman either by inheritance or by spontaneous vocation; in either case, the initial tendency must be confirmed and strengthened by a series of initiatory trials and by instruction in sacred traditions. Attempts have been made to link the shamanic vocation to a psychopathological disposition toward trance and dissociation. The shaman is the focus of the religious life of many peoples of Central and North Asia and plays a lesser role in many other societies. Some shamans typically appear in costumes whose components symbolize their diverse and impressive abilities (magical flight, mediation of the three cosmic zones, gathering of spirits, etc.). BIBLIOGRAPHY: M. Eliade, *Shamanism: Archaic Techniques of Ecstasy* (1964, tr. W. R. Trask).

[E. V. GALLAGHER]

SHAME, SENSE OF. (1) In a general sense, shame has been described as fear of a base action or condition and of the disgrace attached. It is associated with sin either as a fear of being caught in the act and so embarrassed or as an aspect of remorse or psychological guilt over a deed already done. Aristotle (*Ethics* II, 7; IV, 9) classifies it as a laudable emotion, but not as a virtue. St. Thomas Aquinas deals with it first as a form of fear (ThAq ST 1a2ae, 41.4), then as an adjunct of virtue (*ibid.* 2a2ae, 144). The connection with virtue in general is clear: the *honestas* characteristic of all virtue is uprightness, nobility of intent; withdrawal from the ignoble is the negative side of this. Thus one enured to sin is shameless, no longer having any sense of moral turpitude nor sensitivity to disgrace. There is a special connection of shame with temperance as a kind of emotional predisposition for what temperance puts into intended practice. This virtue keeps a person's appetites set on moderation and controlled against excesses that would debase an intelligent human being. But virtues that overcome fear can also moderate shame: where shame itself is exaggerated, so that fear of failure or even of attracting attention would deter a person from the pursuit of good and noble goals. (2) Shame in its most restricted sense can be referred to sexual *modesty or to purity, as the Lat. *pudicitia* (pudicity) etymologically suggests. There is an innate reticence and modesty about sex that enhance its use and restrain its abuse; there is, consequently, a virtue that in its negative function deliberately exercises restraint with regard to the many forms of sexual exposure: dress, comportment, physical contact. This virtue, purity or pudicity, safeguards the primary virtue, *chastity. The norms of this modesty are relative, in great measure dependent on convention and culture. But both prudery and lewdness are recognizably its extreme violations.

[T. C. O'BRIEN]

SHAMGAR (Samgar), Israelite "judge" or "deliverer" succeeding Ehud (Jg 3.31). Apparently only a fragment of the original story remains, giving no information except that he was the son of Anath and that he killed 600 Philistines, a feat similar to that of Samson (Jg 15.14–16) and Shammah (2 Sam 23.11–12). The name is not Semitic, but possibly Hurrian. S. was perhaps from the Canaanite town Bethanath, a Galilean town bearing the name of a Canaanite goddess Anath. The Song of Deborah mentions a S. (Jg 5.6), but the reference includes no information about him, only that "caravans ceased" during his time, apparently indicating a breakdown of law and order.

[T. EARLY]

SHAMMAI, see HILLEI AND SHAMMAI.

SHAMMAI, SCHOOL OF, followers of the Jewish scholar Shammai, who lived in the time of Herod the Great. Shammai and Hillel were the last of the five *zugoth,* pairs of scholars who transmitted the Pharisaic tradition. Little is known of Shammai except that he was a native of Judea and that he taught a rigorous interpretation of the law, in contrast to the more liberal Hillel. His school was perhaps founded before Hillel's since he is mentioned first in reports of their controversies. A dispute between the two schools lies behind the question on divorce put to Jesus (Mt 19.3), the school of Shammai insisting that only adultery was grounds for divorce.

[T. EARLY]

SHAMMÂS (minister), a common Arabic term designating: (1) a (hieratic) deacon; (2) a lesser cleric or a layman ministering in sacred rites, even in the role of an absent deacon. The *shammâs* in the latter sense is often called a subdeacon in Western languages. He wears the stole in the manner traditionally that of a subdeacon, but he is not a subdeacon in the strict sense.

[A. CODY]

SHAMMĀSHĀ, Syriac word used by the East Syrians in reference to the deacon in the strict sense. *MᵉSHAMMSHONO*

[A. CODY]

SHAMMASHUTĀ, East Syrian liturgical booklet containing the texts proper to the deacon, extracted from the *taksā.*

[A. CODY]

SHANKARA (*c.*788–*c.*820), Indian religious teacher, regarded by many as India's greatest philosopher. As the foremost representative of the *Vedanta system of Indian thought, he wrote commentaries on the *Upanishads, the *Vedanta Sutras,* and the *Bhagavad Gita.* His teaching, which was not intended as speculation, but as directed toward salvation or the liberation (moksha) of the self, is extensive and subtle, but there are some major emphases. Ultimately, the absolute transcendent reality (*Brahman) and the self at its deepest level (*atman: the transcendent ground of experience) are one and identical. Thus Shankara's version of Vedanta is called advaita (the nondualist position). Brahman and the ultimate self (together with the whole phenomenal world) only appear to be distinct because of ignorance (avidya) or a kind of inevitable illusion (maya). This is how things are perceived ordinarily, according to a lower, phenomenal level of knowledge or consciousness. Moksha or liberation is to be achieved through a higher inward knowledge or realization (jnana), a pure consciousness, transcending the dichotomy of subjective and objective, aided by the ultimately valid wisdom of the Upanishads. BIBLIOGRAPHY: S. N. Dasgupta, *History of Indian Philosophy*, v. 1–3 (1951–52); T. Organ, *Hinduism* (1974) 97–124; 241–269; G. Thibaut, *Vedanta-Sutras with the Commentary by Shankaracarya (Sacred Books of the East* v. 34, 38, 1904).

[D. P. EFROYMSON]

SHAPCOTE, LAURENCE (1864–1946), English Dominican, administrator, missionary. Born in the Orange Free State, S. was educated in France and Spain, elected provincial of the English Dominicans in 1904, and established his order in South Africa. He was the anonymous translator who singlehandedly produced the literal translation of Thomas Aquinas's *Summa theologica* (20 v., 1911–13) and the *Summa contra gentiles* (4 v., 1923) by "the English Dominican Fathers."

[T. GILBY]

SHAPED-NOTE HYMN, early American religious song using a system of solmization in which each of the four syllables, *fa, so, la, mi,* was represented by a different, shaded note head. Thirty-eight collections of such hymns were published in America in the first half of the 19th century. BIBLIOGRAPHY: W. J. Reynolds, *Survey of Christian Hymnody* (1963).

[M. T. LEGGE]

SHAPIK (W Arm., *shabig*), the Armenian liturgical tunic, like the Western alb or Byzantine sticharion. The *shapik* of the celebrant is always white. That of the deacon and of the lesser ministers may be of any color, with a darker piece, originally a shoulder-cape, applied over the shoulders in front and back; it also has the more specific name *patmoudjan*.

[A. CODY]

SHARAGAN (East Arm., sharakan), in the Armenian Church: (1) a hymn of several strophes, sometimes but not always metrical, sung in the Eucharistic Liturgy or in the Divine Office; (2) a hymnal containing such hymns for the Divine Office (but not those for the Eucharistic Liturgy, which are found in the *tagharan*).

[A. CODY]

SHARED TIME, a recent educational experiment with roots in the late 19th cent., in which pupils in private or parochial schools, by mutual administrative agreement, share such public school facilities as auditoriumn gymnasium, laboratories, and audio-visual equipment, yet attend classes in religious and academic subjects in their own school. It is based on the recognition of the rights and responsibilities of family, Church, and State in education, in opposition to the view that the State's right in education is total and that the complete secularization of education is desirable. Concerned with the need of taking some action against religious illiteracy, many look on shared time as a compromise solution that preserves intact the private and the public school, both of which are acknowledged to be necessary in a pluralistic democratic society. Some parents are opposed to the plan because it seems to them to encroach on their right to choose the education they wish for their children. Others consider it an undesirable weakening of emphasis on Catholic education. On the other hand, many of secularist persuasion object to it as a threat to public education. Although accepted in varying degrees in 25 to 30 states, shared time is still an isolated experiment with an uncertain future. BIBLIOGRAPHY: G. S. Reuter, Jr., ''Shared Time, a New Approach in American Education,'' *Congressional Record* (Feb. 1, 1962).

[M. B. MURPHY]

SHARIDEN (''Hall to store Sacred Ashes'') in the Japanese Zen temple Enkakuji, Kamakura (1281), the oldest (1285) and purest example of *karayō* (Chinese style) Zen architecture, becoming a model for all later Zen monasteries.

[M. J. DALY]

SHASHKEVYCH, MARKIIAN (1811–43), Ukrainian scholar and poet who made a major contribution to Ukrainian language and literature. He was ordained in 1838 in the Catholic Ukrainian rite. A member of the ''Ruthenian Trio,'' he studied native folklore and Ukrainian history. The Trio published a collection of poetry in 1833 called *Syn Rusi*, in which the essay, ''Word to Teachers of the Ruthenian Language,'' carried S.'s conviction that the literature of the Ukraine was their cultural responsibility. *Azbuka i abecadlo* (1836) was a defense of native literature. A poem *Rusalka Dnistrova* (1837) established S. as a considerable poet. In all his writings he promoted a renaissance of Ukrainian literature.

[J. R. AHERNE]

SHAW, GEORGE BERNARD (1856–1950), Irish dramatist, essayist, and critic. A long struggle with poverty developed an interest in socialism and he became a member of the Fabian Society. His major plays are dramas of ideas, chiefly concerned with need for change from dead systems and outworn morality to a vital approach to life. Before the Committee on Stage Censorship (1909), he claimed the right in a civilized society for complete freedom of thought. Many consider his finest play to be *Saint Joan*, revealing high comic powers with strong convictions. His lucid style, full of wit, flippancy, and a certain belittlement of serious issues is confusing for many. His master formula was ''Find the right thing to say, and then say it with the utmost levity.'' He has 36 volumes of collected works. BIBLIOGRAPHY: G. K. Chesterton, *George Bernard Shaw* (repr. 1926); H. Pearson, *George Bernard Shaw: A Full Length Portrait* (1942); C. B. Purdom, *Guide to Plays of George Bernard Shaw* (1963); M. Meisel, *Shaw and the 19th Century Theater* (1963); I. Brown, *Shaw and His Time* (1966).

[M. M. BARRY]

SHAXTON, NICHOLAS (*c.*1485–1556), bp. of Salisbury. He received his bishopric after approving Henry's divorce. He showed a remarkable talent for adapting his doctrinal position to changing circumstances and ended as suffragan to the bp. of Ely under Mary and examiner at the heresy trials. BIBLIOGRAPHY: DNB 17:1390–92.

[V. SAMPSON]

SHEA, JOHN DAWSON GILMARY (1824–92), American Church historian, editor. Though his life was a struggle against poverty, nothing has supplanted the fruits of his dedicated, meticulous scholarship in the writings of later historians. His admiration of Bancroft led him to write a series of articles in the *United States Catholic Magazine* in 1846 and 1847. Though admitted to the bar, he entered the Society of Jesus in 1848 but left in 1852. Meanwhile he had come under the influence of the Canadian Jesuit historian Felix Martin, author of the biography of St. Isaac Jogues, a work S. would translate into English many years later. In 1852 S. published *Discovery and Exploration of the Mississippi Valley,* which won him respect from historians. He was invited to become a corresponding member of the historical societies of Massachusetts, Maryland, and Wisconsin. There followed years of feverish writing necessitated by lack of money. An incredible number of magazine articles flowed from his pen, popular but well written. He wrote a number of historical textbooks for Catholic schools, contributed to encyclopedias, edited *The Library of American Linguistics* (1860–1874), and wrote a history of the archdiocese of New York for Abp. John J. Hughes. He was a cofounder of the American Catholic Historical Society which he served for a time as editor and president. In 1854 Shea published *History of the Catholic Missions among the Indian Tribes of the United States, 1529–1854,* and from 1857 to 1887 he edited 26 volumes of **Jesuit Relations.* His crowning achievement was the four-volume *History of the Catholic Church in the United States,* certainly the most considerable critical history of the American Church ever written. S.'s last years were marked by great poverty. He was not at any point in his life given the credit due him for his scholarship, even by Catholics. Though the Council of Baltimore in 1884 voted him some financial support, it was not sufficient. It is sad to contemplate thus outstanding professional historian of the American Church writing a letter to Abp. Michael Corrigan in 1889, begging for a clerkship.

[J. R. AHERNE]

SHEAR-JASHUB, symbolic name of Isaiah's son (Is 7.3; see also 8.18). Meaning "a remnant will return" (from exile), it could have been intended in the positive sense that the promise to David would be maintained (2 Sam 7.16), or in the negative sense that only a remnant would return (Is 10.22). *REMNANT OF ISRAEL.

[T. EARLY]

SHEBA, see SABA.

SHEBA, QUEEN OF, see SABA, QUEEN OF.

SHECHEM (Sichem), biblical name: (1) Hivite who raped Jacob's daughter Dinah (Gen ch. 34); (2) descendant of Joseph (Num 26.31); (3) son of Shemida, of the tribe of Manasseh (1 Chr 7.19); (4) Canaanite city that became an important Israelite center, modern Tell el-Balatah (Gen 12.6; Jos 24). Jacob bought land there from "the sons of Hamor, Shechem's father" (Gen 33.18–19; see also 35.4). Shechem was in the pass between Mounts Gerizim and Ebal, site of Israelite cultic ceremonies (Dt 27.11–26; Jos 8.30–35). Its importance ended when the northern capital was moved to Tirzah (1 Kg 12.1, 25; 15.33). *SYCHAR.

[T. EARLY]

SHEED, FRANK J. (1897–   ), publisher, lecturer, and theologian. An Australian by birth, S. spent most of his life in England and the United States. His early experience in public discussion and defense of Catholicism took him to Hyde Park in London and Union Square in New York and began a lifelong career on the lecture platform. With his wife Maisie Ward he launched the publishing house of Sheed and Ward in London, later branching out to New York. The house signalled a revolution in Catholic publishing. Under its imprint of a stag at running waters, the firm published giants of the English Catholic world and introduced great Continental writers to an English-speaking public totally unaware of their greatness. It could be said that this cross-fertilization created a renewal in Catholic thinking for the twentieth century. S. himself could write with the best of them. S.'s own *Communism and Man* (1945) was so objective in its unfolding of Marxist doctrine that it was used (in part) by Marxists themselves. *A Map of Life* (1944) is a lucid introduction to Catholicism. Two books, *Theology and Sanity* (1945) and *Society and Sanity* (1953), deserve to be read and reread. Though he never accepted the extremist viewpoint of some post-conciliar writers, he shows in *The Church and I* (1974) a Newmanesque acceptance of change that retains traditional theology. BIBLIOGRAPHY: W. Sheed, "Frank Sheed and Maisie Ward," *New York Times Book Review* (April 7, 1972).

[J. R. AHERNE]

SHEEHAN, PATRICK AUGUSTINE (1852–1913), Irish novelist. A native of Cork, he studied at Maynooth and was ordained in 1895. A succession of pastoral assignments brought him ultimately to Doneraile where he became the beloved "Canon of Doneraile." His early novels, *Geoffrey Austin, Student* (1895) and *The Triumph of Failure* (1898), are fine insights into the problems of young Irish Catholics. His most popular novel, *My New Curate,* appeared first in serial form in *The American Ecclesiastical Review* (1898 ff.) and is an astute study of Irish clerical life. *Luke Delmege* (1905) and *The Blindness of Dr. Grey* (1909) are well developed and compassionate stories that demonstrate S.'s awareness of the society of his times. His pictures of common folk in Ireland drew the admiration of Tolstoy. No other writer in English has shown greater understanding of clerics and given more realistic insight into their lives. BIBLIOGRAPHY: H. Heuser, *Canon Sheehan of Doneraile* (1917).

[J. R. AHERNE]

SHEEN, FULTON JOHN (1895–   ), abp., preacher, writer. The most celebrated preacher in the U.S. (if not the most notable orator generally) in the 20th cent., S. was the most widely known Catholic clergyman of the age. A native of Illinois, he was ordained in 1919 for the Diocese of Peoria, Illinois. After 5 years of study in Europe, he published *God and Intelligence* (1925), which was awarded the Card. Mercier International Prize for Philosophy by the Univ. of Louvain, the first such award to an American. In 1926 he became a member of the philosophy faculty at The

Catholic Univ. of America, and taught there for the next 24 years. His brilliant career as a preacher began in 1925 in England, continuing there over a period of 6 years. In the U.S. his fame grew through years when he was the Lenten preacher in New York at the Paulist church and St. Patrick's Cathedral, New York City. S. was the most popular speaker on the NBC Catholic Hour beginning in 1931; his addresses drew as many as 6,000 letters a day. Perhaps his greatest popular triumph occurred in the 1950s with the radio and television program *Life Is Worth Living,* a phenomenal success which made S. one of the best–known figures in television.

In 1950 he ended his teaching career at Catholic Univ. to become national director of the Society for the Propagation of the Faith and in 1951 was consecrated auxiliary bp. of New York. S. has been a lifelong and articulate foe of communism and a number of his books center on opposition to the philosophy and practice of communism, e.g., *Communism and Religion* (1937). His periodical articles and books constitute a vast outpouring, many of them collections of his addresses. Among his books were *The Life of All Living* (1929), *The Mystical Body of Christ* (1935), *Old Errors and New Labels* (1931), and *Preface to Religion* (1947). A man of extraordinary personal magnetism as well as keen intellect, S. was responsible for bringing a number of distinguished Americans into the Catholic Church. Among them were Heywood Broun, newspaper columnist, Claire Booth Luce, playwright and congresswoman, Jo Mielziner, scene designer for the theater, Fritz Kreisler, concert violinist, Henry Ford II, and Grace Moore, opera star. In 1966, S. was named bp. of Rochester, N.Y., a position from which he resigned in 1969. In retirement he received the personal title of archbishop. Few clerics have had his extraordinary influence on Catholics and non-Catholics in the U.S.

[J. R. AHERNE]

SHEERAN, JAMES B. (1819–81), Confederate chaplain. Born in Ireland, he came to the U.S. in 1833 by way of Canada. Married and a widower, S. taught at a Redemptorist school in Michigan before entering the order; he was ordained in 1858. At the Redemptorist church in New Orleans he became an ardent Southerner and secessionist. A Confederate chaplain in the Civil War, he served with the Army of Northern Virginia. His war journal is an invaluable eyewitness account of several of the great battles and of life as a Confederate soldier. After the war, S. served in New Orleans and ministered to the victims of yellow fever in the epidemic of 1867. Leaving the Redemptorists, he joined the Diocese of Newark, N.J., and served as a pastor.

[J. R. AHERNE]

SHᵉḤÎMŌ (Maronite *Shᵉḥîmtō;* Arab. *Sheḥîm*), West Syrian liturgical book containing the common texts of the Divine Office for ferial days.

[A. CODY]

SHEKINAH, the awesome and loving nearness of God to his people; the abiding presence. The word shekinah, from *shakan*, to dwell, does not occur in Scripture. It does occur in *Targum and in rabbinic commentaries on those biblical passages that treat of the ways in which God has made his presence felt: the ark of the covenant; the tent of meeting; the pillar of cloud by day, of fire by night. The rabbis would also use "shekinah" to explain such biblical ideas as God putting his name in a special place; or bidding the people to seek his face, his glory, his spirit. One rabbi taught that when two sit together, and words of the Law pass between them, the shekinah rests between them. This evokes the promise of Jesus in Mt 18.20 concerning his presence among those gathered in his name. An allusion to the shekinah is found in John's prologue: "The Word became flesh and dwelt among us . . . and we have beheld his glory . . ." The Greek word that is here translated "dwelt" could literally be "pitched his tent," and has the same consonantal structure as "shekinah": a poignant reminder of the Aramaic roots of John's Gospel. *OMNIPRESENCE OF GOD.

[E. J. DILLON]

SHEMA, ancient Jewish confession of faith made up of three passages from the Pentateuch: Dt 6.4–9; 11.12–21; and Num 15.37–41. It serves in the synagogue service in much the same way as the Creed does in Christian worship. It is also recited privately on other occasions by devout Orthodox Jews. The word is taken from *Shema Yisrael* (Hear, O Israel; Dt 6.4) with which the confession begins.

[P. K. MEAGHER]

SHEMONEH ESREH (eighteen benedictions), called also *tephillah* (prayer) and *amidah* (standing, because it is recited while standing), a form of daily community prayer in use among the Jewish people from *c.*200 B.C. Its form and structure varies somewhat according to the occasion (Sabbath, weekday, or festival), and it is incorporated as a central feature in various particular forms of prescribed prayer. The *shemoneh esreh* is thought to have exercised a formative influence on early Christian communal prayer, and through this upon the Divine Office.

[P. K. MEAGHER]

SHEN, PILLARS OF, impressive pair of pillars—funerary monuments from the Chinese Han period (206 B.C.–221 A.D.). They marked the entrance to the "spirit road" leading to the tomb mound of the official Shen, dated by inscription, in the form of lookout towers with pagoda roots carved in stone—the high relief under the eaves depicting horsemen and figures in combat, and Atlantean full forms at the corners; the superstructure supported on rectangular columns with low-relief animals of the four directions: tiger (W), dragon (E), phoenix (S), tortoise-snake (N). Extensive iconography and technical excellence determine the Pillars of Shen the finest funerary monuments from Han times.

[M. J. DALY]

SHENESIT-CHENOBOSKION, see CHENOBOSKION.

SHENOUTE OF ATRIPE (Schenoudi; d. *c*.450), abbot of the White Monastery in Egypt. S. entered this monastery as a child under the care of his uncle, the abbot, and became abbot himself *c*.383. He is reputed to have died at the age of 118, and during his long rule governed his monks and nuns, numbering up to 4,000, with an iron hand. Although never so venerated by the Church, S. was regarded outside his monastery as a saint, and his counsel was sought far and wide. His many journeys to combat heresy included one to the Council of *Ephesus with St. Cyril of Alexandria in 431. After *Pachomius, S. is the greatest organizer of Egyptian monasticism and the outstanding Christian Coptic author. Many sermons and letters are extant but not in a critical edition. Works, Lat. tr. H. Wiesmann, in CSCO 96, 109, 129 (1951–54). BIBLIOGRAPHY: A. G. Gibson, NCE 13:169–170; Quasten 3:185–187.

[R. B. ENO]

SHEOL, (ABODE OF THE DEAD). The Hebrew writings do not contain a formal doctrine of the dead since their fate was considered to be one of the secret things that belong to God. When the biblical tradition speaks of the dead, it uses the common poetry and symbolism of traditional Semitic folklore. The dead have an existence, but they forget their earthly life. They are accessible to God but do not experience his presence, so they do not praise him. They are bereft of earthly pleasures but also freed from earthly sorrow. They are in darkness and in silence, and although they retain earthly rank, they are weary and powerless. Their abode is called the ditch, the pit, the earth, the dust, the nethermost earth, ruin. Its location is sometimes under the earth, under the oceans, under the mountains, or in the West with the setting sun. Death is often personified as an insatiable demon with wide-open throat and gaping jaws. All this is the common folklore of the Semitic Near East. Sheol is the only Hebrew word for the abode of the dead that has no counterpart in other cognate languages. Perhaps it comes from the verb *saal,* to ask or inquire. It could originally have meant the place whence *oracles are sought. Nowhere is the abode of the dead described as a place of torment, a concept that came into Judaism during the Hellenistic period and probably derives from Persian dualism.

[E. J. DILLON]

SHEPEY, JOHN DE (d.1412), English canonist. A doctor of canon law at Oxford by 1367, he was an advocate of the court of Canterbury (1367), and dean of Lincoln (1378–1412). As king's clerk he served on various embassies. Of his writings, all that remain are some notes from 12 lectures at Oxford on the Decretals. BIBLIOGRAPHY: Emden Ox 3:1683–84.

[L. E. BOYLE]

SHEPHERD OF HERMAS, an early apocryphal apocalypse generally classified among the writings of the Apostolic Fathers. Nothing is known about the author apart from the scant biographical data contained in the book itself, and these are unreliable as historical evidence for they (including the author's name) are probably fictitiously devised to provide a setting for the revelations. The *Muratorian Fragment* declares that the author was a brother of Pope Pius I (d. *c*.154), although internal evidence suggests that he was a contemporary of St. *Clement I (d. *c*.101). Many modern scholars date the final redaction of the work *c*.150, but grant that its original form may have appeared as much as a half cent. before. Until the 4th cent. the work was widely accepted in the East as canonical Scripture, a prestige it did not enjoy in the West where already in the 2d cent. the Muratorian Canon rejected it. The work consists in a series of revelations made to Hermas by different heavenly visitors and is divided into visions, Commandments, and Parables (Similitudes). Against the rigoristic view then current, it shows that the forgiveness of post-baptismal sin is possible and it encourages sinners to do penance while there is yet time. Crit. ed. M. Whittaker, *Der Hirt des Hermas* (GCS 48, 1956). Tr. ed. J. Kleist (ACW 6, 1948). Text and tr. ed. K. Lake, Loeb (*Apostolic Fathers* 2). BIBLIOGRAPHY: S. Giet, *Hermas et les pasteurs* (1963).

[R. B. ENO]

SHEPPARD, HUGH RICHARD LAWRIE (1880–1937), Anglican vicar. S. became pastor of St. Martin-in-the-Fields, London, in 1914. His winning personality and religious enthusiasm endeared him to people in all walks of life, esp. after the development of radio. He was among the first to recognize the possibilities of religious broadcasting. His unique parish magazine, *St. Martin's Review,* made his church the best known in the British Empire. He was also active in church reform. He resigned his charge in 1926 because of illness, devoting the last years of his life to pacifism. BIBLIOGRAPHY: C. Jenkins, DNB 1931–40, 809–810.

[M. J. SUELZER]

SHEPTYTS'KYĬ, ANDRIĬ (1864–1944), Ukrainian metropolitan, bishop. A native of a former Ukrainian province, at that time incorporated in Poland, S. learned that he was not Polish and not a member of the Latin rite. In 1888 he became an Eastern rite monk in the Order of St. Basil the Great. For 7 years he taught theology and worked as a missionary. In 1898 he was named bp. of Stanislavov and in 1901 abp. of Lvov and Metropolitan of Galicia. S. ministered to Ukrainian Catholics, largest segment of Eastern Catholics, throughout the world. In 1907 he established a Greek Catholic diocese in the U.S. (now two dioceses) and in 1912 one in Canada. A number of parishes in Brazil owe their foundation to him. S. encouraged the study of Greek church history, liturgy, and the Fathers. For a time after the Revolution of 1917, it seemed that S. would effect a union of Ukrainian Orthodox and Rome, but the Bolshevik revolution ended the hope. Twice arrested, once by the Czarist regime and again by the Polish government, he was released. S. was responsible for the establishment of many institutions that served the Ukrainians.

[J. R. AHERNE]

SHERBERT *v.* **VERNER,** a decision of the Supreme Court of the U.S. (374 U.S. 398 [1963]), one of a series of stands taken by the court reflecting the problems involved in the interpretation of the First Amendment. The case began in the courts of South Carolina where the plaintiff contended that Adell Sherbert, a Seventh-Day Adventist, forfeited her right to unemployment compensation because on religious grounds she refused to work on Saturday. The majority opinion written by Mr. Justice Brennan held that the requirement to work on Saturday was an infringement of Sherbert's religious freedom. The minority opinion held that South Carolina could exempt such claimants from Saturday work but did not accept that the state was compelled to do so. Two points of interest emerge from *Sherbert v. Verner:* whether the state can be required to exempt persons from what the state regards as elements of public interest on grounds of religious belief; whether the decision departs from the no-aid-to-religion which the court has defended. The underlying assumption of the Sherbert decision is that aid to religion is acceptable so long as it does not include direct governmental involvement with religion. Jurists, however, do not find in the decision what may constitute involvement. BIBLIOGRAPHY: *Religion and the Public Order* (ed. D. Gianella, 1963) 3–40.

[J. R. AHERNE]

SHERBORNE, ABBEY OF, former Benedictine monastery in Sherborne, Dorset, England. When St. Aldhelm established a West Wessex see here in 705, with a church and school, there may already have been a house of secular canons dating from the time of King Cenwalh (643–674). In 978 Bp. Wulfsey introduced the Benedictine Rule, he himself becoming the first abbot. When Roger, bp. of Salisbury, joined the priory of Horton to Sherborne, he made Sherborne an exempt abbey (1122). Destroyed by fire and rebuilt in 1436, it was dissolved by Henry VIII in 1539. The townspeople purchased the abbey church for their parish church. The conventual buildings were added to the school, which was refounded in 1550 with a new charter from Edward VI. BIBLIOGRAPHY: Cottineau 2:3027.

[E. J. DILLON]

SHERIDAN, PHILIP HENRY (1831–88), Civil War general. One of the three outstanding Catholic generals in the Civil War (the others being General Sherman of the Union Army and General Beauregard of the Confederate) S. came of Irish immigrant stock. His career at West Point was a stormy one, interrupted by a year's suspension for moving against a cadet officer with a fixed bayonet. Returning, he was commissioned finally and began his military career. Early in the Civil War he became a colonel of cavalry and within a month, by reason of his brilliant command, he was promoted to brigadier-general. His magnificent charge at Missionary Ridge contributed importantly to Grant's victory, and was the beginning of lifelong friendship with Grant. The latter made S. commander of all the cavalry in the Army of the Potomac. The cavalry raids which he directed cut Confederate lines around Richmond and contributed significantly to the destruction of Lee's army. S., upon orders from Grant, devastated the Shenandoah Valley which for years had been a supply source for the Confederate forces. An incident celebrated in the poem "Sheridan's Ride" illustrates the magic of his leadership. S. was twenty miles away when Early's troops attacked and routed the cavalry at Cedar Creek. S. sped to the scene, reorganized the routed troops, and won the ultimate victory. His relentless pressure on the army of Lee led to the retreat and surrender at Appomattox. After the Civil War S. was a stern enforcer of the Reconstruction in Louisiana and Texas. Eventually, in 1884, he became commander-in-chief of the army and was named general of the army by Congress. S. was a brilliant cavalry officer with such devotion to the welfare of his troops that he earned their enthusiastic loyalty. BIBLIOGRAPHY: J. Hergesheimer, *Sheridan* (1931).

[J. R. AHERNE]

SHERMAN, ELLEN EWING (1824–88), wife of General William Tecumseh Sherman, but renowned herself for her active support of Catholic charities and missions. She was the daughter of a U.S. senator and cabinet minister, Thomas Ewing of Lancaster, Ohio. Married to Sherman in 1850, during both his years of failure before the Civil War and his success as a military man, she remained a steadfast wife and mother (six children) and devoted her energies to the work of the Church and its charities.

SHERMAN, THOMAS EWING (1856–1933), Jesuit priest, son of Ellen and General William T. Sherman. He had completed undergraduate and graduate studies when he joined the Jesuits. After ordination he became well known as a preacher of missions and a lecturer-apologist. From 1896 he was afflicted by periodic psychological collapses and from 1911 on he lived in virtual retirement from active work.

SHERMAN, WILLIAM TECUMSEH (1820–91), Civil War general. S.'s connection with Catholicism is tenuous, but a brief sketch of his career seems justified here. Taken in by the family of Thomas Ewing when his father died in S.'s 9th year, he was baptized. In his last hours he received the last rites of the Catholic Church. He seems not to have had affiliation with Catholicism during most of his life. S., dogged by failure in many fields, found his place in history as a Union officer in the Civil War. His years in the South and his love of Southerners made him deeply sympathetic, but his devotion to the Union was paramount. In the course of the War he became one of the ablest generals on the Union side. S. was the first modern general. He believed that the anguish of the conflict could only be ended by measures which would bring the war home to the supporting civilian population. His conquest of Atlanta and the march to the sea made him a hated figure in the Confederacy. S. himself tried to avoid involving civilians but he was unable to control many of the elements let loose by his campaign. After the Civil War he opposed the harsh Reconstruction Acts and strove to reconcile North and South by leniency. He succeeded Grant as commander-in-chief-of the army. A popular figure in the North, he steadfastly refused the nomination for the presidency. There is little question that he stands with Grant and Sheridan as one of the great generals of the Union in the Civil War. BIBLIOGRAPHY: B. H. Liddell Hart, *Sherman-Soldier, Realist, American* (1929); L. Lewis, *Sherman Fighting Prophet* (1932).

[J. R. AHERNE]

SHERWIN, RALPH, ST. (*c.* 1550–81), protomartyr of the English College, Rome. S. studied at Exeter College, Oxford, and, after being reconciled with the Church, at Douai where he was ordained (1577). He spent some time at the English College, Rome, but set out for England (1580) with Edmond *Campion and others. Within 4 months, S. was arrested; he was imprisoned in Marshalsea, tortured in the Tower, and executed at Tyburn. Leo XIII beatified him in 1886; he was canonized in 1970. BIBLIOGRAPHY: Butler 4:464–466; N. Del Re, BibSanct 11:1013–14. *MARTYRS OF ENGLAND AND WALES.

[T. M. MCFADDEN]

SHESHBAZZAR (Sassabasar), Babylonian Jew whom Cyrus made the first governor of post-exilic Judah (Ezra 1.11; 5.14). Cyrus gave him the temple vessels seized by Nebuchadnezzar (2 Kg 24.13; Ezra 1.7–8), and he began the rebuilding of the temple (Ezra 5.16). He was possibly the Shenazzar who was a son of the captured King Jeconiah (1 Chr 3.17), and thus an uncle of Zerubbabel (Hag 1.1; Ezra 5.1–2). Some scholars have suggested, however, that S. and Zerubbabel were the same person.

[T. EARLY]

SHIBBOLETH, in Jg 12.6, the password devised by the Gileadites, followers of *Jephthah, in order to identify the Ephraemites, who were unable to sound ''sh.'' The passage indicates a difference of dialect between eastern and western Palestinians.

[T. C. O'BRIEN]

SHIELDS, JAMES (1806–79), soldier, public official. A native of Ireland, he arrived in the U.S. in 1826 after undergoing shipwreck and settled in Illinois to practice law. His first military service was in the Black Hawk War. As state auditor he saved Illinois from bankruptcy. Charges against him traced to Miss Todd (future wife of Lincoln) and another caused S. to challenge Lincoln to a duel. The matter was settled off the field, and he and Lincoln became friends. Named to the Illinois Supreme Court, he proved a strong jurist. President Polk appointed him commissioner of the

land office in Washington, D.C. A brigadier general in the Mexican War, he served with distinction and suffered serious wounds. S. served in the U.S. Senate from 1849 to 1855. Accepting a land grant in Minnesota Territory, he encouraged Irish colonization there. The Civil War saw him involved as a brigadier-general compaigning in the Shenandoah Valley. S. was a sought-after lecturer on Irish affairs, charitable causes, and Catholic issues.

[J. R. AHERNE]

SHIELDS, THOMAS EDWARD (1862–1921), priest and educator. The son of Irish immigrants, S. studied at St. Francis Seminary, Wis., and St. Thomas Seminary, Minn., and was ordained in 1891. He received his doctorate in biology at Johns Hopkins University in 1895. From 1902 until his death, he was on the faculty of The Catholic University of America, first as instructor of psychology and from 1909 as chairman of the department of education, which he founded that same year. He also founded the first summer school for sisters, the Sisters' College, and the *Catholic Educational Review*. He wrote several textbooks on religion for Catholic schools connected with the University Affiliation Program, and authored *The Education of Our Girls* (1907); *The Making and Unmaking of a Dullard* (1909), the story of his youth; and *The Philosophy of Education* (1917). He is regarded as one of the foremost Catholic educators of his time. BIBLIOGRAPHY: J. Ward, *Thomas Edward Shields* (1947).

[M. B. MURPHY]

SHIITES (Arab., *shî'a*, which is abbreviated from *shî'atu 'Alî*, i.e., the party of Ali), a major division of *Islam, often referred to as the *Imâmîya* or Imamites, embracing almost all nonorthodox Muslims. Typically the Shiites hold that 'Alî ibn abî Ṭâlib, the cousin and son-in-law of *Mohammed, was his only proper and legitimate successor and that the spiritual leadership (the Imamate, see IMAM) of the Muslim community rests in his descendants. In varying degrees the Shiite sects see Ali as a supernatural figure (of greater importance than the Prophet) and hold that the Imamate is passed down to his descendants through specific designation *(nass)*, father to son. They hold in particular veneration Ali's younger son, Husayn (d. A.D. 680), whose death they celebrate as a quasi-salvific event. The earliest Shiite religious (as opposed to purely political) movement was of those who supported Mohammed ibn al-Ḥanafîya as the fourth Imam. Subsequently there arose the *Zaidis and the *Ismailis. The largest Shiite sect is known commonly as the ''Twelvers'' (in contrast to the ''Seveners,'' i.e., the Ismailis), since they hold that Mohammed al-Mahdî (874) was the 12th and last Imam. Though there has been considerable dispute over the series after Mûsâ al-Kâzim (d. 799), the series of Imams is usually given as: (1) Ali, (2) Hasan, son of Ali, (3) Husayn, son of Ali, (4) 'Alî Zain al-'Âbidîn, (5) Mohammed al-Bâqir, (6) Ja'far al-Ṣâdiq, (7) Mûsâ al-Kâzim, (8) 'Alî al-Riḍâ, (9) Mohammed al-Tâqî, (10) 'Alî al-Nâqî, (11) al-Ḥasan al-'Askarî, (12) Mohammed al-Mahdî. They hold that al-Mahdî did not die but still lives on earth, hidden, and will return at the end of the world to establish justice and announce the coming judgment. Since he is ''God's Light,'' which is creative, if he were to die, the world would, they say, be annihilated. The period of his hiddenness they divide into two parts, the first (the Lesser Hiddenness), that during which he communicated to the faithful through designated agents, the Safîrs, ending in 941, and the second (the Greater Hiddenness), which is to extend until his return, during which, lacking an Imam, they will practice neither *jihad nor perform the Friday prayer (see ISLAM). The present state religion of Iran is that of the Twelver Shiites. BIBLIOGRAPHY: D. M. Donaldson, *Shiite Religion* (1933); H. Laoust, *Les Schismes dans l'Islam* (1965). *ASSASSINS; *DRUSES; *FATIMIDS; *KARMATIANS; *NIZARIS; *NUSAIRIS.

[R. M. FRANK]

SHILOH (Silo), city where Israel's *ark of the covenant was kept from the time of Joshua to the time of Samuel. It was in the area allotted to Ephraim and E of the road running from Bethel north to Schechem (Jg 21.19). Excavations at the site, Khirbet Seilun, have revealed occupation from *c.* 2100 to *c.* 1600 B.C., but not from then until the time of the Israelites' coming (*c.* 1200 B.C.). It became a place of assembly for the Israelites after the Conquest, and they set up the tent of meeting there (Jos 18.1). After representatives went out from Shiloh to get descriptions of the land, Joshua cast lots there to apportion the areas for each tribe (Jos 18.8–10; 19.51). The Israelites gathered at Shiloh to make war (Jos 22.12), and they held a yearly religious feast there (Jg 21.19). The men of Benjamin obtained wives by seizing the ''daughters of Shiloh'' who came out to dance (Jg 21.21), perhaps in a fertility rite. Eli and his sons were priests at Shiloh, and Samuel's mother, making a regular visit there, was promised the birth of a son. She later brought Samuel to stay with Eli (1 Sam 1). Samuel received his vision and became known as a prophet at Shiloh (1 Sam 3). The ark was taken to Ebenezer during a battle with the Philistines, who captured it (1 Sam 4.1–11). When they returned it, the Israelites took it to Kiriath-jearim (1 Sam 7.2), and Shiloh ceased to be an Israelite shrine (Ps 78.60; Jer 7.12; see 1 Kg 14.2, however).

Christian interpreters, on the basis of some versions of the obscure prophecy in Gen 49.10 (see, e.g., King James Version) have often given Shiloh a Messianic association.

[T. EARLY]

SHINTO, the faith of 80,000 *jinja*, or Shinto shrines, an institutional adaptation of the archaic religion of Japan. Through many vicissitudes it has persisted as a major faith into the present. Shinto represents collectively the cultus of all these shrines. Each shrine is a repository of local customs of faith and festiva centering on the worship of the *kami*, or Shinto deity, who is patron of the locality. The real basis of Shinto is sociological. The *kami* of major shrines were originally patrons of clans and their territories. Worship in the average shrine today is offered mainly by persons who belong to families of which the deity of that shrine is considered patron. Certain shrines, however, have also developed a traditional clientele among members of various trades or persons with particular types of petitions. Others, like the Grand Shrine of Ise, patronal shrine of the imperial family, are considered appropriate pilgrimage sites for all. The *kami* of each shrine is not necessarily different. Although anciently this may have been the case, for various historical reasons the majority of shrines are now affiliated with one of several great ''families'' of shrines and consider their deities to be one with those of the mother shrine of the chain. Examples are the Inari system, distinguished by the colorful red gates and stone fox guardians of all its shrines and favored for prayers for prosperity; and the Hachiman system dedicated to a triad of deities, usually father, mother, and child. Each shrine is now locally governed by a board of lay trustees who elect the priest. Before World War II the incumbent was appointed by the government, and before the Meiji Restoration of 1868, priesthood was usually hereditary. Most shrines today are members of the national shrine association, which has endeavored to establish liturgical norms and to supervise clerical education.

The Shinto shrine edifice typically has an inner sanctuary where the token of the divine presence—a mirror, a sword, a stone, etc.—is kept behind closed doors. There is no physical representation of the deity, but a mirror and a wand or two with paper streamers as signs of divinity may be placed before the doors. The whole building is set in a yard containing a font for purification and a sacred tree. The precincts are demarcated from the workaday world by the *torii*, the characteristic Shinto gate. The essence of Shinto cannot be appreciated apart from the *matsuri* or festival. These colorful rites usually have two parts: the slow liturgical offering of foodstuffs and branches to the *kami* in the shrine, and a subsequent popular celebration, with a rapid carrying of the deity through the streets in a palanquin, a sacred dance, perhaps a communal meal, and carnival attractions. Apart from the festival, most shrines are continually visited by private worshipers.

Although the pattern of Shinto worship has remained quite stable through the centuries, its relation to the total culture has passed through many stages. The word Shinto (''The Way of the Gods'') seems to have been adopted early to distinguish the indigenous faith from Buddhism. Shinto institutions, both in the court and in the shrine system, were standardized in the early Middle Ages as means of preserving something of the archaic heritage in the face of the imported faith. But in practice Shinto and Buddhism developed a close interrelationship for 1000 years prior to the Meiji Restoration of 1868. The same priests commonly served both altars, and the *kami* were considered guardians or even manifestations of the Buddhas. However, Shinto and its myths (preserved in the *Kojiki,* 712 A.D., and the

Nihongi, 720 A.D.) bore the tradition of a divine origin and mission for Japan and the Imperial House. The royalist reformers and their intellectual precursors in the 19th cent. seized upon Shinto as a symbol and vehicle for their cause. A draconic purification of Shinto from Buddhist influence was effected in 1868, with Shinto acquiring a special place in the structure and ideology of the State. Shinto was declared "nonreligious," and shrines were regarded as sites for mandatory expression of loyalty to sovereign and State. In 1945 all relation between Shinto and the State was abolished.

Shinto thought has likewise found several voices from pantheistic idealism to ultranationalism. Contemporary Shinto thinkers seem to be moving away from these traditions to emphasize that the polytheism of Shinto can provide a symbol for a pluralistic, relativistic universe compatible with ideals of progress, cooperation, and situational ethics.

[R. S. ELLWOOD]

SHIPMAN, ANDREW JACKSON (1857–1915), lawyer, scholar, humanitarian. A native of Virginia, S. became a convert to Catholicism while a student at Georgetown College (1874–78). He worked as superintendent of mines in Ohio, where he became interested in the welfare of Slavic workers and learned their dialects. He became a champion of Greek Uniate and Ruthenian Catholics who found little help from Latin rite priests. Having earned a law degree at New York Univ., S. became a noted lawyer with special interest in labor cases and the business of Greek, Ruthenian, and Slavic peoples. S. was an expert in Eastern European languages and worked to bring Eastern rite clerics to serve the Catholics of that rite. He strove to bring understanding between the Orthodox Church and the Catholic Church. His writings on the Eastern Churches appeared in *The Catholic Encyclopedia* (1907–1914) and in many prominent magazines. In 1911 he made the first English translation of a Greek liturgical book, *The Holy Mass According to the Greek Rite.* S. was a friend and advocate of Bp. S. S. Ortynsky of the Ukrainian Catholic Church when most Latins suspected the orthodoxy of Ukrainian Catholics. BIBLIOGRAPHY: *Memorial of Andrew J. Shipman: His Life and Writings* (ed. C. Pallen, 1916).

[J. R. AHERNE]

SHIRLEY, JAMES (1596–1666), playwright, poet. Educated at Oxford and Cambridge, S. took Anglican orders and was appointed headmaster of St. Albans. He became a convert to Catholicism and shortly thereafter embarked on a long and productive career as a playwright. His audience was the court and its followers rather than the so-called common theater. S. was fluent and graceful, a poet of considerable gifts. If he was not of the stature of predecessors like Ben Jonson he was a skilled dramatist. Of the 31 extant plays he wrote, probably *The Cardinal* and *The Traitor* are best in the area of tragedy, and *The Lady of Pleasure* antici-

pates Restoration comedy. The closing of the theaters in 1642 by the Puritans ended a competent and prolific career in the theater. BIBLIOGRAPHY: A. H. Nason, *James Shirley, Dramatist* (1915).

[J. R. AHERNE]

SHIRWOOD, JOHN, (d. 1493), theologian, English humanist; archdeacon of Richmond 1465; bp. of Durham 1484–93; king's proctor at the Roman Curia under Edward IV; envoy to Rome for Richard III and Henry VII. A scholar with a knowledge of Greek, he amassed a very interesting library including Greek MSS and books. BIBLIOGRAPHY: Emden Ox 3:1692–93.

[C. D. ROSS]

SHITENNŌ SCULPTURES, 7th-cent. Japanese wood carvings in the Golden Hall of Hōrūji. The Shitennō Guardians of the Four Directions and the Law, standing on demons and carrying appropriate attributes, bear an inscription of Oguchi-no-Atai. Shallow drapery and the cylindrical forms of bodies bestow a spiritual serenity related to that of the Kudara Kannon in the same temple.

[M. J. DALY]

SHITENNŌJI, OSAKA, Japanese Buddhist temple built by Prince Shōtoku to the Four Guardians (Shitennō) in gratitude for victory (588). The original structure, greatly modified, still reveals the monastery pagoda, Golden Hall, and Lecture Hall in archaic N-S axial arrangement.

[M. J. DALY]

SHOFAR (SHOPHAR), ancient Hebrew instrument made from a ram's horn and used in Jewish worship down to the present day. It is the oldest type of horn for which there are authentic records. BIBLIOGRAPHY: H. W. Schwartz, *Story of Musical Instruments* (1941).

[M. T. LEGGE]

SHOLOKHOV, MIKHAIL ALEXANDROVICH (1905–), popular Soviet writer; regional novelist of the Don Cossacks, whom he portrays in nearly all his works. His masterpiece, *Tikhy Don* (The Quiet Don, 4 v., 1928–42; tr. 2 v., *And Quiet Flows the Don,* 1934, *The Don Flows Home to the Sea,* 1940), describes with realism and deep understanding the life of the Don Cossacks during World War I and the ensuing Revolution and Civil War. Like *War and Peace,* to which it has often been compared, the novel is both a family chronicle and a historical epic. It was awarded the Stalin Prize for literature in 1941 and has been hailed in the U.S.S.R and abroad as a classic of Soviet realism. It is unfortunate that ideological revisions by the author in 1953 and 1957 somewhat diminished the objectivity and lack of political partisanship that distinguished the novel in its original form. S. is also the author of several collections of short stories; a Five-Year Plan novel, *Virgin Soil Upturned* (1932–33), which is more valuable as a social document of the era of collectivization than as a novel; and a fragmentary war-novel about the defense of Stalingrad, *They Fought for Their Country* (1943–44; 1949–54). He was awarded the Nobel Prize for literature in 1965. BIBLIOGRAPHY: E. J. Simmons, *Russian Fiction and Soviet Ideology* (1958) 163–252; D. H. Stewart, *Mikhail Sholokhov* (1967).

[M. F. MCCARTHY]

SHORT SERVICE, see SERVICE (MUSIC).

SHORTER CATECHISM, one of the two *Westminster Catechisms, written in 1647; a Presbyterian *doctrinal standard.

[T. C. O'BRIEN]

SHORTHOUSE, JOSEPH HENRY (1834–1903), novelist. He was an English Quaker who embraced Anglicanism. S. became the unlikely author of a celebrated novel, *John Inglesant,* on religious and political intrigue in 17th-cent. England and Rome, as well as the religious experience of its hero. Affected by the Pre-Raphaelites and the Romanticism of the 19th cent. (1880), he worked on the novel for 10 years. A private printing brought it to the attention of Mrs. Humphrey Ward, who forwarded it to the head of the Macmillan Company. It was published by Macmillan in 1881. Success was immediate and S. became a famous literary celebrity. The novel has charm and fine delineation of scene but has many deficiencies, and some of it was plagiarized. S. published also *Sir Percival* (1886), *Little Schoolmaster Mark* (1883), and *Countess Eve* (1888), all minor works.

[J. R. AHERNE]

SHOURTCHAR, an Eastern liturgical vestment similar to the chasuble used in the Latin rite, though resembling the full cope without its head. It is the outer vestment worn by a priest of the Armenian rite when celebrating Mass. Its colors do not vary according to the different liturgical seasons, as do vestments in the Western Churches, but the shourtchar is of a brilliant color for joyous celebrations at Easter and of a somber color for penitential celebrations during Lent. BIBLIOGRAPHY: L. Arakelian, *Armenian Liturgy with an Outline of Armenian Church History* (1951); N. Liesel, *Eucharistic Liturgies of the Eastern Churches* (1963).

[R. A. TODD]

SHOWBREAD (Shewbread in the AV), bread placed on a table before Yahweh in the tabernacle and temple. The Kohathites, a group of Levites, prepared it every Sabbath (1 Chr 9.32), setting it on a golden table (2 Chr 13.11). It was also called bread of the presence—literally, bread of the face (Ex 25.30; 1 Sam 21.6; 1 Kg 7.48), the continual bread (Num 4.7), and holy bread (1 Sam 21.4). Twelve loaves were placed on the table each Sabbath, with the priests eating the bread as it was replaced (Lev 24.5–9; but see 1 Sam 21.1–6; Mk 2.25–26).

[T. EARLY]

SHRIFT, a word, now obsolete, formerly used to signify a penance imposed in sacramental confession. Such a penance normally implied absolution, and hence the word came to be used for absolution and for the sacrament of penance itself.

[P. K. MEAGHER]

SHRINE OF OUR LADY OF MARTYRS (Auriesville, N.Y.), the national shrine of the *North American Martyrs, SS. Isaac Jogues, René Goupil, and John Lalande. It stands on the site of the Mohawk village where Ven. Kateri Tekakwitha was born, W of Albany, New York. Opened in 1884 by the Jesuits, it now comprises 600 acres with chapels, shrines, and a spacious coliseum. The shrine honors the place where the first American martyr, René Goupil, was executed by the Iroquois in 1642. His companion Isaac Jogues escaped from imprisonment and returned as a missionary with the lay associate, John Lalande, in 1646; the two were martyred that same year. The three martyrs were canonized in 1930.

[J. R. AHERNE]

SHRIVE, an obsolete word meaning to impose sacramental penance upon someone, and hence to give absolution, to administer the sacrament of penance, to hear a confession. In the passive it means to make one's confession.

[P. K. MEAGHER]

SHROUD, HOLY, the famous relic preserved and venerated since 1578 in Turin, Italy, and believed to be the actual burial cloth of Jesus; it is sometimes called the Shroud of Turin. Tests to date show that the two images, the front and back of the human body of a 6-foot tall male, are not likely to be the work of an artist. The images are true negatives and date from before the discovery of photography had made men familiar with the characteristics of a negative image. Therefore it is far more likely that they are the result of the chemical reaction of powdered aloes sprinkled on the cloth and urea in the sweat that covered the dead body. Accordingly, the imprint would have been left by a body beaten from head to foot, whose head was pierced in many places, whose hands and feet had been pierced, whose side had been pierced, and whose eyes were closed in death. There are indications of rigor mortis. Carbon 14 tests for the exact dating of the shroud will be necessary to answer conjectures that some unfortunate victim, centuries after Jesus, may have been maltreated in the way Christ was during his Passion, to simulate the wounds of Christ. There is no reference to a shroud during the early Christian era. References to a shroud with the imprints of the Passion of Christ are found in the Mozarabic rite, and may date from the 7th century. Replicas of such a shroud have been used in the

Byzantine liturgy from the 7th cent. to the present day. In the 12th cent. it was believed that the original shroud was preserved in the imperial palace in Constantinople. During the Crusades this much revered relic may have been brought to France at a time when the fall of Constantinople to the Orientals was feared imminent. It eventually came into the custody of the House of Savoy and was moved to Turin in 1578.

[E. J. DILLON]

SHROVE, an obsolete word, probably connected with *shrive, used in reference to the Sunday, Monday, and esp. the Tuesday immediately preceding Ash Wednesday. These days made up what was known as Shrovetide, no doubt because of the custom of going to confession in preparation for Lent.

[P. K. MEAGHER]

SHUNEM (Sunem), town of Issachar (Jos 19.18) where the Philistines encamped before the battle of Mount Gilboa (1 Sam 28.4).

[D. J. BOURKE]

SHUNNING, in Mennonite usage another term for the penalty of *avoidance, a consequence of excommunication.

[T. C. O'BRIEN]

SHÛSHEPPŌ (East Syrian, *shûsheppā*), the generic name for any (covering) veil in Syriac. It is the word used always by East Syrians, and occasionally by West Syrians, for the veil covering chalice and paten which is normally called the *annaphûrō* by the West Syrians.

[A. CODY]

SHUWAIRITE ORDER, see BASILIAN ORDERS OF MEL-KITE RITE.

SIAM, see THAILAND.

SIBERT OF BEKA (d. 1332), Carmelite theologian. Having become a Carmelite *c.*1280, he served as prior at Geldern and Cologne. In 1318–20 he was regent of theology at the Univ. of Paris where he had received his master's degree. He served three terms as provincial prior in Germany. In 1326 he had the bull *Super cathedram* extended to the Carmelites; this gave them the privilege of preaching and hearing confessions. S. headed the commission investigating the charges against Meister Eckhart. In the struggle between John XXII and the Emperor Louis IV, he supported the former by his tract refuting the *Defensor pacis* of Marsilius of Padua. His other writings include an ordinal adopted by the Carmelite general chapter and used for 200 years. BIBLIOGRAPHY: D. Andreini, NCE 13 189–190.

[M. J. FINNEGAN]

SIBYLLINA BISCOSSI, BL. (1287–1367), Dominican tertiary. In her childhood Sibyllina was a servant. Becoming blind at 12, she was received by the Dominican tertiaries. Later with a companion she lived in a cell next to the church. During her long life she practiced severe penances and counseled many persons. S. was beatified by Pius IX and is the patron of servant girls in Italy. BIBLIOGRAPHY: Butler 1:665–666; P. Lazzarini, BiblSanct 3:196; M. J. Finnegan, NCE 13:190.

[M. J. FINNEGAN]

SIBYLLINE ORACLES, responses given by a priestess inspired by a god, usually Apollo, to questions submitted to her. The name is from a supposed ecstatic woman called Sibyl and originated in Asia Minor; evidence suggests high antiquity for the Sibyl's origin. The term came to refer to various Sibyls, prophetesses, the most famous and consulted of whom were the Sibyl of Delphi and the Sibyl of Cumae. Throughout late antiquity collections of Sibylline Oracles were widely circulated and figured in Roman politics. Virgil (*Eclogus* VI) relies on the Cumaean Sibyl's authority for his prediction of the advent of a messianic child. A collection of her oracles was kept at Rome and consulted during times of stress. In a more specific sense "Sibylline Oracles" is the title given to 14 books in Greek hexameter composed by anonymous Jews and Christians during the period from the 2d cent. B.C. to the 2d cent. A.D., dealing with historical, political, and religious matters in a frequently unintelligible manner. They had an influence on liturgical hymns, literature, and art during the Middle Ages and Renaissance. BIBLIOGRAPHY: *Oracula sibyllina* (ed. J. Geffken, 1902); *New Testament Apocrypha* (ed., McL. Wilson, tr. A. J. B. Higgins et al., v. 2, 1965).

[M. J. COSTELLOE]

SICARD, CLAUDE (1677–1727), French Jesuit missionary. S. worked in Syria (1706–08) and then in Egypt, where he sought to win Copts to union with Rome. His letters and the reports of his journeys to Upper Egypt, the Delta, and Sinai are valuable for archeology, natural history, ethnology, and the history of monasticism. BIBLIOGRAPHY: H. L. Müller, LTK 9:730.

[M. J. SUELZER]

SICARDUS OF CREMONA (*c.*1150–1215), canonist, historian, liturgist, bishop. Apart from a distinguished career as bp. of Cremona, where he won independence for the city from Frederick Barbarossa and built fortifications, S. was a prolific writer. Some early works are not extant, but his surviving writings show him to have been a man of wide interests. He wrote an influential work of liturgy, *Mitrale*, in 1200; in 1213 he completed a *Chronica universalis*, the earliest Italian example of a history beginning from the creation. Primarily he was a canonist. His *Summa decretorum*, written at Mainz, was the fruit of about 10 years spent teaching at Paris. His great merit is that he was one of the first to break away from the rigid divisions of Gratian's *Decretum*, which hitherto few had dared tamper with. By a use of *Distinctiones*, S. was able to dwell upon and develop points within Gratian's text; by a use of the *Quaestio* method, he was enabled to pick out certain topics in the *Decretum* and to give them a fuller treatment than was normally possible in more rigid commentaries. BIBLIOGRA-PHY: E. Brocchieri, *Sicardo di Cremona e la sua opera letteraria* (1958); L. E. Boyle, NCE 13:190–191.

[L. E. BOYLE]

SICHAR, see SYCHAR.

SICHEM, see SHECHEM.

SICILIAN VESPERS, the revolt (1282) which politically separated the "Two Sicilies"—the island itself and the realm of Naples—for more than 2 centuries. It was directed against French colonization and the fiscal rigors of Charles of Anjou, who had extinguished the *Hohenstaufen cause on the mainland. The actual outbreak, which was unpremeditated, was sparked off by a fracas when a French soldier allegedly molested a young married woman outside a church near Palermo when the bell was ringing for Vespers on Easter Tuesday. It spread like wildfire round the island, and thousands of the Angevin party were massacred. Charles was on the point of mounting an expedition against the Eastern Empire, and was unsuccessful in the war that followed; the free communes of Sicily submitted to the feudal domination of Pedro III of Aragon, who, supported by Byzantium though opposed by the Pope, successfully established the Aragonese dynasty. BIBLIOGRAPHY: S. Runciman, *Sicilian Vespers* (1958).

[T. GILBY]

SICILY, Italian island, off the SW "toe" of mainland Calabria; the largest island of the Mediterranean. Phoenicians had bases in Sicily from the 8th cent. B.C., and Greek colonies were established shortly thereafter. Rome took Sicily in the first Punic War (264–241 B.C.). Paul stopped at the W port city of Syracuse on his voyage to Rome (Acts 28.12), but the origins of Christianity on the island are not clearly known. It had several bishoprics in the 3d cent. and took an active part in 4th–cent. controversies over Donatism and Arianism. After conquest by the Vandals in 455 and Theodoric the Goth in 491, it was taken by Belisarius in 535 and held by the Byzantines for 3 centuries. The bp. of Rome had extensive properties in Sicily, and in the 7th cent. several popes were Sicilian. But Emperor Leo III (717–741) transferred the Sicilian Church to the jurisdiction of Constantinople. Through wars lasting from 827 to 902, the Arabs took Sicily but lost it to the Normans in the 11th century. From his base in Sicily, Charles of Anjou attempted to conquer Constantinople but had to desist after the *Sicilian Vespers (1282). After various changes of sovereignty, Sicily was ruled by the Bourbons of Naples until taken by Garibaldi in 1860.

[T. EARLY]

SICK, APOSTOLATE OF THE, see APOSTOLATE OF THE SICK.

SICK, OIL OF THE, see OILS, HOLY.

SICKENBERGER, JOSEPH (1872–1945), German biblical scholar, patrologist. S. was ordained in 1896. He taught patrology and exegesis at the Univ. of Munich, Würzburg, and Breslau. A number of articles in *Biblische Zeitschrift* between 1903 and 1929, as well as his longer works, established him as a leading exponent of the two-source theory of biblical exegesis. Among his writings are: *Commentary on First and Second Corinthians and Epistle to the Romans* (1919); *Explanation of the Apocalypse of John* (1942); and *Short Introduction to the New Testament* (1916).

[J. R. AHERNE]

SICKINGEN, FRANZ VON (1481–1523), German knight, Reformation figure. As a humanist polemicist, he defended J. *Reuchlin on the eve of the Reformation. His enthusiasm for Luther's ideas was more politically than religiously motivated. He became the leader of a financial and military alliance of German knights against the cities, and fell in battle against the forces of the Swabian League at his castle in Landstuhl.

[T. EARLY]

SIDGWICK, HENRY (1838–1900), English philosopher of broad interests, but known chiefly for his work in the field of ethics. A native of Yorkshire, S. was educated at Rugby and at Trinity College, Cambridge, where he taught classics and, after 1869, philosophy, esp. ethics. He is remembered less for his original contributions to moral theory than for his critical analyses of British ethical thinking, chiefly in its intuitionist, utilitarian, and egoistic forms. Though he held that moral science should reach its conclusions through reason, he nevertheless believed that the type of effort the human mind has made to define the ideal of rational behavior must end in failure, because all such historical attempts depend for their unity and coherence upon the existence of some supreme power which rewards or punishes. Evidence for the existence of such a power, in S.'s judgment, was not to be found. S.'s two most influential works were: *Methods of Ethics* (1874) and *Outlines of the History of Ethics* (1886). BIBLIOGRAPHY: C. D. Broad, *Five Types of Ethical Theory* (1930); idem, *Ethics and the History of Philosophy* (1952); J. B. Schneewind, EncPhil 7:434–436.

SIDNEY, SIR PHILIP (1554–86), English Renaissance gentleman, courtier, and man of action. Of aristocratic background, a courtier with strong Puritan leanings, S. was sent by Elizabeth I on many diplomatic missions, banished by her for opposition to her prospective marriage, reconciled, knighted in 1583, and died of wounds at Zutphen. He exhibits the early Renaissance attitude toward learning as a means to fashion a gentleman for active life. Sidney viewed the poet (*An Apology for Poetry,* c.1583) as a moral teacher stronger than the historian or philosopher since the poet could charm and so lead to virtuous living. He objected to the popular taste of his time in poetry and drama as morally dangerous. For S. all writing was a great vocation which transfigured ordinary experience in the light of his Platonic and Christian view of perfection. Works: ed. A. Feuillerat, 4 v. (1912–26). BIBLIOGRAPHY: M. W. Wallace, *Life of Sir Philip Sidney* (1915).

[M. M. BARRY]

SIDON, a Phoenician city situated on the Mediterranean coast about 25 miles N of Tyre. In biblical genealogies Sidon is listed as the firstborn of Canaan, attesting to its prestige and antiquity. It was a center for fishing and trade, and famous for its purple dye derived from the murex shells that abound along the coast. From the Amarna Letters (Tell el Amarna) one learns of Sidon's attempts to be independent of Pharaoh; and in succeeding centuries Sidon maintained an independence in the face of successive invasions by Hittites, Hapiru, and "Sea Peoples." The biblical narratives often link Tyre and Sidon as near neighbors who yet were never under Israelite control. Both cities received the brunt of the doom oracles of Israel's Prophets because of perceived arrogance and the seductive and corrupting influence of the Phoenician religion centered on a cult of fertility, involving the male and female deities Baal and Astarte. The Assyrians succeeded in bringing both these cities under tribute. Under Esarhaddon the Assyrians went further and destroyed Sidon in 677 B.C. They attempted to repopulate it with people deported from the Persian Gulf area. But the city survived, maintaining its identity through successive dominations by the Egyptians, Babylonians, and Persians. A terrible destruction was brought upon the city by their unsuccessful revolt against the Persians in the mid-4th cent. B.C., and in the year 351 B.C., 40,000 Sidonians lost their lives. This sent shockwaves through Phoenicia, and when it came the Greeks' turn at empire 18 years later, Sidon surrendered to Alexander without battle in 333. After the Greeks came Seleucid and then Roman rule. During the latter period Jesus visited the area of Tyre and Sidon, preached there (Lk 6.17), and discovered the great faith of the Syro-Phoenician woman who asked "to eat the crumbs that fall from the children's table" (Mk 7.24, 31). Jesus foresaw a more favorable judgment for these Phoenician cities than for the cities of Galilee where so many wonders had been performed (Mt 11.21–22).

[E. J. DILLON]

SIDONIUS APOLLINARIS, ST. (c.432–c.480), bp. and poet. Born of a prominent Christian family in Gaul, he received a sound classical education in Lyons, Arles, and Vienne where he had Claudianus Mamertus as a teacher and friend. He married c.450 and began a political career, helped in its earlier stages by the fact that his wife was the daughter of Avitus, prefect of Gaul and later, (455–456) emperor. After the overthrow of Avitus he managed to prosper politically through several changes of government. He was elected bp. of the city now known as Clermont-Ferrand, probably in the hope that he would be useful against the Visigoths under Euric. However, the city fell in 475, and S. was banished till the following year when he returned and resumed his duties. He was a good bp., fostering monastic life and using his wealth generously in helping the poor. Before becoming bp. he wrote 24 poems that have survived. These, although done in correct style and in good Latin, are not greatly esteemed as poetry. A collection of 147 of his letters is also extant and is of some value for its contribution to the picture of the times. Works: PL 58:435–752; text and tr. ed. W. Anderson, Loeb (1936). BIBLIOGRAPHY: Altaner 598–599.

[R. B. ENO]

SIEDENBURG, FREDERIC (1872–1939). A native of Ohio, S. entered the Jesuits and was ordained in 1907. In 1914 he founded the first American Catholic school of social work at Loyola Univ. of Chicago and was its dean for the ensuing 18 years. He was a director of the National Catholic Welfare Conference, member of the National Conference of Catholic Charities, and the Illinois Board of Public Welfare and Social Work; S. also founded and was president of the Illinois Catholic Historical Society. Later he was named chairman of the Detroit Regional Labor Board and president of the Michigan Conference of Social Service. He made notable contributions to the professionalization of Catholic social work.

[J. R. AHERNE]

SIEGBURG, ABBEY OF, Benedictine abbey of St. Michael and St. Maurice, located on Michaelsberg in the town of Siegburg, which grew up around it, in North Rhine (Westphalia), at the influx of the Agger River into the Sieg River, just NE of Bonn, West Germany. Founded 1064 by St. Anno, abp. of Cologne, it was colonized by Frutturia, suppressed in 1802, and restored by the congregation of Subiaco in 1914. BIBLIOGRAPHY: Cottineau 2:3029–30.

[E. J. DILLON]

SIENKIEWICZ, HENRYK (1846–1916), novelist. Born in Poland, S. studied philology. His career in journalism carried him through Europe to Canada and the U.S. Though his style is realistic, S. was essentially a romanticist who celebrated Poland's historic past. He became an encouraging voice to his fellow Poles, subjugated by Russia. Through the novels, S. became a world figure in literature, winning the Nobel Prize in 1905. After writing a number of short stories, he published a trilogy: *With Fire and Sword* (tr. 1890), *Deluge* (tr. 1891), and *Pan Michael* (tr. 1893). Set in the time of Poland's greatness in the 17th cent., they became a patriotic statement. His most famous novel, *Quo Vadis* (tr. 1896) quickly became a world classic. S.'s *Knights of the Cross* (tr. 1900) was based on the conflict between Poland and the Teutonic Knights in the 15th century. His collected works run to 81 volumes.

[J. R. AHERNE]

SIEYÈS, EMMANUEL JOSEPH (1748–1836), French Revolutionary leader. Ordained a priest in 1773, though a skeptic, S. had a rapid rise, becoming councilor for the Estate of the Clergy. A bitter foe of aristocrats and the monarchy, he wrote a pamphlet, *What Is the Third Estate?* (1789) that contributed to popular dislike of the nobility. Elected a deputy from Paris, he helped turn the Estates General into the National Assembly. He managed to survive the Reign of Terror and with the fall of Robespierre reentered public life in 1795. He became a member of the Committee of Public Safety and the Council of Five Hundred. S. took part in peace negotiations with the Dutch and as minister to Prussia assured Prussian neutrality. Finally, as a member of the Directory, the executive arm of government, he engaged in a *coup d'état* with Bonaparte, who then assumed dictatorial powers. Napoleon adopted S.'s views on vesting authority in the ruler. Named president of the senate and a count of the empire, he was forced into exile when Napoleon fell in 1815. After the Revolution of 1830 he returned to Paris.

[J. R. AHERNE]

SIFFRIN, PETER (1886–1963), German Benedictine liturgist who made a complete alphabetical index of the *initia* of the Latin prayers of the medieval liturgical books. He also collaborated with K. Mohlberg in editing the Leonine and Gelasian sacramentaries, the *Missale Francorum,* the *Missale Gallicanum vetus,* and the *Missale Gothicum.* He produced helpful concordances for these sacramentaries. BIBLIOGRAPHY: L. Eizenhöfer, EphemLiturg 78 (1964) 63–65; *idem.* NCE 13:204.

[N. KOLLAR]

SIGEBERT OF AUSTRASIA, ST. (631–656), Merovingian king. On the death of his father, Dagobert I, S. succeeded to the throne of Austrasia (638); his brother Clovis ruled the rest of the Frankish kingdom. An attempt to put down a revolt in Thuringia ended disastrously for Sigebert and his army. He seems to have been zealous in founding churches and monasteries and in good works for the poor. BIBLIOGRAPHY: K. Kunze, BiblSanct 11:1035–37; Butler 1:229.

[G. M. COOK]

SIGEBERT OF GEMBLOUX (c. 1030–1112), historian and hagiographer. S. entered the monastic life as a child, was schooled by Abbot Olbert (d. 1048), and soon went to Metz where for two decades he taught school and began writing with the *Lives* of the saints of Metz. In 1070 when he returned to Gembloux, he began to write local history and hagiography. *The Passion of the Theban Martyr Legion* in hexameters, *Life* of Wicbert, the *Gesta,* the *Chronica,* and the *De viris illustribus* are from this period, the last two often considered his best works. At the time of his death he was an influential writer from the Northern group that was hostile to the reforms of Gregory VII and was strongly royalist. BIBLIOGRAPHY: S. Williams, NCE 13:204; DTC 14:2035–41; É. De Moreau, *Histoire de l'Église en Belgique* (2d ed., 1945) 2:95–99; 156–158, 277–281.

[S. WILLIAMS]

SIGER OF BRABANT (c. 1240–c. 1284) Belgian scholastic philosopher, native of the duchy of Brabant. Few facts are known about his life and these concern his career as a master of philosophy at the Univ. of Paris. In that role, he was identified with an extreme or heterodox Aristotelianism which earned him the censure of SS. *Bonaventure in 1267–68 and *Thomas Aquinas in 1270. Moreover, the abp. of Paris, Étienne Tempier, condemned a number of his teachings in 1270, and again in 1277; further the papal legate, Simon de Brion, reprimanded him in 1275. Finally, the French Inquisition summoned S. to appear in 1276, but he fled to Italy and probably appealed to the Papal Curia at Orvieto. Tradition reports his death there.

These events took place during the period when Greek philosophy and science in Latin translation were being introduced into the universities of the West, often with Arabic commentaries, notably those on Aristotle by the Muslim-Spanish philosopher, *Averroës (1126–98). As a result, there arose at Paris and elsewhere a growing rationalistic movement in philosophy, sometimes called *Latin-Averroism, which claimed to present reasoned demonstrations of conclusions openly opposed to Christian doctrine. S. became associated with this trend, possibly as one of its leaders, and has been charged by some with holding the theory of the double truth—one for reason and one for faith, both true and yet contradictory. This particular accusation is not supported by satisfactory documentary evidence, and is confirmed by nothing in his extant works. There is in fact evidence to show that S. remained a devout Christian and finally openly professed the superiority of faith over reason, despite his interest in the unorthodox interpretations of Aristotle by Averroës and others. S.'s philosophy includes such positions as: the indirect emanation of all being from God through a single creature—the first intelligence; no real distinction between essence and existence in creatures; the necessity and eternity of the created world; one intellect or intellective soul for all mankind (monopsychism); as a corollary of the foregoing, one will for all men; and the denial of individual immortality for man. The lack or obscurity of relevant information and the enigmatic character of the man and his writings account for the fact that the issues with which he has become identified continue to provide dispute and speculation. BIBLIOGRAPHY: *Siger de Brabant et l'averroïsme latin au XIIIe siècle,* (ed. P. Mandonnet, 2d ed., 2 v., 1908–11); É. Gilson, *Dante, The Philosopher* (tr. D. Moore, 1949); F. van Steenberghen, *Aristotle in the West* (tr. L. Johnston, rev. ed., 1955).

[J. T. HICKEY]

SIGFRID, ST., (d. c. 1045), missionary bp. in Norway and Sweden, honored as the apostle of Sweden. The evangelization of Sweden is a subject of much dispute, and there are conflicting narratives regarding S.'s career. He may have been a priest of York or Glastonbury, who may have accompanied two other English missionary bps. to Norway at the invitation of the Norwegian King Olaf. After laboring in Norway, S. moved on to Växjö, Sweden, under the protection of the abp. of Bremen. He is depicted carrying the three heads of his martyred nephews, who had been his chief assistants. He is buried in the church at Växjö. Butler 1:342–343; F. Caraffa, BiblSanct 11:1038.

[E. J. DILLON]

SIGISMUND, ST. (d. *c.*524), king of Burgundy. Converted from Arianism by St. Avitus, bp. of Vienne, he became king of Burgundy in 516. In reparation for the death of his son, strangled by his orders, S. practically reestablished the monastery of Saint-Maurice in the Swiss canton of Valais. About 523 the three sons of Clovis, desirous of annexing Burgundy and revenging their grandfather Chilperic, defeated S., who fled to the area around Saint-Maurice. For a time he led a hermit's life, but was soon taken prisoner and put to death at Orléans. BIBLIOGRAPHY: Butler 2:209–210; Hefele-Leclercq, 2.2:1017–22, 1031–42; H. Platelle, BiblSanct 11:1043–44.

[J. M. O'DONNELL]

SIGISMUND, HOLY ROMAN EMPEROR (1368–1437), king of Hungary (1387); king of the Romans (1410); king of Bohemia (1419); Holy Roman Emperor (1433). S.'s aim was double: political unity in Europe, the Empire; ecclesiastical unity, the end of the great Western Schism. In the first he was only partially successful; troubles in Eastern Europe where he first came into power through his wife Maria, heir to Hungary, resulted from defeats by the Turks in 1396 and 1426; difficulties with Wenceslaus IV of Bohemia, his step-brother, caused failure in intrigues to succeed him. In 1414 he was finally crowned German king at Aachen.

In his attempts to mediate church strife he was more successful. He convoked two Councils, that of Constance (1414–18) at which the several claimants to the papacy resigned; and, with Pope Martin V, that of Basel (1431) which condemned John Hus of Bohemia.

S. never really gained power over the German princes, although, when he was crowned Holy Roman Emperor by Pope Eugene IV (1433), Bohemia formally recognized him as king. His failure to unite Western Christendom under his rule was also a failure against the threat to the West of the Ottoman Turks. At his death he was succeeded by the Habsburg Duke Albert V of Austria, husband of his only daughter, Elizabeth. BIBLIOGRAPHY: A. Main, *Emperor Sigismund* (1903); *Council of Constance* (tr. L. R. Loomis, ed. J. H. Munday and K. M. Woody, 1961).

[M. E. DUFFY]

SIGN OF JONAH, see JONAH, SIGN OF.

SIGN OF THE CROSS, the Christian gesture that traces the lines of the cross over objects, people, or oneself. It was already in common use among Christians at the end of the 2d century. Originally an act of private devotion, it came to be widely employed in the liturgy. The action has many uses, with some difference of significance in different contexts; it may be, e.g., a confession of faith, or a sign that something or someone is sealed or consecrated to Christ, or a gesture of blessing, or an exorcism, or the beginning and conclusion of something done to the honor of God. In the early Church an individual customarily signed himself by making a small cross on his forehead with his thumb. In reaction to Monophysitism the gesture was given Trinitarian and Christological significance by folding back the little and its adjacent finger into the palm of the hand (to confess faith in the two natures of Christ) and by extending the two remaining fingers and the thumb, all joined together (to confess faith in the Trinity of Persons). At about the same time, perhaps to make the gesture more obvious, a larger sign of the cross, in which the hand moved from head to breast to shoulders, replaced the small sign made on the forehead. This manner of making the sign has been retained in the East, where the shoulder movement of the hand is from right to left. The same right-to-left movement may also have been used in the West as late as the 12th cent., but there is some question of whether Innocent III, who prescribed a right-to-left movement, had in mind the large sign of the cross or the smaller sign such as one might trace upon his forehead or upon some object. In any case it is clear that before the end of the Middle Ages the large sign of the Cross in the West was made with the hand open and all its fingers extended, with the final movement of the hand from left to right. BIBLIOGRAPHY: E. Beresford-Cooke, *Sign of the Cross in the Western Liturgies* (1907); H. Thurston, CE 13:285–287; C. Meinberg, NCE 4:475–479.

[P. K. MEAGHER]

SIGNORELLI, LUCA (1441–1523), Italian painter of the Umbrian school, pupil and collaborator with Piero della Francesca. Of the fresco *Madonna and Child with SS. Jerome and Paul* (1474) only the St. Paul figure remains. After 1479, S. executed many commissions, judged models for the façade of the Duomo, Florence (1491), and drew cartoons (rejected) for the pavement at the cathedral of Siena (1506). Most important are S.'s frescoes in the cathedral of Orvieto (chapel of S. Brizio) begun with Frau Angelico in 1499, but completed alone, depicting the *Antichrist, Resurrection of the Dead, The Damned,* and *The Elect,* with a self-portrait and likeness of Fra Angelico. S.'s studies of the nude are forerunners of Michelangelo's Sistine figures, the latter culmination of Quattrocentro anatomic investigation. S.'s nudes though more fully anatomic than Pollaiuolo's, remain stiff, lacking fluid articulation, yet in certain poses (souls catapulting through space, riding on backs of demons), he evidences an advanced grasp of the human figure in action. S. painted (1502–23) many major altarpieces: *Crucifixion with SS. Anthony Abbot and Eligius,* many Madonnas with Child and saints, *Baptism, Eucharist, Coronation of the Virgin* (1523) with his usual heavily crowded composition and ornament. S.'s influence on High Renaissance art was strong, both Michelangelo and Raphael deriving from him. A. Pollaiuolo and S. in their early studies of the nude made possible the dynamic *contraposto* of the fully realized, supremely graceful articulations of Michelangelo. BIBLIOGRAPHY: M. Salmi, *Luca Signorelli* (1953).

[M. J. DALY]

SIGÜENZA Y GÓNGORA, CARLOS DE (1654–1700), Mexican scholar and priest. For a brief time (1660–67) he was a Jesuit. Later he was a professor at the Univ. of Mexico. By New World standards, he was a pioneer in the field of astronomy. His writings also reflect a keen interest in the native Indian as well as the Spanish culture of Mexico.

[E. J. DILLON]

SIKHISM, a sect of reformist Hindus that began with Nānak (1469–1538) and developed under the guidance of the nine gurus who succeeded him until Gobind Singh (1666–1708), the self-proclaimed last of the 10 Sikh patriarchs. While Sikhism differs from Hinduism, many of its major features have Hindu counterparts. The authority of the Ādi-Granth replaced the *Vedas; Gurmukhi replaced Sanskrit as the sacred language. While idolatry was forbidden, veneration of the Granth, the Holy Book, was often idolatrous. Although maintaining great reverence for the true name of God, the Sikhs rejected the ceremonial repetition of names. By abolishing sacrifice, they eliminated the class of priests. By rejecting nonviolence, they lost scruples against killing and eating animals. The history of the patriarchal period of Sikhism reflects a gradual shift, under the increasing hostility of the Muslims, from the pacifism of Nānak toward the political and militaristic character the movement acquired under Gobind Singh. Nānak, considered an incarnation of God with the 16 avatara signs of Rama and Krishna, is believed to be incarnated in the other gurus. Nānak's theism is considered by some to be a synthesis of Ramanuja and Islam. Amardas (1469–1574), the third guru, sought to abolish caste distinctions. Ramdas (1534–1581), the fourth guru, built the Golden Temple at Amritsar, which became the center of Sikhism. The fifth guru, Arjun Dev (1563–1606), Ramdas's son, began to compile the *Adi-Granth*, the sacred writings of Sikh gurus and other saints and reformers. Har-gobind (1595–1645), the sixth guru, was the first to organize the Sikhs into a military brotherhood. Gobind Singh (1675–1708), the tenth, wrote the *Dasam Granth* (Tenth Granth) along with much poetry in Punjabi. By instituting the Khalsa or Sikh Council of those who were pure of faith, and establishing the Granth as the lasting sacred book of the Sikhs, he eliminated the need for future gurus. He began worship of the terrible goddess, Durga, and imparted some of his violent and martial personality to the movement. His infamous agent, Banda, sacked towns, destroyed mosques, and massacred people throughout the Deccan. After Gobind Singh's

death at the hand of a Pathan assailant seeking revenge for his father's murder, the history of the Sikhs continued violent and warlike. The Golden Temple was destroyed during a long inconclusive war with the Afghan chief Ahmad Shah Durrani. Under Ranjit Singh (d. 1839) the Sikhs, with French aid, established their hegemony over all of Punjab and rebuilt their Temple. Fierce wars with the British followed his death. Sikh nationalism continues today in the Punjab, finding expression in the deathless movement, Akāli. Yet, other strains of Sikhism which retain the influence, character, and teaching of Nānak have survived, as have sects which are dedicated to the continued study and theology of the *Ādi Granth*.

[R. J. LITZ]

SILAS (SILVANUS), one of the leading men of the Jerusalem Church. Called a prophet, he is associated with both Paul and Peter in the apostolic missions. It is all but certain that the man called Silas in Acts (15.22) is the man referred to as Silvanus in the letters of Paul (2 Cor 1,19; 1 Th 1.1; 2 Th 1.1) and 1 Peter (5.12). Luke retains the name known in the Jerusalem community; Paul and 1 Peter use the latinized form used in Roman and Hellenistic circles. S. comes on the scene in the Jerusalem Church as the companion of Judas Barsabbas, when the two are sent to Antioch to bring the news of the Jerusalem council's decision concerning the binding force of Jewish Law on gentile Christians. S. was a man of Hellenistic culture, apparently not sympathetic to Judaizing influences, and yet perhaps conciliatory in approach. Paul found him more compatible than Barnabas, whom S. replaced as Paul's companion on the subsequent journey from Antioch through Galatia to Macedonia. S. was imprisoned with Paul at Philippi and suffered through the riots with him at Thessalonica and Beroea. S. stayed at Beroea while Paul went on to Athens. S., Paul, and Timothy were reunited at Corinth where S. remained after Paul's departure. S. may later have evangelized in the north country of Pontus and Cappadocia, because 1 Peter, which originates there, mentions him. He may be coauthor of that letter, just as he may have authored parts of the letters of Paul to the Thessalonians.

[E. J. DILLON]

SILBERMANN, family name of two brothers, founders of a German family of organ builders, clavichord and piano makers. **Andreas** (1678–1734) built the organ in the cathedral in Strasbourg and 29 others. **Gottfried** (1683–1753), the more famous, built the organ of the cathedral in Freiburg and 46 others. He also built magnificent clavichords and was the first German piano maker.

[M. T. LEGGE]

SILENCE, PRACTICE OF. (1) A primary meaning is the ascetical restraint from talking and the creation of a condition of quiet for the purpose of greater thoughtfulness and prayerfulness. Silence in this sense is a kind of symbol of the monastic life itself as a withdrawal from the turmoil of the world in order singlemindedly to seek union with God; as such it became part of the rule of all religious communities. A degree of silence in this sense is necessary for all who seek a life of prayer and study. (2) Silence has also a more universal meaning and a connection with the life of virtue, i.e., of a life lived humanly, not mindlessly. It is characteristic of the virtue of truthfulness to speak in a manner befitting the circumstances and decencies of human communication; that often involves a sensitive reticence. The virtue of modesty as it names a properly modulated manner of comportment implies restraint from chatter and keeping down the noise level. The virtue called by Aristotle *eutrapelia* (*Nichomachean Ethics* 2, 7 & 4, 10; see also 4, 3 for a picture of the "strong, silent type") also means moderation, a manner of acting in such a way as to be pleasant to one's companions; that implies knowing when to keep still. (3) Silence may also be an evil when the demands of justice or charity require speaking out to prevent or correct evil (see SIN, COOPERATION IN).

[T. C. O'BRIEN]

SILLON, a Catholic movement originating in France in 1894, at first literary, then designed to pursue social reform. The idealists who made up the circle, led by Marc Sangnier and Étienne Isabelle, were well intentioned but their ignorance of Catholic doctrine led them to a secularism contrary to church doctrine. In 1910 Pope Pius X condemned the errors and demanded they reorganize under the bishop. They submitted, but the group soon dissolved.

[J. R. AHERNE]

SILO, see SHILOH.

SILOAM INSCRIPTION, a Hebrew inscription of 6 lines found on the wall of the tunnel built by order of Hezekiah (see 2 Chr. 32, 2–4; 2 Kg 20.20) in anticipation of the siege of Jerusalem by Sennacherib, King of Assyria; important as evidence of Hebrew script *c*.700 B.C. The tunnel was built as an underground aqueduct to send water from the spring of Gihon outside the battlements, to the Pool of Siloam inside. The word *Siloam* is the Septuagint Greek transcription for the Hebrew *Shiloah*, which means "sender" (of water) and probably originally referred to the aqueduct, not the pool. The pool is associated with the incident in John's Gospel (9.7) in which Jesus healed the man born blind. The inscription of Siloam was removed in 1880 to the Imperial Museum at Istanbul. Apparently it commemorated the breakthrough in the tunnel's excavation: the point at which the two teams of miners met each other, one snaking its way from outside the wall, the other from inside. When their picks met (according to the inscription) the water started flowing. The inscription gave the measurements of the tunnel as 1200 cubits in length, under 100 cubits of rock at the point of intersection (a cubit is approximately 17–22 inches—depending on the length of the forearm of the person measuring).

[E. J. DILLON]

SILOS, ABBEY OF, Benedictine monastery in S Burgos in Old Castile, founded in 954 by Fernán González. Originally named San Sebastián, it was restored in 1041 by St. Dominic of Silos, who was buried there in 1073. His tomb became the most important pilgrimage center in Castile and it was natural to name the monastery after him. After prospering in the 12th and 13th cent., it declined in subsequent years until it joined the Congregation of Valladolid in 1512. It was suppressed along with other religious orders in 1833 and was restored by the efforts of French monks under Abbot Guépin in 1880. It is a flourishing member of the Congregation of Solesmes. The Romanesque church was largely destroyed during the course of 18th-cent. renovations carried out in the Baroque style. Luckily, the Romanesque cloister survives as a virtual storehouse of Romanesque art. BIBLIOGRAPHY: Cottineau 2:3036–37.

[E. J. DILLON]

SILVA, ATENÓGENES (1848–1911), bishop. A Mexican by birth, S. was ordained in 1871. In 1884 he was appointed theologian of the cathedral of Guadalajara. A notable orator and charitable spirit, S. became bp. of Colima in 1892 and abp. of Michoacán in 1900. Appointed to the Mexican Academy of the Language in 1895, he was also named to the honor of an Arcadian of Rome. An ardent devotee of the Virgin of Guadalupe, he preached her influence on Mexican culture. In 1908 King Alfonso XIII of Spain conferred on S. the Grand Cross of Isabella the Catholic. In 1898 his writings were published as *Obras literarias, pastorales y oratorias*.

[J. R. AHERNE]

SILVA, BEATRICE DA, ST., see MENESES, BEATRICE DA SILVA, ST.

SILVA, DUARTE LEOPOLDO E (1867–1937), Brazilian abp., historian. Ordained in 1892, S. was made bp. of Curitiba in 1904 and first abp. of São Paulo in 1907. He was a promoter of social movements and established exemplary historical archives in his see. In the civil upheavals of Brazil in the 1930s, S. avoided taking sides. As a historian he gained membership in the Instituto Histórico e Geográfico de São Paulo with such works as *Notas de história eclesiástica* (1916–1937), *O clero e a independência do Brasil* (1922), and *O padre Feijó. Sua ação na independência* (1921).

[J. R. AHERNE]

SILVACANE, ABBEY OF, see SAUVECANNE, ABBEY OF.

SILVANUS, TEACHINGS OF, see APOCRYPHA (NT), 60.

SILVEIRA, GONÇALO DA, VEN. (1523?–61), early Jesuit missionary, martyr. A Portuguese who entered the Society of Jesus in 1543, S. was appointed by St. Ignatius

Loyola provincial of the Jesuits in India in 1556. Transferring to Africa in 1559, he established a mission among the Monomotapa. Through Muslim influence he was martyred by strangulation in 1561.

[J. R. AHERNE]

SILVERIO OF ST. TERESA (Julian Fernández Gómez; 1876–1954), general of the Discalced Carmelites (1947–54), prolific writer on their history and spirituality. He edited the works of St. Teresa of Ávila (1915–25) and St. John of the Cross (1927–30); the *Biblioteca mística carmelitana* (20 v.); the *Historia del Carmen Descâlzo* (15 v.); *La Carmelita perfecta* (3 v.). He also published hundreds of journal articles and other studies. Throughout his life he served as a superior and administrator in his order; he died during his visitation in Mexico at Mazatlán.

[T. C. O'BRIEN]

SILVERIUS, ST. (d. 537), **POPE** from 536. He was the son of Pope *Hormisdas (514–523) and a subdeacon on the death of his predecessor, *Agapetus. Theodahad, Ostrogoth King of Italy, saw S. as a likely person to deal successfully with the imperial intrigue and imposed him on the Roman clergy. It is thought that he was not rightfully pope until his final acceptance by the Roman Church. His whole reign was caught in the cross fire of Ostrogothic and Byzantine attempts to control Rome. Forged letters were brought forward to implicate S. in a plot to deliver Rome to the Goths; he was seized, declared deposed, and sent in exile to Patara in Lycia, and *Vigilius was proclaimed Pope—the same Vigilius whom *Boniface II had tried to name as his successor. The Emperor Justinian ordered S. returned to Rome but, en route, he died on the island of Palmaria, near Naples, where a resignation is thought to have been extorted from him (Nov. 11, 537). His remains are still on Palmaria. BIBLIOGRAPHY: J. Chapin, NCE 13:327; T. G. Jalland, *Church and the Papacy* (1944).

[P. F. MULHERN]

SILVESTER GUZZOLINI, ST. (1177–1267), abbot, founder of the Silvestrine (Blue) Benedictines. Renouncing his benefice some years after his ordination, S. became a hermit; but after disciples joined him, he founded a monastery at Montefano, giving it an austere rule based on that of St. Benedict. His order spread widely. Today, greatly reduced in numbers, it is still active in Italy and India. BIBLIOGRAPHY: Butler, 4:422–423; Zimmermann 3:358–360; N. DelRe, BiblSanct 11:1075–77.

[M. A. WINKELMANN]

SILVESTRI, FRANCESCO, see FERRARIENSIS.

SIMEON, biblical name. (1) A patriarchate and tribe. The tribe descended from the second son of Jacob and Leah (cf. Gen 29.33; 35.23) seems, together with those of Reuben and Levi, to have entered Canaan earlier than the main Israelite invasion (13th cent. B.C.), but to have failed to retain its hold on the territory thus acquired, which apparently lay in the relatively rich region of Shechem. This episode may be reflected in the story of Simeon and Levi's taking revenge for the rape of their sister Dinah (Gen 34.25–30). As a punishment for their ferocity on this occasion, they are said to have been scattered throughout Israel (Gen 49.5–7). Subsequently, Simeon figures as a minor tribe, subordinate to Judah, and inhabiting the extreme S region of the Negeb desert. By the time of the monarchy the tribe appears to have been absorbed by Judah and no longer to exist as a separate entity. (2) In the NT, the aged and pious temple devotee "waiting for the consolation of Israel," who met Mary with her child, took Jesus in his arms, and uttered the inspired canticle, *Nunc dimittis,* in token of the fact that Jesus was indeed the consolation of Israel for which the piety of the Old Law had been waiting (Lk 2.25–35).

[D. J. BOURKE]

SIMEON BARSABAE, ST. (d. 344), martyr in Karkha de Ledan, Mesopotamia. In 326, he succeeded Papas as bp. of Seleucia and Ctesiphon on the Tigris, the ninth Katholicos of that region. He was among the first group of Persian martyrs put to death under the Sassanid Dynasty. The cruelty of the persecution renewed by Saper II is attested by Sozomen and other reliable Byzantine historians. S.'s surname (Barsabae) means: son of the dyer, which may give some hint of his social origins. BIBLIOGRAPHY: Butler 2:141–142.

[E. J. DILLON]

SIMEON OF DURHAM (d. *c.*1130), English Benedictine chronicler. His history of the bishopric of Durham, *Historia ecclesiae Dunelmensis,* relies heavily upon Bede. Only the last part of the *Historia regum,* a history of the English from 732, is now attributed to Simeon. BIBLIOGRAPHY: H. S. Offler, *Medieval Historians of Durham* (1958).

[F. D. BLACKLEY]

SIMEON I, THE GREAT, (also Symeon), king of Bulgaria, 893–927. His reign coincided with the golden age of Preslav, when Bulgaria attained its greatest limits: from the Transylvanian Alps almost to the Mediterranean and from the Black Sea to the Adriatic. The real possibility of Bulgarian control over the Byzantine Empire was lost by S.'s successors. It was the same national assembly that proclaimed Christianity the state religion, adopted the Slavic language, replaced the Byzantine with the Slavic rite, and Vladimir (son of Boris I) with his brother Simeon. The latter successfully fought the Byzantines three times (894–897, 913–914, 919–924). After his decisive victory over Leo VI the Wise (896) he arranged a peace whereby Constantinople paid tribute. He went on to defeat the Magyars, assumed the title of tsar, replaced Greek bps. with men of Slavic origin, named the abp. of Preslav patriarch of Bulgaria, assumed the title of tsar of the Romans and the Bulgars (925), and was even crowned by the Byzantine patriarch Nicholas. He ordered the building of schools, churches, and monasteries and fostered the work of translating Byzantine classics into the Slavic tongue—a feat which was to influence the later Slavic literatures of Rumania, Russia, and Serbia. Both his new capitals, Preslav in the East, and Ochrida in the West, were centers of cultural renaissance.

[E. J. DILLON]

SIMEON OF POLIRONE, ST. (d. 1016), a native of Armenia who became a hermit, made pilgrimages to great shrines, and ended his days as a Benedictine monk in the monastery of Polirone. He was once charged with heresy in Rome but was exonerated by Pope Benedict VII. BIBLIOG - RAPHY: Butler 3:140; F. Caraffa, BiblSanct 11:1114–15; Zimmermann 2:500–501.

SIMEON THE STYLITE, ST., (c.389–459), the first and most famous of the *stylites, Christian ascetics who lived on the tops of pillars. Born at Sis, on the boundary between Syria and Cilicia, he tended his father's sheep as a boy and then entered the monastery founded by Eusebonas at Teleda. Forced to leave it some 10 years later because his extreme penances disturbed the common life of the monks, he became a hermit at Telanissos (or Tellneshin), about 20 miles NW of the modern Aleppo. To escape the importunities of the people who asked his prayers, he went up a neighboring mountain and about the year 423 mounted a pillar. As his fame increased, so did the height of his pillar until it reached some 60 feet. After his death in 459 his remains were taken with great solemnity to Antioch. His life was written by his contemporary Theodoret, his disciple Antony, and by Syrian monks in the vicinity. Between c.476 and c.490 a large basilica was built about his pillar. The imposing ruins of this most important Christian edifice prior to the erection of the *Hagia Sophia by Justinian are still to be seen at Qa 'al Sem'an. BIBLIOGRAPHY: H. Delehaye, *Les Saints stylites* (1923) 1–34. H. Leclercq, DACL 15.2:1697–1718; D. Stiernon, BiblSanct 11:1116–38.

[M. J. COSTELLOE]

SIMEON OF SYRACUSE (SIMEON OF TREVES), ST. (c.970–1035), monk and hermit. Although born in Sicily, S. was of Greek parentage and at the age of 7 returned with his father to Constantinople. In the Holy Land he was ordained deacon and entered the monastery of Mt. Sinai. He was sent to Normandy (1027) to collect alms. His journey involved him in much peril, in which he narrowly escaped death. S. visited Rome and Treves, and it was to Treves he returned in 1030 to spend the last 5 years of his life as a recluse. His vita, written by Abbot Eberwin, is a valuable historical source with regard to early pilgrim routes. BIBLIOGRAPHY: AS June 1:85–104; Butler 2:441–442; E. Brouette, BiblSanct 11:1157–60.

[W. A. JURGENS]

SIMEON, CHARLES (1759–1836), leader of the *evangelicals of the Church of England. Educated at King's College., Cambridge, he spent his life as vicar of Holy Trinity Church in Cambridge. He was one of the founders of the *Church Missionary Society (1799) and active in the *British and Foreign Bible Society. Not only did he spread *low-church influence in the C of E by his evangelical preaching, but he was able to place other evangelicals as parish vicars by securing the right of *advowson. BIBLIOG - RAPHY: P. Smyth, *Simeon and Church Order* (1940).

[T. C. O'BRIEN]

SIMEONI, GIOVANNI (1816–92), cardinal, diplomat. A Roman, sponsored by the powerful Colonna family, S. served in the nunciature in Madrid and as secretary to the Congregation for the Propagation of the Faith. Nuncio to Spain (1875–76), he was named cardinal and was secretary of state under Pope Pius IX from 1876 to 1878. His last years were spent as prefect of the Congregation for the Propagation of the Faith.

[J. R. AHERNE]

SIMON, APOSTLE, ST., one of Jesus' 12 Disciples. The name is Greek and is the equivalent of the Hebrew name, Simeon. S. is mentioned in all the NT lists of the *Apostles (Mt 10.4; Mk 3.18; Lk 6.15; Acts 1.13). He is called the "Cananean" in Mt and Mk, and the "zealot" in Lk and Acts. The terms are equivalent, zealot being the Greek for the transliterated Aramaic qan'ānai, and probably refer either to S.'s enthusiasm for the Jewish law or his membership in the *Zealot sect. He may be the same as Simon the brother of Jesus (Mt 13.55; Mk 6.3). The apocryphal Acts of Simon and Jude presents him as preaching in the Near East and martyred by being sawed in two. BIB - LIOGRAPHY: F. Spadaforda, BiblSanct 11:1169–73; Butler 4:213–214.

[T. M. MCFADDEN]

SIMON OF AULNE, BL. (d. 1229), Cistercian laybrother, mystic. He entered the Cistercian abbey of Aulne-sur-Sombre (Belgium) as a laybrother, though of noble birth. He had gifts of prophecy and discernment of spirits and was reputedly consulted even by Pope Innocent III. BIBLIOGRA - PHY: L. J. Lekai, NCE 13:220; M.-A. Dimier, BiblSanct 11:1175–77.

[L. J. LEKAI]

SIMON BALLACHI, BL. (c.1258–c.1329), Dominican lay brother. His entrance into the Dominican community occurred at Rimini when he was 27. He was assigned to work in the monastery garden and to catechize young children. His life was remarkable for its holiness, humility, and bodily discipline. At the age of 57, he became blind and bore this affliction with such cheerful courage that he was honored as a saint. BIBLIOGRAPHY: Butler 4:254–255; P. Burchi, BiblSanct 2:709–710.

[J. M. O'DONNELL]

SIMON OF BISIGNANO, 12th–cent. *decretist, known from his *Summa* (*c.*1170), on *Gratian's *Decretum*, a work important for its establishment of the principle of a systematic updating of canon law and for its wide use by subsequent medieval canonists.

[T. C. O'BRIEN]

SIMON BREDON (d. 1372), astronomer and mathematician, wrote also on philosophy, poetry, and medicine. He studied arts, medicine, and theology at Oxford, to whose colleges he bequeathed many books; held various ecclesiastical benefices; served Richard, earl of Arundel; and attended Joanna, queen of Scots, as physician. His writings remain mostly in MSS. BIBLIOGRAPHY: Emden Ox 257–258.

[R. W. HAYS]

SIMON OF CRAMAUD (*c.*1360–1422), cardinal. Trained in law at Paris, he rapidly gained fame as canonist and orator. He served as bp. of Agen, Béziers, and Poitiers, and was named abp. of Sens in 1390. He was appointed administrator of Avignon by Clement VII. In 1409 he became abp. of Reims; he acted as president of the Council of Pisa; and was made cardinal by John XXIII in 1413. He was a fervent advocate of temporal authority and openly opposed the Hussites. His influence on ecclesiastical affairs waned under Martin V, and he spent his remaining years as administrator of the Diocese of Poitiers. BIBLIOGRAPHY: F. D. Lazenby, NCE 13:221; K. A. Fink, LTK 9:765–766.

[F. D. LAZENBY]

SIMON OF CYRENE, the man who was enlisted to carry the cross of Jesus on his way to Calvary (Mt 27.32; Mk 15.21; Lk 23.26). Mark further identifies him as "the father of Alexander and Rufus" (cf. Rom 16.13).

[M. A. MCNAMARA]

SIMON DE GHENT (d. 1315), English theologian and bishop. He incepted at Oxford as regent master of theology (*c.*1290–91) and he became chancellor of the university (1291–93). Consecrated bp. of Salisbury in 1297, he worked with indefatigable zeal for the spiritual and temporal good of his diocese. BIBLIOGRAPHY: Emden Ox 2:759–760.

[J. A. WEISHEIPL]

SIMON HINTON, English Dominican theologian; regent master of Oxford Dominicans *c.*1248–50; provincial of England (1254–61), when he was deposed and sent to teach in Cologne. Some biblical commentaries of his are extant, but his best work is a *Summa ad instructionem iuniorum,* written probably when he was provincial as a handbook of pastoral theology. BIBLIOGRAPHY: Emden Ox 2:937.

[L. E. BOYLE]

SIMON ISLIP (d. 1366), English churchman. After studying both laws at Oxford, he practiced in ecclesiastical courts and held offices in Lincoln and Canterbury dioceses. He served Edward III as keeper of the privy seal and, as abp. on diplomatic missions and at Edward's request was made abp. of Canterbury (1349). Measures taken to counteract the effects of the Black Death, esp. his freezing of clerical salaries, earned him a reputation for strictness and parsimony. He founded (1361) Canterbury Hall, Oxford, for monks and secular scholars, later reorganizing it as a secular college (1365). He settled a long-standing dispute with York and was victorious in a jurisdictional dispute with the bp. of Lincoln. BIBLIOGRAPHY: F. D. Logan, NCE 13:222.

[R. W. HAYS]

SIMON LANGHAM (d. 1376), English ecclesiastic and statesman. Monk of Westminster by 1340, he studied at Oxford (1346–48) and became prior and then abbot (1349). Energetic and financially astute, he was treasurer of the exchequer (1360–63), bp. of Ely (1361–66), and chancellor of England (1363–67). As abp. of Canterbury (1366–68), he legislated against pluralism. Appointed cardinal, he resigned his archbishopric, joining the papal court at Avignon, where he served as diplomat, became cardinal-bishop of Palestrina (1373), and accepted plural English benefices. He is accounted second founder of Westminster Abbey, where his striking tomb commemorates his vast bequests. BIBLIOGRAPHY: D. Nicholl, NCE 13:222.

[R. W. HAYS]

SIMON MACCABEUS (*c.*200–135 B.C.), Hasmonean high priest of Judea. He was the second of Mattathias's five sons and became high priest following the death of his brother Jonathan *c.*142 B.C. (1 Macc 13.8). He achieved independence for the nation, and documents were issued with the inscription, "in the first year of Simon, the great high priest and commander and leader of the Jews" (1 Macc 13.41–42). He was made governor and high priest with right of hereditary succession granted to his descendants (1 Macc 14.41–49). He was successful in establishing treaty relations with Rome and Sparta and furthering the national life. He was killed, however, *c.*135 B.C. by his son-in-law and rival Ptolemy, son of Abub. Two of his sons were killed with him, but one, John Hyrcanus, escaped and succeeded him.

[T. EARLY]

SIMON MAGUS, Samaritan magician converted by Philip (Acts 8.9–24). He subsequently offered Peter and John money if they would give him the power to bestow the Holy Spirit—whence the term *simony. There is some suggestion in Acts that he headed a Gnostic sect. Legends concerning him proliferated during the early Christian centuries.

[T. EARLY]

SIMON MEOPHAM (Mepham, d. 1333), English archbishop. S. studied at Oxford, where he earned a master's degree by 1295 and a doctorate in theology by 1315. He was a key figure in Edward III's attempt to free himself from the domination of Roger Mortimer. S.'s services led to his elevation in 1328 to the archbishopric of Canterbury in preference to Mortimer's candidate. His term was a troubled one: in 1329 he was suspended by John XXII for refusing to install the abp. of Naples as rector of Maidstone; and he was excommunicated the following year because of a conflict with the monks of St. Augustine's Abbey, Canterbury. He died under excommunication but was posthumously absolved and buried in Canterbury cathedral. The attribution of *Speculum Regis Edwardi* to S. was disproved by L. Boyle in 1963. BIBLIOGRAPHY: T. F. Tout, DNB 13:260–263; Emden Ox 2:26.

[J. L. GRASSI]

SIMON DE MONTFORT (1208–65), earl of Leicester; English political leader; youngest son of the famous Crusader against the Albigenses. Henry III encouraged S., a royal favorite, to enter a controversial marriage (1238) with Eleanor, the King's sister. Later S., losing royal favor, fled England to Crusade in the Holy Land (1240–41). He returned only after brilliant military and administrative service in France (1242–52). Although reconciled with Henry, S. led a coalition of magnates in an attempt to limit royal authority by the *Provisions of Oxford* (1258). His army defeated royal forces at Lewes (1264), and a year later S. summoned the so-called Model Parliament. The King's army rallied and destroyed S. and his party at Evesham (1265). Adam Marsh and Robert Grosseteste, his friends, probably inspired Simon's attempts at governmental reform. BIBLIOGRAPHY: C. Bémont, *Simon de Montfort* (tr. E. F. Jacob, new ed. 1930).

[J. E. WRIGLEY]

SIMON DE MONTFORT L'AMAURY (c.1160–1218), earl of Leicester, best remembered for his leadership of the Crusade against the *Albigensians. From 1208 until his death he campaigned with ruthlessness, skill, treachery, and considerable success. He was besieging Toulouse when he died of wounds. BIBLIOGRAPHY: M. A. Mulholland, NCE 13:234.

[V. BULLOUGH]

SIMON OF SAINT-QUENTIN (*fl.* mid-13th cent.), French Dominican missionary and author. He wrote *Fratris Simonis historia,* an account of a journey to Tatary. He is known only through the *Speculum historiale* of *Vincent of Beauvais. His mission to Tatary lasted from 1245 to July 1248 or 1249, and included three other Dominicans and two Franciscans. BIBLIOGRAPHY: Quétif-Échard 1.1:122; M. Daunou, *Histoire littéraire de la France* 18 (1935) 400–402.

[J. A. WEISHEIPL]

SIMON STOCK, ST. (d. 1265), English Carmelite. Nearly all details of his life are uncertain. Said to have graduated at Oxford after profession as friar, he became prior general of the order, perhaps through election by the chapter in London (1254). Convents at Oxford, Cambridge, Bologna, and Paris were probably founded during his term of office. He is best known for his supposed vision at Aylesford, in which the BVM appeared holding the Carmelite scapular and assured him that all who wore it would be saved. He is venerated there and at Bordeaux, where he died. BIBLIOGRAPHY: L. Saggi, BiblSanct 11:1188–91.

[R. W. HAYS]

SIMON OF SUDBURY (d. 1381), prominent churchman and political figure. He was made bp. of London in 1365, abp. of Canterbury in 1375, and chancellor in 1380. He reluctantly took action against Wycliffe and was responsible for the imposition of a poll tax in 1380. In the Peasants' Revolt of 1381 he was an object of popular hatred. Seized in the Tower of London, where he had taken refuge with the king, he was beheaded by the mob. BIBLIOGRAPHY: W. L. Warren, "Reappraisal of Simon of Sudbury." JEcclHist 10 (1959) 139–152; Emden Ox 3:2218; W. Hunt, DNB 19:146–149.

[J. L. GRASSI]

SIMON OF TOURNAI (c.1130–c.1201), theologian at Paris, important for his use of Aristotle and for the formation of scientific procedure in theology. His *Summa theologica* or *Institutio in sacra pagina* and his *Disputationes* were his most substantive works. BIBLIOGRAPHY: A. Piolanti, EncCatt 11:638–640.

[T. C. O'BRIEN]

SIMON OF TRENT (1472–75), allegedly the victim of a ritual murder, venerated for long at Trent, Italy, as a blessed and sometimes called saint. At a time when anti-Semitic feeling was strong in Trent in consequence of the preaching of *Bernardine of Feltre, the mutilated body of this child was discovered in a ditch. The circumstances of time (it was Easter Sunday morning) and place (the ditch adjoined the property of a Jewish family) caused suspicion to fall upon the Jews of three households. Thirty persons were arrested and under the leadership of Prince Bishop John Hinderbach were interrogated under torture. Despite the intervention of Archduke Sigismund of Tirol and the commissary sent by Sixtus IV, who was critical of the procedure, the prosecution went forward. Confessions were extorted; 15 persons were found guilty and executed. Hinderbach then organized a propaganda campaign with the help of the local Franciscans to stir up a cult of the child-martyr. Stories of wonders and miracles were put into circulation. Sixtus IV forbade the cult in 1478 under penalty of excommunication on grounds that it was too much of a mushroom growth and the motive of the killing had not been clearly enough established. Nevertheless, the de facto cult continued and grew. Baronius, on the basis of the existing cult, included mention of S. in the Roman Martyrology (1548); and Sixtus V in

1588, at the request of Card. Madruzzo, bp. of Trent, authorized the local celebration of the feast. This concession had some of the effects of beatification, although if formal canonization were to be attempted, a thorough investigation of the whole affair would have been necessary. The cult continued down to modern times. In addition to the annual feast, there was a more splendid celebration every 10 years until 1955. Many believed the child was truly a victim of ritual murder for no better reason than that the process was so heavily documented. But beginning in the early part of the 19th cent., scholars (e.g., G. Menestrina, G. Volli, and P. W. Eckert) have sifted the documents critically. The ''confessions'' were discounted as having been wrung from the victims by harrowing torture. Discrepancies and contradictions in the presentation of facts were noted, and a different picture of the whole shameful affair has emerged. Abp. A. M. Gottardi of Trent, with the assent of the Holy See, abrogated the cult, and S. was dropped from the calendar of the saints. BIBLIOGRAPHY: I. Rogger, BiblSanct 11:1184–88.

[P. K. MEAGHER]

SIMON OF TRESK (fl. *c.*1256–90), English architect of the famous Angel Choir of *Lincoln Cathedral, one of the crowning glories of English Gothic, its sculptured angels related to the Westminster school.

[M. J. DALY]

SIMON TUNSTED (d. 1369), English Franciscan provincial, astronomer, and musical theorist. He is said to have written a number of works including a commentary on Aristotle's *Meteora* and the important *De quattuor principalibus musicae* with its description of musical forms and definition of musical terms. BIBLIOGRAPHY: A. G. Little, *Grey Friars in Oxford* (1891); H. Davey, DNB 19:1244–45.

[F. D. BLACKLEY]

SIMON, YVES RENÉ MARIE (1903–61), philosopher prominent in the neo-Thomistic tradition in the U.S. Born and educated in France, he was a professor at the Univ. of Lille before coming to the U.S., where he taught at the Univ. of Notre Dame and the Univ. of Chicago. His interests centered on political philosophy (*Philosophy of Democratic Government*, 1951; *General Theory of Authority*, 1962; *Tradition of Natural Law*, 1965), and on the nature and objectivity of human cognition (*Introduction à l'entologie du connaître*, 1934, various essays on the epistemology of the sciences). *Freedom of Choice*, a Thomistic explanation of free will originally published in French, appeared in 1969.

[T. C. O'BRIEN]

SIMÓN DOMINGUEZ, PEDRO (1581–after 1627), Spanish Franciscan missionary in Hispanic America and chronicler. After working among Indians near Tunja, he served as inspector of convents in Santo Domingo, Venezuela, and Puerto Rico (1612–13). He became provincial of his order in 1623. His *Noticias historiales de las conquistas de tierra firme* (Pt.I, 1627; all 3 parts later pub. 1882–92; II and III, republished 1953; I, amended, 1963) incorporates a philosophy of history which considered human actions the free expression of human will under divine supervision. The section on Venezuela is based on first-hand information as well as a MS of Aquado.

[R. J. LITZ]

SIMONETTA (FAMILY). The brothers **Francesco** (1410–80) and **Giovanni** (*c.*1415–91) served the Sforza dukes of Milan, but when Ludovico Il Moro came to power in 1479, Francesco was executed and Giovanni exiled. **Bonifacio** (d. 1492), their nephew, abbot of S. Stefano Corno, was the author of *Christianae persecutiones* (1496). **Giacomo** (1475–1539), son of Giovanni, served as a lawyer at the Council of the Lateran V, became bp. of Pesaro in 1529 and a card. in 1535. The most prominent member of the family in church history is **Ludovico** (1506–68), nephew of Giacomo and his successor (1537) as bp. of Pesaro. Ludovico was identified with the reform movement during the pontificate of Paul III; he was present during the first period of the Council of Trent (1546–47). In 1561 he was named card. and one of the five papal legates of Pius IV to Trent during its third period.

[T. C. O'BRIEN]

SIMONS, MENNO, see MENNO SIMONS.

SIMONY, so called from Simon Magus who tried to purchase the gift of the Holy Spirit from the Apostles (Acts 8.18–24), the deliberate will to buy or sell for a temporal price things that are spiritual in themselves, such as the sacraments, prayers, indulgences, or things closely connected with the spiritual, such as benefices, sacred vessels, and relics. In order to commit the sin of simony, it is sufficient to have only the resolve of so doing. In order to commit the canonical crime of simony, there must be some external agreement with another person (see CIC cc. 2195, 2218, 2228). The fault lies in so equating the spiritual with the material that it is treated as commercial or negotiable merchandise. Simony is directly opposed to the virtue of *religion. A major problem in the Middle Ages, when the Church was a vested temporal interest on a large scale, simony was popularly and authoritatively condemned, and the abuse has been lessened since the reforms of Trent. BIBLIOGRAPHY: ThAq ST 2a2ae, 100 (esp. in Lat-Eng ed., v. 40, ed. T. A. O'Meara).

[C. NEELY]

SIMOR, JÁNOS (1813–91), abp. of Esztergom, primate of Hungary from 1867, cardinal in 1873. He had taught theology from 1839 and served in the imperial ministry of public worship at Vienna from 1850 when he was named bp. of Györ, Hungary, in 1857. His rule as primate was marked by his efforts to return the Church to closer ties with Rome after the disruption of *Josephinism, and to defend church independence against anticlerical state ministers. At Vatican Council I he was an anti-infallibilist on grounds of the definition's being inopportune and a hindrance to reconciliation of schismatics in Hungary, but accepted the Council's decision and published the definition in Hungary, and objected to government interference with the promulgation.

[T. C. O'BRIEN]

SIMPLICISSIMUS, title character of *Der abenteuerliche Simplicissimus* (1668–69), a novel in five books by Hans Jakob Christoffel von Grimmelshausen (1625–76). Against the background of the Thirty Years' War, the novel, which owes much of its baroque character to the picaresque tradition, reflects the hero's growth to spiritual maturity. BIBLIOGRAPHY: *Adventures of a Simpleton*, (tr. W. Wallich, 1963); W. Rose, *Men, Myths, and Movements in German Literature* (1964) 85–107.

[M. F. MCCARTHY]

SIMPLICITY, (1) a moral quality included in the meaning of the virtue of *truthfulness, disposing towards candor and openness in word and comportment. Simplicity rules out any form of deceit, hypocrisy, or pretense; it describes the kind of image a person intends to communicate to others by being himself, and means quite the opposite of modern advertising's image-making. As a person observes decorum, propriety, and good taste in dress and manner, simplicity also enters the meaning of *modesty; (2) the centering of one's life and intent upon the one thing necessary, the love of God above all. Simplicity is the objective of those seeking spiritual progress by the reduction of desires and attachments that could scatter spiritual energies, and distract them from the search for union with God. BIBLIOGRAPHY: ThAq ST 2a2ae, 109.2 ad 4.

[T. C. O'BRIEN]

SIMPLICITY OF GOD, in classical theology, the designation of the absence in God of any kind of composition. While to state that God is ''simple'' is a function of theology's *via negativa*, the divine simpleness rests upon the meaning of the divine perfection. Every creature is at least ontologically composite because of the real distinction between *essence and *esse*; because God is his own *esse* unreceived, he is absolutely unperfectible; there is no possibility of composition through the development of a potentiality by the accretion of an added actuality to be integrated into the divine, substantial being. Simplicity means, further, that pantheism or panentheism (SEE PROCESS PHILOSOPHY) are impossibilities. God cannot ''enter into'' an entitative union with the creature or evolve with the process of the created universe. The received is limited by the receiver. The significance of the divine simplicity enters into the theology of the Trinity, in the affirmation of the single nature of the three Persons; of the Incarnation, in the rejection of *monophysitism; and into the theology of grace, in the affirmation that the union of grace with God must be an operational union with God as object known and loved (see GRACE, SUBSTANTIAL), not an entitative union.

[T. C. O'BRIEN]

SIMPLICIUS, ST. (d. 483), **POPE** from 468. The Western Empire fell to the barbarians during S.'s pontificate, the Ostrogoth Odoacer becoming king of Italy in 476. In the East with the contrivance of Acacius, Patriarch of Constantinople, *Monophysite bishops were placed in the Sees of Alexandria, Jerusalem, and Antioch, the *Henoticon was issued (382), and thus the seeds of the *Acacian Schism were sowed. S. made valiant efforts to defend the teaching of *Chalcedon and to be kept informed, but his letters (PL 58:893–967) were for the most part ignored. He extended papal authority in Spain by delegating Zeno, bp. of Seville, to see to the observance of papal decrees. S. built four churches in Rome, among them S. Stefano in Rotondo and S. Bibiana, and arranged for the clergy in Rome to minister to churches of the catacombs outside the city. He was buried in the portico of St. Peter's. He has been commemorated in the martyrology since the 9th century. BIBLIOGRAPHY: T. G. Jalland, *Church and the Papacy* (1944) 314–317; Butler 1:545–546.

[P. F. MULHERN]

SIMPLICIUS (1st half of 6th cent. A.D.), Neoplatonic philosopher, a pupil of Damascius, and one of the last members of the Platonic Academy at Athens. He was primarily concerned in his commentaries with establishing a harmony between Plato and Aristotle. He considered that there were only apparent differences in their basic teachings. He followed *Plutarch of Athens in his interpretation of Aristotle's noetic and was opposed to the view that the Platonic undetermined dyad should be identified with matter. He was a representative of a strictly monistic Neoplatonism. He was hostile to Christianity and attacked *Ioannes Philoponus as a renegade. On the closing of the philosophical schools at Athens in 529 A.D., he went to Persia with Damascius and others, but returned to Roman territory in 533 A.D. BIBLIOGRAPHY: P. Merlan, LexAW 2802–03; CHGMP 316–318; Ueberweg 1:634–635.

[M. R. P. MCGUIRE]

SIMPSON, RICHARD (1820–76), journalist. He graduated from Oriel College, Oxford (1843), was Anglican vicar in Surrey until he became a Catholic (1846). Because of his wide interests he became a writer for the *Rambler* and the *Home and Foreign Review* (editor 1858–59). With Lord Acton and John Henry Newman he tried to reconcile Catholic thought with current developments. Most of the English hierarchy opposed many of his views. Through pamphlets Simpson debated Bp. William Ullathorne (1863) and with Acton, composed a reply to Card. Manning on the topic of papal infallibility. After the demise of the *Home and Foreign Review* (1864), he published *Edmund Campion* (1867), and hereafter concentrated his efforts on the study of Shakespeare. BIBLIOGRAPHY: J. L. Altholtz, *Liberal Catholic Movement in England*, (1962); B. McElrath, NCE 13:232–233.

[G. J. RUPPEL]

SIMULATION, a deception in deed, as a lie is a deception in speech. It is governed by the same moral rules; a wrong is done to a person when you palm off to him a falsehood instead of a truth to which he has a right. Custom and convention, social good manners and good sense generally enable a person to discern easily what is proper and what is not. It is agreed that a policeman may wear plain clothes to gain information, but not to act as an agent provocateur; that you may wear a wig or have your false teeth simulate real ones, but not that you may play a part, e.g., of *faux bonhomme*, in order to gain an advantage you do not deserve. Still less, of course, to do a treacherous wrong. The ethics of simulation do not apply to the stage: the more convincing the illusion, the higher the art. Simulation has a specific application to the discipline of the sacraments. A person lacking priestly ordination who simulates celebrating Mass or absolving incurs excommunication (CIC c. 2322, n. 1). A minister sins gravely who falsifies the formula or action of a sacrament without the knowledge of the supposed recipient, e.g., a penitent. The dissimulation of a sacrament is with the supposed recipient's knowledge and consent in order to protect the person against others' knowing the sacrament was denied: e.g., a priest hearing confessions in an open place may simply impart a blessing, when he cannot absolve; observers take the blessing as absolution. BIBLIOGRAPHY: S. F. Parmisano, NCE 13:233.

[T. GILBY]

SIMULTANEUM, a legal term in German ecclesiastical history, short for *simultaneum exercitium religionis*. In its first use in the 16th cent., the Latin phrase referred to the right of simultaneous practice of two or more faiths in the same territory (see TERRITORIAL CHURCH). *Simultaneum* came more often to refer to a right to the use of the same buildings (called therefore "simultaneous churches") by congregations of different faiths. Such a right to use RC churches was conceded to *Old Catholics in Prussia after 1870, but was resisted by Rome. BIBLIOGRAPHY: EncRelKnow 10:431–432.

[T. C. O'BRIEN]

SIN, an act or state that violates the will of God for communion between himself and man. As it is usually understood, both in the language of the Bible and in common parlance, sin is often taken as an ethical category. To sin is to do something contrary to the divinely legislated code for proper conduct. "Whosoever committeth sin transgresseth also the law; for sin is the transgression of the law" (1 Jn.3.4). The OT, with its manifold legislation about the ritual and moral conduct of the Israelite, often identifies sin with transgression of this legislation. Yet biblical religion does not make this definition of sin decisive of itself, for the law whose transgression makes an act sinful is not first of all a written code (even though it is also a code and is eventually written), but the revealed will of the creator. Breaking the law, therefore, means acting deliberately in disobedience to him and in rebellion against his intention for his creatures. This rebellion, not the overtly immoral "living in sin," is what makes sin such a serious business in biblical and in Christian theology. The law, e.g., the Decalogue, is intended as a means of discovering that the will of God has been violated, for "through the law comes knowledge of sin" (Rom 3.20); but it is a moralistic distortion to define sin exclusively in the terms of law, even of divine law.

The deepest insight of Christian faith into the nature of sin has been the recognition that sin is an act of severing, or at least of jeopardizing, the intimate relation between creator and creature. As the positive form of that relation is never simply one of conformity to the prescriptions of a book of rules but is always one of fellowship with God himself, so the negation of that relation is inevitably defined in personal terms. A vivid metaphor for the violation, esp. prominent in the prophecy of Hosea but audible in large parts of the OT, is that of the unfaithful wife who has, by a deliberate and wanton act, cut herself off from her loving husband. This personal dimension of sin attends even the expressions of guilt brought on by the remembrance of a moral wrong. Thus Ps 51.4, attributed to David after his adultery with Bathsheba, makes clear that the sin has violated a relation with God: "Against thee, thee only have I sinned." Conversely, the forgiveness of sins is not merely the removal of moral guilt, but the restoration, by God himself as the injured party, of this personal relationship. The liturgical and penitential practice of the Church has aimed to emphasize this dimension of sin in the language it has used for confession and in its pleas for mercy.

In their discussions of sin, theologians have introduced several distinctions aimed at clarifying its nature. The most basic is the distinction between *original sin and actual sin: actual sin is the term for those deeds in which a man disobeys the will of God; original sin describes a state brought on by the fall of man in which man lost his original sanctifying grace. Theology has distinguished between mortal sin and venial sin (see 1 Jn 5.16–17): mortal sin is so designated because it kills the soul by bringing about the loss of grace; venial sin, though by no means a trifle, does not cause such a loss of grace. The distinction made by theologians between sins of commission and sins of omission is based upon their relation to the law: a sin of commission is a transgression against an express prohibition of the law of God; a sin of omission is a failure to fulfill what that law demands. In all of these distinctions, too, the understanding of sin as the violation of a personal bond with God, not only as a wicked deed, is an essential component.

The central elements of this doctrine of sin are the common property of most Christian denominations, but differences both of emphasis and of content have arisen between Eastern and Western theology and among various schools of Protestant thought. The prominence of St. Augustine in the doctrinal history of the West has been visible in the language about sin used, not only by St. Thomas Aquinas, but by Martin Luther and John Calvin. In Eastern Orthodoxy the Augustinian emphasis upon inherited sin is often absent, but there is a strong sense of sin as dominance by the demonic. Modern Western theology, both Roman Catholic and Protestant, has subjected the traditional Western view of original sin to critical scrutiny. BIBLIOGRAPHY: R. Niebuhr, *Nature and Destiny of Man* (1941–43); E. Brunner, *Man in Revolt* (1939).

[J. PELIKAN]

SIN (IN THE BIBLE). The complexity of the OT conception of sin is reflected in the number of words for sin in Hebrew, each of which expresses a slightly different aspect of it. Thus *hattat* indicates a failure to attain what is due, a missing of the mark; *awon* connotes distortion or "twisting out of the true," and conveys the idea of crookedness or deformity, a turning aside from the true way laid down for man by God which alone can bring him to the happiness he needs and longs for; *pesah* signifies rebellion; *ma'al* means infidelity, a failure to fulfil one's personal obligations to another, esp. those incurred by the covenant with Yahweh freely entered into by the people; *seker*, a lie, conveys that element of falsity which is present in all sin, for all sin implies being false to one's true nature or one's position in relation to God. Sin is also called folly in the sense of being the outcome of a culpably stupid decision that can only lead to disaster.

Sin can only bring trouble, and that not upon the perpetrator alone but on his descendants and family and all those connected with him. Thus, e.g., the sin of one individual, Achan, brings disaster and defeat upon the Israelite army (Jos 7). This aspect of sin is expressed by the word *awen*, which includes in its meaning not only the sin itself but its evil effects.

Hebrew writers, esp. Jeremiah, are acutely aware of how deeply rooted sin is in the heart of man, which is prone to evil from the very first. "Behold I was brought forth in iniquity and in sin did my mother conceive me" (Ps 51.5). The writings of Qumran and the traditions of the rabbinical schools, too, reflect this preoccupation with the *yeṣer hara'*, the evil inclination which is innate in man. But at least according to the J tradition of the Pentateuch, this disposition to sin was no part of man's original condition. Rather it was introduced by the original rebellion of the first parents and intensified by the proliferation of sin in the primordial history of the world so that the inclination to sin became universal and endemic (Gen 3–11).

New Testament. In the Synoptic Gospels little is said about the nature of sin as such, though here, too, Jesus insists that it has its origin in the heart (Mt 15.18–19; Mk 7.20–22), and that it consists in going astray and voluntarily separating oneself from God. This is the plain meaning of the relevant part of the parable of the Prodigal Son (Lk 15.18,21). Sin is disobedience and rebellion (Mt 7.23; 13.41), and the effect of obstinate and unrepented sin will be final exclusion from the kingdom of God.

In the Johannine writings it is, perhaps, significant that sin is spoken of in the singular rather than the plural. Christ has come to take away the sin of the world (Jn 1.29; cf. 1 Jn 3.5). Jesus takes the collective burden of guilt upon himself in order to reconcile the world to God and to bring it back from its state of godlessness (1 Jn 3.4) and subjugation to the Prince of this world. For there is a radical opposition between the works of Satan and the works of God, the children of Satan and the children of God; and it is this that chiefly characterizes the Johannine theology of sin. All sin is regarded as a lie and proceeds from the father of lies (Jn 8.44). As such it is radically opposed to the truth which Jesus himself represents and embodies; and it seeks to murder this truth (Jn 8.44). This murderous intention is characteristic of sin as such. It manifests itself in hatred of one's brother just as love of one's brother is a sign that one is engrafted into the truth and endowed with eternal life (1 Jn 3.10; Jn 13.35).

Paul develops still further the idea of sin as an evil force that dominates the world. All, Jew and gentile alike, have voluntarily, and therefore culpably, submitted to its bondage, and rendered themselves liable to the curse of death which it entails. Furthermore, all the descendants of Adam are subject to the condition of sin which Adam's original act of sin produced (Rom 5.12–21). It is precisely by submitting himself to this curse of death and rendering it lifegiving in a new and unheard of sense to believers that Christ frees men from this bondage to sin. He is the new Adam, and his redemptive act is the symmetrical opposite of the death-bringing act of the first Adam. BIBLIOGRAPHY: A. Ligier, *Péché d'Adam et péché du monde* (2v.; 1960–61); S. Lyonnet, *De peccato et redemptione* 1 (1958).

[D. J. BOURKE]

SIN, COOPERATION IN, being party to the sinful action of another, not, as in *scandal, simply placing a possible occasion for another's spiritual harm. (1) In general, cooperation can take place in any area of morality where one person can directly contribute to the intent and the action of another. Cooperation is sinful because it involves both sharing in the sinful intent of another and in some way making possible the other's sin. The degree of culpability corresponds to how much the sinner is abetted by the cooperator. The cooperation may be immediate, positive, direct, or may be remote, negative, indirect. Thus one having control over other persons and ordering them to commit sinful acts bears a greater guilt than one who merely keeps silent when he could forestall a sinful act. To be culpable, further, cooperation must positively share in the sinful intent and contribute to the commission of sin as such; such cooperation is termed "formal"; a merely de facto and unintended cooperation is termed "material" cooperation. At times a person must accept being a material cooperator, but that requires precise moral conditions: the situation must be inescapable; the evil act of the sinner cannot be intended; the material cooperator's part cannot itself be an act that is sinful. The situation of material cooperation is regulated by the principle of *double effect. (2) In regard to matters of *justice cooperation in the unjust act of another is a theme that has received special development because of the obligation of *restitution. Kinds of cooperation in sins of injustice are classified under two headings: direct or positive cooperation, namely command, advice, consent, approving praise, harboring or protecting, and sharing in ill-gotten gains; indirect or negative cooperation, namely not protesting, not preventing, not revealing. All cooperators, in any of these ways, have an obligation to make restitution for unjust gains or damage done. The obligation rests first on whoever is the actual unjust *possessor. Such restitution not being made, then the cooperator by way of command has the unqualified obligation to complete restitution. He failing, other cooperators are bound to complete restitution, or, where all contribute to the restitution, each is obliged to a share proportionate to the manner of his cooperation.

[T. C. O'BRIEN]

SIN, DESERT OF, wilderness area where the Israelites murmured against Moses and received manna and quails to eat (Ex ch. 16). The location is uncertain. The Exodus account places it between Elim and Sinai, and records that the Israelites reached it before getting to Dophkah, Alush, and Rephidim (Num 33.11–15; Ex 17.1), but none of those locations is known with certainty. Some scholars, connecting it with the ancient Egyptian mining region of Serabit el-Khadim, place Sin at Debbet er-Ramleh.

[T. EARLY]

SIN, GRAVITY OF. "You judge the specific end of a sin from what it turns to, and its gravity from what it turns from" (ThAq ST Lat-Eng 2a2ae, 148.5 ad 2, v.43, ed.T. Gilby, p. 131). The moral objective of a sinful act may be designated as "the lack-of-good-as-meant" (*ibid.* v.18, 167). That implies that a sin is a defective choice: the turning to some good at the cost of neglecting a higher good or the true relation of what is chosen to the full moral good. Thus the seriousness of a sin depends on the good that it subverts. On an abstract level of moral analysis there is a gradation: all sins are not equally disordered; one is worse than another even as one illness is worse than another. A sin that goes directly against the final end is more subversive of moral goodness than one against a subordinate end; a sin against God, worse than one against self or neighbor. Among sins against others, one that injures the person is worse than one injuring his property. Sins that upset the spiritual good are worse than carnal sins. Such a scale mea-

sures sins by reference to their moral objective. Seriousness may also vary by reason of the cause of sin that may increase or diminish *voluntarity; by *circumstances, or by foreseeable, resulting harm; or by the station of the sinner or the one sinned against. (See ThAq ST 1a2ae, 73). More concrete is the theological evaluation, i.e., one based on the revealed meaning of *grace and *charity. Gravity then is a question not simply of moral disorder, but, as the distinction between mortal and venial sin indicates, of total spiritual death, the destruction of the life-principle in the sinner. Grace and charity put a person into a relationship with God as he communicates the filial new being that is supernatural life. A sin is mortally grave when it shatters that vital communication and blocks its sustaining influence. Since the life in grace is a total gift, its loss cannot be remedied by the sinner. That is the mortality of sin, which only divine forgiveness and reconciliation can remedy. Mortality is not the same as the moral disorderliness deriving from the "lack-of-good-as-meant"; identifying sins as mortal from their moral objective means determining that some moral goods are essentially connected with the continuance of charity. BIBLIOGRAPHY: ThAq ST (Lat-Eng, v.27, ed. T. C. O'Brien 1974) app. 2, "Mortal Sin."

[T. C. O'BRIEN]

SIN, HABITUAL, see HABITUAL SINNER.

SIN, MATERIAL AND FORMAL, an application by analogy of the matter-form distinction that runs throughout Aristotelian natural, metaphysical, and moral philosophy, and is taken into moral theology. The material principle is the subject which is given a specific character by the formal principle; a unity is composed from the duality. The stock example, body and soul, is not entirely accurate, but it will serve. This distinction considers a deed objectively wrong as the matter of a sin, the subjective culpability of the agent as the form. The two do not always go together, for a person can do the first and yet be blameless because of unavoidable *ignorance; or again, he may commit the second under the mistaken *conscience of doing something he believes to be objectively wrong. Despite the verbal likeness, the distinction is not the same as the more technical one used by scholastic authors between the formal element in sin (*formale peccati*) and the material element (*materiale peccati*). The first is the essential constitutive of sin, namely the *privation or moral disorder in a human act, e.g., the practice of sexuality between a couple without committed love (which may be considered either as formal or material sin, in the sense of the first distinction). The second is its basis in the act as physically and psychologically real, e.g., the intercourse of a man and a woman, which as such is morally neutral and spells no privation, but rather the reverse. BIBLIOGRAPHY: ThAq St 1a2ae, 18.4 (esp. in ed. Lat-Eng, v. 18, *Principles of Morality*, ed. T. Gilby, 1967).

[T. GILBY]

SIN, MORTAL AND VENIAL (Lat. *mortale*, deadly, and *veniale*, pardonable, respectively), a division that concerns the effect of a *sin called guilt (*reatus*), not its specific character; for example, it may mark the difference between driving a car recklessly in heavy traffic or on an open road, but not between driving a car recklessly and fornicating. The theological argument goes as follows. Some wrongful acts strike so deeply as to determine a person's whole attitude; on a grave issue he has knowingly and willingly turned away from God by preferring something else instead, usually himself in some guise, and so long as he acquiesces in that posture, he cannot be counted among God's friends, and so, having deprived himself of grace and the habit of *charity, and cut himself off from the source of Christian life, he is now by analogy dead. Other wrongful acts, however, do not imply such a tragic crisis; though quite indefensible and indeed inexcusable, either because they are about petty or at least not considerable matters, or because ignorance and emotion have darkened and confused the decision, the person who does them does not will to be cut off from God. His act, of course, is not an actual loving of God; indeed it is a faltering or a missing of the way to God, but it is directly rather against the activity than the habit of charity, and he is, in various degrees, to be called ill, not dead, in respect to the Christian life.

The division, which is not without its academic difficulties for a teleological theology of human acts, and which is rejected by some of the more uncompromisingly black-or-white and simplistically salvational Christian bodies, goes back at least to Tertullian, is clearly present in St. Augustine, is certainly not unscriptural, and is rooted in the working consciousness of Catholic Christianity. It has been criticized, not altogether unfairly, for leading to a preoccupation about how to avoid mortal sin, coupled with an indifference to smaller failings. No reputable moral teacher countenances carelessness about venial sin; quite the contrary, for all warn us, as Chaucer did, how ''skippeth venial into deddlie synne.'' Properly understood, the division encourages confidence in God, not too strait-laced a response to his call, and a robust candor about our failings. Of course on the relative incidence of these two degrees of sin no prudent theologian will pontificate.

Three conditions are required for mortal sin. First, grave matter, for in the spiritual life, as elsewhere, you cannot make molehills into mountains. Second, full advertence as to both what you are doing and its being gravely wrong, for *ignorance may affect the voluntary quality of a human act. Third, perfect consent, for compulsive force or a rush of passion may lessen its freedom. Absence of any one of these conditions operates to make a sin less than mortal.

The category called theological imperfection by some spiritual authors of the last few centuries is not found in the classics of patristic and scholastic moral theology. BIBLIOG - RAPHY: ThAq ST 1a2ae, 72.5 (esp. in ed. Lat-Eng, v. 25, *Sin*, ed. J. Fearon, 1969); 88–89 (v. 27, *Effects of Sin* . . . ed. T. C. O'Brien, 1974) app. 2, ''Mortal Sin.''

[T. GILBY]

SIN, OCCASIONS OF, people, places, circumstances, objects that either general moral judgment or individual past experience indicates to be influences towards sin. They are called occasions and not causes of sin in the sense that nothing outside a person's own will can directly cause sin, since it must by definition be voluntary. Depending on the degree of influence to be expected or that has been experienced, an occasion is designated as remote or proximate. Depending on the reason a person confronts it, an occasion is designated as necessary or voluntary. As pastoral norms it is clear that: to involve oneself in a proximate, voluntary occasion of sin is itself sinful, an unnecessary risking of moral failure; to be confronted with a necessary occasion, requires the intent to keep its influence remote. The second norm indicates how persons faced with an occasion of sin concomitant with their work or means of livelihood must be guided: the requirement is not to give up the work or means of livelihood, but to take whatever measures are possible for self-protection. *OCCASIONISTS.

[T. C. O'BRIEN]

SIN, ORIGINAL, see ORIGINAL SIN.

SIN, PERSONAL. The scholastic psycho-theological analysis of personal or actual sin picked up from the old Greek controversy as to whether moral failure could be resolved into an unfortunate mistake due to ignorance, as Socrates thought, or whether it also introduced a culpable defect of affectivity, as Aristotle thought. It worked with a delicate psychology of human activity, and was constantly alert to the setting of biblical revelation and to St. Augustine's teaching on transgression of divine and indeed eternal law.

Nature. A sin (*peccatum*) is an *evil in acting, not in being. It is a failure of an activity to reach its purpose, an action that miscarries or goes amiss (cf. Gr. *hamartanō,* to miss the mark). The notion by extension may be applied also to non-intelligent beings, which do not always succeed in their natural activities. However, sin takes on a special and its usual sense when applied to *human acts, namely of doing wrong, not right, and through our own *fault (*culpa*). It should be conceived in terms less of substantives and adjectives than of verbs and adverbs; less of a right or a wrong in a juridical sense, than of acting well-directly or ill-directly toward God who is the ultimate aim of human life. This teleological reference is essential for a moral meaning, and in particular for that of sin.

To sin is to fail to go out to God; it sets up a wickedness (*malitia*), a deprivation of a true good that should be man's, and induces a condition of vice (*vitium*), the opposite of virtue. The term *malitia* undergoes a further development, which will be noticed later.

Basic Source. How does it come about that a man fails? It does not spring from the nature of things, not even from the nature of *freedom, which lies in the ability, not to choose between good and evil, but to be uncompelled by any particular good. It is a consequence of the present human predicament. In his environment, the only object which a man's will can love without any hesitation, is goodness, subsistent and complete. However, this is not immediately presented to him as a thing, namely God clearly seen; it exercises its appeal in the pervasive abstraction called happiness, the concrete exemplification of which is broken up into bits and pieces. Were the objects that take man to God the only attractions, were those which lead him away simply distasteful, there would be no problem. As it is, since God himself is an imperative held only as a principle in the darkness of faith or as an inference in the light of reason, and since the objects that take man to him on occasion prove more tedious than those which take him away, he is very open to deflection from his course. Along these lines the problem of moral evil can be represented as the problem of too many and conflicting goods.

For—and here the general consensus of theologians echoes the teaching of the Pseudo-Dionysius—nobody chooses evil for the sake of evil; a man could not do so even were he so crass as to try. Even the cult of vice is a sort of protest against the smugness of virtue, and those who make a parade of it are commonly amateurs in the matter, whereas the real professionals are not conspicuously full of themselves. Human beings can be beastly or devilish, and not human, in their wickedness; but all the same they are pursuing some odd and twisted form of good, though in the single complex of human factors they are judged to be doing evil.

Now evil is more than a negation of good. Were it no more than that, a man would be bad for not being affectionate and considerate about somebody he has never met or is likely to meet. Evil is the privation of good, the lack of it when it should be present, as when a man is not affectionate and considerate with his nearest and dearest. How does this privation come about? By another good elbowing out the due good, thus causing a man to forsake the good he ought to pursue for the pleasure of something else. In fact moral evil is never an evil pure and simple, but, like a weed, which is a plant out of place, or dirt, which is matter out of place, it is a good out of place. All this is said, not by way of extenuation, but to help toward an impersonal appreciation that keeps the subject in proportion.

Accordingly there is in sin the turning away (aversio) from the true good, and the turning to (conversio) another and seeming good in its place. The offense offered to God is the aversion from him; nobody in his senses would do this sheerly for its own sake; what the sinner does is to turn to something else instead of God—"instead" being the operative term. This attachment to a creaturely type of good implying a detachment from uncreated good gives to each kind of sin its specific character, and it accounts also for differences in the degree of malice to be found in different sins.

Causes. Sin rises from a creature who is radically eversible, liable to topple or overturn. That he does so is because of some factor either energetic enough to upset the balance of the whole or inhibiting the action of forces that would maintain it. These causes are both inside and outside man.

Internal causes. The sinner of whom we speak is man, not in a hypothetical state of pure nature, which has never been historical, but in a state of fallen nature; even when he is forgiven through Christ and lives in God's friendship, he still bears the wounds of *original sin, is not yet restored to the integrity of *original justice. Within him there is *ignorance, part inherited, part his own fault; within him is a *sensuality easily inflamed against spiritual values; within him there is a proclivity of will toward proximate and present goods at the expense of more ultimate and necessary goods: this last is called malice in the old sense of the term, a badness not to be confused with "maliciousness," a shriller and narrower term. Hence the common division of sins from ignorance, from weakness, and from malice. The mainspring of sin is the human will, yet the trouble is not exclusively there, but may lie in the mind or sensorium; indeed the true interior cause is the whole personality as the source of voluntary activity.

External causes. God is in no sense the cause of sin, either directly or indirectly, though from him comes all that is positively real in the act. To catch a glimpse of the truth here we have to reflect on the double face of sin already alluded to, namely the negative aversion and the positive conversion which together produce the privation: the matter, however, belongs to the natural mystery of divine *premotion and the supernatural mystery of efficacious *grace. No other outside cause can effectively act on the human will except by way of suggestion and persuasion. Here the unanimous tradition of theologians for centuries includes the *devil, who has a declared interest in the question, and the wickedness of other men.

We should not be in a hurry to blame the parents of the human race, for original sin, which is racial not personal, is our sin as well as theirs, and is to be distinguished from the first actual sin they committed.

Though some sins bring a brood of other sins, and are called capital sins by St. Gregory the Great, there is no intrinsic connection between the vices as there is between the virtues; their effect is anarchic, and it is reassuring to be taught that we can refer to the kingdom of evil only in metaphorical sense.

Effects. The primary effect of sin is an estrangement from God. We speak of his being offended and angry, but there again our language is figurative. He is not hurt; we are. "Venial sin" is like a stumble—we are not going to God when we are doing it; "mortal sin" is like a fall—we have gone away from God when we have done it. The result of estrangement is called *guilt, and more exactly the guilt for punishment (reatus poenae). This penalty should be regarded less as arbitrarily inflicted, as in a human court of law, than as following intrinsically from the wrongdoing. I choose not to look for God, and then, but for his mercy, I surely will not find him, and perhaps for ever, which will be *hell.

Another effect of sin is to make the sinner like the objects he is addicted to; his drunkenness may make him a soak, his avarice may turn him into a sort of human cash-register, and so forth. This is called the stain of sin (*macula peccati*), which expression, though sometimes the occasion of bad pulpit rhetoric, is a fair enough metaphor from bright things being dulled or dirtied by contact with things less precious.

Division. Sins have been divided, with various degrees of popular acceptance and attention to the logic of division, into sins of commission and omission; into those of thought, word, and deed; into those of the flesh and of the spirit; into those against God, one's neighbor, and oneself. The most scientific division, however, is that adopted by St. Thomas Aquinas, namely as a corollary to his classification of the virtues.

However unfaithful its motives and catastrophic its effects, sin is a reality that does not exceed God's power and mercy to deal with. He is never baffled, thwarted, nor even disappointed. Forgiveness of the fault is entirely his without any deserving on man's part. "Turn thou me, and I shall be turned, for thou art the Lord my God" (Jer 31.18). Then also the effects are abolished by Christ's atonement. To share in that is the burden of our following him. BIBLIOGRA-PHY: ThAq ST la, 48; 1a2ae, 21; 1a2ae, 71–85 (esp. in ed. Lat-Eng, v. 8 *Creation, Vanity, and Evil* ed. T. Gilby, 1967; v. 18 *Principles of Morality*, ed. T. Gilby, 1966; v. 25 *Sin*, ed. J. Fearon, 1969; v. 26, *Original Sin*, ed. T. C. O'Brien, 1965; v. 27 *Effects of Sin*, ed. T. C. O'Brien, 1974).

[T. GILBY]

SIN, REMISSION OF, see REMISSION OF SIN.

SIN, UNFORGIVABLE, see UNFORGIVABLE SIN.

SIN OFFERING (IN THE BIBLE). Sacrifices for sin in the OT are divided into 'ăsam sacrifices (guilt offerings) and ḥaṭṭaṭ sacrifices (sin offerings), although the precise significance of the distinction is not clear. The ritual of these offerings is set forth in Lev 4. This type of sacrifice is divided between Yahweh and the priests. No portion of it is consumed by the offerer. A special feature of this type of sacrifice is that some of the blood is actually smeared on the horns of the altar so that contact with the deity is conceived of as particularly close. This may be compared with the ritual of the Day of *Atonement, where blood is sprinkled on the "mercy seat" or *kapporet*, the cult object most directly associated with Yahweh's presence. In the same way, the sin offering appears to have been thought of as particularly holy and charged with numinous power, so that the priests could not leave the "holy place" until they had consumed their portion of it. The purpose of the sin offering is to achieve *purification, i.e., to secure the readmission of the offerer to his due place in the sphere of holiness created by the divine presence, from which he or she has been temporarily debarred by some ritual contamination whether through childbirth, disease, or sexual disorder, or some accidental breach of the cultic rules. BIBLIOGRAPHY: R. de Vaux, *Studies in Old Testament Sacrifice* (1964) 91–112.

[D. J. BOURKE]

SINAI, mountain where the Israelites received the Law, including the Ten Commandments, following their flight from Egypt (Ex ch. 19–35). The people camped at the foot of the mountain while Moses went up the mountain to receive the Law from Yahweh.

The location of Mt. Sinai is unknown. No Jewish tradition concerning the site exists, but Christian tradition since the Byzantine period locates it in the mountains at the S end of the Sinai Peninsula. A natural place for an encampment is in front of Ras es-Safsaf, the NW summit of the range. The higher SE summit is Jebel Musa (*c*.7,500 feet), and SW is Jebel Katarin (*c*.8,500 feet). Tradition names Ras es-Safsaf as *Horeb and Jebel Musa (Mountain of Moses) as Sinai. Horeb was the name used for Sinai in the *Elohist and Deuteronomic traditions (Ex 3.1; Dt 1.6; 1 Kg 19.8). Sinai was the name used by the Yahwist and the Priestly traditions (Ex 19–24).

Assertions that thunder and lightning occurred while the Israelites were at Sinai (Ex 19.16), and that fire, smoke, and quaking were associated with the occasion (19.18) have led some to assume that a volcanic eruption lies behind the tradition. That would suggest a different location, perhaps NW Arabia (Jg 5.4). Others, however, regard the events as weather phenomena or as metaphorical statement. Similar phenomena are reported in connection with Elijah's visit (1 Kg 19.11–12).

Sinai is of special importance for biblical theology as the place where the covenant relation between Yahweh and Israel was established, with the Law regulating the form the relationship would take. BIBLIOGRAPHY: M. Noth, *History of Israel* (1958; tr. P. R. Ackroyd, 2d ed. 1960).

[T. EARLY]

SINAI, MONASTERY OF, a monastery at the foot of Mt. Sinai founded by the Emperor *Justinian I in the 6th cent., and named after St. *Catherine of Alexandria who had suffered martyrdom in the 4th cent. and whose supposed relics repose in the monastery's church of the Transfiguration. This church, built by Justinian, is one of the oldest Christian churches and is outstanding for its grandiose style. On one of its frescoes can be seen a mosaic of the Emperor and his wife, Empress Theodora. Because of its relative isolation, the church escaped the ravages of the controversies over *iconoclasm, and there are more than 400 well-preserved icons throughout the monastic buildings. Two of the most ancient icons in the world are located there: one of the Mother of God and one of the Apostle Paul, both done no later than the 5th or 6th century. The church also contains a great number of relics including those of SS. *Ephrem the Syrian and *John Climacus, one-time abbot of St. Catherine's. The monastery library contains about 3,000 ancient MSS in Arabic, Coptic, Georgian, Greek, Slavonic, and Syriac as well as many other documents and scrolls. While there are fragments of texts that date from the 5th and 6th cent., most of them date from the 8th cent. or later. Among the many codices preserved there, the best known is the *Codex Sinaiticus* (4th cent.) discovered by the German scholar C. Tischendorf and Archimandrite Porfiry Uspensky. A center of early Christian monasticism, the monastery continued to attract both pilgrims and monks and gradually attained autocephalous status in the Orthodox Church (see SINAI, MT., ORTHODOX CHURCH OF). BIBLIOGRAPHY: M. H. L. Rabino, *Le Monastère de Sainte Catherine du Mont Sinai* (1935).

[S. SURRENCY]

SINGENBERGER, JOHN BAPTIST AND OTTO, American church musicians. **John** (1848–1924) was born in Switzerland. He graduated from Innsbruck, spent some time as a choirmaster, then resumed study at Regensburg under F. X. Witt and F. X. Haberl. He came to the U.S. in 1873 as music director for the Normal School at St. Francis, Wisconsin. Modeling it on the one he had established at Grisons seminary, S. cofounded (with Rev. Joseph Salzmann) the American Caecilian Society. He became the first president as well as the founding editor of its publication, *Caecilia* magazine. An able teacher, conductor, and composer of Masses, hymns, and motets, S. was awarded the Papal Cross in 1905 by Pius X and was knighted by Popes Pius X and Pius XI. **Otto** (1883–1944), son of John, was, throughout his lifetime an organist in various cathedrals and churches. After his father's death, he was editor, for a time, of *Caecilia*. He directed the singing at the International Eucharistic Congress in Chicago in 1926, and from 1929–1938 was music supervisor of the Milwaukee Catholic schools. Otto composed Masses, motets, hymns, and other church music. Like his father, he endeavored to compose music practical for singing by congregations and ordinary church choirs. BIBLIOGRAPHY: E. E. Nemmers, *Twenty Centuries of Catholic Church Music* (1949) 174–175.

[M. T. LEGGE]

SINGIDUNUM, MARTYRS OF. SS. Hermylus and Stratonicus, martyred during the persecution of Licinius (308–323), are associated with the ancient city of Singidunum near Belgrade. Montanus and Maxima, although decapitated in Sirmium, are also associated with Singidunum.

[E. J. DILLON]

SINGING, see HYMNS AND HYMNALS.

SINGMESSE, a Ger. term for a Mass during which vernacular hymns were sung, first at the proper of the Mass, then also at the Ordinary. The practice began, partly in imitation of the effectiveness of Lutheran hymnody, in the 17th century. Under *Josephinism in Austria, the simplification of the liturgy, a reaction to the elaborate symphonic Masses of the Classical period, included imposition in 1783 of a hymnal by Johann Kohlbrenner for use in the

Singmesse. In modern times the tradition of the Singmesse was a positive influence in the movement toward vernacular liturgy.

[M. T. LEGGE]

SINGULARI NOS, encyclical letter of Gregory XVI (June 25, 1834), condemning *Lamennais' doctrine as delirious insanity, the product of a frenzied desire for novelty and not a desire for truth. Gregory had previously censured Lamennais' views and his journal *L'Avenir* as advocating the suppression of the freedom of the Church, rebellion against the Church, and separation of Church and State. *Singulari nos* was a reaction to Lamennais' *Paroles d'un croyant* (1834), which impugned the principle of obedience and taught indifferentism and freedom of conscience.

[J. P. REID]

SINNER, HABITUAL, see HABITUAL SINNER.

SINNER, PUBLIC, in canon law and moral theology, one who has been excommunicated by name or whose life of grave sin is notoriously well known. According to present canonical discipline the meaning of "public sinner" is relevant to the issue of administration of the sacraments (see SACRAMENTS, REFUSAL OF; also CIC, c. 855; 1240, § 1 on denial of Christian burial; c. 1066 on marriage). The meaning of the term, however, is being reconsidered as the Church's canon law is in the process of revision and the penal law of the Church is being reevaluated. In the contemporary social patterns and esp. in urban settings the meaning of "public sinner" has lost some of its point and the penalties some of their relevance. While the canonical discipline in itself has not been changed, in this matter pastoral interpretation has become considerably broadened.

SINNICH, JOHN (1603–66), Irish-born theologian of the Jansenist movement. He received all of his academic degrees from Louvain where he collaborated in the publication of Jansenius's *Augustinus*, served as president of the College of the Holy Spirit (1641), member of the theological faculty (1642) and occasionally its dean, and semestral rector of the university (1643). From 1643 to 1645, he participated in the Jansenist controversy as pamphleteer and personal advocate, defending Jansenius in Rome. *Sanctorum Patrum Trias* (1648) is S.'s best-known work.

[R. J. LITZ]

SINS, CAPITAL, see CAPITAL SINS.

SINS, NUMBER OF. The numerical distinction of sins became a prominent issue in moral theology because of the Council of Trent's requirement that each and every mortal sin of which a penitent is aware must be confessed (D 1679–80; 1705). Obviously acts that differ in kind also differ numerically; but the kind of moral good or evil characterizing an act derives from its moral objective. It is thus possible that a sinful act that is deformed on two counts amounts to two distinct sins; adultery, e.g., is both unchastity and injustice. Similarly, a person who kills several people by an act of terrorism is guilty of multiple homicide. A further basis for numbering sins is the continuity of willful engagement in a sinful act. A continuity interrupted by first revoking the sinful intention then renewing it means two distinct acts. On the other hand an act that takes some time to bring about the intended end, e.g., a series of petty thefts in order to steal a large amount, is morally a single sin. The numerical distinctness among internal thoughts or desires is less easy to determine than that of outward actions. The essential point of the sacrament of penance is, of course, *contrition. It is a distortion to regard the moral life as only a series of numerically isolated deeds. The general shape and habitual intent of a person's life are a more telling index than is a mere numerical recitation of sins.

[T. C. O'BRIEN]

SINS AGAINST THE HOLY SPIRIT, *despair, *presumption, impenitence, obstinacy in sin, resistance to the known truth, envy of another's gifts of grace. The enumeration was developed from a considerable patristic literature (Athanasius, Chrysostom, Ambrose, Augustine, Gregory, for example), prompted by the expression in Mt 12.31, "the sin of blasphemy against the Holy Spirit will not be forgiven." These specific sins are singled out because they imply a resolute wickedness or *malice that impugns the sources of salvation and forgiveness, the workings of the Holy Spirit in the soul. Despair destroys regard for God's mercy; presumption, for his justice; impenitence is a fixed purpose against repentance; obstinacy, to continue to sin; resistance to the known truth is a blinding of self against the malice of sin in order to sin with more abandon; envy of grace in another is a loathing of grace itself and its workings. Such sins are said to be unforgivable, not because God is powerless to forgive, but because they are a direct obstacle to and contempt for grace, and because, unlike sins of *weakness or *ignorance, these have no mitigating element and deserve absolutely never to be forgiven. BIBLIOGRAPHY: ThAq ST 2a2ae, 14.

[T. C. O'BRIEN]

SINS CRYING TO HEAVEN FOR VENGEANCE, willful murder, sodomy, the oppression of the poor, and defrauding laborers of their wage. In Gen 4.10 Yahweh speaks to the first murderer, "What have you done? Listen to your brother's blood crying out to me from the ground." The background of this expression seems to be the primitive belief that exposed blood is seen by God and avenged. This is reflected in Gen 37.26 when the brothers of Joseph in plotting his murder plan to cover the blood with the earth. Job 16.18 prays, "Cover not my blood, O earth," and Ezek 24.8 says, "The Lord makes His anger overflow to take revenge by putting blood on the naked rock." Isaiah 26.21 says, "The earth will reveal its blood and no longer hide its

slain." The sin of *sodomy is also included in the list of sins crying to heaven for vengeance in the expression of Gen 18.20–21, "The outcry against them has come up to me." The oppression of the poor is also considered from the expression of Ex 2.23, "The sons of Israel groaning in their slavery cried out for help and from the depths of their slavery their cry came up to God." Finally, defrauding laborers of their wages listed in Jas 5.4, "The laborers mowed your field and you cheated them. Listen to the wages that you kept back calling out; realize that the cries of the reapers have reached the ears of the Lord of Hosts."

[U. VOLL]

SINZIG, PEDRO (1876–1952) Franciscan writer. Born in Germany, S. became a friar in Brazil and was ordained in 1898. A prodigious worker for Catholic cultural causes, he was a journalist associated as founder or editor with a dozen periodicals, among them *Música Sacra,* established in 1941. S. was a novelist of note and a critic. Among his novels was *Pela mão de uma Menina* (1913). Two critical works were *Em Plena Guerra* (1912) and *Através dos Romances* (1928). The influence of S. on Brazil's cultural life was profound.

[J. R. AHERNE]

SION, see ZION.

SIRACH, BOOK OF, in the RC canon of the Bible, one of the deuterocanonical books; for Jews and Protestants, one of the apocrypha, i.e., a non-canonical book. Sirach is part of the name of the author, Joshua or Jesus, son of Eleazar, son of Sira (see 50.27). The Wisdom of Jesus Son of Sira is sometimes given as the title, because of this verse and a subscript to 51.38. In the 3d cent. in the Latin Church, the book received the title Ecclesiasticus (The Church Book), from its frequent ecclesiastical use, and possibly because the Church accepted its canonicity. The book is a Greek translation written in 132 B.C. of a Hebrew original composed by the translator's grandfather, Sira, c.180 B.C. Substantial fragments of the Hebrew original have been pieced together from a number of MSS that have been discovered, amounting in all perhaps to three-fifths of the total work. These exhibit notable departures from the Greek version which we actually possess.

The purpose of the author seems to have been to provide his fellow Jews, who were in danger of being over-impressed by Hellenistic wisdom, with an alternative rooted in their own biblical tradition. Thus the wisdom and skill that a man needs to apply in the ordinary circumstances of practical living in the world are regarded as deriving from the divine wisdom, which was planted, took root, and flourished at Zion (see ch. 24), and which is identified with the Law (24.23–34). The topics treated of are similar to those of Proverbs: patience in times of affliction (2.1–18), obedience to parents (3.1–16), friendship (6.1–17), relations with women (9.1–13), the treatment of slaves

(30.24–31), the virtues of silence (20.1–8), correct behavior at banquets (31.12; 37.29). The principal virtues extolled are prudence, temperance, self-restraint, and circumspection, and above all devotion to the Law. The most striking feature of the book is perhaps the hymns to wisdom interspersed through it, (esp. ch. 24, but also 1.1–20; 4.11–19; 14.20–15.8; 51.13–29), and the "praise of the fathers" from Enoch to Nehemiah, who are presented as examples of virtue and wisdom (44.1–49.19). But Sira includes in this the less worthy figures of the past as well, and forthrightly condemns the sins of Solomon, Roboam, Jeroboam, and the other kings who led Israel astray. He appears to have been an ardent ritualist with a great love of the temple, and one of his most lyrical passages is a description of the High Priest Simeon arrayed in his robes for the ceremonies of the Day of Atonement (ch. 50). H. Duesberg, *Les Scribes inspirés* II (1939) 232–440; P. Winter, "Ben Sira and the Teaching of 'Two Ways'," VT 5 (1955) 315–318; A. M. Dubarle, *Les Sages d'Israël* (1946) 147–185; T. H. Weber, JBC 1:541–555.

[D. J. BOURKE]

SIRICIUS, ST. (d. 399), **POPE** from 384. S. became pope despite the ascetic party and St. *Jerome, whose hostile view of him probably accounts for S.'s exclusion from the calendar of the saints until the 18th century. His pontificate was marked by a strong assertion of papal authority. A letter of his to Spanish bishops, condemning the "rebaptism" of heretics and enforcing celibacy on clerics in major orders, is the first extant collection of papal decrees (see D 181–185). He spoke of St. Peter's bearing the burdens of the Church in his person. In 386 he presided over a synod of 80 bps. at the Vatican, the decrees of which were sent to the bps. of North Africa. In 390 he presided over a synod that condemned *Jovinian's contention that virginity and celibacy were useless. S. contributed to the healing of a schism at Antioch; by his influence Flavian was accepted by the Council of Caesarea as the rightful bishop. S. consecrated the first basilica of St. Paul-outside-the-Walls (390). He was buried in the cemetery of Priscilla. BIBLIOGRAPHY: J. S. Bruscher, *Popes Through the Ages* (1959); Butler 4:424–425.

[P. F. MULHERN]

SIRLETO, GUGLIELMO (1514–85), Italian card., librarian, and editor. For his friend Card. Cervino, later Marcellus II, then presiding officer at the first period of the Council of Trent, S. prepared in Rome memoranda on questions before the Council; he later worked closely with G. *Seripando. He was chief editor of the Roman Cathechism, official texts of the Vulgate and LXX, the *Corpus iuris canonici*, the Breviary and revised Missal, all decreed by Trent. As head of the Vatican Library he was responsible for having the library's entire collection of Greek MSS catalogued.

[R. J. LITZ]

SIRMIUM, city of Roman Pannonia on the Sava River; modern Sremska Mitrovica, Yugoslavia. It was taken by Rome during the reign of Augustus. The *Four Crowned Martyrs were among early Christians of Sirmium. In the Arian era Bp., Photinus championed radical Arianism and was deposed by a moderate synod held there in 351. But the high point of official acceptance of Arianism was reached at another council there in 357 with a doctrinal subordinationist decision that *Hilary of Poitiers called the blasphemy of Sirmium (see HOSIUS OF CÓRDOBA). Through Hilary's *De synodis* the documents of the synods of Sirmium entered Latin theology's discussion of the Trinity. After the Avars destroyed the city, which had been the metropolitan see for W Illyricum, it was rebuilt around the monastery of St. Demetrius and called Dmitrovica. Pope Adrian II unsuccessfully attempted to form an archdiocese of Sirmium in 869. Gregory XI made it a diocese in 1229. Clement XIV unified the dioceses of Bosnia and Sirmium in 1773, with both names used at the new seat of the diocese at Djakovo.

[T. EARLY]

SIRMOND, JACQUES (1559–1651), French Jesuit historian and patrologist. In his earlier years as a teacher in Paris, S. numbered St. Francis de Sales among his students. After 18 years in Rome as secretary to the Jesuit general, *Acquaviva, S. returned in 1608 to his teaching in Paris. His numerous scholarly publications included new editions of many ancient and medieval texts. Especially important are his editions of Eusebius of Caesarea, Fulgentius of Ruspe, and Theodoret of Cyr. Among his own writings are learned works on several questions in the history of dogma such as his treatise on the Pseudo-Dionysius. BIBLIOGRAPHY: F. X. Murphy, NCE 13:260–261; E. Peterson, Enc Catt 11:760.

[R. B. ENO]

SIS, CATHOLICATE OF, the see of the Armenian catholicos from 1293. After the foundation of the independent catholicate in *Echmiadzin (1441), which in time became the main center of the Armenian Church, the importance of Sis fell into decline. Some of the later catholicoi of Sis were in communion with Rome, e.g., Gregory IX Mausapekian (1440–50), Khatchadour (1560–84), Aenis de Tchouga (1584–1602), Gregory X d'Adana (1689–91). How others stood with regard to Rome is doubtful; some were frankly hostile. The jurisdiction of Sis extended mainly to the Asiatic part of Turkey, except for the Armenians of Aghtamar and Jerusalem. The establishment of the patriarchate of Constantinople with civil authority over the Armenians (1460) proved to be a source of continuous tension among the different Armenian jurisdictions. In 1921 the catholicos and most of his faithful fled from the persecution being carried on by the Turks and settled in Lebanon. BIBLIOGRAPHY: L. Arpee, *History of Armenian Christianity* (1946).

[J. MEIJER]

SISERA, Canaanite who fought against the Israelites (Jg 4.2). His defeat by Barak and Deborah ended the major Canaanite uprisings against the Israelites (Jg 4.10). After the battle, S. fled to the tent of Jael, who killed him in his sleep (Jg 4.17–22). The Song of Deborah, generally dated earlier than the other material in the Book of Judges, gives a poetic account of the same events (Jg ch. 5). Sons of S. were later listed as temple slaves (Ezra 2.53).

[T. EARLY]

SISINNIUS (d. 708), **POPE** for 20 days in 708. A Syrian, S. was elected on the death of John VII by the clergy and nobility of Rome, as was then the custom. In that short time he gave orders for the reinforcement of the walls of the city, which was threatened by Lombards from the north and by Muslims from the south. S. is buried in St. Peter's. BIB-LIOGRAPHY: M. A. Mulholland, NCE 13:261; Mann 1.2:124.

[P. F. MULHERN]

SISINNIUS I (d. 427), **PATRIARCH OF CONSTAN-TINOPLE** (426–427). A priest serving in the outskirts of Constantinople, he was made patriarch by acclamation. His selection represented a defeat for *Philip Sidetes, the church historian, and *Proclus, secretary to the deceased Patriarch Atticus (406–425). S. appointed Proclus as bp. of Cyzicus, Asia Minor, but popular opposition kept him from occupying the see. Emperor Theodosius II chose Nestorius (428–431) of Antioch to succeed after S.'s sudden death; and Proclus finally became patriarch in succession to Maximianus (431–434). S. is recognized as a saint.

[T. EARLY]

SISINNIUS II (d. 998), **PATRIARCH OF CON-STANTINOPLE** (996–998). He succeeded Nicholas II, after a 4-year period when the office lay vacant. S.'s writings include a work on the Archangel Michael, a tribute to the martyrs Kerykos (Cyriacus) and Julitta, and a tome on marriage. He forbade the practice called *charisticium*, whereby monasteries and their properties were turned over to laymen. The intention of the practice was to provide for better handling of a monastery's secular affairs, but the administrators came to dominate the monasteries. Though forbidden by S., the practice was later accepted by Patriarch Sergius II (1009–19).

[T. EARLY]

SISTER, RELIGIOUS. Strictly, the title applies only to a religious woman professed of simple vows, temporary or perpetual, in a religious congregation. Most of the congregations whose members are properly called sisters were established during and since the 19th century. Making public profession of the vows of poverty, chastity, and obedience, the religious sister assumes the obligation of seeking Christian perfection by the observance of the rule and constitutions of her community. According to the apostolic purpose and work of her community, religious sisters engage in the education of youth, the care of the sick and aged, and social work, both at home and in mission lands. In popular speech the term sister refers to any woman religious. *NUN.

[C. J. NOONE]

SISTER FORMATION MOVEMENT, see RELIGIOUS FORMATION CONFERENCE.

SISTERS OF CHARITY OF PROVIDENCE, otherwise known as Daughters of Charity, Servants of the Poor, a congregation founded in 1843 at Montreal, Canada, for religious women who wished to devote themselves to the spiritual and corporal works of mercy. It was founded by Mme. Emilie Tavernier Gamelin, a widow, under the direction of Bp. Ignace Bourget. The community's first concern was the care of Irish cholera victims on Canada's eastern shore. Since then the sisters have spread throughout Canada, the U.S., and Argentina. In 1961 the congregation established Providence Heights College of Sister Formation, the first institution of its kind in the West. In 1975 the Sisters numbered 2,844 in 199 houses.

[R. C. CLIGGETT]

SISTERS OF DIVINE PROVIDENCE OF KEN-TUCKY, congregation originally founded in Lorraine, France (1762) by Bl. John Martin Moyë, a parish priest of the Diocese of Metz. Its purpose was to instruct neglected children in isolated areas. The sisters were exiled during the French Revolution but returned to France in 1803, and their numbers grew steadily. In 1888 they extended their work to the U.S. and established Mt. St. Martin Convent, Newport, Kentucky. Since 1919 St. Anne Convent, Melbourne, Ky., has served as provincial house and novitiate. The constitutions were approved in 1943, and teaching and nursing became the principal works of the congregation. In 1977 there were 48 houses with 344 sisters engaged in the states of Kentucky, Ohio, West Virginia, New York, Maryland, Rhode Island, and Washington, D.C.

[R. C. CLIGGETT]

SISTERS OF DIVINE PROVIDENCE OF RIBEAUVILLÉ, congregation founded in 1783 at Molsheim in Alsace by Louis Kremp, a secular priest, for the apostolate of teaching. The houses of the congregation are mainly in Alsace, but by 1964 the sisters were teaching in public schools elsewhere in France and in the Congo on almost all levels and in all types of education. In 1807 Bp. Peter Saurine of Strasbourg gave approbation to the congregation. The motherhouse is in Ribeauvillé (dept. Haut-Rhin). In 1975 the sisters numbered 1,354 in 190 houses.

[R. C. CLIGGETT]

SISTERS OF ST. MARIE MADELEINE POSTEL, founded by the saint originally as the Sisters of the Christian Schools of Mercy, a congregation established in 1807 at

Cherbourg, France, to promote Christian education. The sisters follow the Rule of St. John Baptist de La Salle and are bound by simple perpetual vows. The motherhouse is located at Saint-Sauveur-le-Vicomte, Normandy. The community works in five other countries in Europe, in Asia, and in Africa. In 1975 they totaled 753 members in 73 houses. An independent branch of the original community was formed in 1862 by a group of German sisters at Heiligenstadt, and are now known as the Heiligenstadt Schoolsisters. They moved the motherhouse to Bergkloster and in 1975 had 901 members and 88 houses.

[R. A. TODD]

SISTINE CHOIR, popular name of *Il Collegio dei Capellani Cantori della Capella Ponteficia*, a choir, consisting in 1976 of 32 voices, which sings at all solemn services in St. Peter's Basilica at which the pope officiates. The name derives from the Sistine Chapel, built by Sixtus IV (1474–81). The choir traces its history back to St. Gregory the Great's *schola cantorum*. The Julian Choir, named for Julius II, which also sings at St. Peter's, is sometimes mistakenly taken to be the same as the Sistine Choir.

[M. T. LEGGE]

SIT-INS, a technique used in the Civil Rights Movement to make public facilities, previously denied to a discriminated-against section of the community, accessible to all. A protesting group of Negroes would enter premises customarily restricted to a privileged section and ask to be served. On being refused they would continue to sit there instead of leaving as they were requested to do. Their number was large enough for their removal by the police to attract public attention: often they offered no resistance and had to be dragged away. The resultant publicity led to the banning of the segregation of public facilities and was an important milestone in the Negro Revolution in the U.S. The massive entrance into previously forbidden areas was practiced in churches, on beaches, and swimming pools, causing variations of the word such as "kneel-in," "wade-in," "swim-in." The technique is practiced also by nonracial groups, e.g., students or workers, allegedly as a "nonviolent" form of direct action to remedy grievances.

[G. A. VANDERHAAR]

SITUATION ETHICS, the view that an action can be judged to be right or wrong only by the personal character manifested and the personal values released (or not) in a given particular and concrete case, without reference to an outside and impersonal law. Its positive insistence on the importance of unique and individual factors has served as a timely protest against the tyranny of legal and somewhat mechanical abstractions in morals; and it agreed in this with the traditional allowance for the relevance of *circumstances, though the method called that of *contextual ethics is, not surprisingly, more prominent in the Aristoteleanism of the *Summa* of St. Thomas than in later RC

manuals conceived as expositions of the Ten Commandments and the laws of the Church.

It is by its negativeness, its exclusion of other moral determinants, notably of those arising from the objective nature and moral "kind" of an act in question, that pure situationalism lays itself open to criticism and can scarcely be reconciled with Christian theory. To hold that action is to be decided solely by the "existential" realization of one's authentic self can easily be made to look like a thoroughgoing antinomianism and disconnected individualism. Living in community means embracing common norms, and these are not given by responding merely to the incident here and now. For these and other reasons, including the educational and preventive roles of law, situationalism is judged to be a somewhat one-sided system of ethics.

[T. GILBY]

SITWELL, DAME EDITH (1887–1964), English poet and critic, sister of Sir Osbert and Sacheverell Sitwell. Her work, along with that of her brother Osbert, began to appear in an Oxford avant-garde anthology called *Wheels* (1916–21). In 1922 she achieved stormy notoriety with *Facade*, poems with music by William Walton, which she read publicly in London clad in medieval costume. Early work of fantasy changed to tones of horror at cruelty and social evils in *Gold Coast Customs* (1928) and *The Shadow of Cain* (1947). Her trend toward pessimism was offset in the 1940s and 1950s by the quickening of her interest in religion. She became a Roman Catholic in 1955 and was created Dame of the British Empire in 1954. Her early work is experimental with striking conceits, new rhythms, and confusing private allusions. Her later poetry is more Christian in symbolism but retains verbal intensity and an oracular quality. She has written some critical prose. BIBLIOGRAPHY: See her autobiography, *Taken Care Of,* published posthumously (1965); *Celebration for Edith Sitwell* (ed. J. G. Villa, 1948).

[M. M. BARRY]

SIVA (Sanskrit, auspicious), great god of India who has assimilated many of the attributes of the earlier *Rudra. He is usually listed (with *Brahma, the "creator," and *Vishnu, the "pervader") as one of three major gods; here he is the destroyer of the universe at the end of each yuga or age. Those who worship him as supreme generally accept this characteristic of disintegration, but emphasize it as symbolic of the (ascetic or yogic) annihilation of conditioned individual identity, of everything that would stand in the way of true identity or of union with the divine. This aspect of Siva, as the lord of *yoga, is in dynamic tension with his other aspect as lord of unbridled energy (e.g., as Nataraja, or lord of the dance) and sexuality (symbolized in the lingam, or sacred phallus); each aspect is potentially both creative and destructive. Siva is sometimes distinguished from his *Shakti (energy), understood alternately as another facet of himself or as his consort. Also named as his consorts are the destructive *Kali or Durga, and the more restrained *Parvati. The cult of Siva (Saivism; Sivaism; especially the Saiva Siddhanta and Virasaiva sects) has developed an intense form of *bhakti (loving devotion), is militantly monotheistic, sometimes antiritualistic, and emphasizes the gap between Siva's graciousness and human unworthiness. BIBLIOGRAPHY: W. D. O'Flaherty, *Hindu Myths* (1975) 116–74; idem, *Asceticism and Eroticism in the Mythology of Siva* (1973); A. Daniélou, *Hindu Polytheism* (1964) 188–231; A. K. Ramanujan, *Speaking of Siva* (1973).

[D. P. EFROYMSON]

SIX ARTICLES, "An Act abolishing diversity of opinions," passed by Parliament in 1539 under leadership of the Duke of Norfolk and lay peers, in reaction to recent liberal tendencies of the King's reforming churchmen (see TEN ARTICLES). It affirmed, with heavy penalties for opinions to the contrary, *transubstantiation, communion in one kind, clerical celibacy, vows of chastity, private Masses, and auricular confession. Its opponents called it "the whip with six strings." Because of it, two bps., Latimer and Shaxton, resigned, and Abp. *Cranmer had to send his wife back to Germany for a time. BIBLIOGRAPHY: H. Gee and W. J. Hardy, *Documents Illustrative of English Church History* (1896) 303–319; J. Ridley, *Thomas Cranmer* (1962) 178–198.

[M. H. SHEPHERD]

SIX HUNDRED AND SIXTY-SIX, the number of the beast, the anti-Christ of the Apocalypse, who wages war against the Lamb and against the saints. According to Rev 13.18, "anyone who has intelligence may work out the number of the beast. The number represents a man's name, and the numerical value of its letters is six hundred sixty-six." In some MSS the number is rendered six hundred sixteen, as it seems also to have been known to Irenaeus. From Irenaeus on, attempts have been made to compute the numerical values of various people's names according to the numerical value of the letters in the Greek and Hebrew alphabets. The most happy conjecture is that the name of the beast is "Neron Caesar"—the Emperor Nero. That name in Greek and Hebrew adds up to 666. Drop the "n" from "Neron" to "Nero", in conformity with Latin usage, and the sum of the letters is 616. This way all MS traditions can be justified. However, the history of criticism of this text provides many other conjectures to suit diverse tastes and purposes.

[E. J. DILLON]

SIX POINTS, the liturgical usages advocated in the 19th cent. by the ritualists, a wing of the *high-church party in the Church of England: altar lights, eucharistic vestments, eastward position of the priest at the altar, wafer bread, mixing water with wine in the chalice, and incense. The points were proposed and approved in 1875 at the annual meeting of the Church Union, even though many of them had been declared contrary to English law in 1871. *RITUALISM.

[T. C. O'BRIEN]

SIXTUS I, ST. (d. 125), **POPE** from *c.*115. According to the *Liber pontificalis,* he was a native Roman, and as Pope decreed that the sacred vessels should be touched only by clerics, and that the laity should recite the *Sanctus* with the priest at Mass. He is traditionally venerated as a martyr, but the ancient sources provide no information regarding his martyrdom. BIBLIOGRAPHY: Butler 2:18–19; M. da Alatri, BiblSanct 11:1254–56.

[R. B. ENO]

SIXTUS II, ST. (Xystus; d. 258), **POPE** from 257, martyr. S. sought to restore relations with *Cyprian and others in North Africa and Asia Minor who had been in conflict with his predecessor, *Stephen I, over the question of the *rebaptism of heretics. While sustaining the Roman view, at the urging of *Dionysius of Alexandria the Pope did not interfere with the divergent customs of other Churches. According to the martyrology, S. and four deacons were seized while celebrating the Eucharist in the cemetery of Praetextatus, and beheaded during the persecution of Valerian. Contrary to *Rufinus, he is not the author of the *Sentences of Sextus. One of the most venerated of the early martyrs, he is the Sixtus mentioned in the *Canon of the Mass. BIBLIOGRAPHY: Quasten 2:239; E. Weltin, *Early Popes* (1964) 136–137; S. Carletti, BiblSanct 11:1256–61.

[R. B. ENO]

SIXTUS III, ST. (d. 440), **POPE** from 432. Successor to St. Celestine I in the papacy, S. was a Roman whose mild temperament restrained him from the vigorous attack upon the heresies of the day that some of his contemporaries advocated. His mildness and conciliatory attitude provoked the unjust charge that he favored Nestorianism and Pelagianism. Nevertheless, at the urging of Leo (the Great, then a deacon and soon to succeed him in the papacy), he refused in 439 to reinstate *Julian of Eclanum, and he took a firm stand against the jurisdictional encroachment of Proclus, bp. of Constantinople, warning the bps. of Illyricum against heeding certain demands of Proclus, and cautioning Proclus to accept no appeals from the bps. of Illyricum. He himself refused to hear an appeal by the bp. of Smyrna against Proclus, thus making clear his determination to stand by the established spheres of jurisdiction. In memory of the Council of *Ephesus, he restored the Liberian Basilica (St. Mary Major on the Esquiline) and dedicated it to the Virgin Mary. There is no record of his cult before the early Middle Ages. BIBLIOGRAPHY: E. G. Weltin, *Ancient Popes* (1964) 344–54; J. Chapin, NCE 13:271–272; Butler 3:355–356.

[R. B. ENO]

SIXTUS IV (Francesco Della Rovere; 1414–84), **POPE** from 1471. He had been a Conventual Franciscan, teacher, and renowned preacher, minister general of his order before being made card. in 1467. As pope he showed great favor to the Franciscans, and advanced their espousal of the dogma of the Immaculate Conception. But his reign is notorious for his scandalous nepotism and the machinations of his family (see PAZZI CONSPIRACY). There was an abortive attempt in 1482 to force him to answer to a church council for his actions. S. was a patron of artists, had the Sistine chapel decorated, whence its name, and sponsored other projects of beautification in Rome.

[R. H. SCHMANDT]

SIXTUS V (Felice Peretti; 1520–90), **POPE** 1585–90, influential reformer of the College of Cardinals and the Papal States. Coming from a lower class background, S. did not fully share the aristocratic tastes of other Renaissance prelates. As a Franciscan he became a noted preacher in Rome. He was a stern Inquisitor in Venice (1557, and 1560), served on papal diplomatic missions, and was made bp. in 1566, card. in 1570 by Pius V. When he was elected pope to succeed Gregory XIII whose favor he had not had, S. was faced with church abuses, financial bankruptcy and lawlessness, which had grown under the pontificate of Gregory XIII. He attacked these problems with his ability as an organizer and administrator. In short time order was restored to the countryside around Rome and the papal treasury was more secure. His greatest work, however, was the reorganization of the College of Cardinals. On December 3, 1586 he issued *Postquam verus,* which specified strict qualifications for membership, as to age, theological training, and moral uprightness. Nepotism was restricted. His selection of new cardinals on merit was noteworthy. S. established fifteen curial congregations of cardinals—six with spiritual duties and nine with administrative tasks. His reform of the cardinals was instrumental in paving the way for a more thorough Counter Reformation. BIBLIOGRAPHY: Pastor, 12, 13; M. O'Connell, *The Counter Reformation* (1974).

[C. T. EBY]

SIXTUS OF SIENA (1520–69), Scripture scholar. S. was a Jewish convert who was convicted of heresy, but was persuaded to recant by Michael Ghislieri, the future Pius V. S. is noted for his *Bibliotheca sacra ex praecipuis catholicae Ecclesiae auctoribus collecta* (2v., 1566), a pioneering comprehensive and scientific introduction to biblical study. BIBLIOGRAPHY: DB 5.2:1799–1800; A. Smith, NCE 13:275.

[T. M. MCFADDEN]

SKARGA, PIOTR (1536–1612), Jesuit preacher and apologete, inspirer of Polish piety and patriotism. He became a Jesuit subsequent to his ordination in 1564; after studying in Rome devoted his life to preaching and writing. He founded colleges not only in Poland but in all the Baltic states. He also established charitable brotherhoods in many Polish cities. He is credited with making possible the Ruthenian reunion with Rome in the Union of Brest (1596). His hagiographical and devotional writings in Polish became abiding classics that shaped Polish piety, and his *Sermons Preached to the Diet* is regarded as a principal inspiration of the Polish sense of national identity and destiny. In the last quarter-century of his life. S. was court preacher for King Zygmunt II at Cracow. BIBLIOGRAPHY: G. M. Godden, *P. Skarga, Priest and Patriot* (1947).

[T. C. O'BRIEN]

SKEPTICISM, an attitude of doubt or disbelief. The Greeks developed the West's first and most complete philosophical skepticisms. Although having its origins in pre-Socratic thought, Greek skepticism was first systematically formulated by two later schools, the Academic and the Pyrrhonian. Arcesilaus (c.315–241), the founder of the Middle Academy, developed Platonism's skeptical tendency, in existence since Socrates claimed to know only that he knew nothing, into a complete suspension of judgment in theoretical matters. Pyrrhonism, after Pyrrho of Elis (c.360–c.270 B.C.), received its theoretical formulation from Aenesidemus, probably of Alexandria, in the 1st cent. B.C.; he attacked both the dogmatists and the academics. It found its most complete expositor in Sextus Empiricus (c.200 A.D.), for whom skepticism was the mental capacity, first, to see both the contrariety and the equal validity of all appearances and judgments, thence to achieve complete suspension of judgment, and last to attain thereby perfect mental tranquillity or peace of mind.

Such an absolute categorical skepticism has been unmatched by subsequent thought. Often the suspension of judgment was restricted to one type of knowledge, not for the sake of quietude, but to make the mind more receptive to another type of knowledge. Thus while the Platonic and, increasingly, Aristotelian orientation of philosophy and theology in the Middle Ages had but little room for absolute skepticism, a skeptical understanding of the limitations of the unaided human intellect was often placed in the service of mysticism and fideism. This, present from St. Augustine's *Contra academicos,* intensified with the spread of Ockhamism in the later Middle Ages and exploded in the anti-Aristotelianism of the Renaissance. The *De docta ignorantia* of Nicholas of Cusa (1401–64), the *De libero arbitrio* of Desiderius Erasmus (1467–1536), and the *Essais* of Michel Eyquem de Montaigne (1533–92) are major expressions of the profound effect of skepticism as an instrument of faith upon religious thought, an effect present to this day.

With the scientific revolution another restricted skepticism arose, this in the service of the new mathematico-physical sciences. Not content with the removal of the illegitimate intrusions of metaphysics into the domain of experimental science, early modern skepticism eliminated all philosophical approaches to nature. Notable here are the *Exercitationes paradoxicae adversus Aristoteleos* of Pierre Gassendi (1592–1655), the scientific work of Blaise Pascal (1623–62), and the *Dictionnaire historique et critique* of Pierre Bayle. Eventually such a skeptical scientism lost its fideistic ties and aimed its weapons beyond philosophy to religion itself. This process was already well begun in the *Dialogues Concerning Natural Religion* of David Hume (1711–76) and in *L'Essai sur les moeurs* of Voltaire (1691–1778), and continues unabated in the 20th cent. in the *Why I Am Not A Christian* of Bertrand Russell (1872–1970) and elsewhere.

Skepticism is not the destruction of human speculative hopes. On the one hand, unrestricted categorical skepticism is self-destructive; it is impossible to know that one knows nothing. And a restricted categorical skepticism has no force against knowledge well founded. On the other hand, skeptical suspension of judgment does have a very positive role to play. The skeptic has traditionally goaded the nonskeptic into better founding his theories or even into discarding false ones. But further, contemporary theory, and not only the phenomenological and analytical schools, has followed the lead of René Descartes (1596–1650) in developing a methodological suspension of judgment, the express purpose of which is to render knowledge, once scrutinized, more certain.

[R. E. HENNESSEY]

SKEPTICISM (ANCIENT). There are two main forms, the Pyrrhonian and the Academic. Pyrrho of Elis (*c.*360–270 B.C.), who is regarded as the founder of Greek skepticism proper, and his pupil Timon of Phlius (*c.*320–230 B.C.), sought, as typical representatives of Hellenistic philosophical individualism, to give men peace of mind (*ataraxia*) by advocating skepticism as a basic philosophy of life. They taught that we can know only how things appear to us—and they may appear differently to others. We cannot trust sense-perception, nor human reason. The wise man, therefore, must withhold judgment. He cannot help participating in practical life, but he is resigned to follow probable opinion, custom, and law, always conscious of the fact that he cannot obtain absolute truth. Pyrrho did not found a school, and the new Pyrrhonianism of Aenesidemus had a nominal connection only with him.

Plato raised an epistemological problem in holding that the objects of sense are not the objects of true knowledge, but he sought a solution of the difficulty in his Dialectic. Logical skepticism, however, appears in systematic form in the Middle and New Academies. *Arcesilaus (315–241 B.C.), the founder of the Middle Academy, attacked the Stoic epistemology and maintained that we can be certain of nothing—not even of the fact that we are certain of nothing. Suspension of judgment (*epochē*) must be adopted. *Carneades of Cyrene (214–129 B.C.), the founder of the New Academy, likewise attacked the Stoic epistemology from all angles and with elaborate arguments. However, he rejected complete suspension of judgment, and developed a theory of probability (*pithanotēs*). He recognized various degrees of probability and admitted that we can approximate the truth, but we can never attain certainty. The Academy maintained an epistemological theory of probability throughout its subsequent history, although this philosophical tenet was practically rejected by certain members of the school under the influence of eclecticism.

Pyrrhonian skepticism was revived by Aenesidemus of Cnossus, a contemporary of Cicero. He wrote a work in eight books, *Pyrroneioi logoi*, and he may be considered the founder of a school. All judgments and opinions must be viewed as relative. He realized that men had to act in practice, so, while maintaining a skeptical attitude, they should follow tradition, custom, and law. To support his skepticism, Aenesidemus compiled a list of ten *tropoi* or arguments. These ten were reduced to five by Agrippa, who wrote somewhat later than Aenesidemus, and were ultimately reduced to two: nothing can be made certain through itself, and nothing can be made certain through anything else. The last of the major Skeptics, and the one who has furnished us with details on Skeptic teaching, is the physician-philosopher, *Sextus Empiricus (fl. last half of the 2d cent. A.D.). He denied the validity or possibility of syllogistic proof and opposed the notion of cause. The Skeptic School attacked the Stoic doctrine of Providence and elaborated arguments to show that there was no ground for believing in Providence at all. BIBLIOGRAPHY: OCD 799; L. A. Barth, NCE 11:1054–55; V. Cauchy, NCE 13:275–279; LexAW 2810–12; Copleston 1:413–417 and 442–445; E. Bevan, *Stoics and Sceptics* (1913); M. M. Patrick, *Greek Sceptics* (1930).

[M. R. P. MCGUIRE]

SKEVOPHYLAX, a Greek term meaning guardian of the vessels. From the 6th cent. onward an official with that title was charged with the care of the valuable liturgical vessels and other paraphernalia at the *Hagia Sophia in Constantinople. A skevophylax seems to have been appointed in other churches only if they were rich in precious appointments; in less wealthy shrines the caretaker of such equipment was not so titled. The skevophylax took his place during liturgical services at the door of the treasury or sacristy, ready to supply sacred vessels, vestments, candles, etc., as they were needed. He was also responsible for the scheduling of divine services. In later centuries he was always a deacon and was entitled to a seat in the patriarchal council.

[V. J. POSPISHIL]

SKOPTSY (Eunuchs), a Russian sect, offshoot from the Khlysty, founded in 1770 by Andrei Selivanov. To free the soul from sensual desires, taking literally Mt 19. 12, they practiced emasculation.

[F. WILCOCK]

SKOUPHOS (Gr., cap; Sl., *klobuk*), a shorter version of the black cylindrical *kamilafkion* used by clergy in minor orders and by monks. It is always brimless and like the *kamilafkion* is covered by a black veil for monks above the rank of rasophore. The name is often used popularly, although incorrectly, to refer to the *kamilafkion*.

[J. FRANCAVILLA]

SKREFSRUD, LARS (1840–1910), Norwegian Protestant missionary. S. received an inner call to the missions while serving a prison term (1859–61). He tutored himself in languages, attended the school of the Gossner Mission Society in Germany (1861–63), and was then sent to Chota Nagpur, India. Four years later he left the society to found a mission in Santal. He was ordained in 1882. S. was a gifted linguist and a powerful preacher. BIBLIOGRAPHY: E. Amdahl, RGG 6:105.

[M. J. SUELZER]

SKY AND SKY GODS, typically described as creators and sources of order and cosmic law. Anu (Sumer), Horus (Egypt), Zeus (Greece), Jupiter (Rome), T'ien (China), Varuṇa (India), Ahura Mazda (Iran), and numerous gods in tribal societies are, to various extents, personified celestial deities. Many tribal sky gods are thought to have withdrawn from active participation in terrestrial affairs; they are described as "asleep" or "very old" and receive little or no cultic worship. Other sky gods seem to have been replaced by younger, more vigorous deities. In Mesopotamia, for example, Marduk replaced Anu in the New Year festival; and in India the great Aśhvameda sacrifice was offered successively to Dyaus, Varuṇa, and Prajāpati. Combinations with other deities, as in the primordial Sky (male)–Earth (female) pair, were also common. Fr. Wilhelm Schmidt and other ethnologists unsuccessfully attempted to demonstrate a primitive monotheism based on the prevalence of sky gods throughout human society. BIBLIOGRAPHY: M. Eliade, *Patterns in Comparative Religion* (tr. R. Sheed, 1958) ch. 3.

[E. V. GALLAGHER]

SLACHTA DE ZADJELI, MARGIT (1884–1974), first woman member of the Hungarian Parliament, foundress of the Sisters of Social Service and of the Independent Christian Women's Party in Hungary. Her vigorous championship of working women and the rights of women generally characterized her public life. She was twice a member of Parliament in 1920–1922 and again in the short-lived government of 1945–1947. Her defense of the independence of Catholic schools in the latter session caused her expulson from Parliament. In 1950 she transferred the generalate of her community to Buffalo, N.Y., under pressure from the Communist government. S. is credited with having given asylum to great numbers of Jews when Nazism forced them to flee from Austria. The abortive Freedom Fighters takeover in Hungary was supported by S., who was regarded as next to Card. Mindzenty in influence for good. BIBLIOGRAPHY: Sisters of Social Service, *Star of the Three Magi* (1975).

[J. R. AHERNE]

SLATER, THOMAS (1855–1928), canonist, theologian. An English Jesuit, S. was ordained in 1888. A professor of canon law and moral theology in the Jesuit scholasticate in Wales, he was an authority on canon law before the CIC, which finally ended the confused state of that art. In 1898 he published *De justitia et jure*, distinctive in its presentation of the topic within the framework of English law and custom. *Principia theologiae moralis* appeared in 1902. At the request of American editors, S. prepared *Moral Theology* (2 v., 1908), a pioneer work in English which brought contemporary problems and views into the discussion of principles. *Cases of Conscience* (2 v., 1911) and *Questions of Moral Theology* (2 v., 1915) emphasized practical application of theory. *Foundations of True Morality* (1920) was perhaps his most widely read work.

[J. R. AHERNE]

SLAVERY, a social institution by which human adults are treated as pieces of property. The term has German roots, which originally referred to subject Slavonians in central Europe. The system may vary greatly according to the title of ownership, e.g., capture in war, inheritance of a slave-labor force, legal allotment of a criminal; according to its permanence, e.g., by contractual indenture or hereditary bondage; according to the extent of the dominion, e.g., unrestricted power over mere chattels or some protection from the public authority; and according to the manner in which it is administered, e.g., with kindness and respect or with cruelty or wantonness. But the Christian presumption is that slavery in substance represents an unnatural and undignified human condition, which, like the infliction of involuntary physical evil or punishment, calls for very strong extrinsic reasons indeed before it can be at all countenanced. Never are innocent persons to be reduced to the condition of things or utilities. Nevertheless, a moralist, even one of extremely liberal sentiments, will not be too credulous about identifying social with political freedom, and that with the forms of parliamentary democracy. Neither the universal suffrage nor the classless society are imperatives of the Gospel and Christian theology. One may fight slavery, too, without thereby becoming a political egalitarian or even a desegregationist.

Slavery was equably regarded in classical and biblical times, and though the cumulative effect of Christian influences was to suppress it eventually, for many centuries it was accepted as a social fact, though a steady pressure was kept up to ameliorate its conditions. No moralist defended treating men as beasts. Aristotle thought that some were born to be slaves; St. Augustine, more searchingly, that slavery, like private property, was because of sin, and it ought to be accepted, if wryly, as part of God's plan. It was not a feature of the Jewish economy—in which the sedentary conditions which depend on the maintenance of a toiling class were lacking —and there is no condemnation in the OT. The NT prescribed no new social institutions, but a kingdom in which there was no distinction between bond and free (Gal 3.28).

The inhumanity of what has been called "parasitic slavery," where on one side there is exploitation for private satisfaction and on the other an appropriate servile viciousness, was condemned by the Church from the beginning when it began to take social action. But "symbiotic slavery," in which both sides worked together in one household, with mutual respect and even friendship, was not so much directly opposed as transformed from within. The process was hastened by the infusion of vigorous sentiments of personal freedom from the Germanic tribes and by the genius of church administration open to all the talents. Slavery no longer existed in European Christendom by the 13th century. It should be sharply differentiated from feudal serfdom in the West, which implied reciprocal human rights between a lord and his man.

A recrudescence of slavery came with the opening of America and Africa in the 16th century. Colonial governments and even the missions got involved in it. The substitution of African slaves for Indian workers, as being better fitted to work in the mines, was suggested by Bartolomé de *Las Casas, the great protector of the Indians. He was opposed by the Cardinal Regent *Ximénes, but gained his point, and lived to regret it. The establishment of the slave trade, which constituted a powerful vested interest, has left a grievous heritage for the present generation. Its inhumanities were mitigated by the action of Christians, but its abolition was largely the work of men of the Enlightenment and of the social reformism of Quakers and Evangelical Protestants; its condemnation by Gregory XVI (1838) was, to say the least, somewhat belated.

An internal trade in slaves in Africa and for export to Arabia and Persia persisted until the present century. It was largely in the hands of the Arabs—the Koran does not prohibit possessing slaves, though it enjoins their good treatment and encourages manumission as an act of piety—and was vigorously proceeded against by the colonial powers. Slavery has been abolished in Ethiopia and the rest of Africa, but it still exists in Arabia, and is a matter of concern to the United Nations (see Reports 1951; Draft Convention, 1956).

Slavery, of course, is no plain and simple term, and in certain economic and social situations it is masked under euphemistic names. BIBLIOGRAPHY: W. L. Westermann, *Slave Systems in Greek and Roman Antiquity* (1955); G. MacNunn, *Slavery through the Ages* (1938); G. Freyre, *Masters and the Slaves* (1946); C. W. W. Greenidge, *Memorandum on Slavery* (1954); *idem, Slavery and the United Nations* (1954); N. Turchi et al., EncCatt 11:48–58.

[T. GILBY]

SLAVERY (IN THE BIBLE). Slave labor was not a decisive factor in the agricultural life of the ancient Near East, including Palestine. The land was tilled largely by free small farmers, and secondarily by dependent sharecroppers and tenant farmers. In industry as well, the skilled artisan was the rule. Slaves, for the most part, were found as domestic servants in the large households of the rich. Nevertheless, the institution of slavery was an integral part of the economic and social life of the Near East, and is attested to by law codes, private and court documents from the third millennium to NT times. Palestine was part of this social, economic, and legal tradition, as can easily be judged by a reading of the three clusters of biblical legislation concerning slaves found in Ex 21, Lev 25, and Deut 15. The earliest term meaning "slave" refers to males and females of a foreign country, usually war captives. Traffic in foreign slaves was a normal part of merchant activities. It was punishable by death to kidnap and sell one of your own people into foreign slavery (as in the Joseph story); and gravely wrong to extradite a fugitive slave who has made it back to his own people. State slavery fed on military victories. The Israelite monarchy used this kind of total slavery in the mines of the Arabah and on other grandiose projects in imitation of the other great monarchies of the Near East. Sanctuaries shared in the war booty, including captives, and thus there were temple slaves, branded with the symbol of the god they served. The basic supply source for temporary slaves was hunger, debt, or inability to compensate for a theft. The slave would be released after a prescribed time of service. In Israel there is no evidence of parents selling their children, a common practice in the Near East. Biblical laws punish masters for maiming or killing slaves. Slaves must have Sabbath rest. The Jubilee Year was an attempt to abolish perpetual slavery. The prophet Joel foresaw the pouring of God's spirit upon slaves (Jl 2.29). In the NT Paul teaches that in Christ there is neither slave nor free, just as there is neither Jew nor gentile, male nor female (Gal 3.28). However, the difficulty of going from ideal to practice on the level of human culture can be judged from his letter to Philemon, in which he summons all his tact and gift of persuasion to urge his friend to accept the runaway slave (Onesimus) as a brother and not to punish him (Philem 15–17).

[E. J. DILLON]

SLAVERY, ISLAMIC. Like Judaism and Christianity, *Islam found slavery an already established institution and accepted it as part of the natural order of things. According to the *Koran and the *hadith, the person of the slave is no less valued before God than is the free man. He is under the same universal human obligation (*taklif*) to worship God and is offered the same destiny in the next life, being distinguished only by the determinations of his social status, in accordance with which his duties and obligations under the religious law may be reduced or modified. With slaves, as with all men, the major differentiation is whether a person be a Muslim or a nonbeliever.

The capture of prisoners in war provided the normal source of slaves. *Islamic law forbids the enslavement of believers under any circumstances, and tradition recommends the manumission of a slave who converts to Islam. The great majority of male slaves have served as troops or as palace or personal guards while women were most commonly employed as domestics or as legal concubines. Islamic law gives the slave a mixed status, i.e., as being at once person and property. The slave is entitled to good treatment and adequate sustenance, and the enforcement of this falls under the jurisdiction of the *muḥtasib*, an official responsible for the control of weights and measures, public sanitation, etc. A person who is unable to provide adequately for the material needs of his slave is obliged to sell him or set him free, according to the provisions of the different schools of law. A slave may not hold a position of public authority but may function as *imam and, with the permission of his owner, direct a commercial enterprise, either his own or that of his owner. Slaves may contract valid marriages with the owner's consent (the owner's authority in this matter being analogous to that of a father over his minor children) and when married may not be forcibly separated from their families. A slave, however, cannot contract marriage with his or her owner. In contrast to the Jewish and Christian traditions, Islam recognizes the legality of concubinage with one's own slave-woman, though not in the case of a slave who is the common property of several owners, and a man may not cohabit with his wife's slave or with his own slave-woman if she is married. The children born of legal concubinage are the legitimate children of their father and so are free and equal heirs with his children by his wife; and their mother becomes free upon the death of the father. Manumission may be effected by contract, according to which the slave purchases his freedom (generally in installments) with the earnings of his own labor. The freeing of slaves, however, is a pious act (explicitly prescribed as expiation for some infractions of the religious law) that is recommended in many hadiths, and it was a common practice for an owner to free his slaves at his death. The promise of such manumission is considered to be irrevocable. Since most slaves thus were freed in one way or another, there was a constant need to replenish the supply, and slave trade in Islam, up to modern times, was widespread and flourishing. Under pressure from the European powers, Islamic governments began to restrict trade and abolish slavery in the second half of the 19th cent., until today it has almost vanished altogether, save in the Arabian Peninsula where some authorities among the ultra–conservative *Wahhabis feel that to outlaw the practice would be contrary to the religious law. BIBLIOGRAPHY: R. Brunschvig, EncIslam², s.v. " 'Abd''; S. D. Goitein, *Mediterranean Society* (1967) 130–147.

[R. M. FRANK]

SLAVIC RELIGION, animistic worship originating with the Slavic people. Slavic religion was deeply involved with Slavic daily life: house and family, the land, hunting and fishing, as well as daily life's natural surroundings—forests, rivers, and lakes. The forces of nature were thought magical powers; spirits living in the woods and fields were offered sacrifices, since the acquisition of their goodwill was very important. Slavs believed in a life after death, and funerals were conducted with elaborate ceremonies like the *tryzna*, or funeral banquet. Ancestral spirits were worshiped, since the Slavs venerated the mystery of death—and the life succeeding it—very highly. Corpses were at first cremated; later, under Christianity's influence, ordinary burial became the accepted procedure. Like the Egyptians, Slavs buried tools, animals, sometimes even slaves and wives, with the corpse in the belief that these things would be needed in afterlife. Above the ordinary spirits of household and out-of-doors ranked a number of supreme deities: Perun, god of storms, thunder, and lightning; Svarog, god of sun, fire, and light; and Volos (or Veles), god of cattle and perhaps also of agriculture. Eastern Slavic tribes worshiped Striborg, god of wind, and Mokos (probably the Slavic Mother Earth) particularly. The attributes of these gods are not well known, though they all bear resemblances to deities contained in the Persian and Vedic religious pantheons. There were no priests of Slavic paganism. Worship usually proceeded under the direction of family elders. However, Slavic tribes of the Baltic area, and the Slavic tribes of Russia had both a priestly caste and large temples for worship. BIBLIOGRAPHY: J. Vendreyès, E. Tonnelat, and B. O. Unbegaun, *Les Religions des Celts, des Germains, et des anciens Slaves* (1948); O. P. Sherbowitz-Wetzor, NCE 13:288.

[D. H. BRUNAUER]

SLAVOPHILES, Russian intellectuals of the 19th cent. (esp. 1840–70) who held that the means to Russia's greatness were inherent in the Russian spirit (*Geist*), which they equated with orthodoxy, autocracy, and nationalism (*narodnost'*). Like the *Westerners, they idealized the Russian peasant and hoped for a better balance between agrarianism and industry; unlike them, they sought to achieve their goals by spiritual reform. Leaders of the movement included A. S. Khomyakov (1804–60), I. V. Kireyevski (1806–56), P. V. Kireyvski (1808–56), K. S. Aksakov (1817–60), and I. S. Aksakov (1823–86). BIBLIOGRAPHY: *Russian Philosophy* (eds. J. M. Edie et al., 1965) 1:271–424.

[M. F. MCCARTHY]

SLAVS, a distinct ethnic group of the Eastern Indo-European family. Although present Slavic nations differ greatly because of diverse historical development and migration, evidence exists of a root language common to all, a circumstance leading to attempted political exploitation of *Pan-Slavism. Originally, Slavs settled E of the Carpathian mountains within the Pripet and Dniester valleys; northward to the Vistula and Bug; and westward to the Oder and Elbe rivers. Migration divided them into three groups: (1) Eastern Slavs, who include Russians, White Russians, Ukrainians, numbering today nearly 200 million people; (2) Western Slavs, who number about 50 million: Poles, Czechs, and Slovaks in Central Europe, and such related groups as the Kashubes on the Baltic, and Wends in the

Spree River valley; (3) Southern Slavs who include about 30 million: Bulgarians, Serbs, Croats, and Slovenes in the Balkan peninsula. Slavic migrations began in the 1st cent. A.D., and by the 6th and 7th cent., they were established in the basin of the Oder and Elbe rivers, in Bohemia, Moravia, the Danube valley, Illyricum, and the Balkans, reaching as far as the Adriatic, Macedonia, and Thrace. Those who settled in N and Central Europe came under Roman-German influence; those in the Balkan areas felt Byzantine influence, while those living between the Balkan and Black Seas were exposed to Scandinavian, Iranian, and Turko-Mongol cultures. Slavic tribes in Moravia, Bohemia, and lower Austria early developed a national self determination, establishing a state under the Frankish merchant, Samo (d. 658). In the 9th cent. Great Moravia attained prominence for its unusual Christian culture, the legacy of SS. Cyril and Methodius. Although overpowered by the Magyars in 906, Slavic awareness found expression in Bohemia under Przemyslide leadership. By the 7th cent. the Southern Slavs were becoming organized in the Balkans, largely under Bulgarian leadership. By the 9th and 10th cent., the Russians under Scandinavian rulers and the Poles were beginning to form national entities. Slavic political structure followed closely the familial social pattern, but gradually adopted many Byzantine as well as some Western institutions. The 9th & 10th cent. saw the definitive conversion of the Slavs to Christianity, the West Slavs, the Croats, and Slovenes embracing Latin Catholicism, while most of the South Slavs and the East Slavs formed part of the Byzantine Church but employed their own language, Slavonic, in the liturgy. BIBLIOGRAPHY: F. Dvornik, *Slavs: Their Early History and Civilization* (1956); *idem, Slavs in European History and Civilization* (1962).

[L. NEMEC]

SLEEPING PILLS, sedatives which are used by about 20 million people in the U.S. The commonest and most effective form of these, the barbiturates, are valuable for inducing sleep or quieting anxious patients, but they are also subject to abuse. When taken in excess of the prescribed amounts, they become very addictive with great risk to the user, for there is a limit to the number of pills that the body can endure. Each year, overdose of sleeping pills claims the lives of about 3,000 people. They are usually taken orally, but the contents of the pill can be injected into a vein. Sleeping-pill intoxication results in mental sluggishness, confusion, and emotional instability which can lead to aggressive acts. Abrupt withdrawal of the drug may cause violent, even fatal, illness. Their use under the direction of a competent physican is morally justified; but their abuse, which jeopardizes the health and life of the user, or which produces an effect analogous to sinful intoxication (see DRUNKENNESS) is indefensible. BIBLIOGRAPHY: H. F. Isbell, ''Addiction to analgesics and barbiturates'' *Pharmacological Review* (1950) 355–397; J. Cashman, *LSD Story* (1966) ch. 9.

[P. SMITH]

SLEIDANUS, JOHANNES (Sleidan; 1506–56), the first historian of the Reformation. Born at Schleiden near Aachen, educated in classics and law, he became a Calvinist. In 1544 through M. *Bucer's influence he was appointed by Philip of Hesse to be annalist of the Reformation. His work *De statu religionis et rei publicae Carolo V Caesare commentarii* (2v., 1555) is regarded as distinctive for its impartiality; it is also valuable as a chronicle of Reformation documents and events beginning in 1517; both religious and political elements are carefully recorded. S. spent some time in England in 1551 under the auspices of T. *Cranmer. He also represented some of the South German cities at the Council of Trent (1551–52), and ended his career as professor of law at Strassburg (1554–56). BIBLIOGRAPHY: Léonard HistProt 1:242, bibliog.

[T. C. O'BRIEN]

SLESSOR, MARY (1848–1915), Scottish missionary. A factory worker, S. volunteered to the Foreign Mission Board of the United Presbyterian Church in 1875 and sailed for West Africa the following year. She gained great authority among the natives and persuaded them to forego tribal abuses like twin-murder, human sacrifice, and witchcraft. In 1905 the government invested her with the powers of a magistrate, which she exercised until her death. BIBLIOGRAPHY: W. P. Livingstone, *Mary Slessor* (1915).

[M. J. SUELZER]

SLOTH, the Eng. substitute for the term *acedia (Gr. *akedia*, lack of care, heedlessness, torpor) in the classic list of *capital sins; in this sense, the spiritual sin of apathy toward living the life of grace. Sloth as indolence is listed among the effects of acedia (ThAq ST 2a2ae, 35.4 ad 3). This laziness (*pigritia*) can mean a vice or sin against *prudence, specifically as an aspect of *negligence, being lackadaisical about what serious moral action requires. As an indulgent succumbing to feelings of fatigue, laziness may mean a sort of *pusillanimity, a failure to withstand physical and emotional resistance to accomplishing the virtuous good (see COURAGE); torpor is often the reaction of escape from hardships unpleasant to the sensory and physical side of human nature. Drowsiness or excessive sleeping, it should be noted, may be the effect of neurotic depression, and as such not be culpable.

[T. C. O'BRIEN]

SLOVAK EVANGELICAL LUTHERAN CHURCH, a body formally organized among Slovakian Lutheran immigrants in 1902, and since 1959 named the *Synod of Evangelical Lutheran Churches.

SLUTER, CLAUS (*c.*1340–1405), Dutch-Burgundian sculptor working for the Duke of Burgundy in Dijon, was the greatest innovator in the N in the 14th and 15th centuries. E. Panofsky identifies S. as the exponent of ''Burgundian sculpture of the 15th century.'' After his earliest seated Prophets for the Brussels Town Hall, showing his interest in texture and highly individualized figures, S., until his death, was engaged at the Chartreuse de Champmol, Dijon. From 1385, he worked for Philip the Bold, under the sculptor Jean de Marville, taking the master's place on his death (1389), creating freestanding figures for the portal, with the Virgin and Child of the *trumeau,* and the kneeling donor Philip the Bold and his wife Margaret of Flanders with saints, whose forms, independent of the architecture, are an innovation in their time. S.'s famous *Well of Moses,* the support of a Calvary in the center of the cloister, polychromed and gilded by Jean Malouel, depicts the prophecy of the Passion with the event—OT figures in Sluter style, stocky, heavy of head, highly individualized, with amplitude of drapery beneath mourning angels whose wings are corbels for a Crucifixion now in fragments (a bust of Christ is in the Dijon Museum). S. began (1385) the tomb of Philip the Bold (completed by his nephew Claus de *Werve in 1411), evidencing S.'s theatrical realism in the famous *pleurants* (weeping monks), three of which are in the Cleveland Museum of Art. Other fragments are in the Dijon Museum of the Fine Arts. BIBLIOGRAPHY: H. David. *Claus Sluter* (1951); E. Panofsky, *Early Netherlandish Painting,* 2 v. (1953).

[M. J. DALY]

SMALCALD, see SCHMALKALDIC.

SMALL CATECHISM, Martin Luther's *Enchiridion,* or *Der Kleine Catechismus,* written in 1529 for the instruction of the laity; a Lutheran confessional standard. *CATECHISMS, LUTHER'S.

SMARAGDUS OF ST. MIHIEL (d. after 825), Benedictine, probably of Irish origin, abbot of St. Mihiel, France, Diocese of Verdun, from *c.*809. He was a defender of the Frankish introduction of the *filioque* into the Creed, writing a defense of the doctrine for a council at Aachen in 809, and, as a member of the unsuccessful delegation sent to Rome with this objective by Charlemagne, urging Leo III to adopt the practice. S. wrote a commentary on the Latin grammar of Donatus, a basic text in medieval education. Of special historical interest is his *Expositio in Regulam S. Benedicti* because of its account of 9th-cent. monastic life. He also wrote commentaries on the NT readings for the liturgical year.

[T. C. O'BRIEN]

SMART, PETER (1569–*c.*1652), English Puritan theologian. S. became rector of Boldon and a prebendary of Durham cathedral (1609). He opposed the introduction of high-church ceremonial and in 1628 preached an inflammatory sermon afterwards published as *The Vanity and Downfall of Superstitious Popish Ceremonies.* In 1631 he was suspended and then imprisoned for refusal to pay a fine. Ten years later the Long Parliament restored him. BIBLIOGRAPHY: A. Gordon, DNB 53:392–393.

[M. J. SUELZER]

SMEDT, CHARLES DE (1831–1911), Bollandist. He entered the Jesuit novitiate at Tronchiennes in 1851 and was ordained in 1862. After teaching church history at the Jesuit college in Louvain, he was appointed to the Bollandists and served as their president (1882–1911). The critical acumen he brought to this assignment was invaluable for the progress of the *Acta sanctorum.* With William van Hoof and Joseph de Backer he founded the *Analecta Bollandiana* in 1882, a quarterly publication to gather and report scholarly research on the saints treated in the *Acta.* BIBLIOGRAPHY: AnalBoll 30 (1911) i–x; M. Coens DSAM 3:629–630.

[H. DRESSLER]

SMET, EUGÉNIE DE, BL. (Marie de la Providence; 1825–71), foundress. Upon advice of the Curé d'Ars, S. decided to establish a congregation of religious women devoted to works of charity and to the souls in purgatory, by prayer and labor. In 1856 at Paris the congregation was established, with a rule based on that of the Jesuits. S. shared the impoverished living conditions of those among whom she worked. She was beatified in 1957.

[J. R. AHERNE]

SMITH, ADAM (1723–90), Scottish economist and moral philosopher. After studies at Glasgow (1737–40) and Oxford (1740–46), he became a professor at Glasgow in 1749. Except for 2 years (1764–66) touring the Continent, he remained there until he was appointed commissioner of customs for Scotland in 1778. He achieved contemporary fame through his *Theory of the Moral Sentiments* (1759), but his *Inquiry into the Nature and Causes of the Wealth of Nations* (1776) became his best-known work. The outstanding economist of his period, he is remembered particularly for his belief that a laissez-faire economy would be most favorable to the general welfare. He understood this sort of economy, however, as effective within a legal and moral framework that provided for the equal rights and opportunities of all. It is erroneous to regard his teaching as a charter for the 19th-cent. exploitation of the laissez-faire principle. BIBLIOGRAPHY: *Adam Smith's Moral and Political Philosophy,* (ed. H. W. Schneider, 1948); O. H. Taylor, *History of Economic Thought* (1960).

[T. EARLY]

SMITH, ALFRED EMANUEL (1873–1944), Catholic political leader. Born in New York City, he had little formal education and began his political career (1895) as a clerk and server of jury notices. After election (1903) to the New York State Assembly, he rose to speaker of that body (1913). As governor of New York (1918–20, 1922–28), he won wide respect for his reforms and became the Democratic presidential candidate (1928). The bitter anti-Catholic bias of the campaign helped to defeat him. Unsuccessful in winning the nomination in 1932, he supported F. D. Roosevelt's victorious campaign, but later denounced him and the New Deal and endorsed the Republican candidates in 1936 and 1940. However, during World War II, S. supported Roosevelt's foreign policy and urged aid to the Western allies. S. was associated with various business ventures, including the Empire State Building, County Trust of New York, and New York Life Insurance. BIBLIOGRAPHY: O. Handlin, *Al Smith and His America* (1958); E. A. Moore, *A Catholic Runs for President: The Campaign of 1928* (1956).

[M. CARTHY]

SMITH, HENRY IGNATIUS (1886–1957), Dominican preacher and educator. A native of New Jersey and ordained in 1910, S. became a professor at The Catholic Univ. of America, heading the school of philosophy from 1936. He established the Preachers' Institute there. As dean of the school of philosophy, he did much to make it a leading force in the Thomistic revival and contributed liberally to journals treating aspects of that philosophy. He was founder and editor of the magazine, the *Torch*, and national director of the Holy Name Society and edited the *Holy Name Journal*. A genial and well-known figure on the Catholic Univ. campus, S. influenced generations of students for the priesthood. He was a nationally renowned pulpit orator, with a distinctive rhetorical style.

[J. R. AHERNE]

SMITH, JOHN TALBOT (1855–1923), journalist and author. A native of New York, S. was ordained for the Diocese of Ogdensburg, N.Y. in 1881 but soon removed with his bp.'s consent to New York City. S. wrote a number of novels, short stories, and two diocesan histories. He served as editor of the weekly *Catholic Review* for 3 years. Two books of note were *History of the Catholic Church in New York* (1906), and *Our Seminaries* (1896) highly critical of American seminaries, which occasioned violent criticism but was substantially true. S. founded the Catholic Summer School of America (1905), the Catholic Writers Guild (1920), and the Catholic Actors Guild (1914).

[J. R. AHERNE]

SMITH, JOSEPH (1805–44), founder of the Church of Jesus Christ of Latter-day Saints. S. was born in Vermont and brought up on small farms near Palmyra and Manchester, N.Y., where his parents scratched out a marginal living. Writing his own story in 1838, he claimed that two personages identified as God the Father and Jesus Christ appeared to him as a young man in 1820, and that several years later an angel called Moroni visited him and disclosed the existence of a set of plates inscribed with writing in Reformed Egyptian characters, and the Urim and Thummim, crystal spectacles for deciphering the writing. S. reported that he was allowed to dig up the plates in 1827 from the Hill Cumorah, where they were buried. The translation of the plates revealed the history of the extinct original inhabitants of the Americas and the establishment of a Church by Jesus Christ in the W hemisphere after his Resurrection. This work was published (1830) as the *Book of Mormon*. S.

later composed *Doctrines and Covenants* and the *Pearl of Great Price*, which became standards of doctrine in the Mormon Church. S. organized a Church in 1830 that eventually took the name Church of Jesus Christ of Latter-day Saints, often called simply the Mormon Church. He declared that all other Christian Churches had apostatized and lacked authority to baptize or teach. Claiming that he had received the restored priesthood in 1829 from John the Baptist and from Peter, James, and John, S. assumed the title of president of the Church, and also the titles Prophet, Seer, and Revelator. Headquarters of the new Church were moved from Fayette, N.Y., to Kirtland, Ohio, in 1831, to Missouri in 1838, and to Nauvoo, Ill., in 1840. In Nauvoo, S. began construction of a temple, elaborated a secret ritual drawn mainly from Masonic sources, headed a private army called the Nauvoo Legion, in which he held the rank of lieutenant general, and declared his candidacy for the U.S. presidency. Nauvoo became the largest city in Illinois, and converts arrived from many places, including some from England and the Scandinavian countries. S. had married Emma Hale in 1827; rumors that he had introduced polygamy into the Church encouraged critics to initiate a newspaper in Nauvoo to oppose him. S. destroyed their press and was arrested and taken to a jail in Carthage nearby. A mob attacked the jail and murdered him and his brother Hyrum. Most of the Mormons accepted the leadership of Brigham *Young and went W to establish the Church in the valley of the Great Salt Lake. BIBLIOGRAPHY: F. M. Brodie, *No Man Knows My History, the Life of Joseph Smith, Mormon Prophet* (1935); E. C. McGavin, *How We Got the Book of Mormon* (1961).

[W. J. WHALEN]

SMITH, RICHARD (1500–63), first Regius professor of divinity at Oxford (1535), first chancellor of the Univ. of Douai (1562). He was a fellow of Merton College, Oxford, when Henry VIII established the chair of divinity and appointed R. to it. Under Edward VI, S. retained his position by doctrinal evasiveness for a time, but was replaced by *Peter Martyr Vermigli in 1548 after a public disputation with the Reformer. S. was forced to take refuge on the Continent until Mary Tudor's accession. He then recovered his professorship, was a witness against T. *Cranmer, engaged in debate with Nicholas Ridley and Hugh Latimer, and preached a sermon on the occasion of their execution. Under Elizabeth I. he was arrested, but succeeded in escaping and again reaching the Continent. He became dean of St. Peter's, Douai, then in the Spanish Netherlands, before his appointment to the university at its foundation. S. wrote many polemical works in both English and Latin, directed against teachings of such Reformers as Peter Martyr, Melanchthon, Calvin, and Luther.

[R. J. LITZ]

SMITH, RICHARD (1569–1655), second vicar apostolic of England (1625–31), titular bp. of Chalcedon. Leaving

Oxford after converting to Catholicism, he studied at the English College in Rome and was ordained in 1592. He taught philosophy and theology at the English colleges in Seville and Valladolid before returning to England to serve on the English mission at Sussex from 1603. In 1609 he acted as agent in Rome to secure greater power for the secular clergy in England, and came into conflict with the Jesuit R. *Persons. S. then took up residence in Paris where he was a founder of Arras College, a circle of English priest-polemicists. In 1611 he became theological advisor to Card. Richelieu until being named vicar apostolic and consecrated bishop. On returning to England he claimed the full jurisdiction and status of a residential bp.: Benedictines, Jesuits, and many Catholic laymen objected on grounds of his drawing unwanted attention to Catholics with consequent harshening of measures against them. Rome ruled in 1627 against S.; and after continuing clashes he resigned in 1631, returning to Richelieu's service until the cardinal's death in 1642. S. spent the remainder of his life at a convent of English Augustinian canonesses in Paris.

[R. J. LITZ]

SMITH, SYDNEY FENN (1843–1922), journalist. An Englishman converted from Anglicanism, S. entered the Jesuits. As a convert and a man of conciliating attitude, S. had considerable influence in winning other converts and maintaining good relations with Anglicans. A member of the staff of the Jesuit review, *The Month* for 30 years and its editor for 4 years, S. wrote extensively in defense of the Church, always with courtesy and understanding. A former scripture professor, he published a widely used series, *Scripture Manuals for Catholic Schools.*

[J. R. AHERNE]

SMITH, WILLIAM ROBERTSON (1846–94), Scottish theologian and biblical scholar. S. studied in Germany where he was influenced by A. *Ritschl and J. *Wellhausen. In 1870, he became OT professor at the Free Church College, Aberdeen, but his liberal exegetical views made him a center of controversy and he was forced to resign (1881). He became editor-in-chief for the 9th edition of the Encyclopaedia Brittanica, and in 1883 was appointed professor of Arabic at Cambridge. He defended Wellhausen's theories in *The OT in the Jewish Church* (1881) and *The Prophets of Israel* (1882), and proposed the concept of sacrifice as communion with God in his *Religion of the Semites.* BIBLIOGRAPHY: DNB (1898) 53:160–162; ODCC 1265.

[T. M. MCFADDEN]

SMITHFIELD (originally Smoothfield), an area in the ward of Faringdon-Without in the City of London which was originally an open space used for pasture and fairs and was the site of execution of common traitors and burning of heretics, esp. during the reign of Mary Tudor when roughly 300 perished; it is now site of London's main meat markets.

[J. L. GRASSI]

SMOTRYTS'KYĬ, MELETTĬ (c. 1578–1633), Ukrainian author, Orthodox bp., advocate of church union. In *Threnody* (1610), his best-known polemic, he complains about the state of the Orthodox Church in the Ukraine following the conflicts of the Union of *Brest and mass conversions to Catholicism. His Orthodox partisanship began to shift during discussions in the Polish parliament, where he sat as a representative, on the matter of church reconciliation. After fleeing persecution by Polish officials, he returned to the Ukraine advocating church union through compromise, joining the Uniates in 1627. He was denounced (1628) by the Orthodox Council at Kiev.

[R. J. LITZ]

SMYRNA, city on the Aegean coast of Asia Minor, N of Ephesus; modern Izmir, Turkey. Inhabited as early as 3000 B.C., it was an important Hellenic city when it was destroyed by Lydia c.580 B.C. One tradition made it the birthplace of Homer. It was rebuilt c.288 B.C. by Lysimachus of Thrace and from 129 B.C. was under Roman rule as part of the province of Asia. Residents worshiped various Greco-Roman gods, while Asiatic religions also found adherents. Smyrna contained a Jewish community, and a Church was established there in the apostolic period, perhaps during Paul's stay at Ephesus (Acts 19). Smyrna, warned of coming tribulation, was one of the seven Churches of Rev 2.8–11. St. *Polycarp, who was bp. of Smyrna and martyred there c.155, led in honoring *Ignatius of Antioch when he stopped at Smyrna en route to martyrdom in Rome. St. *Irenaeus was sent to Gaul from Smyrna, and the city retained importance as a metropolitan see through the Byzantine period. It was taken by the Seljuk Turks, later captured by the Ottomans, acquired by Genoa in 1261, burned by Timur (Tamerlane) in 1402, and brought under Ottoman rule again in 1425. BIBLIOGRAPHY: C. J. Cadoux, *Ancient Smyrna . . . to 324* A.D. (1938).

[T. EARLY]

SMYTH, JOHN (Smith; c.1544–1612), regarded as a founder of the Baptists. Educated at Christ's College, Cambridge, and ordained in the C of E (1594), he soon came under the influence of the *Independents and in 1602 became pastor of a *Separatist church, Congregationalist in organization, at Gainsborough. To escape persecution, S. led a group of followers to Holland, probably in 1607, and there found Mennonite teaching congenial to his religious feelings and accepted the need of rebaptism (see BELIEVER'S BAPTISM). To establish his "Brethren of the Separation of the Second English Church at Amsterdam," he first baptized himself—hence he is called the "Se-Baptist" (self-baptizer)—then Thomas *Helwys and other followers. Before his death, S. was of a mind to join his group to the Mennonite Church; Helwys and others, however, returned to England and established the first Baptist Church there. S.'s writings put the rule of inner religious experience above Scripture and the outward Church, insist on the individual's freedom to choose salvation (see ARMINIANISM), and thus reject original sin and Christ's atonement. His works have been published (ed. W. T. Whitley, with biog., 2 v., 1915). BIBLIOGRAPHY: W. H. Burgess, *John Smith the Se-Baptist* (1911); R. M. Jones, *Studies in Mystical Religion* (1923) 407–411; bibliog. for Baptists.

[T. C. O'BRIEN]

SNAKE HANDLERS, cultists in the southern U.S. who, taking Mk 16.17–18 literally, pick up rattlesnakes as part of their religious services. The practice was begun (1909) by George Went Hensley in Tennessee. It was outlawed there, and also in Kentucky and Virginia, after several fatal incidents; but the practice still continues and another fatality occurred in Va. in 1969. Snake Handlers also follow the teaching of *Pentecostalism, but they are repudiated by Pentecostals. BIBLIOGRAPHY: J. T. Nichol, *Pentecostalism* (1966) 151–157.

SOAN, city of ancient Egypt, strategically located in the E section of the Delta, S of Lake Menzaleh, and near the land of Goshen where the Israelites settled. It was known as Avaris when it was the capital city of the Hyksos; renamed Pi-Ramses (City of Ramses) when it was the capital and residence for Ramses II; and called Tanis after 1100 B.C. Tanis is the Greek way of rendering the same Egyptian name which was rendered in Hebrew as Soan. The city was sacked by Assurbanipal of Assyria in 668 B.C. Among its ruins can still be seen Hyksos fortifications, the great structures of Ramses, and a stele commemorating the 400th anniversary of the city's foundation. Since the stele dates from 1320–1310 B.C. the city's foundation was apparently between 1720–1710 B.C. Numbers 13.22 notes parenthetically that the city was built 7 years after Hebron. The city is almost certainly one of the two mentioned in Ex 1.11 as the site of the Israelites' forced labor under the Pharaoh that knew not Joseph. The Prophets and Psalms refer to the ''fields of Soan,'' which is similar to the Egyptian idiom for this area around Tanis. The Hebrew tradition of piety did not forget that the wonders Yahweh performed for his people began here.

[E. J. DILLON]

SOBNA (SHEBNA), the scribe who was among the officials sent by Hezekiah to negotiate with the Assyrian command during the siege of Jerusalem under Sennacherib. After conferring with the Assyrian commander the same team brought the commander's threats to Isaiah who then dispatched them with Yahweh's word to Hezekiah: neither to tremble nor take refuge in some futile anti-Assyrian alliance. This account occurs both in 2 Kg ch. 18 and 19, and in Is ch. 36 and 37. The office of scribe here credited to S. may have been equivalent to secretary of state. The name Shebna is a shortened form of Shebeniah which means, ''Return (now), O Yahweh,'' and may well have been a common name during times of crisis when the people felt

abandoned. This Shebna is sometimes thought to be the same as the one mentioned as majordomo in Is 22.15–19, whom the prophet threatened with exile and deposition from office for building himself a magnificent tomb.

[E. J. DILLON]

SOBORNOST (from the Russian *sobor,* assembly), a theological notion reflected in the thought of N. *Berdyaev and others, but most explicitly associated with A. *Khomyakov. He interpreted *sobornost* as communal unity or the free association of men united with Christ esp. as it was found in the early Church (Acts 2.42) and can be identified with the Greek term *koinōnia.* Emphasizing the superiority of love to juridical values, Khomyakov believed that Russian Orthodoxy's principle of *sobornost* provided a mediating position between the absolute authoritarianism of Catholicism and the individualism of Protestantism. A somewhat ambiguous notion, it suggests a conciliatory spirit involving both laity and hierarchy, the harmony of the individual within society, and provides a criterion of truth whereby decisions are made by the Christian community united in love. BIBLIOGRAPHY: G. Florovsky, ''Sobornost in the Church of God,'' *Anglo-Russian Symposium* (1934) 53–74; N. Zemov, *Three Russian Prophets: Khomyakov, Dostoievsky and Soloviev* (1944).

[F. T. RYAN]

SOBREVIELA, MANUEL (d. 1803), missionary, explorer. A Spanish Franciscan, S. directed the Colegio de Propaganda Fide in Ocopa, Peru, for 8 years. He made great strides in building missions, founding schools and shops in the Peruvian Amazon territory. With help from others he mapped the Amazon Basin. In his writings, S. gave precise accounts of other missions operated by the Franciscans in the Peruvian wilds with much detail concerning territories, rivers, tribes, and passages there. Much of his reporting appeared in the *Mercurio peruana* in Lima.

[J. R. AHERNE]

SOBRIETY, the moral quality of observing due measure. This is connoted in the probably fanciful etymology sometimes given: from Lat. *bria,* a rare word meaning a wine measure or vessel; thus the two words connected with drinking wine, *sobrietas* and *ebrietas* (drunkenness). More probably *sobrietas* comes from the Gr. *sōphrōn,* being sensible or of sound mind. In a general sense sobriety applies to all forms of virtuous moderation: being prudent in moral judgment; restrained in emotion; decorous in comportment. As a distinct moral virtue, however, it is a specific form of *temperance, concerned with moderating the pleasures attendant on drinking intoxicants. It does not mean total abstinence, but an abstemiousness that avoids *drunkenness. The need for such a virtue rests on the power of alcohol to impair or abolish moral judgment. BIBLIOGRAPHY: ThAq ST 2a2ae, 149.

[T. C. O'BRIEN]

SOBRINHO, JOÃO, see CONSOBRINO, JOÃO.

SOCIAL ACTION, an organized effort to improve the social order. It embraces all areas in which injustice can operate, e.g., labor conditions, housing, race relations. Both the private sector and government must collaborate to achieve the object of social action, creation of a just society. In Catholic social thought a clear emphasis is placed on the necessity to create such a favorable environment that good moral lives may be possible for all. The complexities created by the industrial revolution, the perverse effects of *laissez-faire economics, the failure of private charity to cope with the problem, call for an organized effort to bring about needed changes in society. In the Christian framework, a sense of the unity of mankind and the responsibility of every Christian to respond to injustice wherever it exists dominate Catholic thinking today.

For many reasons the Church as a whole was slow to act in the area of social justice. The 19th century relegated religion to being an innocuous dedication to personal piety. Though individual bishops and priests made strenuous efforts to call the attention of society to the injustices rampant, there was little concerted action. In Germany with Bishop von Ketteler, in the U.S. with Cardinal Gibbons, but most effectively in the work of Cardinal Manning in England progressive steps were taken. The American Church was all but submerged in the task of providing churches and schools for the flood of immigrants. Nevertheless, the hierarchy in the U.S. gave support to the *Knights of Labor and a number of individual bishops strove to provide help to blacks. Though the programs in the social order provided by the German organizations in the U.S. were at first directed to German immigrants, they kept alive the concept of Catholic involvement in the social question.

A new era in Catholic concern for the condition of society began with Pope Leo XIII and the encyclical *Rerum novarum*. In France annual *Semaines sociales* and a number of organizations for workers, youth and families emerged in the late 19th and early 20th centuries. In addition, the 20th century has seen the creation in Europe of political parties with Catholic orientation, which gave serious attention to social problems. A feature of all these movements was the emerging role of the laity. In 1919 the National Catholic War (later Welfare) Council, influenced by the great voice of American Catholicism on social matters, J. A. *Ryan, issued a document *On Reconstructing the Social Order* which set the direction of the Church in the U.S. A Social Action Department of the NCWC headed by Ryan sponsored annual conferences on industrial problems, in which labor and management participated. The National Catholic Rural Life Conference, founded after World War I considered problems of farm workers and others. Through the enlightened work of the Jesuit John La Farge the Catholic Interracial Council was founded in New York to awaken Catholics to the plight of blacks. A local group in the beginning, the movement is now national (Catholic Conference for Interracial Justice). A development of the mid-20th century has been increasing collaboration of Catholic, Protestant and Jewish groups working in the social area, a direction encouraged and augmented by Vatican II. World War II drew the attention of Catholics in the U.S. and elsewhere to the problems of the Third World. Catholic War Relief Services operated on a worldwide basis. Encyclicals by Pope John XXIII (*Pacem in terris*) and Pope Paul VI (*Populorum progressio*) have stimulated concern for all humanity. In more recent years the Church as a whole and especially of the U.S. has responded to the problem of hunger in many parts of the world by significant efforts to ameliorate that problem.

The initiatives indicated have taken on a new significance and their reason for being part of the Church's mission have taken on a new urgency in the post-Vatican II era. The rationale of Catholic social action is summed up in the document issued by the 1971 Synod of Bishops, *Justice in the World*. That document itself has behind it the recent encyclicals mentioned above and the landmark Pastoral Constitution on the Church in the Modern World, *Gaudium et spes*, promulgated by Vatican Council II (see esp. Part II, with its chapters on the various social communities, economic, political, and international). *Justice in the World* also reflects the increased and intense participation of the bishops of the Third World in the life of the Church. The oft-quoted key statement of the synodal document concludes its Introduction: "Action on behalf of justice and participation in the transformation of the world fully appears to us as a constitutive element of the preaching of the Gospel, or, in other words, of the Church's mission for the redemption of the human race and its liberation from every oppressive situation" (USCC tr. p.34). Later in the same document the Synod expresses the precise, theological reason for its ministry of justice: "The Church has received from Christ the mission of preaching the Gospel message, which contains a call to man to turn away from sin to the love of the Father, universal brotherhood and a consequent demand for justice in the world. This is the reason why the Church has the right, indeed the duty, to proclaim justice on the social, national, and international level, and to denounce instances of injustice when the fundamental rights of man and his very salvation demand it" (ibid; USSC tr. p. 42). Social action is not a belated Catholic adoption of the *Social Gospel, which in fact was a displacement of the Gospel of grace; rather it is a ministry because the meaning of the gifts of grace and charity demand as one element in their effective fulfilment a recognition of the dignity and rights of neighbor (ibid.). The theological and salvific basis of social action is sometimes relegated to the background by activists, but that is not the course chartered by church teaching. Still, as the discussions during the 1974 Synod of Bishops and the resultant *Evangelii nuntiandi* of Paul VI demonstrate, there is not consensus on the relationship between evangelization and human development.

Since Vatican II in the U.S. the episcopal conference,

NCCB, and the USCC have been intensively pursuing the ministry of justice and have issued a number of documents on the rights of minorities. The bishops also sponsored the bicentennial consultations that led to the Detroit Call to Action justice conference in 1976. As a result the May 1978 meeting of the NCCB approved a new program of social action in the pursuit of justice. BIBLIOGRAPHY: J. C. Haughey, *The Faith that Does Justice* (1977); V. P. Mainelli, *Social Justice: The Catholic Position* (1975); J. Gremillon, *The Gospel of Peace and Justice: Catholic Social Teaching since Pope John* (1976); *Call to Action* (USCC, 1976); NCCB, *To Do the Work of Justice* (1978).

[J. R. AHERNE]

SOCIAL CONTRACT, in political theory, a term applied to the compact or agreement by which it was supposed the State was first instituted among men. The notion of an original contract was premised on a belief in natural law and as such served as a convenient springboard in discussions that sought to justify or condemn specific governments. Distinctions could be drawn between the rights belonging to individuals and the powers properly exercised by the State. Though social-contract theories enjoyed their greatest vogue, and only reached their full development, in the 17th and 18th cent., they can be traced back to the Greek Sophists. In the Middle Ages Thomas Aquinas made use of the concept in arguing that the exercise of authority must not only conform with natural law but that, being conferred, it could, if misused, be revoked. Both Protestants and Catholics regularly relied on the idea to buttress their pro- or anti-government stances during the see-saw political struggles resulting from the Reformation. The three most celebrated theories concerning the origin of the State were those advanced by T. *Hobbes, J. *Locke, and J. J. *Rousseau. According to Hobbes, in the *Leviathan* (1651), the social contract was entered into because man's life in a state of nature was so solitary, selfish, competitive, and amoral that it amounted to continual warfare, the only law being the law of the jungle. To escape this anarchy men agreed to form the State, which would guarantee them order and security, in return for which they would relinquish their individual liberties and pledge absolute obedience to the sovereign. The right of self-preservation alone could justify rebellion. Hobbes' theory was thus used in support of absolute monarchy. By contrast, Locke in his *Two Treatises on Civil Government* (1690) posited a state of nature in which men were free and not altogether egotistical, but who nevertheless felt insecure regarding their property. They therefore created the State as a sort of disinterested arbiter whose responsibility it would be to protect private property and to confirm them in their individual rights. These Locke saw as inalienable. Thus, if the State disregarded individual liberties or usurped them, the basis for the contract was nullified and the people thereby freed to establish a less arbitrary government. Locke's theory was a classic argument for constitutionalism and as such constituted a major influence on American con-

stitutional development. Rousseau's *Social Contract* (1762) was not so much an explanation of how the known State had originated but a Utopian version of what it might be. For Rousseau, man in his original condition was an unwarlike, free, and creative being, naturally predisposed to good and supported in his inclination to virtue by a benevolent nature and God. Evil, far from being fundamental to his nature, resulted from the perversions introduced by false social institutions. The social contract for Rousseau was a means whereby the individual, through surrendering his individual freedom of action to the community at large, for the mutual benefit of all, could actually achieve greater freedom and a higher morality. The sovereign would then be the general will, its authority derived from the people as a whole and resting on the consent of the governed. The underlying assumption here was that the general will (or majority) would necessarily be directed to the common good and that individual citizens would assume their legislative responsibilities, as in a direct democracy, rather than supinely surrendering to the supremacy of a totalitarian State. Social-contract theories obviously played an important part in the evolution of democratic ideology, but with the advance of historical and anthropological knowledge inevitably were found less acceptable as valid explanations of the origins of real States. BIBLIOGRAPHY: *Essays by Locke, Hume, and Rousseau* (ed. E. Barker, 1948); C. B. Macpherson, *Political Theory of Possessive Individualism: Hobbes to Locke* (1962).

[E. M. GATES]

SOCIAL CREED OF THE CHURCHES, a statement adopted in 1912 by the *Federal Council of the Churches of Christ in America, inspired by doctrines of the *Social Gospel and modeled on the Social Creed of the Methodist Episcopal Church (1908). The document esp. opposed the capitalistic exploitation of the working class and advocated many of the reforms adopted in later American social legislation. The adherence of many of the Churches to the Social Creed directly contributed to the progress of such legislation.

[T. C. O'BRIEN]

SOCIAL ETHICS, as an academic and philosophic discipline, the study of norms and their application with a view to right order and beneficent life in society. In objective content such a study is concerned with the requirements and implications of *legal justice, which looks to the common good. Theories of social justice must, therefore, vary according to the diverse theories of the origin and basis of *right and rights (see also ETHICS, HISTORY OF). One common characteristic in the methodology and mode of discourse, however, is that the actual ethical consensus, social ethics as practiced, is one source for determining ethical norms. Aristotle is, in a way, the classical example of the social ethician. For him the primary moral science is the science of politics, i.e., of just and equitable life within the polis, the civil society. And his primary guide for ethical judgment, as well as his basis for argumentation to what is good and right, is the opinion, the consensus of right-minded and right-willed citizens. From a Christian perspective such a model can be followed as an abstraction, i.e., the actual life and laws of a society and a community consensus provide a valid, if incomplete, standard; the presupposition is that there is a natural human orientation to the good that can be developed by the pursuit of justice. A truly ethical, i.e., nontheological but philosophically reasoned, theory of social living can rightly build its norms and conclusions on rationally interpreted experience and observation. Obviously for the Christian the theology, both of the nature of man and of the roots and ultimate direction of morality, at times must supply a more rudimentary concept of right and wrong than community consensus; it must see that consensus can need correctives as human sinfulness comes into the evaluation. But to recognize the value of social ethics is also consistent with a theology that recognizes and preserves the truly created, natural and human values with which God has invested the world. BIBLIOGRAPHY: ThAq ST (Lat-Eng v. 8, ed. T. Gilby, Creation) introd.; idem, Political Theory of Thomas Aquinas (repr. 1973); J. Maritain, Moral Philosophy (tr. M. Suther et al., 1964); J. Messner, Social Ethics: Natural Law in the Modern World (tr. J. J. Doherty, 1949). *SOCIAL GOSPEL.

[T. C. O'BRIEN]

SOCIAL GOSPEL, an attempt to apply the teachings of the Christian faith to problems created by industrial capitalism. The Social Gospel permeated much of American Protestantism in the beginning of the 20th cent., modifying traditional concepts and developing a distinctive theology of social action. In its widest significance, the Social Gospel was a rejection of earlier emphasis on individual salvation and a renewed appreciation of the corporate nature of the Christian commitment. Social Gospel writers stressed the immanence of God, working out his purposes in the world of men. They emphasized the brotherhood of men as children of God and saw a just social order as a preparation for the coming of his kingdom on earth. For many exponents, notably W. *Rauschenbusch, the doctrine of the kingdom of God was a dominant motif in formulating an approach to social problems. The coming of the kingdom implied an ethical ideal in terms of society as a whole, and the Social Gospel proposed a new view of sin in terms of the implications of a solidaristic understanding of society. In approaching social evils, the Social Gospel was fundamentally optimistic, believing firmly in a progressive development of social justice that was, in fact, the working out of God's providence. Its sources were many. The *liberal theology of Horace *Bushnell prepared the way for men like W. *Gladden who followed up the implication of Bushnell's rejection of Protestant individualism. Others drew their inspiration from the Anglican tradition and particularly the social theology of F. D. *Maurice.

The Social Gospel movement rose largely in response to the rapid urbanization and industrialization that threatened to isolate Protestantism from the working class. The *institutional church, settlement houses operated by church groups, and city mission work attempted to bring the Church to the urban poor. Personal experience of the evils of the changing city stimulated the formulation of the Social Gospel. For this reason it was often clearer in its critique of capitalism than in its blueprint for the Christian social order. In Applied Christianity (1886) Gladden found the injustice of employers one of the main reasons for the drift of working men from the Churches. George Herron's "Message of Jesus to Men of Wealth" (1890) indicted a society based on greed for rejecting the doctrine of *stewardship. The failure of capitalism to provide a just social order led others, such as W. D. P. Bliss, to stress the NT basis for a cooperative society in formulating their *Christian Socialism. The need for fraternal cooperation to replace divisive competition as a basis for a Christian social order was also a keynote in the writings of Rauschenbusch. Sin was seen more in its social aspect, as the ultimate barrier to cooperation. In Social Religion (1913) Scott Nearing argued that the majority of men would be virtuous if given the opportunity to lead decent lives, and he called on the Churches to help provide that opportunity. The Social Gospel inspired Christians to take an active role in promoting reform movements of various kinds, supporting social welfare projects, and advocating industrial democracy. In some cases, the Social Gospel provided a bridge between rich and poor Christians and between Christians of different denominations for cooperative ventures (these contributed to the rise of the ecumenical movement). In others, it provided a religious statement of prevailing evolutionary views of society, which avoided the harsher alternatives of Social Darwinism. BIBLIOGRAPHY: C. H. Hopkins, Rise of the Social Gospel in American Protestantism (1967); S. E. Mead, Lively Experiment (1963) 177–183.

[R. K. MacMASTER]

SOCIAL JUSTICE. All justice of its nature is social, in that it is a rendering of what is due to another. However, the tightening and formalization of intercommunity relations, the greater solidification of the political community, or at least of its officials, and the assumption of wider and more searching powers by government have produced new social dimensions that are not completely met by the customary division of commutative justice, which relates individual to individual, of general or legal justice, by which an individual serves the common good, and of distributive justice, originally described in terms of the proper allocation by authority of dignities and burdens. It is now generally accepted, in degrees that vary according to the economic centralization and political temper of a country, that official agencies must undertake the work of caring for its people, esp. the weak and helpless, previously discharged by smaller groups, families, neighborhood groups, free associations, charitable organizations, and religious foundations. Moreover the very size and complications of the problem of securing fair returns from the whole when the units of production are so concentrated and exchanges cannot be left to sectional control has meant the massive entrance of the State or of state-sponsored corporations to regulate the fair give-and-take of justice. This, not only as the affair of officials but of all citizens who actively participate in the social and political life of their country, marks the specific difference of social justice, though its exercise supposes commutative and general justice, for which it is no substitute, despite the current tendency to the contrary.

It was proclaimed by *Quadragesimo anno. Its concern is less directly with purely political forms, economic schemes, or juridical rights and duties than with the natural social decencies that can be threatened by the apparatus of a modern industrialized society and even obscured by its immediate advantages and by what it considers amenities. It works for an equitable ratio between the rewards and responsibilities of workers, owners, and managers, lest one sectional interest should prevail. It holds that gains should be directed to the good of an industry, of the general economy, and the social order. This demands the maintenance of inalienable rights, for instance, to life, security, intellectual and religious freedom, family privacy, and to work according to one's capacity.

We tend to speak of justice as something to be claimed rather than rendered, but in truth justice, and social justice, starts from giving, not receiving. The days of regional autarky are over; economic rationalism is obsolete now that para-political forces are driving us into one world-community. So in the social justice preached by *Mater et magistra, *Pacem in terris, and the Constitution of Vatican II on the Church and the Modern World the help to be given to undeveloped nations plays a large part. Only a shallow cynicism would see in this a religious epiphenomenon to a dialectic of economics.

[T. GILBY]

SOCIAL PSYCHOLOGY, the branch of psychology that deals with the behavior of people in groups. A part of philosophical speculation for centuries, the questions of social behavior were submitted to empirical methods of study for the first time by A. Comte in the 1850s. Beginning with groups of two, and proceeding to more complex groups, this science examines the conditions under which stable interpersonal relations are established, how individuals function in social units, and how groups change. Natural social units like the family, nation, race (and ethnic subgroup), and culture (and subcultures) are examined as well as more arbitrary groupings such as large organizations (business firms, military units, political parties) and institutions (churches, universities).

[M. E. STOCK]

SOCIAL THEOLOGY, the study of the social or community aspect of Christian doctrine and life. As a special branch of theology it arose as a reaction to the individualistic outlook of much postmedieval and modern theology and the reign of individualism in Western thought. It was fostered by the rise of ecclesiology and recently of the doctrine on the Church as the mystical body of Christ and, with Vatican II, as the People of God, with a stress on the community aspects of faith and grace. As study of the social dimensions of Christian dogma and life, it is a theology of society, natural and supernatural. BIBLIOGRAPHY: H. de Lubac, Catholicism (tr. L. C. Sheppard, 1958); E. G. Kaiser, "Theology and the Social Sciences," CCTSD 4 (1958) 70–87.

[P. De LETTER]

SOCIALISM, a term used to denote either a social, political, and economic system based on the collective ownership and control of the means of production and distribution, or a theory of such a system. Since the early 19th cent. when the term first came into general use, it has been employed in very diverse and sometimes contradictory ways. Its meaning has usually included opposition to individualism and capitalism, support for democratic and collective control of economic development, and emphasis on equality and cooperation.

The first Socialists contrasted the disharmony and physical misery of early 19th-cent. industrialization with the possibilities of a more humane and rational society of the future centered around cooperation. The Comte de Saint-Simon (1760–1825), Robert Owen (1771–1858), and Charles Fourier (1772–1837), the most prominent of the early Socialists, formulated criticisms of the competitive societies of their day by posing diverse alternatives—e.g., the centralized planning and scientific administration of an entire society or the creation of many cooperative and voluntary small settlements of producers. A central theme for these writers, who had considerable intellectual and even some practical impact on their contemporaries, was the unjust exploitation of the many by a nonproducing few. This theme developed into an explicitly anticapitalist position in later socialist theory.

While many individuals contributed to the development of socialism in the 19th cent., Karl Marx (1818–83) and Friedrich Engels (1820–95) redefined the very meaning of the term and their ideas still shape socialist thought and practice. Rejecting earlier socialist thought as utopian, since it compared contemporary social conditions with some imagined just and equal society, their "scientific socialism" suggested that history was a series of class conflicts—struggles between those who controlled the means of production and those who did not. The mode of production of each period ultimately determined its culture, ideas, law, and religion, and these generally coincided with the interests of the ruling classes. Under modern capitalism, the ruling class, or bourgeoisie, creates an ever-expanding class of propertyless workers, the proletariat, who survive only by selling their labor power for subsistence wages. The contradictions between the social production of ever greater wealth by an increasingly large proletariat and the private appropriation of that wealth by a bourgeoisie diminishing in number could only be resolved by a proletarian revolution, the first revolution in history aimed at a transfer of power to the class that contained a majority of the population. In theory the ensuing historical stage of socialism would see the rule of the proletariat leading to an abolition of class exploitation, thus making political coercion (and therefore the State) eventually unnecessary and preparing the way for true communism. Marx and Engels placed greatest emphasis on capitalism's creation of a new revolutionary class, the proletariat, not on such future developments as the details of the socialist transition itself. They even raised the possibility of parliamentary transfers of state power to the proletariat in some cases. This aspect of their work, along with developments after their deaths, has permitted a diversity of positions and parties to claim them as patron saints.

The later development of socialism has involved so many millions of people, such diverse national expressions, and political reactions varying from toleration to violent repression that any simple summary is impossible. Many different socialist movements and parties developed in the late 19th and early 20th centuries. By World War I the socialist movement had begun to split between those who emphasized the need for proletarian revolution (called Communists or, later, Marxist-Leninists) and those who argued that socialism might gradually develop out of capitalism (evolutionary socialists). This split deepened first over the question of socialist participation in or rejection of the war, and, second, in reaction to the establishment of the first socialist State, the USSR, in 1917, by Russian Bolsheviks led by V. I. Lenin (1870–1924). By the 1950s and 1960s communist parties had come to power in a number of Eastern European countries, in China, North Korea, Vietnam, Cuba, and Cambodia; they were influential forces in some countries, though suppressed in others. In many developed capitalist societies, the other tendency of socialism has been more important. Evolutionary socialism (often explicitly non- or anti-Marxist) heavily influenced the course of such parties as the British Labour party and the West German Social Democratic party. While in some case the creation of the "welfare state" was seen as only an intermediate step in the creation of true socialism, in other cases such parties have abandoned that goal in favor of social democracy, a movement to reform capitalism rather than overthrow it.

While usually in conflict, evolutionary socialism and revolutionary communism have sometimes been united in alliances such as popular fronts and electoral coalitions. New political positions and forms of movements have also appeared (e.g., the "Eurocommunism" of the 1970s in France and Italy) standing in some intermediate position by seeking participation in government without renouncing socialist goals. In a few industrialized countries, particularly the U.S., the socialist movement has been more sporadic, with movements such as the Socialist party before World War I and the Communist party in the 1930s experiencing brief periods of growth and influence followed by repression and internal factionalizing.

Many movements for national liberation and economic development in the Third World have also described themselves as socialist. Some blend nationalism and indigenous cultural traditions with the ideal of a cooperative socialism, often placing emphasis on other social classes, particularly the peasantry, as working with the proletariat in building socialism. In a few cases, movements have used the popular appeal of the label of socialism as a mask for seizing state power, most notoriously in the case of German "National Socialism" under Hitler, which eschewed the egalitarian and democratic themes of most modern socialisms. Other groups have blended socialist goals of equality and cooperation with various religious, moral, or aesthetic ideals. BIBLIOGRAPHY: G. D. H. Cole, *History of Socialist Thought* (5v., 1953–60); G. Lichtheim, *Short History of Socialism* (1970); M. Harrington, *Socialism* (1972).

[G. W. DOWDALL]

SOCIALISM, FRENCH. French socialism has its roots in the tradition of the French Revolution. In the revolution of 1848, sentiment arose favoring such social reform as the implementation of Louis Blanc's plan for national workshops to alleviate the abuses of the developing industrial system. For revolutionaries like Louis Augusti Blanqui, however, the condition of the workers would improve only after the complete overthrow of the state. Blanquist ideas prevailed in the Paris Commune of 1871, the suppression of which set back the development of French socialism. Marxist theories found support in France only during the 1880's and contributed to a further splintering of the movement. The various factions united into a single party only in 1905, largely through the influence of the outstanding socialist leader, Jean Jaurès. Jaurès was an outspoken defender of Captain Alfred Dreyfuss, who had been convicted of espionage by an army court-martial partly on the basis of a forged document. Since the French Catholic Church defended the army in this affair, anticlericalism intensified and the French Socialists supported the radicals in legislating the separation of Church and State in France. This anticlericalism has continued to characterize the French socialist movement, as when it supported the abolition of the French embassy to the Vatican in February 1925. Although no significant religious question arose while the socialist Léon Blum was premier in 1936–37, their anticlerical attitude cost the Socialists Catholic support when they occupied the pivotal position in French politics following World War II. BIBLIOGRAPHY: George Lichtheim, *Marxism in Modern France* (1966).

[R. J. GIBBONS]

SOCIALISM, GERMAN. The originators of socialism in Germany were Ferdinand Lassalle (1825–64) and Karl Marx (1818–83). Lassalle agitated for democracy so that the working class might influence the State toward social reform. Marx's philosophy advocated a revolutionary seizure of power by the proletariat as the solution to capitalist oppression. Followers of these two influences merged in 1875 to form the Social Democratic party of Germany. The alarming growth of the party led to the enactment of the antisocialist law of 1878, but when it failed to curtail the growth of the socialist movement, the law was repealed in 1890. The period of suppression, however, intensified the bitterness between classes while unifying the burgeoning German proletariat in support of the Social Democratic party. Because of its size and tradition, the German Social Democratic party thus became the dominant influence on European socialism, but it was completely powerless within the political system of Imperial Germany. This gulf between the working class and bourgeois society was manifested in the antagonism of Socialists and the Churches, but during the last year of the German Empire the Social Democratic party developed a close relationship with the Catholic Center Party in their common pursuit of peace. These two parties became the strongest supporters of the Weimar Republic and the most effective opponents of the rising tide of National Socialism. As coalition partners they were able to resolve points of conflict such as the regulation of religious schools. Although outlawed by the Hitler government in 1933, the Social Democratic party regained its support in post-World War II Germany. By moderating its ideology, the party has broadened its political base and now represents one of two major forces in German politics. BIBLIOGRAPHY: C. Landauer, *European Socialism* (1959).

[R. J. GIBBONS]

SOCIALIST REALISM, the official doctrine of Soviet literature and art since 1932, requiring that the artist portray reality truthfully and historically in its revolutionary development, i.e., that he incorporate the ideals of *partiynost'* (identification with the aims of the Communist Party), *ideynost'* (progressive ideas of revolutionary development), and *narodnost'* (national or "folk" character). Though it emphasizes realism, the doctrine does not exclude a certain romanticism, e.g., the positive hero in undaunted pursuit of the ideological goals of communism. BIBLIOGRAPHY: M. Slonim, *Soviet Russian Literature* (1964).

[M. F. MCCARTHY]

SOCIETIES, CONDEMNED, see SECRET SOCIETIES.

SOCIETY. Vatican Council II in summarizing Catholic teaching recalled certain essential points about the traditional position of the Church. Society primarily means the political, cultural, and economic association of people to achieve a common purpose, designated as the "common good." Citing St. Thomas Aquinas (*In Ethic* 1, lect. 1) the Council indicates that society exists because human beings are by nature social, i.e., stand in need of a life in social consort with others (Vat II ChurchModWorld 25). The need regards the common good, "the sum of those conditions of social life which will allow social groups and their individual members relatively thorough and ready access to their own fulfilment" (ibid. 26). An essential Catholic emphasis on the meaning and reason for being of society is this: "the subject and goal of all social institutions is and must be the human person" (ibid. 25). Thus a true and legitimate society must "serve the rights and duties of the individual, which are universal and inviolable. Therefore there must be made available to all men everything necessary for leading a life truly human, such as food, clothing, and shelter; the right to choose a state of life freely and to found a family; the right to education, to employment, to a good reputation, to respect, to appropriate information, to activity in accord with the upright norm of one's own conscience, to protection of privacy and to rightful freedom in matters of religion" (ibid. 26). A further dimension of the contemporary meaning of society is that it embraces not simply the distinct nations and states of the world, but also humankind, so that, because of the interdependence of peoples, the common good takes on an increasingly interrelated complexion and consequently involves rights and duties with respect to the whole human race. Every social group must take account of the needs and legitimate aspirations of other groups, and even of the general welfare of the entire human family" (ibid.). The dynamics of society in all its scope means a constant effort at betterment; the foundation of the process is "truth, built on justice and animated by love; in freedom society should grow every day toward a more humane balance" (ibid.).

One further element, articulated by Pius XII in *Quadragesimo anno* and repeated in the Church's social teaching since, and by Vatican II is the principle of subsidiarity (ibid.86). This principle involves the recognition that while the state or nation is the principal form of human society the competency of subordinate social units to achieve their proper ends must be respected; the function of the more specific social unity should not be absorbed by the greater. The principle also has entered into the Church's understanding of its place vis à vis the State, which requires the mutual recognition and respect of each towards the other. The concept of society, however, has been reckoned as a less appropriate model for expressing the inner nature of the Church since the ecclesiology of Vatican II.

The Church recognizes that sociology has competence in its empirical examination and conclusions about the functioning of society. But a sociology that rejects the philosophical and theological interpretation of the meaning of society is a form of pure positivism that is unacceptable.

[T. C. O'BRIEN]

SOCIETY (METHODIST), J. *Wesley's designation for a group of persons desiring "to flee from the wrath to come." He laid down rules governing its members. Individual societies later became the Churches in the various Methodist denominations in the U.S., as well as in England. Religious societies had existed in the C of E before Wesley's time. BIBLIOGRAPHY: J. S. Simon, *John Wesley and the Religious Societies* (1921).

[F. E. MASER]

SOCIETY FOR PROMOTING CHRISTIAN KNOWLEDGE (SPCK), an organization founded in England in 1698 by T. *Bray with the help of four Anglican laymen. Its purpose was to encourage the establishment of charity schools in England and Wales and to promote Christian knowledge in England and abroad by the distribution of Bibles and religious tracts. In 1701 the *Society for the Propagation of the Gospel (SPG) took over its foreign missionary involvement, leaving SPCK to concentrate upon the education of poor children at home and the publication of religious literature. The Society maintains a publishing house that has served with distinction, esp. in the field of religious publishing.

SOCIETY FOR THE PROPAGATION OF THE GOSPEL (SPG),

Anglican missionary organization, founded in 1701 largely through the efforts of Thomas *Bray, Commissary of the Bp. of London for Md., with the active support of the abp. of Canterbury (T. Tenison) and the bp. of London (H. Compton). Bray had previously organized (1698) the *Society for Promoting Christian Knowledge (SPCK), and this body aided in the organization of the new society, which was originally named the Society for the Propagation of the Gospel in Foreign Parts. In 1703, the SPG sent a former Quaker, George *Keith, on an exploratory mission to the British plantations in America. After visiting most of the colonies, he made an extended report. The chaplain of the ship on which he sailed, John Talbot, joined him in his travels and later became the Society's first settled missionary at Burlington, New Jersey. Throughout the colonial period, the SPG aided in the support of ministers in colonies where the C of E was not established, and in some where it was but where the legal stipends were insufficient. As its original charter restricted its operations to "His Majesty's dominions," it was obliged to cease work in the U.S. after the Revolution. It continued work in Canada and the West Indies and, with the growth of the British Empire, extended its efforts to India and Africa. After an amendment of the charter, it entered China, Japan, and other countries, developing a worldwide mission. In 1965, it merged with the Universities Mission to Central Africa to become the United Society for the Propagation of the Gospel. BIBLIOGRAPHY: H. P. Thompson, *Into All Lands* (1951).

SOCIETY OF BROTHERS

(Bruderhof), intentional Christian communities. Drawn together in 1920 by Eberhard *Arnold, who had been the scholarly executive of the Student Christian Movement in Germany, the Society set out to be a fellowship based on the Sermon on the Mount: mutual love, pacifism, hospitality to all, no use of money among members, frequent worship, equal value of all work. The pattern was influenced by Christoph F. Blumhardt (1842–1919), whom Arnold esteemed highly, and by Hutterite principles; he briefly joined the *Hutterian Brethren in the Dakotas in the early 1930s. First at Sannerz, Germany, then on a large farm in the Rhoen hills, the Bruderhof flourished. Under Nazi pressure the Bruderhof moved to Devonshire, England, then because of wartime anti-German unpopularity, to the Primavera Peninsula in

Paraguay. There, after Mennonite colonies helped the pioneering venture, three groups in Paraguay and one in Uruguay gathered some 1,000 members. Later most of these moved to the U.S., after a schism in the early 1960s caused many of the members to withdraw. In 1969 there were about 800 members, all in three communes: Norfolk, Conn., Rifton, N.Y., and Farmington, Pennsylvania. Firm economic roots were put down as the Bruderhof began to manufacture "community playthings," expensive, very well-constructed wooden items for schools and playgrounds. A provision that all young members spend a trial period in "the world," and choose whether to return afterward has resulted in some attrition, even among descendants of the earliest members, but there is continuing dynamism in the common industrial production task, the serious tradition of corporate worship and chorale singing, and the witness to peace and simplicity. BIBLIOGRAPHY: E. Arnold, *Salt and Light* (1967); *idem, Torches Together* (1964); *idem* et al., *Heavens Are Opened* (1974).

[J. O. NELSON]

SOCIETY OF COMMON LIFE,

a form of the pursuit of Christian perfection by men or women in community, observing the evangelical counsels and their own proper constitutions or rule, but without making public vows (i.e., vows accepted in the name of the Church). The members are not religious in the strict canonical sense (CIC c.673 1). Such a society may be clerical or lay, i.e., made up of priests or of those not in orders. Vatican Council II includes societies of common life, as well as *secular institutes, in its decree on the renewal of religious life, as a form of life dedicated to Christian perfection (n.1). Many mission societies, after the example of the Paris Foreign Mission Society, are societies of common life (e.g., Mill Hill Fathers, Columbans, Maryknollers); other well-known societies of men are the Oratorians, Vincentians, and Sulpicians. The Daughters of Charity of St. Vincent de Paul also were a society of common life. The evolution of this form of evangelical commitment in the Church is explained by complex forces, among them the concepts that the religious life required solemn vows and that a distinctive garb or habit was a sign of the religious. Because of social and political forces operating against the religious life as such, those desirous of living a common apostolic life did so in such a way as not to be classified as religious. The ratification of this form of life in the Church came about formally in the Code of Canon Law of 1917.

[T. C. O'BRIEN]

SOCIETY OF FRIENDS, see RELIGIOUS SOCIETY OF FRIENDS.

SOCINIANISM,

Unitarian doctrine partly rationalistic, partly evangelical, developed in the 16th and 17th centuries. Through the theological leadership exercised after 1579 by F. Sozzini (see SOCINUS), Socinianism became the doctrine of the Minor Reformed Church, which had existed in Poland from 1556. The Socinian center was Raców, near Kraków, where there were a school and a press to diffuse Sozzini's ideas. Among the aristocracy, there were other small congregations and schools. RC reaction led to the closing of the Gymnasium at Raców (1638) and to the proscription of the Socinians (1658). Thereafter, apart from a few scattered communities (e.g., in Transylvania and East Prussia), Socinianism existed only in its individual representatives scattered throughout Europe. Especially in Holland (the *Bibliotheca Fratrum Polonorum* was published in Amsterdam in 1688) its adherents freely circulated their liberal and rationalist ideas. As a result, Socinianism spread to England and America, where it was absorbed into *Unitarianism, and in Europe it served as a preparation for the *Enlightenment.

The distinctive tenets of Socinianism (as in the *Racovian Catechism), though not imposed on adherents, were evangelical and rationalistic. The NT was the sole rule of faith and the only source for knowing God; but reason was autonomous in judging the meaning of revelation. Socinianism was a rejection of the Trinity, the Fall, the Incarnation, the expiatory Redemption, the Resurrection of the body, and the natural immortality of the soul (see CONDITIONAL IMMORTALITY). Christ was held to be essentially a man, divine only in the sense of sharing in the power of the Father. The two sacraments, baptism and the Lord's Supper, were mere symbols to show a desire to imitate Christ's obedience in death. Socinians shared the Lutheran and Calvinist concept of the Church's nature and organization but held the Church to be independent of the State. There was no civil power to coerce heretics; neither, however, was civil oppression to be resisted; tolerance was supreme. BIBLIOGRAPHY: L. Cristiani, DTC 14:2326–34; S. Kot, *Socinianism in Poland* (tr. E. M. Wilbur, 1957); G. Pioli, *Fausto Sozzini* (1953); F. Socinus, *Opera* (2v., 1964); E. M. Wilbur, *History of Unitarianism* (2v., rev. ed., 1965), v.1, *Socinianism and its Antecedents*.

[T. C. O'BRIEN]

SOCINUS, from which the name *Socinianism is derived, the Latinization of the patronymic of Lelio and Fausto Sozzini. (1) **Lelio Francesco Maria Sozzini** (1525–62), Italian anti-Trinitarian, uncle of Fausto, was a rationalist in his biblical and theological views. After 1544 he resided in Germany and Switzerland and was in contact with *Bullinger, *Calvin, and *Melanchthon. Visiting Italy (1552), he made a strong impression upon his nephew. He prepared the way in Poland (1556–59) for Fausto'future coming and bequeathed to him his own theological papers. Lelio's biography (*Vita L. S.*, 1814) was written by C. F. Ilgen. (2) **Fausto Paolo Sozzini** (1539–1604), nephew of Lelio, was the theologian of Socinianism in Poland. A jurisconsult in the family tradition, S.'s predilection was for religious studies. He adhered early to his uncle's views, left Italy (1559) for Lyons, and went to Zurich (1562) to claim Lelio's papers. His *Explicatio primae partis primi capitis evangelii Ioannis* (1562), like most of his works published

anonymously, already expressed his anti-Trinitarian thought. A letter of 1563 defended *conditional immortality. Outwardly a Catholic, he served at Francesco de' Medici's court in Florence (1563–74), then devoted himself to study at Basel (1574–78). His *De Jesu Christo servatore,* denying Christ's divine nature, was completed in 1578, but published only in 1594. S. went to Poland in 1579 and, after initial difficulties, won acceptance by the Polish Brethren (or Brethren of Christ). Fusing his own ideas with their Anabaptist views, he became a kind of theologian for these anti-Trinitarian groups among the Polish aristocracy around Kraków. He composed the first draft of the *Racovian Catechism. Though RC reaction under King Stephen Bathory forced S. to leave Kraków (1583) and led to a public burning of his books and manuscripts there (1598), he was otherwise left to spend the rest of his life quietly in the neighboring village of Luclawice. BIBLIOGRAPHY: *Francesco Sozzini, Opera* (2v., 1964); G. Pioli, *Francesco Sozzini* (1953); bibliog. for SOCINIANISM.

[T. C. O'BRIEN]

SOCIOLOGY OF RELIGION, see RELIGION, SOCIOLOGY OF.

SOCIOPATH, a person who lacks wholly or partly a sense of right and wrong, and therefore feels no internal restraints against violating the rights of others and of society. Some authors prefer the word sociopath to psychopath since it indicates the social dimension of the behavior in question, a dimension that varies from society to society. Behavior condemned by one society may be condoned or encouraged by another. Other authors prefer psychopath, since it focuses attention on the psychological disorder characterized by failure to develop moral sense according to the norms of the society of which the individual is part. *PSYCHOPATHIC PERSONALITY.

[M. E. STOCK]

SOCKMAN, RALPH WASHINGTON (1889–1970), United Methodist clergyman, radio preacher, and recipient of the First Annual Award by the World Commission for Christian Broadcasting for service to America's religious life. Born at Mt. Vernon, Ohio, he secured his higher education at Ohio Wesleyan and Columbia Universities. A prolific writer and a lecturer at numerous universities and colleges, he had the unique distinction of having served only one pastorate throughout his life—Christ Church, New York City (1917–61). He became an international figure through his preaching for 36 years on the National Radio Pulpit. He was also noted for his efforts toward world peace, serving as president of the Carnegie Foundation's Church Peace Union, as president of the Methodist Board of World Peace, and as a member of the Central Committee of the *World Council of Churches. BIBLIOGRAPHY: *Encyclopedia of World Methodism*, 1974.

[F. E. MASER]

SOCRATES (469–399 B.C.), Athenian philosopher, and one of the greatest and most influential of ancient personalities. He himself wrote nothing. Our knowledge of the man and his activity comes from three primary sources: Aristophanes, Xenophon, and Plato. The S. of Aristophanes' *Clouds* is a caricature. Xenophon supplies valuable data in his *Memorabilia,* but he was not close to S., nor did he have more than a superficial comprehension of his thought. Plato is incomparably the most reliable source. He knew S. in person, was deeply influenced by the personal contact, and more than any other had a full appreciation of the man and his teaching. Plato's *Apology, Crito,* and *Phaedo* furnish a uniquely vivid and authentic account of S.s' career, trial, and death. It is a disputed question, however, to what extent the views ascribed to S. as a character in other dialogues of Plato, and in particular in the middle and later dialogues, are really those of the historical S., and not rather those of Plato himself.

He was a small man of rather ugly features, but of strong physique and possessing unusual powers of endurance. He showed conspicuous courage in his military service, and even greater moral courage in his refusal to condemn the generals after the battle of Arginusae (406), in his refusal, after the fall of Athens, to obey the unjust orders of the Thirty Tyrants, and, finally, in his uncompromising defense of his conduct that led to his condemnation to death. Late in life he married a certain Xanthippe, and had children by her. Her complaints about the family's poverty at this time were probably justified, and her shrewishness has very likely been exaggerated.

As a young man, S. seems to have studied cosmological questions, but from middle life on he devoted himself to the investigation of the right conduct of life and the means of attaining it. His decision was undoubtedly motivated by the intellectual crisis of the last half of the 5th cent., esp. at Athens. The traditional norms of morality of the Greek city-state were being challenged or repudiated, and in the ideological conflict between oligarchy and democracy, the opinion was gaining ground that according to the true law of nature the right belonged to the strong. There was as yet no formal code of private ethics, and conduct was still determined by the traditional customs and laws of the city-state itself. Socrates considered his investigation of right conduct and the means of its attainment a divine mission. This is the significance of the consultation of the Oracle of Delphi and the application of its answer to him.

He maintained that the chief business of man is to take care of his soul and to make it as good as possible. He is the first of ancient thinkers to regard the soul as the intellectual and moral personality. This concept of the soul marks an epoch in the history of thought and henceforth plays a central role in Greek and later philosophy. Socrates believed that the world is ruled by divine powers who are good and who order all things for the best. The soul, therefore, should strive towards the good, which, however, he does not define more precisely. It remained for Plato to make the Good a fundamental part of his system. The health and goodness of

the soul can only be attained when the soul really knows goodness. When the soul knows what is truly good, right action will necessariy follow true knowledge. For him virtue is knowledge, but a knowledge from which ignorance and error under the guise of truth have been eradicated.

He believed that true knowledge could be attained by a method of questioning. In the process, assumed knowledge on the part of one regarding himself as an expert in his profession is repeatedly challenged, and in the end the man questioned is in a state of *aporia* or perplexity. He is then led by further discussion to recognize true knowledge or virtue and to act accordingly. In all probability S. thus laid the foundation for the development of Plato's dialectic.

The mysterious "voice" or "sign" or *daimon,* which from his youth, as S. claimed, gave him warnings or imposed prohibitions against given actions, seems best explained as coming from his own highly developed and sensitive conscience. His fits of long abstraction are best interpreted, too, as being due to intense mental concentration, and not as mystical phenomena. He seems to have been absolutely sincere in his piety and in his adherence to the traditional religion of Athens. It is difficult to determine whether he believed in the immortality of the soul and a future life, but his observations in the *Apology* would seem to indicate that he wanted at least to believe in both.

S. was tried on the charges of having introduced new gods and of corrupting the youth. He refuted both charges, but his accusers could not forget that the young intellectuals flocked around him, although he disclaimed that he was a teacher and received no fees, and that among them were men like Alcibiades and Critias who, however, did not follow his path to virtue. Instead of pleading for mercy, as was customary, he maintained his innocence and his right to pursue his mission, even suggesting that the Athenian State support him, for, like a gadfly stinging a lazy horse, he was stirring men to right action. He could easily have escaped from Athens—and this, too, was probably desired by the majority of those who voted against him—but he held that it was his duty to obey the law and submit to its penalty. He died for uncompromising loyalty to his principles and to the laws of Athens.

Socrates exercised a unique influence on the development of human thought, but an equally great influence through his own personality. He was conscious of his duty and he had the courage to perform it even if it cost him his life. He left an indelible impression on one of the young intellectuals in particular, namely, Plato, for whom he was the lifetime inspiration, and who was destined to give him immortality as the leading character in so many of his dialogues. It is not surprising that the Christian Fathers often regarded S. as a pagan prototype of Christ. BIBLIOGRAPHY: OCD 845–846; A. H. Armstrong, *Introduction to Ancient Philosophy* (3d ed. 1959) 24–32; Copleston 1:96–115; W. Jaeger, *Paideia* (1943) 2:3–76; R. Guardini, *Death of Socrates* (tr. B. Wrighton, 1948); E. Benz, "Christus und Sokrates in der alten Kirche," ZNTW 43 (1950–51) 195–224.

[M. R. P. MCGUIRE]

SOCRATES (HISTORIAN) (*c*.380–450), church historian. S. was called also Socrates Scholasticus because he was a lawyer in his native Constantinople. He was the most accurate of the continuators of *Eusebius' Historia ecclesiastica* (see SOZOMEN; EVAGRIUS SCHOLASTICUS; THEODORET OF CYR). S.'s continuation covers the period from 305 (resignation of *Diocletian) to 439. Of the seven books, one covers the short reign of Julian and Jovian; each of the others is devoted to one emperor of the period. The first edition survives only in a few fragments of an Armenian translation; the surviving edition (PG 67:29–872 [Eng. tr. A. Zenos], NPNFC ser. 2, v. 2:1–178) is a revision S. made after discovering inaccuracies in one of his prime sources, *Rufinus. While not of high literary merit, the work is valuable for its objectivity and because it contains quotations from many contemporary documents. BIBLIOGRAPHY: Altaner 276–288; Jedin-Baus 12; Quasten 3:532–534.

[R. B. ENO]

SODALITIES OF OUR LADY, NATIONAL FEDERATION OF, see NATIONAL FEDERATION OF SODALITIES OF OUR LADY.

SODALITIUM PIANUM (Sodality of Pius V), a secret society, French name Sapinière, founded (1909) by U. *Benigni, Italian priest-journalist, to support throughout Europe the campaign called *Integralism against *Modernism. The full nature of the Sodalitium has not yet been documented thoroughly, but it clearly used witch-hunting tactics—accusation by pseudonymous or anonymous letters, insinuation of guilt by association—against reputable Catholic scholars to make them appear to be Modernists; it published its smears in the newsletter, *Correspondenza di Roma*, also founded by Benigni (1909). The discovery of documents during World War I baring some of the Sodalitium's methods, and increasing outrage against Integralism, led to suppression of the Sodalitium by the Holy See in 1921.

[T. C. O'BRIEN]

SODALITY, as a generic term, a pious union of laity for the promotion of their Christian life and worship. "The Sodality" as a proper name referred to the Sodality of Our Lady, established at Rome by the Jesuits in 1563 and fostered by them throughout the world. In the U.S., E. F. *Garesché, SJ and D. *Lord, SJ particularly promoted the Sodality with the magazine, *The Queen's Work,* and by developing in members a spirit of fidelity to the Sodality rule of life.

The successor to the Sodalities is the Christian Life Communities, following a rule of life and program of spirituality revised in accord with Vatican Council II. Paul VI approved the revision in 1971. The U.S. central office of the federation of Christian Life Communities is in St. Louis, Missouri.

SODALITY OF ST. PETER CLAVER FOR AFRICAN MISSIONS (SSPC), also called Missionary Sisters of St. Peter Claver, a congregation founded in 1894 by Maria Teresa Ledóchowska for aiding the African missions, esp. by means of the apostolate of the press. The congregation received papal approval in 1910; the motherhouse is in Rome and the community is under the jurisdiction of the Congregation for the Propagation of the Faith. The sisters are engaged in spreading knowledge about and securing aid for the African missions, and in writing, publishing, and diffusing in Africa itself Catholic newspapers and magazines, written principally in the local languages. They also operate modern printing and editorial centers in Africa, to which are attached catechetical centers, houses for retreat, and hostels for African students. The congregation was established in the U.S. in 1914. In 1975 worldwide there were 142 members in 14 houses.

[C. J. NOONE]

SODEN, HERMANN FREIHERR VON (1852–1914), NT scholar. S. taught at the Univ. of Berlin, and is best noted for his *Die Schriften des Neuen Testament in ihrer ältesten erreichbaren Gestaltung* (1902–10). S. proposed a complex classification system for NT MSS, and concluded to a common but no longer extant source for the MSS now available. Since he often accepted a text as accurate if two of the three main traditions with which he worked agree, his conclusions are generally regarded as an oversimplification. BIBLIOGRAPHY: JBC 2:583; D. W. Martin, NCE 13:411.

[T. M. MCFADDEN]

SÖDERBLOM, NATHAN (1866–1931), Lutheran abp. and ecumenical theologian. Born at Trönö, Sweden, he studied at Uppsala Univ., and received the doctorate in theology at the Univ. of Paris in 1901. After a Paris student pastorate among Swedish Lutherans, he became professor of comparative religion at Uppsala (1901–14), then at the Univ. of Leipzig (1912–14). As abp. of Uppsala and thus primate of Sweden (1914–31), and as confidant of the royal family, he prompted a revival of Sweden's church life, while becoming one of the several key leaders of the movement that led to formation of the World Council of Churches in 1948. He called the first universal conference on *Life and Work (Stockholm, 1925) and guided the *Faith and Order conference at Lausanne (1927). At the beginning of World War I, he drafted a message signed by leading Western churchmen urging Christian solidarity against war. He was given the Nobel Peace Prize in 1925. Two of his books, *The Living God* (Gifford Lectures, 1933) and *The Nature of Revelation* (1933), received wide international circulation. Combining profound scholarship in comparative religion, expertness as churchman and preacher, and a passion for Christian unity, he earned the title "prophet of ecumenism." BIBLIOGRAPHY: H. G. G. Herklots, *Nathan Söderblom, Apostle of Christian Unity* (1948).

[J. O. NELSON]

SODOM AND GOMORRAH, cities that became proverbial for such wickedness that God destroyed them (Is 1.9; Mt. 10.15; 2 Pet 2.6). Told of the impending destruction, Abraham asked God to spare Sodom for the sake of his nephew Lot, who lived there (Gen 13.12; 18.16–33). Apparently not even 10 righteous men could be found in Sodom, however, so after two angels led Lot and his family out, the cities were destroyed (Gen 19.15–25). The vice of sodomy is named from the attempt of the men in the city to assault the angels (Gen 19.4–11). Some scholars speculate that the cities may have been in the area now covered by the S end of the Dead Sea. Others doubt this, or that it is possible to locate the cities. The biblical account as it stands is more a portrayal of Yahweh's punishment of the wicked than an actual historical episode.

[T. EARLY]

SODOMA (GIOVANNI ANTONIO BAZZI; 1477–1549), Italian painter. At 13 a student in glassmaking, then a cobbler (1497), S. finally settled in Siena (1501) and perhaps visiting Milan knew Leonardo whose haunting sweetness is seen occasionally in S.'s work. He painted a *Descent from the Cross* (1502, Siena) juxtaposing symmetric setting with agitating draperies, and at the Benedictine monastery of Monte Olieveto Maggiore finished 31 frescoes of the life of St. Benedict, abandoned (1498) by Signorelli. In Rome (1507) s. decorated a part of the ceiling of the Stanza della Segnatura, in 1518 began the decoration of the S. Bernardino Oratory, and in 1525 painted the life of St. Catherine for the chapel in S. Domenico, Siena, showing handsome figures of intense fervor awkwardly composed. Despite disparate settings, S.'s figures are often forcefully posed (*St. Sebastian*, 1525).

[M. J. DALY]

SODOMY, in moral theology, anal or oral sexual penetration. Because of the account in Gen 19, 1–11, in its first meaning sodomy is taken as an act between males; in a second meaning it is heterosexual, sodomitic congress that includes ejaculation by the male. A consummated sexual act between females involves the same kind of moral disorder. Sodomy is designated as an unnatural sin or a sin against nature, since it is not coital in a proper sense. In canon law sodomy by clerics is grounds for the penalty of *infamy (CIC, c. 2359, § 2).

[T. C. O'BRIEN]

SOFIA, capital city of Bulgaria and see of the patriarch of Bulgaria. The city existed from pre-Roman times as the main settlement of a tribe of Thracians called Serdi—hence its ancient name Serdica (Sardica). An episcopal see from 316, it was one of the centers of church life in the Balkans. During the Arian crisis the important Council of Sardica assembled there in 343. The city became part of the Bulgarian State in 809, following a westward thrust of Khan Krum, and as a Bulgarian city came to be known as Streditsa (Triadits), a Slavic corruption of Serdica. During the Second Bulgarian Empire (1185–1393) the city became a metropolitan see and was called Sofia from the name of its cathedral church, a 5th–6th-cent. building of basilical form, still in use today. Under the Turks Sofia became the administrative center of the whole European portion of the empire, but later was left to deteriorate to the condition of a large, predominantly Turkish, village. Because of its central position in the territory inhabited by Bulgarians, it was chosen as the capital of the newly independent Bulgarian State in 1878. This made the ancient city the center of the political, cultural, and religious life of the country. When the Bulgarian exarchate in Constantinople was abolished de facto after the Balkan Wars (1912–13) and the death of the last exarch (1915), Sofia, already a metropolitan see, became the ecclesiastical center of the Bulgarian Orthodox Church. The metropolitan of Sofia obtained the title of exarch (1945) and then that of patriarch of Bulgaria (1953). The chief institutions of the Bulgarian Orthodox Church are in Sofia, including the Holy Synod and the Theological Academy of St. Clement of Ohrid. It possesses some of the oldest and most beautiful churches in the country: St. Alexander Nevsky (largest Christian church in the Balkans), St. Nedelja, the cathedral of St. Sophia, and the round church of St. George which is built on Roman foundations.

[G. ELDAROV]

SÔGÎTŌ (East Syrian *sôgîtā*), Syrian poetic composition consisting of a series of metric strophes, lyrical, and often involving dialogue.

[A. CODY]

SOGLIA, CERONI GIOVANNI (1779–1856), cardinal, papal secretary of state. A member of the household of Piux VII, he accompanied the Pontiff when the latter was imprisoned by Napoleon. In 1839 he was created cardinal, Latin patriarch of Constantinople, and secretary of the Congregation of Bishops and Regulars by Pope Leo XII. S. was also bp. of Osimo and Cingoli. Pope Pius IX named him secretary of state and president of the Council of Ministers of the Papal States in 1848. When Pius IX fled Rome in 1848, S. confined himself to administering his diocese.

[J. R. AHERNE]

SOHAG, MONASTERIES OF, recently restored Coptic monasteries, centers of ancient and medieval Coptic learning, located in the town and governate of Sohag in the Nile Valley of Upper Egypt, on the Nile's west bank, between modern Asyūt and Jirjā. The so-called Red Monastery, with a basilica church, is located 4 miles NW of the more famous White Monastery, with a late-5th-century basilica church surrounded by a wall of white calcite. During the 4th and 5th cent., there were over 2,000 monks living at the latter site. An indication of its importance both to the Coptic and to the universal Church is the fact that one of its abbots was St. Senute of Atripe, the greatest of all the Coptic theologians of the pre-Chalcedonian Church. He was theological consultant to St. Cyril of Alexandria, whom he accompanied to the Council of Ephesus. According to Coptic and Ethiopian tradition the monastic settlements at Sohag have nearly apostolic origins and were long believed to house the relics of St. Bartholomew. BIBLIOGRAPHY: O. F. A. Meinhardus, *Christian Egypt—Faith and Life,* (1970) 198 and *passim*.

[E. J. DILLON]

SOISSONS, COUNCILS OF. Soissons in the north of France was the site of councils in 853, 866, and 1121. In 1121 Abelard was ordered to burn his work on the Trinity and to confess the Athanasian creed. BIBLIOGRAPHY: G. Dumas, NCE 13:413–414 (for bibliog.)

[B. L. MARTHALER]

SŌKA-GAKKAI (the Value-Creating Society), easily the most influential of the many new (in some sense) religions coming to the fore in Japan after World War II. Its proponent was Tsunesaburu Makiguchi (d. 1944), a Tokyo schoolteacher. Its organizing apostle was Josei Toda (d. 1958). The name of the society refers to Makiguchi's theory of value: life's primary end is happiness, resulting in value; the substance of value is beauty, goodness, and profit. Socially and politically potent, as well as religiously, Soka-Gakkai may be styled an interpretation of Buddhism: technically it is the lay arm of what was formerly a minor Buddhist sect (the Nichiren Shoshu), although Soka-Gakkai itself has a further appendage, political, known as Komeito, or the Clean Government Party. In 1967 this party was the third largest of five blocs in the House of Councillors, the Japanese Diet's upper chamber. Soka-Gakkai doctrinally differs from the time-established religions in that, along with many of Japan's new religions, it holds that man's nature is not sinful and that temporal benefits will come to its faithful. Such optimism is not found in Buddhism generally. Characteristic of Soka-Gakkai, however, is its intolerance of other religions and its political action. Soka-Gakkai's spiritual headquarters are in Taisekiji, at the base of Mount Fuji, but its regular headquarters are in Tokyo. Some observers estimate the membership at 8 to 10 million; its leaders claim 15 million. BIBLIOGRAPHY: J. Kitagawa, *Religion in Japanese History* (1966) 327–331.

[E. A. WEIS]

SOKOLSKIJ, JOSEPH (b. 1786), archbishop. As abbot of Gabrovo near Constantinople, S. was a member of the delegation that announced to the apostolic delegate of Costanza the conversion of about 2,000 Bulgarians to the Catholic Church. In 1861 he was consecrated as abp. by Pope Pius IX and soon afterwards disappeared mysteriously from Constantinople. He was said to have been kidnapped by the Russian ambassador and immured in a monastery in Kiev. BIBLIOGRAPHY: H. K. Steinhausen, DE 3:912.

[M. J. SUELZER]

SOLA FIDE, SOLA GRATIA, SOLA SCRIPTURA, three phrases suggesting essentials of Reformation teaching and its critique of the Renaissance Church. Each phrase points to an emphasis upon the exclusiveness of the factors that the men of the Reformation saw as crucial for the renewal of the Church and Christian life. *Sola Fide* refers immediately to the Pauline thesis stated in Rom 1.17: "The just man will live by faith alone." Thus runs Luther's translation, which he defends as authentic in the context of Paul's thought. He sees the phrase to mean, therefore, that by faith alone is man saved, to the exclusion of "works of the law" or *good works done with a view toward man's pleasing God on his own. *Sola gratia* points to man's absolute need of having God take the initiative to save him. The phrase is used with less discomfort by Roman Catholics since it is echoed in the description of man's situation by the Council of Trent. *Sola Scriptura* is originally identified more with the *Reformed branch of the Reformation. In recent times, however, it can be labeled simply as "Protestant" insofar as it bespeaks the notion that the exclusive source and criterion of knowledge about God is the Bible. The phrase rejects as rules of faith esp. what Roman Catholics ordinarily call *tradition or the *magisterium of the Church. BIBLIOGRAPHY: R. McAfee Brown, *Spirit of Protestantism* (pa., 1965) 57, 214–216.

[M. B. SCHEPERS]

SOLANO, FRANCIS, ST. (1549–1610), Spanish Franciscan missionary to Peru. He made his profession as a Franciscan in 1570, after which he labored 20 years in Spain where he gained fame for his work among the plague-stricken in Montoro. Then for another 20 years he was a missionary in the Americas, first in Argentina, then in Peru. He became Franciscan superior in Lima and Trujillo. His spirituality led others to consider him another Francis of Assisi (*Franciscus redivivus*). He was beatified in 1675 and canonized in 1726.

[E. J. DILLON]

SOLANO, VICENTE (1791–1862), Ecuadorian Franciscan scholar. At age 9 he entered the Franciscan Order and studied in Quito. He became a professor of philosophy even before being ordained in 1814. An authority in natural science, S. wrote ceaselessly and collaborated in founding many newspapers and periodicals. His four volume *Obras* were published in Barcelona in 1892. His letters published in 1902 by the abp. of Quito (Manuel Maria Polit) are a valuable source for reconstructing the history of their period.

[E. J. DILLON]

SOLEMN COMMUNION, see COMMUNION, SOLEMN.

SOLEMN LEAGUE AND COVENANT, a document on church reform in the British Isles. Overtures made by Parliament in the Civil War of 1642 encouraged the Scottish

*Covenanters to hope that the English would reciprocate for the aid they wanted by the acceptance of reformation on the Presbyterian model. The Solemn League and Covenant, drafted by Alexander Henderson and approved by the Scottish Assembly and Convention, was accepted in England in Aug. 1643 by Parliament and by the *Westminster Assembly in September. Those who subscribed it pledged themselves to extirpate *episcopacy from England and popery from Ireland and bring the Churches of the three kingdoms "to the nearest conjunction and uniformity in Religion." In part a defensive bond, in part the seal of an aggressive Presbyterianism, the Covenant proved more divisive than unifying. BIBLIOGRAPHY: Schaff Creeds 1:689–694; bibliog. for Church of Scotland.

[J. A. R. MacKENZIE]

SOLEMN MASS, a term to indicate a form of the former Tridentine *Mass in the Roman rite celebrated and sung by a priest assisted by a deacon and a subdeacon, or by priests' fulfilling these respective roles. Like the *high Mass, it was originally derived from the *pontifical Mass. With the revision of the liturgy of the Mass by Vatican Council II, such distinctions as solemn, *low, or *high Mass are no longer applicable. BIBLIOGRAPHY: J. A. Jungmann, *Mass of the Roman Rite* (rev. ed., tr. F. A. Brunner, 2 v., 1950–55); J. H. Miller, *Fundamentals of the Liturgy* (1959). *MASS, ROMAN.

[N. R. KRAMER]

SOLER, MARIANO (1846–1908), bp., intellectual. An Uruguayan ordained in 1872, S. became the leading Catholic intellectual of Uruguay. Founder of the Liceo Universitario in 1875, he combatted the liberal forces in his country. In the daily, *El Bien Publico,* S. conducted a defense of religion against government attacks. The church of which S. was pastor was the center of opposition to the government. In 1891 S. was consecrated bp. of Montevideo, and abp. in 1897. S. was a skilled polemicist and staunch defender of Catholicism.

[J. R. AHERNE]

SOLESMES (*Solesmensis*), Benedictine abbey. Originally a priory dependent on the abbey La Couture du Mans, Solesmes was founded *c.*1010 in honor of St. Peter by Geoffrey of Sablé on the border between Maine and Anjou. Sacked by the English in 1425, it was restored and its church decorated with famous groups of statues called the Saints of Solesmes. The priory was amalgamated with the congregation of Saint-Maur in 1664, reconstructed in 1732, and sold as a national property in 1790. Prosper *Guéranger purchased it in 1883, and it was shortly thereafter established as an abbey by Gregory XVI. It became head of the Benedictine Congregation of St. Peter of Solesmes, which now numbers 781 monks grouped in 19 monasteries. Solesmes has been famous for its work in the restoration of Gregorian chant (see SOLESMES [MUSIC]), for its promotion of the liturgy, and for its editions of theological studies. In 1901 the monks restored Quarr Abbey on the Isle of Wight. BIBLIOGRAPHY: Cottineau 2:3055–57.

[J. DAOUST]

SOLESMES (MUSIC). Under Dom Prosper *Guéranger the Benedictines of Solesmes undertook the work of restoring Gregorian chant and published, in 1904, the *Editio Vaticana*. Officially recognized by the Church, this version was the result of years of investigation, collection, and comparison of MSS done under Doms Guéranger, Pothier, Jausions, and *Mocquereau. In addition to establishing the true text, Solesmes set out to define, through a quarterly publication begun in 1889 and called *Paléographie musicale*, the authentic method of performance. Called the "Solesmes method," it has received wide acclaim as well as criticism. The recognition given in recent times, to the artistic significance of plainsong is due in large measure to the work of these monks. This labor continued in various publications (*Revue grégorienne, Études grégoriennes*) under Dom Joseph Gajard (1885–1972). Solesmes continues to remain in the forefront of liturgical renewal. Abbot Jean Prou helped to shape the *Constitution on the Sacred Liturgy* of Vatican Council II. The need for chant books for the new rites is being met by a new *Graduale Romanum* (1974) and *Antiphonale Romanum* (1970).

[M. T. LEGGE]

SOLICITATION (CANON LAW), a confessor's abuse of his office by seduction of a penitent to serious sexual sin. The abuse must be connected with the administration of the sacrament of penance and involve seeking to lead the penitent into an objectively grave sinful act with the confessor. The most stringent penalties, even *degradation, may be imposed on a confessor proved guilty (CIC c.2368 § 1). The penitent so approached is under grave obligation to denounce the confessor to the bps. or other church authority (c. 904). To accuse a confessor falsely of this crime is to incur excommunication reserved to the Holy See. The sacredness of the confessor-penitent relationship and the good of the whole church community explain the seriousness that the law attaches to the crime and to false accusation.

[T. C. O'BRIEN]

SOLIFIDIANISM, the doctrine of *justification by faith alone (*sola fide*). The term is applied esp. to this doctrine as proposed by Martin Luther.

[T. C. O'BRIEN]

SOLIGNAC (SOLEMNIACUM), ABBEY OF, Benedictine abbey. Founded *c.*631 in the Diocese of Limoges (Haute-Vienne, France) by St. Eligius (Eloi) in honor of the Apostles Peter and Paul, the abbey was a foundation made from Luxeuil under St. Remaclus, who ruled as abbot 632–642. It was destroyed, or burned, or plundered and ravaged a number of times during its history—twice by

Saracens (735, 793), by the Normans (c.860), by the English (1388), and by Calvinists (1568). The Maurists restored it in 1635 and lived there until the Revolution. The present buildings which date from the 17th cent. are now a seminary for the Oblates of Mary Immaculate. The domed church (12th cent.) with its extending porch encasing a belfry (early 13th cent.) is a notable example of the Romanesque style of Périgord. BIBLIOGRAPHY: Cottineau 2:3058–59.

[J. DAOUST]

SOLIMENA, FRANCESCO (1657–1747), Neapolitan painter and architect. S. studied with his father, developing a bold decorative style seen in frescoes in the chapel of St. Anne in Gesù Nuova (1677), S. Paola Maggiore (1689–94), and further paintings in the Gesù Nuovo (1725).

[M. J. DALY]

SOLLERIUS, see DU SOLLIER, JEAN BAPTISTE.

SOLLICITUDINEM NOSTRAM, a *motu proprio* of Pope Pius XII, promulgated Jan. 6, 1950. It contains the procedural law for the Oriental Church, which was particularly needed among Catholic Orientals of the Near East where the decisions of church tribunals in matters of family relationships were and still are recognized by civil law. BIBLIOGRAPHY: V. J. Pospishil, NCE 10:763–766; F. Galtier, *La Procédure judiciaire en droit oriental* (1954).

[E. EL-HAYEK]

SOLMINIHAC, ALAIN DE, VEN. (1593–1659), Canon Regular of St. Augustine, abbot, bp. of Cahors, monastic reformer. As abbot, A. rebuilt the battlements and throughly reformed the spiritual life of his community at Chancelade. He became noted for his reform activities and was asked to visit several monasteries by Card. François de *la Rochefoucauld. In 1637 he became bp. of Cahors, and in his 22-year episcopate achieved major reforms. He promoted diocesan missions, conducted mainly by Jesuits and Lazarists; established a seminary, orphanages, and a general hospital; and made nine visitations of his entire diocese. He was a strongly against *Jansenism. Some of his activities may have been influenced by his friendship with St. *Vincent de Paul. S.'s cause was introduced in 1783; the decree of heroicity of virtue was granted in 1927. BIBLIOGRAPHY: A. de Solminihac, *Lettres, Documents* (ed. E. Sol, 1930); E. Sol, *Le Ven. Alain de Solminihac* (1928).

[P. K. MEAGHER]

SOLOGUB, FYODOR (Fydor Kuzmich Teternikov; 1863–1927), Russian symbolist, author of poems, novels, short stories, and plays that present psychopathic, decadent, and perverse themes in conventionally classic forms. His preoccupation with insanity and death exercises an almost hypnotic influence on the reader, as does his dualistic and satanic view of the world. Art enables man to escape from

God's world, which is evil, into Satan's world of peace and beauty. His most famous work in this vein is the novel *The Little Demon* (1907). BIBLIOGRAPHY: G. Donchin, *Influence of French Symbolism on Russian Poetry* (1958); R. Poggioli, *Poets of Russia: 1890–1930* (1960) 105–111.

[M. F. MCCARTHY]

SOLOMON, son of David and Bathsheba (2 Sam 12.24) and successor of David as king of Israel (1 Kg 1.32–40). He reigned c.960–920 B.C. S. was crowned at the direction of David. With the backing of his mother, the prophet Nathan, the general Benaiah, and the priest Zadok, S. ousted David's older son Adonijah, who was supported by the general Joab and the priest Abiathar (1 Kg ch. 1). Later S. had Adonijah and Joab killed (1 Kg 2.24–25, 28–35) and Abiathar banished (1 Kg 2.26). S. was praised for his wisdom and his wealth. When Yahweh appeared to him at Bigeon, asking what he would request, S. asked for "an understanding heart" (1 Kg 3.9; see also 1 Kg 3.16–28; 4.29–34; 10.1–10). Much of the OT Wisdom literature was subsequently attributed to him (Pr, Ec, S of S). S. made alliances with several nations through marriages— Pharaoh's daughter having priority (1 Kg 3.1; 9.24) among his 700 wives and 300 concubines (11.3). He was condemned for establishing cultic centers for his wives to worship their gods (1 Kg 11.7–13), an aspect of his reign omitted in the Chronicler's idealized account (1 Chr ch. 28–2 Chr ch. 9). His proverbial wealth (Mt 6.29) was in part a result of peaceful conditions, tribute from vassals (1 Kg 4.21), sea trade conducted in alliance with Hiram of Tyre (1 Kg 9.26–28), and trade in horses and chariots (1 Kg 10.29). His extensive building program culminated in the Temple (1 Kg 6.37–38), but the required taxation and forced labor (1 Kg 5.13) contributed to the division of the kingdom after his death (1 Kg 12.17–20).

[T. EARLY]

SOLOMON, ODES OF. This pseudepigraphical work comprises 42 psalms similar in type to the canonical psalms. It appears to be the work of a Christian author or authors of the 2d cent. A.D., and the original language was probably Greek, although the substance of the work has only survived in a Syriac version in combination with the *Psalms of Solomon. This was discovered and published by J. Rendel Harris in 1909. Prior to this only five of the Odes had been known, having been included in the Coptic *Gnostic work known as the *Pistis Sophia*.

Although the more heretical aspects of Gnosticism (notably the radical dualism which ascribes the Creation of the world to some kind of demiurge hostile to the supreme God) seem to have been avoided, the Odes as a whole are markedly Gnostic in tendency and outlook. Thus, e.g., Ode 38 refers to the marriage of the infernal aeons on earth and to the cup of confusion with which they seduce the world. As compared with the NT there is a marked absence of the name Jesus and no mention at all of the Church. Again the

word sin appears to have been avoided, and a definite diminution of the ethical teaching of the NT is apparent. The central point in the Odes is not the saving power of the Passion, death, and Resurrection of Christ, but rather the overcoming of "error". The Odes display marked affinities with the so-called *Gospel of Truth*, one of the Egyptian Gnostic writings recently discovered at *Nag-Hammâdi.
BIBLIOGRAPHY: J. R. Harris, *Early Christian Psalter* (1909); J. H. Bernard, *Texts and Studies VIII,* No. 3 (1912); R. H. Connolly, "Odes of Solomon: Jewish or Christian?" JTS 13 (1912) 298–309.

[D. J. BOURKE]

SOLOMON, PSALMS OF. These are 18 psalms composed in the same style as the canonical psalms. There seems to have been great uncertainty in the early Church as to whether they should be included in the canon of Scripture. However they seem to have had little influence on early Christian literature and were only rediscovered, after centuries of oblivion, at the beginning of the 17th century.

Originally composed in Hebrew, they have survived only in Greek translation, of which eight MSS are now extant, as well as a Syriac translation of the Greek. In this last they are combined with a further collection of poems, the so-called Odes of *Solomon, from which they must be clearly distinguished. The Odes emanate from Christian-Gnostic circles of the 2d cent. A.D.

The historical allusions contained in the Psalms of Solomon suggest that they were composed c. 60–30 B.C. Thus after a period of prosperity and peace Judah has been subjected to invasion and Jerusalem has been captured. Psalms of Solomon 2,8,17 provide strong indications that this was the occasion of the overthrow of the Hasmoneans by Pompey in 63 B.C. There is a reference in the Psalm of Solomon 17.7 to the "man that is alien to our race"; this may be Pompey himself, though others take it as referring to Herod (37–4 B.C.). In Psalm of Solomon 8.26–37 there seems to be an allusion to Pompey's murder in Egypt.

The style conforms to the main psalm-types established by Gunkel for the canonical psalms. Thus the hymns (e.g., Psalm of Solomon 2.30,33–37; 3.1–2), laments, both collective and individual (e.g., Pss Sol 2.19–25; 7; 8.22–34; 16.6–15), thanksgivings (e.g., Pss 13.1–4; 15.1–6; 16.1–5, combined with a lament as often in the canonical psalms) and wisdom poems (e.g., Pss Sol 3.3–12; 6) are found here also. On the whole, however, the types are less clearly defined, and more frequently intermingled one with another, which indicates a certain decadence in the techniques of psalm composition. Moreover the element of reflective moralizing is more prominent than in the canonical psalms. Some of the headings, notably *eis nikos-lammenaṣṣeah* (from the collection of the master of music) and certain technical directions such as the mysterious *selah* (*dia psalma,* e.g., Pss Sol 17.31; 18.10) also occur, indicating that these psalms too were used in the liturgy and cult.

With regard to their doctrinal content we may notice particularly a belief in the Resurrection (e.g., 3.12; 13.11; 14.9–10) and in free will (9.4), as well as an ardent messianism which finds expression particularly in Pss 17 and 18. These refer to the expectation that a king of David's race is to arise once more, one who is well pleasing to God. And they earnestly entreat that this may soon be brought to reality. In more general terms the Psalms of Solomon envisage two radically opposed groups, the sinners and the just, and this division, more than any other single factor, constitutes the central theme of the ensemble. For this reason the two groups are commonly identified with the opposed parties of the Sadducees and the Pharisees respectively, and the psalms are held to reflect the opposition between them, known to have been particularly fierce at the time when they appear to have been written. Moreover the specific doctrinal points mentioned above represent characteristic tenets of the Pharisees, and for this reason it has been inferred that the psalms themselves were written by members of this particular faction. While this view has much to recommend it, it should not be pressed too far. The Pharisees were not the only ones who believed in free will and the Resurrection, nor who were upheld by ardent messianic hopes. The ideas contained in these psalms are representative of a wider circle and should not be confined exclusively to that particular party. Moreover it is clear that the psalms were composed by several different hands, and certain differences of outlook and interpretation can be discerned in them.

These psalms also reflect a particular concern with retribution in history. Thus the overthrow of Jerusalem by the Romans under Pompey is regarded as a just punishment for the nation's sins and for the sins of the Hasmonean dynasty in particular. But then the harshness of the Roman invaders and their lack of true religion come to be realized and the ultimate death of Pompey himself is also interpreted as an act of divine retribution. BIBLIOGRAPHY: Charles APOT 2:625–652; M. Aberbach, "Historical Allusions of Chapters IV, IX and XIII of the Psalms of Solomon," JQR 41 (1950–51) 379–396; H. H. Rowley, *Relevance of Apocalyptic* (2d ed. 1947).

[D. J. BOURKE]

SOLOVYEV, VLADIMIR SERGEYEVICH (Solov'ev; 1853–1900), religious thinker, philosopher, mystic and writer, the most influential and original Russian religious philosopher of the 19th century. A religious and intellectual family atmosphere together with an imaginative temperament favored his mystical experiences, which began at the age of 9 with his vision of the divine Sophia. This vision was to be repeated twice in 1875 while he was a student travelling in London and in Egypt, and inspired one of his most common religious symbols. He saw in Sophia the wisdom of God, the principle of creation, the Eternal Feminine, the world soul, Christ's body, and many other similar but not identical principles. He led a scholarly life as a student and as a teacher in Moscow and St. Petersburg.

His lectures on *Bogochelovechestvo* (Godmanhood), delivered in St. Petersburg in 1877 and attended by the St. Petersburg intellectual elite, including Dostoevsky and Tolstoy, embody one of his essential theories, the primacy of the Incarnation and Godmanhood as a point of ultimate union for the world. In politics he believed in a free theocracy based on Christian principles, and advocated the pardon of Alexander II's assassins. This gesture cost him his academic career, caused his disappointment with official Russian Orthodoxy, and proved a turning point in his life. During his last 20 years he grew closer to Roman Catholicism, to the point of making a profession of faith before a Catholic priest, though he received the last sacraments in the Orthodox Church. He worked for reunion between the two Churches as part of his goal to achieve total unity of mankind through Godmanhood. Though S. was accused of pantheism and dogmatism, esp. in his earlier works, his later ones, *Foundations of Theoretical Philosophy* (1897–99) and *Tri razgovora (Three Conversations*, 1900), a Platonic dialogue, show moderation and maturity. His thought has been influenced principally by Plato and Hegel, as well as by Russian writers such as Tchadaayev and Khomiakov, whose religious doctrine of *sobornost* he carried to its logical conclusion. He was fascinated by organic systems and by the Trinity; often expressing his thought in triads. He envisioned the ultimate unity of mankind in history. BIBLIOGRAPHY: N. O. Lossky, *History of Russian Philosophy* (1951), 81–133.

[I. M. KASHUBA]

SOMAGLIA, GIULIO MARIA DELLA, see DELLA SOMAGLIA, GIULIO MARIA.

SOMASCHI, religious of an order founded at Venice in 1528 by St. Jerome Emiliani. The formal title is Order of Clerics Regular of Somascha (CRS). The popular title derives from the town near Bergamo where the founder made his headquarters and where he died in 1537. The Somaschi, along with contemporary groups like the Theatines and the Barnabites, were indications of the rising current of the Counter Reformation. At first a community, they were made a religious order by Pope Pius V in 1568. Their apostolate was directed esp. towards the poor, for whom they founded orphanages and schools. In 1975 there were 401 members of the order in 60 houses, located primarily in Italy and Latin America. There are also Somaschi Sisters and a related society, Sisters of the Mother of Orphans. BIBLIOGRAPHY: P. Bianchini, NCE 13:424–425; G. B. Pigato, EncCatt 11:952–954.

[D. NUGENT]

SOMERVILLE, HENRY (1889–1953), editor. An Englishman who studied political science at Oxford, S. went into newspaper work and helped to organize the Catholic Social Guild in 1913, thus beginning a lifelong dedication to Catholic social thought. From 1915 to 1919 he edited the *Catholic Register* in Toronto, Canada. In 1919 returning to England, S. founded the Catholic Workers' College at Oxford. Again in Canada he edited the *Catholic Register* which in 1942 merged with four other Catholic weeklies and became the *Canadian Register*. Among his published works were *The Catholic Social Movement* (1933) and *Employers and Workers* (1945).

[J. R. AHERNE]

SOMMERVOGEL, CARLOS (Marie Nicolas Charles; 1834–1902), Jesuit bibliographist, author-editor of *Bibliothèque de la Compagnie de Jésus* (4 v., 1890–1900). This standard reference work records all the writings composed by Jesuits, whether published or in MSS form, since the beginning of the Society. The work is S.'s redaction and revision of an earlier *Bibliothèque des écrivains de la Compagnie de Jésus* (7 v., 1851–63), with whose editors, A. and L. de Backer, he had collaborated. S.'s work was brought up to date and given an index by P. Bliard and E. Rivière (3 v., 1909–32). The whole work was reprinted in 1960.

[T. C. O'BRIEN]

SON, GOD THE, Second Person of the Holy Trinity. God is not one person only, for Yahweh, the God of Israel, is the eternal Father of an eternal Son. Such is the core of the message revealed by Christ to the world, a message that changed the destiny of men and their vocation, a message as difficult for Christ to convey as it was for his Jewish hearers to understand. That a man, whose background and surroundings they knew, whose life they had witnessed or shared, claimed to be the Son of God, equal to him in all things, appeared unacceptable for it seemed to contradict the monotheist faith of Israel in Yahweh their God. Yet, Christ claimed exactly this. He did so not merely by taking or accepting the title Son of God. By itself this title was not sufficient to sustain Christ's claim, for the OT had called Son of God Yahweh's chosen people, and more esp. their king, his representative among them. Christ however, by making himself Yahweh's equal, claimed for himself a unique Sonship. He declared himself one with Yahweh in an unprecedented manner (Jn 10.30, 38); he made clear that, though sent on an errand by Yahweh, he shared his plane of existence.

Thus, from the mystery of Christ the early Church was compelled to ascend to the mystery of the Son of God. If through his Incarnation the Son of God has become sharer in human nature, he is, prior to this, eternally begotten by the Father and shares with him the divine nature. Therefore there exists in God eternal generation and sonship. That the Son be coeternal with his Father, equal to him in all things yet truly originated from him, is beyond human reason. The mystery of God the Son was bound to be challenged. It was challenged from the early times of Christianity but the Christian Church has always stood by it. In the course of time against the natural tendencies to make the Son inferior to the Father, it became necessary to enunciate the mystery in precise terms. Decisive in this process of explicitation is the definition of the first ecumenical council, that of Nicaea I (A.D. 325), according to which the Son of God is "of one substance (Gr. *homoousios*) with the Father" (D 125). Thus, against Arius who saw God's Son as his first creature and as the instrument of God's creative act, the Church upheld the strict consubstantiality of Father and Son. The mystery could not be tampered with for the sake of an easy conformism with philosophical thought, for in it the Christian vocation was at stake. BIBLIOGRAPHY: DBT 491.

[J. DUPUIS]

SON OF DAVID, a messianic title, refers to Jesus in his fulfillment of the promise made to David through Nathan the Prophet (2 Sam ch 7). In the eschatological context of a covenant the promise transcends the material order: "I have made a covenant with my chosen one, I have sworn to David my servant: Forever will I confirm your posterity and establish your throne for all generations" (Ps 89.4–5). The yearning for restoration of second Davidic kingdom embracing all nations heightened the expectations of the oppressed and dispersed chosen people. In their expectations the son of David as prince of peace would be for them a nationalistic messiah who would restore the dynasty in its pristine splendor. The Synoptics used the title (e.g., Mt 1.1), but Jesus sought to turn men's hearts to a more spiritual concept. Paul calls the man of Davidic lineage the Son of God (Rom 1.3–5). In the primitive Church the title son of David was rejected as heretical by the Epistle of Barnabas. In accord with the teaching of Jesus himself, the Savior is called by it the Son of God. Jesus transcends any earthly kingship by right of lineage from David (words of Jesus before Pilate, Jn 18.33–38). His kingdom is not of this world. His reign is proclaimed in the ancient creeds and announced by the angel to Mary: ". . . and the Lord God will give him the throne of David his father, and he shall be king over the house of Jacob forever; and of his kingdom there shall be no end." (Lk 1:32–33). BIBLIOGRAPHY: B. van Iersel, "Fils de David et Fils de Dieu," *La Venue du Messie* (Recherches bibliques 6, 1962).

[E. G. KAISER]

SON OF GOD, a concept and title that is applied to men and gods of many religious forms. Among the primitive nature tribes the most common name for the god is that of father, and the basic primitive prayer relation with the god is that of son and father. Zeus (or Jupiter) as father derives from the Father Heaven of the Indo-Germanic sources. In Homer, Zeus is the father of men and gods. Throughout, the relation of sonship suggests dependence for life and existence on the god as father with recognition of this dependence tempered by filial confidence in approaching him. In the ancient Near East the relation of sonship to a particular deity is widespread. Among the Greeks the title son of god is applied genealogically to heroes, families, and clans held

to be descended from divinity. The ancient Egyptian kings as also the later Hellenic rulers and men of singular stature (Apollonios of Tyana) are unblushingly proclaimed sons of god. The Stoa contributes much toward the broadening of the concept to include all men. In the mystery religions, man by his own act attains rebirth and becomes a son of god, endowed with divine nature.

In the OT the angels are called sons of God (Job 1.6 and elsewhere) probably because they form the heavenly court and function as messengers and servants of God, not because of any preconceived genealogical derivation, an idea completely alien to Jewish OT thought. When men are referred to as sons of God it is rather that Israel itself (Ex 4. 22–23 and elsewhere) enjoys a special relation to Yahweh. Israel, its king as its representative (Ps 2.7; 2 Sam 7.14), and even the devout Israelite (in later Judaism) enjoyed such sonship because Yahweh graciously elected to adopt the chosen people by a special covenant. This sonship of holiness does not derive from or resemble Egyptian models. It is indeed unique.

In the NT the title is applied to Jesus 100 times, though it reflects neither Hellenic nor OT background. Rather it rests on the revealed word itself as proclaimed in the paschal event by the Apostles and firmly accepted by the primitive Church as characterizing the Savior. The Synoptics (who use the title 31 times) indicate the unique character of Jesus as sent by the Father. As Son of God, possessed of the Spirit of God, Jesus fully realizes the sonship of Israel, and represents the Father to mankind. In the Epistles Jesus is proclaimed the preexistent Son of God, Redeemer through his death, supreme high priest, center of all creation, to whom all creatures owe reverence and submission. As Son in the Father's house he surpasses even the angels, who are only ministering spirits. The divine sonship is the basis for the adoptive sonship of all the redeemed, who through fellowship with Jesus attain to the Father (Col 1.15–29). Similarly in John, the Son is the source of salvation and eternal life, which is brought to men through faith in him. His sonship is the source of the adoptive sonship of men. Because of his intimate union with the Father he receives from him life and the power of judgment over all man as well as his own glorification. His intercession, his saving acts, his whole mediatorial action is efficacious for mankind. Biblical theology here offers systematic theology the basis for profound dogmatic penetration, as became evident in the great Christological debates and definitions. BIBLIOGRAPHY: G. T. Montague and E. G. Hardwick, NCE 13:427–431; G. T. Montague, *ibid*. 435–436; A. Gelin, et al., *Son and Saviour* (tr. A. Wheaton, 2d ed. 1960).

[E. G. KAISER]

SON OF JOSEPH, SON OF MARY, names of Jesus in the NT: Jesus is named "Son of Joseph" four times (Lk 3.23; 4.22; Jn 1.45; 6.42) and "son of Mary" once (Mk 6.3). As with other references to parents and family, these texts witness to the humanity of Jesus and represent the earliest traditions of Christianity. In the light of the virgin birth, the designation ''son of Joseph'' must be considered either as unnuanced (excepting Lk 3.23) or representative of the unawareness of the contemporaries of Jesus. Mark 6.3, however, seems influenced by the virgin birth tradition (cf. Mt 13.55). BIBLIOGRAPHY: L. Sabourin, *Names and Titles of Jesus* (tr. M. Carroll, 1967); V. Taylor, *Names of Jesus* (1962).

[J. J. CUNNINGHAM]

SON OF MAN, the most expressly Semitic title of Jesus in the Gospels. Of all titles the most associated with Jesus, it represents one of the earliest NT Christologies and the belief and expectation of the Palestinian Christian community. This community was responsible for the eschatologically dominated *Q Source, which teaches that Jesus as Son of Man exalted in heaven was imminently to return in judgment to bring to fulfillment the kingdom he preached while on earth. Paradoxically this earliest Christology and the title itself were fairly early set aside in favor of titles more comprehensible to a community increasing its gentile membership and facing the fact that the return of Jesus was not to be imminent. The origins, content, and use of the title by Jesus and the early Christian community is one of the most discussed questions in contemporary scholarship.

OT Background. The phrase ''Son of Man' is a literal translation of the Hebrew *ben 'ādām* (Aramaic *bar' ĕnāsh*, Greek *huios anthrōpou*), a periphrastic expression meaning ''man,'' ''human being.'' The expression is found in poetic parallelism with more usual words for ''man'' in the Bible (e.g., Num 23.19; Is 51.12; 56.2; Ps 8.5). The Prophet Ezekiel is addressed by God with this title almost 90 times, a usage that underlines man's lowliness before the majesty of God. The most important OT incidence and the ultimate origin of NT usage is found in Dan 7.9, 10, 13, 14, passages that, because of their metric structure, are to be distinguished from the remainder of the chapter. In the context of Dan 7, the four beasts emerging from the sea (Dan 7.1–7) and representing the succession of world empires, are judged and the Ancient of Days invests ''one like a son of man'' with dominion, glory, and kingship. The human figure represents a collectivity, ''the holy ones of the Most High,'' almost certainly the Maccabean martyrs, coming to their reward for the sufferings they endured under Antiochus IV. It would seem that the Son of Man usage in Daniel did have a prehistory in non-Israelite speculation, and consequently scholars have proposed numerous possibilities from the history of religions for the origin of the Son of Man figure—and most recently to the Canaanite mythology found in the Ugaritic texts. No hypothesis has gained a scholarly consensus thus far.

It would be an oversimplification to maintain that pre-Christian Judaism offers a formal concept of an apocalyptic Son of Man or that expectation of a Son of Man was preeminent among forms of Jewish eschatology. Apocalyptic literature, illustrated by 1 Enoch (Ethiopian Enoch) and 4

Ezra, presents simply a variety of pre-Christian Son of Man usage. Since Son of Man is not used as a title in the apocalyptic midrash in 4 Ezra 13, it can be seen that only the use of Dan 7 stands as the point of contact between 1 Enoch's use of the term and 4 Ezra. Son of Man expectation in pre-Christian Judaism stands in tension with other forms of expectation, e.g., this-worldly hope for a Davidic messiah, the return of ideal figures like Elijah and Moses, expectation of salvation in which there is no central savior figure. What 1 Enoch, 4 Ezra, and other apocalyptically oriented texts testify to is the survival in Judaism of a hope for a climactic series of events that will lead to the final eschatological intervention of God into human history to bless the faithful and to punish the wicked.

NT Usage. With the exception of Acts 7.56, Heb 2.6, Rev 1.13, 14.14, Son of Man is a title found only in the Gospels, where it always appears in a saying of Jesus. Scholars commonly group the Son of Man sayings into three categories: apocalyptic sayings in which Jesus refers in the third person to a future Son of Man coming as eschatological judge (e.g., Mk 13.26); sayings in which Jesus speaks of himself as a present Son of Man active in his ministry (Lk 9.58); sayings in which Jesus speaks of himself as a suffering, dying, and rising Son of Man (Mk 8.31). It is to be noted that this third category of sayings occurs first in the Marcan material and not in the older Q Source. While it is clear that the origin of NT Son of Man usage is Dan 7.13–14, the origin of the expectation of the exalted Jesus coming from heaven as Son of Man is disputed. While not excluding other scholarly theories or variations on theories, three approaches to the question of the connection between Daniel and Q may be offered: Jesus proclaimed the coming Son of Man as eschatological judge without identifying himself with that figure, and later the early Church in the light of its resurrection experience identified Jesus with the coming Son of Man; Jesus actually thought of himself as the coming Son of Man as well as identified himself in some fashion with an existing and acting Son of Man in his public ministry; the early Church itself arrived at the expectation through an interpretation of its resurrection experience in the light of OT texts, esp. Ps 110.1 and Dan 7.13–14, but Jesus himself did not speak at all of a coming eschatological Son of Man. Scholars who follow the first approach would place particular emphasis on the following apocalyptic Son of Man sayings, which they would hold to be authentic: Lk 12.8–9; 17.24,26,28–30; 11.30; 12.40; Mt 10.23; 19.28; Mk 13.26. Scholars who follow the second approach would stress the following Son of Man sayings, which have a present reference: Lk 7.34 (Mt 11.19); Lk 12.10 (Mt 12.32); Lk 9.58 (Mt 8.30); Lk 6.25 (Mt 5.20); Lk 19.10; Mt 13.37; Mk 10.45; 2.10,28. One passage commonly listed among the apocalyptic sayings of Jesus has been omitted, namely Mk 14.62, the ''I am'' confession of Jesus before the high priest. A growing number of scholars are convinced that the account of the night trial before the Sanhedrin (Mk 14.55–65) is a Marcan composition, one which brings his Christological concerns to a climax, breaking the messianic secret through Christ's acknowledging that he is Messiah, Son of God as Son of Man. While there is small measure of agreement about the connection of Jesus with the Son of Man title, there is agreement that it is perhaps more important to understand the theological usage of the Son of Man tradition made by the Evangelists in their Gospels.

Mark. Just as Mark is the major figure in the creation of that unique literary form known as "gospel," so also is he the major figure in the creative use of the Son of Man tradition in the NT period. Three theological concerns are the axes of his Gospel: the imminent parousia, Christology, and discipleship amid tribulation. Mark's audience were men and women of the Church caught up in a resurgence of apocalyptic expectation, which the author shares, occasioned by the circumstances of the Jewish war (66–70 A.D.), but led astray by false Christological teaching coming from false messiahs and prophets, some perhaps even claiming to be the risen Jesus himself (Mk 13.5b–6, 21–22). Mark writes to encourage his readers to await in hope the returning Jesus and to instruct them that they too as Disciples must accept suffering as part of the definition of being a Christian. The most important Christological title in the Gospel is Son of God, the superscription of the Gospel and the climactic Christological statement of the centurion (Mk 1.1; 15.39). Mark uses the figure of the Son of Man to interpret and to give content to his conception of Jesus as Son of God in order to correct prevalent false ideas of Jesus as Son of God. This may be seen from the balanced structuring of the two titles throughout the Gospel. Two occurrences stressing the authority (*exousia*) on earth of the Son of Man (2.10, 28) are balanced by two emphasizing that Jesus exercises his authority on earth as Son of God (3.11; 5.7); the titles "Christ" and "Son of Man" juxtaposed in the confession of Peter at Caesarea-Philippi (8.27–34) are immediately followed by the reference to "my beloved son" at the Transfiguration (9.7). Further, Christ, Son of God, and Son of Man are juxtaposed at the trial before the Sanhedrin (14.55–65) and Son of God is the title in the confession of the centurion (15.39). In Mark the Christology expressed by the use of the Son of Man emphasizes: Jesus' authority (*exousia*) on earth (2.10, 28), his apocalyptic authority at the final judgment (8.38; 13.26), and the necessity of his (and the Disciples') suffering before entering glory (8.31; 9.31; 10.33–34).

Matthew. The Gospel of Matthew does not have the Marcan imminent expectation of the Son of Man, but centers in Jesus as the Son of God, Christian discipleship as the higher righteousness, and a concern for the gentile mission. That Son of Man is a principal Christological title for Matthew may be seen in the fact that he increases considerably the number of references to the Son of Man (Mt 17.12; 26.2; 10.23; 13.41; 16.28; 24.30; 25.31). The most striking feature about Matthew's use is that it assumes a totally "public" as opposed to a "confessional" character in that it serves to describe Jesus in terms of his relationship to the world, Israel first and then the gentiles, and esp. as he interacts with the crowds and his opponents. Accordingly, in his encounters with the people (16.13–15; 13.37–38a) and the religious authorities (8.19–22; 9.2–3, 8; 11.19; 12.23–24,32,38–40), Jesus openly refers to himself as the Son of Man, and in his Passion predictions he foretells what his enemies in fulfillment of Scripture will do to him (17.12, 22–23; 20.18–19; 26.2,24–25,45). Following Easter, Jesus Son of Man stands before the world as a king before his kingdom; and at the end of time he will confront all the nations (13.38,41–43; 24.30; 25.31–46), Israel and the gentiles (24.32–39; 26.59, 64), as their judge, bestowing eternal life upon the righteous and consigning the accursed to eternal punishment (25.31–46). The counterpart to the title Son of Man in Matthew is naturally his primary title for Jesus, Son of God. The title Son of God has for Matthew an exclusively "confessional" character; it conveys for his Church the deepest mystery concerning the person of Jesus, namely, that Jesus' origin is in God and it is in him that God dwells with his people. The only persons who can utter this title are the Disciples of Jesus (16.13–20) and the confessing Roman soldier by revelation of God. As the Son of God Jesus presides over and resides in his Church until the end of the age, at which time he will confront both the Church and the world again as the Son of Man.

Luke is very sympathetic with the tradition that equates Jesus with the Son of Man, but in his judgment Mark's emphases did not adequately meet the current needs of Christian communities disturbed by enthusiasts who claimed to know the divine timetable for apocalyptic events, or by others who questioned the promise of Jesus' return or his identity as Son of Man. For this reason, he eliminated Mark's apocalyptic association of John the Baptist with Elijah from his own presentation of his public ministry (7.27–30) and by linking Elijah loosely with Jesus, Luke directs attention away from any comparison of Jesus' presence or credentials with intermediary apocalyptic figures and events. Instead, the messianic and apocalyptic hopes are merged in the person of Jesus. While Luke follows Mark in many Son of Man passages (Lk 5.24; 6.5; 9.22; 18.31; 21.27), he has also made significant omissions (9.9; 14.41; 10.45) and alterations (9.26,44; 22.69) in the Marcan material as well as additions from his special source (9.58; 11.30; 12.8,10; 17.22,24,26,30; 18.8). These last additions to the Son of Man passages point to his interest in the apocalyptic problem, illustrating his own two-stage echatology. Thus, Luke teaches that the kingdom of God is not to be confused with an apocalyptic movement, for it is present in the activity of Jesus (17.21) and the Church, but will come again in a definitive second phase as the term of all history with suddenness (17.24). In Lk 12.8,10, he endeavors to adapt to fresh circumstances a Q saying by offering a corrective: it is not a word spoken against the Son of Man but one uttered against the Holy Spirit that will not be forgiven, thus doing justice to his teaching on repentance and to his instruction on hardness of heart (8.10; 24.25–31).

John. In the fourth Gospel, Passion and glorification are both referred to in the Son of Man passages, but here the tendency is to unite the two concepts more strictly in accordance with John's Christology, to the extent of seeing in the Passion the beginning of Christ's glorification. This union can be seen in the "lifting up" passages (3.14; 8.28; 12.34). In all, there are 12 Son of Man passages in the fourth Gospel (1.51; 3.13; 5.27; 6.27; 6.53; 6.62; 9.35; 12.23; 13.31), all occurring in the Book of Signs except 13.31. Although Jesus speaks often of his return in the last discourse, he does not use the Son of Man in such references. BIBLIOGRAPHY: C. Colpe, *Ho huios tou anthrōpou*, Kittel TD 8:400–477; F. Danker, *Jesus and the New Age* (1974); R. H. Fuller, *Foundations of New Testament Christology* (1965); W. Kelber, *Kingdom in Mark* (1974); N. Perrin, *Modern Pilgrimage in NT Christology* (1974); E. Schweizer, JBL 79 (1960) 119–129; NTS 9 (1962/63) 256–261; E. Sjöberg, *Der Menschensohn im äthiopischen Henochbuch* (1946); H. E. Tödt, *Son of Man in the Synoptic Tradition* (1965); B. Vawter, *This Man Jesus* (1973).

[T. J. RYAN]

SONATA DA CHIESA, a 17th-cent. term meaning church sonata, a piece for strings and keyboard. The title, originally designating the place of performance, came to denote a composition in four movements—a slow introduction, a quick fugal movement, a slow, expressive movement, and another quick movement.

[M. T. LEGGE]

SONCINAS, PAOLO, see BARBO, PAOLO.

SONG OF SOLOMON, OT book, also called the Canticle of Canticles and the Song of Songs, i.e., the greatest of all songs. This collection of love poems assembled in late post-Exilic times is extremely difficult to interpret. The collection as a whole has been interpreted as a symbolic representation of Yahweh's relationship with Israel through history (allegorical interpretation), or alternatively as a marvelously beautiful and candid account of human love and desire leading to marriage. This literal interpretation is the most widely accepted nowadays, although obviously it does not exclude further allegorical meanings. Analogies have been found to the poems of this collection in the love poetry of Egypt, and what is perhaps an even more significant analogy, in the marriage customs of Syria. While the importance of these analogies should not be pressed too far, they do make it more probable that it was the goodness and beauty of human love and marriage that the anonymous authors of these poems had primarily in mind. But subsequently they did come to be applied in an allegorical sense to the relations between Yahweh and Israel, or, in early Christian tradition, between Christ and the Church. This obvious application must have been made at a very early stage, and without it the songs would never have been in-

cluded in either the Jewish or the Christian canons. St. Bernard of Clairvaux, St. John of the Cross, and others used the imagery of the poems to describe mystical union with God. BIBLIOGRAPHY: D. Buzy, *Le Cantique des Cantiques* (1950); J. Winandy, *Le Cantique des Cantiques. Poème d'amour mué en écrit de Sagesse* (1960); R. Murphy, JBC 1:506–510.

[D. J. BOURKE]

SONS OF GOD, the title and status in being given in the NT to those who receive Christ and are reborn by the will of the Father (see Jn 1.12). St. Paul gives prominence to the theme in Gal 3.32; 4.4–6; Rom 8.12–18,23; 9.4. There is strong patristic witness to the truth that as Christ is the Son of God by nature, those joined to him by grace become adoptive sons of the Father. Thus, Clement of Alexandria: "Baptized we are enlightened, enlightened we are adopted as sons; being adopted we are made perfect; perfect we are made immortal" (*Paedgogus* 1.26.1); Athanasius: "The Son of God became the Son of Man so that the sons of the man Adam become the sons of God . . . The Word called himself the Son of Man so that men might call God, Father, Our Father . . . He is therefore the Son of God by his nature, we by grace. To him it belongs to be the Son of God, to you, to become the son of God, for you have this title not by nature but by adoption" (*Catechesis* 3.14); Ambrose: "Christ through his own self is pleasing to the Father, we are so through Christ; in those in whom God beholds his own Son as in an image, through the Son he adopts into the grace of sonship" (*De fide* 5.7); Augustine: "He who justifies deifies, because by justifying he makes us sons of God . . . If we are made sons of God we are also made gods; but this comes from the grace of the one who adopts us, not from the nature of the one who gives us our nature" (*Enarrat. in Ps*. 49.2); "The only Son of God by nature by mercy has become for our sake the Son of Man, so that we, by nature sons of man, by grace might through him become sons of God" (*De civitate Dei* 21.15). The literalness of this identity to which the Fathers attest rests on Jesus' being the revelation of God as Father, not simply as a source of beneficence, but as one who draws man into personal communion. Sonship is "a likening through grace and charity to the Word's in the unity he has with the Father" (ThAq ST 3a, 23. 3); "By the act of creation God communicated his own goodness to all creatures through a kind of resemblance; by the act of adoption he communicates likeness to the natural sonship of the Word" (*ibid*. 23.1 ad 2). Jesus himself is the "firstborn," in him human nature is drawn up into personal union with the only begotten Son, the Word. By faith and grace anyone joined to Jesus is in an analogous, but still literal, relationship with the Father. Because it is patterned on and derived from the natural sonship of Jesus, that relationship is one of sonship and is called adoptive because there is only one hypostatic union, only one Son by nature. The reality of the divine adoption is carried out in the meaning of the sacrament of baptism as this is a rebirth, and the grace given is configured to the filial, hypostatic grace of Jesus. The living of the grace life consists essentially in the expression of adoptive sonship through faith, hope, and charity, modeled on the relationship of Christ to the Father.

[T. C. O'BRIEN]

SONSHIP, the relationship to the Father given by grace. The natural sonship of Jesus is the grace of *hypostatic union whereby he is the natural Son of the Father because his humanity is conjoined to the person of the Word. The adoptive sonship conferred by grace is that because grace is patterned after and derived from Jesus and makes the recipient to be the child of the Father. *SONS OF GOD; *PARTAKER OF THE DIVINE NATURE.

[T. C. O'BRIEN]

SOPHISTS, the founders of formal education, and popularizers of knowledge in the Ancient Greek, and Greco-Roman World. As the life of the Greek city-states became increasingly complex in the 5th and 4th cent. B.C., the need for better trained leaders became acute; and this need was met by the appearance of professional itinerant educators, who were called sophists, and who claimed that they could actually teach various skills or proficiencies, although traditionally it was held that *aretē* (skill or proficiency) had to be inherited and could not be acquired. This is the burden of the aristocratic tradition as reflected, for example, in the Odes of Pindar. Since leadership in the city-state depended primarily on the ability to speak eloquently and persuasively, the sophists developed the art of political and forensic oratory, but they also prided themselves on the acquisition of numerous other skills or forms of proficiency and in their ability to teach these to others. They were not interested in the education of the masses, but rather in the training of leaders and the elite, charging high fees for their instruction. They maintained that nature (*physis*) is necessarily the foundation for education. However, anyone possessing adequate natural endowment can be taught any form of *aretē*, and especially the ability to speak effectively by training (*mathēsis*), as inculcated by teaching (*didaskalia*) and practice (*askēsis*). They made use of grammar, dialectic, and rhetoric and mathematics (harmony and astronomy) as the formal disciplines of instruction, and thus laid the foundation for the curriculum of the liberal arts, or *Enkuklios paideia,* as subsequently elaborated by Isocrates and transmitted to the Hellenistic Age and to the Romans as the typical form of humanistic education. Many of the Sophists were virtuosos and as a group— perhaps as yet unaware of its basic importance—gave too little attention to moral education or even ignored it. Furthermore, although they regularly are given a chapter in histories of Greek philosophy, they were not primarily philosophers in any strict or professional sense, but they came under the influence of the conflicting philosophical currents of their age. Hence they tended to adopt a kind of skeptical attitude on basic philosophical questions and at times to adopt views that challenged the whole political, religious, and social tradition of the Greek city-state. By disseminating radical views on the origin of law and order, political society, and religion, they helped to produce the great intellectual crisis of the late 5th and 4th centuries. Some, for example, spread the doctrine that the laws of the state did not have a divine origin, but were purely relative, and that the true law of nature was the law of the stronger, that might is right. It is this sophistic superficiality in the field of political theory, religion, and ethics, that underlies the sharp criticism of the sophists by Socrates, Plato, and Aristotle, and led Plato and Aristotle to place political theory on a new and solid foundation and to create formal systems of ethics. Among the Sophists of the Classical Period the following deserve special mention: Gorgias of Leontini (c. 483–370 B.C.), who questioned the validity of knowledge and its communication by language and founded artistic prose; Protagoras of Abdera (c.480–c.410), who expressed his relativity of knowledge in the dictum "Man is the measure of all things" and was an agnostic in respect to the gods; Prodicus of Ceos (fl. 2d half of 5th cent.), a specialist in the right use of words and author of the famous myth, "The Choice of Heracles"; Hippias of Elis (a contemporary of Protagoras), famous for his proficiency as a teacher in numerous fields, but especially in mathematics; Antiphon of Athens (late 5th cent.), who advocated among other things the equality of all men; Thrasymachus of Chalcedon (fl. c.430–400 B.C.) who taught that might is right.

The term sophist is used also to designate the professors of rhetoric and lecturers who enjoyed such great prestige from the 2d cent. A.D. to the end of antiquity in East and West, among whom must be mentioned: Aelius Aristides (c.117–189); Apuleius of Madaura (c.125, d. after 162); the Philostrati (2d and 3d cent.), Libanius (c.314–393) who probably had among his pupils, SS. Basil, Gregory of Nazianzus, John Chrysostom, and Theodore of Mopsuestia; Eunapius of Sardis (c.345–414). The Sophists under the Empire were champions of the traditional culture and hostile to Christianity. BIBLIOGRAPHY: OCD 848; LexAW 2831–33; Copleston 1:81–95; W. W. Jaeger, *Paideia: The Ideals of Greek Culture* (tr. G. Highet, 2d ed. 1945–   ) 1:286–331; H. I. Marrou, *History of Education in Antiquity* (1956) 46–60.

[M. R. P. MCGUIRE]

SOPHONIAS, APOCALYPSE OF, see ZEPHANIAH, APOCALYPSE OF.

SOPHONIUS, BOOK OF, see ZEPHANIAH, BOOK OF.

SOPHRONIUS, ST. (c.560–638), **PATRIARCH OF JERUSALEM** from 634, probably identified with the Sophronius styled "the Sophist." A native of Damascus, S. was a friend and fellow monk of *John Moschus with whom he traveled extensively to learn more of ascetical practice and doctrine. John dedicated to him his *Spiritual Meadow*. S. became a champion of orthodoxy against the monothelitism accepted by Cyrus, patriarch of Alexandria. He went to Constantinople in an unsuccessful effort to win the Patriarch Sergius I over from the same error. Upon his election to the patriarchate of Jerusalem he wrote his celebrated *Synodal Letter* to the other patriarchs, clearly distinguishing the operations of the two natures in Christ. S. died the year after the surrender of Jerusalem to the Saracens. His writings included a no longer extant florilegium of passages from the Fathers in support of his diothelite position; 23 of his odes and 11 of his sermons are extant. WORKS: PG 87.3;3147–4014. BIBLIOGRAPHY: Altaner 628–629; M. R. P. McGuire, NCE 13:439; Butler 1:557–558.

[R. B. ENO]

SOPHRONIUS OF BETHLEHEM (d. after 392), Greek ecclesiastical writer, mentioned by St. Jerome in his *De viris illustribus*. Jerome refers to him as eminently learned and speaks of a youthful work by S. in praise of Bethlehem and of a recently composed, impressive polemic against the cult of Serapis. He also mentions a book on virginity dedicated to Eustochius and a life of the monk Hilarion, without making it clear that these are works by Jerome translated into Greek by Sophronius. Jerome does explicitly state that S. was responsible for a very creditable translation into Greek of Jerome's Latin rendition from Hebrew of the Psalter and the Prophets. BIBLIOGRAPHY: PL 23, *De viris illustribus* ch. 134.

[E. J. DILLON]

SOPRANO, highest of the women's voices. The term is also used to designate the highest member of certain families of instruments. The unchanged voice of the boy and the falsetto of the man are similar in range to the female soprano.

[M. T. LEGGE]

SORA (SOR), ABBEY OF, Benedictine foundation near the city of Sora in the province of Caserta SE of Rome, in the Diocese of Aquino, Pontecorvo, and Sora. It was built on the site of a Ciceronian villa by St. Dominic of Sora, monk of Monte Cassino, at the request of the Lombard duke Pietro di Rainerio (c.1011). Consecrated in 1104 by Paschal II, the abbey declined rapidly and was made a dependency of the Cistercians of Casamari by Honorius III in 1222. In the 19th cent. Ferdinand II, the Bourbon King of Naples, granted its revenues to the Chapter of St. Peter's in the Vatican. BIBLIOGRAPHY: Cottineau 2:3062.

[E. J. DILLON]

SORAZU, ÁNGELES (Florencia; 1873–1921), mystic. A Spanish nun of the Franciscan convent of the Purissima Concepción, S. was elected abbess in 1904 and held that office until her death. She is known for her mystical writings published after her death. Among them were *La vida espiritual coronada por la triple manifestación de Jesucristo* (1924), *Autobiografía* (1929), and three volumes of letters to her spiritual director (1942–58). Her writings have been compared in quality to those of St. Teresa of Ávila.

[J. R. AHERNE]

SORBON, ROBERT DE, SEE ROBERT DE SORBON.

SORBONNE, COLLEGE OF THE, a 13th-cent. college associated with the Univ. of Paris. It was founded in 1257 by Canon *Robert de Sorbon as a counterpart of the mendicant colleges for clerics, by providing a residence for 16 needy theology students. Students were accepted from the different nations, an international integration that contributed considerably to the college's prestige; in the 15th cent. admission was restricted to French scholars. In time the number of students was increased to 36. Government was vested in the archdeacon and chancellor of Paris assisted by the rector and faculty officials; administration was entrusted to the priors and resident students, elected at a general assembly. After suffering a decline during the Protestant Reformation, the Sorbonne was enlarged in 1629 by Card. Richelieu, and again became a center of intellectual activity, although it was not much touched by the spirit of scientific inquiry prominent at the time. The college was closed from 1792 until 1821 when it reopened with three faculties: theology, science, and letters. It was ceded to the city of Paris in 1852, and incorporated in the Univ. of Paris, by the end of the 19th cent.; the faculty of theology was dissolved in favor of science and the Sorbonne became a secular institution. BIBLIOGRAPHY: H. Rashdall, *Universities of Europe in the Middle Ages* (ed. F. M. Powicke and A. B. Emden, 3 v. 1936).

[M. B. MURPHY]

SORETH, JOHN, BL. (1395–1471), Carmelite reformer. He entered the Carmelite monastery at Caen, studied theology in Paris, and was superior of the province of Francia, 1440–51. In 1451 he became general of the order and held that position for the rest of his life. Under his administration, the reform movement already under way in certain Carmelite houses received official status. In 1462 at the Brussels chapter, he promulgated new constitutions which renewed the observance of poverty and the common life and limited outside activity. His *Expositio paraenetica in regulam carmelitarum* (1625) emphasized the contemplative ideal of the rule and evidenced some affinity with the *Devotio moderna*. After Nicholas V gave permission for the establishment of Carmelite monasteries for women (1452), S. founded several women's communities in the Low Countries and, with Bl. *Frances d'Amboise, in France. He thus became the founder of the Carmelite Second Order. He was beatified in 1866. BIBLIOGRAPHY: G. Meesters, "Carmelite

Spirituality according to Blessed John Soreth,'' *Sword* 16 (1953) 323–335; M. Arts, ''Work of John Soreth,'' *ibid.* 15 (1952) 457–466; E. de la Nativité, *Catholicisme*, s.v. ''Jean Soreth.''

[J. C. WILLKE]

SORGE, REINHARD (1892–1916), German dramatist. A convert to Catholicism (1913), S. was one of the religiously oriented writers of the expressionist school in Germany in the first quarter of the 20th century. In the last years of his short life he wrote religious plays. BIBLIOGRAPHY: J. Kroll, *Reinhard Sorge* (1941).

[I. MERKEL]

SORIN, EDWARD FREDERICK (1814–93), founder of the Univ. of Notre Dame. A native of France and ordained a diocesan priest in 1838, S. joined the newly formed Congregation of the Holy Cross in 1840. S. with six brothers came to the Diocese of Vincennes, Indiana in 1841 and at the instance of the bp. began building a college at South Bend, Ind. in 1842. In 1844 the Univ. of Notre Dame was chartered by the state legislature and held its first commencement exercises. S. served as president until 1865 and is chief architect of the Notre Dame tradition. At the same time he was provincial of the congregation, which served missions in Indiana, Illinois and Michigan. Through him the Sisters of the Holy Cross came from France and in a short time became a large community with many schools; S. established the present motherhouse at South Bend and brought to the congregation Mother Angela, who became the leading influence of the community. In 1865 S. founded the monthly magazine *Ave Maria*. Elected superior general of the Congregation, he exercised worldwide influence.

[J. R. AHERNE]

SORROW, distress at the loss of some valued good. Pain may be taken in a strict sense to mean bodily affliction; sorrow or sadness is rather the internal emotional or volitional experience caused by pain or by any other loss of what is valued. Since the loss of a good is an evil, sorrow as such is connatural and good. It is morally good when a truly human good is lost, and when it is controlled proportionately to the good lost. The virtue of *courage moderates emotional sorrow, not by suppression, but by keeping the person steadfast in the pursuit of good in spite of sorrow. In the Christian life sorrow has a special place. While charity leads to joy in its love for God, it also causes a kind of sorrow because the fullness of union with God is not yet reached, and because of the threat to that union that past sins or the possibility of future sins represent (see CONTRITION). A sorrow that is opposed to the joy proper to charity is the vice of *acedia, an apathy, even a kind of paralyzing regret at what loving God costs.

[T. C. O'BRIEN]

SORROWS OF MARY (SEVEN DOLORS), seven events in the life of Mary in which her compassion with Jesus caused her particular sorrow. Today they are enumerated as the prophecy of Simeon, the flight into Egypt, the search for the boy Jesus, the carrying of the cross, the Crucifixion, the descent from the cross, and the burial. In the NT, Simeon's prophecy refers to a sword that would pierce Mary's soul (Lk 2.35), and Jn 19.25 narrates that Mary stood at Jesus' cross. The earliest patristic literature simply acknowledged Mary's sorrows in commenting upon the scriptural texts. In the East from the 6th to the 10th cent., after an initial period in which Origen's interpretation of the sword in Simeon's prophecy as indicating some loss of faith during the Passion was widely held, this theme of Mary's compassion and spiritual martyrdom was greatly elaborated. A similar elaboration took place in the West during the 11th and 12th cent., and various devotions to the seven sorrows began in the 14th century. The *Servite Order, dedicated to this devotion, was granted (1607) the exclusive right to establish confraternities of the seven sorrows. Two liturgical feasts were placed in the Roman calendar although, since 1960, only one remains (September 15th). BIBLIOGRAPHY: É. Bertaud, DSAM 3:1686–1701; A. Liguori, *Glories of Mary* (1931). *CO-REDEMPTION.

[T. HEATH]

SORTES BIBLICAE, a Christian practice of divination, of a random consultation of the Bible, evolved from the pre-Christian practice of opening at random a book inspired by the Muses: Homer, Hesiod, or Virgil, in the hope of finding application to one's own life. In his *Confessions*, Augustine describes his own resorting to this practice in the famous *tolle et lege* incident. He later came to have second thoughts about such consultations. The Scriptures were widely consulted in this fashion into the Carolingian period, even for such matters of public policy and decision as the election of bishops. The danger to public life became apparent and the custom died out. Its private application survived as an individual's private superstition.

[E. J. DILLON]

SOSTHENES, a name that appears twice in the NT. S., the head of the Jewish synagogue at Corinth, was beaten by the bystanders before the tribunal of the proconsul Gallio after the latter had refused to listen to the accusations brought by the Jews against St. Paul (Acts 18.17). In writing to the Corinthians, St. Paul sends greetings along with ''Sosthenes our brother'' (1 Cor 1.1). In the early Church there was a tradition that this S. was one of the 70 Disciples of Christ (Eusebius, *Eccl. Hist.* 1.12.1). Others have maintained that he is to be identified with the S. mentioned in Acts 18.17, but this seems to be rather doubtful. BIBLIOGRAPHY: DB 5.2:1849–50; A. Penna, EncCatt 11:1000.

[M. J. COSTELLOE]

SOTER, ST. (d. 175), **POPE** from *c*.166, martyr. He is remembered chiefly for his letter to the Corinthian Church under Bp. *Dionysus. According to an untrustworthy source he also wrote a treatise against the *Montanists. He is venerated by the Church as a martyr, but nothing is known of the circumstances of his martyrdom. BIBLIOGRA-PHY: Butler 2:144; A. Amore, BiblSanct 11:1327–28.

[R. B. ENO]

SOTERIOLOGY, an academic term from the Greek *sōtēria* (salvation) meaning a study of salvation. It is used to designate the part of dogmatic theology that seeks to penetrate the meaning of God's action in concrete human history to reconcile man to himself. Specifically it has been used to refer to the theological speculation on the causal relationship between the redemptive events of Christ's life, death, Resurrection and the final union of man with God.

As a speculative theological study it has undergone a considerable development throughout its history. The variety of expressions used in the NT to convey the meaning of Christ's saving acts provided the Fathers of the Church with rich source material from which they constructed their theories of salvation. Although the heresies with which they were confronted concerned primarily the nature of Christ and gave them little occasion for a systematic study of soteriology, nevertheless one does find in the Fathers an underlying concern that is soteriological as they refuted those who denied certain doctrines concerning aspects of Christ's humanity. One finds all the Fathers invoking one sound soteriological principle: What was not assumed (i.e., whatever of humanity was not united in Christ with the Divine person of the Word) was not healed. For the Fathers each Christological heresy was seen not only as falsifying the reality of Christ but also as threatening the truth of man's salvation by Christ. Renewed interest in the Fathers of the Church has revealed in their exegesis the variety of ways in which they viewed salvation: as an illumination by the law, teaching, and example of the Word Incarnate; as a victory of Christ over Satan, sin, and death; as a liberation of man from the power of Satan, sin, and death; as a ransom paid in the blood of Christ; as an expiatory sacrifice offered by Christ on man's behalf; as a mediation reconciling man with the Father in the new covenant; and as a physico-mystical solidarity between the Father and mankind in his Son Jesus Christ.

In the 11th cent. St. Anselm of Canterbury, Doctor of the Church, elaborated the satisfaction theory of salvation in precise legal terms, and so it became part of the comprehensive treatment of the summits of the Middle Ages. The later commentaries on St. Thomas Aquinas's treatment expanded this theory. The theological textbooks of more recent times limited their consideration of the meaning of salvation to one that overemphasized the analogy with a legal transaction, one as it were between God and man, involving so much pain from Christ to make up for so much

sin in man. This theology of salvation in terms of satisfaction, rewards, and merits tended to obscure the more dynamic historical perspectives that had opened up such rich interpretations for the Fathers of the Church.

The contemporary renewal of dogmatic theology, brought on in part by the study of the Scriptures in the light of modern scholarship, is developing a much more balanced theological speculation in the area of salvation. The biblical work of scholars such as F. Durrwell and P. Benoit has brought the saving role of Christ's Resurrection, Ascension and sending of the Holy Spirit to bear on the contemporary understanding of the economy of salvation. L. Cerfaux, A. Feuillet, and others have helped to uncover the soteriological riches in the writings of St. Paul and St. John and thus have provided dogmatic theologians with a more complete framework on which to build a soteriology that reflects the dynamic implications of the revealed message of salvation. Theologians now work to include in their understanding of the divine plan the whole paschal mystery, taught so well by the Fathers, the Pauline idea of man's physical incorporation into the life of the risen Christ, as well as man's communal solidarity and the cosmic aspects of salvation. The application, moreover, of historical perspective by today's scholars helps them round out their understanding of the theology of salvation. BIBLIOGRAPHY: R. Barr, *Main Currents in Early Christian Thought* (1966); J. M. Carmody and T. E. Clarke, *Word and Redeemer* (1966); L. Cerfaux, *Christ in the Theology of St. Paul* (tr. G. Webb and A. Walker, 1959); J. Dupont, *Essais sur la Christologie S. Jean,* (1951); F. X. Durrwell, *Resurrection* (tr. R. Sheed, 1960); A. Feuillet, *Johannine Studies* (1964); P. Benoit, "L'Ascension," RevBibl 56 (1949) 161–203; Y. Congar, "*Christ in the Economy of Salvation and Dogmatic Tracts,*" (*Concilium* 2, 1965).

[J. C. MURRAY]

SOTIR (SAVIOR), see ZOE.

SOTO, DOMINGO DE (1494–1560), Spanish Dominican philosopher and theologian. A Castilian, S. studied at Alcalá and Paris, where he entered deeply into the logical questions of the day, and moved from nominalism to realism, and after returning to Alcalá, he adopted a critical Aristotelianism. Advised by a Benedictine retreat master to join the Dominicans, he was professed in 1525, and taught dialectics at Segovia and theology at Salamanca. He was a major figure at the Council of Trent in his dual role of imperial theologian and proctor of the master general of the Dominicans. On his return to Spain he became confessor to the Emperor Charles V and succeeded Melchior *Cano in the *cátedra de Prima* at Salamanca. A Thomist of the very first rank, he is remarkable as a theologian for considering an unconscious drive within man for the vision of God (*On nature and grace,* 1547); and as a natural philosopher, who opened up questions from Aristotle's *Physics,* historians of science are beginning to discover in him significant anticipations of later theories. BIBLIOGRAPHY: Quétif-Échard 2.1:171–174; V. Beltrán de Heredia, DTC 14.2:2423–31.

[T. GILBY]

SOTO, PEDRO DE (1500–63), Dominican theologian with a special interest in the Fathers and church councils. An Andalusian, S. became a trusted adviser to the Emperor Charles V, esp. in the affairs of Germany, and was mainly instrumental in engineering his political alliance with the papacy. The association lapsed, however, when he advocated a stiffer attitude toward the Protestants than was helpful or even feasible. He succeeded in restoring the chair of theology at the Univ. of Dillingen, with the help of his friend, Card. Truchses of Augsburg, and taught there. Later he was regius professor of divinity at Oxford under Philip and Mary. He died as Pius IV's theologian at the Council of Trent. BIBLIOGRAPHY: Quétif-Échard 2.1:183–184; V. D. Carro, DTC 14.2:2431–43.

[T. GILBY]

SOUBIRAN, MARIE THÉRÈSE DE, BL. (1834–89), foundress. Born near Carcassonne in France, she came under the spiritual direction of her uncle, Canon L. de Soubiran, under whose guidance she made a vow of virginity at the age of 14 and at 20 spent a year at a *béguinage* in Ghent. The following year she established a similar type of house at her native Castelnaudry, which developed into a religious congregation, the Society of Mary Auxiliatrix, in Toulouse in 1866. This was granted diocesan approval in 1867 and that of the Holy See in 1869. The community prospered for a time, despite some dispersion of its members during the Franco Prussian War. Worse trouble came from within in the person of Mère Marie Françoise de Borgia, who was incautiously received into the community in 1868 without the investigation that might have revealed that she was a married woman who had left her husband. Mère Françoise quickly became influential and was made assistant superior general. Dominating and ambitious, she exerted pressure to force upon the community policies that proved disastrous, but she put the blame for the failure upon Mère Thérèse, whom she succeeded in driving from the congregation in 1874. The Sisters of Notre Dame of Charity received Mère Thérèse in their community and admitted her to profession in 1877. After Mère Thérèse's death, Mère Françoise was herself deposed and expelled. Mère Thérèse was exonerated and in 1946 was beatified. BIBLIOGRAPHY: Butler 4:157–161; G. Mathon, BiblSanct 1329–31.

[P. K. MEAGHER]

SOUBIROUS, BERNADETTE, ST. (1844–79), a native of *Lourdes in SW France who as a girl of 14 witnessed 18 apparitions of the Blessed Virgin at the grotto known as Massabielle near Lourdes. Upon reporting her experience she met with much disbelief, but gradually, as word of the event spread abroad and wonders were told of cures at the grotto, the incredulity gave way to belief and Lourdes became a great center of pilgrimage. B., whose health was frail, was much distressed by the attention focused upon her, and to protect her from it the Sisters of Charity and Christian Instruction at Nevers took her in; in 1866 she was received into the community; in which she lived a life of quiet retirement, faithfully performed her humble duties, and endured her physical afflictions with exemplary patience. She was beatified in 1925 and canonized in 1933. BIBLIOGRAPHY: Butler 2:108–112; A. Combes, BiblSanct 8:1036–41.

[P. K. MEAGHER]

SOUFFLOT, JACQUES GERMAIN (1713–80), French architect. Trained at the French Academy in Rome, S. visited Sicily and Asia Minor, did influential work in Lyons and Paris, where he held important posts including the directorship of the Gobelin tapestry factory. His best-known building in Paris is the Church of Ste. Geneviève (Panthéon), designed in the classical-baroque style. S.'s interest in archeology and geometry promoted the transition from late French Baroque to Neoclassicism.

[K. B. NEILSON]

SOUILLAC, ABBEY OF, Benedictine monastery founded in 930 in the Diocese of Cahors (Lot, France). The 11th cent. was its most prosperous period, when more than 80 churches or priories in Haut-Quercy were included in its property. The monastery was sacked during the Hundred Years' War by the Great Companies, and later by the Calvinists. In 1659 it became affiliated with the Congregation of Saint-Maur and the commendatory abbot, Abp. Henri de la Mothe-Houdancourt, restored the conventual buildings. The abbey was closed permanently during the Revolution. The abbey church, which now serves the parish, has a nave with three cupolas (early 12th cent.). The portal (11th cent.) is a masterpiece of Romanesque sculpture. BIBLIOGRAPHY: Cottineau 2:3069.

[J. DAOUST]

SOUL (IN THE BIBLE), the principle of life. Thus, in traditional Catholic philosophy, the human soul is the principle of human life. In biblical tradition the word has a different history and meaning. In Hebrew the word *nephesh* is often translated "soul." But such phrases as "Save my soul, O Lord" could as easily be translated: "Save my life ...", or possibly "Save my neck" or even "Save me." The Hebrew intuition of man was that of a unity, an indivisible being, not as having a body, but as being a living body; not as having a soul, but as being a living soul. The classic text is Gen 2.7, in which God breathed on the clay he had fashioned, and man became "a living soul" (*nephesh*), meaning "a living being." To speak of the body means self as bodily and physically present to others; to speak of the soul means self as the subject of appetite or emotion. To speak of the heart, means this same self as the subject of thought, decision, and volition. To speak of the spirit, means the same self again as graced with life, vitality, and energy. There is a dichotomy that can emerge between spirit and flesh. The first refers to man when God turns to him, smiles on him, and imparts life to him; the second means man in his fragility and confusion, left to die when God turns his face away and withdraws the gift of life. The Greek versions continue this dichotomy with their use of spirit (*pneuma*) and flesh (*sarx*). Another dichotomy can be found in Paul's writings, when he contrasts psychic man to spiritual man. This lends itself to the later natural–supernatural dichotomy. There was to emerge in Greek Christian tradition the dichotomy of soul (*psychē*) and body (*sōma*), in which the former is by nature immortal. This is a departure from the Greek NT, which is faithful to Jewish apocalyptic tradition: that if man overcomes death, it is because God wills it, not because of an immortal soul that of its nature necessarily survives death. In the NT as in Jewish apocalyptic, one hopes for the resurrection of the just as the gracious act of God.

[E. J. DILLON]

SOUL, FACULTIES OF THE, see FACULTIES OF THE SOUL.

SOUL, HUMAN, an important anthropological term referring to the inner, vital, or spiritual principle in man. This term has a complex history and a great variety of meanings.

Nonphilosophical thought and intuition in all cultures and civilizations point to some mysterious reality in man that is relatively independent of his body or that is an intrinsic force or principle of movement and life, including perception, volition, and intellection.

In philosophy and religion the views on the human soul have a wide range. (1) Materialism reduces it to the manifestations or epiphenomena of living matter and denies any possibility of an immaterial, spiritual, or immortal principle or substance in man. (2) An extreme dichotomy in different views holds a spiritual and immaterial principle or soul (spirit) in man that is imprisoned in the human body (matter) for its sins and that can be redeemed from it either by some purification or expiation (Orphism, Neoplatonism, Manichaeism) or by loss of its individuality (usually after many transmigrations or metempsychoses) and merger with an Absolute (Brahmanism, primitive Buddhism). (3) The Thomistic view mediates between the two extremes and is most commonly accepted. According to this hylomorphic presentation man is one being substantially composed of two metaphysical parts: body and rational soul (matter and form), which is man's one substantial form and which performs all vegetative, sensitive, and intellective functions. It as a whole informs the whole body and each part of it. It is essentially and quantitatively simple and completely immaterial, i.e., a subsistent and spiritual form that is natur-ally incorporeal, incorruptible, indivisible, and immortal. It does not have existence before the body, but is created with it and for it by God.

In theology there is no unanimous Christian teaching on the human soul. The solemn magisterium teaches that the Trinitarian God created man "constituted, as it were, alike of the spirit and the body" (D 800); "that man has one rational and intellectual soul" (D 657), which is "immortal . . . and multiple" (D 1440), and "the form of the human body in itself and essentially" (D 902). The ordinary magisterium tends to the Thomistic view and, accepting an essential difference between matter and spirit (D 3891, cf. 3022–24), defends man as a psychosomatic whole. Thus the human soul is the vital (D 2833) and constitutive principle of man's being, i.e., one, spiritual, simple (see, e.g., D 791, 801, 900), immaterial, relatively independent of matter (D 1007, 3002), and immortal (D 1440), because it continues in an incomplete existence in heaven, purgatory, limbo, or hell (see, e.g., D 857–858), expecting the resurrection of the body (see the creeds and, e.g., D 443, 493) to receive reward (D 1000) or punishment (D 443, 780) or suffering and purification (D 1304, 1580). Recent development of biblical anthropology initiated a return from an excessive Hellenic dichotomy to the primitive Christian view concerning the unity of man (which has priority before his parts and dimensions) in his origin (creationism), life, and final destiny (resurrection). BIBLIOGRAPHY: J. Bainvel et al., DTC 1.1:968–1041; J. Haekel et al., LTK 9:566–574; F. Hartmann, RGG 4:287–291; I. C. Brady et al., NCE 13:450–464; C. Fabro, EncCatt 1:1290–1307; ThAq ST 1, 75.1–90.4; A. Ahlbrecht, *Tod und Unsterblichkeit in der evangelischen Theologie der Gegenwart* (1964); D. R. G. Owen, *Body and Soul* (1956); M. Schmaus, *Katholische Dogmatik* (5 v. in 8, 5th ed. 1953–59) 2.1 pars. 128–130; C. Tresmontant, *A Study of Hebrew Thought* (tr. M. F. Gibson, 1960) 83–114.

[P. B. T. BILANIUK]

SOUL, HUMAN (IMMORTALITY), see IMMORTALITY.

SOUL, HUMAN (ORIGIN OF). Although there are no absolutely decisive scriptural references for this issue (Gen 2.7; Wis 15.11; Ec 12.7), a consensus formed within the Catholic tradition that the human soul could not have developed from matter by a purely evolutionary process. No reordering or combination of matter can produce what is essentially diverse from it (D 1440). The rational soul which endows humans with the possibility of self-transcendence is an essentially new and spiritual reality that comes into being only through the act of creation proper to God alone (see INFUSION). However, since the divine creative plan is not in itself temporal nor constituted by successive volitional decisions, the creative act from which the first human being resulted may be understood as part of an unfolding plan or process within time and need not be construed merely as an intervention. The excluded evolutionary transformism is one that does not relate the genesis of corporal beings with the potential for knowing and loving to a divine initiative. When Vatican Council I said that God created out of nothing the human creature composed of spirit and body, it implied that the first human soul, by which human nature was essentially constituted, was due to a distinct divine creative act (*Dei Filius* ch. 1; cc. 4 and 5: D 3002 & 3024–25); it explicitly rejected any notion of pantheistic emanation.

There has been ongoing theological discussion about the manner in which God's creative activity is related to the creative act of parents in which ovum and sperm fuse to form a new, genetically differentiated, living reality. The love of parents which is expressed and perfected through the marital act (see PROCREATION) is seen as a participation in God's own creative act (Vat II ChurchModWorld 49–50). Parents truly generate human life in cooperation with the love of God the Creator. Yet the opinion that they generate both the body and the soul (*traducianism), which was held by Tertullian, following the Stoics in making the soul a material stuff, is not acceptable Catholic doctrine (D 360, 1007, 3220). Catholic theology holds that each human soul is created directly by God (*Humani generis*; D 3896). This position is traceable to Hilary, Ambrose, and Jerome. Augustine remained open to the possibility that the soul of a child is produced by the parent's soul through a special God-given power (Ep. 166; cf. 190). Only by such a spiritual version of traducianism could he adequately explain the handing-on of *original sin. A. *Rosmini's proposal of a kind of *generationism was declared erroneous in 1887 (D 3220; cf. D 1007). How parental generation of the living substance of a new human being, prescinding from the moral context, is related to God's activity is not perfectly clear. Some have referred to parents as disposing the material body for the creation of its soul by God. Although the human soul is something new that transcends any created cause, God works in parents as causes of a genuine natural event. The exact moment of the creation or infusion of the soul has been debated. The Platonic notion of *preexistence, which was adopted by Origen, was formally rejected by synods in Constantinople and Braga during the 6th cent. (D 403, 456). *Thomas Aquinas (ThAq ST 1a, 118.2) and other medieval theologians, following Aristotle, believed that the fetus developed through inferior vegetative and animal stages before it was finally prepared to be informed by a rational soul in a substantial union. The ancients said this occurred about the 40th day for male fetuses and about the 80th day for female fetuses. Rosmini's proposal that a sensitive soul is transformed into a rational soul by an extrinsic divine illumination was declared unacceptable (D 3220–21). In 1679, the Holy Office acceded to the request of the Baianists from Louvain and condemned the laxist position: that the rational soul began to exist only at birth so that no abortion is homicide (D 2135). Although some contemporary authors propose a concept of "individuality," which they judge not to be present until the 14th

day after conception, the majority of Catholic theologians in recent times have held for creationism at the moment of conception. Such an opinion was presupposed by Popes Alexander VII and Pius IX in their discussion of the Immaculate Conception (D 2017, 2803).

[B. P. PRUSAK]

SOUL-BODY RELATIONSHIP. "Though made of body and soul, man is one" (Vat II ChurchModWorld 14). Such insistence continues the OT vision, which ascribed equal importance to "flesh" (Heb. *bāśār*) and "spirit" or "breath" (*nefeš, rūah*). God did not create body and spirit but a human (Gen 2.7; cf. Ps 63.1). Such a view supported the concept of bodily resurrection that later emerged (Dan 12; 2 Macc 7). Only when Platonic thought influenced later Judaism was the body seen as a limiting vehicle from which the soul yearned to be freed through contemplation (Wis 9.15; cf. 8.19–20; Ec 12.7). The NT books teach that to be human is to be embodied by their emphasis upon the Incarnation and bodily Resurrection of Christ, in which believers share as members of Christ's body (Jn 1.14; 1 Cor 6.14–15). At the same time the body (Gr. *sōma*) is contrasted with the soul (*psychē*) as the mortal with the immortal (Mt 10.28). Paul (1 Thess 5.25), and such apostolic fathers as Justin Martyr, distinguished spirit (*pneuma*), soul (*psychē*), and body (*sōma*). The body is not evil in itself; it can be the medium of the sin of an individual. Only when the *psychic* flesh (*sarx*) becomes *spiritual* does the body become incorruptible (Rom 6–8, Gal 5). Irenaeus countered Gnostic pessimism regarding the body and the material world by stressing the Incarnation and Resurrection. Subsequent attempts to devalue Christ's full humanity (*Apollinarianism and *Monophysitism) were rejected. Yet, because early Christian theology developed in a Platonic atmosphere, it became tinged by negative attitudes toward the body. The Alexandrians, particularly Origen, introduced such attitudes, which then colored monastic spirituality. Along with the Stoic notion of *apatheia* they passed into Western theology and spirituality via *Pseudo-Dionysius and *John Cassian. Although God's grace and Jesus' saving action were directed to the total person, some would speak of "saving souls."

During the medieval period the Aristotelian doctrine of *hylomorphism prevailed: every physical being is constituted by matter and form; the soul is the substantial form of the human body. Adapting such philosophical insights *Thomas Aquinas reiterated the substantial unity of the human being. The union is such that it is contrary to the nature of the soul to be without the body (ThAq CG 4.79; ST 1a, 75.4; 76; cf. D 902). In current theology the body is considered the substantial expression of the soul or of spiritual personality. The free decisions of an incarnate spirit, what one is or wishes to become, are actualized in the body. Matter is a condition of possibility for the human spirit, which cannot know and love without the body. Whatever is in the intellect was in the senses. Love or fellowship cannot be actualized without the mediation of language, signs, and gestures. God's own self-communication (revelation) requires deeds and words (Vat II DivRev 2). Thus Jesus proclaimed the kingdom by table fellowship with sinners and outcasts (Mk 2.15; Mt 11.17–19). Precisely as an embodied People of God the Church itself is a sacrament or sign and instrument of union with God and of the union of all humanity (Vat II ConstChurch 1–17). As including physical gestures or actions the seven sacraments communicate or effect the spiritual dimension which they symbolize. The transcendence proper to a spiritual soul must be bodily expressed, since it is an essentially embodied human being that acts. Our bodies are the medium of all personal communication and encounter in which communion with God and other persons is established. If by interior qualities a human being outstrips the whole sum of material things, nevertheless, through bodily composition man gathers to himself the elements of the material world (Vat II ChurchModWorld 14). The potential of the incarnate spirit must be actualized in material time and space. Whenever a human freely decides to transcend self and achieve fuller personhood in communion with an embodied "other," thus imaging God's communion with us, the spiritual soul becomes more embodied (1 Jn 1.6–7; 4.20–21). To be fully human is to be a truly incarnate spirit feeding the hungry and clothing the naked (Mt 25.34–36). A certain tension between the bodily and spiritual dimensions must be respected. One achieves personhood not by appetitive spontaneity but by an active self-transcendence interior to finite beings. One becomes a person by rising above natural necessities and inertia, by consciously opting for the openness that leads beyond the finite self. The soul is an openness to the infinite and transcendence. Although the body can be identified with *concupiscence, understood either as a natural drive to possess or as an inertia preventing the achieving of spiritual self-transcendence, it is also the only means by which the soul or spiritual dimension can fulfill or concretely realize the human potential.

[B. P. PRUSAK]

SOUL OF THE CHURCH, a phrase used in several senses. (1) Primarily it refers to the Holy Spirit. In keeping with the theme that the Church is the mystical body of Christ, the Holy Spirit, who is the Spirit of Christ, is described in this image as vivifying and sanctifying the members of Christ's body by grace and charisms. The expression in modern times was taken up by Leo XIII in *Divinum illud munus* (1897), developed at length by Pius XII in *Mystici corporis* (1943), and incorporated into the ecclesiology of Vatican Council II, which pointed out patristic use of the phrase (Vat II ConstChurch 7, and n. 17). Sanctifying the Church is seen as a primary work of the Holy Spirit, and a question currently discussed by RC theologians is whether this work is a personal mission of "the Lord and giver of life." (2) Some theologians, notably C. *Journet in *L'Église du Verbe Incarné* (1951), 2:522ff., have distinguished the uncreated soul, the Holy Spirit, from the created soul of the Church, charity. Charity is received from Christ and is the source of conformity with Christ, i.e., it is derived from the sacraments of Christ and is directed toward the fullness of ecclesial unity. (3) After Vatican Council I some theologians spoke of those who lived in grace and charity but outside visible membership in the Church as belonging to the soul of the Church. This usage ceased after *Mystici corporis*. *MEMBERSHIP IN THE CHURCH.

[M. B. SCHEPERS]

SOUTANE, commonly called a cassock, an ankle-length garment worn by clerics and usually acolytes serving Mass or assisting at other services. Commonly of black cloth, cassocks in color designate hierarchical rank in the Church. The pope wears white, bishops wear purple, cardinals red, and other prelates are entitled to wear purple. A "house cassock" for prelates is black trimmed with red piping.

[C. J. NOONE]

SOUTER, ALEXANDER (1873–1949), NT and patristic scholar. For 8 years he served as professor of NT Greek at Mansfield College, Oxford. In 1911 he succeeded W. M. Ramsay as regius professor of humanity at Aberdeen, a position he held till 1937. While well-known for work in NT Greek, S.'s, main contributions are in patristic studies and late Latin. He was editor-in-chief of the *Oxford Latin Dictionary*. His *Glossary of Later Latin*, intended originally as an appendix to the *Dictionary*, was published separately in expanded form shortly after his death. BIBLIOGRAPHY: K. Schäfer, LTK 9:899; M. L. W. Laistner, *Speculum* 25 (1950) 418–419.

[H. DRESSLER]

SOUTERLIEDEKENS, a collection of monophonic psalm-tunes intended for use in the home, published in the Netherlands in 1540, and having more than 30 editions. The texts are the earliest rhymed translations into the vernacular of the complete psalter. The music was taken from popular and folk melodies of the time.

[M. T. LEGGE]

SOUTH CAROLINA, S Atlantic state admitted to the Union (1788) as the 8th of the original Thirteen States. The English were the first to colonize successfully, settling first at Albemarle Point and in 1680 at the present site of Charleston. French Huguenots arrived the same year. The first Catholic congregation in South Carolina under the direction of John *Carroll was assembled (1788) by Matthew Ryan. When the Diocese of Charleston was erected (1820), John *England was named first bishop. In 1822 he founded the *U.S. Catholic Miscellany*, the first Catholic newspaper in the U.S. Widely quoted in Catholic newspapers throughout the country during the 1830s and 1840s, it extended England's reputation far beyond the boundaries of his jurisdiction. England's attempts to supply educational facilities to Negroes failed when opposition forced him to abandon the venture. The diocese is a suffragan of the metropolitan see of Atlanta. In 1976 South Carolina's Catholics numbered 51,561 or 1.8% of the total state population. The major Protestant denominations are the Southern Baptist Convention, with 28.4% of the total population in 1972, and the Methodist Church with 9.9%. Other Protestant denominations comprise 12.3% of the population. The Jewish population (1968) was 7,285, or 0.28%. There are no Catholic colleges in South Carolina, but 5 Catholic high schools enroll a total of 1,469 students and 31 Catholic elementary schools care for some 6,532 pupils. BIBLIOGRAPHY: D. D. Wallace, *History of South Carolina* (4 v. 1934); *South Carolina: A Short History, 1520–1948* (1961).

[J. L. MORRISON; R. M. PRESTON]

SOUTH DAKOTA, a N central state admitted to the Union (1889) as the 40th state. The French laid claim to the region after 1742, but habitation was confined largely to Indians and fur traders. The U.S. acquired the territory in the Louisiana Purchase (1803). Except for the efforts of P. J. *De Smet, Christian Hoecken, and Augustine *Ravoux (1839–40), little missionary activity occurred in South Dakota prior to the Civil War. After the war, missionaries arriving to work among the Indians included the Episcopal Bp. W. H. Hare, the Presbyterian minister J. P. Williamson, the Congregationalist minister T. L. Riggs, and the Catholic priest Martin Marty. Marty became the vicar apostolic of Dakota (1879) and first bp. of the Diocese of Sioux Falls (1889). Today the state has two ecclesiastical jurisdictions, the Dioceses of Rapid City and Sioux Falls, both of which are suffragans of the Archdiocese of St. Paul, Minn. In 1976 Catholics numbered 135,792 or 20.6% of the total state population. The major Protestant denominations are the American Lutheran Church, with 17.3% of the total population in 1971 and the Methodist Church, with 8.6%. Other Protestant denominations comprise 23.0%. The Jewish population (1968) was 520, or 0.08%. There are 2 Catholic colleges in S.D., with a total enrollment of 960 students. Five Catholic high schools serve the educational needs of 1,641 students, while 28 Catholic elementary schools are attended by 5,294 pupils. BIBLIOGRAPHY: H. S. Schell, *History of South Dakota* (1961); C. Duralschek, *Beginnings of Catholicism in South Dakota* (1943).

[J. L. MORRISON; R. M. PRESTON]

SOUTH INDIA, CHURCH OF, see CHURCH OF SOUTH INDIA.

SOUTHERN BAPTIST CONVENTION, largest Baptist body in the U.S., organized in 1845. Prior to 1755, Baptists in the South were few, but after the arrival of Shubael *Stearns, a New England *Separate Baptist, revivalistic measures multiplied their numbers to many thousands by 1800. Their organization was limited to local *associations until 1814, when they combined with North-

ern Baptists to form the Triennial Convention for the support of foreign missions (see AMERICAN BAPTIST CONVENTION). Disputes over slavery and church *polity resulted in the formation of the separate Southern Baptist Convention in 1845. Southern Baptists adopted a plan for a *convention that would incorporate home and foreign mission boards, thus laying foundations for a more unified denomination. Influenced by the hardening sectional spirit of the Reconstruction era, Southern Baptists persisted in remaining separate from those of the North after the Civil War. Devastated by the war, their churches struggled to sustain their missionary activities, and by 1890 had overcome most of the obstacles. The Convention recommends the *New Hampshire Confession to its churches; it has had a tradition of conservative theology.

Interest in education began with the founding of Furman Univ., Greenville, S.C., in 1827; today there are more than 30 Southern Baptist colleges and about 20 junior colleges, most of which are owned by state conventions. The Southern Baptist Theological Seminary was founded in 1859 at Greenville, S.C., but was removed to Louisville, Ky., after the war. There are five other seminaries today, each directly under the control of the Convention. From Southern Baptists have come notable preachers (G. W. Truett, R. G. Lee), biblical scholars (J. T. Sampey, A. T. Robertson), and theologians (E. Y. *Mullins, W. T. Conner). In 1965, the Foreign Mission Board reported work in 60 countries, with a staff of 1,769 missionaries. The Home Mission Board engages in diverse types of ministries, employing more than 2,500 missionaries, and having an annual budget of about $8,000,000. The Sunday School Board and the Broadman Press do a multimillion dollar business each year. The Christian Life Commission seeks to inform the consciences of constituents on social issues. State conventions operate hospitals, children's homes, and homes for the aged. During World War II, as southerners migrated to industrial centers of the North, Southern Baptists demanded churches of their own kind, and today they exist in all 50 states. Because the South has retained a more homogeneous population, predominantly agrarian, revivalistic methods have continued to be successful. Between 1940 and 1965, Southern Baptists almost doubled their membership. In 1975 they numbered 12,297,346 members. Although cooperating with other Christians in some endeavors (a Southern-Baptist-Roman Catholic biconsultation has been in progress since 1971), they have resisted membership in the National and World Councils of Churches. BIBLIOGRAPHY: W. W. Barnes, *Southern Baptist Convention, 1845–1953* (1954); R. G. Torbet and S. H. Hill, Jr., *Baptists—North and South* (1964); *Baptist Advance* (ed. D. C. Woolley, 1964).

[N. H. MARING]

SOUTHERN HARMONY, one of the most famous of the *shaped-note hymnals (published 1835). This collection is a rich source of folk hymns, several of which are appearing in contemporary hymnals. BIBLIOGRAPHY: L. Ellinwood, *History of American Church Music* (1953, repr. 1969).

[M. T. LEGGE]

SOUTHERN METHODIST CHURCH, a small denomination organized in 1939 by a group of laymen who refused to accept the merger of the Methodist Episcopal Church, the Methodist Episcopal Church, South, and the Methodist Protestant Church. They believed that there was infidelity and apostasy in the Methodist Episcopal Church. The Southern Methodist Church claims to be a continuation of the old Methodist Episcopal Church, South, although the courts have overruled this contention in regard to property rights and name, The Church defends segregation. It has no bps. but does have a quadrennial *general conference; churches are owned by the local congregations. In 1968 the denomination had 52 churches, about 4,000 members, and 21 ordained clergy. BIBLIOGRAPHY: L. Corbett, *What, Why, How?—History, Organization, and Doctrinal Belief of the Southern Methodist Church* (1956); HistAmMeth 3:592–593.

[F. E. MASER]

SOUTHWELL, NATHANAEL (Bacon; 1598–1676), English Jesuit bibliographer and secretary. He studied humanities at St. Omer, was ordained in Rome (1622) after study at the English College. Southwell (an assumed name) was then sent to England, but was recalled to Rome to serve as procurator and minister of the College, and in 1637 became its confessor and spiritual director. From 1646 to 1668 at the Gesù he was secretary to five generals of the Jesuits, and during this time compiled a *Journal of Meditation* (1669; tr. Edward Harvey, alias Mico) and continued and revised Pedro de Ribadeneyra's great bibliographical work, *Bibliotheca Scriptorum Societatis Jesu* (1676).

[R. J. LITZ]

SOUTHWELL, ROBERT, ST. (c.1561–95), English poet, martyr. S. studied on the Continent because a Jesuit, and was ordained in 1584. He and Henry Garnet left for England in 1586. He worked principally in London and lived for a time at Arundel House in the Strand. He was captured in 1592, tortured, and executed for his priesthood at Tyburn. Chief among his prose works are *An Epistle of Comfort,* expanded from letters addressed to Philip Howard in prison, and *A Short Rule of Life* printed at the secret press he and Henry *Garnet directed. S.'s poetry was written during his 6 years on the English mission. His poetry aimed at service rather than self-expression. He was enabled by his inner suffering to achieve an objectivity not usually associated with lyric writers. He was canonized in 1970. Works: *Poems of Robert Southwell,* SJ, (ed. J. McDonald and N. P. Brown, 1967). BIBLIOGRAPHY: C. Devlin, *Life of Robert Southwell Poet and Martyr* (1967); P. Janelle, *Robert Southwell the Writer* (1935); Butler 2:386–391; N. Del Re, BiblSanct 11:1332–34.

[V. SAMPSON]

SOUTHWORTH, JOHN, ST. (1592–1654), English martyr. Ordained at Douai, he went to the English mission in 1619. After his arrest in Lancashire in 1627 he appears to have spent most of his time in prison until at least 1640, with a few intervals of freedom. With Henry Morse he labored heroically during the London plague (1636–37), serving the Catholic poor who were excluded from public assistance. He was arrested in 1654 and executed at Tyburn. He was canonized in 1970. BIBLIOGRAPHY: E. E. Reynolds, *John Southworth* (1962); N. Del Re, BiblSanct 11:1334–36; Butler 2:662–664.

[V. SAMPSON]

SOUVAY, CHARLES LÉON (1870–1939), Scripture scholar and superior general of the Vincentians. He was professor of Sacred Scripture, Hebrew, and church history in seminaries in France and St. Louis, Mo., where he became rector in 1926. In 1933 he returned to Paris as superior general of the Vincentians. His work on Sacred Scripture, which comprises many articles as well as his thesis, *The Metre of the Psalms,* and other publications, is devoted mainly to the Psalms.

[I. M. KASHUBA]

SOUVIGNY, ABBEY OF, former Benedictine monastery located in Souvigny at the confluence of the Queune and the Picoiseau in Allier, France. It was founded in 920 in what was then the Diocese of Clermont by Adhémar, an obscure progenitor of what came to be the illustrious Bourbon line. The priory became a pilgrimage center after the burial there of two abbots of Cluny, St. Majolus (d.994) and St. Odilo (d.1049). Bourbon rulers were buried there from the time of Duke Louis II (d.1410). Made commendatory in the 16th cent., the priory experienced a revival in the 17th cent. under prior Nicolas des Mesgrigny. Suppressed in 1791, it was demolished in 1793. BIBLIOGRAPHY: Cottineau 2:3073–75.

[E. J. DILLON]

SOVEREIGNTY, ultimate political authority in a validly formed state. In religious thought it is grounded in divine sovereignty and dependent for its legitimacy on conformity to divine principles of right order. *LAW.

[T. EARLY]

SOVIET LITERATURE, as distinct from Russian literature a political term referring to literary works produced in the U.S.S.R. since 1917 and reflecting, though with notable exceptions (e.g., Pasternak), the political, social, and economic ideals of the Communist party. During the period of militant communism (1917–21), when controls were negligible, the quasi-mystical glorification of the Revolution by the Scythians and the avant-gardist rejection of traditional forms and language by the Futurists coexisted with the propagandistic literature of the *Proletkult* (Proletarian Cultural and Educational Organizations). The relative freedom that still existed under the NEP (New Economic Policy, 1921–28) is reflected in the diversity of three main groups of writers: LEF (Left Front), founded by the Futurists in 1923; VAPP (All-Russian Association of Proletarian Writers), organized in 1925; and fellow travelers (non-Communist sympathizers with the aims of the Revolution). The "planned economy" of the first Five-Year Plan (1928–32) was reflected in a stricter control of literature and the formation of the Russian Association of Proletarian Writers (RAPP), which succeeded the VAPP in 1928. In the Stalin era of dictatorship (1932–41), the Central Committee of the Communist Party suppressed the RAPP and formulated for the new Union of Soviet Writers (1932) the official doctrine of Socialist Realism. War novels and patriotic literature appeared briefly during the period of the Great Patriotic War (1941–45), but were suppressed, by order of A. Zhdanov (1896–1948), in the post-war era (1946–53) in favor of a strict observance of Socialist realism (Zhdanovism). The post-Stalin era (1953–62) was characterized by a relative relaxation of literary controls (the so-called thaw). Since 1962, periods of control have alternated with periods of relaxation. BIBLIOGRAPHY: M. Slonim, *Soviet Russian Literature* (1964).

[M. F. MCCARTHY]

SOWERBY, LEO (1895–1968), American organist and composer. S. studied piano with Calvin Lampert and composition with Arthur Olaf Anderson, but as an organist he was self-taught. The first American Prix de Rome-fellow for music, he returned from Italy to teach at the American Conservatory in Chicago, where later he became organist-choirmaster at St. James Episcopal Cathedral. In 1962 he founded and until his death was dean of the College of Church Musicians at the Washington Cathedral. S. wrote music of all categories except opera.

[M. T. LEGGE]

SOZOMEN (5th cent.), church historian. Born in Bethelia, near Gaza, in Palestine of a prominent Christian family, S. settled, after much travel, at the practice of law in Constantinople. An interest in religion acquired from the monastic circles in which his youth was spent led him to the writing of a compendium of Church history in two books, a work now lost. Later he conceived the plan of continuing the great historical work of *Eusebius. This he accomplished in nine books written between 443 and 450. These covered the history of the Church between 323 and 425. He depends heavily but not exclusively on *Socrates. Photius thought S.'s work superior to that of Socrates. He is less original, but his style is simpler and clearer. Works: PG 67:843–1666; Eng. tr. NPNFC, ser. 2, v.2:236–427. BIBLIOGRA - PHY: Quasten 3:534–536.

[R. B. ENO]

SOZZINI, see SOCINUS.

SPAIN, predominantly Catholic country of SW Europe. Paul expressed an intention to visit Spain (Rom 15), part of the Roman Empire by his time, but whether he did is unknown. Irenaeus and Tertullian report the presence of Christians in 2d–cent. Spain, and the persecution of Diocletian claimed martyrs there. After 5th-cent. invasions by Alans Vandals, and Suevi, the Visigoths entered and achieved a dominant position, establishing a capital at Toledo in 554. Formerly Arian, the Visigoths were brought into the Catholic Church upon the conversion of King Recared in 587. The 7th cent. became a golden age for Catholic Spain, producing such notable figures as St. *Isidore of Seville (d. 636). The Hispana Canons, later incorporated in the *False Decretals, were probably compiled in this period. In the 8th cent., the Visigothic kingdom fell quickly to the Arab invaders, but the Church continued much as before. The Arabs governed from Córdoba and established a caliphate there (929–1031). Arab and Jewish learning, including knowledge of Greek philosophy, began reaching W Europe through Spain. Reconquest by Christians from NW Spain, taking inspiration from Compostela, extended to Toledo in 1085, and began its final phase with the marriage of Isabella of Castile to Ferdinand of Aragon. They ruled Castile jointly from 1474 and Aragon from 1479. The Inquisition, which dates from the 13th cent., became a powerful weapon for consolidation of power by these "Catholic kings," and they effected an orthodox reformation. In 1492 they captured the last Moorish province, Granada, and at the initiative of the Inquisitor T. de *Torquemada expelled all Jews except converts, called Marranos. A forced conversion of Muslims came in 1502, and expulsion of these Moriscos in 1609. Also in 1492 Columbus, operating on Spanish funds, discovered a New World where Spain soon built a vast and profitable empire, extending Spanish Catholicism to these new realms. The empire was lost as a result of the Napoleonic Wars, the Latin American wars of independence, and the Spanish-American War. Spain's Charles V, the Holy Roman Emperor, and his successor, Philip II, led Catholic Europe in resisting both the Reformation and the Ottoman advance. Charles began the Habsburg dynasty of Spain that lasted till 1700. Spaniards important in the renewal of Catholic life included Card. *Ximenez, SS. Ignatius of Loyola, John of the Cross, and Teresa of Avila. Also important were El Greco (1548?–?1614) in painting and Cervantes (1547–1616) in literature. After the defeat of the Spanish Armada (1588) and Philip's death (1598), Spanish power declined. The Bourbons ruled Spain from 1700 until the exile of Alfonso XIII in 1931. Bourbon "regalism," royal domination of the Church, led Philip V to break relations with the papacy in 1709. A concordat of 1753 granted extensive royal rights, the *patronato real, in return for minor concessions to the Church. The republic established in 1931 was overthrown in the 1936–39 Civil War that ended in the dictatorship of F. *Franco (1892–1975). On his death Alfonso's grandson, Juan Carlos, became king. The greater political freedom in Spain is paralelled by a much broader spread of opinion in ecclesiastical and political issues in the Spanish Church.

[T . EARLY]

SPAIN, SEVEN APOSTLES OF, see SEVEN APOSTLES OF SPAIN.

SPALATIN, GEORG (Burkhardt; 1484–1545), German Reformer, one of Martin Luther's first disciples. He was born in Bavaria, at Spalt (thus the name he assumed), and developed an interest in law and humanist studies at Erfurt and Wittenberg. After teaching for a time at Georgenthal, he was ordained and became (1509) tutor, librarian, and from 1516 adviser and chaplain to Frederick III, Elector of Saxony, whom he strongly influenced in favor of Luther. S. participated as visitator in the introduction of the Reformation throughout Saxony. Luther wrote frequently to him. S. was one of the theologians who assisted P. *Melanchthon in drafting the *Augsburg Confession (1530). He died as pastor at Altenbert.

[T. C. O'BRIEN]

SPALDING, CATHERINE, MOTHER (1793–1858), cofoundress. A daughter of Maryland whose family migrated to Kentucky, S. became in 1813 one of the first Sisters of Charity of Nazareth, founded in Bardstown by Bp. Flaget and John David. S. was elected first superior. Working in the fields, weaving their own clothing, and living in a log cabin, the sisters led a frugal existence. In 1818 they founded a small school at Bardstown, one of the first in the frontier country. S. established St. Vincent's Academy and directed the Academy of St. Catherine. In a second term as superior, 1825–31, she founded Presentation Academy, Louisville's first Catholic school, St. Vincent's Orphanage (1833), and in 1836 St. Vincent's Infirmary, both also in Louisville. A woman of physical and spiritual beauty, she died as a result of a mission to the sick.

[J. R. AHERNE]

SPALDING, JAMES FIELD (1839–1921), educator. A native of Massachusetts, S. taught at private schools and was ordained in 1869 in the Episcopal Church. Twelve years of pastoral activity followed. In 1891 he entered the Catholic Church. He was professor of literature at Boston College from 1899 to 1903; he lectured extensively at many Catholic schools and contributed frequently to literary periodicals. He wrote *The Teaching and Influence of Saint Augustine* (1896) and *The World's Unrest and Its Remedy* (1898).

[J. R. AHERNE]

SPALDING, JOHN LANCASTER (1840–1916), first bp. of Peoria, Ill., churchman, and writer. Descendant of an old Maryland Catholic family that had migrated to Kentucky and was noted for its priestly vocations, S. studied in the U.S. and at the Univ. of Louvain, where he was ordained in 1863. He labored in the Diocese of Louisville, where he became secretary to the bp. and chancellor. In 1866 as a theologian he attended the Second Plenary Council of Baltimore. He left Louisville for New York City in

1872, in order to engage in research and writing, and in 1877 was named bp. of Peoria. S. was an able administrator and a force leading the growth of the new diocese. But his influence went far beyond his own see. He was of the party of Card. James Gibbons and Abp. John Ireland in the controversies that divided the American Church. At the Third Plenary Council of Baltimore (1884) he was a leading figure and perhaps the primary advocate for the establishment of The Catholic Univ. of America for which he obtained the founding endowment of $300,000 from M. G. *Caldwell. A gifted essayist, he contributed many pieces, esp. on education to the *Catholic World, The American Catholic Quarterly Review,* and *The Educational Review*. He published books on that subject, as well as on philosophy, religion, and social problems: *Essays and Reviews* (1876); *God and the Soul* (1901); *Education and the Higher Life* (1890); *Means and Ends of Education* (1895); *Socialism and Labor and Other Arguments* (1902; 1905). In 1902 President Theodore Roosevelt appointed him to a commission to arbitrate the strike of the anthracite coal miners, and S.'s efforts had much to do with a solution favorable to the miners. He was intensely involved in furthering independent, Catholic parochial education; in this connection he opposed the *Faribault Plan, approved by his friend Abp. Ireland. S. incurred the antagonism of conservative American bps. and to some extent of Roman officials by his ardent patriotism, e.g., by his address at the cornerstone laying of the Catholic Univ. in 1888, for his praise of the American system of separation of Church and State; and by a sermon in praise of his country at the Church of the Gesù, Rome, in 1900. But in no sense did he fit the description of an adherent of the European-invented *Americanism, condemned by Leo XIII. S.'s last years were spent in retirement following upon a stroke.

[J. R. AHERNE]

SPALDING, MARTIN JOHN (1810–72), apologist for Catholicism, able bishop, and a leading force in the American Church. A Kentuckian, ordained in 1834, S. devoted his early years to pastoral work in Bardstown, Ky., giving special care to blacks. He edited the *Catholic Advocate* and founded its successor, the *Louisville Guardian* (1858). A popular lecturer, S. spoke throughout the U.S. and Canada. Named vicar general of Louisville (to which the Bardstown See had been transferred in 1841), he conducted with another cleric a series of lectures published as *General Evidences of Catholicity* (1847). In 1848, S. was consecrated coadjutor with the right of succession to Bp. Flaget of Louisville. His administration of the diocese provided schools, an orphanage, churches, a cathedral. In 1852 he brought financial assistance to John Henry Newman, heavily fined as a result of the *Achilli trial. S. introduced into his jurisdiction the Xaverian Brothers, Franciscan Conventuals, Ursulines, and Sisters of Notre Dame. When the Know-Nothings attacked the German and Irish section of Louisville in 1855 and murdered over 100 people, S. displayed both courage and tact and prevented additional violence. He was active in promoting the American College at Louvain (1857) and later the North American College in Rome. He was a leader in urging a national Catholic university for the U.S. During the Civil War, S. was strictly neutral and aided both sides with charitable services. His essay *Dissertazione della guerra civile Americana* (1863) had influence on European opinion. Named abp. of Baltimore in 1864, he was a major factor in the Second Plenary Council of Baltimore (1866). A number of institutions were added to the archdiocese, including the headquarters for the Josephite Fathers, devoted to black missions. S. took part in Vatican Council I where he supported the definition of papal infallibility and played a significant role as a member of several commissions. A prolific writer, he published among other works: *Sketches of the Early Catholic Missions of Kentucky* (1844); *History of the Protestant Reformation* (2 v., 1860), *Miscellanea* (1855), a series of essays noted for skillful defense of the Church, and an introduction and notes to *General History of the Catholic Church* (4 v., 1865–66) by J. E. Darras. BIBLIOGRAPHY: J. Spalding, *Life of the Most Rev. M. J. Spalding* (1873).

[J. R. AHERNE]

SPANGENBURG, AUGUSTUS GOTTLIEB (1704–92), Moravian bishop. Born in Klellenberg-Hohenstein, Germany, the son of a Lutheran pastor, he studied law, turned to theology, and in 1733 became Count *Zinzendorf's assistant at *Herrnhut. He served (1735–39) in America—first in Georgia, where he had talks with John Wesley, and then in Pennsylvania. He worked in England for a time, and after consecration as a bp. at Herrnhut in 1744, returned to America. From 1762 he was back at Herrnhut, holding posts of leadership.

[T. EARLY]

SPANHEIM, family name of Swiss Calvinist brothers. Both were born in Geneva and studied theology in Leyden, where their father had gone as a professor in 1642. **Ezechiel** (1629–1710) later taught eloquence at Geneva, tutored at the Heidelberg court, and then served as a diplomat for the Palatinate and Brandenburg. **Friedrich** (1632–1701) taught theology at Heidelberg from 1655 to 1670. He then succeeded J. *Cocceius as professor of theology at Leyden. He strongly supported orthodox Calvinism against *Arminianism. He later became professor of ecclesiastical history and published historical works.

[T. EARLY]

SPANISH INQUISITION, see INQUISITION, SPANISH.

SPCK, see SOCIETY FOR PROMOTING CHRISTIAN KNOWLEDGE.

SPECIAL EDUCATION, CATHOLIC, the education of children who so deviate from the so-called normal that the standard school curriculum cannot satisfy their needs, e.g., deaf or hard-of-hearing; blind or partially seeing; mentally retarded; intellectually gifted; emotionally and/or socially maladjusted; speech and orthopedically handicapped. Inspired by Christ's teaching and example, the Church has interested itself from early years in the care of such individuals through individuals or religious societies. (For an account of asylums established under church auspices for the care of the blind, see R. M. McGuinness, NCE 2:615–617). The earliest account of a systematic attempt to teach the deaf goes back to Venerable Bede who wrote of a cure by St. John of Beverly (d. 721), known as the first teacher of the deaf. A Spanish Benedictine monk, Pedro Ponce de León, in the 16th cent. was famous for oral education of the deaf. (See R. F. Panara, NCE 4:681–682.) In the same century attempts were made to devise methods of reading for the blind. St. Vincent de Paul's Daughters of Charity (17th cent.) in France, and other religious congregations since, have dedicated their services to the multiple-handicapped. The 19th cent. brought the introduction of formal education for the mentally defective. In the U.S., outstanding early Catholic institutions are Lavelle School for the Blind, Bronx, N.Y. (1904); St. Edmund's Home for Crippled Children, Rosemont, Pa. (1916); Cushing Hall, Boston, Mass., for the emotionally disturbed (1945); Tekakwitha Hills High School for Girls in Philadelphia, Pa., for the socially maladjusted (1850); and St. Coletta School for Exceptional Children (retarded) in Jefferson, Wisconsin (1904). BIBLIOGRAPHY: E. H. Behrmann, NCE 13:551–554; *Directory of Catholic Facilities for Exceptional Children* (1955).

[M . B . MURPHY]

SPECIES, EUCHARISTIC (from the Lat. *species*, the outward appearance). According to the defined dogma of Trent, after the consecration of the bread and wine Jesus Christ is truly, really, and substantially contained *sub specie*, i.e., under the appearance of those sensible things, the bread and wine; there is a conversion of the whole substance of the bread and wine into the substance of the Body of Christ. The conversion is called *transubstantiation; the species of the bread and wine are the appearances of bread and wine. The substance is the existing thing, and this changes; the species are the accidental properties of the substance that manifest it to sense and scientific experience. These remain. The word species is sometimes translated into English as ''form.'' BIBLIOGRAPHY: C. Vollert, ''Transubstantiation,'' NCE 14:259–261.

[E. A. WEIS]

SPECULATIVE THEOLOGY (from Lat. *speculari*, to spy out, observe), a type of theology characterized by its speculative, philosophical, or argumentative method that with the help of philosophy and everyday experience attempts to penetrate intellectually, to analyze scientifically, and to attain a deeper understanding of the findings of *positive theology concerning the deposit of faith or the divine (self-)revelation (*fides quaerens intellectum*). Two concrete forms of speculative theology are: meditation (i.e., a deep, continued, and comprehensive reflection on some specific topic) and conclusion (i.e., a rational a priori deduction from a philosophical principle or a dogma of faith or both). Analogy plays an extremely important role in speculative theology because a comparison of the mysteries of faith among themselves or with the elements of natural reality (i.e., things, qualities, laws, relationships) helps one to discover some similarity, proportion, interrelationship, connection, or order, and as a result of that to acquire a deeper understanding of the divine revelation and of its salvational significance for man. Thus speculative theology by methodical, systematic, and scientific study of its auxiliary sciences raises the simple understanding of the revealed truth of the faithful (*intellectus fidei*) to a scientifically developed and methodically synthesized level. Speculative theology originates from the intellectual and inquisitive quality of the human spirit and from contemporary cultural, philosophical, and religious trends. But it must rely upon positive theology as its foundation because both types of theology are integral parts of the one theological science. By establishing with the help of philosophy intelligible and orderly patterns of understanding of the divine revelation, speculative theology lays the groundwork for systematic theology and a possible theological synthesis of the revealed truth. BIBLIOGRAPHY: G. F. Van Ackeren, NCE 14:39–49; J. B. Metz, LTK 10:62–71; Y. M. J. Congar, *La Foi et la théologie* (1962); M. Schmaus, *Katholische Dogmatik* (6th ed., 1960) 1:46–51.

[P. B. T. BILANIUK]

SPECULUM HUMANAE SALVATIONIS (Mirror of Human Salvation), a 14th-cent. MS of important scenes in the life of Christ, with additional pictures from the OT and expository texts in Latin and German, which became a most important block book in the early 15th century.

[M. J. DALY]

SPECULUM VIRGINUM (Mirror of the Virgin), 12th-cent. book for the edification of young Christian women by Conrad of Hirsau, containing 12 chapters, each prefaced with a drawing. The earliest extant example is in the British Museum (Arundel 44), London. BIBLIOGRAPHY: A. Watson, ''The Speculum Virginum'' with Special Reference to the Tree of Jesse,'' *Speculum 3* (1928).

[M. J. DALY]

SPEDALIERI, NICOLA (1740–95), philosopher, political theorist. A Sicilian priest, S. taught for some years in the seminary at Monreale, Sicily, but withdrew to Rome to lead a scholar's life for 10 years in 1773 when he received a benefice at the Vatican basilica. Among his works were a treatise on the art of government (1779) and one on the influence of Christianity on civil society (1779). He wrote a

refutation of Gibbon's thesis that Christianity destroyed the Roman Empire *Confutazione . . . dal sig. E. Gibbon* (1784). S.'s chief work was *Dei diritti dell' uomo* (1791), a critique of the French Revolutionary proclamation of the rights of man. S. reiterated the doctrine of St. Thomas and Suárez that all political authority rests radically in the people and originates from God. The book created a storm of opposition from monarchists and the Cartesians. There is suspicion that S. was poisoned by his enemies.

[J. R. AHERNE]

SPEE, FRIEDRICH VON (1591–1635), German Jesuit, professor of moral theology, poet. He died of a fever contracted while nursing victims of the plague in Trier. His pastoral work among persons condemned for witchcraft inspired him to a courageous protest against the witch hysteria of the age, his *Cautio criminalis* (1631). His poems, written in German and already well known before his death, were published in two volumes in 1649, *Güldenes Tugend-Buch* and *Trutz-Nachtigall*. They are genuinely religious, often mystic, in tone and anticipate, to some extent, the nature poetry of the next century. Their style, though baroque, is free from artificial conventions and attentive to verse and word accent. BIBLIOGRAPHY: M. R. P. McGuire, NCE 13:558–559.

[M. F. MCCARTHY]

SPEECH, FREEDOM OF, see FREEDOM OF SPEECH.

SPEECH, INDECENT AND VULGAR. The standards measuring the coarse (vulgar) or unseemly (indecent) in language vary with time, place, and idiom. In any set of circumstances, however, some standard for what is acceptable in speech does exist. To offend against it disregards many virtuous proprieties that should regulate civilized social intercourse: the virtue of civility or courteousness towards others; of decorous moderation in manner and comportment (*modestia*); of sensitivity to moral beauty (*honestas*) and moral ugliness (*verecundia*). Such moral irregularities are not in themselves gravely sinful, but they are out of keeping with human dignity and esp. with Christian ideals. If they are connected with scandal or with a disordered sexual intent, in the case of indecent language, they may become serious (see OBSCENITY). Often use of bad language becomes almost a reflex, and while the acquiring of the reflex may have involved moral fault, the actual use of such language may be altogether inadvertent.

[T. C. O'BRIEN]

SPEER, ROBERT ELLIOTT (1867–1947), Presbyterian layman, secretary (1891–1937) of the Board of Foreign Missions of the Presbyterian Church in the U.S.A. (now United Presbyterian Church in the U.S.A.). He participated in the organization of the *International Missionary Council and in the conferences that led to the organization of the World Council of Churches. In 1927 he was elected *moderator of his denomination, and played a role as reconciler in the fundamentalist-modernist controversy. He was the author of numerous articles and more than 60 volumes, including *The Finality of Jesus Christ* (1933).

[J. H. SMYLIE]

SPELLMAN, FRANCIS JOSEPH (1889–1967), abp. of New York, cardinal, diplomat. A native of Whitman, Mass., he was ordained (1916) in Rome. By 1925 he was attached to the Vatican secretariate of state where he was to know well the future Pius XII. When Pius XI made the first worldwide radio address in 1931, S. followed on the air with the English translation. An episode that made him world-famous was his smuggling of the encyclical of Pius XI against fascism out of Rome to Paris where it was published. Consecrated auxiliary bp. of Boston in 1932, he served in the archdiocese for 7 years when the newly elected Pius XII named him abp. of New York. In that position he was to exercise a public role similar to that of Card. Gibbons in Baltimore. Closely associated with and an adviser of Franklin D. Roosevelt, S. helped guide the course that led to the appointment of a U.S. representative to the Vatican. He was frequently called to the White House and Hyde Park for consultation with the dynamic President. They were cordial friends, although some of the decisions agreed to at Yalta caused S. to question the ailing Roosevelt's wisdom. During World War II and the years that followed, his dedication as military vicar of the Armed Forces carried him across the world many times. Named a cardinal (1946), S. continued his work as a shrewd administrator of his archdiocese and a man prominent in national affairs. His indefatigable devotion to Americans in military service continued to bring him each year to the time of his death to installations on every continent. Often a controversial figure, he maintained a consistent goodwill through a crowded and productive lifetime. BIBLIOGRAPHY: R. I. Gannon, *Cardinal Spellman Story* (1962).

[J . R . AHERNE]

SPENCER, FRANCIS ALOYSIUS (1845–1913), Scripture scholar. A convert to Catholicism, S. became a Paulist and later a Dominican. He held several administrative posts in the order and was elected provincial (1880) of St. Joseph's Province. His translation of the NT from Greek was published posthumously (1937).

[T. M. MCFADDEN]

SPENCER, HERBERT (1820–1903), English philosopher and author. Largely self-educated in science, S. served as teacher, engineer, and journalist before writing his ''Synthetic Philosophy.'' He projected the latter as a master synthesis uniting the general truths of the specialized sciences. His central tenet is a theory of universal evolution as expressed in *The Development Hypothesis* (1852), prior to Darwin's *Origin of Species*. His 20 volumes sought to apply evolution to science universally, but his primary interest lay

in its reference to ethics. S. desired to establish a scientific basis for moral conduct, using evidence supplied by fields such as psychology and sociology. He theorized that to survive, man had developed certain instinctual accommodations to his surroundings: what was conducive to the preservation of life came to be accepted as morally good; what pointed to death, as morally evil. While egoism overcomes altruism in man's early moral formation, an inborn moral sense guides him to an ideal balance, based on mutual sympathy for the aims of all. S. maintained that the goal of all ethical conduct is a society of permanent peace composed of perfect and happy humans. His view is hedonistic in that it presents immediate pleasure as consistent with ultimate happiness. God exists as an unknowable Absolute behind all phenomena, but man's moral relation to him is unclear. S. optimistically foresees the eventual emergence of a single moral code, a common creed, and an eternity of life. For detailed treatment see *First Principles* (1860–62) and *Principles of Ethics* (1879–93).

[J. T. HICKEY]

SPENCER, STANLEY, SIR (1891–1959), English painter. Student at the Slade School of Art, London, who painted religious panels depicting distorted massive figures set in his native village, Cookham, Berkshire, effecting a mystical atmosphere. S. painted murals, *Resurrection of the Soldiers* (1926–32) for a chapel at Burghclere, Berkshire. *Christ Carrying the Cross* (1920), *Resurrection* (1927) and *Resurrection* (1950) are at the Tate gallery, London. His late work moved toward a savage symbolism.

[M. J. DALY]

SPENER, PHILIPP JAKOB (1635–1705), German Lutheran theologian, father of *Pietism. S. studied at Strassburg and was profoundly influenced by the doctrines of M. *Bucer and John *Calvin. He became superintendent of Strassburg in 1663 and of Frankfurt in 1666. In the latter city he introduced new practices, such as confirmation and catechetical instruction. Following an idea of Bucer, he gathered a group of parishioners who held devotional meetings twice weekly in his home. These *collegia pietatis* were the origin of the name and ideas of Pietism. His *Pia desideria* (1675; Eng. tr. T. G. Tappert, 1964) called for thorough Bible study; awareness of the priesthood of all believers; prayer and exemplary conduct; moral, religious, and practical guidance of seminarians; edifying rather than learned sermons; and study of the mystics. Because his clergy objected to his activities, he was happy to accept a post in Dresden in 1686 as chief court chaplain. In 1691 he went to Berlin as provost and consistorial councilor of St. Nicholas Church. He was influential in the founding of the Univ. of Halle, which soon became the center of Pietism. About 7 years before his death S. withdrew from the controversies provoked by Pietist deemphasis of dogma and devoted himself to purely pastoral work.

[M. J. SUELZER]

SPENGLER, OSWALD (1880–1936), philosopher of history. An extraordinary student of the history of man from the Greeks to modern Germany, S. represents a unique view of the story of civilized man and his cultures. A scholar who lived a precarious economic existence, he is known for one highly influential but flawed work, *Der Untergang des Abendlandes* (*Decline of the West*; 2 v., 1918). There is no question that the overtones of pessimism in the study were colorations from the disaster of German defeat in World War I. It seems indisputable that S.'s writings provided an intellectual basis for both the hero-worship and anti-Semitism of Nazi Germany. He died in 1936, embittered by the failure to recognize his substantial contribution to the philosophy of history. His thesis calls for rejection of both the ancient-medieval-modern arrangement and the linear interpretation of history, popular in his time. History, as he views it, calls for a morphological approach; a culture (the orientation of a group of people who have a common approach to their world in art, religion, philosophy, politics and economics) grows, matures, and dies like a plant. The concept of space in which they live is the prime symbol of a culture. Classical man views himself as living in a local limited space. Art, architecture, the city-state fit this pattern which he calls Apollinian. The Faustian concept of Western man is expansionist, reflected in Gothic architecture, Christianity, and Western painting and music. Egyptian culture is narrow and one-dimensional; Russians (non-Western) have a flat-plane culture; Arab culture (called Magian) is filled with the sense of mystery. S. denies that one culture can ever influence or be influenced by another. S. compares the development of cultures to seasonal cycles. An early heroic period largely agricultural constitutes their spring. Summer is an age of towns, of great individual artists such as Shakespeare and Michelangelo, a time of the uncorrupted intellect. Autumn brings cities, commerce, centralized monarchies, and a rationalism that challenges religion. Winter is the epoch of the huge cities, the proletariat, skepticism, and materialism; it is an age of imperialism, tyranny, and incessant warfare. In Western Europe the 20th cent., which he compares to Julius Caesar's Rome, marks the winter of the Faustian culture.

Criticism of S.'s theory rightly charges him with forcing history to suit his thesis. The scientific bases of his theory are at best incomplete and at worst unproved. His defenders have claimed that the Spenglerian hypothesis is a poetic vision rather than a philosophy of history. It would be difficult, however, not to deny his positivistic prejudice and ignoring of human causality. This essential flaw in his theory, however, is the claim that one culture cannot understand another—a claim that nullifies his own efforts. BIBLIOGRAPHY: W. Dray, EncPhil 7–8:527–530.

[J. R. AHERNE]

SPERANDEA, ST. (*c.*1216–76), Italian Benedictine nun. Noted for rigid observance of the ascetic life, she traversed central Italy for 10 years preaching penance. After restoring the Benedictine convent of St. Michael at Cingoli in 1265, she served as its abbess. Shortly after her death she became patron saint of Cingoli. BIBLIOGRAPHY: AS September 3:890–903; Zimmerman 3:42–45; I. Mannocci, BiblSanct 11:1345–46.

[F. D. LAZENBY]

SPEUSIPPUS (d. *c.*339 B.C.), nephew of Plato and first scholarch of the Academy (347–339). Our knowledge of his doctrine depends on passing allusions in Aristotle and on isolated quotations or references in later authors. He seems to have substituted numbers for Plato's forms and to have considered reality as made up of separate systems of numbers, magnitudes, and soul. However, he does not explain their interrelationship. He is most original in maintaining that there is a One beyond being and higher than being, but not to be identified with the Good. He was the first to make a distinction between a twofold One, a higher and a lower. His notion of the One beyond being is one of the basic sources for Neoplatonism. BIBLIOGRAPHY: Copleston 1:263–264; P. Merlan in CHGMP 30–32.

[M. R. P. MCGUIRE]

SPEYER, DIETS OF, three meetings of the imperial Diet convoked by Charles V at Speyer, in W Germany, important to Reformation history. (1) The Diet of June 1526 helped the growth of the Reformation by setting aside enforcement of the Edict of Worms (1521; see WORMS, DIET OF) and allowing rulers to control religious affairs in their territories according to their own consciences. (2) The Diet of Feb. 1529 marked the beginning of the use of the name "Protestant," as a minority entered a "protest" against majority legislation revoking toleration to Lutherans in Catholic territories. (3) The Diet of Jan. 1544 made concessions to the Schmalkaldic League and a promise that religious questions would in future be solved, not in Rome, but in a "free Christian council of the German nation." Pope Paul III severely criticized this last provision. BIBLIOGRAPHY: G. R. Elton, *Reformation in Europe 1517–1559* (pa., 1966); Jedin Trent 1:247–248, 494–499.

[P. DAMBORIENA]

SPG, see SOCIETY FOR THE PROPAGATION OF THE GOSPEL.

SPIEGEL, FERDINAND AUGUST (1764–1835), abp. of Cologne. Early adherent of the 18th-cent. Enlightenment, S. became a priest in 1799. In 1813 Napoleon named him bp. of Münster. He served as adviser to von Hardenberg at the Congress of Vienna, where he championed the freedom of the hierarchy from the State. Briefly an advocate of the national-church group led by von Wesenberg, S. abandoned the movement as a defender of episcopal independence from civil authority. Though he was appointed by the government as abp. of Cologne in 1821, S. refused to accept the post until confirmed by the Holy See and assured of independence in 1824. His administration of the archdiocese gave it new life. S. was opposed to state policy on mixed marriages and only because he was led to believe that the brief of Pope Pius VIII of 1830 sanctioned it did he sign the Berlin Convention of 1834, permitting solemnization of mixed marriages in church without the guarantee of Catholic upbringing of children. Through S. the independence of the Church in West Prussia was a fact long before recognized by law.

[J. R. AHERNE]

SPINA, ALFONSO DE, Spanish Franciscan preacher and scholar. A Jewish convert to Catholicism, he was the author of a polemic against Jews, Muslims, and other "enemies of the Christian faith," known as the *Fortalitium fidei*. It probably appeared *c.*1458 and was very popular through the 16th cent. but is now an embarrassing anachronism. Not much is known about the author. He originated in Valladolid, studied at Salamanca, and served as superior of the Friars Minor house of studies there. He was named bp. of Thermopylae in Greece *c.*1491 and must have died shortly thereafter.

[E. J. DILLON]

SPINA, BARTOLOMEO (*c.*1480–1546), Dominican theologian, master of the sacred palace from 1544 under Paul III. At Rome he was a member of the papal commission appointed to prepare the theological agenda for the doctrinal discussions at the Council of Trent. A learned but irascible man, he offered a strongly partisan opposition to Franciscan promotion of the inclusion of the doctrine of Mary's Immaculate Conception in the conciliar decree on original sin. To that end he had reissued an anti-Immaculatist treatise written by J. de *Torquemada a century earlier at the Council of Basel. S.'s edition, distorting the original at many points, led to controversy with A. *Catharinus, a Dominican Immaculatist. The two in fact were old antagonists, since, when Catharinus had been appointed bp. in 1542, S. had drawn up a list of 50 errors taken from his confrère's works and sent them to Paul III. Catharinus successfully replied to the charges.

[T . C . O'BRIEN]

SPINA, GIUSEPPE (1756–1838), diplomat, cardinal. An Italian lawyer in the service of the Holy See, S. was ordained in 1796 and named a titular abp. in 1799. He prepared the way for the Concordat with France adopted in 1801 and was created cardinal and abp. of Genoa in 1802. When the States of the Church were restored in 1819, S. resigned as abp. of Genoa, served as papal legate to Bologna from 1818 to 1824 and represented the Vatican at the Congresses of Laibach in 1821 and Verona in 1822. S. was an opponent of Austrian ambitions in Italy.

[J. R. AHERNE]

SPINELLO ARETINO (Spinello di Luca; *c.*1346–1410), Italian Florentine painter. A native of Arezzo, pupil of A.

Gaddi, he was influenced by A. Orcagna and Nardo di Cione. S. painted an altarpiece for Monte Oliveto (1385; dispersed), and cycles of frescoes in S. Miniato al Monte, Florence (1386–87), Camposanto, Pisa (1391–92) and in the Palazzo Pubblico, Siena (1408–10), *Pope Alexander III and Frederick Barbarossa*), with some murals in S. Francesca, Arezzo. He is one of the finest of late Giottesque painters in freshness and vigor of style.

[M. J. DALY]

SPÍNOLA, CHRISTÓBAL ROJAS DE (1626–95), bishop. A Spaniard educated in Germany, S. entered the Franciscans and was elected provincial in Spain. In 1661 he became advisor to Emperor Leopold I in Vienna. Appointed bp. of Knin in 1668 and of Wiener-Neustadt in 1686, S. was a vigorous champion of efforts to unite Protestants and Catholics. A plan of reunion submitted to a meeting of Protestant theologians in 1683 was approved by them, but French opposition and S.'s concessions prevented Pope Innocent XI from approving. In 1691 the Emperor named S. commissary general for reunion in Austria-Hungary. His concessions, though acceptable in today's Church, were turned down by the Holy See.

[J. R. AHERNE]

SPINOZA, BENEDICT (BARUCH; 1632–71), Dutch rationalist philosopher. A descendant of Spanish Jews who had fled the Inquisition to seek the greater religious freedom of the Netherlands, S. began Talmudic studies early under a rabbi who favored the rationalistic exegesis of Maimonides, and who introduced him as well to the Cabala and to Crescas. Although he knew the works of Giordano Bruno and had some acquaintance with scholastic thought, chiefly through manuals, the dominant influence in his formation was Descartes. S.'s independence of mind and heterodox views of God led to his formal excommunication by the synagogue of Amsterdam in 1656. He had many Christian friends, esp. among the Mennonites, but never joined a Christian sect. His early death from tuberculosis was perhaps hastened by his labors as a lens-grinder.

S.'s writings, esp. his *Ethics*, are an effort to develop with a rigor like that of mathematics (*more geometrico*) a completely integrated rationalistic metaphysics founded on Descartes' "clear idea" of substance. It is his triumph and his failure that he followed rigorously the logical consequences of the principle to their conclusion in pantheism. He admitted no conflict, for there is no point of contact between the Scriptures and philosophy in attaining the truth. The Scriptures demand of the believer the affirmation of God's existence and the practice of justice and charity. All other truth, speculative or practical, is the realm of philosophy.

From Descartes' definition of substance as that which needs nothing else for its existence, S. establishes first of all that substance exists necessarily, that it is infinite, and that it is unique. This is God or Nature (*Deus sive natura*); the *sive* denotes equivalence. S. gives no proof of God's existence nor requires any, for the clear idea of substance as necessarily existing establishes this (a variant of the Anselmian argument). As infinite, God is constituted by an infinity of attributes, of which only two are known to us: thought and extension. But, for S. as for Descartes, our world is constituted by thought and extension. In God (*natura naturans*) they are attributes; in the world (*natura naturata*) they are modes which show forth the attributes. The modes evolve from God by a series of intermediate emanations, a position which evokes Plotinus. S. calls this process creation, but it is a necessary action, not a free one. God is eminently, even supereminently, free, but the world cannot be other than it is, for if it were God would not be immutable and, therefore, would not be perfect.

In his view of man, S. rejects the body-soul dualism of Descartes. The modes of thought and extension evolve in parallel, and thus the individual soul and body are but manifestations of the one substance. S. thus met the difficulty that Malebranche answered by occasionalism and Leibniz by "pre-established harmony." Man cannot be free under the inexorable evolution, but S. constructs a moral system which, in the nature of the case, is descriptive, not normative. Virtuous men are those who know true values and practice them. Will and intellect are not two faculties, but two aspects of the one mode: thought. The happy man is one who, through clear and distinct ideas, achieves an intuition of the eternal truths and comes to an intellectual love of God. Here, S. holds for a sort of personal immortality. So for the wise and the good. Other men have inadequate ideas, which beget passions, which lead in turn to sorrow and thus unhappiness. In the social order, these latter are guided by the good and wise to the ends of order and public peace.

S.'s system stands or falls as a whole. He faced unflinchingly the consequences of his rationalist premises—even to pantheism. He is not a pantheist in the Eastern sense, nor an atheist in any sense. The Jewish heritage is strong in him and Novalis' description fits him best, "the God-intoxicated man." BIBLIOGRAPHY: H. A. Wolfson, *Philosophy of Spinoza* (1958); A. MacIntyre, EncPhil 7:530–541.

[W. B. MAHONEY]

SPIRATION, a term (from *spirare* to breathe) coined to describe the mode of origin of the Holy Spirit in the Trinity. Unlike the Son's origin from the Father, (Jn ch. 1) the mode of origin of the Holy Spirit does not have description in the NT convenient for theological elaboration. Spiration by way of analogy with the Son's proceeding as Word is explained as a procession in love. Faith holds that the Spirit does not originate by way of generation; it does not determine further the mode of his mysterious procession. The order of origin of the Spirit is however specified by the faith, even though this is conceived differently by the Eastern and the Western traditions. Whether the Spirit proceeds from the Father through the Son or from the Father and the Son as from one principle (cf. Denz 1300–01), one thing is certain and agreed upon by both traditions, though differently expressed

by each: the Spirit is last in the order of origin, for not only the Father's personal action but the Son's as well contributes to his divine origin. The NT speaks of the Spirit as issuing from the Father (Jn 15.26), a term, it must be noticed, that refers to the sending of the Spirit into the world rather than to his eternal procession. The glorified Christ, too, sends the Spirit from the Father (Jn 15.26). Both Persons exercise their influence on the mission of the Spirit because both contribute, even though differently, to his eternal procession. The Father breathes forth the Spirit as last origin of all things in God. The Son receives from the Father all he is, including his influence in the eternal origin of the Spirit. BIBLIOGRAPHY: R. L. Richard, NCE 14:295–306.

[J . DUPUIS]

SPIRIT, HOLY, in general an image for certain divine actions in creation. The holy spirit of God is a powerful and frequent image in the mind of the OT writers who knew and often experienced the mysterious and terrifying wind of the Palestinian desert. This terrifying wind was the breath of Yahweh, the vital force of all creation. The spirit or *ruah* of God hovers over the waters of creation (Gen 1.2). God breathes his *ruah* into the nostrils of man and man lives. The vital force of all creation is the spirit of God, his breath, his wind, his power. The *ruah* of God takes hold of Samson (Jgs 13.25), Gideon (Jgs 6.34), and David (1 Sm 16.13). It is the same spirit of God that inspires the Prophets (Is 61.1). The concept of the spirit of God pervades the OT. It is the power by which God manifests his presence to men, a power both mysterious and terrifying like the desert winds of Palestine.

Although the spirit of Yahweh is described in the OT as outside him, it is his self-extension. The *ruah* Yahweh is essentially the seat of feelings and intelligence—Yahweh's intelligence manifesting his will to men. With the few exceptions of God's creative spirit working in nature, the *ruah* Yahweh is a moral and intellectual force touching the hearts and minds of men. It is the spirit of God that moves men to knowledge and fear of Yahweh; that mediates the covenants through his prophet; and that moves men to do God's will. Sometimes in the OT the spirit of God is personified. However, never is the spirit of God presented in the OT as a spiritual and intellectual personality apart from Yahweh Elohim.

With regard to the spirit of God in the NT, it can be said that the *pneūma hagion* or Holy Spirit is used in the same way as it is in the OT. In the Synoptic Gospels and the Acts there is no reference to the Holy Spirit as a separate Person with the exception of Mt 28.19. Also it should be pointed out that nowhere in Scripture is the name of God given to the Holy Spirit nor does Scripture speak of the Holy Spirit as eternal.

The personality of the Holy Spirit as a specific Person comes through more clearly in the writings of St. Paul. In Paul the Holy Spirit takes his place with Christ in sanctifying the Church. The Holy Spirit is presented as an active person who pours the love of God into the hearts of men (Rom 5.5). The body is the temple and dwelling place of the Holy Spirit (Phil 3.2). Paul speaks of justification through Christ (Gal 2.17) and justification through the Spirit (1 Cor 6.11). Sometimes the distinction between Christ and the Holy Spirit is not clear in Paul.

St. John is the clearest in his reference to the Spirit as a Person. After the Ascension the Holy Spirit is another sanctifier who takes the place of Christ as teacher in the Church (Jn 14.26; 16.12). The Holy Spirit calls to mind what Jesus had already taught (Jn 14.26).

A certain ambiguity remains, however, in the NT references to the Holy Spirit. He is not called God nor is he referred to as eternal. It was left to later generations of Christians to clarify the personality of the Holy Spirit. Under the influence of the Greek Fathers in conflict with early heresies of Modalism and Macedonianism, the Christian teaching concerning the threefold personalities within the Holy Trinity takes more precise shape. BIBLIOGRAPHY: B. Piault, *What is the Trinity?* (tr. R. Haughton, 1959); L. Dewart, *Future of Belief* (1966); J. Macquarrie, *Principles of Christian Theology* (1966) 294–312.

[W. J. DUGGAN]

SPIRITISM, a neologism coined by A. *Kardec as a title for his religious system.

SPIRITS, DISCERNMENT OF, see DISCERNMENT OF SPIRITS.

SPIRITUAL CHILDHOOD, the spirituality of simplicity and self-surrender to the loving Father typified by St. Thérèse of Lisieux, the Little Flower (Thérèse of the Child Jesus). Her life was esp. marked by the gift of *piety; her spirituality draws attention to the essential meaning of the life of grace as an attitude of child to Father, since grace means adoptive sonship patterned after the sonship of Jesus.

SPIRITUAL COMBAT, title of a wk. by the enigmatic Theatine, L. *Scupoli, a classic on the Christian spiritual life. The work was first published anonymously in 1589, then under the author's name in 1610, the year of his death. The original consisted of 24 chapters, but they were expanded in various versions of the work by other writers, not always happily. Scupoli's work is a perceptive description of the ascesis of the will and other faculties necessary for intimate union with God. The Italian *Spiritual Combat* was constantly read and recommended by St. Francis de Sales (see *Devout Life* pt. 2, ch. 17) who turned it into French. It has appeared in many tongues; in English, 1944 rev. of J. Murphy's ed. (n.d.) which includes also Scupoli's *The Peace of the Soul and the Happiness of the Heart*. Other American editions were in 1945 and 1952.

[T. C. O'BRIEN]

SPIRITUAL COMMUNION, a private eucharistic devotion; a prayer to receive Christ spiritually in a way analogous to receiving him sacramentally. The devotion represents a kind of holy communion by desire when sacramental communion is not possible, e.g., it can normally be received only once a day. The devotion was more common in an earlier era when reception of the sacrament and eucharistic devotion generally were more objectified than contemporary (and ancient) understanding of sacraments and liturgy views them. The reform of the liturgy has emphasized the act of holy communion itself as integral to the dynamic liturgical celebration that expresses the active presence of Christ, the communion of his members with him and with one another in the bond of charity, and the whole mystical body's worship of the Father. The Eucharist remains in its abiding effect as a source of the continuous presence of its meaning in the life of the faithful. Further, the Eucharist, like all the sacraments, presupposes the contact or communion of living faith by which Christ's members are joined to their head. These truths make the old understanding of spiritual communion as a private devotion seem superfluous and a distraction from the full significance of the Eucharist. BIBLIOGRAPHY: *Rites of the Catholic Church* (Eng. tr. by the International Commission on English in the Liturgy, 1976) "Holy Communion and Worship of the Eucharist outside of Mass," n. 6.

[T. C. O'BRIEN]

SPIRITUAL DIRECTION, in contemporary understanding this should be classified and spoken of as a form of ministry by which one person guides another in the way of evangelical perfection. The Catholic concept of ministry has been enriched immeasurably since Vatican Council II, so that every form of service within the Church is an expression of the Church's own mission to sanctify and to serve. The multiformed ministries in the Church are radically exercised in virtue of baptism, which makes the People of God a priestly and witnessing community. Particularly critical in the renewed understanding of ministry is the recognition of charisms, the diversity of gifts that exists in and builds up the community of faith and love (VatII ConstCh 7, 12, 32, 34, 40–42). The need for the ministry of spiritual direction is more urgent because, since the Council's affirmation of the universal call to holiness in the Church (*ibid*. 39–42) there is a manifest intensification of spirituality. That call to holiness rests on the faithful's incorporation into Christ; holiness is the forming of Christ in his followers. The very existence of the community called to such holiness creates the sure expectation that within the community there will be gifts of ministry as resources enabling the members to respond to the call.

That supposition simply states in Vatican II's ecclesiological terms a reality in the Church's life since its earliest days. Early on there were "fathers" in the Church, mentors for those who would live a more intense Christian life. The Fathers of the desert were responsible for the beginnings of monasticism as those eager to grow in holiness sought out and put themselves under the guidance of holy men. The ideal of St. Benedict was that the abbot should be spiritual father to his monks. The whole subsequent progress of religious life included the founders' and their saintly followers' development of programs for spiritual formation. The idea of a spiritual director for individual souls, however, became a more explicit element of Christian spirituality through the dissemination of St. Ignatius of Loyola's *Spiritual Exercises*. St. Teresa of Avila emphasized the need that confessors be sound theologians. The call to holiness for the laity and direction in its pursuit are particularly associated with the life and writings of St. *Francis de Sales. From the 18th cent. on the function of the spiritual director became more and more programmed, and the office of spiritual director institutionalized in seminaries.

In the Post-Reformation evolution of spiritual theology it must be recognized that there was a diminution of the theological and ecclesial character of personal holiness. The structure of programs of spirituality, and so of spiritual direction, were conceived and structured in ways that were somewhat individualized; the world of holiness, devotion, prayer, and asceticism was in many ways separated from the liturgical life of the Church. Often the primacy of grace and charity in their full theological force was conventionally acknowledged, but in fact superseded by the elements distinctive of one or another "school of spirituality." The character of Christian holiness by reason of Vatican II has been again perceived as ecclesial, integrated, that is, with what constitutes the Church—the Word of God and the sacraments. The spiritual life is again seen as inherently linked to the Bible, the liturgical and sacramental life, and to the communitarian nature of the Church with its openness to the diverse gifts given for the building up of all its members. Spiritual direction has its meaning determined by these essentials of Christian life and holiness.

"Discernment" is the term that captures the need for and the essence of spiritual direction. The word has the connotation of the long-used meaning of the "discernment of spirits"—a recognition and evaluation of special gifts and spiritual qualities; but discernment in current usage has a broader meaning—it is a perception of the theological identity and direction of a person or of a community. Discernment is judgment of how to respond to the call to holiness. The first spiritual director, the one who aids in such discernment, for every Christian and for the Christian community is the Holy Spirit, who is the Spirit of Christ. The force of that truth has been very simply put by St. Thomas Aquinas: the essential power of the New Law is the grace of the Holy Spirit given through faith in Christ (ThAq ST 1a2ae, 106.1). The Holy Spirit moving through grace is the one who literally bends and guides (cf. Sequence for Pentecost, *flecte quod est rigidum, rege quod est devium*) toward whatever is consonant with the identity of the child of the Father—"For as many as are led by the Spirit of God, they are the sons of God. For we have not received the spirit of

bondage again to fear, but . . . the Spirit of adoption whereby we cry *Abba, Father*. The Spirit himself bears witness with our spirit that we are the children of God" (Rom 8.15–18; cf. 26–30). The source of living the Christian life, therefore of responding to the call to holiness, is not, radically, a plan or program to be consulted; it is not a law, or another human being. The source is the inner capacity, the bent, and the sensitivity for responding to what saves and sanctifies. The way in which responsiveness is shaped and expresses itself is channelized by the paths towards which charity and the other virtues incline. They are the *pondus amoris*, love's weighting of will and appetites, that enable a person to discern what is right, what is to be done (ThAq ST 1a2ae, 106.1 ad 2; 107.1 ad 2; 108.1 & ad 2). The continually formative and at once expressive milieu favorable to the direction of the grace of the Spirit within is the liturgy in which the Word of God is proclaimed and the mystery of Christ's multiformed presence is a reality (see *Rites*, "Holy Communion and Worship of the Eucharist outside of Mass," n. 6).

Spiritual direction before all else derives from these realities. Each person's discernment and empowerment for living the life of the gospel has the further support of the gifts of the Holy Spirit. They lead to an inner perceptiveness and impetus towards the ways of sanctification needed in times of crisis. In the assurance of the graces of the Spirit, no one will fail in what is necessary for salvation (ThAq ST 2a2ae, 8.4 ad 1).

Why then a spiritual director? The answer is that the way of salvation is incarnational. Christ saved *humano modo*. It is altogether consonant with that truth that gifts be given in the community of Christ that match the human pattern of his saving. The wisdom and experience of some are to be expected for the building up of others. The human pattern also includes the truth that God has "left man in the hands of his own counsel" (Sir 15.14). But the counsel of each needs to include taking counsel from others. The basis and the meaning of spiritual direction as rooted in the presence of the Holy Spirit given by grace are keys to what spiritual direction entails. The discernment of the director must correspond to the power of discernment given by the Holy Spirit. That means that spiritual direction must be theological in two senses: because it is based on theological learning; but theological also because it is addressed to the primacy of the theological virtues. These are in the "client" of the spiritual director the essential resources for a sense of identity as the child of the Father and the direction toward whatever, concretely, expresses and ratifies that identity. Both senses of theological direction can only be effectively present when the spiritual director exercises discernment on the basis of sharing in the attunement of grace.

The discernment of the director must also be charismatic. The term is not restricted to the way it is applied to the Catholic charismatic renewal or Neo-Penteostal movement. Rather it means that ministry in the Church is based on gifts given for the life of the community. The new appreciation of that reality brings with it an awareness that spiritual direction, counsel, discernment can come from many sides. There is a growing exercise of the ministry of spiritual direction by those not ordained in the Church. There should be an expectation that spiritual direction can come from the Church community as such. The sense of spiritual direction as charismatic discernment applies to both the counsel given and its purpose. The spiritual director has need to rely on the Spirit for the gift of being perceptive here and now. The designation or choice of a spiritual director has to be based on recognition that charismatic gifts are needed for this ministry. Discernment is of a kind prepared to recognize in the individual the possibility or the actuality of special gifts for the life of the Church. The expectation must always be that the spiritual direction is part of that life, that the person seeking to live a life of holiness does so within the vocation given by baptism and for the sake of the mission of the Church.

[T. C. O'BRIEN]

SPIRITUAL DRYNESS, see ARIDITY.

SPIRITUAL EXERCISES, as a proper name, the spiritual masterpiece of St. *Ignatius of Loyola, the handbook of his distinctive spirituality; as a common noun, literal tr. of *exercitia spiritualia*, a retreat, whether made according to the Ignatian model or not. The two uses are connected because of the strong Jesuit emphasis on making retreats. The term exercises refers to the programmed drill or practice of specific meditations and prayers. Ignatius gradually composed the *Spiritual Exercises* from notes, quotations from spiritual writers, and reflections on his own spiritual experiences. He probably had a completed version, written in Spanish, by 1534. Most modern versions are based on a Lat. text printed in 1548, designated the *vulgata* (Eng. tr. T. Corbishley, 1963). The *Exercises* are designed for use under the guidance of a director, thus literally a "retreat master," and to be adapted to the personal needs of the retreatant or other user. (On the specific program of the *Exercises*, see IGNATIAN SPIRITUALITY.) Because of the plan and influence of the Jesuit retreat, until recently retreats were structured with a basic program of conferences, meditations, and personal consultation. More recently, however, retreats have been marked by more spontaneity and dialogue, with individual consultation taking the place of formal conferences.

[T. C. O'BRIEN]

SPIRITUAL REGULATION (Peter the Great, 1721), one of the many radical reforms enacted by Peter the Great of Russia, in this case at the expense of the Orthodox Church which was hostile to many of his reforms. The regulation deprived Orthodoxy of its last bit of freedom and independence from the State, reducing it to an administrative arm of the government. The legislation, an offshoot of German Protestant ecclesiastical thought, was inspired and drafted by one of Peter's most trusted advisers, Feofan Prokopovich (1681–1736), abp. of Novgorod. The measure abolished the patriarchate, which was not revived until 1917 under the Bolsheviks, and replaced it with the Holy Synod, a collegial body whose 12 members were appointed by the tsar and presided over by a civil procurator. The reform met divided resistance from the clergy, and was most vociferously opposed by the Old Believers who considered Peter the Great antichrist.

[D. DIRSCHERL]

SPIRITUAL SENSE OF SCRIPTURE, a meaning that, over and above the meaning of the words (the *literal sense), the actual realities signified by those words convey. God, the divine author of Scripture, can imbue these realities with a significance beyond that expressed in the literal sense, and it is this that is known as the mystical or spiritual sense (see SENSES OF SCRIPTURE). Thus Isaac is held by Paul to be a type of the gentile community (Rom 9.7; 4.28–31). This is a typical sense, the most important of the three subdivisions of the spiritual sense. The other two are the anagogic sense, according to which the things, persons, institutions, or events recorded in the Bible are interpreted as types of heavenly realities in the future; and the moral or tropological sense, in which they are taken to contain a moral lesson and guide to right conduct.

[D. J. BOURKE]

SPIRITUAL THEOLOGY, the branch of theology concerned with the nature of Christian perfection, the elements of the spiritual life, and the stages or degrees of its development from the beginning to the height of perfection. This branch of theology has been known by various names: ascetical and mystical theology (G. B. Scaramelli; P. Parente; A. Tanquerey); theology of Christian perfection (A. Royo); spiritual theology (J. Heerinckx; J. Aumann); spiritual life (J. Schrijvers; A. Tanquerey); interior life (A. Meynard); devout life (St. Francis de Sales); supernatural life (C. de Smedt); spirituality (P. Pourrat; M. Viller). Although there is no agreement among the authors who use the term ascetical and mystical theology, these adjectives usually refer to the phase which extends from second conversion to the beginning of passive purgation and infused contemplation (ascetical) and the phase which extends from that point to confirmation in grace and transforming union (mystical). Since the writings of Scaramelli appeared in the 17th cent., among the various questions discussed and disputed among the theologians of the spiritual life are the following: Are all Christians called to the perfection of charity, which is the essence of Christian sanctity? Is perfection the same for all Christians or is there an ascetical perfection which terminates in the excellence of the virtues working through ordinary grace and a mystical perfection which is a *gratia gratis data* and therefore an extraordinary grace? What constitutes the mystical act and the mystical state? Are all saints mystics? Is contemplation identified with mysticism? Are all souls called to infused contemplation? Do the gifts of the Holy Spirit constitute the mystical act and state and, if so, do they always produce infused contemplation?

Spiritual theology depends on dogmatic theology for the truths about God which immediately relate to man's life of grace and glory: the indwelling of the Trinity in the souls of the just; redemption by Christ; grace of headship in Christ, who is dispenser of all grace; the theology of the sacraments, and so forth. Even more intimately is spiritual theology related to *moral theology, which treats of man's ultimate end and the means which lead to it. It differs from moral theology by being more experimental and descriptive, since it applies the general and speculative principles of moral theology to the precise question of the spiritual perfection of the individual. Thus, De Guibert defines spiritual theology as "the science which deduces from revealed principles the nature of the perfection of the spiritual life and the means of attaining it" cf. Theology of the Spiritual Life (tr. P. Barrett, 1953, n.9). Since it is experimental and descriptive as well as speculative, spiritual theology likewise draws upon the testimony of the saints and mystics who have reached the perfection of the Christian life.

As a branch of theology which contains much that is practical and experimental, spiritual theology must be both speculative and practical, deductive and inductive. Too exclusive a use of the descriptive method would reduce spiritual theology to religious psychology; it would also give undue importance to phenomenology. Too much emphasis on the speculative approach, on the other hand, would lead to an a priori theology of the spiritual life and this could result in a contradiction between theory and practice. Therefore, the proper method of studying spiritual theology would seem to consist in a study of the pertinent dogmatic and moral truths found in revelation and speculative theology, a deduction from these truths to the nature of Christian perfection and the laws which govern the growth of a soul from the beginning to the terminus of perfection, and finally a verification of these conclusions as found in the testimony of the saints and mystics who have described their own experiences.

The sources to be used for the study of spiritual theology are theological and experimental. Under the theological sources the following can be listed: Sacred Scripture, tradition and magisterium of the Church, dogmatic and moral theology, autobiographical writings of saints and mystics, hagiography, and the history of spirituality. The experimental sources include the following: religious psychology, normal and abnormal psychology, and personal experience.

The division of the study of spiritual theology varies with different authors. Some divide the material on the basis of the three traditional ways: purgative, illuminative, and unitive (A. Saudreau; J. G. Arintero; A. Tanquerey). Those who defend the doctrine of the two distinct types of perfection usually treat of the three stages in both the ascetical and mystical phases (Scaramelli, Naval). St. Teresa of Avila treats of the spiritual life and its growth from the practice of prayer and St. John of the Cross uses the active and passive purgations as his basis. Others avoid a chronological presentation and divide the matter according to more strictly theological titles (R. Garrigou-Lagrange, J. de Guibert, J. Schrijvers). Among more recent theologians there is a tendency to divide spiritual theology into general spiritual theology (doctrinal principles) and special spiritual theology (special questions and applications) or to treat first of the theological principles, then the nature and means of Christian perfection, and finally the phenomena of the mystical state. BIBLIOGRAPHY: R. Garrigou-Lagrange, Christian Perfection and Contemplation (tr. T. Doyle, 1945); idem, Three Ages of the Interior Life (tr. T. Doyle, 1947); J. G. Arintero, Mystical Evolution in the Development and Vitality of the Church (tr. J. Aumann, 1949–51); A. Royo, Theology of Christian Perfection (tr. and ed. J. Aumann, 1962); J. de Guibert, Theology of the Spiritual Life (tr. P. Barrett, 1953); A. Saudreau, Degrees of the Spiritual Life (1907); A. Tanquerey, Spiritual Life (1948).

[J. AUMANN]

SPIRITUALISTS, adherents of a religious movement based on the fundamental belief that communication between the natural world and the spirit world is possible. It began in 1848 with the spirit manifestations reported by the *Fox sisters at Hydesville and Rochester, N.Y., and the publicity resulting from their lecture tours. The ideas and terminology of Spiritualist thought owe their origin to the writings of Andrew Jackson *Davis, particularly his book The Principles of Nature, Her Divine Revelations, and A Voice to Mankind, published at New York in 1847. The fame of the "Rochester rappings" and the demonstrations of psychic phenomena by the Fox Sisters gained numerous converts, who then turned to the pages of *Nature's Divine Revelations for a better understanding of their faith. Horace Greeley opened the columns of the New York Tribune to spiritism and Robert Dale Owen, the noted reformer, lectured on spirit phenomena. Seances and discussions of Spiritualism became commonplace in the U.S. and England in the 1850s. Materialism and scientific-technological developments had shaken the faith of many in traditional religious beliefs. Spiritualism had a strong appeal to these individuals by grounding its belief in the afterlife and the supernatural in verifiable experiments, rather than in simple faith.

Davis made the first move to organize Spiritualism as a religious sect when he established a progressive lyceum, or Spiritualist Sunday school, at Buffalo, N.Y., in 1863. Spiritualism has tended to remain a somewhat amorphous movement as the influence of the individual medium is decisive in gathering or dispersing an individual congregation. The Davis association lasted only until 1872. A more permanent effort to unite the Spiritualist movement began in 1893 with the formation of the National Spiritualist Association, now known as the National Spiritualist Association of Churches. It has aimed at establishing minimum standards for the licensing of churches and ministers and prepared the *Spiritualist Manual* as an aid to worship services. It has represented the more churchly, orthodox wing of the movement. The National Spiritual Alliance of the U.S.A., founded in 1913, and the International General Assembly of Spiritualists, formed in 1936, have similar aims and activities. Many Spiritualists are outside these major national groups, and many have harmonized their beliefs with those of other religious bodies. There were an estimated 24,174 members of Spiritualist churches in 1968.

The beliefs of Spiritualists center on the possibility of contact between the world of the spirits and the world we know. Spiritualists believe in Infinite Intelligence and that both physical and spiritual reality are expressions of Infinite Intelligence. They also believe that personal identity and individual existence survive the apparent death of the body. In his writings, Andrew J. Davis posited a rather elaborate cosmology of the world of the spirits. In his view, man is composed of a mortal physical body, an immortal spirit, and a soul, which is the form of the spirit and clothes it with a quasi-immaterial body recapitulating the physical body. After the death of the physical body, spirit and soul pass into the "Summer-land" of the after-life, progressing through a series of concentric spheres from the lower level of the Summer-land to the Philosopher's Sphere, the Love Sphere, and the Christ Sphere. The beginning point for each one is determined by his previous life, but progress is constant toward a universal redemption. Other writers have adopted slightly different views, and a minority of Spiritualists teach rebirth, but the teachings of Davis are generally accepted. Spiritualist understanding of traditional Christian beliefs may also vary considerably. Their doctrine of God as Infinite Intelligence leaves the individual free to accept or reject much of Christian theology, and they do not emphasize the atonement by Jesus Christ or the Bible as the word of God. Some Spiritualists may profess the doctrines of traditional Christianity, but there is no compulsion to do so, and they often reinterpret these doctrines in their own sense, seeing Jesus Christ as a *medium and the gospel as an account of spirit phenomena. Spiritualist worship services often include scriptural readings and a sermon, as well as congregational hymn singing and pastoral prayer, but the messages from the spirit world delivered by a medium are of paramount interest.

[R. K. MACMASTER]

SPIRITUALITY, the form or manner of living the Christian life in such a way as to advance in Christian perfection, mainly through the practice of prayer. The term itself is used esp. in RC literature, where reference is made to Benedictine, Carmelite, Dominican, Ignatian, Sulpician, and other types of spirituality. The idea, however, is broader than this use of the term. Christian theology generally recognizes the life of grace as a call to live according to the spirit and not according to the flesh (Gal 3.3–6; Rom 8.4–13). The means by which such a call can be fulfilled consti-

tute spirituality. It has taken on a generic meaning because of varying emphases: some forms of RC spirituality stress the pursuit of simple, even mystical, contemplation; others stress the ascetical practice of active virtues in the works of the apostolate; some have developed systematic methods of prayer; others prefer more simple ways of prayer. The Reformation repudiation of good works, monasticism, and many RC devotional practices suggests also the repudiation of spirituality. Yet Luther's own life and writings are deeply concerned with means of living the Christian life (see Wicks). The discipline designed by Calvin was also a spirituality, a quest for conformity to the sovereign will of God. Simply by their concern with perfection, personal experience, and the means to a devout life, however, Pietism and Methodism more obviously are forms of spirituality. There is also a rich spiritual doctrine in the writings of the *Caroline Divines, esp. those of Lancelot *Andrewes. The ideals of the Christian life proposed by groups directly or indirectly belonging to the so-called left wing of the Reformation also may be viewed as forms of spirituality. Great emphasis was put on inner experience, even *mysticism, the practice of meditation, and quiet prayer. The practice of *nonconformity and a nonworldly regulated form of life were meant as a means to deepen the inner life. BIBLIOGRAPHY: L. Bouyer, *History of Catholic Spirituality* (1963); R. Garrigou-Lagrange, *Christian Perfection and Contemplation* (1937); R. N. Jones, *Spiritual Reformers in the 16th and 17th Centuries* (pa., 1959); J. Wicks, *Man Yearning for Grace* (1968).

[T. C. O'BRIEN]

SPIRITUALITY, DOMINICAN, see DOMINICAN SPIRITUALITY.

SPIRITUALS (also spiritual song), the sacred folksongs or folk hymnody of America. It arose in New England, spread through the Middle Atlantic states, and developed in the Mid-South and Deep South in three forms: the Negro spiritual type of *Afro-American religious music (see SPIRITUALS, NEGRO), the generalized white spiritual, and the more localized Pennsylvania-German spiritual. Certain types of 18th–cent. New England *psalmody contributed significantly to the spiritual: "psalm tunes" (based on OT texts), evangelical hymns, and fuguing tunes. Congregational participation was increased through such practices as lining out, non-trained vocal technique, and an increasing use of secular folk melodies, often of a modal nature, while singing schools and traveling singing masters began to bring religious music to a popular level. Specialized notation systems such as shape-notes were introduced. With the camp meetings of the Great Revival beginning around 1800, Baptists, then Methodists and others, cemented the spiritual tradition with the introduction of the revival hymn. The chief investigator of white religious folksong, George Pullen Jackson, contrasted three types of the non-Negro spiritual: religious ballad, folk hymn, and the true spiritual song. These last perpetuated the folk style of singing, the use of folk melodies, the simplification of text, and the dominance of chorus over verse. Called the unwritten music, few spirituals appeared in print at inception, but printed versions of the white versions (at first with texts only) began to appear around 1805 and flourished just prior to the mid-19th century. Collections with texts and music were published by country singing masters who appreciated the effect and popularity of the revival spirituals, in effect preserving them for later appreciation. Revulsion over the content and technique of spirituals by denominational publishers and establishment hymn compilers such as Lowell *Mason served to strengthen the spiritual tradition among rural whites. It spread to such specialized sects as the Shakers and Mormons. The later Holiness Revival, beginning around 1890, marked a resurgence of camp-meeting activity, and hymn writers like John R. Sweney wrote popular revival hymns with little text simplification or folk melodification in a tradition largely dependent on print and then recordings. Southern, white folk groups adapted many of these later gospel and sacred songs, while the spiritual, shape-note, and lining out traditions lingered in certain areas. BIBLIOGRAPHY: G. P. Jackson, *White Spirituals in the Southern Uplands* (repr. ed., foreword by D. *Yoder, 1964); *Another Sheaf of White Spirituals* (1952).

[J. C. HICKERSON]

SPIRITUALS, FRANCISCAN, ideological descendants of the Zelanti, a faction within the Franciscan Order that was in the process of formation even during the lifetime of St. Francis. They believed that the order's first function was to perpetuate the way of life exemplified by the founder and his earliest companions. Every attempt to adapt the life of the friars to the realities of organized existence was to this group of primitivists a betrayal of the Franciscan ideal. They were particularly unyielding in the matter of poverty, holding that the order and all its members were bound to the *usus pauper,* the use of only absolutely necessary things. In an attempt to preserve peace and union within the order, the popes of the 13th cent. issued a series of bulls in which they attempted to clarify disputed sections of the rule. Efforts to enforce these papal pronouncements only served to harden the zealots' resistance. Bl. John of Parma, who sympathized with their aims, was forced to resign as minister general in 1257 because of his involvement in *Joachimism, a form of *apocalypticism to which the persecuted rigorists were strongly attracted. The Zelanti began to be known as Spirituals during the generalate of St. Bonaventure (1257–74). He sought to steer a middle course by opposing both the intolerance of the rigorists and the abuses of the laxists, but his efforts to establish equilibrium and proportion had no appeal for the Spirituals, who began to demand the right to separate themselves from the main body of the order so that they could observe the rule in its primitive severity. Between 1274 and 1317 a bitter battle raged between the Spirituals and the Communitas, as the moderate majority

was called. Each side was guilty of excesses in its attacks upon the other. In 1312 there was a papal condemnation of some of the Spirituals' doctrines; the petition for separate, autonomous existence was denied.

Three geographically separated groups of Spirituals functioned independently. Each was headed by a talented and determined leader: *Peter John Olivi in Provence, *Ubertino of Casale in Tuscany, and *Angelus Clarenus in the March of Ancona. In 1317 John XXII launched a determined program to suppress the Spirituals. Many of them returned to the order, some were imprisoned, and a few were burned as heretics. The hard core became *Fraticelli. By 1325 the Spirituals ceased to be a faction of any significance. BIBLIOGRAPHY: D. Douie, *Nature and Effects of the Heresy of the Fraticelli* (1932), with extensive bibliog.; *idem,* NCE 13:610–611, with selected bibliog.; L. von Auw, *Angelo Clareno et les spirituels franciscains* (1952); T. MacVicar, *Doctrine of the Franciscan Spirituals* (1963); D. Mussey, *Spiritual Franciscans* (1907); M. Lambert, *Franciscan Poverty: The Doctrine of the Absolute Poverty of Christ and the Apostles in the Franciscan Order, 1210–1323* (1961). *POVERTY CONTROVERSY.

[C. J. LYNCH]

SPIRITUALS, NEGRO, the religious folk songs of the American Negro. Though many seem to be based on the so-called white spirituals sung at revivals and camp meetings by 19th-cent. evangelistic Protestants and printed in such volumes as *The Southern Harmony* (1835) and *The Sacred Harp* (1844), Negro spirituals are a folk product whose origins are complex and controversial. Claimed by some musicologists to be based exclusively on white Anglo-American counterparts and by others to be fundamentally of African origin, they are, more probably, a product of the meeting of the two cultures. Negro spiritual music is characterized by extensive use of a five-tone scale, flat sevenths, ''neutral'' thirds, syncopation and offbeat phrasing, and many vocal effects difficult if not impossible to notate. There is a prevalence of ''call and response'' type songs and ''long-meter'' hymns sung according to the old lining-out practice. A source of inspiration in the black people's quest for freedom and identity, spirituals were, more often than not, biblically based and were used as work songs as well as at religious meetings. Considered by many musicologists to be among the finest of the American folk songs, they have, since the Civil War, been the subject of much scholarly interest and of extensive use, in harmonized and ''refined'' arrangements, in concerts throughout Europe and America. Because of the deep and personal religious feeling which they express, spirituals have been well represented in many recent hymn collections. BIBLIOGRAPHY: G. P. Jackson, *White and Negro Spirituals, Their Life-Span and Kinship* (1943); G. Chase, *America's Music* (1955); H. Roach, *Black American Music: Past and Present* (1973); J. S. Roberts, *Black Music of Two Worlds* (1972).

[M. T. LEGGE]

SPIRITUS PARACLITUS, Benedict XV's encyclical on biblical studies, issued on the 15th centenary of St. *Jerome's death (1920). The encyclical seeks to promote bible reading and study, extols Jerome's example, and enumerates the practical benefits and effects of a greater knowledge of the Bible. Benedict affirms the inspiration and inerrancy of the whole Bible and cautions against the use of hermeneutical principles such as implicit quotations, pseudo–historical narratives, and literary forms to maintain that the sacred author was ignorant of the truth and simply set down false contemporary opinions. A defensive attitude toward *Modernism and higher biblical criticism was prevalent among Catholics at this time and is reflected in the encyclical. BIBLIOGRAPHY: Benedict XV, "Spiritus Paraclitus," AAS 12 (1920) 385–422; tr. *Rome and the Study of Scripture* (5th ed., 1953); JBC 2:625, 628.

[T . M . MCFADDEN]

SPITTA, (JULIUS AUGUST) PHILIPP (1841–1894), German musicographer. S. studied at Göttingen. In the course of his lifetime, he held several important teaching and other positions. Among them were those of professor of musical history in Berlin Univ. and perpetual secretary of the Academy of Arts in Berlin. His authoritative biography of J. S. Bach, in two volumes (1873, 1880), is the basis of all later research and criticism. He also published shorter biographies of Bach and Schumann, contributed to many important publications, such as *Grove's Dictionary of Music and Musicians,* and was a prominent figure in the publication, among other works, of *Denkmaler deutscher Tonkunst* and *Monatshefte für Musik-Geschichte.*

[M. T. LEGGE]

SPLENDOR OF HIS GLORY, the light of revelation of the glory of God, which shines in the face of Jesus Christ, and which shines also in us through the Spirit of the Lord that is given to us. This Pauline Christology is expressed most explicitly in 2 Cor 3 and 4, in a context in which Paul explains that this splendor in Christ outshines and surpasses the former glory revealed to Moses at the giving of the Law at Sinai. Paul's account of Christ's glory is no doubt influenced by his experience on the road to Damascus, when he was blinded by luminous glory; but it is in harmony with Luke's teaching that God has glorified his servant Jesus, and that Christ has been taken up in glory and has entered the divine glory; and with the Joannine teaching that Christ shares with us the glory that was his before the creation of the world. In Paul, the splendor of Christ's glory not only surpasses the Mosaic dispensation, but it is the light of a new creation, which the light that came into existence on the first day of creation merely prefigured. "For the same God who said, 'Out of darkness let light shine,' has caused His light to shine within us, to give the light of revelation—the revelation of the glory of God in the face of Jesus Christ." (2 Cor 4.6).

[E. J. DILLON]

SPONDANUS, HENRI (DE SPONDE; 1568–1643), French author, bp., who early in life served Henry of Navarre as *maître des requêtes.* He converted from Calvinism to Catholicism in 1595, moved to Rome (1600), and was ordained (1606). After working in the Roman Curia, then acting as rector of St. Louis des Français, in 1626 he was made bp. of Pamiers (Ariège), where he sought the conversion of Protestants and church reform until 1637, when he retired to Paris. Among his works are pastoral essays, apologetics, history, and biography, the most notable being his *Les Cimetières sacrés* (1597, 1638), his *Epitome* (1613) of his friend Caesar *Baronius's *Annales,* and an *Annalium . . . continuatio* (1641) down to 1639.

[R. J. LITZ]

SPONDE, JEAN DE (1557–95), French humanist and poet who, born a Protestant, converted to Catholicism with Henry IV, under the influence of Card. du Perron (1593). His father, secretary to Jeanne d'Albert, mother of Henry IV, was slaughtered by members of the Catholic Holy League at Palays (1594). Made lieutenant-general of the Sénéchausée of La Rochelle (1592), which he later exchanged for the office of master of petitions or requests, S. was attacked for his conversion in Agrippa d'*Aubigné's *Confessions de Sancy.* His works include: humanistic editions of Homer, Hesiod, Aristotle; his *Declaration des principaux motifs qui induisent le sieur de Sponde à s'unir à l'église catholique* (1594), a personal apology for his conversion; *Réponse au traité des marques de l'église* (1595), a refutation of the Reformer Theodore *Beza; and poetry, considered his best work, of religious inspiration and reflecting neo-Stoic tendencies. Newly rediscovered, it is contributing to the reevaluation of French mannerist and baroque poetry. BIBLIOGRAPHY: F. Ruchon and A. Boase, *La Vie et l'oeuvre de Jean de Sponde* (1949); M. Richter, "Il processo spirituale e stilistico nella poesia di Sponde," *Aevum* 26 (1962) 284–318.

[R. N. NICOLICH]

SPONGE (Gr., *spongia*; Sl., *gubka*), in the Byzantine liturgy a small sponge sometimes cut in a triangular shape and pressed perfectly flat, used to purify the fingers of priest and deacon. It is also used to conduct the bread into the chalice and to cleanse the sacred vessels. Although the sponge is usually left plain, the Melkites often cover it with red silk. When not in use it is placed in the folded antimension on the altar, although a second sponge is sometimes kept at the prothesis table.

[J. FRANCAVILLA]

SPONSA CHRISTI (bride of Christ), a NT image to describe the relationship of Christ and the Church; also an apostolic constitution of Pius XII (1950) dealing with changes in the canonical status of contemplative nuns. The image of the Church's being betrothed to Christ (2 Cor 11.2; Eph 5.27–32; Rev 21.9; 22.17) echoes the OT practice of presenting the love between the Israelites and God under the figure of an engagement or marriage (e.g., Hos 2.21; Jer 3.1). The term conveys a sense of strong personal love and concern, fruitfulness, and exclusivity. In the apostolic constitution of this title Pius XII outlined the origins and excellence of contemplative orders of nuns, and established several new statutes directing their way of life. A minor papal cloister was introduced, federation of monasteries encouraged, and provision for monastic self-support through various apostolic works established. BIBLIOGRAPHY: J. J. O'Rourke, JBC 2:287; Pius XII, "Sponsa Christi," AAS 43 (1951) 5–37; F. B. Donnelly, "Changes in the Status of Contemplative Nuns," HPR 51 (1951) 734–738.

[T. M. MCFADDEN]

SPONSORS, in the sacraments of baptism and confirmation those who present the candidate and promise to promote the candidate's fidelity to the sacrament's meaning. The role of the sponsor (godparent) is most clear in the baptism of infants, where the sponsor speaks for the infant in petitioning for the sacrament, in responding to the baptismal promises, and in affirming the articles of faith; the sponsor's pledge to be a godparent means the assurance that the baptized's Christian upbringing will be assured if the natural parents become incapable or remiss. The beautiful revised rituals of baptism for infants (1969) and for adults (1972) give new emphasis and dignity to the office of sponsor. The restored catechumenate for adults gives the sponsor a part in the instruction of the catechumen and in passing judgment on the candidate's manifestation of faith (*Rites*, n.11); the sponsor accompanies the candidate as the delegate of the Christian community at the time of election to the catechumenate and becomes the catechumen's counsellor and aid during the process of initiation (n.42; n.71). The actual rite of admission to the catechumenate includes the sponsor's pledge of readiness to help the candidate to know and to follow Christ (n.77) and the sponsor's testimony to the candidate's decision to choose Christ as Lord (n.81); the sponsor signs the senses of the candidate, after the minister, with the sign of the cross (n.85). The role of the godparent at the rite of election, proximate preparation for baptism, is described as the godparent's first act of ministry: to testify to the whole community as to the candidate's worthiness (n.136, n.144–145). In the series of scrutinies that take place during Lent, the sponsor places a hand on the candidate's shoulder during the prayers (n.163, n.170, n.176). At the baptism itself the sponsor's hand is on the shoulder of the recipient, and from the sponsor the newly baptized receives the white garment and candle (n.221, n.225, n.226). When the Eucharist follows the baptism the sponsors are mentioned by name during the Eucharistic Prayer and with the newly baptized receive communion under both kinds (n.233,234). During the post-baptismal catechesis (*mystagogia*), the godparents continue their role (n.235). These same elements are adapted even when the baptism takes place according to the simple rite (n.240) or in the baptism

of infants; the decree of promulgation stresses that the latter rite should clearly express the responsibilities of the sponsors. The general instruction on Christian initiation indicates that a sponsor should: be mature enough for his or her responsibility; have received baptism, confirmation, and the Eucharist, be a Catholic canonically free of penalties that would prevent fulfilling the office. One godparent is required; if there are two, they are to be a man and a woman; a Christian of another communion is permitted (n.10).

In the new (1971) rite of confirmation a sponsor is required who will present the candidate and aid the candidate to fulfill the baptismal promises ratified by confirmation. Abrogating CIC c.796,1, the document recommends that the sponsor at baptism also be the sponsor at confirmation; it also allows the parents to be the sponsors, or a sponsor different from the baptismal sponsor. The sponsor for confirmation must have the same qualifications as those of the baptismal sponsor. In the sacramental rite of confirmation the candidate is presented by the sponsors who announce the candidate's name and rest a hand on the candidate's shoulder at the moment of anointing (n.22, n.26). BIBLIOGRAPHY: *Rites of the Catholic Church* (Eng. tr. by the International Commission on English in the Liturgy, 1976), "Christian Initiation" n. 3; "Baptism for Children" nn. 16–18; "Christian Initiation of Adults" nn. 42–43; "Confirmation" nn. 5–6.

[T. C. O'BRIEN]

SPOON, LITURGICAL, a spoon used in most Eastern liturgies (except the Armenians, East Syrians, and Maronites) in communicating the sacred species in the Eucharistic Liturgy.

[A. CODY]

SPORER, PATRITIUS (*c.*1620–83), German Franciscan of the Strict Observance, moral theologian. Ordained in 1644, he served as penitentiary and preacher in the cathedrals of Passau and Augsburg, taught theology at Dettelbach (1653–65). In moral theology he was a proponent of *probabilism; his textbooks stressing pastoral practice were in use for over a century. They include: *Tyrocinium theologiae moralis . . .* (1660–61); *Seraphim moralis . . .* (1662); *Tyrocinium sacramentale practicum . . .* (1681–82). The last compendious edition and revision was published, I. Bierbaum, ed., in 1901–05.

[R. J. LITZ]

SPORTELLI, CAESAR, VEN. (1702–50), first Redemptorist novice. An Italian lawyer, S. was drawn to St. Alphonsus Liguori and became his first novice. The earliest associate of St. Alphonsus, S. became a celebrated preacher and pastor. He founded several houses of the Redemptorists. Three years after his death his body was still in a state of complete preservation. S. was declared Venerable in 1899.

[J. R. AHERNE]

SPORTS, see LEISURE.

SPORTS, BOOK OF, see BOOK OF SPORTS.

SPOUSE OF BLOOD, an epithet pronounced in exclamation by Zipporah, wife of Moses, as recounted in Ex 4.24–26. The entire episode is obscure. It is difficult to give a clear rendition of what happened. According to the text: "Yahweh met Moses, meaning to kill him . . ." Then Zipporah "picked up a sharp flint, cut off her son's foreskin, and touched him with it, crying out, 'You are a spouse of blood to me'." It is not apparent from the text why such an epithet should apply to Moses, nor is there any hint why his son's circumcision should save Moses' life. The text merely states "So Yahweh let Moses alone." Yahweh has been placated or even warded off like a demon of the night. The passage ends with a slight attempt at explanation: "Then she said, (or: therefore women say,) 'Spouse of blood by circumcision'." The episode would seem to have it that the rite of circumcision came into the cult of Yahweh linked with Passover by its kindred motif of an urgent need to ward off a potential destroyer.

[E. J. DILLON]

SPRINGER, MAX (1877–1954), German organist, composer, and writer on church music. S. studied at the Univ. of Prague. He became organist-choirmaster at the Benedictine monastery of St. Emmaus and, in 1910, was appointed professor of church music at Klosterneuberg. He wrote various books on church music such as *The Art of Accompanying Plain Chant,* and composed Masses, organ works, choral music, two symphonies, and other instrumental compositions.

[M. T. LEGGE]

SPURGEON, CHARLES HADDON (1834–92), English Baptist preacher. Born at Kelvedon, Essex, the son of a Congregationalist minister, he became a Baptist in 1850. At age 20 he became pastor of a London church and soon drew such crowds that the 6,000-seat Metropolitan Tabernacle was built for him. He preached there until his death. In 1887 he left the Baptist Union in protest against its liberal tendencies. He founded several institutions, including a college for ministers.

[T. EARLY]

SPY WEDNESDAY, the Wednesday of Holy Week, by custom so named to refer to Judas's looking for an opportunity to betray Jesus.

[J. DALLEN]

SPYRIDON, ST. (Spiridion; d. *c.*348), Cypriot bp. and confessor of the faith. According to the story told of him, he was a shepherd who was chosen bp. of Tremithus on the Island of Cyprus. A poor man in a poor community, he continued even as a bishop to tend sheep. He is said to have endured the same kind of mutilation in the persecution under Galerius as is reported of *Paphnutius, a victim of the same persecution. He is also said to have been among the bps. present at the Council of Nicaea, but this is doubtful. Legend had made much of his rustic simplicity. BIBLIOGRAPHY: Butler 4:556–557.

[R. B. ENO]

SQUARCIALUPI, ANTONIO (1416–80), Italian organist and composer. None of S.'s works remain. Known only are the facts that his compositions existed and that he was a contemporary of Dufay.

[M . T . LEGGE]

SQUARCIONE, FRANCESCO (1397-*c.*1468), Italian artist-teacher in Padua, whose importance lies, not in his painting, but in his having conveyed to N Italian students an interest in classical antiquity, knowledge of Florentine artists and of Padua's native son, Donatello. His chief pupil was Mantegna, though he further influenced Crivelli and Bellini.

[M. J. DALY]

SQUARE NOTATION, the notation of the school of Notre Dame, a group of polyphonic composers, *c.*1200. They were the first to use square shapes for their notes rather than the less definite symbols of earlier periods.

[M. T. LEGGE]

SRI LANKA (formerly Ceylon), an independent island state within the British Commonwealth, SW of the S end of India (25,332 sq mi; UN est. pop. 1975, 13,990,000, 70% of whom are Singhalese and Aryan, and 20% of Dravidian and Tamil stock). Ceylon has been subject to a succession of occupations, earlier by Indian invaders, and in modern times by European powers. The Portuguese held important coastal positions from the beginning of the 16th cent.; they were gradually displaced by the Dutch in the 17th cent.; and in 1796 the British seized the occupied areas, making Ceylon a crown colony in 1802. Buddhism is the religion of 61 per cent of the people (mostly Singhalese); Hinduism of 22 per cent (mostly Tamils), Christianity 9 per cent, Islamism 7 per cent. The country became independent in 1948, but remained in the British Commonwealth. Franciscans were active in missionary work on the island from 1518 and were later joined by Augustinians, Dominicans, and Jesuits. The evangelization was relatively successful, but when the Dutch came into control, missions were closed, missionaries were expelled, churches burned, and Catholics who chose to stand firm in their faith suffered grievous persecution. The survival of Catholicism was largely the result of the labors of Oratorians from Goa, esp. Joseph Vaz (d. 1711), at the time of whose death the Catholic community numbered more than 70,000. The British granted freedom of religion, and in the 19th cent. the Oblates, who arrived in 1847, contributed much to the missionary effort. By the end of the century Rome created the Ceylonese hierarchy and established a pontifical seminary that became a great training center for Ceylon and India. The missions in Ceylon have made an excellent contribution toward the education of the people. The hierarchy at the present time comprises an ecclesiastical province with an archbishop-cardinal at Colombo and suffragan sees at Jaffna, Kandy, Chilaw, Batticaloa (Trincomalee), and Galle. The national clergy is numerous and there are many well-organized groups of the laity active in the apostolate. Catholics number about 985,581. During the years 1961–63 the government took restrictive measures against Catholic education, and steps were taken toward the expulsion of foreign missionaries and sisters. The situation has greatly improved. Protestant historians have accused the Dutch Calvinists of striving to suppress Catholicism rather than to introduce Protestantism while they were in power. Most of the effective Protestant missionary work was done by British Churches, Anglican, Methodist, and Baptist, the Anglicans being the most successful. Of late the Pentecostals have been very active. An effort is being made to form a national organization patterned on that of the Church of South India. The total Protestant community numbered about 95,000 in the 1960s. BIBLIOGRAPHY: F. de Queyroz, *Temporal and Spiritual Conquest of Ceylon* (tr. S. G. Perera, 3 v., 1930); W. L. A. Peter, *Studies in Ceylon Church History* (1963).

[P. DAMBORIENA]

SRI LANKA, ART OF, prehistoric finds in the former Ceylon, related to those of India include megalithic forms, stone cremation urns, and pottery. Caves with animal paintings in red and yellow ochre and engraved pictographs are still inhabited by aborigine Aryan Veddas who came from N India in the 6th cent. B.C. In the 3d cent. B.C. Buddhists from India built great stupas and many monasteries of which the most famous is the Mahavihāra near *Anuradhapura. After the Tamil conquest (2d cent. B.C.) the Ruvanvali dagoba and the Mahā-Pāsāda palace with copper roof were built. The largest stupa, the Tetavana (3d cent. A.D.), is in Andrha style with sculptured friezes, and colossal Buddha images are dated 4th–5th centuries. A royal fortress at Sigiriya is decorated with paintings echoing *Ajanta. In the late Anuradhapura period an 8th-cent. Buddha with "flaming" *uṣṇiṣa* and other elegant bronzes merge Pallavan and Sinhalese styles in a new motion. The Chola invasion destroyed Anuradhapura (1017), introducing octagonal, seven-storied stepped stupas with huge portrait sculpture of the donor king. At rock-cut Gal Vihara is a colossal sorrowing Buddha with conventional figures of drooping lids and narrow foreheads in flawless execution. Excess marked a decline with the last capital at Kandy (16th cent.) and 18th-and 19th-cent. painting reflecting the Rajput school in India during a period of British domination. BIBLIOGRAPHY: V. A. Smith, *History of Fine Art in India and Ceylon* (3d rev. ed., 1961).

[M. J. DALY]

STABAT MATER (MUSIC), a poem usually attributed to Jacopone da Todi (*c.* 1228–1306). It was added to the liturgy in 1727 as a sequence for the feast of the Seven Sorrows of Our Lady (Sept. 15). In addition to the chant version, there are numerous musical settings done by composers of all periods, among them A. Scarlatti, Pergolesi, Boccherini, Haydn, Rossini, Verdi, and Dvořák.

[M. T. LEGGE]

STABILITY, the permanence in one monastery vowed by a Benedictine monk. Stability is an element inherent in the meaning of monasticism as a life of contemplation removed from the world and as distinct from apostolic forms of religious life. Even in the desert fathers there was an emphasis on remaining in one place as a way and a sign of concentrating on the one goal of union with God, esp. in their warnings of restlessness and wandering as symptoms of *acedia, a distaste for the things of the spirit. The monk's intent to remain in the monastery of his profession is conditioned by the willingness to obey the abbot should a transfer be necessary to the common good.

[T. C. O'BRIEN]

STADION, CHRISTOPH VON (1478–1543), bp. of Augsburg from 1517. A descendant of Swabian nobility, he was considered one of the more learned prince-bishops by his contemporaries, and was a correspondent of Melanchthon and Erasmus. Seeking to reconcile Catholics and Reformers, he was willing to concede communion under both kinds, vernacular liturgy, the abolition of clerical celibacy and fasting, but resisted the revolutionary theology of Luther. To counteract it, he summoned Urbanus Rhegius to preach at the Augsburg cathedral and convened three synods, one of them at Dillingen, proscribing Luther's works; and he circulated the 1520 bull *Exsurge Domine* censuring Luther's teachings. S. participated in the imperial diets at Augsburg (1530) and Nuremberg (1543).

[R. J. LITZ]

STADLER, MAXIMILIAN (1748–1833), Austrian Benedictine, composer and music scholar. S. completed his musical education at the Jesuit college in Vienna. In 1766 he became a Benedictine and, in 1786, was made abbot of Lilienfeld, then of Kremsmünster. S. also spent many years as a parish priest. A friend of both Haydn and Mozart, he took care of Mozart's musical effects after his death. S. composed an oratorio, Masses, a Te Deum, as well as other church and secular music.

[M. T. LEGGE]

STADLMAYR, JOHANN (1560–1648), German composer. S. served in the court at Salzburg and at Innsbruck. His compositions were all for RC church services. Written for the most part for several voices, his works were at first purely vocal, and then for voices with instruments. He wrote Masses, Magnificats, hymns, and others.

[M. T. LEGGE]

STAËL, MADAME DE (1766–1817), precursor of French Romanticism and 19th-cent. literary criticism. Anne Louise Germaine Necker, the daughter of the Swiss banker who was Louis XVI's minister of finance, she married the Swedish ambassador to the court of France: the union was neither faithful nor fond. Her salon was an influential political center, usually in opposition to any government that threatened moderate and constitutional liberalism: she welcomed the Revolution but fled the Terror; quarreled with the Directory but was exiled by Napoleon. An early feminist, she was both generous and taxing in her loves and friendships, which at one time were given to Talleyrand. Her Protestantism of the Enlightenment was later colored by her taste for medievalism; she exalted the Christian, romantic, sensitive, and melancholy North over the pagan, classical, sensuous, and serene South; her diffused fideism blended mysticism with the ethics of sensibility, and was attracted by the *Quietist writers of spirituality. She has been justly entitled the mistress to an age. BIBLIOGRAPHY: J. C. Herold, *Mistress to an Age* (1958); W. Andrews, *Germaine: A Portrait of Madame de Staël* (1964).

[T. GILBY]

STAFF, EPISCOPAL, the liturgical pastoral staff (Gr. *poimantikē rabdos, baktēria, pateritsa*; Sl., *pastushki posokh, djezl*) in the Byzantine Church is carried by all bishops, even titular ones, and by certain other dignitaries as well. It is shorter than the Roman crozier and is surmounted by an orb topped by a cross with two stylized serpents, heads facing each other, near the top of the orb. It is usually made of metal, but other materials such as wood or ivory are sometimes incorporated. The two serpents symbolize the prudence that the shepherd of the flock should possess. At the place where the staff is held by the bishop there is sometimes placed a veil of silk, often embroidered; it was originally used to protect the metal from perspiration, a practice reminiscent of the Roman *sudarium*, which served a similar purpose. Many Catholic bishops of Eastern rites other than the Byzantine have adopted the Roman crozier as have also non-Catholic Armenian bishops. The vardapets of the Armenian Church employ the Byzantine style of pastoral staff. Besides the liturgical pastoral staff, a shorter staff (*chazranion*, derived from Turkish and Arabic) is used by Eastern prelates as a walking stick. It is usually made of black ebony wood with silver, gold, or enameled decorations. It is carried on formal, nonliturgical occasions and on occasions when the bishop is abroad in *rason*.

[A. J. JACOPIN]

STAFFORD JOHN (c. 1388–1452), English prelate and statesman. A natural son of Sir Humphrey Stafford of Southwick (Wiltshire), a doctor in canon law (Oxford) by 1413, S. rose as lawyer and administrator in the service of Abp. Chichele of Canterbury. He then passed into the service of Henry V and Henry VI, becoming keeper of the privy seal (1421–22), treasurer (1422–26), and chancellor (1432–50), and was rewarded by preferment to the sees of Bath and Wells (1424–43) and Canterbury (1443–52). An An able civil servant and diplomat, he seems also to have been a conscientious and respected bishop. BIBLIOGRAPHY: E. F. Jacob, ''Archbishop John Stafford,'' *Trans. Royal Historical Society,* series 5, 12 (1962) 1–23.

[C. D. ROSS]

STAGEL, ELSBETH (c. 1300–60), Dominican nun. She entered the convent at Toss, Switzerland, at an early age and became its first chronicler. She wrote biographies of some 40 nuns who lived in the convent from its founding in 1233 until 1340. But she is primarily noted for her correspondence with *Henry Suso, who told her of his mystical experiences. Her recording of these, together with their correspondence, forms Suso's *Life* and *Book of Letters*.

[T. EARLY]

STAINER JOHN (1840–1901), English organist, composer, teacher, and scholar. At the age of 7, S., already an accomplished player and singer, became a choirboy at St. Paul's Cathedral in London, where he remained until 1856, playing the organ and studying harmony and counterpoint. At 16 he was made organist at St. Michael's College in Tenbury; then later, at Oxford, where he earned degrees in music and art. He returned to St. Paul's as organist and, in his forties, became professor of music at Oxford. Knighted by Queen Victoria in 1888, S. held numerous positions of importance in the fields of music and music education in England. He also engaged in research, wrote articles and textbooks, and composed music (services, anthems, hymns, etc.) for the Anglican Church. Popular among his compositions are *The Daughter of Jairus* (1878) and *The Crucifixion* (1887).

[M. T. LEGGE]

STALIN, JOSEPH (1879–1953), Soviet dictator. Originally named Iosif Vissarionovich Djugashvili, he adopted the pseudonym Stalin (man of steel) while engaged in revolutionary activities. Born in Gori, near Tiflis, Georgia, S. was directed toward the priesthood by his deeply religious mother, widowed when S. was eleven. He attended the Orthodox seminary in Tiflis (1894–99), but rebelled against the discipline, grew interested in Marxism, and was expelled when he did not take examinations. Subsequently involved in various efforts to overthrow the czar, aligned with Lenin's Bolsheviks from 1903, he escaped from several imprisonments but was exiled in Siberia when the 1917 Revolution began. Returning to Petrograd, he was appointed to the Bolshevik executive committee and helped prepare for a seizure of power. In 1922 he became general secretary of the party, and though Lenin's will called for his removal, he succeeded Lenin in 1924. His wholesale brutalities alienated many Westerners sympathetic to the aims of the Revolution. The Churches endured severe repression until World War II, when Stalin made concessions to gain their aid. After the war his extension of Soviet domination brought Church-State conflict to other E European countries. He was posthumously condemned by N. Khruschev (1956). BIBLIOGRAPHY: A. B. Ulam, *Stalin* (1973).

[T. EARLY]

STALLS, fixed rows of seats flanking both sides of the choir of a church, usually conventual churches and cathedrals, with a long book-rest in front of each row and with arm-rests dividing the individual seats. The stalls are often carved and occasionally canopied. They are reserved for clergy, church officers, members of special orders such as the Knights of the Garter in England, and most commonly for those who sing the offices.

[R. J. LITZ]

STALPAERT VAN DER WIELE(N), JOANNES BAPTISTA (1579–1630), Dutch poet of the Counter Reformation. He left the practice of law to study theology at Louvain, was ordained (1606), became a doctor of theology in Rome, then parish priest (1617), and in Delft (1620), superior of the monastery of St. Agatha and head of the Béguinage. His corpus of ardent Counter Reformation prose and poetry includes: baroque poems on earthly transience; satirical works such as *Roomsche Reys,* (Roman Journey, 1624), and *Extractum Catholicum tegen Verwarde Hersenen* (A Catholic Summary against Addled Brains, 1631); lyrical celebrations of saints' lives; and works for religious reflection, which spiritualize commonplace items of experience.

[R. J. LITZ]

STANBRIDGE, JOHN (d. *c.* 1510), schoolmaster and grammarian. Scholar and then fellow of New College, Oxford (1480–86), he became usher and headmaster of Magdalen College School (1487–94) and canon of Lincoln (1509–10). His grammatical textbooks, including *Vulgaria,* won him great reputation as an educator, and three of his pupils became leading grammarians. BIBLIOGRAPHY: Emden Ox 3:1754–55.

[C. D. ROSS]

STANBROOK ABBEY, monastery of Benedictine nuns located at Powick near Worcester, England, in the Diocese of Birmingham. First founded in 1625 in Cambrai, Flanders, by Dame Gertrude More and other kinswomen of Thomas More and other English martyrs, it remained under the jurisdiction of the English Black Monks. Dispossessed by the French Revolution, the community spent 18 months in prison in Compiègne before returning penniless to England, finally settling in Stanbrook in 1838. The new monastery with full monastic observance was completed by 1880. In 1911 the community was able to help establish the Benedictine community of Santa Maria in São Paulo in Brazil. BIBLIOGRAPHY: Cottineau 2:3083.

[E. J. DILLON]

STANDARD CONFESSION, a *confession of faith of *General Baptists in London, drafted in 1660. The confession was prompted by a desire to present a statement of Christian orthodoxy to Charles II at the time of the *Restoration, since Baptists had been active in the *Commonwealth army, and were accused of being subversive. The name Standard Confession dates from 1663, when the 1660 statement was revised and reconfirmed by a general assembly of the General Baptists. This confession was a source of Baptist unity during the oppression of *Dissenters. BIBLIOGRAPHY: *Baptist Confessions of Faith* (ed. W. L. Lumpkin, 1959).

[T. C. O'BRIEN]

STANDARD OF LIVING, the average, thus normative, level of material comforts and cultural advantages prevailing in a country; or their level as proportionate to an individual's means and station in life. Taken in the first sense, a standard of living is a measure for the aims of *social justice. Law as well as economic theory and practice by right must take the community standard of living into account in regard to *just prices, equality of employment opportunity, a *living wage, housing, and other areas of social consequence. The standard of living is a mean; what it exacts in justice is not extreme egalitarianism or social uniformity. This mean, however, does work as an economic factor setting the cost of the necessities of life, and therefore is an index of the minimum requirements for a decent human life in any given human society; it therefore determines the true mean that justice honors. An individual's standard of living bears on the obligation in charity to give help to those in dire need. That obligation regards wealth in excess of what is required for the necessities of a life in keeping with one's own status, i.e., with the individual's standard of living. There is no obligation to lower this in order to give aid; but such a standard cannot rightly mean hoarding wealth, sheer luxury, or extravagance. The obligation is of ancient Christian affirmation; for being dictated by charity it is not of a lighter urgency, but is central to the Christian meaning of life (see ThAq ST 2a2ae, 32.5 & 6).

[T. C. O'BRIEN]

STANDING, the basic Christian liturgical posture, seen as symbolic of freedom in grace and of readiness to do the Lord's will. Kneeling, initially a penitential posture and now seen as a gesture of reverence, and sitting, a more passive posture of waiting or listening, are secondary. Many Eastern and European churches still lack pews and kneelers.

[J. DALLEN]

STANDING CONFERENCE OF CANONICAL ORTHODOX BISHOPS IN THE AMERICAS, a nonjurisdictional agency formed in 1960 as a means for inter-Orthodox discussion and cooperative action. The Standing Conference (SCOBA) was begun on the initiative of Abp. Iakovos Coucouzes, Exarch of the Ecumenical Patriarch in

North and South America. While it does not exercise canonical authority, SCOBA does represent the majority of Orthodox believers in the U.S., and serves as a clearing house for many Orthodox interests. Member Churches of the conference are the: Albanian Orthodox Diocese of America (Ecumenical Patriarchate), American Carpatho-Russian Greek Catholic Diocese, Antiochian Orthodox Christian Archdiocese of New York and All North America, Bulgarian Eastern Orthodox Church, Greek Orthodox Archdiocese of North and South America, Orthodox Church of America, Romanian Orthodox Missionary Episcopate in America, Serbian Orthodox Church in the U.S. of America and Canada, Ukrainian Orthodox Church of America (Ecumenical Patriarchate), Holy Ukrainian Autocephalic Orthodox Church in Exile.

[T. BIRD]

STANISLAUS OF CRACOW, ST., (*c.*1030–79), patron of Poland. He was educated in the cathedral school of Gniezno, then capital of Poland. Pope Alexander II named him successor to Lambert as bp. of Cracow in 1072. He was slain for treason by King Boleslaus II, S. having favored the uprising led by the King's brother Ladislaus. In response, Pope Gregory VII laid the country under interdict, which hastened the King's fall from power. S. was revered as a martyr, canonized by Pope Innocent IV in 1253, and is buried in Cracow's cathedral, which now bears his name.

[E. J. DILLON]

STANYHURST, RICHARD (1547–1618), Irish historian. Born in Dublin to a Protestant family, he studied at Oxford and Lincoln's Inn. He returned to Ireland and collaborated with Edmund *Campion on a history of Ireland published as part of Holinshed's *Chronicles*. After the death of his wife in 1579, he went to the Netherlands, where he became a Catholic and continued his writing. After his second wife died, he was ordained and became chaplain to Archduke Albert of Austria.

[T. EARLY]

STAPHYLUS, FRIEDRICH (1512–64), German theologian, studied at Cracow, Padua, and Wittenberg. In 1546, while teaching theology at Königsberg, he debated with W. Gnaphaeus for his Anabaptist leanings, and later engaged A. *Osiander in a controversy that shifted S. closer to the support of Roman Catholic tradition. In 1553, after converting to Catholicism (1552), he published his argument that only the Church with its tradition could provide a true interpretation of Scripture. As a Catholic spokesman at the Disputation of Worms (1557), he opposed Melanchthon. He charged the Protestants with disunity in his *Theologiae M. Lutheri trimembris epitome* (1558). He maintained that acceptance of a single biblical text, the Greek Vaticanus, would resolve most Protestant-Catholic conflicts.

[R. J. LITZ]

STAPLETON, THOMAS (1535–98), English theologian and controversialist. Educated at Oxford, S. left England at the accession of Elizabeth I and studied theology first at Louvain and then at Paris. Back in England in 1563 he refused to repudiate papal authority and withdrew with his near relatives to Louvain. From 1568 he was associated with W. *Allen in the establishment of the English College at Douai, where he taught theology. In 1584 he entered the Jesuits but left without completing his novitiate and returned to Douai. In 1590 he succeeded M. *Baius as professor of Scripture at Louvain. S. was a man of remarkable talent and erudition, who shared Allen's conviction that the vigorous defense of Catholic doctrine would lead to the return of England to the Catholic faith. BIBLIOGRAPHY: Gillow BDEC 5:526–529, with list of S.'s writings; M. O'Connell, *Thomas Stapleton and the Counter Reformation* (1964).

[R. B. ENO]

STAPULENSIS, JACOBUS FABER, see LEFÈVRE D'ÉTAPLES, JACQUES.

STAR OF BETHLEHEM, the star seen by the wise men from the East in Matthew's Infancy Gospel (Mt 2.1–12). They interpreted its first appearance as the sign of the birth of an infant king of the Jews. After they had vainly sought the infant in Jerusalem, it appeared to them again and led them to the birthplace of Jesus. Interpretations vary from miraculous to legendary. Many hold for a natural phenomenon, stressing the contemporary astrological and messianic beliefs. Others tend to underline the midrashic style of the infancy narrative.

[M. A. MCNAMARA]

STAR OF DAVID (Magen David or Shield of David), the hexagram, a symbol, now associated almost exclusively with Judaism. The six-pointed star is of extremely obscure origins, found in use in Bronze-Age civilizations from Mesopotamia to Britain, during the Iron Age in India, and in Iberia before the Roman conquest. The oldest undisputed example is from Sidon in 7th cent. B.C. Probably used decoratively, possibly in magic, the two equilateral triangles superimposed at their centers to make a hexagram has no biblical or Talmudic authority. Some Arab sources identify the symbol as the "seal of Solomon" and stress its magical use, indicating power over demons. The later association of the symbol with David may originate in either Judaism or Islam. The seals of 10th- and 11th-cent. kings of Navarre contained the symbol, along with *pentagrams. Alchemists of the 17th cent. used the symbol to denote harmony between antagonistic fire and water. Mentioned by a 12th-cent. Karaite, Judah Hadassi, it did not become widely accepted as a Jewish symbol until the 19th cent., when its use was advocated to serve the same function for Judaism as the cross does for Christianity. Adopted by the Zionist Organization at their first congress (1897), it later became incorporated into the national flag of Israel.

[R. J. LITZ]

STARETS, Russian for old man or elder, a term signifying a monk, not necessarily a priest, who because of his wisdom was sought out for spiritual guidance, not only by the inhabitants of the monastery and its surrounding area, but also by those at great distances. This happened not infrequently under Russian monasticism. The ancient custom depended neither on the official position of the religious nor upon his age. He was singled out by the people for his obvious gifts of the Holy Spirit. The most notable of these men include Paissius Velichkovsky (1722–94), SS. Tikon of Zadonsk (1724–82), and Seraphim of Sarov (1759–1833). Optina Pustyn, the most famous monastery of this tradition, was the center of spiritual counseling for many important 19th–cent. Russian thinkers. Zossima, Doestoevsky's elder in *The Brothers Karamazov*, is the most famous personification of the Russian starets.

[D. DIRSCHERL]

STATE, THE, a term derived from the Latin *status,* standing, or, more fully, *status rei publicae,* the establishment which is of public concern. For the Romans this was a matter more wide-spreading than the Greek city-state or *polis,* studied in Aristotle's *Politics,* the first systematic treatment of the organized body-politic, and still an indispensable text. The simple term was used by *Machiavelli and came into English late in the 16th cent., when the notion of the State in all its panoply as separate from the Church and as an earthly commonwealth supreme and self-sufficient had been effectively embodied after the decline of the papal-imperial diarchy and the fragmentation of Christendom.

A State requires the occupation of a territory by a population that accepts common laws and a unified sovereign authority possessing the plenitude of civil power and a monopoly in law enforcement. It is also to be distinguished from the notion of a nation, namely a people with a common language, traditions, and customs, and supposed to derive from a common stock (racial origins need to be treated with critical care by the social and political historian); one nation may overlap the frontiers of one State, as in the Netherlands, Belgium, and South Africa, or again, one State may contain several nations, thus the English, Scots, and Welsh in Great Britain. Nor is it to be identified with the governing body, though the logic of administration tends to create a class of experts who control the organs of State, whether as permanent officials or as politicians, and who are not uncommonly regarded by subjects as "the powers that be"; St. Augustine repeats the Roman teaching that the State is the whole people—*populus* here does not mean the populace—knit together by custom and law. General usage treats the State as synonymous with the country, yet in fact there are differences, for as a more formalized and juridical structure it calls for one's rendering to the State that part of justice which is called *respect (observantia),* and *obedience (obedientia),* rather than the more unpremeditated loyalty and *patriotism (pietas)* owed to one's own folk and land. In this connection it may be remarked that the State comes midway between and shares in character of a community bound together by ties that lie deeper than contract and of a free association of equals; it will be healthy if its laws are grounded on an instinctive unanimity and promote an open society of persons.

What sort of entity is the State? Is it a real organism or just an artificial construction? Here the answer falls between the extremes of corporatism (which we have come to call *totalitarianism) and of *individualism. The legal fiction of personality was credited to corporations by *Innocent IV, and was later enlarged by political philosophers as the feudal order moved into a system where the State seemed to have a life of its own, which became all-embracing with Fichte and Hegel and exacted its victims under *communism, *Nazism, and *fascism. The historic tradition of *liberalism has been to limit the pretensions and powers of the State. To Catholic philosophy, persons are the irreducible "things," and a human group is one person or one body only in a legal, metaphorical, or mystical sense. It is not a substantial but an accidental whole: "accidental" here means in the category of *relation, not "incidental," such as a chance heap of stones, or, as Aristotle notes, a collection of people who happen to dwell within the same boundaries. However, an accidental whole can be a natural whole, e.g., a family, and is not necessarily an artificial whole, e.g., an oil company. At this point we may remark the split that shows itself in the Christian tradition, between the "Augustinism" that State institutions and in particular sanctions exist because of sin and that the State would wither away were human nature to recover its innocence, and the Aristotelianism that association in a State springs from the very condition of human nature, which is to be a *zoön politikon,* a social and political animal. BIBLIOGRAPHY: T. Gilby, *Between Community and Society, A Theology of the State* (1953).

[T. GILBY]

STATE CHURCH, commonly a synonym for *national Church or *established Church, but more precisely any Church that is legally recognized as the official religion of a particular state. As such, the term applies to Roman Catholic, Protestant, or Orthodox Churches, where these have such recognition. The term is also used in another sense to signify a Church that exists in direct subordination to the State (see ERASTIANISM). By this meaning, a contrast is suggested with a Church–State, i.e., a Church–State partnership in which the former is dominant, as in a theocracy.

[N. H. MARING]

STATED CLERK, an official of governing bodies in Churches of Presbyterian polity. Although the *session (governing unit) of each local congregation elects a clerk, the term "stated clerk" is generally used only in larger administrative units—*presbytery, *synods, and *general assembly. It involves responsibility for maintaining records and is normally not a full-time position for bodies other than the general assembly. The stated clerk of the general assembly, however, is a full-time official in the major Presbyterian Churches. He gives general supervision to the administrative work determined by the general assembly, and in some ways is regarded as the leader of the denomination. Authority, however, rests with the general assembly, over which an elected moderator presides.

[T. EARLY]

STATEMENT OF FAITH (United Church of Christ), a testimony, in broad areas of Christian teaching, of the belief of this Church. It is not a *doctrinal standard, nor can it be imposed on local churches or used as a test for members or ministers. The preparation of a brief statement of faith was the first task of the Church after its formation in 1957. An appointed committee of members in equal numbers from the uniting denominations prepared the text, and it was accepted substantially by the Second General Synod in 1959. Written in modern language, descriptive rather than definitive, lyrical rather than theological, the statement was designed for liturgical use in worship services and has had wide acceptance for this purpose. The affirmations are so phrased and arranged as to accommodate even a non-Trinitarian understanding of Christian teaching.

[R. F. G. CALDER]

STATES OF LIFE, the distinction common in Roman Catholic usage between the several stable vocations in life, each having its proper mode of living with certain privileges and responsibilities peculiar to itself. The three main states are the lay, clerical, and religious states. From the earliest times the faithful in general were known as the laity from a word signifying the people [of God]. Gradually those who served at the altar and governed the Christian community were distinguished as clerics. A third classification was added when large groups of the faithful began to devote themselves to lifelong observance of the evangelical counsels. With the development of monasticism, esp. in the 4th and 5th centuries, the men and women who consecrated themselves to monastic life came to be known as religious. In popular speech the laity are often distinguished as pertaining to the married or single state, and the notion of a special state seems to be accurately attributed to the married, but its application to the unmarried, whose condition is unstable and changeable at will (at least when the condition is not deliberately adopted as a way of life) is to be understood in a looser sense. In a yet looser sense the term state of life is sometimes used by moral theologians in reference to one's social position and status in the community, as when they speak, e.g., of expenditures, etc., in accordance with one's state. *STATES OF PERFECTION.

[P. F. MULHERN]

STATES OF PERFECTION, a technical term in canon law that clearly includes the religious communities, societies of common life, and *secular institutes. Pius XII's *Provida Mater Ecclesia* of 1947, including secular institutes among the states of perfection, clearly pronounced these to be the three states of perfection. The force of "state" is that the form of life is a dedicated and constant condition of striving for the perfection of charity according to the three evangelical counsels of poverty, chastity, and obedience (not necessarily vowed) and the observance of the constitutions or rule approved for the specific way of life. St. Thomas Aquinas includes episcopacy as a state of perfection because of the stability and dedication required (ThAq ST 2a2ae, 184.5–7). It is disputed whether the life of secular clergy is to be regarded as a state of perfection. Vatican Council II gives a more positive meaning to the place of laity in the Church, esp. in underlining the universal call to holiness in the Church. Thus while the clerical or the lay state may not be canonically states of perfection, their proper ways of life are ideally a constant striving for perfection and a witness in the Church.

[T. C. O'BRIEN]

STATES OF THE CHURCH, the lands in Italy over which the popes had both temporal and spiritual sovereignty. From the earliest centuries of Christianity, the bps. of Rome had been the recipients of territorial grants, but the major acquisition of land came in 756 when Pepin the Short, having defeated the Lombards, made his famous Donation of a large part of central Italy to the Papacy. During succeeding centuries, papal temporal sovereignty increased or diminished, depending on the prestige of the Holy See. During the Avignon Papacy, the Italian possessions had to be reconquered and rehabilitated.

The era of the French Revolution and Napoleon saw not only the annexation of papal territories to the French Empire but also the dissemination of the principles of the French Revolution. Although the Congress of Vienna (1815) restored the Papal States to the Holy See, the Risorgimento eventually destroyed papal sovereignty. After the defeat of Austria in 1859, the papal territories of the Romagna and the Marches were annexed by Piedmont, which became the Kingdom of Italy in 1861. In 1870, when the French troops who had been guarding Rome for almost a decade were withdrawn to take part in the Franco-Prussian War, the troops of King Victor Emmanuel II marched into Rome, thereby ending the existence of the States of the Church.

BIBLIOGRAPHY: P. Partner et al., NCE 13:655–662.

[E. A. CARRILLO]

STATIONAL CHURCH, a particular church in which upon a fixed day the faithful gather for the celebration of the bishop's liturgy. The name stational is derived from the Latin *statio*, this being from early times the term for Christian assemblies of worship. The custom of repairing to particular churches on certain days is frequently witnessed to in early Christian literature; it undoubtedly developed from the desire of bps. to visit the increasing number of churches under their jurisdiction. Rome has preserved the most complete account of its stational churches, although many Christian centers, esp. Jerusalem and Constantinople, give evidence of a like practice. On some occasions, the stational church was reached and the stational liturgy begun with a solemn procession which brought the pope or bishop, the clergy, and the laity to the particular church appointed for that day. Gregory the Great was primarily responsible for organizing the stational schedule, and the Roman Missal still carries his designations of the stational church for a particular day. The practice flourished well into the 13th cent., but fell into disuse as a result of the Avignon exile of the popes, and was continued thereafter only on a diminished scale. In our own day, John XXIII in 1961 resumed the visit of stational churches in the parishes of Rome. The establishment of the stational churches and liturgies was intended to continue and symbolize the original model of Christian worship in which the bishop celebrated the Eucharist as the shepherd in the midst of his flock, thereby demonstrating the unity of the liturgical community. BIBLIOGRAPHY: H. Leclercq, DACL 15.2:1653–57; R. F. McNamara, NCE 13:662–664.

[B. ROSENDALL]

STATIONS OF THE CROSS, see WAY OF THE CROSS.

STATISTICS OF RELIGIOUS BODIES, numerical reports for Churches and other religious organizations on such items as membership, number of congregations, and financial contributions. Such reports are difficult to secure for the total world picture and present special problems of interpretation. Many religious bodies have a loose organizational structure, with no personnel employed to gather accurate statistics. Particularly in the emerging nations of the world, religious bodies may not have the resources or the training, or sometimes may be lacking the interest, needed to keep complete and detailed records. Further difficulties result from a lack of uniformity among the various bodies in methods of gathering statistics and defining terms. Some Churches include children who have been baptized but not confirmed, while others do not. Still others do not baptize infants, and that must be considered in comparing their numerical strength with other groups. Statistics on Jews generally include all who are Jewish by birth. Few religious bodies attempt to distinguish between nominal and active membership. Statistical reports, therefore, do not indicate whether significant percentages of the reported membership may have ceased to participate in worship and other expressions of religious life. Enthusiastic devotees, sometimes unconsciously, may exaggerate the following of their group. Occasionally such figures can be corrected by the studies of more objective, outside institutions, such as government agencies or polls by private organizations. Since some people object to governmental questioning of citizens about their religion, however, government agencies often remain aloof from that area. In the U.S. no government census of religious preference has been taken since 1936. By and large, therefore, those who gather statistics on religious bodies are dependent on the reports given by those bodies.

A further difficulty is estimating the number of people who identify with a particular religious group although they do not have formal affiliation. People may be in general agreement with the teachings of the group and participate to a considerable extent in its community life without becoming formally identified. In mission areas such adherents may comprise a significant number, particularly if the missionaries require thorough preparation prior to baptism. Warnings against undue emphasis on statistics are frequently given; nonetheless, some consideration of statistics seems essential for church planning, finances, and representation in ecumenical bodies. Statistical trends of growth or decline are subject to varying interpretations and cannot be automatically equated with the growth or decline of religion's influence on society. See, for general compilations of statistics, along with some discussion of the difficulty of securing them, *World Christian Handbook* (eds. H. W. Coxill and K. Grubb, 1968); and *Yearbook of American Churches* (ed. L.B. Whitman, annual).

[T. EARLY]

STATIUS, PUBLIUS PAPINIUS (*c*.45–c.96 A.D.), a principal Latin poet of the silver age of Latin literature. Born at Naples where his poet-father was a teacher of literature, S. settled in Rome where he gave recitations from his works and became the friend of the leading men of his day, including Domitian. Toward the end of his life he retired to Naples after a humiliating defeat in a poetry contest. Among his extant works are the epic poems *Thebaid,* the work of 12 years, and the unfinished *Achilleid.* Thirty-two occasional poems addressed to his friends comprise the *Silvae.* S.'s verse is fluent and polished but highly rhetorical and full of learned allusions; his debt to Virgil, both in language and incident, is great. The epics were much admired in antiquity and the Middle Ages, when for some unexplained reason he was believed to have been a Christian. (Dante, *Purg.* 21–27). BIBLIOGRAPHY: E. Wood, OCD 858.

[F. J. MURPHY]

STATTLER, BENEDICT (1728–97), Bavarian Jesuit, philosopher at the Univ. of Ingolstadt. He was the defender of C. Wolff's system against Kant in his *Philosophia methodo scientiis propria explanata* (1769–72). S. also wrote *Dissertatio logica de valore sensus communis tamquam criterio veritatis* (1780) and *Anti Kant* (1788). He is classified as a semirationalist because of his *Demonstratio catholica* (1775), put on the Index for its obscuring of the distinction between faith and reason. In defending Wolff's philosophy, in vogue at the time, S. proposed the principle of sufficient reason as the proof of everything. BIBLIOGRAPHY: J. E. Gurr, *Principle of Sufficient Reason in Some Scholastic Systems: 1750–1900* (1959).

[T. C. O'BRIEN]

STATUTA ECCLESIAE ANTIQUA, a 5th-cent. compilation of canons attributed to Gennadius of Marseilles that became part of many canonical collections. It contained both disciplinary canons and ritual prescriptions and formulas; it is important to the study of the history of the Gallican liturgy.

STAUDENMAIER, FRANZ ANTON (1800–56), German theologian, typical of many who studied and taught at Tübingen, in his speculative bent: attempting to speak in the idiom of the various contemporary German philosophical systems and lacking strong attachment to the traditions of the Church Fathers or of the medieval Doctors of the Church. Born in Württemberg, he was ordained in 1827, taught dogmatic theology at Giessen and Freiburg in Breisgau, was cofounder of the *Jahrbücher für Theologie* and *Zeitschrift für Theologie;* author of *Der Geist des Christentums* (1835), *Enzyklopädie des theologischen Wissenschaft* (1834), and the unfinished *Die Philosophie des Christentums oder Metaphysik* (1844–52). His major concern was to respond critically to the idealism of Hegel.

[E. J. DILLON]

STAUFFENBERG, CLAUS VON (1907–44), German general and leader of the anti-Nazi resistance movement. S. was born into an old Swabian noble family with a long Catholic tradition. He believed that this elite status imposed a special responsibility for service to the community. In 1926 he joined the German army as an officer cadet. His determined pursuit of military training brought rapid advancement and his acceptance into the Staff College in 1936. After a two year course there he was assigned to a cavalry division as a staff officer in charge of logistics. The capacity for organization and hard work which he displayed earned him promotion to the General Staff. His experiences in the General Staff made him increasingly critical of Adolf Hitler's leadership, on both military and moral grounds. At the beginning of 1943 he was assigned to a tank in Africa, where he lost his right hand, two fingers of his left hand, and his left eye. After his recovery he became chief of staff to the commander of the reserve army, General Frederick Olbricht. In this capacity S. devoted all of his energies to the conspiracy to overthrow Hitler. Olbricht secretly prepared the reserve army to seize control in Berlin following the assassination of Hitler planned by the conspirators. The assassination attempt occurred on July 20, 1944, when S. carried a briefcase containing a time bomb to the briefing session at Hitler's headquarters. After placing the briefcase near Hitler and activating the bomb with the three fingers of his left hand, he left the conference and returned to Berlin. The explosion injured but did not kill Hitler. The news that Hitler was still alive ended the coup d'état. S. was tried by a summary court-martial and shot the next day. BIBLIOGRAPHY: J. Kramarz, *Stauffenberg* (1967).

[R. J. GIBBONS]

STAUPITZ, JOHANN VON (*c*.1468–1524), German Augustinian, theologian, counselor of the young Martin Luther. S. entered the Augustinian Order in 1490; became a doctor in Scripture in 1500. Invited by the Elector Frederick III of Saxony to reorganize the Univ. of Wittenberg, he became first dean of its theology faculty (1503–12). Elected vicar general of his order in 1503, he became Luther's spiritual adviser and appointed Luther his successor in the chair of Scripture at Wittenberg. Luther gave credit to S. for aiding him in his torments of conscience by turning his thoughts to Christ's love; in his last letter Luther (1523) told S. that he had led him to the light of the gospel. After Luther's attack on indulgences, however, S. drew apart from the controversies, and would not renounce his own loyalty to Rome. He resigned as vicar general in 1520 and accepted an invitation to be court chaplain at Salzburg. There in 1532 he joined the Benedictines, dying as abbot of St. Peter's. BIBLIOGRAPHY: E. Wolf, RGG 6:243–343; R. Weijenbourg, LTK 9:1026.

[M. J. SUELZER]

STAUROPEGIUM (Gr., fixing a cross), the rite of erection of a cross in that spot of a future church where the altar would be located. When it is performed at the order of the patriarch, this subtracts the church, monastery, or institution (hospital, orphanage) from the jurisdiction of the bishop, conferring thereby the right of patriarchal exemption to the place and all the persons connected with it. The law of the Eastern Catholic Churches regulates the stauropegium in ClerSanc, c.263. The Orthodox patriarchs of Constantinople and Antioch have in the past conferred the stauropegial exemption even upon lay confraternities in Poland and the Ukraine in the 16th cent. to enable them to resist bishops who had decided to join the Catholic Church. Pope Clement XI permitted the continued existence of the Confraternity of Lvov (1709) but subjected it to the local bishop as his delegate. BIBLIOGRAPHY: V. J. Pospishil, *Law on Persons* (1960) 133–135, 299–302.

[V. J. POSPISHIL]

STAVELOT, ABBEY OF (*Stabulense, Stabuletum*), Benedictine abbey, founded *c*.648 in the Ardennes, Diocese of Liège (Belgium) by St. Remaclus (d. *c*.664) with the aid of King Sigibert II of Austrasia and the mayor of the palace, Grimoald. With Malmédy it formed a double monastery under a single abbot. Destroyed by the Normans in 881, restored by St. Odilon in 938, it became an imperial abbey (962), and its abbots were princes of the Holy Roman Empire. Abbot Popponius (1021–48) constructed a huge abbey church. Abbot Wibald (1130–80) was an outstanding monastic figure of his time. In the 16th cent. it joined the Congregation of Bursfeld. The abbey was suppressed in 1797. Certain portions of the buildings are still standing. BIBLIOGRAPHY: Cottineau 2:3085–88.

[J. DAOUST]

STEARNS, FOSTER (1881–1956), librarian, member of U.S. Congress. A member of an old Yankee family of Massachusetts, S. was ordained an Episcopalian minister but resigned to enter the Catholic Church in 1911. In 1917 he was state librarian of Massachusetts. After distinguished service in World War I he entered the foreign service, was stationed in turn in Washington, Constantinople, and Paris. Leaving the diplomatic corps, he engaged in library work, planning and acting as director of the Dinand Library, College of the Holy Cross, Worcester, Mass., (1925–30). He was elected to the U.S. Congress and for three terms (1939–45) as a Republican supported the New Deal foreign policy. S. contributed many valuable works from his own library to various libraries. Among his writings were a translation of Felix Klein's *Madeleine Semer: Convert and Mystic* (1927) and a work on Edward Everett Hale in the American Secretaries of State Series.

[J. R. AHERNE]

STEARNS, SHUBAEL (1706–71), Baptist revivalist. Reared a Congregationalist in Boston, Mass., S. was influenced by the preaching of George *Whitefield *c*.1745. In 1751 he became a Baptist and was ordained a minister. His preaching was highly emotional and proved effective among the frontier inhabitants of N.C., where he and Daniel *Marshall organized the Sandy Creek Church in 1755. By 1758, several other congregations had been constituted, and the Sandy Creek Association was begun. The type of revivalistic preaching represented by Stearns, Marshall, and other *Separate Baptists from New England was not readily accepted by the older Baptist Churches of the South, but it led to rapid Baptist expansion and laid the foundations for their subsequent predominance in that section. BIBLIOGRAPHY: W. L. Lumpkin, *Baptist Foundations in the South* (1961).

[N. H. MARING]

STEFAN (SEMEN IAVORSKĬ, 1658–1722), Russian theologian. He studied at Kiev, Lvov, and at Jesuit schools in Poland where he accepted Roman Catholicism for a time (1684–87). Returning to Orthodoxy he became a monk and changed his name from Semen to Stefan. He taught at Kiev; under his rectorship the school officially became an academy in 1701. That same year S. was named patriarchal exarch of Moscow and, through his influence, the Academy of Moscow was staffed by Latinizing theologians from Kiev. He became first president of the *Holy Synod of Russia when the Moscow patriarchate was suppressed in 1721. His chief work *Petra fidei* (*Kamen' very; Rock of Faith*), written in 1773, was a polemic against the Protestantizing of Feofan *Prokopovich. Displeased by the work, Czar Peter the Great suppressed it, and it was not published until 1778. S. relied heavily on the method, content, and even language of St. Robert Bellarmine's theology. His writings had considerable influence on A. *Khomyakov. BIBLIOGRAPHY: J. Ledit, DTC 14.1:326–329.

[F. T. RYAN]

STEFANO DA VERONA (1375–1438), Italian painter wrongly called "da Zevio." In *Adoration of the Magi* (1435) and *Madonna of the Rose Garden,* S. shows linear rhythms of great sophistication in fluid figures and realistic plants and animals, which determine him an International Gothic artist related to Cologne and Prague masters rather than to the Italian school. His many frescoes in Verona are now lost.

[M. J. DALY]

STEFFANI, AGOSTINO (1654–1728), Italian composer and diplomat. S. studied in Munich and Rome and, later in Paris. He was ordained in 1680 and made a titular abbot in 1882. S., who had early success as an organist and composer, held important musical and diplomatic positions with the courts of Munich and Hanover. He composed many operas and cantatas, several fine duets, madrigals, gavottes, minuets, and other secular and church music. The best known of his works is probably his "Stabat Mater." S.'s artistic influence has been seen in the music of Handel and of other German composers.

[M. T. LEGGE]

STEIN, EDITH (1891–1942), Carmelite nun and philosopher. A native of Breslau, Silesia, she came from a devout Jewish family. She studied philosophy at Freiburg and at Göttingen under the phenomenologist E. *Husserl and became a leading member of the phenomenological school. Having lost faith in her ancestral religion, she first learned of Catholicism through M. Scheler, a pupil of Husserl. After several years of study and doubt, she was deeply impressed by a biography of St. Theresa of Avila and decided to become a Catholic. Giving up her university appointment, she accepted a teaching position at a Dominican sisters' school in the Rhineland. She was appointed a lecturer at the Education Institute in Münster (1932) but lost her position the following year because of anti-Semitic legislation. She entered the Carmelite Order at Cologne that same year and there completed her synthesis, begun several years earlier, of Thomist philosophy and modern thought, *Finite and Eternal Being*. Anti-Jewish persecution forced her to flee to a convent in Echt (Holland) in 1938, and there she wrote *Science of the Cross*, the life of St. John of the Cross from a phenomenological point of view. Arrested and deported, she died in an Auschwitz gas chamber in 1942. BIBLIOGRAPHY: H. Graef, *Scholar and the Cross* (1955).

[J. P. REID]

STEIN, ERNST (1891–1945), Austrian Byzantine historian. At the rise of Hitler, S., who had taught at the Universities of Vienna and Berlin, left Germany and became a member of the Oriental Institute of Brussels. As a visiting professor he taught at The Catholic University of America (1934–36). He was given a chair at Louvain in 1937 but once again was forced to flee by the German invasion of 1940, this time to Switzerland where he spent the war years. Beginning his career with studies in Roman history and epigraphy, he later gave much of his attention to Byzantium, concentrating on social questions and institutions. The first volume of his most famous work, the *History of the Later Roman Empire*, appeared in Vienna in German in 1928; the second was published posthumously in French in 1949. BIBLIOGRAPHY: M. Higgins, NCE 13:687.

[R. B. ENO]

STEIN AM RHEIN, ABBEY OF, Schaffhausen, Switzerland. Originally Benedictine, it was founded on the Hohentwiel in the 10th cent. and later moved to Stein. During the Reformation Stein was suppressed. The abbey's German property was taken over in 1698 by the abbey of Petershausen. Since 1927 the monastery has been used as a museum. BIBLIOGRAPHY: P. Volk, NCE 13:687.

[M. J. FINNEGAN]

STEINER, RUDOLF (1861–1925), founder of the Anthroposophical Society. Born in Karlovic, Hungary, he received a scientific education, studying at the Technical University in Vienna, but his interests lay in philosophy. In 1886 he published *Goethe's Theory of Cognition,* and during the years 1890–97 he helped edit the Weimar edition of Goethe's works. He became interested in Christianity and in *Theosophy and in 1902 founded the German Theosophical Society. Ten years later he established the Anthroposophical Society for the study of human evolution in the light of the Christ-Event. In 1913, because of S.'s opposition to the Hinduism of Annie *Besant and the Adyar Theosophists, the German Theosophical Society was expelled and its members were absorbed into the Anthroposophical Society. In the same year at Dornach, Switzerland, S. built the Gotheanum, a center of his own architectural design, for his followers. He developed Anthroposophy as a system of thought and way of life whereby man could spiritualize his existence; S.'s doctrine did not include theism. His later years were devoted in writings on the social order and to fostering experimental theater and music. His writings are extensive on theosophic and philosophic subjects. BIBLIOGRAPHY: A. P. Shepherd, *Science of the Invisible* (1954). *ANTHROPOSOPHY.

[R. K. MacMASTER]

STEINMANN, JEAN (1911–63), biblical scholar. A French parish priest, S. studied and wrote extensively on exegesis. Attempting to lead Christians to a realization of the wealth in biblical lore, he traveled with groups of laymen and women in the Near East, as well as in Mexico and Europe, to teach the variety of cultures in the world. He was drowned in a flood in Palestine during one of these expeditions. His many works include *Le Prophète Isaïe* (1955), *Le Livre de Job* (1955), *David, roi d'Israel* (1948), *Les Plus anciennes traditions du Pentateuque* (1954) and *Une Foi chrétienne pour aujourd'hui* (1967). *Vie de Jésus* (1959) was placed on the Index in 1961.

[J. R. AHERNE]

STEINMEYER (FARMER, FERDINAND; 1720–86), a Jesuit who entered the society in 1743, and came to the U.S. in 1752, laboring in Eastern Pennsylvania, New Jersey, and New York. Attached to St. Joseph's Church, Philadelphia, in his missionary efforts he traveled widely. S. was an astronomer well known in Europe; he was also one of the first trustees of the University of Pennsylvania. J. Kirlin, *Catholicity in Philadelphia* (1909).

[J. R. AHERNE]

STELZHAMER, FRANZ (1802–74), Upper Austrian poet of ingenious natural talent. In his dialect poems he dealt with the life of the peasant and human existence in general. He was the son of a farmer, and his rural surroundings became the natural environment for his works. He tried his hand at several professions but could not cope with the growing urbanization of the time.

[B. F. STEINBRUCKNER]

STENDHAL (pseudonym of Henri Beyle; 1783–1842), French writer and diplomat. Trained in science, S. held posts in the Napoleonic armies, spent the Restoration years in private life, and after 1830 was French consul at Civitavecchia in the Papal States. Intellectually a disciple of the encyclopedists and ideologists, but temperamentally a romantic, he possessed the formers' terse, ironical, analytical style (e.g., *De l'Amour*, 1822); and the latter's feeling for Italy and enthusiasm for new literary forms (*Promenades dans Rome*, 1829; *Racine et Shakespeare*, 1823). His posthumously published autobiographical works—*La Vie de Henri Brulard, Souvenirs d'égotisme* and his *Journal* (tr. as *Private Diaries of S.,* 1962)—show S. as anticlerical, indifferent to religious symbolism, and skeptical, one who summarized his personal philosophy, ''Beylisme,'' as a passionate epicurean's quest for happiness. A disdain for religious subjects occasionally marred his aesthetic judgment as his *Histoire de la peinture en Italie* (1817) reveals. His novels, though primarily studies in the crystallization of love, reflect a liberal intellectual's view of religion in Restoration France and Italy. Julien Sorel, the protagonist outsider of *Le Rouge et le Noir* (1830) selects the priesthood (the black) as a surer means of advancement than the army (the red), while Fabrizio del Dongo in *La Chartreuse de Parme* (1839) passes through worldly adventures and love affairs before becoming a disillusioned, ascetic archbishop of Parma. *Armance* (1827) casts in a minor role Lacordaire's correspondent Mme. Swetchine, whose quaint mysticism S. mocks under the guise of a Mme. Bonivet. These novels, along with *Lucien Leuwen* (begun 1834, but left unfinished), depict a society steeped in religious hypocrisy because of the union of throne and altar and the pervasive influence of the Congregation of the Blessed Virgin, Ultramontanists in conflict with Gallicans and Jansenists, politics manipulated by stereotyped Jesuit intriguers, and unflattering portraits of seminary life and candidates for the priesthood—a cynical picture only occasionally redeemed by an admirable ecclesiastical figure. BIBLIOGRAPHY: F. M. Albérès, *Stendhal et le sentiment religieux* (1956).

[G. E. GINGRAS]

STEPHEN (PROTOMARTYR), ST., the first Christian martyr, whose brief career of ministry, ending in martyrdom outside Jerusalem, is outlined in chapters 6 and 7 of Acts. The story of Stephen is used by the author of Acts to introduce the period of savage persecution of Christians unto death, beginning in Jerusalem with S., spreading throughout the Empire, and ending in Rome. It is easier to see the scheme of things into which the author fits S., than it is to figure out exactly how S. might have fitted into the early Jerusalem Church. He is introduced during a seemingly minor incident in the life of that Church. The widows of the Hellenists were being overlooked in the daily distribution of the Christian community; Greek-speaking men of good reputation were chosen to rectify this imbalance. But what follows is a solemn ordination event presided over by the Twelve; and the seven newly ordained, far from waiting on table, are presented preaching the Word with power. S.'s ministry of the Word is described in terms parallel to the account of Jesus' own ministry. Full of grace and power, S. began to work great miracles and signs among the people. False accusation was brought against him, alleging that he was speaking blasphemously against the Temple, Moses, and the Law. At his trial when he mentioned seeing the heavens opened and the Son of Man coming, his audience could not bear the blasphemy, and they carried him outside the city and stoned him. S.'s final words—"Lord Jesus, receive my spirit" and "Lord, do not hold this sin against them"—echo the final words of Jesus on the cross in the gospel version of Luke. The sermon of S. to his accusers (ch. 7) is the longest of the many sermons contained in Acts. It gives a complete account of Israelite-Jewish history. The tone of this account (v. 1–50) could be viewed as quite similar to the many disapproving homilies in the Deuteronomic history, which in turn borrowed from the outlook of the great Prophets. The closing verses (51–53), however, represent a tragic step further. No longer is it a brotherly rebuke. It now reflects a complete rupture, and no doubt derives from the experience of Pauline communities throughout the Mediterranean world. Now it is "we who have been forced to break away" against "you apostates," who culminate a history of apostasy by betraying and murdering the Righteous One. Saul (Paul) was present at the stoning of S., and approved it. He later got authorization from the High Priest to persecute the synagogues of Damascus. This would seem to indicate that a more correct description of the divisions in Jerusalem of that time would identify the tension as existing between the temple party of collaboration with Roman authority, and those Jews of various types (including Hellenists) who looked for the liberation of Jerusalem. BIBLIOGRAPHY: M. Liverani, BiblSanct 11:1376–92; Butler 4:616–617.

[E. J. DILLON]

STEPHEN I, ST. (d. 257), **POPE** from 254, successor of St. *Lucius. The letters of St. *Cyprian (65–75, CSEL 3.2:738–827) attest to continued controversy with this Pope. The disputes are important as early evidence of the Roman See's exercising primacy over other Churches. S. reinstated Martial of Merida and Basilides of Leon Astorga, bishops who had been deposed as *Libellatici*; Cyprian and other African bishops urged the Spanish Churches to ignore the Pope's act. When S. hesitated to act against Marcian, bp. of Arles, accused of being a *Novatianist, Cyprian wrote in protest. A more significant issue, however, concerned *baptism of heretics. S. defended the Roman practice, followed also at Alexandria and Palestine, of recognizing such baptisms, and reconciling those so baptized by simple absolution. Cyprian rejected baptism by heretics in a treatise written c. 255 and through the enactments of councils at Carthage in 255 and 256. S. negated these decrees, forbidding rebaptism of heretics, with the words "Should anyone return to you from any sort of heresy, let nothing be introduced beyond established practice, namely penance through the laying on of hands." The Pope addressed himself similarly to the Churches of Asia Minor, and particularly to Fermilian, bp. of Caesarea, who in turn wrote to Cyprian attacking the Pope. Cyprian convoked a new council in September of 456, which renewed the earlier condemnations. The conflict was unresolved when a persecution under the Emperor Valerian in 258 intervened. There is no certainty as to whether S. died a martyr. BIBLIOGRAPHY: E. Weltin, *Early Popes* (1964).

[R. B. ENO]

STEPHEN [II], elected pope on the death of St. *Zachary in 752 but never consecrated because his own death followed within 3 days of his election. Since 1961 the *Annuario Pontificio* in its list of the popes adverts to this Stephen in a footnote, explaining that he is omitted from the list in conformity with the canon law of the time, according to which a pope's pontificate began, not with his election, but with his consecration. In modern canon law, the pontificate begins with the election, and perhaps for this reason the *Annuario* adds to the traditional numeration of each of the succeeding Stephens a parenthetical ordinal indicating the number as it would be if Stephen [II] had been accorded a place on the list, e.g., Stephen II (III). This practice has not been generally accepted and is not followed here. BIBLIOGRAPHY: R. Poole, "Names and Numbers of Medieval Popes," EHR 32 (1917) 465–478; Mann 1.2:290–291; P. J. Mullins, NCE 13:695.

[P. F. MULHERN]

STEPHEN II (d. 757), **POPE** from 752. When S. became Pope, *Aistulf, King of the Lombards, had already taken Ravenna and was threatening a move on Rome. The Eastern Emperor, Constantine V (740–775), immersed in war with the Saracens and in trouble at home because of his *iconoclasm, looked to S. to save Ravenna, seat of the exarch.

Although the Pope went in person to treat with Aistulf, his pleas for peace were in vain. He therefore crossed the Alps in the winter of 753, consecrated Pepin and his sons, naming them kings and patricians of Rome, and persuaded the Franks to come to the aid of the Holy See. Twice Pepin led his armies into Italy, finally taking from Aistulf by arms the papal and imperial lands that the Lombards had appropriated. Pepin summarily refused Constantine's demand that the territory of the exarchate thus liberated be returned to him. Pepin, looking upon these lands as spoils of the war he had undertaken "for love of St. Peter," made them over to the Church. In a dramatic gesture he had the keys of the conquered cities laid on the tomb of the Apostle. This came to be known as the Donation of Pepin. As it seemed to promise the Holy See independence of temporal rulers, S., shortly before his death, wrote to Pepin of the great good he had done the Church. BIBLIOGRAPHY: L. Duchesne, *Beginning of the Temporal Sovereignty of the Popes* (tr. A. Mathew, 1908); Einhard, *Life of Charlemagne* (tr. S. Turner, 1960); P. J. Mullins, NCE 13:695.

[P. F. MULHERN]

STEPHEN III (d. 772), **POPE** from 768. A native of Sicily and a monk, S. entered the papal service under St. *Zachary. Thirteen months intervened between the death of his predecessor, St. Paul I, and S.'s own consecration. The intrigues, first of a Roman faction and then of certain Lombard officials, had put successively into the chair of Peter two improperly elected occupants. The first, Constantine, was made pope by means of force by his brother Duke Toto of Nepi. Christopher, an official under the late Pope, persuaded the Lombards to send armed forces to rectify the situation. Constantine fled to sanctuary, Toto was slain, and the Lombards had a monk called Philip elected. Christopher, however, induced Philip to resign, and at a new election S. was chosen. After his election but prior to his consecration, S.'s supporters took fearful vengeance upon certain of those involved in the preceding elections. A council at the Lateran (769) confirmed the status of S., ordered Constantine (already blinded) imprisoned for life, and to safeguard future elections decreed that none but the Roman clergy were entitled to vote in a papal election. When S. opposed Charlemagne's proposed marriage to the daughter of *Desiderius, the latter came to Rome, and Christopher, fearing his wrath, mustered an armed defense. S., however, appeased the King's anger by turning Christopher over to the Lombards, who put him to death. S. claimed he had learned that Christopher was plotting to take his life. BIBLIOGRAPHY: Mann 1.2:361–393; W. Ullman, *Growth of Papal Government in the Middle Ages* (1962); C. M. Aherne, NCE 13:695–696.

[P. F. MULHERN]

STEPHEN IV (d. 817), **POPE** from 816. A deacon of the Roman Church, S. was elected without imperial interference and, in conformity with the decree of the Roman Council in 796, by clerical electors only. A noble, of the family that was later to give *Sergius II and *Adrian II to the papacy, S. was able to unite contending parties and thus heal the divisions that had afflicted the reign of his predecessor, *Leo III. Although elected without imperial interest, S. recognized the Emperor's rights as patrician of the Romans; he exacted of the Roman nobles an oath of fidelity to Louis the Pious and sent a cordial announcement of his election to the Frankish court. In 816, S. journeyed to France where he solemnly consecrated and crowned Louis and his Queen, Ermengarde. Those exiled from Rome as a result of the disturbances in the reign of Leo III (799 and 814) were pardoned by S. and his short reign was peaceful. BIBLIOGRAPHY: Mann 2:111–121; L. Duchesne, *Beginnings of the Temporal Sovereignty of the Popes* (tr. A. Mathew, 1908).

[P. F. MULHERN]

STEPHEN V (d. 891), **POPE** from 885. S., a Roman, was elected without the approval of the weak Emperor, Charles the Fat (885–887), who attempted to depose S., challenging the validity of his election, but was unable to overcome the vehement opposition of the Romans to his maneuvers. When Charles was himself deposed by his own people in 877, contention for the imperial crown forced S. into politics. S. tried unsuccessfully to induce Arnulf of Germany to accept it and was forced to crown Guy of Spoleto who personified the anti-papal traditions of the Lombards. After the death of St. Methodius (885) S., yielding to the wishes of the German bps., forbade the use of the Slavic liturgy in Moravia, although this had been sanctioned by *John VIII and *Adrian III. The part played by S. in the second deposition of Photius is a matter of dispute. BIBLIOGRAPHY: Bihlmeyer-Tüchle 2:59–60; P. Mullins, NCE 13:969.

[P. F. MULHERN]

STEPHEN VI (d. 897), **POPE** from 896. He had been consecrated bp. of Anagni by Pope *Formosus. Probably under pressure from Lambert of Spoleto, claimant of the imperial crown, S. presided over the infamous *Cadaveric Synod which tried the dead Formosus and declared him to have been an illegitimate occupant of the papal see on the ground that he was translated from the See of Porto to that of Rome. Such a transfer was considered uncanonical at that time. The same argument forestalled the charge that S. himself was not legitimately pope, for in his own case there was no real translation from one see to another because his consecration as bp. of Agnani was invalid if Formosus was not truly pope. To lend credibility to the argument, all the Holy Orders administered by Formosus were declared invalid. S., while yet living, was subjected to a degradation like that he had inflicted on the dead Formosus. When Lambert left Rome, the people took matters into their own hands; in the tumult, S. was stripped of his papal insignia and strangled. BIBLIOGRAPHY: L. Duchesne, *Beginnings of the Temporal*

Sovereignty of the Popes, A.D. 854–1073 (tr. A. Mathew, 1908); Mann 4:76–85; P. Mullins, NCE 13;696.

[P. F. MULHERN]

STEPHEN VII (d. 931), **POPE** from 929. A Roman, S. was cardinal priest of Sta. Anastasia, when chosen to succeed *Leo VI. He is thought to have been a creature of *Marozia, who had brought about the death of *John X in 928. All that is recorded of S.'s brief reign is that he granted a number of privileges to the Cluniac monasteries which St. Odo was establishing in France and Italy. BIBLIOGRAPHY: Mann 4:189–190; M. A. Mulholland, NCE 13:696.

[P. F. MULHERN]

STEPHEN VIII (d. 942), **POPE** from 939. Having been educated in Germany, S. became a priest after his return to Rome. He rose to the papacy through the influence of Alberic II. A man of virtuous life, S. strove earnestly as pope to make and keep peace in a time rife with war and threats of war. Through the influence of his legate he persuaded French and Burgundian nobles to give up a rebellion against the King, Louis IV; in Italy, using the good offices of St. *Odo as his predecessor had done, he composed the differences between Alberic and Hugh, King of Italy. He also continued the encouragement given by his predecessors to the Cluniac reform. BIBLIOGRAPHY: Mann 4:212–217; M. Mulholland, NCE 13:697.

[P. F. MULHERN]

STEPHEN IX (Frederick of Lorraine, *c.*1000–58), **POPE** from 1057. Having studied at Liège and served as canon and archdeacon of St. Lambert's, he went to Rome with Pope Leo IX. There he became chancellor and librarian of the Roman Church and cardinal priest of St. Chrysogonus (1057). Elected pope during the minority of Emperor Henry IV, he continued the reform and centralization of the Church, dealing in synod with problems of simony and clerogamy. His influence on the Church was decisive, living on in the work of his aides, Peter Damian, Humbert of Silva Candida, and Hildebrand. BIBLIOGRAPHY: A. Fliche, *La Réforme grégorienne* (v. 1, 1924); G. Despy, "La Carrière lotharingienne du pape Etienne IX," *Revue belge de philosophie et d'histoire* 31 (1953) 955–972.

[O. J. BLUM]

STEPHEN (*c.* 1096–1154), **KING OF ENGLAND** from 1135, grandson of William the Conqueror. Despite his oath (1126) to support Matilda, Henry I's daughter, Stephen seized the throne. To win the support of his brother, Henry, bp. of Winchester, he granted a charter of liberties (1136) allowing clergy to be subject only to church courts. He himself was tried (1139) for violating this charter. Further quarrels with the Church served to increase its autonomy. His long struggle against Matilda ended with the treaty of Wallingford (1153) in which S. kept his throne but recog-

nized Matilda's son, Henry, as his successor. BIBLIOGRAPHY: H. F. C. Davis, *King Stephen* (1967).

[F. D. BLACKLEY]

STEPHEN I, KING OF HUNGARY, ST. (*c.*975–1038), first king of Hungary (from 998), founder of the Hungarian state and the Hungarian Church. A descendant of Árpád, S. (Hungarian, István), son of Duke Géza, ruler of Hungary, married Gisela, daughter of the Duke of Bavaria, and on his father's death was confronted with a formidable pagan revolt. Riding under the banner of St. Martin, he vanquished the rebels in 998, when he assumed the royal title. Maneuvering skillfully to avoid being drawn into the power struggle of the Eastern and Western Empires, S. requested Pope Sylvester II to send him the royal crown. S.'s reign was harmonious and prosperous, and while on the throne he put into effect a constitution that gave Hungary a Western character (e.g., the division of the nation into counties and the regulation of the institution of private property). He gave vast material assistance to various Catholic orders, particularly to the Benedictine monks. Under him, Catholicism became a primary unifying force in Hungary. S. gave asylum to the exiled sons of Edmund Ironside. His daughter Agatha married Prince Edward; thus S. became the grandfather of Edgar the Aetheling and St. Margaret, queen of Scotland. S.'s only son and heir to the throne, St. *Imre (Emery, Emeric), died at the age of 24. This left the problem of succession to the crown in grave doubt. S. was canonized in 1083. His sacred right hand is still Hungary's most cherished relic. Hungary, in its 944 years as a Christian monarchy, was officially the property "of the sacred crown of St. Stephen." The crown of St. Stephen, symbol of Hungarian nationhood, was returned (1978) to Hungary by the U.S., which had held it since recovering it from the Nazis in World War II, in spite of protest by Hungarian patriots against the crown's falling into Communist hands. BIBLIOGRAPHY: I. Lukinich, *History of Hungary* (tr. C. Dallas, 1937); Butler 3:466–468; E. Páztor, BiblSanct 12:19–22.

[D. H. BRUNAUER]

STEPHEN I NEMANJA, KING OF SERBIA (1114–1200), founder of the Nemanjid dynasty which ruled the Serbian Empire for more than 2 cent., beginning in 1180 with the death of the Byzantine Emperor Manuel I Comnenus. The political center of the Serbs had shifted from Zeta (modern Montenegro) to Rascia (Raška). Sometime after 1165 S. assumed the title of grand župan of Rascia. He then built on the achievements of two Serbian leaders of the previous cent., Prince Stephen Vojislav and King Constantine Bodin, who had ruled in Zeta independently of both the Bulgarian tsar and the Byzantine emperor. Before retiring to a monastery in 1196, S. had absorbed the kingdom of Zeta as well as territory along the Adriatic and obtained recognition of autonomy from Byzantium.

[E. J. DILLON]

STEPHEN II NEMANJA, THE FIRST CROWNED,
Serbian king of the Nemanjid dynasty (1196–1228). Son
and able successor of Stephen I, he solidified the unity of
the new Serbian state, obtained a royal crown from the
papacy, and received from the exiled Byzantine emperor an
independent abp. for the Serbian Church. The abp. was the
king's younger brother, St. Sava, who was to become the
patron of the national Church of Serbia.

[E. J. DILLON]

STEPHEN OF BOURBON (*c.*1190–*c.*1261), French
Dominican. S. entered the order at Lyons and began to
serve as preacher and inquisitor in 1230. In the interests of
preachers he wrote *De VII donis Spiritus Sancti,* which
scholars consider a mine of information on the cultural
milieu, the sects, and the superstitions of France. BIBLIOG-
RAPHY: G. Gieraths, LTK 9:1043.

[M. J. SUELZER]

STEPHEN OF CONSTANTINOPLE (Stephen the
Younger; 713–764), abbot and martyr. He was born and
died in Constantinople. The Emperor Constantine V Cop-
ronymus named him leader of the anti-iconoclasts, imprisoned him with 300 monks, and then put him to death after
many tortures. An early 9th-cent. biography by Deacon
Stephen of Hagia Sophia is a primary source for the history
of the iconoclast controversy. BIBLIOGRAPHY: P. Rouillard,
BiblSanct 11:1402–03.

[E. J. DILLON]

STEPHEN OF DIE, ST. (Stephen of Châtillon; d. 1208
or 1213), Carthusian bishop. He joined the Carthusians at
Portes near Belley, where he became prior. In 1207 he was
popularly acclaimed bp. of Die, a position he accepted reluctantly. He was venerated for his austere life. BIBLIOGRA-
PHY: AS Sept. 3:175–201; É. Brouette, BiblSanct
11:1396–98.

[L. J. LEKAI]

STEPHEN OF GRAVESEND (d.1338), English
ecclesiastic and politician; bp. of London (1319). His episcopate was marked by political and ecclesiastical controversy. Courageous and honest, he supported the barons
against Edward II, but protested his deposition and worked
to free Edward III from Roger Mortimer's control. BIBLIOG-
RAPHY: R. W. Hays, NCE 13:698–99.

[R. W. HAYS]

STEPHEN HARDING, ST. (d.1134), third abbot of
Cîteaux. S. was placed as an oblate by his parents in Sherborne abbey, Dorset, England. After the Norman Conquest
he fled to Scotland and later continued his studies in Paris.
He went on a pilgrimage to Rome and on his return, stopped
at Molesmes abbey, where, edified by the abbot, St. Robert,
he decided to remain as a monk. In time, he was one of the
band of 20 monks chosen by Hugh, abp. of Lyons, to insti-

tute a foundation devoted to a stricter observance of the
Benedictine rule at Cîteaux. He was elected abbot (1109)
and kept the struggling community together until St. Bernard arrived with his companions. S. was interested in revising the text of the Latin Bible with the aid of Jewish scholarship. BIBLIOGRAPHY: M. A. Dimier, BiblSanct 11:1398–
1402; Butler 2:114–116.

[R. T. MEYER]

STEPHEN LANGTON (d. 1228), scholar, cardinal, abp.
of Canterbury. A native of Lincolnshire, S. studied at the
Univ. of Paris and taught there for more than 20 years. He
wrote commentaries on the Bible, a theological *Summa*, and
Questiones disputatae. He also devised the division—still in
use—of the books of the Vulgate into chapters. Scholars
generally credit him with the composition of the *Veni
Sancte Spiritus*. He was called to Rome by Innocent III,
who had known him in Paris, and made cardinal in 1206.
Succession to the archbishopric of Canterbury came under
dispute, the monks of the chapter preferring one candidate,
the king and suffragan bps. another; and Innocent settled the
matter by securing the election of S. by representatives of
the monks. S. was consecrated and given the pallium; but
because King John refused to accept him, an interdict was
imposed on England (1208) and the King was excommunicated (1209). When it seemed that Philip Augustus, King of
France, was prepared to invade England to enforce John's
deposition, John sued for reconciliation and acknowledged
S. as abp. of Canterbury. S. then returned to England
(1213) where he shortly became involved in the struggle
between the King and his barons. S. encouraged the barons
to demand constitutional reform and freedom from tyranny
in both civil and ecclesiastical matters. It is not known that
he had a personal hand in drafting the Magna Carta, but
there is no doubt that the document owed much to his inspiration. Innocent was displeased with S.'s part in the matter,
annulled the Magna Carta, and ordered S. to excommunicate the disturbers of the peace. Because he thought the
Pope misunderstood the situation, S. refused to declare the
excommunication. On his way to Lateran Council IV he
learned that the Pope had suspended him from office (1215).
After several months he was absolved but was not permitted
to return to England until 1218 when peace had been restored in England under Henry III. BIBLIOGRAPHY: F. M.
Powicke, *Stephen Langton* (1928); L. Antl, NCE 13:699–
700; W. H. Kent, CE 8:791–793.

STEPHEN OF LEXINTON (d. 1260), Cistercian abbot.
S. came of a distinguished family of Nottinghamshire,
studied in Paris and Oxford, and in 1221 joined the Cistercian abbey of Quarr (Isle of Wight). He was soon made
abbot of Stanley, later (1229) of Savigny (France), and
finally (1243) of Clairvaux. He reformed the decadent Irish
Cistercians and founded the College of St. Bernard in Paris
(1244), a controversial action for Cistercians. In 1256 he
was deposed by the Cistercian general chapter and retired to

Ourscamp abbey. See much of his important correspondence edited by B. Griesser, "Registrum epistolarum Stephani de Lexinton," AnalOCist 3 (1946) 1–118; 8 (1952) 181–378. BIBLIOGRAPHY: C. H. Lawrence, "Stephen Lexington and the Cistercian University Studies in the 13th Century," JEcclHist 11 (1960) 164–179.

[L. J. LEKAI]

STEPHEN OF MURET, ST. (*c.*1045–1124), hermit, founder of the Order of Grandmont. Influenced by the Gregorian reform movement, with which he became acquainted through Bp. Milo of Benevento (under whose care he passed some time in his early youth) and perhaps through some years of residence in the Rome of Gregory VII, S. established a hermitage at Muret (N of Limoges, France), lived an austere life, and attracted a number of disciples. His order exemplifies the eremitical development that took place in Western monasticism in the second half of the 11th century. Attributed to him are a rule and a collection of teachings (*Liber sententiarum*) containing his spiritual doctrine, a work of some importance in the history of spiritual literature. The stress he lays on poverty, inspired by Gregory the Great, anticipates the poverty of the mendicant orders. BIBLIOGRAPHY: H. Platelle, BiblSanct 11:1406–08; Butler 1:282; J. Becquet, DSAM 4.2:1504–14.

[V. BULLOUGH]

STEPHEN OF NARBONNE, ST. (also known as Stephen of Saint-Thibery; d. 1242), Franciscan martyr. He was appointed inquisitor by Pope Gregory IX in 1237. In carrying out this function in Avignonet, which was sympathetic to the Cathari, S. and 10 associates were murdered. Pope Pius IX approved the cult of these martyrs Sept. 1, 1866. BIBLIOGRAPHY: Wadding Ann 3:78–79; J. Guiraud, DHGE 5:1154–62; S. M. Bertucci, BiblSanct 2:647–649.

[H. DRESSLER]

STEPHEN OF OBAZINE, ST. (d. 1159), Cistercian abbot. Of humble origin, S. was first a secular priest, then a hermit, and finally a Benedictine. In 1142 he founded and became first abbot of Obazine near Limoges, France, and later made several other foundations. In 1147 he and his followers joined the Cistercian Order. BIBLIOGRAPHY: Butler 1:527–528; L. J. Lekai, NCE 13:701.

[L. J. LEKAI]

STEPHEN OF PERM, ST. (1345–96), a monk at Rostov for some 13 years. He was ordained and departed for missionary work among the Zyrians near the Ural Mountains. He invented an alphabet for their language and used it for biblical and liturgical translations. In 1383 he was named bishop; he founded schools and seminaries and was fearless in defending his people against government oppression. BIBLIOGRAPHY: I. Dujčev, BiblSanct 12:8–9; Butler 2:167.

[G. T. DENNIS]

STEPHEN OF SALAGNAC (*c.*1210–91). Having joined the Dominicans at Limoges in 1230, he later served as prior there (1249–59) and at Toulouse (1259–61). His chief importance as a writer is his work on the achievements of the Dominican Order, *De quatuor in quibus Deus praedicatorum ordinem insignivit* (ed. T. Kaeppeli, 1949).

[L. E. BOYLE]

STEPHEN OF TOURNAI, (1128–1208), canonist, theologian, and bp. of Tournai. A native of Orléans who studied at Bologna and served as adviser to Philip II Augustus, he was abbot of the Canons Regular at Sainte-Geneviève-de-Paris. His best–known work is *Summa decreti* (ed. J. F. von Schulte, 1891); but many letters and sermons also survive. BIBLIOGRAPHY: J. A. Corbett, NCE 13:701.

[V. BULLOUGH]

STEPHEN, REVELATION OF, see APOCRYPHA (NT), 61.

STEPHENS, JAMES (1882–1950), Irish poet and fiction writer. Born in the Dublin slums, S. became one of the leading figures of the Irish Renaissance. Unlike other authors in the movement, his works were not connected with the Irish theater. In his poetry and fiction he made wide use of Irish folklore and peasant life. It is for his highly colorful prose writings that he is best known. In 1912 he wrote two masterpieces: *The Charwoman's Daughter* (entitled *Mary, Mary* on this side of the Atlantic), and *The Crock of Gold*, a brilliant fantasy that has since become a minor classic. In the same year he produced his second volume of poetry, *The Hill of Vision*, his first being *Insurrections* (1908). *Reincarnations* (1918), a volume of free translations from Gaelic poets, has been considered his greatest single achievement in verse. *The Demi-Gods* (1914) and *The Crock of Gold* are his best-known books. He was only a clerk in a lawyer's office when *The Crock of Gold* established his fame. Other prose works are *Irish Fairly Tales* (1920), *Deirdre* (1923), and *In the Land of Youth* (1924), all based on Irish legend and folklore. After he went to London in 1925, he was less productive. With the exception of *Collected Poems* (1926), he wrote only three works: *Etched in Moonlight* (1928), containing some excellent short stories in the Irish tradition, *Strict Joy* (1931), and *Kings and the Moon* (1938), two volumes of abstruse verse that are pessimistic in tone possibly because of the Eastern mysticism which had supplanted his earlier Protestant faith. He is credited with having a most agile mind, as being a sort of literary acrobat. S. was a broadcaster in London from 1939 until his death in 1950.

[S. A. HEENEY]

STEPHENS, THOMAS (1549–1619), English Jesuit missionary to India, poet. He entered the Society at Rome (1575), having left England after converting to Catholicism.

He left Lisbon (1579) for Goa, via Cape of Good Hope, and sent an account of the voyage to his father in England. This account, including a description of Portuguese commerce in the East, was widely circulated and was included in the travel narratives of Haklyut, Purchas, and John Hamilton Moore. For the sake of the people in his mission, he composed a grammar (c.1640), a doctrinal handbook (c.1622) in the native dialect, Konkani. Seeking to provide a native Christian literature to replace traditional Hindu texts, S. wrote an epic narrative in literary Marathi of Christ's entrance into the world, the *Krista-Purana, Discorso sobre a Vinda Jesus Christo* (1616; *The Christian Purana*, ed. J. L. Saldanha, 1907).

[R. J. LITZ]

STEPINAC, ALOJZIJE (ALOYSIUS; 1898–1960), Yugoslav cardinal. Born in Krasic, Croatia, to a peasant family, he attended the gymnasium in Zagreb and was then drafted into the Austrian army, serving as a 2d lieutenant in World War I. He was captured by the Italians and later joined the South Slav volunteers against the Habsburgs. After the war he studied agriculture in Zagreb, but then went to Rome for doctorates in philosophy and theology. He was ordained in 1930 and in 1937 became abp. of Zagreb, Yugoslavia's largest Catholic diocese. After the 1941 German conquest of Yugoslavia, an independent Croatian state was established under German and Italian sponsorship by the Ustachi (insurgent) party, a nationalist group that used fascist and terrorist methods. It carried out executions of Jews and forced conversions and executions of Orthodox Serbs. After the war, S. was arrested (1946) by the *Tito government and accused of collaboration with the Ustachi regime. In the first of several widely publicized trials of Catholic prelates by the new Communist governments of Eastern Europe, a Zagreb People's Court found him guilty and sentenced him to 16 years hard labor. The Vatican announced excommunication of all those who helped bring about his conviction. In the U.S. and other non-Communist countries S. was honored as a victim of Communist tyranny. He was released in 1951 but confined to his native village. When Pius XII named him a cardinal in 1952, Yugoslavia broke diplomatic relations with the Vatican, which have since been restored.

[T. EARLY]

STERCKX, ENGELBERT (1792–1867), Belgian abp. and cardinal. Born at Ophem, Brabant, of a peasant family, he was ordained in 1815 and then taught until 1821 at the seminary of Mechelen (Malines). After filling pastoral and administrative posts, he was appointed in 1832 as abp. of Mechelen (now Mechelen-Brussels), becoming a card. in 1838. Rejecting *ultramontanism, S. argued for Catholic acceptance of liberal provisions in the 1830 Belgian constitution. S. contributed significantly to the intensification of the priestly and lay apostolates, to the reopening of the

Univ. of Louvain, and to the cause of state support of religious education.

[T. EARLY]

STERILITY, an incapacity to bring about conception by reason of some physical disorder on the part of husband or wife. Unlike *impotence, sterility does not constitute an impediment to marriage. Nor is it grounds for annulment. The attempt to determine causes and to remedy sterility does not justify the use of means that are immoral in themselves; there are other effective medical techniques that are permissible.

[T. C. O'BRIEN]

STERILITY PILLS, see ANOVULANTS.

STERILIZATION, the medical procedure of making a person permanently or temporarily incapable of reproducing. It may be considered as it is in some way voluntary on the subject's part, or as it is involuntary, i.e., inflicted by law for eugenic or for punitive reasons. (1) Sterilization may be the indirectly voluntary, but justifiable side-effect of a surgical procedure required for the preservation of the patient's life (see HYSTERECTOMY; ORCHIECTOMY; OVARIOTOMY). Directly intended solely as a contraceptive measure, whether by X ray, surgery, or drugs, sterilization involves a temporary or permanent *mutilation that is morally unjustifiable, since no threat to the patient's overall bodily health is verified (see TOTALITY, PRINCIPLE OF). Particularly in this matter it is a moral principle that the body's integrity has a relationship not only to individual well-being but also to the forces of nature in virtue of which sexual intercourse is possible and reproductive. The Holy See has addressed the question of contraceptive pills and ruled out their purely contraceptive use; they may, however, be used in anticipation of the unjust aggression of rape, or as regulatory of the menstrual cycle (see HUMANAE VITAE). (2) Involuntary sterilization that is imposed by law on the innocent for purely eugenic reasons cannot be justified morally; human law does not have such power over the human rights of the innocent (see ThAq ST 2a2ae, 104.5). Eugenic sterilization of the mentally defective became the law in many states of the U.S. during the early part of the 20th cent.; advances in medical science as well as Nazi horrors have made such laws largely a dead letter. Sterilization as punishment for crime, esp. the castration of males, may be justified as a purely punitive measure; whether it has any preventive or remedial effect to deter others from crime is a moot issue.

[T. C. O'BRIEN]

STERN, HENRY AARON (1820–85), missionary to the Jews. Born in Germany of Jewish parents, S. received Christian baptism in London in 1840 and 2 years later began to prepare for mission work. For about 10 years he was active as an itinerant missionary among Jews in Mesopotamia, Persia, and Kurdistan. He was ordained in 1849 during a visit to London. The next decade he spent largely in Constantinople but also made journeys to Abyssinia. There he was successful among the black Falasha Jews until anti-European sentiment caused his imprisonment (1864–68). After his release he was active among the Jews in London until his death.

[M. J. SUELZER]

STERN, RAFFAELE (1774–1820), Italian architect in Rome, known for the new wing (1817–22) to the Vatican sculpture museum, a distinguished example of the classicist style in the first half of the 19th century.

[M. J. DALY]

STERZINGER, FERDINAND (1721–86), German Theatine, church historian. Born at Lichtwehr, Tyrol, S. entered the Theatine Order in 1740 and taught at several of their houses. In 1759 he became a professor at Munich and remained there until his death. He became controversial for his criticism of witchcraft trials then current in southern Germany, particularly for his book, *On Common Prejudice Concerning the Effectiveness of Witchcraft* (1766).

[T. EARLY]

STEUART, ROBERT (1874–1948), English Jesuit spiritual writer. Born at Reigate, Surrey, England, of Scottish descent, he sought a career in the Royal Navy, but was prevented from realizing it on medical grounds. He thereafter joined the Jesuits and during World War I was a military chaplain. He became a noted retreat master and extended his influence through such writings as *Inward Vision* (1929); *Temples of Eternity* (1931); *Diversity in Holiness* (1937). His *Spiritual Teaching* was presented in a collection (ed. K. Kendall, 1952). S. also made a noteworthy, pioneering contribution to the development of *secular institutes as a form of the life of Christian perfection. He was superior of the famed Jesuit community at Farm Street, London, from 1926 until 1935. BIBLIOGRAPHY: K. Kendall, *Father Steuart: A Study of His Life and Teaching* (1950).

[T. EARLY]

STEUERNAGEL, CARL (1869–1958), OT scholar. S. taught Scripture at the German Univ. of Halle, Breslau, and Greifswald. A follower of J. *Wellhausen, he published several well-received studies on the Pentateuch, a Hebrew grammar, and an OT introduction. He edited the archeological findings of G. Schumacher and was editor of the *Zeitschrift des Deutschen Palästina-Vereins*.

[T. M. MCFADDEN]

STEVENS, GEORGIA, MOTHER (1871–1946), music educator. Descendant of a well-known Yankee family of Massachusetts, S. became a convert to Catholicism in 1895 and entered the Society of the Sacred Heart (RSCJ). Her significant training in music fitted her for her life work.

Liturgical Music at Manhattanville College, then in New York City, she pioneered in the U.S. a dedication to Gregorian chant and other forms of liturgical music. S. wrote a series of texts for elementary schools, *Tone and Rhythm* (1935–45).

[J. R. AHERNE]

STEVENSON, JOSEPH (1806–95), Scottish historian. Originally Presbyterian, he took Anglican orders (1842), became Roman Catholic (1863), and, after his wife's death (1869), a Jesuit priest. He edited numerous medieval historical MSS for the Public Record Office, other government agencies, and private societies, and was important in the inception of the Rolls Series. He also worked for the British government in the Vatican archives. BIBLIOGRAPHY: T. Cooper, DNB 18:1127–29.

[R. W. HAYS]

STEVENSON, ROBERT LOUIS (1850–94), Scottish author, son of an Edinburgh engineer. Travels in France, where he met Fanny Osbourne, are reflected in *An Inland Voyage* (1878) and *Travels with a Donkey* (1879). In 1880 he married Mrs. Osbourne in San Francisco. His long, courageous struggle with tuberculosis ended in Samoa where he lived his last 5 years, well liked by the natives and called by them "Tusitala," (Teller of tales). Literary popularity came with *Treasure Island* (1883) and *Kidnapped* (1886). Excellent in romantic adventure, he also wrote *A Child's Garden of Verses* (1885), essays and fugitive pieces in *Virginibus Puerisque* (1881), and critical studies in *Familiar Studies of Men and Books* (1882). His natural courage, generosity, and hatred of injustice appear in his answer to an unjust attack on Father Damien, the leper priest of Molokai (*Father Damien: An Open Letter*, 1890). BIBLIOGRAPHY: G. K. Chesterton, *Robert Louis Stevenson* (1955); J. C. Furnas, *Voyage to the Windward: the Life of Robert Louis Stevenson* (1952).

[M. M. BARRY]

STEWARDSHIP, the concept, based on such NT passages as 1 Cor 4.1–2, 9.17, that man must live as the faithful trustee of what he has received from God and must render an account. The term, most often used by Protestants but since Vatican II adopted by Catholics (there is now a National Catholic Stewardship Council), is sometimes given as the theological basis for *tithing, but stewardship of time and of talents is also recognized. Stewardship has been invoked as a justification for great material possessions, which, however, also beget humanitarian obligations. The term was prominent in the *Social Gospel movement; its most recent application has been to describe the Christian's vocation to concern for the world, for the "secular city." BIBLIOGRAPHY: V. Ely, *Stewardship* (1962); T. Kantonen, *Theology of Christian Stewardship* (1964); F. J. McConnell, *Christian Materialism* (1936); H. Cox, *Secular City* (1965).

[F. E. MASER]

STICHARION, a vestment in the Eastern Church resembling the Latin rite alb. That of a priest is white with narrow sleeves, while that of a deacon has shorter and wider sleeves and is the same color as the priest's *phelonian*.

STICHERON, the equivalent in Byzantine church music of the psalm tropes, i.e., interpolations between the verses of a psalm. A collection of *stichera* is called a *sticherarion*.

[M. T. LEGGE]

STICHOMETRY, the ancient system of measuring the extent of a work by the number of lines (*stichoi*) that it contained. Works written in verse were numbered as they are today. However, a problem arose in connection with the copying of prose works, and a unit had to be established for controlling the accuracy and honesty of the scribes and for the convenience of determining their compensation. The Greek hexameter of 16 syllables and of 34–38 letters was ordinarily adopted as the unit, and it became customary to speak of works in terms of the number of line units (*stichoi*) it contained. A prospective purchaser of a text would normally check the number of *stichoi* to be sure the work was complete. Diogenes Laertius tells us that the writings of Aristotle, for example, comprised 445,270 *stichoi*. According to Diocletian's *Edict on Prices,* a scribe was paid 25 or 20 denarii per 100 *stichoi*. Stichometry is found in wide use among Christians as well as pagans. BIBLIOGRAPHY: F. G. Kenyon, OCD 859; V. Gardthausen, *Griechische Paläographie* (2 v., 2d ed., 1913) 2:70–82; E. M. Thompson, *Introduction to Greek and Latin Palaeography* (1912) 67–71; R. Devreesse, *Introduction à l'étude des manuscrits grecs* (1954) 61–65.

[M. R. P. MCGUIRE]

STIFTER, ADALBERT (1805–68), Austrian novelist. Characterized by the attitude toward life of the Biedermeier period, S. had a sense of the beauty of nature and man's place in what he termed "the gentle law" (*das sanfte Gesetz*) of existence (see preface to *Bunte Steine*). Born in the Bohemian forest country of middle-class parents, he received a humanistic education from the Benedictines at Kremsmünster, spent several years in Vienna studying law and natural sciences, and worked as tutor in aristocratic houses. In 1850 he became school superintendent in Linz and retired in 1865. Although a faithful Catholic, he tried to take his own life under stress of illness, emotional strain, and financial trouble; but he died with the last rites of the Church. He has received some attention recently as representing the timeless Christian humanism that sees both man and nature as guided by the Divine, and the harmony of being expressed in seemingly small things, an unselfish life rather than in violent passion or stormy creation. Although his style is somewhat slow-moving for the modern reader, his technique is still appreciated. The best known of his works are the collected short stories in *Studien* (6 v., 1844–50) and *Bunte Steine* (1853). He also wrote two novels, *Nachsommer* (1857), a story of gradually maturing love, and *Witiko* (1865–67), a historical novel of 12th-cent. Bohemia. BIBLIOGRAPHY: E. A. Blackall, *Adalbert Stifter, Critical Study* (1948).

[B. F. STEINBRUCKNER]

STIGAND OF CANTERBURY (d. 1072), last Anglo-Saxon abp. of Canterbury (1052–70). A careerist with few loyalties, S. was a royal priest under Canute. Deprived of Elmham before consecration (1043), he obtained Winchester (1047), holding it in plurality with Canterbury (1052), after the expulsion of Abp. Robert of Jumièges. Excommunicated by several popes, his primacy seldom recognized (only in 1058 and 1067–70), he was deposed (1070) by a legatine council at Winchester. Of cultured tastes and unblemished private life, S. had no interest in reform and represented the worst in the late Anglo-Saxon Church. BIBLIOGRAPHY: F. Barlow, *English Church 1000–1066* (1963).

[F. D. BLACKLEY]

STIGMATIZATION, a mystical phenomenon, the marking of a person's body with the wounds Jesus suffered in his Passion, called the *stigmata,* marks or signs. The marks appear suddenly and without external causes; the experience is usually accompanied by suffering, sometimes with actual bleeding. The stigmatization may be by one wound, several, or all—head, hands, feet, side. The marks may be permanent, intermittent, or transitory; they may be visible or invisible to others. The first recorded instance of stigmatization is that of St. Francis of Assisi, Sept. 17, 1224, at Alvernia. Some 300 other cases have been recorded as part of the lives of the saints since then; the most famous contemporary case is that of Padre Pio, the Capuchin friar, in San Giovanni Rotondo, Italy. There have also been fraudulent claims and, of course, the whole idea has been ascribed to pathological causes by nonbelievers. Stigmatization is only one part of the total mystical experience of the recipient; nor is it a phenomenon universal or even common in the mystical life. Its meaning is consonant with the character of the whole Christian life as one of being conformed to Christ in his paschal mystery (cf. Phil 3,10) and of participating in his suffering (cf. Col 1.24). For this reason it is charismatic (a *gratia gratis data*), i.e., a gift to teach others; it may also be part of and an expression of the intensity of the stigmatic's own grace of union with Christ in love or as a *victim soul. The actual occurrence of the phenomenon is not a matter of faith.

[T. C. O'BRIEN]

STILE ANTICO (It., old style), in church music, the strict contrapuntal style of *Palestrina (16th and 17th centuries).

[M. T. LEGGE]

STILE MODERNO (It., new style), the monodic, declamatory musical style of the early 17th century. *(see SECONDA PRATTICA)

[M. T. LEGGE]

STILLA, BL., 12th–cent. ascetic. Little is known of her life other than the substantiated fact that she constructed a church at Abenberg, Germany. She died before establishing a monastery which she had hoped to enter. According to the Bollandists, 55 miracles have been attributed to her. BIBLIOGRAPHY: C. M. Aherne, NCE 13:714; K. Kunze, BiblSanct 12:33–34.

[F. G. O'BRIEN]

STILLINGTON, ROBERT (d.1491), political prelate, a canonist with a doctorate from Oxford; bp. of Bath and Wells (1466–91); keeper of the privy seal (1460–67); chancellor of England (1467–70, 1471–73). A timeserver in politics, he declared Edward IV's children illegitimate on behalf of Richard III. Described by Comines as "ce mauvais évêque," he visited his diocese only twice. BIBLIOGRAPHY: Emden Ox 3:1777–79.

[C. D. ROSS]

STILPON (*c*.380–300 B.C.), Megarian philosopher. He was the third head of the *Megarian School and was esp. distinguished as a teacher and for his proficiency in dialectic. *Zeno of Citium, the founder of Stoicism, was one of his pupils. He rejected the Platonic theory of forms and universal concepts in general. He himself taught that the copula marks an identity between subject and predicate. Of his numerous dialogues, a few titles only have been preserved. He adopted an attitude of *apatheia* and may be regarded as a moderate Cynic in this respect. BIBLIOGRAPHY: OCD 860; LexAW 2927.

[M. R. P. MCGUIRE]

STIMMEN DER ZEIT, Jesuit monthly journal of opinion published in Germany since 1915. Its roots go back to *Stimmen aus Maria Laach,* which the German Jesuits began in 1871 at their house at the old Rhenish monastery of that name. Several decades after the Jesuits left Maria Laach, they changed the journal's name and published it from Munich and Freiburg. The National Socialist government suppressed it between November 1935 and April 1936, and again after May 1941; it resumed publication in the fall of 1946. *Stimmen der Zeit* publishes serious articles on leading political, social, and cultural issues. Most prominent German Jesuit writers have contributed to its pages. BIBLIOGRAPHY: L. Koch, *Jesuiten-Lexikon* (2 v., 1962) 2:1694.

[R. H. SCHMANDT]

STINIAN, ST., see JUSTINIANUS, ST.

STIPENDS, a monetary offering made to a priest on the understanding that he will celebrate Mass for the intention specified by the donor. The custom of making offerings to priests on the occasion of their performing the services of their ministry goes back to biblical times. Both OT (Lev 2.3; 5.13; 6.8–10) and the NT (1 Cor 9, 13) recognize the need of priests, whose main, if not only, source of sustenance is the service he renders, to receive adequate income.

But until the early Middle Ages there is no evidence that stipends were offered for celebrating Mass for the intention of an individual. However, it can be argued that the offering of a stipend had earlier precedent. One theory of stipends, e.g., relates them to the earlier type of offering made by the faithful as a normal part of their participation in the Eucharistic Liturgy, viz, at the offertory of the Mass. Another sees in stipends an opportune fulfillment in part of the obligation, already recognized generically in NT times, to support one's pastors. The practice of receiving stipends has never been condemned by the Church, despite the occasional occurrence of abuses. The present Code of Canon Law (cc. 824–844) has, and in its revision will have, regulations governing the proper procedures to be followed regarding stipends. The priest who accepts one incurs a grave obligation to apply the fruits of the Mass according to his agreement with the donor, although the exact nature of this application and its effect is subject to debate. A stipend may be a "manual" stipend, i.e., given *ad hoc* for a particular intention, or a "foundation" stipend, i.e., the interest or gain on money or property that is to be used for an annual Mass or Masses. Sometimes a priest may request additional recompense for unusual circumstances, such as when he must travel to a distant place or celebrates Mass at a difficult hour. The legislation on stipends was modified by Pope Paul VI by the *motu proprio, Firma in traditione* (AAS 66 [1974] 308–311). Currently there is considerable dissatisfaction with the stipend system on the part of some notably the Canon Law Society of America, and various proposals have been made to make provision for the support of the priests in other ways. BIBLIOGRAPHY: P. M. Boyle, NCE 13:715 (bibliog.).

[C. NEELY]

STOBAEUS, IOANNES (5th cent.), a compiler from Stobi in Macedonia. His work in four books was addressed to his son Septimius and was prepared for his instruction. At a later date, in spite of the unity of the work, it was divided under the titles *eklogai* and *anthulogion.* It is an orderly presentation of extracts from some 500 Greek writers of prose and poetry, from Homer into the 4th cent. A.D. Formal attention is given to the respective literary genres in both prose and poetry. Philosophical writers and ethical materials seem to be emphasized in the period from the 2d cent. A.D. In some respects, it is likewise a kind of encyclopedia in the arrangement of material and topics covered. The work is of major importance because it contains excerpts from writers whose works, otherwise, are not extant in any form. In this respect, it may be compared to the compilations of Suidas and Photius. The best edition is that of C. Wachsmuth and O. Hense (1884–1923). BIBLIOGRAPHY: OCD 862; LexAW 2928; W. Schmid and O. Stählin, *Geschichte der griechischen Literatur* (1924) 2.2:1087–89.

[M. R. P. MCGUIRE]

STOCK, LEO FRANCIS (1878–1954), historian, educator. A native of Pennsylvania, S. taught at several colleges before becoming a member of the division of historical research of the Carnegie Institution, Washington, D.C., to which he devoted 35 years. S. taught at The Catholic Univ. of America, Mt. St. Joseph College in Emmitsburg, Md., and Trinity College, Washington. He was the author of numerous articles in the *Catholic Historical Review* and served on its editorial staff from 1921 to 1939. Among his published works were *Proceedings and Debates of the British Parliament Respecting North America* (5 v., 1924–41) and *United States Minister to the Papal States, Instructions and Despatches, 1848–1868* (1933).

[J. R. AHERNE]

STOCKHOLM CONFERENCE, the first international conference of the *Life and Work movement, held at Stockholm, Sweden, Aug. 19–30, 1925. The conference found a working model in an earlier conference at Birmingham, Eng., on the application of Christian principles to politics, economics, and citizenship (the so-called COPEC meeting). The Stockholm Conference considered the Church's obligation in view of God's purpose for the world; the Church and economic and industrial problems; the Church and social and moral problems; the Church and international relations; the Church and Christian education; and methods of cooperative and federative efforts by the Christian communions. Under these general headings the delegates studied housing, crime, alcoholism, youth, sex, education, family life, war, race problems, and international law. The reports were not voted on, and the "message" issued by the conference was general in tone, stressing the pressing need for Christian education in social and economic problems and calling for a united effort to build the kingdom of God on earth by working for social justice. BIBLIOGRAPHY: *Stockholm Conference 1925* (ed. G. K. A. Bell, 1926).

[D. CODDINGTON]

STÖCKLEIN, JOSEPH (1676–1733), Jesuit historian. After serving as the Austrian Prince Eugene's chief field chaplain in Serbia (1714–18), he became a preacher at the court and rector of Vienna-Neustadt College (1720–23). He began a compilation of the mission reports of Jesuits sent back from 1624 to 1726 and published the first volume of *Der Neue-Weltbott* in 1726 (see *c.* *GOBIEN). He then collected material for the three volumes published in 1736. Other Jesuits continued Stöcklein's work until 1761. *Der Neue-Weltbott* is a chief primary source on Catholic missions of that period.

[R. J. LITZ]

STODDARD, CHARLES WARREN (1843–1909), American poet. S. taught for several years as a professor at Notre Dame Univ. and at The Catholic Univ. of America. An extensive and well-seasoned traveler, he is best known for *South Sea Idyls* (1873), a book of sketches considered to be of superior literary quality.

[S. A. HEENEY]

STODDARD, SOLOMON (1643–1729), Congregationalist; grandfather of Jonathan *Edwards. S. served as pastor at Northampton, Mass., from 1669 until his death. After the New England Congregationalists, under the *Half-way Covenant, began to baptize the children of baptized but noncommuning members of the Church, S. developed the theory ("Stoddardeanism") that the Lord's Supper was instituted as a means of regeneration and that persons could and should come to it even though they knew themselves to be in an unregenerate state. He opened the Supper to all and, by attempting to use it as an *ordinance for conversion, became, according to some interpreters, the first American revivalist.

[J. H. SMYLIE]

STOGLAV (Sl. for 100 chapters), the decrees, chiefly disciplinary and liturgical, of the synod held by Metropolitan Makary in Moscow in 1551 in an attempt to reform the Russian Church. BIBLIOGRAPHY: E. Duchesne, *Le Stoglav ou les cent chapitres* (1920).

[G. T. DENNIS]

STOHR, ALBERT (1890–1961), bp. of Mainz from 1935, a leading figure in the German hierarchy before and after World War II, distinguished for his zealous promotion of the youth apostolate, the liturgical movement, and ecumenical dialogue.

[N. KOLLAR]

STOICISM, the most influential of the Greek philosophical schools from *c.*300 B.C. to the rise of Neoplatonism in the early 3d cent. A.D. It was a philosophico-religious system, a way of life well suited to an age of individualism and cosmopolitanism. Its founder, *Zeno of Citium, created a fully developed new philosophy. Stoicism is essentially a materialistic monism which, however, was modified in various respects in the long period in which it flourished. Three phases must be distinguished in the history of ancient Stoicism: early, middle, and late. The Greeks were preoccupied with Stoic cosmological speculation as well as with Stoic ethics, but the Roman interest was chiefly in the ethical doctrine.

Early Stoicism. Its leading representatives were Zeno of Citium (335–263 B.C.), Cleanthes of Assos (331–232), and Chrysippus of Soli (*c.*280–207), the last being considered the second founder of the school because of his elaboration and systematization of its doctrines. Cleanthes' beautiful *Hymn to Zeus* is extant, but of Zeno and Chrysippus only fragments remain.

Stoic Physics (cosmology, physics, psychology, and theology). All reality is corporeal and made up of two principles—that which acts and that which is acted upon. The acting principle has a teleological character and is thought of as a first cause, Zeus, nature, providence, destiny, reason (*logos*), law, fire, aether, or breath. The *logos* is the container of the active forms of all things that are to be, the *logoi spermatikoi*, or "seminal reasons," which were destined to have an important and fruitful influence in the whole history of philosophy. The teaching that the world is produced from fire is borrowed from Heraclitus, but the eternal cycle of identical world-revolutions and world-destructions by universal conflagration is a peculiarly Stoic doctrine. Absolute necessity or destiny (*heimarmenē*) governs the cyclic process and is identified with the divine reason (*logos*) and providence. The Stoics had to face the problem of reconciling cosmological determinism with their doctrine of inner freedom. Divine providence is regarded as benevolent and the Stoic *Weltanschauung* is essentially optimistic. Physical evils are apparent only, and they may ultimately be goods. Moral evil is viewed as the deprivation of right order in the human will—a lack of harmony with right reason.

Man is a microcosm, his soul being an emanation of the fiery soul or *logos* of the universe. The Stoic soul is a corporeal unity and all its faculties are regarded as rational: "man feels, knows, and wills with his whole soul." The dominant part of the soul (*hēgemonikon*) is placed in the heart by Chrysippus. The soul survives the body only until the time of the next world-conflagration. Universal reason operates as the principle of "cohesion" (*hexis*) in inanimate objects, of "nature" (*physis*) in plants, and of "soul" (*psychē*) in animals—the last having powers of "imagination" (*phantasia*) and "appetition" (*hormē*).

Stoic Logic and Epistemology. Aristotle's 10 categories are reduced to 4: subject matter, essential quality, mode or accident, relation or relative mode. All knowledge is founded on sense-perception of particular objects, which make an impression (*typōsis*) on the soul. After the act of perception a memory (*mnēmē*) remains, and experience (*empeiria*) is based on the accumulation of memories of impressions. While the Stoics may be classified as empiricists, or nominalists, they also teach that there are general ideas (*koinai ennoiai* or *prolēpseis*) that are antecedent to experience. Their criterion of truth is "apprehensive perception" (*phantasia prolēptikē*) or representation. This criterion of truth, accordingly, is in the perception itself; and clear perception should, ordinarily, compel the assent of the soul. However, difficulties arose in the application of this criterion, and they were never solved completely. The Stoics were preoccupied with definition of terms in their dialectic and rhetoric; and they made important contributions to the differentiation of the parts of speech, and inflections, and to the building up of grammatical and philosophical terminology in general. They adopted a rationalistic attitude toward the traditional polytheism, yet they were able to incorporate it into their thought by a process of modification, rationalization, and esp., of allegorization of religious myths. This approach is already found in Democritus, but the Stoics developed allegorical interpretation into a system. They regarded the heavenly bodies as superior rational beings and hence were prepared to give a fateful welcome to Greek and Oriental astrology.

Stoic Ethics. This is the most important and influential part of the Stoic system. Philosophy itself is regarded by the Stoics primarily as the science of conduct. Happiness is the end of life and is identified with virtue, i.e., with living and acting according to nature, with thought and action in conformity with right reason. Stoic determinism is modified in practice through the recognition of a conscious choice of good on the part of the wise man and of a willing submission to the divine law. Hence there is a place in Stoic ethics for moral exhortation. Virtue is good in itself and possessed in its entirety, or not at all. The Stoic cardinal virtues—moral insight (*phronēsis*), courage, self-control or temperance (*enkrateia*), and justice—are all possessed, if one is possessed. There is a corresponding teaching in respect to vice and vices. In Early Stoicism no degrees in virtue or vice are admitted. What is neither morally good nor morally bad is regarded as indifferent (*adiaphoron*). Morally indifferent things are classified into those in accord with nature and therefore valuable; those contrary to nature and therefore without value; and those having neither value nor "disvalue." Right intention is stressed in all action, and virtuous action or conduct (*kathorthōma*) is strictly the fulfillment of duty or "what is proper" (*kathēkon*). All passions and affections—pleasure (*hēdonē*), sorrow (*lupē*), desire (*epithymia*), and fear (*phobos*)—are regarded as irrational and contrary to nature. Habitual passions and affections, which are really illnesses of the soul, must be eradicated and replaced by an attitude of apathy (*apatheia*).

Mankind is divided into fools and wise men. The genuine wise man is free, happy, master of emotion and desire, truly a king not inferior to Zeus himself through his inner sovereignty. Action not in conformity with right reason is considered to be sin and folly. The pride of righteousness in the Stoic conception of virtue is in marked contrast to the Christian ideal of goodness combined with humility and love. The Stoic doctrine of individual self-sufficiency and of the wise man was borrowed from the Cynics, but the emphasis on the rational, active, and responsible role of the individual in a cosmopolitan or universal society was apparently Zeno's own contribution. According to him, all men are born for society since there is a natural and rational impulse in mankind to live in society, there is really only one country and law for all men, the wise man is not a citizen of an individual state, but a citizen of the world and sharing this citizenship with all men, Greek or barbarian, slave or free. The ethical basis for this cosmopolitanism is sought primarily in the concept of *oikeiōsis*, "self-love" or "self-preservation," and through the extension of *oikeiōsis* to include all who are connected with one's self, however remotely. Man, as master of himself, is permitted, under certain circumstances, to commit suicide.

Middle Stoicism. This exhibits marked modifications in Stoic teachings, owing in large part to the influence of the Platonic and Aristotelian schools. The chief representatives are Panaetius of Rhodes (*c*.185–109 B.C.) and Posidonius of Apamea (*c*.135–51 B.C.). Panaetius visited Rome in 144 B.C. and became closely identified with the Scipionic circle, upon which he had a marked influence. He abandoned the Stoic doctrine of world-conflagration, adopted the Platonic and Aristotelian teaching on the eternity of the world, rejected astrology and divination, the doctrine of apathy, the equality of vices, and the ideal of the Stoic wise man. He emphasized, on the other hand, the importance of external goods, the performance of ordinary duty, and propriety. His threefold division of theology was adopted by Q. Mucius Scaevola and by M. Terentius Varro. Perceiving the practical bent of Roman thought, he developed the concept of *humanitas* and ethical teaching, stressing the more appealing virtues of magnanimity, benevolence, and liberality rather than the traditional Stoic virtues of fortitude and justice. Cicero's *De officiis* is based essentially on one of his works.

His most distinguished disciple, Posidonius, established a school at Rhodes in 97 B.C. His great importance has been established by modern scholarly research, although only scanty fragments of his vast writings are extant. He fused pre-Socratic, Platonic, Aristotelian, and Stoic elements into a closely knit system. As opposed to the Early Stoic monism, he adopted a dualism that was influenced by that of Plato's *Timaeus* but not identical with it. His tripartite division of the soul is Platonic. He regarded God as divine fiery breath and active providence and located him in the aethereal regions, especially in the sun. Man's intellect, as the rational part of man's soul, is an emanation of the divine substance in the sun. He retained, however, the Early Stoic doctrine of world-conflagration.

He distinguished two divisions in the cosmos, the supralunar and infralunar worlds. He taught that there are grades of being from the lowest inorganic substances of the mineral kingdom, through the organic kingdoms of plants, animals, and man, reaching the zenith in the super-organic Divine. The whole system is bound together in world sympathy and world harmony by God, i.e., absolute reason, active providence. Man, as the "bridge being" or bond between the supralunar and infralunar worlds, is the highest being in the corporeal order and the lowest in the spiritual order. Demons (*daemones*) or higher spiritual beings exist and form an intermediate hierarchy between God and man. He was an advocate of divination in its various forms and assigned important roles to visions, dreams, and oracles as a means of knowing the future and of communicating with the *daemones*. He believed that the soul in sleep or ecstasy has a clearer knowledge, and the power to penetrate the future. He identified politics and ethics and held that political activity was a religious duty. He wrote voluminously in history and science to support or demonstrate his speculative teachings. He exercised a great influence on subsequent writers through the universality of his speculation and learning. His attempts to combine dualism and monism is one of the main stages on the road to Neoplatonism.

Late Stoicism. This is characterized, at least in its main representatives, L. Annaeus *Seneca (*c*.5 B.C.–65 A.D.), *Epictetus of Hieropolis (*c*.50–120 A.D.), and the philosopher-emperor *Marcus Aurelius (121–180 A.D.; emperor 161–180) by an almost exclusive preoccupation with ethics. In the writings of these men there is a more personal approach to God, a genuine warmth and sympathy for one's fellow man that one misses in the earlier stages of Stoicism.

The Stoic school lost its formal identity with the rise of Neoplatonism, but it had exercised a considerable influence on Middle Platonism in the 2d cent. A.D., esp. in the field of terminology. The Early Christian writers were influenced to a marked degree by Stoic ethics in particular, and Stoicism enjoyed a revival in the Renaissance, and again at the turn of the 16th and 17th cent., esp. in France. BIBLIOGRAPHY: K. von Fritz, OCD 861–862; LexAW 2929–32; Copleston 1:385–400, 421–437; M. Pohlenz, *Die Stoa* (2 v., 2d ed., 1955); E. V. Arnold, *Roman Stoicism* (1911; repr. 1958); M. Spanneut, NCE 13:719–721; *idem, Le Stoicisme des Pères de l' Église de Clément de Rome à Clément d' Alexandrie* (1957).

[M. R. P. McGUIRE]

STOLBERG, FRIEDRICH LEOPOLD VON (1750–1819), German writer. Born at Bramstedt, Holstein, the son of a Danish count, he was reared in an atmosphere of Lutheran *Pietism. Studying law at Göttingen, he joined the poetic circle, *Hainbund,* and later published various poetic works. After conversion to Catholicism in 1800 he wrote a 15-volume history of Christianity, *Geschichte der Religion Jesu Christi*. (The work was later extended to 54 volumes, completed in 1853). He was influential in the movement of German Romantics to the Catholic Church.

[T. EARLY]

STOLE, a long narrow band of material worn at all liturgical services by bps., priests, and deacons. In the Roman rite the stole is put on over the alb and worn around the neck: by the deacon, over his left shoulder and crossed under his right arm; by the priest and the bp. crossed draped down in front to the knees or waist. In the Eastern liturgies the stole has become a broad band with a hole for the head and is worn hanging down in front. The origin of the stole is uncertain. It appeared in the East by the 4th cent. as an insignia for the clergy and later in the non-Roman West (Gaul and Spain in the 6th to 7th cent.) and finally in Rome by the 12th century. BIBLIOGRAPHY: H. Norris, *Church Vestments: Their Origin and Development* (1950).

[T. M. McFADDEN]

STOLE FEES, offerings given to clergymen on the occasion of their performance of certain rites, particularly baptisms, marriages, and funerals. The term originated from the fact that the clergyman normally wears a stole while performing those ceremonies. Though such gifts are often made to ministers of other churches, the term is more commonly used in the RC Church, in which the practice is regulated by canon law. BIBLIOGRAPHY: W. A. Ferry, *Stole Fees* (1930).

[T. EARLY]

STOLTZER, THOMAS (*c*.1475–1526?), German Renaissance composer. S. was Kapellmeister for King Louis of Hungary and Bohemia. His compositions, many of which have been reprinted in modern editions, number psalm-settings, motets, and tunes for both Latin and German hymns.

[M. T. LEGGE]

STOLZ, ANSELM (1900–42), Benedictine theologian. A monk from 1918 and ordained in 1924, S. taught theology at S. Anselmo in Rome from 1928 and served as librarian. Inaugurating *Studia Anselmiana* in 1933, he contributed his first work, *Glaubensgnade und Glaubenslicht nach . . . Thomas von Aquin*. In 1934 he published *Gottes leben Sein Erkennen und Wolle*. His observations on mysticism given in lectures at the Univ. of Salzburg were published in 1936 as *Theologie der Mystik*. In 1937 S. published *Alselm von Canterbury*; in 1938 appeared in translation his *Doctrine of Spiritual Perfection*. His course in theology, *Manuale theologiae dogmaticae,* appeared between 1939 to 1943. His emphasis was on the Fathers, monastic theology, and the medieval Doctors. He regarded much later theology to be excessively dependent on reasoning and insufficient in mystical and biblical orientation.

[J. R. AHERNE]

STOMER (STOM), MATTHIAS (*c.*1600–51), Flemish painter, student of Honthorst, whom he followed so closely as to confuse attribution though S.'s work is more dramatic and stronger in chiaroscuro, his Sicilian works closer to Caravaggio. In 1631 S. painted a Passion series in S. Efremo Nuovo, and is recorded in Messina and Palermo.

[M. J. DALY]

STONE, BARTON WARREN (1772–1844), one of the four founding fathers of the Christian Churches (Disciples of Christ). A lifelong frontiersman, S. was a pioneer in Christian union. Educated in David Caldwell's log college at Guilford, N.C., and licensed as a Presbyterian minister, he migrated to Bourbon Co., Ky. (1796). By his agency the *Kentucky Revival reached its climax on the grounds of his Cane Ridge church in Aug. 1801. A feature of this *camp meeting was the subordination of doctrinal disputes to the spirit of cooperation among Methodists, Presbyterians, and Baptists. He withdrew from the Presbyterian Church in 1804, determined to own "no name but Christian,"to acknowledge "no creed but the Bible," and to pursue Christian union. He did not accept the doctrine of the Trinity or of Christ's vicarious atonement. Churches under his persuasion called themelves Christian Churches. They spread throughout Kentucky, Missouri, Indiana, Illinois, and Ohio. With Christian union as his polar star for life, his greatest success was the merging of his followers with "the Reformers" (Disciples) of Alexander *Campbell in 1832. BIBLIOGRAPHY: autobiog. (1847); lives by C. Ware (1932) and W. G. West (1954).

[D. E. STEVENSON]

STONE, DARWELL (1859–1941), prominent theologian of Anglo-Catholicism. Born in Denbighshire, educated at Owens College, Manchester, and Merton College, Oxford, librarian and principal of Pusey House, he wrote many books upholding Catholic teaching, which include the massive *History of the Doctrine of the Holy Eucharist* (2v., 1909). His responsibilities prevailing over his natural reserve, he was drawn into an unequalled position of influence merited by both his knowledge and abilities. More guarded than other Anglo-Catholics in his admiration for the *Caroline Divines and for the specific difference of Anglicanism, he thought that the Anglican Church should be understood only as a fragment of the Church universal. With his venerable beard and his measured and exact mode of speech, he was a familiar Oxford character, the subject of many anecdotes, and was loved and revered for the manifest devotion of his religious faith, his disregard for personal ambition, and his fairness in controversy. BIBLIOGRAPHY: life by F. L. Cross (1943).

[T. GILBY]

STONE, JAMES KENT (1840–1921), American Passionist. Born in Boston, son of Dean J. S. Stone of the Episcopal seminary in Cambridge, he became an Episcopal priest in 1866, following service in the Civil War. After the death of his wife, S. converted to Catholicism (1869), joined the Paulists, and received Catholic ordination in 1872. Seeking a more austere life, he joined the Passionists in 1877, taking the name Fidelis of the Cross. S. served many years in Latin America, establishing Passionist foundations in Chile, Argentina, and Brazil. He was named Passionist provincial for South America in 1908. His last labors before retirement in 1917 were in Cuba and Texas. S. left an account of his conversion in *An Awakening and What Followed* (1920).

[T. EARLY]

STONE, JOHN, ST. (d. *c.*1539), English martyr. He became an Augustinian, probably at Canterbury. He was the only friar there (1538) who resisted the Act of Supremacy. After imprisonment in the Tower, he was executed at Canterbury. He was canonized in 1970. BIBLIOGRAPHY: Butler 2:292.

[V. SAMPSON]

STONING, standard form of capital punishment in ancient Israel. The OT decreed stoning for several offenses: idolatry (Dt 17.2–5), inciting to idolatry (Dt 13.1–10), sacrificing a child to *Moloch (Lev 20.2), being a medium or wizard (Lev 20.27), blasphemy (Lev 24.16), violation of the Sabbath (Num 15.32–36), rebellion against parents (Dt 21.18–21), "playing the harlot" (Dt 22.21), and, presumably, adultery (Dt 22.22; cf. Jn 8.4–5). In other cases where the death penalty was prescribed, stoning likely was the method (Ex 21.28–32), though other methods of capital punishment were used. Stoning was also used against the ox that gored

(Ex 21.28). Enraged mobs resorted to stoning (1 Kg 12.18). David (1 Sam 30.6) and Jesus (Jn 10.31) were threatened, and Stephen, the first Christian martyr, was killed by stoning (Acts 7.59–60). Though not killed, Paul was stoned and left for dead (Acts 14.19). The whole community participated in the stoning, which took place outside the city (Lev 24.14; Acts 7.58), with the witnesses laying their hands on the head of the one being stoned. The witnesses cast the first stones (Dt 17.7; Jn 8.7). Jesus referred in one of his parables to unjust stoning (Mt 21.35). In his famous lament over Jerusalem he spoke of the city's record of stoning those who had been sent to it (Mt 23.37). He particularly condemned the stoning of Zechariah "by command of the king" in the "court of the house of Yahweh" (2 Chr 24.21; Lk 11.51).

[T. EARLY]

STONYHURST, a Jesuit college in Lancashire, England, providing education for boys at the pre-university level. The college from which its origin is derived was founded (1593) at St. Omer, France, by Robert Persons, S.J., who obtained permission from Philip II of Spain to establish an English college in Flanders (then under Spanish rule) to provide Catholic education banned in England by the penal laws. As a result of political turmoil, the college suffered many hardships and was forced to relocate several times until 1794, when alumnus Thomas Weld provided a definitive site at Stonyhurst Hall, Lancashire. The college offers an educational opportunity comparable to that provided by the English public school. Attached to the college are the Stonyhurst Observatory, built in 1883, a museum, and a library housing 40,000 volumes and many valuable MSS and incunabula. Enrollment averages about 600. BIBLIOG-RAPHY: J. Gerard, *Stonyhurst College* (1894).

[M. B. MURPHY]

STORCH, NICHOLAS (d. 1530), radical Reformer and agitator. S., a weaver, was one of the *Zwickau Prophets. He was a fanatic, possibly deranged. He preached a doctrine of individual inspiration, and also the establishment of a new kingdom of God by violent revolution. After expulsion from Wittenberg in 1522, he became a wandering preacher in Poland and Bavaria. He is sometimes classified as an Anabaptist because he rejected *infant baptism and argued for rebaptism.

[T. C. O'BRIEN]

STORER, FRANZ (1617-after 1658), Jesuit missionary to India, traveler through Asia Minor and Persia. After entering the Society (1635), he served as professor of Hebrew and mathematics at Ingolstadt before leaving for his Eastern mission. He is known to have journeyed to Ethiopia in 1656; but his last letter was written in 1658.

[R. J. LITZ]

STOSS, VEIT (*c.*1447–1533), German master sculptor, painter, engraver, engineer, architect trained in Nuremberg, invited to design and execute the high altar in St. Mary's Church, Cracow, (1477) where as "Wit Stwosz" he stayed for 19 years doing tombs for King Casimir IV (1492) and Abp. Zbigniew Oleśnicki (1493). Returning affluent to Nuremberg (1496) S. was cheated of his savings, tried to regain them by forgery, was found guilty of fraud and deprived of civic rights (1503) but restored to citizenship by Emperor Maximilian (1506). He executed his renowned *Annunciation* group (1517–19), a *Crucifixion* for St. Sebald (1520), and an altar never completed because of the Protestant Reformation. The Cracow altarpiece, most spectacular of his works for complexity and detail (requiring 12 years in execution), depicts in High Gothic style the Passion of Christ and death of Mary with innumerable figures, the central triptych alone having 50 painted wooden figures. The Nuremberg *Annunciation,* novel in its oval form (12 ft by 10 ft), pendant on a slender cable from the vault, a wreath of roses, a hanging rosary, medallions, and musician angels suspended in the open spaces, is a tour de force of Gothic sculpture. S., one of the greatest of European wood carvers in supreme virtuosity and flamboyance of form marks the climax of late Gothic sculpture. BIBLIOGRAPHY: E. Lutz, *Veit Stoss* (1952).

[M. J. DALY]

STOUP (OE stéap, a vessel), the holy water font placed at the entrance of a church. Fountains for washing hands and face before services were placed in the atrium of the early Roman basilicas. But the origin of the stoup is better traced to the 9th cent. when the practice of sprinkling the faithful at Sunday Mass with holy water began. The blessed water was left in an appropriate vessel for the use of those unable to be present at the Mass, or for those who wished to take the water home. At least until the 15th cent., the hand was not placed directly into the holy water; an aspersorium or sprinkling device was used. All RC churches have holy water fonts at the principal entrances, and the practice is followed in some Anglican churches.

[T. EARLY]

STRACHAN, JOHN (1778–1867), first Anglican bp. of Toronto, Canada. Born in Aberdeen, Scotland, he emigrated to Canada in 1799 and received ordination in 1803. He served as a parish rector, then as archdeacon and from 1839 as bp. of the newly created diocese of Toronto. He became the first president of King's College but resigned when it was secularized in 1850 and became the Univ. of Toronto. He then founded the Univ. of Trinity College as an Anglican college. He was intent throughout his life on church unity, and church control of education.

[T. EARLY]

STRACHEY, GILES LYTTON (1880–1932), English biographer, critic, and essayist. He inaugurated a new school of biography with his brilliant character studies: *Eminent Victorians, Queen Victoria, Elizabeth and Essex,* and *Portraits in Miniature*. S., fascinated by personality and motive, aimed to create a work of art rather than to record events, yet this desire to paint a portrait sometimes led to inaccuracies, even caricatures. His great weakness is his belief that politics is merely intrigue, religion a stupid anachronism, and that the only important facet of life is personal relationships. Thus his view is clear but narrow, and he is unable to grasp accurately a complex character. He is preeminent for his humor and wit, his elegant, slightly ironical style, and his power of vivid portrayal. BIBLIOGRA-PHY: M. Beerbohm, *Lytton Strachey* (1943).

[M. J. BARRY]

STRACK, HERMANN (1848–1922), Talmudic scholar. With P. Billerbeck, S. published *Kommentar zum neuem Testament aus Talmud und Midrasch* (5 v., 1922–28), a NT commentary from rabbinic sources which has become an indispensable guide for understanding the interaction of Semitic and Greek NT influences. S. taught at the Univ. of Berlin and founded the Institutum Judaicum there. BIBLIOG-RAPHY: Hermann Strack, *Introduction to the Talmud and Midrash* (authorized tr., 1931; 2d ed., 1959).

[T. M. MCFADDEN]

STRAHOV, MONASTERY OF, a Premonstratensian abbey in Prague, Czechoslovakia, also known as the Czech Mt. Sion. Established by Bp. Henry Zdík of Olomouc in 1140 and confirmed by Ladislaus II, it became the motherhouse for many other foundations. Burned in 1258, and destroyed by the Hussites in 1420, it was restored by Abbot Johann Lohelius (1586–1612). In 1627 Abbot Caspar of Questenberg had the relics of St. Norbert transferred to Strahov from Magdeberg. Always known as a cultural center, the abbey library numbered in its collection 110,000 volumes, 2,000 MSS, and 1,200 incunabula. Displayed in its unique art gallery were 1,100 paintings of the great masters. The abbey always expressed a distinct Czech character, and its members assumed many important roles in the life of the Czech nation. The Czechoslovak Communists suppressed the abbey in 1950, dispersed the community, and turned the confiscated library into a state museum. BIB-LIOGRAPHY: A. Huber, LTK 9:1102–03; L. Nemec, *Church and State in Czechoslovakia* (1955). Rich material may be found in the numerous Czech historical and artistic literary contributions. *cf.*, T. Ekert, *Posvátná místa Král. hl. města Prahy* (1883) 1:116–185.

[L. NEMEC]

STRAMBI, VINCENZO MARIA, ST. (1745–1824), early Passionist and bishop. Under the influence of St. Paul of the Cross he entered the Pasionists and was ordained in 1768. He filled a number of positions in his congregation and in 1801 was named bp. of Macerata and Tolentino. A man of great zeal, he renewed his diocese. In 1808, refusing to take the oath of allegiance to Napoleon, S. was expelled from his see. Returning in 1813 he had to contend with

Murat who occupied Macerata as Napoleon's ally. S. saved the city from destruction when the French were about to destroy it and withdraw. At the death of Pope Pius VII S. resigned his see, but Pope Leo XII brought him to Rome as his confidential adviser. S. was canonized in 1950. BIB-LIOGRAPHY: F. dell'Addolorata, BiblSanct 12:1178–80.

[J. R. AHERNE]

STRANGER (IN THE BIBLE). There are several words connoting the idea of alien or foreigner in the OT (*zār, nokrī, toshav, gēr*), but the most frequently used, *gēr,* often has a technical sense and is important theologically and sociologically. The basic meaning of *gēr* is that of an outsider who may have certain rights and responsibilities within the country. He is not considered a complete foreigner, *nokrī,* nor is he native-born. In context he may be a guest (Ps 39.12), a sojourner (Ps 119.19), a displaced person (Ru 1.1). Most often he is a resident alien. The term may apply to nations, Israel in Egypt (Ex 22.20), to non-Israelites in Palestine (Ex 20.22–23), or even to Israelites outside their tribal territory (Jg 19.16). The Levites were considered as *gērīm* since they did not have their own territory (Dt 12.12); the Patriarchs were *gērīm* in Palestine (Gen 12.10); Moses was a *gēr* in Midian (Ex 2.22) and David in Philistia (1 Sam 27.2–3). Technically, "resident alien" seems to be the closest translation, but the term also embraces the poor and homeless stranger who is dependent on Israelite charity just as are the widow and the orphan. In post-Exilic times *gērīm* are full citizens, akin to naturalized aliens. The LXX translation of *gēr* by *prosēlutos* indicates that they were considered as prospective converts. The background of this term is important for the understanding of several NT passages (Mt 25.35; Eph 2.19; 1 Pet 2.11). BIBLIOGRAPHY: EDB 2332–34.

[M. A. MCNAMARA]

STRASBOURG, UNIVERSITY OF, a national institution of higher learning in Strasbourg, France. It developed from the merger of three existing schools (among them, the Lutheran theological school, in which Calvin taught 1539–41), under the direction of the German humanist and educator J. Sturm (1507–89), whom Lutheran critics later deposed (1581). In 1567 Maximilian II officially recognized the school as an academy, and in 1621 Ferdinand II gave it university rank. Strasbourg's reunion with France in 1681 and the establishment of a Catholic university there in 1701, caused the Lutheran university's decline. Both institutions were suppressed during the French Revolution and reopened in 1808 under Napoleon as the Académie de Strasbourg, a part of the Université de France. Suspended during the Franco-Prussian War, the university was restored under German rule as the Kaiser Wilhelm Universität (1872). It exerted a strong influence on German Lutherans and French Protestants under prominent teachers such as É. Reuss (1804–91), H. J. Holtzmann, J. Ficker, and Albert *Schweitzer. The Catholic faculty of theology, incorporated in 1903, in turn strongly influenced religious thought through theologians such as Cardinal Michael Faulhaber (1869–1952), professor of OT, and Karl Adam (1876–1966). When Strasbourg was retaken by the French in World War I, the German university was replaced by a French university but two theological faculties were maintained. Evacuated to Clermont-Ferrand during World War II (1939–45), the university was reestablished in Strasbourg in 1945. It comprises faculties of law and political science, medicine, sciences, letters, and pharmacy. Enrollment averages 17,545; teaching staff, 855. The library houses 3,000,000 volumes, 5,446 MSS, 4,541 papyri, 3,877 rare books of the 16th to 18th cent., and 1,971 incunabula. BIBLIOGRAPHY: H. Rashdall, *Universities of Europe in the Middle Ages* (ed. F. M. Powicke and A. B. Emden 3 v. 1936).

[M. B. MURPHY]

STRASSMAIER, JOHANN NEPOMUK (1846–1920), German Jesuit Assyriologist. Most of his life was spent in London, where he worked on cuneiform inscriptions at the British Museum. His *Alphabetisches Verzeichnis* (1886), his published and unpublished Babylonian texts, and works co-edited with J. *Epping opened the way to the development of Assyriology.

[T. C. O'BRIEN]

STRATA FLORIDA ABBEY (in Welsh, *Ystrad Fflur*), a monastery founded as a Cistercian daughter monastery of Whitland by Robert fitz-Stephen, castellan of Earl Roger of Hereford, in the Clare lordship of Cardigan, Wales, in 1164. On Robert's defeat, Rhys ap Gruffydd became its second founder; and he and his descendants, its most generous benefactor. Strata Florida is closely associated with the Welsh struggle for independence; and became the last resting place of many of the Welsh nobility. In it were written a version of *Annales Cambriae* and *Brut y Tywysogion*. A magnificent new monastery was built *c.*1200 on the banks of the Teifi or Taf. Among its daughter houses are Aberconway (1186) and Caerleon (1179 or 1189). It was dissolved in 1539. BIBLIOGRAPHY: J. F. O'Sullivan, *Cistercian Settlements in Wales and Monmouthshire, 1140–1540* (1947); J. E. Lloyd, *History of Wales* (2 v., 1948).

[C. MCGRATH]

STRATFORD, JOHN DE, see JOHN STRATFORD.

STRATON OF LAMPSACUS (d. 270–268 B.C.), outstanding physicist of the Peripatetic School. A pupil of Theophrastus, he succeeded him as head of the school (286–270 or 268). He wrote on logical, ethical, and historical subjects, but his main concern and his primary importance in the history of philosophy are in the field of physical science. He rejected Aristotle's concept of a transcendent deity and replaced it completely by nature. *Nous* in man is regarded as a purely biological phenomenon, and immortal-

ity of the soul is denied. The cosmos is not a living being, but is governed by unconscious corporeal forces or qualities only. In brief, he reduced the Aristotelian philosophy of nature to a monistic materialism. His most original contribution deals with space. He denied the continuous void of Democritus and maintained that vacuum is found only in the interstices separating the molecules that constitute substance. This theory of space had a great influence on ancient medicine and mechanics. BIBLIOGRAPHY: OCD 863–864; LexAW 2941; Copleston 1:425–426; P. Merlan, CHGMP 111–112.

[M. R. P. MCGUIRE]

STRAUSS, CHRISTOPH (1580–1631), Austrian composer, one of several generations of his family in the service of the Habsburgs. S. composed a series of 36 motets for 5–10 vocal and instrumental parts and 16 Masses for 8–20 parts. His music is a mixture of old German and newer Italian styles.

[M. T. LEGGE]

STRAUSS, DAVID FRIEDRICH (1808–74), a principal representative of the *Tübingen School of NT interpretation. He was a student of F. C. Baur and F. D. E. *Schleiermacher; the dialectical philosophy of G. W. *Hegel became a determinative element of his own thought. In his life of Jesus (*Leben Jesu*, 2 v., 1835–36; Eng. tr. M. Evans, repr. 1970) S. proposed that the Gospels did not portray the historical Jesus, but the Christ of faith, a synthesis of the myths evolved by the early Christian community. The fragments of fact in the Gospels are so few and scattered that a life of the historical Jesus is impossible to write. S.'s mythical interpretation undermined the confidence of many biblical scholars in the historical character of the NT; it was a direct influence on the demythologizing theme of R. Bultmann.

[T. C. O'BRIEN]

STRAVINSKY, IGOR (FEODOROVICH; 1882–1971), Russian-born master of modern music composition. Son of a famous bass singer, S. grew up in an artistic environment. Encouraged by Rimsky-Korsakov, with whom he would later study, S. discontinued the study of law at the Univ. of St. Petersburg to take up that of music composition and early manifested a mastery of technique. In 1909 Diaghilev commissioned him to write a ballet and thence began the association that produced, among others, the ballets *Petrouchka* (1911) and *Le Sacre du printemps* (1913), both of which marked turning points in music composition. The latter, indeed, being a complete break with traditional harmony, is hailed by many composers as the beginning of a new era. Following his stay in Switzerland during the war years (1914–18), S. returned to Paris and worked for Diaghilev, but soon entered upon a new compositional trend, his so-called Neoclassical period, characterized by a return to the past, esp. to the Baroque in style and form. Some of the better-known works of this period are the opera-oratorio *Oedipus Rex* (1927), the *Symphony of Psalms* (1930) for chorus and orchestra, and the opera, *The Rake's Progress* (1951). Thence followed still another radical change, a use of serial techniques as manifest in such compositions as *Canticum sacrum* (1955), a work for chorus and orchestra, and *Threni* (1958), a cantata. The works of his last years, *Abraham and Isaac* (1963), *Elegy for J.F.K.* (1964), and others are marked by brevity and a certain austerity. Though he became a French citizen in 1934, S. left France in 1939 and settled in the U.S., becoming an American citizen in 1945. S. made numerous tours, as a guest conductor, in Europe and America. In 1962, having already been given many honors by other countries, S. was invited back to his native Russia, where he was received with great enthusiasm. The catalogue of S.'s works is long and includes operas, ballets, vocal, choral and orchestral works, concertos, chamber and piano music. His sacred works, some of which were already mentioned, include a Mass, for which in 1963 Pope John XXIII bestowed on him the Papal Knighthood of St. Sylvester, an honor very rarely given any other than a Roman Catholic. An intensely religious man, S. gave evidence of his profound spirituality in the reverence and religious sentiment of his sacred works. He will probably be regarded by future historians as one of the most influential figures of 20th-cent. music. BIBLIOGRAPHY: E. W. White, *Stravinsky, The Composer and His Works* (1969); R. Vlad, *Stravinsky* (tr. F. and A. Fuller, 2d ed., 1967); P. H. Lang, *Stravinsky, A New Appraisal of His Work* (1963).

[M. T. LEGGE]

STRAWBRIDGE, ROBERT (d. 1781), Methodist lay preacher who is thought to have organized the first Methodist *society on the Wesleyan plan in North America, probably in 1764. An emigrant from Ireland, he settled on Sam's Creek, Frederick Co., Md., using his house as a preaching center. He itinerated through the Eastern Shore of Maryland, Delaware, parts of Pennsylvania, and Virginia, establishing societies and licensing local preachers. BIBLIOGRAPHY: HistAmMeth 1:75–76; F. E. Maser, "Robert Strawbridge, Founder of Methodism in Maryland," *Methodist History* (Jan. 1966) 3–21.

[F. E. MASER]

STREIT, KARL (1874–1935), founder of the Cartographical Institute (1930) for study of geographical and statistical aspects of the Catholic Church. Born at Dittersbackel, Czechoslovakia, he entered the Society of the Divine Word and spent much of his life at Steyl, Holland. In 1906 he published *Katholische missionsatlas,* which gave statistics on Catholic mission work. In 1913 he published *Atlas hierarchicus* (2d ed., 1929), surveying all Catholic dioceses of the world.

[T. EARLY]

STREIT, ROBERT (1875–1930), pioneer in study of Catholic mission work. Born in Fraustadt, Germany, he entered the Oblates of Mary Immaculate and after ordination became editor of the Oblates' mission journal. He led in the movement to establish mission study as a science and published seven volumes of *Bibliotheca missionum,* a bibliography with detailed annotation. His collaborator, J. Dindinger, continued the project after S.'s death.

[T. EARLY]

STRIGEL, VICTORINUS (1524–69), theologian prominent in the doctrinal controversies of second-generation Lutheranism. He studied under Melanchthon at Wittenberg. In the *Synergistic Controversy, he maintained that original sin did not destroy man's power for good and that in conversion there is some human cooperation with grace. His teaching was rejected in the *Formula of Concord (Art. 1). From 1563 he lectured at Leipzig, but was forced to leave because of his Calvinistic interpretation of the Lord's Supper. In 1567 he openly adopted Calvinism and became professor of ethics at Heidelberg. BIBLIOGRAPHY: G. Kawerau, EncRelKnow 11:113–114.

[M. J. SUELZER]

STRIGOLNIKI (Russ., shearers), the first heretical sect to originate in Russia. They flourished in Novgorod and Pskov in the 14th century. Scripture-oriented, antiliturgical, and moral rigorists, they held Russian Orthodox sacraments and hierarchy invalid because simoniacal. They elected "teachers" from among themselves but since laymen could not administer sacraments, they abolished all except penance. They devised "confession to the Earth," later adopted by some Russian sectarians.

[T. BIRD]

STRIKES, temporary stoppages of work by employees acting collectively to put pressure on the employer to grant their demands. These may be, for instance, higher wages, improved working conditions, shorter hours, recognition of an organization to represent them. Their significant appearance dates from the growth of 19th-cent. industrial capitalism. At first they met with serious opposition in the form of criminal prosecution or civil suits on the grounds that they were illegal conspiracies or breaches of contract. Courts often upheld these charges and outlawed the unions. Violence frequently accompanied strikes in those early days, often resulting from the clash between the workers and "strikebreakers" brought in by the employers. Gradually workers became better organized, their unions came to be protected by law, and agencies of government intervened to mediate between labor and management.

Since a strike seriously affects the living interests of both employers and employees, and of consumers and users in the community at large, questions arise about the morality of strikes as means of redressing grievances. Moral theologians generally hold that a strike may be just from the point of view of commutative justice when there is no breach of a fair labor contract and when no unreasonable demands are imposed; and from the point of view of social justice when the sectional benefit sought is notable enough to compensate for the damage inflicted on the community. The application of these principles is in the actual economy not clear cut. Moreover, all other means of settling the dispute must have failed, there must be a genuine prospect of a successful outcome, and the means used by the strikers must not be unlawful. BIBLIOGRAPHY: L. C. Brown, NCE 13:733–739.

[G. A. VANDERHAAR]

STRIPPING OF THE ALTAR, see ALTAR STRIPPING.

STRITCH, SAMUEL ALPHONSUS (1887–1958), cardinal, abp. of Chicago. Ordained for the Diocese of Nashville, Tenn., in 1910, S. was for a number of years secretary to the bp., to the chancellor of the diocese, and to the superintendent of schools. He was successively bp. of Toledo (1921), abp. of Milwaukee (1930–39), and abp. of Chicago (1939–58). He was a dedicated promoter of liturgical music; he labored to improve social conditions for workers, esp. blacks and Puerto Ricans. Catholic charities received a strong impetus from him. S. was chairman of the National Catholic Welfare Conference in 1945. In 1946 he was created cardinal. Appointed to head the Congregation for the Propagation of the Faith in Rome, he died before taking office.

[J. R. AHERNE]

STROMATA, also *strōmateis,* Gr. words meaning coverlets, carpets, tapestries, and in a metaphorical sense miscellanies. Like other picturesque titles such as meadows, honeycomb, and discoveries, *strōmata* was a word used to describe literary works into which a variety of topics were woven without any great attention to plan or systematic development of a theme. The Latin grammarian L. Caesellius Vindex composed a *stromateus*, and a *strōmateis* was falsely ascribed to Plutarch. *Strōmateis* is also the name of one of the most important works of Clement of Alexandria. In seven books (the origin of the eighth is disputed), he traces the relation of Christianity to secular culture. BIBLIOGRAPHY: Aulus Gellius, *Noctes Atticae*, pref. 4–10; Quasten 2:12–14.

[M. J. COSTELLOE]

STROPHICUS, in plainchant, a *neume of the "ornamenting" class, a group of two or three signs of identical pitch. Though actually indicating a quick reiteration, it is now usually sung simply as a sustained note.

[M. T. LEGGE]

STROSSMAYER, JOSIP JURAJ (1815–1905), leader of Croatian nationalism and Catholic bishop. Born at Osijek, Croatia, of German descent, he studied at Djakovo and Budapest and was ordained in 1838. After receiving a doctorate in theology at Vienna, he taught at the Djakovo seminary, served as court chaplain in Vienna (1847–49), and became bp. of Djakovo in 1849. An advocate of Catholic-Orthodox reunion, he opposed the dogma of papal infallibility at Vatican I, but later accepted it. He saw in the doctrine an obstacle to church reunion, esp. with the Russian Orthodox Church. Throughout his life he labored for good relations with all the Orthodox in his territories. He also was a staunch patriot, striving to achieve Croatian autonomy within the Austro-Hungarian Empire.

[T. EARLY]

STROZZI, a Florentine family noted for its role in supporting Renaissance scholars and artists. **Palla** (1372–1462) patronized scholarly efforts in classical philology, gathering and supporting scholars such as Manuel Chrysoloras. Plutarch's *Lives,* Aristotle's *Politics,* and Plato's works were among the MSS they collected and studied. Exiled by the Medici to Padua, Palla himself translated Greek works into Latin. **Filippo the Elder** (1426–91), the banker, began construction of the Palazzo Strozzi, memorial of the family and lasting example of Italian Renaissance architecture in Florence. **Giovanni Battista,** Filippo's son, (1488–1538), engaged in the continuing struggle with the Medici for control of the city. He remained at the French court in the 1530s as papal legate. When his military efforts to regain the city failed at Montemerlo (1538), he was imprisoned in the Florentine citadel where he committed suicide. **Leone,** Giovanni's son, (1515–54) was sent by Henry II of France to help protect Mary Queen of Scots against Elizabeth. **Carlo** (1587–1671) is known primarily for his work on the family's history. **Isabella Acquaviva** (1703–60), also of the family, assisted the apostolate of St. *Leonard of Port Maurice.

[R. J. LITZ]

STRUMI, ABBEY OF, former Vallombrosan monastery dedicated to San Fedele, near Poppi in the Province of Arezzo, Italy. It was founded first at Strumi by Count Teugrimo of the Guido family in the 10th cent. for Benedictine monks. These were replaced by Vallombrosans at the end of the 11th century. The abbey itself was abandoned a century later during the struggles between Guelfs and Ghibellines. A new one was built at Poppi. This was given in commendation to the abp. of Florence in the 15th cent., was restored to Vallombrosan control in 1510, and was suppressed in 1809. The abbey church at Poppi still exists. BIBLIOGRAPHY: Cottineau 2:3097.

[E. J. DILLON]

STUART, so written by Mary Queen of Scots, but also written Stewart and Steuart, the name of a family, founded by the son of a Norfolk baron of Breton ancestry, who became steward or seneschal of Scotland in the second half of the 12th century. From it descend, through marriage with Robert Bruce, the reigning sovereigns of Scotland since 1371; through marriage with Margaret Tudor, of England and Ireland since 1603. The hereditary title of the present ruling house in the United Kingdom derives from the marriage of a Stuart princess to a German elector. The last Stuart sovereign was Queen Anne, d. 1714. Many of them combined an attachment to Catholicism and to beautiful women, few of them were dull, or possessed of political good sense, most were tragic figures but gifted with a charm that captured and held the loyalty of their followers even when the cause was lost. For 2 cent. after the Reformation they were the rallying point for Catholics in the British Isles. The final defeat came with the failure of the '45 and the hunting of Bonnie Prince Charlie as a fugitive over the heather. The royal line (that is from James II) died out in 1807, with his brother, Henry Benedict, Cardinal Duke of York.

[T. GILBY]

STUART, HENRY BENEDICT MARIA CLEMENT (1725–1807), cardinal, last male heir of the Stuarts. S. was the son of the Old Pretender (called by his followers James III of England) and younger brother of Charles Edward, the Young Pretender to the English throne. In the view of the Stuart supporters, S. was Duke of York. Ordained a priest, he was named bp. of Ostia, Velletri, and Frascati and in 1747, cardinal. In 1759 he was appointed abp. of Corinth by Pope Clement XIII and in 1761 bp. of Tusculum. His revenues decreased during the French Revolution, the cardinal sacrificed incredible sums to help pay the ransom of Pius VI demanded by Napoleon. Dispossessed in 1799 by the Revolutionists, S. fled to Padua and Venice, completely impoverished; King George III generously rescued him from poverty. With S.'s death the male Stuart line ceased. He was a man of great prudence and amiability, and of more balanced judgment than his father and brother.

[J. R. AHERNE]

STUART, JAMES EDWARD FRANCIS (1688–1766), claimant to the throne of England and Scotland as James III of England and VIII of Scotland; also known as "the Old Pretender." A devout Catholic, he was doomed by the determined Protestantism of England and Scotland to spend a lifetime in vain attempts to gain the throne to which he had legitimate claim as son of James II. He was born in the year of the *Glorious Revolution, which deposed his father and imported the Protestant William of Orange to replace James II. When his father fled England the infant Prince and his mother were sent to St. Germain in France. Louis XIV made a secret agreement with William that the Prince should succeed to the throne on the latter's death on condition that he be reared as a Protestant. James II objected to the condition and the arrangement fell through. The French king promised James II that his son would succeed.

But by the Act of Settlement of 1701 male heirs of the Stuarts were barred from the throne of England, and by a special act the Prince was excluded from succession. The first serious attempt to restore S. to the throne occurred in 1705. Louis XIV outfitted a strong fleet and troops, which, with the Prince aboard, made for Scotland. Typically a combination of weather, English espionage, and misinformation made the expedition a failure and the French forces returned to Dunkirk. The death of Louis XIV and the provision of the Treaty of Utrecht barring the Pretender from living in France were blows to his fortune. S. moved to Bar-le-Duc in Lorraine which was to be his permanent base for the future. In 1715 the Scottish Earl of Mar attempted a rising for S. but the defeat at Preston ended hopes for an English rising. At Sheriffmuir in Scotland the battle was indecisive, but the report sent to France made it seem a Jacobite victory. The Prince in disguise came to Scotland where the Earl of Mar and others proclaimed him king of England and Scotland. S. set up court at Scone Palace and seemed to have widespread support. Threatened by an army from the south led by the Duke of Argyll, Mar and S. left Scotland, the Pretender deciding to do so to save his followers. The desertion left great bitterness, esp. among the Highland chiefs. An attempt to have Charles XII of Sweden intervene was ended by the death of the Swedish king. Spain outfitted an expedition in 1719 led by the Duke of Ormonde and the Earl Marischal. This, too, came to nothing. In 1719 S. in Madrid was married by proxy to Princess Maria Clementine Sobieska of Poland. S.'s subsequent history in France is a sad story of intrigues and quarrels within his official household. His wife deserted him, and the Prince became less and less able to take action. He demonstrated throughout his career a sadness and lack of energetic purpose. Nevertheless he was essentially compassionate, a devout Catholic in spite of some dissipation, and a man for whom thousands in England and Scotland exhibited a fierce loyalty. He was essentially a victim of anti-Catholic feeling and the inability of his followers to pursue firm and united action. He died in Rome.

[J. R. AHERNE]

STUART, JANET ERSKINE (1857–1914), educator, writer. An English convert to Catholicism in 1879, S. entered the Society of the Sacred Heart in 1882. She was superior vicar of England and in 1911 was named superior general of the Society. S. founded a number of convents in Scotland and England and made a worldwide visitation of her congregation. Devoted to education, she wrote *Education of Catholic Girls* (1911). Other publications included *Highways and Byways in the Spiritual Life* (1923) and *Poems* (1924).

[J. R. AHERNE]

STUBBS, WILLIAM (1824–1901), historian, bishop. Born and educated in England, S. became an Anglican priest in 1850 and served in a country parish. Here he studied the sources of medieval English history and laid the foundations of a knowledge that made him the leading scholar of his age. In 1861 he edited the medieval document *De inventione Sanctae Crucis* and began his contributions to the *Archeological Journal*. As Lambeth librarian from 1862 he had great research resources available to him. In 1864–65 appeared his two-volume *Chronicles and Memorials of Richard I*. S. was appointed regius professor of history at Oxford in 1866. While never in agreement with Oxford's teaching system, S. was still a creative professor. Of the many solid historical studies he published 19 volumes in the Rolls Series. His masterwork, however, was the *Constitutional History of England* (3 v., 1873–78), a massive work which remained standard for 50 years. In 1884 at the instance of Gladstone, S. was made bp. of Chester and in 1888, bp. of Oxford. In both sees he proved a zealous administrator, more at ease with large issues than petty details. S. was of the high church party and greatly devoted to Pusey. BIBLIOGRAPHY: *Letters of William Stubbs, Bishop of Oxford* (ed. W. Hutton, 1904).

[J. R. AHERNE]

STUDD, CHARLES THOMAS (1862–1931), English missionary who worked in China with the China Inland Mission, in India, and in Central Africa. In Africa he founded (1913) the Heart of Africa Mission, and conceived the idea of the Worldwide Evangelization Crusade (WEC, originally called Christ's Etceteras by S. himself), which has since extended its activities to many countries. For a historical sketch of the WEC and a statement of its objective, principles, organization, and activities, see D. J. Cornell in *Encyclopedia of Modern Christian Missions* (ed. B. L. Goddard, 1967) 707–710. BIBLIOGRAPHY: N. P. Grubb, *Charles Thomas Studd* (1933).

[P. K. MEAGHER]

STUDION, see STUDIUS.

STUDIORUM DUCEM, an encyclical letter of Pope Pius XI (June 29, 1923) endorsing the approval given to St. Thomas Aquinas by his predecessors, esp. Leo XIII and Pius X, and by himself in *Officiorum omnium* (Aug. 1, 1922), stating that the Church adopts the philosophy of St. Thomas as its very own. He reminds professors, esp. those in schools for major clerics, of the prescription of canon law (CIC c. 1366.2) to teach rational philosophy and theology in accordance with the method, doctrine, and principles of the Angelic Doctor, so that all can truthfully call him their teacher. BIBLIOGRAPHY: AAS 15 (1923) 323 ff.; D 365–367.

[J. H. ROHLING]

STUDIOUSNESS, the moral virtue of devotion to learning. It is quite typical of St. Thomas Aquinas's own spirit to recognize that a right devotion (*studium*) to the pursuit of knowledge channels an instinct of mind and will that are as connatural to man as the instinct toward the pleasures of the body. He thus allies studiousness as a moral virtue to *temperance (see also DOCILITY). Its direct concern is the ordering of the quest for knowledge toward its rightful purpose and through rightful means. Its secondary function is to overcome the physical and emotional shirking from the hard work of learning (ThAq ST 2a2ae, 166.2 ad 3). Studiousness controls an unchecked inquisitiveness (*curiositas*) that consists in pursuing trivia to the neglect of knowledge required for one's life or profession; or looks for knowledge from false sources; or seeks to know about creatures to the exclusion of God; or exceeds a person's mental capacities (*ibid.* 167.1).

[T. C. O'BRIEN]

STUDITES, those monks who lived in the monastery of *Studius from the time of St. Theodore the Studite or who, living in other monasteries around Constantinople from the early 9th cent. onward, observed the Rule of St. Theodore. This rule emphasized the liturgical life and urged the monks to go to confession and receive the Holy Mysteries at least on Sundays. Other particular aspects of Studite monasticism involved the need for fasting; weekly instructions on the ascetical life were given by the abbot himself. Stress was laid on the importance of learning, and a significant role was played in every Studite monastery by the monks assigned to the copying of manuscripts. Studite monasteries were instrumental in defending the Orthodox faith against the Iconoclasts even when the latter enjoyed the support of imperial power; a number of monks died in this cause. The absolute authority of the abbot of the monastery as well as the unconditional obedience of the monks was insisted upon, for St. Theodore firmly believed that only in complete submission could the monk hope to achieve success in the practice of asceticism. Beck 127, 209, 491–496.

[S. SURRENCY]

STUDIUM GENERALE, a medieval term for a university, i.e., an organized center of learning—arts, law, canon law, theology—attended by students from various countries and qualified to grant a license to teach anywhere. In many instances the *studium* evolved from a grouping of students around an outstanding master or masters, e.g., Salerno, Bologna, Paris. Before the 13th cent. recognition was commonly established through royal or imperial approval; after the 13th cent. it was customary to seek recognition from the pope, not only because his approbation was a better guarantee that the license to teach would be accepted universally, but also because rights and privileges conferred by the Holy See provided some protection against local tyranny and interference.

[M. B. MURPHY]

STUDIUS (STUDION), MONASTERY OF, perhaps the most famous and influential monastery in Constantinople. Dedicated to St. John the Baptist, the monastery and attached church (built in 463) were soon called by the name of the founder, the prominent patrician Studius (*Stoudios*) and were referred to as *ta Stoudiou*, the property of Studius. The well-endowed monastery flourished until the monks were expelled by the Iconoclastic emperors in the 8th century. But it soon recovered and became the most important center of monasticism in the Byzantine capital, counting some 700 monks. This was due largely to its most famous abbot, St. *Theodore, whose wise and humane organization of the community life appealed to many candidates. A school and a hospice for the poor were attached to the monastery. In contrast to most other monasteries, that of Studius stressed the education of the monks for the service of the Church. It became a center for the study of liturgical music, hymnography, painting of icons, and esp. the copying of MSS; this last was considered such an important service that it dispensed one from the Divine Office. To the end of the empire the monastery retained its fame and significance, although the Latin occupation (1204–61) proved almost fatal. Its *typikon* (rule) became a model for monasteries throughout the Christian East, notably among the Slavs. Under the Turks the church was made into a mosque (Imrahor Djami), and practically nothing is now left of either church or monastery. BIBLIOGRAPHY: E. Candal, LTK 11:1441–42.

[G. T. DENNIS]

STUMPF, JOHANNES (1500–78), Swiss Protestant theologian and historian. S. studied at Heidelberg and Strassburg and entered the Order of St. John in 1521. The following year he became prior of his order and people's priest in Bubikon. The date of his conversion to Lutheranism is not known; but he continued as Protestant pastor at Bubikon until 1543, when he took a church in Stammheim. Though usually conciliatory, S. resolutely defended Zwingli's view of the Eucharist. He wrote numerous historical, geographical, and theological works, and his Swiss chronicle (1548) remained authoritative into the 18th century. Another of his treatises, *Reformationschronik,* contains the first biography of Zwingli.

[M. J. SUELZER]

STUNDISTS (STUNDO-BAPTISTS), an evangelical Christian group which emerged sometime between 1858 and 1864 in the Ukraine in S Russia, presently the most influential body of Russian non-Orthodox Christians with adherents numbering nearly half a million. Pastor Bonekampfer is considered the founder. The group was born when native Russians began attending the devotional hours (Ger. *Stunden*) of the Lutheran, Reformed, and Mennonite communities in the German colony at Rohrbach; the movement was also rationalistic. The Baptist influence dominated and prompted an iconoclastic reaction against Orthodox relics, icons, rejection of any elaborate ritual and worship, and of the sacraments. During the 19th cent. these Stundo-Baptists became increasingly puritan in outlook and

behavior and Baptist in religious orientation. Suspected by the Russian government of harboring German sympathies, the group suffered persecution from 1867. Their right of association was sharply restricted by the Ministry of Internal Affairs (1894). The Stundists are now part of the Russian All Union Council of Evangelical Christians and Baptists established in 1944. BIBLIOGRAPHY: S. BolshaKoff, *Russian Nonconformity* (1950).

[R. J. LITZ]

STURM UND DRANG (STORM AND STRESS), the "Geniezeit," a German literary movement (1765–85) which stressed originality and freedom from literary conventions. The name is derived from the drama *Der Wirrwarr, oder Sturm und Drang* (1776) by Friedrich Maximilian von Klinger (1752–1831). Under the influence of Rousseau, Klopstock, Herder (whose *Von deutscher Art und Kunst* [1773] is considered a manifesto of *Sturm und Drang*), Hamann, and Shakespeare, the youthful dramatists (among them Klinger, Wagner, Lenz, Leisewitz, and Maler Müller) produced prose tragedies of middle-class life around themes of violence, conflict, murder, and rape. The lyric poets—Claudius, Bürger, and the poets of the Göttinger Hainbund—glorified friendship, virtue, patriotism, and liberty in an emotional and sentimental poetry that owed its inspiration to Klopstock. The early works of Goethe and Schiller were the best products of this period, which influenced such later literary movements as romanticism, realism, and naturalism. BIBLIOGRAPHY: J. G. Robertson, *History of German Literature* (4th ed., 1962) ch. 7–9.

[M. F. MCCARTHY]

STURMI, ST. (744–779), Benedictine abbot. A Bavarian disciple of St. Boniface, S. worked as a missionary among the Hessians. At Boniface's command he founded the monastery of Fulda, becoming its first abbot. Because of a jurisdictional argument with Abp. Lull of Mainz, S. was exiled by King Pepin between 763 and 765, but the King then acknowledged Fulda's rights. S. established Fulda's internal life on a firm basis from his experience in visiting key Italian monastic centers. He brought the abbey to a flourishing state in religion, education, culture, and economy. Possession of Boniface's relics enhanced its fame. Charlemagne planned to use S. and his 400 monks for the Christianization of Saxony. BIBLIOGRAPHY: K. Kunze, BiblSanct 12:43–46; *Bavaria sancta* (ed. G. Schwaiger, 3v., 1970–73) 3:33–47.

[R. H. SCHMANDT]

STURZO, LUIGI (1871–1959), Italian Catholic priest, political leader, social theorist. Born in Caltagirone, Sicily, he was ordained in 1894 and later taught in his native town and served as mayor (1905–20). In 1919 he led in founding the Partito Popolare, precursor of the Christian Democratic Party. But in 1923 the Vatican, under pressure from Mussolini, withdrew support. From 1924 to 1940 Sturzo lived in exile in England, and then until 1946 in the United States. He was made a senator for life by the president of Italy in 1952. Among S.'s influential writings are: *International Community and the Right of War* (1930); *Church and State* (1939); *True Life* (1943); *Inner Laws of Society* (1944).

[T. EARLY]

STYLIANOS OF NEOCAESAREA (9th cent.), Byzantine abp., also known as Mapas. He was a leader of the "Little Church" that refused association with Patriarch *Photius (858–867; 877–886) or bps. consecrated by him. After the deposition of Photius by Emperor Leo VI, S. refused to accept the Emperor's brother, Stephen, as patriarch (886–893), since Stephen had been ordained a deacon by Photius. But S. was later reconciled to the official Church, perhaps in 899.

[T. EARLY]

STYLITE, a Christian ascetic living on the top of a column or pillar (*stulōs*). This remarkable form of eremitical life was originated by St. Simeon the Stylite, who mounted a pillar in the mountains of N Syria *c.*423 to escape the importunities of the crowds who came to seek his prayers and advice. It spread through Syria, Egypt, Greece, Palestine, Anatolia, and Mesopotamia but never found favor in the West. Its popularity may partially be explained by the fact that it combined three earlier forms of penance: stability, the living in a single place; rooflessness, or living out in the open; and standing upright for long periods of time. The practice became so common that it had to be regulated by canonical and liturgical prescriptions. Among the more famous stylites were St. Daniel, who took up his residence on a column near Constantinople in the year 460; St. Simeon the Younger, who lived on a pillar near Antioch and died in 592; and St. Alypius, who stood for 53 years on his pillar near Adrianople and then, after losing the use of his feet, lived there for 14 more years on his side. The columns of these heroic men frequently became the centers of monasteries and the objects of pilgrimages both during their lifetime and after their death. BIBLIOGRAPHY: H. Delehaye, *Les Saints stylites* (1923); *Les Moines d'Orient* (ed. A. J. Festugière, 1961) v. 2.

[M. J. COSTELLOE]

SUÁREZ, FRANCISCO (1548–1617), Spanish Jesuit scholastic philosopher and theologian. S. studied at Salamanca and subsequently taught at several Jesuit colleges in Spain and at Coimbra (1597–1615). He was a prolific writer whose collected works fill 28 volumes in their Paris edition. His scholarly influence was great both during and after his lifetime (see SUAREZIANISM), and he is usually considered the greatest Jesuit scholastic theologian. As a philosopher, S. was fundamentally Thomistic although he differed in several important areas from Thomas Aquinas. He rejected *nominalism and the formalism of *Duns Scotus, but maintained that there is not a real but a rational distinction between essence and existence. Even in the crea-

ture, therefore, existence becomes identified with essence, and the concretely existing individual is the realization of its essence. This identification of essence and existence does not make the creature infinite because the very nature of created being is to be contingent. Some of his other important philosophical positions are that metaphysics is the study of being as being, not being in abstraction; that being is analogical not univocal as Scotus held; and that a metaphysical proof for God's existence can be constructed from the principle of efficient causality. The key to his metaphysics seems to be the concept of participation in being which in his theology is translated into the utter dependence of creatures upon God. Theologically, S. was an advisor to the Jesuits in the Molinist controversy (see MOLINISM); composed long treatises in Mariology and Christology, holding that the Incarnation would have happened even if Adam had not sinned; and wrote *De defensione fidei* in response to Pope Paul V's request to refute the errors of King James of England. He emphasized the absolute transcendence of the supernatural order and allowed an active *obediential potency in man for the supernatural. S. was also a highly influential and original thinker in the philosophy of law, and contributed to the transition from the medieval to the modern conception of political power. The state is a natural entity with power from the community of citizens for their good. The form of government is a choice of the people, and the medieval ideal of imperial power is rejected. BIBLIOGRAPHY: *Opera omnia* (28 v., Paris ed. 1856–78); J. Dalman, NCE 13:751–754; J. Mourant, EncPhil 8:30–33.

[T. M. MCFADDEN]

SUAREZIANISM, a scholastic philosophical tradition that derives its orientation and name from the Spanish Jesuit, Francisco *Suárez (1548–1617). The Suarezian system is basically Thomistic, although scholars disagree concerning its faithfulness to Thomas and the validity of its acknowledged innovations. Suárez was most influential during his life, and soon after his death chairs of Suarezian philosophy were established at several Spanish universities (e.g., Valladolid, Salamanca, Alcalá). His metaphysics dominated thought at Catholic and many Protestant German and Dutch universities of the 17th and 18th cent., and many scholastic authors wrote their works *ad mentem Suarezii.* *Descartes is said to have carried a copy of the *Disputationes* with him; C. *Wolff's ontology is greatly dependent upon this system; *Leibniz read Suárez extensively, as did *Schopenhauer. Among the chief features of Suarezianism are the conception of the individual as the object of direct divine and human intellectual cognition, the pure potentiality of matter, and the conceptual but not real distinction between essence and existence in created being. Suarezianism departs from strict Thomism regarding the relationship between the natural and supernatural by holding an active *obediential potency in man for the supernatural. BIBLIOGRAPHY: Copleston 3:353–406; A. J. Benedetto, NCE 13:754–756.

[T. M. MCFADDEN]

SUBCINCTORIUM (Lat., *subcingulum,* also *succingulum*), a kind of cincture worn over the alb to which a maniple-like piece of material is attached at the wearer's right side. This may have derived from a sort of pocket in the form of a purse of some practical use to the celebrant at certain liturgical functions. Once the use of the subcinctorium was general among bps. in the Western Church, but since the 13th cent. this article of liturgical apparel has been reserved to the pope.

[P. K. MEAGHER]

SUBDEACON, until recently, one who had advanced in holy orders to the grade below that of deacon. The subdiaconate was introduced in the early 3d cent., and the ministry was conferred in an ordination rite that did not include an imposition of the hands, generally regarded as an essential element in the sacrament of orders. Nevertheless it was long considered a major order in the Western Church. Today, however, theologians look upon the rite of the subdiaconate as a sacramental instituted by the Church. The ministry of the subdeacon was to assist the deacon in the solemn Liturgy of the Eucharist. For as long as the ministry was recognized in the Western Church because of its classification as a major order, with ordination to the subdiaconate, one assumed the obligation of celibacy as well as the duty of reciting the Divine Office, the official prayer of the Church. In the Eastern Church the subdiaconate was considered a minor order, although as late as the Council of Trullo (692), subdeacons were not permitted to marry. Today in the Eastern Church subdeacons may marry and commonly do before ordination to the diaconate. In the Western Church, with the revision of orders by Paul VI, the minor orders and the order of subdeacon were abolished on Sept. 14, 1972, by the apostolic constitution *Ministeria quaedam* (dated Aug. 15, 1972, AAS 64 [1972] 532). This was done in accordance with the desire of Vatican Council II, which declared that the diaconate constituted the lower level of the hierarchy. BIBLIOGRAPHY: A. Michel, DTC 14.2:2459–66; P. de Puniet, *Roman Pontifical: A History and Commentary* (tr. M. Harcourt, 1932).

[P. F. PALMER]

SUBINTRODUCTAE, see AGAPETAE.

SUBJECTIVISM, as a religious attitude, a tendency to place individual reason and personal experience above objective, external authorities. Luther and Calvin have been blamed for teaching the right of *private judgment, but both in fact believed in an objective authority. It was the 18th cent. that brought about a crisis in epistemology that undermined old authorities. After Hume had cast doubt upon the causal nexus, Kant announced in his *Critique of Pure Reason* that one cannot know reality-in-itself, but only appearances. Therefore religion must rest upon man's inner sense of right and wrong, from which God's existence and human immortality may be deduced. F. *Schleiermacher located the essence of religion in "a feeling of absolute dependence upon God." *Liberal theology, deprived of an infallible Bible, grounded authority in God-consciousness, the conscience, or other forms of religious experience. Without intending to do so, *Pietism, *revivalism, and *evangelicalism reinforced the tendency toward subjectivism by stressing the "conversion experience" above creeds, Church, ministry, and sacraments. Scientific method, depth psychology, and sociology further contributed to a relativism that permeated every area, including religion. The *Bultmann School's existentialist approach to the NT (see EXISTENTIAL THEOLOGY) and the neo-orthodox separation of the Jesus of history from the Christ of faith are evidences of the lack of confidence in external authorities. In ethics, older systems were supplanted by situational (or contextual) ethics (see NEW MORALITY). Thus the growing tendency toward subjectivism has made modern man tend to be antidogmatic, skeptical of authority, and reliant upon his own religious and ethical judgments.

[N. H. MARING]

SUBLAPSARIANISM, the doctrine, held by some Calvinists and affirmed by the Synod of *Dort (1618–19), that God after the creation and Fall of man decreed the salvation of the elect and the reprobation of the wicked according to his inscrutable will. *CALVINISM; *SUPRALAPSARIANISM; *PREDESTINATION.

[J. A. R. MACKENZIE]

SUBLIMATION, a psychological process in which drives and energies are expended on goals which are considered more noble, moral, spiritual, and humane than the earthier or grosser purposes to which they seem primarily directed. In Freudian psychoanalysis, sublimation has often been considered a simple diversion of instinctual sexual and aggressive drives to substitute purposes of a more acceptable social nature, and thus sublimation counts as a mechanism of defense, i.e., a mode of releasing the pressure of dangerous drives. This concept empties higher human pursuits of much of their intrinsic validity. Contemporary psychoanalysis leans in the direction of more traditional views in which sublimation is considered as a focusing of intellectual and emotional energies on higher goals with a consequent diminution of interest in and desire for more mundane purposes, partly because attention and energy are focused elsewhere and partly because the higher gratifications compensate for the relinquishing of the lower. Nevertheless, even in this view, the element of truth contained in Freud's formulation may be admitted, e.g., a labor union leader fighting management for economic justice may also be gratifying repressed aggression. Counsellors and spiritual directors should take into account their clients' capacities for sublimation as they advise them on the most appropriate means to balance off their hopes and ambitions against the pressures of their needs and frustrations. BIBLIOGRAPHY: R. Dalbiez, *Psychoanalytical Method and the Doctrine of Freud* (1941).

[M. E. STOCK]

SUBMERSION, see IMMERSION.

SUBORDINATIONISM, an erroneous and heretical explanation of the mystery of the Trinity that maintains the Son to be inferior (subordinate) to the Father, and the Holy Spirit to the Father and the Son. A certain amount of subordinationism is to be found in Hermas, Justin Martyr, Irenaeus, Clement of Alexandria, and Origen. It was explicitly taught by Arius and his followers, who held that the Son was not eternal but begotten by the Father as an instrument for the creation of the world. The heresy was condemned by the Council of Nicaea in 325 and again by that of Constantinople in 381. Its origins may be traced to an exaggerated defense of monotheism, a one-sided interpretation of such biblical passages as Pr 8.22 and Jn 14.28, and an excessive rationalism under the influence of Gnostic and Neoplatonic teachings, which postulated a series of lesser beings to bridge the gap between God and his visible creation. BIBLIOGRAPHY: G. Bardy, DTC 15.2:1625–29; C. Vagaggini, EncCatt 11:1465–68. *ARIANISM.

[M. J. COSTELLOE]

SUBORDINATIONISTS, early Christians who held that the Word, esp., is inferior to the Father. Orthodox Christianity holds that the three Persons of the Trinity are co equal because consubstantial. The first important subordinationist was *Origen (c.185–253/4), who implied that the Son is somehow inferior to the Father because he comes forth from him; yet at the same time Origen seems to hold that the Word is the Father's utterly perfect image. Thus Origen seems to be merely a hierarchichal subordinationist —the Word is second to the Father in order, but not inferior to his being. The most important subordinationism is *Arianism; *Arius (c.289–336) taught that the Word is the highest creature, made by the Father from all eternity. The most radical subordinationists were the *Anomeans (4th cent.), who held that the Son is simply "unlike" the Father. The *Macedonians and the *Pneumatomachians subordinated the Holy Spirit.

[R. R. BARR]

SUBPRIOR (SUBPRIORESS), assistant superior to the prior or prioress in older orders, e.g., the Augustinian. In the Benedictine and other monastic traditions, the subprior comes after the abbot and the prior in authority.

SUBSEMITONIUM, see SUBTONIUM.

SUBSIDIARITY, PRINCIPLE OF, respect, as opposed to usurpation, of each entity's proper competence. Based on the Christian philosophy formulated by popes in modern times, it is consonant with the radical changes in social conditions and concern for the common good. The principle (though not so named) appears in Pope Leo XIII's *Immortale Dei* and *Rerum novarum* (it had already found place in Aquinas's writings on the law and the state; see NCE 13:645). Pius XI first enunciated the principle in *Quadragesimo anno* (n. 79; see NCE 13:380; Vat II Church-ModWorld 86, Abbott 300 note) that what can be done by the smaller body is not to be usurped by the larger. Pius XII stated it as a valid principle for the Church "without prejudice to its hierarchical structure" (AAS 38 [1946] 145); he quoted his predecessor Pius XI, as did also John XXIII. Pope John, with his Council, confirmed and deepened understanding of it; it is clear in the documents of Vatican Council II (as ChurchModWorld 86; ChrEduc 3, 6; Const-Church 27). Paul VI has continued in their spirit (esp. noteworthy in ecumenical approach to the Eastern Churches [cf. *Concilium* 48:124–129]).

The principle of subsidiarity has particular relevance: to the increasing social consciousness of the Church and of civil governments (cf. *Concilium* 45:8, note 11; 48:124); to religious communities; to the profession of the individual person as a function in society (cf. *Concilium* 45:14–19), with his objective product (*perfectio operati* subordinate to the artisan value, *perfectio operantis*); to the person's awareness of the meaning and purpose of the task performed bringing joy and heightened individual initiative (cf. *Concilium* 44:66; 45:21, note 13); to education, preventing state monopoly (see Vat II ChrEduc 3,6), yet upholding government's beneficent role (cf. *Concilium* 45:18); to the Eastern Churches, in which the role of the patriarch is supported (cf. *Concilium* 48:124, note 3–129). BIBLIOGRAPHY: Abbott; *Encyclicals and Other Messages of John XXIII* (ed. J. F. Cronin et al., 1964) 263, 267, 279, 289; *Concilium*, esp. v. 44, 45, 48.

[M. R. BROWN]

SUBSISTENCE (Lat., *subsistentia*), a term that came into use somewhat late in the history of the development of Christian dogma. It seems to have been coined by Rufinus of Aquileia (d. 410) to make up for the relative poverty of the Latin tradition in expressing the concept of person. While the Greek tradition understood *hupostasis* as referring to the person, the Latins understood *substantia* (which could appear to be the Latin equivalent of *hupostasis*) in the sense of nature. To express the idea of person, the Latins had only the word *persona*, which was not entirely satisfactory because its connotation had long been phenomenological rather than ontological. *Persona* was originally the personage which an actor puts on in a stage play. Subsistence was introduced to provide a better Latin equivalent for the Greek *hupostasis*. It is found in the Trinitarian and Christological councils to signify the ontological person. However, the term *subsistentia* underwent a certain evolution in the late scholastic period. No longer used of the person, it came to designate the formal ontological perfection by which a person subsists, i.e., his act of existence as a whole and uncommunicated substance. Hence the term is beclouded by some ambiguity even today. According to its original meaning there are three subsistences in God, the three Persons; later usage, however, permits the affirmation of one subsistence only, i.e., the subsistence of the divine nature itself.

BIBLIOGRAPHY: T. U. Mullaney and T. E. Clarke, NCE 13:763–766. *HYPOSTASIS.

[J. DUPUIS]

SUBSTANCE. For Aristotle, to ask of anything what it is, is to ask about its substance (*Metaph*. 1028b2). Because of this, the search for substance involves the search for the senses in which anything may be said to be. Aristotle is emphasizing precisely the fact that a substance refers to this individual thing here as individual and that it deals with the question of why this individual should be at all. The question of substance is the question of what is. In answering this question Aristotle distinguishes two senses of the word substance: primary and secondary substance. By primary substance is meant precisely the concrete, individual thing; while by secondary substance is meant anything like genus or species which results from an abstraction from the concrete individual. Secondary substance depends upon primary substance for its meaning. Yet, in the sense in which a secondary substance is a subject, it may be said to possess the same attributes as a primary substance.

Aristotle insists upon the priority of the notion of substance. It is prior to all other categories in three ways. (1) It is prior because it can exist apart, whereas all other categories depend upon substance for their existence. (2) It is prior because it can exist apart, whereas all other include a definition of the substance which grounds the category. (3) It is prior in knowledge because to know of something what it is is superior to knowing any other relations which it might have.

Aristotle suggests four senses in which the word substance (*ousia*) may be understood: (1) as essence; (2) as universal; (3) as genus and species; and (4) as substratum. Of these four senses the primary and proper understanding of substance is essence. By essence Aristotle means what a thing is by its very nature, that which gives it its individuality and makes it what it is, namely, this individual thing here. In this sense of the word substance, it must be understood in relation to change as the total being which undergoes changes, and not as that which remains the same throughout change.

In contrast to Aristotle, Descartes saw substance as being that in which sensible qualities were grounded, an underlying substratum which supported the characteristics of a thing. He defines substance as ''a thing in which this something that we perceive or which is present objectively in some of our ideas, exists formally or eminently.''

It is precisely this notion of substance, and not Aristotle's, which John Locke attacked in *An Essay concerning Human Understanding*, arguing that this must be an empty notion, suggested to us by the fact that we find it difficult to conceive of the characteristics which constitute a thing existing together without something holding them together. But, as Locke suggests, there is nothing which can be said of this substratum except that the characteristics which it is said to support exist together.

Immanuel Kant modified the notion of substance even further, suggesting that rather than describing some characteristics of things as they are in themselves, it was only one of the categories in terms of which the human mind organized phenomena, and that therefore its support was not in some external reality, but rather as a necessary structure of the mind. BIBLIOGRAPHY: L. Foss, ''Substance, Knowledge and *Nous* in Aristotle,'' *New Scholasticism* 43 (1969) 379–399.

[F. J. CUNNINGHAM]

SUBSTANTIAL CHANGE. In scholastic philosophy, it is the change of a complete mobile or material being into another mobile being. Examples of substantial change would be the burning of wood which would yield carbonaceous ashes or the death of an animal, leaving behind the inanimate chemicals. Substantial change is contrasted to accidental change wherein such changes as in color, size, or shape occur. In substantial change, however, there is an unqualified coming-to-be in which a new material being comes into existence. Scholastic sacramental theology, the theology of *transubstantiation drew on the meaning of substantial change to articulate the way in which Christ's body and blood come to be present in the Eucharist.

[F. T. RYAN]

ṢÛBṬÂ, the East Syrian service of preparing the Eucharistic offerings.

[A. CODY]

SUBTLETY, the quality of a glorified body (i.e., a body in heavenly glory), whereby it is not hindered in its passage through material impediments. Theologians have been brought to infer its existence from the gospel descriptions of Our Lord's post-Resurrection appearances (Jn 20.19,26).

[E. A. WEIS]

SUBTONIUM, the tone below the *final* of a church mode. From the 16th cent. on, it has meant, more specifically, a whole tone as distinct from a half tone below the final, which is called *subsemitonium*. The use of a subsemitonium to replace what would normally be a subtonium (e.g., C# instead of C in the Dorian mode) was called *musica ficta*.

[M. T. LEGGE]

SUBUNISTS, the Catholics opposed to the *Utraquists in 15th-cent. Bohemia. The Subunists defended holy communion under one species (*sub una specie*); they were also called Unists. *HUSSITES.

[T. C. O'BRIEN]

SUBURBICARIAN DIOCESES, seven dioceses within a 40–mi. radius of Rome, since the 12th cent. sees of cardinal bps.: Albano, Frascati, Ostia, Palestrina, Porto e San Rufino, Sabina, Velletri. In 1962 John XXIII made them merely titular sees of cardinals, with residential bps. having actual jurisdiction over them. The designation passed into church usage from Roman law; it is used in CIC c. 236, §§ 3 & 4.

SUCCENTOR, the subcantor, i.e., the assistant to the precentor. The name survives now only as an honorary title of a canon in some cathedral chapters.

SUE, EUGÈNE (1804–57), French writer, born Marie-Joseph Sue, whose serialized novels dramatizing social problems had mass audience appeal. Originally a ship's surgeon, S. became a celebrated Parisian dandy and author of fashionable society fiction. He evolved toward socialism, was a deputy after the 1848 Revolution, but went into permanent exile with Napoléon III's *coup d'état*. In his later novels describing society's lower depths, he coupled democratic and socialist ideals of reform with an anticlerical, anti-Catholic, and esp. anti-Jesuitic polemic. These works, his best known, include *Les Mystères de Paris* (1842), *Le Juif errant* (1845–47), *Les Sept péchés capitaux* (1847–49) and *Les Mystères du peuple* (1849–56). BIBLIOGRAPHY: J. Moody, *Les Idées sociales d'Eugène Sue* (1938); J.-L. Bory, *Eugène Sue. Le Roi du roman populaire* (1963).

[G. E. GINGRAS]

SUETONIUS, (Gaius Suetonius Tranquillus; *c.* A.D. 70–145), Roman historian and biographer. At first a lawyer and friend of Pliny the Younger, he became secretary to Hadrian but was dismissed *c.* 121. S. was a man of wide erudition and wrote on a great variety of subjects, but his only extant works are portions of his *De viris illustribus,* "On Famous Men," which served St. Jerome as a model for a similar work, and nearly the whole of his *De vita Caesarum,* biographies of the emperors from Caesar to Domitian. S.'s lives are replete with curious information collected from a wide variety of sources. He wrote clearly and with feeling, but without any trace of rhetoric. His influence on later writers has been great. BIBLIOGRAPHY: J. W. Duff, *Literary History of Rome in the Silver Age* (3d ed., 1964) 501–512.

[M. J. COSTELLOE]

SUFFERING, the conscious, reflective experience of physical or mental pain. Happiness, or blessedness, is described by St. Thomas Aquinas as belonging to intelligent beings: they have the capacity to recognize their own possession of the fulfillment of their desires; are aware that things can go well or badly for them; and have mastery over their own activities (ThAq ST 1a, 26.1). Suffering can be taken as the opposite: an intelligent being's awareness of the deprival of the good desired, through pain and adversity making things go wrong, and in a way from which there is no escape, over which there is no mastery. Any sentient being experiences pain and the emotion of sorrow; but it is the reflective power of intelligence that gives the experience of pain and sorrow the full dimension of suffering. The Latin root of the term means undergoing; it is particularly the helplessness, the inability to escape from or diminish pain, to change things, that is the essence of suffering, whether the pain is an excruciation of body or an anguish of mind or spirit.

Suffering is what "creates" the problem of *evil. For the question connatural to the sufferer, or to the observer of suffering, is: Why? The helplessness that is at the core of suffering wrenches the question from the sufferer or the observer. The power to reflect that suffering is a brute fact; that it need not happen; and that the mastery once experienced over life and self has changed to impotence—these create the question of why and the perception that it is unanswerable. Evil is a problem because of the harrowing experience that it has no meaning. That experience is suffering, personal or vicarious.

St. Thomas also makes the disconcerting statement that in human affairs every evil is either the evil of sin or the evil of punishment. The implication is that all evil in human life has a moral quality, since not only sin but also punishment has a moral meaning—it is the moral consequence of guilt. The distinction often suggested in discussing evil, between moral evil and physical evil, according to St. Thomas's statement, does not apply to evil as personally undergone (*ibid.* 48.5). Evil that is the cause and object of suffering is the evil of punishment—the unwilling loss of what a person holds dear—health, fortune, friends, life itself. There is but one escape from the brutality of the experience of suffering. Christ absorbed suffering as the evil of punishment redemptively, as expiation and atonement. That takes away the helplessness, the unwilling subjection that constitutes suffering. The evil of punishment by charity's submission and acceptance is transferred into redemptive and expiatory suffering (*ibid.* 1a2ae, 87.6; 3a, 48.2 & 3). The mystery of the suffering Christ is the only divinely given response to the why that is wrenched from the sufferer. The power communicated by faith in Christ is the only resource that keeps the sufferer from despair and blasphemy. Because the loss of all that is held dear is the inevitable fate of every person, every one must face the ultimate challenge of faith, the total acceptance of sharing in Christ's lot. Only in the experienced survival through Christ of that challenge will anyone receive the answer to the why that suffering imposes. *Patientia*, a Latin term linked to suffering, describes a virtue that is the condition for the survival of charity. This is why both Augustine and Aquinas describe it as a virtue, the virtue of suffering which means so much more than "patience," proper to the Christian and impossible without grace (*ibid.* 2a2ae, 136.3). BIBLIOGRAPHY: ThAq ST 1a2ae, 87 esp. in Lat-Eng (v.27, ed. T. C. O'Brien) app. 1.

[T. C. O'BRIEN]

SUFFICIENT REASON, PRINCIPLE OF, the principle according to which whatever is existent and whatever is true have sufficient reason for being so. G. W. *Leibniz gave it the first of many and various formulations. Just as the principle of contradiction was the principle upon which all reasoning about the necessary was to be based, so the principle of sufficient reason was the principle upon which all reasoning about the factual and contingent was to be based. Leibniz's formulation was at least doubly ambiguous. First, it indiscriminately unites an ontological principle about real existents with a logical principle about truths about existents; this is nothing but the rationalist identification of the structures and relations of the real with those of the conceptual. Secondly, his principle of sufficient reason is laden with the determinism of his entire metaphysics, in which all is radically necessary and contingency is but apparent, arising out of human ignorance of the factors of necessity. From Leibniz the principle of sufficient reason made its way through the scholasticism of Christian *Wolff into the critical philosophy of Immanuel Kant. Kant saw the principle of sufficient reason as the fundamental synthetic a priori proposition, with the principle of contradiction being the fundamental analytic a priori proposition. The principle of sufficient reason functioned, in Kant's severe conceptualism, as the means by which the human knower imposed intelligibility upon the phenomenal world. Modern and contemporary Neo–Scholasticism, unifying both rationalist and Kantian elements with those of classical Aristotelianism, has tried to integrate the principle of sufficient reason with the first principles of the earlier tradition. But this attempt is paradoxical. On the one hand, if the principle of sufficient reason is not purged of the ambiguities of the Leibnizian and Wolffian rationalism and of the skepticism of Kantianism, then it is incompatible with the fundamental tenets of Aristotelico-scholastic realism. On the other hand, if so purged, the principle of sufficient reason is reduced to two theses already integral parts of Aristotelico-scholastic realism. One, ontological, holds that everything that exists exists per se or as caused by another. The other, logical, is that every true proposition is true per se or its truth is derived from one or more prior true propositions. BIBLIOG - RAPHY: J. E. Gurr, *Principle of Sufficient Reason in Some Scholastic Systems: 1750–1900* (1959).

[R. E. HENNESSEY]

SUFFRAGAN BISHOP, bp. of a suffragan see, i.e., a diocese as part of an ecclesiastical province, with an archdiocese being the metropolitan see. The CIC gives certain rights of oversight to the metropolitan abp. (CIC, c. 274), but the suffragan bishop has full episcopal responsibility and jurisdiction for his own see. Vatican Council II declared that ecclesiastical provinces should be strengthened for the more effective pastoral ministry of bishops (see Vat II BpPastOff 39–41).

SUFFRAGES FOR THE DEAD, see DEAD, PRAYERS FOR THE.

SUFFREN, JEAN (1571–1641), confessor, royal counselor. A French Jesuit, S. taught successively at Dôle, Avignon, and Lyon. He was a celebrated preacher and became confessor to Marie de Médicis, the Queen Mother, in 1615.

He steered a prudent course through the court intrigues of the age, influencing King Louis XIII but remaining loyal to the Queen Mother. S. was instrumental in preventing war between France and Austria in collaboration with Lamormaini, confessor to Emperor Ferdinand II. He followed Marie into exile in London, vainly striving to reconcile Card. Richelieu and the Queen Mother. S. wrote a series of meditations, *L'année chrétienne*. . . . (5 v., 1640), which attained considerable popularity.

[J. R. AHERNE]

SUFISM, Islamic mysticism. The term is taken from the Arab. noun ṣûfî, one who practices mysticism (taṣawwuf) and is commonly held to be derived from the garment of coarse wool (ṣûf) worn by mystical ascetics. Sufism or mysticism proper is normally to be distinguished from simple asceticism (zuhd), though historically the latter grew out of the former. The *Koran contains frequent calls to the rejection of the values of this world in favor of total devotion to God and even in the earliest period of Islam there were a number of Muslims who led genuinely ascetic lives. By the mid-9th cent. the ascetic (zâhid) was already a fairly common figure in the cities, as teacher and preacher. Some, particularly those known as the quṣṣâṣ (sing., qâṣṣ, literally a recounter of stories or history) fell into ill repute because of the fantastical elaborations of their histories and eschatalogical tales, but others had wide influence in all strata of the community. Among them, Ḥasan al-Baṣrî (d. 728) was one of the most important and influential religious figures of early Islam; members of his circle were instrumental in the development of movements as diverse and opposed as those of the *Mutazilites and the Sufis. Within the following century the characteristics of Muslim mysticism take on more definitive form in the writing and teaching of a large number of important persons such as Rabâḥ ibn 'Amr al-Qaysî (d. 796) or the woman mystic, Râbi'a al-'Âdawiya (d. 801), who composed poetry on her love for God. 'Abd al-Wâḥid ibn Zaid (d. 793) founded a cenobitic community at 'Abbadan, and Ibn Karrâm (d. 869) founded a number of schools through which his disciples propagated his theological and mystical teaching. It is at this period that the golden age of earlier Islamic mysticism begins. Al-Muḥâsibî (d. 857), a follower of the teaching of Ḥasan al-Baṣrî and a brilliant moral theorist, wrote many important tracts on the examination of conscience. More important in the development of strictly mystical doctrine, however, are Dhû 1-Nûn, an Egyptian (d. 859), who was probably the first to distinguish the stages (maqâmât) and states (aḥwâl) of the soul in its progress toward religious perfection; al-Tirmidhî (d. 898), known as al-Ḥakîm (the Sage), who systematically elaborated and expanded the theology of Ibn Karrâm; abû Yazîd al-Bisṭâmî (d. 874), who sought, through the most rigorous asceticism, to rid his consciousness of all beings save God so as to stand altogether alone in the presence of his creator; and al-Junaid (d. 910), whose teaching considerably advanced the theories of the mystical union. The Sufi masters of this period tended not to teach publicly since they were frequently denounced by the theologians (*mutakallimîn*) for rejecting the rational understanding of the faith in favor of a more immediate and intuitive knowledge of God, and accused, esp. by the canonists and traditionists (see HADITH) of belittling the law (Sharia) in favor of the interior judgment of conscience and noncanonical devotions, and for their ecstatic utterances. Al-*Ḥallâj, the greatest of all Muslim mystics (d. 922), who insisted on preaching publicly and who openly laid claim to a mystical union with God, was put to death for his teaching.

From the time of al-Ḥallâj, the teaching of the Sufis came progressively under the influence of Neoplatonic philosophy and the gnosticizing doctrines of the *Ismailis. Though there are a number of important orthodox writers in the later period, most notably al-*Ghazzâlî, one of the foremost theologians and reformers of medieval Islam (d. 1111) and 'Abd al-Qâdir al-Jîlânî (d. 1166), the founder of the Qâdirîya order (see DERVISHES), the dominant writers show a marked progress from the earlier doctrine of the ''unity of witness'' (*waḥdat al-šuhûd*) to one of the ''unity of being'' (*waḥdat al-wujûd*); and from teaching a union (*ittiṣâl* or *it-tiḥâd*) of the soul with God to one of a fusion (*ḥulûl*) of God with the creature. Important among later writers are Shihaâb al-Dîin al-Suhrawardî, who taught an elaborate doctrine of illumination (*išrâq*) by the divine light and, charged with being a *Karmatian agent and of claiming prophetic knowledge and powers, was put to death by the famous *Saladin in 1191. By far the most important and influential of the later writers was Muḥyî 1-Dîn Ibn 'Arabî (b. Murcia, Spain, 1164; d. Damascus, 1240, where his tomb is still a place of pilgrimage), a prolific writer who expounded, often in highly symbolic language, an elaborate monism. A large quantity of great mystical poetry was also produced by later Sufis, particularly by Ibn al-Fâriḍ (d. 1235); the Persian Jalâl al-Dîn Rûmî, the founder of the Mawlawîya order of dervishes (d. 1273); and 'Abḍ al-Karîm al-Jîlî (d. 1428). In contrast to the pure asceticism and contemplation of the early mystics, one finds among many of the later Sufis a tendency to employ various artificial means, most commonly the *dhikr* (see DERVISHES), to induce a state of ecstasy. It is in this later period, too, that the great Sufi confraternities (*ṭuruq*; sing., *ṭarîqa*) were formed and came to penetrate all segments of Islamic society. BIBLIOGRAPHY: A. J. Arberry, *Sufism* (1950); L. Gardet, *Mystique musulmane, aspects et tendances, expériences et techniques* (1961).

[R. M. FRANK]

SUGER OF ST. DENIS (c.1081–1151), abbot, statesman, and historian. Of humble origin, S. was offered to the monastery of St. Denis (c.1091) where King Louis VI was also a student. He was appointed abbot of St. Denis (1127) and not only began but completed the reformation of the abbey. A patron of the arts, he rebuilt the monastic church in a new style (later called Gothic), which spread rapidly throughout the kingdom and the Western world. S. was a friend and constant adviser of Louis VI and Louis VII. During the latter's absence on the Second Crusade, S. was appointed regent of the kingdom, which he administered ably (1147–49). His writings provide insight into his administration of the abbey, the building of the church, and, more importantly, into the lives of Louis VI and Louis VII. BIBLIOGRAPHY: E. Josi, EncCatt 11:1488–90.

[R. A. FOULK]

SUHARD, EMMANUEL CAELESTINUS (1874–1949), cardinal abp. of Paris. S. was ordained in 1898. He was professor of theology at Laval's seminary until being named bp. of Bayeux and Lisieux in 1928. He became abp. of Reims in 1930, S. received the red hat in 1935 and was appointed abp. of Paris in 1940. He suffered harassment during the German occupation of Paris and refused to join the national council of the Vichy government. Much disturbed by the dechristianization of France, he proposed to the French bps. in 1941 the creation of the Mission de France, a cooperative plan that would make priests equally available to all dioceses and bind the French dioceses together. In 1943 he addressed the clergy of Paris on the subject of the state of Catholicism in France, later publishing his thesis in the book *France a Mission Country?* He also formed the Mission de Paris, out of which grew the priest-worker movement. In 1947 S. published *Growth or Decline? The Church Today* (tr. J. A. Corbett, 1948). Called to Rome, he defended the priest-worker movement. Traditional Catholics in France opposed him and Rome eventually condemned the movement. Another influential work was *Priests among Men* (tr. L. Bégin, 1949). His last pastoral letter exhorted young Christians to combine scientific exactness, technological efficiency with faith in God and confidence in man. BIBLIOGRAPHY: *Encyclopedia Universalis* 20:1847–48.

[J. R. AHERNE]

SUICER, JOHANN KASPAR (1620–84), Swiss Reformed professor at Zurich, author of *Thesaurus ecclesiasticus e Patribus Graecis* (2 v., 1682) that became an established resource for the study of the language of the Greek Fathers.

[T. C. O'BRIEN]

SUICIDE, the deliberate taking of one's own life. Catholic moralists commonly distinguish between direct and indirect suicide. It is direct when the self-destruction is the intended object of the act, regardless of whether this is desired as an end in itself or as a means to an end. It is indirect when self-destruction is not intended in itself, but is simply foreseen as a more or less probable consequence of an act aimed at another objective (as when an individual exposes himself to great danger in caring for victims of a plague). Both types of self-destruction can be accomplished by either positive or negative means: positive, when one does something to cause death; negative, when the lethal effect is accomplished by inaction rather than action, i.e., by failing to do what is necessary to preserve life.

Suicide has at all times attracted the attention of philosophers, most of whom have expressed disapproval, e.g., Plato and Aristotle among the Greeks, but not the Stoics; the encyclopedists and Kant, but not Nietzsche.

Unlike philosophy, the Bible has little to say on the subject of suicide. There is, of course, the commandment "Thou shalt not kill," but there is nothing to spell out unequivocally to the doubter its applicability to the act of self-destruction. The Bible records several instances of suicide—Abimelech (Jg 9.53–54), Saul and his armorbearer (1 Sam 31.3–5), Zambri (1 Kg 16.18), Macron (2 Macc 10.13), Judas (Mt 25.5; Acts 1.18)—without expressing condemnation, and the act of Razis, who fell on his own sword, is mentioned with something like respect (2 Macc 14.37–46).

But from the beginning, Christian tradition took a strong stand against any direct form of self-destruction. While some few applauded Christians who voluntarily reported themselves to pagan authorities in order to suffer martyrdom, the mainstream of Christian thought strongly opposed such misguided zeal. Augustine attacked the Donatists for their stand in this matter, and his views did much to shape the traditional opposition to direct suicide. Canonical documents forbidding the admission of suicides to Christian burial are traceable to the 6th cent., a prohibition still in effect in RC canon law (CIC c. 1240.1.3).

Apart from this penalty and that of *irregularity ex delicto imposed on those who attempt suicide (CIC c. 985.4), there is little documentary evidence of the teaching of the magisterium with regard to suicide. The Catechism of the Council of Trent applies the commandment against killing to suicide. Pius XII in several addresses restated the traditional doctrine of theologians, e.g.: " [It is] a fundamental principle of Christian and natural law . . . that man is not the master and possessor of his body and his existence; he is only the beneficiary with regard to both." (AAS 39 [1957] 129). However, the want of more abundant evidence indubitably stems not from any weakness of conviction but rather from the unanimity with which the doctrine is recognized and taught by Catholic moralists.

Theologians commonly support the position with three arguments drawn from reason: (1) Suicide is an infringement of the Creator's supreme dominion over his creation; man belongs more intimately to his Creator than he does even to himself. (2) Suicide is a violation of one of the profoundest tendencies of nature, namely, to preserve itself in existence. (3) Suicide is an offense against the community because an individual through it withdraws on his own initiative from the social body to which he is essentially obligated.

Catholic theology's condemnation of suicide, however, extends per se to direct suicide only. Indirect suicide, or the exposure of oneself to probable or even certain death in the performance of a deed of great importance, provided all the conditions necessary for the legitimate application of the principle of the *double effect are satisfied, is considered not only permissible but in some circumstances an act of great virtue.

The law requiring the denial of Christian burial to those who die by suicide is generally interpreted benignly, not so much to avoid adding to the grief of surviving relatives, but more out of practical recognition of the probability that the deceased was not sufficiently *sui compos* in taking his own life to be held responsible for his act. Suicide is commonly an effort to escape intolerable stress and strain; consequently there is, even apart from other evidence, a certain probability that a person who has taken his life did so in a state of mental and emotional unbalance in which his judgment was beclouded and his will lacked the freedom necessary to truly responsible action. BIBLIOGRAPHY: T. C. Kane, NCE 13:781–783; M. Van Yve, "La Mort volontaire," *Revue philosophique de Louvain* (1951); P. L. Landsberg, *Le Problème moral du suicide* (1951).

[P. K. MEAGHER]

SUIDAS, the most comprehensive Byzantine lexicon, composed in the late 10th century. It now seems certain that Suidas is not the name of a person but the title of the work signifying a "rampart" (of information). It is a kind of combined dictionary and encyclopedia covering biographical, geographical, theological, and literary material derived from earlier sources. However, it contains also some information not found elsewhere, the citations from authors whose works are not extant being esp. valuable. BIBLIOGRA - PHY: R. J. Schork, NCE 13:783; PW 4A1, 675–717.

[M. R. P. MCGUIRE]

SUIDBERT, ST. (d. 713), Anglo-Saxon Benedictine missionary bp. who worked for the conversion of the Bructeri of the upper Rhineland. He labored first in Frisia in 690 and then was selected by his associates to go to Britain, where he labored in Mercia in the footsteps of St. Wilfrid. He was consecrated bp. in 693 and returned to the Continent among the Bructeri. He founded the illustrious monastery at Kaiserswerth on an island in the Rhine given him by Pepin d'Heristal and lived out his life there. The only reliable source on S.'s life is the Ven. Bede, who termed him a mild-mannered and tender-hearted man. He has always been much revered in Germany.

[E. J. DILLON]

SUKKOT, see TABERNACLES, FEAST OF.

SÜLEYMAN I (1497–1566; reigned from 1520), the greatest of the Ottoman emperors. Under him Turkish expansion reached its highest point. He captured Belgrade in 1521 and won a decisive victory over the Hungarians of Mohacs in 1526. Three years later he laid siege to Vienna, but he withdrew with the coming of winter. In 1532 he advanced again and ravaged Styria. After the death of

Zapolya in 1540, he annexed south and central Hungary. During 1547–48 and 1553–54 he was occupied with maintaining his position in Persia. He died as he was besieging Szigetvar in Hungary. He was a pious Muslim with a high sense of his responsibility as a ruler. His success in Eastern Europe, however, was made possible in part by the rivalries and wars of European kings who did not scruple to seek his aid in their own plans. He gave Ottoman administration its definite form, as is reflected in the designation *Qanuni* (Regulator) given him by the Turks. Turkish civilization in his age enjoyed a great flowering, and because of the splendor of his person and the brilliance of his court his traditional title in the West is "The Magnificent". BIBLIOGRA - PHY: J. A. Williams, NCE 13:783–784; R. B. Merriman, *Suleiman the Magnificent 1520–1566* (1944); V. J. Parry, "The Ottoman Empire, 1520–1560," CModH² 2 (1962) 511–533.

[M. R. P. MCGUIRE]

SULLIVAN, ARTHUR SEYMOUR (1842–1900), English composer. S. was a choir boy in the Chapel Royal Academy of Music and at the Leipzig Conservatory. He soon became known as a composer of worth and, in 1866 was appointed professor of composition at the Royal Academy. The following year saw the first of the comic operas for which he and, later, Sir W. S. Gilbert would become famous. In addition to his works for the theater, S. composed oratorios and cantatas and edited two books of hymns, for which he wrote some of the tunes (that of "Onward! Christian Soldiers" was one).

[M. T. LEGGE]

SULLIVAN, HARRY STACK (1892–1949), psychiatrist. Born in New York State, S. suffered much from isolation in his youth because of his Irish Catholicism. The experience would lead to one of his important theories in psychiatry, i.e., a child's preadolescent experience is crucial to later mental health. At the age of 17 and again at 24, S. underwent psychiatric treatment. His significant work with schizophrenics began at St. Elizabeth's Hospital in Washington, D.C., and continued at Sheppard Pratt hospital in Baltimore. He taught for a time at Georgetown Univ., in 1938 founded the journal *Psychiatry,* and established with two social scientists the Washington School of Psychiatry. S. saw schizophrenia as curable; its victims had failed in interpersonal relations and to cure them the ability to deal with others had to be restored. Treatment consists of bringing the patient into a relationship with a sympathetic therapist. The chief merit of S.'s work is to have joined psychiatry and the social sciences.

[J. R. AHERNE]

SULPICIAN SPIRITUALITY. Father Jean Jacques Olier, founder of the Society of Saint Sulpice, intended his seminary to be above all a school of holiness. Sanctity for the Sulpician is primarily the holiness of any Christian in the Church: the personal intense response to God giving himself

in all the realities of the Christian mystery. Olier was convinced that in the Church the priest is like a living Christ. The events of Christ's life are mysteries, and the heart of each mystery is the interior state or disposition of Christ in the mystery. Of all these states the most central is Christ's state of "infinite servitude" to God. The priest's total commitment to Christ means total abnegation of self-centeredness. The Sulpician's primary emphasis must be upon the sanctifying value of his ministry. To be a source of holiness for the Sulpician himself, the Sulpician ministry must be lived in the spirit of Christ. The two qualities designating the specific character of Sulpician ministry are the collegial direction of the seminary and community life. BIB - LIOGRAPHY: E. A. Walsh, *Priesthood in the Writings of the French School: Bérulle, de Condren, Olier* (1949); P. Pourrat, *Christian Spirituality,* (tr. W. H. Mitchell et al. 4 v. 1953–55) 3:332–401; H. Daniel-Rops, *Church in the Seventeenth Century* (1963).

[T. O. WOOD]

SULPICIANS. Father Jean Jacques Olier founded the Society of Saint Sulpice at Paris in 1642. Official state recognition of the society was decreed in 1645, and the society's constitutions, drafted by Olier's successor, received formal Church approval in 1664. Late in 1641, accompanied by Fathers François de Caulet and Jean du Perrier, Olier had moved into the small rectory left vacant by the parish priest in the village of Vaugirard at the edge of Paris. Candidates for the priesthood came to live there with the priests, sharing in their life of prayer, study, and work. Probably in March 1642, the little band at Vaugirard identified itself as a society for the training of future priests. When Olier became pastor (Aug., 1642) of Saint Sulpice, Paris, he and his companions took up residence in the parish rectory. Their parishoners spoke of them as the Priests of the Clergy, but history would know them as the Priests of the Society of Saint Sulpice. Along with their spiritual and academic formation, Olier's seminarians participated actively in all phases of the pastoral life of the parish. Before his death (1657), Olier sent to Montreal four of his colleagues whose work laid the foundations of the society's Canadian Province. The beginnings of the Sulpicians' U.S. Province date to the opening of St. Mary's Seminary (1791) in John Carroll's new See of Baltimore. Today there are the three Provinces (French, Canadian, American), working with about 650 priests on six continents and they staff seminaries across the world from Vietnam and Japan to South America and Africa. BIBLIOGRAPHY: P. Pourrat, *Father Olier: Founder of St. Sulpice* (tr. W. S. Reilly, 1932); C. G. Herbermann, *Sulpicians in the United States* (1916); H. Daniel-Rops, *Church in the Seventeenth Century* (1963).

[T. O. WOOD]

SULPICIUS OF BOURGES, SS., two early medieval bps. of Bourges. (1) Sulpicius "Severus" (d. 591), who as bp. of Bourges (584–591), convoked a provincial synod at Clermont (585–588?) and attended the synod of Mâcon

(585). Gregory of Tours praises his rhetorical and poetic skill. (2) Sulpicius "the Pious" (d. *c*.647), bp. of Bourges (624–*c*.647), is best known as the titular saint of St. Sulpice in Paris and patron of the Sulpicians. BIBLIOGRAPHY: G. M. Cook, NCE 13:787; H. Platelle and M. O. Garrigues, BiblSanct 12:62–66.

[G. M. COOK]

SULPICIUS SEVERUS (*c*.363–*c*.420), historian and hagiographer. He came of an influential family of Aquitania, received an excellent education (perhaps at Bordeaux), practiced law, and married the daughter of a wealthy family. After his wife's early death, upon the advice of his friends Paulinus of Nola and Martin of Tours, S. gave up his law practice, embraced an ascetical life in solitude, and may have become a priest. S.'s best-known works and models for medieval hagiography center about Martin of Tours: the *Life of St. Martin,* substantially completed during the saint's lifetime; and three letters and two dialogues concerning the saintly bishop. His two books of chronicles are a summary of history from creation to A.D. 400. This work, stylistically influenced by Sallust and Tacitus, is S.'s most polished work. Its concluding chapters are valuable for the history of Priscillianism. BIBLIOGRAPHY: Altaner 278–279; J. Fischer, LTK 9:1161–62.

[H. DRESSLER]

SULPRIZIO, NUNZIO, BL. (1817–36), an Italian youth who bore with patience harsh treatment as an orphan. S. was broken in health by his guardian; the few years of his adult life were spent as an invalid. He was beatified in 1963. BIBLIOGRAPHY: D. Rossio, BiblSanct 12:66–67.

[J. R. AHERNE]

SULTAN (Arab., *sulṭân*), a Muslim ruler. The original sense of the term is authority or power, religious or governmental, a meaning that it often retains. It was also used to designate one who holds such power and in the 11th cent. came to be used as a title, though not an official one, applied sometimes to the *caliph or to a quasi-independent prince. It was made the official title of the Seljuk Tughril Beg in 1055; and among *Sunnites became from that time the common title of an independent ruler, sometimes granted by the caliph and often simply taken by an independent prince. Thus, it was used, for example, by *Saladin and later by the Mamluk rulers of Egypt. Among Ottoman rulers it was first taken by Orkhan (d. 1360) and from Ottoman times has been commonly used by minor provincial rulers.

[R. M. FRANK]

SULZER, SALOMON (1804–90), Austrian synagogue music scholar. S. was a renowned cantor and precentor of the synagogue at Vienna from 1825. He studied composition in Vienna and then set about reforming the Jewish service by giving new rhythm and harmony to the old melodies. His best known works are *Schir Zion,* a collection of Jewish hymns widely used in Austria, Germany, Italy, and America, and *Dudaim,* a collection of home and school songs.

[M. T. LEGGE]

SUMER, ancient nation in lower Mesopotamia, the area later known as Babylonia. Of unknown origin, the Sumerians appeared in the area *c*.3300 B.C. Non-Semitic, they spoke a language unrelated to any other known to modern scholars. Sumer was conquered by the Akkadians under Sargon I *c*.2300 B.C. A Sumerian revival occurred, however, *c*.2100–1720 B.C. Among the outstanding rulers of the latter period were Gudea of Lagash and Ur-Nammu of Ur, who founded the Third Dynasty of Ur and is known for his law code. Sumer finally succumbed to the Amurru (Amorites) from the West and the Elamites from the East. The latter captured Ur and carried off its last king, Ibi-Sin. An inter-city struggle for dominance followed, ending with the rise of Hammurabi. The earliest known civilization of the Near East, Sumer, had a decisive cultural influence on Akkad, Assyria, and Babylonia, where the Sumerian cuneiform was used as a "scholarly" language almost until the Christian era. Lost to view until the 19th cent., Sumerian culture is important for biblical studies because of the apparent origin of the patriarchs in Ur (Gen 11.31) and the parallels found in Sumerian literature to such biblical accounts as the Flood story. BIBLIOGRAPHY: S. N. Kramer, *Sumerians* (1963).

[T. EARLY]

SUMERIAN RELIGION, see MESOPOTAMIAN RELIGION.

SUMMA, see SENTENCES AND SUMMAE.

SUMMA PARISIENSIS, a *summa*, important to the history of canon law, on the *Decretum of Gratian, dated *c*.1160 and composed at Paris.

SUMMER SCHOOLS, CATHOLIC, formal summer classes or courses offered for laymen and religious in Catholic institutions of higher learning. Programs of study of this kind were introduced in the U.S. in the early 1900s, although before that time religious teaching congregations of both men and women provided lectures, seminars, and discussion periods in teacher education for their members. The Catholic Univ. of America sponsored the first Catholic teacher institute in New York City in 1902. In 1909 Marquette University inaugurated its first summer session, followed in 1911 by The Catholic Univ., with summer courses for laymen and a Sisters' College. Catholic dioceses soon followed suit with formal summer sessions by 1919 in Portland, Ore., Cleveland and Toledo, Ohio, and San Francisco, California. Catholic institutions of higher learning in many states entered the field, offering 6-weeks' programs in the summer in the liberal and fine arts, philosophy, theology, science, teacher education, and nursing, to qualified religious and laymen. Work done at such sessions can generally fulfill, entirely or in part, the requirements for the baccalaureate or for a master's or doctoral degree. There are at present in the U.S. approximately 240 Catholic colleges and universities for men and women offering summer programs. BIBLIOGRAPHY: R. J. Deferrari, *Some Problems of Catholic Higher Education in the United States* (1963).

[M. B. MURPHY]

SUMMI PONTIFICATUS, encyclical of Pius XII, Oct. 20, 1939, the first of his pontificate, on principles for a right social order. Directed against the evils that had led to the outbreak of World War II, it stressed natural-law evidence and the teaching of revelation on the unity of mankind and the universality of right moral values. It repudiated state absolutism, as well as social and economic injustice.

[T. C. O'BRIEN]

SUN (IN THE BIBLE), the great light placed in the firmament on the 4th day of creation, to light the earth in daytime and to regulate the seasons (Gen 1.14–18). At the end of the present era, when all things revert to primordial chaos, the sun will be darkened. At the final triumph of Yahweh, when a new order is brought to birth, the sun will be sevenfold as bright as it is now. The Israelites were surrounded by peoples who included the sun in their pantheons, and the cult of the sun was part of surrounding cultures. Mannasseh encouraged such a cult in Israel and built model horses and chariots and placed them at the entrance to the sanctuary to symbolize the "chariot rider" deity that traverses the heavens each day. Deuteronomy forbids such a cult, and King Josiah proscribed it; but it was apparently still popular at the time of Ezekiel. Hebrew folklore borrows heavily from its neighbors. Even the word sun, *shemesh*, can be masculine or feminine, reflecting differing traditions among Semites regarding the gender of the solar deity. The widespread representation of the solar deity as a winged disc finds an echo in Malachi's vision of the rising of the sun of righteousness with healing in its wings. The motif of the sun standing still, quoted in Joshua from the lost Book of Jashar, or the motif of the sun reversing its course for Hezekiah as found in 2 Kg, are common motifs in folklore. The idea of the midday sun as a demon (Ps 91.6) is widespread, and probably derives from common-sense experience. The darkening of the sun at the Crucifixion of Jesus, mentioned in all four Gospels, is also a common note in folklore, attesting nature's homage at the death of a hero.

[E. J. DILLON]

SUN WORSHIP, the rendering to the sun, or a god identified with the sun, or personifying the sun, of divine honors and reverence. Already in primitive stages of cultural development, men felt some numinous force in the sun because of its apparent self-movement and because of the dependence of all earthly life on its presence. The sun's regular rising and setting lends itself to association with the cycle of life and death in all nature, and its constant rising

after setting has led men to look to solar divinity for help given to the dead in finding their way to a new place of light in the afterlife. In the solar worship of primitive men sympathetic magic is important, with disks representing the sun run through fields to assure their fertility, or, in an effort to help the sun itself assure its vital presence, by constructing solar wagons meant to bear the sun in its voyage across the skies, or by building bonfires to help the sun when natural phenomena cause its light to dim.

In higher cultures, with their tendency to personify the sun as a god with human behavior, one finds mythological opposition between a sun god and the powers of darkness and evil.

Although sun worship in some form or other is found throughout the history of religion, it was above all in the religious systems of the Aztecs with their cult of Tonatiuh and of the Egyptians with their cult of Re that sun worship was the heart and center of an official and widespread religious system.

Among the ancient Semitic peoples the sun was worshiped as a personified god or goddess. In Israel, sun worship, expressly condemned along with worship of other astral bodies in Dt 4.19; 17.3, was certainly included in the idolatrous practices introduced in Jerusalem by King Manasseh after 687 (2 Kg 21.3, 5; Jer 8.2), then abolished by King Josiah a half century later (2 Kg 23.5) in the reform that included the removal of model horses and chariots for the sun, which had been standing at the entrance to the Temple (2 Kg 23.11). The motif of the sun standing still as it occurs in Jos 10.12 is epic rather than mythological, although it has mythological parallels. The winged solar disk, a symbol of the sun god in the Ancient Near East, seems to be the image underlying the "sun of righteousness . . . with healing in its wings" in Mal 4.2. In the Greco-Roman world, sun worship was little practiced in early times, but it grew in importance, esp. with the spread of originally Oriental cults like that of the Syrian *Sol Invictus*, until it became the principal cult of the Roman Empire in the 3d cent. A.D. BIBLIOGRAPHY: F. Boll, *Die Sonne im Glauben und in der Weltanschauung der alten Völker* (1922); M. Eliade, *Patterns of Comparative Religion* (tr. R. Sheed, 1958) 124–153.

[A. CODY]

SUNDAR SINGH (1889–1932), Indian Christian mystic. A *Sikh reared in the ancient Hindu and Islam traditions from boyhood, esp. in Yoga discipline, in 1905 he was converted to Christianity because of a vision a year earlier: "I saw the form of the Lord Jesus Christ" (see Underhill). His wealthy parents, strongly averse to Christianity, threatened and even tried to poison him. After Anglican baptism (1905), his attempt to train for holy orders failed, and he withdrew to become an undenominational lay missionary, adapting his Indian religion to Christianity. His apostolate took him not only through India, Tibet, and the Himalaya region, but to China, Japan, England and N

Europe. An admirer of *Francis of Assisi and R. *Rolle, he had an ecstatic faith; his reading consisted in the Scriptures and the *Following of Christ.* Underhill considers him "the first Indian mystic of the Christocentric type." His work, *At the Master's Feet,* appeared in English in 1922 (repr. 1977). BIBLIOGRAPHY: E. Underhill, *Mystics of the Church* (1964, repr. pa., 1971) 243, 253–256; N. Turchi, EncCatt 11:1520 with extensive bibliog.

[M. R. BROWN]

SUNDAY, BILLY (1863–1935), American revival preacher. Born in Ames, Iowa, of German parents, originally named Sontag, S. had a successful career as a major league baseball player, (1883–91). Converted in 1887 after hearing an itinerant evangelist, he left baseball and took a full-time position in the YMCA in Chicago. His career as an evangelist began in 1895. He received ordination to the Presbyterian ministry in 1903. He was famous for his emotional appeals and his use of baseball terminology to describe the struggles of the soul to accept the grace of conversion. He fully developed D. L. *Moody's use of business techniques to advertise and conduct revivals. A Presbyterian himself, S. relied on the financial support of all local denominations to mount his crusades. His opposition to liquor made him a valuable ally of prohibition advocates. He reached the peak of his influence in 1908–10. Many criticized his methods as theatrical and sensational and disparaged the conversions he elicited as ephemeral. An expensive failure in New York City made his work more difficult, and after World War I he was less influential. BIBLIOGRAPHY: W. G. McLoughlin, *Modern Revivalism* (1958); idem, *Billy Sunday Was His Real Name* (1955).

[R. K. MACMASTER]

SUNDAY, the name of the first day of the week. The nominal association of this day with the sun is of pagan origin and was introduced in Rome, along with the observance of the Egyptian week, during the 1st and 2d cent. A.D. Among Christians, esp. for liturgical purposes, the day has been called the Lord's Day (*dies dominica*), possibly with scriptural warrant (Rev. 1.10). Sunday began in apostolic times to replace the Jewish Sabbath as the day of worship, although it is erroneous to speak of a transfer of the obligation to worship from the Sabbath to Sunday, since the Jewish law was primarily concerned, not with public assembly for worship, but with rest (see Gen 2.1–3), whereas the Christian Sunday is primarily dedicated to public worship and only in a secondary and accessory way to rest. The obligation of the Sabbath has been regarded by all but a few Christians as abrogated under the New Law (see Col 2.16). There is, however, mention of eucharistic celebration on the first day of the week (Acts 20.7; possibly also in 1 Cor 16.1). The writings of the early Fathers put it beyond reasonable doubt that from the 1st cent. onward an assembly for worship was commonly held on the first day of the week; by the 4th cent., attendance at this service was generally thought to be part of a Christian's duty; the earliest explicit church legislation prescribing such attendance is from the first years of the 4th century. The association of the day with rest began with the purpose of providing opportunity for worship. In justification of the common Christian choice of Sunday as the day devoted above others to public worship, it is usual to point to Christ's resurrection and the descent of the Holy Spirit as having taken place on the first day of the week. In the liturgy, the association of the day with the resurrection is esp. important. Liturgically, Sunday is regarded as a little Easter, standing in relation to the week as Easter itself does to the year as a whole.

In common usage one Sunday is distinguished from another by its order in relation to certain seasons (Lent, Advent) or to the Epiphany, Easter, and Pentecost. Some Sundays also have popular names derived from the first word of the entrance hymn, or introit, of the Latin liturgy (thus Gaudete, Rorate, and Laetare Sundays), or from the topic of the Gospel of the day, or from some practice observed (Dominica in albis), event commemorated (Palm and Easter Sunday), or mystery celebrated (Trinity Sunday) on that day. BIBLIOGRAPHY: W. J. Sherzer, NCE 13:797–798; M. Herron, NCE 13:799–802.

[P. K. MEAGHER]

SUNDAY, ORTHODOX, see ORTHODOX SUNDAY.

SUNDAY AND HOLY DAY OBSERVANCE IN EASTERN CHURCHES. Ancient local synods in the East demanded that the faithful attend the liturgy on Sundays and holy days, but the Christian East never developed a system of compulsory attendance. Eastern Christians do not feel obliged to be present at church every Sunday and holy day. They tend to take the view that the clergy and the monks are their representatives before God. But on the other hand they have preserved more liturgical rites within the family circle. When some groups reunited themselves with the Church of Rome, they mistakenly thought themselves obliged by the decrees of Lateran Council IV enforcing Sunday observance, and by custom or synod, norms were enacted similar to those of the Latin rite. Only the Catholic Byelorussians, Ethiopians, Malankars, and Russians never developed a definite obligation. Vatican Council II recognized that each Catholic Eastern Church had the authority to determine the days of religious observance and to define the obligation, esp. whether it could be satisfied by attending other services than the Eucharistic Liturgy, or be fulfilled by attendance on Saturday evening and the eves of feast days (Vat II EastCath 15). The introduction of the concept of "substantial" satisfaction of positive church laws, as employed by Pope Paul VI in connection with fast and abstinence, softens the obligatory character of this law also. Catholics can satisfy their obligations by attending Mass in any rite, and they are dispensed from it when they occasionally assist at Eastern Orthodox liturgies; when there is no Catholic church available, they are even urged to attend such services (*Ecumenical Directory,* 1967, art. 47).

[V. J. POSPISHIL]

SUNDAY LETTER, another name for the *dominical letter.

SUNDAY OBSERVANCE, the law or custom found in most Christian Churches urging or obliging the faithful to participate in worship and to abstain from servile work and certain public affairs on Sunday. The Christian observance of Sunday was strongly influenced by the Jewish observance of Saturday, or the Sabbath, as a day consecrated to God. The third commandment made this explicit: ''Keep holy the Sabbath'' (Ex 20.8). The sanctification of this day involved abstention from work, and participation in religious instruction and special worship. The early Christians clearly knew they were not obligated by these Jewish practices, but the abrogation of the Sabbath observance left a void in the week that very soon came to be filled by Sunday. The development of the two elements of Sunday observance, worship and rest, occurred at different times. During apostolic times Sunday was regarded as particularly sacred because it was the day on which Christ's resurrection took place, and it was very soon known as the Lord's Day (Gr. *kyriakē hēmera;* Lat. *dies dominica*). The Christian assemblies generally seem to have celebrated their Eucharist on Sunday, and it is probable that they met for instruction and worship every Sunday. Certainly the practice of the Sunday Eucharist was firmly established early in the 2d cent., but it was only very gradually that attendance at the Sunday liturgy came to be looked on as obligatory. In the 4th cent. the Council of Elvira enforced attendance under pain of excommunication. Thereafter ecclesiastical legislation became more and more strict, and by the mid-12th cent. it had become part of the law of the Roman Church. The Eastern Church has never considered such attendance as obligatory, although some groups in union with Rome may do so. Observance of Sunday as a day of rest was a later development. As more insistence was laid on attendance at church, and as the services grew longer, it became more desirable to have the day set aside for rest from ordinary work. As early as 321 Constantine had decreed a weekly holiday on Sunday. There also seems to have been a general feeling that the rest on the Jewish Sabbath had been transferred to Sunday. After having been enjoined by many local councils, the Sunday abstinence from work was made binding in the Western Church by Pope Gregory IX in 1234.

The same general trend may be observed among the Protestant Churches. In several Protestant societies, particularly Calvinistic and Puritanical ones, attendance at Sunday worship was stressed and sometimes enforced by the secular authority. In a number of Churches not only has abstinence from work been obligatory, but a rigorist prohibition against recreational activities on Sunday has been prominent, the remnants of which still exist in the ''Blue Laws'' found in several states. In general, however, most Protestant Churches encourage attendance at worship and abstinence from work on Sunday but do not regard it as binding in conscience. Many RC theologians now give a broader interpretation of the Sunday obligation. Vatican Council II stresses the ideal of Sunday as the day for Christ's faithful to come together and, by hearing the word of God and participating in the Eucharist, call to mind the passion, resurrection, and glorification of the Lord. Sunday should be observed as a day of joy and freedom from work (Vat II SacLit 106). Greater freedom has been given to the faithful in some regions to fulfill the obligations to hear Mass on a day other than Sunday. BIBLIOGRAPHY: H. Dumaine, DACL 4.1:858–994; M. Herron, NCE 13:799–802. *SABBATA - RIANS.

[G. T. DENNIS]

SUNDAY SCHOOLS, the principal institutional agency developed by Protestants to provide general religious education, esp. for the young. Although there is record of earlier examples of local attempts to operate schools for religious instruction, the Sunday school movement began with Robert Raikes (1735–1811) of Gloucester, England, who in 1780 opened a school to teach poor and neglected children the Bible and elementary school subjects as well. Classes were held on Sundays and also on week days. His efforts met opposition: some feared that the education of the poor might lead to revolution; others objected to the violation of the Sabbath. But his effort was successful. Hannah More (d. 1833) and others became interested in the work and established similar schools elsewhere. News of these developments soon reached the U.S., and by 1791 projects of a like kind were undertaken in New York City, Boston, and Philadelphia. In 1816 two important societies were founded in New York City to promote Sunday schools and a third in Philadelphia in the following year. The Philadelphia society—the Sunday and Adult School Union—soon overshadowed the New York City societies in importance, and the latter associated themselves in an auxiliary capacity with the Philadelphia Union, which thereupon took the name American Sunday School Union. For the next 40 years the American Union was the dominant influence in the Sunday school movement. Under its leadership there was an enormous expansion in the number of Sunday schools in the U.S. and in their enrollment. The Union published a great number of books for use in the schools, as well as periodicals for children and teachers. Eventually mounting denominational opposition—the establishment of denominational organizations to promote strictly denominational schools and provide denominational literature for use in them—weakened the position of the Union. Leadership in the field as a whole passed from the Union to national (later, international) Sunday school conventions, beginning in 1859. From 1875 until 1914 these conventions were held every 3 years, and after 1914, every 4 years. After 1905 effective leadership passed into the hands of permanent boards or councils of officials who, generally speaking, have been people of notable professional competence, with more clearly defined educational objectives and sound ideas about how they should be achieved.

Objectives and methods of the Sunday schools have developed during these different periods. Before the formation of the Union the schools aimed at providing general rudimentary as well as specifically religious education, and their sessions therefore tended to take up from 5 to 8 hours of the day. The schools at this time sought primarily to impart doctrinal instruction in religious matters, and the method was usually catechetical. Under the Union, the development of secular schools freed the Sunday schools from the need to provide other than religious instruction, and it was possible to reduce the ordinary Sunday session to a much shorter period of time. It also became feasible to concentrate less effort upon the poor and to extend the program to include children from all social classes. Doctrinal instruction and catechetical recitation gave way to the memorizing of passages from Scripture. At first these passages were chosen somewhat haphazardly; in time the Union's *Select Passages* put a measure of order and comprehensiveness in the coverage of biblical material, although memorization continued to be used as the test of mastery. Under the Conventions, effective steps began to be taken toward the training of teachers. Institutes were established in various places from 1861, notable among them the Chatauqua Sunday School Assembly for Teachers (1874; see CHATAUQUA MOVEMENT). With better-trained teachers available, memorizing of biblical texts began to fall from favor. The teachers were given more scope to explain and apply the scriptural texts. A uniform system for the study of the same texts on given Sundays over a fixed period of time was adopted, but with rather more stress on specific content than was later considered desirable. Under the later leadership of boards and committees, and esp. with the programming in the hands of professionally oriented educators, there has been a shift of emphasis from a content-centered to a pupil-centered curriculum: the overall aim has moved away from the communication of specific information and has come to focus more directly upon evoking in the pupil a religious response to the gospel message that will find expression in actual Christian living.

The contribution of Sunday schools to the religious vitality of Protestant denominations has been enormous. They have been established everywhere in the U.S. and have been remarkably well attended. Through the missionary work of the Churches they have spread to other lands, where they also enjoy a splendid record of accomplishment. The involvement of the laity in the work is a circumstance that speeds the development of independent, self-sufficient Churches in mission areas, staffed by indigenous leaders and teachers. With the recognition of the importance of the work of the Sunday school, and the development of its aims and methods, the institutional distinction between Church and Sunday school is less clearly drawn than in former times. In recent years with the general secularization of society, attendance has decreased somewhat in U.S. Sunday schools. This has been a matter of concern to those who see the importance of the work of the Sunday school for the continuing vigor of Christian Churches. The system has been subjected to close scrutiny in the hope of strengthening it to the better performance of its work. Among the criticisms leveled against the schools in the present situation are the following: (1) the lack of adequately trained teachers and leaders; (2) the brevity of the sessions, which generally last no longer than an hour on a Sunday morning; (3) an overemphasis on teaching older adults with a consequent loss of interest among teenagers and young adults; (4) inadequate and outdated curriculum materials, although writers and planners are seeking to move forward with the times and are striving to make use of the best modern educational methods; (5) generally poor discipline and order, a situation that tends to discourage serious study and faithful attendance. BIBLIOGRAPHY: *Westminster Dictionary of Christian Education* (ed. K. B. Cully, 1963); E. W. Rice, *Sunday School Movement, 1780–1917* (1917); J. M. Price et al., *Survey of Religious Education* (1959); G. P. Albaugh, *Encyclopedia of Religion* (ed. V. Ferm, 1945) 744–749.

[P. K. MEAGHER]

SUNEM, see SHUNEM.

SUNG, JOHN (1901–44), Chinese Protestant missionary. S. worked in the mission field of China, Thailand, and neighboring territories. In the midst of political change he created groups of lay missionaries and strove for a Christian Church independent of Western connections. He is reputed the greatest Protestant missionary of China. BIBLIOGRAPHY: J. Lorch, RGG 6:527.

[M. J. SUELZER]

SUNNITES (Arab. *sunnî*), orthodox Muslims (see ISLAM). The term Sunni is most commonly used to designate orthodox Muslims as distinct from the *Shiites and other heterodox Islamic sects. The term is derived from the word *sunna* which originally meant simply "behavior" and more specifically, even in pagan times, the customary behavior of the community as it is constitutive of the moral norm for its members. It occurs in the *Koran in this sense. In Islam *sunna* came to denote the normative belief and practice of the community as modeled on that of the Prophet Mohammed. From the early centuries of Islam one finds the expression *ahl al-sunna wal-jamâ‘a* (those who follow the *sunna* and the community [consensus]) used by those who would set themselves apart, as orthodox, from any kind of heresy (*bid‘a*, [blameworthy] innovation), whether in matters of dogma or law. The term Sunna is often used, particularly in later and modern times, to designate the corpus of prophetic tradition (see HADITH) on which it claims to be based and sometimes also to refer to the law of the four orthodox schools or rites (see ISLAMIC LAW).

[R. M. FRANK]

SUÑOL, GREGORIO MARÍA (1879–1946), authority on Gregorian chant. A Benedictine of Montserrat, he studied at the abbey of Solesmes. He was in charge of the monastic choir at Montserrat from 1907–28, and prior, 1915–31. He became president of the Associación Gregoriana of Barcelona and in 1931 head of the Scuola

Superiore di Musica Sacra in Milan. From 1938 he served as president of the Pontificio Istituto di Musica Sacra in Rome. Among his published writings were *Método completo de canto gregoriano, Introducción a la paleografía gregoriana* (1925), and *Antiphonale missarum juxta ritum sanctae ecclesiae mediolanensis* (1935).

[J. R. AHERNE]

SUPEREGO. In Freudian theory there are three "structures" in the human psyche, the *id, the *ego, and the superego. The superego comprises unconscious moral norms and ideals. It is represented as being formed principally as a result of the resolution of the *Oedipal conflict. To resolve this conflict, the 6 year-old must abandon or repress passionate yearnings for parents and jealous rages and hostilities. This involves an *identification with the parents; that is, an internalization of the parental images. Generally speaking, such internalization facilitates the giving up of passionately loved objects; nevertheless, the child identifies mentally with the moral attitudes and aims of the parents as they are expressed by word, gesture, or look, or in exhortations, prohibitions, threats, and urgings, etc. This forms the nucleus of the child's own future sense of morality, his conscience, and his ideals. In Freud's words, the superego is "a precipitate in the ego" and constitutes "the higher, moral, supra-personal side of human nature."

The superego remains largely unconscious throughout life, a characteristic explained by its origin in repressive reactions and unconscious identifications. But whenever a person violates one of its prescriptions or falls away from the ideal it expresses, he feels "guilt," often acutely, just as he did when, as a child, he incurred parental disapproval. Conversely, when he lives up to superego prescriptions, he feels a virtuous satisfaction, as if his parents were applauding. The superego therefore performs a self-watching, self-censoring, and self-punishing mental role, which on the one hand assists the ego in controlling id impulses and on the other hand restricts its choice of possible activities. A rigorous, superego is a general cause of neurosal conflict.

Psychoanalysis has found origins for the superego other than the Oedipal conflict, for instance, in prior parental influences, esp. in the period of toilet training. Later experiences even in adulthood can further modify the superego. Critics of psychoanalysis, esp. from a Christian point of view, have objected to the identification of the superego with moral *conscience. Conscience is an intelligent, conscious evaluation of behavior in the light of consciously realized moral norms from which reasonable judgments of right and wrong are drawn; whereas the superego is a nonrational, unconscious set of fantasies from which irrational guilts and self-approbations are generated. BIBLIOGRAPHY: S. Freud, *Ego and the Id* (1923).

SUPEREROGATION, WORKS OF, acts of virtue not required for the very existence but for the betterment and increase of virtue. The term derives from the Lat. Vulgate words in the parable of the Good Samaritan, *quodcumque supererogaveris* (whatever you shall spend besides; Lk 10.35). The meaning of such works involves the distinction between precepts and the evangelical *counsels; that distinction itself was developed because of Christ's recommending renunciation of all possessions and Paul's praise of virginity. The distinctions are eminently in keeping with the New Law as it consists essentially in the interior grace of the Holy Spirit and as it is lived in the freedom of children of the Father. Thus appropriately the Christian may freely embrace better courses of action in order more fully to express the totality of charity's love for God and to be more singly intent on that love. The New Law, however, is not a law of ethical *perfectionism; and the essence of the Christian life remains the fulfilment of the precept of charity itself, at least to the minimal extent of not doing anything contrary to it. The evangelical counsels of poverty, chastity, and obedience are primary works of Christian supererogation, but other practices of the better good freely undertaken all come under the term. Reformation rejection of the counsels and such practices as fasting stemmed from the position that undue emphasis was put on good works, to the detriment of the truth that *justification is by faith alone.

[T. C. O'BRIEN]

SUPERINTENDENT (Lutheran), a church official in continental Lutheranism. The Reformation, esp. in Hesse and Saxony, was put into practice by superintendents who conducted visitations of, and often prepared church orders for, the *local churches. In the Reformation of Denmark and Norway, J. *Burgenhagen substituted superintendents for bishops and ended any continuation of *apostolic succession. In Germany the office of superintendent as an administrator and pastoral official in a region and territory has continued, but increasingly under control of the*synod.

[T. C. O'BRIEN]

SUPERINTENDENT (Methodist), the original title given to the leaders of the Methodist Episcopal Church in the U.S., Francis *Asbury and Thomas *Coke, who were elected at the *Christmas Conference (1784). The title was soon changed to "bishop," but the *district superintendent remains an important official in Methodist polity.

[T. C. O'BRIEN]

SUPERIORS, RELIGIOUS. (1) Canonically, the religious superior is either a major superior, one to whose care is committed a province, an abbey (or equivalent legal entity) or even a whole religious institute; and a local superior, one having care of the religious of one convent or house. The superior has the power to govern in all that concerns the purposes of the institute and the approved means for achieving its purposes. By vow the subject owes obedience to commands appropriate to the superior's juridic competence. (2) In the theology of the religious life the historical prototype of the religious superior is the "father" of desert monasticism, the holy one who was the mentor of his followers. St. Benedict gave to monasticism the ideal of the abbot, father to his monks in their quest for holiness, one to guide and, if necessary, to reprove them in their following of Christ. The history of monasticism saw the development of the "lord abbot" as a kind of feudal prince or even as equivalently a bp. in his own territory. But the paternal ideal was never lost sight of; in explaining the meaning particularly of religious obedience, St. Thomas Aquinas draws on the analogy between God's spiritual fatherhood and the function of the superior, and points to the fittingness of submitting to a human guide and mentor in the "school of salvation" through obedience (ThAq ST 2a2ae, 104.1; 186.5). The postmonastic forms of religious life, from the mendicants on, kept obedience as primary among the religious vows, and the idea of the father and the mother superior. A further analogy introduced by the Jesuits and adapted in various ways by other post-medieval religious institutes is the military one, with the superior's being compared to an army officer able to exact absolute obedience. The purpose of the idea was the effective disposal of resources at the service of the Church and the apostolate. Whatever the analogies employed, the office of superior means power and therefore it has been abused; but that is merely a historic inevitability.

The renewal of religious life proposed by Vatican Council II and the subsequent reflection of religious communities on conciliar directives and on their own life have brought out new evaluations of the religious superior's role. As with many other elements of the Church's life—and even with regard to the Church's own nature—there has been a recognition that the palest analogue for describing the nature of a religious community is that of the merely human, juridical social unit. Comparison with a "perfect society" has the merit of pointing out that in any social unit authority is necessary to achieve the intended goals. The weakness of the comparison is that whether the analogue is a civil, military, or even commercial social unit, the exercise of authority is concerned with external, effective functioning in order to achieve an external, common goal. The religious community, however, exists on the basis of an inner union of charity among the members and as a way of life meant to express more vividly the inner life of the Church itself as the mystical body. The purpose of the community is the intensification of that interior union and thereby of the union of each person with Christ; the apostolate of the community has as its purpose, in turn, the inner life of those served. Religious obedience is lived as an evangelical counsel, as the living, inner choice to follow another's will because that is a way of loving God and neighbor. The superior's office is not that of a manager; the superior is not an autocrat, nor just a juridic head. There is a contemporary awareness that as the community itself exists by reason of the continuing choice of the members to live its life, so, too, there is a more participatory mode of life in all that concerns the community. The superior is sometimes described as an "animator," as one whose function is to enliven the community as it is a community of charity; other currently proposed designations are "moderator" or "director." These titles do not mean to supersede the rights and obligations accepted as part of religious profession; it is rather a case of keeping foremost the theological inspiration of religious life. There has been encouragement in the Church's directives on renewal toward a return to the spirit of each community's foundation. That means the task of deformalizing or de-institutionalizing in favor of an interiorizing of the elements of religious life. The origins of every religious institute are explained by the voluntary association and commitment of a group of motivated people around a founder. The "observances" were not "practices" to be preserved; they were the ways of living in voluntary commitment to the sanctifying and apostolic purposes of the spontaneous association of members. The role of the superior is being fruitfully understood as that of recreating the original spontaneity or reanimating the mode of life proper to the community and in ways that make it a living out of the life of charity.

[T. C. O'BRIEN]

SUPERNATURAL, a term used in Catholic theology to indicate what transcends all created nature. The mystery of the supernatural, a basic dogma of the Catholic faith, lies in man's existence in an order in which he is called to a life and endowed with powers that are above the order of his creaturehood and which, without destroying what pertains to his natural life and powers, enables him to share in the divine life. Etymologically, the term, which is not scriptural but patristic and scholastic, expresses the fact that, in relation to nature, what is called supernatural is above the claims and powers of nature. Man is not strictly in need of the supernatural to be a man, nor can he effect or conquer it by himself. The paradox lies there: the supernatural perfects man (he secretly yearns for it) in a manner he could never conceive or achieve by himself (he could do without it); yet when it is offered as he is now, he is not free but obliged to accept the offer. Of this complex relation of the supernatural to nature, the Catholic faith holds that the supernatural is a gratuitous gift of God, or grace, not man's achievement; and that man's obligation to welcome it is based in the obedience a creature owes to the Creator, who determines man's (supernatural) destiny. Theology seeks to explain the natural desire for the supernatural while maintaining the gratuity of the supernatural. The desire does not amount to a claim or right; it is ineffective but for God's free self-gift.

In itself the supernatural consists in God's self-gift to his rational creature, resulting in a union and assimilation with Him called in Scripture and tradition sharing in the divine nature, divine adoptive filiation, divine indwelling, or divinization. M. de la Taille has expressed this transforming union by the phrase "created actuation by Uncreated Act," meaning that God, Uncreated Act, unites himself to the rational creature and so produces a change, or "created actuation." The divine self-gift to man takes place primarily in the Incarnation and further in the life of grace and glory.

In grace and glory, God unites himself to man as object of knowledge and love (St. Thomas Aquinas) and also in an intersubjective relationship, distinct from man's creaturely relationship to God. Scripture teaches that through grace men are sons of the Father, brothers of the Son, and temples of the Spirit. These personal relationships to the Trinity are so many signs of the gratuitous and transcendent character of the supernatural. BIBLIOGRAPHY: O. H. Pesch, LTK 10:437; J. P. Kenny, NCE 13:812–816.

[P. DE LETTER]

SUPERNATURAL DESTINY, the Catholic doctrine that all men are destined for a supernatural end to be anticipated in this world in the life of grace and attained in the other life. No one can achieve full happiness and perfection in this world, nor can anyone attain it by purely human means. There is no natural destiny in the sense of final goal for any man. Since the end commands all action and principles of action, this point of faith determines the meaning of human existence. Its denial is naturalism.

The doctrine of faith holds that man's ultimate destiny lies in the possession and vision of God. What existential experience suggests somehow, namely, that only the Infinite can satisfy man's basic aspirations, the faith reveals as an actual possibility for those who accept God's will and his help to do it. The vision of God, which is beatific, or achieving bliss, is conceived by theologians in two ways. Intellectualists, after St. Thomas Aquinas, stress the cognitive aspect, the intuition of the divine essence and Trinity, an intuition that is not comprehensive. Voluntarists, after St. Bonaventure and Scotus, place the emphasis on love and the happiness flowing from love. These views are complementary rather than contradictory, resting on a physical and ecstatic concept of bliss. Heaven means both possession and surrender. Mind and heart find in God their ultimate fulfillment.

Three further aspects of the supernatural destiny should be noted. Grace and glory come to men through Christ, in whom they attain their final destiny: it is Christological. The vision of God is a personal encounter with Father, Son, and Holy Spirit; the final destiny of men is Trinitarian. They reach their destiny as members of the body of Christ and of the people of God; their final destiny is social, or communitarian. Those who refuse God's final self-gift condemn themselves to fail to reach their supernatural destiny and to be deprived of the bliss of life eternal. BIBLIOGRAPHY: Vat II ConstChurch 1–69; John XXIII, *Mater et magistra* (AAS 53:401–464); Paul VI, *Ecclesiam suam* (AAS 56:609–659).

[P. DE LETTER]

SUPERNATURAL EXISTENTIAL, a kind of supernatural orientation postulated by some theologians as given by God to all men prior to grace. Since this is given to all men, there can be no purely natural order. The basis for this opinion is the doctrine of God's universal salvific will conceived as ever active (see K. Rahner, LTK 3:1301). Since this divine will must have a created effect, even before grace is offered and accepted there must be in all men a "supernatural existential." This explains their duty to accept grace, when this is offered. All concede that it is difficult to say in what precisely this "existential" consists. Other theologians such as E. Schillebeeckx and H. de Lubac (*The Mystery of the Supernatural,* 1967) reject the supernatural existential as an unnecessary postulate; man's natural openness to the supernatural suffices to explain his duty to welcome it. They object that the supernatural existential entails some extrinsicism of the supernatural, instead of providing a closer link between nature and grace.

[P. DE LETTER]

SUPERNATURAL LIFE, VOCATION TO, see VOCATION TO SUPERNATURAL LIFE.

SUPERNATURAL ORDER, the ensemble of effects and causes whereby man is raised to and operates within a mode of existence that surpasses the endowments proper to his own essence and is thus ordered to the divine life. The term supernatural admits of various applications. It is possible to speak of a supernatural being (God), supernatural acts (Christian faith and charity), supernatural effects (miracles), and a supernatural finality (the beatific vision). When used as referring to a supernatural order, the term signifies the total structure of created reality in its actual state, i.e., redeemed by Christ and ordered to a level of existence that is proper to God alone. This structure or order shall be explained both negatively by contrasting it with its antithesis, the natural order, and positively.

Nature may be understood as the principle of life and operations in any being, rooted in its essence, from which all of its activities proceed. A natural order therefore would be that disposition of reality which pertains to, arises from, or is conformable to nature. By contrast the supernatural order would encompass everything which does not belong to, or is not founded upon the essence of a thing. The fundamental characteristic of the supernatural order, therefore, is its gratuity, a gratuity which goes beyond the gratuity involved in creation itself. Because of this gratuity we know of the supernatural order only through revelation. Granted that revelation, speculative theology may in turn reflect upon the characteristics of man's supernatural elevation and the nature of man as it would be without the gift of grace (*pure nature).

An exclusively negative presentation, however, entails several possible misinterpretations. First of all, it must be emphasized that the supernatural order is the *de facto* state of actual existence. The state of pure nature never existed and may be known only by reflecting upon the gratuity of the supernatural order. The nature that man has phenomenologically experienced is suffused with the supernatural. We do not encounter man in a self-enclosed natural state and speculate upon the supernatural as an order of reality lying beyond our experience. It would also be incorrect to think of the supernatural order as an extrinsic adornment to the human soul, an elevation limited to a particular human faculty. Man's supernatural vocation is not partial but invests him with a totally new dignity and mode of existence. This vocation so deeply affects man's inmost being that he shares in the divine nature itself. The supernatural order, therefore, must be described as affecting a radical transfiguration in man. It permeates his total being and raises it to the plane of a higher nature, a participation in the Divine Life. BIBLIOGRAPHY: H. de Lubac, *Mystery of the Supernatural* (tr. R. Sheed, 1967); B. Lonergan, "Natural Desire to See God," *Proceedings of the 11th Annual Convention of the Jesuit Philosophical Association* (1949) 31–43; M. Scheeben, *Nature and Grace* (tr. C. Vollert, 1954). *NATURAL ORDER; *SUPERNATURAL EXISTEN-TIAL.

[T. M. MCFADDEN]

SUPPLICATION, a term bringing out the quality of prayer as imploring God's help humbly and reverently; (see OB-SECRATION). St. Thomas Aquinas assigns a particular meaning to supplication: a kind of prayer petitioning God's help in a general way, rather than for some particular need; the second he designates as *postulatio* (ThAq ST 2a2ae, 83.17). In classical Roman religion the *supplicatio* was a public prayer or occasion of special solemnity observed in times of either triumph or need.

[T. C. O'BRIEN]

SUPPLICES, the opening word of the ninth prayer of the *Canon of the Mass after the *Sanctus*. The English text begins, "Almighty God, we pray that your angel. . . ." It is a prayer for the acceptance of the sacrifice with the consequence that the communicants be filled with every grace and blessing. Two details are ambiguous. Some have thought that the angel to which the prayer refers is Christ; others have understood it to mean a creature or creatures of the angelic order. The altar from which we receive may be the earthly altar or the heavenly altar mentioned in the preceding sentence, or it may be the two conceived as one. The English translators have not attempted to resolve either point of obscurity. The thought expressed by the word *supplices* itself is not directly translated, perhaps because it is adequately expressed in the inclination made by the priest as he recites the prayer. Some would see in this prayer the remnants of an *epiclesis*.

[P. K. MEAGHER]

SUPPORT OF PASTORS, one of the commandments of the Church (CIC, c. 463), Juridically every Catholic is a member of a parish, or the equivalent, and is urged by church law to assist at the liturgy in the parish church. The obligation to contribute to the support of the pastor corresponds to the pastor's right to receive the necessities of life from those to whom he ministers; the supposition is that in devoting' himself to the ministry he has no way of providing

for his own support. The parishioners are obliged to contribute in a way commensurate with their own means. In the U.S. and in other countries where clergy are not supported by the State, the obligation of the parishioners extends to the support of the parish plant, personnel, and activities. As the concept of ministry is undergoing change, the whole question of parish support will undoubtedly change as well; that change will probably include some variation of the priest-worker idea.

SUPPOSIT, see SUBSISTENCE.

SUPRALAPSARIANISM, in contrast to *sublapsarianism, the doctrine held by some Calvinists that the decree of *election and the decree of *reprobation are antecedent to the Fall of man. The Fall is merely the means by which the previous decrees are carried out, the elect saved, and the reprobate left to perish. Though this doctrine was repudiated at the Synod of *Dort (1618–19), it was often and widely held in later Calvinism.

[J. A. R. MacKENZIE]

SUPREMACY, ACT OF, see ACT OF SUPREMACY (1534).

SUR (SHUR), WILDERNESS OF, the barren steppes SW of Palestine, E of Egypt, and N of the deserts of the Sinai peninsula. According to the narrative in Ex 15, after the crossing of the Sea of Reeds, Moses led the people out into the wilderness of Sur, where they traveled for 3 days without finding water. In the account of Hagar's flight from Sarah, Gen 16.7, the angel of the Lord found her by a spring of water "in the wilderness on the way to Sur." In Gen 20.1, Abraham is depicted living as an alien in Gerar, having journeyed by stages into the Negeb, and having settled "between Kadesh and Sur." According to Gen 25.18, the sons of Ishmael, Abraham's son by Hagar, inhabited the land "from Havilah to Sur, which is E of Egypt an the way to Asshur." Saul cut the Amalekites to pieces "all the way from Havilah to Sur on the borders of Egypt" (1 Sam 15.7). It was they who inhabited the country S of the Philistine cities "all the way to Sur and Egypt" (1 Sam 27.8). Since the word suggests the word wall, it is thought it may have originally referred to a line of fortresses constructed by Egypt to protect its eastern frontier. The "way of Sur" must refer to the ancient caravan route going out away from Egypt E and then N.

[E. J. DILLON]

SURGERY, COSMETIC, see COSMETIC SURGERY.

SURIANO, FRANCESCO (1549–1620?), Italian composer. S. studied with Palestrina, was choirmaster at various churches and finally at St. Peter's in Rome. He composed madrigals, motets, Masses, canons, a Magnificat, and a Passion.

[M. T. LEGGE]

SURIN, JEAN JOSEPH (1600–65), French Jesuit spiritual writer and mystic. A Jesuit from 1616 and a tertian under L. *Lallement, he began his ministry as a preacher at La Rochelle in 1630. He was commissioned in 1634 to exorcise Mère Jeanne des Anges, superior of the Ursulines of Loudon in Poitou. He spent three years in this mission, offering himself to God to suffer the pains of possession in substitution for the nun. The experience caused him psychological hardship, and for the next 20 years he suffered deep depressions and felt himself to be diabolically tormented. At the same time his own spiritual life intensified. The last 8 years of his life brought tranquillity and profound mystical experiences. His spiritual doctrine, deriving from St. Ignatius Loyola and Lallement, influenced other Jesuit writers of the 18th century. S. advocated contemplation in awareness of the presence of God, active purification of the senses, passivity to the divine will in a *disinterested love, absolute reliance on the inspiration of the Holy Spirit. S.'s most celebrated work is his *Catéchisme spirituel*; in 1659 it was published without his knowledge and under Calvinist auspices; through pressure from Jansenists it was put on the Index in 1695; a later revised edition, (1730) was not censured. Other works, all posthumous, are: *Les fondements de la vie spirituelle* (1674); *Dialogues spirituelles* (1695); *Triomphe de l'amour sur les puissances de l'enfer* (1929); *Sur l'amour de Dieu* (1930).

[R. J. LITZ]

SURIUS, LAWRENCE (1522–78), German Carthusian, spiritual writer, editor. At Cologne, where he received his M. A. (1539), he returned to Catholicism and entered the Carthusians (1540). His *De probatis sanctorum historiis* (6 v., 1570–75) was a surprisingly objective work for the period. It was revised and reissued many times, the edition gaining widest acceptance being a 12-volume work of 1618 that the *Bollandists used as a basic model and source for their own work. S. contributed to the growth of Counter Reformation spirituality by a book of meditations on the life of Christ and by editions and translations of the writings of Henry Suso, J. Tauler, J. van Ruysbroeck, and other Rhenish mystics. His reply, *Commentarius brevis rerum in orbe gestarum 1500–65* (1566), to J. *Sleidanus's history of the Reformation provoked Protestant wrath; others continued the work down to the year 1673. S. also edited *Conciliorum collectio* (1567) and works of the Church Fathers.

[R. J. LITZ]

SURPLICE, a loose–fitting garment extending to the knees, with large sleeves reaching well below the elbow and worn over the cassock. It originated during the 11th cent. as a loose, ungirded alb to cover the garment made of hides that was worn during the cold winter N of the Alps. Late in the 16th cent. the surplice began to be shortened, and it became customary to ornament it with lace, a practice that has been rather commonly abandoned in the 20th century.

[N. KOLLAR]

SURREALISM, a movement in poetry (Aragon, Breton, Éluard, Gérard), theater (Buñuel, Cocteau), and art (Arp, Dali, Ernst, Masson, Miró, Man Ray, Magritte, Tanguy), based directly on the work of Apollinaire and the Dadaists. Surrealism dominated Europe between World wars I and II. André Breton, who wrote the first Surrealist manifesto (1924), was one of the first to publish the work of Freud, whose discoveries the Surrealists utilized in the systematic application of the irrational and the subconscious as a primary source of their art, presenting dream images, the bizarre and fantastic as credible through sharp-focus realism exploiting a shock value. *Collages* (foreign materials applied to picture surface) and *frottages* (rubbings), and ''pure, psychic automatism'' were thought fundamental in expressing a superreality or surreality. Surrealism was a major revolution in the development of modern art. BIBLIOGRAPHY: M. Jean, *History of Surrealist Painting* (1960); M. Nadeau, *History of Surrealism* (1965).

[S. N. BLUM]

SUSANNA wife of Joakim and legendary heroine of the Greek versions of the Book of Daniel (chapter 13), accepted as an historical figure and revered as a saint in the early Church. Her ordeal was a common motif in catacomb frescoes, in one of which she is depicted symbolically as a lamb between two wolves. The name Shoshanna is the Hebrew word for lily, which in turn is the traditional symbol for the just man; it is an obviously appropriate name for the heroine of a pious *haggadah*, or edifying story, whose theme is the vindication of the righteous who prefer death to sin. The story has themes common to folklore: that of the faithful wife calumniated and later vindicated; that of the wise young person who overturns an unjust verdict. A variation on the latter theme is found in the story of Ali Chadsa in *A Thousand and One Nights*. It was natural for the story to attach itself eventually to the figure of Daniel, whose name means God is my Judge. It may have served the Pharisees in their polemic against the Sadducean reliance on two witnesses in capital cases, without cross-examination. However the false witnesses in the Susanna story are undone by less stringent criteria than that required by the Pharisees. The story was not quite satisfactory to either party in this dispute, and this may explain its ultimate exclusion from the Daniel of the Jewish canon.

[E. J. DILLON]

SUSATO, TIELMAN (TYLMAN; d. *c.*1561), German composer and music publisher. S., who settled in Antwerp, was for some time one of the five musicians employed by that city. In 1543 he began printing music of his own and, by 1561, had put out over 50 volumes of motets, madrigals, Masses, etc., many containing works of his own composition.

[M. T. LEGGE]

SUSO, HENRY, BL., see HENRY SUSO, BL.

SUSPENSION (CANON LAW), a *censure, but sometimes also a vindictive (punitive) penalty barring a cleric from an office or *benefice (CIC, c. 2278, § 1). Suspension from office bars any exercise of the power of *holy orders or of *jurisdiction (*ibid.* 2279, § 1); but there are modified forms, among them: suspension *a divinis*, i.e., from the ministerial exercise of any order received; suspension of jurisdiction, e.g., from the right to hear confessions and absolve (for other types, see *ibid.* § 2, nn. 3–9). Suspension from a benefice deprives the cleric from its income, but not from the use of the house attached to the benefice (*ibid,* c. 2280, § 1). Suspension may also be inflicted in a clerical religious community, either as a whole or on its guilty parties (*ibid.* c. 2285, § 1). *Corpus iuris canonici,* bk. 4 on canonical processes, gives a local ordinary (e.g., a diocesan bp.) the right to suspend *ex informata conscientia*, i.e., at his own conscientious discretion (*ibid.* c. 2186, § 1). The law calls it an extraordinary remedy; the power can only be invoked where it is the only course to correct an evil (*ibid.* § 2). The suspension cannot be perpetual; the facts of the case and of invoking this right must be recorded by the ordinary (*ibid.* c. 2188). The cleric need not be given reasons for the suspension (*ibid.* c. 2193); he has the right to appeal to the Holy See, and the ordinary must provide proof of the crime for which he inflicted the suspension (*ibid.* c. 2194).

[T. C. O'BRIEN]

SUSPICION, a thinking evil of another on the basis of very slight evidence. The causes of suspicion are deep: (1) an ego sickness or at least an immaturity, so that one's own faults are projected to others; (2) a bad relationship with another, such as hatred, anger, or envy, which inclines one to believe what one wishes to be true; (3) the long experience of human wickedness, although old age is obviously an excusing cause. Since even in the sanctuary of conscience, others should be innocent until proven guilty, suspicion can be a vice, small enough when it is only a question of doubting the goodness of another, but more serious when one proceeds to a rash judgment that attributes positive evil to another (Mt 7.1), and most serious when actual condemnation in word or deed follows. Obviously the material itself must be grave for the sin to be grave. (See ThAq ST 2a2ae, 60.3, 4.)

[P. F. MULHERN]

SUSPICION OF HERESY. In canon law, a *delict connected with that of heresy that those who although not explicitly professing heresy nevertheless by their manner of speaking or acting commit. The CIC has six generic or specific ways in which this delict is committed; among them, for example, the simoniacal administration or reception of the sacraments or of orders. The censures attached to this delict are enumerated in c. 2315. BIBLIOGRAPHY: DDC 5:1107–08.

[E. A. WEIS]

SÜSSMAYR, FRANZ XAVER (1766–1803), Austrian conductor and composer. S. was a pupil of A. Salieri and of Mozart, with whom he formed a deep friendship. It was S. who completed Mozart's *Requiem*. He also composed operas, operettas, and instrumental music.

[M. T. LEGGE]

SUTCLIFFE, EDMUND FELIX (1886–1963), Jesuit Scripture scholar. S. taught OT at St. Beuno's and Heythrop Colleges, England. He wrote numerous articles for theological journals, a Maltese grammar, and three books: *The OT and the Future Life* (1947); *Providence and Suffering in the Old and New Testaments* (1955); and *Monks of Qumran* (1960). He was the OT editor for the first edition of *Catholic Commentary on Holy Scripture* (1953).

[T. M. MCFADDEN]

SUTHERLAND, GRAHAM (1903–   ), one of the leading English painters. After studying at the Univ. of London, he exhibited meticulously representative prints in 1925. Teaching (1930), S. began to paint in 1933, exhibiting symbolic landscapes in London and New York (1938–46). In 1946 he painted for St. Matthew's Church, Northampton, the austere, disturbing, powerful *Crucifixion* reminiscent of Grünewald's *Isenheim Altarpiece. Portraits of S. Maugham, Sir Winston Churchill, and Lord Beaverbrook brought him fame. He exhibited internationally at the Venice Biennale (1952), in Paris, London, and the São Paolo Bienal (1955), receiving in 1960 the British Order of Merit. In 1962, S.'s magnificent and controversial 74 ft long tapestry of *Christ in Majesty* was hung in Conventry Cathedral. His earlier work is related somewhat to Blake and S. Palmer, with technique recalling H. Moore; in 1944 S. introduced his distinctive entangled, horny, spiked shapes suggesting the claws and teeth of malevolent beasts, literally deduced from the thorny growths in his native landscape. BIBLIOGRAPHY: D. Cooper, *Work of Graham Sutherland* (1962).

[M. J. DALY]

SUTRA (Sanskrit; *Sutta*, Pali), in *Buddhism the fundamental unit of Scripture or a generic reference to particular quotations, ancient verses, or precepts of monastic discipline. The titles of sutras can indicate the subject of a discourse, the place where a dialogue or teaching was delivered, or even the names of the participants in a dialogue. The root meaning of sutra is "thread" or "to sew," from which arose the sense of the word as a particular "thread" of discourse or the "weaving" of dialogue on a given subject.

[R. J. LITZ]

SUTRAS (Hinduism), concise, pithy, aphoristic expositions of some aspect of the orthodox Hindu tradition such as customs, rites, philosophy or law, often mnemonically using only a few suggestive words. For example, the four traditional aims of Hindu life are presented in sutras or in expansions upon sutras called sastras: the *kamasutras* dealing with pleasure and sensual existence; the *dharmasutras* covering the laws of dharma; the *artha* concerning economic improvement; and *moksa* on liberation. The major sutras were composed as manuals during the classical Hindu period from about the fifth cent. B.C. to 500 A.D. The term is sometimes used to indicate the last Vedic period (500–100 B.C.) even though it specifically refers to a writing style dating from 200 A.D. This sutra style by its superb verbal economy provides a way to condense, almost beyond comprehension without commentary, many aspects of the Hindu tradition.

[R. J. LITZ]

SUTRI, COUNCILS OF, in the 11th cent. two reform councils convoked at Sutri, a diocesan seat north of Rome. The first in 1046 deposed Pope Gregory VI despite his claim that he bought the office to reform it. The second in 1059 was called to confirm the claims of Pope Nicholas II against the anti-pope, Benedict X. BIBLIOGRAPHY: R. Kay, NCE 13:828.

[B. L. MARTHALER]

SUTTNER, BERTHA VON (1843–1914), Austrian writer whose peace novel, *Die Waffen nieder* (1889), wielded great influence. Czar Nicholas II was inspired by it to issue his peace manifesto of 1898. In 1905 she was awarded the Nobel prize. She also served as vice president of the international peace bureau in Switzerland. BIBLIOGRAPHY: K. Kupisch, RGG 6:534.

[M. J. SUELZER]

SUTTON, CHRISTOPHER (c.1565–1629), devotional writer. Canon of Westminster and Lincoln, S. wrote in the tone of Jeremy *Taylor and Thomas *Ken, and his books were well loved in their day. His *Godly Meditations upon the Most Holy Sacrament of the Lord's Supper* (1613) takes a position midway between that of Trent and that of *Zwingli, and together with *Learne to Die* (1600) and *Learne to Live* (1608) was reissued by the Tractarians, with prefaces signed by J. H. N. (i.e., *Newman).

[T. GILBY]

SUTTON HOO, TREASURE OF (c.630 A.D.), a rich burial deposit in a 90 ft ship of the pre-Viking age (c.630 A.D.), believed to be the monument of an East Anglian king, excavated in Suffolk, England (1939). The gold jewelry, silver plate, weapons and armour, symbols of office, and items of domestic use, in design partly Jutish, with Scandinavian, Celtic, and Frankish elements (a new style flourishing in E Anglia in the 7th cent.) constitute the most important archeological document of its era in Europe. The treasure is housed in the British Museum. BIBLIOGRA-

PHY: R. L. S. Bruce-Mitford, *Sutton Hoo Ship-Burial, a Provisional Guide* (1947).

[R. L. S. BRUCE-MITFORD]

SÛYYÂKĒ (Endings), one or two *hûllālē* preceding the vigils (*qālē d-shahrā*) in East Syrian night Offices of Sundays and Lent.

[A. CODY]

SVETLOV, PAVEL IAKOLEVICH, (1861–1942) Russian theologian. He wrote many books and articles on dogmatic and moral theology, apologetics, and exegesis. He also favored religious unity among Catholics, Anglicans, and Orthodox, and adopted a conciliatory position on controversial doctrinal points. He supported religious liberty in Russia and reform in the Russian Orthodox Church. His religious works, in general influenced by A. *Khomiakov, include: *Christian Doctrine Presented in Apologetical Form* (1912); *Idea of the Reign of God in Its Significance for a Christian Concept of the World* (1905); *On the Reform of Religious Teaching in Russia* (1906).

[I. M. KASHUBA]

SWASTIKA, a cross with arms at right angles of equal length, usually clockwise. It has appeared in the cultures of the Hindus, Buddhists, Incas, and early Christians. In Nazi Germany, the black swastika was the official flag of the Third Reich because to Hitler in his *Mein Kampf,* the swastika was the sign of the struggle for the victory of Aryan man and his creativity which is forever anti-Semitic.

[F. H. BRIGHAM]

SWEARING, taking an *oath; i.e., invoking God as witness to the truth of an assertion or promise. Usually, however, the term denotes a wrongful use of God's name in asserting some frivolous matter. A fully deliberate act with the intent to treat God lightly would gravely offend against the reverence due to his truthfulness, universal knowledge, and providence. Usually, however, "cursing and swearing" simply mean profanity. Even if in content some expression may be irreverent towards God, or even *blasphemy, the speaker does not advert to or intend this. Then the morality is to be judged as that of indecent or vulgar *speech.

[T. C. O'BRIEN]

SWEDEN, predominantly Lutheran country of Scandinavia; a constitutional monarchy with capital in Stockholm. The first–known Christian missionary to Sweden was St. *Ansgar in 830. He later became abp. of Bremen-Hamburg, and this see claimed jurisdiction over Sweden. King Olaf I accepted baptism from Sigfrid c.1000, and though resistance came from the paganism centered at Uppsala, by 1100 the Church was fairly well established. Eric (r. c.1160) became the national saint. From 1104 Lund served as primatial see of Scandinavia. Cistercians established the first monastic houses in the 12th century. Uppsala, now primatial see of Sweden, became an archdiocese in 1164. The outstanding literary figure of medieval Sweden was St. Bridget (c. 1303–73), foundress of the Bridgettines. Margaret of Denmark (r. 1387–1412) united Norway and Sweden under the Danish crown. In 1523 Gustavus I defeated Christian II of Denmark and became king of Sweden, which included Finland until Russia took it in 1809. Gustavus gave his support to the Lutheran Reformation, led in Sweden by Luther's pupil, Olaus *Petri, and Olaus's brother, Laurentius, abp. of Uppsala (1531–73). As a concession to opponents of the new order, the Swedish Church retained much of its pre-Reformation tradition, including episcopal succession. But the considerable land holdings of the Church were taken by the crown and nobility. During the 30 Years' War, King Gustavus II Adolphus (1611–32) became a champion of Protestantism. His daughter, Christina, converted to Catholicism in 1654 and abdicated. As a reaction to Enlightenment influences, *Pietism and nonconformist, evangelical denominations gained some strength in the 18th and 19th centuries. Several Swedish churchmen have attained international prominence in the 20th cent.—among them, Abp. N. *Soderblom and Bps. G. *Aulén and A. *Nygren. A RC vicar apostolic was appointed to Stockholm in 1783; it received its diocesan status in 1953. In 1975 there were 8 churches, 29 diocesan and 67 religious priests, 231 religious women, and some 73,000 Catholics.

[T. EARLY]

SWEDENBORG, EMANUEL (1688–1772), Swedish scientist and religious thinker. Born in Stockholm, the son of a Lutheran bp., he was graduated from the Univ. of Uppsala in 1709 and studied Newtonian physics and natural sciences during a prolonged stay in England. He was appointed to the Swedish Royal Board of Mines in 1716 and held other scientific posts, while writing extensively on science. His major scientific works include his *Principia* (1734) and *The Economy of the Animal Kingdom* (1740). He grew more interested in religious mysticism, and in 1745 he published *The Worship and Love of God*. In 1756 the eight volumes of *Arcana Coelestia* appeared, followed in 1758 by *The New Jerusalem and Its Heavenly Doctrine*. His many published works on mathematics, geology, anatomy, and cosmology gave him a considerable reputation as a theoretical scientist. His religious writings claim to represent revelations made to Swedenborg in frequent visits by spiritual beings and visions of heaven and hell that he personally experienced. He was the unique channel for this revelation and, through his writings, was to provide the basis for the teachings of a new Christian Church. He did not personally found the *Church of the New Jerusalem, but is regarded by its members as a divinely illuminated seer. His sense of the correspondence of the spirit world with the natural world enabled him to develop a personal religion that he felt consistent with science and reason. BIBLIOGRA-

PHY: S. Toksvig, *Emanuel Swedenborg: Scientist and Mystic* (1948); C. O. Sigstedt, *Swedenborg Epic* (1952).

[R. K. MACMASTER]

SWEELINCK, JAN PIETERS (1562–1621), Dutch organist, composer, and teacher. S. studied with and succeeded his father as organist of the RC Old Church of Amsterdam. He kept this post until his death when he was in turn succeeded by his son Dirck. S.'s vocal compositions, principally his settings of French psalms and his Latin *Cantiones sacrae* (1619), place him among the last of the great Renaissance composers of the Netherlands school. As an instrumentalist, however, he is regarded as belonging more to the 17th than to the 16th century. The Baroque style is evident in his organ works, particularly his fantasies, toccatas, and variations on secular tunes. Teacher of numerous important organists of the time, S. was also influential in the great school of German organ music of the 17th century. S.'s complete works, edited by Max Seiffert, were published in 12 volumes (1895–1903). BIBLIOGRAPHY: Reese MusR.

[M. T. LEGGE]

SWENEY, JOHN R. (1837–99), American hymn composer. S. was among those composers who laid the foundations of American gospel hymn writing. He wrote over 1,000 sacred songs, many of which were translated into other languages. In addition, he was editor or associate editor of 60 or more other hymn books.

[M. T. LEGGE]

SWETCHINE, ANNE SOPHIE (1782–1857), Russian emigrée to Paris, noted for her salon which drew many intellectuals. Born in Moscow to the wealthy Soymanov family, enjoying connections with the czarist court, she married Gen. Nicholas Swetchine, governor of St. Petersburg. Originally Russian Orthodox, she became a Catholic in 1815, influenced by the French minister to Russia, J. de Maistre. After losing favor at court, the family moved to Paris in 1816. Among the members of her Paris circle were De *Tocqueville, *Montalembert, and *Lacordaire. BIBLIOGRAPHY: M. V. Woodgate, *Madame Swetchine: 1782–1857* (1948).

[T. EARLY]

SWIFT, JONATHAN (1667–1745), English prose satirist, dean of St. Patrick's, Dublin. A friend of Pope, Addison, Arbuthnot, and Bolingbroke, S. reluctantly left London for Dublin. Staunchly C of E, he looked with disfavor on Presbyterians and Dissenters. He was a foe of injustice and sought to do what he could to change the deplorable economic conditions in Ireland under English rule. His best-known work, *Gulliver's Travels* (1726), a terrifying and challenging book, satirizes courts, statesmen, Churches, and in general the behavior of mankind. His *Journal to Stella* reveals his daily activities (1710–13) and his devotion to Esther Johnson. His private life was tragically unhappy. His skill as a satirist consists in the casual tone with which he marshalls facts and arguments to an inexorable and devastating conclusion. BIBLIOGRAPHY: R. W. Jackson, *Jonathan Swift, Dean and Pastor* (1939); S. Gwynn, *Life and Friendships of Dean Swift* (1933); K. Williams, *Jonathan Swift and the Age of Compromise* (1958); P. Harth, *Swift and Anglican Rationalism* (1961).

[M. M. BARRY]

SWINBURNE, ALGERNON CHARLES (1837–1909), English poet and critic. He left Oxford without a degree, published blank verse drama, *The Queen Mother* and *Rosamond* (1860); a lyrical tragedy, *Atlanta in Calydon* (1865); and *Poems and Ballads* (1866). The last gained him immediate popularity for new melodies and severe criticism for sensuality and paganism. Robert Buchanan attacked him and other Pre-Raphaelites in the *Contemporary Review* in 1871, using the phrase "the fleshy school of poetry." S.'s muse was always a spirit of revolt against conventions and restraints in government, Church, society, and moral life. As a critic he is stimulating and suggestive but lacks reasoned judgment. He revolutionized English prosody, breaking away from the bondage of iambic meter. His philosophy of life, defiant rebellion with no real purpose, is weak and destructive. He was a voluminous writer. BIBLIOGRAPHY: J. V. Nash, *Religious Life of Swinburne* (1923); H. Nicolson, *Swinburne* (1926); J. A. Cassidy, *Algernon Charles Swinburne* (1964).

[M. M. BARRY]

SWINT, JOHN JOSEPH (1879–1962), bishop. A native of West Virginia, S. was ordained for the Diocese of Wheeling in 1904. As a pastor and missionary in W. Virginia, he showed extraordinary zeal for the next 17 years. He was named auxiliary bp. of Wheeling in 1922 and succeeded that same year to the see. His years as bp. reflected zeal and administrative competence; in his 40 years at the head of his diocese, he built over 100 churches, 35 elementary schools, 8 high schools, a college, and several hospitals, nursing schools and homes for the aged. A notable preacher, S. published three volumes of sermons.

[J. R. AHERNE]

SWISS AMERICAN CONGREGATION, see BENEDICTINES.

SWISS BRETHREN, a name designating the Swiss Anabaptists, followers of C. *Grebel, G. *Blaurock, and F. *Manz. They called themselves simply "Brethren." BIBLIOGRAPHY: J. H. Yoder, *Täufertum und Reformation in der Schweiz* (1962); bibliog. for Anabaptists.

[T. C. O'BRIEN]

SWISS GUARDS, corps of Swiss soldiers employed to guard the pope or, in intervals between popes, the college of cardinals. The present arrangement dates to Pope Julius II (1503–13), although papal armies had included Swiss even earlier. The Guards are noted for their colorful uniforms, including one reportedly designed by Michelangelo. Three other papal units—the Noble Guard, the Palatine Guard, and a police corps—were disbanded in 1970, and a civilian security corps added.

[T. EARLY]

SWITHBERT, ST. (also known as Suidbert, Suitbert; d. *c*.713), Anglo-Saxon bp. and missionary in the Netherlands. Northumbian by birth, he studied under Egbert in Ireland. He accompanied Willibrord to Frisia in 690. In 693 Wilfrid of York consecrated him bishop. He labored in the area NE of the Rhine. A pagan reaction forced him back to the abbey of Kaiserswerth. He was apparently a scholar and there is evidence to show that he was bp. of Dorostat, now Wijk-bij-Duurstede on the Rhine. BIBLIOGRAPHY: Butler 1:452–454; M. Bateson, DNB 19:155; H. Farmer, BiblSanct 12:49.

[J. DRUSE]

SWITHIN, ST. (d. 862) bishop. He served as counsellor to King Egbert of Wessex and was tutor and ecclesiastical adviser to his son, Ethelwulf. It was during the latter's reign that he became bp. of Winchester in 852. Though legendary even in his lifetime for his charity, humility, and zeal, S. did not attract a cult for more than 100 years after his death. But his translation in 971 was the occasion for numerous tales of miracles to spring up in connection with his name. He remained patron of the cathedral until 1538, when his shrine was vandalized at the time of the Reformation.

[E. M. GATES]

SWITHIN'S DAY, ST., feast, July 15, commemorating the day in 971 when the remains of St. Swithin, the 9th-cent. Anglo Saxon bp. of Winchester were transferred from an obscure grave in the cathedral close to a position of honor within the restored church, which at this time adopted him as its patron saint. Legend has it that rain or shine on St. Swithin's Day will determine whether there will be rain or shine over the next 40 days.

[E. M. GATES]

SWITZERLAND, republican federation of 22 cantons (3 subdivided, making 25 units) in central Europe; capital at Berne. It is about half Catholic and half Protestant. Swiss history begins with the Roman period, when Julius Caesar subdued the Helvetians, a Gallic tribe in the West, and Augustus conquered the Rhaetians and other tribes in the East. Christianity won its way in the area gradually, beginning perhaps in the 3d cent. The record of bps. begins from the 4th century. In the 5th cent. Rome settled Arian Burgundians in W Switzerland as a buffer against Germanic tribes such as the pagan Alamanni then coming into central Switzerland. German remains the predominant language in areas taken by the Alamanni, whereas the West is French-speaking; Italian prevails in certain areas adjacent to Italy; the Romance dialects of Romansh and Ladin survive in Rhaetian valleys that resisted the Alamanni. Christianity was not totally eliminated in Alamannia, but the area was regained for the Church only slowly—6th to 9th centuries. By 1033 all of present-day Switzerland was incorporated in the Holy Roman Empire. In 1291 the cantons of Schwyz, Uri (locale of the William Tell legend) and Nidwalden formed a defensive league against the Habsburgs. Other cantons later joined them, and in 1499 they won virtual independence from Emperor Maximilian I. Switzerland's formal independence was recognized by the Peace of Westphalia (1648) and reaffirmed by the Congress of Vienna (1815). Its permanent neutrality was guaranteed by the 2d Treaty of Paris (1815). H. Zwingli, based in Zurich, led the Reformation among German Swiss. But some areas remained Catholic; and in 1847 the Catholic rural cantons, allied in a Sonderbund, were defeated by the Radical party, which established a more centralized government under the constitution of 1848. In French-speaking Geneva, J. Calvin became the preeminent figure of Reformed Protestantism and made Geneva the chief Protestant center. BIBLIOGRAPHY: W. Martin, *Switzerland from Roman Times to the Present* (6th ed., 1971).

[T. EARLY]

SWORD OF THE SPIRIT, English Catholic movement. Proposed by Christopher *Dawson, it was founded in 1940 by Card. A. Hinsley, abp. of Westminster, to further Catholic cooperation with non-Catholics in support of the war and postwar goals. Full membership was restricted to Catholics, and non-Catholics formed a counterpart group, Religion and Life. The movement declined after the war, but in 1950 was revived as an agency for educating Catholic laity in international affairs. In 1965 it became the Catholic Institute for International Relations.

[T. EARLY]

SYCHAR (Sichar), Samaritan city near which Jesus talked with a Samaritan woman (Jn 4.5, the only appearance of the name in the Bible). It was said to be near a field Jacob gave to Joseph (Gen 33.19; 48.22; Jos 24.32), and Jesus sat at a well known as Jacob's Well (Jn 4.6). Scholars have disputed whether Sychar is to be identified with *Shechem. Jerome regarded Sychar as a scribal misspelling of Shechem, and modern excavations have supported the identity of Sychar and Shechem.

[T. EARLY]

SYENE, Egyptian village on the E bank of the Nile, opposite the island Elephantine; the modern Aswan. The southern boundary of ancient Egypt, it was mentioned for its remoteness (Ezek 29.10; 30.6; Is 49.12).

[T. EARLY]

SYLLABIC STYLE, in plainchant, a setting having one note to each syllable of the text, with an occasional syllable having two or three. The settings of the *Credo*, for example, are in syllabic style.

[M. T. LEGGE]

SYLLABUS OF ERRORS, a compilation of 80 propositions issued by Pius IX with the encyclical *Quanta cura*, Dec. 8, 1864. He had previously condemned these propositions in allocutions, encyclicals, and apostolic letters dealing with pantheism, naturalism, rationalism, religious indifference, socialism, communism, certain secret, biblical, and clerical-liberal societies, rights of the Church, civil society, relations of Church and State, natural and Christian ethics, Christian marriage, temporal power of the popes, and liberalism. The manner in which each proposition is censured can be gathered from the document in which the error had first been condemned. BIBLIOGRAPHY: D 2901–80; W. F. Hogan, NCE 13:854–856.

[J. H. ROHLING]

SYLLOGISM, an inference or argumentation in which, from an antecedent premise set of, basically, two propositions, a consequent proposition, the conclusion, is derived. The central focus of traditional logic, the syllogism is of two kinds, the categorical and the hypothetical, first discovered and analyzed by Aristotle and the Stoic logicians, respectively. The categorical syllogism is a syllogism the propositions of which are each categorical, i.e., absolute, simple, and free from conditions. An example is the following:

All birds are animals.

But all crows are birds.

Therefore, all crows are animals.

The third proposition, of course, is the consequent and conclusion. The first proposition is the major proposition, containing as it does the major term, the predicate of the conclusion. The second, as it contains the subject of the conclusion, or minor term, is the minor proposition. The major and minor propositions, linked by the mediating or middle term, together compose the antecedent premise set. The basis of the syllogism is the *dictum de omni et nullo*: whatever is universally affirmed or denied of some subject must be affirmed or denied of all included under that subject. But traditional logic also elaborated a set of more immediate rules by which the validity of a purported syllogism can be judged. (1) The syllogism has three and only three terms, each appearing twice and in two different propositions. This rule entails that there are but four possible "figures," or arrangements of the terms of the syllogism. With S designating the subject term of the conclusion, P its predicate term, and M the middle term, they are as follows:

I. M is P.	II. P is M.	III. M is P.	IV. P is M.
S is M.	S is M.	M is S.	M is S.
S is P.	S is P.	S is P.	S is P.

(2) Whatever term is distributed, in the conclusion or taken in its full extension or universally, must have been distributed in the premises; and the middle terms must be distributed at least once. (3) If one premise is negative or particular, the conclusion must also be; if both premises are particular or negative, then there is no conclusion (a particular proposition is one in which only some of the subjects are included, e.g., "Some men are rational").

The hypothetical syllogism is one in which the major premise is a non-categorical proposition, being conditional, disjunctive, or alternative. Most important are the so-called *modus ponens* and *modus tollens*. Letting p stand for one proposition and q for another, they are:

modus ponens	*modus tollens*
If p, then q.	If p, then q.
But p.	But not-q.
Therefore q.	Therefore not-p.

Traditional logic's reliance upon largely intuitive rules for determining the validity of hypothetical syllogisms has now been replaced by the use of the rigorous axiomatic system of the propositional calculus. Also, with its beginnings in the later Middle Ages, the tendency of modern and contemporary logic has been to reduce the logic of the categorical syllogism to being but a derivative of the logic of the propositional calculus.

[R. E. HENNESSEY]

SYLLUCIANISTS, early 4th cent. subordinationists, many of them influential bps. who, probably with Arius, had been disciples of *Lucian of Antioch (d. 312). Lucian had founded the exegetical school of Antioch (c.260) and was one of the earliest and most influential subordinationists. The Syllucianists supported Arius in his controversy (318?–323?) with Alexander of Alexandria, but their efforts failed against the antisubordinationist majority at the Council of *Nicaea I (325) where Arius' doctrine was condemned. *ANTIOCH, SCHOOL OF; *SUBORDINATIONISM.

[R. R. BARR]

SYLVESTER I, ST. (d. 335), **POPE** from 314, the first to accede to that office after the Edict of Milan. Little is known of his life or pontificate, perhaps because he was so completely overshadowed by Constantine whose initiative and influence even in ecclesiastical matters commanded greater attention. The legend that S. baptized Constantine at the Lateran and cured him of leprosy is without historical foundation. So also is the story that the Emperor in gratitude gave the provinces of Italy to the Church (the so-called *Donation of Constantine). S. did not attend but was represented at the Councils of Arles (314) and Nicaea (325), but there is no record of what he himself did in connection with these councils or with the other affairs of his day. Constantine gave the palace of the Laterani, which had re-

cently become an imperial property, to the Church as a residence for the bp. of Rome, adapted a great hall of the palace as the first Lateran Basilica, and began construction of the famous baptistery. BIBLIOGRAPHY: E. Weltin, *Ancient Popes* (1964) 163–176; Butler 4:644–645; J. Chapin, NCE 13:857–858.

[R. B. ENO]

SYLVESTER II (c.945–1003), **POPE** from 999. He came of a lower class French family and was known as Gerbert until his election to the papacy. From early years educated by monks, and possibly a monk himself, he became one of the most learned men of his time. After studying in Spain under the patronage of a Spanish count, Gerbert was introduced to the papal court of John XIII (965–972), who sent him to the imperial court of Otto I (963–973) to lecture. Later he became an instructor in the cathedral school at Reims and secretary to the abp., with whom he traveled to the court of Otto II (973–983), adding to his scholarly renown and writing numerous letters wherever he went. Otto II was so impressed with his learning that he made him abbot of Bobbio in N Italy, but he resigned from that office on Otto's death and returned to his teaching in Reims. There he became involved in politics, influencing the election of Otto III as emperor (983) and the choice of Hugh Capet as king of France (987). After becoming king, Hugh, under the influence of Otto, attempted to oust the abp. of Reims and put Gerbert in his place. Both John XVI (985–996) and Gregory V (996–999), the latter a cousin and nominee of the Emperor, refused to sanction the illegal action. Gerbert then became a teacher at the imperial court where he remained until Otto named him abp. of Ravenna, now with the approval of Gregory V, who sent him the pallium. The following year, on Gregory's death, the Emperor succeeded in inducing the Romans to accept Gerbert as pope. Taking the name Sylvester II, he was the first Frenchman to hold the papal office. His 4-year reign was perhaps less productive than might have been expected of one of his scholarly attainment. He made no headway toward mastering the Romans. Indeed, with Otto he was driven from Rome in 1001 and was able to return only after Otto's death in 1002. But there were some accomplishments. S. gave Poland its first metropolitan organization. In Hungary he bestowed the royal crown on St. Stephen I and established the metropolitan system there also. In the regular synods S. conducted, he insisted on clerical celibacy, denounced simony and nepotism, and promoted reform throughout the Church by encouraging local synods. Like other popes of the period, he helped to forge instruments of reform in the 11th cent. by strengthening monastic foundations. In his writings he gave mathematical sciences equality with grammar and dialectics. He was a practical teacher and constructed material aids to learning—e.g., globes, rhetorical charts, and an abacus. In philosophy he emphasized problems of definition and classification. His many letters on almost every aspect of his wide interest—mathematics, MSS, science, politics, ecclesiastical administration—give a good picture of an otherwise poorly documented period. BIBLIOGRAPHY: *Letters of Gerbert, with his Papal Privileges as Sylvester II* (tr. H. Lattin, 1961); O Darlington, "Gerbert, the Teacher," *American Historical Review* 52 (1956–57) 456–476; Mann 5:1–120.

[P. F. MULHERN]

SYLVESTER III (John of Sabina; d. 1046), **POPE** (antipope?) from 1045. Formerly bp. of Sabina, at the instigation of the Crescentian faction he was promoted to oppose Benedict IX. He is generally considered to have been an antipope. After a few weeks Benedict overcame his opponent, who returned to his diocese. S. was formally considered an interloper by the synod of Sutri (1046) where Henry III deposed Gregory VI and installed Clement II. BIBLIOGRAPHY: P. Brezzi, *Roma e l'impero mediovale* (1947) 206–211; F. X. Seppelt, *Geschichte der Päpste* (1955) 2:414–417.

[O. J. BLUM]

SYLVESTER, JOHANNES, Latin name of the Hungarian Dominican scholar, János Serestely, who is credited with a translation of the NT into Hungarian, using sound philology. It was published in 1541 and again in 1574. S. was one of three Hungarian disciples of Erasmus who were forerunners of the ensuing era of Hungarian national literature. S. was also the author of the first Hungarian poem, written in heroic couplet to show the adaptability of classical forms. He is credited also with the first Hungarian grammar.

[E. J. DILLON]

SYLVESTRINES, see BENEDICTINES, SYLVESTRINE.

SYLVIUS, FRANCISCUS (vernacular form, François Du Bois; 1581–1649), Belgian theologian. He studied at Louvain and Douai and began teaching at Douai in 1613. He became a canon in 1618, dean of the chapter, and vice-chancellor of the university in 1622. Among his writings are a well-known commentary on the ThAq ST, a textbook of pastoral theology, biblical commentaries, and a work against C. *Jansen. BIBLIOGRAPHY: É. Amann, DTC 14:2923–25.

[R. B. ENO]

SYMBOL, the primal and fully expressive representation in which one reality renders another present. The symbol is the reality in which a person attains knowledge of the being that expresses itself in the symbol. Thus a symbol allows what it symbolizes to be present insofar as the symbol is the vital and not merely arbitrary speaking forth of the reality it represents. Several contemporary theologians, esp. P. *Tillich and K. *Rahner, have insisted upon this understanding of symbol and have pointed out the essential, although often neglected, difference between symbol and sign. A sign is

arbitrary in the sense that the meaning of most types of sign is determined by a factor extrinsic to the reality itself. A human observer decides that a red light is a sign for stop. A sign has a secondary relationship to the reality it points to; it is not necessarily joined with the object signified and has no inexorable connection with the very nature of that object. The operative factor of a symbol, however, is that it is the proper expression of another reality. A man, for instance, affirms himself in his actions, which may be considered the symbol of all that he is. The sacraments are signs, but their deeper reality consists in their function as symbols, i.e., historical expressions of God's dealings with man.

This notion of symbol differs from that of C. G. *Jung, who noted the recurrence of certain symbols in dreams and artistic expressions. Jung postulated a collective unconscious to explain this recurrence, and reasoned that symbols, esp. religious symbols, are products of man's inherited psychological tendencies. E. *Cassirer, on the other hand, emphasizes the unity that exists between the symbol and the symbolized to the degree that they are joined into an essential oneness. According to Cassirer, it is not so much that the symbol represents the symbolized, as unites with it to form a single entity at least as perceived by consciousness.

Philosophers of comparative religion have also been concerned with the meaning of symbols. M. *Eliade in particular emphasizes that the religious symbol is a substitute for the sacred or *holy and serves as a means for establishing a relationship with the sacred. Thus a thing or an action is transformed into something other than it appears to be in profane experience because the holy has expressed itself in it, making it a symbol. The symbol, therefore, is not chosen by man as a sign would be; it is the vehicle whereby transcendent reality embodies itself and demonstrates the essential unity of the cosmos. BIBLIOGRAPHY: Rahner ThInvest 4:221–253; P. Tillich, "Theology and Symbolism," *Religious Symbolism* (ed. F. E. Johnson, 1955); E. Cassirer, *Philosophy of Symbolic Forms* (tr. R. Manheim, 3 v., 1957); C. G. Jung, *Psyche and Symbol: A Selection from the Writings of C. G. Jung* (ed. V. de Laszlo, 1958); M. Eliade, *Images and Symbols* (1961).

[T. M. MCFADDEN]

SYMBOL OF FAITH, a summary formula of the truths of Christian faith. The Gr. *symbolon* (sign) was used for a token of identity such as a signet ring or legal bond. This source of the term was given by some of the Fathers, since the symbol of faith was the mark by which the catechumen was recognized as acceptable for baptism, and was also a sign of uniformity of faith among Christians. The term was applied to early creedal formulas at least from the 3d cent. (e.g., by St. Cyprian, d. 259). The formulas themselves were developed in conjunction with the baptismal ritual, one of the most ancient being the *Apostles' Creed (*Symbolum Apostolorum*). Generally the terms symbol and creed are accepted as synonymous and, although some disagree with the usage, are applied not only to the so-called *ecumenical creeds but also to later RC professions of faith, e.g., that of the Council of Trent, and to the Protestant *confessions of faith. The theological discipline concerned with the study of such documents is called comparative symbolics.

[T. EARLY]

SYMBOLICS, also called symbolic theology and *comparative symbolics, a study of the *confessions of faith or *doctrinal standards of Churches. *SYMBOL OF FAITH.

SYMBOLISM (IN RUSSIAN LITERATURE), dominant literary movement in Russian literature, esp. poetry, from about 1890 to 1910. Developed under the influence of the Russian poet and philosopher Vladimir Solovyev (1853–1900) and the French symbolists, it enriched Russian poetry by its greater freedom in the use of verse forms, its musicality, and its emphasis on aesthetic values. Leading symbolists were Merezhkovski, Bryusov, Hippius, Sologub, Blok, and Biely. BIBLIOGRAPHY: G. Donchin, *Influence of French Symbolism on Russian Poetry* (1958); O. A. Maslenikov, *Frenzied Poets: Andrey Biely and the Russian Symbolists* (1952).

[M. F. MCCARTHY]

SYMBOLISM, THEOLOGICAL. In Christian theology two areas stand out in which symbolism and the study of it are prominent: typology, in which personages, places, and events of the OT foreshadow those of the New; and sacramentalism, in which the sign value of the sacraments is enriched by the multidimensional and multivalent signification of the numerous symbols to be found in the Christian liturgies. With the notable exception of St. Ambrose of Milan, in his treatises *On the Mysteries* and *On the Sacraments,* the Fathers of the West were satisfied to regard the sacraments as natural religious symbols of spiritual rebirth, growth, nourishment, healing, etc. This tradition of the West finds classic expression in the rationale for the seven sacraments in the Decree for the Armenians (D 1310). St Thomas Aquinas, to whom the framers of the Decree are indebted, added other dimensions. Thus the sacraments are not only the signs of present grace; as symbols they recall the Passion and death of the Lord and are the pledge of eschatological glory (cf. ThAq ST 3a, 66.3) and Aquinas's Eucharistic hymn *O sacrum convivium*). The Fathers of the East were more disposed to explore the OT for types of the Christian mysteries and to develop by way of analogy and allegory the symbolism of the sacraments. Examples may be found in the catechetical and mystagogic lectures of St. Cyril of Jerusalem, Theodore of Mopsuestia, and St. John Chrysostom. Theologians today, more interested in the sign value of the sacraments, are rediscovering the rich overtones and the multiple resonances of sacramental signification in the Bible and in the more developed liturgies of the early Church. BIBLIOGRAPHY: G. Coulon, NCE 13:873–

875; J. Daniélou, *Bible and the Liturgy* (1956); *Religious Symbolism* (ed. F. Johnson, 1955).

[P. F. PALMER]

SYMBOLOFIDEISM (symbolic fideism; critical symbolism), the theory that all dogmatic and theological formulations are symbols or reflection of subjective religious experience; that, like religious experience itself, dogma is essentially and interminably evolving. The view is associated particularly with a school of Protestant theologians at Paris in the 19th cent., led by A. *Sabatier. It rested upon basic themes of *liberal theology and had its influence upon *Modernism among Roman Catholics. *FIDEISM.

[T. C. O'BRIEN]

SYMEON, see SIMEON.

SYMMACHAN FORGERIES, documents actually composed *c*.500 by followers of Pope *Symmachus, but purporting to be enactments by or about earlier popes. They were meant to supply precedents for Symmachus's position in the Laurentian Schism. Their main point was that the pope was above judgment by any human authority. Their content followed the teaching of the *Gelasian Letter concerning papal authority. BIBLIOGRAPHY: Altaner 553–554; W. Ullmann, *Growth of Papal Government in the Middle Ages* (1962).

[T. C. O'BRIEN]

SYMMACHIANS, a small Judeo-Christian sect existing until the 5th cent. and considered a Western branch of the Ebionites. Augustine and other Latin authors mention their existence in Africa and Italy. The connection of their name with the Bible translator Symmachus the Ebionite is obscure. BIBLIOGRAPHY: J. Schmidt, LTK 9:1217; F. J. Bacchus, CE 14:378–379, s.v. "Symmachus the Ebionite"; EncRelKnow 11:212.

[J. FANG]

SYMMACHUS, ST. (d. 514), **POPE** from 498. S., a native of Sardinia, was elected to succeed St. *Anastasius II, but a Byzantine faction elected the archpriest *Laurentius. S. was approved by Theodoric the Great, king of Italy, who sent Laurentius to Nocera as bishop. In 501 the latter returned to Rome and his claims to the papacy led to the Laurentian schism, which brought 5 years of turmoil and bloodshed to Rome. The pronouncements of S. during the strife included a prohibition of electioneering for a successor to a living pope, and an insistence that the pope could be judged by no human authority. In support of this teaching, the *Symmachan Forgeries were composed by his followers. In spite of many attempts, S. made no real progress towards healing the *Acacian Schism. Under him *Caesarius of Arles became papal vicar of Gaul, and was the first abp. outside of Italy to receive the *pallium. S. built many churches and also the earliest papal residence at the Vatican.

BIBLIOGRAPHY: Altaner 553–554; T. G. Jalland, *Church and the Papacy* (1944).

[P. F. MULHERN]

SYMMACHUS, QUINTUS AURELIUS (*c.*340–*c.*402), Roman rhetorician and statesman. S. became proconsul of Africa in 373 and prefect of Rome in 384. He lived to see his family's prestige, which was bound up with Rome's pagan glory, eclipsed by two events: the triumph of Christianity and the threat of barbarian invasion. As consul in 391 he led the party that succeeded for a short time in restoring paganism. His longest and greatest struggle was with his relative Ambrose in a futile attempt to restore the altar Augustus had set up before the statue of Victory at the curia entrance. S.'s extant writings are 10 books of letters to prominent contemporaries, 2 panegyrics, and fragments of other elaborately ornamented speeches. Text: O. Seeck, MGH, *Auctores antiquissimi* 6.1. BIBLIOGRAPHY: F. H. Dudden, *Life and Times of St. Ambrose* (2 v., 1935).

[M. J. SUELZER]

SYMPATHY, from late Lat. *sympathia* (Gr. *sumpatheia*), a suffering with or fellow-feeling. The term enters into theology in connection with *affective knowledge, thus experiencing divine things rather than knowing about them; with *compassion (Lat. *compassio*, a literal and earlier translation of the Greek) commiseration; with *mercy; and with real or supposed affinities, either manifest or occult, which may affect human conduct, for instance the powers of sympathetic medicine and magic, or the influence of the heavenly bodies.

[T. GILBY]

SYNAGOGUE, Jewish congregation and the place where it meets. Its origin was the Babylonian Exile when Judean refugees were allowed to gather to hear prophetic messages and to pray from their sacred writings. After the Temple was rebuilt, Jews continued to congregate in localities away from Jerusalem to learn their written and oral traditions and to praise and petition God through psalms. Thus, the synagogue kept alive and fertile Jewish learning and liturgy throughout the Diaspora. As is evident from early Christian documents (Acts of Apostles and Pauline Epistles) and from present archeological knowledge, there were synagogues in all the important towns of the Mediterranean basin in the 1st Christian century. Synagogal worship and government, in fact, greatly influenced the liturgy and structure of early Christian Churches. In recent times Jews have come to call the synagogue a temple, or, among the Yiddish Orthodox, a *Schul* (school). The synagogue's basic character has not drastically changed for 2 millennia, except that many Reform synagogues no longer use Hebrew as the sacred liturgical language.

[J. F. FALLON]

SYNAGOGUES, CONSERVATIVE WORLD COUNCIL OF, see WORLD COUNCIL OF SYNAGOGUES, CONSERVATIVE.

SYNAXARION, in the Christian East, an introduction to the Liturgy. All feasts and Sundays have their proper Synaxarion. In this introduction there is given the predominant idea upon which the faithful should meditate. The theme of the day is the purpose of the Synaxarion.

[P. MORLINO]

SYNAXARY, in the Eastern Churches: (1) a liturgical book used in the Liturgy of the Hours at Morning Prayer (*Orthros*) and containing in chronological order for the days of the year brief lives of the saints; (2) a *Menologion*, i.e., a book of short lives of the saints; (3) a calendar of saints' feast days, the small synaxary. The first sense applies to the Synaxary of Constantinople, known to date from at least the 9th cent. and important to the history of Byzantine liturgy, esp. in regard to the honoring of saints. Other Eastern Churches have their own books that correspond to the Byzantine liturgical synaxary.

[T. C. O'BRIEN]

SYNAXIS (Gr. assembly), a term referring: to gatherings of Christians for divine worship in early Christian times; to a celebration at a specified place in the Byzantine rite to commemorate a feast, e.g., the Synaxis of St. Joachim and Anne; to the counsellors of the abbot in a Byzantine monastery.

[J. R. AHERNE]

SYNCELLUS (Gr. *synkellos*), literally one who shares a cell, in the Eastern Church an ecclesiastic who lived with a bishop, the secretary of a bp. or a titular bp. In the West it referred to a counsellor who in time succeeded to the office of the prelate.

[J. R. AHERNE]

SYNCRETISM, a term applied disparagingly by A. *Calov to G. *Calixt's proposals for Christian reunion. Calixt sought to overcome doctrinal differences by reducing *credenda* (fundamental articles of faith) to a minimum based on the *consensus quinquesaecularis*. Calov and others insisted that this was a dilution of orthodoxy, an extreme *irenicism that disregarded truth and the criterion of the *confessions of faith as in accord with biblical revelation. Syncretism is used contemporarily in ecumenical discussions to indicate any similar attempt at unity through a disregard or diminution of doctrines or confessions distinctive of the Churches. Such a position is not generally considered a sound principle of ecumenism.

[T. C. O'BRIEN]

SYNCRETISM, RELIGIOUS. The term, a transliteration of Greek *synkrētismos,* was first used by Plutarch to indicate a "federation of Cretan cities" for mutual defense. By a rather strange etymological and semantic development, the word is now employed in the historical study of religion to designate the fusion of various religious cults or practices. This fusion can have a popular political, or religio-philosophical foundation. When two polytheistic societies, e.g., were brought into close relation by peaceful intercourse or by conquest, there was a tendency to equate the gods of one society with those of the other; or, under the influence of religio-philosophical thinking, to merge the gods of both groups into a new and more cosmopolitan synthesis, which often tended in the direction of universality or monotheism. The ascendency of Marduk and Ashur in Mesopotamia is to be explained in terms of the political ascendency of Babylon and Assyria respectively. Assyrian pressure was undoubtedly responsible for the introduction of the worship of Ashur into the cult of the Temple of Jerusalem under Manasseh. In Egypt the supremacy of Thebes led to the fusion of the cult of Amon at Thebes and of Ra at Heliopolis into the imperial cult of Amon-Ra. Among the Greeks, Apollo and Dionysius were originally foreign divinities who were incorporated into Greek religion and who were destined to play central roles in official as well as popular cult. The Romans adopted important divinities from the Etruscans, but esp. Greek divinities, among them Apollo and Dionysius. Furthermore under Greek influence they transformed their old *numina* into anthropomorphic divinities to whom they assigned the attributes of the Olympian pantheon.

It was, however, in the Hellenistic and imperial ages that syncretism reached its fullest development in Greco-Roman antiquity. In the interests of national unity the first Ptolemies promoted the development of the syncretistic cult of Serapis and Isis. This Hellenized cult, in which Isis soon became dominant, spread rapidly throughout the ancient Greco-Roman world. Isis came more and more to be worshipped as a universal divinity, identified with numerous other goddesses. She is addressed, "Thou of a thousand names." In the famous inscription set up by Antiochus I of Commagene (69–68 B.C.) at Nemrad-Dagh, Greek, Egyptian, and Persian divinities are combined and reflect the syncretistic religion of the ruler. *Plutarch and *Apuleius furnish striking examples of the syncretistic tendencies of the Imperial Age. Plutarch, for instance, maintains that the various religions of mankind all worship the same God under various names. On the political side it should be noted that the paganism which the Emperor Julian attempted to revive and promote was syncretistic in character, including even institutional features borrowed from Christianity itself! The Orphic and Hermetic literature constantly bears testimony to religious syncretism, as is evident from *Orphic Frg.* 239 (Kern), which in praising Isis says: "there is only one hymn . . . only one mystery, for there is, finally, only one god in all things." The philosophico-religious tendency towards syncretism and universality is esp. marked also in *Gnosticism, *Neopythagoreanism, and *Neoplatonism. *Iamblichus, in particular, gave ancient paganism a kind of systematic theology and made wide use of allegory in the elaboration of his religious syncretism. As an interesting example of a syncretistic religion that was formally developed as such since the close of the 19th cent. in Vietnam, see CAODAISM. BIBLIOGRAPHY: E. Des Places, NCE 13:881; Prümm 852–854; Hastings ERE 12:155–157; F. C. Grant, *Hellenistic Religions: The Age of Syncretism* (1953).

[M. R. P. McGUIRE]

SYNDERESIS, "a habit containing the precepts of natural law, i.e., the first principles for man's actions" (ThAq ST 1a2ae, 94.1). The term, Latinized form of the Gr. *syntērēsis,* became prominent in medieval theology because of one single text from the commentary of St. Jerome on Ezekiel 1.57 (PL 25:22), in which he refers to the term in Plato's *Republic* (4.439) and renders its meaning as *scintilla conscientiae,* the spark of conscience. St. Thomas, in bowing to the conventional use of Jerome's text, developed his own explanation reflected in the definition given above. Two connected points are implied: the explanation of synderesis follows a direction in Aristotle's thought, but is not derived from Aristotle; the meaning given belongs to the Christian view of the moral life. The Aristotelian direction consists first of all in a rejection of any innate ideas, and secondly, in the need for connaturally grasped first principles of thought as a fixed point of departure for the discursive movement of reasoning (Aristotle, *Posterior Analytics* I, ch. 1–3). St. Thomas develops the meaning of synderesis by comparing the directive function of human reason (reason as practical) to the purely cognitive function of reason (reason as theoretical). The reasoning process of the purely cognitive function begins with immediately grasped first principles of knowing, habitually retained for use by the habit or intellectual virtue called in Lat. *intellectus,* insight; correspondingly, a process of reasoning meant to reach decision about human action also ought to have a set of first principles as an irreducible starting point; their retention for use is the function of synderesis (ThAq ST 1a, 79.12; 2a2ae, 47.6). However scholastically articulated, this affirmation of a universal grasp of basic moral precepts is grounded on a Christian view of man, as having a given final end and a divinely endowed nature that makes known right and wrong (see Augustine, *De libero arbitrio* II, 10; PL 32.1256). Thus, St. Thomas before identifying synderesis as the habitual knowledge of the precepts of natural law, indicates that natural law itself is a kind of impress of the divine light in us (*ibid.,* 1a2ae, 91.2). Aristotle's ethics has no such "ontological" point of view, nor, correspondingly, method of moral discourse. The *nous* of which he speaks in *Ethics* VI, 11.1143a35–b15, is not synderesis, nor is his conception of the apprehension of the good based on a given ultimate end that sets up a corresponding moral order. In St. Thomas's conception the function of synderesis is to express the right moral ends or objectives for which the virtue of *prudence determines and measures its concrete judgments about what is right in a particular instance (*ibid.,* 2a2ae, 47.6). What is often missed in St. Thomas's thought, however, is that like prudence, the rightness of whose judgments depends on the moral virtues' rendering the appetites amenable to right action, the first moral principles or precepts depend for their formation and their imperative quality on the rudimentary order of appetite to the good.

In explaining the origin of natural law Aquinas keeps to his parallel between reason as cognitive and reason as directive. Because reason is essentially cognitive, its first thought is of being and its first immediately grasped principle is based on insight into being. The first apprehension of reason as directive is said to be "good"; its first principle, "The good ought to be done." But this initial apprehension of good occurs not by intellectual insight, but because the mind functions at the service of one who is to act, and the apprehension of the good is based on the appetitive drives to action. The first principle is an imperative, as are other rudimentary moral principles, not because of intellectual analysis, but because the precepts reflect appetitive drives, the exactions of ends. The primary moral precepts retained by synderesis have their origin and function as imperatives directive of prudence because they express the connatural orientation of human appetite to what is good for the person. Between the effective functioning of these first precepts and the imperative formed in the particular by prudence the habituation of the moral virtues keep the connatural orientation towards the good from being diverted. BIBLIOGRAPHY: T. Deman, *Somme théologique: La Prudence* (1949) 426–448; *Aristotle, L'Ethique à Nicomaque* (ed. R. A. Gauthier, 1970) 2.2:563–566; ThAq ST (Lat-Êng, v.36, ed. T. Gilby, *Prudence,* 1974).

[T. C. O'BRIEN]

SYNDIC, APOSTOLIC, a layman who administers the property of the Franciscans by authority of the Holy See. The rigid concept of poverty imposed by St. Francis of Assisi on his followers proved in time to be impractical as the friars grew in numbers and spread throughout Europe. The Holy See made itself the guardian and owner of Franciscan property. There is a syndic who administers the property of the whole order and of its provinces and houses. *POVERTY CONTROVERSY.

[J. R. AHERNE]

SYNEISAKTOI, see VIRGINES SUBINTRODUCTAE.

SYNERGISM (Gr. *syn,* together, *ergon,* work; *synergos,* working with; see 1 Cor 3.9), a term historically applied to a theory that the human will actively cooperates with grace in the act of conversion; its opposite is *monergism.* Primarily it was used in the *Synergistic Controversy (1550–77) regarding the doctrine of Philipp *Melanchthon; it has also been applied to one aspect of RC teaching on *justification, and to *Arminianism (see DORT, SYNOD OF). Melanchthon first completely accepted the ideas of Luther on unconditional predestination and the abiding sinfulness and impotence of fallen nature (see AUGSBURG CONFESSION, Art. 18). Successive revisions of his theological text, *Loci communes,* manifested a change, and that of 1548 stated that the causes of conversion are the Holy Spirit, the Word, and the will of man "not wholly inactive in its own weakness." Melanchthon did not regard the cooperation of the will,

however, as a coordinate, equal cause; human consent was itself caused by the Holy Spirit and the Word. In the ensuing Synergistic Controversy other Lutherans censured synergism as a betrayal of justification by faith alone, in favor of a revived *Semi-Pelagianism, or of a crypto-Catholicism (see GNESIOLUTHERANISM; FLACIUS ILLYRICUS, M.). The *Formula of Concord (Art. 2) is addressed to this controversy; it accepts only two causes in man's conversion, the Holy Spirit and the Word, but affirms that the regenerated will "cooperates in the works which follow."

In RC teaching, the decree of Trent on justification affirms that man's cooperation with grace is necessary and real. Grace invites free cooperation and makes it possible and effective. But God and man are not equal partners; human cooperation is itself a gift of grace, since grace brings about free consent. (D 1551–55). Thus RC synergism is not in basic opposition to the *sola gratia* of Luther.

[T. C. O'BRIEN]

SYNERGISTIC CONTROVERSY, a doctrinal dispute among Lutherans from *c.*1550, settled in Art. 2 of the *Formula of Concord. Influenced by the teaching of P. *Melanchthon, such synergists as G. *Major and V. *Strigel defended fallen man's power to cooperate in a limited degree in his conversion. They were opposed by N. *Amsdorf, M. *Flacius Illyricus, and others, who maintained that Martin Luther taught that fallen man is utterly helpless and is a merely passive recipient of grace. The Formula of Concord seeks to express a mediate position. *SYNERGISM.

[T. C. O'BRIEN]

SYNESIS, the moral virtue of coming to a sound practical judgment, the conclusion of a process of deliberation. A virtual part (*pars potentialis*) of the virtue of prudence, it is expressed in an act of right and sincere *conscience, that this should be done or that avoided. It precedes, though it does not ensure, the effective carrying out of the decision through prudence in the most proper sense of the term. This requires the executive command (*imperium*) of the reason and the application (*usus*) of the will to the matter in hand.

[T. GILBY]

SYNESIUS OF CYRENE (*c.*370–*c.*414), Neoplatonist writer and bp. of Ptolemais. A native of Cyrene, S. studied first at Athens, then at Alexandria, where he became a devoted pupil of *Hypatia. The citizens of his province chose him as their ambassador to the Emp. Arcadius to plead for a reduction of taxes. After accomplishing this mission he married a Christian. Again distinguishing himself for public service by putting to flight desert marauders, he was elected bp., although at the time he was apparently not yet baptized. When he hesitated to accept the office, unwilling to abandon either wife or philosophical position, the Patriarch Theophilus consecrated him without requiring that he give up either. Almost all of his surviving works are of a nonreligious nature. Only 12 of his 156 extant letters deal with ecclesiastical matters. He wrote several philosophical essays, one of which is of interest because it defends the moderate enjoyment of pleasure against the demands of exaggerated asceticism. Extant also are 10 hymns that manifest a fusion of Christian and Neoplatonist thought. Works: PG 66:1021–1756; *Letters of Synesius of Cyrene* (tr. and ed. A. Fitzgerald, 1926); *Essays and Hymns of Synesius of Cyrene* (tr. and ed. A. Fitzgerald, 1930).

[R. B. ENO]

SYNGE, JOHN MILLINGTON (1871–1909), Irish poet and playwright. Educated at Trinity College, Dublin, S. studied music in Paris, but was persuaded by W. B. *Yeats to return to Ireland to concentrate on literature and explore the primitive Gaelic language of the people of the Aran Islands off the coast of Galway. S. gleaned sufficient material in his close contact with the people to provide subject matter for his first published play, *Riders to the Sea* (1903), one of the greatest modern tragedies. Other plays include *In the Shadow of the Glen* (1904), *The Well of the Saints* (1905), *The Playboy of the Western World* (1907), *The Tinker's Wedding* (1908), and the posthumous, unfinished *Deirdre of the Sorrows* (1910). All these are considered masterpieces of the Celtic renaissance. S. was the Abbey Theatre's first great discovery, and he wrote for it until his early death. He is considered, with Sean O'Casey, an Abbey playwright of major importance. S.'s writings reveal his genuine lyric quality and his sensitive ear for Anglo-Irish speech, and he passes with honor tests of universality of appeal and of genuine characterization, of skill in the interweaving in the beauty of his prose, of characters, setting, and incident with the perceptible beat of poetic rhythms. BIBLIOGRAPHY: M. Bourgeois, *John Millington Synge and the Irish Theatre* (1965); D. Corkery, *Synge and Anglo-Irish Literature* (1931).

[S. A. HEENEY]

SYNOD (Gr. *sunodos,* a coming together), in general historical usage, an assembly of bishops. The terms "synod" and "council" were used interchangeably until the time of Nicaea (325). Then council came to be used for the ecumenical council, and synod for regional meetings of bishops. The term synod, however, in the RC Church still is sometimes used as an alternate term in conciliar documents of ecumenical councils (see GENERAL COUNCIL). In the Eastern Churches, the synod exercises supreme and decisive authority. In the RC Church, synod is used more specifically for the diocesan synod, which is composed of priests under the presidency of the bishop. Its competence is limited to matters of diocesan discipline, and it has only a consultative function (CIC c. 352–356). Vatican Council II urged greater use of the synod by the bishops of the Church (Vat II BpPast-Off 36). The following articles deal with other specific uses of the term.

[T. C. O'BRIEN]

SYNOD (Diocesan), a consultative body convoked by the diocesan bp every 10 years to recommend legislation for the betterment of the diocese (CIC, c. 356). Such recommendations are enacted into law by the sole power of the bp. (*ibid*. c. 362). The vicar general, diocesan consultors, rural deans, a pastor from each deanery, all pastors of the cathedral city, and superiors representing clerical religious institutes in the diocese, must be included; others may be invited (*ibid*. c. 358).

[T. C. O'BRIEN]

SYNOD (Lutheran), a term used in several senses in Lutheran polity. (1) In Germany it is a body for doctrinal as well as administrative supervision. In Luther's idea the synods of pastors were to safeguard discipline and fidelity to the Scriptures. The synod in its modern sense developed in the 19th cent. with the abandonment of the idea that the civil ruler was also the head of the Church (*summus episcopus*). Church synods are composed of clerical and lay representatives of the local congregations, as well as of delegates from theology and law faculties. (2) In the U.S. the term was first used to designate a whole group of Lutheran congregations organically united. This is the sense of the term in the title, Lutheran Church—Missouri Synod. Many American Lutheran bodies, however, have dropped this use of the term, but the synod as a regional unit within the general church body is retained. (3) An administrative body for a whole Lutheran body, or for one of its districts. The synod represents the local congregations in matters of common concern with regard to ministerial training, educational, social works, and finances. Members are clerical and lay representatives of the local churches.

SYNOD (Moravian), the highest governing body of the *Moravian Church. It is a legislative assembly of clergy and laity meeting at intervals that vary in different regions from 3 to 5 years. Each of the 17 provinces of the Church has its own synod for the election of executives and bishops and for the enactment of legislation to be carried out by the congregations during the intersynodal periods. Executives and administrators of the Church's institutions are responsible to the synod. A worldwide synod, meeting every 10 years, is authoritative in matters of doctrine and coordinates international mission efforts. BIBLIOGRAPHY: W. H. Allen, *Who Are the Moravians?* (1966); *Book of Order, Moravian Church in America* (1954).

[J. R. WEINLICK]

SYNOD (Old Catholic), legislative body for the Church. The Synod governs each national Old Catholic Church; the bishop is chairman of the Synod; members include both priests and laymen representing the parishes. The Synod is empowered to elect the bishop by majority vote. The scope of its rule extends only to administrative affairs of the Church, not to matters of doctrine. Meetings are held annually; an executive council is chosen for the interim, and is composed of the bishop, three priests, and five laymen.

[T. C. O'BRIEN]

SYNOD (Presbyterian), an ecclesiastical governing body in Churches of presbyterian polity. The term is applied both to governing bodies in particular geographical districts in some *Reformed Churches (hence called particular synods in the *Reformed Church in America), and to the corresponding bodies in Presbyterian Churches (called sometimes regional synods). Membership in the regional synod consists of representative clergymen and *elders from the district. It ranks in authority above the *consistory court or *church session of the local congregation and the *classis or *presbytery, and below the general synod (Reformed) or *general assembly (Presbyterian). The presiding officer, who may be an elder, is usually elected annually and is designated the moderator. The synod meets annually; in practice it is often considerably less important than most classes or presbyteries. This framework of presbyterian government originated in the Calvinist churches during the 16th century. The basic principle is that of representative government at each of the four levels. While the general synod or assembly possesses supreme authority in ecclesiastical matters, its authority rises from the local congregations, passes through the classis or presbytery and the regional synod, and is settled finally in the national body. This principle is best illustrated by the fact that the laws the national body passes must receive the approval of the classis or presbytery. Both the regional and general synod exercise a judicial function, receiving and handling appeals from classes or presbyteries. Their other main function is legislative. Both types of synod also administer missionary, evangelistic, and other kinds of Christian activity. The general synod has the additional task of administering the ecumenical relationships of the national body.

[E. EENIGENBURG]

SYNOD (Protestant Episcopal Church), the governing body for the provinces of the Church. There are eight such provinces, into which the dioceses and missionary regions are grouped. These elect as members of the synod one bishop, four priests, and four laymen.

SYNOD, THE HOLY, is the ruling body of the Greek Orthodox Church and its patriarchates. Faith and discipline are the responsibility of the holy synod. Of late development and modeled after the Holy Synod of Russia (1721), they have become a limiting influence on the patriarchs and have at times brought the Church under civil control.

[J. R. AHERNE]

SYNOD OF BISHOPS, a deliberative body in the RC Church constituted by Pope Paul VI's motu proprio, Apostolica sollicitudo, Sept. 15, 1965 (AAS 57 [1965] 775–780) in conformity with Vatican II's teaching on episcopacy in the life of the Church (see Vat II ConstChurch 22). The Council also explicitly recognized the role of the Synod as it ''demonstrates that all bishops in hierarchical communion share in the responsibility for the universal Church'' (Vat II BpPastOff 5; cf. VatII ConstChurch 23). *Apostolica sollicitudo* determined that 85 per cent of the synodal participants were to be elected by the national or regional episcopal conferences. The rest of the body was to be made up of curial officials, representatives of religious institutes, and personal appointees of the Supreme Pontiff. The Synod of Bishops was to be convoked and its agenda set by the pope. The *ordo celebrandi* was set by the Secretariat of State Dec. 8, 1966 (AAS 59 [1967] 91–103), and modified by the Council for the Public Affairs of the Church June 24, 1969 (AAS 61 [1969] 525–539), and further c. Aug 20, 1971 (AAS 63 [1971] 702–704). Five Synods, preceded by consultation in the various episcopal regions in the Church, have been held: 1967, 1969, 1971, 1974, 1977. The 1969 session is considered an extraordinary meeting, therefore the other Synods are enumerated: The First General Assembly of the Synod of Bishops, 1967; The Second, 1971; The Third, 1974; and The Fourth General Assembly, 1977. The Synods have had an impact on the life of the Church, notwithstanding Roman ambivalence about giving collegiality and the Synod as its expression full implementation. The *ordo celebrandi* and its modifications place the assemblies under absolute papal control.

The 1967 Synod, coming soon after the Council, devoted itself to the internal life of the Church: the revision of the CIC, seminaries, liturgy, marriage. The discussions had their impact on subsequent papal and curial directives in these areas. The 1969 Synod was concerned largely with a study of the Synod's own functioning.

The 1971 Synod issued two documents on the topics of its concern: the priesthood and the Church's role in promoting justice and peace. The document *The Ministerial Priesthood* led to further theological reflection in the Church on the pastoral role and vocation of the priest and their adaptation to the times. There is a strong reaffirmation of the discipline of celibacy. The document *Justice in the World* marked a further intensification of the postconciliar Church's new concern and commitment to social justice. One statement particularly has become almost a slogan on the lips of those having special commitment to this ministry: ''Action on behalf of justice and participation in the transformation of the world fully appear to us as a constitutive dimension [*ratio constitutiva*] of the preaching of the Gospel, or in other words, of the Church's mission for the redemption of the human race and its liberation from every oppressive situation'' (USCC ed. p. 34).

The phrase was not received with universal approval, as the discussions of the 1974 Synod made clear. The theme of this, The Third General Assembly, was evangelization. Much of the synodal debate concerned the relationship between evangelization and human development or liberation. The discussions are reflected in the ''Declaration'' made by the Synodal Fathers at the close of the assembly (USCC *Synod of Bishops, 1974*, 18–20). The direction of the debates in both the 1971 and 1974 Synods, esp. on the issue of facing the problems of human rights and human development, reflects the greater presence and voice of the Third World Churches in the universal Church. The 1974 Synod did not issue any document like those of the 1971 Synod. Rather it put its recommendations and discussions into the hands of the Holy Father. The response was Pope Paul VI's last major document, the apostolic exhortation *Evangelii nuntiandi*, Dec. 8, 1975. The exhortation acknowledges the input of the bps.; it addresses the connection of preaching the gospel with the ministry of justice; and it has had marked influence in the life of the Church. In 1977, the International Theological Commission issued a temporizing interpretation of the text from *Justice in the World*, and the controversy on the relationship between evangelization and human liberation goes on.

The 1977 Synod was devoted to the theme of catechetics and catechesis. The assembly is considered to have been less "newsworthy" than the two preceding. Those in the field of catechetics, however, consider the Synod to have made a solid contribution. The Synod did not offer any specific teaching document, but did submit "Message to the People of God" (USCC, *Synod of Bishops 1977*, 5–16) and a set of proposals for the consideration of Pope Paul VI. BIBLIOGRAPHY: Synod 1971, *Ministerial Priesthood; Justice in the World* (USCC 1971); *Synod of Bishops 1974* (USCC 1975); *Synod of Bishops 1977* (USCC 1978); *Living Light* 15 (1978) 1–127, whole issue on Synod 1977; G. Caprile, *Il Sinodo dei vescovi* 1971, 2 v. (1972); *idem, Il Sinodo dei vescovi, 1974* (n.d.); Paul VI, *On Evangelization in the Modern World* (USCC 1976). D. Wuerl, *Priesthood: Catholic Concept Today* (on the 1971 Synod, n.d.).

[T. C. O'BRIEN]

SYNOD OF EVANGELICAL LUTHERAN CHURCHES, a small American Lutheran body organized in Pennsylvania in 1902 as the Slovak Evangelical Lutheran Church. Slovak Lutherans migrated to the U.S. in the latter part of the 19th cent. and shortly after their arrival began to form congregations, the first being in Illinois, Pennsylvania, and Minnesota. Neglected by the mother Church in Europe, they grew but slowly. In 1894, however, preliminary steps were taken to unite the various congregations in the United States. The Synod declared its adherence to the confessions and doctrines of the Lutheran Church and its full agreement in doctrine and practice with the Lutheran Church—Missouri Synod. It joined the *Lutheran Synodical Conference of the Evangelical Lutheran Church in 1908, but it is not a member of the *Lutheran World Federation. It continues to work closely with the Lutheran Church—Missouri Synod, through which it distributes its missionary funds, although it has a mission board of its own. Its teachers and pastors are educated in the colleges and seminaries of the Missouri Synod. For administrative purposes the Synod of

Evangelical Lutheran Churches is divided into three general districts. Synodical meetings are held every 2 years. The denomination's periodical is the *Lutheran Beacon*. BIBLIOGRAPHY: J. Daniel, EncLuthCh 3:2317–18.

[F. E. MASER]

SYNODAL EXAMINERS, see EXAMINERS, SYNODAL.

SYNODICAL CONFERENCE, see LUTHERAN SYNODICAL CONFERENCE.

SYNODS, EARLY CHURCH, meetings of bps., presbyters, and other church leaders to debate and decide on disciplinary, doctrinal, and liturgical issues as they arose. The apostolic council of Jerusalem (Acts 15; Gal 2), on the question of gentiles and the Law, is usually regarded as the first such meeting. In the latter half of the 2d cent., the *Easter controversy (see QUARTODECIMANS) necessitated synods in Palestine, Rome, Gaul, and elsewhere (Eusebius, *Hist. eccl.* 5.23); the *Montanist movement occasioned others (*ibid.* 5.16.10). Several synods seem to have dealt with the NT canon, and, at least in Greece, with "all the important questions" (Tertullian, *De pudicitia* 10; *De jejunio* 13,6). Third-century Carthage held synods on the rebaptism of heretics as early as 220 (Cyprian, *Ep.* 71,4; 73,3), and held seven between 251 and 256 on the same issue and on the question of penance for those who had lapsed during persecution (Cyprian, *Ep.* 55; 57; 64–65; 70–75; see NOVATIANISM). Synods at Rome, Antioch, and perhaps elsewhere dealt with Christological issues associated with *Sabellius and *Paul of Samosata (Eusebius, *Hist. eccl.* 7.27–30). The 4th cent. saw the rise of the ecumenical councils or synods, beginning with Nicaea in 325 (followed by Constantinople in 381, and, in the 5th cent., Ephesus and Chalcedon). The 4th-cent. synods are also important as the first whose canons, or decisions, have been preserved. Among the more significant: Elvira (309), Arles (314), Ancyra (314), Antioch (341), Sardica (343), and Gangra (c.343). Many of the synods seem to have borrowed the procedures of the Roman senate or of municipal government: a typical procedure included a statement of the issue or case to be debated (the *relatio*); the participants' expression of opinion; statement, when possible, of the consensus of the members (the *sententia*); the recording of individual decisions (*placita*). In some cases, synodal letters were sent out to other provinces, communicating the decisions reached. BIBLIOGRAPHY: Hefele-Leclercq v. 1; H. Marot et al. *Le Concile et les conciles* (1960) 19–109; S. Laeuchli, *Power and Sexuality: Emergence of Canon Law at the Synod of Elvira* (1972); H. Hess, *Canons of the Council of Sardica* (1958).

[D. P. EFROYMSON]

SYNOPTIC GOSPELS, the name used to indicate the first three Gospels: Matthew, Mark, and Luke. They share so much of the same material that, for purposes of comparative study, they can be printed in parallel columns in such a way that their correspondences can be seen at a glance. This "seeing together" is the meaning of the Greek word *synopsis,* which was first applied to the Gospels when J. J. Griesbach published them in this three-column form in 1776. Similar though they are, they present surprising divergences, too, and this strange combination of similarities and differences is at the bottom of what is known as the Synoptic Problem.

[J. J. CASTELOT]

SYNOPTIC PROBLEM, the question of the literary interdependence of the three *synoptic Gospels (Mt, Mk, and Lk). The problem arises from the fact that considerable parts of these Gospels are so similar in content, and often in actual language too, that in effect either one or two must be dependent upon the third, or else either two or all three of them must be dependent upon a prior common source or sources. The possible interconnections are so varied and so complex that it is unlikely that any one wholly satisfying explanation will ever be arrived at. Of the various hypotheses so far put forward, no one does complete justice both to the similarities and to the divergences between these Gospels. Broadly speaking, however, the suggested solutions to the problem fall into three main classes: the partial literary dependence of Mt and Lk upon Mk; the partial dependence of all three Gospels upon one or more prior documentary sources; the partial dependence of all three Gospels on a single common fund of oral tradition.

There is widespread agreement that Mk is prior to, and independent of, the Greek Mt and Lk, at any rate in their present form, and that these are dependent upon Mk for their general framework and for at least some of their narrative material. It is also widely held that another prior and independent source has to be postulated to account for the areas—chiefly in the discourse material—in which Mt and Lk agree to some extent against Mk. This source has been called "Q." This "two-source" theory, as it has been called, is radically limited by its failure to allow for the influence of oral tradition not only in the earliest stages of gospel transmission, but also side by side with written tradition right down to the time when the three Gospels were fixed in writing in their present form. Thus two recent scholars, L. Vaganay and X. Léon-Dufour, have in effect renounced the classic "two-source" theory with its exaggerated emphasis on literary interdependence, and formulated in its place a far more complex theory. According to this a single basic gospel was progressively expanded and modified by the interplay of oral and written tradition until three distinct versions of this basic gospel emerged to become our three Synoptic Gospels. While this theory is open to many objections, it does have the merit of being broad and flexible enough to allow for other influences besides purely literary ones, and probably comes somewhat closer to solving the problem. BIBLIOGRAPHY: B. F. Streeter, *Four Gospels. A Study of Origins* (1924); W. R. Farmer, *Synoptic Problem* (1964); F. Grant, *Earliest Gospel* (1943); W. L. Knox, *Sources of the Synoptic Gospels I-II* (1953); X. Léon-Dufour, *Les Évangiles et l'histoire de Jésus* (1963); *idem, Études d'évangile* (1965); L. Vaganay, *Le Problème synoptique* (1954); F. McCool, NCE 13:886–891; J. Cambier et al., *La Formation des évangiles, Recherches Bibliques* (2 v., 1958).

[D. J. BOURKE]

SYON, ABBEY OF, English *Bridgettine house dedicated to the Holy Savior, Our Lady, and St. Bridget and chartered as a double monastery at Isleworth in Middlesex (1415) by Henry V. A center of resistance to Henry VIII's religious policies, it alone refused to surrender. After its suppression in November 1539, many members continued to live in smaller communities and were briefly reestablished under Queen Mary. After dispersion under Elizabeth, the nuns' community survived on the continent; some nuns returned to London from Lisbon in 1811. The nuns' community formally returned to England in 1861 and is now settled at Marley, Devon. BIBLIOGRAPHY: Cottineau 2:3042.

[E. J. DILLON]

SYRIA, predominantly Muslim country of the Middle East, with capital in Damascus. Most of the Muslims are Sunnis, though Shiites form a significant minority. The country also contains important Druse and Christian communities. Monophysite and Melkite (both Orthodox and Uniate) patriarchates are based at Damascus. In past centuries the name "Syria," of uncertain relation to "Assyria," has designated a larger area. The Septuagint used "Syria" for the Hebrew "Aram," and English translations of the OT follow this usage. The ancient Syrian city of Ugarit dates to the 5th millennium B.C., and Semitic culture came to the area with the Amorites in the 3rd millennium. The area has been continuously assaulted by world conquerors—Assyrians in the 8th cent. B.C., Babylonians in the 7th, Persians in the 6th, and Alexander the Great in 333. And over the centuries, Egypt has periodically made its presence felt. The Seleucids moved the capital from Damascus to Antioch, which served as the Roman provincial capital after Pompey conquered Syria in 64 B.C. In the NT, Syria refers to this province. Followers of Jesus were first called Christians in Antioch, and Paul was converted en route to Damascus. After the fall of Jerusalem in 70 A.D., Antioch became the principal Christian center of the region and gained recognition as one of the four patriarchates of the East. Its school of theology became noted for its historical method of biblical study, contrasting with the allegorical method favored by Alexandria. When the Roman Empire divided, Syria came under Eastern, Byzantine rule. Edessa (now Urfa, Turkey) became a major center of Syrian Christianity. Syria became a stronghold of *Monophysitism, identified with Syrian nationalists, while the Greek-oriented supporters of the orthodox line upheld by the emperor became known as Melkites (emperor's men). Nestorius was from Antioch, and

Syria provided much of the strength for *Nestorianism. After the Arab conquest (633–640), a majority of Syrians became Muslims. But the period of Umayyad rule from Damascus (661–750) also produced St *John Damascene. Most Syrian Christians who were not Monophysite or Nestorian allied with Constantinople following the schism of 1054, though the *Maronites have been formally in union with Rome since 1182 and a Uniate hierarchy of Melkites has existed since 1684. Syria was conquered by the Seljuk Turks in the 11th cent., Saladin in the 12th, and Mongols in the 13th. Mamelukes ruled from 1260 to 1516, and then the Ottoman Turks until World War I, when the area was divided between France and England. After World War II it was divided into four states—Syria (independence 1944), Jordan, Lebanon, and Israel.

[T. EARLY]

SYRIAC LANGUAGE IN LITURGY. Syriac, the Eastern Aramaic language originally centered in Edessa, is the classical liturgical language of both the West and East Syrian Churches and the Maronite Church, and was long used, parallel to Greek, in the Byzantine patriarchate of Antioch. Today, it is retained by all the properly Syrian, non-Byzantine, Churches for the entire Divine Office. It is being replaced, in varying degrees by various Churches, with Arabic in the eucharistic and sacramental rites, except in certain W Syrian parishes in the Syrian Djéziret and East Syrian parishes in N Iraq and Iran, containing the surviving speakers of vernacular Syriac dialects. *ARABIC LANGUAGE IN LITURGY.

[A. CODY]

SYRIAN CATHOLIC CHURCH, the Church formed by former members of the W Syrian (Jacobite) Church who have united with Rome. Latin missionary activity had already won a number of Jacobites to the union when a Catholic bishop, Andrew Akhijian, succeeded in obtaining recognition of the Turkish sultan as patriarch of the Syrian nation (*millet*) in 1656. The Jacobites as a whole resisted this step, in which the French consul in Aleppo had a hand; and with Akhijian's episcopal successor the unionistic hierarchy dwindled until, in 1781, four of the six Jacobite bishops elected the Catholic, but formerly Jacobite, Bp. Michael Jarweh as Syrian patriarch. The anti-unionistic party elected another patriarch, who succeeded in obtaining the Sultan's recognition as head of the Syrian nation, and the split of the W Syrian Church into Jacobites and Syrian Catholics was an accomplished fact. Rome confirmed Jarweh as the first Catholic "patriarch of Antioch of the Syrians" in 1783, but it was not until 1830 that the Turkish authorities recognized the independence of the Catholics from the civil jurisdiction of the Jacobite patriarchs. The Catholic center became Sharfeh in Lebanon, location of a seminary and the official residence of the patriarch, although his actual residence for most of the year is Beirut. The W Syrian liturgy and ecclesiastical discipline are re-

tained, but Latinizing influences, evident already in earlier years, succeeded in replacing many Syrian usages with Latin ones in the Synod of Sharfeh (1888). Conversions from the ranks of the Jacobites were numerous in the 19th cent. and the early years of the 20th but have decreased in latter years. The Syrian Catholics today number about 80,000. BIBLIOGRAPHY: W. de Vries, LTK 9:1256. *WEST SYRIAN CHURCH.

[A. CODY]

SYRIAN CHANT. Though research is limited, ancient Syrian melodies not having usually been committed to writing, it is very probable that Syria possessed a body of chant very early in the Christian era and that it flourished from the 3d to the 7th century. Syrian chant was influenced by that of Palestine and it, in turn, influenced the music of both Byzantium and the West. From the time of Severus, patriarch of Antioch (6th cent.), the Syrians had the system of *Oktoechos, a classification, shared with the Byzantines, of melodies into eight groups. Generally regarded as equivalent to the ecclesiastical *modes, they were, however, not "scales" but melodic formulas that had been put together and then concentrated into eight main groups. The Syrians are credited with introducing antiphonal and responsorial singing into their services, a practice which was eventually adopted in the West. A second important influence was the Syrian penchant for singing praise in versified poetry. This singing of hymns became very popular in the East and the West. The Syrian, St. Ephraim, was among the first whose hymns were used in the liturgy. BIBLIOGRAPHY: Reese MusMA.

[M. T. LEGGE]

SYRIAN (JACOBITE) CHURCH OF ANTIOCH, an American archdiocese of the *West Syrian or "Jacobite" Church. There are about 4,000 faithful in five parishes and the archbishop, who resides in Hackensack, N.J., is dependent on the Syro-Jacobite Patriarch of *Antioch.

[F. T. RYAN]

SYRIAN CHURCH IN INDIA, a general term to designate the native Christians, non-Latin Catholics and non-Protestants, in the present state of Kerala. They often call themselves the St. Thomas Christians because of the tradition that the Apostle Thomas established Christianity in India. It is certain that there were Christians in that region before the 6th cent. and quite possibly about the 4th century. Strongly influenced, and perhaps dependent upon, the Church in Persia, they used the Syriac language in their liturgy and consequently came to be known as Syrian Christians. Not much is known of their early history, but with the arrival of the Portuguese (1498), the native Christians in India spontaneously renewed communion with Rome, which had never been formally broken. Difficulties soon arose, however, because the Portuguese insisted on placing the Church under royal control (Padroado); and the W bishops, distrustful of the Syriac ceremonies and suspicious of *Nestorianism, subjected the native Church to Latin prelates and introduced Latin elements into their liturgy. In 1653 a number of them broke away. Those who still remained in union with Rome, known as *Malabars, were without a bp. of their own for centuries. They now have their own native bps. and ecclesiastical organization; their rite is being restored to its true form; and the vernacular, Malayalam, is replacing Syriac in the liturgy. At present the Malabar Church is very flourishing with about a million and a half faithful. The group which separated from Rome in 1653 turned to the *West Syrian Church from which they receive their bishops. In the course of the 19th cent., several groups broke away and formed various Protestant Churches, some of which have recently reunited in the Church of South India. In 1930, another group returned to union with Rome and are known as *Malankars. Those still not in union with Rome, numbering perhaps a million, are divided into several small groups. BIBLIOGRAPHY: L. W. Brown, *Indian Christians of St. Thomas* (1956); E. Tisserant, *Eastern Christianity in India* (1957).

[G. T. DENNIS]

SYRIAN RITE, the rite of the Syrian Catholic Church of the patriarchate of Antioch, which goes back to the split of the Monophysites from the orthodox church in the 5th cent. Though contacts existed with the Roman Church by individual patriarchs and bps. since the 13th cent., a separate Catholic Syrian Church with a hierarchy of its own came into being only with Andrew Akidjian, bp. of Aleppo from 1656, and patriarch of all Syrians from 1662. Because of persecution from the non-Catholic Syrians, only with the election of Abp. Michael Jarweh of Aleppo as patriarch for the Catholics, and of another one for the Orthodox (Jacobites), did the Church begin to consolidate its life. Because of persecution from the Ottoman government, the Syrian Catholic patriarch resided successively at Sharfeh (Lebanon), Aleppo (Syria), Mardin (Turkey) and Beirut (Lebanon), where the patriarchate was transferred by the famous Syriac scholar and liturgist Mar Ignatius Ephrem II Rahmani. The great reorganizer of the Church was Patriarch Ignatius Tappouni (1929–1967), the first Syrian cardinal. Many Orthodox Syrians joined him together with their Abp. Mar Hanna Gandour (d. 1961). Since the visit of the Orthodox Patriarch Mar Ignatius Yacoub III to Rome in October 1971, the relations between the two branches of the Syrian Church of Antioch have become cordial. Patriarch Ignatius Antun II Hayek heads this church of 80,000 faithful in nine dioceses or patriarchal vicariates.

[J. MADEY]

SYRIAN TEXT, see BIBLE TEXTS.

SYRIANUS (5th cent. A.D.), Neoplatonic philosopher. He was scholarch of the Platonic Academy at Athens (431 A.D.) and he was the teacher of *Proclus. He composed commentaries on works of Plato and Aristotle and was sharply critical of Aristotle in defending Plato's theory of ideas against him. Under the influence of Iamblichus he tried to establish a harmony in the teachings of Plato, the Pythagoreans, Orphics, and the *Chaldaean* and related theurgic literature. BIBLIOGRAPHY: P. Merlan, LexAW 2965–66; Copleston 1:477–478; Ueberweg 1:624–625.

[M. R. P. MCGUIRE]

SYRO-MALABAR, a term relating to the Christians native to the region called Malabar along the SW coast of India. Sometimes they are called Thomas Christians, since they claim to be descendants of the early Christian Church formed by the Apostle. The original Malabar Christians are believed to have been converts of the missionary efforts of the East Syrian Church. From the earliest times, they made use of the Chaldean rite, with Syriac as the liturgical language. Traditionally they received bps. from Babylon (Bagdad), Mesopotamia. After the Synods of Goa (1585) and Diamper (1599), the use of the Syro-Malabar rite was more or less discontinued. Ancient books containing the liturgy of Mesopotamia were destroyed and many Western rites and formulas were translated into Syriac. To the present day, the liturgy is celebrated in a westernized form of the Chaldean rite using Syriac and Malayalam. The Syro-Malabarese have jurisdiction over two archdioceses, 14 dioceses and one exarchate. Their total membership is approximately 3 million. BIBLIOGRAPHY: Orient Catt 379–392; D. Attwater, CCE.

[R. A. TODD]

SYROPOULOS, SYLVESTER, Byzantine ecclesiastic and historian, who accompanied Joseph II, patriarch of Constantinople (1416–39) to Italy for the Council of Florence. S. was apparently forced by the Emperor to sign the decree of union, but on returning to Constantinople he was an ardent foe of the decree. He is chiefly known for his Memoirs, edited in 1660 by the Anglican bp., Robert Chreyghton, entitled *Vera historia unionis non verae* (an authentic account of a union that was not authentic). His point is that the decree was signed under duress. It is an important source for understanding the Council, esp. the backstage intrigue among the Greeks. There is no record of S.'s life after the fall of Constantinople (1453). BIBLIOGRAPHY: J. Gill, *Council of Florence* (1959).

[E. J. DILLON]

SYSTEMATIC THEOLOGY (Gr. *systēma,* from *synistanai,* to place together), a type of theology that methodically and in the light of faith tries to organize all divinely revealed truths and their explanations according to some form of regular, intrinsic, and rational plan, connection, interdependence, etc. It is usually based on a comprehensive exhibition of essential principles, or dogmatic, historico-salvational, moral, existential facts, and attempts to form one organized and intelligible whole, i.e., a theological system, or a synthesis. Systematic theology is not an arbitrary creation of man because it has profound roots in the unity of the natural and supernatural orders and of the divine economy of salvation. Thus its task is also to detect the nexus between the mysteries of faith and to establish harmony between faith and reason by illumining the unity among the ontological, logical, and semantic orders. Since the time of *John Damascene (c.650–c.750) and his work *Pēgē gnōseōs* (including *De fide orthodoxa*), systematic theology, by integration and reduction to one synthesized system of the results of all sciences, tended to an ideal of an all-embracing wisdom. However, perfect wisdom or a perfect theological system cannot be reached because the divine revelation as a historic fact and a salvific message expresses infinite and incomprehensible truths concerning being and the objective historico-salvational facts. In different branches of theology, different types of systematization are possible: e.g., dogmatic theology uses a historic (also economic) or logical plan (i.e., logical concatenation of the revealed mysteries). Moral theology has been systematized, for example, according to the Decalogue, the virtues, the gifts of the Spirit, modern personalist phenomenology, etc. Oriental Christianity elaborated a twofold synthesis: theology (i.e., Trinity, or the necessary mystery of God in himself) and economy (i.e., God in his free mystery or activity, *ad extra*: Christ, Church, Sacraments, *eschata*). BIBLIOGRAPHY: G. F. Van Ackeren, NCE 14:39–49; A. Menne, s.v. System, LTK 9:1264; Y. M. J. Congar, *La Foi et la théologie* (1962); M. Schmaus, *Katholische Dogmatik* (6th ed., 1960) 1.1.

[P. B. T. BILANIUK]

SYZYGY (Gr. *Syn*, together; *Zygon*, yoke), a term in *Gnostic, and esp. *Valentinian thought, for the union or coupling of any two of those heavenly principles or archons (usually one masculine and one feminine) that emanate from the Absolute and that account for the origin of the material world and the human predicament in it. BIBLIOGRAPHY: W. Foerster, *Gnosis* (2 v., 1972, 1974).

[D. P. EFROYMSON]

SZÁNTÓ, ISTVÁN (Arator; 1541–1612), Hungarian Jesuit, missionary, writer. He helped create the Hungarian College at Rome, which became part of the Collegium Germanicum-Hungaricum. From 1579 until 1600 he worked as part of the Jesuit mission seeking to revive the Church in Transylvania. After expulsion of the Society from Transylvania, S. spent the remainder of his life at Olmütz, Austria, working on a translation of the Bible into Magyar and on other literary projects.

[R. J. LITZ]

SZARZYNSKI, STANISLAUS (Stanislaw Sylwester; 17th–18th cent.), Polish composer. S. was a Cistercian monk and composer of a Mass, motets for voices and instruments, a masterly sonata, and other compositions that have been lost.

[M. T. LEGGE]

SZEPTYCKY, ANDREAS (1865–1944), metropolitan of Lvov in the Catholic *Ukrainian rite. Having discovered that his boyar family had abandoned its Ukrainian heritage to become Latin rite Poles, S. returned to his ancestral rite, entered the *Basilians, and took the name of Andrew. Consecrated bp. of Stanislavov in 1899, he was appointed abp. of Lvov in 1901, a position he filled with distinction until his death. After Pope Piux X's elevation, S. received what amounted to patriarchal rights enabling him to foster the growth of the Eastern Catholic rites. He established a Greek Catholic diocese for Slavs in the U.S. in 1907, another in 1912 for Canada and Brazil, and at the end of World War I, a Russian Catholic exarchate. He was one of the few Catholic Orientals in his day who realized the problems of *latinization, and by his European tour in 1921, he helped to make others aware of them. A pilot program of progressive delatinization was centered around his Studite monks, founded at Sknylov in 1906. Convinced that Eastern Catholics by holding more firmly to Orthodox forms would serve as a guarantee that union did not mean abandoning an ancient and valid liturgical and cultural heritage, he sought Western help. Efforts to further this work and to assist in the formation of these Studite monks led S. to become involved with Lambert *Beauduin, Michel *d'Herbigny, and Cyril *Korolevsky. Today only a handful of his Studites remain in a Roman suburb, but his efforts at delatinizing contributed to a better understanding between East and West. BIBLIOGRAPHY: C. Korolevsky, *Le Métropolite André Szepticky* (1921); E. Borschak, *Un Prélat Ukrainien le Métropolite Chaptickyj 1865–1944* (1946).

[S. QUITSLUND]

T

TAANACH, see THAANACH.

TABB, JOHN BANISTER (1845–1909), American poet. When the Civil War broke out, T. enlisted in the confederate army, was taken prisoner in 1864, and while in the "Bull-Pen" at Point Lookout formed an enduring friendship with Sidney Lanier. Released in 1865, he went to Baltimore to study music. Here he met Alfred Curtis, an Episcopalian minister, who later entered the RC Church and who was instrumental in T.'s conversion to Roman Catholicism (1872). T. entered St. Mary's Seminary (1881) and was ordained in 1884, after which he returned to St. Charles College as an English teacher. He privately published a small volume in 1882, but for the most part his poetry appeared in various periodicals. Editors at first rejected his poems because they did not understand them, but after 1890 his poems were welcomed. The collection entitled *Poems* (1894) was acclaimed immediately. His poems, collected into five volumes, are permeated by his devoutness and illuminated by his highly cultivated and gifted mind. BIBLIOGRAPHY: F. A. Litz, *Father Tabb: A Study of His Life and Works* (1928); A. Meynell, *Selection from the Verses of John B. Tabb* (1910); J. B. Tabb, *Letters—Grave and Gay, and other Prose* (ed. F. E. Litz, 1950).

[S. A. HEENEY]

TABEEL, name of two persons: (1) The father of the man whom Rezin of Syria and Pekah of Israel sought to make king of Judah instead of Ahaz (Is 7.6–7); Isaiah told Ahaz that God would not let the plan succeed. (2) The official who wrote Artaxerxes complaining of the Jews' rebuilding Jerusalem (Ezra 4.7).

[T. EARLY]

TABENNISI, a settlement in the Thebaid of upper Egypt on the E bank of the Nile, where St. *Pachomius (*c.*320) founded his first monastery. There he developed his rule for the common life; eventually Tabennisi had more than 1,000 monks. All dwelt behind the same walls, but within the monastery the community was divided into groups of 20 according to their work. By the time of Pachomius's death, eight other monasteries had been founded from Tabennisi. BIBLIOGRAPHY: Palladius of Helenopolis, *Lausiac History* (ed. C. Butler, 1898–1904); F. van der Meer and C. Mohrmann, *Atlas of the Early Christian World* (1958).

[R. B. ENO]

TABERNACLE, from the Latin *tabernaculum* (tent), a term with two distinct meanings, one with reference to Jewish, the other to Christian usage.

The Jewish tabernacle was the portable shrine or tent-like sanctuary of ancient Israel, constructed under Moses and used during the wanderings in the wilderness and until the erection of a permanent temple at Jerusalem under Solomon. It was considered the dwelling of Yahweh and was held to embody the presence of God in the midst of the Israelite people. The biblical foundations of the tabernacle and an account of its structure are to be found in Ex 25–31 and 35–40. The tabernacle consisted of a court and an inner shrine where the Ark of the Covenant was kept.

Tabernacle in the Christian sense refers to the shrine, generally a conspicuous and sometimes highly ornamental receptacle, used to contain the sacred vessels in which the Blessed Sacrament is reserved. The custom of reserving the Blessed Sacrament in churches began about the 4th cent. for the purpose of giving communion to the sick, but until the 16th cent. there was no uniform practice as to how it was to be kept. Sometimes it was reserved in the sacristy or kept in a movable vessel suspended before the altar. In the 16th cent. it became customary to reserve it in a repository fixed to the main altar, a custom that was sanctioned by law in 1614, although other forms of reservation were not forbidden until 1863. Since the reform of the liturgy by Vatican II, it is agreed that the best place for reserving the Blessed Sacrament is in a chapel suitable for the private devotion of the people. If this is not possible, reservation should be at a side altar or other appropriately adorned place. In either case, the tabernacle should be safe and inviolable, of a size and construction appropriate to the church, and prominent yet not obtrusive.

[B. ROSENDALL]

TABERNACLES, FEAST OF, the greatest Israelite feast, called sometimes the feast of Yahweh, or simply the feast. There are two aspects to the feast: the Canaanite and the Israelite. Israel assimilated Canaanite festive traditions and gave them a distinctively Israelite interpretation. An early Canaanite name for this feast was "Feast of Ingathering." It was the original pilgrimage festival and the principal harvest festival, coming at the end of the season at vintage time. The grape festival was the time of rejoicing par excellence for agricultural peoples. Israel had its yearly feast of the Lord at Shilo, a time of special yearly sacrifices. The outlines of such a feast can be discerned in the Books of Judges and Samuel, and was apparently marked by the great number of sacrifices and a spirit of vintage revelry. At an early date Israel chose this high point of the agricultural year to celebrate its own covenant-renewal feast of Yahweh. Gradually this tent festival of covenant renewal, typical of nomadic peoples, became joined with the Canaanite festival of booths, named after the makeshift booths constructed of branches and serving as guardposts during the olive harvest and left standing during the grape harvest. Tents gave way to booths, and the traditional "tent of meeting" gave way to the temple at Shilo and later at Jerusalem. The dedication of the temple, as narrated in 1 Kings, coincided with the feast of Tabernacles. The solemn public reading of the Torah was also linked with that feast. In fact the feast was probably linked with all the key elements of Israelite faith and history: the Covenant, the Torah, the choice of Zion and Zion's King, the Temple, and the gift of the Land, and incidentally with the period of desert wandering when Israel lived in tents. Tabernacles was probably also linked with the New Year celebration and the Day of Atonement; only after the Exile were these latter feasts celebrated separately. New Year then fell on the 1st day of Tishri (September); Atonement on the 10th day; Tabernacles began on the 15th day and lasted 7 days, with 2 extra days, culminating in the Simhath Torah, the Joy of the Law. Readers of the NT will discern the presence of the feast. A prominent aspect of it was the joyful processions during the singing of the Hallel, with celebrants carrying branches of palms bound together into festal plumes with citrus fruit attached. The branches were waved aloft at the cry for salvation in Ps 118, called *Hoshianah Rabbah.* Prominent rites centered on water brought from the pool of Siloam, and there were recurrent all-night festivals of light. The Canaanite heritage with its basic nature mysticism endured, with water and light symbolizing fertility and life. This symbolism is taken up by the Gospel of John in chapters 7 and 8, when on the Feast of Tabernacles Jesus refers to faith as living water and to himself as the light of the world.

[E. J. DILLON]

TABLATURE, a method of musical notation (*c.* 15th–16th cent.) in which figures, letters, or other signs were used as opposed to the system of placing notes on a staff (notation). There were different systems in different countries as well as various systems for the same instrument. The most important tablatures were those for the keyboard and for the lute. Tablatures, directing the placement of the fingers rather than telling the performer what notes to play, are in use today for such instruments as the guitar and the ukulele.

[M. T. LEGGE]

TABLE OF THE NATIONS, traditional name for the list in Gen ch. 10 (see also 1 Chr 1). The table, which continues the genealogy of Gen ch 5, attempts to organize the then-known peoples of the world in terms of descendants of Noah. It lists first the descendants of Japheth, then those of Ham, and concludes with those of Shem, ancestor of Abraham and the Hebrew people. Although the table is not altogether in harmony with the conclusions of modern ethnographers, it is considered remarkable as the first attempt to show ethnic relationships on so wide a scale. Among its notable aspects is the assumption of a common ancestry for the entire human race.

Scholars who analyze the table according to the *documentary hypothesis conclude that verses 8–19 and 25–30 are from the *Yahwist (J) and most of the remainder from the *Priestly source (P). Blending of the sources has resulted in some inconsistencies. Havilah, for example, is listed as a son of Cush, a Hamite, in verse 7, but a son of Joktan, a Shemite, in verse 29.

The nations covered in the table extended from Transcaucasia to Ethiopia and from Iran to the Aegean. As descendants of Japheth it named Cimmerians (Gomer), Medes, Ionians (Javan), Scythians (Ashkenaz), Cypriotes (Elisha and Kittim), and others. They were generally nations along the north of the Fertile Crescent and extending to the west. The main subdivisions of the Hamites are Cush, Egypt (Mizraim), Canaan, and Put (perhaps Cyrene). Egypt was called the father of the Philistines and the Cretans. They had no language or ethnic connection, however, so the connection was probably made for geographic and political reasons.

The Shemites (Semites) comprise the Assyrians, Aramaeans, and various tribes of Arabia. The unrelated Elamites are included possibly for geographic reasons. Babylon is unaccountably omitted. The identity of Arpachshad (verse 24), ancestor of the Hebrews (Eber), is unknown.

The table's primary interest is the Hebrews; therefore, Shem is listed last, although he was the eldest son of Noah. The descendants of Eber's son Peleg are not given, but the following chapter (11.10–26) lists the direct descent from Shem to Abraham. Chapters 10 and 11 provide the background for the story of Abraham, which begins with chapter 12.

Lists for each of the three groups conclude with variations of the same formula: "These are the sons of Japheth in their lands, each with his own language, by their families, in their nations'' (verse 5; cf. verses 20 and 31).

Composition of the table in its present form dates possibly from the Exile, though the general ideas reflected in it were current earlier. Some scholars judge that it reflects the world situation of c.1200–1000 B.C. Canaan, e.g., was under nominal Egyptian control c.1500–1200 B.C. and was perhaps listed with Egypt as a Hamite nation for that reason (verse 6).

[T. EARLY]

TABLÎTŌ, in West Syrian churches, a tablet of wood or stone, consecrated by a bishop, placed on the center of the altar and covered by a large square of colored cloth, usually over two smaller ones. On it the sacred vessels rest (among the Jacobites, even from one ceremony to the next). It does not contain relics.

[A. CODY]

TAB‘Ō (seal), the West Syrian eucharistic bread, also called *bûkrō* (firstborn), *perîstō* (cake), and (esp. Syrian Catholic) *pûrshōnō* (separation, Arabic *burshânah*). Among the Jacobites it is still a leavened cake some three-eighths of an inch thick, with a little olive oil and salt added to the dough; while among the Syrian Catholics today, it is usually a thin unleavened wafer with a little salt but no oil in the dough. In either case it is about three inches in diameter, with the upper surface divided into 12 sections by two perpendicularly intersecting diameters and four alternating radii extending from an inner circle. The sections are marked with a cross and called *margōnîtō* (pearl) or *gemûrtō* (live coal) and are separated in the rite of fraction.

[A. CODY]

TABOO, from the Polynesian term *tapu* (*ta,* to mark or strike; *pu,* exceedingly), meaning certain traditional prohibitions that must be observed because of the power and sacred significance which some things possess. Thus any object, action, or person which has or acquires force of a more or less uncertain nature is or becomes taboo. This power (*mana*) is seen to be ultimately derived from the *holy or numinous, and thus regarded with awe. Many primitive societies have rules concerning situations such as pregnancy, birth, initiation, death, or even eating in the presence of the chieftain. In addition to the taboos given by tradition, there are those which are made by chieftains and persons who have *mana*, in order to protect their property or rights they claim for trees and other objects. While a priest is taken into possession by the godhead, it becomes taboo to work, to make fire, etc. Taboos work by themselves, i.e., the one who breaks them will automatically be punished by the power he abused (lack of success, illness, death), although occasionally their observance may be enforced by society. Since similar phenomena of prohibition can be observed in other cultures, the term taboo is no longer restricted to the Polynesian situation. It is used as a collective term for those socially effective prohibitions demanded for

no other reason than that of an immanent sanction and the integrity of the symbolic world structure. The ambivalence of the sacred, subconscious fears, the need for social stability, and magical certainty and power are a few instances that account for the taboo-conscience as a crosscultural phenomenon, not restricted to any particular segment of mankind. BIBLIOGRAPHY: J. G. Frazer, *Golden Bough* (3d ed., 1911); S. Freud, *Totem and Taboo* (1918); F. Steiner, *Taboo* (1956); M. Eliade, *Patterns in Comparative Religion* (tr. R. Sheed, 1963) 14–19. *SYMBOL; *SACRED AND PROFANE.

[W. DUPRÉ]

TABOR, MOUNT, the modern Jebel et-Tor, an isolated hill less than 1850 feet high, located in the NE corner of the Valley of Jezreel, 6 miles E-SE of Nazareth, 12 miles W-SW of the S end of the Sea of Galilee. Because its sides rise steeply out of the plain to a dome-shaped summit, it has a striking appearance and was considered comparable in majesty to the much higher mountains Hermon and Carmel. Tabor dominates two important routes: the E-W route connecting the Valley of Jezreel and the Sea of Galilee; the N-S road between Beth-shan and Damascus. Tabor is first mentioned by name in Joshua (19.22) in the description of the borders of the various tribal territorial allotments. Tabor is a border point common to Issachar, Naphtali, and Zebulun. Barak selected it as a base from which to rally Naphtali and Zebulun against Sisera (Jg 4). The Midianite kings killed the brothers of Gideon there (Jg 8). There was a sanctuary to Yahweh there (Hos 5.1). During Hellenistic times the Syrian tyrants fortified Tabor. Christian legend associates it with the unnamed mount of the Transfiguration (Matt 17.1). The summit of the mount has seen many churches. The present Basilica of the Transfiguration was completed by the Franciscan Fathers in 1923. BIBLIOGRAPHY: C. Kopp, *Holy Places of the Gospels* (1963) 242–247.

[E. J. DILLON]

TABORGA, MIGUEL DE LOS SANTOS (1833–1905), abp. of Sucre, Bolivia, politician and historiographer. After serving as parish priest, T. made his mark on the political scene as a delegate to various legislatures and as a twice-elected senator from Chuquisaca. When anti-Catholic sentiment manifested itself in Bolivia late in the 19th cent., he fought against criticism of the Church and the secularization of Bolivian society and government in the weekly newspaper *El Cruzado*, published in Sucre. In 1898, T. was named abp. of Sucre, in which office he served until his death. However, his most permanent contribution to Bolivia was made in the field of historiography. His careful studies of basic source materials helped clarify both the major facts and dates in Bolivian history. Among his most important works are: *Documentos para la historia de Bolivia; Aclaraciones sobre el 25 de Mayo; Crónicas de la catedral de Sucre; Idea de una introducción a la historia de Bolivia.* BIBLIOGRAPHY: L. Paz, *Estudios históricos de Monseñor Taborga* (1913).

[T. J. RYAN]

TABORITES, a sect of Hussite extremists. The name comes from the theocratic hill town near Prague where they settled. The teaching of the Taborites went far beyond the *Utraquists, for they advocated a communistic society, denied the *Real Presence, and rejected all the sacraments except baptism and the Lord's Supper (see D 1259). Among them also, there were undercurrents of *Adamite and *Picardian doctrine. The Taborites were crushed and scattered by the combined Utraquist and Catholic forces in 1434; but adherents and ideas of the sect influenced the beginnings of the Bohemian Brethren. BIBLIOGRAPHY: Bihlmeyer-Tüchle 2:442–443; F. G. Heymann, *John Žižka and the Hussite Revolution* (1955). *HUSSITES.

TACCHI VENTURI, PIETRO (1861–1956), Jesuit ecclesiastical historian. Born in San Severino, Marche (Macerata), Italy, he entered the Society of Jesus in 1878 and in addition to his studies in philosophy and theology obtained a doctorate in letters from the Univ. of Rome in 1891. Assigned in 1896 to write the history of the Jesuits in Italy, he began the meticulous research that resulted in two volumes published in three parts, bringing his account of the Society to the death of Ignatius Loyola (1556). In addition to his historical work he wrote for *La Civiltà Cattolica*, served as the secretary of the Society (1914–21), acted as an intermediary for the Holy See in the negotiations with the Italian government before the Lateran Treaty (1929) and during the crisis over Catholic Action (1931). He also served on the editorial board responsible for the publication of the *Enciclopedia Italiana* and *Genio italiano all' Estero*, on the committee of the *Istituto di studi romani*, and as executive editor for *Storia delle religioni* (1934). He also wrote the well–received *Lo stato della religione in Italia alla metà del secolo XVI* (1908) and *Opere storiche del P. Matteo Ricci* (1911–13), which remains an indispensable work. BIBLIOGRAPHY: M. Scaduto, AHSJ 25 (1956): 755–756.

[T. J. RYAN]

TACHÉ, ALEXANDRE ANTONIN (1823–94), Oblate of Mary Immaculate, abp. of St. Boniface, Manitoba. After his ordination (1845), he was sent to the Manitoba Indian missions. He was made coadjutor to Bp. Provencher in 1851 and succeeded him as bp. of St. Boniface in 1853. While at Vatican Council I, he was forced by the Red River Rebellion (1869–70) to return to his diocese. He devoted himself to securing a just peace settlement and took the case of the Métis to government commissions. In 1871 he was made archbishop. BIBLIOGRAPHY: J. P. A. Benoît, *Vie de Msgr. Taché* (2 v., 1904).

[R. K. MacMASTER]

TACITUS, CORNELIUS (c.55-after 115 A.D.), Roman historian. He began a political career under Vespasian and continued it under his successors, becoming consul in 97 under Nerva, and proconsul of Asia under Trajan, probably in 112–113. His earliest extant work, the *Dialogus de oratoribus*, treats of the status of oratory. The *Agricola* and *Germania* are monographs on his father-in-law and Germany respectively. His *Historiae* recorded the events from the death of Nero to that of Domitian and his *Annales* those from the death of Augustus to that of Nero. Large sections of these latter works, upon which T.'s reputation as a historian rests, have been lost. T. aimed at writing objectively (*sine ira et studio—Annales* 1.1), but the terrors of Domitian's reign seem to have warped his outlook, making him interpret earlier events in too pessimistic a fashion. He has a tendency to neglect social, economic, and political factors and to interpret everything in the light of personal motives. This adds to the interest of his narrative but hardly to its impartiality. He imitated the asymmetry of Sallust and Thucydides and is a master of irony and the sententious phrase. BIBLIOGRAPHY: R. Syme, *Tacitus* (1958).

[M. J. COSTELLOE]

TACTUS, Renaissance musical term, a complete lowering and raising of the hand, the time of a beat. The tactus was represented by a *semibreve* (whole note) and is estimated to have been at a metronome speed of 60–80. Whereas the beat varies, the tactus was a constant, normal pulse. BIBLIOGRAPHY: Reese MusR 179–180.

[M. T. LEGGE]

TADDEO DI BARTOLO (1362–1422), Sienese painter who introduced the Northern International Gothic style into Tuscany. T.'s early work, based on Duccio and Simone Martini, is marked by hieratic figures, with voluminous drapery, the somber forms turned inward in the manner of B. di Fredi, with gold on garments (after 1393) as used by Barnata da Modena (*Crucifixion*, 1395). T. began the International Style (1397) in a *Baptism* with Gothic convoluted draperies, reaching a climax in his masterpiece, the frescoes of the Palazzo Pubblico, Siena, in the *Life of the Virgin*, showing animated figures and deeply sculptured drapery in refined and elegant compositions. In a final period (1409–22) T. is related to Giotto (*St. Christopher,* 1412) though the ponderous works lack grandeur (*Volterra Altarpiece*). A bland uniformity because of many assistants contributed to T.'s decline. BIBLIOGRAPHY: E. Borsook, *Mural Painters of Tuscany* (1960).

[M. J. DALY]

TAGHAKAN, Armenian parish council, composed of laymen elected by the parish.

[A. CODY]

TAGHARAN (Tal'aran), Armenian hymnal containing the variable songs of the Eucharistic Liturgy, sung by the clerics forming the choir.

[A. CODY]

TAGORE, RABINDRANATH (1861–1941), Bengali poet. Born in Calcutta, after his education at St. Xavier's Univ. there and at the Univ. of London, this greatest of modern Bengali authors of prose and poetry began his literary career in 1880. The publication in English of *Gitanjali* (1912), a collection of some of his Bengali songs, and the award of the Nobel prize for literature (1913) facilitated the translation of other volumes of his poetry (e.g., *The Gardener, The Crescent Moon, Fruit Gatherings*), his plays (e.g., *Chitra, The Post Office,* and *The King of the Dark Chamber*), and his novels (*The Home and the World* and *Gora*). After World War I, he not only lectured throughout the world but founded an international center at Shantineketan. Inspired by Gandhi, he wrote the play *Mukta-Dhāra* (1922), affirming spiritual values in the face of growing technology, and later composed *The Child* (1931) after prophetically envisaging the possible martyrdom of Gandhi. He painted and continued his writing almost to the end of his days, a poet of love, nature, God, and man. BIBLIOGRAPHY: *Collected Poems and Plays* (1956); K. R. Kripalani, *Rabindranath Tagore: A Biography* (1962).

[T. J. RYAN]

TAGRÎT (Arab., Takrît, colloquially Tikrît), town on the Tigris, *c.* 30 miles upstream from Baghdad, the metropolitan see of the West Syrians in the East (629–1156). The city was also the center of a type of W Syrian liturgy with marked local particularities (often shared with Nestorians), which is still in evidence in certain Jacobite centers of Iraq. Some usages have been adopted in the Syrian Catholic festive offices. Tagrît is often identified (erroneously) with Maipherqat, another city of Christian historical interest in the area. BIBLIOGRAPHY: J.-M. Fiey, *L'Orient syrien* 8 (1963) 299–341.

[A. CODY]

TAIGI, ANNA MARIA, BL. (1769–1837), Trinitarian tertiary and mystic. Born in Siena, she was brought to Rome by her family in 1774 and there grew up in circumstances of suffering, hard labor, and degradation. In 1789, she married Domenico Taigi, a valet at the Palazzo Chigi, to whom she was to bear seven children. She joined the Third Order of the Trinity in 1790 and from that time was favored with extraordinary graces, including the experience of a "mystic sun," a luminous globe surrounded by a crown of thorns in which she could read future events. To her voluntary austerities undertaken for the conversion of sinners and the needs of the Church, she brought to bear a heroic patience in caring for a hot–tempered husband, a sickly mother, and in suffering periods of spiritual aridity and darkness of spirit. She was frequently consulted by Popes Leo XII and Gregory XVI as well as by Napoleon's mother and uncle, Card. Fesch. She was beatified May 30, 1920. BIBLIOGRAPHY: C. Salotti, *La Beata Anna Maria Taigi, secondo la storia e la critica* (1922); AAS 11 (1919) 55ff; 133ff.

[T. J. RYAN]

TAILO, ST. (6th cent.), monk from S Wales, who must have been an important figure in his day. His ministry must have centered in the monastery at Llandeilo Fawr in Car-

marthenshire. His cultus is evidenced by the abundance of places and churches named for him throughout S Wales and also in Brittany at Landeleau in the diocese of Quimper.

[E. J. DILLON]

TAINE, HIPPOLYTE (1828–93), French philosopher, critic, and historian. Although he remained a theist, T. lost his Catholic faith by the age of 15. He sought to fuse positivistic elements with German idealism in formulating a philosophy to synthesize experience by extending the method of the natural sciences to other disciplines. In aesthetics he explained literature and art mechanically as the interaction between the artist's dominant synthesizing faculty and the determining factors of race, environment, and historical moment. Religious and philosophical systems also result from such forces; they have no absolute value and reflect only a particular culture's *Weltanschauung*. Scientific history will show man to be governed by laws as determining as those regulating the material universe. He posited a physiological basis of personality, concluding that mental and physical acts are two aspects of the same process and that the self is not a fixed substantial entity but a series of mental events. If statements like "virtue and vice are only products like vitriol and sugar" give a mechanistic tone to his ethics, T. nevertheless considered moral responsibility to be compatible with philosophical determinism. Under the influence of Hegel and Spinoza, he conceived God as an immanent force working through the historical process in a Nature constituted by a hierarchy of necessities. He hoped his method would eventually yield a scientific metaphysics. Despite his initial hostility to Christianity, provoked largely by personal experience of clerical interference, T. came to acknowledge the Church's creative and beneficent role in French history. He continued, however, to view clericalism as an obstructive force, although the experience of the Paris Commune (1871) reinforced his middle-class conservatism and the conviction that revolution and radicalism were the real enemies of the nation. He saw some possibility of a reconciliation between positivism and a theology of liberal Protestant hue. He was repelled by Puritanism but attracted to Anglicanism, and he requested burial according to a Protestant rite, although he adopted no particular creed. BIBLIOGRAPHY: S. J. Kahn, *Science and Aesthetic Judgment: A Study of Taine's Critical Method* (1953).

[G. E. GINGRAS]

TAIWAN (FORMOSA), island 110 mi E of the Chinese mainland; the territory held by the Republic of Free China (36,000 sq mi; pop [1976 est.] 15,338,995). Spaniards and Portuguese began to occupy Taiwan in the 16th cent.; at the end of the 17th cent., it became part of China. It was ceded to the Japanese after the Sino-Japanese War in 1895 but was formally returned to China in 1945. When the Communists overran the mainland of China in 1949, the Nationalist government moved to Taiwan and made Taipei its capital. Taiwan's religion, like that of China, is a fusion of Confucianism, Buddhism, and Taoism. The first efforts at evangelization were made in 1621 by Dominicans from the Philippines, but their work was wiped out by Dutch Calvinists. A new epoch for the missions began in 1859. During the Japanese occupation, evangelization was forbidden. In 1946 there were only 17 priests and 8 sisters on the island whose Catholic community numbered about 6,000. By 1958 there were 170,000 Catholics in addition to 80,000 catechumens. Taipei, seat of the Catholic Univ., was made an archdiocese in 1952. There are now six suffragan sees, all occupied by native bishops. In 1976 the Catholics numbered 293,819, priests 738, men religious 624, women religious 1,258.

Protestantism was long represented by Presbyterians. After World War II more than 70 missionary agencies entered Taiwan, along with church workers fleeing mainland China. There are two denominational colleges, two universities, one junior high school, three middle schools, five seminaries, and a number of hospitals and social service centers. In 1968 the reported Protestant membership was 459,343.

[P. DAMBORÍENA]

TAIZÉ COMMUNITY, Protestant monastic community founded by Roger Schutz in 1944. In 1939, while studying theology at Lauzanne, Schutz organized study clubs from which sprang the Taizé idea. In August 1940 he moved into a house in the village of Taizé, close to Cluny, in Burgundy, France. Here he devoted himself to prayer, meditation, and community action. After an absence of 2 years in Switzerland, Schutz, accompanied by several companions, returned to Taizé in 1944. On Easter Sunday, 1949, seven men made their profession, agreeing to live in celibacy, to hold property in common, and to submit to authority. By 1968 there were close to 70 members, drawn for the most part from Western Europe, and of the Lutheran and *Reformed Churches. *The Rule of Taizé* was edited by Roger Schutz in 1952–53 and was developed further in 1960. The Rule describes community activities, spiritual discipline, commitments (celibacy, etc.), the duties of the prior, and the work of mission brothers. After a novitiate of 2 or 3 years devoted to the study of the Bible, church history, and sociology, the candidates make their profession, donning a silver ring, the only outward distinguishing mark of their membership in the community. Members of the community reside either in Taizé or are "on mission" in the U.S., France, Germany, Uruguay, North Africa, or the Middle East. Those on mission return annually to Taizé for retreats. The brothers work as physicians, architects, ministers in churches, in the arts, in factories, and on community projects. Seminars are conducted on sociological topics in an effort to bring the community into close touch with current problems. The spirit of ecumenism pervades Taizé, a spirit nurtured by Schutz, who made retreats in RC monasteries, visited Anglican religious communities, kept in close touch with RC parish priests and worker-priests, attended the sessions of Vatican

Council II, and did his licentiate dissertation on *The Monastic Ideal until Saint Benedict and its Conformity with the Gospel*. Taizé is best described as a contemplative community working in the world. BIBLIOGRAPHY: J. Heijke, *Ecumenical Light on the Renewal of Religious Community Life: Taizé* (1967); R. Schutz, *Living Today for God* (1961).

TAJ MAHAL (1632–54), one of the world's most beautiful buildings. A masterpiece of Islamic art erected in the first half of the 17th cent., which saw the flowering of Muslim architectural genius, this exquisite mausoleum was built outside Agra, India by the Mogul emperor Shah Jahan, as memorial to his beautiful wife, Arjumand Banu Begum, called Mumtaz-i-Mahal. With weightless, elegantly contoured dome rising 200 ft above the base—the white marble walls broken by deep, shadowy, cool, translucent recesses—the entire building seems to float. A poetic reverie is induced by the long reflecting pool, tree-lined in dark green, accenting the cool whiteness. The interior is inlaid with precious stones. A companion mausoleum planned for the Shah himself was never built. Legend states that the Emperor ordered the architect blinded to ensure that he would never plan a rival structure. The magnificent Taj Mahal surpasses the Alhambra in subtle sophistication.

[M. J. DALY]

TAKSĀ, East Syrian liturgical book containing the common parts of the Eucharistic rite, with the texts of the three anaphoras, generally with baptism and other sacramental rites added as a supplement.

[A. CODY]

TALBOT, EDWARD STUART (1844–1934), of Christ Church, Oxford, first Warden of Keble, which in the face of snobbishness, social and religious, he raised to a position of esteem. He was a close associate of Charles Gore and, like many of the Tractarians of the second generation, felt deeply involved in the social problem. Asked what was his party, he replied, "Conservative—with a bad conscience." Leaving the academic life behind (1888), he was successively vicar of Leeds, bp. of Rochester, of Southwark, of Winchester. He was a conspicuously fair administrator and kept order in the troubles between Ritualists and Evangelicals. His sons were distinguished: Edward Keble became superior of the Mirfield Fathers, Neville Stuart bp. of Pretoria, and Gilbert was killed at Ypres (1915). Talbot House was founded in Gilbert's memory.

[T. GILBY]

TALBOT, JAMES (1726–90), vicar apostolic of the London District (1781–1790). Born at Isleworth, Middlesex, brother of the 14th earl of Shrewsbury, he was educated at Douay College and ordained there on Dec. 19, 1750. For several years he lectured in theology and philosophy until chosen as coadjutor to Bishop Challoner of the London District in 1759. He was the last Catholic priest to be indicted in an English court for celebrating Mass (1771). He was buried in Hammersmith Church, but in 1901 his remains were transferred to the seminary of Old Hall, Ware. BIBLIOGRAPHY: *Biographies of English Catholics in the Eighteenth Century* (eds. J. H. Pollen and P. E. Burton, 1909) 228.

[T. J. RYAN]

TALBOT, MATT (1856–1925), Irish laborer, reformed alcoholic, ascetic. Born in Dublin, into a large and impoverished family, T. received little education and spent his young manhood as a laborer for the Port of Dublin and fell to excessive drinking. At the age of 28, he underwent a remarkable conversion of life, which included a return to prayer and the sacraments and the taking of what came to be a lifelong pledge to refrain from alcohol. Further, until his death, he led a life of extraordinary penance, abstaining from meat 9 months of the year, sleeping but 3½ hours nightly, wearing chains, which at his death were found embedded in his flesh. He died on Trinity Sunday on the way to Mass. He was buried as a Franciscan tertiary in Glasnevin Cemetery. The diocesan informative process for his beatification began in Dublin in 1931; the apostolic process began in 1947. BIBLIOGRAPHY: E. J. Dougherty, *Matt Talbot* (1953); M. Purcell, *Matt Talbot and His Times* (1955).

[T. J. RYAN]

TALBOT, PETER (1620–80), abp. of Dublin. He was employed on diplomatic missions on behalf of the exiled Charles II, related difficulties of which necessitated his amicable resignation from the Jesuits in 1659. After being appointed abp., disputes arose that compelled him to leave Ireland and England temporarily. In 1678, after being permitted to return, he was arrested on false charges connected with the Titus Oates plot and was imprisoned until his death.

[P. J. HENNESSEY]

TALEBEARING, the carrying of reports on private matters, a form of backbiting when done maliciously, though often done for the satisfaction of vanity—the thrill of being first with the news—or of idle curiosity, and sometimes done in order to curry favor or somewhat priggishly to reflect credit on oneself. Adults should not lower standards held by children, for whom a tell-tale or tattle-tale is a term of contempt. The vice seems compounded of failures with respect to truthfulness, friendliness, magnanimity, honor, and modesty. *SECRETS.

[P. F. MULHERN]

TALITHA CUMI, the Greek transliteration of the Aramaic *talîtā' qumi*, "Girl, rise up." Jesus addressed these words to the dead daughter of Jairus when he raised her to life.

[J. J. CASTELOT]

TALL BROTHERS (fl. end of 4th cent.), four brothers, monks of the Egyptian desert, of exceptional height, whose names were Dioscurus, Ammonius, Eusebius, and Euthymius. Exiled under the Arian Emperor Valens (364–378) for their orthodoxy, they were honored by *Theophilus, patriarch of Alexandria, who consecrated Dioscurus bp. of Hermopolis Minor. Later (*c*.400) when they gave sanctuary to a priest unjustly excommunicated by Theophilus, the latter in anger excommunicated them as *Origenists. Driven thus from Egypt, they went first to Palestine and finally to Constantinople where they appealed to the Patriarch *John Chrysostom (402), who welcomed them but withheld communion to avoid offending Theophilus. Dioscurus and Ammonius died about the time of the Synod of the *Oak in which Theophilus proceeded against Chrysostom. BIBLIOGRAPHY: V. Monachino, Enc-Catt 5:1717.

[R. B. ENO]

TALLAGHT, ABBEY OF, near Dublin, Ireland, a monastery founded in 774 by St. Máel-Rúain, which became the center of his reform movement. In 1111 it was included in the Diocese of Glendalough, and in 1214 became an episcopal manor, up to and after the Reformation when Protestant abps. began residing there. In 1822 the government bought the property and demolished the building. It is also famous for the valuable *Martyrology of Tallaght* (ed. R. I. Best and H. J. Lawler, 1931), composed *c*.800. BIBLIOGRAPHY: E. Ball, "Descriptive Sketch of Clondalkin, Tallaght . . .," *Journal of the Royal Society of Antiquaries of Ireland* 29 (1899) 83–108; Kenney, s.v.

[C. MCGRATH]

TALLEYRAND, ALEXANDRE-ANGÉLIQUE, (1736–1821), cardinal, abp. of Reims and Paris, uncle of C. M. Périgord Talleyrand. A royalist, T. advanced from chaplain to the king and vicar general of Verdun in 1762 to become abp. of Reims in 1777. Elected to the Estates General in 1789, he took part in the Constituent Assembly, defending vigorously the rights and privileges of the Church. Compelled by the cataclysmic events of the Revolution to leave France for Germany, he attached himself even more closely to the retinue of the exiled monarchy, refusing to resign his see after the Concordat of 1801, returning to France in 1814 with Louis XVIII, and fleeing again with him during the Hundred Days. Instrumental in effecting the Concordat of 1817, he was created cardinal abp. of Paris that same year by Pope Pius VII and sometime later imposed upon his clergy the acceptance of an oath favorable to Jansenism. BIBLIOGRAPHY: S. Furlani, EncCatt 2:1711–12.

[T. J. RYAN]

TALLEYRAND-PÉRIGORD, CHARLES MAURICE DE (1754–1838), French statesman. A member of an important French aristocratic family, T. was ordained in 1779, appointed spokesman for the clergy, and named bp. of Autun in 1788. A freethinker whose philosophy was that of the *Enlightenment, he sat in the Revolutionary Estates General, actively helping to destroy the old French Church and to create a new schismatic one (see CIVIL CONSTITUTION OF THE CLERGY). He consecrated the first bps. of the Constitutional Church, then abandoned the clerical state. After living abroad during the Reign of Terror, he returned to become minister of foreign affairs in 1797, a post he also held under Napoleon from 1799 to 1807. He represented Louis XVIII at the Congress of Vienna. Although he was officially laicized, T. had married only civilly; he was reconciled with the Church on his deathbed. BIBLIOGRAPHY: A. D. Cooper, *Talleyrand* (1958).

[R. H. SCHMANDT]

TALLIS, THOMAS (c.1505–85), English Renaissance organist and composer. T. was organist at Waltham abbey until the 1540 dissolution. He then went to Canterbury for a while, before being appointed a gentleman of the Chapel Royal, where he served for some 40 years. With William Byrd, he was organist there and the two were given a licence, 1575, as sole printers and publishers of music in England. In the same year they dedicated to the Queen a joint collection of motets (*Cantiones sacrae*) that evidence the contrapuntal skill of both composers. In addition to motets, T. composed 2 Masses, 2 Magnificats, a remarkable song in 40 parts, "Spem in alium," and other compositions with Latin text. Among the first to compose music with English words for the Anglican Church, he contributed *Preces* and Responses, Psalms, Services, and several anthems. T. also composed some secular and instrumental works. Very little of T.'s music was published in his lifetime. His complete works may be found in v. 4 of *Tudor Church Music* (1928).

[M. T. LEGGE]

TALMUD, the great reservoir of Jewish teaching stemming from the oral law said to have been given to Moses at the same time as the written law, and passed on, commented upon, redacted, and discussed ever since. There are two literary works referred to as the Talmud: the Babylonian Talmud and the Erez-Israel or so-called Jerusalem Talmud. Post-dating the Erez-Israel Talmud by about 2 cent. and by far a larger, more interesting version, the Babylonian Talmud is taken as authoritative. The oral tradition, including vast exegesis of Scripture and discussion among teachers, was eventually systematized into tractates and chapters by *Hillel and subsequent scholars and given authoritative form in 220 A.D. by Rabbi Judah Ha-Nasi under the title "Mishnah" ("teaching"). The intense studies and discussions at academies in Palestine and Babylon became part of the tradition and were called Gemara because they complemented the Mishnah. Together, Mishnah and Gemara constitute the two Talmudic texts. The Erez Israel Talmud was redacted in 400 A.D. or earlier; the Babylonian was completed c.500 but supplemented in the 6th and 7th centuries. Although the oral law was not to be written down, because of persecutions, private MSS eventually committed the entire Talmud to writing. Manuscripts of the Talmud became the object of a purge in 1240 when a disputation purportedly proved that the Talmud contained blasphemies against Jesus, and Louis IX of France ordered all copies burnt. Similar burnings occurred elsewhere. The only complete surviving MSS are the Erez Israel of the Leyden Codex and a copy of the Babylonian Talmud in the Munich Codex (1334). Daniel Bomberg printed the first complete edition of both versions in Venice in the 1520s. Each page of Bomberg's Babylonian Talmud has the Mishnah and Gemara text in the center surrounded by commentary by Rashi, supplemented by *Tosephta comments. Translations of individual tractates and finally of the whole Talmud into Latin were made in the 18th century. The first complete German translation of the Babylonian Talmud was done by L. Goldschmidt (1897–1935); and the first scholarly English translation was done under the editorship of I. Epstein (1935–52). The Talmud provides *halakhah,* the law or way to walk, as well as *aggadah,* inspirational suggestions, ethical insight, legend, and history. For some, study of the Talmud is fulfillment of duty for its own sake, an immersion of the whole self in the "sea of Talmud." For Reformed Jews, the Talmud is not binding, but merely reflects a phase of Jewish history. For all Jews, however, it signifies the continued presence of the rabbinic tradition.

[R. J. LITZ]

TALON, NICOLAS (1605–91), French Jesuit author of *L'Histoire sainte* (4 v., 1640–54), a popular OT bible history; a parallel work on the NT was less well received.

[T. C. O'BRIEN]

TAMAMUSHI SHRINE, 7th-cent. Japanese shrine in the Horyuji, Nara, decorated with irridescent wings of *tamamushi* (beetles), painted in lacquer with Buddhist guardian figures and two scenes from Jatakas (tales) of the Buddha, the earliest example of narrative pictures in Japan, reflecting the art of Northern Wei China in the sinuous grace and elegance of slender figures.

[M. J. DALY]

TAMBURINI, MICHELANGELO (1648–1730), 14th general of the Society of Jesus. A professor of philosophy at Bologna and of theology at Mantua for 12 years, T. successively became rector of several Jesuit colleges, provincial of the Venetian province, secretary general, vicar general, and finally general of the Society (January 3, 1706). During his generalate, Jesuit missionary activity flourished with the Reductions of Paraguay, new missions in the Near East, and with Constant Beschi's continuation of the tradition of Brahman Christianity initiated by Robert de Nobili in India. But T.'s administration was also troubled by Jansenist charges that the Jesuits had failed to follow Rome's directives for adapting Christianity to non-European cultures, and by Pope Clement XI's condemnation in the *Chinese Rites controversy, abolishing certain native ceremonial customs Jesuit missionaries had held permissible in China and India.

[T. J. RYAN]

TAMBURINI, PIETRO (1739–1827), Italian theologian, "promoter of the faith" at the Jansenist Synod of Pistoia, advisor of Bp. S. de Ricci. T., ordained in 1760, studied for 3 years in Rome before teaching at Pavia. He prepared, directed formulation and propagation of the Pistoian teachings. After the Synod he held a chair in moral theology at Pavia. He died apparently reconciled to the Church, but made no formal retraction when the Synod's decrees were condemned in 1794. His main work was *Ethica Christiana* (4 v., 1783); he followed *Baius's teaching on grace, *Gallicanism in regard to Church-State relations; opposed *probabilism and was anticurial in discussions on the papacy.

[T. C. O'BRIEN]

TAMBURINI, TOMMASO (1591–1675), Italian Jesuit, casuist, exponent of *probabilism. He was professor of moral theology at Messina and Palermo. His first work, *Methodus expeditae confessionis* (5 v., 1647) was widely used and to it T. added a complete moral theology text, *Expeditae decalogi explicationes* (1654) and *Expedita juris divini, naturalis et ecclesiastici moralis explicatio* (3 v., 1661). His moral solutions were accused of favoring *laxism. Among the laxist propositions condemned by the Holy Office in 1665–66 (D 2021–65) and 1679 (D 2101–67), several are traceable to the *Decalogi explicationes,* but neither decree of condemnation attributes them to T., and they were used by other authors out of context. The full title of the work mentioned indicates that it solves all cases with as much "benignity" as is permissible; and the "principle of benignity" was T.'s own chief defense against charges of laxism. He wrote a polemical response to the charges as levelled by the Dominican V. *Baron in 1666.

[T. C. O'BRIEN]

TAMETSI, the title of decree in which the Council of Trent in 1563 imposed the observance of a certain form in the celebration of marriages—viz., that they should be contracted in the presence of the local pastor, or ordinary, or of some priest delegated by either pastor or ordinary, and in the presence also of at least two other witnesses. The Council made this observance necessary to the validity of marriages. This legislation was intended to put an end to marriages contracted in such secrecy that satisfactory evidence of their having taken place could well be wanting. However in many areas this decree was not officially published, and in those places it was not binding. That situation was rectified by Pius X's decree *Ne temere*, which was issued in 1907 and became effective on Easter Sunday, 1908. This extended the invalidating ban on clandestine marriages to the whole of the Latin Church. *CLANDESTINE MARRIAGES.

[P. K. MEAGHER]

TAMMUZ, Mesopotamian deity resulting from a divine personification of the cyclic vanishing and recurring creative powers of springtime. His name was originally Sumerian, Dumuzi, abbreviated from Dumi-zid-abzu, Faithful Son of the Cosmic Ocean. He was a principal figure in a myth wherein he was abducted to the underworld of death, only to be followed by his sister and wife, Ishtar, who rescued him after being imprisoned there herself. The descent of Tammuz and Ishtar to the underworld represented mythically the departure of life and fertility on earth; their resurrection, the return of new life and fertility. The re-enactment of the myth entailed a sexual union (*hieros gamos*) of the king and a temple-prostitute, representing the creative union of Tammuz and Ishtar (the goddess of fertility). The act was meant to assure the fertility of fields and flocks. A striking ritual element was the weeping for the dead Tammuz, mentioned in Ezek 8.13–13. BIBLIOGRAPHY: E. Dhorme, *Les Religions de Babylonie et d'Assyrie* (1945) 115–119; S. Langdon, *Tammuz and Ishtar* (1914); *idem, Sumerian and Babylonian Psalms* (1909).

[A. CODY]

TANCHELM (Tanchelin; d. 1115), heresiarch, a native of the Netherlands, possibly a renegade monk. T. was used by Count Robert II of Flanders against the Diocese of Utrecht in the interests of Franco-Flemish policy. At Rome, where T. sought aid from Paschal II, he absorbed the spirit and principles of the reform papacy. Later, he preached anticlerical doctrines at Utrecht, Bruges, and Antwerp, and developed a large following, choosing also a small band of disciple-bodyguards. He rejected the Eucharist and all the other sacraments, and advised the populace not to pay tithes to the clergy. He proclaimed himself to be the Holy Spirit and entered a "mystical marriage" with the Virgin Mary, promoting a personal cult about himself. Following a violent attack on the clergy, he was killed by an enraged priest. Facts about his teaching are hard to separate from exaggerations of hostile clerics and unsympathetic chroniclers, who also accuse him of sexual license. Still, T.'s teachings perdured for years, since St. Norbert of Xanten had to preach against them at Antwerp in 1124. BIBLIOGRAPHY: W. Mohn, "Tanchelm van Antwerpen," *Annales universitatis saraviensis,* 3 (1954); *Vita Norberti,* MGHS 12:690–691; C. J. Kirkfleet, *History of St. Norbert.*

[N. F. GAUGHAN]

TANCRED (*c.*1185–*c.*1234), canonist, writer, archdeacon of Bologna. The author of an *Ordo judiciarius* (1214–16), he also wrote a *Summa de sponsalibus et matrimonio* and commentaries on the first three of the *Quinque compilationes antiquae*. To him Honorius III entrusted the gathering of the pope's own letters which was promulgated by Honorius in 1226 and later became the *Quinta compilatio*. BIBLIOGRAPHY: A. M. Stickler, DDC 6:1132–44.

[L. E. BOYLE]

TANERETZ (Dzikhater), among the Gregorian Armenians, that priest whom a particular family chooses among the priests of the parish to take care of the family's religious needs.

[A. CODY]

TANEY, ROGER BROOKE (1777–1864), U.S. Supreme Court chief justice. Born in Maryland of a Catholic family, T. studied law, built a successful practice, and entered political life in his native state. Having supported Andrew Jackson's presidential campaign, T. received from him an appointment as U.S. attorney general in 1831 and an interim appointment as secretary of the treasury in 1833. Although unconfirmed at Treasury, he turned the tide of public opinion against the Bank of the United States. In 1836 Jackson made him chief justice of the Supreme Court. T.'s defense of slavery in the Dred Scott decision cast a shadow over his reputation that has only recently begun to lift. BIBLIOGRAPHY: L. Friedman and F. L. Israel, *Justices of the United States Supreme Court, 1789–1969* (4 v., 1969) 1:635–713; W. Lewis, *Without Fear or Favor: A Biography of Chief Justice Roger Brooke Taney* (1965).

[R. H. SCHMANDT]

TANKEI (1173–1256), renowned Japanese sculptor and oldest son of the master Unkei. Though Unkei and Kankei influenced T., his works are less dynamic, more serene (e.g., *Bishamon Triad*, Sakkeiji, Kochi perfecture).

[M. J. DALY]

TANNER, EDMUND (*c.*1526–79), bp. of Cork and Cloyne, Ireland. He became a Jesuit at 39 but had to resign because of ill health. Appointed bp. in 1574, he was imprisoned for a short time by Sir William Drury, president of Munster. His premature death was speeded by hard labor and want.

[P. J. HENNESSEY]

TANNER, HENRY OSSAWA (1859–1937), American Negro artist, student of T. Eakins, working after 1891 in Europe because of prejudice in the U.S. In Paris, after earlier academic genre pieces *(The Banjo Lesson)*, T. painted *The Annunciation* (1895) and *Disciples Healing the Sick* (1930–35), romantic religious works in dramatic light and dark contrasts, rich impasto and warm, glowing tones, his Rembrandtesque interpretation of Scripture, enriched by his spiritual, poetic insight. T.'s *Annunciation,* acquired (1899) by the Philadelphia Museum of Art, has been honored as the featured Christmas painting at the entrance to the Museum.

[M. J. DALY]

TANNER, MATTHIAS (1630–92), Jesuit educator and author. Born in Pilsen, he taught and was rector at the

Charles Univ., Prague, and wrote volumes of Jesuit biographies, works concerning the Blessed Sacrament, and accounts of Jesuit martyrs in England.

[P. J. HENNESSEY]

TANNER, PHILIP (1577–1656), Swiss Capuchin preacher. He was well-loved by the needy and spent his life promoting devotion to Mary.

[P. J. HENNESSEY]

TANQUEREY, ADOLPHE ALFRED (1854–1932), French Sulpician, professor of theology at St. Mary's Seminary, Baltimore, Md. (1887–1902). T. became a Sulpician in 1878 after his ordination and taught theology at the seminary of Rodez before being assigned to St. Mary's. During his tenure there he published for the use of seminarians two manuals of dogmatics, *Synopsis theologiae dogmaticae* (2 v., 1894; Eng. tr. 2 v., 1959) and *Synopsis theologiae fundamentalis* (1896); for moral theology, *Synopsis theologiae moralis* (2 v., 1902, v. 3, 1905). These works, long standard in seminaries, were marked by solid, clear, and pastorally oriented presentation. During T.'s subsequent career in France, as professor, superior of the Sulpician novitiate, and assistant to the general, he also published his respected, somewhat eclectic, *Précis de théologie ascétique et mystique* (1923), *Spiritual Life* (tr. H. Branderis, 1947), as well as other works and articles on the spiritual life.

[T. C. O'BRIEN]

TANTRAS, (Sanskrit, unfolding?), body of Indian and Tibetan literature regarded as authoritative in *Tantrism or *Vajrayana Buddhism, though looked on as heretical and dangerous by other Hindu and Buddhist traditions. Its principal components are manuals of instruction, largely in the use of *mantras (chanted words or syllables for meditation), mandalas (sacred symbolic designs for use in ritual and meditation), and meditations and rituals for various duties. They are written in "twilight" or "intentional" language (*sandhabhasa*), obscure or unintelligible to outsiders, but quite evocative to the initiated. BIBLIOGRAPHY: C. Chakravarti, *Tantras: Studies in Their Religion and Literature* (1963).

[D. P. EFROYMSON]

TANTRISM, esoteric mystical and ritual tradition (dating from *c.*600 A.D.) of N India, Nepal, and Tibet, including both Hindu and Buddhist (*Vajrayana) versions. The name derives from its literature (*Tantras), largely manuals of instruction. The tradition's central tenet is the claim that while absolute reality is ultimately one, it is to be achieved or expressed only in terms of a conceptual, intuitive, and ritual polarization of opposites (esp. male and female). Thus Tantrism makes extensive use, in ritual, meditation, and art, of the earlier Indian polarization of deities (e.g., *Siva and his Shakti, or "energy," symbolized as his consort) or personified forces. Through magical-ritual and meditative identification with these deities or forces, by use of mandalas (symbolic diagrams), *mantras (symbolic chants), and mudras (ritual gestures), the initiated adept (under the instruction of a guru) "becomes" that which is symbolized and thus transcends the duality of ordinary experience. The heavily sexual dimension of some of the ritual and symbolism, together with allegations of libertine practices (eating meat, drinking wine, and "overcoming passion by means of passion") led to condemnation of Tantrism by many outsiders. BIBLIOGRAPHY: A. Bharati, *Tantric Tradition* (1965); J. Blofeld, *Tantric Mysticism of Tibet* (1970).

[D. P. EFROYMSON]

TANTUM ERGO, a hymn in praise of the Eucharist, widelyknown because of the prescription that it be sung at Benediction of the Blessed Sacrament. It is part, the fifth or penultimate verse (although almost always used in combination with the final verse), of a much longer hymn, the *Pange lingua gloriosi*. This was composed most likely by Thomas Aquinas *c*.1264 as the Vesper hymn for the Office of the feast of Corpus Christi, but it is also widely used for eucharistic processions. The entire hymn is highly regarded for its poetic inspiration and doctrinal exactitude relative to the Eucharist.

[B. ROSENDALL]

TANUCCI, BERNARDO (1698–1783), antipapal, anti-Jesuit chief minister of the Kingdom of Naples. As head of the Council of Regents for Ferdinand, son of Charles III of Spain, T. directed the policy of hampering religious orders, subjecting Church to State, and above all of suppressing the Jesuits. He had them expelled from Naples in Nov. 1767, and worked with the other Bourbon ministers to force papal suppression, which came in 1773 under Clement XIV. T. fell from power after King Ferdinand married Marie Caroline of Austria and allied Naples with the Habsburgs.

[T. C. O'BRIEN]

TANUCCISM, named from Bernardo Tanucci (1698–1783), all-powerful minister of state in the Kingdom of Naples, who was more successful in asserting state control over the Church and in expelling the Jesuits—in circumstances of brutality, 1767—than in his fiscal and foreign policies vis-à-vis the British Navy. As a movement, it was the Neapolitan counterpart to *Pombal and an anticipation of *Josephinism and *Leopoldinism; as might have been expected from its locale, it was less streamlined and more subject to the patchy play of personalities.

[T. GILBY]

TAOISM, one of the three main philosophical and religious traditions of China, together with *Confucianism and *Buddhism. Its history has been extremely checkered. Although fundamentally a worshipful reverence for nature and a search for a harmonious relationship between man and the universe, Taoist sects have at various times adopted animism, polytheism, "magicism," and an elaborate ritualism. The founder of Taoism is popularly regarded as *Lao Tsu, reportedly an older contemporary of *Confucius, born in 604 B.C., and the author of the *Tao Teh Ching* (The Way and Virtue Classic), a compilation of 81 short poems which remains the basic text of Taoist thought to this day. An understanding of Tao is crucial to the interpretation of Lao Tsu's classic, although Lao Tsu warned that the Tao is an unfathomable mystery. Tao is regarded as the first principle of being, the intelligence of the universe, life-giving, immanent, and eternal; it informs and transforms all things. The Tao is nonbeing, in the sense that nonbeing implies that there must be something before all other beings came into existence. This nonbeing is the Ultimate and the First; its activity is distinguished by nonaction, i.e., it never acts and yet through it, all is done and things are allowed to follow their own course. There is nothing higher than the Tao and man is called to pattern his life after it, "Man models himself on the earth, the earth models itself after heaven, the heaven models itself after Tao, but Tao models itself by that which is so by itself" (Tao Teh Ching 1:25). Virtue (Teh), therefore, follows from the complete harmony between man and heaven, and in man's adaptation to nature's beat and rhythm. The cardinal virtue is humility. There is a recurrent theme of gentleness, resignation, the futility of contentions, the strength of weakness, and the importance of failure. Lao Tsu elevated man's inner being or spirit rather than his strength, pride, and acquired knowledge. His value system was directly opposed to that of Confucianism, which stressed action and achievement.

In addition to Lao Tsu, many other religious thinkers have been responsible for the forms which Taoism has adopted in its long history. Yang Chu (440–336 B.C.), a naturalist philosopher, taught personal integrity and self-protection against the inroads of an autocratic state. Chuang Tzu (d. *c*.295 B.C.) formulated many of Lao Tsu's original insights into a speculative system, interpreting the Tao as the ground of all being. A naturalistic monism appeared in the 3d cent. B.C., which regarded the Tao's power as made up of two types of energy: *Yin,* a concentrating force which is seen as dark and evil, and *Yang,* an expanding force regarded as bright and good. From this combination of *Yin* (the female principle) and *Yang* (the male principle), the universe was produced. Buddhism had a strong influence upon the later development of Taoism, which began in the 2d cent. A.D. to copy the Buddhist ritualism, hierarchical structures, and pantheon of gods. The Amida sect of the 5th cent. was a reaction against this tendency, seeking to return Taoism to its original simplicity and adopting a type of monotheism.

Taoism has consistently been divided by sects and secret societies. Among the more important are the Principle One sect, characterized by monasticism, spiritism, and devotion to a high priest; the Perfecting the True sect, which was extremely syncretistic in its efforts to combine Taoism, Buddhism, and Confucianism; the Pervading-Unity Tao sect, which stressed the ultimate teleological unity behind all earthly change; and the White Lotus society, a religious organization which formed into many political revolutionary secret groups. Although the present Communist government suppressed many of the Taoist sects and societies, it seems to be encouraging the Taoist traditions in general or at least to be using them in the political re-education of the Chinese people. BIBLIOGRAPHY: P. J. Maclagan, Hastings ERE 12:197–202; J. A. Hardon, *Religions of the World* (1963) 177–187; W. Chan, *Religious Trends in Modern China* (1953).

[V. T. JOHNSON]

TAPARELLI D'AZEGLIO, LUIGI (Prospero; 1793–1862), Italian Jesuit, brother of the Risorgimento hero, Massimo, editor, early promoter of the Neo-Scholastic revival. He was one of the first Jesuit novices admitted after the restoration of the Society in 1814. From 1824 he was rector of the Collegio Romano; in 1829 he became provincial of Naples; from 1833–50 he was professor of philosophy at Palermo; the rest of his life he spent in Rome as an editor of *Civiltà Cattolica*. As rector in Rome and as provincial in Naples he took steps, not without meeting strong resistance, to reform the program of studies, then in a chaotic state of eclecticism, by a return to scholastic philosophy; he continued to write in this cause as an editor. In social and political thought T. is regarded as a man ahead of his times by his anticipation of internationalism, the urgent need of which has come to be fully realized in the late 20th century. His principal work—in addition to continuous articles in *Civiltà Cattolica*—is *Saggio teoretico di dritto naturale appoggiato sul fatto* (1843; many revised editions). One of the controverted points of his socio-political teaching was his concept of nationality.

[T. C. O'BRIEN]

TAPIA, GONZALO DE (1561–94), Spanish Jesuit, founder of missions in the present state of Sinaloa, Mexico, where he converted thousands of natives. He was martyred there at Tavoropa. From his pioneering work the Jesuit missions spread through Baja California and Arizona.

[T. C. O'BRIEN]

TAPPERT, RUARD (Tappaert; 1487–1559), theologian at Louvain, dean and chancellor there, university representative (1551–52) at the Council of Trent. He was one of the most quoted theologians of the era and at Trent looked on as a leader. On his return to Louvain he dealt vigorously with the errors of his former student, Michel du Bay (see BAIUS AND BAIANISM). The most celebrated of T.'s writings developed out of his work as Inquisitor General for the Low Countries, a post he held from 1537 and which he carried out not by use of force but by the power of teaching. He developed a symbol of faith for circulation among the faithful, containing a series of dogmatic propositions. It was published in 1545; T. developed a long commentary on these propositions, published as his *Explicationes* (2v., 1555–57). The work presented an exposition of Catholic teaching, Protestant objections, the author's replies. T. also published other works against Reformation teaching.

[T. C. O'BRIEN]

TARASIUS, PATRIARCH OF CONSTANTINOPLE, ST. (d. 806). An imperial secretary and well-educated layman, he was named patriarch in 784 by the Empress Irene to put an end to *iconoclasm. He restored friendly relations with Rome and presided over the Council of Nicaea II (787) which condemned iconoclasm. He showed great moderation in dealing with bps. who had favored the heresy and for this he was criticized in some circles.

[G. T. DENNIS]

TARDINI, DOMENICO (1888–1961), Italian cardinal and papal secretary of state. Ordained 1912, he became professor of sacramental theology and liturgy at the Roman Seminary and Propaganda College. During the pontificates of Pius XI and Pius XII, he was named to several congregations, including the Papal Congregation for Russia. Under John XXIII, T. became a cardinal and secretary of state. When John decided upon an ecumenical council, T. worked indefatigably for its preparation. Although known primarily as a diplomat, T. was also interested in social problems. He founded Casa Nazareth, a home for orphans, and he strongly supported John XXIII's *Mater et magistra*.

[E. A. CARRILLO]

TARGUM, Aramaic translation or paraphrase of the OT. When the Jews came to speak Aramaic after the Exile and the ordinary worshiper no longer understood Hebrew, a translation would be given after the Scripture reading. The translations were placed in the margin alongside the Hebrew text. The most famous targums are those of Onkelos on the Pentateuch and Jonathan on the Prophets. BIBLIOGRAPHY: P. E. Kahle, *Cairo Geniza* (2d ed., 1959).

[T. EARLY]

TARPHON, RABBI (d. *c.* 123 A.D.), a Jewish teacher. He was dean of the Academy of Jabneh and Lydda. In his youth he served in the Temple in Jerusalem, and his sayings reflect a nostalgia for the beauty of that place, destroyed forever under Titus. A student of the school of Shammai, he also studied under Gamaliel the Elder and Johanan ben Zakkai. Among his students were Akiba ben Joseph and Judah ben Ilai. T., called in his time "father of Israel," rendered many of the opinions on interpreting the Law that are recorded in the Talmud.

[E. J. DILLON]

TARSHISH, see THARSIS.

TARSICIUS, ST. (3d cent.). The oldest source of information on T. is the 4th-cent. poem of Pope Damasus. He states that T. was assaulted and killed by a pagan mob while carrying the Blessed Sacrament through the streets of Rome. According to a later tradition dating from the 6th cent., T. was a young acolyte slain while bearing the Eucharist to Christians imprisoned in the persecution of Valerian, but his youth and his status as acolyte are uncertain. A reference to St. *Stephen in the poem of Damasus might suggest that T. was a deacon, and indeed it was among the ordinary duties of the deacon to carry the Eucharist from the liturgical celebration to the sick, although during times of persecution acolytes or Christians of any status might be called upon to perform that service. Indeed in earlier times, it was not uncommon for a Christian to keep the Eucharist in his home. BIBLIOGRAPHY: Butler 3:335; A. Amore, EncCatt 11:1776–77.

[R. B. ENO]

TARSUS, a city, perhaps the oldest in the world, in the Turkish province of Cilicia on the SE coast of Asia Minor and the birthplace of St. Paul the Apostle, "Saul of Tarsus" (Acts 9.11). With a continuous history of about 6 millennia, it was founded in Neolithic times, fortified in the 3d millennium B.C., active in coastal trade during the Trojan era (c. 2300 B.C.), mentioned in Hittite records, invaded by Sea Peoples (c. 1200 B.C.), resettled by Mycenean Greeks in the diaspora following the Trojan War, captured by the Assyrian Shalmaneser III (832 B.C.), subsequently held by the Persians, Alexander (333 B.C.), and the Seleucids. Capital of a Roman province, of which Cicero temporarily served as governor, it opposed Cassius after the death of Caesar, and was rewarded by Mark Anthony (41 B.C.) when Cleopatra made her grand entrance into the city. Augustus restored full rights to its mixed Anatolian, Roman, Greek, and Jewish people. Tarsus was the center of a strong native intellectual life and home of many philosophers, most notable being Athenodorus, Augustus' tutor.

[R. J. LITZ]

TARTAGLIA, NICCOLÒ (c. 1500–57), Italian mathematician and military engineer. His youth was spent in poverty and hardship. Though his family name was Fontana, during the French sack of Brescia in 1512, he sustained a serious wound which impaired his speech and earned his nickname tartaglia, "the stutterer." It has been suggested that his pyschological resentment toward war contributed to his various studies of ballistics and military fortifications such as *Nuova scienzia* (1537) and *Quesiti invenzioni diverse* (1546). He is credited, for example, with the discovery that the range of a projectile is greatest at a 45° angle. Yet his most important and controversial mathematical study was his solution to the cubic equation. After secretly revealing it to a colleague, Girolamo Cardan, T. learned that Cardan published the equation and claimed most of the credit. T. also published translations of works by Euclid and Archimedes. His academic achievements were esp. noteworthy because he possessed almost no formal education. BIBLIOGRAPHY: E. T. Bell, *Development of Mathematics* (1945); *Mechanics in the Sixteenth Century* (ed. S. Drake, 1969).

[C. T. EBY]

TARTAN, official of the Assyrian army. The office dates at least from the time of Adad-nirari II (911–891 B.C.). The Bible refers to tartans of Sargon II (Is 20.1—"commander-in-chief") and Sennacherib (2 Kg 18.17).

[T. EARLY]

TARTARUS, the dark subterranean region in Greek mythology where Chronos and the other Titans were imprisoned. It is said that Tartarus is as far below the earth as heaven is above and that it would take a falling anvil nine days to reach its depths. The personification of the place was the son of Chaos and he sired the monsters Typhoeus and Echidna. Tartarus became associated with torment and punishment, opposed to the Elysian fields where happiness prevailed. This name is sometimes used (e.g., Prov. 30.16) in the LXX to translate the Hebrew word for infernal hell, "Sheol," and in 2 Pet 2.4 it is used to designate a place of torment for the fallen angels.

[R. J. LITZ]

TAS (East Ar.., das), in Armenian churches the choir, located between the *pem* (elevated sanctuary) and the *adyan* (nave).

[A. CODY]

TASCHEREAU, ELZÉAR ALEXANDRE (1820–98), abp. of Quebec. Ordained in 1842, T. did parish work, taught in the Quebec seminary, and served as rector of Laval Univ. before his consecration (1871) as abp. of Quebec. When the Canadian hierarchy condemned the Knights of Labor (1885), T. issued a circular letter warning Catholics against the trades union movement. Leo XIII made him the first Canadian cardinal (1886). One of the founders of Laval Univ., T. remained interested in Catholic education throughout his life. BIBLIOGRAPHY: H. Têtu, *Les Évêques de Québec* (1889); P. G. Roy, *La Famille Taschereau* (1901).

[R. K. MacMASTER]

TASSELS (IN THE BIBLE), a number of threads twisted together at the end of a single cord and sewed to the four corners of a cloak. These tassels were prescribed to be worn by all Israelites (Dt 22.12) to remind them to live by the commandments of the Lord (Num 15.39). Probably the practice was originally superstitious and was changed in meaning as the Mosaic religion developed. The gospel records indicate that Jesus wore such tassels. The sick sought to touch "the fringes" of his garment (Mt 9.20; 14.36) in the hope of being cured. Jesus criticized the scribes and Pharisees for making their tassels unusually long to attract special attention (Mt 23.5). BIBLIOGRAPHY: F. J. Stephens, "Ancient Significance of Sisith," JBL 50 (1931) 59–70.

[C. P. CEROKE]

TASSILO CUP, Merovingian chalice of gold, enameled and chased, presented by Tassilo, Duke of Bavaria, to the abbey of Kremsmünster between 777 and 788, a deep and fulsome cup-shape wisely revived in the present day, with a beauty of proportions esp. harmonious with 20th-cent.

ecclesiastical, architectural forms, as opposed to the unrelated tall, narrow shape of the Gothic chalice. More important is the consciousness that in all periods of high accomplishment, the minor arts have confirmed and intensified the architectural aesthetics through perfect harmony, as well as impressive craftsmanship.

[M. J. DALY]

TASSO, TORQUATO (1544–95), Italian Renaissance poet, best known for his epic masterpiece *La Gerusalemme liberata*, T. spent his early years in Naples but in 1554 followed his poet-father into political exile to Rome. His education took him to several other cities, but it was probably in Urbino, as a student at the Della Rovere court, that he developed his lifelong attachment to courtly life and to the chivalric ideal. That attachment, together with the philosophy and classical literary standards he acquired as a student of law at the Univ. of Padua, set the stage for his career and orientation as a poet. In 1562, still only 18, he published his first important work, *Rinaldo,* a romantic poetic essay, which enjoyed immediate critical success. In 1565 he entered the service of Card. d'Este in Ferrara, becoming in 1571 court poet to the d'Este Ruler, Duke Alfonso II. Here, amidst the splendors and intrigues of one of the most brilliant Renaissance courts, T.'s genius flourished. In 1573 T. completed the pastoral drama *Aminta* (published 1581), still considered one of the best examples of its type. Its classically inspired plot and lyrical evocation of the joys of rustic simplicity must have appealed strongly to its court audience, both for the chivalric values it projected and for its suggestion of a lost golden age. T.'s greatest work, *La Gerusalemme liberata,* a romantic epic in 20 cantos dealing with the Crusaders' siege and capture of the Holy City from the Saracens in 1099, was completed in 1575. This enormous undertaking joins the heroic epic form of Homer and Virgil with the chivalric romances of Ariosto, and creates out of these disparate elements a new whole, infused by Christian morality and at least loosely based on historical fact. If not totally successful, the poem nevertheless represents a noble attempt, which, for its linguistic beauty, high-minded themes, well-realized characterizations (especially of women), and colorful, romantic episodes, richly deserves its high reputation in Italian literature and readily explains its popularity among the poet's contemporaries. Ironically, the epic brought T. nothing but distress. Unfavorable criticism from both literary and religious sources led him first to delay its publication, then to develop excessive anxieties over the poem's orthodoxy, and finally to be victimized by paranoid delusions and a complete mental collapse. Thus, in 1579, after a violent attack on his patron, he was confined as a madman to a hospital, where he remained virtually a prisoner for the next seven years. (This tragic episode later inspired the legend that Tasso had been imprisoned owing to the poet's passionate love for Alfonso's sister, Leonora d'Este.) Yet even in these circumstances T. managed to write, both prose and poetry, and in

1581 a corrected edition of *Gerusalemme* was published in Ferrara, though it had not been authorized by its creator and was in fact later repudiated in favor of a much inferior, rather spiritless version, *La Gerusalemme conquistata* (1593). Upon his release in 1586, T. spent a year at the court of Duke Vincenzo Gonzaga in Mantua, where he completed the tragedy *Re Torrismondo*. He then traveled widely in Italy and wrote *Monte Oliveto* and a number of philosophical and moral dialogues. In Rome, after the publication of *Gerusalemme conquistata*, he was granted a pension by Pope Clement VIII, but he died before bestowal of the promised honor of poet laureate. T. also produced some 2,000 minor poems, letters, pieces of literary criticism, and a somewhat longer poem depicting the world's creation. Both for range and lyric quality, he easily ranks among his country's greatest poets.

[E. M. GATES]

TATIAN (b. *c.*120), Christian apologist. T. was born of pagan parents in eastern Syria. A pupil of Justin Martyr and convert to Christianity, he returned to the East (*c.*172) and started his own school, which advocated severe asceticism. Modern scholars challenge Irenaeus's statements (Eusebius, *Hist. eccl.* 4.29) regarding T.'s founding the Encratites and his affinity with Gnosticism. Of T.'s works only two survive. The *Diatesseron,* his most important work, is a harmony of the four Gospels. His *Discourse to the Greeks* is a vehement polemic against Greek culture and civilization. BIBLIOGRAPHY: G. Bardy, DTC 15.1:59–66; A. Hamman, LTK 9:1305.

[H. DRESSLER]

TATWINE OF CANTERBURY, ST. (d. 734), a Mercian monk of Breedon (Leicestershire) who was consecrated ninth abp. of Canterbury (731). T. was known for his godliness and learning. Forty riddles (in acrostic technique) and a grammar by him survive. BIBLIOGRAPHY: W. Hunt, DNB 19:389–390; W. Bolton, *History of Anglo-Latin Literature,* (1967).

[W. A. CHANEY]

TAULER, JOHN (*c.*1300–61), preacher and mystic. He entered the Dominican Order in his native city of Strassburg at the age of 13 and did his early ecclesiastical studies there. He completed them at Cologne *c.*1325–29. In both places he was probably under the tutelage of Meister *Eckhart. Following his studies, T. returned to Strassburg, remaining there until the local authorities exiled the Dominicans (who went to Basel) for obeying the papal interdict of 1326 in defiance of Louis of Bavaria. T. returned to Strassburg from Basel in 1347. In both cities T. carried on a vigorous preaching apostolate and became renowned as a spiritual director and a leader of the *Friends of God. Rulman Merswin, a wealthy merchant of Strassburg and a writer of spiritual treatises, was one of his penitents. Among his friends were the Dominicans Henry Suso, Margaret Ebner of Maria Medingin monastery, Christiana Ebner of the monastery of Engeltal, the secular priest Henry of Nördlingen, and probably the Flemish mystic Jan van Ruysbroeck. T. probably corresponded with the Italian Dominican mystic Venturino of Bergamo. His only authentic surviving letter was sent to Margaret Ebner. Most of his 83 extant sermons were preached to nuns and were taken down by his hearers. His warm personality was marked by deep thought, moderation, and humility. His vivid, picturesque sermons were illustrated by examples from everyday life. His spiritual doctrine was influenced by the themes of Eckhart, but T. was more practical, plain, direct, and marked by lack of hyperbole. Though advocating resignation to the will of God and stripping of personal interests and desires, T. insisted on an active, laborious, and virtuous life. His pretended conversion by the legendary ''Friend of God'' of the Oberland is a fiction. BIBLIOGRAPHY: F. Vetter, *Die Predigten Taulers* (Deutsche Texte des Mittelalters 11, 1910); an English anthology with introduction by Eric Colledge and Sr. M. Jane, *John Tauler, Spiritual Conferences* (1961); *John Tauler, ein deutscher Mystiker. Gedenkschrift zum 600 Todestage* (ed. E. Filthaut, 1961).

[W. A. HINNEBUSCH]

TAUNTON, ETHELRED (1857–1907), English ecclesiastical writer. Born in Rugeley, Staffordshire, he was educated at Downside, trained in music, and was for 6 years (1880–86) an Oblate of St. Charles at Bayswater. He left to serve the mission at Stoke Newington in N London until physical injury permanently incapacitated him for pastoral work. He turned to writing, produced numerous articles and several books, translated some works and founded the short-lived *St. Luke's Magazine* during his convalescence at Bruges (1888–90). In church music and liturgy, he was considered something of an authority. Inaccuracy and prejudice against the Jesuits, manifested in his controversial *The History of the Jesuits in England* and his article on the Jesuits in the 11th ed. of the *Encyclopedia Britannica,* made him a controversial figure.

[T. RYAN]

TAUROBOLIUM, a religious rite that originated in Asia Minor and passed over to Rome in the early 2d cent. A.D., where it became associated through religious syncretism with the worship of Cybele, or the *Magna Mater,* and from there spread throughout the West. In the performance of the rite, a ditch was dug and covered with a grating. The recipient descended into the ditch as a symbol of his death and burial, and a bull was sacrificed over him. He came out covered with blood in a kind of rebirth or resurrection. The beneficiary was adored by those who had gathered for the event: ''Mortal, you have become a god.'' The ceremony became extremely popular in the Late Empire. BIBLIOGRA-PHY: F. Cumont, *Les Religions orientales dans le paganisme romain* (4th ed., 1929) 63–68.

[M. J. COSTELLOE]

TAUSEN, HANS (1494–1561), the first preacher of the Reformation in Denmark. T. entered the Order of St. John of Jerusalem at Antvorskov and subsequently studied at Rostock, Copenhagen, Louvain, and Wittenberg, where in 1523 he adopted Luther's teaching. When he returned to Antvorskov and announced his conversion, he was sent away to Viborg. There he so favorably impressed his abbot that he was at first permitted to preach the new doctrine. Soon, however, he was expelled from his convent. At this juncture King Frederick I gave him a letter of protection, and the citizens of Viborg opened their largest church to him. In 1526 equal rights were given to Catholics and Lutherans, and the King called T. to preach in Copenhagen. T. helped draft the 43 articles presented to the Diet at Copenhagen (1530). In the changes of fortune that the two religions continued to experience he showed himself tolerant and even magnanimous. His translation of the Pentateuch appeared in 1535. After the death of the King, T. entered into a compromise with the bp. of Roskilde that harmed his reputation among Lutherans. As a consequence, he was passed over when evangelical superintendents were being named to replace the Catholic bishops in 1536 at the formal establishment of the Reformation. In 1538 he became professor of theology in Roskilde, and in 1542 he was made bp. of Ribe. BIBLIOGRAPHY: J. M. Jensen, EncLuthCh 3:2324.

TAVANT, FRESCOES OF, in the French church, at first a priory of Marmoutier (987), rebuilt as the church of St. Nicholas (11th–12th cent.), remarkable murals in the choir and semidome of the apse (discovered 1945–46), showing Christ in majesty with symbols of the Evangelists, eight angels below, and Infancy scenes. Most important is the series in the crypt, in expressive and iconographical aspects, the most unique Romanesque fresco cycle ever created, presenting in direct and forceful brushwork a *Psychomachia* of symbolic Virtues and Vices from Prudentius's poem, the mystery of Christ, Adam and Eve, scenes of the Deposition, and Limbo. All work is by the same hand and dates between 1125 and 1175. BIBLIOGRAPHY: P. H. Michel, *Les Fresques de Tavant* (1944).

[M. J. DALY]

TAVERNER, JOHN (*c.* 1495–1545), English organist and composer. T. was, for about 3 years, choirmaster and organist at Cardinal College in Oxford. During this period, it is supposed that he wrote his fine church music since, in 1528, he was accused of Lutheran heretical views, and, although subsequently released, he had undergone a complete change of religious conviction that ended his musical career; he became agent of T. *Cromwell in the dissolution of the monasteries. One of the finest church composers of the early Tudor period, T. followed Fairfax and just preceded Tye and Tallis. His works, contained in v. 1 and 3 of *Tudor Church Music* (1928), comprise Masses, Magnificats, motets, a *Te Deum,* and other sacred and secular compositions.

[M. T. LEGGE]

TAVERNER'S BIBLE, English translation issued in 1539 by the lawyer Richard Taverner (*c.*1505–75), who was proficient in Greek. It was a revision of *Matthew's Bible (1537). Since Coverdale's *Great Bible also appeared in 1539, Taverner's never became popular, although some of its phrases were used in the NT of the Authorized Version.

[T. EARLY]

TAX COLLECTOR, see PUBLICANS.

TAXATION, the process of imposing, by legitimate authority, a pecuniary charge on persons or property to acquire revenue to be spent for public purposes. In developing countries, taxation is a form of forced saving which diverts income from the consumption stream and channels it, by government spending, into the formation of productive and social overhead capital. In developed countries, the tax dollar supports a multitude of public services that no private individual or group could adequately provide, e.g., national defense, highway construction and maintenance. Taxes are levied on property and income (personal and corporate), on sales of some specified groups of retail or manufacturing establishments (sales tax), or on the sale of some particular good or service (excise tax). In the payment of taxes, there need not be a specific connection to the public service from which the taxpayer benefits, such as is the case in the payment of a highway toll. Taxes are proportional if they apply at the same rate to all incomes. They are progressive if they apply at a higher rate to higher incomes; the rates increase as the tax base (the object against which the tax is levied, in this case the amount of taxable income received) increases. A regressive tax, strictly speaking, would apply at rates which decline as the tax base increases. However, the term ordinarily applies to taxation which takes a larger percentage of total income from low than from high income groups. For example, a poor person ordinarily spends a higher percentage of his total income on groceries than a rich person does. A sales tax on grocery purchases is therefore called "regressive."

In his encyclical letter "On the Development of Peoples" (*Populorum progressio*, 1967) Pope Paul VI invited wealthy Christian nations to consider their obligations toward the poor nations of the world. Addressing individual Christians the Pope said, "Let each one examine his conscience, a conscience that conveys a new message for our times. Is he prepared to support out of his own pocket, works and undertakings organized in favor of the most destitute? Is he ready to pay higher taxes so that the public authorities can intensify their efforts in favor of development?" (n. 47). It is unlikely that this idea will be enthusiastically received by Christian taxpayers for many years to come. Most Catholic moral theologians hold that citizens are bound by legal and social justice to obey just tax laws. Since tax laws are of their nature onerous, it is morally right to take advantage of every legal means to pay no more than what the laws exact. BIBLIOGRAPHY: R. A. Musgrave, *Theory of Public Finance: A Study in Public Economy* (1959).

[W. J. BYRON]

TAXIL, LEO (pseud. of Gabriel Antoine Jogand-Pagès; 1854–1907), French author. Despite a Catholic rearing and a Jesuit education, T. became one of the most notorious religious hoaxes of the 19th century. He attacked the Catholic clergy in his first books, *La Soutane grotesque* (1879); *Les Bêtises sacrées* (1881); *Les Amours secrètes de Pie IX* (1881); *Les Borgia* (1881); *L'Empoisonneur Léon XIII* (1883). He also founded an antireligious publishing house and a daily newspaper, *L'Anti-clérical,* which catered to a league of freethinkers that reportedly numbered 17,000. Rejection of T. by the Freemasons prompted him in 1885 to repent apparently and return to the Church. Absolved of the excommunications against him and having closed his publishing firm under the pseudonym Leo Taxil, he attacked Freemasonry bitterly, particularly in a series of pamphlets with the general title *Révélations complètes sur la Franc-Maçonnerie.* Eventually the fabrications in these pamphlets were revealed with T. publicly gloating over his exploitation of Catholic credulity. Forced to leave Paris, he maintained his anticlerical stance until his death.

[T. J. RYAN]

TAYLOR, ALFRED EDWARD (1869–1945), British philosopher, whose teaching career was unusually varied, as were his interests—Greek philosophy, ethics, metaphysics, and the philosophy of religion. His thought lay roughly within the tradition of British Neo-Hegelianism, with other influences. He had a firm and lasting attachment to a theistic and spiritualistic interpretation of reality. He attempts to move from acts of moral experience to religious metaphysics. In the concrete experience of the world, facts and values are never separate but are given together. This moral aspect of experience must be seen to point beyond itself to theism and ultimately to religion. Value in concrete moral experience transcends the form of temporality and points to an eternal good. This striving is not frustrated but is responded to by the initiative of the eternal, a divine grace that makes possible moral fulfillment. This minimum philosophical theology itself seeks fulfillment in the concreteness of an actual historical religion. For T., Christian revelation esp. fulfills this expectation. BIBLIOGRAPHY: A. E. Taylor, *Plato: Man and His Work* (1926); *idem, Commentary on Plato's Timaeus* (1928).

[J. MCFADDEN]

TAYLOR, EDWARD BURNETT (1832–1917), founder of cultural anthropology. An Englishman, T. worked as a clerk until 1855 when he travelled to the U.S. and in Mexico, publishing in 1861 *Anahuac,* or *Mexico and the*

Mexicans, Ancient and Modern, a statement on the evolution of human culture. His most important work was *Primitive Culture* (1871), which treated of the relation of primitive man and modern man. In 1896 T. became the first professor of anthropology at Oxford. His theory postulates that the belief of man in non-material spirits originated in the phenomena of dreams. Primitive man saw himself as a dual being: body and soul; the body died but the spirit continued to live in a disembodied state. The same duality was characteristic of animals, whose spirits also survived death. Souls live on, either in close proximity to the living or in a special place.

[J. R. AHERNE]

TAYLOR, FRANCES MARGARET (1832–1900), foundress of the Poor Servants of the Mother of God. Born in Stoke-Rockford, Lincolnshire, England, as a young woman influenced by the Oxford Movement, T. was for a short time a member of Miss Sillon's Anglican sisterhood. While serving as a nurse during the Crimean War in a hospital ward of Irish Catholic soldiers, T. came into contact with Mother Mary Francis Bridgeman of the Sisters of Mercy and shortly thereafter converted to Roman Catholicism. In 1861, she entered the novitiate of the Sisters of Charity, Rue de Bac, Paris, but her superiors and Card. Manning urged her to return to London. There she founded the Poor Servants of the Mother of God and served as superior until her death. She was also active as a writer, as editor of the *Lamp,* and as a collaborator in the start of the English edition of the *Messenger of the Sacred Heart* and the *Month.* BIBLIOGRAPHY: M. Geraldine, NCE 13:952–953.

[T. J. RYAN]

TAYLOR, HUGH STOTT (1890–1974), chemist, Catholic lay leader at Princeton University. Born and educated in England, he joined the Department of Chemistry at Princeton in 1914 and served there until his retirement in 1958; from 1945 until 1958 he was Dean of the Graduate School of the university. In World War II he worked on the Manhattan Project; from 1958, he was president of the Woodrow Wilson Fellowship Foundation for the support of graduate students. He was knighted by Queen Elizabeth II in 1953. All through his life he was closely identified with the Catholic presence at Princeton and was the friend of J. *Maritain during the latter's tenure there. In 1953 T. was honored by the Pope with the title of Knight Commander of the Order of St. Gregory.

[J. R. AHERNE]

TAYLOR, JAMES HUDSON (1832–1905), English physician, founder of the China Inland Mission. He was devoted from 1853 to the evangelization of China and founded the China Inland Mission in 1865 as an interdenominational society of Protestant missionaries united in the common purpose of teaching the Bible. During T.'s lifetime and until the Communist regime, the China Inland

Mission had a successful history. T. himself was a man of apostolic dedication and personal holiness.

[T. C. O'BRIEN]

TAYLOR, JEREMY (1613–67), Anglican bp. and spiritual writer. Born and educated at Cambridge, T. was ordained in 1633. His charm and eloquence attracted the attention of Abp. W. *Laud, through whose favor he received rapid preferment, becoming chaplain to Charles I *c.*1635. He served as chaplain in the Royalist army and lived out the Commonwealth in Wales as chaplain to the earl of Carbery. After the Restoration he was made bp. of Down and Connor in Ireland (1660) and administrator of Dromore (1661), the Irish rather than an English appointment being due to some suspicion of his orthodoxy stemming from his attack upon Calvinist doctrine in his *Unum necessarium* (1655), and also from his friendship with C. *Davenport, the Franciscan. Of his theological works the best known are his *Liberty of Prophesying* (1647), a plea for tolerance for all whose religious views were not subversive to the state, and his *Ductor dubitantium* (1660), intended as a manual for confessors, the first complete work on casuistry in the English language. His fame rests chiefly upon his spiritual writings, esp. his *Rule and Exercise of Holy Living* (1650), and his *Rule and Exercise of Holy Dying* (1651). These are spiritual and literary classics, putting forth practical religious wisdom in ornate prose, rich with beautiful cadences and delicately wrought images. The abundance of detail and argument, which is a defect in his theological works, proves well suited to the reflective reading of devotion. He urges moderation, cheerfulness, contentment, and hopeful dependence on the goodness of God, and draws often from the Greek and Latin moralists of antiquity. Another spiritual work, *The Golden Grove* (1655), is a manual of instruction and prayers. Works: *Whole Works,* (ed. R. Heber, rev. C. P. Eden 10v., 1847–54). BIBLIOGRAPHY: C. J. Stranks, *Life and Writings of Jeremy Taylor* (1952).

[P. K. MEAGHER]

TAYLOR, JOHN (1694–1761), English biblicist. Educated at Whitehaven, he was ordained by dissenting ministers and worked at Norwich where he founded the Octagon Chapel (1754). In 1757 he was appointed divinity tutor at Warrington Academy. His greatest work of scholarship was his *Hebrew Concordance* (1754–57), based on that of J. Buxtorf and marking an important advance in the study of Hebrew roots. Theologically he tended toward an Arian view of the person of Christ and to a denial of the fact of original sin. His *Scriptural Doctrine of Original Sin* had a wide circulation, particularly in the U.S., where it prepared the way for the Unitarian Movement in American Congregationalism.

[T. J. RYAN]

TAYLOR, MYRON CHARLES (1874–1959), industrialist and diplomat who served as personal representative to the Vatican for Presidents Roosevelt and Truman. He was an executive of the U.S. Steel Corp., and in 1932 succeeded J. P. Morgan, Jr., as chairman of the board. In 1939 President Roosevelt gave T., an Episcopalian, the rank of ambassador and appointed him personal representative to Pius XII. He was charged particularly with facilitating cooperation in the interest of peace and alleviation of wartime suffering. He retained the position under President Truman until 1950, after which he performed other governmental missions. BIBLIOGRAPHY: T.'s *Wartime Correspondence between President Roosevelt and Pope Pius XII,* with introduction and notes (1947).

[T. EARLY]

TAYLOR, NATHANIEL WILLIAM (1786–1858), American Congregationalist theologian, professor at Yale Divinity School. After graduation from Yale, T. studied theology under T. *Dwight and was ordained in 1812 as pastor of the First Congregational Church, New Haven. He encouraged *revivalism in his church and was a founder of the *American Bible Society. His liberal Calvinism, termed the New Divinity or *New Haven theology, was foreshadowed by his 1819 sermon on "Salvation Free to the Willing." His more famous *Concio ad clerum,* a sermon preached at Yale in 1828, explained *total depravity to mean not man's nature but his own act, consisting of a free choice of some object rather than God as his chief good. T. was involved in controversy with both Unitarians and the conservatives in his own denomination and wrote voluminously on the disputed questions of predestination and freedom of the will. His classroom *Lectures on the Moral Government of God* (2v., 1859), defending a moral system created by God in which free agents are able to sin, became his major published work. "Taylorism" greatly contributed to the revivalism dominant in pre-Civil War American Protestantism. BIBLIOGRAPHY: S. E. Mead, *Nathaniel William Taylor* (1942); R. H. Bainton, *Yale and the Ministry* (1957); *Theology in America* (ed. S. E. Ahlstrom, 1967) 211–249.

TAYLOR, VINCENT (1887–1968), Methodist minister and NT theologian. After serving in numerous churches, he attained his Ph.D. in 1922 and his D.D. in 1926 from the Univ. of London. A long association with the Univ. of London (1931–43) as examiner in biblical languages and theology was followed by lectureships in NT Greek at Cambridge (1948–53) and Oxford (1951–52). His numerous works include: *The Atonement in the New Testament* (1945), *Forgiveness and Reconciliation* (1946), *The Formation of the Gospel Tradition* (1935), *The Names of Jesus* (1962).

[T. J. RYAN]

TAYLOR, WILLIAM (d. 1423), Lollard heretic; principal of St. Edmund Hall, Oxford (1405–06). After a long history of heretical activities, T. was degraded and burnt.

He held that prayer should not be directed to the saints or even to Christ under the aspect of his humanity. BIBLIOGRAPHY: Emden Ox 3:1852.

[F. D. BLACKLEY]

TE DEUM LAUDAMUS, canticle of praise almost certainly to be attributed to Nicetas, bp. of Remesiana (*c.*5th century) although by legend it was credited to St. Ambrose. The traditional chant melody is a composite creation, rare in Gregorian chant. The *Te Deum* became part of the Roman liturgy for Matins on Sundays and feast days and is used on special occasions as a most appropriate expression of joy and thanks. It has been a favorite text for composers of all periods.

[M. T. LEGGE]

TE IGITUR, the opening words of the First Eucharistic Prayer (Roman Canon). The English version begins, "We come to you, Father . . ." It was probably introduced into the Canon during the 4th century. It asks that the Father bless and accept the gifts offered, and declares the purpose for which they are offered; namely, that God watch over the Church, guide it, grant it peace and unity. Where the Latin text could be understood to mean that these gifts are offered in union with the pope, the bp., and those who hold and teach, etc., the English translators have taken it to mean that the gifts are offered for the pope, the bishop, etc.

[N. KOLLAR]

TEACHER, THE, a commonly used name for Jesus—24 times in the Synoptics alone. It should be considered with the related "Rabbi" (Mk 9.5; 11.21; 14.45; Mt 26.25), "Rabbuni" (Mk 10.51) and "Master" (Lk 5.5; 8.24,45; 9.33,49; 17.13). John states that "Teacher" (*didaskalos*) translates the Aramaic "Rabbi" (1.38) and "Rabbuni" (20.16). The latter are titles of respect used for teachers of the Law and undoubtedly represent a form of address used by the contemporaries of Jesus. Luke betrays his sense of their inadequacy in his use of "Master." For the same reason none of the four titles received wide usage and are not found in the rest of the NT. BIBLIOGRAPHY: L. Sabourin, *Names and Titles of Jesus* (tr. M. Carroll, 1967); V. Taylor, *Names of Jesus* (1962).

[J. J. CUNNINGHAM]

TEACHING AUTHORITY OF THE CHURCH, see MAGISTERIUM.

TEACHING OF JESUS, the message of the earthly Jesus, taught to his Disciples and countrymen prior to his Crucifixion. The use of the term intends a distinction both from the message about Jesus, proclaimed and taught by those who believed in his Resurrection after his Crucifixion and from the account of his message written by the four Evangelists for the early Church from their perspective of resurrection faith. The teaching of Jesus is still the subject of serious dispute. Critics and historians with impressive credentials manage to differ fundamentally in establishing what can reliably be accepted as the teaching of Jesus and in the meaning they assign to those words of Jesus they agree to accept. The range of divergence rather widens than narrows with time. The recent tendency among believing scholars has been to emphasize the theology of the Evangelists, viewed in their role as editors sifting and shaping earlier traditions, and to put off indefinitely the task of getting beyond the traditions of the first Palestinian Christian communities to the teaching ministry of Jesus. Furthermore, it seems evident that the teaching of Jesus was a matter of little significance to important elements of the early Church. One searches in vain, for example, among the writings of Paul for a reference to the teaching of Jesus to help solve the many thorny questions of faith and morals that fill his letters. Acts contains many examples of early Christian preaching, attributed to Peter, Paul, Stephen, and others, and addressed to Jew and Gentile, but has scarcely a reference to the teaching of Jesus. It is not clear whether Paul ever knew Jesus and he may have been deliberately vague on the subject. He preached Christ as the risen Lord who gives the Spirit to those who believe him risen and able to save them from sin; he preached only Christ crucified and raised from the dead. For his communities that became the core of the gospel message. In such communities, if a word from the Lord is invoked to settle an issue, the reference is to a word from the risen Christ spoken through a Christian prophet at a Spirit–filled gathering. The role of such prophets is easily understated by modern Christians, since the phenomenon fell into disfavor during the 2d cent. because of Montanist aberrations. For the Pauline communities the Church is founded on the Apostles and the Prophets, Apostles being originally primarily those to whom God had revealed Jesus as the Risen One who would soon come again as the Christ (i.e., those graced with resurrection experiences) and Prophets being those Spirit-filled Christians who revealed the mind of the Risen One and through whom the Christ gave instruction and guidance to the New Israel. The Pauline letters, the Gospel of John, and the Book of Revelations contain, in large part, revelations of the risen Christ through the Christian prophets. But in the early Christian communities, there were other dynamics, linked more to the historical Israel than to the historical Jesus and especially represented by the traditions incorporated into the Synoptic Gospels. Through them come echoes first of the Aramaic, Palestinian, and Jewish Christian communities, and by reflection, echoes of the teaching ministry of Jesus. In the account of Jesus' miracles and teaching found in these traditions, no title is so frequently used in addressing Jesus as "teacher" or "rabbi." Here Jesus acts as a teacher of the Law, gathering disciples, expounding biblical texts, and being asked questions typically asked of rabbis: Is it lawful to divorce your wife for any reason? Which is the greatest commandment? Who is my neighbor? How many will be saved? What will the resurrection be like? Who sinned, this man or his parents, that he should be born blind? He taught like a fully accredited rabbi, with the privilege of introducing novel modes of interpretation, not like an elementary teacher. His pattern of public retort and private explanation was a familiar rabbinic one. He taught in the synagogue, in the Temple, and in the open air. However, he was also viewed as having a special quality, as a teacher with the power of healing and as one with the spirit of the ancient Prophets, esp. Elijah, to whom miracles had also been attributed. He is perhaps best known for his use of parables, an apt polemical device before a diversified audience; but the Gospels also preserve his sayings and exhortations, blessings and woes. The sayings reflect varied cultural traditions, prophetic and apocalyptic, as well as timeless wisdom. In his prophetic utterances, with his careful use of parallelism typical of Hebrew poetry, he matched the power and grandeur of the ancient Prophets. Some parables, such as those on the Prodigal Son or the Good Samaritan, easily transcend their historical moment and retain power in any religious tradition. Some aspects of Jesus' message have proven to be stumbling blocks to many: the note of apocalypse, the urgent eschatology, and even the central theme of God's coming reign by which he will transform the world by his saving power. Yet Jesus' call to repent, to forgive and be forgiven, to believe the gospel, can only be understood in the context of urgent eschatology, and the special moment in Jewish apocalyptic introduced by the ministry of John the Baptist. The needs of the primitive Church determined which teachings of Jesus would be remembered and how they would be modified, arranged, and edited. In the last analysis it is now virtually impossible to separate the teaching of Jesus from the proclamation and catechesis of the early Church. The effort to do so must continue, but the results will always be incomplete and subject to dispute. To some, that will present more of a problem than to others, and not one likely soon to disappear. BIBLIOGRAPHY: A. Schweitzer, *Quest for the Historical Jesus* (1910); R. Bultmann, *History of the Synoptic Tradition* (1926); J. Jeremias, *Rediscovering the Parables* (pa. 1966).

[E. J. DILLON]

TEACHING SISTERS OF THE HOLY CROSS (Menzinger Sisters), a congregation of religious women founded for educational and charitable works, in Switzerland in 1844 by the Capuchin Theodosius Florentini (1808–65) and Mother Maria Bernarda Heimgartner. They conduct elementary and secondary schools, hospitals, homes for the aged, the poor, and the handicapped. The community has foundations in Europe, Africa, and Latin America. In 1975 they had 3,335 members in 384 houses.

[J. R. AHERNE]

TEBROUTIUN, book containing extracts from the Armenian liturgy for the use of the faithful.

[A. CODY]

TECHNOLOGY in the broad sense encompasses the practical arts or applied sciences and deals with the methods and tools created by man for manipulating and dominating the total human environment. In the plural form of technologies or techniques, the reference is to bodies of skills, knowledge and procedures for creating, using, and developing tools to achieve useful things. Technology always refers to action rather than contemplative knowledge. As a tool, a technology or a technique is the concrete instrument created and used by man to obtain certain ends. From this perspective the history of technology can be considered as the history of inventions, developments, and improvements of mechanical means. Technologization and mechanization are sometimes identified. As a method, technology represents the totality of the processes, rationally arrived at, which supposedly assure absolute efficiency in every field of human activity. From this point of view, technology represents more than the manipulation of the natural environment; it is almost a re-creation of the environment. Technology and environment are so inseparably connected that the extension and nature of the former will depend on man's actual concept of the latter. Techniques created for manipulation of environment will then be determined by the cosmology developed at a given time in a given society. But a technique which changes environment also creates the need of another technique to cope with this new environment, and so on indefinitely. Technology in this sense can be considered as the most important source of societal change and historical development.

The magical use of religion is a technique; such was the case in primitive society when environment was considered to include hostile spirits against which man had to defend himself. Magic was a technique invented for the manipulation of this animist environment. The primitive magical mind is generally hostile to the development of a rational, material technology because it fears the invisible reality which continues to dominate its image of the environment. Thus it is opposed to the modern technological mind because of its view of the environment through a different cosmology even though both magic and technology are tools for dealing with the environment.

Modern Western technology, certainly the most advanced and inclusive form of technology ever developed, finds its origin in: (1) the Judaeo-Christian belief in the creation of the world by God which thus liberates the natural environment from the presence of irrational spirits, and also rejects magic as a tool for manipulating the supernatural and transforms nature into a rationally organized material environment capable of being mastered by rational means; (2) the continuous transmission of cultural heritages and technologies through successive generations; this permitted the accumulation of skills and knowledge that creates in turn the acceleration of the mutual transformation of environment and technology. The changes have been cumulative, not repetitive, in Western history. Present technological society then can be defined as that stage of development in which the environment has become more technicized than natural. Today man lives in a completely new environment, no longer the natural, God-created world, but an artificial, rationalized, man-created technological world. Environment does not therefore appear hostile to man because he recognizes himself in it.

This is why the technological world is not only one in which the environment has been transformed but a world in which man and environment tend to be identified. This represents a danger for man's freedom. Technology's existence requires a new theology of the co-creative vocation of man with God in the general framework of the divine economy of creation and salvation. This new theology should be of man himself who, in a technological world, can become the slave of his own rational powers to rationalize life. What he needs is a renewed awareness of the Christian call to freedom, for he will be free only when he masters his own technology. In rejecting it he retreats to magic. Man can, then, dominate technology by transcending it in a renewal of a strong belief in the individual vocation offered by the Christian message. BIBLIOGRAPHY: J. Ellul, *Technological Society* (1967); L. Mumford, *Technics and Civilization* (1963); *idem, Technics and Human Development (Myth of the Machine* v. 1, 1967).

[G. FRAGNIÈRE]

TECHO, NICOLÁS DEL (1611–85), Jesuit missionary and historian. Born in Lille, France, he served in the Guarani missions in Paraguay for most of his life. He wrote the *Historia provinciae paraguariae Societatis Jesu* and *Decades virorum illustrium paraguariae Societatis Jesu.*

[P. J. HENNESSEY]

TEGERNSEE, ABBEY OF, Benedictine monastery of the Holy Savior, located on Lake Tegern between the Isser and the Inn in SE Bavaria, founded (746) by its first abbot Adalbert and his brother Otkar, counts of Warngau and Tegernsee. Completely destroyed in the Magyar invasion of 907, it was restored in 979 by Otto II and Abbot Hartwich, a former monk of St. Maximin of Trier and reformed by St. Godard (d. 1038), becoming a center of monastic reform, famous for its production of stained glass. After declining in the 14th cent., the abbey revived under Abbot Caspar Ayndorffer (1426–68), who reformed it in the pattern of Melk. In 1684 the abbey became the head of the Bavarian Benedictine Union and its abbot was titled "primate of Bavaria." After the abbey's suppression in 1803, its library was transported to the National Library of Munich. BIBLIOGRAPHY: Cottineau 2:3127–29.

[E. J. DILLON]

TEILHARD DE CHARDIN, PIERRE (1881–1955), French Jesuit, scientist, poet, theologian, and writer. T. studied at the Jesuit College of Notre Dame de Mongré, near Lyons; entered the Jesuits (1899); and taught physics and chemistry at Ismailia, Egypt (1905–08). In 1912 at

Paris, he worked under the renowned paleontologist, Mercellin Boule, and became a confirmed evolutionist under the influence of Henry Bergson's *Creative Evolution*. He served as corporal in the medical corps during World War I; became professor of geology at the Institut Catholique in Paris; began (1923) a series of geological excavations for the French government in China; and lectured (1933) throughout North America. In 1939, he was interned in Peking for the duration of World War II, and it was during this period that he wrote his most significant work, *Phenomenon of Man*. When he returned to France after the war, Roman ecclesiastical officials refused permission for the publication of *Phenomenon of Man* since it seemed to them to contradict *monogenesis and the gratuity of the *supernatural. In view of his outstanding work in geology, paleontology, and anthropology, however, T. was elected (1950) to the French Academy of Sciences. But because his religious ideas were regarded with suspicion, he was asked to leave Paris by his superiors and in 1951 he went to New York at the request of the Wenner-Gren Foundation for Anthropological Research. Except for several expeditions to S Africa, he remained in New York until his death.

The major thrust of T.'s thought was the synthesis of mind and matter. According to T., mind and matter share the same primitive origin and are two manifestations of a primal stock or world stuff. This primal matter moved up an axis of complexity-consciousness. Under the pressure of an explosively expanding universe subatomic particles formed atoms, atoms formed molecules, micro-molecules formed mega-molecules, inorganic compounds formed living organisms. This progressive complexity of matter was accompanied by an intensification of consciousness within matter. The high point of the process presently is man whose closely knit molecular structure is capable of self-reflective consciousness. At the apex of the axis of complexity-consciousness is the *Omega Point*. Omega is that point toward which the human species is evolving. It is a point at which the total organism of thinking particles will become superpersonalized. Omega is both a point drawing all matter to superpersonalization and a point buried deeply within the evolutionary process pushing matter toward its evolutionary goal. Theologically Teilhard makes Christ and Omega identical. Christ is Omega drawing all conscious matter to unity with him and through him with God.

In addition to *Phenomenon of Man* (1959), T.'s works include *Divine Milieu* (1960), *Making of the Mind* (1961), *Man's Place in Nature* (1961), *Hymn of the Universe* (1961), and *Future of Man* (1964). BIBLIOGRAPHY: C. Cuénot, *Teilhard de Chardin* (tr. V. Colimore, 1965); H. DeLubac, *Teilhard de Chardin, The Man and His Meaning* (tr. R. Hague, 1967).

[W. J. DUGGAN]

TEKAKWITHA KATERI, VEN. (1656–1680), Mohawk Indian and candidate for canonization. Baptized by the Catholic missionary Jacques de Lamberville in 1675, she was forced by the hostility of the tribe to live among Christian Indians in Canada. There she lived a life of great austerity until her death at the age of 24. Her cause was introduced in Rome in 1932. BIBLIOGRAPHY: M. C. Buehrle, *Kateri of the Mohawks* (1954).

[J. R. AHERNE]

TEKOA (Thecue), section of the Judean wilderness and a city of that area about 10 miles S of Jerusalem. Known particularly as the home of Amos (1.1), it is mentioned several times in OT history (2 Sam 14.4; Neh 3.5; 2 Chr 11.6).

TELEOLOGY, theory that the universe or parts of it are directed toward an end or goal. It is distinguished from mechanistic theories that assert the universe can be explained only in terms of its processes. Though the term was perhaps first used by C. Wolff in 1728, teleology was taught by Aristotle and St. Thomas. It found popular expression in W. Paley's *Evidences* (1794). Darwin's theory of natural selection invalidated the concept for many philosophers, but others contend the universe as a whole can still be interpreted in terms of the goal toward which it moves. BIBLIOGRAPHY: W. R. Mathews, *Purpose of God* (1936).

[T. EARLY]

TELEPATHY (from the Gr. *tēle*, afar, and *patheia*, feeling), the transmission and/or reception of impressions from one mind to another independently of the recognized channels of sense, and therefore classed among the extrasensory phenomena, ESP, and included by parapsychologists among psi- phenomena, i.e., actions emanating from the mind. In the past, extraordinary instances of communication were either ascribed to supernatural or preternatural ''powers'' or dismissed as not worthy of rational investigation. However, they are taken for granted in some regions, e.g., the Hebrides, where the phenomenon is generally referred to as ''second sight.'' Tests conducted under scientific controls confirm their existence but do not explain how the power is present and how it functions.

[C. P. SVOBODA]

TELESIO, BERNARDINO (1509–88), pioneer in the empirical study of nature. He was a man of letters and of philosophical interests, but never formally a teacher. His main work, *De rerum natura juxta propria principia* (1586), as its title indicates, is a study of nature based on experimental observation of its own workings. In inspiration it was directed against Aristotle, whose *Physics* T. criticized for being based on abstract ideas, not on concrete observation. T.'s chief importance is the direction he gave toward use of the empirical method that was followed by such figures as Galileo, T. Campanella, F. Bacon, and other leaders in the history of the sciences. T. was not a crypto-rebel against the Church or the Christian faith; he thought his own teaching to be in harmony with biblical teaching on creation.

[T. C. O'BRIEN]

TELESPHORUS, ST. (d. 136), **POPE** from 125, martyr. St. *Irenaeus lists T. as the 7th successor of St. Peter and states that he always observed Easter on Sunday (see QUAR-TODECIMAN CONTROVERSY). The same witness (*Adv. haer.* 3.3) also makes T. the first of the early popes whose martyrdom is established with certainty. The introduction of the *Gloria* into the Mass is ascribed to T. by the *Liber pontificalis*, but this is a baseless legend. BIBLIOGRAPHY: É. Amann, DTC 15:82; Butler 1:33; A. Frutaz, EncCatt 11:1872.

[R. B. ENO]

TELESPHORUS OF COSENZA, the author, probably pseudonymous, of a volume of millennialist prophecies composed (*c.*1356–65) during the Great Schism and which predicted that the Schism would end in 1393. The author drew heavily on earlier apocalyptic literature, esp. the works attributed to Joachim of Fiore. BIBLIOGRAPHY: Pastor 1:152–155.

[J. MULDOON]

TELLO, ANTONIO (d. 1653), Spanish Franciscan, chronicler of his order's missions in Mexico and California in *Cronaca miscelanea de la sancta provincia de Xatisco*. The work existed only in MSS until the 19th cent.; parts have been lost; a modern edition of those extant has been published.

[T. C. O'BRIEN]

TᵉLŌIṬŌ (erection), West Syrian indication that a prayer is to be said by the celebrant aloud and without inclination.

TEMERITY, in a moral sense, a contempt for rule, guidance, or counsel (ThAq ST 2a2ae, 53.3 ad 2). One manifestation goes against *prudence—foolhardiness, i.e., precipitateness in a situation calling for step-by-step deliberateness (*ibid.*). Rashness is also a quality that causes unjust judgment about the actions of others, one based on flimsy reasons or mere suspicion (*ibid.*, 60.2 & 3). Temerity may also amount to arrogance, a prideful claim to endowments not possessed (*ibid.*, 112.1 ad 2). As it names reckless daring, temerity is an unreasonable disregard of risk or peril, the contrary of true moral *courage (*ibid.*, 123.4; see 1a2ae, 45 on daring). Among the theological "notes" or qualifications applied to statements not conformed to the teachings of faith, one censure is "temerarious and false"; the meaning is that the censured statement, while not heretical, does go counter to a conclusion, proved or commonly agreed upon by theologians of repute; thus a statement contrary to a "certain theological conclusion."

[T. C. O'BRIEN]

TEMPERAMENT, in common usage, the total of an individual's basic tendencies and characteristics that are the result of his innate physical and mental organization. It differs from character because character includes what a person is by acquired habit, disposition, and inclination. Both concepts are obviously useful in the evaluation of moral and religious behavior. The oldest and best-known attempt to classify types of temperament is that made by Galen (d. *c.*201 A.D.), who distinguished four temperaments—the choleric, the melancholic, the phlegmatic, and the sanguine—and attributed the difference between them to the relative proportions in different individuals of the four humors or vital juices that enter into the composition of the human body. Galen's physiology was accepted in the Middle Ages and the differences of temperament he noted were well known to moralists, ascetical writers, and preachers. As useful summations of common observation, the four temperaments described by Galen have survived the naive physiology with which they were associated. In modern times attempts have been made to correlate differences of temperament with other physiological and anatomical differences. The German psychiatrist, E. Kretschmer, proposed three types: the asthenic (long and lean in physique), the athletic (muscular and tough), and the pyknic (round and short). The first two types were claimed to tend toward schizoid personalities, and the last toward the cycloid type characterized by alternating enthusiasm and depression. The American anthropologist, W. Sheldon, proposed similar basic components, and called the physical types ectomorphic, mesomorphic, and endomorphic, which are respectively sensitive, muscular, and visceral. These he correlated with three psychological types, namely, cerebrotonic (withdrawn and moody), somatotonic (aggressive and tough), and viscerotonic (sociable and comfort-loving). An Italian theory based on work begun by A. de Giovanni, proposes types on the basis of hyper- or hypo-functioning of various endocrine glands, e.g. hyper- and hypothyroid, hyper- and hypoadrenal, etc.

The material brought to light by depth psychology shows the importance of early life experiences upon an individual's basic and ostensibly inborn characteristics. To some extent this weakens the assumption of a marked correspondence between physical and psychical types and perhaps even invalidates the concept of temperament as defined above. Two modern classifications of psychological types, unassociated with biotypology, have proved useful in the study of human behavior, namely, Freud's oral, anal, and genital types; and Jung's introversion-extraversion classification. BIBLIOGRAPHY: E. Martínez, NCE 14:352–353; M. Stock, NCE 13:983–985.

[M. E. STOCK]

TEMPERANCE (Lat. *temperantia*; Gr. *sōphrosunē*), the virtue of moderation in the desire for pleasures, chiefly those of the sense, commonly recommended by all sages. To the Latin Stoics virtue lay in an aloofness from passion of any sort; while the patristic and ascetical authors were inclined to echo dutifully the puritan ideals of philosophers they admired, they were addressing themselves, not to an ethical élite, but to ordinary people struggling to be good Christians in the flesh. Temperance was treated as a general condition of all virtue, a restraint manifested in a certain poise and decency of comportment, austere and even spare in its wants, modest and unaffected, grave and, above all, well-ordered.

When Aristotle was recovered in the 13th cent. a more systematic moral theology was developed, together with a more specialized notion of temperance, though the general notion was retained (*temperantia metaphorica*) and even expanded by the spiritual writers, who were aware of pleasures more subtle and beguiling than those of the flesh, under such captions as undue attachment to creatures and spiritual fornication. Temperance as a special virtue was described, and sometimes morosely, in terms of the bodily pleasures, of which the most primitive and deepseated, the most important for the preservation of the individual and the race, and the strongest and most likely to be upsetting to the rule of reason, were those connected with what they called the sense of touch (*tactus*); this should be rendered as a diffused body-sense not restricted to skin contacts or any one particular organ, but basic to all sensation. And so by antonomasia temperance was defined in this field: the cardinal virtue at work among these pleasures in keeping the course of reason between two extremes—one, by excess, the various forms of dissoluteness; the other, by defect, the various forms of unfeelingness (*insensibilitas, apatheia, anaisthesis*). This narrowing down, though open to the occupational hazard of a somewhat coarse fixation on the gullet and the genitals, is in fact, as will be suggested, a delicate attempt to localize the topic accompanied by a modest recognition of its limits.

The parts of a cardinal virtue fall into three groups: (1) its component elements or integrating parts; (2) its associated virtues, i.e., virtual or potential parts; and (3) its subspecies or subjective parts.

(1) Sensitiveness to shame (*verecundia*) and a sense of honor (*honestas*), as described by the *Nicomachean Ethics*, Cicero, and St. Ambrose, are treated as appropriate elements in temperance; of themselves they are emotions that do not amount to virtue, yet by their fastidiousness and gallantry enter into its makeup.

(2) The virtues allied to temperance, described more fully under their separate entries, are as follows: *Continence, a virtue of will-power which masters the passion of lust, without, however, composing it, as temperance does. Meekness and clemency moderate the pleasures of anger and punishing respectively. Modesty is a generic heading for temperance in behavior, and rather loosely covers: *humility; *studiousness, the right pursuit of knowledge (*studiositas*); playfulness (*eutrapelia*); being neither over- nor under-dressed. All these are virtues of temperance about pleasures in a field much wider than that of temperance in its most specific sense.

(3) Most specifically, temperance is a well-controlled attitude in a man's power of emotional desire (the concupiscible appetite, *epithumētikon*) toward the pleasures of the body-sense. This appetite requires regulation to keep it in accord with the reasonable needs of this life. Temperance is not as such directly engaged in the higher pleasures nor with the wilder shores of love. It ranks well below the theological virtues, and after the other three cardinal virtues, prudence, justice, and courage—a thought usually slurred over in pastoral instruction and homiletic literature.

The emphasis on the comparative earthiness of temperance is continued in the classification of its kinds, which are concerned with the natural functions of nutrition or reproduction. Eating and drinking are sufficiently distinct human occupations, whatever the dietetics of the question, to warrant discrimination between abstemiousness (*abstinentia*) and sobriety (*sobrietas*).

Both Aristotle and St. Thomas were of the opinion that the pleasure in eating relevant to morals lay in the body-sense rather than in the taste; all the same, if it is not in the palate, neither is it in the belly, for the contrary vice of gluttony, if more a matter of being a gourmand than a gourmet, lies in being greedy, not in being stuffed. The student will pursue his own researches beyond this summary, bearing in mind that the normal subject for gluttony is a fairly well nourished person, not a Lucullus nor a half-starved tribesman before a freshly killed buffalo. One principal act of abstemiousness is called fasting (*jejunium*).

The grounds for discerning a special kind of temperance in sobriety are slightly more complicated, yet they remain those according to ordinary usage and not that of any particular school of physiology or psychology. Sobriety is not concerned with drink as such, but with intoxicating drink, and it seems difficult to relate this to the body-sense directly, and not to the nose and palate, or even the eye. Here again the opposite vice of drunkenness lies in the over-indulging, not in the after-effects, which are governed by other moral considerations. Both psychologically and morally, a drunkard has to be distinguished from an alcoholic, whose predicament is not intemperate indulgence in pleasure. The use of tobacco is governed by the principles affecting sobriety; had pleasurable smoking existed in the days of St. Thomas, he would doubtless have found a special name and slot for its pleasurable use and abuse. Many other forms of drug-taking, however, seem to lie outside the special field of temperance, and call for treatment, perhaps under its virtual parts, perhaps under courage or justice.

In matters of sex the virtue of temperance is called chastity (*castitas*) where complete venereal satisfaction is concerned, and purity (*pudicitia*) in the matter of thoughts, words, and deeds more or less closely related to it. Virginity is an exceptional yet admirable type of chastity, to which it is compared as magnificence to liberality. The vice opposed to chastity is called *luxuria,* lechery, lewdness, lasciviousness, and is traditionally divided into fornication, seduction, rape, incest, adultery, sacrilege, and other aberrancies, autosexual, homosexual, heterosexual, some of which stray outside humanity. All these matters, both good and bad, should be seen with a sense of proportion. A human streak towards the bawdy and obscene lends them a compulsive interest, yet the space given them in some textbooks is beyond the measure of their importance.

The resolute keying down of temperance to the animal levels of life is part of a process of establishing a moral typology apart from individual situations and personal intentions, though these are of no less importance for the complete picture. The purpose of placing chastity under the special virtue of temperance is to tackle some of the common difficulties arising from sex, and to uncover some of the rules for the behavior of a man and a woman together, not directly to mediate their relationship as persons, nor consequently to discuss the mystery and the problem of sex. Yet persons are individual examples of human nature, and it is in their animality that their sexuality is rooted as well as their pleasures with meals and strong drink. BIBLIOGRAPHY: ThAq 2a2ae, 141–154, (Lat-Eng, v. 43, ed. T. Gilby); T. Gilby, NCE 13:985–987.

[T. GILBY]

TEMPERANCE MOVEMENT, the organized crusade against use of alcoholic beverages that began in the early 19th cent. as one of many expressions of the religious and humanitarian impulses of that period. In an era when many tended to concentrate upon one reform as the panacea for all human ills, abstention from intoxicants was frequently thought of as the remedy for poverty, vice, ill-health, marital discord, etc. The first organized groups were limited to families or segments of congregations, but a national movement to combat intemperance was initiated (1812) by the preaching of Lyman *Beecher (1775–1863). The American Society for the Promotion of Temperance, founded (1826) at Boston, Mass., sponsored reform publications and revivalistic-type meetings across the U.S. and was the model for a similar organization in Canada. As the cause gained in popularity, local societies sprang up; an effort at coordination was made with the creation (1833) of the U.S. Temperance Union, later the American Temperance Union. The first World Temperance Convention was held in London, England (1846), and was attended by American delegates Beecher and William Lloyd Garrison, abolitionist leader. RC interest in temperance grew also, and independent groups were founded in Boston and elsewhere, encouraged by the approval of the bps. at the Provincial Council of Baltimore (1840). Converts to the cause of total abstinence increased as a result of the Catholic–Protestant-sponsored American tour (1849) of the Irish Capuchin preacher Theobald Mathew. However, the national controversy over slavery, Civil War, and the problems of the Reconstruction era brought about a temporary decline in public interest in the temperance movement.

The organization of the *Woman's Christian Temperance Union (1874) revived the cause, and emphasis shifted from temperance to total abstinence and a full-scale attack upon the saloon. The major thrust, however, was initiated by the formation of the Anti-Saloon League of America (1895), an agency manned by socially progressive Protestant churchmen and assisted by a number of liberal Catholics. The revivalistic doctrines of *Christian perfection and *sanctification, as well as commitment to the *Social Gospel for the betterment of the working man, inspired the crusade. By 1900, five of the forty-five states had adopted laws banning the manufacture and sale of intoxicating beverages, while others had made provision for local option. Meanwhile, general RC interest in total abstinence had revived and many RC societies had been founded, including the Catholic Total Abstinence Union of America (1872), a moderate, nonprohibitionist organization that generally avoided politics and confined its activities to moral suasion. However, the drive to suppress the liquor traffic had strong support, and it eventually became a great crusade of many Protestant, and esp. Methodist, Churches. By April 1917, more than 25 states had gone "dry," and before the end of the year a constitutional amendment prohibiting the manufacture, transportation, and sale of alcoholic beverages had been passed by Congress and submitted to the states for ratification. The 18th Amendment became effective in Jan. 1920, but the enforcement procedures established were widely disregarded; a general disrespect for law ensued, with an increase in organized crime. The 21st Amendment (1933) repealed the 18th, ending the unsuccessful national experiment in prohibition. Subsequently, temperance groups devoted themselves to promoting their cause through educational programs and state legislation. Some, like Alcoholics Anonymous (1935), relied heavily on religious motivation and the fellowship of other victims. BIBLIOGRAPHY: J. Bland, *Hibernian Crusade: The Story of the Catholic Total Abstinence Union of America* (1951); J. R. Gusfield, *Symbolic Crusade: Status Politics and the American Temperance Movement* (1963); J. H. Timberlake, *Prohibition and the Progressive Movement, 1900–1920* (1963); A. Sinclair, *Prohibition, the Era of Excess* (1962); HistAmMeth 3:329–343.

[M. CARTHY]

TEMPIER, ÉTIENNE, (d. 1279), bp. of Paris from 1268 until his death. He is esp. known for his activity against radical Aristotelianism and Latin Averroism at the Univ. of Paris. As bp., he condemned 13 philosophical errors related to Averroism (Dec. 10, 1270) and 219 propositions taken from the writings of masters of the faculty of arts among whom was Thomas Aquinas (March 7, 1277). BIBLIOGRAPHY: M. de Wulf, *History of Mediaeval Philosophy* (tr. E. C. Messenger, 1937) 1:320; P. Glorieux, DTC 15:99–107.

[J. J. SMITH]

TEMPIETTO, name given to the martyrium of S. Pietro, in Montorio, Rome. Designed in severe, Roman Doric order by D. *Bramante in 1502, this small but monumental, centrally planned shrine with deeply "sculptured wall" has exerted a tremendous influence on the history of Western architecture. Built to commemorate the spot where St. Peter was erroneously believed to have been crucified the "Tempietto" embodies the High Renaissance ideal of totally rationalized space and integrated forms.

[L. A. LEITE]

TEMPLARS, the first of 12 military religious orders of knights to flourish in the high Middle Ages. Their ruthless suppression at the hands of Philip IV (the Fair) of France and the Avignon pope, Clement V, remains one of the most debated events of medieval history. The Templars were established during the Crusades in the early years of the (Frankish) Kingdom of Jerusalem and were founded *c*.1119–20 by eight or nine French knights led by Hugh of Payens and Godfrey of Saint-Omer. They formed a religious community committed to defend and guide Christian pilgrims along the often dangerous routes to the holy places in Palestine. The knights were given quarters by King Baldwin II in a wing of the royal palace in Jerusalem, in the area of the former Jewish Temple, hence the name Templars. They were also popularly called Poor Brothers of the Temple. Their official Latin name was *Pauperes commilitones Christi templi Solomonici*, which could be translated, Poor Fellow-knights of Christ (and) of the Temple of Solomon. Their head was known as the Grand Master of the Temple of Jerusalem; their rule was written by Bernard of Clairvaux, whose favor enhanced their popularity throughout Europe. At first they avoided all pomp as well as the wearing of any distinctive garb. Under the Cistercian Pope Eugene III the Templars were permitted to wear the white mantle of the Cistercians with a distinctive red cross. Originally members had the prerogative to leave at will after entry; later they could only leave to enter a stricter order. At first members were knights drawn from the nobility. Later priests were admitted as chaplains, and "sergeants" were admitted from the wealthy bourgeoisie. The fact that they were subject only to the pope, that they were free from the tithe, and that they amassed great wealth and lands all over Europe made them the objects of envy and hostility. As long as the defense of the Holy Land was in question attacks on them were unsuccessful. The final ousting of the Christians in 1291 spelled doom for the Templars. King Philip IV of France undertook an intensive propaganda campaign against them, arrested their entire membership on the same day (Oct. 13, 1307), occupied their lands, and sequestered their properties. In lands free of French control—England, Scotland, Ireland, Aragon, Castile, and Germany—they were found innocent of all charges, including heresy and immorality. Within Philip's sphere of influence—France, Provence, the Kingdom of Naples, and the Papal States—they were found guilty as charged. Pope Clement V, who owed his election to Philip and was eager to appease him in the aftermath of the disastrous policies of *Boniface VIII, suppressed the order by papal provision in 1312. Having obtained confessions by torture, Philip managed to have the Grand Master and the highest dignitaries burned at the stake in 1314;

before dying they repudiated their confessions and asserted the innocence of the order. Their lands were turned over by the pope to the Knights Hospitallers and similar groups. The Templars' policy of absolute secrecy concerning internal business, including their rites of initiation, made them vulnerable to the propaganda campaign of the French king. This fact has not prevented subsequent secret brotherhoods, including the Freemasons, from imitating them. It has never been completely explained how a military brotherhood such as the Templars, with four times the wealth and holdings of the king of France, could go down to such complete defeat without putting up any resistance. BIBLIOGRAPHY: G. Grosschmid, NCE 13:992–994.

[E. J. DILLON]

TEMPLE, WILLIAM (1881–1944), abp. of Canterbury. The son of F. Temple (1821–1902), bp. of Exeter and afterward abp. of Canterbury, he was a Balliol man, president of the Oxford Union, and later a fellow of Queen's. Nominated bp. of Manchester (1920), he became abp. of York (1929) and then of Canterbury (1942). Through the *Faith and Order and *Life and Work movements he became a strong advocate of social and national righteousness. Yet though he entered into and respected the proper medium of reform, to such an extent that he was commonly regarded as a socialist, he always believed that the cause was secondary to the fundamental truths of the gospel. He was the chosen leader of the Life and Liberty movement to secure independence for the C of E, if need be by *disestablishment. He also was a pioneer in the ecumenical movement, acting in concert with the cardinal of Westminster and the moderator of the Church of Scotland. In public he was a formidable leader, not given to caution; in private he was loved for his kindliness and candid humor. It was said of him that he was too much of a theologian for philosophers and too much of a philosopher for theologians. His philosophy moved away from the Neo-Hegelianism he had learned from E. Caird; his theology was objectively Christ-centered and stressed the incarnation rather than the redemption. The Gifford Lectures for 1934, *Nature, Man, and God,* if not the most widely read, form probably the most enduring of his writings. BIBLIOGRAPHY: Life and Letters, by F. A. Iremonger (1948).

[T. GILBY]

TEMPLE TAX, annual payment required of all Jews 20 years old or above to support the temple services. It presumably originated with the half-shekel ransom or atonement money stipulated when Moses took a census (Ex 30.11–16). The payment may have been intended to atone for the presumption of numbering God's people (2 Sam ch. 24). The "shekel of the sanctuary," specified as weighing 20 gerahs, was perhaps an older weight, heavier than the shekel used in post-Exilic times (Ex 30.13). In Nehemiah's time the tax was only one-third of a shekel (10.32), leading some scholars to conclude that the half-shekel in the Pentateuchal references was anachronistically inserted later. Though asserting that "sons" are free from the tax, Jesus had Peter pay it for the two of them to avoid giving offense (Mt 17.24–27). Vespasian had the Jews continue paying the tax even after the Temple was destroyed (Josephus, *Jewish War*, 7.6.6). *WEIGHTS AND MEASURES.

[T. EARLY]

TEMPLIN, PROKOP VON, (*c.*1607–90), Capuchin preacher and author. During his years in Berlin (1620–25) he was converted to Catholicism and became a Capuchin in 1628. His very original sermons, most of them given in Austria and Bohemia, his deeply religious hymns show him as a rare master of the German language. Twelve of his songs were incorporated in the romanticist collection of songs *Des Knaben Wunderhorn.* T. was a forerunner of Abraham of Santa Clara. Among his numerous books are sermons, meditations, a catechism, and other pious writings, e.g., *Lignum vitae* (1665), *Mariale* (1667). BIBLIOGRAPHY: A. Zawart, *History of Franciscan Preaching and Franciscan Preachers* (1928) 510–512; A. Kober, *Mariengedichte des Prokop von Templin* (1925).

[S. A. SCHULZ]

TEMPORAL POWER. The Church has held civil authority both in governing States of the Church in Italy and in exercising sovereignty as an institution. The Church's temporal power, established particularly after Christianity became the official religion under Emperor Theodosius (d. 395), increased in the early Middle Ages with the conflation of secular and religious spheres and the growing role of churchmen in governments. Further, papal temporal rule over the duchy of Rome was expanded to include most of the Byzantine Exarchate of Ravenna by the Donation of Pepin (756), which established the Papal States. The forged Donation of Constantine (*c.*750), attributing to Emperor Constantine (d. 337) the grant of political authority over the Western Empire to the Papacy, provided a juridical, if false, basis to papal temporal power for centuries. Gregorian reform (11th–12th cent.) and ecclesiastical participation in feudalism augmented this power, which was elaborated theoretically by canonists and glossators. While the Church's temporal power has declined generally in modern times, the Lateran Treaty (1929) restored papal sovereignty over Vatican City (108.7 acres), a remnant of the Papal States. BIBLIOGRAPHY: W. Ullmann, *Medieval Papalism* (1949); *idem, Growth of Papal Government* (1962); G. Tellenbach, *Church, State and Christian Society* (1948).

[W. A. CHANEY]

TEMPORAL POWER (OF THE CHURCH), not the civil power exercised by the pope in Vatican City, but the general authority claimed by the Church in certain matters and affairs that touch upon and affect the temporal order. This power is not claimed as something distinct from the spiritual power; it is the spiritual power as exercised in an existential human order in which the spiritual and the tem-

poral are inseparably intertwined. The infliction of temporal penalties and the possession of temporal goods are the chief examples of the exercise of a temporal power claimed by the Church. As to the infliction of penalties, this right (long asserted but never defined) is claimed in CIC c. 2214.1: "It is the innate and proper right of the Church, independent of every human authority, to correct its delinquent subjects by penalties both spiritual and temporal." The acknowledgment of this right, however, does not oblige the Catholic to hold that its exercise in given situations is always prudent. There has been much disagreement among theologians and canonists about the extent of this right and about the manner in which penalties can be legitimately inflicted. The Church's right to possess temporal goods is asserted in CIC c. 1495: "The Catholic Church and the Apostolic See innately have the right freely and without dependence on civil authority to acquire, retain, and administer temporal goods in the attainment of its proper goals." The claim to temporal power supposes that the Church is a reality in this world, working among men as they are in this world, sanctifying them through human and material instrumentalities that can never be completely disembodied. If it is to carry on the work with which it has been charged, it must have the independence to procure and administer what is necessary to its mission. BIBLIOGRAPHY: G. Glez, DTC 12.2:2670–2772; H. Tüchle, LTK 6:26–265; A. Scheuermann, *ibid*. 269–271; J. Lederer, *ibid*. 279–283; H. Rabb and J. P. Michael, *ibid*. 288–300.

[S. E. DONLON]

TEMPORAL PUNISHMENT, according to RC teaching, the purification which must be undergone for sins either on earth or in *purgatory. It is to be distinguished from the eternal punishment of *hell. This teaching is based upon a doctrine of salvation which maintains that even after personal conversion to Christ an individual is not necessarily free from all imperfections. Thus a certain interior purification is necessary through a gradual maturation into the fullness of Christ. Since an inclination to evil remains even after sin has been forgiven, man experiences the struggle to accept grace and to overcome the resistance which he encounters because of human sinfulness as a suffering or punishment. Reformation theology generally opposes this teaching on the grounds that conversion to Christ totally justifies the sinner because of God's infinite goodness, not man's subsequent state of perfection. BIBLIOGRAPHY: P. Fransen, "The Doctrine of Purgatory," ECQ 13 (1959) 99–112; Rahner-Vorgrimler 391–392.

[T. M. MCFADDEN]

TEMPORALITIES, material possessions involved in an ecclesiastical office, such as revenues from a benefice.

[J. R. AHERNE]

TEMPTATION, in Christian life, a trial consisting in the experience of the attractiveness of the objects of sin. Temptation is an essential concomitant of Christian life as that means an imitation and following of Christ who was tempted. Christ's temptations were really of two kinds: the temptations by the devil in the desert (Mt 4.1–11); the temptation he experienced from within in the agony in Gethsemane (Mt 26.36–45). The first illustrates the divine permission of Satan's influence for evil, which Christian faith recognizes (see DEVIL AND SIN). The second illustrates the tension from within between the appetites for created goods and charity's choice of God above all. It is because, like Christ, the Christian in charity chooses God's will above all else that temptation is possible. The commitment of a person to follow his own desires unrestrainedly is the choice of self as absolute and ultimate; there is no issue of temptation because there is nothing to contradict or conflict with self-will and indulgence. The Christian significance of temptation is that charity is a continual and ever-renewed choice, a responsiveness to the Father's love. Its meaning involves at once the affirmation of the true good in all created things as objects of desire and the choice of a higher good, God himself. The experience of temptation is the experience of the way of salvation: Christ's whole life was a struggle against the power of sin in human life, and his Passion and Resurrection the ultimate triumph over that power. Baptized in Christ and become with Christ the child of the Father, the Christian dies to sin, but the process of salvation remains a struggle to reach the final victory. Baptism gives the new being of grace that charity expresses dynamically in the love of the Father, but *concupiscence remains, with temptation its stimulus. Through the grace of Christ the struggle against the power of sin is the process of salvation, and the Christian finally dies to sin in Christ by making the struggle an imitation of the Passion and by thereby coming to share in Christ's Resurrection.

[T. C. O'BRIEN]

TEMPTATION (IN THE BIBLE). The Bible speaks of temptation in three ways: God tempts or tests man; man tempts or tests God; and man is tempted or attracted to evil by *Satan, worldly desires, or his own sinful inclinations. (1) The OT often speaks of God's trying particular men or the Israelites as a whole to determine their obedience and faith. The classic examples are Abraham (Gn 22.1–19) and Job, who submit to God's will even in the face of incomprehensible suffering. In the NT infancy narratives, Zachary, Joseph, and Mary are all tested by God. Indeed, all men face the supreme test of affirming faith in the risen Jesus (Mk 16.16). In this sense, therefore, temptation is a gift from God. (2) Man also tempts God. The Israelites try God's patience during the Exodus by not acknowledging his power or his salvific will in their regard (Ex 14.10–12; 15.24–25; 16.1–5). The Scribes and Pharisees often tempt Christ, i.e., they challenge him in their doubt and unbelief (Mk 8.11). (3) Temptation in the sense of inducement to evil is attributed to the *serpent in Paradise, Satan, or even to natural disasters and wealth. In the NT, temptation is said to come both from within a man by the sinful desires of his heart, and from without by those who have rejected the Word. Indeed, this state of temptation is characteristic of the Christian life (1 Cor 10.13; Gal 6.1). In the Lord's Prayer (Mt 6.13; Lk 11.4), Christ instructs his Disciples to ask God to keep them from enticements to evil by ungodly powers. James 1.13 is significant in that it forbids calling God the author of temptation, since he cannot be tempted to do evil nor does he lead anyone into sin. BIBLIOGRAPHY: H. Seesemann, Kittel TD 6.23–36; EDB 2401–05. *TEMPTATION OF JESUS.

[T. M. MCFADDEN]

TEMPTATIONS OF JESUS, trials experienced by Jesus during his earthly ministry. The three Synoptic writers refer to a special time of testing at the beginning of Jesus' public ministry after his baptism in the Jordan, when he was led by the Spirit into the wilderness to be tempted by Satan. The latter, whose name means Adversary or Accuser, was identified in the NT Book of Revelations with the serpent of Paradise that led the whole world astray (12.9–10). The Synoptic accounts use the title "devil" and "Tempter," in harmony with rabbinic tradition that knew him as the enemy who stirs up the evil impulse in man, seduces him into sin, denounces him before God, and then punishes him with death. The spirit and technique of this figure can be assessed from Matthew's and Luke's elaboration of three temptations that test Jesus concerning the role revealed to him in a special way at his baptism, that of chosen instrument of God's reign. Each of the temptations—to turn stones into bread, to demonstrate his trust and God's protective care by hurling himself down from the pinnacle of the Temple, and to seek political power and the glory of worldly dominion,—is rebuffed with a quote from Deuteronomy (6.13,16; 8.3). All three Deuteronomic texts are from the same homiletic elaboration on the Shema, the most sacred text of Judaism: "Hear, O Israel, the Lord is our God, one Lord . . ." (6.4ff) and are meant to evoke the entire homily with its dominant theme that the vocation of Israel is to love the Lord with all one's heart and soul and strength and to serve him alone. When these temptations proved fruitless, the tempter departed, biding his time (Lk 4.13). A more awesome time of testing was yet to come, the hour of testing (Lk 22.40) when the Prince of this world would come (Jn 14.30), having been given leave to sift all Jesus' band like wheat (Lk 22.31). Jesus urged the leaders of his band to pray that they might be spared the test (Mk 14.37–38) and he himself was overcome with terror and dismay (v.33). He confided to his disciples that his heart was ready to break with grief; he entreated them to keep vigil with him while he prayed that the hour might pass him by (Mk 14.33–36). The Letter to the Hebrews contains a meditation on this event; this was the way for Jesus to become the perfect high priest, compassionate and loyal (2.16–18), who became like "these brothers of his" in every way, sharing their flesh and blood so that he might break the power of him who had death at his command (the devil), and liberate those who, through fear of death, had all their lifetime been in servitude (2.14–15). He is able to bear patiently with the ignorant and erring, since he knows what it is to be clothed in weakness (5.1–2); son though he was, he learned in the school of suffering what it means to obey (5.8–9). Since he himself has passed through the test of suffering, he is able to help those who are meeting their test now (2.16–18). Because of his likeness to us he is able to sympathize with our weakness, having himself been tempted in every way, only without sin (4.15–16).

[E. J. DILLON]

TEMPTING GOD (Lat. *tentatio Dei*), a type of irreverence toward God and therefore against the moral virtue of *religion. Tempting here means putting to the test, trying something out of which we are not certain in order to see what happens. The sin lies in asking or taking steps to enter dangers without need in order to find out whether God will deliver us. So Our Lord rebuked Satan (Mt 4.7) when invited to cast himself down from the parapet of the Temple by quoting Scripture: "Do not put Yahweh your God to the test as you tested him at Massah" (Dt 6.16), which was where Moses struck the rock because of the grumblings of the thirsty sons of Israel (Ex 17.1–7). Apart from its setting in Scripture, the sin formally considered might seem to be a rather recherché and curious piece of irreligiosity; in fact, however, and interpretatively, it twines closely with a not uncommon childishness on occasions when a man should say to himself, "Be your age." Thus exploring a tooth to find out whether it will start aching again, scab picking, playing with fire, dare-you games such as racing across the road before an oncoming car. Tempting God transfers some of this deep-seated dubiety into our relations with him; it may strain for signs and wonders instead of taking his loving Providence as it is, or expose oneself to morbid imaginings and self-torturing about what one would do when faced with martyrdom. It is a case of sticking out your head, when, in the deepest and most literal sense, we should play safe with God. His grace will be sufficient for us; in the meantime we should not jump our fences until we come to them. The solicitude of theologians about this weakness, though not indulgent, is gentle. BIBLIOGRAPHY: ThAq ST 2a2ae, 97 (esp. in ed. Lat-Eng, v. 40, ed. T. A. O'Meara, 1967).

[T. GILBY]

TEMPUS, in music the 13th-cent. equivalent of the Renaissance *tactus. It was a beat at the metronome speed of about 80 and was represented by a *brevis,* the shortest value note then in use.

[M. T. LEGGE]

TEN ARTICLES, a doctrinal formulary issued in July 1536 by King Henry VIII of England, with the consent of *Convocations, "to establish Christian quietness and unity," with statements on the creeds, the Sacrament of the Altar, baptism, penance, justification, images, the saints and their invocation, ceremonies (holy water, lights, ashes, etc.), and purgatory. They were ambiguously composed to defend traditional beliefs and practices while placating Lutheran sentiment. The King was probably assisted in drafting them by Edward Fox, Bp. of Hereford, who had recently returned from an embassy to the German Lutheran princes. The articles were taken up and expanded in the *Bishops' Book of 1537. BIBLIOGRAPHY: C. Lloyd, *Formularies of Faith Put Forth by Authority during the Reign of Henry VIII* (1856 ed.); *English Historical Documents 1485–1558* (ed. C. H. Williams, 1967) 795–805.

[M. H. SHEPHERD]

TEN COMMANDMENTS, see COMMANDMENTS, TEN.

TEN THOUSAND MARTYRS, THE, a title applicable to two quite legendary companies of martyrs commemorated by the Roman Martyrology. On June 22 one entry records the crucifixion on Mt. Ararat of that number of Christian soldiers, together with their commander Acacius, for refusing to sacrifice to the gods. The other commemoration on March 18 seems to refer to the martyrdom of many Christians in Nicomedia at the beginning of the persecution of Diocletian in 303, but the number 10,000 is certainly a legendary exaggeration.

[R. B. ENO]

TENCIN, PIERRE GUÉRIN DE (1680–1758), ambassador of France to the Holy See, 1721–24, 1739–42; abp. of Embrun, 1724, cardinal, 1739, abp. of Lyons, 1740; minister of state, succeeding Card. *Fleury, 1742–51. His name is particularly linked with the anti-Jansenist Council of Embrun, which he convoked in 1727 and which deposed the Jansenist appellant, Bp. Soanen of Senez. Among T.'s other measures against Jansenism was a pastoral instruction of 1721 that declared the bull *Unigenitus* (condemning P. *Quesnel's work) to be dogmatic teaching that must be accepted. He issued a continuous series of polemical instructions against every point of Jansenist theology.

[T. C. O'BRIEN]

TENEBRAE (darkness), the name given to the manner of celebrating *Matins and *Lauds on Holy Thursday, Good Friday, and Holy Saturday before the Holy Week reforms of 1955. As these hours were then anticipated the previous evening, they were celebrated in darkness, a practice beginning in the Middle Ages. During the service lighted candles were extinguished after the recitation of each psalm, a practice that was allegorically interpreted as the Disciples' desertion of Christ and finally his own death and burial. BIBLIOGRAPHY: D. Stevens, NCE 13:1007–09.

[B. ROSENDALL]

TENEBRISTS, a name given to those baroque painters, mostly of the 17th-cent. Neapolitan, Netherlandish, and Spanish schools, whose work is characterized by highly dramatic violent contrasts of light and dark, after the manner of Caravaggio, and, therefore, also called Caravaggisti. BIBLIOGRAPHY: W. Schöne, *Über das Licht in der Malerei* (1954).

[L. A. LEITE]

TENNENT, GILBERT (1703–64), Presbyterian clergyman of Irish origin. While a pastor at New Brunswick, N.J., he fell under the influence of Theodore *Frelinghuysen, who has been credited with beginning the *Great Awakening in the Middle Colonies. A friend of Jonathan *Edwards and Jonathan *Dickinson, and a great admirer of George *Whitefield, T. soon became one of the most ardent preachers of the Awakening. In his polemical sermon "The Danger of an Unconverted Ministry" (1740), he attacked the hypocrisy of ministers who resisted the spiritual ferment of the times; the discourse helped cause the Old Side and *New Side division within American Presbyterianism (1741–58). His pamphlet "The Peace of Jerusalem" contributed to the restoration of unity. His ecumenical spirit is suggested in one of his chief tracts, *Irenicum ecclesiasticum* (1749).

[J. H. SMYLIE]

TENNESSEE, a south central state, admitted to the Union (1796) as the 16th state. The first Catholic missionaries visited the area in 1541 and later explorers included *Marquette, Joliet, and *La Salle. Claimed at various times by France, Spain, and England, Tennessee was acquired by the U.S. in 1783. Baptist and Methodist *circuit riders subsequently covered the state in search of converts, their proselytizing encouraged by the Great Revival of 1799–1800. Presbyterians also grew in numbers and founded several early institutions of higher learning.

Few Catholics could be found in Tennessee during the early national period. When the Diocese of Nashville was founded (1837), it had only about 300 Catholics, no priests, and one church. The first bp., R. P. Miles, OP, was responsible for establishing Catholicism in Tennessee. He founded 13 churches and 9 schools and brought the Dominican Sisters to the diocese. By 1860, when J. Whelan became Nashville's second bp., the number of Catholics had increased to 12,000. The Diocese of Nashville, and the Diocese of Memphis (1970), are suffragans of the Metropolitan See of Louisville, Ky. In 1976 Tennessee's Catholics numbered 100,307 or 2.4% of the total state population. The major Protestant denominations are the Southern Baptist Convention, with 27.9% of the total population in 1971, and the Methodist Church, with 9.9%. Other Protestant denominations comprised 9.9% of the population. The Jewish population (1968) was 16,710 or 0.4%. There are two Catholic colleges and one junior college in Tennessee, with a total enrollment of about 1,226 students. Some 5,832 students attend the state's 10 Catholic high schools, while 11,429 pupils attend 43 Catholic elementary schools. BIBLIOGRAPHY: S. J. Folmsbee et al., *History of Tennessee* (4

v., 1961); *Catholicity in Tennessee, 1541–1937* (ed. G. J. Flanigan 1937).

[J. L. MORRISON; R. M. PRESTON]

TENNO, Chinese pronunciation of a Japanese word meaning "emperor." The term is often used to designate a cult in Shinto, the indigenous Japanese religion, of emperor worship, in which it is believed that the present emperor is descended from Amaterasu, the Sun Goddess, through the first human emperor, Jimmu Tenno. Manipulated by Japanese militarists and nationalists during the 1930s, the traditional Shinto Way of the Gods or Kami was identified with the Imperial Way, channeling the popular mood and spirit of racial, ethnic, and spiritual superiority of the Japanese people into identification with the emperor and his causes. One consequence of the Japanese defeat in 1945 was a forced disavowal on the part of Emperor Hirohito that the emperor was divine and the admission that this divinity rested only on legend and myth.

[R. J. LITZ]

TENNYSON, ALFRED (1809–92), English poet. Son of a brilliant though erratic father, an Anglican clergyman of some literary talent, T., in collaboration with his brothers, published his first poems in *Poems by Two Brothers* (1827). Educated at Trinity College, Cambridge, he formed a close friendship with Arthur Henry Hallam, a talented young intellectual. His own first works, *Poems Chiefly Lyrical* (1830) and *Poems* (1832) reveal his gifts of musical versification and reflect his concern for Victorian moral and social problems. Harsh attacks by critics plus his irreparable loss at the sudden death of Hallam (1833) caused his withdrawal from publication for almost 10 years. New and revised poems in the 2v. edition of *Poems* (1842) established his reputation, and in 1850 he was named poet laureate. In that year he published his major work, *In Memoriam,* an elegy in memory of Hallam, which comprises a series of short lyric poems written over a period of 17 years and reveals the intensity of his grief and of the spiritual torment in his attempts to reconcile the death of Hallam with the existence of a beneficent God. He was able ultimately, however, to return to his faith in God and the immortality of the soul, as articulated in *In Memoriam*. T. produced a wide variety of works: lyric and narrative poetry, monodrama, dramatic monologues, ballads of adventure and patriotism, dialect poems, and dramas of lesser consequence including poetic drama and a series of historical tragedies, only one of which, *Becket,* enjoyed great success, though posthumously. The then current revival of interest in the Middle Ages and in the Arthurian legends turned T. to the writing of the *Idylls of the King* in which he had for years been interested. T. enjoyed unparalleled popularity for decades, except for the period 1870–80 when he competed with the works of newer poets such as Browning, Swinburne, Morris, and Rossetti. *Ballads and Other Poems* (1880), and four additional collections of poems were published during his last years. After his death his reputation suffered a tremendous attack as critics concentrated on his weaknesses. Recent criticism has, however, accorded him his rightful place among English poets. BIBLIOGRAPHY: C. Tennyson, *Alfred Lord Tennyson,* the standard biography (1949).

[S. A. HEENEY]

TENOR, a term having several meanings, the most common of which is that of the highest natural male voice or its counterpart in a musical instrument, e.g., tenor horn, etc. In chant, the tenor is the recitation (''held'') note; in four-part writing, it is the second lowest part; in the writing of the polyphonic period (*c.* 13th–17th cent.), it denoted the voice of the *cantus firmus,* the part to which the other contrapuntal voices were set.

[M. T. LEGGE]

TENOR MASS, a polyphonic setting of the Mass in which a *cantus firmus,* i.e., one certain melody—frequently taken from plain chant, and used in the *tenor—is the basis of all the movements.

[M. T. LEGGE]

TENORIO, GONZALO (1602–*c.*82), Peruvian Franciscan, theologian, author of an unpublished Mariological treatise that also was marked by its extolling of native Peruvian culture and a prediction of a millennial era when Peru would become the center of the Church. BIBLIOGRAPHY: J. L. Phelan, *Millennial Kingdom of the Franciscans in the New World* (1956).

TENT OF MEETING, also called Tent of the Testimony, the privileged locus of divine revelation during the Israelites' desert sojourn. As often as the pillar of cloud descended to the door of the tent, God met with Moses (Ex. 33.7–11). It was also a tribunal of justice where Moses sat as judge in the presence of Yahweh. Anyone for whom some matter was in dispute or doubt could seek the face of God, inquire of God, bring his cause to God, come and stand before God and lay his case before him. It was the first of the recurring ways for God's tabernacling Presence to be felt among his people, and may also have been the first depository for sacred law. It reminds one of the tent which later housed the ark of the covenant, another locus of the Presence, which made it possible for pilgrims to stand before the Lord at Shilo. According to the Chronicler God dwelt from tent to tent until the time of Solomon. When Solomon built the Temple with a tabernacle suitable to house the ark and also to serve as a depository for the code of sacred law, the Temple then became heir to both previous traditions of the tabernacling Presence. *HOLY OF HOLIES; *SHEKINAH.

[E. J. DILLON]

TEPIDITY, see LUKEWARMNESS.

TEPL, MONASTERY OF, a monastic foundation made by Bl. Hroznata in 1193 for the Premonstratensian monks who came from the abbey of Strahov in Prague. It survived the Hussite wars and the rebellion of some of the monks under the impact of Protestantism in 1525. For the most part, the abbots concentrated their efforts to combat Lutheranism. Destroyed by fire in 1659, Tepl was rebuilt primarily to provide pastoral care for German Catholics. The abps. of Prague gave extensive jurisdiction over many parishes to the abbots and entrusted many schools to their care. The present cloister was built by Abbot Raymond Wilfert (1688–1724). The monks excelled in scholarship and their rich library built by Abbot Gilbert Helmer (1900–44) included in its collection over 600 MSS and 500 incunabula. The abbey, predominantly German, was annexed to the German Reich in 1938. After 1945 it was administered by the Czech prior, Herman Tyl, whose attempts to restore the abbey to its former prestige were foiled by the Czechoslovak Communist suppression of the religious community in 1950. The monastery is at present a state museum. BIBLIOGRAPHY: B. Grassl, *Geschichte und Beschreibung des Stiftes Tepl* (1910); L. Nemec, NCE 13:1013.

[L. NEMEC]

TEPOTZOLTAN, CHURCH AT, formerly the Jesuit seminary of S. Martín, founded in 1584 near Mexico City. The present church (1670–82) with magnificent Churrigueresque façade added (1760–62), after the expulsion of the Jesuits (1767) became the Virreinato Museum—a national monument housing 3 centuries of Mexican-Spanish art. The façade was executed by someone close to L. Rodríguez in style; the sumptuous interior boasts gilded woodcarving and retables of great splendor—those in the nave possibly by I. V. Balbás (1750s), with chapels of great richness and an 18th cent. *camarín* (church treasure house). BIBLIOGRAPHY: J. A. Baird, Jr., *Churches of Mexico, 1530–1810* (1962).

[M. J. DALY]

TER DOEST, ABBEY OF, monastery, entitled All Saints, in the town of Lissewege, Belgium, founded in 1106 as a Benedictine priory dependent on Saint-Requier. In 1176 it became a Cistercian daughter abbey of Les Dunes, located near Bruges in what was then W Flanders. Acquiring extensive land holdings and famous for its prosperous wool industry, Ter Doest was united to the bishopric of Bruges in 1559, was pillaged and burned by the Calvinists in 1571 and 1578, was purchased from government authorities by the monks of Les Dunes at the time of the Revolution and given to the Diocese of Tournai (today Bruges). The 13th-cent. structures still stand. BIBLIOGRAPHY: Cottineau 2:3134.

[E. J. DILLON]

TERAH (Thare), name of: (1) the father of Abraham (Gen 11.24–32); he started from Ur toward Canaan, but stopped at Haran and died there; according to Joshua, he "served other gods" (24.2); (2) the place, location now unknown, where the Israelites camped on their way to Canaan (Num 33.27–28).

[T. EARLY]

TERAPHIM, idols mentioned in the OT. Little is known about them, but they were small and apparently household gods (Gen 31.34). David seems to have had a larger one in his house, but they were later condemned (2 Kg 23.24; Zech 10.2).

[T. EARLY]

TERBRUGGHEN, HENDRICK (ter Brugghen; 1588–1629), only Dutch master of the Utrecht School who knew Caravaggio, major inspiration of the Utrecht painters. He studied the Caravaggesque style while at Rome, 1604–14. T.'s *Crowning with Thorns* (1620) and *Four Evangelists* (1621) are important half-length figure compositions. His *Calling of St. Matthew* established the table-group as standard composition in Utrecht. Honthorst's candle light is seen in T.'s works (1623), esp. in the magnificent *St. Sebastian Tended by Women* (1625). Late paintings have a more subtle color range (*Liberation of St. Peter*). T.'s contribution to Dutch art as a member of the Utrecht School is important. BIBLIOGRAPHY: L. J. Slatkes, *Hendrick Terbrugghen in America* (1965).

[M. J. DALY]

TERESA, MOTHER (1910–   ), founder of Calcutta-based order for service to the most impoverished. Of Albanian descent, she was born in Skopje (now in Yugoslavia) and baptized Agnes Gonxha Boyaxhiu. In 1928 she joined the Sisters of Loretto, and after a brief period in Ireland went to teach in India. Impressed with the needs of the poor, she took a nursing course and then moved into the Calcutta slums. The order she founded there, Missionaries of Charity, which received canonical sanction in 1950, initially devoted itself to taking in the sick and dying from the streets. It later added ministries to lepers, cripples, and the blind, while also founding schools and orphanages. In time, the order branched out to other parts of India and to several other countries. Among her numerous honors, Mother Teresa received the Padnashri (Lord of the Lotus) award from the Indian government in 1963, and in 1971 Paul VI gave her the first John XXIII peace prize.

[T. EARLY]

TERESA OF AVILA, ST. (1515–82), Carmelite reformer and mystic. Of a pious and respected family, she entered the Carmelite monastery of the Incarnation at Avila in 1535. After 18 years of undistinguished religious life, she was converted to the pursuit of perfection and began frequently to experience unusual favors in prayer. Her raptures and visions increased, to the consternation of her confessors and the townspeople of Avila. SS. Francis Borgia in 1555 and Peter of Alcántara in 1560 reassured her of God's will and encouraged her contemplative prayer. Her mystical experience deepened and matured throughout her life and was marked by ecstasies, transverberation, and spiritual marriage. Because the atmosphere at Incarnation failed to support her desire for a life of austerity and perfection, she founded in 1562 St. Joseph's monastery, a small community of nuns from Incarnation whose rule was based on the primitive tradition of Carmel and the reform inaugurated among the Franciscans by St. Peter of Alcántara. After substantial opposition in beginning the reform, Teresa enjoyed 5 years of relative calm during which she wrote *The Way of Perfection*, which counseled her nuns on the pursuit of virtue and the practice of prayer.

From 1567 until her death T. worked to spread the reform through the establishment of many monasteries for the nuns and friars of Carmel. With the collaboration of St. *John of the Cross, her efforts prospered; but she encountered fierce opposition and harassment from the parent branch of the order, a struggle which ended in the separation of the two observances in 1580. Her contemplative life, maintained in the midst of incessant labor and continuing conflict, is given detailed description in her autobiography, written at the request of her directors. With frequent use of metaphor and unexpected clarity, she delineates the various stages of prayer and their characteristics from discursive meditation to ecstatic union. In her most mature work, *The Interior Castle*, the castle is the soul. Its progress toward God is a journey through various rooms (each representing a stage in prayer) until the soul penetrates the innermost room or the very center of itself where deepest intimacy with God and fullest integrity as a human being is achieved. She was canonized in 1622, and, together with St. *Catherine of Siena, was declared a Doctor of the Church by Paul VI, Oct. 15, 1967. BIBLIOGRAPHY: *Complete Works* (ed. Silverio de Santa Teresa and E. A. Peers, 3 v. 1946); E. A. Peers, *Mother of Carmel: A Portrait of St. Teresa of Jesus* (1946); Alphonse de la Mère des Douleurs, *Practice of Mental Prayer and of Perfection according to Saint Teresa and St. John of the Cross* (tr. J. O'Connell, 6 v., 1910–20); O. Steggink and S. Ramge, NCE 13:1013–17.

[J. C. WILLKE]

TERESA MARGARET OF THE SACRED HEART, ST. (1747–70), discalced Carmelite nun and mystic. Born Anna Maria Redi at Arezzo of a noble Tuscan family, she entered the Discalced Carmelite convent in Florence, Sept. 1, 1764, taking the religious name of Teresa Margaret of the Sacred Heart because of her devotion to the Sacred Heart, SS. Teresa of Ávila, and Margaret Mary Alacoque. In the community, she served as sacristan and infirmarian, but her importance to the Church was as herald of devotions to the

Sacred Heart, not only in Carmel, but in Tuscany and Italy, where Jansenism attempted to bring the devotion into disrepute. Since her early death her body has remained incorrupt. She was canonized by Pope Pius XI on March 19, 1934. BIBLIOGRAPHY: *Ephemerides Carmeliticae* 10 (1959); S. V. Ramge, NCE 13:1017.

[T. J. RYAN]

TERILL, ANTHONY (Bonville, 1621–76), Jesuit moral theologian. Born in Canford, England, he was converted to Catholicism in 1636. He taught at Florence, Parma, and the English College, Liège, also serving at the latter as director of studies and as rector. Among his theological works, *Fundamentum totius theologiae moralis seu tractatus de conscientia probabli* earned him a controversial reputation. In it he offers an explanation of how a person does not violate the law of God by transgressing a law of which he is ignorant.

[P. J. HENNESSEY]

TERMINISM, the more suitable name for Ockamist conceptualism or nominalism. The philosophy of *William of Ockham is often described as conceptualism, because he at one time recognized not only spoken or written terms, but also mental terms or concepts. Such a scheme allows universals to have mental existence, as objective products of mental activity. However, with his later estimation that mental terms or concepts are simply to be identified with the subjective, concrete, and individual acts of thinking, the *Venerabilis inceptor* would rather exclude conceptualism in favor of a more parsimonious nominalism that admits no true universality. At any rate, Ockhamism opposes realism. Thus rejected is Platonic or extreme realism's thesis that universals have an independent and extramental existence. But it is further denied, against Aristotelian or moderate realism, that universals have even a basis in reality. Thus Ockham insisted that science was not of things themselves, but of the terms standing for them; whence Ockhamist nominalists were quite naturally called *terministae*.

Terminism's preoccupation with terms continues in contemporary linguistic analysis and its investigation of language, both "ordinary" and "formal." But linguistic analysis, like terminism, does not escape the tendency to substitute the means, a very valuable means, for the end of philosophical activity.

[R. E. HENNESSEY]

TERRIEN, JEAN-BAPTISTE (1832–1903), Jesuit theologian. Born at St. Laurent-des-Autels, Maine-et-Loire, France, he entered the Society of Jesus in 1854, taught philosophy and dogmatic theology at the seminaries of Laval (1864–80), St. Helier (1880–88), and at the Institut Catholique of Paris (1891–94). His most significant theological works are those intended for the Catholic population at large, *La Dévotion au Sacré Coeur de Jésus d'après les documents authentiques et la théologie* (1893); *La Grâce*

et la gloire ou la filiation adoptive des enfants de Dieu (1897); *La Mère de Dieu et la mère des hommes d'après les pères et la théologie* (1900, 1902).

[T. J. RYAN]

TERRITORIAL CHURCH (Ger. *Landeskirche*), a term applied to the German Churches that developed during the Reformation. Since no unified German state then existed, it was impossible to establish a single, united Lutheran Church. Therefore each of the nearly 300 political entities established its own autonomous Lutheran Church. The *Augsburg Confession and Luther's Small Catechism (see CATECHISMS, LUTHER'S) furnished a common doctrinal character, but each territorial Church was independent of any power outside its own political boundaries. Having to provide some means of administration to assume functions formerly exercised by bps., Luther advised that civil rulers temporarily take on these duties. Although Luther was not entirely satisfied with such an arrangement, the system became permanent, especially with the establishment of the principle *cuius regio, eius religio* (Peace of Augsburg, 1555). The territorial prince in each domain considered himself the *summus episcopus,* having broad powers of jurisdiction but without the right of preaching the word or administering the sacraments. So long as princes were devout members of the Church, some of the worst features of this form of *Erastianism were avoided. As the concept of the State became more secularized, losing its character as one of God's created orders, the Church became increasingly subordinated to political interests. BIBLIOGRAPHY: A. L. Drummond, *German Protestantism since Luther* (1951).

[N. H. MARING]

TERRITORIAL PARISH, in the discipline of the Latin Church a parish in the fullest canonical sense: a subdivision of a diocese with its own boundaries and its own pastor, who has the care of souls for the faithful living within those boundaries. This is distinguished from a parish that is called "personal," i.e., for a group of people of one language or family, such as are the national parishes in the U.S., which were set up for care of the various ethnic groups of immigrants. A mixed parish is one established for a distinct group of people within one territory.

[T. C. O'BRIEN]

TERRITORIALISM, a concept of Church-State relationship, based on the natural-right theories of H. Grotius (1583–1645) and C. Thomasius (1655–1725). In practice it is the equivalent of *cuius regio eius religio*. The theory itself, however, rests on the conception that the State originates in the members' natural right to form a society, which includes their ecclesiastical association. Thus the State (or its head) as reflecting this will has power over the Chuch. *Collegialism puts the origin of the Church in a will of the members to associate, distinct from the will that originates the State. The two theories agree, however, in rooting authority of both Church and State in the will of the members to form a society. BIBLIOGRAPHY: EncRelKnow 11:303.

[T. C. O'BRIEN]

TERSTEEGEN, GERHARD (1697–1769), German author of devotional works and hymns. After undergoing a severe religious crisis (1719–24) and withdrawing from the Reformed Church, Tersteegen devoted his full time to spiritual activities: speaking at prayer meetings, translating the works of mystics and quietists, composing devotional works, and offering spiritual guidance, though without founding a new sect. His hymns and religious poetry are among the best literary fruits of Pietism. BIBLIOGRAPHY: J. Julian, *Dictionary of Hymnology* II (1957) 1142–45.

[M. F. MCCARTHY]

TERTIAN, a member of a religious order or congregation in the stage of his formation known as the third year of novitiate, or tertianship. Sometimes described as the *schola affectus*, tertianship in the Society of Jesus comes for priests sometime after ordination but prior to solemn profession or assumption of definitive status in the order; for brothers there is a corresponding period of formation. All at this time again make a 30-day retreat. In many institutes for religious men and women approved after the Jesuits, similar usage is found. BIBLIOGRAPHY: *Societatis Jesu constitutiones et epitome instituti* (Rome, regularly revised and reissued by the curia of the general).

[E. A. WEIS]

TERTIARY, a member of a *third order, i.e., an association affiliated as such to some religious order (e.g., Dominican, Franciscan). A third order offers its members encouragement, opportunity, and direction helpful in the pursuit of Christian perfection; and it provides a rule of life patterned on that of the order to which it is affiliated. Those tertiaries who embrace a community life and take vows are known as regular tertiaries (see THIRD ORDERS REGULAR); they are religious in the strict sense of the word. The term is generally restricted to secular tertiaries who continue to live in the world and take no formal religious vows. BIBLIOGRAPHY: CIC 702.1.

[J. C. WILLKE]

TERTULLI, see PSYCHOPNEUMONES.

TERTULLIAN (*c*.160–*c*.240), ecclesiastical writer, controversialist, and the most important theologian in the West before Augustine. The son of a *centurio proconsularis,* T. was educated at Carthage, and lived for a time in Rome. His knowledge of history, archeology, medicine, Aristotelian philosophy, oratory, and jurisprudence, combined with his literary talents, forceful personality, and theological interests, made him one of the leading apologists of the early Church. He was converted to Christianity *c*.195, won over it seems by the sight of the constancy of the Christian mar-

tyrs. According to St. Jerome he became a priest even though he was married, but this has been questioned by a number of scholars. After his conversion, he dedicated himself to the defense of Christianity against pagans, Jews, and heretics, combining great skill in argumentation and brilliant aphorisms with bitter sarcasm and relentless attack. Because of his choleric and impetuous nature, he became disaffected with the Church *c*.206 and left it to become a *Montanist. T. was a prolific writer, but most of his works are fairly short. They are of an apologetic, polemical, and practical nature. In the first he defends the Church against the attacks of the pagans; in the second he refutes the arguments of heretics and expounds the truths of faith; and in the third he gives rules and exhortations for living a Christian life. In general his apologetic and polemical works belong to his Catholic period and his practical works to his Montanist period. There are 31 authentic treatises still extant; at least 12 others have been lost. Among the most important are the following.

Apologetic Works. In the *Ad nationes* (early 197), Tertullian reproaches the pagans for their culpable ignorance of Christianity and their unjust treatment of the Christians. In the *Apologeticum* (end of 197), addressed to the provincial governors, he repeats many of the arguments of his earlier work but with renewed vigor and in greater detail. This passionate defense of Christianity, despite its vehemence, is without doubt one of the classics of ancient Christian literature. The *De testimonio animae,* written shortly after the *Apologeticum,* argues somewhat paradoxically that, since the pagans believe in the unity of God, the survival of the soul, and the existence of evil spirits, the "soul is naturally Christian" (see *Apologeticum* 17). The *De pallio* (*c*.210) is a personal apology for his adopting the pallium of a philosopher in place of the more common toga. The *Ad Scapulam* (211 or 213) is a brief letter to the proconsul of Africa describing the sufferings endured by the Christians. It defends their right to profess their faith and threatens the governor with divine vengeance for his treatment of the Christians. The *Adversus Judaeos* (*c*.207) shows how the law of Moses has been replaced by that of Christ.

Dogmatic and Polemical Writings. These are longer and more detailed than his apologetic works, and they firmly establish him as an original thinker and able theologian. In the *De praescriptione haereticorum* (*c*.200), Tertullian applies to heretics the *praescriptio*, a technical device in Roman law to disqualify an opponent before he can even bring his case to trial. Since the Scriptures belong to the Church and have belonged to it from the beginning, delivered to it by the Apostles, heretics have no right to argue from Scripture. The *Adversus Hermogenem* (*c*.201) defends the doctrine of creation against the teachings of a Gnostic painter of Carthage. The *Adversus Marcionem* (3d rev., 207) is by far Tertullian's longest work. It treats of the unity of God, the messianic mission of Christ, and the continuity of the OT and NT. The *Adversus Valentinianos* (*c*.208) is an attack on Gnosticism. The *Scorpiace* (211 or

213) is "a remedy against the sting of the scorpion" of Gnostic heresy, which denied the value of martyrdom. The *Adversus Praxeam* (213 or 217) was directed against the patripassian Praxeas and presents the clearest teaching in the Church on the doctrine of the Trinity before the Council of Nicaea. In another series of antiheretical works, Tertullian attacked particular doctrines. The *De baptismo* (*c*.200) upholds the necessity of this sacrament and discusses its symbolism, minister, matter, and form. The *De carne Christi* and *De resurrectione carnis* (both 210 or 212) refute the Docetists who denied the resurrection of the body. The *De anima* (*c*.210) is the first Christian psychology. It treats of the nature, origin, and functions of the soul even when separated from the body.

Practical Questions. The *Ad martyres* (197) is an ardent exhortation to the confessors to persevere. The *De spectaculis* (197 or 200) gives numerous reasons why it is not lawful for Christians to attend the circuses and games. The *De oratione* (198 or 200) is an instruction for catechumens on prayer and gives an explanation of the Our Father. The *De patientia* (200 or 203) sets forth the meekness of the Savior as an example to be followed and as a preparation for martyrdom. The *De paenitentia* (203) discusses two types of conversion, that of baptism, and that of canonical penance, which is permitted only once after baptism. The *De cultu feminarum* (197–201) condemns female luxury and the use of cosmetics. In his *Ad uxorem* (*c*.203) he asks his wife to remain a widow after his death or at least marry a Catholic so that there will be a community of faith and affection. The *De exhortatione castitatis* (before 207) and the *De monogamia* (*c*.217) oppose second marriages. The *De virginibus velandis* (*c*.207) is an exhortation to a life of virginity and demands the wearing of a veil by virgins in church and in public. The *De corona* (211) proscribes military service for Christians. The *De idolatria* (*c*.212) forbids any contact with pagans that might give an appearance of idolatry. The *De fuga in persecutione* (*c*.212) describes flight in time of persecution as a kind of apostasy. The *De ieiunio adversus psychicos* (*c*.217) is a defense of rigorous fasts against the more lenient practices of the Catholics. The *De pudicitia* (*c*.220) denies the power of the Church to forgive serious sins. It may have been directed in part against an edict of Pope Callistus I (217–222).

Doctrine. Tertullian is the founder of the theology of the West. He gave to it not only its language but also its special character. In contrast to the contemporary Eastern theologians, Tertullian was not a philosopher. Though he had some harsh things to say about this science, he accepted it insofar as it agreed with Christian truth. He maintains, for example, that the existence of God and the immortality of the soul can be proved from natural reason. His training as a lawyer enabled him to give a precise definition to his theological speculations. In his exposition of the Trinity he formulated the classical definition: "*Trinitas unius divinitatis, Pater, Filius et Spiritus Sanctus*" (*De pudic*. 21). He affirms the duality of natures in the one person of Christ in terms later adopted by Leo the Great and eventually in-

corporated into the definitions of the Council of Chalcedon. He makes specific mention of baptism, confirmation, and the Eucharist. Despite departures, e.g., his belief in a coming millennium, his teaching on traducianism, his rejection of the virginity of Mary *post partum*, and his ultimate apostasy, Tertullian is without doubt one of the greatest figures of the early Church. Among the later writers he influenced was St. Cyprian, who read something from Tertullian every day and frequently said to his secretary, "'Give me the master!' meaning Tertullian" (Jerome, *De vir. ill.* 53). BIBLIOGRAPHY: A. d'Alès, *La Théologie de Tertullien* (1905); G. Bardy, DTC 15:130–171; M. Pellegrino, EncCatt 11:2025–33; W. Le Saint, NCE 13:1019–22; J. Morgan, *Importance of Tertullian in the Development of Christian Dogma* (1928).

[M. J. COSTELLOE]

TERTULLIANISTS, members of a sect founded in the early 3d cent. in Carthage by *Tertullian upon Montanistic principles. After brilliantly serving the Church with his pen, Tertullian became disaffected with what he considered to be its laxity. He openly broke with it *c*.207 and became a Montanist. While retaining the ethical rigorism of this Phrygian heresy, he purged it of its local and provincial character and gave it a more definitive theology. He never mentions Pepuza (see PEPUZIANS), which was to have been the site of the parousia; he rarely refers to Montanus himself; and he excludes women entirely from the office of preaching and teaching. The sect that he thus founded persisted down to the time of St. Augustine, when the few surviving Tertullianists at Carthage returned to the Church and handed over their famous basilica to the Catholics. BIBLIOGRAPHY: St. Augustine, *De haeres*. 86; A. Mayer, EncCatt 8:1345–46. *MONTANISTS.

[M. J. COSTELLOE]

TESHBÛḤṬŌ (East Syrian, *teshbôḥtā*), glory; used of various laudatory compositions in the Syrian churches, e.g., a form of the *Gloria in excelsis Deo* ("*teshbûḥtō* of Mar Athanasius") or the East Syrian *Nûhrā*.

[A. CODY]

TESHMESHṬŌ (East Syrian, *teshmeshtā*), service; a Syriac liturgical technical term signifying: (1) one of the hours of the Office; (2) a nocturn of the East Syrian Office (also called *qawmō* or *'eddōnō*); and (3) a short West Syrian service beginning with verses of a psalm or canticle with halleluyah intercalated after the first hemistychs, continuing with a *ḥûssōyō*, and concluded with a *qōlō*. The *teshmeshtō d-kōhnê* (*teshmeshto* of priests) is sung for departed clerics at the end of Compline on Saturday evening, in the *beiṭ qadd îshê* if the church has one.

[A. CODY]

TEST ACT, an English law of 1673 enacted to prevent "dangers . . . from popish recusants." The Act deprived Catholics and *Nonconformists of rights. It came in the wake of the *Declaration of Indulgence (1672), which had produced anti-Catholic fear instead of more toleration. Suspecting that the King expected eventually to make England Catholic again, and that the Declaration was a first step, Protestants of many parties united to oppose it. Parliament also objected to it because the Declaration was an attempt to set aside laws by royal proclamation. Besides taking oaths of allegiance and supremacy, persons holding civil and military offices were to deny belief in *transubstantiation. Among those excluded from office by this act was Charles's brother James, who had been Lord High Admiral of the Fleet. The Act was abrogated by the Catholic Relief Act of 1829. BIBLIOGRAPHY: H. Gee and W. J. Hardy, *Documents Illustrative of English Church History* (1921); H. W. Clark, *History of English Nonconformity* (2 v., 1911–13) v. 2.

[N. H. MARING]

TEST-OATH (MISSOURI). As part of the violent reaction against the South after the Civil War (1861–65), a constitutional convention, assembled in St. Louis, Mo. (January, 1865), required a test-oath as a prerequisite for exercising political or civil rights. The oath defined loyalty to the United States so narrowly that no one on the Southern side of the War could ever again participate in public life, even including preaching or teaching, whatever their ''persuasion, sect or denomination.'' The Constitution, itself, effective July 4, 1865, could be voted upon only by those eligible to take the oath.

The Catholic Church in Missouri was threatened with paralysis, since very few priests or sisters could swear that they ''had never manifested by word or deed adherence to the cause of the enemies of the United States, foreign or domestic [i.e., South], nor desired their triumph, nor sympathized with their rebellion.'' In response Abp. Peter Richard Kenrick wrote a pastoral letter (July 28, 1865) to his priests directing them to contact him at once if pressured to take the oath.

John A. Cummings, a young priest in Louisiana (City), Mo., offered Mass and preached on Sunday, September 3, 1865 without taking the oath. He was indicted, arrested, tried, and imprisoned. His condemnation was appealed to the Supreme Court of Missouri where the oath was upheld, but it was later condemned by the Supreme Court of the United States (January 14, 1867). Meantime, Father Cummings fell ill after his brief imprisonment, became insane, and died. John Hogan, later bishop of Kansas City, Mo., was also arrested and brought to trial over the test-oath but was freed as an effect of the Supreme Court's decision. Eight Sisters of Loretto who continued teaching while refusing to take the oath were indicted, but only three were arrested: Sister Angela Augusta Nesbit, Sister Margaret McAuley, and Sister Olympia Wimsatt.

While not specifically directed against the Catholic Church, the test-oath deeply affected it, because large numbers of priests and sisters (one estimate says three-fourths) disqualified from taking it, were in effect forbidden to function in Missouri until the Supreme Court's decision overturned it. BIBLIOGRAPHY: W. T. Johnson, CE 14:538–539.

[C. M. AHERNE]

TESTAMENT, term that as a designation for the parts of the Christian Bible, the *New Testament and the *Old Testament, is a translation, through the Vulg. *testamentum*, of the Gr. *diathēkē*. The biblical books were grouped under this title as taken in the primary sense that *diathēkē* has in the Bible, an agreement or *covenant; the two testaments contain the revelation of God's covenants with his people. Such a use of the term testament or covenant is found in the Scriptures themselves: 1 Macc 1.57 refers to persecution of those possessing ''the book of the covenant''; St. Paul in 2 Cor 3.14 mentions those who ''read the old covenant.'' Jesus referred to the ''New Covenant of my blood'' at the Last Supper (Lk 22.20; 1 Cor 11.25); the superiority of the new over the ''first or former'' covenant is stated in Heb 9.15 (see 2 Cor 3.6). The designation of the two parts of the Bible as OT and NT dates from the early Christian centuries. Melito of Sardis refers to the Jewish Scriptures as the Old Testament; the first recorded use of the term New Testament is in Tertullian, *c.*200. This usage was reflected in the Old Latin and Vulgate translations, *Vetus Testamentum* and *Novum Testamentum*. *BIBLE.

[T. C. O'BRIEN]

TESTAMENT (IN THE BIBLE), the unique meaning of the word as used in the phrase, Old Testament or New Testament. The word is a hallowed misnomer for covenant and refers to the covenant with Moses on Sinai and to the new covenant mentioned in Jeremiah and believed by Christians to have been fulfilled in Christ. The English word testament, from the Lat. *testamentum*, actually refers to the unilateral disposition of one's goods after death or, more strictly, to a written instrument by which a person disposes of his estate, effective at death. This would correspond to the word *diathēkē* in classical Greek. Unfortunately, the LXX translators used *diathēkē* to translate the Hebrew word *b'rith*, covenant. The latter is a two-party arrangement in which one is bound by oath; it means an agreement or pact, a kind of partnership. The Greek *synthēkē* would have been more accurate and would have been rendered by *foedus* in Lat. and ''covenant'' in English. More than just a semantic loss was at stake, because the covenant idea was at the heart of Judaism and the idea of partnership between God and His people has not come through intact in the people of the New Testament. BIBLIOGRAPHY: A. Yonick, NCE 13:1022; G. E. Mendenhall IDB 4:575.

[E. J. DILLON]

TESTAMENT OF OUR LORD IN GALILEE, an apocryphal work, also known as the ''Epistle of the Apostles,'' of *c.*150 A.D., purporting to record conversations between the Apostles and the risen Christ. BIBLIOGRAPHY: M. R. James, *Apocryphal New Testament* (1924) 485–503.

[D. J. BOURKE]

TESTAMENTUM DOMINI, a Syrian apocryphal work, originally written in Greek, whose full Latin title is *Tes-*

tamentum Domini Nostri Jesu Christi. This 5th-cent. Monophysite treatise was discovered in 1899 by the Syrian Patriarch Rahmani, and published by him in Syriac and Latin. Versions exist in Ethiopian, Coptic, and Arabic, languages of areas accepting Monophysitism. J. A *Jungmann, in his *Early Liturgy*, lists it as one of the ten most important literary sources for reconstructing the ancient liturgy and its evolution. It contains an *anamnesis* adapted from the Apostolic Traditions of Hippolytus. It is related to the so-called Clementine Liturgy, the oldest complete Mass text existing. The importance of the *Testamentum Domini* is explained in detail in Jungmann's *The Place of Christ in Liturgical Prayer*. In this Syrian document we find for the first time a prayer to Christ in the eucharistic liturgy. Until then the ancient tradition had been for the eucharistic prayer to be addressed to the Father, through Christ, with him, and in him. The way of addressing Christ exemplified in the *Testamentum Domini* had been forbidden for the Western Church at two African synods of the late 4th century. BIBLIOGRAPHY: J. A. Jungmann, *Pastoral Liturgy*, (1962) 14; *Early Liturgy* (1959) 7 and *passim; Place of Christ in Liturgical Prayer* (1965) 15–21 and *passim*.

[E. J. DILLON]

TESTEM BENEVOLENTIAE, an apostolic letter of Pope Leo XIII to Cardinal James Gibbons (Jan. 22, 1899) disapproving *Americanism, in the sense that the Church should accommodate itself, its teachings, and its discipline to the spirit of the age by recasting certain traditional formulas of faith and glossing over unpopular doctrines. The Pope insisted that Catholic doctrine is a sacred deposit of divinely revealed teachings that must be faithfully safeguarded in their entirety. BIBLIOGRAPHY: *Great Encyclical Letters* (ed. J. J. Wynne, 1903) 441–453; D 3340–46; T. T. McAvoy, *Great Crisis in American Catholic History 1895–1900* (1957); *idem*, NCE 1:443–444; W. F. Hogan, NCE 13:1022–23.

[J. H. ROHLING]

TESTIMONIA, Messianic proof-texts; OT passages cited in witness to the Christ event. In the Gospel of Matthew we find one kind of testimonia: an OT passage is cited rather fully to show that some event in the life of Jesus had been foreseen by the prophets of Israel (e.g., 4.15–16; 12.18–21). It may not have been uncommon during the intertestamental period to form such anthologies of OT Messianic texts as have been found in the library at Qumran. Such collections would have shaped and nourished the Messianic or Zionist hope. Such collections could serve as proof-texts once it was believed that the hope had been realized. Such collections probably also existed in the early Church. There is evidence that St. Cyprian revised and expanded one such earlier work. It need not have entailed as much artificial reasoning as might appear. Jesus and his disciples were formed by biblical culture and those who nurtured the apocalyptic hope would be especially drawn to such writings as Daniel, Second Isaiah, Joel, and the Messianic Psalms. Those works colored the consciousness of Jesus and his disciples and gave them their symbols and vocabulary. It was natural that the texts would later be cited more formally to explain and validate what had been accomplished in the events of the Christian dispensation. BIBLIOGRAPHY: C. H. Dodd, *According to the Scriptures* (1953).

[E. J. DILLON]

TETRAGAMY (Gr., four marriages), a term of historical importance in connection with an ecclesiastical and political dispute over the four marriages of the Byzantine Emperor Leo IV. His first two wives died without leaving a male heir to the throne. In Byzantine canon law third marriages were forbidden and penalized but not considered invalid. Despite this, Leo married Eudocia Baiana in 900, and within a year she too died, leaving Leo still without an heir. Byzantine canon law absolutely prohibited fourth marriages and considered them invalid. In 905 the Emperor's mistress, Zoe Carbonopsina, bore him a son, the future Constantine VII Porphyrogenitus. Patriarch *Nicholas Mysticus under pressure from the extremist faction in the Byzantine Church legitimatized the child but demanded that Leo separate from Zoe. When the Emperor brought Zoe back to his court, the patriarch refused them the sacraments. Leo countered by appealing to Rome. Pope Sergius III, declaring his respect for Byzantine law, nevertheless thought the good of the State justified a dispensation and granted it. Nicholas resigned under pressure and the synod elected Euthymius who persuaded most of his bishops to accept Rome's decision. However, he refused to crown Zoe or to put her name on the *diptychs. This divided the Byzantine Church as strife raged between the Nicholaites and Euthymians. When Leo died (912) his brother Alexander deposed Euthymius and reinstated Nicholas, who punished his opposers, accused the Holy See of approving adultery, and struck the Pope's name from the diptychs. A reconciliation between the Euthymians and Nicholaites was partially achieved at a synod in 920. Because a strong minority demanded papal intervention, Nicholas prevailed upon Rome to send legates to repeat the original decision of Pope Sergius III. The event is significant as evidence that during this time there still existed among some in the Byzantine Church a recognition of the primacy of Rome. This disappeared during the ensuing 75 years. BIBLIOGRAPHY: S. Salville, DTC 9:365–379; Ostrogorsky 208–209; M. J. Higgins, NCE 2:943–944.

[G. T. DENNIS]

TETRAGRAMMATON, the four consonants YHWH, properly pronounced ''Yahweh,'' used in the Hebrew OT to write the sacred personal name of God. Before destruction of the First Temple (586 B.C.), judging from the near-contemporary Lachish letters, this name was spoken regularly, yet by the 3d cent. B.C., other names such as Adonai, Adonai Elohim, or the Greek Kyrios were being substituted for YHWH in order to avoid verbalization of the Holy Name. Some scholars claim that YHWH is a verbal variant of *hyh* (by way of *hwh*), an old Hebrew verb meaning "to be," thereby justifying the folk etymology of the name found in Ex 3.14, where God speaks to Moses identifying himself as "I Am Who I Am." Others claim that YHWH is from the simple "Yah," which means "it is he." Others offer the meaning: "He brings into existence whatever exists." "Yah" is found in many names and liturgical expressions, e.g., *hallelu-yah*; the more philosophical explanation of YHWH, however, does convey the idea of creator. The name Jehovah arose from an improper hybridization of the vowels from Adonai and the consonants of the tetragrammaton to YeHoWaH by European Christian scholars of the early medieval period.

[R. J. LITZ]

TETRAKTYS, a figure regarded as sacred by the Pythagorean philosophers consisting of a pyramidal arrangement of 10 points with one at the summit, two below that, then a row of three and another of four. See PYTHAGOREAN SCHOOL.

TETRAPOLITAN CONFESSION (*Confessio tetrapolitana*, Confession of the Four Cities), a Reformation *confession of faith, composed in 1530 and published in 1531. The document presents the Zwinglian beliefs of the S German cities Strassburg, Constance, Memmingen, and Lindau. M. *Bucer and W. *Capito composed it during the sessions of the Diet of Augsburg (1530), at which the four cities were not represented. The 23 chapters correspond generally in subject matter to the *Augsburg Confession. Chapter 18 on the Lord's Supper attempts a compromise between Zwinglian and Lutheran doctrine. The Confession was never widely accepted or used. BIBLIOGRAPHY: Schaff Creeds 1:526–529.

[T. C. O'BRIEN]

TETRARCH, a petty ruler or dependent prince; the ruler of one district of a great empire. When the term was originated in Macedonia it had as its literal meaning, "ruler of a fourth part." It is also literally appropriate for Luke to apply it to Herod Antipas and his brother Herod Philip (Lk 3:1), because together they inherited one-half of the territory ruled by their father, Herod the Great. Usually the term was not intended literally, and the privileges and limitations of various tetrarchs must have varied from place to place. But generally speaking, in descending order of prestige and dignity, the titles of honor bestowed on dependent princes could include that of king, ethnarch, or tetrarch, with tetrarch the least.

[E. J. DILLON]

TETRARDUS, early (*c.* 9th century) musical term for what are now called the mixolydian and hypomixolydian modes.

The term, of Greek origin, means fourth, the final of these modes being the fourth of the basic finals. (d, e, f, g).

[M. T. LEGGE]

TETZEL, JOHANN (1465–1519), German Dominican, opponent of Luther in the *indulgence controversy. T. served as prior at Glogau and was inquisitor for Poland in 1509. From 1504, he was an indulgence preacher; in 1516 he was made subcommissioner in Meissen for the indulgence available to those who contributed money for the rebuilding of St. Peter's in Rome. T. preached the erroneous belief that indulgences can be gained for the dead independently of the spiritual dispositions of the person gaining them and can be applied absolutely to a specific soul in purgatory. Luther replied with the "Ninety-Five Theses" (1517). T. answered him with 122 antitheses, drafted by K. Wimpina, and also printed a refutation of Luther's position in 1518. T. was boastful, flamboyant, and not learned, but the charges that he begot illegitimate children were fabrications of polemicists. Luther wrote kindly words to him during T.'s last illness. BIBLIOGRAPHY: J. P. Dolan, *History of the Reformation* (1965) 234–237.

[M. J. SUELZER]

TEUTONIC KNIGHTS, popular name for the German military order, originally Order of St. Mary's Hospital of the German House. It developed from a hospital founded by German crusaders at Acre in 1190. In 1198 it became a military order using the Knights Templars' rule. Through crusade and negotiation it acquired lands in Prussia and Livonia. Constant warfare against the non-Christian peoples of these areas changed into disastrous conflicts when strong national states emerged as its neighbors. At the Reformation the Prussian branch became Lutheran. Suppressed by Napoleon, the order later revived, giving up military activity and concentrating on pastoral and charitable endeavors. Its headquarters are in Vienna. BIBLIOGRAPHY: M. Tumler and U. Arnold, *Der deutsche Orden von seinem Ursprung bis zur Gegenwart* (3d ed., 1974); K. H. Lampe, *Bibliographie des deutschen Ordens bis 1959* (1975).

[R. H. SCHMANDT]

Ṭ WÎLAITĀ, Nestorian equivalent of the West Syrian *tabl ˀitō*, in recent times replaced by the *prāsā*.

[A. CODY]

TEWKESBURY, ABBEY OF, former Benedictine monastery near the Severn at Tewkesbury, Gloucestershire, England, dedicated to St. Mary (Theotokos), and going back perhaps to a monastic settlement founded in 715 by Odon, duke of Mercia. Staffed by Benedictines from Cranborne Abbey (Dorset) in 980, it was restored in 1102 under the Normans in reparation for the burning of the cathedral of Bayeux by Henry I. It acquired vast holdings and is second only to Westminster in the number of the powerful interred within its walls. Suppressed in 1540 under Henry VIII, its last abbot (John Wakeman) was consecrated bp. of Gloucester the following year. The abbey church with its magnificent Norman tower and western arch was completed and consecrated in 1123 and is now the parish church of Tewkesbury. BIBLIOGRAPHY: Cottineau 2:3141.

[E. J. DILLON]

TEXAS, a southwestern state, admitted to the Union (1845) as the 28th state. A succession of Spanish expeditions explored the area in the 16th cent., including those of Alonso de Pineda, Alvar Nuņez Cabeza de Vaca, and Francisco Vasquez Coronado. The first major settlement was made at Ysleta, near the present site of El Paso. Since Texas was located on the periphery of the Spanish Empire, little colonization took place until the 19th cent., when Anglo-Americans moved into the area. S. F. Austin founded the first permanent Anglo-American settlement at San Felipe de Austin (1821). Thereafter the American population increased considerably, and Texas declared itself independent (1836). The admission of Texas to the Union 9 years later led to a war between Mexico and the U.S. and American conquest of a vast empire in the SW.

The first mission established in the area was probably the Mission San Francisco de los Tejas, situated near modern Nacogdoches and founded in 1690. By 1745 the Franciscans had established a number of missions in the territory. In the 19th cent., Vincentians served the few Catholics of Texas. They were led by J. M. *Odin, who was appointed vice prefect of Texas (1839), vicar apostolic (1841), and bp. of the new Diocese of Galveston (1847). At the time of his consecration, there were 10 priests and as many churches in Texas. After Odin was transferred to New Orleans (1860), C. Dubuis was appointed as the second bp. of Galveston. He supported new Polish and German parishes and welcomed the arrival of the Sisters of Divine Providence and the Sisters of Charity of the Incarnate Word. Both orders have continued to serve Texas' educational and medical needs.

The Diocese of San Antonio, which eventually became the metropolitan see for the entire province of Texas and Oklahoma, was founded in 1874. Its first bp., A. D. Pellicer, presided over 40,000 Catholics until his death in 1880. His successor, J. C. Neraz, invited the Oblates of Mary Immaculate to do mission work in the W part of the diocese and encouraged the Brothers of Mary to construct St. Mary's University. Neraz died in 1894 and was succeeded by J. A. Forest, under whom the number of Catholics in the diocese grew to 100,000. To meet the needs of this expanding population, Forest built numerous missions, stations, and schools.

J. W. Shaw served as bishop of San Antonio from 1911 until his transfer to New Orleans in 1918. He expanded educational facilities and founded a diocesan seminary. In 1926, under his successor, A. J. Drossaerts, San Antonio was raised to the status of an archdiocese. Its suffragan sees are the Dioceses of Amarillo, Austin, Beaumont, Bronwsville, Corpus Christi, Dallas, Fort Worth, Galveston-Houston, San Angelo, all in Texas, and Oklahoma-Tulsa in Oklahoma.

Under R. E. Lucey, abp. (1941–69), the Archdiocese of San Antonio continued to receive help for its missionary activity among Mexican-Americans. Among the major contributors of this aid are the Lyons Council of the Propagation of the Faith, the Catholic Church Extension Society, the American Board of Catholic Missions, and the Commission for Catholic Missions Among the Colored and Indians. The archdiocese has also attempted to help Mexican-Americans by publishing dual-language newspapers, and by providing a headquarters for the Bishops' Committee for Hispanic Affairs. San Antonio is the hub of much of the Church's work for Hispanics, their ethnic rights, religious and cultural needs. The Mexican-American Cultural Center is justly renowned for its work in this regard. Catholic Action and the Confraternity of Christian Doctrine have received particular emphasis in the archdiocese. The archbishop since 1969 has been the Most Rev. Francis Furey, D. D.

In 1976 the Catholics of Texas numbered 2,159,224 or 17.7% of the total state population. The major Protestant sects are the Southern Baptist Convention, with 21.1% of the population in 1971, and the Methodist Church, with 7.6%. Other Protestant denominations comprised 8.5% of the population. The Jewish population (1968) was 65,520 or 0.6%.

There are 6 Catholic colleges in Texas, with a total enrollment of 11,353 students. Some 18,759 students attend the state's 52 Catholic high schools, and over 64,465 pupils attend 245 Catholic elementary schools. BIBLIOGRAPHY: L. W. Newton and H. P. Gambrell, *Texas Yesterday and Today* (1949); C. E. Castañeda, *Our Catholic Heritage in Texas, 1519–1936* (7 v., 1936–58).

[J. L. MORRISON; R. M. PRESTON]

TEXTUAL CRITICISM, the science of evaluating the various surviving ancient MSS and *versions of the Bible, and also the citations from the Bible found in other ancient writings, in order to establish as accurately as possible, the reading of the original text. Between original autographs and the earliest or most accurate extant MSS lies a long period of copying and recopying, translating and retranslating the originals, with the inevitable human error and interference. The task of the text-critic, therefore, is to recognize and discern the human limitations of copyists and translators, to isolate and set aside as far as possible all the interferences, deliberate or accidental, which caused them to depart from the original, and so to restore the text as far as possible to its original state. The text-critic thus has two basic tasks, viz, to establish which are the earliest MSS, and which are the most reliable, as far as this can be determined by comparing different MSS independently reproducing the same text. In order to establish the factor of independence, the text-critic has to assure himself that the common reading found in several MSS is not to be explained by the fact that one has been copied from another, or that several have been copied from an earlier common archetype other than the original itself. The further back he can establish independent agreement on a given reading, therefore, the more likely that reading is to be the one initiated by the original author. Thus antiquity and independent witness are the two prime objectives in MSS research, by means of which the text-critic traces his way back through copies, translations, and ancient citations to the original text.

To facilitate research of this kind, MSS are organized on the basis of their dependence upon or derivation from one another, into "families" tracing their origin back to a common "ancestor," from which they have been copied either directly or indirectly. In the case of translations the text-critic's work becomes more complex, since he often has to reconstruct the original language that underlies a given reading. In the case of the OT, the ancient Greek and Latin versions often offer invaluable independent readings; they bear witness to independent Hebrew texts which would otherwise be lost, systematically rejected, or destroyed by the Masoretes in order to achieve an artificially uniform Hebrew text. The supreme importance of the *Qumran biblical MSS consists precisely in the fact that they bear witness to pre-Masoretic Hebrew texts that antedate the earliest extant Masoretic MSS by at least 1000 years.

The epoch-making researches and discoveries of P. E. *Kahle, more than those of any other scholar, changed the course of modern OT textual criticism. Kahle demonstrated that not all the MSS of the existing Hebrew Bible go back to a single archetype, that diversity in readings existed earlier than had originally been thought, and that even within the Masoretic tradition, different and rival schools existed. In the NT field the most notable critics have been K. von *Tischendorf, B. F. *Westcott, his collaborator F. J. A. *Hort, H. von *Soden, E. *Nestle, and A. *Mark. BIBLIOGRAPHY: F. G. Kenyon, *Our Bible and the Ancient Manuscripts* (rev. ed., 1958); J. Renmann, *Romance of Bible Scripts and Scholars* (1965); O. Eissfeldt, *Old Testament: An Introduction* (tr. 1965); M. Noth, *Old Testament World* (1966); J. H. Greenlee, *Introduction to New Testament Textual Criticism* (1964); K. Lake, *Text of the New Testament* (6th ed., 1943); B. M. Metzger, *Chapters in the History of New Testament Textual Criticism* (1963).

[D. J. BOURKE]

TEXTUS RECEPTUS (Lat., the received text), the Greek text of the NT that was accepted from the time of the first printed editions in the 16th-cent. until better textual traditions were established in the 19th. The text was that used by Erasmus's edition in 1516 and revised in the edition of Robert Étienne (Stephanus) in 1546. The phrase *textus receptus* is from the preface of the 2d ed. of the Greek NT of

T. *Beza by the Elzevir brothers in 1633. The Hebrew text of the *rabbinical Bible of 1525 sometimes is referred to as the *textus receptus* for the OT. BIBLIOGRAPHY: P. W. Skehan et al., JBC 2:581–583.

[T. EARLY]

THAANACH (TAANACH), an ancient Canaanite city located near the site of Megiddo in the Plain of Esdraelon. Its earliest occupation must go back at least to the 26th cent. B.C., as the ruins of a tomb that resembles Egyptian tombs of the 3d Dynasty in its style of masonry and techniques of construction attest. Archeological evidence seems to indicate that whenever Thaanach flourished, its neighbor Megiddo lay in ruins, and vice versa. Not until the time of Solomon were both sites occupied simultaneously. A number of cuneiform letters have been discovered at the site, dating from 100 years before the *Amarna Letters, which they resemble in character. These letters show that in the middle of the 2d millennium B.C., Thaanach was the residence of an Egyptian governor. It is also mentioned in an Egyptian account of the capture of Megiddo by Thutmose III in his campaign against a Syro-Palestinian coalition of princes in 1468 B.C. According to the Song of Deborah (Jg 5.19), Thaanach was the site of a glorious Israelite victory, when Barak and Deborah successfully rallied Israel against the Canaanite kings, at a time when Megiddo apparently lay unoccupied. According to Jg 1.27, the Canaanites held their ground in both Thaanach and Megiddo, as they must generally have maintained control of the Plain of Esdraelon. It may be that the two cities did not effectively come under Israelite control until the monarchy. Thaanach is mentioned in Jos 12.21 as a Levitical town of the tribe of Manasseh, but its actual Israelite history must have been brief. Its name appears on an Egyptian list of Palestinian cities conquered and destroyed in 918 B.C., shortly after Solomon's reign.

[E. J. DILLON]

THABOR, MOUNT, see TABOR, MOUNT.

THADDEUS, see JUDE THADDAEUS, ST.

THADDEUS, ACTS OF, see APOCRYPHA (NT), 62.

THAILAND, a country of SE Asia (208–148 sq. mi.; pop. est. 1974, 41,020,000). Known as Siam until 1949, Thailand was converted from an absolute to a constitutional monarchy in consequence of a bloodless coup in 1932. During recent decades, military oligarchies have been in control of the government. People of the Thai ethnic group migrated southward from W China from the 7th to the 14th cent., occupying the land and driving the earlier inhabitants to the mountains and border areas. Buddhism is the state religion and the faith of more than 90% of the people. Portuguese Dominicans first introduced Christianity in

1554. Franciscans, Jesuits, and members of the Paris Foreign Mission Society followed them. Bp. Laneau brought letters from the Pope and the French King. As a result the ruler of Siam entered into a trade agreement with France and made concessions favorable to the missioners. However, the Siamese people protested the foreign settlements at Bangkok and Mergui, dethroned the king, and destroyed the promising Christian community. In 1816 French missionaries again entered Siam, and after 1865 conditions became more favorable for the Church. Salesians, Redemptorists, Betharram Fathers, and Jesuits now teach and evangelize. As of 1976 there were 2 archdioceses, 8 dioceses, 8 bps., 218 parishes; 165,349 Catholics, 327 priests, 350 male religious and 1,166 sisters.

Baptists and Presbyterians have been working in Thailand for more than 100 years. The latter have formed the Church of Christ in Thailand with some 7,000 members. Adventists and the Christian and Missionary Alliane have done pioneering medical work. Among new arrivals are Pentecostals, Southern Baptists, and the Worldwide Evangelization Crusade. In 1968 the total Protestant membership was 30,816.

THAÏS, ST., the heroine of a morality play, which enjoyed great popularity in the Middle Ages, with versions existing in Greek, Latin, and Syriac. The setting of the story was 4th- cent. Alexandria, and the drama centered on the conversion of a famous courtesan named Thaïs through the impression made on her by a hermit variously named Paphnutius, Serapion, or Bessarion. After being sealed in a cell in a convent for three years in prayer and penance for her former worldliness, she was released to join the life of the convent, only to die two weeks later. The discovery of two mummified remains at Antinoë in Egypt at the beginning of this century, with the names Serapion and Thaïs attached to the graves, caused a stir. But it remains dubious that there is any shred of historical truth behind this stereotypical morality play.

[E. J. DILLON]

THALASSIUS, (fl. c.650 A.D.), Libyan monk and Byzantine ascetical writer, renowned in N Africa for his science and virtue, author of four spiritual centuries. These are groups of one hundred maxims, dealing mostly with the purification needed to rise to the higher degrees of prayer and contemplation. Although he shows a marked dependence on Neoplatonism, his main links are to Maximus the Confessor, with whom he had copious correspondence, and to Evagrius Ponticus, whose mystical doctrine until then had been subject to official criticism. Each group of maxims culminates in thoughts of dogmatic content such as the Incarnation, God, and the Trinity. The compilation must antedate the Monothelite controversy, since there is no hint of it in the collection. Basically T.'s work represents the mainstream of Byzantine monastic spirituality.

[E. J. DILLON]

THALES OF MILETUS (1st half of 6th cent. B.C.), pioneer natural philosopher, later honored as the first of the Seven Wisemen of Greece. He maintained that the origin (archē) of the earth and of all things is to be found in water and that the earth itself floats on water. According to Herodotus (1.74), he predicted the solar eclipse of 585 B.C. He observed the phenomenon of magnetism and explained it as a living force or soul in the magnetic metal. On a visit to Egypt, he tried to find a natural explanation for the Nile floods. He wrote nothing, but he is rightly regarded as the founder of both science and philosophy in the strict sense. BIBLIOGRAPHY: Copleston 1:22–24; LexAW 3023–24; Guthrie 1:45–72.

[M. R. P. McGUIRE]

THALHOFER, VALENTIN (1825–91), German liturgist and exegete who was responsible for kindling interest in genuine liturgical research in 19th-cent. Germany. His insistence upon sound historical method is reflected in his well–known Handbuch der katholischen Liturgik (2 v., 1883–93).

[N. KOLLAR]

THANGMAR OF HILDESHEIM, (c.950–1024), historian. At one time head of the cathedral school of Hildesheim, T. also served as librarian and dean of the cathedral. A distinguished scholar and statesman, he taught Bernward of Hildesheim (whose biographer he became) and Emperor Henry II. His Vita Bernwardi, one of the finest biographical pieces of the Middle Ages, reveals its author as an eye-witness and as an active participant in much that it relates. BIBLIOGRAPHY: O. J. Blum, NCE 14:2–3.

[O. J. BLUM]

THANKSGIVING PSALMS, see HODAJOTH.

THARE, see TERAH.

THARSIS (TARSHISH) a place name, occurring often in prophetic oracles and difficult to identify. In genealogies, Tharsis is a descendant of Japheth (Gen 10.4) and son of Jediael (1 Chr 7.10). In the prophets, Tharsis is a daughter of Tyre, associated with far-off places like Put and Lud; associated also with merchants dealing in precious metals and fabulous trade. The psalmist (Ps 72.10) invites Tharsis and the islands to worship with gifts the messianic king. One suggestion is that the word Tharsis was originally not a place name at all, but a common name for a refinery: a place where metal is melted and refined. It may be a Phoenician loan-word and was used preeminently of one particular Phoenician refinery, perhaps the one in their colony on the island of Sardinia. The famous ''ships of Tharsis'' would originally have been refinery ships constructed for the transport of such heavy cargo as smelted metal. Whatever the original meaning, in poetry and symbol it came to be the name of a fabulous far-off place whose wealth was legendary (see 1 Kg 10.22; Ps 48.8; Is 2.16; Eg 27.25).

[E. J. DILLON]

THARTHAN, see TARTAN.

THAYER, JOHN (1758–1815), American missionary priest. Born in Boston, Mass., the son of Unitarian parents, he attended Yale for three years and was awarded an A.B. in 1779. After serving as chaplain for the militia on Governors Island in Boston Harbor for a year, he made his way to Europe where contact with former Jesuits (the Society having been suppressed) as well as the canonization process of St. Benedict Joseph Labre prompted his conversion to Roman Catholicism in 1783. His published account of his conversion was widely read. After studies at the English College in Rome and at the Seminary of St. Sulpice in Paris, T. was ordained June 2, 1787. Returning to America, he was assigned by Bp. John Carroll to Boston where he became involved in the dissension between French and Irish Catholics in that region. His temperament judged unsuitable for the Boston mission, T. left in 1792 and undertook during the next twelve years a series of assignments that brought him to Albany, New York, Canada, and the Kentucky missions, where he championed the abolition of slavery long before conditions made it practicable. In 1804, he again went to Europe and finally retired in Limerick in 1811. Upon his death, his estate passed, by his will, to the priest who had replaced him in Boston, F. R. *Matignon, for the purpose of founding an Ursuline convent and school there. BIBLIOGRAPHY: R. H. Lord et al., *History of the Archdiocese of Boston* (1945).

[T. J. RYAN]

THEANDRIC ACTS OF CHRIST, those operations of the Savior in which both divine and human natures cooperate and which are therefore distinctive, or characteristic, of the God-man alone. The term, with its origin in Pseudo-Dionysius and its historic association with Monotheletism and the stress on a single energy or operation in Christ, has received an entirely orthodox and fruitful interpretation. This rests on the two distinct natures with their distinct wills and modes of action, the human and divine united in the one Divine Person. Manuals of theology distinguish three kinds, or levels, of operation in Christ. There is the purely divine, such as the creation of the world (in union with Father and Holy Spirit), and the Trinitarian personal processions in the Godhead, which are not at all theandric. There is the purely human (e.g., walking, breathing), which belongs to the Logos only insofar as it is the Divine Person *(principium quod),* the ''who'' to whom the acts in the human nature *(principium quo)* belong. These in turn are theandric only in the broadest sense, though their importance in the doctrine of the Savior's redemptive merit, satisfaction, sacrifice, may not be ignored. And finally, there are the strictly theandric, or mixed, operations, in which the two natures inseparably produce one common effect as joint cause, the divine power being the principal, the human power, the instrumental cause. The miracles are such theandric acts: walking on the water, healing the sick by a mere word or gesture, or by means of prayer. Most significant is the redemptive theandric operation: the prayer, the suffering, the death, the Resurrection, the Christ action in the mystical body, the priestly acts in eternal glory. BIBLIOGRAPHY: C. J. Moell, NCE 14:4–5; P. Galtier, *De Incarnatione ac Redemptione* (9th ed., 1947) 136–141; I. Solano, STS BAC 3:427–432.

[E. G. KAISER]

THEATINES (Order of Clerks Regular), an order of men founded (1524) by St. Cajetan, bp. of Thiene (hence the name), with several associates (one became Pope *Paul IV) to promote reform in the Church of the 16th century. An austere community, the Theatines worked among the poor and the sick. The community was approved by Pope Clement VII in 1524 and the constitutions by Pope Clement VIII in 1604. An early work of the Theatines was liturgical reform, evidenced by their aid in revising the liturgical books. The Theatines experienced great growth in Italy and spread to France, Spain, Germany, Austria, Poland, and Portugal. Missionary activity took them to Russia and India. The 19th cent. witnessed decline through political unrest, but Pope Pius X restored the order. Latin America and the U.S. were new ventures in the 20th century. In the U.S. their work centered in Denver, Colo., and the W missions. BIBLIOGRAPHY: P. Hallett, *Catholic Reformer: A Life of St. Cajetan of Thiene* (1959).

[J. R. AHERNE]

THEBAID, the birthplace of Christian monasticism. This region, which derives its name from the ancient city of Thebes, extends along the Nile south from Antinoë (modern El Sheykh 'Ibâda) to the first cataract near Aswân. The Thebaïd around *Tabennisi was the site of St. Pachomius's first cenobite community. From Tabennisi, cenobite monasticism first spread up and down the Nile valley, then to the rest of the Christian world. The Sahidic or Theban dialect of Coptic developed in the Thebaïd as did early Coptic art. BIBLIOGRAPHY: O. Meinardus, *Atlas of Christian Sites in Egypt* (1962).

[D. W. JOHNSON]

THEBAN LEGION, a Roman legion, believed to have been composed entirely of Christians and martyred together *c.*287 A.D. at Agaunum in modern Switzerland. The legion is named after the city of Thebes in Upper Egypt because it was believed to have been recruited in that area. The legion formed part of the greater army under Maximian Herculius, at whose command its soldiers were executed. One version has them refusing to offer sacrifice when the army arrived at Octodurum, Martigny on the Rhône above Lake Geneva. Instead, they withdrew to Agaunum, St. Maurice-en-

Valais, their place of martyrdom. Another version has them refusing to kill other Christians. The legion commanders were Maurice, Exuperius, and Candidus. The fact of their martyrdom is attested by the 4th-cent. church built at Agaunum by Theodore, bp. of Octodurum. The principal source of knowledge about them is St. Eucherius, bp. of Lyons (434–450). Their cult enjoyed tremendous popularity in the Middle Ages, esp. in Germany, many of whose towns claimed their patron to be numbered among the legion's members. They are known in the Western Church as St. Maurice and his companions. This same Maurice, besides being patron of innumerable European towns, is the patron of Savoy and Sardinia.

[E. J. DILLON]

THÉBAUD, AUGUSTUS (1807–85), French educator, writer. T. was ordained a diocesan priest, entered the Jesuits in 1835, and volunteered for the American missions. In 1838 he was assigned as rector at St. Mary's College, Kentucky, moving thence to St. John's College, Fordham, in 1846, where again he served as rector until 1852. After parish work in Troy (1852–60) he was again rector at Fordham, pastor and rector of St. Francis Xavier, N.Y., and was assigned to other Jesuit foundations. T. contributed many valuable essays to Catholic magazines, including ''Superior Instruction in Our Colleges'' and ''Freedom of Worship in the United States,'' both appearing in the *American Catholic Quarterly Review* (Oct. 1882 and April, 1885). Among his books were *The Church and the Gentile World at the First Promulgation of the Gospel* (2 v., 1878) and *The Church and the Moral World* (1881). Posthumously published were two memoirs, *Forty Years in the United States of America* (1904) and *Three-Quarters of a Century* (2 v., 1912–13).

[J. R. AHERNE]

THEBES: (1) No-Amon, ancient city of Upper Egypt, capital of Egypt from the Middle Kingdom until Ashurbanipal's Assyrian invasion (c. 661 B.C.). It rose during the 11th Dynasty (c. 2133–1992 B.C.) to become capital and the world's first monumental city. Thebes, like Diospolis, is a Greek name for what Egyptians variously called ''the City,'' because of its prominence; ''the Southern City,'' since it is 300 miles south of modern Cairo; or ''City of Amon,'' having been cult center for the worship of Amon. Thebes declined with the Hyksos invasion at the end of the Middle Kingdom, revived with the rise of the New Kingdom. The mention of Thebes in Nah 3.8–10 refers to the utter sacking of the city by Ashurbanipal. Numerous monumental temples surround Thebes: temples of Amon, Khons, Monthu, and Mut are in Karnak; the temple of Amon-Min, built by Amenophis III and Ramses II is at Luxor; in the necropolis on the west bank, where pharaohs of the 18th, 19th, and 20th Dynasties are buried, are the temples of Queen Hatshepsut, Seti I, and Ramses II. Even under Muslim rule Thebes remained a Christian monastic

center. (2) Greek city, now Thebai or Thivai, NW of Athens in S Boeotia. It was powerful from Mycenean until classical times. ''The leg'y Cadmus,'' with the aid of his Phoenician or Canaanite warriors conquered the native Aonians and Hyantes to found the city of Thebes. The dynasty he began there included the dramatically celebrated Oedipus.

[R. J. LITZ]

THECLA, ST. (d. c. 790), Benedictine abbess. A nun of Wimborne, England, Thecla became a member of St. Boniface's mission to Germany at his request and worked there with her relative Lioba at Bischofsheim. T. was made abbess of Ochsenfurt and later, according to tradition, abbess of Kitzingen. BIBLIOGRAPHY: Zimmermann 3:182–183; Butler 4:122.

[W. A. CHANEY]

THECUE, see TEKOA.

THEFT, the taking of something belonging to another without his knowledge and against his reasonable will, with the intention of keeping it as one's own. It differs from *robbery which, because of the element of violence or its threat, does outrage to another in his person as well as in his property. The right to possess *property belongs to human beings by both natural and divine law, and stealing is sinful because it is an attack on this right. The malice attaching to theft is serious as a general rule. It is an act forbidden by the commandment of God (Ex 20.15), and according to St. Paul, ''thieves are among those who will not inherit the kingdom of heaven'' (1 Cor 6.10). Various circumstances may lessen the sin in particular cases, however, as when the thing stolen is of little value, or its owner is not notably unwilling to be deprived of it. Still the theft of a thing of small value in itself can be gravely sinful if the owner has great need of it, or if the thief intends his act as a partial realization of larger aims. What is of great value to one person may be hardly missed by another. Nevertheless, moralists agree that at some point in the scale of ascending values a thing or sum of money is of such importance in itself that its theft would be gravely sinful, regardless of whether or not the owner felt the loss. Things or sums having such value constitute what moral theologians call absolutely grave matter for theft. The determination of the sum necessary for absolutely grave matter is reached, not by an estimation of the harm done to a particular owner, but by consideration of the social disorder that would prevail if the theft of so large a sum were generally regarded as a trivial offense. Under ordinary circumstances the malice of an act of theft is estimated by a relative rather than an absolute standard. That is to say, an act is to be judged seriously sinful when the owner suffers a serious loss by being deprived of what is stolen. Thus, if the owner is very poor or in grave need of what the thief takes, the act does him a serious injury and is to be considered a grave sin, even if the sum involved is small. The absolute standard is only applied when a relative standard becomes meaningless because, e.g., the wealth of the injured party (a very rich man, a large corporation) makes it improbable that the loss will be seriously felt. In the application of the relative standard to ordinary people in ordinary circumstances, there has been some agreement among moralists that the loss of a day's wage or its equivalent is to be accounted a serious injury. Whatever is stolen from another continues to belong to its rightful owner and the thief is obliged to restore what he has taken (see RESTITUTION).

The need of the person who steals also exercises a modifying influence on the morality of the act. One who is in extreme need of something belonging to another and who takes it to keep from starving, for example, is not in the strict sense and from a moral point of view to be accounted a thief at all, because the owner can be presumed to be willing to give such desperately needed help to a fellow man in an emergency of that kind. And even should the owner be indifferent to his neighbor's need, his unwillingness to give the necessary help would be unreasonable. Hence the act would not be theft as defined above. Grave, though lesser need on the part of one who takes another's property, would not absolve the taker from guilt, but his guilt would be diminished in proportion to the seriousness of his need and the unavailability of other means of meeting it. BIBLIOGRA - PHY: ThAq ST 2a2ae, 66; A. Doolan, NCE 14:8; Davis MorPastTh 2:298–310.

[P. F. MULHERN]

THEFT (IN THE BIBLE), taking the property of another without his knowledge or consent, the misappropriation of another's goods committed to one's safekeeping or temporary use. The vital social importance of the injunction against theft can be gauged from its place in the Decalogue. Among social obligations, only the honoring of parents and the prohibition of murder and adultery rank higher. In Assyrian and Babylonian law life and property were commensurable. Loss of life could be compensated with money, and there was capital punishment for theft. The laws governing theft in Ex 22 do not go so far, but they are severe. A man must pay back five oxen for every one he steals, and four sheep for every sheep. If he cannot pay, he himself is to be sold into slavery and the price given to the injured party. It is not murder to fatally wound a burglar caught in the act, unless the break in occurs after sunrise. In Lev 19.11–18, there is the priestly tradition's elaboration of the commandment: "You shall not steal." It breathes a humane and virile spirit: it forbids stealing, cheating, and deception; it is wrong either to rob or oppress or to keep back a hired man's wages until morning; it is wrong either to favor the poor or be subservient to the rich; it is wrong to spread slander or take sides recklessly when a capital offense is involved. The correct thing is to reprove a neighbor openly for an offense, not to nurse hatred or seek revenge. In short, the passage concludes, "You shall love your neighbor as a man like yourself." The various injunctions of Deuteronomy show

more concern for the poor who "will always be with you in the land" (Dt 15.11) and for the need to be open-handed with countrymen than with injunctions against theft. The dominant social concern of the entire prophetic tradition was the violence of the rich against the poor.

[E. J. DILLON]

THEGLATH-PHLASAR, see TIGLATH-PILESER III.

THEINER, AUGUSTIN (1804–74), Polish historian, canonist. After a period away from the Church, he returned and became an Oratorian in Rome. Through a pronounced Romanophile viewpoint in his historical works, T. won the favor of Pope Pius IX, who appointed him in 1850 to the Vatican Archives. Despite his severely criticized and acutely anti-Jesuit *Geschichte des Pontifikats Clemens XIV* (1853), T. retained the favor of Pius IX, who appointed him in 1855 prefect of the Vatican Archives. This trust it was later learned he had betrayed. He retained in his personal possession transcripts of the *acta* of the Council of Trent, despite prohibition by the Pope; these were published after T.'s death. At Vatican Council I he betrayed information about other documents related to the Council of Trent to Card. G. A. Hohenlohe and other bps. opposed to the definition of papal infallibility. This action led to his dismissal from the Archives in 1870. His editions of canonical sources and the 3-v. continuation of Baronius are his only works of lasting value. BIBLIOGRAPHY: É. Amann, DTC 15:1:217–218; H. Rumpler, NCE 14:9.

[T. J. RYAN]

THEISM, belief in the existence of God as both transcendent and immanent. Though it is opposed to atheism and agnosticism and normally implies monotheism, theism does not necessarily entail belief in the Christian doctrine of God or Trinitarianism. Unlike pantheism, however, it asserts that God is not identified with the universe; and unlike deism, it asserts that God is not totally removed from the universe. Generally the term is used in philosophical discussions of total world views, and ordinarily by those who think a reasoned proof of the position can be given. It is therefore normally discussed in works of *natural theology. It is less emphasized by those theologians who base all theology on revelation. Theism does not deal with such central Christian doctrines as the Incarnation and the Atonement, and because its teaching about God is not tied to Christology, some theologians question whether its God is the same as the one whom Christians know in faith as the God and Father of Jesus Christ. Theism has been greatly influenced by the Christian theological tradition, however, and though theists understand God in various ways, they generally conceive him as a being in some sense personal, with whom man can enter into relationship.

The term was perhaps first employed by R. Cudworth in the preface to his *Intellectual System* (1678) as the opposite to atheism. But the general approach has been widely adopted wherever men admitted the validity of a philosophical defense of religious belief.

The classical support of theism has been the ontological, cosmological, and teleological proofs for the existence of God. Though the first is found initially in Anselm, the other two have been a part of Western intellectual history since at least the time of Plato. Discussion has centered around whether and in what sense they demonstrated the existence of God. Of special importance have been the five proofs of St. Thomas, the first four of which are versions of the cosmological and the fifth of the teleological argument. St. Thomas rejected the ontological argument, but several notable thinkers, such as Descartes, found it valid. W. *Paley's *Evidences* (1794) was a famous expression of the teleological argument, contending that the design of the world shows an arrangement leading toward a goal or purpose, and that only the action of God can explain such design.

Immanuel Kant (1724–1804) contended that all arguments for the existence of God were defective as far as pure reason is concerned. He asserted that the feeling of duty necessitates the existence of freedom and immortality, which entail the existence of God, thus he bases belief on the practical reason. Kant's approach is known as the moral argument, and some form of it has been characteristic of much modern theism. The argument from experience starts from some inward state that is held to necessitate a religious explanation.

Theists using the argument from design have necessarily had to deal with what appears to be negative evidence, the existence of evil, and so have been concerned with theodicy. Some theists, such as Leibniz, have held that God is limited by possibilities in some sense outside himself, and therefore creates the best of all possible worlds, though not one absolutely perfect. The perennial dilemma has been expressed: either God is all-powerful and able to prevent evil but not all-loving and so does not, or he is not all-powerful and therefore not the ultimate power.

Theism has received less attention in recent years. In part that has been because theists have found that their ''proofs'' did not in fact convince unbelievers. Vatican I asserted that man by natural reason can know the existence of God, but experience has shown that whether he in fact does so depends on many extra-rational factors. Meanwhile, philosophy has turned to the study of language (linguistic analysis) or analysis of man and his decisions (existentialism), and theology has emphasized revelation and the meaning of the Christian life. One popular modern theism, however, has been the system of P. Teilhard de Chardin, who asserted that God is the end toward which the universe moves in its evolution. BIBLIOGRAPHY: E. L. Mascall, *He Who Is* (rev. ed., 1966); C. C. J. Webb, *Studies in the History of Natural Theology* (1915); J. Macquarrie, *Twentieth-Century Religious Thought* (1963).

[T. EARLY]

THEMISTIANS, followers of Themistius, a 6th-cent. deacon of Alexandria, the founder of a Monophysite sect who claimed that Christ had no knowledge of the last day because of Mk 13.32; Jn 11.34. For this reason they were also called Agnoetae (''to be ignorant of''). The teaching was condemned by Pope Gregory I. BIBLIOGRAPHY: A. Vacant, DTC 1:586–596; A. Michel, *ibid.* 14.2:1628–65.

[F. H. BRIGHAM]

THEOBALD OF CANTERBURY (d. 1161), Anglo-Norman ecclesiastic; Benedictine monk of Bec Abbey; abbot (1137); abp. of Canterbury (1138). Inevitably involved in the English civil war, T., while remaining primarily loyal to the papacy, sided with King Stephen against Matilda and devoted much attention to problems of cooperation between Church and State. Stephen exiled him for attending Eugenius III's council at Reims (1148), but reconciliation followed and he became papal legate. Known for administrative ability and piety, T. defended archiepiscopal prerogatives against the Canterbury monks, was friendly with Bernard of Clairvaux, and included in his household John of Salisbury, Vacarius, and Thomas Becket.

[R. W. HAYS]

THEOBALD OF ÉTAMPES (d. after 1132), a Norman secular cleric largely responsible for the Oxford schools. He taught theology at Oxford for some 30 years. Of Theobald's five surviving letters, one, *Improperium cuiusdam in monachos,* is an apologia for secular canons as opposed to monks. BIBLIOGRAPHY: Emden Ox 3:1754.

[F. D. BLACKLEY]

THEOBALD OF PROVINS, ST. (1017–1066), Camaldolese priest and hermit. With another nobleman, Walter, T. built cells for themselves in the forest of Pettingen in Luxembourg. The necessary manual work included making charcoal for the forges, and T. is patron saint of charcoal burners. When his reputation for sanctity grew, he retired to a woody place near Vicenza, Italy and once again attracted many followers. The bishop there ordained him a priest so that he could better serve the spiritual needs of his disciples. Before his death T. made his profession to an abbot of the Camaldolese hermits. He was canonized by Pope Alexander II in 1073. BIBLIOGRAPHY: D. S. Buczek, NCE 14:12; AS June 7:540–556; G. Cacciamani, BiblSanct 12:196–197; Butler 2:678–679.

[M. C. BRADLEY]

THEOBALD OF VAUX-DE-CERNAY, ST. (c. 1200–47), French abbot. Eldest son of Burkhard de Montmorency, T. abandoned knighthood and the royal court in 1225 to join the Cistercians at Vaux-de-Cernay (Versailles). Ten years later he was elected abbot. It was through his efforts that Louis IX was reconciled with Queen Margaret, his wife. BIBLIOGRAPHY: C. H. Talbot, NCE 14:12.

[J. E. WRIGLEY]

THEOCENTRISM, (Gr., *theos,* God + *kentron,* center), a view or system of doctrines that accords to God a central importance. The term can be used in an absolute or a relative sense.

In the absolute sense, it is used without expressed or implied comparison. In this sense any genuine theism is theocentric both as an entire system and in each of its aspects considered in relation to its ultimate premises. Thus for Christianity, Judaism, and Islam God is the creator on whom all creatures depend for their existence, the ultimate goal toward which they all tend, and the absolutely perfect norm of truth, beauty, and goodness.

In the relative sense, the term theocentrism has special application to Christian theology: doctrinal, moral, and spiritual. Although the term thus used is opposed to *Christocentrism, it is not a question of choosing, as it were, between God and Christ. The apparent opposition is possible only because Christ is God, and it is a question of the relative emphasis given in a particular case to the transcendent Godhead as such or to the Incarnate Son.

Thomistic theology is an example of relative theocentrism, as the term is used here. It begins with God as known from revelation or from reasoned demonstration. It then proceeds to relate all creatures, all theoretical doctrines, and all moral and spiritual norms, to God in such a way that the Divinity himself is, as such, the center of the entire theological framework.

A Christocentric outlook, on the other hand, such as that elaborated by É. Mersch, begins with the God-man as he is made known to men in the Gospels. It immediately introduces the Godhead as the ultimate principle shining forth in Christ (2 Cor 4.5–6) and affirms the identity of the evangelical Christ and the transcendent Divinity. But it continues, throughout its development, to emphasize the mediation of Christ as its unifying principle. BIBLIOGRAPHY: ThAq ST, *Prima pars*; P. M. Daffara, ''La teologia come scienza nella Somma Teologica di S. Tommaso,'' *Sapienza* 1 (1948) 12–22; J. A. Jungmann, *Christus als Mittelpunkt religiöser Erziehung* (1939); É. Mersch, ''L'Objet de la théologie et le Christus Totus,'' RechSR 10 (1936) 129–57.

[M. D. MEILACH]

THEOCRACY (Calvinism). Though the political organization of Geneva in the period of *Calvin is commonly termed a theocracy, Calvin himself rejected the idea that the political organization of the Jewish people could be repeated in Geneva, or that the Church is ever to be equated with the whole of society. The Church for Calvin is witness to the reign of God and to the restoration of man's humanness in Christ; the political order has been created by God with external constraints that maintain a relative order and morality. Calvin assumed that ecclesiastical and secular authorities collaborate in the government of the State and that both alike have a balanced responsibility to implement the will of God in the life of the people. Rulers are responsible to God to do his business and are answerable to him; they are also responsible to their subjects, whom they are to defend against the injuries of the wicked (*Commentary on Romans*, 13.4). The political doctrines of Calvin find ex-

pression beyond Geneva particularly in Oliver *Cromwell's *Commonwealth and in Scotland after the Reformation. BIBLIOGRAPHY: R. E. Davies, *Problem of Authority in the Continental Reformers* (1946); W. A. Mueller, *Church and State in Luther and Calvin* (1954).

[J. A. R. MACKENZIE]

THEODARD OF NARBONNE, ST., (*c.* 840–893), archdeacon, then abp. of Narbonne (885–893). He received the pallium from Pope Stephen V in 886. T. did much to repair damages done by the Saracens and came to the aid of the suffering, even using church treasures to ransom Christian captives. He was buried in Montauriol, his place of birth, in the Benedictine Abbey of St. Martin, which later came to be named after him. His cultus dates from the mid-10th cent.

[E. J. DILLON]

THEODICY, that part of natural theology which explains the goodness and omnipotence of God against the objections raised by the presence of evil in the world. The name was coined by G. W. *Leibniz (1646–1716), as the title of his *Essais de théodicée sur la bonté de Dieu* (1710). As the justification of God's providence, theodicy can be traced to the ancient prophets of Israel, e.g., the Book of Job, and to the patristic age of Christianity, e.g., *De praedestinatione sanctorum* of St. Augustine. Since the time of Augustine, the basic solution to the problem has been to explain evil by the creature's abuse of freedom. This was a reaction to Manichaeism that entered Christian circles from Zoroastrian sources and which postulated two ultimate principles of creation, a good deity that produced everything spiritual and an evil deity responsible for the material universe. With the rise of Calvinism, the focus shifted; human freedom was in effect denied as a consequence of Adam's fall and grace was declared irresistible. Leibniz inherited both problems: the perennial one raised by the Manichaeans and the new one introduced by Calvin. His solution evidenced the shift in explanation from human freedom to the providential design of the Creator. He projected an extremely optimistic view of the world which, according to Leibniz, is the best possible. Evil thus becomes a necessary element in the universe, like the shadows in a picture which throw into relief the beauty and the harmony of the whole.

By the 19th cent., theodicy came to be applied by some authors to the whole field of natural theology. Used in this sense, it refers to the knowledge of God attainable by the light of human reason. This wider use of the term, however, is not accepted by many philosophers who prefer to restrict it to the consideration of providence and the problem of evil. BIBLIOGRAPHY: G. W. Leibniz, *Theodicy: Essays on the Goodness of God, the Freedom of Man and the Origin of Evil* (1952); J. F. Donceel, *Natural Theology* (1962); G. Smith, *Natural Theology* (1951).

[T. M. MCFADDEN]

THEODORA I (495–548), **BYZANTINE EMPRESS,** co-ruler with her husband Justinian. A former actress and a concubine of the governor of Africa Pentapolis, as empress she observed faithfully all feasts and fasts, founding a monastery to rehabilitate prostitutes. She showed herself courageous in the Nika taxation riots. She favored the Monophysites, sheltering their bps. and helping them found churches and monasteries in Constantinople, but in general promoting the moderates among them. She was successful in having Pope Silverius deposed for treason, replacing him with Vigilius. She favored the Edict of the *Three Chapters, and was instrumental in inducing Vigilius, probably under duress, to condemn the three Chalcedonian theologians whose works were at issue in that decree. Estimates of her work vary. Two years after her death, Paul Silentiarius called her St. Theodora. A millennium later the great Baronius referred to her as a pupil of the devil and a citizen of hell.

[E. J. DILLON]

THEODORA II (810–867), **BYZANTINE EMPRESS** (842–855) during the childhood of her son Michael III. He was able to force her to abdicate and proclaimed himself emperor. She had been the wife of the Emperor Theophilus, who reigned 829–842. Theodora continued secretly to venerate icons during the reign of her husband who was an ardent iconoclast. At his death, she convoked a synod (843) which deposed the iconoclastic patriarch, John the Grammarian, elected the monk Methodius as his successor, confirmed the decisions of Nicaea II, and condemned the iconoclastic leaders and their heresy. This victory is commemorated annually by the Feast of Orthodoxy (the first Sunday of Lent). T. was canonized because of her role in restoring icon veneration.

[E. J. DILLON]

THEODORA THE ELDER (d. *c*.926), wife of *Theophylactus, who played a precious part in the faction politics of Rome to the detriment of papal respectability. By one account, her morals were vile; by another, perhaps written ironically, she was pious and virtuous. The mother of *Marozia, T. exercised undue influence on Popes Sergius III and John X. BIBLIOGRAPHY: Fliche-Martin, 7:29–38.

[G. T. DENNIS]

THEODORE I (d. 649), **POPE** from 642, a native of Jerusalem, but of Greek ancestry. The immediate confirmation of his election on the death of John IV by the Emperor Constans II through the exarch of Ravenna, may have been due to the fact that T. was a Greek. But throughout his pontificate T. was in conflict with the Emperor, who for political reasons was favorable to the *Monothelites. At T.'s urging Constans withdrew the *Ecthesis but substituted in its place the *Typos, which forbade discussion of the question of one or two wills and operations in Christ. This was condemned by T.'s successor, Martin I. BIBLIOGRAPHY: P. J. Mullins, NCE 14:16; Mann 1:369.

[P. F. MULHERN]

THEODORE II (d. 897), **POPE** for 3 weeks in 897. T., a Roman, was ordained by Pope *Stephen VI, but he revealed none of the anti-Formosan venom that characterized the acts of Stephen. On the contrary, in his brief pontificate he did what he could to right the wrong Stephen had done. He presided at a synod that restored to office the clerics degraded by Stephen and recognized the validity of the orders conferred by Pope *Formosus. In a solemn ceremony he returned the body of Formosus to its place in St. Peter's. Although positive evidence to support such a conclusion is lacking, scholars have speculated that T.'s forthright action and the brevity of his pontificate were interrelated. BIBLIOGRAPHY: L. Duchesne, *Beginning of the Temporal Sovereignty of the Popes*, A.D. *754–1073* (tr. A. Mathew, 1908); Mann 4:88–90; P. Mullins, NCE 13:17.

[P. F. MULHERN]

THEODORE ASCIDAS (d. 558), Origenist monk, theological advisor to Justinian I. Born in Jerusalem, he had been abbot of the New Laura near Tekoa, Palestine, before being introduced to the court society of Constantinople. Through the backing of the Empress Theodora he was promoted to be abp. of Caesarea in Cappadocia without the obligation of residence. His main concern seems to have been to prevent the condemnation of Origen. To stay in favor he had to sign the edict of Justinian against Origen (543) and after the condemnation of Origenists at the Council of Constantinople II (553), he gave up his defense. At first T. emerged as a defender of Chalcedon against the extreme Monophysites; later he sided with Justinian in his *Three-Chapters policy to such an abrasive extent that Pope Vigilius was moved to excommunicate T. and his coterie. By his apologies and retraction, T. was reconciled to the Pope before Constantinople II. At the council he was a leading figure and probably set the council agenda.

[E. J. DILLON]

THEODORE BALSAMON, see BALSAMON, THEODORE.

THEODORE OF CANTERBURY, ST. (*c*.602–690), abp., organizer of the Anglo-Saxon Church. A Greek from Tarsus, T. studied at Athens and was learned in philosophy, literature, and law. Pope Vitalian appointed him abp. of Canterbury, provided that Abbot Hadrian, who had refused the office, would accompany him to guarantee Roman orthodoxy. Consecrated in 668, T. reached Canterbury in 669. He restored order to the English Church, filling vacant sees, establishing Roman orthodoxy, and dividing dioceses. He summoned the first synod of the whole English Church (Hertford, 672) and with Hadrian established the famous school of Canterbury. BIBLIOGRAPHY: Bede, *Ecclesiastical History* 2.3, 4.1; W. Hunt, DNB 19:602–606; Butler 3:598–601.

[W. A. CHANEY]

THEODORE OF EUCHAÏTA, ST., ancient martyr of Pontus, whose cult and legend enjoyed incredible popularity in East and West and grew with the centuries. He was venerated as one of the great "warrior saints" and his legendary exploits are portrayed in 38 of the stained glass windows of Chartres. The Byzantine liturgy still mentions him, along with fellow dragon-slayer St. George, and the other warrior saint, St. Demetrius. Not much that is historically certain can be culled from the heroic legends. He may or may not have been a Roman soldier; his alternate name, Theodore Tiro (from the Latin word for young recruit) is thought to indicate he may have been a newly enlisted man sent into winter quarters in Pontus where he met martyrdom under Diocletian (c.306?). His ashes were given burial at Euchaïta by a lady named Eusebia. The church at the site was rebuilt by the Emperor John Zimiskes; at the same time the town was renamed Theodoropolis in gratitude for victory over the Russians in 971, which the Emperor attributed to the powerful intercession of the warrior saint. There is also an ancient church at the foot of the Palatine hill in Rome named after him.

[E. J. DILLON]

THEODORE OF ICONIUM, 6th-cent. bp. of Iconium, who is credited with writing the Acts of SS. Cyricus and Julitta. His are not the acts declared spurious by Pseudo-Gelasius, but nonetheless are scarcely creditable, in view of the critical works attempting to get to the origins of the widespread cult of those two supposed martyrs.

[E. J. DILLON]

THEODORE LECTOR (fl., 520–530), Byzantine church historian, reader (anagnōstēs, hence, lector) of Hagia Sophia Church of Constantinople. He wrote two significant ecclesiastical histories in Greek: the so-called Historia tripartita and the Historia ecclesiastica. The former, written between 520–530, consisted of four books (books three and four are preserved only in fragments) and deals with the history of the Church from the reign of Constantine I up to 439. It is a collection of extracts from the estimable church histories written in the 5th cent. by such historians as Socrates Scholasticus, Sozomen, and Theodoret of Cyr. T.'s critical estimate of the various sources of these authors is still of value. The second work also consists of four books and continues the history from 439 to the reign of Justin I; only fragments are preserved in citations by other writers.

[E. J. DILLON]

THEODORE OF METOCHITES, (c.1266–1332), leading Byzantine scholar and statesman. He was born in Nicaea; his father, George Metochites, was the leading advocate of union with the Latin Church under Michael VIII Palaeologus. T. was a principal literary and philosophical figure who used his various public roles—grand chamberlain, chancellor, prime minister, and diplomat—to foster the arts and sciences. His own writings cover a wide spectrum, including mathematics, astronomy, history, and philosophy. His "Embassy Papers" (Presbeutikos) contain valuable information concerning the diplomatic overtures made by the Byzantines to the Slavic rulers to offset Ottoman advances. His commentaries on Plato's Dialogues influenced the 15th-cent. Platonic renaissance. In his major work (Personal Comments and Annotations), known in the West by its Latin title, Miscellanea philosophica et historica, he preserved, paraphrased, and annotated 120 essays drawn from ancient historical and philosophical writings. He directed the material and artistic restoration of the Chora Monastery (now called Kahriye Djami), considered the acme of 14th-cent. Byzantine mosaic art. At the fall of his patron, the Emperor Andronicus II Palaeologus, in 1328, he was deprived of his wealth and briefly exiled.

[E. J. DILLON]

THEODORE OF MOPSUESTIA (350?–428), the most notable of Antiochene exegetes and theologians. Born in Antioch c.350, he had *Libanius as his mentor for rhetoric and literature and *Diodore of Tarsus for exegesis and theology. His fellow student and friend, St. *John Chrysostom, persuaded him to enter and persevere in monastic life. Ordained in 383, he was consecrated bp. of Mopsuestia in 392. During his lifetime he distinguished himself by his preaching, learning, and orthodox teaching. A few years after the Council of *Ephesus, serious charges of Nestorianism were brought against his teaching on the Incarnation by St. *Cyril of Alexandria and *Marius Mercator. Temporarily vindicated by the letter of *Ibas of Edessa at the Council of Chalcedon in 451, T. was condemned in his person and his writings by the Council of Constantinople II in 553 as the first of the *Three Chapters. Since the publication of the Syriac text of his Catechetical Homilies in 1932, his complete orthodoxy has been attested by several scholars. However, some still regard his teaching as basically Nestorian.

While he wrote commentaries on most of Scripture, the only complete text in Greek is his commentary on the minor prophets. There is a Syriac version of his commentary on St. John's Gospel and a 5th-cent. Latin translation of a commentary on the ten shorter Pauline Letters. His biblical commentaries reflect sound principles of exegesis and literary criticism. His most important and most quoted theological work is On the Incarnation. The Syriac version was discovered in 1905 and was lost during World War I. Latin, Greek, and Syriac fragments survive. However, his Catechetical Homilies mentioned above are the best source for his teaching on doctrine, ethics, and liturgy. BIBLIOGRAPHY: Quasten 3:401–423.

[F. H. BRIGHAM]

THEODORE OF PHARAN, bp. of the town of Pharan in Arabian Sinai during the first half of the 7th cent., thought to be the first proponent, and perhaps the founder, of the Monenergist heresy, and thus a forerunner of *Monotheletism. Both the Lateran Council of 649 and Constantinople III, 680–681, cite against him excerpts from his letter to Sergius of Arsinoë in Egypt and from his commentary on patristic texts. Scholars variously characterize him as a Monophysite or a Chalcedonian. He is currently thought to be identical with the subtle Theodore of Rhaithu. Maximus the Confessor seemed to indicate that T. was led into his error by Sergius I of Constantinople.

[E. J. DILLON]

THEODORE OF RHAITHU, 6th-cent. theological writer, monk and priest of a monastery at Rhaithu (at-Tûr), a port in S Arabia. The last of the Neo-Chalcedonian authors T. is currently thought to be identical with *Theodore of Pharan, accused of being the first proponent of Monenergism. Writing during a time of theological peace, T. (while a monk–scholar, 580–620) composed his *Proparaskeue* (or *Praeparatio*) in an attempt to harmonize Chalcedon with the terminology of St. Cyril of Alexandria; and to demonstrate how the Church follows the moderate ground between heresies in its doctrine of the Incarnation. He may have been the author of another work, *De sectis* as well.

[E. J. DILLON]

THEODORE OF STUDIUS, ST. (759–926), Byzantine monastic leader and theologian. After a thorough education he became a monk under his uncle, Abbot Plato, at the Saddacum monastery and became abbot himself in 794. In 796 he was exiled to Thessalonica for opposing the adulterous second marriage of Constantine VI (see MOECHIAN CONTROVERSY), but returned a year later. T. moved his monks to the monastery of *Studius at Constantinople in 799, but was again banished in 809 over a recurrence of the Moechian dispute. He returned to the capital in 811 only to suffer a third exile when he defended the veneration of images against the iconoclastic Emperor Leo V (813–820). Leo's successor, Emperor Michael II, was more tolerant, but T. was not permitted to return to avoid further political turmoil. His greatest contribution was in the field of monastic legislation, principally contained in two catecheses. BIBLIOGRAPHY: É. Amann, DTC 15.1:287–298; A. Gardner, *Theodore of Studium* (1905).

[F. T. RYAN]

THEODORE OF SYKEON, ST. (d. 613), Byzantine archimandrite, ascetic revered as a miracle worker, and for a time bp. of Anastasioupolis. Born in Sykeon, Anatolia, in the mid-6th cent., he was ordained a priest at the age of 18, so impressed was Bishop Theodosius of Anastasioupolis with the T.'s asceticism. Later, after serving as bp. for eleven years, T. resigned the office and returned to his monastery at Sykeon.

[E. J. DILLON]

THEODORE OF TARSUS see THEODORE OF CANTERBURY, ST.

THEODORET OF CYR (393–466), most versatile writer of the *Antiochene school. He was born and educated in Antioch at one of its monastic schools and became well versed in classical tradition. First a monk at Apanea, he became bp. of Cyr in 423. In this capacity, he worked tirelessly for all in his district. As a theologian, he played a significant role in the complexities of the Christological controversies of the 5th century. He defended the Antiochene school and *Nestorius as he charged the 12 anathemas of St. *Cyril of Alexandria with containing *Appollinarism; he opposed the Council of *Ephesus for its condemnation of Nestorius in 431 by defending duality in Christ and calling Mary *theotokos* (Mother of God) in the figurative sense. However, in 433 he not only assented to the Act of Union between St. Cyril of Alexandria and *John of Antioch but probably formulated its creed. Because he opposed the Monophysite teaching of *Eutyches as contrary to that of Nestorius, he was condemned by the *Robber Synod of Ephesus in 449 and exiled to the monastery of Apamea by decree of the Emperor *Theodosius II, even though he composed another creed affirming unity of Christ and condemning all who did not accept Mary as *theotokos*. After T. appealed to Pope *Leo I and agreed to the Christology of Leo's *Tome to Flavian* (see TOME OF LEO), the Emperor *Marcion brought him back to his see and invited him to the Council of *Chalcedon in 451. This Council declared him an ''orthodox father'' after he had anathematized Nestorius. The Council of *Constantinople II (553) condemned his writings against Cyril and the Council of Ephesus together with those sermons and letters included in the *Three Chapters*. There is continuing scholarly dispute about his Christology.

Apart from his dogmatic Christological writings he distinguished himself as an apologist with a brilliant synthesis, *The Cure of Pagan Evils*, contrasting classical and Christian responses to fundamental philosophical and theological questions. As an exegete, with his clear and balanced Antiochene interpretation of several OT books and the Epistles of St. Paul; and as historian with his *Church History*, a continuation of the *Ecclesiastical History* of *Eusebius from 323–428. While most of his sermons are lost, his letters are an important historical source for the 5th century. BIBLIOGRAPHY: P. Canivet, NCE 14:20–22; Quasten 3:536–554.

[F. H. BRIGHAM]

THEODORIC BORGOGNONI OF LUCCA, (1205 or 08–1298), Dominican bp., a medical genius who advanced the art of medicine on a variety of fronts, but was esp. a pioneer in the practice of surgery. Born in Lucca or Parma, he died at Bologna. He learned surgery and medicine from his father Hugh of Lucca and practiced all his life. He entered the Dominicans at Bologna in 1226, was consecrated bp. of Bitonto in 1262, and became bp. of Cervia in 1266. His most famous work, *Chiurgia* (1266), anticipated many procedures whose value was only vindicated in modern times, esp. the need for aseptic surgery. His methods were successfully applied by his student Henry of Mondeville, but then fell into disuse for centuries. There is a two-volume, modern (1955–60) English translation of T.'s work on surgery, translated by E. Campbell and J. Colton.

[E. J. DILLON]

THEODORIC OF ECHTERNACH (d. after 1192), chronicler. Entering the Benedictine Order very young, Theodoric, noted for his learning, was probably a *schoasticus,* one entrusted with the direction of the scholarly activities of the monastery. He was respected for his chronicle (*Liber aureus*) and for his defense of the abbey's independence against Emperor Henry IV in 1191. The text of his *Libellus de libertate Epternacensi propugnata* is in MGS 23:38–72. BIBLIOGRAPHY: C. J. Ermatinger, NCE 14:22.

[M. E. DUFFY]

THEODORIC OF FREIBERG (Thierry de Fribourg; *c.*1250–1310), German Dominican philosopher and theologian. He was a student in Paris in 1276, provincial of Germany in 1293, and possibly a master at Paris from 1297. In his theological writings he influenced Meister Eckhart and Johannes Tauler. In his many philosophical opuscula he rejects St. Thomas Aquinas's teaching on the real distinction between *essence and esse*. T. was also a precursor of modern science, both by the general methodology followed in his study of optics, and by his explanation of the rainbow through investigation of the refraction of light rays. BIBLIOGRAPHY: W. A. Wallace, NCE 14:22–24.

[T. C. O'BRIEN]

THEODORIC THE GREAT (*c.*455–526) king of the Ostrogoths from 475; of Italy from 493 to 526. T. spent his youth as a hostage at Constantinople. Commissioned by the Byzantine emperor Zeno, he overthrew and succeeded the usurper Odovacer as king of Italy. He successfully kept himself free of eastern entanglements and surrounded himself with Roman counsellors like Boethius, Cassiodorus, and Ennodius, bp. of Pavia. He looked upon his rule as a continuation of the Roman and did not disturb the Catholic establishment but created an Arian church alongside it. Under him occurred a reflowering of the Roman spirit. He strengthened his position through political marriages; saw to the security of the public roads; restored canals, harbors, and aqueducts; enacted legal, social, and economic reforms; befriended the arts; and gave to Germanic legend the figure of Dietrich von Bern (Theodoric of Verona, so called for the city in which he loved to sojourn). He restored public monuments esp. at Rome and Ravenna and erected new structures. Yet his efforts to govern the Romans were not wholly successful: he had to punish a conspiracy by executing its leaders, among whom was the philosopher-statesman Boethius. BIBLIOGRAPHY: A. Nagl, PW 5.2:1745–71; W. Ensslin, *Theoderich der Grosse* (2d ed., 1959).

[M. J. SUELZER]

THEODORIC OF NIEHEIM (Deitrich of Niem; 1340–1418), canonist, historian, advocate of *Conciliarism. Of Westphalian origin, T. was a papal notary at Avignon; then,

returning (1377) to Rome with *Gregory XI, *abbrevitor in the Papal Chancellery. At the Council of *Constance (1414), T. renounced his original support of *John XXIII (antipope), against whom he published his *Invectiva in fugientem e Concilio Constantiensi Joannem XXIII*. Besides advocating disciplinary reforms in the Church, T.'s other works strongly defend the supremacy of the general council and the concept of a papal authority delegated by the Church to the Pope. These works include *Nemus unionis* (1408), *De schismate* (1410), *Avisamenta de unione et reformatione membrorum et capitis fienda* (1414). He also wrote two earlier works on curial practice. BIBLIOGRAPHY: Bihlmeyer-Tüchle 2:379–380, 390; *De schismate* (ed. S. Erler, 1890); E. F. Jacob, "Dietrich of Niem," *Essays in the Conciliar Epoch* (1943) 24–43; J. Leuschner, LTK 3:386, s.v. "Dietrich von Niem," bibliog.

[T. C. O'BRIEN]

THEODORIC, TOMB OF, Ravenna, mausoleum of Theodoric the Great, king of the Goths, erected by his daughter outside the walls near the NE corner of the city. A circular building it is remarkable for a monolithic dome, 36 ft in diameter, with "handles" carved from the same block, probably used for hoisting into position. Barbaric interlace adorns the structure; a porphyry basin forms the sarcophagus.

[M. J. DALY]

THEODORUS THE ATHEIST (*c.*330–270), Cyrenaic philosopher. He maintained that individual acts are indifferent, and that contentment of mind is the only true happiness. He seems to reflect one aspect of early Sophistic teaching in holding that circumstances only, and not nature, make lack of patriotism, stealing (including robbing of temples), and adultery wrong. In his work *On the Gods* he rejected completely belief in the existence of gods of any kind; hence, his sobriquet *atheos*. He is one of the extremely few persons in antiquity who are formally identified as atheists. LexAW 3046; Copleston 1:122; Ueberweg 1:171, 176.

[M. R. P. McGUIRE]

THEODOSIAN CODE, the legal code ordered by Emperor Theodosius II, published in 438–439. It contained only the general laws decreed by Constantine and his successors including Theodosius II. The few and incomplete MSS of this code, largely of Western origin, pose a problem of authenticity and interpretation. BIBLIOGRAPHY: *Theodosian Code and Novels* (eds. and trs., C. Pharr et al., 1952).

[E. EL-HAYEK]

THEODOSIUS II, BYZANTINE EMPEROR (401–450), reigned from 408. T.'s reign witnessed great theological controversies and prevailing opinion of Church-State relations necessitated his intervention. T., however, never tried to enforce his own theories; he provided opportunity for solemn ecclesiastical debate and then accepted the decisions rendered there. He convoked the Council of

*Ephesus in 431 to consider *Nestorianism, but in condemning both Nestorius and his opponent Cyril, the Council confronted him with a dilemma. Ultimately he condemned Nestorianism. The Monophysite dispute led him to summon another council at Ephesus in 449, that upheld Monophysitism. Theodosius accepted its decision despite Pope Leo I's protests (see ROBBER SYNOD). The Council of *Chalcedon clarified the situation, but only after Theodosius' death. T. also was responsible for the Theodosian Code, important to the history of *Roman Law. BIBLIOGRAPHY: Fliche-Martin v. 4; P. Hughes, *Church in Crisis: History of the General Councils, 325–1870* (1961).

[R. H. SCHMANDT]

THEODOSIUS I (345–395), **ROMAN EMPEROR** from 378. Flavius Theodosius was proclaimed by his troops in 378 and made co-Augustus by Gratian in 379. He was pious, impressionable, and mild, yet capable of crime when enraged. A case in point is his massacre of dissident elements in Thessalonica in 390, for which Ambrose excommunicated him until he repented. An excellent soldier, T. pacified the Goths and settled them in Thrace. Upon the murder of Gratian in 383, he came to the aid of the former's half-brother, the boy emperor Valentinian II, who was threatened by the usurper Maximus and later by Eugenius. It was Theodosius who completed the transformation of the Roman empire into a Christian state. He convoked the Council of Constantinople in 381 in an effort to put an end to Arianism. In 384 he blocked the attempt of *Symmachus and other pagans to restore the altar which had stood near the statue of Victory in the curia. He forbade public financial support for pagan worship and proscribed public sacrifices and related practices. About 394 he permanently closed the Olympic Games. Towards the end of his life he installed his older son Arcadius as ruler in the E and bequeathed the W to his second son, Honorius. The division of rule was in theory administrative only; but in practice it separated into two distinct empires, regions that had always differed in culture and in language. BIBLIOGRAPHY: H. Leclercq, DACL 15.2 2265–71; N. Q. King, *Emperor Theodosius and the Establishment of Christianity* (1960).

[M. J. SUELZER]

THEODOSIUS, MONOPHYSITE PATRIARCH OF ALEXANDRIA (d. 566). He became patriarch through the favor of the Empress Theodosia in 535; but Justinian I had him brought to Constantinople in 537, and T. remained an exile for the rest of his life. He had considerable influence, however, as the leader of the Monophysites; he journeyed twice throughout the Byzantine Empire; consecrated *Jacob Baradai as a bp.; and urged the formation of a Jacobite Church. T. also wrote numerous treatises, following the line of Severus of Antioch. Justinian II offered him the opportunity to return Alexandria, but T. died before being able to do so.

[T. C. O'BRIEN]

THEODOSIUS I BORADIOTES (1179–83), **PATRIARCH OF CONSTANTINOPLE** from 1179. He was patriarch at the end of the reign of Manuel I Comnenus and continued during the struggle for power of Andronicus I during the minority of Alexis II.

[P. J. HENNESSEY]

THEODOSIUS OF THE CAVES, ST., (the Cenobiarch; 423–529). Born at Garissus in Cappadocia, he was a disciple of St. Simeon Stylites and an antagonist of the Eutychian heresy and its patron, the Emperor Anastasius. In his 106th year he died in the monastery he founded south of Jerusalem and was buried nearby in the cave where he had begun his monastic pilgrimage. The two principal sources for his life are the biography written by his disciple Theodore, bp. of Petra, and a shorter account by Cyril of Skythopolis.

[E. J. DILLON]

THEODOSIUS OF PALESTINE, ST., (c.423–529), monastic leader. Born in Cappadocia, he became a monk and lived at several monastic sites near Jerusalem and Bethlehem, and was elected archimandrite of the cenobite monks of Jerusalem (493). He became famous for the shelters he built for the aged, the poor, strangers, and travelers. Exiled by Emperor Anastasius I for his opposition to Monophysitism, he returned to his monastery at the death of the Emperor. Three early biographers, including his student (Theodore of Petra), attest to his virtues.

[E. J. DILLON]

THEODOSIUS THE DEACON, COLLECTION OF, a compilation of canonical and historical material by an unknown deacon, found solely in the Verona Chapter Library Codex LX, and dating from c.700, first published by S. Maffei in 1738. The material contains 27 documents relating to early E and N African councils and other church matters, including some important ones not found elsewhere: a letter from a Roman synod (c.372) to the bishops of the East; the canons of a synod at Carthage in 419; a paschal cycle; two letters from Athanasius to the Church at Alexandria; a letter from the Council of Sardica; and an official diary of the Alexandrian Patriarchate from 346–368. The large quantities of Carthaginian and Sardican material causes speculation that the collection might have resulted from an early 5th-cent. African inquiry into the nature of the Council of Sardica.

[E. J. DILLON]

THEODOTIANS, see THEODOTUS THE TANNER.

THEODOTION (fl. 2d cent. A.D.), according to ecclesiastical tradition a translator of the OT into Greek. Irenaeus states that T. was a proselyte from Ephesus; Epiphanius, that he was a native of Pontus; and Jerome, possibly confusing him with Symmachus, that he was an Ebionite. The name actually covers a large body of recensional material of the 1st cent., as may be seen from quotations in the NT and from fragments of the Minor Prophets from Nahal Hever in the Judaean desert. This version formed the sixth column in Origen's Hexapla. BIBLIOGRAPHY: J. W. Wevers, InterDB 4:618–619; JBC 570–572.

[M. J. COSTELLOE]

THEODOTUS, 2d-cent. *Gnostic teacher of the school of *Valentinus, several of whose sayings or teachings have been preserved by Clement of Alexandria in his *Excerpts from Theodotus*. Theodotus is usually associated with the Eastern tradition of the school, as opposed to the Western or Italian Heracleon. BIBLIOGRAPHY: W. Foerster, *Gnosis* 1 (1972), 146–153, 222–233.

[D. P. EFROYMSON]

THEODOTUS OF ANCYRA (d. *c*.446), bp. of Ancyra (Ankara, Turkey), who accused Nestorius of heresy at the Council of Ephesus (431) and supported St. Cyril of Alexandria. Four of T.'s sermons, often quoted by later writers, are extant in the acta of Ephesus. He also wrote a commentary on the creed of Nicaea I that claims Nestorius's heresy to have been already condemned by Nicaea.

[T. C. O'BRIEN]

THEODOTUS THE TANNER (the Elder; the Cobbler; 2d cent.), teacher at Rome of a dynamic *Monarchianism. T. came from Byzantium *c*.190; he was condemned by Pope *Victor I for proclaiming that Jesus was not divine but became the Christ at his baptism. T. was probably defending himself from the charge that he had apostatized during persecution, by claiming that he had not in fact denied God (cf. Augustine, *Haer*. 33). His followers, called Theodotians, included Theodotus the Younger, also called the Money Changer; they set up a short-lived Church, with their own bishop, Natalis, first anti-pope. Epiphanius (*Panar*. 54) refers to them as *Melchisedechians. BIBLIOGRAPHY: Altaner 147; G. Bardy, DTC 10:513–516, s.v. "Melchisédeciens"; Bihlmeyer-Tüchle 1:159.

[T. C. O'BRIEN]

THEODULF OF ORLÉANS (d. 821), poet, archbishop. An exile from Spain, T. took refuge among the Franks and won Charlemagne's favor as one of the foremost poets and intellectuals of the Carolingian Renaissance. Named bp. of Orléans *c*.800, T. strove to improve education and to inculcate an appreciation of art, of which he was a connoisseur. His theological writings are the *Libri Carolini*, an edition of the Vulgate, and treatises on baptism and the Holy Spirit. His poetry celebrates both secular and religious themes. He served Charlemagne on political missions and remained in royal favor under Louis the Pious until 817, when the emperor, perhaps unjustly, deprived him of his see. BIBLIOGRAPHY: A. Freeman, "Theodulf of Orléans and the *Libri*

Carolini," *Speculum* 32 (1957) 663–705; M. Laistner, *Thought and Letters in Western Europe A.D. 500–900* (rev. ed., 1957).

[R. H. SCHMANDT]

THEOGNIS OF NICAEA (d.*c*.343), a disciple of Lucian of Antioch and one of the most enthusiastic followers of Arius. Though he signed the symbol of faith at Nicaea, he worked with others to weaken its effects. Deposed from his See of Nicaea, he was sent into exile in Gaul by Constantine (325). Recalled after 3 years, T. led the battle against Athanasius and the Homoousians, becoming the recognized leader of Arianism after the death of Eusebius of Nicomedia until his own death in 342 or 343. BIBLIOGRAPHY: W. Ensslin, PW 5.2: 1984–85; A. van Roey, LTK 10:55; A. Amore, EncCatt 11:1955; Quasten 3:193–194.

[M. J. COSTELLOE]

THEOGNOSTUS (fl. 250–280), head of the catechetical school of Alexandria in succession to *Dionysius. He produced a work in seven books entitled *Hypotyposeis*. This seems to have been written with no pretense of originality but, according to Photius, in regrettable fidelity to the errors of Origen. St. Athanasius, however, thought better of it. BIBLIOGRAPHY: L. B. Radford, *Three Teachers of Alexandria* (1908) 1–43; LexAW 3049–50.

[R. B. ENO]

THEOGONY, an account of the origin of gods (Gr. *theogonia*, birth of gods). Many peoples have developed such mythological accounts, which are inseparable from cosmogonies. The material gathered in Hesiod's poem, the *Theogony*, was the earliest and most authoritative in classical antiquity. Hesiod recounts the genealogy of successive generations of gods starting from Chaos (Space) and Gaia (Earth). Certain features of his treatment, such as the story of Ouranos, Gaia, and Kronos, are now recognized as ancient material found also in Mesopotamian epic. Later Greek theogonies, like the Orphic, used Hesiodic material combined sometimes with folk motifs, sometimes with original speculation. Plato's *Timaeus* is the most important philosophical work in the tradition. In later antiquity Gnostic, Hermetic, Neoplatonic, and Neopythagorean speculation combined Greek with OT and Oriental themes in complex theogonies. BIBLIOGRAPHY: M. L. West, *Hesiod: Theogony* (1966) 1–48; H. Schwabl, "Weltschöpfung" PWSuppl 9, the only modern comprehensive treatment.

[Z. STEWART]

THEOLEPTUS, METROPOLITAN OF PHILADELPHIA, (*c*.1250–*c*.1326), controversial Byzantine spiritual writer, charismatic teacher, and promoter of *Hesychasm. After being appointed abp. of Philadelphia in Lydia, he became a renowned pastor and director of souls. Shortly after the reunion of Rome with the Byzantine Church was concluded at the Council of Lyons in 1274, he organized the opposition to this policy in Bithynia and at one point was imprisoned and maltreated by the pro-union Emperor Michael VIII for this opposition. Around 1275, T. left the wife he had recently married, retired from the diaconate, and practiced Hesychastic spirituality in solitude, following the teachings of Nicephorus the Athonite. T.'s writings provide the link between the Hesychasm of Nicephorus and *Gregory Palamas. After appointment as archbishop in 1285, T. became even more involved in political and religious struggles; he wrote against the followers of John XI Beccus, attacked the theory of the procession of the Holy Spirit taught by Gregory II Cyprius, patriarch of Constantinople, and helped rally his city against a Turkish siege.

[E. J. DILLON]

THEOLOGIA CRUCIS (theology of the cross), a theme in Martin Luther's reform of theology. Beginning with the Disputation at Heidelberg in 1518 Luther opposed this theme to the *theologia gloriae* of the scholastics. He rejected their concentration on the reasonable ascent to knowledge of God through his works in nature. Luther wished to turn theology away from speculation to the Bible, and to the search for God in the hiddenness, suffering, and powerlessness revealed in Christ and the cross. The theologian in his quest for knowledge of God must be imbued with a sense of the cross's contradiction to natural and human values, even as the believer must not seek righteousness in good works. BIBLIOGRAPHY: U. Saarnivaara, *Luther Discovers the Gospel* (1951).

[T. C. O'BRIEN]

THEOLOGIA GERMANICA (*Theologia deutsch*), a German ascetical and mystical treatise written c.1400. Its author, whose name is unknown, was a *Friend of God, a priest, guardian of a house of Teutonic Knights near Frankfurt-on-Main. The earliest known MS, discovered in the 19th cent., is dated 1497 (ed. F. Pfeiffer, 1900). Luther supervised the first printed edition (1516 and 1518); he was interested in the work because of the support it appeared to give to his doctrine on good works. Later the Pietists valued it highly. Although a Latin translation by S. *Castellio (d. 1563) was put on the Index in 1612, the *Theologia Germanica* is Catholic in content and inspiration. Against the *Brothers and Sisters of the Free Spirit, it seeks to define the true friend of God. The work reflects the mysticism of Meister *Eckhart and J. *Tauler. The experience of God in nonconceptual vision is placed as a goal to be attained by detachment from all creatures, esp. from self-will. The work is pious rather than speculative; its language is simple and often imprecise. Union with God in being is confused with union with God in knowledge and love. Descriptions of obedience and resignation are somewhat quietistic. Text: Eng. tr. of Pfeiffer's crit. ed., S. Winkworth, rev. J. Bernhart (1949). BIBLIOGRAPHY: J. Paquier, *Un Mystique allemand au XIV siècle* (1922).

[T. C. O'BRIEN]

THEOLOGIAN. The term in its Christian use has both historical and functional connotations. Historically, the early Christian writers understood the term *theologos* according to its usage in Greek culture: the *theologoi* were authors who gave religious, usually meaning mythological, explanations of the universe and its origin (theogonies). The term came also among the Stoics to mean those devoted to *theologia,* a rational account of the working of the gods as personifications of the forces of nature. There was among Christian writers, then, an initial, unfavorable contrast between the *theologoi* and Christian teachers who treated of the mystery of God himself. By the time of Eusebius of Caesarea (d. c.340), however, there was acceptance of the term theology as teaching about the divine, an intellectual elaboration of the doctrine of faith. It is noteworthy, however, that Pseudo-Dionysius used the term *theologoi* in his writings to refer to the authors of the biblical books. When the presentation of Christian teaching developed more and more along systematic lines, the term theologian was not in common use. The medieval division of thinkers and writers about the matters *sacra doctrina* dealt with was into *sancti* and *philosophi*; the first were the believers, Fathers and Christian writers; the second, the pagans. But even as the term *theologia* came to replace *sacra doctrina, sacra scriptura, sacra pagina,* so *theologi* came to replace *sancti,* and to indicate those professionally engaged in the study and teaching of theology. Whatever the title used, the function of the theologian from the beginning has been understood to be a concern for the intellectual elaboration of the truths of revelation. But specialization has come to particulate theology into many functions and has created a connotation of functional diversity in the force of the word theologian. The theologian is set apart from the philosopher by object, principles, purpose, and method. But the theologian is often understood as one who is primarily concerned with the rational systematization of the teachings of faith; he is the systematic (dogmatic) theologian, or, in some circles, the philosophical theologian. One who is concerned with a similar, rationally based study of morality has to be specified as a moral theologian; and within that area, further as an ascetical, mystical, or pastoral theologian. One concerned with the history of Christian doctrines is a historical theologian. One concerned with patristic studies is a patrologist. One concerned with the confessions of faith is a symbolic theologian. One who concentrates on biblical expressions, categories, and themes is a biblical theologian. All, in turn, are distinct from the biblical scholar, the exegete, hermeneuticist, or textual critic. At the practical level, the vastness of the body of learning makes such distinctions of concentration, therefore of title, necessary. Ideally, however, the distinction of functions can exist within an epistemological recognition of the inherent unity of theology. The unity is one of purpose: the search for understanding of the mysteries of faith. But there is also a unity of internal coherence of all the functions of theology. It is a unity derived from the intelligibility of the one concern of theology, God as he has revealed himself. That establishes a common note of intelligibility: if meaning is communicated to man, then the meaning is open to the mind's resources to penetrate, to reflect, to defend, to elaborate. The source of God's revelation is the biblical word as continuously and vitally understood by the believing community. That calls for all the positive functions of theology, the biblical and symbolic studies, the study of the Fathers as the witnesses to the living word of God. The body of knowledge opened to the mind is to be treasured by theoretical penetration, but also is a directive for action, the pursuit of the salvation revealed. All of these functions, however specialized in exercise, have their specific unity from the multifaceted but one, intelligible word of God. A sense of that unity is involved in a second, functional connotation of the title theologian, the ecclesial function. Because theology is concerned with the word of God, it is a science of salvation in the Church and for the Church. The theologian is not the embodiment of the teaching Church; the office of the magisterium is exercised by the pastors set apart by sacred orders as teachers, pastors, rulers, the bishops, and their coworkers, priests. But the theologian is one who exercises a service in the Church to the teaching office, and in principle can rely on charismatic gifts to fulfill his office. The faith that enlightens his whole effort is the faith that joins all the members of the Church to Christ and to one another. That faith also joins the body of theologians, with their diverse functions, to one another so that theology itself becomes a communal effort. Theologians putting their own labors at the service of the faith contribute to the ever-deepening understanding in the Church of the words and realities that the Church is ever handing down (See Vat II DivRev 8).

[T. C. O'BRIEN]

THEOLOGICAL CONCLUSION, the intellectual advance from a truth explicitly contained in revelation to another truth not found as such in revelation, by means of a valid and certain deductive process. By such deduction, revelation is explained, applied, and developed. This process is not merely the explication of truths formally contained in revelation, nor simply the application of irrefutable logic to revealed truths. It is rather the expression of a reality that pertains to the essence of the revealed truth and that cannot therefore be denied without negating the data of revelation itself. For example, Jesus Christ is truly a man (revealed truth); but man has free will (a truth of reason based upon an essential attribute of man); therefore Jesus Christ has free will (theological conclusion). Theologians differ as to whether such conclusions constitute dogmas, and whether they are to be believed as divinely revealed truths or as certain teachings of the Church. BIBLIOGRAPHY: Y. M. J. Congar, DTC 15.1:341–502; *La Foi et la théologie* (1962); F. Marín-Sola, *L'Évolution homogène du dogme catholique* (1925); G. B. Mondin, NCE 14:30.

[T. M. MCFADDEN]

THEOLOGICALLY CERTAIN, the theological note applied to religious propositions the truth of which is guaranteed by their intrinsic connection with revealed doctrine, although the Church's teaching authority has not yet made definitive judgment on their validity. Theological certainty is to be distinguished from revealed certainty, where the only criterion is the word of God revealing. It is also distinguishable from merely rational certainty, where the only norm is human reasoning. Moreover, there is absent in theological certainty the critical element of infallible definition by the Church that a proposition is true.

Essentially, therefore, a doctrine is theologically certain when the norm of certitude is bivalent, i.e., partly God's revelation and partly human reason. The technical term for this bivalence is "intrinsic connection with revealed truth." By this is not meant a simple restatement in synonymous words of something formally revealed, e.g.,: Christ is one person or one individual. It must be such an extension of revealed truth that a positively new element enters the proposition, namely some principle that has not been supernaturally revealed.

Examples of such nonrevealed truths that may enter into composition with revealed doctrine are the mind's capacity for knowledge and certitude, the existence of corporeal beings, the essential difference between intellect and senses, the basic difference between transient phenomena and the enduring reality that produces them. These and similar premises are the common patrimony of the human race and, when joined with revealed doctrine, lead to conclusions that give theological certainty. Such conclusions cannot be denied without rejecting either the revealed truth from which they are derived or a fundamental principle of human knowledge.

Some writers prefer to call this kind of conclusion implicitly—and not just virtually—revealed. They would reserve the term theologically certain for conclusions in which one premise was revealed but the other was known from human experience and not reason. More commonly, however, these are called dogmatic facts. They include a wide variety of contingent data, like the orthodoxy of a certain person, the validity of a sacred rite, or the inspiration of a piece of writing.

Accordingly the terminology differs among scholars on the extension of the phrase theologically certain. But there is no dispute on the importance of the concept behind the terminology. Most of the Church's defined teaching originally belonged to this category of conclusions, which were jointly derived from revelation and from another premise that was not revealed but came from human reason or experience. BIBLIOGRAPHY: E. J. Fortman, NCE 10:523–524; G. B. Mondin, *ibid.*, 14:30; S. Cartechini, *De valore notarum theologicarum* (1951).

[J. A. HARDON]

THEOLOGY, a word, found in English 20 years before its use by Chaucer, that comes from Lat. and Gr. *theologia,* literally talk about God, which sense is to be maintained through its various later elaborations, popular and academic, despite appearances to the contrary. Before coming to them it will be well to distinguish it from certain related notions. *Revelation, the source of theology, is God's act of disclosing himself by his "word" and mighty deeds in history, with respect both to his mysteries, which are quite beyond our own powers to attain, and to the "natural truths of religion," which we might come to ourselves but for our congenital muzziness of mind and heart, the legacy of *original sin. *Faith is our reception of this revelation, our utter cleaving to God's truth, which even when considered as an act of the mind according to the analysis of the schoolmen, still more of course, when taken in its full Pauline and in its Lutheran sense, is an assent breaking free from all bonds of thought. Holy *Scripture is the record of revelation. *Articles of faith are the dogmas or credal declarations made by the Christian Church to safeguard our authentic witness to God; they are not what we believe "in," but rather what we believe "through"; nevertheless they are permanent, not interim, structures for the corporate faith of the Church. Though, as will be indicated, one office of a theologian will be to reflect on these, there can be no more question of his doubting them than of a medical practitioner questioning the blessing of good health: neither will get anywhere unless he starts from definite premises. Revelation, heavenly vision, earthly faith, Scripture, articles of faith, all these comprise at varying strengths the principles from which theology derives: they are not theology itself.

The mention of "theologian" may suggest a professional expert. Let it be said at once, and firmly, that the word should never lose its common ring, even when it is extended to the refined tones of esoteric disciplines. This is a special vocation for some, but all the people of God, to the extent they are called upon to think at all, are called upon to think theologically, for all issues, except those of improvisation to immediate circumstances, are at bottom theological. Indeed it will be a mark of a master to respect, and even to envy, the ease and confidence of ordinary folk. Are they set down just as people of simple faith? Better not, for it is a pretentious patronage to equate the lack of sophistication and a technical vocabulary with a failure to translate the faith into human experience, or to suggest that the experience of those whose faith is simple is limited. Cajetan was equably prepared to admit that his washerwoman was not only a better believer than himself but also a better theologian.

So then theology is to be defined essentially, if rather generically, as the overspill of divine faith into all the levels of human reasonableness, its wit, humor, poetic imagery, sense of analogy, power of coordination, openness to be taught, and search for reasons why, whence, how, and what is it all about. It engages all that makes the theologian other than God and other than the angels and the beasts. We are not to suppose that God is a theologian himself, or that angels are—except, according to Augustine, as a minor and evening avocation (of ThAq ST 1a,58.6). Animals certainly are not, though occasionally you stray across some that wear the air. It was in this crowded but tight enough sense

that the patristic and medieval writers took the term: it was humanity complete and entire engaged with divinity, asking the proper questions and half-getting the answers. And divinity was all about us, not a diffused unknown x, but the Father, Son, and Spirit revealed to us in the Scriptures and borne witness to by the Church.

The term theology does not occur in the Scriptures. The early Christians jibbed at it because of its pagan associations, preferring gnōsis until that was spoilt for them. It was generally adopted by the Greek Fathers from the time of Origen, though it referred to the study of the divinity, whereas the term economy (oikonomia) denoted that of the humanity of Christ, and the restoration of friendship between God and man in the Word made flesh (Logos sarx egeneto). It is not prominent in St. Augustine, and though it appeared in Erigena's influential translation of the Dionysian De mystica theologia, it was not until Abelard that it was popularized in Latin: even with him it stood for a dialectical discipline. It was identified with sacra scriptura by the Victorines, and with the sacra pagina by other medievals—the slight increase of accuracy we may read back into the phrase was probably unconscious. The term adopted by St. Thomas Aquinas was sacra doctrina, holy teaching, and despite the title of his Summa, the word theology appears only fugitively in that work, and then in its Aristotelian sense.

However, the first question, which defines the scope of Christian theology, remains a locus classicus. Important is its inclusion of symbol, myth, metaphor, indeed of all the genialities of human communion with God's world. Nevertheless, the author was of too Aristotelian temper to leave matters at that; accordingly, he sought how theological investigation could adopt intellectual processes, not merely dialectical but also scientific, and form a body of knowledge, an epistēmē which worked with its own proper severity of discourse and could conduct an argument or dialogue in which human reasons communicated in a civilis conversatio. From this sprang the divisions of theological disciplines to be looked at later. Henceforward theology was to be regarded—if disapprovingly by those acquainted only with physico-mathematical models—as truly a science. The effort of scholasticism to this effect can be caricatured, and not altogether unfairly, for a naked deductivism, but in St. Thomas at least it sprang from his view that revelation was published to the people of God, that a people, not just a race-group or caste-group and so forth, really communicate when there is an agreed currency of thought and values, and that only on this agreement can there be a progressive development. This is not an argument for any one school of theology, but for a thinking theology, and one prepared to elaborate and explain. Such a science is no more to be ripped from its living roots than are the political and legal institutions of a state from the deeper and more indeliberate factors of a country's social unanimity. Indeed, theology is the Church thinking aloud, and here, it may be remarked, the people, not the professionals, have sometimes led the way—the distinction is not that between laity and clergy.

Accordingly, Christian theology takes place within the household of the faith. To look at divine revelation from outside, in so far as that be possible, would not be theology, but a detached and critical philosophy of religion, and the same may be said about "natural theology," called "theodicy" since Leibniz, when treated merely as a part of natural, moral, and metaphysical philosophy out of its context in salvation history. The qualification, "in so far as that be possible," is added because the true Light enlighteneth every man that cometh into the world (Jn 1.9), and nothing but formal rejection of faith can cut a person off from thinking theologically in a Christian sense, though none of that may be consciously recognized.

For this reason theology is single in its root, whatever its ramifications. The growth may seem luxuriant and wild, for like Scripture it takes in the jungle as well as the cultivated patches of human experience, yet all is from and for the revelation of God. It is on God himself that St. Thomas centers his theological science, and though not unsympathetic to earlier views fixing on the sacraments, the works of salvation, of the mystical body, it is not preoccupationally kerygmatic or eschatalogical. It springs from faith, and faith is a prelude to the *beatific vision, and of both God himself is the object. Its impulse, in St. Anselm's phrase, is faith seeking understanding.

What sort of understanding can be expected? Clearly not the seeing of God face to face or glorious *theophanies so long as we walk in the darkness of faith, as we must until the day of our death. Rather it will be the insight that comes from affinity (connaturalitas, sumpatheia), such as is wrought in us by the gift of the Spirit, understanding, knowledge, and wisdom. And this will be supplemented by the theological effort to listen to the resonances in God's creation, to catch glimpses of how things hang together, of taking the truths of faith into "profane" experience and conversely, of being open-minded and ready to grasp analogies, of being sturdy and spirited about difficulties, in short of being a person of distinct uncommon sense. Such a discipline will give us a synoptic view, rare enough for an individual to attain to, but easier in the team-thinking of the Church. So theology takes philosophy and literary and historical criticism in its stride, for nothing that is of and for God is to be rejected; so theologians, somewhat primly though excusably, speak of the ancillary sciences; so, more equivocally, did some of the earlier of them mutter about spoiling the Egyptians. The constant aspiration is to reach to understanding beyond the ratiocination, a content of mind when our volubiles cogitationes, as St. Augustine calls them, are stilled. Yet its proper act is not an act of faith, nor is its proper object an article of faith, but rather a *theological conclusion, though the term need not here be narrowed to its formal meaning according to the procedures of the Holy Office. Finally, though he knows better, a theologian may feel more pleased than otherwise when he is told that most of his science adds up to little more than an anthropology about God. It is the little more that counts.

As responses to the pressures of history, the divisions of theology are not altogether tractable to the logic of classification; some schools can be treated as period pieces, faded ancient and fading modern, or be regarded good-humoredly as special pleadings. This outline may begin by adopting the Hellenist distinction between pure and pragmatic knowing, theōria and praxis, and make its first division between contemplative and practical theology, respectively that which seeks to know the truth for its own sake and that which seeks to know what we should do about it. Contemplative theology may be divided into positive and systematic theology. The first, which seeks to establish the true meaning of the facts, may be subdivided into biblical theology (of which exegesis is a function), historical theology (engaged with patristic, conciliar, and papal authorities), and dogmatic theology (more concerned with the contemporary content of the articles of faith than with how they have developed). This last shades off, however, into systematic theology which relates or coordinates these meanings and develops them. Both have been called, somewhat unhappily, "speculative" theology, a Latinism which has lost its original strength and carries the suggestions of being remote, conjectural, or dabbling in stocks and shares; both are worthily represented, and not for historical reasons alone, by the title "scholastic theology."

To turn to practical theology: this may be comprehensively called, quite simply, moral theology, and shades back according to the old tradition, now being recovered, into contemplative theology, for as anyone who has fallen in love knows, and that without being bemused, it is difficult to draw the line between a state of being and a condition of being. A manualist tradition tended to cut it off from its sources, and even to commit to canon law, too closely for the health of either. Then also a past vogue made three disciplines: moral theology, how to avoid sin; ascetical theology, how to advance in virtue; mystical theology, how to respond to the rarer and miraculous manifestations of grace. It is the compartmentation, not the nomenclature that is criticized. But an emphasis on diverse functions can, of course, break a single science into appropriate sections, and so can diverse applications; thus we have pastoral theology, educational theology, inner-city theology. Affective theology as a rhetoric belongs here, but as engaged really with the heart of the matter it is part of contemplative theology, and, not least, of systematic theology, which might be expected on a superficial view. All the above rough headings should mark no exclusion: a biblical and historical theologian will need to be a dogmatic theologian and work back to origins from meanings as they are at present in the mind of the Church, and a scholastic theologian will be all the better for a well-informed sense of history. BIBLIOGRAPHY: ThAq ST 1a,1 (Lat-Eng., v. 1), *Christian Theology*, ed. T. Gilby, (1964) cf. appendices; Y. M. J. Congar, DTC 15.1:346–447; E. L. Mascall, *Words and Images* (1957); G. F. van Ackeren, NCE 14:39–49.

[T. GILBY]

THEOLOGY, APOPHATIC, see APOPHATIC THEOLOGY.

THEOLOGY, DISPENSATIONAL, see DISPEN-SATIONALISM.

THEOLOGY, DOGMATIC, see DOGMATIC THEOLOGY.

THEOLOGY, EXISTENTIAL, see EXISTENTIAL THEOLOGY.

THEOLOGY, EXPERIENCE, see EXPERIENCE THEOLOGY.

THEOLOGY, FUNDAMENTAL, see FUNDAMENTAL THEOLOGY.

THEOLOGY, HISTORICAL, the expository and interpretative study, employing a historical method, of Christian dogmas and of their diverse theological explanation and defense. The term historical distinguishes it from *systematic theology. While usually set apart as an academic discipline, historical theology ideally is one function within the epistemological unity of theology as a whole. The principles of theology are the articles of faith, and these express God's revelation as an entrance into and commentary on human history. Further, the community of believers is a historical community; the understanding of the truths of faith is sustained in it by the assistance of the Holy Spirit present throughout time. The believing community's understanding at any period is a necessary part of theology's assessment of its own principles.

[T. C. O'BRIEN]

THEOLOGY, LUNDENSIAN, see LUNDENSIAN THEOLOGY.

THEOLOGY, NATURAL, see NATURAL THEOLOGY.

THEOLOGY, POLEMICAL, see POLEMICAL THEOLOGY.

THEOLOGY, SOCIAL, see SOCIAL THEOLOGY.

THEOLOGY, SYSTEMATIC, the discipline concerned with a reasoned reflection on and interpretation of the main tenets of Christian faith; the equivalent of what in Catholic curricula was called dogmatic as distinct from moral theology. The designation systematic usually distinguishes this branch of theology from biblical theology, from positive theology, which includes patristics and symbolic theology (study of the confessions of faith), or from *historical theology. In its strongest meaning systematic theology implies both a faith or confessional commitment and the choice of an intellectual or philosophical system, i.e., the acceptance and discursive application of an epistemological and ontological viewpoint as best suited to defend, articulate, and elaborate upon the articles of belief. The term philosophical theology has a narrower usage, signifying at times *natural theology or at times a theology developed exclusively through philosophical categories. Systematic theology incorporates elements from Scripture, the Fathers, symbols of faith, and historical theology.

[T. C. O'BRIEN]

THEOLOGY AND FAITH, the theme of the relationship between believing and seeking an understanding of what is believed. In the mainstream of Christian history that relationship has been viewed, albeit in different ways, as positive; there has, however, always been resistance, in the name of the sacredness and transcendence of God's word, against any attempt to articulate the meaning of revelation through mundane terms and categories. The interpretation here given of the positive relationship between theology and faith rests on the teaching of St. Thomas Aquinas, his own development of Augustine's phrase, "faith seeking understanding" to describe theology; or St. Anselm's *credo ut intelligam*. The act of faith, belief, and the act of theologizing are distinct. In essence, belief is a gift of grace, and it is a simple, nondiscursive assent to God revealing. The act of theology is in itself the natural exercise of the mind reflecting on what faith assents to. That comparison suggests the distinction between theology and other ways in which the contents of faith are expressed. Revelation as conveyed by the biblical authors is not theology: their human thought and literary expression come under the direction of *inspiration. Church proposals of dogmatic formulas as sound ways in which revealed truths are to be understood transcend theology, however much theology may have prepared the way for them. The act of the teaching Church comes under the grace of the Holy Spirit's direct guidance of the believing community. Theology is a human discipline; but it exists and must exist because the truths that faith accepts stand before the human mind, which connaturally seeks some understanding of them. In the description of belief as "to ponder with assent" (*cum assensione cogitare*), the stimulus to a theology exists. The pondering inherent to belief is the unsatisfied questing of the mind for understanding. The effort to understand, however, can mean two different things. One puts theology in opposition to belief. It is a refusal to assent to any truth except on grounds of human reasoning; it requires that understanding precede belief, instead of belief preceding understanding, when namely a person is willing to believe only what he can discern by his own reason (ThAq *In Boethii De Trin*. 2,1). In the order consonant with faith as this is, an assent to what God reveals as true, the act of theology is, as it were, suspended from that assent. The search for ways to grasp how what is revealed is true does not mean questioning whether it is true. That search has basically two paths to follow. The one is negative; the *via negativa* consists in denying the creaturely connotations of every human word and concept when chosen to express divine realities. The second is positive: because what is believed is true, because faith rests on God's guarantee of that, then the mind can develop positive, though limited, expressions of that, consonant with the truth. Faith always guides the choice of such attempts. Right theologizing depends on belief, never proposing as an expression of its meaning what, because it is intellectually counterfeit, is unworthy of the truth that faith assents to on God's word. BIBLIOGRAPHY: ThAq ST (Lat-Eng, v. 31, ed. T. C. O'Brien) app. 4.

[T. C. O'BRIEN]

THEOLOGY AND LITURGY. A relationship of mutual dependence and enrichment between *theology and *liturgy has always been acknowledged in the Church. This is esp. evident when theology is taken in a broad sense to include the study of Scripture, the spiritual life, and the liturgy itself. But this relationship exists between liturgy and dogmatic theology as well. The ancient axiom, *lex orandi, lex credendi* (a criterion of prayer is a criterion of faith), testifies that the liturgy is an important instrument in the transmission of true doctrine. The believing community expresses its faith commitment through its acts of worship. Thus, for example, the meaning of Christ and the nature of his sacrificial death are clearly demonstrated in the actions and texts of the Mass. The papal bull *Ineffabilis Deus* frequently refers to liturgical texts to support the doctrine of the Immaculate Conception. But the liturgy, even though it is a source of the Church's teaching, must consistently turn to theology to seek a deeper understanding of the realities which it celebrates. BIBLIOGRAPHY: J. J. von Allmen, *Worship: Its Theology and Practice* (1965); G. Diekmann, *Come, Let Us Worship* (1961); C. Vagaggini, *Theological Dimensions of the Liturgy* (tr. L. Doyle, 1959).

[T. M. MCFADDEN]

THEOLOGY AND PHILOSOPHY, the theme of the use within theology of categories, principles, and modes of discourse developed by human reason. The theme presupposes that the two are distinct human disciplines and that this distinctness is discernible within theology's employment of philosophy. The distinction rests on the objective intelligibility that engages each. Philosophy in all its parts considers its topics as they manifest themselves to connatural power of the human mind. Theology is engaged by the "divinely revealable" (ThAq ST 1a, 1.3), i.e., by the new intelligibility that divine revelation as faith assents to it, gives to who God and man are, and to their relationship. While distinct from the theological act of knowing, the assent of faith conditions theology internally (see THEOLOGY AND FAITH); the aim of theology is not to ask whether what God reveals is true, but how it is true; its incorporation of philosophical resources serves that aim. Theology so understood is not a "philosophical theology," i.e., an attempt to establish both an *epistemology and a set of philosophical conditions to which the fact of belief and the acceptability of what is believed must conform. That enterprise subjects *God and faith* to the measures of human reason; it is not a theology but a rationalist philosophy (ThAq *In Boethii de Trin.* 2.3).

A positive relationship between theology and philosophy, however, can exist and in fact has existed since the earliest Christian ages. Such a relationship presupposes that the one true and truthful God (a presupposition of faith) is the source of the natural range of truths open to the human mind and of the truths accepted by faith. On that conviction rests theology's bringing philosophical truths and procedures into its service. In the Middle Ages a positive relationship between the two disciplines marked the progress of each, in the varying forms of scholastic thought (see SCHOLASTIC PHILOSOPHY). Roman Catholic theology has been marked by the intent to continue the spirit of medieval theology and even its form and content; but more recently new lines and modes of theological discourse have emerged. In truth, no philosophy imposes itself upon the theologian; his one imperative criterion is that the appropriation and application of philosophical resources genuinely serve belief as assent to truths guaranteed as such by God.

[T. C. O'BRIEN]

THEOLOGY AND PRAYER, two areas of human spiritual effort, between which special relationships exist. The problems in understanding these relationships arise from the fact that theology as a science is the speculative or historical study of Christian doctrine, whereas prayer is the seeking after union with God, the raising up of the mind and heart to him. Both activities result from faith. How are they mutually beneficial? History gives the answer. In the ancient Church theology meant a manner not of knowing but of praying: a contemplative attitude towards mysteries revealed in Jesus Christ; a thanksgiving, praise of the Father in the Spirit; a discourse made to God, about God, under the inspiration of God. The proclamation of God's word was a witnessing to the truth marvelled at in prayer. Such was the conception held by the Fathers of the Church and the Western monastic tradition until the 13th century. Knowledge was love, as was said: "It is by love that we know God. Love is itself an act of knowing."

With Abelard in the 12th cent. greater emphasis began to be given to intellectual, dialectic research. Theology was more frequently discussed, even "disputed," in the schools. In the 13th cent. St. Thomas Aquinas and St. Bonaventure maintained harmonious equilibrium between prayer and intellectual research in theology but in later scholasticism they came to be separated. Today the tendency is to reconcile sacred study and doctrine with the spiritual life.

In fact the origin of all intellectual research about God should be living faith animated by love, which inspires the desire for deeper knowledge of the loved one. Thus faith is a stimulus to theology as a science: historical research and speculation by means of critical methods. This deepened knowledge should give rise to theology as prayer: contented consent, wondering admiration, humble adoration, joyful thanksgiving, exultant praise, ardent supplication—the whole impelling to the fervent giving of self to God and men. This conception of theology helps one to understand St. Thomas. It was the bond of common experience of God linking the undivided Church in W and E before the days of separation. Today it is the clergy's best preparation for pastoral activity, which should be the fruit of a savory, happy, and enthusiastic knowledge of the mystery of God. Thus study and apostolate conduce to prayer. This is the Church's final purpose and finds its best expression in its liturgy.

BIBLIOGRAPHY: J. Leclercq, *Theology and Prayer* (1963); *idem*, NCE 14:64–65.

[J. LECLERCQ]

THEOLOGY AND SCIENCE. This is a variation, with special difficulties which will appear, on the more general theme, faith and reason, theology being taken as faith articulated in reasoned reflection. Christian theology is usually meant when a contrast or conflict is implied; though, as will be noted, natural theology, now somewhat more in abeyance among believers than it was, or even than it is elsewhere, plays a key role. But first, some clarifications as to the terms.

The main activity of theology is to gain some insight into the truths of faith; St. Anselm puts it succinctly: it is faith seeking understanding. This it does by deepening the sense of what they mean, by showing how they hang together, by extending their implications, and, when the matter allows, by demonstrating, at least negatively and indirectly, that objections against them are not cogent. It embraces the critical study of sacred history, above all as recorded in the Bible, the literary evaluation of symbol and metaphor, and the development of the resources of philosophical reasoning. Its processes are conducted throughout according to the full exigences of scientific method, and accordingly it deserves the title of science; indeed it is the queen of the sciences as being concerned with the original and ultimate questions of human interest. So then it is to be contrasted with "science," not, as is often done, as opening out into a world of fancy, feeling, and ineffable convictions inaccessible to hard scientific thinking things out; but more as a synoptic, metaphysical, and normative science is to be contrasted with a particular and descriptive science.

That it does not prove its assumptions or principles does not invalidate its status as a science, for such is the case with all the other sciences. That the articles of faith themselves lie beyond the rational evidences for them puts theology in a special category; but the fact, while not unnaturally baffling and indeed irksome to our positivist mentality, should not prove a stumbling-block to one well acquainted with the way in which science works and with the boundaries it recognizes.

We turn to the second term of our title, namely, science. We may begin by defining it as comprehending the disciplines practiced by those we call scientists—a circular definition, it must be admitted, yet scarcely to be avoided. Rather less than a century ago it would have been easy to classify them as the empirical and inductive sciences, but even then

the temptation would have been one to be resisted; for as is clearer now, their progress follows a dialectic which jumps beyond observation and experiment, relies on deductive and even *a priori* forms of thought, enters into high abstract theory, and does not disdain an inspired guesswork which bears some resemblance to an act of faith. Such is the development of some of them even as specialist disciplines; it characterizes them still more when they are regarded as convergent disciplines forming a true university rather than a polytechnic of the sciences. Still, this being admitted, when all is said and done, it remains true that science represents a spirit of seeking evidences within the field of human life and turning these to serve human living as we know it, even if it means voyaging into outer space. Moreover, in seeking the sort of exactness it needs for its rational, if provisional, plans, it measures its objects according to mathematics, more explicitly in some branches than in others. On these grounds its contrast with theology, the "science of faith" which appeals to an authority outside the universe, will be pronounced.

The matter would be less difficult if we could strike a condominium and agree that science is fixed on this world and theology on the next. Some do this, though of course they do not state their position according to such simplistic dimensions; they see no grounds of conflict, and are at once first-rate scientists and convinced and thoughtful Christians. A more comprehensive view of theology, however, is not content with an eschatological relegation to the hereafter; it sees his eternity as now, the kingdom of God as already among us, and every truth, at least by implication, as coming from and leading to God and as a concern for the science of salvation. Hence it must enter into the field of the anthropological sciences, and yet it must do this without intruding into the particular sciences in such a way as to smudge their own proper evidences. In other words, for the sake of its own freedom to range without offering violence, it should possess a knowledge which is virtually a philosophy of science, or at least about science.

Since many of the truths of natural religion and morality are preparatory antecedents of the truths of faith, and provide the terms in which these last are articulated, and since these truths are also reached out to by natural science, it is here that we may look for the area where theology and science may meet. It is here, also, that we may look for some sort of common grammar without detriment to proper and regional usage. There is gain to neither side, nor, which is more important, to the unity in complexity of human experience, when theology and the sciences all pursue their separate courses without speaking together. The problem of communication will not prove insoluble once it is grasped that analogy is not just a figure of speech but also an instrument of thought.

We end with four headings which express traditional Catholic convictions on the relationship between theology and science. First, no contradictory opposition can arise between them so long as each is working in its own proper medium. Second, nor is contrary opposition possible with the same proviso; yet because each is seated in one and the same thinking subject, who can be played upon by opposing evidential influences, a tension may well arise between a theological and a non-theological conclusion: it is this which will require careful thinking out and possible re-statement on one side or the other. Third, no science can ever disprove a truth of faith; indeed a believer who shares in the Church's reaction to the *double-truth theory will be confident that any attempt can be defused, though he may lack the technical ability to do so himself: in this matter mere logic often goes a long way. Fourth, nor can any science prove a supernatural truth of faith. Inspection will usually show that the debate is being conducted in the marches of natural philosophy between sacred doctrine and descriptive science. A conflict not rarely arises between the values that are more ultimate and the advantages that are more immediate, which is a way of saying what St. Augus-tine saw, that utilities have to be watched lest they spoil our enjoyment of things. The internal combustion engine and smog are examples. Another is that while good medicine will always be good morals, and conversely, bad morals, or morals inadequately rendered, can be bad medicine, and conversely. BIBLIOGRAPHY: ThAq ST 1a,1 (esp. in ed. Lat-Eng., v. 1, *Christian Theology*, ed. T. Gilby, 1964).

[T. GILBY]

THEOLOGY AS SCIENCE. The phrase has, first of all, a historical reference: the development of Christian theol-ogy as an intellectual discipline. From the earliest centuries, church writers viewed the data of faith as affording a world view superior to and defensible against the wisdom of the philosophers, esp. the Greek philosophers. "For now the true Master teaches us and so thanks to the Word henceforth every place is Athens and Greece for us," wrote St. Cle-ment of Alexandria (*Protreptikos* 112). From the age of the Apologists through Augustine and up to the Middle Ages the wisdom of human philosophy was employed in the reflection on the teachings of faith. But the formalization of an epistemology that located the reflection on and develop-ment of the meaning of faith in relationship to other intellec-tual disciplines is a properly medieval development. With the West's full acquisition of Aristotle's works, the issue "theology as science" came gradually to mean the standing of *sacra doctrina*, holy teaching, as compared to the notion of *epistēmē,* as set forth in Aristotle's *Posterior Analytics*. There were, from the earliest application of dialectics (logic) to the study of the *sacra pagina* and the texts (*auc-toritates*) received from church writers (see SCHOLASTIC METHOD), always resisters (e.g., St. Peter Damian; St. Ber-nard of Clairvaux): the "science of salvation" should not be measured by logical canons of human invention, since its measure and sole criterion are the word of God; its purpose, sanctification. But there was also a line of men confident because the mind that believes and the mind that thinks is the one mind, created by the one God of truth. The line includes St. Anselm and Abelard, and, perhaps less boldly, Peter Lombard and Hugh of St. Victor. But the most rigor-ous and fruitful resolution of the issue came with St. Thomas Aquinas. In the first question of the *Summa theologiae* he deals with the ways in which *sacra doctrina* has its own irreducible principles, organic unity, distinctive subject matter, resources for defensible conclusions. He vindicates the full nature of theology as a wisdom acquired by study, evolving out of and reflecting on the articles of faith and supported by its continuity, through the pervasive assent of faith in its procedures, with the "science of God and the blessed." Obviously in this history, then, theology was not understood as science in the sense of the empirical sciences; it was, however, shown to be a soundly grounded intellectual discipline. Later in scholasticism the integral conception of theology as wisdom was impoverished as "theology as science" came to be more narrowly under-stood as "speculative" or "scholastic" theology—in con-trast with biblical studies and "positive" theology (study of sources)—and to mean deductive argumentation from re-vealed principles to their implied conclusions. The history of the theme, it must also be noted, includes a new strain of anti-intellectualism, that introduced by Luther's repudiation of reason as he had seen its uses in decadent scholasticism. In that lay a spirit that led to the relegation of theology to a realm apart from the human disciplines, that left the world of hard reality to the secular disciplines.

In its contemporary setting the phrase "theology as sci-ence" has infinite resonances: infinite because the epis-temological possibilities that the phrase contains are literally endless. That, too, has its historical reasons, deriving from the intellectual evolution of the modern era. There cannot be a consensus on theology as science, even as a starting point for discussion, because there is no consensus on the mean-ing of theology. Obviously it is not "science" in the sense of mathematics or physics. But it is a widely shared conces-sion that Kant has shown in consequence that theology or any metempirical form of knowledge has no defensibly ob-jective referent or truth value. If, then, theology has any status or reason for being, their grounds are to be sought within the human spirit and its exigencies. Any reflection on the nature of theology for generations now has taken, therefore, as its starting point the philosophic impossibility of any epistemological realism in any form. A notable reac-tion to the *liberal theology developed on that premise is K. *Barth's "theology of crisis," a strong affirmation of realism, to be sure, but at the cost of the resounding "NO" of the word of God against any construct of human reason to articulate the meaning of his word.

A second conditioning of the impossibly elusive sense of the phrase "theology as science" is a loss of another kind of realism: realism about the significance of faith. The patristic and medieval presupposition accepted faith as an assent to the reality who is God and to the reality of the history of salvation, thus of the meaning of the world. Some of the truth about God and the world was expressed in the biblical word. The intellectual reflection that theology names, thus, had its data, and its procedures were suffused with the originating assent of faith to the truth. Such realism has largely been put aside as ''dogmatism'' or ''supernaturalism.'' Thus theology does not begin with its own data, nor does it enjoy the criterion that its procedures must develop in ways consistent with the truth who is God. Rather, theology must establish its object, largely anthropocentrically, if it is to be a ''philosophical theology''; if it is also to retain a biblical base and focus, it must also establish the relevance of the biblical word that is something other than biblical historicity or truth bearing value (see DE-MYTHOLOGIZING).

Roman Catholic theology has never lost completely its historical continuity with its patristic and medieval antecedents; the issue of theology as science has retained, therefore, the sense that theology ought to be an intellectually sound discipline, consistent with and worthy of the truth to which faith assents. The status of RC theology has also been determined by RC ecclesiology: that the word of God means the ''deposit of faith,'' truth to be faithfully transmitted and safeguarded. Yet there is undoubtedly in contemporary RC theology a strain on both sources of its strength. Pluralism has always been characteristic of RC theology, even though there has been a juridically sanctioned ''party line.'' But that pluralism always included a commitment to intellectualizing that remains in conformity with the truth-content of faith. That criterion is less respected today; in the name of the inadequacy of any set of human categories to capture the full truth of God's revelation, many maintain that no philosophical system or set of categories is incompatible with the truth of revelation. There is, as well, a questioning of the Church's magisterium and of the need for a continuity in the development of doctrine. Because of these factors ''theology as science'' has a less agreed upon force in RC circles and on the part of many receives a response that is a Catholic neo-Pietism. The second represents a despair of theology as an intellectual discipline and an escape in the name of ''keeping the faith'' to a spirituality split off from theology. BIBLIOGRAPHY: Y.-M. Congar, *History of Theology* (1968); M.-D. Chenu, *Is Theology a Science?* (1959); *idem, La Foi dans l'intelligence* (1964); ThAq ST (Lat-Eng), v. 1, ed. T. Gilby, *Christian Theology* (1964) 58–87; v. 31, ed. T. C. O'Brien, *Faith* (1974) 195–216; T. C. O'Brien ''Sacra Doctrina,'' *Thomist* 41 (1977) 475–509.

[T. C. O'BRIEN]

THEOLOGY OF THE CROSS, see THEOLOGIA CRUCIS.

THEONAS OF ALEXANDRIA, ST. (d. *c.*300), patriarch from 281. He ruled over the Church in Alexandria during the period of tranquillity that preceded the outbreak of the last great persecution; he labored zealously to consolidate the Christian community, converting many pagans and constructing churches throughout the city. The learned *Pierius was head of the catechetical school during that time. A letter supposed to have been written by him to Lucian at the court of Diocletian (PG 10:1567–74) is no longer regarded as authentic. BIBLIOGRAPHY: AS June 7, p. 27 ff.; H. Leclercq, DACL 8:2773–75.

[R. B. ENO]

THEOPASCHITES, a group of Scythian (Gothic) monks led by John Maxentius and Leontius who insisted that the words ''one of the Trinity suffered for us in the flesh'' (Gr. *ena tēs hagias triadas pepothenai*) be added to the *Trisagion to thwart the pro-Nestorian teaching of some bishops. When the Roman legates at Constantinople refused to endorse it on the grounds that it had Monophysite support, the monks presented their case to Pope Hormisdas at Rome (520). Despite the intercession of Dionysius Exiguus, the Pope refused to give a favorable decision. BIBLIOGRAPHY: E. Amann, DTC 15.1:505–512; G. Kruger, PW 19:658–662.

[F. H. BRIGHAM]

THEOPASSIANS, a group of heretics who believed that the Divinity had suffered with Christ on the cross. They are mentioned and given this name by Danaeus in his edition of Augustine's *De haeresibus* (1576; see PL 12:1203), but they are not otherwise identified. The doctrine, however, at least in an implicit form, is to be found in the teachings of Apollinaris.

[L. G. MÜLLER]

THEOPHANES. Several important figures in the Eastern Church bore the name. **Theophanes Graptos** (*c.*775–845), monk. Born at Kerak, T. and his brother Theodore entered the monastery of St. Sabas near Jerusalem (*c.*797). In 813, the brothers went to Constantinople, where they became embroiled in the struggles of the second outbreak of iconoclasm. After the death of Theodore of Studios (826) they emerged as the leading figures of the iconodule opposition. They were scourged and exiled by the iconoclast Emperor Leo V (813–820), again banished by Michael II (820–829), and at last branded upon the forehead with doggerel iambics by Theophieod (829–842); hence the name *Graptoi*. Following the restoration of image worship in 843, T. was made abp. of Nicaea. A prolific hymnographer, he wrote 19 idomela and 162 canons. BIBLIOGRAPHY: S. Vailhé, *Revue de l'Orient chrétien*, 6 (1901): 313–345, 611–641; W. Christ-M. Paranikas, *Anthologia Graeca Carminum Christianorum*, 236–242; Sophronios, *Nea Siōn*, Jerusalem, 339–344, 403–406, 618–623.

Theophanes Protothronos, abp. of Caesarea of Cappadocia in 886. According to Nicetas the Paphlagonian, a partisan of the Patriarch Ignatius (847–858, 867–878), T. assisted Ignatius's rival, the Patriarch Photius (858–867, 878–886), in the forging of an illustrious genealogy of the Emperor Basil I (867–886), a scheme which brought about the reinstatement of Photius as patriarch in 876. Several of Photius's extant letters are addressed to Theophanes. He appears to be the author of three *Encomia* of SS. Theodore and Theophanes Graptoi, SS. Menas, Hermogenes and Eugraphos, and the Prophet Elijah. BIBLIOGRAPHY: Nicetas the Paphlagonian, *Vita Ignatii*, PG 105:565–569; F. Halkin, BHG, 577c, 1271d, 1745z.

Theophanes Kerameus. Under this name there are extant 90 Italo-Greek homilies of the 13th century. The author was probably the monk and philosopher Philagathos, who flourished at Rossano under Roger II (1130–54) and William I (1154–66). When his works were collected in Byzantium where the ecclesiastical situation in Italy was then little known, they were wrongly ascribed to the 9th-cent. Theophanes Kerameus, abp. of Taormina. Sixty-two of the 90 homilies have been edited. BIBLIOGRAPHY: PG 132:49–1077.

Theophanes, 14th-cent. abbot of the Batopedion Monastery, later Metropolitan of Peritheorion, biographer of the celebrated Athonian monk Maximos Kausokalybes (d. *c*. 1365), author of a discourse against the Latins. BIBLIOGRAPHY: F. Halkin, BHG, 1237.

Theophanes III, metropolitan of Nicaea from 1366 until his death (*c*. 1380), friend of the Emperor John VI Kantakuzenos (1347–54), staunch supporter of the Palamites. A voluminous writer, T. composed an apology of Christianity against the Jews of his time, who, he argued, had nothing in common with those of biblical days. He also wrote two works concerning Palamite Theology, a tractate against the Latin doctrine on the procession of the Holy Spirit, and three homilies, the last of which comprises a virtual compendium of the dogma of the Eastern Church. BIBLIOGRAPHY: L. Allatius, *Joannes Henricus Hottingerus fraudis et imposturae convictus circa Graecorum dogmata* (1661), 187–191; PG 150:288–349.

[J. FEATHERSTONE]

THEOPHANES THE CONFESSOR, ST. (*c*. 752–*c*. 818), Byzantine chronicler. He retired to a monastery which he built on the Sea of Marmora at Sigriane near Cyzicus. He participated in the Second Council of Nicaea in 787. In 815 he was summoned to Constantinople by the Emperor Leo V the Armenian for opposing iconoclasm, imprisoned for 2 years, and then sent into exile on the island of Samothrace, where he died. He is the author of a chronicle covering the period 284–813. It is esp. important for the years 769–813. His work was much used and continued by a number of later chroniclers. It was translated into Latin by *Anastasius the Librarian in the late 9th cent. and thus became a valuable source to the West for Byzantine history. BIBLIOGRAPHY: P. Charanis, NCE 14:68–69; Ostrogorsky 79–80; *idem*, PW 5A² (1934) 2127–32.

[M. R. P. MCGUIRE]

THEOPHANES THE GREEK (fl. 1378–1405), Byzantine fresco and icon painter, colleague (perhaps teacher) of Rublëv. The fresco (1378) in the Church of the Transfiguration, Novgorod, a virtuoso piece of late-antique illusionism,

is the only work attributed to T. with certainty. He worked (1405) with Rublëv and Prochor of Gorodets on the fresco cycle (destroyed) for the Cathedral of the Annunciation, Moscow, and on the iconostasis, executing with apprentices the dëesis tier. *The Virgin of the Don* (*c*. 1380) is attributed to T., who, astonishingly, worked without models.

[M. J. DALY]

THEOPHANY (EPIPHANY), an awe-inspiring self-manifestation of God to man (Gr. *theophania*, from *theos*, God, and *phainō* to make shine, to show). A classic theophany occurs in the narrative of Exodus, preceding the giving of the Law to Moses and the Israelites at the holy mountain of Sinai. This descriptive account apparently borrows heavily from traditional, liturgically reenacted theophanies of a mountain god or a storm god. Such a god would reveal himself amid peals of thunder and flashes of lightning, amid dense cloud and a loud trumpet blast (cf. Ex 19.16). Another classic theophany, in the Elijah saga of 1 Kg, esp. 19.8–13, shows how the prophetic tradition altered the conventional imagery of theophany, giving primacy to the divine Word. When Elijah went as commanded and stood on the holy mountain, Horeb (corresponding to Sinai), he encountered first a great wind that shattered rock, but the Lord was not in the great wind. Then followed first an earthquake and then a great fire, but the Lord was in neither. Then came a low murmuring sound as of a gentle breeze; Elijah on hearing it hid his face in his cloak. Then in the ensuing silence came the voice of the Lord. This prophetic reworking of the imagery of theophany presages the later rabbinic tradition of the *Shekinah, the awesome and loving nearness of God to his people, God's tabernacling presence throughout history in various ways, but esp. in the assembly of the just who seek to be faithful to his Law. Somewhat akin to this is the Christian Johannine concept of the epiphany: the Word of God made flesh, which dwelt among us, so that we have seen his glory (Jn 1.14).

[E. J. DILLON]

THEOPHILANTHROPY, religious cult founded in Paris in 1796 as a substitute for Catholic beliefs and practices by Jean Baptiste Chemin-Dupontes, who drew his inspiration principally from Voltaire and Rousseau. Gaining the support of Revellière-Lepeaux, a member of the Directory, this group was permitted the use of Notre Dame Cathedral as well as numerous other Parisian churches for services. The cult had little appeal to the majority of the people but attracted a number of the intelligensia, scientists, politicians, and artists, including Jacques David. Theophilanthropy never became the state religion but was used by the Directory to oppose Catholic teaching. By 1799, the sect was in complete decline and by 1802 was legally prohibited. Theologically, theophilanthropy was a form of deism, its god Voltaire's god of reason, and its concept of the afterlife excluded the resurrection of the body. Its morality was based upon tolerance of others and loyalty to the French

republic. Its services included readings from the writings of world religions, the classics, and French authors, esp. Voltaire and Rousseau. Homage was paid to the great humanitarians of the world. There were also simple rites for baptism, marriage, and burial. The principal purpose of theophilanthropy was the establishment of a religious sect completely free from doctrine and any but the most general moral principles. BIBLIOGRAPHY: J. Brugerette, DTC 15:1; 518–523; L. Cristiani, EncCatt 2:1949–50; M. Lawlor, NCE 14:70.

[T. J. RYAN]

THEOPHILUS (Gr., beloved of God), person to whom Luke addressed his Gospel (1.1–4) and Acts (1.1). Nothing is known about him other than that he was a concrete person. He was called ''most excellent,'' leading some to speculate that he was an official, possibly a Roman involved in Paul's trial.

[T. EARLY]

THEOPHILUS, BYZANTINE EMPEROR (829–842). He was the son of Michael II, of the Phrygian dynasty, the principal promoter of the 9th-cent. Byzantine renaissance of learning, and the last emperor to attempt to revive iconoclasm. T.'s interest in Arab culture and architecture and his zeal for *iconoclasm both derive from his teacher and ally, John the Grammarian, who in 823 became the patriarch of Constantinople. Able soldier, financier, and builder, T. was generally a benevolent ruler, imitating the learned Persian Caliph Hārūn ar-Rashīd of Baghdad by informally hearing grievances of the oppressed in the streets of Constantinople. His iconoclastic decrees were enforced severely against the monks, however. In one case he branded the brothers Theodore and Theophanes by burning iconoclastic verses into their foreheads. The people remained overwhelmingly attached to the icons, however, and he was even opposed secretly by the beautiful Theodora, whom he had married in 821. It is an irony of history that it was under the rule of this lover of Muslim culture that the Byzantine empire suffered some of the most severe setbacks in its history at the hands of the Muslims. Ground was lost to the Venetians and the Franks as well.

[E. J. DILLON]

THEOPHILUS (RUGERUS) (fl. early 12th cent.), Benedictine, author of *De diversis artibus*. In three books he covers a wide range of medieval arts and crafts and describes techniques with a sureness of detail that could only come from firsthand knowledge. In the preface to book three in particular, he expounds a theology of art. For him the artist serves the basic purpose of man, namely, to give glory to God. Art not only produces works of beauty, but is to be thought of as an act of piety and worship. BIBLIOGRA-PHY: M. R. P. McGuire, NCE 14:70–71; *Theophilus* (ed. C. R. Dodwell, tr. from the Lat. with intro., notes, and

bibliog., 1961); E. De Bruyne, *Études d'esthétique médiévale*. 2 (1946) 413–417.

[M. R. P. MCGUIRE]

THEOPHILUS OF ALEXANDRIA (d. 412), patriarch of Alexandria (385–412), predecessor and uncle of St. *Cyril. He crushed the remnants of paganism in his city, demolishing the famous Serapeum in 391. He was a man of violence and determination and apparently without scruple in furthering the prestige of his see. His efforts to that end included an anti-Origenist campaign and a persecution of *John Chrysostom, then patriarch of Constantinople, for which he was excommunicated by Innocent I. Little remains of his literary output save a few letters and fragments, which can be found in PG 65:33–68, 401–404. BIBLIOGRAPHY: Quasten 3:100–106.

[R. B. ENO]

THEOPHILUS OF ANTIOCH (2d cent.), native Mesopotamian, convert to Christianity, bp. of Antioch, apologist. His chief work consists of three books addressed *To Autolycus* (c. 180; PG 6). The first treats of the divine nature and providence; the second attacks pagan myths and the immoralities of the gods; the third refutes calumnies against Christians. In most respects similar to the other apologists of the time, T. was the first Christian writer to use the term ''Triad'' of God, and is notable for his development of the doctrine of the Logos. His other works—treatises against Marcion and Hermogenes, catechetical books, scriptural commentaries—are lost. BIBLIOGRAPHY: Quasten 1:236–242; Quasten Init 1:267–273.

[R. B. ENO]

THEOPHILUS OF CORTE, ST. (1676–1740), Franciscan, ascetic. Born in Corsica, Biagio de' Signori Corte, of noble parentage, he nevertheless entered the Corsican Franciscan Observants at Corte in 1693. He was ordained in 1700 and embraced the austere life of the convent of retreat at Civitella. His entire ministry was spent in the retreat apostolate, for thirty years at Civitella and then at Palombara. In both houses, he held the offices of guardian, rector, confessor, and preacher. In later life he founded two convents of retreat, at Zvani in Corsica and at Fucecchio, Tuscany, where he died. He was beatified by Pope Leo XIII, (1895) and canonized by Pope Pius XI (1930). BIBLIOGRA-PHY: J. B. Wuest, NCE, 14.71–72.

[T. J. RYAN]

THEOPHRASTUS OF LESBOS (372–286), Aristotle's successor as head of the Lyceum (327–286). Through his *Enquiry into Plants* and his *Aetiology of Plants,* he founded the science of botany. He was the author of a *History of Natural Philosophy (phusikōn doxai)* from Thales to Plato and wrote voluminously, not only on scientific subjects, but also on logic, rhetoric, poetics, style, and the history of religion. His *Characters,* a literary work which describes 30 different types, had a considerable vogue in the Renaissance. He defended Aristotle's doctrine of the eternity of the world against the Stoics, but he seems in his *Metaphysics* to be inclined to replace Aristotle's concept of a transcendental deity by that of nature. On the history and value of religion he wrote, among other treatises, *On Piety,* (*peri eusebeias*), preserved in part by Porphyry. He rejected animal sacrifices and the eating of flesh-meat and maintained that all men are related. He is a typical representative of the Peripatetic School with its preoccupation with science and erudition. With the exception of the *Characters,* most of his works are preserved in excerpts or fragments only. BIBLIOGRAPHY: K. O. Brink, OCD 896; LexAW 3057–58; Copleston 1:369–370; P. Merlan, CHGMP 107–111; O. Regenbogen, "Theophrastos," PW Suppl. 7 (1940) 1354–1562.

[M. R. P. McGUIRE]

THEOPHYLACT OF BULGARIA (d. *c.*1108), Greek theologian and abp. of the Bulgarian see of Ohrid in Macedonia. A pupil of Michael Psellos, he wrote numerous exegetical, polemical, and other works. In the East-West controversy of the time, he took a middle position on the points under discussion between Rome and Constantinople. In his life of St. Clement of Ohrid, he gives the best detailed account of the collapse of the Moravian mission of SS. Cyril and Methodius and the new revival of Slavic Orthodoxy in Bulgaria. BIBLIOGRAPHY: Beck 649–651.

[G. ELDAROV]

THEOPHYLACTUS (d. *c.*926), first count of Tusculum, head of the aristocratic party that actively opposed the followers of Pope *Formosus. An unscrupulous politician, T. exercised a great influence on Pope Sergius III. BIBLIOGRA-PHY: Fliche-Martin, 7:29–38.

[T. GILBY]

THEOPHYLACTUS (1050–*c.*1108), abp. of Ohrid in Yugoslavia. After studying at Constantinople T. was made bp. among the Bulgars, a move which he considered an exile from the land of scholarship. In this enforced retreat he wrote extensive commentaries on the NT. He also wrote a *History of the Fifteen Martyrs* and the *Life of St. Clement,* his predecessor. From his teacher Psellus he believed that the Holy Spirit proceeds from the Father alone. He also rejected papal supremacy and clerical celibacy.

[R. T. MEYER]

THEOPHYLACTUS SIMOCATTA (d. after 638), Byzantine historian whose 8-book history of the Emperor Maurice (582–602), dealing mainly with the war in the Balkans and written between 628 and 638, is a unique source for the 6th- and 7th-cent. history of Greek relations with the Slavs and the Persians. Born in Egypt of an upper-class family, he was introduced to Byzantine court society, found a patron in the Patriarch Sergius I, and was prefect and imperial secretary under Emperor Heraclius (610–641). Thus T. had access to excellent sources, to both Persian and Byzantine leaders, to foreign ambassadors, and to the Byzantine archives.

[E. J. DILLON]

THEOPONITAE, those who taught that in Christ the divinity suffered the crucifixion. The belief is implicit in the teachings of *Apollinaris of Laodicea and was taken up by some of his followers. Without name, both Filaster (*Haer.* 75) and Augustine (*Haer.* 92) mention adherents of this teaching. The name Theoponitae comes from *Praedestinatus* (1:75).

[L. G. MÜLLER]

THEOSIS (Gr., deification or divinization), the Greek Christian doctrine that salvation consists in becoming God. In its extreme form (e.g., in *Origen, John Scotus Erigena) theosis is difficult to distinguish from pantheism. At the opposite pole lies the metaphorical, extrinsic divinization proper to Western theology and spirituality and generally absent from Eastern tradition. Between the two poles is an orthodox theosis which is neither pantheistic nor metaphorical. Patristic in its explicit origins, theosis remains a part of Orthodox soteriology down to the present day.

Theosis in its orthodox form is the doctrine that man (or all creation) becomes God literally and intrinsically, but in a finite way, by participating in God's activities (energy, energies) and characteristics without confusion of substance, hence without the loss of personal identity. By the end of the patristic era the doctrine had become very highly systematized. Maximus the Confessor (*c.* 580–662) proclaims a gradual assimilation to God through the exercise of the virtues and contemplation in this life, and total deification "in so far as this is possible" in the next. The creature's mode of existence, esp. in the life to come, is conceived of as a perichoresis (analogous to the perichoresis of the Chalcedonian Christ, total interpenetration without mixture), wherein the soul in heaven (and the body-soul composite after the general resurrection) performs no operations of the will or intellect other than those of God, and has no qualities or attributes other than God's, within the limits of finitude proper to the creaturely nature. The latter, together with its faculties, remains intact and operative, but its operations, like its qualities, are divine.

The doctrine evolved very gradually. *Ignatius of Antioch (*c.* 110) merely invokes St. Paul on incorruptibility and immortality, an emphasis resumed by *Justin Martyr (*c.* 101–*c.* 165) and other *apologists. Theophilus of Antioch (2d cent.) finally dared to use the expression "become God." Irenaeus (*c.* 138–*c.* 202) is the first to discuss the concept *ex professo.* Clement of Alexandria (*c.*149–*c.*210) introduces the importance of certain virtues and (especially) *gnôsis* (cf. Maximus's contemplation as a means to deification). *Origen (c. 185–253 or 254) teaches the ultimate deification of all spiritual creation, perhaps rather pantheistically; like Clement, he emphasizes intellectual activity. By the 4th cent. theosis became so axiomatic that *Athanasius (295–373) could appeal to it as a universally acceptable premise to argue the full divinity of the Word, the deifier, against the *Arians: God became man so that men might become gods. *Basil the Great (c.329–379) and *Gregory of Nazianzus (330–390) developed Athanasius' emphasis on the roles of the Incarnation and the Spirit. *Gregory of Nyssa (332–394) created the first genuine dogmatic synthesis, and *Cyril of Alexandria (c. 382–444) made further important synthetic contributions. In Denis the Areopagite (490?), theosis became still more highly organized, if somewhat idiosyncratically, and he was the first to employ the word. His main emphasis was on contemplation. Maximus the Confessor created the final patristic synthesis. The foremost post-patristic exponents of theosis were probably Erigena, then Gregory Palamas and the Palamists of his day and ours.

[R. R. BARR]

THEOSOPHY, a doctrine that attempts a synthesis of religious, philosophic, and scientific insights drawn from many traditions, but primarily from Hindu philosophy and occult science. In 1875 at New York City the Theosophical Society was founded by Helena Petrovna *Blavatsky, Henry Steele Olcott, and William Q. Judge ''to collect and diffuse a knowledge of the laws which govern the universe.'' This secret lodge of occultists sought to explore ''secret laws of nature familiar to the Chaldeans and Egyptians.'' The theosophical movement early divided into several independent groups, but there has been a general unanimity on doctrinal points. Theosophy does not accept the idea of a personal God. It is pantheistic in its starting point; God is held to be wholly immanent in the world. He does not create in the traditional Christian sense, but is a part of his creation, which emanates from him. God is the Absolute Principle of Hindu pantheism, impersonal and unknowable. The Logos, who is three in one, in the forms of creator (Brahma), preserver (Vishnu), and destroyer (Shiva), is described as the Supreme Beings who sustain the solar system and are the fount of authority of an extensive occult hierarchy. This hierarchy includes Jesus and other great thinkers who have passed through the cycle of rebirths and attained the state of divinity. Reincarnation is a central teaching, as is the evolution of the soul, for salvation comes by evolution and there is no need for an atonement. Evolution is thought of as a process of self-realization carried on by the cosmic life through repeated incarnations. All matter is held to contaiin consciousness that is evolving in accord with the divine plan in a twofold movement involving descent into matter and ascent into spirit. The adept can speed up or direct their own courses by observing the hidden rules of nature known to theosophy. Death brings rebirth, liberating the human spirit from its physical body to enjoy the life

of the astral world. The astral world is not the true heaven, except for grosser men. Only after repeated incarnations can the true heaven or mental world be reached. Evolution, reincarnation, and karma thus create the rhythm of the universe.

In 1878 the Theosophical Society transferred its headquarters to Adyar, near Madras, India; in 1880 it began publishing *The Theosophist* at Madras. In 1888 Mme. Blavatsky went to London, where she issued *The Secret Doctrine* and formed an Esoteric Section of the Theosophical Society devoted to occult lore. Following her death in 1891, Annie *Besant succeeded her as leader of the Adyar Theosophical Society and greatly increased the role of Hindu thought in Theosophy as well as the occult sciences. William Q. Judge, one of the three founders of theosophy and president of the American branch, became involved in controversy with the Adyar leadership in 1892 and in 1895 established the fully independent Theosophical Society in America. It made its headquarters first at Chicago, later at Altadena, California. Those loyal to Annie Besant formed the Theosophical Society of New York. Other independent groups include the Temple of the People, founded at Syracuse, N.Y., in 1899, now at Halcyon, Calif., and the Universal Brotherhood, an outgrowth of the Judge group, with its headquarters at Point Loma, California. Opposition to Annie Besant in Germany led to the separation of the Anthroposophical Society formed by Rudolf *Steiner in 1912. In several books, Mrs. Besant advanced the theory that Jesus was an incarnation of the Buddha. In 1908–11 she created further stir by revealing that the Christ was alive and would reappear. She identified a Hindu youth, Jeddu Krishnamurti, as the reincarnate Jesus/Buddha. The formation of the Order of the Star in the East (1911) and the *Liberal Catholic Church (1915–16) was closely connected with the new avatar.

In a more general sense, theosophy may refer to any esoteric explanation of the universe based on mystical, usually pantheistic intuition, reserved to initiates. BIBLIOGRAPHY: C. J. Ryan, *What is Theosophy?* (1944); L. W. Rogers, *Elementary Theosophy* (1950).

[R. K. MacMASTER]

THEOTIMUS OF TOMI, ST. (d. 403), bp. of Tomi from 392. Born in Scythia, of Hunnish descent, he was educated in Greece where he took the Greek name meaning ''god-fearing'' and worked for the conversion of his own people. According to the Byzantine historian Sozomen, the Huns dubbed T. ''God of the Romans'' because of the wonders he performed. He defended John Chrysostom and refused to condemn the works of Origen, opposing Epiphanius of Salamis in this matter.

[E. J. DILLON]

THEOTIMUS THE VALENTINIAN, 2d-cent. Gnostic writer, of whom nothing is known beyond the one intriguing reference to him by Tertullian in his work against the Valentinians: "Theotimus worked hard about the images of the Law" (*Adv. Val.* 4). The context is a discussion, rich in Tertullian sarcasm, of Valentinus, his followers, and similar Gnostic speculators. Specifically at issue were the elaborate theories about the various aeons and their relation to God, as well as of the names and numbers given to them. T. is mentioned with Heraclean, Secundus, and the magician Marcus, as developing Valentinus's schema to include the aeons in the very essence of the Deity.

[E. J. DILLON]

THEOTOCOPULI, DOMENICO, see GRECO, EL.

THEOTOKARION, liturgical book of the Greek Church containing songs in honor of the Blessed Mother (*Theotokos*) that are distributed throughout the 8 weeks in accordance with the eight tones of the liturgical calendar. The hymns are divided into eight groups, and each one of these contains seven songs for each day of the week. The most famous of the hymnographers are SS. Andrew of Crete, John of Damascus, Theodore the Studite, and Theophane Graptos.

[L. PEANO]

THEOTOKOS, meaning God-bearer, or Mother of God, a Greek term that became a central title for the Virgin Mary. The earlier affirmations that Jesus was truly born of Mary and that this Jesus, born of Mary, is truly God were summed up in the single term Theotokos. The earliest evidence of its use dates from the writings of Alexander of Alexandria in 319 (PG 18:568). It was used frequently in the 4th cent. as a precise theological expression, e.g., in Athanasius, Eustathius of Antioch, Gregory of Nyssa, and Eusebius of Caesarea. About the same time it became part of popular Marian devotion. The Greek equivalent of the still contemporary liturgical antiphon *Sub tuum praesidium confugimus* (We fly to your patronage) contains the term; it dates from the 4th (or possibly the 3d) century.

In the 5th cent. Nestorius questioned the correctness of the term, at least in its full sense. Nestorius argued that Jesus and the Word are two hypostases, or persons, and that Mary should properly be called *Christotokos* (Christ-bearer) or *Theodokos* (God-receiving) rather than *Theotokos*. The reaction, led by St. Cyril of Alexandria, culminated in the definition at the Council of Ephesus (431) of the unity of Person in Christ and of the divine maternity. This doctrine was repeated in the Council of Chalcedon (451) and has been a central fact of Mariology ever since. In the Latin Church the term *Dei genetrix* is usually preferred to *Deipara*, which is connected etymologically with *theotokos*. BIBLIOGRAPHY: J. M. Carmody, NCE 14:75; W. J. Burghardt, "Theotokos: The Mother of God," *Mystery of the Woman* (ed. E. D. O'Connor, 1956) 5–33; H. Merklebach, *Mariologia* (tr. and ed. P. Arenillas, 1954) 65–86.

[J. HENNESSEY]

THEOTONIUS, ST. (1082–1162), cofounder and first prior of the famous Santa Cruz monastery in Coimbra, Portugal. Born in Ganfei, in Portuguese Galicia, he was canonized a year after his death by the provincial council of Coimbra. Pope Alexander III confirmed the decision in 1630. He had first been canon and prior of the cathedral chapter at Viseu; and after two pilgrimages to the Holy Land, he joined his former teacher, the Archdeacon Tello, in founding the new monastery, following the Rule of St. Augustine and the customs of St. Ruf. Theotonius' reputation for sanctity and the favor of Portugal's first king (Alfonso Henriques) made the monastery famous.

[E. J. DILLON]

THERAPEUTAE (Gr., devotees), Jewish monastic group living in Egypt toward the end of the 1st cent. B.C. They are known only from Philo (*De vita contemplativa*), who contrasted them as contemplatives with the more active *Essenes. Practicing celibacy and poverty, they lived in individual huts, and except for celebrations each 50th day, gathered only for Sabbath services. Living above Lake Mareotis, near Alexandria, they fasted 6 days a week, taking only one meal, eaten after sunset. Except for prayers at dawn and sunset they gave the entire day to meditation, particularly on the Scriptures. Students of monasticism have been interested in them as a pre-Christian monastic group. Some have thought that they formed a connection between the Essenes and Christian monasticism.

[T. EARLY]

THERAPHIM, see TERAPHIM.

THERAVADA BUDDHISM (Pali *vāda*, the way or teaching; *thera*, of the elders), the name of that form of *Buddhism predominant in SE Asia. This school has traditionally claimed fidelity to the teaching of the historical Buddha, though this has been disputed by other schools. Historically, it seems to have spread from a center in Ceylon from about 240 B.C. and may be traceable back to archaic or original Buddhism through an earlier Indian school, the Sthaviras (Sanskrit, the elders). Doctrinally, Theravadins share the general Buddhist teaching on the Four Noble Truths, the Eightfold Path (esp. the cultivation of "mindfulness" or awareness, leading to wisdom), and Nirvana. There is emphasis on the historicity of the Buddha, who is to be followed as teacher and exemplar, rather than worshiped. The Sangha or monastic community is a highly visible center of reference. Theravadin practice is characterized by a reciprocal merit-producing interaction between monks and laity and by an intimate relationship between government and Sangha. BIBLIOGRAPHY: E. Conze, *Buddhist Thought in India* (1967); R. C. Lester, *Theravada Buddhism in Southeast Asia* (1973).

[D. P. EFROYMSON]

THÉRÈSE DE LISIEUX, ST. (1873–97), Carmelite nun, known popularly as the Little Flower. Born in Alençon, France, T. was devoutly religious from infancy, and after a "conversion" experience shortly before her 14th birthday, conceived a strong desire to enter the Carmelite convent in Lisieux. She applied for admission, but because of her age there was a year's delay before she was finally permitted to enter. Her life as a religious was marked by exemplary fidelity in the observance of the rule and the performance of her duties, but was in no other outward respect remarkable. Only through reading her autobiography, published after her death, did many even of those who had lived with her in the convent become aware of the intensity and fervor of her interior life. This work, despite minor defects attributable to the literary conventions and tastes with which T. was familiar, quickly became popular throughout the world. With disarming simplicity and candor it told of the Little Way of approaching God in the ordinary things of life. The autobiography quickly gained recognition as a spiritual classic, and T.'s cult was widespread, esp. in the 1920s and 30s. She was beatified in 1923 and canonized in 1925. BIBLIOGRAPHY: *Autobiography* (tr. R. Knox, 1958).

[P. K. MEAGHER]

THERESIA, BL. (d. 1250), daughter of Sancho I of Portugal. She was beatified with her sister Sancia in 1705. The cult of a third sister, Mafalda, was confirmed in 1793. T. and Sancia founded Cistercian cloisters at Lorvão and Villabuena. T.'s two daughters became Cistercians as well. Her own marriage to her cousin Alfonso IX of Leon (1191) was annulled *c*. 1196. In 1230 she renounced her daughters' rights to succeed to the throne. She and Sancia refused to surrender castles in Portugal to their brother Alfonso II (1211–23). Her exploits are discussed in the chronicles of Roger of Hoveden, Lucas of Tuý, and Rodrigo Ximenes.

[E. J. DILLON]

THERRY, JOHN JOSEPH (1790–1864), Irish missionary priest. Educated at St. Patrick's College, Carlow, and ordained in 1815, T. volunteered to work in the British penal colony of New South Wales. Until the passage of the Catholic Emancipation Act in England (1829), he struggled with the authorities to secure religious liberty and equality of status for Catholics and protested the abuses of the penal system. He built the first Catholic churches and schools in Australia. With the arrival of the first bp. (1835), T. served as a parish priest in Sydney, Hobart, and Melbourne. He was buried in the crypt of St. Mary's Cathedral which he founded.

[T. J. RYAN]

THERSA, see TIRZAH.

THESSALONIANS, LETTERS TO, two NT letters addressed to the Christian community established by Paul at Thessalonica on his second missionary journey (Acts 17.1–9).

1 Thessalonians, the 13th book of the NT canon, probably the first Pauline letter. The first epistle to the Thessalonians (1.7) indicates that it was written at Corinth (cf. Acts 18.1–7). It is to be dated with a high degree of certainty in A.D. 51–52. Paul's anxiety over the harassment experienced by the community (cf. Acts 17.5–10) led him to send Timothy back to it upon his arrival in Athens (3.2). Timothy's report prompted the writing of this letter (3.6). Despite opposition from their fellow citizens (2.14), the Thessalonians remained loyal to their new faith (1.3, 8–9). In writing them, Paul accomplished three main objectives: to show his concern for them, to encourage them to persevere, and to counteract an overemphasis on the parousia that caused some in the community to grieve excessively over their dead (4.13) and induced idleness in others (5.14). The apostle's identification of himself with those hoping to be alive at the time of the parousia (4.15, 17) has caused extensive exegetical discussion. While some scholars have sought to explain Paul's language as the mere expression of a personal hope, others have insisted that the apostle held a proximate parousia, i.e., the appearance of Christ to terminate human history (cf. 1.10), as a doctrinal certainty. Better understanding of the thought of the NT Church as a whole and of the teaching of Jesus himself rather indicates that the possibility of the proximate parousia was an element of Christian hope entertained by the Christian communities of the first generation, since the teaching of Jesus did not distinctly foreclose this possibility (cf., e.g., Acts 1.11; see PAROUSIA). Here in 1 Th (4.13–18), while Paul assumes the possibility of the proximate parousia, his main objective is to teach that the Christian dead are to arise prior to this event and will join the living as the witnesses of it. The Thessalonians, therefore, have no reason to mourn as if death deprived its victims of the initial joy of the parousia event. The Apostle further urges that the Thessalonians maintain themselves in a constant state of readiness, since, as they have been instructed, the exact time of the parousia is unknown and its occurrence will be sudden (5.1–11). In addition to the parousia, 1 Thessalonians makes allusions to other Christian doctrines such as the virtues of faith, hope, and love (1.3), the Holy Spirit (1.5), the divine sonship of Jesus (1.10), and holiness as intrinsic to the Christian life (3.13; 4.3) that reveal the actual amount of content and instruction undertaken by Paul and his companions in the formation of a Christian community. This epistle is so well attested in early Christian tradition and its style so clearly Pauline that modern scholarship no longer feels justified in questioning its authenticity.

2 Thessalonians. The comparison of 2 Thessalonians with 1 Thessalonians reveals certain difficulties that have caused a minority of modern scholars to question Paul's authorship of this epistle. There are parallel passages between the two epistles, some of which are in verbal agreement. The second letter may be understood to place the parousia in a more remote future by comparison to the assumption of its proximity in the first letter. The second letter does not refer to the first letter. Despite these difficulties the majority of modern Pauline scholars accept 2 Thessalonians as authentically Pauline. Their position is that the unknown circumstances behind the second letter may account for its apparent oddities by comparison to 1 Thessalonians, that 2 Thessalonians is even better attested by early Christian tradition as Pauline than the first letter, and that no plausible hypothesis for the origin of 2 Thessalonians other than its Pauline authorship has been advanced. According to 2 Th 2.1–2, the opinion was being spread in the community that the parousia was imminent, i.e., an occurrence to be anticipated from day to day, not merely proximate as in 1 Th 4.13–18. The apostle declares this opinion to be a deception on the ground that the parousia cannot be considered imminent until the occurrence of a great apostasy and rebellion against God, as he has already taught them (2.3–5). He adds that a restraining power (the nature of which he does not specify) is at work preventing the outbreak of the force that is anti-God (2.6–7). The parousia is to occur only in conjunction with this religious rebellion which Christ will then put down (2.8–9). BIBLIOGRAPHY: B. Rigaux, *Saint Paul: Les Épitres aux Thessaloniciens* (1956); W. Neil, in the Moffatt NT Commentary (1950).

[C. P. CEROKE]

THESSALONICA (Saloniki, ancient Thermai), the chief city and port of Macedonia founded *c.*315 B.C. It was an important Roman city located on the Via Egnatia, linking Italy with Constantinople and the East. St. Paul preached the gospel there twice (Acts 17, 20) and addressed two of his epistles to the Christians of the city. During the Byzantine period it was the second city of the empire, noted not only for its commercial prosperity but also as an intellectual and artistic center. Despite capture by the Arabs (904), the Normans (1185) and the French (1205), it maintained its commercial and political importance. The 14th cent. was marked by the controversy over *Hesychasm, the seizure of power by the "Zealots," and the massacre of the nobles in 1345. Definitively taken by the Turks in 1430, it remained under their rule until its liberation by the Greeks in 1912. Thessalonica has always been an important religious center and is still noted for its Byzantine churches, esp. that of St. Demetrius, patron of the city. Present population is about 200,000, of whom the majority are Greek Orthodox. BIBLIOGRAPHY: O. Tafrali, *Topographie de Thessalonique* (1913); A. Vakolopoulos, *Historia tēs Thessalonikēs* (1947).

[G. T. DENNIS]

THETFORD, PRIORY OF, former Benedictine monastery of St. Mary's and St. Andrew's at the confluence of the Thet and the Little Ouse at Thetford, Diocese of Norwich, Norfolk, England; a Cluniac foundation established in 1103–04 by Roger Bigod, the steward of Henry I, and Bp. Herbert of Losinga, with monks from Lewes. At first, settling in the former cathedral of Thetford and then moving

to new buildings in 1114, the foundation acquired the dependencies of Horkesley and Wangford but never quite achieved independence from Cluny. It was suppressed in 1540. BIBLIOGRAPHY: S. Wood, NCE 14:88; Cottineau 2: 3145; ODCC 982.

[E. J. DILLON]

THEUDAS (THEODAS), revolutionary leader referred to in Gamaliel's speech (Acts 5.33–40). Gamaliel recalled that T. had failed, and he argued to the Sanhedrin that the Apostles would likewise fail if their work was not of God. The speech put T. prior to the census (6 A.D.). Josephus reported a messianic leader named T. who was decapitated by Cuspius *c.*44 A.D. Some scholars conclude that the reference in Acts is an anachronism, while others suppose the records refer to different men.

[T. EARLY]

THEURGY, a form of philosophico-religious magic. The first theurgist—and he may have coined the term *theourgos*—was a certain Iulianus who, in the late 2d cent., composed, or at least compiled and cast into verse form, the *Chaldaean Oracles*. They were presented as divine revelations which furnished rules for the evocation of the gods, for entering into intimate communication with demons and gods, and for acquiring divine power on the part of the theurgist himself. From Middle Platonism, theurgy passed into Neoplatonism where it had a major role. Plotinus, the founder of Neoplatonism, either had no knowledge of or no interest in theurgy, but his pupil Porphyry adopted a wavering attitude. He warned against its dangers but admitted that it could purify the spiritual soul and "prepare it for the reception of spirits and angels and for seeing the gods" (as quoted in Aug. *De civ. Dei* 10.9). *Iamblichus, however, made it the very center of his system and deals at length with theurgy and its techniques in his *De mysteriis*. *Proclus goes so far as to define theurgy as "a power higher than all human wisdom, embracing the blessings of divination, the purifying powers of initiation, and in a word all the operations of divine possession" (*Theol. Plat.* p. 63). Theurgy was an elaborate system of irrationalism in which salvation was sought, not through reason, but through magic ritual. E. R. Dodds has well characterized it as "the refuge of a despairing intelligentsia which already felt the *fascination de l'abîme*" (*op. cit.* p. 288). BIBLIOGRAPHY: E. R. Dodds, *Greeks and the Irrational* (1951) 283–311; H. Lewy, *Chaldaean Oracles and Theurgy* (1956); P. Boyancé, "Théurgie et télestique néoplatonicienne," *Revue de l'histoire des religions* 147 (1955) 189–209.

[M. R. P. MCGUIRE]

THIEL, BERNARDO AUGUSTO (1850–1901), second bp. of San José, Costa Rica. Born in Elberfeld, Germany, he became a Vincentian. Ordained in Paris, he was sent by his superiors in 1874 to Ecuador, where he taught in the seminary. Political upheaval after the death of García

Moreno (1876) compelled him to leave for Costa Rica. In 1880 he was consecrated bp. of the long vacant see of San José, but political opposition to the Church led to both his and the Jesuits' expulsion from Costa Rica in 1884. After a two-year exile in Europe, he was granted amnesty and permitted to return to his diocese. He restored the seminary, rebuilt the archiepiscopal residence, and founded the review, *El Mensajero del Clero*. His historical interests resulted in the publication in 1882 of his notes on Costa Rican Indian lexicography. In 1896 he began to prepare his *Datos cronológicos para la historia eclesiástica de Costa Rica durante el siglo XIX*. His other works include: *Términos de origen costarricense que se encuentran en documentos de los siglos XVII y XVIII; explicación del catecismo de la doctrina cristiana*, a sacred history, pastoral letters, and other short treatises. BIBLIOGRAPHY: L. Lamadrid, NCE 14:88–89.

[T. J. RYAN]

THIEMO, BL. (*c*.1040–1102), popularly venerated as a martyr because he died on a Crusade at the hands of the Seljuk Turks. He had been abbot of Sankt Peter in Salzburg, then abp. of that see. As abp. he engaged in warfare against the rival imperial bp. of Moosburg and had spent five years as a prisoner before he was freed; then he joined the Crusade.

[T. C. O'BRIEN]

THIERRY OF CHARTRES (Theodoric of Chartres; d. before 1155), French theologian, philosopher, teacher of the arts. He defended *Peter Abelard at his trial for heresy. He taught at Paris and at Chartres, where he became chancellor in 1142. A short time after the Council of Reims in 1148, which he attended, he became a monk. Among his students were *John of Salisbury and possibly Abelard. He vigorously defended the ideal of classic culture and contributed to the Platonic tradition of the Latin Middle Ages. T. was the first in the West to foster Arabian science and in cosmology and cosmogony he strove to harmonize Plato's *Timaeus* with the scriptural accounts of creation. His theology and philosophy employ a Pythagorean-Platonic dialectic of arithmetic speculation on the theme of unity-multiplicity as applied to the Trinity and the relationship of the Creator and creation. His stress upon the unity of the Godhead tended to confuse the distinction of Persons. He saw God as the form of things, not as involved in their matter, but as causing them by his presence to be what they are. Thus, since God is oneness, all things are one, despite their multiplicity. His teaching, understood in its proper context, was neither anti-Trinitarian nor pantheistic. BIBLIOGRAPHY: Gilson HCP 145–148.

[J. T. HICKEY]

THIERRY OF FLEURY (*c*.950–*c*.1018), Benedictine hagiographer who lived at the time of Abbo of Fleury. T. compiled his *Libelli duo de consuetudinibus et statutis monasterii Floriacensis*, which describes the customs of that abbey. In Rome he composed a life of Pope Martin I, of SS. Tryphon and Ruspicius, the Forty Martyrs of Sebaste, and St. Anthimus of Nicomedia. At Monte Cassino he wrote a biography of Firmanus, Abbot of Fermo. He produced his best-known work, the *Illatio sancti Benedicti* at Amorbach. Included in his other writings are a hymn in honor of St. Maurus and an explanation of the Catholic Epistles, which has survived only in part. BIBLIOGRAPHY: A. G. Biggs, NCE 14:90.

[M. C. BRADLEY]

THIERS, JEAN-BAPTISTE (1636–1703), erudite French parish priest, who from the relative obscurity of a country parish wrote painstaking, well-researched critiques of popular piety. Born in Chartres of a poor family, he was a teacher for a time at the Collège du Plessis in Paris. From 1666 he was parish priest in Champrond and then from 1692 until his death was in Vibray. T. wrote a long series of treatises on the abuses in popular piety of relics and holy days, of the sacraments, and in the cult and exposition of the Blessed Sacrament. His concern was to restore a liturgical usage free of superstition that would make the people aware of the historic, biblical, and Christian tradition. His works were received with dismay in many circles, and many sections were placed on the Index. His classic work is a 4-volume work combining several treatises on superstitions in the light of Holy Scripture, the councils, the Fathers, and the theologians; he appended a special treatment of superstitions in the use of the sacraments. In some ways he was ahead of his time, working from within as parish priest with responsibility to the people in his care, intent on purifying belief.

[E. J. DILLON]

THIERS, LOUIS ADOLPHE (1797–1877), French statesman and historian. A native of Marseilles, he studied law at Aix-en-Provence before turning to political journalism in Paris after 1821. His successful 10-volume *Histoire de la révolution française* (1823–27), which by eulogizing the Revolution constituted an indirect attack on the reactionary regime of Charles X, early established his reputation. In 1830 he helped found the influential opposition paper *National* and after the July Revolution had brought Louis Philippe to the throne, T. entered parliamentary politics directly. Under the liberal Orléanist regime (1830–48), Thiers twice served as premier, but both in 1836 and 1840 was dismissed by the king for embracing risky foreign policies. The Chamber of Deputies provided his forum for opposition to the government over the next 8 years, though much of this time went into his massive 20-volume recreation of the Napoleonic era, the *Histoire du consulat et de l'empire* (1845–62). When the revolution of 1848 toppled the July monarchy, T. supported Louis Napoléon in his bid for the presidency, but turned against Louis after the *coup d'état* of 1851 transformed the Second Republic into the Second Empire, with Louis as Emperor. Exiled briefly by the Emperor, T. abandoned active politics for writing for more than a decade, only returning to the legislative arena in 1863. He played his most important role during and immediately following the disastrous Franco-Prussian War (1870–71). Though he failed to obtain support for France among the other powers, he did succeed in obtaining an armistice and a viable peace settlement from Bismarck. As chief of the executive power of the provisional government in Bordeaux, T. was called on to deal with the revolutionary Commune of Paris which had been set up in opposition. His savage suppression of the insurgents in May 1871 not only dealt the working classes a lethal blow, but left a lasting legacy of class hatred in France. He was far more effective as the architect of France's postwar recovery; his economic policies permitted the relatively speedy liberation of the national territory from German occupation. President of the nascent Third Republic during its most critical days, he was forced from office by the monarchist and clerical majority in the National Assembly in 1873. A moderate liberal throughout his career, T. shared the strengths and weaknesses of the bourgeoisie. He was not doctrinaire: though personally drawn to constitutional monarchy, he twice accepted a republic instead. He took a similar position in regard to the Church: though often opposed to its interests, as when he refused to protect the Papal States from annexation by Italy, he yet saw in it institutional support for the established social order, and thus favored its control over primary education. An admirer of the Revolution of 1789, he nonetheless balked at the socialist revolution of 1848 and was absolutely pitiless toward the even more extreme communards of '71. In short, T. could be flexible except where his limited class outlook warped his vision. This failure, detracting from his undeniable achievements as a statesman, was unfortunately to leave its mark on the 70-year regime he helped establish.

[E. M. GATES]

THIETMAR (DIETMAR) OF MERSEBURG, (975–1018), bp. and chronicler. Of the noble Walbeck family related to the Ottonian house, T. was ordained in 1004 and appointed bp. of Merseburg in 1009. He began a chronicle of Merseburg important as a history of the Ottonian Empire, and a unique 11th-cent. source for the Church in its relations with the West Slavs. BIBLIOGRAPHY: O. J. Blum, NCE 14:90.

[O. J. BLUM]

THILS, GUSTAVE (1909–), theologian. T. was born in Brussels, studied at the seminary in Malines and at Louvain Univ. (1931–37), taught Scripture at Malines (1937–47), and has held the Chair of fundamental theology in the Catholic University of Louvain since 1947. T. has written extensively in the field of ecclesiology, ecumenism, and spirituality. Among his works translated into English are *Christian Holiness: A Précis of Ascetical Theology* (1961) and *Diocesan Priest: Nature and Spirituality of the Diocesan Clergy* (1964).

[T. M. MCFADDEN]

THINKING, the discursive intellectual activity, i.e., moving from idea to idea in pursuit of meanings and explanations. As such, thinking is a peculiarly human activity. God knows all things and does not have to think them out; angels, according to classic theology, know through species infused by God. Brute animals lack intelligence in the strict sense and therefore cannot think, although higher animals can learn from experience if it builds on their instinct patterns. Human culture and civilization are the products of thinking, for men think about everything they do and devise ways of doing things better, from eating, drinking, and home building to politics, science and art. The drive behind thinking, even when there are no practical problems to be solved, is man's insatiable curiosity to know. Man's cognitive activities develop through several stages. In infancy, his "thinking" consists in the development and coordination of useful sensory-motor patterns of behavior. Through childhood he develops the capacity to perceive reality as it is, to organize and classify data, to manipulate simple data mentally and to solve simple problems, but his thinking is still largely restricted to concrete objects as concretely perceived and remembered.

In adolescence, a person becomes capable of thinking hypothetically, i.e., of handling thoughts of objects as if they were other than they are, of conceiving of possibilities of things. Thinking becomes more abstract, more universal, and more a search for the ultimate answers to problems. In maturity a person becomes aware of the enormous complexity of reality and of his own liability to bias, and seeks to check his ideas and conclusions more thoroughly, i.e., his thinking has become judicious. Thinking comprises many operations at many different levels of abstraction: description, the accurate detailing of the appearances and activities of things; definition, the elucidation of the essential nature of things; division, the separation of things into parts and kinds; reasoning, the discovery of the causes and purposes of things; analogy, the detection of similarities in the dissimilar; extrapolation, the extension of known patterns into the unknown, etc. Some thinking is concrete, i.e., dealing with the solution of actual individual problems; some, general, dealing with broad areas of data; some universal, dealing with all the cases of a given class. The last-mentioned is called abstract thinking and is used in the pure sciences, mathematics, and metaphysics in the classical sense. Of special note is scientific thinking, which begins with observable and measurable data, and constructs hypotheses which suggest and are checked against further data, and produces explanatory theories as supported by data. It is a powerful intellectual tool wherever applicable.

Of great value also is creative thinking, which depends on special conditions in the mind of the thinker, e.g., thorough acquaintance with the materials in question, freedom from stereotyped thought patterns, willingness to entertain bizarre notions, etc. Examples of errors in thinking are generalizations from insufficient data (over-simplification), assumption of causality on the basis of mere sequence (*post hoc, propter hoc*). The actual causes of errors in thinking are often passion, custom, prejudice and bias rather than simple, intellectual mistakes.

[M. E. STOCK]

THINKING WITH THE CHURCH, a phrase for the correct intellectual attitude of Catholics as conceived by *Ignatius of Loyola in his 18 "Rules for Thinking with the Church," which he appended to his *Spiritual Exercises*. They are a counterpart and continuation of his more basic rules for the discernment of spirits. Through these rules Ignatius sought to establish practical guidelines so that the 16th-cent. Catholic could remain faithful to the Church and free from what Ignatius saw as the errors of the Protestant Reformation. The rules admonish Catholics to avoid any private interpretation of the Bible, receive the sacraments often, venerate the saints, and abide by the Church's laws. Rule 13 praises unconditional submission to the Church because of its divine guidance, "What seems to me white, I will believe to be black if the hierarchical Church so defines." Ignatius also stressed complete loyalty to the pope. BIBLIOGRAPHY: H. Rahner, *Ignatius the Theologian* (tr. M. Barry, 1968); P. Rivera, NCE 14:92–93. *IGNATIAN SPIRITUALITY.

[P. MISNER]

THIOFRID OF ECHTERNACH (d. 1110), Benedictine abbot and hagiographer. As abbot of Echternach, he restored regular observance and improved the monastic buildings. His biographical writing, frankly credulous of the miraculous powers of his pre-Carolingian heroes, is noteworthy for the simplicity of its style and its use of cursus and rhymed prose. His chief work includes the lives of Bps. Liutwin and Basinus of Trier and of St. Willibrord. BIBLIOGRAPHY: O. J. Blum, NCE 14:93.

[O. J. BLUM]

THIONVILLE (DIEDENHOFEN), COUNCILS OF. Thionville, near Metz, was the location for synods in 821, 835, and 844. Their primary purpose was to settle the recurrent quarrels among the descendants of Charlemagne. BIBLIOGRAPHY: L. E. Boyle, NCE 14:93.

[B. L. MARTHALER]

THIRD HEAVEN, the highest of the superterrestrial levels and the dwelling place of God. St. Paul seems to use the term in this sense (2 Cor 12.2–4), and Thomas Aquinas maintains (ThAq ST la, 68.4) that there are a sidereal, a crystalline, and an empyrean heaven—only the last of which is heaven in the proper sense. The Pauline usage follows from the OT designation of heaven and the heaven of the heavens (Dt 10.14; 1 Kgs 8.27). Later rabbinical literature, influenced by Babylonian speculations, often spoke of seven heavens. BIBLIOGRAPHY: EDB 949.

[T. M. MCFADDEN]

THIRD ORDERS REGULAR, religious communities or congregations made up of religious who live a common life under vows and are affiliated with an order to which a third order is attached. Such congregations have been established either by devout members of a *third order secular who chose to leave the world and follow their rule under vows, or by the affiliation of a congregation to an order privileged to grant it that status. Members of third orders regular are religious in the full sense of the term.

[J. C. WILLKE]

THIRD ORDERS SECULAR, associations of the faithful, living in the world and unbound by public vows, who are affiliated in a special way to certain religious orders. Such associations exist to give their members a rule of life in keeping with the spirit of the orders to which they are affiliated, to permit a sharing in the spiritual advantages deriving from that spirit and fellowship, to encourage prayer and good works, and to provide opportunities for instruction and guidance. The members of third orders secular, as distinguished from *third orders regular, are not religious in a canonical sense of the term. Indeed, only in a loose sense can the term "order" be applied to their society, i.e., inasmuch as their rules and constitutions, their habits (usually worn only in token form such, e.g., as the *scapular), their novitiate and profession, their officials with titles corresponding to those of the orders to which they are affiliated, give them a certain likeness to an order. The associations are called "third" orders to distinguish them from the first and second orders having the same family name, the first being the order of religious men, and the second the associated order of cloistered women.

Third orders are analogous to, but not derived from, groups of devout persons sometimes associated with monastic establishments before the mendicant orders were founded. The first third order to be organized under definite rule (approved 1221) was that of St. Francis. Similar groups of layfolk came under Dominican influence in the same century, some of whom were originally brothers and sisters of penance following the Franciscan rule. The groups that associated themselves with the Dominicans came to be called the Militia of Christ; no special rule was drawn up for them nor was the nature of their affiliation with the Dominicans precisely defined until 1285 when a rule was composed for them closely patterned on that of St. Francis. But it was not until 1406 that the aggregation of this society to the Dominican Order received papal approval. Similar approval was given to the Carmelite third order (1452), the Augustinian (1400 and 1470), the Minims (1435), the Servite (1424), the Trinitarian (1584), and the Marist (1850).

Local units of a third order are called sodalities in Church law; among the Franciscans they are known as fraternities, and among the Dominicans as chapters. Usually members are received in and through local units, but private membership is generally permissible if aggregation to a definite local unit is impractical. To found a local unit of a third order, the competent religious superior, with the consent of the local ordinary, issues a decree of establishment. Generally, the first officials and council of a newly established unit are appointed; thereafter they may be elected. The moderator or director is appointed by the competent religious superior of the first order if the unit is annexed to a church or oratory of the order; otherwise he is appointed by the local ordinary (CIC c. 698.1). To be eligible for membership one must be a Roman Catholic, unaffiliated with any condemned society, free of ecclesiastical censure, and not known to be of evil life. Professed members of a religious order or congregation may not belong to a third order, nor may one belong to two third orders at the same time without the special permission of the Holy See. Transfer from one third order to another, however, is permissible for a reasonable cause, and so also is transfer from one local unit to another of the same third order. BIBLIOGRAPHY: CIC cc. 702–706; S. Hartdegen, NCE 14:93–96. *OBLATES, *OBLATES OF ST. BENEDICT.

[J. C. WILLKE]

THIRLBY, THOMAS (1506?–70), English bp. during the religious revolution of the mid-16th century. While studying at Cambridge, T. became a protégé of T. *Cranmer who helped him to royal favor. He was a member of the convocation that accepted the ecclesiastical supremacy of Henry VIII (1534) and signed the decree annulling the King's marriage with Anne of Cleves (1540). In 1540 he was made the first (and last) bp. of Westminster, the abbey having been suppressed in 1539. When the bishopric was in turn suppressed (1550), he was given the see of Norwich. During the reign of Edward VI he reluctantly accepted the Prayer Book, but because of his known opposition to Protestantizing trends he was permitted to remain in office under Mary (as bp. of Ely from 1554) and was called upon for diplomatic missions and other services to the crown. He assisted at the degradation of his onetime patron, Cranmer (1556). At the accession of Elizabeth he shook off the ambiguity that had marked his earlier career, refused the Oath of Supremacy, was deposed and imprisoned (1560) until his death. BIBLIOGRAPHY: DNB 56:135–138.

[R. B. ENO]

THIRTEEN ARTICLES, a document prepared in 1538 as a *confession of faith of the Church of England. While never adopted formally, the Thirteen Articles influenced the later *Forty-Two Articles and the *Thirty-Nine Articles. The 1538 statement was drawn up during the discussions (1535–38) between Anglican and Lutheran theologians. The Articles followed the order of the first 13 articles of the

*Augsburg Confession, and adopted some of its language. BIBLIOGRAPHY: Schaff Creeds 1:612–613, 623–627.

[T. C. O'BRIEN]

THIRTY-NINE ARTICLES, in the C of E a counterpart of the continental *confessions of faith. This has been questioned within the Anglican Communion, but the contemporary writings of the framers, the subtitle of the Articles, and the requirement of some form of assent by the clergy down to the present, make it clear that officially the C of E is a confessional Church. The first version of the Articles was agreed upon by *Convocations in 1562; the accepted form in which they now appear in the Book of Common Prayer was not achieved until 1571 (see TEN ARTICLES; BISHOPS' BOOK; SIX ARTICLES; KING'S BOOK; FORTY-TWO ARTICLES). They are characterized by brevity, dealing only with fundamentals of faith and with points disputed at the time; by clarity, in their positive doctrinal statements and rejection of heresy; by *comprehensiveness, admitting within limits differing interpretations as allowed by Scripture.

Historically three theological streams contributed to the Articles: the pre-Tridentine tradition of the West; the Lutheran tradition, and the Reformed or Calvinistic tradition. Articles 1–5 and 8 evidence the Trinitarian and Christological doctrines of the West and the *ecumenical creeds. The Reformation *formal principle or doctrinal norm, the primacy of Scripture, is established in the C of E by Articles 6 and 7. Lutheran doctrine on justification, the Church, and the distinction between ecclesiastical and temporal power is reflected in Articles 9–24, 31–34, 36–39. The Calvinistic influence is more decisive in the infralapsarian doctrine of *predestination in Article 17; and Articles 25–30 reject RC, Lutheran, and Zwinglian views in favor of a Reformed doctrine on the sacraments (although Article 28 on the Lord's Supper has also been interpreted as allowing for the *Real Presence).

The *Lambeth Conference of 1968 examined the status of the Articles, since throughout the Anglican Communion there are major parties that do not conform to them. It is doubtful, e.g., whether current preoccupation with the *historic episcopate as essential to the Church of Christ is compatible with their letter and spirit; yet radical theological views are clearly excluded. In the Protestant Episcopal Church of the U.S., while they are largely neglected by clergy and laity alike, the Articles still have an official confessional-liturgical status. Even though specific subscription to them is not necessary, the Constitution of the Church (Article X) requires their use; ordinands solemnly engage to conform to the doctrine of the Church; and the ordination vows of the Book of Common Prayer are all based on the doctrine of the Articles. BIBLIOGRAPHY: J. C. Ryle, *Knots Untied* (1964) ch. 4; E. J. Bicknell, *Theological Introduction to the Thirty-Nine Articles of the Church of England* (1924); H. E. W. Turner, *Articles of the Church of England* (1964).

[J. H. RODGERS]

THIRTY YEARS' WAR, political and religious conflict, 1618–48, involving nearly all of the major European countries and after which France emerged as the dominant power. The Thirty Years War was not a sudden event, but rather the explosion of political, religious, economic, and social forces that had been operating within Europe since the 16th century. After several false starts such as the formation of the Catholic and Protestant Leagues and the Julich-Cleves Dispute, the war was sparked by a nationalist revolt in Bohemia in 1618, in part a response to renewed religious pressure by Ferdinand II. A Calvinist, Frederick V, was elected to the throne of Bohemia, but Frederick was soon driven back to his Electorate of the Palatine when he was defeated by Catholic forces under Tilly at the Battle of White Mountain in 1620; imperial control of Bohemia was achieved. Protestant princes tried to resist Catholic forces, and the entrance of Christian IV of Denmark opened the Danish phase, which lasted from 1625 to 1629. In 1629 the highpoint of Catholic power was reached in the *Edict of Restitution. In 1630 Gustavus Adolphus arrived in Germany and the Swedish phase commenced. The death of Adolphus in 1632 prepared the way for France's participation in 1635. The treaties at Westphalia in 1648 ended the war with the exception of the conflict between Spain and France, which lasted until 1659. Historical interpretations of the causes and results of the Thirty Years War widely vary. BIBLIOGRAPHY: J. V. Polisensky, *Thirty Years War*, (tr. R. Evans, 1971); *Thirty Years' War* (ed. T. K. Rabb, 1964).

[C. T. EBY]

THNETOPSYCHITAE, see ARABACI.

THOLUCK, FRIEDRICH (1799–1877), German Lutheran theologian of the Protestant "awakening" movement. While a student of biblical languages and theology at the Univ. of Berlin, T. was attracted to the Pietist movement and in 1824 while teaching at the Univ. of Berlin, he wrote *Guido und Julius*. His *Die Lehre vom Sünder und vom Versöhner oder Die wahre Weihe des Zweiflers* (1823, 9th ed. 1870), against the rationalism of his day, was a work widely read in Pietist circles throughout the world. He became professor of theology at Halle in 1826, and university preacher in 1833, devoting much time to counseling students. His influence was decisive on men such as Martin Kähler and Julius Schuiewind. His numerous writings include exegesis of Old and New Testament works, studies in 17th and 18th cent. church history, and collections of sermons.

[T. J. RYAN]

THOMAR (TOMAR), MONASTERY OF, a monastic establishment located in central Portugal in the district of Santarem. It was the seat of the Templars in Portugal and of the Order of Christ. It contains elements of the best Portugese architecture from the 12th to the 17th centuries. The convent palace of the Knights of Christ includes a church and cloister dating from the 12th cent., two cloisters and chapter house added in the 15th cent. by Prince Henry the Navigator, and several other buildings of lesser importance. The convent claims Flemish and Portugese paintings of the Grao-Vasco school dating from the 16th cent., as well as the works of other masters. It serves as witness to a glorious past, having no religious significance in the present. BIBLIOGRAPHY: EB (1910) 5:436–437; E. P. Colbert, NCE 14:100–101 (bibliog.).

[L. NEMEC]

THOMAS, ST., APOSTLE, one of the Twelve, as listed in the three synoptic Gospels (Mt 10:2–4; Mk 3:16–19; Lk 6:14–16) and in Acts (1:13). "Thoma" is the Aramaic word for "twin." In John's Gospel the addition of the Greek word for twin, *Didymus*, to the name Thomas (Jn 11.16; 20.24; 21.2) indicates that this Apostle was also known as "The Twin" to the Greek communities to which the fourth Gospel was addressed. Both Greek and Aramaic tradition knew him by his nickname, not by his name. In the NT itself his real name and the identity of his twin are not settled. Syriac Christian tradition knew him as Judas the Twin. The 3d- or 4th-cent. apocryphal *Acts of Thomas* call him Judas Thomas and portray him as the twin of Jesus, traditions accepted by the Mesopotamian Church and still taken seriously in some scholarly circles. In the 4th cent. Eusebius mentions in his *Historia ecclesiastica* that Thomas was a missionary in Parthia. The Acts of Thomas also relate his martyrdom in India and the translation of his body to Mesopotamia. John's Gospel contains three scattered utterances of Thomas: "Let us also go, that we may die with him" (11.16); "Lord, we do not know where you are going, so how can we know the way?" (14.5); "Unless I see the mark of the nails on his hands, unless I put my finger into the place where the nails were, and my hand into his side, I will not believe it." (20.25). This is the biblical portrait of Thomas. On the basis of this it would seem that resurrection faith, when it finally dawned (Jn 20.28), came to one with a nature at once skeptical, stubborn, and loyal.

[E. J. DILLON]

THOMAS AGNI (d. 1277), Sicilian Dominican, bp., patriarch of Jerusalem. He entered the Dominicans *c.*1220, founded San Domenico priory (Naples, 1231), was provincial (Rome, 1255), bp. of Bethlehem (1255), Messina (1262), and Cosenza (1267), and patriarch of Jerusalem (1272). He received Thomas Aquinas into the order (*c.*1243), arbitrated quarrels like the Jerusalem kingship, and wrote a biography of Peter Martyr. BIBLIOGRAPHY: DizBiogItal 1:444–445.

[R. I. BURNS]

THOMAS AQUINAS, ST. (*c.*1225–74), Doctor of the Church, patron of schools, called the Angelic Doctor, and *Doctor communis*. He was born at Roccasecca, near Monte Cassino, and entrusted to the abbey for his early education

(1231). At the Univ. of Naples (1239–44) he first became acquainted with the writings of Aristotle and the commentaries of Averroës. He received the habit of the Dominicans in 1244 at S. Domenico in Naples, and, after withstanding family opposition, was able to settle into the Dominican life by 1245. In 1245 or 1246 he became the student of St. Albert the Great, at Paris or Cologne, and at Cologne 1248–52 was Albert's assistant while beginning his own literary output with short philosophical treatises and scriptural commentaries. As a candidate for the doctorate at the Univ. of Paris he was reader of the *Sentences* (1252–56), and his own commentary on Peter Lombard's work as well as a major treatise *De ente et essentia* are from this period. Because of opposition from the secular masters, he was only begrudgingly granted the doctorate in 1257. During his first professorship at Paris (1256–59) the major work was the *De veritate*, the first of his *Quaestionis disputatae*. He was again in Italy (1259–68) at Dominican houses near the papal court, at Anagni, Orvieto, and Viterbo. But in 1265–67 he was regent and planned the course of studies at the convent of Sta. Sabina in Rome. To this period belong: the completion of his *Summa contra gentiles*, as an aid to disputations with the Mohammedans and Jews in Spain; his *Catena aurea*, evidencing his broad patristic knowledge; the conception of the plan of his masterwork, the *Summa theologiae*; and the completion of its First Part. During this time he also instigated new translations of Aristotle by William of Moerbeke and began his own Aristotelian commentaries. During his second Paris tenure (1269–72), he engaged in polemics against *Siger of Brabant and the Latin Averroists, esp. in his *De unitate intellectus*, another of the *quaestiones disputatae*. He also continued his philosophical and scriptural commentaries, the *De virtutibus*, the Second Part of the *Summa theologiae*, and 30 questions of the Third Part. The last phase of his professional career was at the Dominican studium at Naples (1272–74), where he continued his Aristotelian commentaries and ended his work on the *Summa theologiae* with question 90 of the Third Part (the so-called Supplement was added to complete the plan by Reginald of Piperno). After a mysterious experience at prayer on Dec. 6, 1273, he ceased altogether from writing. Four months later he died, after being taken ill on his way to the Council of Lyons II. Canonized in 1323, T. was extolled by the popes through the centuries for the soundness and clarity of his teaching. His thought is directly reflected on the dogmatic decrees of the Council of Trent. The *Summa theologiae* became the classic RC theological text from the 16th cent., and has remained a lapidary reference for theology ever since. The restoration of Thomism inaugurated officially by Leo XIII's encyclical letter, *Aeterni Patris* of 1879, gave rise to a century of intensive Thomistic studies, which however, have abated in the post-Vatican II atmosphere of theological pluralism. The terms of ecclesiastical approbation and the focus of research that it prompted led to a modern emphasis on St. Thomas Aquinas, philosopher. For historical and apologetic reasons, attention centered on his

logical orderliness, his confidence in the essential integrity of human reason, and in a harmony between nature and grace. The symmetry of his intellectual synthesis and the power of his metaphysical and psychological insights are beyond question. But he was a theologian before all else. Beneath the techniques and categories of his scholastic method, his vision goes deeply into the salvific history and existential dimension afforded by faith. This is above all apparent in the Second Part, the so-called moral part, of the *Summa theologiae*. Here his genius has no equal precedent; here the depths in actuality of his evangelical insights remain unsounded. This summation of T. *Gilby is unsurpassed in any language as it reaches to the inner essence and movement of the *Summa theologiae* and its author's spirit: "Philosophical theology enters into the substance of the *Summa*; its arguments, however, are the ground bass to the movement of *sacra doctrina* not the whole. Otherwise the *Summa* would be like other works of human wisdom, a statement of the conflict between essence and existence, a protest of men confined within themselves, perhaps a plea for reason and dignity. An undercurrent from the tragic sense of life in the poets and philosophers runs through the *Summa*, but their experience has moved into a new dimension. The same phenomena remain and the natures they manifest are not obliterated. The ideas are not shadowed by the appearance, as for the Platonists; the logos is not remote from sensibility, as for the Stoics; the touch of divinity is not rare, like the good fortune of the Eudemian Ethics. The Word is made flesh and has come into history, and now meaning and deed are conjoined, *sacramentum* is translated into *res*, creatures are real as both things and signs, and as real they are held in God in whose Image they are both expressed and created. The feelings that stir are taken into the charity which is the root, mother, and mover of all fair love, the sevenfold Gift of the Spirit is not a stroke of genius but a permanent condition, for the Son and the Spirit are sent to God's people and have taken up their abode and the kingdom of heaven is already with us though we have yet to rejoice in its glory. This is the reality, compact of time and eternity, bearing still the wounds received on earth and transfigured in heaven, this is the *causa* for the knowledge of the blessed from which *sacra doctrina* derives." (ThAq ST Lat-Eng, v. 1, ed. T. Gilby, app. 1, p. 130). BIBLIOGRA -PHY: W. A. Wallace and J. A. Weisheipl, NCE 14:104–115 for complete list of works and bibliog.; J. A. Weisheipl, *Friar Thomas d'Aquino* (1974); V. J. Bourke, *Aquinas's Search for Wisdom* (pa. 1965). *THOMISM.

[T. C. O'BRIEN]

THOMAS OF BAYEUX (d. 1100), abp. of York from 1070. A well-educated Norman, T. came to England with Odo of Bayeux. As abp., he resisted the claims of Canterbury to the primacy of England and would consecrate Anselm only as metropolitan, not as primate. BIBLIOGRAPHY: W. Hunt, DNB 19:640–643.

[F. D. BLACKLEY]

THOMAS À BECKET, ST., see BECKET, THOMAS, ST.

THOMAS BELLACI, BL, known also as Thomas of Florence, (c.1370–1447), Franciscan lay brother. He entered the Franciscans of the Observance at Fiesole, after having repented of a dissolute youth. He assisted in opposing the heretical Fraticelli. Captured when he went to join Albert of Sarteano in the East, he was ransomed by Eugene IV and returned to Rome in 1445. BIBLIOGRAPHY: F. D. Lazenby, NCE 14:115; R. Lioi, BiblSanct 12:580–582; Butler 4:200–201; Wadding Ann 11:336–346.

[F. D. LAZENBY]

THOMAS OF BERGAMO (Thomas of Olera; c. 1559–1631), Capuchin lay brother and mystic. Born probably in Olera near Bergamo, of the Acerbi family, he entered the Capuchins in Verona in 1580; lived at various times in Vienna, Munich, and Salzburg; and died in Innsbruck. His tomb is in the Capuchin cloister there. He assisted Joan Mary of the Cross (Bernardina Floriani, born Maffeotta) in founding the Claretian Cloister in Rovereto. BIBLIOGRAPHY: L. von Ebersberg, LTK 10:137.

[E. J. DILLON]

THOMAS BRADWARDINE (c.1290–1349), Abp. of Canterbury, theologian and mathematician, known as *Doctor profundus*. In the *Canterbury Tales* Chaucer ranked him alongside St. Augustine. His great theological work, *De causa Dei adversus Pelagium et de virtute causarum* (completed 1344) was directed against *Nominalist theologians, *William of Ockham and *Robert Holcot among them. T.'s condition stressed grace and neglected nature; his deterministic explanation of the efficacy of God's causality was taken up by *John of Mirecourt, *Nicholas d'Autrecourt, and J. *Wyclif. BIBLIOGRAPHY: Gilson HCP 793–794; Knowles ROE 2:81–82, G. Leff, *Bradwardine and the Pelagians* (1959); J. J. Przezdziecki, NCE 14.116.

[T. C. O'BRIEN]

THOMAS OF BUCKINGHAM (c.1290–1351), English scientist and theologian, a fellow of Merton College, Oxford, by 1324; a master in arts by 1331; a doctor in theology by 1346. As a theologian he was largely concerned with the problem of free will and opposed the theological determinism of Abp. Bradwardine. He wrote *Quaestiones* on the *Sentences* of Peter Lombard (1333–38). BIBLIOGRAPHY: EmdenOx 1:298–299.

[C. D. ROSS]

THOMAS OF BUNGEY (fl. 1270s), Franciscan theologian. T. was the eighth minister provincial of the English province of Franciscans (1272–75) and was the first provincial described in the lists as *magister*. He was tenth Franciscan master at Oxford (1270–72), and fifteenth Franciscan master at Cambridge (1275–79). Writings attributed to him are: 33 *Quaestiones,* (MS Assisi, 158); a commentary on *De coelo et mundo*; a *Commentary on the Sentences* (now lost); a commentary on the Epistle to the Romans. BIBLIOGRAPHY: C. Walmesley, "Extracts from an Unknown Work of Thomas de Bungeye," *Annali dell'Istituto Superiore di scienze e lettere S. Chiara*, 5(1954) 217–238; T. C. Crowley, NCE 14:116–117.

[J. J. SMITH]

THOMAS OF CANTELUPE, ST. (c.1218–1282). After studies in the faculty of arts at Paris before 1245, he enrolled in the faculty of law at Oxford, and was chancellor in 1261–63 and 1273–74. In 1275 he became bp. of Hereford, acquiring a reputation as a reformer. Although he had favored the barons against Henry III, he was a trusted adviser of Edward I from 1275. Excommunicated by John Pecham, he died at Orvieto while seeking justice from the Pope. There is evidence of a cultus at Hereford shortly after his death; and he was canonized in 1320. BIBLIOGRAPHY: Emden Ox 1:347–349; H. Farmer, BiblSanct 12:566–567.

[L. E. BOYLE]

THOMAS OF CANTIMPRÉ (1201–c.1272), Belgian hagiographer and philosopher, also called Thomas of Brabant. T. was born of a noble family, his father having taken part in the Third Crusade. At 15, he received instruction at Liège, where he heard the sermons of Jacques de Vitry. At 16, T. was an Augustinian novice at Cantimpré, near Cambrai, but in 1230, joined the Dominicans at Louvain and was sent to the Univ. of Cologne, where he studied under Albert the Great and knew Thomas Aquinas. In 1237, he went to the Collège of St. Jacques at the Univ. of Paris for theology, returning to Louvain in 1240. The writings of T. fall into three categories: hagiography, with a life of Blessed Lutgard as the best known; naturalist writings, as would follow from a student of Albert the Great, more than 20 books; and moralistic, such as *Bonum universale de apibus*, commenting upon the life of bees, with sociological, political, and moral applications for human society. BIBLIOGRAPHY: H. de Vocht, *Biographie Universelle de Belgique* 25:27–34.

[N. F. GAUGHAN]

THOMAS OF CAPUA (d. 1243), a bp. of Naples (1215), cardinal-priest of St. Sabina (1216). T. served the papacy as secretary, drafting important papal correspondence. A poet, he wrote part of the office for St. Francis of Assisi. His handbooks for official correspondence, *Ars dictandi* and *Summa dictaminis,* are important in the history of Latin prose style. BIBLIOGRAPHY: *Die Ars dictandi* (ed. E. Heller; 1929); W. A. Ernest, NCE 14:118.

[M. A. WINKELMANN]

THOMAS OF CELANO (d. 1260), Franciscan hagiographer. Received into the order by St. Francis himself, at whose deathbed he may have been present, and at whose canonization (1228) he certainly was, he wrote *Vita prima*

(1229) and its epitome *Legenda ad usum chori* at Pope Gregory IX's request; he composed *Memoriale in desiderio* (commonly called *Vita secunda*) before 1247. The *Vita prima* is based on personal knowledge and reliable witnesses, though its value has been questioned. The *Dies Irae* has been attributed to him. For discussion of these problems, see J. R. H. Moorman, *Sources for the Life of St. Francis of Assisi* (1940).

[J. L. GRASSI]

THOMAS OF CHARLTON (d. 1344), English royal official, governor of Ireland (1338–40), bp. of Hereford from 1327. He was an Oxford doctor of civil law (1317); entered the royal service under Edward II; under Edward III was treasurer of England and fulfilled ambassadorial missions. In Ireland he was the firm executor of crown policy. He received the bishopric as a benefice and honor rather than as a pastoral office.

[T. C. O'BRIEN]

THOMAS OF CLAXTON (fl. early 15th cent.), English Dominican theologian at Oxford who in 1411 participated in the condemnation of J. *Wycliffe's teachings and in the deliberations of the Council of Constance (1415) against Wycliffe and J. *Hus. T.'s works, among them a set of *quaestiones* on Peter Lombard's *Sentences* and a *quodlibet*, reflect a fidelity to such key teachings of St. Thomas Aquinas as the real distinction between essence and *esse* and the analogy of being.

[T. C. O'BRIEN]

THOMAS OF COBHAM (d. 1327), scholar, bishop. He held degrees from Paris, Oxford, and Cambridge. His election to the see of Canterbury (1313) was frustrated by royal opposition, but he was provided with the bishopric of Worcester instead (1317). He endowed a congregation house and library at Oxford. BIBLIOGRAPHY: E. H. Pearce, *Thomas de Cobham* (1923); J. L. Grassi, NCE 14:119.

[J. L. GRASSI]

THOMAS OF CORBRIDGE (d. 1304), abp. of York. He was a graduate of Oxford, chancellor of York *c.* 1280, and succeeded to the see of York in 1299. Most of his energies as abp. were directed to diocesan affairs; he almost completed two thorough visitations in his short episcopate. He is described as exemplary, profound, deeply learned, and an incomparable professor of all the arts. BIBLIOGRAPHY: J. Raine, *Fasti Eboracenses* (1863); *Register of Thomas Corbridge* (Surtees Society, ed. W. Brown and A. H. Thompson); J. L. Grassi, NCE 14:119.

[J. L. GRASSI]

THOMAS CORSINI, BL. (*c.* 1260–1343), Servite lay brother, born of noble parentage in Orvieto. When the Virgin appeared to him, asking him to espouse her cause, he attributed the vision to hallucination; but when she reap-

peared, he joined the Servite Brothers. Preferring the contemplative life, he also begged alms for his community. BIBLIOGRAPHY: F. D. Lazenby, NCE 14:119; A. M. Rossi, LTK 10:146.

[F. D. LAZENBY]

THOMAS OF DOVER (Thomas Hales; d. 1295), English Benedictine and reputed martyr. A member of the community of St. Martin at Dover, he was killed by marauders from France in 1295 while defending the church. Although he had a local cult until the Reformation, attempts in the late 14th cent. to have him canonized failed. BIBLIOGRAPHY: P. Grosjean, AnalBoll 72 (1954) 167–191.

[L. E. BOYLE]

THOMAS OF ECCLESTON (fl. 13th cent.), English chronicler, Franciscan at Oxford and London friaries. T. is known only through his valuable history of the English Franciscans, *De adventu Fratrum Minorum in Angliam* (2d ed., A. G. Little, 1951). He studied at Oxford and possibly at Paris and spent 26 years gathering material for his book. BIBLIOGRAPHY: Emden Ox 1:623–624; R. B. Brooke, NCE 14:119–120.

[R. W. HAYS]

THOMAS OF FARFA, ST. (d. *c.* 720), abbot. While on a pilgrimage from his native Savoy to Rome and the Holy Land, he is said to have been directed by Our Lady to rebuild the monastery of Farfa in Spoleto, founded by St. Lawrence Siro in the 4th cent., which had later fallen into ruins. This he did with the help of the Lombard duke of Spoleto. T.'s reputation for holiness attracted many vocations and the abbey flourished. BIBLIOGRAPHY: S. Baiocchi, NCE 14:120.

[G. M. COOK]

THOMAS GALLUS OF VERCELLI, (d. *c.* 1246), French-born mystical theorist, also known as Thomas of Saint-Victor, Augustinian Canon of the Abbey of Saint-Victor in Paris; and first abbot of Sant'Andrea di Vercelli in Piedmont. He wrote exhaustively on the Dionysian mysticism of *Pseudo-Dionysius the Areopagite, attempting to harmonize this doctrine with the biblical mysticism of such books as the Song of Songs and Isaiah. His mystical thought emphasized, as did Hugh of St. Victor's, the necessity of the transcendence of God and renunciation. He was known personally to St. Anthony of Padua, had an influence on Franciscan spirituality, and is often cited by Bonaventure and Alexander of Hales. Because of his loyalty to his Ghibelline cardinal patron, he was deposed by the apostolic visitor in 1243 and died excommunicated and in exile. His tomb is in Sant'Andrea di Vercelli. T.'s *Compendiosa extractio*, a paraphrase, is contained in the modern edition of the Latin translations of Dionysius' works, *Dionysiaca* (ed. Ph. Chevalier, 2 v., 1937, 1950).

[E. J. DILLON]

THOMAS HÉLYE, BL. (1187–1257), teacher and preacher. As a young man T. taught catechism in his native Biville in Normandy. After being ordained deacon by the bp. of Coutances, he made several pilgrimages and then entered the Univ. of Paris. Four years later he was ordained priest. He spent his life catechizing and preaching near Biville. BIBLIOGRAPHY: F. D. Lazenby, NCE 14:120; H. L. Müller, LTK 10:142–143.

[F. D. LAZENBY]

THOMAS OF JESUS (DE ANDRADA; 1529–82), Portuguese Augustinian, preacher and spiritual writer. After a successful preaching apostolate in Portugal, he went with King Sebastian on an expedition (1578) against the Moors in N Africa, was captured, and imprisoned. During his confinement he wrote *Os trabalhos de Jesus* (2 parts, 1602–09; first American ed. 1841, *Sufferings of Our Lord Jesus Christ*), a collection of meditations and a guide to mental prayer. Freed himself, he stayed on to minister to Christian slaves in Morocco, where he died from illness brought on by hardship and privation.

[T. C. O'BRIEN]

THOMAS OF JESUS (DÍAZ SÁNCHEZ DE ÁVILA; 1564–1627), Discalced Carmelite, promoter of the spread of his order, spiritual writer. Already a doctor of law and theology at Salamanca, he entered the order in Granada, where St. John of the Cross was prior, and made profession in 1587. In Spain T. was responsible for setting up at Belarque (1593) and Las Batuecas (1599) the first Carmelite "deserts" (priories for the eremitical life). He was called to Rome by Paul V in 1607, became a member of the Italian Congregation of the Discalced, and inaugurated their first missionary activity, his work becoming a forerunner of the Congregation for the Propagation of the Faith. Under his leadership new Carmelite foundations were established in Belgium, France, and Germany; he was provincial of the Belgian province (1617–23) before returning to Rome as general definitor. He wrote on the mystical life, history, and missiology, notably his *De procuranda salute omnium gentium*.

[T. C. O'BRIEN]

THOMAS JORZ (d. 1310), English Dominican theologian. Regent master of the Oxford Dominicans (c. 1292), and prior of the Dominican house there (1294–97), T. was provincial of England (1297–1304). While on a royal mission to the papal curia at Lyons in 1305, he was made a cardinal by Clement V. His only extant writings are some extracts from a commentary on the *Sentences*. He died at Grenoble while on a papal mission to Henry VII of Germany. BIBLIOGRAPHY: Emden Ox 2:1023.

[L. E. BOYLE]

THOMAS À KEMPIS (c. 1380–1471), writer on the spiritual life. Born at Kempen near Cologne (hence his name; his family name was Hammerken); he studied (c. 1392–c. 99) at the Deventer school of the *Brethren of the Common Life under *Florentius Radewijns. T. then entered Mt. St. Agnes, a new monastery of the Canons Regular of St. Augustine, where his older brother John was prior. He spent the rest of his life with the community, serving for a time as master of novices and in 1425 and 1448 as superior. The *Devotio moderna* classic, *Imitation of Christ* (c. 1427), is generally attributed to him. He also wrote several other treatises and conferences on the ascetical life, as well as biographies of Gerard Groote and Florentius. BIBLIOGRAPHY: R. R. Post, *Modern Devotion* (1968). *IMITATION OF CHRIST.

[T. EARLY]

THOMAS DE LA MARE (1309–96), abbot of St. Albans, the premier abbey of England (1349–96). Of a distinguished family, privately educated in letters by his parents, T. became a monk at 17 at Wymondham, and later at Tynemouth where he was prior. When Abbot Michael of Montmore died in the plague, the Black Death, in 1349 at St. Alban's, T. was elected his successor at the age of 40. Although his two predecessors were scholars, he was of a more practical bent. Privy Councillor to Edward III, personal counselor to the Black Prince, and a contemporary of Wycliffe, Langland, and Chaucer, he was an energetic monastic lawmaker. For 20 years he was president of the Black Monks, drawing up statutes for the province and constitutions for his own house. He has been called the greatest and last of the abbots of the age of monastic magnificence. He was a great builder at St. Albans. Jealous of abbatial rights, he cared little for personal luxury and display and assiduously kept the monastic rule, esp. emphasizing a devout liturgy. Weakened by the plague in its second visitation (1361–62), T. still continued his tasks, although he did try to resign. For the last nine years he was a complete invalid from various maladies that made him helpless in body and weakened in intellectual abilities. BIBLIOGRAPHY: D. Knowles, *Saints and Scholars* (1962) 123–133.

[N. F. GAUGHAN]

THOMAS OF MARLEBERGE (d. 1236), English Benedictine chronicler, book-collector, architect, and craftsman. After studying in Paris, lecturing at Oxford, and practicing canon law, T. entered Evesham Abbey (c. 1199). He successfully conducted the case arising from Evesham's claim for exemption (1202–05) from official visits by Bp. Mauger of Worcester, engineered the ouster of the corrupt abbot Roger Norreys, and became sacristan, prior, and (1230) abbot. *Chronicon abbatiae de Evesham* (ed. W. D. Macray, Rolls Series 29, 1863) contains his surviving writings. BIBLIOGRAPHY: Emden Ox 2:1223–24.

[R. W. HAYS]

THOMAS OF PAVIA, (c. 1212–betw. 1280 and 1284), Franciscan Chronicler. T. was a lecturer in theology in

Bologna, Parma, and Ferrara, and provincial of Tuscany province (1258–70). His writings include: *Assidua*, legend about St. Anthony of Padua; *Dialogus de gestis ss. Fratrum Minorum* (c. 1245), a collection of miracles; *Dictionnarium bovis* (c. 1254), a source book for preachers; *Tractatus sermonum; Gesta imperatorum et pontificum*, a chronicle (ed. Boehmer, *Fontes rerum Germanicarum*, 4:609–672). T. did not believe in the Immaculate Conception. Salimbene characterizes him as holy, wise, judicious, humble, and meek, but verbose in his writings. BIBLIOGRAPHY: E. Longpré, AFH (1923) 16:3–33; J. Cambell, NCE, 14:122.

[J. J. SMITH]

THOMAS OF STRASSBURG (c. 1275–c. 1357), Augustinian theologian, prior general from 1345. He taught at Strassburg and at Paris, where he was in 1337. As a philosopher he belonged to the line of *Giles of Rome, supporting the position of St. Thomas Aquinas on many points, e.g., the real distinction between essence and *esse*; departing from it on others. In theology T. wrote a commentary on Peter Lombard's *Sentences*, which contained an original view of the doctrine of predestination. As Augustinian general he pursued a program of reform of the order's discipline.

[T. C. O'BRIEN]

THOMAS OF SUTTON (c. 1250–c. 1315), English Dominican, early Thomist at Oxford. He completed two of St. Thomas's unfinished commentaries, *Perihermeneias* and *De generatione et corruptione*. In his original works, esp. 4 *Quodlibeta* and 36 *Quaestiones disputatae*, he ably defended teachings of St. Thomas Aquinas against Duns Scotus and others. BIBLIOGRAPHY: J. J. Przezdziecki, NCE 14:123.

[T. C. O'BRIEN]

THOMAS OF TOLENTINO, BL. (d. 1321), Franciscan martyr. Sent to Armenia in 1290, T. made many conversions. He was dispatched by Pope Clement V on missions to Tartary and China, but, en route, he was captured by Muslims in India and decapitated. His body was discovered by Bl. Odoric of Pordenone. His head is in Tolentino. BIBLIOGRAPHY: F. D. Lazenby, NCE 14:123; G. Fussenegger, LTK 10:148–149; A. Matanić, BiblSanct 12:587–589.

[F. D. LAZENBY]

THOMAS OF VILLANOVA, ST. (1487–1555), Spanish Augustinian and abp. of Valencia. He was named professor of philosophy at the Univ. of Alcalá at age 26. In 1516 he entered the Augustinian Order and was ordained in 1518. T. was provincial of Andalusia from 1527 to 1529 and of Castille from 1534 to 1537. In the latter capacity he sent the first Augustinians to the New World to work in Mexico (1533). In 1542 Charles V nominated him to the archbishopric of Granada, which he declined. When in 1544 the Emperor named him to the see of Valencia, T. protested

but had to accept the appointment. At Valencia T. earned the title "father of the poor," leading by his example as a religious who refused to change the simple way of life he had followed before. T.'s charity was astounding, whether exercised for the sick or for a recalcitrant cleric. He did not attend the Council of Trent, but was represented by a suffragan bishop; his influence on the Castilian bishops also made his interest in church reform known at the Council. A renowned preacher, T. left a collection of discourses, published in 1881–97, and other writings, published in 1885, under the title *Opúsculos castellanos*. He was canonized in 1658.

[J. R. AHERNE]

THOMAS WALEYS (c. 1287–1349), Oxford Dominican who lectured on the *Sentences* (1314–15) and was regent master of theology (c. 1318–20). At Bologna he preached against the Franciscan doctrine of poverty and at Avignon he opposed the view of *John XXII on the beatific vision. Because of these opinions and charges brought against him by the Franciscan *Walter of Chatton, he was imprisoned without trial for 11 years. Soon after 1342 he was released and returned to England. BIBLIOGRAPHY: J. A. Weisheipl, NCE 14:124; Quétif-Échard 1.2:505, 597–602; Emden Ox 3:2054.

[J. A. WEISHEIPL]

THOMAS OF WILTON (Thomas de Wylton; d. c. 1327), English theologian. A graduate of Oxford, T. lectured in theology in Paris (c. 1312–22) and appears to have been much under the influence of Duns Scotus. In 1320 he was named chancellor of St. Paul's, London, and he functioned in that capacity from 1322 to 1327. BIBLIOGRAPHY: Emden Ox 3:2054–55; J. A. Weisheipl, NCE 14:124.

THOMAS OF YORK (d. c. 1260), Franciscan philosopher, theologian. T. became a master of theology at Oxford (1253–56) and then the sixth master at the Franciscan house of studies at Cambridge. His writings are: *Sapientiale*, an encyclopedic philosophical treatise in seven books, which aims to be a concordance between the philosophers and theologians; *Comparatio sensibilium; Manus quae contra omnipotentem*, a defense of the position of the mendicants in the controversy on poverty between the regulars and seculars. T. accepted the Aristotelian doctrine of nature but follows Augustine on the origin of human knowledge. In the Augustinian tradition he held that philosophy must be directed by the truths of revelation; otherwise philosophy is doomed to error. BIBLIOGRAPHY: J. P. Reilly, "Thomas of York and the Efficacy of Secondary Causes," MedSt 15 (1953) 225–233; E. Longpré, AFH (1926) 19:875–930.

[J. J. SMITH]

THOMAS II OF YORK (d. 1114) archbishop. Son of Samson (later bp. of Worcester), brother of Bp. Richard of Bayeaux, and the nephew of Abp. Thomas I of York (d.

1100), who provided for his education, T. was destined to rise. He was in line for the vacant see of London, when Henry I nominated him (1108) to York, but T.'s refusal to recognize the primacy of Canterbury delayed his consecration till 1109 when he submitted. Reputedly religious, liberal, of good disposition, he was learned and eloquent. He died young. BIBLIOGRAPHY: W. Hunt, DNB 19:643–645; R. W. Southern, *Saint Anselm and His Biographer* (1963); O. J. Blum, NCE 14:125.

[O. J. BLUM]

THOMAS, CHARLES AMBROISE (1811–96), French composer. T., who learned music from his earliest years, studied privately with J. F. *Lesueur and others and attended the Paris Conservatory. He there gained many prizes and early manifested great promise as a composer. T. produced many works for the Opéra Comique, notably his opera *Mignon*. Professor of composition at the Paris Conservatory from 1852, he became its director in 1871. T. was made a member of the Institute in 1851 and received the Grand Cross of the Legion of Honor in 1896. In addition to his operas and other secular works, he composed a *Messe de Requiem,* a *Messe solennelle,* and a *Marche religieuse.*

[M. T. LEGGE]

THOMAS, DYLAN (1914–53), Anglo-Welsh poet and prose writer. T.'s *Eighteen Poems* (1934) created controversy but brought him immediate fame, which became greater with the publication of *Twenty-five Poems* (1936) and *The Map of Love* (1939). His complex imagery derives from many sources—Welsh legend, witchcraft, Christian symbols, astronomy, and Freudian symbols—all of which made his early poetry hard to understand. Readers are attracted by his love of life, his humor, and his mastery of sound: a prodigal use of alliteration, internal rhyme, and assonance. He is recognized as a major poet. T.'s highly individualistic prose comprises stories and sketches, many autobiographical, all with some trace of fantasy. There are several collections of his prose, e.g., *Portrait of an Artist as a Young Dog* (1940). He wrote for radio *A Child's Christmas in Wales* (published 1954). His play, *Under Milk Wood* is a striking drama, characterized as "a fantastic, funny, exuberant celebration of one spring night and a day in a Welsh sea-town." He became even more famous through his readings and recordings in the U.S. and his broadcasts for the BBC. He enjoyed his success and lived recklessly until his early death. BIBLIOGRAPHY: S. Fraser, *Dylan Thomas* (1957); J. P. Clancy, NCE 14:125–126.

[S. A. HEENEY]

THOMAS, ACTS OF, see APOCRYPHA (NT), 63.

THOMAS, APOCALYPSE OF, see APOCRYPHA (NT), 64.

THOMAS, GOSPEL OF, see APOCRYPHA (NT), 65.

THOMAS CHRISTIANS, see ST. THOMAS CHRISTIANS.

THOMAS SUNDAY, see ANTIPASCHA.

THOMASIUS, CHRISTIAN (1655–1728), German jurist, leading naturalist, philosopher in the *Enlightenment, yet also the philosopher of *Pietism. He began his teaching career at Leipzig in 1682; in this phase of his thought he defended the absolute independence of reason from dogma, of philosophy from theology, and the subordination in the practical sphere of Church to State. Such views, anathema to orthodox or scholastic Lutheranism, forced his departure in 1690 from Leipzig to Halle, where the Prussian government was more favorable. He founded the Univ. of Halle in 1693, taught law there for the remainder of his life, and served as rector. In 1694, in part from association with A. *Francke the Pietist leader, in part from a siege of intellectual despair, T. became a Pietist. His opposition to Lutheran scholasticism, to episcopal *polity, to dogmatic creeds, as well as his views on the absolute need of grace for true knowledge or upright living and the mysticism of his metaphysics, made his ideas an accepted norm for Pietism. His influence led to Pietist domination in the universities of Germany until the ascendancy of C. *Wolff's system a generation later. T.'s works reflecting his pre-Pietist thought are his *Introductio ad philosophiam aulicam* (1688), a system of education for those entering royal service; introductions to logic, *Einleitung zu der Vernunft-Lehre* (1691) and to ethics, *Einleitung zur Sitten-Lehre* (1692), and other texts in both subjects. These vernacular works, as well as his lecture practice, brought about abandonment of Latin in university courses. T.'s writings from this period all advocate an agnosticism about metaphysics, a purely pragmatic evaluation of philosophical learning. The Pietist phase is expressed in his *Confessio doctrinae suae* (1695), a kind of repudiation of past error, and the *Versuch vom Wesen des Geistes* (1699), the statement of his mystical, vitalistic metaphysics. T.'s name is important as well to the study of law, esp. for his theory of a basic, rationally perceptible and immutable natural law and for his ideas on tolerance and on state supremacy. Among his representative works on law are: *Institutiones jurisprudentiae divinae* (1688); *De jure principis circa adiaphora* (1695); *Vindiciae juris majestatis circa sacra* (1701); *Fundamenta juris naturae et gentium ex sensu communi deducta* (1705).

[T. C. O'BRIEN]

THOMASIUS, GOTTFRIED (1802–75), German Lutheran theologian of the *Erlangen School. His Christology proposed that the *Logos* emptied himself of his divinity in the Incarnation (see KENOSIS). T.'s *Christi Person und Werk* (3 v. 1852–61) was the first Lutheran church dogmatics of the 19th century.

[T. C. O'BRIEN]

THOMASSIN (LOUIS D'EYNAC; 1619–95), French Oratorian theologian, important to the RC development of historical (positive) theology. He taught at Saumur and at Paris. His published works include: *Dogmatica theologica* (3v., 1680–89); *Traites historiques et dogmatiques sur divers points de la discipline de l'Eglise et de la morale chrétienne* (7v., 1680–97).

[T. C. O'BRIEN]

THOMISM, a blanket term for a body of philosophical and theological convictions set forth by Thomas Aquinas in the 13th cent. and since developed and variously stressed by numerous disciples. The whole is represented: sometimes as a fixed system, deductively complete, virtually closed, and requiring only explicitation in the light of fresh factual information; sometimes as an assemblage of conclusions most of which are acceptable within their frame of reference; sometimes as an organic unity open to further syntheses and homogeneous evolution. Hence the division between juridical, eclectic, and true-blue Thomists. Further subdivision is possible; thus the first include those who repeat their master rabbinically, who treat him as dwelling in a world of essences, ontological, aloof, and intricately divisible, who are devoted to him as a subject in medieval history or archeology, or who use his teachings mainly for administrative needs; the second applaud a prodigious pioneer effort, but in greater or lesser degree replace elements of his construction from elsewhere; the third include cerebral metaphysicians of a Spanish temper, semineoplatonists, and existentialists more in sympathy with the contemporary flux. These interests can be disentangled only rather tentatively, for the living history of Thomism is that of their intertwining. Curiously only the first and second treat their cause as a system; the third are uncomfortable under the name, and paradoxically it is on them that this article concentrates.

Their thought does not develop geometrically but follows the analogies implied by the singleness in variety of being and supplied by exuberant human experience. It is accepted without shrug or apology that the half-real is real, the not wholly perfect sufficiently perfect—jejune phrases that suggest a rare quality for a metaphysician, not, of course, for one who comes to terms with the world on a lower level. The notion of "being potential" is taken to a height and depth only faintly prophesied by Aristotle. God alone is the purely actual; the inference is not drawn, however, that he is the all and only; instead it is because of his infinite transcendence that he can produce other real beings. Creatures are things in themselves, though not from or for themselves. The metaphysics of creation, which lies at the heart of Thomism and is its greatest contribution to Christian thought, is explicated by the distinction between essence and existence, and ramifies into all its characteristic teachings: the reality of matter, of individual things, and of secondary principal causes. Univocation is not possible for discourse about pluralism at this depth, and metaphor is not enough, unless it be sublimated in philosophical analogy. And so this becomes the central method and explains the constant burdens in Thomism, of distinguishing in order the

reunite, of being chary about an "either-or" and preferring the "both-and."

Thomism is primarily a theology, though this cannot be understood without its philosophy. It is possible, however, to perform an excision, and to take the philosophy without the theology; in fact this has been accepted by many thinkers who have not shared the beliefs of Roman Catholics or even Christians. Such a philosophy stands as complete as any purely rationalist or humanist account of the world can be expected to be. Accordingly we indicate: first, some of the philosophical principles in Thomism; second, some consequences when they are lifted up into theology. The customary apparatus used is the logic of Aristotle. By induction (which here means an abstractive insight rather than an inductive argument) from sense experience, reasoning proceeds deductively from effect to cause, and vice versa. Physical substances are essentially composed of matter and form, but this hylomorphism is not applied to spiritual substances. Man is a psycho-physical unity, and the embarrassments for the doctrine of the immortality of soul that it is the single substantial form of the body are candidly faced. Moral philosophy is eudaemonistic, directed toward human happiness. The epistemology is one of direct realism, free from the correspondence theory of Descartes.

The development is continuous from philosophy into a theology that is rooted in this world but open to and vivified by the word of God. It observes a tidal movement of ebb and flow from creatures and the creator. Yet though the world shows forth his glory, and Thomism is committed to a demonstrable theism, carefully steering its course by the aid of analogy between anthropomorphism and agnosticism, or even the old *theologia negativa,* its theology is set above all on God for himself, not as the integrator of the universe. His grace is a sheer gift beyond the rights of human nature, yet offers no violence to it. The harmony of grace and nature, faith and reason—and, it may be added, of *agape* and inborn appetites—is a major theme: it was composed under the stresses of the double truth controversy from which Thomism was born. A supplementary theme is the intrinsic efficaciousness of divine grace: the phrase dates from the great debates on predestination in the century following the Reformation (see CONGREGATIO DE AUXILIIS). Free will is seen as operating within God's universal causality with respect to all existence and action from beginning to end, and as contributing nothing that is entirely the creature's own except sin. Thomists were called Jansenists, yet with as little truth they might have been called Pelagians. It is noteworthy how unanxious was the spirituality that fed on their doctrine of grace, and how full of a joyous abandon to the will of God. Their moral theology remained comparatively immune from the legalisms that dominated the age of casuistry; to be happy rather than to be dutiful is man's final purpose, and duty itself is more a matter of equity than of a code.

The whole is very ordered and strangely open, and the tightening of Thomism into a closely knit school occurred only a century or more after the master's death; once again it is now loosening out, and with no real loss of continuity and identity. Its history may be outlined under four periods, high medieval, late medieval, Renaissance and Baroque, and post-Vatican I: each era with its catalogue of noble names. Three years to the day after his death in 1274, Thomas was condemned by ecclesiastical authority, in effect for making the human spirit too soil-bound. His old master, Albert the Great, rallied to his support, and he was followed by young Dominicans, notably in England and France. Though they secured the backing of the order, got the condemnation quashed and Thomas himself canonized by the first quarter of the 14th cent., they were too independent, too engaged in forming their own minds, and too close to him to treat him as an oracle and form a school in the narrow sense of the word. But they were men who knew where their intellectual loyalties lay and were fighting for the same cause. In fact, in those early years the name of Albert was as potent as that of Thomas, and in Germany the stream of Neoplatonism ran strong, where, as in Meister Eckhart, the movement might well be called Albertino-Thomism.

After the Black Death the medieval universities became more stiff and sectarian in their ways, and Thomism became but one of several schools in the same league, each staffed by members of the same religious order, the Franciscans being the most versatile, since they could be Augustinians, Scotists, or Ockamists. A more classical glow came with the opening of the 16th cent.; it moved from the Italy of Cardinal Cajetan to the Rhineland, and Louvain, and settled in Spain. Teachers such as Francisco de Vitoria, Domingo de Soto, Domingo Báñez, and John of St. Thomas are part of the imperial glory of that country. In an earlier age Francisco de Suárez would have been called a Thomist, but not then, when even Thomism was sometimes called *Báñezianism. With the decline of the Spanish Empire it lingered like an elderly don in a cloister, and was all but destroyed at the French Revolution. But it formed the core for the revival of scholasticism under Leo XIII in the later half of the 19th cent. and grew to become the quasi-official philosophy and theology for ecclesiastical power, so much so indeed that there were times when a Thomist who was a yogi rather than a commissar could have wished that the *Summa* might be put on the Index in order that its thought might be freed from such bureaucracy. Fortunately times have changed; Thomism has survived both the patronage and the manuals of instruction that accompanied it, and is now weathering the storms partly occasioned by them both. BIBLIOGRAPHY: É. Gilson, *Christian Philosophy of St. Thomas Aquinas* (tr. L. K. Shook, 1956); *idem, Spirit of Thomism* (1964); J. A. Weisheipl, NCE 14:126–135, with bibliog.

[T. GILBY]

THOMISM, TRANSCENDENTAL, a 20th-cent. philosophical approach which seeks to affirm the classical insights of Thomas Aquinas through analyzing the implications of human understanding. Among its proponents are some of the leading RC philosophers-theologians of this century: Bernard Lonergan, Karl Rahner, Maurice Blondel, Josef Maréchal, and Emerich Coreth. The approach owes much to I. Kant: "I call every knowledge transcendental, which occupies itself not so much with objects, but rather with our way of knowing objects insofar as this is to be possible a priori." Thus transcendental Thomism is a way of reflecting upon the previous or a priori conditions for the very possibility of any act of knowledge; it is an attempt to understand understanding by examining the operations of the conscious subject. Such an analysis reveals an unlimited horizon within which all knowledge of finite objects proceeds. Thus, absolute being is the implicit term in every act of human knowing and willing. Such conclusions pave the way for the religious standing-before absolute being as the culmination of human existence and "define" human beings as hearers of the word, i.e., as awaiting in history a possible word of revelation. BIBLIOGRAPHY: O. Muck, *Transcendental Method* (1968); B. Lonergan, *Insight: An Enquiry into Human Understanding* (1957); K. Rahner, *Hearers of the Word* (1969); E. Coreth, *Metaphysics* (1968); W. J. Hill, *Knowing the Unknown God* (1971) 59–88; *idem*, NCE 16:449–454.

[T. M. MCFADDEN]

THOMIST THESES, the 24 theses approved by the Sacred Congregation of Studies (July 27, 1914) as expressing the basic principles of Thomistic philosophy prescribed by *Doctoris angelici* of Pope Pius X (June 29, 1914). Without excluding other interpretations of St. Thomas, the same Congregation stated (March 17, 1916) that these 24 theses are true to his philosophy and are proposed as safe and directive norms. Benedict XV decided (*Quod de fovenda*, March 19, 1917) that not all the theses need be held so long as they are proposed as safe and directive. BIBLIOGRAPHY: AAS 6 (1914) 383–386; D 3601–24; J. A. Weisheipl, NCE 12:1168, s.v. "Scholasticism 3."

[J. H. ROHLING]

THOMPSON, FRANCIS (1859–1907), English poet and essayist. His father was a convert to Catholicism through Henry Edward Manning. Starving in London, having attempted suicide, he was befriended by Wilfred Meynell, to whose magazine *Merrie England* he had sent a poem. Alice Meynell's kindness to him was repaid by his finest verse in *Poems* (1893), published by the Meynells. This volume was praised by Coventry Patmore. *Sister Songs* (1895) and *New Poems* (1897) confirm his strange inventiveness in diction. His poetry is intensely religious, sometimes verbose, and sentimental, but he can be very simple as in "The Daisy." His best-known poem is "The Hound of Heaven" with its magnificent image of pursuit of the soul by Christ. He wrote some biographical essays and a treatise on the ascetic life, *Health and Holiness*. BIBLIOGRAPHY: P. van K. Thomson,

Francis Thompson (1961); J. C. Reid, *Francis Thompson: Man and Poet* (1960).

[M. M. BARRY]

THOMPSON, WILLIAM (1733–99), first President of the Wesleyan Methodists of England after the death of John *Wesley (1791). T. was born at Fermanagh, Ireland, and became a Methodist preacher in 1756. A sound administrator, in 1795 he drew up the Plan of Pacification, which settled the question of the relationship between the Methodists and the Church of England.

[F. E. MASER]

THOREAU, HENRY (1817–62), American essayist, poet, and naturalist. A graduate of Harvard (1837), he taught in his brother's school (1837–41). T. became a very close friend of Ralph Waldo Emerson and lived for some time in his home, supporting himself on the wages of a man of all work. He also helped Emerson to edit *The Dial*, the organ of of the Transcendentalists. In addition he earned some money by surveying. In 1845 T. built a cabin for himself on the shore of Walden Pond, near Concord, where he lived for more than two years, on very little money. He sought an existence that was "free from the world, concentrated, and simple." *Walden; or Life in the Woods"* (1854), his best-known book and a classic, relates an account of his life at Walden Pond. His purpose was to write, but he found difficulty in attracting a reading public. He himself had to publish *A Week on the Concord and Merrimack Rivers* (1849) and had 706 copies returned by the publisher. The only other book published in his lifetime was *Walden*. BIBLIOGRAPHY: H. D. Thoreau, *Writings* (ed. B. Torrey and F. B. Sanborn, 20 v., 1960); F. O. Matthiessen, *American Renaissance* (1941); W. Harding, *Days of Henry Thoreau* (1965).

[S. A. HEENEY]

THORGILSSON, ARI (1067–1148), Icelandic historian. T. was educated at Haukadalr and ordained. Only one of his works is extant, a short history of Iceland from *c*.870 to 1120, which may have been produced in connection with the establishment of ecclesiastical law in 1125. He was the first to employ Icelandic for scholarly writing. BIBLIOGRAPHY: A. Salvesen, NCE 1:790–791.

[M. J. SUELZER]

THORLÁK THÓRHALLSSON, ST. (1133–1193), monk; bp. of Skálholt (1178–93). A canon regular of St. Augustine, T. was educated in Iceland, France, and England, then became superior of a house of his order until elected bp. of Skálholt (1174), and consecrated four years later. Like many others, the bp. asserted the rights of the Church and objected to encroachments by the State; again, like many, not always successfully. Regarded locally as a saint, his cult after his death was confined to Iceland. BIBLIOGRAPHY: Butler 4:602–603; *Book of Saints* (compiled by

the Benedictine Monks of St. Augustine's Abbey, 1966); H. Bekker-Nielsen, NCE 14:140; H. Bekker-Nielsen and O. Widding, BiblSanct 12:458–459.

[M. E. DUFFY]

THORN, COLLOQUY OF, a conference held in Thorn, W Prussia, in 1545, under the auspices of King Vladislav IV of Poland and aimed at religious peace (*colloquium caritativum*). Roman Catholic, Lutheran, and *Reformed theologians participated, but factions and divisions made the meeting a failure. It is notable for contributing to the syncretistic controversy, esp. because of the opposition between the Lutherans A. *Calov and G. *Calixt (see SYNCRETISM), and for a Reformed declaration of faith drawn up by the Reformed theologians and later adopted by some Reformed Churches. This declaration strongly asserts agreement in faith with the early creeds and councils. BIBLIOGRAPHY: Schaff Creeds 1:560–563.

[P. DAMBORIENA]

THORN IN THE FLESH, the vivid, yet enigmatic, symbol of affliction mentioned briefly by Paul during an intriguing self-revelation found in 2 Cor 12.1–10. Obliged to boast in order to defend his credentials against detractors, Paul writes first of "visions and revelations granted by the Lord." He apparently is referring to an experience 14 years before when he was "caught up as far as the third heaven . . . into paradise," where he "heard words so secret that human lips may not repeat them." To keep him from being inflated by the magnificence of such revelations, he was given "a thorn in the flesh which came as Satan's messenger to bruise him." He begged the Lord three times to rid him of it but received the answer, "My grace is all you need; power comes to its full strength in weakness." In order that the power of Christ might be an abiding thing in him, he learned to be content "with weakness, contempt, persecution, hardship, and frustration." The phrase, "thorn in the flesh," conjures up a very physical image and indeed has provoked commentators to imagine a variety of chronic physical afflictions for Paul. It is curious to note that Paul himself ends the account with a list of external afflictions encountered during his missionary efforts. But that may be his way of turning attention away from a physical ailment that was still a source of shame as well as physical pain. This would not be untypical of Paul's enigmatic style of self-revelation, which conceals while it reveals.

[E. J. DILLON]

THORNEY, ABBEY OF, former Benedictine monastery of St. Mary and St. Botulph, earlier known as Ancarig, in the Diocese of Ely (formerly Lincoln), Cambridgeshire, England. It was founded *c*.972 by Ethelwold of Winchester and King Edgar the Peaceful, on the site of a hermitage whose origins may date from King Sebert (604) and Abbot Saxulph (*c*.662), and which was destroyed by the Danes in 870. Nine Saxon saints are buried there. The abbey was known for its active scriptorium and its special school of calligraphy. Its first abbot was Godeman. Renovations occurred under Abbot Gunther (1085–1112) and again under Abbot David in the 13th century. It was suppressed in 1539. The nave of the abbey church continued in use as a parish church. BIBLIOGRAPHY: Cottineau 2:3153.

[E. J. DILLON]

THOROUGH BASS, see FIGURED BASS.

THOTH, Egyptian god of number and measure and, finally, of all writing and language. From him came laws, ritual, and medical prescriptions, and all sorts of mysterious knowledge. He is often a moon god, but his characteristic form is that of a man with an ibis head. In his best–known representation he stands in the Hall of Judgment tabulating the results of the weighing of the dead person's heart against justice. The Greeks identified him with Hermes. BIBLIOG - RAPHY: H. Bonnet, *Reallexikon der ägyptischen Religionsgeschichte* (1952) 805–812.

[A. CODY]

THOURET, JOAN ANTIDA, ST. (1765–1826), French foundress of the Sisters of Charity of St. Joan Antida. Having joined the Daughters of Charity in Paris in 1787, Joan was compelled to return home after the dispersal of religious communities caused by the French Revolution. After the fall of Robespierre, she entered a new Congregation of Charity in Switzerland and for 2 years shared this group's hardships. In 1799, she went to Besançon and founded there a school for poor girls and a hospital. Soon joined by other young women, Joan Antida founded a religious institute, whose rules and constitutions were approved by the archbishop of Besançon. The work of her institute soon spread to Italy through the generosity of the mother of Napoleon. However, her devotion to the Holy See and the approval of her congregation by Pope Pius VII in 1819, resulted in bitter opposition to her and her institute from the Gallican-oriented clergy of Besançon. She died at the Regina Coeli convent in Naples and was buried there. Joan Antida was beatified on May 23, 1926, and canonized on Jan. 14, 1934.

[T. J. RYAN]

THREAT, a declaration of intent to inflict some loss, pain, penalty, or damage in retribution for or conditionally upon some course of action. Its rightness or wrongness will depend on both sides: the competence of the utterer to back up a command by such a menace, and the nature of the project entertained by the one open to it. Good laws are to be obeyed, and if need be enforced, but there should be a proportion between their importance and their sanction; and to threaten an evil beyond one's authority is an unjust aggression. Then also, though the consequences of a good course of action may be some deprivation, nobody has the right to impose the painful pressure of its anticipation as a dissuasion.

[T. GILBY]

THREE CHAPTERS, Justinian's edict of 544, condemning the pro-Nestorian positions of *Theodore of Mopsuestia and his works, *Theodoret of Cyr writing against *Cyril of Alexandria, and *Ibas of Edessa in his letter to Maris. Later the term Three Chapters came to signify these condemned opinions together with those who defended them. Justinian was convinced by *Theodore Ascidas, a Monophysite and an Origenist, that by condemning these pro-Nestorians and their writings, he could win over the powerful Monophysite faction. Pope *Vigilius vacillated in approving the edict because the Western bps. considered this to be detrimental to the Council of *Chalcedon, but under pressure from the Emperor, he issued his *Iudicatum* of 448, condemning the Three Chapters and upholding Chalcedon. Amid strong protest from the West, he retracted this statement. In 553, the Council of Constantinople II condemned the Three Chapters at the direction of Justinian. In 554, Vigilius approved the council's action in his decree *Constitutum* and his successor, Pelagius I, agreed. This resulted in a serious schism in Africa and Italy which ended under Sergius I (687–701) with the reconciliation of Aquileia. BIBLIOGRAPHY: É. Amann, DTC 15.2:1868–1924; Bihlmeyer-Tüchle 1:292–295.

[F. H. BRIGHAM]

THREE CHILDREN, the companions of Daniel who miraculously survived the ordeal of the fiery furnace after refusing to worship the king of Babylon's idol. The deuterocanonical "hymn of the three men" (Dan 3.52–90a) is inspired by this episode. BIBLIOGRAPHY: F. Zorell, "Canticum trium juvenum (Dan 3:52–90)," *Verbum Domini* 1 (1921) 296–299; C. Kuhl, *Die drei Männer im Feuer* (1930). *SHADRACH, MESHACH, ABEDNEGO.

[D. J. BOURKE]

THREE HOLY HIERARCHS, in the Byzantine liturgy a special title honoring SS. Basil, John Chrysostom, and Gregory the Theologian (Nazianzus), the three holy hierarchs or bishops, who lived in the 4th century. In the 11th cent., a dispute arose as to which of the three was the greatest. The question was ended when according to legend the three appeared to a holy bishop and told him that they were equal in glory and asked that a single day, Jan. 30, be assigned when all Christians would honor them together.

[A. MOHRBACHER]

THREE HOURS (*Tre Ore*), the devout practice popular in some places of spending the hours between noon and 3 P.M. on Good Friday in meditation upon the passion of Christ. In some churches it has been customary to hold public services during those hours, with discourses upon the seven last words of Christ and the Stations of the Cross. In many places the practice has been discontinued since the publication of Pius XII's Holy Week Ordinal (1956) because it would distract from the proper observance of the restored rites. The devotion appears to have been started by the Jesuits in Lima, Peru, in 1687. The duration of three hours is based on a reconciling of Mk 15 and Jn 19.

[M. F. MCNAMARA]

THREE MARYS, the three women who, in the Johannine account, stood near the cross where Jesus hung crucified (Jn 19.25–26). Their names according to this account were: Mary, the mother of Jesus; her sister Mary, wife of Clopas; Mary of Magdala. There are discrepancies between this and the Markan account, which has been followed with minor variations by Luke and Matthew. According to Mark (15.40–41) there were many women "looking on from afar," who had followed him when he was in Galilee, ministered to him, and had come up with him to Jerusalem. Mark singles out by name Mary Magdalene, Mary the mother of James the Younger and of Joses, and Salome. Some of them must still have been keeping vigil when Joseph of Arimathea came to take the body of Jesus for burial, because Mary Magdalene and Mary the mother of Joses saw where he was laid (Mark 15.47). When the Sabbath was past, Mary Magdalene, Mary, mother of James, and Salome bought spices and went early to the tomb to anoint the body (Mark 16.1). Matthew mentions the mother of the sons of Zebedee in place of Salome at the crucifixion; he mentions only Mary Magdalene and "the other Mary" observing the place of burial and the coming after the Sabbath to anoint the body (Mt 27.55–56, 61; 28.1). Luke, perhaps conscious of discrepancies, omits names throughout the account until the actual reporting of the fact of the empty tomb to the Apostles. He then mentions that it was Mary Magdalene and Joanna and Mary the mother of James and the other women with them who brought the report (Lk 24.10).

[E. J. DILLON]

THREE STUDIES FOR A CRUCIFIXION, powerful, climactic work (1962) by Francis Bacon (1910-   ), most important Irish-born figure painter in the British Isles. A series of studies on the Crucifixion theme produced the famous *Magdalene* (1945–46), the solid figure, bent double, rooted in Giotto, a weird animal form with mouth opened in an unending wail of grief (recalling Masaccio's *Expulsion, c.*1425), revealing Bacon's superb painting and strong sense of tradition. He transforms masterworks of the past into monstrous, deformed interpretations of the present world. In 1950 the *Portrait of Pope Innocent X* by Velasquez inspired a "Pope" series which, despite its horrifying impact, evidences B.'s beautiful painting and grandeur of conception. In the 1962 triptych (a framework suggesting the traditional altarpiece), *Three Studies for a Crucifixion*

(each panel 6 ft by 6 in by 4ft 9 in) with sides of beef (deriving from Rembrandt through Soutine), appearing heraldicly on the wings in Bacon's large space, the central nude. Within the secret room (windows shaded) a bleeding cadaver could suggest beatings to death in concentration camps or other monstrous ravages of man—Crucifixions for our time.

[M. J. DALY]

THRONE, in the Old and New Testaments the proper and formal seat of a ruler, whether human or divine, and of those who share power and honor with him (2 Kg 3.10; Mt 5.34; Rev 3.21;4.4). It also signifies in later Christian literature the elevated chair of a bishop, esp. at a liturgical function, or figuratively, in either sense, the power or dignity that the occupant of the seat possesses.

[E. A. WEIS]

THRONE, EPISCOPAL, a fixed seat of honor, with chair, steps, and canopy, in the sanctuary of cathedral and abbey churches. It may be occupied only by the ordinary of a diocese, a cardinal or abbot, in their own respective jurisdictions.

[J. R. AHERNE]

THRONE NAME, the name given to a king upon his accession to the throne. It is not known to what extent this ancient Near Eastern custom, still in vogue in papal tradition, was followed by the kings of Israel or Juda. The Egyptians certainly seem to have imposed the custom when Pharaoh Neco made Josiah's son, Eliakim, king in place of his father and gave him the name Jehoiakim (2 Kg 23.34). The Babylonians seem to have done the same when Nebuchadnezzar deported Jehoiachin to Babylon and made his uncle Mattaniah king in his place, giving him the name Zedekiah (2 Kg 24.17). The custom may not have been previously unknown in Juda. It is even intriguing to speculate that David may be the throne name of the hero Elhanan, who is cited in 2 Sm 21.19 as the warrior from Bethlehem who slew Goliath.

[E. J. DILLON]

THRONES, one of classes of angelic beings named in the Pauline writings. Colossians 1.16 reads: "For in him were created all things . . . whether Thrones or Dominations. . ." BIBLIOGRAPHY: O. Schmitz, Kittel TD 3:160–167; Arndt-Gingrich 364–365.

[E. A. WEIS]

THUILLIER, VINCENT (1685–1736), French Benedictine. After being director of novices and subprior, T. was called to continue the work of J. *Mabillon. He at first supported Jansenism and opposed *Unigenitus*, but *c.*1723 began actively to defend the bull. He also labored to restore harmony among the pope, the king, and the Maurists. BIB-LIOGRAPHY: G. Heer, LTK 10:173.

[M. J. SUELZER]

THUNDERING LEGION, a name given to the Roman Twelfth Legion. A story credited by some early Christian writers (Tertullian, Eusebius, Apollinaris of Hierapolis, and others) traces the title to an event that occurred miraculously in answer to the prayer of its Christian legionaries. In A.D. 174 the legion was engaged, under Marcus Aurelius, in a campaign against the Quadi in a land seared at the time by drought. The legion was exhausted by thirst and in peril from the enemy when a sudden thunderstorm saved the day by bringing water and frightening off the barbarians. A letter of the Emperor to the Senate gave credit to the Christians, whose further persecution he had forbidden by decree, and he bestowed the title *fulminata (fulminea, fulminatrix)* upon the legion. No doubt some storm did help the Romans, perhaps decisively, in the campaign, for such an event is pictured on the Antonine Column in Rome. But the Emperor's letter to the Senate, appended to the *Apology* of Justin, is admittedly a later interpolation, and it is an established fact that no change occurred in the Roman policy of persecution at that time. The pagan Dio Cassius attributed the "miracle" to the incantations of an Egyptian magician named Arnuphis and to prayers addressed to Hermes. He also claimed that the title went back beyond the event in time, for even in the reign of Augustus the shields of the legion were marked with the device of Jupiter brandishing the thunderbolt. BIBLIOGRAPHY: M. Ott, CE 14:711; A. Amore, EncCatt: 7:1073–74.

[R. B. ENO]

THUREAU-DANGIN, JEAN GENEVIÈVE FRANÇOIS, (1872–1944), French Assyriologist. During his long association with the Louvre, he authored many works dealing with the writing, history, religion, and mathematics of Babylonia, including many volumes of the *Textes cunéiformes du Louvre* (1910–32), *Rituels accadiens* (1921), and *Textes mathématiques babyloniens* (1938). With Vincent Scheil, he served as one of the directors and principal contributors to the *Revue d'assyriologie et d'archéologie orientale* from 1910 until his death and was involved in the excavations of and the publications of the inscriptions from Tell Ahmar and Arslan Tash in Syria (1927–31). His greatest contributions were in the first publication of a large corpus of unilingual Sumerian historical texts in transliteration and translation, *Les Inscriptions de Sumer et d'Accad* (1905), and in the establishment of a standard method for transliterating cuneiform characters into Roman letters, *Le Syllabaire accadien* (1926) and *Les Homophones sumériens* (1929). BIBLIOGRAPHY: J. A. Brinkman, NCE 14:147.

[T. J. RYAN]

THURIBLE, see CENSER.

THURIFER, (Lat., incense, *t(h)ūs*; bearer, *ferre*), in the Roman liturgy, the minister who carries the thurible or censer. The thurible is a small metal pot suspended on chains, in which is placed lighted charcoal for burning incense during Mass and some other liturgical functions.

[J. DALLEN]

THURIFICATI, a class of *lapsi* seeking reconciliation after having offered incense (Lat. *thus, thuris*) to pagan gods because of the persecution of Christians during the reign of Decius (249–251). BIBLIOGRAPHY: *LIBELLATICI; *SACRIFICATI.

[T. C. O'BRIEN]

THURMAYR, JOHANNES, see AVENTINUS.

THURSTAN OF YORK (d. 1140), abp. of York. Son of a married priest, T. succeeded to the See of York in 1114, but his unwillingness to subordinate himself to Canterbury prevented his taking possession of his see until 1121. As abp. he fostered the development of the Augustinian Canons and the Cistercians in his territory, established the Carlisle diocese (1133), enjoyed some reputation as an ascetic and spiritual director, and actively promoted the resistance to the Scots that culminated in the Battle of the Standard (1138). BIBLIOGRAPHY: D. Nicholl, *Thurstan, Archbishop of York* (1964); *idem.,* NCE 14:147; Knowles MOE 230–239.

[J. L. GRASSI]

THURSTON, HERBERT (1856–1939), English Jesuit hagiographer and apologist. A Jesuit from 1874, ordained in 1890, he spent his career from 1894 as a member of the staff of the periodical, *The Month*. For it he wrote over 700 pieces; he also contributed more than 100 entries for the *Catholic Encyclopedia*. Through these publications and above all by his revision of Butler's *Lives of the Saints* (4 v., 1926–38; repr. 1977), T. earned his reputation as the most critical and scientifically exacting historical and hagiographical writer of the English-speaking Church. His apologetic writing was particularly directed against spiritualism, in vogue during his lifetime. Posthumously published were some of his works on psychic phenomena as compared to spiritual and mystical phenomena proper to the life of grace.

THUTMOSE III (1490–36 B.C.), the pharaoh of the Eighteenth Dynasty of Egypt who established on a firm foundation the Egyptian military, political, and economic hegemony in the neighboring Asian lands of Canaan, Phoenicia, and Syria. T. came to power in the wake of the successful Egyptian expulsion of the Hyksos, the Asiatic foreigners who had until then exercized dominance in Egypt. There was a surging of nationalist spirit which found expression under T.'s reign in military imperialism. Not content with cultural superiority and traditional Egyptian preeminence in trade, in all he led 17 military campaigns into Asia. The various towns and principalities of Syria and Palestine formed a far-flung coalition against Egypt, the like of which they would never again quite manage to duplicate despite recurrent attempts. They were no match for T.'s Egyptian forces. The leading city of the confederation was Kadesh on the Orontes in Syria. His enemies' place of muster was the Canaanite town of Megiddo in the Valley of Jezreel. When T. defeated them, he stripped them of their horses and chariots, the produce of their harvests, and other possessions; he forced them to take an oath of fealty to the Egyptian pharaoh. T. demonstrated his administrative genius in setting up the apparatus of the Asian empire, establishing resident garrisons throughout the provinces, appointing Egyptian high commissioners, and setting up a courier service which made for an effective communications network. Thus, the cedar groves of Lebanon became an Egyptian preserve; there is record of his finding sport in an elephant hunt in the marshes of Syria; the famed Mediterranean ports were available for Egyptian exploitation. The pharaoh maintained local princes on their thrones, but took their sons and brothers to Egypt to be brought up at the Egyptian court. There they served first as hostages and later became the kind of successors to the provincial thrones who would be loyal to Egypt and wedded to Egyptian culture. T.'s fame endured in Syria for a century, and in Egypt his throne name gave magical authority to scarabs for a millennium.

[E. J. DILLON]

THYATIRA, city of west Asia Minor, in Lydia. It was the home of Paul's convert Lydia (Acts 16.14), and one of the seven Churches addressed in Revelation (2.18–29).

[T. EARLY]

THYMIATERION, Greek term (Sl. *kadilo*) for the vessel in which incense is burned during liturgical services. The bowl is usually smaller than the Western thurible and the chains are considerably shorter. It is swung at full length rather than doubled up in front as in Western fashion. The Russians leave the censer plain, but the Greeks ornament the chains by attaching 12 small silver bells symbolizing the Apostles. The censer is often made in the shape of a small church surmounted by a cross. The Oriental form and the method of holding and swinging it are very ancient and once were prevalent in the West. During the liturgy it is the deacon who usually performs the incensation. The name is also applied to a smaller censer that has a small handle instead of chains. It is used chiefly in Greek homes before the holy icons. This form was used in ancient Egypt as well as in Christian times.

[A. J. JACOPIN]

THYRAUS, HERMANN (1532–91), German Jesuit received (1556) while a professor at Rome by St. Ignatius Loyola; professor and preacher in Germany; author of *Con-*

fessio Augustana (1567), an apologetic critique of the *Augsburg Confession.

[T. C. O'BRIEN]

TIARA, the tall, beehive-shaped headdress, or triple crown, worn by the pope at his coronation and on such other solemn occasions as processions and public pronouncement of dogmas, as an emblem of his princely power to teach, to rule, and to sanctify. It is to be distinguished from the episcopal miter which is worn during the performance of liturgical functions. The tiara proper developed out of the simple white Phrygian cap adopted during the 7th or 8th cent.; in the 10th or 11th, the headpiece was stiffened and a single diadem placed around it; the two lappets, or pendanta, attached to the rear probably appeared in the 13th. Under Boniface VIII (1294–1303), a second coronet was added, while by 1315, still a third one formed part of the vestment. The tiara assumed its final shape and costly, jewel-encrusted character during the Renaissance. Paul VI gave the tiara to Card. Spellman; it is on display at the National Shrine in Washington, D.C., and visitors contribute to the work of Mother Theresa of Calcutta. Pope John Paul I and Pope John Paul II did not have a coronation.

[E. M. GATES]

TIBERIAS, city on the west shore of the Sea of Galilee; modern et-Tabariyeh. Named for Tiberius Caesar, it was built by Herod Antipas (*c*.25 A.D.) as the capital of his tetrarchy of Galilee and Perea. It is mentioned only once in the NT (Jn 6.23). A Gentile city in Jesus' time, it later became a Jewish center where the Palestinian *Talmud was developed. The name was sometimes also given to the Sea of Galilee (Jn 6.1; 21.1).

[T. EARLY]

TIBERIUS II, BYZANTINE EMPEROR from 578–582. A pleasant, extravagant ruler, T. was no religious fanatic, yet he allowed the continuation of the persecution of the Monophysites that had begun under his predecessor, Justin II. Yielding to the demands of public opinion in Constantinople, he authorized repressive measures against Arians as an expression of anti-Germanic sentiment. His patriarch, Eutychius (552–565; 577–582), engaged in theological controversy with St. *Gregory the Great, then the papal representative in the capital. Tiberius, asked to moderate the debate, sided with Gregory. BIBLIOGRAPHY: J. B. Bury, *History of the Later Roman Empire* (2 v., 1889); G. Every, *Byzantine Patriarchate, 451–1204* (1947); F. H. Dudden, *Gregory the Great* (2 v., repr. 1967).

[R. H. SCHMANDT]

TIBERIUS III, BYZANTINE EMPEROR from 698–705. He rose to power in a military coup against *Justinian II. During his own reign T. suffered the loss of much territory to the Arabs, esp. in N Africa. He himself was overthrown in turn by Justinian and was executed. T. was at odds with the papacy as he tried to enforce the decrees of the *Quinisext Council, but a degree of reconciliation was achieved through the efforts of Pope John VI.

[T. C. O'BRIEN]

TIBERIUS CLAUDIUS NERO (42 B.C.–A.D. 37), **ROMAN EMPEROR**, stepson, adopted son, son-in-law, and successor of Augustus in A.D. 14. After a brilliant military career, T., piqued by Augustus' preference for his direct descendants as potential heirs, withdrew to Rhodes in 6 B.C. and returned to Rome only in A.D. 2. Of an austere, difficult, and obscure temperament, T. was misunderstood by his contemporaries and by later historians, notably Tacitus, who interpreted all he did in a sinister light. As Emperor he followed in general the program of Augustus but with greater economies and the refusal of any form of divine honor. His reign was marred by revolts of the legions, numerous trials for treason, and his withdrawal under the influence of Sejanus to Capreae (Capri) in A.D. 26. Though little credit should be attached to the tales of debauchery circulated about his life, he may well have been somewhat demented during his last years. BIBLIOGRAPHY: F. B. Marsh, *Reign of Tiberius* (1959).

[M. J. COSTELLOE]

TIBET, country of central Asia (470,000 sq. mi.; pop. est., 1976, 2,000,000). Intermittently controlled by China for 12 centuries, Tibet was completely absorbed by Communist China in 1959. It is now officially known as Tibet Region and Chamdo (Changtu) Area. Its religion is Lamaism, a corrupt form of Buddhism. For centuries Catholic missioners dreamed of evangelizing the land. Jesuits crossed it on their way to China. In 1704 the territory was entrusted to Capuchins, who dispatched three expeditions and even established a monastery in Lhasa before the Chinese forced them to withdraw. The Paris Foreign Mission Society tried again in 1845. After persecution and withdrawal, missioners were readmitted to Tibet under the Treaty of Tientsin (1862). This time it was the Buddhist monks who drove them out and destroyed their stations. Tibet is now without missionaries, and the status of the few thousand Christians is not known.

Protestant missionaries have never settled in Tibet; but the Central Asian Mission, the Moravian Church, and the Evangelical Alliance Mission work with Tibetans on the Indian border and with refugees. BIBLIOGRAPHY: E. D. Maclagan, *Jesuits and the Great Mogul* (1932); E. R. Hambye, NCE 14:151–152.

[P. DAMBORIENA]

TIECK, JOHANN LUDWIG (1773–1853), German writer, one of the founders of early (Jena) romanticism. Under the influence of W. H. Wackenroder (1773–98), he published his *Phantasien über die Kunst* (1799), an important document of romantic aesthetics. His early works (e.g., *Volksmärchen von Peter Lebrecht*, 3 v., 1797) reveal a typically romantic preoccupation with the Middle Ages, the role of the supernatural, and the ironic disruption of form. His later works (after 1822) consist chiefly of realistic novelle and critical writings. BIBLIOGRAPHY: P. Matenko, *Ludwig Tieck and America* (1954); E. H. Zeydel, *Ludwig Tieck, the German Romanticist* (1935).

[M. F. MCCARTHY]

TIEFFENTALLER, JOSEPH (1710–85), Jesuit missionary in Hindustan, N India. He began his missionary work in 1743 and after the suppression of the Jesuits in 1773 continued his apostolate. Besides works on Hinduism and on the natural sciences, he made valuable contributions on the history and geography of Hindustan particularly on the Ganges River, published in Berlin by J. Benoulli, *Des P. J. Tieffentallers . . . historisch-geographische Beschreibung von Hindustan* (3 v., 1785–87).

[T. C. O'BRIEN]

TIENTO, an organ composition (16th–17th cent.), Spanish in origin, similar to the Italian *ricercare*.

[M. T. LEGGE]

TIEPOLO, GIOVANNI BATTISTA (1697–1770), Venetian painter, great master of illusionistic ceiling decoration and whose earliest works show sharp contrasts of light and dark after Magnasco (*The Sacrifice of Abraham*, 1715–16). In 1720–25 he began the ceiling decorations ideally suited to rococo architecture, which made him famous, unsurpassed in their *di sotto in su* perspective (from below upward), remarkable in their aerial space (*Glory of St. Teresa*). T., 1731–40, introduced transparent colors rather than the dark 17th-cent. palette, often creating more quiet, spiritual pictures *vs.* his baroque theatrical ceilings (*The Road to Calvary*, 1738–40, of more impetuous composition). *The Miracle of the Holy House of Loreto* (1743–44) was T.'s major religious fresco (destroyed, 1915). The Cleopatra cycle (1745–50) for the Labia Palace is magnificently clear and defined in decoration. T. is at his height in the ceilings of the Kaisersaal and staircase at the Episcopal Residenz. Würzburg (1751–53)—Europe's finest 18th-cent. frescoes, which established his fame beyond the Alps. In Madrid (1762–70) he decorated the new Royal Palace, his genius commanding an inexhaustible variety of sky, clouds, and airy spaces, peopled by historical and mythological figures with a grace and felicity which influenced the youthful *Goya (1766). BIBLIOGRAPHY: V. Crivellato, *Tiepolo* (1962).

[M. J. DALY]

TIERNEY, RICHARD HENRY (1870–1928), Jesuit journalist. He was a native of the state of New York, entered the Jesuits, and was ordained in 1907. He became a professor at Woodstock, Md., and was a frequent contributor to periodicals. He published *Teachers and Teaching* in 1914. In the same year he became a member of the editorial staff of *America* magazine and within a few months, its editor. T. took many controversial stands but was regarded as an outstanding spokesman for U.S. Catholics. He advocated neutrality before the entrance of the U.S. into World War I, defended the Church in Mexico against Carranza and Villa, supported the Irish Free State, and opposed prohibition.

[J. R. AHERNE]

TIFLIS, the capital of ancient Georgia, founded in 458 or 455 A.D. when the capital was transferred from Mtskheta. It is now called Tbilisi and is the capital of the Georgian Soviet Socialist Republic. Located on the Kura River, it owes its stormy history to its strategic location, controlling the route between western and eastern Transcaucasia. During the 6th and 7th cent. it was conquered successively by the Persians, the Byzantines, and the Moslem Arabs. In 1122 it regained autonomy under David II, the Builder, who captured it and restored it as the capital. In 1234 it fell to the Mongols. In 1386, it was sacked by the Islamic Timur Lenk (Tamerlane). The Ottoman Turks captured it several times. In 1795 the Persians burned it to the ground. In 1801 it was captured by the Russians, and has grown in importance since, until in 1921 it became the capital of the modern Georgian republic.

[E. J. DILLON]

TIGLATH-PILESER (THEGLATH-PHALASAR) III, King of Assyria, actual founder of the empire of the Sargonides, as the kings of his family are called. His name in Akkadian means, "my trust is (in) the son of (the temple) Esarra." He came to power through a coup d'état whose details are not known. Having replaced a succession of weak kings, he established during his reign (745–727 B.C.) policies that were to endure for 100 years. He initiated the large-scale transplantations of conquered peoples, decided not to rely on loyal native puppet rulers, and instead favored complete annexation of subject territories under the rule of Assyrian officials. At the death of the loyal king Nabunasir of Babylon, T.-P. made himself king of Babylon under the throne name Pulu. The virtual disappearance from history of the Israelites of Galilee and Gilead serves as an example of his policy of transplanting conquered rebels. It was a direct result of the disastrous Syro-Ephraimite coalition under King Pekah of Israel and King Rezin of Damascus in their futile rebellion against Assyria. The terrible devastation of Damascus in 732 B.C. was another result. Under T.-P.'s rule, Assyria definitively replaced Egypt as the sovereign overlord of Syria and Palestine, with the king of Juda among the many princes paying tribute.

[E. J. DILLON]

TIKHON, PATRIARCH OF MOSCOW (Vasili Ivanovich Belyavin; 1865–1925), the first patriarch of Moscow and All Russia (elected 1917) for more than 200 years. He excommunicated the Bolsheviks in 1918, denouncing their cruelty and suppression of faith and liberty. He was imprisoned for a year and released in 1923 after signing a "confession" not to interfere with the new government. In his will of 1925 he called for neutrality in political affairs and exhorted the faithful to work with the regime for the common good.

[T. BIRD]

TIKHON OF ZADONSK, ST. (1724–83). Named bp. of Voronezh at the age of 39, T. encountered serious difficulties in dealing with the clergy and laity of his diocese. His constant attempts to improve the situation met with little success, and broken health forced him to resign in 1767. The rest of his life was spent at the monastery of Zadonsk, devoted to the spiritual and temporal assistance of the people who came to him. His numerous instructional and spiritual writings were extremely popular and influential. BIBLIOGRAPHY: N. Gorodetzky, *St. Tikhon Zadonsky* (1951).

[G. T. DENNIS]

TILLEMONT, LOUIS SÉBASTIEN LE NAIN DE (1637–98), French ecclesiastical historian. Ordained in 1676, he never assumed ecclesiastical office. Persecution because of his Jansenism forced him to change locations frequently until he retired to Tillemont in 1679, where he remained, except for short trips, for the rest of his life. His work on church history was at first censored, but he was able to publish a part, one volume of *Histoire des empereurs* (6 v., 1690–1738), and more liberal censors later permitted publication of the entire work, unchanged, under the title: *Mémoires pour servir à l'histoire ecclésiastique des six premiers siècles* (16 v., 1693–1712). The work remains indispensable for its comprehensiveness and attention to detail. Another work, *Life of St. Louis*, was not published in its original form until 1847–51.

[P. J. HENNESSEY]

TILLICH, PAUL JOHANNES (1886–1965), Protestant theologian. T. was born in Starzeddel, a village in the German province of Brandenburg, where his father was a Prussian territorial church minister. T. received his Ph.D. from Breslau in 1911 and a licentiate in theology from Halle in 1912. He was ordained in 1912 by the Evangelical Lutheran Church, served 2 years as a pastor, and then spent the war years as an army chaplain. Following World War I, T. began his academic career as *Privatdozent* of theology at Berlin (1919–24), later teaching at Marburg (1924–25), Dresden (1925–29), and Leipzig (1928–29). He was professor of philosophy at Frankfurt from 1929 until 1933, when he was dismissed because of his criticism of Nazism. Through the efforts of Reinhold *Niebuhr he came to the U.S. and taught philosophical theology at Union Seminary, New York (1933–55). From 1955 to 1962 he taught at Harvard, and from 1962 until his death, at Chicago.

Prior to his emigration T. published numerous works in

German, including *Die religiöse Lage der Gegenwart* (1926), which appeared in the U.S. in 1932 as *The Religious Situation* with translation and introduction by H. Richard *Niebuhr, making available T.'s thought to American readers. Among his later books were *The Courage to Be* (1952), *Love, Power, and Justice* (1954), *Dynamics of Faith* (1957), and *Christianity and the Encounter of the World Religions* (1963). His most substantial work was his *Systematic Theology* (3 v., 1951, 1957, 1963). He took as the norm of his theology "New Being in Jesus as the Christ," and used the method of analyzing the questions involved in human existence and correlating them with the answers given by theology. He saw his theology as apologetic, in contrast with the *kerygmatic theology of K. *Barth.

T. was deeply influenced by the German philosophical tradition, particularly Schelling. Through contact with Heidegger he developed an existential approach to theology, though he did not accept existentialism as a philosophy. He combined a conservative appreciation for the history of Christian thought with a desire sometimes to reformulate it radically in modern terms. He emphasized the *Protestant principle, which he interpreted as the criticism of all expressions of religion, including Protestant Christianity, its dogmas, and its forms of church life, in the light of the ultimate. He accepted biblical criticism and held that the foundations of faith, which he defined as "ultimate concern," were beyond the reach of historical criticism. T. worked to relate theology to cultural and political questions. In Germany he was an active supporter of religious socialism. He was also interested in modern painting and in psychotherapy stemming from Freud. Toward the end of his life he developed a special interest in comparative religions, which he saw as the basis for future developments in theology. BIBLIOGRAPHY: *Theology of Paul Tillich* (eds. C. W. Kegley and R. W. Bretall, 1952); D. H. Hopper, *Tillich: A Theological Portrait* (1968).

[T. EARLY]

TILLMAN, FRITZ (1874–1953), German Catholic theologian and biblical scholar. He was professor of theology at the Univ. of Bonn from 1913 until his retirement. T.'s most noteworthy contribution was in the field of biblical ethics. His works include *Jesus und das Papsttum* (1910); *Die Idee der Nachfolge Christi* (1934, 1953); *Die Verwicklung der Nachfolge Christi* (1935–36; 1951–53). BIBLIOGRAPHY: *Brockhaus Enzyklopädie* 18:705.

[T. J. RYAN]

TILLOTSON, JOHN (1630–94), abp. of Canterbury, preacher, polemicist. T. was the son of Puritan parents, educated at Clare Hall, Cambridge, and ordained in 1661. He participated in the *Savoy Conference on the *Nonconformist side. As a preacher of practical, moral sermons, he not only won renown, but was also imitated by many. He was dean of Canterbury (1670), later canon (1675) and dean (1689) of St. Paul's, London. In 1691 he agreed, with reluc-

tance, to accept election as abp. of Canterbury. His polemics were directed against Roman Catholicism (e.g., in his *Rule of Faith*, 1666) and "atheism" (i.e., rationalism). He sought unsuccessfully to broaden membership in the C of E to include all Nonconformists except Unitarians. BIBLIOGRAPHY: *Golden Book of Tillotson* (ed. J. Moffatt, 1926).

[T. C. O'BRIEN]

TILLY, JOHANN TSERCLAES (1559–1632), military commander, Count of the Holy Roman Empire. Born in Brabant (1559), educated by the Jesuits and destined for an ecclesiastical life, T. chose soldiering instead in the school of the great Parma and the Spanish *tercios* and served in the Low Countries and fought against the Turks. A loyal servant of the House of Austria and of Bavaria and commander of the polyglot forces of the Catholic League, he was the foremost general during the first period of the Thirty Years' War. He was pictured as an ogre by Protestant publicists because of the Sack of Magdeburg (1631), though in justice it should be recorded that he strove to arrest, and not unsuccessfully, the destruction, for which he should be blamed no more than Wellington for Badajoz. Devotedly religious and beloved by his men, he held them to a discipline comparing favorably with that of his enemies in a war of mingled punctilio and beastliness. His infantry, aided by the cuirassiers, the famous "Pappenheimers," of his lieutenant Count Pappenheim, were the victors in many a fight, until, confronting the superior tactical flexibility of Gustavus Adolphus and out-metalled by the Swedish artillery, they were defeated at Breitenfeld. "Stout Tilly" was mortally wounded a few months later when contesting the passage of the Lech and died in Ingolstadt. BIBLIOGRAPHY: C. V. Wedgwood, *Thirty Years' War* (1939).

[T. GILBY]

TIME (CANON LAW). Among the general norms of canon law, CIC, Book 1, Title 3, cc. 31–35, includes rules for interpreting terms expressing time in the law or in other canonical documents. Excluded are matters determined in liturgical laws (CIC, c. 31). Time is to be reckoned by the following understanding of time-terms: "day" means 24 hours, beginning at midnight; "week" means 7 full days; "month" means 30 days; "year" means 365 days. If, however, an actual calendar date for day, month, and year is specified, the terms are taken in accord with the calendar, e.g., if a stipulation is made "for two years, Jan. 1, 1978 to Feb. 29, 1980" (c. 32). As to determining the time of day for fulfilling an obligation, e.g., to fast, a person may use the local time, true (sun) time, or mean (Greenwich) time, or "legal" time, e.g., Eastern Standard Time or Eastern Daylight Time. Otherwise the customary, i.e., "clock" time is followed (c. 33). The remaining canons give precise rules for time computation in regard to various ecclesiastical acts. Their application and observance is important esp. in cases where fulfillment of the specification of law is required for the validity of an act. One such norm is that should the beginning of the period stipulated for an act not coincide with the beginning of the day, the first day of the period is not counted; thus a novitiate-period of 1 canonical year begun at 9:00 A.M. on Jan. 1, 1978 would not be completed until the beginning of Jan. 2, 1979. (c. 34 3 n. 3). Two other classifications of time are given in c. 35: *tempus utile* in a canonical document means the time actually available to a person, so that time during which he was unaware of or unable to exercise a right, does not count; *tempus continuum* refers to running, noninterruptable time.

TIME (IN THE BIBLE). The concept of time in the OT is radically conditioned by the overriding idea of God implementing a preconceived plan in and through history. Despite all obstacles, betrayals, failures or rebellions on the part of the denizens of the world, he intervenes in history and causes it to advance inexorably and irresistibly towards the predestined consummation he has designed for it. More specifically the covenant people, from the moment in world history when the covenant was first instituted, are advancing toward that point in time predetermined by God at which his plan will have attained its goal, his glory will have been manifested, and his people's happiness in the deepest and widest sense will have been achieved. This sense of an irresistible advance *from* a specific point in the past *through* the present *to* a specific point in the future gives rise to a conception of time as essentially *linear*, and of history as advancing in a straight line towards its goal. By a further projection this process is regarded as starting, not with the institution of the covenant, but with the creation of the world, and in the minds of the later writers as ending with the realization of the plan of God, not in history but at the end of history, bringing the present world order to an end and initiating a new and radically different era. Thus *eschatology is born. But this sense of linear time, as it has been called, is radically modified by certain other considerations. The first of these is that within the general flow of time, certain specific points constitute the "right time for" some specific activity, whether human or divine. Thus there is a "time of love" (Jer 1.16 etc.), "the time of Yahweh's house to rebuild it" (Hag 1.2), ". . . a time for everything under heaven" (Ec 3.1–8), etc. In the case of Yahweh these "right times for" are mysterious and unpredictable. Any given moment may be decreed by Yahweh as the time of judgment or decision when he intervenes directly and decisively to determine man's fate. The individual must maintain himself in a state of constant watchfulness for this mysterious and unpredictable "right time for" or *kairos* of God. Otherwise when it comes, it may import final condemnation and perdition for him instead of salvation. It is this sense of time that underlies the parables of the guest without a wedding garment (Mt 22.11–14); the thief in the night (Mt 24.43; Lk 12.39); the ten virgins (Mt 25.14–30), etc.

A further factor radically affecting Hebrew man's sense of time is his awareness of the cyclic and rhythmic pro-

cesses of the natural order and, as a formalized expression of this, the cyclic and regular recurrence of the seasonal festivals and the return of the year to its starting-point. Cultic or rhythmic time, therefore, is essentially cyclic, involving an endless return to the origins. This sense of cyclic time is characteristic of pagan mythology. Its influence on Hebrew thought has undoubtedly been exaggerated and overgeneralized.

The distinctively Hebrew sense of time, therefore, is one which combines both linear and cyclic time, and is also pervaded by a sense of the "right time for" or *kairos* of Yahweh's action. Primarily it has in view the linear development of sacred history towards its predestined consummation. But this process does admit of intermediate *kairoi*, points at which Yahweh intervenes directly to visit, to judge, and to reimpose the right order of his will. Each of these intermediate *kairoi* partakes of the nature of the final consummation and carries sacred history a stage further toward it. It follows that the various *kairoi*, taken as a series, correspond to and resemble one another, and all in their various ways foreshadow the final consummation to which all correspond. It is this that provides the only sound and objective basis for *typology. But this means that the sense of time involved is neither totally and exclusively linear nor totally and exclusively cyclic, but rather spiral. The course of Israel's life is predestined and purposeful, moving towards its ultimate goal in a series of spirals, each of which culminates in the achievement of an intermediate goal, and each of which reproduces the essential elements of the previous spirals while projecting the whole course of history irrevocably nearer to its last end. BIBLIOGRAPHY: J. Barr, *Biblical Words for Time* (1962); T. Boman, *Hebrew Thought Compared with Greek* (Eng tr. 1960); J. Marsh, *Fullness of Time* (1952); O. Cullman, *Christ and Time* (tr. F. V. Filson, rev. ed. 1964).

[D. J. BOURKE]

TIME SETTING, calculation and determination of the day of Christ's second coming. It has usually been a feature of *adventism in its various forms. From the "signs of the times," as well as from complex, often numerological interpretations of Scripture, time setters seek to discover and predict the moment of an impending disaster that will mark the destruction of the wicked and the beginning of the millennial reign of Christ and the just. *MILLENARIANISM; *DISPENSATIONALISM; *JEHOVAH'S WITNESSES.

TIMON, JOHN (1797–1867), bishop. The son of Irish immigrant parents, T. was born in Conewago, Pa., entered the Vincentians, and was ordained in 1826. He was assigned to the missions of the Southwest, traveling much in Missouri and Texas. Named vicar apostolic of Texas after rejecting appointment as coadjutor of St. Louis, he ministered in Texas, Indiana, and Colorado. In 1847 he was appointed first bp. of Buffalo. In New York, he scotched the *trusteeism that had evicted him from his cathedral, founded a number of charitable institutions, including three orphanages, a hospital, a Magdalen home, and the first American Catholic refuge for unmarried mothers. In 1848 he established the Vincentian seminary (later Niagara Univ.); in 1849 St. Joseph's College; in 1856 the school for the deaf (later Le Couteulx) also in Buffalo. In 1862 he published *Missions in Western New York* and *Church History of the Diocese of Buffalo*. The esteem in which he was held by Bp. Francis P. *Kenrick is evident in the latter's proposing T. for the sees of Baltimore and Philadelphia. BIBLIOGRAPHY: C. G. Deuther, *Life and Times of Rt. Rev. John Timon, D. D.* (1870).

[J. R. AHERNE]

TIMOTHEUS I, PATRIARCH OF ALEXANDRIA, 381–385, unanimously elected to succeed Peter II as patriarch. He served briefly and uneventfully and was succeeded by Theophilus. An elderly man and a disciple of Athanasius, T. became patriarch in time to attend the Council of Constantinople I in 381 and may briefly have presided over that council in the interval between the resignation of Gregory of Nazianzus, whom T. opposed, and the election of Nectarius, as bp. of Constantinople. T. cannot have been overjoyed by that council's canon placing Constantinople ahead of Alexandria in the order of dignity among patriarchates, but he did not break away from Catholic communion.

[E. J. DILLON]

TIMOTHEUS I (d. 518), **PATRIARCH OF CONSTANTINOPLE** from 511, selected by the Emperor Anastasius to replace the deposed Macedonius II. T. generally followed the policy urged by the Emperor of placating the Monophysites. At first he refused to comply with the request of the patriarch of Alexandria that he explicitly condemn the Council of Chalcedon and the *Tome of Leo; he ended by accepting the acts of the Synod of Tyre (514–515), which did abrogate Chalcedon. He expressly condemned Chalcedon in letters to Elias and to John of Jerusalem. T. is responsible for having the Nicene Creed recited regularly in the liturgy, instead of only on Good Friday as formerly. Many of the people of Constantinople did not accept the deposition of the former patriarch, and they rioted when the Emperor tried to introduce into the *Trisagion the Monophysite formula, "crucified for us."

[E. J. DILLON]

TIMOTHEUS I (d. 823), **NESTORIAN PATRIARCH** from 780–823. Born in Ḥazzā in the area of modern Iran, he studied under Abraham bar Dāshāndād. He was first a monk, then bp. of Bēth-Bāghāsh, and finally patriarch of the Nestorian Church until his death in Baghdad. Highly regarded by the Moslem Caliphs, he was allowed to carry on impressive missionary activities in India, Turkestan, China, Yemen, and the region around the Caspian Sea. His tenure was decisive in separating the Persian hierarchy from the See of Rome. He was a prolific writer in Syriac; his

works reflect a keen interest in Aristotelian philosophy and include a commentary on the writings of Gregory of Nazianzus.

[E. J. DILLON]

TIMOTHY, ST., associate of the Apostle Paul. Paul included T. as a co-writer of 2 Cor, Phil, Col, 1 and 2 Th, and Philemon. He used T. as an emissary (Phil 2.19; 1 Cor 4.17; 16.10–11; 1 Th 3.1–6); referred to him as a fellow worker (Rom 16.21); and commended him for his service (Phil 2.22). According to Acts, T. was the son of a Jewish Christian mother and a Greek father and was living in Lystra (16.1). Paul found him there on his second missionary journey (16.3; 17.14; 18.5; 19.22; 20.4). The epistles 1 and 2 Tim were purportedly from Paul to T., but some scholars question their Pauline authorship. According to tradition, T. was martyred in A.D. 97 and his remains moved to Constantinople in 356.

[T. EARLY]

TIMOTHY AELURUS (d. 477), **MONOPHYSITE PATRIARCH** of Alexandria since 457. His condemnation of the Council of Chalcedon was not accepted by the majority of bishops; therefore he was banished by Emperor Leo I in 460. During his exile he wrote much to propagate Monophysitism, but, unlike Eutyches, he held that the body of Christ was of the same substance as other human bodies. Recalled from exile and reinstated in 475 by Emperor Basiliscus, and finally, exiled again by Emperor Zeno, he died before the decree of banishment could be carried out. In the Coptic Church he is commemorated as a saint on July 31.

[L. PEANO]

TIMOTHY OF JERUSALEM, priest, author of homilies on the Song of Simeon and the Presentation in the Temple, and perhaps also of works wrongly attributed to others. His life is variously placed, either in the 4th or 5th cent. (DTC) or somewhere between the 6th and the 8th centuries (LTK). T.'s importance rests on his clear reference to the Assumption of Mary into heaven, although it is not clear whether his use of the word "immortal" precludes the possibility of Mary's having died before being taken up. The exact reference is found in his comments on the words of Simeon, "your own soul a sword shall pierce." Some see in this, according to T., an indication that Mary was martyred by the sword, as were so many Christians. But, he says, this is not so: "The Virgin guiltless above all, and holy in every way, was taken up to the higher places by him who had his dwelling in her . . . (she is) immortal to this day" (PG 86:245–248). BIBLIOGRAPHY: B. Kotter, LTK 10:200; DTC 15:1140ff.

[E. J. DILLON]

TIMOTHY, LETTERS TO, two books of the NT that, with Titus, are designated Pastoral Letters (on the reason for this designation and the problem of authorship, see PAS-TORAL LETTERS).

Timothy is one of Paul's most faithful disciples (Acts 16.1–5), now raised to the position of "elder-in-charge" or chief presbyter (the position does not yet amount to that of bishop in the full sense) over the other presbyters in the Church at Ephesus. Basically these epistles are designed to instruct him in how to guide those under his charge, how to defend them from false teachers (1 Tim 1.3–20; 4.1–11; 6.3–10, etc.), and how to keep both himself and them steadfastly faithful to the true teaching of apostolic tradition (1 Tim 6.3).

In content the two epistles cover much the same areas:

(1) False teachers, Judaizers broadly similar to those in *Galatians, indulge in fables and genealogies of a type encountered in the apocryphal literature (cf. 1 Tim 1.3–4); they attach a distorted value to the Law (1 Tim 1.3–7), failing to recognize its true place in the Christian dispensation (1 Tim 1.8–11). They distract their hearers from the authentic faith as embodied in the apostolic tradition (2 Tim 2.14–26), and taught to Timothy by Paul himself (cf. 2 Tim 1.6, 13; 2.1–2, 8–9; 3.14, etc.).

(2) The purpose of instruction is "that there should be love proceeding from a pure heart, a clear conscience and a sincere faith" (1 Tim 1.5). It should be based on the teaching handed on to Timothy by Paul and also on the Scriptures (2 Tim 3.14–17). Timothy must adhere undeviatingly to the truth preserved and taught by the Church (1 Tim 3.15–16), the gospel of "Jesus Christ risen from the dead, sprung from the race of David" (2 Tim 2.8).

(3) Timothy himself must be fearless, firm, and resolute in preserving this truth (1 Tim 1.18–20; 2 Tim 1.6–14; 6.11–14), using the gifts of his calling to this end (1 Tim 4.12–14; 2 Tim 1.6–13), and making a blameless and virtuous life the basis of his authority (1 Tim 4.11–14), even though this may entail suffering and even danger. (2 Tim 1.15–18; 3.1, 10–13, etc.). He must strive to guide his flock by gentleness and charity rather than by harsh correction (1 Tim 5.1–2; 2 Tim 2.22–26).

(4) Timothy, responsible for the whole Church at Ephesus, must have knowledge of the qualifications, duties, rights, and privileges of each of its officials and of all the classes within the community. He has to give an example to all by the blamelessness and virtue of his personal and family life (1 Tim 3.1–7). Similar criteria apply to deacons and their counterparts among the women (1 Tim 3.8–13). Presbyters must be defended from false accusations, yet fearlessly rebuked when they deserve it (1 Tim 5.17–21). Care must be taken to provide them with the material sustenance which is their due (1 Tim 5.18). Widows formally "enrolled" as such must likewise be women of advanced years, blameless, dedicated in their way of life, and genuinely left without relatives to support them (1 Tim 5.3–16). Slaves must respect their masters (1 Tim 6.1–2). The rich must be beware of pride in riches and selfishness (1 Tim 6.17–19), and all should preserve an attitude of detachment toward material wealth (1 Tim 6.6–10). Official prayers should be offered for the whole Church, and also for the preservation of the existing political and social order, so that Christians may be free to live their faith to the full in stability and peace (1 Tim 2.1–2). These epistles, Paul's testament to Timothy in the evening of his life (2 Tim 4.6–8), clearly presuppose a Church with some degree of hierarchical organization, though such terms as *episkopos* and *diakonos* cannot be taken as referring to bishops and deacons in the developed and sacramental sense which these designations subsequently came to acquire. For bibliography see PASTORAL EPISTLES.

[D. J. BOURKE]

TIMUR (TAMERLANE; c.1336–1405), Muslim conqueror. Also called Timur Lang (Timur the Lame), he began his career by freeing his native Transoxania (modern Russian Turkestan) from the Mongol nomads who had overrun it in the time of Genghis Khan. Presenting himself as the champion of the settled Muslims against the nomads, he gained the support of the Muslim clergy of Samarkand and proclaimed himself sovereign there c.1370. Though fighting the Mongols, he married Mongol princesses and claimed descent from Genghis Khan. He freed Khwarizm (Khiva) and the Oxus Valley in campaigns of the 1370s. Then beginning in 1381 with an attack on Persia, T. carried out campaigns in all directions, conquering such important cities as Moscow, Delhi, Damascus, and Baghdad. He became noted for the cruelty with which he treated defeated peoples, even those of his own faith. He almost obliterated Nestorian Christianity. He encouraged art, science, and building, however, and carried off scholars and artisans of conquered cities to adorn Samarkand. He died while initiating a campaign against the Ming Dynasty of China. His empire was divided after his death, but under the Timuri Dynasty, descended from him, Persian Islamic culture experienced a revival in eastern Iran.

[T. EARLY]

TINCTORIS, JOHANNES (1435–1511), Renaissance cleric, musician, mathematician, and professor of law with a passion for learning, its systemization, and transmission. Born near Brussels, he finally settled in Naples, and proceeded to make its musical life as excellent as possible after the manner of French and Flemish models. His desire and ability to condense huge quantities of contemporary music theory in superbly organized form resulted in his 12 treatises covering the whole spectrum of musical thought and practice of his day. The first treatise is a dictionary of musical terms, the first ever printed; in the third treatise on modes, T. even intuits the eventual formation of a new, non-modal tonal system. The most famous treatise is the ninth, on *counterpoint: of and for the Renaissance, it doubts the worth of music more than 40 years old, extols contemporary musicians, and explains their methods. T. also left at least four Masses, two motets, and his *Lamentations,* printed in 1506, as well as some secular works. BIBLIOGRAPHY: H. Hüschen, MGG 13:418–425; Reese MusR.

[P. DOHERTY]

TINDAL, MATTHEW (1655–1733), English deist who wrote several rationalistic treatises that aroused great opposition. His final work, *Christianity as Old as the Creation, or the Gospel a Republication of the Religion of Nature* (1730), became the chief manual of deism. It argued that the Gospel added nothing to the great eternal law of nature common to all rational creatures. BIBLIOGRAPHY: L. Stephen, DNB 56:403–405.

[M. J. SUELZER]

TINEL, EDGAR (1854–1912), Belgian composer, T. studied music with his father until, at the age of 9, he entered the Brussels Conservatory where he studied with many prominent musicians of the time. He had a brief career as a concert pianist but, having won the Prix de Rome in 1877, decided to devote himself to composing music. He became director of the School of Religious Music at Mechlin (1882), then professor (1896) and later, director (1909) at the Brussels Conservatory. In 1910 he was made master of the Royal Chapel. T. composed an oratio, "Franciscus," some stage music, settings for the *Te Deum*, a Mass in honor of Our Lady of Lourdes, "Songs of Mary" for mixed chorus, and other religious music. He also published a work on Gregorian chant and another on St. Pius X.

[M. T. LEGGE]

TINTERN, ABBEY OF, English Cistercian monastery near Hereford on the River Wye, founded in 1131 by monks of the French l'Aumône. The abbey after a humble beginning was magnificently rebuilt during the 13th century. The ruins of the great church are still imposing, featuring a 245-foot nave, a 110-foot transept, and arches 70 feet high. Growing population and prosperity enabled the monks to establish two other houses Kingswood (1139), and Tintern-Minor (1200). At the time of the dissolution, Tintern had 13 monks under Abbot Richard Wych. It is with Fountains Abbey, the most beautiful ruin in England, inspiring Wordsworth's poem, *Tintern Abbey*. BIBLIOGRAPHY: O. E. Craster, *Tintern Abbey* (1963); F. A. Gasquet, *Greater Abbeys of England* (1903) 190–197; C. H. Talbot, NCE 14:168–169.

[L. J. LEKAI]

TINTESSAKAN, Armenian diocesan council of laymen.

TINTORETTO JACOPO ROBUSTI; (1518–94), son of Giovanni Battista Robusti, a dyer *(tintore;* Tintoretto, little dyer) from 1548 leading Venetian painter. He kept a large workshop in which his children, Domenico, Marco, and Marietta worked as assistants. Of exceptional gifts, T. produced numerous works owing to his eagerness, low prices, immediacy of execution, and haste—distinctive of his inventive style. He also modified his style to match other artists' works (*Miracle of the Lame,* 1559 to relate to the work of Pordenone; *Assumption* after Veronese). Yet T. is not eclectic but unmistakingly personal in swift brushstrokes and brilliantly improvised lighting which shines from behind his figures toward the spectator, rendering the forms in dramatic silhouette. His chiascuro space-design (*Presentation in the Temple,* 1551 and *Crucifixion*) is spectacular in *Miracles of St. Mark* (1562) in which appears T.'s Renaissance signature in eight self-portraits in the crowd. His pictures with sensuous, luminous nudes include the great *Susanna and the Elders.* T.'s chief claim to fame rests on the monumental decoration of the Scuola di S. Rocco (1564–88) where, among the famous paintings of the *Annunciation* and *The Flight into Egypt,* the great *Crucifixion* is to be found. These works exhibit his characteristic style of crowded composition, full of movement, daring foreshortenings, unexpected perspectives and phosphorescent color. Between 1590–92, with the help of his son Domenico and assistants, he completed his most ambitious painting, *Paradise* (Doge's Palace, Venice) which covers the entire 80-ft wall of the Hall of the Grand Council. BIBLIOGRAPHY: E. Newton, *Tintoretto* (1952); H. Tietze, *Tintoretto* (1948).

[M. J. DALY]

TIPTOFT, JOHN (*c.* 1427–70), Earl of Worcester, patron of humanists, and book-collector. As constable of England under Edward IV, his severity won him the nickname of "Butcher of England." Unusual amongst contemporary English noblemen for his interest in humanism, he studied in Italy (1459–61) and bequeathed a valuable library to Oxford University. BIBLIOGRAPHY: R. J. Mitchell, *John Tiptoft* (1938).

[C. D. ROSS]

TIRIDATES III (d. *c.* 330), Armenian King, first a persecutor of the Church under Diocletian, then after conversion by St. Gregory the Illuminator, Christianizer of his kingdom, venerated as a saint by the Armenian Church.

TIRON, ABBEY OF, former Benedictine monastery of the Holy Trinity, located near the Tironne in the commune of Thiron-Gardais, Diocese of Chartres, Eure-et-Loire, France; founded (1109–14) by Bp. Ives and its first abbot, St. Bernard of Tiron, former prior of Savigny and monk of St. Cyprien of Poitiers. When Bernard settled there in the forest of Le Perche with his 500 disciples, they followed a strict observance of the Benedictine Rule but gradually assimilated what was for them the less austere Cluniac usages. In the course of the 12th cent. the abbey founded 9 abbeys in France, 5 in Scotland, and nearly 100 priories, becoming the head of the Congregation of Tiron. Burned by the English in 1428 and by Huguenots in 1562, it was united to the Maurists in 1629 and was suppressed in 1790. The abbey church and a few buildings survive. BIBLIOGRAPHY: Cottineau 2:3162–63.

[E. J. DILLON]

TIRRY, WILLIAM (1609–54), Irish martyr. An Augustinian who studied at Valladolid and Paris, T. returned to Ireland (*c*.1640) where he became prior of Fethard, provincial secretary (1646), and prior of Skryne (1649). He was arrested during the Cromwellian persecution, condemned, and executed.

[V. SAMPSON]

TIRZAH (THERSAH), name of: (1) one of Zelophehad's five daughters (Num 26.33); (2) Canaanite city (Jos 12.24) and capital of the northern kingdom of Israel from the time of Jeroboam I (1 Kg 14.17) until the time of Omri (1 Kg 16.23–24).

[T. EARLY]

TISCHENDORF, KONSTANTIN VON (1815–74), NT textual critic. A German Lutheran, T. studied theology at Leipzig (1834–38), developing a special interest in philology. Nominally a member of the Leipzig faculty from 1845, he spent his life largely searching through libraries of Europe and the Near East for biblical MSS., publishing the results of his studies. His most famous accomplishment was the discovery and publication of the Codex Sinaiticus. T. also published critical editions of Codex Ephraemi rescriptus (1843–45), Codex Amiantinus (1850), and Codex Claromontanus (1852). From 1841 he published editions of the NT, giving a full critical apparatus of the variant readings. The eighth edition (3 v., 1869–94) became a standard authority. All textual critics acknowledge their indebtedness to him.

[T. EARLY]

TISO, JOZEF (1887–1947), Slovakian Priest and political leader. Recipient of a doctorate in theology from Vienna's Pazmaneum, T. nevertheless devoted many years to parish work and was rural dean of Banovce. Success as a Catholic publicist led to a position of leadership in the Catholic conservative and autonomist Slovak People's Party. In 1925 he was elected as deputy and in 1927 became Minister of Public Health. Eventually becoming party leader in 1938, he favored full autonomy for Slovakia rather than independence, but was moved to espouse the cause of independence in 1939 because of the Nazi threat and fear of Hungarian occupation. He was president of Slovakia, 1939–45. Surrendering to the Americans in Austria, T. was returned to Bratislava to stand trial, was condemned, and executed as the Slovak ''Quisling'' despite appeals for clemency. BIBLIOGRAPHY: W. B. Slottman, NCE 14:173–174.

[T. J. RYAN]

TISSERANT, EUGENE (1884–1972), Orientalist, biblical scholar, cardinal. Ordained (1907) in his native France, T. in 1908 was brought to Rome as professor of Assyrian languages and librarian at the Vatican. He studied American document holdings in the U.S. at the invitation of the Carnegie Foundation in 1927. Named a cardinal in 1936, he served in Vatican administrative posts under three popes. T. was a master of Oriental languages, an expert on Eastern liturgy, and an able interpreter of early Christian documents. In 1961 he was elected to the French Academy. In his later years he was dean of the College of Cardinals.

[J. R. AHERNE]

TISSOT, JAMES JOSEPH JACQUES (1836–1902), French painter and etcher. He was student of Lamotte and Flandrin (1857), showing in the Salon of 1859. T. moved to London (1871), painting English society with considerable acclaim. Returning to Paris, he changed to mystical religious paintings and etchings, publishing the Tissot Bible (1896), 865 compositions from studies made in Palestine. His religious works were influenced by the English Pre-Raphaelites and Japanese graphics.

[M. J. DALY]

TISSOT, JOSEPH (1840–94), French spiritual writer. A member of the Missionaries of St. Francis de Sales and eventually their superior general, he wrote *Flore mystique de S. François de Sales* (1873), *Les Abeilles mystiques* (1880), *La Journée de Philothée* (1893), but is best known for his publication of *La Vie intérieure simplifiée* of the Carthusian, François de Sales Pollien. BIBLIOGRAPHY: P. K. Meagher, NCE 14:174.

[T. J. RYAN]

TITCOMB, H. EVERETT (1884–1968), American organist and composer. T. held the position of organist-choirmaster of St. John the Evangelist Episcopal Church in Boston, instructor in liturgical music at the school of music of Boston University. He composed a *Te Deum* at the close of World War II, many anthems, and organ works. He also wrote *a Choirmaster's Notebook on Anglican Services and Liturgical Music* (1950). BIBLIOGRAPHY: L. Ellinwood, *History of American Church Music* (1953) 235.

[M. T. LEGGE]

TITELOUZE, JEAN (1563–1633), French organist and composer. Born to a musical family of English origin, T. received a fine education, probably at the Walloon Jesuit College. He was appointed organist of the church of St. Jean at Rouen (1585) and, later, at the cathedral there (1588). Considered the founder of the French school of organ playing, T. contributed some of the finest organ music of the early Baroque period. Among his compositions are *Hymnes de l'église,* a volume of settings for hymns of the liturgy, and *Magnificat,* a volume of settings for that Vesper canticle.

[M. T. LEGGE]

TITIAN (TIZIANO VECELLI OR VECELLIO, *c*.1488–1576), Italian painter giant of the Venetian School, one of the greatest masters in the history of Western art, the most prodigious and prolific of Veneitan painters. He enjoyed an international reputation numbering among his most enthusiastic patrons both the Holy Roman Emperor, Charles V, and his son, Philip II of Spain. Commanding a wide variety of subjects including religious scenes, portraits, and mythological subjects, T. created a vast number of paintings during his long career. He studied under both Gentile and Giovanni Bellini, and was a fellow-student with Giorgione. A splendid example of his early Giorgionesque style is *Sacred and Profane Love* (*c.* 1515, Galleria Borghese, Rome), although even here he evidenced his interest in solid forms modeled in clear, bright colors. His *Assumption of the Virgin* (1516) combined heavenly and terrestrial zones, the silhouetted, raised arms in a Renaissance convention of transition (e.g., Raphael's *Disputa*). The embodiment of High Renaissance ideals in Venice, T. constructed his compositions on dynamic diagonals as seen in the *Madonna of the Pesaro Family* (1519–26; Sta. Maria dei Frari, Venice). As his style evolved T. increasingly muted and modulated his palette producing extraordinary nuances of color which he used as the sole means of constructing form, in a distinctive Venetian mode. One of his most significant contributions to Western painting was the creation of painterly techniques, manipulating the texture of the pigment with as much subtlety as its color. Painting from an innovative dark ground, he restored the lights by an application of white lead, over which he painted luminous transparent colors, a method followed by later Venetians. He exploited the expressive qualities of painterly technique most profoundly in his late paintings, e.g., the magnificent *Christ Crowned with Thorns* (*c.*1573–75; Alte Pinakotek, Munich) with its shimmering lights and spiritualized, dematerialized forms. T. restored and exalted the sensuous beauty of Venus in great mythological panels: *Venus of Urbino* (1530), *Perseus and Andromeda* (1550), *Venus with a Mirror* (1555), and left a formula for the skillfully composed, psychological portrait of great depth in: *Man with a Glove* (1520), *Pope Paul III* (1543), *Pope Paul III and His Grandsons* (1546), and the forceful *Self-Portrait* (1550), copied by El Greco in *Cleansing of the Temple* (*c.*1575). BIBLIOGRAPHY: R. Pallucchini, *Tiziano* (1969); E. Panofsky, *Problems in Titian, Mostly Iconographic* (1969); H. Wethy, *Paintings of Titian* (3 v., 1970–77).

[S. CONWAY]

TITLE OF THE CROSS. On the way to the place of crucifixion, the criminal carried a placard suspended from a cord about his neck. On it were written his name and the crime for which he was being executed. It was such a placard that was put on the cross over Jesus' head, but at the order of Pilate, the criminal charge was replaced, rather ironically, with the title, King of the Jews. It was written in three languages: Aramaic, the language of Palestine; Greek, that of the Greco-Roman empire; and Latin, that of the Roman government. The actual wording differs slightly from Gospel to Gospel: "This is Jesus, the King of the Jews" (Mt 27.37); "The King of the Jews" (Mk 15.26); "This is the king of the Jews" (Lk 23.38); "Jesus the Nazarene, King of the Jews" (Jn 19.19).

[J. J. CASTELOT]

TITTLE, ERNEST FREMONT (1885–1949), Methodist clergyman noted mainly for his profound prayer life and his advocacy of international peace and good will. He was born at Springfield, Ohio, and received his higher education at Ohio Wesleyan Univ. and Drew Theological Seminary. His largest and most influential pastorate was at First Church, Evanston, Ill., (1918–49). A lecturer at numerous universities and colleges, he made his chief contribution to world peace as chairman of the World Peace Commission of the *Methodist Church and as a member of three major commissions of the former Federal Council of Churches: the Federal Council Commission to Study the Basis of a Just and Durable Peace; the Federal Council Commission on War in the Light of the Christian Faith; and the Federal Council's Department of International Justice and Goodwill. He participated in numerous conferences, wrote nearly a dozen books, including a book of *Pastoral Prayers,* and a number of pamphlets and articles. BIBLIOGRAPHY: *Encyclopedia of World Methodism* (1974).

[F. E. MASER]

TITUS, ST., companion and helper of the Apostle Paul. He is mentioned in Gal 2.1–3, where Paul says he took T. on his visit to Jerusalem and that T. was not compelled to be circumcised, despite being a Greek. Paul also refers to him as a messenger to Corinth (2 Cor 7.5–16; 8.6, 23; 12.18). T. seems to have replaced *Timothy, who is mentioned in 1 Cor as Paul's messenger. The Letter of Titus purports to be from Paul to Titus, but many scholars date it later than Paul. According to it, Paul had sent T. to supervise the churches of Crete (1.5). Authentic Pauline references to T. may be preserved in Tit 3.12 and 2 Tim 4.10. According to tradition, T. died at Crete, was buried at the capital, Gortyna, and his remains brought to St. Mark's, Venice, in the 9th century.

[T. EARLY]

TITUS OF BOSTRA (fl. 2d half of 4th cent.), bp. of Bostra in Arabia in 362 when *Julian the Apostate wrote urging the people there to revolt against him. He continued in his see despite this, and the following year signed a statement at the Council of Antioch accepting the *homoousios* of the Nicene Creed. He wrote a treatise against the Manichaeans, part of which has survived in Greek, but the complete text only in Syriac. There exist also some fragments of his homilies on the Gospel of Luke. Works: PG 18:1065–1204. BIBLIOGRAPHY: Quasten 3:359–362; P. Canivet, NCE 14:181.

[R. B. ENO]

TITUS, APOCRYPHAL EPISTLE OF, see APOCRYPHA (NT), 66.

TITUS, LETTER TO, NT book that with 1–2 Tim is one of the Pastoral Letters (on this designation and the question of authorship see PASTORAL LETTERS).

Titus, a faithful and trusted disciple of Paul (cf. Gal 2.1; 2 Cor 8.6, 16, 23) had apparently been left behind in the course of one of Paul's missionary journeys to organize the Church at Crete (cf. 1.5). This epistle, like 1–2 Tim, represents the final instructions which Paul hands on at the close of his life to one who is to succeed to a measure of his responsibilities. It is primarily concerned to instruct and exhort an "elder-in-charge" of a local Church so that he will be able to guide, admonish, and instruct those under him according to their various callings and positions in the Church and in the world, to ward off from them the evil influence of false teachers, and to show them how to preserve true faith and Christian living despite the difficulties of the times.

As in 1–2 Tim, the false teachers appear to be Judaizers who try to seduce their hearers with vain and idle speculations and to insist on the retention of such observances as the dietary laws of Judaism (cf. 1.10–16). Against this Paul reiterates the necessity of adhering without deviation or compromise to the true message of the Christian religion (cf. 2.11–15; 3.4–7). All members of the community, the presbyters (1.5–9), the elderly of both sexes (cf. 2.2–3), young women (cf. 2.4–8), slaves (cf. 2.9) and all the faithful in general (3.1–3) must concentrate, to the exclusion of all irrelevancies and distortions, on practicing the Christian virtues appropriate to their particular state. Titus himself must spare no pains to ensure that this is carried out (3.8–10), and that the holiness proper to the people of God as a whole pervade the life of each individual (2.11–15). For bibliog. see PASTORAL EPISTLES.

[D. J. BOURKE]

TIXERONT, JOSEPH (1856–1925), French Sulpician patrologist. His *History of Dogmas in Christian Antiquity* (tr. 1926–30), first published in 3 v. (1905–12), was long the standard work for the study of the subject in RC seminaries. T. was a disciple of L. Duchesne; he taught at Lyons (1884–98) and at Louvain (1898–1925). Other publications include: the texts, *Précis de patrologie* (1918) and *Mélanges de patrologie et d'histoire des dogmes* (1921), studies on the life and discipline of the early Christian centuries, on the preaching of St. Irenaeus, and a renowned work on sacrament of penance, *Le Sacrement de pénitence dans l'antiquité chrétienne* (1904).

[T. C. O'BRIEN]

TOBA SOJO (KAKUYŪ: 1053–1140), Japanese painter, abbot of Miidera of the Tendai sect near Kyoto, who was thought to have executed with skill, humorous and satirical sketches in *Animal Caricature Scrolls* and *Shigisan Engi Scrolls*. These attributions have recently been questioned.
*ANIMAL SCROLL.

[M. J. DALY]

TOBEY, MARK (1890–   ), American painter. T. studied at the Chicago Art Institute and with Henry S. Hubbell and Kenneth Hayes Miller. Inspired by European modernism and a serious student of Oriental calligraphy (1923) and Zen philosophy (1934), by the mid-1930s T. developed a unique abstract style, with strong religious overtones, sometimes referred to as "white writing" placing him among the pioneer leaders of American abstract expressionism. T. worked in terms of his religious experience, with passionate convictions of the void, not as vacuum but charged with energy, of cosmic and terrestrial forces invisible to the eye, but infinitely important. BIBLIOGRAPHY: C. Roberts, *Mark Tobey* (1959); W. C. Seitz, *Mark Tobey* (1962); W. Schmied, *Mark Tobey* (1966).

[F. S. GRUBER]

TOBIA THE AMMONITE, (1) the father of a group of returned exiles who could not prove their Israelitish descent (Ezra 2.60; Neh 7.62). (2) the opponent of Nehemiah (Neh 2.10). He may have been the same person as the preceding, though he is called an Ammonite. He was associated with *Sanballat in opposition to Nehemiah's project of rebuilding the Jerusalem walls. They questioned Nehemiah's political loyalty (Neh 2.19), ridiculed his efforts (Neh 4.3), sought to harm him (Neh 6.1–2), and hired Shemaiah to frighten him (Neh 6.10–13). T. could have been descended from the Israelites who fled to Ammon after the defeat of Judah (Jer 41.15). He was connected with the priest Eliashib, who gave him a room in the temple area while Nehemiah was away. Nehemiah threw him out when he returned (Neh 13.4–9). Many of the nobles also had ties with T. (Neh 6.17–19).

[T. EARLY]

TOBIT, BOOK OF, a moral tale or novel, probably entirely fictitious, of a Jewish exile at Nineveh who, after a lifetime of charitable and pious works, becomes poor and blind in old age. He sends his son Tobias to collect a debt from a friend at Ecbatana with a trustworthy companion who subsequently turns out to be the angel Raphael. Guided and strengthened by Raphael, Tobias succeeds in capturing a fish, parts of which have curative properties. On arriving in Media they stay with Tobias' kinsman Raguel, and with the help of Raphael succeed in overcoming a demon which has killed all those who have previously attempted to marry Raguel's daughter Sarah. As a reward for his piety and obedience to Raphael's instructions, Tobias does enter into a happy marriage with her, succeeds in recovering the debt, and on his return, loaded with riches, restores his father's sight and the whole family's fortunes, again with Raphael's guidance. The story was mainly circulated in Greek, which may explain its exclusion from the Jewish canon of Scriptures; or it had great appeal among Jews trying to be faithful to their tradition of prayer and piety in a hostile, non-Jewish environment. The events of the story are represented as taking place during the deportations from Israel in the reign of Shalmaneser of Assyria. The story was actually written many centuries later, between 200–170 B.C. It is probably of Palestinian or Syrian origin, perhaps originally written in Aramaic and then translated into both Greek and Hebrew. It must date from before the period of terrible persecution, and there is no mention of the resurrection of the just. The book is full of prayers reflecting a piety of praise and thanksgiving, and of honoring God among the gentiles. The wisdom it recommends is that piety and good works give strength in adversity during a life lived in the Dispersion. Good works exemplified include burying the dead even at personal risk; almsgiving; cleanliness; perfect fidelity in marriage. Other distinctive motifs include affliction by the demon Asmodeus, the hidden guidance of the angel Raphael, and miraculous cures in favor of the just. The book was much loved and quoted in the early Church. BIBLIOGRAPHY: R. Pautrel, *Le Livre de Tobie,* (2d ed. 1957); R. Brunner, *Tobias, Vater und Sohn* (1950); T. F. Glasson, "Main Source of Tobit," ZATW 71 (1959) 275–277.

[D. J. BOURKE; E. J. DILLON]

TOCCATA, musical term for a type of keyboard composition, esp. for organ, characterized by running passages, full chords and, in some toccatas, alternating contrapuntal sections. The toccata flourished in the 17th cent. under Gabrieli, Frescobaldi, Merlo, Buxtehude, Bach, and others.

[M. T. LEGGE]

TOCQUEVILLE, ALEXIS CLÉREL DE (1805–1859), historian. Born in Paris and educated in law, T. received a judicial position at Versailles in 1827, entered the Chamber of Deputies in 1839, and held the ministry of foreign affairs briefly in 1849. Of aristocratic origins, T. observed the rise of democracy in the Western world, and this tension permeated all his thinking. His *De la démocratie en Amérique* (1835–40) records his observations of government and society during his visit to the U.S. in 1831. His *Souvenirs,* written in 1850–51, but published only in 1893 gives his interpretation of the revolution of 1848, while his *L' Ancien Régime et la Révolution* (1856) is a study of the first French attempt at a democratic society. Whether he was a believing Christian is a disputed point. BIBLIOGRAPHY: E. T. Gargan, *Alexis de Tocqueville: The Critical Years, 1848–1851* (1955); J. P. Mayer, *Alexis de Tocqueville: A Biographical Essay in Political Science* (1960).

[R. H. SCHMANDT]

TOGO, African republic (21,853 sq. mi.; pop. [est. 1976] 2,221,189). Togo was a German colony from 1894 to 1914 and was then variously mandated until it achieved independence in 1960. Divine Word missioners from Germany entered the area in 1892. After World War I they were replaced by African Missionaries of Lyons. Conversions are fairly numerous. The hierarchy, created in 1955, consists of an archbishopric at Lomé (former Togo); suffragan sees at Sokodé and Atakpamé; and a prefecture at Dapango.

Catholics in 1976 numbered 442,441. There were 22,227 catechumens, 169 priests, seminarians, 22,252 sisters, 1 archdiocese, 3 dioceses, 60 parishes. Native priests are still few.

Protestantism was introduced in 1847 by the N German Mission and was furthered by Eng. Methodists, Scotch Presbyterians, French Protestants, and Pentecostals, with a combined membership of 99,890 in 1968. BIBLIOGRAPHY: R. M. Wiltgen, NCE 14:186–187; *Bilan du Monde* 2:853–855.

[P. DAMBORIENA]

TOLAND, JOHN (1670–1722), Irish Deist. T. became a Protestant in 1687. He produced the chief writing of deism, *Christianity Not Mysterious* (1696), in which he asserted that neither God nor his revelation is beyond human reason and that the mysteries of Christianity are merely pagan conceptions and priestcraft. When the book was condemned by the Irish parliament, T. fled to London. He also traveled extensively on the continent and was welcomed at German courts. In his crowning work, *Pantheisticon* (1720), he proposed a free philosophical community for the cultivation of pantheism and provided for it a liturgy modeled on Christian services but excerpted from pagan writings. BIBLIOGRAPHY: M. Schmidt, RGG 6:931–932.

[M. J. SUELZER]

TOLEDO, FRANCISCO DE (1532–96), theologian and first Jesuit cardinal. Born in Cordova, T. studied philosophy at Valencia, theology at Salamanca under Domingo de Soto, joined the Society of Jesus, and was brought to Rome by St. Francis Borgia, where he first taught philosophy and then theology at the Roman College. A man of great talents and extraordinary energy, for despite his employment on diplomatic missions to Poland, Germany, and the Low Countries (where he received the abjuration of *Baius), and his office as preacher to the papal court, to which he had been appointed by Pius V and which he held for 24 years, he wrote many works on philosophy, theology, and Scripture. Of these the most significant is his commentary on the *Summa theologiae* of St. Thomas Aquinas. He parted company on many points with Cajetan, then its most esteemed expositor. He was the first to teach predestination after the foreseeing of merits, which was the augury of acrimonious debates to come. He was created a cardinal at the instance of Henry IV of France, in whose reconciliation with the Church he had acted as intermediary; but he used his position to interfere, neither successfully nor happily for his later reputation, in the internal policies of the Jesuits.

[T. GILBY]

TOLEDO, COUNCILS OF, 18 national synods of some 80 Spanish sees held the following years: 400, 531, 589, 633, and 636; 638, 646, 653, 655, and 656; 675, 681, 683, 684, and 688; 693, 694, and 702 (acts not extant). *Elvira (*c.* 306) and Saragossa I (380) and III (691) may also rank as national; Toledo XI (675) was merely provincial. At Toledo III (589) the Arian Visigoths became Catholic with little resistance; and their Erastian kings expected the solidly established Catholic episcopacy to support royal authority, recently enhanced by *Leovigild (d. 586). The irregular dates of councils reflect the needs of the kings and not the state of society. Except for *Leander and *Isidore of Seville, the councils gave the bishops of Toledo a national primacy, formally recognized in 681. Independence of Rome developed, only eight papal letters arriving 604–711. A minority of lay nobles (15–20 as opposed to 20–60 bps.) attended the councils, which dealt with civil affairs also. Religious influence raised the level of law, which was based on rational proof rather than on Germanic compurgation and ordeal. The kings presided or instructed the councils by a tome; royal decrees confirmed the canons and punished infractions by confiscations that accrued to the royal fisc. Spanish bps. did not object to royal direction, which included the appointment of bishops. BIBLIOGRAPHY: A. K. Ziegler, *Church and State in Visigothic Spain* (1930).

[E. P. COLBERT]

TOLERANCE, in the widest sense, a willingness to put up with the affirmation and practice of belief that is in conflict with one's own. It is used in reference both to an attitude on the part of an individual and to a policy of a state.

The Bible provides no explicit solution to the modern problem of pluralism. The Jewish theocracy, though scarcely permissive, was less intolerant than many contemporary civilizations (cf. Dt 10.18 and Ruth *passim*). Interference by the State in religious matters was indeed expressly condemned in 1 Macc 2.19–22, but there the threat came from a pagan political power. Jesus refused unequivocally to make use of political influence in support of faith (Mt 4.8–10; Jn 6.15) and allowed believers and unbelievers to live side by side (Mt 13.30, 40–42). Religion and politics are two totally different sides of human life, whose spheres of authority must not be equated (Mt 22.21).

As long as Christians were persecuted they demanded tolerance from the state authorities. Toleration was introduced and extended to all forms of divine worship through the Edict of Milan (313). But soon some Christian factions called for a privileged position for their faith. Already in the course of the 4th cent., intolerance, esp. toward heretics, became more widespread. The medieval theology of the two swords, which placed pope above emperor, often led to an abuse of political power in support of ecclesiastical claims. Christians generally adopted the view that they ought to be intolerant of error; that since their faith was the true faith, it alone had the right to exist; and that the toleration of false belief was equivalent to the error of *indifferentism. Moreover, political as well as religious considerations seemed to require intolerance. Unity of faith was a cohesive force that helped hold the State itself together; and what threatened this unity was a threat also to peace, order, and the stability of civil government itself.

Neither the Reformation nor the Counter Reformation brought any immediate change in this attitude. But influences were already at work that were to lead to the acceptance of religious pluralism as politically feasible and indeed inevitable, for it became clear in many places that uniformity of belief could not be enforced. The power of churchmen to call for the persecution of heretics diminished. With the Enlightenment of the 18th cent., tolerance moved forward, although often as a consequence of indifference toward all forms of religious truth. The pace of change quickened in the 19th cent. in many countries through disestablishment. Roman theologians did not look favorably on liberalism, though some, in order to reconcile old theory with contemporary politics, maintained a dualism not beyond criticism, holding fast on the one hand to the old view that the State must be subservient to truth, but counterbalancing it on the other with the hypothesis that in the given circumstances it was best to let things be as they were.

With Vatican Council II there was a shift of emphasis from the tenets or opinions people held, to their behavior and their readiness to live in harmony. The old principle that only truth, not error, has any right no longer stiffened the stand against toleration.

The Council did not speak about toleration, which implies a judgment of values, but about freedom of conscience. It pronounced "on the right of the person and of communities to social and civil freedom in matters religious" as follows: "This freedom means that all men are to be immune from coercion on the part of individuals or of social groups and of any human power, in such wise that in matters religious no one is to be forced to act in a manner contrary to his own beliefs. Nor is anyone to be restrained from acting in accordance with his own beliefs, whether privately or publicly, whether alone or in association with others, within due limits. The Synod further declares that the right to religious freedom has its foundation in the very dignity of the human person, as this dignity is known through the revealed Word of God and by reason itself" (Vat II RelFreed, 2).

This now renders nugatory the charge that Catholics, if they are in the minority, demand toleration on the basis of principles held by their opponents, and when they are in power refuse tolerance on the basis of their own principles. BIBLIOGRAPHY: A. Hartmann, *Toleranz und chrislicher Glaube* (1955); J. C. Murray, E. Schillebeeckx, et al., *La Liberté religieuse. Exigence spirituelle et problème politique* (1955); A. F. Carillo de Albornoz, *Roman Catholicism and Religious Liberty* (1959); *idem, Le Concile et la liberté religieuse* (1967); J. Hamer et Y. Congar, *La Liberté religieuse* (1967).

[T. EARLY]

TOLERATION ACT, in England, an act of Parliament in 1689 granting a degree of *religious freedom. Toleration was granted to *Dissenters, provided they believed in the Trinity, but not to RC *recusants. The penalties prescribed by the Conventicle Act of 1670 were rescinded, on the condition that Dissenters make a declaration rejecting transubstantiation and swear oaths of allegiance and supremacy (Quakers were permitted to make a simple affirmation). The Toleration Act left in force the *Test Act (1673) barring Dissenters from civil office. For freedom in their ministry, dissenting ministers were required to subscribe to the *Thirty-Nine Articles, except the two on *infant baptism. While the granting of limited toleration was prompted by a desire to unite all Protestants politically in the loyalty to the King, William III, the Act did represent progress in the cause of religious liberty and brought relief from the persecutions long suffered by English Baptists, Quakers, and others. The Act also brought greater religious freedom to minority groups in the American colonies.

[R. B. ENO]

TOLERATION ACTS OF 1639 AND 1649 in Maryland, legislative provisions for religious liberty. The Maryland Charter created by the first Lord Baltimore, based on the Privileges of Durham whereby the king exempted the colony from English statute and gave authority to make its own laws to the Maryland assembly, required legislative implementation. Both the second Lord Baltimore as proprietor and the assembly advanced plans which included a form of toleration. The assembly adopted its own law in 1639, extending toleration to all Christians and affirming all the rights and privileges of the great charter, which would include non-Christians. The latter provision was not in accord with Lord Baltimore's thinking. A third enactment avoided condemnation of blasphemy, sorcery, and sacrilege, thus indicating a separation of Church and State. The Maryland assembly, composed largely of Catholics, thus espoused what English Catholics believed about nonestablishment.

The Act of 1649 was restrictive of the spirit of the Act of 1639 by limiting rights to Trinitarian Christians. Even so it was more liberal than the legislation of most colonies at the time. The effect of the act was to protect Catholics and Protestants who were non-Puritan. Up to 1700 the protection of the Act of 1639 was successfully invoked by members of the Maryland colony.

[J. R. AHERNE]

TOLKIEN, JOHN R. R. (1892–1973), British novelist, poet, scholar. Also a philologist and critic of note, T. is best known for creating a mythology of his own in the novels, *The Hobbit* (1937); and the trilogy, *The Lord of the Rings* (1954), *The Two Towers* (1954), and *The Return of the King* (1955). This trilogy, revealing him as a masterly story-teller, yields diverse meanings to his readers and critics. T. is also numbered among the chief collaborators in translation and literary revision for the *Jerusalem Bible*. BIBLIOGRAPHY: *Tolkien and the Critics* (eds. N. Isaacs and R. Zimbardo, 1968).

[S. A. HEENEY]

TOLOMEI, BERNARD, see BERNARD TOLOMEI, BL.

TOLOMEO DA LUCCA, see PTOLEMY OF LUCCA.

TOLOSANUS (Pierre Grégoire; *c.*1540–97), French canonist at Toulouse, important to the development of the jurisprudence proper to canon law in such works as: *Syntagma iuris universi* (1582); *Commentaria seu annotationes in decretalium praemium* (1592); *Totius iuris canonici partiones . . .* (1594).

[T. C. O'BRIEN]

TOLSTOY, ALEXEY KONSTANTINOVICH (1817–75), Russian author. His finest works include nature and love lyrics, a comic *History of the Russian State* (1868), a majestic paraphrase of St. John Damascene's prayer for the dead (1858), and numerous works glorifying the Russian past: ballads modeled on the Russian *byliny* (folk epic); the historical novel, *The Silver Prince* (1863); and a trilogy of historical dramas, of which the second, *Tsar Fyodor Ioannovich* (1868), is the best. BIBLIOGRAPHY: D. S. Mirsky, *History of Russian Literature* (1927) 286–289; M. Slonim, *Soviet Russian Literature* (1964) 140–150.

[M. F. MCCARTHY]

TOLSTOY, LEV (LEO) NIKOLAYEVICH, (1828–1910), great Russian author and moral thinker. His works reflect, in varying degrees, his constant wrestling with moral, religious, and ethical problems. Despite the so-called Christian anarchy that led to his condemnation of all organized forms of government and his rejection of and by the Russian Orthodox Church (he was excommunicated in 1901), he remained, all his life, a fanatical seeker after truth. His belief that social progress depended, not on socialism or Marxism, but on the spiritual reform of each individual, led him to a life of asceticism. "Tolstoyanism," the religion of non-resistance that he gradually evolved and which won him many followers, was a rationalistic religion based on the moral teachings of Christ, whose divinity, however, T. denied. T.'s spiritual conflict is reflected in numerous essays of the 1880s and 1890s, esp. the *Confession* (1878–79), *What Do I Believe?* (1883), the *Criticism of Dogmatic Theology* (1880–84), and *The Kingdom of God Is Within Us* (1894). His preoccupation with the thought of death inspired the short masterpieces *Three Deaths* (1858) and *The Death of Ivan Ilyich* (1886); his deeply rooted conviction that sexual activity is permissible only for procreation is incorporated into such works as *The Kreuzer Sonata* (1890), *Father Sergius* (1898), and *Resurrection* (1899); his certainty that the key to moral goodness lay in the simple life of the Russian peasant appears in numerous works, e.g., in the naturalistic drama *The Power of Darkness* (1886). Many of his short masterpieces incorporate positive aspects of his moral and ethical thinking, e.g., *God Sees the Truth but Waits* (1872), *What Men Live By* (1881), and *Evil Allures, But Good Endures* (1885). In them, as in the great novels, *War and Peace* (1863–69) and *Anna Karenina* (1873–77), Tolstoy achieves the perfect synthesis of art and moral content that is the hallmark of good and universal literature. BIBLIOGRAPHY: E. J. Simmons, *Introduction to Tolstoy's Writings* (1968); H. Troyat, *Tolstoy* (translated from the French by N. Amphoux, 1968).

[M. F. MCCARTHY]

TOMB OF OUR LADY, the site in the Valley of Cedron, near Jerusalem, where Mary's body was laid until her *Assumption. A 5th-cent. church commemorates the traditional place. The church is in the form of a cross, and a small cubical in the center of the eastern arm is regarded as the tomb itself. Several early apocryphal works attest to Mary's burial in Jerusalem, and by the 5th cent. it had become a popular place for pilgrimages. A rival tradition, placing Mary's tomb in Ephesus where she was supposed to have journeyed with St. John the Evangelist, seems to be based upon a faulty gloss in an early manuscript. BIBLIOGRAPHY: B. Meistermann, CE 14:774–775.

[T. M. MCFADDEN]

TOME OF LEO, the letter sent by Pope Leo I (*Ep.* 28) to Flavian, Patriarch of Constantinople, on June 13, 449, called also *Epistola dogmatica*. Leo supported Flavian during the Eutychian controversy by sending legates with the Tome to the Council of Ephesus in 449, which developed into the famous Robber Synod. Based on the teaching of the Fathers, esp. Tertullian and St. Augustine, Leo exposed very clearly the doctrine of the Latin Church on the Incarnation: Jesus Christ is one person, the Divine Word in whom there are two natures, the divine and the human, inseparably united although unconfused and unmixed. Each one of these natures has its own faculties, its own operation but within the unity of the one person; the unity of person entails what is termed *communicatio idiomatum*, so that it can truly be said that the Son of Man descended from heaven and also that the Son of God was crucified. This letter, always regarded as a dogmatic document of exceptional value, was directed against the heresy of Eutyches. It received formal recognition by the Council of Chalcedon (451). BIBLIOGRAPHY: Grill–Bacht Konz; P. T. Camelot, *Éphèse et Chalcédoine* (1962).

[P. FOSCOLOS]

TOME OF UNION (433), a document containing the terms of agreement that partially settled the Christological controversy between John of Antioch and Cyril of Alexandria. The tome was occasioned by the schism that had occurred 2 years earlier over the orthodoxy of Nestorius. On June 22, 431, Cyril of Alexandria had opened the Council of Ephesus, which had been summoned by the Emperor Theodosius II, and immediately proceeded to condemn and depose Nestorius as a heretic and to proclaim Mary "Theotokos," "Mother of God," and not merely "Christotokos," as was maintained by Nestorius. John of Antioch arrived 4 or 5 days later with a delegation of Eastern bishops, who then held their own synod (with 43 or 53

present), which denounced the condemnation of Nestorius and deposed Cyril. On July 11, the papal legates, who had also arrived late approved the measures adopted under the guidance of Cyril. In August the dissenting bishops approved a formula explaining their own position; drafted by Theodoret of Cyr, this was sent to the Emperor. Through the intervention of the latter and of Pope Sixtus III, who wrote to John, and of Acacius of Beroea, who obtained some explanations of Cyril's anathemas from Cyril himself, an understanding was reached. After making a few slight changes, John sent the original document of Theodoret to Cyril (contained in *Ep.* 38 of Cyril's correspondence), who received it with obvious expressions of joy (*Ep.* 39). In signing the document, John made some generous concessions, not the least of which was his acceptance of the condemnation of Nestorius. Cyril, on the other hand, in accepting it, showed himself much more conciliatory than he had been at Ephesus, not insisting upon some of his favorite expressions such as "one nature" and "hypostatic union" which had been a cause of alarm to the Antiochians. He also accepted some of the latters' favorite expressions such as "one person (*prosopon*)" and "union (*enōsis*; Lat. *unitio*), of two natures." But essentially he was vindicated: the doctrine of Mary's divine maternity was upheld and the distinction of two natures in one person was maintained. Unfortunately, many of the followers of both John and Cyril were afraid that in the agreement there had been sacrifices of doctrine along with that of terminology. As a result the Tome of Union was only partially successful. BIBLIOGRAPHY: Cyril, *Epp.* 38, 39, 47 (PG 77:169); É. Amann, DTC 11.1:120–127; Bihlmeyer-Tüchle 1:271–275.

[M. J. COSTELLOE]

TOME OF UNION (920), a temporary agreement reached between two dissident groups within the Greek Church over the question of fourth marriages. It is of more general import because both parties recognized the authority of the Pope in this dispute. In the East there had been a long tradition that, though marriage was lawful, a second marriage was a concession to human weakness, and a third and esp. a fourth, unlawful. When the Emperor Leo VI lost three wives in rapid succession, he married the grandniece of the historian Theophanes, Zoë Carbonospina and was excommunicated by the patriarch Nicholas the Mystic. Both parties to the dispute then had recourse to the Holy See, and Pope Sergius III in reply sent legates to Constantinople upholding the validity of the Emperor's marriage since there was no condemnation of fourth marriages by the Church at large. BIBLIOGRAPHY: Mann 4:131–134; Fliche-Martin 7:123; A. A. Vasiliev, *History of the Byzantine Empire* (1964) 1:334; Mansi 18:336–341.

[M. J. COSTELLOE]

TOMKINS, THOMAS (1572–1656), English organist and composer. One of a very large family of musicians, T. studied with William Byrd and earned his degree in music at

Oxford. He was organist at the Worcester cathedral and at the Chapel Royal. T. ranks high among the 16th-cent. English polyphonic writers. His works include fine madrigals as well as "Musica Deo sacra" (a collection of services and 95 anthems) and other church music.

[M. T. LEGGE]

TONALE (tonary, *tonarium, tonarius*), medieval music book which contained the formulas of each of the psalm tones assigned to the eight Gregorian modes and in which were listed, according to their mode, the various antiphons, responsories, Introits, etc., of the liturgy. BIBLIOGRAPHY: Reese, MusMA.

[M. T. LEGGE]

TONE, see PSALM TONE.

TONES IN GREGORIAN CHANT, the formulas for the chanting of the *psalms *and *canticles. There is a psalm tone to correspond to each of the eight *church modes plus the *tonus peregrinus* (pilgrim tone), the *tonus in directum* (for psalms sung without an antiphon) and the paschal tone (for certain psalms during the Easter season).

Each formula, or psalm tone, contains six elements: (1) the *intonation,* a brief melodic formula leading to the tenor or dominant; (2) the *dominant* or *tenor,* the reciting note for all the words between the intonation and the mediant cadence; (3) the *flexa,* a melodic inflection where the length of the verse demands an interruption for breath; (4) the *mediant cadence,* a closing figure for the first half of the verse; (5) the *caesura,* the whole bar dividing the two halves of the verse; (6) the *dominant* or *tenor,* the reciting note for the second half of the verse; (7) the *final cadence,* the closing figure for the second half of the verse. (The following illustration is the simple setting for Tone V:)

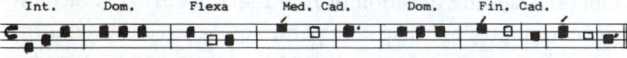

BIBLIOGRAPHY: L. F. Heckenlively, *Fundamentals of Gregorian Chant.*

[M. T. LEGGE]

TONGA ISLANDS (Friendly Islands), a part of *Polynesia. The Tongas consist of about 150 small islands (270 sq. mi.; pop. [1976] 98,200). They were discovered by the Dutch in 1606 and charted in the 1770s by Capt. James Cook, who named them for the friendliness of the natives. They were annexed by Great Britain in 1900. Marist Fathers landed in 1837 but were soon expelled. Further efforts at evangelization in 1842 were also thwarted; but a treaty of friendship with France provided religious liberty in 1855. A vicariate was organized in 1937. Tonga became a vicariate apostolic along with Niue in 1957. In 1966 the hierarchy was established. In 1976 Catholics numbered 14,372.

Almost 80% of the Tongans belong to the Methodist Overseas Mission and the Free Church of Tonga. Angli-cans, Adventists, and Mormons are also active on the islands. BIBLIOGRAPHY: *Bilan du Monde* 2:856–857.

[P. DAMBORIENA]

TONGERLOO, ABBEY OF, a Premonstratensian abbey near Antwerp in Belgium. Founded in 1130 by Giselbert of Kasterlee, it served 59 churches. It was held *in commendam* by the episcopal See of Hertogenbosch. The order's college in Rome, founded in 1618, was supported by Tongerloo. The abbey in the years 1786–96 served as the seat of the Bollandists. It was suppressed in 1796, and the church and most of the buildings were razed. It was restored in the years 1835–40, in 1868 again became an abbey, and was rebuilt (1928) after a fire. In 1964 it had 265 members. BIBLIOGRAPHY: Backmund 2:330–335.

[N. BACKMUND]

TONGIORGI, SALVATORE (1820–65), Italian Jesuit, professor of philosophy at the Gregorian Univ. in Rome. His textbook, *Institutiones philosophicae* (3 v. 1861–62), contributed to the neo-scholastic revival of the 19th century.

[T. C. O'BRIEN]

TONGUES, GIFT OF (BIBLICAL), glossalalia, a charism of prayer manifesting the presence and power of the Holy Spirit in the early Church and thereafter, a striking phenomenon cited in the NT writings of Paul and Luke. The meaning of this *charismatic gift appears to differ in 1 Cor 12–14 and in Acts 2, and the history of interpretation has been largely a history of attempting to reconcile these two sets of texts. The older view, dating back to the Church Fathers, conceived the phenomenon as one of speaking real languages in whole or in part, e.g., foreign languages or dialects of known languages. The contemporary view is that glossolalia in both the texts of Paul and Luke refer to ecstatic prayer, i.e., involuntary utterance of rapid sequences of inarticulate sounds perhaps in chanting cadence. Some prefer to designate this form of prayer as "pre-conceptual" rather than ecstatic. Speaking in tongues was apparently so well known at Corinth and elsewhere that Paul felt no compulsion to explain or describe the phenomenon. In fact, because of an exaggerated emphasis upon glossolalia at Corinth, Paul was forced in 1 Cor to situate the charism in its proper relationship to the greatest gift, love, and to coordinate its use with the more communally oriented gifts of interpretation and prophecy (1 Cor. 14.5). While ecstatic behavior may have accompanied the gift, contemporary exegetes stress that there is little scriptural evidence that the glossolalist be in a trance-like state or out of control. Those who possess the gift can use it or not, seemingly at will (1 Cor 14.26–28, 32–34), as Paul himself does (1 Cor 14.18), and can employ it for the edification of the church assembly (1 Cor 14.27f, 32,40). The first Epistle to the Corinthians (14:14) clearly describes glossolalia as a prayer of one's spirit (*pneuma*) rather than one's mind (*nous*), which remains empty. It is thus a form of praise (1 Cor 14.16f) without readily intelligible content, but since the gift is capable of being interpreted, some prefer to describe it as preconceptual rather than non-rational. In Paul's judgment, the gift of glossolalia is a genuine gift of the Spirit (1 Cor 14.2), a means of genuine personal growth (1 Cor 14.4), which he desires for all members of the community. Since glossolalia evidence the divine presence in the community, they are a sign to unbelievers (1 Cor 14.22). Tongues are not to be forbidden (1 Cor 14.39); on the contrary, they are one of the gifts to be sought (14.1). In fact, Rom 8.26–27 appears to confirm, albeit indirectly, Paul's positive evaluation of preconceptual prayer. On the other hand, the exercise of glossolalia had to be regulated because of the exaggerated emphasis placed upon it by the enthusiasts at Corinth. When Paul lists the gifts of the Spirit, glossolalia are mentioned last (1 Cor 12.10, 30; 14.19). Their use must be determined by their value in building up the Church "in love" (1 Cor 13; 14.4–5, 17–19). The gift of tongues should be accompanied by the gift of interpretation (1 Cor 14.27–28) and the glossolalist should pray for this gift since he has a responsibility to the community as a whole (1 Cor 14.13–14).

Other references to tongues in the Acts of the Apostles exclusive of chapter 2 (Acts 10.44–56; 19.6) lead to the same conclusion concerning the nature of the phenomenon as that found in 1 Corinthians. The narrative of Acts 2 is a Lucan composition based upon a historically significant and formative event in the life of the Christian community, namely, the first time Christ was preached publicly under the influence of the Spirit. The oral tradition reporting this event very likely recalled Jesus' disciples proclaiming Christ and praising God in tongues in such manner as to persuade listeners of the presence of the Spirit. Luke reinterpreted this scene in two ways: by situating the event on Pentecost; by changing glossolalia to "other tongues" (Acts 2.4). Situating this first apostolic proclamation on Pentecost is significant since scholars today more readily agree that the feast was associated in Judaism before the second century A.D. with a commemoration of the making of the covenant at Sinai. This association had already been made in certain Jewish circles before the Christian era (Jubilees 6.17–21; 1 QS 1,2) and may well have become more widespread in Judaism after the destruction of the Temple in 70 A.D. Luke has reinterpreted these Jewish traditions about Pentecost, seeing in the proclamation and glossolalia the inauguration of a new covenant of the Spirit offered to all nations, a new Sinai. It was also Luke's "witness-mission" theology which prompted him to reinterpret Pentecostal glossolalia in terms of intelligible speech, "in other tongues." Acts 2.9–11 accurately reflects the Lucan perspective concerning the effects of this witness, this new Spirit covenant offered to all men. The gift of tongues is no longer seen as momentary and largely incomprehensible prayer, but the apostolic proclamation becomes the inauguration of a truly universal preaching that will unify men, transcending every boundary of nationality and speech, reversing the divisions among men begun at Babel (Gen 11.1–9). However, in spite of Luke's reinterpretation, certain elements of his account can only be explained in terms of glossolalia. If the crowd understood what was happening, there would have been no need for Peter's sermon. Furthermore, the cynical reaction of certain witnesses is hard to explain if the apostles were really speaking in foreign tongues, but would be natural if their speech was glossolalia.

Consciousness of the difference between the Pauline and Lucan presentations of glossolalia provides, not only deeper insight into the manner of NT composition, but also lends a needed biblical perspective to contemporary pentecostal experience. BIBLIOGRAPHY: G. Montague, *Spirit and His Gifts* (1974); *idem*, *Holy Spirit* (1976). *GLOSSOLALIA.

[T. J. RYAN]

TONGUES SPEAKING, a phrase commonly used as an equivalent for *glossolalia, the charismatic gift of speaking in strange languages, which is emphasized esp. in *Pentecostalism.

[T. C. O'BRIEN]

TONIOLO, GIUSEPPE (1845–1918), Italian socioeconomist, considered a founder of Christian Democracy in Italy. He spent most of his career as a professor of economics at the Univ. of Pisa. His most influential and programmatic work is *La democrazia cristiana* (1900). In the cause of providing an order of social justice inspired by Christian ideals, he established several organizations and the *Revista internazionale di scienze sociali*. T. favored the principle of subsidiarity in the cooperative harmony of Church and State and in the structuring of the social order. His thought is regarded as having had influence on Leo XIII's landmark encyclical *Rerum novarum*. He was an exemplary Catholic and his cause for beatification was introduced.

[T. C. O'BRIEN]

TONSURE: (1) formerly a ceremony signifying, by a clipping of the hair, admission to the clerical state and separation from the world; abolished by Paul VI's *motu proprio*, *Ministeria quaedam* (1972), which also suppressed minor orders and the subdiaconate; (2) the hair-style of clerics and monks. The first was also called a *corona* (Lat., crown) and was a shaved spot at the crown of the skull. The monk's or friar's tonsure (Lat., *rasura*) amounted to a shaving of the pate, with a circle of hair left below; variations were often imaginative, sometimes bizarre. The tonsure was not worn in the U.S., except by some Trappists; it is now everywhere obsolescent.

TONUS (Lat.) or tone, in music a term denoting: (1) a musical sound as opposed to a noise; (2) the quality of a musical sound; (3) the interval of a major second (whole tone); or (4) a psalm-tone in Gregorian chant.

[M. T. LEGGE]

TONUS PEREGRINUS, in plainchant a psalm tone peculiar to Ps 114 (113) for *In exitu Israel*, having a different *tenor (recitation note) for the first and second parts; also a name for the Aeolian mode (the natural minor scale beginning on A).

[M. T. LEGGE]

TOOROP, JAN THEODOOR (1858–1928), Dutch painter. T. studied at the Academies of Amsterdam and Brussels. After periods in Holland, London, and Paris, influenced by Manet and Ensor, T. painted in dark tones, in the style of the Hague School and the Belgian painter Vogels, subjects inspired by social problems of the days. After 1890 T. moved toward symbolism and a mystical point of view. Becoming a Catholic (1905) he began a series of religious works austere and angular in line. T.'s important work in the 1890s is symbolic in theme relating to Art Nouveau (*The Three Brides*, 1893) embracing book design and posters. BIBLIOGRAPHY: R. Siebelhoff, *Jan Toorop* (1970–71).

[P. H. HEFTING]

TOPHET (THOPHETH), the *high place in the valley of Gehinnom near Jerusalem where human sacrifices were offered to Molech (2 Kg 23.10). In Is 30.33 and Jer 19.11–14, this name is used to signify "place of burning" for corpses and unclean things, and Jeremiah threatens that Jerusalem itself will become a "tophet" in this sense.

[D. J. BOURKE]

TORAH, the Law as the will of Yahweh revealed through the priests. The people came to the priests for knowledge of God, to seek instruction. The Law gives life, so that when the priests do not faithfully impart Torah to the people, the priests bear the heaviest burden of judgment (Hosea, Amos, Jeremiah), but the people also perish. Originally Torah may have referred to the divine oracle revealed by lot; *Urim and Thummim. The etymology of the word suggests this, since it probably comes from the verb *yarah*, "to throw or cast" (lots). The blessing of Moses pronounced on Levi is instructive (Deut 33.8–11). The first prerogative of Levi is the custody of Urim and Thummim; but the fully developed priestly role is also envisioned: "They observe your word and keep your covenant; they teach your precepts to Jacob, your Law (*Torah*) to Israel." The meaning of Torah expanded and deepened from the simple oracular casting of the lot to a more diversified divine commandment and response communicated by the priests, to priestly instruction in general, and to the priestly version of the national epic. This included compilations of laws and traditions, which came to be the ultimate meaning of Torah, the Book of Moses. In Ezra-Nehemiah, the heart of Judaism is this written Torah, in definitive form, interpreted by scribes who are descendants of priestly families and learned in the Torah. From beginning to end, Torah is bound up closely with priestly tradition. In the prologue of Sirach the reference to "the Law and the Prophets" is the first occurrence of a phrase that was in common usage at the time of Jesus. The usage is evidence that the received tradition of sacred writings was understood as the combined heritage of the priests and the prophets.

[E. J. DILLON]

TORCULUS, a *neum in *Gregorian chant notation signifying a succession of three notes, the second higher in pitch than the other two.

[A. DOHERTY]

TORELLO, BL. (d. 1282), penitent and hermit. He lived for 50 years in obscurity at Avallaneto near Poppi in the diocese of Arezzo, Tuscany. His name is probably a shortened form of Victoriello. He is invoked as a protector of children and of women in childbirth and is represented in art as a hermit with a wolf and a small child. The simple austerity of his life is reminiscent of St. Francis' love of his wilderness hermitage. The abbot of the Vallombrosian Abbey of San Fedele in Poppi was T.'s spiritual director. He took the habit of a penitent from this abbot, but he belonged to no order. His cult was approved by Benedict XIV.

[E. J. DILLON]

TORGAU ARTICLES, the basis for the second part (Art. 22–28) of the *Augsburg Confession, dealing with matters of worship and discipline. The Articles were drawn up in March 1530, on instructions of John Frederick I, Elector of Saxony, in preparation for the Diet of Augsburg, by Luther, P. *Melanchthon, J. *Jonas, J. *Bugenhagen. They are named for the place where they were presented to the elector. BIBLIOGRAPHY: Schaff Creeds 1:229. *SCHWABACH ARTICLES.

[P. DAMBORIENA]

TORNIELLI, BONAVENTURE, BL. (1412–1491), Servite missionary. A late vocation, T. swiftly progressed in his spiritual life, marked by fervor and austerities. After ordination he was assigned to preach in the great cities of Italy. His desire to enter a hermitage was thwarted when Sixtus IV appointed him apostolic preacher. He continued his missionary apostolate and died while preaching Lenten sermons at Udine. Pius X beatified him in 1911. BIBLIOGRAPHY: A. Serra, *Ricerche sul Beato Bonaventura da Forli* (1964); A. M. Serra, BiblSanct 3:287–290.

[J. M. O'DONNELL]

TORO, GABRIEL DE, see GABRIEL DE TORO.

TORQUEMADA, JUAN DE (*c.* 1563–1624), historian of Mexico. He entered the Franciscans in Spain and was sent to work in their missions in Mexico, where he became associated with the convent of Santiago Tlatelolco. He was a pupil of the Franciscan historian Juan Bautista and he himself continued the tradition of the Franciscan historians of New Spain. T.'s major work is the huge *Monarquía Indiana* (1613), which incorporated much material from Jerónimo de Mendieta's *Historia eclesiástica Indiana* and other authors. Torquemada also wrote the *Vida de fray Sebastián de Aparico* (1605). BIBLIOGRAPHY: R. Ricard, *Spiritual Conquest of Mexico* (tr. L. B. Simpson, 1966).

[R. H. SCHMANDT]

TORQUEMADA, TOMÁS DE (1420–98), Spanish inquisitor. Of noble birth, he was Dominican prior of Santa Cruz in Segovia (1452–74), and confessor-counselor to Isabella and Ferdinand. His negligible role in the Spanish Inquisition's origins grew to one of importance. As Grand Inquisitor (1483), his legislative-administrative reorganization set its permanent character. Somewhat discredited at Rome (1494), he retired to Santo Tomás monastery, the Renaissance gem he built at Avila. Intransigent, fearless, studious, devoid of personal ambition, not a cruel man nor an anti-Semite, his rigorous intolerance sprang from ideological rather than psychological roots. Legends and exaggerations distort his biography. BIBLIOGRAPHY: A. Michel, DTC 15.1:1239.

[R. I. BURNS]

TORRES, BARTOLOMÉ DE (1512–68), Spanish theologian who taught in Salamanca, accompanied Philip II to England for a time, and who was bishop of Las Palmas in the Canary Islands from 1566 until his death. Born in Burgos, he studied in Salamanca where he seems to have been influenced by Francisco de Vitoria. He then taught philosophy there (1542–43), held the Scotus chair in theology (1543–47), and expounded the theology of Thomas Aquinas (1547–51), on whose *Summa theologiae* he wrote commentaries still extant in part.

[E. J. DILLON]

TORRES, FRANCISCO (Turrianus; *c*.1509–84), patrologist, appointed papal theologian by Paul IV for the Council of Trent, Jesuit from 1567. From 1540, after studies at the Univ. of Alcalá, he was in Rome, a member of the household of Card. Salviati and edited works of several Eastern church writers, among them St. John Damascene. During the first period of Trent he published a work against A. *Catharinus, taking the position that episcopal residency is of divine law. At the Council in 1562 he was a leading spokesman for that view and made leading contributions to the discussions on other disciplinary reforms and on the Eucharist and holy orders. His *De Summi Pontificis supra concilium auctoritate* (1551) was a notable study on the Church as well as a polemic against the Lutherans.

[T. C. O'BRIEN]

TORRES, LUIS DE (Turrianus Complutensis; 1562–1635), Spanish Jesuit theologian, professor at Alcalá for most of his career. He published *Disputationes in II^{am} II^{ae}*

D. Thomae (1617), a *Tractatus de gratia* (1623), and *Selectarum disputationum . . . partes duae* (1634), which was ordered withdrawn from circulation by the Jesuit general. T. was imprisoned by the Inquisition (1602–03) for permitting a student to defend as a hypothetical thesis that it is not a matter of Catholic faith that a particular pope is the successor of St. Peter.

[T. C. O'BRIEN]

TORRES BOLLO, DIEGO DE (1551–1638), founder of the Reductions of Paraguay. Born in Spain, he went to Peru after being ordained. After serving in several posts, he founded the vice-province of New Granada (1605) and the province of Paraguay (1607).

[P. J. HENNESSEY]

TORRIGIANI, PIETRO (1472–1528), Italian sculptor, fellow-apprentice with Michelangelo (whose nose he broke). Fleeing Florence (1492), T. worked in England on the tomb of Henry VII (1512–19) showing affinity to Benedetto da Maiano. In Seville (1521) he moved from the High Renaissance style of *The Virgin and Child* to a mannerist *St. Jerome* (1525). Realism, agonized *contraposto*, and *terribilità* of spiritual force in these polychromed terracottas may have influenced Velásquez and Zurbarán. BIBLIOGRAPHY: M. Soria, *Art and Architecture of Spain and Portugal and Their American Dominions (1500–1800)* (1959).

[M. J. DALY]

TORRITI, JACOPO (fl. *c*.1280–96), Italian painter and mosaicist of the 13th-cent. Roman school who signed the apse mosaic in St. John Lateran (1291) and in Sta. Maria Maggiore (1295 or 1296); half-figures of Christ, the Virgin, John the Baptist and St. Francis in the second vault from the transept in S. Francesco, Assisi, are attributed to T. on a stylistic basis—an apotheosis of late Italo-Byzantine mode of great elegance, grace, and delicate colors. "Restoration" at St. John Lateran has destroyed much. At Sta. Maria Maggiore the design for redecoration under Nicholas IV (1288–92) depicting the *Coronation of the Virgin* in star-studded mandorla within a field of vine scrolls is of earliest iconographic type, while below an idyllic River Jordan and *putti riding dolphins and fishing are reminiscent of Roman wall paintings and mosaic designs. T.'s graceful, aristocratic style is couched in a reduced plasticity which adds to the spiritual effect. F. Rusuti, follower of T., executed the façade mosaic of Sta. Maria Maggiore. BIBLIOGRAPHY: A. Nicholson, "Roman School at Assisi," *Art Bulletin* 12 (1930); G. Coor-Achenbach, "Earliest Italian Representation of the Coronation of the Virgin, *Burlington Magazine* 99 (1957).

[M. J. DALY]

TORRUBIA, JOSÉ (1698–1761), missionary, historian. Of Spanish birth, T. entered the Franciscans in 1714 and went to the Philippines in 1719. He became known as a writer but suffered from the jealousy of some Franciscans and others. In Spain in 1733 he cleared himself of their charges. In 1752 T. was named archivist and chronicler of his order. He continued the *Chronica* begun by Damien Cornejo, contributing the most scientific history to that work. In 1759 T. published his significant *I Moscoviti nella California . . .* His final work, on natural science, *Aparato para la historia natural española*, appeared in 1754.

[J. R. AHERNE]

TORTURE, the deliberate infliction of excruciating pain, an act that may be prompted by a number of different reasons.

Its motive might be ritualistic, for instance, in the service of a god requiring such inhumanity; or even quasiethical, e.g., to provide a respected enemy with an opportunity to display his endurance, a compliment to his imperturbability that he could probably do without.

It could be imposed as a means of gratification, e.g., to gloat over the agony of a victim because it appeases the torturer's desire for revenge, or because he is so depraved that he takes delight simply in inflicting pain. To take pleasure in hurting is a beastliness and savagery that is the worst form of intemperance (see ThAq ST 2a2ae, 159.2).

Torture may be imposed as a form of *punishment, whether as an accompaniment to capital punishment, or stopping short of death, as a maiming that expresses revengeful hatred for the offender or the community's execration of the offense; or whether it is adopted as a deterrent; or whether it is used to administer a swift and sharp tonic. Torture as part of retributive punishment may have satisfied a rougher age's sense of poetic justice but has now been replaced by neater methods, even in countries where the notion of retribution survives. If we condemn our forefathers on this point, we may well ask whether modern society is altogether guiltless in its own reprobative action by the casual tolerance of subtler psychological tortures. That some sort of inflicted pain acts as a warning to others is generally admitted by penologists; the debate centers on where the line should be drawn and is to be settled by reasons of humane utilitarianism. Few would countenance mutilation, but more would advocate flogging for certain offences, and are not thereby to be ruled out as lacking Christian charity. As for the curative infliction of pain, that scarcely amounts to the torture here under discussion.

The fourth and main consideration is the use of torture to further the administration of law by extracting a confession from the accused, or by securing evidence about a crime, or to be forewarned about a danger to the community. Quasijudicial torture was not employed by the Jews nor is it mentioned in the OT. Greece and Rome approved its use, and held that it was an effective way of getting at the truth. Christian sentiment was opposed to it, though if regretted it was also considered necessary, and with the reception of the Roman law, the ecclesiastical authorities, though forbidding its use by clerics, came to endorse and profit from its practice by the secular arm. It was only after the Enlightenment that they came to have much of a conscience about it. The Inquisition may be grudgingly allowed the grim merit of a clinical approach; its instructions, which were less objectionable than its actual conduct, drew a distinction between the methods used to extort a confession and to incriminate an accomplice. Torture was defended more by the jurists than by the moralists. The latter could not be altogether easy in their minds about it. The arguments advanced in the apologias of both must be judged to be insufficient.

The use of torture was not at first recognized in the Christian lands north of the Alps. The appeal to God's judgment which is a feature of the *ordeals and the English development of trial by jury rendered unnecessary the extraction of a confession. In the common law, innocence was presumed, whereas in Roman law a credible accusation established a presumption of guilt. In England the legality of torture was never acknowledged, and Edward I administered the snub direct to the pope who directed him to employ it against the Templars. However, with the growth of state absolutism it was allowed by prerogative, and by the time of Elizabeth, its incidence, if less common, was scarcely less abominable than in countries which had received the Roman law. The *peine forte et dure* may be noticed as a form of torture: if the accused remained "mute of malice" and refused to plead, weights were piled on him until either he changed his mind or was pressed to death. This was undergone by Margaret *Clitherow at York (1586) because she was suspected of harboring priests, and by Giles Cory at Salem, Mass. (1692), on suspicion of witchcraft. Formal torture was abolished in England in the mid-17th cent. and in Scotland, where it was part of judicial procedure and equipped with a formidable array of instruments, 50 years later. It had never been part of Irish law. By the end of the 19th cent. it had been generally abandoned in Europe; *Beccaria was the most potent single influence in this reform.

Torture as such is morally offensive, being an *abuse of the nature and functions of a human creature. Self-torture as a cult or ascesis is not demanded of us by the service of God or the rule of right reason, notwithstanding the bizarre and strained mortifications described by hagiographers and some of them on the basis of fact. As an indulgence, a taking of pleasure in hurting, it is vicious in a peculiarly nasty way. As punishment, a moral theologian will view it with wary suspicion and with downright condemnation in its more atrocious forms, though if he is tender without being sentimental, he will not allow emotional repugnance to discredit totally the core idea of the rightful infliction of pain to serve a greater good. As a judicial method it is open to criticism even within the medium of pure law and politics as being ineffective and futile. Again, it is liable to revolting abuse. Moreover, it imposes pain as tantamount to penalty when guilt has yet to be proved, and by treating the innocent as a means to State purposes degrades the nature of a free person. It is therefore rightly rejected as a legal instrument, though we have no cause to consider our age enlightened in this respect, for it has made systematic use of torture and with techniques and devices more accurately called fiendish than beastly. Whether grievous pain can be applied, or the threat of it, to get vitally necessary information when the common good is seriously threatened is not for discussion in general terms, and if, in a particular case those charged with protecting the common good should think resort to torture necessary, their ruthlessness should not be established as a precedent. BIBLIOGRAPHY: G. R. Scott, *History of Torture throughout the Ages* (1940); P. K. Meagher, NCE 14:208–209.

[T. GILBY]

TOSEPHTA (Tosefta, pl. Toseftoth), collection of Tannaitic traditions related to the *Mishnah. The term is Aramaic for additions, and the work consists of Mishnaic material along with supplementary explanations. In organization it resembles the Mishnah, with generally the same orders and tractates. The Tosephta sayings are part of the *Baraithoth. In general it is considered closer to the Palestinian *Talmud than to the Babylonian.

[T. EARLY]

TOSTADO, ALONZO (1400?–55), theologian and exegete. He taught theology, philosophy, and law at Salamanca until Pope Eugene IV condemned him for heresy (1443), which he retracted. Briefly a Carthusian at Scala Dei, he became royal chancellor (1444) for John II of Castile and then bp. of Avila (1449). He wrote 70 theological and exegetical works. BIBLIOGRAPHY: E. Mangenot, DTC 1.1:921–923.

[R. I. BURNS]

TOSTI, LUIGI (1811–97), Benedictine of Montecassino, historian, proponent of *Neo-Guelfism. Among T.'s purely historical works are histories of Monte Cassino (1842), Boniface VIII (1846), the Lombard League (1848), Abelard (1851), the Council of Constance (1853). He also wrote *La Contessa Matilde e i Romani Pontefici* (1859) and *I Prolegomeni alla storia universale della Chiesa* (1861). His plan for a federation of Italian states under the presidency of the pope (i.e., Neo-Guelfism) he outlined in *Il Veggente del secolo XIX* (1848). He was a friend of *Gioberti, leader of the Neo-Guelfs, and also a close friend of Pius IX, whom he urged to abandon temporal power during the pope's exile in Gaeta in 1849. T. also acted as an intermediary between Mazzini and Pius. His pamphlet of 1887, *La Conciliazione*, was a program for peace between the kingdom of Italy and the papacy.

[T. C. O'BRIEN]

TOTAL ABSTINENCE, the principle and practice of absolute renunciation of alcoholic drink. Abstinence from all strong drink was included in the rules of the Nazarite in the OT (Num 6.3), and the Nazarite vow continued into the

Christian era (Acts 21.23–26). Total abstinence is a precept of Islam. It is also a tenet of many Christian bodies, esp. those classified as evangelical or fundamentalist. To some extent this is explained by the preaching and promotion of this ideal as a remedy against drunkenness among the poor, laboring classes. Part of the evangelization by John *Wesley among the poor of England was preaching total abstinence; Theobald *Mathew preached the same ideal to combat drunkenness among the Irish in Ireland and among Irish immigrants in the U.S. (see also *TEMPERANCE MOVEMENT.) Moral theology describes *temperance as the virtue of moderation; a specific form of temperance is *sobriety, necessary because of the special power of alcohol to impede psychological and moral judgment. Total abstinence can mean a higher form of sobriety, embraced in order to eliminate the danger of alcohol completely, esp. as this might detract from the intensity and direction of the life of charity. In the case of the confirmed alcoholic, sobriety means total abstinence; that is the only way virtuous moderation can be observed.

[T. C. O'BRIEN]

TOTAL DEPRAVITY, a description of the sinful condition of man caused by the Fall. The particular historical association of the phrase is to the Calvinism taught by the Synod of *Dort (1619) against *Arminianism (see. FIVE POINTS OF CALVINISM). The Canons of Dort, like other Protestant *confessions of faith (e.g., *Augsburg Confession, Art. XVIII; Second *Helvetic Confession, c. IX; *Westminster Confession, c. VI), acknowledged that human nature and its own power for truth and goodness are not destroyed by original sin. "Depraved nature" means rather a concrete incapacity actually either to live an upright ethical life or, more importantly, to cooperate in the process of salvation. Arminianism took the position that man can and does cooperate in his conversion; Arminian optimism became a characteristic of the teaching of John *Wesley and of American *revivalism. Human depravity was affirmed by Dort (3d and 4th Heads of Doctrine, Art. III–IV, X–XII), denying such cooperation. It is not simply a denial that anything positive can come from man's powers by which he prepares himself for salvation. Rather, the process of salvation is so described that grace and the Holy Spirit supply the operation of the will in conversion. The powers of man are not in their inherent nature really salvaged by grace; they remain corrupt. This position contrasts with RC teaching: under grace man does consent and cooperate in his own conversion; i.e., grace heals and elevates the power for good inherent in man's natural powers even after sin, so that the act of conversion does come vitally from them. When a doctrine of total depravity is attributed to the Reformation generally, it is because salvation by faith and grace alone was presented as excluding human cooperation even under grace in the process of salvation. The acts of man are in themselves, at worst, as Luther claimed, continuously sinful or, at best, irrelevant to salvation.

[T. C. O'BRIEN]

TOTALITARIANISM, a term coined in the 1920s from an elision of ''totality'' and the adjectival suffix ''-arian.'' It was used to refer to the political practice and theory of Russia under Leninist communism and later of Germany under Nazism. The sturdy good sense, culture, and sophistication of the people, and the presence of counterforces, notably the Church and family-feeling, prevented its effective realization in Italy under fascism. In any case, an authoritarian state is not necessarily totalitarian, for both *absolutism and dictatorship may operate within an avowedly limited field; they may acknowledge a higher or divine law and a fundamental or customary law; and they may tolerate or even foster the political rights of associations they do not control. Totalitarianism, on the other hand, is, as the term indicates, quite engulfing, and marks a lapse into tribal and non-civil conditions engineered by a ruthless minority actuated by a mixture of motives. These range from high to low, from a protest against competitive industrialism to the determination to be the bosses.

At some sub-human biological levels, the full organism appears to be the group, not the units composing it, the hive not the bee, the colony not the ant. So also in some ''primitive'' societies there is no life for the individual apart from the tribe. Even in Greece the *polis* was predominant. Yet thence sprang the ideals of citizenship, which were reinforced by the gospel preaching of personal dignity, responsibility, and immortality, backed by a Christianized Roman law, and energetically defended by the Church. Nor did the Church hesitate to make friends of the mammon of iniquity, at first for Augustinian and later for Aristotelian reasons, to fight any suggestion of State omnicompetence. Group personality was then a figure of speech or a legal fiction; the individual person was the unabsorbable ''thing,'' the ultimate substantial unity or *whole (though composed of essential, integral, and virtual parts); the community to which he belonged was a unity of order, whether natural, such as a family, or artificial, such as a guild, or both, such as a Nation-State. There was then no question of the State's being regarded as a ''thing'' with a life of its own, or even of its functionaries' being regarded as ''them,'' except in a partisan sense according to which they could be, and often were, circumvented. There was then also no question of reifying the ''mystical body'' or ''the people of God'', or even of reducing theology to the status of social science.

Yet Leviathan still lurked and began to emerge during the wars of nationalism against Napoleon with the deification of the Prussian State. Even so he still appeared a fairly domesticated monster, and it was not until the present cent. that the totalitarian State, armed with modern techniques of surveillance and compulsion, has tried to engross every human interest. Its characteristic features are the centralized monopoly of coercion and control over every instrument of power, communication, indoctrination, and psychological suggestion exercised through a party machine, the suppression of all values not included in its own interest, the treatment of criticism as a crime, and the transference of worship from God to itself, complete with the appropriate ritual and hierophants. Whether it will ever evolve out of itself remains to be seen. It has never been a polity or civilization; but Pius XI, who did not mince his words, condemned it in several encyclicals on theological grounds—*On Christian Education* (1929), *Non abbiamo bisogno* (1931), *Mit brennender Sorge* (1937), and *Divini Redemptoris* (1937).

[T. GILBY]

TOTALITY, PRINCIPLE OF, a rule invoked in moral theology to discern the morality of certain deliberate *mutilations of the living human body. In substance the principle states that one is allowed to sacrifice a part of the body when such privation is required for the total good of the person who suffers the loss. It is consequently a principle certainly applicable to most surgical procedures employed by physicians for the benefit of their patients. Thus, e.g., in instances of acute appendicitis, appendectomy is medically indicated and morally justifiable for the one reason that it is necessary for the preservation of life; whereas wanton amputation of a healthy limb is both medically and morally abhorrent because of lack of justifying reason.

In their efforts to refine the theological implications of the principle of totality, contemporary theologians have engaged in various speculations of an entirely legitimate kind. Thus, e.g., relative to the *transplantation of human organs from living donors, question was once raised whether one might, as member of the mystical body or of the broader world community, consider himself and his bodily components as integral parts of those totalities and thus subordinated to their communal good. Pius XII rejected this interpretation of bodily member as that term occurs in the principle of totality, but without pronouncing on the morality of organic transplantation *inter vivos*.

Even more recently it has been suggested that the total good of an individual so transcends his physical and psychic welfare as to include also his ascetical growth, and that application of the principle of totality should be broadened accordingly, thus facilitating favorable solution of the problems of organic transplants and human experimentation. It remains yet to be seen whether this theory as proposed will withstand the test of prolonged scrutiny by theologians.
BIBLIOGRAPHY: J. J. Lynch, NCE 14:211; M. Nolan, ''Principle of Totality in Moral Theology'' *Absolutes in Moral Theology*? (ed. C. E. Curran, 1968) 232–248.

[J. J. LYNCH]

TOTEM POLE, tall—often 70 feet or more—carved wooden post with elaborate social and religious heraldry, particularly associated with the Haida people of the Queen Charlotte Islands, British Columbia. Kinship patterns and the privileges of chiefs are represented in the masklike segments of the poles that emphasize the relationships of the clan and chief with their totem animals. These Pacific Northwest totem poles are relatively modern, dating from about the 18th cent.; the styles changed with the availability of metal tools. Quite different are the Tnatantja poles of the Arunta people of Australia. These totem poles can be long, short, thin as a spear, or stout as a fasces; decorated and fitted with cross poles, they are an essentially male object. They serve an important function in structuring Arunta society, indicating patrimony. When a pregnant woman first notices fetal quickening, she is believed to be impregnated by the spirit associated with a Tnatantja to which has been attached a bullroarer, a noise-maker constructed from a thin blade on a cord. *TOTEMISM.

[R. J. LITZ]

TOTEMISM, a complex of ideas, practices, legend, fears, and kinship patterns, relating to the connection of humans and animals or plants. The word totem has been borrowed by anthropologists from the Ojibwa Indian languages of North America; *ototeman* (he is my relative) indicated kinship lines and defined the limits of marriageability. Durkhein and Radcliffe-Brown however argue that Australian aborigines demonstrate the nature of totemism better than the Ojibwa. Totemism is a world-view in which no sharp distinction is made between humans as a species and other things, animal, vegetable or mineral; humans are simply creatures in the scheme of things. It is a world-view in which environment dominates humans and in which humans maintain spiritual relationships with the elements of their environment. The belief that the whole world has spirit, similar to that of humans, is at the heart of totemism; the totem objects themselves provide categories by which relationships based in personal revelation, religious experience, or membership in a specific group can be distributed. Association of an animal or plant with a group does not necessarily indicate totemism; a football team and its mascot are not an example of a totemic relationship. Elements of the above-mentioned world-view and the distinctive use of symbolic animals or plants to indicate the associations which tie a person to a community and the world are essential to a definition of a culture as totemic. The theory that totem animals were associated with the dietary habits of different clans has been disputed and abandoned. The major theorists on totemism have been J. G. Frazer (1910), who catalogued totems; E. Durkheim (1915), who saw totemism as the general basis of "dementary" religion; S. Freud (1919), who offered his psychoanalytic impression that fear of animals, particularly among children, is a displacement of fear of the father onto the totemic animal; A. R. Radcliffe-Brown (1929), who approached the subject functionally; and C. Lévi-Strauss (1962), who reviewed and extended the discussion. Recent writers, such as W. Stanner, have seriously questioned the utility of such a broad concept.

[R. J. LITZ]

TOTH, ALEXIS (1854–1909), priest immigrant of the Catholic Ukrainian rite who in 1891 put many Ukrainian Catholic parishes in the U.S. under the jurisdiction of the Russian Orthodox bp. of San Francisco. T. drew his people away from Rome on grounds of the Latin hierarchy's disregard for the rites and customs proper to the Ukrainians.

[T. C. O'BRIEN]

TOTIES QUOTIES, a qualification attached to an indulgenced practice (see INDULGENCES) meaning that an indulgence may be gained as often as the practice is performed, with all the *usual conditions fulfilled. The Latin phrase, meaning "as often as," distinguishes the practice to which it is attached from others that are indulgenced once a day, once a year, or the like.

TOUL, COUNCILS OF, a series of local synods, largely of local interest, held at Toul, France, in the 9th century. Later diocesan assemblies gathered in 1123, 1359, and 1515. Cf. R. Kay, NCE 14:213.

[B. L. MARTHALER]

TOUMLILENE, ABBEY OF, a Benedictine monastery in the Atlas mountains of Morocco, the scene of international Catholic-Muslim conferences of considerable influence. In 1952 fifteen choir monks and 5 lay brothers went there from the Abbey of Encalat in S France, with Dom Denis Martin as their prior. Tioumliline (an alternate spelling) is the name of a spring and of a narrow ridge transected by the spring's waters. In the valley below lies the town of Azrou; to the NW is the royal city of Meknes; to the N, the sacred city of Fez; to the W lies Casablanca. The building, of stone and mortar designed by a Dutch lay brother, is a simple, modern blend of Benedictine and Moorish. This contemplative community of strict silence lies in a fervently Islamic area, with ragged holy men and Berber tribesmen. As a work of mercy the monks built a small dispensary and soon found themselves treating 200 Berber tribesmen a day. They adopted several Moroccan orphan boys and soon were running a small school for languages and useful trades. Local Arabs and Berbers called them "true Muslims." The community grew to more than 30 and became an independent priory the same year Morocco gained independence (1956). The monastery had been a sanctuary for independence leaders, even fugitives, and a hospitable haven for Muslim university students. The spirit of natural dialogue led to the important conferences, including the impressive one of August 1957, sponsored by the Sultan (now King) of Morocco, the abp. of Rabat, and the ambassadors of France, Spain, and the United States. BIBLIOGRAPHY: J. Kritzeck, "Moslem-Christian Dialogue," *Commonweal* (December 13, 1957) 282–285.

[E. J. DILLON]

TOURAINE REFORM, a Carmelite reform movement of the 17th cent. that originated in the province of Touraine. The Touraine Reform, part of the general spiritual revival that marked the Counter Reformation period, was an effort to improve the religious and spiritual life of the Carmelite friars by a renewed appreciation of stricter observance and a revival of the contemplative ideal. Pierre Behourt (1564–1633), who inaugurated the movement, sought to restore the old observance of the rule. Leadership gave way, however, to Philip Thibault (1572–1638) and a group of younger friars who had learned the newer currents of reform at Paris. Thibault's moderate and diplomatic direction avoided any rupture with the order, but sought to adapt the traditional ideal of Carmel to the needs and newer currents of the age. In the years 1608–15 the reform was given legal form and official approval. From the monastery at Rennes, it spread throughout France, Belgium and Germany. In 1645 the general chapter prescribed the Touraine constitutions for all reformed monasteries of the order. Touraine spirituality is characteristically 17th cent. in its points of emphasis, e.g., individual piety, interior prayer, special devotional practices, and rigorous method and regulation. In the 18th cent. the Touraine reform declined and virtually disappeared after the Fr. Revolution. Its influence, however, is still apparent in the present constitutions of the order. BIBLIOGRAPHY: P. Janssen, NCE 14:215–216.

[J. C. WILLKE]

TOURNÉLY, ÉLÉONOR FRANÇOIS DE (1767–97), French émigré priest who established the Society of the Sacred Heart of Jesus in 1794 at the former Jesuit house, Egenhoven, near Louvain, Belgium. T.'s purpose was to reinstitute the Jesuit form of life during this period of the Society of Jesus' suppression. The Society of the Sacred Heart merged with the *Paccanarists in 1799, and most of the members eventually joined the Jesuits after their restoration (1814). T.'s premature death of smallpox, in Vienna, forestalled execution of his plan for a Jesuitlike institute for women, but through his associate, J. Varin d'Ainville, St. Madeleine Sophie Barat did found the Sacred Heart Society (Madames of the Sacred Heart), which reveres T. as a founder.

[T. C. O'BRIEN]

TOURNÉLY, HONORÉ DE (1658–1729), theologian at the Sorbonne (1692–1716). His theological writings include a defense of the bull *Unigenitus against P. *Quesnel: *Relation fidèle des assemblées de Sorbonne touchant la constitution Unigenitus* (1716), and a monumental cursus of theology, *Praelectiones theologicae* . . . (16 v., 1725–30; 10 v. abridgement, 1731–46). In his teaching on grace T. is noted for his theory, against Jansenius, that the efficacy of grace consists in its pleasing attraction overcoming the will's resistance and drawing its consent. As each of the parts of his work appeared it was subjected to violent attack by the Jansenists. T. was also an exponent of *Gallicanism, particularly on the need of the consent of the whole Church to give infallibility to papal doctrinal pronouncements.

[T. C. O'BRIEN]

TOURNUS, ABBEY OF (Trenorchium), former monastery, founded probably in the 9th cent., in the present diocese of Autun, France. In 875 the Benedictine monks, driven from Noirmoutier by the Normans, settled there, bringing with them the relics of St. Philibert, who then became, after Our Lady, the secondary patron of the monastery. A center of learning from the 10th to the 13th cent., the abbey was plundered by the Huguenots in 1562, given to secular canons in 1627, and suppressed in 1785. The buildings of the abbey, constructed between the 10th and 12th cent., are remarkable for originality and purity of style. BIBLIOGRAPHY: Cottineau 2:3188–89.

[J. DAOUST]

TOURON, ANTOINE (1686–1775), French Dominican historian whose main work on the order's history is *Histoire des hommes illustrés de l'ordre de Saint-Dominique* (6 v., 1743–49). He also published *Histoire générale de l'Amérique depuis sa découverte* (14 v., 1768–70), and apologetic works against the deists and rationalists of the French Enlightenment.

[T. C. O'BRIEN]

TOURSCHER, FRANCIS EDWARD (1870–1939), patristic scholar, historian. A native of Pennsylvania, T. entered Villanova College in 1892 and in 1895, the Augustinians. His entire life was spent as a scholar in the field of the Fathers, esp. St. Augustine, and in American church history. T. prepared a textbook series of the writings of St. Augustine. He was a frequent contributor to the *American Ecclesiastical Review* and *Records* of the American Catholic Historical Society of Philadelphia and edited the *Diary and Visitation Record of Rt. Rev. Francis P. Kenrick, 1797–1863* (1916). He also published *The Hogan Schism and Trustee Troubles in St. Mary's Church, Philadelphia, 1820–1829* (1930).

[J. R. AHERNE]

TOWER OF BABEL, the tower in the legend recorded in Gen 11.1–9. The legend explains how the ancient city in the land of Shinar came to be called Babel: a name which would have reminded both the story teller and his audience of the Hebrew word *balal*, ''to mix, confuse.'' That there actually were such towers constructed of bricks can reasonably be deduced from isolated remains, from structural plans in cuneiform, and from the descriptive account of Herodotus. Apparently a *ziggurat* (tower) customarily stood next to a Mesopotamian temple. Herodotus describes the *ziggurat* Etemenanki, built in seven layers, each a different color of brick, with a small shrine at the summit. The name apparently meant ''house of the foundation of heaven and earth,'' and it stood next to the temple of Marduk. It may have symbolized the cosmic mountain, similar to the one portrayed on Mesopotamian seals with a god emerging from it. Perhaps those whom the Genesis account describes as coming upon a plain in the land of Shinar had formerly been mountain dwellers who worshiped their god(s) in ''high places.'' At any rate, in the *Yahwist account, the act of building such a city with a tower ''with its top in the heavens'' provoked the Lord to confuse their speech so that they could not understand one another. Otherwise, ''nothing they have a mind to do will be beyond their reach'' (11.6). According to the story, the building of the tower is the origin of the dispersion of humankind over the face of the earth, their language a babble of tongues.

[E. J. DILLON]

TOWIANSKI, ADREAS (1799–1878), influential Polish mystic and social theorist. Born in Antoszwiniec, Lithuania, he was a lawyer in Vilna from 1818 to 1826, emigrated after the Polish insurrection of 1831, and eventually lived in Paris in 1835, where he came under the influence of Saint-Simon. In 1841 he began his conferences on mystical messianism, the transforming of the social order through spiritual renewal and advanced mysticism, to be spearheaded by people of the Slavic tradition. In 1842, and again in 1848, he was forced to leave France. He lived for a while in Rome, then in Switzerland. His teaching is presented in the 2-v. work of his disciple, the Polish Romantic A. Mickiewicz: *L'Église officielle et le messianisme* (1842–43). BIBLIOGRAPHY: V. Bugiel, *La Grande Encyclopédie*, 31:256.

[E. J. DILLON]

TOWYN MONASTERY, Celtic monastery in Merioneth, Wales. Founded by St. Cadfan *c.*500, Towyn was one of the most notable monasteries in all Wales, and mother church of the whole commot of Ystum Anner (located at Llanfihangel y Pennant). It survived till the end of the 13th century. BIBLIOGRAPHY: A. W. Wade-Evans, *Welsh Christian Origins* (1934); J. E. Lloyd, *History of Wales* (2 v., 1948).

[C. MCGRATH]

TOYNBEE, ARNOLD J. (1889–1975), historian. In his 12 volumes entitled *A Study of History* (1934–61), he attempted to interpret history on an extraordinarily imposing scale. A tutor of ancient history at Oxford (1914), T. sensed a similarity between the outbreak of World War I and the outbreak of the Peloponnesian War in 431 B.C. This foreboding led him to the comparative study of civilizations in order to determine how they arise, grow, break down, and disintegrate. Civilizations, he believed, arise and grow by making creative responses to a series of challenges, but the eventual failure of creativity leads to breakdown and a social schism culminating in disintegration. Modifying this cyclical view of history, however, is his contention that higher religions arise from the breakdown of civilizations. He steadfastly refused to predict, as O. *Spengler had, the downfall of W civilization. Instead, T. preached salvation through a coalescence of the four existing ''Universal Churches'' into a worldwide brotherhood. His concern for international harmony was reinforced by his participation in the Paris Peace Conference in 1919 and by his position as Director of Studies at the Royal Institute of International Affairs. In that capacity he edited the annual *Survey of International Affairs* until his retirement in 1955. Thus he alternated between the past and the present in working on the two grandiose literary projects that occupied a major portion of his life.

T. was widely praised for his learning and literary accomplishments, but his interpretation of history has been strongly criticized by historians and philosophers. Although he presented an enormously detailed narrative, specialists have detected some fundamental misrepresentations in the support for his basic arguments. Others have pointed to such underlying conceptual problems as his attempt to discover laws of human behavior while espousing a belief in free will. Religious speculation played an increasingly dominant role in T.'s thought during the latter part of his life. Although he never repudiated his membership in the Church of England, he admitted that ''I should not pass the most elementary tests of Christian orthodoxy.'' Even so, his speculations concluded that ''the true end of man is self-sacrificing love.'' It was in fact his infusion of unorthodox spiritual significance into his work that has made it most problematical for scholars. BIBLIOGRAPHY: A. J. Toynbee, *Study of History* (abr. ed. D. Somervell, v. 1–6, 1947; v. 7–10, 1957); (ed. M. A. Montagu, *Toynbee and History: Critical Essays and Reviews* (1956); R. N. Stromberg, *Arnold J. Toynbee: Historian for an Age in Crisis* (1972); O. K. Rabinowitz, *Arnold Toynbee on Judaism and Zionism: A Critique* (1975).

[R. J. GIBBONS]

TOZZO, ST., bp. of Augsburg, Germany, from *c.*772 to *c.*778. Little is known of his life and nothing of his episcopacy. He seems to have been a Benedictine monk of Murbach, to have helped Magnus, first abbot of Füssen, establish the church and monastery there, and to have labored as pastor at nearby Waltenhofen. T. must have succeeded Wikterp as bp. of Augsburg, where he is buried in the church of St. Afra.

[E. J. DILLON]

TRA LE SOLLECITUDINI, *motu proprio* issued in 1903 by Pius X, an instruction on, and regulations governing, the music for the RC liturgy. Having stated some general principles, the document lists several points to be observed: the kinds of sacred music to be used, preeminence being given to Gregorian chant and the classic polyphony of the Roman school; use of Latin as the language of the liturgical functions, the text of which is not to be altered in any way; the rules governing the form of sacred compositions, the singers, the use of instruments (the organ only, with rare exceptions), and the length of the various chants. The document ends with an exhortation to cultivate good performances, particularly of the Gregorian chant, and to establish *scholae cantorum* wherever possible. BIBLIOGRAPHY: E. E. Nemmers, *Twenty Centuries of Catholic Church Music* (1949) 197–206.

[M. T. LEGGE]

TRACHONITUS, area NE of the Sea of Galilee. Ruled by Herod the Great till his death, it became part of his son Philip's tetrarchy (Lk 3.1). Part of the region known in the OT as *Bashan, its most noted feature is a 350-square-mile mass of black basalt, congealed volcanic lava.

[T. EARLY]

TRACT, in the Roman Mass prior to recent reforms, the short responsory substituted for the Alleluia before the Gospel during the penitential season (from Septuagesima Sunday to Easter); also in Masses for the dead.

[J. DALLEN]

TRACT (MUSIC), in the Latin Mass, the part of the Proper of the Mass used instead of the Alleluia during Lent, on various penitential days, and at the Requiem. It consisted of several uninterrupted verses of a psalm and was centonized, i.e. sung to a specific number of standard phrases according to a prescribed scheme. The melodies of the Tracts reflect a very early stage in the development of the Gregorian chant.

[M. T. LEGGE]

TRACT 90, the last of J. H. *Newman's *Tracts for the Times,* published Feb. 27, 1841. In *Tract 90* Newman applied a historical method of interpretation to certain passages in the *Thirty-Nine Articles and showed that they could be subscribed to in a Catholic sense since they did not condemn the Council of Trent and were directed less against the formal teaching of the Holy See than against the abuses of popular religion. A Protestant clamor arose questioning his honesty; he refused to withdraw his assertion and retired into lay communion with the Church of England.

[T. GILBY]

TRACTARIANISM, the *Oxford movement; more precisely the tenets and practices set forth in *Tracts for the Times, by Members of the University of Oxford,* started by J. H. *Newman in 1833 and brought to a close by him in 1841, with the controversial *Tract 90* on the Thirty-Nine Articles. The tracts comprised brief pamphlets and also extended treatises, such as that by E. B. *Pusey on baptism. The Tractarians, an extreme wing of the *high church party, stood for a conservative return to ancient doctrine and discipline, and operated within the larger setting of the Oxford movement and certainly of *Anglo-Catholicism, which soon displayed, like contemporary Romanism, a vitality of its own in adapting itself to new environments. Tractarianism, less formally and courteously called Puseyism (which term, now out of date, suggested the extravagances of *ritualism to 19th-cent. Protestant sentiment), still lingers to mean a learned, mellow, and historically minded devotion to patristic and conciliar orthodoxy and traditional *church order.

[T. GILBY]

TRACTATUS ORIGENIS, a collection of 20 homilies ascribed to Origen by 10th- and 12th-cent. MSS but now conceded to be the work of St. Gregory of Elvira (late 4th century). All but one of the sermons is based on OT texts. The collection was first published by P. Batiffol and A. Wilmart in 1900.

[R. J. LITZ]

TRACTS FOR THE TIMES, a series of pamphlets and books—E. *Pusey's contribution on baptism was an elaborate treatise—launched by Newman and his friends, hence Tractarians, to recall the C of E to its Catholic witness, apostolic descent, and *via media*. The first three appeared Sept. 9, 1833; the last was the famous *Tract 90* (1841), catastrophic in its effect. They were greeted with surprise, dismay, ridicule, and abuse from Protestants and bps. of the C of E but met with eager sympathy from many, and were so sought after that printers could not meet the demand.

[T. GILBY]

TRADE UNIONISTS, ASSOCIATION OF CATHOLIC, organization founded in New York in 1937 for the purpose of fostering Catholic social teaching as it concerns workingmen in home, school, factory, and community. Not itself a labor union, the ACTU has worked to educate laborers in organizational procedures and legal rights and to help them in union affairs. From 1968–72 it conducted three labor educational institutes in the Spanish language. It also has advised congressional committees on abuses in both union and management policies. Although the ACTU once counted 11 active chapters, it has presently only 5 chapters and affiliates.

[J. C. WILLKE]

TRADE UNIONS, combinations of workmen of the same trade or of several allied trades, for the purpose of securing by united action favorable wages, improved working conditions, better hours of labor, and righting grievances against employers. Beginning with the encyclical *Rerum novarum* of Pope Leo XIII, the Church has recognized that the free establishment of trade unions is among the basic rights of the human person. Another ancillary right is the taking part in the activities of trade unions without reprisal. Through such participation, according to their proper abilities, workers can enter into economic and social growth.

[F. T. RYAN]

TRADITIO LEGIS, the handing over of the authority to rule by Christ to the Apostles, a common theme symbolically portrayed in early Christian art on catacomb walls and on sarcophagi. Especially noteworthy is the sarcophagus in the Arles Museum on which Christ is depicted handing to Peter a little scroll with the words, *Dominus legem dat*—the Lord gives the Law; hence, *Traditio legis*—the handing over of the Law. Just as Moses is often depicted receiving the Torah (Law) on a mountain to be given to the people, so Jesus is portrayed on a mountain surrounded by Apostles, esp. Peter and Paul, transmitting to them power to rule the Church and exercise authority in his name. It is a translation into the Roman idiom of rule by Roman law of the Jewish rabbinic teaching mandate as found in Mt 28.18–19.

[E. J. DILLON]

TRADITIO SYMBOLI, a step in the catechumenate of the early Church, literally, the handing over of the Creed. When candidates prepared for baptism they were given doctrinal instruction in a special place outside regular services. The baptismal creed served as a summary of these talks and was presented to them in a special celebration, the *Traditio symboli*. This was distinct from the formal recital of the Creed (*Redditio symboli*) which came at the end of the period of preparation, just before baptism. Both rites are reflected in the new liturgy for the baptism of adults with its restoration of the catechumenate. BIBLIOGRAPHY: *Rites of the Catholic Church* (1976) 20–30.

[E. J. DILLON]

TRADITION, in the religious sense, the body of Christian teaching and practice handed down whether in oral or written form, separately from, but not independently of, Sacred Scripture. Practically all Christian theologians acknowledge tradition as operative in all Christian denominations, but they do not explain its significance in the same way. In RC doctrine and theology, tradition constitutes a source and *rule of faith, i.e., it contains in a real sense divine revelation. The Council of Trent (1546) affirmed both the Bible and tradition as divine sources of Christian doctrine but left unclear the relationship between them. Vatican II in Ch. 2 of its *Dogmatic Constitution on Divine Revelation (Dei Verbum)* declared that Scripture and tradition form a unity in the transmission of divine revelation; they are not, therefore, two independent sources of revelation. Further, the Council conceived tradition in a dynamic fashion as "growth in the understanding of the realities and words which have been handed down." This concept of tradition as dynamic rather than static accounts for the undeniable development of doctrine in Christian thought, while it allows at the same time for the setting aside of past tradition that later understanding perceives not to have been adequate (see MAGISTERIUM). Within Protestantism the view of tradition most widely held conforms to the position of the *Thirty-Nine Articles of the C of E, where tradition is presented as essential to the Christian faith, but only insofar as it is judged to be in explicit accord with the Bible. Thus for Protestantism generally, doctrine such as the RC teaching on the Immaculate Conception and the Assumption of the Virgin Mary does not pertain to divine revelation and is not of faith, since it is not unmistakably identifiable in Scripture.

Each of these positions on tradition has manifested its own inherent dangers: within Roman Catholicism the tendency, largely dissipated by Vatican II, was to depreciate the role of Scripture in Catholic thought and practice; within Protestantism the trend was to overly restrict divine revelation to the Bible. Under the impulsion of Vatican II Christian theologians have begun to listen to one another unde-

terred by denominational barriers; their dialogue can bear nothing but good fruit for growth in the understanding of the relationship between the Bible and tradition. BIBLIOGRAPHY: G. Moran, *Scripture and Tradition* (1963); J. P. Mackey, *Modern Theology of Tradition* (1960); C. Hanson, *Tradition in the Early Church* (1962).

[C. P. CEROKE]

TRADITION, ISLAMIC, see HADITH.

TRADITIONALISM, the 19th-cent. theory developed by some RC philosophers and theologians that the human mind cannot acquire knowledge of natural truths, whether metaphysical or moral, without divine revelation, passed on by oral instruction or tradition. It was a reaction to the uncertainties caused by rationalism and to the upheavals of the French Revolution. Principal exponents were Louis de Bonald (1754–1840), A. Bonnetty (1798–1879), F. de Lamennais (1782–1854), and J. de Maistre (1753?–1821). Two encyclicals of Pius IX *Mirari vos* (1832) and *Singulari nos* (1834), were directed against Lamennais's political and traditionalist doctrines. Vatican Council I condemned the position that unaided human reason could not attain knowledge about God (see D 3004, 3026).

[T. C. O'BRIEN]

TRADUCIANISM (from Lat. *tradux*, offshoot, sprout), sometimes called generationism, a group of theories dealing with the mystery of the origin of the human soul from the parents, i.e., either through the material act of generation out of an animate or inanimate matter (material traducianism), or as an offshoot of the substance of the parental soul (spiritual traducianism, or generationism). Sometimes it denotes the secondary creative power of the parental soul received from the Creator to produce another soul and to transmit it to the child through generation. Traducianism entered Christian thought from Stoicism through Tertullian (*De anima* 23–41), because it facilitated the explanation of original sin; i.e., it explained how all human souls were somehow present in Adam. The Church teaches *creationism and rejects traducianism as opposed to the spirituality and simplicity of the human soul and the transcendent dynamism of the Creator (D 360–361, 1007, 3220). BIBLIOGRAPHY: P. B. T. Bilaniuk, NCE 14:230; A. Mitterer, LTK 4:668–669; H. Vorgrimler, LTK 10:302; G. Oggioni, EncCatt 12:414–416; P. Overhage and K. Rahner, *Das Problem der Hominisation* (1961); G. Sauser and M. Vodopivec, "Gott in Welt," *Festschrift K. Rahner* (ed. H. Vorgrimler, 1964) 2:850–872.

[P. B. T. BILANIUK]

TRAFFIC LAWS, civil regulations governing automotive movement on public roads. Once thought purely penal, obliging only to penalties for their infraction, today such laws are considered binding in conscience. Their observance is regarded as necessary to avoid injury to persons and property. Pius XII taught that police power by itself is not enough to prevent the evils that would happen if all drivers ignored traffic regulations. The obligation of drivers, moreover, to respect the lives of others, the Pope saw as serious. In 1958, the Catholic bps. of Australia compared drivers to a man carrying a loaded gun. Thus, authorities agree that disregard of traffic laws which might result in serious injury to self or others is gravely sinful, unless there is an excusing cause proportionately important. For example, deliberately to go through a red light at a busy intersection, to travel at high speed in a crowded area, to operate a vehicle which is notably unsafe are all grave transgressions of a driver's obligation to respect others' rights. Lesser violations, e.g., illegal parking, which constitute no danger to self or others would, at most, be venially sinful and *epikeia might excuse from all fault in such a case. BIBLIOGRAPHY: W. Conway "Moral Law in Dangerous Driving," IER 88 (1957) 344–346; P. F. Mulhern, NCE 14:230–231.

[P. F. MULHERN]

TRAINI, FRANCESCO (fl. 1321–1350/75), important Pisan painter of the signed altarpiece in Sta. Caterina, Pisa (1345), depicting four scenes from the life of St. Dominic. T.'s major works are the frescoes in the *campo santo* (1350), badly damaged in World War II, since detached from the wall, transferred to canvas and restored, revealing precious underdrawings (*sinopie*). Depicting the *History of the Anchorites* and eschatological scenes *(The Triumph of Death)* this is the most impressive fresco cycle from the 14th cent. in Italy. T.'s work, in the violent, emotional, melodramatic style of the period after the Black Death (1348), is the medieval message of the folly of pleasure, the inevitability of death—the Florentine-Sienese visual engagement with the realism of a mortal world but emphasizing its ineluctable evanescence. A *Madonna and Child with St. Anne* (Princeton Univ.) and a fresco of *St. George Killing the Dragon* (Parma) are noteworthy. BIBLIOGRAPHY: M. Moiss, *Painting in Florence and Siena after the Black Death* (1951).

[M. J. DALY]

TRAJAN (Marcus Ulpius Traianus; 53–117), **ROMAN EMPEROR.** He was born in Spain and adopted by Nerva, in 97 after he had distinguished himself in the army and served a term as consul. Acclaimed emperor after the death of Nerva in 98, he won the title of *optimus princeps* because of his popularity with the army, the people, and the senate. His military conquests in Europe, Africa, and Asia brought the empire to its maximum extent. He sponsored a wide variety of public works, erected numerous buildings in Rome and in the provinces, and kept a strict control over provincial governors, as can be seen in his correspondence with Pliny the Younger. A rescript which he sent to Pliny on the manner of dealing with Christians established a policy that was generally followed during the 2d century (Pliny, *Ep.* 10.97). BIBLIOGRAPHY: R. Paribeni, *Optimus Princeps* (2 v., 1926–27).

[M. J. COSTELLOE]

TRANCHEPAIN, MARIE ST. AUGUSTIN, MOTHER (d. 1733), missionary. A native of France and brought up as a Protestant, T. became a Catholic and joined the Ursulines in 1677. In 1727 she and 10 other Ursulines arrived in New Orleans. Under her direction the first boarding school for girls on American soil was opened and the first free school. She and her sisters worked with whites, blacks, and Indians as well as wealthy families of New Orleans.

[J. R. AHERNE]

TRANQUILIZERS, the general name for a large group of nonbarbiturate sedatives now widely used. Medically, their primary use is for patients suffering from excessive worry or tension. The relief of tension and the pleasant drowsiness they induce is somewhat similar to the effect of alcohol and sleeping pills. Legally available only by physician's prescription, they can be obtained easily on the black market. While in ordinary doses they are safe and nonaddicting, taken in large doses and over an extended period of time, they represent the danger of *drug addiction. Moreover, large quantities can result in loss of consciousness, shock, and even death. If taken with large amounts of alcohol or ordinary amounts of barbiturates, the danger is greatly increased. If the drug is abruptly withdrawn from an addict, he suffers tremors, anxiety, vomiting, convulsions, but rarely death. A number of auto accidents have been attributed to lethargy and the failure of coordination resulting from tranquilizers. Under the direction of a competent physician, the use of tranquilizers for mental balance is certainly good. However, immoderate use is to be avoided as immoral because of the danger of loss of self-control and possible threat to life itself. BIBLIOGRAPHY: L. S. Goodman, *Pharmacological Basis of Therapeutics;* (5th ed., 1975).

[P. SMITH]

TRANSCENDENCE AND IMMANENCE, GOD'S. Transcendence is a condition attributed to divinity as beyond the limitations characterizing creatureliness and as beyond comprehension by any created mind. The term sums up the attributes of divine being; rules out the possibility of pantheism, i.e., the teaching that the divine becomes a component of creation; it rules out any limits from the divine goodness and perfection; it excludes divine perfectibility, failure, or defectibility; it rules out subjection to time, space, or any other extrinsic measure; it rules out the possibility of any relationship in which God and creatures act as two coordinated, partial causes of an effect. With regard to human (or angelic) knowledge of God, transcendence implies the classical, apophatic theology: the divine perfections can be known and affirmed as to what they are; they cannot be known in their proper mode of being and can be affirmed only in terms which fall short in their mode of signifying. Thus the treatise "On the Divine Names" that became part of the tradition of Christian theology through *Pseudo-Dionysius' work of that title must include always the *via negativa*: whatever can be said about God as to the perfection signified must be denied as to mode of signifying. The divine transcendence thus also rules the theological use of *analogy, since the analogous are alike in the most enfeebled sense. Further variations on the theme of transcendence are the *theologia crucis* of Luther and K. *Barth's crisis or dialectical theology.

The area of theology in which divine transcendence is currently discussed most is the topic of God's involvement in the working of creation, Classic theology always has affirmed along with transcendence God's immanence as well. The relationship of the two can best be weighed in connection with the issue of God's causal presence in creation. The classic teaching maintained that God is both transcendent and immanent, i.e. omnipresent in all creation. That position is being rejected by many, including Catholic theologians, in favor of process philosophy and process theology. For the tradition of a real transcendence and a real immanence those who have followed A. N. *Whitehead's line of thought have substituted a "bipolar theism." God in his antecedent nature is absolutely transcendent; God in his consequent nature is completely immanent in creation developing the divine antecedent possibilities through and in the evolving process of creatures, which is the sum of all reality. The position of bipolar theism is reconcilable with any orthodox meaning of God's transcendence only by recourse to the mind-bending device of a rejection of the principle of noncontradiction and of the distinction between potentiality and actuality. The absolute, antecedent nature of God seems, in effect, to be no more than a logical contrivance, a matrix against which the dialectics of process teaching can be carried out.

The causal presence of God, particularly as developed in the thought of St. Thomas Aquinas, is required by the dependence of whatever has being on the divine, continuous causation of being as such. Because being as such (*esse*; see ESSENCE AND ESSE) is the proper effect of God alone and because *esse* is the inmost reality of every being, God is said to be "in" every creature. Because there is no intermediary between God and either his own causative action or the existent effect, God in his own "essence" or substance is said to be present in every being that exists. The language is spatial; the meaning is an attempt to assert the absolute dependence of creation on God's continually being "there." The difficult and often missed step in the explanation of the divine omnipresence is that between God and the existents he causes there is no intermediary; there is no "action" or "energy" passing out of God. The divine causality itself is totally the mind and will of God, one with the divine being, Thus there are two realities: God himself in himself; all other beings. The "innerness" of God, the divine immanence, is the being of the creature as dependent on God's causality, which is God (see ThAq ST 1a,25.1 ad 3,54.1 ad 3, capital texts). Such an understanding is an affirmation at once of God's transcendence—nothing "goes out" of God to become mingled with the creature—and God's immanence because the being of and in all beings is the presence of God to them. One of the criticisms leveled against St. Thomas's idea of God's transcendence has been that it makes God "absent" and uninvolved. A particular point of weakness, it is said, is evident in the teaching that creatures have a real relation of dependence upon God, but that God's relation to creatures is a "relation of reason," one posited for the sake of knowledge, but not real. Thus to say that God is creator is to *think of him* as related to creation, but he is not *really* so related (see *ibid*. 13,13.7). The point of this position, however, is that to be the creative and sustaining cause of all being does not add a new quality (the predicate "relation") to God; God is not related to creatures by anything added when they come into being; in his being and acting, which are one with himself, he is freely, yet totally related to creation. This is the force of saying that God is present by essence, power, and presence—the expression taken from St. Gregory the Great (*ibid* 8,3). The involvement of God is the very being and working out of creation; the being and action of creatures are real and actual divine effects; they are the reality of God's being immanent. When theology further enriches this concept in view of the doctrine on the Trinity, then it sees the working out of creation to have as its pattern the eternal actuality of the relations of the divine persons to each other (*ibid*. 45,6).

The divine transcendence and immanence take on a sublimer meaning in reference to the presence of God to the just in the living of the life of grace. The consideration goes beyond the divine causal presence to the special presence of God as object known and loved (*ibid*. 8.1). The transcendence of God becomes the measure for trying to express the marvel that is God's self-gift through grace. For union in being with God, an interpenetration of the creature's and God's being is impossible. Union in person is not; that is what the *hypostatic union brought about in Christ. Union in knowing and loving is not; that is what grace given through Christ brings about. Because that union with God as the one who is known and loved unmediatedly is made real by grace, then the immanence of God means the indwelling of Father, Son, and Holy Spirit, The recipient "possesses" or "enjoys," not just a divine, created gift, but the Divine Persons themselves (*ibid* 43.3,6; cf. CG 3.51; 4.21). BIBLIOGRAPHY: ThAq ST (Lat-Eng, v. 7, ed., T. C. O'Brien, *Father, Son, and Holy Spirit*, app. 3; *idem*., v. 14, *Divine Government*, app. 1; *idem*., v. 31, *Faith*, app. 2).

[T. C. O'BRIEN]

TRANSCENDENTALISTS, in the U.S., those participating in the movement arising (1830s) in New England as a revolt against the rationalistic philosophy of the *Enlightenment and the rigor of conventional Protestantism. The tenets of the American Transcendentalists are indirectly traceable to German idealism—the view that ultimate reality transcends phenomena and is apprehended by intuition—and certain mystical elements of *Romanticism, but more immediately to the influence of Thomas Carlyle and Samuel T. Coleridge. Associated with the movement at one time or another were most of the literary, religious, and social-reform leaders of New England, including such prominent figures as Ralph Waldo Emerson (1803–82), George Ripley (1802–80), Orestes Brownson (1803–76), Bronson Alcott (1799–1888), and Henry David Thoreau (1817–62). Basically eclectic, the Transcendentalists held widely differing views but were bound together by their belief in an "order of truths that transcends the sphere of the external senses." And since "the truth of religion does not depend on tradition, nor historical facts, but has an unerring witness in the soul," they rejected all external authority. For a short period they organized a community of their own at *Brook Farm. BIBLIOGRAPHY: W. R. Hutchinson, *Transcendentalist Ministers* (1959); *Transcendentalists: An Anthology* (ed. P. Miller, 1960).

[M. CARTHY]

TRANSEPT, part of a cruciform church lying at right angles to the nave. The area where the transept intersects the nave is known as the crossing and is often surmounted by a dome or tower. A transept normally crosses the nave just in front of the choir, though a second transept is sometimes placed behind the choir.

[T. EARLY]

TRANSFERENCE, a psychological phenomenon, first detected by Freud, that occurs in *psychoanalytic, therapeutic, and *counseling situations. It is an emotional or attitudinal relationship arising from the unconscious of the patient or counselee and attaching to the doctor or counselor. The relationship does not arise as a product of the interviews but represents rather a displacement or "transference" of a relationship the person had early in life towards a parent or parent substitute. As such, it is valuable insofar as it reveals unconscious attitudes and provides a trust and dependency rapport on the basis of which therapy becomes effective. Jung sees it as unavoidable, but the client-centered therapy of Rogers pays little attention to it. Experience of countertransference, i.e., the counselor's subconscious reaction to the patient, also shows the importance of taking it into account as a factor in the therapeutic process. BIBLIOGRAPHY: K. Menninger, *Theory of Psychoanalytic Technique* (1958); J. Dominian, *Psychiatry and the Christian* (1962) 87–88.

[M. E. STOCK]

TRANSFIGURATION, etymologically signifying a change in appearance, is an expression used in the NT to designate the incident in Christ's life when the divine glory shone through his humanity (Mt 17.1–13; Mk 9.2–13; Lk 9.28–36; cf. 2 Pt 1.16–19). While traditionally the place of this miracle is at Tabor, it may possibly have been *Hermon; the Gospels say simply a high mountain. Its purpose, according to Leo the Great (PL 54.310), seems to be the heartening of the disciples for the approaching scandal of the cross; the careful placing of the incident by the evangelist immediately after the first Passion-prediction bears this out. Peter, James and John are the chosen inner circle to witness this glory as they will be witnesses of the

*Agony in the Garden. With the transfigured Jesus appear Moses and Elia who not only represent the *Torah and the prophets, but the mystics of the OT who had some vision of the sanctity of God manifesting itself through his glory. They speak with Jesus about his *exodus,* that is, his Passover (Lk 9.31). Peter suggests making tents which may be a recollection of the tabernacles of the desert. Mark (9.6) and others legitimately criticize Peter, as the hesychiasts were later to be legitimately criticized, for making the promise something permanent. The vision of Transfiguration is temporary; it is a foreshadowing of the glory of the Resurrection and the parousia, and the way to these is the way of the cross. BIBLIOGRAPHY: J. de Fraine, "Transfiguration," EDB, 2487–89; ThAq ST 3a, 45.

[U. VOLL]

TRANSFORMING UNION, a technical term used by RC mystical theologians for the cleaving to God which is the final stage of Christian perfection in this life and is the immediate prelude to the beatific vision. Sometimes described as the "mystical marriage," it marks the highest peak of the spiritual life. Though still in the darkness of faith, the sharing by grace in the divine nature which comes with divine grace now, in the transforming union, is not only glimpsed but also experienced in a manner beyond that of the "conforming union." As described by St. Teresa, this culmination of the Christian life is different in degree from the earlier stages of prayer through which the soul has passed by its awareness of the permanence of the mutual love between God and self (*Interior Castle,* "Seventh Mansions," ch. 1, 2). After the sufferings of the purgative and illuminative ways the soul now enjoys with only brief interruptions an almost constant realization of his presence, and a lasting peace which nothing can disturb. Self is of no concern, forgotten now in the greater absorption in God's majesty. Suffering counts for nothing in the reliance on his will, even the wish to die and to be with him is now replaced by a willingness to remain in life for many years if thereby one can help souls through Christ to the Father.

TRANSFORMISM, the gradual succession of varying external structures in which these forms pass in succession from the less complex to the more complex. There is an accumulation of paleontological evidence to substantiate the fact of transformism, but it is difficult to substantiate the process itself since within it the material traces of one species passing into another are lost. We are confronted with the species of origin and the species of term, but the intermediary species are lost. The law of the suppression of peduncles means that intermediary species are too weak to leave paleontological traces of themselves, whereas the original species and the terminal species are sufficiently fixed. Biologists and paleontologists have generally limited their consideration of transformism to the exterior structures of matter. *Teilhard de Chardin, however, also considers transformism to be operative on the psychological level, causing an evolution from less intense to more intense forms of consciousness. BIBLIOGRAPHY: Teilhard de Chardin, *Phenomenon of Man* (1959); *idem*, *Future of Man* (1964). *COMPLEXIFICATION.

[W. J. DUGGAN]

TRANSIGNIFICATION, a term some contemporary RC theologians have substituted for *transubstantiation; transfinalization is similarly used. For some theologians the change in terminology implies a denial of any ontological or real change in the bread and the wine in the Eucharist. For the more traditionally rooted theologians, however, the new terms avoid belaboring the philosophical aspects of the dogma and simply bring out the long-neglected sign value or significance of the Eucharist. To paraphrase Irenaeus of Lyons, writing in the 2d cent., the Church's gift of bread and wine, the fruits of the earth, are not rejected, they are transformed, changed in their signification and in their reality (see PG 7:1125–27). Transignification intends to express that the meaning of bread and wine as physical nourishment is transformed as they become spiritual nourishment. BIBLIOGRAPHY: Encyclical of Paul VI, *Mysterium fidei*, AAS (1965) 753–774; J. Powers, *Eucharistic Theology* (1967); E. Schillebeeckx, *Eucharist* (1968).

TRANSJORDAN, modern designation for the area E of the Jordan River, sometimes called beyond the Jordan in the Bible (Jos 12.1). It embraces the OT regions of Bashan, Gilead, Ammon, Moab, and Edom, together with some desert area beyond them. In NT times the area comprised Gaulanitis, most of Decapolis, Perea, and part of the Nabatean Kingdom. The region has been settled since the 3d millennium B.C. The tribes of Reuben and Gad and the half-tribe of Manassah received allotments in the area at the Conquest (Jos 13.8). Control of the region fluctuated, with David and Solomon maintaining Israelite authority. In 732 B.C. it became a part of the Assyrian Empire. After periods of rule by Babylonia (604–536) and Persia (536–332), it was conquered by Alexander the Great, after which numerous Greek colonists settled in the Decapolis. The Nabateans meanwhile were pushing north, and during the Maccabean period Jews settled in Perea. Muslims overran the area in the 7th cent., and it subsequently came under the rule, successively, of the Latin Kingdom of Jerusalem, the Egyptian Mamelukes, and the Ottoman Empire. After World War I Great Britain administered it under a League of Nations mandate, terminated in 1946.

[T. EARLY]

TRANSLATION, a term used for the moving of the relics or remains of a saint from one place to another, usually to a new shrine. In some cases the event was commemorated by a liturgical feast under the title "Translation of"; such feasts were dropped from the liturgy in the 1969 revision of the Roman Calendar.

TRANSMIGRATION OF THE SOUL, the belief that after death the soul will assume a new form of earthly existence. Transmigration has been interpreted in various ways. Either the whole soul or parts of it, e.g., the name-soul of the Eskimos, may be reborn in the descendants (see REINCARNATION), or may change into an animal, a tree, or some other object (see METEMPSYCHOSIS), or it may be stored in a spirit-home from which it will eventually return to the womb of a pregnant woman. In the pre-Aryan traditions of India there is a kind of cosmic transmigration. The elements of man are carried to heaven by the smoke of his funeral pyre. Returning to earth by rain, the elements are transformed into semen and thus become again a human being. In Greece (Orphic and Pythagorean traditions; Eleusian mysteries; Plato, etc.) and in sects such as the Manichaeans and the medieval Cathars, transmigration was interpreted as punishment for sin, thus serving as a means and mechanism of purification. According to the samsāra theory of Hinduism, the soul goes through all stages of existence before it finds salvation. Bad souls are punished by being reborn in a stage inferior to the one previously reached. Buddhism connected the idea of transmigration with the doctrine of *karma, i.e., the inherent effectiveness of human deeds as an explanation of consciousness. When the complexities of the body vanish at death, karma remains as the "germ of consciousness" and thus becomes the force responsible for the wheel of life and its chain of rebirth. BIBLIOGRAPHY: Hastings ERE 12:425–440; J. G. Frazer, *Belief in Immortality and the Worship of the Dead* (3 v., 1913–1924): H. S. Long, *Study of the Doctrine of Metempsychosis in Greece from Pythagoras to Plato* (1948); A. Jensen, *Myth and Cult among Primitive Peoples* (tr. M. T. Choldin and W. Weissleder, 1963).

[W. DUPRÉ]

TRANSPLANTATION OF ORGANS, see ORGANIC TRANSPLANTS.

TRANSUBSTANTIATION, in RC teaching the technical term for the eucharistic change. Reflecting Aristotelian philosophy, the term affirms a change of the substance of bread and wine into the substance of Christ's body and blood, without any change, however, in the accidents, or appearances, of bread and wine. The fathers of the Council of Trent adopted the word "transubstantiation" as "apt" to describe the reality of such a change, without canonizing the philosophical system that helped to coin the expression. The substantive issues with which Trent was concerned were two: (1) the meaning of Christ's words, "This is my body," is that "this" is no longer bread but is my body; (2) if this be so, the "no longer bread" is verifiable only in the ontological order, known to faith, and not in the empirical order, or the order of appearances (see D 1642).

In the Ante-Nicene Church, Ignatius of Antioch, Justin Martyr, Irenaeus of Lyons, Hippolytus of Rome, and Cyprian of Carthage are all witnesses to the belief that the bread is the body of Christ, that the bread becomes, or is made, the body of Christ. To cite Justin: "... just as, through the word of God, our Savior Jesus Christ became incarnate and took upon himself flesh and blood for our salvation, so we have been taught, the food which has been made the Eucharist by the prayer of his word ... is both the flesh and blood of that Jesus who was made flesh" (*1 Apol.* 66). After Nicaea (325) further precision was introduced by reference to the change, or transformation, of the elements of bread and wine into the body and blood of the Lord. It might have been argued that bread and wine are made, or become, the body and blood of Christ without ceasing to be bread and wine, just as in the incarnation the Word was made flesh, without ceasing to be the Word. The possibility is removed by the word "change." Thus, Cyril of Jerusalem states the essentials of the doctrine of transubstantiation in language free of all technicality: "Of old in Cana of Galilee, he changed water into wine of his own will. Is he less worthy of credence when he changes wine into blood ...? Therefore, look not upon the bread and wine as bare elements, for they happen to be, according to the Lord's assurance, the body and blood of Christ; for even though the senses suggest this to you, let faith make you certain and steadfast. Do not judge the matter by taste, but by faith rest assured without any misgivings that you have been deemed worthy of the body and blood of Christ" (*On the Mysteries* 4.2.6). In the medieval period Lanfranc in his reply to Berengarius can use the words "substance" and "appearances" in the nontechnical sense that "the earthly substances ... are transformed ... into the essence of the Lord's body, the appearances (*species*) of these same remaining along with certain other qualities" (PL 150:430). "Substance" and "appearances" are essential words in the traditional nomenclature of the East and the West and as such are in no sense to be confused with the Aristotelian categories of substance and accidents. The actual term "transubstantiation" came into use in the West in the 12th cent.; in the 13th it was used officially by Lateran Council IV (D 802) and the Council of Lyons II (D 860), and by all theologians. In the 14th cent. John Wycliffe, and in the 16th cent. all the Reformers rejected transubstantiation. BIBLIOGRAPHY: P. F. Palmer, *Sacraments and Worship* (1955); J. M. Powers, *Eucharistic Theology* (1967); E. Schillebeeckx, "Transubstantiation, Transfinalization, Transfiguration," *Worship* 40 (1966) 324–338; C. Vollert, NCE 14:259–261. *REAL PRESENCE; *CONSUBSTANTIATION; *VIRTUALISM.

[P. F. PALMER]

TRANS-VOLGA ELDERS, see NIL SORSKY.

TRANSYLVANIA, that part of western Romania bounded on the E, N and S by the Carpathian Mountains and on the W by the Apuseni Mountains. Originally, the country formed part of Hungary but was ceded to Romania in 1918. The majority of the inhabitants are Romanians, descendants of the veterans of Trajan sent in the 2d cent. A.D. to colonize the two Roman buffer provinces of Dacia. Transylvania was evangelized in the 3d and 4th centuries. *Nicetas of Remesiana was an early bishop of the region. Romanians are basically Latin in race and language and may have originally used a Latin liturgy of which no trace has survived. Christianity became Byzantine in form and the Cyrillic alphabet was adopted, largely under the influence of the Serbs and the Bulgarians. Some Romanians have maintained that while Orthodoxy took hold in Romania, Transylvania, which at that time was part of the Hungarian kingdom, remained Catholic. This was due, it is believed, to the presence of German Catholic peasants who had been brought in by the Habsburg monarchs to ease the tension between the Hungarians and the Romanians. The reunion movement among the Orthodox of Transylvania began under the Metropolitan Athanasius Angelus Popa of Alba Julia (1697–1713), who in 1700 at a synod solemnly accepted and proclaimed the Union. (See ALBA JULIA, UNION OF). Thus came into being the second largest group of Byzantine rite Catholics in Eastern Europe. *ROMANIAN RITE.

[A. WALKER]

TRAPPISTS, popular name for the Order of Cistercians of the Strict Observance. The Cistercian Order itself began in 1098 as a reform movement seeking to return to the original simplicity of the *Benedictine rule. After initial growth, decline set in, and Abbot Denis Largentier of *Clairvaux began (1615) a more simple and rigoristic observance. Largentier's "strict observance" quickly spread to other monasteries, which adopted their own constitutions (1623) while remaining an integral part of the Cistercian Order. The reform was carried a step further by Abbé Armand de *Rancé (1626–1700) of La Grand Trappe (from whose name the word Trappist is derived) who, inspired by the Desert Fathers, introduced even greater rigors into the monastic life. The strict observance reached its most severe expression under Augustine de Lastrange, a former novice master of La Trappe, who founded La Val Sainte Abbey in Switzerland during the French Revolution. With the revival of the Cistercians in Europe after Napoleon's fall, the Trappists formed three separate congregations: Westmalle (Belgium), La Trappe, and Sept Fons, which were united (1892) under the auspices of Leo XIII to form the Order of Cistercians of the Strict Observance, thus making it distinct from the Cistericians of the Common Observance. The order today comprises some 86 houses of men and 45 of women spread throughout the six continents. With the post-Vatican II return of the order to the spirit and aims of its original Cistercian founders, the Trappist name can no longer be considered apt. The Special General Chapter of the Order (1969) set forth its present-day ideal as the following of the gospel practically interpreted through the Rule of St. Benedict. A sense of the divine transcendence and the lordship of Christ pervades the Cistercian life, directing it totally toward an experience of the living God. Through the word of God, vigils, fasting, and an unceasing conversion of life, the monk aims to become more disposed to receive the gifts of pure and continual prayer. This search for God, presided over by a rule and under the direction of an abbot, is carried out in a community and lives in an atmosphere of silence and separation from the world, which fosters and expresses its openness to God in contemplation. T. Merton, *Waters of Siloe* (1949); L. J. Lekai, *Seventeenth-Century Rise of the Strict Observance* (1968), *The Cistercian Spirit: A Symposium* (ed. M. B. Pennington, 1969); M. R. Flannagan, NCE 14:261–264. *CISTERCIANS; *LA TRAPPE, ABBEY OF.

[M. B. PENNINGTON]

TRAUBE, LUDWIG (1861–1907), medieval Latin philologist, paleographer. He earned his Ph.D. at the Univ. of Munich and then spent his university career there. His publications include: the *Poetae Latini Aevi Carolini,* (3 v., 1886–96) in MGH; *Textgeschichte der Regula S. Benedicti* (1898); *Perrona Scottorum* (1900), a classic in Latin paleography; *Nomina sacra,* a monumental contribution to the history of Latin abbreviations. BIBLIOGRAPHY: L. Traube, *Vorlesungen und Abhandlungen von Ludwig Traube,* (ed. F. Boll, 3 v., 1909–20). This work has an excellent biographical introduction and bibliography.

[J. J. SMITH]

TRAVELING PREACHER, a layman licensed to preach in a Methodist *annual conference. Admission to the office by the annual conference amounts to a 2-year ''admission on trial'' under the supervision of a bishop. At the end of the probation the candidate is examined according to norms established by John *Wesley for his preachers. If approved, he is admitted fully to the ministry. Ordination is conferred only on those approved as preachers. BIBLIOGRAPHY: N. B. Harmon, *Understanding the Methodist Church* (rev. ed., 1955).

[T. C. O'BRIEN]

TRAVERSARI, AMBROSE, BL. (1386–1439), Camaldolese theologian and humanist. He was prominent in the circle of those renewing the study of classical and patristic literature in Florence. He was a friend of Cosimo de' Medici, at whose urging he translated the writings of Diogenes Laertius and other Greek works into Latin. As general of his order he promoted its reform. In his *Hodoeporicon (Itinerarium)* he gave in abundant detail an account of his visitation of various houses of his order. The work is important for documenting the contemporary decline in the religious life. At the Council of Basel he defended the primacy of the pope in opposition to conciliarist theory, and at the Council of Florence he strongly supported the reunion of Eastern and Western Churches. He was venerated in his order as a blessed; however, his cult was never officially approved. BIBLIOGRAPHY: A. Dini-Traversari, *Ambrogio Traversari e i suoi tempi* (1912).

TRDAT II, a name shared by two men of antiquity: a late 1st-cent. B.C. Parthian prince and the King of Armenia who ruled from 217–*c.*238 A.D. Both names are also rendered Tiridates II. The Parthian Trdat was a contemporary of Caesar Augustus. He revolted against King Phraates IV and drove the latter into Scythian exile. Then Phraates returned and it was Trdat's turn to seek asylum in Syria. After an unsuccessful invasion of Mesopotamia, he took refuge with the Emperor Augustus in Spain. He seems never to have regained his homeland. The Armenian Trdat II is also known as Khosrow the Great. He was recognized as king by the Romans after they had unsuccessfully attempted to annex the country. T.'s resistance to Sasanian Persia resulted in his eventual assassination by a Persian agent.

[E. J. DILLON]

TRE FONTANE, ABBEY OF, Cistercian abbey in Rome, known also as the monastery of SS. Vincent and Anastasius. It was founded originally for the Benedictines by Pope Honorius I and was located on the site hallowed, according to tradition, by the martyrdom of St. Paul. There three fountains were claimed to have sprung up—hence the monastery's name. In 1140 the house was transferred to Cistercians under Abbot Bernard Paganelli, who soon became Pope Eugene III. Another famous abbot was Ferdinando Ughelli (1639–70), scholar and historian. The abbey was suppressed under Napoleon but was given to Trappist Cistercians in 1868. BIBLIOGRAPHY: A. Barbiero, *L'Abbazia Nullius dei SS. Vincenzo e Anastasio alle Tre Fontane* (1938); M. B. Morris, NCE 14:267.

TRE ORE, see THREE HOURS, THE.

TREACLE BIBLE, popular name given to the *Great Bible (1539), because of its use of the word ''triacle'' (obsolete form of ''treacle,'' in the old sense of a medicinal salve) in Jer 8.22 where other English versions have ''balm.''

TREASURY OF THE CHURCH (Treasury of Merits), a metaphor to express one element in the meaning of the communion of saints, namely the vital beneficence of the good done by one member of the Church upon the other members. Sometimes the metaphor has been pushed to extremes in rather mathematicized explanations of the doctrine of *indulgences. The central meaning of the metaphor is more sublime; it is based on the truth that the Church in its entirety is Christ together with those joined to him by a living charity, or at least by faith, on earth and by glory in heaven. The vitality of the Church begins with and in Christ and is a communion of love between him and his brothers and sisters and a communion among those so joined to Christ. The effectiveness of that love as a whole is intended by ''treasury.'' The Church is not a third reality that becomes, as it were, a depository; the Church is the whole Christ, Christ and his members, and the effectiveness of their love exists in that whole reality. The supreme and originating source is what Christ's own love accomplished;

the derivative resources are the mutual benefits that those vitalized by his love accomplish. The idea of "merits" enters with the theological meaning that grace and love are given as the resources for progress towards the gift of eternal life as a reward. Christ merited for all who are joined to him that they can share in the process of their own salvation through his grace. Those who do share in his grace are friends bound to the Father with Christ and with one another. Their life of love is acceptable to the Father and in reward can be of assistance to others in the community of charity. Thus by prayer and by virtue of their love, the saints in heaven assist those on earth; because of that same love, those on earth contribute to one another and to the building up of the body of Christ.

[T. C. O'BRIEN]

TREATISE CONCERNING THE POWER AND PRIMACY OF THE POPE (*Tractatus de potestate et primatu papae*), a confessional document written by P. *Melanchthon in 1537. The *Treatise* was incorporated in the *Book of Concord because it was thought to be an appendix to the *Schmalkaldic Articles; in fact it had been written as a supplement to the *Augsburg Confession, which had no article on the papacy. The assembly of the Schmalkaldic League at Schmalkalden in Feb. 1537 had as its purpose a statement of Lutheran doctrine in view of the general council summoned by Pope Paul III to meet at Mantua in May. The Schmalkaldic Articles prepared by Luther were not approved as a confessional document; Melanchthon's treatise was. In signing the articles, he had attached a conciliatory statement in regard to the papacy. The *Treatise*, however, reflecting the view of the assembly, was adamantly antipapal. The first part considers the pope; the second, the bishops. Papal primacy by divine right over the Church and secular princes is rejected, as is the necessity to accept the primacy in faith and obedience. The power exercised by bishops is condemned as a usurpation, and the *Treatise* teaches that episcopacy is not essential to the nature of the Church. BIBLIOGRAPHY: G. Gieschen, EncLuthCh 3:2183–89; *Book of Concord* (ed. T. G. Tappert, 1959) 319–335; R. Stupperich, *Melanchthon* (pa., 1965).

TREBIZOND (Trabzon), city and port on the NE Black Sea coast of Turkey. Founded as the Greek colony of Trapezus *c*.1000 B.C., it became commercially important because of its location on the maritime and land trading routes to the East. After the Latin conquest of Constantinople in 1204, *Alexis I Comnenus fled to Trebizond, where he assumed the title of emperor and where his descendants ruled over a small but commercially and intellectually important realm until its capture by the Turks in 1461. Prosperous under the Ottoman Empire, it has since declined. BIBLIOGRAPHY: W. Miller, *Trebizond, the Last Greek Empire* (1926).

[G. T. DENNIS]

TREBIZOND, GEORGE OF, see GEORGE OF TREBIZOND.

TREBNITZ, ABBEY OF, convent of Cistercian nuns near Breslau in Silesia, founded in 1202 by Duke Henry I and his wife, St. Hedwig (d. 1243). It became Hedwig's home after the death of her husband. The church in transitional style is the oldest surviving architectural monument in that province. After the disasters of the Thirty Years' War, the nuns' quarters were rebuilt in Baroque. The abbey was secularized in 1810, although the church continued to serve the local parish. The other buildings were purchased (1889) for the motherhouse of the Sisters of Mercy of St. Charles Borromeo. BIBLIOGRAPHY: E. D. McShane, NCE 14:267; K. Engelbert, LTK 10:331; A. Bach and A. Kastner, *Geschichte des Klosterstiftes Trebnitz* (1859).

[L. J. LEKAI]

TRECY, JEREMIAH (1824?–88), missionary. Born in Ireland but brought as a child to the U.S., he studied for the priesthood and was ordained for the Diocese of Dubuque by Bp. Mathias Loras in 1851. In the interest of the effort at Catholic colonization in the Midwest, T. explored areas of Nebraska and Iowa, settling on a tract near Sioux City, which he designated as St. John's City, St. Patrick's Colony, Nebraska Territory. Promising in its start, the colony suffered from the rigors of the frontier and from T.'s absence on missionary journeys, and it ceased to exist in 1860. T. then went to Alabama, where for two years he was regimental chaplain for General William Rosecrans during the Civil War.

[J. R. AHERNE]

TREDIAKOVSKI, VASILI KIRILLOVICH (1703–69), Russian poet, philologist, and literary theoretician. He is remembered for his *New and Brief Introduction to the Composition of Russian Verses* (1735), which advocated the use of syllabotonic, as opposed to syllabic, prosody in long lines of Russian verse; for his translations of Boileau's *L'Art poétique* and Horace's *De arte poëtica*; and for his introduction of French Pseudo-Classicism into Russia. BIBLIOGRAPHY: T. Lindstrom, *Concise History of Russian Literature* (1966) 47–48; *Handbook of Slavic Studies* (ed. L. I. Strakhovsky, 1949) 379–381.

[M. F. MCCARTHY]

TREE OF KNOWLEDGE, the tree in paradise, whose fruit the first man and woman were forbidden to eat (Gen 2.16–17). The *Yahwist recounts the story, without giving any clear definition of the meaning of this tree; nor of the serpent, nor of the other tree mentioned: the tree of life. Both the serpent and the tree of life (Gen 3.22) are common motifs in ancient legend and tradition among various peoples. The tree of knowledge has no parallel, however, so it is all the more enigmatic. It is called variously: the tree in the middle of the garden; or the tree of knowledge good and evil. Syntactically, ''good'' and ''evil'' could be expected to be what Hebrew grammar terms the construct state, so as to be translated: the knowledge *of* good and evil; but they are not. The phrase must be translated: the tree of knowledge good and evil, which does not quite make sense. The best advice perhaps is not to look too closely at the symbols and concentrate instead on the way they participate in the drama of the story. To eat the fruit seemed to man and woman to mean becoming more like God. Instead it destroyed the harmony between humankind and God, brought shame and guilt, and then expulsion from the place of abundant and harmonious life. Man and woman experienced disharmony within themselves and without. The drama also suggests that it is not the tree of life that brings the full genuine life man seeks. Obedience to God brings it; disobedience brings all the evil man is heir to.

[E. J. DILLON]

TREES, SACRED, those trees which in almost every religion are considered as symbols of sacred realities. Although trees are an extremely common religious image, their significance varies, e.g., the Indian consideration of the tree as an image of the cosmos obviously differs from the May tree used in spring festivals as a symbol of renewed life. Many different types of trees are regarded as sacred: the Japanese reverence the sakati tree; the Buddhists, the bodhi tree; the Indians, the asvattha; and other cultures, the olive, palm, cedar, and fig trees. Although scholars differ on the point, some insisting that the primitive veneration of trees is only a type of *animism, a coherent pattern does seem to emerge: trees were not regarded as sacred in themselves but as symbols of the sacred. They were so regarded because of their obviously vital powers: they reach the heavens, grow, die, and come back to life. The tree, therefore, enacts the whole structure of the cosmos itself. It can be taken as a symbol of the universe in its relationship with the holy, and as the center of the world from which all life flows. The tree of the knowledge of good and evil (Gen 2.9) is open to a variety of interpretations, but basically it is linked with the recurrent theme of man's search for immortality, which in Genesis is seen as a usurpation of Yahweh's unique dominion over life. BIBLIOGRAPHY: M. Eliade, *Patterns in Comparative Religion* (tr. R. Sheed, 1963) 265–331; T. Barns, Hastings ERE 12:448–457.

[T. M. MCFADDEN]

TREJO Y SANABRIA, FERNANDO DE (1553–1614), bp. of Tucumán, founder of the Univ. of Córdoba in Argentina. A Franciscan, he was born in Paraguay and devoted his life to converting unbelievers and promoting culture. Toward these ends he established a seminary in Santiago del Estero and the monastery of Santa Catalina in Córdoba, as well as the university.

[P. J. HENNESSEY]

TREMELLIUS, JOHN IMMANUEL (1510–80), Protestant biblical translator. T. and his son-in-law, Franciscus Junius, published (1575–79) at Frankfurt-am-Main a Latin translation from Hebrew of the canonical books of the OT, and from Greek, of the deuterocanonical books. T. also translated the NT into Latin from a Syrian version. This, together with the OT translation mentioned, was published in England in 1580.

[P. J. HENNESSEY]

TRENT, COUNCIL OF. The imperial city of Trent, situated in the Alps near the S end of Brenner Pass, was the scene for the most important assembly of Catholic prelates in modern times. It came as a tardy response to Luther's demand for a ''free Christian council on German soil.'' In *Laetare Jerusalem,* the bull announcing the Council, Pope Paul III directed it toward three goals: (1) to heal the schism; (2) to reform the Church; and (3) to take precautions against the Ottoman Turks. Despite its limited success in these tasks, Trent emerged as a dominant influence on church history over the next 4 centuries. The history of the Council, written over a period of 18 years, has three distinct chapters: Dec. 13, 1545 to Feb. 16, 1548; May 1, 1551 to April 25, 1552; and Jan. 18, 1562 to Dec. 4, 1563. In all, 25 solemn sessions were held.

Sessions 1–10 (1545–48). After several delays because of poor attendance and political upheaval, the Council opened on a note of controversy. The papal forces wanted to begin with the doctrinal issues, whereas the Emperor Charles V's supporters insisted that church reform be the first order of business. Three sessions were spent on this and other procedural questions before a compromise was reached. It was finally decided that questions of doctrine and reform were to be considered side by side in separate commissions and reported out alternately in the plenary sessions. The fact remains, however, that the early discussions on reform were inconclusive, and the important declarations in this phase of the Council were primarily doctrinal. One decree issued (April 8, 1546) at the fourth session was the Catholic answer to the Protestant *sola fide, sola gratia, sola scriptura.* It enumerated the books of the OT and NT canon; endorsed the Latin Vulgate; and insisted on reverence for tradition (D 1501–08). The Catholic position regarding various aspects of *original sin was defined in session 5 (June 17, 1546; D 1510–16). The sixth session came at the end of months of debate (Jan. 13, 1547). It addressed the critical issue of *justification, which had become the touchstone of Luther's doctrinal position. The conciliar decree sought to repudiate Reformation teaching on the subject without at the same time condemning any of the divergent opinions held by Thomists, Scotists, and Augustinians (D 1520–83). The notion and nature of the seven sacraments were clarified in the seventh session (March 3, 1547; D 1600–30). On March 11, 1547, at the eighth session, the papal supporters seized upon an outbreak of typhus as a reason for transferring the council to Bologna. The move further antagonized Charles V, who was already bitter over the direction of the Council. After two solemn sessions in Bologna, at which no important decrees were issued, Paul III suspended the Council.

Sessions 11–16 (1551–52). Soon after he was elected in 1550, Pope Julius III summoned the Council back to Trent the following year. New overtures were made to the Lutherans, who conditioned their participation in the Council on three points: (1) questions of doctrine that had already been considered were to be discussed anew; (2) Lutheran representatives were to have equal voice and vote with the Catholic prelates; and (3) the pope's legates should no longer preside over the proceedings. The council fathers extended safe-conduct to a delegation of the German princes, but were unable to meet their other demands. The most important contribution of this second phase was the Council's doctrinal statement on the Eucharist. In the 13th session (Oct. 11, 1551) it defined the Real Presence in terms of transubstantiation (D 1635–61). Catholic teaching on the sacraments of penance and extreme unction was clarified in the 14th (Nov. 25, 1551; D 1667–1719). War in Germany forced another suspension of the Council in the spring of 1552. More than 10 years elapsed before it met again.

Sessions 17–25 (1562–63). When convoking the Council in 1560, Paul IV was purposely silent on the question whether it was to be a continuation of the previous sessions or a new Council. The council fathers gave their answer by voting to take up the deliberations from where they had left off in 1552. Sessions 21 and 22 were devoted to eucharistic doctrine and practice: the first (July 16, 1562) dealt with holy communion, giving the rationale for denying the chalice to the laity (D 1725–34); the second (Sept. 17, 1562) explained the sense in which the Mass is a sacrifice (D 1738–59). In discussing the sacrament of orders, the 23d session (July 15, 1563) brought to a head the debate over the episcopacy. Already in 1546 the Council had discussed the obligation of bps. to be resident in their sees; in 1563 the debate turned on the source and, by inference, the seriousness of the obligation. Though Trent's decree on holy orders did not settle all questions, it contradicted the Protestants on several points by declaring the priesthood to be truly a sacrament (D 1763–78). It also directed bps. to establish seminaries for the training of priests.

The crucial issue of reform continued to divide the Council. The papal forces were pushing to end the Council, but the Spanish, French, and imperial bps. were unwilling to adjourn before some substantive reform was legislated. The non-Italians suspected that the Roman Curia would be satisfied with token measures. Their fears were in large part allayed by Card. Morone, the papal legate newly appointed to preside over the Council. In the summer of 1563, he drafted a comprehensive program of reform that took cognizance of the complaints submitted by the Spaniards, the French, and the emperor. Morone's proposals served as the basis for discussion. After extensive revision it was passed

by the Council in sessions 24 (Nov. 11, 1563) and 25 (Dec. 3 and 4, 1563). Despite the juridical nature of the reform decrees, they were prompted by pastoral concerns. They established qualifications for cardinals, bishops, and all the clergy; the manner of life, duties, and procedures for appointing them to office were spelled out. Bishops were directed to conduct visitation of their sees; diocesan and provincial synods were to be held regularly. Some of the exemptions from episcopal jurisdiction enjoyed by religious orders in pastoral matters were curtailed. General norms were set down regarding the admission of candidates to religious orders. Stringent laws governing the cloister had lasting effect on orders of women. The important decree *Tametsi* reforming marriage legislation was also passed at the 24th session. It prohibited clandestine weddings and laid down certain forms and procedures required for the validity of a marriage (D 1813–16). The concluding session lasted 2 days (December 3–4, 1563). In addition to the work it did on reform, it approved committee reports on indulgences, purgatory, and the veneration of images; and finally it made arrangements to take care of unfinished business. The Council called upon the Pope to commission new editions of the Index of Prohibited Books, the breviary, the Roman Missal, the catechism, and the Latin Vulgate. Although the Sixto-Clementine edition of the Vulgate appeared only in 1592, the other works were published within a decade after the Council ended. Together with the decrees of the Council itself, these works became the principal instruments of "the Tridentine reform." The *Catechism of the Council of Trent* (1566) proved to have an extraordinary effect in disseminating Catholic doctrine as defined by Trent. It was not a catechism in the usual sense of the word, but rather a manual of instruction for pastoral clergy.

Pius IV gave formal approval to Trent in the bull *Benedictus Deus* (Jan. 26, 1564; D 1847–50). The Pope did not alter the canons and decrees, but he maintained that the Apostolic See alone has the right to interpret them. In Aug. 1564 Pius created a special commission to safeguard and explain the decrees of Trent. It was continued with expanded responsibilities under his successors as the Congregation of the Council. Initially, the success of the Council depended upon acceptance of the reform measures by the Catholic governments. Italy, Portugal, and Poland accepted them immediately. Ferdinand I approved them for his hereditary possessions, but the decrees were never published for the empire as a whole. Nor were they ever promulgated officially in France. In Spain they were published with the saving clause, "without prejudice to royal authority." The Catholic powers were willing to accept the doctrinal teaching of Trent, but when its reform measures ran contrary to national law or privilege, they were reserved.

Historical Perspective. In terms of the mandate given to it in *Laetare Jerusalem*, the Council of Trent was only a limited success. It set the stage for reform within that segment of Western Christendom that remained in communion with Rome, but it did not bridge the gap between Catholics and Protestants. Before a final appraisal of Trent can be made in ecumenical terms, another question must be answered: to what extent was it responsible for the ensuing polemics and controversies? Historical evidence suggests that the spirit at Trent itself was more irenic than the post-Tridentine spirit. The council fathers made an effort to get a first-hand knowledge of the Protestant confessions; unlike earlier councils, it condemned errors, but not persons; and in making room for the divergent opinions within Catholicism itself, it did not present the Church as a monolithic structure. From a historical perspective, it is now recognized that Trent was handicapped by the small number of representatives it attracted and that no one seems to have seen the problem whole. Despite the fact that a principal occupation of both papal and theological writings in the 14th and 15th cents. was ecclesiology and that the chief underlying concern of Protestant Reformers in the 16th cent. was the nature and mission of the Church, Trent never confronted this issue directly. It said a great deal about the teachings of the Church, but nothing on the Church itself; much on the sacraments, but nothing on the Church as the great sacrament. Nor was the Council well served by its critics, for they too had a limited vision. Despite the piecemeal approach, however, the Council became the focal point and symbol of post-Reformation Catholicism. Both its apologists and critics are one in admitting Trent's importance in shaping church history in the West. BIBLIOGRAPHY: *Conciliorum oecumenicorum decreta* (ed. G. Alberigo, 1962) 633–775, a critical edition of the official text of canons and decrees first published in Rome in 1564; H. Jedin, NCE 14:271–278, with bibliog.; Jedin Trent; H. J. Schroeder, *Disciplinary Decrees of the Council of Trent* (1937).

[B. L. MARTHALER]

TRENT CODICES, MS collection, of 15th-cent. polyphonic music. Six of the seven volumes were discovered in the library of the cathedral of Trent, N Italy, by F. Q. Hoberl. The seventh, discovered later, contains mainly duplicates. The MSS represent works of some 75 composers and contain over 1500 compositions, many of which have been published in the *Denkmäler der Tonkunst in Österreich.*

[M. T. LEGGE]

TRENTO, VITTORIO (1761–1833), Italian composer, mainly of ballets and operas, who also wrote oratorios, including ''The Deluge'' and ''The Maccabees.''

[M. T. LEGGE]

TRESHAM, prominent English Catholic family: **Thomas** (d. 1471), speaker of the House of Commons. He was knighted after serving Henry VI in the War of Roses. As speaker, he accused the Duke of York and later was himself accused of high treason when the Yorkists prevailed. A pardon was followed by another arrest, another pardon, and

final beheading. **Thomas** (d. 1559), grand prior of England in the Order of Knights Hospitallers of St. John of Jerusalem. Grandson of the first Sir Thomas, he was knighted in 1530, served in Parliament, and for four terms was sheriff of Northhamptonshire. He attended Queen Mary on her entrance into London in 1553, hence his appointment as grand prior. **Thomas** (1543?–1605), prominent recusant, grandson of second Sir Thomas. Knighted in 1570, he served as sheriff of Northhamptonshire. He was reared as a Protestant but was converted to Catholicism, after which he was arrested for harboring Edmund Campion and charged regularly with recusancy.

[P. J. HENNESSEY]

TREVAUR, JOHN (d. *c.*1357), Welsh ecclesiastic, bp. of St. Asaph (1346). Prince Edward pressed the canons of St. Asaph to elect an English bp. (1345). They resisted, choosing John, a papal servant, whose provision by Clement VI, the first clear instance of such action there, vindicated papal and Welsh rights. BIBLIOGRAPHY: Emden Ox 3:1898; G. Williams, *Welsh Church from Conquest to Reformation* (1962) 125–126.

[R. W. HAYS]

TREVAUR (TREFOR), JOHN (d. 1410), Welsh ecclesiastic, doctor of canon and civil law from Oxford, bp. of St. Asaph (1395). After serving at the Roman Curia and the courts of Richard II and Henry IV, T. joined the rebel Owain Glyndwr and fled the realm. Patron of Welsh bards, he may have written on heraldry and history. BIBLIOGRAPHY: G. Williams, NCE 14:280; Emden Ox 3:1898–99.

[R. W. HAYS]

TREVISA, JOHN DE (d. by 1402), English translator. Fellow of Exeter College, Oxford (*c.*1362–69), he progressed during the year 1370 from acolyte to subdeacon, deacon, and priest. He was fellow of Queen's (1369–79), vicar of Berkeley (Gloucester) in 1387, chaplain to Thomas, Lord Berkeley, and from *c.*1389, canon of Westbury-on-Trym. His translations of Latin works into English included Higden's *Polychronicon* and, according to Caxton, the Bible. BIBLIOGRAPHY: Emden Ox 3:1903.

[C. D. ROSS]

TRIAD, a special and even sacred fullness or wholeness made up of three components, a recurrent notion in magic, religion, and philosophy. By reason of such fundamental perceptions as the distinction in time in present, past, and future; in the world, in the upper world, earth, and the lower world or in heaven, earth, and hell; and in the family, in father, mother, and child, there emerged in Egypt the divine family of Osiris, Isis, and Horus. The divine triad is widespread; in India: Brahma, Vishna, and Siva; in Greece: Zeus, Athena, and Apollo; in Rome: Jupiter, Juno, and Minerva or Jupiter, Mars, and Quirinus. Then there are the lesser triads: three Fates, three Graces, and three Furies; and the more mundane and magical threefold repetition of formulas, rituals, and invocations.

[E. J. DILLON]

TRIAL OF JESUS, that process by which Jesus was judged guilty and condemned to death by the Jewish Sanhedrin and Pontius Pilate. The four Evangelists present substantially the same account, but there are variations. These differences demonstrate that the trial narrative, like the rest of the NT, is a theological reflection, an attempt to demonstrate the significance of the events, not to report them in their merely factual dimension. Concerning the discrepancy in dating the crucifixion (the Synoptics place it on the 15th day of the Jewish month of Nisan and John on the 14th day), two solutions are proposed: that the Synoptics followed the Pharisee's liturgical calendar and John followed that of the Sadducees, or that Jesus followed the solar calendar of the Qumran community, celebrating the Passover on Wednesday and the Last Supper on that Tuesday evening. Thus the latter solution places the arrest on Tuesday evening rather than the traditional Thursday.

Five events within the juridical process are narrated by one or more of the Evangelists: (1) The interrogation by Annas—after his arrest, Jesus was brought to Annas who, although he was not high priest that year, retained that title and wielded great influence. This was a hasty interrogation concerning Jesus' disciples and teaching. (2) The morning trial before the Sanhedrin presided over by the high priest, Caiphas—this was a more formal trial in which witnesses, according to Jewish court procedure, brought evidence against the accused. Since the witnesses could not agree, Caiphas elicits a ''blasphemous'' response from Jesus: that he will sit in judgment at God's right hand. Scholars differ about whether the Sanhedrin had the power of capital punishment; at any rate, they needed Roman confirmation. (3) The first hearing before Pilate—the issue is now a political one of sedition. (4) Herod's questioning—since Pilate found sufficient evidence lacking, he sent Jesus to Herod as to a court of higher appeal. (5) The second appearance before Pilate—the final scene before the flagellation and crucifixion. Pilate continues to recognize Jesus' innocence. The offer to release Barabbas, a Zealot revolutionary, entails a play on words. Barabbas (in Aramaic, son of the father) is chosen over Jesus, the true Son. Pilate finally succumbs to pressure and condemns Jesus. The narrative, whose purpose is to affirm Jesus' legal innocence, probably softens Pilate's attitude since he was extremely harsh toward revolutionaries. The flagellation, rightly placed by Mk after the sentence of condemnation, was regularly connected in Roman practice with execution by crucifixion.
BIBLIOGRAPHY: JBC 2:55–57; 110–112; 160–161; J. Blinzler, *Trial of Jesus* (1959); P. Winter, *On the Trial of Jesus* (1961); T. E. Crane, NCE 14:281–284.

[T. M. MCFADDEN]

TRIBES OF ISRAEL, the tribal confederation, united by an allegiance to Yahweh, the Lord of Sinai, in whose name, mighty in battle, was achieved the conquest of the land of Canaan. Israel has been compared to the association among neighboring Greek city-states (amphictyony), but it can be doubted whether there ever was a stable confederation along those lines in Israel. Israel was a confederation of seminomadic tribal groups, whose shifting fortunes moved them into fluctuating patterns of alliances. There may have been successive alliances involving now some, now other tribes over a period of centuries during which various seminomadic tribes gradually settled in Canaan as the new masters of that land. A clue to the pattern of successive waves of would-be conquerors can be found in the Jacob saga, which relates the births of the eponymous heroes of the twelve tribes of Israel and their return with Jacob in separate groupings to the land of Canaan. On his way to meet his brother Esau, Jacob received from God the name Israel. There are five subgroupings of tribes in the narrative (Gen 35.22–26). First come the early Leah tribes: Reuben, Simeon, Levi, and Judah. This group may have tried to enter Canaan from the south. Reuben, Simeon, and Levi were eventually driven back, and their remnant was absorbed by Judah or other later tribes who successfully entered Canaan from the east. Next come the Bilhah tribes (named after Rachel's handmaid): Dan and Naphtali, of whom little is known, since they had little significance for the biblical writers. Thirdly, come the tribes of Zilpah (named after Leah's handmaid): Gad and Asher, who took no part in the victory celebrated in the ancient Song of Deborah (Jg 5). Next come the later Leah tribes: Issachar, Zebulun, (and Dinah). The Song of Deborah praises Issachar and Zebulun for answering the call to fight alongside the Rachel tribes. Lastly come the Rachel tribes, Joseph and Benjamin; or, as they came to be called, Ephraim, Benjamin, and Manasseh. Manasseh (Machir) had a temporary preeminence along with its cult center at Shechem. Benjamin may actually have crossed the Jordan first as outriders of the Rachel group and at a terrible cost in lives. By the time the story of Joshua and Judges is told, the tribe of Benjamin is greatly reduced and lives in the shadow of the Canaanite ring of cities that separate Judah from Ephraim. Ephraim is the key tribe in the alliance, the dominant tribe of Israel. From Ephraim came Joshua and later Samuel. In the territory of Ephraim are most of the ancient cult centers mentioned in the Deuteronomic history: Shiloh, Bethel, Mizpah, etc. The prophetic books use the names Ephraim and Israel interchangeably. Rather than a stable confederation of twelve tribes, Israel was very soon divided in two: Ephraim and Judah (north and south); Bethel (replacing Shiloh and Shechem) and Jerusalem. Tribal customs and tribal religious ideals continued to exist even after the institution of the monarchy, alongside traditions and values borrowed from the Canaanite way of life. This was a source of creative tension that perdured in Israel down at least to the time of the Babylonian conquest.

[E. J. DILLON]

TRIDENTINE, the adjectival form of reference to the Council of Trent (from *Tridentum,* the town of Trent in northern Italy); e.g., the Tridentine Catechism is the *Catechism of the Council of Trent;* the Tridentine reform is that instituted by the decrees of Trent.

TRIDUUM, a three-day period of prayer, devotions, and preaching in preparation for a feast day, a kind of abbreviated *novena. The reform of the liturgy seeks to bring all such devotions into line with the calendar, rites, and biblical readings of the liturgy. (Vat II SacLit 13).

TRIEST, ANTOINE (1576–1657), bp. of Bruges from 1616, of Ghent from 1620, defender of C. *Jansen (Jansenius) against attacks on the *Augustinus*. T. was an exemplary bp., putting into effect the reforms of the Council of Trent and devoting himself to the needs of the poor. He wrote his *Raisons* (1647) in defense of Jansen, whose memory he revered and whose teachings he judged to be misrepresented. For a brief period T. himself was under censure from Rome because of his stand.

[T. C. O'BRIEN]

TRIEST, PETER JOSEPH (1760–1836), Belgian priest at Ghent, founder of the Sisters of Charity of Jesus and Mary (1803) and of the Brothers of Charity (1807) for the care of orphans, the sick, and the aged; of the Brothers of St. John of God (1823), a nursing community; and of the Sisters of the Holy Childhood (1835), dedicated to the care of foundlings. T. was referred to as the St. Vincent de Paul of Belgium because of his ministrations to the physical and spiritual needs of his people in the aftermath of the French Revolution.

[T. C. O'BRIEN]

TRIFORMIANS, those who taught that God is of three "forms," or parts: Father, Son, and Holy Spirit are partial beings; the three together make up the perfection of the Trinity. The belief was described by Filaster (*Haer.* 93) and Augustine (*Haer.* 74). The name *Triformii,* or *Triformiani,* was invented by Danaeus in his edition (1576) of Augustine's *De haeresibus* (PL 12:1205).

[L. G. MÜLLER]

TRIGAULT, NICOLAS (1577–1628), Belgian Jesuit missionary in China, promoter of the missions, and of the views of M. *Ricci in the *Chinese Rites Controversy. A Jesuit from 1594, T. began his apostolate in China in 1610, but 2 years later was sent to Europe to advance the interests of the missions. To this period belongs his Latin translation of Ricci's work *De christiana expeditione apud Sinas . . . ex P. Ricci commentariis* (1615; Eng. tr. L. J. Gallagher, *China in the 16th Century,* 1953); the work greatly heightened European awareness of the missions. In the cause of missionary *adaptation, T. received from Paul V in 1615 a brief allowing the use of Chinese instead of Latin in the liturgy. He traveled as spokesman and recruiter throughout Europe, returning to China only in 1619 but with

44 missionary recruits. He spent his years mainly in writing, translating Chinese classics, and defending Ricci's position.

[T. C. O'BRIEN]

TRIGON, *neume found in the MSS of St. Gall (9th–10th centuries). It consisted of three dots in the form of a triangle and probably signified a staccato performance of the *torculus* (a figure of three notes, such as e, f, d or b, c, a).

[M. T. LEGGE]

TRIKERION (Tricerion), a liturgical candlestick with three candles accompanied by the dicerion (a two-branched candlestick). They form a set used by the bp. in the Byzantine Rite. This one represents the Trinity. These are used when the bp. gives a blessing. The origin of this set of candles is probably the candle carried in front of the bp. as a sign of honor, as well as to give light in the church for him to read the liturgical text.

[P. MORLINO]

TRINE IMMERSION (Triune Immersion), a ritual for baptism in which the recipient kneels in water and is immersed three times, in the name of the three Persons of the Trinity. This method of baptizing is esp. characteristic of the *Brethren Churches.

TRINITARIAN PROCESSIONS, a credal and theological term expressing the internal nature and life of the triune God in light of the data of Christian revelation. Though the doctrine of the Trinity is the result of centuries of theological reflection on the precise meaning of Christian monotheism, the Bible itself contains an implicit trinitarian understanding of the one God who has disclosed himself to man in history by sending his Son and the Spirit of his Son (*Gal.* 4.4–6). God as he acts in time (economic Trinity) is God as he really is in himself apart from created history (immanent Trinity). Thus, if God sends forth his Son and his Spirit through an external outpouring of love toward man (soteriological Trinity), this act must be rooted in an internal capacity to love that is proper to God alone (ontological Trinity). This series of reflections gradually led Christian thinkers to speak of an eternal generation of the Son from the Father and of a timeless spiration of the Spirit from the Father and the Son. These terms, later to be adopted by the whole Church, had their origin in the theology of Augustine, who used the model of man's own psychological nature to elucidate the twofold procession in the being of God; the generation of the Son from the Father is analogous to the generation of thought from man's spiritual faculties; the spiration of the Spirit corresponds to the process by which the human will, once it perceives an intellectual good, embraces and enacts it. Thus the Son is the personal Word whom the ungenerated Father eternally conceives and realizes in the divine community; the Spirit is the expression of the mutual act of love that the Son wills with the Father. Since the divine love actually "spirates" a new personal reality within the Godhead, the Spirit both binds the Father and the Son in internal peace and grounds their ability to express their love externally towards created reality. Theological reflection on the trinitarian processions thus attempts to guarantee man's own spiritual existence as knower and lover of the triune God in nothing less than the Trinity's own internal knowledge and love. BIBLIOGRAPHY: M. Scheeben, *Mysteries of Christianity* (1941; tr. 1946); K. Rahner, *Trinity* (1974); G. Sloyan, *Three Persons in One God* (1964).

[P. J. ROSATO]

TRINITARIANISM, the belief or the theology affirming that the one God is three Persons, Father, Son and Holy Spirit. The term is frequently used in opposition to Unitarianism.

TRINITY, HOLY, the mystery of the three Divine Persons—Father, Son, and Holy Spirit—in one divine nature. Together with that of Christ, the mystery of the Trinity forms the core of the Christian message. Both mysteries are inseparable, one being implied in the other; for Christ is the eternal Son of the eternal Father, himself made man and filled with the Spirit in order to communicate his divine sonship to sinful men. Far from being a mere puzzle for the intellect, the mystery of the Trinity is therefore of great importance in the order of God's personal relations with men.

Old and New Testaments. Yahweh's deeds for the salvation of Israel mark the first stage of God's self-disclosure: not only did he enter into a covenant relationship with the people of his choice, but he proved himself a Father whose loving kindness is unequalled and whose forbearing endurance is without repentance. Through his Word he spoke to them and acted in their favor; his Spirit inspired the Prophets and presided over the destiny of the people. However, the OT never conceived the idea of a plurality of Divine Persons; though literarily hypostatized, the Word and the Spirit were understood as dynamic expressions of Yahweh's selfmanifestation. The new dispensation is God's decisive revelation. Christ is Son of God in a unique and transcendent manner. Related as Son to the Father, he belongs to Yahweh's own sphere of existence. Sent by the Father, the Word incarnate promises in turn to send the Spirit. Pentecost is the public manifestation of the Spirit; it ushers in the present era of salvation, the Church era. The heavenly Father, Jesus Christ his true Son, the Spirit of God truly personal: such is the Trinity of Divine Persons contained in the writings of the NT.

Development. Through the first cent. of Christianity, the Church has grown in its awareness of the mystery of the Trinity. The approach of the early tradition remains fundamentally that of the Scriptures: from the economy of the divine selfmanifestation in the history of salvation, the Christian reflection ascends to the ontology of God's inner life. That Jesus Christ is the Son of God incarnate implies in God an eternal relationship of Father and Son; similarly the

manifestation of the divine Spirit leads up to his eternal existence. The three—Father, Son, and Spirit—are one God. The reversed process from unity to plurality represents a further stage in the theological reflection: one God is three—Father, Son, and Spirit. St. Augustine is in the 4th cent. the main representative of this approach. The term Trinity (Gr., *trias*) made its appearance as early as the 2d cent. (Theophilus of Antioch), but a long evolution was to take place before a precise theological terminology could be elaborated. The meaning of the terms known to the philosophies of the time evolved progressively toward the dogmatic distinction of nature and person: God is one nature and three Persons. The Council of Constantinople II (553; D 421) enunciates the dogma and fixes its technical expression, bringing to completion the work of the first two ecumenical councils, in which the divinity of the Son and of the Spirit had been clearly affirmed. Against Arius's denial, Nicaea I (325) had stated clearly the "consubstantiality" of the Son with the Father (D 125); Constantinople I (381) had affirmed against various heretics (Pneumatomachians and others) that the Spirit must be adored and glorified together with Father and Son (D 150). Later, the Council of Lateran IV (1215) will confess with Peter Lombard that "there is one highest, incomprehensible, and ineffable reality that is truly Father, Son, and Holy Spirit" (D 804).

From a logical standpoint the mystery can be approached in two opposite directions: either the mind ascends from what is plural in God to what is one—from Persons to nature—or vice versa. Far from being mutually exclusive, these two ways complete each other: both views stress different and complementary aspects; each needs the help of the other to avoid the onesidedness that leads to error. The Trinitarian heresies also fall into two opposite categories: (1) those affirming the plurality of Persons to the prejudice of the unity of nature (among which are subordinationism, tritheism); (2) those that stress the unity of nature but fall short of the plurality of Persons (modalism and others). The Christian faith overcomes the antinomy of those extreme and opposite positions; it combines strict monotheism with the Trinity of the Divine Persons. Father, Son, and Holy Spirit are three distinct subjects and one divine reality. The Second Person originates from the first by way of generation; this means that there is eternal fatherhood and sonship in God. The Third Person is even more mysterious than the others; the name given him by divine revelation, Spirit (Heb., *ruah*; Gr., *pneuma*), suggests little concerning the manner of his divine origin. However, his place and order of origin among the three is clear, though it is expressed differently by the Western and the Eastern traditions. According to the Western tradition the Spirit proceeds from the Father *and* the Son as from one principle; according to the Eastern tradition he proceeds from the Father *through* the Son. Both formulations are guaranteed by the Council of Florence (D 1300–01), not in the sense that both are identical or exactly equivalent but because they complete each other. As stated by the same Council of Florence (D 1330), in God "all things are one, except where there is opposition of relationship." Father, Son, and Spirit are distinct through relationships only; they are the same divine reality in threefold relational hypostasis; or, to put it the other way round, they represent three hypostatic modes of being one God. The mystery of the Trinity reveals the inner riches and fecundity of the divine life: though unique God is not a solitary monad, for his inmost self is made of a communion of Persons. Indeed, each Divine Person is constituted in existence by his relationship to the others. This means that each is entirely for the others and turned to them. All egocentrism is metaphysically impossible in God, for self-realization coincides here with substantial selfgiving. The Father knows himself in the Son; the Spirit is the communion of love of Father and Son, their togetherness hypostatized. Sharing the same reality in relational distinction, the three are not only equal in divinity but mutually inclusive.

Theology. For centuries Christian theology has dwelt on the data of the faith. Among the various theological insights into the mystery of the divine life, the one developed by St. Augustine and further elaborated by St. Thomas Aquinas seems the most adequate. It is based on the revealed message where St. John speaks of the Word that was with God at the beginning (Jn 1.1) and identifies the Son with the Word. After St. Augustine, St. Thomas explains that in God the Second Person proceeds by way of intellection and concludes that, since there are only two immanent acts in God, understanding and loving, it necessarily follows that the Third Person proceeds by way of volition. The Son is the immanent result, or the fruit, of the divine act of selfconsciousness: God knows himself in his Word. The Spirit is the loving communion of Father and Son, their togetherness in love, their we-ness hypostatized.

God's inner life defies human understanding. But, however mysterious it may be, it is nonetheless supremely relevant to man's understanding of himself and has a deep significance for his own life. Not only does it throw new light on what man is as a person, a subject who attains selfpossession by communicating with other men, it also affects deeply the history of mankind. The economy of God's dealings with men reflects the ontology of his inner life. Salvation history as it unfolds itself is marked with a Trinitarian rhythm, each person exercising his proper influence according to his order of origin. The Council of Vatican II repeatedly stresses the Trinitarian nature of the history of salvation: the Father's saving design is accomplished in the Son's Incarnation and carried out through the sending of the Spirit (Vat II ConstChurch 2–4). Thus the Church "takes its origin from the mission of the Son and the mission of the Holy Spirit in accordance with the decree of God the Father" (Vat II MissAct 2). The history of God's personal dealings with each man also is marked with a Trinitarian rhythm: God gives himself through Christ in the Spirit; life in the Spirit imparts upon man through Christ the sonship of the Father. Thus the Christian view of life and of the world is bound to the Trinity. The analogous doctrines found in other religious traditions (as for instance the Hindu doctrine of Trimurti) cannot be identified with the Christian dogma. They may, however, be incomplete perceptions of the mystery of a God who intervenes personally, though in a hidden manner, in the life of every man of good will. BIBLIOGRAPHY: H. de Lavalett et al., LTK 3:543–560; R. L. Richard, NCE 14:295–306.

[J. DUPUIS]

TRINITY COLLEGE (UNIVERSITY OF DUBLIN), coeducational institution of higher learning in Dublin, Ireland, founded as the College of the Holy and Undivided Trinity by Queen Elizabeth in 1591. By royal charter, the body corporate was composed of a provost and at least three fellows and three scholars. As the first five provosts were Cambridge men, the early bias was strongly Puritan; policy later changed to Anglican. The college first admitted Catholics in 1793 but did not abolish the religious test until 1873. The library houses 900,000 books and 3,000 MSS, including the Book of Kells, the Book of Armagh, and the Brehon MS. Enrollment numbers 3,154 men and women; the teaching staff, 355.

[M. B. MURPHY]

TRINITY SUNDAY, feast celebrated on the Sunday after Pentecost. The theme of this feast is not altogether clear. It may be a celebration of the dogma of the Trinity or a solemn celebration of all the Paschal mysteries. As a feast, it is of non-Roman origin and began as a votive Mass in the 8th century. The Benedictines, especially those of Cluny, fostered the feast. John XXII in 1334 approved and extended its celebration to the whole Latin Church. It is esp. popular in the Church of England. Both the C of E and the Lutheran Church, reckons its Sundays after Trinity rather than Pentecost, as until recently was the practice of the Carmelites and Dominicans of the Roman Rite. BIBLIOGRAPHY: R. Cabie, *La Pentecôte: L'évolution de la cinquantaine paschale au cours des cinq premières siècles* (1965); N. M. Denis-Boulet, *Christian Calendar* (1960); A. A. McArthur, *Christian Year and Lectionary Reform* (1958).

[N. KOLLAR]

TRIO SONATA, a Baroque chamber music form employed by most of the composers of that period. It was written in three-part harmony—two upper parts of the same range with a figured bass support. Though the instrumentation varied, some trio sonatas having been composed for organ alone, some even for orchestras, the form basically retained its three-part texture.

[M. T. LEGGE]

TRIODION, in the East, a liturgical book of hymns composed by holy men for the guidance of the faithful. Triodion means "song of three odes," the symbol of the Trinity. One of the main themes of the Triodion is that of the love of God from Creation throughout salvation history to the fulfillment of God's promise through Christ.

[P. MORLINO]

TRIPITAKA, the "three baskets" (Pali), i.e., the collections of Buddhist scripture making up the *Pali canon. The *Vinaya-pitaka* (the "Book of Discipline") is largely narrative material concerning the establishment of the Buddhist community and the rules governing it. *Sutta-pitaka* (Pali; Sanskrit *sutra*, thread of discourse) is the discourses and dialogues of the Buddha and certain of his disciples. *Abhidhamma pitaka* consists of abstract, analytic, and systematized doctrine. Among Pali works of great weight, though not included in the canon, are the *Questions of King Milinda* and the *Path of Purity* by Buddhaghosa. The term *Tripitaka* is also conventionally used to describe significant collections of Mahayana *sutras* (preserved in Sanskrit, Chinese, and Tibetan versions and not in the Pali canon), like the *Prajnaparamita* ("perfection of wisdom") literature, including the *Diamond* and *Heart sutras*; the *Pure Land*, *Lotus*, and *Vimalakirti sutras*; and the *Path of Enlightenment* by Santideva. The Chinese *Tripitaka* would also include the ("Platform") treatise of Hui-neng and that of Huang-po (the "Transmission of Mind"), both important in the Chinese (Ch'an) and Japanese (Zen) traditions. BIBLIOGRAPHY: K. Ch'en, *Buddhism* (1968), 211–235; *idem.*, *Buddhism in China* (1964) 365–386.

[D. P. EFROYMSON]

TRIPLUM, in the early polyphonic works of the Notre Dame school, the part above the *tenor.

[M. T. LEGGE]

TRIPTYCH, a painting or bas relief sculptural group in three unequal sections shaped so that the two smaller side panels, turning on hinges, can be folded over the center. During the Gothic period many altar pieces took this form, with triptychs most often serving as portable altars. The central panel bore the main subject, which the outer wings then continued or complemented. Depending on the use of the triptych, the backs of these might also be decorated, frequently by means of a whole series of smaller paintings in boxes, so that when closed the triptych displayed a quite different obverse. The principal panel commonly rested on a painted base, the predella. Though large triptychs were generally created out of wood or stone, miniature triptychs in ivory, enamel, and gold also enjoyed popularity.

[E. M. GATES]

TRISAGION (Gr., thrice holy), the brief hymn found in the rites of all ancient Churches, whose Greek text, because of the syntax involved, must be translated "Holy (is) God, holy (and) strong, holy (and) immortal; have mercy on us." In form, the first part is an acclamation to be understood in the third person singular; while the conclusion, "Have mercy on us," is an impetration in the second person singu-

lar imperative. Failure to make this distinction between the two loosely connected parts has led to the initial acclamation's being put clearly into the second person by West Syrian translators, or to its understanding as a vocative by the East Syrians, Armenians, Copts, and Ethiopians as well as by the Slavonic and Romanian Byzantine translators. The Trisagion is clearly inspired by the triple "Holy" with which the angels acclaim God in Is 6.2–3 and Rev 4.8, but its origin is unknown. It makes its first documentary appearance in the Acts of the Council of *Chalcedon (451). Around 470 the Antiochene patriarch Peter the Fuller, who followed Monophysitism, had the phrase "who was crucified for us" added to the end of the acclamatory part, thus making the hymn Christological and insisting (legitimately, but with a polemic emphasis) that it was "God," named thus in the acclamation, who suffered crucifixion. A lasting controversy then arose between the orthodox party, insisting that the acclamation is Trinitarian, and the monophysite party, insisting that it refers to the Son. In fact, the original sense is neither explicitly Trinitarian, nor is it originally addressed to the Son. The West Syrians, Armenians, Copts, and Ethiopians still retain the incise of Peter the Fuller, the Armenians having three alternate forms for various seasons and feasts; the Copts and Ethiopians having expanded the incise itself into several clauses. In the Roman liturgy the trisagion is sung on Good Friday, and the *Sanctus of the Mass has a similar foundation in Is 6:2–3. BIBLIOGRAPHY: A. Baumstark, "Trisagion und Queduscha," JBLit 3 (1923) 18–23.

[A. CODY]

TRISTAN L'HERMITE, FRANÇOIS, see L'HERMITE, FRANÇOIS.

TRITHEISM, any teaching that sees in the Trinity, besides a distinction of persons, also one of natures or substances. Thus there would be not one God, but three Gods. Historically, tritheism has not been a heresy taught explicitly, but rather an implication of the philosophical expressions used by certain theologians in discussing the Trinity. In this sense the following are classified as tritheists: John Philoponus (fl. 6th cent.), because he identified nature and person; Roscellin (d. *c*.1125), by teaching that there could be no nature common to many persons; Gilbert de la Porrée (1076–1154), by asserting that the common nature was a fourth distinct reality in the Trinity (D 745); Joachim of Fiore (*c*.1132–1202), by teaching that the three Persons had a collective nature (D 803–806). A. Günther (1783–1863), employing Hegelian language, taught that the three divine Persons were distinct substances, the one divine consciousness being the only bond of unity (D 2828).

[E. A. WEIS]

TRITHEMIUS, JOHANNES (family name, Zeller; 1462–1512), Benedictine abbot and scholar. Becoming abbot at the early age of 23, T. sought zealously to bring about the reform of his monastery and to promote learning among the monks. He was a friend of many of the learned men of his time, assembled a notable collection of books, but eventually lost favor with his community by his efforts to improve discipline. In 1503 he joined the Scottish monastery of St. Jacob at Würtzburg where he was again elected abbot. Of the many works he wrote, only some have appeared in print: *Joannis Trithemii opera historica* (1601), and *J. T. opera pia et spiritualia* (ed. Johannes Busaeus, 1604). Despite his scholarship, he took a keen interest in the occult, witchcraft, and cryptography. BIBLIOGRAPHY: P. K. Meagher, NCE 14:311–312; P. Lehmann, *Merkwürdigkeiten des Abtes Trithemus* (1961).

[J. R. SCHULZ]

TRITONE, a musical interval consisting of three whole tones or six semitones, for instance F–B. In traditional harmony it is considered a dissonant or unstable interval, one requiring resolution to a stable interval. As such, it is often a component of the next-to-last chord of a musical phrase; its harmonic tension is resolved by the final chord, conveying a sense of completion. It was considered esp. problematical by medieval and renaissance musicians, who termed it *diabolus in musica* (the devil in music) and went to great lengths to avoid it.

[A. DOHERTY]

TRITTA, GIACOMO (1733–1824), Italian composer. T. studied at the Conservatorio della Pietà dei Turchini at Naples and later became a teacher there and assistant to his former professor, Cafaro. When the Conservatorio was transformed into the Collegio Reale di Musica, T. became one of the first directors. He was also maestro at the Royal Chapel from 1816. T. composed 50 operas, wrote some theoretical books, and produced a good amount of church music: Masses, a Passion, a *Te Deum*, motets, cantatas, etc., none of which were printed.

[M. T. LEGGE]

TRIUMPH, a ceremonial procession at Rome in honor of a general victorious over a foreign foe. During the Republic the honor was conferred by the Senate according to a number of fixed rules. Under the Empire it became an imperial prerogative, though victorious generals were allowed to wear triumphal insignia on state occasions. During the elaborate parade, which passed from the Porta Triumphalis to the Capitolium, the *triumphator* rode in a chariot drawn by four horses. Dressed in a special robe and with his face painted red, he was accompanied by his children and by a slave who whispered to him: "Remember you are a man." BIBLIOGRAPHY: A. Momigliano, OCD 926.

[M. J. COSTELLOE]

TRIUMPHALISM, an abstraction bandied about since Vatican II, mainly as a pejorative term—triumph, like charity and prudence has come down in the world—for the insolence incidental to, but not uncommon in, the exercise of ecclesiastical power, the RC assumption of superiority over other religious bodies, the proclamation of rights and privileges before charity and the service of our neighbor, the exaltation of a clerical caste, the retention of what are felt to be obsolete and regal trappings in liturgical and para-liturgical functions, the authoritarian accents of rulers confident in their divine commission and not prepared to submerge their office in the current social dialectic, and, in brief, a religious jingoism that stalks on its way, as they say, regardless.

So far so good, and the term has its relevance. But the concept is not new, and, which may come as a surprise to those out of sympathy with the past, it has been harbored not least by those in the seats of power, and is symbolized, to take one instance at random, by the burning flax and the *sic transit* at a papal coronation. In our days its emotive fringes tend to displace its meaning, so that it becomes a slogan, a rabble-rousing sound, that often betrays a lopsided theology of the reign of the Spirit, a millenarianism that has been the *Doppelgänger* of the Church down the ages, and a somewhat callow sense of history indifferent alike to the grandeurs and miseries of our ancestors.

For there are triumphs to be celebrated, and they are to be found in the Scriptures, in the Fathers, and in the sacred liturgy: above all God's majesty should be acclaimed in doxologies which do not stop at words, and the standards of the King, of Christ the victor over evil and death, should go forth with more splendor than the royal Trooping of the Colour or the *joyeuse entrée* of a Burgundian duke. Honor and fame and glory are genuine human values, from which only the mean-spirited abstain, and their expression answers genuine human needs: it is not from Jung alone that we learn the value of archaic myths among the forces of social cohesion. And it is right that the premonitions and anticipations of divinity already manifested in the history of the Church should be solemnized, and this without lessening the bitter-sweet appreciation of its commitment to the human imbroglio, of God's writing straight with crooked lines, of the whole mixture of motives that clusters round the best of causes, and of the b.o. that goes with the *esprit de corps* of the marching Church.

For the rest it is largely a question of style and sense of proportion, which seems to be tackled more easily by simple and cultivated people than by those betwixt and between; it is significant perhaps that the poor in fact as well as in spirit are less resentful about pomp than others who can afford to live in the suburbs, and less inclined to grumble with Iscariot, *Ut quid perditio haec?* The plain needs for human decency must first be met in the name of social justice, but afterwards no apology is needed for that aristocratic fling from human nature which spends itself on works of art for God without thought of self-betterment, a lordliness carefree and without illusion, for it knows its effects are relatively tawdry.

Not everybody is required to have a taste for the splendors of the Gothic or the apotheoses of the Baroque, or to be well-informed about or grateful for the contribution of proud prelates to our legacy of civilization and culture. Anybody can be sardonic if he likes about the haberdashery of Neo-Byzantinism and the sonorities of pontifical documents. Yet a particular Providence drops him in one place and period, and there his charity begins; then as his experiences and affections ripple out to wider regions and ages, without yet reaching the shores of eternity, he finds objects for his patriotism (*pietas*) and worship (*dulia*), which are parts of justice, for the magnificence which is part of courage, and for the display of honor which is part of temperance: all belong to the life of grace. There is something missing if he is not a partisan for something short of St. Augustine's City of God. He need be a bigot because he is proud of being a Papist no more than a ninny because he recognizes, with Nurse Cavell, that patriotism is not enough. Of course there are occupational diseases here, as there are in religion itself, for as the one can be spoilt by superstition, so can xenophobia, racialism, nationalism, sectarianism, class-warfare, absurd punctilio, and sheer bad manners enter into any glorification of the non-sacred. But he is a sad fellow, though he may be a sufficient Christian, who does not kindle to earthy triumphalism of some sort, to the drums and fifes of the Irish Brigade at Fontenoy, to Handel's *Messiah*, to the *Battle Hymn of the Republic*, to Leo at the gates of Rome, or Hildebrand at the castle of Canossa, to the thunder rolling round the dome at Vatican I. Are they Dunkirks? Perhaps, and none the worse for that. Men become Christians because of them. And who, knowing the Scriptures, would decry the fact? BIBLIOGRAPHY: ThAq ST 2a2ae, 101–103; 129–135; 145.

[T. GILBY]

TRIVIUM AND QUADRIVIUM, in medieval education the seven liberal arts: the trivium grouped under *logic comprised grammar, rhetoric, and dialectic; the quadrivium, grouped under mathematics, comprised arithmetic, music, geometry, and astronomy. The seven were regarded as the instruments indispensable to the study of philosophy and theology. BIBLIOGRAPHY: *Didascalicon of Hugh of St. Victor* (ed. J. Taylor, introd. 7–19, repr. 1968).

[T. C. O'BRIEN]

TRIVULZIO, a noble Milanese family of soldiers, churchmen, and political magnates which has flourished since the 13th century. **Gian Giacomo** (d. 1518) gained prominence during the regency for Gian Galeazzo *Sforza. He supported the French connection which became traditional in the family, several members of which became marshals of France. Five became cardinals: **Antonio** (d. 1509), as a concession to Louis XII of France; **Agostino** (d. 1548); **Scaramuzza** (d. 1527), learned in law and advisor to Louis XII; **Antonio II** (d. 1559), who performed various missions for the Pope; and **Teodoro** (d. 1657), who was much favored by Philip III and Philip IV of Spain. A family collec-

tion of MSS, letters, and books was preserved by the efforts of two brothers, **Alessandro** (d. 1789) and **Teodoro** (d. 1763). One of the great private collections of Europe, it was acquired by the city of Milan in 1935 and was housed in the Sforza castle.

[N. G. WOLF]

TRNOVO, capital city of the Second Bulgarian Empire (1185–1393) and see of the Bulgarian patriarchate (1235–1394). Trnovo acquired political and ecclesiastical prominence with the liberation of the Bulgarians from Byzantine dominion in 1185. The new Bulgarian State appealed for support to the see of Rome, which recognized the autonomous Bulgarian Church (1204), and granted the abp. of Trnovo the rank of primate of Bulgaria and Valachia. The Latin occupation of Constantinople, however, led the Bulgarians and Byzantines to improve their relations, while those with Rome deteriorated. In 1235, the patriarch of Constantinople (then residing in Nicaea) recognized the autonomy of the Bulgarian Church and the rank of patriarch for the abp. of Trnovo. Schism with Rome followed as a result. The Patriarchate of Trnovo played a significant role in the development of Slavic letters, particularly in the time of Patriarach Evtimi (1375–93). The see was abolished after the Turkish conquest in 1393, and its territory was incorporated into the Patriarchate of Constantinople. When the autonomous Bulgarian Church was established again in 1870–72, Trnovo became one of its metropolitan sees. The city still contains impressive ruins of its past, including the interesting church of the Forty Martyrs with two rare inscriptions of the First and of the Second Bulgarian Empires.

[G. ELDAROV]

TROARN, ABBEY OF, former Benedictine monastery of St. Martin, located near the Dives in Troarn, Diocese of Bayeux, Calvados, France, founded in 1022 for canons by Roger of Montgomery, but settled by Benedictine monks from Conches under Roger's son (*c*.1050). The first church was dedicated in 1059 under Abbot Durandus of Troarn. The abbey secured freedom from secular control in 1190 and flourished until the 16th century. Pillaged by its own tenants in 1562, it declined under commendatory abbots in the 17th cent. and was suppressed in 1790. A few ruins remain. BIBLIOGRAPHY: Cottineau 2:3220.

[E. J. DILLON]

TROELTSCH, ERNST (1865–1923), German theologian and religious sociologist. After studies at Erlangen, Göttingen, and Berlin, he was for 3 years a Lutheran pastor in Munich. His professional career was spent mainly at Heidelberg, as professor of systematic theology (1894–1915); and at Berlin, as professor of philosophy (1915–23). His major work, *Die Soziallehren der christlichen Kirchen und Gruppen* (1912; Eng. tr. O. Wyon, *The Social Teaching of the Christian Churches*, 2 v., 1931), became a classic, esp. in its interpretation of the forms of Christianity under the classifications Church, sect, and mysticism. The work is a comprehensive historical presentation of the relation of the Churches to the process of social change, and the development of Christian social teaching. T. was also concerned with the claim that Christianity is an absolute and unique doctrinal and moral teaching. Influenced by the thought of A. *Ritschl and Kant, his own terms of inquiry led him to a relativism: claims to absolute value are a reflection of aprioristic thought patterns; the forms and ideas of Christianity were to be accounted for by their historical and environmental source. BIBLIOGRAPHY: I. Ludolphy, EncLuthCh 3:241–247; H. Benkert, RGG 6:1043–48.

[T. C. O'BRIEN]

TROITSKAYA LAURA (also known as Sergius's Foundation), Russian monastery in Zagorsk NE of Moscow, founded in 1340 by St. Sergius of Radonezh, and serving as a model for Russian monastic life. After its resistance to a Polish siege in the 17th cent., it became the center of patriotic fervor as well and thus a unique pilgrimage center for all of Russia. It achieved the status of Laura in 1744 and even after its secularization in 1764 continued to be the richest monastery in Russia, with icons, vestments, an extensive library, and other treasures. From 1814 the Moscow Theological Academy was located there. In 1920 the Laura was turned into a museum of history by the Soviet government. After World War II, in gratitude for the patriotic solidarity of church leaders, the Stalinist regime allowed it to become again a religious and theological center on a reduced scale.

[E. J. DILLON]

TROLLOPE, ANTHONY (1815–82), novelist. A product of the English middle class, T. led an unhappy life as a boy and as a young civil servant in London, and emerged from his loneliness and boredom only when appointed postal inspector in Ireland (1841–59). His early novels were failures, but with *The Warden* (1855) he achieved popular success. The sequel to *The Warden* was *Barchester Towers* (1857), perhaps his most widely read novel. These and four other books of provincial life in England constituted valuable commentary on life in the towns of Victorian England. Among his political novels are: *Phineas Finn, the Irish Member* (1869); *The Eustace Diamonds* (1873); *The Prime Minister* (1876). A novel of the civil service, *The Three Clerks* (1858) and *Orley Farm* (1862) are representative of his novels of society. In spite of his popularity, T. was not a great novelist, though he drew an interesting portrait of his age. BIBLIOGRAPHY: M. Sadleir, *Anthony Trollope, a Commentary* (1927). *BARCHESTER CHRONICLES.

[J. R. AHERNE]

TROMBELLI, GIOVANNI CRISOSTOMO (1697–1784), Italian theologian. He became a member of the Canons Regular of the Most Holy Savior in 1713. A teacher of theology at Bologna for 15 years, he was named abbot in

1737 and abbot general of the congregation in 1760. The author of many theological works, T. published his most important study in 1740, *De cultu sanctorum dissertationes decem* in six volumes. Among other writings may be mentioned *Beatae Mariae Virginis vita ac gesta* (6 v., 1761).

[J. R. AHERNE]

TROMP, SEBASTIAN (1889–1975), Jesuit theologian at the Gregorian Univ., Rome. Born in Beek, the Netherlands, and teaching in Rome since 1929, he carried on the theology of Bellarmine, Franzelin, and Billot in his treatises on revelation and inspiration. He also developed the theology of the mystical body which went into Pius XII's encyclical of 1943. In the preparations for Vatican II, he was secretary of the important theological commission under Cardinal Ottaviani. BIBLIOGRAPHY: J. N. Bakhuizen van den Brink, *Gregorianum* 57 (1976) 365–372.

[P. MISNER]

TRONA, JOHN BAPTIST, VEN. (1682–1750), Italian Social reformer. Ordained in 1705, he entered the Oratorians the same year. He labored during an age of crisis in N Italy, demonstrating zeal in pastoral care and devotion to the victims of war. T. was a strong voice reminding employers of their obligations to workers.

[J. R. AHERNE]

TRONSON, LOUIS (1622–1700), French Sulpician superior. He was a canonist ordained in 1647 and became chaplain to Louis XIII. He resigned in 1656 to enter the Sulpicians. In 1676 he was elected the superior general of the society. A foe of Jansenism and Gallicanism, he was a firm adherent of the papacy. Two of T.'s writings were *Règlements de la Compagnie* (1680), constitutions of the Society of St. Sulpice, and *Examens particuliers sur divers sujets propres aux écclésiastiques*. He is credited with helping to devise the Sulpician method of mental prayer, followed in Sulpician seminaries by all seminarians and so with a lasting influence on priestly formation.

[J. R. AHERNE]

TROPARION, a short hymn celebrating the event or saint commemorated in the Greek Liturgy and Office. Compositions in poetic form are attested as early as c.400. Later the Troparia developed into one-strophe hymns that were sung in a variety of tones. Among the types of *troparia* is the *Theotokion, containing Marian hymns.

[L. PEANO]

TROPE, in broad terms, an interpolation into the liturgical chant, a practice traced back to at least the 9th century. Troping was done in any one of three ways: adding texts to an already existing *melisma; composing an altogether new text and melody and appending it to a chant; adding a newly composed melody to an existing chant. The process was abused to such an extent that there was hardly a portion of the liturgy that was not affected. In 1562, the Council of Trent, in revising the liturgy, eliminated all of the tropes. Though many were corruptions of chant, some were of artistic merit and have survived in other forms. From the middle of the 10th cent., for example, the *Quem quaeritis* trope of the Easter Introit was detached from its context in the Mass and dramatized as the first medieval religious play.

[M. T. LEGGE]

TROPER (*troparium*), a book of *tropes. The earliest that have been found date from the 10th–11th centuries. Of particular interest is an English MSS called the *Winchester Troper*, important as a source of early *organum.

[M. T. LEGGE]

TROPHIMUS, SS., name of the first bp. of Arles in France and also of the Gentile companion of Paul whose presence with Paul in Jerusalem (Acts 21.29) was the occasion of the latter's arrest. Since the former Trophimus was erroneously identified with the companion of Paul, the latter has no feast day of his own. St. Gregory of Tours in the mid-6th cent. mentions Trophimus as the first bp. of Arles and one of six bishops from Rome to accompany St. Dionysius of Paris in the mid-3d century. In a letter to the bps. of Gaul in 417 Pope St. Zosimus mentions a Trophimus who was sent into Gaul by the Holy See and whose preaching at Arles was the source of faith of the surrounding countryside. Paul's companion, whose Greek name means "nutritious," met Paul at Troas on Paul's final visit to Jerusalem. Together with Tychicus, he represented the Asian Churches in the presentation of the collection for the Church at Jerusalem. When Jews from the province of Asia saw Paul and Trophimus together, they supposed Paul had taken him beyond the temple barrier separating the court of the Gentiles from the court of Israel. The riot that broke out led to Paul's arrest. The Trophimus mentioned in 2 Tim 4.20—"Trophimus, I left ill at Miletus"—may be a third one since, according to Acts 27.7–8, Paul did not pass through Miletus on his trip from Jerusalem to Rome.

[E. J. DILLON]

TROPHY OF THE APOSTLES, monument commemorating the victory of a martyr–apostle, usually involving a tomb and a basilica and often located near the supposed site of martyrdom. The phrase "trophies of the Apostles" is found in a celebrated passage of Eusebius in which he quotes the words of a "certain ecclesiastical writer by the name of Gaius." The latter, whose birth Eusebius dates during the time Zephyrinus was bp. of Rome (198–217), was disputing with Proclus, the leader of "the Phrygian sect" (the Montanists). Eusebius cites the words of Gaius concerning "the places where the earthly tabernacles of the . . . Apostles are laid." "I (Gaius) can show you the trophies of the Apostles. Indeed, if you wish to come to the Vatican or to the Via Ostia, you will find the trophies of those who have founded this Church." Eusebius had al-

ready mentioned that Paul was thought to have been beheaded at Rome and Peter to have been crucified under Nero, a fact confirmed (notes Eusebius) by the existence of memorials of Peter and Paul in the cemeteries of that city to his day. In Greece, a trophy (*tropaion*) was a memorial of victory set up on the field of battle at the spot where the enemy had been routed (from the Greek *tropē*, "rout"). The Romans called any triumphal arch or column a trophy. The use by Gaius seems more closely to approximate the Greek usage. BIBLIOGRAPHY: Eusebius, *Hist. eccl* 2, 25; M. Guarducci, *Tomb of St. Peter* (1960) 39 and *passim*.

[E. J. DILLON]

TROPOLOGY, the moral or ethical sense of a biblical passage, thought to be a deeper, hidden, figurative, and spiritual meaning of the text. To arrive at it probably involves more art than science and cannot be properly appreciated outside the Alexandrian context of biblical scholarship from which it derives. It all began when the ancient schools of Alexandria became so addicted to rationalism that they found the traditional Greek mythology distasteful in its literal sense, and so developed the art of allegorical interpretation to give the myths back some respectability. Philo, the Alexandrian Jewish scholar (25 B.C.– A.D. 40), then applied the method to the Jewish sacred writings. Next the Alexandrian Christian scholar, Origen (185–254 A.D.) applied the same interpretive method to the Christian Bible with a thoroughness that gives him claim to be the father of an approach to biblical interpretation that remained dominant for more than 1,000 years. Interpreters of this tradition would find, routinely, three deeper meanings in a given passage, beyond the literal sense, which was often disparaged. They spoke of getting beyond the flesh of a text to its soul and spirit. Although the Antiochene tradition, with its stressing of the historical and literal sense, made a strong protest, the triumph of allegory was all but complete. John Cassian formulated for his monks at Marseilles (*c*.425) a terminology that remained in vogue for a millennium. Thus a text has its historical sense and three spiritual senses: allegoric, anagogic, and tropologic. To the successors of Origen, allegory was the meaning the text has for Christology or ecclesiology; *anagogē* provides the meaning the text has for the eschatology of the individual; tropology applies the text to moral or ethical living. A later Latin scholastic mnemonic summed it up along the same lines, too wordy perhaps in translation: "The letter teaches the events, allegory what you are to believe, tropology what you are to do, *anagogē* in what direction you must strive." To call something "tropology" must in itself be a play on words, since the Greek *tropos* can mean either "figure of speech" or "moral character"; and tropology came to mean the figurative sense that applies to moral character. Jewish *Midrash strives to give a hidden meaning of a text. Jewish *halakhah is even closer to Alexandrian tropology, since it specifically tries to find for a biblical passage a meaning that makes it relevant to moral conduct. In the NT itself, the

Letter to the Hebrews may be an example of the Alexandrian method of figurative interpretation of OT texts.

[E. J. DILLON]

TROTSKY, LEON (1879–1940), Russian revolutionary leader. He was born into a prosperous Jewish farming family in the S Ukraine. At school and the university in Odessa, he was attracted to literature and mathematics and exposed to cosmopolitan influences. The freedom and civilization of the West seemed to him the antithesis of the reactionary Russian Empire. On his first contact with socialist ideas in Nikolayev in 1896 he rejected them, but within a few months changed his mind and joined a revolutionary organization. He was soon arrested and imprisoned, then sent to Siberia. In 1902 he escaped to England, where he worked with V. I. Lenin editing the revolutionary newspaper *Iskra*. In the Revolution of 1905 T. returned to Russia and organized and presided over the Petrograd Soviet, where the display of his power as an orator added to his fame. After the defeat of this revolution he again went into exile in W Europe. During World War I he played a major role in the Zimmerwald movement of socialists opposed to the war. T. returned to Russia in July 1917 to join the Bolsheviks and became a leader in their taking power in November. He became War Commissar and organized the new Red Army, which successfully defended the Bolshevik regime in the Russian Civil War. Thus by 1921 he was second only to Lenin. After Lenin's death in 1924, however, Joseph Stalin tightened his control over the party apparatus and gradually isolated T., whose theories were attacked at party congresses and whose most important powers were removed. Following an abortive uprising on the 10th anniversary of the Bolshevik Revolution, T. and his followers were expelled from the party and in 1929 he was deported. In exile he wrote a history of the Russian Revolution, an autobiography, a biography of Stalin, and several other works attacking Stalin and defending the positions he had taken during the great controversies of the 1920s. He also attempted to organize parties of his followers under the aegis of the so-called Fourth International. The 1937 Moscow Purge Trial condemned T. in absentia as an "enemy of the people," and a Stalinist agent assassinated him in Mexico in August 1940. BIBLIOGRAPHY: Isaac Deutscher, *Trotsky*, (3 v., 1954–63).

[R. J. GIBBONS]

TROUBADOUR, term used properly to designate a composer of songs of all genres, esp. in Provençal. In French *trouvère*, and *trobador* in Provençal and Catalan, the etymon may be the word "to find (appropriate verses, rhymes)" or a verb from *trope*. The troubadour composed according to rich and demanding genres and patterns; *trobar ric* (complex), *trobar clus* (hermetic), and *trobar leu* (simple) were basic categories of style. Usually attached to one or more noble patrons, the troubadour composed and performed for them songs of praise, exhortations to valor, argument poems (*tensos*), and complaints and invectives. His songs could take the theme of begging for a horse or clothing, lament for nobility, spring campaigns, lists of annoyances, dawn songs (*albas*), etc. The first-known troubadour was William IX, Duke of Aquitaine (fl. 1100); others were intellectuals, clerks, even vagabonds. The Goliardic tradition (11th and 12th cent.), though largely Latin in composition, was an important background for troubadour poetry. BIBLIOGRAPHY: H. J. Chaytor, *Troubadours* (1912).

[J. P. WILLIMAN]

TROY, JOHN THOMAS (1739–1832), abp. of Dublin. He became a Dominican in 1754 and was ordained in Rome in 1762, serving at the Irish priory of San Clemente as regent of studies and prior. T. was named bp. of Ossory, Ireland, in 1776. A consistent foe of rebellion, T. defended the legitimacy of the existing British rule. Appointed abp. of Dublin in 1786, T. continued his opposition to rebellion, particularly during the uprisings of 1798. Swayed by British assurance that persecution of Catholics would cease, he supported the Union of Britain and Ireland in 1801 and pledged that only candidates friendly to the government would be appointed bps. in Ireland. Many of T.'s stands were unpopular among Irish patriots. He was a jealous and effective pastor, and his guidance was sought by many of his colleagues in the episcopacy.

[J. R. AHERNE]

TRUCHSESS VON WALDBURG, family name of two ecclesiastics, uncle and nephew, prominent in German Reformation history. **Otto** (1514–73) became abp. of Augsburg and an influential religious and political figure during the early Counter Reformation. While completing his studies in Italy, Otto came into contact with the growing spirit of reform. Unlike several other aristocratic German bps., he became an enthusiastic supporter and, although he has been criticized for overtaxing his finances, attempted to correct religious abuses in Augsburg. In 1546, for instance, he laid the foundations for the famed Univ. of Dillingen with the intent of improving the quality of his clergy. His participation in the imperial and papal disputes surrounding the first period of the Council of *Trent, however, overshadowed his other work. Having been made an imperial councillor in 1541, Otto was deeply loyal to the emperor. Yet, as a cardinal (1544) and later papal legate (1556), he was intimately involved in papal affairs. Since he firmly believed that the unity of the Church depended upon the close cooperation between the emperor and the pope, he constantly acted as a mediator. His several missions to Germany aided the opening of Trent. He was largely responsible for convincing German leaders that the Council was not an empty gesture or a papal political move, but rather a serious plan of reform. Finally, he also worked for an alliance between the Habsburgs and Catholic Bavaria. BIBLIOGRAPHY: B. Schwarz, *Otto Truchsess* (1932); H. Jedin Trent.

Gebhard (1547–1601) was archbishop-elector of Cologne (1577–83), whose Protestant conversion threatened Catholicism in the lower Rhine. The nephew of the famous Otto von Truchsess, Gebhard seemed assured of a successful church career. When Salentin von Isenburg resigned his office in 1577, Gebhard was elected to replace him as archbishop-elector of Cologne. He was not a particularly religious man. In fact, soon after his election he married his mistress, Agnes von Mansfeld, and converted to Protestantism. In violation of the "ecclesiastical reservation" of the Peace of Augsburg, he refused to resign in 1582, and the Archbishopric of Cologne tottered on the brink of Protestantization. Gregory XIII deposed Gebhard in 1583 and replaced him with Ernest of Bavaria. The Pope's choice in the light of needed church reform was wrong because Ernest was as immoral as Gebhard. Yet Ernest was a Catholic and his claims were supported by the political might of his brother, William V, Duke of Bavaria. The Protestant aid promised to Gebhard did not come, and he was forced to flee to the Netherlands. His defeat insured that the important episcopal territory of Cologne remained Catholic. BIBLIOGRAPHY: H. Holborn, *Reformation (History of Modern Germany* 1, 1959); M. Lossen, *Der Kölnische Krieg, 1565–1586,* (2 v., 1882, 1897).

[C. T. EBY]

TRUDO OF BRABANT, ST. (TROND; d. *c.*698) Benedictine abbot. A holy youth, sent to be educated at St. Stephan-Protomartyr in Metz (his relics are there), T. later founded a convent near Bruges and a monastery (St. Trond) near Louvain. Although his cult was practically forgotten by the 11th cent., his sanctity and early devotion to him are recalled in the abbey that was named for him and that promoted his cult. BIBLIOGRAPHY: Butler 4:413; *Book of Saints* (compiled by the Benedictine Monks of St. Augustine's Abbey, 1966); É. Brouette, BiblSanct 12:683–685.

[M. E. DUFFY]

TRUDPERT, ST. (d.*c.*643). There are no reliable sources for the life of this saint. According to the vita, he lived in a cell in the Black Forest and was murdered there by his servants. The Benedictine abbey of St. Trudpert, subsequently erected on the site, was dissolved in 1806. BIBLIOGRAPHY: W. A. Ernest, NCE 14:323; AS April 3, 424–440; K. Kunze, BiblSanct 12:686–688.

[M. F. McCARTHY]

TRUE DOCTRINE, see NOTES, THEOLOGICAL.

TRULLENCH, JUAN AEGID (d. 1644 or 45), Spanish moral theologian. His primary works were *Opus morale in decem decalogi et quinque ecclesiae praecepta* and *Praxis sacramentorum.*

[P. J. HENNESSEY]

TRULLO, COUNCILS IN. Two councils are styled *in trullo* because they were held in the *trulos* (Gr.), a vaulted meeting hall of the imperial palace in Constantinople. The first was Constantinople III, the sixth general (ecumenical) council, held in 680–681. The second was called the *penthekti* (Quinisext, 5th–6th), because it completed the work of Constantinople II (553) and III, the fifth and sixth general councils respectively; it is one of the principal sources of the Eastern tradition in canon law. It was summoned by Justinian II to deal with disciplinary questions and was held in the fall of 691. BIBLIOGRAPHY: K. Baus, LTK 10:381–382.

[E. A. WEIS]

TRUSTEE, a legal term used in the American Church to refer to lay members of a parish as a legal corporation, the only legal existence it has in the eyes of the law. Ironing out the legalities came as the result of the episode called *trusteeism in American church history. In practice, the role of the trustee has usually been perfunctory. More important than the legal corporation ecclesiologically are the parish council and the liturgical committee as these were inspired by Vatican Council II. Ideally, members of these bodies will share in the life of the parish as an ecclesial, worshiping community and will be given true responsibility for the life of the parish as this is the Church in its local presence.

TRUSTEEISM, a controversy in the history of U.S. Catholicism that involved lay trustees' making legal claim to property rights over churches and the right of appointment and dismissal of their clergy. Based on the Protestant system of administering church property, which was accepted in U.S. civil law, the trustee system created major problems between its proponents, lay and clerical, and the hierarchy from the end of the 18th cent. to the last years of the nineteenth. In 1785 the laymen who established St. Peter's in New York City incorporated as a group of trustees. Bp. Carroll appointed the Capuchin Charles Whelan as pastor and another Capuchin, Andrew Nugent, as assistant. The trustees demanded the dismissal of Whelan in favor of Nugent, but Carroll denied their right to patronage. Nugent soon outraged the trustees, left the Church, and claimed the property of St. Peter's. Civil courts restored the property to the trustees. The typical pattern of refractory clerics' favoring trustees' claims was repeated in all cases of trusteeism in Philadelphia, Pa., Baltimore, Md., Buffaló, N.Y., Charleston, S.C., New Orleans, La., and St. Louis, Missouri. The Hogan schism at St. Mary's in Philadelphia, poorly handled by Bp. H. *Conwell, moved Rome to intervene. Both Pius VII and Leo XII issued briefs condemning Trusteeism (1822 and 1828). Bp. J. *England of Charleston showed how an alert ordinary could maintain control. The First Provincial Council of Baltimore in 1829 addressed the problem by asking local ordinaries to obtain deeds to church property, by denying the right of lay patronage, and by levelling penalties against clergy or laity who opposed these decrees. Later provincial councils and the First Plenary Council of Baltimore (1852) amplified the condemnation of Trusteeism. The nativist Know-Nothings in the 1850s secured legislation in New York and elsewhere upholding lay trustees in civil law, but the pioneering New York Act of 1863 led the way to incorporation of parishes in a way acceptable to the bps., calling for an aggregate corporation made up of the diocesan bp., vicar general, pastor, and two lay trustees. This model was accepted by the Third Plenary Council of Baltimore in 1884. This effectively ended the problem, except in a few isolated cases in national parishes. BIBLIOGRA - PHY: P. Dignan, *History of the Legal Incorporation of Catholic Church Property in the United States, 1784–1932* (1933).

[J. R. AHERNE]

TRUTH. From the myriad meanings the term has been given, St. Thomas Aquinas covers three that can serve for one exposition of the theological bearing of "truth." The same Latin word, *veritas*, may signify truth in being, truth in knowing, truth in speaking or acting. The third is a moral meaning and for Aquinas is the moral virtue, *veritas* or *veracitas,* truthfulness, a self-manifestation that squares with a person's inner identity and attitudes; among its opposites are lying, deceit, pretense, boasting (ThAq ST 2a2ae, 109–113). The first two meanings in their philosophical development are discussed here.

Philosophical Meanings. St. Thomas has one brief statement of the terms in which he discusses truth in being and truth in knowing. "Truth is defined in terms of conformity between a mind and a reality (being)" (*ibid*. 1a, 16.2). (1) Truth in being ("ontological" truth) is the conformity of a being to the exemplar or idea on which it depends. A sculpture is true, i.e., right, when it matches the sculptor's idea or rightly portrays its subject. All of being is true in that it matches the divine intelligence, its cause. An allied meaning is that all being is true in relation to the human mind because the consistency or coherence of being is "apt" to allow the mind to have true knowledge about it. The truth that is inherent in being measures the truth or falsity of knowledge about it. (2) Truth in knowing or truth as known is the knowing conformity of mind to being. The meaning is elusive. The force is not that the mind in a kind of self-enclosed act contemplates its own idea, then somehow assents that the idea corresponds to the real existent. Rather the knowledge of truth is itself the cognitional "exercise" of the existence of what is known. The act of knowing truth is called "judgment"; it is the mind's assent to the real existence of the way subject and predicate are cognitively joined. The formation of the judgment is described as an act of joining or of separating (affirmation-negation, *compositio-divisio*). But the assent as symbolized by the copulative that joins or separates subject and predicate is an assertion of identity: that which exists as subject is that which exists as predicate; the existing as human is the existing as white—this is the truth-act in the statement "The man is white" (*ibid*. 85.5 ad 3; cf. 1a, 13.12 & ad 3; 14.14). The verification of the truth claim is a further step. The fact, however, of asserting existential identity is what makes the distinction between truth and falsity possible. The ultimate

measure, criterion, is the "truth in being" of the existent on which the judgment centers. The vindication of the mind's capacity to know truth is the task of *epistemology. The radical criterion of truth in knowing is truth in being. The implication is that there must be some primitive judgment, assent to the existent, that is an experience of immediate verification, in which "being" is so transparent that the truth value of the assent is self-vindicating. For St. Thomas the first experience of mind is that of being and the first judgment that a being cannot be itself and not itself at the same time (*ibid*. 1a2ae, 94.2). For St. Thomas, in fact, the meaning of both truth in being and truth in knowing rests on the basic conviction that being cannot be incoherent, inconsistent; that to be is to be something definite. That conviction rests ultimately on the identity of being and knowing in God, the identity therefore of truth in being and truth in knowing, and the impossibility of the irrational, the absolutely indeterminate, being the first cause. Put another way, it is impossible for the divine to exist unintelligibly or to know incoherently. The difficulty with coming to grips with the metaphysics of truth and being is that truth has come to mean simply facts or data; at the same time philosophical certitude about reality has only limited scope; there is as well a whole area of human experience, esp. in the area of moral decision, that cannot be known with mathematical certitude.

Theological Applications. The meaning of truth in being and its roots in the divine exemplarity can be taken in what is disparagingly referred to as an "essentialist" view. This is rejected in favor of a view that is existential, dynamic, and historical, and one that is more in accord with the character of biblical revelation. The view of truth given, however, recognizes itself as an abstraction and as an incomplete account. The analysis is an attempt to reach certain irreducible points of intelligibility; it is, in fact, a defense of intelligibility itself. The attempt is in no way incompatible with the recognition that the unfolding of being is historical; that it develops according to the design and mysterious determinations of God's plan of salvation. The unfolding of being is contingent and has a history because it does depend on the mystery of divine "counsel" and free choices. For some theologians and in various contexts, including that of morality, the consequence of that contingency is that the truth in being is ever in process, ever developing. Because of that there is no possibility of a truth in knowing, but only of a knowledge reaching out to a not-yet-realized or even determined truth. The metaphysics of "ontological truth" defends as a setting for the contingency of history, even salvation history, and the teachings of faith, the absolute coherence of the divine being and knowing, and the requirement of ontological coherence in all the actualizations of being wherein God shapes his creation. However short human knowledge falls from grasping the whole meaning of being and of truth, it has the support of the irreducible consistence of being as measure of its search.

There is a second implication in the defense of the relevance of a metaphysics of truth to theology. Theology is the science of faith. One of the meanings of faith is that it is assent to the truth of what is believed. The motive of faith is not the human insight into, or analysis of the terms in which the truths of faith stand before the human mind (e.g., in the articles of the Creed). The motive of faith is the truthfulness of the Word of God. But because theology does exist in dependence on faith, the presupposition that faith is assent to truth guides theology's tasks. Thus it is significant that wherever in the *Summa theologiae* one of the major mysteries of faith—the Incarnation, the Eucharist, the Trinity—is the topic, the function St. Thomas identifies for theology is that it show that what is taught is not impossible: it does not require the mind to renounce intelligibility (*ibid*. 1a, 1.8; 2a2ae, 2.10). That contains another form of assurance. Because the Word of God has been communicated in human language, open to the human mind, then the presupposition is that the terms and propositions of faith are not irrelevant to the divine realities they express. The task of theology is to pursue their truth, even though proper, intrinsic meaning of the mysteries of faith can only be known to the divine mind and to those who share in the beatific vision. The ultimate presupposition of this meaning of theology is that to be a *scientia de Deo,* or a human discipline linked to faith, it cannot propose the irrational, the incoherent, the contradictory to be the meaning of faith. What would be an insult to human intelligence is a far more unworthy insult against the God who is truth in being and in knowing. BIBLIOGRAPHY: ThAq ST (Lat-Eng v. 31, ed. T. C. O'Brien, app. 1 & 2.

[T. C. O'BRIEN]

TRUTH (IN THE BIBLE). Recent scholars have emphasized that the Semitic concept of truth differs profoundly from that of our Western civilization, and more particularly from the Augustinian concept of truth as *adaequatio rei et intellectus.* To the Hebrew mind, the true is that which is solid and genuine, that which can be relied upon to be what it purports to be and to which, therefore, one can give one's belief. By contrast, that is false which cannot stand up to testing and examination. It does not continue steadfastly to be that which it purports to be in time of stress. Evidently these ideas apply primarily to persons and only in a secondary and derived sense to things. The true man is one who deserves to be trusted and relied upon, one who is worthy of the personal commitment of another in faith. The liar, on the other hand, is one who claims this personal commitment from another and then abuses it by deviating in some way from his initial self-presentation, almost always for the sake of his own personal gain. To the Hebrew mind, therefore, truth is essentially the object of belief and trust. To the Greek mind, it is far more the object of intellectual knowledge. It is the essential quality of the idea which informs the mind correctly. The NT concept of truth stands somewhere between these two, some instances being closer to the Semitic concept, while others owe more to the Greek. In the

Johannine writings in particular, the word true as applied to Christ has a special sense. When Jesus says that he is the true light (Jn 1.9), the true vine (Jn 15.1), or that his body and blood are true food and true drink, he is saying, in effect, that they have a genuineness, a credibility which is deeper than that which belongs to this world, a truth which derives from the heavenly dimension to which he belongs, with its immutability and absolute immunity to all that is corrupt or transient. It is due to the various aspects of his salvific work that he has the quality of absolute truth, or rather *is* the absolute truth in this sense, that he can claim the total and all-embracing assent of faith from his followers. Truth in John's sense, therefore, has itself the power to liberate (Jn 8.32) from the bondage of sin. It is the truth that comes direct from God and is made present to men in Christ. By men's response to it, they reveal where they themselves stand, whether they are "of the truth" and so hear his voice (Jn 18.37) or whether they are of the devil, the father of lies, and therefore seek to suppress the truth by murdering Jesus.

In the Pauline epistles truth is often equated with the gospel, and the manifestation of the truth is the proper activity of the apostle (2 Cor 4.2). From all these passages it is clear that truth is the reality of God himself as manifested to the world, and the NT teaching on truth represents a drawing out of the implications of this central conception. BIBLIOGRAPHY: O. Loretz, *Truth of the Bible* (1968); I. de la Potterie, "L'Arrière-fond du thème johannique de vérité," *Studia evangelica* (1959) 277–294.

[D. J. BOURKE]

TRUTH, DIVINE, an attribute of God inasmuch as he is the first cause and measure of all reality. The Hebrew *'emet* expresses the OT idea of truth, and is used to designate an object, person, or statement worthy of confidence (see TRUTH, IN THE BIBLE). The word has connotations of personal commitment, dependence, and objective reliability rather than merely intellectual assent. In this sense, the OT presents God as true: he is faithful and reliable, merits man's trust, and is a firm foundation upon which man may base his life. In the NT, a more intellectual notion of truth is introduced in accordance with the predominant Hellenistic philosophy of the time. Truth becomes, although not exclusively, a reality to be intellectually apprehended rather than believed. Thus God is true as opposed to unreal (1 Th 1.9); his word is truth itself (Jn 8.45). In John's gospel, "true" is often combined with a description of Jesus: he is the true light (1.9), the true vine (15.1), true food and drink (6.55). The sense here seems to be that Jesus is true because he shares the qualities characteristic of God: constant, incorruptible, worthy of trust. In John, Jesus is full of truth (1.14) and the truth itself (14.6) in the sense that he manifests in his word and person the saving reality of God which is truth.

Speculative theology speaks of God as truth itself (ThAq ST 1a, 14.4; 16.5). Truth is of the divine essence because in him all that is true finds its perfect realization. God is true insofar as he is; since he is without limit, he is truth without limit. It is of his nature to be true because it is of his nature to be. Moreover, since he has caused all things to be and is their exemplary cause (see EXEMPLARITY OF GOD), anything is true to the degree that it conforms to him. He is the first truth—the measure of all other truth. BIBLIOGRAPHY: L. Hartman, EDB 2498–2502; A. Michel, DTC 15:2675–87.

[T. M. MCFADDEN]

TRUTHFULNESS, or veracity, the virtue of speaking the truth; that is, saying in speech what one honestly believes to be true. Truth in general means agreement between the mind and objective reality. A statement is said to be objectively true when it agrees with the facts. An individual is said to be truthful in speaking, when his words agree with what he thinks. Truthfulness can be applied to any of the meanings of truth, but it is most commonly used of this agreement of responsible speech and thought. Its opposite is lying. According to traditional Catholic theology, lying is always sinful. When one gives every indication of intending to speak what he truly believes, he must speak the truth. This does not mean that he is always obliged to say all that he thinks. One must conceal secret knowledge. And often, even when the knowledge or opinion is not strictly secret, charity and social fairness still demand that it not be stated. BIBLIOGRAPHY: D. Hughes, NCE 14:335–336. ThAq ST. 2a2ae. 109–110. *MENTAL RESERVATION; *LYING; *SECRETS.

[J. J. FARRAHER]

TRYPHON, the murderous tyrant of Antioch, whose treachery toward the Jewish leaders of the mid-2d cent. B.C. is recounted in I Macc 11–13. Tryphon (meaning ''reveler'') is the surname of Diodotus, who held the office of ''king's friend'' under Alexander Balas, and later managed to proclaim Antiochus VI Dionysius king at Antioch and himself regent. He then had this boy king confirm Jonathan as high priest of the Jewish people. T. later invaded Palestine, trapped Jonathan by treachery, held him for ransom, and killed him. T. assassinated Antiochus VI and proclaimed himself ''autocrator'' of Syria. The brother of Demetrius II (Antiochus VII) was finally able to expel the tyrant, who fled and then, according to Strabo (XIV. 5.2), committed suicide.

[E. J. DILLON]

TSCHAN, FRANCIS J. (1881–1958), historian, educator. Born in Germany and educated in the U.S., T. studied at Loyola Univ., Chicago, Ill., and received a doctorate from the Univ. of Chicago. He taught also at Chicago, Yale Univ., Carnegie Institute of Technology, Pittsburgh, Pa.; and 21 years at Pennsylvania State College (later University). He was president of the American Catholic Historical Association (1929–30). Among his published works were his translation, *The Chronicle of the*

Slavs by Helmold, Priest of Bosau (1967), a text; *Western Civilization* (in collaboration); and his 3-v. *Saint Bernard of Hildesheim* (1942, 1951, 1952; *Medieval Studies Series*, No. 12, 13, Univ. of Notre Dame); his posthumous *Adam of Bremen, History of the Archbishops of Hamburg-Bremen* (1959).

[J. R. AHERNE]

TSENG–TSIANG, LOU (PIERRE CELESTIN; 1872–1949), statesman, monk. Son of a Protestant catechist in Shanghai, T. became a diplomat, married a Catholic while at the legation in St. Petersburg, and became acquainted with many Catholic scholars and political figures. In 1912 he entered the Church. He was part of the revolutionary effort which, under Sun Yat-sen, unseated the emperor in 1912. For most of the succeeding 8 years, T. was foreign minister of the new Republic of China; he was prime minister for a brief period. When the Japanese issued a humiliating ''Twenty-one Demands'' to China in 1915, it was T. who negotiated and reduced the burdensome demands. He represented China at the Versailles Peace Conference, but Japanese pressure blocked the aspirations of China and he refused to sign the treaty. In 1927 after the death of his wife, he became a Benedictine monk in Belgium.

[J. R. AHERNE]

TUAM, ABBEY OF, a monastery founded *c.*560 by St. Jarlath, which became important only in 11th cent. when the O'Connor kings of Connaught transferred the center of their rule to this district. In 1152, at the Synod of Kells, Cardinal Paparo granted archiepiscopal status to Tuam; and Toirdelbach O'Connor had the church rebuilt in a style worthy of the new honor. It was probably at this time that Tuam lost its monastic character. BIBLIOGRAPHY: J. Ryan, *Irish Monasticism* (1931); E. A. D'Alton, *History of the Archdiocese of Tuam* (2 v., 1928).

[C. MCGRATH]

TUAS LIBENTER, a letter of Pius IX (Dec. 21, 1863) to the abp. of Munich, occasioned by a meeting of theologians at Munich under the leadership of Johannes J. I. Döllinger (Sept. 1863). Concerned about their orthodoxy, the Pope wrote this letter stating norms for dealing with sacred sciences and warning that to preserve the integrity of revealed truth, human reason must not venture beyond the limits set by obedience to the Church's divinely instituted magisterium and must avoid not only heresy, but also opinions that would deserve other theological censures. BIBLIOGRAPHY: D 2875–80.

[J. H. ROHLING]

TÜBINGEN SCHOOL, 19th-cent. group of radical NT scholars. It was founded by F. C. *Baur (1792–1860), professor at the Univ. of Tübingen from 1826 until his death. Though he came from the Orthodox Lutheran tradition, he developed a radical point of view toward the origins of Christianity. Applying the Hegelian philosophy to the early Church, he contended that two parties, one following Peter and the other led by Paul, were in conflict and that the resulting synthesis was Catholicism, which emerged in the 2d and 3d centuries. Little of the NT was apostolic, according to the theory; and Mark, though it was the earliest Gospel, was dated after the time of Justin Martyr. The NT, therefore, could not give reliable historical information. Prominent members of the school included E. Zeller, editor of the *Tübinger Theologische Jahrbucher* (1842–57), and A. Hilgenfeld (1823–1907), who continued it as *Zeitschrift fur wissenschaftliche Theologie* (1858–1914). Theories of the school were asserted most prominently in A. Schwegler's *Nachapostolisches Zeitalter* (1846). At the height of its influence in the 1840s, the school declined thereafter as scholars concluded that its theories could not be sustained by historical evidence.

[T. EARLY]

TUBULAR PREGNANCY is a fertilized ovum in the fallopian tube, the passage leading from ovary to uterus. It is classified as an ectopic pregnancy since it occurs outside the normal place, the uterus. The important medical fact for the moral issue is that an impregnation in such a place very soon brings about a serious pathological condition. The reason is that the tube, unlike the uterus, is neither anatomically nor histologically equipped to handle this type of invasion. Often enough the fetus will rupture into the tube and be carried through the tube into the peritoneal cavity. Rupture of the tube itself may also occur. Either the invading villi will perforate the tube or the wall may weaken from within because of the pressure of the growing fetus.

Usually by the time the tubular pregnancy is discovered, the damage to the tube has progressed so far that it constitutes a serious threat to the life of the mother. When this occurs, according to the now common opinion of RC moral theologians, the tube may be removed as pathological tissue to save the life of the mother. The principle of the double effect would apply here and the death of the fetus would be incidental (neither an end or a means) to saving the life of the mother. The means to the mother's safety would be the removal of the pathological tube.

It may be that in a rare case one will encounter a tubal pregnancy only in an advanced stage, when the fetus is approaching viability. At this stage the element of proportionate reason becomes very important. One must weigh the danger to the mother against the chances of delivering a viable fetus. Unless the danger to the mother is quite immediate, expectant treatment would be called for, esp. in a situation in which the mother could get rather immediate attention in case of emergency.

Moralists in the past have implied that when surgery is indicated in tubal pregnancies, the non-viable fetus must be left *in situ* until the tube has been excised; otherwise there would be question of direct abortion. This does not seem to be necessary. As long as the whole procedure is aimed at removing a pathological tube, once the tube has been clamped off, there would seem to be no objection to opening it and removing the fetus before excising the tube. Once the fetal blood supply has been cut off, the fetus is no worse off outside the tube than in it. Also, if only a part of the tube is in serious pathological condition, there would seem to be no need to remove the whole tube. For a thorough and competent treatment of this problem, see T. L. Bouscaren, *Ethics of Ectopic Operations* (1943); T. O'Donnell, *Morals in Medicine* (1959) 199–206.

[J. R. CONNERY]

TUDESCHIS, NICOLAUS DE (Panormitanus; 1386–1445), canonist. After canonical studies in Bologna (under Antonius de Butrio) and at Padua (under Franciscus Zabarella), he taught at Bologna, Parma, Siena and Florence. Chief among the ecclesiastical dignities and offices he held were the abbacy of the Benedictine abbey of Sta. Maria de Maniaco (whence his appellations *abbas, abbas siculus, abbas modernus*) and the archbishopric of Palermo (whence Panormitanus). He also represented Pope Eugene IV at the Council of Basel but later changed his position and, as the envoy of Alfonso V, found himself on the opposing side and actually presided over the session which decreed the suspension of Eugene IV. When the Council elected the antipope Felix V, T. was rewarded by him with the cardinalate. Of special significance among his works is the *Commentarium* on the decretals of Gregory IX, his *Lectura in sextum, Lectura in Clementinas,* the *Consilia,* and the *Quaestiones.* T.'s political activities in connection with the Council of Basel resulted in a number of polemical writings supporting positions not altogether consistent with those espoused in his canonical treatises. BIBLIOGRAPHY: C. Lefebvre, "L'Enseignement de Nicolas de Tudeschis et l'autorité pontificale," *Ephemerides iuris canonici* 14:312–339; *idem, Dictionnaire de droit canonique* 6:1195–1215; K. Nörr, *Kirche und Konzil bei Nicolaus de Tudeschis* (1964); J. F. von Schulte, *Die Geschichte der Quellen und der Literatur des kanonischen Rechts* (1875–80) 2:312–313; A. Van Hove, *Commentarium Lovaniense in codicem iuris canonici* 1:497.

[J. E. BIECHLER]

TUDOR, a house which supplied all five sovereigns to 16th-cent. England, when state absolutism and Protestantism were established. The family fortunes started with a Welsh squire, Owen Tudor, who came to the court of the infant Henry VI, attracted the attention of the Queen Mother, Catherine of Valois, and "dwelled with the said queen." Five children were born, one became a Benedictine monk, the eldest, Edmund (b.c. 1430) was declared legitimate and made Earl of Richmond. Edmund married Lady Margaret Beaufort, who descended from the issue, subsequently legitimized, of John of Gaunt, and therefore from Edward III. Their only child, who was posthumous, became

Henry VII, after the Battle of Bosworth (1485). His mother's name is still held in benediction for her munificence to Oxford and Cambridge, in which she was advised by St. John *Fisher. On his father's side he was an upstart; even on his mother's side the Plantagenet strain ran rather thin, and it was to be thinned out again with the matrimonial adventures of his son, Henry VIII. He took the precaution of marrying Elizabeth, daughter of Edward IV; the Tudor emblem was a rose which combined his red rose of Lancaster with the white rose of York.

[T. GILBY]

TUKI, RAPHAEL (1701–87), Coptic scriptural scholar. An Egyptian of the Uniate Coptic Church, T. labored in Egypt before being called to Rome. There named bp. of Arsinoe, he was charged with supervising the printing of books of the Coptic liturgy: the *Missal* (1746), the *Psalter* (1749), *Breviary* (1750), *Pontifical* (1761), *Ritual* (1763), and *Theotokia* (1764).

[J. R. AHERNE]

TULSĪDĀS (1543?–1623), Hindu sacred poet. His Rāmcaritmānas (Lake of the Acts of Rāma; 1574–77), the greatest literary work in medieval Hindi, was primarily responsible for the shift to the cult of Rām in northern India. T. worshipped Rām himself, but accepted the traditional polytheism of his country.

[P. J. HENNESSEY]

TUMA, FRANTISEK ANTON IGNACE (1704–74), Bohemian violist and composer. He studied with J. J. *Fux in Vienna, where he spent most of his life. T. wrote church music of great musical and devotional worth. Outstanding among his compositions are his Masses in D minor and in E minor.

[M. T. LEGGE]

TUNICLE (Lat. *tunicella, tunica, dalmatica minor,* tunic), the outer liturgical garment worn by the subdeacon. It appears to have developed from the Roman tunic of late imperial times. Although its use as a distinctive clerical garment was suppressed at Rome by Pope Gregory I (d. 604), it was restored *c.* 1000 and thereafter its development closely paralleled that of the dalmatic, from which in time it became indistinguishable. It is desirable, however, that the sleeves of the tunicle be narrower than those of the dalmatic, and that it have no *clavi,* or at least that its *clavi* be unjoined by a horizontal stripe (see DALMATIC). Since 1960 the rubrics no longer require that the bp. wear the tunicle under the chasuble when he pontificates. BIBLIOGRAPHY: H. Norris, *Church Vestments: Their Origin and Development* (1950).

[P. K. MEAGHER]

TUNISIA, republic in N Africa (63,362 sq. mi.; pop. [census 1976] 5,564,000). Ruled successively by Phoenicians, Romans, Vandals, Arabs, and Turks, Tunisia became a French protectorate in 1881 and a republic in 1956. Arabic is the official language. The religion of the majority is Islam, but freedom of religion is assured under the constitution. In antiquity Christianity flourished in the area, but Arab conquerors wiped it out completely. The efforts of Franciscans, Trinitarians, Mercedarians, and Dominicans in the 13th cent. and the work of Capuchins and Lazarists in the 17th yielded no results. A new mission era began with the French protectorate. The Prefecture Apostolic of Tunisia was erected in 1884 and *Lavigerie was made abp. of Carthage and primate of Africa. Pastoral care was directed mostly to Europeans by White Fathers, Assumptionists, Marianists, Christian Brothers, and Salesians. After the departure of almost 300,000 Europeans in 1960, the Catholic community in Tunisia was reduced to less than 1% of the population. The Archdiocese of Carthage was suppressed and replaced by a prelature at Tunis. Only a few churches remain open; more than 100 have been given over to the state for civil use. Islamization and the state's full control of education make a direct apostolate almost impossible; but missioners are welcomed as teachers and social workers. In 1976 the Catholics numbered about 18,000.

Protestantism is represented in Tunisia by Anglicans, Methodists, Adventists, and members of the African Mission, with a total membership in 1968 of 1,737. BIBLIOGRAPHY: L. Lopetegui, *Islam y Cristianismo* (1946); J. Cuoq, NCE 14:341–342.

[P. DAMBORIENA]

TUNSTALL, CUTHBERT (Tonstall; 1474–1559), English bp., conservative during the Reformation. During his term as bp. of London (1522–30), he was useful to Henry VIII as an ambassador to France. As bp. of Durham, he retained Henry's favor in spite of his objections to the Protestant reformers but was arrested by Edward VI for opposing Protestantism. His release and restoration by Mary Tudor were only followed by a second imprisonment when Elizabeth assumed the throne. He is also known for two works: *De veritate corporis* . . . and *De arte supputandi,* a textbook on arithmetic.

[P. J. HENNESSEY]

TURA, COSIMO (*c.* 1430–95), Italian painter, founder of the school of Ferrara, many of whose earlier works are lost, though later paintings for churches survive: *Two Saints* (Philadelphia Museum of Art), *Madonna with Sleeping Child, Madonna in a Garden* (Washington, D.C.), the mature *Roverella Altarpiece* (*c.* 1474), *St. Anthony* (1484), and others. It is thought he did not fresco the Schifanoia Palace (today the gift of U.S. ambassador Myron Taylor as an American Academy of Art). T.'s mannered style in enamel-like color with moving lines shows the influence of A. Mantegna, R. van der Weyden and A. Pisanello. Forgotten for a time, T.'s nervous stylization and brilliant color have revived interest in his work in the 20th century. BIBLIOGRAPHY: E. Ruhmer, *Tura: Paintings and Drawings* (1958).

[M. J. DALY]

TURBA, the term used in a sung Passion or oratorio for the choral part representing the crowd.

TURGENEV, IVAN SERGEYEVICH (1818–83), Russian novelist and playwright; leading representative of poetic realism. In six novels, *Rudin* (1856), *A Nest of Gentlefolk* (1859), *On the Eve* (1860), *Fathers and Sons* (1862), *Smoke* (1867), and *Virgin Soil* (1877), he documented the frustrated idealism of the liberal and radical "superfluous men" of the 1840s to 1870s. The term nihilist, with which he described Bazarov, the materialistic hero of his masterpiece *Fathers and Sons,* was appropriated by Pisarev. Turgenev is also the author of short stories, esp. *A Sportsman's Sketches* (1852); several plays, which anticipate Chekhov's dramatic technique, e.g., *A Month in the Country* (1850); and *Poems in Prose* (1879–83). His works are characterized by lyrical descriptions of nature and love; psychological portrayal of characters, esp. women; conscious artistry; balanced and objective treatment of social themes; and melancholy pessimism. BIBLIOGRAPHY: R. H. Freeborn, *Turgenev: the Novelist's Novelist* (1960); A. Yarmolinsky, *Turgenev, the Man, His Art and His Age* (rev. ed., 1960).

[M. F. MCCARTHY]

TURINI, FRANCESCO (1595–1656), Italian composer. He was trained at Venice and Rome and became chamber organist to Emperor Rudolph II in Prague. Later he went to Brescia as organist of the cathedral. T. published a Mass, motets, and madrigals. The theme for one of his canons was the subject of compositions by Handel, Bach, and others.

[M. T. LEGGE]

TURKEY, a country of SE Europe and Asia Minor (301,380 sq. mi.; pop. [1976 government est.] 36,270,000). From the fall of Constantinople in 1453, Turkey formed part of the Ottoman Empire until its dissolution after World War I. It was proclaimed a republic in 1923 and during the ensuing decade the country underwent sweeping reforms that transformed it from a medieval Islamic state into a modern democracy. The region had been evangelized by the Apostles Paul, Philip, and John; Christianity had flourished there under the Byzantine Empire. In Turkey of the present day, 98% of the inhabitants are Muslim; Christians, Orthodox and Catholic, constitute only a very small minority (26,328, 1976). In the 16th and 17th cent. some Capuchins and Jesuits settled in the country but little headway was made. Between 1913 and 1922 Turkey was the scene of one of the most severe persecutions of modern times. Armenian Christians—600,000 of whom were massacred or deported—suffered the most; but Jacobites, Maronites, and Chaldeans also bore the brunt of Turkish reaction to the revolutionary movements in the Balkans that were attributed to interference by the Christian countries of Europe. Armenian Christians have an archbishopric at Istanbul and at Mardin, with suffragan sees at Adana, Amida, Ankara, Caesarea, Erzerun, Karput, Marasc, Melitene, Musc, Prusa, and Trabson. Catholics of the Latin rite have a vicariate apostolic and an exarchate in Istanbul, and a metropolitan at Izmir. There are Chaldean and Syrian sees at Amida and Mardin.

Protestantism is represented by the American Board, American Baptists, Disciples, Brethren, Quakers, and Adventists. Their two best known institutions are Robert College for boys and the American College for girls, both at Istanbul. Protestant membership reported in 1968 was about 10,000. BIBLIOGRAPHY: S. Bates, *Religious Liberty, An Inquiry* (1945); *Bilan du Monde* 2:863–871.

[P. DAMBORIENA]

TURKOKRATIA (Gr., rule of the Turks), the period of Turkish domination over the former Byzantine Empire, particularly in Greece, from the 15th to the 19th centuries. The Turks generally followed the Muslim policy of not directly persecuting Christians under their rule, but subjected them to severe social and religious restrictions. The church structure became the civil structure for the Greeks, known as the *Rum Millet* (Turkish, Roman nation), under the administration of the Orthodox patriarch, the *ethnarch or *milletbashi. While this enabled the Greeks to survive as a people, it also made impossible any distinction between Church and nation far more than had been the case in the Byzantine period, and its effects are quite noticeable today. The hierarchy was caught up in a degrading system of bribery and simony, since the Sultan had to be paid before a patriarch or bp. could assume office, and often these positions were openly sold to the highest bidder. The patriarch was also used by the Turks to control other Christians under their rule, so that the decline of the Turkish Empire brought with it independent national Churches in the Balkans resentful of the patriarch of Constantinople. The Turkish occupation resulted in intellectual stagnation in the Church, a conservatism from which it is only now emerging. The few theologians of the Turkish period were forced to study in W Europe in Catholic or Protestant schools. Although this period witnessed many apostates to Islam, it also saw many martyrs, referred to as the *New Martyrs. While corruption was rampant in the ecclesiastical administration, the average Greek clung stubbornly to his faith. Christianity survived 4 cent. of oppression, but in a sense that was all it did; and it is this period, perhaps more than the millennium of flourishing Byzantine Christianity, which has left its mark on Greek Orthodoxy today.

[G. T. DENNIS]

TURMAIR, JOHANNES, see AVENTINUS.

TURMEL, JOSEPH (1853–1943), French historian of dogma, Modernist. Ordained in 1882, he early repudiated the faith but continued to operate within the Church, becoming one of the most determined adherents of Modernism. Like others in the movement T. believed that scientific discovery would in time destroy the credibility of Christianity. Nonetheless he contributed a number of historical studies to the *Revue du clergé fran˛cais,* and his two-volume *Histoire de la théologie positive* (1904–06) initiated the series *Bibliothèque de théologie historique* published by the Institut Catholique of Paris. His work was placed on the Index in 1910, as were many later writings. For years T. wrote, under a variety of pseudonyms, attacks on Catholic doctrine, all placed on the Index; his authorship was not proved until 1929. In 1930 he was excommunicated and deprived of clerical status.

[J. R. AHERNE]

TURNEBUS, ADRIANUS (1512–65), classical scholar. Born in Normandy, he taught at the Univ. of Toulouse and assumed the chair in Greek philosophy at the Collège de France. For a while he was, with Guillaume Morel, editor of all Greek publications from the Royal Press. Among his works are translations from Greek to Latin and French and editions of classical authors. He also wrote *Ad Sotericum gratis docentem,* a satire on the Society of Jesus.

[P. J. HENNESSEY]

TURNER, CUTHBERT HAMILTON (1860–1930), critical historian of early Church documents. T. spent the whole of his mature life at Oxford as a student, lecturer, research fellow, and professor of exegesis. His major work, *Ecclesiae occidentalis monumenta juris antiquissima* (2 v., 1899–1913), is a critical edition of the early collections of Western canon law. Many of his essays on biblical criticism and early church history are collected in his *Studies in Early Church History* (1912). BIBLIOGRAPHY: H. N. Bate, DNB Suppl (1922–30) 861–864; H. A. Larroque, NCE 14:347.

[T. M. MCFADDEN]

TURNER, WILLIAM (1871–1936), professor of philosophy, 6th bp. of Buffalo, New York. Irish-born, educated in Ireland and in Rome, T. was ordained in 1893 for the diocese of St. Augustine, Florida. He taught philosophy (1906–19) at The Catholic Univ. of America; his *History of Philosophy* (1903) was long a standard text in seminaries. He was chosen bp. of Buffalo in 1919; his episcopacy was marked by the growth of works of charity in that diocese.

[T. C. O'BRIEN]

TURPIN OF REIMS (748 or 749–794), monk, archbishop. Known as one of Charlemagne's paladins in the *Song of Roland*, he was a historical person. Originally a monk of St. Denis, he became abp. of Reims (753). He took part in a Lateran synod (769) held under Stephen III. Writings about Charlemagne and St. James of Compostela are erroneously attributed to him. BIBLIOGRAPHY: P. Kirbe, NCE 14:347.

[A. CABANISS]

TURRETINI, three Reformed theologians at Geneva, originally from Lucca in Italy. (1) **Benedetto** (1588–1631), pro-

fessor from 1612, wrote a defense of the Bible translations made at Geneva. (2) **Francesco** (1623–87), son of Benedetto, was the best known in the U.S., where the family name is usually given as Turretine. His scholastic exposition of strictly orthodox Calvinism, *Institutio theologiae elencticae* (3 v., 1679–85), became the standard text at Princeton Theological Seminary under A. *Alexander. (See HODGE, C.; PRINCETON THEOLOGY.) (3) **Giovanni Alfonso** (1671–1737), son of Francesco, brought about a moderation of adherence to the rigid Calvinism of the Synod of *Dort and the *Helvetic Consensus Formula and strove for union between the Reformed and Lutheran Churches. BIBLIOGRAPHY: EncRelKnow 12:42–44.

[T. C. O'BRIEN]

TUSCULANI, medieval Italian political family which reached the height of its power during the first half of the 11th century. The name derives from the ancient hill town of Tusculum, SE of Rome. Their partisan support of the emperor put them in direct opposition to the Crescentii, who fought for the independence of Rome. Emperor Otto III rewarded **Gregory** of Tusculum for his loyalty by giving him the title *praefectus navalis*. Gregory's son **Theophylactus** became pope, taking the name Benedict VIII. Another son, **Romanus,** carried out imperial policy in Rome with the office of *patricius Romanorum* and later he became pope as John XIX. The last of the Tusculani popes was the notorious Benedict IX, who bought and sold the papacy several times. When he was removed from office the last time (1048), the family's ecclesiastical role diminished. They continued to use their political influence to oppose the *Gregorian reform and independence from the emperor. Only in 1170 did Alexander III regain Tusculum for the Papal States. BIBLIOGRAPHY: G. Fasoli, EncCatt 12:646–647.

[E. J. DILLON]

TUTIORISM, a moral system that arose in reaction to *probabilism, esp. in its laxist form (see LAXISM). In case of doubt, according to tutiorism, one must always abide by the law. In place of the fundamental laxist principle (*lex dubia non obligat* i.e., a doubtful in the sense of a not absolutely certain law never obliges), tutiorism substituted a principle of its own, namely, that there is no such thing as doubtful freedom. Where there is the slightest doubt as to whether one is free or not, one is automatically deemed bound by the law. In its most extreme form, this teaching is also called moral rigorism and has been condemned by the RC Church (see D 2303). A mitigated form (moderate tutiorism) according to which it is permissible to follow a less safe line, but only provided that the case in its favor is most probable, has not been condemned, although almost all RC moral theologians reject it as too rigorous. BIBLIOGRAPHY: B. Häring, *Law of Christ* (1965) 162; J. Connell, NCE 14:348.

[S. WILLIAMS]

TWELFTH DAY, the twelfth day after Christmas, Jan. 6. Formerly it was also observed as *Epiphany. In the East it was associated in the Eastern Churches with Christ's baptism, and in the West with the visit of the Magi.

[T. EARLY]

TWELFTH NIGHT, the eve of *twelfth day. In many areas it has been a time of popular observance, marking the end of the Christmas season.

[T. EARLY]

TWELVE, THE, the special band of Disciples chosen by Jesus. They formed a college and presided over the fledgling Church after he was taken from them. Their names are listed in the first three Gospels and in Acts, but the lists are not in harmony. Their role is sharply detailed in Luke's account in Acts where they teach, speak, and perform signs and wonders in the name of Jesus and preside over the distribution of goods. They are defined as the Disciples chosen by Jesus who were with him from the beginning, that is, from the baptism of John on, and empowered to be witnesses of his Resurrection. Luke also calls them Apostles, a name that became identical with the Twelve, although originally they were more than (and even other than) apostles. Their number calls to mind the tribes of Israel and Jesus promised them a part in the judgment of the tribes of Israel (Mt 19.28; Lk 22.30). He also "sent" them (hence, apostle): first during his ministry in Galilee, empowered to cast out demons, to heal diseases, and to announce the kingdom; later as witnesses of the Resurrection, empowered with the Holy Spirit to preach repentance, to make disciples, and to baptize. Both in the Gospels and in Acts, Peter enjoys a preeminence in the group and often speaks and acts in their name. Only one of them was lost (Judas) and his place was filled by the election of Matthias (Acts 1.26).

[E. J. DILLON]

TWELVE, GOSPEL OF THE, title of two apocrypha: (1) A heterodox work referred to by Origen (*In Luc. Hom.* 1.5, 2–4); the majority of critics today would identify it with the Gospel of the Ebionites. (2) The (Kukean) Gospel of the Twelve. According to some scholars, the Kukeans were gentile Christians of the region of Edessa strongly influenced by Parsism, who produced a Gnostic gospel under this title. They seem to have corrupted and distorted the NT to fit in with their own tenets, yet left the OT intact (thus Maruta of Maiperkat). BIBLIOGRAPHY: E. Hennecke, *New Testament Apocrypha*, v. 1 (ed., tr. W. Schneemelcher, 1963) 1:264–265.

[D. J. BOURKE]

TWELVE ARTICLES, *Claims of the Whole Peasantry,* a declaration of their demands made by the peasants of Swabia for religious and social reform (Feb. 1525). The Twelve Articles were composed by S. *Lotzer, although they have also been attributed to B. *Hubmaier. The document, which became the manifesto of the *Peasants' War, claimed as divine rights, sanctioned by Scripture, the election and dismissal of pastors, as well as freedom from serfdom and taxes on water, forests, and pasture lands. In April 1525 Luther replied in *Appeal for Peace, Touching the Twelve Articles of the Swabian Peasants*, warning against the use of violence by the peasants. BIBLIOGRAPHY: Bihlmeyer-Tüchle 3:30–31; Léonard HistProt 1:104–105; bibliog. for the Peasants' War.

[T. C. O'BRIEN]

TWELVE PATRIARCHS, TESTAMENTS OF THE. It is generally held that a substantial nucleus of this work must go back to a Hebrew or Aramaic original, probably of the 2d cent. B.C., and that the latest material included in it would have been composed before the destruction of the temple in A.D. 70. It is also regarded as assured that in spirit, outlook, doctrinal content, and even language the work reflects the traditions of the Essenes; and this has been confirmed by the discovery of substantial fragments of two of the original Testaments among the sectarian writings of *Qumran. Special difficulties arise, however, from the inclusion of specifically Christian elements, and even of apparent allusions to Jesus himself. Are these due to early Christian editors who altered and added to a pre-Christian original? Or is it rather that the work was actually composed by Christians who took as their model certain isolated Jewish testaments (notably that of Levi) and compiled the remainder on this basis? In spite of a formidable weight of opinion to the contrary, the balance of the evidence seems to favor the latter view.

The Testaments themselves purport to be the last words addressed by each of the sons of Jacob in turn to their own descendants assembled round their deathbeds. The work as a whole seems to be inspired by Jacob's blessing as set forth in Gen 49. Each Testament comprises three main elements: a pseudohistorical introduction recalling the events in the life of the particular patriarch concerned, a didactic section in which he recommends his descendants to emulate his virtues or avoid his faults and sins, and a messianic and apocalyptic conclusion. As a whole, the work may be said to be haggadic in tendency: it consists largely of edifying meditations on the text of Scripture amplified and embellished with further legendary material. This is designed to confirm the faith of the reader and his messianic hopes and to inculcate virtue and morality. Thus Reuben recalls with shame his sin with his father's concubine, Bilhah (Gen 35.22; cf. 49.4), and warns his descendants against unchastity and the beguilements of women. Simeon draws a warning against jealousy from the episode in which he and his brothers sought to kill Joseph and recalls that he himself was held captive in Egypt by Joseph as an act of divine retribution (cf. Gen 42.24). In the longest and most elaborate of the Testaments, Levi relates how he was taken up into the seventh heaven so that he and his descendants might be invested with the priesthood, but also recalls the vengeance he exacted on behalf of his sister Dinah (Gen 34). He exhorts his sons to wisdom and reverent devotion to the Law. He also foretells that his later descendants will bring disgrace upon the priesthood until at last the sinless and glorious Messiah arises from his stock to overcome the power of evil and to inaugurate the final age of bliss. Judah recalls his feats of valor, but also the sins of his youth as recorded in Gen 38, which he ascribes to passion and love of wine. He exhorts his sons to avoid these and to submit to the direction of the tribe of Levi. He predicts the future exile and restoration, and the advent of the Messiah of Judah who, however, is to be subordinate to the Messiah of Levi. In the Testament of Issachar, the virtues of the simple countryman are recommended on the basis of Gen 49.15. Zebulun is taken as an example of compassion, though the tradition on which this is based is unknown to us. Dan, Simeon, and Gad are held to have been esp. full of anger and hatred against Joseph; and in their Testaments, anger and lying are seen, in the light of their own past histories, to lie at the roots of all human wrong-doing. Naphtali appears as an example of harmonious relationships with one's fellows. He exhorts his sons to a pure, simple, and kindly attitude to others. Asher plays upon the meaning of his own name, happy, and extols the virtues of simple kindness. The Testament of Joseph elaborates upon the original story in Genesis with all kinds of haggadic embellishments and recalls how his chastity was vainly put to the severest tests in Egypt. Benjamin declares that he no longer wishes to be known as a "ravenous wolf" (Gen 49.27). Rather he is one who works for the Lord and "divides the spoil" according to his decrees. He admonishes his sons to preserve purity of conscience and holds up his full brother Joseph to them as an example of chastity.

A particularly important feature in the ethical teaching of this work is its insistence on the duty of forgiveness and love of neighbor which appears to represent a significant advance on any of the relevant OT teachings on the subject. Personal resentments and hatreds must be banished, and even the guilty must be forgiven and readmitted to the community. To the extent that we achieve this we reflect the attitude of God himself and his forgiveness. Love of God and love of neighbor are in fact brought into significant correlation, as is seen from such expressions as "Love the Lord and your neighbor" (Test Iss 2), "Love the Lord through all your life and one another with a true heart" (Test Dan 3). The same ideal of generous and forgiving love appears in such sayings as "When envy goes a man's mind is lightened and he can enjoy the well-being of his former rival" (Test Sim 3.5, 6). The references to the gentiles are inspired by the same basic attitude. The Law was given to enlighten every man and the gentiles are to be saved through the example and teaching of Israel (Test Lev 16.4).

The distinctive messianism of this work is also important. The priestly Messiah of Levi is to walk in meekness and justice and to be sinless (Test Jud 24.1). He is to be a mediator to the gentiles (Test Lev 8.14), and to overthrow the forces of evil, not only Israel's earthly enemies, but the demonic hosts of Beliar or antichrist as well (Test Reub 6.12), delivering the souls of the saints taken captive by him (Test Dan 5.11) and opening paradise to the righteous (Test Lev 18.10). The sphere of his everlasting dominion is to be this present earth, where his reign is to usher in a general resurrection first of the OT heroes and Patriarchs and then of all men, divided into the righteous and the unrighteous (Test Ben 10.6–8). BIBLIOGRAPHY: Charles APOT 2:282–367; M. de Jonge, *Pseudepigrapha Veteris Testamenti Graece* I, *Testamenta XII Patriarcharum* (1964).

[D. J. BOURKE]

TWELVE-TONE MUSIC, music based on a technique devised early in the 20th cent. by Arnold Schoenberg (1874–1951). Having rejected, with others of the Viennese school, the major-minor tonality which had dominated the music of two cent., Schoenberg, out of his search for an organizing principle of composition, contrived the *dodecaphonis* or twelve-tone system, a technique that was subsequently adopted and used, in greater or lesser degrees, by Alban Berg, Anton Webern, Ernst Krenek, Milton Babbitt, and many others. Compositions according to this technique begin with the establishment of a "tone row," a series of intervals in which each of the twelve tones of the chromatic scale is used in an order chosen by the composer, with the restriction that no tone may be repeated until the other eleven have been used. The tone row may be modified by using the octave position of any tone, by inverting the row, by retrograde, by retrograde-inversion, or by the transposition of any of the above to any other step of the chromatic scale. The 48 modifications thus made available are used in either melodic or choral forms or in a combination of these. Subdivision of the row may be made only within specific limits. The use of the twelve-tone system has by no means been limited to secular subjects. Stravinsky's *Threni-id est Lamentationes Jeremiae Prophetae* (1958) and *Abraham and Isaac* (1965), and Schoenberg's *Moses und Aron* (1932) are but a few compositions with a religious theme that, along with the works of A. Webern, O. Messiaen, K. Stockhausen, E. Krenek, and others incorporate twelve-tone techniques. BIBLIOGRAPHY: G. E. Wittlich, *Aspects of Twentieth-Century Music* (1975); W. W. Austin, *Music in the 20th Century* (1966); J. Machlis, *Introduction to Contemporary Music* (1961); H. H. Stuckenschmidt, *Twentieth Century Music*, (1969); G. Tremblay, *The Definitive Cycle of the Twelve-tone Row*, (1974). *SERIAL MUSIC.

[M. T. LEGGE]

TWENTY-FIVE ARTICLES OF RELIGION, a *doctrinal standard prepared by John *Wesley for U.S. Methodists. At the *Christmas Conference (1784) T. *Coke presented the Articles. Along with Wesley's *Notes on the New Testament* and the *Standard Sermons*, they were adopted for the newly organized Methodist Episcopal

Church. The Conference added one Article to the 24 prepared by Wesley, numbering it the 23d ("Of the Rulers of the U.S.A.") and renumbering the original. Wesley's document was an adaptation of the *Thirty-Nine Articles of the C of E; his deletions and modifications were designed to remove any Calvinistic, RC, or ritualistic elements. The Articles have continued unaltered throughout the history of the Methodist Episcopal Church and the Methodist Church. BIBLIOGRAPHY: H. Wheeler, *History and Exposition of the Twenty-Five Articles of Religion of the Methodist Episcopal Church* (1908), bibliog. and parallel textual comparison with the Thirty-Nine Articles; N. B. Harmon, *Understanding the Methodist Church* (rev. ed., 1955) 25–79, text with commentary.

[F. E. MASER]

TWENTY PRINCIPLES OF RELIGION, a Congregational statement of faith, which constituted an important part of the Declaration of Faith and Order agreed upon in 1833 by the Congregational Union of England and Wales. It was the first statement of faith formulated by Englis Congregationalism since the *Savoy Declaration (1658). The statement, which was not authoritative, was without great merit in form or substance. Mainly it signifies a drift from traditional Calvinism, manifested more in a weakening of the original conviction than by an assertion of any alternative. This is particularly true with regard to its pronouncements about the sacraments.

[R. F. G. CALDER]

TWO-SEED-IN-THE-SPIRIT PREDESTINARIAN BAPTISTS, a Baptist group originating in the second half of the 18th cent. as a result of Daniel Parker's protests against *Arminianism. They believe that in the Garden of Eden two seeds entered the life stream of humanity, a good seed implanted in the spirit by God, and an evil seed implanted in the spirit by the devil. Each person is born with one seed or the other and therefore is absolutely predestined. They oppose missions, have no paid ministry, and follow congregational polity. They have all but disappeared in the 20th century.

[J. C. WILLKE]

TWO SWORDS, DOCTRINE OF THE, authoritative teaching devised during the Middle Ages to rationalize the use of papal power in both the spiritual and temporal spheres. It found its most authoritative articulation in the papal bull, *Unam sanctam*, promulgated by Boniface VIII, Nov. 18, 1302. Boniface expressed papal policy that reached back at least to Gregory VII and that reached its zenith during the series of powerful canonist popes, beginning with Innocent III (1198–1216). The symbol of the two swords derives from the enigmatic passage in Lk 22.35–38, in which the disciples make reference to possession of two swords. Boniface was able to assert that two swords were here given to Peter and that anyone who denies the temporal

sword to the pope does not understand this Scripture. The king wields the temporal sword on behalf of the Church, under the direction of the priest; the spiritual power is above the temporal and should instruct it and judge it. "Whosoever resists this highest power ordained of God resists God Himself. It is altogether necessary to salvation for every human creature to be subject to the Roman Pontiff." A year earlier, Dec. 5, 1301, in a letter, *Ausculta Fili,* to Philip IV, the Fair, Boniface had applied to himself the words of God to Jeremiah, "God has placed us, unworthy though we be, over kings and kingdoms in order that we shall root out, destroy, disperse, build up, and plant in His name and by His doctrine. Do not allow yourselves to think that you have no superior and that you are not subject to the head of the ecclesiastical hierarchy. Whoever thinks this is a madman; whoever supports him in this belief is a heretic" (Jer 1.10). This was a uniquely Western variation on the theme of Caesaropapism, which had been the continuous reality in the Christian world, East and West, since the days of the Emperor Constantine I, the Great (d. 337). Its most stable expression was found in the Byzantine world where the head of state (the emperor) was also the head of the Church, the vicar of Christ, and the supreme judge in religious matters. However, authoritative Byzantine theologians (Chrysostom, Maximus the Confessor, and John of Damascus) still denied imperial power over the Church. Even Constantine's apologist, Eusebius of Caesarea, would grant imperial dominance only in such "external" matters as managing administrative affairs, presiding over councils, appointing patriarchs, and defending the Church. The ideal was interdependence, with mutually recognized autonomies. Justinian described the relationship between the *sacerdotium* and the *imperium* as a symphony. Only Leo III, the Iconoclast, assumed the title of priest as well as king. In practice, in East and West, the Church has been subordinated time and again to the State: under Charlemagne, Henry VIII, Ivan the Terrible, Peter the Great, and in post-Reformation Germany. In the W patriarchate (Rome), however, the pope had to fill a virtual vacuum left in the wake of the emperor's move to Constantinople; thus preparing the way for the medieval papacy, in which the pope became heir to the imperial role. The more successful popes in this role were the pragmatic predecessors of Boniface, who left room for royal autonomy by giving importance to the theory that papal interference in secular affairs is only valid *ratione peccati* (by reason of sin). Boniface, by his inflexible arrogance, is considered to have hastened the decline of the papal empire and the rise of autonomous nation states. The Constantinian model of collaboration between *imperium* and *sacerdotium* still has vestiges in the canon law of East and West, and in the historrty of the Holy See's temporal sovereignty.

[E. J. DILLON]

TYARD (or THIARD), PONTUS de (1521?–1605), French Renaissance poet, member of the *Pléiade, and one of the first French sonnet writers. A competent Latinist, mathematician, astronomer, and theologian, T. was canon of the cathedral of Mâcon, prothonotary apostolic, almoner of Henri II, and bishop of Châlon-sur-Saône (1578–94), from which post he resigned under pressure from the Catholic Holy League. His works, of considerable Platonic influence, include: *Les Erreurs amoureuses* (1549–73); a translation (1551) of Leone Ebreo's *Dialoghi d'amore*; and *Discours philosophiques* (1587). BIBLIOGRAPHY: H. Chamard, *Histoire de la Pléïade* (4 v., 1939–40); R. V. Merrill, ''Platonism in Pontus de Tyard's *Erreurs amoureuses* (1549)'' *Modern Philology* 35 (139–158).

[R. N. NICOLICH]

TYBURN, also called Tyburn Tree and Deadly Never Green, the place of the Middlesex Gallows, a stone's throw from the present Marble Arch in London. Among those executed here were many Catholics who were hanged, drawn, and quartered for their faithfulness to the Mass and the pope.

[T. GILBY]

TYCHĒ, see FORTUNE, CULT OF.

TYCHICUS, resident of Asia Minor, possibly an Ephesian, who accompanied Paul on part of his third missionary journey (Acts 20.4). He later performed missions for Paul (Eph 6.21; Col 4.7; 2 Tim 4.12; Tit 3.12).

[T. EARLY]

TYCHON OF AMATHUS, ST. (AMATUS; fl. 5th cent.), early bp. of Amathus (modern Limassol) in Cyprus, venerated there as the Wonder-worker and the patron of vinegrowers. His feast and the blessing of the grape harvest take place together on June 16. German scholars, e.g., H. Usener, identify T. with the pagan god Priapus because of the link with vintage folk-culture. There was, however, very likely a 5th-cent. bp., perhaps consecrated by Epiphanios of Salamis, whose tomb was a famous shrine by the end of the 6th century. His fellow Cypriote, St. John the Almoner, patriarch of Alexandria (610–620), wrote T.'s biography in elegant Byzantine Greek. In the 9th cent. St. Joseph the Hymnographer composed an office in his honor.

[E. J. DILLON]

TYCHON OF SADONSK (1724–83), Russian Orthodox monk. A man of learning in the Russian Orthodox Church and a monk in a community which condemned learning, he studied the Fathers. Named bishop of Voronezh, a barbarian region, he unsuccessfully strove to educate the illiterate clergy and reform the monks. T. resigned after 4 years to resume his monastic life, enduring quietly the petty persecution of his community. After his death his writings had a lasting influence on Russian spirituality.

[J. R. AHERNE]

TYCONIUS (d. *c.*400), Donatist, lay theologian and exegete. In two works now lost, *De bello intestino libri tres* and *Expositiones diversarum causarum*, T. departed from pure Donatism by maintaining that the Church was a universal body and included both the good and the wicked. He was condemned by a Donatist Council at Carthage (*c.*380). He strongly influenced later, esp. medieval, scriptural studies. His *Liber regularum,* with seven basic rules of hermeneutics, was partially incorporated by Augustine in the *De doctrina christiana*; and his commentary on Revelation, preserved in part in the writings of Beatus of Liebana (*c.*776), gave prominence to the use of the spiritual sense in scriptural exegesis. BIBLIOGRAPHY: F. C. Burkitt (ed., *Book of Rules of Tyconius* 1894); *Turin Fragments of Tyconius' Commentary on Revelation* (ed. F. Lo Bue, 1963).

[R. B. ENO]

TYE, CHRISTOPHER (born *c.*1500), English composer of sacred music. Many details of his life and works are uncertain, but it is known that he was choirmaster at Ely Cathedral (1541–61) and was ordained in 1560. T. was an important and influential figure in English church music. Called the ''father of the anthem,'' he established in his English works a simple, direct manner of writing that contrasted with his more elaborate Latin church music (Masses, Magnificats, and many pieces whose musical text is incomplete). His main contributions are his English anthems and ''The Acts of the Apostles,'' a popular setting for voices and lute of his own translation of the text into English verse.

[M. T. LEGGE]

TYLDEN, THOMAS, see GODDEN, THOMAS.

TYNAN, KATHARINE (Hinkson; 1859–1931, Catholic poet and novelist. Her birth date, usually given as 1861, is confirmed as 1859 by a certificate of baptism from Our Immaculate Lady of Refuge Church, Rathmines, Dublin. She was one of the writers active during the Celtic Renaissance. Her poems fall essentially into three categories: on religious themes, on Irish legends and folklore, and on nature. Besides her poetry, she also turned out a stream of mediocre novels. Her autobiography in five volumes, is valuable for its eyewitness accounts of Irish life and for details about contemporary literary and political figures. *Twenty-five Years* (1913) and *Memories* (1924) are two of the series. Some volumes of her poetry in which Gaelic themes are dominant are *Shamrocks* (1887), *Ballads and Lyrics* (1890), and *Irish Poems* (1913); other works are *Flower of Youth* (1915) and *Collected Poems* (1930). She was considered one of the best Irish poets of her time and she was the only one who reflected in her work her deep religious faith. BIBLIOGRAPHY: F. I. Moloney, *Katharine Tynan Hinkson: A Study of Her Poetry* (Univ. of Pennsylvania, 1952); E. Boyd, *Ireland's Literary Renaissance* (1916, repr. 1968).

[S. A. HEENEY]

TYNDALE, WILLIAM (c. 1491–1536), English Protestant martyr whose translations formed the basis for the *Authorized Version of the Bible. He studied at Oxford (c. 1506–15), was ordained, and at Cambridge became acquainted with Erasmus's Greek NT. T. began his translation of the NT from Greek into English in 1520; unable to get support in England and suspected of heresy, he left England for Germany in 1524. He came in contact with Luther, many of whose views he shared. Printing of his translation was begun at Cologne in 1525, but was stopped by the authorities; two editions were published in Worms in the same year. T. also translated the Pentateuch (1530) and Jonah (1531), and published his final revision of the NT in 1535. T. was executed as a heretic at Vilvorde in Brabant, because of his anti-Roman writings. His Bible translations set the language and style of subsequent English versions. BIBLIOGRAPHY: *Works of William Tyndale* (ed. G. E. Duffield, 1964).

[T. C. O'BRIEN]

TYNDALE'S BIBLE, translation (c. 1523–36) of the Bible, which had an impact not only upon the early phases of the English Reformation, but also upon English as a literary language. It was the result of the painstaking scholarship of William Tyndale. Inspired by such contemporary works as Erasmus's New Testament and Luther's German Bible, Tyndale greatly improved upon the older Lollard versions produced by J. *Wycliffe and his followers. Tyndale's skills in Latin, Greek, and Hebrew, were evident throughout his translation. But his personal determination also contributed to the Bible. After leaving England in 1524, he completed the New Testament in 1525. Constantly hounded by church and civil authorities, he almost finished the Old Testament before his execution for heresy on October 6, 1536. The English language is heavily indebted to Tyndale's Bible. The Authorized Version of 1611, which serves as the basis for modern English, was founded almost entirely upon Tyndale's work. BIBLIOGRAPHY: C. H. Williams, *William Tyndale* (1969); J. F. Mozley, *William Tyndale* (1937).

[C. T. EBY]

TYNEMOUTH, PRIORY OF, former Benedictine monastery of St. Mary and St. Oswin in Northumberland, England. It was founded c. 1085 in the Diocese of Durham by Robert de Mowbray, count of Northumberland, on the site of an earlier monastic settlement, which contained the tomb of St. Oswin, King of Deira (d. 649) and which was destroyed by the Danes in 875. The new foundation was given to the Abbey of St. Albans, which retained it as its foremost dependency despite rival claimants. The priory declined during the 15th cent. and was suppressed in 1539. BIBLIOGRAPHY: Cottineau 2:3237.

[E. J. DILLON]

TYPE AND ANTITYPE, see ANTITYPE.

TYPIKON, (Gr., according to a model), originally the rule of a monastery, sometimes imposed by the founder, even if he did not join the community. It had two parts: a liturgical one setting the norms for divine services (days, kinds, frequency, etc.), and a disciplinary one, defining the rights and duties of the superior, the members, officials, the management of temporal goods, ascetical advice, etc. The liturgical typika of some monasteries were taken over by entire Churches, as that of the Laura of St. Sabbas near Jerusalem. Consequently, the term typika refers today primarily to the rules describing the liturgical services throughout the year, adding also advice in respect to abstinence, metanies (prostrations), etc., and can be compared to the *ordo perpetuus* of the Latin rite. The typikon is consulted by the clergy and religious if the liturgical books containing the texts do not offer sufficient information.

[V. J. POSPISHIL]

TYPOLOGY, that approach to the interpretation of the OT which finds in the persons, events, institutions, and things there recorded a basic correspondence with the person of Christ and the events of his life and work as recorded in the NT. The NT itself authorizes this approach in principle. Christ is said to be the new Adam (Rom 5.14), the new Moses (Heb 3.2–6), the new high priest (Heb 4.14), the new Melchizedek (Heb 6.20); the manna of the desert wanderings is taken as a type of the Eucharist (Jn 6.48–51); the crossing of the Red Sea as a type of baptism (1 Cor 10.1–2); the sacrifices of the Day of Atonement as a type of the sacrifice of Christ on the Cross (Heb 9.11–14); Isaac is a type in reference to gentile Christianity (Gal 4.28–31).

The typological approach was brought into disrepute by the arbitrary, strained, and artificial correspondences asserted by those of the Fathers who were influenced by Origen and the Alexandrine school. Many of the types and figures proposed are totally irreconcilable with the literal sense as established by modern scholarship. A sound and objective basis for typology can be found in the essential unity of God's plan for the salvation of mankind, commencing with the creation and culmination in Christ as its goal and consummation. Because they are elements in God's salvific plan, the realities referred to in the OT are radically and essentially orientated to Christ as their final consummation, and have that intrinsic and objective conformity to him which typology is designed to express. The salvific plan as a whole derives its unity from its ultimate goal, and the intermediate stages on the way to that goal, being of their nature radically conformed to it, have a perceptible similarity to that goal. When revelation or the understanding of revelation makes that similarity clear, it is safe to see in the realities of the OT types of Christ. BIBLIOGRAPHY: G. von Rad, "Typologische Auslegung des Alten Testament" *Evangelische Theologie* 12 (1952) 17–33; A. Kerrigan, *St. Cyril of Alexandria, Interpreter of the Old Testament* (1952), esp. ch. 2.; J. Coppens, *Les harmonies des deux Testaments. Essai sur les divers sens des Écritures et sur* *l'unité de la Révélation* (2d ed., 1949). *SENSES OF SCRIP-TURE.

[D. J. BOURKE]

TYPOS (Gr., type or model), the decree of Emperor Constans II in 648 forbidding further discussion on the wills or operations of Christ (see MONOTHELITISM). Since previous efforts had failed to heal the breach in the empire caused by the Monothelite controversy, Constans published his rule of faith as a compromise measure. Since it permitted the continuance of Monothelitism, however, it failed to satisfy the anti-Monothelites led by St. *Maximus the Confessor. Pope Martin I condemned both Monothelitism and the *Typos* at a Lateran synod (639), whereupon Maximus and Martin were abducted to Constantinople, severely mistreated, and exiled. The controversy continued until Emperor Constantine IV summoned the ecumenical council of *Constantinople III in 680 and had Monothelitism condemned and outlawed. BIBLIOGRAPHY: É. Amann, DTC 15.2:1945–48.

[R. R. BARR]

TYRANNICIDE, the killing of a tyrant, a somewhat vexed question, which some distinctions will help to clear: first, between a sentence of death inflicted by the people or a body representing it and an assassination; second, between a "tyrant by usurpation" and a "tyrant by oppression." The first unjustly displaces the legitimate ruler; the second abominably abuses his power. The moral and legal standing of each is rather different (though one person may combine them both) and will be touched on below, where also applications of the first distinction will appear.

A usurper can be considered either in the making of his attempt to gain power or after he has succeeded. In the first phase, he is a criminal, and as a traitor can be rightly put to death by legitimate authority according to due forms of law. If this is not possible, then respected theologians hold that an individual may have a tacit mandate to despatch him more informally, though others will not allow this right unless the usurper is his actual aggressor. In the second phase, that is, after the prescriptive period has run its course and the usurper is in "peaceful possession," then there is nothing else for subjects to do than to acquiesce in the state of affairs to the extent of not using violence and exposing their country to the miseries of civil war. They are not bound to change their attachment to the old regime and may work for its restoration through peaceful means. This is their problem, about which it is difficult to lay down general rules, or to avoid the suspicion that even in morals nothing succeeds like success, or the historical reflection that ruling power is often old robbery writ large. Then also it should be remembered, if we are to keep the matter in historical perspective, that at some periods usurpers were killed, as they also killed possible pretenders, as standing for a family, not a national interest.

We turn now to tyrants by oppression. The early Middle Ages took a robust view of the rights of the people with respect to a ruler, whose power came through them, and to dispose of him when his wickedness was flagrantly and obstinately violating the common good. (Thus, *John of Salisbury, humanist of Chartres and friend of St. Thomas Becket). This changed with the growth of courtly privilege, unitary regalism, and conceptions of the "sacred person" of the "Lord's anointed." Already a hardening against upsetting the public peace in order to redress grievous wrongs can be perceived in St. Thomas Aquinas, though he was no supporter of absolutism. By the 16th cent. the privileged position of rulers by divine right was common form. Then came the bombshell—with a delayed action: the Jesuit, Juan *Mariana, published his *De rege et regis institutione* (1599), in which he argued with many qualifications his personal judgment that when all else had failed, a subject could remove a monstrous tyrant by open means, and, a grim yet salutary note, that princes should be educated with this in mind. It was a touchy subject, for already there were rumors of Catholic plots to kill Elizabeth of England; and Henry III of France, who, whatever his shiftiness about the Catholic cause, was no tyrant, had been assassinated (1588) by the Dominican, Jacques Clément. Yet such was the irony of history that the book appeared under the aegis of ecclesiastical authority and the court in Spain. The explosion came when well-loved Henry IV of France was assassinated by Francois Ravaillac, who had tried without success to become first a Cistercian and then a Jesuit and who had never read the book. This, in the general outcry, was repudiated by the Society.

Many of the Reformers, for instance Luther, Melanchthon, Junius Brutus, John Knox—who urged the English to kill Mary Queen of Scots—taught that rulers could be executed by their subjects. The Puritans succeeded in what many regarded as the judicial murder of Charles I of England. In our own days a group of men, of upright and Christian character, attempted to do away with A. Hitler. Yet in these days it seems that the most rigorous steps should be taken to prevent or punish private attempts to kill men in public office when no mandate of any sort can be claimed in any court of morals or law. BIBLIOGRAPHY: F. Alluntis, NCE 14:354, bibliog.

[T. GILBY]

TYRANNY, absolute political rule, unchecked by law or constitution; or absolute rule usurped and/or exercised for personal ends, not for the public good. Aristotle particularly describes it as the opposite of true kingship (*Ethics* VIII, 10–11). The overthrow of such a rule, which in modern terms would be called an abusive dictatorship, is not *sedition, St. Thomas Aquinas teaches: tyranny is contrary to justice; the overthrow, however, must not mean an upheaval more harmful than the tyranny itself to the people (ThAq ST 2a2ae, 42.2 ad 3). The Neoplatonic theme, the wicked life of the tyrant vs. the virtuous life of the philosopher, is reflected in Greek patristic literature, e.g., in *Pseudo-Dionysius. Satan is often compared to the tyrant; the beneficent power exercised over men by the angels is contrasted with satanic tyranny.

[T. C. O'BRIEN]

TYRE, the southernmost Phoenician city, which in ancient times was close to the border of the northernmost Israelite territory of Asher. Its navigators and merchants were legendary. Its wealth and arrogance provoked the prophets to denunciation (see esp. Ezek 26–28). Tyre was situated on an island off the Phoenician coast and was able to escape complete conquest until Alexander built a mole a half mile long linking the mainland to the island. By the 10th cent. Tyre had replaced Sidon as the leading city of Phoenicia. Hiram of Tyre lent craftsmen to David and Solomon to build David's palace, Solomon's temple, and the Israelite fleet at Ezion-geber in the Gulf of Aqaba. Solomon gave Hiram 20 cities in Galilee (which did not please him). A later king of Tyre (Ethbaal), who was also priest of Astarte (the female deity), married his daughter Jezebel to Ahab, King of Israel. Her daughter Athaliah married Joram, King of Judah. Through these marriages the religion of Tyre (Baal and Astarte) was able to gain prominence in Israel and found a worthy opponent in the prophet Elijah. This was a time of cultural imperialism for the people of Tyre. In that same century they colonized N Africa and Spain, bringing their religion along with them. During NT times, when Tyre was under the control of the Roman legate in Syria, Jesus withdrew there as to a place of relative safety. He preached there (Lk 6.17), found great faith there Mk 7.24ff), and forecast a more benign judgment for the Phoenician cities than for those of his homeland (Mt 11.21–22). Paul found Christians there and stayed with them a week while his ship's cargo was unloaded (Acts 21.3). Today (called Sur) it is a village of 6,000 inhabitants.

[E. J. DILLON]

TYRE, MARTYRS OF, several Christians of Egypt, some of whom had settled in Palestine, others at Tyre. The historian Eusebius (*Hist. eccles.* 6, 13) mentions their martyrdom *c.*304 and presents himself as an eyewitness to their ordeal. The Roman Martyrology commemorated them on February 20 in a reference to "... blessed martyrs whose number the wisdom of God alone can tell." The names mentioned (Tyrannio, Silvanus, Peleus, Nilus, and Zenobius) may be Christians of similar background who met similar fates, but at different times and places. St. Tyrannio, for example, was bp. of Tyre at the time of the martyrdoms at issue and may have encouraged them in their ordeal. He himself was taken to Antioch 6 years later and executed. Eusebius mentions Peleus and Nilus as Egyptian bps. who were among the martyrs of Palestine. The Bollandists place the death of Silvanus at Emesa, that of Zenobius at Antioch. BIBLIOGRAPHY: Butler 1:379–380.

[E. J. DILLON]

TYRIE, JAMES (1543–97), Scottish Jesuit theologian. Among his many accomplishments were helping to found Clermont College, contributing to the preparation of an edition of the Jesuit *Ratio studiorum,* and acting as consultant to Clement VIII and Scottish Earls in negotiating support for an attack against the Kirk (1594). Early in his career, an attempt to restore his brother to Catholicism involved him in a controversy with John Knox.

[P. J. HENNESSEY]

TYRRELL, GEORGE (1861–1909), English Jesuit theologian, the apostle of *Modernism in the English-speaking world. He was born in Dublin, of Anglican parents, and was influenced by a Calvinist aunt; he studied at Trinity College, Dublin, became devoted to the *high-church movement, and later became a Roman Catholic (1879). A year later he entered the Jesuits, was ordained in 1891, and taught moral theology at Stonyhurst until 1896, when he went to the Jesuit Church of Farm Street in London as a curate. He published three popular books of devotion, *Nova et Vetera* (1897), *Hard Sayings* (1898), and *On External Religion* (1899). His thought then took on immanentist qualities because of the influence of F. von Hügel and his reading of Loisy, Blondel, Bergson, and other 19th-cent. French writers. His rebellion against scholasticism and the exterior formalism of Catholicism appeared in his article "The Relation of Theology and Devotion," and one month later in "A Perverted Devotion" in the *Weekly Register* (1899). He had the former article reprinted in 1907 and insisted it was the matrix of his thought. It was concerned with keeping the immanent apprehension of the divinity from being overwhelmed by the structure of belief and external forms. These articles led to his removal from Farm Street and to retirement. He wrote *Oil and Wine* (1900), but it was held up by his superiors for 2 years before it was published. His *The Faith of Millions* appeared in 1901 and the *Lex Orandi* in 1903. He published *A Much Abused Letter* (1906), which resulted in his being suspended by the Jesuits, but he continued to write. *Lex Credendi* appeared in 1906, *Through Scylla and Charybdis* in 1907, and two letters of protest against the encyclical *Pascendi*, which resulted in his excommunication in 1907. His two last works were *Medievalism* (1908), an attack on the neo-Thomist revival, and *Christianity at the Cross-Roads,* published posthumously in 1909. Tyrrell was a brilliant speaker and writer with a large following. He was devoted to Christian spirituality but his belief in the immanentist philosophies of 19th-cent. France put him outside the structure of traditional Catholicism. He felt finally that Christianity was the beginning of a major world religion but did not of itself contain all that was necessary to be universal. He died with the last rites of the RC Church, but Henri Bremond, the French spiritual writer, was suspended for conducting T.'s funeral (Ratté, 167). BIBLIOGRAPHY: A Vidler, *Modernist Movement in the Roman Catholic Church* (1934); J. Ratté, *Three Modernists* (1967).

[J. P. WHALEN]

TYUTCHEV, FYDOR IVANOVICH (1803–73), Russian metaphysical poet. His 300 short lyrics, which have won him a place in literature next to Pushkin, include nature lyrics, imbued with his own tragic concept of the irrationality of life and the isolation of man in a world where Cosmos and Chaos are constantly merging with one another; love poems of singular poignancy; and political poems, which reveal his Slavophilic sympathies. BIBLIOGRAPHY: R. A. Gregg, *Fedor Tiutchev, The Evolution of a Poet* (1965); M. Slonim, *Epic of Russian Literature* (1949) 245–249.

[M. F. MCCARTHY]

TZAKISMA (Klasma), in the Cucuzelian musical system of Byzantine notation, a sign used in conjunction with the *gorgon* to mark a dotted quaver followed by a semiquaver.

[M. T. LEGGE]

U

UBACH, BUENAVENTURA (1879–1960), biblical scholar. A Spanish Benedictine, U. taught Oriental languages at San Anselmo in Rome. After some years in the Holy Land, he established the Biblical Museum of Monserrat (Spain). His work as editor of *La Biblia de Monserrat* represents U.'s principal achievement. This series was a Catalan version of the Bible with exegesis; to it he contributed volumes containing the Pentateuch, historical books, and the Psalms.

[J. R. AHERNE]

UBAGHS, GERHARD CASIMIR (1800–75), Belgian philosopher, leader in the ontologico-traditionalist movement at the Univ. of Louvain. There U. edited the *Revue catholique,* the official organ of ontologism. In 1843 the Congregation of the Index ordered a retraction of some of his teachings, and in 1861 the Holy Office censured a series of his propositions (D. 2841–47).

The basic position of ontologism holds that the object producing the idea in the human intellect is God himself, so that the mind contemplates God directly and sees in him the truths or objective ideas of which human knowledge is a mere weak reflection. Traditionalism states that the acquiring of metaphysical and moral truths depends upon divine teaching and its oral dissemination, and that reason can then comprehend and even demonstrate these truths. Ontologico-traditionalism is rooted in a distrust of reason, yet sees reason as capable of directly confronting eternal truth or the divine essence. BIBLIOGRAPHY: M. De Wulf, *Histoire de la philosophie en Belgique* (1910) on ontologism at Louvain; for U.'s life see Jacobs in *Annuaire de l'Université de Louvain* (1876).

[J. T. HICKEY]

UBALD D'ALENÇON (Leo Louis Berson; 1872–1927), Capuchin historian. A Capuchin from 1891, he had poor health throughout his life and consequently devoted himself to research in Franciscan and Capuchin history. He contributed frequently to *Études Franciscaines* and *Annales Franciscaines* and published numerous monographs in his field.

[T. C. O'BRIEN]

UBALD OF GUBBIO, ST. (c.1080–1160), bishop. Of Germanic parentage and orphaned early, he was educated at the cathedral in Gubbio, where he became a canon regular. Ordained in 1114, he was made prior of the cathedral chapter in 1117 and bp. in 1129. Canonized in 1192, his body was found incorrupt and was translated to the pilgrimage chapel at Colle Ingino, built to entomb his relics, in 1194. He is a patron against diabolic possession and mental illness. BIBLIOGRAPHY: AS May 3:625–650; P. Cenci, *Vita di s. Ubaldo* (1924); N. Del Re, BiblSanct 12:732–735; Butler 2:325–326.

[W. A. JURGENS]

UBALDI, PAOLO (1872–1934), Italian classical scholar and patrologist. An orphan at age 10, U. was educated by St. John Bosco and ordained in 1895. At first he taught classical Greek literature at Turin and Catania, but later his interests turned more explicit to patrology which he taught at the Catholic University at Milan and at the major seminary of Venegono. He published critical texts of Homer, Plato, Pindar, and Aeschylus; and in patrology, he edited texts of Palladius, Tatian, Methodius of Olympas, and Athenagoras. His influence contributed to the revival of interest in early Christian literature in Italy. BIBLIOGRAPHY: F. X. Murphy, NCE 14:360; P. Barale, EncCatt 12:655–656.

[R. B. ENO]

UBERTINO OF CASALE (1259–c.1330), a leader of the Franciscan *Spirituals. U. was born at Casale in the Diocese of Vercelli and entered the Franciscan Order in 1272. After 9 years of study and lecturing at Paris, he returned to Italy and engaged in an effective preaching apostolate, during which he came in contact with John of Parma, Peter John Olivi, and other ardent Spirituals. He espoused their cause and became leader of the movement in Tuscany. His most important writing, *Arbor vitae crucifixae* (1305), mercilessly castigated high-living prelates and lax friars. Its argumentative style and *Joachimism caused U. to be accused of spreading heresy and promoting schism within the order. He took a prominent part in the acrimonious debate on Franciscan poverty between 1309 and 1322. Because of U.'s intransigence, John XXII ordered him to transfer to the Benedictines. When another charge of heresy was lodged against him in 1325, he fled Avignon. The remainder of his life is shrouded in mystery. BIBLIOGRAPHY: D. Douie, *Nature and Effects of the Heresy of the Fraticelli* (1932); E. G. Salter, "Ubertino da Casale," *Franciscan Essays* 1 (ed. A. G. Little, 1912), 108–123. *POVERTY CONTROVERSY.

[C. J. LYNCH]

UBIQUITARIANISM (Lat. *ubique*, everywhere), a designation for the teaching that the body of Christ shares in the divine omnipresence. Such a position was held earlier, e.g., by John Scotus Erigena, Amalric of Bène, William of Ockam, but it is particularly associated with early Lutheranism. Martin Luther taught such a doctrine in refutation of Sacramentarian denial of the possibility of the Real Presence (*Confession Concerning the Lord's Supper*, 1528). The *Formula of Concord makes the same point (Art. VII). Luther did not, however, base his affirmation of the Real Presence on the ubiquity or omnipresence of Christ. Johann Brenz (1499–1570), who espoused an absolute omnipresence, was opposed by Martin Chemnitz (1522–86), who held for a simple multipresence of Christ, effected by his will, as in the Eucharist. In some form, ubiquitarianism remained a part of Lutheran orthodoxy up to the 18th century.

[T. MANTEUFEL]

UBIQUITY, the "everywhereness" of God (Lat. *ubique*, everywhere); another term for the divine *omnipresence.

UCCELLO, PAOLO DI DONO (1397–1475), Italian painter of the early Renaissance, Florentine School, obsessed by perspective, painting in a conservative manner using multiple vantage points. This conservatism is largely the product of a series of visual games the artist plays with the viewer's eye. His greatest work, in which he manipulates a thoroughly consistent Albertian system of perspective to unify and dramatize space, is the fresco of the *Deluge* (1445–47), originally located in the Chiostro Verde at Sta. Maria Novella in Florence, where he had already painted Creation scenes (*c.* 1431). U. executed four Prophets and provided cartoons for the Nativity and Resurrection stained-glass windows (1443) in the cathedral. His last documented work is a predella for the Urbino Confraternity of the Holy Sacrament (1465–69). BIBLIOGRAPHY: J.

Pope-Hennessy, *Complete Works of Paolo Uccello* (1950); J. White, *Birth and Rebirth of Pictorial Space* (1957).

[S. CONWAY]

UDALL, JOHN (*c.* 1560–92), Puritan pamphleteer. During his curacy at Kingston-on-Thames (1585–88) U. was sued for criticism of the episcopacy, but this did not deter him from publishing anonymously several widely read pamphlets. In 1590 he was convicted of the authorship of one of them. His pardon was procured, but he died before release from imprisonment. U. also published several volumes of sermons and a Hebrew grammar and dictionary. BIBLIOGRAPHY: S. Lee, DNB 58:4–6.

[M. J. SUELZER]

UDALL, NICHOLAS (*c.* 1505–1556), English playwright, translator and schoolmaster. He is best known for his comedy, *Ralph Roister Doister,* thought to be the first such in English. His period as a schoolmaster was marked by severity and a dishonorable termination resulting from his apparent homosexual relations with some of his students. U.'s work as a translator served as an outlet for his sympathies for the Reformation. His best-known translations are of Erasmus, *Apopthegmes* (1542), and a paraphrase of Luke (1548). In spite of his Protestantism, his plays assured his favor even at Mary Tudor's court. Other works attributed to him include: *A Newe Mery and Wittie Comedie . . . , Jacke Jugeler, Respublica,* and *Ezechias.*

[P. J. HENNESSEY]

UDO, mid-to-later 12th-cent. theologian at Paris, author of a *Summa super sententias Petri Lombardi,* preserved in 15 MSS and written *c.* 1165. This *Summa,* systematic treatment of the 4 books of the Lombard's *Sentences*, affords a good picture of the theology of its time on such dogmatic questions as the Trinity, Christology, and the Redemption.

[E. J. DILLON]

'UGAB, name given in the *Talmud for one of the first instruments mentioned in the Bible. It was probably a vertical-type flute. BIBLIOGRAPHY: J. Gelineau, *Voices and Instruments in Christian Worship* (tr. C. Howell, 1964) 300.

[M. T. LEGGE]

UGANDA, MARTYRS OF. In 1886, about 100 Africans were murdered by their king, Mwanga, in his attempt to stamp out Christianity in Uganda. Mwanga was the successor to Mtesa who had permitted the White Fathers to bring Christianity into the country in 1879. When certain of his pages refused to comply with the king's homosexual demands, Mwanga started a reprisal. Fifteen boys and young men were taken to Namugongo, a place of execution. Three died en route and the rest of them were wrapped in reed mats, placed on a large pyre, and burned to death, 1886.

Persecution then spread indiscriminately among the Christians in Uganda before dying out. Twenty-two were beatified in 1920, canonized in 1964. BIBLIOGRAPHY: AAS 12 (1920) 272–281; C. Salotti, *I martiri dell' Uganda* (1921); M. Hallfell, *Uganda, eine Edelfrucht . . .* (1921); A. E. Howell, *Fires of Namugongo* (1948).

[P. K. MEAGHER]

UGANDAN ORTHODOX CHURCH. Two Ugandans left the Anglican Church and in 1932 were ordained priests of the African Orthodox Church. In 1946 the Greek Patriarch of Alexandria adopted them, creating a diocese of Irinoupolis under a Greek bishop to care for them and local Greeks. They have spread to Kenya and their numbers have grown to several thousand.

[F. WILCOCK]

UGARIT, ancient city-state on the coast of northern Syria. Excavations, which began there in 1929, turned up a considerable literature, some in Ugaritic, most in Akkadian. These were of immense importance for biblical studies, both because of insights into pre-Israelite Canaanite culture and because of linguistic kinship between Hebrew and Ugaritic.

[T. EARLY]

UGARITIC RELIGION, see CANAANITE RELIGION.

UGHELLI, FERDINANDO (1595–1670), Italian Cistercian, abbot (1639) of SS. Víncenzo ed Anastasio (now Tre Fontane, Rome), church historian. He was notable for his *Italia sacra sive de episcopis Italiae* (9 v., 1642–48), an attempt at a complete and documented catalogue of bps. in Italy up to his time.

[T. C. O'BRIEN]

UGOLINO DA SIENA (fl. 1295–*c.*1339), Italian painter, according to Vasari pupil of Cimabue, and follower of Duccio in Gothicized forms though not so in composition as seen in *Way to Calvary*—a panel from the polyptych (now dispersed) for the high altar of Sta. Croce, Florence.

[M. J. DALY]

UGUZO, ST. (also Lucio di Val Cavargna; d. before 1200), popular Lombardian saint, patron of cheesemakers. By legend a shepherd near Cavargna, he gave his savings to the poor. Dismissed by his master, he went into the service of another employer who prospered from that moment. Consequently the first employer killed him. BIBLIOGRAPHY: A. Rimoldi, BiblSanct 8:283–284.

[F. D. LAZENBY]

UKRAINIAN METROPOLIA, (U.S.A.) the common title for the Ukrainian Orthodox Church of the U.S.A., and the largest of the Ukrainian jurisdictions in America. The metropolia came into existence in October 1950 with the merger of two previously independent dioceses that had been headed by Metropolitan John Theodorovich and Abp. Mystyslaw Skrypnyk respectively. Theodorovich, originally consecrated in 1921 by Basil Lipivisky, was reconsecrated in 1949 in an irregular manner and, thus, the metropolia is not recognized by other Orthodox bodies. The Ukrainian Metropolia does not belong to the *Standing Conference of Canonical Orthodox Bishops in the Americas but is in communion with the Ukrainian Greek Orthodox Church of Canada. There are approximately 79,000 faithful in 95 parishes.

[T. BIRD]

UKRAINIAN RITE, one of the Eastern Catholic rites, also called Ruthenian (see RUTHENIAN RITE). Originating in Kievan-Russia, this rite comprises many national groups: Ukrainians, Byelorussians, Hungarians, Slovaks, Yugoslavs, and those who emigrated from their homeland. The first mission of SS. *Cyril and Methodius extended from the Black Sea to Kiev, but the Christian faith did not officially come to the Ukraine until the conversion of St. *Vladimir, Prince of Kiev, in 988. Christianity spread throughout the kingdom, and Vladimir with his son Yaroslav set up statutes regulating the relations of Church and State. The first metropolitan of Kiev was Ivan, a Greek, and it was not until 1051 that a native Ukrainian, Ilarion, was appointed. After the East-West *Schism, the see of Kiev was held at one time by those opposed to Rome, at another by those who were friendly. Attempts to bring unity to the Ukrainian Church were made at the Council of *Florence (1439). This temporary reunion resulted in the formation of a metropolitanate in Moscow, thereby dividing the Kievan jurisdiction. Because of increasing difficulties in both the Catholic and Orthodox Churches, a second step at reunion was made in 1594 when bishops Ipaty Potiy and Kyrylo Terleckij were sent to Rome with letters of submission in the name of Metropolitan Rahoza of Kiev. In 1595 Clement VIII issued the bull of union, *Magnus Dominus,* and the apostolic letter, *Decet pontificem romanum*. The following year marked official reunion with the synod of Brest-Litovsk (see BREST, UNION OF). At the same time, however, an anti-union group became the Orthodox Church in the Province of Kiev. One of the bps., Meletius Smotrytskyi, became a Catholic after the martyrdom of St. *Josaphat Kuntsevych in 1623. By the end of the 17th cent., the Carpatho-Ukraine as well as the bishoprics of Galicia and Peremyshl were reunited to Rome, with Lvov and Lutsk following shortly thereafter. Continued efforts at union were accompanied by a renewal of internal organization that was strengthened by the Synod of Zamost in 1720. The legislation of this synod was approved by Benedict XIII in 1724 and became the canon law for the Ukrainian rite. By the 18th cent. two-thirds of the Ukrainian and Byelorussian peoples were Catholic, but the union of the Ukrainian Church was jeopardized by the partitioning that placed the Ukraine and Byelorussia immediately under Russian rule and Galicia under Austrian. A general suppression of the union in the Ukraine followed for about a century, but in Galicia Catholicism continued to develop. The metropolitan see of Halych-Lvov, reestablished by Pius VII in 1807, contributed to a renewal of this part of Ukrainian Catholicism. Metropolitans such as M. Levyckyj, S. Sembratovych, A. Szeptyckyj, and J. Slipyj figured prominently in church development. In 1934 there were three eparchies and an apostolic administrature; a theological academy was founded under Szeptyckyj and a number of religious congregations were established. Some interritual problems were settled between the Ukrainian and Polish (Latin) hierarchies by the Concordat of 1859. From the 18th to the 20th cent., several dioceses were created in the Austro-Hungarian Empire for emigrant Carpatho-Ukrainians, Hungarians, Croatians, and Macedonians. Russia temporarily seized Galicia in 1914 and imprisoned Metropolitan Szeptyckyj. After final occupation of Galicia and Carpatho-Ukraine during World War II, the Russians determined to destroy the Catholic Ukrainian rite. Those who refused to accept Orthodoxy were either deported or killed, and all the bps. died in prison except the present Card. Josyf Slipyj, who spent 18 years in Siberia. In Galicia and Carpatho-Ukraine a new Orthodox hierarchy was imposed by the patriarch of Moscow and is distinct from the Ukrainian Autocephalous Orthodox Church, which broke away from the Muscovite regime. No accurate figures are available on the number of native Ukrainian Catholics, but in 1974 it was estimated that there were about 4,355,095 members located in Russia, Galacia, Poland, the U.S., Canada, Australia, Brazil, Argentina, England, Wales, Germany, and France. In 1972 efforts and claims by Card. J. Slipyj and other prelates for the establishment of a patriarchal system for all Ukrainian Catholics throughout the world were opposed in a document signed by Card. Jean Villot and sent to the apostolic nuncios and delegates in countries with Ukrainian bishops. It stated that ''the Ukrainian Church has not been erected as a patriarchate . . .'' In 1975, the Holy Father again informed Card. Slipyj of his negative decision, adding ''at least for now,'' which was accepted by the majority of Ukrainians, who understood the reason that at this time a patriarch could not function according to canon law in the Ukraine. The Roman decision reflects concern to maintain whatever church freedom exists in Communist countries of Eastern Europe. BIBLIOGRAPHY: M. Andrusiak, DTC 14.1:382–407; B. Boysak *Fate of the Holy Union in Carpatho-Ukraine* (1963); I. Wlasovsky, *Outline of the History of the Ukrainian Church* (1956–).

[S. BERDAR; F. T. RYAN]

ULENBERG, KASPAR (1548–1617), German priest, theologian, writer, and translator. His Lutheran parents wanted him to become a minister. After preliminary studies he enrolled in the Univ. of Wittenberg where he was trained by leading Lutheran theologians. It has been conjectured that psychological rather than theological reasons caused his conversion to Catholicism in about 1572. From August 1572 to December 1575 he studied at Cologne and eventually was ordained. His early parish work was uneventful. In 1583 he returned to Cologne and began an active career. Among his achievements were a catechism, translations of works by Thomas à Kempis, a theological treatise entitled *Erhebliche Ursachen . . .*, and a German translation of the Bible. His debate with the Calvinist minister in Cologne, Johannes Badius, was also noteworthy. Between 1600 and 1606 he was a tutor to the two sons of the Margrave of Baden and in 1610 was appointed rector at the Univ. of Cologne. U. was representative of the revived spirit of German Catholicism in the late 16th century. BIBLIOGRAPHY: J. Solzbacher, *Kaspar Ulenberg: Eine Priestergestalt aus der Zeit der Gegenreformation in Köln* (1948); A. Franzen, *Der Wiederaufbau des kirchlichen Lebens im Erzbistum Köln unter Ferdinand von Bayern, 1612–50* (1941).

[C. T. EBY]

ULFILAS (Gothic, Wulfila; *c.*311–382 or 383), Arian bishop from 341 and apostle of the Visigoths, at first N of the Danube, then, with permission of Emperor Constantius, in Moesia. At the Council of Constantinople (360) Ulfilas supported the homoiousian doctrine. His most lasting monument is his translation of the Bible into Gothic. BIBLIOGRAPHY: G. Bardy, DTC 15.2:2048–57. *GOTHIC BIBLE.

[M. F. MCCARTHY]

ULLATHORNE, WILLIAM BERNARD (1806–89), English Benedictine and bishop. Of an old English Catholic family and a descendant of St. Thomas More, U. entered the Benedictines and was ordained in 1830. He served in Australia as vicar general for 10 years. Out of his experience came the pamphlet ''Horrors of Transportation,'' a denunciation of British attitudes toward the prisoners shipped to Australia. Returning to England, he was named vicar apostolic of the W district in 1846 and in 1848 vicar apostolic of the central region. He played a key role in the restoration of the English hierarchy in 1850, when he was appointed bp. of Birmingham. In 1888 he resigned. U. was a moving force in the 19th-cent. revival of Catholicism in England. A pamphleteer, he engaged in numerous controversies, and his letters are a prime source for historians of Vatican Council I (See C. Butler, *Life and Times of Bp. Ullathorne, 1806–86,* 2 v., 1926). As the bp. in whose diocese the Birmingham Oratory was located, U. was a true friend to J. H. Newman.

[J. R. AHERNE]

ULLERSTON, RICHARD, (d. 1423), English theologian. A fellow of Queen's College, Oxford (1391–1402), he wrote (1408) at the request of Robert Hallum, bp. of Salisbury, a tract called *Petitiones pro ecclesiae militantis reformatione* which the English bps. used at the Council of

Pia (1409). Other works include a treatise on the Creed (1409), a commentary on the Psalter, and a *Defensorium dotationis ecclesiae* against the Lollards. BIBLIOGRAPHY: Emden Ox 3:1928–29.

[L. E. BOYLE]

ULLMANN, REGINA (1884–1961), Swiss writer. A convert to Catholicism, U. is one of a group of Swiss novelists and poets who constituted a Catholic literary revival. U. wrote of everyday life which, while not free of evil, gives witness to the ascendancy of good, the mystery of love and goodness (see her *Von einem alten Wirtshausschild*).

[J. R. AHERNE]

ULRIC OF AUGSBURG, ST. (890–973), German bishop. Born of a noble family, attended school at Sankt Gallen, returned to the service of his uncle, Bp. Adalbert of Augsburg, U. was consecrated bp. in 924. Until his death, he built up the monastic life of the diocese, constructed walls of the city, and defended it from the Hungarians, and for Otto I made several journies to Rome. A letter opposing clerical celibacy was falsely attributed to him and was much used by Protestant reformers in later times. BIBLIOGRAPHY: N. Del Re, BiblSanct 12:796–798; U. Schmid, CE 15:123; H. Thurston, CE 3:486a; Butler 3:16–17.

[S. WILLIAMS]

ULRIC OF STRASSBURG, 13th-cent. Dominican philosopher and theologian, whose *Summa de summo bono* enjoyed great popularity in the 15th century. Born Ulrich Engelberti, he was a fellow student with Thomas Aquinas at Cologne under Albert the Great (1248–52). He lectured at Strassburg for many years and was provincial of the German province of his order (1272–77). U. must have died in Paris soon after arriving to lecture on the *Sentences* and to obtain a Master's degree. His unfinished *Summa*, known as *Summa de bono*, was contemporary with that of Thomas Aquinas and probably was the vehicle by which Albert's doctrine on God and his attributes, with its distinctive blend of Plato and Aristotle, came to influence the later Rhineland mystics. A critical edition of the work is being prepared at St. Joseph's College, Hartford, Conn., under the Rev. Francis Lescoe.

[E. J. DILLON]

ULRIC OF ZELL, ST. (1029–93), Cluniac monk. Godson of Emperor Henry III, U. participated in the march on Rome and then made a pilgrimage to Palestine. He became a monk at Cluny in 1061. He was prior in four monasteries; the last, at Zell, is now called Sankt Ulrich. He wrote a treatise on the organization of the Abbey of Cluny. BIBLIOGRAPHY: L. Kurras, NCE 14:380; Butler 3:101.

[M. J. FINNEGAN]

ULRICH, ST., see WULFRIC, ST.

ULTRAMONTANES (Lat. *ultra,* beyond, *montes,* mountains), advocates of strong papal authority. The term reflects the location of Rome as viewed from France, Germany, and England. Ultramontanes were those who opposed *Gallicanism, *Febronianism, *Josephinism, and also who defended the pope against 19th-cent. attacks in Italy on the temporal power of the papacy. The term was frequently used in reference to champions of papal infallibility at *Vatican Council I.

[T. C. O'BRIEN]

UMAYYADS, the first great Islamic dynasty, which came to power in Syria and ruled the Empire of the Caliphate from 661 to 750. Although they ruled from Damascus, the Umayyad caliphs belonged to the aristocratic clan of the Banū Umayya, merchants of the Ouraysh tribe centered at Mecca. They had been leaders of the pagan oligarchy who opposed the Prophet Muḥammad and at first resisted Islam. One of their members became a convert and brought family members into prominent administrative positions under Muḥammad and his immediate successors. The Sufyānid branch came to power (661–684) when Mu 'āwiyah, son of Abū Sufyān, emerged victorious over the followers of Muḥammad's son-in-law 'Ali. The Sufyānids were in turn replaced by the Marwānids (684–750). The Umayyad power base remained in formerly Byzantine Syria, backed by half-Christianized Syrian Arabs and Syrian Christians, with Christians in key posts. The Doctor of the Greek Church, John of Damascus, was reared at the Umayyad court. This caliphate is often referred to as the Arab Kingdom, since it was more an expression of Arab nationalism than a world religion. Under the Marwānids the caliphate reached its peak, stretching from Spain to India. Arabization followed apace, with Arabic becoming the official state language and with Arabs replacing Persians and Greeks in the various provincial administrations. They met defeat, however, at the hands of the Byzantine Emperor Leo III (717) and were turned back by the Turks in Anatolia; the Berbers in North Africa; and the Franks at Poitiers. The internal dissension of the Shiites, of the many non-Arab converts to Islam, and of other alienated elements fueled the opposition of the Hāshimīyah, and the 'Abbāsid dynasty overthrew Marwān II (744–750). Members of the disgraced family were hunted down and killed. One member, 'Abd ar-Raḥmān, escaped to Spain and founded the Umayyad dynasty of Córdoba, which reclaimed the imperial title of Caliphate in 929 and survived until 1031. The failure of the Umayyads had been their inability to make the transition from a patriarchal tribal system to a vast, cosmopolitan world empire and a world religion. The polarity tending towards schism between the Umayyads and the Shiites and other pietists persists in Islam to the present day.

[E. J. DILLON]

UNA SANCTA MOVEMENT, name given to the ecumenical efforts of reconciliation in Germany of both Roman

Catholics and Lutherans. These efforts began after World War I, but were based on earlier attempts since the Reformation times. The term was taken from the Nicene Creed (*"Credo in . . . unam sanctam . . . ecclesiam"*) to indicate the desire for reunification. Pioneering attempts began in 1918 with the founding of the Protestant high-church movement (*Hochkirchliche Vereinigung*) by the Berlin pastors Friedrich Heiler and F. Seigmund-Schultze. But it was Max Joseph Metzger (1887–1944) who in his Una Sancta Brotherhood (1928) unified scattered Catholic-Protestant study groups concerned with reunion. Dialogues spread to similar movements, such as the *Berneuchen Circle and the Michaelsbrüderschaft. Suppressed by the Nazis (who executed Metzger), the movement reflourished after World War II, gaining popularity under the leadership of Matthias Laros, a Catholic pastor from the Rhineland. After his death (1965) the Benedictine Abbey of Niederaltaich became the center; there its journal *Una Sancta* (formerly *Rundbriefe*, founded 1946) had been edited (1953–63) by Thomas Sartory and A. Ahlbrecht (1963–   ). The forces inspiring the movement are a new appraisal of Luther research both by Protestants and Catholics (e.g., Josef Lortz, *Die Reformation in Deutschland*, 1939–40), the liturgical movement, a scriptural renaissance, and increasing lay participation in the RC Church; the Nazi persecution of all Christians and the effects of the war, which uprooted people and brought them into closer physical contact, strengthened the movement. Una Sancta has found expression in various forms of dialogue, study groups, theological institutes, conferences, and printed media. The Una Sancta efforts were not always viewed favorably by the RC Church, e.g., the encyclical *Mortalium animos,* 1928, and there were periods of restrictions and mistrust until the 1950s, when official sponsorship by Lorenz Jäger, Abp. of Paderborn, and the participation of prominent theologians (Hugo Rahner, Heinrich Fries, Otto Karrer, and the Lutheran Hans Asmussen) brought it new momentum, later increased by the ecumenical sentiments of Vatican Council II. BIBLIOGRAPHY: S. J. T. Miller, NCE 14:381–382; J. Höfer, LTK 10:463–466; J. Lell, RGG 6:1117–19; L. J. Swidler, *Ecumenical Vanguard: The History of the Una Sancta Movement* (1966).

[J. R. FANG]

UNAM SANCTAM, papal bull issued by Boniface VIII (1302) containing the most famous expression of the claims of certain medieval popes to supreme authority in all of Christendom. This bull demands unequivocally the subjection of the temporal power of kings to the spiritual authority of popes. Since spiritual realities are superior to the temporal, those who possess spiritual authority in Christendom have the duty to judge temporal rulers, but only God judges the pope who possesses supreme spiritual authority. Although written in the context of the medieval feud between civil rulers and popes, *Unam sanctam* seems to go beyond the then current strife with *Philip IV and enounce the principles of the crumbling supranational unity of Christen-

dom which Boniface tried unsuccessfully to maintain. BIBLIOGRAPHY: Brian Tierney, *Crisis of Church and State, 1050–1300* (1964); M. D. Chenu, LTK 10:462.

[P. MISNER]

UNAMUNO Y JUGO, MIGUEL DE (1864–1936), Spanish writer whose essays, novels, and poems emphasized existentialist themes. Of Basque origin, he spent most of his life at the Univ. of Salamanca, where from 1901 he was rector. Out of passionate love for Spain, he opposed the political regime of Primo de Rivera; and after first supporting Franco, he criticized both sides during the Spanish Civil War. The first led to exile (1926–31); the second, to his house arrest before his death. U.'s principal work was *Del sentimiento trágico de la vida en los hombres y en los pueblos* (1913; tr. J. E. Crawford Flinch, *The Tragic Sense of Life,* 1921); the novel, *San Manuel Bueno, mártir* (1933) is of equal importance for an evaluation of U.'s philosophy of life. That philosophy is regarded as existentialist because U. developed his views out of his own experience of the tragedies and conflicts of the human situation, concentrated on the familiar themes of existentialism, and the resolution of life's unresolvable tensions through courage and feeling. Part of such a resolution for him was his adherence to the Catholic faith, for he regarded the conflict of faith and reason as insoluble intellectually. BIBLIOGRAPHY: J. Ferrater Mora, *Unamuno: A Philosophy of Tragedy* (tr. P. Silver, 1962).

[T. EARLY]

UNBELIEF, the act or state of mind of one who does not give assent to God's revealed word. Since, however, the acceptance of God's word admits of growth and development—in extent and intensity, both objectively and subjectively—belief and unbelief can designate contrary rather than contradictory acts and states of mind. An acceptance of God's word attains its fullness only when faith is transformed into vision. The condition of man in his present pilgrim state must ever involve some mixture of belief and unbelief. Unbelief can never be total, for that would involve an absolute rejection of God and a complete repudiation of knowledge and desire. As commonly used, however, the term unbelief indicates non-acceptance of the truth substantially identifiable with the historical revelation made through Jesus Christ.

Theologians distinguish between (1) those who, having once accepted the message, later withdraw their assent and refuse to believe, and (2) those who have never assented to it. In the first class are heretics, schismatics, and apostates. In referring to them, one generally prefers the specific classification to the generic one; they are not normally called unbelievers, nor is their state of mind termed unbelief. In ordinary usage, an unbeliever is a person falling in the second of the above classifications. Unbelief in this sense occurs in three distinct forms. First there is purely negative unbelief (see D 1968). This is the unbelief of one to whom

Christ's message has never been adequately proposed and who has therefore never had the opportunity of deciding for or against it. Second, there is the unbelief of one who has heard the Christian message, examined it, and culpably decided against it. This is called positive unbelief. Finally, there is the unbelief of one who has heard of the Christian message but for one reason or another has neglected to listen to it or to take it seriously. This is called privative unbelief. That men neither listen to nor accept the Christian message may be due to their own fault; but it may also be due to the insufficiency of the ministers of the gospel who, perhaps, by their deeds give the lie to what they preach and thus never succeed in communicating to others authentically and existentially the message of Christ, God made man to save all men.

Contemporary theological speculation has given greater attention to the problem of belief and unbelief of those who belong to religions in which there is no acceptance of God's revelation proclaimed through the Prophets of the OT and through the Incarnate Word. So far as historical revelation is concerned, their state can be rightly called unbelief. But it cannot be affirmed with certainty that they are altogether without revealed truth. The sacred books of historical revelation tell of God speaking with men at the beginnings of humanity. In this sense it is possible to speak of a primitive (perhaps better, a primal) revelation, and to understand it, not in a mere temporal sense, but rather in a supratemporal and supraspatial sense, based ultimately on the creative word of God ever causing and conserving, where good and truth and beauty are concerned. The history of religions suggests the existence of such a revelation, and its recognition is theologically well founded and in harmony with statements of Vatican Council II (e.g., Vat II, NonChrRel 2). It is not unreasonable to hold that elements of this primal revelation have remained intact, or even that they may have a saving and justifying action. The acceptance of these elements can therefore constitute belief, even belief on a supernatural level. These elements are, of course, ultimately referred to God's revelation of himself to Israel and finally to the complete revelation in Jesus Christ. In that sense they are in themselves incomplete and imperfect, and they cannot lead to a fully authentic knowledge of the one, living God. Nevertheless, their acceptance is truly belief, and this must give new comprehension and extension to the theological terms believer and unbeliever. BIBLIOGRAPHY: C. Williams, NCE 14:383–385; É. Cornelis, *Valeurs chrétiennes des religions non chrétiennes* (1965); M. Eminyan, *Theology of Salvation* (1960); E. Drinkwelder, *Vollendung in Christus* (1934).

[C. WILLIAMS]

UNCIAL, script using majuscule letters slightly rounded. Dominant from the 4th to 8th cent., it succeeded square and rustic capitals, and in the time of Alcuin gave way to minuscules. Latin for 1/12, or an inch, the term derives from a statement by Jerome criticizing books written in "un-

cialibus . . . litteris,'' perhaps implying the letters were too large.

[T. EARLY]

UNCONSCIOUS. One of the principal tenets of *psychoanalysis, as Freud developed it, is that the human psyche operates in great measure unconsciously. Although the *ego generally functions consciously, both *id (the source of instinctual drives) and *superego (moral norms and ideas incorporated by identification with parents) function for the most part unconsciously. Freud distinguished not only the conscious (the processes of which one is aware) but also the preconscious (memories and items of habitual knowledge available for deliberate recall) from the unconscious which contains the fantasies, thoughts, and memories which are ordinarily beyond recall even by sustained and intense effort. These are in fact not simply forgotten; they have been repressed. The existence of the unconscious is proved, as Freud sees it, by the fact that conscious processes make better sense when the unconscious is posited. Besides, those psychoanalytic techniques which enable a patient to overcome the resistance which keeps mental contents in the unconscious show, when they bring these materials to awareness, an intermediate functioning of the unconscious. Thus the memories and fantasies elicited from hysterical patients under hypnosis often provide the etiology for their neurotic symptoms. Dreams too—"the royal road to the unconscious"—offer a rich source to the insight of analysis, representing for this theory, the disguised expressions of the attitudes, yearnings, fears, and conflicts of the unconscious. Likewise the analysis of wit, slips of the tongue, and similar phenomena reveal that unconscious motivation influences behavior. Finally, the experiment of post-hypnotic expression, in which the subject is commanded to perform an action after he has emerged from a hypnotic trance and then does perform it, shows the existence of the unconscious.

The unconscious then contains images, thoughts and memories representing actions satisfying the instinctual drives, i.e., actions of sexual gratification, murderous revenge, fantastic orgies, etc. They have been repressed because their obscenity or violence is too great to tolerate even in fantasy and because they provoke intense anxiety, guilt feelings, and fear of possible retaliation. They are continually "worked over" in the mode of functioning called primary processes. This is not reality-oriented, nor verbal, nor logical; it has no reference to past, present, and future, and is without reference to moral norms or rules of decency. It is rather a process entirely ruled by the need to discharge *instinctual drive energy, and its purpose is the production of a representative of instinctual drive aims whose sexual or violent elements are sufficiently disguised to allow them to escape censorship and repression. Two of the main features of this primary process are displacement and condensation. By the first, one image is substituted for another to assume its drive purposes and emotional value. But by condensation, one image or idea substitutes for many, and assumes all their affective and drive charges. The process of symbol analysis is in large part a process of unravelling the course of displacements and condensations.

Unconscious processes, therefore, are not so much those of which we are totally unaware as those which are not yet integrated into the logical, reality-oriented mental processes. In Freud's words, they involve thing-images to which we have not attached word-images, or thing-images from which word-symbols have been detached. While the entire concept of unconscious has been criticized as self-contradictory, as if consciousness and mental were coextensive, the objection can be answered in a conception of the unconscious mind as simply inarticulate. Many thinkers before Freud were somewhat aware of its existence and influence, but his great contribution was in devising effective techniques for exploring the unconscious mind systematically and in developing the first extensive analysis of its dimension and dynamic. BIBLIOGRAPHY: Sigmund Freud, *Unconscious* (1957).

[M. E. STOCK]

UNCREATED LIGHT. The Son of God is described in the Creed as "light from light," an incorporation of the metaphor of light as a description of the divine being (Jn 1.8,12). Pseudo-Dionysius in his *On the Divine Names* extensively develops the theme of "intelligible light" as one of the names proper to the Good, God as enlightening by knowledge and the light of grace (ch. 4; cf. St. Thomas Aquinas *In de divinis nominibus* 4, lect. 4). The Dionysian influence formed part of the background of a particular, historical usage of the theme, Uncreated Light, namely in the mystical movement in the Eastern Church known as hesychasm, and esp. in the theology of Gregory *Palamas. By it he intended to establish that only by uncreated grace can man be truly deified, as deification is taken to mean the proper effect of grace. He applied his distinction between the transcendent divine being and the communicative divine energy to the case of Christ's Transfiguration and describes the illumination surrounding Christ on Mount Tabor as the Uncreated Light of divinity. Similarly, the soul in grace is deified by uncreated grace, the Uncreated Light of the Holy Spirit illumining it. *HESYCHASM.

[T. C. O'BRIEN]

UNCTION, an obsolescent term: (1) for anointing, whether sacramental—as in the former designation of the sacrament of the anointing of the sick as extreme unction, in the ritual anointings of baptism, confirmation, and holy orders; or consecratory—as in the medieval anointing of the Holy Roman Emperor: (2) following scriptural use (2 Cor 1.21; 1 Jn 2.20, 27; Lk 4.18; Acts 10.38), a metaphor about the life of grace, referring to its inner enlightenment and strength in holding fast to the word of God. Thus unction is a term for the quality of writing or preaching that outwardly expresses an inner intensity of grace. St. Thomas Aquinas extends the metaphor by describing the attitude of the devout as an unction or anointing of Christ by tears, devotion, pure intention, praise, and thanksgiving (*In Is* 61).

[T. C. O'BRIEN]

UNDE ET MEMORES, see ANAMNESIS.

UNDERGROUND CHURCH, a movement to create a new form of ecclesial community in place of the *institutional Church. The term "underground," to which some participants object, connotes that the views and practices of groups involved in the movement are at odds with established structures, laws, conventions, and that, consequently, the existence and meetings of such groups are kept secret from ecclesiastical authorities. Participants share generally in the conviction that only by revolution, not simple, gradual adaptation within existing patterns, can there be a Church genuinely relevant to actual human conditions. Among Roman Catholics the underground movement appeared first as the expression of a desire for free liturgical experimentation. While spontaneous liturgical celebration, often at variance with church law, continues to be a mark of underground groups, their objectives have widened into an intense social concern, a desire to discard the parish system, and to change or bypass the basic authority structure of the Church. Among Protestants the underground movement is equally strong and has similar goals. Protestant underground groups have often been motivated by ecumenical and social interests contrary to policies of their denominations. There is in fact little reason to differentiate sectors of the underground movement on any denominational basis. Participants are united in an essential humanism and minimize doctrinal differences separating Christian from Christian, or even Christian from atheist. BIBLIOGRAPHY: *Underground Church* (ed. M. Boyd, 1968). *FLOATING PARISH.

[T. C. O'BRIEN]

UNDERHILL, EVELYN (1875–1941), Anglican authority on mystical theology. Brought up in an agnostic, albeit tolerant atmosphere, at the age of 32 she experienced a sudden conversion at a Catholic retreat which convinced her of the truth of Catholicism. She postponed entrance into the Church because of her fiancé whom she later married, but she resolved not to enter the Church at all when the papal encyclical, *Pascendi*, condemned Modernism with which she sympathized. In 1910 she published her book entitled *Mysticism*, which has become a classical work on the subject. About the same time she came under the influence of F. von *Hügel who led her to active membership in the C of E, then herself undertook to give private spiritual direction. She also wrote books of devout scholarship on religious experience, and under the pseudonym John Cordelier, symbolic interpretations of the stations of the cross and the mysteries of the rosary. In the later years of her life, she conducted retreats and gave lectures on theology which received great academic acclaim. Just before the outbreak of

World War II, she was an ardent pacifist. BIBLIOGRAPHY: J. T. L. James, NCE 14:389; M. Cropper, *Life of Evelyn Underhill* (1958).

[U. VOLL]

UNDERSTANDING (*intellectus*), a gift of the Holy Spirit. It can be described by analogy with the *nous* of Greek philosophy, with the qualification that it is a quality of knowledge less through conceptual judgment than through sympathy in friendship with the divine. It provides an insight within the darkness of faith into what the Christian mysteries do and do not imply both for our thinking and our conduct. Whereas belief is an assent, understanding is rather an appreciation; it complements and endows faith with a certainty and security that is a fruit of the Holy Spirit. According to St. Augustine, it is matched by the sixth Beatitude, ''Blessed are the clean of heart, for they shall see God.'' Its character appears from its opposite vices, indicated by St. Gregory, which rise from preoccupation with the flesh, namely, the blindness (*caecitas*) of mind that fails to recognize spiritual truths, and the more common and remediable obtuseness (*hebetudo*) which cannot penetrate into them. BIBLIOGRAPHY: ThAq ST (Lat-Eng v. 32, ed. T. Gilby).

[T. GILBY]

UNDOING, a psychological defense mechanism discovered by psychoanalysts by which a person tries by ritualistic gestures or behavior to disprove or ''undo'' the harm he unconsciously imagines may be caused by wishes and impulses, whether these are sexual or hostile. Operating unconsciously, it relieves vague guilt feelings. It is often associated with obsessional symptoms, and when found in a person deeply affected by religious sentiments, it may become in fact the motivation behind repetitions of formulas of prayers, genuflections, signs of the cross, etc. It probably has its roots in the magical thinking of childhood when mind and reality were not distinct, and thoughts were believed to be as efficacious as deeds.

[M. E. STOCK]

UNDSET, SIGRID (1882–1949), Norwegian novelist, daughter of a Norwegian archeologist and a Danish mother. Her early novels reflect modern life in Oslo. Her study of archeology and of Christianity in early Scandinavian countries led her to become a Roman Catholic (1925). Her two great historical novels of the Middle Ages, *Kristin Lavransdatter* a trilogy (U.S. ed. 1923–27) and *The Master of Hestviken* a tetrology (1923–36), have been considered as the most beautiful novelistic portrayal of the Catholic spirit of life ever written; they are also superb in their portrayal of medieval life and in their character creation. Later novels handle modern spiritual problems. She married in 1912 and separated from her husband in 1925. She lectured widely in the U.S. against the Nazi occupation of Norway; her son was killed in the war. In 1928 she received the Nobel prize

for literature and in 1947 was the first woman not of the nobility to receive the Grand Cross of the Order of St. Olaf. BIBLIOGRAPHY: A. H. Winsnes, *Sigrid Undset: A Study in Christian Realism* (tr. P. G. Foote, 1953).

[M. M. BARRY]

UNFORGIVABLE SINS, according to Mt 12.31, sins of blasphemy against the Holy Spirit. They are termed unforgivable, not with respect to the power and mercy of God, but because they are sins of *malice, with no mitigating element, and because they are directly contemptuous obstacles to the workings of the Holy Spirit in the soul. BIBLIOGRAPHY: ThAq ST 2a2ae, 14.3.

[T. C. O'BRIEN]

UNGUENTARIUM, antique vessel often of alabaster or faïence, used to contain ointments. The Greek unguentarium was distinguished by a narrow neck for controlling the flow of oil, a witness to the rationale of form and function of that intellectual people. The alabastron, aryballos, and ampulla were shaped in the same manner. In Christian art Mary Magdalen holds an unguentarium, in the form of a jar with lid, for the ointment with which she will anoint Christ.

[M. J. DALY]

UNIATISM, a term often used in a depreciatory sense in reference to the type of union established between certain Eastern Christian Churches or communities and the Roman Church, the methods used to bring such union about, and the subsequent development of those Churches or communities within the Catholic Church. In its pejorative sense it implies in particular a betrayal of the Eastern tradition of those communities as is apparent in the corruption of their original characteristics and in the presence of non-Eastern, mainly Latin and Western, elements. It is frequently decried as a handicap to true reunion and even to good interchurch relations.

Uniatism, however, is a complex phenomenon, which cannot be considered without regard to certain historical, canonical, liturgical, and theological aspects. The historical circumstances existing at the time of a group's entering into union with Rome were in most cases such that the group was politically dependent on a Latin Catholic power capable of exerting moral pressure in favor of the Latin case in the agreed form of reunion. Such was the situation of the Armenian and Maronite Uniates when they entered into union with Rome at the time of the Crusades, of the Italo-Greeks of Southern Italy, the Malabar Uniates of South India under the Portuguese, the Ukrainians under Poland, the Ruthenians and Romanians under Habsburg Austria. Much the same is true of certain unions effected in a non-Catholic country, but with the favor and support of a Western Catholic power (more often France), as was the case with the Bulgarian, Greek, Melkite, Syrian, and Coptic Uniates in the Turkish Empire and the Ethiopian Uniates in

Ethiopia. This uneven partnership has normally persisted and affected the further development of the community. The non-Oriental features tended to increase, while those more genuinely Oriental tended to decrease.

The Uniate community's loss of its original Eastern features seems more rapid in theology, esp. in those areas of legitimate theological difference allowed and even required by the catholic quality of the Church. Often a traditional theological position disappears almost without notice, which may be explained by the fact that reunion frequently occurs after a long period of more or less direct theological influence of the Western Church. Most notable, however, is the loss of Oriental identity in ecclesiastical discipline. Almost always, the Oriental Catholic community loses the broad autonomy it once enjoyed and is reduced to the status of a simple Latin rite diocese as far as its relations with the Holy See are concerned. Notwithstanding explicit safeguards agreed to at the time of reunion, disciplinary matters gradually become adapted to those of the Latin Church or are abandoned, as in the case of the matrimonial discipline of the clergy. The last stage in this loss of canonical identity was probably reached with the Roman codification of Oriental canon law. Ritual and liturgical features are relatively less affected, although serious departures from the original, esp. among the Ukrainians, Ruthenians, and Malabar Christians are easily discernible, and their rites can perhaps be more accurately described as new Catholic liturgical rites rather than as Catholic Byzantine or Malabar rites.

The theological and ecumenical or unionistic evaluation of Uniates is generally negative. To many, both Catholic and non-Catholic, it seems that the principle underlying the ''de-Orientalizing'' process evident in the Catholic communities of Oriental rite, is not only the superiority of the Western form of Christianity but also its normative character for church life and structure. However this principle may have been expressed, in practice it has often guided Roman policy with regard to the Christian East.

Still, there are at least two considerations that favor a more positive appraisal of Uniatism. The Uniate communities have generally come into being in times of notable decadence and internal strife within the original non-Catholic Churches. Reunion with Rome has meant, in most cases, an improvement in the religious life of the community. This naturally led them to imitate features of Western canon law, spiritual and devotional life, the training of the clergy (so essential to the further development of the community), and the wide introduction of clerical celibacy. The other factor to be considered is the objective efficiency to the Uniate body of restored communion. Communion means exchange of ecclesiastical and religious values among those who belong to the same Church. Any attempt to stop this exchange or to put obstacles in its way certainly affects the very unity of the Church. In the union of the far larger Latin Church with the smaller Uniate Churches, it is natural that the exchange should move more frequently and

abundantly from West to East than the other way about. That such has happened is clear from the degree of Latinization existing in the Oriental Catholic Churches. Those bodies whose communion with Rome has been longer appear far more deeply affected by the phenomenon. This can be said without denying that Uniatism itself is an obstacle to reunion today. However, its elimination ought not to bring with it the immediate destruction of the Eastern Catholic communities, as some Catholics would favor and as has already been accomplished by force in some Communist countries of Eastern Europe.

Beginning with Pope Leo XIII, much has been done in the Catholic Church to bring about a better balance in the East-West exchange. There exists an impressive array of documents and laws intended to safeguard the genuinely Oriental elements in the Oriental Catholic Churches. Much has also been done for the purification of Oriental liturgy and canon law. Vatican Council II in its decrees on Ecumenism and on the Eastern Catholic Churches, has also sought to thwart the corrupting inroads of Latinism and to encourage the recovery of the lost or altered Oriental elements of their tradition. Moreover, it provided a rare occasion for the Oriental Catholics to communicate to their Western Catholic brethren those Oriental elements and insights which had been hard to transmit previously. BIBLIOGRAPHY: C. Korolevskij, *L'Uniatisme,* Irénikon-Collection 5–6 (1927). See also the exchange on Uniatism between Orthodox Metropolitan Chrysostom of Myra and Melkite Abp. Elias Zoghby in *Informations Catholiques Internationales,* 256, 267, 278 (1966).

[G. ELDAROV]

UNICITY OF GOD, the divine attribute that precludes a plurality of gods. The divine unity is the unity of God as identical with his own *esse*; because God is unreceived *esse*, the possibility of a numerical plurality of subjects receiving that being is ruled out. A plurality meaning a differentiation in being would require subjects limiting the divine *esse*; a numerical plurality meaning mathematical number would require materiality incompatible with the divine, unreceivable being.

[T. C. O'BRIEN]

UNICITY OF THE CHURCH, the characteristic of the Church that follows from the unique position of Jesus Christ as the one mediator between God and man (1 Tim 2.5), and the consequent mission of the Church to preach the gospel to all men (Mt 28.19). It is to be distinguished from the *unity of the Church, i.e., the internal ecclesiastical unity that binds all Christians together in the life of Christ. The NT presents abundant evidence of the Church's unicity: Christ promised that there shall be but one fold and one shepherd (Jn 10.16); through the Eucharist the Christian participates in the one body of Christ (1 Cor 10.17); there is but one Lord, one faith, and one baptism (Eph 4.4–6). Traditional RC teaching maintains that there are both visible and invisible elements in this unicity: although the one Church of Christ is constituted by the interior action of the Holy Spirit, it is visibly united in adherence to the pope and the bps. in communion with him. Protestant theology teaches either a totally invisible unity according to which the Church is the body of those who have been saved, irrespective of their ecclesial commitments, or an invisible unity that is visibly present where the true gospel is preached and the sacraments administered. The Anglican *branch theory maintains that there are three visible divisions of the one apostolic Church: the Roman, Orthodox, and Anglican. BIBLIOGRAPHY: H. Küng, *The Church* (tr. R. and R. Ockenden, 1967) 285–296; R. Prentes, *Creation and Redemption* (tr. T. Jensen, 1967) 515–546; P. F. Chirico, NCE 14:395–396.

[T. M. MCFADDEN]

UNIFORMITY, ACTS OF, see ACTS OF UNIFORMITY.

UNIGENITUS, a bull (Sept. 8, 1713), elicited from Clement XI on the insistence of Louis XIV, after thorough examination renewing the condemnation of P. *Quesnel's *Réflexions morales,* which had already been placed on the Index in 1708. The *Unigenitus* cited as errors 101 propositions quoted verbatim (D 2400–2502). Quesnel taught that: (1) man's will necessarily obeys whichever attracts more strongly, concupiscence or grace; (2) all acts not motivated by pure charity are evil; and (3) the Church errs in condemning *Jansenism. Almost all French bishops accepted *Unigenitus;* a few refused or hedged. The Sorbonne and Parlement submitted; the Jansenists replied with contention and intrigue. Ensuing controversies split the French Church, fostered irreligion, and engendered revolution. BIBLIOGRAPHY: J. Carreyre, DTC 15.2:2061–2162; J. Thomas, *La Querelle de l' Unigenitus* (1949).

[W. DAVISH]

UNION CHURCH, a type of *community Church that begins with the merging of two (or more) existing congregations or with the organizing of a new Church on a nondenominational basis. It usually has no other affiliations and is strictly independent. Made up of people from diverse religious backgrounds, union Churches vary widely with respect to liturgy, theological complexion, and type of ministry. This kind of Church is common, but it is almost impossible to obtain statistics regarding the number of Churches and their members. When they are listed or discussed, they are usually subsumed under the categories ''community'' or ''independent.'' *INDEPENDENT CHURCHES.

UNION OF BREST, see BREST, UNION OF.

UNION OF CHRISTENDOM, see ECUMENICAL MOVEMENT.

UNION OF FLORENCE. The Council of Ferrara-Florence was the 17th Ecumenical Council of the Latin Church, but is not listed among the accepted councils of the Orthodox Eastern Churches. The Council, convoked by Pope Eugene IV with the consent of the Byzantine Emperor John VIII, was to have met in Ferrara, but because of the outbreak of the plague it was translated to Florence where it met in 1431. The Byzantine Emperor, Patriarch Joseph of Nicaea, Isadore of Kiev, Mark of Ephesus, and the layman philosopher George Scholarios represented the Greek Church. The Patriarchates of Antioch, Alexandria, and Jerusalem were represented by bps. who acted as their procurators. On the Latin side the burden of the discussions was borne by two persons, the bp. Andrew of Rhodes, O.P., the only Latin who spoke Greek, and Cardinal Giuliasco Cesarini.

The five main points separating the Catholic and Orthodox Churches were discussed, and an agreement reached. Bessarion and Isadore were won over by the Latin presentation. The Patriarch Joseph died and Mark of Ephesus had nothing with which to controvert the Latin arguments except to declare the quotations, adduced from the Fathers, to be forgeries and interpolations.

The attacking Turks were coming closer to Constantinople and the Greeks were filled with anxiety. At length, worn out by the Latin arguments, filled with worry about their homeland and heeding the Emperor's desire for union because it meant Western help (which never came) in defending Constantinople, the Greeks either agreed or, like Mark of Ephesus, remained sullenly adamant.

The Emperor did not have the decree of union proclaimed immediately upon his return to Constantinople nor did he curb the activities of Mark of Ephesus who was against the union. When the union was proclaimed in the Cathedral of the Holy Wisdom (Sophia), the church became deserted except for those who were unionizers. Thus, when the Turks attacked the city, its inhabitants were sadly divided religiously. The last Emperor, Constantine XII, died defending his capital and he died in communion with the Latins.

While the Orthodox Churches came in time to reject the union, there exists no genuine evidence of any synod or council that did so. Outside the movement toward union connected with the Synod of Brest-Litovsk in Poland (1596), one in Romania, one in Hungary, and one among the Arabic Melkites in Syria, the Union of Florence bore little fruit in the cause of the reunion because the people were not psychologically and spiritually prepared for it.

[A. WALKER]

UNION OF SOVIET SOCIALIST REPUBLICS, Communist state of E Europe and N Asia. In area it is the world's largest nation, and it ranks third in population, after China and India. The first Marxist state, it was formed by Lenin's Bolsheviks, who took power in Nov. 1917 from the parliamentary democracy formed after the overthrow earlier that year of the Russian czar. The capital was moved from Petrograd (formerly St. Petersburg; now Leningrad) to Moscow. The USSR, officially constituted in 1922, unites 15 republics: *Russia (by far the largest), Estonia, Latvia, Lithuania, Belorussia, Ukraine, Moldavia, Georgia, Armenia, Azerbaijan, Turkmen, Kazakh, Uzbek, Tadzhik, and Kirghiz. From the beginning the USSR has been governed by a party (called Communist from 1918) committed to atheism. Though it generally tolerated worship, it executed and imprisoned many church leaders, confiscated all church property, and took other measures to diminish church influence. But disestablishment of the Orthodox Church following the Revolution improved the relative position of non-Orthodox groups. In addition to Russian and Georgian Orthodox, the USSR includes Baptists, Lutherans, Catholics, Armenians, Jews, Muslims, and Buddhists. While all Churches have benefited from the lessening of repression since Stalin's death in 1953, the government has continued to propagandize against religion while forbidding the Churches to conduct schools for children or evangelize publicly. Restrictions on Jewish communal life have led many Jews to emigrate.

[T. EARLY]

UNION OF UTRECHT, the alliance of Old Catholic Churches adhering to the Convention of Utrecht. Abp. Heykamp of Utrecht summoned and chaired the Utrecht conference of 1889. It included the Old Catholic bps. and theologians from Holland, Germany, and Switzerland. Reaching complete harmony, the conference issued the Convention (Agreement) of Utrecht to effect a union of Old Catholic Churches, according to this plan: First, an assembly of bps. was established for mutual consultation, the abp. of Utrecht being chairman as *primus inter pares;* each Church is independent and regulates its own affairs according to its need; no bp. may consecrate anyone without the consent of all the bps. and without acceptance of the Convention of Utrecht by the candidate. Second, an International Old Catholic Congress was scheduled every 2 years. Third, the bps. issued the Declaration of *Utrecht containing doctrinal principles binding on Old Catholic bps. and priests; an Old Catholic is one who accepts this declaration. The conference's decisions were later accepted by the Old Catholic Church in Austria. The union was joined (1897) by Bp. A. S. Kozlowski's short-lived Polish Old Catholic Church (in the U.S.) and later by the Polish National Catholic Church. In 1908 the Old Catholic Mission in Great Britain entered, but it soon was expelled by the assembly of bps. because Bp. Mathew broke the Convention of Utrecht. The Union admitted the *Mariavites of Poland (1909) but dropped them (1925) because of the abp.'s views. Other members are the Old Catholic Church of Czechoslovakia, the Old Catholic Church of Yugoslavia, and the Polish National Catholic Church of Poland, all of which have suffered adversity since World War II. At the Old Catholic Congress in 1965 the Philippine Independent

Church was accepted by other member Churches into membership in the Union of Utrecht. BIBLIOGRAPHY: U. Küry, *Die Altkatholische Kirche* (1966); C. B. Moss, *Old Catholic Movement* (1966).

UNIONISM, in its religious usage a disparaging term with several applications. (1) The amalgamation of Lutheran and *Reformed Churches first decreed in 1817 by Friedrich Wilhelm I, King of Prussia, but not accomplished until 1833. In this policy he was advised by F. *Schleiermacher. The staunchly confessional Lutherans termed the policy unionism, criticizing its adulteration of historic confessionalism. (2) The attempt in the 19th cent. to develop an ''American Lutheranism,'' led by S. *Schmucker and aimed at closer fellowship with the Protestants, but at the expense of fidelity to the *Augsburg Confession, was denounced by opponents as unionism. As a consequence Lutheran Churches in the U.S. increasingly emphasized their proper confessional heritage. (3) In a more general sense, unionism has been used to criticize attempts at interdenominational and ecumenical cooperative efforts that disregard or dismiss doctrinal differences. *IRENICISM; *SYN - CRETISM; *ECUMENISM.

UNISTS, an alternate name for the Subunists, i.e., those in 15th-cent. Bohemia defending the practice of communion under one kind, in opposition to the *Utraquists, who insisted on communion under both kinds. *HUSSITES.

[T. C. O'BRIEN]

UNIT ORGAN, type of organ popular primarily as a cinema instrument. Developed by American and British builders, esp. Hope-Jones, its principle is that of the fullest use of a comparatively small number of ranks of pipes: one rank is extended upwards and downwards, enabling the tone to be taken from it at four different pitches.

[M. T. LEGGE]

UNITARIAN UNIVERSALIST ASSOCIATION, a religious denomination of liberal persuasion, with Churches in the U.S. and Canada. The denomination is the result of a merger, in 1961, of the American Unitarian Association (founded in 1825; incorporated in 1847) and the Universalist Church of America (initial organizational form, 1779; incorporated in 1866). The two denominations shared common concerns during the 19th cent., yet they remained separate. They drew closer together during the first half of the 20th cent., and the formation, in 1953, of a Council of Liberal Churches (Unitarian Universalist) enlarged departmental cooperation during the decade when full merger was being considered. The merged denomination continues significant traditions that were held in common by the parent movements, such as congregational polity; a programmatic creedlessness; strong social and ethical concerns; the cherishing of freedom of religious belief in a disciplined quest for truth; a deep respect for human dignity (expressed in an early rejection of the doctrine of *total depravity); a strictly humanitarian Christology; acceptance of theists, religious humanists, and agnostics in religious fellowship; and a striving for a worldwide, interfaith, religious community. The creedless character of the denomination distinguishes it from many other religious movements. Individual Churches or fellowships may have covenants or bonds of union, as long as these statements are not used as creedal tests. The association of autonomous Churches and fellowships is governed by a president, a board of trustees, and a general assembly. The constituency, which contains a high proportion of members who have come from other denominations, included, in 1975, a total of 210,648 persons affiliated and 1,019 Churches. The Unitarian Universalist Association is a member of the *International Association for Liberal Christianity and Religious Freedom (IARF); it is a member of neither the National, nor the World, Council of Churches. *UNITARIANISM; *UNIVERSALISM.

[J. C. GODBEY]

UNITARIANISM, as a theological classification, any belief that affirms the one God but rejects the Trinity of persons. Historically, Unitarians have, on biblical and rational grounds, rejected the doctrines of the Trinity, the divinity of Christ, and the *total depravity of man. Unitarianism does not have a creed. In mid-20th cent., it embraces such differing views as Christian liberalism, naturalistic theism, existentialism, and a concern for the development of a scientific theology. Contemporary Unitarians cherish as prime religious responsibilities the critical examination of religious beliefs and the relevant expression of these beliefs in areas of social responsibility.

In the Reformation era, Juan de *Valdés (c.1500–41), Bernardino *Ochino (1487–1564), and Michael *Servetus (1511–53) influenced the rise of historic Unitarianism. It developed indigenously in Poland, Transylvania, England, and the United States. The movement no longer exists in Poland, but it has had a continuing history in each of the other three countries. In Poland, an incipient division in the *Reformed Church was furthered by Italian evangelical rationalists, who came to Poland via Switzerland. After the failure of a conference to reconcile the division, those who were excluded because of their antitrinitarian views formed the Minor Reformed Church of Poland in 1565. Faustus *Socinus (1539–1604) came to Poland in 1579 and was thereafter recognized as the leader of the movement; the Polish and Lithuanian antitrinitarians adopted the name Socinians. After his death, Socinus's followers published the influential *Racovian Catechism (Polish ed., 1605; Latin ed., 1609). Mounting RC opposition to the movement led to the destruction of the Socinian school and printing press at Raków in 1638 and the complete expulsion of Socinianism from Poland by 1660 (see SOCINIANISM). Transylvanian Unitarianism also arose as a division within the Reformed Church when Francis *Dávid (1510–79) began questioning the biblical bases of the doctrine of the Trinity. *The True and False Knowledge of God,* published by Dávid and Giorgio *Blandrata, showed the influence of Servetus's writings in Transylvania. The decree of the Diet of Torda (1568) ensured religious toleration for the Unitarians, and King John Sigismund granted them legal recognition in 1571. Dávid's increasing rejection of the invocation of Christ in prayer, however, threatened to introduce an illegal "innovation," which could have caused the Unitarian movement to be deprived of legal recognition. Hence, Dávid was sentenced and died in prison. After centuries of severe persecution, Unitarianism still exists in Hungary and Romania. The four hundredth anniversary was celebrated in 1968 in Kooszvár (Cluj) and in Budapest.

Unitarianism was first maintained in England by John *Biddle (1615–62) in *XII Arguments Drawn out of the Scripture* (1647) and *A Twofold Catechism* (1654). Unitarians were excluded from the provisions of the *Toleration Act (1689) and were subject to legal penalties until 1813. Samuel *Clarke (1675–1729) and William Whiston (1667–1752) advocated an "Arian" view of Christ as a subordinate being. Theophilus *Lindsey (1723–1808) left the Anglican ministry to affirm a belief in the strict humanity of Christ. He established the first Unitarian chapel in London in 1774. The influence of Joseph *Priestly (1733–1804) and the leadership of Thomas Belsham (1750–1829) marked the ascendancy of a stress on Christ's strict humanity. The British and Foreign Unitarian Association was organized in 1825. James Martineau (1805–1900) was probably the most creative English Unitarian theologian of the 19th century. In 1926, the British and Foreign Unitarian Association merged into the General Assembly of Unitarian and Free Christian Churches.

American Unitarianism arose within New England Congregationalism as a result of the influences of *Arminianism and *antitrinitarianism. Sharp controversy developed in 1805, when Henry Ware, a liberal, became Hollis Professor of Divinity at Harvard. William Ellery *Channing (1780–1842) defended the liberals in 1815 and gave them a clear theological platform in his famous "Baltimore Sermon" of 1819. The American Unitarian Association was founded in 1825. Ralph Waldo *Emerson (1803–82) and Theodore *Parker (1810–60) introduced insights from *transcendentalists into Unitarianism and, by this influence, ensured that Unitarianism, while including a Christian orientation, cannot be limited to that alone. In the 20th cent. the rise of religious humanism has significantly modified the movement. After a period of decline, the American Unitarian Association grew under the presidencies of Frederick May Eliot and Dana McLean Greeley. A "Council of Liberal Churches (Unitarian Universalist)" was formed in 1953 to enlarge departmental cooperation between Unitarians and Universalists. A merger in 1961 resulted in the *Unitarian Universalist Association. BIBLIOGRAPHY: *Bibliotheca Fratrum Polonorum qui Unitarii Appellantur . . .* (8 v., 1656); E. M. Wilbur, *History of Unitarianism* (2 v., repr., 1965); *idem, Our Unitarian Heritage* (1953); G. H. Williams,

Radical Reformation (1962); C. Wright, *Beginnings of Unitarianism in America* (1955); *Transactions of the Unitarian Historical Society* (1916–); *Proceedings of the Unitarian Historical Society* (1925–).

[J. C. GODBEY]

UNITAS ASSOCIATION, an international organization formed in Rome in 1945, under RC auspices, to promote spiritual unity among Christians. The organization was founded by Charles Boyer, a French Jesuit, who became its first president. In spirit the Association is related to the earlier spiritual ecumenism of Abbé Couturier in France and Lewis Thomas *Wattson of the Atonement Friars in the U.S., the two men whose separate apostolates led to the establishment of the annual *Church Unity Octave, or *Week of Prayer for Christian Unity. The Association, which has affiliated groups in European countries and in Canada, sees its work as threefold: promotion of prayer for Christian unity; fostering of fraternal rapprochement between Christians of the East and the West; and exposition of the meaning of Catholicism to Protestants. Through its quarterly review, *Unitas,* published in English, French, and Italian editions, it circulates information about all aspects of the ecumenical movement.

[D. CODDINGTON]

UNITAS FRATRUM (Unity of Brethren), original name of the Bohemian Brethren, organized in 1457. Before formal organization, members used the name Fratres Legis Christi (Brethren of the Law of Christ), but to avoid being thought of as a new monastic order they changed it to simply Brethren. When organization had finally been effected, they assumed the name Unitas Fratrum, or in Czech, Jednota Bratrská. When the almost extinct Brethren became the Moravian Church through its renewal under Count *Zinzendorf, the name Unitas Fratrum was retained; it continues as the official designation of the denomination. BIBLIOGRA-PHY: E. de Schweinitz, *History of the Unitas Fratrum* (1885). *MORAVIAN CHURCH.

[J. R. WEINLICK]

UNITATIS REDINTEGRATIO, see DECREE ON ECUMENISM.

UNITED CHURCH OF CANADA (UCC), Church formed by the union (1925) of the Congregational, Methodist, and Presbyterian Churches. The history of the church chronicles a continual effort to reverse the process of fragmentation besetting the Christian community. Each of its founding communions was itself a product of reunion. The early Presbyterianism of British North America consisted of more than a dozen independent groupings, divided by national origin into Scottish, Irish, and Dutch, by differences in *polity into *free Churches and national Churches, and by a basically political dispute into *Burghers and *Anti-Burghers. To all this was added the natural divisions of geography. Canadian Methodism was likewise greatly

fragmented, the major cause being the cleavage between those congregations founded by the American *Methodist Episcopal Church and those which gave their allegiance to the nonepiscopal, Wesleyan fellowships in England. By and large the divisions within Canadian Congregationalism were geographical. The challenge to achieve effective ministry in a vast new land succeeded in reducing this multitude to essentially three major groupings through the formation of the Presbyterian Church in Canada (1875), the Methodist Church (1884), and the Congregational Union of Canada (1906).

A desire for yet greater unity had resulted in sporadic calls for interconfessional union as early as 1874, but official negotiations did not actually begin until 30 years later. By 1908, however, a Basis of Union had been agreed upon, setting forth the doctrine and polity of the proposed Church. That very year, individual congregations of the three communions, particularly in western Canada, began to effect local amalgamations on this Basis of Union and in anticipation of the united Church to come. Some 3,000 such local unions preceded the formal merging of the mother Churches. The final consummation was delayed by the outbreak of World War I and was not achieved until June 1925. Although a substantial number of Presbyterians remain separated, the merger nevertheless represented the first major union of differing traditions within Protestantism and, as such, was a significant event in the ecumenical movement. Since 1925 several additional Protestant communions have joined the UCC, the Evangelical United Brethren being the latest (1968).

The thought and life of the UCC reflect its history with its fundamental doctrine (as set forth in the 20 articles of the Basis of Union) presenting the essence of a faith common to all Reformation communions. The Bible is acknowledged as the supreme authority, but tradition is also recognized, specifically in the "great creeds of the ancient Church" and in the confessions of the *Reformed Churches. A careful balance is observed between the Presbyterians' Calvinist heritage and the *Arminianism of John *Wesley. Moreover, the Presbyterian emphasis upon loyalty to the doctrine of the Church is united with the Congregational insistence upon the individual's freedom in matters of faith. Candidates for ordination are required only to be "in essential agreement" with the stated doctrine.

Worship in the UCC is marked by the Reformation emphasis on the reading and exposition of the word of God. The regular service is composed of hymns, prayer, Scripture, and a meditation but does not routinely involve the celebration of the Lord's Supper. A deepening interest in liturgy is apparent, yet there still remains the Protestant concern for simplicity in worship. Although freedom in prayer and in the selection of Scripture is still the custom, the *Book of Common Order, adopted by the Church in 1932 as a guide for the conduct of worship, usually sets the pattern in most congregations. It is closely followed for the sacraments and special services of the Church.

The UCC recognizes only two sacraments, baptism and

the Lord's Supper, or holy communion. *Infant baptism is the normal practice and is usually administered as a congregational rite at the regular Sunday morning service. The sacrament of holy communion is dispensed a minimum of four times per year and is understood more as a eucharistic and fellowship meal than as a sacrifice, although the latter theme is also expressed in the liturgy. Marriage, confirmation, and ordination are recognized as rites of the Church but, in keeping with Reformation theology, are not regarded as sacraments.

The polity of the UCC is a synthesis of elements from its threefold heritage. Authority, as in each of the founding communions, is invested in a hierarchy of *courts rather than a hierarchy of persons. (All ministers have the same rank and differ only in office.) From Congregationalism comes the recognition of the whole congregation as the supreme local authority rather than the *session or *elders as in Presbyterianism. This authority is also greater in relation to the higher courts than in the Calvinist tradition. The next court, the *presbytery, consists of some 25 to 50 pastoral charges and is responsible for the general supervision of church life. The *Conference, composed of perhaps 10 presbyteries, comes from the Methodist tradition. It meets annually and is responsible for the placement of ministers and for the examination and ordination of candidates for the ministry. Its exercise of the former function again reflects its complex heritage. Congregations retain the right to call a minister, as in Congregational and Presbyterian practice, but the authority to confirm such appointments rests with the "settlement" committee of the Conference, thereby continuing the tradition of the Methodist "stationing" committee. The settlement committee is charged, wherever possible, to respect the wishes of ministers and congregations. The supreme court of the Church is the General Council, presided over by a moderator, who acts as titular head of the Church for the 2-year period between sessions of the Council. It alone has the authority to legislate on matters of faith and discipline. All courts, other than the congregation, have equal numbers of clergy and laity. Laymen may assume any office in the Church with the exception of Conference president, since the latter serves as the ordaining officer of the Conference. All offices of the Church, including the ministry, are open to women as well as men. The UCC is a member of the World Council of Churches and of the World Methodist Council, the Alliance of Reformed Churches, and the International Congregational Council. BIBLIOGRA-PHY: G. C. Pidgeon, *United Church of Canada* (1949); G. W. Mason, *Legislative Struggle for Church Union* (1956); J. W. Grant, *Canadian Experience of Union* (1967).

[J. C. HOFFMAN]

UNITED CHURCH OF CHRIST, denomination formed in June 1957, through the union between the General Council of Congregational Christian Churches and the *Evangelical and Reformed Churches. The United Church of Christ (UCC) has significance in the ecumenical movement in that it combines two forms of polity: *Con-

gregationalism and *Presbyterianism. It also reflects the noncreedal position that was part of the history of the two merging bodies. First steps toward union were taken in 1941; by 1944 a Basis of Union had been prepared. After the plan had been circulated within each body and independently accepted (with some resistance), a joint meeting in Cleveland, Ohio, in 1957 accomplished the union. In 1959 a *Statement of Faith was formulated at Oberlin, Ohio. Agreement was still needed on a constitution; this was reached at Philadelphia, Pa., 1961, when permanent officials also were elected. Membership in 1975 was 1,867,810, in 6,617 churches. The UCC is a member of the World and National Council of Churches, as well as the International Congregational Council and the World Alliance of Reformed Churches. Unity efforts of the Church continue by participation in the *Consultation on Church Union and through discussions with the Christian Churches (Disciples of Christ) and the *Community Churches.

The Statement of Faith represents an affirmation of agreement in broad areas of Christian teaching; it cannot be imposed as a *doctrinal standard or for subscription by local congregations or individuals. Its standing in the Church conforms to the noncreedal tradition of the Congregational, Christian, and Evangelical and Reformed Churches. Baptism and the Lord's Supper are accepted as sacraments; ordination is the setting aside by prayer and the laying on of hands for ministry in the whole Church. The autonomy of the *local church stands as a cardinal and inviolable principle. Doctrine, worship, and participation in the connectional life of the whole Church rest with the local congregation. This connectional life is maintained through associations of local churches in a region; through conferences uniting associations; and through a general synod of the whole Church, meeting biennially. The general synod, presided over by a moderator, establishes what are called "instrumentalities" of the Church, i.e., agencies for foreign and home missions, education, welfare, social action, and ecumenism. There is an executive council appointed by the general synod for current affairs of the Church. BIBLIOGRA-PHY: D. Horton, *United Church of Christ: Its Origins, Organization and Role in the World Today* (1962). *CONGRE-GATIONAL CHRISTIAN CHURCHES, NATIONAL ASSOCIATION OF.

[R. F. G. CALDER]

UNITED METHODIST CHURCH (U.S.), the 1968 union of the *Evangelical Brethren Church and the *Methodist Church; it involved more than 11 million members. Its basic ecclesiology is catholic, evangelical, and ecumenical: "The church is a community of all true believers under the Lordship of Christ. It is the redeemed and redeeming fellowship in which the Word of God is preached by men divinely called, and the Sacraments are duly administered according to Christ's own appointment. . . . The Church of Jesus Christ exists in and for the world" (*Constitution*, "Preamble"). Creedally the Church accepts the cardinal doctrines of historic Christianity, emphasizing the universality of the atonement and the freedom of every person through faith to enter the way of salvation. Its polity provides for connectional structures and an ordered ministry. Organization for mission is expressed through *conferences: general, jurisdictional, central, annual, and charge. Bishops, elders elected by jurisdictional and/or central conferences and consecrated to administer such structures, preside over annual, jurisdictional, central, and general conferences (*Plan of Union*, # 51). Order for ministry is held to be derived from the ministry of Christ: "All Christians are called to ministry and theirs is a ministry of the people of God within the community of faith and in the world" (# 301). But "there are persons, within the ministry of the baptized, who are called of God and set apart by the church for the specialized ministry of Word, Sacrament, and Order" (# 302)—namely, deacons and elders (# 307). The act of ordination includes prayers and the laying on of hands (# 310); deacons are ordained by a bp., elders by a bp. assisted by other elders in the laying on of hands. Appointment of ministers to charges is done by the bp. after consultation with district superintendents (# 59).

Christian practice stems from the tradition of an earnest and patient attempt to embody "the life of Christ" on earth. Understanding itself to be a part of the Church universal, the United Methodist Church has determined to implement the conviction that "all persons, without regard to race, color, national origin, or economic condition, shall be eligible to attend its worship services, to participate in its programs, and, when they take the appropriate vows, to be admitted to its membership in any local church in the connection. . . . No conference, or other organizational unit of the church shall be structured so as to exclude any member or any constituent body of the church because of race, color, national origin, or economic condition" (# 4). To this same end the Church has amplified the Methodist Social Creed of 1908, which was a prophetic landmark in the enunciation of Christian conviction on economic issues, into a generous and sensitized concern for the material, as well as the spiritual, welfare of all people. Thus the teaching on ministry is ordered to mean practical servanthood in every phase of human life.

At the time of the merger in 1968 the Church also took a new attitude on the use of tobacco and alcoholic beverages. No longer are ministers required to take an oath of total abstinence or agree to shun the use of tobacco, as in the former Methodist Church. Instead, ministers are asked "to make a complete dedication of themselves to the highest ideals of the Christian life . . . and to this end agree to exercise responsible self control by personal habits conducive to bodily health, mental and emotional maturity, social responsibility, and growth in grace and the knowledge and love of God." A footnote in the *Discipline* points out that "the changes . . . do not relax the traditional view concerning the use of tobacco and beverage alcohol . . . . rather they call for higher standards of self discipline . . ." At the General Conference of 1972—4 years after union—a Com-

mission on Doctrine and Doctrinal Standards presented a report that was accepted. It stressed that the Articles of Religion of the former Methodist Church and the Confession of Faith of the former Evangelical United Brethren Church "are not to be regarded as positive, juridical norms for doctrine, demanding unqualified assent on pain of excommunication." Rather the Articles of Religion and the Confession, together with John Wesley's *Standard Sermons* and *Explanatory Notes Upon the New Testament* are landmark documents and "we should interpret them . . . to appropriate the contributions of our Christian past even as we also stretch forward toward the Christian future." Guidelines for interpretation are found in four sources: Scripture, tradition, experience, and reason. "The United Methodist Church expects all its members to accept the challenge of responsible theological reflection." BIBLIOGRAPHY: *Plan of Union of the Methodist Church and the Evangelical United Brethren Church* (1967); *Book of Discipline of the United Methodist Church* (1968).

[A. C. CORE]

UNITED NATIONS (UN), an international organization established to promote world peace and maintain principles of international law and justice. It embraces efforts to solve international disputes, and to protect human rights. Headquarters are in New York City, with offices in Geneva, Switzerland, and other areas of the world. After a series of preliminary steps, the UN was formally established after the San Francisco Conference of 1945. All nations willing to conform to the UN Charter are eligible for membership. Key provisions of the Charter affirm equal sovereignty of nations; the right of individual nations to maintain their own national concerns without outside interference; peaceful settlement of international disputes; observance of sanctions against nations who violate the principles laid down by the Charter; condemnation of the use of force. The two crucial organs of the UN are the General Assembly and the Security Council. The General Assembly, composed of representatives of all member nations, is the principal deliberative body. It has wide powers but may not make recommendations on matters before the Security Council except where lack of concurrence of permanent members on the Security Council makes peace action impossible. The Security Council is made up of five permanent members (China, France, the Soviet Union, United Kingdom, and the U.S.) and six members elected every 2 years. The Council is the executive arm of the UN and its principal agent for keeping the peace. Its actions depend on unanimity among the permanent members. The chief executive officer of the UN is the Secretary General, elected by the General Assembly for a five-year term. He is empowered to call attention to threats to international peace. One momentous action of the General Assembly was the 1948 Universal Declaration of Human Rights affirming basic human rights based on dignity and equality. The Vatican maintains a permanent observer of the UN; in 1965 Paul VI addressed the General Assembly in the cause of world peace.

The UN Educational, Scientific and Cultural Organization, UNESCO, established in 1946, has a Basic Program which has developed major projects in education and cultural activity. Examples are promotion of teacher preparation in order to expand elementary education and participation in international scientific research. The Program of Assistance to Developing Countries pursues its goal through conferences, regional centers, special projects, technical assistance, and publications. A third program fosters cooperation among nations through conventions and action. Since 1952 the Holy See has had a permanent office for liaison with UNESCO.

United Nations Children's Fund (UNICEF) was set up in 1946 to care for children who were victims of war in Europe. In 1950 the purpose was enlarged to meet the needs of children everywhere, but particularly in underdeveloped countries. UNICEF enlists support from many nongovernmental organizations, a number of them Catholic.

The United Nations Conference on Trade and Development (UNTAD) is an increasingly important force working on behalf of the developing nations.

[J. R. AHERNE]

UNITED NATIONS CHILDREN'S FUND (UNICEF),

a specialized agency of the UN. It grew out of the UN International Children's Emergency Fund created in 1946 to deal with war-related problems. In 1953 it became a permanent body under its present name but retained its UNICEF trademark. Its area of concern became the eradication of endemic diseases affecting children in primitive areas; it conducted highly successful campaigns against tuberculosis, yaws, and trachoma. In cooperation with the countries where it operated, the Fund formulated programs aiming to educate adults in aspects of child care such as birth assistance, nutrition, day care centers, and improved schooling.

[R. H. SCHMANDT]

UNITED NATIONS EDUCATIONAL, SCIENTIFIC AND CULTURAL ORGANIZATION (UNESCO),

intergovernmental organization related to the United Nations but operating under its own charter and with its own bureaucracy and budget. UNESCO's purpose is to promote peace by "collaboration among nations through education, science, and culture." Membership is separate from the UN but most UN states also join UNESCO. Its principal organ is a biennial general conference. An executive board elected for 4–year terms under a director general, with staff headquarters in Paris, administers the programs endorsed by the Conference. Each member nation is obligated to maintain a commission or cooperating body to serve as a liaison between UNESCO and its own related national groups. Traditionally free of political controversy, UNESCO experienced unusual problems in 1976 when its Arab state members attempted to expel Israel and exclude its citizens from participation in international conferences. Education, formal and vocational, has been the major area of UNESCO concern, chiefly in the underdeveloped parts of the world. It has set as a goal the elimination of illiteracy from the world and to that end it has promoted teacher training, expansion of school systems, development of libraries and bookmobiles, the production of books and other forms of reading matter, and numerous vocational institutes. UNESCO does not engage in scientific research but it encourages and cosponsors conferences for the dissemination of data and the examination of problems of worldwide significance. It has promoted ambitious programs of cooperative study in geophysics, oceanography, water resources, agriculture, earthquakes, atomic energy, and environment. The RC Church maintains an International Catholic Coordinating Center at UNESCO.

[R. H. SCHMANDT]

UNITED PRESBYTERIAN CHURCH IN THE U.S.A.,

a denomination formed as a result of a union between the United Presbyterian Church of North America and the Presbyterian Church in the U.S.A. in 1958. The first, the smaller of the two bodies, was formed in 1858 by a union of two types of Scottish Presbyterianism, the Covenanters and the Free Church of Scotland, members of which had immigrated to America. While this denomination attempted to preserve such practices as *closed communion and Psalm singing, its Presbyterianism gradually became more and more American, making union with the larger body possible.

The older and larger body of Presbyterians, with predominantly English, Scottish, and Irish roots, along with some continental influence, was organized in its first *presbytery in 1706, its first synod in 1716, and in its *general assembly in 1789. The denomination has accepted under various subscription formulas the *Westminster Confession and Westminster Catechisms as *doctrinal standards, a Presbyterian form of government involving government by elders in representative *judicatories (beginning with the session of the local congregation), and the two sacraments of the Lord's Supper and baptism, including the baptism of infants. In worship, the denomination was influenced in the past by the Puritan and revivalistic traditions. By the mid-19th cent. the Church began to draw upon the richness of the *Reformed liturgical tradition, and since 1906 it has used a *Book of Common Worship. The work of the denomination between meetings of judicatories has been done by boards, which are now four in number and are known as the Board of Christian Education, the Board of Home Missions, the Commission on Ecumenical Mission and Relations, and the Board of Pensions. The executives of the denomination, including the *moderators and *stated clerks of the various judicatories, have a functional, not sacerdotal, status.

The Church is committed in its ecclesiology to the ecumenical movement. Its own history has been marked by division and then often by reunion, e.g., the "New Side" and "Old Side" (1741–58), the "New School" and "Old

School'' (1838–69), and the Cumberland division, partially healed in 1906. The ''North'' and ''South'' division of 1861 has not been healed (see PRESBYTERIAN CHURCH IN THE U.S.A.). The denomination has been a strong supporter of and a participant in the World Alliance of Reformed Churches, the International Missionary Council, the World Council of Churches, the Federal Council of Churches, and the National Council of Churches. In recent years it has engaged in conversations with Lutherans and Roman Catholics, and has been one of the leading promoters of the *Consultation on Church Union.

The United Presbyterian Church has been concerned with problems of the social order. Its members were deeply involved, e.g., in the movement for American independence, the antislavery cause, and the *Social Gospel, although Presbyterians have also been a strong conservative force in American life. Recently the denomination has stimulated discussion of Church-State relations, civil rights, the Vietnam war, and international affairs involving rich nations and poor nations of the world. After the union of the two denominations (1958), Presbyterians adopted a new confessional position in a Book of Confessions that still included the Westminster Confession and the *Confession of 1967. This new confession emphasizes God's reconciling work, man's ministry of reconciliation, and the fulfillment of reconciliation. In this Confession the Church deals with the implications of reconciliation for the problems of war, race, poverty, and sex in modern life. The most aggressive Presbyterian body in America, the United Presbyterian Church numbers about 8,732 (1975), congregations, 2,908,958 communing members. BIBLIOGRAPHY: L. Trinterud, *Forming of an American Tradition* (1949); L. Loetscher, *Broadening Church* (1954).

[J. H. SMYLIE]

UNITED PRESBYTERIAN CHURCH IN THE U.S.A., CONFESSION OF 1967 OF, see CONFESSION OF 1967 (UNITED PRESBYTERIAN CHURCH IN THE U.S.A.).

UNITED STATES, MARONITE CHURCH IN, see MARONITE CHURCH IN THE UNITED STATES.

UNITED STATES CATHOLIC CONFERENCE, INC. (USCC), a corporation founded after Vatican Council II as the executive agency of the National Conference of Catholic Bishops. Its purposes are ''to unify, coordinate, encourage, promote and carry on all Catholic activities in the United States; to organize and conduct religious, charitable and social welfare at home and abroad; to aid in education; to care for immigrants and generally to enter into and promote, by education, publication and direction, the objects of its being.'' The successor to the National Catholic Welfare Conference, USCC has a general secretariat and three major departments: education, communication, and social development and world peace. Departments are headed by an episcopal chairman and members both episcopal and non-episcopal. Each department is administered

by a secretary, under the supervision of the general secretary. The U.S. Bishop's Advisory Council of 60 drawn from priests, religious, and laity of the U.S. assists the USCC administrative board.

[J. R. AHERNE]

UNITED STATES CATHOLIC MISSION COUNCIL, successor to the Mission Secretariat, an agency founded by the National Conference of Catholic Bishops in 1969, for coordination of missionary interests of the American Church. The executive board is made up of representatives from the five committees that constitute the Council, the NCCB, the Conference of Major Superiors of Men, the Leadership Conference of Women Religious, the National Council of Catholic Laity, and the pontifical mission aid societies. The Council fosters the missionary activity of the Church in keeping with the direction given by Vatican Council II, and specifically through educational and publicity programs on missions, missiological studies, missionary formation programs, and ecumenical liaison with other Christian missionary bodies. The headquarters are in Washington, D.C.

[T. C. O'BRIEN]

UNITED SYNAGOGUES OF AMERICA, an association of synagogues of the Conservative branch of Judaism. Founded in 1913 by Solomon Schechter, it grew from 22 congregations to over 800. In 1918 Mrs. Solomon Schechter founded the National Women's League. Later, the National Federation of Jewish Men's Clubs was established, as well as the United Synagogue Youth, and *Atid* for people of college age. The United Synagogue Commission on Education publishes textbooks for the religious schools and sets standards and curricula for Conservative schools. It operates the National Academy for Adult Jewish Studies and promotes the development of an adult education program. Two publications, *Guide to Standards for Congregational Life* (1952) and *Statement of Standards for Synagogue Practice* (1959), became binding on member congregations. A commission on Social Action brings principles of Judaism to the social question. In 1959 the United Synagogue organized the World Council of Synagogues comprising representatives from 22 countries.

[J. R. AHERNE]

UNITIVE WAY, third of the three states in the process and progress of charity or Christian perfection, the first two being the purgative way and the illuminative way (way of purgation and way of enlightenment). The three stages traditionally so named designate the degrees of charity's intensification; since charity is essentially union with God, the highest stage takes the name ''unitive'' as marked by this union par excellence. Characteristic of the spiritual life of those who have reached the unitive way are virtues practiced heroically, intense operation of the gifts of the Holy Spirit, a kind of habitual and more passive submission to the control of the Holy Spirit, passive purification of the soul, prayer of union, with the dominance of the gift of wisdom. The typology of the three ways is, of course, an abstraction: concretely, elements of the three occur in each, and the spiritual life of each person will have its own patterns and individuality.

[T. C. O'BRIEN]

UNITY, one of the most traditionally stated characteristics of the Church. It has been approached in different ways and for different purposes throughout the centuries. In the NT literature, the Gospel of John reflects the teaching of Jesus that he is the one shepherd of the one fold (Jn 10.11) and his prayer that all his followers will be one as he and the Father are one (Jn 17.20–21). Other NT passages list some of the elements pertaining to the unity of the community: one God and Father of all, one Lord, Spirit, faith, baptism (Eph 4.3–6), or the teaching of the Apostles, common life, the breaking of the bread, and prayer (Acts 2.42–46). Unity basically characterizes the new common life in Christ, the gift received from the Father to be lived in the Spirit, and variously acknowledged and expressed by the local communities of believers.

As the many different forms of the early Christian creeds expressed belief in the one God and his one only Son, they also testified to the Church as one. In the formulation of the Nicene Creed, it is one, holy, catholic, and apostolic (cf. D 1–76). Unity was thus a vital property or dimension in the Church's self-understanding, professed by faith and asserted dogmatically.

Following the great schisms and divisions in the Church in the East and West, apologists in the 16th and 17th cent. viewed unity and other characteristics of the Church variously as signs, marks, notes, demonstrations, etc., of the true Church. Unity as a note of the Church was conceived as a positive absolute, e.g., the Catholic Church alone is one; or as a negative absolute, e.g., the one true Church is not the visible Church; or as a matter of comparison, e.g., the Roman Catholic Church is more perfectly one than other communions.

With the growth of the ecumenical movement in modern times, what has been foremost in men's minds is the lack of unity between the Churches and the disastrous consequences this situation brings on all Christians. Unity in the ecumenical movement is recognized both as a gift already received by the Church, essential to its nature, and as a goal, i.e., a task yet to be fulfilled and manifested responsibly. In clarifying the relationship between the one Church and the Churches, it has generally been acknowledged that unity is neither uniformity nor bureaucratic unification, that one Church with diversity is not to be a superchurch, and that unity means joint service and mission as much as uniting existing institutional bodies.

The ultimate foundation is in God himself. For Christians that unity has been made known through the one Lord, Jesus Christ, and is lived in the one Spirit who animates the body of believers in Christ, the Church. BIBLIOGRAPHY: *History of the Ecumenical Movement* (eds. R. Rouse and S. C. Neill, 2d ed., 1967); G. Thils, *Histoire doctrinale du mouvement oecuménique* (2d ed., 1963); *idem*, "Marks of the Church (Properties)," NCE 9:240–241; *idem*, "Unity of the Church," NCE 14:450–451.

[L. B. GUILLOT]

UNITY OCTAVE, ordinary way of referring to what is formally entitled the *Week of Prayer for Christian Unity, an annual period of prayer for Christian unity, Jan. 18–25, inaugurated by Lewis Thomas *Wattson. *WEEK OF PRAYER FOR CHRISTIAN UNITY.

[T. C. O'BRIEN]

UNITY OF FAITH, an expression that may refer to the unity of the act of faith in the individual believer, or it may refer to the socio-religious unity of a body of believers. It may also refer in both senses to the unity of the believer(s) with the object of belief. Neither are major world religions nor Catholicism and Protestantism among them agreed in the analytic understanding of the nature of faith and the norms of right expression (orthodoxy) of faith. Consequently, many contemporary theologians and scholars of comparative religion have adapted a functional approach to the understanding of the nature of faith as it operates within different religious groups and within each man, whether such be expressly theistic, professing an explicit belief, or not.

In the more traditional, ontological understanding of faith, to believe is to see with the eyes of God, to share in God's view of himself. Faith is a supernatural gift, lifting man above himself. In the act of faith, the finite is united with the infinite. Human words, e.g., preaching, and various media, e.g., sacraments, serve to incarnate the divine light and life grasped by faith. Because faith is social and a unity of believers is constituted or expressed through the adherence to and use of such language and sacramental media, the matter of teaching authority and orthodoxy, in word and action, takes on a special importance in any religious tradition.

For Roman Catholics, the unity of faith is a supernatural bond uniting all the faithful who accept divine revelation. Fundamentally, this is mediated through entrance into the body of believers with the sacrament of baptism. In this tradition, however, only those persons who accept the RC Church and its teaching authority and who are able to celebrate the Eucharist in union with a bp. in apostolic succession are considered fully united in faith.

In reaction to this emphasis on human teaching authority and the necessity of sacramental media, the Protestant tradition has emphasized the quality of faith as gift (*sola gratia, sola fides*) and the transcendence of God as the giver and object of belief. Consequently, the invisible unity of believers has often received greater stress than their visible unity and the social expressions of such unity, e.g., creeds and rites.

Medieval scholastic theology, mainly Thomistic, and Catholicism from the time of the Counter Reformation have accented the qualities of faith as an intellectual virtue. The analysis of faith tended to be an objectivistic delineation of the parts of the *preambula fidei* and faith itself, the intellect, will, and emotions, the objects of faith (*fides quae*) and motivating forces of faith (*fides qua creditur*). Doctrines, the "deposit" of faith, and the absoluteness of the truth to be believed on the strength of the one revealing it were emphasized in this intellectualist approach.

Protestantism and more recent Catholic theology have balanced this view with attention to the personal and wholistic qualities of faith. All the dynamics of personal psychological life, including tensions, inner conflicts, and doubts are part of the experience and expression of faith. This is true not only of the individual but of the social body. Unity of faith does not eliminate personal and social differences, nor is uniformity of expression in every respect a condition of its healthy existence.

The union of the believer and the object of his belief is also more than an act of intellect. It is a personal-social reality, dynamic and wholistic. In the Christian tradition, faith is communion with a personal loving God as well as adhesion to truths revealed by him.

In all the types and expressions of faith in different religious traditions, there is an underlying unity: the movement of man as an intelligent social being, incomplete and seeking fulfillment, searching for, grasping, and surrendering himself to that which is ultimate, personal or no, theistic or no, for him. Faith is not some kind of special knowledge which cannot be proved, or for which there is no evidence. It is not simply the will to believe. Nor is it to be identified totally with any one of its many expressions. It is the concern for, orientation towards, and communion with that which is ultimate for man, individually and socially. BIBLIOGRAPHY: P. F. Chirico, NCE 14:450–451; M. D. Chenu, *Faith and Theology* (1968); P. Tillich, *Dynamics of Faith* (1957).

[L. B. GUILLOT]

UNITY OF THE BRETHREN, a denomination of some 32 congregations and 6,000 members, organized at Granger, Tex., in 1903 by Czech immigrants whose ancestors had belonged to the *Unitas Fratrum. In Europe the same people had more recently belonged to Lutheran and *Reformed Churches. Originally called the Evangelical Unity of Czech-Moravian Brethren of North America, the Church adopted the shorter name in 1959. The group tends to identify with the Presbyterian tradition, but because of a common *Hussite heritage is also in close fraternal relations with the *Moravian Church. Most of its ministers have studied either at Austin Presbyterian Theological Seminary or at Moravian Theological Seminary. BIBLIOGRAPHY: J. Barton, *Texas Brethren* (1949).

[J. R. WEINLICK]

UNITY OF THE CHURCH, together with holiness, catholicity, and apostolicity, one of the attributes predicated of the Church in the Nicene Creed: "I believe in one, holy, catholic, and apostolic Church." The Church is one because Christ is one. Therefore, she is "eager to maintain the unity of the Spirit in the bond of peace. There is one body and one Spirit, just as you were called to the one hope that belongs to your call, one Lord, one faith, one baptism, one God and Father of us all, who is above all and through all and in all" (Eph 4.3–6). The threat of division or *schism in the Church is therefore countered with the rhetorical question "Is Christ divided?" (1 Cor 1.13.) If he is not, then neither should his Church be. Christ is not only the sign and the model of the unity of the Church; he is also its foundation and its source. Whatever other factors may be at work in the establishment and preservation of church unity, it is the common bond of allegiance to his lordship that is, in the Holy Spirit, the tie that binds Christians together within the fellowship of the Church. Yet the NT makes it clear that this allegiance is no simple emotion of personal loyalty but an obedience to a common body of truth as revealed in Christ. Both the narratives in the Acts of the Apostles and the exhortations in the Epistles describe the unity of the Church as a unity in doctrine. The most nearly complete statement of Christian doctrine in the NT, the Epistle to the Romans, warns in its concluding paragraphs (Rom 16.17): "I appeal to you, brethren, to take note of those who create dissensions and difficulties, in opposition to the doctrine which you have been taught; avoid them." Unity in Christ is therefore unity in teaching. The term *heresy is used in the NT primarily for the party-spirit that creates divisions within the Church, but its specific application by the Fathers to the false teaching that has this effect is a logical development of this usage.

Unity in doctrine has as its corollary a unity in church life and structure. Christians of various traditions are not in agreement about the necessity and the proper form of such unity. Roman Catholicism maintains that the unity of the Church is both expressed and achieved through unity with the See of Peter, while both Eastern Orthodox and Protestant theologians assert that the Church is one even if it does not owe fealty to a single visible head. In some forms of Protestant ecclesiology this assertion has taken the form of the doctrine of the Church as essentially invisible; the evident disunity, error, and infidelity of the visible empirical Church do not vitiate the true unity, which can be seen only by faith (see INVISIBLE CHURCH). Even the RC position, moreover, is less monolithic than it appears to be; for it also postulates the existence of those who, while not externally affiliated with the Roman Catholic Church, are already one with it in faith, hope, and love. Thus the full scope of the Church's unity is, through baptism, wider than its institutional boundaries (see Vat II ConstCh 13–15). As the reference to baptism suggests, the sacraments occupy a special place in the theological understanding of unity. Baptism is the rite of initiation into the Church; therefore, it is also the source and the sign of its unity: "one Lord, one faith, one baptism." But it is esp. the Eucharist that functions as a force to unite believers. In the exposition of its meaning in 1 Cor, ch. 10–12, the Eucharist is seen as the most intimate and meaningful articulation of oneness in Christ. The relation of the Eucharist to church unity is, however, two-directional. For while it is theologically sound to describe the Eucharist as an activity that fosters true unity, there is also a measure of unity that must be present before Christians share in the Eucharist. The necessity of this is the reason for the anomalous situation arising, esp. in ecumenical relations, that Christians may find themselves united in everything except the sacrament that is intended to unite them, which thus becomes a divisive force (see INTERCOMMUNION).

Counterbalancing this emphasis upon unity in doctrine and in structure is the recognition of the inevitable variety that is evident throughout the Church. From the very beginning there have been differences in forms of worship between various regions, due in part to linguistic peculiarities. Church structure likewise manifests both development and diversity, even when the unity of visible Christendom has been preserved. Nor is the area of doctrine a place where unity is tantamount to uniformity; already in the NT it is possible to speak of a Pauline theology or a Johannine theology, beneath and beyond the unity in the doctrine of the gospel. The relation between the unity of the Church and such diversities has become esp. important since the growth of the *ecumenical movement, which has compelled the Churches and their theologians to ask all the ecclesiological questions in a new way and with a new urgency. BIBLIOGRAPHY: A. C. Outler, *Christian Tradition and the Unity We Seek* (1957); *History of the Ecumenical Movement 1517–1948* (eds. R. Rouse and S. C. Neill, 2d ed., 1967); J. Pelikan, *Riddle of Roman Catholicism* (1959).

[J. PELIKAN]

UNITY SCHOOL OF CHRISTIANITY, one of the largest and most influential of the *New Thought groups. It was founded by Charles and Myrtle (Page) *Fillmore in 1887 at Kansas City, Mo., although the Unity School of Practical Christianity, the local Kansas City center, was not chartered until 1903 and the Unity School of Christianity was incorporated only in 1914. During a residence in Pueblo, Colo., the Fillmores had come to know Emma Curtis Hopkins, who was also instrumental in the development of the *Church of Divine Science. They had long been building up an eclectic theology and had taken more than 40 courses from different New Thought centers. In 1889 the Fillmores began the magazine *Modern Thought,* which became *Unity* in 1891 and gave its name to their movement. Originally, Unity teachings were offered to members of any or no denomination, without any effort to develop a membership or denominational organization. Its earliest function, Silent Unity, is a worldwide prayer movement, to which those in need may send a request for prayer. Through Silent Unity, a counseling service is also available to anyone who writes for help. Silent Unity has been particularly devoted to requests for healing. Unity has many close affinities to both Christian Science and the wider New Thought movement.

While accepting many of the doctrines of traditional Christianity, Unity interprets them in its own way, harmonizing them with its commitment to reincarnation and the regeneration of the body by successive rebirths. God is thought of as impersonal Life, Mind, and Spirit. In the attribute of Mind is the meeting ground of God and man. God is immanent and is dwelling within his creatures. Unity teaches the doctrine of the Trinity, however, and the divinity of Jesus Christ, but also sees earlier incarnations of Jesus in the prophets and lawgivers of the OT. The significance of the Cross is the overcoming of mortal beliefs that hold us thrall to disease, sin, and death; salvation consists in the recognition of our sinlessness and incorruptibility. The promise of eternal life is seen as literal immortality. Both are attained by breaking out of the cycle of births and reaching the level where the true spiritual body replaces the physical body and man puts on Jesus Christ in a new life. Unity stresses the Bible and encourages its reading but often understands the text in an allegorical sense. As in Christian Science, health is considered the natural state of man, and healing is by affirming health in the body. Affirmation, rather than belief, is the means of developing Christ-consciousness in the individual, who is also counseled to strive for absolute sinlessness and to turn away from carnality. While not demanding compliance of its followers, Unity definitely discourages sexual intercourse, allowing the use of sex only for procreation, if at all, and urges abstention from meat, tobacco, drugs, and intoxicants as well. The emphasis in Unity is not negative, but on the positive influence of religion as a constant factor in daily life. The adoption of a creedal statement in 1921 and the opening of Unity Training School for ministers in 1930 indicated the beginning of Unity's development as a separate denomination, but its influence is much wider than its own local Unity Centers or their membership.

[R. K. MacMASTER]

UNIVERSAL, that which is common to many existents. Putting aside the rather special notion of the universal cause, a cause capable of specifically different effects, there are two important modes of universality, often insufficiently distinguished. The first is that of that nature which is common to many individuals. The second is that concept by which many are understood. Since the time of the Greek philosophers the status of both the common nature and the universal concept by which it is understood have been controverted. There have been two major problems, one ontological and one epistemological, corresponding to the two modes of universality. The ontological problem is that of determining the exact relation between the individual existent and the common nature which it shares with other existents of the same kind. The epistemological difficulty is seeing the precise manner in which scientific knowledge, being both universal and necessary, could be a knowledge of the changing and singular existent of experience.

The problem of universals, receiving particularly penetrating analyses in medieval scholasticism, has seen three major solutions competing throughout the history of thought. Two positions, ultrarealism and antirealism, are polar opposites. Plato was the definitive ultrarealist. For him, only the common nature, or form, is truly real; the changing singular is left with but a shadowy existence, participating, in his terminology, in the reality of the form. The form itself, existing independently of the singulars, beyond space and time, is that which is the object of scientific knowledge. The singular is the object of opinion. In spite of Aristotle's criticism to the effect that the Platonic notion of participation was but metaphorical and that a knowledge of the forms would in no way yield a knowledge of the existents of experience, Platonic ultrarealism has survived and even prospered. From St. Augustine, Boethius, Joannes Scotus Eriugena, William of Champeaux, and John Duns Scotus to Hegel and Alfred North Whitehead, theoreticians have defended the objective reality of universals. Nominalistic and conceptualistic antirealism deny real universality. For the former, only words have universality; for conceptualism, universal terms do refer to universal concepts, but to this universality there corresponds nothing in reality. Only individuals, or bare particulars, enjoy real existence. Thus, while ultrarealism jeopardized the reality of the singulars, antirealism can hardly hope to explain the common natures of things; much less can it provide a solid foundation for scientific knowledge. This strain of thought became immensely influential in the late Middle Ages, with William of Ockham as its most notable representative, continued strong in modern philosophy, largely through the influence of John Locke, David Hume, and Immanuel Kant, and dominates Anglo-American philosophy of the 20th cent. in the form of linguistic analysis.

The middle position, that of moderate realism, attempts to safeguard both the singular existent and the common nature by avoiding both extremes. Aristotle was the major proponent of moderate realism. He thought the primary existents to be the concrete singulars but that these primary existents provide a real basis for the universality of concepts. The form or essence common to many singulars is not in itself individuated, but is individuated by its existence in matter. By virtue of its immateriality, the human intellect is able to derive the universal from the singulars through abstraction. The bases of the Aristotelian position have been adopted by St. Thomas Aquinas, following St. Albertus Magnus, and by the Thomistic tradition since then. In this way it maintains a presence now. But it is also true that the position of moderate realism is sometimes rediscovered independently.

[R. E. HENNESSEY]

UNIVERSALIS ECCLESIAE, the bull of Julius II (July 28, 1508) conferring on the rulers of Castile and León the right to present candidates for offices and benefices in cathedrals, major (collegiate) churches, and monasteries; thus part of the history of the *patronato real*.

UNIVERSALISM, the doctrine affirming the ultimate salvation of all men (see APOCATASTASIS). This view has tradi-

tionally been grounded on a doctrine of God that stresses divine love and divine desire to bring all men to holiness and happiness. Modern Universalism, however, includes both theistic and nontheistic views. Clement of Alexandria, Origen, and John Scotus Erigena were earlier advocates of universalist doctrines. Universalism developed greater influence in the modern era. Gerrard *Winstanley, Samuel Richardson, and Jane Lead were early influential English writers. Both English and American Universalists were strongly influenced by John William Petersen, George Klein-Nicolai (pseudonym, Paul Siegvolck), John David Schaeffer, Christopher Schuetz, and Ferdinand Oliver Petitpierre. James Relly (1720–78) left George *Whitefield in 1750 to proclaim Universalism. Relly's treatise, *Union* (1759), argued thus: since all souls (not only the elect) were in an indissoluble union with Christ, Christ was thereby guilty of the sins of the race; Christ was punished, therefore there is no more punishment. John Murray (1741–1815), Relly's disciple, brought this theology from England to America in 1770. He became the pastor of a Universalist congregation in Gloucester, Mass., which dedicated its church in 1780. George de Benneville (1703–93) came in 1741 from Germany to Pennsylvania, where he gave personal leadership to a variety of groups that espoused universalist doctrines (e.g., Schwenkfelders, Quakers, mystics). Many persons in these groups had been influenced by Klein-Nicolai's *Everlasting Gospel*, Schuetz's *Golden Rose*, and Schaeffer's *Everlasting Gospel*. Charles *Chauncy, pastor of the First Congregationalist Church in Boston, published his influential *The Salvation of All Men* in 1784. Elhanan Winchester (1751–97) asserted the finite, future punishment of sinners and the eventual salvation of the race in his *Dialogues on the Universal Restoration* (1788). Hosea *Ballou became the most important leader of early American Universalism, primarily through his *A Treatise on Atonement* (1805), in which he asserted that the atonement was moral, not legal, in nature. As a determinist, Ballou denied that man can resist God's loving will to save all men. He explicitly rejected the doctrine of future punishments. In his treatise, Ballou also asserted that Christ was human and not divine.

The early organizational pattern of American Universalism was the development of state or regional conventions. In 1803, the New England ministers met at Winchester, N.H., to adopt a general statement of agreement, the *Winchester Profession of Belief. The New England Convention went through several changes before it became the Universalist General Convention in 1866. In the interim some believers in future punishment temporarily seceded (1831–41) to form the Massachusetts Association of Universal Restorationists. In 1942 the name of the national movement was changed to the Universalist Church of America, which merged with the American Unitarian Association in 1961 to form the *Unitarian Universalist Association. Clarence Skinner (1881–1949) was the leading Universalist theologian in the 20th century. BIBLIOGRAPHY: R. Eddy, *Universalism in America* (2 v., 1884–86); J. H.

Allen and R. Eddy, *History of the Unitarians and Universalists in the United States* (American Church History Series, v. 10, 1894).

[J. C. GODBEY]

UNIVERSALIST CHURCH OF AMERICA, see UNITARIAN UNIVERSALIST ASSOCIATION; UNIVERSALISM.

UNKEI (d.1223), famous Japanese sculptor, carving the thousand-armed Kannon (1164), Kyoto. His greatest works are in the Tōdaiji and Kōfukuji in Nara. Two gigantic fierce guardian figures at the South Gate of the Tōdaiji made by U. and Kaikei evidence the vitality of the period. U. executed imaginary portrait statues of 5th-cent. Buddhist theologians: Mujaku (Kōfukuji, Nara), and Seshin, the realism permeated by gentle, serene, contained spiritual essence.

[M. J. DALY]

UNLEAVENED BREAD (IN THE BIBLE), the distinctive food of the agricultural feast of thanksgiving at the beginning of the harvest. It is the name of the feast as well as the food—in Hebrew, *mazzoth*; in Greek, *azyma*. It was the universal custom for the settled peoples of the Mediterranean and the Near East to mark the beginning of the harvest, when the first green blades appear, with such a feast. The Canaanites probably introduced Israel to the tradition. The ritual observance linked to the feast had a powerful simplicity. The rhythm of seasons with their recurring cycle of fertility from seed time to harvest was never taken for granted but inspired a fundamental awe. The first green sprouts from the earth in the spring were received as coming directly from the deity and must be offered to the deity in thanksgiving before man can use the remainder. The Feast of Unleavened Bread was the first of the three great agricultural feasts of the year and was celebrated in the first month of the year (springtime). Its distinctive observance was the complete abstention from the use of leaven for a week. The cakes (bread) to be eaten were to be made entirely from the first shoots of grain of the new spring. Any leaven would be foreign and profane and therefore a kind of impurity. At an early date the feast was combined with the pastoral feast of Passover, which involved the firstborn of herd and flock. This combined feast acquired a historical significance, celebrating the deliverance of Israel from slavery in Egypt. In some ancient biblical texts, the Feast of Unleavened Bread is given this historical meaning even without mention of the concurrent feast of Passover. As the Jewish tradition of worship evolved, *mazzoth* became a subordinate part of the celebration of Passover.

[E. J. DILLON]

UNNI OF HAMBURG, ST. (d. 936), a monk of Corvey, consecrated by King Conrad in 918. In an area and at a time when paganism and Christianity were contending for the favor of Slavs, Hungarians, and Northmen, U., with the aid of the pagan Harald Bluetooth, and Emperor Henry I carried Christianity northward. BIBLIOGRAPHY: AS October

9:373–396; G. Spahr, NCE 14:472–473; E. Weise, LTK 10:521.

[S. WILLIAMS]

'ŪNNŌYŌ, responsory or antiphon given at the beginning of certain Syrian metrical compositions (a *bō'ûṯō* or a *madrōshō*), consisting of one or two strophes, rarely more, normally repeated in whole or in part at the end of the piece. In the East Syrian *madrāshā* it consists regularly of a single strophe which is still supposed to be repeated after each strophe of the *madrāshā*.

[A. CODY]

UNTERLINDEN, CONVENT OF, former monastery of Dominican nuns, an important center of mysticism in Colmar, France, in what is now the Diocese of Strasbourg. Unterlinden was founded in 1232 by Agnes of Mittelnheim and Agnes of Herkenheim and incorporated into the Dominican Order in 1245 by Innocent IV; the convent church was consecrated in 1269 by St. Albert the Great. The community was in close contact with Meister Eckhart and other mystics. The religious experiences of the nuns are described in the *Vitae sororum* of Catherine of Geberschweier (d. 1346). Reformed by Schönensteinbach in 1419, it was dissolved in 1792.

[E. J. DILLON]

UPANISHADS (lit., to sit down near, from Sanskrit *upa*, near, *ni*, down, and *sad* to sit), Indian philosophical and religious texts dating approximately from the 9th to 4th centuries B.C. They are considered by Hindus, esp. *Vedantists, to be the basis and standard of Hindu tradition; *Shankara (probably in the 9th cent.) established the canon of orthodox Upanishadic texts and the advaitic (nondual) interpretations which are generally accepted as the most authoritative exegesis. The number of Upanishads and their interpretations, however, vary among the great Indian commentators: *Ramanuja, Madhva, and *Radhakrishnan. In *The Sacred Books of the East*, Max Müller collected twelve Upanishads; to this collection, Robert Ernest Hume's edition adds the Mandukya Upanishad, and S. Radhakrishnan's edition adds the following: Subāla, Jābāla, Paingala, Kaivalya, Vajrasūcikā.

Throughout, the various Upanishads emphasize the unity of the empirical world (or maya), including the empirical self (or jiva), with *Brahman (or "one without a second"). This emphasis on the unity or oneness of reality has remained an essential ingredient throughout the history of *Indian philosophy, but when interpreted in the context of the earlier *Vedic hymns, its religious and cultural significance are no less apparent. See translations and commentaries by M. Müller (1879, 1884; 2d ed., 1962); R. E. Hume (1877; 2d ed., 1931); and S. Radhakrishnan (1953).

[R. A. MCDERMOTT]

UPPER ROOM, also called cenacle (*caenaculum*, a small dining place), the place where Jesus celebrated the Last

Supper, the Passover meal, with his friends; the term is often used also symbolically as a place, or even as a mental, inner "sanctuary," for meditation.

UPPER VOLTA, a republic in W Africa (105,869 sq. mi.; pop. [1973 est.] 5,490,000). This was French territory from 1897 until its independence in 1960. Evangelization began in 1900 with the coming of the White Fathers from Sudan and the Sahara. Despite government opposition, the pioneer organizer, Bp. Hacquard, established strong missions (1915–20). In 1921 Ouagadougou became a vicariate and, when the hierarchy was erected in 1955, the metropolitan see, with suffragan sees at Koudougou, Bobo-Dioulasso and Nouna. Other suffragan sees were added later: Koupéla (1956), Ouahigouya (1958), and Fada N'Gourma (1964). The missionary priests active in the country are White Fathers and Redemptorists. In 1973 the number of Catholics had increased from the c.63,500 of 1949 to 313,844. There were about 369 priests and some 900 religious brothers and sisters working in the area. The contribution of the mission to education and the care of the sick has been outstanding.

The chief Protestant denominations in Upper Volta are Pentecostals, Assemblies of God, and the Christian and Missionary Alliance, whose combined membership in 1968 was c.29,700. BIBLIOGRAPHY: J. R. de Benoist, NCE 14:474; *Bilan du Monde* 2:440–444.

[P. DAMBOORIENA]

UPPSALA ASSEMBLY, fourth general assembly of the World Council of Churches (WCC), July 4–20, 1968, at Uppsala, Sweden. Its theme was "Behold, I make all things new"; in attendance were 701 delegates from 238 Churches. At this assembly, the emergence of a new emphasis on secularity and relevance brought conflict between the more theologically oriented conservatives and those who emphasized social ethics and Christian involvement in the strategies of economic development and revolution. The report of section I, "The Holy Spirit and the catholicity of the Church," was more conservative but put emphasis on the quest for the unity of mankind. Such questions of current interest as the war in Vietnam and the population explosion occupied the delegates. The shift in interest from theology to secularity was indicated by several features: the slogan that the Church should let the world's agenda be its own; the presence of President Kaunda of Zambia, Negro novelist James Baldwin, and economist Barbara Ward as speakers, and the increasing importance of the youth delegates. RC participation became more pronounced as Roberto Tucci delivered a major address on relations between the RC Church and the WCC. Several RC theologians were accepted as full members of the Commission on Faith and Order.

[R. B. ENO]

UR, ancient city of S Babylonia, located just a few miles from the mouth of the Euphrates, and about 200 miles SSE

of modern Baghdad. At the site of the ancient city, Tell Mugheir, a long and careful archeological investigation was undertaken jointly by the British Museum and the Univ. of Pennsylvania, 1922–34. The results constitute an immense contribution to knowledge of the history and culture of ancient Mesopotamia. During the fourth millennium B.C., Ur was a satellite city of Uruk, the biblical Erech. Then during the course of the third millennium, Ur was the leading metropolis of Mesopotamia, exercising hegemony during three different dynasties comprising the reigns of fifteen kings. The third and last dynasty came at the end of the millennium, during a Sumerian renaissance, following a period of Akkadian dominance. The famous ziggurat discovered at Ur, one of the best preserved, dates from the third dynasty. It is a brick step-tower of the type that must have inspired the biblical legend of the tower of Babel. It stood in the corner of a great temple complex dedicated to the cult of the moon god and his consort. At the end of the third millennium Ur and all Sumer came under Amorite domination in what came to be called the first dynasty of Babylon. Ur then gradually passed from history. At the beginning of the biblical account of Hebrew history Ur is mentioned as the homeland of Abraham's forefathers. Abraham's father and clan migrated from Ur to Haran, where Abraham received God's call to leave his father's house and move on to Canaan. The biblical phrase "Ur of the Chaldees" is anachronistic, however, since the period of Chaldean dominance in southern Mesopotamia was still a thousand years away.

[E. J. DILLON]

URANIUS, 5th-cent. bp. of Emesa, succeeding Pompeianus in that office sometime after 445. He was a loyal friend of Theodoret. The same *Latrocinium* (Robbers' Synod) that deposed Theodoret made a lengthy accusation against U., alleging his consecration to have been defective, probably because he had signed the act of deposition of Eutyches and because of his friendship with Theodoret. U. attended the Council of Chalcedon and subscribed to the *Tome of Leo.

[E. J. DILLON]

URARTU, the biblical Ararat, known best through Assyrian sources, where the Urartu people are first mentioned in the 13th cent. B.C. and from the 9th to the 7th cent. are presented as a persistent rival to Assyrian power. Their name was given to the mountainous region SE of the Black Sea and SW of the Caspian Sea, centered in the mountains of Armenia around Lake Van in modern Turkey. During the heyday of the Urartian kingdom (840–612 B.C.), the people borrowed heavily from the high culture of Assyria, developing their own distinctive counterparts to elements of Assyrian culture. Taking advantage of a period of Assyrian decline (823–745), they acquired an empire that stretched from W of the Euphrates to within 20 miles of Aleppo in N Syria. The Assyrians and later the Cimmerians gradually drove them back to their mountain homeland. They were replaced by the Armenians during the course of the 6th century. Their influence was considerable. They attained an excellence in rock cutting, masonry, the building of aqueducts and irrigation systems, which, together with certain characteristics of their statecraft, literature, and art, were taken over by the Persians and the Medes. Through trade they influenced the developing art of Greece and Italy. Mt. Ararat in the ancient territory of the Urartu was chosen as the likely spot for the ark of Noah to touch land (Gen 8.4). Although Assyrian records do not corroborate this, Ararat is mentioned as the land of refuge for Sennacherib's sons after they had murdered their father (2 Kg 19.37; Is 37.38). The mention of Ararat in Jer 51.27 reflects the restlessness of the Urartu, the Scythians, the Medes, and the Manneans as they anticipated the fall of Babylon. What was the ancient land of the Urartu is now divided between modern Turkey, Russia, and Iran. The archeological and historical investigation of that people and culture, as of the Armenians who replaced them, has been relatively neglected. BIBLIOGRAPHY: M. S. Miller and J. L. Miller, *New Harper's Bible Dictionary* (rev. 8th ed., 1973).

[E. J. DILLON]

URBAN I, ST. (d. 230), **POPE** from 222, successor of *Callistus I. The scant details on U. in the Roman Martyrology and the *Liber pontificalis* are apocryphal. The schism of *Hippolytus continued during his pontificate. The discovery of a fragment of his tomb in the 19th cent. confirmed the tradition that he was buried in the catacomb of Callistus. Whether he was martyred is not certain. BIBLIOGRAPHY: Butler 2:389; E. Weltin, *Early Popes* (1964) 92–95.

[R. B. ENO]

URBAN II, BL. (Odo of Châtillon-sur-Marne; c.1042–99), **POPE** from 1088. Born of a noble family, he studied under St. Bruno at Reims and was named archdeacon of that city. Between 1067–70 he embraced monastic life at Cluny where he became prior. Pope Gregory VII made him cardinal bp. of Ostia and sent him as legate to Germany in 1084. Elected to the papacy, U. showed himself dedicated to the Gregorian reform. He dealt tactfully with the problems confronting his pontificate and searched for ways to restore relations with the Byzantine Church. Of the numerous councils at which Pope U. presided, the following are esp. noteworthy: the Council of Melfi (1089) which renewed the prohibitions against simony, lay investiture, and the marriage of priests; the Council of Piacenza (1095), where norms were established to deal with those who had received sacred orders from schismatic and simoniacal bishops. The Council of Clermont, convoked in November of the same year, forbade a bp. or priest to swear the feudal oath to a king or any layman. This Council is more widely known, however, for U.'s call to the First Crusade. Though the actual wording of the call is uncertain and widely divergent interpretations of the pope's motives in issuing the call have

been suggested, the proclaimed objective of the expedition was Jerusalem. This goal was attained when the crusaders entered Jerusalem on July 15, 1099. Two weeks later the Pope died. The veneration shown to U. "from time immemorial" (*Roman Martyrology*, July 29) was ratified and confirmed by Pope Leo XIII on July 14, 1887. BIBLIOGRAPHY: *Roman Martyrology* (English tr. J. B. O'Connelly, 1962); Jedin-Baus (1966) 3.1:442–450; J. Richard, NCE 4:506–507.

[H. DRESSLER]

URBAN III (Uberto Crivelli; d. 1187), **POPE** from 1185. Before his election he was abp. of Milan. Because of troubled conditions U. spent most of his pontificate at Verona where he was besieged by Frederick Barbarossa. Many decisions rendered by this Pope came to have an important place in medieval collections of Decretals. BIBLIOGRAPHY: E. Amann, DTC 15.2:2285–88; J. Powell, NCE 14:478; Jedin-Baus (1968) 3.2:108–109.

[H. DRESSLER]

URBAN IV (Jacques Pantaléon; c.1200–64), **POPE** from 1261. The son of a cobbler, U. completed his university studies at Paris and began a notable career as canon of Lyons; then at Laon (1227); archdeacon at Liège (1242); legate to Silesia, Poland, Prussia, and Pommerania (1247–49); archdeacon at Laon (1249); legate to the German princes, bp. of Verdun (1253), and from 1255 to his papal election, was patriarch of Jerusalem. Significantly, he was consecrated at Viterbo and lived at Orvieto and Perugia without ever entering Rome. His great concern was to wipe out Ghibelline influence in Tuscany and Lombardy and to substitute French power for the Hohenstaufens. He revoked the grant of Sicily made to Henry III of England by his predecessor, and after offering it to Louis IX, who declined, he made an accord with Louis' brother, Charles of Anjou (Aug. 1264) to conquer it. In the struggle of the English barons, he supported King Henry. For the Church, he added six French cardinals, but his design for the Eastern empire was frustrated by Michael VIII's mistrust of papal friendship with the menacing Charles of Anjou. He made into a universal feast the local Lowland celebration of Corpus Christi. BIBLIOGRAPHY: H. Wieruszowski, NCE 14:478–479; G. Mollat, EncCatt 12:907–908; H. Schmidinger, LTK 10:544–545; Mann 15:131–206; F. M. Powicke, *13th Century* (2d ed., 1962) 120 *passim*.

[S. WILLIAMS]

URBAN V, BL. (Guillaume de Grimard; c.1310–70), **POPE** from 1362. Entering the Benedictines at an early age, U. studied law at Paris and Bologna and taught at Montpellier and Avignon. In 1352 be became abbot of Saint-Germain, Auxerre, and in 1361 of Saint-Victor, Marseilles. After being elected pope at Avignon, he decided to return to Rome in 1366, but having reached Viterbo he was finally forced, because of hostility in Rome, to return to

Avignon in 1370. A noted educator, he lived austerely and had a high reputation for sanctity. He was beatified in 1870. BIBLIOGRAPHY: E. Baluze, *Vitae Paparum Aninionensium* (ed. G. Mollat, 1914) 1:349–414; G. Mollat, *Popes at Avignon, 1305–78,* (tr. J. Love, 1963).

[L. E. BOYLE]

URBAN VI (Bartolomeo Prigano; 1318–89), **POPE** from 1378. He had served as abp. of Aceranza (1363), of Bari (1377); and chancellor of Gregory XI. Never a cardinal himself, his attempts to reform the College of cardinals probably caused the Great Schism. A group of cardinals, mainly French, elected Robert of Geneva as Clement VII on Sept. 20, 1378, but U. kept the allegiance of most of Christendom until his death some 10 years later. BIBLIOGRAPHY: G. Mollat, *Popes at Avignon, 1305–1378* (tr. J. Love, 1963).

[L. E. BOYLE]

URBAN VII (Giambattista Castagna; 1521–90), **POPE** from Sept. 15 to Sept. 27, 1590. After becoming a *doctor utriusque juris,* he spent his career in the papal service, beginning, in 1551 as auditor of the papal legation to Henry II of France. In 1553 he was made bp. of Rozzano; he was in turn governor of Fano (1150) and of Perugia and Umbria (1559). At the Council of Trent (1562–63), where he was president of several theological commissions, he addressed the conciliars on the subject of the derivation of episcopal power from the pope. He became nuncio in Spain at the court of Philip II until 1572. In 1573 he resigned his episcopal see and became nuncio to Venice and governor of Bologna. He was named cardinal-priest by Gregory XII in 1583; in the following year, papal legate to Bologna; in 1586, inquisitor general of the Holy Office. He was elected pope to succeed Sixtus but died of malaria before coronation; he had, however, already planned administrative reforms in the States of the Church.

URBAN VIII (Maffeo Barberini; 1568–1644), **POPE** from 1623. He entered the papal service after obtaining (1589) a doctorate in civil and canon law at Pisa. Before his pontificate he served as papal nuncio to France (1604), having been consecrated with the title, abp. of Nazareth; he was made a cardinal in 1606, bp. of Spoleto in 1608; legate for Bologna and prefect of the Signatory of Justice in 1617. He was elected pope by a nearly unanimous vote. For the internal life of the Church his pontificate included many canonizations and beatifications, esp. of Christians of the Counter Reformation era. He reformed the church calendar and the Breviary, approved the foundation of the Vincentians in 1632, and vigilantly enforced the Tridentine disciplinary decree on episcopal residence. His pontificate is important to the history of missions because of his promotion of the work of the Congregation for the Propagation of the Faith (now also called Congregation for the Evangelization of Peoples) and his foundation in 1627 of the Collegium Ur-

banianum (now the Pontificia Università Urbaniana) for the education of missionaries. In 1639 he proscribed slavery in Brazil, Paraguay, and the West Indies. It was also U.'s bull *In eminenti* (1642) that began, by proscribing the *Augustinus,* Rome's repudiation of Jansenism. The second trial of Galileo also took place during his pontificate. He supported *Bernini's work on St. Peter's Basilica and other projects of beautification in Rome; but he stripped the Pantheon of its bronze in order to make guns for use against the Duke of Parma. In politics U. tried to follow a policy of neutrality in the Thirty Years' War, but is blamed for failing the Catholics of Germany and for the disadvantageous Peace of Westphalia. In a life otherwise blameless and a reign marked by religious zeal in many ways, he was nevertheless flagrantly guilty of nepotism, creating two of his unqualified nephews cardinals and allowing other family members to enrich themselves through ecclesiastical office.

URBAN, JAN (1874–1940), Polish Jesuit editor. U. entered the Society the year after his ordination (1899); twice he spent extended periods of time in Russia (1902–03; 1907–10), ministering to persecuted Catholics there and organizing groups of Catholics of the Oriental rite. He founded several journals, among them *Oriens* (1933), aimed at uniting Eastern Christians with Rome. He died as the result of sufferings caused by the Nazi invasion.

[M. J. SUELZER]

URBAN CHURCH HISTORY, a study of the impact that cities have made on the Christian Church and the influence the Church has had on cities. A highly specialized branch of the general field of urban history, it is of current interest because of the changing character of Western civilization. Whereas in 1800 approximately 5% of the population of Europe and the U.S. lived in cities, recent U.S. census figures indicate that 75% of Americans live in urban areas. If the present trend continues, it appears that by the year 2000 approximately 95% of the people of the Western world will live in cities.

Urban historians point out that the Church began as a movement among the people of the Roman cities and that it was an urban institution when it became the Empire's official religion. In subsequent centuries, however, the strongly rural character of western Europe left its mark on the Church, which, however, did not lose all urban characteristics. The rise of cities, the Renaissance, and much of the Reformation were urban influences. The Industrial Revolution found the Church still a predominantly rural institution, and much of the writing of urban church historians deals with its adjustment to an urbanized society. In the U.S. the pioneering work on urban church history is C. H. Hopkins, *Rise of the Social Gospel in American Protestantism, 1865–1915* (1940). This was followed by A. I. Abell, *Urban Impact on American Protestantism* (1943), and H. F. May, *Protestant Churches and Industrial America* (1949). Numerous publications in the general field of urban history touch on this subject, but a great deal of research is still needed on the specific question of the Church and the city. Application of social history to the study of American Catholicism is an important recent development typified by the work of Professor Jay Dolan of the Univ. of Notre Dame. BIBLIOGRAPHY: J. Dolan, *Catholic Revitalism: The American Experience* (1978); A. Greeley, *American Catholic: A Social Portrait* (1977).

[A. W. SKARDON]

URDANETA, ANDRÉS DE (1508–68), Spanish Augustinian priest and explorer. He is best known for discovering and mapping the return route from the Philippines to New Spain, which was later used by the Manila fleet.

[P. J. HENNESSEY]

URFÉ, HONORÉ D' (1567–1625), French writer. Of ancient nobility, he participated actively in the French religious wars with the Catholic "Holy League," and was twice imprisoned. In order to marry his sister-in-law, Diane de Chateaumorand, whose marriage to his brother had been annulled (1598), he left the Order of Malta (1599), which he had entered young and probably without vocation. While his *Épîtres morales* (1598) shows influences of Renaissance Platonism and Stoicism, his fame rests on his immensely long pastoral, *L'Astrée* (1607–27), one of the first such novels to achieve great popularity. With the attention d'U. gave in it to the Neoplatonist theories of love in which he was influenced by contemporary religious moralists, *L'Astrée* marks the evolution of a tradition of secular ethics away from dogmatic morality. Its lengthy discourses on love reveal the influence on d'U. of, among others, Ficino, Bembo, Pico della Mirandola, and St. Francis de Sales. He was also writer of a poem, *La Sireine* (1611) and a 5-act pastoral, *La Sylvanire* (1625). BIBLIOGRAPHY: J. Ehrmann, *Un Paradis désespéré: l'amour et l'illusion dans L'Astrée* (1963); Anthony Levi, *French Moralists: Theory of the Passions, 1585 to 1649* (1964).

[R. N. NICOLICH]

URIEL, (1) a Kohathite who helped David bring the ark to Jerusalem (1 Chr 6.24; 15.5, 11); (2) father of Micaiah, the mother of Abijah (2 Chr 13.1–2). The name is also given in apocalyptic literature to an angel of God's throne.

[T. EARLY]

URIM AND THUMMIM, devices used by the Israelites to get divine answers to their questions. Little is known concerning them, however. The high priest carried them in his *breastplate (Ex 28.30), an indication that they were small. Questions that allowed only two answers were put to them, Urim signifying one answer and Thummim, the other (1 Sam 14.41–42). The devices were perhaps used when the Israelites "inquired of Yahweh" (Jg 1.1) or made choices by a process of elimination (Jos 7.14). These names were

given by Joseph *Smith, Mormon founder, to the spectacles used to translate the Book of Mormon.

[T. EARLY]

UR–MARCUS, according to a theory of E. Wendling and others, an earlier, primitive form of the Gospel according to St. *Mark. The existence of Ur-marcus is inferred from alleged signs of revision in the existing text of Mk, and also from the study of the other two Synoptic Gospels which, so it is argued, give indications of a knowledge of this more primitive version. The theory never gained wide allegiance and has been largely abandoned by more recent scholars. BIBLIOGRAPHY: V. Taylor, *Gospel According to St. Mark* (2d ed., 1966); P. Parker, *Gospel Before Mark* (1953). *SYNOPTIC PROBLEM.

[D. J. BOURKE]

ÛRŌRŌ (East Syrian, *ûrārā*), Syrian stole, of which the following types and manners of wearing must be distinguished: (1) sacerdotal—like the Byzantine *epitrachilion* in form, but always sewed together in front; (2) diaconal—worn over the left shoulder, the two lengths falling to the hem of the *kûṯînō* in front and back among West Syrians, but among East Syrians and Maronites drawn over and fastened at the right waist; (3) subdiaconal (the style also of lesser clerics fulfilling the diaconal role): West Syrians take the back of the diaconal stole, pass it loosely under the right arm and throw it back over the left shoulder; East Syrians loop the stole around the neck before letting the two lengths fall from the left shoulder (one in front, the other behind); (4) West Syrian lesser ministers: the stole is placed over the left shoulder with the greater length in back; this is drawn across the back from shoulder to right waist, then around the front waist from right to left passing over the front length of itself, then brought up across the back and over the right shoulder and down perpendicularly at the right, under the horizontal portion already formed. Thus on the wearer's back it appears crossed, on his front as a cincture holding in place the two ends falling from the shoulders.

[A. CODY]

URQUHART, DAVID (1805–77), British diplomatist of vast experience who worked tirelessly for the establishment of international law to govern nations and to prevent the great powers from violating the sovereignty of small nations. He fought courageously for the independence of Greece, then fought diplomatically for the integrity of Turkey in the face of encroachment by Russia and the other European powers. A persistent critic and foe of Lord Palmerston, U. wrote in periodicals, often founding them to provide himself with a platform. Though he was born at Braelangwell, Cromarty, Scotland, he was educated in France, Switzerland, and Spain, and worked as a farmer and an ordinary workman in an arsenal. He seemed to be able effortlessly to sympathize with diverse cultural and national communities. Among his writings the one with the most overtly religious consequence is his *Appeal of a Protestant to the Pope to Restore the Law of Nations* (1868). He even attended the Vatican Council I as an observer, but was not able to get his concern on the agenda. BIBLIOGRAPHY: DNB 20:43–45.

[E. J. DILLON]

URRÁBURU, JUAN JOSÉ (1844–1904), Spanish Jesuit philosopher prominent in 19th-cent. scholastic revival. He taught at the Gregorian Univ. in Rome (1878–87) and at several Jesuit colleges in Spain. His *Institutiones philosophicae* (8 v., 1890–1900) and *Compendium philosophiae scholasticae* (5 v., 1902–04) are typical of the period. U.'s attempt to present the thought of St. Thomas Aquinas is marked by his own alien presuppositions.

[T. C. O'BRIEN]

URSACIUS (d. before 375), bishop of Singidunum (Belgrade), promoter of *Arianism in the West. A pupil of *Arius, he, with *Valens of Mursa, first opposed *Athanasius at the Council of Tyre in 335, and was one of those responsible for the banishment of Athanasius after the Synod of Jerusalem. Excommunicated by the Council of *Sardica in 343, U. retracted his errors and his attacks against Athanasius. Soon, however, he again took up Arian positions, yet changing from one Arian party to another (see ANOMOEANS and HOMOEANS) to suit the will of the Emperor *Constantius II. U. took part in all of the Arian-dominated councils in the West: at Sirmium, Arles, Milan, and Rimini. He was excommunicated by Pope *Damasus I c.369 and then disappeared from history. BIBLIOGRAPHY: Bihlmeyer-Tüchle 1:253–254.

[R. B. ENO]

URSICINUS OF RAVENNA, ST. (d. 537 or 538), bishop and martyr. He was abp. of Ravenna from 534 until his death; little else is known of him. He is not to be confused with another Ursicinus of Ravenna, a martyred physician of the 2d century. The relics of the martyred bp. are in the altar of the basilica of San Vitale in Ravenna. BIBLIOGRAPHY: AS Sept. 2:535–536; Peter Damian, *Carmina sacra et preces,* PL 145:950.

[W. A. JURGENS]

URSINUS (Ursinicius; d. after 381), **ANTIPOPE.** On the death of Liberius (366), U. was chosen pope by the strong but small faction that had supported the antipope, Felix II (355–357). U. caused deep division in Rome, even to street-fighting and bloodshed, until he and his deacons, Amantius and Lupus, were exiled by the prefect. An imperial pardon permitted their return, but the resulting violence led to further exile. Established in Milan (370–372), U. was supported by some Arian bishops and together they charged Pope *Damasus I with foul crimes. The last-known mention of U. is in a letter to the Emperor from the Council of Aquileia (381), warning against the intrigues of the anti-

pope. BIBLIOGRAPHY: M. R. P. McGuire, NCE 4:624–625; P. Brezzi, *Papacy* (1958) 181.

[P. F. MULHERN]

URSINUS, ZACHARIAS (1543–85), Protestant theologian, a principal author of the *Heidelberg Catechism. He studied at Breslau and at Wittenberg (1550–57), where he formed close ties with P. *Melanchthon. After visiting Zurich and Geneva, where he met John *Calvin, he adopted Calvinist theology, esp. with regard to the Lord's Supper. In 1561 he was placed in charge of the Collegium Sapientiae at Heidelberg by the Elector of the Palatinate, Frederick III; and in 1562 he was given the chair of theology. At this time U. composed a *Summa theologiae* and a *Catechismus minor,* which served as preparations for his collaboration with C. *Olevianus on the Heidelberg Catechism. Against his own temperament, U. was continually drawn into controversy at Heidelberg; he had to defend both the Catechism and the *Reformed teaching officially adopted in the Palatinate, against the Lutherans. His proposals in *Monitum Ursini* (1568) for church discipline similar to that of Geneva earned him many enemies among his colleagues. After the death of Frederick and the closing of the Collegium Sapientiae (1577), U. taught at Neustadt-am-Hard (near Worms) in the Collegium Casimirianum. Here he wrote *De Libro concordiae, admonitio christiana* (1581), a Calvinist critique of the *Formula of Concord and *Book of Concord.

[T. C. O'BRIEN]

URSMAR, ST. (d. 713), abbot-bp. of Lobbes. He was made abbot of *Lobbes c.690 and shortly thereafter elevated to the episcopate. A founder of monasteries and an ardent preacher in N France and Flanders, he broke his health by his zealous labors. As a consequence, resigning c.711, he was succeeded by St. *Ermin. BIBLIOGRAPHY: Wattenbach-Levison 2; Butler 2:129.

[A. CABANISS]

URSPRUNG, OTTO (1879–1960), German musicologist. U. studied at the Univ. of Munich and later became a professor there. He was a specialist in medieval and Renaissance music and editor of the works of Jacobus de *Kerle.

[M. T. LEGGE]

URSULA, ST., commemorated under the rubric St. Ursula and her maidens, martyrs; their date is unknown. They were the subjects of a legend that grew substantially with the cent. into the Middle Ages and gained widespread popularity. At the height of the story their numbers grew to 11,000 virgin martyrs, who died at the hands of unbelieving barbarians. In the Church of St. Ursula at Cologne there is a stone bearing a Latin inscription, cut in the late 4th or early 5th cent., according to which a certain Clematius, of senatorial rank, rebuilt a ruined basilica in honor of some virgins who had been martyred in that place. There is no word about numbers, names, time, or circumstances of suffering. And that is all really certain about the actual events that gave rise to the cult.

[E. J. DILLON]

URSULINA VENERII, BL. (1375–1410), virgin. Encouraged by a divine visitation she claimed to have had at the age of 15, she worked tirelessly, though unsuccessfully, for the conclusion of the Western Schism. She journeyed to Avignon to persuade Clement VII to renounce his claim to the papacy, and to Rome to see Boniface IX for the same purpose. A pilgrimage to the Holy Land was followed by exile from her native Parma. Her peaceful death occurred at Verona. BIBLIOGRAPHY: Butler 2:49–50; H. L. Müller, LTK 10:575; D. S. Buczek, NCE 14:490.

[J. M. O'DONNELL]

URSULINES (Company of St. Ursula, Order of St. Ursula, OSU), a community of religious women founded in Italy by St. Angela Merici in 1535, devoted to education. The Company of St. Ursula, following the Rule of St. Augustine, was approved by Pope Paul III in 1544. In the early years of their history, the members of the congregation lived individually, coming together for common exercises and teaching duties but not wearing a distinctive habit. St. Charles Borromeo invited the society to Milan, brought them together in common living, and conferred the status of an enclosed order. At this time a distinctive garb was adopted. The Ursuline Congregation of Paris, which became a famous center, was constituted an order (i.e., a group taking solemn vows) with papal cloister. Spreading to other countries of Europe, Ursulines followed two designs: the congregated (who followed the original plan) and the religious Ursulines (a cloistered community taking solemn vows). The Ursulines experienced rapid growth in France before the French Revolution. During the Terror, 35 nuns endured martyrdom. In addition to France the order flourished in a number of European countries including Germany, the Netherlands, and Belgium. Missionary activity has carried Ursulines to Canada, the U.S., including Alaska; to Cuba and Brazil; to Australia and India; to China, Taiwan, and Thailand; to South Africa and the Congo.

America. In 1639 Mother Mary of the Incarnation led a group of Ursulines to Quebec, the first foundation in the New World. Presently in Quebec is the *Canadian Union of the Order of St. Ursula* with 800 members in 61 houses. Another Canadian group is the *Chatham Union* with 324 members in 30 houses. An independent branch, with 76 members in 9 houses, is in Bruno, Saskatchewan.

Ursulines of New Orleans. First nuns to come to the continental U.S. were from the Rouen convent and from other French foundations; in 1727 they came to New Orleans at the behest of Nicolas Ignace Beaubois, superior of the Louisiana Jesuits. The Ursulines added to their primary apostolate of education, hospital and other charitable activities. The group was led by Sr. Mary Augustine Tranche-

pain. With the transfer of the territory of Louisiana to the U.S. in 1803, the community dwindled drastically. In Montpellier, France, Mother St. Michel Gensoul, informed of the plight of the New Orleans group, volunteered to go to the city and arrived there, accompanied by a small group of nuns, in 1810. Soon after the War of 1812 the Ursulines confined their work to education, directing the celebrated Ursuline College and Academy. The statue of Our Lady of Prompt Succor, brought to New Orleans by Mother St. Michel, is the center of a popular shrine in the church attached to the convent.

Ursulines of Brown County, Ohio. Shortlived foundations were in New York and Boston; in Brown County, Ohio, the congregation established a lasting foundation. In 1845 the bp. of Cincinnati, J. Purcell, brought to Ohio a group of Ursuline nuns from Paris. Under the superiorship of Mother Julia of the Assumption an academy for girls was established. Other schools followed and from Ohio new foundations were established in Santa Rosa, Calif. and Columbia, South Carolina.

Ursulines of Texas. During the Mexican War, Ursulines from New Orleans opened a convent in Galveston, Tex. (1847) and an academy, later establishing two more schools. During the yellow fever epidemic and the Civil War their convent served as a hospital. More schools followed in Dallas, which became in 1900 the motherhouse.

St. Louis Ursulines. Founded by Austrian Ursulines, led by Mother Magdalen Stehlin, in 1848, a new undertaking began in St. Louis, Mo., with the establishment of a convent school. Later the complex was moved to Kirkwood, Mo., the present motherhouse. The Ursulines staff a number of parochial schools in the Archdiocese of St. Louis and in the Ozark Mountains Arcadia College and Ursuline Academy. From Kirkwood other communities have been founded in Illinois, Kansas, Montana, and New York.

Ursulines of Cleveland, Ohio, a membership of 407 nuns in 26 houses. Brought by Bp. Rappe from Boulogne-sur-Mer in France to Cleveland in 1850, Ursuline nuns under the leadership of Mother Mary of the Annunciation established an academy and served parochial schools of Cleveland, then opened schools in Youngstown and Toledo. In 1871 they were empowered to offer college degrees in Cleveland, but pressure of demands of elementary and secondary teachers caused them to abandon collegiate work until 1922 when Bp. Schrembs authorized the opening of Ursuline College.

Ursulines of Toledo, Ohio, have 212 nuns in 20 houses. The congregation, founded from that of Cleveland, under the direction of Mother des Seraphims, established itself in Toledo, Ohio, in 1854; some came also from the Paris Congregation. They established an academy, taught in parochial schools, and in 1922 founded Mary Manse College (see M. Mattimore, NCE 9:394–395), which no longer operates.

Ursulines of New York. Founded from St. Louis, Mo., by Mother Magdalen Stehlin, the New York foundation dates from 1855. In New York the community operates academies and parochial schools.

Ursulines of Louisville, Ky. number 437 nuns in 48 houses. Upon invitation of Bp. John Spalding of Louisville Bavarian Ursulines, with Mother Mary de Sales Reitmeyer as superior, were with some from the Paris Congregation established in Louisville in 1858. In that city they operated academies, parochial schools, and orphanages. From Louisville they founded schools and orphanages in Omaha, Neb.; Evansville, Ind.; Columbus, Ohio; Cumberland, Md.; and Wheeling, W. Va. as well as in towns in Pennsylvania. In more recent times, they have conducted schools in Baltimore, Altoona, Grand Rapids, and Indianapolis.

Ursulines of Columbia, S.C. The Ursulines returned to South Carolina in 1858 under the superiorship of Mother M. Baptista *Lynch, another group having left Charleston in 1847. The academy in Columbia became famous throughout the South but was destroyed in the burning of the city at the end of the Civil War. A new school and convent were established just outside Columbia. A third location in the city followed 20 years later. In 1891 the third location, now the motherhouse, was occupied.

Ursulines of Alton, Ill. Founded in 1859, the first superior being Mother M. Josephine Bruiding of St. Louis, Mo., this community conducts a number of schools in Illinois.

Ursulines of Mt. St. Joseph, Ky. have 401 nuns in 61 houses. The congregation was established in 1874 in Davies County where a boarding school for girls was opened in 1880. The special work of this community has been education of the rural population. Its pioneering superior was Mother M. Aloysius Willett. The Owensboro independent motherhouse is Mt. Saint Joseph in Maple Mount, Kentucky.

Ursulines of Youngstown, Ohio, have 143 nuns in 13 houses. Founded in 1874 from Cleveland, with Mother Mary Theresa as superior, the group founded numerous schools serving N Ohio. The motherhouse is at Canfeld, Ohio.

Ursulines of Frontenac, Minn. Coming from Alton, Ill., in 1887, under direction of Mother Liguori Curran, the Ursulines established a new community in Lake City, Minnesota. Villa Maria Academy in 1891 in Frontenac became their motherhouse.

Ursulines of New Rochelle, N.Y. Becoming an autonomous foundation in New York City in 1891, with Mother Seraphine Leonard as first superior, the congregation opened academies and schools in the Archdiocese of New York. In 1904 Castle School was opened, the first Catholic college for women in the state of New York (now the College of New Rochelle).

Ursulines of Great Falls, Mont. Founded in 1884 by a band of nuns from Toledo, Ohio, led by Mother Amadeus Dunne, the new congregation established a number of Indian schools in Montana as well as academies in several localities. In 1905 the Montana Ursulines established a foundation in Alaska. The convent at Great Falls is the motherhouse for E Montana. The provincial headquarters was established at St. Ignatius Mission, Montana.

Ursulines of Waterville, Me. A foundation from the Ursulines of Québec (1888), the congregation of Maine operates academic and parochial schools in that state. The motherhouse is Mt. Merici Convent in Waterville.

Ursulines of York, Neb. Established in 1890 by a group of German Ursulines in exile, led by Mother Clare, the Nebraska Ursulines conduct schools and a college in several dioceses of Nebraska.

Ursulines of St. Ignace, Mich. Founded from Canada in 1897 under the leadership of Mother Angela, the St. Ignace community operates schools in the diocese of Marquette, the motherhouse being at St. Ignace.

Ursulines of Cincinnati, Ohio, have one house with 48 members. One offshoot of the Brown County Ursulines, the Cincinnati congregation was founded by Mother Fidelis Coleman in 1910 and operates schools in the Archdiocese of Cincinnati.

Ursulines of Kenmare, Neb. Established by a group of Ursulines from Germany, led by Mother Leonie Rodgers, with motherhouse at Kenmare, this community operates schools in the Dioceses of Bismarck and St. Cloud.

Ursulines of Caldwell, Ohio. Formed by nuns from Germany, the first superior being Mother M. Salesia, this community was established in 1915 and in 1925 became an autonomous congregation. The nuns conduct schools in the Diocese of Columbus and maintain the motherhouse in Caldwell.

In 1900 Leo XIII proposed a Roman Union with motherhouse in the Holy City (1975 membership: 5,141 in 212 houses). Mother St. Julian was first prioress general. In the U.S. those NA congregations affiliated with the Roman Union were organized into four provinces: Eastern (Bronx, N.Y.—336 members); Central (Crystal City, Mo. —489); Western (Santa Rosa, Calif.—119); Northeastern (Dedham, Mass.—157). Independent Ursuline groups in the U.S. (from European motherhouses) number 1,983. Also in the U.S. are Ursuline congregations of Tildone, Belgium (Roman Union; U.S. address at Blue Point, Long Island, N.Y.); of Blackrock, Cork, Ireland (at Columbus, Ga.); and of Mt. Calvary (at Belleville, Illinois). BIBLIOGRAPHY: M. McKiernan, *Order of St. Ursula* (1945).

[J. R. AHERNE]

USCC, see UNITED STATES CATHOLIC CONFERENCE.

USE (Lat. *usus*), a word with two special meanings in religious and philosophical literature. (1) In liturgy it signifies a variant usage, i.e., a habitual, customary, or prevailing practice within a rite, which is not of sufficient importance to constitute a special rite. In this sense one speaks of the old Dominican "use" or variation of the Roman rite, although this variation has often been popularly, if imprecisely, referred to as the Dominican rite. (2) In moral theology, use designates a terminal phase in the analysis of the human act. This occurs when an object has passed from being wished for, resolved on, or chosen (phases pertaining to the order of intention), and is actually being laid hold of, employed, or possessed (phases pertaining to the order of execution).

The object in question may itself be transitional to a further object, or it may be final or completive within the system of reference adopted, a difference that may be taken here as equivalent to that between a means and an end. The former is a utility (*utile*) and in the most specific sense is said to be used. The latter is to be enjoyed (*delectable*); it is relished for its own sake, and in that sense is too likable just to be used. The thought lies behind St. Augustine's celebrated antithesis of *uti* (to use) and *frui* (to enjoy), which may be developed to mean that one should not take his pleasures sadly or work too hard at them, nor contrariwise, should one make a song or dance about the jobs of work he is given (see ABUSE).

However, some ambiguity may arise on a point of terminology. Classical authors, St. Augustine himself, and later theological writers occasionally refer to the enjoyment of an object as its *usus*. Thus, e.g., the phrase *usus feminae*, and its translation in medieval English and later, does not mean treating a woman as a convenience, but getting to ''know'' her in the OT sense.

To St. Thomas Aquinas, who was the first to compose a comprehensive psychologico-moral analysis of a *human act, the word *usus* also has a delicately defined technical sense. It is, first, the *usus activus,* the will's executive application to a deed or work following the practical reason's command or *imperium,* which may result from choice. Thereafter it is the *usus passivus*, the carrying out of the action by the appropriate powers, abilities, or faculties. BIBLIOGRAPHY: ThAq ST 1a2ae, 16 (esp. in Lat-Eng ed., v. 17, ed. T. Gilby, 1970).

USENER, HERMANN (1834–1905). German classical scholar. He spent most of his career as a professor at the Univ. of Bonn. In philology he stood for the view that there was an underlying unity to the discipline. U. was also a student of comparative religions, his most important published work being *Die Götternamen . . .* (1896).

[J. R. AHERNE]

USHAW COLLEGE (College of St. Cuthbert), a combined college and seminary near Durham, England. It was founded to accommodate students obliged to leave Douai by the closing during the French Revolution of the English college located there. The uprooted academic community settled briefly first at Tudhoe, then at Pontop, villages near Durham, then in 1794 at Crook Hall in the same vicinity, and finally in 1808 at Ushaw. The college followed the Douai system that provided for the education of both lay and clerical students. The curriculum, strong in the classics, included humanities, philosophy, and theology. The college

is governed by a board composed of the bps. whose dioceses it serves. The library contains valuable collections of rare books and MSS. Among Ushaw's prominent alumni were Cardinals Wiseman, Bourne, and Merry del Val; the historian, John Lingard; Wilfred Ward, editor of the *Dublin Review*; and the poet, Francis Thompson.

[M. B. MURPHY]

USPENSKY, PORPHYRIUS (1804–85), Russian bp., archeologist, discoverer of the Codex Sinaiticus. He published many volumes on his travels in the Orient and an 8-vol. autobiography. BIBLIOGRAPHY: A. Ferrua, DE 3:1249.

[M. J. SUELZER]

USUAL CONDITIONS, a stipulation attached to an indulgenced prayer or act of devotion that means the indulgence may be gained provided that the person has received the sacraments of penance and the Eucharist, has the intention of gaining the indulgence, makes the prescribed visit to a church, and prays for the pope's intentions.

[T. C. O'BRIEN]

USUARD (d. *c.*875), Benedictine monk who produced the most celebrated of medieval martyrologies, commonly known as the *Martyrology of Usuard* (PL 123–124). BIBLIOGRAPHY: H. Thurston, CE 15:235.

[P. K. MEAGHER]

USURY (Lat. *usura*, a using), restricted by Christian writers to a wrongful profiting from money-loans, which, together with heresy, was a most execrated crime in the Middle Ages. In a formally defined and crystallized sense it was condemned in church councils culminating in Lateran V (1515); the teaching was reaffirmed by Benedict XIV in the encyclical, *Vix pervenit* (1745). The financial economy of the world may have changed, but not the theological doctrine of the Church; however, it may be argued that this, in the present case, has to have so fine a point put upon it as no longer to be generally applicable to modern conditions. A brief review will make the matter clearer.

The OT strictly forbade the exacting of interest among the people of Israel, and the spirit of the NT is expressed in the command, ''Lend without hope of return, and your reward shall be great'' (Lk 6.35). Plato held that it upset the balance in the city; Aristotle, followed by Cicero and Seneca, that money was essentially barren. Roman law allowed charging for money-loans a limited toleration. The consensus of the Fathers was dead against it: its origin was greed; its effect, the oppression of the poor. It was forbidden to clerics at Nicaea (325) and soon the prohibition was extended to laymen; Vienne (1311) applied to it the sanctions against heresy. Eventually it was not merely rapacious and exorbitant interest that was attacked, but the charging of any interest for moneylending as such: we shall return to the point in a moment.

However, with the rise of mercantilist capitalism, the principle began to go into eclipse. Though the great Anglican divines still maintained the medieval position, Calvin and others permitted the lending of money for profit. Civil legislation, which had hitherto followed canon law, began to allow for moderate charges. Money was no longer treated as a fungible, or token means of exchange, but as capital productive of wealth like any other property; a distinction was drawn between a loan for production and consumption, and the term usury was limited to excessive rates. Nevertheless, there are political economists of our own day whose diagnosis is that this admission of the fruitfulness of money lies at the root of the troubles in a capitalist society.

The old argument was simple, though it needs to be taken exactly. The injustice of usury consists in selling what does not exist, namely, the use of the money as apart from the money itself, and this in virtue of its being lent. This last qualification was essential, because it was agreed that a charge could be made because of outside factors. These ''extrinsic titles'' validating interest, as they were called, began to be listed under five headings: first, *damnum emergens,* the positive damage suffered by the lender because he had not the money in hand; second, *lucrum cessans,* the loss of a reasonable profit for the same reason; third, *periculum sortis,* the unforeseen risks he incurred; fourth, *poena conventionalis,* a penal cause for nonrepayment by the agreed date according to contract; and fifth, *titulus legis civilis,* a charge set by the laws of a country to encourage commerce and the flow of money.

What was in question was the loan of a fungible, that is, a good which is consumed in being used so that the return required is not of the identical thing but of its equivalent, as when you oblige your neighbor with ten dollars or a bottle of whisky for the evening, but not with your motor car. Here we are speaking, not of charity, but of justice; there a money profit for the lending of some things may be not just mean but downright unfair as well. A loan of this sort is defined as the temporary concession of a fungible; hence, it differs from a deposit, a gift, a sale, an exchange, and an investment. Investing money in a venture is not usury so long as you do not both levy a charge and demand your money back whatever the outcome. BIBLIOGRAPHY: ThAq ST 2a2ae, 78; B. N. Nelson, *Idea of Usury* (1949); R. H. Tawney, *Religion and the Rise of Capitalism* (1926); J. T. Noonan, *Scholastic Analysis of Usury* (1957); T. F. Divine, *Interest: An Historical and Analytical Study in Economics and Modern Ethics* (1959).

[T. GILBY]

USUS PAUPER, the observance of the vow of poverty by the use of only what is absolutely necessary. In history the phrase was prominent during the *Poverty Controversy among the Franciscans. In theology the *usus pauper* connotes a practice of the spirit of poverty. It is distinguished against a merely literal observance of the vow, ''use with permission,'' a concern for securing the permission of superiors, but not for renunciation in the use of temporalities. *POVERTY.

[T. C. O'BRIEN]

UT QUEANT LAXIS RESONENT FIBRIS, opening of the liturgical hymn for the feast of St. John the Baptist. The first syllables in the half lines of the first stanza were used by Guido d'Arezzo to name the plainsong notes to which the syllables were sung. He proposed as a musical scale this aid to the tonal memory for sight singing. This is the antecedence of the names of the notes in the do-re-mi-scale.

[M. T. LEGGE]

UTAH, a Rocky Mountain state, admitted to the Union (1896) as the 45th state. The most significant event in the modern history of Utah was the arrival of the Mormons (Church of Jesus Christ of Latter-Day Saints). After a succession of unsuccessful settlements in New York, Illinois, and Missouri, the Mormons were led on a torturous journey to their permanent homesite by Brigham *Young in 1847. The following year Utah was acquired by the U.S. in the Treaty of Guadalupe Hidalgo. Until this time the area had been part of Spanish Mexico. Several Franciscan friars had visited the territory in 1776–77, but few Catholics had settled there before the coming of the Mormons.

In 1866 E. Kelly opened a chapel in Salt Lake City, and in 1871 Patrick Walsh became the first permanent Catholic missionary assigned to Utah. He was replaced (1873) by L. *Scanlan, who became vicar apostolic (1887) and bp. of the new Diocese of Salt Lake City (1891). The diocese is a suffragan of the metropolitan see of San Francisco, California.

In 1976 Utah's Catholics numbered 51,819, or 4.3% of the total state population. The major non-Catholic denomination for more than a century has been the Church of Jesus Christ of Latter-Day Saints, with 74.5% of the total population in 1971. Other Protestant denominations comprised 3.6% of the population. The Jewish population (1968) was 1,650, or 0.16%. There are no Catholic colleges in Utah. The 3 Catholic high schools in the state are attended by more than 777 students; 1,789 pupils attend 9 Catholic elementary schools. BIBLIOGRAPHY: W. Sultan, *Utah: A Centennial History* (3 v. 1949); G. O. Larson, *Outline History of Utah and the Mormons* (1958).

[J. L. MORRISON; R. M. PRESTON]

UTHRED OF BOLDON (d. 1396), Oxford theologian who was censured for his doctrine of the ''clear vision'' between personal death and judgment. Although he was at Oxford by 1337, he interrupted his studies in 1342 to become a Benedictine at Durham, returning for his doctorate in theology, which he obtained in 1357. Depending heavily on the writings of *Nicholas of Autrecourt, he opposed John

*Wycliffe and the mendicancy of the friars. BIBLIOGRAPHY: Knowles ROE v. 2; *idem,* "Censured Opinions of U. of B.," *Proceedings of the British Academy* 37 (1951) 305–342; Emden Ox 1:212–213; F. D. Blackley, NCE 14:503.

[J. A. WEISHEIPL]

UTICA, MARTYRS OF, perhaps to be identified with the group of North African martyrs commemorated under the rubric Massa Candida, a place name in North Africa meaning White Farm. Prudentius mentions the many who were martyred together at Carthage; Augustine places the event near Utica, 25 miles from Carthage. The event is dated during the persecution of Valerian and Gallienus.

[E. J. DILLON]

UTIEŠENOVÍC, JURAJ, see MARTINUZZI, GYÖRGY.

UTILITARIANISM, a theory of ethics and social reform prominent in 19th cent. England. It is based on the principle of utility, i.e., the principle that personal moral conduct and civil legislation should ever aim at the greatest happiness of the greatest number. Jeremy Bentham (1743–1833), a legal and economic theorist, was its founder; John Stuart Mill (1806–73), a logician, economist, and member of Parliament, its ablest and most influential exponent. At that time the effects of the Industrial Revolution were acutely apparent; squalor, poverty, and abuses of labor abounded, and Parliament was failing to provide remedies. Utilitarianism, calling attention to the social values and disvalues of human action, probably helped to refine the moral judgment of men of its generation, and certainly inspired many much needed legislative changes.

According to Bentham, the standard of all morality and the end of human action are expressed in the principle of utility. The welfare of the individual is bound up inextricably with the well-being of the group, and it is only in promoting the general happiness of all that an individual can realize his own. Actions are morally good to the extent that they advance the general happiness; they are morally evil to the extent they impede or retard it. Happiness is taken to mean pleasure and the absence of pain. A proposed action should receive the exact measure of approval or condemnation warranted by the pleasures and pains it promotes. Only quantitative considerations, in Bentham's view, should form the basis for the evaluation of the pleasures considered in the process of moral appraisal. These, as Bentham thought, can be precisely calculated so as to give ethics the accuracy of an exact science. All relevant aspects of the pleasure (or pain) must, of course, be taken into consideration—its intensity, duration, certainty, proximity, fecundity, and purity must be weighed. These are the governing criteria of unit values to be totaled in the "felicific calculus." The social extent of given pleasures and pains, i.e., the number of persons affected by them, must also be computed. With the principle of utility, Bentham's single master principle, he hoped to sweep aside the complexity of personal ethical decision and the accumulated intricacies of legal processes by placing both areas of human judgment on what he conceived as a simple, rational foundation.

In his essay, *Utilitarianism,* Mill confirmed Bentham's basic tenets, esp. the principle of utility and the identification of pleasure with happiness. However, according to Mill, pleasures have not only a quantitative but also a qualitative value. Men share bodily pleasures with brute animals, but rational delight is reserved to man alone. Therefore, Bentham's quantitative norm was defective, unless it is modified by a qualitative norm, when used as a standard of moral judgment. Details, such as what choice should be made between a qualitatively superior but quantitatively inferior pleasure and one which is qualitatively inferior but quantitatively superior, were not elaborated convincingly. It was enough to say that existence should be as rich in pleasure and as devoid of pain as possible.

Nevertheless, Mill succeeded in making Utilitarianism a truly altruistic form of hedonism by defending it against the charge of self-interest notable in its original form. He stressed the fact that the principle of utility champions the beatitude of all and showed that men could sacrifice their personal advantage for the welfare of others in the effort to put that principle into practice. For Mill, an act of this kind is the essence of virtue. Not only does it serve the interests of others, but it redounds to the happiness of the individual by the feeling of well-being with which it enriches him. Thus Mill based his form of Utilitarianism not, on egoism, but on the social sentiments of mankind, which yearn for human unity and cooperation. One must be wholly impartial when his own interests appear to be in conflict with those of others.

The attempt to make ethics an exact discipline cannot be described as successful. Ultimately the value of Utilitarianism lay, not in the practicality of its claim to have discovered a method to give precision to moral thought, but in the effective insistence of its advocates that the good of every man is equally precious under the social and legal institutions of society. This insistence made itself felt at a time when that principle needed strong emphasis, and it played an important part in preparing a climate of thought in which the social message of the gospel could command the concentrated attention of many Christian thinkers. BIBLIOG-RAPHY: J. Bentham, *Fragment on Government: Introduction to the Principles of Morals and Legislation* (ed. 1948); J. S. Mill, *Utilitarianism, On Liberty, Essay on Bentham, Together with Selected Writings of Jeremy Bentham and John Austin* (ed. with intro. by M. Warnock, 1962); H. Sidgwick, *Outlines of the History of Ethics* (ed. 1946); A. J. Ayer, "Principle of Utility," in *Philosophical Essays* (1954).

[J. T. HICKEY]

UTOPIA AND ITS LITERATURE. The word utopia was the creation of St. Thomas More in the 16th cent. and means literally "no place," but can also designate "good place." The notion of an ideal society can be traced to Plato's *Republic*, a society dominated by the philosophers and their wisdom. St. Augustine's *City of God* has aspects of the utopian, the viewpoint being the supernatural rather than the natural order. Thomas More revived the Platonic concept and has had numerous imitators, such as the Lutheran Johann Andreä (*Christianopolis*, published in 1619) and Tommaso *Campanella, in *The City of the Sun* (1623). There is a utopian element in the incomplete *The New Atlantis of Lord Bacon* (1627). In the 19th cent. the most celebrated utopian work was *Looking Backward* (1888) by Edward Bellamy, which makes utopia a socialist society and is notable also because in spite of the title it is futuristic. H. G. Wells carried the genre into the 20th cent. with *A Modern Utopia* (1905) and *Men Like Gods* (1925). Wells vacillated between enforcing the primary of the individual and the claims of the state. A contemporary utopia is B. F. Skinner's *Walden Two*, portraying a society dominated by psychology. Anti-utopias are more characteristic of the 20th century. Most notable pictures of a repulsive society are Aldous Huxley's *Brave New World* (1932) and George Orwell's *1984* (1949). Most utopias have been humanist documents emphasizing man's capacity to live rationally. Some were theistic, but the prevailing tone is one of dependence on man's own powers. The anti-utopias depend on a distrust of man's capacity to make reason prevail. BIBLIOGRAPHY: C. Walsh, *From Utopia to Nightmare* (1962).

[J. R. AHERNE]

UTRAQUISTS, the moderate party of the *Hussites. The name denotes their position that all must receive holy communion under the forms of both bread and wine (Lat. *sub utraque specie*). The Utraquists were also called Calixtines (Lat. *calix,* chalice). They were not as anti-Roman doctrinally, or as extreme politically, as the *Taborites. The Utraquist practice was sanctioned by the *Compactata (1433) but was suppressed by the Edict of *Restitution (1629). BIBLIOGRAPHY: Bihlmeyer-Tüchle 2:441–444; bibliog. for Hussites.

[T. C. O'BRIEN]

UTRECHT, DECLARATION OF, see DECLARATION OF UTRECHT.

UTRECHT, SCHISM OF, see SCHISM OF UTRECHT.

UTRECHT, TREATY OF, the collective name for a group of treaties signed at Utrecht, Rastatt, and Baden in 1713–14, ending the War of the Spanish Succession. France recognized the Hanoverian dynasty in England that, with Austria, acknowledged the Bourbon dynasty in Spain, perpetually separated from France. England guaranteed the integrity of the Spanish Empire, but received commercial concessions there. Spain surrendered the Belgian Netherlands, Milan, Naples, and Sardinia to Austria, Sicily to

Savoy, and Gibraltar and Minorca to England. France gave up Newfoundland, Nova Scotia, and the Hudson's Bay area to England. Prussia became a monarchy. Minor boundary adjustments were made by France. BIBLIOGRAPHY: C. A. Petrie, *Earlier Diplomatic History, 1429–1713* (1949); J. B. Wolf, *Emergence of the Great Powers* (1951).

[R. H. SCHMANDT]

UTRECHT, UNION OF, see UNION OF UTRECHT.

UTRECHT PSALTER (*c.*820–835), most extraordinary of all Carolingian MSS, attributed to the Reims School probably under the aegis of Abp. Ebbo. The 108 folios of vellum, written in late-antique (Roman) *capitalia rustica* with uncial headings, are particularly remarkable for 166 pen drawings in brown ink in the nervous, vibrant, expressive line significant of the Reims School, which ensures each psalm a true poetic richness and drama beyond the merely narrative illustration proper to other books of the Bible. The Reims style continued to influence succeeding generations (*Lindau Gospels,* 870).

[M. J. DALY]

UTRECHT SCHOOL, 17th-cent. school of Dutch painting in Utrecht, a Catholic center, characterized by the influence of Caravaggio. Having begun (1524) with Jan van Scorel, it flourished under J. Wtewael, and Master A. Bloemaert, whose students Honthorst and Terbrugghen, returning from Rome (1610–20), painted religious works of relentless realism *(Incredulity of St. Thomas, Calling of St. Matthew)* in strong contrasts of light and dark. The school made Utrecht one of the chief centers of Caravaggesque Baroque in Holland.

[M. J. DALY]

UTTO BL. (d. *c.*800), Benedictine abbot, also called variously Otto, Othon, Odon. He was baptized and reared by Bl. Gamelbert, lord of Michaelsbuch, on whose land he founded the monastery of Metten in Lower Bavaria. He must first have been a monk at Reichenau, near Constance, since the first monks of Metten came from there.

[E. J. DILLON]

UZHOROD, UNION OF, ecclesiastical union of the Ruthenians of the Byzantine-Slavonic rite in the NE part of the former Kingdom of Hungary. At the beginning of the 17th cent. they were Orthodox. Their religion was only tolerated, clergy were treated as serfs. At the same time the landlords of Mukacevo tried by various means to win them to Protestantism. In such conditions the idea of a union with the Catholic Church arose. Promotors were Bp. Basil Tarasovich and the Fathers of St. Basil. The Union took place in the chapel of the Castle of Uzhorod, April 24, 1646, in the presence of Latin-Catholic Bp. George Jakusic of Agris (Eger) and 63 Ruthenian priests. They made the profession of the Catholic faith under three conditions: that their rite be kept; that they preserve the right to elect their bishop, who would then be confirmed by the pope; that their clergy would be equal with the Latin clergy in sharing civil rights. These conditions were approved by the Primate of Hungary, George Lippay. The fulfilment of the third condition depended on the landlords. Because some of them opposed it, Emperor Leopold I, in 1692 issued the *Diploma Leopoldinum* granting the requested civil rights. The Union of Uzhorod soon spread among the Subcarpathian Ruthenians. The Orthodox hierarchy ceased to exist in 1733. According to a report of Bp. Manuel Olsavsky to Rome, in 1759 there were no more Orthodox Christians. Even the Union of Uzhorod is a rare example of a complete union. The movement against the Union began among the immigrants in the U.S. in 1891, with Rev. Alexis *Toth, who with his congregation in Minneapolis, Minn., passed again to Orthodoxy, and after him many others. In 1950 they were about 300,000. Some people who returned to their homeland spread this idea in Subcarpathia and in Slovakia. Also because of political reasons, about 120,000 persons abandoned the Union there. The adherents to the Union in 1945 totaled about 1,350,000. Soon after, the Union was forcibly suppressed: in Romania (1948), in Subcarpathia (1949), in Czechoslovakia (1950). It remained in Yugoslavia, in Hungary, and of course, in the USA and Canada. In Czechoslovakia it was reestablished in 1968. In the USA in 1969 the Ruthenian Metropolitan Province of Munhall, Pa. was established. BIBLIOGRAPHY: M. Lacko, *Unio Uzhorodensis*, (2d ed., 1965; *idem*, "Union of Uzhorod;" *Slovak Studies* 6 (1966): 7–190; *idem* "Forced Liquidation of the Union of Uzhorod;" *Slovak Studies* 1 (1961): 145–185.

[M. LACKO]

V

VACANDARD, ELPHÈGE FLORENT (1849–1927), French priest and church historian, author of many learned and critical studies in hagiography and church history. His findings were not well received by highly placed churchmen and he spent the last fifty years of his life as an obscure chaplain of the Lycée Corneille in Rouen. He wrote concerning the origins of the sacrament of penance, the workings of the Inquisition, and countless articles for the DTC and the *Dictionnaire des connaissances religieuses*. He edited *Études de critique et d'histoire religieuse*.

[E. J. DILLON]

VACANT, ALFRED (1852–1901), founder and first director of the *Dictionnaire de Théologie Catholique*. V. studied theology at Saint-Sulpice (Paris), and later taught at the diocesan seminary in Nancy (1876–1901). He wrote several apologetical works on revelation and the natural knowledge of God as well as an important analysis of Vatican I's apostolic constitution *Dei Filius*, dealing with the relationship between faith and reason. His emphasis on the historical development of theology and its precision as a science is consistently evident in the DTC. BIBLIOGRAPHY: E. Amann, DTC 15, 2447–2462.

[T. M. MCFADDEN]

VACARIUS (d. after 1198), glossator of Roman law. A Lombard civilian lawyer, trained at Bologna, he went to England (*c*.1139–45) and joined the household of Abp. Theobald of Canterbury. He lectured on Roman law at Oxford as early as 1149, thereby evidencing the existence of that university prior to 1167. His judicial activities in England and his anti-Becket associations indicate that he was not responsible for the introduction of studies in canon law into that country. His writings include the *Liber pauperum* (*c*.1149); *Summa de matrimonio* (*c*.1157–59); *De assumpto homine*; and *Liber contra multiplices et varios errores* (1177). BIBLIOGRAPHY: S. Kuttner and E. Rathbone, "Anglo-Norman Canonists of the 12th Century," *Traditio*

7 (1949–51) 279–358; B. Paradisi, "Diritto canonico e tendenze di scuola nei glossatori da Irnerio ad Accursio," *Studi medievali*, 3d ser. 6 (1965) 155–287; O. J. Blum, NCE 14:509–510.

[O. J. BLUM]

VACATIO LEGIS, in canon law, the suspension of a law during the interval between its *promulgation and the date of its coming into effect. In the case of laws of the Holy See this is a three-month period following the date of promulgation in the *Acta Apostolicae Sedis*, the official organ of the Holy See (CIC, c.9). For episcopal laws there is ordinarily no *vacatio legis* (c.335, § 2).

[T. C. O'BRIEN]

VADIANUS, JOACHIM (Von Watt; 1484–1551), Swiss humanist, Reformer at Sankt-Gallen, historian. He wrote commentaries on works of Pliny, Dionysius Afer, and Pomponius Mela. He also became a doctor of medicine and was appointed city physician at Sankt-Gallen in 1518, Bürgermeister in 1526. He was largely responsible for Protestantizing the city. His prime historical work is *Grosse Chronik der Abte von Skt. Gallen*. Though unpublished until the 19th cent. V.'s works influenced other historians and were marked by a degree of objectivity uncommon in the polemical atmosphere of his time.

[T. C. O'BRIEN]

VAET, JACOB (d. 1567), Flemish composer. V. was Kapellmeister to Maximilian II from 1554. A composer almost exclusively of church music, he is, perhaps, best known for a magnificent *Te Deum* for eight voices. Copies in MSS of his Masses, motets, etc. may be found in various libraries of Europe. M. Steinhardt in *Denkmaler der Tonkunst in Osterreich* undertook a complete edition of his works.

[M. T. LEGGE]

VAGAS (East Arm., vakas), the distinctively Armenian amice. To the top of the linen humeral part is attached a long stiff band of colored or decorated material some 4 inches high, which remains visible on the celebrant's shoulders and back, over the *shourtchar*. In older usage, the word *vakas* referred to a stole.

[A. CODY]

VAIN OBSERVANCES, a classification of *superstitions contrary to the virtue of *religion. Superstition is a wrong way of worship, either in that worship is offered to some object other than God, or is offered in unwarranted ways. Vain observances come under the second excess: they transgress the ways God prescribes for worship (ThAq ST 2a2ae. 92,1 & 2). Their basic disorder consists in seeking knowledge or even physical effects from an appeal to imagined demonic powers. Among the forms are: black magic; consulting astrological shapes and figures; consulting artifacts, numbers or words; incantations, amulets, and esoteric inscriptions; fortune telling. (*ibid.*, 96,1–4). Serious participation in the practices of occultism, in astrology, or in spiritualism fall within this category of sin. The wearing of religious medals or relics sometimes becomes a superstition; the rightful purpose, however, is to express confidence in God and in the intercession of the saints, not in the physical object worn. See IMAGES, VENERATION OF.

[T. C. O'BRIEN]

VAINGLORY (*inanis gloria*), the fault of immoderately desiring to manifest good qualities and to have them acclaimed. This is to be distinguished from the healthy desire to be justly esteemed (Mt 5.6) and from a relatively harmless vanity about one's appearance. Aristotle already noticed the occupational hazard of the magnanimous man to put too high a price on glory (*Nicomachean Ethics*, 4.3), and, as might have been expected, the patristic moralists found vainglory even more inimical to Christian virtue. However, though alive to its kinship with pride (Gregory the Great treats the two as one, which he considers a capital sin), they were not disposed to make too much of it. John Chrysostom represents this attitude, and Thomas Aquinas developed him in holding that human respect and the craving for it, which constitute the matter and motive of vainglory, are not important enough in themselves to strike directly at the heart of charity. Yet it can breed seven daughters, most rather worse than itself. These are boastfulness, hypocrisy, disobedience, obstinacy, quarrelsomeness, discord, and the itch for novelty. BIBLIOGRAPHY: ThAq ST 2a2ae, 132 (esp. in ed. Lat-Eng, v. 42, ed. A. Ross and P. Walsh 1964).

[T. GILBY]

VAISHNAVISM, a Hindu religion, probably originating as a bhakti cult during the 1st and 2d cent. B.C. among certain non-Aryan tribes. The defining concern is ritual devotion to *Vishnu and his two major incarnations, *Rama and Krishna. Its history and origin are linked with the obscure ancient Pañcharātra sect. Its primary features are: an emphasis on total surrender of self to God, in whom one must have absolute faith; devotion to God through simple ritual and image-worship without the intermediation of priests or knowledge; a distinctive ritualism that includes caste-marking; a strident antipriestly, anti-Brahmanic attitude (later somewhat softened by Shankara [788–838], the Vedantic philosopher who commented on the *Bhagavad Gita*), and displacement of Sanskrit by such vernaculars as Marathi, Tamil, and Hindi. The major works of Vaishnava literature are: the *Pañcharātra Āgamas*, samhitas (final compilations) of Sandilya and his followers (*c.*100 A.D.) which comprise the first systematic treatment of five primitive doctrines into a syncretistic monotheism of Vishnu; the *Mahabharata* (*c.*500 A.D.), an epic poem, probably the world's longest at 220,000 lines, which embodied three earlier works, the *Nārāyanīya*, the *Anugītā*, and the *Harivamsa*; hymns of early Tamil poet-saints, the Alvārs (*c.*650 A.D.); the *Bhagavad Gita* (*c.*750), by an unknown writer, which became ch. 25–42 of the *Mahabharata*; the *Vishnu Purana* (*c.*800); and the *Bhagavata Purana* (*c.*900), which incorporates vast quantities of supernatural lore and legends about Krishna. The great number of Vaishnavite figures in religion and literature and the numerous Vaishnavite subsects all testify to the rapid development and growth of Vaishnavism since the Hindu medieval period.

[R. J. LITZ]

VAISON, COUNCILS OF. Of the two early councils convoked at Vaison in SE France, the second in 529 was of more lasting importance. Five canons regulated the education of future clerics; encouraged preaching everywhere; introduced the chanting of the *Kyrie Eleison*; prescribed the reading of the pope's name in the liturgy; and inserted the phrase, "as it was in the beginning," into the minor doxology. BIBLIOGRAPHY: J. Rath, LTK 10:592 for bibliog.

[B. L. MARTHALER]

VAJRAYANA, the "diamond" or "thunderbolt" (Sanskrit *vajra*), vehicle (*yāna*) of salvation. It is a Buddhist tradition of N India, Nepal, and esp. Tibet (see TANTRISM) resulting from the incorporation (*c.*600 A.D.) of the cult of Indian goddesses (esp. Tara, a savior-goddess, and *Shakti, as *Siva's "energy" or consort) and sexual polarity, with certain emphases of the *Mahayana (esp. the possibility of enlightenment here and now, and Nagarjuna's *sunyata*, the "emptiness" or relativity of all things, even the distinction between *samsara and *nirvana). Through extensive use of aids to enlightenment (*upaya*, skill in means)—chants (*mantras), symbolic diagrams (mandalas), and ritual gestures (mudras), together with symbolic and ritual unification of polar opposites (god and goddess, active and passive principle)—one "identifies" with the principle, force, or deity. This leads to or constitutes the transcending of the ordinary, conditioned "self" (the illusion of a "self" is, for Buddhism, the root of all suffering and evil), and the realization or achievement of that *vajra-self* (= Buddhahood) which is transcendent consciousness, wisdom, and freedom. BIBLIOGRAPHY: A. Bharati, *Tantric Tradition* (1965); J. Blofeld, *Tantric Mysticism of Tibet* (1970).

[D. P. EFROYMSON]

VALADES, DIEGO DE (1533–79?), Franciscan missionary, historian, author and artist. He wrote *Retórica christiana*, the first Mexican book published in Europe. It is a description of Indian culture and history.

[P. J. HENNESSEY]

VALAMO, MONASTERY OF, a monastic foundation located on one of the Valamo Islands near Lake Ladoga, in the Karelo-Finnish Republic in Russia. Its founders are believed to have come from Athos in 1329, and to have established the abbey as a center for Greek Orthodox missions. Dissolved in 1618, when Karelia united with Sweden, it was restored by Tsar Peter the great in 1718. It attracted many members, numbering about 500 monks in 1914. Statistics indicate a sharp decline in recent times. Of interest is the fact that church Slavonic was employed as the liturgical language, indicating a strong Cyrillomethodian cultural influence in the past. After 1918, the abbey came under the autonomous Orthodox Church of Finland, Following the Finnish War, this territory was annexed to Russia and the religious community was divided: some members moved to Heinävesi, an independent priory in Finland, while others remained at Valamo. Here the abbey continues in existence despite Communist political control. BIBLIOGRAPHY: L. I. Denisov, *Pravoslovnye monastyri rossinskij imperii* (1909); J. Meyendorff, *Orthodox Church* (1962) 104, 118, 181.

[L. NEMEC]

VALDÉS, FERNANDO DE (1483–1568), Spanish abp. and inquisitor general. Doctor and professor of canon law at Salamanca, he was bp. of Huelva (1524), Orense (1529), Oviedo (1533), and Sigüenza (1539) before becoming abp. of Seville and inquisitor general in 1546. His only rival in power was the abp. of Toledo (Bartolomé de Carranza) whom he bested in a famous dispute which led to the latter's arrest and trial for heresy. In 1558 V. instigated a raid on Protestants which resulted in the capture of their leaders. He published his own Index of forbidden books (1551, 1554, 1559), and lavished his enormous wealth on colleges (Oviedo and Salamanca) and good works. He also built the great church in his home town where he is buried. His *Instructions to the Holy Office* were published posthumously (1612). BIBLIOGRAPHY: R. O. Ausenda, EncCatt 12:964.

[E. J. DILLON]

VALDÉS, JUAN DE (*c*.1495–1541), Spanish humanist and religious writer. Born in Castile, he studied at Alcalá.

During his early years, the influence of Erasmus on him was strong, but his mature religious thought derived more from an indigenous Spanish Catholic piety. His *Dialogue on Christian Doctrine* (1529) and two works by his brother Alfonso incurred the hostility of the Spanish Inquisition because of their Erasmian tendencies, and he went to Italy. From 1531 until his death Juan remained there, first as chamberlain to Pope Clement VII, and after 1534 employed by Cardinal Ercole Gonzaga at Naples. During the latter period he wrote *The Christian Alphabet* as a spiritual guide for Giulia Gonzaga. In these last years he also wrote *One Hundred and Ten Considerations* and commentaries on the Psalms, Romans, Corinthians, and Matthew. While he never repudiated the RC Church or the seven sacraments, he did subordinate ceremony and forms to personal experience of sin and guilt, faith and repentance, and works of love as the fruits of the indwelling Holy Spirit. Through direct contacts V. exerted a profound influence on many prominent persons, and his fame became more widespread after the posthumous publication of his works. Most studies of V. are in languages other than English. An exception is E. Boehmer, *The Lives of Alfonso and Juan de Valdés* (1882). Easily accessible is an introduction to his life and thought, along with excerpts from three important works, in A. M. Mergal, ed., "Evangelical Catholicism as Represented by Juan de Valdés," *Spiritual and Anabaptist Writers* (ed. G. H. Williams, v. 25, LibCC, 1957). BIBLIOGRAPHY: F. C. Church, *Italian Reformers, 1534–1564* (1932) 50–54.

[N. H. MARING]

VAL-DES-ÉCOLIERS, MONASTERY OF, former abbey of canons regular in the Diocese of Langres, France. Its name "Valley of the Scholars" derived from the fact that it was formed *c*.1200 by professors from Paris seeking a life of prayer. The canons modeled their rule on that of the Abbey of Saint-Victor in Paris. It flourished as a center of prayer and study and established many daughter houses until the 17th cent. when it fell under the harmful effects of a *commendation. The monastery, including its great library, was ravaged by the French Revolution and the community ceased to exist.

[T. C. O'BRIEN]

VALDIVIA, LUIS DE (1561–1642), Spanish Jesuit, defender of the Araucanian Indians of Chile against slavery and military attack, author of an Araucanian grammar and dictionary, a catechism, and a guide for confession. He worked among them from 1597, pleaded their cause in Spain in 1609, and again in 1620. His untempered zeal in their behalf antagonized the government and forced his retirement in Spain in 1621.

[T. C. O'BRIEN]

VALDIVIESO, RAFAEL VALENTIN (1804–78), abp. of Santiago in Chile from 1845. Born in Santiago, he did not think of becoming a priest until he was 29; because of his education and family background he was ordained the following year. Before becoming abp., he was an aide to Abp. Larraín, first dean of theology in the Univ. of Chile, and director of *Revista Católica*. As archbishop he viewed himself in the role of Thomas à Becket, founding the St. Thomas of Canterbury Society to defend the prerogatives of the Church against the State. He was a participant of Vatican Council I.

[E. J. DILLON]

VALENCE, COUNCILS OF. For the most part the councils held at Valence in SE France legislated in disciplinary matters. Two, however, took up doctrinal questions: *c.*530, St. Caesarius of Arles was called to account for his teaching on grace; *c.*854, the question of predestination was discussed. BIBLIOGRAPHY: R. Kay, NCE 14:515 for bibliog.

[B. L. MARTHALER]

VALENCIA, MARTÍN DE (*c.*1473–1534), Spanish Franciscan, from 1524 leader of the first Franciscan missionaries to Mexico, the so-called Twelve Apostles of Mexico; custos of the Mexican mission.

VALENS, (328–378), **ROMAN EMPEROR** of the East from 364. Flavius Valens was taken as coregent by his elder brother Valentinian I upon his election after the death of Jovian. Valens, last of the Arian emperors, followed policies dictated by Eudoxius, bishop of Constantinople and his successor, Demophilus of Beroea. He exiled Catholic bishops—Athanasius among them—and opposed the reunion of the Semi-Arians with the Catholics. In 376 he acceded to the petition of the Visigoths, who were threatened by the Huns, and settled them on crown lands in Thrace. When, however, the Visigoths used force to obtain provisions denied them and enlisted the aid of other barbarians, Valens went to war against them. He died on the battlefield of Adrianople in a defeat as severe as that at Cannae. The consequent loss of Thrace and Moesia proved to be a turning point in the fortunes of the empire. BIBLIOGRAPHY: N. H. Baynes, CMedH² 1:218–249.

[M. J. SUELZER]

VALENS (d. after 367), bishop of Mursa, promoter of *Arianism in the West. Both V. and *Ursacius were disciples of Arius and joined in the condemnations of *Athanasius in Councils at Tyre in 335, Arles in 353, and Milan in 355. At Sirmium in 357 V. was with the extreme Arian party, the Anomoeans, but by 359 at the Synod of Rimini had gone over to the Homoeans. He constantly suited his doctrine to the will of the Emperor *Constantius II. Nothing is known of V. after his excommunication in 367 by Pope *Damasus I. St. *Hilary of Poitiers opposed both V. and Ursacius in *Adversus Valentem et Ursacium* (CSEL 65 [1916] 39–193).

[T. C. O'BRIEN]

VALENTINE, SS., the name of two and perhaps three saints of antiquity. The least famous, and but also least controvertible, is the later one, a 5th-cent. missionary bp. in Rhaetia, patron of many ancient churches in the Tirol. First buried at Mais in the Tirol, his remains were later translated to Trent *c.*750, then to Passau in 768. These facts are based on such early reliable testimony as that of Eugippius, Venantius Fortunatus, and Arbeo of Freising. The earliest Valentine is more famous, but his vita is of dubious value. There is an early Roman cult of a priest martyr, decapitated Feb. 14 and buried on the Flaminian Way. A basilica was erected as early as 350; a catacomb was later formed on the spot; his remains were subsequently removed (perhaps to St. Praxedes). The date of martyrdom may have been 269 in the persecution of Claudius the Goth. However, the Roman Martyrology mentions two Valentines martyred the same day by decapitation on the Flaminian Way. One is also associated with Interamna (Terni). There is early local cultus in both places. Perhaps the bp. of Interamna, as he is called in the *Hieronymianum* (Martyrology of St. Jerome), was taken to Rome after his arrest and put to death. Maybe it is the same Valentine with two different cults arising from the two different communities that knew him: Interamna where he was bishop and Rome where he was martyred. *VALENTINE'S DAY, ST.

[E. J. DILLON]

VALENTINE (d. 827), **POPE** for no more than 40 days. V. spent his life in the service of the papal curia, and was made a cardinal deacon by Paschal I (817–24). In accord with the Constitution of Lothair, accepted in 824 by Eugene II, V.'s predecessor, which set aside the election decrees of 796, the lay nobility participated in V.'s election. He was reputed to be a man of great piety and charity. BIBLIOGRAPHY: Mann 2:183–186; L. Duchesne, *Beginnings of the Temporal Sovereignty of the Popes* (tr. A. Mathew, 1908); M. A. Mulholland, NCE 14:517.

[P. F. MULHERN]

VALENTINE OF PASSAU, ST. (d. 440?) bishop. Only fragmentary knowledge of V. exists. He was a bp. in Rhaetia, venerated locally after his death. His remains were transferred to Passau in 768.

VALENTINE'S DAY, February 14, feast commemorating the martyrdom of two early Christian saints of the same name but observed since the Middle Ages as a day for romantic customs. The practice probably derived from the pagan belief that it was at this time of year that the birds began to mate. Little is known of the Valentines whose names were later associated with love and courtship, except that one was a Roman priest and the other bp. of Interamma (now Terni), both of whom were persecuted under the Emperor Claudius and apparently buried the same day on the Flaminian Way. The Church of St. Valentine in Rome, dating to the 4th cent., was supposedly built upon the martyr's grave, and near here, in the 19th cent., fragments inscribed with his name were discovered.

[E. M. GATES]

VALENTINI, GIOVANNI (d. 1649), Italian organist and composer. V. was court organist for Ferdinand II of Austria. He taught organ and composed motets, madrigals, Masses, Magnificats and other sacred music.

[M. T. LEGGE]

VALENTINI, PIER FRANCESCO (d. 1654), Italian composer. V. was court organist for Ferdinand II of Austria. He taught organ and composed motets, madrigals, puntal music, esp. canons, one of which, based on a line of the Salve Regina, has over 2000 possible resolutions.

[M. T. LEGGE]

VALENTINIAN I (321–375), **ROMAN EMPEROR** of the West from 364. An officer in the emperor Jovian's guard, Flavius Valentinianus was elected emperor by the military and civil authorities and took his brother Valens as coregent in the East. He continued to direct the army personally, repelling barbarian attacks from Britain to the Danube. He repudiated Julian's anti-Christian legislation but prided himself on impartiality and permitted pagan worship except for bloody sacrifices. To demonstrate his neutrality further, he successively confirmed the Arian Auxentius and the Catholic Ambrose in the see of Milan. At his court in Trier he was host to Martin of Tours, and he enacted many laws pertaining to church privilege and clerical abuses. BIBLIOGRAPHY: A. Nagl, PW 7.2:2158–04; J. R. Palanque et al., *Church in the Christian Roman Empire* (tr. E. C. Messenger, 1949).

[M. J. SUELZER]

VALENTINIAN II (c.371–392), **ROMAN EMPEROR** of the West together with his brother Gratian from 375. Son of Valentinian I, he was under his mother Justina's regency until he was 12. He was just, abstemious, and "one who laughed at things strong men fear" (Ambrose). During his reign two prominent pagans held high office: Symmachus was prefect of Rome and Praetextatus prefect of the pretorian guards. In 387 the British usurper Maximus, who had overthrown Gratian in the North, crossed the Alps and threatened Milan. V. fled with his mother to the protection of Theodosius in the East, who restored him to his throne the following year. He was slain in 392, probably by the Gothic general Arbogast. BIBLIOGRAPHY: W. Ensslin, PW 7.2:2205–32; R. J. Palanque et al., *Church in the Christian Roman Empire* (tr. E. C. Messenger, 1949).

[M. J. SUELZER]

VALENTINIANS, followers, continuators, and in many cases modifiers of the systematic doctrines of the Gnostic teacher *Valentinus. Of those whose names have been recorded, the most important are probably: Ptolemy (whose *Letter to Flora* has been preserved by Epiphanius); Heracleon (author of the first known commentary on John's Gospel); Theodotus (whose sayings are preserved in Clement of Alexandria's *Excerpts from Theodotus*); and Marcus. There seem to have been divergent eastern (Theodotus) and western or Italian (Heracleon) traditions. BIBLIOGRAPHY: W. Foerster, *Gnosis* 1 (1972).

[D. P. EFROYMSON]

VALENTINUS, most influential Gnostic teacher-theologian who seems to have come to Rome from Alexandria c.140 A.D. He nearly became leader of the Roman community, but eventually separated from it and taught independently. Most of what is known of him and his teaching comes from later anti-Gnostic opponents: Irenaeus, Clement of Alexandria, Tertullian, Hippolytus, and Epiphanius, although some of the writings recently discovered at Nag Hammadi may be V.'s own or contain his teaching (perhaps the *Gospel of Truth, On the Resurrection, Exegesis on the Soul* and the *Gospel of Philip*). The teaching seems to have undergone significant modification even during his life, but at its most distinctive stage (probably late, and at its greatest distance from the more common Christian teachings) the following elements seem prominent. There is a supreme and unknowable God, beyond the creator-God of the Bible. Between this God and the material world intervenes a series of emanations of spiritual principles (*aeons; archons*), the last of which (usually *Sophia*, wisdom) fell because of curiosity and desire to know the Unknowable. The material world and human confinement within it are due to this fall. The human predicament consists in the imprisonment or exile of men's spirits in material bodies and in a material world, forgetful of their true and spiritual identity. Salvation consists essentially in *gnōsis*, the special knowledge of their true identity, brought to humans by Jesus, a non-human redeemer, from the spiritual world from which humans have fallen and to which they are destined to return. BIBLIOGRAPHY: W. Foerster, *Gnosis* (2 v., 1972, 1974); *Le origini dello gnosticismo* (ed. U. Bianchi, 1967); H. Jonas, *Gnostic Religion* (1963); R. McL. Wilson, *Gnostic Problem* (1958); R. M. Grant, *Gnosticism and Early Christianity* (1966).

[D. P. EFROYMSON]

VALERIAN, ST., 5th-cent. bp. of Cemenelum, now called Cimiez, near Nice, in southern France; commemorated on July 23; he must have died c.460. He took part in synods at Riez (439) and Vaison (442), as well as in the jurisdictional dispute settled at Arles (455) between the bp. of Fréjus and the abbot of Lérins. V. joined with the other bps. of the region in their request to the pope to restore metropolitan privileges to the See of Arles. Twenty brief homilies of Valerian are extant, reflecting his love of asceticism and his severe morality; some view him as a Semipelagian, despite his concurrence with Pope Leo I's dogmatic epistle to Flavian. V.'s warm and lengthy letter to the monks of Lérins may indicate he himself had been a monk there before becoming bishop.

[E. J. DILLON]

VALERIAN (Publius Licinius Valerianus; d. *c*.260), **ROMAN EMPEROR** from 253. V. became consul in 238 and was proclaimed emperor by his troops and the Roman senate. Towards the end of his reign he became hostile to the Christians, possibly under the influence of Macrianus. In August 257, he forbade Christian assemblies, confiscated church properties, and ordered the Christians to observe the ceremonies of the state cult. In 258 another edict provided for the degradation of Christian nobles and the execution of ''bishops, priests, and deacons.'' Among the martyrs of his persecution were Sixtus II in the cemetery of Calixtus at Rome, Cyprian of Carthage, and Fructuosus of Tarragona. Valerian was captured in an expedition against the Persian King Sapor in 259 and apparently died soon afterwards. BIBLIOGRAPHY: P. J. Healy, *Valerian Persecution* (1905); U. Wickert, PW 13:488–495; A. Amore, EncCatt 12:986.

[M. J. COSTELLOE]

VALERIO OF BIERZO (fl. 675), Visigothic ascetic and author in NW Spain. He is important for his autobiographical writings, surely an unusual literary genre in 7th-cent. Spain. He wrote three treatises about himself: *Ordo querimoniae, Replicatio*, and *Residuum*, several other treatises: one on Egeria, a charming 4th-cent. nun who made a pilgrimage to the Holy Land *(Vita et epistola beatissimae Egeriae)*, important for establishing the correct spelling of her name; he described several accounts of visions of heaven and hell, and a treatise, *De genere monachorum* for the monks of the Abbey of San Pedro de Montes with which he had some dealings, but was not a member, nor abbot. He probably had no cult, the epithet *sanctus* on his tomb being a designation at that time for any of the faithful. He is an important source for the existence in Visigothic Spain of proprietary churches, i.e., churches completely controlled by landed proprietors who sometimes had serfs ordained to serve the estate church. BIBLIOGRAPHY: *Obras* (ed. R. F. Pousa, 1944); C. M. Aherne, *Valerio of Bierzo, an Ascetic of the Late Visigothic Period* (1949); AS Feb. 3:490.

[C. M. AHERNE]

VALÉRY, ST., see WALARICH, ST.

VALÉRY, PAUL (1871–1945), French poet and essayist. He came under the influence of Huysman, Mallarmé, and the Decadents in 1889. The influence of Mallarmé was profound, though V. published no collection of poetry until 1917. It was Gide who insisted that he collect poems published in obscure magazines years before. Reluctantly V. acceded after years of delay, and *La Jeune Parque* appeared in 1917. An unknown, V. suddenly became a celebrated poet. His best work *Le Cimitière marin* (1920; tr.

Graveyard by the Sea) added to his fame. A student of architecture, V. published in 1923 *Eupolinos:* or, *The Architect*, a prose work. Between 1924–44, under the title *Variété* (tr. *Variety I,* 1927, and *Variety IV,* 1938), he published five collections of essays. Numerous other collections of essays came out in the years 1926 to 1939, among them *Poésie et pensée abstraite* (1939). V.'s poetry has the condensed and obscure characteristics of Impressionism.

[J. R. AHERNE]

VALESIANS, a sect whose existence in 3d cent. Achaea was reported by Epiphanius (*Panarion*, 58), who said that its adherents resorted to castration as a means of serving God, and also attributed other heretical and depraved doctrines to them. However, Epiphanius is the only early source of information about them, and their historical existence has never been established beyond doubt. BIBLIOGRAPHY: G. Bareille, DTC 5:1516–21, s.v. ''Eunuques ou Valésiens.''

[L. G. MÜLLER]

VALESIUS, HENRICUS (1603–76), French patristic scholar. He studied law but turned to a life of scholarship. Among other works he prepared Greek texts with Latin translations of and commentary on the historians Eusebius of Caesarea (1659), Socrates, and Sozomen (1668), and on Theodoret and Evagrius Scholasticus (1673). His studies, reprinted in Migne's *Patrologia Graeca*, contributed significantly to the study of early church history.

[J. R. AHERNE]

VALFRÉ, SEBASTIAN, BL. (1629–1701), confessor. Born in Piedmont, Italy, V. joined the Congregation of the Oratory and was ordained in 1652. His life as preacher, confessor, master of novices, and superior of the Oratory at Turin, Italy, was that of a model religious. His influence over the most miserable inhabitants of the area was great, as was his impact on Victor Amadeus, future king of Sardinia. V. was beatified in 1834.

[J. R. AHERNE]

VALIDITY, in canon law and in theology the state of truly existing as a sacrament or as a contract; distinguished against licitness (in ecclesiastical jargon sometimes termed ''liceity''). Thus a sacrament or a contract may be valid but illicit, i.e. in some way contravene the requirements of positive law. A sacrament is valid when it is celebrated by use of the proper matter and form by the proper minister, having the proper intention. A contract is valid when it is entered into by a competent person: capable of consent, and of fulfilment; possessing the knowledge of the essentials in the contract; not forced or gravely intimidated. The essentials for the validity of the sacraments are determined by the magisterium of the Church (see e.g. D 1312; 1611; 3859–61). In the case of such major contracts as religious profession or marriage the CIC makes explicit the conditions required for validity.

[T. C. O'BRIEN]

VALIGNANO, ALLESANDRO (1539–1606), Italian Jesuit missionary to the Far East. He was born in Chieti (Abruzzi) into an influential family and studied for the law at Padua. After an unspecified religious experience, he entered the Society of Jesus in 1566. His missionary work began in 1573 when he was sent to the Far East to supervise the growth of the Jesuit missions. He remained there for most of the rest of his life, and did much to spread Christianity. Nowhere, however, was his influence as great as in Japan, where his missionary work included not only a plan for the development of self-supporting missions, but also the blending of national customs and culture with Christian precepts. His success is attested to not only by his organizing the first diplomatic mission from Japan to Europe (1582–90), but also by his legacy of approximately 300,000 Christians in Japan at the time of his death.

[P. J. HENNESSEY]

VALLA, LORENZO (1407–57), Italian humanist. Educated in Rome and ordained in 1431, he taught eloquence at the Univ. of Pavia (1429–33), became secretary to King Alfonso V of Aragon and Sicily (1437), and eventually was made apostolic secretary to Pope Nicholas V (1448). He first achieved fame through two works: *De voluptate* (1431) and *Elegantiarum linguae latinae libri sex* (1444). The former, a set of three dialogues presenting Stoic, Epicurean, and Christian ethical values, often construed as representing Renaissance paganism, was an attempt to show that the true Christian life is pointed toward pleasure and happiness. The latter treatise reveals his interest in philology and linguistics and expresses the stock humanist disgust with the Latin of the Middle Ages. V. also attacked scholasticism, but rather ineptly. He launched Renaissance biblical scholarship with his *Adnotationes in Novum Testamentum* (edited by Erasmus, 1526), wherein he applied to the sacred texts the methods used for pagan authors. The *De libero arbitrio* (1493) was esteemed by Martin Luther. His famous *De falso credita et ementita Constantini donatione declamatio* (1440), begun under the auspices of King Alfonso, was a decisive attack on the validity of the document known as the Donation of Constantine, on which the Church largely based her claim to temporal power. This work also has been cited by historians as evidence of V.'s skepticism and his critical spirit. The work, which also challenged papal temporal power, was in reality an attempt to help Alfonso secure Naples. V. soon found himself before a tribunal composed of his enemies and was able to escape punishment only through his protector's intervention. While visiting Rome in 1446 he was again surrounded by enemies and forced to flee for his life. When Pope Nicholas V was elected, he forgave V. and made him apostolic secretary. V.

has been regarded as a forerunner of the Reformation or even as a pure skeptic. RC scholars, however, regard his attempt at a synthesis of antiquity and Christianity, of theology and philology, as intended to serve the Catholic faith.
BIBLIOGRAPHY: J. Leuschner, RGG 6:1227–28; R. Montano, NCE 14:522–523, with bibliog.

[D. G. NUGENT]

VALLADOLID, the name of a province in NW Spain, and also of the capital city of that province. Part of the Tierra de Campos or "granary of Spain," the province is usually considered part of Old Castile, but is also sometimes placed in León. The city lies SW of Burgos where the Río Pisuerga meets the Esqueva. Originally an obscure Moorish town named Belad Ulid, it was conquered by the Christians in the 10th century. First mention of it in Christian writings occurs in a letter of Alfonso VI (1074). The town then grew in importance to become the seat of the Castilian and then of the Spanish court from Alfonso VII to Philip II, and again under Philip III. It was a vital center of the Renaissance in Spain. One of Spain's oldest universities was founded here in 1346. Isabella and Ferdinand were married here in 1469. Philip II was born here in 1527. Christopher Columbus died here in 1506. Cervantes lived here from 1603 to 1606. The city suffered extensive damage during protracted conflict with the French during the Peninsular War (1808–14).

[E. J. DILLON]

VALLARSI, DOMENICO (1702–71), patristic scholar. An Italian cleric, V. spent his life in scholarship at Verona. His chief work is an edition of the writings of St. Jerome, published in the years 1734–42 in 12 volumes, *S. Hieronymi opera omnia* . . . The work is incorporated in PL 22–30; V. also contributed an edition of Rufinus, part of which was reproduced in PL 21; and he collaborated with F. Maffei on the *opera* of St. Hilary of Poitiers (PL 21).

[J. R. AHERNE]

VALLGORNERA, TOMÁS DE (*c.*1595–1665), theologian and spiritual writer. He joined the Dominicans in Barcelona; later he declined the office of provincial of Aragon to which he was twice elected, though under obedience he was to serve as vicar-provincial for the temporarily detached Catalan priories. His major work, *Mystica theologia divi Thomae*, written in an exact and sometimes glowing style to counter the lingering illuminism of the *alumbrados, still remains a respected standard text (last republished Turin, 1924); it assembles the spiritual doctrine of St. Thomas Aquinas and divides it according to the customary purgative, illuminative, and unitive ways.

[T. GILBY]

VALLISCAULIANS, an order of monks (established in Val-des-Choux, France) in the 12th cent. by a Carthusian brother named Viard. Essentially Carthusian, the order was approved by Pope Innocent III in 1205. The Duke of Burgundy built a monastery and chapel for the monks in the late 12th century. The abbey once had 30 dependent houses, mostly in France, but with three established in Scotland. By the 18th cent., numbers at Val-des-Choux had declined to just a few monks, and the order was joined to the Cistercians.

[J. R. AHERNE]

VALLOMBROSA, ABBEY OF, monastery of the Holy Trinity, founded by the Florentine, St. John Gualbert, in 1039. Located on the wooded slopes of Monte Secchieta 22 mi from Florence, Italy, in the Diocese of Fiesole, it was the chief monastery of the Vallombrosans, a new congregation of Benedictine monks, approved in 1070. Favored by the popes, it received generous donations from the Countess Matilda of Tuscany and others of the nobility. The abbey buildings were constructed in the 15th cent. under Abbot Francesco Altoviti. In 1529 it was sacked by the army of Charles V. A century later it was enlarged by Abbot Averardo dei Niccolini. Napoleon confiscated its lands; it was suppressed in 1810–1817 and again in 1866 by the Italian government. Only recently was it restored to the monks, and it is now the residence of the abbot general of the Vallombrosans. BIBLIOGRAPHY: Cottineau 2:3286–87.

[E. J. DILLON]

VALLOMBROSANS, a reform congregation of Benedictine monks founded near Florence, Italy, in 1035 by the abbot St. John Gualbert. The purpose of the congregation was to restore Benedictine life in its pristine rigor. Devoted to poverty, the community refused appointment to church offices and stressed rigorous preparation of candidates for sacred orders; many were trained for Italian dioceses. From the original foundation other autonomous monasteries were set up and ruled by abbots elected by the community and approved by the abbot of Vallombrosa. Abbots served life terms. In 1300 there were upwards of 80 abbeys in the congregation. In the 13th cent. a community of nuns was established, dependent on the male congregation. By 1540 the Vallombrosans had deteriorated and joined the Cassinese Congregation of the Benedictines. Suppression by Napoleon and later by the Italian government in the 19th cent. reduced the Vallombrosans to two abbeys at Livorno and Vallombrosa (since 1961) and a small body of monks. There are three priories in Italy, one in São Paolo, Brazil. There are four houses of Vallombrosan nuns.

[J. R. AHERNE]

VALLOTTI, FRANCESCO (1697–1780), Italian organist, composer and theorist. Maestro at the Church of St. Anthony at Padua from 1730 until his death, V. was one of the greatest organists of his time. He composed a great quantity of church music and was the author of a learned theoretical work in four volumes dealing with the principles of Rameau and Tartini.

[M. T. LEGGE]

VALOIS, a region of Picardy, part of the government of the Ile-de-France, which gives its name to three cadet branches of the Capetian kings of France, the original from 1328, the Orléans from 1498, and the Angoulême from 1515 to 1589. The Valois title to the crown was challenged by the English in the Hundred Years War, and vindicated by St. Joan of Arc.

[T. GILBY]

VALOR ECCLESIASTICUS, the appraisal of all church properties and revenues in England made by royal commissioners in 1535. The legislation by which Henry VIII became (1534) supreme head of the Church in England made him recipient of a large portion of ecclesiastical and monastic revenues. The evaluation made proved a prelude to the *dissolution of the monasteries. These records, sometimes called the ''King's Books,'' provided a survey of the ecclesiastical establishment of the time, which is valuable to the historian. They were published in 6 volumes, 1810–34, by the Records' Commissioners in England. BIBLIOGRAPHY: Hughes RE 1:282–283.

[T. C. O'BRIEN]

VALPARAISO, CATHOLIC UNIVERSITY OF, a coeducational institution of higher learning in Chile. It was founded in 1928, was officially recognized by the Chilean government in 1929, and since 1951 has been under the direction of the Jesuits. It was canonically erected as a pontifical university in 1961 with the approval of John XXIII. The bp. of Valparaiso is the institution's grand chancellor and administration is in the hands of the rector, who is assisted by the university council. The university comprises faculties of physics and mathematics; architecture and town planning; law and social science; economics and commerce; philosophy and education; and agriculture. It also operates a technical and other institutes, began the first educational television station in Chile, maintains a pilot plant for industrial fishing research, and offers adult courses for workmen. The library contains 155,000 vols. Enrollment numbers *c.* 7,500; the teaching staff, 1,000 full-time and part-time members.

[M. B. MURPHY]

VALUE, PHILOSOPHY OF, a general designation, relating to many different fields, for a concern with axiological problems having to do with the definition, identification, and understanding of the good and the bad, as well as with the process and consequences of decision making. The notion of a distinct philosophy of value, as such, did not become current until the end of the 19th century. Ethics and aesthetics are usually the first disciplines to be considered dedicated to a philosophy of value, yet other fields, including sociology, anthropology, jurisprudence, political science, economics, education, psychology, even logic and epistemology also actively pursue this inquiry into value. Philosophers have always discussed the differences between the good and the bad, the true and false, the beautiful and ugly, obligation and prohibition, but until the 19th cent. when Lotze, Nietzsche, and Ritschl expanded the usage, the term "value" was used primarily as an economic indicator of worth. By the late 19th and early 20th cent., the broader sense of "value" as a common subject of many fields had been established, initially by A. Meinong, C. von Ehrenfels, and other disciples of Franz Brentano. The notion of a general theory of value was maintained in England by Neo-Hegelians such as Bosanquet, Sorley and others; and in the U.S., during the 1910s and 20s, J. Dewey, R. B. Perry, E. W. Hall, D. W. Prall, D. H. Parker and others were also developing the notion. S. C. Pepper and P. W. Taylor, both Americans, later explored it further. The vague and often ambiguous way in which "value" and "valuation" can be and are used has made some, like C. I. Lewis, restrict value problems to the sub-discipline of ethics, while at the same time, others like Ralph Barton Perry, seek common elements of all value problems regardless of their subject matter, whether it be economics or aesthetics. Recent philosophies of value follow two major lines, normative and metanormative theories: the former dealing with value judgments and specific platforms defending particular definitions and descriptions of the good or right; the latter dealing with the analysis of how and why a value judgment is made. Normative theorists, in defining the good or the final end toward which man and nature tend, have arrived at numerous definitions of the good: pleasure (Epicurus, utilitarians); satisfaction (Dewey, Lewis); divine communion (Augustine, Aquinas); self-realization (Bradley); power (Nietzsche); knowledge (Spinoza); superb activity or eudaemonia (Aristotle); love, friendship, harmony, enlightenment, justice, beauty, truth, etc., all of which are seen as intrinsically good, ends worthy of themselves. The metanormative theorists, recognizing that humans continually make value judgments, ask questions about the basis of those judgments and the manner in which they are made, and demand justification either in linguistic, empirical, or intuitional terms for the content and method of those judgments. Among these theories, basically critiques of normative theories, there are many in the 20th century which question even the basis and justification for making metanormative theories.

[R. J. LITZ]

VALUE, THEOLOGICAL, the validity of a proposition in theology, judged by its objective consistency with divine revelation. As in any other science, so in theology, there are theses and hypotheses. The former are affirmations provable by their agreement with known declarations of divine faith. The latter are suppositions that are either debatable, because their agreement with the faith is only conjectured, or even untenable, because they are inconsistent with established principles of Catholic Christianity. In the area of doctrinal affirmations, the theological value of a thesis qualifies it on the scale of the Church's authoritative teaching, which ranges from solemn definition to simple (and often silent) acceptance by the magisterium.

On a broader scale, the history of dogma is almost a history of dialogue on the value of theological hypotheses. Here the value assigned to a speculative theory serves to distinguish it first of all from doctrinal positions that are certain and not hypothetical. Such terms as probable and more (or less) commonly held are familiar. But it may also identify a theory as rash or improbable, where analogy of faith shows a conflict with the main body of Christian truth.

Development of doctrine is reflected in the changing theological value of theses and hypotheses. New insights may raise the value of established theses, and raise or lower the value of hypotheses. Guided by the Church's teaching, this value becomes an index of genuine dogmatic progress.
BIBLIOGRAPHY: E. J. Fortman, NCE 10:523–524; S. Cartechini, *De valore notarum theologicarum* (1951); R. Latourelle, *Theology of Revelation* (1966) 249–314.

[J. A. HARDON]

VALVERDE, VICENTE DE (d. 1541), Spanish Dominican, first bp. of Peru, where he surveyed and reported on the land that had been captured by the Spanish.

[P. J. HENNESSEY]

VALVERDE TÉLLEZ, EMETERIO (1864–1948), Mexican bp., bibliographer. He was ordained in 1887; in 1909 he became bishop of Leon. A promoter of Catholic education and devotion to Christ the King, he addressed notable pastorals to his diocese. V. wrote in the field of philosophy (e.g., *Apuntaciones históricas sobre la filósofia en Mexico*), mysticism (*Poema del amor divino*), and an important 3-v. *Bio-bibliografía eclesiástica mexicana (1821–1943)*, referring only to bishop and priest writers of independent Mexico, (1949).

[J. R. AHERNE]

VAN CALOEN, GERARD, see CALOEN, GERARD VAN.

VANDALISM, the wanton destruction of the property of another individual or moral person. It is a sin against justice, an *injury to another's rights; it is precisely an act of causing *damage, and requires restitution. Where the vandals are juveniles, parents may share in the obligation to make restitution, simply because minors are still under parental care. The principles governing cooperation in *sin come into play to determine the extent of a parental obligation to restitution.

[T. C. O'BRIEN]

VANDALS, Germanic people originally living along the Baltic, who reached the area of the Oder and the Vistula by the 1st cent. B.C. and later spread farther east. Recruited into the Roman army, some of the Vandals attained high positions. Stilicho, for instance, c.400 became the most powerful individual in the Roman Empire. In 406 the Vandals, along with the Suevi and other tribes, crossed the Rhine boundary into Gaul and entered Spain 3 years later. Under Geiseric they built a fleet, mastered Africa by 431, and soon annexed the islands of the western Mediterranean. In 455 they sacked Rome. Tyrannical but illiterate, they left administration in the hands of the subject Romans. They disappeared from history soon after their defeat in 533 by Justinian. BIBLIOGRAPHY: L. Schmidt, *Geschichte der Germanen: Vandalen* (1944).

[M. J. SUELZER]

VAN DER BROECK, THEODORE (1783–1851), missionary. A Dutch priest ordained in 1808, V. entered the Dominicans in 1817. Coming to the U.S. in 1832 he served at Green Bay, Wis. among the Indians and whites. At Little Chute, V. taught the Indians to read, built a church, and ministered among the Menominee and Winnebago Indians 200 miles away. In addition to working for their conversion, he taught the Indians to work with tools and to cultivate the land. In 1848 V. journeyed to his native Holland and brought back a number of Dutch immigrants who settled in NE Wisconsin.

[J. R. AHERNE]

VAN DER SCHRIEK, LOUISE (1813–86), educator. She was educated in Belgium where she entered the Sisters of Notre Dame de Namur. In 1840 she was one of a group of eight to bring the community to Cincinnati, Ohio. From 1848 until her death. V. was superior of Notre Dame houses E of the Rocky Mountains. An able administrator, she was responsible for 25 houses being founded during her regime. Among innovative projects were schools for black girls in Cinncinnati and Philadelphia, and night schools for adult immigrants.

[J. R. AHERNE]

VAN DOREN, MARK (1894–1972), American poet, teacher, and critic. Brother of Carl (1885–1950), V. was educated at the Univ. of Illinois and at Columbia, where he later taught. *Collected Poems* (1922–1938) earned him a Pulitzer Prize in 1940. Studies in Dryden, Hawthorne, and the metaphysical poets are included in the canon of his works, as are several novels, collections of lectures, and one of short stories (1962). He published his autobiography in 1958.

[R. M. FUNCHION]

VAN DYCK, ANTHONY (1599–1641), noted Flemish painter of portraits and scenes, religious and mythological. Gifted pupil and collaborator with Rubens (1618–20), V. was in England (1620), Italy (1621–27), and Holland (1628–29), then finally returned to London (1632), where he was knighted and appointed court painter to Charles I. Very early studies by V. are elegant but melancholic, with strong value contrasts. The *Martyrdom of St. Peter* and *Martyrdom of St. Sebastian* are in a free, rhythmic style.

The *Descent of the Holy Ghost* and *Christ Crowned with Thorns* were done in the years of work with Rubens. In 1617–21 V. produced numerous distinguished portraits influenced by the Venetians and the eclectics. Though remaining Flemish, he added a personal touch of increased elegance and hauteur to the Rubensian image. Settled in London (1632), he recorded with distinction the royal family and nobility in beautifully decorative panels rather than in deeply felt character studies, with a style that influenced British portraiture for 200 years. BIBLIOGRAPHY: H. Vey, *Die Zeichnungen Anton van Dyck* (2 v., 1962); A. Neppi, EncCatt 12:1017–19.

[M. J. DALY]

VANGADIZZA, ABBEY OF, former Benedictine monastery of Santa Maria, 15 mi. from Rovigo on the bank of the Adige, in the Diocese of Adria, Veneto, Italy. Dating from at least the mid-10th cent., it was richly endowed by popes and emperors. By order of Innocent III it passed from the Benedictines to the Camaldolese in 1213. After a period of decline, it was placed in commendation by Eugene IV in 1435, and was suppressed in 1808–10. Some impressive ruins remain. BIBLIOGRAPHY: Cottineau 2:3294.

[E. J. DILLON]

VAN HOVE, ALPHONSE (1872–1947), Belgian canonist. H. was professor of canon law at the Univ. of Louvain. Besides writings on historical and political questions, he produced the *Commentarium Lovaniense in Codicem juris canonici* (5 v., 1928; v.1 repr. 1945), one of the most esteemed commentaries on the *Normae generales* of the *Code of Canon Law*. BIBLIOGRAPHY: W. Onclin in EphemThLov (1948) 5–22, with complete list of H.'s works; L. Guizard, *Catholicisme* 5:995–996.

[T. C. O'BRIEN]

VANINI, GIULIO CESARE (1584–1619), natural philosopher who held that nature is the first cause and that it has the stature of a divinity.

[P. J. HENNESSEY]

VANITY, see VAINGLORY.

VANN, GERALD (1907–63), English Dominican theologian and writer. He entered the order in 1923 and was ordained in 1929. From 1934–52 he taught at Blackfriars School, Laxton, a Catholic public school. He lectured widely in the U.S. and served as a visiting professor at The Catholic Univ. of America, Washington, D.C. from 1959 to 1962. V. was the author of a number of books which had wide circulation in England and the United States. Among them were *Morality and War* (1939), *The Heart of Man* (1944), *The Divine Pity* (1945), and *The Paradise Tree* (1959), *The Temptations of Christ* (with P. K. Meagher, 1957). V. was both a profound Thomistic moralist and perceptive to human values and anguish; he was able to bring theology to the devotional and pastoral level, to the great advantage of his many readers and students.

[J. R. AHERNE]

VANNE, ST., see VITONUS, ST.

VAN NOORT, GERARD (1861–1946), Dutch theologian. A teacher at the seminary of Warmond, he became known for his *Tractatus apologetici et dogmatici* (1898–1908) in 10 volumes, which were highly regarded for the study of apologetics.

[P. J. HENNESSEY]

VAN QUICKENBORNE, CHARLES FELIX (1788–1837), missionary, educator. A Belgian educated for the priesthood, V. was ordained in 1812 and because of his interest in the U.S. missions entered the Jesuits in 1815 and came to the U.S. in 1817. He labored in parish ministry in Maryland with special care for the poor and the blacks. In 1823 he was named superior of the Jesuits setting out for Missouri and established the center of a new province at Florissant, Mo., founding a parish, a seminary for Indians, and two schools. V. established St. Louis College in 1828 (see VERHAEGEN, P.). He travelled into the territories of the Osage, Potawatomi, and Kickapoo Indians, setting up in 1836 a mission with a resident priest among the Kickapoo and then among the Potawatomi. V. was the pioneer missionary of Missouri, Iowa, and Illinois. Among his disciples were P. *De Smet and C. *Hoecken.

[J. R. AHERNE]

VAN RAALTE, ALBERTUS CHRISTIANUS (1811–76), principal founder and developer of the Dutch immigrant colony at Holland, Mich. in the mid-19th century. He joined others in 1834 in revolt against the repressive policies of the Netherlands government in its enforcement of a *state Church. Ordained in 1836 by the Free Reformed Church, in 1846 he led many to the U.S. as a haven from persecution. In 1850 V. represented the immigrant group in securing union with the Reformed Dutch Church of the eastern United States. His labors furnished a foundation for the whole western section of the *Reformed Church in America, largely through the establishment of Hope College (1851) and Western Theological Seminary (1866), both in Holland, Michigan. BIBLIOGRAPHY: life by A. Hyma (1947).

[E. EENIGENBURG]

VAN ROSSUM, WILHELM MARINUS (1854–1932), Redemptorist theologian, cardinal. Born in the Netherlands, V. entered the Redemptorists in 1874 and was ordained in 1879. In 1896 he became consultor of the Holy Office in Rome. He was named cardinal in 1911 and president of the Pontifical Biblical Commission in 1914, where he contributed to Benedict XIV's encyclical *Spiritus Paraclitus,* summarizing the Church's position on Scripture. From 1918

on, V. served as Prefect of the Congregation for the Propagation of the Faith, and greatly intensified the missionary planning and activity of the Church. V. was author of *De essentia sacramenti ordinis* (1914).

[J. R. AHERNE]

VARANGIANS, (probably from the Russian *warjag,* tradesman), term used to designate the Scandinavian invaders who set up trading posts on the Baltic coastlines, and along the Volga and Dnieper Rivers. They came into contact with the populations of the East-European continent from the 7th to the 10th century. The first Varangian route, that of the Volga, united the Baltic sea coast with the shores of the Caspian Sea. Between 854 and 860 the Great Route of the Varangians to the Greeks was opened, by way of the Neman, Dvina and Dnieper Rivers. The Varangians advanced into the Ukraine, established the principality of Kiev, the *Rus* state that incorporated Slavic societies evolving from tribal to political status. Under Varangian influence the word "Russian" soon came to mean a people, a state, a Christian rite, and a civilization essentially Slavic.

[L. PEANO]

VARDAN, MAMIKONIAN, ST. (d. 451), Armenian commander of the resistance against. Yazdgard II, the Persian ruler who sought to impose Zoroastrianism on the Christian Armenians. V. fell in battle at Avarair after preparing himself and his troops for martyrdom by the reception of the Eucharist.

[L. PEANO]

VARDAPET (VARTAPED), Armenian tr. of the NT word *didaskalos*, teacher. Since the 12th cent. the term also meant theologian. The degree of Vardapet was granted after the fulfillment of the 14 required steps of scholarship. This once highly cherished degree has, since the 18th cent., become merely an honorary title granted by the bps. of the Armenian Church.

[L. PEANO]

VARELA Y MORALES, FÉLIX (1788–1853), patriot, philosopher, educator. Born in Havana, Cuba, he studied for the priesthood and was ordained in Havana in 1811. Appointed to the chair of philosophy at the college and seminary of San Carlos in Havana at age 23, he proved an inspiring and progressive educator. As a philosopher he did not adhere to scholasticism but was influenced by 18th-cent. empiricists. He was also devoted to scientific experiments. Among his published philosophical works were *Institutiones philosophiae eclecticae ad usum studiosae juventutis editae* (1812–14), and *Las lecciónes de filosofía* (4 v., 1818–20), the latter his most notable work. When Spain became a constitutional monarchy V. lectured on the new constitution and wrote a widely acclaimed *Observaciones sobre la constitución politica de la monarquía Espanõla* (1821); a year later he was elected to the Cortes in Madrid.

Among other achievements there, he worked for the abolition of slavery in Cuba and greater autonomy for the Spanish colonies. When the absolute monarchy returned in 1823, V. fled to the U.S., laboring in Philadelphia and New York, continuing his prolific writing and living in danger of assassination for his attacks on the Spanish monarchy. V. published *Cartas á Elpidio sobre la impiedad, la superstición y el fanatismo* (2 v. 1835–38), a defense of Christianity. An active priest serving the poor, V. was co-administrator of New York twice on the absence of the bp. and was vicar-general from 1839 till his death. BIBLIOGRA - PHY: DAB 11:224–225.

[J. R. AHERNE]

VARGAS Y MEXIA, FRANCISCO DE (1484–1566), Spanish diplomat and jurist. He presented the celebrated protest of Charles I against the removal of the Council of Trent to Bologna and was a Spanish representative at the second period of the Council of Trent (1551–52).

[P. J. HENNESSEY]

VARIAE PRECES, one of the liturgical books published by Solesmes in 1901. It is a useful source for hymns, antiphons and sequences not included in the standard publications.

[M. T. LEGGE]

VARIATA, the edition of the *Augsburg Confession prepared by Philipp *Melanchthon in 1540. Because of differences from the earlier editions (1530 and 1531), this came to be disparaged by Lutherans as the Altered Augsburg Confession, and was disowned by the *Formula of Concord in distinction from the *Invariata*, the unaltered. The *Variata* reflects Melanchthon's *synergism, and particularly in art. 10, a toning down of the Lutheran doctrine of the Real Presence in an attempt at concord with Zwinglian and Calvinistic eucharistic teaching. The *Invariata* is the edition accepted by Lutherans as their primary *confession of faith. *CRYPTO-CALVINISM; *GNESIOLUTHERANISM.

[T. C. O'BRIEN]

VARIN D'AINVILLE, JOSEPH-DÉSIRÉ (1769–1850), French religious founder. He entered the new Society of the Sacred Heart of Jesus and was ordained in 1796. He succeeded the founder as superior of the congregation in 1797. When it merged with the *Paccanarists in 1799 he supervised the French houses. When they were disbanded in 1804 by Napoleon, V. worked in the parish ministry. With the restoration of the Jesuits in France (1814) he entered the Society. In an effort to offset the damage done by the French Revolution, V. organized catechetical missions and retreats. V. aided St. Madeleine Sophie *Barat and St. Julie *Billiart and their Congregations, and in the founding of the *Sisters Faithful Companions of Jesus.

[J. R. AHERNE]

VARNHAGEN, FRANCISCO ALDOLPHE DE (1816–78), Brazilian historian. Born of a German father in Sorocaba, São Paolo and raised in an atmosphere of European culture, V. was yet also a patriotic Brazilian nobleman, who had an enormous influence on Brazilian historiography. After his education in Portugal he began his historical research in the Jesuit letters at São Paolo. His entrance into the diplomatic service in 1842 enabled him to consult Portuguese, Spanish, Dutch, Paraguayan, and Austrian archives. His thorough searches uncovered many fundamental sources for the history of colonial Brazil, esp. 16th-cent. chronicles and diaries, documents on the 17th-cent. Dutch War, and Metternich's correspondence with Baron de Mareschal relating conversations with Pedro I concerning the Brazilian independence movement. In addition to publishing critical editions of many of these documents and several specialized studies, he wrote the *Historia general do Brazil* (1854–57). Although frequently criticized for its deficiencies in synthesis and conceptualization, this work presented, as a result of V.'s assiduous research, a thoroughly detailed treatment of Brazilian history from the European discovery to the declaration of independence. BIBLIOGRAPHY: E. Bradford Burns, *Perspectives on Brazilian History* (1967).

[R. J. GIBBONS]

VARRO, MARCUS TERENTIUS (116–27 B.C.), greatest of ancient Roman scholars. Trained in the method of the Alexandrian philologists, he became thoroughly versed in Greek philosophy through his studies in Athens. In philosophy, like his contemporary Cicero, he was an eclectic. His scholarly production was voluminous and encyclopedic in character, comprising some 74 works on political, social, and literary history, religion, philosophy, agriculture, geography, rhetoric, law, music, medicine, and architecture, and also satires and dialogues. Of these works only *Rerum rusticarum libri III*, and 6 books of his *De lingua latina* are extant. His *Antiquitatum rerum humanarum et divinarum libri XLI* is particularly important. In the last 16 books, *Res divinae*, Varro dealt with priests, temples, shrines, festivals, games, public and private worship, and the gods. St. Augustine drew heavily on Varro's *Antiquitates* in his *De civitate Dei* and made effective use of his data and philosophical interpretation of Roman religion in refuting the pagan charges against Christianity. Augustine is the chief source for the contents of the *Antiquitates* and for the extant fragments of that work. BIB - LIOGRAPHY: M. R. P. McGuire, NCE 14:540; J. P. Enk, OCD 937; H. Dörrie, LexAW 3183–85; H. Dahlmann, PW, Suppl. 6 (1935) 1172–77.

[M. R. P. MCGUIRE]

VASARI, GIORGIO (1511–74), Italian painter and architect of the Florentine School. Though he worked in the prevailing Mannerist style (e.g., his design for the Uffizi,

1560, which purposely distorts classical proportions), V. is noted primarily as the first systematic biographer of artists. His enormous work, *Le Vite de' più eccellenti architetti, pittori et scultori italiani, da Cimabue insino a tempi nostri*, encyclopedic in scope, was first published in Florence in 1550, with a second edition in 1568. Although somewhat less reliable in the treatment of early artists, tending to be a collector of fact and legend, V. is extremely informative about his contemporaries, esp. his most highly regarded friend, Michelangelo. V.'s *Lives* are invaluable to the student of Renaissance art. BIBLIOGRAPHY: A. Del Vita, Enc-Catt 12:1036–37.

[S. CONWAY]

VASCHALDE, ARTHUR ADOLPHE (1871–1942), Orientalist. V. was on the staff of The Catholic University of America, Washington, as an editor for the *Corpus scriptorum Christianorum Orientalium*. In addition to his scholarly contributions to this series, V. published important indices to publications of Coptic biblical texts for the Rev-Bibl (1919–22), and *Le Muséon* (1930–33). BIBLIOGRAPHY: R. J. Scollard, NCE 14:541–542.

[T. M. MCFADDEN]

VASECTOMY, the surgical ligation of the two tubes (*vasa deferentia*) through which the spermatazoa pass from the testicles into the seminal fluid at ejaculation. This relatively simple and painless procedure is more and more being urged as the most effective form of contraception, since it renders the male's ejaculate sterile. But contraception is a purpose that does not justify this form of *mutilation morally, since vasectomy is not done to preserve the man's life. The forced sterilization of many men by this means during World War II raised the canonical question of whether an irreversible vasectomy gives rise to the canonical marriage impediment of *impotence. After a long period of debate the final consensus of moralists and canonists came to be that it does not. This position was affirmed officially on May 11, 1977 in a decree of the Congregation for the Doctrine of the Faith, issued in August, 1977.

[T. C. O'BRIEN]

VASEY, NICHOLAS JOSEPH (1875–1931), Augustinian provincial superior. Ordained in 1898, V. served his order for many years at Villanova College, Villanova, Pa., including a term as vice president. Elected provincial in 1918, he transformed the province and its work in his 8 years as major superior. Until his tenure, the order was confined to the Atlantic seaboard with the exception of a high school and parish in Chicago. During the years 1918 to 1926 Vasey established a parish and high school in Illinois, three parishes in Michigan, and a preparatory school in Tulsa, Oklahoma. In California he created three parishes and two high schools. In the East, the order's work was expanded by the addition of a preparatory school, a house of philosophy

and a parish in Pennsylvania, a postulate, a novitiate, two parishes in New York, and a theologate in Washington, D.C. The extraordinary growth represented by these 19 new foundations changed the nature of the Augustinian apostolate in the United States.

[J. R. AHERNE]

VÁSQUEZ, FRANCISCO XAVIER (1703–85), Peruvian Augustinian. V. was made general of his order in 1753 and became noted as a builder. BIBLIOGRAPHY: DE 3:1273.

[M. J. SUELZER]

VÄSTERÅS (WESTERAS), ORDINANCE OF, decree of the Diet of Västerås in Sweden, 1527, turning over, at the order of King Gustavus Vasa, church property to the nobles in order to gain their support. The expropriation was part of Gustavus's plan of state domination over the Church, a step toward the Lutheran state Church that emerged a decade later in Sweden.

[T. C. O'BRIEN]

VATABLE, FRANÇOIS (*c.*1485–1547), Hebraist. V. was the first professor of Hebrew at the Collège de France; his lectures were so significant that he is credited with restoring Hebrew studies in France. Students' notes from his exegetical lectures, condemned by the Sorbonne professors in their original inaccurate form, were revised and included in Robert *Estienne's Latin translation of the Bible. They are an example of precision and attention to the literal sense that was unusual at the time. BIBLIOGRAPHY: DB 5.2:2378–79; C. L. Souvay, CE 15:276; L. F. Hartman, NCE 14:543.

[T. M. MCFADDEN]

VATELOTTES, see CHRISTIAN DOCTRINE (NANCY), SISTERS OF.

VÄTH, ALPHONSE (1874–1937), German Jesuit missionary in Bombay, India, for many years. He taught for 6 years at St. Francis Xavier College in Bombay. From 1918 to 1925 he was editor of *Catholic Missions*. V. published many books and made a number of contributions to scientific journals. Among his books were *German Jesuits in India* (1920), *St. Thomas the Apostle of India* (1925), and *Picture of the World Church* (1932).

[J. R. AHERNE]

VATICAN, the residence of the pope and the immediate territory of the Vatican City State; the central authorities of the RC Church and its administration; the papacy. BIBLIOGRAPHY: F. X. Murphy, NCE 14:543–551; J. Carcopino and A. I. Marrou, DACL 15.2:3291–3346.

[F. H. BRIGHAM]

VATICAN ARCHIVES, the official collection of the acts and documents of the government of the RC Church established by Pope Paul V in 1612. Appropriate archival materials prior to this were stored separately in the Bibliotheca secreta, Castel Sant'Angelo, the Apostolic Camera and other offices. More documents continue to be maintained in what has become the Central Papal Archive. However, other documents belonging to the Holy Office, the Propagation of the Faith, the Sacred Penitentiary, the Congregations of Ceremonies and for Extraordinary Ecclesiastical Affairs are still kept apart from the Central Archives. Pope Leo XIII made the archives available for scholarly research in 1881. BIBLIOGRAPHY: K. A. Fink NCE 14:551–555.

[F. H. BRIGHAM]

VATICAN CITY, STATE OF (Lo stato della Città del Vaticano), the name given to the independent State established by the Treaty in the Lateran Pacts of 1929. This international treaty declared that this territory was under the absolute sovereignty of the pope, completely independent of the government of Italy. The Republic of Italy renewed this commitment in 1948. The territory includes 108.7 acres to the right of the Tiber, bounded on all sides by walls dating from the Middle Ages with the exception of the East which is lined by the open side of St. Peter's Square and Colonnade. The Treaty also provided for the jurisdiction of the Vatican beyond its immediate boundaries to areas and buildings including the major basilicas of St. John Lateran, St. Mary Major and St. Paul Outside the Walls, other office buildings, the transmitting center of Vatican Radio, and the papal palace at Castel Gandalfo. It has its own constitution regulating its administrative, economic, and business activities. BIBLIOGRAPHY: L. Barbarito, NCE 14:555–559; F. Hayward, *Pope and Vatican City* (tr. B. Ward, 1950); J. Neuvecelle, *Vatican, Its Organization, Customs and Way of Life* (tr. G. Libaire, 1955).

[F. H. BRIGHAM]

VATICAN COUNCILS. The great Renaissance edifice, St. Peter's basilica in Vatican City, was the theater for two modern councils of exceptional importance. Although they were nearly a century apart, there were certain similarities between them: both were called to address problems arising from a changed intellectual and social milieu in which the Church found itself; the number of conciliar fathers far surpassed the attendance at any previous council; Vatican Councils I and II were catholic in the sense that they drew a large proportion of their representatives from non-European countries; and each in its own way was primarily concerned with ecclesiological issues.

Vatican Council I (1869–70). Between the solemn opening on Dec. 8, 1869, and the suspension of its activities on Sept. 1, 1870, the Council met in three other solemn sessions and 89 general congregations. Taking part in it were 774 prelates, from five continents. Two short doctrinal constitutions were promulgated, and much business was left undone. Pope Pius IX first proposed an ecumenical council to a closed meeting of cardinals on Dec. 6, 1864. He an-

nounced it publicly at the end of June 1867, and a year later issued the bull *Aeterni Patris,* formally convoking it. The bull of convocation was addressed to bishops, abbot-presidents, and generals of religious orders. In September 1868 papal briefs were sent to the patriarchs of the Orthodox, Armenian, Jacobite, and Coptic Churches inviting them to attend; but, displeased by the wording of the invitations, they refused. Pius's public appeal "to Protestants and all non-Catholics" to return to the true fold was also rebuffed and widely resented.

In the spring of 1867 the Pope appointed a steering committee, the "Central Commission," which in turn appointed five sub-committees to prepare materials for the Council. These subcommittees, taking into consideration proposals and suggestions sent in by the bishops, drafted 51 schemata. Shortly before the Council opened Pius IX issued an apostolic letter, *Multiplices inter* (Nov. 27, 1869), governing the Council's procedures. Based on an important memorandum drafted by Bp. Hefele, it established four deputations, elected by the Council, to prepare final drafts on faith, ecclesiastical discipline, Eastern Churches, and religious orders. Though every conciliar father enjoyed the right to speak in the general meetings, only the pope, as head of the Council, could introduce topics to the agenda. Later, in an effort to speed up the work of the Council, the procedures were somewhat modified by another rescript, *Apostolicis litteris* (Feb. 20, 1870). The Central Commission spent much time weighing the possibility of a definition of papal *infallibility. The spectrum of Catholic opinion ranged from those who strongly opposed a definition to those who would set no limits to it whatever. When the showdown came, the Council itself seemed to be divided between the "infallibilists" who, with varying degrees of enthusiasm, favored the definition, and the "inopportunists" who, for one reason or another, thought the definition inadvisable. The eventual outcome of the debate was predictable because the infallibilists led by Abp. Manning of Westminster, among others, succeeded in electing to the deputation on faith only those known to favor a definition of papal infallibility. Moreover, the infallibilists had the backing of Pius IX. Although 51 schemata were drafted by the preparatory committees, only six were discussed in the general congregations. The two dogmatic constitutions ultimately passed by the Council, *Dei filius* and *Pastor aeternus*, represented modified versions of the original proposals. *Dei filius*, approved in the third solemn session (April 24, 1870), is a dogmatic statement, divided into four chapters treating: (1) God the creator of the universe; (2) the possibility for man to know God and the need for divine revelation; (3) the nature of faith; and (4) the twofold order of knowledge found in faith and reason (see D 3000–45). *Dei filius* is a revision and abridgment of only the first part of the original schema on the Catholic faith, *Apostolici muneris*.

The issue of papal infallibility, which overshadowed the proceedings of the Council from the very beginning, was after much debate resolved in the dogmatic constitution *Pas-*

tor aeternus (D 3050–75). In the form finally approved in the fourth session (July 18, 1870), it consists of a prologue and four chapters: (1) the institution of papal primacy; (2) its continuation; (3) its extent; and (4) the solemn definition of papal infallibility. The original schema on the Church, *Supremi pastoris*, distributed to the fathers on Jan. 21, 1870, consisted of 15 chapters; it made no mention of infallibility. *Pastor aeternus* represents a recasting of chapters 11 and 12 of *Supremi pastoris*, together with a distillation of many amendments proposed by the fathers of the Council. The outbreak of the Franco-Prussian War in July and the Italian occupation of the Papal States in September brought the Council to an abrupt standstill. On Oct. 20, 1870, Pius IX formally suspended it *sine die*, but the seed sown by the Council did not wither and die. The encyclicals of Leo XIII on ecclesiological questions and on relations of Church and State drew heavily on the archives of Vatican I. Though the Council promulgated no disciplinary decrees, changes in church law proposed by the preparatory committees made their way into the reform legislation of Pope Pius X and the Code of Canon Law (1918).

Vatican Council II (1962–65). Over a period of 4 years, the Council met in 168 general congregations and 10 public sessions. Present at the opening on Oct. 11, 1962, were 2,540 prelates, and the attendance held well above 2,000 throughout. In addition, the number of delegate-observers from Orthodox and Protestant Churches reached 93 in the last year of the Council. Vatican II issued 16 formal statements and was the occasion for uncounted volumes of study documents and published speeches. On Jan. 23, 1959, 3 months after his election, Pope John XXIII announced his intention of calling an ecumenical council. On Pentecost (May 17) he appointed a planning committee to consult with bishops, the curia, and faculties of theology and canon law with an eye toward organizing an agenda. A year later (June 5, 1960), Pope John issued a motu proprio, *Superno Dei nutu*, establishing a Central Committee, 10 preparatory commissions, and two secretariats to draft schemata; in all, 73 documents were prepared in advance of the Council. The formal convocation came with the bull *Humanae salutis* on Christmas, 1961. The motu proprio *Appropinquante concilio* (Aug. 6, 1962) gave guidelines for the organization and procedures of the Council. It established an international steering committee of 10 cardinals, who also took turns presiding over the general congregations. Ten commissions, roughly corresponding to the preparatory commissions, were set up for: (1) the doctrine of faith and morals; (2) bishops and government of dioceses; (3) the discipline of the clergy and Christian people; (4) religious; (5) the discipline of the sacraments; (6) the liturgy; (7) studies and seminaries; (8) the Oriental Churches; (9) the missions; and (10) the lay apostolate, communications media, and entertainment. Each commission was to have a chairman, 8 members were to be appointed by the pope, and 16 were to be elected. A parliamentary maneuver by Cardinal Lienart of Lille in the very first general congregation

wrested the initiative from the curialists and made it possible to elect truly representative commissions. Pope John appointed nine members instead of the prescribed eight, and Pope Paul VI later increased the size of the commissions to 30.

Another crucial move in the early days of the Council was Pope John's decision to make the *Secretariat for Promoting Christian Unity under Cardinal Bea equal in status to the ten commissions. The secretariat had arranged for several Orthodox and Protestant communions to send delegate-observers. Although they were not permitted to speak or vote in the general congregations, the delegate-observers were able to make their views known to the conciliar commissions through Bea's secretariat. Although Pope John died after the first period of the Council, Oct. 11–Dec. 8, 1962, his influence was felt throughout. In an address on opening day John expressed the pastoral concern and the hope for unity among all men that were to dominate all the subsequent discussions and proceedings. The first public statement of his successor, Paul VI, announced the continuation of the Council. Before it reconvened Pope Paul revised some of the procedural rules and invited laymen, representing Catholic agencies in various parts of the world, to attend. Later, lay and religious women were welcomed into the Council as auditors. Under Paul Vatican II met over 3 years. While the work of the commissions was continuous, the full Council met only in the fall: Sept. 29–Dec. 4, 1963; Sept. 14–Nov. 21, 1964; Sept. 14–Dec. 8, 1965. By the time the Council adjourned in December 1965 it had issued four constitutions, nine decrees, and three declarations, totaling more than 100,000 words. The tone of the conciliar statements is positive and the style straightforward. The Council made a conscious effort to avoid rigid definitions and condemnatory anathemas and, wherever possible, to couch its teaching in biblical language rather than scholastic or juridical terms. The constitutions, even the ones labelled "pastoral," are primarily doctrinal statements expressing the common faith of the Church about itself. The decrees have more immediate practical significance and deal with particular aspects of church life. The declarations express general principles and guidelines normative for the Church in its relations with other societies.

The Council's statements with their official Latin titles and the dates of promulgation are as follows:

Constitution on the Sacred Liturgy (*Sacrosanctum concilium*). Dec. 4, 1963.

Dogmatic Constitution on the Church (*Lumen gentium*). Nov. 21, 1964.

Dogmatic Constitution on Divine Revelation (*Dei Verbum*). Nov. 18, 1965.

Pastoral Constitution on the Church in the Modern World (*Gaudium et spes*). Dec. 7, 1965.

Decree on the Instruments of Social Communication (*Inter mirifica*). Dec. 4, 1963.

Decree on Ecumenism (*Unitatis redintegratio*). Nov. 21, 1964.

Decree on Eastern Catholic Churches (*Orientalium ecclesiarum*). Nov. 21, 1964.

Decree on the Bishops' Pastoral Office in the Church (*Christus Dominus*). Oct. 28, 1965.

Decree on Priestly Formation (*Optatum totius*). Oct. 28, 1965.

Decree on the Appropriate Renewal of the Religious Life (*Perfectae caritatis*). Oct. 28, 1965.

Decree on the Apostolate of the Laity (*Apostolicam actuositatem*). Oct. 28, 1965.

Decree on the Ministry and Life of Priests (*Presbyterorum ordinis*). Dec. 7, 1965.

Decree on the Church's Missionary Activity (*Ad gentes*). Dec. 7, 1965.

Declaration on Christian Education (*Gravissimum educationis*). Oct. 28, 1965.

Declaration on the Relationship of the Church to Non-Christian Religions (*Nostra aetate*). Oct. 28, 1965.

Declaration on Religious Freedom (*Dignitatis humanae*). Dec. 7, 1965.

Even before Vatican II ended Pope Paul took steps to ensure implementation of the conciliar directives. By a series of motu proprios, he set up the administrative structures to carry on the work of reform and renewal called for by the Council: *Sacram liturgiam* (Jan. 25, 1964) instituted a commission to implement the Constitution on the Sacred Liturgy; *In fructibus multis* (April 2, 1964) established a commission for the communications media; *Integrae servandae* (Dec. 7, 1965) reorganized the Holy Office into the Congregation for the Doctrine of the Faith; *Finis concilii* (Jan. 11, 1966) created five more postconciliar commissions, a new Central Committee to coordinate their work, and gave permanent status to the Secretariats for Promoting Christian Unity, for Non-Christian Religions, and for Non-Believers. The five postconciliar commissions corresponded to the commissions of the Council itself, for (1) bishops and the government of dioceses; (2) religious; (3) the missions; (4) Christian education; and (5) the apostolate of the laity.

Historical Perspective. The century bracketed by the two Vatican Councils was a period of revolutionary upheaval. Empires fell and national borders were redrawn, and in that 100 years men became aware that every frontier of human experience—social, cultural, economic, political and scientific, emotional, psychological and intellectual— had changed. The Councils illustrate the difference. Pope Pius IX announced Vatican I on Dec. 6, 1864, 2 days before he published the encyclical *Quanta cura*; he intended the Council to address itself to the issues outlined in the *Syllabus of Errors*. When Vatican II took up the problems of the Church in the modern world a century later, there was an entirely different life-style. The questions were new, and the style of the answers seemed as important as the content to men of the 20th century. Vatican II became a symbol of many important changes, but most importantly it seemed to symbolize the Church's willingness to accept change. In the face of the unknown future, the openness of Vatican II won the sympathy of all honest searchers after truth. The concern to reestablish unity within the Christian community proved inspirational to all believers in Christ. The catholicity of the Council, bringing men together from all over the world, gave it truly ecumenical appeal. BIBLIOGRAPHY: for Vatican I, C. Butler, *Vatican Council* (2 v., 1930; abr. ed., 1962); H. Jedin, *Ecumenical Councils of the Catholic Church* (1961), 143–180; J. J. Hennesey, NCE 14:559–563; *idem, First Council of the Vatican: The American Experience* (1963); BIBLIOGRAPHY: for Vatican II, R. F. Trisco, NCE 14:563–572; *Documents of Vatican II* (ed. W. M. Abbot, 1966); H. Vorgrimler, *Commentary on the Documents of Vatican II* (5 v., 1967–69); *Council Daybook: Vatican II* (ed. F. Anderson, 3 v., 1965–66); Xavier Rynne, *Vatican Council Two* (1968); *American Participation in the Second Vatican Council* (ed. V. A. Yzermans, 1967); *Dictionary of the Council* (eds. J. Deretz and A. Nocent, 1968); *Council Speeches of Vatican Two* (eds. H. Küng et al., 1964).

[B. L. MARTHALER]

VATICAN LIBRARY, the library that dates in its current form back to the 15th cent. and the patronage of Nicholas V (1447–55). Its present building was erected by Sixtus V in the 16th century. Vatican Greek and Latin MSS are its most notable collections, making it foremost as a MS center. Pope Leo XIII was responsible for opening the archives of the library to scholars in 1881, and Pope Pius XI made it more accessible and expanded its collections. Pius XII in 1952 allowed over 11 million pages of Vatican MSS to be photographed and housed in the Pius XII Library, St. Louis, Missouri. BIBLIOGRAPHY: N. Vian, NCE 14:572–577.

[F. H. BRIGHAM]

VATICAN OBSERVATORY, the Specola Vaticana, was established by Pope Gregory XIII in 1576 to assist in calendar reform. Its recent history began when Pope Leo XIII restored it to its original site, the "Tower of the Winds." It has been directed by the Jesuits since the appointment of J. G. Hagan in 1906 by Pope Pius X. After 1930, its director, Joannes Stein, transferred it to its present location, the papal summer palace at Castel Gandolpho and outfitted it with new telescopes and other required equipment. That section of the Astrographic Catalogue assigned to the Vatican charting the location of one-half million stars was completed in 1928 with its final charts released in 1957, under its current director, D. J. K. O'Connell. It continues to monitor the positions of stars in the Vatican zone of the sky by conducting photographic studies and photoelectric photometry of variable stars together with research of interstellar polarization. BIBLIOGRAPHY: D. J. K. O'Connell NCE 14:577.

[F. H. BRIGHAM]

VATICAN RADIO, the station established by Pius XI in 1931 which broadcasts by shortwave in 31 languages around the clock. The programming consists of news, religious themes, and special events at the Vatican; prayers are also broadcast in the various languages.

VAUDREUIL, PHILLIPE DE RIGAUD DE (*c*.1643–1725), governor of New France (1703–25). A native of France, V. rose rapidly in the army, coming to Quebec in 1687 as commander of marine troops in New France. Administrator of Montreal, he participated in the defense of Quebec against the British in 1690. In 1703 V. was named Governor of New France and a marquis. Through skill and luck he maintained a successful military position against the British, but fared badly as civil administrator because of economic problems.

[J. R. AHERNE]

VAUGHAN, the name of an old Herefordshire family of landed gentry, settled at Courtfield in the marches between England and Wales, remarkable for their faithfulness to the old religion, their devoutness, and their theatrical good looks. These qualities came out strongly in the 19th cent., when six sons and five daughters were given to the RC church. **Bernard John Vaughan** (1847–1922), a Jesuit, was perhaps the best known preacher of his day; he moved in high society and sought publicity, yet was a simple religious whose first interest was social reform and work in the London slums. His eldest brother, **Herbert Alfred *Vaughan,** (1832–1903), third abp. of Westminster and cardinal, the intimate of and successor to H. E. Manning whose ultramontanism he continued: he had bought *The Tablet to* promote this cause. He was the founder of the *Mill Hill missionaries, and of the great cathedral of Westminster designed by J. F. Bentley. He was unresponsive to the ethos of Anglicanism, and secured the papal letter, *Apostolicae curae* which denied the validity of its orders. The next brother, **Roger Bede Vaughan,** (1834–1883) was a Benedictine who became second abp. of Sydney, Australia. His death was followed by the hegemony for 50 years of Irishborn bishops in Australia. But he had been an effective leader and honor was done to him when his remains were returned from England, where he had died, and reburied in his cathedral at Sydney when this epoch was closed. He was the author of a monumental life of St. Thomas Aquinas (1872).

[T. GILBY]

VAUGHAN, HENRY (1622–95), a Welsh metaphysical poet of secular and religious works. He was influenced by both Donne and George Herbert but lacks their precision and intensity. In 1648 he experienced a religious conversion resulting from political problems and personal illness, but most from the influence of Herbert's holy life. His volume *Silex Scintillans* (1650–55), contains his best poems. He also wrote fine devotional prose. Vaughan is concerned with the dichotomy between body and soul, and expresses the exiled soul's longing to return to its heavenly home. He anticipates Wordsworth's interest in childhood as being close to divinity and laments the adult's loss of the sense of God. His finest images combine light with peace, majesty, security, and control: "eternity . . . like a great *Ring* of pure and endless light." BIBLIOGRAPHY: F. E. Hutchinson, *Henry Vaughan: A Life and Interpretation* (1947).

[M. M. BARRY]

VAUGHAN, HERBERT ALFRED (1832–1903), English card., abp. of Westminster. Descendant of an old Catholic family of *recusants, V. studied for the priesthood (as did five of his brothers), was ordained in 1854, and became vice president of St. Edmund's College, Ware, in 1857 joined H. E. *Manning's Oblates of St. Charles, but left them when a dispute in 1861 imperiled the community. V. was fired with an ambition to aid the foreign missions and spent two years traveling in mission countries and elsewhere, raising funds for their support. His journey took him to Panama (where he faced arrest for ministering to victims of an epidemic), to San Francisco, then to South America, through Chile and Peru and thence around the Horn to Brazil. Recalled to London, V. founded St. Joseph's College at Mill Hill for missioners. The *Mill Hill Fathers grew rapidly and were assigned by the Holy See to work among blacks in the U.S. (see JOSEPHITE FATHERS). V. came to America and travelled through most of the South, learning the missionary situation. Back in London, he bought *The Tablet* and was its editor for three years (1868–71), championing papal infallibility. In 1872 he was named bp. of Salford in Lancashire. He opened the Pastoral Seminary for newly ordained priests in 1875 and in 1880 St. Bede's College, Manchester. V. brought a whole new efficiency to his diocese esp. in the area of financial management. Alert to loss of faith by Catholic children in Protestant institutions and homes, he established the Rescue and Protection Society. Marshalling thousands of volunteer workers and maintaining seven homes for children, V. achieved complete success. At Salford he inaugurated a strong campaign to have Parliament acknowledge the obligation of the state to support voluntary schools (private) as well as boarding schools (public). He continued the campaign even after he went to London. He was appointed abp. of Westminster to succeed Card. Manning in 1892, and made cardinal the next year. It is ironic that among the English bps. it was V. who led the way in requesting the Holy See to approve a Catholic chaplaincy at Oxford and Cambridge; it was he, with Manning, who had bitterly opposed Card. Newman's proposal of the same project 30 years before. The petition was approved by Leo XIII in 1895. In the controversy over *Anglican orders, V. played a large part. The petition for Rome's recognition of validity was the work of a group of Anglicans desiring corporate reunion between the Church of England and the Roman Catholic Church. V. regarded this as unfortunate meeting ground because it depended upon historical fact rather than doctrine, but he urged the pope to appoint an international commission to investigate. The result was Leo XIII's *Apostolicae curae* denying the validity of Anglican orders. A major work of V. was the building of Westminster Cathedral, long envisioned but never started. The ultimate design, a combination of Romanesque and Byzantine styles, he approved. He laid the cornerstone in 1895; the cathedral was opened June 25, 1903, sadly enough, for V.'s funeral. Another of his major concerns was to achieve recognition by the Parliament that all school children were equally the charge of the state for educational support. He worked with the Abp. of Canterbury and other church leaders, but it was V.'s advocacy that won the battle; the Education Act of 1902 accepted his philosophy. Both in Manchester and London, V. was a competent administrator, a careful manager of finances, and a notable public figure. Never a scholar or theologian of note, he was a simple, idealistic, plainspoken man; his faith was great and his zeal exemplary. His devotional writings were extremely popular. BIBLIOGRAPHY: Snead-Cox, *Life of Cardinal Vaughan* (1910).

[J. R. AHERNE]

VAUGHAN WILLIAMS, RALPH (1872–1958), English composer. He studied at the Royal College of Music in London and at Cambridge. His early interest in English folk music both gave these materials new life and, along with the music of the Tudor period, became a source of stimulation and inspiration from which he developed a highly personal and often distinctively English style. He served with the British army in World War I. Afterwards, among other things, he became professor of composition at the Royal College of Music in London and paid three visits to the U.S., both conducting and lecturing at Bryn Mawr College and at Cornell and Yale. He completed the last of his nine great symphonies at the age of 85. Other of his works include orchestral suites, chamber music and numerous stage and choral works. Some of his well known sacred compositions are *Mass in G Minor* (1923), *Fantasia on Christmas Carols* (1912), a *Benedicite*, a *Magnificat* and several contributions to *The English Hymnal* (e.g. "For All the Saints"). BIBLIOGRAPHY: D. Ewen, *The World of Twentieth Century Music* (1968).

[M. T. LEGGE]

VAUVENARGUES, LUC DE CLAPIERS, DE (1715–47), French moralist. After a disappointing military career which ruined his health, V. settled in Paris and, befriended by Voltaire and Marmontel, devoted himself to writing. His main work, *Introduction à la connaissance de l'esprit humain suivie de réflexions et de maximes* (1746) consists of maxims, portraits, reflections on writers and other subjects. In spite of his sufferings, V. worked out a system of optimism derived from the rehabilitation of sentiment contrasting with La Rochefoucauld's and Pascal's pessimism. V. remains a fine example of moral courage and fortitude. BIBLIOGRAPHY: M. Wallas, *Luc de Clapiers, Marquis de Vauvenargues* (1928); Fernand Vial, *Une*

philosophie et une morale du sentiment: Luc de Clapiers Marquis de Vauvenargues (1938).

[A. S. CRISAFULLI]

VAUX, ROLAND DE (1903–1971), Dominican archeologist and biblical scholar. He was responsible for many significant excavations in the Holy Land. His most important work was *Ancient Israel: Its Life and Institutions*. From 1933 his life was spent at the École Biblique a Jerusalem; he was its director (1945–65) and editor of its journal, *Revue biblique* (1938–53).

[P. J. HENNESSEY]

VAUX-DE-CERNAY, ABBEY OF, French Cistercian monastery near Versailles, was founded in 1118 by monks of Savigny, with whom it joined the Cistercians in 1147. The abbey prospered for two cent. and actively opposed Albigensianism. Ruined in the wars of the 14th–16th cent. and unable to recover under commendatory abbots, the community of 12 monks joined the Cistercian Strict Observance in 1624, but it was suppressed during the Revolution (1791). The ruins of the 12th-cent. Gothic church are among the finest Cistercian architecture. BIBLIOGRAPHY: M. Aubert, *L'Abbaye des Vaux-de-Cernay* (1934); L. J. Lekai, NCE 14:580.

[L. J. LEKAI]

VAZ, JOSEPH (1652–1711), apostle of Ceylon. A native of Goa, India, ordained in 1676, V. labored in India until he formed a group of Oratorians in 1685 to go to Ceylon, then under persecution by the Dutch. Going alone, disguised as a beggar, V. had considerable success despite persecution. When the King of Kandy granted religious freedom through V.'s influence, he brought other Oratorians to Ceylon, and the group had great success in making converts.

[J. R. AHERNE]

VÁZQUEZ, FRANCISCO JAVIER (1703–85), Peruvian Augustinian, prior general from 1733, polemicist. After ordination in Peru he spent the rest of his life in Rome, filling administrative posts for his order. He was a staunch defender of the position of H. *Noris in controversies on the efficacy of grace. He was also an implacable opponent of the Jesuits, sympathetic to their Jansenist enemies, and a significant contributor to suppression of the Society in 1773.

[T. C. O'BRIEN]

VÁZQUEZ, GABRIEL (1549–1604), Spanish Jesuit, theologian. A member of the Society from 1569, he taught theology in Madrid (1577–79), Alcalá (1579–85), Rome, succeeding F. *Suárez at the Collegio Romana (1585–91), and again in Alcalá (1591–1604). V.'s writings, in the form of brief expositions of the text of Aquinas's *Summa* followed by long "disputations, i.e., the author's personal interpretations, were published in 10 v., 1598–1616. In

1617 M. de la Llana published *Disputationes metaphysicae*, a philosophy textbook culled from V.'s writings. All through his teaching career, V. engaged in controversy and sometimes in personal exchanges with Suárez. Near the end of his career V. was briefly imprisoned by the Inquisition for permitting at Alcalá an academic disputation on the hypothetical thesis that it is not a matter of faith that any particular pope is the successor of St. Peter. As a commentator on Aquinas at almost every point in dogmatic theology V. took positions diametrically opposed to those of the *Summa* and adverse to St. Thomas's overall viewpoint. V.'s works are marked by a thorough use of conciliar documents and the writings of St. Augustine. In moral theology his work belongs to the history of the origins of *probabilism. A mark of the tentativeness of his defense of using a less probable opinion as a guide is what may be described as his own *tutiorism (that in cases of doubt the safer course must be followed). In fact this reservation is a relic of the traditional moral position that to be good an act must be judged so by the moral agent; probablism requires a merely extrinsic justification—someone else's opinion. The acceptance of probabilism, not the gesture towards the classic tradition, was the side of V.'s moral thought that prevailed.

[T. C. O'BRIEN]

VÁZQUEZ DE ESPINOSA, ANTONIO (*c.* 1570–1630), Spanish Discalced Carmelite and chronicler of Spanish America. The author was born in Jérez de la Frontera, and after entering the Carmelites he sailed to Spanish America and reached Mexico by 1612. He may have traveled as far south as Chile before returning to Spain after 1626. His important MS *Compendio y descripción de las Indias Occidentales* was recently discovered in the Vatican Library (1931) by Charles U. Clark. The work consists of acute and objective observations of all aspects of life in Spanish America at the height of the empire's prosperity, including descriptions of nature, the economy, and the workings of Church and State.

[E. J. DILLON]

VÁZQUEZ DE HERRARA, FRANCISCO (1647–1712?), historian. A Guatemalan, V. entered the Franciscans in his native land and was ordained in 1670. A teacher of theology and censor for the Inquisition, he was appointed chronicler of his order's province in Guatemala in 1681. Though not a trained historian, V. proved to be a conscientious chronicler with a sense for the use of original documents. His principal work was *Crónica de la provincia de Santísimo Nombre de Jesús . . .* (ed. L. Lamadrid, 4 v., 1937–44).

[J. R. AHERNE]

VÁZQUEZ SANTA ANA, HIGINIO (1899–1962), editor, educator. A native of Mexico, V. was inspector general of education of the city of Durango and later director general of education for the state of Michoacán. A journalist, he was an editor of several periodicals such as *Juventud Liberal, Revista de Revistas* and *Sursum*. In 1939 he began studies for the priesthood and was ordained in 1942; he did pastoral work in Mexico City. Among books and pamphlets written by V. were important studies of Mexican folklore such as *Cantares y corridos* and *Danzas mexicanas*.

[J. R. AHERNE]

VEDANTA (Sanskrit, the end or goal of the Vedas), often used in literary references to the Upanishads, but commonly refers to one of the six so-called orthodox systems of Indian philosophy (technically darshanas, or points of view). Vedanta lays great stress on the teaching of the *Upanishads and of the *Vedanta Sutras,* as well as the *Bhagavad Gita*. There are three versions or schools of Vedanta. The system of *Shankara stresses the identity or oneness, at its deepest level, of the ''self'' (*atman*) and ultimate reality (*Brahman*). Thus his position is called advaita (nondualist) Vedanta. The way to liberation (*moksha*) is through a higher knowledge or inner realization (*jnana*). The system of *Ramanuja posits some distinction between the self and ultimate reality, which, for Ramanuja, is a personal God, *Ishvara (Supreme Lord). This position is classified as a qualified nondualism (*vishishtadvaita*); in it love or devotion (*bhakti*), directed usually to *Vishnu or esp. Krishna, leads to salvation. The marginal system of A. Madhva is usually described as dualist (*dvaita*). BIBLIOGRAPHY: S. N. Dasgupta, *History of Indian Philosophy,* v. 1–4 (1951–55); T. Organ, *Hinduism* (1974) 97–124; 241–86.

[D. P. EFROYMSON]

VEDANTA SOCIETY, a religious body cultivating the Vedas, sacred writings of Hinduism. The society was established in the U.S. in 1898 by the Swami Vivekananda (1863–1902), who had introduced his ideas at the World's Parliament of Religion held in Chicago in 1893. He stressed esp. the idea, derived from Ramakrishna-Paramahansa (1834–86), that all religions are in essence one, expressions of many ways for man to achieve full self-realization. The Vedanta teachings and methods of achieving wisdom are a form of *theosophy. The headquarters of the society are in Calcutta, India; there were 13 centers in the U.S. in 1975, each largely independent; combined membership was *c.*1000. The principal center is the Vedanta Society of New York.

[F. E. MASER]

VEDAS, the hymns, treatises and other writings comprising the sacred canon of Brahmanic *Hinduism, recognized as authoritative in all orthodox Hinduism; composed in Vedic, an archaic form of Sanskrit. The root of the word, *vid,* means know, and the *amnaya* or sacred text of the Vedas is believed to be the revealed knowledge, existing eternal and perfect from the beginning of time, of the all-knowing Brahman as "heard" by inspired ancient rishis who handed it down orally. From a disorderly mass of verses, the sage Vyasa salvaged as much as possible and organized the material in four groups, each of which came under the care of one of Vyasa's leading disciples. These four parts are: the *Rig-Veda, 1,028 hymns addressed to the gods; Sama-Veda, an anthology of verses from the Rig-Veda gathered for liturgical purposes; Yajur-Veda, an arrangement of sacrificial formulae and portions of hymns from the Rig-Veda for ritual purposes; and the Atharva-Veda, the spells, hymns, verses, and prose containing the magical lore of the Atharvans, a class of priestly magicians. These hymns or mantras are metrical songs of praise composed during the Vedic period of Hinduism, from the second millennium B.C. to 800 B.C. The *Brahmanas*, prose works which were added to the four major Vedic hymns, include exegesis of the hymns and instructions for ritual sacrifice. *Aranyakas*, also called the "forest treatises" after the sages who taught in their forest retreats, are appendices to the *Brahmanas*. These additional treatises merge with the theologically and philosophically significant *Upanishads, which mark the end of the Vedic canon. Lesser Upanishads, composed after the classical Upanishads, while important to the Vedanta School, are not considered part of the canon. The classical Upanishads were composed between 800 and 400 B.C. The essence of Upanishadic teaching was summarized in the *Brahma-Sutra*.

[R. J. LITZ]

VEDAST OF ARRAS, ST. (Vaast; d. *c.*540), bishop. After living sometime as a recluse, V. became a priest at Toul, where he is said to have prepared Clovis for baptism. V. assisted St. Remigius in converting the Franks at Reims until Remigius consecrated him bp. of Arras (*c.*500). He was also charged with the see of Cambrai. During 40 years of episcopal labor, V. revived an almost extinct Christian community. BIBLIOGRAPHY: G. M. Cook, NCE 14:585; Butler 1:262–263.

[G. M. COOK]

VEDRUNA, JOAQUINA DE, ST. (1783–1854), foundress of the Carmelite Sisters of Charity. A native of Barcelona, V. spent 17 years as wife and mother of 8 children. She was a widow for 8 years before she founded her congregation in 1843, for the apostolates of teaching and nursing. Under her direction the community established schools and hospitals throughout Catalonia. V. was beatified in 1940 and canonized in 1959.

[J. R. AHERNE]

VEGA, ANDREAS DE (1490–1549), Franciscan of the Observance, a leading theologian at the Council of Trent. He was already a professor at Salamanca when he became a Franciscan there in 1538. At Trent he was the theologian of Card. Pedro Pacheco, bp. of Jaén and head of Charles V.'s imperial delegation to the first sessions of the Council. V. and Domingo de *Soto were the foremost theologians during this first period of Trent. V. was deeply attached to St. Thomas Aquinas and differed with the Conventual Franciscan theologians on many points in the debates on *justification, esp. in standing for the sufficiency of inherent grace (see DOUBLE JUSTICE) and against the certitude of salvation. With Soto he held faith to be the formal cause of justification and the dispositions to justification to express a kind of psychological typology, not a uniform or exhaustive description of every case. In the earlier decree on the canonical Scriptures V. was a leader in the discussions because of his knowledge of biblical languages, and the final decree adopted reflects his thought. He returned to Salamanca in 1549. He published *De justificatione universa libris 15 absolute tradita* (1548), a defense of the Tridentine teachings, the last two books being directed against J. Calvin's *Acta synodi Tridentinae cum antidoto;* V.'s work, together with his earlier *De justificatione, gratia, fide, operibus, et meritis* (1546) was edited and issued in 1572 by St. Peter Canisius.

[T. C. O'BRIEN]

VEGA, LOPE DE (Vega Carpio, Lope Felix de; 1562–1635), Spanish poet and playwright, creator of the Spanish *comedia*. His tempestuous life began in Madrid. The son of an embroiderer, he was given the opportunity for a good education, studying first with the poet Vicente Espinel and then at several universities with an eye toward the priesthood. After a period of military service, he met his first love, Elena Osorio, whom he pursued vainly for several years, and climaxed by his exile from Madrid for eight years because out of jealousy, he had published libels about her. He took with him a girl, Isabel de Urbina, whom he was pressured to marry. During his exile, he enthusiastically began his writing career, and, returning to Madrid after his wife died, he found that his name was becoming well known. In 1598 he married Juana de Guardo, with whom he was apparently happy, although in 1601 he established another household for Micaela de Lujan, by whom he also had children. He had lost both of these women through death by 1613, and, having developed strong religious concerns, V., with the same irrepressible fervor that characterized his writing and his love of women, entered the priesthood. He soon found celibacy beyond his capacities, however, and consequently disgraced his order. Sometime later he met his last love, a married woman, Marta de Nevares, with whom he remained until her death in 1632, her last years made agonizing by blindness and the loss of her reason. V.'s sorrows climaxed in 1634 through the death of his favorite son and the abduction of his youngest daughter. Tortured by regrets, he died the next year, deeply mourned by the Spanish people. V. is probably the most prolific writer ever known. The plays alone certainly his number more than 400, and the sonnets almost 1600. Some estimates set the number much higher. With such an output, it is not surprising that only a small percentage has much literary merit. During his life, his work was tremendously popular, but most of it has not withstood time. *La Dorotea* (1632), a dialogue inspired by his unrequited love for Elena, is generally hailed as his best work. It is also cited because it gives an insight into the principle behind V.'s plays, the *comedia,* as explained in his treatise in verse, *Arte nuevo de hacer comedias en este tiempo.* The *comedia,* though it is, in Spanish, the generic term for drama, has a specific application as a result of V.'s work. Departing from traditional notions of universals in drama, which appealed only to an elite audience, the concerns of the *comedia* were determined by popular issues and emotions, and thus altered fundamentally according to time and location. Among V.'s best known works are *Arcadia* (1598), a novel, and the two poems, *Laura de Apolo* and the 6000 stanza, *Jerusalén conquistada* (1609).

[P. J. HENNESSEY]

VEGETARIANISM, exclusion of meat from human diet. Various degrees of strictness are practiced, sometimes excluding fish and in some cases animal products such as milk and eggs. Supporters of vegetarianism argue both that meat is physically unhealthy and that it is morally destructive, some contending that it stimulates man's animal nature. Vegetarianism is also based on a feeling of reverence for life and a conviction that none of God's creatures should harm others. Advocates emphasize that in the beginning God gave man "every plant yielding seed which is upon the face of all the earth, and every tree with seed in its fruit" (Gen 1.29), but not meat. It was only after the Flood that God declared man could eat animals, but even then he was not to consume the blood, in which the life was believed to exist (Gen 9.3–4). Isaiah's vision of the future Messianic Age, furthermore, includes a condition where all earth's creatures live together in harmony (11.6–9). Though vegetarianism was taught by some in ancient Greece, as well as by certain Hindu and Buddhist groups, as a modern movement it arose in the mid-19th cent., particularly in Britain and the U.S. The *Seventh Day Adventists, who arose at that time, adopted the practice and continue to maintain it.

[T. EARLY]

VEGETATION CULTS, see FERTILITY CULTS.

VEGHAR (Vel'ar), the black hood distinctive of the Gregorian Armenian celibate clergy and bishops. It is veil-like in form and pointed on top to fit over the *pakegh.* The Catholicos of Etchmiadzin wears a rhinestone cross on the front of his *veghar.*

[A. CODY]

VEGHE, JOHANNES (1431 or 32–1504), preacher, one of the foremost exponents of the *Devotio moderna.* He was educated by and became a member of the Brethren of the Common Life. He published one Latin work on the mystical

life, *Lectulus noster floridus* (mod. ed. H. Rademacher, 1938), and many others in German.

[P. J. HENNESSEY]

VEGIO, MAFFEO (VEGIUS, MAPHEUS, 1406–58), Augustinian humanist, educator, and poet. Educated at Pavia, he was at one time secretary of papal briefs, apostolic datary, and canon of St. Peter's. As an educator, he believed the end of education to be a sound moral and Christian character. He recommended the study of the classics, prescribed thorough moral and religious instruction, insisted that children be ruled by love and judicious praise, and advocated practical training for girls in the domestic arts. His writings include *De educatione liberorum et eorum claris moribus (On The Education of Children and Their Moral Training),* his most important work, and numerous Latin poems, both religious and classical. BIBLIOGRAPHY: V. Staudt Sexton, NCE 14:588–589.

[M. B. MURPHY]

VEGLIARE CON SOLLECITUDINE, address of Pope Pius XII to the Union of Italian Midwives on Oct. 29, 1951, frequently cited in subsequent papal documents. Urging his addressees to medical competence for their work, the Pope admonished them to counsel their patients in their duties as mothers. The address reaffirms the opposition of the Church to sterilization, abortion, and artificial birth control. It repeats the doctrine that procreation is the primary purpose of marriage. The address also condemns artificial insemination as a subordination of the human to the biological. Finally there is emphasis on abstinence in sexual life as an exercise in virtuous moderation.

[J. R. AHERNE]

VEHE, MICHAEL (1480–1539), German Dominican. V. studied at Heidelberg and in 1513 acquired his doctorate in theology. He played an important role as "Inquisitor for Germany" in the Reformation and participated in the Diet of Augsburg in 1530. In 1537 he published a *New Little Hymnbook,* the first Catholic hymnal of the Reformation era. Its selections are based on old German hymns with some new texts and melodies he, with G. Witzel, J. Hofmann and others supplied.

[M. T. LEGGE]

VEIL, HUMERAL, see HUMERAL VEIL.

VEIL, LENTEN, see LENTEN VEIL.

VEIL, RELIGIOUS, a traditional symbol worn by Christian women to express their religious vocation, status, or role. In ancient Rome the veil was given to newly wed women to symbolize constancy and conjugal fidelity. The Vestal Virgins, and then Christian virgins, adopted the veil to symbolize the rejection of marriage itself. The Christian custom was usually, in the beginning, a private family affair. Widows also took the veil to signify their intention of remaining without the consolation of sexual union after the death of their husbands. Public imposition of such veils by priests or, more solemnly, by bishops gave the vocation a more obviously communal dimension. With the passing of the centuries the custom became more complex, with the proliferation of a variety of veils: a white one to indicate probation for novices in convents; a special one for the professed; another one for those professed who act equivalently as deaconesses, intoning the Office and reading the homilies in choir; the veil of an abbess to signify the special authority; and even more. Vatican Council II's norms on the renewal of religious life directed a simplifying of the garb of religious; as a result religious women's communities have adopted veils that conform to this directive (Vat II RenRel-Life n. 17), but retain the veil as a sign of the consecrated life.

[E. J. DILLON]

VEIL OF THE TEMPLE, the fabric dividing the holy place of the temple from the holy of holies. The high priest alone was allowed to go beyond the veil, and he only once a year on the Day of Atonement (Lev 16). Present in the tabernacle (Ex 26.31–35), the veil was apparently absent from Solomon's temple (1 Kgs 6.31), but used in the second temple and Herod's temple. The account given by the Chronicler (2 Chr 3.14) perhaps reflects the situation of his own time. The NT records that the veil was rent at the time of the Crucifixion (Mk 15.38). The author of Hebrews used the symbolism of the temple veil to interpret the ministry of Jesus (6.19–20; 10.19–20).

[T. EARLY]

VEITH, JOHANN EMMANUEL (1787–1870), preacher. Member of an Orthodox Jewish family, V. studied medicine and was director of the Institute for Veterinary Medicine in Vienna. Under the influence of St. Clement *Hofbauer he became a Catholic in 1816. Joining the Redemptorists he was ordained in 1821. A famous preacher, he ultimately left the Redemptorists and became cathedral preacher at St. Stephen's in Vienna, a position he held from 1831 to 1845. Active in organizing, V. was a founder of the Katholikenverein and the newspaper *Volksblatt für Glauben, Freiheit und Gesittung* (1848).

[J. R. AHERNE]

VELASCO, PEDRO DE (1581–1649), Mexican Jesuit missionary. Ordained in 1604, V. labored in the Indian missions in Sinaloa for 27 years. Later he was provincial of the Jesuit province (1646). He founded in the same year a college in Guatemala. V. represented the Jesuits in a bitter controversy with the bishop of Puebla. As a result of V.'s prudent work, the bp. was recalled to Spain and removed from his see by the pope.

[J. R. AHERNE]

VELASCO Y PETROCHE, JUAN DE (1727–92), Ecuadorian Jesuit historian. He entered the Society of Jesus in 1744 and after ordination taught in Popayán, in present-day Colombia. Expelled with his colleagues by the decree of 1767, he went to France. There he wrote a history of Ecuador in three volumes, *Historia del reino de Quito,* finished in 1789 but not published until 1841–44. In his work *El Manuscrito de Faenza,* V. created the first history of Ecuadorian literature.

[J. R. AHERNE]

VELÁZQUEZ, DIEGO RODRÍGUEZ DE SILVA Y (1599–1660), great Spanish master, painter of portraits, genre, landscape, mythological and religious subjects. V. was a master of Spanish realism eschewing Italian classicism as pretentious. Early tenebrist works include *Christ in the House of Martha and Mary* (1618) with the religious scene relegated to the background, and *The Adoration of the Magi* (1617–19) with crossing diagonals related to Zurbarán. V.'s appointment to the court of Philip IV (1623) restricted his religious commissions. After a trip to Italy (1629–31) V. developed mastery of subtle half-tones and freer brush work (*Christ at the Column,* 1629). In 1634, equestrian portraits of the royal family followed (*Balthasar Carlos*) and the historic masterwork, *The Surrender of Breda.* In penetrating portraits, the so-called Fraga *Philip IV* (1644) and the humble *Court Jester* (c. 1628), equally distinguished, V. evidences a ritualistic formality in the flattering royal studies and in nonroyal subjects, a profound psychological insight in interpretations of great dignity, even religious feeling, in his immense love of the individual. *Innocent X* (1650) is one of the greatest portraits of all time in psychology and painterly surface, and a last portrait of the King (1655) is intimate and sad. In the world-famous group portrait of the Infanta with her retinue of ladies and dwarfs, *Las Meñinas* (1656), V. reaches an apogee of luminous atmosphere and freedom of brush stroke, anticipating Impressionism, which is esp. evident in landscapes (*Medici Gardens),* and *The Weavers* (1657) perhaps his masterpiece. V.'s genius asserts itself in first impressions of simplicity which yield new insights and delights with successive addresses. BIBLIOGRAPHY: J. A. Gaya Nuño, *Bibliografía crítica y antoógica de Velásquez* (1963); J. Lopez-Rey, *Velázquez . . .* (1963).

[J. A. LEITE]

VELEHRAD, city in Czechoslovakia traditionally regarded as the first see of St. Methodius (d. 885) in Great Moravia and the place of his interment. Recent archeological discoveries have focused attention on these traditions but thus far have failed to produce conclusive evidence. Beginning in 1863 the annual celebrations here honoring SS. Cyril and Methodius have continued to keep Velehrad a center of their heritage and cult. Under Antonin Cyril Stojan (d. 1923) abp. of Olomouc, Velehrad became an important center for Unionistic Congresses (1907–47). BIBLIOGRAPHY: M. Gordillo, *Velehrad ed i suoi congressi unionistici* (1957).

[L. NEMEC]

VELITCHOVSKY, PAISSY (1722–94), founder, Russian spiritual writer. A monk and hermit, V. attracted to the monastery on Mt. Athos many followers. In Moldavia V. founded a monastery, placing it under the Mt. Athos rule of St. Basil and St. Theodore the Studite, which eventually became two monasteries with 1,000 monks. V. directed his monks to translate, copy, and revise Greek and Latin patristic texts. His own work *Dobroto-liubie* laid down a special form of asceticism. V. influenced the spirituality of the Slavs from his own time to the Russian Revolution in 1917.

[J. R. AHERNE]

VENAISSIN (Comtat, Comtat Venaissin), the former name of a region along the Rhone, consisting of two-thirds of the present Department of Vaucluse, France. It was bounded by Dauphiné, Provence, and Languedoc. Its capital was originally Pernes; after 1320, Carpentras. V. was acquired by the papacy at the end of the Albigensian War (1229), but papal rule did not begin until 1274. The French Assembly annexed it in 1791. BIBLIOGRAPHY: G. Mollat, NCE 14:593.

[J. E. WRIGLEY]

VENANTIUS FORTUNATUS, see FORTUNATUS, VENANTIUS HONORIUS CLEMENTIANUS.

VENANTIUS OF TOURS, ST. (d. 5th cent.), abbot. Leaving Bourges, V. became a monk at Tours. He was later elected abbot and gained renown for his sanctity. He is credited with miracles and is patron against fevers.

[G. E. CONWAY]

VENANTIUS OF VIVIERS, ST. (d. 6th cent.), bishop. According to an 11th- or 15th-cent. panegyric, he was son of King [St.] Sigismund, became a monk, and then was bp. of Viviers. He attended the synods of Epaon (517) and Clermont (535). Little else of fact is known of him. BIBLIOGRAPHY: G. M. Cook, NCE 14:594 (bibliog.).

[G. M. COOK]

VÉNARD, JEAN THÉOPHANE, BL. (1829–61), missionary of the Paris Foreign Missionary Society, martyr. He was ordained in 1852; in 1854 he entered Tonkin Province (now in North Vietnam) secretly because Christianity was proscribed. He ministered to the persecuted Christians at great peril, often forced into hiding, until he was betrayed by a Christian at Kimbang in Nov. 1860. He was imprisoned in a bamboo cage and tortured during his captivity and the journey to Hanoi. There he was condemned and beheaded on Feb. 2, 1861. He was beatified as one of the Martyrs of Tonkin in 1909.

[T. C. O'BRIEN]

VENCE, CHAPELLE DU ROSAIRE (MATISSE CHAPEL), Dominican convent chapel outside Vence, consecrated in 1951, erected almost opposite the villa of the great contemporary genius Henri *Matisse, who designed all its appointments: stained glass, sculpture, painting, vestments. In a message to Bp. Rémond on the day of dedication Matisse called the chapel his "masterpiece," an apotheosis in the achievements of his "entire, active life." Becoming involved through Sister Jacques (novice at Vence) who had been his nurse at Nice, with L. B. Rayssiguier (a Dominican novice-architect in Vence for his health) supplying liturgical and architectural knowledge, the well-known ecclesiastical architect A. *Perret acting as consultant, and L. Milon de Peillon as architect, Matisse designed the nun's choir, nave for the laity, and sanctuary with altar placed on a diagonal so as to be seen by all. Remarkable are the gloriously luminous full-length stained-glass windows of the sanctuary, choir, and nave (inspired by Rev 21.19–21; 22.1–3) in a brilliant tree-of-life pattern of yellow and blue leaves on a bright green ground, and decorative black linear forms on white tile (a truly Dominican color-scheme) depicting on inner walls *St. Dominic,* the *Virgin and Child* amid flower-like shapes, and *Stations of the Cross* in one continuous narrative. The latter provocative images without faces address themselves easily to pure souls who define them in the innocent, grace-illumined reaches of their souls. To determine them for others was to Matisse an arrogance and domination he denounced. Matisse further designed the bronze altar crucifix, and dramatically decorative motifs of the chasubles. Termed a "painter's architecture," the entire work, an exposition of creative genius, ranks with *Ronchamp and *Assy as one of the greatest religious art expressions of this century. BIBLIOGRAPHY: H. Matisse, *Chapelle du Rosaire des dominicaines de Vence* (1951); *Les Chapelles du Rosaire à Vence par Matisse et de Notre-Dame-du-Haut à Ronchamp par Le Corbusier* (ed. M. A. Conturier et al, 1955).

[M. J. DALY]

VENDÔME, ABBEY OF (Sainte-Trinité), Benedictine monastery founded in 1034 by Geoffrey, count of Angers, and his wife. The founder bequeathed to it a gift he had from Emperor Henry III, namely what was claimed to be the "holy tear" shed by Christ over the tomb of Lazarus. Geoffrey of Vendôme, abbot 1093–1132, obtained from Urban II the monastery's exemption from all other ecclesiastical authority save that of the Holy See. The abbey united with the Congregation of Exempt Benedictines in 1579, and was occupied by the Maurists from 1620 until the Revolution. The church (1306-early 16th cent.) has a magnificent free-standing bell tower and a façade in the flamboyant style (early 16th cent.) by the famous Jean de Beauce. The original chapel of the monks (11th cent.), the 14th-cent. chapter room, a wing of the cloister (14th–15th cent.), and a large building that now serves as a museum, are still standing. BIBLIOGRAPHY: Cottineau 2:3317–19.

[J. DAOUST]

VENDVILLE, JEAN (1527–92), bp. of Tournai. Born in Lille, France, he began his career as a professor of canon law at the University of Douai, not entering the priesthood until 1581, after his wife died. He devoted his life to proposing the establishment of a seminary for missionaries in Rome, a dream realized only after his death in the founding of the College of the Propaganda (1627).

[P. J. HENNESSEY]

VENERABLE BROTHER, the form of address used by the Pope in communicating with a bishop. Sometimes it was also used of brothers in nonclerical religious institutes.

VENERATION OF THE CROSS, *worship offered to a representation of Jesus crucified; a special instance of the veneration of *images. The rightness of this veneration has as its principle that honoring the representation is honoring the one represented, not the material artifact. The special meaning of venerating the cross is that it is *latria,* i.e., the adoration due to the divine person who is the one imaged and venerated. On the supposition that there existed relics of the actual cross on which Jesus died, medieval theologians agreed that *latria* was offered to them because of their contact with Jesus' body (ThAq ST 3a, 25.3 & 4).

[T. C. O'BRIEN]

VENERINI SISTERS (Maestre Pie Venerini), a congregation founded by Bl. Rosa Venerini in Italy (1685). Devoted to education, the Institute Venerini received approval of the Holy See in 1836. The sisters came to the U.S. in 1909 and conduct day nurseries, primary and secondary schools in New York State and New England. In 1975 their worldwide membership was 438. The generalate is in Rome. BIBLIOGRAPHY: S. Mattei, EncCatt 7:1805–06.

[J. R. AHERNE]

VENETIAN SCHOOL (MUSIC), a group of 16th-cent. Flemish and Italian composers headed by Adrian Willaert, choirmaster at St. Mark's in Venice, and including Andrea and Giovanni Gabrieli, Cipriano de Rore, Claudio Merulo, Gioseffo Zarlino and others. Though contemporaneous with the great polyphonic schools, the Venetian school, with its new ideas and developments in chromatics, harmony, etc., extended its influence well into the Baroque period and may be said to mark the beginning of modern music. With the passing of Willaert, the secular influence in music began to grow and, though St. Mark's continued to produce such important musicians as Monteverdi and Carissimi, true church music ceased after the two Gabrieli.

[M. T. LEGGE]

VENEZUELA, predominantly Catholic republic of N South America, on the Caribbean between Colombia and Guyana; capital, Caracas. The population is about 65 per cent mestizo, 20 per cent white, 8 per cent black, and 7 per cent Indian. When the explorer Amerigo Vespucci found an island where Indians built villages above the water on stilts, he called it Venezuela (little Venice) and the name was later applied to the mainland. Settlement began early in the 16th cent. by the Spanish, though it was interrupted for a generation after Charles V gave rights in the area to the Welsers, German bankers. After they withdrew, Catholic missionary orders played a key role in development of the country. Many Venezuelan towns developed from missions and the converted Indians associated with them. Panama, most of Colombia, and Venezuela constituted New Granada, whose governmental center was established at Bogotá in 1549. The rest of Colombia and Ecuador were included when New Granada became a viceroyship in 1717. Later Venezuela became a separate political unit. A revolt against Spanish rule broke out in 1795 but did not achieve success until after Napoleon occupied Spain. F. de Miranda led a Venezuelan revolution that began in 1810, and independence was declared the following year. But separation from Spain was not finally secured until 1821, following intervention from Colombia by the Venezuelan Simon Bolívar. Venezuela then formed part of Greater Colombia until it won independence in 1830. Its constitution of that year stripped the Church of many privileges, including control of education. Anticlericalism peaked under Guzman Blanco, dominant figure in Venezuelan politics from 1870 to 1888. Direct popular election of a president came only in 1947, and the first elected president was replaced by a military dictatorship in 1948. A new democratic constitution was adopted in 1961. Though most of the population is Catholic, there is no established Church. BIBLIOGRAPHY: Edward Lieuwen, *Venezuela* (2d ed., 1965).

[T. EARLY]

VENGEANCE, the retaliation or punishment afflicted for an injury received; the moral act or attitude involved in such retaliation. Punishment inflicted has its moral rightness or wrongness from this act or attitude. Vengeance can be virtuous as it comes under the form of *legal justice called "vindicative," or under the virtue called in Lat. *vindicatio* by Cicero (*Rhetorica* II, 53). In justice it belongs to a judge to impose punitive sentences attached to crimes by the law (ThAq ST 2a2ae, 67.4; 108.2 ad 1). As a virtue, vengeance controls a private person's sentiments of retaliation for wrongs against him (*ibid.*). In either case an attitude or act of sheer revenge, i.e., the naked will to inflict injury, is morally wrong; to redress an injury is right, however, when the intent is to contain and correct evil, and the punishment is both proportionate to the offense and effective of the right intent (*ibid.* 2). Right intent includes zeal for God's honor, or for the correction of the one punished, or for deterring others from wrongdoing. The meaning of vindicative justice and vengeance also implies that not every punishment is medicinal or remedial for the one punished, but that simply the rectification of wronged justice is a sound reason for punishing (*ibid*. 1a2ae, 87.4 ad 2; 7). Vengeance may be tempered by the virtue of *clemency, where mitigation seems to be the virtuous course. The private avenging of grievances can never mean taking the law into one's own hands; it is tempered as well by the evangelical counsels of *meekness and of love for one's enemies. BIBLIOGRAPHY: ThAq ST Lat.-Eng, v. 27, T. C. O'Brien, ed., Appendix 1, ''Guilt and Punishment.''

[T. C. O'BRIEN]

VENI CREATOR SPIRITUS, hymn to the Holy Spirit, attributed with some probability to Rabanus Maurus. It is used at Tierce on Pentecost and at ordinations, canonizations, and as a prayer of devotion to the Holy Spirit. In addition to the original Latin and chant versions, there have been numerous translations and musical settings. BIBLIOGRAPHY: W. Douglas, *Church Music in History and Practice* (1937).

[M. T. LEGGE]

VENIAMINOV, INNOCENT (1792–1879), Ivan Evseevich Popov was a renowned missionary who, with his wife, worked (1824–68) among the Eskimos, Aleuts, and Indians in Alaska. He translated the liturgy, a catechism, and portions of the Scriptures into Aleut, and upon becoming a widower in 1840, was named bp. of Kamchatka, the Kuriles, and the Aleutians. The first Orthodox bishop in America, his administration witnessed the greatest period of evangelization in Alaska's history. He wrote scientific treatises on the culture and ethnography of the Aleuts. In 1868 he was elected metropolitan of Moscow and there founded the Orthodox Missionary Society.

[T. BIRD]

VENICE, LEAGUE OF, alliance, formed April 1, 1495, of the papacy, the Holy Roman Emperor, the King of Aragon, Milan and Venice against France during the early Italian Wars. In February 1495 Charles VIII of France completed his conquest of the Kingdom of Naples. The other Italian states, shocked by this easy victory, decided to unite and to crush Charles before he could return to France. The treaty was signed in Venice by the Venetian Doge, Ferdinand, the King of Aragon, Maximilian, the Holy Roman Emperor, Pope Alexander VI, and Ludovico Sforza, the Duke of Milan. Sforza's adherence to this union was particularly ironic because he had initially invited the French to conquer Naples in hopes of overthrowing his rival, Ferrante. The League of Venice failed in its objective. Charles VIII was able to defeat its troops at the Battle of Fornovo on July 6, 1495 and safely retreat to France. BIBLIOGRAPHY: L. Batiffol, *The Century of the Renaissance* (1916); M. P. Gilmore, *The World of Humanism, 1453–1517* (1952).

[C. T. EBY]

VENTURA DI RAULICA, GIOACCHINO, (1792–1861), an Italian Jesuit theologian (1809–17) who joined the

Theatines (1818) after the Jesuits were suppressed in the Kingdom of Naples. V. became superior general of the Theatines (1831–33). A theologian and philosopher of considerable acumen, V. spent most of his career in Rome and later in Paris. A moderate liberal who was influenced by Lamennais (though repudiating the latter's rebellion against the Holy See), de Maistre, and de Bonald, V. had mixed relations with the Vatican. Two of his writings were disapproved, yet he enjoyed the favor of the popes. A renowned orator, he gave the panegyric at the funeral of Pope Pius VII. His political liberalism was not shared by Pius IX, but V.'s publication *Opinion sur une chambre des pairs dans les États pontificaux* (1848), recommending a confederation of Italian states under the presidency of the pope, led Pius IX to give a constitution to the people of Rome. V. came ultimately to espouse complete separation of the spiritual and the temporal. As a philosopher V. was a seminal force. Among his other works are *La Raison philosophique et la raison catholique* (1852–59) and *La Tradition et les semipélagiens de la philosophie* (1856). In the former work he espouses the view that reason unaided can study and elaborate revelation but it cannot discover revealed truth. In the latter work, V. takes the position that just as man cannot penetrate to the essence of the material world, neither can he grasp the essence of spiritual things through human reason. It is absurd to believe that man, without benefit of God's word, could fashion a concept of the nonmaterial world, as absurd as to attribute to man the capacity to build without materials. He also published *La philosophie chrétienne* (3 v., 1861). BIBLIOGRAPHY: P. Sejourné, DTC 15. 2:2635–39.

[J. R. AHERNE]

VENTURI, ADOLFO AND LIONELLO. Adolfo (1856–1941), Italian art historian, active in museums in N Italy and in Rome, where he taught in the University. At first influenced by Morelli, V. later came to regard connoisseurship and a sense of aesthetic quality as essentials in art criticism. His 22-volume *Storia dell'arte italiana* (1901–36) is a classic. **Lionello** (1885–1961), Italian theorist and art historian, son of Adolfo, born in Modena, professor of art history at the Univ. of Turin (1915–31). An anti-Fascist, V. emigrated to France and later to the U.S., where he lectured and wrote on Renaissance, 19th-cent. French, and modern art, returning to Rome in 1945. BIBLIOGRAPHY: R. U. Montini, EncCatt 12:1241–42.

[K. B. NEILSON]

VENTURINO OF BERGAMO (1304–46), popular Dominican preacher and writer on ascetical and mystical themes. He entered the Dominicans in 1319. He became a popular preacher in Italy. As if to prove his zeal, he accepted a commission from Clement VI to preach a Crusade in Italy (1344), having been called a hypocrite by a previous pope, Benedict XII, and exiled to France. He died in Smyrna while on crusade, having sailed there with thousands of Italian recruits. V.'s *De profectu spirituali* is a treatise expressive of his own mystical experiences and personal asceticism.

[E. J. DILLON]

VENUS OF WILLENDORF (*c.*15,000–10,000 B.C.) most famous small female statuette (4⅜ in high), found at Willendorf, Austria, dating from the Aurignacian period, symbol of fertility, the highly exaggerated breasts, abdomen, and buttocks, in bulbous, almost abstract shapes, quite distinct from the precise realism determining animal forms of the same period.

[M. J. DALY]

VENUSTIANS, see PATERNIANS.

VERA, JACINTO (1813–81), missionary, bishop. Born in Brazil and educated in Buenos Aires, V. was ordained in 1841, returned to Uraguay and became vicar apostolic there. A zealous leader, he came into conflict with the Republic over his jurisdiction in 1862 and was exiled. The revolutionary government of 1863 recalled him to Montevideo. In 1864 he was named bp. of Megara and in 1879 first bp. of Montevideo.

[J. R. AHERNE]

VERA CRUZ, ALONSO DE LA (1504–84), theologian, scholar of the Order of Hermits of St. Augustine at the Royal and Pontifical Univ. of Mexico from 1553. He had come from Salamanca, where he was a professor in the philosophy faculty, to join the missionary effort in Mexico, attracted by the appeal of Fray Francisco de la Cruz. V. devoted himself exclusively to the university and his work is credited with introducing Christian humanism into the New World. His works include: *Recognitio summularum* and *Dialectica resolutio*, treatises in logic, and a study in philosophical psychology, *Physica speculatio*, known as *Los libros del alma* (on Aristole's work *De anima*).

[T. C. O'BRIEN]

VERACITY, see TRUTHFULNESS.

VERANUS OF CAVAILLON, ST. (d. after 589), bp. Both Gregory of Tours and an anonymous legendary biography ascribe to V. miraculous powers of healing. He was present at the Council of Mâcon (585), and was one of the three bps. sent by King Guntram to investigate the murder of Praetextatus of Rouen. BIBLIOGRAPHY: J. Daoust, NCE 14:608.

[G. M. COOK]

VERARKOU, a black ankle-length garment with wide sleeves worn in public by all degrees of Gregorian Armenian clerics, except when specifically liturgical garb is prescribed. The Catholic Mekhitarists use the *verarkou* as a choir-cloak.

[A. CODY]

VERBIEST, FERDINAND (Nan Huai-Jen; 1623–88), Belgian Jesuit missionary and astronomer. Assigned to China, he succeeded Adam Schall von Bell in 1666 as president of the Imperial Board of Astronomy. His knowledge in various fields made him influential with the Chinese government.

[P. J. HENNESSEY]

VERBIST, THÉOPHILE (1823–68), Belgian missionary, founder of the Scheut Fathers. Ordained in 1846 for the Archdiocese of Mechelen, he became national director of the Holy Childhood Association in 1860. Desirous of establishing a mission in China, he was encouraged by Rome to found a mission congregation, at Scheut, near Brussels, in 1862 and began the Congregation of the Immaculate Heart of Mary. He became superior general. Named pro-vicar apostolic of Mongolia, he arrived in China in 1865. With a number of his associates in the community he had founded, V. established orphanages, gave instruction to Christians, and trained a native clergy. Unfamiliar with the language of his area, V. did not attempt to convert the non-Christians of the vicariate. He died during a visitation of his vicariate; his remains were brought to Scheut in 1931.

[J. R. AHERNE]

VERCELLONE, CARLO (1814–69), textual critic and Bible editor. V. is significant for his work on the various editions of the *Codex Vaticanus,* publishing both the original and revised edition as prepared by Card. Angelo Mai, assisting Tischendorf in his translation, and collaborating with G. Cossa-Luzi in a still more critical edition. Even more valuable are his critical studies of the Latin Vulgate which paved the way for subsequent revisions. BIBLIOGRAPHY: C. L. Souvay, CE 15:349–350; H. Lesetre, DB 5.2:2396; D. W. Martin, NCE 14:610–611.

[T. M. MCFADDEN]

VERDI, GIUSEPPE (1813–1901), Italian operatic composer. A precocious pupil, V. even as a boy succeeded his teacher, the village organist, at his post. He studied at Busseto and Milan. Considered unfit for the conservatory there, V. later studied privately with Vincenzo Lavigna at La Scala. He subsequently took various posts at Busseto and began the composition of opera, for which he is best known. His early works met with unequal success. *Aida, Otello,* and *Falstaff,* however, mark him as a master of the Italian operatic style. His production of religious but nonliturgical music was limited to a Requiem Mass in honor of A. Manzoni, two Ave Marias, a Te Deum, a Stabat Mater, a Pater Noster, and a hymn to the Virgin. During the last third of his life V. became again a practicing Catholic.

[M. T. LEGGE]

VERDIER, JEAN PIERRE (1864–1940), cardinal abp. of Paris. A Sulpician, ordained in 1887, he headed the

Institut Catholique of Paris and was elected superior general of the Sulpicians in 1929. In the same year he was named to the See of Paris and cardinal by Pope Pius XI. An advocate of Catholic action, V. labored to create a strong clergy in his archdiocese. With the coming of World War II, V. was an outspoken defender of the Allied cause and several times denounced Nazi Germany as barbarous. A foe of communism, he supported the Socialist government of Léon Blum in the interest of France. He gave aid to persecuted Jews fleeing Germany and appealed to all Christians to take their part.

[J. R. AHERNE]

VERDUN SUR MEUSE, ABBEY OF (also called St. Vanne), former Benedictine abbey founded in 952 by Bp. Berengar and really taking root in Verdun under the reform abbot Richard (1004–46). It was enclosed within the fortified citadel of Verdun after 1552, became head of the Benedictine Congregation of Lorraine in 1604, and in 1613 founded the Congregation of St.-Maur at St.-Augustin de Limoges. Later, deeply affected by Jansenism, it was suppressed in 1791. BIBLIOGRAPHY: Cottineau 2:3334–35.

[E. J. DILLON]

VERECUNDUS OF JUNCA (d. after 534), bp. of Junca, in the North African province of Byzacena. According to two references to him in the chronicle of his compatriot, Victor of Tunnuna, V., like so many North African bishops who opposed Justinian's politico-religious campaign against the *Three Chapters, was summoned to Constantinople by the Emperor in 551 to give an account of his faith, but V. fled to Chalcedon where he died in 552. Extant writings of his include a commentary on nine OT canticles, written while he was still a priest, sometime after 534, since he refers to the devastations of the Vandals as a thing of the past; also selected treatises on the *acta* of the Council of Chalcedon, mostly written with the view of defending the Three Chapters; and a long penitential poem.

[E. J. DILLON]

VEREMUNDUS, ST., (*c.*1020–92?), Benedictine abbot. As a youth of 10 he joined the Benedictines of Hyrache, then directed by his uncle, Abbot Munius, whom he was elected to succeed (*c.*1052). Under V. the monastery rose to the height of its spiritual and temporal fame. Called to Rome by Alexander II, he was commissioned to reform the Church in Spain, esp. in its liturgy. BIBLIOGRAPHY: AS March 1:794–798; J. Pérez de Urbel, *Semblanzas benedictinas* (1925) 1:95–99; O. J. Blum, NCE 14:612; Butler 1:526–527.

[O. J. BLUM]

VERGER, RAFAEL (1722–90), missionary, bishop. Born in Spain, V. joined the Franciscans and was ordained in 1746. A volunteer for the missions of New Spain, he came to Mexico in 1750. A teacher in and administrator of San Fernando College, Mexico, a center for Franciscan missionaries, he became superior of the missionaries there. With Junípero Serra, he was a chief influence in the establishment of the California missions. In 1783 V. was appointed bishop of Nuevo León, transferring the see to the city of Monterrey (now Monterey).

[J. R. AHERNE]

VERGER (Lat. *virga,* rod), a term with two main meanings: (1) one who carries a mace (verge) or other symbol of authority before dignitaries as they enter a cathedral, church, or university gathering; and (2) a person who has responsibility for caring for the interior of the church, combining the functions of usher and sexton.

VERGERIO, PIER PAOLO (1370–1445), Christian humanist, canonist, statesman. and educator. After studies at Padua, Florence, and Bologna, V. was secretary to Innocent VII, Gregory XII, and later, Emperor Sigismund. The first Italian Renaissance educational theorist, he saw as the true aim of education the fusion of the highest standards of learning with sound Christian principles, considered literature the foundation of all learning, and thought history, moral philosophy, and eloquence the essentials of a liberal education. His educational treatise, *On the Manners of a Gentleman and Liberal Studies (De ingenuis moribus)*, outlines the training of a prince, emphasizing the importance of moral discipline, courtesy, and respect for parents and elders. The treatise greatly influenced the Christian humanist and schoolmaster, *Vittorino da Feltre. BIBLIOGRAPHY: W. H. Woodward, *Vittorino da Feltre and Other Humanist Educators* (1921).

[M. B. MURPHY]

VERGIL, POLYDORE (c. 1470–1555), humanist, historian. Ordained in Italy by 1496, V. was in England in 1502 as a deputy collector of Peter's Pence. The renown of his two works, *Proverbiorum libellus* and *De rerum inventoribus*, induced Henry VII to commission him to write a history of England. He became an English subject in 1510. The climate of the court of Henry VIII was less agreeable. V. was at first employed by Wolsey in the negotiations for obtaining the cardinalate, but by 1515 he was imprisoned in the Tower for opposing Wolsey. His *Anglica historia* first appeared at Basel in 1534. The viewpoints of later English historians were shaped by this work and through them Shakespeare's portrayal of England's past. V. signed the rejection of papal supremacy (1536) and the declaration for the administration of communion under both kinds (1547), even though he was not committed to the new order. The religious changes under Edward VI prompted his departure from England for Italy where he spent his remaining years. BIBLIOGRAPHY: D. Hay, NCE 14:614–615; *idem, Polydore Vergil: Renaissance Historian and Man of Letters* (1952).

[J. M. O'DONNELL]

VERHAEGEN, PETER JOSEPH (1800–68), educator, missionary. A Belgian who came to the U.S. in 1821, V. studied for the priesthood in the Society of Jesus in Maryland and with the pioneering group went to Florissant, Mo., where he was ordained in 1825. Named rector of their college in St. Louis, Mo., V. brought it to flourishing condition and in 1832 had the institution chartered as St. Louis University. Superior of the Indian missions served by the Missouri Province of the Jesuits, he published an article on these missions which did much to interest Europe in the region. V. became provincial of the Maryland Province in 1844, and as president of St. Joseph's College, Bardstown, Ky. from 1847 gave it new life. From 1850 V. was a pastor in St. Charles, Missouri. A man of brilliance and scholarship, V. contributed to the development of schools and Indian missions.

[J. R. AHERNE]

VERISM, following World War I, an art movement all over Europe seeking objective realism (Neue Sachlichkeit, Magic Realism, Verism); a reaction against Expressionism, Cubism, Dada, and abstraction. V. arose, esp. in Germany, from the involvement of artists and their need to express the chaotic political and social situations in the world. The social verists—Gross, Dix, and Max Beckmann—expressed a violent opposition in anarchic, cynical imagery, a weapon of offense and defense. A second version, in Italy, was modified by national pictorial traditions of the *Quattrocento*. In this realism there may be aspects of magic experience in the world of the objects (*Pittura Metafisica* of Giorgio de Chirico), or a more lyrical, simplified, primitive realism—as in Rosai. A third variation evidences a factual realism combined with fantastic, magic imagery, relating to Surrealism (Max Ernst). Similar developments in America can be seen in the works of Ivan Albright, Peter Blume, Philip Evergood and Stephen Greene.

[P. H. HEFTING]

VERJUS, ENRICO BATTISTA STANISLAO (1860–92), Italian Missionary of the Sacred Heart. He entered the congregation in 1872, was ordained in 1883, and reached New Guinea the following year. He was named coadjutor bp. of New Guinea in 1889. Later he returned to Italy to obtain additional recruits but died before the date on which they were to depart. His cause was introduced in 1949.

[M. J. SUELZER]

VERKADE, WILLIBRORD (Jan; 1868–1946), Dutch Benedictine priest, painter, author. Student in the Academy at Amsterdam (1887–89), V. met Gauguin and Sérusier in Paris (1891), and joined the *Nabis (prophets), whose interest in theosophy and the occult attracted him. Impressed by the Catholic Nabi M. *Denis, after visits to Pont-Aven and Holland, V. was baptized a Catholic (Aug. 26, 1892). Attracted by Beuronese art and the works of Fr. Desiderius *Lenz, V. became a Benedictine monk (Willibrord) in Beu-

ron (1894), took the name Willibrord, and was ordained in 1902. Though not accepting fully the theories of D. Lenz, V. was influenced by the neo-Byzantine mode of the Beuronese school. As priest and artist he was most active in the revitalization of contemporary religious art. He translated and edited works of Ruysbroeck and Gertrude the Great. BIBLIOGRAPHY: Dom W. Verkade, *Die Unruhe zu Gott: Erinnerungen eines malermönches* (1920); W. Verkade, *Yesterdays of an Artist Monk* (tr. J. Stoddard, 1930); J. P. du Ry, "De la beauté à Dieu: Willibrord Verkade "in F. Lelotte, *Convertis du 20e Siècle* (1953–   ) 87–102.

[M. J. DALY]

VERLAINE, PAUL (1844–96), lyric poet, considered the fountainhead of modern French Catholic poetry and credited with giving French verse greater freedom and musical quality. His life was turbulent and pathetic. A Bohemian existence with Rimbaud destroyed his marriage and led to violence and prison. Remorseful, he converted to Catholicism (1874), and religion sustained him for several years during which he wrote the distinctly Catholic poetry of *Sagesse* (1881). Thereafter until his death he experienced alternately periods of religious fervor and debauchery, which found their echo in parallel collections of spiritually inspired verse (e.g., *Amour*, 1888; *Liturgies intimes* 1891) and of sensual, even obscene poems (*Jadis et naguère*, 1884; *Parallèlement*, 1889). A priest attended him at death and a crowd of artists and writers honored the vagabond poet's funeral at Saint-Etienne-du-Mont. V. had abandoned the plastic forms of the early *Poèmes saturniens* (1866) for an impressionistic art emphasizing music, mood, and suggestion. Perfected in the poems of *Fêtes galantes* (1869), *La bonne chanson* (1870), and *Romances sans paroles* (1874), the poetics was ideally suited to render subtle nuances of religious sentiment. V. authored several prose works: *Les Poètes maudits* (1884) publicized the symbolist revolution and advocated the moral autonomy of the art object; and *Mes prisons* (1893) emotionally narrates his conversion in prison. BIBLIOGRAPHY: L. Morice, *Verlaine, le drame religieux* (1946); L. and E. Hanson, *Verlaine, Prince of Poets* (1958); O. Nadal, *Paul Verlaine* (1961).

[G. E. GINGRAS]

VERMEERSCH, ARTHUR (1858–1936), Belgian Jesuit, moral theologian, and canonist. He was a doctor of law from Louvain before becoming a Jesuit in 1879. After completion of his theological studies in Rome he taught moral theology and canon law at the Jesuit college, Louvain, 1893–1918. From 1904 he was a consultor and collaborator in the preparation of the *Codex juris canonici* (1917), and specifically prepared the legislation for religious. From 1918 until 1934 he was professor of moral theology at the Gregorian Univ. in Rome. In the field of canon law V. published, in collaboration with J. Creusen, SJ, *Epitome juris canonici cum commentariis* (3 v., 1921–

23), one of the most highly respected works of its kind. In moral theology he published his *Quaestione de justitia* in 1900 and a 2d ed. in 1904; his chief moral work was *Theologiae moralis principia, responsa, consilia* (4 v., 1922–24), a work of notable insight into the moral thought of Aquinas. V. was founder-editor (1912) of the journal *Periodica de re canonica, liturgica, morali;* he was a prime contributor to the *Catholic Encyclopedia* and to periodicals on ecumenism, social justice, and papal social teaching. Apart from the interests directly involved in his teaching, throughout his life he was a strong voice for the need of social and racial justice, and notably for the Belgian Congo. He published several works on social questions in Belgium: *Manuel social* (1900); *La question congolaise* (1906); *Guide social belgique* (1911). Another important work was his *Tolerance* (1912), on relations of Church-State and on religious freedom.

[T. C. O'BRIEN]

VERMIGLI, PIETRO MARTIRE, see PETER MARTYR VERMIGLI.

VERMONT, a New England state, admitted to the Union (1791) as the 14th state. A French expedition under Samuel de *Champlain laid claim to the area in 1609: the first permanent English settlement was made at Ft. Dummer, now Brattleboro, in 1724. Conflict between the French and English claims ended with the British victory in the French and Indian War. In 1778 Vermont established a state government and proclaimed the principle of religious freedom. Until that time Congregationalism had been the dominant and quasi-established religion in Vermont.

When the Diocese of Burlington was created (1853), Louis de *Goesbriand was appointed as first bp. of the diocese, which is still coextensive with the boundaries of the state. Goesbriand founded 68 churches and 24 schools to serve a population of 20,000 Catholics. He was succeeded by J. S. Michaud (1899), J. J. Rice (1910), M. F. Brady (1938), E. F. Ryan (1945), R. F. Joyce (1957) and J. A. Marshall (1971). The diocese is a suffragan of the metropolitan see of Boston, Massachusetts. In 1976 Vermont's Catholics numbered 149,797 or 31.8% of the total state population. The major Protestant denominations are the United Church of Christ, with 6.5% of the total population 1973, and the Methodist Church, with 5.2%. Other Protestant denominations comprise 7.7% of the population. The Jewish population (1968) was 2,330 or 0.52%.

There are 3 Catholic colleges in Vermont, with a total enrollment of 2,468 students. Some 1,461 students attend 3 Catholic high schools in the state, while over 3,349 pupils attend 15 Catholic elementary schools. BIBLIOGRAPHY: E. Fuller, *Vermont: A History of the Green Mountain State* (1952); V. B. Maloney and J. K. Durick, eds., *1853–1953: One Hundred Years of Achievement by the Catholic Church in the Diocese of Burlington, Vermont* (1953). D. W. Johnson, P. R. Picard, B. Quinn, *Churches and Church*

Membership in U.S. (1974); "Catholic Schools and Students in U.S." *Catholic Almanac* (1977); *Jewish Yearbook* (1974).

[J. L. MORRISON; R. M. PRESTON]

VERONA FATHERS (Sons of the Sacred Heart, FSCJ), a congregation of priests and brothers founded in 1867 by Bp. Daniele Comboni in Verona, Italy. At first a secular institute for the African missions, the society became a congregation in 1885 with the name Congregation of Sons of the Sacred Heart. The Holy See created a second society, Missionary Sons of the Sacred Heart in 1923. The community staffs missions in the Sudan, Ethiopia, Uganda, and Mozambique in Africa, and in Brazil, Mexico, and Ecuador. The Verona Fathers established their American branch in Cincinnati, Ohio, in 1940 and work among blacks, Indians, and Mexicans in Ohio, Kentucky, Georgia, and California.

[J. R. AHERNE]

VERONESE, PAOLO (Paolo Caliari, 1528–1588), one of the greatest Venetian painters. He excelled in large wall paintings which contain, in classical architectural settings and serene landscapes bathed in the mildest of airs, a great number of beautiful figures engaged in noble or festive actions. The operatic splendor of his works is always modified by a lyrical gentleness and a quiet, understated ease in the presentation of many of his actors. As a result, his pictures often are singularly believable and affecting. In his *Marriage at Cana* (Louvre), Christ and Mary are at first hardly noticed in the multitude of guests at the wedding, yet they are at the center of the composition and with their quiet presence lend an air of sacredness to the music of the whole work. A *Last Supper* was objected to by the Inquisition because of the seeming frivolity of his decorative apparatus of a huge company of diners and their attendants. A compromise eventually led to the change of the title of the picture (*The Feast in the House of Levi,* Academy, Venice). V.'s finest secular work is the decoration of Palladio's *Villa Maser*. He is also well known for his sensitive portrait paintings. BIBLIOGRAPHY: *Tutta la pittura di Paolo Veronese* (1969).

[P. P. FEHL]

VERONICA, a woman for whom, acc. to earlier legend, Jesus miraculously caused his likeness to appear upon a cloth. This story, recorded in apocryphal Pilate literature, gave way in the 14th cent. to a new legend that identified V. as a compassionate woman who wiped the face of Jesus on his way to Calvary. The name Veronica was given both to the woman and to a representation of the cloth with the face of Christ depicted on it. BIBLIOGRAPHY: P. K. Meagher, NCE 14:625; Butler 3:82–83.

[M. F. MCNAMARA]

VERONICA MASTER (fl. 1410–20), German painter of *St. Veronica Holding the Miraculous Veil* (Munich), one of the most important works of the early Cologne school; it is noted for delicacy and enamellike colors. *The Madonna with Pea Blossom* and a *Martyrdom of St. Ursula* are attributed to him. He influenced the master Stephen Lockner.

[M. J. DALY]

VEROT, JEAN PIERRE AUGUSTIN MARCELLIN (1805–76), bp. and missionary. A French Sulpician ordained in 1828, V. came to Baltimore in 1830, taught at St. Mary's Seminary and later as a pastor showed deep concern for the slaves and the poor. Named vicar-apostolic of Florida in 1858, he found it a wretched area with three or four priests in a few parishes. He worked heroically to build up the Church in his vicariate; he established schools, brought in a number of priests and sisters and Christian Brothers from Europe. He appealed to U.S. and European Catholics to migrate to Florida. A Southern sympathizer, he worked to assure better care for slaves and in a widely published sermon in 1861, *A Tract for the Times: Slavery and Abolition*, he attacked the slave trade, outlined a code of rights and duties of masters but defended their property rights. The pamphlet was suppressed by secretary of state Seward. In 1861 V. became bp. of Savannah, Ga., but remained in charge of Florida. He ministered to Union prisoners at Andersonville and supplied sisters as nurses in military hospitals. Postwar years saw him rebuilding a ravaged diocese, building churches and schools, establishing aid for blacks, begging in the N for financial help. At Vatican Council I he was a stormy figure, scolding the council, advocating recognition of blacks, and opposing the definition of papal infallibility. When St. Augustine, Fla., was made a diocese, V. accepted it, leaving the more important see of Savannah.

[J. R. AHERNE]

VERROCCHIO, ANDREA DEL (1435–88), painter, goldsmith, and after Donatello, the most renowned Florentine sculptor of the second half of the Quattrocento. V. received (1463–67) the commission for his famous bronze, *Christ and St. Thomas,* a masterpiece of his distinctively noble interpretations, cast the copper ball for the lantern, cathedral of Florence (1471, destroyed by lightning), executed tombs of Piero and Giovanni de' Medici (1472), and Card. Niccolò Forteguerri (1473), worked on the famous bronze equestrian *Colleoni* (1479, cast by Leopardi, 1489)—a model for equestrian statues of all time, the bronze *David* (1476) and the silver *Beheading of the Baptist* (1480). V.'s command of anatomy lacked mastery of fluid movement, but expressed his noble instinct and penetrating insight into character. Though teacher of masters Perugino, Botticelli, and Leonardo, V. produced paintings inferior to his carvings, the historic *Baptism of Christ* (1470–75), in crisp ''sculptured'' lines, treasured for evidences of Leonardo's work in a gracious attendant angel and the lyrical landscape. BIBLIOGRAPHY: J. Pope-Hennessy, *Italian Renaissance Sculpture* (1958); C. Seymour, *Sculpture in Italy, 1400–1500* (1966).

[L. A. LEITE]

VERSET, a short organ piece used to replace a verse of a psalm, canticle or other portion of a liturgical text. The practice, popular from the 16th to the 18th cent., esp. in France, was practically abolished by *Tra le sollecitudini*, motu proprio of Pius X (1903). Introduced to relieve the monotony of psalm singing, the custom encouraged organ composition and gave rise to many collections or organ versets, notable among which are the early publications of P. Attaignant (1530) and G. Cavazzoni (1542).

[M. T. LEGGE]

VERSICLE, a short verse, followed by a response, esp. in the Liturgy of the Hours. The versicle is frequently taken from the psalms, e.g., V. ''Our help is in the name of the Lord''; R. ''Who made heaven and earth'' (Ps 123.8).

[J. DALLEN]

VERSIONS OF THE BIBLE, see BIBLE VERSIONS.

VERSTEGAN, RICHARD (Rowlands; *c.*1550–1640), writer, publisher, engraver. Son of a Dutch immigrant living in London, V. attended Oxford but could not earn a degree because he was a Catholic. In London V. became a publisher and engraver. His publication of Catholic works forced his flight to Paris, where he again published Catholic writings. He was arrested to oblige the English, but his release was secured by Card. Allen. In 1587 he went to Antwerp where he was an agent and publisher for the *Recusants in England. A prolific writer in various fields, V. published, among many writings *Theatrum crudelitatum* (1587) on the English martyrs, *Primer or Office of the Blessed Virgin Marie* (1599), and a collection of verse, *Odes* (1601). In addition V. wrote *Restitution of Decayed Intelligence in Antiquities* (1605).

[J. R. AHERNE]

VERTOT, RENÉ AUBERT DE (1655–1735), French historian. A member of the Premonstratensians, he wrote *Histoire de la conjuration de Portugal* (1690), *Histoires des révolutions de Suède* (1695), *Révolutions romaines* (1719), and a history of the Knights Hospitallers of St. John (1726).

[P. J. HENNESSEY]

VERUELA, ABBEY OF, former Cistercian monastery in the diocese of Tarazona, Saragossa province, in Aragon (Spain), a daughter house of Scala Dei, in the lineage of Morimond. In 1146 Pedro de Atarés, who is buried there, gave the site and the surrounding land to French Cistercians from Scala Dei in return for perpetual prayers. The Romanesque church, which resembles Clairvaux, was consecrated in 1248. Countless abbots and dukes of Villahermosa are buried there. The abbey was suppressed in 1835; the buildings have been partly restored by Jesuit initiative since 1877. BIBLIOGRAPHY: Cottineau 2:3349–50.

[E. J. DILLON]

VERVOORT, FRANCESCO (1500–55), Franciscan ascetical theologian at Malines, scholar of ascetical and mystical works of his own and ancient times. Most of his own works were published anonymously. BIBLIOGRAPHY: A. Ampe, EncCatt 12:1310–11.

[P. J. HENNESSEY]

VERWYST, CHRYSOSTOM ADRIAN (1841–1925), missionary, linguist. Born in the Netherlands to a family which migrated to the U.S. at the behest of a Dutch missionary and took up land in 1855 at a Dutch settlement in Wisconsin, V. entered the seminary in Milwaukee and was ordained in 1865. After 13 years at various parishes in Wisconsin, he was sent to Indian territory around Lake Superior. In 1882 he entered the Franciscans and spent most of the rest of his life working out of Bayfield, Wisconsin. V. was an expert on the Chippewa language, published a monthly magazine in Chippewa, and the book *Chippewa Exercises: Being a Practical Introduction into the Chippewa Language* (1901). To mission history he contributed *Missionary Labors of Fathers Marquette, Ménard and Allouez in the Lake Superior Regions* (1886) and *Life and Labors of Rt. Rev. Father Frederic Baraga* (1900).

[J. R. AHERNE]

VERZERI, TERESA EUSTOCHIO, BL. (1801–52), foundress of the Daughters of the Sacred Heart of Bergamo. A native of N Italy, V. entered a convent of Benedictine nuns three times and left three times. She felt called to establish a community to care for neglected children and young women and to serve in retreat centers for women. In 1847 the Holy See approved her congregation. The community flourished in the brief period of her remaining years. V. was beatified in 1946.

[J. R. AHERNE]

VESPASIAN (A.D. 19–79), Roman Emperor from 69. Son of a tax collector, Titus Flavius Vespasianus became *consul suffectus* in 51. He fell into disfavor with Nero in 66 but was recalled the following year for service in the Jewish War. The legions of the East proclaimed him emperor in 69 and on the death of the short-lived Emperor Vitellius the Senate formally accepted him. He returned to Rome, leaving his son Titus to conclude the Jewish conflict with the capture of Jerusalem in 70 and the destruction of the temple. Vespasian created financial stability by an increase in provincial taxation, new tariffs, retrenchment, and resumption by the State of land unlawfully occupied. He improved defenses, founded colonies, and erected many public buildings. He made "Caesar," which was a family name among the Julio-Claudians, his official title and conferred it on his son so that it came to be the accepted designation of the heir to the principate. BIBLIOGRAPHY: G. H. Stevenson and A. Momigliano, CAH 10:808–865; M. P. Charlesworth, CAH 11:1–45.

[M. J. SUELZER]

VESPUCCI, AMERIGO (1451–1512), Florentine navigator and controversial explorer. The crucial part of his career began in 1492, when he went to Seville as an agent of the Medici family to work for Giannotto Berardi, a merchant who fitted out ships, and to take over when Berardi died. Here V. helped to prepare for Columbus's second and third voyages. V. is known to have made two voyages to the New World between 1497 and 1504, but it is questionable whether he made two others. Because he wrote letters chronicling his explorations and giving descriptions, he was often credited with being the discoverer of the New World, particularly as a result of his 1502 voyage, which established that the land mass was indeed new and not part of the Asian coast, as had been previously thought. In 1507, Martin Waldseemüller first suggested that the new lands be named America for Vespucci.

[P. J. HENNESSEY]

VESSELS, SACRED, those used in the Eucharistic liturgy, esp. the chalice with paten, which is consecrated by a bishop. Blessed vessels include the ciborium, used for distributing holy communion, the monstrance and lunette (glass container for the host), used for exposition of the Blessed Sacrament; the pyx, used for bringing communion to the sick. Current practice more readily allows the nonordained to handle sacred vessels than formerly was the case.

[T. C. O'BRIEN]

VESTAL VIRGINS, Roman priestesses in the service of Vesta, the patron goddess of the public hearth located within the Temple of Vesta in the Roman forum. In historical times they were six in number. Chosen by the *pontifex maximus* between the ages of 6 and 10, they were obliged to tend the sacred fire of the goddess for 30 years. Afterwards they were free to marry, but since this was considered to be unlucky, few took advantage of the permission. The vestals could be scourged by the *pontifex maximus* for neglect of duties. For violations of chastity they were interred alive in an underground chamber near the Colline Gate. Though the vestals received many honors and privileges, the Roman nobility at the time of Augustus were reluctant to see their daughters chosen for the office. In the late 4th cent. St. Ambrose compared the small number of Vestals with the great number of Christian virgins (*Ep.* 18.11–12). BIBLIOGRAPHY: K. Latte, *Römische Réligionsgeschichte* (1960) 108–111.

[M. J. COSTELLOE]

VESTIARIAN CONTROVERSY, in 16th-cent. England a dispute over Puritan resistance to the use of vestments. The first manifestation was during the reign of Edward VI, when John Hooper refused (1550) to wear surplice and rochet for his consecration as bp. of Gloucester, feeling that they were remnants of popery. The matter was settled by compromise, with Hooper agreeing to the vestments for his induction and for his first sermon before the King. The controversy arose again after the Act of Uniformity (1559) of Elizabeth I; Puritans, many of them under the influence of Geneva from their exile there during Mary Tudor's reign, again objected to the prescribed use of vestments. The *Book of Advertisements (1566) sought to enforce uniformity and met with bitter opposition. The issue became secondary in the broader program of Puritan reform of the Church throughout the 17th century.

VESTMENTS. The liturgical dress of the Roman clergy was originally ordinary secular clothing: the long tunic, a loose undergarment tied at the waist (now the alb), and the mantle, an outer garment wrapped around the body (now the chasuble). This was the practice as late as the 4th century. As fashions changed, the clergy kept the old style and vestments developed with their symbolic significance. Such vestments were decorative by their fullness and natural folds; but the Middle Ages began adding decorations and using brocades, which required abbreviating the vestments to permit movement. By the end of the 18th cent. vestments were ornaments rather than clothing. The 19th cent. began the movement to restore the more ample and aesthetic cut of the ancient (misnamed ''gothic'') vestments.

Vestments are of two major kinds: undergarments, usually of linen—amice (optional), alb, and cincture (optional); and outer garments of better material and various colors—the stole (reserved to deacons, priests, and bishops); the dalmatic (for the deacon); the chasuble (Mass vestment for priests and bishops). These are the most common. The stole is increasingly being worn over the other vestments and a combination alb-chasuble is now permitted. BIBLIOGRAPHY: E. A. Roulin, *Vestments and Vesture* (1950); R. Lesage, *Vestments and Church Furniture* (1960).

[J. DALLEN]

VESTRY, in Anglican usage, a group of persons responsible for parish business; also one of their meetings. The name comes from the fact that meetings were held in the vestry, the church room for vestments and vesting. In the C of E the vestry became less important with the formation (1921) of parochial councils; it still administers poor relief. In the U.S., parishes of the Protestant Episcopal Church have vestries consisting of *rector, *churchwardens, and vestrymen. The number of vestrymen, their duties, and methods of election vary in different dioceses, but in general they serve as trustees representing the religious corporation in matters of property and in relations between parish

members and clergy, esp. regarding the appointment of a rector. BIBLIOGRAPHY: D. Stevick, *Canon Law: A Handbook* (1965).

VETANCOURT, AGUSTÍN DE (1620–1700), missionary, historian. A Mexican Franciscan, V. served as pastor of an Indian parish in Mexico City for 40 years. He taught philosophy, theology, and the native tongue, Nahuatl. Appointed chronicler of the Franciscan Province of the Holy Evangelist, he wrote a significant history called *Teatro mexicano*, a four-part work dealing with natural history, pre-Cortés Mexico, the conquest by Cortés, and a chronicle of the Franciscan Province of the Holy Evangelist.

[J. R. AHERNE]

VETO POWER IN PAPAL ELECTIONS, see EXCLUSION, RIGHT OF.

VETTER, PAUL ALEXANDER (1850–1906), scripture scholar. A specialist in writers of the Armenian Church, V. was professor of OT at the Univ. of Tübingen, Germany. He wrote on the Pentateuch problem, on inspiration, and on biblical literary forms.

[J. R. AHERNE]

VETUS LATINA, see OLD LATIN VERSION.

VEUILLOT, LOUIS (1813–83), the leading lay apologist for Ultramontanism and editor of *L'Univers*. Belligerent, satirical, imprecatory, and not rarely intemperate in style, he authored a prodigious literary output to defend the temporal power of the papacy, to fight against Gallicanism and Liberalism, and to secure the Church's preponderance in the educational structure of France. ''The Perfume of Rome'' (1861) attested his attachment to the Holy See, ''The Smells of Paris'' (1866) his repulsions: these included the liberal Catholicism of *Montalambert and *Dupanloup. He preferred the 1848 Revolution to the July Monarchy, but swung to the support of Louis Napoleon's *coup de'état* though later he fell foul of the Second Empire's Italian policies. He lobbied for an extreme position concerning infallibility at Vatican I. Generally respected for his sincerity, and esp. influential among the country clergy, he was disliked in many quarters for his manners. On his retirement his brother, Eugène, rallied *L'Univers* to the conciliatory policies of Leo XIII, but after his death his sister, Élise, founded *La vérité française* to continue his tradition of intransigence.

[T. GILBY]

VEUSTER, JOSEPH DE, see DAMIEN, FATHER.

VEXILLUM, see BANNER.

VÉZELAY, former Benedictine abbey with a 12th-cent. church that is considered the masterpiece of Burgundian

Romanesque, in the diocese of Sens (formerly Autun), Burgundy, France. It was founded by Duke Girart on his lands at Vézelay in 858–859 as an abbey for Benedictine nuns. In 877 the pope approved the replacement of nuns by monks. Completely destroyed by the Normans in 886–887, it was rebuilt above the valley where the village of St.-Pierre is now located. Reformed in 1037 by Abbot Geoffrey, it became independent of Cluny in 1159. Because the relics of Mary Magdalen were believed to be there, it became an important pilgrimage center and a stop-off place on the way to Compostela. Bernard of Clairvaux preached the Second Crusade at Vézelay; Richard I of England and Philip II of France met there on their way to the Third Crusade; King St. Louis of France visited it in 1248. Thomas à Becket was at Vézelay when he excommunicated Henry II of England in 1166. Bloody conflict occasionally broke out between the wealthy abbey and the strong bourgeois community that grew up around it. Secularized in 1537–38 and damaged in the Wars of Religion, it was restored almost from ruin by Viollet-le-Duc (1840–60).

The central tympanum (1120–32) of the Church of La Madeleine is one of the greatest masterpieces of medieval sculpture, uniting in iconographic richness the *Ascension of Christ* and the *Mission of the Apostles* (Acts 1.4–9) who were to preach, heal, and save all nations. With the expected encyclopedic contribution of the Middle Ages, here is an amalgam of religious and secular thought from classical antiquity and the East in reliefs of healing, drawing out of devils, zodiacal signs (calendars from andient Chaldees), labors of the months, and fanstastic creatures of the pseudo-science of Isidore of Seville, the *cynocephaloi,* large-eared, and snouted faces of "unknown" lands. Stylistically (as at Autun) abrupt line, windblown drapery, elongation, angularity, agitated poses, decorative calligraphic line of whorls and zigzags, rooted in MSS and ivories, are delightfully distinct from sculpture of S France—rooted in a noble but visually determined classical antiquity. Capitals at Vézelay (1120–40) depicting profane, biblical, allegorical, and hagiographical subjects, related to those at Saulieu and Autun, are probably from the same workshop. In rosy stone, the vast nave full of light from huge windows and the varied capitals—all evidencing clarity of organization—effecting an interior of great beauty. Certainly the spirit of the Crusaders inspired the iconography. The conquest of Jerusalem, in turn, introduced the Burgundian style into Palestine and Syria, churches at Tortosa, Beirut, and Jerusalem relating to Vézelay. BIBLIOGRAPHY: F. Salet and J. Adhémar, *La Madeleine de Vézelay* (1948); K. J. Conant, *Carolingian Romanesque Architecture, 800–1200* (1959). A. Katznellenbogen, "The Central Tympanum at Vézelay . . .," *Art Bulletin* 26, 3(1944).

[E. J. DILLON; M. J. DALY]

VEZZOSI, ANTONIO FRANCESCO (1708–83), historian, theologian. A native of Florence, Italy, V. joined the Theatines in 1732. After 14 years as professor in Bergamo and Rome he was appointed professor of church history at the Sapienza in 1751 by Pope Benedict XIV. V. served two terms as superior general of the Theatines (1756–59 and 1774–77). He edited the liturgical works of Giuseppi Tommasi and wrote *I Scrittori dei chierici regolari detti theatini* (2 v., 1780).

[J. R. AHERNE]

VIA DOLOROSA, term in use since the 16th cent. to designate a suggested path of Christ from the Antonia to Calvary following a forced itinerary through the streets of the walled city of Jerusalem. Each station has its own particular history (i.e., date and localization). At the beginning of the 17th cent. the way terminated with the seventh station. The present way of 14 stations was influenced by the practice in Flanders of adding the episodes of Calvary and the Holy Sepulchre. The path of the Via Dolorosa depends on the theory that Pilate judged Christ at the Antonia. This idea is rejected by some modern scholars who hold that the praetorium was permanently located at the royal palace of Herod in the NW corner of the city wall.

[M. A. MCNAMARA]

VIADANA, LODOVICO GROSSI DA (1564–1645), Italian composer. V., who became a Franciscan in 1596, was twice *maestro di cappella* at the cathedral of Mantua as well as at Fano and Venice. He published Masses, psalms, Magnificats, motets, etc., but is probably best known for his "Cento concerti ecclesiastici," a collection of motets with organ accompaniment in which he provided a real *basso continuo*, i.e., an organ bass that did not simply duplicate the lowest melodic line of the vocal arrangement.

[M. T. LEGGE]

VIALAR, ÉMILIE DE, ST. (1797–1856), French religious foundress. She suffered persecution from her family because she refused to marry. From 1818 to 1832 she devoted herself to the care of children, the sick, and the poor in her father's home. An inheritance gave her independence in 1832, and at Gaillac, Archdiocese of Albi, she laid the foundations of the Sisters of St. Joseph of the Apparition, receiving episcopal approval in 1835. The congregation, devoted to the education of children and care of the sick, spread to North Africa, Malta, the Balkans, and the Near East. Both in N Africa and France, V. encountered many setbacks, which led to her finally settling the motherhouse at Marseilles. Her own vigorous leadership was responsible for the growth of the congregation to 40 houses, including foundations in Burma and Australia. V. was canonized in 1951.

[J. R. AHERNE]

VIANNEY, JEAN BAPTISTE MARIE, ST. (1786–1859), patron of parish priests, known as the Curé of Ars.

The poverty of his family, aggravated by the disorders of revolution and war that kept his native France in turmoil during the years when he was growing up, made it impossible for V. to obtain much basic schooling. Under the direction of Abbé Balley, pastor of Écully, he began his studies for the priesthood, but progress was slow and difficult. From 1811 to 1814 he studied in a minor and major seminary, only to be dismissed as hopelessly incapable of qualifying academically. Abbé Balley resumed his tutoring, and in 1815, after a special examination, he was ordained. He was appointed to assist Abbé Balley at Écully, and in 1818 was sent to the village of Ars-en-Dombes where he worked first as local chaplain and from 1821 as pastor. He lived a life of great personal austerity and worked tirelessly to quicken the religious fervor of his flock. The spiritual demands he made of his people were rigoristic, but he softened these somewhat as he grew older and more experienced. His fame spread abroad and multitudes of people came to Ars to see him, to beg his help, and to make their confessions to him. He was credited with an ability to read hearts; many miracles and wonders were attributed to him; and he was plagued for 30 years by hostile preternatural phenomena. BIBLIOGRAPHY: F. Trochu, *Curé of Ars* (tr. E. E. Graf, 1927); H. Ghéon, *Secret of the Curé d'Ars* (tr. F. J. Sheed, 1948); Butler 3:285–292; R. Fourrey, BiblSanct 6:1040–45.

[P. K. MEAGHER]

VIATICUM, the name given to the Eucharist when received by someone who is near death. Holy Communion received as viaticum is considered as one of the *last sacraments and should be received after confession and anointing. The Church binds all capable to receive the last Eucharist. Bringing the Eucharist to those too sick to be present at Mass is a practice dating from ancient times, and was regarded as food for the Christian's journey into the afterlife. The availability of the Eucharist for the sick has historically been the primary reason for Eucharistic reservation. In the late Middle Ages the Eucharist was carried even to those too sick to receive the Host, so that the sick person, before his death, could make an act of faith in Christ eucharistically present before him. Because the Eucharist is both fulfillment of sacramental life and foretaste of eternal life, Vat II SacLit 74 stipulates that viaticum be received following the other last sacraments. The 1972 *Rite of Anointing and Pastoral Care of the Sick,* ch.3 (93–114) enriched the liturgy of viaticum and provides rules for its reception both within and outside of Mass. BIBLIOGRAPHY: *Eucharist Today* (ed. R. Tarte, 1967); J. J. Hannon, *Holy Viaticum* (1951); G. Grabka, "Christian Viaticum: A Study of Its Cultural Background," *Traditio* 9 (1953) 1–43; *Rites of the Catholic Church* (Eng. tr. The International Commission on English in the Liturgy, 1976).

[J. J. FLOOD]

VIATORIANS (Clerics of St. Viator, CSV), a congregation of men founded in Lyons, France, in 1831 by Louis Querbes and approved by the Holy See in 1846. The Viatorians' principal work was instruction in Christian doctrine and education on the elementary, secondary, and higher levels. In 1903 the Viatorians left France because of the antireligious laws, migrating to Belgium and Canada. The earliest foundation in the U.S. was at Carondelet, Mo., in 1842. Forced by circumstances to leave there in 1857, Viatorians founded schools in Illinois. St. Viator's College in Bourbonnais, Ill., became their leading institution (1868). Two fires and financial crises closed the college in 1938. Viatorians administer and teach in a number of high schools, mostly in Illinois, and operate parishes. Their provinces exist in the U.S., Canada, France, and Spain. They number (1975) 1,365 (of whom 476 are clerics) in 116 houses, with a motherhouse in Rome.

[J. R. AHERNE]

VIAU, THÉOPHILE DE (1590–1626), French mannerist-baroque poet, often known simply as Théophile. Born of a Huguenot family, V. received a solid Protestant formation at Saumur (1611) and Leiden (1615), but showed an early spirit of independence which evolved, under the influence of Vanini, to epicurean freethinking. A friend of *Boisrobert, Maynard, Des Barreaux, and *Saint-Amant, winning the patronage of noble protectors, and gaining prominence for his poetry, he became a leader of the *libertins*. His poetic theory which is a reaction against *Malherbe's rules, and insists on natural temperament, represents this same defense of freedom. Having abjured Protestantism, out of convenience, before Louis XIII's confessor, Père Séguiran (1622), V. was charged (1623) with complicity in the publication of the antireligious *Parnasse satyrique* (1622). Sentenced to death in absence and burned in effigy (1623), he attempted escape from France, was arrested near the frontier, but was eventually released with a nominal sentence of exile (1625), and died shortly thereafter, his health ruined by imprisonment. One of V.'s accusers had been the Jesuit, Garasse, who attacked him in his *Doctrine curieuse des beaux esprits du temps, ou pretendus tels* (1623). V.'s *Oeuvres* (1621, 1623, 1625, and collected 1626), include poetry, a tragedy, *Pyrame et Thisbé* (publ. 1623), and a *Traicté de l'immortalité de l'âme ou la mort de Socrate.* BIBLIOGRAPHY: A. Adam, *Théophile de Viau et la libre pensée française en 1620* (1936, repr. 1965).

[R. N. NICOLICH]

VIAUD, LOUIS MARIE JULIEN, see LOTI, PIERRE.

VICAR, in general, one who is the official representative of another. In England the term was originally applied to the cleric who exercised the functions of a parish priest as the delegate of the proper rector or of the religious community to whom the church was entrusted. In such a case the tithes, or a major portion of them, went to the rector or the religious community represented by the vicar. In later usage the term has been applied to the incumbent of any church whose tithes are impropriated or appropriated. The vicar in this sense enjoys all the spiritual jurisdiction that would be his if he were a rector in the full sense of the term. *RECTOR; *CURATE.

[P. K. MEAGHER]

VICAR APOSTOLIC, a priest with special delegation from the bp. to assist him in the administration of the diocese. He has the jurisdiction of all matters temporal and spiritual assigned by ordinary law to the bishop.

[F. H. BRIGHAM]

VICAR CAPITULAR, the administrator of the diocese during a vacancy caused by the death or resignation of the bishop, in dioceses where there is a cathedral chapter (*capitulum*) of canons. One of the canons must be elected to administer the see within eight days of the vacancy (CIC c. 432). In the U.S. and elsewhere where there are no cathedral chapters, the diocesan councillors must elect an administrator upon the occurrence of the see's vacancy.

VICAR FORANE, see DEAN, RURAL.

VICAR OF CHRIST, papal title since the pontificate of Innocent III (1198–1216) and emphasizing the pope's jurisdiction as the successor of St. Peter with vicarious powers received from Christ.

[F. H. BRIGHAM]

VICARI, HERMANN VON (1773–1868), abp. of Freiburg-im-Breisgau, Germany. He was ordained in 1797. From Constance, where he was a member of the diocesan curia, he was appointed to the cathedral chapter at Freiburg, becoming chapter dean in 1830. Auxiliary bishop in 1832, he was nominated for the archbishopric in 1836, but the government of Baden and the Roman Curia disapproved. In 1842 his election was not opposed by the government, but was only reluctantly approved in Rome. A defender of the rights of the Church in education, marriage regulation, freedom from state approval of bishops, and property rights, V. led the province bishops in a series of demands for recognition of canon law in these matters. Memoranda expressing the demands, at V.'s insistence, were addressed to the government in 1848, 1852, and 1853. After 1853 V. ignored the civil restrictions and followed canon law. In May, 1854, he was held house prisoner for 8 days. The conflict with civil authority was still in progress at the time of V.'s death at age 95.

[J. R. AHERNE]

VICARIATE, the provisory status of an ecclesiastical territory: a vicariate apostolic prior to diocesan status; a territory of a religious institute prior to its becoming a province.

VICARIATE OF ROME, the curia that administers Rome, the see whose bishop is the pope. The head of the vicariate is the cardinal vicar; he exercises actual episcopal jurisdiction in the diocese. The vicar continues in office during a vacancy of the Holy See. Vatican City is not included in the vicariate but has its own. The vicariate of Rome comprises four sections: offices of divine worship; of discipline; of administration; and a chancery with its own courts.

VICE, a voluntarily retained and exercised propensity towards sinful action; the opposite of virtue. On the basis of virtue's consisting in the "happy medium," the opposition of vice to virtue is either excess or deficiency. The implication is that the objects of moral choice are generally classifiable as the hierarchized goods perfective of the human person. A virtuous choice is the choice that respects the hierarchized value of the good chosen; a sinful choice is a failure that either exaggerates or absolutizes its good object, or falls short of its true value; an act of greed exaggerates the worth of money; an act of wastefulness wantonly disregards that worth. A typology of the moral life, therefore, is possible, e.g. the Second Part of St. Thomas Aquinas's *Summa theologiae,* by delineating the virtues and the two kinds of vice opposed to each. The idea of vice as an abiding propensity, a *habit, rests on the way human moral powers are oriented connaturally towards the good. The will itself is the overall inclination of human nature towards its good; the sensory appetites are drawn naturally towards some good beneficial to, or shrink from some evil threatening, particular sides of human nature. Because the will and the other appetites follow upon knowledge, there is a connatural and imperative apprehension of the good towards which the will and appetites are bent (see SYNDERESIS). But the virtues themselves are not innate and the actual use of right moral knowledge requires the right tempering of their inclinations. The moral life develops by the continuous process of making choices; these result inevitably in a bent of appetite reflecting the choices made: in virtues, the amenability of appetite towards the true good; or in vices, the unrestrained and unmeasured quest for what pleases them, and the distortion of moral judgment. The vices, then, are ingrained sources for wrong moral choices. But they are properly vices only when they are voluntarily retained; that alone gives them their quality as morally evil. Thus a person who seeks to rectify his life, and concretely a Christian who repents, does not lose the conditioning of appetite towards wrong, but that conditioning is no longer a vice; rather it becomes the occasion for the struggle against sin (see TEMPTATION) and for the development of the virtues.

[T. C. O'BRIEN]

VICEGERENT OF ROME, an abp., assistant to the cardinal who heads the *vicariate of Rome; there are two vicegerents appointed by the Holy Father and exercising episcopal jurisdiction in the Diocese of Rome.

VICELINUS OF OLDENBURG, ST. (c. 1086–1154), missionary, bp., apostle of the Wends. Having been a canon and schoolmaster at Bremen, V. was ordained by St. Norbert. In 1126 he began a long period of missionary labors among the Wends and other Slavonic tribes. He made monastic foundations at Holstein, Högersdorf, and Segeberg. He became bp. of Oldenburg in Holstein in 1149; three years later he was attacked by the long illness that caused his death. BIBLIOGRAPHY: Butler 4:547; O. Scheib, BiblSanct 12:1074–75.

[M. J. FINNEGAN]

VICENTINO, NICOLA (1511–72), musical theorist, composer. V. was a disciple of the famous musician, A. Willaert, and after ordination served as music director for the chapel of the Ferrara court and of Card. Ippolite II d'Este at Rome. He is important for his significant contributions to the development of new harmony forms and for his madrigals. He strove to unfetter musical composition from its traditional forms. The result of controversy over his views was his work: *L'Antica musica ridotta alla moderna prattica.* BIBLIOGRAPHY: K. G. Fellerer, NCE 14:644.

[J. M. O'DONNELL]

VICO, GIAMBATTISTA (1668–1744), philosopher, historian, jurist. V.'s strongly humanistic formation moved him away from his initial Cartesian orientation. He makes his greatest impact in his study of the history of law. Codified laws had been considered the products of reason and will. V.'s work *Scienza nuova d'intorno alla commune natura delle Nazioni* (1725, 1730, 1744) opened a new epoch in historiography. He saw codified laws as being crystallizations of vast bodies of historical experience involved in the development of institutions and of the human mind itself. *Scienza nuova* reconstructs human presence and social process in history. The reconstruction of human presence is an epistemological vindication of the practical effectiveness of imagination and the passions. But the deployment of the human presence through time is in the collective consciousness rather than in the individual. Hence, the historical document is not simply a written record but a living social process. History, accordingly, is not merely a science, but the universal matrix of significant human discourse. Further, the course of history is subject to *corsi i ricorsi*, the cyclical theory of history for which Vico is best known. Finally, Providence provides the principle of rectification between the course of nations' history and ideal, eternal history. There is much contemporary interest in V.'s contribution to philosophical hermeneutics. BIBLIOGRAPHY: G. Vico, *New Science* (tr. T. G. Bergin and M. H. Fisch [from 3d. ed. 1744] 1948); *idem, Diritto universale* (3 v., 1720–22); P. Gardiner, EncPhil 8:247–251.

[J. MCFADDEN]

VICTIM SOUL, the designation of one chosen by God and accepting his role, who sacrifices himself and all he is or has, after the example of Christ, for the good of the Church or humanity or an individual.

[J. R. AHERNE]

VICTOR I, ST., (d. 198 or 199), **POPE** from 189, successor of *Eleutherius. The principal event of his pontificate was the *Quartodeciman controversy, in which he sought to exercise the primacy of Rome over all the Church. The fact that a congregation of Eastern Christians in Rome always observed Easter on the 14th Nisan of the Jewish calendar, whatever the day of the week, led V. to direct that synods on the question be held throughout the Church, and to convoke a council at Rome. He insisted that *Polycrates of Ephesus and other Eastern bps. conform to the Roman practice of keeping Easter only on Sunday. Though he threatened them with excommunication, the pope was dissuaded from such severity by *Irenaeus. V. also excommunicated *Theodotus, a Byzantine leather merchant, who was propagating *monarchianism at Rome (see MELCHISEDEKIANS). The belief that V. died a martyr is unfounded. BIBLIOGRAPHY: Butler 3:201; E. Weltin, *Early Popes* (1964) 92–95.

[R. B. ENO]

VICTOR II (Gebhard; d. 1057), **POPE** from 1055. He was made bp. of Eichstätt in 1042 and became imperial chancellor to Henry III. He was appointed pope by Henry after the death of Leo IX in Sept., 1054, but delayed his canonical election and coronation for 6 months. He continued the reform begun by his predecessor and served, like him, as a kind of "imperial vicar" for Italy. In October of 1056 Henry III died in Victor's arms, commending to him his son, a minor, and the interests of the Empire. After crowning young Henry in Aachen, Victor returned to Rome to hold his last synod in the Lateran. His death ended the 10-year period of imperial-papal reform. BIBLIOGRAPHY: J. Haller, *Papsttum* (1955) 2:307–310; Mann 6:183–206; E. Amann, DTC 15.2:2863–66; O. J. Blum, NCE 14:646–647.

[O. J. BLUM]

VICTOR III, BL. (Dauferius; 1027–87), **POPE** from 1086. After living for several years as a hermit, he entered the Benedictine Order, taking the name Desiderius. In 1058 he succeeded Frederick of Lorraine (Stephen IX) as abbot of Monte Cassino and during his tenure rebuilt the abbey and stimulated an artistic and literary renaissance. Following the death of Gregory VII and a year of disorder, he was elected to the papacy. As pope, he was more conciliatory to the empire than his predecessor, but continued the Gregorian policy against lay investiture. An expedition sent by him against the Saracens in Tunis anticipated the First Crusade of the next decade. BIBLIOGRAPHY: J. Haller, *Papsttum* (1955) 2:430–433; Mann 7:218–244; H. Bloch, "Monte Cassino, Byzantium, and the West," *Dumbarton Oaks Papers* 3 (1946) 163–224.

[O. J. BLUM]

VICTOR, SS., the name of four saints and one blessed contained in Butler. (1) Victor, St., Pope and martyr. He was pope, *c.*189–199, but there is no good reason to suppose him martyred. What is known of him comes from Eusebius and the *Liber pontificalis*. He was a native of Africa and was said by Jerome to have been the first in Rome to celebrate the liturgy in Latin. (2) Victor of Marseilles, St., Christian officer in the Roman Army. He was martyred at Marseilles *c*.290, under Maximian and became one of the most celebrated martyrs of Gaul. According to St. Gregory of Tours and Venantius Fortunatus V.'s tomb in Marseilles was one of the best known places of pilgrimage on French soil. (3) Victor Maurus, St., so-called to distinguish him from other holy Victors, since he was from Mauretania. Ambrose names him as one of the patrons of Milan, decapitated there *c*.303 under Maximian. Having been a soldier in the praetorian guard and a Christian from youth, he was arrested and martyred in old age. His tomb is mentioned by Gregory of Tours. (4) Victor the Hermit, St., the subject of two panegyrics by St. Bernard, born at Troyes, died *c*.610. (5) Victor III, Bl., (Pope) 1086–87. Born of the Lombard family of the dukes of Benevento, he was a hermit, wandering monk, and finally abbot of Monte Cassino before becoming pope.

[E. J. DILLON]

VICTOR OF ANTIOCH, 5th-cent. biblical exegete, a scholiast of the Antiochene school, with its concern for the literal meaning of biblical texts and for historical and geographical detail. Virtually nothing is known of him beyond quotations in a certain number of exegetical chains (*catenae*). The most important is probably the chain of scholia on Mark's Gospel, although many others exist pertaining to the OT and NT books. These collections of marginal comments reflect the state of the scriptural commentary at that time.

[E. J. DILLON]

VICTOR EMMANUEL II (1820–78), King of Piedmont 1849–61 and of Italy from 1861. Assuming the crown in 1849 after the abdication of his father Charles Albert, he retained the constitution issued in 1848. His premier during most of the years 1852–61 was *Cavour, whom he disliked and resented. Nevertheless the two worked to achieve the unification of Italy during this period. After the death of Cavour, V. E. was more forceful in asserting his monarchical authority. Excommunicated by Pius IX in 1860 for invading papal territories, he was reconciled to the Church in 1869 during an illness. The Roman Question, created by the unification of Italy at the expense of the Church, remained unresolved. With the permission of the Pope, V. E. was given a religious burial in the Pantheon. BIBLIOGRAPHY: D. Mack Smith, *Italy, A Modern History* (1959).

[E. A. CARRILLO]

VICTOR OF PLANCY, ST. (d. 6th cent.), hermit. Although he was ordained and served as a priest, V. became a hermit in Plancy near Troyes. His sanctity and miracles attracted crowds to his hermitage. After his death his cult spread under the name St. Vittre, and was so popular in the

12th cent. that St. Bernard of Clairvaux composed an office of St. Victor. BIBLIOGRAPHY: É. Brouette, NCE 14:649; Butler 1:426–427.

[G. M. COOK]

VICTOR OF TUNNUNA (d.*c*.567) North African bp. who defended the Three Chapters against Justinian and Justin II; he suffered imprisonment in the Balearics, Egypt, and Constantinople. Only the last years (443–566) of his general chronicle are extant; it deals with religious controversies and events in Rome, Carthage, the Eastern patriarchates, and on the imperial frontier. V.'s chronicle, continued by John Biclarensis, was superseded by that of Isidore of Seville.

[E. P. COLBERT]

VICTOR OF VITA (5th cent.), bp. in the N African province of Byzacena. He wrote a history of the persecution under the Arian Vandal kings Genseric and Hunneric of Catholics in the Province of Africa (439–489) which provides information of value concerning the political and religious situation in Africa at that time. The *Passion of the Seven Monks* was added by a later author. V. also wrote *Notitia provinciarum et civitatum Africae*, a work important for its listing of Catholic bps. of the Vandal realm in North Africa. Works: PL 58:180–216; crit. ed. M. Petschenig, CSEL 7 (1881). BIBLIOGRAPHY: G. Bardy, DTC 15:2881–82; Bihlmeyer-Tüchle 1:230.

[R. B. ENO]

VICTORIA, TOMÁS LUIS DE (1549–1611), master of the Spanish polyphonic school. V. went, at an early age, to Rome. It is supposed that he studied there with Palestrina whom, in 1571, he succeeded as *maestro di cappella* at the Roman College. He was also associated with the German College, as student and as *maestro,* was ordained in 1575 and became a chaplain at the Church of S. Girolamo della Carità, the site of St. Philip Neri's foundation of the Oratory. V. returned to Spain *c.* 1598 to become chaplain to the Empress Maria, and subsequently to her daughter at the Convent of the Descalzas Reales in Madrid. Though it bears the influence of Palestrina and the Roman school, V.'s music reflects his Spanish inheritance in its dramatic vigour and its mystical and emotional intensity. His works, including motets, Masses, Magnificats, psalms, and hymns, held a wide reputation in his own time and are regarded, along with the compositions of Palestrina, as representative of the high point of religious polyphonic music.

[M. T. LEGGE]

VICTORIA AND ANATOLIA, SS., virgin martyrs whose cultus extended to various parts of Italy. The date and circumstances of their martyrdom are not known. Their *passio* is spurious and presents an offensively negative view of marriage, of the sort once commonly incorporated into homilies in favor of virginity.

[E. J. DILLON]

VICTORINES, SPIRITUALITY OF, the spirituality associated with the Abbey of St. Victor after it was founded (1108) by William of Champeaux, who emphasized Scripture and the Fathers of the Church in his study. Among its leaders were Adam of St. Victor, Hugh of St. Victor, Richard of St. Victor and Walter of St. Victor. BIBLIOGRAPHY: H. C. Van Elswijk, NCE 14;650–651; A Forest, *Le mouvement doctrinal du XIe au XIVe siècle* (Fliche-Martin, 13; 1951) 112–123.

[F. H. BRIGHAM]

VICTORINES, THEOLOGY OF, the approach to God through the unity of mind and heart as taught by Hugh of St. Victor and his successors. All knowledge was the way to a better grasp of the Scriptures, the source of true spiritual life and mysticism. BIBLIOGRAPHY: H.C. Van Elswijk, NCE 14:650–651; J. Chatillon, *Théologie, spiritualité et metaphysique dans l'oeuvre oratoire d'Achard de St. Victor,* (*Études de Philosophie Médiévale,* 1969).

[F. H. BRIGHAM]

VICTORINUS, ST. (d. *c.* 304), bp. of Pettau (now Ptuj in NE Slovenia), martyr. According to Jerome, he was a Greek by birth, and was the first exegete to write in Latin, in which he achieved no distinction of style, for it was not his native tongue. He commented on many books of the Bible, although his commentary on Revelation is the only exegetical work that has survived. A portion of a treatise *De fabrica mundi* is also extant. He was among the proponents of Millenarianism. V. was martyred in the persecution of Diocletian, but there is no evidence that he enjoyed a special cult in antiquity. Works: PL 5:281–344; crit. ed. J. Haussleiter, CSEL 49 (1916). BIBLIOGRAPHY: Quasten 2:411–413.

[R. B. ENO]

VICTRICIUS OF ROUEN, ST. (*c.*330–*c.*407), bp. Probably of a military family, and he himself a soldier from an early age, V., after becoming a Christian, had doubts about the lawfulness of his profession and laying down his arms one day he asked for a discharge. For this he was flogged and barely escaped execution as a deserter. As bp. of Rouen he strove to convert the pagans, still numerous in his diocese, esp. in its more rural areas. He was conspicuously devoted to the saints, writing in their honor his *On the Praise of the Saints*, and being at some pains to gather their relics. He traveled to Britain in response to an appeal for help in the settlement of an ecclesiastical dispute (*c.*396), and to Rome to clear himself of a charge of heresy (404). He received from Pope Innocent I the *Liber Regularum*, an important document in the history of canon law in the West. Most of what is known of him is gathered from his correspondence with *Paulinus of Nola. Works: PL 20:443–458. BIBLIOGRAPHY: Butler 3:275–276.

[R. B. ENO]

VICTURIUS OF LE MANS, ST. (d. 490), bp. of Le Mans NW France, from 450, also called Victorius or Vic-

tor. He assisted at the synods of Angers (453) and Tours (461). Soon after his death he was referred to as "venerable confessor" by Gregory of Tours, who also attributed to his sanctity the cures at his tomb in the cloister of the Twelve Apostles which V. had built. Since the 7th cent. he has been venerated in the basilica dedicated to him at Le Mans.

[E. J. DILLON]

VIDA, MARCO GIROLAMO (*c.*1485–1566), bp. of Alba, Italian poet and Church reformer. He wrote a successful epic on the life of Christ in six volumes, *Christiad* (1535), as well as other sacred and secular poetry. After being appointed bp., he was known for the enthusiasm with which he pursued heretics and endeavored to improve disciplinary standards within the Church.

[P. J. HENNESSEY]

VIDI AQUAM, the opening of the antiphon that may be sung during the Paschal season in place of the *Asperges, during the sprinkling of the congregation with holy water, a rite which may replace the penitential rite at any Mass on Sunday or anticipated Masses on Saturday. The antiphon is based on Ezek 47, 2 and is followed by the first verse of Ps 117. The prayer is the one used throughout the year.

[R. B. ENO]

VIEBAN, ANTHONY (1872–1944), professor of theology. A French Sulpician ordained in 1895, V. came to the U.S. and from 1898 was a professor of theology at St. Mary's Seminary, Baltimore, Maryland. In 1917 he joined the school of theology at The Catholic University of America, and in 1919 became superior of the Sulpician novitiate. He also served as rector of the University's Theological College. He was a contributor to Theological journals and to A. *Tanquerey's *Dogmatic Theology*. V. also held many offices in Sulpician administration.

[J. R. AHERNE]

VIEL, PLACIDA, BL. (Victoria Eulalia Jacqueline; 1815–77), religious superior. Child of a poor French family she joined a small congregation, the Sisters of the Christian Schools of Mercy. The foundress and superior general, St. Mary Magdalen Postel, trained V. to be her successor, entrusting her with considerable responsibility and naming her mistress of novices. In 1846 V. was elected superior general. Her vigorous administration and fund-raising strengthened the young community which grew, under her leadership, from 150 to 1,000 members, with houses increasing from 37 to 105. V. was beatified in 1951.

[J. R. AHERNE]

VIENNA, CONCORDAT OF (1448), an agreement which resolved a dispute between the Holy See and the Council of Basel and established ecclesiastical policy for Germany. It dealt primarily with ecclesiastical appointments.

[P. J. HENNESSEY]

VIENNA, CONGRESS OF, a peace conference necessitated by the disordered state of Europe after the fall of Napoleon Bonaparte, beginning in September, 1814, and ending in June, 1815. Though dominated to a degree by the four great powers, Austria, Prussia, England, and Russia, the Congress was influenced by France and Spain and to a lesser extent by less powerful countries such as Portugal and Sweden. Count Metternich of Austria was the brilliant figure who guided the conference, the most elaborate negotiation for a new order prior to the League of Nations. Other prominent representatives who participated were Lord Castelreagh of Britain, von Hardenburg of Prussia, Czar Alexander I of Russia, and ultimately Talleyrand of France, representing Louis XVIII. Card. Consalvi, papal secretary of state, represented Pope Pius VII. The decrees comprised 17 agreements, each signed by the states involved. The Final Act of June 9, 1815, summarized the treaties. Among significant outcomes were the partition of Poland between Russia and Prussia, the restoration of the papal states in Italy, creation of an independent Netherlands, setting up of the German Confederation, and restoration of a number of Italian kingdoms. Whatever its faults, the Congress of Vienna established a European order, broken only twice in a period of almost 100 years. BIBLIOGRAPHY: H. Nicholson, *Congress of Vienna* (1948).

[J. R. AHERNE]

VIENNE, COUNCIL OF. In 1308 Pope Clement V announced a council to discuss the Knights Templar, the recovery of the Holy Land, and church reform. It met Oct. 16, 1311 to May 6, 1312 at Vienne on the Rhone. Although Clement, after consulting with King Philip the Fair of France issued invitations to 231 carefully screened prelates, the council is customarily listed as an ecumenical council. Despite the efforts of the French king, the council refused to condemn the memory of his implacable enemy, Pope Boniface VIII; but Clement and the conciliar fathers did yield to Philip's demands in suppressing the Knights Templar. The crusade to the Holy Land discussed at the second and third sessions never materialized. The reform decrees, about 38 in number, touched on a wide variety of topics from the internal affairs of the Franciscan Order to hospitals, usury, and the teaching of biblical languages (D 891–898; 906–908). The council also denounced an opinion which held that the rational soul is not *vere et per se* the form of the human body (D 902). BIBLIOGRAPHY: J. Lecler, *Histoire de conciles oecuméniques—Vienne* (1964); M. François, NCE 14:660.

[B. L. MARTHALER]

VIENNESE SCHOOL (MUSIC): (1) one of the three main centers of symphonic composition in Germany. Of the period immediately preceding Haydn and Mozart, it included the composers Monn, Wagenseil, Gassman and Michael Haydn; (2) school of composition in *twelve-tones, including the composer Arnold Schoenberg and his pupils, Alban Berg and Anton Webern. BIBLIOGRAPHY: D. J.

Grout, *History of Western Music* (rev. ed., 1973) 461–463; R. Leibowitz, *Schoenberg and His School* (1949).

[M. T. LEGGE]

VIERZEHNHEILIGEN ("Fourteen Saints"), **CHURCH OF** (1743–72), one of the most splendid German rococo churches near Bamberg by J.B. *Neumann (1687–1753), architect to the Schönborns of Würzburg, and of Bamberg. Dedicated to 14 saints who appeared to a shepherd in the 15th cent., it is the third church erected on the site. Only the undulating bays of the sober façade hint at the interior, with its ingenious groundplan of tangent ovals and circles, the fluid space in continuous motion of dematerialized, interwoven intricacies in a bewildering vista of variety and surprise, as light through numerous windows glances off white, pale, and gilded surfaces, so that the very boundaries of architecture, sculpture, music, and painting dissolve in a visionary unity. The earlier Gnadenaltar of J. J. Küchel stands in the central oval space, while ceiling frescoes of G. Appiani, and stucco ornament, statues and *putti* of J. M. Feuchtmayer and J. G. Ubelhör of Wessobrunn confirm the ecstasy of the luminous masterwork. BIBLIOGRAPHY: R. Teufel, *Vierzehnheiligen* (1957); H. Reuther, *Die Kirchenbauten Balthasar Neumann* (1960). *FOURTEEN HOLY HELPERS.

[M. J. DALY]

VIETNAM, since July 2, 1976, the Socialist Republic of Vietnam, combining the former North Vietnam (Democratic Republic of Vietnam), 63,334 sq mi and South Vietnam (former Republic of Vietnam) 66,000 sq mi; the combined population is 45,311,000 (1977 est.). The Southern government surrendered on April 30, 1975; a new national government was elected in April 1976. Occupied by China from the 2d to the 9th cent., it continued long thereafter as a suzerain state of the Chinese Empire. The Portuguese settled in a few places along the coast in the 16th century. From 1884 to 1949 the region was a French Protectorate. Buddhism is the dominant religion. Franciscans and Dominicans came there at the close of the 16th century. The most renowned missioner was the Jesuit, Alexander de *Rhodes (1591–1660), who was the first to use catechists to assist him and pioneered in training native priests. By 1639 Christians numbered 82,000; but Confucian scholars and Buddhist\monks inaugurated severe persecutions which continued sporadically throughout most of the 19th century. Approximately 100,000 Christians, 45 missionaries, and 115 native priests suffered martyrdom. Missioners continued to enter Vietnam, however, and Trappists and Carmelites founded monasteries for contemplation. World War II and the civil war of the mid-20th cent. in Vietnam have retarded mission work. In North Vietnam, despite claims of religious freedom, Christianity fell into eclipse. Episcopal sees were vacant; some priests were in prison or in hiding; and most churches were closed. Children were required to study antireligious Marxist doctrine. In South Vietnam, the Church fared better; in addition to native

South Vietnamese Catholics there were more than 650,000 Catholic refugees from North Vietnam settled in the country. The hierarchy consists of 3 archdioceses and 22 dioceses. There are 2,392 priests, 1,125 men religious, and 7,130 women religious. The total Catholic population is about 2,750,000. Since Communist unification of the country little is known about internal affairs and about the conditions under which the Church exists. For a time the only Protestant denomination in Vietnam was the Christian and Missionary Alliance. Then also came Adventists, the Worldwide Evangelization Crusade, and the Wycliffe Bible Translators. In 1968 the total Protestant membership was 55,677.

VIGIL, FRANCISCO DE PAULA GONZALEZ

(1792–1875), political figure, polemicist. Enigmatic and erudite, V. was a Peruvian ordained in 1818. Refusing pastoral work he taught at the Colegio de Independencia. Elected a member of Congress in 1825, he aided in subordinating the Church in Peru to the State. Leaving Congress in 1835, he was named director of the National Library in 1836, a position he held for most of his remaining years. His principal work in two parts was *Defensa de la autoridad de los gobernos contra las pretensiones de la Curia Romana* (6 v., 1848–49) and *Defensa de la autoridad de los obispos contra las pretensiones de la Curia Romana*. The works asserted limitation of the authority of the pope to purely spiritual matters; in 1851 Pius IX condemned them. V.'s writings became more and more anticlerical and scarcely Christian. A man of good character and liberal social views, he died outside the Church.

[J. R. AHERNE]

VIGIL, a day before certain feasts or holy days which included prayer and penance. The General Roman Calendar of 1969 lists vigil Masses for Easter, Christmas, Pentecost, the Feasts of the Birth of St. John the Baptist, Feast of SS. Peter and Paul, and the Assumption of the Blessed Virgin. The *Easter Vigil has special rank and solemnity in the liturgical year. The former penitential observance of vigils, and the special designation as a type of liturgical day no longer obtain.

[F. H. BRIGHAM]

VIGIL, EASTER, see EASTER VIGIL.

VIGILANTI CURA, encyclical on motion pictures issued by Pope Pius XI June 29, 1936. The first major papal encyclical devoted to this subject, *Vigilanti cura* was directed primarily to the American hierarchy as an expression of approbation for their work in this area. The document acknowledged the cultural significance of movies, their value for popular education and recreation, while drawing attention to their potential danger to public morality. It established guidelines to direct the Church's concern and recommended for all countries the measures undertaken by

the American bishops: a national office to coordinate activity and a pledge of support from the laity.

[R. SCHMANDT]

VIGILANTIUS (d. after 406), adversary of St. *Jerome. A native of Calagurris in Aquitaine, V. appears first in history as the bearer of a letter from *Paulinus of Nola to Jerome in Bethlehem. Jerome received him kindly but a discussion with Jerome's brother Paulinian and other companions of his host terminated in a quarrel. Upon his return to the West, V. accused Jerome of *Origenism, to which charge Jerome quickly replied with a letter (n. 61) calling attention to the deficiencies of V.'s background and education. V. was serving as a priest in Southern Gaul in 404 when he was denounced to Jerome by a neighboring priest, Riparius, for attacking the cult of the saints and relics. Jerome wrote asking for further information and copies of V.'s writings. On the receipt of these in 406 Jerome in one night dictated his *Contra Vigilantium*. None of V.'s writings have survived. According to Jerome's hasty and perhaps exaggerated polemic, V. denied the intercession of the saints, the cult of relics, and opposed clerical celibacy as well as certain other ascetical practices being introduced in the West at that time. BIBLIOGRAPHY: G. Bardy, DTC 15:2992–94; E. Peterson, EncCatt 12:1414.

[R. B. ENO]

VIGILIUS (d. 555), **POPE** from 537. A native Roman, V. served as papal apocrisiarius in Constantinople. Some evidence suggests that the Empress *Theodora prevailed upon him to agree to further the cause of *Monophysitism. Back in Rome he was chosen to succeed Pope Silverius who had been deposed by the Byzantine general Belisarius. But instead of favoring Monophysitism he reaffirmed the doctrine of *Chalcedon. The Emperor *Justinian in an effort to win over the Monophysites by condemning the *Three Chapters had V. brought to Constantinople. After some resistance the Pope yielded to imperial pressure by condemning the Three Chapters in his *Judicatum* of 548. Although he expressly stated his adherence to Chalcedon, the Western reaction was so violent that he had to withdraw the document. He then refused to take part in the council called by the Emperor to condemn the Three Chapters. After much harassment, including the threat of his own condemnation by the council, V. issued a condemnation of the Three Chapters and their supporters. BIBLIOGRAPHY: F. X. Murphy, NCE 14:664–667; É. Amann, DTC 15:1868–1924.

[G. T. DENNIS]

VIGILIUS OF AUXERRE, ST. (d. 684 or 689), bishop. He was born of a noble family noted for its sanctity. Beyond the fact that he built a monastery which was given first to the Augustinians and ultimately to the Premonstratensians, little else is known of him. He is credited with building a hospital for the poor. He was murdered in a forest near Compiègne and his body was returned to his see at Auxerre. BIBLIOGRA - PHY: C. M. Aherne, NCE 14:667.

[F. G. O'BRIEN]

VIGILIUS (fl. *c*.500), N. African bp. of Thapsus, writer. Nothing is known of his life save that he participated in the Carthaginian conference of 484 between the Catholics and the Arian Vandals, held under the auspices of the Vandal king Hunneric. Of the works attributed to V. (PL 62:93–544) a *Dialogue against Arians, Sabellians and Photinians* and five books against *Eutyches, in which he defends the *Tome of Leo and the Council of *Chalcedon, against the *Monophysites, are certainly authentic; the rest are not. BIBLIOGRAPHY: Altaner 587; G. Bardy, DTC 15:3005–08.

[R. B. ENO]

VIGNIER, JEROME (1606–61), Oratorian scholar. Born at Blois, France, he was a convert to Catholicism. After entering the priesthood, he studied languages, genealogy, and numismatics. He wrote *La Véritable origine des maisons d'Alsace de Lorraine et d'Autriche* (1649) and *Endiatessaron, histoire et harmonie de l'évangile* (1662). He also edited St. Augustine's *Contra Julianum, opus imperfectum.*

[P. J. HENNESSEY]

VIGNOLA, GIACOMO BAROZZI (Il Vignola; 1507–73), Italian architect, member of the Accademia Vitruviana in Rome (1534), in France (1537–39) with Primaticcio, and architect of civic projects in Bologna (1541). V. enjoyed the patronage of the Farnese family (Rome), executing the Oratory of S. Andrea (1554), and palaces (the Villa di Papa Giulio, but esp., the Palazzo Farnese at Caprarola, 1558) revealing a mastery of movement in exploiting the topography in monumental ramps and stairs, a style unique in the 16th cent. He published the *Regola delli cinque ordini d'architettura* (1562) and succeeded Michelangelo at St. Peter's (1564). V.'s designs for the Gesù (1568) and Sta. Anna dei Palafrenieri (1573), became models for Counter Reformation building throughout the Catholic world. BIBLIOGRAPHY: J.P. Coolidge, *Studies on Vignola* (1948).

[L. P. SIGER]

VIGNY, ALFRED DE (1797–1863), French writer. Disillusioned with his military career, he sought refuge in fledgling Romanticism, producing major works in drama, fiction, and poetry, many of which illustrate stages of that movement's confrontation with Christianity. Royalist, conservative, and Catholic, V. gradually adopted Republican ideals, became a religious skeptic with a humanitarian creed and welcomed the 1848 Revolution. A philosophical poet embodying his thought in symbolic figures, V. explored in the collections *Poèmes antiques et modernes* (1822–26–37) and *Les Destinées* (1864) problems in theodicy: an unjust God demanding sacrifice and striking both innocent and guilty (*La Fille de Jephté* and *Le Déluge*), indifferent to

man's anguish (*Moïse*), silent before Christ, his tormented Son (*Le Mont des Oliviers*), giving man the illusion of freedom (*Les Destinées*) and ultimately abandoning him to forge his own destiny (*La maison du berger* and *La sauvage*). The biblical epic *Eloa* depicts an angel, born of Christ's grief, forsaken by God, trying to redeem a romanticized Satan. In the poems of mystical elevation, *Paris* (1831) and *Les Amants de Montmorency* (1832), V. envisaged a new apostolate blending elements of Saint-Simon, Lamennais, and the Enlightenment. Themes typical of Romantic historicism's treatment of religion are reflected in certain novels, tales, and plays: a sinister Richelieu prosecuting "the devils of Loudon" (*Cinq-Mars*, 1826); the majesty of Pius VII's office humbling Napoleon (*Servitude et grandeur militaire*, 1835); a gentle Quaker preaching justice to Christians immured in materialism (*Chatterton*, 1835). *Stello* (1832) and *Journal d'un poète* (1867) show V. choosing the religion of honor and advocating the saintly silence of stoical resignation. Despite generally antiChristian views, 15 days before his death V. received absolution stating "I am a Catholic, I die a Catholic." BIBLIOGRAPHY: A. Whitridge, *Alfred de Vigny* (1933).

[G. E. GINGRAS]

VIGOUROUX, FULCRAN GRÉGOIRE (1837–1915), biblical scholar and editor. V. taught Scripture at the Institut Catholique in Paris before becoming the first secretary of the *Pontifical Biblical Commission (1902). He is best known for his editorship of the important *Dictionnaire de la Bible* (1895–1912), a generally conservative reference work but one that went far to advance Catholic scholarship at a time marked by a highly negative attitude toward higher criticism. His *Manuel biblique* (5 v., 1876), which went through many editions, is an example of the traditional exegesis characteristic of contemporary RC scholarship. BIBLIOGRAPHY: JBC 2:598; P. F. Chirico, NCE 14:668.

[T. M. MCFADDEN]

VIKTRING, ABBEY OF, former Cistercian abbey in Carinthia, Austria, Diocese of Gurk. Founded in 1142 by Count Bernard of Spanheim, Duke of Carinthia, in what was then the Diocese of Salzburg, it was settled by monks from Villers-Betnach in Lotharingia. The Romanesque church was consecrated in 1202. The stained glass, considered Austria's most famous, dates from 1380–90. The abbey was suppressed by Joseph II in 1783 or 86 and the part of the church that escaped destruction was used as a parish church. BIBLIOGRAPHY: Cottineau 2:3363–64.

[E. J. DILLON]

VILATTE, JOSEPH RÉNÉ (1854–1929), a bishop numbered among the *episcopi vagantes. Born in Paris, V. came to North America, where he took part in the religious services of various denominations in Canada and the U.S., settling finally in Wisconsin. Ordained deacon and priest in 1885 by Dr. Herzog, Old Catholic bp. in Switzerland, he worked for a while among Belgian immigrants in the Green Bay area. After making various inquiries of Episcopalian and Orthodox authorities in the hope of receiving episcopal orders, he finally journeyed to Ceylon, where he was consecrated bp. in May 1892 by Abp. Alvares of the "Independent Catholic Church of Goa and Ceylon," a prelate of dubious standing in the Jacobite Church. This consecration was allegedly performed on the authority of a bull of Patriarch Ignatius Peter III of Antioch. Because of doubts surrounding this action, both Indian Jacobite and American Episcopalian authorities have denied the validity of the consecration. V., however, continued to ordain and consecrate others. In 1898, he sought to be reconciled to Rome, but he was formally excommunicated in 1900 after consecrating an Italian priest for the "Italian Episcopal Church." He continued his activities in the U.S. until retirement in 1920. He was succeeded by Bp. Frederick Lloyd, whom he had consecrated in 1915, the date of the official incorporation of his followers as the "American Catholic Church." After being reconciled to Rome in 1925, he died in France in 1929. BIBLIOGRAPHY: H. R. T. Brandreth, *Episcopi Vagantes and the Anglican Church* (2d ed., 1961) 47–54; P. Anson, *Bishops at Large* (1964).

[R. B. ENO]

VILLA-LOBOS, HEITOR (1887–1959), Brazilian composer. Aside from study with Agnello Franca and Benno Niederberger, he had almost no formal musical education. As a member of the Rio de Janeiro symphony, he became acquainted with the music of many composers, but, upon returning from a year in Paris in 1923, V. decided to devote himself to compositions based on folk-like themes and written in non-traditional forms. Thus followed his popular *Choros* and *Bachianas Brasileiras*. V. L. returned to Paris for three years in 1927, spent some years in pedagogical activities in his native Brazil, and visited the U.S., dividing the last years of his life among these three places. His religious contributions number, among a few other pieces, a Tantum Ergo, a Mass and a Magnificat.

[M. T. LEGGE]

VILLANI, GIOVANNI (*c.*1275–1348), chronicler. After an active business and political career, he compiled a universal chronicle, books 7–12 of which provide a valuable history of Florence during much of its formative period (1266–1348). BIBLIOGRAPHY: G. Villani, *Chronicle: Selections* . . . (ed. P. Wicksteed, tr. R. Selfe, 1906).

[J. MULDOON]

VILLARD DE HONNECOURT (fl. *c.*1225–*c.*1250), French architect. V. who traveled widely sketching architecture and sculpture, is renowned for his notebook (*c.*1240) of plans, elevations, ornament, animals, figure sculpture, technical drawings, and figures drawn from life, preserved in the National Library, Paris.

[M. J. DALY]

VILLARROEL, GASPAR DE (*c.*1590–1665), Augustinian abp., writer. Born in Quito, Ecuador, he taught at the monastery of San Agustín of the University of San Marcos in Peru. As procurator of the province of Peru, he went to Madrid in the 1620s where he served as court preacher to Philip IV and on the Council of the Indies. Returning to New Spain, he was bp. first of Santiago de Chile (1637), then of Arequipa in Peru (1651), and finally archbishop of Charcas (1660). His work on eccesiastical polity and royal powers, *Gobierno ecclesiástico* . . . (2 v. 1656–57), is an important record of the period.

[P. J. HENNESSEY]

VILLARUTIA, JACOBO DE (1757–1833), jurist, editor. Born in Santo Domingo, educated in Spain, V. became a lawyer. In 1792 he was named a judge of the *audiencia* in Guatemala and in 1805 that of Mexico. Transferred to Spain for political reasons, he served in Seville and Barcelona. When Mexico achieved independence, V. returned and held political office, ultimately a position on the supreme court. V. was a liberal in social and political views but an orthodox Catholic. He directed a number of newspapers and journals in Spain, Mexico, and Guatemala. Among published works were his *Estatutos para una academia téorico-práctica de jurisprudencia en la ciudad de Valladolid* (1780) and *Reglamento general de artesanos*.

[J. R. AHERNE]

VILLEGAIGNON, NICOLAS DURAND DE (*c.*1510–72), member of the Order of Malta who led a French expedition in attempt to establish a colony in Brazil. After taking part in many military campaigns, he organized 600 men, largely from French prisons, to leave for Brazil in 1555. The presence of two Huguenot ministers in a later expedition to the same colony encouraged much conversion to Protestantism, and V. resorted to tyranny in order to maintain his leadership. He nevertheless had to resign in 1559 and return to France, shortly before the colony disbanded.

[P. J. HENNESSEY]

VILLEHARDOUIN, GEOFFREY OF (*c.*1150–*c.*1213), the first major French chronicler, he used his position as warrior on the Fourth Crusade (1202) to explain the events of that expedition. More important, his record is an attempt to justify the armies' digression to the sack of Constantinople, a scandal which Villehardouin does not alleviate. Made marshal of Romania, he died in the Eastern Empire. Text: G. de Villehardouin, *La Conquête de Constantinople,* (ed. and tr. E. Faral, 2 v. 1938–39).

[J. P. WILLIMAN]

VILLENEUVE, JEAN MARIE RODRIGUE (1883–1947), Oblate of Mary Immaculate, abp. of Quebec, cardinal. After his ordination (1907), V. taught at the Univ. of Ottawa 1907–1919 and then served as superior of the Oblate scholasticate until he became bp. of Gravelbourg, Saskatchewan, in 1930. He was made abp. of Quebec in 1932 and cardinal in 1933. His administration of the archdiocese brought improved understanding between the Church and the labor movement and the development of programs for New Canadians. He suffered from poor health in his last years and died in retirement.

[R. K. MacMASTER]

VILLENEUVE-BARGEMONT, JEAN PAUL ALBAN (1784–1850), French political economist. As a member of a leading literary noble family of Provence, the Viscount de Villeneuve-Bargemont entered the civil service of the French Empire. He held several posts in the prefectorial administration during the Napoleonic and Restoration periods, but refused to take the oath to support Louis Philippe following the Revolution of 1830. He sat in the Chamber of Deputies as a legitimist, 1830–31 and 1840–48, but he spent most of this period on his studies of poverty. His *Économie politique chrétienne* (3 v., 1834) has been described as a forerunner of Christian Socialist views. He opposed the ideas of Saint-Simon on inheritance, of Malthus on population, and of the entire Manchester School on laissez-faire economics. Instead he sought such remedies for the social evils of industrialization as the extension of charitable relief, workers savings associations, compulsory free education, and the provision of a "sufficient wage" before profits. His research into the causes and the extent of poverty was impressive, but his primary solution, a reinvigoration of agriculture through the establishment of farm colonies for the poor, naively ignored the economic forces stimulating industrialization. He achieved more success in his attempts to reform the laws affecting poverty. He was one of the chief authors of the 1841 law limiting child labor, which he enthusiastically and convincingly presented to the Chamber. It was "a reaction against that economic system which is only a science of wealth, unmindful that the true wealth of a country consists above all in the strength of its population, in their intelligence, and in their morality." BIBLIOGRAPHY: M. I. Ring, *Villeneuve-Bargemont: Catholic Social Protagonist* (1935).

[R. J. GIBBONS]

VILLENEUVE-LÈS-AVIGNON, ABBEY OF, a Benedictine monastery founded atop Mount Andaon, on the right bank of the Rhone, opposite Avignon. It was reestablished in 976 by Garnier, bp. of Avignon. In 1292 King Philip IV the Fair gave a charter of exemption to its territory and the village around the abbey received the name of Villeneuve. Between 1262 and 1368 the kings of France incorporated the monastery within the vast fortress of Saint-André. The Maurists occupied the abbey from 1635 until the Revolution. Only the Romanesque chapel of Our Lady of Belvezet remains today, a structure noted for the purity of its lines. BIBLIOGRAPHY: Cottineau 2:3393–94.

[J. DAOUST]

VILLERS, ABBEY OF, Cistercian monastery near Namur, Belgium, founded in 1146 by St. Bernard of Clairvaux. The flourishing establishment numbered 400 monks by the 13th cent. and was a famous center of mysticism. Destroyed in 1544, the abbey was soon rebuilt and experienced a new era of prosperity. It was secularized during the French Revolution (1796). The ruins of the church are among the finest examples of Cistercian Gothic in Belgium. BIBLIOGRAPHY: L. J. Lekai, NCE 14:677; E. de Moreau, *L'Abbaye de Villers aux 12e et 13e siècles* (1909); T. Ploegaerts and G. Boulmont, *Histoire de l'abbaye de Villers du XIIIe siècle à la Révolution* (1926).

[L. J. LEKAI]

VILLON, FRANÇOIS (1431–after 1463), Middle French poet, vagabond, and criminal. Raised by an uncle, whose last name he adopted, Villon received the master's degree from the Univ. of Paris. He rapidly moved from student pranks to criminal undertakings, and wrote many poems in underworld jargon. His first major work, *The Legacy,* announces his heart's death at the cruelty of love, and is a series of bequests—satirical, imaginary or sincere. A later, longer work of the same format, *The Great Testament,* is richly varied with *ballades* and other longer poems: the beautiful "*Ballade* to pray Our Lady," for his mother; the "*Ballade* of Ladies of Bygone Days"; under sentence of death, Villon wrote the "*Ballade* of the Hanged Men" to ask the prayers of his "human brothers" who would pass the gallows. Villon was reprieved but banished from Paris, and, after a final poem for his jailer, disappeared. BIBLIOGRAPHY: D. B. Wyndham Lewis, *François Villon: A Documented Survey* (1928).

[J. P. WILLIMAN]

VIMALAKIRTI, legendary disciple of the Buddha, subject of a 1st-cent. Sūtra. Of great learning, influential in developing lay Buddhism in China and Japan, V. is frequently pictured in debate. His association with learning drew many *wen-jen* or scholar-gentlemen-painters of China.

[M. J. DALY]

VIMPA, a silk veil covering shoulders and hands of servers carrying mitre and cross in a pontifical ceremony.

VINCENT OF BEAUVAIS (*c.*1190–1264), French Dominican encyclopedist. While a student at the University of Paris *c.*1220, V. entered the Dominicans there. Transferred to Beauvais *c.*1233, he became the lifelong friend of King Louis IX, who expressed interest in, and provided financial assistance toward, the completion of an encyclopedic *Speculum maius* that Vincent had begun. Vincent was also appointed lector at the Cistercian monastery of Royaumont (1250) and at the royal court. His connections with the royal family motivated his lesser works. The *Epistola consolatoria super morte filii* he sent to Louis in 1260 when the Dauphin Louis died. For Queen Marguerite he wrote a treatise on the manner of educating princes: *De eruditione filiorum nobilium* (1260–61). He composed his *De morali principis institutione* (part of a planned *opus universale* that remained unfinished) at the urging of Louis, King Theobald of Navarre, and his own master general, Humbert of Romans.

The *Speculum maius,* a three-part work: *Speculum naturale, historiale,* and *doctrinale,* comprised 80 books (9,885 chapters). Its first version appeared *c.*1244, followed by a second *c.*1247, and by a third after 1250. The *naturale* is an encyclopedia of nature orientated around the biblical account of creation, the fall, and the redemption of man. Into this account Vincent weaves chapters on optics, astronomy, meteorology, geology, botany, and other branches of science. The *historiale* relates the history of mankind from creation to 1254 (final version). The *doctrinale* summarizes all the learned arts: mechanical and practical (moral philosophy and medicine). It includes such diverse topics as grammar, logic, music, husbandry, political affairs, trades and professions, weights and measures, and surveying. Included is a dictionary of some 3,200 entries. A spurious *Speculum morale,* based on the works of Thomas Aquinas, was added by an anonymous author between 1310 and 1325. Though the *Speculum maius* makes no claim to originality and contains the defects inherent in a work of such nature and scope, its influence was wide and deep. It circulated in many manuscripts, seven printed editions, and several vernacular translations. It is truly monumental and the best encyclopedia produced by the Middle Ages. Apart from these major works, Vincent wrote a *Speculum vel imago mundi* (*c.*1244). Several ascetical and theological treatises ascribed to him are insufficiently authentic. BIBLIOGRAPHY: *De eruditione filiorum nobilium* (ed. A. Steiner, 1938); A. Gabriel, *Educational Ideas of Vincent of Beauvais* (2d ed., 1962), esp. helpful for bibliog.

[W. A. HINNEBUSCH]

VINCENT FERRER, ST. (*c.* 1350–1419), Catalan Dominican preacher whose prodigious effort as a wandering preacher of repentance throughout Spain, France, Lombardy, and Switzerland is considered a second evangelization of Christendom. Born in Valencia, he died in Vannes, Brittany, was canonized by Calixtus III in 1455. In his early career he was a teacher of the natural sciences, dialectician, logician, prior of a convent, and teacher of theology. He came to prominence as a strong supporter of the Avignon claimants to the papacy, Clement VII and Benedict XIII. The latter, dubbed the "mule of Aragon," had ordained V. and been his patron. V. became his chaplain and adviser at Avignon. When V. set out on his twenty years of wandering, preaching repentance and imminent judgment, Benedict gave him power of legate *a latere* to reconcile any and all sinners who came for absolution. Reliable witnesses attest to the charismatic atmosphere that attended his preaching effort, the miracles, the gifts of tongues, and the extraordinary response of the people. In all he preached 6,000 sermons, each three hours long. His sermons were apocalyptic and scriptural. Many theologians took advantage of the schism in the Church to downgrade the excessive role of the papacy and attempted to democratize the structure. V.'s role tended to exalt even more the role of the papacy. He eventually lost all faith in Benedict, rose from a sick-bed to denounce him publicly, and hastened the latter's downfall. V. was called upon to act as mediator in the Hundred Years' War, just as he was called on to heal the schism in the Church. In the end his company of priests and penitents were felt to have transformed Europe. BIBLIOGRAPHY: Life, H. Ghéon (tr. F. J. Sheed 1939); M.-M. Gorce, DTC 15:3033–45.

[E. J. DILLON]

VINCENT OF LÉRINS, ST. (d. *c.*445), a monk of Lérins in Gaul, formulator of the so-called Vincentian canon. His fame rests on his two *Commonitoria,* written *c.*434, only one of which has survived. The work is celebrated for its enunciation of the canon or criterion of orthodoxy *quod ubique, quod semper, quod ab omnibus creditum est:* the orthodoxy of a doctrine is to be judged on the basis of its geographical and historical universality; that is Catholic truth which has been held always, everywhere, and by all the faithful. Many see in V.'s work an attack upon Augustine's anti-Pelagian writings, or at least upon an extreme interpretation of them, and consider V. to have been a Semi-Pelagian. V. has had some veneration as a saint, but there is evidence to show that his cult is not an ancient one. Works: critical edition, A. Juelicher (2d ed., 1925); translations, R. Morris, FathCh 7 (1949), 255–332, and G. McCracken, LibCC 9 (1957), 23–89. BIBLIOGRAPHY: Butler 2:382–383.

[R. B. ENO]

VINCENT MADELGARIUS, ST. (*c.*615–*c.*677), abbot. His biography is an accumulation of hagiographical plagiarisms from the lives of other saints. It is recounted that *c.*653 he and his wife Waldetrud separated, she to found a convent at Mons, he a monastery at Hautmont. Later, desiring more complete solitude, he took the name Vincent and went to his estate at Soignies where he may have founded an abbey. The first historical mention of the Abbey of Soignies is 870; here the saint's relics are venerated in the collegiate church. BIBLIOGRAPHY: H. Roeder, *Saints and Their Attributes* (1955); *Book of Saints* (compiled by the Benedictine Monks of St. Augustine's Abbey, 1966); Butler 3:607–608; É. Brouette, BiblSanct 12:1177–78.

[M. E. DUFFY]

VINCENT DE PAUL, ST. (1581–1660), founder of the Vincentians and the Daughters of Charity; called the Apostle of Charity. Son of a peasant family of Pouy (now renamed Saint-Vincent de Paul) in Gascony, France, he became a priest in 1600. His earlier career, from 1609 onwards, he spent in Paris, seeking out and obtaining a series of benefices. He was received into the circle of the wealthy, becoming chaplain of the Gondi family in 1618; a counsellor of Louis XIII, and, after the king's death in 1643, of the regent Anne of Austria, and of Card. Richelieu. V. fell out of favor with Card. Mazarin after 1654. From early ambition and after a struggle with doubts of faith, V. gradually was converted to a life of heroic charity. His friendship with P. de *Bérulle and St. *Francis de Sales were important to his spiritual conversion and formation. Through St. Francis de Sales he became associated with St. Jane Frances de Chantal, assisted in the foundation of the Visitandines, and was their superior from 1622 until his death. V. was also associated with the Abbé de *Saint-Cyran and the *Arnauld family, but became alienated by their conflict with Rome. V. is regarded as one of the main opponents of *Jansenism in France. As part of V.'s works of charity toward the poor he established in 1617 at Châtillon the Confraternity of Charity, an association of laywomen to assist the poor and sick; similar associations spread throughout France. The Congregation of the Missions, called also Vincentians and Lazarists, was founded in 1625, with the assistance of the Gondi family, to evangelize the rural population of France. In the same period he established retreats and institutes for the training of priests that directly contributed to the development of the seminary system of ecclesiastical training. With St. *Louise de Marillac, with whom he had been associated in work for the sick poor since 1625, V. founded the *Daughters of Charity in 1633. Canonized in 1737, V. was declared patron of works of charity in 1885. BIBLIOGRAPHY: P. Coste, *Life and Works of St. Vincent de Paul* (3 v., tr. J. Leonard, 1952); H. Daniel-Rops, *Monsieur Vincent* (tr. J. Kernan, 1961).

[T. C. O'BRIEN]

VINCENT OF SPAIN, influential medieval canonist whose numerous writings remain in MS form. He understood Roman law, studied and taught canon law at Bologna (1210–15), and was the first commentator of the *Decretals* of Gregory IX. One of his students was the future pivotal papal figure, Innocent IV. Nothing else is known of V. for certain. He may have been a Portuguese ecclesiastic, and after becoming a bp., may have returned to Portugal. BIBLIOGRAPHY: A. Moreschini, EncCatt 12:1435–36.

[E. J. DILLON]

VINCENT, LOUIS HUGUES (1872–1960), Dominican scholar of the École Biblique in Jerusalem, renowned authority on Palestinian archeology. He was a pioneer in RC biblical criticism, the collaborator of J. M. *Lagrange. V.'s greatest works were *Jerusalem: Recherches de topographie, d'archéologie et d'histoire* (8 v., 1912–26), and *Jerusalem de l'Ancien Testament* (2 v., 1954–56).

[T. C. O'BRIEN]

VINCENTIAN, ST., French hermit, also known as St. Viance. Unfortunately there is no solid evidence that he

ever existed, except that his cult flourished in the Diocese of Toul. An 11th-cent. fabrication of his life is summarized in Butler 1:22.

[E. J. DILLON]

VINCENTIAN CANON, the criterion proposed by *Vincent of Lérins for testing the orthodoxy of a doctrine claimed to be of Christian faith. It is found in his *Commonitorium* (2.5): "We must take great care to hold to what has been believed everywhere, and always, and by all, for that in the true and proper sense is catholic." (*Magnopere curandum est, ut id teneamus, quod ubique, quod semper, quod ab omnibus, creditum est, hoc est enim vere proprieque catholicum.*) The canon is incontestably valid if understood in an affirmative sense, i.e., if it is taken to mean that what has been the object of universal consensus is certainly catholic truth. But if it is understood in a negative sense so as to exclude from Catholic faith all that has not been explicitly the object of such consensus, it is not valid, for in that case it would leave no room for the legitimate development or unfolding of doctrine. BIBLIOGRAPHY: H. G. J. Beck, NCE 14:681–682.

[R. B. ENO]

VINCENTIAN SISTERS OF CHARITY (VSC), a congregation of papal approbation founded in Austria (1835) by the daughter of Franz I, Emperor of Austria, to teach children of the poor and to care for the sick. Under the leadership of Mother M. Emerentiana Handlovits, a foundation was established in the U.S. (1902) in the Diocese of Pittsburgh, Pa., where their motherhouse is located. In 1928 a new branch was founded in the Diocese of Cleveland at Bedford, Ohio. The elder branch numbered (1976) 327 professed sisters and the Bedford branch, 110. Represented not only in Pennsylvania and Ohio, they are in Georgia, Alabama, and Missouri. They also have foundations in Canada, in Toronto, and in St. Catherine, Ontario.

VINCENTIAN FATHERS (Congregation of the Mission, Lazarists; CM), a congregation of men religious, founded in 1625 by St. Vincent de Paul. The first residence was at the priory of St. Lazare in Paris. The purpose of the society was primarily to establish mission churches, particularly in rural areas. Other goals are education of seminarians, foreign missions, staffing parishes, and conducting schools. Approved by the Holy See in 1632, the congregation operated 550 missions at the time of St. Vincent's death (1660). The Vincentians combine the nature of secular clergy and religious in community who take simple, private vows. They are governed by a superior general elected for life by an assembly of provincials and elected delegates. In 1953 Pope Pius XII sanctioned new constitutions for the congregation. The Sisters of Charity of St. Vincent de Paul are under the jurisdiction of the Vincentian superior general and find spiritual direction from members of the congregation of religious men.

Actively spreading in France, the community established foundations in Italy and Poland in the 17th cent. and served on the perilous English and Scottish missions. Work in Algeria among the Christian slaves of the Moors in Algeria followed. The missions in Madagascar claimed so many lives of Vincentians that they withdrew, to return at the close of the 19th century. In the 18th cent., Vincentians labored in Bulgaria and the Near East. After the suppression of the Jesuits, a group of Vincentians took over missions in China. They suffered persecution under the Empire and were finally driven from China by the Communists. They work today in Japan, India, the Philippines, and other areas of the Far East. Vincentians operate a number of provinces in Latin America.

The congregation came to the U.S. in 1816, labored in Bardstown, Ky., briefly, then proceeded to St. Louis, Missouri. In 1818 the American motherhouse was established at Perryville, Missouri. From there the Vincentians did pastoral work in Arkansas, Mississippi, Illinois, and Indiana. The society gave the American Church a number of bishops: Joseph Rosati (St. Louis), Leo De Neckere (New Orleans), John Odin (Galveston, Tex., and New Orleans), John Timon (first provincial and bishop of Buffalo), John Lynch (Toronto, Canada) and Michael Domenec (Pittsburgh). In 1867 provincial headquarters were transferred to St. Vincent's Seminary, Germantown, Philadelphia. A foundation in Brooklyn (1868) grew into St. John's University. In 1875 at Chicago, Ill., was founded a parish and the nucleus of De Paul University. The Vincentian college in Niagara assumed university rank in 1883 and the status of a pontifical university under Pope Pius XII. In 1888 the American province was divided into an Eastern and Western province, the Eastern centered in Germantown, the Western in St. Louis. The Seminary Church in Germantown became the shrine of the Miraculous Medal (revealed to St. Catherine Labouré in Paris in 1830). Father Joseph Skelly in 1915 established the Central Association of the Miraculous Medal. The perpetual novena was begun at Germantown in 1930. A celebrated Vincentian, Thomas *Judge, founded two missionary communities to work in the South. Vincentians opened centers in Maryland, North Carolina, and Alabama.

The Western province operates from St. Louis, with a vice-province in California and one in New Orleans. The province has staffed seminaries in St. Louis; Denver, Colo.; Los Angeles, Calif.; Kansas City, Mo.; San Antonio and Houston, Texas. Like their colleagues in the Eastern province, those of the West maintained missions in China until the Communist takeover. The Western province operated motor missions in rural areas and inaugurated in 1937 the Catholic Correspondence Course, culminating in the Catholic Information Bureau of St. Louis, Mo., supported by the Knights of Columbus.

Vincentians operate throughout the world in 64 countries. An important part of their work remains the conducting of diocesan seminaries (in 1960 nearly 100 such institutions).

BIBLIOGRAPHY: *La Congregation de la Mission* (1927); S. Delacroix, *Histoire universelle des missions catholiques* (4 v., 1956–59).

[J. R. AHERNE]

VINCI, LEONARDO (1690-1730), Italian composer. V. composed some church music, but his main work was in the field of opera. His manner of treatment of themes in the aria had important implications for the successive development of the concerto and the symphony.

[M. T. LEGGE]

VINCIBLE IGNORANCE, see IGNORANCE.

VINDICIANUS OF CAMBRAI-ARRAS, ST. (c.620–712?), early bp. of the Low Countries. He completed the Abbey of Saint-Vaast (685). This monastery was richly endowed by King Theodoric III in reparation for the murder of Bp. Leodegar of Autun by his official, Ebroin. His body now rests in the cathedral of Arras. BIBLIOGRAPHY: C. M. Aherne, NCE 14:689.

[F. G. O'BRIEN]

VINE, SYMBOLISM OF THE. In the OT the vineyard is a frequent symbol for Israel, occasionally symbolic of a spiritually fruitful people (Is 27.2–6), more often of a people spiritually unproductive and disappointing to God (Jer 5.10; 12.10–11). The distinction between the people as vineyard and vine in the OT is not cut and dried as the imagery sometimes shifts from one image to the other (cf. Ps 80.9, 13) or becomes mixed with other figures. Thus, in the writings of the prophets, God is both spouse and dresser of the vine. For Hosea, Israel is a fruitful plant that credits her productivity to others than the God who is her spouse through the covenant (Hos 10.1; 3.1). As vinedresser, God has done everything for his vine, but instead of the anticipated fruit of justice, the harvest has yielded bloodshed and the cry of the oppressed; nothing remains but to give over the vineyard to those who would despoil it (Is 5.1–7). For Jeremiah, Israel is a chosen plant become degenerate and barren (Jer. 2.21; 8.13) to be uprooted and trampled (Jer. 5.10; 12.10). Ezekiel employs the comparison of the once-fertile vine that dries up and is burned to represent Israel unfaithful to its God (Ezek 19.10–14; 15.6) and its king unfaithful to a sworn covenant (Ezek 17.5–19). Yet in spite of past lack of fruitfulness, there will come an era when the vine will again flourish under God's watchful care (Is 27.2–3). It was in this hope that Israel called upon God's covenant love to save the vine, which will henceforth be faithful to him (Ps 80.9–17). Hence it is not surprising to find the vine as the symbol of the nation on the coins of the Maccabean period, nor to find the vine used as a symbol for the Messiah in the Syriac Apocalypse of Baruch, nor even to find the divine wisdom itself likened to a vine (Sir 24.17–23).

In the NT, the Synoptic Gospels draw upon the OT vineyard symbolism, particularly Isaiah's song of the vineyard (Is 5.1–7). Such is obviously the case in Mk 12.1–7 (cf. Mt 21.33–41), an allegory of God's dealings with his people aimed particularly at the Jewish religious leadership, which was killed the prophets in the past and finally the vineyard owner's son, in order to teach that the Gentiles (''other tenants'') have now become the renewed Israel, God's people. Mt presses this theme home in the Parable of the Two Sons, only one of whom obediently works in the vineyard (Mt 21.28–32). At the same time, the Synoptic writers esp. Mt, insist upon the totally gratuitous character of God's rewards for the workers (cf. Mt 20.1–16). The fourth Gospel develops the image of the vine to its full theological and Christological dimensions. The idea of the tree of life (Rev 22.2), the OT imagery of Israel as the vine, the concept of wisdom as a life-giving tree or vine (Sir 24.17–21), and the Eucharist itself supplied the background for John's unique metaphor of the vine and the branches (Jn 15.1–17). The basic meaning of the comparison is clear. Jesus is the life-giving vine; the believer must remain in Jesus as a branch remains on the vine. Believers have become branches through faith and baptism, having been given life from above. To make them bear more fruit, it is necessary that Jesus' commandment of love express itself more and more in their lives. The person and word of Jesus as vine is an active force that is both spirit and life for the believer and that, just as the Eucharist, deepens union with Jesus and the heavenly Father, who as in the OT, remains the vinedresser, who takes away the worthless and prunes the fruitful branches. BIBLIOGRAPHY: R. E. Brown, *Gospel According to John* (1970) v. 2:669–684; X. Léon-Dufour, *Dictionary of Biblical Theology* (1973), 629–30; C. H. Dodd, *Interpretation of the Fourth Gospel* (1953).

[T. J. RYAN]

VINEGAR BIBLE, popular name given to a folio edition of the Bible printed in 1716–17 by John Baskett. The name derives from a quaint misprint in the caption for Lk ch. 20, ''The Parable of the Vinegar'' in place of ''The Parable of the Vineyard.''

[D. J. BOURKE]

VINES, RICHARD (c.1600–56), Puritan theologian and controversialist. He was a member of the *Westminster Assembly (1643) and a drafter of the *Westminster Confession; master of Pembroke College, Cambridge (1644), until dismissed for upholding the monarchy in 1649. He also held various parish livings as rector. V.'s main reform objective was in favor of *Presbyterianism and the abolition of episcopacy; but he was equally opposed to the *congregationalism of the Independents.

[T. C. O'BRIEN]

VINET, ALEXANDRE RUDOLF (or RODOLPHE) (1797–1847), Swiss Reformed theologian and literary crit-

ic. Born at Ouchy, near Lausanne, he studied theology at Lausanne, but then taught French language and literature at Basle, 1817–37. He was ordained in 1819, and on leaving Basle returned to Lausanne as professor of practical theology. In 1845, protesting state interference in church affairs, he resigned his professorship and led in formation of the Free Church. A theological liberal, V. wrote important books in support of freedom of conscience and separation of Church and State. Because of his emphasis on individual experience in religion, he was sometimes called the Swiss or the French Schleiermacher. He was also influential in intellectual circles through his studies of French literature. Several volumes of his literary studies were published posthumously from his lecture notes. An important study of Pascal appeared in 1848. BIBLIOGRAPHY: P. T. Fuhrmann, *Extraordinary Christianity: The Life and Thought of A. Vinet* (1964).

[T. EARLY]

VIOLATION, profanation of a church or cemetery that has been blessed. This profanation occurs because of the violent shedding of blood or by using the place for base practices; a cemetery is also violated by the interment of one who has no right to Christian burial. Violation requires a ritual reconciliation before the church or cemetery can again be used for sacred purposes (CIC, c.1207). *DESECRATION.

VIOLENCE, as here understood, physical force exerted to compel a person to do something against his will. The interest of moral theologians in violence taken in this sense centers either upon the voluntariness and imputability of what is done under its influence, or upon the rights and wrongs of its application. (1) Violence is one of the traditionally recognized impediments to voluntariness (*hostes voluntarii*). An act brought about by violence (*violentum; to biaion*) does not issue from the will of the person upon whom the violence is exerted, but from the will of the person who exerts it. It is therefore to the latter rather than to the former that the action must be imputed. If, however, an action is brought about not by violence but by threat of it, the operating influence is *fear rather than violence, and the voluntariness of what is done should be estimated accordingly. (2) It is generally admitted that the vindication and maintenance of justice by constituted authority may be backed by punishment, which is essentially a form of violence, since it is against the will of the person who is punished. Again, it is commonly agreed that the commonwealth may engage in a just war, that force may be used by parents and educators in pursuance of good discipline, and that a private person may toughly defend his rights. On the other hand, violence accompanying a breach of commutative justice adds a special criminality which a civilized society will not hesitate to deal with draconically. Even more dangerous to the public peace is mob violence, and more indefensible, for a mob has no moral standing at all, though the causes that have produced it, or have allowed for it, may well be serious matters of conscience. BIBLIOGRAPHY: ThAq ST 1a2ae, 6.4–5 (esp. in Lat-Eng ed., v. 17, ed. T. Gilby, 1970).

[T. GILBY]

VIOLLET-LE-DUC, EUGÈNE EMMANUEL (1814–79), French architect and writer on medieval architecture. He restored many Romanesque and Gothic buildings, notably through the application of color to the stonework (e.g., the abbey church of *Vézelay, the Sainte Chapelle, and Saint-Denis, Paris). His *Dictionnaire raisonné de l'architecture française du XIe au XVIe siècle* (1854–68) is famous. BIBLIOGRAPHY: P. Gout, *Viollet-le-Duc: Sa vie, son oeuvre, sa doctrine* (1914).

[K. B. NEILSON]

VIRET, PIERRE (1511–71), French Reformation preacher and author. A friend of Calvin, he helped to spread the Reformation in France and Switzerland and to establish an academy at Lausanne.

[P. J. HENNESSEY]

VIRGA, in *Gregorian chant notation, one of the two signs for a single note. Probably derived from the grave accent, in the early MSS it generally took the form of a slanting line, sometimes thickened at the top. Later it assumed the square shape with a descending stem still used in modern printed chant books. It originally signified a note relatively high in pitch, while the *punctum indicated a relatively low note. This distinction has been suppressed in the modern editions; the punctum is used for all single notes, while the virga is used only in combination with other neumes.

[A. DOHERTY]

VIRGIL (Publius Vergilius Maro; 70–19 B.C.), Roman poet born of a modest family at Andes near Mantua and educated in Cremona, Milan, and Rome. Though he was of a rather retiring temperament, had a rustic appearance, and suffered from poor health, V. won the friendship and patronage of the wealthy Maecenas and even of the Emperor himself. In 42 B.C. he seems to have lost his family estate in the confiscation of lands for distribution to Octavian's veterans but then to have regained it through the help of his powerful friends. He spent the latter years of his life near Naples. In 19 B.C. he went to Greece with the intent of staying there for some time. He met Augustus in Athens and was persuaded to return to Italy with him. Falling ill at Megara, he was brought back to Brundisium, where he died. His remains were taken to Naples and interred in a tomb on the road to Puteoli.

A collection of 14 shorter, and 5 longer poems known as the Appendix Vergiliana has been attributed to Virgil from antiquity. Of uneven quality, their authenticity has been seriously challenged. It may well be, however, that at least some were written by Virgil in his youth. Between 42 and 37 B.C. he composed ten Eclogues, or Bucolics, pastoral poems in dactylic hexameters freely modeled on Theocritus. Between 36 and 29 B.C. he wrote the Georgics, his most finished work, a didactic poem in four books of hexameters dealing with the cultivation of crops, the growing of fruit trees, the care of animals, and the keeping of bees. His inspiration for this came from Hesiod's *Works and Days,* the Georgics of Nicander of Colophon, the agrarian reforms of Augustus, but above all from his own experiences in, and love for, the Italian countryside.

The last 11 years of his life Virgil spent on the Aeneid, the story of the wanderings of the Trojan Aeneas and his conquest of the Rutulians for the eventual founding of Rome. Despite the fact that Virgil was never able to put the finishing touches on this epic, it is still the greatest of Roman poems and the national poem of a noble race. The beauty of its form, melody of its lines, and deep human insights have given it a truly universal appeal. It immediately became a classic and remained popular throughout the Middle Ages. An inspiration for Dante and countless others, Virgil is still today one of the most widely read and deeply loved poets of all time. BIBLIOGRAPHY: B. Otis, *Virgil, a Study in Civilized Poetry* (1963).

[M. J. COSTELLOE]

VIRGIL (FERGAL) OF SALZBURG, ST. (c.710–784), Irish abbot, bishop, mathematician, venerated as the apostle of the Slovenes. He went to the court of Pepin the Short in 743 and was appointed bishop of Salzburg in 745, but, although he ruled the diocese from that time, he was not in fact consecrated bishop until 755 (or 767?). He was responsible for the construction of the Salzburg cathedral that was destroyed in the 16th century, sent missionaries to Carinthia and Styria, and erected a number of monasteries. St. Boniface viewed him with some suspicion and twice denounced him to Rome: once for not requiring the re-baptism of persons he discovered had been baptized by an unlearned priest who distorted the words of the baptismal rite into ungrammatical form, and once for teaching that there was an antipodal world inhabited by men (see ANTIPODES). The Pope supported V.'s position in the dispute about re-baptism, but declared that if a synod found him guilty in the other matter, he was to be excommunicated. The precise details of V.'s views about the antipodes are unknown, nor is there record of further action on the charge. In any event, V.'s career was in no way blighted by the incident. Pope Zachary's statement that the opinion of which he was accused was "wicked and perverse, offensive alike to God and his own soul," has been occasionally cited as an example of the fallibility of papal pronouncements upon scientific fact. However, it was not so much V.'s belief in the existence of antipodes as the implication such belief then carried that the human race had no single origin, no common inheritance of original sin, and no common redemption, that was considered censurable from the point of view of faith. BIBLIOGRAPHY: Butler 4:436–437; F. S. Betten, *St. Boniface and St. Virgil* (1927).

[P. K. MEAGHER]

VIRGILIUS OF ARLES, ST. (mid-6th cent.–*c*.610), archbishop of Arles. V. became abbot of St.-Symphorien, abp. of Arles, and apostolic vicar to the court of Childeric II. The Venerable Bede speaks of him in connection with Augustine of Canterbury, and some correspondence exists between V. and Pope Gregory I. BIBLIOGRAPHY: Duchesne FÉ 1:252.

VIRGILIUS MARO, THE GRAMMARIAN (fl. 7th cent.), one of the most enigmatic figures in medieval Latin literature. He deliberately assumed the name of the great Latin poet, and gave similar names to his real or imaginary teachers and friends. His 12 *Epitomae*, or short grammatical treatises, and his 8 *Epistulae* are filled with fantastic explanations, false etymologies, and bizarre words coined by himself. He claimed to distinguish 4 genders and 12 different varieties of Latin. He even concocted a kind of cryptic language. Whether his work actually reflects cultural decline, or is a satire or parody on grammatical treatises—as P. Lehmann suggested—is not certain. At any rate, he was taken seriously, esp. in Ireland, and was used by a number of medieval writers before the 12th century. BIBLIOGRAPHY: M. R. P. McGuire, NCE 14:691; Laistner, 176–177; Manitius 1:119–127; P. Lehmann, *Die Parodie im Mittelalter* (1922) 21–22.

[M. R. P. MCGUIRE]

VIRGIN, APOCALYPSE OF, see APOCRYPHA (NT), 67.

VIRGIN, CONSECRATION OF A, an ancient and solemn ceremony of the Latin rite to bless and consecrate women who oblige themselves by public vow to perpetual *virginity. The most ancient form of the consecration is to be found in the *Sacramentarium* and *Missale Francorum*. The rite was common in monastic communities of women in the earlier Middle Ages, but following the lead of nuns of the Cistercian and mendicant orders, newer congregations did not take it up and many older ones abandoned it. However it continued in use among Carthusian and Norbertine nuns and some communities of Benedictines. The rite itself closely paralleled that of ordination, even involving, with the Carthusians, the conferral of maniple and stole. (See A. Vermeersch, CE 15:458–459.) For the new rite of consecration, see VIRGINITY, RITE OF CONSECRATION TO.

VIRGIN BIRTH, the belief that Mary, the mother of Jesus, conceived her Son through the power of God and not by a human father. This topic is dealt with in the article PERPETUAL VIRGINITY OF MARY. In Catholic usage the term "virgin birth" is often taken to mean Christ's birth of a

virgin in the sense of one who was a virgin before, during, and after the birth of her son (*ante, in*, and *post partum*), and therefore includes the virginity of Mary in its broadest dimensions.

[P. K. MEAGHER]

VIRGINES SACRATAE, consecrated virgins, to whom had been administered a rite of solemn consecration approximating the ordination of deacons. It was esp. applied to deaconesses in the early Church. The rite belongs to the *Pontificale Romanum* and can be performed only by a bishop. There is no indication before the 4th cent. of any liturgical ceremony of consecration. It is found first in Africa, then Milan, and then Rome and Gaul. In the West it was marked by the taking of the veil. There is a recent *Rite of Consecration to a Life of Virginity* (1970). *VIRGINITY, RITE OF CONSECRATION TO.

[E. J. DILLON]

VIRGINES SUBINTRODUCTAE, Lat., virgins secretly brought in, a term roughly corresponding to the Greek *parthenoi syneisaktoi*: virgins brought in with (men), and used to refer to women, usually virgins (also called *agapētai*, beloved) who, in the early Church, shared living quarters with men in a variety of contexts. One practice, the spiritual, i.e. nonsexual, marriage or union, is found in the 2d cent. and later (even earlier, if 1 Cor 7.36–38 refers to it; this, however, is doubtful): the *Shepherd* of Hermas (Sim. 9, c.11) refers to it approvingly (as does, perhaps, *Didache* 11, 11), but it is severely criticized as frequently leading to sexual immorality and as at least dangerous and scandalous (e.g. by: Irenaeus *Adv. haer* 1.6.3; Cyprian *Ep.* 4; the *Synodal Letter* condemning Paul of Samosata and his companions, in Eusebius, *Hist. eccl.* 7.30.12–13; Jerome *Ep.* 22,14; and two letters of John Chrysostom, *PG* 47:495–532). Several synods of the 4th cent. (e.g. Elvira, can. 27; Nicaea, can. 3; cf. also Ancyra, can. 19) demand that clerics must have no women dwelling with them except mother, sister, etc.; this may attempt to prevent the abuse of so-called spiritual unions, but may also only refer to caution in the choice of female domestics. Tertullian probably refers to a different practice when he recommends that a widower might take a widow "whose age is her adornment" as a "spiritual wife," as a remedy for loneliness and to help with domestic duties (*De ex. cast.* 12; *Monog.* 16). BIBLIOGRAPHY: P. de Labriolle, *Revue Historique* 137 (1921) 204–225; R. Kugelman, F. X. Murphy, NCE 14:698–699.

[D. P. EFROYMSON]

VIRGINIA, a south Atlantic state and the 10th of the original Thirteen States to ratify the Constitution (1788). After receiving a charter from James I, the Virginia Company established its first settlement at Jamestown (1607). Throughout the 17th and 18th centuries, Anglicans were dominant in Virginia, but lack of hierarchical structure, as well as the power exercised by local economic and political leaders, prevented the Anglican Church from maintaining complete control over religious matters in the colony. During the Great Awakening of the 1740s, Presbyterianism, German Pietism, and Lutheranism all developed without serious challenge from the official religion.

Except for some Jesuit missionary activity prior to 1607, there was little Catholicism in Virginia throughout the colonial period. At the time of the American Revolution, there were only 200 or 300 Catholics in the state. When the Diocese of Richmond was erected (1820), its first bishop, Patrick Kelly, was transferred (1822) to Waterford and Lismore in Ireland. For the next 19 years the diocese was administered by the abp. of Baltimore. R. V. Whelan, who was appointed second bp. (1841), concentrated his efforts in the western part of Virginia, while T. O'Brien administered the eastern portion of the state. In 1850 J. McGill became bp. of Richmond. The diocese is a suffragan of the metropolitan see of Baltimore, Md.

In 1976 Catholics numbered 263,133 or 5.6% of the total state population. The major Protestant denominations are the Southern Baptist Convention, with 13.8% of the total population in 1971, and the Methodist Church, with 10.7%. Other Protestant denominations comprised 13.5% of the population. The Jewish population (1968) was 37,350 or 0.8%. The one Catholic college in Virginia has an enrollment of 610 students. Over 5,612 students attend the state's 16 Catholic high schools, while 17,939 pupils attend 55 Catholic elementary schools. BIBLIOGRAPHY: W. Hemphill, M. Schlegel, and S. Engelberg, *Cavalier Commonwealth: History and Government of Virginia* (1957); W. W. Sweet, *Virginia Methodism, A History* (1955); F. J. Magri, *The Catholic Church in the City and Diocese of Richmond* (1906); J. H. Bailey, II, *A History of the Diocese of Richmond: The Formative Years* (1956).

[J. L. MORRISON; R. M. PRESTON]

VIRGINITY (Lat. *virginitas*; Gr. *parthenia*), related to fresh and verdant (*virens*), and by some to heroine (*virago*), the condition of a woman who has not surrendered to sexual passion, and later, extended so as to apply to men as well as women, the dedicated purpose of maintaining sexual reserve. Virginal values seem almost instinctively honored in many cultures, and are sometimes invested with a religious cult; that they are usually restricted to women may be explained by the fact that female more than male chastity is important for a family line. A dedicated state of virginity was unknown in the OT, but, inspired by our Lord's teaching that some make themselves eunuchs for the kingdom of heaven, virginity came to be exalted by the Fathers, both Greek and Latin, whose praise of it was sometimes accompanied, as in St. Jerome, with a depreciation of sex; and taking the veil was invested with solemn liturgical ceremonies. The reasons were partly ascetical, in order to free the mind for the contemplation of divine things and the loving service of others (1 Cor 7); partly mystical, the imita-

tion of the flesh of Christ and of his virgin mother. The tradition was upheld during the Protestant Reformation by the Council of Trent, which declared that virginity is better and more felicitous than matrimony (D 1810). Some remarks on the theology of the matter may help to bring it into perspective. First, the Council makes a flat comparison between states considered in themselves, and there, in the abstract and ideally, the more heroic the love the nobler the state. What love is greater than that of chosen persons, who for the sake of loving God and their neighbor the more, deny themselves the blessings of marital companionship and children? This can be said despite the occupational hazards, pointed out by the Fathers, notably St. Augustine, of becoming old maids (male or female), of hugging themselves for their escape from the chores and anxieties of marriage, of false conceit in their immunity, and of consequent spiritual sterility.

Second, virginity is a special vocation for some, not the ordinary rule for living in God's friendship and reaching to Christian perfection. If, as may be questioned, more virgins than others have been canonized, this is because their fame profits from a more efficient system of public relations; and anyhow holiness and canonization are not convertible terms. The Council never thought that a celibate was better than a non-celibate, or that in each concrete case, indeed in the vast majority, marriage was a second best.

Virginity is an extreme type of chastity, like magnificence compared to liberality, or martyrdom to courage, and is not for everybody. It is accorded an eminence in the realm of chastity, yet other virtues are ranged above it, and they include the vowed service of the community through poverty and obedience. It should be noted that merely physical integrity is quite incidental to virginity. Its material is the absence of a deliberate sexual climax, and its shaping form is the constant resolve to deny oneself venereal pleasure, of which only the former once lost can never be recovered. BIBLIOGRAPHY: ThAq ST 2a2ae, 152, (Lat-Eng v. 43, ed. T. Gilby); P. T. Camelot, NCE 14:701–704.

[T. GILBY]

VIRGINITY, RITE OF CONSECRATION TO. The Latin text of the *Rite of Consecration to a Life of Virginity* was issued in 1970; the authorized English verson, in 1975. The rite is part of the *Roman Pontifical,* its celebration being reserved to a bishop. Formerly this consecration was reserved to cloistered nuns. The new rite is intended for laywomen, active or contemplative. The rite has two forms, one for laywomen, another for religious. In both cases the recipient must never have been married. With regard to laywomen the admission to consecration must be given by the bp. and be based on solid evidence of the candidates' suitableness and dedicated life. The instruction urges that the rite be held in the cathedral with the attendance of the faithful so that the sign value of virginity and the Church's ancient esteem for it will be proclaimed through this ceremony. The rite ordinarily is celebrated within a ritual Mass appropriate to the occasion. The pledge of consecration is received by the bp. after the Liturgy of the Word. The bp. may bestow insignia, e.g., veil or ring, on the recipients.

For religious the rite is integrated with final, perpetual religious profession and takes place after the pronouncing of vows, again within a ritual Mass. Only religious of communities where the consecration has been the custom or those whose petition for it is approved by the bp. may receive consecration.

The rite is not widely known in the U.S. and since its issuance few uses of it have been made. BIBLIOGRAPHY: International Commission on English in the Liturgy (ICEL), *Rite of Consecration to a Life of Virginity* (1975).

VIRTUALISM, the teaching of John Calvin and the *Reformed Churches that in the Holy Eucharist the life-giving power (Lat. *virtus*) of Christ's glorified humanity becomes present to one receiving with faith. The position avoids RC and Lutheran affirmations of the actual presence of Christ's body and blood in the Eucharistic elements, as well as the Zwinglian reduction to a simply symbolic presence. Virtualism proposes a dynamic presence of Christ, in the communication of the saving effectiveness of his flesh and blood. *REAL PRESENCE; *TRANSUBSTANTIATION.

[T. C. O'BRIEN]

VIRTUE, a habit of good action. Man is good in his being and if he is to achieve happiness he must be good in his acting as well. For this he is equipped by his active capabilities (*potentiae*), faculties, grouped as his powers of cognition and appetition, principally those of his spiritual soul (intellect and will), but also those of the body-soul composite (sense and feeling). These, however, do not manifest an instinctive determinism to any one object amid the welter of his environment, and their pliancy is given a settled bent towards this or that type of activity by a disposition or quality called a *habitus*, mistranslated "habit" if that suggests a mechanical reflex, for a *habitus* becomes second nature in that it enhances the "from withinness" or voluntariness of its activity. A virtue is a good *habitus*, a vice a bad *habitus*.

The OT progressively discloses the notion of virtue (in the Septuagint, *aretē*) as inner responsiveness rather than external legalistic conformity; this thought also runs strongly in Greek philosophy. The first systematic study of the virtues is found in the *Nicomachean Ethics* of Aristotle. There a distinction is drawn between the intellectual and moral virtues. Of the former the fivefold enumeration has become traditional: for matters of theory, insight or *nous*, scientific knowledge or *epistēmē*, and wisdom or *sophia*; for matters of practice, prudence or *phronēsis*, and art or *technē*. They suffice to adapt a man to a certain phase in his experience, but not to put him in harmony with the whole business of living, as, e.g., in the case of one who by insight knows what should be done and yet does nothing about it. Consequently moral virtues, dispositions implying

a right appetitional attitude or, as we say, goodwill and qualities of character, are also required before we can speak of a downright good man. In this Aristotle is criticizing the Socratic reduction of virtue to knowledge and vice to ignorance. Their four main types, prudence, justice, courage, and temperance, have been called cardinal virtues since the days of St. Ambrose. It will be noticed that prudence holds a place under both headings. This is because it is not only the practical wisdom of knowing what should be done, but also fills the imperative role of carrying it into execution. It differs from art because it is concerned with human doing, not human making, and a moral reference is implied in a human act well done, but not, directly, in a work well made.

The index of the virtues according to the Latin Stoics and the patristic moralists who followed them (Cicero, St. Gregory, and John Cassian are representative authorities) was more detailed and descriptive if less analytical, and the tendency was to treat the life of virtue as a single *Gestalt* while tracing its various general conditions; thus all courage was temperate and all justice prudent. It was not until the thought of Aristotle was recovered in the 13th cent. that the whole field was systematically mapped by St. Thomas Aquinas, and his work, which coherently relates together without suppressing the mixed teachings tradition, remains the classical typology of the virtues.

Their parts fall into three classes. First, the components (*partes integrales*), or the elements that go to make up the virtue; thus memory and circumspection enter into prudence. Second, the sub-species (*partes subjectivae*) of a generic type of virtue; thus sobriety and chastity are distinct kinds of temperance. Third, allied virtues (*partes potentiales*), which are half like and half unlike the main virtues with which they are ranged; thus religion goes with justice in rendering what is strictly due, and yet differs in that it sets up a relationship not between equals. Of these associated virtues, 22 come up for separate discussion in the *Secunda secundae* of St. Thomas' *Summa theologiae*. The principle of differentiation is this: where a distinct specific interest (*objectum formale*) is engaged, there a distinct specific virtue may be isolated. For instance, the challenge to the good life from our emotional fears and our desires for pleasure are not the same, hence the distinction between courage and temperance, and within the scope of temperance the distinction scales down to the pleasures of food, drink, and sex and thus provides basis for the difference between abstemiousness, sobriety, and chastity. Here we may notice that the vices, differentiated along the same lines, are more numerous than the virtues, since they may be in conflict with them either by excess or defect; thus rashness and cowardice are against courage and are diametrically opposed to each other.

The moral virtues follow a measured course (*medium virtutis*) for right living in this world. Taken as the City of Reason, they are the natural virtues, better called the acquired virtues, since they are not innate but are learned by repeated acts; taken as the City of God already present, then they are the supernatural or "infused" virtues which are among the endowments of sanctifying grace. Within their respective dimensions these two sets offer counterparts to one another at every point. How far the natural virtues can flourish by themselves or whether the activity of these supernatural virtues is merely that of the natural virtues though oriented towards a higher end are matters of controversy. Note, however, the norm for a Christian theologian is man as open to grace; pure nature is not a historical condition, but an abstraction serving methodic consideration of the working of natural virtue as the material substructure to the workings of Christian virtues, of the decencies that remain after grace has been lost, and of the dynamism in the growth of virtue.

So far we have been speaking of moral virtue, but there are virtues which do not rest within the frame of right living but break out, as it were, to reach directly to God. These are the three theological virtues, faith, hope and charity. Already Plotinus had looked beyond morality to divine and exemplar virtues, and the Christian theologians developed the doctrine of virtues not to be measured according to not-too-much and not-too-little, and not content with any creaturely value, but extravagant in their manner, and finding nothing less than God Himself as their object. The difference appears from a comparison between the moral virtue of religion concerned with divine worship and the theological virtue of charity in love with the very goodness of God.

The enumeration of the virtues in systematic theology may convey the impression, not allayed by the knack in scholastic Latin of reification, that they represent so many different compartments, but in fact they are like shorthand headings to show the versatility of the good life. Its singleness is well recognized, alike in the patristic teaching on the interpenetration of the virtues, in Aristotle's that the moral virtues are knit together by prudence, and in the general consensus that, unlike the vices which can be quite disjointed, all the virtues are quickened and reach their goal through charity. BIBLIOGRAPHY: ThAq ST 1a2ae, 55 ad 67 (esp. in Lat.-Eng ed., v. 23, ed. W. D. Hughes 1968).

[T. GILBY]

VIRTUE, HEROIC, virtue that in manner and excellence seem superhuman, beyond ordinary expectation. The term has both a general and a technical sense. In general any exceptionally good moral action may be called an act of heroic virtue, whether because of what it is objectively, or because it exceeds the expectable capacities of the one who acts. St. Thomas Aquinas takes the expression *virtus heroica vel divina* from the Latin text of Aristotle (see *Ethics* 7,1.1145a20) and refers it to the Gifts of the Holy Spirit (ThAq ST 1a2ae.68,1 ad 1;2a2ae. 159,2 ad 1). The point is that sometimes superhuman way of acting—either objectively or subjectively—is needed to achieve the goal of the virtues; for this the *instinctus*, the special movement and assistance of the Holy Spirit, is given; the Gifts of the Holy

Spirit are a receptivity to that; the corresponding act is of superhuman quality. In a more technical sense heroic virtue is a requirement in the life of one proposed for beatification or canonization (CIC c. 2102; 2104); the heroicity of virtue for the nonmartyr is as the counterpart of the martyr's death (*ibid.*). The requisite of heroic virtue is part of the formalization of the canonization process by Benedict XIV, written before his pontificate (*De servorum Dei beatificatione et beatorum canonizatione*, 1734–38). The virtue in question refers to the theological and cardinal virtues, the intense practice of which marks the pattern of the saint's life.

[T. C. O'BRIEN]

VIRTUES, INFUSED, the theological and moral virtues that are the concomitants of *sanctifying grace. Infusion is a metaphor, portraying God's bestowal of grace as an outpouring of his gifts upon the soul. Acquired virtues are those that, at least in abstract theory, can be developed by repeated good acts. The infused virtues cannot be so developed, faith, hope, and charity clearly mean resources that make possible a union with and relationship to God that only his gift of grace can explain. The infusion of these three theological virtues is stated as the effect of God's justifying grace by the Council of Trent (D 1530). St. Thomas Aquinas expresses their reason for being by comparing the supernatural resources given to man to the natural endowments of the soul. The identity that grace itself gives the recipient as the child of God is a new being that brings with it the capacities for a living expression of this being in knowing by faith and in loving by hope and charity (ThAq ST 1a2ae.62,1–3; 110,2–4). He also maintains that there are infused moral virtues. In name they correspond to the four cardinal virtues. They are distinct from acquired virtues because the *ordinatio* of charity means a new set of moral values, a new measure of moral good (*ibid.*, 63,3 & 4). They are more effective than acquired virtues because of the indefectible power of grace; yet they may lack the ease of operation that virtues developed by repeated acts can have.

[T. C. O'BRIEN]

VIRTUES, THEOLOGICAL, those supernatural gifts which, as habitual dispositions of the intellect and will, have God as their immediate object. They are *faith, *hope, and *charity. Theological virtues are supernatural rather than natural, i.e., they transcend all human virtue and belong to man only insofar as God has called him to divine life. They are distinguished from the intellectual and moral virtues insofar as they relate directly to God; it is He in whom man must believe and hope, and whom he must love. BIBLIOGRAPHY: T. C. O'Brien, NCE 14:704–709.

[T. M. MCFADDEN]

VISCH, CHARLES DE (*c.*1600–66), Flemish Cistercian bibliographer. He taught theology at Eberbach, was chaplain of the Cistercian nuns of Val Celeste and finally became prior of Les Dunes. His great work was *Bibliotheca scriptorum S. Ordinis Cisterciensis* (1649).

[P. J. HENNESSEY]

VISCHER FAMILY, Nuremberg sculptors, active from the mid-15th- to the mid-16th cent., esp. noted for bronze casting. **Hermann the Elder** (d. 1488), founder of the workshop, was succeeded by his son, **Peter the Elder** (*c*.1460–1529), the outstanding member of the family, who, first employed by Philip the Elector-Palatine (Heidelberg), returned to Nuremberg, undertaking tomb projects for Abp. Ernest of Magdeburg (1494–5) and Bp. John IV, Breslau (1496). The masterpiece of the Vischer foundry is the shrine of St. Sebald (1508–19) in Nuremberg, by Peter the Elder—the figures in strong classical postures—demonstrating a mastery of casting techniques in most intricate and complex forms, an eminence further evidenced in Peter's monument to Maximilian at Innsbruck. The work of his sons is not certain, monuments at Regensburg and Aschaffenburg credited to Hans, work on the Eisen Memorial in the Agidienkirche to Paul, while Peter the Younger is thought to have done the monument for Prince Frederick the Wise. BIBLIOGRAPHY: G. Dehio, *Geschichte der deutschen Kunst* (1919–34).

[R. E. FLEISCHER]

VISCONTI, ruling family of Milan, 1277–1447. The Visconti appear as a powerful force in Lombard politics from the 11th century. Their control of Milan began with the election (1262) of Ottone Visconti (d. 1295) as abp. and it became permanent upon his return from exile (1277) and at the ending of opposition to Visconti domination. Politically, the Visconti strove to control N Italy and perhaps to create a Visconti kingdom. This policy was first developed by Giovanni (d. 1354) who brought Bologna and Genoa under Milanese control. After a period of disunion following his death, Visconti power was unified again and brought to its apex by Gian Galeazzo (d. 1402) who acquired the title of duke and married his daughter, Valentina, to the brother of the king of France. His sons, however, were mediocre rulers at best and with the death of the last of them, Filippo Maria (1447), power ultimately passed to Francesco Sforza, the husband of Filippo's illegitimate daughter, Bianca Maria. BIBLIOGRAPHY: D. Muir, *History of Milan under the Visconti* (1924).

[J. MULDOON]

VISDELOU, CLAUDE DE (1656–1737), French missioner, writer. He joined the Jesuits in 1673 and was sent to China in 1685. In the Chinese rites controversy he alone among the Jesuits opposed adaptation. The papal legate, Charles de Tournou, who also condemned the Chinese rites, named V. vicar apostolic of Kwei-Chou in 1707, and V. was consecrated bp. of Macao in 1708. He spent his remaining years, however, with Capuchins in retirement in Pondicherry, India, where he wrote extensively on the Chinese rites and Chinese history. His most important work is *Histoire de Tartarie*.

[J. R. AHERNE]

VISHNU, the god of India who pervades the universe, holding it together. He is conventionally named (with *Brahma, the creator, and *Siva, the destroyer) as one of the three major gods, but for his devotees (Vaishnavas; Vishnuites) he is supreme. Devotional emphasis is placed on his liberality and beneficence toward humans. He has a consort (either Lakshmi, good fortune, or Shri, prosperity). But most characteristic are his many *avatars, his incarnations or descents in various forms for the sake of the protection or the guidance of the human race. Principal among these (all of which had an independent mythical or literary existence before they became understood as Vishnu's incarnations) are his appearances as a fish (who saves the first man in the deluge), a boar and a dwarf (who each preserve the earth for humans); as *Rama (the epic hero-king of the *Ramayana*) and esp. as *Krishna (the incarnate god of the later parts of the *Mahabharata*, and the originally quite distinct divine-human lover of the *Bhagavata Purana*); as the Buddha (though Buddhists, of course, do not accept this claim); and finally, at the end of this present age, as the evil-destroying Kalki. BIBLIOGRAPHY: J. Gonda, *Aspects of Early Visnuism* (1954); idem, *Visnuism and Sivaism* (1970); W. D. O'Flaherty, *Hindu Myths* (1975) 175–237; A. Daniélou, *Hindu Polytheism* (1964) 149–187.

[D. P. EFROYMSON]

VISIBILITY OF THE CHURCH, the composite of all the external, sensibly perceptible elements by which the Church exercises its role as the universal sacrament of Christ in the world. These elements correspond to the Church's triple function of bringing grace to men and of leading them to God in the spheres of faith, ritual, and Christian conduct. On all three levels the Church is visible as a sign of Christ's continued presence among His people and of their responsive devotion to him.

Its visibility in faith is seen in the communication of revealed truth by means of the Bible and tradition or, taken together, of the Church's constant authoritative teaching of the Word of God. The faithful are thus offered in easily discernible form the substance of what they are to believe in order to be saved. They are assured divine guidance through the Church's magisterium, the hierarchy under the bishop of Rome. Correspondingly they can show their allegiance to Christ through the visible means of professing the faith offered by the Church and thereby receive from Christ that supernatural enlightenment that is the foundation of the Christian life.

The Church's visibility in ritual spans the sacramental system and the Mass, along with the whole liturgical practice of Catholicism. Always the sacraments are perceptible signs that show forth the continued action of Christ in sanctifying his people, infusing or increasing his grace in them singly and socially. His purpose is to give them an ever greater share of his own divine life in anticipation of their eternal life with him at the end of time. Here the visibility is causally related to sanctity, since the right use of these sacramental signs is essentially tied in with the reception of the blessings which they signify.

Similarly the faithful show forth the visible nature of the Church every time they use the sacraments and participate in the liturgy. The sacraments are thus as much Christ's encounter with His people as their encounter with Him. He is visibly present to them in the objectively effective channels of grace that he instituted, as they are visibly present to him in their subjective readiness to profit from this contact with the divinity become human and operating in their favor.

Christian conduct is visibly directed by the Church's authority through its lawfully constituted pastors under the visible leadership of the vicar of Christ. In a way, this third form of visibility comprehends all three because without it the Church's visibility might seem to be only instructive (for teaching), declarative (for the sacraments), and recommended (for conduct), whereas it is divinely prescriptive on all these levels where essentials of faith, liturgy, and morals are concerned.

The Church's authority, no less than its magisterium and sacramental system, is visible. But here the visibility carries the added connotation of voluntariness that is only implicit in the other two. It means that human beings are believed to be vested with Christ's authority and that their expressions of will—under proper conditions—are an expression of the divine will. The biblical warrant for this prerogative is Christ's promise to the Apostles as a group and to Peter alone that whatever they bind on earth would be considered bound in heaven, and whatever they loose on earth would be considered loosed in heaven (Mt 16.19; 18.18).

Again the Church's authority exercised by visible persons in perceptible words has its counterpart in the Church's obedience offered to visible spokesmen in answer to perceptible directives. The fusion of these two constitutes the strongest binding force that unites the Church as a visible society—between the Apostles under Peter and the faithful in the early Church, as between the bishops under the pope and the faithful at the present time.

Accordingly, ''the visible structuring of the Church is no less the Church than her invisible reality. The sacramental Church is the spontaneous result of grace which, like love, seeks visible expression and identifies with it. The grace of Christ in which the Church is created is not imprisoned in the visible structure of the Church, but neither is it independent of her. For the Church is a sign or sacrament of grace. This means that the grace of the Lord, requiring visible presence among us (even as did he), is . . . expressed through the institutional structures of the Church and is inseparable from them'' (*The Church in Our Day, A Collective Pastoral of the American Hierarchy* [1968] 26).

The Church's visibility, therefore, is an extension of Christ's visible humanity; the Mystical Body is the continuation of the work of the God-man. Its relation to the Church corresponds to Christ's human nature in the Incarnation.
BIBLIOGRAPHY: P. F. Chirico, NCE 14:715; J. A. Möhler, *Symbolik* (1832); M. Schmaus, *Katholische Dogmatik*, 5 v. in 8 (5th ed. Munich 1953–59; 6th ed. 1960–) 3.1:391–409.

[J. A. HARDON]

VISIBLE CHURCH, an expression contrasting the Church as an empirical, imperfect, organized institution, with the invisible Church, the true Church as spiritual community. Such a distinction, made by many Reformers, is still maintained by some Protestant bodies; it has always been rejected in RC teaching, which regards the Church as a single reality with visible and invisible aspects. *INVISIBLE CHURCH.

[T. C. O'BRIEN]

VISIGOTHIC RITE, the liturgical rite characteristic of the Church in Spain and dominant there until the 11th century. it is also called the *Mozarabic Rite, probably because it survived in the parts of Spain where Arabic influence remained strong, and in churches of marked Arabesque style. It was also known as the Rite of Toledo since the Roman Rite gradually replaced it in all but six churches of Toledo. It is appropriately called the Visigothic Rite, however, since it can trace its beginnings to the coming of Visigothic rule to Spain in the 6th century. It underwent alterations because of Roman conciliar interventions and through the impact of preachers from Rome, but it remained typical of Spain until the Council of Burgos (1080) imposed the Roman Rite on Spain, not without popular resistance. It is perpetuated to this day only in the Toledo cathedral, in the chapel built for this purpose by the 15th-cent. Abp. Garcia de Cisneros.

[E. J. DILLON]

VISIGOTHS, a division of the Goths, the Germanic people who lived in what is now Sweden and moved eastward by A.D. 200 to the north coast of the Black Sea. The separation of Goths into East and West (Ostrogoths and Visigoths) occurred in the following century. In 332 Constantine settled the Visigoths in Dacia to defend the Danubian border. When the Huns pushed them across the Danube, they sought a closer alliance with Rome. Rejected, they invaded the Empire and slew Valens in battle in 378. Theodosius formally permitted them to remain in Moesia. A few years later they moved through Greece, Italy, Gaul, and Spain. In 410 they sacked the city of Rome. At their greatest extent the Visigoths held all of Spain and Gaul to the Loire. The Arabs destroyed their kingdom in 731. The Visigoths were converted to Christianity by prisoners from Cappadocia and natives of the Black Sea coast; and they brought their Arian faith to the Ostrogoths, Burgundians, and Vandals. BIB-

LIOGRAPHY: M. Bang, M. Manitius, and L. Schmidt, CMedH 1:183–217; 250–292; A. K. Ziegler, *Church and State in Visigothic Spain* (1930).

[M. J. SUELZER]

VISIONS. Apparitions as signs of God's presence or intervention (see THEOPHANIES) occurring through the Scriptures indicate that visions are part of the divine way of guiding men in the way of salvation. Parallel to the biblical record, but not having such authentication, is the history of visions claimed for the saints throughout the Christian centuries as a recognized mystical phenomenon. In discussing the nature of visions, theology has assigned various explanatory elements. The scripturally narrated visions are connected with the history of salvation and in that sense are supernatural, i.e., related to grace. Any vision by definition may be classified as "preternatural," i.e., occurring as to manner and–or content outside the normal course or range of human knowing. The term "vision" may be further clarified as denoting either the recipient's act of perception or the content ("message") perceived. The possibility of the occurrence of visions in either sense can be assigned on the basis of the meaning of the *beatific vision. As the supernatural destiny of man, the beatific vision means the immediate contemplation of God himself and of all else in God's being. Thus the mind that now perceives by faith in darkness is ultimately intended for clear vision; it is possible, therefore, that some momentary act of vision can be received. In the divine being or essence, as to content, there is eternally present the whole panoply of the history of salvation down to its individual details. Thus God can communicate a vision of some element belonging to the history of salvation, whether past, present, or future. The nature of the visionary's experience, finally, may be purely "internal" a vision in the imagination or mind of the beholder, whether sleeping, awake, or in rapture; the vision may be "outside" in the way, e.g., Bernadette's visions at Lourdes are depicted.

Such are the possibilities; verification of a genuine, divinely given vision is another matter. The fact and the content of the biblical visions of the Patriarchs, Prophets (see PROPHECY), and Apostles are accepted in the general acceptance of the veracity of Scripture. The private visions claimed throughout the Christian era have no such general authentication. The Church has sanctioned some indirectly in approving devotions or shrines that have resulted from reported visions, e.g., at Lourdes, Fatima, the shrine of the Miraculous Medal, Rue de Bac, Paris (see CATHERINE LABOURÉ, ST.). But even with ecclesiastical recognition (which basically means that there was nothing hallucinatory or fraudulent in the visionary's experience and that the content reported is not in conflict with the faith) that any vision has in fact occurred is not a matter of faith.

[T. C. O'BRIEN]

VISITANDINES, see VISITATION NUNS.

VISITATIO SEPULCHRI, a designation for the *Quem quaeritis* trope after it has been detached from the Introit to be performed as a play. It is essentially the confrontation of the angel and the three Marys at the empty tomb after Christ has risen, but the term is also used to cover later additions, like the visit of Peter and John to the sepulcher. Karl Young applies the designation *Visitatio sepulchri* to all Easter plays except four very elaborate texts which he groups under the name *Ludus paschalis*.

[E. C. DUNN]

VISITATION NUNS (VHM; Sisters of the Visitation of Holy Mary), an order founded by St. *Jane Frances de Chantal, under the direction of St. *Francis de Sales, in Annecy, France, in 1610. Originally intended to take simple vows and devote itself to visiting the sick, in actuality the community became an institute whose members took solemn vows and were cloistered. The contemplative life or a mixed regimen where schools were conducted in conjunction with the convent evolved. The spirit of St. Francis de Sales is evident in the emphasis on less rigorous ascetical practices enjoined by the rule, approved by Pope Urban VIII in 1626. The order spread throughout France by the 19th cent. and elsewhere in Europe in the 18th. It was St. Margaret Mary Alacoque, a member of the community at Paray-le-Monial, France, who became the apostle of devotion to the Sacred Heart. Each convent is an independent house, though that of Annecy held a primacy of honor. Foundations spread from France to most countries of Europe, to Syria, Latin America, the U.S., and to Mexico. For a brief period (1951–63), all Visitation communities were united in a confederation with a mother general residing in Annecy. There were 20 regional federations. The office of mother general was abolished and only the federations remain today.

Visitation Nuns in the U.S. Georgetown Visitation was the first American foundation, dating back to 1816, though the group who were affiliated as Visitandines in that year had lived a community life and operated an academy since 1799. Mother Teresa Lalor was superior when the first group took solemn vows and assumed the Visitation habit. Visitation Academy has had a distinguished, if at times endangered, history. The War of 1812 and the Civil War were times of great difficulty for the nuns.

Mobile Visitation of Holy Mary Monastery, founded from Georgetown, D.C., in 1833, operates Visitation Academy. Baltimore Visitation was established in 1837 from Georgetown under the direction of Mother Juliana Matthews; they operate there, too, the Visitation Academy. St. Louis, Mo. Visitation was originally (1833) established at Kaskaskia, Ill., by Mother Mary Agnes Brent from Georgetown. When the convent was destroyed by floods in 1844, the community was united with one recently founded in St. Louis, where it conducts an academy. Wheeling, W. Va. Visitation was founded from Baltimore in 1848 by Mother Eleanora Walsh; the community opened an academy during the Civil War. Parkersburg, W. Va. Visitation was established in 1864 from Georgetown and Frederick, Md., under the leadership of Mother Appolonia Diggs; the community operates an academy. Wilmington, Del. Visitation was founded in 1868 from Keokuk, Iowa, but the convent had to close. Mother M. Alexandrine de Butler was first superior. The academy in that city was likewise closed in 1893. Dubuque, Iowa Visitation was established in 1871 from St. Louis and directed by Mother Mary Genevieve King. The community conducts an academy. Georgetown, Ky. Visitation was founded in 1875 from a convent at White Sulphur, Ky., removed to Rock Island, Ill., and was finally established at Georgetown, Ky., where an academy is conducted. Tacoma, Wash. Visitation was founded in 1891 from Paris, Ky. under the leadership of Mother Mary Gonzaga Carreher. They conduct Visitation Villa Academy. Rock Island, Ill. Visitation is a community which moved to Rock Island from Maysville, Ky., under the leadership of Mother Francis Borgia Nolan. The community conducts Villa de Chantal Academy. Wytheville, Va. Visitation was founded by removal from Abingdon, Va., in 1902; the group conducts Villa Maria Academy. Springfield, Mo. Visitation was founded in 1906 from St. Louis, Mo., by Mother Jane Francis Fletcher; the community operates St. de Chantal Academy. Philadelphia, Pa., Visitation was founded by nuns in exile from Mexico City in 1926, led by Mother Margaret Mary Semple. The Mexican foundation, made from Mobile, Ala., had conducted a distinguished academy in the Mexican capital for nearly 30 years. Other Visitation convents are located in Catonsville, Md.; Brooklyn and Riverdale, N.Y.; Richmond, Va.; and Toledo, Ohio.

[J. R. AHERNE]

VISITATION OF MARY, story recorded by Lk (1:39–56) describing Mary's visit to her cousin Elizabeth in the hill country of Juda after the annunciation. In the structure of Lk's infancy gospel this incident plays a transition role between the announcement stories and the births of John and Jesus. Mary's stay of 3 months indicates she was present for the birth of John even though her return home is recorded before the birth of John. Lk often finishes with one topic (Mary's visit) before starting a new one (John's birth). The joyful reception of Mary by Elizabeth stresses the faith of Mary in accepting the word of the Lord and typifies the reception which Israel should give to its promised Messiah. For Mary's response see CANTICLE OF OUR LADY. The event has been celebrated by a special feast in the Western Church since the 14th century.

[M. A. MCNAMARA]

VISITATION OF THE SICK, one of the corporal works of mercy. The understanding of its Christian meaning is expressed in the Introduction to the Rites for Anointing and Care of the Sick, issued in 1972 (Eng. tr., International Committee on English in the Liturgy, 1974). Sickness itself is placed within the setting of Christian imitation of Christ in his suffering. Ministering to the sick is commended to all Christians as a sharing in Christ's and the Church's love for those who suffer. By visiting and "comforting them in the Lord, all can show brotherly help in their need" (42). This ministry should be seen as an action of the community, and the celebration of anointing and communion of the sick should have a communal dimension (33). All who try to show care and love for the sick should try to help the sufferers to view their illness as a share in Christ's Passion and to sanctify their suffering by prayer. The prayer and thoughts particularly appropriate to the ministry to the sick are the Scriptures, esp. the Psalms and passages on Christ's suffering. The occasion of visitation can always be an opportunity to pray with the patient. Priests esp. have the charge of ministering to the sick, praying with them, the laying on of hands, preparing the sick for the sacraments of anointing and communion. (43–45).

VISTA, see VOLUNTEERS IN SERVICE TO AMERICA.

VITAE SANCTORUM, the expression of patristic and medieval hagiography; the most popular form of literature in those centuries; a variation of the classical heroic biography, in which the saint is the hero whose virtues, miracles, works, and ordeals are held up for the wonder and imitation of the reader. The prototype is the biography of Anthony of Egypt written *c.*357 by St. Athanasius. Of similar impact during the Middle Ages was the life of St. Martin of Tours by Sulpicius Severus. Prosaic history was not the key; rather the miraculous and the legendary were most savored. The masterpiece is the *Legenda aurea*, a compilation of about 200 vitae by the Dominican abp. of Genoa, *James of Voragine. During the Renaissance this literary genre fell into disrepute and in the 17th cent. the *Bollandists began their protracted scientific investigation of the history behind the legends. There is often little history to be discovered after the centuries of legend. The scientific hagiographies lose the major impact of the earlier vitae: namely, the revelation of the aspirations of medieval man and his sense of his destiny and his world. Scientific study into Slavonic, Armenian, Coptic, Arabic, Persian, Ethiopian, and Georgian hagiography still remains to be done. BIBLIOGRAPHY: P. Séjourné s.v. "Culte des Saints," DTC 14:870–978; B. Kötting, s.v. "Hagiographie," LTK 4:1316–21; F. Halkin, "Hagiography" NCE 6:894–897.

[E. J. DILLON]

VITAL DU FOUR (Vitalis de Furno; *c.*1260–1327), pre-Scotist Franciscan philosopher and theologian. He studied at Paris (1285–91), taught in schools of his order at Montpellier and Toulouse. He was involved in the poverty controversy that divided the Franciscans. Serving at the papal court of Avignon, he was created cardinal in 1312, bp. of Albano near Rome in 1321. V. grounds the truthfulness of human intellection in a special, even mystical, divine illumination. The inclusion of many of his disputations in *De rerum principio*, wrongly attributed to Duns Scotus, caused some confusion to historians of Scotism. V. also was the author of theological and scriptural commentaries. BIBLIOGRAPHY: Gilson HCP 346–347.

[T. C. O'BRIEN]

VITALI, PIETRO (d. 1467), Basilian monk. V. became abbot of Grottaferrata in 1432 and was active in restoring and reforming houses of his order in Italy and Sicily. In 1462 he was made head of the Basilian monastery in Messina but was forced to abdicate in 1467 because of calumnies.

[M. J. SUELZER]

VITALIAN, ST. (d. 672), **POPE** from 657. In the letters announcing his election to succeed St. *Eugene I addressed to the emperor Constans II and to Peter, patriarch of Constantinople, V. apparently deliberately refrained from any mention of the controversy over *Monothelitism (SEE MARTIN I TYPOS). This conciliatory attitude pleased Constans, who replied with his approval of the pope's election and the restoration of imperial privileges accorded the Roman See. V.'s pontificate included a struggle with Marus, abp. of Ravenna, who sought to exempt himself from papal jurisdiction. In England the Pope supported the Roman dating of Easter established at the Synod of Whitby (664). His appointment and consecration (668) of Theodore of Tharsus (SEE THEODORE OF CANTERBURY) proved the basis of the organization of the Anglo-Saxon Church around an effective primate. BIBLIOGRAPHY: É. Amann, DTC 15:3115–17.

[P. K. MEAGHER]

VITALIS, ST., the name of two martyrs much venerated in medieval times, or of one martyr about whom two distinct legends developed in antiquity. As associated with Agricola, Vitalis was a slave converted to Christianity by his master (Agricola) and martyred with him at Bologna, probably during the persecution of Diocletian. Their bodies were discovered in a Jewish cemetery and were translated in the presence of St. Ambrose to a Christian church (393). See AS Nov. 2 (1894) 233–253. As associated with Valeria, Vitalis was the father and Valeria the mother of SS. Gervase and Protase. He suffered martyrdom in Ravenna and his wife in Milan, probably in the persecution under Marcus Aurelius. BIBLIOGRAPHY: H. Delehaye, AnalBoll (1928) 50–67.

[R. B. ENO]

VITALIS OF SALZBURG, ST. (d. *c*.730), abbot-bishop. He is supposed to have been a disciple of Rupert of Salzburg, as well as his successor as bishop. Authentic material is not available, and his history is obscure. He is the patron of Pinzgau. His cult was approved for the Abbey of Sankt Peters (1519) and for the archdiocese of Salzburg (1628). BIBLIOGRAPHY: H. Wolfram, NCE 14:724; P. Karner, *Die Heiligen und Seligen Salzburgs* (1913) 54–63.

[J. M. O'DONNELL]

VITALIS OF SAVIGNY, ST. (*c*.1063–1122), founder of the Benedictine monastery and congregation of Savigny. V. was chaplain to Robert, Count of Mortain, brother of William the Conqueror (*c*.1082) and became canon of the Church of St. Evroul of Mortain. Desiring a more austere life, he settled at Dompierre and founded the abbey of Savigny in the forest of Craon in the Diocese of Avranches. Here he lived for 17 years while caring for the spiritual needs of the people in the vicinity, and was famous for his preaching and his untiring zeal. BIBLIOGRAPHY: C. Auvry and A. Laveille, *Histoire de la congrégation de Savigny* (1896–98); E. J. Kealey, NCE 14:724; R. Van Doren, BiblSanct 12:1222–24.

[J. R. RIVELLO]

VITANDUS, in canon law, an excommunicate who is to be shunned, in distinction from the *toleratus,* one who may be tolerated (CIC, c. 2258, § 1). A *vitandus* is one who is excommunicated by name by the Holy See and expressly declared a *vitandus*. If such an excommunicate is present at a divine service, he must be ejected, or if that is impossible, the service suspended (*ibid.*, c. 2259, § 2); the faithful are urged to have no contact in everyday life with the *vitandus,* unless he is a relative or member of the household, or unless there is some serious reason (*ibid.,* c. 2267). In the proposed draft for a revision of the Church's penal code (SEE PENAL POWER OF THE CHURCH) the usage *vitandus-toleratus* is eliminated.

[T. C. O'BRIEN]

VITELLESCHI, MUTIUS (1563–1645), sixth general of the Society of Jesus. Under his direction, the Society expanded continually, although his method of rule has occasionally been criticized.

[P. J. HENNESSEY]

VITONUS, ST. (Vanne; d. *c*.529) bp. of Verdun. By legendary account, V. received his see, which he held for 25 years, from Clovis after St. Firmin died during Clovis' seige of the city. V. is remembered principally by the Benedictine abbey which bore his name. BIBLIOGRAPHY: G. M. Cook, NCE 14:726–727; Butler 4:304.

[G. M. COOK]

VITRUVIUS (Marcus Vitruvius Pollio; fl. 1st cent. B.C.), Roman architect and engineer. V.'s tremendous influence upon the history of Western architecture results from his 10-volume architectural treatise, *De architectura, libri X,* the essential source for a detailed understanding of ancient architecture. V. writes of city planning, waterworks, and strict systems of proportions; defines basic architectural functions and illustrates architectural orders. His work determined the Renaissance architectural theories of L. B. Alberti and Palladio, exerting far-reaching influence throughout Europe, England, and colonial America.

[S. CONWAY]

VITRY, PHILIPPE DE (1291–1361), French musical theorist, bp. of Meaux from 1351. V. was the author of an important treatise, *Ars nova, (c.*1320) whose chief renown lies in its recognition, for the first time, of binary rhythm. Also an excellent poet and composer of motets on historical themes, he was praised by Petrarch and others of his time for his works.

[M. T. LEGGE]

VITTORIA, ALESSANDRO (1525–1608), North Italian architect, sculptor, stucco worker, and medalist of the Venetian school. A follower of Il Sansovino and Palladio, V. designed buildings on the Grand Canal (1582–92), but is more important as sculptor of portrait busts of Venetian dignitaries (*Tommaso Rangone*, 1571), and small bronzes of unique pictorial quality (*St. Jerome*, 1566). V. is credited with having helped to establish the primacy of sculpture over architecture (*Luganegheri altar c.*1600). BIBLIOGRA-PHY: J. Pope-Hennessy, *Italian High Renaissance and Baroque Sculpture* (1963).

[L. A. LEITE]

VITTORINO DA FELTRE (real name, Vittorino de' Rambaldoni, 1318–46), Italian humanist, scholar, educator. Educated at Padua, he studied under *Vergerio, whose educational treatise, *De ingenuis moribus,* deeply impressed him. He taught at Padua but resigned to open a school in Venice. In 1423 Gian Francesco Gonzaga, Marquis of Mantua, entrusted him with the education of his 3 children, a trust he accepted with the provision that he could hold classes at the court and receive other promising children. Called *Casa Giocosa* (happy house), the school is considered the first outstanding Renaissance school. It was modeled on Plutarch's *De liberis educandis,* Quintilian's *De institutione oratoria,* and Vergerio's treatise, to which he added the stamp of his own creativity and experience. Truly Christian in character, the school emphasized the importance of Christian principles and humanism in the development of the whole man, while not neglecting science, the fine arts, and physical education. Vittorino died at Mantua, leaving no written works. BIBLIOGRAPHY: W. H. Woodward, *Vittorino da Feltre and Other Humanist Educators* (1921).

[M. B. MURPHY]

VITUS, ST. (fl. possibly *c.* 300), the saint whose cult together with that of Modestus and Crescentia is ancient and authentic, but of whom virtually nothing is known. St. Vitus was the main beneficiary of the fame accruing to the fantastic legend concerning the three martyrs. His reputed relics made the rounds in France and Germany during the 8th and 9th centuries. Protector of epileptics and those suf-fering from the nervous disorder named after him (St. Vitus' Dance), he was also patron of dancers and actors, invoked against storms, oversleeping, the bites of mad dogs, and serpents, and all injuries to man from beasts. BIBLIOGRA-PHY: Butler 2:545–546; A. Amore, BiblSanct 12:1244–46.

[E. J. DILLON]

VIVA, DOMENICO (1648–1726), an Italian Jesuit theologian. He joined the Jesuits in 1663; he became a theology professor and provincial in Naples in the early 18th century. V. published numerous volumes in his field, the most notable being the anti-Jansenist work *Damnatae theses ab Alexandro VII, Innocentiae XI et Alexandro VIII necnon Jansenii ad theologicam trutinam renovatae juxta pondus sanctuarii* (3 v., 1708) and *Trutina theologica thesium Quesnellianarum* (1716). A more general disquisi-tion was published in 1712, a *Cursus theologiae ad usum tyronum elucubratus* (8 v., 1712); and in 1721, a 4-v. moral series *Opuscula theologica-moralia*. Not an original thinker V. reflects the probabilist approach of Jesuit theologians of the 18th century.

[J. R. AHERNE]

VIVALD, BL. (d. 1320), hermit from San Gemignano, in Tuscany, who lived in a forest eight miles from there. He was beatified by Pius X in 1908. He was a disciple of Blessed Bartolo of San Gemignano, whom he nursed through 20 years of leprosy. He was attached to the third order of St. Francis. A convent was built on the site where he lived and died.

[E. J. DILLON]

VIVALDI, ANTONIO (*c.*1675–1741), Italian priest-composer. Ordained in 1703, he spent from 1704 to 1740 with the Conservatorio dell' Ospedale della Pietà in Venice, of which he was *maestro de concerti* for about 30 years. The Pietà was one of four important Venetian music schools for girls in the 18th century. V. was of frail health and as a result rarely said Mass but was never, as has been claimed, under suspension. He was a master of the concerto, esp. of the violin concerto. Much of his church music has not yet been fully published and the dates of composition are uncer-tain. He composed oratorios, Vesper-settings, music for Mass, and sacred motets. V. wrote for clavier, clavier and strings, oboe, flute, and organ. He composed 39 operas and some of these were performed in Rome, Florence, Mantua, and Ancona as well as in Venice. He left Venice in the last year of his life and died at Vienna. BIBLIOGRAPHY: G. Guerinni, *Vivaldi* (1951).

[J. R. AHERNE]

VIVARINI, the surname of a family of painters, exponents of Gothic painting in Venice. **Antonio** (*c.*1415–betw. 1476 and 1484), oldest of the family, whose earliest major work, *The Adoration of the Magi* (*c.*1441), is completely Interna-tional Gothic, combining gold leaf, linear arabesques, and realistic animals. His masterpiece (in the Accademia, Venice) is the altarpiece executed in 1446 for the Scuola Grande della Carità, gorgeously ornamental, not winged but a single measured space, the details full of jewelry, rooted in Gentile da Fabriano, Jacobello del Fiore, and Masolino. His *Parenzo Polyptych* (1443) is less great. In a late Vatican polyptych (1464) he gestures to A. Mantegna. **Bartolommeo** (*c.*1432–*c.*1499), brother of Antonio, rivaled Mantegna "at age 16." A *St. John Capistrano* (Louvre) and Madonna (1464) are routine, hard and bright, with "quotations" from Mantegna. His most outstanding works are the altarpieces of SS. Giovanni e Paolo (1473), the Frari (1474), S. Giovanni in Bragora (1478), and in the Accademia (1477). **Alvisi**, son of Antonio, though less talented, influenced his pupils L. Lotto and Jacopo de' Barbari, moving from elongated, linear forms to the classical *Capodistria Altarpiece* (1489). He shared with Giovanni Bellini a series of works at the Doge's Palace (1488). A portrait is more psychologically complex than those of Bellini but Alvisi's work lacks atmosphere. BIBLIOGRAPHY: B. Berenson, *Italian Pictures of the Renaissance: Venetian School* (1957).

[M. J. DALY]

VIVARIUM, MONASTERY OF, former Benedictine abbey of St. Martin, founded in 540 by Cassiodorus at his family estate on the Gulf of Squillace. Excavations have uncovered a basilica similar in form to Sant' Apollinare il Nuovo, founded by Theodoric at Ravenna and also dedicated to St. Martin. It was for the monks of Vivarium that Cassiodorus wrote his *Institutiones divinarum et saecularium litterarum*, which is credited with giving the Benedictine movement a scholarly bent, with its stress on the copying of MSS as the highest level of manual labor and on treating the liberal arts as a necessary preparation for the study of theology. BIBLIOGRAPHY: Cottineau 2:3412.

[E. J. DILLON]

VIVENTIOLUS, ST. (d. 523/524). V. was elected bp. of Lyons (*c.*514) on the recommendation of Avitus abp. of Vienne. He attended the Fifth Council of Lyons (*c.*516) and the Council of Epaon (517), and presided at the Sixth Council of Lyons (518). Avitus praises his zeal in the five extant letters he wrote to him. BIBLIOGRAPHY: M. R. P. McGuire, NCE 14:731; DACL 10.1:201–203 (with bibliog.).

[M. R. P. MCGUIRE]

VIVES, JUAN BAUTISTA (1545–1632), Spanish priest, founder of the Urban College in Rome (the Propaganda), renamed in 1962 the Pontificia Università Urbaniana. From the pontificate of Sixtus V in the papal service, V. was appointed an original member of the Congregation for the Propagation of the Faith in 1622 by Gregory V. His main interest was the training of missionary clergy; after several unsuccessful experiments at establishing a seminary, he bought the Palazzo Ferratini and, endowing it for the educa-

tion of 12 students, offered it to Urban VIII. V. himself received the task of preparing the statutes for the seminary and Urban, by the bull *Immortale Dei Filius*, 1 Aug. 1627, formally established the Urban Pontifical College.

[T. C. O'BRIEN]

VIVES, JUAN LUIS (1492–1540), Spanish humanist, educator, a pioneer in the field of psychology. A refugee from the Spanish Inquisition, he studied at Paris, 1509–12, and there developed an antipathy toward the prevalence of disputes over logic, the partisan bickering of scholastics, and arid interpretations of Aristotle that ignored the Philosopher's own reliance on experience and observation. After a period of tutoring and study in Bruges, V. in 1519 became professor of humanities at Louvain, publishing there in 1522, with the encouragement of Erasmus, a commentary, critical of the clergy and the friars, on St. Augustine's *City of God*. The work bore a dedication to Henry VIII of England, and V. was invited there and became a friend of Thomas *More; he tutored at Corpus Christi, Oxford, and was a secretary to Queen Catherine of Aragon. (He later displeased Henry by opposing his divorce from Catherine.) He returned to Bruges in 1524, where he married and where he devoted the rest of his life to writing. He is to be classified as a religious thinker rather than as a philosopher. His spirit was that of the *Devotio moderna*; like Erasmus, he was intent on the moral implications of philosophy, not in scholastic speculation. V.'s strongest appeal was to the "common sense" of mankind as verification of religious and moral truth; his chief concern was the way to eternal salvation and the rising above merely terrestrial goals. He was a strong advocate of measures that would relieve the poverty of the common people; of the education of women; and of a whole pedagogic program that would be practical and spiritually beneficial. His *De anima et vita* (1538) is regarded as one of the earliest attempts at an experimental psychology. His major pedagogical works include: *De disciplinis* (1531); *De institutione feminae christianae . . .* (1523); *Ad animi exercitationem in Deum commentatiunculae* (1538); and *Exercitatio linguae latinae* (1538). V. also wrote in the cause of pacificism, *De concordia et discordia* (1529); an essay on Christian philosophy, *De prima philosophia*; an ascetical work, *Jesu Christi triumphus* (1514); and an apologetics, *De veritate fidei christianae* (posthumous, 1543).

[T. C. O'BRIEN]

VIVIAN, ST., see BIBIANA, ST.

VIVISECTION, any scientific experimentation on living animals, by surgery, injection, or other means. Since justice is a relationship between persons, such experimentation is not a violation of justice. But since human beings have the obligation to treat all creation with respect and care, and to avoid any form of cruelty, vivisection must be carried out only for legitimate benefit to mankind, and with care to render the experimentation as painless as possible.

[T. C. O'BRIEN]

VIZCARDÓ, JUAN PABLO (1748–98), agitator for Latin American independence. Tenuously connected with the Jesuits as a candidate but never ordained, the Peruvian V. wás caught up in the expulsion of the Society from Peru and taken to Spain. Refused permission to return to Peru, by 1781 V. was negotiating with British agents in Italy to mount a fleet and help the rebels against Spain. V. became an English agent in London, but his plan was thwarted when England made peace with Spain. In 1791 while the French Revolution was under way, V. was in France where he wrote *Lettre aux Espagnols-Américains*, which urged the Creoles (of whom he was one) to rebel. V.'s letter was published in Spanish (1801) by the rebel General Miranda who claimed it as Jesuit support of his rebellion.

[J. R. AHERNE]

VLACHS, sometimes called Wallachians, the name of the Latin-speaking peoples of Rumania and N Greece who sought refuge in the mountains during the Slavic invasions of the early Middle Ages. They called themselves Armanou or Arumni, meaning Roman. Originally Latin Christians, they gradually seem to have adopted Byzantine Christianity. In the 13th cent. they migrated to the plains, and a few large groups laid the foundations of modern *Rumania.

[G. T. DENNIS]

VLADIMIR OF KIEV, ST. (980–1015) first Christian ruler of Russia. Although V.'s grandmother, St. Olga, was Christian, he himself was originally pagan, son of Svyotoslav I and his mistress Malushka. V. became Prince of Novgorod in 970, but when his father died 2 years later a long and fierce civil war ensued that ended in 980 with V. as master of Kievan Russia. According to the chronicler Nestor, V. sent envoys to investigate the religions of Christianity, Judaism, and Islam. He finally accepted Christianity partly because his legates were so impressed with the ritual of Constantinople but esp. because the Byzantine Emperor Basil II offered V. his sister Anna in marriage provided he would also become Christian. V. was baptized *c.*988 at Kherson in the Crimea. Returning to Kiev, he brought about the conversion of his subjects and the Christianization of Russia spread rapidly. V.'s reign was marked with endless warfare and nomadic strife, but he contributed greatly to unifying Russia both civilly and religiously. He is considered a saint by both Russian Orthodox and Byzantine Catholics, and his sons, SS. *Boris and Gleb, were murdered by their power-hungry brother, Svyatopolk. BIBLIOGRAPHY: F. Dvornik, *Slavs: Their Early History and Civilization* (1956).

[F. T. RYAN]

VLADIMIR, JOHN BAPTIST, ST. (Vladimir-ović; d. 1016), prince of Zeta (not king of Dalmatia), martyr. V. is reputed founder of the Elbasan monastery (today Orthodox) in present central Albania. In the Elbasan church, since 1215, rest his mortal remains. He was much venerated there; his cult spread to Croatia, where it became known through the writings of G. Kavanjin and A. Kačić-Miošić. After conquest (*c.*993) of his territory (now Salōna, site of an ancient Roman colony, where Diocletian was born in 245 at Dioclea), V. was vassal to Samuel, Bulgarian ruler, whom he respected and the love of whose daughter Teodora-Kosara he won. Samuel's death unleashed bloodshed, and his son who succeeded him was killed. Samuel's nephew Vladislav sought also to eliminate V., whom he lured to his city near Lake Prespa and killed in the church. Aside from information in the *Chronicle* by a priest of Dioclea (see esp. ed. by F. Šišić) which is substantially true, V.'s legend presents the martyr as a holy man and wonder-worker. BIBLIOGRAPHY: F. Dvornik, *Slavs: Their Early History and Civilization* (1956, repr. 1959) 141–144; *idem, Making of Central and Eastern Europe* (2d. ed. 1974) 291, maps pp. 40, 96; A. G. Matanić, BiblSanct 12:1321–23.

[E. D. CARTER]

VLADIMIR, OUR LADY OF, icon of Greek origin, probably dating from the 12th cent. but popularly attributed to St. Luke. Given to Prince George Dolgorouky by the Patriarch of Constantinople in 1155 and placed in the Cathedral of Vladimir (hence its name), it was transferred to Moscow in 1395. It is now in the Tretiakov art gallery (Moscow).

[F. WILCOCK]

VOCATION, in general, one's calling or profession in life; in a restricted ecclesiastical sense, a special call to serve God in the priestly or the religious state. Writers, while not in agreement on many of the aspects of vocation, do agree on the objective elements by which one may be considered called to the more perfect state: (1) aptness, or possession of qualities which fit a person for the clerical or religious life, and (2) a right intention, the will to dedicate self to God's service. A vocation to the priesthood, in particular, has two elements, the strictly internal, an intimate conviction that one is called by God, and the external element, a direct invitation of the bishop to advance to Orders. BIBLIOGRAPHY: J. Sikora, *Calling* (1968) 9–29.

[P. F. MULHERN]

VOCATION TO SUPERNATURAL LIFE, the call of all men to share in the life of grace and glory. As God's design for mankind, this is identical with his universal salvific will. Salvation means not only liberation from evil, sin, or suffering, but also supernatural union with God. It expresses the fact that all men are meant for a *supernatural destiny, namely, to find their fulfillment in communion with the Triune God. This destiny is anticipated in this world in the life of grace, or supernatural life. All men are called to the life of grace. They were called from the beginning, in men's *elevation to the supernatural order. They remained called after the Fall, though then unable to restore themselves to grace. Through Christ the Redeemer, the vocation to supernatural life can become effective again for all those who welcome him. Both in the beginning and after the redemption, the calling of men to supernatural life is socially patterned; they are called, as members of a body, or of the people of God.

This divine plan is carried out in the history of salvation. Before Christ this history comprised the election of Israel, anticipating the new covenant, and for the nations the call to salvation through the cosmic revelation. After Christ, men are called through the proclamation of the gospel. Those who believe and freely welcome it, come to the life of grace and for them the vocation to supernatural life becomes effective. Those who, through no fault of their own, are ignorant of the Christian message can yet, if they live according to their lights and conscience, be "anonymous Christians." By accepting their life's duty and so surrendering to the Absolute (whatever name they may call God), they implicitly, without knowing it, welcome Christ's offer and grace. However, for them too the proclamation of the gospel is necessary to enable them to know what they are and live their Christian life in a normal human way. BIBLIOGRA - PHY: H. de Lubac, *Surnaturel: Études historiques* (1946); *Le Mystère du surnaturel* (1965); T. Deman, BullThom 7 (1943–46) 422–446.

[P. DeLETTER]

VOCATIONAL PSYCHOLOGY, the branch of applied psychology dealing with the talents, experience, and interests of the individual in relation to occupational roles. On the one hand it determines the qualifications demanded for successful and contented performance in a given vocation, and on the other hand, it employs a variety of tests to reveal the individual's capacities and attitudes. Tests of overall intelligence, of verbal vs. mathematical skill, of mechanical aptitude, of achievement in various areas, etc., are employed to evaluate talent. Personality tests, and tests designed to reveal basic interests are used to assess subjective adaptability to a work role. At present there is growing interest in the use of the methods of vocational psychology to assist in judging candidates for religious and clerical vocations. BIBLIOGRAPHY: J. F. Kinnane, NCE 14:738.

[M. E. STOCK]

VOETIUS, GISBERTUS (1589–1676), Dutch Reformed theologian. He was a professor at the University of Utrecht; his writing, *Politica ecclesiastica* and *Diatriba de theologia*, reveal his strict Calvinism. He is known for condemning Cartesian rationalism as atheistic.

[P. J. HENNESSEY]

VOGELSANG, KARL VON (1818–90), Prussian civil servant and social reformer. Conservative by nature and feudalistic in outlook, V. opposed Frederick William IV's Constitution of 1848. After his conversion to Catholicism in 1850, he became actively interested in socio-economic problems. His moving to Austria in 1864 and accepting the editorship of *Das Vaterland*, a journal hostile to industrial capitalism, gave him the opportunity to expound his social theory. In 1879 he founded the *Monatschrift für christliche Sozialreform*. He saw in the existing division of social classes, in which a large segment of the population was being exploited, a danger of disrupting society. V. developed a complete social theory, creating an employer-employee relationship comparable to the corporations of the Middle Ages, which he envisioned as leading to the sharing of profit and ownership between industrialists and laborers. This, he assumed, could be done if Christian ethics were followed. Though seemingly too idealistic, his theories spread and influenced a number of industrialists to take steps toward improving the lot of the laborers. Many of his works were published in *Das Vaterland*, and collected in K. von Vogelsang. *Gesammelte Aufsätze über sozialpolitische und verwandte Themata* (12 v., 1885–86). BIBLIOGRAPHY: P. Jostock, NCE 14:740–741; J. C. Allmayer-Beck, *Vogelsang: vom Feudalismus zur Volksbewegung*.

[M. A. WATHEN]

VOGLER, GEORG JOSEPH (1749–1814), German organist, composer, and teacher. V. was practically self-taught as a musician. Ordained in 1773, he received several ecclesiastical honors and, in 1775, was appointed court chaplain and second *Kapellmeister* at Mannheim. In 1783 he became *Kapellmeister* at Munich and, in 1786, went into the service of the King of Sweden. V. devised his own system of teaching composition, made several innovations in organ building, and spent many years traveling, giving concerts, and founding music schools. His compositions include operas, ballets, secular choral works, a famous Requiem, Masses, hymns, psalms and motets, miscellaneous instrumental music; he also wrote numerous works on musicology.

[M. T. LEGGE]

VOGÜE, EUGÈNE-MELCHIOR, VICOMTE DE (1848–1910), French diplomat and writer. V. held various diplomatic posts (1871–82), including that of secretary to the French Embassy in St. Petersburg. Thereafter through his novels and criticism he influenced the reaction against naturalism and the development of the Catholic Revival. His chief work, *Le roman russe* (1886), described French realism as limited by its philosophical roots in positivism, accounting for a lack of charity toward its subjects, and advocated a mystical novel in the manner of Gogol, Dostoievsky, and Tolstoy equally able to depict man's spiritual and material dimension. He answered his own plea for an idealistic novel with *Jean d'Agrève* (1897), *Les Morts qui parlent* (1899) and *Le Maître de la mer* (1903). His other works deal chiefly with Russia, its history and literary figures. BIBLIOGRAPHY: L. Le Meur, *L'Adolescence et la jeunesse d'Eugène Melchior de Vogüé* (1932); E. W. Gosse, *Portraits and Sketches* (1914).

[G. E. GINGRAS]

VOIGT, GEORG (1827–91), historian. Son of the Prussian nationalist historian Johannes Voight and influenced by Leopold von Ranke, V. turned to the meticulous study of history at an early age. While still a young man he published two major historical works, which established his reputation and earned him successive academic appointments at the universities of Königsberg, Rostock, and Leipzig. The first of these was a biography of Pope Pius II, *Enea Silvio de Piccolomini als Papst Pius der Zweite und sein Zeitalter* (3v., 1856–63). In addition to providing a richly detailed account of the pontificate of Pius II, V. also analyzed the many-sided personality of the humanist pope, describing his activities as poet and speaker, letter writer, editor, geographer, and historian. This interest in humanism led to the second major work, *Die Wiederbelebung des classischen Altertums, oder das erste Jahrhundert des Humanismus* (1859), in which he offered an interpretation of the Renaissance similar to the much more famous one published by Jakob Burckhardt a year later. Although V. was interested mostly just in its psychological effects, his work identified the humanists' revival of antiquity as the dominant element of Renaissance culture. BIBLIOGRAPHY: W. K. Ferguson, *The Renaissance in Historical Thought* (1948).

[R. J. GIBBONS]

VOJTĚCH RAŇKŮV Z JEŽOVA (ADELBERTUS RANCONIS AB ERICINO, OR ADELBERT RANCONIS OF JEŽOV; 1325–88), Czech theologian, reformer. Educated at Prague, Oxford, and Paris where he became professor and rector (1355), he later taught at Oxford before returning to Prague. Here V. was the associate of surrounding scholars, an officer in the chancery of Emperor Charles IV. With John Milíč he advocated the *Devotio moderna* and frequent communion for laymen, founding the Bethlehem Chapel as the center of the movement. Ideas for ecclesiastical reform gathered in Oxford and Paris appealed to him; he protected Czech reformers and is considered by Hussites as their precursor. However, V. always remained faithful to the Church. In his will he gave his estate to provide scholarships for Bohemians at Paris and Oxford. BIBLIOGRAPHY: J. Papini, NCE 14:742.

[M. E. DUFFY]

VOLASENUS, FLORENTIUS (Florence Wilson; 1500–c.1557), humanist. Born in Scotland, V. spent most of his life on the Continent, mainly in Paris and Lyons. His *Scholia in Somnium Scipionis* (1529) and commentaries on the psalms show a predilection for Hebrew and patristic studies. *Commentatio theologica* (1539) reflects the *Devotio moderna*. He was at first a supporter of the English schism, but his writings after 1536 are essentially Catholic. He concerned himself with the spiritual life and avoided controversy. *De animae tranquillitate* (1543) presents St. Paul's view of the cross as the key to interior peace.

[J. R. AHERNE]

VOLKSVEREIN (Volksverein für das katholische Deutschland), a Catholic association founded at Cologne in 1890 to promote social reform along lines of Catholic principles. Its three leaders were Franz Brandts, Franz Hitze, and Ludwig Windthorst. Their program was one of education in social principles applied to the new industrial society of Germany and the directing of Catholics toward greater participation in civic affairs. With a central office at Mönchengladbach, the organization advised on social questions, published two quarterlies, pamphlets and books which circulated in the millions, conducted courses for other groups and a celebrated summer session devoted to social problems. The Volksverein was suppressed by the Nazis in 1933.

[J. R. AHERNE]

VOLTAIRE (Arouet, François-Marie; 1694–1778), French writer and philosopher. V. was educated by Jesuits, but turned early to libertinism. He was twice imprisoned in the Bastille for personal offenses against political figures (1717–18 and 1726). Next sentenced to exile, he spent 3 years in England, but was again forced to flee Paris (1734) when his *Philosophical Letters on the English* (really attacking the French State and Church) were condemned. At the home of Mme. du Châtelet, where he lived off and on until 1749, he spent a period of intense scientific and literary activity, writing in 1738 his *Elements of the Philosophy of Newton*. After the death of Mme. du Châtelet V. went to Berlin at the invitation of Frederick II of Prussia. Following disillusionment, rivalry, and further journeyings, he settled at Ferney, Switzerland, becoming an autocratic but beneficent lord of the village, with a large household managed by his niece. From this vantage point he freely exercised his caustic genius against all forms of tradition. His influence spread throughout Europe, and when he returned to Paris shortly before his death he was triumphantly acclaimed. Devoted to the classics, Voltaire wrote many plays and discovered Shakespeare for the French. As a historiographer (*History of Charles XII of Sweden*, 1731; *The Century of Louis XIV*, 1751) he was original in considering cultures as well as politics. He sought documentation, critical analysis, and impartiality, falling far short, however, in this last. He also produced literary criticism, numerous brochures, and over 6000 letters in the Ferney period alone. His facile and insinuating sarcasm was directed against all who practiced any type of religion. He failed to recognize the role of the Church, notably in the 17th century. A deist himself, V. believed in the existence of God, but denied Providence, the immortality of the soul, the value of prayer, and the possibility of man's glorifying God or having duties. Philosophy for him was not a system but a set of attitudes, largely skeptical. His rationalism was more practical than metaphysical. V.'s *Portable Philosophical Dictionary* presents a summary of his thought in alphabetical order. He was often gravely inconsistent, e.g., sometimes defending free will, sometimes determinism. Early an optimist, he became ever more pessimistic and cynical. Among his most widely read works are the stories, notably *Micromégas* (1752), *Candide* esp. (1759), and *L'Ingénu* (1764). V. may rightly be called the father of rationalism in the 19th cent. and later. His superficiality, frequent incoherence, and departure from truth are recognized by modern critics, but he remains unsurpassed as a master of style. In his own day, no opponents could match him in popular style. However, it must be said that he fought intolerance and influenced social consciousness. His byword ''Ecrasez l'infâme!'' (Crush the infamous) was ambiguous in application, but certainly included all that V. considered prejudice or injustice. He championed certain victims of oppression (Calas, Sirven) and berated many abuses. His ideas in such areas were sound and paved the way for improvement. BIBLIOGRAPHY: F. M. A. Voltaire, *Oeuvres Complètes* (ed. L. Moland, 52 v., rev. ed. 1877–85); *Critical Bibliography of French Literature* (v. 4, ed. D. C. Cabeen); *Eighteenth Century* (ed. G. R. Havens and D. F. Bond, 1951) and *Supplement* (ed. R. A. Brooks, 1968).

[L. TINSLEY]

VOLTERRA, DANIELE DA (Daniele Ricciarelli; 1509–66), Italian painter. V. studied with the Sienese Sodoma, but was influenced more strongly by the Sienese painter and architect B. Peruzzi, executing the fresco frieze (1538) in Peruzzi's Palazzo Massimo alle Colonne. V. though prominent as a mannerist in Rome, is linked servilely with the life and works of Michelangelo. His *Descent from the Cross*, in the Church of Trinità de' Monti derives from Rosso, but copies composition and forms from the *Last Judgment* of the Sistine Chapel. Pope Paul III appointed him superintendent of Vatican works (1549–51) on the advice of Michelangelo. In later years V. engaged in carving (*Murder of the Innocents*, 1557, Volterra) and the equestrian statue of Henry II of France (destroyed in the French Revolution). As companion to Michelangelo, V. wrote the master's letters, was present at his deathbed, and executed a bronze bust of Michelangelo from the death mask. Ironically, V. painted draperies on nudes in Michelangelo's *Last Judgment* on the order of Pope Paul IV (1559) and was called in derision 'Il Bragghetone'' (breeches maker). BIBLIOGRAPHY: M. L. Mez, *Daniele da Volterra* (1935).

[M. J. DALY]

VOLTO SANTO OF LUCCA. The so-called holy face of the 11th or 12th cent., in a small shrine in the cathedral of Lucca, is a Byzantine image of the crucified Christ clothed in the colobium (tunic) with reference in Dante's *Inferno*, 41:28.

[M. J. DALY]

VOLUNTARINESS, the quality of an act as voluntary, i.e., as proceeding from an agent's will. The theological terminology used in this matter by RC moral theologians was sorted out by St. Thomas Aquinas in the second half of the 13th century.

The action of a thing may be natural or not. It is natural when it issues from within according to the proper propensities of a thing; ''nature'' is here taken as the Gr. *phusis,* the inner principle of motion toward an end. When it is not natural it may be looked at from different points of view as violent (Gr. *biaion*) or as artificial (*technichon*), or as preternatural or supernatural. In the last case ''nature'' shifts to meaning a type of being. The point is important when treating of the supernatural action of grace, which is not unnatural in the sense that it is in any way enforced or imposed, and is fully voluntary in the senses to be touched on below.

Now voluntary activity as an intrinsic movement in full measure is a type of natural activity. However, a navigational hazard is to be noted: in classical theological usage, acting through will is sometimes contrasted with acting through nature. For example, we are created freely by God and not by a necessary emanation from his substance. ''Nature'' here suggests a determinism, and, moreover, a blind and therefore not willed appetite, tendency, or gravitation, whereas ''voluntary'' means a bent of conscious desire. It is well, then, in reading theological texts to allow for the distinction between the merely natural and the voluntarily natural.

Next, it should be noted that the knowledge from which voluntary activity issues may be that only of the senses, which arouse a motion of the sensitive appetite, as in non-rational animals. Accordingly the term voluntary is conceded to their non-automatic and non-tropistic reactions. However, in its full and proper sense, which is the normal usage in theological texts, it is reserved to intelligent creatures who are not aware just of particular desirable items, but grasp the meaning of purpose (*ratio finis*) and relate means to ends as such.

The notion of voluntary or spontaneous activity in human beings does not necessarily involve that of free and moral activity, though the terms are commonly treated as synonomous in theological writing, because in fact in man's present condition all his completed voluntary acts are free and performed in a moral setting. For a voluntary act is defined as one that proceeds from the mind perceiving and the will loving an end. Now this end may be so all-embracing a good that there can be no hesitation about a man's wanting it. So, for example, does a man want happiness-in-general, whenever he acts at all; so also would he want God, were he clearly seen. A free act, on the other hand, is one that holds a certain poise of will before an object that is a particular and limited good, and so therefore is not found ''compelling'' to the will as would be a universal and unlimited good. To speak precisely within any frame of reference adopted, choice (Lat. *electio*) is enclosed within the sphere of goods apprehended as limited, whereas volition (Lat. *velle*), and enjoyment (*frui*) are about the end respectively intended and possessed. In other words, a man chooses to be free; he is born to be voluntary. On a point of terminology note that the technical name in moral theology for a free act is a *human act. These refinements are not as idle as they may seem; they apply in practice, as when, for instance, it is observed that a rush of desirous passion increases the voluntariness of a deed yet lessens its freedom and the responsibility, also the blame if it be bad, though not—a nice touch this from St. Thomas—the praise if it be good.

Some useful divisions of voluntary activity are to be noted; in pursuing them it should be noticed that the voluntary is differently opposed by the negative non-voluntary, a condition or act in which the will has no part, and the privative involuntary, an act which is positively against the will.

The first division is between a voluntary commission and a voluntary omission, called by St. Thomas the directly and the indirectly voluntary respectively. Most of the modern authors, however, use these terms to refer to willing an object for itself and willing the effects which may follow. This last is the celebrated *voluntarium in causa* that looms large in *casuistry together with the principle of the *double effect, one good, the other bad. May a therapeutic operation be performed even if it results in an abortion? Yes, given the conditions that the good effect is not caused through the evil effect, that it is warranted by proportionate reasons, and that the intention is good. In practice it may well be found that a robust virtue of prudence can come to a decision without reflection on such rules.

It remains to glance at the forces working against voluntary activity, the *hostes voluntarii*, as they are called. First, force, compulsion, coercion, or violence: this may be imposed upon the will, not in its inner act of volition, but in the outward acts it would otherwise command. Secondly, fear, dread, or *metus*, defined in Roman law as alarm of mind on account of an instant or future evil. This may cause a man to do things against the grain. Both Aristotle and Nemesius regard what is so done as a mixture of the voluntary and the involuntary. St. Thomas recognizes the reluctance, but nevertheless concludes that all-in-all the deed is downrightly, *simpliciter*, voluntary, though involuntary from one point of view (*secundum quid*). Many modern moralists reverse his terminology. Thirdly, it is agreed that a strong emotion of fear or desire may so affect the mind that the element of rational knowledge required for voluntary activity is non-operative or impaired. The fourth obstacle to voluntariness is ignorance. When this is not willed in any way, an action that follows under its influence is involuntary. When it is willed, whether directly or indirectly, one is not exempt from responsibility for its results. BIBLIOGRAPHY: ThAq ST 1a2ae, 6 (esp. in ed. Lat-Eng, ed. T. Gilby, 1970); Merkelbach 1:36–106.

[T. GILBY]

VOLUNTARY (MUSIC), an organ composition played during an English church service. Originally an improvised piece, the voluntary soon assumed a variety of forms and styles, such as those of the prelude, toccata, suite, sonata, etc. Voluntaries, while having no fixed place in the service, are, however, generally played between the psalms and the first lesson, before Communion or as an offertory piece. Though for some time the voluntary was misused, there has been a renewal of effort to employ music of quality and suitability to the liturgical season. Among the composers of voluntaries are Byrd, Gibbons, Blow, Purcell, Wesley, Willan, and many others.

[M. T. LEGGE]

VOLUNTARYISM (voluntarism; voluntary principle), the theory and practice according to which church membership or support is a matter of personal choice, free of civil or even ecclesiastical coercion. Voluntaryism is closely associated with *denominationalism; it stands opposed to any form of *established Church, of *Erastianism, or even of authoritarian ecclesiastical system. The idea clearly emerged in 17th-cent. England in the *gathered Church theory (see INDEPENDENCY; NONCONFORMISTS). Dropping the original qualifying emphasis upon God's initiative in the gathering process, John Locke defined the Church as a purely voluntary organization: "A church then I take to be a voluntary society of men, joining themselves together on their own accord, in order to the public worshiping of God" (*First Letter concerning Toleration*). As a principle of church life voluntaryism clearly emerged in the *Great Awakening in the U.S., and "the voluntary principle in religion has been the great tradition of the American churches" (W. S. Hudson, *The Great Tradition of the American Churches* [1953], 19). The full development of the principle was made possible by the incorporation of religious freedom and separation of Church and State into law in the U.S.; the voluntary principle allowed for the proliferation of sects and denominations; these in turn strengthened the force of voluntaryism in American Christianity. Without an established Church each denomination had to win adherents, raise financial support, and find means of influencing society. *Revivalism proved to be a natural concomitant of voluntaryism as the Churches sought aggressive approaches to win multitudes of churchless people. The success of the Churches in winning converts is apparent from statistics of church membership, attendance, budgets, buildings, and the like.

Voluntaryism affected the dynamics of church life in the form of "voluntary societies." While Americans resolved to separate the spheres of religion and civil government, they did not intend to separate religion from the rest of life. In the early 19th cent., numerous local, state, and national voluntary societies, or associations, were organized to propagate the Christian faith and to reform society. Among the better known were: American Bible Society (1816),

American Colonization Society (1817), American Sunday School Union (1824), American Tract Society (1825), American Temperance Society (1826), American Education Society (1827), American Peace Society (1828), and the American Anti-Slavery Society (1833). Promoters of revival were often linked with reform movements, and many individuals held membership in several societies, forming a network that came to be known as the "Benevolent Empire." Although many members belonged to Churches, they were not official representatives. Thus through informal interdenominational cooperation, the fabric of American political and social life was permeated. Struck by the vitality of religious life in America, many European visitors commented on the good and bad effects of the voluntary principle. Philip *Schaff, after a dozen years in the U.S., explained the benefits of the "so-called voluntary principle" to former compatriots in Germany, pointing out also its limitations. The voluntary principle was not without its critics, who complained that it fostered excessive *individualism and *subjectivism, weakened objective standards of authority and denominational loyalties, and stressed personality traits above theological competence as qualifications for the ministry. BIBLIOGRAPHY: C. I. Foster, *Errand of Mercy: The Evangelical United Front, 1790–1837* (1960); *Voluntary Church: American Religious Life (1740–1865) Seen through the Eyes of European Visitors* (ed. M. Powell, 1967); F. H. Littell, *From State Church to Pluralism* (1926); S. E. Mead, *Lively Experiment* (1963).

VOLUNTEERS IN SERVICE TO AMERICA (VISTA),

a domestic *peace corps, open to volunteers over 18, established in 1964 as part of the antipoverty program. Its members, who receive $50 monthly plus living expenses, contribute their services to domestic projects designed to assist migrant workers, Indians, drop-outs, the aged, and mental patients. BIBLIOGRAPHY: R. Hoopes, *Complete Peace Corps Guide* (1965).

[M. B. MURPHY]

VOLUNTEERS OF AMERICA (VA),

an organization founded in 1896 by Ballington *Booth, son of *Salvation Army founder William Booth, as the result of an effort to make the Salvation Army (SA) more democratic. The VA is similar in most respects to the parent body. Ballington Booth and his wife, Maud Charlesworth Booth, were appointed joint commanders of the American forces of the SA in 1887. They resigned in 1896 when recalled to England, after a long struggle to convince the elder Booth of the need for greater local autonomy, but discouraged any secession from Salvation Army ranks. They founded the VA as a new organization but drew heavily on the experience and methods of the Salvation Army. Officers are chosen democratically, and all with the rank of major or higher form the Grand Field Council, which has direction of the Volunteers under a commander-in-chief whom it elects for a 5-year

term. The VA has the same fundamentalist beliefs and evangelistic, nonliturgical worship as the SA, but it has adopted its own forms for the administration of baptism, the Lord's Supper, and marriage. The VA directs a variety of evangelistic and social work projects, including a special ministry to inmates of prisons, the Volunteer Prison League. There were 45 stations with 40 evangelists and 5,500 members in 1968.

[R. K. MacMASTER]

VOLUSIANUS OF TOURS, ST.

eighth bishop of Tours (488–496). He was reared at Lérins, was married, was of senatorial rank, and was related to his two predecessors. According to Gregory of Tours, he was exiled to Spain by the Visigoths who suspected him of sympathy for the Franks. Later accounts indicate he might have been decapitated in Toulouse c.498. V.'s relics were brought to Foix, where a famous church and cloister, later destroyed by the Huguenots, were erected in his honor. As bp. he was known for his care for the poor and for his wife, whose temper, according to fellow-bishop Ruricius of Limoges, was a terror to all their acquaintance. He was canonized, probably on the grounds of his supposed martyrdom.

[E. J. DILLON]

VON DER HEIDE, HENNIG

(fl. c.1490–1510), German late Gothic master wood-carver in style relating to B. Notke. His masterwork is *St. George and the Dragon* (1504, Lübeck). His *St. John* figure, treasure of the Marienkirche, Lübeck, was destroyed in World War II.

[M. J. DALY]

VONIER, ANSGAR (MARTIN; 1875–1938),

abbot, theologian. Born in Germany, V. joined the English Benedictines of Buckfast Abbey and was ordained in 1898. After teaching in Rome he was elected abbot of Buckfast in 1906, after being saved in a shipwreck that took the life of his predecessor, Abbot Natter. His chief accomplishment as abbot was to restore the ancient abbey buildings, a work that took 32 years to complete. It is as a theologian, however, that he exercised lasting influence. A perceptive student of St. Thomas Aquinas, an able English stylist, V. produced a number of works influential in their time. Among these were *The Human Soul and Its Relation with Other Spirits* (1913), *The Personality of Christ* (1914), *A Key to the Doctrine of the Eucharist* (1925) the most authentic English-language exposition of St. Thomas's sacramental theology, and *The People of God* (1937). V. has been called with justice an intuitive and original theologian.

[J. R. AHERNE]

VOODOO (Vodun),

a mode of African traditional religion, developed among the mixed African peoples of the Caribbean, particularly Haiti, during the 18th century. Though the large cult-centers once associated with Haitian patriarchal families have declined in this century, Vodun remains the dominant religion of the Haitian peasantry. Sorcery, homeopathic medicine, and magic continue to play an important part in popular Vodun. The word Voodoo or Vodun is Dahomean for God or the ultimate protective spirit. Vodun incorporates elements of the traditional religions of the Fon of Dahomey, of the Yoruba, Ibo, and other peoples of West Africa who were brought to the Caribbean as slaves. Given the capacity of African traditional religion to assimilate alien gods, saints, rituals, and concepts, Vodun also deeply incorporates the French Catholicism of the Haitian slave masters. With Haitian independence in 1804, the plantation regime was replaced by an agricultural system that closely resembled the African feudal system; and in the absence of the Catholic Church's central religious authority, Vodun proliferated among the Afro-Haitians in a variety of local sects, each different from the others. Generally speaking, Vodun has two distinct strains, a benevolent one associated with the Arada (or Rada) rites, and another, malevolent strain of the Petro rites. The supreme deity of the Vodun pantheon is referred to as Great Mother or Papa; the other lesser deities are called *loa* (Congolese: power). The most widely honored being of Arada is Damballah-Weda, whose fertility is signified by one or two serpents. Legba, a Fon deity, represented as a cross or crossroad, is an omniscient, omnipresent mediator between the human and spiritual realms, and so all rites involving other *loa* must begin with an invocation of Legba. The goddess Erzulie-Freda is the African transformation of the Virgin Mary. Guede, god of death, is the chief *loa* of the Petro. Human authority in Vodun rests with the male *houngan* or *papoloi* and the female *mambo* or *mamaloi*, who serve the *serviteurs* or followers as priests and priestesses, healers, seers, diviners, and preservers of the tradition. The Vodun sanctuary (*Houmfó*) contains an open area for the public ceremonies that are the outstanding feature of Vodun, a garden with a pool, trees, and a black cross, a special initiation chamber (*djévo*), and the chapel of the gods (*caye-mystère*) with stone altar. The ritual of initiation by which a new Vodun personality is reborn in the candidate is derived from a Yoruba original. Although Vodun was officially suppressed after the revolution, it has always exerted a powerful popular political force in Haiti, from the Oath of Bois-Caiman, which began the revolution, to the rule of the dictator François Duvalier, a self-acclaimed Vodun Messiah. BIBLIOGRAPHY: A. Metraux, *Voodoo in Haiti* (tr. H. Charteris, 1972).

[R. J. LITZ]

VORSTIUS, CONRADUS (Konrad von der Vorst; 1569–1622), German-born defender of *Arminianism. V. studied at Düsseldorf, Cologne, Herborn, and received his doctorate in theology at Heidelberg (1594). His subsequent disputations and teaching in Basel, Geneva, and Steinfurt were praised until he became suspected of *Socinianism, a charge which he confuted at Heidelberg (1599). After J.

*Arminius died, V. was called by J. Uitenbogaert (1610) to Leyden. He then published *Tractatus theologicus de Deo sive de natura et attributis Dei* (1610), a reprint of his disputations of 1602, and *Anti-Bellarminus* (1610). The contra-Remonstrants criticized his *Tractatus,* which was condemned by the Heidelberg theologians, to which he replied in *Protestatio epistolica* (1610). James I of England sided with V.'s critics, had his books burnt, and through the British ambassador forced the States-General at the Hague to dismiss him. The Synod of *Dort (1619) condemned and banished V. as a heretic. He went into hiding. A confession of faith composed before he died stated his lasting Socinian beliefs.

[R. J. LITZ]

VOS, JAN (JOHANN VOSWINI; 14th cent.), a disciple of Gerard Groote (d. 1384). V. was the leader of a group which in 1386 founded the Monastery of Windesheim, the Netherlands, a house of the Canons Regular of St. Augustine, and served as its prior from 1391 to 1424. The monastery became a center of learning and a force in church reform in the 15th century.

[J. R. AHERNE]

VOSS, GERHARD JOHANNES (1577–1649), Calvinist theologian, philologist and historian. Born in Heidelberg of Dutch parents, he studied at Leyden and taught at Dordrecht (Dort), Leyden, and Amsterdam. He also was from 1629–32 attached to Canterbury Cathedral. He concerned himself with Pelagianism and opposed himself to F. *Gomarus and J. *Arminius on the question of predestination. V. is credited with proving that the *Quicumque vult* was not written by St. Athanasius, but was of Western provenance, in his *Dissertationes tres de tribus symbolis* (1642).

[P. J. HENNESSEY]

VOSTÉ, JACQUES MARIE (1883–1949), Scripture scholar. V. taught Scripture at the Angelicum in Rome, became (1929) a member of the *Pontifical Biblical Commission and later (1939) its secretary. As secretary, his response to Card. Suhard on Mosaic authorship and literary genre in the Pentateuch was an important milestone in RC scriptural scholarship. It was also during his term as secretary that *Divino afflante Spiritu* was issued. V. was a prodigious scholar who produced a vast number of articles and books on scriptural studies.

[T. M. MCFADDEN]

VOTING, from the medieval Lat. *votare*, the rendering of a formal decision on a question of public interest, the use of the ballot to express the preference of the members of a group in the choice of public officials or in the ratification of proposed laws or policies of government. In old and settled states, when social cohesion is assured and the public is not very crisis-minded, and where there are strong strains of timocracy, aristocracy, and monarchy (not necessarily associated with the hereditary principle) the duty of the individual citizen to exercise his right of suffrage has not always been regarded as a matter that should weigh heavily upon his conscience. But when a society is more democratically structured, it is more important that a free member of the group should take his share of responsibility for the corporate actions of the community. The obligation appears to be one of justice, and to refrain from registering an opinion seems defensible only when no great issue is involved or when the outcome is so certain that individual votes are of little consequence. RC moralists have been giving increasing attention to this duty of citizenship, which was previously regarded as being serious only in specially urgent situations. Pius XII on several occasions called attention to the obligation. See e.g., his allocution to International Union of Catholic Women's Leagues (AAS 39 [1947], 486).

[T. GILBY]

VOTIVE MASS, in the Roman liturgy, a Mass in honor of a saint or of a particular mystery of the Lord, not called for by the calendar as the Mass of the day but permitted for reasons of piety and devotion when no other celebration is specified for that day. The votive Mass differs from a ritual Mass (accompanying the celebration of a sacrament), from a Mass for the dead, and from a Mass for a particular need or occasion.

[J. DALLEN]

VOTIVE OFFERING, from the Latin, *vovere*, to desire, an external sign of a desire attached to prayer. For example, a votive candle is a sign of one's petition; a plaque left at a shrine is a sign of one's desire to express gratitude. The purpose of any type of votive offering is to give a force to one's prayer, not ideally, at any rate as a bribe to God but as a stimulus to foster in the petitioner the sentiments proper to prayer. It is an act of the virtue of religion by which the offerer expresses a recognition of God's supremacy and, at the same time, submits to his will. BIBLIOGRAPHY: P. F. Mulhern, NCE 4.833–834.

[P. F. MULHERN]

VOTIVE OFFICE, in the Breviary a special office of some mystery or saint differing from the regular office of a given day and allowed to replace the regular office occasionally by reason of a privilege. These votive offices were abolished in 1911, the sole remaining vestige being the Office of the Blessed Virgin Mary for Saturday.

[R. B. ENO]

VOUET, SIMON (1590–1649), French painter of religious subjects, history, and portraits. Pupil of his father, after travel V. settled in Rome (1614), showing the influence of Michelangelo and Caravaggio in *Scenes from the Life of St. Francis*. After 1620 he commanded a mildly ecstatic baroque in *The Virgin Appearing to St. Bruno*.

Returning to Paris (1627) at the request of Louis XIII, V. painted in a broad, elegant, decorative style. At Fontainebleau (1644) and in the Palais Royale, Paris (1643–47), V. established a formula of mannerist Roman baroque which dominated the French school for a century. In illusionism V. relates to Correggio and Tiepolo, though his portraits are harshly realistic. He influenced profoundly Eustache LeSueur, Pierre and Nicholas Mignard, and Charles Le Brun.

[M. J. DALY]

VOWEL POINTS. Since neither the Syriac nor the Hebrew alphabet contains any vowel signs, systems of points and other minute signs arranged in patterns were devised to indicate what the vowel sounds of the scriptural text should be. These vowel points were grouped round the letters of the original consonantal text without disturbing the existing order of the letters. It is probable that the Hebrew "Tiberian" system devised by the Masoretes was influenced by earlier Syriac systems. *MASORA.

[D. J. BOURKE]

VOWS, as understood in Catholic theology, promises made to God. Vows in this sense were familiar to the first Jewish Christians (Act 18.18; 21.23) but, while dedicated virginity was "a way of life" from earliest times, public vows which constituted one in a permanent state did not appear during the first 3 centuries. From the time of St. Basil (d. 379), entrance into religious life after a period of trial was viewed as a lasting commitment. The early monk was "vowed to the monastic life" with the reality if not the name of the three vows. Beginning with St. Benedict (d. after 546), entrants to the monastery "read before all" a promise of "stability, obedience, and *conversio morum*." Until the 13th cent., the religious life generally was founded on this type of single promise to live according to the rule of a community. Meanwhile, private vows as, e.g., the vow to make a pilgrimage, grew common. With Innocent III, "poverty, chastity, and obedience" had become "essential to the religious life," and to render private vows more sacred, their dispensation was limited to episcopal authority. At the time of the Reformation, Wycliffe, Luther, and Calvin declared vows to be void, esp. the vows of the religious life because they thought them derogatory to faith and to baptism; this teaching was rejected by the Council of Trent (D 1622), and popes and Vatican Council II have emphasized the value of vows in the pursuit of Christian perfection and for the good of human society (D 3345). This derives from its excellence as an act of religion, committing a human good to the service of God (ThAq ST 2a2ae, 88.5); for instance, the vow of poverty dedicates to him one's right to personal possessions and the use of material goods.

An act done under vow, considered as a type of act without making individual comparisons, at once proceeds from and promotes a greater subjection to God than the same sort of act not done under vow. Since it calls for a deeper resolve to dedicate a whole series (often a whole lifetime) of acts to God than to perform one or several or many taken singly, a vow is seen as producing a *status*, an established condition of commitment to God persisting throughout the vicissitudes of life. Vows, of course, are implicit in the sacraments of baptism and matrimony, and therefore belong to the Christian life for all. In addition the Church encourages, though with care and prudence, the taking of vows, not as ends, but as instruments to deepen and extend our friendship with God and our neighbor. Christian perfection, however, does not lie in them, but in charity: the classical theological teaching is clear on the point (cf. ThAq ST 2a2ae, 184). The ''state of perfection'' constituted by the vows is little more than a canonical category.

Public vows, those witnessed and attested by religious superiors for the Church, are either solemn or simple. Authorities do not agree on what constitutes the difference. Their legal effects, however, are certainly different. Solemn vows have the canonical effect of rendering certain commitments opposed to the vows invalid as well as illicit, whereas simple vows render such commitments illicit but not invalid. All vows are considered binding in conscience, and to break a vow is an offense against religion, grave or not so serious as the case may be. BIBLIOGRAPHY: Vat II RenRelLife, 1, 5, 12–14; E. C. Butler, *Benedictine Monachism* (1924; repr. 1961); P. F. Mulhern, NCE 14:756–58.

[P. F. MULHERN]

VOYSEY, CHARLES (1828–1912), theist. V. was ordained in the C of E and after holding several curacies served as vicar of Healaugh (1864–71) until his removal from office because of his heterodox views. He withdrew to London and founded the Theistic Church. BIBLIOGRAPHY: D. Wright, DNB 1912–21, 545–546.

[M. J. SUELZER]

VRAU, PHILIBERT (1829–1905), French industrialist and philanthropist. After a university education he went to work in his father's factory in Lille, at that time a rapidly expanding industrial center. Under his management the factory prospered, but V. devoted most of his energies to charitable and religious activities intended to make Lille a ''holy city.'' He helped establish several schools, a seminary, the Univ. of Lille, and a variety of religious societies. While he was president of the Council of the St. Vincent de Paul Society, 161 new chapters were established. He undertook to organize and gained the approbation of Pope Leo XIII for the first Eucharistic Congress, which met in Lille, June 28–30, 1881. V. was also a major supporter of the Catholic press in France; and when the Assumptionists were dissolved in 1900, his Assumptionist nephew, Paul Feron-Vrau, assumed editorship of the Vrau newspapers *La Croix* and the *Bonne Presse*. BIBLIOGRAPHY: A. Mabille de Poncheville, *Deux maîtres d'oeuvre, Philibert Vrau Camille Feron-Vrau*, (1945).

[R. J. GIBBONS]

VULGATE, the principal Latin version of the Bible, done or supervised chiefly by St. Jerome between 383 and 405; the name comes from the 13th-cent. reference to this text as the *editio vulgata,* the edition in general use. After an initial period of opposition, the Vulgate from the time of Charlemagne (*c.*742–814) onwards, came to replace all earlier Latin translations as the official version of the RC Church. Its authoritative status was formally declared and decreed by the Council of Trent in 1546 (D 1506). The work of translation was achieved in stages. In 383–384 St. Jerome, at the wish of Pope St. Damasus, revised the *Old Latin Gospels and Psalms based on the Septuagint (see PSALTER, ROMAN). Jerome's work at this stage was based on better Greek MSS of the NT than those employed, *c.*406, by the unknown revisors of the Pauline epistles, and the rest of the NT.

At Bethlehem, (*c.*385–389) Jerome, basing himself on Origen's *Hexapla, undertook an initial revision of Job, 1–2 Chron, Pr, S of S, and a further revision of Psalms. Most of this work was immediately lost or stolen, but the revision of Psalms is the one incorporated into the Vulgate, and became the official liturgical version throughout practically the whole Latin Church (see PSALTER, GALLICAN). In the years 390–405, dissatisfied with his attempts at revising the *Old Latin version on the basis of the Septuagint, Jerome finally undertook a completely new translation of the protocanonical books of the OT from the original Hebrew. In this he was most successful in the historical books and Job; in the prophetic books his renderings tend to be excessively literal, while Ec and S of S are less polished. He left most of the *deuterocanonical books (which he regarded as apocryphal) in the Old Latin, except for Jdt and Tob, of which he produced somewhat hasty and careless translations. His third version of the Psalter, though of high quality, failed to replace the Gallican Psalter as part of the Vulgate (see PSAL-TERIUM JUXTA HEBRAEOS).

The problems of preserving the Vulgate text from corruption, great even in Jerome's own lifetime, prompted attempts to standardize the text by *Cassiodorus, *Alcuin, and in the 13th cent. by the *Exemplar* of the Univ. of Paris and the *correctoria* of the mendicant friars. The authentic edition commissioned by Trent was published under Sixtus V in 1590, but proved to be full of errors; a revised edition was issued under Clement VIII, 1592–93. This corrected normative edition, known as the Sisto-Clementine Vulgate, has been under critical revision since 1907, and its completion is in the care of the Benedictines of San Girolamo in Rome.

The Vulgate shows the work of a skilled and elegant Latinist who had learned Hebrew well and worked from very early and generally very good MS sources. This fact alone gives it a permanent value as an independent witness to the original texts. Further, because of its universal adoption and use over many centuries by the Latin Church, its influence on the development of theology and liturgy was enormous. BIBLIOGRAPHY: *Novum Testamentum Latine secundum editionem S. Hieronymi I–II* (ed. J. Wordsworth and H. J. White et al., 1889–1954); S. Berger, *Histoire de* la *Vulgate pendant les premiers siècles du moyen-âge* (1893); *Biblia Sacra Vulgatae editionis: Editio emendatissima a cura Monachorum O.S.B.* (1959); *Bibliorum Sacrorum juxta Vulgatam Clementinam nova editio,* (ed. A Gramatica, 1951); B. J. Roberts, *Old Testament Text and Versions* (1951), 260–262; B. M. Peebles, NCE 2:439–457.

[D. J. BOURKE]

VULPES, ANGELO (d. 1647), Italian theologian. He is the author of a compendious Scotistic Mariological work entitled *Sacrae theologiae summa Ioannis Duns Scoti . . . et Commentaria quibus eius doctrina elucidatur, comprobatur, defenditur.*

[P. J. HENNESSEY]

VYSHENSKY, IVAN (d. *c.*1625), Ukrainian polemical writer. An Orthodox monk of Mt. Athos, he opposed union with the Catholic Church in his writings, most of which were not published till the 19th century.

[P. J. HENNESSEY]

W

WAAL, ANTON MARIA DE (1836–1917), German archeologist. After gaining the doctorate in theology in Rome (1869), W. became rector of the Teutonic College of Santa Maria in Camposanto (1873) which he reorganized as a house for priests, esp. those pursuing studies in Christian archeology and history. He devoted much time to the spiritual welfare of Germans in Italy, founding several societies for that work. His fame as an archeologist derives chiefly from his excavations under the basilica of St. Sebastian on the Via Appia. Besides publishing numerous monographs, W. founded two scholarly periodicals: the *Römische Quartalschrift* (1887) and *Oriens Christianus* (1901). BIBLIOGRAPHY: F. Chiovaro, NCE 14:761; J. Gugumus, LTK 10:904–905.

[R. B. ENO]

WACH, JOACHIM (1898–1955), philosopher and sociologist of religion. A native of Germany, W. was professor of the history of religions at the Univ. of Leipzig (1929–35), at Brown Univ. (1935–45), and the Univ. of Chicago (1945–55). W. made significant contributions to the science of religion and the sociology of religion. His approach was comparative, psychological, and sociological. He studied the history of hermeneutics and the empirical aspects of religion; of religion in the rapport of the religious community with ultimate reality as reflected in its religious awareness; of sociology as it reveals the interaction of religion and society. Among his many published works were *Religionswissenschaft: Prolegomena zu ihrer . . . Grundlegung* (1924), *Sociology of Religion* (1944), and *Comparative Study of Religions* (1958).

[J. R. AHERNE]

WADDING, LUKE (1588–1657), Franciscan historian, theologian, and diplomat. Forced by the Penal Laws to leave his native Ireland, he went to Portugal where he became a Franciscan, completed his theological studies, and was ordained a priest. After establishing a reputation for his linguistic ability and learning as lector of theology at León and Salamanca in Spain, he was elected to accompany the Spanish mission to Rome requesting the definition of the Immaculate Conception. He remained at Rome for the rest of his life, devoting his energies and talents to promoting the works of the Church, his order, his province, and the Irish cause. He founded St. Isidore's College for Irish Franciscans, the Ludovisian College for Irish secular clergy, and a novitiate at Capranica. He served five terms as guardian at St. Isidore's; was vice procurator general of the order and vice commissary; a consultor for the Congregations of the Propaganda, Holy Office, Index, and Sacred Rites. Through his efforts the feast of St. Patrick on March 17 was extended to the universal Church. An ardent patriot, as agent and procurator for the Irish Confederation, he collected money and supplies and obtained papal sympathy and support for their cause. A prolific writer, W. compiled, edited and published more than 50 volumes in his lifetime. Beginning his literary career for the purpose of vindicating and restoring the Franciscan reputation for scholarship, he collected and published the first complete and annotated edition of *The Writings of St. Francis*, the first complete and annotated edition of the works of *Duns Scotus, a biography of Scotus, and a bibliography of Franciscan authors (Scriptores Ordinis Minorum) with its syllabus of Franciscan martyrs and confessors. His greatest literary achievement, which established him internationally as a scholar and the greatest Franciscan historian, was his *Annales Ordinis Minorum*, a history of the order from the time of St. Francis until 1540. This monumental work, first published in 8 large volumes and divided into 16 by subsequent editors, is one of the finest works of its kind. W. declined ecclesiastical honors and died revered as much for his deep piety as for his profound learning. BIBLIOGRAPHY: *Father Luke Wadding; Commemorative Volume* (ed. Franciscan Father, 1957); G. Cleary, *Father Luke Wadding and St. Isidore's College, Rome* (1925).

[D. A. MCGUCKIN]

WADHAMS, EDGAR PHILIP (1817–91), bishop. Born in upstate New York, W. left the Presbyterians to become an Episcopal seminarian, later laboring as a deacon. A student of the *Oxford Movement, he became a Catholic in 1846, studied for the priesthood, and was ordained for the diocese of Albany in 1850. Rector of the cathedral and vicar general of the diocese, he was consecrated first bp. of Ogdensburg in 1872. Under his direction, the new diocese grew in numbers and institutions such as schools, orphanages, a house for the aged, and a hospital. BIBLIOGRAPHY: C. A. Walworth, *Reminiscences of Edgar P. Wadhams* (1893).

[J. R. AHERNE]

WAFER BREAD, thin, round pieces of unleavened bread used for communion in many Western Churches, particularly the Roman Catholic. First referred to in the 12th cent., this size and shape became common as unleavened bread became customary in the West (from the 8th cent.) and as frequency of communion declined. Earlier practice (again recommended in the new Roman Missal) used a large loaf that was broken and shared by communicants, symbolizing their unity in Christ (cf. 1 Cor 10:16). The continued use of wafer bread has practicality and custom as its reasons; following the current liturgical recommendation of the loaf will restore the ancient tradition and enhance Eucharistic symbolism.

[J. DALLEN]

WAFFELAERT, GUSTAVE JOSEPH (1847–1931), Belgian theologian and spiritual writer. He taught moral theology at the major seminary of Bruges and became bp. of Bruges in 1894. He was author of *Tractatus theologici de virtutibus cardinalibus* (3 v., 1885–89), *De la science morale* (1894), and *Sur l'obligation en conscience des lois civiles* (1884). In 1896 W. founded the magazine *Collationes Brugenses*. In ascetical theology he published *Meditationes theologicae*, a series (1896–1905).

[J. R. AHERNE]

WAGGERL, KARL HEINRICH (1897–1973), Austrian novelist. W. was a teacher but World War I and his experience as a prisoner of war damaged his health and he had to abandon teaching. He turned to writing novels, which portray the Austrian Alpine village where he lived. The novels are reflective of the little but not uneventful life of the village, a microcosm of the larger human experience. He was Catholic, realist, but also idealist in his approach. The much-appreciated novels *Brot* (1930), *Das Jahr des Herrn* (1934), and *Mütter* (1938) treat of children, of the liturgical year as it measures the life of the villager, and of man's free will. While not blind to the dark forces at work in life, W. brought to his work humor and compassion.

[J. R. AHERNE]

WAGNER, LIBORIUS (1593–1631), German Catholic martyr. Converted by the Jesuits at Würzburg and ordained

(1625), he worked in his first pastorate, began in 1626 near Schweinfurt to reclaim Catholics from Protestantism. Captured during the Swedish invasion of the Thirty Years' War, when he refused to recant his faith, he was tortured and killed.

[R. J. LITZ]

WAHHABIS (Arab. *wahhâbî*), a fundamentalist reform movement in *Islam. Basically of *Hanbalite inspiration, the movement was initiated in the Arabian Peninsula by Mohammed ibn 'Abd al-Wahhâb (1703–87) from whom it takes its name. His principal aim was to restore Islam to its primitive purity by eliminating all innovations introduced after the 3d cent. A.H. (*anno Hegirae*; see HEGIRA); among the chief elements in the program was the total elimination of the cult of the saints, which had been widely spread through the influence of the Sufi congregations. Despite widespread opposition from the *ulema, Ibn 'Abd al-Wahhâb gained strong support in Arabia from Mohammed ibn Su 'ûd (d. 1765) and his son 'Abd al-'Azîz whose forces helped spread the movement in Arabia and later, in the 19th cent., into Syria and Iraq; but in the face of strong opposition from religious authorities and from the Ottoman government the Wahhabi dynasty was able to maintain its sway only in Arabia. The movement spread also to India in the first half of the 19th cent. where the jihad was the central element of its program, but through want of broad popular support in established Muslim communities it had little lasting importance. At the beginning of the 20th cent., with the establishment of the kingdom of Saudi Arabia by the family that had supported the movement since its inception, Wahhabi doctrine became official for most of Arabia. BIBLIOGRAPHY: H. St. John Philby, *Arabia* (1930).

[R. M. FRANK]

WAILING WALL (Western Wall, Heb. *Kotel Maaravi*), all that remains intact of the western supporting wall of the Jerusalem Temple Mount since the destruction of the Second Temple (70 A.D.). The wall has been a Jewish religious site since 135 A.D. when, with the failure of the *Bar Kokhba revolt, the walls of the temple were all that remained for the Jews in diaspora. By *c.*1520 the Wall reached its prominent place in Jewish tradition when it was uncovered and opened to Jews as a place to pray, in keeping with the Midrash, "The Divine Presence never departs from the Western Wall," though that reference more likely refers symbolically to the ruined wall of the Holy of Holies. In modern times the wall has come to represent the continued relationship of a suffering people and their God through prayer. Much of the wall, which was originally 1,580 ft long, remained hidden by surrounding structures; its accessible portion is now about 160 ft and it is 60 ft high. The base remains buried, and at its lowest levels rests on bedrock of the Tyropoeon Valley; other levels date to the Second Temple, over which is a Roman layer from Hadrian's time, and finally some Arab stonework from after the 7th century. Arab-Israeli hostilities have often restricted access to the wall, which adjoins the Haram es-Sherif, a Muslim holy site.

[R. J. LITZ]

WAKE, WILLIAM (1657–1737), abp. of Canterbury from 1716. W. experienced the flood tide of Gallicanism as chaplain to the English ambassador in Paris (1682–85). On returning to England he held several important posts before being named abp. of Canterbury. Liberal and ecumenical, he sought the union of the C of E with the French Church, but without success. He also befriended English Nonconformists. Among his many writings a history of English synods (1703) is the most important. BIBLIOGRAPHY: N. Sykes, *William Wake* (2 v. 1957).

[M. J. SUELZER]

WAKE, a vigil of God's word celebrated for the deceased on a day or days before the body is brought to the church for the funeral Mass. Called one of the "stations" of the rite in the 1970 Rite of Funerals, it may be held at the home or the funeral parlor and even in the church, but then separately from the funeral itself. In the past the common prayer at a wake was the Rosary; the new ritual prescribes (nn. 26–29) a psalm, scripture reading, optional homily, prayers of intercession, the Lord's Prayer particularly. BIBLIOGRAPHY: *Rites of the Catholic Church* (1976) pp. 662–666.

[T. C. O'BRIEN]

WALA, ST. (*c*.755–836), Benedictine abbot and statesman, leader of church reform and promoter of an imperial unity independent of the personalities of the rulers. Cousin of Charlemagne, brother of the Abbot Adelard and St. Ida of Herzfeld, and educated at the palace school, W. served under Charlemagne and Louis the Pious before entering the abbey of Corbie. In England he helped found Corvey and Herford, succeeded his brother Adelard as abbot of Corbie, and consistently played the role of mediator in crises in the imperial family, once enduring exile for opposition to the Empress Judith. From 833 until his death, he was abbot of Bobbio. His remains were translated to Herford in 1060. Only a minor cult developed in the Middle Ages.

[E. J. DILLON]

WALAFRID STRABO (*c*.808–849), abbot, theologian, poet, prominent figure of the Carolingian Renaissance. Educated at the monastery of Reichenau and later under Rabanus Maurus at Fulda, W. became tutor for Charles the Bald and was rewarded for his services by being made abbot of Reichenau (838). He fell into disfavor and was forced to flee because of his support of Lothair I, but in 842 was restored to his abbey where he remained for the rest of his life. His *De exordiis* is a valuable source of information regarding the religious views and liturgical practices of his time. He advocated a moderate veneration of images, explained the ceremonies then in use, saw value in the use of the vernacular in worship, favored the daily celebration of Mass by priests, and described the position of the pope in the structure of the Church. But he is best known for his poetry, which is remarkable for its simplicity and its mastery of intricate forms. His *Visio Wettini,* a poem describing the vision granted to the monk Wettin of a journey through the other world, is the earliest Christian example of that literary theme. His *Hortulus* is a collection of poems on the plants and flowers of his monastery garden. He was formerly credited with the composition of the *Glossa ordinaria* so widely used during the Middle Ages in the study of the text of Scripture, but recent scholarship has shown that little, if indeed any, of it is directly attributable to him. Works: PL 113, 114. Crit. ed. of his verse, MGH Poetae 2 (1884) 259–473. BIBLIOGRAPHY: M. F. McCarthy, NCE 14:768–769; H. Peltier, DTC 15.2:3498–3505.

[M. S. TANEY]

WALARICH, ST. (Valéry; d. 619), hermit. Educated at the monastery of Automnon (Auvergne), he later went to the monastery of Saint-Germain d'Auxerre. From there he was drawn to Luxeuil by the renown of St. Columban. When Theodoric expelled St. Columban, W. set out on a mission to Neustria, where he lived as a hermit. In time the abbey of Leuconay grew up around him, which, with the adjacent town, took his name (Saint-Valéry) in the 9th century. BIBLIOGRAPHY: Butler 2:1–2.

[G. M. COOK]

WALBURGA OF HEIDENHEIM, ST. (*c*.710–779), Anglo-Saxon missionary to Germany, Benedictine abbess, one of the most popular medieval saints, patroness of the sick and esp. of those with affliction of the eyes. She was raised at Wimborne in Dorsetshire, S England and died at Heidenheim, Germany. Each year from October 12 to February 25 oil flows from a deposit on a stone slab near her relics in Eichstätt, is collected in small bottles, and sent upon request to various places as a kind of sacramental to be used with the prayers of the sick for healing. W. (also called Walpurg, Waldburga, Walburg, Waldburgis, and Waldpurgis) went to Germany at the invitation of St. Boniface, entered the double monastery at Heidenheim, and succeeded her sister, St. Winnebald, as abbess. Her long rule was marked by a practical compassion. She esp. favored the education of women.

[E. J. DILLON]

WALDECK, FRANZ VON (1491–1553), count and bp. who favored the Reformation. W. sought to establish a duchy out of the three sees that he held simultaneously, Minden (from 1531), Münster, and Osnabrück (from 1532). To this end he openly favored the Reformers but was thwarted by the cathedral chapters, and the dioceses remained Catholic. During the Anabaptist uprisings at Münster (1533–35), W. besieged and eventually recaptured the city. BIBLIOGRAPHY: H. Börsting, LTK 10:933; bibliog. for Anabaptists.

[T. C. O'BRIEN]

WALDECK-ROUSSEAU, PIERRE MARIE RENÉ (1846–1904), French statesman. During his premiership (1899–1902) France's foreign policy was adventurous, and anticlerical legislation was enacted. The anticlerical policy was supported by the reaction to the Dreyfus affair. Authorized religious congregations were put under state supervision and unauthorized ones made illegal. BIBLIOGRAPHY: D. W. Brogan, *France under the Third Republic, 1870–1939* (1940).

[J. P. REID]

WALDENSES, a body of Christians with origins in southern France in the 12th cent. Historians disregard the claim that the Waldenses go back to apostolic times. They were founded by *Waldo, a merchant of Lyons, who *c.*1170 gave his wealth to his relatives and began a life of evangelical poverty. His followers, who were also called Poor Men of Lyons, *Pauperes Christi, Leonistae, Pauperes spiritu,* and *Insabbatati,* observed strict poverty and preached against the wealth and laxity of the clergy. They were approved in 1179 by Pope Alexander III with the proviso that they obtain authorization from local clergy before preaching. For not complying with this condition they were condemned (1184) by Pope Lucius III and later (1215) by Lateran Council IV. In 1211 more than 80 of them were burned as heretics at Strassburg. Waldensian teaching was similar to that of other medieval lay dissenters. Clerics have no special right to speak in God's name. All Christians can preach since each is a depositary of the Holy Spirit. Only Waldenses preserve the ideals of primitive Christianity, and the Church is the community of Satan. The efficacy of the sacraments depends on the sanctity of the ministers; and the practice of poverty empowers a person to administer all sacraments. Purgatory, indulgences, fasting, and the cult of the saints are to be rejected. Each Holy Thursday the Waldenses celebrated the Lord's Supper in a simple rite, but they did not believe in the Real Presence. Worship services consisted of scriptural readings, sermons, and the Lord's Prayer. Some of their beliefs and practices were borrowed from the *Cathari. Like the Cathari, they were divided into Perfecti and simple believers. The former were celibates who eschewed manual labor and went about as mendicant preachers. The believers were married, and worked to provide for the material needs of the Perfecti. The ministers (*barbes,* uncles) came from the ranks of the Perfecti. At times to avoid persecution Waldenses remained outwardly faithful to the Church. Their modest way of life made them liked by the common people, but their popularity waned with the founding of the Franciscan and Dominican Orders in the 13th cent. In spite of repressive measures against them, the Waldenses survived through the centuries, esp. in remote places. In 1532 they subscribed to some Protestant doctrines; and with the passing of time most adopted Calvinistic theology. In the 17th cent. they were persecuted in RC territories. Napoleon granted them toleration; and in 1848 the Duke of Savoy, in whose domain most of them then lived, gave them full political and religious liberty. The modern Waldenses number about 30,000, almost all of them in Italy. Since the 19th cent. they have conducted a vigorous program of evangelization in Italy and have established a theological school in Rome. BIBLIOGRAPHY: L. Cristiani, EncCatt 12:966–970; Y. Dossat, NCE 14:770–771 with bibliog.

[J. E. LYNCH]

WALDENSTRÖM, PAUL PETER (1838–1917), Swedish Protestant religious leader, writer, and editor. Born in Luleå, he became a convert to a north-Swedish pietist movement similar to the Moravian brethren and influenced by Carl Olof Rosenius Erwecker. W. was a pastor, 1864–82, of the Swedish Church, from 1868 editor of a pietist periodical, and member of parliament, 1884–1905. He wrote many popular inspirational articles. From 1872 he was taken with the problem of reconciliation with God; the realization that his notion of sin was incompatible with orthodox Lutheran notions together with his notion of the Church as fundamentally congregational led to his formal break with the Lutheran Church in 1878, and his support of the establishment of a Swedish Free Church. From 1905 he was the leader of this Church.

[E. J. DILLON]

WALDETRUD, ST., 7th-cent. Belgian holy woman, wife and mother of four, founding abbess of a cloister she had built in Castrilocus in Monte. Around it developed the abbey and town of Mons in the Diocese of Cambrai, Belgium. Her parents were St. Bertilia and St. Walbert, Count of Hainaut; her sister was St. Aldegund, founding abbess of Maubeuge. W. married St. Vincent Madelgarius and her four children entered the cloister and became saints. Her husband retired to Hautmont Abbey, which he had founded, and she retired to Castrilocus in Monte. She is the patroness of Mons and her relics are found in the church named after her there.

[E. J. DILLON]

WALDO (Valdes, Valdesius; d. *c.*1215), wealthy Lyonnaise merchant, founder of the Poor Men of Lyons, or *Waldenses. Little is known about his personal life. Partly as a result of his study of the Gospels, which he had had translated into Provençal, he experienced a spiritual conversion in 1176. In imitation of St. Alexis he left his family, gave his goods to the poor, and took a vow of poverty. As an itinerant preacher he waged a vigorous campaign against worldliness in the Church. His way of life was approved by Alexander III in 1179, but he was forbidden to preach. He ignored this prohibition and was condemned as a heretic by Lucius III in 1184. Nothing is known of his life after that event. From 1368 he was referred to as Peter Waldo by the Waldenses. BIBLIOGRAPHY: L. Cristiani, EncCatt 12:966–970; F. Hayward, *Inquisition* (1965) 29–31; H. Daniel-Rops, *Cathedral and Crusade* (1957) 524–527.

[C. J. LYNCH]

WALDRON, JOHN A. (1859–1937), educator. A native of Ohio, W. entered the Marianists. He was a teacher and writer on educational topics whose chief influence was exerted through the service to, and publications of, Catholic educational associations. From 1906 to 1922 he contributed frequently to the *Bulletin* of the Catholic Educational Association, predecessor to the National Catholic Educational Association, and served as one of the officers of both groups as well as of the executive board of the Department of Education National Catholic Welfare Conference, after 1919. From 1929 to 1937 he was one of the editors of the *Catholic School Journal*.

[J. R. AHERNE]

WALDSASSEN, ABBEY OF, Cistercian abbey, Diocese of Regensburg, Bavaria, Germany; founded *c.*1133 by Margrave Diepold III of Vohburg with monks from Volkenrode in Thuringia. It was granted imperial immunity in 1147 and in turn founded and colonized Sedletz and Ossegg in Bohemia. Called ''prince abbot'' in a charter of Emperor Sigismund in 1434, the abbots took part in imperial diets. Protestant in 1559, secularized in 1571, the abbey was restored by Fürstenfeld Abbey in 1669 and then suppressed in 1803. Cistercian nuns from Seligenthal in Landshut purchased the cloister buildings in 1863 and it became an abbey again in 1925, with both an elementary and a secondary girls' school. BIBLIOGRAPHY: Cottineau 2:3428–29.

[E. J. DILLON]

WALES. The Roman Empire effectively controlled the routes into Wales by the 2d cent. with one legion to the N and another to the S, yet there is nothing to connect Roman rule or the legendary flight of the defeated Britons from the heathen Anglo-Saxons with the coming of Christianity. The country was evangelized by Celtic monks, and by the 5th cent., despite the turbulence of the times, was completely Christian. St. Dewi, or David, the patron saint of Wales, represents a golden age of saints, of monasticism, and of a religious literature among the oldest in Europe, the memory of which, together with a natural sacramentalism that made much of holy shrines and wells, still survives in the national consciousness. Though the Welsh do not warm to the Irish, their kin to the West, their fight has always been with the English from the East. Devoted to Rome, they resented their allegiance's being mediated through Canterbury as it came to be when the Normans' civil and ecclesiastical structures were expanded all over England and Wales. It would, however, be a mistake to picture this as a clash between two national or primatial Churches; it was more between two cultures and disciplines. The Welsh were loosely grouped around houses of monks and hermits; the Anglo-Norman were more tightly organized in territorial parishes and dioceses.

Political nationalism was then no great force, and there was no question of treating the Welsh as a subject people. Their princes could treat on terms of equality with the Lords of the Marches, though eventually they were to be defeated, or more often absorbed. The Welsh bowmen were the decisive arm in the English victories in France during the 100 Years' War. The Cistercian and Dominican outposts of Plantagenet power entered into the feelings of the people about them. Wales was a recruiting ground for the Lancastrians as it was 2 centuries later for the Stuarts, and a Welsh dynasty, the Tudors, ruled in England and Wales for more than a century.

That was when the Reformation came. The Welsh priests were not the same stuff as of old, and lay control had caused grave abuses. The Elizabethan settlement was on the whole equally assented to, and the more easily because it brought a Welsh prayer book (1567) and Bible (1588). Active Catholics went into exile, and if they came back it was often to work in England. It seems that except in pockets to the NE and SE where the gentry remained faithful to the old religion, Catholicism starved to death for lack of priests. Yet it cannot be claimed that the Established Church filled the void. By the 18th cent. it had grown rather formal and an extension of an anglicized squirearchy. Puritan devotion, however, was slow in making a start, and it was not until the Methodist movement that a large part of the Welsh were touched by its enthusiasm. For a long time there was no thought of secession, but partly from the coldness of vested ecclesiastical interests and partly from the desire of the lay preachers to be given sacramental office, the ''connection'' became in 1811 a dissenting denomination which ordained its own ministers. It rejected Arminianism and was called Calvinistic Methodism. Dissent or ''chapel,'' now greatly outnumbered ''Church,'' i.e., Anglicans; with its evangelical piety and choral singing, it presents the most characteristic feature of Welsh religious life.

The Anglican Church was disestablished and disendowed in 1919 to its own content and prosperity; it is named the Church in Wales. The industrialization of the southern valleys brought in large numbers of Irish, and these, together with other immigrants, have formed the Catholic Archdiocese of Cardiff with well over 100,000 people and its more scattered suffragan see of Menevia. One result of the revival of Welsh nationalism, particularly in university and literary circles, has been to look back to the Catholic roots of the national culture.

[T. GILBY]

WALES, CHURCH IN, see CHURCH IN WALES.

WALES, MARTYRS OF, see MARTYRS OF ENGLAND AND WALES.

WALFRID, ST., (d. *c.*765), founding abbot of the Benedictine abbey of St. Peter, Palazzuolo. Born in Pisa of the noble family Gherardesca, he became a prosperous citizen of that city. He and his wife Thesia had five sons and at least one daughter. Later in life W. and his wife decided to withdraw from secular life and live under monastic discipline.

He helped found (754) the monastery for men at Palazzuolo, near Monte Verde in Tuscany and another foundation nearby for women, including wives of those who had become monks. A daughter and one son also entered the cloister, the son succeeding W. as abbot. His biography was written by the son of the man who helped him found his monastery. His cult was approved in 1861.

[E. J. DILLON]

WALL, JOHN, ST. (1620–79), English martyr. After studies and ordination on the Continent and a brief return in England, W. became a Franciscan at Douai (1651). He left for England in 1656 where he labored as a missionary for more than 20 years. With the Oates Plot he was imprisoned in Worcester Castle and then examined by the Privy Council. Though proved innocent of conspiracy, he was condemned for his priesthood (1679) and executed at Worcester. He was canonized in 1970.

[V. SAMPSON]

WALL OF SEPARATION, a phrase used to symbolize the "establishment of religion" clause in the First Amendment to the U.S. Constitution. Jefferson used the expression in 1802. It was cited by Chief Justice Waite in 1878 (*Reynolds v. U.S.*), 98 U.S. 145 but did not affect the decision. The first direct appeal to the phrase in a case was *Everson v. School Board*, 330 U.S. 1,16,18 (1947), which ruled that reimbursing parents of parochial school children for bus transportation was permissible. Quoting the Jefferson reference to a wall of separation, Justice Black gave a clear interpretation of what the phrase meant constitutionally. Through *McCollum v. Board of Education*, 333 U.S. 203,212 (1948) and *Zorach v. Clarison*, 343 U.S. 306 (1952) the "wall of separation" concept became more sharply defined. In spite of the reference, *Tilton v. Richardson*, 403 U.S. 672 (1971) showed the Court to be making a distinction between federal support for secular purposes in four Catholic colleges and support for religion and so to be deciding that federal aid for nonreligious aspects of the institutions was constitutional. There has been criticism of applying the "wall of separation" metaphor to juridic decisions. Members both of the Supreme Court and constitutional authorities contend that the intent of the First Amendment was not to support either secularism or organized religion. *CHURCH AND STATE.

[J. R. AHERNE]

WALLENSTEIN, ALBRECHT WENZEL VON (1583–1634), military leader, statesman. Colorful and enigmatic, W. was one of the most influential generals and political figures of the 16th and 17th cent. in Europe. Though sometimes regarded as a hero in the Catholic cause, he was self-serving and could change sides whenever it was to his advantage. Seldom has a leader been so dominated by venality. Born of Protestant parents in what is now Czechoslovakia, W. became a Catholic in 1606. He made an advan-

tageous marriage with a wealthy Czech widow in 1609. Establishing a lifelong pattern, W. outfitted a mercenary force to aid Emperor Ferdinand II in the war against Venice. Repeating this course when the Bohemian noble revolted against the Habsburgs in 1618, W. emerged with great profit. He was named governor of the kingdom of Bohemia, issuer of coins for Bohemia, Moravia, and Austria, and soon after made a member of the Estate of Princes and finally Duke of Friedland (1625). In that year W. was made commander of Imperial Forces in the Holy Roman Empire and the Low Countries. Raising an army of 70,000 men, W. defeated the Hungarians and Danes. As a reward he was appointed Duke of Mecklenburg, a hereditary fief, in 1629. At this point, W. ceased to be the loyal supporter of the Habsburgs and set out on his own political policy, which included negotiating with Protestant States and disapproval of the *Edict of Restitution (1629) whereby Ferdinand attempted to force restoration of ecclesiastical lands where Protestantism had been established after 1552. The Diet of Regensburg in 1630 forced the Emperor to dismiss Wallenstein. When his successor as commander-in-chief, the Bavarian Tilly, was defeated, Ferdinand had to restore W. to his old position as commander. After initial successes against Gustavus Adolphus of Sweden, W. was defeated at Lutzen in 1632. The Emperor was now free to punish W. as a traitor. His intrigues with other States failing and many of his trusted officers deserting his cause, W. was assassinated in 1634 by soldiers under the command of the Irish general Walter Butler. BIBLIOGRAPHY: L. Von Ranke, *Geschichte Wallensteins* (1869).

[J. R. AHERNE]

WALLINGFORD WILLIAM (d.1492), Benedictine monk, abbot of St. Albans (1476–92). Worldly and not above financial roguery, he was charged in 1490 with simony, usury, wasting the goods of his house, and other crimes and excesses. At St. Albans his building work included the erection of an altar screen and the completion of the chapter house. BIBLIOGRAPHY: Emden Ox 3:1967–68.

[C. D. ROSS]

WALPOLE, HENRY, ST. (1558–95), English martyr. Educated for law, W. was converted to Catholicism and became a Jesuit priest on the Continent. After serving in Lorraine and the Netherlands and teaching at Seville and Valladolid, he was finally permitted to go to the English mission (1593). Within hours after debarking in Yorkshire, he was arrested, imprisoned for a year in the Tower of London (where he was repeatedly subjected to torture), and was then returned to Yorkshire for trial and execution. He was canonized in 1970. BIBLIOGRAPHY: G. Fitz Herbert, NCE 14:779–780.

[V. SAMPSON]

WALRAM OF NAUMBERG (d.1111), bishop. In the investiture struggle he was a supporter of the Emperor as expressed in certain letters (MGHLiblit 2:286–291), but under Paschal II he became reconciled to Rome. He is mentioned in undated letters of St. Anselm of Canterbury. BIBLIOGRAPHY: S. Williams, NCE 14:780.

[S. WILLIAMS]

WALSH, EDMUND ALOYSIUS (1885–1956), Jesuit educator, founder. A native of Boston, Mass., W. was ordained a Jesuit in 1916. In 1919 he founded the School of Foreign Service of Georgetown Univ. and was its regent for 34 years. He was associated with the American Famine Relief Mission to Russia in 1922 and became director-general of the Papal Relief Mission and a negotiator for Catholic interests with the Soviet leadership. He was a lifelong foe of communism. In 1926 he became president of the Catholic Near East Welfare Association. He worked with Dwight Morrow to achieve peace between the Mexican government and the Catholic Church. After World War II he acted as consultant to the chief American counsel in the war crimes trial at Nuremberg.

[J. R. AHERNE]

WALSH, GERALD GROVELAND (1892–1951). Born in Connecticut, he was educated in England and entered the Jesuits there in 1910. He was ordained in the U.S. in 1926. After 5 years at Woodstock, Md., as professor of church history, W. spent most of his career at Fordham Univ., New York City. From 1939 to 1949 he edited the quarterly, *Thought*. A historian and Dante scholar, W. wrote *Emperor Charles IV*, *Medieval Humanism*, and *Dante Alighieri*, coauthored *Philosophy of History* and *Great Religions of the Modern World*. In 1950 he was one of a group of scholars who initiated the series *The Apostolic Fathers*.

[J. R. AHERNE]

WALSH, JAMES ANTHONY (1867–1936) missionary, founder of Maryknoll, writer. Born in Cambridge, Mass. and educated for the priesthood in St. John's Seminary, Brighton, Mass., W. was ordained in 1892. His lifelong interest in the foreign missions found an outlet in 1903 when he became director of the diocesan branch of the Society for the Preservation of the Faith. He began publishing a lively mission magazine in 1907. W. achieved his hope for an American congregation for foreign missions when, with the North Carolina missioner Father Thomas *Price, he founded the Catholic Foreign Mission Society of America, which was approved by Rome in 1911. The society, soon to be known as the Maryknoll Fathers, chose a site near New York City as motherhouse, and W. became first superior. The first missionaries went to China in 1918. The society grew rapidly during W.'s lifetime, extending to Korea, Japan, Manchuria, the Philippines, and Hawaii. He was elected superior general in 1929 when Maryknoll adopted a permanent constitution; in 1933 he was named titular bishop. His influence on Maryknoll and in making the U.S. more mission conscious was extraordinary. In addition to a

constant stream of periodical writing, W. wrote several books, among them *A Modern Martyr* (1905), *Thoughts from Modern Martyrs* (1908), and *Observations in the Orient* (1919).

[J. R. AHERNE]

WALSH, JAMES JOSEPH (1866–1942), physician, writer. A native of Pennsylvania, W. received his M.D. from the Univ. of Pennsylvania in 1895. In 1907 he became acting dean and professor of neurology at Fordham University in New York City. His lectures on the history of medicine and the influence of mind on body were the first of their kind in American medical schools. Medical editor of the *New York Herald* and a contributing editor of the *Journal of the American Medical Association*, W. was also a prolific writer of books on medical, scientific, and Catholic subjects. *The Thirteenth, Greatest of Centuries* (1907) and *The Popes and Science* (1908) were widely read. He spoke out against religious prejudice and was a persistent foe of birth control.

[J. R. AHERNE]

WALSH, JOHN (1830–98), abp. of Toronto. Native of Ireland, W. came to Canada to study for the priesthood and was ordained for Toronto in 1854. Appointed vicar general in 1862, he participated in the Third Provincial Council of Quebec in 1863. Named bp. of Sandwich, Ontario, in 1867, he was invited to and attended the Third Plenary Council of Baltimore in 1884. W. was appointed abp. of Toronto in 1889, where he proved an able administrator.

[J. R. AHERNE]

WALSH, PETER (1615–88), Irish Franciscan priest, born to political intrigue, caught in the Church-State struggles of his time. After studying at Louvain, he taught philosophy and theology at Kilkenny, only to be suspended from preaching for supporting the opponents of the papal nuncio. He openly sided with the bps. and priests who resisted the nuncio's censure. During Puritan rule he was in hiding in England; in 1661 he was named procurator of the Irish clergy. Because of proven independence from Rome he was approached by a group of Anglo-Irish Catholics with the request that he present to Charles II on their behalf a statement of grievances and a petition for protection against persecution, along with a protestation of allegiance to the Crown. This last, called the Remonstrance, proved so offensive to Rome that W.'s defense of it eventually led to his excommunication in 1670. He was received back into communion before his death, after recanting and pledging allegiance to the Holy See.

[E. J. DILLON]

WALSH, WILLIAM, (1512–77), Irish bp. whose career reflects the tumult of the Reformation in England and Ireland. He was a Cistercian at Bective in Meath until forced to flee Ireland during the suppression of the monasteries under

Thomas Cromwell (1537). While in Rome in the capacity of chaplain to Card. Pole, he was able to transfer to the Augustinian Order, and in 1554, when Catholicism was restored in England under Mary I, Pole had W. appointed bp. of Meath. At Elizabeth's accession, he refused the oath of supremacy (1558) and opposed the introduction of the Elizabethan liturgy and the Book of Common Prayer. His status as bp. was successfully challenged in Rome, but he was reappointed by Pius IV in 1564. After being imprisoned in Dublin Castle, 1565–72, he somehow escaped to France and then to Spain, where he was suffragan to the abp. of Toledo. He died in Spain.

[E. J. DILLON]

WALSH, WILLIAM JOSEPH (1841–1921), abp. of Dublin, patriot, and theologian. Born in Dublin, he attended the Catholic Univ. of Dublin during Newman's rectorship, entered St. Patrick's College, Maynooth in 1858, continued there after his ordination in 1867 in the capacity first of professor, then vice president, and finally president. He intervened decisively in the movement for land tenure reform by exposing the abuses of the landlords before a commission appointed by Gladstone. As abp. from 1881 he firmly supported Home Rule and demanded that public funds be used to support training colleges and universities for Catholics. He was elected first chancellor of the National Univ. of Ireland. Generally he was able to interpret Irish problems to Roman officials who had always been too inclined to take the British ruling class's view of Ireland's social problems. W. was the champion of Irish peasants, the advocate of trade unions, women's suffrage, and their admission to the university and the professions. He objected to the Irish Government Bill of 1912 and denounced the partition of Ireland.

[E. J. DILLON]

WALSH, WILLIAM THOMAS (1891–1949), American Catholic journalist, educator, and author. An alumnus of Yale, he worked as a reporter in Philadelphia and Hartford, as well as in his home town of Waterbury, Connecticut. He was professor of English at Manhattanville College, (1933–47). His numerous books written during this latter period reflect a deep interest in Catholic life, esp. Spanish Catholic life, as his biographies of Isabella, Philip II, and St. Teresa of Ávila attest.

[E. J. DILLON]

WALSINGHAM, THOMAS, (*fl.* 1364–1422), English Benedictine and chronicler. Monk of St. Albans by 1364, later precentor and *scriptorarius* of the abbey, and briefly (1394–96) prior of the cell of Wymondham (Norfolk), he produced a series of voluminous chronicles, which form the most important source for English history from 1376 to 1422. Though his merits are chiefly those of the conscientious compiler, he was the last major medieval monastic chronicler. He also wrote a *Gesta abbatum*, a history of

Alexander, and other works. BIBLIOGRAPHY: *Annales Ricardi secundi* (ed. H. T. Riley, 1866); *St. Albans Chronicle, 1406–20* (ed. V. H. Galbraith, 1937).

[C. D. ROSS]

WALSINGHAM, MONASTERY OF, former priory of Canons Regular of St. Augustine in the small town of Walsingham in N Norfolk, at the site of the major shrine of Our Lady in medieval England. The widow Richelde de Fervaques built a copy of the Holy House at Nazareth there *c.*1120 and in 1153 her son Geoffrey established the priory to care for it. The statue of Our Lady was greatly venerated by royalty and other pilgrims, esp. from the 13th cent. on. When Henry VIII and Catherine of Aragon came there on pilgrimage in the early 16th cent., it was the most popular place of pilgrimage in England and the second richest monastery in Norfolk. The shrine was despoiled in 1538, the statue was sent to London and burned, and the priory was dissolved. In recent times pilgrimages to Walsingham, esp. of university students, have been revived. BIBLIOGRAPHY: Cottineau 2:3431.

[E. J. DILLON]

WALTER OF BIERBEEK (BIRBECK), BL. (d. *c.*1206), Cistercian monk. Born at Bierbeek (Birbeck) in Brabant of high nobility, W. served under Duke Henry the Lion until *c.*1182, when he joined the Cistercians at Himmerod (Germany). He was outstanding for his devotion to Mary and his charity to the poor. BIBLIOGRAPHY: M. A. Dimier, BiblSanct 7:423.

WALTER OF BRUGES (*c.*1225–1307), Franciscan theologian; bp. of Poitiers from 1279. He was a staunch defender of the teachings of St. Bonaventure, whose student he had been at Paris, and attacked Thomist departures from the traditional teaching of universal hylomorphism. He left an incomplete commentary on the *Sentences*; 36 *Quaestiones disputatae* were edited by E. Longpré in 1928.

[T. C. O'BRIEN]

WALTER OF CANTELUPE (d. 1266), English bp. and reformer. He was the second son of William, first baron of Cantelupe, the royal steward of King Henry III. Elected bp. of Worcester in 1236, W. appears between 1258 and 1265 as the chief spokesman of those bps. who supported Simon de Montfort's struggle to limit royal authority. He was also important in ecclesiastical reform.

[J. E. WRIGLEY]

WALTER OF CHÂTILLON (b. *c.*1135), humanist poet. He taught at Laon and then Châtillon-sur-Marne, and was also a canon at Reims. W. performed diplomatic service for Henry II of England and was later in the service of Abp. William of Reims (1176–1201) as *notarius* and *orator*. His writings include: the *Alexandreis*, an epic poem in 10 books which shows dependency on Quintus Curtius' history of

Alexander the Great, on Justinus and Josephus, and on Isidore's *Etymologies; Tractatus contra Judaeos; Georgica*, attributed to him, but now in doubt. BIBLIOGRAPHY: Manitius 3:920–936; W. C. Korfmacher, NCE 14:787–788 with bibliog.

[J. J. SMITH]

WALTER OF CHATTON (*c.*1285–1343), English Franciscan scholastic, theologian at the papal court of Avignon. He was at Oxford as master in 1322–23, possibly until 1330; in philosophy and theology he was a follower of Duns Scotus, an opponent of William of Ockham. At Avignon he participated in the *Poverty Controversy and in the formulation of a new Franciscan constitution in 1336. He was named by Clement VI bp. of St. Asaph, Wales, but while the incumbent was still alive, and W. never took possession of the see.

[T. C. O'BRIEN]

WALTER (GAUTIER) OF COINCY (1177–1236), French monk of the abbey of St. Médard, religious writer, best known for his writings on saints' lives and miracles. His collection of *exempla* called *Miracles de la Sainte Vierge* is the best known and achieved of all the ''Miracles de Notre Dame'' genre. Fifty-four miracles, totalling over 30,000 verses, present the most familiar of the miraculous traditions relating to the Virgin. W.'s work was used by Rutebeuf, Villon, Chaucer, and others. BIBLIOGRAPHY: M. J. Hamilton, NCE 14:788–789.

[J. P. WILLIMAN]

WALTER GIFFARD (d.1279), bp. of Bath and Wells (1265–66); abp. of York (1266–79); chancellor of England (1265–66). Brother to Godfrey, bp. of Worcester, W. studied at Oxford and Cambridge. When rebel barons under Simon de Montfort laid waste W.'s lands (1265), Abp. Boniface ordered their excommunication. As abp., W. revived the ancient dispute with Canterbury over primacy. BIBLIOGRAPHY: Emden Ox 2:762–763.

[R. W. HAYS]

WALTER DE GRAY (GREY; d. 1255), English ecclesiastic and politician, was chancellor of England 1205–13 and in 1214, and often acted for Henry III. He became bp. of Worcester (1214) and abp. of York (1216), where he was known for efficient administration, building, and initiation of successful record-keeping, but failed in attempts to assert primatial jurisdiction over Scotland. BIBLIOGRAPHY: Emden Ox 2:807–808.

[R. W. HAYS]

WALTER JORZ (Jorse, Jorsz, or Joyce; d. 1321), English Dominican, abp. of Armagh (1307–11). Brother of Card. *Thomas Jorz, W. was a graduate of Oxford who distinguished himself by his teaching and writing. Fined by Edward I for receiving consecration in Italy, he gave up his

see in favor of his brother Roland after a brief and turbulent tenure and became auxiliary bp. of Lincoln. BIBLIOGRAPHY: Quétif-Échard 1.2:513–514; Emden Ox 2:1023–24.

[J. A. WEISHEIPL]

WALTER MAP (*c.*1140–1209 or 1210), British satirical writer. After studying at Paris, he held minor English church offices, frequented Henry II's court, and attended the Third Lateran Council. His only surviving work, *De nugis curialium* (ed. T. Wright, Camden Society, 1850), is a valuable source for religious and political history. BIBLIOGRAPHY: R. W. Hays, NCE 14:789; G. Karp, LTK 6:1369.

[R. W. HAYS]

WALTER OF MERTON (d. 1277), bishop, chancellor, founder of Merton College, Oxford. A graduate of Oxford where he became the friend of Adam Marsh and Robert Grosseteste, he was chancellor of England (1261–63 and again 1272–74); he became bp. of Rochester in 1274. He founded (1264) Merton College, Oxford which set a pattern for the collegiate system followed since. BIBLIOGRAPHY: D. Nicholl, NCE 14:789–790.

[J. L. GRASSI]

WALTER OF MORTAGNE (*c.*1090–1174), bp. of Laon, theologian. His theology is contained in *Liber de Trinitate, De conjugio*, and ten extant letters on theological topics, including letters to Abélard and to Hugh of St. Victor. The two treatises mentioned became part of the *Summa sententiarum* formerly ascribed to Hugh.

[P. J. HENNESSEY]

WALTER OF POINTOISE, ST. (c. 1025–99), abbot. Although Walter (Gautier, Gualterius) succeeded in reforming his monastery, he was unhappy there either because of difficulties encountered in governing the community or because of a certain instability of temperament. Several times he left his post, hoping to lead the life of a simple monk elsewhere, but was ordered to return as abbot. He promoted the Gregorian reform and is regarded as a patron saint of prisoners because of the legendary story that recounts a successful effort to help a prisoner to escape. BIBLIOGRAPHY: Butler 2:53–54; P. Rouillard, BiblSanct 7:427–429.

[V. BULLOUGH]

WALTER REYNOLDS (d. 1327), abp., administrator. He was a prominent figure in the reign of Edward II but, despite his high offices, was of limited ability and influence; keeper of wardrobe of Prince of Wales, 1301; bp. of Worcester and treasurer of England, 1307; chancellor, 1310–14; abp. of Canterbury, 1313. BIBLIOGRAPHY: F. D. Logan, NCE 14:790.

[J. L. GRASSI]

WALTER OF ST. VICTOR (d. *c.*1190), successor of Richard of St. Victor as prior of the abbey of St. Victor,

Paris, from 1173; known chiefly as an opponent of dialectics in theology and as an anti-intellectual. In his *Contra quatuor labyrinthos Franciae* he particularly attacked Abélard, Peter Lombard, Peter of Poitiers, and Gilbert de la Porrée.

[T. C. O'BRIEN]

WALTER OF SKIRLAW (d. 1406), bp. of Durham from 1388. He studied canon and civil law at Oxford, becoming a doctor of canon law by 1373. As early as 1359 he was secretary to *John of Thoresby, abp. of York. He was an experienced diplomat and lawyer and high in the king's favor. BIBLIOGRAPHY: J. Tait, DNB 18:357–358; Emden Ox 3:1708–10; V. Murdoch, NCE 13:279.

[J. A. WEISHEIPL]

WALTER DE STAPLEDON (d. 1326), bp., administrator, founder. He was graduate of Oxford, papal chaplain, bp. of Exeter 1308, treasurer of England 1320–26. He rebuilt a large part of Exeter Cathedral, founded Exeter College, Oxford, 1314 and made momentous reforms in the Exchequer. He was murdered by a mob in the revolt of 1326. BIBLIOGRAPHY: T. F. Tout, *Place . . . of Edward II in English History* (2d. ed., 1936); N. Denholm-Young, NCE 14:791 (bibliog.).

[J. L. GRASSI]

WALTER, JOHANN (Walther, b. Blankenmueller; 1496–1570), German Lutheran composer and musical adviser to Martin Luther. Nothing is known of W.'s schooling or musical preparation except that he attended a Latin school. In 1517 he obtained a place in the Hofkapelle of Frederick I of Saxony through the good offices of its conductor. He spent three weeks in Luther's home in 1524, working with Luther and K. Rupsch (Rupff) on the music of the Lutheran Church. His first work, *Geystlich Gesangk Buchleyn* (1524), was destined to become the model for almost all Lutheran hymnals. Twenty-three of the 30 hymns, as well as the Preface, were by Luther. The hymnbook was entirely independent of the three other songbooks that appeared the same year, and it was the first to have systematic arrangement. W.'s songs were intended for church, school, and home use, but they did not lend themselves easily to congregational singing. He was the first to set to music Luther's translations of the Bible. BIBLIOGRAPHY: W. E. Buszin, EncLuthCh 3:2455–56.

[M. J. SUELZER]

WALTHAM, MONASTERY OF, former house of Augustinian Canons, dedicated to the Holy Cross and St. Lawrence and located in the county of Essex in the ancient See of London, England. Founded *c.*1038 by the landowner Tovi and enlarged in 1060 by Earl Harold of Wessex, who was buried there after the Battle of Hastings, it was destroyed by Geoffrey de Mandeville in 1144. It was reendowed by Henry II in 1177 as part of his penance for the murder of Becket. The secular canons were replaced with the Canons Regular of St. Augustine. Having attained the status of abbey in 1184 under Walter of Gant and made a privileged abbey in 1199 by Innocent III, it was the most important house of Augustinian Canons in England and the last monastery to be suppressed by Henry VIII (March 1540). The nave of the abbey church continued in use as a parish church. BIBLIOGRAPHY: Cottineau 2:3431.

[E. J. DILLON]

WALTHEOF (WALTHEN), ST. (d. 1159), Cistercian abbot. Son of the English earl Simon de Senlis, he became an Augustinian Canon, then a Cistercian at Wardon, later at Rievaulx, and (1148) abbot of Melrose (Scotland). He was noted for humility and austerity. BIBLIOGRAPHY: AS Aug. 1:248–277; Butler 3:254–255.

[L. J. LEKAI]

WALTHER, CARL FERDINAND WILHELM (1811–87), conservative Lutheran theologian. A native of Germany, W. began the study of theology at the Univ. of Leipzig in 1829, graduated in 1833, and was ordained in 1837. Because of his convictions about pure doctrine and a vital personal faith, he could not accept the growing rationalism in the state Church. With a large body of like-minded people from Saxony, he migrated (1839) to St. Louis, Mo., and became a pastor in Perry Co., Mo.; there he helped form, and taught in a log-cabin college that developed into Concordia Seminary. In 1841 he accepted the pastorate at Trinity Church in St. Louis; after the transfer of Concordia to St. Louis, he was also professor of theology (1850–87). In 1844 he began publishing *Der Lutheraner,* a periodical directed at bringing together Lutheran conservatives; in 1855 he founded the quarterly *Lehre und Wehre,* in which most of his theological writings appeared. He played a leading role in the formation in 1847 of what is now the Lutheran Church—Missouri Synod, which he served as president, 1847–50 and 1864–78. W. communicated to the Missouri Synod an insistence on doctrinal orthodoxy as the first basis of unity in the Church. Although estrangement between the Missouri Synod and other synods resulted from it, W. strongly defended, against *revivalism and *liberal theology alike, man's unconditional dependence upon grace for salvation. BIBLIOGRAPHY: C. F. W. Walther, *Proper Distinction between Law and Gospel* (tr. W. Dau, 1929); W. G. Polack, *Story of Carl Ferdinand Wilhelm Walther* (1947); L. Spitz, *Life of Dr. Carl Ferdinand Wilhelm Walther* (1962).

[R. BEESE]

WALTHER VON DER VOGELWEIDE (*c.*1170– *c.*1228), medieval German *Minnesinger.* He learned the art of *Minnesang* in Vienna (*c.*1190–98), probably under Reinmar von Hagenau. From 1198 to 1220, when he received a small estate in Würzburg from Frederick II, W. went from court to court as a wandering minstrel and close observer of the political scene. His lyric poems praise *daz werde wîp* (''the noble woman''), not the conventional *frouwe* (''lady'') of *Minnesang*. He is author also of a number of *Sprüche*, of several political and patriotic poems, and of religious poems which, despite his political attacks on Pope Innocent III (1198–1216), reveal him as a man of faith. A favorite theme, esp. in his last years, was the transitoriness of earthly joys. BIBLIOGRAPHY: M. O'C. Walshe, *Medieval German Literature* (1962); W. Kosch, *Deutsches Literatur-Lexikon* (1963) 470–471 (bibliog.).

[M. F. MCCARTHY]

WALTMAN OF ANTWERP, BL., (d. 1138), Premonstratensian abbot. Disciple of Norbert of Xanten, W. came as a learned and pious canon with Norbert and 11 other companions to Antwerp in 1124, to combat the heresy of the deceased Tanchelm. The invitation to the city came from the abp. of Cambrai, through overtures made by the canons of St. Michael. With the mission successful, the secular canons in gratitude turned over St. Michael's to Norbert and his Premonstratensian Order. W. became the first abbot (1124–38) and founded abbeys at Averbode and Tongerloo. There seems to be no independent account of his life. BIBLIOGRAPHY: C. J. Kirkfleet, *History of St. Norbert* (1916).

[N. F. GAUGHAN]

WALTON, BRIAN (*c.*1600–61), Anglican bp. and editor of a polyglot Bible. After a pastorate in London and a brief imprisonment for his defense of the clergy's tithing rights, W. moved to Oxford where he enlisted several eminent scholars to help publish the whole Bible in eight versions. The work, *Biblia Sacra Polyglotta* (6 v., 1653–57), is the most valuable of the polyglot Bibles and a significant aid in textual criticism. In recognition of his efforts, W. was named bp. of Chester (1660). BIBLIOGRAPHY: D. S. Margoliouth, DNB 59:268–271; V. Verostko, NCE 14:793.

[T. M. MCFADDEN]

WALTON, IZAAK (1593–1683), English biographer and author of *The Compleat Angler* (1653). He knew the poet Donne and had many other clerical friends. His *Lives* of Donne, Wotton, Herbert, Hooker, and Sanderson, written between 1640 and 1678, are the first English biographies. They are generally accurate for he used letters and verbal information. He has been accused of revealing his own calm strong Christian spirit rather than the personalities of those he wrote about, but this accusation is not just. He venerates the men he wrote about and presents their spiritual strengths rather than their failures, but he shows both humor and irony. *The Compleat Angler* is a poetic pastoral of a quiet England created by a gentle spiritual man in the days of dissension under Cromwell. His motto was ''Study to be quiet.'' See H. Nicolas' biog. prefixed to the 1836 ed. of *Compleat Angler.*

[M. M. BARRY]

WALWORTH, CLARENCE AUGUSTINE (1820–1900), early Paulist. Born in New York State, W. became a lawyer but abandoned practice to study for the ministry of the Episcopal Church in 1842. Influenced by the Oxford Movement, he was a convert to Catholicism in 1845, studied for the priesthood as a Redemptorist, and was ordained in 1848. He preached missions in England and the U.S. before joining his close friend I. *Hecker in founding the Paulists in 1858. His health failing, W. went to the Diocese of Albany, N.Y., where he served for 34 years. Devoted to charitable work, a critic of political corruption, and an advocate of the workingman, W. became a recognized figure. He contributed many articles to periodicals and published a number of books, among them *The Gentle Skeptic* (1863) and *The Oxford Movement in America* (1895).

[J. R. AHERNE]

WANDERING JEW, LEGEND OF THE, an ancient tale relating the fate of a man who scolded Christ and urged him to go faster on his way to Calvary. Christ is said to have replied, ''I am indeed going, but you will wait until I return.'' Hence the man is condemned to wander the earth until the Second Coming. The first written record of the legend is found in the *Flores historiarum* (1235) of Roger of Wendover, who casts Pilate's doorkeeper as the wanderer. The doorkeeper's name was Cartaphilus (much beloved; perhaps a derivation from the legend that John, the Beloved Disciple, would never die), who now lives a saintly life and has taken the Christian name Joseph. The story became popular after the publication (1602) of a German pamphlet which linked the legend with a Jewish shoemaker named Ahasuerus. In this version, Ahasuerus does not convert to Christianity and has been regarded as representing the persecuted Jewish people, dispersed over the earth. BIBLIOGRAPHY: A. F. Remy, CE 9:126–127; S. M. Polan, NCE 14:794.

[T. M. MCFADDEN]

WANDRILLE, ST., (Wandregisilus, *c.*600–663), Benedictine abbot. Of a noble Frankish family, W. served at the court of Dagobert I. Married by parental arrangement, he separated from his wife by mutual agreement, and entered the monastery of Montfaucon. Later he went to Bobbio, Romainmoutier, and then to Rouen. There he was ordained deacon by St. Ouen, and priest by St. Omer. After several years of pastoral activity he founded the monastery of Fontenelle (649), where he served as first abbot. BIBLIOGRAPHY: L. David, *L'Abbaye St-Wandrille de Fontenelle* (1957); O. J. Blum, NCE 14:795.

[O. J. BLUM]

WANINGUS ST. (Vaneng; d. *c.*688), wealthy patron of religious houses. W. was born in Rouen. He became a gamesman and courtier in the entourage of Clotaire III and underwent a conversion after the impact of the biblical text about the rich man, the camel, and the needle's eye. He renounced court life, assisted St. Wandrille in founding the abbey at Fontenelle (649). He founded in the valley of Fécamp a church in honor of the Trinity, with an adjoining nunnery under the direction of St. Ouen and St. Wandrille. Over 360 contemplative nuns sang the Divine Office in relays, night and day without interruption.

[E. J. DILLON]

WAR, JUST, teaching developed in reaction to the ancient plea that war was a necessity or benefit for the State. Where arguments of utility placed no serious restraints on the conduct of war, just-war theory tried to set limits to both its justifying causes and methods. This teaching has evolved from Augustine, through Thomas Aquinas and others, applying the standards of order-peace-justice to Western civilization from the days of the late Roman Empire through medieval Europe to our own perplexing international situation. While ''holy wars'' have been defended, the just war teaching was not their basis. The latter never affirmed that war was something morally good. It rather assumed that war was evil and participation in it morally questionable, but tried to identify the conditions under which it could be tolerated in the effort to avoid some greater injustice. Aquinas summed up the earlier tradition from Augustine and identified three such justifying conditions. To be just, war must (1) be waged by duly constituted authority, (2) for a just cause, and (3) with the intention of establishing a good order or correcting an evil one. To these three, Francisco de Vitoria added a fourth in the 16th cent., namely, that the war must be conducted with proper means. These guidelines served Western civilization for several centuries. They provided an alternative to Renaissance and Machiavellian principles of statecraft, and served as a check on the policies of many Western nations. Applying this standard to the actions of modern States in conflict, many Christians avoided the pitfalls of purely private morality and self-securing sectarianism. They sounded a warning in public affairs, calling for the pursuit of justice rather than vengeance or selfish interest. When war had become the sport of kings in the 18th cent., just-war teaching was employed to temper the evils involved. Little was heard about these guidelines again until the 20th cent., when they encountered a radically changed ideological and technological set of circumstances. All of the formerly acceptable guidelines for personal and public behavior have been drastically revised in recent decades. And just-war teaching was not exempt, coming to center stage following World War II and its wake of nuclear armaments, cold-war tensions, and the ''limited police actions'' in Korea and Vietnam. The situation demanded a reevaluation of all four of the traditional conditions placed on warfare. (1) The appropriate authority condition worked best as applied to medieval princes and kings. But man, mindful of the American and French revolutions, wanted to justify the wars of liberation in emerging countries, even though they were not conducted by ''officially sanctioned

authorities.'' (2) The just cause condition has received little attention since it is broad enough to include many rationalizations. Discussion of this condition focused largely on the differences between aggressive acts of war and national self-defense. With the introduction of the subtlety called anticipatory self-defense and various extensions of the meaning of national welfare and self-interest, the differences between aggressive and defensive war have been blurred. If the distinction has not already become meaningless, it is at least at the point of impasse. (3) The proportionality criterion tolerating war's evil in the interest of a prospective better ordering of life has also been scrutinized. As employed in the 20th cent., it has been used to sanction war against totalitarian forces like Nazism and Communism. The challenges directed to it include questions about the relative advantages of differing forms of government and the pacifistic possibilities of surrender and life under equally imperfect political orders. Concepts of territoriality and sovereignty have also been criticized in the light of international needs and possibilities, creating crises in formerly acceptable meanings of good political order. (4) The fourth condition, concerned with the proper means of war, has been the most widely problematical one in recent decades. Since the advent of nuclear energy, many have questioned whether warfare is ever justifiable. Others tried to discriminate between limited and all-out nuclear war. Still others, with the experience of Korea and Vietnam, turned their attention to the means of war as it affects noncombatant civilian populations. The issues of nuclear and deterrent nuclear arsenals were discussed in Vatican Council II, with a representative sampling of the prevailing differences of opinion and a resultant teaching that adhered to the principles of the just-war doctrine. In an attempt to limit war and build peace, the conciliar statements exhibit some ambiguities which have been debated by some and totally ignored by others as irrelevant. The debate on noncombatants continues with little likelihood of imminent resolution. While an issue in the conduct of World War II, it was not widely discussed until the perplexities of guerilla-type warfare were brought to the fore in Vietnam. One writer has suggested that part of the difficulty with the just-war teaching is that it suffers from lack of exercise. This may be particularly true of the failure of American moralists to apply the conditions rigorously to their own national behavior in the 40s, esp. during the saturation and atomic bombings and unconditional surrenders of that period. Another school of thought believes that we should use the phrase ''last resort war,'' rather than ''just war,'' since the latter implies that war is a necessary alternative or a right granted to nations. This school questions the presumption that war is at all a proper resort to achieve the goals intended. Hence one opinion holds that the just-war teaching is better than nothing, offering some guidelines in an imperfect world which would be worse without them. A second opinion holds that nothing is better than vague principles which have never offered any truly concrete norms, and have generally justified too much. A third opinion suggests we return to the concept of justice, as the common root from which arise the traditional fourfold conditions. These principles are, after all, nothing without the theorem of "integral cause" which generated them. Hence, some believe a reworking of the medieval maxim "good from an integral cause, evil from any defect" would profit us in evaluating the conditions for a just war. War would then be tolerable only by reason of an integrative coincidence of the four conditions, and intolerable if but one were defective. Focus would then shift to the purpose of the principles, namely the maintenance of justice and peace, rather than misdirected attempts to justify war by complying with one or more of the principles detached from all the rest.

[J. F. SMURL]

WARD, in Mormon nomenclature, the local congregation of the Church.

WARD, BERNARD (1857–1920), British bp. and historian. Son of William George Ward and brother of Wilfrid Philip Ward, he studied at St. Edmund's College and Oscott, where he was ordained (1882). Most of his priestly life (1882–1916) was spent at St. Edmund's, where he served as president from 1892 until 1916. He was appointed administrator of the new Diocese of Brentwood, and became its first bishop (1917). He was successful both as college and diocesan administrator. His most important publication was *The Dawn of the Catholic Revival in England* (7 v., 1909–15). Among his other writings were *The History of St. Edmund's College* (1893); *Catholic London a Century Ago* (1905); and *The Priestly Vocation* (1913). BIBLIOGRAPHY: M. Ward, *Wilfrid Wards and the Transition* (2 v., 1934–37).

[G. J. RUPPEL]

WARD, CORNELIUS (d. *c.*1641), Irish Franciscan missionary to the Western Highlands and Scottish Isles. Arrested in London (1629) on his second journey to Brussels on behalf of his mission, he was tortured and imprisoned until 1631. After release he went to Rome, again seeking aid to his mission and returned to work in Scotland (1635) until his ill-health forced him to retire in 1640.

[R. J. LITZ]

WARD, HUGH (Hughboy Macanward; 1580?–1635), Irish Franciscan hagiographer. Entered the order at Donegal, then studied at Salamanca. In 1616 he became first professor of theology at the Irish St. Anthony's College at Louvain. He began searching libraries in France (1623) for material on Irish saints, collaborating with fellow Franciscan Patrick Fleming. He became lector and guardian at St. Anthony's in 1626, the same year he began working on a history of Ireland with which to preface his lives of the Irish saints. His life of St. Rumold (1662) and other works were published posthumously. His collections were the basis for Colgan's *Acta Sanctorum Hiberniae* (1645).

[R. J. LITZ]

WARD, JUSTINE BAYARD (1879–1975), music educator. She was born in Morristown, N.J., the daughter of William Bayard Cutting, a founder of the Metropolitan Opera Company. She studied harmony, counterpoint, form, and composition privately under Herman Wetzler, a prominent N.Y. musician of the time. In 1901 she married and in 1904 was converted to Catholicism. In gratitude for the gift of faith, she vowed to spend her life promoting the cause of sacred liturgical music according to the norms of the 1903 motu proprio of Pius X. A way soon opened to her through a meeting with the Very Rev. Dr. Thomas E. Shields, dean of the department of education at The Catholic Univ. of America. He asked her to compose a complete system of music education for Catholic schools, based on the same principles of modern psychology and Catholic philosophy as the other courses he was preparing. After years of studying pedagogy with him, of experimenting with children, and of further study of chant with Dom André Mocquereau at Solesmes, she began issuing her series, which would span grades 1 through 8. The "Ward Method," as it is called, is an ingenious and fascinating technique, using the chant and other great music of the world, carefully planned and graduated, to teach children how to read, to sing, and to love music. It has had three American revisions; its translations were received enthusiastically abroad, particularly in France and in Holland, where, in the 60s, the method bore fruit in a generation of excellent church music composers. W.'s generosity extended also to higher institutions of learning; she aided in the formation of the Pius X School of Liturgical Music (1918), the Dom Mocquereau Foundation in N.Y. (1928), and the Schola Cantorum of The Catholic Univ. of America (1929). She was decorated for service by Italy and the Netherlands, was honored by the Vatican with the *Bene merenti* and *Pro ecclesia et pontifice* medals, and held an honorary doctorate from the Pontifical Institute of Sacred Music. W. continued for many years to write and publish materials and to supervise school activities and teacher-training in her method. This method, as well as her numerous other works, are a testament to her conviction of the importance of music in the formation of the person. BIBLIOGRAPHY: *New York Times* (Nov. 29, 1975) 30; Sister Cecilia, "Justine Bayard Ward, Crusader Extraordinary," *Musart* 14 (1962) 6; P. Hume, "Valiant Lady of Chant," *Sign* 40 (1960) 24–26.

[M. T. LEGGE]

WARD, MAISIE (Mrs. Francis Joseph Sheed; 1889–1975), author, lecturer, publisher. Daughter of Wilfred *Ward, historian of the 19th-cent. English Catholic revival and Josephine Ward the novelist, W. inherited and grew up in a literary and religious tradition that prepared her for a life as an intellectual lay apostle. She married Frank *Sheed in 1926, like herself an active worker in the Catholic Evidence Guild. W. edited *Catholic Evidence Training Outline*, a notable contribution to apologetics. In 1926 she and her husband founded the publishing house of Sheed and

Ward in London and opened an office of the firm in New York in 1933. It is no exaggeration to say that this publishing house became the mentor of English and American Catholics in the middle period of the 20th century. One notable service Sheed and Ward performed was to bring the best of European Catholic writers to the attention of English speaking Catholics. W. wrote a number of significant books including *The Wilfred Wards and the Transition* and *Insurrection versus Resurrection,* the two forming a history of Catholic thought from 1870 to 1920. The latter volume shows the Catholic revival as an answer to the doctrines of Modernism. Her biography of G. K. Chesterton (1943) is the definitive life of that giant among modern Catholic writers. In addition to innumerable lecture appearances, writing, and publishing, W. was an active supporter of *The Catholic Worker* and the Grail movement. She was a worthy successor to W. G. Ward and Wilfred Ward whose influence on English Catholic thought in the 19th cent. was monumental.

[J. R. AHERNE]

WARD, MARGARET, ST. (d. 1588), English martyr. She served the Whittles, a London Catholic family, and was arrested after helping William Watson, a secular priest, escape from Bridewell prison. After being tortured, she was executed at Tyburn. She was canonized in 1970. BIBLIOG- RAPHY: G. Fitz Herbert, NCE 14:808.

[V. SAMPSON]

WARD, MARY AUGUSTA (Mrs. Humphrey Ward; 1851–1920), British novelist and social worker. Her best known novel, *Robert Elsmere* (1888), embodies her lifelong belief that Christianity can be revitalized only by discarding its miraculous element and emphasizing its social mission. To this end she worked much among the London poor, founded a settlement for popular Bible reading and simplified Christianity, established recreational centers for London children and made the public aware of the needs of the physically defective. Her output of novels was extraordinary. Her early literary work combines serious intellectual interest with vivid descriptive power and skillful presentation of social types, but her later novels, except for *The Case of Richard Meynell* (1911), do not reach her earlier level. See her autobiography, *Writer's Recollections*, and her biography by J. P. Trevelyan (1923).

[M. J. BARRY]

WARD, WILFRID PHILIP (1856–1916), Catholic biographer and journalist. Son of William George Ward, he attended Ushaw College and the Gregorian University. He then began lecturing at Ushaw (1890), became a member of the royal commission on Irish university education (1891), and in 1906 editor of the *Dublin Review*. He was most noted for his biographical studies, among which were: *William George Ward and the Oxford Movement*, 2 v. (1889); *William George Ward and the Catholic Revival* (1893); the

Life and Times of Cardinal Wiseman (1897); *Aubrey de Vere* (1904); and his most important work, the *Life of Newman*, 2 v. (1912). He founded (1896) the Synthetic Society to promote dialogue between Catholics, Anglicans, and Nonconformists. BIBLIOGRAPHY: M. Ward, *Wilfrid Wards and the Transition* (1934).

[G. J. RUPPEL]

WARD, WILLIAM GEORGE (1812–82), English theologian, convert to Roman Catholicism during the *Oxford Movement. Educated at Oxford, he became a fellow of Balliol and a friend of Jowett, his fellow tutor. He took minor orders in the Anglican Church opposed the Evangelicals (Low Church), and believed in strong ecclesistical authority. His defense of J. H. *Newman resulted in the condemnation of his book *The Ideal of a Christian Church, Considered in Comparison with Existing Practice* (1844) and he was degraded from his degrees. Resigning his fellowship, he became a Roman Catholic. Through Cardinal Wiseman he taught at St. Edmund's College, first philosophy and later theology. He edited the *Dublin Review* making it very influential from 1863 to 1878. He defended Pius IX's *Syllabus of Errors*, was an extreme ultramontanist, opposed such liberal Catholics as C. *Montalembert and J. E. *Acton, and even Newman in his hope to see Catholics again at Oxford and Cambridge. BIBLIOGRAPHY: W. P. Ward, *William George Ward and the Oxford Movement* (1889); *idem, William George Ward and the Catholic Revival* (1893); M. Ward, *Wilfrid Wards and the Transition* (1934–37).

[M. M. BARRY]

WARDE, M. FRANCIS XAVIER, MOTHER (1810–84), foundress of the Sisters of Mercy in the United States. Born in Ireland, W. became one of the first associates of Mother McAuley, foundress of the Sisters of Mercy. W. was from 1837 superior and foundress of several convents in Ireland; in 1843 she and six companions came to the U.S. to serve in the Diocese of Pittsburg. She founded schools and charitable institutions there, made foundations in Chicago, W Pennsylvania, and Providence, R.I. Her courage and commanding presence saved the convent at Providence from destruction by the Know Nothings in 1850. With astounding energy she opened schools, hospitals, homes, and other institutions in New Hampshire, Maine, Philadelphia, Pa., Nebraska, New Jersey, and California.

[J. R. AHERNE]

WARDEN, see CHURCHWARDEN.

WARDLAW, HENRY DE (d. 1440), Scottish ecclesiastic and statesman; bp. of St. Andrews (1403). Educated at Oxford, Paris, Orléans, and Avignon, he owed his ecclesiastical preferments to the schismatic antipopes. He founded St. Andrews Univ. (1412), restored his cathedral, and reformed clerical discipline. His moderating influence on James I helped stabilize national politics. BIBLIOGRAPHY: Emden Ox 3:1983–84; V. H. Baxter, *Scots Magazine* NS 33 (1940) 5–14.

[R. W. HAYS]

WARFIELD, BENJAMIN BRECKINRIDGE (1851–1921), Presbyterian theologian. Born near Lexington, Ky., W. studied at the College of New Jersey (now Princeton Univ.), Princeton Theological Seminary, and the Univ. of Leipzig. After ordination (1879) he taught at Western Theological Seminary (now Pittsburgh Theological Seminary) until he was called (1887) to teach theology at Princeton Seminary. He engaged in intense study of many fields, including biblical criticism, patristics, theology, and church history. He defended the orthodox Calvinism of C. *Hodge in highly rationalistic terms and supported what he called evangelical religion (see PRINCETON THEOLOGY). W. helped to define the doctrine of biblical inerrancy as the basis upon which the Presbyterian Church in the United States of America and other sympathetic Christians defined the authority of Scripture. He was chief editor of the *Presbyterian and Reformed Review* (1890–1903), to which he made many contributions, and his posthumous works include, among many others, *Revelation and Inspiration* (1927), *Calvin and Calvinism* (1931), and *The Westminster Assembly and Its Work* (1931).

[J. H. SMYLIE]

WARHAM, WILLIAM (*c.*1450–1532), abp. of Canterbury and lord chancellor of England. After New College, Oxford, (LLD, 1488), he went to London but returned to moderate the school of civil law at Oxford. He was consecrated bp. of London (late 1502) after years of diplomatic and ecclesiastical service. He became abp. of Canterbury and lord chancellor in 1504. In 1506 he was principal negotiator in Henry VII's marriage to Margaret of Savoy; he crowned Henry VIII and Catharine of Aragon (1509). By gifts and patronage he sought to induce Erasmus to settle in England. In 1515, Card. Wolsey, with whom W. struggled throughout their careers, replaced him as lord chancellor. Involved early (1527) in the inquiry into Henry's marriage to Catharine, he gingerly avoided public participation, though in 1530 he too signed the letter to the Pope seeking consent to Henry's divorce. After their submitting to the King's designs, W. finally rebelled in 1532, when he formally protested all acts undermining either the Pope's authority or prerogatives of Canterbury. Henry alleged abuses in W.'s jurisdiction, and the old abp. capitulated in accepting the famous "submission of the clergy," May 1532; he died shortly afterwards.

[R. J. LITZ]

WARIN, BL., (d. 856), Benedictine abbot, disciple of Paschasius Radbertus. He became abbot of Corvey after the death of Adalard (826), initiated the North German missions, to Meppen (834) and Vispek (855). He was the son of the Saxon Count Eckhert and St. Ida of Herzfeld, was brought up in the palace of Charlemagne, and served in the imperial court during his early years before entering the abbey of Corbie. In 822 he was sent to the new abbey of Corvey. When he became its abbot he was given at the same time (by Louis the Pious) the abbey of Rebais. It was at the request of Warin that Paschasius Radbertus (who had given his former disciple the name Placidus Varinus) composed his fundamental work, *Liber de corpore et sanguine Domini*, for the instruction of the recently converted Saxon monks who were not yet well instructed in their faith. BIBLIOGRAPHY: H. Peltier, DTC 13:1630.

[E. J. DILLON]

WARING, GEORGE (1872–1943), army chaplain. Born in England and coming to the U.S. in 1888, W. studied for the priesthood and was ordained for New York in 1903. A chaplain with the U.S. Army in 1904, he later became head of chaplains in military prisons. From 1918 to 1938 W. served as chancellor and vicar general of chaplains in the Armed Forces of the U.S.

[J. R. AHERNE]

WARMUND OF IVREA, BL. (d. between 1010 and 1014). He was named bp. of Ivrea in Piemonte, Italy, by Emperor Otto I in 969. In his public life he was involved in a conflict between the civil and ecclesiastic powers for control of the city. His chief opponent was King Arduin, whom he excommunicated twice between 997 and 999. W. was a poet and devoted to arts and crafts. His building activity included the cathedral of Ivrea, and he introduced the Carolingian script into the scriptorium of his episcopal school. A number of his poems are extant, and likewise MSS prepared under his supervision. His cult was confirmed by Pope Pius IX in 1857. BIBLIOGRAPHY: N. M. Riehle, NCE 14:812; A. P. Frutaz, EncCatt 12:1033.

[M. R. P. MCGUIRE]

WARNING, CANONICAL, in the CIC a penal remedy that the local ordinary directs to a person involved in a proximate danger of committing a canonical crime or about whom official inquiry raises suspicion of crime already committed. The warning may be given secretly or in the presence of witnesses; a record of it must be kept in the diocesan archives. (CIC *c.* 2306–09.)

WARREN, LEONARD (1911–60), opera singer. An American baritone, W. married a Catholic and became a convert. Making his debut at the Metropolitan Opera in New York in 1939, he began a career that took him to the major opera houses in the U.S., Latin America, and Europe. He was a foremost interpreter of Verdi and died while singing the role of Don Carlo in *La Forza del destino* on the Metropolitan Opera stage, March 4, 1960.

[J. R. AHERNE]

WARS OF RELIGION, primarily eight French civil wars involving the *Huguenots and Catholics between 1562 and 1598, but the whole period of religious wars did not end until 1629. The first war (1562–63) began after the Massacre of Vassy (March 1, 1562) and was terminated by the Peace of Amboise (March 19, 1563), which granted the Huguenots liberty of conscience but restricted freedom of worship. An anti-Huguenot "little" League was formed. The second war (1567–68) was equally inconclusive: the Peace of Longjumeau reestablished the terms of the previous settlement. The third war (1568–70) broke out as a result of Catherine de Médicis' plans to seize the Huguenot leaders Condé and Gaspard de Coligny. The Huguenots were defeated at Jarnac (March 1569) and Moncontour (October 1569); their losses were heavy but the Peace of Saint-Germain (Aug. 8, 1570) was favorable, permitting them to garrison four strongholds. In the fourth war (1572–73), which followed the *St. Bartholomew's Day Massacre (Aug. 24, 1572), in which Coligny was murdered, royal forces besieged the Huguenots in their strongholds. The treaty of La Rochelle (July 8, 1573) restricted their freedom of worship to three towns. During the fifth war (1574–76) Francis, Duke of Alençon, brother of King Henry III, joined the revolt with Henry of Navarre; after the defeat of the Huguenots by Henry of Guise at Dormans, the treaty of Beaulieu ("Peace of Monsieur," May 6, 1576) established religious and civil equality and authorized six additional strongholds; this caused considerable resentment and led in 1576 to the formation of the Catholic League. The sixth war (1577) and the seventh war (1580) were local. The eighth war (1586–89) was provoked by the League, which prevailed on Henry III to issue the Treaty of Nemours (July 1585), canceling all previous concessions and in effect banning Calvinism. In this "War of the Three Henries," Henry of Navarre won a victory at Coutras (Oct. 20, 1587), and Henry of Guise and Henry III were murdered. Henry of Navarre then became King Henry IV and reconquered the country. He was reconverted to Catholicism and fought a victorious war against Spain; the war was brought to a close by the Treaty of Vervins (May 2, 1598), which was also the political end of the Wars of Religion. The *Edict of Nantes (April 13, 1598) gave the Huguenots freedom of conscience and civil equality but restricted their freedom to worship. The ensuing period of religious truce was broken by several Huguenot revolts (1615, 1620, and 1625) and by the siege of their stronghold, La Rochelle (1627–28), conducted by Cardinal Richelieu, who destroyed the power of the Huguenot party by imposing, in June 1629, the Peace of Alais. This deprived Huguenots of civil and political rights, and the religious freedom granted by the Edict of Nantes was not honored. BIBLIOGRAPHY: W. J. Stankiewicz, NCE 7:201–204, s.v. "Huguenots," with bibliog.

[W. J. STANKIEWICZ]

WARSAW, UNIVERSITY OF, a Polish state-supported institution under the jurisdiction of the ministry of education. Although a recognized cultural center, 19th-cent.

Warsaw had only two institutions of higher learning: a medical school and a law school established in 1808, and incorporated into the university when it was founded in 1818. Closed by Czar Nicholas I after the 1830–31 Polish uprising, it was reopened in 1861 by Alexander II as a "principal school" which was replaced in 1863 by a Russian university. After the 1915 German invasion of Poland, the university again reopened, entered a period of academic progress, including in its organization faculties of Catholic, Protestant, and Orthodox theology; humanities, which emphasized the classics and history; and science. In 1939 the German invasion closed the institution although some instruction continued to be carried on secretly. After the war the university reopened. By degrees, however, Communist pressure and Marxist infiltration produced internal and external changes: the transfer elsewhere in 1950 of medical and pharmaceutical studies, and the suppression of the faculties of Catholic and Protestant theology, the former merging with that of Cracow at a monastery outside Warsaw; the Christian Theological Academy at Chylice replacing the latter. The university library, founded in 1817, contains 1,550,830 vols., numerous rare books, MSS, and special collections.

[M. B. MURPHY]

WARTBURG, the castle near Eisenach in Thuringia, where Martin Luther, disguised as "Knight George," took refuge in 1521 after the Diet of *Worms. The name also connotes the "Patmos" period in the Reformer's life (May 1521–March 1522), during which he translated the NT into German and wrote many pamphlets and treatises. Disorders aroused by the radical innovations of *Karlstadt and the *Zwickau Prophets, which he had tried to control by incognito excursions, led to his return to Wittenberg. BIBLIOGRAPHY: K. Wessel, *Luther und der Wartburg* (1955); M. Reu, *Luther's German Bible* (1934); M. Gravier, *Luther et l'opinion publique* (1942).

[P. DAMBORIENA]

WARTENBERG, FRANZ WILHELM VON (1593–1661), Catholic organizer and bp. during the Thirty Years' War. In 1621, Elector Ferdinand of Cologne named him political administrator. Elected bp. of Osnabrück (1625), he did not enter the city until 1628. He strove to reorganize the region's politics, education, and religion along Catholic lines, administering the Edict of *Restitution (1629) throughout Lower Saxony, until Osnabrück was taken by the Swedes (1633) and W. fled to Regensburg. He also served as bp. of Verden (1630) and of Minden (1631), vicar apostolic to Bremen (1645), representative of Catholic imperial electors at Westphalia (1648), bp. of Regensburg (1649), and was named cardinal 8 months before his death.

[R. J. LITZ]

WASHING OF THE FEET, a customary and necessary action in the Near East to remove the dust from a man's feet when he entered a house. The OT speaks of it as a gesture of hospitality on the part of a host toward his guests (e.g., Gen 18.4). The Mosaic Law required priests to wash both hands and feet before executing their sacred duties (Ex 30.19). In the NT the neglect of Simon the Pharisee to perform this act for Jesus after having invited him to his house is contrasted by Jesus with the love shown by the woman who washed his feet with her tears (Lk 7.44). At the Last Supper Jesus washed the feet of his apostles and told them to imitate his example of humility (Jn 13.4–20). The washing of the feet was encouraged by Paul (1 Tim 5.10). Probably because of the association of water with baptism the Western Church had the practice from the 4th century to the Middle Ages of washing the neophytes' feet at baptism. In the RC and in the Eastern Churches the rite has been part of the observances for Holy Thursday. For the practice among some Protestant groups, see FOOTWASHING.

[M. A. MCNAMARA]

WASHINGTON, a Pacific Coast state, admitted to the Union (1889) as the 42d state. Among the fur trading companies that exploited the region were the North West Company and John Jacob Astor's Pacific Fur Company. The area became part of the U.S. through the Oregon Treaty of 1846. Missionary activity developed slowly in Washington. The first significant effort was made by Marcus Whitman, a physician employed by the American Board of Commissioners for Foreign Missions, who established a station on the Walla Walla River (1836). He was a Presbyterian. The first major Catholic missionaries, F. N. *Blanchet and Modeste Demers, worked among the fur trappers and Indians after 1838. Blanchet served as vicar apostolic of the area until 1846, when his brother, A. Magloire A. Blanchet, was made bp. of the newly created Diocese of Walla Walla. After the diocese was suppressed (1853), A. Blanchet became bp. of the new Diocese of Nesqually. His successor, A. Junger, founded 20 schools and 60 churches while gaining the assistance of Redemptorists, Benedictines, and Jesuits. After Junger's death (1895), the Diocese of Nesqually was changed to Seattle under his successor, E. J. O'Dea. O'Dea was followed by G. *Shaughnessy and by Thomas A. Connolly, who became Seattle's first abp. (1951–75). Abp. Connolly began the Visitation Retreat House, Blanchet High School, and St. Thomas the Apostle Seminary. The archdiocese has two suffragan sees, the Dioceses of Yakima and Spokane. Abp. Raymond Hunthausen has been the ordinary since 1975. In 1976 Washington's Catholics numbered 466,247 or 13.4% of the total state population. The major Protestant denominations are the Methodist Church, with 3.4% of the total population in 1971, and the American Lutheran Church, with 2.9%. Other Protestant denominations comprised 15.5% of the population. The Jewish population (1968) was 15,485 or 0.45%. There are 4 Catholic colleges in Washington, with a total enrollment of 6,439 students. Over 6,827 students are enrolled in 13 Catholic high schools in the state, while 20,621 pupils attend 92 Catholic elementary schools. BIBLIOGRAPHY: M. W. Avery, *History and Government of the State of Washington* (1961); C. B. Bagley, ed., *Early Catholic Missions in Old Oregon* (2 v. 1932); E. V. O'Hara, *Pioneer Catholic History of Oregon* (4th ed. 1939).

[J. L. MORRISON; R. M. PRESTON]

WASHINGTON, D.C., the capital of the U.S. Its site was chosen in 1790 by a commission appointed by George Washington. Having been carved out of Maryland territory, the Federal District shares its religious history with that state. The city was part of the Archdiocese of Baltimore, Md., until 1947, when it was separated, along with its surrounding suburban counties in Maryland, and made an archdiocese. Card. Patrick A. O'Boyle, appointed as Washington's first abp., has attempted to provide for expanding population by constructing numerous schools and churches, and became a major Catholic spokesman for racial justice and a leading figure in the attack upon urban problems in the U.S. Card. William W. Baum succeeded to the see upon Card. O'Boyle's resignation in 1973. The archdiocese has one suffragan see, the prelature nullius of the Virgin Islands.

In 1976 Catholics of the archdiocese numbered 396,421 or 18.9% of the total population. The Jewish population of the District (1975) was 115,000, or 15.2%. About 18,752 students attend 4 Catholic colleges in the city. There are 28 Catholic high schools in the archdiocese, with a total enrollment of 12,095 students. Over 30,264 pupils attend 84 Catholic elementary schools in the archdiocese. BIBLIOGRAPHY: J. T. Ellis, ed., *Documents of American Catholic History* (2d ed. 1962); H. Philibert et al., *Saint Matthew's of Washington, 1840–1940* (1940); E. J. Long, *America's National Capital* (1959).

[J. L. MORRISON; R. M. PRESTON]

WATCH NIGHT, a gathering for prayer, praise, and exhortation, begun in 1742 by Methodist colliers in Kingswood, England, who before their conversion had spent Saturday nights drinking. John *Wesley encouraged the watch night and introduced it himself in London, April 9, 1742, choosing the Friday night nearest a full moon. Wesley likened it to the vigils of the primitive Church and those mentioned in the Book of Common Prayer. The custom continues in various denominations only on New Year's Eve.

[F. E. MASER]

WATERLAND, DANIEL (1683–1740), a Lincolnshire man, fellow and master of Magdalene College, Cambridge, and canon of Windsor. He maintained the traditional Christian position against *deism and did more than any other divine to halt the spread of *latitudinarianism in the C of E. Wary of mysticism, he rested his case on external evidence; his deep and accurate learning, and his wiry and perspicuous style made him a redoubtable opponent. His publications include considerations of Arianism, vindications of the divinity of Christ, and a critical history of the *Athanasian

Creed, which has been many times reprinted. In the C of E his moderate eucharistic theology won wide approval.

[T. GILBY]

WATERTON, CHARLES, (1782–1865), naturalist and explorer. A descendant of St. Thomas More and a Yorkshire country gentleman of staunch faith, wide charity, deep prayer, and dauntless courage, Squire Waterton of Walton Hall belonged to the great race of English eccentrics: *inter alia* when on pilgrimage to Rome he climbed to the top of St. Peter's dome and danced a jig there to the extreme displeasure of the reigning pontiff; he rode on the back of a cayman in Guyana; he prepared animal specimens without internal stuffing and "elevated taxidermy from a sorry handicraft to an art." See his *Autobiography* and *Wanderings in South America*; DNB 59:449.

[T. GILBY]

WATERWORTH, WILLIAM (1811–82), English Jesuit scholar. Born in Lancashire and educated at Stonyhurst, he was admitted to the Jesuits in 1829. He was ordained a priest in 1836, completed his theology at the Collegio Romano and then taught dogmatic theology at Stonyhurst seminary. In subsequent years he was rector of the church in Farm Street, London, rector of the College of St. George in Worcester, spiritual director of the College of St. Ignatius, London, and superior of the mission at Bournemouth, where he died. He wrote rather extensively on the Jesuits, on the relations between the English Church and the Roman See, on the origin and development of Anglicanism, and on the ancient Church in Ireland. BIBLIOGRAPHY: T. Cooper, DNB 20:908–909.

[E. J. DILLON]

WATKINS, FRANKLIN CHENAULT (1894–), American painter, executing dramatic works of violent pose, fitful lighting, turbulent settings, and excited, mixed techniques (*Suicide in Costume,* 1931), whose later work is religious and symbolic (*The Angel Will Turn a Page in the Book*, 1944, and *Resurrection*).

[M. J. DALY]

WATRIGANT, HENRI (1845–1926), French Jesuit ascetical writer, renowned for giving retreats based on the Exercises of St. Ignatius. Born in Lille, he was ordained in 1880 and labored in the ministry in Lille and near Rheims. From 1902 until his death, he lived in Belgium as a writer and scholar, writing and collecting works centered on the Exercises. A remarkable monument to his efforts is the library founded by him in Belgium, containing 8000 various works written through the centuries and dealing with the Exercises and their spiritual exegesis. It has been a rich resource for Jesuit retreat masters.

[E. J. DILLON]

WATSON, JOHN BROADUS (1878–1958), behaviorist, psychologist. After extensive experiments on animals at Johns Hopkins Univ. in Baltimore, Md., W. published a paper in 1913, "Psychology as the Behaviorist Views It," which laid the foundations for the behaviorist school of psychology. W. contended that human beings as well as animals could be conditioned to become whatever the experimenter wished. He scoffed at home and religion as having any shaping influence on man. Reinforcement by reward could determine human response. His best known among several books, was *Behavior: An Introduction to Comparative Psychology* (1914).

[J. R. AHERNE]

WATTSON, PAUL JAMES FRANCIS (1863–1940), ecumenist, founder of the Society of the Atonement. Born Lewis Thomas in Millington, Md., he studied theology at General Theological Seminary, New York City, and after ordination in the Episcopal Church (1886) worked toward unity between his Church and Rome. He founded (1898) at Graymoor, N.Y., in conjunction with Mother Lurana White, an Episcopal nun, the Society of the Atonement, a group of Franciscan friars and sisters whose prayer and activities were designed to further Christian unity. When he had passed a year in the novitiate of the Anglican Fathers of the Holy Cross, he received the habit of his order, taking the name Paul James. In 1903 he began publication of *The Lamp* and in 1909 inaugurated the period of prayer called the Church Unity Octave. This became the *Chair of Unity Octave and was observed by other Christian Churches as the Universal Week of Prayer for Christian Unity. The Graymoor community was received corporately into the RC Church in 1909, and W. was re-ordained a priest in 1910. He also founded at Graymoor a refuge for homeless men and organized the Graymoor Press and the "Ave Maria Hour" on radio. The Rev. C. V. LaFontaine of the Graymoor Ecumenical Institute has documented W.'s crucial role in the formation of the *Catholic Near East Welfare Association, of which he was vice president (see RACHS 86 [1975] 53–78). BIBLIOGRAPHY: D. Gannon, NCE 14:828; T. Cranny, *Father Paul, Apostle of Unity* (1955).

WAUGH, EVELYN (1903–66), English novelist and critic. Born in London of a publishing family, W. was educated at Lancing and Oxford. He sprang into fame with his first novel, *Decline and Fall*, and extended his reputation with many succeeding books, which include *Helena*, the story of Constantine's mother, the legendary finder of the True Cross, and *Brideshead Revisited*, a nostalgic study of recusant aristocracy in decay. Of his two biographies, that of Edmund *Campion, written for the Oxford Jesuits, remains a classic, and that of his friend, Ronald *Knox, is definitive, though tinctured with a sense of grievance properly the author's. He was a comic writer of first rank, his humor was deeply serious, its expression mordantly satirical, its effect to expose an agnostic worldliness with its own sophistication. He had become a Catholic as an undergraduate, and his faith maintained him through tragedy and a singular capacity for boredom, an effect he was unable to produce on others. He reacted with choler to invasions of the new barbarians, both sacred and profane, and armored himself in old-fashioned ways that were dismissed as affectations by hostile outsiders, but his friends found them endearing, sometimes odd (as, e.g., the great curly trumpet he carried as a hearing aid), but usually they were manifestations of a consistent loyalty to the traditional values of the West. His were the virtues of a partisan; he fought for the blessed mutter of the Latin Mass, and though he had no romantic illusions about it, was prepared to defend Roman *triumphalism to the end. He had a great courage in the face of danger, and many of the incidents in his trilogy, *Men at Arms*, modestly disguise his own exploits in the Royal Marines and Commandoes. BIBLIOGRAPHY: F. J. Stopp, *Evelyn Waugh: Portrait of an Artist* (1958), a recommended study in depth.

[T. GILBY]

WAVE OFFERING, sacrifice offered to Yahweh by Israelites, presumably using a back and forth cultic motion. The gesture perhaps symbolized the gift of the object to Yahweh and his return of it to the priests, who sometimes received it as their food. Wave offerings could include parts of a ram and breads (Ex 29.22–27), first fruits of the harvest (Lev 23.9–11). The act of offering was generally performed by the priests (Num 6.19–20; cf. Lev 8.27).

[T. EARLY]

WAVERLEY, ABBEY OF, the first Cistercian monastery in England, founded 1128 near Farnham, Surrey, by Bp. William Giffard of Winchester and colonized from Aûmone. Between 1133 and 1226, Waverley founded Garendon, Ford, Thame, Bruerne, Combe, and Grâce Dieu. It was one of the few abbeys successfully to oppose the royal privilege of assigning corodies (livings). It was suppressed in 1535–36. Little remains of the site. BIBLIOGRAPHY: Cottineau 2:3435–36.

[E. J. DILLON]

WAX, the beeswax of which candles are made. It was considered a pure, indestructible substance, and as such, a symbol of the flesh of Christ. Even today there are canonical regulations that the paschal candle as well as Mass candles must be of beeswax in greater part. Other candles on the altar should be at least partly wax. In addition to the special symbolism, which dates from antiquity, there is also the traditional liturgical preference for natural over artificial substances in the accoutrements of worship.

[E. J. DILLON]

WAY OF THE CROSS (Stations of the Cross), a pious devotion, honoring the passion and death of Christ, which consists in prayer and meditation successively before 14 stations each representing an event which supposedly occurred on the journey to Golgotha. The devotion originated in imitation of the early Christian practice of visiting the scenes of Christ's passion in the Holy Land. Encouraged by the Franciscans, it became common in the 15th century. While the number and type of stations have varied, the following are accepted in modern times: (1) Jesus is condemned to death; (2) Jesus carries his cross; (3) Jesus falls the first time; (4) Jesus meets his Mother; (5) Simon of Cyrene helps Jesus carry his cross; (6) Veronica wipes the face of Jesus; (7) Jesus falls the second time; (8) Jesus speaks to the women of Jerusalem; (9) Jesus falls the third time; (10) Jesus is stripped of his garments; (11) Jesus is nailed to the cross; (12) Jesus dies on the cross; (13) Jesus is taken down from the cross; (14) Jesus is laid in the sepulcher. The stations are essentially a series of crosses, but usually are accompanied by artistic representations. While commonly found on the walls of churches, they may also be placed out of doors. Erection of the stations follows specific canonical procedures, and numerous indulgences have been granted to the faithful for making the way of the cross. BIBLIOGRAPHY: H. Thurston, *Way of the Cross* (1906); W. Picard, DSAM 2.2:2576–2606; B. Brown, NCE 14:832–835.

[J. C. WILLKE]

WAY, THE TRUTH, AND THE LIFE, THE. In the OT, the "way of truth" is a way of life in conformity with the divinely revealed Law (Ps 86.11; 119.30; Wis 5.6), a way which leads to life (Pr 15.24) and contrasts with the way of death (Jer 21.8). At Qumran also the way of the Spirit of truth is opposed to the way of the Spirit of iniquity (1QS IV:15–16; IX:17–18), a way of strictest observance of the Law as interpreted by the great teacher of the community (1QS IX:21; VIII:12–16). The early Christian Community considered itself "the Way," preparing itself for the return of Christ (Acts 9.2; 19.9, 23; 22.4; 24.14, 22). In Jn 14.6, Jesus presents himself as the "Way," the only means of salvation, because he is the "Truth," the supreme revelation of the heavenly Father. Not only does Jn 14.6 manifest the true nature of Jesus, but the passage also tells what Jesus is in relation to men. If Jesus is the "Way" because he is the "Truth" and the "Life," it must also be stated that "truth" and "life" are not simply coordinate, since life comes to men through the truth. Those who believe in Jesus, the incarnate revelation of the Father, receive the gift of life, since the words and the person of Jesus are the source of life (cf. Jn 6.63; 5.24; 18.37). BIBLIOGRAPHY: R. Brown, *Gospel According to John* (1966, 1970), 2:628–633; I. De La Potterie, NRT 88 (1966) 907–942.

[T. J. RYAN]

WAYNFLETE, WILLIAM (*c.* 1394–1486), master of Winchester College (1429–42); provost of Eton (1442–47); bp. of Winchester from 1447; chancellor of England (1456–60). W. founded Magdalen College, Oxford, for the study of theology and philosophy, an accompanying grammar school, and a school at Wainfleet, Lincolnshire. He also completed the building of Eton College. BIBLIOGRAPHY: Emden Ox 3:2001–03.

[C. D. ROSS]

WAYS, THREE SPIRITUAL, a classical division of the stages (purgative, illuminative, and unitive), whereby a person strives after Christian perfection. The notion of diverse spiritual stages is acknowledged in the NT, e.g., 1 Cor 3.1–3 where Paul speaks of spiritual childhood and maturity, and is also frequently found in patristic sources. Most early writers, however, enumerated only two stages: the active stage characterized by a virtuous life and a gradual rejection of any sinful habits, and the contemplative life in which the mind is habitually oriented to God. The classical division into three stages follows the enumeration of *Evagrius Ponticus (d. 399), who spoke of the active life as a purgation and divided the contemplative life into the illuminative and unitive ways. Following Evagrius, some contemporary writers (e.g., R. *Garrigou-Lagrange, L. Bouyer) stress the mystical orientation of the three ways. The purgative way emphasizes the conquest of sin and vice, the striving after the moral virtues, and meditative prayer. The illuminative way is given to growth in love and initial contemplation with continuing progress in virtue. The unitive way belongs to the perfect, those who constantly enjoy the presence of God, his conscious activity in their lives, and infused *contemplation. The transition from one way to the other is marked by a "night," the first, of the senses, the second, of the spirit, during which the person is prepared for the next stage. Other contemporary writers (J. De Guibert, A. Tanquerey) understand the three ways more ascetically, stressing the characteristics of mortification, interior renovation joined to total abnegation, and finally the stage of perfect charity. All writers agree, however, that each individual's path is unique and no one conforms rigidly to this general pattern of religious development. BIBLIOGRAPHY: R. Garrigou-Lagrange, *Three Ages of the Interior Life* (tr. M. T. Doyle, 2 v., 1947–1948); J. De Guibert, *Theology of the Spiritual Life* (tr. P. Barrett, 1953); L. Bouyer, *Introduction to Spirituality* (tr. M. P. Ryan, 1961).

[M. B. PENNINGTON]

WAZO OF LIÈGE (Wazon, b. *c.*985), bishop. He studied at Lobbes and Liège, served as master at Saint-Lambert of Liège, then as provost. W. was elected bp. in 1042. A strong supporter of Henry III and imperial prerogative against the feudatories, he never hesitated to advocate the superiority of the Church, or its autonomy—a positive reformer before Gregory VII. BIBLIOGRAPHY: D. S. Buczek, NCE 14:836–837; T. Schieffer, LTK 10:970–971; MGHS 7:210–234; *Biographie nationale de Belgique* 27:145–150.

[S. WILLIAMS]

WEAKLAND, REMBERT G. (1927–), musicologist, writer, teacher, monastic leader, abp. W. studied at St. Vincent's Abbey in Latrobe, Pa., and at the Juilliard School of Music, where he majored in piano. Following his theological studies and his ordination in Rome, he pursued doctoral studies in musicology at Columbia University. In 1957, after a year of research in Milan on medieval MSS of Am-

brosian chant, he returned to St. Vincent's to teach in and later to head the music department there until his election as archabbot in 1963. W. is a past-president of the Church Music Association of America; he was chairman of the Music Advisory Board of the American Bishops Commission on the Liturgical Apostolate; he directed the preparation of the music for the English texts in the 1966 *Sacramentary* and was music editor of the *New Catholic Encyclopedia* (1967). From 1967, he served as abbot primate of the confederated Benedictine congregation with residence at Sant'Anselmo, Rome. A composer himself of liturgical music, he continued to lecture and to write on problems of liturgical music and renewal until his appointment as abp. of Milwaukee, Sept. 20, 1977.

[M. T. LEGGE]

WEAKNESS (INFIRMITY), in the theology of sin, one of the causes of sin; also an effect of *original sin. As an inner cause of sin, weakness consists in an inability to resist *passion. Thus sins of weakness are distinguished against sins of *malice; they have a mitigating cause, indicate less voluntariness, and so less moral disorder. (See ThAq ST 1a2ae. 77.3; 78.4). As an effect of original sin, weakness is numbered among the "wounds of nature", along with ignorance, malice, and concupiscence, in an anonymous commentary on the parable of the Good Samaritan (see Lk 10, 30). Weakness in particular describes the diminution of man's forces to pursue the good in spite of the arduousness of the task.

[T. C. O'BRIEN]

WEARMOUTH, ABBEY OF, former Benedictine monastery on the Wear River in Northumbria, at Sunderland, Durham, England. Founded (674) by Benedict Biscop on land given by King Egfrid of Northumbria and dedicated to St. Peter, it was closely associated with the sister foundation of St. Paul 6 or 7 miles away at Jarrow and usually ruled by the same abbot. The Venerable Bede was the celebrated exemplar of the twin foundation's monastic school and scriptorium. Destroyed by the Danes (867–870), and reconstructed (*c.*1074) by Alduin of Winchcombe, neither house attained again its earlier importance, remaining dependencies of Durham until the dissolution in 1539. BIBLIOGRAPHY: Cottineau 2:3444.

[E. J. DILLON]

WEATHER GODS, frequently personifications of one or another attributes of a particular deity. Zeus, for example, is called Bronton ("Thunderer"), Astrapaios ("Sender of Lightning"), Urios ("Sender of Favorable Winds"), and Hyetios ("Rainy"). Thunder, lightning, and rain are often associated with *sky gods, sometimes with the moon; Thor (Scandinavia) and Indra (India) characteristically wield the thunderbolt and cause storms. The Nuer of the upper Nile describe all atmospheric phenomena as manifestations or instruments of Kwoth ("Spirit" or "God"); they have no specific term for rain or lightning but say rather that Kwoth rains or lightnings. Since weather is of supreme importance for agricultural societies, various rites and magical practices develop to insure the desired events. The rainmaking ceremony of the Papago Indians (southern Arizona), for example, centers on the making and drinking of cactus liquor in the hope that the saturation of the participants with liquor will presage the saturation of the earth with rain. The ceremony is conducted by religious specialists and is typically held at the beginning of the rainy season. BIBLIOGRAPHY: M. Eliade, *Patterns in Comparative Religion* (tr. R. Sheed, 1958); M. Riemschneider, *Der Wettergott* (1956).

[E. V. GALLAGHER]

WEATHERS, WILLIAM (1814–95), Welsh-born priest, canon of Westminster (1851), auxiliary bp. to H. *Manning, and one of two English-speaking theologians who participated in the preparatory phase of Vatican Council I. W. had been vice president, procurator, then president of Old Hall, where he himself had studied in preparation for his own ordination in 1838. He was rector of Hammersmith seminary, 1869–92, then lived in Isleworth, Middlesex in virtual retirement, but in the capacity of chaplain to the Sisters of Chanty, until his death.

[E. J. DILLON]

WEBB, SIDNEY JAMES (1859–1947), husband of Beatrice Potter Webb (1858–1943), who in close partnership with his wife was actively dedicated to social and economic reform. They began their collaboration as members of the Fabian Society and took prominent part in building up the British Labour Party. In the interest of their cause they wrote extensively on government, labor, education, and socialism. As advocates of a kind of socialism they were sympathetic to Russian communism. They visited Russia in 1932 and their last major work *Soviet Communism: A New Civilization* (1935) shows some revision of their earlier views. BIBLIOGRAPHY: *Webbs and Their Work* (ed. M. I. P. Cole, 1949).

[M. J. BARRY]

WEBB, THOMAS (*c.*1724–96), layman, prominent in the establishment of Methodism in the United States. He was a captain in the British Army who assisted P. *Embury in N.Y., founded St. George's Methodist Church in Philadelphia (1767), and strengthened Methodist *societies in Del., Md., N.J., and on Long Island. BIBLIOGRAPHY: HistAm-Meth 1.

[F. E. MASER]

WEBER, ANSELM (1862–1921), Franciscan missionary. Born in Michigan, W. entered the Franciscans and was ordained in 1889. In poor health he gave up teaching in 1898 to work as a missionary in Arizona among the Navajos. While laboring as a missioner, W. composed his *English-Navaho and Navaho-English Dictionary* (2 v.,

1912). W. edited *Franciscan Missions of the Southwest* from 1913 to 1921.

[J. R. AHERNE]

WEBER JOSEPH (1753–1831), Bavarian-born philosopher, teacher and writer. He studied with the Jesuits, was ordained a priest, and then taught philosophy and physics at Dillingen and Ingolstadt. He wrote hundreds of articles on religious, scientific, and philosophical subjects. He was influenced by Wolff and Leibniz, and favored Kant over the dogmatism of the scholastics, but defended metaphysics against Kant's critique. He attempted to find in the philosophy of Schelling a way of reconciling philosophy and Christian belief. His works include: *Estne metaphysica possibilis?,* (1795); *Philosophie, Religion, und Christentum im Bunde* (1808–09); *Die Philosophie in einer freien Darstellung* (1911).

[E. J. DILLON]

WEBER, MAX (1864–1920), German sociologist who together with É. *Durkheim and K. *Marx, is considered one of the founders of modern sociology. W. produced influential analyses of power relationships, the sociology of charismatic authority, bureaucratic organization, and social stratification. His comparative studies in the sociology of religion investigated the connections between religion and the surrounding society's polity and economy. He took issue with any monocausal theory of society. Against Marx's position of economic determinism, W. argued that religious phenomena might exert an independent effect upon economic organization. In his examination of the rise of the capitalistic ethos in Europe, W. asserted that certain specifically religious traits of Puritanism were linked to purely economic trends. Disciplined striving for success in one's calling not only was consistent with the teachings of Calvin and other leaders of the Reformation, but also functioned to promote the development of modern capitalism. The religious ideal of "inner-worldly" asceticism thus operated as a major cause of changes in the economic system of Europe (see PROTESTANT ETHIC). W. devoted considerable attention to general theoretical and methodological issues, and regarded sociology as a value-free discipline which rested upon the analysis of the subjective meaning of interaction for the participants. BIBLIOGRAPHY: R. Bendix, *Max Weber: An Intellectual Portrait* (1960); J. Freund, *Sociology of Max Weber* (1968).

[G. W. DOWDALL]

WEBER, MAX (1881–1961), American painter and sculptor, born in Russia, coming to the U.S. in 1891. In Europe (1905–08) he knew H. Rousseau and Matisse. Successively a Fauve, Cubist and Futurist (*Chinese Restaurant*, 1915), W. returned to panels of figure and landscape in a poetic mood. In the late 1930s he expressed intense religious themes of the Jewish-Hasidic mystical sect in symbolic arrangements, Expressionist colors, and linear inter-lacings (*Adoration of the Moon*, 1944).

[M. J. DALY]

WEBSTER, AUGUSTINE, ST. (d. 1535), Carthusian martyr. Educated at Cambridge, W. entered the char-terhouse at Sheen and was chosen prior of Axholme in Lincolnshire. With John Houghton and Robert Lawrence, W. appeared before Thomas Cromwell in the hope of ob-taining a form of oath that would meet the demands of the Act of Supremacy and yet be acceptable to conscience. The three were imprisoned in the Tower and executed at Tyburn. He was canonized in 1970. BIBLIOGRAPHY: L. E. What-more, *Blessed Carthusian Martyrs* (1962).

[V. SAMPSON]

WEDDING CUSTOMS (IN THE BIBLE), the tradi-tional folkways governing the way a man formally took to himself a bride and brought her into his house. The biblical literature presupposes knowledge of these customs, which must not have differed much from age to age. A composite picture emerges from the many allusions to marriage and marriage feasts found throughout the biblical record. The formal marriage contract was drawn up by the parents of the bridal couple. By this the bride was pledged to her groom. The actual wedding celebration might take place several months later, at which time the man publicly took his bride and they came together in the midst of the "grooming feast." The bride, dressed in special attire and wearing her jewels, waited with her girl friends for the coming of the groom to her father's house. The groom, wearing a garland made for him by his mother, came in company with "the friend of the bridegroom" and other "sons of the wedding hall" to fetch his bride. With joyful shouts and songs the bridesmaids and groomsmen accompanied the young couple to the bridegroom's house, where the groom brought the bride into the bridal chamber and raised the veil. The wed-ding celebration usually continued for about a week. A great crowd would be invited and expected to come in festive attire.

[E. J. DILLON]

WEEK, a cycle of seven successive days used as a division of time. It was recognized in the calendar of the Jews, from whom it was adopted by Christian, Muslim, and other peoples. Actually, what the Jews observed was not the week but the recurrence of the Sabbath, as Christians did the Sunday, and Mohammedans the Friday. The approximately 7-day phases of the moon were known to the ancients; but in the OT the weeks run uninterruptedly without regard to the waxing and waning of the moon. The Egyptians employed at times a month made up of a sequence of 7, 8, 8, and 7 days; but their civil calendar divided the month into decades of days. In the OT, traces of this 10-day week occur alongside the 7-day week. The texts of Ugarit prove that the Babylonians knew the 7-day week, yet there is nothing to

show that they governed their work by it as the Jews did. The Greeks divided their month into thirds and seem to have been unacquainted with the 7-day week. In Italy the recur-rence of markets (*nundinae*) every 9th day generated a cycle which was indicated on calendars by a series of letters, *A* through *H*, the first being the day of the *nundinae*. Even at the present in parts of Asia, Africa, and Central America natives use a local week of constant length (3, 4, 5, or 6 days), reckoned from one market day to the next.

Numerous explanations have been proposed to account for the choice of 7 as the length of the week: that 7 is a sacred and mystic number; that the Pleiades total 7; that 7 winds blow from 7 directions. Believers in astrology used the 7-day week in Hellenistic times. They assigned single hours of the day consecutively to the sun and 6 of the planets and then named each whole day for the heavenly body that they thought ruled its first hour. It is not known when Rome adopted this planetary week, but the Latin planet-names for the days are met frequently in texts of A.D. 3d century: *dies Solis, dies Lunae, dies Martis, dies Mer-curii, dies Jovis, dies Veneris, dies Saturni*. The Germanic tribes borrowed the names upon their earliest contact with the Romans but substituted corresponding Teutonic deities for the Roman. It is from them that the Anglo-Saxon day-names derive. In the West and in Egypt Christian writers sometimes followed the Roman practice; but for the most part they kept the Jewish custom of calling the last day of the week "Sabbath" and using numerals as names of the other days, except for one change: they christened the first day of the week *dies dominicus*. Curiously, it is only the astrological name for Sunday that lends itself to Christian interpretation. The rising sun is an early symbol of Christ in his incarnation and in his resurrection. BIBLIOGRAPHY: F. H. Colson, *Week* (1926); De Vaux AncIsr.

[M. J. SUELZER]

WEEK OF PRAYER FOR CHRISTIAN UNITY, or-ganized by Abbé Paul Couturier (1881–1953), an annual period of prayer for Christian unity in which all Christians are invited to pray that unity may come as Christ wills and by the means he wills. In 1932 Couturier visited the Bene-dictine community at Amay, Belg., where he learned about the *Chair of Unity Octave. He introduced the octave in Lyons, his native city, in 1933, but decided that the basis direction of the octave should be changed. In accordance with the theology of the times, the octave then advocated submission and conversion of non-Catholics to the RC Church for the attainment of Christian unity. The Abbé realized that such views did not allow non-Catholic Chris-tians to pray with sincerity because of their contrary beliefs. Holding spiritual ecumenism to be the heart of the ecumeni-cal movement, Couturier substituted a new formula of prayer for unity so that each person could pray according to his own conscience. The World Council of Churches adopted the Couturier formula, and a Joint Working Group of the World Council and the RC *Secretariat for Promoting

Christian Unity now yearly develop a common service for the Week of Prayer, Jan. 18–25, for use according to local circumstances throughout the Christian world. BIBLIOGRA - PHY: M. Villain. *Abbé Paul Couturier* (1959).

[R. MATZERATH]

WEEKS, FEAST OF, second of the three main Hebrew festivals (Ex 23.14–17; Lev 23; Num 28.26–31; Dt 16). Originally a harvest festival, it later commemorated the giving of the Law at Sinai. *PENTECOST.

[T. EARLY]

WEELKES, THOMAS (*c*.1575–1623), English composer and church musician. Although he published a collection of madrigals in 1597 and produced some contributions to the lovely English musical genre, the lute song, W. was basically an excellent contrapuntalist without an extraordinary melodic facility; Weelkes found his metier in the composition of *services and *anthems of a conservative nature with some oddly progressive touches. His failure to secure a truly important church position (although he served at Chichester Cathedral) combined with his miserable personal life perhaps kept him from gaining an initiative to use his creative talents in a monumental way. BIBLIOGRAPHY: D. Brown, *Thomas Weelkes* (1969).

[P. DOHERTY]

WEHRLE, VINCENT DE PAUL (1855–1941), missionary, bishop. Of Swiss origin, W. entered the Benedictines and was ordained in 1882. Coming to the U.S. in that same year, he worked on the missions of Arkansas and Indiana. His chief center was the Dakota Territory where he ministered to the numerous German immigrants. Founder of St. Gall's Monastery, he became its abbot in 1904. Under his direction the abbey became the center of Catholic influence for western North Dakota. He was named first bp. of Bismarck, N.D. in 1910 and became the moving force for Catholic life in the area. In 1939 he resigned as bp. because of age.

[J. R. AHERNE]

WEIGEL, GUSTAVE (1906–64), American theologian, ecumenist. He entered the Society of Jesus in 1922, was ordained in 1933, and completed his theological studies with a doctoral course, 1935–37, at the Gregorian Univ., Rome (S.T.D., 1938). The first phase of his professorial career was as professor of dogmatic theology at the Catholic Univ. in Santiago, Chile, 1937–48. He was appointed dean of the theological faculty in 1942; published *El Cristianismo oriental* (1945) and *La Psicología de la religión* (1946). From 1948 until his death he was professor of theology at Woodstock College, Woodstock, Md. He entered into contact and dialogue with many Protestant theologians, including Paul *Tillich. With his colleague and friend John Courtney *Murray he collaborated in studies of the Church-State problem. He published two philosophical

works: *Knowledge: Its Values and Limits* (1961) and *Religion and Knowledge of God* (1961).

From 1954 onward, after a period of serious illness, W. stood with Murray at the forefront of the movement toward renewal in the RC Church in the U.S. He became the most prominent American RC theologian in the ecumenical movement, and as participant or observer attended the national and international meetings of the World Council of Churches. His ecumenical concentration was reflected in his works: *Catholic Primer of the Ecumenical Movement* (1957); *Faith and Understanding in America* (1959); *American Dialogue* (1960); *Churches in North America* (1961); *Catholic Theology in Dialogue* (1961); and *The Modern God* (1963). As a culmination to this work he was called to Rome to help prepare Vatican Council II's *Decree on Ecumenism. During the Council he acted as a liaison and interpreter for the observers from other Churches. His diary of the beginnings of the Council is preserved in the archives of Woodstock. BIBLIOGRAPHY: *Woodstock Letters* (v. 97, 1968) n.4; W. J. Burghardt, NCE 14:843–844.

WEIGEL, VALENTIN (1533–88), German religious writer. W. was Lutheran pastor at Zschopau. He became well known only after his death when his works were first published (Halle, 1609). He was a precursor of *Romanticism whose influence is seen in J. *Arndt and J. *Boehme. W. believed that man possesses a divine spark, which if developed will eventually supplant Scripture, the means of grace, the ministry, the science of theology, and all historical elements of religion. He felt that the knowledge of God is personal and autonomous, derived more from interior prayer than from the Bible and the sacraments. BIBLIOGRA - PHY: I. Ludolphy, EncLuthCh 3:2464; R. H. Grützmacher, EncRelKnow 12:285–287.

[M. J. SUELZER]

WEIGHTS AND MEASURES (IN THE BIBLE). Though a considerable amount is known about weights and measures in the ancient Near East, a great degree of uncertainty still remains. Standards were, in fact, uncertain at the time, providing opportunities for abuse by the merchants who carried their weight measures in a bag (Mic 6.11; Pr 20.23). Israel used many of the same weights and measures as her neighbors. Those mentioned in the Bible, therefore, are often the same as the ones used in Babylonia, Egypt, and other nations of the area. Though the Bible contains many indefinite expressions, such as "three days' journey" (Gen 30.36), this article deals with only the more specific weights and measures.

For weight the basic unit was the shekel. The phrase "shekel of the sanctuary" (Ex 30.13) perhaps implies that a standard weight was kept at the temple. Apparently a royal standard of measurement existed, somewhat different from the common one (2 Sam 14.26). Presumably it assured the king the desired amount of revenue. Shekel weights found by archeologists show considerable variation, but the general standard seems to have been about 11 grams (.4 ounce). The pim (1 Sam 13.21 RSV) was perhaps two-thirds of a shekel; the beka (Ex 38.26), half a shekel; and the gerah (Ex 30.13), a twentieth. The mina (1 Kgs 10.17) contained 50 shekels (60 in the Babylonian system), and the talent, 60 minas. The weight of the qesitah (Gen 33.19 RSV mg) is unknown.

In the NT the talent of the parables (Mt 18.24; 25.15–28) represented a large but indefinite sum. The same is the case for the pounds of Luke (19.12–25). The pound as a measure of capacity, however, was perhaps the Roman 12-ounce pound (Jn 12.3; 19.39).

Hebrew measures of capacity, like the weights, were never fixed with precision. In general they followed the Assyro-Babylonian system. The standard measure was the homer (Ezek 45.10), estimates of which vary from 11 bushels or 90 gallons down to less than half that. A homer of barley was valued at 50 shekels of silver at one time (Lev 27.16). The cor (1 Kgs 4.22) was equal to the homer. The lethech was perhaps half a homer (Hos 3.2). The ephah (dry measure) and the bath (liquid measure) were one-tenth of a homer (Ezek 45.11). The omer of the daily manna ration (Ex 16.16) was a tenth of an ephah (Ex 16.36). The seah (Gen 18.6 RSV mg) was perhaps a third of an ephah. The hin (Ex 30.24), a liquid measure, was perhaps a sixth of a bath. According to rabbinical tradition the kab (2 Kgs 6.25) was an 18th of an ephah. The log (Lev 14.10), the smallest biblical measure of capacity, was perhaps a fourth of a kab.

NT measures are Greek or Roman. The RSV translates the two or three *metretai* of Jn 2.6 as 20 to 30 gallons. The bushel (Mt 5.15) was about a fourth of an American bushel. The RSV translates the *choinix* (Rev 6.6) as a quart.

For length the cubit was the standard measure among the Israelites, as well as for the Egyptians, Sumerians, and Assyro-Babylonians. It was the length of the forearm, or roughly 18 inches. The long cubit, perhaps an older measure, was a handbreadth longer, with six long cubits making a reed (Ezek 40.5 RSV; compare Dt 3.11 for the common cubit; see also 2 Chr 3.3). The span (Ex 28.16) was the distance between the extended thumb and the little finger, and equal to half a cubit (see Ezek 43.13 where the rim is a span and 43.17 where it is half a cubit). The handbreadth (1 Kgs 7.26) was the width of the hand at the base of the fingers, about three inches. The finger (Jer 52.21) was a fourth of a handbreadth.

The fathom (Acts 27.28) was perhaps four cubits. The stadion (Rev 14.20) was about 400 cubits or 200 yards. The 60 stadia of Lk 24.13 (KJV furlongs) are translated "about seven miles" in the RSV. The mile (Mt 5.41) was probably the Roman mile of *c*.5000 feet. The sabbath day's journey (Acts 1.12) was generally rated at 2000 cubits, though in the Talmud it was 3000 and in the *Zadokite Fragments manual, 1000.

The Hebrew term translated acre (Is 5.10) meant the area a yoke of oxen could plough in a day, probably less than an acre. Land was also measured by the amount of seed required to sow it (Lev 27.16).

The Bible frequently refers to weights and measures in connection with its demands for justice and in symbolic references (Lev 19.36; Amos 8.5; Ps 62.9; Dan 5.27).

[T. EARLY]

WEIL, SIMONE (1909–1943), French Jewish radicalist and religious writer. Impelled by a sharp awareness of suffering and a search for social justice through true human community, W. was a political radical and anarchist. After attaining an agrégée in philosophy at the École Normale Supérieure, she first taught school but soon joined the working classes in France to implement her political ideals. She was an avowed agnostic, but after a visit to Solesmes (1938) became convinced of Christ's love and divinity. She deeply experienced the significance of prayer and the meaning of the Eucharist, but social, historical, and philosophical objections kept her from joining the Church. Determined to share in the privations of World War II, she returned to France from a short trip to the U.S., and died in a state of exhaustion in London. BIBLIOGRAPHY: S. Weil, *Waiting on God* (tr. E. Craufurd, 1951); *Need for Roots* (tr. A. Wills, 1952); J. M. Perrin, NCE 14:845; G. Brée, EncPhil 8:284.

[T. M. MCFADDEN]

WEINGARTEN, ABBEY OF, Benedictine monastery in Württemberg, Germany, founded (934) by Count Henry as a cloister for nuns, later settled by monks from Altomünster in Freising, and established as an imperial abbey by Welf IV, duke of Bavaria, and his wife Judith (1053–56). After 1088 it followed the customs of Hirsau, joined the Swabian congregation of Benedictines in 1603, the Salzburg confederation in 1653, was suppressed in 1803, and restored by monks from Erdington and Beuron (1919–22). The present basilica and cloister reflect the major periods of the abbey's history: Romanesque, late Gothic, Renaissance, and Baroque. BIBLIOGRAPHY: Cottineau 2:3437–39.

[E. J. DILLON]

WEINHEBER, JOSEF (1892–1945), Austrian poet who mastered dialect songs and classical verses equally well. Born in Vienna as the son of a butcher, he lost his parents early and spent several years in an orphanage. In 1903 he received a scholarship at a *gymnasium*, but failing in mathematics, lost it. Bitterly disappointed, he became a postal clerk. After being divorced from his first wife, he left the Church. In 1925 he discovered his poetical talent. In his odes and hymns he draws from antiquity both in form and thought, glorifying mythical powers of the heroic and tragic. Among his works are: *Adel und Untergang* (1934), poems, and *Zwischen Göttern und Dämonen* (1938), poems.

[B. F. STEINBRUCKNER]

WEISMANN, CHRISTIAN EBERHARD (1677–1747), German Lutheran mystical theologian. Educated at Tübingen, W. became deacon at Calw (1701–04); he was next made court chaplain at Stuttgart (1704–07), where he also taught church history and philosophy in the local gymnasium (1707–21). He was called to be professor of theology at Tübingen in 1721 and served after 1729 as provost of St. George's as well. W. was a distinguished preacher and a popular author of hymns. Nourished by Meister *Eckhard, J. *Tauler, and P. J. *Spener, he showed marked sympathy for *Pietism and opposed the *Enlightenment. His theology-centered church history avoids the onesidedness of the *Magdeburg Centuries. BIBLIOGRAPHY: D. Scheib, LTK 10:1006–07; E. Beyreuther, RGG 6:1581.

[M. J. SUELZER]

WEISS, ALBERT MARIA (1844–1925), German theologian, teacher, and writer who, by word and action, anticipated the progressive aspects of the later social encyclicals. Born in Bavaria, he was ordained a priest in 1867 and received his doctorate in theology from the Univ. of Munich in 1870. He collaborated on the second edition of *Kirchenlexikon* (1872–76), joined the Dominican Order in Graz in 1876, taught sociology then fundamental theology at the Univ. of Fribourg in Switzerland (1890–1919).

[E. J. DILLON]

WEISS, BERNHARD (1827–1918), a generally conservative German theologian and NT critic, professor of NT studies at Kiel (1867–77) and Berlin (1877–1908). W.'s *Life of Jesus* (1882; Eng. tr., 1883) was long a standard work. His own long life coincided with an era of marked progress in critical studies of the Bible and of Christian origins. W. is the author of a long series of studies on various NT books; his special interest was the synoptic problem and he held that Mark was the first gospel written, a priority conceded by conservative scholars only at a later time.

[E. J. DILLON]

WEISS, LIBERAT (1675–1716), Bavarian Franciscan missionary, martyred at Abbo, near Gondar, Ethiopia and venerated as a Servant of God after the introduction of his cause in 1933. He became a friar at Graz in 1693, was ordained in Vienna in 1698, joined the Upper Egypt-Ethiopian mission at Rome in 1704. He was named prefect of the Ethiopian mission in 1711 and was welcomed, along with his friars, by King Yustos and Abbot Gregory in 1712. The king supported the friars against the indigenous Monophysite monks, but his successor David III brought the friars to trial for offenses against Monophysite piety. They were stoned to death by the people, led by an Armenian monk.

[E. J. DILLON]

WEISS, PETER (b. 1916), controversial German author of political dramas reminiscent of B. Brecht's political theater. *Marat* (1964) (full title: *Die Verfolgung und Ermordung Jean Paul Marats dargestellt durch die Schauspielgruppe des Hospizes zu Charenton unter Anleitung des Herrn Sade.*) This revolutionary drama was set to music by H.-M. Majewski; songs and dialogues criticize, in a traditional setting, contemporary bourgeois tendencies. Two didactic plays deal with German concentration camps (*Die Ermittlung*, 1965) and the war in Vietnam (*Vietnam Diskurs*, 1968) BIBLIOGRAPHY: J. Milfull, "From Kafka to Brecht: Peter Weiss's Development toward Marxism," *German Life and Letters*, 20 (1966) 61–71.

[S. A. SCHULZ]

WEISSENAU, MONASTERY OF, imperial Premonstratensian abbey near Ravensburg (Württemberg). Founded in 1141 from the abbey of Roth by Gebizo von Wisemburg. It served 15 parishes, owned since 1283 a famous relic of the precious blood, still venerated today. Suppressed in 1803, the beautiful Baroque buildings are now an asylum. BIBLIOGRAPHY: Hugo 2:287–304; Backmund 1:88–89.

[N. BACKMUND]

WELD, THOMAS (1773–1837), English cardinal. Born in London, he was the son of an ancient Catholic family which through the years had generously offered shelter to various religious orders and émigrés of the Revolution. W. married in 1796 and was widowed in 1815. After his daughter's marriage in 1818, he made over his estates to his brother, and was ordained a priest by the abp. of Paris in 1821. After serving as priest in London until 1826, he was consecrated coadjutor to the bp. of Kingston, Ontario, Canada. Because of ill health he was unable to leave London. Instead he later moved to Italy where, in 1830, he was made a cardinal. He died in Rome.

[E. J. DILLON]

WELL-BELOVED, one loved in a special way; uniquely loved. As a form of address the word underwent a complex evolution in meaning in biblical literature. It may have its origin in the liturgy and cult of the Palestinian god of fertility, much invoked by young lovers esp. at festival time. The lovers in Song of Songs call each other "beloved" without necessarily realizing the word they use was once the exclusive name of that amiable deity. Isaiah (5.1–7) takes up the role of ballad singer introducing a new love song at the vintage festival, only to deliver a reproach and a threat in his parable of the vineyard. He refers to the God of Israel as "my beloved." A strikingly similar parable is attributed to Jesus in Mk. 12:1–9, with mention of the "beloved son" sent to collect the produce of the vineyard. Here the beloved is not the God of the prophet, but the unique prophet of God, martyred like so many sent before him. By the time of Jesus it was normal to reflect upon this common fate of prophets. A popular symbol of the coming of the new age was the appearance of the last and unique martyr-prophet at a time of judgment for the world. This may have been a variation on the theme of Second Isaiah in his Servant Songs, in which the prophetic role is Israel's: to be a light to the nations (49:6), at the cost of much suffering (53). In fact, the first Servant Song (42:1) is cited by a voice from heaven to define Jesus in his role at his baptism (Mk 1:11), and again at the Transfiguration (Mk 9:7). In both citations the Greek NT traditions falter between "my son, the beloved" and "only-begotten son." Perhaps both traditions are needed together to do justice to the resonances of the "specially loved," the "uniquely loved." Finally in Paul and other Christian writings, "beloved" becomes a common form of address to believers in whose hearts the love of God has been shed abroad through the Holy Spirit given them (Rom 5:5). The Only-begotten has become the first-born of many brothers. BIBLIOGRAPHY: Kittel TD 1, s.v. "Agapētos."

[E. J. DILLON]

WELL OF MOSES, stone monument by Claus *Sluter in the *Chartreuse de Champmol, Dijon.

WELLESZ, EGON (1885–1974), musicologist and composer. W. was born in Vienna and studied at the Univ. of Vienna, where he was one of the earliest pupils of Arnold Schoenberg. From 1913 W. was lecturer there and, from 1930, professor until he fled the Nazis (1938) and went to Lincoln College, Oxford. There he became university lecturer in 1943 and later reader in Byzantine music until 1956. The university bestowed an honorary doctorate on him, and he retained a fellowship there until his death. W. was a convert to Roman Catholicism. In 1961 John XXIII made him a Knight of St. Gregory. His publications, *Eastern Elements in Western Chant* (1947) and *History of Byzantine Music* (1949), are standard works. He was general editor of *Studies in Eastern Chant,* editor from 1932 of *Monumenta musicae Byzantinae,* and was one of the editors of the *New Oxford History of Music.* As a composer, W. was the last of the Second Viennese School founded by Schoenberg. He wrote operas, ballets, choral works, chamber music, and nine symphonies. For the Latin liturgy, he composed 3 Masses (1934, 1937, 1963), a *Magnificat* (1967), and several other works. BIBLIOGRAPHY: M. Dawney, obituary in *Music and Liturgy* (1975) 1:105–106; Baker, 1778–89.

[M. T. LEGGE]

WELLHAUSEN, JULIUS (1844–1918), German Protestant biblical scholar. He is noted primarily for his theories of the evolution of Israelite religion and the composition of the Hexateuch. Born at Hameln, he studied with G. H. A. Ewald (1803–75) at Göttingen and taught there 1870–72. He then taught at Freifswald for 10 years, but resigned because his views on biblical inspiration differed from those of the school. He taught Semitics at Halle (1882–85), Marburg (1885–92), and Göttingen (1892–1918).

His theory of the Hexateuch, following up the suggestion of K. Graf (d. 1869) that the Law was later than the Prophets, was the best known expression of the documentary theory, asserting that the Hexateuch was not a unity but a weaving together of four basic documents, that the Deuteronomic legislation derived from the time of Josiah,

and that the Hexateuch reached its final form only in the time of Ezra. His view became standard among liberal Protestant scholars and a focus of attack by conservatives. Though subsequent studies have revised his work in many details and rejected his evolutionary interpretation of Israelite religion, his literary theory is still accepted by both Protestant and Catholic scholars, except for the most conservative. During his later years W. devoted himself to a critical study of the NT, particularly the Gospels. Among his most significant books are *History of Israel* (1878; English tr. of 2d ed., 1885); *Komposition des Hexateuchs* (1885); and books on each of the first five NT books.

[T. EARLY]

WELLS, SWITHUN, ST. (1536–91), English martyr. A country gentleman and former schoolmaster, W. became involved in his latter years in the support and service of seminary priests. When priests were apprehended while saying Mass in W.'s London house, he and his wife and several others were arrested. W. was executed and his wife died in prison. He was canonized in 1970. BIBLIOGRAPHY: A. M. Forster, NCE 14:869; Butler 4:532–534.

[V. SAMPSON]

WELLS, HOLY, waters associated with a saint or event in Christian tradition; also part of popular devotion in non-Christian religious. The most famous of such places in Christendom is the grotto of Lourdes. St. Brigid's well in Ireland and St. Winifride's in England are similar places of pilgrimage with long histories.

[J. R. AHERNE]

WELLS CATHEDRAL, English Gothic structure, first building in 1180–1240 (completed 1290–1340). The W front is a vast screen of the finest 13th-cent. English sculpture. The towers were added 1386 (by William de Wynford) and 1424. Important are the chapter house (1290–1315), a fine N porch of the best Early English style, and the remarkable, distinctively English strainer arches at the crossing (c.1320).

[M. J. DALY]

WELSH BIBLE AND PRAYER BOOK, translations into Welsh of the Bible and the *Book of Common Prayer. The NT in Welsh, translated from Greek mainly by W. Salesbury (c.1529–95), appeared in 1567, and formed part of the whole Welsh Bible published in 1588 by W. Morgan (c.1547–1604), bp. of St. Asaph. The Welsh Bible still in use is a 1620 revision of Morgan's translation. The 1559 BCP was translated by R. Davies (1501–81), bp. of St. David's; a Welsh translation of the 1662 BCP was completed in 1664 and, with some revisions, remains in use. The two translations had a definitive influence on the Welsh language.

[T. C. O'BRIEN]

WELTANSCHAUUNG, Ger. term signifying world view in the sense of a comprehensive concept of man and reality. Every man lives by such a world-view in a more or less conscious and consistent manner. This world-view is commanded by his philosophy or religion. The Christian *Weltanschauung,* in keeping with the gospel message of salvation, sees man and world in the light of God's providence leading human world history, which is salvation history, to its fulfillment at the second coming of Christ. It includes a scale of values, different from that of the nonbeliever. It acknowledges all human values and man's earthly tasks, but subordinates them to spiritual and eternal values, not intracosmic but eschatological. The Christian outlook on life is other-world minded in that it does not consider human values as final or supreme; they are, for all their genuineness and necessity, meant to pass and to be taken up in a new creation. At times *Weltanschauung* is meant to signify a time- and place-conditioned world picture of the universe and of mankind. A measure of demythization may be needed to reach the true content of religious doctrine. BIB - LIOGRAPHY: P. Lippert, *Die Weltanschauung des Katholizismus* (1927); G. Söhngen, LTK 10:1027–29.

[P. DeLETTER]

WELTSCHMERZ (literally "world sorrow"), a term coined by Jean Paul (pseud. of Jean Paul Friedrich Richter, 1763–1825) in the novel *Selina* (1827). It designates the cosmic disillusionment, skeptical pessimism, and restless search for happiness that characterize such literary personages as Goethe's *Werther* and Byron's *Childe Harold.* BIB - LIOGRAPHY: W. Rose, *From Goethe to Byron: The Development of Weltschmerz in German Literature* (1924).

[M. F. MCCARTHY]

WENAILUS, ST. (Guénault; d. *c.*580–590), abbot. He became a monk at Landevennec in Brittany where he succeeded his friend, St. Winwaloe, as abbot. W. later resigned his position and for 34 years traveled in England and Ireland founding and reforming monasteries. He eventually returned to Brittany and founded a monastery at Morbihan where he died. His relics were brought to Paris during the Norman invasions, but were later transferred to Corbeil. BIBLIOGRAPHY: J. Evenou, BiblSanct 7:445–447.

[G. M. COOK]

WENCESLAUS IV, KING OF BOHEMIA (1361–1419), son of Emperor Charles IV, crowned King of Bohemia and Germany (King of the Romans) during his father's lifetime. In 1378 the son succeeded as ruler of the empire, and for the first time in 200 years, without contention. The early years of his reign in Bohemia were successful despite his impetuosity and a growing habit of intemperance. The alienated nobles and ecclesiastics imprisoned him in 1394, but his brother John, Duke of Görlitz, soon rescued him. In 1400 the electors and some princes deposed him for negligence and elected Rupert III, thus precipitating a schism in the German monarchy. Eventually his brother Sigismund, King of Hungary, was elected Emperor in 1411. W. retained the title King of the Romans and the Kingdom of Bohemia which he governed poorly until his death. BIBLIOGRAPHY: J. Papin, NCE 14:874.

[J. E. LYNCH]

WENINGER, FRANCIS XAVIER (1805–88), missionary, writer. An Austrian, W. studied for the priesthood, was ordained in 1828, and became professor of theology. He entered the Jesuits in 1834 and taught theology in Jesuit faculties at Linz and Innsbruck until the Society was suppressed in Austria in 1848. W. came to the U.S. in 1850 and from Cincinnati, Ohio, served German immigrants in many areas of the United States. A writer of popular theology and devotional books and pamphlets, he published, among other works: *Summa doctrinae christianae in usum docentium proposita* (1844), *Handbuch der christkatholiscen Religion* (1858), *Catholicism, Protestantism, and Infidelity* (1862).

[J. R. AHERNE]

WENLOCK, ABBEY OF, former Benedictine monastery of St. Milburga in Shropshire beyond the Saverne, in the ancient Diocese of Hereford, England. St. Milburga, youngest daughter of Penda, built it as a double monastery in 680. After destruction by the Danes, it was rebuilt in 1078 by Roger of Montgomery and Cluniac monks. The tomb of Milburga was discovered in 1101. The abbey remained a dependency of Charité-sur-Loire until 1494, setting up dependencies of its own at Dudley, St. Helen's on the Isle of Wight, and Preen. It was suppressed in 1540. Some buildings remain. BIBLIOGRAPHY: Cottineau 2:3442–43.

[E. J. DILLON]

WENRICH OF TRIER (d. *c.*1081), a royalist pamphleteer in the period of the papal reform. All we know of him is that he was a canon at Verdun and a cathedral schoolmaster at Trier (1080–1081), when he sent an apology of Henry IV to Pope Gregory VII (MGHLiblit 1:280–299) complaining that Gregory was too hasty in condemning practices sanctioned by tradition. BIBLIOGRAPHY: DTC 15.2:3528–29; A. Fliche, *La Réforme grégorienne* (1924–37).

[S. WILLIAMS]

WERBURGA, ST. (fl. 7th cent.), a descendant from the royal families of Kent and Mercia. She is patroness of Chester where her body is buried. She was promised in marriage to a prince, but finally overcame all obstacles and entered religion at Ely. She reformed the religious houses of women in Mercia and founded new ones. Her body was found intact after nine years in the tomb, and her brother Kenred, then King of Mercia, resigned to enter religion. BIBLIOGRAPHY: Butler 1:241–242.

[R. T. MEYER]

WERDEN, ABBEY OF, former Benedictine monastery in the Ruhr, Archdiocese of Cologne, Germany. It was founded c.800 by St. Ludger as a base for his mission among the Saxons. Werden received immunity and royal protection later in the century and coinage and market rights in 974; it came directly under imperial control in the 12th century. It declined under the lay abbot, Conrad of Gleichen (1454–74), joined the Bursfeld Reform in 1478, was a leader of the Bursfeld Union, and finally came under Prussian control and was suppressed in 1803. BIBLIOGRAPHY: Cottineau 2:3443–44.

[E. J. DILLON]

WERENFRID, ST. (d. c.726), Anglo-Saxon monk and missionary. A Northumbrian, he accompanied St. Willibrord on the Frisian mission. He preached in Holland and Gelderland and was martyred after his return from a journey to France. His relics were venerated at Elst. BIBLIOGRAPHY: J. Druse, NCE 14:876; W. Levison, *England and the Continent in the Eighth Century* (1946), 61; Zimmerman 2:572–573.

[J. DRUSE]

WERFEL, FRANZ (1890–1945), Austrian novelist, poet, playwright. One of the most prominent writers of German literary Expressionism, he leaned toward Catholicism in his later work without formally joining the Church. Like F. Kafka, W. was born in Prague as the son of a Jewish merchant. After studies and service in the Austrian army during World War I, he married Alma Maria Mahler and settled in Vienna. In 1938 they fled from the Nazis to France and later (1940) to the U.S., where they lived in Beverly Hills, Calif. A number of his novels have won popularity both in English and German, especially his *The Song of Bernadette* (1942), the story of the Lourdes miracle told movingly without being a religious book; it was written as fulfillment of a vow for safe arrival in the U.S. In his play *Der Spiegelmensch* (1920) the hero wins a Faustian struggle between the dual powers within himself through overcoming the selfish "mirrorself" in the spiritual world of the monastery. The novel *The Forty Days of Musa Dagh* (1934) gives a powerful portrait of the brutal extinction of the Christian Armenians by the Mohammedan Turks and is a plea for humanitarianism. Shortly before his death W. completed a novel, *Star of the Unborn* (1946), in which only Catholicism is given a chance to survive in a future world. BIBLIOGRAPHY: *Franz Werfel, 1890–1945* (ed. L. B. Foltin, 1961).

[B. F. STEINBRUCKNER]

WERNER OF OBERWESEL, ST. (c.1273–87), patron of winegrowers. His legend, based on hearings for his canonization (1426), asserts that W., a vineyard worker, was murdered by his Jewish employer. The resulting persecution of the Jews was stopped by Rudolf of Hapsburg. A chapel over W.'s grave became a place of pilgrimage. By winegrowers he is venerated as St. Vernier. BIBLIOGRAPHY: D. Andreini, NCE 14:876.

[M. J. FINNEGAN]

WERNER OF TEGERNSEE (d. after 1195), monk. Exiled for a time to Salzburg, W. returned to become head of the school at Tegernsee as Latin scholar (Werner Scholasticus) and teacher. Broader interests led him to draw a map of the world and to begin a botanical garden, as well as to enlarge the monastery library. His hand is recognized in various codices; he wrote part of the *Annales Tegernseenses*. Scholars are still examining and have not reached agreement upon his contributions to other MSS of the 12th cent. at Tegernsee, nor that he worked as an illuminator. BIBLIOGRAPHY: A. A. Schacher, NCE 14:876–877.

[M. E. DUFFY]

WERNER, ZACHARIAS (1768–1823), German romantic playwright. After a dissolute life, Werner became a Catholic (1810), a priest (1814), and a popular Viennese preacher. His dramas, which reveal the influence of the Baroque stage and of Schiller, are generally mystic treatments of historical subjects (e.g., *Martin Luther, oder die Weihe der Kraft*, 1807; *Attila, König der Hunnen*, 1808. His most famous work, however, is the one-act *Schicksalstragödie* (fate tragedy), *Der 24, Februar* (produced in 1810; published in 1815). BIBLIOGRAPHY: W. Kosch, *Deutsches Literatur-Lexikon* (1963) 482.

[M. F. MCCARTHY]

WERVE, CLAUS DE (d. 1439), Flemish sculptor, nephew and pupil of Claus Sluter, upon whose death W. completed the famous *Well of Moses* at the *Chartreuse de Champmol, carving the weeping angels at the top, and completing (1411) Sluter's tomb of Philip the Bold which influenced many later such monuments. W. was commissioned to carve the tomb of John the Fearless, never realized because of lack of funds. W. died in poverty.

[M. J. DALY]

WESLEY, CHARLES (1707–88), younger brother of John *Wesley; Anglican priest and hymn writer. The brothers were born at Epworth, Lincolnshire, where the father was rector of the parish. In 1716 Charles entered Westminster School, London, and in 1726, Christ Church, Oxford. There, in 1729, he became part of the holy club of students, who in ridicule were dubbed "methodists." He was ordained in 1735, and or the next year served as Gen. Oglethorpe's private secretary in the Ga. colony. Ill and disillusioned over his Ga. mission, W. was back in Eng. in Dec. 1736. Like his brother he had a conversion experience the following Whitsunday, which satisfied the longing, inspired by contact with Moravians in Ga., for a personal saving faith in Christ. He voiced his mood of exaltation in his famous hymn, "Where Shall My Wondering Soul Begin?'' and became an enthusiastic preacher-evangelist of the Methodist revival, itinerating (see ITINERANCY) until 1756, and thereafter preaching regularly at Bristol and at London. He was always a loyal partner and champion of his brother, who was the more prominent authority in the movement. The brothers, however, differed at some points; Charles strongly disapproved of John's 1784 ordinations (see AS-BURY, F.; COKE, T.) and generally showed a fiercer, though not stronger, devotion to the established Church. He wrote more than 6,000 hymns as effective means of evangelizing; they made the Methodists a singing people, and enriched the hymnody of other Churches. More than 500 are of excellent lyrical quality; many are still useful and almost universally known, e.g., ''Jesus, Lover of My Soul,'' and ''Hark! the Herald Angels Sing.'' BIBLIOGRAPHY: C. W. Flint, *Charles Wesley* (1957); J. E. Rattenbury, *Evangelical Doctrines of Charles Wesley's Hymns* (1941); E. Routley, *Musical Wesleys* (1968).

[D. R. CHANDLER]

WESLEY, JOHN (1703–91), founder of *Methodism. Older brother of Charles, W. was born at Epworth in Lincolnshire. His father, Samuel, was a devout and studious parish priest; his mother, Susanna (Annesley), a woman of remarkably independent spirit and high mental gifts. Their legacy to the children was a devotion to the Church, the Bible, and the BCP, a Puritan morality, and esp. a disciplined way of life. In 1709 W. was saved from a fire in the parsonage, and afterward thought of himself as a ''brand plucked from the burning,'' the recipient of miraculous divine intervention for a purpose largely fulfilled by the Methodist revival. He entered Christ Church, Oxford, in 1720, where from *c*.1725 his reading of books by W. Law, J. *Taylor, and Thomas à Kempis gave him ''a settled conviction to become a real Christian.'' This ''alteration of his temper'' was accompanied by the decision to take holy orders; accordingly he was ordained deacon in 1725 and priest in 1728. Periodically he served as his father's curate, and upon returning to Oxford in 1729 became leader of a holy club, a group of serious students who had united with Charles to seek ''inward holiness.'' Strict regularity of life earned them the jeering name ''methodists'' from other students, but they were soon widely known for their good works and their unusual devotion to the Church and the sacraments. In the Ga. colony (1735–38) his parishioners rejected his ministry; the Indians were unreceptive to the Gospel; and the young girl he loved married another man. But his religious desires were deepened by association with some Moravian settlers, who proclaimed the felt assurance of faith to be the very essence of scriptural Christianity.

Back in England he ''preached faith'' with such enthusiasm that he was barred from several pulpits. On May 24, 1738, at a little society in Aldersgate Street in London, he felt his ''heart strangely warmed,'' and he was given the faith in Christ he had been seeking so long. After a summer's visit among the Moravians at *Herrnhut in Germany, W. returned to England and gave himself to the revival then in progress, preaching, organizing societies and classes, and directing all related activities. He adopted the *field preaching introduced by G. *Whitefield, appointed local and traveling lay preachers, opened houses of worship (see FOUN-DRY), and raised funds for the preachers and benevolent causes. As editor and author he prepared grammars (Hebrew, Greek, French, Latin, and English), sermons, poems, hymns, letters, adridgements of classics, *A Christian Library, Rules, Advices,* and *Instructions*, and treatises in theology, politics, science, and medicine. For 52 years W. so dominated the Methodist movement that for the most part it became the creation of his mind and spirit. Many journeys to Scotland, Ireland, and Wales spread his influence widely. Because of his love for the C of E, W. hoped the Methodists would never leave it, but many practical steps he took, particularly the ordinations he himself performed beginning in 1784 (see ASBURY, F.; COKE, T.), broke eccl. law and forced a separation; his lay preachers, appeal to *Nonconformists, and distrust of the parish system (see ITINERANCY) also contributed. In time active opposition to the Methodists gradually lessened, and mob violence, so common earlier, disappeared; in his last years he was honored as ''England's grand old man.'' He died, an Anglican priest to the last, and was buried behind the Methodist City Road Chapel, London.

The spread and organization of the Wesleyan revival combated 18th cent. *deism and rationalism. Although he distrusted extremes both of mysticism and enthusiasm, he encouraged emotionalism and passionately insisted on the primacy of a personal experience of faith and of God's love. His central doctrine, *Christian perfection, which drew away from Luther's view of sinful human nature, inspired *revivalism and the *Holiness movement. His *Arminianism, as opposed to Calvinistic predestination, stressed the universal availability of grace and an optimistic view of every form of human goodness. The minutely disciplined Christian life that he taught against Moravian *antinomianism had a widespread effect on moral standards, both personal and social. Emphasis on the gospel message as communitarian fostered Christian social consciousness. The possibility of a personal experience of sanctification widely affected attitudes toward the mediating role of Church or sacraments. Through such ideas W. has had an impact on Christian thought and life next only to that of Luther and Calvin. BIBLIOGRAPHY: John Wesley, *Journal* (ed. N. Curnock, 8v., 1909–16); *Compend of Wesley's Theology* (eds. R. W. Burtner and R. E. Chiles, 1958); V. H. H. Green, *John Wesley* (1965); Mayer RB 284–294; R. C. Monk, *John Wesley: His Puritan Heritage* (1966); M. Piette, *John Wesley and the Evolution of Protestantism* (tr. J. B. Howard, 1937); J. M. Todd, *John Wesley and the Catholic Church* (1958); M. Schmidt, *John Wesley: A Theological Biography* (v. 1, tr. N. P. Goldhawk, 1962); C. Williams, *John Wesley's Theology Today* (1960).

[D. R. CHANDLER]

WESSENBERG, IGNAZ HEINRICH VON (1774–1860), German Catholic pastoral theologian, liturgical reformer, humanist, man of the Enlightenment. Born in Dresden, W. was influenced by Karl von Dalberg who became his patron, enabling him to become vicar general of Constance while still a subdeacon, ten years before ordination as priest. Rome vigorously resisted various attempts to have W. promoted to bishop. His pastoral and liturgical reforms were hopelessly ahead of his times. The wonder is that he was able to avoid outright condemnation and schism. He promoted continuing education for clergy after ordination, fostered the vernacular in liturgy, esp. vernacular hymns. He also tried to upgrade preaching and biblical studies and fostered leadership and scholarship among the laity. Dalberg named W. his vicar at the Congress of Vienna in 1813, where he tried unsuccessfully to obtain autonomy from Rome for German-speaking Catholics. He was outspokenly against such traditions as pilgrimages, processions, Marian devotions, monasteries, and mendicant orders. Two of his works which were critical of Roman attitudes were placed on the Index. He remained a prolific writer and bequeathed his library to the city of Constance, where it became the basis for that city's university library.

[E. J. DILLON]

WESSOBRUNN, ABBEY OF, former Benedictine abbey in Upper Bavaria, founded *c.* 753 by monks who came from Niederalteich. Here was composed the Wessobrunn Prayer, the oldest monument of German language. The Hungarian invasion destroyed it (1065), only monks came back, and a nunnery was added. It was at all times a cradle of intellectual life and scholarship. In 1803 it was suppressed; in 1810 the church and most of the buildings were pulled down; only the hostelry, a gem of baroque art, remains, now habited by Benedictine nuns. The lands are owned by the monks of St. Ottilien, who have a small priory there. BIBLIOGRAPHY: Hemmerle, *Die Benediktinerklöster in Bayern* (1951) 139–141.

[N. BACKMUND]

WESSOBRUNNER GEBET (often referred to as *The Wessobrunn Creation and Prayer*), two short texts (A and B) in Bavarian dialect found in a 9th-cent. MS (now in Munich) from the monastery of Wessobrunn in Bavaria. Text A, a fragment of alliterative verse (9 lines) about the time preceding creation, contains conventional poetic formulae reminiscent of the pagan Eddic *Völuspá* and, perhaps, of Anglo-Saxon poetry. Text B is a prose prayer to the Creator. The MS heading, *De poëta*, is usually interpreted as a Latinization of the Greek *poiētēs* (Creator). For text, see K. V. Müllenhoff and W. Scherer, *Denkmäler deutscher Poesie und Prosa aus dem 8. bis 12. Jahrhundert* (3d ed. rev. E. von Steinmeyer, v. 1, No. 1, 1892); for commentary, see L. Seiffert, "Metrical Form and Composition of the *Wessobrunner Gebet*," *Medium Aevum* 31 (1962) 1–13.

[M. F. MCCARTHY]

WEST, BENJAMIN (1738–1820), Quaker, American-English artist. He painted portraits in Philadelphia (1756) and in New York, and studied Neoclassical 16th- and 17th-cent. Roman and Bolognese artists in Italy (1760). Settling in London (1763), he became a popular portrait and history painter, the favorite of George III (1768) who wished to knight the artist. Introducing modern costume, W. revolutionized history panels (*Death of Wolfe*, 1771), and remaining expatriate became second president of the Royal Academy (1792). The Neoclassical panels, *Our Saviour Healing the Sick* (1811) and *Christ Rejected by Caiaphas* (1814), with the famous *Death on a Pale Horse* (1817), full of frenzy, presaging French romanticism, mark vigorous last period of finest work. Young American painters studied in W.'s London studio, notably Gilbert Stuart who was to surpass his master. BIBLIOGRAPHY: Philadelphia Museum of Art, *Benjamin West, 1738–1820* (1938).

[M. J. DALY]

WEST SYRIAN CHURCH, the Syrian Monophysite or "Jacobite" Church, formed by those Christians of the Patriarchate of Antioch who did not accept the decisions of the Council of Chalcedon in 451. Its own members do not care for the title "Jacobite" and call it simply the "Syrian Church" or, to distinguish it from the Syrian Catholic Church, the "Syrian Orthodox Church," but the latter expression leads to confusion, being used also by the (Byzantine) Orthodox of the Patriarchate of Antioch.

The original division between Monophysites and Orthodox in Syria, as in Egypt, corresponded largely to a cultural division, Hellenistic Syrians, found esp. in the large cities and along the coast, accepting Chalcedon, representatives of native Syrian culture, predominantly in country districts, joining the Monophysite party, although the nationalist aspect was less pronounced than in Egypt. The Syrian Monophysites were slow to organize because of the vacillation in ecclesiastical politics following Chalcedon. Both the acts of Chalcedon and the conciliatory *Henoticon of the Emperor Zeno were definitively repudiated by a synod held at Tyre in 512 under the leadership of Severus of Antioch, who gave Syrian monophysitism (as well as Coptic and Armenian monophysitism ultimately) its official theological form.

The actual organization of the Monophysite Syrian Church was accomplished by Ya'qôb Burde'āyā (or Burde'ānā; 490–578), generally referred to as Jacob Baradai, one of two bishops consecrated, through the favor of the Empress Theodora, by the Alexandrian Patriarch Theodosius in 542 for the Monophysites of Syria, from whose name the epithet "Jacobite" is derived. A period of vitality ensued, and the Church gained a strong foothold not only in Roman Syria but also in N Mesopotamia, thanks partly to the favor it enjoyed in the Persian Empire through Shirin, Monophysite wife of Khosrow II. The 7th cent. marked the advent of Islam in the Near East. The Jacobites fared reasonably well under the Omayyads, but the doubling of taxes imposed on all Syrian Christians by the Abbasid caliphs shortly after the mid-8th cent. began a slow but steady leakage to Islam, although the number of Jacobites increased in Mesopotamia, mostly at the expense of Nestorianism, with the result that a majority of Jacobites was eventually to be found in Mesopotamia.

After flourishing culturally and religiously 1100–1275 (the "Syrian Renaissance"), the Church began a marked decline, all the more difficult to arrest because of the neglect of clerical learning and discipline, and the internal conflict which was evident in the regional splitting of the hierarchy itself into two (and at times even four) rival patriarchates. It was in this weakened state that it suffered the worst outward persecution of its history, under Tamerlane (1360–1405), with massive apostasy to Islam. In 1665 those East Syrian Catholics of South India who rebelled against the heavy Latinizing imposed upon them by the West united themselves to the Jacobite patriarchate and adopted the West Syrian liturgy. The Church was troubled in the 19th cent. by its definitive split into the traditional Syrian Church and the Syrian Catholic Church, and in the 20th by the efforts of the Indian Jacobites to achieve greater independence; both the conversions to Catholicism and the Indian independence movement have now lost most of their impetus. In earlier centuries the Syrians quarreled often with other Monophysites, esp. the Armenians; relations with the Egyptians have been closer, Syrian patriarchs occasionally arbitrating disputes within the medieval Coptic Church, and one of the centers of medieval Syrian learning being the Monastery of the Syrians in the Nitrian desert. Today all Monophysite Churches recognize one another peacefully.

The patriarchal residence, moved many times over the centuries, is since 1959 in Damascus. Since 1293 all patriarchs take the name Ignatius upon their accession. The present patriarch, Mar Ignatius (XXXIX) Jacob III, has more than 100,000 faithful (not counting the more numerous Indian Jacobites). BIBLIOGRAPHY: M. Jugie, DTC 10:2216–51. The best survey is that of B. Spuler, *Handbuch der Orientalistik* I. viii. 2:170–216.

[A. CODY]

WEST SYRIAN LITURGY, liturgical rites and practices of the W Syrian Church (Jacobite and Catholic), used also in India by the Syrian Orthodox since their union with the Jacobite Patriarchate in the 17th cent. (hence, since the 1930 conversions, also by Catholics of the new Syro-Malankar Rite) with minor variants from group to group. In its origins the liturgy contained Greek elements from Jerusalem and Antioch as well as Syrian ones from Edessa. It was simply the liturgy of the Patriarchate of Antioch, until the split of that patriarchate into a Chalcedonian branch, which eventually adopted the Byzantine liturgy completely, and a Monophysite branch, in which the Antiochene liturgy continued to develop in its own way, with all texts soon in Syriac, thus constituting a liturgy conveniently called W Syrian to distinguish it from the E Syrian use of the Nestorians. The detailed history of its development is yet to be done. It is often difficult to judge whether a given element shared with E Syrian or Greek liturgies is loaned to or borrowed from W Syrian practice or whether a common antecedent lies behind them.

As in other Churches, the number and identity of the Sacraments varied before the medieval period. Bar Hebraeus (1226–86) enumerated five: baptism, Eucharist, laying-on-of-hands (holy orders), consecration of *myron* (chrism, used in confirmation), and burial. Jacobites today hold that there are seven sacraments (*mysteria*), the same seven as in the modern Roman Church, with confirmation represented by the consecration of *myron*. The anointing with *myron* follows baptism immediately, a distinction between the two being made more clearly today than often in the past. The anointing of the sick appeared very late as a sacrament. Private confession is practiced today. The Eucharistic Sacrifice (*qûrrōḇō, qûrbōnō*) has a matrix of prayers and ceremonies remaining constant (the *ordo communis*), into which are inserted variable readings, *sed̲rê, teshb^eḥōt̲ō*, and especially one of the various anaphoras, of which 70 or so are available, but only a dozen are in common use. The most important and most ancient of the anaphoras is that of St. James, the ancient anaphora of the Church of Jerusalem translated into Syriac and showing certain variants from the Greek recension. In Jacobite usage the communion of both priest and people takes place at the very end of the Eucharistic Sacrifice, after the dismissal of the rest of the congregation. Leavened bread is used, and communion is given under both species, the people receiving pieces of the consecrated bread touched with the consecrated wine in the rite of intinction.

The canonical hours are seven: Vespers, Compline, the Night Office, the Morning Office, Terce, Sext, and None. The beginning of the day is still reckoned in Semitic fashion as beginning at sunset; hence what is called "Vespers of Monday" is said Sunday evening by Western reckoning. Set forms of Sext, None, and Compline established for each day of the week are invariable even on feasts; the other hours have proper texts for Sundays and feasts. The Night Office is divided into three "stations" (nocturns), with a long section after the third station which was originally a morning office. The ancient psalmody has been reduced to a minimum, strophes originally meant to be intercalated between the verses of the psalmody having developed into the greater part of the present office.

Two major variants of W Syrian usage are those of the W Syrians in Mesopotamia, which reflects E Syrian influence, and of the Maronites, which is highly eclectic, borrowing and rearranging texts of various W and E Syrian provenance, with considerable Roman influence in vestments, vessels, furnishings, and actions.

The liturgical year begins on the Sunday nearest the last day in October (Sunday of the Hallowing of the Church). BIBLIOGRAPHY: H. W. Codrington, "Syrian Liturgy," ECQ 1 (1936) 10–20, 40–49, 87–99, 135–148.

[A. CODY]

WEST VIRGINIA, an east central state admitted to the Union (1863) as the 35th state. Although the region remained a part of Va. until the Civil War, it had long enjoyed a distinct history, esp. in the matter of religion, for it did not recognize the establishment of Anglicanism in the colonial era. Throughout the 18th cent. numerous Protestant missionaries and immigrants went to West Va. Presbyterians were active there by 1735, while Baptists were present in several eastern counties by 1743.

Few Catholics were among the W. Va. populace during the 18th and early 19th cent. When the Diocese of Wheeling was erected (1850), there were only about 5,000 Catholics, 6 priests, and 7 churches and chapels in the area. R. V. Whelan, Wheeling's first bp., was succeeded (1875) by J. J. Kain, who carried on missionary work in the rural diocese. P. J. Donahue, who became the third bp. in 1893, was succeeded (1922) by J. J. *Swint. Swint, who served Wheeling for 41 years, emphasized institutional development until his death in 1962. The present bishop is J. J. Hodges; his diocese is a suffragan of the metropolitan see of Baltimore, Md. It comprises the State of W. Va. with the exception of certain counties in the eastern panhandle which are under the jurisdiction of the Diocese of Richmond, and it also includes some counties of the State of Va. In 1977 W. Va.'s Catholics numbered about 97,455, or 5.6% of the total state population. The major Protestant denominations are the Methodist Church, with 12.5% of the total population in 1971, and the Am. Baptist Convention, with 8.2%. Other Protestant denominations comprised 14.1% of the population. Jewish population (1968) was 5,233, or 0.3%.

There is one Catholic college in W Va. with an enrollment of 1,041 students. Ten Catholic high schools serve the educational needs of more than 2,800 students, while 37 Catholic elementary schools are attended by 6,825 pupils. BIBLIOGRAPHY: C. H. Ambler and F. P. Summers, *West Virginia: The Mountain State* (2d ed., 1958); J. H. Bailey, II, *A History of the Diocese of Richmond: The Formative Years* (1956); D. W. Johnson, et al., *Churches and Church Membership in U.S.* (1974).

[J. L. MORRISON; R. M. PRESTON]

WESTCOTT, BROOKE FOSS (1825–1901), Anglican bp. and biblical scholar. He graduated from Trinity College, Cambridge, in 1848, and was ordained in 1851. He became assistant master of Harrow in 1852, Regius professor of divinity at Cambridge in 1870, and successor to J. B. *Lightfoot as bp. of Durham in 1890. In addition to doctrinal works and collections of sermons and addresses, he published highly regarded commentaries on John (1881), the Epistles of John (1883), and Hebrews (1889). In collaboration with F. J. A. *Hort, he published *The New Testament in the Original Greek* (1881–82). Their classification of the NT MSS traditions into the Neutral, Alexandrian, Western, and Syrian, while modified by later scholars, became the basis for all modern textual criticism. BIBLIOGRAPHY: A. Westcott, *Life and Letters of Brooke Foss Westcott* (2 v., 1903); P. W. Skehan et al., JBC 2:582–583.

[T. EARLY]

WESTERN RITE. Though a generic name for the liturgical families of W Christianity, it is usually used to refer to the dominant form, the Roman rite. While there were several urban centers of Christianity in the East, only Rome was such in the West and only it could claim association with the Apostles. With the Roman switch from Greek to Latin by the end of the 4th cent., Latin became the sole liturgical language of the West. While the Roman is the only Western rite now in extensive use, the Ambrosian (Milanese) rite also survives, as does a vestige of the *Mozarabic (one chapel of the Toledo cathedral), and some variants of the Roman used by several religious orders. Vatican II's permission for vernacular languages and call for cultural adaptation of the liturgy can be expected to lead to significant variations of the Roman liturgy, particularly in the Third World.

Historically, there have been two major liturgical groupings in the West: the Gallic or Gallican and the Roman-African. The Gallic or Gallican family of rites, of disputed origin, shows many similarities to the W Syrian liturgies of the East and is of various types. (1) The Spanish (Mozarabic or Visigothic), fully developed by the 6th cent., was basically ended by the Islamic conquest, though a vestige of its 15th-cent. revival continues today. (2) Little is known of the Celtic rites of Ireland and Scotland, though they seem not to have been particularly original. (3) The Milanese rite, now heavily Romanized, is the only Gallican liturgy still in extensive use. The fact that it often maintains Roman features later abandoned by Rome has led many scholars to see it as a primitive Roman liturgy. (4) The Gallican liturgy proper is a collective term for a great variety of forms in the Frankish kingdom. These were suppressed by Charlemagne in the early 9th cent. in favor of the Roman, in an effort to unify his kingdom.

Little is known of the Roman-African family, except for the Roman rite. The African was apparently quite similar, as is the Alexandrian family of Eastern rites. The Roman was fixed quite early and has rarely been creative in its later development, though it has borrowed from the East and was much modified as it was being imposed on the Franks by Charlemagne. By the end of the 11th cent. the Gallicanized Roman liturgy returned to Rome and displaced the Roman itself. This is the form which has remained in use since. Twentieth-cent. reforms have been primarily directed at recovering the "soberness and sense" of the Roman rite.

Medieval English rites were only "uses" or local modifications of the Roman, often with strong Gallican features. The most important were those of Sarum, York, Hereford, and Bangor. BIBLIOGRAPHY: T. Klauser, *Short History of the Western Liturgy* (1969); A. King, *Liturgies of the Past* (1959).

[J. DALLEN]

WESTERN SCHISM, see GREAT WESTERN SCHISM

WESTERN TEXT OF THE NEW TESTAMENT, one of the principal MS traditions identified by scholars in their quest for an authentic text of the New Testament. The myriad extant MSS and versions fall into one of several "families" or MS traditions; the most important are: the Antiochian, called A after an ancient MS coded A; the Alexandrian, called B for a similar reason; the Caesarean, represented by MS Ō and Th; and the Western Text, called D after MS D, but of uncertain geographical origin. The Western Text is very ancient, going back at least to the 2d cent., and is represented not only by the Greek MS D, but by the Old Latin and Syriac versions as well. Thus it was widely circulated in Latin and Syriac lands and apparently also in Egypt, since Clement of Alexandria seems to have been familiar with it. It was the old popular Christian text and as such the victim of mediocre editing, reflecting the low level of culture in which it thrived. As a result, its Gospels are characterized by accretions, harmonizations, omissions, and frequent modification of difficult terms. It has a special text of Acts which, by its addition of so many events and details omitted in other texts, can be called a secondary form of the text. The Antiochian text (A) was the official text of the Greek Church from the Greek fathers down to the 19th cent., and only with the insistent scholarship of recent decades has the Alexandrian text (B) replaced it as most ancient and authentic, as well as most intelligently edited. Because of the Western Text's careless editing, it is considered generally more remote than B from the original text, but it still has variants of great value.

[E. J. DILLON]

WESTERN THEOLOGY, the theology of the Western Church. Starting with the datum of revelation and using the law and effort of reason to construct a science of divine things, Western theology tries to arrive at a better technical understanding of God and man's relationship to him. For this purpose it employs rational analogy, a proportionality between the finite and infinite. Though conscious of the limitations of human reason, it opts for a positive use of created perfections in understanding the infinite ones because they reflect God himself, their author. Perhaps the first proponent of the principle that no contradiction exists between natural truth and revelation was St. Anselm of Canterbury, Doctor of the Church commonly called the father of scholastic theology; St. Thomas Aquinas, also a Doctor, was its foremost proponent. Since the 13th-cent. flowering of scholasticism, the Western orientation is toward Christology. Christ is recognized to be the center and total circumference of his mystical Body, the Church. The Church feels the tension between the present and the future, but its major interest is in the present. BIBLIOGRAPHY: P. De Letter, NCE 14:49–58. *EASTERN THEOLOGY.

[J. FICHTNER]

WESTERNERS, Russian intellectuals of the 19th cent. (esp. 1840–70) who believed that the way to Russia's greatness lay in imitation of the West. Though they agreed with the *Slavophiles in promoting agrarian and industrial re-

forms, they were, for the most part, radicals and atheists, whereas the Slavophiles were non-political Christian idealists. Both groups were influenced, though in different ways, by Hume, Proudhon, and the German philosophers Kant, Schelling, Hegel, and Marx. Leaders of the movement included V. Belinsky (1811–48), A. Herzen (1812–70), and M. Bakunin (1814–76). BIBLIOGRAPHY: *Russian Philosophy* (ed. J. M. Edie et al., 1965) 1:155–270.

[M. F. MCCARTHY]

WESTMALLE, ABBEY OF, Trappist Cistercian monastery in Belgium, near Antwerp, founded by monks expelled by the French Revolution. The house was firmly established in 1814 after several futile attempts and became an abbey in 1836, serving until 1892 as the headquarters of the Belgian Trappist Congregation. The abbey has a fine library and the monks print the liturgical books of their order. BIBLIOGRAPHY: B. Bader, LTK 10:1073; CollOCR (1935) 2:19–21.

[L. J. LEKAI]

WESTMINSTER ASSEMBLY, a synod appointed by the Long Parliament in June 1643, for the purpose of remaking the C of E in accordance with the demands of the Puritans, who claimed that the Church had not yet been purified of errors. Among the 151 members of the Assembly were 30 laymen and 120 theologians. Convinced advocates of *episcopacy did not attend, and the field was left to the larger group of Presbyterian sympathizers. The Assembly began by considering revisions of the *Thirty-Nine Articles, but under the influence of the *Solemn League and Covenant, it framed a completely new document, the *Westminster Confession. Under increasing Presbyterian domination, the Assembly was joined by eight commissioners from Scot. The *Westminster Directory for Public Worship, which for a time replaced the *Book of Common Prayer (1645–61), and the two *Westminster Catechisms were also issued. The Assembly met intermittently until 1653 and was never officially dissolved. The Westminster Standards, the documents produced by the Assembly, were in effect only briefly in England, but they are still recognized by the *Church of Scotland and by most Presbyterians. BIBLIOGRAPHY: W. Beveridge, *Short History of the Westminster Assembly* (1904); S. W. Carruthers, *Everyday Work of the Westminster Assembly* (1943).

[R. B. ENO]

WESTMINSTER CATECHISMS, the Larger and Shorter Catechisms, approved in 1648 by the *Westminster Assembly and intended to be, together with the *Westminster Confession, the doctrinal standard of the Presbyterian Churches. The Larger Catechism is based on earlier catechisms, e.g., Luther's *Catechisms and Calvin's *Genevan Catechisms, and more directly on the *Irish Articles (1615) and James Ussher's *Body of Divinity* (1645). Written mainly by Anthony Tuckney (1599–1670) of Emmanuel College, Cambridge, it tends to be philosophical rather than biblical in its definition of God and departs from the evangelical character of the older Calvinist tradition by implying a doctrine of *limited atonement. The Shorter Catechism, also written mainly by Tuckney, is a notable example of later Calvinism at its best in its pedagogical method, its unity of thought, and terseness of expression. Intended "for such as are of a weaker capacity," i.e., for children who found the Larger Catechism too detailed for memorizing, the Shorter Catechism is divided into two main sections, totaling 107 questions and answers: first, doctrines to be believed and, second, duties to be performed. Though the Catechisms are no longer in general use, their influence in and beyond Presbyterianism has been immense. BIBLIOGRAPHY: Schaff Creeds 1:783–787; 3:676–704.

[J. A. R. MACKENZIE]

WESTMINSTER CATHEDRAL, London cathedral church of the Archdiocese of Westminster. Projected by Card. Wiseman in 1865 but not begun until the archbishopric of Card. H. *Vaughan in 1895, it was designed by John Francis Bentley. It carries elements of Gothic, Romanesque, Norman and Byzantine architecture. The exterior is of brick and concrete and is distinguished by an impressive campanile. Gothic type pillars are inside but the exterior is free of outside support. The roof of the main structure is a series of domes. The interior is wide and free of obstructing supports and the sanctuary is Byzantine. The Byzantine is also evident in the mosaics and marble of the interior. To the viewer, a striking feature of the exterior is the pattern of stone bands running through the red brickwork. The facade has a recessed arch over the main entrance, and on each side of the arch tribunes and stairway turrets. Westminster has affinities with St. Mark's of Venice and the style of Constantinople.

[J. R. AHERNE]

WESTMINSTER CONFESSION, the primary *confession of faith for Presbyterianism, and a major *Reformed document. Toward the close of 1640 a document written probably by Alexander Henderson (c. 1583–1646) was presented from Scotland to the English Lords of the Treaty at London, declaring that it was desirable "that there were one Confession of Faith, one form of Catechism, one Directory for all the parts of the public worship of God . . . in all the Churches of his majesty's dominions." In 1642 the English Parliament affirmed its desire for "a most firm and stable union between the two kingdoms of England and Scotland." The General Assembly of the Scottish Church expressed its own desire to agree upon a common Confession of Faith, Catechism, and Directory for worship, and in Aug. 1643 elected commissioners to attend the *Westminster Assembly for this purpose. Drafted in 1646, the confession was published in 1648 with the approval of both Houses of Parliament, but it was never sanctioned in its entirety in England. In Scotland its acceptance was more immediate, the *General Assembly having already in 1647 expressed its

approval, "judging it to be most orthodox and grounded on the Word of God."

The Confession contains 33 chapters dealing with Scripture, God, the eternal decrees, creation and providence, the Fall, sin, the covenant, Christ the mediator, free will, effectual calling, justification, sanctification, faith, repentance, good works, perseverance of the saints, grace, the law of God, Christian liberty, worship, the magistrate, Church and sacraments, censures, synods and councils, and death and judgment. As used by Presbyterians in the U.S., ch. 23 (magistrates) and ch. 31 (synods and councils) have been altered. Hendry lists four characteristics of the Confession: its approach is excessively legalistic; it assumes that every question has a right or wrong answer; it sees everything in terms of black and white; it is individualistic and does not express the social significance of redemption. Yet ch. 1 on Scripture is an excellent statement of the Calvinist position. The "awful decree" of *double predestination is discussed in ch. 3, though few Presbyterian Churches now hold to the doctrine as here expressed. The Confession departs from earlier Calvinism, however, by speaking of two covenants (works and grace); when it discusses the sacraments (ch. 27), not so much as seals of the word of the gospel as seals of our faith in the gospel, it tends to restrict the evangelical character of the covenant of grace.

In Scotland commitment to the Confession became increasingly rigid. From 1690 university teachers and from 1711 *probationers and ordinands were required to subscribe to it as "founded upon the Word of God" and to acknowledge it as the confession of their own faith. The Confession, though held to be subordinate to Scripture, of which it was a summary and guide for interpretation, came to be regarded as the touchstone of Calvinist orthodoxy. There were, nevertheless, remarkably few dissentients, and only in the 19th cent. were certain of its major doctrines seriously questioned. The *Articles Declaratory of the Church of Scotland (1926) distinguished between basic doctrines of the Christian faith and those on which liberty of opinion was permitted, and the formula of subscription to the Confession has been considerably modified in most Presbyterian Churches. BIBLIOGRAPHY: Schaff Creeds 1:753–782; 3:598–673 (text); G. S. Hendry, *Westminster Confession for Today* (1960); E. A. Dowey, Jr., *Commentary on the Confession of 1967 and an Introduction to the "Book of Confessions"* (1968). *AUBURN AFFIRMATION; *CONFESSION OF 1967.

[J. A. R. MACKENZIE]

WESTMINSTER DIRECTORY FOR WORSHIP, the *Directory for the Public Worship of God,* produced by the *Westminster Assembly and imposed by Parliament in 1645 as a replacement for the Book of Common Prayer (BCP) to bring about in worship the uniformity of practice advocated in the *Solemn League and Covenant. The framers of the Directory were mainly English churchmen of Puritan or Presbyterian inclinations. The influence of the BCP and the

*Book of Common Order is evident, and though its use was never widespread in England, the Directory remained a standard of worship in the Church of Scotland until the 1860s, when reforms in worship began to be introduced. In the 1890s similar developments began in American Presbyterianism. The Sunday morning service in the Directory is one of solemn simplicity and strongly scriptural content, with all responses and the Apostles' Creed omitted. The sections on the sacraments, drafted by the Scottish Commissioners at the assembly, preserve the older Scottish tradition. The celebration of communion ("frequently to be celebrated") consists in a warning against unworthy reception and the narrative of institution from 1 Cor 11; the outlines of a prayer of consecration are indicated. For text and commentary see T. Leishman, *Westminster Directory* (1901).

[J. A. R. MACKENZIE]

WESTMINSTER STANDARDS, a collective reference to the Confession, Catechisms, and Directory for Worship formulated by the *Westminster Assembly.

WESTON, WILLIAM (1551–1615), Jesuit missionary. Educated in law, W. became a Jesuit and was ordained on the Continent. In 1584 he returned to England where he became a principal organizer of the Catholic mission. He was arrested in 1586 and endured a long imprisonment in the Clink (1586–88), Wisbech Castle (1588–98), and the Tower (1598–1603), during which time he became a symbol of Catholic resistance. Released into exile in 1603, he died as rector of the English College, Valladolid. BIBLIOGRAPHY: W. Weston, *Autobiography of an Elizabethan,* (tr. P. Caraman, 1955); *Wisbech Stirs* (Catholic Record Society 51, ed. P. Reynold, 1958); DNB 60:378.

[V. SAMPSON]

WESTPHALIA, PEACE OF, the name for two treaties simultaneously concluded on Oct. 24, 1648, ending the Thirty Years' War. The Treaty of Münster was between the Holy Roman Empire and France; that of Osnabrück, between the Empire and the Protestant Estates as well as Sweden. By the political and territorial determinations, Sweden and France were both greatly strengthened, the independence of Switzerland and the Netherlands was recognized, and the Empire was reduced to a shadow of its former prestige and power. The principle *cuius regio eius religio* was extended to the *Reformed Churches. Protestant and Catholic states were to be equals in the Empire. The *Edict of Restitution (1629) was set aside, and the situation prevailing on Jan. 1, 1624 as to ecclesiastical lands was ratified. Religious questions in the Diet of the Empire were to be settled amicably rather than by coercion, and Protestant administrators of church lands were to be seated. A prince who changed his religion was to forfeit his lands. The influence of the papacy on German ecclesiastical affairs was greatly restricted (Pope Innocent X protested against the

treaties in the bull *Zelo domus Dei,* Nov. 16, 1648). By the Peace of Westphalia Protestantism gained strength and official recognition. BIBLIOGRAPHY: C. V. Wedgwood, *Thirty Years' War* (1939).

[F. E. MASER]

WETTE, WILHELM DE, see DE WETTE, WILHELM

WEYDEN, ROGIER VAN DER (1399 or 1400–1464), with Jan van Eyck the most influential early Netherlandish master. Considered a pupil of Robert Campin, W. was appointed city painter of Brussels in 1436. In the holy year of 1450, he made a pilgrimage to Rome. Except for a few extremely elegant portraits (*Francesco d'Este*, New York; *Young Lady*, Washington), W. was a painter of religious subjects marked by serious piety. The major figures, such as Christ and the Virgin, are often isolated against a setting stripped of its usual narrational elements, thereby transforming a familiar scene into a devotional icon (Miraflores altarpiece, Berlin; *Braque Triptych*, Louvre; *Crucifixion*, Vienna). W. was one of the few 15th-cent. painters to express emotion, and his scenes of the Passion display the grief of Christ's followers with an unsurpassed beauty and restraint. BIBLIOGRAPHY: M. J. Friedländer, *Rogier van der Weyden and the Master of Flémalle* (tr. H. Norden, *Early Netherlandish Painting* 2, 1967); J. Destrée, *Roger de la Pasture-van der Weyden* (2 v., 1930).

[S. N. BLUM]

WHARTON, HENRY (1664–95), English divine and author. He assisted William Cave in the *Historia litteraria* (1688), then worked with Thomas Tenison in controversy with Roman Catholics, to which W. contributed four anti-Roman works. After ordination in 1688 he began work on his *Anglia sacra* (1691); the first 2 v. were on English dioceses in the hands of the regular clergy and their bishops up to 1540. A later companion volume on secular administered English sees was never finished. He continued to write critical, religious, and hagiographical works throughout his life. For political reasons his clerical career ended in 1689.

[R. J. LITZ]

WHATELY, RICHARD (1787–1863), Oxford scholar, fellow of Oriel, who was Anglican abp. of Dublin (1831–63). A man of wide-ranging interests, he was the author of the standard text *Elements of Logic* (1826) and probably also of the much more controversial *Letters on the Church by an Episcopalian* (1826). He had considerable influence on Newman during the latter's drift towards stronger anti-Erastian and anti-evangelical positions. Whately was one of the best known Noetics, but he opposed the Tractarians and the *Oxford Movement, urging the condemnation of Newman's Tract 90. As abp. of Dublin, he maintained an active interest in social reform and collaborated with the Catholic abp. in devising religious curricula for the national schools that could satisfy both Catholic and Anglican students.

[E. J. DILLON]

WHETHAMSTEDE, JOHN (*c.*1392–1465), Benedictine writer and abbot of St. Albans (1420–40, 1452–65). Well-versed in classical literature and attracted to Italian humanism, which influenced his Latin style, he wrote several encyclopedias and anthologies, such as *Granarium de viris illustribus,* and was responsible for preparing the St. Albans' chronicles of his day. BIBLIOGRAPHY: Emden Ox 3:2032–34.

[C. D. ROSS]

WHICHCOTE, BENJAMIN (1609–83), a Shropshire man, fellow and tutor of Emmanuel College, Cambridge. His sermons strove to turn men's minds from the form of words to the "inwards of things." Appointed provost of King's College under the *Commonwealth (1644), he was ejected, protesting, at the *Restoration. One of the leading *Cambridge Platonists, he was averse to the pessimism of stiff Puritan doctrine and advanced a freer and more rational spirit in men's converse with God. He was, in consequence, charged at various times with *latitudinarianism, *Arminianism, and *Socinianism. BIBLIOGRAPHY: F. J. Powicke, *Cambridge Platonists* (1926).

[L. J. LEKAI]

WHISPERING, the word generally used to translate what RC moral theologians called *susurratio,* by which they meant the secret reporting of something malicious or slanderous about a person to one or more of his friends in order to make mischief. Charity, justice, truthfulness, friendliness—all may be violated by the whisperer. An analogous use of the word occurs in the expression "whispering campaign."

WHITBY, ABBEY OF (formerly Streoneshalh), a monastery on Northumbrian coast of England. It was founded as a double monastery by Hilda, of the royal house and Abbess of Hartlepool, *c.*657. Here King Oswy summoned the synod of 664 (or 663), in an effort to unite the Celtic and Roman churches of his realm, which decided to adopt the Roman usage. Whitby became the most important monastery in NE England. In it were buried its kings; and it was noted for its learning. Caedmon (d. 680), the father of English poetry, lived here. Whitby was abandoned on account of the Viking onslaughts *c.*867. After the Norman Conquest, Whitby was revived as a Benedictine priory and eventually became an abbey under Henry I. It had six dependencies. Henry VIII suppressed Whitby in 1543. The site has been excavated and its Celtic-type cells and houses in an enclosure unearthed. BIBLIOGRAPHY: G. Young, *A History of Whitby* and *Streoneshalh Abbey* (2 v., 1817); C. R. Peers and C. A. Ralegh Radford, "The Saxon Monastery of Whitby," *Archaeologia* 89 (1943) 27–88; I. G. Sieveking, "St. Hilda and her Abbey at Whitby," *Antiquary* 40 (1904) 327–330.

[C. MCGRATH]

WHITBY, SYNOD OF. Whitby, at the mouth of the river Esk in Yorkshire, was formerly the site of a Benedictine monastery. The synod held there in 664 was decisive for the Church in England. The particular issue was the date of Easter, but the broader issue was whether Latin or Celtic traditions would prevail. Venerable Bede gives a full account of the debate (*Eccl. Hist.* 3.25). The Celtic tradition was represented by King Oswy of Northumbria and the bishops SS. Colman and Chad; they claimed to follow the practice of St. John for dating Easter. The Roman tradition, already observed in the South, was defended by SS. Agilbert and Wilfrid who appealed to St. Peter and to the Council of Nicaea. The authority of St. Peter apparently caused King Oswy to change his position; it was then only a matter of time before Roman customs supplanted Celtic usages in Northern England. BIBLIOGRAPHY: W. A. Chaney, NCE 14:891–892.

[B. L. MARTHALER]

WHITCHURCH, EDWARD (d. 1561), English Protestant printer. W. gave financial aid to M. Coverdale for printing his NT. In 1539 he published the Great Bible at Greyfriars House in London. He also saw to the printing of both the First and Second Prayer Books (1549, 1552). BIBLIOGRAPHY: S. Lee, DNB 61:30–31.

[M. J. SUELZER]

WHITE, ANDREW (1579–1656), missionary. Born in England of a recusant family, W. was educated in Spain and Douai, France, where he was ordained *c.*1605. Returning to the English mission, he was arrested and banished. In Louvain (Belgium), he entered the Jesuits. For about 10 years he taught at various Jesuit colleges in Spain and Flanders. From 1619 to 1629, W. taught theology at Louvain and at Liège. Living in secrecy in England after 1629, he composed for Lord Baltimore a prospectus on colonization published as *Condition of Plantation.* He was appointed to the Maryland mission and went there in 1634, writing later of the mission in his *Relatio itineris in Marilandiam.* He worked among the settlers and the Indians for 10 years, compiling a dictionary, grammar, and catechism in the Indian tongue. When the Puritans rose in Maryland in 1644, W. was sent to England for trial, where once again he was banished. In spite of threat of death he worked again on the English mission.

[J. R. AHERNE]

WHITE, CHARLES IGNATIUS (1807–78), religious author and editor. Of an old Maryland family, W. studied for the priesthood and was ordained in 1830. He became rector of the cathedral in Baltimore and teacher at St. Mary's Seminary; he served as pastor of St. Matthew's Church, Washington, D.C., from 1857 to 1878 and was widely recognised as a preacher and influential cleric in the capital. He established charitable institutions, two of them for blacks, and served the poor of his area. An outstanding writer, he cofounded and edited the *Religious Cabinet* (1842), which became the *United States Catholic Magazine* (1843–1848). In 1853 W. founded and edited the *Metropolitan Magazine*. The quality of his periodicals was high. From 1849 to 1855 he was editor of the diocesan weekly, *The Mirror*. In addition, W. compiled the annual *Catholic Directory*, 1834–57, wrote the popular biography, *Life of Mrs. Elizabeth A. Seton* (1853), and published a number of translations of French Catholic works.

[J. R. AHERNE]

WHITE, ELLEN GOULD (1827–1915), cofounder and prophetess of the *Seventh-day Adventists. As a young girl she joined the Methodist Church but embraced *Adventism after hearing W. *Miller preach. The year after her baptism as a Methodist she was disfellowshiped for her Adventist views. She married James White, an Adventist preacher, in 1846. Along with Joseph Bates they are considered the founders of the Seventh-day Adventists. In 1855 the Whites moved to Battle Creek, Mich., where the first church conference was held in 1863. After her husband died (1881), W. traveled and lectured in Europe (1885–87) and in Australia (1891–1900). At the time of her death the Seventh-day Adventists had 136,879 members. Although never ordained a minister or elected to any church office, W. has been the most influential figure in the history of her Church. Adventists consider her to have possessed the gift of prophecy; her numerous visions were decisive in resolving many problems of doctrine and practice. Her first vision took place in 1844; in it the tiny band of Adventists were described as the remnant of true believers. When in a trance state, W. appeared to suspend breathing, her muscles became rigid, and sometimes she remained deprived of sight for 3 hours. One vision depicted the commandment ''Remember that thou keep holy the Sabbath day'' surrounded by a halo of light. Although her formal education ended at the age of 9 because of a head injury, during her lifetime she wrote 24 books, 4,600 articles, and numerous tracts, pamphlets, and unpublished manuscripts. Her total literary output exceeded 25 million words. Her works include the *Conflict of the Ages* series (5v., 1888–1911) and *Testimonies for the Church* (9v., 1855–1909). In Seventh-day Adventist seminaries and colleges her writings are still studied as inspired. BIBLIOGRAPHY: F. D. Nichol, *Ellen Gould White and Her Critics* (1951); D. M. Canright, *Life of Ellen Gould White* (1919).

WHITE, EUSTACE, ST. (*c.*1560–1591), English martyr. Of a prominent Protestant family, W. converted to Catholicism and was ordained in Rome (1589). He returned to England where he labored in the West until his capture in Dorset (1591). He was imprisoned in Bridewell, examined, tortured, and executed at Tyburn. He was canonized in 1970. BIBLIOGRAPHY: Butler 4:533.

[V. SAMPSON]

WHITE, FRANCIS (1564?–1638), Anglican bp. and polemicist. Ordained in 1588, in his lifetime he became successively bp. of Carlisle (1626), Norwich (1629), and Ely (1631). He is notable for his tracts against Catholicism, esp. *The Orthodox Faith and the Way to the Church* (1617), and his participation in disputations. James I appointed him as debater against the Jesuit John Fisher. At the command of Charles I, W. wrote his *Treatise of the Sabbath Day* (1635) against Sabbatarianism. *SABBATARIANS.

[J. R. AHERNE]

WHITE, HELEN CONSTANCE (1896–1967), American novelist, critic, and educator. A teacher of English for some years, two of which were spent at Smith College, she received her Ph.D. degree at the Univ. of Wisconsin in 1924, where she later became a full professor of English. She held many scholarly posts, at the same time writing historical novels, most notably *Watch in The Night*. W. was also the author of critical appraisals in such works as the *Mysticism of William Blake* and *Metaphysical Poets: A Study in Religious Experience*. There is a strong religious quality in her novels, reflecting her RC faith. BIBLIOGRAPHY: *Commonweal*, May 24, 1935.

[S. A. HEENEY]

WHITE, HENRY JULIAN (1859–1934), Latin and NT scholar, Anglican priest and theologian. W. is best known for his collaboration with John Wordsworth and H. F. D. Sparks in the production over many decades of what still may be the best available edition of Jerome's Vulgate, in the version with the prefatory letter, *Novum opus,* addressed to Pope Damasus, who had commissioned Jerome to translate the Scriptures into Latin. A supplement to this work was their important 7-v. edition of *Old-Latin Biblical Texts* (1883–1923). White was born at Islington, educated at Christ Church, Oxford, ordained deacon in 1885 and priest in 1886. He was elected honorary fellow of Merton College in 1921 and fellow of the British Academy in 1932. He was theological lecturer at Merton College, Oxford, and professor of NT at King's College, London. BIBLIOGRAPHY: DNB 1931–1940: 901–902.

[E. J. DILLON]

WHITE, JOSEPH BLANCO (1775–1841) theologian, polemicist. Born in Spain but of Irish origin, W. entered the seminary at age 12 largely to escape working in his father's business. His remaining career was a series of vacillations, scrupulosity, and rebellion. Doubts about Catholicism plagued him but he was ordained in 1800. After some years of priestly work he became involved with the Spanish Junta in Seville that attempted to resist the Napoleonic invasion. Forced to flee he went to London in 1810 where the first group of the surprisingly kind English friends obtained employment for him as editor of a Spanish periodical. The journal was supported by the British government, which gave White a life pension. By 1814 he had become an Anglican minister. In 1826, now settled at Oxford, he began a career which brought him into friendship with J. H. *Newman and the other leaders of the *Oxford movement. Through his close friendship with Whately he became editor of the *London Review.* Plagued by ill health and a sensitive nature as well as financial worries, W. left Oxford to live with Whately who had been appointed Anglican Abp. of Dublin. His last move theologically, influenced by J. *Martineau was to Unitarianism. He contributed to a number of periodicals such as *The London and Westminster Review, The Quarterly Review,* and *The New Monthly.* Among his published works are *Letters from Spain by Don Leucadio Doblado* (1822), *Practical and Internal Evidence against Catholicism* (1825), and *Observations on Heresy and Orthodoxy* (1835). BIBLIOGRAPHY: DNB 21:63–67.

[J. R. AHERNE]

WHITE, RICHARD, BL., see GWYN, RICHARD, ST.

WHITE, STEPHEN (1575–1647?), Irish Jesuit historian and hagiographer. Graduate of Trinity College, Dublin, and Salamanca, W. taught scholastic theology at Ingoldstat (1606–09), Dillingen, and elsewhere, while continuing his research into Irish MSS on the Continent. At Dilligen (1621) he transcribed Adamnan's life of St. Columba: He contributed much to the biographies of SS. Patrick, Brigid, and others through his manuscript research and transcription. He corresponded and collaborated with Calvinist, James Ussher, Abp. of Armagh. W. returned to Ireland in 1638. His best-known work is his *Apologia pro Hibernia,* written in 1615.

[R. J. LITZ]

WHITE, THOMAS (1563–1676), English priest, theologian, and controversialist; known also as Blackloe and Blacklow. W. studied at the English colleges at Valladolid, Seville, St. Omer, and Douai. After ordination (1617) he was professor at Douai, representative of the English clergy at Rome (1626), and president of the college at Lisbon (1630). W. was a prolific writer on philosophical, theological, and polemical topics. In some of his works he advanced views on purgatory, hell, and papal infallibility that were censured first by the Douai faculty, then by the Inquisition. When works of his were placed on the Index he submitted, but continued to write in defense of himself. BIBLIOGRAPHY: T. Cooper, DNB (repr. 21:79–81) Gillow BDEC 5:578–581, with complete list of W.'s writings.

[T. C. O'BRIEN]

WHITE, WILLIAM (1748–1836), bishop, leader in the formation of the *Protestant Episcopal Church. Graduated from Franklin's College (now the Univ. of Pa.) in 1765, he was ordained in the Anglican Church (deacon in 1770, priest in 1772). As assistant rector and later rector of Christ Church, Philadelphia, W. was prominent among his fellow churchmen who were Whigs during the Revolution; he was chaplain of Congress (1777–1800), and after the war worked to moderate popular antipathy toward his Church. In the reorganization that led to the Protestant Episcopal Church, he helped draw up a constitution that emphasized lay control and the equality of all Churches in a free nation. Consecrated Bp. of Philadelphia (1787), he became first president of the *General Convention in 1789, and in 1795, presiding bishop of the Episcopal Church. His primary contribution to American religion was the application of John Locke's political theories to the polity of the Episcopal Church. BIBLIOGRAPHY: William White, *Case of the Episcopal Churches in the United States Considered* (ed. R. G. Salomon, 1954); W. H. Stowe, *Life and Letters of Bishop William White* (1937); W. H. Manross, *William White* (1934).

[W. S. PETTIT]

WHITE CLERGY, in Eastern Churches secular, or diocesan clergy, often called "popes," usually married. They are called white in distinction from the monks or black clergy. Their robes are usually grey, brown, or purple, but sometimes they are black.

[F. WILCOCK]

WHITE FATHERS, popular title given to members of the Society of Missionaries of Africa because of their traditional white religious garb. Founded in Algiers (1868) by Charles *Lavigerie, abp. of Algiers and later cardinal, the White Fathers were destined exclusively to the apostolate in Africa. From their initial undertaking, the care of destitute and homeless Arab children around Algiers, they soon spread to various parts of Algeria, the oases of the Sahara, Tunisia, and East Central Africa, engaging in educational and health services, and direct or indirect evangelization according to circumstances and possibilities. The society is committed to a policy of missionary *adaptation, and the establishment of seminaries for the training of an African clergy became an essential part of White Father procedure early in its history. Today the majority of the 60 dioceses of North, East, Central, and West Africa in which the White Fathers work are in the hands of African clergy. Though Africa remains the primary focus of the society in terms of orientation, manpower, and resources, additional commitments have been undertaken, notably the seminary training of the Melkite rite clergy in the Near East, and ecumenical work among the Eastern Orthodox Churches. Members of the society, priests and brothers, number over 2,249 and come from most of the countries of Europe and several countries of Africa, as well as Canada and the United States. The U.S. province of the society was erected in 1948. BIBLIOGRAPHY: J. Bouniol, *White Fathers and Their Missions* (1929); G. Kittler, *White Fathers* (1957).

[T. M. MCFADDEN]

WHITE FRIARS, see WHITEFRIARS

WHITE LADIES, formerly the name given Cistercian nuns. More recently it is a name for the Daughters of the Presentation, founded in 1796.

WHITE MONASTERY, an ancient Christian monastery, also known as Deir-el-Abiad, situated 3 miles W of Sohaq, Egypt, on the left bank of the Nile. It was founded at the time of Constantine by Bagoul, a disciple of St. *Pachomius, and became an important center of Eastern monasticism under Shenudi who became superior in 383. Shenudi, who sought to establish a stricter way of life than the prevailing Pachomian discipline, was unpopular among the monks, but his generous hospitality won him the favor of outsiders. He rebuilt the monastery, little of which remains, and constructed (*c.*430) a stone church, one of the first great churches of Egyptian cenobitism, which still stands. Since then, the monastery has followed the commonplace history of Eastern monasteries until today when it is hardly more than a refuge for a few Coptic priests. BIBLIOGRAPHY: P. Cousin, *Précis d'histoire monastique* (1956); J. Leroy, *Monks and Monasteries of the Near East* (tr. P. Collin, 1963); G. Lefebvre, DACL 4.1:459–502.

[M. B. PENNINGTON]

WHITE MONKS, a popular name for the Cistercians, who were so called because of the color of their habit. This appeared as one of the differences between them and the traditional Cluniac monks in the 12th century. The older orders of Black Monks used tailored habits of fine material. The reformed monks, seeking closer conformity to the Rule of St. Benedict (''The monks should not complain about the color or the coarseness of any of these [habits] but should be content with what can be found in the district where they live and can be purchased cheaply'' 55.7) made do with homewoven wool that retained its natural color. BIBLIOGRAPHY: A. Wulf, *Compendium of the History of the Cistercian Order* (1944); L. Lekai, *White Monks* (1953). *TRAPPISTS; *CLUNIAC REFORM.

[M. B. PENNINGTON]

WHITE RUSSIAN S.S.R., see BELORUSSKAYA S.S.R.

WHITE SISTERS (Missionary Sisters of Our Lady of Africa), a congregation of women religious dedicated to work on the African mission. Founded in 1869 by Card. Lavigerie and Mother Mary Salome, the community labors in 13 African countries. A U.S. foundation was established in New Brunswick, N.J., in 1929. In 1975 they had 1,913 members; the generalate is in Frascati, Italy.

[J. R. AHERNE]

WHITEFIELD, GEORGE (1714–70), one of the greatest pulpit orators of the 18th century. W. was born in Gloucester, England; he left school for a year to assist his widowed mother, but continued reading, esp. the Bible and the *Imitation of Christ,* which deeply impressed him. In 1732 he entered Pembroke College, Oxford, as a servitor, working for his education. In 1734 he met Charles *Wesley, who invited him to join the *holy club, and he began a life of severe asceticism. This brought him no satisfaction, but in 1735 he found peace through faith in Christ. He was ordained a deacon at Gloucester, June 20, 1736, and became a popular preacher around London. At the invitation of John *Wesley he went to Ga., where he conducted a successful ministry. Returning to London, he discovered that the strong language in his published *Journal* had hurt his popularity, and some church doors were closed against him. He was ordained priest in the C of E in 1739, and the same year preached in the open fields (see FIELD PREACHING) to large crowds of colliers at Kingswood. At his request John Wesley assisted him, and outdoor preaching became important to the growth of Methodism. Back in the American colonies, 1739–40, he was one of the leading figures in the *Great Awakening and preached effectively along the entire Seaboard. In 1743 in Wales he assisted Howell *Harris in organizing the *Calvinistic Methodists. He split with the Wesleys, favoring the Calvinist doctrine of election against the Arminian doctrine of free will (see ARMINIANISM). He was chaplain for Selina, Countess of *Huntingdon, preaching in her home and chapels to her friends. In all he made seven American preaching tours. The impact of his preaching came not from its content but from his personality. He is not considered a founder of Methodism in America; he disregarded denominational lines. While differing from the Wesleys, he remained their friend and requested that John Wesley preach his funeral sermon. He died, however, in Newburyport, Mass., and is buried there. BIBLIOGRAPHY: S. C. Henry, *George Whitefield: Wayfaring Witness* (1957); *George Whitefield's Journals* (introd. I. Murray, 1960); HistAmMeth 1:69–73.

WHITEFRIARS, written as one or two words, a name applied to Carmelite friars in medieval England, and sometimes, in the plural, to the houses in which they lived. They were so called from the white color of the cloaks the Carmelites wore over their brown habits.

[J. C. WILLKE]

WHITEHEAD, ALFRED NORTH (1861–1947), English logician and philosopher. Educated at Trinity (Newton's college), Cambridge, he became a Fellow. He collaborated with Bertrand Russell on *Principia Mathematica,* a work on the relation between formal logic and mathematics which has influenced that field more than any other in the 20th century. He lectured (1910–24) at the University of London and the Imperial Institute, when his interests were epistemological and cosmological, concerned with problems arising from the new physics. He taught at Harvard (1924–37), and after his retirement from teaching remained at Harvard as a Senior Fellow. W.'s philosophy, which he called ''organism'' and others describe as ''process philosophy,'' exhibits a unity and progress rare in contemporary thought. He is in the perennial tradition ("All Western philosophy," he wrote, "is a series of footnotes to Plato"), avoiding the extremes of realism and idealism. Philosophizing must begin with the given of experience, and must see that all things are related. The Many of the world are related to the One of God, but God is both cause and consequent of creativity, the material ground of all becoming. Some see no personal God demonstrated in W.'s thought, but his preoccupation with religion and the notion of God in the life of man is a constant, not an isolated factor in his work. He was a believing and practicing Christian in the Anglican tradition. BIBLIOGRAPHY: *Dialogues of Alfred North Whitehead* (ed. L. Price, 1954); V. Lowe, *Understanding Whitehead* (1962); EncPhil (1968).

[W. B. MAHONEY]

WHITFIELD, JAMES (1770–1834), bishop. Born in England, W. was a merchant in Liverpool for some years but ultimately studied for the priesthood and was ordained in France in 1809. Entering the Jesuits in England in 1811, he left the Society shortly and at the invitation of his old friend and teacher, Ambrose Maréschal, coadjutor bp. of Baltimore, W. came to Maryland in 1817. He became one of the first priests in the U.S. to receive a doctorate in sacred theology from an American institution (St. Mary's Seminary, Baltimore). Coadjutor to Maréschal in 1828, W. succeeded his friend as abp. of Baltimore in that same year. In his brief tenure, W. spent much of his fortune building institutions for the archdiocese. He inaugurated the Provincial Councils of Baltimore, the first in 1829. During W.'s administration the Jesuits established the Maryland Province; he founded St. Charles College, Ellicott City, Maryland.

[J. R. AHERNE]

WHITFORD, RICHARD (Whytford; 1475–1559), English writer of devotional books who called himself the wretch of Syon. A monk of the Brigittine double monastery of Syon, England, and a friend of St. Thomas More, he is said to have encouraged More in his refusal to take the Oath of Supremacy. He himself opposed the king's agents, but escaped punishment. Nineteen works of devotion are attributed to him, many of them written only for the monks and nuns of his monastery but known and used far more widely. His fame rests chiefly on his *Jesu's Psalter,* a favorite book of English Catholic piety during the Reformation period, and on his translation from Latin into English of the *Imitation of Christ,* which he calls *The Folowyng of Cryste,* the earliest English translation and stylistically still unsurpassed. His writings possess great charm and sweetness. BIBLIOGRAPHY: Emden Camb 635; Gillow BDEC 5:581–582.

[M. J. BARRY]

WHITGIFT, JOHN (c.1530–1604), Abp. of Canterbury; resister of Puritan influence. W. turned to Reformation doctrine even before becoming a student at Cambridge. Having received his M.A. in 1557, he was ordained in 1560 in one of the first ordinations of Elizabeth I's reign. At Cambridge he was made Lady Margaret Professor of Divinity in 1563, and in 1567 master of Trinity College and Regius Professor of Divinity. In 1577 Elizabeth made him Bp. of Worcester, and in 1583 Abp. of Canterbury. Opposition to the Puritans began when W., while master of Trinity and vice-chancellor of the university, had T. *Cartwright deprived of his professorship (1570) for attacking *episcopacy in the Church of England. The abp. sought to enforce ritual uniformity, dealt severely with the circulators of the *Marprelate Tracts, and thwarted Puritan efforts in 1584–85 to abolish episcopacy in the Church. The *Lambeth Articles isssued under his sponsorship in 1595, however, attest to W.'s acceptance of the Calvinistic doctrine on absolute predestination of the elect and reprobation of all others. BIBLIOGRAPHY: V. J. K. Brook, *Whitgift and the English Church* (1957); Hughes RE 3:167–174, 193–201, 206, 228.

[T. C. O'BRIEN]

WHITHORN, PRIORY OF, former Premonstratensian priory at Whithorn, Wigtownshire, Scotland, at the site of a previous monastery called Candida Casa, founded by St. Ninian (d. 432). In 1177 Bishop Christian of Galloway founded Whithorn by replacing the existing cathedral clergy with Premonstratensians. It became a place of pilgrimage and was richly endowed. After the death of its last prior (1569), its revenues were appropriated by the crown and given to the Anglican bishops of Galloway. BIBLIOGRAPHY: Cottineau 2:3452.

[E. J. DILLON]

WHITING, RICHARD, BL. (d. 1539), last abbot of Glastonbury, martyr. Educated at the abbey, W. became abbot of Glastonbury and, as such, was a member of the House of Lords and immediately involved in Henry VIII's divorce proceedings in which he prudently took no stand. In 1534 he and his monks took the Oath of Royal Supremacy. Glastonbury was the greatest of the great monasteries and therefore a target for suppression and destruction and the source of great wealth for the king. Plans of the king's men to find reason to accuse W. and his monks of treason failed. On one of their visitations they ransacked the abbey and found some valuable articles hidden away. They changed treason to robbery as a basis for arresting Abbot Whiting. Without his knowledge, his monks and servants were dispersed throughout the land. After being subjected to harsh interrogations, he was sent to the Tower in London for Cromwell to interrogate him further. He remained adamant in his faith. Secretly and without trial he was condemned to death. He was taken back to Glastonbury, was laid on a hurdle and dragged through the town to be hanged, drawn, and quartered. He was beatified in 1896. BIBLIOGRAPHY: N. Del Re, BiblSanct 12:1403–05; F. A. Gasquet, *Last Abbot of Glastonbury* (1895); Butler 4:461–462.

[S. A. HEENEY]

WHITLAND MONASTERY (or Y Ty Gwyn ar Daf, or Alba Landa), the first foundation of the Cistercian order in Wales. It was established in 1140 at Little Trefgarne by John de Thorynton and patronized by Rhys ap Gruffydd, prince of South Wales; but moved to Whitland, probably in 1151. It was predominantly Welsh in character. Among its eight daughter and granddaughter houses are the Welsh monasteries of Cwmhir (1143), Strata Florida (1164), and Strata Marcella (1170). It was dissolved in 1537. BIBLIOGRAPHY: J. F. O'Sullivan, *Cistercian Settlements in Wales and Monmouthshire, 1140–1540* (1947); Knowles–Hadcock.

[C. MCGRATH]

WHITSUN(DAY), an alternative designation in English for *Pentecost Sunday. It is a corruption of "White Sunday," an earlier name for the feast taken from the fact that those who had been baptized the previous day during the Vigil ceremonies appeared for this day's liturgical services in their white baptismal garments. The exact origins of the usage of this name are uncertain, but it still is sometimes used in the British Isles. BIBLIOGRAPHY: F. X. Weiser, *Handbook of Christian Feasts and Customs* (1952) 246–254; ODCC 1456.

[B. ROSENDALL]

WHITTINGHAM, WILLIAM (1524?–79), English Calvinist, fellow of All Souls, Oxford, one of the leaders in the Frankfort community of English Protestant exiles in the reign of Mary Tudor (1553–58). He and Knox advocated purer Calvinism in Frankfurt against Richard Cox and those who favored traditional English Protestantism, and controversy arose over the use of Edward VI's Book of Common Prayer. W. followed Knox to Geneva when Knox was expelled from Frankfurt. W. became an elder of the Geneva Church (1556), deacon (1558), then minister (1559), though never ordained. He did not return to England with other exiles after Elizabeth's accession, remaining to complete his contribution to the *Geneva Bible. Some of his metrical arrangements of psalms became part of a new Calvinist service-book. After returning to England (1560) he was appointed dean of Durham where his controversial Puritan activities increased; an effort was made to depose him for his refusal to follow the BCP and because he was not validly ordained, but W. died before the issue was resolved.

[R. J. LITZ]

WHOLE DUTY OF MAN, the title of a devotional manual widely used in England. Published *c.*1658 under the *Commonwealth, when high Anglicanism had gone underground, it is composed of 17 moral discourses, "one whereof being read every Lord's Day, the whole may be read over thrice a year." It was probably composed by Richard Allestree, the preface is by Henry Hammond, and John Fell seems to have been associated with its production; all three were Oxford men who inherited and transmitted the noble spirituality of the *Caroline Divines and combined ideals that were exacting with lessons that were practicable.

WIBALD OF STAVELOT (1098–1158), monk, abbot, and statesman, who died en route from Constantinople. He typifies the dynamic nature of Europe's 12th century. Educated at Liège, and having worked in the imperial chancery, he was elected abbot of Stavelot (1130) and later (1138) served as protector of young Frederick (Barbarossa) while Conrad III went on the Second Crusade. BIBLIOGRAPHY: S. Williams, NCE 14:902; F. Hausmann, LTK 10:1085–86; É. De Moreau, *Histoire de l'église en Belgique* (2d ed.) 2:353–354; 3:41–58.

[S. WILLIAMS]

WIBLINGEN, ABBEY OF, a monastery located in what is now a suburb of Ulm, Germany. It was a Benedictine establishment founded 1093 by the counts Hartmann and Otto of Kirchberg, peopled by St. Blasien and famous for its intellectual prosperity at all times. In 1783 a splendid new church was dedicated which still stands. It was suppressed in 1806, the community moved to Poland (Tyniec) and there became extinct. The abbey is now used for offices. BIBLIOGRAPHY: *Handbuch der historischen Stätten Deutschlands* (8v., 1960) 6:692.

[N. BACKMUND]

WIBORADA, ST. (known in French as Guiborat and in German as Weibrath; d. 926), a recluse, commemorated as a virgin martyr on May 2. Born in Klingau, in the Swiss canton of Aargau, of Swabian nobility, she first lived in solitude in her parents' house, then worked as a bookbinder for the monks of St. Gall, where her brother was a priest monk. She was a recluse at St. George (*c.*912–916), then near the Church of St. Magnus at St. Gall. She cared for the sick, was a counselor to rich and poor, was considered a spiritual mother by Ulric, future bp. of Augsburg and by St. Rachildis. Young women came to her for instruction. She was fatally wounded during an invasion of Hungarians and died at St. Gall. She was canonized by Clement II in 1047. A biographical sketch was written by Hartmann, monk of St. Gall, a near contemporary.

[E. J. DILLON]

WICHERN, JOHANN HEINRICH (1808–81); German Lutheran church leader whose initiatives effectively moved the Evangelical Church to organize and act to alleviate the suffering brought on the poor by the Industrial Revolution in Germany; considered to be the founder of the German Home Mission *(Innere Mission)*. Born in Hamburg, he studied theology at Göttingen and Berlin, where he came under the influence of Neander and Schleiermacher. On returning to Hamburg, he was consumed by the desire to provide for the material and spiritual needs of the children of the poor. In 1833 he founded Rauhes Haus for this purpose and later founded a center to train those who would join him in this apostolate. He later edited a periodical which was to become the central organ of all charitable undertakings in German Protestant Churches. At the first Congress of Evangelical Churches at Wittenberg (1848), his initiatives were converted into a basis for what came to be the German Home Mission. In 1857 he was further entrusted with the burden of Prussian prison reform. He and his Brothers also formed the *Felddiakonie* to give assistance to the wounded in the wars of 1864, 1866, 1870–71. In his declining years he returned to his beloved Rauhes Haus to die.

[E. J. DILLON]

WICHMANN OF ARNSTEIN, BL. (d. 1270), Premonstratensian, later Dominican. After entering the Order of Prémontré, he was elected bp. of Brandenburg, but the election was not confirmed. He helped to establish the Dominicans in Magdeburg and in 1224 entered the Order. W. was prior in three convents. Many legends are associated with him. His letters testify to deep spirituality. BIBLIOGRAPHY: P. M. Starrs, NCE 14:902.

[M. J. FINNEGAN]

WICHMANN OF MAGDEBURG (d. 1192), archbishop. Count of Seeburg, educated at Halberstadt and Paris, canon and then provost of Halberstadt, W. became bp. of Naumburg (1149) and in 1152 abp. of Magdeburg. He acted as mediator between Alexander III and Frederick I Barbarossa. He greatly expanded and colonized his archdiocese and codified the laws of Magdeburg. BIBLIOGRAPHY: L. Kurras, NCE 14:902–903; B. Stasiewski, LTK 10:1090.

[L. J. LEKAI]

WIDENFELDT, ADAM (1617–*c*.1677), German jurist. W. wrote a Jansenist treatise on devotion to Mary which caused a great furore and was attacked by Bourdaloue. Debate about his ideas has never been satisfactorily resolved.

[M. J. SUELZER]

WIDOW (IN THE BIBLE). The position of woman in Israelite society was one of total dependence upon her nearest male relative, either father or husband. The widow, therefore, was in a peculiarly defenseless position, and it was a prime duty of all, particularly those in authority and all who exercised judicial functions, to ensure that the rights of widows were protected and that they were not defrauded or oppressed by the more powerful members of the community. The widow, therefore, is regarded as the type of the poor and unprotected who is, in a special degree, the client of Yahweh. Yahweh is the champion of widows and will punish all who wrong them. Deuteronomy in particular legislates for their care (cf. Dt 16.11,14; 14.29; 26.12; 24.19–21). In the NT too the care and succor of widows is regarded as a work of true religion (cf. Acts 6.1; 9.39; 1 Tim 5.3–16; Jas 1.27).

[D. J. BOURKE]

WIDUKIND, PRINCE OF SAXONS (*fl.*775), a shadowy figure of whom little is known. He led prolonged Saxon resistance to Charlemagne during the period 775–785. Other chieftains surrendered, but Widukind continued to escape, always to emerge from hiding and rally his followers. By 785 his leadership had lost its appeal. Acquiescing in capitulation and baptism, he disappeared from record. BIBLIOGRAPHY: H. Hartwig, *Widukind in Geschichte und Sage* (1951); R. E. Sullivan, NCE 14:904.

[A. CABANISS]

WIDUKIND OF CORVEY (d. after 976), monk, chronicler. He was a monk of Corvey, Saxony, whose only extant work is *Rerum gestarum Saxonicorum,* an important source for the history of Germany in 10th-cent. The work was dedicated to Matilda, daughter of Emperor Otto I; text, MGH, 56. BIBLIOGRAPHY: H. Beuman, *Widukind von Korvei* (1950); J. A. Brundage, NCE 14:904.

[J. L. GRASSI]

WIEGER, LEON (1856–1932), Alsatian Jesuit missionary to China; outstanding Sinologist. He had studied and practiced medicine before going to China in 1887. He continued as a doctor there and helped other missionaries acquire a foundation in Chinese language, history, and culture. His activity centered in Sien-hsien until his death there. After 1920 his study centered on problems of modern China. He wrote introductory works for Europeans being initiated into Chinese culture and catechetical works to be used by missionaries seeking to be sensitive to Chinese religious and cultural traditions. His writings show an absorbing interest in the history of China, ancient and modern, in Chinese philosophical literature, and in the history of Chinese religious and philosophical beliefs.

[E. J. DILLON]

WIES, DIE, German pilgrimage church in S Bavaria, a triumph of rococo, housing the miraculous statue of Christ at the Column, begun by the Abbott of Steingaden, who commissioned (1744) from Dominikus Zimmermann a church and priory, consecrated in 1754. Johann Baptist Zimmerman painted the magnificent light, gay frescoes of the curved ceiling. Anton Sturm carved the four Fathers of the Church at nave piers, Aegidius Verhelst, the Prophets and Evangelists; the painting above the altar was executed by Balthasar Albrecht. Light and color dominate the delicate oval interior, elaborate with Zimmermann's distinctive broken curves, the figures ethereally white with gold accents, the columns of pink and blue marbling with much gilding. The modest exterior (in the manner of rococo, a foil for the overwhelming richness of the interior) has a triple bay W end, and a sober E tower linking the church with the priory. BIBLIOGRAPHY: C. Lamb, *Die Wies* (1964).

[M. J. DALY]

WIGBERT OF HERSFELD, ST. (d. *c*.746). Anglo-Saxon monk and missionary. His reputation for sanctity impelled St. Boniface to bring him to Germany in order to reform the monasteries of Fritzlar and Ohrdruf. At Fritzlar he taught St. Sturmi. His grave at Fritzlar became a shrine, and his relics were translated to Hersfeld. BIBLIOGRAPHY: J. Druse, NCE 14:905; W. Levison, *England and the Continent in the Eighth Century,* 235–236; Lupus of Ferrières, *Vita* in MGS 15.1:37–43; Butler 3:322.

[J. DRUSE]

WIGGER, WINAND MICHAEL (1841–1901), bishop. The son of immigrant German parents, W. was accepted as a seminarian for the Diocese of Newark, N.J., and was ordained in 1865. After 15 years in parish work in which he displayed courage, tact, and devotion to the poor, he was named bp. of Newark in 1881. At the Third Plenary Council of Baltimore (1884) W. took a prominent part in support of parochial schools and care for the immigrant. He founded Leo House in New York to aid German immigrants on their arrival in the U.S. W. was a mild advocate of more Germans in the American hierarchy and of national parishes and schools. In 1890 he refused appointment to the See of Milwaukee. An active leader of his diocese, though plagued by poor health, he built a cathedral, parish churches, and schools, labored incessantly for immigrants within his diocese; he also was a strong promoter of temperance.

[J. R. AHERNE]

WIKENHAUSER, ALFRED (1883–1960), Catholic NT exegete; one of the founders of the Regensburg NT series; first editor of *Herder's Theological Commentary on the New Testament*. Ordained a priest in 1907, he taught at Freiburg im Breisgau, Germany, from 1929 until his retirement in 1951. He was one of the first Catholic scholars to apply scientific methods of literary and historical criticism to such areas as Paul's Christology and the Johannine writings, without incurring ecclesiastical censure.

[E. J. DILLON]

WIKTERP, ST. (d. 771), the first historically certain bp. of Augsburg, Germany. Born in Epfach, near Landsberg, he was a contemporary of St. Boniface. W. built many monasteries (Füssen, Benediktbeuern, Wessobrünn, Ellwangen, Polling, Ottobeuren, Kempten) and rebuilt the Church of St. Afra, destroyed by the Huns. He took part with Boniface in synods which introduced the Roman diocesan structure to Germany, where Christian life had till then centered around monasteries. W. was buried in St. Lawrence Chapel at Epfach. In the 12th cent., perhaps in conjunction with his canonization, his relics were translated to the Church of SS. Afra and Ulric in Augsburg.

[E. J. DILLON]

WILAMOWITZ-MOELLENDORFF, ULRICH VON (1848–1931), Greek scholar. Born in East Prussia, he held successive professorships in Greifswald, Göttingen, and Berlin. Combining textual criticism, philology, and a historico-critical outlook, he produced commentaries on the Greek tragedians and studies on Homer, Hesiod, Plato, Aristotle, and Hellenistic poetry. With his stress on the importance of later Greek writing, including the Hellenistic and patristic Greek, he had an influence on the Greek curriculum in German education. He died in Berlin.

[E. J. DILLON]

WILBERFORCE, BERTRAND (1839–1904), English Dominican, preacher, writer. Born at Lavington, Sussex, in the house of his aunt, the wife of H. E. *Manning, afterwards cardinal, W. was educated at Radley and Ushaw. The grandson of the Liberator, he inherited the famous "Wilberforce voice," and was much occupied in giving missions and retreats. Through his translations he was mainly instrumental in introducing the works of the Abbot *Blosius to English readers.

[T. GILBY]

WILBERFORCE, ROBERT ISAAC (1802–57), one of the most learned Tractarian divines. He was the son of the famous statesman and philanthropist William Wilberforce and brother of Samuel Wilberforce, Anglican bp. of Oxford. The two brothers collaborated in writing the 5-v. biography of their father (1838). Oxford–educated, and elected Fellow at Oriel in 1826, W. was close to J. H. Newman and R. H. Froude. After taking orders he was rector in Kent and Yorkshire, canon of York cathedral, and in 1841 was appointed archdeacon of the East Riding. From 1843 on, his extensive theological correspondence concerning the Roman claims with H. E. Manning led eventually to his embracing of Roman Catholicism in Paris in 1854. He had expressed his Anglo-Catholic theology in articles on the Incarnation, baptism, and the Eucharist. Before finishing his studies in Rome in preparation for Roman orders, he died in Albano. His books include *History of Erastianism* (1851) and *Five Empires* (1840).

[E. J. DILLON]

WILBERFORCE, SAMUEL (1805–73), Anglican bishop. After serving 10 years as a rector on the Isle of Wight, W. was made a chaplain at court in 1840. In 1845 he became Dean of Westminster and bp. of Oxford. Conspicuous for his pastoral zeal, he introduced notable reforms in his diocese, promoted education, encouraged the establishment of religious sisterhoods, and founded Cuddesdon Theological College. In 1867 he was transferred to the see of Winchester. BIBLIOGRAPHY: F. Legge, DNB 61:204–208.

[M. J. SUELZER]

WILBERFORCE, WILLIAM (1759–1833), an English philanthropist, convert to Evangelical Christianity, and leader of the movement to abolish slavery in the British Empire. A lifelong friend of the famous Prime Minister Pitt, he had a profound religious influence by his writings and example, esp. by linking the cause of emancipation with the Evangelical movement. He is buried in Westminster Abbey. Three of his four sons were among those who followed John Henry Newman into the Catholic Church during the later *Oxford Movement.

[E. J. DILLON]

WILBUR, JOHN (1774–1856), American Quaker. Born in Hopkinton, R.I., he became the leader of those orthodox Friends who, in the 1840s, gave more emphasis to the traditional Quaker belief in *Inner Light than to evangelical Protestant tenets (see HICKS, E.; GRELLET, S.). These Friends were called Wilburites or Conservatives, as against Gurneyites (see GURNEY, J.) or Evangelicals. BIBLIOGRAPHY: *American Quakers Today* (ed. E. Bronner, 1966) 20–31; bibliog. for Friends.

[T. C. O'BRIEN]

WILBURITES, the 19th-cent. Quakers who followed J. *Wilbur's emphasis on *Inner Light; also the Quaker bodies tracing their separate origin to Wilbur's interpretation of Quaker teaching.

[T. C. O'BRIEN]

WILDE, OSCAR (1854–1900), British author. W. was born in Ireland, educated at Trinity College in Dublin, and then at Oxford (1874–78). His life was probably more scintillating than even his ironic wit and epigram-studded dialogue. It is commonly accepted that W.'s foppish eccentricity of dress and manner has best preserved him as a 19th-cent. curio. The eccentricity of the man stirred the literary roots to a cleverness that might have stayed merely dormant. His skill in combining theme and style is at its best in what is probably his masterpiece, *The Importance of Being Earnest* (1895). Critics are divided on the subject of his sincerity of theme in the problem plays. Likewise, they question his originality of subject in his poetry as well as in its form. W. was a child of his time, a speaker for the decadence which neither Ruskin nor Pater could bless. W. could not strike that "hard gemlike flame" that Pater sought, nor could he sustain the ecstatic moment. W.'s conviction as a sexual deviate has given his name currency in the world of psychology and has probably encouraged much research and many studies of the man and his work. That case followed by a term of imprisonment no doubt hastened his death at 46. W. is remembered for his portrayal of decadence in *The Picture of Dorian Gray,* a novel. Other works are a play, *Lady Windemere's Fan* (1892), and the well-known poem *The Ballad of Reading Gaol* (1898). W. became a member of the Catholic Church in his last days. BIBLIOGRAPHY: H. Pearson, *Oscar Wilde* (1946); R. Merle, *Oscar Wilde* (n.d.).

[R. M. FUNCHION]

WILDGANS, ANTON (1881–1932), Austrian poet, dramatist, representing the Viennese form of literary expressionism. An advocate of the socially deprived classes, he never lost confidence in human goodness. He studied law, a subject which he never liked, was examining magistrate for 2 years, then dedicated himself fully to writing. He was director of the Vienna Burgtheater 1921–23 and 1930–31. Although several unpublished dramas and novels were found after his death, he is mainly a lyricist.

[B. F. STEINBRUCKNER]

WILFRID OF YORK, ST. (634–709), Anglo-Saxon monk and bishop. Originally a monk of Lindisfarne, he traveled to Rome with Benedict Biscop in 654 and studied at Lyons before ordination. He became abbot of Ripon and was the effective leader in the Roman victory at the Synod of Whitby (664). His election as bp. of York involved him in a life of controversy with kings and bps. of England including Theodore of Canterbury. Alternately bp. and exile, he invoked Roman help, converted Sussex to Christianity, built churches at Ripon and Hexham, and strengthened the Benedictine rule in English monasteries. He died as bp. of Hexham. BIBLIOGRAPHY: Eddius Stephanus, *Life of Bishop Wilfrid*, in C. Abertson, *Anglo-Saxon Saints and Heroes,* 89–162; E. Duckett, *Anglo-Saxon Saints and Scholars* (1967), 101–214; Bede, *Hist Eccl.*; Butler 4:96–100.

[J. DRUSE]

WILGEFORTIS LEGEND, widely told romance whose heroine grows a beard so as to avoid marriage. The heroine's name also was rendered as Liberata, Uncumber, Kummernis, Livrade. The legend was popular in Europe in the Middle Ages. The nonexistent "St. Wilgefortis" was widely invoked by wives against the oppression of husbands.

[E. J. DILLON]

WILGIS, ST. (d. *c.*700), Anglo-Saxon monk. He was a Northumbrian and father of St. Willibrord. In his later years he established St. Andrew's chapel on the banks of the Humber, and lived as a hermit nearby. A community gathered, attracted by his sanctity. Alcuin was later prior of this monastery. BIBLIOGRAPHY: J. Druse, NCE 14:908; Stanton, *Menology,* 42–43; Zimmerman 7:152.

[J. DRUSE]

WILHELM VON KÖLN (Master Wilhelm von Köln; d. betw. 1372 and 1378), German painter, documented in Cologne (1358–72). Reference in the Limburg Chronicle to a Meister Wilhelm von Köln as "best painter in German lands" led to the legends of the 19th century. The oldest parts of the *St. Clare Altarpiece* in the choir, Cologne cathedral, may evidence his style.

[M. J. DALY]

WILHELMA (WILHELMINA) OF BOHEMIA (OF MILAN), a woman of high birth, claiming to be daughter of Premysl Otakar (Ottakar) king of Bohemia, who came to Milan c.1270. She appears to have gathered followers, though the doctrine she is supposed to have taught is known only through inquisitorial proceedings involving members of her cult (see MANFREDA OF PIROVANO). She died in 1282 and was buried first in the cemetery of S. Pietro all'Orto, and later in the Cistercian abbey of Chiaravalle near Milan. After the condemnation of her followers on grounds of heresy (1302) her body was exhumed and burned. BIBLIOGRAPHY: L. Oliger, EncCatt 6:1251–52.

[P. K. MEAGHER]

WILHERING, ABBEY OF, Cistercian house on the Danube near Linz, Austria. Founded 1146 by the brothers Ulric and Cholo of the Wilhering family with monks from Reun in Styria, Wilhering founded in turn Hohenfurt, Engelszell, and Säusenstein (1259–1334). It suffered in war with the Turks, almost collapsed at the Reformation, and went on to survive Joseph II and Napoleon. Its revival under Abbot Theobald Grasböck (1892–1915) was impeded by two World Wars and the Nazi suppression. Since 1945 it has experienced a renewal, with monks staffing a school and serving in 9 parishes. BIBLIOGRAPHY: Cottineau 2:3454–55.

[E. J. DILLON]

WILIGELMO DA MODENA (fl. 1098–1110), Italian Romanesque sculptor. His façade friezes and other sculpture at Modena cathedral (c.1110–20) are among the first examples of Romanesque monumental sculpture in Italy. W. may have been trained and employed in Apulia, since the episcopal throne (1098) and the N door of St. Nicholas, Bari, have affinities with his Modena work. BIBLIOGRAPHY: A. Quintavalle, *La Cattedrale di Modena* (1961); R. Salvini, *Il Duomo di Modena* (1966).

[R. C. MARKS]

WILKINS, DAVID (1685–1745), Anglican priest-scholar. Appointed professor of Arabic at Cambridge in 1724, he published a monumental 4-v. work on the Councils of Great Britain and Ireland from the 5th to the 18th cent. and other critical studies in the area of Anglo-Saxon ecclesiastical law.

[E. J. DILLON]

WILL (Lat. *voluntas;* Gr. *thelēma*), the power and activity of loving the *good as such, properly speaking, as known through intelligence; by extension, through the senses. Will in its proper sense appears in theology with the notion of voluntary activity. This means appetition from within which in some way is conscious, by contrast with blind or merely natural appetition. It is credited to animals, and is an essential part of human living, which cannot be sustained by will-power alone, but requires the emotions, preferably charged with the cardinal virtues of *courage and *temperance. These are said to partake of will, to be voluntary by participation, literally to share in will, and the implications

of this are drawn out in Aristotle's ethics and St. Thomas's moral theology. So also, largely from St. *John Damascene, we have the notion of the human will of Christ in his sensitive appetites, the "sensual will" which at Gethsemani shrank from the prospect of his passion (cf. ThAq ST 3a, 18.2).

Will properly so called refers to a spiritual being, the acting of which manifests the twin abilities of knowing what is true as such and of loving what is good as such. These, respectively the mind and the will, are its only two powers of faculties, as they are called, and all other differentiations of function are less radical; thus as the faculty of reason is not distinct from that of understanding, so the faculty of *choice is not distinct from that of simply loving. Mind is open to the entrance of all being as true; will is the readiness to go out to all being as good. Notice that while a thing's being known by mind is a condition of its being loved by will, the motion is not toward its concept or mental condition, but toward the thing as it really is: the principle is of great importance for the dialectic of love in Christian theology. The meaning of will, like that of its object, is allegorical; it includes all manner of values, delights, and utilities, and all degrees of desiring and enjoying. Accordingly it is applied to God with all the due safeguards of the theistic method, and the notion of the divine will, which is declared in Scripture, is carefully refined by theological science.

Here we are concerned with the human will and human willing. Damascene remains a major source in the distinction drawn between simple willing, which he called *thelēsis,* and the early scholastics' will as will (*voluntas ut voluntas*), and deliberate willing, which he called *boulēsis*, and the early scholastics the will as reason (*voluntas ut ratio*). The first is the will as set on its own proper object, namely the all-good which is its end, which objectively is God and subjectively is *happiness (*beatitudo, eudaimonia*) in all its integrity. Were God clearly seen and the will immediately confronted with full happiness there could be no hesitation, no indeterminancy which is the condition of freedom. As it is, in this present life the will is always faced by objects that can be apprehended as less than the all-good; God is an imperative in the darkness of faith and but an inference in the light of reason, and full happiness is no more than a promise. Consequently the will can always hesitate, even if its true good is recognized, for acting for such a good might involve an effort which as a taxing evil it finds itself disinclined to adopt. The impasse can be broken only by an act of self-determination (*boulēsis*) whereby by taking counsel a person makes up his own mind. We speak, of course, on the level of the will itself: lower down there may obviously be physiological and psychological determinisms at work constricting the freedom of what in fact is performed.

The literature on the inter-relations of mind and will is copious: briefly it may be said that the first puts meaning into motion, whereas the second puts motion into meaning. For their comparative importance, a subject of scholastic debates between Dominicans and Franciscans which generated heat as well as light, see *Intellectualism and *Voluntarism. BIBLIOGRAPHY: ThAq ST 1a, 82–83 (esp. in ed. Lat-Eng, v. 11, ed. T. Suttor, 1970); ThAq ST 1a2a, 8–12, (in ed. Lat-Eng, v. 17, ed. T. Gilby, 1970).

[T. GILBY]

WILL OF GOD, in RC theology, the appetitive or volitional capacity and attitude of the divine being with respect to what the divine mind apprehends. That there is will in God is generally admitted by all who conceive him to be a personal being, possessed of intelligence, for knowledge is inseparable from one kind or another of appetitive reaction. But the term as applied to God is recognized to be analogous; one knows that will as it is in God is no more distinct from the divine being than is divine intelligence, and that intelligence and will in God are not in reality distinguished from each other. Still, the human mind, if in its present state it would know God at all, can only grasp him through the medium of ideas that represent distinct and separate realities when applied to creatures. Without losing sight of this essentially analogous character of its conclusions, Catholic theology has speculated much upon the implications of attributing will to God.

The attribution itself is clearly based upon revelation. Scripture teaches explicitly that God's will is manifested in the works of his hand: creation (Gen 1.26); the promise (Gen 28.13–15); man's perfection through the acceptance of the will of God (Rom 12.2). To the Hebrews, the will of God was the supreme cosmic force to which all other forces are subject.

Although the existence of will in God has never been explicitly defined, the fact is manifestly implied in what has been defined: that the three divine persons have but one will (D 501); that the true God is infinite in will (D 3001); that Jesus Christ has a divine as well as a human will (D 500).

The proper object of the divine will is the goodness of God's own being and he loves it necessarily for it corresponds to the total amplitude of his capacity to love. But this also embraces the goodness of all possible reflections of his perfections in created nature. Yet his will, so far as the actual existence of the creature is concerned, is supremely free, because no partial reflection of divine goodness can be so completely satisfying that it compels his creative love. The freedom of the divine will to create has been explicitly recognized by the Church (D 3025).

The divine will differs from the human in this respect that God's will does not presuppose but rather causes the goodness in the creature that he loves, while the human will is essentially passive and responds to the attraction of a good conceived as already existing in some sense.

Although no creature is willed by God as contributing anything essential to the divine goodness, the creaturely goodness that God does will is willed unchangeably from eternity, to make its appearance in the world of time and change. Although God creates out of love for himself and is moved by nothing other than his own goodness, nevertheless he wills the interdependence of created things, timeliness, order, and change, all of which depend upon him, while he depends upon nothing apart from himself. Thus the complex and wonderful order of the universe is a visible revelation of the divine will.

God could have loved and chosen to bring into existence other creatures than those existing in the present economy of things. Why he chose the things that are in preference to things that might have been is veiled in mystery, whatever may be the considerations of fittingness with which we try to account for the choice. Choosing the things he did, he brought them into existence by his love. And, since divine love chooses only the good, the presence of evil in the world must somehow be explained in this frame of reference (see EVIL).

Attempts to reconcile apparent conflict between different statements in Scripture concerning God's will and to correlate the doctrine of revelation with theological positions regarding such matters as evil, divine foreknowledge, divine concurrence in human, even sinful, activity, predestination, and reprobation, certain distinctions have been elaborated and absorbed into theological tradition. Among them are the distinctions between: (1) God's will of good pleasure (*voluntas beneplaciti*) and his will as expressed (*voluntas signi*) in acts such as prohibition, precept, counsel, permission, or actual operation. (2) The divine will considered as efficacious and as inefficacious, a distinction needed to reconcile the fact that God's will is irresistible (see Est 13.9), and yet is not always fulfilled, as when man sins. (3) The absolute and the conditioned will of God, i.e., the actual choice of the divine will, and that choice as it would have been had certain conditions been verified. (4) God's antecedent and consequent will, i.e., God's will viewed before or after his consideration of certain objectively variable circumstances. These distinctions, of course, do not represent real differences in God, who is utterly simple; they reflect rather the multiplicity of concept needed by the human mind in its thought about God. BIBLIOGRAPHY: ThAq (Lat-Eng) 5.2 ad 53; T. C. Donlon, NCE 14:914–917.

[R. J. BUSCHMILLER]

WILL OF GOD, SIGNED, part of a scholastic distinction between the will of God in a literal and proper sense (*voluntas beneplaciti*, the will of good pleasure) and God's will in a metaphorical sense (*voluntas signi*). Only the "will of good pleasure" is truly affirmed as being "in" God, i.e. as being the volitive aspect of the divine being. The "signed will" means rather a "sign of will." The metaphor consists in applying what in human experience are outward expressions of a person's will (e.g. a spoken request or command) to similar expressions as signs of God's will. The traditional enumeration of such signs is: prohibition, precept, counsel, doing, permitting. Terms denoting these five, e.g. in the language of the Bible, do not refer to the simple will of God itself, although the divine will underlies them. The convention of classifying the "signed will" as a metaphor is accepted to acknowledge the supremacy and hiddenness of God's true will (see ThAq ST 3a.1,3).

[T. C. O'BRIEN]

WILL OF GOOD PLEASURE, a theological phrase and concept used in scholastic discussions of the will of God. The will of good pleasure is distinguished from the will of sign (or signed will). The former is the real uncreated will of God, hidden in God, in which God is pleased (hence the name). The will of sign is only an exterior manifestation in the realm of creation, in which we think we find the expression of the real but hidden will of God. The signs mediate prohibitions, precepts, counsels, and permissions. BIBLIOGRAPHY: A. Michel, DTC 15.2:3349.

[E. J. DILLON]

WILLAERT, ADRIAN (*c.*1490–1562), Flemish Renaissance composer who studied in Paris under Jean *Mouton, but spent most of his creative life in Italy, first at Ferrara and Milan in the service of the Este family, then at St. Mark's in Venice, where he was *maestro di cappella* from 1527. He was chiefly responsible for the importation to Italy of the musical culture of the great Franco-Flemish composers of the 15th cent. that resulted in the establishment of the *Venetian School of Music and in Italy's becoming the center of European musical culture in the 16th century. Among W.'s many pupils were Cipriano de *Rore, who succeeded W. at St. Mark's, Costanzo *Porta, *Vicentino, and *Zarlino. Though not the inventor of polychoral composition, W. developed the technique which became a feature of music at St. Mark's. He was a superb contrapuntalist and also experimented with chromaticism. His most significant sacred works are his numerous motets; he also wrote Masses and psalms. Among his secular works his madrigals are outstanding. BIBLIOGRAPHY: W. Gerstenberg, MGG 14:662–676; ReeseMusR.

[P. DOHERTY]

WILLAIK, ST. (d. *c.*725), Benedictine abbot. His country of origin is uncertain. He succeeded St. Swithbert in 713 as abbot of Kaiserwerth. His relics were rediscovered in 1626; since 1403 his head, however, has been preserved at St. Lambert's in Düsseldorf. BIBLIOGRAPHY: J. Druse, NCE 14:918; AS March 1:148–150; Zimmerman 1:274–275.

[J. DRUSE]

WILLEBOLD, BL., pilgrim (d. 1230). Beyond a conjectured relationship to the counts of Calw, nothing is known of Willebold's family. Miracles at the time of his death at Berkheim in Swabia made his grave a place of pilgrimage. Since 1273 his relics have been in the church at Berkheim; ecclesiastical confirmation of his cult is being sought. BIBLIOGRAPHY: D. Andreini, NCE 14:918.

[M. J. FINNEGAN]

WILLEHAD OF BREMEN, ST. (d. 789), missionary, bishop. Last of the great Anglo-Saxon missionaries, he was born in Northumbria and became a friend of Alcuin. After laboring in Frisia, he was sent by Charlemagne to the Saxons of the lower Elbe-Weser region (780). Revolts forced his withdrawal to Echternach, but he returned to the area and became the first bp. of Bremen (787). BIBLIOGRAPHY: Butler 4:297–298.

[W. A. CHANEY]

WILLIAM I (*c.*1028–87) the Conqueror, **KING OF ENGLAND** from 1066. Duke of Normandy (1035) and lord of Maine (1062) and Brittany, W. had defeated France before his victory over Harold II near Hastings (1066). This, combined with papal approval, Norwegian alliance, and claims of being the Confessor's heir, made him first Norman king of England. He suppressed English revolts (1066–70), devastating the north, and combined Anglo-Saxon institutions with Norman feudalism in decisive rule. He appointed Lanfanc of Bec abp. of Canterbury (1070) and supported ecclesiastical reform and monastic revival, asserting royal-ducal control and rejecting papal over-lordship. BIBLIOGRAPHY: D. C. Douglas, *William the Conqueror* (1964).

[W. A. CHANEY]

WILLIAM II (called Rufus; d. 1100), **KING OF ENGLAND** from 1087. He obtained the throne with the help of Abp. Lanfranc, but, on Lanfranc's death (1089), plundered the Church unmercifully. When ill, he appointed Anselm to Canterbury (1093), but soon drove the primate into exile. His religious cynicism and immorality were notorious, but he was a strong king. His brother Robert pawned the duchy of Normandy to him to go on a crusade (1096). The attempt to interpret William's death in the New Forest as a ritual murder is not accepted generally. BIBLIOGRAPHY: C. Brooke, *Saxon and Norman Kings* (1963); DNB 61:301.

[F. D. BLACKLEY]

WILLIAM OF AEBELHOLT, ST. (*c.* 1127–1203), first abbot of Aebelholt, Denmark, canonized in 1224. Born in Paris of noble family, he was educated in France, was canon regular at Sainte-Geneviève-de-Paris, and was called to Denmark (1165) by Absalon of Lund, then bp. of Roskilde, to reform the house of canons on Eskilsø. As first abbot of Aebelholt, founded 1175, he was an important writer and teacher and tried to be a reconciling mediator in Franco-Scandinavian disputes. He worked for peace and for the freedom of the Church.

[E. J. DILLON]

WILLIAM OF ALNWICK (d. *c.*1333), English Franciscan scholastic, bp. of Giovinazzo, Sicily, from 1330. He was a student of Duns Scotus at Paris; taught there and at Oxford, Montpellier, Bologna, and Naples. He is known to have signed the document, *De paupertate Christi*, a protest in 1322 against Pope John XXII. W. received the episcopacy through his friendship with Robert of Sicily. In his writings W. basically reflected Scotus's teachings with the exception of several typical Scotist points. He left a commentary on Lombard's *Sentences*, many *quaestiones disputatae*, and may possibly have prepared Scotus's *Ordinatio*.

[T. C. O'BRIEN]

WILLIAM OF APULIA (fl. *c*.1090–1111), Norman court poet. Though not himself of Norman stock, W. produced a metrical history which gives important information about the activity of the Normans in Italy and Sicily until 1085. BIBLIOGRAPHY: *Le Geste de Robert Guiscard* (ed. and tr. M. Mathieu, 1961).

[G. E. CONWAY]

WILLIAM OF AQUITAINE, ST. (d. 812), Carolingian noble, monastic founder, monk. He was a cousin of Charlemagne, Tassilo, Adalard, Wala. Of his ten children, one was Bernard, court chamberlain of Louis I. Count of Toulouse in 790, W. recaptured Barcelona. He founded the monastery of Gellone and entered it (806). His family and Charlemagne's were closely related by blood and marriage. There are several *Chansons de geste* about him. BIBLIOGRAPHY: J. Calmette, *De Bernardo sancti Guillelmi filio, ?–844* (1902); B. Hamilton, NCE 14:520–521; R. Van Doren, BiblSanct 7:467–470.

[A. CABANISS]

WILLIAM OF ARNAUD, BL. (d. 1242), French Dominican martyr. He was appointed by Pope Gregory IX inquisitor for four dioceses in Provence. W.'s zeal to root out heresy led to his banishment from Toulouse. In 1242, lured to a castle by an officer of Count Raymond VII of Toulouse, W. and 11 companions were assassinated. He was beatified in 1866.

[J. R. AHERNE]

WILLIAM OF AUBERIVE (d. 1180), Cistercian monk of the Strict Observance, abbot of Auberive from 1165. Little is known of him beyond his interest in the symbolism of numbers. He continued the *Analytica numerorum* of Odo of Morimond and wrote a treatise of his own on the sacramental meaning of the numbers from 3 to 12, *De sacramentis numerorum a ternario usque ad duodenarium*. He stopped work on this the year he became abbot, but the work was continued by Gottfried of Clairvaux.

[E. J. DILLON]

WILLIAM OF AUVERGNE (William of Paris; *c*.1180–1249), French theologian and philosopher. He was professor of theology at the Univ. of Paris and in 1228 was consecrated bp. of Paris by Pope Gregory IX. He belonged to the first generation of masters at the university who employed the teachings of the recently rediscovered Aristotle and of Islamic and Jewish philosophers in support of Chris-

tian theology. He was among the first to insist upon the autonomous character of philosophy as a distinct science and one worthy of cultivation as such for the assistance it rendered to Christian theological speculation. But though W. owed much to Aristotle, Maimonides, and Avicenna, and was a precursor of the interest soon to develop in the new philosophy, in his basic theological positions he did not deviate from the Augustinianism that was prevalent in his time. His principal work is *Magisterium divinale* (1228–36). BIBLIOGRAPHY: Copleston 2:218–227; D. Knowles, EncPhil 8:302–303; Gilson HCP 250–258.

[J. T. HICKEY]

WILLIAM OF AUXERRE (*c*.1150–1231), scholastic theologian. W. taught theology at the Univ. of Paris and was commissioned by Gregory IX to revise Aristotle's *Physics* and *Metaphysics* so that they could be inserted into the univ.'s curriculum. His most significant contribution is a theological *summa*, the *Summa aurea*, written betw. 1215 and 1220 and published in several editions. The treatise shows the influence of Augustine, Anselm of Canterbury, and Victorine theology in general. It was a major influence on both W.'s contemporaries and the later scholastics. Although the work covers the whole corpus of theological thought, its most lasting contribution is the analysis of free will, natural law, and the virtues. BIBLIOGRAPHY: G. Gál, NCE 14:921–922.

[T. M. MCFADDEN]

WILLIAM V OF BAVARIA (1548–1626), duke of Bavaria, 1579–1597 or 1598. While his education was limited—two years at the Univ. of Ingolstadt—, W. was an astute and capable politician. After his marriage to Renata of Lotharingia in 1568, he devoted himself to his love of art. His castle at Trausnitz became a showplace of the early baroque filled with art works, books, antiquities and music. William was an extremely pious man and concerned about the Church's welfare. He relied heavily upon the Jesuits during his extensive reform of the Bavarian Church, such as, the re-Catholicization of the district of Hohenwaldeck between 1581 and 1584. Yet his religious policies were closely interwoven with dynastic and territorial interests. His internal reforms clearly prepared the way for the rise of the absolutist state in Bavaria. Foreign policy was also based upon Wittelsbach gain as seen in the election of his brother, Ernest, as abp. of Cologne in 1583. Ernest's election not only halted the threat of Protestantism in Cologne, but also insured Wittelsbach control of this important episcopal territory. W.'s diplomatic ventures and artistic tastes, however, overburdened Bavaria's financial resources and in the interest of the state he voluntarily abdicated on October 15, 1597 in favor of his son, Maximilian I. W. spent the rest of his life in a monastery. BIBLIOGRAPHY: D. Albrecht, "Die Herzoge Wilhelm V. und Maximilian I," *Handbuch der Bayerische Geschichte,* (v. 1, ed. Max Spindler, 1966); R. S. Dunn, *Age of Religious Wars, 1559–1689* (1970).

[C. T. EBY]

WILLIAM OF BOURGES, ST. (1150–1209), archbishop. He entered the Cistercians in 1167 and in 1184 became abbot of Fontaine Saint-Jean. Named abp. of Bourges in 1200, he began a life of strict observance. He died while undertaking a crusade against the Albigenses and was canonized in 1218. BIBLIOGRAPHY: F. D. Lazenby, NCE 14:922; Butler 1:65–66; C. Dupont, BiblSanct 7:459–460.

[F. D. LAZENBY]

WILLIAM OF CHAMPEAUX (*c*.1070–1122), early scholastic philosopher and bishop. W. taught logic at the cathedral school in Paris; founded a house of Augustinian canons at Saint-Victor, also in Paris; and became (1113) bp. of Châlons-sur-Marne. He composed one of the earliest books of theological sentences in an effort to produce a systematic treatment of all theology. He was a logical realist who originally held that the universal was essentially, identically, and wholly realized in each of its particulars. Dissuaded from this position by his pupil, Peter *Abelard, W. later defended a theory of indifference: that the universal is present in its particulars not essentially but without differentiation. Under his influence, the Abbey of Saint-Victor flourished and needed reforms were introduced into his diocese. BIBLIOGRAPHY: D. Luscombe, EncPhil 8:303–304; B. M. Bonansea, NCE 14:922–923.

[T. M. MCFADDEN]

WILLIAM OF CONCHES (*c*.1090–*c*.1160), Platonist master at the school of Chartres. He was there most of his teaching life, leaving *c*.1140 to become tutor to the future Henry II of England and in protest against attacks on his teaching. The "Cornificians" upbraided him for cultivating study of the humanities; the Cistercian William of Thierry, in *De erroribus Guillelmi a Conchis,* for advocating use of philosophy in the study of theology. W. has a twofold importance in the history of scholasticism. He prepared glosses and other works belonging to the medieval trivium and quadrivium. Secondly, he is an important exponent of the Platonism developed at the school of Chartres, chiefly in his treatise *De philosophia mundi* (found in PL 90,1127–28 among the works of Bede; and in PL 172,39–102) with works by Honorius of Autun). The primary inspiration of the works is Plato's *Timaeus*, whose world view W. combines with the Genesis creation account. The encyclopedic *De philosophia* covers the meaning of philosophy, God and spiritual beings, the material universe, the creation of man. W. relates the Trinity to creation by placing in the Word the ideas according to which the Father creates, and by making the Holy Spirit the World Soul; the three persons are the efficient, formal, and final uncreated causes, matter the sole created cause of the universe. In a later work, *Dogmatica,* after being accused by William of Thierry of *modalism, W. posited "nature" as the formal cause of the world.

[T. C. O'BRIEN]

WILLIAM OF CORBEIL (d. 1136), abp. of Canterbury. Clerk of Ranulf Flambard, bp. of Durham, and friend of St. Anselm of Canterbury, W. became the first prior of the Augustinian Canons of St. Osyth's, Essex, in 1119. He was elected abp. of Canterbury in 1123 and although the monks there disputed the election, it was confirmed by Pope Callistus II. Appointed papal legate in 1126, he held legatine councils in 1127 and 1129. He completed and dedicated the Canterbury Cathedral in 1130. Under him Canterbury lost its effective claim to supremacy over York. BIBLIOGRAPHY: T. F. Tout, DNB (repr. 1949–50) 4:1120–23; D. Bethell, *Archiepiscopate of William de Corbeil, 1123–36* (unpublished dissertation, Bodleian Library, Oxford).

[J. L. GRASSI]

WILLIAM OF CREMONA (*c*.1270–1356), bishop. After studying and teaching at Paris, W. was elected prior general of the Augustinians (1326) and later chosen bp. of Novara (1342). His writings include a criticism of Marsilius of Padua. BIBLIOGRAPHY: A. Gwynn, *English Austin Friars in the Time of Wycliffe* (1940).

[J. MULDOON]

WILLIAM OF EDYNTON (Edington; d. 1366), bishop, administrator. He was keeper of the wardrobe (1341), treasurer of England (1344–56), bp. of Winchester (1346), chancellor (1356–63). He introduced William of Wykeham to royal administration and built the west end of Winchester cathedral. BIBLIOGRAPHY: T. F. Tout, *Chapters in Administrative History of Medieval England* (6 v., 1920–29); V. Mudroch, NCE 14:924; Emden Ox 1:629–630.

[J. L. GRASSI]

WILLIAM FIRMATUS, ST. (d. *c*.1095) priest, hermit, and perhaps bishop. W., a gifted citizen of Tours, was appointed a canon of St. Venantius in his youth before he became a soldier and physician. Later he retired into the wilderness with his widowed mother, and after her death lived as a hermit. W. visited the Holy Land, was renowned for his sanctity, and was credited with miracles one of which was the liberation from prison of Count Baldwin of Boulogne, later King of Jerusalem. Stephen of Fougères, bishop of Rennes, wrote his life. BIBLIOGRAPHY: J. C. Moore, NCE 14:924; Butler 2:158–159; P. Rouillard, BiblSanct 7:492–494.

[M. C. BRADLEY]

WILLIAM FITZHERBERT, ST., see WILLIAM OF YORK, ST.

WILLIAM OF GAYNESBURGH (Gainsborough); d. 1307, Franciscan, bishop. He was provincial of the Franciscans (1285–*c*.1292), regent at Oxford (*c*.1292–94), member of the royal council (1295), often an envoy of Edward I, esp. in French negotiations (1295–98), bp. of Worcester from 1302. BIBLIOGRAPHY: *Register of William de Geynesborough* (ed. J. W. Willis Bund, 2 v. 1907–29); Emden Ox 2:750–51.

[J. L. GRASSI]

WILLIAM DE GRENEFIELD (Greenfield; d. 1315), archbishop, chancellor. A nephew of Walter Giffard, abp. of York who maintained him at Oxford and Paris; he was much used as ambassador by Edward I from c.1290 to 1300, was chancellor of England (1302–04) and abp. of York from 1304, after which he devoted himself entirely to his see. BIBLIOGRAPHY: J. Raine, *Fasti eboracenses* (1863); F. Roth, NCE 14:925.

[J. L. GRASSI]

WILLIAM OF HECHAM, Augustinian theologian, W. was master regent at Oxford 1292 when Giles of Rome was teaching in Paris. Because of W.'s excellent education his teaching became a theological study requirement for the members of the order. He took part in numerous public discussions and wrote many *quaestiones disputatae*, remnants of which still exist. Also preserved are two sermons addressed to students at Oxford. He was prior provincial of the Order (1300–07). BIBLIOGRAPHY: Emden Ox 2:899; F. Roth, *History of the English Austin Friars* (2 v. 1961) 1:48.

[A. WARDLE]

WILLIAM OF HEYTESBURY (c.1313–72), English scholastic logician, chancellor of the Univ. of Oxford 1353–54(?) and 1370–72. A fellow of Merton College, W. helped develop the new logic and mathematical physics stimulated by *William of Ockham and *Thomas Bradwardine. His own writings, e.g. *Termini naturales* and *Regulae solvendi sophismata*, were exceptionally influential in universities on the Continent. BIBLIOGRAPHY: Emden Ox 2:927–928.

WILLIAM OF HIRSAU, BL. (d. 1091), reforming abbot. W. became abbot of Hirsau in 1071 and was a zealous supporter of Gregory VII in the investiture struggle. The practice of professing monastic servants at Hirsau is attributed to William. It later spread to a number of abbeys. In 1079 W. was persuaded to adopt the Cluniac reforms and merge them with the existing customs of Hirsau. The result is known as *Constitutiones Hirsaugienses*. The reform attracted so many vocations that a second house was added in 1083. Subsequent foundations were made in Styria, Carinthia, Erfurt, and Magdeburg. W. is also the author of works on music and astronomy. BIBLIOGRAPHY: M. Fischer, *Studien zur Entstehung der Hirsauer Konstitutionen* (1910); Butler 3:17–18; A. Walz, BiblSanct 7:474–475.

[B. F. SCHERER]

WILLIAM OF HOTHUM (d. 1298), English Dominican theologian and abp. of Dublin from 1296. Having studied at Oxford and Paris, W. lectured as regent master at Paris (1280) when he was made provincial of the English province and defended the Thomistic doctrine on the unity of substantial form. BIBLIOGRAPHY: Emden Ox 2:970; DNB 27:414; F. J. Roensch, *Early Thomistic School* (1964) 28–34.

[J. A. WEISHEIPL]

WILLIAM OF JUMIÈGES (fl. c.1070), Benedictine historian of the 11th cent. (surnamed Calculus). W. is famous only for his *Historia Normannorum* in eight books, a chief authority for the history of the Norman people from 851 to 1137. Only seven of eight books are from W.'s own hand; the first four were taken from an earlier work by Dudo of Saint-Quentin but were modified and corrected by W. who made good use of the information provided. Ordericus Vitalis used the *Historia Normannorum* for portions of his work that refer to the Normans. BIBLIOGRAPHY: R. Foreville, NCE 14:926–927; G. C. Alston, CE 15:633.

[M. C. BRADLEY]

WILLIAM OF KILKENNY (d. 1256), English ecclesiastic and royal administrator; elected bp. of Ossory (1231), but resigned unconsecrated (1232); bp. of Ely (1255). Possibly of Irish origin, W. was educated at Oxford and rose in Henry III's administrative and diplomatic service to be keeper of the great seal, with the duties of chancellor. BIBLIOGRAPHY: Emden Ox 2:1048–49; H. Mayr-Harting, NCE 14:927.

[R. W. HAYS]

WILLIAM DE LONGCHAMP (d. 1197), English ecclesiastic and politician; bp. of Ely (1189–97); chancellor of England (1189–97); chief justiciar of England (1189–91); papal legate (1190–94). Of low birth, W. served Richard I before and after he became king. His high-handedness and exclusive devotion to Richard's interests led to his unpopularity and exile (1191). His character has been much disputed. BIBLIOGRAPHY: H. Mayr-Harting, NCE 14:927.

[R. W. HAYS]

WILLIAM OF MACCLESFIELD (d. 1303), English Dominican theologian. W. preached at Paris in 1293–94 and was regent of studies at Oxford 1299–1300. A large number of writings are attributed to him, but only a few are certainly his; his place in the history of Oxford Thomism has not yet been fully established. Unaware of his death earlier in the year, Benedict XI made him a cardinal in 1303. BIBLIOGRAPHY: Emden Ox 2:1200–01.

[L. E. BOYLE]

WILLIAM OF MALEVAL, ST. (d. 1157), hermit, founder. After pilgrimages to Rome and Jerusalem, he became a hermit near Pisa, then moved in 1155 to the desert valley of Maleval near Siena. Here W. and his disciples formed the beginnings of the community of the Hermits of St. William (Williamites) which eventually spread throughout Europe. BIBLIOGRAPHY: S. Mottironi, BiblSanct 7:471–473.

[G. E. CONWAY]

WILLIAM OF MALMESBURY (c.1090–1143), English Benedictine monk and chronicler. Educated at Malmesbury abbey, where he became librarian, W. wrote both historical and devotional works. His *Gesta regum* (1125), an account of the kings of England, is scholarly and readable. Other historical works by W. are his *Gesta pontificum* (1125), a chronicle of the bishops of England, and the unfinished *Historia novella,* concerned with the civil war during king Stephen's reign. His devotional works include lives of Wulfstan, Dunstan, and Aldhelm, and *Miracles of the Virgin* (c.1140). BIBLIOGRAPHY: H. Farmer, "William of Malmesbury's Life and Works," JEcclHist 13 (1962), 39–54; DNB 61:351.

[F. D. BLACKLEY]

WILLIAM OF MANDAGOUT (d. 1321), cardinal from 1312, abp. of Embrun from 1295, of Aix-en-Provence from 1311, canonist, important for his contribution to the *Liber Sextus*, compiled under Pope Boniface VIII; also author of a treatise (c.1294) on canonical elections.

[T. C. O'BRIEN]

WILLIAM DE LA MARE (d. c.1290), English Franciscan, author of *Correctorium fratris Thomae* (1278; revised 1282), a standard of Francisan opposition to Thomism; and of *Correctio textus Bibliae*, a textual study of the Bible outstanding for its time. BIBLIOGRAPHY: D. Callus, NCE 14:928–929. *CORRECTORIA.

[T. C. O'BRIEN]

WILLIAM OF MELITONA, Franciscan theologian. Born in England (hence Melitona/Militona from Middleton?), he studied in Paris c.1245 under Alexander of Hales and was a member of a commission (1248) that proposed the condemnation of the Talmud. He also was part of an effort to publish posthumously the unfinished *Summa* of Alexander of Hales. W.'s principal work was his *Quaestiones de sacramentis,* the most extensive and important treatment of the subject before Bonaventure and Aquinas.

[E. J. DILLON]

WILLIAM DE MELTON (d. 1340) archbishop, administrator. He was a great and zealous abp. of York and a leading figure of his time; keeper of the privy seal (1307–14); keeper of the wardrobe (1314–16); abp. of York (1316); treasurer of England (1325–26 and 1330). BIBLIOGRAPHY: J. Raine *Fasti eboracenses* (1863); L. H. Butler "Archbishop Melton, His Neighbours and Kinsmen," JEcclHist 2 (1951) 54–68.

[J. L. GRASSI]

WILLIAM OF MOERBEKE (c.1215–c.1286), translator of Greek philosophical texts and archbishop. W. belonged to the Dominican priory at Ghent, spent a number of years as a chaplain at the papal courts in various Italian cities, and then lived in Greece and Asia Minor. He was a forceful proponent of reunion between the Greek Orthodox and Rome, and was appointed (1278) abp. of Corinth. He is best known as an extremely competent although precisely literal translator of Aristotle and later Greek philosophers into Latin. His work gave Western scholars a much more accurate text of Aristotle than had been available, and his precise adherence to the literal text enabled the medieval scholastics to distinguish between authentic Aristotelian positions and the Neoplatonic interpretations that had been added to them. Through his translations of later Greek philosophers, esp. *Proclus, W. also influenced the development of medieval Neoplatonism. BIBLIOGRAPHY: E. R. Fairweather, EncPhil 8:305–306; J. C. Vansteenkiste, NCE 14:929–930.

[T. M. MCFADDEN]

WILLIAM OF MONT LAUZUN (d. 1343), Benedictine abbot, canon and civil lawyer, called "most elegant doctor of decrees." Born in Quercy in SW France during the second half of the 13th cent., he studied theology and canon law in Paris, joined the Benedictines at Cluny in 1308, taught canon and Roman law in Toulouse, and perhaps in Paris and Poitiers. He was made abbot of Montierneuf in Poitiers in 1334 by John XXII. An eminent and widely traveled canonist, W. attacked the theological ignorance manifested by many jurists. Many of his writings were published in the 16th cent. or later.

[E. J. DILLON]

WILLIAM DE MONTIBUS (d. 1213), English theologian and chancellor of Lincoln from c. 1191. While teaching at Paris he had a number of outstanding disciples including Giralcus Cambrencis and Alexander Neckham. On his return to England he raised the prestige of the schools at Lincoln to that of Oxford, but he was unable to establish a permanent center of studies. W. made theology understandable to the clergy by his simplified approach and his manuals of instruction. BIBLIOGRAPHY: Emden Ox 2:1298–99.

[J. A. WEISHEIPL]

WILLIAM OF NEUCHÂTEL (c.1150–1231), once commemorated as a saint. His cult was abolished and his name was removed from the Breviary in 1852 because his alleged miracles were unsupported historically. He was born in Paris, claimed English origin, and after being ordained priest, assumed the roles of teacher, canon, provost of canons, and perhaps chaplain, all in the entourage of a count of Neuenbourg.

[E. J. DILLON]

WILLIAM OF NEWBURGH (1136–c.1201), Augustinian canon of Newburgh priory and the finest English historian of his age. His *Historia rerum Anglicarum,* covering the years 1066–1198, is distinguished for its historical criticism and is an important source for the reign of Henry II. W.'s life is obscure, although he was educated and died at Newburgh priory. BIBLIOGRAPHY: DNB 61:360; H. E. Salter, *William of Newburgh* EHR 22 (1907) 510–514.

[F. D. BLACKLEY]

WILLIAM OF NORWICH, ST. (1132–44), an alleged child-martyr whose mutilated remains were discovered in a wood near Norwich. The accusation made by his uncle that he had been ritually murdered by Jews was not credited by local authorities. However, William Turbeville, bp. of Norwich, reopened the case in 1149, and eventually the body of the child, who was receiving some local veneration, was buried in the Norwich cathedral. The charges were never substantiated, despite a credulous investigation by Thomas of Monmouth. This was the first appearance of the charge, common in the later Middle Ages, that Jews ritually murdered Christian children. BIBLIOGRAPHY: C. Roth, *History of the Jews in England* (1941).

WILLIAM OF NOTINGHAM (d. 1336), English Franciscan theologian. He lectured on the *Sentences* at Oxford by 1290, was lector in the Oxford friary (c. 1312–14), and minister provincial of the English Franciscans from 1316 to (c. 1330). At the general chapter of Perugia in 1322 he signed the letter of protest against the decrees of John XXII concerning evangelical poverty. BIBLIOGRAPHY: Emden Ox 2:1377–78; J. A. Weisheipl, NCE 14:931–932.

[J. A. WEISHEIPL]

WILLIAM OF NOTRE DAME DE L'OLIVE, ST. (d. 1240), Flemish hermit. In early life a baker, W. joined the Canons of St. Norbert at Aisne, Fr., but left to live as a hermit at Mariemont, Belgium. There he founded Notre Dame de l'Olive, an abbey for women, which became affiliated with Cîteaux. BIBLIOGRAPHY: E. Brouette, NCE 14:932.

[J. E. WRIGLEY]

WILLIAM OF OCKHAM (Occam; c. 1285–1347), as representative of "the modern way" (*via moderna*), one of the most influential philosophical and politico-theological figures of the 14th century. He was born in Surrey, Eng., became a Franciscan, and studied and taught at Oxford. A robust and prolific controversialist and a complex but unified thinker his work may be considered under the three heads of logic and epistemology, of scholastic theology, and of Church-State relations. Under the first, he is a seminal force in the history of *nominalism; his close and exact analysis of the grammar of scientific discourse, in which he anticipated theorems of modern logic, and his severe economy about the multiplication of entities—"Ockham's razor"—set up a terminism that reduced universals to conceptual modes applied to unique and irreducible things. It was opposed to the critical realism of the Thomist, Scotist, and Augustinian schools, and became prevalent in the universities, notably Paris, Oxford, Heidelberg, Vienna, Erfurt, and Leipzig.

His skepticism about the validity of metaphysics entered into theology; this was marked by a sort of retreat from reason to faith, which, however, was never headlong and brought off its rational baggage intact. The freedom of omnipotence was stressed against the alleged necessitarianism of divine ideas; the universe was conceived as an expression of God's will rather than of his mind. Hence the paradoxes that God could create "impossibilities" and could contradict what men consider to be his moral law. Constant recourse was made to the distinction between the ordinate power (*potentia ordinata*) and the absolute power (*potentia absoluta*) of God. He looms largest, however, in religious history as a leading figure in the fight between the twin establishments of secular and sacred power, and between the last and the poverty ideals of the Franciscan *Spirituals. O. was summoned from Oxford to Avignon by John XXII, no mean antagonist; though many of his propositions were judged open to censure, he was not condemned, perhaps because an assessor, the Dominican Durand of Saint-Pourçain, was himself a stormy petrel. O. threw himself into the support of his minister general, Michael of Cesena, attacked the Pope, and fled to the side of the Emperor, Louis of Bavaria, at Munich. There he conducted a vigorous polemic, giving as much as he took, against papal jurisdiction in temporalities. He was, of course, excommunicated, but those were the days when harsh words broke no bones and ecclesiastics could not be closely and effectively regimented. He was much respected, his title was the *venerabilis inceptor;* he was elected general by the brethren of his party, and died professing his obedience to legitimate authority. His position in the genealogy of Lutheranism, of Pietism, and of positivism calls for very cautious and qualified attribution. BIBLIOGRAPHY: P. Boehner, *Ockham, Philosophical Writings* (1957); G. de Lagarde, *La Naissance de l'esprit laïque* (1956–63) v. 4. and 5.

[T. GILBY]

WILLIAM OF PAGULA (Poul; d. c. 1332), parish priest, canonist. A doctor of canon law of Oxford, and vicar of Winkfield, Berkshire (1314–32), W. is the author of five works, the most influential of which are the *Summa summarum,* a vast compilation of law and theology, and the *Oculus sacerdotis,* a practical handbook of pastoral and sacramental theology. BIBLIOGRAPHY: L. E. Boyle, *Transactions of the Royal Historical Society,* 5th ser., 5 (1955) 81–110.

[L. E. BOYLE]

WILLIAM PERALDUS (Perault; c. 1200–c. 1271), French Dominican theologian, manualist. Of his five extant works the most influential was the *Summa de vitiis et virtutibus,* the *de vitiis* being written in 1236, the *de virtutibus* in 1248–50. It is a work of practical moral teaching, based on scriptural and patristic sources. Some 500 MSS are extant, and it was printed 16 times before 1500. The best study of W. is A. Dondaine, AFP 18 (1948) 162–236.

[L. E. BOYLE]

WILLIAM OF POITIERS (c. 1020–c. 1087), Norman historian. W. attended school at Poitiers whence his surname. After leading the life of a knight, he was ordained and became chaplain to William the Conqueror. W. was the best informed man of his age; he knew the Greek and Latin authors. His only extant work is his life of William the Conqueror, *Gesta Guilelmi II, ducis Normannorum, regis Angelorum I,* which has the value of a contemporary source based on direct testimonies. It exists only in a single MS almost destroyed. As archdeacon of Lisieux, W. wrote sermons and poems, now lost. BIBLIOGRAPHY: R. Foreville, NCE 14:935; L. Bréhier, CE 15:637.

[M. C. BRADLEY]

WILLIAM OF PUYLAURENS, French chronicler. Born near the close of the 12th cent., he was chaplain of Raymond VII, Count of Toulouse. His *Chronicon* covering the years 1099–1272 is an important source for the history of the crusade against the Albigenses. W. was an eye witness of the events from 1223–49. BIBLIOGRAPHY: A. Potthast, *Bibliotheca Historica Medii Aevi* 2:555–556 (2d ed. 1896); J. Guiraud, DHGE 1:1053–54.

[H. DRESSLER]

WILLIAM REDE (d. 1385), English mathematician, astronomer, and bishop. A fellow of Merton College, and a master of theology, he was appointed to the see of Chichester (1368) and was consecrated at Avignon. Although bp. and member of Parliament (1329–80), he retained a lively interest in astronomy and is generally considered the founder of the library at Merton. BIBLIOGRAPHY: C. L. Kingsford, DNB 16:817–819; Emden Ox 3:1556–60.

[J. A. WEISHEIPL]

WILLIAM RISHANGER (*c.*1250–after 1312), English Benedictine chronicler. A monk of St. Albans Abbey from 1271, he continued the chronicles of Roger of Wendover and Matthew Paris from 1259 to at least 1312, or, according to Thomas of Walsingham, to 1322. R.'s most valuable work is his *Chronicle of the Barons' Wars* (ed. J. O. Halliwell, 1840). The only other work assigned to him with certainty is *Gesta Edwardi primi regis Angliae* (ed. H. T. Riley, 1865). BIBLIOGRAPHY: M. J. Hamilton, NCE 14:936; T. F. Tout, DNB 16:1205–07.

[R. W. HAYS]

WILLIAM OF RUISBROEK (Ruysbroeck; fl. mid–13th cent.), Franciscan missionary. In 1252 W. set out for the realm of Sartak accompanied by his confrere Bartholomew of Cremona. The *Itinerarium*, the narrative of his mission, stresses the spiritual nature of the undertaking and in addition gives valuable ethnographic and linguistic information. BIBLIOGRAPHY: A. Wyngaert, *Sinica Franciscana* 1:145–332 (1929); C. Dawson, *Mongol Mission* 87–220 (1955).

[H. DRESSLER]

WILLIAM OF SAINT-AMOUR (*c.*1200–72), secular master of theology at Paris and bitter opponent of the Dominicans and Franciscans there. He began to teach in 1250. His life-long polemic against the mendicants, oc-

casioned by their privileges and the Joachimite agitation aroused by *Gerard of Borgo San Donnino, was a success under Innocent IV. This pope, because of W.'s representations at Anagni, in 1254 severely curtailed the mendicants' academic rights. Alexander IV, however, reversed these decisions in 1255; W.'s work *De periculis novissimorum temporum* was condemned (1256); he was forbidden to teach, and exiled from France. His activities and the condemned work led both SS. Bonaventure and Thomas Aquinas to write defenses of the mendicants. W., after his exile, spent his last years continuing the agitation by his correspondence with Gerard of Abbeville. BIBLIOGRAPHY: A. J. Heiman, NCE 14:936–937; D. L. Douie, *Conflict between the Seculars and the Mendicants at the University of Paris in the Thirteenth Century* (1954).

[T. C. O'BRIEN]

WILLIAM OF SAINT-BÉNIGNE OF DIJON, ST. (962–1031), reform abbot. W. entered the Benedictine monastery at Locedio near Vercelli where he had been a child oblate. Later he joined the Abbot Majolus at Cluny and was entrusted with the reform of the Abbey of Saint-Bénigne of Dijon. In 1001 he began the erection of the Abbey of Fruttuara in Lombardy, whence the Cluniac reform spread through northern Italy and into Germany. Monks from his abbey of Dijon brought the reform into Normandy, Poland, and Hungary. In his 40 monasteries, W. fostered a tradition of learning and encouraged the spread of Romanesque architecture. Never formally canonized, he is honored, however, by the Benedictines. BIBLIOGRAPHY: B. Hamilton, NCE 14:937–938; Butler 1:12; J. Marilier, BiblSanct 7:482–484.

[M. A. WINKELMANN]

WILLIAM OF SAINT-BRIEUC, ST. (William Pinchon; *c.*1175–1234), bishop. W. became bp. of Saint-Brieuc in 1220 but was banished by the duke of Brittany for having opposed him in his dissensions with the Church. He took refuge for two years at Poitiers. Returning to Saint-Brieuc in 1230, he continued work on its cathedral. W. was canonized in 1247. BIBLIOGRAPHY: Butler 3:212–213; H. Platelle, BiblSanct 7:494–495.

[F. D. LAZENBY]

WILLIAM OF SAINT-THIERRY, BL. (*c.*1085–1148), ascetical theologian and abbot. W. probably studied under Anselm of Laon; entered the Benedictines; was appointed abbot of Saint-Thierry near Reims (1119); but resigned (1135) in order to seek a more contemplative life as a Cistercian at Signy. He was a close friend of St. Bernard of Clairvaux, and supported him in the defense of the Cluniac reforms and in his arguments against Peter Abelard. In his major works (*De natura et dignitate amoris; De contemplando Deo; Epistola ad fratres de Monte Dei*), W. considers man's natural capacity for love as disordered by sin and rectified by grace. Man bears the image of God in his soul, and this image can be restored after sin only in stages. The soul must pass through an animal, then rational, and finally a spiritual life in which, through love, it begins to contemplate God and eternal life. The Cistercian menology and the diocese of Reims have honored him with the title "Blessed," but there is no evidence that this ever developed into a liturgical cult. BIBLIOGRAPHY: M.-A. Dimier, BiblSanct 7:484–486.

[T. M. MCFADDEN]

WILLIAM OF SANDWICH, CHRONICLE OF, a spurious eye-witness account, written c.1380, probably by Philip Ribot, a French Carmelite, of the beginnings and spread of the Carmelite Order. Printed by G. Wessels in AnalOCarmC 3 (1914–16) 302–315.

[L. E. BOYLE]

WILLIAM OF SHERWOOD (Shyreswood; d. c.1267): treasurer of Lincoln cathedral from c. 1254. He is often confused with William de Monte, chancellor of Lincoln (d. 1213) and William of Durham (d. 1249). He may have taught in Paris and was considered by Roger Bacon to be a greater logician than Albert the Great. His *Introductiones in logicam* and *Syncategoremata* are significant for illustrating the evolution of the forms of medieval logic.

[E. J. DILLON]

WILLIAM OF TOULOUSE, BL. (c.1297–1369), ascetic theologian and mystic. A member of the Augustinian Order, W. studied at the Univ. of Paris and taught theology there. He had special devotion to the souls in purgatory. Fifty days after death his cult was approved locally, but it was confirmed only in 1893. BIBLIOGRAPHY: D. Andreini, NCE 14:939; Butler 2:343; H. Platelle, BiblSanct 7:486–487.

[J. E. WRIGLEY]

WILLIAM OF TRIPOLI (c.1220–after 1273), Dominican missionary, author. In 1273, shortly after W. had withdrawn from the journey of the Polo brothers to China (1271–95), he composed an influential *Tractatus de statu Saracenorum et de Mahometi pseudopropheta* at the request of Gregory X (ed. H. Prutz, *Kulturgeschichte der Kreuzzüge*, 1883).

[L. E. BOYLE]

WILLIAM OF TURBEVILLE (c.1095–1174), prior and bp. of Norwich (1146–74). As prior, he championed the cult of the child-martyr, allegedly murdered by Jews, *William of Norwich (1144). When bp. (1146), W. encouraged Thomas of Monmouth to record the legendary account of the crime and he himself transferred the remains of the child to the Norwich Cathedral. He was a staunch supporter of Abp. Becket. BIBLIOGRAPHY: D. Knowles, *Episcopal Colleagues of Archbishop Thomas Becket* (1951); C. Roth, *History of the Jews in England* (1941) 9, 13.

[F. D. BLACKLEY]

WILLIAM OF TYRE (c.1130–c.1187), abp., historian. A Palestinian of English or French commercial family W. studied arts and theology in France from 1145, and law at Bologna. After ordination W. returned to the Holy Land (1165) and became archdeacon of Tyre (1167), diplomat to Rome and Constantinople (1169), tutor to the future King Baldwin IV (1170), chancellor of Jerusalem kingdom (1170–1174), abp. of Tyre (1175), and representative to the Lateran Council III (1179). Bitter at missing the patriarchate (1183) and excommunicated by his rival, he died (probably not by poison) at Rome. He is famous as an historian-memoirist of the crusade era. BIBLIOGRAPHY: B. Lacroix, NCE 14:940 (bibliog.).

[R. I. BURNS]

WILLIAM OF VAUROUILLON (c.1390–1463), Franciscan scholastic, Scotist. He taught at Paris, 1429–31, and 1447–49 completed his licentiate and became a master there. He was provincial of the Conventual Franciscans of Touraine, from c.1449 to 1461. He died in Rome while there for questioning about one of his sermons. His works include a commentary on Lombard's *Sentences* and a *Liber de anima*.

[T. C. O'BRIEN]

WILLIAM OF VERCELLI, ST. (1085–1142), abbot, founder of the Williamites, a now extinct Benedictine congregation. As a youth W. entered upon a hermit's life, but after he was joined by companions, he built a monastery at Monte Vergine. Patronized by King Roger II of Naples, he founded several other monasteries in southern Italy. BIBLIOGRAPHY: M. A. Habig, NCE 14:940–941; Butler 2:635–637; G. Mongelli, LTK 7:487–489.

[M. A. WINKELMANN]

WILLIAM OF WARE, late 13th-and early 14th-cent. English Franciscan theologian. Born in Ware, Hertfordshire, c.1255–60, he entered the Franciscans 1270 or 1275, studied at Oxford, was a commentator on the *Sentences* there and perhaps also in Paris, and may have influenced both John Duns Scotus and William of Ockham. Called *Doctor fundatus, praeclarus*, he was the first to introduce and positively defend the Immaculate Conception in university schools. Only his commentary on the *Sentences* is extant, mostly in manuscript form.

[E. J. DILLON]

WILLIAM WAYNFLETE (c.1395–1486), bp. of Winchester. Upon ordination (1426) W. became master of St. Mary Magdalen hospital. He was named provost of newly established Eton College in 1443 and bp. of Winchester in 1447. The following year he founded at Oxford a hall dedicated to St. Mary Magdalen for theology and philosophy, refounded in 1457 as Magdalen College. He was chancellor from 1456 to his resignation in 1460 and acquiesced in the accession of Edward IV. BIBLIOGRAPHY: I. S. Leadham, DNB 60:85–89.

[M. J. SUELZER]

WILLIAM OF WHITTLESEY (d. 1374), archbishop. A nephew of Simon Islip, abp. of Canterbury, who promoted his career at several stages, he was a graduate of both Oxford and Cambridge, chancellor of Canterbury, bp. of Rochester (1361), bp. of Worcester (1364), and abp. of Canterbury (1368). BIBLIOGRAPHY: J. Tait DNB (repr. 1949–50) 21:158–160; F. D. Logan NCE 14:941.

[J. L. GRASSI]

WILLIAM WICKWANE (d. 1285), abp. of York from 1279. His episcopate was tumultuous and he was continually harassed by the metropolitan claims of *John Peckham. As a result of his troubles he left England for the Roman curia, stopping at the Cistercian abbey of Pontigny, where he died of fever. BIBLIOGRAPHY: W. Hunt, DNB 21:178–179.

[J. A. WEISHEIPL]

WILLIAM WOODFORD (fl. 1351–1400), Oxford Franciscan theologian who wrote against the doctrines of *Wycliffe, with whom he had originally been on friendly terms, but whose doctrine he came to recognize as dangerous. BIBLIOGRAPHY: J. E. Healey, NCE 14:942; Emden Ox 3:2081–82; A. F. Pollard, DNB 21:867–868.

[J. A. WEISHEIPL]

WILLIAM OF WYKEHAM (1324–1404), educationalist; chancellor of England (1367–71, 1389–91); bp. of Winchester (from 1367). An important lay-minded royal clerk, he obtained the bishopric of Winchester against the wishes of Urban V. He played an important part at the Good Parliament (1376) and was a political moderate under Richard II. W. made no mark as a churchman, but his two educational foundations (begun in 1378 and 1380) broke with the past. New College was the first Oxford college primarily designed for Arts undergraduates; Winchester grammar school became the first English "public school." BIBLIOGRAPHY: G. H. Moberly, *Life of William of Wykeham* (2d ed., 1893); DNB 63:225.

[F. D. BLACKLEY]

WILLIAM OF YORK, ST., (d. 1154) controversial abp. of York, canonized by Honorius III in 1227. Born William Fitzherbert, he is also known as William of Thwayt and was the son of Count Herbert, treasurer to Henry I. Before being elected abp. of York in 1142, W. had been treasurer of the church of York. His election was contested by Cistercian leaders and others for alleged unchastity and simony. Rome was especially concerned about undue pressure from the king in W.'s behalf. Although consecrated by Henry of Winchester in 1143, W. was eventually caught in the Cistercian politics of Bernard of Clairvaux and Pope Eugenius III, and deposed. He fled to Winchester where he led a penitential life in the cathedral monastery for six years. In 1153 his three main enemies died (Bernard, Eugene III, and Abbot Henry Murdac of Fountain Abbey). W. was able to receive the pallium from Pope Anastasius IV, reentered York in 1154, made restitution at Fountain Abbey for the destruction brought to it by his overzealous defenders, and died a month later. He was commonly believed to have been poisoned by the man who succeeded him. The people always had favored him over his austere critics, were impressed by his troubles, considered him a martyr, and acclaimed the miracles wrought at his tomb. His relics survived the Reformation, but subsequently disappeared.

[E. J. DILLON]

WILLIAM LA ZOUCHE (d. 1352), abp. of York. In the royal service from the beginning of the reign of Edward III, W. was elected abp. of York in 1340. He was harassed by the opposing claimant and kidnaped in Geneva on his way to present his case to the pope. Released and consecrated bp., he returned to York where he was very active against the invasion of the Scots in the north. W. did all in his power to alleviate the shortage of clergy caused by the Black Death. BIBLIOGRAPHY: T. F. Tout, DNB 21:1335–1338; Emden Ox 2:1115–16.

[A. WARDLE]

WILLIAMITES, a name given to three religious orders and to three heretical sects, none of the six any longer in existence. (a) A Benedictine congregation founded by William of Vercelli, approved in 1197, ceased to exist in the 18th century. (b) The Hermits of St. William, named for William of Maleval, were quite numerous in the 13th cent., when they were divided into two congregations, one following the rule of Benedict, the other, the rule of Augustine. They ceased to exist in the 17th century. (c) A supposed Williamite Order of Knights with origins in the 9th cent. is a complete fiction, born of the fact of certain monasteries founded by William of Aquitaine (d. 812). (d) The name Williamites is given to the followers of William of Saint-Amour (d. 1272), an adversary of the Dominican and Franciscan theologians of Paris. (e) Also called Williamites were the heretical followers of *Wilhelma, or Wilhelmina of Bohemia (d. 1282). (f) The name was given also to the followers of Aegidius Cantoris of Brussels (14th century). These last, however, have their name from William of Hildernisse, a priest who was accused of supporting them. BIBLIOGRAPHY: AS Feb. 2:473–486; Heimbucher, *Die Orden und Kongregationen der katholischen Kirche* 1 (2 v., 3d ed., 1932–34) 179, 201, 302, 539; K. Elm, *Beiträge zur Geschichte des Wilhelmitenordens* (1962).

[W. A. JURGENS]

WILLIAMS, GEORGE (1821–1905), founder of the *Young Men's Christian Association (YMCA). He was a young clerk in London when, with 12 fellow workers, he formed the YMCA to assist urban workers to live a good Christian life. From 1886 until his death he was president of the association, which spread throughout the world. During the 50th anniversary of the London YMCA, W. received knighthood from Queen Victoria. He was also active in the

*British and Foreign Bible Society, the Church Missionary Society and other organizations devoted to temperance and mission work.

[T. C. O'BRIEN]

WILLIAMS, JOHN (1796–1839), one of the most remarkable missionaries of modern times, who labored diligently in the Pacific Islands from 1817 until his tragic death in 1839. His scant education as one of the London poor culminated in 7 years of apprenticeship to a London iron-monger. Following a religious experience in 1816, he passed an examination and was accepted by the London Missionary Society (L.M.S.) and was sent by them to the far Pacific the following year. Mary Chauner, whom he married in 1816, was to share in all his missionary labors until his death. At first he worked in the better–known isles, beginning at Eimeo near Tahiti, then branching out to more remote and potentially more dangerous areas, until he came in 1839 to Dillon's Bay, Erromanga. There he was immediately killed and eaten by natives, perhaps in retaliation for cruelties inflicted on them by some English sailors. W., despite minimal academic preparation, worked diligently to acquire the languages he encountered, even attempting to translate portions of the Bible into the Raratongan language. He adapted himself to varying customs and modes of thought with understanding and appreciation of differences. He concerned himself with people's temporal welfare, patiently sharing with them his own skills in farming and industry. As news of his death spread from island to island, the native peoples gave themselves up to inconsolable grief. When news arrived in England, it elicited an outburst of missionary zeal. For years there was a succession of ships named John Williams, employed in furthering the evangelization of the Pacific Islands. An even more precious reminder of the remarkable man is his *Narrative of Missionary Enterprises in the South Sea Islands* (1837), containing considerable autobiographical material. BIBLIOGRAPHY: DNB 21:423–425.

[E. J. DILLON]

WILLIAMS, JOHN JOSEPH (1822–1907), fourth bp. of Boston. Born in Boston of Irish immigrant parents, W. studied for the priesthood and was ordained in 1845. He was vicar general of the diocese of Boston in 1857 and endeared himself to Yankees as well as Irish. Named coadjutor of Boston in 1866, he became bp. immediately, the death of Bp. Fitzpatrick occurring that year. The 40 years of his leadership was largely responsible for the prodigious growth in parishes, schools, and charitable institutions of the period. He became abp. in 1875 when Boston became a metropolitan see. W. built the new cathedral (1875), opened St. John's Seminary (1884), St. Elizabeth's Hospital (1868), and a number of foundations for welfare. He a-droitly managed relations between Irish and other immigrant elements. W. was responsible for the opening of many parochial schools and introduced the Sisters of St. Joseph,

Sisters of the Sacred Heart, Franciscan Sisters, Carmelite Sisters, and Marist Brothers into the diocese. He aided the Jesuits at Boston College and the Augustinians and Redemptorists. W. participated in the various Baltimore Councils as well as Vatican Council I. He was a man of remarkable personal and administrative qualities and a formative influence on a great archdiocese.

[J. R. AHERNE]

WILLIAMS, MICHAEL (1877–1950) editor. Canadian by birth, W. came to the U.S. as a newspaper man, working on the *Boston Post,* the *New York World,* and *New York Evening Telegram*. In 1906 he was city editor of the *San Francisco Examiner* during the great earthquake. A socialist in youth, he returned to the RC Church in 1915 and gave his mature years to its causes. President of the Calvert Associates, devoted to religious freedom, W. founded the *Commonweal*, a liberal Catholic magazine in 1924 and served as its editor until 1938. He was a foremost foe of Nazism, covered the election of Pius XII for the *New York Times,* and the Spanish Civil War for the *New York American*. Among his books were *Book of High Romance* (1918), *Catholicism and the Modern Mind* (1928), and the *Catholic Church in Action* (1935).

[J. R. AHERNE]

WILLIAMS, NORMAN POWELL (1883–1943), Anglican priest, one of the leading Anglo-Catholic theologians of his day. He was elected Fellow of Magdalen College in 1906, was chaplain-fellow of Exeter College from 1909–27, Lady Margaret Professor of Divinity from 1927 until his death. His views were expressed in such essays as "The Origins of the Sacraments" (1927); "The Theology of the Catholic Revival" (1933); and "What is Theology?" (1939); and in such books as *The Ideas of the Fall and of Original Sin* (1927; Bampton Lectures for 1924); and *The Grace of God* (1930).

[E. J. DILLON]

WILLIAMS, ROGER (*c*.1603–83), champion of religious liberty. Born in England and educated at Cambridge, W. was ordained in the C of E but early became a *Separatist and went to Massachusetts Bay in 1631. He alienated pastors and magistrates by his extreme Separatist views, his insistence that only purchase, not royal grants, conferred title to land, and his denial that civil magistrates had any authority in strictly religious matters. Banished from Mass. in 1636, he obtained land from Indians to establish with other associates Providence Plantations, the Rhode Island colony, granting complete religious freedom to all inhabitants. At Providence, W. helped to organize the first Baptist church in America, but he remained a Baptist for only a few weeks. The rest of his life he was a Seeker. Believing that direct *apostolic succession is necessary to a true Church, and that no such ministry had existed since the early centuries, he concluded that there is no true Church on earth. In *The Hireling Ministry None of Christ's* (1652), he published his opinions on this subject. During a visit to England in 1644 he published *The Bloudy Tenent, of Persecution for Cause of Conscience*. After a rebuttal by John *Cotton, he wrote *The Bloudy Tenent Yet More Bloudy* (1652). Williams's writings were revived by Isaac *Backus during his struggle for religious liberty in Massachusetts. Modern historians have portrayed W. as a liberal democrat and an agnostic, who was far in advance of his time. They failed to recognize that his views differed radically from the natural-rights philosophers. In his theology, W. was a Puritan of the Puritans, and his doctrine of religious liberty derived from his Calvinist views on God's absolute sovereignty and predestination and from a typological interpretation of the OT. He held that church membership must be restricted to the regenerate and could not include a whole civic community. An established Church could only be maintained by coercion, which has no place in matters of conscience. Church and State must be kept totally separated. Often acclaimed as the pioneer Baptist in America, by his brief relationship with that body he had little influence upon its development. Baptists honor him, however, because he so well symbolizes their concern for religious freedom. His works are contained in *Complete Writings of Roger Williams* (ed. P. Miller, 7v., 1963). BIBLIOG-RAPHY: P. Miller, *Roger Williams* (1953); L. A. Moore, ''Roger Williams and the Historians,'' *Church History* 32 (1963) 432–451; B. E. Winslow, *Master Roger Williams* (1957).

[N. H. MARING]

WILLIAMS, WILLIAM (1717–91), Welsh theologian and religious poet, also known as Pantycelyn. A convert to Methodism, he was ordained a deacon in 1740 and in that capacity helped establish Methodism on a firm foundation in Wales. He is best known for his countless hymns, some of which can be found in Welsh Catholic hymnals. He is the author of ''Theomemphus,'' called by one Welsh critic the first great European romantic poem. It records the soul's progress in union with Christ and gives a hint of Williams's accomplishment in providing a structure for Nonconformists to grow in a discipline of prayer.

[E. J. DILLON]

WILLIBALD OF EICHSTÄTT, ST. (700–781), Anglo-Saxon monk, missionary to Germany. An account of his journey to the Holy Land (722–730) is to be found in the *Hodoeporicon*, the first English travel book (MGHS 15. 1:86–106; Eng. tr. C. H. Talbot, *The Anglo-Saxon Missionaries in Germany* (1954)). In 730, W. entered the monastery of Monte Cassino. In 740, at the command of Pope Gregory III, he went to assist St. Boniface in Germany. Boniface ordained him priest in 741 and made him bp. of Eichstätt in 742. At Heidenheim, W. shared in the foundation of a double monastery of which his brother, St.

Winnebald, became abbot and his sister, St. Walburga, abbess. BIBLIOGRAPHY: Butler 2:494–496.

[M. F. MCCARTHY]

WILLIBALD OF MAINZ (fl. 8th cent.), an Anglo-Saxon priest appointed as biographer of St. Boniface by Bps. Lull of Mainz and Megingoz of Würzburg. The biography (MGHS rer.Germ 57:90−106; Eng. tr. C. H. Talbot, *The Anglo-Saxon Missionaries in Germany*, 1954), written between 754−768, is based on Boniface's letters and the reports of his disciples. BIBLIOGRAPHY: W. Wattenbach, *Deutschlands Geschichtsquellen im Mittelalter* I (1893) 135–136.

[M. F. MCCARTHY]

WILLIBRORD OF UTRECHT, ST. (658–739), Anglo-Saxon missionary. Son of St. Wilgis, trained as a monk under Wilfrid and Egbert, W. led 11 companions on missions to Frisia. His labors fruitless, he sought aid from France and Rome. The pope supported his work and consecrated him bp. in 695, his see being Utrecht. W. enjoyed close relationships with the early Carolingians, who helped return him to Frisia after his expulsion in 715 by the pagan Radbod. W. eventually retired to the abbey of Echternach, his foundation, and died. He was the first Anglo-Saxon missionary who bound together the Frankish kings and the popes. BIBLIOGRAPHY: Alcuin's *Life*, tr. C. H. Talbot, *Anglo-Saxon Missionaries in Germany* (1954) 3–22; M. Tout, DNB 21:484–486; C. Wampach, *Sankt Willibrord;* Butler 4:286–289.

[J. DRUSE]

WILLIGIS OF MAINZ ST. (d. 1011), archbishop. He was born in Saxony of a humble family and educated by Volkold who introduced him to the service of his pupil, Emperor Otto I. He became chancellor (971), abp. of Mainz and archchancellor (975). He was leading adviser during the minority of Otto III and the decisive influence in the succession of Henry II (1002). His episcopate was somewhat stormy but he allowed great freedom to his suffragans, encouraged the monastic reform movement, founded monasteries and parishes, and rebuilt his cathedral when it burnt down on its dedication day.

[J. L. GRASSI]

WILLIRAM OF EBERSBERG (d. 1085), educated in Bamberg; entered Benedictine monastery of Fulda; in 1048, appointed abbot of Ebersberg by Henry III. Though influenced by Notker Labeo, Williram's allegorical paraphrase and commentary on the Canticle of Canticles (1059–65) is theologically, not humanistically, oriented. It depicts the Church as the Bride of Christ.

[M. F. MCCARTHY]

WILLSON, ROBERT WILLIAM (1794–1866), English RC bishop, church leader, and advocate of prison and hospital reform. The son of a builder, he was ordained a priest by Bp. Milner in 1824, and for 18 years was pastor of Nottingham. Then he was appointed the first bp. of Hobart, Tasmania, then Britain's main penal colony, where he devoted himself to the welfare of convicts, the insane, and orphans. For ten years he fought for reforms and is credited with helping to stop the transporting of convicts.

[E. J. DILLON]

WILMART, ANDRÉ (1876–1941), French Benedictine historian of Latin Christian literature, patristic and medieval. Professed at Solesmes in 1901, he was ordained on the Isle of Wight in 1906 and was assigned officially among expatriated Solesmes monks at Farnborough Abbey until his death. However, his research led him to direct study in libraries in England, Belgium, France, Italy, and Switzerland, including 10 years (1929–40) at the Vatican Library. During World War II he was in Paris at the Bibliothèque Nationale. A master of research and presentation, he is responsible for the production of 377 books and 87 reviews. Notable among his works are studies in Gregory of Elvira and St. Hilary, among early Latin fathers, and St. Anselm and St. Bernard, among medievals.

[E. J. DILLON]

WILMERS, WILHELM (1817–99), German Catholic philosopher and theologian who wrote voluminously and comprehensively on theology, and is considered a pioneer of Neo-Scholasticism. Born in Westphalia, he joined the Jesuits in Switzerland in 1834. He was forced to leave Switzerland when the Society was expelled. Ordained in France in 1848, he taught for over 30 years in various countries: at Issenheim, Louvain, Cologne, Bonn, Aachen, Maria-Laach, Poitiers, St. Helier, and on the Isle of Jersey. He gained fame as Cardinal Geissel's theologian at Cologne's provincial council in 1860 and was present at Vatican Council I in 1870 as Bishop Meurin's theological expert. He died in Holland during the Council. He published a defense against opponents of papal infallibility. His 4-v. *Lehrbuch der Religion* was translated into English and published in 1891.

[E. J. DILLON]

WILPERT, JOSEPH (1857–1944), German archeologist and authority on the catacombs. After his ordination (1883) he went to Rome to study canon law, but under the influence of A. de Wall his interest turned to Christian archeology, esp. primitive iconography. His first studies of the catacombs were pursued under the direction of G. B. de *Rossi. In his scholarly publications he made abundant use of photography to ensure accuracy of reproduction. From 1926 he was a professor of the Papal Institute of Christian Archeology.

[R. B. ENO]

WILSNACK, a shrine near Wittenberg, Germany. In the fourteenth century three consecrated hosts were believed to have miraculously survived a fire in the church at Wilsnack and became the center of pilgrimage where great favors were alleged to have been granted pilgrims. Popes Eugenius IV and Nicholas V accepted the shrine as authentic. In 1552 Wilsnack became Protestant and the hosts were destroyed.

[J. R. AHERNE]

WILSON, THOMAS (1663–1755), the much-revered Anglican bishop of Sodor and Man, who served there for nearly 6 decades (1698–1755). Born in Cheshire, he pursued medical studies at Trinity College, Dublin. In 1686 he was ordained a deacon and the following year was named curate to his uncle in Lancashire. He became the chaplain to the ninth Earl of Derby in 1692. It was at the latter's insistence that he accepted in 1697 the see of Sodor and Man; he was consecrated the following year. It was his vigorous policy to impose public penance on those found guilty of such offenses against public morality as slander and perjury. This policy drew him into legal disputes and in one case led to his brief imprisonment.

[E. J. DILLON]

WILTEN CHALICE, probably one of Henry the Lion's gifts to Wilten Abbey in 1166. The cup, known as the Chalice of Berthold of Andechs, is of silver gilt, embossed and engraved with Old and New Testament scenes. It is now, with its paten, in the Vienna Kunsthistorisches Museum.

WILTON ABBEY, former Benedictine monastery in Wiltshire, England, Diocese of Salisbury. Formerly called Ellandune, it was first established as a college of priests in 773 by Egbert, King of the East Saxons, and then converted into a Benedictine abbey for nuns *c*. 800 by its first abbess, St. Alburga, sister of King Egbert. Rebuilt with stone by Edith, the wife of Edward the Confessor, it was dedicated in 1065 to Our Lady, St. Bartholomew, and St. Edith, the daughter of King Edgar and the Abbess Wulftrude. Royally endowed and fortified, it grew in importance until its abbess ranked as a baroness. It was surrendered to Henry VIII in 1539. Nothing remains of the original buildings. BIBLIOGRAPHY: Cottineau 2:3456–57.

[E. J. DILLON]

WILTON DIPTYCH (*c*.1396), tempera painting representing Richard II kneeling before the Virgin. One of the great masterpieces of the International Gothic style, it is now in the National Gallery, London.

[M. J. DALY]

WILTRUDE, BL. (d. *c*.990), Benedictine abbess. She was perhaps the niece of Emperor Otto I, probably the wife of Berthold, Duke of Bavaria, and widowed in 947. She became a Benedictine nun renowned for her piety and her skill in handicraft. After founding the Benedictine abbey of Bergen, or Baring-bei-Neuburg, in the Diocese of Eichstätt,

she became its first abbess sometime after 976. BIBLIOGRA-
PHY: Butler 1:42.

[E. J. DILLON]

WIMBORNE ABBEY, ancient abbey of nuns in Dorsetshire, England, founded c.713 by St. Cuthberga, sister of
King Ine, famous for its role in the evangelization of Germany. Soon after, it was destroyed, probably by the Danes,
and even its site is unknown. It is not to be confused with
Wimborne Minster, now an Anglican parish church, whose
origins may date from a house of secular canons established
by Edward the Confessor. It was from Wimborne Abbey
that 30 nuns crossed over to Mainz to aid St. Boniface in
response to the letter of request sent by him to Abbess Tetta,
sister and successor of Cuthberga. The missionary sisters
from Wimborne founded innumerable settlements throughout Germany. BIBLIOGRAPHY: Cottineau 2:3457.

[E. J. DILLON]

WIMMER, BONIFACE (1809–97), founder and first
abbot of St. Vincent's Archabbey, Latrobe, Pennsylvania.
He studied for the priesthood and was ordained (1831) in his
native Germany. In 1834 he became a Benedictine at St.
Michael's Abbey, Metten, Bavaria, out of desire for the
missions. In 1846 he led a group of four clerics and 14 lay
brothers to the U.S. and settled near Latrobe, in the Diocese
of Pittsburgh, where he received his companions into the
Order of St. Benedict. He founded St. Vincent's, which
became an abbey in 1855, and there established a college
and a seminary. He became pastor of a parish at Latrobe and
traveled throughout Pennsylvania as a missionary. Under
his guidance St. Vincent's became the founding house of St.
John's Abbey, Collegeville, Minn; St. Benedict's Abbey,
Atchison, Kan.; Belmont Abbey, N.C.; St. Bernard's Abbey, Cullman, Ala; St. Procopius Abbey, Lisle, Ill.; and
Holy Cross Abbey, Canon City, Colorado. W. was named
archabbot of St. Vincent's in 1883. The apostolate to immigrants of many nationalities that his work inaugurated is a
great chapter in American church history.

[T. C. O'BRIEN]

WIMPFELING, JAKOB (1450–1528), German
humanist. In his early schooling he came under the
influence of the tradition of the *Brethren of the Common
Life, and he went on to study at Freiburg, Erfurt, and
Heidelberg (where he served for a time as rector). He was
cathedral preacher at Speyer, 1484–98. He was actively
interested in the revival of classical literature and was leader
of a circle of humanists at Strassburg (1501–15). In his two
educational treatises, *Isidoneus* and *Adolescentia,* he
stressed the value of grammar, literature, and ethical formation in the spirit of the *Devotio moderna*. Despite his fundamental conservatism, W. sympathized with much of
Luther's criticism of the Church. He attacked monastic orders, charging them with decadence; urged the strict observance of priestly celibacy; and called for an end to
simoniacal practices. Yet he remained loyal to the papacy

and was saddened toward the end of his life to see scholars
whom he had helped to educate turning to the Reformation.
BIBLIOGRAPHY: L. W. Spitz, *Religious Renaissance of the
German Humanists* (1963) 41–60; idem, NCE 14:954.

[D. G. NUGENT]

WIMPINA, KONRAD (Koch; 1465?–1531), theologian,
opponent of Lutheranism. As a student at Leipzig, 1479–
86, he became a Thomist; he was rector there, 1494–95,
ordained priest after 1495, became a licentiate in theology
in 1502 and a doctor in 1503. In a dispute over poetry at this
time he accused his former professor, Martin Polich, of
heresy. In 1505 at the invitation of Joachim of Brandenburg, he became the founder and rector of the Univ. of
Frankfurt-am-Oder; there in 1518 J. *Tetzel was his student. It was W. who drafted the theses, 122 at first, pared to
95, that Tetzel defended against M. Luther; many of them
presented mere theological opinions as though they were
Catholic teaching. W. alienated humanists by his attacks on
the arts. He gathered together a collection of numerous
sources and authorities in his *Sectarum errorum* . . . .
Anacephalaeseos . . . librorum partes tres (1528), recapitu-
lations of Lutheran errors as embodying all heresies of all
times, and as immediately traceable to J. Wyclif and the
Hussites. As theologian at the Diet of Augsburg in 1530, he
wrote a refutation of Luther's Schwabach theses; he also
helped write a refutation of the Augsburg Confession. W.
may be taken as an example of the mediocre state of
Catholic theology in Germany at the time of the Reformation.

[R. J. LITZ]

WIMPLE, headdress covering head, throat, and neck, once
a common dress for women, later a feature of the nun's
religious habit until recent modifications. The wimple was
particularly uncomfortable and even unhealthful.

[J. R. AHERNE]

WINCHESTER PROFESSION OF BELIEF, a statement of faith adopted by the New England Convention of
Universalist Churches meeting at Winchester, N.H., in
1803. The Profession contains three articles: that Scripture
contains a revelation on "the character of God" and on
human destiny; that God is one, and is love revealed in
Jesus by the Holy Spirit of Grace, and that there will be a
final restoration of all mankind (see APOCATASTASIS); that
happiness and holiness are inseparably connected. The
document was intended to allow both Trinitarian and Unitarian views, and various interpretations of Universalism
(e.g., those of John Murray, Elhanan Winchester, Caleb
Rich, Hosea Ballou, Abel Sarjent). The Profession was a
statement of principles for all who accepted Universalism
and was not a formula to be imposed as a condition for
membership. BIBLIOGRAPHY: R. Eddy, *Universalism in
America* (2v., 1884–86); Schaff Creeds 1:933–934. *UNI-
VERSALISM.

[J. C. GODBEY]

WINCHESTER SCHOOL, name given to a new style of manuscript illumination developed in the 10th cent. in South England under Benedictines brought to Winchester by Bp. Aethewold. Determined by Carolingian miniscule, narrative scenes in the vivid, agitated style of the school of Reims, together with substantial compositions, daringly colored pages surrounded by lush borders of foliage sprouting from heavy gold frames, are characteristic. The style contributed to English art after the Norman Conquest. BIB-LIOGRAPHY: T. Kendrick, NCE 1:535.

[R. L. S. BRUCE-MITFORD]

WINCKELMANN, JOHANN JOACHIM (1717–68), German archeologist and art historian, who wrote on Greek art and culture as the highest expression of ideal beauty. W. felt that the creative principle of Greek art was a process of idealization—the subordination of particulars in nature to a scheme of ideal beauty that has a perfection beyond the capabilities of nature, a concept held to this day. Through classical texts and curatorial experience, W. had a grasp of the iconography of Greek art. A student of theology and medicine, he interpreted ancient culture as cyles of growth and decline. Among many works, W. published, excavation reports on Pompeii and Herculaneum (1758–62), *History of Ancient Art*—his masterpiece (1764), *Monumenti antichi inediti* (1767–68), which had enormous influence on late 18th-cent. taste.

[K. B. NEILSON]

WINDELBAND, WILHELM (1848–1915), philosopher. A German who taught at Zurich, Freiburg im Breisgau, Strassburg, and Heidelberg, W. was a leading interpreter of I. *Kant. As a historian of philosophy he created the method of study through the grouping of philosophic concepts rather than through simple chronology. W. labored to apply Kantian philosophy to historical sciences and was influenced by the value-philosophy of his time. He differed with Kant, insisting that scientific categories of knowledge were not the only areas of knowledge but that activities of the will and the emotions must also yield knowledge. Among his most influential works were *Präludien* (2 v., 1884) and *Lehrbuch der Geschichte der Philosophie* (1892). BIBLIOGRAPHY: H. White, EncPhil 8:320–322.

[J. R. AHERNE]

WINDESHEIM, MONASTERY OF, former foundation of Canons Regular of St. Augustine, W of Zwolle, the Netherlands. It was founded in 1386 by six pupils of Gerard Groote under the leadership of Johann Goswini Vos, who became the second prior (1391–1424). Advocates of the *Devotio moderna*, the canons may have written or inspired the *Imitation of Christ*. The monastery had close affinity with the *Brethren of the Common life and absorbed the tradition of Groenendals, near Brussels, and the spirituality of Jan van Ruysbroeck. The congregation of Windesheim, established 1393 and approved at the Council of Constance, brought monastic reform to monasteries throughout the Low Lands, the Rhineland, and Switzerland. By 1500 it encompassed 97 monasteries and served as a model for other orders, for the secular clergy, and the laity, fostering eucharistic devotion and intellectual study. Its monastic discipline included manual labor and scholarship, but not pastoral work. It declined during the Reformation and the Revolt of the Netherlands and was dissolved in 1581. The reconstituted congregation survived in Belgium and Germany until 1802. Today there is one monastery left, in Uden, the Netherlands.

[E. J. DILLON]

WINDTHORST, LUDWIG (1812–91), leader of the Center Party in Imperial Germany. After the establishment of the German Empire, W., a former minister of justice in Hanover, became the leader of the Center Party, which existed primarily to defend the interests of German Catholics through parliamentary action. The validity of this concern was demonstrated in 1873 when the Prussian government began the *Kulturkampf,* an attack on the position of the Catholic Church. W.'s leadership helped to unify German Catholics in this struggle, and electoral support for the Center Party increased, making it the second largest party in the *Reichstag*. Moreover, W.'s forensic abilities and astute parliamentary tactics eventually brought the *Reichstag* to repudiate most of the *Kulturkampf* legislation. This political skill in the defense of religious principles not only preserved the rights of German Catholics, but also developed the Center Party into a pivotal factor in German politics. BIBLIOGRAPHY: Erich Eyck, *Bismarck and the German Empire* (1950).

[R. J. GIBBONS]

WINE, RELIGIOUS USE OF. The fermented juice of the grape was a common drink in the ancient world, particularly in Italy, Greece, Palestine, and Syria. As symbolic of strength and joy and as an intoxicant, it was often used in religious ceremonies, public and private, particularly in libations (pouring out as an offering). The cult of Dionysius or Bacchus is the best-known such pagan use. In Israel wine was the common mealtime drink, although priests were to abstain during the time of their service. In the Old Testament it was never used alone as an offering but only to accompany a sacrifice. In later Judaism a precise ritual was determined for its use at the Passover meal. At the Last Supper it was probably the "cup of blessing," the final cup of wine during the grace after meals, which Jesus proclaimed to be the new covenant in his blood.

In the Christian Eucharist the wine is symbolic of union with Christ, the true vine (Jn 15), and with fellow Christians, since wine is produced from many grapes (*Didache* 9). Its presentation, together with bread, is symbolic of the offering to God of creation, of human work (through which it was made), and of human life (which it supports). At Mass a small quantity of water is added, the ancient Greek custom followed in Palestine in Jesus' time. In the RC Church only wine may be used for the Eucharist; some Protestant Churches use grape juice. The alcoholic content is ordinarily 12–18%, although alcoholic priests are permitted to use weaker wine (*mustum,* a barely fermented wine; they may also concelebrate and receive communion under the form of bread alone). Originally all receiving communion received under the forms of both bread and wine. As communion became infrequent and for practical reasons (danger of spilling), communion became customary only under the form of bread and later the cup was prohibited to the laity. This was a source of controversy at the time of the Reformation, which restored the cup. Since the recent reforms of the liturgy, the cup is now permitted to the laity whenever practical (see COMMUNION UNDER BOTH KINDS). BIBLIOGRAPHY: J. A. Jungmann, *Mass of the Roman Rite* (rev. ed., tr. F. A. Brunner, 2 v., 1950–55) 2:37–41.

[J. DALLEN]

WINEBRENNER, JOHN (1797–1860), founder of the Churches of God in North America (General Eldership). Born in Frederick Co., Md., he attended Dickinson College, Carlisle, Pa., and was ordained in 1820 as pastor of Salem German Reformed Church, Harrisburg, Pennsylvania. W. wholeheartedly accepted *camp meetings and *revivalism. His prayer meetings and fellowship with Methodists led to his expulsion from the *Reformed ministry in 1825. He formed "a church on the New Testament plan" with others, taking the Bible as the only rule of faith. His evangelism throughout central Pa. developed a movement among German-speaking Christians similar to that led by Alexander *Campbell. W. published *A Brief View of the Formation, Government and Discipline of the Churches of God* in 1829 and reluctantly accepted denominational leadership as general elder in 1830. He was an active champion of temperance and the abolition of slavery and served as pastor of the Harrisburg congregation until his death.

[R. K. MacMASTER]

WINNOC, ST. (d. early 8th cent.) monk, one of a group of four Britons or Bretons who presented themselves at the monastery of Sithiu (Saint-Omer). The abbot, St. Bertinus, encouraged them to build small huts in the countryside near Dunkirk and quietly practice hospitality and charity. W. survived his companions and directed the establishment until his death. BIBLIOGRAPHY: Butler 4:276.

[A. CABANISS]

WINSTANLEY, GERRARD (1609–*c.*1660), *Leveller, religious and social writer. W. began to write first of his mystical experience of the divine light within man, in his *New Law of Righteousness* (1648); Thomas Coomber, Dean of Durham, writing in 1678, mistakenly called him the founder of the Quakers (see INNER LIGHT). W. next advocated a classless society without private property, e.g., in *The Law of Freedom in a Platform* (1652); he became the

leader of the short-lived Digger movement; his thought turned to materialism and pantheism, and he came to view religion simply as a means for fostering social justice. BIBLIOGRAPHY: *Gerhard Winstanley, Selections from His Works* (ed. L. D. Hamilton, 1944); R. M. Jones, *Studies in Mystical Religion* (1923) 493–500.

[T. C. O'BRIEN]

WINTER, VITE ANTON (1754–1814), Bavarian church historian, liturgical reformer of the Enlightenment. Born in Lower Bavaria, he was ordained a priest in 1778. He taught church history, patristics, catechetics, and liturgy, first in Ingolstadt, then in Landshut. He was a participant in a Bavarian academy that fostered critical research in Bavarian church history, esp. Reformation history. He considered liturgical reform to be the key to true reform in religion and morality.

[E. J. DILLON]

WINTERFIELD, KARL GEORG VON (1784–1852), musicologist. A German lawyer, W. was devoted to musical research and reform of church music. He wrote influential and perceptive studies in music history, among them *J. Gabrieli und sein Zeitalter* (1834), studies on Palestrina (1832) and polyphony, on Luther's hymns and *Der evangelische Kirchengesang* (3 v., 1843–47).

[J. R. AHERNE]

WINTHIR, ST., popular 8th-cent. Bavarian saint, of whom nothing certain is known. He seems to have been one of the numerous wandering ascetics from the North, a mule driver, never a member of any established religious order. He may have settled in Neuhausen, the NW section of modern Munich, since he is invoked as a patron there and is buried there in St. Nicholas Church. He is invoked for good weather and against cattle plague.

[E. J. DILLON]

WINWALOE, ST. (Guénolé; d. *c.*520), Breton monk. He was born a Briton but his family fled to Brittany. At 15 he became a monk at Islevert, and settled at Landevennec (*c.*485), which became one of the chief abbeys of Brittany. His cult was widespread also in Cornwall. BIBLIOGRAPHY: H. Aikins, NCE 14:963; G. H. Doble, *Saints of Cornwall,* Pt. 2, 59–108.; R. Latouche, *Mélanges d'histoire de Cornouaille v^e-xie siècles,* 47–82, 97–112.

[J. DRUSE]

WIPO (d. 1046), writer, priest and chaplain to Emperors Conrad II and Henry III. W. was born in the Swabian area of Burgundy, but little is known of his education, although he seems familiar with classical writers. Much of his verse is lost, but surviving are a *Tetralogus,* a eulogy of Henry II (d. 1024), and *Proverbs,* a series of moralistic maxims for Prince Henry. He is best known for his *Victimae paschali laudes,* the sequence for Easter. His *Gesta Chuonradi II* *imperatoris* is the principal source for the reign of Emperor Conrad II (1024–39). The critical edition of his works is by H. Bresslau, MGHerGerm 57 (1915).

[N. F. GAUGHAN]

WIRCEBURGENSES, name given to four Jesuit theologians at the Univ. of Würzburg, Germany, in the late 18th century. Lectures on most aspects of theology were contributed by individual professors, with no effort to synthesize. First published in 14 volumes in 1766–71, the compilation is entitled *Theologia dogmatica, polemica, scholastica et moralis, praelectionibus academicis accommodata.* It was republished in 10 volumes in 1852–54 and in 1879–80. Traditionally scholastic in method, it shows the influence of the new historico-critical approach and is therefore a valuable document of the transition in theology of the time.

J. Neubauer (d. 1795) contributed in the field of apologetics, A. Kilber (d. 1782) in biblical commentary, T. Holzklau (d. 1783) in scriptural studies, U. Munier (originally Müller; d. 1759) in exegesis and dogma. The massive work is a solid contribution to Catholic theology. BIBLIOGRAPHY: M. Grabmann, *Die Geschichte der katholischen Theologie* (1933).

[J. R. AHERNE]

WIRNT, BL. (d. 1127), Benedictine abbot. In 1108 he became the strict but efficient abbot of Formbach, Benedictine abbey near Passau. He gained wide fame for miraculous cures of the sick. Unfortunately, the only extant vita (attributed to Gerhoh of Reichersberg) affords little more than a record of incredibly superstitious miracles. BIBLIOGRAPHY: PL 194:1425–44 (vita); F. D. Lazenby, NCE 14:964.

[F. D. LAZENBY]

WIRT, WIGAND (1460–1519), acrimonious Dominican polemicist against Franciscan proponents of the doctrine of the Immaculate Conception of Mary. A successive exchange of diatribes that began in 1494 ended with W.'s *Dialogus apologeticus* of 1504 being delated to Rome, where it was condemned in Oct. 1512; W. made public submission at Heidelberg's Holy Spirit Church in Feb. 1513.

[R. J. LITZ]

WIRTH, JOSEPH (1879–1956), chancellor of Germany. Born into a working-class family in Baden, a largely Catholic area with strong democratic traditions, W. became the outstanding leader of the left wing of the Catholic Center Party during the Weimar Republic. After a brief career as a mathematics professor, he entered politics and became finance minister of the Baden state government following the Revolution of 1918. He served a year as German finance minister before assuming the chancellorship on May 10, 1921, under the pressure of the London ultimatum, the deadline the Allies had imposed for German acceptance of a plan to pay reparations at a rate of 3 billion gold marks annually. Although doubtful of Germany's capacity to pay, W. accepted the plan and launched the policy of fulfilment of Allied demands, which he regarded as the only realistic hope for gaining future concessions to Germany. The fulfilment policy did not prevent him from providing funds for secret rearmament in violation of the Versailles Treaty, nor from aligning the country diplomatically with the Soviet Union by the Rapallo Treaty of April 1922. Even so, the policy incurred the enmity of German nationalists, some of whom assassinated W.'s friend and foreign minister, Walther Rathenau, June 24, 1922. Delivering an impassioned tribute to Rathenau in the Reichstag, W. presented a law "for the protection of the Republic" and proclaimed, "The enemy is on the right." Unable to achieve any improvement of the reparations problem or of Germany's financial position, he resigned on November 14, 1922. He remained active in support of the Republic and subsequently served in the cabinets of Hermann Müller and Heinrich Brüning. In March 1933 he followed the party line in voting for the Enabling Law, which assisted the consolidation of the Nazi regime, but he then went into exile in Switzerland. After his return to Germany in 1948, W. advocated German neutrality in opposition to Konrad Adenauer's association with NATO. W. was an excellent public speaker and a tireless and courageous politician, but the crises confronting him exceeded his leadership abilities. BIBLIOGRAPHY: D. Felix, *Walther Rathenau and the Weimar Republic* (1971).

[R. J. GIBBONS]

WISCONSIN, a north central state, admitted to the Union (1848) as the 30th state. Jean Nicolet, who visited Green Bay in 1634, was followed into the area by J. *Marquette and L. Jolliet, D. G. Duluth, and others. After 1660, Jesuit missionaries worked among the Winnebago, Chippewa, Menominee, Fox, and other tribes. England won control of the region from France in 1763, and the U.S. officially acquired the area in 1783. Wisconsin became part of the Old Northwest Territory prior to statehood.

Catholics in 19th cent. Wis. had few clerics to serve them until G. *Richard came to Green Bay (1823). Thereafter a large immigration from Ireland, Germany, and Norway made it imperative that Catholic clergy be stationed in the area. The Diocese of Milwaukee was erected (1843), with J. M. *Henni as first bishop. To refute the attacks of nativists, Henni engaged in a propaganda war, publishing *Facts against Assertions* (1845). He was also involved in educational development, opening numerous multilanguage schools and a new seminary. In 1875 Milwaukee was made an archdiocese, with Henni as abp. until his death (1881). The suffragan sees now include the Dioceses of Milwaukee, Green Bay, La Crosse, Madison, and Superior. Abp. Rembert Weakland, OSB, succeeded to the see in 1977.

M. *Heiss, who succeeded Henni, successfully opposed the Bennett Law of 1889, which imposed compulsory education, including the teaching of English and attendance at a school in one's own district.

In the first 2 decades of the 20th cent. Wis. received large numbers of Polish, Swedish, and Italian immigrants, causing numerous problems for the archdiocese. The *Kuryer Polski,* a Polish daily, carried on a crusade for Polish dioceses for a quarter of a century. In 1916 the state supreme court intervened in support of the bishops' opposition to this crusade. Immigration also required institutional expansion, such as the construction of schools, by the archdiocese and by such orders as the Sisters of St. Francis, the German Dominican Sisters, and the Sisters of St. Agnes.

In 1976 Wisconsin's Catholics numbered 1,519,337 or 33.5% of the total state population. The major Protestant denominations are the Lutheran Church (Missouri Synod), with 8.2% of the total population in 1971, and the Evangelical Lutheran Joint Synod, of Wisconsin, with 5.9%. Other Protestant denominations comprised 19.5% of the population. The Jewish population (1968) was 32,295, or 0.7%.

There are 7,159 students in Wisconsin's 8 Catholic colleges, and 20,677 students attending the state's Catholic high schools, and 11,463 attending 16 Catholic high schools in the archdiocese. Over 105,375 pupils are enrolled in the state's 455 Catholic elementary schools; 50,351 of these pupils attend 177 Catholic elementary schools in the archdiocese. BIBLIOGRAPHY: H. R. Austin, *The Wisconsin Story* (2d ed. 1957); L. Gara, *A Short History of Wisconsin* (1962); P. L. Johnson, *Crosier on the Frontier: A Life of John Martin Henni* (1959); B. J. Blied, *The Catholic Story of Wisconsin* (1948).

[J. L. MORRISON; R. M. PRESTON]

WISDOM, a gift of the Holy Spirit. It can be explained by analogy with the intellectual *sophia* described by Aristotle in the opening of the *Metaphysics* and seated by St. Augustine in the *ratio superior,* a synoptic judgment which embraces in their highest causes all the specialized findings of the *ratio inferior.* This can come only from *charity, which immediately unites the will to the source of all goodness. The gift is not to be treated as though it were dominated by conceptual and discursive processes: divinity, in the phrase of the Pseudo-Dionysius, is not just something to be learned, but undergone. Accordingly the theological treatment of the topic draws on the sapiential literature of the biblical and Neoplatonist tradition. This is the *locus classicus* for the study of the indwelling of the Holy Spirit in the soul and of the mystical life of contemplation, esp. for those authors who hold that the latter is open to all in God's grace. This gift is traditionally associated with the seventh Beatitude, "Blessed are the peacemakers, for they shall be called the children of God." The etymology of *sapiens* from *sapor,* and St. Isidore's derivation of *stultus* (a fool) from *stupor* (state of senselessness) have led ascetical writers to descant in detail on the contrast of wisdom and foolishness in 1 Cor ch. 13.

[T. GILBY]

WISDOM (IN THE BIBLE). (1) Old Testament. Israelite wisdom may very broadly be defined as that practical knowledge which enables a man to live his allotted span in the greatest possible harmony with his fellow men and with the world in which he has been placed by conforming his life down to the last detail with the harmony or order imposed upon the world by God himself. By doing this, the individual concerned is achieving the greatest possible happiness and profit for himself, the greatest respect in the eyes of others, and most of all that peace with God from which alone all happiness springs. At its most exalted, therefore, wisdom is the order or plan with which God created the world, and by which he continues to regulate its movements. That wisdom he has now graciously bestowed upon his people so that they can regulate their human lives by it down to the most intimate and homely details. It tells them how to choose a wife, how to bring up their children etc., how to preserve the ordinary decencies of social behavior (e.g., at parties), the importance of avoiding the folly of intemperance in its various forms, the merits of prudence, diligence, discretion, modesty, and a quiet dignified demeanor. In two famous passages, Pr 8 and Sir 24 this divine wisdom is personified, and its part in the creation, its intimacy with God and the manner in which it came to be bestowed upon his people are described. In its more developed form, too, wisdom is broadened so as to include speculations of a quasi-philosophical kind on the problem of evil, the transience of earthly things, etc., such as are found in Job and Ecclesiastes.

Israelite wisdom springs from two main sources, one indigenous, one foreign. The indigenous wisdom was originally the instruction handed down in the family circle from father to son. In a more developed form it was the instruction given by the country Levites and others, which has left a deep imprint esp. upon Dt and writings of the Deuteronomist tradition. Here, in particular, wisdom comes to be identified with the law. The importance of this indigenous wisdom has only recently been realized. From the time of Solomon onwards the more advanced form of wisdom became necessary in order to cater to the class of professional administrators and courtiers, educated on Egyptian lines, who were needed to administer Solomon's kingdom. This more foreign type of wisdom, which palpably has so many and such close affinities with the wisdom of Egypt and Babylon, was designed to meet the educational needs of the new upper class. It seems possible to infer that from the time of Solomon onwards Israelites were tempted to foreign, and esp. to Egyptian sources for this kind of wisdom. The insistent message of the Israelite wisdom writings is that it comes from Yahweh. It is divinely imparted knowledge bestowed upon Israel by him alone, and diligently to be prized and learned from her sages. The same is true of the more speculative type of wisdom found, for instance, in Job and Ec, which likewise owes much to foreign prototypes.

(2) New Testament. It is the concept of wisdom as secret knowledge of God and of his plan and purpose for the world and mankind that the NT chiefly presupposes. Men of good will recognize that Jesus has this wisdom, though they wonder where he can have obtained it without schooling (Mt 13.54; Mk 6.2). It enables him to provide new and authoritative interpretations of the law. Jesus imparts this new and greater wisdom to the disciples (Lk 21.15). It is a wisdom which is proved authentic and from God by its results (Mt 11.19; Lk 7.35). In the Pauline epistles too wisdom is a charismatic sharing in the unfathomable wisdom of God himself (1 Cor 12.8; Rom 11.33 etc.), and part of the equipment of the apostle (Col 1.28). Christians must distinguish between this true wisdom and the false wisdom of the world (Col 2.23), and must use it to admonish their fellow Christians (Col 3.16) and to deal prudently with non-Christians (Col 4.5). True Christian wisdom is Christ crucified (1 Cor 1.18,22; 2.2). Though the world regards this as folly, in reality it is the spurious wisdom of the world that is folly to God (1 Cor 3.18—). BIBLIOGRAPHY: *Wisdom in Israel and in the Ancient Near East VT Suppl.* 3 (ed. M. Noth and D. W. Thomas 1955); "Didactic and Wisdom Literature," *Ancient Near Eastern Texts Relating to the OT* (ed. J. B. Pritchard 2d ed., 1955) 405–452.

[D. J. BOURKE]

WISDOM, BOOK OF, in the RC canon one of the *deuterocanonical books; in the Jewish and Protestant tradition, one of the *apocrypha. From its title in the LXX it is also called the Wisdom of Solomon. The true author's name is unknown, but the book was written long after Solomon, probably in the first half of the 1st cent. B.C. by a Greek-speaking Jew in Alexandria. The book is chiefly characterized by a firm belief in the after life. This makes it relatively easy for its author to provide a solution to the problem of evil, which proved so baffling to earlier wisdom writers. For the author of this work, the sufferings of this present life constitute a brief period of testing, from which the just emerge victoriously to enter upon an eternity of happiness in God's presence, while the wicked are cast from that presence into eternal destruction. Virtue in this context means adhering to the two complementary ideals of wisdom and the Law.

The basic theme is developed in the three main sections into which the book may be divided: ch. 1–5, a series of contrasts between the virtuous and the wicked; ch. 6–9, a recommendation to strive for wisdom addressed to rulers and judges; ch. 10–19, a meditation on Israel's history and the wonders achieved in it by wisdom. Chapters 7–8 idealize the personification of wisdom, intimately united to God in his plan and purpose for the world. From this position of intimate union with God, wisdom descends into the souls of the just and there becomes the source of all virtues and all happiness. The author has been evidently influenced here by ideas drawn rather from Greek philosophy than from Hebrew tradition. To this extent wisdom is less closely identified with the Law than in other OT wisdom literature. BIBLIOGRAPHY: C. Larcher, *Le Livre de Sagesse* (1965–66);

J. Drouet, *Le Livre de la Sagesse* (1967); J. Geyer, *Wisdom of Solomon* (1963); A. G. Wright, JBC 1:556–568.

[D. J. BOURKE]

WISDOM, DAUGHTERS OF, a congregation of women devoted to the care of the sick poor and the children of the poor. Founded in France in 1703 by St. Louis de Montfort and Louise Trichet, the community grew slowly in the beginning. It gave over thirty martyrs to the Church during the French Revolution. In 1810 the first work outside France was undertaken, nursing wounded soldiers in Antwerp, Belgium. In the 19th cent. the sisters founded communities in eighteen countries. Missions were established in the Congo, Madagascar, Nyasaland, and Colombia. As a result of the anti-religious laws at the beginning of the 20th cent. in France, the Congregation spread to the U.S. in 1904. They operate schools and medical facilities in New York, Virginia, Maine, and Connecticut.

[J. R. AHERNE]

WISDOM LITERATURE (OT), a title under which the OT books of Job, Ec, Sir, and Wis—and often, though less appropriately, S of S—are classified. The close parallels between the wisdom of Israel and that of Egypt, Edom, and Babylon have often enough been noticed. This area of the OT, perhaps more than any other, shows the influence of other ancient Near Eastern cultures upon Israel's thought. These wisdom books consist largely of maxims prescribing how the individual should discipline and train himself in virtue, choose his wife, bring up his family, etc., in order to live wisely, moderately, and harmoniously with the world and his fellow men, and so to attain the maximum of earthly happiness, prosperity, and dignity. In this literature, presented for the most part in the form of brief aphorisms, most normal social and domestic activities are covered. At the same time, emphasis is laid upon the divine origin of wisdom, and upon the fact that it emanates directly from the God of Israel and was most intimately associated with him in the creation of the world. Wisdom is often identified with the Law. BIBLIOGRAPHY: A. M. Dubarle, *Les Sages d'Israël* (1946); H. Duesberg and I. Fransen, *Les Scribes inspirés* (1966); R. E. Murphy, *Seven Books of Wisdom* (1960); *idem, Introduction to the Wisdom Literature of the Old Testament* (1965); *idem,* "Assumptions and Problems in Old Testament Wisdom Research," CBQ 29 (1967), 407–418; *Wisdom in Israel and in the Ancient Near East* VT Suppl. 3 (eds. M. Roth and W. D. Thomas, 1955).

[D. J. BOURKE]

WISEMAN, NICHOLAS PATRICK (1802–65), first abp. of Westminster, cardinal, a central figure in the Catholic revival in England in the 19th century. Born in Spain, educated in Ireland and at Ushaw College (where he came under the influence of John *Lingard), W. pursued his theological studies in Rome as one of the first alumni of the reopened English College. His early interest in Oriental studies—he published an exposition of a Syrian version of the OT in 1827—gave place to his involvement in affairs of the English Church after his appointment (1828) as rector of the English College and ex officio Roman representative of the English bishops. In the 1830s he visited England where he delivered a series of lectures that were favorably received and helped to found the *Dublin Review* (since 1961, the *Wiseman Review*). In 1840 he was named coadjutor to the vicar apostolic of the central district in England and rector of Oscott College. When the vicar apostolic for London died, W. was appointed (1848) to succeed him, and with the restoration of the Catholic hierarchy in England he became abp. of Westminster and cardinal. His pastoral letter *From out of the Flaminian Gate* on the occasion of the restoration of the hierarchy aroused great indignation among non-Catholics, which his later *Appeal to the Reason and Good Feeling of the English People* only partially allayed. During his administration he was bitterly attacked by priests and laymen of the old Catholic tradition, who considered him too ultramontane in his outlook, and these difficulties were aggravated by the ecclesiastical promotion under his patronage of Henry *Manning, whom W. had received into the Church. W.'s dream of an early return of England to the RC Church was not realized. Nevertheless, there was a great growth in number of Roman Catholics in England during his lifetime and a notable increase in the vigor of Catholic life. BIBLIOGRAPHY: W. P. Ward, *Life and Times of Cardinal Wiseman* (2 v., 1897); B. Fothergill, *Nicholas Wiseman* (1963); *idem*. NCE 14:976–977.

[G. RUPPEL]

WISHART, GEORGE (*c*.1510–*c*.1546), leading figure of the early Scottish Reformation, Protestant martyr. Little is known about his early life. He studied at the Univ. of Louvain and was a brilliant student—graduating second out of 133. In 1534 he was accused of teaching the Greek NT to his pupils and was forced to flee to England. Recanting his error in 1539 W. began a career at Cambridge, but soon abandoned it for two years of travel in Switzerland and Germany. When he returned to Scotland, he had become a fervent and vigorous Calvinist preacher. From 1544 to 1545 he actively preached in various Scottish territories where his words moved his hearers to destroy churches. Anticlerical, anti-French feeling was common. W. eventually became involved in political intrigues against Card. *Beaton. In January 1546 he was arrested as a conspirator and later executed for heresy. He exerted a profound influence upon John Knox's religious views. BIBLIOGRAPHY: D. McRoberts, ed., *Essays on the Scottish Reformation, 1513–1625* (1962); E. Percy, *John Knox* (1966).

[C. T. EBY]

WISSEMBOURG, ABBEY OF (Weissemburg), an abbey founded by Dagobert II *c*.624. It is located 40 miles NE of Strasbourg. Wissembourg, Fulda, Kempten, and Murbach, were the four abbeys that enjoyed ducal status in the Empire. Their abbots were ex officio princes of the Holy Roman Empire. Amalgamated with the Congregation of Bursfeld in 1482, Wissembourg was secularized in 1524, the abbot becoming provost of a regular chapter. In 1561 Florent of Flersheim, bp. of Speyer, united Wissembourg to his abbatial property. In the 18th cent. a dean, a custodian, ten canons, and two vicars were responsible for the monastery, which was suppressed during the Revolution. The church (13th cent.), the Romanesque tower, and a wing of the cloister (14th cent.) are still standing. BIBLIOGRAPHY: Cottineau 2:3461–62.

[J. DAOUST]

WITCHCRAFT, from Old English wiccecrãeft, the exercise of human powers in league with spiritual forces to produce effects out of the ordinary run of things and therefore deemed to be preternatural and usually claimed to be magical. That general definition will serve as a preliminary: other elements, however, have to be introduced in order to relate it to the Christian setting. But first as to nomenclature. A witch ordinarily stands for a female magician or sorceress, but it also included a "he witch," also called a wizard, warlock, or sorcerer, and the usage remains in the term "witch-doctor." Then also note the distinction drawn by popular estimation between black magic and white magic: the former is used for a maleficent or offensive purpose and proceeds from "one that hath conference with devils"; the latter is defensive and has harmless or even beneficial effects, such as charming away warts or, as commonly in Italy, casting a love-spell, and it proceeds from one "of good disposition" or "that pretends to deal only with good angels." The demonological or angelological reference is essential to the notion; it meant that scientists, such as Pope Sylvester II or St. Albert the Great, who were ahead of their times in tapping the resources of the physical world, could easily acquire an ambiguous reputation.

The energetic Christian reaction to witchcraft may be accounted for under two headings, historical and doctrinal. Though the genius of the Church in the conversion of the tribes was not to make a clean sweep, leaving them swept and garnished, but to incorporate the old myths and even to baptize the old gods, the process of assimilation was not complete—nor should it have been, for turning to Christ does not demand the displacement of one culture by another. Folk memories of pagan rites, often associated with fertility cults for humans and their stock and crops, stubbornly survived into modern industrialism, and even now are being revived, though suitably packaged, by the techniques of salesmanship stimulating a taste for the occult which grows when human beings have lost a dogmatic faith yet still need reassurance about life beyond. We throw spilt salt over our left shoulders, and so, a more extreme case, the old lady always bowed her head reverently at mention of the devil, "because," as she explained, "you never know, and it always pays to make sure." Now in the change from one religion to another the old god becomes the new devil—it may be etymologically fanciful to treat "devil" as "little god," a diminutive from the root "div'," divine, nevertheless the point will serve. Consequently trafficking with pre-Christian religious agencies quite easily slips into being regarded as having intercourse with the devil, or at least as a form of superstition, or going after strange gods.

This last was the thought of Israel (Ex 2.18; Lv 19.31; 20.6; Dt 18.9–12), and the vanity of such idolatory is the theme of the prophets (cf. Is 2.6; Jer 10.2–3). So sorcery is condemned in the NT; St. Paul goes further and rounds on Elymas the magician, "Thou son of the devil" (cf. Acts 8.9; 13.8; 19.9; Gal 5.20). Among the Church Fathers, Tertullian and Augustine did not doubt the existence and power of the devils working through magic; Hippolytus and John Chrysostom, however, are more reserved. In some regions the Church acted as though magic could only be overcome by counter-magic; Celtic legends are full of saints who beat the old wonder-workers at their own game.

Nevertheless, the profound difference between Christian doctrine and practice, and the science and art of magic was beginning to show itself. Magic was at least a pseudo-science in that it attempted to deal with laws, not merely occurrences. It sought to bend the powers above to human purposes; they were not supposed to be benevolent, or only freakishly so, but they might, as it were, be trapped into doing us good. Such a view was quite opposed to the Christian doctrine of the loving Father whose particular Providence extends even to the life of a sparrow sold for one farthing. Moreover magical and sacramental practice could not be more opposed, for the sacraments are God's free gifts to men. The theological conviction that God is to be neither tricked nor *tempted, and that we should be content with the loving economy of his salvation, and not seek to go outside it, rather than horror at a pact with the devil, lies at the heart of the Christian rejection of magical thinking or practices in religion. And it applies alike to white magic and black.

An anthropologist and student of folklore will not be too quick to set down some proceedings, simultaneously uninhibited and highly formal, or even sexual orgies as instances of depravity. Nevertheless the association of magic with demons in the form of beasts, a bull, dog, or cat in England, but never a goat, as in France and Germany, does suggest a subhumanness, the *theriotes* of the *Nicomachean Ethics* (1149al). Moreover there are authenticated cases of practices sufficiently nasty: queer happenings on the Cheshire moors and in California rival anything among the *curiosa* of the ancient world.

Until the 13th cent. the Church punished witchcraft with ecclesiastical censures alone; Hildebrand was not alone in forbidding the killing of witches. But from then onwards the secular laws took a hand, and though the Inquisition, which, if ruthless, at least insisted on quasi-scientific procedures,

did something to protect poor creatures from mob violence; the 15th cent. saw a mounting hysteria that was to last until the Enlightenment of the 18th. The *Hammer of Witches* (1487) served both to guide forensic procedure, which might include torture, and to inflame popular sentiment. These shameful pages in religious history relate alike to Catholics and to Protestants; though Protestant theology was more hag-ridden by the devil, and in England and America witch-hunting reached its peak under the Puritans. Witchcraft is superstition, but that it should have been so savagely suppressed from superstition is a commentary on how bad Christ's shepherds can be, and how execrably we can treat one another from our fears and ignorances. BIBLIOGRAPHY: M. A. Murray, *Witch-cult in Western Europe* (1921); M. Summers, *History of Witchcraft and Demonology* (2d ed., 1956).

[T. GILBY]

WITCHES' HAMMER, Lat. title, *Malleus maleficarum (maleficas et earum haeresim framea conterens)*, a compendium on witchcraft and witch hunting first published in 1486 by the Dominicans Jakob Sprenger (1436–95) and Heinrich Krämer (Latinized as Institor; *c.* 1430–1505). In 1484 Krämer obtained a bull from Innocent VIII sanctioning the witch hunts of the Inquisition in Germany. The *Malleus* had as its purpose the instruction of judges in the trial of witches. Part I of the work develops the need for such instruction, so that the witches will be recognized as heretics who consort carnally with devils. Part II is a collection of fantastic and bizarre tales about sorcery, incubi and succubi, compacts with devils, and the baneful powers of the witch. Part III discusses judicial proceedings against those suspect of witchery. The wk. went through numerous editions, revisions, and translations into German, French, Italian, and English, through the 17th cent. The witchcraft lore of the *Malleus* was taken with solemn literalness by both Catholics and Protestants as long as witch hunting remained in vogue.

[T. C. O'BRIEN]

WITELO, (b. *c.* 1230), Polish philosopher, mathematician, and physicist. Born in Silesia (then part of Poland), he studied arts at Paris and canon law at Padua, was at the papal court in Viterbo in 1269, and finished his major work *Perspectiva c.* 1270. This was later combined with writings of Alhazen and served as the principal textbook on optics in the West until the 17th century. In W.'s Neoplatonic metaphysics, God is the First Light.

[E. J. DILLON]

WITHAM CHARTERHOUSE, England's first Carthusian foundation, located near Frome in the Diocese of Bath, Somerset, founded *c.* 1178 by Henry II as part of his expiation for the murder of Thomas à Becket. Its motherhouse was the Grande Chartreuse. St. Hugh of Avalon was virtual founding prior, first in the capacity of prior (1180) and then as bp. of Lincoln while retaining charge of Witham's foundation. By the time Hugh died (1200), the permanent buildings were almost complete. During the 15th cent. the number of lay brothers declined. In 1535 Witham accepted the royal supremacy. At its suppression in 1539, it was surrendered by the prior and 13 religious. No trace of the monastic buildings remains. The lay brothers' church survives as Witham parish church. BIBLIOGRAPHY: Cottineau. v. 2.

[E. J. DILLON]

WITHBURGA (WIHTBURH), ST. (fl. mid-7th cent.). Daughter of King Anna of East Anglia (d. 654) and sister of SS. Sexburga, Ethelburga, and Etheldrita, W. was a nun, and perhaps abbess, at East Dereham, according to tradition. Little is known of her life; her remains were translated to Ely (974). BIBLIOGRAPHY: Zimmermann 1:339–340; Butler 3:41.

[W. A. CHANEY]

WITHERSPOON, JOHN (1722–94), Presbyterian clergyman, educator, and statesman. After graduation from the Univ. of Edinburgh, near his birthplace, W. served pastorates in Scotland. He stood with the evangelicals against the moderates, whom he satirized in *Ecclesiastical Characteristics* (1753), a work that brought him considerable attention. In 1768 he assumed the presidency of the College of New Jersey (now Princeton), where he served with distinction, lecturing on theology, moral philosophy, and rhetoric, and where he encouraged the study of Hebrew, French, and science. He was the only clergyman to sign the Declaration of Independence (1776). Through him the Scottish Common Sense Realists were an influence on the *Princeton theology of A. *Alexander and C. *Hodge. BIBLIOGRAPHY: V. L. Collins, *President Witherspoon* (2 v., 1925).

[J. H. SMYLIE]

WITNESS, personal testimony. In secular and biblical literature, the Greek term *martys* signifies the attestation of a person. Personal testimony may express itself in a confession, preaching, prayer, teaching, or martyrdom, but it always conveys, unless it is false, a personal commitment to a fact or truth. In the Bible witness has both legal (Dt 19.15; 2 Cor 13.1; 1 Tim 5.19) and theological significance. Jesus himself is a witness to the Father (Jn 3.11; 5.36; 8.14, 26; 18.37). The Apostles in turn are to testify to him (Lk 24.48; Acts 1.8; Jn 15.27), to his resurrection as well as to his earthly life (Acts 1.22; 4.33; 5, 32; 10.42; 13.31; 22.15; 26, 16). This role of witness to faith in Jesus was taken up by the entire Christian community and was manifested in martyrdom (Acts 22.20); it helped to characterize the age of the Church Fathers. The historicity of the biblical witness has been so debated, almost throughout the Christian era, as to have occasioned methodological questions about history and faith, the Jesus of history and the Christ of faith, factual testimony and the testimony to truth. The outcome of the debate is not yet in sight, but a solution lies in linking fact with significance. The purpose of Christian witness is twofold: to bring the believer to the full realization of his faith, his unique relationship to God, and to win others to Christ (2 Th 1.10). BIBLIOGRAPHY: EDB 2591–94.

[J. FICHTNER]

WITNESSES (LAW), persons called upon to give evidence under oath, as in a court of law or a congressional hearing. If summoned by subpoena, a person is morally obliged to give testimony. Sometimes he may be morally obliged to come forward voluntarily unless excused by a proportionate inconvenience. Ordinarily he is entitled to compensation for expenses and time lost from work, unless he is the culpable cause of the parties being in contention. He is bound to answer truthfully; to strive to be objective; to be certain before identifying another person; not to reveal privileged communications without permission; to show respect and obedience to the presiding officer. He may be required to give evidence that tends to shame or disgrace himself. If he has guilty knowledge he may invoke the Fifth Amendment but he must accept the judicial meaning and limitations of this privilege. If he is unjust he is obliged to restitution or reparation. BIBLIOGRAPHY: ThAq ST 2a2ae, 70.

[R. H. DAILEY]

WITTA, ST. (Hwita, Wizo). The little known about this saint is found in the lives of other Anglo-Saxon missionaries in Germany, esp. St. Boniface and St. Willibald. W. was the first bp. of Hesse, having Buraberg for his see. With Boniface and Burchard he was co-consecrator of Bp. Willibald.

[A. WARDLE]

WITTE, EMMANUEL DE (1617?–1691 or 1692), Dutch painter of history and portraits, noted for recording church interiors. Early a figure painter in Delft and Rotterdam (1652), W. painted various churches in Amsterdam. The *Interior of a Church* (1668) is a composite of the Old Church, Amsterdam and St. Bavo's, Haarlem, whereas *View in the New Church, Amsterdam* (1656?) is an authentic record. W. painted portraits and market scenes but after 1660 was forced to indenture himself.

[M. J. DALY]

WITTENBERG, CONCORD OF, an effort to harmonize Lutheran and Zwinglian teaching on the Eucharist, at a meeting held in Wittenberg in 1536. Martin Luther himself was there; Philipp *Melanchthon presented a document setting forth Lutheran teaching on the *Real Presence. Martin *Bucer, who represented the Zwinglian side and whose efforts at conciliation since the failure of the *Marburg Articles (1529) had brought about the meeting, gave assurance that the doctrine as stated could be accepted by the Churches of S Germany and Switzerland. The hopes of

Wittenberg were dashed, however, when the Swiss Churches rejected the agreement.

WITTGENSTEIN, LUDWIG JOSEPH JOHANN

(1889–1951), philosopher. A native of Vienna W. was a brooding, melancholy, generous man who loved seclusion. He esteemed friendship, but found making friends difficult; his life style was one of simplicity. He was a remarkable teacher, whether the students were 9 and 10 year-old Austrian children or undergraduates at Cambridge (where he taught from 1930 to 1936, 1937–1941, and 1944–1947). A friend of Bertrand Russell, W. ultimately concluded that Russell did not understand his philosophical position. The first of his major works, *Tractatus Logico-Philosophicus* was published in a German annual in 1921 and in a German-English edition in 1922. Though his work has affinities with the logical positivist school of Vienna, W. differed from the group in important ways. The central concept of the complex *Tractatus* is that a sentence is a picture corresponding to reality, to fact. He saw as the cardinal problem of philosophy the distinction between what can be said in propositions (language) and what cannot be said but only shown. Somehow we grasp meaning even if we cannot explain it. A second major work, *Philosophical Investigations*, written in the periods 1936–45 and 1947–49, was published posthumously. It is a system of thought which opposes the position taken in the *Tractatus*. In the latter, W. argued that the elements of language are names denoting simple objects; in *Philosophical Investigations*, he denies this basic view, asserting that the notions of "complex" and "simple" vary according to the language game. The theory that a sentence has meaning because it is a picture is discarded for one which postulates that the meaning of a sentence is its use or application. W.'s work has been influential on contemporary philosophers and theologians in the interpretation of religious language. At the time of his death there was some indication of his own religious interest. BIBLIOGRAPHY: G. E. M. Anscombe, *An Introduction to Wittgenstein's Tractatus* (2d. rev. ed. 1965); I. D. 'Hert, *Wittgenstein's Relevance for Theology* (1975); W. D. Hudson, *L. Wittgenstein: The Bearing of His Philosophy on Religious Belief* (1968); A. Keightley, *Wittgenstein, Grammar and God* (1976); A. Kenny, *Wittgenstein* (1973).

[J. R. AHERNE]

WITTIG, JOSEPH

(1879–1949), German Catholic theologian and popular writer. He studied in Breslau and Rome, attained his doctorate in theology in 1902, and was ordained in 1903. He was recognized as academic lecturer in Ancient Church Studies and Christian Archeology at Breslau in 1909 and became *ordinarius* at Breslau in 1912. The publication in 1922 of his essay "Die Erlösten" (The Redeemed) in the periodical *Hochland* and of his major work *Leben Jesu . . .* (Life of Jesus . . .) led to his suspension and the placing of parts of his works on the Index. In 1926 he was excommunicated. He lived as a layman and a

man of letters until his reconciliation with the Church in 1946. His writings reflect his loyalty both to German cultural values and to Christian faith. His concern had been to make the latter accessible to the German people.

[E. J. DILLON]

WITTOLA, MARK ANTON

(1736–97), pastor, theologian, prolific writer, an effective preacher, and a leading spokesman for the Jansenist movement in the Vienna of his day. Born in Oberschlesien, he studied theology in Vienna, received his doctorate and was named pastor of a church there, and was named a member of the Board of Censors by Empress Maria Teresa. Through the influence of the suffragan bishop von Stock, W. became familiar with Jansenist literature and the schismatic Church of Utrecht. He was drawn in that direction by his conviction that only through a return to the simple, demanding faith of primitive Christianity could the Church recover its world transforming power.

[E. J. DILLON]

WITZ, KONRAD

(Konrat van Rotwil); *c.*1400–*c.*1445), German painter from Rottweil (Swabia), who formed his style in the environment of the Basle Council, revitalizing German art with strong realism, expressed in heavy sculptural figures, sparse architecture and contrasting colors. An early example is the *Heilsspiegel Altarpiece* (*c.*1435) for Basle, based on the *Speculum humanae salvationis*. The Geneva St. Peter altarpiece (1444) shows most intense union of inspired religious narrative with visual verisimilitude, and outside panel painting of the *Miraculous Draught of Fishes* showing the most remarkable landscape of 15th-cent. painting in its rendering of Lake Geneva and optical effects of objects under water. A *Sacra Conversazione* (Capodimonte, Naples) attributed to W. abounds in Netherlandish conventions.

[R. BERGMANN]

WITZEL, GEORG

(1501–73), German Catholic irenicist during the Reformation. In many ways he was a typical product of Erasmian humanism. His dissatisfaction with the deplorable abuses in the Church initially attracted him to Luther, but he could not make the commitment fully to embrace Lutheranism. His life was illustrative of this indecision. In 1524 he left the priesthood, married and became a Lutheran minister. Yet Lutheran doctrine proved unsatisfying and in 1531 he returned to Catholicism. Later W. served as an adviser to such important figures as George of Saxony, Joachim II of Brandenberg and Ferdinand I. Throughout his career W. championed the Erasmian solution to the Reformation: there were no insurmountable differences between the Protestants and Catholics and unity might be maintained if the Church corrected its abuses. Moral reform, not religious dogma was the real issue, he argued. *Methodus concordiae ecclesiasticae* and the disputation *Typus prioris, ecclesiae* were works that reflected Witzel's irenicist attitudes. BIBLIOGRAPHY: J. Lecler, *Toler-*

ation and the Reformation (2 v., tr. T. L. Westow; 1960); J. Lortz, *The Reformation in Germany* (2 v., tr. R. Walls; 1968).

[C. T. EBY]

WIWINA, ST. (Wivina; d. 1170), Benedictine prioress. W. miraculously restored to health a young suitor whom she had rejected. At 23 she became a hermit in a forest near Brussels. In 1120 Count Godfrey of Brabant built the convent of Le Grand Bigard of which she acted as prioress. Many miracles were attributed to her after death. BIBLIOGRAPHY: F. D. Lazenby, NCE 14:985; Butler 4:580–581.

[F. D. LAZENBY]

WOLFF, CHRISTIAN (1679–1754), German rationalist philosopher of the Enlightenment. His early intellectual interest was in mathematics and his philosophical system was to follow a mathematical model. Descartes and Leibniz are the strongest influences on his metaphysical thought, but he was familiar as well with the scholastic theological tradition of Lutheranism, which was markedly Aristotelian, and of Catholicism, reflecting Aquinas and Suárez. W. was a prolific writer, but he showed no great originality either in his mathematics or his philosophy. W. did bring to his writing a sense of method that produced the most coherent philosophical system of the 18th century. His tidy, even too tidy, division of philosophy finds echoes in scholastic manuals even into this century. W.'s first systematic work establishes logic as the art of demonstration (though he had planned as a capstone a treatise on the logic of discovery and invention). His *First Philosophy or Ontology* puts the metaphysics of Descartes and Leibniz in the framework of scholastic Aristotelianism. W.'s psychology accepts the mind-body dichotomy of rationalism and with it Leibniz's pre-established harmony. While insisting that his natural theology is entirely compatible with Christian revelation, W. attempted to prove rationally no more than God's existence. For him the existence of God is demonstrable a priori by the ontological argument, a posteriori most clearly by the cosmological one. W.'s moral philosophy is purely rational. Moral law depends on the structure of being, not on God's will, and can be discovered independently of Christian revelation. W.'s writing and teaching exercised a strong influence on German thought and paved the way for the revolution of Kant. BIBLIOGRAPHY: Copleston 6:101–114; E. Utitz, *Christian Wolff* (1929); G. Tonelli, EncPhil 8:340–344.

[W. B. MAHONEY]

WOLFF, GEORGE DERING (1822–94), editor. A native of W. Va. whose father was a prominent Lutheran pastor, W. studied law but became a minister of the Lutheran Church and served in several congregations before becoming a Catholic in 1871. The following year he was editor of the Baltimore *Catholic Mirror* and in 1873 became editor of the Philadelphia *Catholic Standard and Times,* a position he held until his death. W. was cofounder of the *American Catholic Quarterly Review* of Philadelphia, which first appeared in 1876, and contributed numerous articles on apologetics to that journal.

[J. R. AHERNE]

WOLFF, MADELEVA, SISTER (1887–1964), poet, educator. Educated at St. Mary's College, Indiana, she entered the Congregation of the Holy Cross and taught at the college in early years. Her lyric poetry appeared in prominent magazines of the day. During her years at Berkeley she wrote and published *Knights Errant and Other Poems* and at the end of her doctoral program *The Pearl: A Study in Spiritual Dryness.* In 1925 also appeared *Chaucer's Nuns and Other Essays.* She was the first nun to earn a doctorate at the Univ. of California at Berkeley. She founded (1926) a new college in Salt Lake City, Saint Mary's of the Wasatch. A year at Oxford Univ. put her in touch with the great tradition of Catholic literary life in England. In 1934 she was appointed president of St. Mary's College, South Bend, Indiana. Her wise administration saw the erection of new buildings, a whole new curriculum, and the deliberate effort to make St. Mary's a center of Christian humanism. W. opened the School of Sacred Theology (1943), designed primarily for lay students. She brought to her campus the outstanding Catholic thinkers and writers of the day. She was herself "of the center" as Alice Meynell said Catholic writers should always be. BIBLIOGRAPHY: M. Madeleva, *My First Seventy Years* (1959).

[J. R. AHERNE]

WÖLFFLIN, HEINRICH (1864–1945), Swiss writer on aesthetics, specializing in Renaissance and baroque art. A student of Jacob Burckhardt, W. in his important *Kunstgeschichtliche Grundbegriffe* (*Principles of Art History*, 1915) presents his theory of visual and ideal values in art, maintaining that forms are always conditioned intuitively by factors common to a specific period, and practically established the descriptive terminology of art history today. Other works include *Renaissance und Barock* (1888), *Die klasische Kunst* (1899), *Die Kunst Albrecht Dürer* (1905).

[K. B. NEILSON]

WOLFGANG OF REGENSBURG, ST. (c.924–994), bishop, patron saint of Regensburg; Bavaria. Schooled at Reichenau, W. became head of the cathedral school at Trier in 956, later a monk at Einsiedeln, and eventually bp. of Regensburg in 972. He was occupied not only with monastic settlement and reform but also with the secular churches of Prague and the work of Otto II and III. BIBLIOGRAPHY: A. A. Schacher, NCE 14:987–988; Butler 4:230–231.

[S. WILLIAMS]

WOLFGANG ALTAR (*Coronation of Mary*), major wood sculpture and painting by M. *Pacher in the Church of Sankt Wolfgang am Ambersee, Austria.

[M. J. DALY]

WOLFHARD OF VERONA, ST. (d. 1127), Camaldolese hermit. The account of his life is early but filled with legend. Trained as a saddlemaker at Augsburg, and known for his piety, he went to Verona as a journeyman in 1097. He soon retired from the world and lived as a hermit in a forest on the Adige River. Prevailed upon to return to Verona, he entered the Camaldolese monastery of San Salvatore as a recluse and died there. In 1507 the brotherhood of saddlers made him their patron. In 1602 some of his relics were taken to Augsburg, where they are preserved in the Church of St. Sebastian. BIBLIOGRAPHY: M. R. P. McGuire, NCE 14:988; Zimmermann 2:127–129; Butler 2:200–201.

[M. R. P. MCGUIRE]

WOLFHELM, BL. (d.1091), theologian and abbot of the Benedictine monastery at Brauweiler from 1065 until his death. W. is known to have opposed the views of Berengar of Tours on the matter of the Eucharist. W. was himself attacked for his position of the compatibility of pagan philosophy and Christian doctrine. BIBLIOGRAPHY: Butler 2:147.

[B. F. SCHERER]

WOLFRAM VON ESCHENBACH (c.1170–c.1220), greatest epic poet of the German Middle Ages; author of several extant lyric poems and three courtly epics: *Parzival, Willehalm,* and *Titurel.* Nothing is known of his life except what can be gleaned from his works. He seems to have enjoyed the patronage of the Lords of Durne and the Counts of Wertheim and is known to have been at the court of Landgrave Hermann of Thuringia. His *Parzival* (c.1210), based largely on Chrétien de Troyes' *Li Contes del Gral,* combines the Arthurian and Grail legends into what has been called the first German *Entwicklungsroman* (''developmental novel''): the story of Parzival's spiritual ascent to a full Christian maturity which embodied the chivalric, not the monastic, ideal. A no longer extant French *chanson de geste, La Bataille d'Aliscans,* was Wolfram's source for the unfinished epic *Willehalm,* which he began c.1210 after the completion of *Parzival.* The *Titurel,* begun at about the same time and likewise unfinished, relates in two fragments of lyric beauty the love story of Schionatulander and Sigune. BIBLIOGRAPHY: M. F. Richey, *Studies of Wolfram von Eschenbach* (1957).

[M. F. MCCARTHY]

WOLGEMUT, MICHAEL (1434–1519), German painter and designer of woodcuts, after his *Wanderjahre* (1450), probably working with Hans Pleydenwurff (c.1460–70). W. painted the six-winged altar of the Marienkirchen, Zwickau (1476–79), the high altar at the Heiligenkirche, Nuremberg (1486), and the extensive piece at the Stadtkirche of Swabach (1506–08). Dürer at 15 (1486) entered W.'s shop, valued his teaching highly, and painted his portrait (1516). W. was the first to explore the woodcut medium, raising it from illustration to an artistic creation. His workshop produced some of the greatest 15th-cent. works in *Schatzbehalter* (1491) and the famous *Schedelische Weltchronik* (1493) of 645 cuts in 1809 illustrations, all of which formed the basis for the supreme woodcuts of Dürer's *Apocalypse and Passion* series.

[M. J. DALY]

WOLSEY, THOMAS (1471–1530), archbishop of Canterbury, card., papal legate, chancellor of England under Henry VIII. In many ways his career typified the corruption in high church office in the 16th century; W. was representative of the belief that the Church was primarily a source of employment and secular advancement. Coming from a merchant background, he was educated at Oxford where he showed little ability for either theology or scholarship. His connections with influential patrons secured him several posts until in 1509 he was attached to the king's court. In six years he became abp. of Canterbury and chancellor. W.'s impressive talents as an administrator and his capacity for hard work cemented his relations with the often fickle Henry VIII. His overbearing attitudes, however, antagonized his subordinates. He was a failure as a diplomat because England's involvement in French wars and with the papacy proved costly and unrewarding. He was also a pluralist, simultaneously holding such bishoprics as Canterbury, York, Durham, and St. Albans. His fall in September 1529 was prompted by his inability to secure the king's divorce. Some historians argue that W.'s mistakes led to the English Reformation; others maintain he cannot be held responsible for Henry VIII's later actions. BIBLIOGRAPHY: A. F. Pollard, *Wolsey* (1929); J. J. Scarisbrick, *Henry VIII* (1968).

[C. T. EBY]

WOLTER, MAURUS (1825–90), liturgist, founder. A native of Germany, W. studied for the priesthood and was ordained in 1850. After heading several schools he joined the Benedictines in 1857. W. founded the monastery of Beuron in 1863, taking over the former Augustinian monastery there and became its first abbot. A follower of Dom Guéranger at Solesmes, France, W. actively supported a program at Beuron of liturgy, Gregorian chant, and art. He published a 5-v. work on the Psalms, *Psallite sapienter* (1871–90), and wrote on Benedictine life *Praecipua ordinis monastici elementa* (1880). W. was founder of the Beuronese Congregation of Benedictines and established houses in Belgium, England, Prague, and Styria.

[J. R. AHERNE]

WOLTER, PLACIDUS (1828–1908), German Benedictine abbot and leader of the modern Benedictine renewal, brother of Maurus. He was ordained priest (1851), entered the Benedictines (1855), and went to São Paolo that same year. He returned to Germany in 1860 to help his brother Maurus rebuild Beuron. W. was prior and then abbot (1878) at *Maredsous, Belgium, and finally succeeded his brother as archabbot of Beuron in 1890. In subsequent years he presided over the remarkable growth of the Beuron Congregation throughout Germany, in the Holy Land, in Portugal, and Brazil. BIBLIOGRAPHY: U. Engelmann, LTK 10:1221.

[E. J. DILLON]

WOMAN CLOTHED WITH THE SUN, the woman referred to in Rev. 12.1–6. She is clothed with the sun, with the moon under her feet, and wears a crown of 12 stars; she gives painful birth to a male child whom a dragon seeks to destroy but who escapes to the throne of God. The woman is then said to flee to a place prepared by God in the desert. The patristic biblical commentators identified the woman with the Church, although in the Middle Ages it was widely held that she represented Mary. Almost all modern exegetes adopt the older interpretation. John is speaking of the coming of the Kingdom as a birth; Israel and the Church, used interchangeably, have given birth to the Messiah in pain and with persecution, but the Messiah has triumphed and is at the right hand of God. A Marian interpretation may be admitted insofar as Mary is the type of the Church. BIBLIOGRAPHY: JBC 2:482–483; E. F. Siegman, NCE 14:1000–01.

[T. M. MCFADDEN]

WOMEN IN CHRISTIAN TRADITION. The recent and rapid evolution of the status of women in Church and in society has drawn attention to the issue between the "environmentalists," those who say that woman's role has been thrust upon her and the protagonists of the "eternal feminine" school who see woman's nature as a given which determines her actions and status. But the issue need not be defined as a man-woman confrontation. The status that women have come "from" is not as important as the goal that is to be achieved: full dignity and equality that rest on human personhood, of which womanhood is one constitutive expression.

In the Ancient East women generally possessed no legal rights and were subjugated to male dominance. Woman's status in ancient Greece and Rome was also one of subjection, though to a lesser extent. The Hebrew Scriptures show some women achieving prominence in a patriarchal society, but in ancient Israel it was motherhood rather than womanhood that merited respect. Christianity's moral revolution should have effected an appreciation of woman as person; Christ's law of love and the responsible freedom flowing from the gospel was to extend to all regardless of sex. Jesus' own encounters with women and his explication of the spirit of the law teach positive respect for women. The double standard of morality was repudiated in principle; the dignity and stability of marriage affirmed. The Christian woman's free choice to witness to Christ as a virgin was now respected. But spiritual insights are learned slowly, and neither religious teaching nor the Church itself exists in a vacuum. In fact acculturation frequently involves the acceptance of thought patterns which obscure the full implication of Christ's teaching. Thus, while Paul affirms that in Christ there is neither slave nor freeman, male nor female (Gal 3.28), he also reflects his times in his opinion of woman as inferior.

Living in areas where women were denigrated, the Fathers of the Church, too, are frequently misogynist. Although they generally fail to recognize in their writings woman as totally equal to man in her human nature, yet deaconesses played an important role in the early Church.

The Christian Middle Ages did not penetrate the scope of what it meant to be "in Christ." Thomas Aquinas was influenced by Aristotle's view of woman as a defective being. According to the limited scientific knowledge of the day, man was thought to be the active principle in generation and Christians were, therefore, to love father more than mother (ThAq ST 2a, 2ae, 26.10). These positions, based on biblical exegesis common at that time, stand in contrast to Aquinas's statement on the dignity of the human person as image of God and on growth in God's likeness which contain an implicit attestation to the equality of the sexes. However, the emphasis on disparity prevailed.

The Industrial Revolution has been hailed as the catalyst that led to the restructuring of modern life and greatly influenced the emancipation of women. In the long view this is true. In its early stages the Industrial Revolution lured women from the home to work under inhuman conditions. Through protests and the pressuring of lawmakers, women were emancipated from economic slavery. Political recognition in the right to vote and hold office followed. Women have not yet secured professional equality with men even in the U.S. despite the Civil Rights Act of 1964 which prohibited discrimination in employment on the basis of sex. The movement for economic and political equality was largely extra-Church. During the pontificate of John XXIII, however, one finds forthright and consistent acceptance of the changed and changing position of woman. John saw women demanding "rights befitting a human person" (*Pacem in terris* 41), and spoke of a fading "superiority complex which had its roots in socio-economic privileges, sex, or political standing" (*Pacem in terris* 43). *Gaudium et spes* of Vatican II also recognizes that discrimination based on sex is "to be eradicated as contrary to God's intent (Vat II ChurchModWorld 29). The 1971 Synod of Bishops' *Justice in the World* repeats the same sentiments.

There is a great deal of variation in RC circles regarding the status of women although statements since John XXIII leave the way open for a development of doctrine that might culminate in the ordination of women. Theologians and the Pontifical Biblical Commission see no obstacles. It has also been asserted that the position of woman is intricately bound up with, and dependent on, the ultimate resolution of the birth control question. Regardless of their views on the above issues, there is a growing realization on the part of men and women that they are morally bound to use their intelligence in the interest of the whole human family and this necessarily includes a reconsideration of the status of woman.

It has also been proposed that the use of the masculine gender in reference to God who is Spirit has had a deep effect on the psyche of both man and woman with attendant ramifications relative to the *de facto* position of woman. This practice is no doubt contributory to the problem, but a condition that has perdured so long is likely to have multiple and deep-seated causes. K. Horney notes a significant psychological problem. With the aid of sociological and anthropological data she shows that societies and "even men who consciously have a very positive relationship with women and hold them in high esteem as human beings, harbor deep within themselves a secret distrust of them. . . . Man's fear of woman is deeply rooted in sex, as is shown by the simple fact that it is only the sexually attractive woman of whom he is afraid and who, although he strongly desires her, has to be kept in bondage." (p. 112).

Another author (Callahan) holds "Woman's subordination . . . arose because, as an embodied projection of sexuality, she was considered mysteriously different and inferior. Only when sexuality is demythologized, accepted, and enjoyed, can women and woman's sexual functions be calmly accepted" (p. 14). Whether merely considered "mysteriously different and inferior" or "feared" the demythologizing of sex would seem for some to be the remedy needed if women are to be accepted as persons in the full sense of the word. It has become evident, therefore, that greater cooperation between theological and behavioral scientists is a prerequisite to the actual living of the radical NT teaching with its proclamation of freedom for all in Christ.

Discrimination against women still characterizes our male-centered and male-oriented culture. While battles rage in feminist circles, the Church has just begun to assess its own attitude toward women. Women admitted to sessions of Vatican II were accepted as observers only, even when major decisions regarding communities of religious women marked the agenda. The Church through local ordinaries in the U.S. has appointed women religious (as well as lay men) as extraordinary ministers of the Eucharist, with permission to distribute holy communion in case of emergency and within specific areas. The Congregation for the Doctrine of the Faith in 1977 repudiated the possibility of women's ordination. Nor may women receive institution to the lay ministries of reader or acolyte (Paul VI *motu proprio, Ministeria quaedam,* 1972). Yet in fact women, esp. religious women, are exercising a variety of ministries in the Church, as campus ministers, counsellors, ministers to the sick; some serve as vicars for religious, and in team ministry, with the title of "associate pastor."

Today, woman's traditional housewife and childbearing roles are in process of rapid occupational decline. Technology has provided woman with free time since World Wars I and II forced men to reassign many profitable industrial roles of amazing variety to her. For centuries Christianity's most revered image has been the image of Madonna and Child. Man esteemed woman as the necessary and glorious procreative function of society. Her human dignity stemmed chiefly from this role. While the "mother of many" achieved great status in human society, birth control, abortion, infanticide, and child abandonment or abuse were almost universally considered crimes against nature with appropriate punitive measures for prevention. Now, it seems that mankind has concluded from a threatened overpopulation that the uncontrolled fecundity of woman is "out" and abortion "in." Meanwhile the women's liberation movement and feminist groups like NOW (National Organization for Women, with an ecumenical task force on women and religion), Women's Ordination Conference, and the Catholic organization St. Joan's International Alliance, are attempting to prepare women for the heaviest burden known in history—the burden of their own freedom, a status to be gained through real political, legal, and economic equality.

BIBLIOGRAPHY: EDB 2594; P. Ketter, *Christ and Womankind* (tr. I. McHugh, 1952); S. C. Callahan, *Beyond Birth Control: The Christian Experience of Sex* (1968); M. Daly, *Church and the Second Sex* (1968); K. Horney, *Feminine Psychology* (ed. H. K. Kelman, 1967); *CTSA: Report on the Status of Women in Society: Considered in the Light of the Question of Women's Ordination* (ed. S. Butler, 1978); *Role of Women in Ecclesial Ministry: Biblical and Patristic Foundations* (ed. A. Cunningham, 1976); Pontifical Biblical Commission, *Report Origins* (1977) 92–96; Congregation for the Doctrine of the Faith, *Inter insigniores* (tr. *Declaration on the Question of the Admission of Women to the Ministerial Priesthood,* 1977); *Sexism and Church Law: Equal Rights and Affirmative Action* (ed. J. A. Coriden, 1977); *Women Priests, a Catholic Commentary on the Vatican Declaration* (ed. L. and A. Swidler, 1977); ThSt 36n.4 (1976), entire issue; Leadership Conference of Women Religious, *Status and Role of Women: Another Perspective* (1976); N. Foley, "Women Religious, Diagonal Communities," *Origins* 5 (1975) 180–187; C. Safilios-Rothschild, *Women and Social Policy* (1974); idem, *Women Working* (1978).

[M. F. R. CARTON; J. MORGAN]

WOMEN'S CHRISTIAN TEMPERANCE UNION (WCTU), a society for the encouragement of personal total abstinence based on Christian principles, and for the abolition of the liquor traffic. The idea for such a society came at a *Chautauqua meeting; organization was completed in Cleveland, Ohio, in 1874. Frances E. Willard (1839–98), who was first corresponding secretary, then president (1879–98), established branches throughout the U.S., and in 1883 formed the World's WCTU. She was a Methodist, and the organization received the strong support of the Methodist and other Protestant Churches. The WCTU, in spite of the setback represented by the repeal of the 18th Amendment, continues to work for its objectives. There are units in all the states and organizations for all age groups. Headquarters are in Evanston, Ill., where the Frances E.

Willard Memorial Library for Alcoholic Research is also located. BIBLIOGRAPHY: M. Earhart, *Frances Willard: From Progress to Politics* (1944). *TEMPERANCE MOVE-MENT.

[T. C. O'BRIEN]

WOODFORD, WILLIAM, see WILLIAM WOODFORD.

WOODHOUSE, THOMAS, BL. (d. 1573), English martyr. Ordained during the reign of Mary, W. resigned his parish because of Elizabeth's religious policy. Arrested while saying Mass, he was committed to the Fleet in 1561 where he remained. After negotiating by mail his admission to the Society of Jesus (1572), he was moved to write to Lord Burghley, exhorting him to persuade Elizabeth to submit to the pope. He was the first priest executed for high treason on solely religious grounds during the reign of Elizabeth. BIBLIOGRAPHY: Butler 2:587–588.

[V. SAMPSON]

WOODLOCK, THOMAS FRANCIS (1866–1945), journalist, financier. Born and educated in England, W. came to the U.S. in 1892 to join the Dow-Jones News Service and became editor of the *Wall Street Journal* in 1902. In 1905 he left the paper to become a member of the New York Stock Exchange for the next 13 years. He was appointed to the Interstate Commerce Commission in 1925 and left the commission in 1930 to return to the *Wall Street Journal* as a columnist. In addition to books on railroad economics, W. wrote *The Catholic Pattern* (1942). He contributed frequently to the archdiocesan weekly of New York, *The Catholic News* and to other Catholic periodicals. He was a recipient of the Univ. of Notre Dame's Laetare Medal.

[J. R. AHERNE]

WOOLLEY, CHARLES LEONARD (1880–1960), archeologist. W. devoted his life to archeological investigations in the Near East. He is best noted for his excavations at *Ur in southern Iraq, where he unearthed traces of the first settlement there in *c.*3700 B.C. and demonstrated the advanced state of Sumerian civilization. He wrote several scientific and popular books reporting his studies. BIBLIOGRAPHY: T. W. Buckley, NCE 14:1010.

[T. M. MCFADDEN]

WOOLMAN, JOHN (1720–72), American Quaker preacher. He was born in New Jersey, which was his home for most of his life. A tailor and shopkeeper, he became a minister in 1743, and thereafter made numerous journeys as a preaching Friend, becoming noted for his opposition to various social evils, esp. slavery. His *Some Considerations on the Keeping of Negroes* (1754) was one of the first antislavery works. To further his cause he traveled to England in 1772, and died at York. He is principally known for his *Journal* (1774), which records his "Life, Gospel-Labors, and Christian Experiences" after 1756. By virtue of its simplicity and strong religious feeling, it is considered a preeminent expression of the Quaker life. BIBLIOGRAPHY: *Journal and Essays of John Woolman,* ed. with a biographical introduction by A. M. Gummere (1922).

[T. EARLY]

WORCESTER, WILLIAM (1415–betw. 1480–83), English antiquarian. Secretary to Sir John Fastolf (d. 1459), W. was a prolific collector of historical and topographical materials and compiled a unique survey of his native Bristol. He also translated Cicero's *De senectute* from the French and wrote a *Boke of Noblesse.* BIBLIOGRAPHY: K. B. McFarlane, "William Worcester," *Studies Presented to Sir Hilary Jenkinson* (1957) 196–221.

[C. D. ROSS]

WORD OF GOD, key theme in the Judaeo-Christian revelation. To the Semitic mind, the spoken or written word has a quasi-sacramental force, i.e., it not only signifies, but in some sense renders present, permanent, and effective that which it signifies, giving it a reality that is abiding and irrevocable. In the word the psychic power of the speaker's own person is projected into the world. This is esp. true when the word concerned is a statement of his decision in some solemn matter such as a covenant or contract, and supremely true of vows, curses, and blessings, which, in various ways, have the power of determining the future. Thus Isaac could not revoke the blessing which he had pronounced upon Jacob (Gen 27). The woman suspected of adultery had to absorb into her own person the "bitter water" containing the words of the conditional curse that had been washed into it together with dust from the floor of the tabernacle. Again in its force as designating or signifying some object, it actually imparts a fulness of reality which that object would not otherwise possess. This is the function of the word as name.

All this applies with far greater force to the words of Yahweh, and esp. as uttered by his inspired prophets. Indeed "word" in this particular sense is the distinguishing prerogative of the prophet, as instruction is the prerogative of the priest, and counsel that of the sage. It is the word of revelation either as addressed by Yahweh to the prophets or as proclaimed by them in his name and by his power. The word of God in this sense embodies Yahweh's own power to create and to destroy. It is like a burning and irrepressible fire (Jer 20.7–9), like a sword (Is 49.2) or hammer (Jer 23.29); it is able "to pluck up and to break down, to destroy and to ruin, to build and to plant" (Jer 1.9–10). It endures forever (Is 30.8), is irrevocable (Ps 89.35–38; Jer 4.28), does not return to Yahweh "in vain" (Jos 21.45; 23.14; Is 45.23; 55.10–11). The fact that it is Yahweh's word guarantees that he personally will fulfil it of his own "faithfulness" (Num 23.19; Dt 9.5; Is 44.26).

The word is used to designate the most sacred elements of the law, esp. the decalogue (Ex 34.28; Dt 4.13), and law in general, esp. written law, is referred to as the "word of God" from Dt onwards. It is by his word in this sense that Yahweh creatively shapes the entire life of his people as a whole, and the lives of each individual member (Dt 30.19). The word as blessing has a creative and life-giving effect upon the people. It is a source of salvation to them (cf. Ps 119.25,49,107,154 etc.). The same word that rules Israel as her law dominates nature, too (Ps 147.15–18). It was by his word that Yahweh created the world and all that it contains (Gen 1 passim; Ps 33.6, 9, etc.), and by it he upholds and guides all the natural forces of the cosmos (Job 37.5–13; Ps 147.15–18).

Revelation, then, as imparted through the prophets, is designated as the word of God, and by extension the authors of Scripture themselves in their inspired writings convey this word of revelation, so that the canonical writings too come to be known as the word of God. In Mt and Mk the word of God, though referred to only infrequently, signifies the gospel of Jesus himself conceived of as the successor to the law and the prophets, the supreme revelation of Yahweh's will and purpose. In Lk this usage is more frequent (e.g., 5.1; 8.11,21; 11.28), and in Acts the phrase is often applied to the gospel as preached by the apostles (4.4,29–31; 6.4; 8.4; 10.44; 11.1,16; 10.36; 13.44,48; 13.26; 16.6,32; 17.11; 18.5 etc.). It is spoken of as something with an intrinsic vitality of its own. It grows and gains strength (Acts 19.20). Like the gospel it has power to save (13.26), to impart grace (20.32) and life (5.20), and the apostles are its ministers (6.4).

In Paul, too, the word of God is primarily the gospel (1 Cor 14.36; 2 Cor 2.17; 6.7; Gal 6.6; Eph 1.13; Phil 1.14 etc.). Here, too, the word has an active force in those who receive it by faith (1 Thess 2.13). It seems to be thought of as a prolongation or further projection of the event of salvation into the lives of believers. It is a seed planted in them in virtue of which they are born anew (Jas 1.21; 1 Pet 1.23).

In the Johannine writings, the phrase "word of God" refers not so much to the gospel as a whole, but to the words of the Father given to Jesus and actually uttered by him (cf. Jn 8.55; 12.47–50; 14.24; 17.8, etc.). But this word is also, in a peculiar sense, Jesus' own (Jn 5.24; 8.43,51; 12.47–50; 14.23; 15.20 etc.). This is an application of the distinctive Johannine teaching on the special unity between Jesus and the Father based ultimately on the conception enunciated in the prologue that Jesus himself is the Word. All the creative force attributed to the word of God in the OT achieves its final consummation by becoming incarnate in Jesus. Here the word is not merely mediated through a human intermediary as of old, but is actually uttered directly by the Father into this present world, to be the fulness of grace and truth. The background to this conception is to be sought initially and primarily in the Bible itself and not (except in a very secondary sense) in those extra-biblical writings that are often, but unconvincingly, invoked as precedents. BIBLIOGRAPHY: R. J. Tournay, A. Robert, J. Starcky, C. Mondésert, "Logos", DBSuppl. 5:425–497; G. Auzou, La Parole de Dieu (3d ed., 1962); P. R. Ackroyd, Vitality of the Word of God in the Old Testament, Annual of the Swedish Theological Institute 1 (1962) 7–23. *LOGOS.

[D. J. BOURKE]

WORDS OF INSTITUTION. The Church has solemnly defined that Christ instituted all seven sacraments (D 1601). And it is of faith that He immediately instituted them. Such institution involved establishing the rite and giving it the efficacy to bestow grace. Whether the institution was specific or generic as far as some of the sacraments are concerned is discussed among theologians. The words of institution would be, first of all, those words uttered by Christ in the act of establishing the sacraments. In English usage, moreover, "words of institution" is a phrase that refers to that part of the sacramental form that repeats the words that Christ used in the institution of the sacrament, e.g., This is My Body. BIBLIOGRAPHY: OED 5:354.

[E. A. WEIS]

WORDSWORTH, JOHN (1843–1911), Anglican bp. of Salisbury, Latin scholar, ecumenist. Elder son of Christopher Wordsworth, bp. of Lincoln, he was educated at Winchester and New College, Oxford, became a fellow of Brasenose College (1867), prebendary of Lincoln (1870), Bampton lecturer (1881); first Oriel Professor of the Interpretation of Holy Scripture, (1883–1885), bp. of Salisbury from 1885. He worked over 30 years to produce a critical edition of the Vulgate New Testament. As bp. he worked for reunion of the C of E with the Swedish and Old Catholic Churches, published two treatises on the validity of Anglican Orders, and in 1897 composed the Latin response sent by the abps. of Canterbury and York in reply to Pope Leo XIII's negative evaluation of Anglican Orders in *Apostolicae curae*.

[E. J. DILLON]

WORDSWORTH, WILLIAM (1770–1850), English poet, poet laureate (1843–1850). He had a daughter through a liaison with Annette Vallon in France (1791), but, prevented from returning to France by war, settled with his sister Dorothy at Racedown. Having settled matters with Annette, he married Mary Hutchinson (1802). Friendship with Coleridge crystallized his philosophy and stimulated his creative ability. With him he published Lyrical Ballads (1798), which contains some of his finest poems. The "Preface," 1800, and the poems themselves acted as a manifesto of the Romantic poets. His statement of the origin of poetry as "emotion recollected in tranquility" is valid when he recreates experience in language so that the reader relives the experience and feels the emotion, as in Michael (1800), and in parts of the autobiographical *Prelude* (1805–1850). His sonnets are among the best in English. BIBLIOGRAPHY: G. M. Harper, *William Wordsworth* (2 v., 1929); M. Moorman, *William Wordsworth, a Biography* (2 v., 1957–65).

[M. M. BARRY]

WORK, the labor or activity in which a person engages seriously, generally as a means of supporting himself and his dependents. Genesis represents creation as God's work (2.2), and man's work as a kind of continuation of God's creative activity (1.28). Even in the state of original happiness there was work to be done, and with the fall its performance became burdensome and painful by way of penalty (3:17–19). However, man's association with God in his work continued. For its accomplishment, he depends upon God (Ps 127:1–2) and prays for God's blessing upon it. Recognition of the obligation of work is thus deeply rooted in Judaic tradition; later rabbis, even though they were occupied in the study of the law, did not think themselves privileged to depend upon others for their support. In the NT Jesus himself appeared as a worker (Mk 6.3). Work was part of his obedience to his Father that accomplished our salvation. The NT goes beyond the OT in affirming that we are co-workers with God (1 Cor 3.9; 2 Cor 6.1; Mk 16.20). Work is seen as a service not only to men but to God also (Col 3.22–4.1; Eph 6.5–9) and a means of exercising the virtue of charity (Eph 4.28).

Philosophers have generally shown themselves antagonistic to physical work in the biblical sense. The harsher slavery of Greek and Roman civilization made physical toil seem a degrading thing. Both Platonism and Neoplatonism, which conceived man as a spirit tangled up with matter, urged him to free himself from his physical bonds and return by way of contemplation to his origins. This opposition between thought and action long marked Western tradition and vestiges of it remain, e.g., the traditional distinction between servile and liberal work employed by moralists and canonists in their interpretation of the obligation to rest on Sunday. In many monastic rules work was made obligatory, less however as a thing of value in itself than as an ascetical practice and as a means of earning one's livelihood.

Karl Marx proclaimed the ideal of restoring, not abolishing, work as a value: "until now the philosophers have been satisfied to contemplate the world; from now on, it is rather a question of transforming it."

The Fathers and schoolmen developed no satisfactory theology of work, although in scattered places there is evidence of their appreciation of certain ideas basic to the development of such a theology (see, e.g., Augustine, *De opere monachorum*, PL 40.547–580; ThAq ST 2a2ae, 187.3). St. Thomas wrote pregnantly on work (*opus*) as the proper interest of man as an artist (cf. ThAq ST la2ae, 57.3–4, esp. in ed. Lat-Eng, ed. W. D. Hughes, 1969), and the distinction between *opus*, which is in no sense a curse,

and *onus* or *labor* is highly relevant to the conditions of a leisure society brought about by automation.

A contemporary treatment of work must respond to the completely new experience of an industrial civilization, and will have to draw less on scriptural texts and past philosophical and theological writings, but on the broad lines of revelation and salvation history for its systematization. Such a theology of work should be concrete and not abstract; it should be normative; it should give pride of place to a new understanding of the dynamic unity of nature and grace by transcending the Augustinian theory of giving work a value by the devout intention of the worker; finally, it should base itself on an anthropology that rejects any implied opposition of body and soul. Man created to the image of God shares in his divine work within and recapitulates the work of the Son in coming to earth and leading men back to the Father. Thus the theology of work would be based on the biblical vision of eschatology and the theological teaching of hope. In the Christian view, work must be seen as something that brings together the people of God in order that they may be led into glory. BIBLIOGRAPHY: A. Richardson, *Biblical Doctrine of Work* (1952); M. D. Chenu, *Theology of Work* (tr. L. Soron, 1963); *Work* (ed. J. M. Todd, 1958); E. G. Kaiser, *Theology of Work* (1966).

WORKER PRIESTS, a phenomenon of postwar France and Belgium (1944–1954), wherein a number of priests took jobs as workers. They labored mostly in factories, set aside their clerical garb, and shared the living conditions and the social and economic problems of workers. Some were diocesan, some religious priests. They lived alone or in small communities of two or three and supported themselves through their labor. They attempted to form Christian cells among the workers on the job, joined whatever unions effectively enhanced the workers' situation, shared in various manifestations of solidarity in the struggle for decent working conditions, wages, and housing, and were partners in the broader struggle against racism and for peace. The experiment had many origins: the experience of the young priests who clandestinely joined the French youth who were deported to the factories of Germany during the Nazi occupation, (see Henri Perrin, *Prêtre-ouvrier en Allemagne* [1945]; Eng. tr., *Priest-Workman in Germany* [1947]; the experience of the special mission to the working–class neighborhoods (Mission de France), (as reflected in Abbé Godin's electrifying report, *France pays de mission?*), and in the writings and teachings of intellectuals such as J. Maritain and Card. E. Suhard of Paris, who were keenly aware of the chasm separating the Church and modern man. The worker priests were part of a broader movement that included the Young Christian Workers of the 30s, movements of adult lay Christians, secular institutes, and the new religious communities inspired by the life and spirituality of Charles de Foucauld. Although the priest workers were given assistance by Card. Suhard and although those who entered the "experiment" considered it a vocation entered upon for life, the hostility was such, from conservative lay and clerical quarters and from the Roman Curia, that Rome intervened, under Pius XII in 1953–54, to stop the experiment. The Roman intervention directly affected the French priests, indirectly the Belgians. The priest workers were stopped, but the mission to the workers continued; and in some respects the original experiment continued in low profile or went underground. The French bishops were also unobtrusive in their guidance of the renewed Mission de France. Rome, under John XXIII, felt constrained to intervene again in 1959 to further restrict the kinds of work deemed suitable for priestly ministry. In 1965 Paul VI approved the concept of priest workers in extremely modified form. The extent and intensity of the opposition to such a limited movement, never numbering more than 100 priests, shows the depth of both lay and clerical attachment to a clerical subculture of dignity, leisure, and privilege and to the existing, formalized apparatus of ministry. Still the experiment is not ended. At a congress of the renewed Mission de France held in 1974, it was found that of the 325 priests in this apostolate to workers, 85% were themselves working, in a variety of jobs including work in factories, hospitals, the merchant marine, and schools; that this was an increase from the 15% who had held jobs in 1964; that the movement had spread beyond France to Algeria, black Africa, and Latin America, where priests were often involved in liberation movements, living in teams, either serving Christian communities or still waiting for such communities to emerge. Independently from the French and Belgian experiment, a Spanish movement became apparent in 1967, when 10 priests were arrested during student and labor demonstrations. It was divulged that at least 50 priests were working as taxi drivers, bricklayers, miners, and factory workers in Madrid, Bilbao, Barcelona, and smaller industrial centers in Asturias, Galicia, and Barcelona. Bishops were willing to support them if they maintained a low profile. Seminarians would join them during vacations or weekends. The abp. of Oviedo set up a diocesan center for them. Opposition from the Spanish upper-class and from middle-class intellectuals was intense. Even lay leaders considered the approach outdated. The priests insisted they preferred to earn their own bread and not add to the burdens of workers by living on free-will offerings. BIBLIOGRAPHY: J.-M. Ploux, *Études* 34599 (1974) 614; J. Somnet, *Month* 223 (1967) 363–367; G. Siefer, *La Mission des prêtres-ouvriers: Les faits et conséquences* (1963).

[E. J. DILLON]

WORLD (IN THE BIBLE), Old Testament. It is generally regarded as significant that Hebrew contains no single word for world or cosmos in the sense conceived of in Western civilizations from that of ancient Greece onwards. Even the phrase heaven and earth is not equivalent to cosmos in our sense. In place of the Greek conception of the unified and harmonious cosmic order Hebrew man tends to think of the world he knows as the center and sum of a number of conflicting forces. If we could reconstruct any unified conception of the world from the relevant passages (many of them representing different, and often conflicting traditions) it might be summarized somewhat as follows:

Earth is conceived of as a flat disc or expanse (cf. Ps 136.6) supported on pillars (1 Sam 2.8; 2 Sam 22.16; Ps 75.3; Job 9.6). Beneath it are the waters of the lower abyss or subterranean ocean (cf. Ex 20.4; Ps 136.6, etc.; 24.2, etc.), while above it are the waters of the upper abyss, from which are drawn the rain and dew that irrigate the earth. Originally these two "waters" constituted a single vast primeval ocean, but they were divided from one another and are kept apart by the "firmament of heaven." This is conceived of as a vast inverted lapis lazuli bowl based upon the extremities of the earth. At these outward extremities lie the "islands of the nations" (cf. Is 40.15), the "eternal hills" (Dt 33.15; Hab 3.6), between which the sun and moon rise and take their alternate courses (Ps 19.5 ff.; Hab 3.11; Job 9.7), and in which are the storerooms of snow, hail storm, clouds, etc., (Job 38 *passim*). In the extreme north is located a mountain which is raised high above the rest, reaching right up to the dwelling place of God himself (Is 14.13; Job 26.7). In the firmament are fixed the stars and planets (cf. Gen 1.6–8; Ex 24.10; Is 34.4). Above it and the heavenly sea of the upper abyss is the dwelling-place of God himself (Ps 33.13–14; 104.3; Is 63.15). Below the waters of the lower abyss lies the underworld or Sheol, the dwelling-place of the dead.

It is only in the later Wisdom books, where Greek influences are already at work that the word cosmos appears. The concept of God as creator (cf. 2 Macc 7.23; 13.14; Wis 9.9, etc.) and ruler (cf. 2 Macc 7.6; 12.16) of the world is still retained, but now emphasis is laid on the fact that the entire universe has a unified and harmonious structure (cf. Wis 7.17) and on the fact that it is actively engaged in God's war against wickedness (cf. Wis 5.21). In other passages it is clear that cosmos signifies not the entire universe but earth alone, which man has been created to preside over (cf. Wis 9.3), but which has been invaded by death and idolatry (cf. Wis 2.24; 14.14). Finally the word cosmos is also used in contexts where it clearly signifies humanity, as when we are told that Adam is the father of the world (Wis 10.1), Noah its hope (Wis 14.6) and the wise its salvation (Wis 6.24).

New Testament. Perhaps the fullest expression of what cosmos means in the NT occurs in Acts: "The God who made the world and everything in it, being Lord of heaven and earth . . ." (17.24), "the heaven and the earth and the sea and everything in them" (Acts 4.24). The cosmos was made through the Word (Jn 1.10). A more developed idea of creation *ex nihilo* than any found in the OT appears to underlie such passages as Col 1.15–17. The cosmos had a beginning (Mt 24.21) or foundation (Mt 25.34; Lk 11.50; Jn 17.24; Eph 1.4; Heb 4.3 etc.) and is, of its nature, transient and destined to pass away (cf. Mt 3.40; Eph 2.2; 1 Cor

7.31, etc.). It is therefore valueless in comparison with the salvation of the soul (Mt 16.26; Mk 8.36; Lk 9.25). The world is also thought of as the scene of human life and activity, as consisting of kingdoms (Mt 4.8) and nations (Lk 12.30), as identical with mankind itself, to which the apostles are sent (Mt 26.13; Mk 16.15; cf. Rom 1.8).

Cosmos also has a pejorative connotation. It stands for the world of men as alien or even hostile to God, so that it becomes a Christian's duty to "keep himself unspotted from the world" (Jas 1.27), and to recognize that "friendship with the world is enmity with God" (Jas 4.4). The values of the world are so radically false that "the wisdom of this world is folly with God" (1 Cor 3.19; cf. 1.20–21, 26–28). It has been corrupted and made subject to condemnation by reason of the sin introduced into it by Adam (Rom 5.12) and now pervading it throughout.

The opposition between the world and God is still more sharply stated in John. Christ came into the world (Jn 3.17; 9.39 etc.) to fulfill the loving decision of his Father to save it (Jn 3.16—). He is its light (Jn 1.9; 3.19, etc.), the Lamb who takes away its sin (Jn 1.29) and who gives it his life (Jn 6.33). Yet the world is in darkness, ruled over by a power hostile to God (Jn 16.11), hating Jesus (Jn 7.7; 15.18) and refusing to acknowledge either himself or his Father (Jn 1.10; 17.25).

The message of the NT, therefore, is that the Christian must live in the world and, in spite of its hostility, maintain unswervingly the attitude of love that Christ showed toward it. Yet he must never allow himself to adopt its attitudes or values. BIBLIOGRAPHY: H. Sasse, Kittel TD 3:867–896 s.v. "kosmos"; C. R. North, InterDB (1962) 4:873–878.

[D. J. BOURKE]

WORLD ALLIANCE OF REFORMED CHURCH-ES, a shorter alternate title for the Alliance of the Reformed Churches throughout the World Holding the Presbyterian Order; it is also named the World Presbyterian Alliance.

WORLD CONGRESS OF THE LAY APOSTO-LATE, an organization founded after the First World Congress of the Lay Apostolate held in Rome in 1951 to carry out the resolutions of that meeting. The Permanent Committee for World Congresses of the Lay Apostolate was established by the Holy See in 1952. Subsequent congresses have met in Rome in 1957, 1967, and 1975. There have been spinoff regional conferences. The 1967 assembly created controversy by its recommendation to the concomitant 1967 Synod of Bishops. The 1975 meeting was milder and convened as the World Consultation on the Laity. The Second World Congress met in 1957. John XXIII in 1959 appointed a nine-member, lay board of directors for the organization. Vatican II's emphasis on the laity has increased the importance of these congresses. Any future assemblies will be held under the direction of the Pontifical Council on the Laity.

[J. R. AHERNE]

WORLD CONVENTION OF CHURCHES OF CHRIST, an agency formed in 1930 for communication and fellowship for the Christian Churches (Disciples of Christ) throughout the world. Membership of the churches served by the World Convention was over 2,500,000, in 33 countries, in 1968. The organization also serves the aim of unity with other Christians on a NT basis. Assemblies of the World Convention are held every 5 years; headquarters are in New York City.

[T. C. O'BRIEN]

WORLD COUNCIL OF CHRISTIAN EDUCATION (WCCE), a service agency founded in 1907 to link together the Christian church bodies of all countries dealing with religious education. With 71 member units and 5 associated regional organizations, WCCE is devoted to the development of more effective educational programs and competent leadership by the provision of educational aids and training materials, by educational consultations and studies, and by international educational institutes. Its program revolves esp. around improved biblical studies and the encouragement of interdenominational cooperation toward Christian unity. In 1967 it presented to the Bristol meeting of the World Council of Churches' *Faith and Order Commission a detailed program for ecumenical commitment in Christian education.

[D. CODDINGTON]

WORLD COUNCIL OF CHURCHES (WCC), an international, interconfessional organization of Christian Churches designed to facilitate unity in fellowship, service, and mission. Headquarters are in Geneva, Switzerland. The WCC at its beginning defined itself as "a fellowship of Churches which accept our Lord Jesus Christ as God and Savior." In 1961 at the *New Delhi Assembly this was expanded to "a fellowship of Churches which confess the Lord Jesus Christ as God and Savior according to the Scriptures and therefore seek to fulfill together their common calling to the glory of the one God, Father, Son, and Holy Spirit." The WCC was formally constituted Aug. 23, 1948, at the *Amsterdam Assembly. Groundwork for the organization had been laid at a 1938 meeting in Utrecht, but World War II intervened, and until the Amsterdam Assembly the letterhead of the organization carried the line "in process of formation." At Utrecht, Abp. W. *Temple (1881–1944) was elected chairman of the Provisional Committee, and W. A. Visser't Hooft, secretary; in 1948 the latter became the first general secretary of the WCC. The WCC represented the union of two lines of ecumenical development, *Life and Work and *Faith and Order. Life and Work, led initially by Abp. N. *Söderblom, sponsored the *Stockholm (1925) and *Oxford (1937) Conferences, which sought a unity of Christian efforts, despite doctrinal differences, toward the solution of various problems of society. Faith and Order, led initially by Bp. C. H. *Brent (1862–1929), sponsored the Lausanne (1927) and Edinburgh (1937) Conferences, which sought to deal with doctrinal differences. At the Oxford and Edinburgh Conferences both groups, which included many of the same individuals, decided that the two aspects of the ecumenical movement could not properly be separated, so plans were laid that led to the organization of the WCC; the name was suggested by S. M. Cavert, an American ecumenist. At the New Delhi Assembly a third line of ecumenical development, represented by the *International Missionary Council (IMC), merged with the WCC, becoming the Division of World Mission and Evangelism.

The highest authority of the WCC is the General Assembly, which normally meets every 7th year. Between assemblies the WCC is guided by a central committee of 100 members, normally meeting once a year, and a smaller executive committee, which normally meets twice a year. The WCC has a presidium composed of six presidents, who are chosen to give broad representation, geographically and confessionally. The full-time executive staff is headed by the general secretary. Eugene Carson Blake, former Stated Clerk of the United Presbyterian Church, succeeded Visser't Hooft as general secretary in 1966. The WCC is not itself a Church; nor does it exercise the authority of a Church. Membership in the WCC does not require that a Church recognize other member communions as Churches in the full sense, that it accept the full validity of their ministries, or that it practice *intercommunion with them. The WCC is an organizational means for the members to work together in service projects, to meet together for deeper fellowship and mutual understanding, and to present a more united witness in preaching the gospel. The WCC continues the work of those lines of ecumenical development that it incorporates, sponsors such projects as the Christian Student Movement and Church World Service, and maintains the Ecumenical Institute at Chateau de Bôssey, near Geneva. Statements on various subjects issued by the WCC are not binding on the member bodies.

The membership of the WCC currently embraces most of the Christian Churches of the world, about 225 in 1968, including most of the Eastern Orthodox Churches. Some conservative groups have chosen not to seek membership, fearing that it would mean compromise of doctrinal conviction and that the WCC might become a centralized, authoritarian organization that would endanger freedom. In the U.S. the Southern Baptist Convention, the Lutheran Church—Missouri Synod, and several smaller conservative bodies have remained outside. Liberal groups, such as the Unitarians, are prevented from belonging because they do not meet the WCC requirement of belief in Jesus Christ as God and Savior. Some conservatives, although they favor ecumenical cooperation, oppose the WCC because its leadership includes some whom they consider too liberal in doctrine, and because they object to positions taken by WCC leadership on contemporary social issues (see WORLD EVANGELICAL FELLOWSHIP; INTERNATIONAL COUNCIL OF CHRISTIAN CHURCHES).

Roman Catholics, although invited to attend the Amster-dam Assembly, were forbidden to do so by a *monitum* of the Holy Office. In 1928 after the Stockholm and Lausanne Conferences, Pius XI declared, ''The Apostolic See can by no means take part in these assemblies nor is it in any way lawful for Catholics to give such enterprises their encouragement and support. If they did so, they would be giving countenance to a false Christianity quite alien to the one Church of Christ.'' With the coming of Vatican II, however, and the change of atmosphere associated with John XXIII, official RC observers were sent to the New Delhi Assembly, and WCC observers were invited to, and attended, Vatican II. In 1965 Paul VI and the WCC established a joint continuing committee to work on a regular basis for dialogue and cooperation. Nine of the official RC observers at the Uppsala Assembly (1968) were elected to membership on the Faith and Order Commission. On a visit to WCC headquarters at Geneva on June 10, 1969, Paul VI stated that the question of RC membership in the WCC was not yet mature. RC participation increased at the Nairobi Assembly (1975). This Assembly considered as themes: Jesus Christ Who Frees and Unites; the African Challenge; Unity; Faith; Women in a Changing World; Liberation; Technology and Human Survival. BIBLIOGRAPHY: official reports of the Assemblies ed. by W. A. Visser't Hooft and D. M. Paton, *Breaking Barriers Nairobi, 1975* (1976); G. K. A. Bell, *Kingship of Christ* (1954).

[T. EARLY]

WORLD COUNCIL OF CHURCHES, ORTHODOX PARTICIPATION IN, the impact of the Orthodox communions on the formation and progress of the World Council of Churches (WCC). Eastern representatives were in on the formative conferences from the start, esp. in the *Faith and Order conferences. Between the world wars, ecumenical discussions continued to attract members of various Orthodox communions. Many of the Russian diaspora sought allies in their struggle against hostile government policies. By the time the WCC was formally created (1948), however, only the Patriarchate of Constantinople and the Church of Greece joined, with the Russian-dominated communions holding aloof. In 1961 the Patriarchate of Moscow applied for membership, and the other autocephalous Churches followed suit. The Orthodox representatives have repeatedly affirmed their basic conviction that the basis of unity among Christians is the primitive apostolic faith from which the Orthodox Churches have never departed. Their presence in the WCC is to facilitate and enrich discussion among all Christians concerning the best way of restoring the lost unity, and concerning problems of common action and witness in the modern world. No aspect of the WCC is untouched by the special impact of the Orthodox experience of faith.

[E. J. DILLON]

WORLD COUNCIL OF CHURCHES, UNITED STATES CONFERENCE FOR THE, an organization of the Churches in the U.S. that are members of the *World

Council of Churches (WCC). It is a continuation of the American Comm. for the WCC established in 1938, when plans were first laid for the formation of the WCC. When the WCC was formally constituted at the 1948 *Amsterdam Assembly, the Committee was renamed the Conference of U.S.A. Member Churches of the WCC, and the name was later changed to its present form. The Conference meets annually and is composed of the delegates and alternates from the U.S. Churches to the preceding general assembly of the WCC. Normally one of the presidents of the WCC is American and serves as chairman of the Conference. The Conference employs a full-time staff—the only regional conference of the WCC to do so—and its offices are at 475 Riverside Drive, New York City. The Conference promotes the work of the WCC in the U.S. and works to raise the U.S. portion of the WCC budget (currently about $600,000 annually, more than half the total), as well as its own budget of about $100,000. The Conference serves as the coordinating link between WCC headquarters in Geneva and the U.S. member Churches. It is to be distinguished from the *National Council of Churches, which cooperates with the WCC and has generally the same membership but is an independent organization.

[T. EARLY]

WORLD COUNCIL OF SYNAGOGUES (CONSERVATIVE),

an international organization of synagogues, an expression of the Conservative movement in Judaism, which embraces like-minded synagogues all over the world. In its biennial meetings it brings together synagogue leaders of 22 different countries and observers from many more, to discuss problems of mutual interest. The association was organized in 1957 by the United Synagogue of America, an association of Conservative synagogues in the U.S. and Canada which was itself founded in 1913 by Solomon Schechter, president of the Jewish Theological Seminary, in the hope of strengthening "historical Judaism" in the U.S. and as far as possible unifying the entire Jewish community. Maxwell Abbell (1902–57), who had been president of the United Synagogues of America (1950–53), was a key founder of the World Council of Synagogues (1957). The council maintains offices in N.Y., Argentina, and Israel. The existence of the organization has facilitated the movement of Conservative rabbis from one country to another.

[E. J. DILLON]

WORLD EVANGELICAL FELLOWSHIP,

an association formed at Woudschoten, Holland, in 1951. The Fellowship regards the *World Council of Churches as too liberal, and the *International Council of Churches as reactionary. Headquarters in 1968 were maintained in Don Mills, Ont., Canada, with an editorial office in London. Among the affiliates are the *Evangelical Alliance and the *National Association of Evangelicals.

WORLD HEALTH ORGANIZATION (WHO),

United Nations agency with responsibility for the improvement of world health conditions; headquarters are in Geneva. Its constitution was drafted at a New York conference held in 1946 at the request of the UN Economic and Social Council, and it came into formal existence in 1948 after ratification by the 25th-member government. WHO was established as a successor to the Health Organization of the League of Nations (established 1923) and the International Office of Public Health, Paris (established 1909). The constitution defines its objective as "attainment by all peoples of the highest possible level of health," which it calls "one of the fundamental rights of every human being without distinction of race, religion, political belief, economic or social condition." WHO's constitution also declares that health is "a state of complete physical, mental, and social well-being and not merely the absence of disease or infirmity." The organization provides governments with information related to health, stimulates research, conducts programs to eradicate disease, seeks to improve sanitation standards, promotes adherence to uniform standards in such areas as health statistics, and works to strengthen public health programs, particularly in Africa, Asia, and Latin America. Religious organizations, including the Vatican, have associated themselves with its work in a variety of ways.

[T. EARLY]

WORLD METHODIST COUNCIL,

a federation of Methodist bodies for promoting ecumenical, evangelistic, educational, and historical emphases among autonomous Methodist bodies in 86 different countries. The functions of this agency are fraternal and cooperative, and it has no legislative powers. Named the World Methodist Council in 1951, it is the successor to the Ecumenical Methodist Conference, which convened at 10-year intervals from 1881. Permanent secretaries were established in 1951, one in England and one in the U.S., and a slate of officers and representatives was chosen as a World Executive Committee to sponsor a World Methodist Conference every 5 years and to carry on the work of the organization in the interim. Headquarters were established at Lake Junaluska, N.C., in 1953. Among its activities the Council has helped sponsor a series of publications including *Who's Who in Methodism* (1952) and published *World Encyclopedia of Methodism* (2v. 1974). The Council supervises ministerial exchanges among Methodists of different countries, and has established the Oxford Theological Institute, a quadrennial meeting of 100 selected Methodist theologians at Lincoln College, Oxford. The Council named the Methodist observers to Vatican Council II. Its official periodical is *World Parish*.

[F. E. MASER]

WORLD METHODIST HISTORICAL SOCIETY

has a fivefold purpose which includes sponsoring periodic conferences among Methodist and Methodist-related bodies who are interested in Methodist history. It was first organized in 1911 under the name of the Methodist Historical Union. In 1947 it became known as The International Methodist Historical Society, and in 1951 it began quinquennial meetings, usually at the site of the World Methodist Conferences sponsored by the *World Methodist Council. Over the next two decades the Society aided in the publication of numerous scholarly works on Methodist history and in the preservation of several important Methodist landmarks.

In August 1971 at a meeting in Denver, Colorado, the organization was renamed the World Methodist Historical Society and a new constitution was approved. Its organization included a president and five vice presidents representing different parts of the world. Frederick E. Maser was elected its executive secretary. The quinquennial meetings were continued, and in the interim, regional conferences were held in various sections of the world. In December 1971 a news bulletin was launched. The current executive secretary is Dr. John H. Ness, Jr. Headquarters of the Society are in the World Methodist Building, Lake Junaluska, North Carolina, U.S. BIBLIOGRAPHY: "International Methodist Historical Society," *Encyclopedia of World Methodism* (1974); F. Baker, "Origins of the World Methodist Historical Society," *News Bulletin WMHS*, v. 1, No. 1 (1971).

[F. E. MASER]

WORLD PARLIAMENT OF RELIGIONS, 17-day gathering held in Chicago in September 1893, bringing together representatives of the major world religions. It was organized as part of the Chicago Fair (World's Columbian Exposition) commemorating the 400th anniversary of Columbus's discovery. The gathering was important in helping Americans become better acquainted with Eastern religions and forms of religious thought. Among the visitors coming to the U.S. for the event was the Hindu Swami Vivekananda of India, who remained to found the Vedanta Society in 1897; *Bahai was also first brought to the U.S. through the Chicago gathering.

[T. EARLY]

WORLD PRESBYTERIAN ALLIANCE, shortened title of the *Alliance of the Reformed Churches throughout the World Holding the Presbyterian Order.

WORLD-SOUL. The idea of the world being animated and governed by spiritual forces is found not only among primitive peoples, but from the early days of Greek philosophy. The notion of a world-soul (*anima mundi*) was developed esp. by Plato in his *Timaeus*. The world-soul has an intermediary role between the Ideas and the material world. This soul is the principle of order and life governing the material world, but is superior to the latter in origin and nobility. It presides also over the movement of heaven and the stars and is the source from which the Demiurge derives individual souls (*Tim.* 41D–42). The Stoics made the *pneuma* the physical and rational principle of order and generation in the world, which is supported by a power they call *animum mundi* (Cic. *De nat. deor.* 2.7.19) and identify with God.

From this principle the Stoics derive their *logoi spermatikoi* or "seminal reasons" (*rationes seminales*). In Neoplatonism, beginning with Plotinus, the world-soul is made the connecting link between the suprasensory world and the sensory world, between the *Nous* and matter. In its higher part it turns its gaze upon the *Nous,* but in its lower part it looks down to the world of Nature; creates the world of Nature in accordance with the ideas contemplated in the *Nous* (*Enneads* 3.8.4). The Early Christian writers and Fathers were familiar with the concept of the world-soul that permeated all later Hellenic philosophical and religious thought. The Greek Fathers found a parallel for the Holy Spirit in the world-soul of the Neoplatonists, but the Latins, and esp. Augustine, were much more reserved in this respect. In the Renaissance, there was a marked revival of the concept of the world-soul, beginning with M. *Ficino. It was stressed as an active and autonomous principle of Nature, and esp. by *Agrippa, *Paracelsus, G. *Bruno, and T. *Campanella. In the 17th cent., the doctrine in one form or another was held by a number of thinkers throughout Europe. A special impetus was given to the doctrine by the alchemists and other pseudo-scientists and scientists before the rise of modern chemistry. The basic teaching of *Panpsychism is somewhat related to the doctrine of the world-soul. BIBLIOGRAPHY: T. Gregory, G. Tonelli, NCE 14:1027–29; Eisler 3:509–511; T. Gregory, *Anima Mundi* (1955); A. J. Festugière, *La Révélation d'Hermès Trismégiste.* 2, *Le Dieu cosmique* (1949). *MACROCOSM AND MICROCOSM.

[M. R. P. MCGUIRE]

WORLD STUDENT CHRISTIAN FEDERATION, a union of national student Christian movements organized at Vadstena, Sweden, in 1895 to aid in building and strengthening a multiracial, ecumenical witnessing-community of Christians in institutions of higher learning throughout the world. With headquarters in Geneva, Switzerland, it now embraces student organizations in more than 75 countries. It is affiliated with the international YMCA and YWCA, as well as with the World Council of Christian Education and the World Council of Churches; it maintains relations with other international student groups, such as Pax Romana and the World Union of Jewish Students, and enjoys consultative status in the United Nations' Educational, Scientific, and Cultural Organization (UNESCO).

[D. CODDINGTON]

WORLD UNION FOR PROGRESSIVE JUDAISM, international organization founded at London in 1926 to unite and foster Reform (Progressive, Liberal) Judaism. It comprises congregations and associations with about 1,100,000 members in 25 countries. The majority of members are in the U.S., whose Reform congregations organized the Union of American Hebrew Congregations in 1873. The World Union assists new congregations, publishes literature, holds biennial international conferences, and carries out various other activities to further its aims. Headquarters were in London from 1926 to 1960; since then they have been in New York.

[T. EARLY]

WORLD UNION OF CATHOLIC WOMEN'S OR-GANIZATIONS, an association of Catholic women's groups from around the world. From small beginnings in 1910, the Union has grown to nearly 40,000,000 members. The purpose of the organization is to represent the Catholic view, esp. in areas of concern to women, and to bring to bear the influence of Catholic women on international bodies, such as the United Nations, where the Union has consultative status with the Economic and Social Council, UNESCO, UNICEF, the Food and Agricultural Organization and the International Labor Office. It is represented also on the Council of Europe and the Organization of American States.

Internal structure calls for each affiliated organization to elect delegates to the general meeting each two years. A board of directors meets twice a year. There is a permanent secretariat located in Paris.

[J. R. AHERNE]

WORLDLINESS. The double-meaning of ''world'' in the Scriptures, the one in opposition to God, the other ''so loved'' by him, has set up a tension between world-rejection and world-acceptance running throughout Christian thought and practice, and now thrusting to this side, now to that. The dialectic still continues. Christ's kingdom is a challenge to this world, which killed him, though to its own defeat or, rather, reformation. He warns us against gaining the world and losing our soul (Mt 16.26), and St. Paul repeatedly commands us not to be conformed to it (e.g. Rom 12.2). To Johannine and patristic theology it is a vast and threatening conspiracy of evil influences (cf. 1 Jn 5.20). Nowadays ''worldliness'' means something much more trivial, though when this is systematically diffused by our apparatus of persuasion, the effect, if less dramatic, is scarcely less sapping. So Christians are urged not to be of this world, though they are in it. However, spiritual writing has its journalese and, understandably, a rhetoric that can be somewhat over-shrill about vile and pernicious worldly influences: sometimes the other-worldliness inculcated turns out to be still a this-worldliness, though prim and protected and stocked with sacred rather than profane images. The worldly, *mundanum, kosmikon*, is not a key-notion for St. Thomas Aquinas: he takes notice of St. Paul on the ''prudence of the flesh'' (Rom 8.7) and St. John on all in the world being ''the lust of the flesh, and the lust of the eyes, and the pride of life'' (1 Jn 2.16); but the true problem appears in his analysis, thoroughly non-Manichean, of moral evil. This is not just a negative, a turning away from God, but a privative, constituted by a turning to a creaturely good instead: the adverb is crucial. The sin lies in the attachment as a substitute for the loving God. What is wrong in worldliness

are the idols it sets up. The two great commands of charity (Mt 22.37–39) state the right order: we should love God's world in him. That is to love things as they really are, namely creatures. If we are totally committed to him, we shall be found no less engaged than others with his world. It is a case, not confined to the religious situation, of being detached and of thereby being more attached. In this ''holy worldliness,'' as it has been called, with more accuracy than geniality, we are esp. aided by the gifts of the Holy Spirit, notably ''knowledge'' (ThAq ST 2a2ae, 9), to which theological tradition attaches the beatitude, ''Blessed are they that mourn, for they shall be comforted'' (Mt 5.4). ThAq ST 1a2ae, 75 and 77 (esp. in ed. Lat-Eng v. 27, ed. J. Fearon, 1969); R. Gregory Smith, *Secular Christianity* (1966), D. Bonhoeffer, *Letters and Papers from Prison* (3d ed., 1967).

[T. GILBY]

WORLD'S CHRISTIAN ENDEAVOR UNION, an agency formed in 1895 to coordinate the activities and interests of the member organizations of the Christian Endeavor movement throughout the world. *CHRISTIAN ENDEAVOR, INTERNATIONAL SOCIETY OF.

[T. C. O'BRIEN]

WORMS, CONCORDAT OF, the compromise agreement in 1122 between Pope Calixtus II and Emperor Henry V ending the *investiture struggle. Each side retreated from previous extreme positions and granted concessions. Elections of bishops and abbots were to be free and canonical; in Germany the emperor could attend and resolve disputes. He was permitted to invest churchmen with their properties and civil responsibilities, but consecration and investiture with spiritual authority could come only at the hands of proper church officials. In Germany, investiture was to precede consecration; in Italy and Burgundy, to follow. In sum, the Concordat distinguished between the civil and the spiritual rights and duties of bishops.

[R. H. SCHMANDT]

WORMS, COUNCIL OF, site for a long series of councils and diets during the period of the Holy Roman Empire. The council of 1122 arranged the Concordat of Worms between the Emperor Henry V and Pope Callistus II, settling the investiture controversy. At the Diet of 1521, Martin Luther defended his position before the Emperor, Charles V. When Luther refused to recant, the diet issued the famous Edict of Worms which formally condemned his writings. BIBLIOGRAPHY: E. P. Colbert, NCE 14:1029–30.

[B. L. MARTHALER]

WORMS, DIET OF, in Reformation history the sessions of the Imperial Diet, Jan. 27–May 25, 1521, before which Martin Luther was summoned to defend his teaching. That this civil body sat in judgment on doctrinal issues was not in accord with papal views or wishes, but it served the national interest to solve the problems raised by Luther in Germany. The papal legate at Worms, Aleander, urged the implementation of the excommunication of Luther already given at Rome (see EXSURGE DOMINE). Luther appeared in the presence of Emperor Charles V, on April 17–18. On the first day, before a small committee of the Diet, he requested more time to deliberate about his own subscription to what he had written, esp. against the sacraments and the primacy of the pope. On the second, before the whole assembly, he made his refusal to recant in a statement that tradition quotes in the words, "Here I stand. I can do no other," rejecting popes and councils and appealing to his conscience, captive to the word of God. On May 25 the Edict of Worms was signed by the Emperor, making Luther liable to punishment by burning for subverting the established order. But before that Luther had been given refuge in the *Wartburg.

[T. C. O'BRIEN]

WORMS, DISPUTATION OF, conference on reunion held at the Diet of Worms between Catholics and Protestants, begun in Nov. 1540 and terminated in Jan. 1541. Most of the time was spent on procedural matters. Finally, with J. *Eck the spokesman for the Catholics and P. *Melanchthon for the Protestants, a discussion based on the *Augsburg Confession was conducted. A formula of agreement on *original sin was reached, but the Emperor Charles V transferred the discussion to the Conference of *Regensburg. BIBLIOGRAPHY: Jedin Trent 1:374–377.

[T. C. O'BRIEN]

WORSHIP, the exhibition to God by some act of mind or body, or both, of the honor and reverence due to him by reason of his supreme dominion. Such acts may be private or public and communal. Different forms of worship include, with varying emphasis, confession and repentance for sin, praise, petition, and thanksgiving. Among Roman Catholics the term has been applied not only to the cultic acts due to God alone (*latria*), but also to those rendered to his saints because of their special relationship to him (*dulia*). In later usage, however, the term is more commonly restricted to the kind of reverence shown only to God, and, to avoid misleading ambiguity, the honor exhibited to the saints is generally spoken of as veneration. Among Protestants the word is sometimes used to distinguish one form of service from another, e.g., a worship, as distinguished from a preaching, service; in Catholic practice the specific forms of service are generally designated by their proper names.

[P. K. MEAGHER]

WORSHIP, BOOK OF, see BOOK OF WORSHIP (METHODIST).

WORSHIP IN THE BIBLE, homage, here restricted to man's cultic expression of his dependence on God.

In the OT. The usual Hebrew word for worship is *'abodah*, "service." In Israelite faith true worship con-sisted in humble submission to Yahweh and his commands. With this basic criterion the people could change and develop their rites or outward forms of worship and enrich them by borrowing from the rituals of other religions. Thus the patriarchs worshiped at holy places, which probably were already pagan sanctuaries, but which they reconsecrated by erecting an altar to Yahweh, e.g., Shechem, Bethel, Oak of Mamre (Gen 12.6–8; 13.18–20)—a practice continued by David at Jerusalem (2 Sam 24.18–25). Worship at these shrines was performed by the head of the family or clan in response to an act of God's love or to a command.

In Egypt the people asked to go into the desert to "serve Yahweh." After the exodus and the covenant between Yahweh and his people, to serve Yahweh meant to recall with gratitude his mighty acts of delivery and to observe the covenant lovingly. From this relationship definite forms of worship developed together with a priesthood and calendar of feasts. Exodus 20.24 gives Yahweh's prescription for worship: "You are to make me an altar of earth, and sacrifice on this the holocausts and communion sacrifices from your flocks or herds. In every place in which I have my name remembered, I shall come to you and bless you." Following this prescription the Israelites realized that Yahweh could not be confined to any one place. They worshipped him at the traditional shrines of the patriarchs and at other places esp. where he appeared; e.g., Ophra, Carmel, Sinai-Horeb, Gibeon, Shiloh, Jerusalem.

Israelite cultic institutions also changed according to their way of life. In the desert wanderings the Tent (Ex 29.42–46) and the Ark of the Covenant (Ex 25.10–16; Num 10.35–36) represented Yahweh's presence in the midst of his people. They were not attached to places but moved with the people. Even after the Israelites were settled in Canaan and the monarchy established, David failed in his ambition to build a permanent dwelling for Yahweh and centralize all worship in Jerusalem (2 Sam 7.1–17). When Solomon went ahead with David's plans (1 Kg 5–6), it caused a division in the kingdom and ended in the Babylonian captivity. With permanent institutions the people could go through formal rituals while neglecting the essential feature of true worship: humble submission to Yahweh and his command to love one's fellowman. The prophets complained that if the people and priests did not amend their behavior, Yahweh would destroy the Temple and refuse their sacrifices (Jer 7; Am 5.21–26; Hos 8.11–13). After the exile, the Temple was rebuilt in Jerusalem as the center of a restored theocracy where Yahweh would dwell with Israel (Ez 37.23–28; 41.1–7), and became the only place where sacrificial worship could legally be performed.

The priesthood was now organized for Temple worship (Lev 1–7; 1 Chr 23–26), instead of priests being attached to the different sanctuaries. They performed the daily services of the Temple, which consisted of two holocausts, one in the morning and one in the evening; the Sabbath service; and the monthly service of the New Moon (Ex 29.38–42; Num 28.2–15). They also observed a calendar of feasts developed throughout the history of the people, from the more ancient feasts of the Passover and Unleavened Bread, the Feast of Weeks and the Feast of Tents (Ex 12–13; 23.16,22; Dt 16.13,16), all of which involved an annual pilgrimage to Jerusalem, to the later feasts of Yom Kippur or Day of Atonement (Lev 23.27–32), and the Feast of Hannukah or the Renewal (1 Macc 4.36–59). All sacrifices ceased with the destruction of the Temple in A.D. 70, but worship in the synagogues continued with secondary cultic acts of readings and prayers.

In the NT. The first Christians continued Israelite worship to Yahweh, but added a new dimension: the worship to Jesus whom God has made "both Lord and Christ" (Acts 2.36). The Gospels show that Jesus and his parents conformed to the Temple worship and Jewish cultic practices. Jesus was circumcised, presented in the Temple with the usual sacrificial offering, and at 12 made the annual pilgrimage to Jerusalem for the Passover (Lk 2.21–24, 41–42). The major events of Jesus' public ministry are placed in a cultic setting. Many of his cures and discourses took place in the synagogue, in the Temple, or on the Sabbath (Lk 4.16–22; 6.1–11; 19.45–48). This becomes so pronounced in the Fourth Gospel that the Gospel may be divided according to the Jewish liturgical year and its principal feasts.

At the same time, the evangelists present Jesus in polemic with the religious authorities of the Jews and their religious observances, and Jesus asserted that he himself is the focus of a religion, restored "in spirit and truth" (Jn 4.24). He insisted that the "sabbath was made for man, not man for the sabbath; so the Son of Man is master even of the sabbath" (Mk 2.27–28). In the Fourth Gospel Jesus replaces the Temple and other Jewish institutions with his own person (2.19; 6.1–21; 8.12). He is made equal to Yahweh by the use of the same phrase, "I am," that Yahweh used to reveal himself in Ex 3.14 (Jn 6.35; 8.12,24,58; 13.19; 18.5,8). The Last Supper not only took place in a paschal setting, but was intended to fulfill the promises inherent in the Passover story, and to establish a new covenant (Lk 22.14–16; 1 Cor 11.25). Whether the Last Supper was itself a Paschal meal or not, the Eucharist was presented as the New Passover. Just as the Passover was the *zikkaron* or memorial, the thankful re-enactment of the central event of the OT, the Passover from slavery to freedom, so now Jesus asked that the Eucharist be a memorial of the final saving deed of God's love: his Passion, death and Resurrection (1 Cor 11.23–27; Lk 22.19–20).

This tension between the observance of the old Israelite worship and its replacement by the new worship that Jesus was instituting was evident in the practice of the early Christians. The disciples continued "to go up to the Temple to pray" (Acts 3.1), "but met in their houses for the breaking of bread" (Acts 2.46). They proclaimed the Good News both in the Temple and in private houses (Acts 5.42; 19.8–10). They developed their own rites to express the worship in spirit and truth proclaimed by Jesus: baptism in the name of Jesus Christ for the forgiveness of sins and to receive the gift of the Holy Spirit (Acts 2.38), and the breaking of bread

(Acts 2.42), together with sharing their goods. Christian observance continued side by side with Israelite worship, and Peter and the Judeo-Christians did not resolve this tension until Paul refused to hold his Gentile converts to Jewish observance. Christian worship then came into its own, giving prominence to the Lord's Day instead of the Sabbath.

The NT tells little about the rites of Christian worship. Baptism was called for as man's expression of faith in response to the Good News (Acts 2.37–41; Rom 6.1–11). John the Baptizer had practiced the rite and Christ himself had submitted to it (Lk 3.3–21), but now it became the special initiation rite of Christians. It seems to have been performed any place and by any disciple once the candidate had accepted the Good News (Acts 8.36–39; 10.48; 19.5). The Eucharist became the central act of worship just as the Passover was for the Jews. It was a family meal at which the community thanked God by recalling Jesus' redemptive act. Unlike the Passover, however, the Lord's Supper was not made a yearly feast, but a more frequent celebration. Acts 20.7–12 describes such a celebration that took place "on the first day of the week" (see also 1 Cor 11.17–34). There is no indication of a need for a priesthood in such a celebration nor for any special sanctuary in which to meet. The NT insists more on the worship of the word which consists in the proclamation and acceptance of the Good News in faith and love rather than on cultic institutions. The Apostles saw themselves more as ministers of the word than as priests (Acts 6.2; 1 Cor 1.17). BIBLIOGRAPHY: J. Plastaras, *God of Exodus* (1966); De Vaux, AncIsr 271–515; O. Cullmann, *Early Christian Worship* (tr. A. S. Todd and J. B. Torrance 1962); W. O. E. Oesterley, *Jewish Background of the Christian Liturgy* (1965).

[E. CABEY]

WORSHIPBOOK, liturgical aid produced at the initiative of the United Presbyterian Church and with joint participation by the Cumberland Presbyterian Church and the Presbyterian Church, U.S. (Southern). It marks the first time American Presbyterians have produced a complete book of services and music for use of all worshippers. However, it was not adopted officially and use is voluntary. *The Worshipbook—Services* was issued in 1970 and *The Worshipbook—Services and Hymns* (including service music) in 1972. A preliminary step was introduction of provisional services in a 1966 edition called *The Book of Common Worship*, the title of a United Presbyterian predecessor of 1946. In addition to a Service for the Lord's Day and services for other occasions, *The Worshipbook* includes a lectionary, prayers and readings for the Christian year, litanies and special prayers. The Lectionary uses, with a few modifications, the readings of the Catholic lectionary issued after Vatican II. The Lord's Prayer and creeds conform to versions prepared by the International Consultation on English Texts. Contemporary English is used throughout, and Scripture passages are taken from modern translations. *The Worshipbook* considers normative a service of both word and sacrament for each Lord's Day, although

Presbyterian churches have commonly celebrated communion less frequently. BIBLIOGRAPHY: Horace Allen, "Catching Up to Calvin: Liturgical Developments Among Presbyterians," *Worship* (v. 10, no. 10, 1974) 580–594.

[T. EARLY]

WORTHINGTON, THOMAS (1549–1627), third president of Douai College. Of a prominent English Catholic family, he was ordained on the Continent and worked on the English mission from 1578 until his capture and banishment in 1585. He became president through the influence of his friend and advisor, Robert *Persons, and his administration (1599–1616) was marked by a pro-Jesuit policy that aggravated discord between the English seculars and Jesuits. BIBLIOGRAPHY: J. L. Whitfield, CE 15:713–714; T. H. Clancy, NCE 14:1035.

[J. C. WILLKE]

WOUNDS OF OUR LORD have in general the same theological significance as that of the Crucifixion. As a visible token of the new covenant sealed in his blood, the eternal source of purification and life, the wounds remain forever engraved in the flesh of the risen Lord (Jn 20.20, 25–27; Rev 5.6; Heb 7.25). It is the wounded side of Christ that is emphasized in the NT (Jn 19.34–37). The symbolic intent is clear: Jesus having breathed forth his spirit at last, blood and water pour from his open side (Jn 19.30, 34; cf. 1 Jn 5.8). The symbolism is sacramental and ecclesial, referring to the outpouring of the messianic Spirit, the formation of the new Eve, and the Sacraments of initiation. The blood shows that the Lamb has been truly sacrificed for the life of the world (Jn 6.51). The water, symbol of the Spirit (Is 43.19–20; Ezek 47.1–12; Jn 7.37–39), shows that Christ's sacrifice is the source of grace. There is a nuptial significance at work: Christ gives saving reality to and weds the Church, his bride. Jeremiah 2.2 sees the prototypical paschal event as climaxing in the betrothal of Israel to Yahweh. The new Israel is made ready for her marriage by water that Christ gives (Eph 5.26) and is delighted by water that flows from the throne of the Lamb of God (Rev 22.1). The patristic and liturgical tradition joins this to the Adam-Christ parallel (Rom 5.12–19) and sees the Church, mother of all the living, sprung from the open side of the sleeping Christ and fructified with the power of the Holy Spirit through the water and the blood (baptism and the Eucharist for many of the Fathers). This figurative interpretation is copiously documented by S. Tromp.

   The reality of the wounds of Christ assures the primitive Church of the historical reality of the Resurrection, and their witness leads it, like the Apostle Thomas, to confess the master who has died and is risen, as "Lord and God" (Jn 20.28). BIBLIOGRAPHY: J. P. Schanz, NCE 14:1036–37; S. Tromp, *Corpus Christi quod est ecclesia* (tr. A. Condit, 1960) 32–63.

[C. REGAN]

WOUNDS OF OUR LORD, DEVOTION TO, honor given to the wounds in Christ's hands, feet, and side as signs of his redemptive sacrificial death (Eph 1.7) and as signs of his triumph over death (Jn 20.26–27). As signs of his love for humankind, they evoke a response of love and gratitude from Christians. With the development of the medieval emphasis on the Passion at the time of the Crusades, special devotion developed to the five wounds (and later to the wounds of the scourging and the crown of thorns). It was at this time that the crucifix, representing the crucified Christ, came into common use. Various hymns and prayers have come into use since medieval times to honor the wounds of Christ, although there is no feast honoring them in the revised universal calendar. Devotion to the Sacred Heart may be considered a contemporary form of such devotion.

[J. DALLEN]

WOUTERS, LOUIS (1864–1933), Redemptorist moral theologian, highly regarded as a casuist. His 32 listed works include mostly topical articles, but also a *Tractatus dogmatico-moralis de virtute castitatis et de vitiis oppositis* (1928; 1932), and *Manuale theologiae moralis* (2 v., 1933). Born in Vessem, Holland, in the Diocese of Bois-le-Duc, he made his profession as a Redemptorist in 1882, was ordained priest in 1888, taught moral theology at Wittem and at the Alphonsianum in Rome, and was provincial of his order in Holland (1924–33). Under his direction the order founded retreat houses and an ambitious apostolate for youth. BIBLIOGRAPHY: M. de Meulemeester, *Bibliographie générale des écrivains rédemptoristes* (1935), 2:473–474.

[E. J. DILLON]

WOYWOOD, STANISLAUS (1880–1941), canonist. Born in Germany, W. came to the U.S. in 1897, entered the Franciscans, and was ordained in 1906. After 3 years of study of canon law in Rome, W. taught at various Franciscan houses. He served as editor of the National Catholic Almanac of many years. W. made the first English paraphrase of the 1917 CIC. His *Practical Commentary on the Code of Canon Law* (1925) was a standard reference in the field. W. was a commentator on church law for the *Homiletic and Pastoral Review* from 1918 until 1941 and was highly esteemed as a consultant.

[J. R. AHERNE]

WRATH OF GOD. Anger is a desire for revenge because of a hurt done, for which punishment should be inflicted. It is primarily a passion of the soul and can be predicated only metaphorically of God. Divine wrath is a figure of the judgment of justice. God, who is infinite goodness and the cause of all created goodness, must of necessity will only the good. The deliberate defection from goodness by a free creature requires, in justice and mercy, a punishment for such sin. God wills to take vengeance on sin in order to preserve the divine good through his justice. This justice of God, which man fears, is the will of God to preserve the true good. Historically, God has threatened man with punishment and given reason for this evidence of his anger. He has punished, but punishment always ceases with repentance. He will punish sin for eternity in his place of wrath unless there is repentance.

Divine wrath, as God's judgment of justice, presupposes perfect love. It can be understood only in the light of his perfect love. BIBLIOGRAPHY: InterDB.

[R. J. BUSCHMILLER]

WREDE, WILHELM (1859–1906), German theologian and biblical scholar. Professor of NT at Breslau from 1895 until his death, he became famous for demonstrating the significance of the motif of the messianic secret in the Gospels. His thesis, expounded in *Das Messiasgeheimnis in den Evangelien* (1901), was that Jesus did not claim to be the messiah and was not considered such by his disciples during his lifetime; to hide this fact, Mark invented the motif of the messianic secret, a key theological concept in his Gospel, and borrowed by the other Synoptic writers. A second important book by W. appeared in 1905, *Paulus*, in which he sets forth his thesis that the Christian religion as we know it should be attributed to Paul, who radically transformed the historical religion of Jesus. The influence of W.'s works can be gleaned from Schweitzer's work on the quest for the historical Jesus, whose original German title should be translated ''From Reimarus to Wrede''.

[E. J. DILLON]

WREN, CHRISTOPHER (1632–1723), English architect. Already an established mathematician and architect while professor at Oxford, he was commissioned to help in the rebuilding of London after the fire of 1666. St. Paul's in London is his most famous building, but he also designed 52 other London churches as well as many secular buildings, esp. the Sheldonian Theatre at Oxford and the Trinity College Library, Cambridge. His churches with their graceful spires are admired for strength and the elegance of their style; many were destroyed or damaged in World War II. W. was knighted in 1673.

[T. C. O'BRIEN]

WRIGHT, FRANK LLOYD (1869–1959), internationally renowned American architect. Largely self-taught, W. worked in the firm of Sullivan and Adler, Chicago. He acknowledged his debt to Sullivan in *Genius and the Mobocracy* (1949). In 1893 he worked independently, was in Japan (1905) and Europe (1910–11), returning to Japan (1916–22). Most notable of W.'s houses of horizontal emphasis for Chicago suburbia was the Robie house, lavishly decorated with polychrome brick (1909), a culmination of his prairie-style house phase. In Trinity Church, Oak Park, Madison, Wis. (1906–07), W. introduced reinforced concrete, with corner block reserved for circulation and utilities. A chief work was the Imperial hotel (Tokyo, 1915–22, demolished 1967), its floating cantilever construction withstanding the earthquake of 1923. W. engaged (1931–35) in planning Broadacre City and garden towns of low-cost housing. A classic example of W.'s great genius in adaptation to site, is Fallingwater, Bear Run, Pa. (1936) a stunning conception, its dramatic cantilevered terraces and tower of natural stone hovering over the waterfall, patterned by shadow lines of surrounding woods, is enmeshed with the landscape, magically assuming tones from season to season in unfailing topographical harmony. W. designed the Unitarian Church, Madison, Wis. (1947); Beth Sholom Synagogue, Elkins Park, Pa. (1959), a dramatic Sumerian ziggurat rising as the ''holy mountain'', enriched with copper traditionally used by the ancient Semitic peoples to sheathe their temples; and the provocative circular Guggenheim Museum, N.Y. (1957–59), a continuous spiral ramp effecting one of the greatest architectural spaces of the 20th cent. comparable to St. Peter's or the Roman Pantheon. A genius, W., through his mastery of site and space, with intuitive engineering created a poetic, authentic 20th-cent. statement. BIBLIOGRAPHY: F. L. Wright, *Autobiography* (1932, rev. 1943, repr. 1976); J. L. Wright, *Appreciation of Frank Lloyd Wright (1960)*.

[M. J. DALY]

WRIGHT, WILLIAM (1563–1639), English Jesuit. After teaching theology at Vienna and Graz, he was sent (1606) to the English mission where he was soon captured and imprisoned. He escaped and concealed himself in Leicestershire where he established the Jesuit mission. He published several notable controversial works. BIBLIOGRAPHY: Gillow BDEC 5:596–598; T. Cooper, DNB 21:1050–51.

[V. SAMPSON]

WU LIANG TOMBS, 2d cent. Chinese tombs of the Wu family in the Shantung Province, mentioned in Sung literary sources, and discovered in the 18th cent., yielded engraved slabs important for the study of the Han dynasty, preserving legends and histories in lively engraved silhouettes of full forms distinctive of the period—in horizontal registers crowded in a *horror vacui*, with texts—providing authoritative records highly significant to Chinese history. BIBLIOGRAPHY: T. Sekino, *Sepulchral Remains of the Han Dynasty, Shantung* (1916); W. Fairbank, ''Offering Shrines of Wu Liang Tz'u,'' *Harvard Journal of Asiatic Studies* 6 (1941).

[M. J. DALY]

WULF, MAURICE DE, see DE WULF, MAURICE

WULFILA, see ULFILAS.

WULFLAICUS, ST. (Vulfiliac, Wulphy, Walfroy; d. *c.* 594), hermit of Lombard origins. St. Gregory of Tours cites an encounter with W. *c.*585. His relics were translated in 979 to Yvois (Carignan, near Sedan), which Gregory had described as W.'s place of hermitage. Apparently, after a visit to the tomb of St. Martin of Tours, W. built a hermitage near Yvois, worked miracles through the intercession of St. Martin, won the local inhabitants away from the worship of Diana, and would have imitated Simon Stylites in his search for seclusion by living atop a pole had it not been for the dissuasion of neighboring bishops.

[E. J. DILLON]

WULFRAM OF SENS, ST. (d. late 7th cent.), a wealthy courtier, who endowed the monastery of Fontenelle with land. During the exile of Bp. Amatus of Sens, he was consecrated bp. (c. 682). Perhaps because he questioned the canonical propriety of his election, he resigned and devoted himself to the evangelization of the pagan Frisians. BIBLIOGRAPHY: Butler 1:642–643.

[A. CABANISS]

WULFRIC, ST. (Ulrich; d. 1154), English anchorite. His enclosure in a cell at Haselbury Plucknett (Somerset) took place about 1125. He was famous for prophecies and miracles. His cell, in which he was buried, was a popular place of pilgrimage in the Middle Ages. BIBLIOGRAPHY: Butler 1:382–383.

[M. J. SUELZER]

WULFSTAN OF WORCESTER, ST. (c.1008–95), Benedictine abbot and bp. of Worcester from 1062. He sided with Harold of Wessex but submitted to William in 1066 and became a trusted advisor of the King. When William died, Wulfstan was one of two native prelates surviving under Norman rule. A man of great personal holiness, he was canonized in 1203 by Innocent III. His life was preserved by William of Malmesbury (*Vita Wulfstani*, R. R. Darlington, Camden Society 40, 1928; tr. J. H. F. Peile, 1934). BIBLIOGRAPHY: F. M. Stenton, *Anglo-Saxon England* (2d ed., 1947); D. Knowles, *Monastic Order in England* (1949); Butler 1:121–123.

[M. M. BARRY]

WULFSTAN OF YORK (d. 1023), Benedictine preacher, reformer, lawmaker; bp. of London 996–1002; bp. of Worcester 1003–16; abp. of York 1003–23. He is best known for his sermon c.1014 *Sermo Lupi ad Anglos* blaming the English for faintheartedness and slackness. In law his great accomplishment is *Institutes of Polity*, an attempt to clarify the relationship of Church and State and to define the duties of various classes of men. He was trusted advisor to Kings Ethelred and Canute. BIBLIOGRAPHY: *Homilies of Wulfstan* (ed. D. Betherum, 1957); W. Hunt, DNB (repr. 1949–50) 63:174–176; S. B. Greenfield, *Critical History of Old English Literature* (1965).

[M. M. BARRY]

WULMAR, ST. (d. c. 710), hermit, abbot. After his marriage was annulled, he entered a monastery at Hautmont. Later he was ordained priest and allowed to retire to a hermitage in Picardy. He founded two monasteries, one for women, the other for men, and was abbot of the latter until his death. The monastery was later renamed Saint-Vulmer in his honor. BIBLIOGRAPHY: E. Brouette, NCE 14:1048.

[A. CABANISS]

WULPHILDA, ST. (Wulfhilda; d. c.980), Benedictine abbess. Of West Saxon nobility, she was abbess, apparently simultaneously, of convents at Horton (Dorsetshire), which she founded on her estates, and Barking (Essex), rebuilt after Viking raids. Tradition asserts she was driven from Barking by King Edgar's widow, Elfthryth, but was later restored. BIBLIOGRAPHY: AS, Sept. 3:454–460; Zimmermann 3:33–37.

[W. A. CHANEY]

WUNDERLE, GEORG (1881–1950), Bavarian priest, philosopher, and theologian who taught philosophy in Eichstätt, and apologetics, comparative religions, and Eastern church art in Würzburg. His numerous writings attempt a synthesis between Catholic faith and modern culture and a better understanding between religious traditions. They include pioneer efforts on the subjects of prayer, the philosophy, psychology, and history of religion, pedagogy, and Eastern church art.

[E. J. DILLON]

WUNDT, WILHELM (1832–1920), German physiologist, physician, philosopher, esp. remembered for his pioneer work in the field of scientific psychology and its methodology. His entire professional life was devoted to research, writing, and teaching at the universities of Heidelberg, Zurich, and Leipzig (where he founded the first laboratory of experimental psychology in 1879). Though chiefly reputed as a psychologist, W. was deeply interested in philosophy, in which he took an eclectic position. Nevertheless, the influence of German idealism is apparent in his opposition to sensationalism, materialism, and the relativity of values in ethics. BIBLIOGRAPHY: A. Wellek, EncPhil 8:349–351, bibliog.; Copleston 7:381–383.

[J. T. HICKEY]

WÜRTTEMBERG CONFESSION, a Lutheran *confession of faith, prepared in 1551 by Johannes Brenz (1499–1570) for presentation at the Council of *Trent. Like the *Saxon Confession, it was prepared to satisfy the wish of the Emperor and Duke Christopher of Württemberg for representation of Lutheran teaching at Trent. The delegation presenting the document, Jan. 24, 1552, had no success. The Württemberg Confession follows closely the *Augsburg Confession, but it was not incorporated into the *Book of Concord. It was consulted in the preparation of the *Thirty-Nine Articles of the Church of England. BIBLIOGRAPHY: Schaff Creeds 1:343–344, 627–628.

WÜRZBURG, RESIDENZ, magnificent German residence of the prince-bishops of Würzburg, built (1720–44) by the master architect B. *Neumann, witness to the collaboration of substantial patronage, coordination of architectural design by one architect enhanced by the genius of superb decorators. Johann Philipp Franz von Schönborn, prince-bishop (1719) began the construction; Friedrich Karl von Schönborn continued it (1729); the superb decoration of the great stairs and the main Kaisersaal were accomplished under Karl Philipp von Greifenklau (1749–54) and all work completed in 1765. The architectural plan is essentially Neumann's, the oval pavilions by M. von Welsch, J. L. von Hildebrandt of Vienna contributing the garden front and chapel interior. The surpassingly beautiful frescoes of the Kaisersaal: *Apollo Conducting Beatrice of Burgundy to Barbarossa* (ceiling), *Wedding of Barbarossa* and the *Investiture of Bishop Harold* (walls) with the magic *trompe l'oeil* of the stair hall depicting the exotic regions of the world—all by G. B. Tiepolo—are Europe's finest 18th-cent. frescoes (1751–53), happily spared in World War II bombing of the Residenz itself.

[M. J. DALY]

WUST, PETER (1884–1940), German Catholic layman and philosopher. He became a critic of the intellectual life in Germany, author of many works reflecting a personalist metaphysics derived from M. Scheler, partner of Bp. von Galen of Münster in the latter's resistance to National Socialism. Born in Saar, W. studied at Berlin and Strassburg, took his doctorate at Bonn, and was professor of philosophy at Münster.

[E. J. DILLON]

WUTZ, FRANZ XAVER (1882–1938), biblical scholar. W. taught OT at the major seminary in Eichstätt, Germany; published an important study of Jerome's *Onomastica sacra*, and several volumes of textual criticism based upon the theory that the original text of the Hebrew Bible could be reconstructed from a comparison of the Septuagint and the transcribed Hebrew words in several other MSS. Such a reconstruction is no longer regarded as possible. BIBLIOGRAPHY: M. Rehm, LTK 10:1277–78; O. G. Loretz, NCE 14:1050.

[T. M. MCFADDEN]

WYATT, JAMES (1746–1813), English architect, synthesizing the styles of Robert Adam, later Palladianism, Classic and Gothic styles at Fontill Abbey (1796), an offshoot of Lee Priory (1783) leading to Ashridge Park (1808) of Gothic style, and great Neoclassic houses in Ireland.

[M. J. DALY]

WYATT, THOMAS (1503–42), English diplomat and poet, employed by Henry VIII on missions to Francis I, to the papal court in Rome, and to Venice. He was high marshall of Calais (1528–1530). His intimacy with Anne Boleyn (not proved) was probably the reason for his brief arrest of one month as an attempt to incriminate her. After Thomas Cromwell's death he was again imprisoned on charge of correspondence with Card. Reginald Pole, but was freed by the intercession of the queen, Catherine Howard. He wrote lyrics, satires, and free paraphrases of the penitential psalms. He introduced the sonnet form into England but his own sonnets are stiff and strained. Many of his lyrics were published in the first English anthology in 1557,

Songes and Sonettes (Tottel's Miscellany). BIBLIOGRAPHY: DNB 63:187.

[M. M. BARRY]

WYCLIFFE, JOHN (Wiclif, Wyclif, etc.; *c.*1320–84), English reformer. A native of Wycliffe-on-Tees in Yorkshire, W. received appointments as parish priest of Fillingham (1361), Ludgerhall (1368), and Lutterworth (1374). His life, however, was passed mainly in the academic world of Oxford, where he developed those teachings that were later condemned as heretical by the Council of *Constance (1415; see D 1151–95). His title "Morning Star of the Reformation" rests primarily upon his denial of *transubstantiation and upon his *ecclesiology. W. was not a profound philosopher or theologian; no philosophical position except that of extreme realism in regard to universals shaped his religious thinking. His denial of transubstantiation was a purely speculative consequence. The substance of bread and wine could not be changed, much less annihilated as the Scotists taught, because, like everything that exists, these substances were participations in the eternal, necessary, and real universals existing in the divine mind. Transubstantiation would mean God's negating himself. However obscure his own explanation of the Real Presence, W. did not anticipate later Zwinglian, Calvinistic, or Lutheran teaching; nor did he deny that the Mass is sacrificial.

A theological determinism derived from Thomas Bradwardine (*c.*1290–1349) enabled W. to look at the Church the way he looked at the world of universals; it was the *universitas praedestinatorum*, neatly determined through the infallible workings of faith in the predestined. They were surely guided interiorly to interpret the gospel, which was the sole and sufficient rule of faith; and they had no insuperable need for a sanctifying ministry. It was, then, no problem for W. to do away with the teaching and sanctifying ministry of the Church. This he did through his theory of *dominium*, lordship, in *De dominio divino* (1375) and *De civili dominio* (1376). These are the first two of the collection of treatises called his *Summa theologiae* (written 1374–84; of its other treatises, the *De ecclesia* [1378], *De potestate papae* [1379], and the *Trialogus* [1382] were much used by Jan *Hus). He was also a popular preacher and pamphleteer; instituted his "poor priests," itinerant and unlicensed lay preachers (see LOLLARDS); and the Wycliffe Bible was a part of this campaign of popular instruction. W.'s theory and applications on lordship must also be taken against the background of his political and reform activities. From 1374 onward he several times favored the civil over the eccl. powers in conflicts on provisions, papal tithes, and the law of sanctuary. The theory itself was derived from Richard Fitzralph, and fitted W.'s practical resistance to eccl. jurisdiction. Lordship meant feudal suzerainty; it belonged properly to God alone, was shared through grace by all the predestined, and by them only, and was lost by mortal sin. He extended the notion to include the teaching and sanctifying power of the Church, and, esp. after the *Great Western Schism (1379), rejected the papacy outright as a diabolical usurpation. W. also inveighed against the religious orders (he called them "sects"), but this seemed to have been a reprisal for their opposition to his Eucharistic doctrine.

In 1377 Gregory XI condemned a series of W.'s propositions (D 1121–39) and called for an inquiry, which never took place. A synod held at Blackfriars, London (1382) censured 24 propositions from W.'s writings; W., however, was supported by the Univ. of Oxford and suffered little inconvenience. The instruction of Constance that his bones be exhumed and scattered was finally carried out in 1428. W.'s chief impact was not upon the English, but upon the Continental Reformation, through Hus and the *Hussites (see JEROME OF PRAGUE). BIBLIOGRAPHY: Bihlmeyer-Tüchle 2:435–437; J. Dahmus, NCE 14:1050–52; Gilson HCP 771–772; M. Spinka, *Advocates of Reform from Wyclif to Erasmus* (1953); S. P. H. Thomson, EncPhil 8:351–352; H. B. Workman, *John Wycliffe* (2v., 1926).

[T. C. O'BRIEN]

WYCLIFFE BIBLE TRANSLATORS, INC., a society for translating the Scriptures into all languages now in use. It had its beginning in a Summer Institute of Linguistics organized in Sulphur Springs, Ark., in 1934 by William Cameron Townsend and L. L. Letgers. In 1935 the first translation team was sent to Mexico. In 1942 the Institute was moved to the campus of the Univ. of Oklahoma. There are now three such institutes in the U.S. and four in other countries. More than 1,500 workers are involved in translating the Bible into 330 languages. The Wycliffe Bible Translators cooperate with other *Bible societies and with all Christian Churches. In 1947 it established a Jungle Aviation and Radio Service, Inc., a department to service its linguists in remote areas. This division also renders valuable aid to natives, esp. in emergencies. The doctrinal views of the organization, as contained in the articles of incorporation, include belief in the divine inspiration of the Scriptures; the Trinity; man's Fall and redemption by Christ; justification by faith; the resurrection of the body; and eternal reward or punishment.

WYCLIFFITES (Wyclifites), a term used, esp. in late medieval ecclesiastical documents, to designate not only *Lollards but anyone accepting the teachings of John *Wycliffe or similar doctrines. BIBLIOGRAPHY: D 1151–95; 1247–79.

[T. C. O'BRIEN]

WYKEHAM, WILLIAM OF, (1324–1404), powerful English ecclesiastical politician, who served as chancellor under Edward III and Richard II, and was bp. of Winchester (1366–1404). Born at Wickham, Hants, he was educated at Winchester and accumulated a large number of benefices without cure of souls before being ordained. He was briefly out of favor as a result of pressure from an anticlerical group influenced by John of Gaunt; and when W. came back to

power under Richard II, he seemed to have lost his taste for politics and was a moderating influence in such matters as the persecution of the Lollards. He is mainly remembered for founding two colleges dedicated to St. Mary: one at Oxford founded in 1379, and formally opened in 1386, which came to be called New College; the other a grammar school at Winchester, whose papal charter dates from 1378 and whose royal charter dates from 1382. It opened in 1394 to prepare poor boys for later studies at Oxford. This was the first independent, self-governing school in the country.

[E. J. DILLON]

WYNNEBALD, ST. (Winnebald fl. 8th cent.), Anglo-Saxon missionary to Germany. W. met St. Boniface in Rome and returned with him to Thuringia (739) where he was ordained priest. He seems to have spent three years in Bavaria and some time in Mainz (c.747) before retiring to Heidenheim, where he built a monastery and became its first abbot. BIBLIOGRAPHY: the vita in MGHS 15.1:106–117 by the nun Hugeburc (Hygeburh) of Heidenheim; see also E. S. Duckett, *Anglo-Saxon Saints and Scholars* (1967); Butler 4:582–583.

[M. F. MCCARTHY]

WYNTOUN, ANDREW OF (d.c.1422), Scottish historian. W. was a canon of the Augustinian cathedral priory of St. Andrews and elected prior of St. Serf, one of its dependencies (c.1393). He wrote *De Orygynale Cronykil of Scotland*, a metrical history, valuable to philologists and students of medieval Scotland BIBLIOGRAPHY: *Original Chronicle of Andrew of Wyntoun* (ed. F. V. Amours, 6v. 1903–14); A. Mackay, DNB 21:1181–82; L. MacFarlane, NCE 14:1053.

[R. W. HAYS]

WYOMING, a Rocky Mountain state, admitted to the Union (1890) as the 44th state. Among the inhabitants of the area before the coming of the Europeans were the Sioux, Cheyenne, and Crow Indians. The first white men to reach Wyo. were probably François and Louis Joseph de la Vérendrye (1742–43). Protestant missionaries to the traders and Indians of the area included the Methodists, J. and D. Lee, and the missionary physician, M. Whitman. The first Catholic missionary in Wyo. was P. *De Smet (1840); later, Jesuits worked among the Indians, traders, and trappers until the Diocese of Cheyenne was erected (1887). The first bp., M. F. Burke, transferred to St. Joseph, Mo., in 1893, was succeeded by T. M. Lenihan (1897). The diocese, coextensive with the boundaries of the state, is a suffragan of the metropolitan see of Denver, Col. In 1976 Wyo.'s Catholics numbered 45,000 or 13.2% of the total state population. The major Protestant denominations are the Church of Jesus Christ of Latter-Day Saints, with 8.7% of the total population in 1971, and the United Methodist Church, with 4.9%. Other Protestant denominations comprised 20.4% of the population. The Jewish population (1968) was 710, or

0.2%. There is no Catholic college in Wyo.; one Catholic high school enrolls 198 students, while 8 Catholic elementary schools are attended by about 1,842 pupils. The Confraternity of Christian Doctrine is active in areas lacking parish schools. BIBLIOGRAPHY: F. Beard, *Wyoming from Territorial Days to the Present* (3 v. 1933); Federal Writers' Project, *Wyoming: a Guide to its History, Highways, and People* (1941).

[J. L. MORRISON; R. M. PRESTON]

WYSZYNSKI, CASIMIR, VEN. (1700–55), Polish priest, member of the Marian Fathers, credited with bringing about the spiritual renewal of that order in his successive roles as master of novices, local superior, superior general, and procurator general in Rome. He was born near Warsaw with the name Jeziora Wielka and took the name Casimir of St. Joseph when he entered the Marian Fathers novitiate. He died in Portugal after going there to found a monastery of his order.

[E. J. DILLON]

X

XAINCTONGE, ANNE DE, VEN. (1567–1621), foundress. A native of Dijon, France, X. saw the need of better education of girls and established a community of women religious, non-cloistered, in 1606, a time when cloister was regarded as essential for nuns. The Society of St. Ursula of the Blessed Virgin was the first non-cloistered teaching community of women. The congregation conducts schools in Europe, Africa, and America.

[J. R. AHERNE]

XANTHOPULUS, NICEPHORUS CALLISTUS (c.1260–c.1335), Byzantine priest and ecclesiastical writer. A member of the clergy of Santa Sophia, he was a teacher of grammar and rhetoric in the patriarchal school. His writings were occasioned by his experiences as a pastor and teacher. Among his liturgical writings may be mentioned synaxaries, an Office of Our Lady as the Source of Life, Marian poems, and prayers. Among his works of exegesis, rhetoric, and history, the most significant is his *Ecclesiastical History* in 18 books covering from the beginnings of Christianity to the death of the Emperor Phocas (618). In spite of charges of plagiarism made against it, it is valuable because it contains excerpts from writers no longer extant. The practical needs of his teaching led him to compute also catalogues of the Fathers of the Church, emperors, patriarchs, melodists, and saints. BIBLIOGRAPHY: V. Laurent, NCE 14:1057; Beck 705–707.

[M. R. P. MCGUIRE]

XAVERIAN BROTHERS, congregation of lay religious founded in Bruges, Belgium, by Theodore Ryken in 1839 for the education of young men. Ryken's original plan was to establish schools for American Indians, among whom he had served. He was persuaded to change the purpose of the new society to education of American children. The foundation met with difficulties from the start and it was not until 1846 that the first member took vows. A school in Bruges and one in England opened. In 1854 the Xaverians came to Louisville, Ky., to establish two schools. Ryken's direction was not altogether successful and he resigned, to be replaced by Brother Vincent Terhoeven, under whose administration (1860–95) the society made great progress. The English schools, largely elementary, contributed much to the cause of Catholic education. It was in the U.S., however, that Xaverian education flourished. Louisville, Baltimore, Massachusetts, and Virginia were locations where a number of schools were staffed. There was a gradual transition in the 20th cent. from elementary to secondary education. The Belgian province led the way to missionary activity by the congregation with missions in the Congo. The American provinces operate in Kenya, Bolivia, and Uganda. The generalate of the congregation is in Rome. BIBLIOGRAPHY: Bro. Julian, *Men and Deeds* (1930).

[J. R. AHERNE]

XAVIER, FRANCIS, ST., see FRANCIS XAVIER, ST.

XENOCRATES OF CHALCEDON, second scholarch of the Academy (339–314). He seems to have been especially impressed with Plato's preoccupation, in his last years, with numbers and astral religion, but he goes beyond Plato in some of his doctrines. He identified the One, Mind, and the Good as the single supreme principle, and as the male generative principle of the universe. He recognized also the Indeterminate Dyad, which he regarded as the supreme female principle, and as containing the forms-numbers, produced by a union with the One. The World-Soul is presented as a self-moving number. He distinguished three worlds—the sublunar, the heavenly, and the supercelestial, all of which are peopled with a hierarchy of good and bad daemons. Like Plato, he believed that the heavenly bodies were living and intelligent beings. In respect to the soul, he held that even the irrational parts do not perish with death. Accordingly, he opposed the eating of meat because that might lead to the dominion of the irrational over the rational in the soul. Like *Speusippus,

Xenocrates exercised a definite influence on some of the basic doctrines of Middle Platonism and Neoplatonism. BIBLIOGRAPHY: A. H. Armstrong, *Introduction to Ancient Philosophy* (1957) 67–68; Copleston 1:264–265; P. Merlan in CHGMP 32–37, fundamental.

[M. R. P. MCGUIRE]

XENODOKIA, (Gr. *xenos*, stranger) inns for travelers; it was an institution of Christian charity attached first to the *diakonia*, to provide a specific form of assistance to help pilgrims on long journeys to the sanctuaries of faith. Constantine I encouraged the systematic erection of xenodokia and the Council of Nicaea (325), c. 75, declared that in every city separate facilities were to be provided for pilgrims, the sick, and the poor. The name increasingly signified shelter for the sick and in time *xenodokium* became synonymous with *hospitale* (Latin). Up to the 9th cent. in the West *xenodokion* was used in the Byzantine sense. The Latin word *hospitale*, however, was gradually preferred.

[L. PEANO]

XENOGLOSSY (Xenolalia), the ecstatic utterance of a strange language (Gr. *xeno*, strange, foreign; *glossa*, tongue; *lalia*, talking) by a person who had no previous knowledge of that language. Among Pentecostals *glossolalia usually occurs as sounds, inarticulate or articulate, that are not identifiable as a language. Cases of xenoglossy, however, have also been reported. BIBLIOGRAPHY: N. Bloch-Hoell, *Pentecostal Movement* (1964) 141–145.

[T. C. O'BRIEN]

XENOPHANES OF COLOPHON (*c.*570–470), the first Greek philosophical theologian. As a professional rhapsode, he composed and recited verse, and late in life settled at Elea in South Italy. Fragments of his own compositions in verse are preserved in later writers. He was opposed to the anthropomorphic conception of the gods and their conduct as portrayed in Homer. He maintained that there is "One god, the greatest among gods and men, neither in form like unto mortals, nor in thought", who "abideth ever in the self-same place, moving not at all; nor doth it befit him to go about now hither and now thither" (*Frgs.* 23 and 26). However, a critical examination of his fragments and the testimony of Aristotle (*Meta.* 986b18) indicate that he identified God with the world, and that he was a monist, not a monotheist. His monistic view of divinity may have had an influence on the anti-pluralism of the Eleatics, and he was definitely a pioneer in the development of Greek theological thought. BIBLIOGRAPHY: Copleston 1:47; LexAW s.v.; Guthrie 1:360–402.

[M. R. P. MCGUIRE]

XEROPHAGY (Gr. *xeros*, dry and *phagein*, to eat), the practice of eating dry food or meals, without meat, gravy, juicy fruit, or wine. In his *Montanist period Tertullian in his treatise *On Fasting* (*De jejunio* 1) defends the practice, which was opposed as excessive by his Catholic or *psychic opponents. BIBLIOGRAPHY: T. Barnes, *Tertullian* (1971) 130–142.

[D. P. EFROYMSON]

XIMÉNEZ DE CISNEROS, FRANCISCO (often written Jiménez in modern style; 1436–1517), cardinal, statesman, patron of learning, a glory of the golden age of Spain. A Castilian, he graduated at Salamanca, held high preferment in the Church, but, seeking greater solitude for prayer, at the age of 48 became a Franciscan. Then his grand career opened. Adviser to Queen Isabella I, he was created abp. of Toledo and primate of Spain. He was one of the great reformers and renewers of Christian life in Spain in the era before Trent. He was the founder of the Univ. of Alcalá de Henares and its splendid benefactor, and financed the famous polyglot Bible, the first to provide the printed Greek text, known as the *Complutensian Polyglot*, called so from the Latin name, *Complutum*, of Alcalá. He saved the Mozarabic rite from extinction, and though he ordered the burning of copies of the Koran, he preserved the Moorish books of medicine, philosophy, and history. He was governor of Castille after the short reign of poor Juana, and personally directed the conquest of Oran in North Africa. He held together the realms of Isabella and Ferdinand, suppressed factions, improved agriculture, lowered taxation, supported the humane policies of *Las Casas in the Indies. He protected Spain from misgovernment from Flanders, and prepared it for the reign of the Emperor *Charles V. With all this he lived in a style of severe personal poverty, and though something of an autocrat, left a reputation for sanctity.

[T. GILBY]

XIMÉNES DE RADA, RODRIGO, (*c.*1180–1247), abp. of Toledo, statesman, historian, linguist, reformer. Born in Puente la Reina, Navarre, he was a graduate of Bologna and Paris (1201–05), bp. elect of Osna and abp. of Toledo, 1208–09. He became chief adviser of Alfonse VIII and Ferdinand III of Castile and was appointed by Honorius III papal legate in Spain for battle against Islam. He aided in the reconquest of Andalusia and promoted religious renewal there and in Morocco. Known as a protector of the Jews, he acquired for Toledo the chancellorship of Castile in 1230, the primacy of Spain in 1239, and jurisdiction over La Mancha in 1243. He took part in the reforming Lateran Council IV in 1215, began to build the present magnificent cathedral and abp.'s palace in 1227, wrote the estimable *Historia Gothica*, based on Christian and Moslem sources, and other histories, including the unpublished *Breviarium historiae catholicae*.

[E. J. DILLON]

XP, see CHRISMON.

Y

YAHWEH, the name of God revealed to Moses from the burning bush as he was sojourning in the land of the Midianites near the holy mountain of Sinai (Ex 3). The sacred name has four consonants YHWH, and traditionally it was so vocalized in English translation as to be pronounced Jehovah. Now it is generally conceded that a correct vocalization would result in the name Yahweh, pronounced ''YAH-way.'' The origin of the name, its derivation, and its primitive meaning are obscure and the subject of much dispute. A plausible theory of origin is the so-called ''Kenite hypothesis'': that the cult of Yahweh originated among the Kenites, a clan of the Midianites in whose territory Mount Sinai is located. Moses would have been introduced to the cult when he fled Egypt and sojourned in the land of Midian, where he married the daughter of Jethro, priest of Midian. Attempts have been made to show from Arabic cognates that the name Yahweh means ''storm-god'' or ''the passionate one.'' From Ugaritic cognates some construct the meaning ''he who speaks.'' Apparently the enigmatic dialogue of Ex 3.14 admits of various translations. Thus, ''I am who I am'' would be an evasive answer; ''I cause to be what comes to be'' would be a claim to be the Lord of history, a prominent Egyptian theological motif at the time and consonant with later Israelite prophetic consciousness. Whatever its former meaning, from the prophetic consciousness of Moses it came to mean the One who brought Israel out of the land of Egypt, the place of slavery (Ex 20.2; Dt 5.6). Whereas the forefathers (the patriarchs) invoked the name El Shaddai (God the Almighty), from the time of Moses Israel learned to call upon the name Yahweh (Ex 6.2–3). Just as all peoples walk each in the name of his god, Israel will walk in the name of Yahweh forever (Mic 4.5). ''This is my name forever; this is my title in every generation'' (Ex 3.15). When Yahweh pronounced his name to Moses, the latter experienced the presence of a god compassionate and gracious, constant and true (Ex 34.5; cf. Ex 33.19). The priests are instructed to pronounce the name over the Israelites so that they too may experience his graciousness and kindness, and receive his peace (Num 6.24–27). Yet Yahweh does not leave unpunished the one who takes his name in vain (Ex 20.7; Dt 5.11).

[E. J. DILLON]

YAHWIST TRADITION (Jahwist), one of the documentary sources involved in the composition of the Pentateuch; designated by the code letter J (see DOCUMENTARY THEORY). The oldest of the four sources (9th cent. B.C. or possibly earlier), J is named from its use of Yahweh, rather than Elohim, to refer to God. Among the passages belonging to J are some of the key parts of the OT, e.g., the Fall, the Deluge, the call of Abraham, the stories of Isaac, Jacob, Esau, Joseph, Moses; the exodus up to the death of Moses. The unity and destiny of Israel and God's intervention in history are themes of the J Narratives. BIBLIOGRAPHY: O. Eissfeldt, *Old Testament, an Introduction* (3d ed., 1965).

[T. C. O'BRIEN]

YAKUSHI, NARA, Japanese Buddhist temple, originally (686–697) outside Nara, relocated in 718 within the ancient city. Only the E Pagoda has survived fires and typhoons. A large bronze triad of the Yakushi (''Healing'') Buddha with attendants and a bronze *Sho Kannon (Avolokiteśvara)*—excellent examples of Nara art—reflect the Chinese T'ang style.

[M. J. DALY]

YAKUSHI BUDDHA (''Healing Buddha''), massive wood sculptured figure (*c*.793) in the Jingoji temple near Kyoto, holding a medicine jar in the left hand. The austere figure with deeply cut drapery is an example of the somber dignity of early Heian style.

[M. J. DALY]

YAMAMOTO, SHINJIR (1867–1942), Japanese Catholic layman, rear admiral in the Japanese navy under

Fleet Admiral Count Heihachiro Togo in the Russo-Japanese War. After retiring from the navy he taught French to Emperor Hirohito while the latter was Crown Prince and accompanied him to Europe in 1921, then toured Europe himself again in 1937 to explain to European Catholics the Japanese version of the recent hostilities with China. He died in Tokyo during the height of World War II.

[E. J. DILLON]

YANEZ DE LA ALMEDINA, FERNANDO (fl. 1506–31), Spanish painter from La Mancha. Y. studied with Leonardo da Vinci in Florence, collaborated in the Valencia cathedral on 12 monumental paintings (1507–10) evidencing Italian *sfumato*, architectural settings, and perspective. Y.'s *St. Catherine* has the suave, subtle, feminine beauty of Leonardo, though retaining a Spanish spatial isolation.

[M. J. DALY]

YARMUK, one of the tributaries of the Jordan, flowing east to west across Transjordania and entering the Jordan River a short distance south of the Sea of Galilee. Now called wâdī el-Yarmūk, most of its course forms the boundary between modern Syria to the N and Jordan to the South. It is the northernmost of four somewhat parallel streams cutting Transjordan into five highland regions, mutually separated by the deep gorges formed by these streams, and accounting for the distinct peoples and place names given (from N to S) to Bashan, Gilead, Ammon, Moab, and Edom. It rises on the lava plain of the Hauran range in SW Syria at a point where three drainage systems converge. After 50 miles of convolutions it enters the Jordan at a point 830 feet below sea level. Its deep gorge, containing masses of limestone, is marked by hanging valleys and gorgeous cascades, since some of its tributaries have not yet cut through the overlying volcanic rock. Although not mentioned in Scripture, it has acquired religious meaning for Islam, since it is the site of the decisive victory of the Arabs over the Byzantines (August 20, 636) that opened the region to 900 years of Arab dominance and 1300 years of Islamic history.

[E. J. DILLON]

YAROSLAV I, THE WISE, the chief prince of Kiev (1019–54), during the time of widest expansion of the first East Slavic state in Russia. Y.'s reign was a time of cultural renaissance, following on the military and dynastic successes of his father Vladimir's long reign. Y. promoted Christian civilization in Russia by having Greek religious classics translated into Slavic, founding churches and monasteries, fortifying and beautifying Kiev with the "Golden Gate" and the cathedral of St. Sophia. He maintained trade and diplomatic relations with Western countries.

[E. J. DILLON]

YAZILIKAYA (14th-13th cent. B.C.), Hittite rock sanctuary near Boghazkeuy, Turkey, with impressive relief carvings of warriors wearing high caps, short skirts, and shoes with upturned toes, a god embracing a young king, and a huge dagger with hilt symbolically ornamented.

[M. J. DALY]

YEAR, fundamental unit for measuring lifetimes and other long durations of time, based primarily on the phenomenon of the recurring seasons in nature. The year was sacred because the seasons were sacred; and the gift of the year was the gift of life, vitality, and fertility. To celebrate the New Year was to celebrate this gift. The recurring seasons and years were computed by the recurring planting and harvesting of the various crops in succession. The spring or autumn equinox might have been the day for celebrating the New Year and yet lunar computations must have interfered with this schema. The 12 months (originally moons) of the year have had a long evolution. The moon goes through its phases in approximately 29½ days. The Tyrians and Egyptians rationalized this phenomenon, devising a solar calendar made up of 12 moons of 30 days, with 5 extra days added. This served as an international calendar, adopted and adapted by the Greco-Roman and the Christian world. The religious calendar adopted by the Jews and still in use was based on the lunar calendar of Assyria and Babylon; it involves much more complex computation. A year made up of 12 moons adds up to approximately 354⅓ days. For basic harmony with the solar year and the seasons, it is necessary to add an extra month (moon) slightly more than once every three years. Various calendars might have been in use simultaneously and might have vied for acceptance. Even today, of course, the year and its seasons defy mathematical symmetry. BIBLIOGRAPHY: J. Morgenstern, InterDB 4:923–924; *New Westminster Dictionary of the Bible* (ed. H. S. Gehman, 1970) 1007–09.

[E. J. DILLON]

YEAR OF GRACE, the Jubilee Year, every 50th year; the sabbath year of sabbath years, coming on the year following seven times seven years; called Jubilee after the ram's horn (in Hebrew, *yōbēl*) *with whose loud blast the* year was ushered in on the Day of Atonement. Accordingly, in post-exilic Jewish usage, the trumpet blast would proclaim liberty to all Israelites who were in bondage to any of their countrymen and the return to their ancestral lands for any who had been forced to sell them. The land was to lie fallow as in a sabbath year. There is no evidence that the Jubilee Year was ever literally practiced. The legislation and accompanying texts are of late date, and reflect a period when Jews lived under gentilic rule. The Jubilee tradition would serve to awaken the ancient Israelite ideal of justice and brotherhood and God's gift of the land to all the nation. The impressive use of the Jubilee tradition by the prophet whose oracle is preserved in Is 61.1–3 has had far reaching impact. It was used by Jesus to explain his prophetic ministry and to describe the redeeming act of God which was about to transform human history. According to Lk 4.18–19,

Jesus cited the prophecy as summarizing his saving mission. The Septuagint version of the Isaian text uses the phrase "acceptable year of the Lord", which can also be rendered "Year of the Lord's grace (or favor)". Thus every subsequent year of the Christian dispensation is labeled: anno Domini, in the year of the Lord. Each liturgical year is called a year of grace, as celebrating and renewing the redemptive event of Christ's victory over death. BIBLIOGRAPHY: J. Morgenstern, "Jubilee," InterDB. *JUBILEE; *HOLY YEAR.

[E. J. DILLON]

YEATS, WILLIAM BUTLER (1865–1939), Irish poet, playwright, and critic. Y.'s first book of long poems, *The Wanderings of Oisin* (1889), reveals the strong impact upon him of the Young Ireland movement. His intense nationalism was fed by his association with the young Irish patriot, Maud Gonne, whom he loved passionately but who refused his offers of marriage. He used symbolism freely as evidenced in *The Wind Among the Reeds* (1899), though the poetry of his middle years showed less dependence upon symbolism and became somewhat satirical and realistic. Among his best poems, less intensely mystical, were his last: *The Tower* (1928) and *Last Poems* (1940). In 1898 he founded with Lady Augusta Gregory, Edward Martyn, and George Moore, the Irish Literary Theatre (later the Abbey Theater), whose first production was Y.'s *The Countess Cathleen*. Among his other dramas written for the Abbey Theater is *Cathleen ni Houlihan* (1902), the finest of his plays. One of Y.'s great services to the Irish theater was his success in inducing J. M. *Synge to return to Ireland from France to study the primitive Irish and their language and to write plays for the Abbey Theater. It was Y.'s aim, as well as that of other writers of the Celtic Renaissance of whom he was the leader, to provide a body of Irish literature written in English and to explore for preservation, literature that was in the oral tradition only. *The Celtic Twilight* (1893), prose tales, is the result of his deep interest in Irish folklore.

The Protestantism of Y.'s early youth having been shattered by the impact of science, he felt that he had to make up a "new religion" out of the works of poets and painters. However, he was absorbed by an awareness of the forces of Christianity as revealed in Byzantine art and in the intellectual history of the Western world.

He was the winner of the Nobel Prize for Literature in 1923. By that time he had earned the respect of his countrymen and had become a member of the Irish senate. He is credited with being the greatest lyric poet that Ireland had produced and, at his death, was regarded as the greatest poet writing in English. BIBLIOGRAPHY: A. G. Stock, *W. B. Yeats, His Poetry and Thought* (1961); R. Ellmann, *Yeats, The Man and the Masks* (1948).

[S. A. HEENEY]

YEMEN, country in SW Arabia. With some 75,000 square miles, it has a population of about 5 million. It embraces the areas of the ancient Sabean and Minean kingdoms. Following the Sabean period, numerous Jews and Christians lived there for a time, but a persecution in 523 by Yusuf 'as'ar Yat'ar (Masruk Dhu-Nuwas) decimated the Christians. Islamic forces gained control of the area in 628. From 893 until the Yemen Arab Republic was proclaimed in 1962 imams governed the nation. Sana is the capital, and Hodeida a major port on the Red Sea. About 60% of the population is nominally Sunnite Muslim, with most of the remainder Zaydi (Zeidi) Shiites. Some 50,000 Jews migrated from Yemen to Israel between 1948 and 1950.

[T. EARLY]

YEMIPORON, see EMIPORON.

YERETZ, (Eretz), generic word for priest in Armenian (= *qahana*).

[A. CODY]

YEROVI, JOSÉ MARÍA (1819–67), Ecuadorian priest, lawyer, politician who became a Franciscan and finally bp. of Quito. He began by studying law at the Univ. of St. Thomas and was ordained less than a year after receiving the title of attorney. He was interested in pastoral renewal and found it natural to involve himself in social and political struggles. After serving in two parishes and as chaplain of a monastery, he became deputy in the Constitutional Assembly (1850). During a time of religious and political upheaval, he was forced to resign as vicar of Guayaquil (1853) and fled to Pasto (1854). Eight years later he entered the novitiate at the Franciscan monastery of Cali. After his profession at Lima, he was appointed apostolic administrator of Ibarra, then coadjutor bp. of Quito with right of succession. He was consecrated in 1866 and died the next year. He was widely mourned as one whose zeal in pastoral renewal had surpassed that of all who came before him.

[E. J. DILLON]

YESIRAH, BOOK OF (Hebrew, *seper y'ṣîrâ*, "Book of Creation"), a brief, about 1600-word, enigmatic text of systematic speculations on cosmology and cosmogony, traced by some to the late 2d or 3d cent., but more likely dating from the 6th. The earliest extant Hebrew text of its kind, it influenced Jewish Cabala and mysticism. The unknown Palestinian author of the work declares that God created the world by means of "32 secret paths of wisdom" and that these 32 paths incorporate the 22 elemental letters of the Hebrew alphabet and 10 numbers, called *sephiroth*. The paths were probably intended to indicate a metaphysical order in the stages of creation, and supplanted the more common numerical designation *misparim*. The *sephiroth* were interpreted by cabalists and others as indicating a theory of emanations. There are three strata to the cosmos—world, time, human soul—filled by all the real beings that came into existence by way of the "231 gates," a number reflecting the combined internal pairings of all

22 letters of the alphabet. Thus, all beings contain linguistic elements that are founded on one mystical name, either the Tetragrammaton or a name including the entire alphabet. Specific parts of anatomy as well as celestial and terrestrial objects are accounted for by a complicated system of linguistic-alphabetic numerology. The whole book, especially the *sephiroth* doctrine, suggests the influences of Gnostics, Stoics, and neo-Pythagoreans. Commentaries on the book began in the 6th cent. and continue into the 20th. The Hebrew *Seper Yeṣirah* was first published in Mantua (1562); the most popular Hebrew edition in Warsaw (1884). A Latin tr. was done by G. Postel, a Christian mystic (Paris, 1552), and another with commentaries by S. Rittangel (1652). English translations: I. Kalisch (1873); A. Edersheim (1883); W. Westcott (1911); K. Stenring (1923); and *The Book of Formation*, Akiva ben Joseph (1970). There are also translations in other modern languages.

[R. J. LITZ]

YEVELE, HENRY (d. 1400), English architect at Canterbury Cathedral (1375), worked at Westminster Abbey (1395). Y. probably designed the Black Prince's tomb designed in the nave of Canterbury Cathedral, vaulted in 1400, the highest achievement in English Perpendicular style. Among England's greatest architects Y., enjoying royal patronage, perfected the most English of all styles.

[M. J. DALY]

YEZIDI RELIGION, faith of a Kurdish tribe centered in the Mosul area of N Iraq. Of uncertain origin, it shows influences from Christianity, Islam, and other traditions. Through confusion, Yezidis have been called Satan worshippers. A principal belief is that Satan has repented and been restored as the chief of the angels. The existence of hell and evil are denied. The name perhaps derives from the Persian *ized*, meaning angel or deity. The chief angel, Malak Ta'us (Peacock Angel), rules the universe with six other angels. The supreme God takes no interest in the universe. Yezidis have a religious center north of Mosul at a place named for their national saint, Shaykh 'Adi (d. *c.* 1162), a Sufi (see SUFISM), and an annual pilgrimage is made to the area. Though most adherents speak Kurdish, their Scriptures are in Arabic—two short books: *Book of Revelation* and *Black Writing*.

[T. EARLY]

YIN-YANG, famous Chinese symbol of the principle of duality: male-female, active-passive, hot-cold, wet-dry, etc., symbolized by a circle divided by an S-shaped line through the center, into two equal parts, one half black, the other, white.

[M. J. DALY]

YOGA, a mode of physical, mental, and spiritual discipline that is a feature of nearly all types of Hindu contemplation and that has been adopted by other contemplative traditions,

including the Christian. Mention of yoga disciples is found in material relating to the early Indus civilization, yet as one of the six orthodox Hindu philosophical systems it is held to have been founded by Yajnavalkya, codified in the *Yoga-sutra* by Patanjali, and identified with the Samkhya school of Hindu thought. The word itself probably derives from *yuj*, meaning to join or yoke, and was applied to the joining of the human to the universal soul. Depending on what form of power, enlightenment, or salvation is sought, a different path of yoga is prescribed, each with its own stages and practices: *hatha-yoga*, through physical discipline; *raja-yoga*, through spiritualism and physical discipline; *jnana-yoga*, through knowledge; *mantra-yoga*, through mantras and spells; *bhakti-yoga*, through faith; *karma-yoga*, through works; and *laya-yoga*, through elevation of *chakras* of the body. The most common type, *hatha-yoga*, has eight stages in developing physical control: 1) *yama*, external control and self-restraint; 2) *niyama*, internal control and meditative peace; 3) *asana*, body control and postures; 4) *pranayama*, breath control; 5) *pratyahara*, sense control; 6) *dharana*, meditation; 7) *dhyana*, contemplation; 8) *samadhi*, heightened consciousness. The path of dedicated yogis, *raja-yoga*, incorporates the stages of *hatha-yoga* into its more elevated spiritual and mental disciplines. An even higher, more contemplative form and path, *maha-yoga*, eliminates external techniques.

[R. J. LITZ]

YOM KIPPUR, see DAY OF ATONEMENT.

YON, PIETRO ALLESSANDRO (1886–1943), organist and composer. Y., Italian by birth, studied extensively in Milan, Turin, and Rome. In 1907, after two years as an organist in Rome, he immigrated to the U.S. (he became a citizen in 1921). He was organist first at St. Francis Xavier Church, then at St. Patrick's Cathedral in N.Y. City, and was successful both as a recitalist and composer. His works include Masses, motets, songs, an oratorio, and piano and organ pieces, one of which, *Gesù Bambino* (1917), became very popular as a carol in various vocal and instrumental arrangements.

[M. T. LEGGE]

YORK, ANCIENT AND MEDIEVAL SEE OF. There was a See of York in Roman Britain in the early fourth century but it disappeared when the Saxons conquered the province. With the second evangelization of Britain by St. Augustine of Canterbury in the 7th cent., York was established as a diocese. In 734 it became a metropolitan see. The Norse invasions of the 9th cent. saw York occupied and its suffragan dioceses destroyed. Durham, though a subordinate see, was wealthier and more powerful than metropolitan York in the Middle Ages. Once again during the Norman Conquest York suffered catastrophe. The dispute that arose in the 11th cent. over the primacy of England pitted York against Canterbury. For three hundred years it remained a conflict, the question being finally settled by Innocent VI (1352–62) when the abp. of Canterbury was named Primate of All England and the abp. of York, Primate of England. The abps. of York were powerful in ecclesiastical as well as temporal matters, the most celebrated being Cardinal Wolsey in the 16th century. The most memorable contribution of York to civilization is York minster or cathedral. There were in fact two great minsters, one built in the 11th cent., razed in the 13th, and supplanted by the present church, begun in 1227, and which has the richest treasure of medieval stained glass extant in England. In the 8th cent. York had a flourishing school and the finest library in Europe. Early monasticism in the territory of York produced SS. *Cuthbert of Lindisfarne and *Bede the Venerable. The school of York by producing *Alcuin contributed to the Carolingian renaissance in 9th-cent. Europe. *CONVOCATIONS OF CANTERBURY AND YORK.

[J. R. AHERNE]

YORK RITE, a term used to designate the liturgical ritual in use in the northern province of England prior to the Reformation. The name derives from the cathedral of York, whose abp. was metropolitan of the province. Gradually modified over the years, the rite came to approximate very closely the Sarum rite. The same term also designates an order of Freemasonry. Third degree Masons may rise through a system of York rite steps to the Order of Knights Templar or, in the Scottish rite, to the 33d degree. Only Christians may become Knights Templar or, in the Scottish rite, receive the 14th or higher degrees.

[T. EARLY]

YORKE, PETER CHRISTOPHER (1864–1925), writer, controversialist. Born and educated in Ireland, Y. volunteered for the diocese of San Francisco and was ordained in the U.S. in 1887. He was chancellor of San Francisco from 1894 and editor of the diocesan weekly *The Monitor* from 1895. An able theologian, orator, and pastor, Y. was also a fiery polemicist. Among his published works were *Lectures on Ghosts* (1897), an attack on bigotry; the *Roman Liturgy* (1903); and *The Mass* (1921). Founder of the Catholic Truth Society in San Francisco (1897), Y. fought bigotry on the W coast. He was a friend of labor and mediated several strikes. A champion of Irish freedom, he collected money for Dr. Hyde's Gaelic League and in 1902 established the Irish weekly *The Leader,* whose columns he used to deliver his caustic and wide-ranging comments. As an educator he composed a series of texts in religion for parochial schools, served as vice president of the National Catholic Educational Association (1918, 1921–1923), and in 1902 was appointed to the board of regents of the Univ. of California.

[J. R. AHERNE]

YOSHIDA SHIGERU (1878–1967), prime minister of post-war Japan. Y. was the son of a samurai family which had played a leading role in the Meiji Restoration of 1868, a turning point in the development of modern Japan that Y. often compared to the post-World War II revival. After graduating from the Imperial Univ. in Tokyo, he embarked on a diplomatic career. While he was consul general in Mukden, his sharp tongue and contemptuous wit earned him the hostility of the Kwantung Army leaders who asserted the need for direct and forceful Japanese control of Manchuria. Y. served as ambassador to Rome and London, but the antipathy of the increasingly influential militarists blocked his proposed appointment as foreign minister in 1936 and forced his retirement in 1939. For him the basic principle of Japanese foreign policy consisted of close political and economic relations with Great Britain and the United States, and he sharply criticized the departure from this principle which led to war. Because of his criticism of the militarists, his experience in government, and his knowledge of English, Y. was an obvious candidate for political leadership during the American occupation of Japan. As newly elected leader of the Liberal Party, he became prime minister in May 1946 and held that post for 7 of the next 8½ years. He introduced agricultural and educational reforms, ended economic controls while stabilizing the value of the yen, established the National Police Reserve, and vehemently opposed Communist influence in Japan. In 1951 Y. successfully negotiated the Peace Treaty, which ended the occupation, while resisting American pressure for Japanese rearmament. He provided for Japan's defense instead by concluding the Security Treaty with the United States. Thus the foundations of Japan's democratic society, economic strength, and ties to the free world were laid under his auspices. BIBLIOGRAPHY: Yoshida Shigeru, *Yoshida Memoirs* (1962).

[R. J. GIBBONS]

YOUNG, BRIGHAM (1801–77), Mormon leader and colonizer. Although he had only 11 days of formal schooling, Y. became one of America's great colonizers and religious leaders. Born in Whitingham, Vt., he worked as a carpenter and glazier as a young man. He joined the Methodist Church at 21 but read the *Book of Mormon, accepted its authenticity, and was baptized in the Mormon Church in 1832. Y. joined the Mormon prophet Joseph *Smith and the infant Church in Kirtland, Ohio, and rose to the rank of apostle. He accompanied the Mormons to Missouri and to Nauvoo, Ill.; in 1840 he left Nauvoo for a mission assignment in England. When Smith was murdered in 1844, Y. was seeking converts in the eastern states. He hurried back to the Mormon city and assumed leadership of most of the stricken Mormons. He directed the epic march to the valley of the Great Salt Lake and established the Mormon theocracy in Utah. He was appointed governor of the Utah territory in 1850, but aroused the hostility of the federal government and many non-Mormons when he openly preached the doctrine of *plural marriage after 1852. Federal troops threatened to occupy Salt Lake City (1857–

58), but Y. countered by making plans to burn the city and the military action was abandoned. Y.'s superb administrative abilities enabled the Mormons to survive and prosper in their western sanctuary. He married 27 wives, who bore him 56 children. His 27th wife filed suit for divorce and toured the nation denouncing polygamy. Y.'s theological views are elaborated in the volumes of his *Journal of Discourses*. Contemporary Mormons venerate him as a prophet but may not share all his views on polygamy, plurality of gods, blood atonement, and other doctrines. BIBLIOGRAPHY: M. R. Werner, *Brigham Young* (1925); R. B. West, Jr., *Kingdom of the Saints: The Story of Brigham Young and the Mormons* (1957).

[W. J. WHALEN]

YOUNG CHRISTIAN STUDENTS, an organization for high school and college students, founded by Canon (later Card.) Cardijn in Belgium in 1925. A form of specialized Catholic Action, it uses the "cell" technique effectively utilized by the Communist movements. Meetings involve New Testament readings, followed by the "see", "judge", and "act" steps which apply Christian principles to student life and the wider area of the milieu in which students find themselves. International in membership, YCS has a national character in the U.S. with headquarters in Chicago. Like its counterpart, Young Christian Workers, it has proven an effective agency of the lay apostolate.

[J. R. AHERNE]

YOUNG CHRISTIAN WORKERS (YCW; *Jeunesse Ouvrière Chrétienne*, JOC), an international social movement, organized for the benefit of young working people or those planning to work. YCW originated under the title of Jeunesse Syndicaliste at Laeken, near Brussels, Belgium, in 1912, when Abbé Joseph Cardijn gathered together a group of young men and women; he worked to prepare them as Christians able to face all types of responsibilities in the working world. The organization seeks to support and engage all young workers to participate actively in the solution of common labor problems that involve their domestic, moral, social, and spiritual living and to prepare them to fulfill their responsibilities as Christian workers, citizens, and apostles of the movement. In 1925, YCW reached the national level and several years later became internationally active. It received papal recognition and the support of Pius XI, Pius XII, John XXIII, and Paul VI. By 1964, the apostolate had reached missionary dimensions, sending lay workers of all races and nationalities into all parts of the world, establishing the movement in 103 countries and territories of Africa, Asia, Europe, the Americas, and the South Pacific Islands. In 1971, Tran Ngoe Khiet, president of the YCW in Vietnam, reported a grave situation to working women in his country in a letter to headquarters: "in the spirit of the Gospel and of the decisions of the Bishops' Conference in Manila, we have taken up the struggle for justice and human dignity at the side of the working women." BIBLIOGRAPHY: M. De la Bedoyère, *Cardijn Story: A Study of Msgr. Joseph Cardijn and the Young Christian Workers Movement . . .* (1958); E. Boland, "Cardinal Cardijn: His Principles and Methods," *Catholic Educator* 35 (1965) 862–864.

[R. A. TODD]

YOUNG ITALY, a movement founded by Giuseppe Mazzini in the early 1830s for the purpose of achieving the unity and independence of Italy under a republican form of government. Composed for the most part of earnest young men under 40 drawn from the middle classes, Young Italy carried out its work through a paper, *La Giovine Italia*, which was printed in Marseilles and clandestinely circulated throughout the Italian peninsula. Mazzini proclaimed as articles of faith for Young Italy the alliance of politics with religion and a new religious synthesis based on a belief in God and people. Not all of his disciples accepted this creed, and as the organization expanded many joined it from personal ambition. The masses were apathetic or hostile. The chief value of Young Italy was that it kept alive the cause of Italian unification by means of raids and revolts during the years 1833–45.

[E. A. CARRILLO]

YOUNG MEN'S CHRISTIAN ASSOCIATION (YMCA), an interdenominational Protestant group, whose aim is to provide an opportunity for spiritual, physical, and educational development in a wholesome atmosphere. It was founded in London in 1844 by George Williams (1821–1905), then a 22-year-old clerk, in order to provide a center for young working men to hold Bible study classes and prayer meetings. The movement grew rapidly and spread to different parts of the British Empire. In 1850 the first North American branch was organized at Montreal. The following year the YMCA movement reached the U.S. with the formation of a branch at Boston by T. J. Sullivan. In 1852 other branches were established at Washington, D.C., New York City, Philadelphia, and other cities; the movement had also spread in continental Europe. In 1855 an international meeting at Paris unified the previously amorphous movement into a single worldwide organization.

One practical effect of the revival movement that spread through urban America, 1857–59, was a remarkable growth in the YMCA movement and the strong support for religious centers for city workers. Several outstanding young businessmen became full-time YMCA workers; among them were Dwight L. *Moody, who became secretary of the Chicago YMCA, John Wanamaker, secretary of the Philadelphia YMCA, and Robert R. McBurney, secretary of the New York City YMCA. James Mercer Garnett formed the first campus unit of the YMCA at the Univ. of Virginia in 1858. By 1868 there were more than 500 separate YMCA branches in the United States. R. R. McBurney is generally credited with the development in the 1860s and 1870s of the characteristic YMCA programs of gymnasiums, swimming pools, and athletic events. In the later 19th cent. the YMCA also became a center for courses in practical and academic subjects. Acceleration of this trend in the first quarter of the 20th cent. led to the founding of several institutions of higher learning that eventually broke off from the parent YMCA. Another longtime YMCA program has been the providing of inexpensive living and dining facilities for young men in urban centers.

Fundamental to the YMCA has been its religious program. The Association Press has been an important adjunct of this effort by publishing religious books of many types. As a non-denominational religious body, the YMCA has been a valuable auxiliary for Protestant missions in Africa, Asia, and Latin America. Only active members of an evangelical Protestant Church were eligible for YMCA membership under the rules adopted at Paris in 1855 and reaffirmed in 1914, but this rule was relaxed in the 1920s. Under the leadership of John R. *Mott, the YMCA Student Department of the U.S.A. played an important part in ecumenical concerns, particularly through the Student Christian Movement (see WORLD STUDENT CHRISTIAN FEDERATION). The ecumenical spirit of the YMCA contributed to the foundation of the World Council of Churches. In 1955 the YMCA had more than 4,000,000 members in all parts of the world. In 1968 there were some 5,200,000 members in the U.S., and 1,800 local branches. Local Ys are independent, but in 34 nations they are associated in national councils; the movement worldwide is represented by a service agency, the World Alliance of the YMCA, with headquarters at Geneva, Switzerland. BIBLIOGRAPHY: C. H. Hopkins, *History of the YMCA in North America* (1951).

[R. K. MACMASTER]

YOUNG WOMEN'S CHRISTIAN ASSOCIATION (YWCA), a nondenominational Protestant group, intended to provide a means for young Christian women and girls to develop a healthy spiritual, physical and moral outlook. It was formed, on the model of the *Young Men's Christian Association, in London in 1855 under the patronage of Lady Mary Kinnaird. In 1858 the movement spread to the U.S. with the formation of the first American YWCA in New York City by Mrs. Marshall O. Roberts, the wife of a steamship magnate. The earliest efforts of the YWCA closely followed the YMCA pattern, chiefly providing wholesome places of residence and recreation for young women working in urban centers. In 1894 the World's Young Women's Christian Association was formed to unite the movement internationally. It repeated the YMCA commitment to evangelical Protestantism and reiterated the same fundamental stance in its 1913 reorganization. It has worked closely with Protestant missionary efforts in many lands. In 1911 Frances Gage and Anna Welles, two Americans, developed a YWCA movement in the Ottoman Empire and the Balkan countries. The YWCA was also active in war relief and refugee efforts during both World Wars. In 1928 there was a serious division in the international

movement on the question of admitting Roman Catholics to membership. Finland and South Africa withdrew their YWCAs at this juncture. In 1951 the YWCA made a complete commitment to ecumenism. The American and Latin American branches have been open to Catholics for 40 years, while a vigorous movement began in Italy and eastern Europe between the World Wars. In Scandinavia and Germany the YWCA is usually organized on a parish basis and works closely with the Churches. In 1968 there were some 4,000,000 members around the world and an estimated 2,200,000 in the U.S. BIBLIOGRAPHY: M. S. Sims, *YWCA: An Unfolding Purpose* (rev. ed., 1965).

[R. K. MACMASTER]

YOUTH FEDERATION, INTERNATIONAL CATHOLIC, see INTERNATIONAL CATHOLIC YOUTH FEDERATION.

YOUVILLE, MARIE MARGUERITE D', BL. (1701–71), Canadian foundress of the Grey Nuns. Born Marie Lajemmerais, she was widowed (1730) and devoted much of her time to charities while operating a family business. In 1737 she formed her first group of followers to nurse the sick poor. Her efforts to reopen the general hospital at Montreal (1749) led to the founding of the Grey Nuns (1753). She remained their superior until her last years. BIBLIOGRAPHY: M. P. Fitts, *Hands to the Needy* (1950).

[R. K. MACMASTER]

YSARNUS, ST. (d. 1043), Benedictine monk, abbot of Saint-Victor in Marseilles. Y. attracted many vocations by his virtue, charity, and supernatural gifts. Reforming his abbey, he also reformed monasteries in central France and Catalonia. Although ill, he went to Spain to discuss with the Muslims the freedom of some imprisoned monks. His tomb is located in the crypt of the abbatial church. BIBLIOGRAPHY: E. Brouette, NCE 14:1082; AS Sept. 6:728–749.

[M. C. BRADLEY]

YSELIN (ISELIN; d. 1513), German wood sculptor. Y. carved the choir stalls and altar at St. Gall Church, Bregenz, busts for pews of the Kloster St. Katherinental, and Prophets and Apostles for the Constance cathedral, all in his Expressionistic style.

[M. J. DALY]

YUGOSLAVIA, a federal republic in SE Europe (99,079 sq. mi.; pop. [est. 1975] 21,330,000). All the territory of Yugoslavia formed part of provinces of the Roman Empire. Sirmium on the Sava and Salona (Split) on the Adriatic coast were the most important ecclesiastical centers. Roman civilization and Christianity were nearly obliterated by the incursions of the Avars and the immigration of the Serbs, Croats, and Slovenians c. 600. Western influences and Latin Catholicism took root in the West among the Croats and Slovenians, while the influence of Constantinople, through the cultural media provided by the Cyrillo-Methodian missionary activity in the 10th cent. reached the Macedonians and Serbs. The highly developed ecclesiastical organization of the Latin rite Church in Slavonia, Bosnia, Herzegovina was destroyed by the advance of the Turks, while that of Croatia, Dalmatia, the Croatian Coast, and Slovenia survived. The E part of Yugoslavia became the domain of the Serbian Orthodox Church. Islam penetrated with the Turks and left behind two groups: the Croato-Serbian Muslims in Bosnia-Herzegovina and the Albanian Muslims in Serbia and Macedonia.

Since 1918 Yugoslavia embraces all the southern Slavs (Serbs, Croats, Slovenians, Macedonians) except the Bulgarians, in addition to Albanians, Hungarians, Turks, Slovaks, Romanians, Czechs, and Italians. Those of the population who admitted religious affiliation were, according to the semiofficial estimate of 1971: 42% Orthodox, 32% Roman Catholic, 1.14 other Christians, 12% Muslim, and .04% Jewish. In the 1953 census 13.6% of the total population declared themselves atheists.

In Croatia are the archdiocese of Zagreb (former titulars, A. *Stepinac, and J. Šeper) and the dioceses of Senj, Djakovo, and Križevci; the archdiocese of Zadar and the dioceses of Dubrovnik, Hvar, Kotor, Krk, Poreč-Pula, Rijeka, Šibenik, Split-Makarska. Slovenia has the archdiocese of Ljubljana and the diocese of Maribor. In Serbia is the archdiocese of Belgrade. The Catholics of Macedonia are under the bishop of Skopje, those of Bosnia-Herzegovina under the archbishop of Sarajevo and the bishops of Banjaluka and Mostar. The few Latin rite Catholics of Montenegro are in the archdiocese of Bar. In 1978 there were 2,531 Catholic parishes in Yugoslavia, 2,712 diocesan and 1,318 regular priests, 2,089 male and 6,664 female religious.

The relationship of the Communist government towards the Churches has been for a number of years one of hostile disinterestedness or total detachment rather than of open conflict. Diplomatic relations with the Vatican were resumed in 1967. BIBLIOGRAPHY: M. Lack, NCE 14:1083–89.

[V. J. POPISHIL]

YULE, an ancient Teutonic designation, meaning revelry, of a pagan feast which in Christian times in England became identified with the Christmas season. The word was also used as a joyous Christmas greeting or exclamation.

[J. R. AHERNE]

YUMEDONO, main hall of the Japanese Buddhist temple. That of Horyuji, near Nara, built by the priest Gyoskin for Prince Shotoku (7th cent.), one of the oldest buildings in the world, was restored extensively in 1230. The octagonal structure on a double stone terrace, with surmounting bronze finial, houses portrait sculptures of Gyoshin and others, together with the Yumedono Kannon.

[M. J. DALY]

YUMEDONO KANNON, 7th-cent. Japanese wood sculpture in the Horyuji, Nara. Also known as the "world-saving Kannon" (Kuze Kannon), the figure—tall, slender, and faintly smiling—having been wrapped in layers of silk until the 19th cent., is excellently preserved.

[M. J. DALY]

YÜN-KANG ("Cloud-Terrace") **CAVES,** complex of Buddhist caves (450–550 A.D.) in the Shansi Province, China, W of Ta-t'ung, capital of the Tatar Northern Wei dynasty that persecuted Buddhists from 444 to 453 A.D., then accepted them. The 40 cave temples hollowed out of the sandstone cliffs (460–494 A.D.) with a few fashioned later (500–535 A.D.) are one of the most famous Buddhist monuments in Asia, the figures of benign and gentle loveliness, softly rounded, combine with acanthus, vines, and Hindu iconography in a Sino-Indian symbiosis of great iconographic and decorative richness. An early seated Buddha, 45-ft high (cave 20) modeled on the colossal Buddha of Bāmiyān, Afghanistan, is Central-Asian in style. The late 5th-cent. caves of Chinese style are sumptuous, deep chapels with sculptured zones of numerous Buddha and Bodhisattvas. Later figures are more attenuated as at *Lung-mên. BIBLIOGRAPHY: S. Mizuno and T. Nagahiro, *Yün-Kang, the Buddhist Cave Temples of the Fifth Cent. A. D. in North China* (16 v., 1951–56).

[M. J. DALY]

Z

ZACCARIA, FRANCESCO ANTONIO (1714–95), Jesuit theologian, historian, and prolific writer. One of the most erudite men of his time, he was responsible for the publication of well over 150 works, including a 22-v. collection of dissertations on church history (1792–97) and the 13-v. *Thesaurus theologicus*. Born in Venice, he joined the Jesuits in Austria (1731), was ordained in Rome (1740), and was soon caught up in the intrigues among Jesuits, Jansenists, and Febronians. After the suppression of the Jesuits in 1773, a pension granted him by Clement XIII as recompense for his work in defense of the papacy was stopped and his MSS were confiscated. For a time he was imprisoned in Castel Sant'Angelo but was soon restored to favor by Pius VI, who appointed him professor of church history at the Sapienza and director of the Academy of Noble Ecclesiastics.

[E. J. DILLON]

ZACCHAEUS, tax collector of Jericho (Lk 19.1–10). Short in stature, he climbed a sycamore tree to see over the heads of the crowd; Jesus showed his disregard of Jewish prejudice by inviting himself to dine with the tax collector. Z. consequently vowed to restore fourfold what he had taken wrongfully and to give half his goods to the poor. A soldier by the same name is mentioned in 2 Macc 10.19.

[T. EARLY]

ZACHARIA, see ZECHARIAH.

ZACHARIAE, JOHANN (*c.*1362–1428), Augustinian theologian, "Hussomastix." After a lectorship at Oxford and doctoral studies in theology at Bologna, Z. went to the Univ. of Erfurt in 1410. He preached at the Council of Constance and is said to have convicted John Huss. As provincial of the Augustinians in Saxony, Z. headed the general chapter at Asti. He wrote a commentary on the Apocalypse and *Notabilia* on Matthew, Luke, and Mark. BIBLIOGRAPHY: F. Roth, NCE 14:1105.

[M. J. FINNEGAN]

ZACHARIAS, ST. (d. 631), **PATRIARCH OF JERUSALEM** (609–628). Priest and guardian of the sacred vessels in Hagia Sophia at Constantinople, he held the patriarchate of Jerusalem during troubled times. During the Persian invasion of 614 he attempted to resist the capture of Jerusalem and the massacre of its people, but was captured and exiled to Persia until liberated by Heraclius in 628. During exile he remained in touch with his people by encyclical letter. During his absence St. John the Almsgiver, patriarch of Alexandria, undertook the restoration of the ancient monuments.

[E. J. DILLON]

ZACHARIAS, BOOK OF, see ZECHARIAH, BOOK OF.

ZACHARY, see also ZECHARIAH.

ZACHARY, ST. (d. 752), **POPE** from 741. Born of Greek parentage in Calabria, Z. succeeded Gregory III in the papacy at a time when Rome was threatened with invasion by Lombards. By his personal influence he prevailed upon King Liutprand to make peace with Rome and to restore four cities he had taken, and also to desist from his attack upon Ravenna. He consolidated papal authority in the North by encouraging the missionary work of St. Boniface, whom he made papal legate to a Frankish council (742), and by his approval of the decision of Pepin to assume the kingship of the Franks. He sought to persuade the Emperor in Byzantium to abandon his policy of supporting Iconoclasm. Z. translated the *Dialogues* of Gregory the Great into Greek. BIBLIOGRAPHY: M. C. McCarthy, NCE 14:1106; Mann 1.2:225–288; Hughes HC 2:132–134; Butler 1:596–597.

[R. B. ENO]

ZACHARY THE RHETOR (Zacharius Scholasticus; 465–536), church historian and metropolitan of Mitylene. Born near Gaza, Z. was one of the Gaza Triad together with

3799

*Procopius and *Aeneas of Gaza. He was educated in philosophy at Alexandria, but later moved to Constantinople where he was well-known at court and as a practicing lawyer. His *Ecclesiastical History* is an important source for Egyptian and Palestinian history between 450 and 491. Other writings include a *Life of Severus of Antioch*, a *Life of the Monk Isaac*, a *Life of Peter the Iberian*, and a dialogue *De opificio mundi*. BIBLIOGRAPHY: *Syriac Chronicle* (tr. F. J. Hamilton and E. W. Brooks, 1899).

[F. H. BRIGHAM]

ZACHARY, CANTICLE OF, see BENEDICTUS.

ZADOK (Sadoc), priest in the time of David and Solomon. For a while he was in charge of the Ark of the Covenant jointly with Abiathar (2 Sam 15.24). In the conflict over David's successor, Abiathar supported Adonijah, and Z. supported Solomon (1 Kg 1.22–39). Z. consequently became the sole head of the priesthood, and his descendants formed the dominant priestly family (1 Kg 4.2; 2 Chr 31.10; Ezek 40.46). His genealogy was traced to Eleazar, Aaron's oldest son (1 Chr 6.1–8). Several other biblical figures bore the name. (1 Chr 12.28; 2 Kg 15.33; 1 Chr 6.12; Neh 3.4; 10.21; 13.13; Mt 1.14).

[T. EARLY]

ZADOKITE FRAGMENTS, documents found in 1896–97 in the Ibn-Ezra Synagogue genizah, Old Cairo. They are the remains of two medieval copies of a Jewish sectarian manual in Hebrew. S. Schechter, who edited them in 1910, gave them the name, believing they were extracts from a Zadok book. Portions of the manual have since been found at *Qumram, however, and scholars believe it originated in the same movement that the Qumram community represents. It is also called the Damascus Document/Fragments because it describes a group that goes to Damascus (perhaps a symbolic expression for leaving orthodox Judaism) and enters into a new covenant.

[T. EARLY]

ZAHM, JOHN AUGUSTINE (1851–1921), scientist, educator, writer. A native of Ohio, Z. entered the Congregation of the Holy Cross and was ordained in 1875. He was a teacher at the Univ. of Notre Dame (Ind.) the better part of his life and also was procurator general in Rome for his congregation (1896–98), and provincial superior (1898–1905). A prolific writer, Z. contributed to many periodicals and published a number of books. His earlier works included *Catholic Science and Catholic Scientists* (1893), *Bible, Science and Faith* (1894), and *Evolution and Dogma* (1896). Extensive visits to South America resulted in four volumes of valuable history on the South American republics (1910–1917). He accompanied Theodore Roosevelt on one of the expeditions. At a time when most RC writers were fearful of science and the theory of evolution, Z. took a more positive (but controversial) stand.

[J. R. AHERNE]

ZAHN, THEODORE VON (1838–1933), Scripture scholar. Z. taught NT at several German universities, and was a leading proponent of biblical conservatism. He published numerous biblical treatises; edited and contributed extensively to the *Kommentar zum Neuen Testament* (18 v., 1903–26) in which he rejected the conclusions of liberal biblical scholarship. BIBLIOGRAPHY: J. Schmid, LTK 10:1306; L. A. Bushinski, NCE 14:1109–10.

[T. M. MCFADDEN]

ZAHUR, RAPHAEL (1759–1831), writer and scholar of Egyptian affairs. Upon Napoleon's conquest of Egypt, Z. was appointed to the Egyptian Institute and, in 1803, was named professor of Arabic at the Institut de Langues Orientales in Paris. He later (1816) became director of the National Printing Press in Cairo. He wrote books on a wide variety of subjects, notably an Italian-Arabic dictionary, a study of Arabic music, and a chronology from Adam to Christ based upon Roman, Greek, and Persian sources. BIBLIOGRAPHY: L. Malouf, NCE 14:1110.

[T. M. MCFADDEN]

ZAIDIS (Arab., *al-Zaydîya*), a *Shiite sect which traces its origins to Zaid ibn 'Alî, a grandson of al-Husayn ibn 'Alî, who led a revolt against the Umayyad government and was killed in 740. The Zaidis did not, however, become a cohesive group until later under the direction of two Alids, al-Hasan ibn Zaid (d. 864) and al-Qâsim al-Rassî (d. 860). The Zaidis, unlike the rest of the Shiites, do not recognize the inheritance of the Imamate. Their *Imams, consequently, do not represent a single unbroken series and they recognize the theoretical possibility of there being no imam or more than one for a brief period of time. Their theology, derived from that of al-Qâsim, is akin to that of the *Mutazilites and their law is sometimes recognized as a fifth school (see ISLAMIC LAW). Zaidi rule in Yemen, only recently replaced by a republic, was established by Yahyâ ibn al-Husayn, a grandson of al-Qâsim al-Rassî. BIBLIOGRAPHY: R. Strothman, EncIslam[1], s.v. "Zaidîya"; W. Madelung, *Imam al-Qâsim ibn Ibrâhîm und die Glaubenslehre der Zaiditen* (1965).

[R. M. FRANK]

ZALVIDEA, JOSÉ MARIA DE (1780–1846), Spanish Franciscan missionary who spent 40 years ministering to the Indians in California, until his death at Mission San Luis Rey. Born in Bilbao, Vizcaya, Spain, he joined the Franciscans in 1798 and was sent to the College of San Fernando in Mexico in 1804, where he spent a year in preparation for service in California.

[E. J. DILLON]

ZAMBONI, GIUSEPPE (1776–1846), Venetian priest, physicist. He is credited with inventing the Zamboni pile, a motor activated by the reaction of discs coated with zinc and manganese binoxide, and also with developing an electrical clock. Having studied in a seminary in Verona, he was ordained in that city and taught physics at the lyceum there. He died in Venice.

[E. J. DILLON]

ZAMOMETIČ, ANDREA (d. 1484), Croatian Dominican who attempted a conciliarist *coup-de-main* against Sixtus IV. As novice-master at Padua, he had been a friend of Francesco della Rovere, the future pope; but later on coming to Rome as abp. of Krajina (Albania) and imperial envoy, he lashed at the venality, rapacity, and nepotism he discovered there, and was thrown into Sant'Angelo. After his release, smarting under the humiliation, he attempted to rally the enemies and critics of the papacy, which included the league of Milan, Florence, and Naples, and the Universities of Paris, Louvain, Cologne, Erfurt, Kraków, and Vienna. In a singular sense of defiance in the cathedral of Basel (1482), he called for the reconvention of the reforming Council of Basel and summoned the Pope to defend himself at its bar. His supporters backed away at so extreme a step, and in particular the city-fathers, who at first had welcomed the project as good for the economy, were alarmed at the effects of an interdict. They put the abp. in chains. He acted dauntlessly until, 2 years later, he hanged himself in his cell. The story is commemorated by the Botticelli in the Sistine Chapel depicting justice being executed on Korah for his rebellion against Moses.

[T. GILBY]

ZAMORA, ALFONSO DE (*c*.1474–*c*.1531), Hebraist. Converted to Christianity from Judaism, Z. taught Hebrew at *Salamanca, contributed extensively to the Complutensian *polyglot Bible, wrote a Hebrew grammar and dictionary, and a Christian apologetic addressed to Roman Jews. BIBLIOGRAPHY: S. M. Polan, NCE 14:1111.

[T. M. MCFADDEN]

ZAMORA, ALONSO DE (1635–*c*.1717) Colombian Dominican historian. Entering the order in 1651, and ordained in 1659, he was made provincial chronicler (1688) and provincial (1698). From 1691 to 1696, using available archives, he completed a work of civil and ecclesiastical history begun by José de Caldas, *Historia de la provincia de San Antonio del Nuevo Reyno de Granada del Orden de Predicadores* (1701; prefaced by Caracciolo Parra, annotated by Andrés Mesanza, 1930; 4 v. ed., 1945). Book I focuses on flora and fauna, Book II–V are chronicles covering 1528 to 1696.

[R. J. LITZ]

ZAMORA CATHEDRAL (1152–74), Spanish church of Muslim, Poitevin, and Burgundian flavors, the exaggerated crossing tower with lantern, inspired by the Church of the Holy Sepulchre, Jerusalem (1149), the dome, French and Muslim. Oriental-romanesque sculptures of the Bishop's Door, 15th-cent. choir stalls, and marble tombs of Juan Mella and Canon Juan de Granada are notable.

[M. J. DALY]

ZANHOUR, RAPHAEL, see ZAHUR, RAPHAEL.

ZAPATA DE CARDENAS, LUIS (*c*.1515–1590), Spanish Franciscan, abp. of Bogatá, Colombia, from 1570. He entered the diocese in 1573; his primary effort was to make missionary work effective, and to this end he sought native Creole and mestizo clergy. He had Miguel de Espejo write a catechism to serve as a practical guide to pastors; the work includes important guides on native culture and social customs. Z. redistributed the Indian doctrinas, and in 1583 established the first seminary in Colombia, Colegio-Seminario de San Luis, where he himself taught the Muysca language to future pastors of the natives. His policy of promoting native clergy put him at odds with the missionaries of Spanish religious orders.

[R. J. LITZ]

ZAPATA Y SANDOVAL, JUAN (d. 1630), Mexican Augustinian, bishop. Of an aristocratic family, Z. became an Augustinian in Mexico City in 1590. Ordained a priest, Z. taught at Colegio San Pablo and the Univ. of Mexico. From 1602 to 1613 he taught in Valladolid, Spain. Named bishop of Chiapa, Mexico, in 1613 he returned to Mexico in 1614. In 1621 Z. was appointed bp. of Guatemala. Z.'s published work *De justitia distributiva* (1609) was a strong plea for placing colonial natives in civil and ecclesiastical positions in Spanish possessions rather than reserve offices for Spaniards alone. He is credited with having opened the door to Creole advancement in New Spain.

[J. R. AHERNE]

ZARATHUSHTRA, see ZOROASTER.

ZATVORNIK, THEOPHAN (1815–94), Russian Orthodox bp., spiritual leader, and writer. Born George Vasilievich Govorov and ordained in Kiev in 1841, he became a monk, taking the name Theophan. He taught in Kiev, Novgorod, and St. Petersburg. He left Russia in 1847 and lived in Palestine for 7 years, studying Greek and the Fathers. He returned to Russia and was consecrated bp. of Tambov in 1857; then was transferred to Vladimir in 1863. He resigned in 1866, however, and passed the rest of his life in a monastery. The fruits of his prayer and study are his many works on spiritual theology, commentaries on Scripture and monastic rules, and volumes of letters of spiritual direction. These writings reflect a mind and spirit steeped in patriotic thought and also in the writings of Aquinas. Z.'s doctrine is in the genuine Catholic tradition, although he was no partisan of the Church of Rome. He is rightly regarded as one of the soundest modern representatives of Eastern Christian tradition. BIBLIOGRAPHY: G. A. Maloney, NCE 14:1113–14.

[L. PEANO]

ZAVATTARI FAMILY. Six Milanese painters (fl. 1404–79) who signed, in the Monzo Cathedral, the large fresco cycle of the *Life of Theodolinda* (1444), the most monumental International Gothic painting in Lombardy.

[M. J. DALY]

ZEAL, in general, energetic and intense devotion to a cause; theologically, a spirit of dedication to the works of religion shown by a willingness to help promote projects which aid the Church. It is a desirable or undesirable quality depending at once on the merit of its cause and the prudence which rules it. A pejorative connotation is sometimes associated with the word because the enthusiasm which it engenders often is self-defeating. Frequently, zeal makes of the enthusiast a zealot, of the believer a bigot, of the patriot a flag-waver. Zeal in a good cause, however, when moderated by prudence makes a Christian a better one. BIBLIOGRAPHY: R. Knox, *Enthusiasm* (1950).

[P. F. MULHERN]

ZEALOTS (Greek, *zēlotai*), those "zealous" for God and his Law. Because of a certain ambiguity in ancient usage, the term has come to be used loosely to refer to a broad front of Jewish politico-religious activity against Rome *c.* 6–70 A.D. Two uses should be distinguished. Self-designated Zealots formed one of the nationalistic and revolutionary Jewish parties that pressed the war against Rome (66–70 A.D.) and against Jewish collaborators and moderates (Josephus, *War* 4:161); in this technical sense the Zealot party seems to have come into existence only during the war, and must be distinguished from other revolutionary groups (*ibid.* 7:262–270) including the *Sicarii* ("dagger-men" or assassins). In a less technical sense, the "zealots" were any Jews who were "zealous" for God and Law, whose religious motivation was based on the intense belief that no one but God was to rule Israel, that accepting Roman rule, paying Roman taxes, or offering sacrifice for the emperor was tantamount to idolatry, and who would rely on force in support of this belief. The attitude goes back to the example of the Maccabees and perhaps Elijah and Phineas (1 Kgs 18 and 19 and Num 25 with 1 Macc 2); it becomes esp. manifest in the revolutionary activity of Judas the Galilean (whom Josephus lists as the leader of the "fourth philosophy," i.e. in addition to Pharisees, Sadduccees, and Essenes: *War* 2:118; *Ant.* 18:9,23; Josephus does not use the designation "Zealots" to name the "fourth philosophy"). Thus many could be called "zealots" (e.g. Simon, the "zealot", the disciple of Jesus, Mk 3,18; Lk 6,15), without belonging to the (apparently later) Zealot party. BIBLIOGRAPHY: D. M. Rhoads, *Israel in Revolution 6–74 C.E.* (1976); M. Smith, *Harvard Theological Review* 64 (1971), 1–19; M. Hengel, *Die Zeloten* (1961).

[D. P. EFROYMSON]

ZEBEDEE, the fisherman father of the Apostles James and John (Mt 4.21; Mk 1.19).

[D. J. BOURKE]

ZEBULUN (Zabulon), sixth son of Jacob and Leah and ancestor of the tribe of Zebulun (Gen 30.20). The tribe numbered 57,400 at the first census (Num 1.31) and 60,500 at the second (Num 26.27). After the Conquest it received territory in the center of Palestine, between the Sea of Galilee and the Mediterranean (Jos 19.10–16). The tribe of Zebulun was closely associated with Issachar, the fifth son of Jacob and Leah (see Gen 49.13–15; Dt 33.18–19). It was summoned to fight with Barak (Jg 4.6) and Gideon (Jg 6.35). The judge Elon was from the tribe of Zebulun (Jg 12.11). Capernaum was in the territory of Zebulun, and Jesus' visit there was cited as a fulfillment of prophecy (Is 9.1; Mt 4.13–15).

[T. EARLY]

ZECHARIAH (Zachary), father of John the Baptist (Lk 1.5–79; 3.2). A priest of the Abijah division (1 Chr 24.7–19), he was burning incense in the Temple when the angel Gabriel announced to him that his barren wife Elizabeth, who was related to the mother of Jesus (Lk 1.36), would have a son, who was to be called John. Skeptical, Z. asked for a sign and consequently was struck dumb until the child was born, when he uttered the hymn known as the Benedictus (Canticle of Zechariah).

[T. EARLY]

ZECHARIAH, BOOK OF. Zechariah ch. 9–14 is certainly by a different and later hand than that which wrote Zech 1–8 in 520–518, shortly before the dedication of the second temple. This first section, Zechariah proper, consists mainly of eight nocturnal visions combined with exhortations to repentance, summons to the exiles to return, and promises of restoration. These are followed by a symbolic account of the coronation of Zerubbabel (although the name of Joshua the high priest has subsequently been interpolated). The central question in this first part of Zechariah is the rebuilding of the temple and the restoration of the people as a whole to messianic peace and well-being. This is to be presided over by the two anointed ones or messiahs, Joshua the high priest and the 'branch' of the Davidic house ruling together in perfect harmony (6.11–13). The nations will be defeated and will come as subordinates to the chosen people assembled about the temple where Yahweh will take up his abode.

Zech 9–14 is likewise messianic in character, but the unknown author, who probably wrote *c.*315, is no longer concerned with Joshua and Zerubbabel or with the rebuilding of the temple. Points that stand out in this group of oracles are the punishment of the foolish shepherds of Judah (11.4–17), the destruction of the nations advancing upon Jerusalem (ch. 12–14) and the renewal of the house of David in the person of a humble and "meek" messiah (9.9–10). BIBLIOGRAPHY: M. Bic, *Das Buch Sacharja* (1962); A. Gelin, *Aggée, Zacharie, Malachie* (3d ed., 1960); R. Brunner, *Sacharja* (1960); P. Lamarche, *Zacharie IX–XIV. Structure littéraire et messianisme,* (1961); H. G. May, "A Key to the Interpretation of Zechariah's Visions," JBL 57(1938) 173–184.

[T. M. MCFADDEN]

ZEDEKIAH, KING OF JUDAH (Sedecias), last of the kings of Jerusalem (597–587). Son of Josiah, he was appointed by Nebuchadnezzar in place of his nephew Jehoiachin (hence he may not have been regarded by all as true king). In spite of the warnings of Jeremiah (24.8–10) he proved too weak to resist the pressures and intrigues of the anti-Babylonian faction at his court and was drawn into the rebellion which led to his own and his city's ruin. After the conquest of Jerusalem he was blinded and taken captive to Babylon where he died.

The name was borne also by a prophet mentioned in 1 Kg 22.11; and by a false prophet castigated by Jeremiah (29.21).

[D. J. BOURKE]

ZEGADO, ESCOLÁSTICO (1813–71), educator. Born in Argentina, Z. was ordained in 1836. He founded the Colegio de Educandos, a normal school in Jujuy in 1858. Responsible for bringing Vincentian sisters and priests to the area, he established schools for boys and girls. In 1850 he built and endowed the San Roque hospital. Z. was the founder of *Recoba*, a society with social and economic goals. Named provincial governor of Jujuy, he took part later in the constituent parliament of 1855. Z. wrote an important work *Instrucciones cristianas*, used as a text in the schools of Argentina.

[J. R. AHERNE]

ZELANTI (Zealots), the party of *Franciscans which insisted in the 13th cent. on a strict interpretation of the rule, especially in regard to poverty. The Zelanti became the *Spirituals. *POVERTY CONTROVERSY.

[T. C. O'BRIEN]

ZEN BUDDHISM, an intuitive, experiential school of Mahayana Buddhism in China and Japan. Zen is the Japanese pronunciation of the Chinese *ch'an,* a transliteration of Sanskrit *dhyana*, meditation. The roots of Zen reach back to Indian Buddhist Yoga with its discipline of mind and body and the practice of meditation. When Indian Buddhism first entered China (1st cent. A.D.) the philosophy and practice of meditation were welcomed by Taoists, and the synthesis of Buddhist meditation and Taoist quietism later produced Zen. The legendary transmitter of Zen to China was Bodhidharma (6th cent. A.D.), the 28th patriarch in the Mahayana tradition and the 1st Zen patriarch. He provided the model for the subsequent development of Zen by his teachings, his extreme meditational practices, and his paradoxical and iconoclastic religious attitudes. However, the man most responsible for the formation of Zen as a distinctive Chinese school was the 6th patriarch, Hui-neng (d. 713), the "2d founder of Zen in China." Following his time it split up into several sects, the leading two being *Lin-chi* and *Ts'ao-tung*, with the former gaining greater popularity. The golden age of Zen extended from the 8th to the 12th century, during which time it interfused with the Pure Land School to give Chinese Buddhism its distinctive character. Zen was the most creative force in the culture of that age and was one element in the formation of Neo-Confucianism. However, it gradually declined after the 13th cent., and since 1949 has probably ceased to exist as an organized movement in China.

Zen was introduced to Japan from China in the 7th cent., but it did not become a separate movement until the 12th. A Japanese priest, Eisai (d. 1215), transmitted the *Lin-chi* sect known in Japan as *Rinzai*. The *Ts'ao-tung* sect, known in Japan as *Soto*, was introduced by a priest, Dogen (d. 1253), and it achieved great popularity in Japan. Zen's most influential period was the 13th to the 16th cent. during which it became the religion of the *samurai* ruling class; and during Japan's "dark ages" (14th–16th cent.) it provided vitality and creativity not only in religion but also in education, government, foreign trade, and culture. Neo-Confucianism was introduced and propagated by Zen priests, and the "Way of the warrior" (*bushido*) was a product of Zen and Neo-Confucianism. A third Zen sect, *Obaku,* was introduced from China in 1654. Basho (d. 1694), a Zen layman, made the 17-syllable *haiku* verse popular as a vehicle of Zen sentiment. Hakuin (d. 1768) was the most creative Zen thinker since Dogen and was known as the "2d founder of *Rinzai*." In 1965 there were 23 Zen sects with a membership of 9½ million households. *Soto* accounts for 6½ million; and *Rinzai*, 2½ million. Zen was introduced to the West in the 20th cent., mainly through the writings of a *Rinzai* Buddhist, D. T. Suzuki. Since World War II it has aroused the religious and scholarly interest of many Westerners and has been one of the main channels for the influx of Eastern thought, practices, and artistic ideals to the West.

Zen considers itself to be true to the spirit of the teachings of the Buddha, and tradition claims that it began with his enlightenment experience. Zen stands within the framework of Mahayana Buddhist thought with its emphasis on the final unknowability of Ultimate Reality, but it has received from Chinese thought an acceptance and affirmation of the world of nature and of everyday life. A verse attributed to Bodhidharma provides the model for Zen thought: "A special tradition outside the scriptures; No dependence upon words and letters; Direct pointing to the soul of man; Seeing into one's own nature and the attainment of Buddhahood." The key to Zen thought and experience is enlightenment (Jap. *satori*). Man's basic problem is his ignorance about the true nature of reality. He views himself and the world in abstract, dualistic terms, and he tries to understand reality intellectually and thereby misses the direct experience of life. The solution to his problems is enlightenment, the direct, intuitive insight into reality, i.e., the Buddha Nature inherent in all persons and things. Reality is the fundamental, original unity that transcends yet pervades all dualities of the world. It lies beyond all dichotomies such as subject–object, self–other, and good–bad. The Buddha Nature is identical with man's mind, so that enlightenment comes by insight into the identity of the Buddha Nature and one's own self. Once man realizes this truth, he is set free from dualistic illusion and he lives in composure, creativity, and spontaneity. Enlightenment is the acquisition of a new viewpoint that leads to a new style of life. Zen rejects all asceticism or world-denying philosophies because it affirms that everyday life and the world of nature are the Buddha Nature. Therefore, for the enlightened man, cooking rice or chopping wood is just as religious as prayer and meditation. Since enlightenment is a direct experience, Zen rejects all external authority and indirect attempts to apprehend reality.

Any technique that leads one to enlightenment is valid, although certain ones have been proved by time and usage to be more effective. Zen has always taken care to avoid replacing its true goal, enlightenment, by any technique. All Zen techniques are based upon the conviction that reality can be found only within man, and that enlightenment lies beyond words and intellect. The most common technique is sitting cross-legged in meditation (Jap. *zazen*), which is esp. emphasized in *Soto*. *Zazen* has been found to provide ideal physical and mental discipline to prepare the way for enlightenment. While sitting, one may empty his mind of all dualistic content and attempt to grasp the Buddha Nature within himself (*Soto*), or he may search for the solution to a paradoxical riddle (*Rinzai*). In *zazen* one does not enter a hypnotic trance or gain supernatural powers. He does not become something different; he simply apprehends what he is and has always been—the Buddha Nature. *Soto* also emphasizes worship and the study of scriptures as useful techniques, and it views enlightenment as a gradual and lifelong process of moral and spiritual growth.

The *Rinzai* techniques are more dramatic. Since *Rinzai* holds that enlightenment comes as an instantaneous experience of intuitive self-knowledge, many of its techniques have the purpose of shocking the disciples. A response from a master to a disciple's question may be a shout, "*katsu*," or a physical blow with the hand or a stick. The purpose of these techniques is not to punish the disciple but rather to shock him out of his ordinary dualistic thinking. Such techniques are used only in the intimate master-disciple relationship of love and trust. A *Rinzai* technique of mental shock is the paradoxical, rationally-insoluble riddle (*koan*) posed by the master (e.g., "What is the sound of one hand clapping?"). The *koan* is beyond logical or rational solution, so the disciple is finally driven to a psychological impasse. The only solution is to make an intuitive leap, and it is by a similar transrational process that one attains enlightenment. There is a collection of about 1,700 *koan*, and the master chooses an appropriate one for each disciple, who may struggle with it for years before gaining enlightenment or receiving a new *koan*. Other similar methods are private interviews between master and disciple (Jap. *sanzen*) when there may be a question-answer dialogue (Jap. *mondo*). Both *Soto* and *Rinzai* insist that although enlightenment is a personal experience, the master–disciple relationship is an absolute necessity for the journey toward enlightenment. Both also insist upon the usefulness of group discipline in a

monastery in which manual labor always stands as a corrective for "other-worldly" asceticism. The possibility of enlightenment is not denied to laymen, but they must live as disciplined a life as possible, and most monasteries provide facilities for laymen to study and practice meditation.

Zen shows an appreciation for both the cultural life of man and the world of nature. Since Zen is primarily a direct participation in everyday life, it has been one of the most creative forces in the development of Chinese and Japanese culture. Much of the sculpture, painting, and poetry in Sung China (960–1279) was inspired by Zen. The transmission of Sung culture to Japan was due primarily to Zen monks, who became the cultural leaders in Japan after the 13th century. Zen's influences in Japan can be seen in the tea ceremony, flower arranging, gardening, architecture, poetry (esp. *haiku*), *No* drama, painting, fencing, and archery. Zen art is characterized by simplicity, creativity, profundity, serene composure, and unthinking spontaneity. BIBLIOGRAPHY: H. Dumoulin, *History of Zen Buddhism* (tr. P. Peachey, 1965); C. Humphreys, *Zen Buddhism* (1958); D. T. Suzuki, *Essays in Zen Buddhism* Series I, II, III (new eds., 1958), and numerous other titles; A. W. Watts, *Spirit of Zen* (3d ed., 1958).

[C. H. HAMBRICK]

ZENO OF CITIUM (335–263 B.C.), founder of Stoicism. Coming to Athens from Cyprus in 313, Z. studied under Polemon the Academic and Diodorus the Megarian, and was converted to Cynicism by Crates of Thebes. His *Politeia* or *Republic* (not extant) was written in his Cynic period. He was greatly influenced by the personality of Socrates as presented in the writings of Xenophon and Plato, by the teachings of Antisthenes, and by Heracleitus, and, to some extent, by Aristotle. He founded his own School, the Stoa (named after the *Stoa Psikile* in Athens, where he lectured) *c*. 300 B.C. He created a full system of philosophy, comprising logic and epistemology, physics, and ethics. In his physics, he drew heavily on Heraclitus; in his logic and epistemology, he was influenced chiefly by Antisthenes and Diodorus. He is esp. important as the founder of Stoic ethics. He taught that the only true good consists in virtue and that the only real evil is moral weakness. The wise man, through the possession of virtue, is truly independent and happy. BIBLIOGRAPHY: K. von Fritz, OCD 965; LexAW 3326–27; E. Bevan, *Stoics and Sceptics* (1913).

[M. R. P. MCGUIRE]

ZENO OF ELEA (c.490–d. after 440 B.C.), the disciple and friend of Parmenides, and the founder of dialectic. In defending the position of Parmenides regarding Being, and his denial of becoming, change, and motion, he refuted the arguments of his opponents by drawing contradictory conclusions from their premises. Through his paradoxes, with their concrete illustrations, he became, according to Aristotle, the inventor of dialectic. The following example may be cited as typical of his method: Achilles can never overtake the tortoise since, when he reaches its starting point, the tortoise is a little farther on, and so *ad infinitum*. BIBLIOGRA - PHY: OCD s.v.; Copleston 1:54–59; LexAW s.v.; Guthrie 2:80–118.

[M. R. P. MCGUIRE]

ZENO OF VERONA, ST. Thought to be a native of Africa, Z. was bishop of Verona, c.362–372. Local tradition does not support St. *Gregory the Great's claim that Z. was a martyr. His sermons (PL 11:253–528, not all of which are authentic), reveal classical and ecclesiastical learning, the flourishing state of his diocese, and his activity against paganism and *Arianism. The miraculous preservation of Verona from flood in 598, attributed to Z.'s intercession, greatly increased his cult. BIBLIOGRAPHY: Altaner 432; Butler 2:77–78; M. F. Stepinach, *Christology of Zeno of Verona* (1948).

[R. B. ENO]

ZENZELINUS DE CASSANIS (d. 1334), medieval French civil and canon lawyer, an important defender of papal authority during the political and religious controversies preceding the Great Schism. Born in SW France, he taught civil and canon law at Montpellier until 1318, occupied several curial posts at the Avignon papal court, and died there. His extant writings exist mainly in manuscript.

[E. J. DILLON]

ZEON (Gr. boiling), the small amount of hot water which is blessed by the celebrant in the Byzantine liturgy and poured into the chalice by the deacon or the priest after the breaking of the holy bread and directly before the communion of the clergy. It symbolizes the heat and fervor of the Holy Spirit communicated by the participation in the precious blood of Christ. Its use is often omitted by Eastern Catholics. The name is also used for the small vessel used to contain the hot water.

[A. J. JACOPIN]

ZEPHANIAH, APOCALYPSE OF. Known only in fragmentary form from citations by Clement of Alexandria (*Strom* 5:11, 77), and from a Sahidic fragment (to these an anonymous apocalypse in the Akhmîmic dialect should probably also be added), this work relates how Zephaniah was carried up into the fifth heaven, privileged to witness the worship of the angelic hosts, and accorded a vision of hell. The state of the saved, and also of the damned, is described. The citations by Clement of Alexandria show linguistic connections with 1 Cor 8.6, and the work as a whole is akin to other pseudepigrapha, notably the *Apocalypse of Peter* and the *Ascension of Isaiah*. BIBLIOG - RAPHY: G. Steindorf, *Die Apokalypse des Elias, eine unbekannte Apokalypse, und Bruckstücke des Sophonias- Apokalypse* (1899); H. P. Houghton, *Coptic Apocalypse* I: "Sahidic 'Sophonias' Apocalypse'", II: "Akhmîmic 'Anonymous Apocalypse'", *Aegyptus* 39 (1959), 40–91.

[D. J. BOURKE]

ZEPHANIAH, BOOK OF. The oracles contained in this book were in substance delivered during the first part of the reign of Josiah (c.640–622 B.C.) when the idolatrous practices that had flourished under his apostate predecessors (e.g., star worship cf. 1:5) were apparently still prevalent. The book has been subjected to considerable editing and expansion since then, and in its existing form appears to fall into four short sections: (1) the day of Yahweh (1.2–2:3), (2) oracles against the nations (2.4–15), (3) against Jerusalem (3.1–8), and (4) promises of restoration (3.11–18a). Verses 9–10 and 18b–20 probably constitute a later interpolation. Although Zephaniah is often said to have been influenced by, or even to have been a disciple of Isaiah (principally because he, too, envisages a righteous remnant surviving Yahweh's punitive destruction of Judah and Jerusalem to become the new messianic people of God, cf. Zeph 2.1–3; 3.11–13), he is in fact both in language and ideas far closer to Hosea, Jeremiah, and Deuteronomy. He envisages a total destruction of Jerusalem and Judah which will obliterate not only the sinners but beasts, birds, and fishes, too, leaving only the humble ''trusters in Yahweh'' to survive and repeople the land. The occasion of this is the ''day of Yahweh'' depicted in 1.14–18, an idea which Zephaniah took over from Amos, but which he radically reshaped to fit in with his own ideas of the occasion of the divine judgment. BIBLIOGRAPHY: A. George, *Michée, Sophonie, Nahum* (2d ed., 1958); G. Gerlemann, *Zephania (textkritisch und literarisch untersucht)*, (1942); L. Pettibone Smith and E. R. Lacheman, ''The Authorship of the Book of Zephaniah,'' *Journal of Near Eastern Studies* 9 (1950) 137–142.

[T. M. MCFADDEN]

ZEPHYRINUS, ST., POPE (d. 217). Z. succeeded *Victor I in 198 or 199; there is no proof of his alleged martyrdom. He is coupled with his deacon and successor, St. *Callistus, in the attacks of St. *Hippolytus. The claim, repeated by A. *Harnack, that Z. was a Modalist, is unfounded. Z. gave the land which is the site of the Cemetery of St. Callistus (see CATACOMBS). BIBLIOGRAPHY: Bihlmeyer-Tüchle 1:162; D 105; Butler 3:406; Jedin-Baus 201, 258; Quasten 1:279–280.

[R. B. ENO]

ZERED (ZARED), brook flowing into the SE corner of the Dead Sea and marking the boundary between Edom and Moab. The Israelites crossed it on their way to Canaan (Num 21.12). It is possibly the Brook of Willows (Is 15.7).

[T. EARLY]

ZERUBBABEL, grandson of Jehoiachin, exiled king of Judah. His name means ''seed[scion] of Babylon,'' but to the Jews in exile he was the chosen servant of Yahweh, the focus of messianic hope because of his Davidic lineage. The prophets Haggai (2.21–23) and Zechariah (4.6–10) encouraged the people to think along such lines during the months following the death of Cambyses and the accession of Darius. The latter actually appointed Z. governor of Jerusalem. He was possibly leader of one of the first parties of the returning exiles (Ezra 2.2; Neh 7.7; 12.1). As such, and in league with the high priest Joshua, he spurred on the restoration of the ruined temple and environs, which had been begun by his uncle Sheshbazzar, and was completed in the sixth year of Darius. The work was accomplished despite legal harassment by the descendants of those who had never left the province of Judah, and whose faith had not matured in the light of the experience of exile to Babylon. The biblical record is silent about the end of Z.'s governorship and about his death. Some read into this silence the possibility he may have suffered disgrace because of the messianic hopes he engendered. It is even speculated that he is the historical figure behind the portrait of the suffering servant in Is 53. At any rate his memory was revered in later Judaism; in Sirach he is celebrated as one of Israel's renowned men; he figures in haggadic legend and in a Hanukkah hymn. The Evangelists Matthew and Luke both include him in Jesus' genealogy.

[E. J. DILLON]

ZERVANISM, a form of ancient Persian religion in which "Time" was worshipped as the supreme god. There is no reference to *Zervan* in the *Gâthâs,* but Berossus in his *Babylonica* (4th cent. B.C.) mentions a "mythical king Zerovanus," and Eudemus of Rhodes (2nd half of 4th cent. B.C.) speaks of a philosopher under the name of Zervanus in a passage preserved in the late Neoplatonic philosopher Damascius (5th–6th cent. A.D.). However, it is clear from the excerpt that, while the supreme and sole principle is called Time, Space is also used to designate the "infinite and intelligible all." Zervanism as a form of astral fatalism seems to have been revived or at least developed in Iranian circles under Greco-Babylonian influence. It enjoyed a great vogue under the Arsacid, but esp. under the Sassanid, dynasties. Whether Zervanism at any time replaced Mazdaism in practice is a disputed question. Perhaps Zervanism and Mazdaism were cultivated side by side through a process of accomodation. *Zervan* was regarded as infinite and as a god of the three ages of man and of death. There is a close parallel between him and the Hellenistic divinity *Aiōn* and the old myth was revived that Ormazd and Ahriman were the twin sons of Zervan. The religio-philosophical speculations connected with *Zervan* exercised a marked influence on Gnosticism, but particularly on Manichaeism. The supreme god of Manichaeism is Zervan; and this fact would seem to indicate that the cult of Zervan had a greater vitality than the official cult of Ormazd in the 3rd cent. A.D. BIBLIOGRAPHY: J. Duchesne-Guillemin, NCE 14:1119; *idem, La Religion de l'Iran ancien* (1962), esp. 184–189 and 302–307; R. C. Zaehner, *Zurvan: A Zoroastrian Dilemma* (1955).

[M. R. P. MCGUIRE]

ZEUS, TEMPLE OF, OLYMPIA (486 B.C.–460 or 456 B.C.), Greek temple designed by Libon of Elis. One of the largest Doric temples on the mainland, its famous sculptured W pediment and metopes of Parian marble depicting the *Battle of Lapiths and Centaurs,* and the *Labors of Hercules* are magnificent examples of early classical Greek form. Within the cella was the renowned chryselephantine statue of *Zeus Olympieios* by Phidias. The temple was destroyed in the Byzantine period but impressive fragments remain.

[M. J. DALY]

ZEUSS, JOHANN KASPAR (1806–56), Celtic philologist. Born at Vogtendorf in Bavaria, educated at Würzburg and Munich Universities, Z. never held an academic position because of his being Catholic. Teaching in the Gymnasium at Munich, he nevertheless produced scholarly works on ethnography and local history. In 1853 he produced his monumental *Grammatica Celtica,* based on the examination of the oldest extant records of the six Celtic languages.

[R. T. MEYER]

ZHAMAKARKOUTIUN (Zhamakarqouthiun), Armenian Catholic breviary or office-book, containing in one volume the *zhamakirk,* the *sharagan,* and those texts of the *djashotz* which are needed for the Divine Office.

[A. CODY]

ZHAMAKIRK (Zhamakirq; East Arm., *zhamagirk*), Armenian liturgical book containing the ordinary parts of the Divine Office without the hymns or the lessons.

[A. CODY]

ZIEGELBAUER, MAGNOALD (1689–1750), Swabian–born Benedictine historian, author of the 4-v. history of Benedictine letters, published posthumously (1764). He made his profession at the abbey of Zweifalten (1707), was ordained in 1713, taught theology at Reichenau until 1726 and moral theology at Göttweig (1732–33). He died in Olmütz where he had been active in the quietly effective *Societas eruditorum incognitorum,* a learned society.

[E. J. DILLON]

ZIEGLER, ALOYSIUS KIERAN (1895–), medieval historian. Born in Adell, Wis., of Louis and Mary Elizabeth (*née* Kenna) Z., he attended Adell Public School and St. John's, Plymouth, Wis., studying from 1908–19 at St. Francis Seminary, Wisconsin. He was ordained in 1919 and received his B.A. that year, an M.A. at the Univ. of Wisconsin in 1925, S.T.D. from The Catholic Univ. of America for which he wrote *Church and State in Visigothic Spain* (1930), an epoch-making work in a little-known period of Spanish history. He was sent abroad to specialize in medieval studies at the École Nationale des Chartes, during which he wrote *Histoire de la géomancie latine*, a work which took him to most of principal archival collections of Western Europe, and won for him (1934) the degree of *Archiviste palaéographe*; (there were only two others in the U.S. at this time). He also received the degree L.H.D. (*honoris causa*). His articles, ''Pope Gelasius I and the Relations of Church and State,'' *Catholic Historical Review* (1941) and ''History of Medieval Latin Literature,'' in NCE (1967) are definitive works in their respective areas.

But Z.'s greatest contribution by far was his training of graduate students during his career as professor of medieval history and medieval Latin literature (1934–76). He directed 25 doctoral dissertations, mostly in the internationally renowned series: *Studies in Medieval History,* several of them in Visigothic Spanish history, two in Medieval English, two in French, one in music. His skill was in direction and formation of scholars who have themselves won international reputations, e.g., Francis X. Murphy, CSSR; Sister Elizabeth (formerly Thomas Aquinas) Carroll, RSM; Edward P. Colbert; Jeremiah J. Smith, OFM Conv; Anselm Biggs, OSB; Sr. Germaine McNeill, CSJ; to mention a few. Msgr. Ziegler retired in 1976 to St. Anne's Residence, 3800 North 92nd St., Milwaukee, Wisconsin.

He served as chairman of the Department of History at The Catholic Univ. of America, Washington, D.C., from 1944 to 1964; was associate editor of *The Catholic Historical Review,* editor of *The American Ecclesiastical Review,* dean of the Catholic Sisters' College and for many years chaplain of Trinity College, Washington, D.C.

An early champion of women's rights, he expressed his esteem for them by granting them no special favors, giving no quarter, and developing their potential *pari passu* with men. His seminars, held on Saturday mornings from 10 to 12 regularly ran until 1 o'clock; only the hardiest student dared to ask to be excused at 10 minutes of 1 and then only for a matter of life or death.

[C. M. AHERNE]

ZIERIKZEE, CORNELIUS OF (1405–*c*.1470), Dutch Franciscan Observant, leader of seven friars sent to Scotland (1447) to establish Franciscan life. Highly popular, Z. gained noble and educated members for the order and administered friaries at Edinburgh, St. Andrews, and Perth. He left Britain in 1462 and died at Antwerp. BIBLIOGRAPHY: J. Cambell, NCE 14:1119–20.

[R. W. HAYS]

ZIGGURAT (ZIKURAT), typical Mesopotamian shrine or temple ''rising to the heavens'' simulating a sacred mountain. The important Neo-Sumerian ziggurat at Ur (2125 B.C.), dedicated to the moon by King Urnammu, is constructed of batten walls of mud-brick laid in reed mats, dipped in bitumen found, according to Herodotus, in lumps in the stream Is, tributary to the Euphrates, eight days journey from Babylon. Upon a massive 50-foot base, three suc-

cessively recessed stories with shrine, were faced with flashing, glazed tiles in colors symbolic of the underworld, earth, and heavens, with ceremonial stairways and ramps (Citadel of Sargon II, Khorsabad, 706 B.C.), and terraces gay with trees and gardens (Hanging Gardens of Babylon) made possible in the arid area by an elaborate system of irrigation analyzed by Herodotus (*History*, I, §193). The tower of Babel is thought to have been a ziggurat. BIBLIOGRAPHY: H. J. Lenzen, *Die Entwicklung der Zikkurat von ihren Anfängen bis zur Zeit der dritten Dynastie von Ur* (1941).

[M. J. DALY]

ZIGLIARA, TOMMASO (1833–1893), Dominican cardinal, philosopher, and theologian. He was a Corsican, a friend and trusted adviser of Leo XIII, and helped to prepare important encyclicals, including *Rerum novarum*. A leading figure in the Leonine revival of Thomism, he was the director of the critical edition of the works of St. Thomas Aquinas and wrote the notes in vol. 1. Although deeply involved in the disputes about the alleged *ontologism of *Rosmini, he was singularly untouched by controversial odium. His *Summa philosophica* (3 v. 1876), for some decades a standard text, was written in a leisurely and rounded style. His most important work was to explore the philosophical grounds of systematic theology.

[T. GILBY]

ZILBOORG, GREGORY (1890–1959), psychiatrist and author. Born in Russia to Orthodox Jewish parents, Z. received his M.D. at St. Petersburg, served in the Russian army, and participated in the February Revolution. Forced to leave the U.S.S.R. in 1919, he came to the U.S. and in 1925 became an American citizen. He received an M.D. from Columbia in 1926 and later practiced psychiatry in New York. He wrote, lectured widely, and taught at several schools. After coming to the U.S. he joined the Society of Friends, then in 1954 became a Roman Catholic. Against Freud he defended the validity of a religious point of view. BIBLIOGRAPHY: his *Psychoanalysis and Religion*, edited by his wife (1962).

[T. EARLY]

ZIMMER, PATRICK (1752–1820), German Catholic philosopher and theologian. His many volumes of systematic treatises in theology reflect a persistent anti-Kantian polemic and a certain affinity for the pantheistic notions of F. Schelling. Born in Württemberg, Z. studied at Ellwangen and Dillingen, was ordained a priest in 1775, was professor of dogmatic theology at Dillingen from 1783 until 1791. He was then named pastor at Steinheim. He again became a professor of theology at Ingolstadt and then Landshut from 1799 until becoming professor of exegesis in 1807. In 1819 he was both rector of the university and a deputy in the Bavarian parliament. He died in Steinheim.

[E. J. DILLON]

ZIMMERMAN, OTTO (1873–1932), Jesuit theologian and spiritual writer. Born in Switzerland, he entered the upper German province of the Jesuits in 1908. From 1905 on he was a collaborator of the review *Stimmen der Zeit*. He wrote many books on asceticism, including his *Lehrbuch der Aszetik* (1930), which became the leading book of its kind in German.

[E. J. DILLON]

ZIMMERMANN, BENEDICT MARY OF THE CROSS (1859–1937), priest, scholar, linguist, and historian of the Order of Discalced Carmelites. His major work is the history of his order in England, *Carmel in England* (1899). He also edited various works of St. Teresa and St. John of the Cross and other important Carmelite documents. He was born George Rudolph Zimmermann, in Switzerland, the son of a Zwinglian pastor; was converted to Catholicism in 1877; joined the Carmelites in London in 1885; was ordained priest 1889. He was novice master (1891–1903), then was elected prior and held that office until his death.

[E. J. DILLON]

ZIMMERMANN, DOMINIKUS (1685–1766), Bavarian architect. At first a stuccoist, he executed six altars for the abbey in Fishingen, Switzerland, and did decorative work for the Rathaus, Landsberg, Germany. A prolific architect, Z.'s masterpieces are the pilgrimage churches at Steinhausen and at Wies, the extreme lightness and delicacy seen in the oval of the former, reaching an apotheosis with the blending of Bavarian and French elements (from Cuvilliés) in the exquisite oval church of "Die Wies," upper Bavaria (1745–54), one of the finest spatial designs of the mid-18th cent., a ceiling resting on paired free-standing supports, the oval structure a configuration more complex and fluid than that at Würzburg. **Johann Baptist** (1680–1758), German stuccoist and fresco painter. He worked for Cuvilliés at the Nymphenburg (1721) and other palaces, in the tradition of the Asam brothers, though in a more airy rococo style, and collaborated with his brother Dominikus in the decoration of the churches at Steinhausen and at Wies. BIBLIOGRAPHY: S. L. Faison, "Dominikus Zimmermann," *Magazine of Art, 45* (1952).

ZINGERLE, PIUS (1801–81), Syrian scholar. Z. taught theology at the Benedictine Abbey of Marienberg, except for a brief period as professor of Arabic at the Sapienza College in Rome. He published numerous volumes of Syriac texts in German translation and is esp. noted for his translations of St. *Ephrem. BIBLIOGRAPHY: L. F. Hartman, NCE 14:1121–22.

[T. M. McFADDEN]

ZINZENDORF, NICHOLAS LUDWIG VON (1700–60), Pietist leader and founder of the Renewed *Moravian Church. Count Zinzendorf, born into nobility at Dresden, was, by his father's early death, brought under the care of his maternal grandmother, a prominent Pietist. His precocious piety was deepened by 6 years at A. *Francke's preparatory school at Halle. Yielding to family pressure, he spent 3 years studying law at Wittenberg and in 1721 entered state service. His own choice would have been a career in the Church. Married to a woman who shared his religious interests, he opened his Dresden home to Pietist meetings. With inherited money he purchased an estate, including the village of Berthelsdorf, with a Lutheran church, near the home of his grandmother, and proceeded to build a manor house. His intention of making this estate a religious center was quickened by the arrival of refugees from Moravia seeking freedom to worship in the manner of their forefathers, the *Bohemian Brethren. They established their village of *Herrnhut in 1722, a mile from the village church. Attending the church for preaching services and the sacraments, they also held their own religious meetings at Herrnhut under the direction of the Count. Within a decade Herrnhut was a flourishing Pietist center with missionaries throughout the world and diaspora evangelists in the churches at home. Z. kept a tight rein on this development and soon left state service (1727). He was ordained a Lutheran clergyman in 1734 and received episcopal consecration from a Moravian bp. in 1737. During the years 1736–47 he was banished from Saxony for unorthodox religious activities. His travels extended his influence, and in that period he spent 14 months in America, where he took part in the Moravian settlement of Bethlehem, Pa., in 1741. Though he was free to return home in 1747, work in England, Holland, Switzerland, and W Germany kept him away. Only during the last 4 years of his life did he direct the Church from Herrnhut. He lived long enough to see as the fruit of his activities new life in state Churches all over Europe; Moravian Churches on the Continent, in England, and in America; and converts on the mission field from Greenland to Africa. It had been Z.'s intention that his society remain as a vivifying influence within the Lutheran Church; circumstances, esp. missionary development, led to the emergence of the separate Moravian Church. The Christ-centered theology of his many writings emphasize a deeply-felt faith in the creator, savior, and preserver of all. This *Herzens-religion,* a religion of warmth and experience, influenced church life in Germany and, through its effect on F. *Schleiermacher, the subsequent course of theology. As an 18th-cent. hymn writer, Z. was second only to Charles *Wesley in the number of hymns composed. BIBLIOGRAPHY: J. R. Weinlick, *Count Zinzendorf* (1956).

[J. R. WEINLICK]

ZION (SION), the fortified mountain that was an ancient Jebusite stronghold before becoming the fortified city of David. The mount of Zion is probably the lesser, eastern hill of Jerusalem, near the spring of Gihon; and not the higher, western summit. Strictly speaking, Zion is the fortified hill; Jerusalem is the city-state whose peace derives from the strength of Zion; and Judah is the southern province of the

Israelite confederation. These distinctions can become blurred in the poetic imagery of prophetic oracles. There were some sacred traditions of Zion taken over by the Davidic monarchy from the Jebusite inhabitants of Jerusalem. These traditions probably include the belief that Zion is a holy mountain fortified by God who will never let it be completely destroyed; that the king of Zion is God's anointed and brings justice and peace to Jerusalem. The high-priest who is also king in the manner of Melchisedek may have its origin in Zion tradition. The prophet Isaiah couched his oracles of judgment and hope in the imagery of this tradition. From him derive the Zionist themes central to later messianism and the Jewish apocalyptic era.

[E. J. DILLON]

ZION, DAUGHTER OF, a poetic phrase of frequent use by the prophets of Juda as a synonym for Jerusalem and its inhabitants. It is especially recurrent in Isaiah and the Book of Lamentations. The same phrase as used in Zechariah 9.9 is quoted in Mt 21.5 and Jn 12.15, and applied to the people of Jerusalem welcoming Jesus' entry to that city "humble and mounted on an ass." It was common usage to refer to cities, towns, and villages as "daughters" of a larger entity: a tribe, a nation, a land, or a metropolis. At first glance it might seem strange, therefore, that the larger entity (Jerusalem) should be called the daughter of the smaller entity (Zion), until one recalls that Zion, the holy mountain, Yahweh's stronghold, the fortified city of David wherein dwell Jahweh and his anointed, is the source of life, security, well-being, and peace for outlying Jerusalem and the Judean countryside.

[E. J. DILLON]

ZIONISM, a movement founded by nationalistic Jews in the late 19th cent. to establish a Jewish nation with its own territory and independent government. In 1948 the effort seemed to succeed in the recognition of the state of Israel by a majority of the United Nations. The term derives from one of the names of David's city, Jerusalem, the capital of his empire, which became a symbolic, messianic name under the influence of Israelite prophets, esp. Is 1 and 2 which foretold a spiritual and political rebirth of Israel after the destruction of Jerusalem, and Israel as a nation, in 587 B.C.

Until the 18th cent. the mass of Jewry existed in quasi-autonomous enclaves in metropolitan areas of Europe, but when Jews began to live apart from the ghetto in the emancipation movement of the 19th cent., many of them became disturbed by the growing assimilation to gentile ways and culture, and the violent anti-Semitism that they encountered. In 1897 at Basel, under the leadership of a Viennese journalist, Theodor Herzl, political Zionism was founded at the First Zionist Congress as an attempt to establish a Jewish state that would have international recognition, preferably in Palestine. Despite great opposition from assimilated, and then, religiously scrupulous Jews, the movement received support, mainly from the youthful and persecuted Jews of

Eastern Europe. The World Zionist Organization with Herzl's guidance set up a financial trust to buy land in Palestine and attempted to gain the backing of the great powers, esp. England, Germany, and Russia. Turkey, the country then ruling Palestine, however, remained strongly opposed to having a powerful Jewish enclave in its empire.

After Herzl's death in 1904 a more practical Zionism fostered a limited agricultural and urban colonization in Palestine, and a nationalistic rebirth of Hebrew language and culture. During World War I, Zionists, led by Chaim Weizmann, won the Balfour Agreement from the British, which spoke of the desirability of a Jewish national home in Palestine but without prejudice to the rights of the native Palestinians. Under the post-war Palestinian Mandate, the Zionist Jewish Agency for Palestine attempted to have the Balfour Agreement implemented to a much greater degree than was ever intended by the British government, who had also committed itself to the establishment of independent Arabian states or state in the same territory. The resulting friction led to constant unrest in Palestine, culminating in the war between the native Arabs and their allies and the immigrant Jews who made up the state of Israel, which has been going on since 1948. Since then Zionism has persistently aided in colonizing Palestine until now there is a Jewish population of foreign origin of almost 2 million people. In the meantime a population of more than a million and a quarter native Palestinians live in various refugee camps on the fringes of their native land supported by the UN. The Arab states have never accepted or recognized Israel as a political entity, but claim it to be the most extreme example of Western imperialism, in which foreign people of greater wealth and military skill and resources almost completely expel the native population to make room for colonists. The situation is one of the major sources of international disunity and friction in the present world.

[J. F. FALLON]

ZIRC, ABBEY OF, Cistercian monastery in Hungary in the diocese of Veszprém founded in 1182 by monks from Clairvaux. It prospered until 1526 when the Turks completely destroyed its building. It was rebuilt in Baroque style in the 18th cent. by German Cistercians of Heinrichau. During the 19th cent. the abbey became the flourishing center of the Hungarian Cistercian Congregation numbering over 200 monks, who operated 5 gymnasia and 15 parishes throughout the country. The abbey and all its institutions were suppressed by the Communist government in 1950. Monks from Zirc founded Our Lady of Dallas Abbey (1958), Texas. BIBLIOGRAPHY: L. J. Lekai, NCE 14:1124; T. von Bogyay, LTK 10:1380–81; K. Horváth, *Zirc története* (1930).

[L. J. LEKAI]

ZITA, ST. (1212–1272), virgin. At the age of 12, Zita became a domestic for the Fatinelli family in Lucca. She humbly and industriously discharged her duties for 48

years. A deep spirit of prayer and charity for the poor marked her life. She overcame the antagonism and opposition of her fellow-workers by her meekness and amiability. Innocent XII confirmed her cult in 1696. On Sept. 26, 1953, she was made the patroness of domestic workers. BIBLIOGRAPHY: Butler 2:173–174; N. Del Re, BiblSanct 12:1483–84.

[J. M. O'DONNELL]

ŽIŽKA, JOHN (*c.*1376–1404), Bohemian patriot, leader of the *Taborites. Z. was the military leader in the victories of the people of Prague during the first Hussite wars (1420–23) against the Emperor Sigismund and the crusades authorized by Pope Martin V. He was also one of the heads of the Taborite community and during 1423 successfully led it in the civil wars against *Utraquists and Catholics. BIBLIOGRAPHY: Bihlmeyer-Tüchle 2:442.

[T. C. O'BRIEN]

ZOBOR, ABBEY OF, monastery located near Nitra in Slovakia. Founded by Bp. Viching of Nitra for the Benedictine monks in 882, it was richly endowed by Prince Svatopluk. It became a center for monastic training, and at Benedict's martyrdom in 1012, it became a national shrine. In 1468, the monks were dispersed by the bp. of Nitra who confiscated the abbey for his residence. In 1691, Bp. Jalkin of Nitra restored it and gave it to the Camaldolese monks. It was suppressed by Emperor Joseph II in 1782. In 1936, it was given by the bp. to the Divine Word Congregation. The Communists liquidated it (1950), and it now serves as a museum. BIBLIOGRAPHY: B. Hřín, "Benedictine Monasteries in Slovakia," *Slovak Studies* 1 (1961) 51–60; L. Nemec, NCE 14:1124; B. Chropovský, "The Situation of Nitra in the light of Archeological Findings," *Historica* (1964) 8:5–32, for recent literature concerning this abbey.

[L. NEMEC]

ZOE (Gr., life), a brotherhood similar to Catholic secular institutes founded by Archimandrite Eusebius Matthopoulos in 1907 to make Christianity more relevant and intelligible for the masses of Greek Orthodox. Members of this brotherhood take solemn promises of poverty, chastity, and obedience (not vows, however), and usually live in common while engaging in a great diversity of activities. One fourth of the approximately 200 members are monks, and the rest are laymen. The majority possess a university degree in theology and engage directly in some form of teaching or preaching. They publish books, pamphlets, and newspapers for all classes of Greek Christians. Zoe operates 2,300 catechetical Sunday schools with more than 200,000 students. Since 1929 it has published more than 400,000 copies of the Bible in five editions. Twelve other associations affiliated with Zoe aim at evangelizing particular sections of the population. In 1960 a conservative group, fearing the liberal tendencies of the younger Zoe theologians,

broke away to form a similar brotherhood called *Sotir* (Savior).

[G. A. MALONEY]

ZOËGA, JÖRGEN (1755–1809), Danish archeologist and numismatist, who is considered (along with W. Winckelmann and Visconti) to be the founder of scientific archeology. Through his work on Egyptian monuments in Rome, he advanced our knowledge of ancient Egypt and wrote on the pharaohs, obelisks, hieroglyphs, and the more recent Roman and Coptic periods. Born in Daler, Schleswig, he studied in Altona, at Göttingen and Leipzig; and later studied numismatics in Vienna. He was converted to Catholicism in 1783 and through his patron, the future Cardinal Stefano Borgia (then Secretary of Propaganda Fidei), he was interpreter of modern languages at the Propaganda. In 1798 he was Danish consul general to Rome; in 1802 professor at Kiel; in 1806 elected to the academies of science of Rome and Vienna. He was commissioned by the Danish government to work on a study of medals and ancient coins at Copenhagen, Munich, and other cities. He collaborated on the first modern Icelandic-Danish dictionary. He died in Rome.

[E. J. DILLON]

ZOËRARDUS AND BENEDICT, SS., late 10th- early 11th-cent. Slovak hermits; patrons of the Diocese of Nitra (Czechoslovakia), declared saints in the time of Ladislaus I. Born in Silesia, they came to Slovakia during the reign of St. Stephen of Hungary (1002–03). Zoërardus, also known as Andrew, and whose Slovak name was Svorad, was a monk in Zobor, Hungary, then a center of Benedictine life. With his disciple Benedict, whose Slovak name was Stojislav, he lived a life combining aspects of the Camaldolese and the Benedictine tradition. The master died in 1009; the disciple was killed by robbers in 1012, near the cave in Skalka which had been their cenobitic hermitage. The relics of both are in the cathedral of Nitra. BIBLIOGRAPHY: F. G. Holweck, *Biographical Dictionary of the Saints* (1924).

[E. J. DILLON]

ZOHAR (Heb. "brightness"), Jewish mystical commentary on the first five books of the Bible and other biblical books, stemming from the 13th-cent. Spanish cabalistic school and attributed mostly to Moses de Leon (d. 1305). It became very popular among the Jews expelled from Spain in the 16th cent., who settled at Safed in Palestine. Although remaining essentially Hebraic in character, it betrays much influence of Gnosticism and Neoplatonism. Hasidic and Sephardi Jews still hold it in great honor.

[J. F. FALLON]

ZOÏLUS OF ALEXANDRIA, Patriarch, 540–551. Though a staunch follower of the Council of Chalcedon against the Monophysites, he was compelled to sign the

Edict of Justinian I opposing the Three Chapters. He sent messengers to Pope Vigilius early in 546 to protest that he had signed under duress and to excuse his weakness. He was forced to flee Alexandria and Justinian deposed him in July 551 because of his refusal to condemn the Three Chapters.

[L. PEANO]

ZOLA, GIUSEPPE (1739–1806), N Italian Jansenist theologian. As a young man he taught moral theology at the seminary of Brescia until the bp. of Brescia relieved him of that duty for his rigorism. A few years later he was teaching church history at Pavia and was also director of the German College there. At the death of the Emperor Joseph II, the Lombard bps. re-established their episcopal seminaries and Z. was again dismissed, along with his friend *Tamburini. After the annexation of the Cisalpine Republic to France under Bonaparte (1796–99), Z. occupied the chair of diplomatic law at Pavia, a position he was able to keep after the formation of the kingdom of Italy.

[E. J. DILLON]

ŻÓŁKIEWSKI, STANISLAW (1547–1620), Polish military leader. A nobleman who had been educated at the Univ. of Lvov, he served the Polish kings Stephan Bathory and Sigismund III in a number of diplomatic and administrative posts. His greatest achievements, however, came as Field Hetman when he led the armies of Poland to victories over the Cossacks, Swedes, and Muscovites. Z. hoped to establish a voluntary union of the crowns of Poland and Russia and, following his brilliant victory at Klushino in 1610, he agreed with the Russian boyars to guarantee freedom of the Orthodox faith in return for the election of Ladislas, Sigismund's son, as tsar. When Sigismund insisted on his own election as tsar, this policy of conciliation collapsed and a protracted religious and national war between the two countries ensued. Z. suffered from the neglect of his prudent advice again when Polish intervention in the Thirty Years War left the country vulnerable to Turkish invasion. He died in the battle of Cecora while heroically defending the frontiers with inadequate forces. BIBLIOGRAPHY: *Cambridge History of Poland* (ed. W. F. Reddaway *et al.*, (1941–50).

[R. J. GIBBONS]

ZOLLI, EUGENIO (1881–1956), Semitic scholar and Jewish convert to Christianity. After studies in Florence, Z. was chief rabbi of Trieste, taught Hebrew at the Univ. of Padua, and in 1940 became chief rabbi of Rome. During the German occupation, he went into hiding but continued to exercise his leadership. He became a Catholic in 1945, influenced by a life-long interest in the person of Christ and by the charity of Pius XII. From 1945 he taught Semitics at the Univ. of Rome and the Pontifical Biblical Institute. BIBLIOGRAPHY: E. Z., *Nazarene* (tr. C. Vollert, 1950); *idem*,

Before the Dawn: Autobiographical Reflections (1954); G. Wood, NCE 14:1128–29.

[T. M. MCFADDEN]

ZONARAS, JOHN (d. after 1160), Byzantine historian and canonist. After a career as a court official he entered a monastery c.1118 and there wrote his history and other works. His *Epitomē Istoriōn* is a world chronicle to 1118. In richness of content and in quality of presentation it is superior to most of the other Byzantine universal chronicles. He made use in part of sources no longer extant and quoted at length from them. For example, the complete text of Cassius Dio was available to him. His *Epitomē* was much utilized by later Byzantine writers. It was translated into Old Slavonic and, in the Renaissance, into Latin, French, and Italian. His elaborate commentary on the *Apostolic Constitutions*, the synods, and Fathers of the Church is one of the most important contributions to Byzantine Canon Law. BIBLIOGRAPHY: R. Browning, NCE 14:1129; É. Amann, DTC 15.2:3705–3708; Beck 656–657.

[M. R. P. MCGUIRE]

ZONE (Gr., belt, girdle), the equivalent of the Roman cincture worn by bishops and priests in the Byzantine Church to gird the *sticharion* (alb). It is a belt-like vestment usually but not necessarily made of the same material as the *phelonion* about three inches wide and marked with a cross in the middle of the front. The zone is fastened in the back with long tapes or sometimes by an ornamented buckle. The *epitrachelion* (stole) is also worn beneath the zone along with the *sticharion*. The Ruthenians, however, have the custom of placing the *epitrachelion* on top of the zone, perhaps to distinguish themselves from Orthodox priests.

[A. J. JACOPIN]

ZOOLATRY, worship of a particular kind of animal. This phenomenon was esp. prominent in the religion of ancient Egypt, where it had a complex history and evolution. In various times and places such worship involved the jackal, the jackass, the cat, the hawk, the ram, the cow, the vulture, the crocodile, the lioness, the ibis, and the scorpion. It is not always clear whether such worship was directed toward the animal as the representative of a natural force, the incarnation of some deity, or the symbol of some power or protector, such as a tribal ancestor. The word itself (zoolatry) is from the late Latin *zoolatria*, which is itself a direct borrowing from the Greek for "animal-worship."

[E. J. DILLON]

ZORELL, FRANZ (1863–1947), German Jesuit biblical scholar, Orientalist, and lexicographer, best known for his immensely erudite Bible lexicons. Even before entering the Society of Jesus in 1884 he was deeply immersed in humanistic studies, including Semitic languages. His first monumental work was his Greek NT lexicon, published in

1911, the product of twelve years' intensive effort. He began immediately an even more ambitious product, a Hebrew and Aramaic OT lexicon. Its final fascicule was readied for publication just before his death. Editing and revision delayed final publication until 1954. From 1923 on, Z. also taught Armenian and Georgian at the Pontifical Biblical Institute in Rome.

[E. J. DILLON]

ZOROASTER (ZARATHUSHTRA), the prophet and religious reformer of ancient Persia. Owing to the nature of the sources available, it is practically impossible to separate the man and his work from legend and determine his actual teaching as distinct from the later modifications and additions of Zoroastrianism. It is generally agreed that the *Gāthās* are authentic hymns of Zoroaster and contain vague but reliable data on his life and doctrine. He grew up apparently as a small landowner in the early 6th cent. B.C. in NE Iran, and during his lifetime his religious reform seems to have been largely confined to this area. He should be regarded primarily as a prophet and religious reformer rather than the founder of a new religion in any strict sense. He inherited the belief in *Ahura Mazda* as the Wise Lord, but also traditional beliefs in other divinities and in the efficacy of magic. The main tenets of his teaching would seem to be the following: Man must make a choice between good and evil and he will be rewarded or punished according to his choice of good or evil and the conduct of his life in thought, word, and action. *Ahura Mazda* must be recognized as the one supreme god, the Wise Lord, the Good Power, the creator of light and darkness, heaven and earth, and the entire universe and its movements. The worship of the demons (*daēvas*) is forbidden and abuses in sacrifices are to be removed. Emphasis is placed on the cult of fire as the great purifier and as a symbol of divine justice. BIBLIOGRAPHY: J. Duchesne-Guillemin, NCE 14:1133–34; *id.*, *La Religion de l'Iran ancien* (1962, esp. 135–146, 202–207); W. Eilers, RGG 6:1866–68 (esp. for bibliog.); R. C. Zaehner, *Dawn and Twilight of Zoroastrianism* (1961); G. Widengren, *Die Religionen Irans* (1965).

[M. R. P. MCGUIRE]

ZOSIMUS, ST. (d. 418), **POPE** (417–418) during whose short pontificate two incidents of note took place: (1) Z. granted to Patrocles, bp. of Arles, the title of papal vicar in Gaul and made him metropolitan of the provinces of Vienne and Narbonne. This disturbance of the status quo evoked strong protests from the bps. of Gaul, and Z.'s successor revoked the appointment. (2) In the Pelagian controversy, *Pelagius and *Caelestius, after having been condemned by the African councils of Carthage and Milevis (approved in their decisions by Pope Innocent I), appealed to Z.., who absolved them as falsely accused. The outrage of the African bps. at this action caused Z. to issue his *Epistola tractoria,* in which he set forth the history of the whole controversy and condemned anew the Pelagian doctrine; he also condemned Caelestius and Pelagius personally as the African councils had done. Though Z. clearly recognized the rights and duties of the Holy See, he did not always exercise them happily. Works: PL 20:639–704. BIBLIOGRAPHY: Altaner 417.

[R. B. ENO]

ZOSTRIANUS, APOCALYPSE OF, a Gnostic work in Coptic, discovered in 1946 at Chenoboskion in Upper Egypt, 30 miles N of Luxor. It was one of 48 treatises contained in 13 codices, all in Coptic, and provisionally dated from the 3d or 4th century A.D. Besides various apocalypses these works included apocryphal gospels, epistles, dogmatic treatises, prayers, and cosmogonies. Apocalypses such as this one of Zostrianus were very popular in Christian Egypt and elsewhere. They tended to become more and more fantastic, guided tours of heaven and hell and other occult areas by those who had been there; in marked contrast to the two canonical apocalyptic books: Daniel and Revelations, which focus on the hidden meaning of the historical crisis at hand at the time of writing. The Church's polemic against Gnosticism was due in part to the latter's neglect of historical reality.

[E. J. DILLON]

ZOUAVES, PAPAL, a corps of volunteer soldiers serving in the papal army during the period of struggle between the Papal States and the Kingdom of Italy, over the question of the political unification of the Italian peninsula (1861–1870). They were drawn from various militantly Catholic and generally right-wing segments of Europe, and were convinced that the future of the Church and the papacy hinged on the fate of the Papal States. There were 5,000 Austrian foot-soldiers (light infantry), 4,000 Swiss, 3,000 Irish volunteers, and finally a motley group of Franco-Belgian volunteers who brought with them the title *zouaves*, a name borrowed from an infantry corps created for the colonial wars in Algeria. The corps was organized by F. de *Mérode, a priest friend of Pius IX, who had formerly been a Belgian army officer. It was led by a succession of legitimist, monarchist, old regime, and former colonial officers, and was no match for the Italian army. The papal army was defeated at Castelfidaro in 1860 and surrendered at Ancona in 1861. The zouaves, after reorganization of the army in 1865, did probably prevent the outbreak of revolution in the Papal States whose people chose instead to wait for liberation by the Italian armies. After the surrender of Rome in 1870 the papal zouaves were repatriated. The zouaves became a symbol of Catholic loyalty to the papacy and the zouave costume on dolls or even children part of the symbolism.

[E. J. DILLON]

ZSCHOKKE, HEINRICH (1771–1848), German-born writer, statesman, and political journalist who became an effective spokesman for the awakening democratic Swiss national consciousness. He was born in Magdeburg, his full name, Johann Heinrich Daniel Zschokke. His early studies were in Lutheran theology and in philosophy. In 1796 he settled in Switzerland, and through his much loved stories, novels, dramas, and studies in nature and history, he promoted among the people an emerging Liberal consciousness. His articles appeared in newspapers and periodicals. Their edifying tone and appeal crossed denominational barriers and allowed him to play a decisive part in the creation of the new Swiss Canton of Aargau.

[E. J. DILLON]

ZUCCARI (ZUCCARO), FEDERICO (1542–1609). Italian painter and art theorist. Z. painted scenes from the Life of St. Eustace (c.1560) in a neo-Raphaelesque style. In 1563 he executed a Moses cycle in the Vatican, the *Adoration of the Magi* (1564, Venice), traveled and worked in the English court (1574). Criticized for his painting of the cupola of the cathedral, Florence, and for the *Procession of St. Gregory* (Bologna), Z. executed in retort his satirical *Porta Virtutis* (1581), whereupon he was exiled from the papal states. Patronized by the Duke of Urbino and painting in Venice (1582), when reinstated in Rome he completed the Pauline frescoes in the Vatican. Upon the invitation of Philip II of Spain, he painted the high altar at the Escorial (1586–88). Returning finally to Rome (1589), Z. taught and examined the arts in reference to scholastic thought in his *Idea de' pittori, scultori e architetti* (1608).

[M. J. DALY]

ZUCCONE (''pumpkin head''; 1423–25), one of five forceful, sculptured prophet figures (1416–35) by Donatello for the cathedral of Florence. Zuccone is a triumph of characterization in Donatello's most original harsh realism—the bony, bald, uncouth, awkward figure, with spastic hand clutching the crumpled garment deeply undercut—not just a ''mirror of life,'' but the magnificent aesthetic essence of distortion, Donatello's unique, acutely personal contribution to the history of sculpture in this discrete expression of the Italian Renaissance.

[M. J. DALY]

ZUMÁRRAGA, JUAN DE (c.1468–1548), missionary, bishop. A Spanish Franciscan, Z. was provincial superior of Concepción from 1520 to 1523. In 1527 he was named bishop-elect of Mexico. He operated in Mexico for 5 years before being consecrated. The organizing of the vast territory—present Mexico to the S limit of Guatemala—was a demanding task that Z. successfully accomplished. He verified and approved the apparition of Our Lady of Guadalupe. Appointed protector of the Indians, Z. experienced opposition from civil authorities and was called to Spain where the King accepted Z.'s defense of his role and had him consecrated bp. in 1533. Returning to Mexico, Z. promoted church discipline and founded schools and colleges. With Viceroy Mendoza, he built the first seminary

and high school in America (1536), laid the groundwork of the Univ. of Mexico (actually established in 1553). With the Viceroy Z. established the first printing press in the New World in 1539, published a number of books in Mexican and Castilian, and wrote several himself, e.g., *Regla christiana* (1544). Through his efforts four new dioceses were created. Z. called provincial meetings of bishops of Mexico City, producing much benefit. Appointed inquisitor, Z. made his share of mistakes and was removed. Regrettably, out of misplaced zeal, he permitted the destruction of ancient temples and writings. Z. is one of the great figures of Spanish colonial history. BIBLIOGRAPHY: *Don fray Juan de Zumárraga: primer obispo y arzobispo de Mexico* (4 v., 1947).

[J. R. AHERNE]

ZUR'AT BEN TIBBĀN AS'AD, see DHŪ-NUWĀS MAS-RUĶ.

ZURBARÁN, FRANCISCO DE (1598–1664), Spanish Baroque artist known for paintings of monks and religious works of deep spiritual feeling. Z.'s style, characterized by a dramatic tenebrism merged with an extreme realism, evokes strong emotional responses (*Christ on the Cross*, 1627; *St. Serapion*, 1628). He is famed for his white-robed monks in monastic cycles—*Life of S. Pedro Nolasco* (1628), and *Life of S. Buenaventura* (1629)—remarkable for large areas of dark color and brilliantly lighted simple forms. His great Baroque altarpieces (*Triumph of Thomas Aquinas*, 1631) inbue intense naturalism with deep mystical feeling. Under Murillo's influence Z.'s work became sentimental (*Way to Calvary*, 1653), his later Holy Families and penitent saints, meditative and lyrical. He further explored the dramatically spotlighted subject against a dark background in still life paintings rendered extraordinary by an almost obsessive insistence on volume and surface texture, e.g., *Still Life with Oranges* (1633) at Norton Simon Foundation, Los Angeles.

[S. CONWAY]

ZURICH CONSENSUS (*Consensus Tigurinus*), a document of agreement between Zwinglian and Calvinistic parties of the Reformed Church. Luther, who insisted that the body and blood of Christ were actually present in the bread and wine (see CONSUBSTANTIATION), condemned *Zwingli's doctrine of Christ's spiritual presence in the Eucharist. Calvin tried to mediate between these positions with his concept of Christ's real spiritual presence for the elect who received the elements in faith. In 1549 he and G. *Farel worked out with H. *Bullinger a harmonizing statement in the *Consensus Tigurinus*. It maintains that in the Lord's Supper the body and blood of Christ are not received carnally, but that by the power of the Holy Spirit the elect receive Christ spiritually. BIBLIOGRAPHY: Schaff Creeds 1:471–473.

[N. H. MARING]

ZURLA, GIACINTO PLACIDO (1769–1843), Italian Camaldolese monk who became cardinal vicar for three popes. Born in Legnano, he entered the Camaldolese in Venice when he was eighteen. After Napoleon suppressed the order's college where he had been teaching theology and philosophy, he taught for a while at a nearby seminary, then moved to Rome in 1821, where he was prefect of studies at the Collegio Urbano. In 1823 he became a cardinal and was cardinal vicar to Leo XII, Pius VIII, and Gregory XVI. He may have had a special interest in cartography and geography, since he published studies on mapping, including one that traced the journeys of Marco Polo.

[E. J. DILLON]

ZWEIFALTEN, CHURCH AT (1740–65), Benedictine pilgrimage church near Zweifalten, S Germany, a joyous, exuberant rococo masterpiece, overwhelming in 18th-cent. beauty and richness in a final flowering in Bavaria and Swabia, designed by Johann Michael Fischer, with ''illusionistic'' painting by F. J. Spiegler. Chapels line the nave between blue and pink marble columns, and choir stalls of lustrous walnut and maple are delicate with shells, tendrils, and gold reliefs of the lives of Christ and the Virgin.

[M. J. DALY]

ZWEIG, STEFAN (1881–1942), Austrian essayist, biographer, dramatist, poet, who is mostly known for his psychological biographies of great figures of literature and history. Born in Vienna as the son of a well-to-do Jewish manufacturer, Z. studied philosophy in Berlin and Vienna and lived there as independent writer. Being a pacifist, he spent the years of World War I in Switzerland and then in Salzburg, until he emigrated to England in 1934, and in 1941 to Brazil. Depressed by personal problems and the political fate of Austria he ended his life a year later. A prolific writer and gifted translator, Z. was strongly influenced by S. *Freud's psychoanalysis and used this approach in his controversial historical monographs and essays (e.g., *Joseph Fouché*, 1929; *Marie Antoinette*, 1932; *Maria Stuart*, 1935). His works reveal his tolerant and cosmopolitan humanism. In his last book, which some consider his best, *Die Welt von Gestern: Erinnerungen eines Europäers* (1942) he recalls the past era of the Habsburg monarchy. *Complete Works,* tr. E. and C. Paul (1949–   ). BIBLIOGRAPHY: J. Romains, *Stefan Zweig, Great European* (tr. J. Whitall, 1941).

[B. F. STEINBRUCKNER]

ZWEMER, SAMUEL (1867–1952), American missionary. With J. Cantine, Z. founded the Arabic Mission of the Reformed Church in America and during his years in Bahrein (1890–1912) traveled extensively to promote the work. He wrote more than 30 books and served as professor at Cairo Theological Seminary (1912–29) and Princeton Theological Seminary (1929–38). BIBLIOGRAPHY: R. P. Beaver, RGG 6:1949.

[M. J. SUELZER]

ZWETTL, ABBEY OF, a Cistercian monastery near Krems, Lower Austria, in the diocese of St. Pölten, formerly Passau, founded from Heiligenkreuz in 1138 by Hadmar I of Kuenring. From 1348 it began to decline, suffered at the hands of the Hussites in 1427, and declined further during the tensions of the Reformation; it began a revival under Abbot Ulrich Hackl (1577–1607). In the 1960s the monks served in 13 parishes and conducted a retreat house. The buildings reflect the Romanesque, Gothic, and Baroque periods of its history. BIBLIOGRAPHY: Cottineau 2:3485–86).

[E. J. DILLON]

ZWICKAU PROPHETS, agitators, esp. T. *Münzer and N. *Storch, who at Zwickau in Saxony preached a religion of inner inspiration and a chiliastic kingdom of God to be established by force. Expelled from Zwickau, they had some success in Wittenberg (1521–22), impressing Philipp *Melanchthon and converting *Karlstadt. The latter, along with the Prophets, had to flee before Luther's wrath when he returned to Wittenberg in March 1522.

[T. C. O'BRIEN]

ZWIEFALTEN, ABBEY OF or Zwiefaltach, former Benedictine monastery in Württemberg, above Ulm in the Swabian Alps, founded as a double monastery in 1089 by Counts Cuno and Liutold of Achalm, colonized by Hirsau; and made independent in 1091. Dedicated to SS. Stephen and Aurelius, it remained a double monastery until the 13th cent. and produced estimable copyists, illuminators, and chroniclers. In the 15th and 16th cent. it helped reform Weingarten and Reichenau. The monks studied and taught at the Univ. of Tübingen, Dillingen, and Salzburg in the 16th and subsequent centuries. It was secularized in 1802. The abbey church became the Catholic parish church. BIBLIOGRAPHY: Cottineau 2:3486–88.

[E. J. DILLON]

ZWIERLEIN, FREDERICK JAMES (1881–1960), historian. A native of New York State, Z. was ordained for the diocese of Rochester, N.Y., in 1904. From 1907 to 1938 he taught church history and art at St. Bernard's Seminary, Rochester. Z. published a number of historical studies, the outstanding one being the *Life and Letters of Bishop McQuaid* (1925–1927), a pioneer work in the field of American church history. Another study concentrated on Church and State in the Philippines after the Spanish-American War, *Theodore Roosevelt and Catholics, 1888–1919* (1956).

[J. R. AHERNE]

ZWINGLI, HULDRYCH (Ulrich; 1484–1531), Swiss Reformer and patriot. Following humanistic studies at the Univ. of Basel, he was ordained at Constance in 1506 and sent to serve in the parish of Glarus. At that time he was affected by the three forces that formulated his theological thinking and his career: a series of sermons by Thomas

Wyttenbach, who impressed him with the supremacy of the Scriptures in the life of the Christian; a chaplaincy with the Glarus mercenaries at Rome, where he became disillusioned with Roman liturgy as well as the mercenary system (he experienced the defeat of the Swiss at the Battle of Marignano in 1515); and an enlivened interest in the *New Learning, leading to his friendship with *Erasmus. He was removed from Glarus to a retreat in the monastery of Einsiedeln (1516) because of his strong opposition to sending Swiss mercenaries abroad. There he studied the Greek NT, the Fathers, and the *Enchiridion* of Erasmus. In 1518 he was chosen people's priest for the Great Minster at Zurich through the influence of his friend Oswald *Myconius, and against the stern resistance of some who found fault with his love of music and with his life, which he admitted to be unchaste. His preaching was lauded, and in 1522 he published the *Archeteles* and the *Sixty-Seven Conclusions*, attacking church ceremonies and proposing radical reforms. In 1524 images were removed and the Mass abolished. In this year he announced his marriage to the widow, Anna Reinhard, to whom he had been secretly married for 2 years. In April 1525 the first celebration of the Lord's Supper according to Zwinglian principles was held in the cathedral. He brought about (1525) persecution of the Swiss Anabaptists who resented his alliance with the civil magistrates (see GREBEL, C.; MANZ, F.). In the intense civil warfare between Zurich and the Catholic cantons Zwingli was slain in the Battle of Kappel. Although in Switzerland the Reformation gradually become Calvinistic, Z. had great influence on Reformation theology. His theory of the Eucharist esp. continues to be accepted by many Churches.

In accord with the theological trend of the Reformers, Z.'s thought was basically bibliocentric, setting Scripture as the sole guide of belief. Thus he dismissed the need for an authoritative interpretation of the Bible outside individual religious experience. He taught further that faith was an internal implant, placed in the Christian by Christ and only indirectly stimulated by the external words of revelation. His own tendency to interpret the Scriptures rhetorically furthered the importance of subjective response. His theology was also primitivist in character, rejecting scholasticism and the elaborate liturgy that grew from the Middle Ages and reaching back to the simpler practices of the primitive Church, as indicated in the testimony of the Fathers. This interest in the Fathers was in part influenced by his contact with Erasmus and his writings. The religious belief of Zwingli in summary form was a revolt against the hierarchical structure of the Church and the preeminence of the bishop of Rome. To Z. the Church was a body both visible, embracing all members signed with baptism, and invisible, incorporating the elect of God. Its visible design, though admitting no hierarchy, did call for pastors, who were not only teachers of the word, but recipients of inspiration and charism. Its polity was congregational but with a strong reliance upon the lay authority (Council of the Canton) for cooperation in religious policies and for the enforcement of penalties for transgressions, including those meriting removal from the church community.

Z. acknowledged only baptism and the Eucharist as sacraments instituted by Christ. These, moreover, were not productive of grace when rightly performed and under conditions of proper intention but were mere tokens (*signa nuda*) of divine favor, like the rites of circumcision and the Passover ceremonies of the OT. His stand on the symbolic presence of Christ in the species of bread and wine became a prominent theory in the sincere but fruitless attempts at doctrinal compromise among the Reformers. While Luther denied the Mass but affirmed a Real Presence in the Eucharist, Zwingli denied both, and Luther vehemently opposed this view (see MARBURG ARTICLES). Zwingli's theory of divine providence and predestination was fatalistic to an extreme. Man, since Adam's fall, is helpless to will what is good and, as the victim of sin, is completely at God's pity. God thus becomes an inexorable deity who has fixed the fate of men, foreordaining them to election or damnation. In this divine plan God is glorified in his goodness by the chosen, and in his justice by the reprobated. BIBLIOGRAPHY: *Zwingli and Bullinger* (ed. G. W. Bromiley, 1953), a compilation including Zwingli's *Exposition of the Faith*; J. V. Pollet, *Huldrych Zwingli et la Réforme en Suïsse* (1963); O. Farner, *Zwingli the Reformer* (tr. D. G. Sear, 1952).

[E. D. MCSHANE]